CONCISE ENCYCLOPEDIA OF ISLAM

[redacted]

CONCISE ENCYCLOPEDIA OF ISLAM

EDITED ON BEHALF OF THE ROYAL NETHERLANDS ACADEMY

H.A.R. GIBB AND J.H. KRAMERS

FOURTH IMPRESSION

BRILL ACADEMIC PUBLISHERS, INC.
BOSTON • LEIDEN
2001

Library of Congress Cataloging-in-Publication Data

H.A.R. Gibb and J.H. Kramers
Concise encyclopedia of Islam edited on behalf of the Royal Netherlands Academy by H.A.R. Gibb and J.H. Kramers.
p. cm.
Previously published as: Shorter encyclopaedia of Islam.
Includes bibliographical references and index.
ISBN 0-391-04116-9
1. Islam—Dictionaries. I. Gibb, H.A.R. (Hamilton Alexander Rosskeen, Sir 1895–1971). II. Kramers, J.H. (Johannes Hendrik, 1891–1951). III. Shorter encyclopaedia of Islam

BP40 .C66 2001
297'.03—dc21

2001035754

ISBN 0-391-04116-9

PRINTED IN THE UNITED STATES OF AMERICA

The Sanctuary at Mecca with the Kaʿba, seen from the East

The "Concise Encyclopedia of Islam" includes all the articles contained in the first edition and Supplement of the *Encyclopaedia of Islam* which relate particularly to the religion and law of Islam.

The majority of the original articles have been reproduced without material alteration. A number of articles have been shortened or revised, and a few new articles have been added. In most cases, additional entries have been made in the bibliographies in order to bring them up to date.

ABBREVIATED TITLES OF THE MOST OFTEN QUOTED WORKS

Ash'arī, *Maḳālāt* = *Maḳālāt al-Islāmiyīn*, ed. H. Ritter, Istanbul 1929-30.
Baghdādī = *al-Farḳ bain al-Firaḳ*, Cairo 1328.
Balādhurī = *Futūḥ al-Buldān*, ed. J. de Goeje, Leiden 1866.
Brockelmann = Geschichte der arabischen Litteratur, second ed., Leiden 1943-49.
Brockelmann, *S.* = the same work, Supplementbände, Leiden 1937-42.
Ibn al-Athīr = *al-Kāmil*, ed. C. J. Tornberg, Leiden 1851-76.
Ibn Ḥazm = *al-Faṣl fi 'l-Milal*, Cairo 1317-20.
Ibn Hishām = *Sīra*, ed. Wüstenfeld, Göttingen 1859-60.
Ibn Khallikān = *Wafayāt al-A'yān*, ed. F. Wüstenfeld, Göttingen 1835-50.
Mas'ūdī = *Murūdj al-Dhahab*, ed. Barbier de Meynard, Paris 1861-77.
Nawawī = *Tahdhīb al-Asmā'*, ed. F. Wüstenfeld, Göttingen 1843-48.
Shahrastānī = *al-Milal wa 'l-Niḥal*, ed. W. Cureton, London 1846.
Ṭabarī = *Ta'rīkh*, ed. J. de Goeje and others, Leiden 1879-1901.
Wensinck, *Handbook* = *Handbook of early Muhammadan Tradition*, Leiden 1927.

ABBREVATIONS FOR PERIODICALS ETC.

Abh. G. W. Gött = Abhandlungen der Gesellschaft der Wissenschaften in Göttingen
Abh. K. M. = Abhandlungen f. d. Kunde des Morgenlandes
Abh. Pr. Ak. W. = Abhandlungen d. preuss. Akad. d. Wiss.
Afr. Fr. B = Bulletin du Comité de l'Afrique française
Afr. Fr. RC = Bulletin du Com. de l'Afr. franç., Renseignements Coloniaux
AIEO = Annales de l'Institut des Etudes Orientales de l'Université d'Alger
AM = Archives marocaines
And. = Al-Andulus
Anth. = Anthropos
Anz. Wien = Anzeiger der philos.-histor. Kl. d. Ak. der Wiss. Wien
AO = Acta Orientalia
ArO = Archiv Orientalní
ARW = Archiv für Religionswissenschaft
As. Fr. B = Bulletin du Comité de l'Asie française
BAH = Bibliotheca Arabico-Hispana
BASOR = Bulletin of the American School of Oriental Research
Bell. = Türk Tarih Kurumu Belleten
BFac. Ar. = Bulletin of the Faculty of Arts of the Egyptian University
BEt. Or. = Bulletin d'Etudes Orientales de l'Institut Français de Damas
BGA = Bibliotheca geographorum arabicorum
BIE = Bulletin de l'Institut Egyptien
BIFAO = Bulletin de l'Institut Français d'Archéologie Orientale au Caire
BR.Ac. Esp. = Boletín de la Real Academia de Historia de España
BSOS = Bulletin of the School of Oriental and African Studies
BTLV = Bijdragen tot de Taal-, Land en Volkenkunde van Ned.-Indië
BZ = Byzantinische Zeitschrift
EI (1) = Encyclopaedia of Islam, 1st ed.
GGA = Göttinger Gelehrte Anzeigen
GJ = Geographical Journal
GMS = Gibb Memorial Series
Gr. I Ph. = Grundriss der Iranischen Philologie
GSAI = Giornale della Soc. Asiatica Italiana
Hesp. = Hespéris
IA = Islâm Ansiklopedisi
IBLA = Revue de l'Institut des Belles Lettres Arabes
IC = Islamic Culture
IG = Indische Gids
IRM = International Review of Missions
Isl. = Der Islam
JA = Journal Asiatique
JAfr. S = Journal of the African Society
JOS = Journal of the American Oriental Society
JAnthr. I = Journal of the Anthropological Institute
JASB = Journal and Proceedings of the Asiatic Soc. of Bengal
JE = Jewish Encyclopaedia
JNES = Journal of Near Eastern Studies
JPHS = Journal of the Punjab Historical Society
JQR = Jewish Quarterly Review
JRAS = Journal of the Royal Asiatic Society
JSFO = Journal de la Société Finno-ougrienne
KCA = Körösi Csoma Archivum
KS = Keleti Szemle (Revue orientale)
Mash. = Al-Mashriḳ
MDOG = Mitteilungen der Deutschen Orient-Gesellschaft
MDPV = Mitteilungen und Nachr. des Deutschen Palästina-Vereins
MFOB = Mélanges de la Faculté Orientale de Beyrouth
MGG Wien = Mitteilungen der geographischen Gesellschaft in Wien
MGMN = Mitt. z. Geschichte der Medizin und Naturwissenschaften
MGWJ = Monatsschrift f. d. Geschichte u. Wissenschaft des Judentums
MI = Mir Islama
MIE = Mémoires de l'Institut Egyptien
MIFAO = Mémoires publiés par les membres de l'Inst. Franç. d'Archéologie Orientale au Caire

MVAG = Mitteilungen der Vorderasiatisch-ägyptischen Gesellschaft
MMAF = Mémoires de la Mission Archéologique Franç. au Caire
MMIA = Madjallat al-Madjmaᶜ al-ᶜIlmī al-ᶜArabī, Damascus
MO = Le Monde oriental
MOG = Mitteilungen zur osmanischen Geschichte
MSFO = Mémoires de la Société Finno-ougrienne
MSL = Mémoires de la Société Linguistique de Paris
MSOS Afr. = Mitteilungen des Sem. für oriental. Sprachen, Afr. Studien
MSOS As. = Mitteilungen des Sem. für oriental. Sprachen, Westasiat. Studien
MTM = Millī Tetebbüᶜler Medjmūᶜasī
MW = The Muslim World
NC = Numismatic Chronicle
NGW Gött. = Nachrichten d. Gesellschaft d. Wiss. Göttingen
OA = Orientalisches Archiv
OC = Oriens Christianus
OLZ = Orientalistische Literaturzeitung
OM = Oriente Moderno
Or. = Oriens
PEFQS = Palestine Exploration Fund. Quarterly Statement
PELOV = Publications de l'école des langues orientales vivantes
Pet. Mitt. = Petermanns Mitteilungen
PRGS = Proceedings of the R. Geographical Society
RAfr. = Revue Africaine
RCEA = Répertoire chronologique d'Epigraphie arabe
REJ = Revue des Etudes Juives
Rend. Lin. = Rendiconti della Reale Accad. dei Lincei, Cl. di sc. mor., stor., e filol.
REI = Revue des Etudes islamiques
RHR = Revue de l'Histoire des Religions
RI = Revue Indigène
RMM = Revue du Monde Musulman
RO = Rocznik Oryentalistyczny
ROC = Revue de l'Orient Chrétien
ROL = Revue de l'Orient Latin
RRAH = Rev. de la R. Academia de la Historia, Madrid
RSO = Rivista degli studi orientali
RT = Revue Tunisienne
SBAk. Heid. = Sitzungsberichte der Ak. der Wiss. Heidelberg
SBAk. Wien = Sitzungsberichte der Ak. der Wiss. in Wien
SBBayr. Ak. = Sitzungsberichte der Bayrischen Akademie der Wissenschaften
SBPMS Erlg. = Sitzungsberichte d. Phys.-medizin. Sozietät in Erlangen
SBPr. Ak. W. = Sitzungsberichte der preuss. Ak. der Wiss. zu Berlin
TBGKW = Tijdschrift van het Bataviaasch Genootschap van Kunsten en Wetenschappen
TOEM = Tārikh-i ᶜOthmani (Türk) Tarihi Endjümeni medjmūᶜasī, Revue Historique publiée par l'Institut d'Histoire Ottomane
TTLV = Tijdschrift v. Taal-, Land- en Volkenkunde
Verh. Ak. Amst. = Verhandelingen der Koninklijke Akademie van Wetenschappen te Amsterdam
Versl. Med. Ak. Amst. = Verslagen en Mededeelingen der Koninklijke Akademie van Wetenschappen te Amsterdam
WI = Die Welt des Islams
Wiss. Veröff. DOG = Wissenschaftliche Veröffentlichungen der Deutschen Orient-Gesellschaft
WZKM = Wiener Zeitschrift für die Kunde des Morgenlandes
ZA = Zeitschrift für Assyriologie
Zap. = Zapiski
ZATW = Zeitschrift f. alttestamentliche Wissenschaft
ZDMG = Zeitschrift der Deutschen Morgenländischen Gesellschaft
ZDPV = Zeitschrift des Deutschen Palästinavereins
ZGErdk. Berl. = Zeitschrift der Gesellschaft für Erdkunde in Berlin
ZK = Zeitschrift für Kolonialsprachen
ZOEG = Zeitschrift f. Osteuropäische Geschichte
ZS = Zeitschrift für Semitistik

A

AARON. [See Hārūn.

ABĀḌITES. [See Ibāḍites.

al-**ʿABBĀS** b. ʿAbd al-Muṭṭalib, surnamed Abu 'l-Faḍl, uncle of Muḥammad. He was only three or, according to Ibn Ḥadjar, two years older than the latter. He was a merchant and made a large fortune; according to Ibn Hishām (p. 953) and Ṭabarī (i. 1739), he took in his commercial travels the style of a descendant of the ancient kings. It is reported that the right of supplying drink to pilgrims was conferred upon him and that he put dried raisins from his garden at Ṭā'if in the Zamzam water. The traditions agree in representing him as opposed to the religious movement initiated by Muḥammad, as long as the latter lived at Mecca. But he did not belong to the implacable adversaries of the Prophet, and, when Abū Ṭālib died and he thereby became the protector of his nephew, it is not impossible that he defended his cause in the assembly of ʿAḳaba as tradition has it. An awkward fact is that he fought in the ranks of the Meccans at Badr and was taken prisoner. But it was asserted that he had been forced by the Meccans to take part in this campaign against his will. Further, the story was embellished with different traits in his honour; e.g. it was said that he was taken prisoner by the help of an angel and that Muḥammad could not sleep from thinking that his uncle was in chains. Ibn Hishām uses the convenient method of passing over the story of his ransom in silence. It is further certain that, having paid his ransom, the returned to Mecca; tradition explains this by asserting that he had really accepted Islām, but from motives of a pecuniary nature temporarily kept his conversion secret. He not only protected in Mecca the followers of the Prophet but also revealed to his nephew the plans of campaign of his fellow-citizens. As a matter of fact it is not only possible but quite probable that he regarded with increasing sympathy the rapid development of his nephew's power. When Muḥammad visited Mecca in the year 7/628-9, ʿAbbās gave him his sister-in-law Maimūna [q.v.] to wife. The following year, when Muḥammad marched upon Mecca, ʿAbbās joined him before his arrival in front of the town; but the story that he then took Abū Sufyān under his protection is apocryphal. At Mecca Muḥammad confirmed him in his right to supply pilgrims with drink. In the battle of Ḥunain he kept at the Prophet's side, who was beholden to the power of his uncle's voice for the happy turn the fight took. According to Wāḳidī, he contributed from his purse to the fitting out of the great campaign against the Byzantines; he also took part in washing the Prophet's dead body. There is very little mention made of him after this. He accompanied Fāṭima when she went to Abū Bakr to claim her part of inheritance. He had his share in the great endowments of ʿUmar. In the reign of this caliph, he made a present of his house for the purpose of enlarging the mosque of Madīna. Considering how old he was at that time, it is very doubtful whether he was present in the Arab army east of the Jordan; but, it is said, he dissuaded ʿUmar from going in person to the theatre of war against the Persians. He fruitlessly endeavoured to make ʿAlī accept his advice not to have any share in the election of ʿUmar's successor. He died at Madīna in the year 32/652-3 or, according to others in the year 34 at the age of 88. The ʿAbbāsid caliphs descended from his son ʿAbd Allāh [q.v.].

Bibliography: Ibn Hishām, *passim*; Ibn Ḥadjar, *Iṣāba*, ii. 668 *sq.*; Nawawī, p. 331 *sq.*; Ṭabarī, i. *passim*; Balādhurī, p. 6, 28, 56, 255; Yaʿḳūbī (ed. Houtsma), ii. 47; Wāḳidī, *Kitāb al-Maghāzī* (ed. Wellhausen), *passim*; Ibn Saʿd, iv[a]. 1—21; Goldziher, *Muhamm. Stud.*, ii. 108 *sq.*; Nöldeke, in *ZDMG*, lii. 21—27; Buhl, *Das Leben Muhammeds*, p. 247 *sq.*, 306 *sq.*

ʿABD (a.), slave, servant.

I. IN THE SOCIAL AND LEGAL SENSE.

a. *Slavery in ancient Arabia.*

It is known that Islām retained the ancient Arabian institution of slavery, the legality of which the old Biblical world admitted. Muhammedanism allows its followers to appropriate to their own use the infidels of any country which is neither subject to nor allied with the Islamic empire, and the slave-trade was for long an important business for the Muslim countries.

A male slave is generally called in Arabic *ʿabd* (plur. *ʿabīd*) or *mamlūk* [q.v.] a female slave *ama* or *djāriya.*

Prisoners of war, including women and children, taken in the wars of the Prophet against the Arab tribes, were, unless ransomed, reduced to slavery, according to the ancient Arab custom. Thus in the campaign against the Banu 'l-Muṣṭaliḳ, a very considerable number of women fell into the hands of the Muslims. One of them was Djuwairīya bint al-Ḥārith, who formed part of the booty of Thābit b. Ḳais. Thābit agreed with her to set her free for nine or ten ounces of gold; when that had been arranged she went to the Prophet and implored his aid. She was very beautiful, and the Prophet paid her ransom and demanded her in marriage. This induced the Muslims to set free the other women who had fallen into their hands; for, said they, it is not fitting that the women of a tribe to which our master has become allied should be our slaves.

In Arabia slaves were also obtained by purchase or by brigandage. For example Zaid, one of Muḥammad's slaves — the first who embraced Islam, — came from the noble tribe of the Banū Kalb. One day his mother, wishing to pay a visit to her tribe, took Zaid, who was still an infant, with her. Some horsemen surprised them and Zaid fell into their hands. They put him up for sale at ʿUkāẓ, where he was bought by Khadīdja, who presented him to her husband after her marriage with Muḥammad. After some time, some Kalbites saw Zaid at Mecca, and told his father they had discovered him, and he at once hurried to Mecca. "Give him his liberty for the ransom we will pay", said he to the Prophet; but Zaid declared that he preferred to remain with Muḥammad.

There were at that time many Arabs amongst the slaves. But even earlier, in the time of paganism, slaves were kept, some black, others white, who had been brought from Africa and the northern countries (comp. G. Jacob, *Altarab. Beduinenleben*, 2d ed., p. 137; ʿAntara, *Muʿallaḳa*, verse 27, ed. Arnold, p. 153). The caliph ʿUmar, it is said, was the first to lay down the principle that an Arab could not be a slave, even though purchased for money or a prisoner of war; only foreigners could be reduced to slavery (comp. A von Kremer, *Kulturgesch. des Orients unter den Chalifen*, i. 104). In any case canonical law forbids the Muslim to make his coreligionists slaves. Parents are therefore not allowed to sell their children (comp. however, E. W. Lane, *Modern Egyptians*, i, ch. vii: *Domestic life*; *the lower orders*), and a creditor may not sell his Muslim debtor into slavery, as the Roman law permitted. If, however, slaves embrace Islām later — and they mostly do so — they remain in servitude.

b. *Ḳurʾān and Ḥadīth.*

The conditions of slavery in early Islām are reflected in the several Ḳurʾānic passages that deal with slaves. The low condition of slaves appears clearly from the parable in S. xvi, 75 and in the prescriptions concerning retaliation in S. ii, 178 (a free man for a free man, a slave for a slave). On the other hand, the Ḳurʾān recommends their good treatment (S. iv, 36; xvi, 71) and includes them among those who are to benefit from pious gifts (*ṣadaḳa*), cf. S. ii, 177; ix, 60. Here slaves are alluded to as *riḳāb*, plural of *raḳaba*, the metaphorical expression which is also used in the passages where the liberation of a slave is prescribed as atonement for the killing of a believer (S. iv, 92) or the breaking of an oath (S. v, 89). The rules given for modest behaviour towards slaves in S. xxiv, 31 and 57 presuppose honorable and friendly relations between them and the other members of the Arabian household. Slave girls may not be compelled to prostitution (S. xxiv, 33). Manumission of slaves is recommended in S. xxiv, 33. An islamic novelty is that a pious slave is to be preferred in marriage to an infidel (S. ii, 220), though the general rule remains, that sexual intercourse with slave girls (*mā malakat aimānukum*) is allowed, with the exclusion of marriage (S. iv, 3, 25; xxiii, 6). S. xxiv, 32 includes slaves and slave girls in the general recommendation to contract marriages.

In the *Ḥadīth* collections the only chapters dealing especially with slavery are those on manumission and its consequences (*ʿitḳ* and *walāʾ*; *mukātab*). But incidentally the entire canonical tradition furnishes many proofs of the real importance of the institution of slavery for the private and public life of early Islām. The sayings of the Prophet insist on good treatment of slaves, who are the Muslims' brothers; he who beats a slave can only expect forgiveness if he sets him free. A special point is made of the punishment of slaves in different circumstances. The complications connected with the selling of slaves and their marriages foreshadow the more systematic treatment of these subjects in canonical law (cf. Wensinck, *Handbook*, s.v. *Slaves*, *Manumission*, etc.). In dealing with manumission many traditions refer to the case of the slave girl Barīra, whom ʿĀʾisha wanted to buy in order to set her free; her masters, however, would give their consent only on condition that her patronage (*walāʾ*) should remain with them. The Prophet opposed this condition by his saying: *innamā 'l-walāʾ liman aʿtaḳa*, and further prohibited generally the selling or the giving away of the patronage right. It is clear that the new Islamic attitude induced the Prophet on several occasions to take unwonted decisions. Once he received homage from a slave without knowing his true condition; after learning that he had had to do with a slave, he purchased him from his master and set him free.

c. *Legal position of slaves according to the terms of the canonical law. Concubinage and marriage.*

In the *fiḳh* literature, just as in the *ḥadīth*, the prescriptions concerning slaves are scattered over a variety of chapters. Modern hand-books have grouped together the chief features in one section (cf. Juynboll, *Handleiding*, p. 232 *sqq.*; Bergsträsser, *Grundzüge*, p. 38 *sqq.*; Santillana, *Istituzioni*, p. 111 *sqq.*).

Theoretically slaves have no legal rights whatever; according to Mohammedan law they are merely things, the property of their owner. The latter can alienate them as he likes, by sale, gift, dowry, or in other ways. In the eyes of the law they are incapable of making any enactment, can therefore neither alienate, nor undertake responsibilities, nor make wills, and therefore cannot be guardians or testamentary executors; what they earn belongs to their master. Neither can a slave appear as witness in a court of Justice. He can, however, at the order of his master (e.g. as shop-assistant) make contracts concerning property and accept liabilities (he is then *maʾdhūn lahu*, as he is styled in the Muslim law books).

Between slaves and their masters, according to the terms of the law, marriage is impossible and only concubinage is permitted, but in all other cases even for slaves marriage is recognized as legal. Slaves may marry with the consent of their masters. According to most jurisconsults, slaves may have only two wives (slaves or free women), but according to the Mālikites they may have four like free Mohammedans. The slave, like the freeman, is obliged to give a dowry and must work for it. The dowry due to female slaves, however, belongs to their owner, since a slave, as such, cannot acquire property. The slave may only repudiate his wife twice. The waiting term (*ʿidda*) for female slaves is the same as for free women with the following difference: if a female slave loses her husband by death, she must observe a waiting time of 2 months and 5 days only, and if she loses him through any other cause, it is of 2 *ḳurʾ* only, instead of 3 *ḳurʾ*.

The children of a married female slave belong to her master.

A freeman may also according to the law contract a marriage with the female slave of another master. The serious part of this is that the children of such marriages become the slaves of the mother's master. For this reason marriage between a freeman and female slave is, according to most jurisconsults, permissible only under the following conditions: 1) that he is not yet married; 2) that he does not possess the required dowry for a free woman; 3) that he may be exposed to the danger of unchastity if he remains a celibate; 4) that the female slave is a Mohammedan (comp. Ḳurʾān, iv. 25). Only the Ḥanafites permit such marriages also with a Jewish or Christian slave and do not insist on the 2ᵈ and 3ᵈ stipulations. That female slaves are married by freemen is "a case that happens more frequently than might be expected" (*Mekka*, ii. 136).

If a master by virtue of his right of ownership begets a child of his slave, the child belongs to its father's class and is therefore free. This principle was first laid down in Islām. Amongst the ancient Arabs the rule was *partus sequitur ventrem*. The best known case is probably that of the poet ʿAntara. In the earliest times of Islām, the true Arabian mind was shocked at the idea that slaves should bear "their own masters", i.e. free children, and that even caliphs could be descended from slaves (see J. Wellhausen, *Die Ehe bei den alten Arabern*, in *NGW Gött. Phil.-hist. Kl.*, 1893, p. 440; A von Kremer, *loc. cit.*, ii. 106; G. Jacob, *loc. cit.*, p. 213; *Aghānī*, vii. 149; comp. J. L. Burckhardt, *Notes on the Bedouins and Wahabys*, London, 1831, i. 182). The slave who has borne her master a child is called *umm walad* [q.v.], i.e. "mother of [his] child". On the death of her master she recovers her freedom. On this account a master can neither sell nor pawn his *umm walad*.

The master may have sexual relations only with his Mohammedan, Christian or Jewish slaves, not with unbelievers, and according to the Shāfiʿite school, the modern Christians and Jews are to be placed in the same category as other unbelievers, with whom concubinage is absolutely forbidden on account of the "forged" books of revelation.

Anybody who has obtained a female slave, by purchase or in any other way, may not cohabit with her before he has ascertained that she is not pregnant, so that no doubt shall arise concerning the paternity of the child. In Arabic this is called *istibrāʾ* (i.e. waiting or examination as to whether the uterus of the slave is free). To this end the law ordains a certain period of probation.

d. *Liberation* (*ʿitḳ*) *and patronage* (*walāʾ*).

The liberation of slaves is looked upon in Islām as a good work (*ḳurba*), and gives right to a reward in the other world. "He who sets free a Muslim slave, shall be freed from the fires of Hell", Muḥammad is said to have declared.

If a slave is the common property of several persons and one of the latter gives him his freedom, the slave becomes entirely free if his liberator is able to pay the co-owners the value of part due to them; otherwise the slave is only partly free. Such a slave is called *mubaʿʿaḍ*, literally "a divided one".

The *umm walad*, as already mentioned, becomes free on the death of her master. Anybody also who becomes the property of his nearest relative becomes *eo ipso* free. According to the Shāfiʿite school, only the direct relatives in descending or ascending line of the owner can become free in this way; according to the Mālikites, also his brothers and sisters, and according to the Ḥanafites, every person who stands in such blood-relationship to the owner that marriage between them would be illegal (i.e. every *dhu-'l-maḥram*).

If anyone says to his slave: "When I die you shall be free", this is called "*tadbīr*" liberation. According to most jurisconsults (Ḥanafites and Mālikites), the owner cannot recall the *tadbīr* and the slave (i.e. the *mudabbar*) is unalienable. According to the Shāfiʿites, the owner may cancel the *tadbīr* like any other testamentary disposition, e.g. by selling the *mudabbar*, the *tadbīr* being thereby annulled. In any case all are unanimous that on the death of the owner, the *tadbīr* is to be considered as a testamentary enactment.

The *kitāba* is a form of buying oneself free, which Islām has taken over from the old Arabian custom (comp. above the case of Djuwairīya and Ḳurʾān, xxiv. 33). It is a contractual liberation, and a *sine qua non* of it is that the slave pays his owner a certain equivalent for his freedom — according to the Shāfiʿite opinion, in at least 2 or 3 instalments. This contract cannot be cancelled by the owner (*mukātib*), but the slave (*mukātab*) alone can annul it if he wishes. The owner must allow the slave to obtain property, whilst the slave binds himself to pay the price agreed upon. The *mukātab* is inalienable.

It is praiseworthy to help the slave in his efforts to obtain freedom, and according to the Shāfiʿites, the owner should grant the *mukātab* a reduction on the purchase price of his freedom. A portion of the poor-rates (*zakāt*) is to be specially set aside for the *mukātab*. If a slave asks for the *kitāba*, it is praiseworthy of the owner to grant it, but not obligatory.

The slave is called *ḳinn*, if he or she is neither *mukātab*, nor *mudabbar*, nor *umm walad*, nor *mubaʿʿaḍ*, but entirely unfree.

A legal consequence of every liberation is the "clientship" or "patronage" (*walāʾ*). The freed slave is the client of the liberator; if he dies without heirs, his patron inherits his estate, or if the latter be dead, then the latter's male heirs (*ʿaṣabāt*) inherit him. On the death of the patron, his patronage is transferred to his *ʿaṣabāt*, and besides the right of inheritance it gives its holder certain other prerogatives. The patron is "bridal attorney" (*walī*) for the freed female slave, and he receives the blood-money if the freed slave is murdered etc.

II. IN THE RELIGIOUS SENSE.

The relation *ʿabd-rabb* is frequently met with in the Ḳurʾān as an image of the relation of man towards Allāh. Here the common Western Semitic meaning of *ʿabd*, "slave, worker" has been qualified by its opposition to *rabb* in the sense of "the Lord" (vide RABB). This use of *ʿabd* is already pre-islamic, as is attested by many proper names in pagan times, composed with *ʿabd* as their first member and the name of a deity as second member (cf. Wellhausen, *Reste arabischen Heidentums*, p. 1 sqq.). Also ʿAbd Allāh, one of the most frequent Islamic names, is pre-islamic. The composition of *ʿabd* (and also *ama*) with one of the many "beautiful names" of Allāh in Islamic times consequently reposes on ancient tradition, just as in the case of the Syriac Christian names composed with *ʿebed*. In the Ḳurʾān the plural *ʿibād* is reserved for the pious and believing; in Sūra xxv, 63 and xliii, 19 *ʿibād-al-Raḥmān* looks like a preamble to the later so frequently occurring name ʿAbd al-Raḥmān. The use of the verb *ʿabada* in the sense of "to worship" is essentially ḳurʾānic (cf. Sūra cix) and derived from the religious meaning of *ʿabd*.

In mystic terminology the term *ʿubūdīya*, as opposed to *rubūbīya*, denotes the condition of the devoted, self-containing, complacent Muslim (*Dict. of Techn. Terms*, p. 948); *ʿubūdīya* conveys the idea of a much more complete surrender to the Lord than the derivation *ʿibāda*, which, on the whole, is reserved for the performance of the duties prescribed in Muhammadan law (cf. ʿIBĀDĀT). The religious use of *ʿabd* is also at the base of the injunction, found in the ḥadīth, that a master should not say *ʿabdī*, but *fatāya* or *ghulāmī* (places in Wensinck, *Handbook*, p. 217).

ʿABD ALLĀH B. AL-ʿABBĀS, surnamed Abu 'l-ʿAbbās, cousin of the Prophet. His birth is said to have taken place when the Hāshimids were blocked in al-Shiʿb, a couple of years before Muḥammad's emigration to Madīna. According to al-Bukhārī, he and his mother had already been converted before his father al-ʿAbbās [see AL-ʿABBĀS B. ʿABD AL-MUṬṬALIB] accepted the Islāmic faith. He began to come into prominence under ʿUthmān. The caliph entrusted him with the leadership of the pilgrimage in the fateful year 35/655-6, and it was to this that he owed his fortunate absence from Madīna when the caliph was murdered. He then went over to ʿAlī, who frequently employed him as an ambassador and appointed him governor of Baṣra. When ʿAlī was obliged to accept arbitration at Ṣiffīn he wanted to make ʿAbd Allāh his representative, but his own followers refused to accept this arrangement. Nevertheless he accompanied Abū Mūsā, and was in Dūmat al-Djandal with him. When ʿAlī lost Egypt, he consoled him with words of friendship. A fact which is confirmed on all sides is that he took a large sum of money (some say 6 million dirhams) from the state treasury of Baṣra and then left the town. But, whereas several authorities, as for instance al-Madāʾinī, ʿUmar b. Shabba and Balādhurī, make this incident happen before the assassination of ʿAlī, others, as Abū ʿUbaida and al-Zuhrī, place it during al-Ḥasan's caliphate, and represent it as being much more reprehensible, since, according to their version, ʿAbd Allāh went over to Muʿāwiya, and got the latter to secure the stolen sum for him as a reward for his treachery. At the same time it is true that this perfidy is ascribed to ʿAbd Allāh's brother ʿUbaid Allāh by al-Madāʾinī, Balādhurī, and Yaʿḳūbī; yet it can hardly be doubted that this is a later distortion of the facts. The fact that after al-Ḥasan's abdication he recognized the rule of the godless Umaiyad could not be denied even by the ʿAbbāsid historians. Al-Madāʾinī makes him protest, in company with the four candidates for the caliphate, against Muʿāwiya's efforts to secure the sovereign authority for his son Yazīd, but this is certainly a merely harmless fiction. After Muʿāwiya's death he quietly did homage to Yazīd on perceiving that the latter had a majority on his side. He died in Ṭāʾif in the year 68/687-8, or, according to some, in the year 69 or 70.

ʿAbd Allāh does not owe his fame to his political activity, but to his greatly admired knowledge of profane and sacred tradition, of jurisprudence and exegesis of the Ḳurʾān. He is celebrated as the Doctor (Rabbi) of the Community (*ḥibr al-umma*), and is called "the sea". Tradition contains the most exaggerated accounts of his infallible scholarship and of the interest the Prophet took in this infant prodigy. He can not be held responsible, as earlier criticism often has done, for the many evidently forged traditions which go under his name.

Bibliography: al-Bukhārī (ed. Krehl), i. 339, 341; Ibn Saʿd, ii^b., 119—124; Ṭabarī, i. 3040, 3273, 3285 *sq.*, 3312, 3327, 3333, 3354, 3358 *sqq.*, 3412, 3414, 3453, 3455 *sq.*; ii. 2, 7, 176, 223; iii. 2335—2338; Masʿūdī, *Murūdj* iv. 353 *sq.*, 382; Yaʿḳūbī, ii. 204, 220, 221, 255; de Goeje, in *ZDMG* xxxviii, 392 *sq.*; Wellhausen, *Das arab. Reich und sein Sturz*, p. 69 *sq.*; do., *Reste arabischen Heidentums*, 2nd ed., p. 14; Ibn Ḥadjar, *Iṣāba*, ii. 802—813; Nawawī, p. 351—354; Sprenger, *Das Leben und die Lehre des Moḥammad*, iii. cvi—cxv; Caetani, *Annali dell' Islām*, i. 47—51. — For the commentary to the Ḳurʾān ascribed to ʿAbd Allāh, see Brockelmann, *GAL*, *Suppl.* i. 331; Goldziher, *Richtungen der islamischen Koranauslegung*, 65—74.

ʿABD ALLĀH B. IBĀḌ (ABĀḌ) AL-MURRĪ AL-TAMĪMĪ. [See IBĀḌITES.]

ʿABD ALLĀH B. MAIMŪN, according to historical sources not older than the IV/X^th century, a Shīʿite sectarian propagandist. He instigated and organized the Ismāʿīlī movement, the first outbreak of which was the rebellion of the Ḳarmaṭians and afterwards the rise of the Fāṭimid power. The gist of the many versions of his career is that he came from al-Ahwāz, where his father Maimūn practised as an oculist (*ḳaddāḥ*). Under various influences, of which are named the Bardesanians and the Khaṭṭābites, he evolved a religious system of his own and founded, by means of esoteric propaganda by secret missionaries, a religious-political party, which was to follow one of the ʿAlids. After having worked in ʿAskar Mukram and Baṣra he went to Salamīya in Syria, where his death is calculated to have occurred towards 261/875. His real ambition would have been to put himself in the place of the ʿAlid and there was a general belief that he was the real progenitor of the Fāṭimid dynasty, who indeed came from Salamīya.

Recent researches by W. Ivanow have made it highly probable that the career of this personage is nothing but a myth, which originated from false identifications and more or less conscious falsifications in Sunnite and non-Ismāʿīlite Shīʿite circles. The most ancient source for it is Ibn al-Razzām, who is the authority for the version given in the *Fihrist* and who lived in the first half of the IV/Xth century. It appears from Shīʿite *ḥadīth*-collections, notably al-Kulīnī's *Kāfī*, that Maimūn and his son ʿAbd Allāh were faithful retainers of the imām Muḥammad al-Bāḳir and his son Djaʿfar al-Ṣādiḳ and that they were authorities for many sayings of the latter. They are said to have been maulā's of the Banū Makhzūm. ʿAbd Allāh was a contemporary of Djaʿfar and may have died about 165/780. The surname Ḳaddāḥ can better be explained as a maker or a man in charge of bowls (*ḳadaḥ*) or perhaps as a parer of arrow-rods (cf. Ṭūsī, *List of Shīʿa books*, no. 425). The connection of Maimūn and his son with a religious movement may have been brought about by the existence of a sect called Maimūnīya, called so after Maimūn, surname of Muḥammad, son of Djaʿfar's son Ismāʿīl; this Muḥammad's son was also called ʿAbd Allāh. Their relation with the Khaṭṭābīya [q.v.] could be a result of the modelling of the myth of Ibn al-Ḳaddāḥ on the story of Abu'l-Khaṭṭāb himself, who had had friendly relations with the imām Djaʿfar, but was afterwards repudiated by him on account of his dangerous fanaticism, abhorred by "orthodox" Shīʿites and Sunnites alike. That ʿAbd Allāh was made a Bardesanian seems to be due to a misunderstanding caused by a wrong identification with a certain Bardesanian (so much as heretic or dualist), called ʿAbd Allāh, who is mentioned in early tradition as an opponent of the imām Djaʿfar. Finally certain details given in ʿAbd Allāh's career may be explained by the activity of the descendents of Ismāʿīl, the seventh imām of the Ismāʿīlites.

These results have left the origin of Ismāʿīlism and the Ḳarmaṭian and Fāṭimid movements much more in the dark than was assumed before. The descent of the Fāṭimids from ʿAbd Allāh b. Maimūn can in no way be maintained. See also ISMĀʿĪLĪYA.

Bibliography: W. Ivanow, *The alleged Founder of Ismailism*, Bombay 1946; *Fihrist*, ed. Flügel, p. 186 *sqq.*; Niẓām al-Mulk, *Siyāsat-Nāme*, p. 184; Maḳrīzī, *Khiṭaṭ*, i. 391 *sqq.*; Ibn al-Athīr, (ed. Tornberg), viii. 21 *qqs.*; de Sacy, *Exposé de la religion des Druses*, Préface; de Goeje, *Mémoire sur les Carmathes du Bahrain et les Fatimites*, Leiden 1880; B. Lewis, *The origins of Ismaʿilism*, Cambridge 1940.

ʿABD ALLĀH B. MASʿŪD. [See IBN MASʿŪD].

ʿABD ALLĀH B. ʿUMAR B. AL-KHAṬṬĀB, eldest son of the caliph ʿUmar I, and one of the most respected of all Muḥammad's companions, generally called Ibn ʿUmar. ʿAbd Allāh was born several years before the Hidjra, his mother's name being Zainab bint Maẓʿūn. He became a convert to Islām in his boyhood at the same time as his father. At the battles of Badr and Uḥud he was kept in the background by Muḥammad, because he was still too young, but he took part in the campaign of the Ditch and fought in all the battles of the Prophet. Subsequently also his name is often mentioned in connection with military expeditions. First of all he followed Khālid b. al-Walīd in the latter's expedition against the rebellious tribes in the interior of Arabia, then he took part in the battle of Nihāwand, the date of which is usually given as 21/642. He was further amongst the Madīnian reinforcements, which ʿUthmān sent to ʿAbd Allāh b. Saʿd b. Abī Sarḥ, his governor in Egypt, to subjugate the rest of North Africa, and soon afterwards — in the year 30/650-1 — he marched to Ṭabaristān under the command of Saʿīd b. al-ʿĀṣ. Again in the year 49/669 Ibn ʿUmar took part in an expedition against the Byzantines, which was led by Yazīd b. Muʿāwiya. As to home politics, ʿAbd Allāh took up a strictly neutral position amongst the different parties which fought for supremacy. When ʿUmar on his death-bed appointed six trustworthy men to elect a new ruler, he nominated his son ʿAbd Allāh as consultative member. In the year 38/658-9 the latter was present at the court of arbitration that was appointed to settle the dispute between ʿAlī and Muʿāwiya, without, however, himself making any claim to the caliphate. He was indeed one of the candidates proposed by Abū Mūsā al-Ashʿarī, but was not considered suitable. After ʿUthmān's death, ʿAlī had required Ibn ʿUmar to do homage to him, a thing the latter energetically refused to do, declaring he would only pay homage to him when all Muslims did so. Later on Muʿāwiya received the same answer when he demanded homage for his son Yazīd. When, however, the latter ascended the throne, Ibn ʿUmar made no difficulties, but at once took the oath of allegiance. ʿAbd Allāh b. ʿUmar was personally a religious man, who was everywhere held in great esteem on account of his noble and unselfish character. He is moreover esteemed as one of the most trustworthy authorities on the earliest history of Islām. His traditions were handed down to posterity by his sons and other disciples. ʿAbd Allāh b. ʿUmar died at Mecca in the year 73 (beginning of 693) or 74 after the pilgrimage, at the age of 84 according to general report.

Bibliography: Ibn Saʿd, iii. 1st part, introduction; iv. 1, 105 *sqq.*; Ṭabarī, i. 1358 *sqq.*; Nawawī, p. 357 *sqq.*; Muir, *The Caliphate, its Rise, Decline and Fall* (new ed. of Weir); Wellhausen, *Muhammed in Medina*; Balādhurī; Masʿūdī, *Murūdj*, iv; Lammens, *Etudes sur le règne du calife omaiyade Moʿâwia Ier* (*MFOB* 1908); further bibliography by Caetani and Gabrieli, *Onomasticon Arabicum*, ii. 986.

ʿABD ALLĀH B. WAHB AL-RĀSIBĪ, a Khāridjite, bore the surname of the "Man with the callosities" (*dhu 'l-thafināt*), because he had received callosities from his many prostrations. ʿAbd Allāh belonged to the prominent men amongst the first Khāridjites, so that he was chosen to be imām by his followers, when they had separated from ʿAlī (37/658). He fell in the same year in the bloody battle of Nahrawān.

Bibliography: Mubarrad, *Kāmil*, p. 558 *sqq.*; Ṭabarī, i. 3363 *sqq.*; Dīnawarī (ed. Girgas and Rosen), p. 215 *sqq.*; Brünnow, *Die Charidschiten*, p. 18 *sqq.*; Wellhausen, *Die religiös-politischen Oppositionsparteien*, p. 17 *sqq.*

ʿABD AL-ḲĀDIR AL-DJĪLĪ (GĪLĀNĪ) MUḤYI 'L-DĪN ABŪ MUḤAMMAD B. ABĪ ṢĀLIḤ ZENGI DŌST, preacher and Ṣūfī, after whom the Ḳādirī order is named, born in 470/1077–8, died in 561/1166. The numerous biographies of this personage teem with fictions, out of which some history may be gleaned. Thus his pedigree is traced on the father's side to al-Ḥasan, grandson of the Prophet, in the direct line. But this is contradicted by the foreign name of his father, and the fact that the shaikh was called ʿAdjamī (foreigner) in Baghdād, and indeed the pedigree was shown to be a fabrication of his grandson, the ḳādī Abū Ṣāliḥ Naṣr, to whom some more fictions may be traced. His mother is said to have been Fāṭima daughter of ʿAbd Allāh al-Ṣawmaʿī, both, we are told, saints; and the name of the village where he was born is given as Nīf or Naif, in the district of Gīlān, south of the Caspian. He was sent to Baghdād at the age of eighteen to study, and was there at first supported by his mother. He attended the philological classes of Tibrīzī (d. 502/1109), and learned Ḥanbalite (and according to some, Shāfiʿite) law from a number of shaikhs: in his works he usually quotes traditions from Hibat Allāh al-Mubārak and Abū Naṣr Muḥammad b. al-Bannāʾ. Little is known of his life between 488/1095 and 521/1127, except that he appears to have gone on pilgrimage during that period, and that he also married, since of his forty-nine children one was born in 508/1114-5. According to some authorities, he was guardian of the tomb of Abū Ḥanīfa. He learned Ṣūfism from Abu 'l-Khair Muḥammad b. Muslim al-Dabbās (d. 525/1131), a saint of sufficient eminence to be included in Shaʿrānī's list, by whose gaze he was converted on the occasion of a visit when one or other of them had caught a falcon (in consequence whereof ʿAbd al-Ḳādir was surnamed al-Bāzi 'l-Ashhab, according to Damīrī). Training by al-Dabbās involved considerable hardship, and it would seem that the other Ṣūfī aspirants resented the intrusion of a jurist amongst them. After a time, ʿAbd al-Ḳādir was considered worthy to receive the Ṣūfī livery called *khirḳa*, which was given him by the ḳādī Abū Saʿd Mubārak al-Mukharrimī, the head of a school of Ḥanbalite law near the Bāb al-Azadj in Baghdād, which ʿAbd al-Ḳādir appears to have attended. In 521/1127, on the advice of the Ṣūfī Yūsuf al-Hamadhāni (440—435/1048—1140), he began to preach in public, at first to a small audience, which gradually increased, till he took a chair in the oratory at the Ḥalba gate of Baghdād, and owing to the constant increase of his hearers, he found it necessary to go outside the gate. There a *ribāṭ* was built for him; and in 528/1133-4, by public subscription the school of Mubārak al-Mukharrimī (probably then dead or retired) was enlarged by taking in the space occupied by the neighbouring buildings, and ʿAbd al-Ḳādir was installed as its head. The nature of his courses was probably similar to those of Djamāl al-Dīn al-Djawzī which are so vividly described by Ibn Djubair. On Friday mornings and Monday evenings ʿAbd al-Ḳādir preached in his school, on Sunday mornings in his monastery. Of his numerous pupils many were afterwards famous as saints, while some (like the biographer Samʿānī) acquired distinction of another sort. His sermons are said to have effected the conversion of many Jews and Christians to Islām, as well as of many Muslims to the higher life. Presents, often in the form of vows, were sent him from the numerous regions whither his fame penetrated: one day's such receipts often amounted to more than one dīnār. These enabled him to keep open house for aspirants. Legal questions were addressed to him from all parts, and these he is said to have answered impromptu. Caliphs and viziers are supposed to have figured among his clients.

ʿAbd al-Ḳādir's works are all religious in character, and largely consist of reports of his sermons or addresses; the following are known: 1) *al-Ghunya li-ṭālibī ṭarīḳ al-ḥaḳḳ*, a ritual and ethical treatise (Cairo 1288). 2) *al-Fatḥ al-rabbānī*, 62 sermons preached in the years 545—546/1150—1152 with appendix (Cairo 1302). MSS. sometimes bear the title *Sittīn madjālis*. 3) *Futūḥ al-ghaib*, 78 sermons on various subjects, compiled by the shaikh's son ʿAbd al-Razzāḳ, followed by his dying injunctions, his pedigree on the father's and mother's side, proof of his connection with Abū Bakr and ʿUmar, his creed, and some of his poems, (on the margin of al-Shaṭṭanawfī's *Bahdjat al-asrār*, Cairo 1304). 4) *Ḥizb bashāʾir al-khairāt*, mystical prayer (Alexandria 1304). 5) *Djalāʾ al-khāṭir* (mentioned by Ḥādjdjī Khalīfa), a collection of sermons of which the first bears the same date as the 59th and the last the same as the 57th of No. 2; perhaps it is another title for the same work. 6) *al-Mawāhib al-raḥmānīya wa'l-futūḥ al-rabbānīya fī marātib al-akhlāḳ al-sanīya wa'l-maḳāmāt al-ʿirfānīya* quoted in *Rawḍāt al-djannāt*, p. 441; possibly identical with 2 or 3. 7) *Yawāḳīt al-ḥikam* (mentioned by Ḥādjdjī Khalīfa). 8) *al-Fuyūḍāt al-rabbānīya fi'l-awrād al-ḳādirīya*, collection of prayers (Cairo 1303). 9) Sermons included in the *Bahdjat al-asrār* and other biographical works (MS. 622 in the India Office Catalogue is an imperfect copy of this work, and Persian writers speak of them generally as *Malfūẓāt-i ḳādirī*).

In these works ʿAbd al-Ḳādir figures as a capable theologian, and an earnest, sincere, and eloquent preacher. Many a sermon is introduced into his *Ghunya*, which also contains an account of the 73 Islāmic sects, grouped in ten divisions. He occasionally refers to the grammarians, such as Mubarrad, more frequently to the old commentators on the Ḳurʾān and the Ṣūfī saints. His doctrine in this work is strictly orthodox, and the tone uniformly sober: there are however some mystic interpretations of the Ḳurʾān, and the practice of repeating certain formulae fifty or a hundred times is recommended. The sermons included in No. 2 are some of the very best in Muslim literature: the spirit which they breathe is one of charity and philanthropy: the preacher would like "to close the gates of Hell and open those of Paradise to all mankind". He employs Ṣūfī technicalities very rarely, and none that would occasion the ordinary hearer much difficulty, though one visitor to his courses declared that he could not understand a word. The general theme of the sermons is the necessity of a period of asceticism during which the aspirant can wean himself from the world, after which he may return and enjoy his portion while converting others. The Ṣūfī doctrine that everything, whether it be the prizes of this world or the next, is a veil between the aspirant and the Deity, and that the aspirant's thoughts should be directed to the Deity only, is also a leading topic. The hearers are urgently advised to bestow their good on the saints even to the exclusion of their own families. The preacher says little about himself, and that in no very arrogant strain; where he calls himself "the touchstone of the people of the earth", the meaning is only that he can easily discern the serious from the triflers among his audience. On the other hand he emphatically claims to speak only after divine authorization.

The accounts of ʿAbd al-Ḳādir by his disciples ʿAbd Allāh b. Muḥammad al-Baghdādī, ʿAbd al-Muḥsin al-Baṣrī, and ʿAbd Allāh b. Naṣr al-Ṣiddīḳī (called *Anwār al-nāẓir*, quoted in *Bahdjat al-asrār*, p. 109) are not at present accessible: in the dictionary of Samʿānī the name of the shaikh is mentioned s.v. Djīl, with an empty space left after it. An account of the shaikh by Samʿānī's son is preserved, which is respectful, but not enthusiastic; in another by Muwaffaḳ al-Dīn ʿAbd Allāh al-Maḳdisī, who was with him the last fifty days of his life, we are told that he was highly respected by the people of Baghdād, and miracles were attributed to him, but the narrator had himself seen none. He and another were at the time the shaikh's only pupils. His contemporary Abu 'l-Faradj b. al-Djawzī speaks of his success as a preacher, many of his hearers dying of emotion; this writer's grandson in *Mirʾāt al-zamān* records some miracles which the shaikh performed. In the works of Ibn ʿArabī (born 560/1165), ʿAbd al-Ḳādir is mentioned as a just man, the *ḳuṭb* of his time (*al-Futūḥāt al-Makkīya*, i. 262), "the ruler in this path, the authoritative judge of the men" (*ib.*, ii. 24), "one of the Malāmatīya" (iii. 44); he is also quoted for the statement that ʿAbd al-Ḳādir praised God in the womb, and that he had a rank which placed him over all beings save God. The *Bahdjat al-asrār*, by an author who died in 713/1314, contains the narrative of many miracles performed by the shaikh, and authenticated by chains of witnesses: whence Ibn Taimīya (d. 728/1328) declared that they satisfied the requirements of credibility, though others were less credulous: the book is, e.g., condemned by Dhahabī as containing frivolous tales, whereas Ibn al-Wardī (*Taʾrīkh*, ii. 70, 71) copies it. Much more offence was given by the arrogant claims put in the shaikh's mouth: thus the *Bahdjat al-asrār* begins with a list of persons who heard him say "My foot is on the neck of every saint", and he is similarly made out to have claimed the possession of seventy gates of knowledge, each one of them broader than the distance between heaven and earth, etc. Late followers of ʿAbd al-Ḳādir (such as the author of the Persian treatise *Makhāzin al-ḳādirīya*, MS. Brit. Mus., Or. 248), while endeavouring to restrict the universality of the first of these sayings, try to show that ʿAbd al-Ḳādir was justified in uttering it; and pious writers (such as Damīrī, i. 320) only find in it evidence of ʿAbd al-Ḳādir's dignity. Sayings of this sort do not seem to be found in the genuine works of the shaikh (though there are parallels to them in the poems ascribed to him), and are probably due to the enthusiasm of his followers. With them his fame has in some places nearly displaced that of the Prophet Muḥammad, and he is regularly styled the Sulṭān of the Saints, nor is his name ever uttered without one of the following epithets: *Mushāhid Allāh, Amr Allāh, Faḍl Allāh, Amān Allāh, Nūr Allāh, Ḳuṭb Allāh, Saif Allāh, Firmān Allāh, Burhān Allāh, Āyat Allāh, Ghawth Allāh, al-Ḳaws al-aʿẓam* [see ḲĀDIRĪYA]. The growth of the legend was probably aided by his many sons, of whom eleven are mentioned in the *Bahdjat al-asrār* as following in their father's steps: ʿĪsā (d. 573/1177-8 in Egypt), ʿAbd Allāh (d. 589/1193 in Baghdād), Ibrāhīm (d. 592/1196 in Wāsiṭ), ʿAbd al-Wahhāb (d. 593/1197 in Baghdād), Yahyā and Muḥammad (d. 600/1204 in Baghdād), ʿAbd al-Razzāḳ (d. 603/1207 in Baghdād), Mūsā (d. 618/1221 in Damascus), ʿAbd al-ʿAzīz (migrated to Djiyāl, a village of Sindjār, d. 602/1205-6), ʿAbd al-Raḥmān (d. 587/1191), and ʿAbd al-Djabbār (d. 575/1179-80). Some authorities add a few more names. Of these ʿAbd al-Wahhāb inherited his father's school, in which he was succeeded by his son ʿAbd al-Salām (548—611/1153—1215), who was followed by his cousin Abū Ṣāliḥ Naṣr, son of ʿAbd al-Razzāḳ (564—633/1168—1236). During the reign of Nāṣir the family of ʿAbd al-Ḳādir were temporarily exiled from Baghdād, according to Sibṭ b. al-Djawzī at the demand of Abū Yūnus, vizier of Nāṣir. Some of them perishedwhen Baghdād was taken by the Mongols, but the headquarters of the society (except for the brief interval mentioned) have always been in that city.

Bibliography: A list of biographies of ʿAbd al-Ḳādir is given by Ahlwardt, *Verz. der arab. Handschr.*, Nos. 10072—92; of these the following have been published: al-Shaṭṭanawfī, *Bahdjat al-asrār* (Cairo 1304); Muḥammad b. Yaḥya 'l-Tādafī, *Ḳalāʾid al-djawāhir* (Cairo 1303); Muḥammad al-Dilāʾī, *Natīdjat al-taḥḳīḳ* (Fās 1309), translated by Weir, in *JRAS*, 1903. Further, *Ghibṭat al-nāẓir*, ascribed to Ibn Ḥadjar (not in Ahlwardt's list), edited by E. D. Ross (Calcutta 1903). Probably the best extant biography is that in Dhahabī's *Taʾrīkh al-Islām*, largely based on Ibn al-Nadjdjār (published in *JRAS*, 1907, p. 267 *sq.*). Shaikh Sanūsī is said to have recently written the biography of ʿAbd al-Ḳādir. Modern European writers dealing with ʿAbd al-Ḳādir and the Ḳādirīs are: L. Rinn, *Marabouts et Khouan* (Paris 1884); A. Le Chatelier, *Confréries Musulmanes du Hedjaz* (Paris 1887); Depont et Coppolani, *Confréries religieuses musulmanes* (Algiers 1897); Carra de Vaux, *Gazali* (Paris 1902); W. Braune, *Die Futūḥ al-Gaib des ʿAbd al-Qādir*, Berlin 1933; M. A. Aïni, *Un grand saint de l'Islam, Abd al-Kadir Guilani*, Paris 1938; G.W.J. Drewes and Poerbatjaraka, *De mirakelen van Abdoelkadir Djaelani*, Bandoeng 1938; Brockelmann, *GAL* ², i. 560 *sqq.*; *Suppl.* i. 777 *sqq.*

ʿABD AL-ḲĀHIR AL-BAGHDĀDĪ. [See AL-BAGHDĀDĪ.]

ʿABD AL-KARĪM B. IBRĀHĪM AL-DJĪLĪ, celebrated Muslim mystic from Djīl in the district of Baghdād, born about 767/1365-6; the date of his death is uncertain (811—820/1408—1417). No exact data concerning his life have been handed down to us; in his works he mentions as his shaikh Sharaf al-Dīn Ismāʿīl b. Ibrāhīm al-Djabartī, with whom he lived in Zabīd; at the same time he gives the following dates: 796/1393-4, 799/1396-7, 805/1402-3. ʿAbd al-Karīm followed the mystic ideas of Muḥyī 'l-Dīn b. ʿArabī [see IBN AL-ʿARABĪ], whose works he commented, but whom he now and then contradicts in some details. Of his numerous works (see list in Brockelmann, *GAL* ², ii. 264) his *al-Insān al-kāmil fī maʿrifat al-awākhir wa 'l-awāʾil* has been printed. He himself borrowed from Ibn ʿArabī the idea and the name of the "perfect man", who as a microcosmos of a higher order reflected not only the powers of nature but also the divine powers "as in a mirror" (cf. the γενικὸς ἄνθρωπος of Philo); he endeavours (in the 60ᵗʰ chapter) to allegorize Muḥammad as such an ideal man. The souls of the remainder of humanity possess the divine powers, as ʿAbd al-Karīm is fond of putting it, only as "a copy" (*nuskha*). ʿAbd al-Karīm often interweaves mystic fictions into the presentation of his theories; in the introduction he has incorporated a *maḳāma*. His work has had great influence in the moulding of religious ideas in the greater part of the Islamic world and especially in Indonesia [cf. AL-INSĀN AL-KĀMIL].

Bibliography: Brockelmann, *GAL* ², ii. 264; *Suppl.* ii, 283 *sq.*; al-Djīlī, *al-Insān al-kāmil*, ii. 46; Ḥādjdjī Khalīfa (ed. Flügel), No. 10989; *India Office Cat.*, No. 666; Vollers, *Leipz. Katal.*, p. 69; Schreiner, in *ZDMG*, lii, 520; C. Snouck Hurgronje, *Verspr. Geschr. IV*, ii, 107; R. A. Nicholson, *Studies in Islamic Mysticism*, Cambridge 1921, p. 77—142.

ʿABD AL-MUṬṬALIB B. HĀSHIM, the Prophet's grandfather. The only tradition concerning him which is perhaps of historical value is that which relates how he looked after his grandson after the death of his son ʿAbd Allāh.

All other stories about him are Meccan or Madīnian fictions. His real name is said to have been Shaiba. It is told of his mother Salma, who belonged to the Banu 'l-Nadjdjār in Madīna, that she had stipulated with his father Hāshim that she should give birth to her child in Madīna. Hāshim died shortly after while travelling, and Shaiba grew up in Madīna till he was recognized by the family and brought to Mecca by his uncle al-Muṭṭalib, whence he received the name ʿAbd al-Muṭṭalib, i.e. Muṭṭalib's servant. Another uncle of Shaiba's, Nawfal, wished to withhold his inheritance from him, but was compelled by Shaiba's relatives on his mother's side to give it up. Advised by a vision, he excavated the choked up Zamzam spring and, in spite of the opposition of the Ḳuraishites, was able to make good his ownership. He consequently possessed the privilege of giving drink to the pilgrims (cf. also the art. SHAIBA). In the Abraha legend he is the Shaikh of the Ḳuraishites and as their ambassador was treated with great respect by Abraha. Still more exaggerated legends about him are to be found in Yaʿḳūbī (ed. Houtsma, ii. 8 *sq.*); he has even become a religious reformer who introduces many customs afterwards confirmed by the Ḳurʾān and Ḥadīth. — Abu 'l-Ḥārith is given as his *kunya*. Remarkably enough al-Masʿūdī in the *Murūdj* (ed. Paris, iv. 121) gives amongst the Meccan tribes the Banu 'l-Ḥārith b. ʿAbd al-Muṭṭalib as being subordinate to the Banū Hāshim and the Banu 'l-Muṭṭalib, whilst they, being according to the common genealogy a branch of the Hāshimids, are coordinate with the Banū 'l-Muṭṭalib. Sprenger has on this account set it down as questionable whether ʿAbd al-Muṭṭalib is not possibly a mythical personage. The second part of the name without doubt designates an old Arabian divinity.

Bibliography: Ṭabarī, i. 937 *sqq.*, 980, 1082 *sqq.*, 1087 *sq.*; Ibn Hishām, i. 33 *sqq.*, 71, 91 *sq.*, 107 *sq.*; Ibn Saʿd, i[a]. 48 *sqq.*; Sprenger, *Das Leben und die Lehre des Moḥammad*, iii., p. cxliv.; Wüstenfeld, in *ZDMG*, vii. 30—35; Caussin de Perceval, *Essai sur l'histoire des Arabes avant l'islamisme*, i. 259; Muir, *The Life of Mahomet* (1st ed.), i., p. ccli. *sqq.*; Caetani, *Annali dell' Islām*, i. 110—120; Buhl, *Das Leben Muhammeds*, p. 113 *sqq.*

ABDĀL. [See BADAL.]

ʿABDUH. [See MUḤAMMAD ʿABDUH.]

ABEL. [See HĀBĪL.]

ABRAHAM. [See IBRĀHĪM.]

ABŪ BAKR ʿABD ALLĀH, with the surname of ʿATĪK, variously interpreted by tradition, the first caliph. It is not related why he was given the surname of Abū Bakr (i.e. "father of the camel's foal"), which his enemies mockingly twisted into Abū Faṣīl "father of the weaned young of a camel"). His father ʿUthmān, also called Abū Ḳuḥāfa, and his mother Umm al-Khair Salmā bint Ṣakhr both belonged to the Meccan family of Kaʿb b. Saʿd b. Taim b. Murra. According to the current account, Abū Bakr was three years younger than Muḥammad. He lived as a well-to-do merchant in Mecca. He belongs to Muḥammad's oldest supporters, even though it remains doubtful whether he was the first male believer, as many maintain. He soon took an important position in the newly formed community. Especially characteristic of him was the unshakable, blind faith with which he considered Muḥammad as the chosen instrument of divine revelation. On occasions when others doubted, e.g. after the Prophet's account of his journey at night, or when they did not know what to make of his conduct, as on the occasion of the Ḥudaibiya covenant, he remained unshaken. It is this faithfulness which, according to Ibn Isḥāḳ, gained him the surname of *al-Ṣiddīḳ* [q.v.], which has constantly remained attached to him throughout the historical tradition of Islam. His was a gentle character. During the reading of the Ḳurʾān he shed tears and as his daughter related, he wept with joy at the news that he might accompany Muḥammad in his emigration. At the same time he was of an open, right-thinking nature and was several times able to restrain Muḥammad from rash actions by his sensible advice. He was very susceptible to the purely moral thoughts in the Prophet's preaching, proving this by purchasing the freedom of several slaves and by other similar actions. If, after the impressive conduct of the Jew al-Zabīr, he really uttered the bigoted words: "He will meet his beloved ones again in Hell!", it must be explained by his complete absorption in the religious ideas with which his friend inspired him. No sacrifice was too great in his eyes for the sake of the new faith. Thus it came about that of his considerable fortune, estimated at 40,000 dirhams, he brought to Madīna the small sum of 5,000 dirhams. Amidst the greatest dangers he faithfully stood by his friend and master, and was among the few who during the worst period did not flee to Abyssinia. But once, during the exclusion of the Hāshimids from the Meccan community, he is said to have lost his courage. He therefore quitted Mecca, but soon returned under the protection of an influential Meccan, and from that time forward remained in the city although his protector left him in the lurch. His life attained its apogee when Muḥammad chose him to accompany him when he emigrated from Mecca, and his self-sacrificing friendship was rewarded by his name being immortalized in the Ḳurʾān as "the second of the two" (S. ix. 40). His family also went to Madīna with the exception of his son ʿAbd al-Raḥmān, who had remained a heathen and fought at Badr against the faithful, till he too finally was converted and migrated to Madīna. In this new home Abū Bakr set up a modest household in the suburb of al-Sunḥ. Through his daughter ʿĀʾisha, whom Muḥammad had married shortly after the emigration and greatly loved, the tie between the two men was strengthened still more. Abū Bakr was nearly always with the Prophet and accompanied him on all his campaigns. On the other hand he was very seldom employed as a leader of military enterprises; e.g. in the Tabūk campaign he was entrusted with a standard. But the Prophet sent him in the year 9/631 to Mecca to conduct the pilgrimage, and it is quite possible that it was he and not ʿAlī, as traditions maintain, who on this occasion read out the act of separation to the heathens. When Muḥammad fell ill, Abū Bakr had to conduct the *ṣalāt* in the mosque to the Muslims in his stead. This distinction made it possible for ʿUmar and his friends, after Muḥammad's death on the 8th June 632, to propose Abū Bakr as the head of the community, thus preventing the threatened split. In no way did Abū Bakr represent new ideas or principles. In this manner he was able, in spite of all mutual antipathies, to hold together the talented men who had gathered round Muḥammad. Through his absolute lack of originality and his simple but sturdy character he became a reincarnation of Muḥammad, conducted the young religious community through the most difficult and dangerous times, and left it at his death in such a firm position that it could support the rule of the powerful and talented ʿUmar. He gave a proof of his scrupulous obedience to Muḥammad's orders first after the latter's death, by sending, in spite of the threatening state of affairs in Arabia, the young Usāma with an army on a quite unimportant expedition to the country east of the Jordan. Meanwhile the tribes in the country round about began to rise up against the political centralization in Madīna. Abū Bakr indignantly rejected the demand for the remission of the taxes. When Usāma's army had returned home, he marched out against Dhu'l-Ḳaṣṣa and was lucky enough to choose the talented general Khālid b. al-Walīd as commander of his forces. This latter defeated the Asad and Fazāra at al-Buzākha, subjugated the Tamīm and finally, after the bloody battle at Aḳrabāʾ in the Garden of Death, brought the Banū Ḥanīfa under the power of Islām, a thing that even Muḥammad had not succeeded in doing. His fortune in war made it possible for other generals to suppress the revolts in Baḥrain and ʿUmān, and finally also Yemen and Ḥaḍramawt were again brought under the dominion of Madīna by ʿIkrima and al-Muhādjir. Following his master's example,

Abū Bakr treated the vanquished mercifully and probably thus helped to re-establish peace in the country; cruelties, as for instance on some women who had sung parodies on Muḥammad's death, or the burning of al-Fudjā'a, but seldom occurred. After the subjugation of Arabia, which was complete in less than a year, he sent Khālid and other tried generals on a campaign of conquest against Persia und Byzantium. It can safely be assumed that the energetic men who were behind him originated this idea in order, by means of a campaign made in common and promising rich booty, to put an end to home troubles and to teach the Arabs in a practical manner the unity of Islām. Abū Bakr had the satisfaction of seeing during his short rule the first great victories of the Arabian army on both theatres of war: in Persia the conquest of al-Ḥīra in May or June 633, and in Palestine the battle of Adjnādain in July 634. Shortly after this latter success he died on the 22nd Djumādā II 13/23rd August 634, and was buried beside Muḥammad. In order to mark him out as a martyr, a tradition makes him die of poisoned food. His short reign, which was mostly taken up in wars, did not bring about any epoch-making changes in ordinary life. On his share in the first compilation of the Ḳur'ān, see AL-ḲUR'ĀN. As to the division of the spoils of war, he kept to the dictum of the Ḳur'ān, that all true believers had equal rights, a principle which ʿUmar later abandoned. As caliph he lived as simply as before, at first in his house in al-Sunḥ and subsequently, when the distance became inconvenient, in the town itself. Tradition relates many anecdotes of his modesty and his aversion to enrich himself at the expense of the State. It also gives a good description of his appearance: a lean, somewhat bent form, with ungraceful, loosely hanging clothes; a narrow face with a high forehead and sunken eyes; hair prematurely grey and beard dyed red with ḥinnā'; thin hands with knotted, swollen veins. The impression which his character made can be seen from several of the speeches attributed to him, which he delivered on different occasions (see Ibn Hishām, ed. Wüstenfeld, p. 1017; Ṭabarī, i. 1845 *sq.*; Mubarrad, *Kāmil*, p. 5 *sq.*).

Bibliography: Ibn Hishām, p. 245 *sq.*, 264, 692, 919 *sqq.*; Ibn Saʿd, iiia. 119—152, 202, 208; Ṭabarī, i. 1165 *sq.*, 1496, 1827, 1886, 1890, 2127 *sq.*; Ibn Ḥadjar, *Iṣāba*, ii. 828—835, 839; Nawawī, p. 656-669; Balādhurī, p. 96, 98, 102, 450; Masʿūdī, *Murūdj*, iv. 173—190; Nöldeke-Schwally, *Gesch. d. Qorâns*, ii, 81 *sqq.*; Nöldeke, in *ZDMG*, lii. 19 sq.; Sachau, in *Sb. Pr. Ak. Wiss.*, 1903, i. 16—37; Caetani, *Annali*, III 1,81—119; F. Buhl, *Das Leben Muhammeds*, p. 150 *sq.*, 337 *sq.*

ABŪ DJAHL, properly Abu 'l-Hakam ʿAmr b. Hishām b. al-Mughīra, also named Ibn al-Ḥanẓalīya after his mother, an influential Meccan of the illustrious Ḳuraishite family of Makhzūm. According to one anecdote he was of about the same age as the Prophet. The traditions concerning him possess but little historical value; in any case it is evident from them that he was one of Muḥammad's most embittered opponents amongst the aristocrats of Mecca. He persecuted the Prophet himself with his abuse and was only prevented by miraculous visions from doing him bodily harm. Some commentators connect this, though wrongly, with Ḳur'ān, xcvi. 6 *sq.*, whereas Ḳur'ān, xvii. 60 and xliv. 43 are said to have been called forth by his mockery at Muḥammad's description of Hell. In the conference of the Ḳuraishites shortly before Muḥammad's emigration he advised them to have him killed by men from every family in Mecca. When hostilities broke out between Muḥammad and the Meccans he met a host sent out under Ḥamza's command, but it did not come to a battle. It is nevertheless put down to his pugnacity that a fight did take place at Badr. On this occasion ʿUtba b. Rabīʿa gave him the nickname of "the man with the perfumed buttock". By his prayer before his battle: "Perish the man who has done most to cut the tie of blood-relation", he, according to tradition, called down his own destruction. In the battle he was wounded and killed by Muʿādh b. ʿAmr b. al-Djamūḥ and Muʿawwidh b. ʿAfrā'. When Muḥammad saw his corpse, he is said to have called him "the Pharaoh of his people". His picture, naturally drawn very one-sidedly by tradition, is completed by the mourning songs of the Meccans on him, in which he is called "the Meccan chief, the noble-minded man, never vulgar nor greedy".

Bibliography: Ibn Hishām, *passim*; Ibn Saʿd, iiib. 55; viii, 193; Ṭabarī, i. *passim*; Yaʿḳūbī, ii. 27; Nawawī, p. 686; Sprenger, *Das Leben und die Lehre des Mohammad*, ii. 115; F. Buhl, *Das Leben Muhammeds*, p. 169; 243.

ABŪ ḤAFṢ ʿUMAR AL-NASAFĪ. [See AL-NASAFĪ.]

ABŪ ḤANĪFA, AL-NUʿMĀN B. THĀBIT B. ZŪṬĀ, leading fiḳh scholar and theologian in ʿIrāḳ, after whom the madhhab of the Ḥanafites [q.v.] has been named. He was born about 81/700 in Kūfa, where his grand-father, who had been taken prisoner at Kābul, had been brought as a slave, to become afterwards a maulā of the Taim Allāh tribe. Some biographical sources make him a descendant of the ancient Persian kings. His father Thābit probably belonged to the supporters of the ʿAlids, as it is stated by al-Nawawī (p. 699) that ʿAlī blessed him and his descendants.

Abū Ḥanīfa is said to have devoted the whole of his life to the sacred science and gathered many auditors around him. He made his living as a cloth merchant. Most of his later biographers relate that he persistently refused to accept the office of ḳāḍī, which the Umaiyad governor in Kūfa, Yazīd b. ʿUmar b. Hubaira, and later the caliph al-Manṣūr wanted him to accept. By his refusal he is said to have incurred corporal punishment and imprisonment, so that he died in prison in the year 150/767. The same is related of other pious men of the epoch, who deemed it wrong to enter the service of the impious rulers (Goldziher, *Muh. Stud.* ii. 39). Another reason for his imprisonment and death is given in Zaidite sources, according to which Abū Ḥanīfa was a supporter of the Zaidite imām Ibrāhīm b. Muḥammad, who in 145/760 rose in Baṣra against the ʿAbbāsids (van Arendonk, *De opkomst van het Zaidietische imamaat*, p. 288). It is probable that Abū Ḥanīfa, descending from a pro-ʿAlid family in Kūfa, had at first sympathised with the revolutionary movement instigated by the ʿAbbāsids, but later joined in the disappointment of the adherents of ʿAlī's family and so turned against the new dynasty. Other accounts of his life, however, do not mention his death in prison.

Although authentic writings of Abū Ḥanīfa are not extant and probably never have existed, his influence as an authority on legal questions has resulted in the rise of the ʿIrāḳian law school. The rationalistic method of establishing rules in matters of fiḳh, namely by making a large use of the personal view (*ra'y*), which is characteristic for the Ḥanafite school, may go back to Abū Ḥanīfa himself, but the attacks on him by later Ḥidjāz scholars, who reproached him for persistent neglect of tradition, are unfounded. The so-called *Musnad Abī Ḥanīfa* is a collection of traditions, compiled by his disciples and later Ḥanafites, which the imām of their madhhab had used and elaborated in his teaching. It is perhaps better to speak of a series of *Musnads* of this kind, of which about ten are still extant (*GAL, Suppl.* i. 286-7); their compilation was due to the wish of the Ḥanafites to prove to their opponents the use their master had made of traditional material (Goldziher, *Muh. Stud.* ii. 230).

Abū Ḥanīfa has exercised a considerable influence on the dogmatics of Islām; his tradition has been kept up especially in the school of al-Māturīdī [q.v.] and its adepts in Samarḳand. The only authentic document by Abū Ḥanīfa wich has come down to us is his letter to ʿUthmān al-Battī (unedited), in which he defends his Murdjiʾitic [cf. AL-MURDJIʾA] views in an urbane way.

The *Fiḳh Akbar* (II) which is ascribed to him in the *Fihrist* and by later tradition, is an *ʿaḳīda* representing an early stage of scholastic theology, possibly composed in the first half of the tenth century A.D. This work must be distinguished from another *Fiḳh Akbar* (I), the text of which has not come down to us in an integral form, but embedded in a commentary, which needs no discussion here (text and commentary printed at Ḥaidarābād 1321).

Detached from the commentary this *Fiḳh Akbar*, which in order to distinguish it from the later work of the same name, may be numbered I, appears to consist of ten articles of faith delineating the orthodox position as opposed to the Khāridjites, Ḳadarites, Shīʿīs and Djahmites. Polemics against the Murdjiʾites as well as against the Muʿtazilites are lacking. This means that the author was a Murdjiʾite who lived before the rise of the great Muʿtazilī movement.

A second work in which the *Fiḳh Akbar* I was embedded is the *Fiḳh Absaṭ* (unedited), a work consisting of answers to dogmatical questions propounded to Abū Ḥanīfa by his pupil Abū Muṭīʿ al-Balkhī (d. 183 = 799). In this work all the articles of the *Fiḳh Akbar* I are to be found, except one.

This state of things is of a nature to leave no doubt of the authenticity of the *Fiḳh Akbar* I, not as a composition, but as to the provenance of its enunciations. It was not long before the ten articles of this creed proved to require revision and enlargement. This was done in a completely new work, which received the title *Waṣīyat Abī Ḥanīfa* and which, in some MSS., has been put in the form of a last admonition of Abū Ḥanīfa to his disciples. The *Waṣīya* seems to represent the theology of Aḥmad b. Ḥanbal.

The *Fiḳh Absaṭ* contains, apart from nine of the articles of the *Fiḳh Akbar* I, utterances of Abū Ḥanīfa on a number of dogmatical questions such as were debated in his days.

Of the *Kitāb al-ʿālim wa'l-mutaʿallim* only some citations seem to have been preserved. Citations from this and other writings ascribed to Abū Ḥanīfa were composed in several collections, all of which refer to the same subjects.

Bibliography: Al-Khaṭīb al-Baghdādī, *Taʾrīkh Baghdād*, xiii. 323-425; Al-Ashʿarī, *Maḳālāt al-Islāmiyin*, i. 138-9; Ibn Khallikān no. 736 (transl. de Slane, iii. 555—565); A. v. Kremer, *Culturgesch. des Orients unter den Chalifen*, i. 491—497; I. Goldziher, *Sitz. Ber. Wien*, xxviii. 500 *sqq.*; do., *Die Zahiriten*, p. 3, 12 *sqq.*; Snouck Hurgronje, *Verspr. Geschr.* ii. 46, 55, 312 *sqq.*, 323; A. Sprenger, *Zeitschr. für vergl. Rechtswissenschaft*, x. 15 *sqq.*; F. Kern, *MSOS*, As., 1916 p. 141 *sqq.*; Wensinck, *The Muslim Creed*, Cambridge 1932; J. Schacht, *The origins of Muhammadan Jurisprudence*, Oxford 1950; Brockelmann, *GAL*² i. 176 *sqq.*; *Suppl.* i. 284 *sqq.*

ABŪ HURAIRA, a member of the Sulaim b. Fahm clan of the South-Arabian tribe of Azd, a companion of the Prophet and a zealous propagator of his words and deeds. He is generally known by his *kunya* Abū Huraira; the most divergent statements concerning his real name in heathendom and in Islām have been handed down. In the most trustworthy accounts his name wavers between ʿAbd al-Raḥmān b. Ṣakhr (see Nawawī, ed. Wüstenfeld, p. 760) and ʿUmair b. ʿĀmir (Ibn Duraid, *Kitāb al-Ishtiḳāḳ*, p. 295); the surname of "the father of the little cat" is supposed to have been given him on account of his tenderness to cats. He came to Madīna in the year of the battle at Khaibar (7/629), joined Muḥammad and thenceforward lived with him. At first he is said to have earned his sustenance as a labourer. His constant intercourse with the Prophet encouraged him after the latter's death to transmit a greater number of ḥadīths in his name than the other companions; the number of those that are supposed to come from him is estimated at 3.500, but certainly a great part of them have been foisted on him. Amongst those who handed down the sayings transmitted by him are to be found the names of the most respected members of the oldest Islāmic community. Legend justifies the air of infallible memory, with which he imparted his numerous traditions, by inventing the tale that the Prophet had with his own hands wrapped him in a cloth spread out in front of them during their conversation and that by this means he assured the faithful remembrance of what he had heard — a fabulous trait which is also to be met with as a symbol of intimate friendship. On account of his great renown as an interpreter of the sayings and deeds of the Prophet ʿUmar was able to appoint him prefect of Baḥrain. After his deposal, he refused the caliph's offer to restore him to the office, and preferred to remain for a length of time in Madīna as a private citizen. It is very improbable that Marwān, who favoured him in many other ways, appointed him as his lieutenant in the governorship of Madīna. Abū Huraira died in the year 57 or 58 (676—678) at the age of 78.

The humorous temperament (*mazzāḥ*) of Abū Huraira, which gave rise to numerous anecdotes (Ibn Ḳutaiba, ed. Wüstenfeld, p. 142), is often reflected in the way he gave his ḥadīth communications, in which he enveloped the most unimportant things in pathetic language. The inexhaustible stock of information which he always had in hand (the Abū Huraira ḥadīths take up no less than 313 pages in the *Musnad* of Ibn Ḥanbal, ii. 228—541), appears to have raised suspicion of their trustworthiness in the minds of his immediate auditors, nor did they hesitate to give utterance to their suspicions in ironical form (cf. also Bukhārī, *Faḍāʾil al-aṣḥāb*, Bāb 11). He had several times to defend himself against the charge of idle talk. These facts give our criticism every reason to be prudent and sceptical. Sprenger calls Abū Huraira "the extreme of pious humbug". At the same time we must take into account the fact that most of the sayings of which tradition makes him the originator were probably foisted on him at a later date.

Bibliography: Muslim, *Ṣaḥīḥ*, v. 202 (Bukhārī and Tirmidhī have no separate paragraphs about *faḍā'il* of Abū Huraira); Ibn Saʿd, ii^b. 117—119; iv^b. 52—64; Ibn al-Athīr, *Usd al-ghāba*, v. 315; Sprenger, *Das Leben und die Lehre des Moḥammad*, iii., lxxxiii.; Goldziher, *Abh. zur arab. Philologie*, i. 49; do., in *ZDMG*, i. 487; D. S. Margoliouth, *Mohammad*, p. 352.

ABU 'L-ḲĀSIM. [See Muḥammad.]

ABŪ LAHAB ("father of the flame", i.e. man of Hell), the surname, by which an uncle and at the same time violent opponent of Muḥammad is designated in the Ḳur'ān (cxi. 1) and called chiefly by the Muslims. His real name was ʿAbd al-ʿUzzā b. ʿAbd al-Muṭṭalib, the heathen character of which shocked Muḥammad. Until his death he sided with the most resolute adversaries of Muḥammad in Mecca. This fact may be explained by the fact that his wife, Djumail bint Ḥarb b. Umaiya, was the sister of Abū Sufyān, the prominent leader of Muḥammad's adversaries in Mecca till the year 8. In any case she showed much hostility to the Prophet, for in the above-mentioned sūra her torments and humiliation in Hell are indicated also. — This sūra reads as follows: 1) "Perish the hands of Abū Lahab and perished is he. 2) His fortune and all that he hath acquired profited him not. 3) He will roast in a glowing fire (*dhāta lahab*). 4) And his wife carries the wood. 5) On her neck a rope of bast".

The sequence shows that verse 4 means that in Hell she must gather the wood for the glowing fire (cf. Baiḍāwī, *ad loc.*), and that other interpretations do not hold. (Cf. for example Ṭabarī, *Tafsīr*, xxx. 192, and Baiḍāwī, *ad. loc.*). — As a motive for this hostile prediction the following is related by several Arab traditionists in the name of Ibn ʿAbbās: "After verse 214 of sūra xxvi. ("Warn thy tribe, those that stand near thee") was revealed, Muḥammad addressed from mount Ṣafā (according to some from Minā) his relations in Mecca in the following terms: 'If I announced to you an approaching enemy would you not believe me?' — 'Yes', they answered. — 'Well' said he, 'I caution you against a great punishment!' At that time Abū Lahab came up towards him and said: 'Perdition on thee (*tabb^{an} laka*)! is it for this that thou hast convoked us here?' Therefore sūra cxi. (*tabbat yadā* etc.) was revealed". Materially not much different is the account of Ibn Isḥāḳ in the name of ʿAbbād. According to another account of Ibn Isḥāḳ, however, reproduced by Ibn Hishām, Abū Lahab expressed himself with scorn against Muḥammad on another occasion, before Hind bint ʿUtba, adding the imprecatory word *tabb^{an}*. The sūra is generally considered as a Meccan one (the preterite *tabbat* used for the prediction of the future perdition; cf. Baiḍāwī to Ḳur'ān, xi. 14); Nöldeke counts it amoungst the oldest Meccan sūras. Still the wording of verse 2: *Mā aghnā ʿanhu māluhu* shows, according to the consistent usage of the Ḳur'ān, something that had already happened (cf. Ḳur'ān, vii. 48; xv. 84; xxvi. 207, *passim*), for in the case of future events the imperfect tense (*yughnī*) is always used; neither is there any parallel to the usage of *mā aghnā* as a preterite future. In accordance with this wording therefore this sūra contains a cry of triumph at the death of Abū Lahab (see below), and could have been composed only some time after the battle of Badr. Abū Lahab did not personally take part in that battle, because, according to some, he was sick, according to others, he was afraid of ʿĀtika's bad dream. He sent in his place ʿĀṣī b. Hishām, whose fortune he had won in an arrow game, and whom he had enslaved as his debtor. Abū Lahab's great-greandson, the poet al-Faḍl b. al-ʿAbbās al-Lahabī, boastingly mentions the latter fact in a verse (*Aghānī*, xv. 7). The news of the unhappy issue of the battle threw him into such anger that he behaved with violence towards the bearer of the news and his wife. Shortly afterwards (7 days according to Ibn Hishām) he died of smallpox. The hatred of the Muslims was satisfied by the fact that his sons feared to touch his corpse, which was left to putrefy, and when they were ordered to remove it, it was buried with indignity (Ibn Isḥāḳ in *Aghānī*, iv. 33 *sq.*; Baiḍāwī ad Ḳur'ān, cxi. 2).

Abū Lahab is depicted as a large, corpulent "heavy" man, prompt to anger. He had acquired considerable wealth, in order, according to Muḥammad's opinion, to assure himself against adversity (Ḳur'ān, cxi. 2). His son ʿUtba had before Islām married a daughter of Muḥammad but when the latter proclaimed himself a prophet, he divorced her, and he himself embraced Christianity. Cursed by Muḥammad, he is said to have been torn by a lion or a hyena while on a journey to Syria. This story, however, is not in accordance with the statement that he went over to Islām in the year 8, nor with another that he died as late as the year 80 /699-700. Possibly there is a confusion with another son of Abū Lahab. The poet al-Faḍl b. al-ʿAbbās b. ʿUtba (see *Aghānī*, xv. 2—11) was a grandson of ʿUtba.

Bibliography: Ibn Hishām, i. 69, 231 *sqq.*, 244, 430, 461; Ṭabarī, i. 1170, 1204 *sqq.*, 1329; iii. 2343; Wāḳidī, *Kitāb al-Maghāzī* (ed. Wellhausen), p. 42, 351; Baiḍāwī, ad Sūra cxi; Ṭabarī, *Tafsīr*, xxx. 191 *sq.*,; Baghawī (*Tafsīr*), Bukhārī and Wāḳidī in Sprenger, *Das Leben und die Lehre des Moḥammad*, i, 526; Nöldeke-Schwally, *Gesch. d. Qorâns*, i, 89 *sq.*; A. Fischer, *Die Wert der vorhandenen Koran-Übersetzungen und Sura 111*, in *Berichte ü. d. Verh. d. Sachs. Ak. d. Wiss.*, 89, 1937, Heft. 2; F. Buhl, *Das Leben Muhammeds*, p. 168.

ABU 'L-MAʿĀLĪ. [See al-Djuwainī.]

ABŪ SUFYĀN (or Abū Ḥanẓala) Ṣakhr b. Ḥarb b. Umaiya, of the Kuraishite family of ʿAbd Manāf, a leader of the aristocratic party in Mecca hostile to Muḥammad. According to the usual statement regarding his death (see below), he was a few years older than Muḥammad, according to others, however, he was ten years older. Abū Sufyān was a rich and respected merchant, who repeatedly led the great Meccan caravan. Like most of the great merchants he took up a hostile attitude to the movement brought about by Muḥammad, which touched him personally inasmuch as his daughter Umm Ḥabība had married a follower of the Prophet's and emigrated with him to Abyssinia. Against his desire he brought about the fateful battle at Badr; the army, which had hastened up at his cry of distress, would not return without striking a blow, although he ordered it to do so once he had got his caravan into safety. His eldest son Ḥanẓala fell in the fight; another son ʿAmr was taken prisoner but exchanged subsequently for one of Muḥammad's followers, who a as pilgrim had fallen into Abū Sufyān's hands. After the battle of Badr, he took over the command of the Meccans. We are not at all clear as to the facts concerning his oath of vengeance after the defeat and the miraculous campaign he undertook to fulfil his vow (the *sawīḳ* campaign). The battle of Uḥud afforded great satisfaction both to himself and to the Meccans, but he neglected the opportunity of thoroughly humiliating his dangerous opponent. Equally obscure is the tale of the meeting arranged after the battle of Uḥud for the following year at Badr and of his non-appearance at the rendez-vous. Whether Muḥammad really, as Ibn Hi<u>sh</u>ām relates, sent assassins to Mecca to kill Abū Sufyān after the murder of <u>Kh</u>ubaib and of Zaid, is very doubtful. In the year 5/627 during the "campaign of the Moat", he led one part of the great army that advanced against Madīna; as however after some time he saw the hopelessness of the siege, he ordered his troops to march back and soon the whole army melted away. During Muḥammad's campaign which was concluded by the treaty of Ḥudaibiya, he kept entirely in the background. When the treaty was broken by the quarrel between Bakr and <u>Kh</u>uzāʿa he feared the consequences for his town and proceeded to Madīna to arrange the matter. This may explain why Muḥammad at the beginning of the campaign against Mecca proclaimed that anybody who took refuge in Abū Sufyān's house should enjoy complete immunity. It is true that Abū Sufyān's wife Hind cried shame on her husband's weakness, but her fury was as unsuccessful as the armed resistance attempted by a few irreconcilables. By his respectful treatment of Abū Sufyān, Muḥammad admitted how much he owed to the latter's cunning surrender. Abū Sufyān accompanied him on his campaign against the Hawāzin tribe. After the victory also he received "for the winning of his heart" such a generous share of the booty that he had every reason to be satisfied. At the siege of Ṭāʾif, behind whose walls another of his daughters was living, he lost an eye (according to Ṭabarī, i. 2101, this accident happened in the Yarmūk battle). Abū Bakr made him governor over Na<u>dj</u>rān and Ḥi<u>dj</u>āz (thus Balā<u>dh</u>urī, ed. de Goeje, p. 103; cf. Ibn Ḥa<u>dj</u>ar, *Iṣāba*, ii. 477, where the statement that the Prophet had already placed him over Na<u>dj</u>rān is contested). The other tales concerning him are of no value as they show too distinctly anti-Umaiyad party interests. Thus it is very doubtful whether, as is related in Ṭabarī, i. 1827 *sqq.*, he opposed Abū Bakr's election and was on this account reprimanded by ʿAlī. Still more clearly is this tendency shown in an account which represents Abū Sufyān as having been delighted at every advantage gained by the enemy of the Muslims at the Yarmūk battle. As a matter of fact there is another tale, according to which he called on Allāh for help during the battle. That he took part in the battle is also mentioned elsewhere (Balā<u>dh</u>urī, ed. de Goeje, p. 135; Saif even makes him a *ḳāṣṣ* on this occasion: Ṭabarī, i. 2095), but it is rather remarkable as he was then some 70 years old. According to the generally received account he died at the age of 88 in the year 31/651-2; but others give the years 32, 33 or 34 (652—655).

Bibliography: Ṭabarī, i. *passim*; Ibn Hi<u>sh</u>ām, i. 463 *sq.*, 543 *sq.*, 583, 666, 753, 807, 993; Ibn Saʿd, viii. 70; Balā<u>dh</u>urī, p. 56, 135; Ibn Ḥa<u>dj</u>ar, *Iṣāba*, ii. 477 *sqq.*; Nawawī, p. 726; Masʿūdī, *Murū<u>dj</u>*, iv. 179 *sq.*; Caetani, *Annali* i, ii, iii, see Index; F. Buhl, *Das Leben Muhammeds*, p. 239 *sqq.*, 306 *sqq.*

ABŪ ṬĀLIB ʿAbd Manāf b. ʿAbd al-Muṭṭalib, Muḥammad's uncle. He took charge of his orphaned nephew when the latter's grandfather [see ʿabd al-muṭṭalib] died. According to tradition Muḥammad accompanied him on his business journeys. As Abū Ṭālib was poor and had a numerous family, Muḥammad is said to have shown his gratitude to him by bringing up his son ʿAlī in his own house; but this is perhaps only a later legend, especially as it does not agree with what is elsewhere related of Abū Ṭālib's conduct. Thus when the Meccans began to persecute Muḥammad on account of his attacks on their religion, he, as head of the family, took his side and in spite of the repeated protests of the Meccans would not relinquish this parental duty. His example was followed by the other Hā<u>sh</u>imids with the exception of Abū Lahab, and when the Ḳurai<u>sh</u>ites made the declaration of ostracism, they all retired to the quarter of the town inhabited by them (the *<u>sh</u>iʿb* of Abū Ṭālib), and lived there for a length of time in a very depressed condition. It was therefore a severe blow to Muḥammad when his faithful uncle died 3 years before his emigration to Madīna, and 10 years after his prophetic mission. It is not astonishing that tradition fastened on this man, who had been so intimately connected with the Prophet and of whom so little was known. In one tradition he has become the Saiyid of the Ḳurai<u>sh</u>ites. *Ḳaṣīdas* were composed and put into his mouth. More especially was the question discussed whether he was converted before he died or whether he died an infidel. Party interests had their influence in this case; the general and certainly correct view was that, whilst remaining quite faithful to his nephew, he yet considered his preaching as a delusion. This was very unpalatable to the ʿAlid party and they therefore manufactured several traditions which asserted the contrary with more or less vigour. The consequence was that the opponents of the ʿAlids came forward with other traditions, in which the Prophet himself speaks of the torments, even through moderate, which his pagan uncle had to suffer in Hell.

Bibliography: Ṭabarī, i. 1123, 1174 *sqq.*, 1199; Ibn Hi<u>sh</u>ām (ed. Wüstenf.), i. 115, 167 *sq.*, 172 *sq.*; Ibn Ḥa<u>dj</u>ar, *Iṣāba*, iv. 211—219; Caetani, *Annali dell' Islām*, i. 308; Goldziher, *Muhamm. Stud.*, ii. 107; Nöldeke, in *ZDMG*, lii. 27 *sq*; F. Buhl, *Das Leben Muhammeds*, p. 115—118, 171, 175, 181.

ABŪ ʿUBAIDA b. al-<u>Dj</u>arrāḥ, more properly, ʿĀmir b. ʿAbd Allāh b. al-<u>Dj</u>arrāḥ, of the Balḥāri<u>th</u> family, one of the ten believers to whom Muḥammad is said to have promised Paradise. He embraced Islām very early and distinguished himself by his bravery and unselfishness, on account of which the Prophet named him al-Amīn. He hastened to the Prophet's help in the battle of Uḥud, accompanied him on all his campaigns, and commanded the troops in several expeditions. Later on he was sent to Na<u>dj</u>rān, there to train in Islām the tribes which had submitted; he also played a prominent part in the election of the first caliph. He was sent by the latter, at the head of a number of troops, to Syria, and when ʿUmar became caliph, he even received the supreme command over the Syrian army, and conquered Damascus, Ḥimṣ (Emesa), Antioch, Aleppo, etc. He died of the pest in the year 18/639 at Amwās. His tomb is said to be in the <u>Dj</u>āmiʿ al-<u>Dj</u>arrāḥ in Damascus.

Bibliography: Ibn Saʿd, iii[a]. 297 *sqq.*; Ibn al-A<u>th</u>īr, *Usd al-<u>gh</u>āba*, iii. 84; v. 249; Sprenger, *Das Leben und die Lehre des Mohammad*, i. 432 *sqq.*; Lammens, *Le Triumvirat Abou Bakr, ʿOmar et Abou ʿObaida*, dans *MFOB*, iv, p. 113 *sqq.*

ABŪ YAZĪD. [See al-Bisṭāmī.]

ABŪ YŪSUF. [See Ḥanafites.]

ʿĀD, an ancient tribe frequently mentioned in the Ḳurʾān. Its history may be learned only from sporadic indications; it was a mighty nation that lived immediately after the time of Noah, and which became haughty on account of its great prosperity (Ḳurʾān, vii. 69; xli. 15). The large edifices of the ʿĀdites are spoken of in Ḳurʾān, xxvi. 128 *sqq.*; cf. in lxxxix. 6—7 the expression "ʿĀd, Iram of the pillars", where *Iram* [q.v.] may designate either a tribe or a place. According to Ḳurʾān, xlvi. 21, the ʿĀdites inhabited *al-Aḥḳāf* (the sand dunes). The prophet sent to them, their "brother" Hūd, was treated by them just as Muḥammad was later treated by the Meccans and on account of that they were, with the exception of Hūd and a few pious men, swept away by a violent storm (vii. 65 *sqq*; xi. 58; xli. 16; liv. 19; lxix. 6). Finally, in Ḳurʾān, xi. 52 is said that they suffered from a drought. These indications gave rise to many legends, ascribed to the Prophet. It cannot be said with certainty what more ancient elements there are in these legends. The ancient poets knew ʿĀd as an ancient nation that had perished (Ṭarafa, i. 8; *Mufaḍḍalīyāt*, viii. 40; Ibn Hishām, ed. Wüstenfeld, i. 468; cf. Zuhair, xx. 12 and the article LUḲMĀN), hence the expression, "since the time of ʿĀd" (*Ḥamāsa*, ed. Freytag, i. 195, 341). Their kings are mentioned in the Dīwān of the Hudhailites (lxxx. 6) and their prudence in that of Nābigha (xxv. 4). The mention of the ʿĀdite Aḥmar by Zuhair (*Muʿallaḳa*, verse 32) and in the Dīwān of the Hudhalites (p. 31) merits consideration, as Muslim legend connects this (Ḳudār) al-Aḥmar with the Thamūdites [q.v.]. Whether there really existed, and where, a nation called ʿĀd is still an unanswered question. The genealogies of the Arabs relating to the ʿĀdites are naturally valueless, just as is their locating of that nation in the large uninhabitable sandy desert between ʿUmān and Ḥadramawt. The identification of Iram with Aram, adopted by the Arabs and several modern scholars, is not at all sure. Among the latter, Loth identified ʿĀd with the wellknown tribe of Iyād; on the other hand, Sprenger sought for the ʿĀdites in the Oadites, who, according to Ptolemy, lived in Northwestern Arabia, which recalls the Iram well in Ḥismā (Hamdānī, p. 126; Sprenger, *Die alte Geogr. Arabiens*, § 207). But Wellhausen remarked that instead of "since the time of ʿĀd" the expression *min al-ʿād* also occurs, and therefore he supposed that originally ʿĀd was a common noun ("the ancient time"; adj. *ʿādī* = very ancient) and that the mythical nation arose from a misinterpretation of that word.

Bibliography: Ṭabarī, i. 231 *aqq.*; Hamdānī, *Ṣifa*, p. 80; Sprenger, *Das Leben und die Lehre des Moḥammad*, i. 505—518; do., *Die alte Geogr. Arabiens*, § 199; Caussin de Perceval, *Essai sur l'histoire des Arabes avant l'islamisme*, i. 259; Blochet, *Le Culte d'Aphrodite-Anahita chez les Arabes du Paganisme*, 1902, p. 27 *sqq.*; Loth, in *ZDMG*, xxxv. 622 *sqq.*; Wellhausen, in *Göttinger Gelehrte Anzeigen*, 1902, p. 596; J. Horovitz, *Koranische Untersuchungen*, Berlin u. Leipzig 1926, p. 125 *sq.*; H. Gliddon in *BASOR*, no. 73 (Feb. 1939), 13 *sqq.*

ʿĀDA, (A.; P., T. and others Ādat, Ādet = habit, custom), a legal term designating a prescriptive right, which is, in Islāmic countries, given currency independently of the canon law (*sharīʿa*) in those juridical cases which are not closely connected with the religious ordinances. The practical validity of this right, which often is in disagreement with the theologically established law, divided in many countries the jurisdiction into a spiritual and a secular one. We are now in possession of several collections of *ʿāda* laws. In literature, *ʿāda* is sometimes replaced by the term *ʿurf*, or *ḳānūn*. [Lee ADAT LAW].

Bibliography: I. Goldziher, *Die Ẓāhiriten*, p. 204 *sq.*; Snouck Hurgronje, *Verspr. Geschr.* ii 70 *sqq.*, 314; iv, i, p. 259 *sqq.*; T. W. Juynboll, *Handleiding*, p. 8 *sqq.*; *Medjelle*, artt. 36—45 and commentary; for bibliography of Indian and North-African *ʿāda* see: *Preussische Jahrbücher*, 1905, p. 290—292; for India: *Customs in the Trans-Border Territories of the North-West Frontier Provinces* (*Journ. As. Soc. Beng.*, lxxiii., pt. iii. 1904, *Extra Number*, p. 1—34); for North-Africa: Saïd Boulifa, *Le Kanoun d'Adni* (in *Recueil de Mémoires et de Textes*, Algiers 1905, p. 151—179); Decambroggio, *Kanoun Orfia des Berbères du Sud-tunisien* (in *Revue tunisienne*, ix. 346—356).

ĀDAM, surnamed *Abu 'l-Bashar*, "the father of mankind", and *Ṣafī Allāh*, "the one chosen by God", the Biblical Adam. His creation is related in the Ḳurʾān in the following terms: "We created man of dried clay of black mud formed into shape" (xv. 26). According to Muḥammadan legend, however, the angels Gabriel, Michael, and Asrafīl had, each in his turn, received the order of God to take from the seven layers of the earth seven handfuls of sand. The earth had refused to give it; ʿAzrāʾīl then, having received the same order, tore away by force a quantity of earth sufficient to create a man of it. This legend, with some modification, was borrowed from Jewish literature (see Targūm of Jerusalem to *Gen.* ii. 7; Bab. Tal. *Sanhedrīn*, p. 38ᵃ; *Pirḳē R. Elīʿezer*, ch. xi.). God caused a rain to descend for several days on that clay in order to make it soft, then, after it had been kneaded by angels, God himself made the mould of it, which He left to dry for a long time before animating it. Masʿūdī, referring to the above mentioned passage of the Ḳurʾān, states that Ādam's body had remained formless during 80 years, and then 120 years longer without being animated (cf. *Berēshīt Rabba* ad *Gen.* ii. 7, and *Abōt de R. Nātān* (ed. Schechter), p. 22). After Ādam had been created, God commanded the angels to prostrate themselves before him; all of them obeyed with the exception of Iblīs (Satan), who by his rebellion brought about his own and Ādam's fall (Ḳurʾān, ii. 36; vii. 12; xvii. 60 and elsewhere). As to the legend that God had established Ādam as the king of the angels, the Ḳurʾān followed the Christian Syriac Midrāsh (see Bezold, *Schatzhöhle*, p. 3 *sqq.*; text, p. 14). Ādam passes for the first prophet to whom God revealed books (alluding to the Book of Adam). God showed Ādam all the generations of men with their prophets; having learned that David was to live a very short time, Ādam, the duration of whose life should have been 1.000 years (equal to one day of God), gave him 40 years of his own life, thus Ādam lived 960 years (Ṭabarī, i. 156 *sqq.*; Ibn al-Athīr, i. 37). Cf. *Berēshīt Rabba* ad *Gen.*, iii. 8, and *Bemidbar Rabba* ad *Num.*, vii. 78, where, depending on *Gen.* v. 5, it is said that Adam gave David 70 years of his life. Having been driven from Paradise, Ādam alighted upon the island Sarandīb (Ceylon), where he stayed 200 years separated from his wife, spending his time in doing penitence (Ḳurʾān, ii. 36; cf. Bab. Talm, *ʿErūbin*, p. 18ᵇ). There is on the island a mountain called by the Portugese Pico de Adam, where, according to legend, the imprints of Adam's feet 70 cubits long are seen on a rock. After Ādam had repented, Gabriel brought him to Mount ʿArafāt near Mecca, where he met his wife. According to Ṭabarī (i. 122) and Ibn al-Athīr (i. 29), God ordered Ādam to build the Kaʿba, and Gabriel taught him the pilgrimage ceremonies. — Ādam died on Friday the 6th Nīsān, and was buried in the Cave of Treasures (*maghārat al-kunūz*), at the foot of Mount Abū Ḳubais (Yaʿḳūbī, ed. Houtsma, i. 5). According to other authorities, his corpse was brought by Melchizedek to Jerusalem after the flood.

Bibliography: Ṭabarī, i. 115 *sqq.*; Kisāʾī, *Ḳiṣaṣ al-anbiyāʾ* (ed. Eisenberg), i. 23 *sqq.*; Thaʿlabī, *al-ʿArāʾis* (Cairo 1297), p. 23 *sqq.*; Nawawī (ed. Wüstenf.), p. 123 *sqq.*; Masʿūdī, *Murūdj* (ed. Paris), i. 115 sqq.; Ibn al-Athīr (ed. Tornb.), i. 19 *sqq.*; Weil, *Biblische Legenden der Muselmänner*, p. 12 *sqq.*; G. Sale, *The Koran*, i. 5, notes; ii. 83, notes, 410, notes; Grünbaum, *Neue Beiträge zur semit. Sagenkunde* (Leyden 1893), p. 54 *sqq.*; *ZDMG*, xv. 31 *sqq.*; xxiv. 284 *sqq.*; xxv. 59 *sqq.*; J. Horovitz, *Koranische Untersuchungen*, Berlin 1926, p. 85.

ADAT LAW. In the languages of the Muslim peoples of the Eastern Archipelago *adat* (sometimes with dialectical modifications), derived from the Arabic *ʿāda*, is the word in general use for "custom, practice, use and wont". The application of the word is extended to all that a community or an individual has become accustomed to; even an animal has his adat. In the little community within which the Indonesian usually spends his life, harmony is only secured if every one of the members observes the traditional customs or those that are felt to be traditional. An adat can never be neglected without misgivings for the community or the individual; unforeseen harmful results might ensue. Since Islām has penetrated into Indonesia, the adat of the islamized communities has more or less incorporated elements of the Islamic institutions, especially the rules for marriage and family law; to a certain extent also legal procedure.

Adat Law as a term applies to that section of the adat which covers the legal relations of man in state and society and with which legal issues are associated. The first to give this clearer definition of the term was C. Snouck Hurgronje. It has come into general use by the researches and the work of C. van Vollenhoven. The term is also applied to non-Muslim peoples and extended to the whole area where Indonesian law is in force. So it includes, in addition to Indonesia proper, the Philippines, Malakka, Formosa and Madagascar.

The Muslim peoples of Indonesia themselves are often conscious of the difference between the Islamic parts of their adat and the native adat. The two elements are contrasted as *hukum sarat* and *adat* in the narrower sense. Although the binding force of the former is recognized in theory, practice takes account of it only as far as it has become part of the customary law. As, in the course of the xixth century, the institutions of Islām became better known in Indonesia owing to increased contact with Arabia and other Islamic countries, there have come into existence, in several parts of Indonesia, movements aiming at the better application of the pure *sharīʿa*. Against these the adat parties held up their ancient customs, as for instance in Minangkabau on the Western coast of Sumatra, where the ancient matriarchal institutions are wholly incompatible with the tenure of Islamic family law. These oppositions have led in several instances to fanatical outbursts and conflicts. The adat law itself has often been subject to changes under influence of the conflicting tendencies. After the adat law had become better known, its application was regulated and circumscribed by colonial legislation.

The adat law is not easy to discover and collect. The native written sources are in the first place edicts of the chiefs, of which there are a number in existence. Descriptive works of adat are of less value because they take the word adat in its widest sense and record the most important events in the life of man with all the ceremonial associated with them. The so-called law-books are not to be judged according to western ideas. They are the work of jurists who lay down in them their own opinions, not always in agreement with customary law. Compiled at the instigation of chiefs, they give the laws regulating the relations of chief to subject, traditional wisdom in the guise of legal opinions.

After, in the course of the xixth century, several Dutch colonial officials had shown understanding for the customary legal institutions in connection with government policy, Snouck Hurgronje was the first to emphasize in his book *De Atjehers* (1892-3), the importance of customary law. Later there appeared van Vollenhoven's *Het adatrecht van Nederlandsch-Indië*, in which for the first time adat law was treated as a complete system of law. The book confines itself to the adat law of the Muslim and non-Muslim peoples of the Dutch Indies. The fact that much material for the study was to be found in older writings of a geographical and ethnological nature, in official documents and memorials of all kinds, if only it could be dug out, resulted in the publication, at van Vollenhoven's instigation, of the *Adatrechtbundels*, which appeared regularly from 1910 up to 1943 in 42 volumes. This series has the double purpose of making older scattered material readily accessible and of adding new discoveries. The material is ample, but there are many lacunae. We are thus left with society itself as an important source, and observation of how it lives and is ruled.

The investigation of the sources of adat law cannot afford to neglect ethnology. While for example marriage is contracted according to the *sharīʿa*, it is frequently followed by a celebration. Although from an Islamic point of view the validity of the marriage is completely secured by following the *sharīʿa*, the omission of the second part often brings about invalidity. Here adat law comes into contact with ethnology; but if certain conduct is punished coram populo by the authorities because it injures the spirits, it may be disputed whether we have to do with adat law or ethnology.

The Islamic admixture in adat law is not the same everywhere in Indonesia. The *zakāt*, on encountering native systems of taxation, could become no more than a voluntary offering. Family law has generally speaking been remodelled in keeping with the demands of the *sharīʿa*. Funerals also are performed with Muḥammedan rites. Institutions imported with Islām, like the *waḳf*, retain generally their legal character, but may have undergone changes by adaptation to circumstances. For the rest the pre-Islamic has only rarely completely been driven out in the spheres governed by the *sharīʿa*.

The question of codification, which had started already in the xviiith century, retained its importance at a later date, because the principle was maintained that the natives were to be left in enjoyment of their own customary law. But as the liquid character of adat law is incompatible with codification, this method was later abandoned. Shortly before the last war the colonial government made an attempt to ascertain some of the principles of adat law in force in one juridical division — called in Dutch *rechtsgauw* —, by which is meant an area in which one and the same adat law prevails; about twenty different areas of adat law were then distinguished in Dutch Indonesia. There exist also special descriptions of the adat in such divisions by indigenous jurists.

In recent times the Indonesian nationalists have manifested a dislike for an excessive regard for adat law and its study, as it seems uncompatible with the modern institutions they wish to introduce.

Bibliography: C. Snouck Hurgronje, *The Achenese*, Leiden 1906; C. van Vollenhoven, *Het Adatrecht van Nederlandsch-Indië*, 3 vols., Leiden 1918—1933; do., *De Ontdekking van het Adatrecht*, Leiden 1928; *Adatrechtbundels* i-xlii, The Hague 1910-43 (continued; vol. xvi and xxi contain contributions to the adat law of the Philippines); *Pandecten van het Adatrecht*, vols. i-x. Amsterdam-Bandoeng 1914-36 (these are divided according to the subjects of Adat Law); *Dictionnaire de termes de droit coutumier indonésien*, Amsterdam 1934; B. ter Haar, *Beginselen en Stelsel van het Adatrecht*, 1939 (English translation by A. Schiller and A. Hoebel: *Adat Law*); J. Prins, *Adat en Islamietische Plichtenleer in Indonesië*, The Hague 1948.

ʿA<u>DH</u>ĀB (A.), "torment, suffering, affliction", inflicted by God or a human ruler, and in so far as it expresses not only absolute power but also love of justice, also "punishment, chastisement (*ʿuḳūba*)". The divine judgments, which are often mentioned in the Ḳurʾān, strike the individual as well as whole nations in the life of this world as well as in the life to come. It is mainly unbelief, doubt of the divine mission of the prophets and apostles, rebellion against God that are punished in this manner [see ʿĀD, FIRʿAWN, LŪṬ, NŪḤ, <u>TH</u>AMŪD, and others]. With respect to the punishments in the life to come, which begin already in the grave (*ʿa<u>dh</u>āb al-ḳabr*), see <u>DJ</u>AHANNAM, MUNKAR WA-NAKĪR.

The punishments established in Muslim law (*<u>sh</u>arīʿa*) are of four kinds:

1. *Ḳiṣāṣ*, i.e. retaliation. The guilty one may, by virtue of the right of retaliation, be killed, wounded or mutilated [see ḲIṢĀṢ].

2. *Diya*, i.e. blood money, which has to be paid if the plaintiff gives up his right to *ḳiṣāṣ*, or if retaliation is either impossible or not permitted [see DIYA].

3. *Ḥadd*, i.e. the punishment exactly defined by the law, which may neither be reduced nor augmented, e.g. lapidation, a fixed number of lashes, crucifixion, and cutting off the hands or the feet [see ḤADD].

4. *Taʿzīr*, i.e. the punishment inflicted by the judge at his discretion. It may for instance consist of imprisonment, exile, corporal punishment, boxing on the ear, a reprimand or any other humiliating proceeding. The judge may for instance blacken the face of the culprit, cut his hair or have him led through the streets, etc. [see TAʿZĪR].

The punishment is considered in Muslim law either as the right of God (*ḥaḳḳ Allāh*) or as the private right of a man (*ḥaḳḳ ādamī*). In the latter case the punishment is applied only at the desire of the injured party (or of the latter's relatives or heirs). The punishment, e.g. retaliation, is inflicted upon the culprit as the personal right of the plaintiff.

In the case of a transgression against God, the punishment consequently being then a *ḥaḳḳ Allāh*, a peculiar principle in the law applies. God, it is supposed, is forbearing and, in fact, desires not at all the punishment of the transgressor.

Punishment was considered in the beginning of Islām, just as in Arabian paganism, as a purification from sin. So for instance a certain Māʿiz b. Mālik came to the Prophet and said to him: *ṭahhirnī*, "purify me", i.e. punish me! — Cf. I. Goldziher, *Muhamm. Stud.*, i. 27, note 1; do., *Das Strafrecht im Islam* (*Fragen zur Rechtsvergleichung, gestellt von Th. Mommsen, beantwortet von H. Brunner, c.s.*), p. 101, 104, note 2. But the Prophet is stated to have said: "God will forgive the sins of every believer except when the sinner himself makes them known. God loves those of his servants that cover their sins".

On the ground of this tradition, there is a prescription in the Muslim law books that when the punishment is to be considered as a *ḥaḳḳ Allāh* the transgressor should hide his guilt as much as possible and not confess it, and even when he does confess it revoke this confession. He should rather turn himself to God in stillness, for God accepts his conversion when his intention is pure.

The witnesses too are recommended not to testify to the detriment of the accused person, and it is meet that the judge should show the latter all the circumstances extenuating his guilt and the validity of revoking his confession. The judge may even entirely remit the punishment except when the right of a man is also injured at the same time and the latter demands the punishment of the guilty one.

Only in the case of a punishment established by the law (*ḥadd*) the judge has no choice and must execute the punishment. With regard to the latter punishments even an intercession on behalf of the culprit is not allowed, while otherwise it is recommended. But in order to establish the guilt of the culprit in these cases a very difficult legal proof is always required. In fact the rules of the Muslim canon-law offer everybody the opportunity for escaping such punishments. Practically there is only one ground on which the legal evidence and the execution of "determined punishments" may be based, namely the confession of the culprit himself; so that in this respect the "determined punishments" have the character of penitence.

It is hardly necessary to remark that eastern despots were never satisfied with these legal punishments. Very often by mere arbitrariness they inflicted quite cruel and barbarous punishments for real or supposed misdeeds. In particular there was nothing more usual than that disgraced viziers or other dignitaries were subjected to torture in order to extort money from them before they were executed.

Bibliography: Besides the *fiḳh* books of the various schools, see for the <u>Sh</u>āfiʿite rite: E. Sachau, *Muhamm. Recht nach schafiitischer Lehre* (Berlin 1897), p. 757—849; Snouck Hurgronje, in *ZDMG*, liii. 161 *sqq* (= *Verspr. Gesch.* ii, 408 *sqq.*); do., *Mr. L. W. C. van den Berg's beoefening van het Mohamm. recht*, ii. 49—61 (= *Verspr. Geschr.* ii, 188—201). For the Ḥanafite rite: J. Krcsmárik, in *ZDMG*, lviii 69—113, 316—360, 539—581; L. W. C. van den Berg, *Le droit pénal de la Turquie* (in *La législation pénale comparée*, Berlin 1893); G. Bergsträsser, *Grundzüge des Isl. Rechts*, Berlin 1935, p. 96 *sqq.*; J. P. M. Mensing, *De bepaalde straffen in het Hanbalietische recht*, Leiden 1936; A von Kremer, *Culturgesch. des Orients unter den Chalifen*, i. 459—469, 540 *sqq.* For the Mālikite rite: M. B. Vincent, *Etudes sur la loi musulmane (rite de Malek)*; *Législation criminelle* (Paris 1842); I. Goldziher, in *Zum ältesten Strafrecht der Kulturvölker. Fragen zur Rechtsvergleichung, gestellt von Th. Mommsen, beantwortet von H. Brunner, c.s.* (Leipzig 1905), p. 102 *sqq.*; J. Kohler, in *Zeitschr. für vergl. Rechts-Wissensch.*, viii. 238—261; O. Procksch, *Uber die Blutrache bei den vorislamischen Arabern und Muhammeds Stellung zu ihr* (Leipzig 1899); J. Wellhausen, *Reste arabischen Heidentums* (2nd ed., Berlin 1897), p. 186 *sqq.*

ADHĀN (A.), "announcement", a technical term for the call to the divine service of Friday and the five daily *ṣalāts*.

According to Muslim tradition, the Prophet, soon after his arrival at Madīna (1 or 2 years after the Hidjra), deliberated with his companions on the best manner of announcing to the faithful the hour of prayer. Some proposed that every time a fire should be kindled, a horn should be blown or a *nāḳūs* (i.e. a long piece of wood clapped with another piece of wood; with such a *nāḳūs* the Christians in the East used at that time to announce the hour of prayer) should be used. But one Muslim, ᶜAbd Allāh b. Zaid, related that he saw in a dream somebody who from the roof of the mosque called the Muslims to prayer. ᶜUmar recommended that manner of announcing the *ṣalāt*, and as all agreed to it, this adhān was introduced by order of the Prophet. From that time the believers were convoked by Bilāl, and up to our days the adhān is called out at the time of the *ṣalāt*.

The adhān of the orthodox Muslim consists of seven formulas, of which the sixth is a repetition of the first:

1. *Allāhᵘ akbar*: "Allāh is most great".
2. *Ashhadu an lā ilāhᵃ illa 'llāh*: "I testify that there is no god besides Allāh".
3. *Ashhadu anna Muḥammadᵃⁿ rasūl Allāh*: "I testify that Muḥammed is the apostle of Allāh".
4. *Ḥaiya ᶜala 'l-ṣalāt*: "Come to prayer"!
5. *Ḥaiya ᶜala 'l-falāḥ*: "Come to salvation"!
6. *Allāhᵘ akbar*: "Allāh is most great".
7. *Lā ilāhᵃ illa 'llāh*: "The is no god besides Allāh".

The first formula is repeated four (by the Mālikites two) times one after the other, the other formulas are repeated twice each, except the last words: *lā ilāhᵃ illa 'llāh*, which are pronounced only once. The 2nd and 3rd formulas after being pronounced twice are repeated a third time in a louder voice. This repetition (*tardjīᶜ*) is generally considered as recommended by the law, only the Ḥanafites forbid it. At the morning prayer (*ṣalāt al-ṣubḥ*) the words *al-ṣalāt khair min al-nawm* ("prayer is better than sleep") are added in the adhān. This formula, also pronounced two times and called *tathwīb* (repetition), is inserted between the 5th and 6th formulas, but the Ḥanafites pronounce it at the end.

The adhān of the Shīᶜites differs from that of the Sunnites in that the former has an eighth formula (inserted between the fifth and the sixth): *Ḥaiya ᶜalā khair al-ᶜamal*, "Come to the best work!" These words have at all times been the shibboleth of the Shīᶜites; when called from the minarets in an orthodox country, the inhabitants knew that the government had become Shīᶜite (cf. Snouck Hurgronje, *Mekka*, i. 63; S. de Sacy, *Chrestomathie arabe* i., text, p. 60; transl., p. 169). The Shīᶜites pronounce also the final formula two times.

The Muslims who hear the adhān must repeat its formulas, but instead of the fourth and fifth, they recite: *lā ḥawlᵃ wa-lā ḳuwwatᵃ illā bi-'llāh*, "there is no strength nor power but in Allāh", and instead of the *tathwīb* formula in the morning adhān, they say: *ṣadaḳta wa-bararta*, "thou hast spoken truthfully and rightly".

The adhān is followed by formulas of glorification which are recommended and precisely determined by the law. They are omitted only after the call to the *maghrib-ṣalāt* [see ṢALĀT], because the interval between the adhān and the second call (*iḳāma*) to this prayer is very short.

There is no fixed melody for the adhān. Every adhān may be modulated at will with any known tune, provided that the right pronunciation of the words is not impaired by it. Cf. Snouck Hurgronje, *Mekka*, ii. 87: "In Mecca one hears different airs at the same time. Like the recitation of the Ḳur'ān, the singing of the adhān is in Mekka a highly developed art". Only among the Ḥanbalites there are doctors who do not allow any melody for the adhān.

Every Muslim who, whether alone or with his family, recites the above-mentioned *ṣalāts* at home or in the field must pronounce the adhān in a loud voice as is recommended by the law (cf. Snouck Hurgronje, *Mekkanische Sprichwörter und Redensarten*, p. 87 = *Verspr. Geschr.* v. 83).

The call to the other public *ṣalāts*, e.g. those of the two feasts, those at sun and moon eclipses, etc., has only one formula: *al-ṣalāt djāmiᶜatᵃⁿ*, "come to the public prayer"! This formula is said to have been current already in the time of the Prophet (cf. I. Goldziher, in *ZDMG*, xlix. 315).

Important information on the modifications of the adhān formulas introduced at various times and in various places from the beginning of Islām is to be found in Maḳrīzī, *Khiṭaṭ*, ii. 269 *sq.*

Owing to the profession of faith frequently occurring in the adhān, the Muslims pronounce it in the right ear of a child shortly after its birth (cf. Lane, *Arab. Society in the Middle Ages*, p. 186; Snouck Hurgronje, *Mekka*, ii. 138) as well as in the ear of people supposed to be possessed of *djinn* (evil spirits).

Bibliography: Bukhārī, *Ṣaḥīḥ*, *Kitāb al-Adhān* (French translation of O. Houdas and W. Marçais, i. 209 *sq.*); A. N. Matthews, *Mishqâtul-masâbîh*, i. 141 *sqq.*, and other tradition collections and *fiḳh* books.

ᶜADĪ B. MUSĀFIR. [See YAZĪDĪS.]

ᶜADL (A.), "equitableness", a maṣdar also used as an adjective (= *ᶜādil*), "equitable", "blameless", therefore ᶜadl designates in the *fiḳh* a person whose testimony is valid; antithesis: *fāsiḳ*; cf. Juynboll, *Handleiding tot de kennis van de Moh. wet*, p. 293 *sq.*; Dozy, *Supplément*, ii. 103. In numismatics ᶜadl means "of full weight", and therefore this word (often abridged to ᶜ) is stamped on coins to show that they have the just weight and are current (*ᶜadlī*).

AGHA KHĀN. [See KHŌDJAS.]

AHL AL-KITĀB (A.) = "the people of the Book". Muḥammad calls so the Jews and Christians, in distinction from the heathens, on account of their possessing divine books of revelation (*Tawrāt* = *Torah*; *Zabūr* = Psalter; *Indjīl* = Gospel), which it is true, they transmit in a falsified form, but the acceptance of which gives them a privileged position above followers of other religions. In contradistinction to the heathens Muḥammad granted them (Ḳur'ān, ix. 29) after their submission free public worship against payment of a poll-tax (*djizya*; q.v.). The punctual observance of the special conditions laid upon them ensures them the unconditional protection of the Muslim authorities (as *muᶜāhadūn* or *ahl al-dhimma* = protégés in accordance with an agreement). Violation of this defensive alliance with the Ahl al-Kitāb is considered as a heinous perfidy. Of course the proceedings of the Prophet with regard to the Banū Naḍīr and Banū Ḳuraiẓa cannot be taken as a model. Against all fanatical sentiment expressed in odious terms the following principle was established, in the form of a saying of Muḥammad's: "He who wrongs a Jew or a Christian will have myself (the Prophet) as his accuser on the day of judgment" (Balādhurī, p. 162). Likewise in the ancient instructions for generals setting out on expeditions of conquest as well as for administrators of the provinces it is always stressed that the subjected Ahl al-Kitāb must not be disturbed in their public worship and must be treated with humanity. To be sure after the death of the Prophet, who had begun himself with the expulsion of the Jews, permanent stay in Arabia itself was forbidden to them. The Muslims based themselves on a saying supposedly uttered by the Prophet in his last hour, according to which "two religions may not dwell together in the Arabian Peninsula" (*Muwaṭṭa*ʾ, iv. 71; cf. Zarḳānī's commentary as to the geographical limits), a principle which is claimed to have been applied already by Abū Bakr in his message to the Christian inhabitants of Nadjrān (Ṭabarī, i. 1987, $_{13}$). The restrictive special conditions, which became always more oppressive in proportion to the increasing spirit of intolerance, are codified in their oldest form in a document which passes for the *ʿAhd ʿUmar* "the treaty of ʿUmar" (with the Christians of Jerusalem), but which is certainly a production of a later epoch (de Goeje, *Mémoire sur la conquête de la Syrie*, 2nd ed., p. 140 *sqq.*). This document is the basis of the interconfessional legislation in Islām, and it has been further developed in the codifications according to the ruling opinions of their respective authors. Within the right of free public worship the following question remained the most practical: To what extent may the Ahl al-Kitāb erect new prayer houses or restore old ones? It always gave rise to renewed negotiations. One may conceive that in different law schools, in spite of the maintenance of common principles, differences as to the treatment of the Ahl al-Kitāb from the point of view of religious law may be manifested. The principal differences appear in the questions of the *dhabāʾiḥ ahl al-kitāb* (if the Muslim may partake of what they slaughter) and of the *munākaḥāt ahl al-kitāb* (to what extent a Muslim is allowed to marry a wife of them). The assumption that the books which the Ahl al-Kitāb possess are falsified and that they concealed their true contents (Ḳurʾān, ii. 75; iii. 71; v. 13; vi. 91), as well as the belief that Muḥammad, his mission and the victory of the Arabs and Islām are foretold in the Holy Scriptures of the Jews and Christians and that the Ahl al-Kitāb obscured these prophecies by false interpretation, called forth an extensive polemical literature, the materials for which the Muslim theologians received in the first place from converts. With regard to the Jews a particular subject of polemics rose out of the assertion of the *naskh al-sharīʿa*, i.e. the abrogation of the divine laws affirmed by the Muḥammadans and denied by the Jews; cf. also NAṢĀRĀ; YĀHŪD.

Islām extended very early the circle of the Ahl al-Kitāb beyond its original limits. Supported by the statement that Muḥammad accepted the *djizya* from the Parsis in Hadjar (Baḥrain), the Muslims included the Madjūs too in that class. In the time of Caliph Maʾmūn (215/830) the heathens of Ḥarrān succeeded in suggesting to the Muslims that they were the Ṣābiʾūn [q.v.] mentioned frequently in the Ḳurʾān among the believing nations, and that they possessed books of revelation brought to them by ancient prophets (Chwolson, *Die Ssabier*, i. 141). In the xivth century a Muḥammadan prince in India allowed the Chinese, against payment of a *djizya*, to keep up a pagoda on Muslim territory (Ibn Baṭṭūṭa, iv. 2). The inner state of affairs in India brought it about that even veritable idolaters were considered as *ahl al-dhimma* (*ibid.*, p. 29, 223). Such extensions could be made, however, only in the matter of concession of religious toleration. The two questions alluded to above (the laws of food and marriage) were never taken into consideration beyond the circle of the original Ahl al-Kitāb.

Bibliography: T. W. Juynboll, *Handleiding*, p. 341—346; Wensinck, *Mohammed en de Joden te Medina* (Leyden 1908); A. S. Tritton, *The Caliphs and their non-Muslims subjects*, 1930. On the legislation with regard to the Ahl al-Kitāb: *JA*, 1852; Bethäuser, in *REJ*, xxx. 6 *sqq.*; R. Gottheil, *Dhimmis and Moslems in Egypt* (in the *Old Testament and Semitic Studies in Memory of W. R. Harper*, Chicago 1908, ii. 351 *sqq.*); D. Künstlinger in *R O*, iv (1926), p. 238—247; R. Brunschvig, *Conquête de l'Afrique du Nord*, in *Annales de l'Institut d'Études Orientales* VI (1942—47), Algiers, p. 108 *sqq.* Polemics: Steinschneider, *Polem. und apologet. Liter. in arab. Sprache*, in *Abh. K. M.*, vi., No. 3; Goldziher, in *ZDMG*, xxxii, 341—387; further sources in the *Jewish Encyclopaedia*, vi. 658. Customs and usages: *REJ*, xxviii. 75 *sqq.*

AHL AL-ṢUFFA is the name given to a group of muhādjirūn [q.v.] and other Muslims who settled in Madīna with Muḥammad or after the hidjra. Having no proper dwelling-place in that city, they were lodged in a roofed-in corner (*ṣuffa*) of the mosque. They were in a miserable state, and in the Ḳurʾān (sūra ii. 267, 273) they were commended to public charity. When the *ḳibla* [q.v.] was turned towards Mecca, the ṣuffa remained nevertheless at the southern wall of the mosque (cf. al-Batanūnī, *al-Riḥla al-Ḥidjāzīya*, 2nd ed., Cairo 1329, the plate opposite p. 250 as compared with that opposite p. 244). In course of time Muḥammad was able to make provision for the poor *muhādjirūn*. Ahl al-Ṣuffa remained nevertheless a title of nobility held in respect by later Islām. The term ṣuffa has the meaning of saddle-cushion; *sofa* in several European languages goes back to it.

AHL-I ḤAKK, "men of God", a secret religion found especially in Western Persia. The name ʿAlī-Ilāhī, given them by their neighbours, is an misleading nickname, as ʿAlī is not the principal figure in their religious system.

The Ahl-i Ḥakk has no canonical unity as a church and represents rather a confederation of affiliated movements. In theory there are twelve *khānadān* or *silsila* [cf. below] but there are divisions outside of this list, like the Saiyid Djalālī and the Tūmārī (a group which has diverged considerably!). For the moment we are best acquainted with the Ātash-begī division, and the following exposition will be based mainly on Ātash-begī documents, supplemented by statements from the *Firḳān*, the author of which was a Khāmūshī (?).

The Dogmas. The central point in the dogmas of the Ahl-i Ḥakk is the belief in the successive manifestations of the Divinity, the number of these being seven. The manifestations of God are compared to garments put on by the Divinity: "to become incarnate" means "to come (to dwell) in a garment" (*libās*, *djāma*, *dūn* < Turk. **don*).

Each time the Divinity appears with a following of Four (or Five) Angels (*yārān-i čār-malak*) with whom he forms a close group.

The table of theophanies given by the MS. of the *Sarandjām* enumerates seven theophanies with the names given to them and to their angels.

In pre-eternity (*azal*) the Divinity was enclosed in a Pearl (*durr*). He made his first external appearance in the person of Khāwandagār, the Creator of the world. The second avatar was in the person of ʿAlī. From the beginning of the third epoch the list becomes quite original and typically Ahl-i Ḥaḳḳ. The first four epochs correspond to the stages of religious knowledge which in the first epoch was the *sharīʿa*, in the second the *ṭarīḳa*, in the third the *maʿrifa*, and in the fourth the *ḥaḳīḳa* "Real Truth". The religion culminates in the epoch of Sulṭān Ṣohāk who is the fourth theophany and who is recognised by all the Ahl-i Ḥaḳḳ as the founder of their religion. On the other hand, several differences of opinion regarding the successors of Sulṭān Ṣohāk are recorded.

Just as the divine essence reappears in each of the seven "garments", the angels are avatars of one another. The angels are emanations of the Divinity: the first of them was produced by Khāwandagār from his armpit, the second from his mouth, the third from his breath, the fourth and fifth from his perspiration and his light respectively (cf. the *Sarandjām*).

The angels are usually said to be four in number (in some lists and in certain periods this number is reduced to three) but in fact a fifth angel is especially charged with the supervision of worship. This angel's symbolical name is Razbār, Raẓbār or Ramzbār ("entrusted with mysteries") and her feminine character is indisputable; but the sex in Razbār is not emphasised.

Metempsychosis and Eschatology. The belief in the reincarnation of the theophanies finds its parallel in the general belief in metempsychosis. "Men! Do not fear the punishment of death! The death of man is like the dive which the duck makes".

Human beings must pass through the cycle of 1.001 incarnations, in the course of which they receive the reward of their actions. According to the *Firḳān* (i. 32, 35, 57, 68), however, the possibilities of purification are essentially limited by the very nature of beings; of whom some, created out of yellow clay (*zardagil*), are good, and the others, created out of black earth (*siyāh-khāk*), are evil. "The more (the former) go through the world of garments and the more they suffer, the more they approach God and the more their luminous state increases", while the "Dark ones" shall never see the Sun. As a complement to these beliefs, the Ahl-i Ḥaḳḳ eagerly await the advent of the Lord of Time who shall come "to accomplish the desires of the Friends and embrace (*iḥāṭa*) the Universe". There are a number of prophetic *kalāms* which announce the coming of the Messiah. The scene of the Last Judgment (*sān* "review") will be the plain of Shahrizūr or that of Sulṭānīya, where the "sulṭāns shall be exterminated". According to the *Firḳān*, i. 57, the Good shall enter the Paradise (which is the contemplation) of the beauty of the Lord of Generosities, while the Wicked shall be annihilated (*maʿdūm*).

Rites. The Ahl-i Ḥaḳḳ have a number of practices which are quite original.

1. We find little mention of individual prayer; on the other hand, the Ahl-i Ḥaḳḳ attach tremendous importance to assemblies (*djam* < *djamʿ*) in which "all difficulties find their solution". The life of the community is eminently collective and the assemblies are held at fixed intervals and in connection with all important events. *Kalāms* are recited at them to the accompaniment of music.

2. On solemn occasions sessions of *dhikr* [q.v.] are held. Specially qualified dervishes to the sounds of music (*sāz*) enter into a state of ecstasy, accompanied by anaesthesia, which enables them to walk over burning coals, to handle them, etc.

3. The indispensable features of these assemblies are the offerings and the sacrifices: *nadhr wa-niyāz* (raw offerings, uncooked, including animals of the male sex, oxen, sheep, cocks, intended for sacrifice) or *khair wa-khidmat* (cooked or prepared victuals, like sugar, bread, etc.). The *Firḳān*, i. 74 counts fourteen kinds of bloody or bloodless sacrifices (*ḳurbānī-yi khūndār wa-bī-khūn*). The ritual of sacrifice is regulated and the flesh is separated from the bones, which are buried. The boiled meat and the other offerings are distributed among those present and dedicatory formulae (*khuṭba*) are repeated. The term *sabz namūdan*, "to render green, i.e. living, to reanimate", is applied to the ceremony (*Notes*, p. 210 [90]).

4. "Just as every dervish must have a spiritual director (*murshid*) so the head of every Ahl-i Ḥaḳḳ has to be commended to a *pīr*". In the course of this ceremony (*sar-sipurdan*) the persons symbolizing the "Five (sic!) Angels" stand round the infant. A Muscat nut (*djawz-i buwā*) is broken by the celebrant as a substitute for the head. It is then worn as an amulet, with a piece of silver called *hawīza* bearing the Shīʿa form of the profession of faith (*hawīza* from the Shīʿa town of Hawīza in Khūzistān cf. *Notes*, p. 227 [107]). Links recalling blood relationship are established between him whose head is commended and the line of the Shaikh to whom the head has been commended. This spiritual relationship carries with it the prohibition of marriage between the individual dedicated and the family of the *pīr*.

5. With the object of attaining moral perfection special unions (nuclei) are formed between a man (or several men) and a woman who are called brother and sister (*sharṭ-i iḳrār*). The union is said to be formed in anticipation of the Day of Resurrection (*Notes*, p. 230 [110]; cf. the *ākh wa-ukht al-ākhira* among the Yazīdīs [q.v.].

6. Fasting is rigorously observed but lasts only for three days, as among the Yazīdīs [q.v.]. It takes place in winter and is followed by a feast. Among the divisions of the sect, only the Ātash-begī do not observe the fast, "for the days of the (final) advent are near" and instead of fasting they say one ought to feast.

For the other rites and customs see *Notes*. The rites are usually based on the precedents established in the epoch of Khāwandagār and especially in that of Sulṭān Ṣohāk. This is amongst others the case with the so-called "commendation of the head". The fast is intended to commemorate the death in the storm of the men called *ḳabaltāsān* who were endeavouring to join the King of the World (cf. *Notes*, p. 219 [91]). The sacrifice of the cock was instituted in commemoration of the death of the young Saiyid Iskandar who died of his own free will to expiate the sin of Muṣṭafā (*Notes*, p. 211 [91]). The fraternal unions seem to be based on the relations which had existed between Razbār and

Muṣṭafā Dowdān (these two individuals are sometimes regarded as one).

Firḳān al-akhbār. The author of this treatise was Ḥādjdjī Niʿmat-Allāh of Djaiḥūn-ābād near Dīnawar (1871—1920) who belonged to the Khāmūshī division and who believed the time had come to reveal the Real Truth (*ḥaḳīḳat*). His son Nūr ʿAlī Shāh (b. 1313/1895) wrote the biography of his father and an introduction to the *Firḳān* under the title of *Kashf al-ḥaḳāʾiḳ*. While confirming much that was already known, the *Firḳān* represents a tradition different from that of the Ātash-begī in as much as it makes no mention of "seven" epochs and reserves a special position for Khāwandagār and Sulṭān Ṣohāk.

Distribution. The principal centres of the Ahl-i Ḥaḳḳ are in the west of Persia, in Luristān, Kurdistān (land of the Gūrān east of Zohāb, town of Kirind) and in Ādharbāidjān (Tabrīz, Mākū, with ramifications in Transcaucasia). Little colonies of Ahl-i Ḥaḳḳ are found almost everywhere in Persia (at Hamadhān, Ṭeherān, at Māzandarān, Fārs and even in Khurāsān. In the ʿIrāḳ there are Ahl-i Ḥaḳḳ among the Kurd and Turkoman tribes of the region of Kirkūk, of Sulaimānīya and probably at Mōṣul.

Very little is known of the connection between the Ahl-i Ḥaḳḳ and the sects popularly known under the name of ʿAlī-Ilāhī or by contemptuous terms like *čirāgh-söndürän* ("extinguishers of lights"), *khurūs-kushān* ("slaughterers of cocks") etc. In any case, it is a striking fact that the direct influence of Ahl-i Ḥaḳḳ preachers of the district of Zohāb could be traced among the ʿAlawī (Ḳizilbash) of ʿAintāb. Cf. Trowbridge, *The Alevis*, in *Harvard Theological Review*, ii (1909), 340—55 (also in *M W*, 1921, p. 250—66).

Religious History. The Ahl-i Ḥaḳḳ possess a wealth of legends arranged according to the manifestations of the Divinity. The collections of these legends are known as *Sarandjām*. The epoch of Khāwandagār is interesting only for its cosmogonic myths. The traditions relating to the epoch of ʿAlī (which does not in any way form the central point) are inspired by the extreme Shīʿa. The epoch of Khoshīn, the fourth theophany, is placed in a typically Lur environment. The fourth epoch is placed in the land of the Gūrān close to the river Sīrwān. The sayings attributed to Sulṭān Ṣohāk are in Gūrānī which is the sacred language of the Ahl-i Ḥaḳḳ (cf. the *Firḳān*, i. 3). The greatest sanctuaries of the sect: Bābā-Yādegār and Perdiwer, are situated in the same region. In the later epochs the scene is transferred to Ādharbāidjān and the *kalāms* relating to these epochs are in "Āzarī Turkish". From these facts it may be concluded that the stages of propagation and development of the religion have been: Luristān — land of the Gūrān — Ādharbāidjān.

Exact dates are naturally difficult to obtain and we shall endeavour to proceed from the known to the unknown. Khān-Ātash, the seventh theophany, born at Adjari (north of Marāgha) and buried in the village of Ātash-beg in the district of Hashta-rūd, north-east of Mount Sahand, is said to have lived at the beginning of the xviii[th] century (*Notes*, p. 41 [27]). This line was continued by his direct descendants of whom the seventh was called Saiyid ʿAbd al-ʿAẓīm Mīrzā (Aghā-bakhsh) and lived at Garrabān (also called Dorū) on the Gāmāsāb to the south of Bisūtūn where O. Mann visited him. He died in 1917 and was succeeded by his son Muḥammad Ḥasan Mīrzā. The popularity of the Turkish poems of Shāh Ismāʿīl Ṣafawī is significant; the *kalām*, known as *Ḳuṭb-nāma*, calls Shāh Ismāʿīl the "*pīr* of Turkistān" (= Ādharbāidjān where Turkish is spoken). The spread of Ahl-i Ḥaḳḳ doctrines among the Turkoman tribes seems in any case to go back to an earlier period, that of the Ḳara-Ḳoyunlu rulers. The remnants of these Turkomans who live in a district in the centre of Mākū are Ahl-i Ḥaḳḳ. Similarly in Transcaucasia the Ḳara-Ḳoyunlu in the region of Gandja live in the close neighbourhood of the G'öran (< Gūrān!). Djahānshāh (1437—67), who is regarded by the Sunnites as a terrific heretic, was entitled among his adherents *sulṭān al-ʿārifīn*, "ruler of the gnostics". Shāh Ibrāhīm, whom many of the Ahl-i Ḥaḳḳ regard as the successor of Sulṭān Ṣohāk, and who lived in Baghdād and whose acolyte angel was Ḳushči-oghli (author of the Turkish *kalāms*), was perhaps responsible for the dissemination of Ahl-i Ḥaḳḳ teaching among the Turkomans north of the Tigris.

Tradition places immediately before Shāh Ibrāhīm the famous Sulṭān Ṣohāk who (outwardly) was the son of Shaikh ʿĪsī and Khātūn Dāyira, daughter of Ḥasan Beg Djald, chief of the tribe of Djāf-i Murād. His real name is said to have been Saiyid ʿAbd al-Saiyid. Barzindja, north of Sulaimānīya, is said to have been his birthplace. The leaders of the Kākāʾī of Taʾūḳ pretend to be his direct descendants. Shaikh Maḥmūd, who after the war of 1914—18 proclaimed himself "King of Kurdistān", wished to be considered as descendant of the brother of Sulṭān Ṣohāk in the twelfth generation. His genealogy does not allow us to put Sulṭān Ṣohāk's time further back than the xv[th] century (personal information of C. J. Edmonds).

The Elements of the System. The religion of the Ahl-i Ḥaḳḳ is typically syncretist. At its foundations we find Shīʿa extremism. It should be noted that the Ahl-i Ḥaḳḳ always speak of the 12 imāms and so ought not (at least directly) to be connected with Ismāʿīlism. According to the *Firḳān*, the "religion of Truth" simply re-establishes the contents of the 10 *djuzʾ* which were suppressed in the received text of the Ḳurʾān but in fact the Ahl-i Ḥaḳḳ deviate from the orthodox Shīʿa to the extent of forming a separate religious system. The religion of the Ahl-i Ḥaḳḳ has in common with those of the Druzes and the Nuṣairīs the worship of ʿAlī, but ʿAlī is completely overshadowed by Sulṭān Ṣohāk.

The other obvious element in the formation of the Ahl-i Ḥaḳḳ is the rites of the Ṣūfī dervishes: election of the *pīr*, agapes with *dhikr* and distribution of food, brotherly unions.

From the social point of view, the religion of the Ahl-i Ḥaḳḳ is professed particularly by the lower classes, nomads, villagers, inhabitants of the poorer quarters, dervishes etc. From this probably comes the hope that on the day of the last judgment "the sulṭāns" will be punished (*Notes*, p. 44 [31]). On the other hand, the eminently popular character of the religion is apparent in the exuberance of the miraculous and folklore element in the traditions of the Ahl-i Ḥaḳḳ. The Divinity enclosed in the Pearl is a Manichaean idea like the belief in the purification of the "Luminous" in the course of their transmigrations. The belief in metempsychosis cannot be directly Indian for it was already in existence in Ismāʿīlism. The division of beings into two distinct categories is perhaps a later development of Zoroastrian ideas. The sacrifice of the cock has been several times connected with the corresponding Jewish rite while the Biblical names (Dāwūd, Mūsī) may have come through the intermediary of the

Ḳur'ān. The alleged Christian influence ought not to be exaggerated: if the Ahl-i Ḥaḳḳ in their conversations with missionaries talk of Jesus and Mary, it should be remembered that, apart from these possibly being simply reminiscences of the Ḳur'ān, the Ahl-i Ḥaḳḳ regard them merely as avatars of their own pantheon. For the agapes it is not necessary to go farther back than the known dervish practices (e.g. the Bektas̲h̲ī). The elasticity of the system of metempsychosis is responsible for the appearance of unexpected names such as Malak Ṭā'ūs in the myths.

Bibliography: V. Minorsky, *Materiali dl'a izučeniya persidskoy sekti "L'udi Istinî" ili "Ali Ilahi"* (in Russian with French compilation), Moscou 1911 (*Trudi po vostokovedeniyu izdavayemîye Lazarevskim institutom*, Tome xxxiii); do., *Notes sur la secte de Ahlé-Haqq*, in *RMM*, xl (1920), 20—97 and xlv (1921), 205—302; [cf. the review by F. Cumont in *Syria*, iii (1922), 262]; do., *Un traité de polémique Béhai-Ahlé-Haqq*, in *JA* 1921, p. 165—167; do., *Études sur les Ahl-i Haqq "Toumari" = Ahl-i Ḥaqq* in *RHR*, xcvii (1928), 90—105; Dr. Saeed Khan, *The Sect of Ahl-i Haqq*, in *MW*, xvii (1927), 31—42; Gordlevsky, *Kara-koyunlu*, in *Izw. Obščestva izučeniya Azerbaydjama*, Baku 1927; Adjarian, *Gyorans and Toumarians, a newly founded religion in Persia*, written in English in *Bulletin de l'Université d'Erivan* (French translation by F. Macler, *Une religion nouvelle. Les Toumaris*, in *RHR* (1926), 294—307); M. F. Stead, *The Ali-Ilahi sect in Persia*, in *MW*, 1932, p. 184—89.

AḤMAD b. Muḥammad b. Ḥanbal, known by the name of Ibn Ḥanbal, celebrated Islāmic theologian, a member of the Arab clan of S̲h̲aibān, born at Bag̲h̲dad in Rabīʿ I 164/November 780. During his studies in his native town (till 183/799) and on very extensive student travels, which led him through ʿIrāḳ, Syria and Ḥid̲j̲āz to Yemen, he aimed chiefly at acquiring a knowledge of *ḥadīt̲h̲* [q.v.]. After he returned home, he took lessons from al-S̲h̲āfiʿī in *fiḳh* and its *uṣūl* (195—197/810—813). His religious turn of mind was in creed and law unalterably determined by the old traditional views. He had occasion to display them, when under the caliphs al-Ma'mūn, al-Muʿtaṣim and al-Wāt̲h̲iḳ (218—234/833—849) the Muʿtazilite definition of the dogmas was raised to a *confessio fidei* prescribed by the State and criminal proceedings were introduced against acknowledged theologians who would not without reserve profess the doctrine of the "creation of the Ḳur'ān". Ibn Ḥanbal too was brought before the inquisition (*miḥna*). As he was being led to Ṭarsūs in chains to al-Ma'mūn, he received the news of the caliph's death. Under the latter's successor he patiently submitted to corporal punishment and imprisonment, without being moved even to any softening of the rigid traditional form of confession. Only when under al-Mutawakkil return to orthodoxy was demanded by reasons of State Ibn Ḥanbal's trials ceased; he was on several occasions distinguished by the caliph and invited to the Court, even a pension was without his knowledge allowed his family. The fame of his learning, piety and unswerving faithfulness to tradition gathered a host of disciples and admirers around him. He died at Bag̲h̲dād on the 12th Rabīʿ I 241/31st July 855. His burial is the subject of fabulous description by biographers. His tomb, associated with stories of miracles (cf. Goldziher, *Muhamm. Stud.*, i. 257), in the Bag̲h̲dād cemetery of martyrs (*maḳābir al-s̲h̲uhadā'*) in the Ḥarbīya quarter, was for a long time venerated as that of a saint. After it had been destroyed towards the end of the viith (xiiith) century by the inundations of the Tigris, the veneration was transferred to the tomb of his son ʿAbd Allāh in the Ḳurais̲h̲ cemetery near the Straw Gate, which Tīmūr had restored in 795/1392—3. After that time the tomb of the son was confounded with that of the father, and the cult of the latter was transferred to the former (G. le Strange, *Baghdad during the Abbaside Caliphate*, p. 166).

Among Ibn Ḥanbal's works, the great encyclopaedia of traditions, *Musnad*, compiled by his son ʿAbd Allāh from his lectures and amplified by supplements (*zawā'id*), containing 28,000—29,000 traditions, acquired great renown (printed in Cairo 1311, 6 vol.; cf. Goldziher, in *ZDMG*, l., 465—506; M. Hartmann, *Die Tradenten erster Schicht im Musnad des Aḥmad ibn Ḥanbal*, (in *MSOS*, year 9, part ii., Berlin 1906). The son also supplemented his *Kitāb al-zuhd* ("the book of ascetism"). The *Musnad*, around which a respectable series of secondary works and adaptations grew up, has continually been the subject of pious reading. From the xiith (xviiith) century we have the statement that a pious society read this work to the end in 56 sittings at the Prophet's tomb in Madīna (Murādī, *Silk al-durar*, iv. 60). The traditions of the *Musnad* have been used in Wensinck's *Handbook* and are made accessible in the *CTM*.

Besides the *Musnad* there has been published Ibn Ḥanbal's *Kitāb al-ṣalāt wa-mā yalzam fīhā*, on the discipline of prayer (lithographed in Bombay, n.d.; printed in Cairo [K̲h̲ānd̲j̲ī] 1223). A polemical treatise by Ibn Ḥanbal, written in prison, is frequently quoted in works of Ḥanbalite dogmatists: *al-Radd ʿala 'l-Zanādiḳa wa 'l-D̲j̲ahmīya fī mā s̲h̲akkat fīhi min mutas̲h̲ābih al-Ḳur'ān*, in which he refutes the *ta'wīl* [q.v.] explanation introduced by the Muʿtazilites. — Likewise a book of his entitled *Kitāb ṭāʿat al-rasūl* is quoted; in it he discusses the line one must follow in those cases where the *ḥadīt̲h̲* seems to be in contradiction with the text of certain Ḳur'ānic passages. He formulated his dogmatic confession in his *Kitāb al-Sunna* (printed at Mecca).

As Ibn Ḥanbal occupied himself more with the sources of the *ḥadīt̲h̲* than with the derivation of the law, some representatives of jurisprudence, as for instance al-Ṭabarī, do not consider him an authoritative *fiḳh* authority; hence the great animosity of Ibn Ḥanbal's followers towards al-Ṭabarī (Kern, in *ZDMG*, lv. 67; his edition of the *Ik̲h̲tilāf*, p. 13 *sq.*). To be sure Ibn Ḥanbal established no *fiḳh* system of his own; but in his answers to his pupils' questions he made pronouncements on specific disputed points of law. There are cited for instance: *Masā'il Ṣāliḥ* (questions put to him by his son Ṣāliḥ and his decisions with regard to them) and answers to the questions of his pupil Ḥarb (Ibn Ḳaiyim al-D̲j̲awzīya, *al-Ṭuruḳ al-ḥikmīya fi 'l-siyāsa al-s̲h̲arʿiya*, Cairo 1317, p. 251, 293 *sq.*). His *Fatāwī*, accessible still to the author just mentioned, amounted to about 20 books (*sifr*; cf. *Hidāyat al-ḥayārā*, Cairo 1323, p. 121). Even in his lifetime some of his disciples systematized his legal teaching, especially Abū Yaʿḳūb Isḥāḳ al-Kawsad̲j̲, who in doubtful cases applied to Ibn Ḥanbal for oral instruction (D̲h̲ahabī, *Tad̲h̲kirat al-ḥuffāẓ*, ii. 105), and a little later Abū Bakr al-K̲h̲allāl, who died in Bag̲h̲dād in 311/923—4 ("Mu'allif ʿilm Aḥmad b. Ḥanbal wa-d̲j̲āmiʿuhu wa-murattibuhu"; *ibid.*, iii. 7). The latter's work is still quoted by Ibn Ḳaiyim al-Djawzīya (d. 751/1350), in his *Aʿlām al-muwaffaḳīn* (see the appendix to al-Ṭabarānī's *al-Muʿdjam al-ṣaghīr*, p. 271), but certainly not from autopsy. The system of doctrine developed under the guidance of Ibn Ḥanbal's ideas was recognized by the *idjmāʿ* of the orthodox Sunnites as one of the four authoritative *madhāhib*: it is that of the Ḥanbalites. Ibn Ḥanbal, as an adherent of the Ahl al-Ḥadīth [see FIḲH], makes concessions to *raʾy* only under pressure of sheer necessity and where possible derives every law from traditional sources. This compels him to be very indulgent to the *ḥadīth* and sometimes to admit very feeble traditions as the basis of his decisions. In none of the recognized rites has the prohibition of the *bidʿa* [q.v.] been pushed to such extremes as in the *madhhab* named after Ibn Ḥanbal. Thence a far extending rigorousness resulted in all ritual and social connections and a more intolerant attitude than in the general orthodoxy. In dogmatic theology his school clings to the pre-Ashʿaritic orthodoxy; even al-Ashʿarī himself was compelled, in order to gain a footing in the general conceptions of the Muslims, to make several concessions to it in the definite formulation of his dogmatics, nay even to declare expressly that he was in full harmony with the teaching of Ibn Ḥanbal and that he avoided everything that was in contradiction to it (Ibn ʿAsākir; Spitta, *Zur Gesch. al-Aśʿarī's*, p. 133). The essence of the Ḥanbalite dogmatics may be found in the most concise manner in ʿAbd al-Ḳādir al-Djīlī's *al-Ghunya li-ṭālibī ṭarīk al-ḥakk* (Mecca 1314), i. 48—66.

The Ḥanbalites, who represent now the smallest Islāmic *madhhab*, were till the viii[th] (xiv[th]) century much more widely spread in the countries of Islām. Muḳaddasī finds them in Persia: in Ispahān, Raiy, Shahrazūr and other places, where their religious system seems to have been characterized by extravagances of various kinds. Above all they displayed in those places a particular predilection for the memory of the Caliph Muʿāwiya (ed. de Goeje, p. 365, 13, 384, 14, 399, 6, 407, 13). Their attachment to the memory of this Umaiyad may of course not be intended for his merit as a pious man, but for the caliph recognized by the orthodox Sunna. The favourable attitude towards Yazīd, found precisely among the Ḥanbalites, is to be interpreted from the same point of view (illustrations for which in *ZDMG*, liii. 646, note). In Syria and Palestine, where the Ḥanbalite *madhhab* was introduced in the vth (xi[th]) century by ʿAbd al-Wāḥid al-Shīrāzī (*Kitāb al-ins al-djalīl*, p. 263), it was represented till into the ix[th] (xv[th]) century (cf. *ZDMG*, viii. 364). Mudjīr al-Dīn (d. in 927/1521), a Ḥanbalite himself, enumerates in his just mentioned *Kitāb al-ins al-djalīl* (p. 592 *sq.*) the most renowned representatives of Ḥanbalism in Palestine from the vi[th] to the ix[th] (xii[th]—xv[th]) centuries. It was also in this period that the appearance of Taḳī al-Dīn b. Taimīya (661—728/1263—1328) in Syria caused a great sensation. He took up anew the fight for the Ḥanbalite theology (refutation of the rationalistic explanation of the Ḳurʾān and traditions — *taʾwīl* —, rejection of all innovations, as for instance visiting tombs, venerating the saints etc.; cf. Schreiner, in *ZDMG*, lii. 540—563; liii. 51—67) against the dogmatics that had dominated for a long time. But as he offended in this way the requisitions of the orthodox *idjmāʿ* he was persecuted. By his fall the prestige of Ḥanbalism suffered a considerable decline. Until the establishment of Turkish predominance in Islām all the four schools, including the Ḥanbalite, were represented officially by ḳāḍīs in all Islāmic centres. The predominance of the Ottomans dealt Ḥanbalism a very severe blow; since then it has continued more and more to dwindle away, although in its isolated apparitions it has retained acceptance as an element of Sunnite orthodoxy. In the Azhar Mosque it is, of course in a relatively small number, represented by teachers and students (*riwāḳ al-Ḥanābila*); in 1906 there were 3 Ḥanbalite teachers and 28 pupils (out of a total of 312 teachers and 9,069 students). On the other hand in the xviii[th] century, it appeared in a new and vigorous form, namely in the movement of the Wahhābites [q.v.], in which the after-effects of Ibn Taimīya's exertions have been demonstrated.

The following are the eminent Ḥanbalite teachers in successive epochs: Abu 'l-Ḳāsim ʿUmar al-Kharaḳī (d. in 334/945—6), whose compendium of Ḥanbalite *fiḳh* is extant; ʿAbd al-ʿAzīz b. Djaʿfar (282—363/895—974), whose *Muḳniʿ* has been for centuries the groundwork for compendiums and commentaries (printed: *al-Rawḍ al-murtiʿ fī sharḥ zād al-mustaḳniʿ*, Damascus 1303; cf. *Mashriḳ*, iv. 879); Abu 'l-Wafāʾ ʿAlī b. ʿAḳīl (d. in 515/1121—2), who was celebrated as head of a productive school; ʿAbd al-Ḳādir al-Djīlī (471—561/1078—1166), whose central importance as a Ṣūfī was combined with faithful adherence to Ibn Ḥanbal; Abu 'l-Faradj b. al-Djawzī (508—597/1114—1200); ʿAbd al-Ghanī al-Djammāʿīlī (d. 600/1203—4); Muwaffaḳ al-Dīn b. Ḳudāma (d. 620/1223), who appended his much studied *Mughnī* as a commentary to Kharaḳī's compendium (printed with the commentary of Shams al-Dīn Ibn Ḳudāma [died 682/1183—4] in 12 vols. Cairo 1346—48); the celebrated controversialists Taḳī al-Dīn b. Taimīya [see above] and his faithful pupil Muḥammad b. Ḳaiyim al-Djawzīya [see above], both known for the harshness of their dogmatic system and their intolerant controversy against those who believe and think otherwise. Of the works of the latter two Ḥanbalite teachers numerous writings have recently been published in the printing houses of Cairo; in these may be studied the doctrinal ideas of the Ḥanbalite school. Still in the xi[th] (xvii[th]) century some eminent Ḥanbalite scholars came from the little place Buhūt (district of Maḥallat al-Kubrā): ʿAbd al-Raḥmān al-Buhūtī (d. 1051/1641—2) and his pupil Muḥammad al-Buhūtī (d. 1088/1677—8); both lived and taught in Cairo. In the Azhar Mosque the *Nail al-maʾārib* (a commentary on the *Dalīl al-ṭālib* of Marʿī b. Yūsuf, otherwise known as epistolographer, d. in 1030/1621) of ʿAbd al-Ḳādir b. ʿUmar al-Dimishḳī (d. in 1035/1625—6) — printed in Būlāḳ 1288 — is taken as the basis of Ḥanbalite instruction.

Abu 'l-Faradj ʿAbd al-Raḥmān b. Radjab (d. in 795/1392—3) wrote *Ṭabaḳāt al-Ḥanābila*, which is extant in manuscript (see Vollers, *Kat. Leipzig*, No. 708). The *Ṭabaḳāt al-Ḥanābila* of Ibn Abī Yaʿlā (died 526/1131—2) are now accessible in the Damascus edition of 1350 (1931). The literature of Ḥanbalite law is most copiously registered in the catalogue of the Cairo manuscripts, iii. 293—301. Cf. further W. M. Patton, *Aḥmed ibn Ḥanbal and the Miḥna* (Leyden 1897) and in connection with it: Goldziher, in *ZDMG*, lii. 155 *sq.*; do., *Zur Gesch. der ḥanbalit. Bewegungen* (*ibid.*, lxii.); H. Laoust, *Essai sur les doctrines. . . . d'Ibn Taimiya*, Le Caire 1939, esp. p. 76; Brockelmann, *GAL*, i. 181 *sq.* (2nd ed. i, 193); *Suppl.* i, 309.

AḤMAD AL-BADAWĪ, SĪDĪ, who has for centuries been considered the greatest saint in Egypt, is said to have been a descendant of ʿAlī. His forefathers are said to have emigrated to Fās about the year 73/692 in consequence of the troubles in Arabia. Aḥmad was born at Fās in the *Zuḳāḳ al-Ḥadjar*, probably in the year 596/1199—1200, and he seems to have been the youngest of seven or eight children. His mother was called Fāṭima; the position of his father is not mentioned. His full name was Aḥmad b. ʿAlī b. Ibrahīm and his genealogy was traced up to ʿAlī, and even to Maʿadd and ʿAdnān. He bore several surnames, of which some are explained in the sources and some are not. He was called al-Badawī because like the African Bedouins he wore the face-veil (*lithām*). Further in Mecca he was called al-ʿAṭṭāb, "the intrepid horseman" (some sources misunderstand this Maghribī expression); the same meaning underlies, as it seems, his name Abu 'l-Fityān, although the sources do not say so. In Mecca he was also called al-Ghaḍbān, "the furious, raging one"; further Abu 'l-ʿAbbās, which might come from Abu 'l-Fityān by *taḥrīf* (miswriting). In his position as a Ṣūfī he was called al-Ḳudsī, al-Ḳuṭb ("the pole") and the Silent, and in more recent times Abū Farrādj ("liberator" ,namely of prisoners).

When still a child he set out with his family on a pilgrimage to Mecca, where they arrived after four years of travelling. This is placed in the years 603—607/1206—1211. His imposing reception among the Bedouins is spoken of, but Egypt is not mentioned. In Mecca his father died and was buried near the Bāb al-Maʿlāt. As a grown youth Aḥmad is said to have distinguished himself in Mecca as a daring horseman and a merry wild fellow, whence his above surnames al-ʿAṭṭāb and Abu 'l-Fityān. Then about 627/1230 he must have undergone an inner transformation. He read the Ḳurʾān according to all the seven *aḥruf* (readings) and studied a little Shāfiʿite law. He gave himself up to devotion (*al-ʿibāda*) and declined the offer of a marriage. He withdrew from men, became taciturn, made himself understood by signs only, and often fell into trances (*walah*). According to some authorities the journey to Mecca was undertaken after a vision, but others mention here three consecutive visions, which summoned Aḥmad (Shawwāl 633/June—July 1236) to visit ʿIrāḳ, where Aḥmad al-Rifāʿī (d. 570/1174—5) and ʿAbd al-Ḳādir al-Gīlānī (d. 561/1165—6) had been worshipped as the greatest saints for two generations. Aḥmad emigrated thither in the company of his eldest brother Ḥasan. From that time onward the reports become very fabulous and vague. The brothers visited, besides the tombs of the two "poles" mentioned above, a great many other saints, amongst them being al-Ḥallādj (d. 309/921—2) and ʿAdī b. Musāfir al-Hakkārī Abu 'l-Faḍāʾil (d. 558/1162—3). Under the impression of these visits Aḥmad's religious consciousness entered on a new phase. Al-Rifāʿī and al-Gīlānī, the "owners of the keys of the countries", invited him to share in this possession. But Aḥmad refused the offer saying that he would accept the "keys of the countries" from none but God. In ʿIrāḳ he subdued also the indomitable Fāṭima bint Barrī, who had never yet surrendered to any man, and refused her offer to marry him. In the *Djawāhir* and elsewhere this incident has been turned into a highly romantic story. A year later (634/1236—7) Aḥmad had another vision which induced him to visit Ṭanditā (Ṭanṭā, Ṭanta) in Egypt, where he stayed till his death. His brother Ḥasan returned from ʿIrāḳ to Mecca. In Ṭanditā Aḥmad entered on the last and most important period of his life. His mode of life is described in the following way: "He climbed in Ṭanditā on to the roof of a private house, stood there motionless and looked up into the sun so that his eyes went red and sore and looked like two fiery coals. Sometimes he would maintain a prolonged silence, at other times he would indulge in continuous screaming. He went without food or drink for about forty days". Traits of this and similar nature have evidently been borrowed from the lives of Indian ascetics (*yogis*). In Ṭanditā and its neighbourhood he met with both friends and adversaries. In his search of a cure for his sore eyes he came across ʿAbd al-ʿĀl, who at that time was still a boy and afterwards became his confident and *khalīfa* (successor). He worked miracles and signs (*karāmāt wa-khawāriḳ*), many of which are described at some length in the authorities. Those saints who were still reverenced at the time of his arrival in Ṭanditā found themselves eclipsed. Ḥasan al-Ikhnāʾī refuses to acknowledge him and leaves the place; Sālim al-Maghribī submits to him and is for that reason allowed to remain in Ṭanditā. Wadjh al-Ḳamar is cursed by Aḥmad and his abode is deserted and falls to ruin. His contemporary al-Malik al-Ẓāhir Baibars is said to have venerated him and to have kissed his feet. His disciples were called *Suṭūḥīya* or *Aṣḥāb al-saṭḥ* from their habit of living on the roof. In the night he used to read the Ḳurʾān; in his prayers he was joined by two imāms. Concerning his state of mind it is said: *ḥuḍūr*ᵘ*hu akthar*ᵘ *min ghiyābihi*, "he was oftener in his senses than in a trance". After he had lived and worked in this way at Ṭantā for nearly 41 years, he died on the 12ᵗʰ of Rabīʿ I 675/Aug. 24, 1276, that is on the anniversary of the Prophet's death.

Judged by his conduct Aḥmad al-Badawī is a representative of the yogi-like type of the dervishes. The following have been handed down to us as the productions of his mind:

1. A prayer (*ḥizb*); *Berlin Cat.*, iii. 411, 3881.
2. *Ṣalāts*, on which a commentary was written by the celebrated Ṣūfī of the xiiᵗʰ (= xviiiᵗʰ) century ʿAbd al-Raḥmān b. Muṣṭafā ʿAidarūs (1135—1192/1722—1778) under the title of *Fatḥ al-Raḥmān* (*Cairo Cat.*, vii. 88).
3. His spiritual testament (*waṣāyā*), addressed principally to his first *khalīfa* ʿAbd al-ʿĀl. The sayings and admonitions it contains are of such a general nature, are so little individual and so exactly identical with the fundamental ideas of Islāmic asceticism of all times, and part of them even similar to those of non-Islāmic asceticism and mysticism, that it is doubtful whether they can be considered as the spiritual production of Aḥmad al-Badawī, and whether they may be ascribed to his moral personality.

After his death ʿAbd al-ʿĀl, who had known him since his boyhood and had lived with him for forty years, became his *khalīfa* and the possessor of the Master's insignia: the red cowl, the veil and the red banner. He ordered a chapel to be built on Aḥmad's tomb, which in course of time developed into a large mosque. He seems to have kept his adherents under strict rule, arranged the ceremonies (*ashāʾir*) and died in 733/1332—3.

The celebration of Aḥmad's *mawlid* and the veneration of the saint abroad seem to have increased rapidly, though not without opposition, strife and reaction. The opponents were partly scholars, who were averse to all Ṣūfism; partly politicans who objected to the Ṣūfīs as rulers of the people. This may account for the fact that twice a *khalīfa* of al-Badawī was murdered (Ibn Iyās, ii. 61, 15 *sq.*; iii. 78, 14). Amongst the scholars who were at first hostile to Aḥmad but afterwards believed in him are mentioned Ibn Daḳīḳ al-ʿĪd (d. 702/1302—3) and Ibn al-Labbān (d. 739/1338—9). Already under the first *khalīfas* one hears of quarrels between the followers of al-Badawī. In 850/1446—7 mention is made of the restoration of the *mawlid* which had sunk into neglect (Ibn Iyās, ii. 30, 5). An ardent venerator of Aḥmad was Sulṭān Ḳāʾit Bey, who visited his tomb in 888/1483 and ordered the sanctuary to be enlarged (*ibid.*, ii. 217, 7, 301, 15). In the processions of the Mamlūk sulṭāns the *khalīfa* of al-Badawī appeared at the side of the principal ecclesiastical dignitaries of the realm. Under Ottoman rule the outward splendour of his cult seems to have diminished, because it annoyed the powerful orders of the Turks. But this political attitude could not prejudice his veneration amongst the Egyptians. He has been for a long time the greatest saint of Egypt and a deliverer from all troubles. The deliverance of Muslim captives out of the hands of the Christians is supposed to have been one of his earliest achievements, to which he owes his name of *Mudjīb al-asārā min bilād al-naṣārā* [cf. above Abū Farrādj]. No less than three *mawlids* are celebrated every year in Egypt in honour of him, the dates of which are noteworthy from the point of view of the history of religion. As a matter of fact the festivals have been arranged according to Coptic dates or (generally speaking) according to the solar year, to wit: the principal *mawlid* is in Misra (August); the middle one, also called *mawlid* of Shurunbulālī, is in Barmūda (March-April); and the least important one, also called *mawlid al-radjabī* or *laff al-ʿimāma*, is in Amshir (February). The small and the middle *mawlid* are essentially big fairs, whereas the principal *mawlid*, apart from its commercial importance, is a politico-religious celebration in the grandest style with offerings, prayers, vows, *dhikrs* and sermons; it ends with the *rakbat* (or the *rukūb*) *al-khalīfa*, i.e. the solemn procession of the *khalīfa* with his retinue through the town of Ṭanṭā.

The followers of al-Badawī are called *Aḥmadīya* and are found all over Egypt and beyond. Their badge is the red turban. The Baiyūmīya, the Shinnāwīya, the Awlād Nūḥ and the Shuʿaibīya are looked upon as branches (*furūʿ*) of this order.

For a long time Aḥmad has ranked as a *ḳuṭb* in Egypt together with ʿAbd al-Ḳādir al-Gilānī, Aḥmad al-Rifāʿī and Ibrahīm al-Dasūḳī, in what is called the *ḳiṭāba*.

One of his greatest venerators was ʿAbd al-Wahhāb al-Shaʿrāwī (d. 973/1565), whose family, like Aḥmad al-Badawī, came from the Maghrib, but had settled down in Egypt. Al-Shaʿrāwī called himself al-Aḥmadī after him (Vollers, *Cat. Leipzig*, No. 353); he often went on a pilgrimage to his tomb, counted him amongst the greatest Ṣūfīs and conversed with him in visions (cf. *Revue Africaine*, xiv. [1870], 229).

It is altogether impossible to account for the historical importance of Aḥmad al-Badawī by his individuality; it can only be explained by supposing that, both as a Ṣūfī and as a saint, he had become the point of crystallisation of many wants and tendencies of his own time and of those which came before and after him. It has already been noticed by Maspero, Ebers and Goldziher, that old Egyptian elements have been mixed with the cult of Aḥmad. In addition to the immoral features of his cult, which have been narrated by Goldziher, may be mentioned what al-Shaʿrāwī relates of his pilgrimage to the tomb of al-Badawī. Being one day at the tomb of the saint in the company of his newly married wife Fāṭima, whom he had not yet approached, he was summoned by the (dead) Aḥmad to deflower her before him at his tomb. The summons to this act and its ensuing execution are just as much in keeping with the cult and the spirit of Aḥmad, as they are opposed to the character of al-Shaʿrāwī, whose feelings were very delicate in matters of sex.

All over Egypt prayers are addressed to Aḥmad, and feasts are celebrated in his honour not only in Ṭanṭā but also often in Cairo by the Aḥmadīya, and even in small villages, e.g. Berumbāl (ʿAlī Mubārak, ix. 37, 24). It is more difficult to ascertain whether the tombs and chapels which bear the name of al-Badawī have anything to do with him. J. L. Burckhardt (*Syria*, p. 166) mentions a saint of this name near Tripoli (Syria); there is another one near Ghazza (Goldziher, *Muh. Studien*, ii. 328; *ZDPV*, xi. 152, 158). The traditions concerning Aḥmad are quite reliable, though tinged with a legendary colouring. All the oldest authorities refer to an account of Aḥmad's brother Ḥasan, who still lived with him in Mecca and parted from him after the journey in ʿIrāḳ. Aḥmad's importance in the ix[th] (xv[th]) century can be concluded from the fact that al-Maḳrīzī and Ibn Ḥadjar al-ʿAsḳalānī devoted biographical articles to him (cf. *Berlin Cat.*, iii. 218, 3350, 6; ix. 483, 10101; also al-Suyūṭī, *Ḥusn al-muḥāḍara*, Cairo 1299, i. 299 *sqq.*). The account which al-Shaʿrāwī gives of him in his *Ṭabaḳāt* is written with fervent piety (lithogr. Cairo 1299, i. 245—251).

In 1028/1619 a certain ʿAbd al-Ṣamad Zain al-Dīn, employed at the *maḳām* of the saint, wrote his *al-Djawāhir al-sunnīya* (*sanīya*?) *fi 'l-karāmāt wa'l-nisba al-aḥmadīya*, in which he brought together everything on the subject which was worth knowing (printed and lithographed Cairo 1305 etc.). He drew not only from the above mentioned sources, but from unknown authorities besides, e.g. Abu 'l-Suʿūd al-Wāsiṭī, Sirādj al-Dīn al-Ḥanbalī, Muḥammad al-Ḥanafī and the "genealogy" (*nisba*) of Yūnus (elsewhere Yūsuf) b. ʿAbd Allāh, called Ezbek al-Ṣūfī. The anonymous *Nasab* of al-Badawī (127 fol.), mentioned in the *Cairo Catalogue*, v. 167, may be the work of this Ezbek. ʿAbd al-Ṣamad gives an account of Aḥmad's life and states his authorities; next comes a description of the homage of the novices and of the *khalīfas*; at the mention of Aḥmad's death the elegies of his brothers and sisters are given; then he writes of the *mawlid*, his miracles, his *waṣāyā*, and adds numerous *ḳaṣīdas* on him, arranged alphabetically, by Shihab al-ʿAlḳamī, Shams al-Bakrī, ʿAbd al-ʿAzīz al-Derīnī (d.c. 690/1291), ʿAbd al-Ḳādir al-Danōsharī and others; finally he treats of his followers and of the eight words of his first years after which he became *ṣammāt* (taciturn). Much less important is the work of ʿAlī al-Ḥalabī (d. 1044/1634—5) *al-Naṣīḥa al-ʿalawīya fī bayān ḥusn ṭarīḳat al-sāda al-aḥmadīya* (*Berlin Cat.*, ix. 484, 10104). The author's principal aim is to praise asceticism and the *fuḳarāʾ* of Aḥmad. A London MS. (*Brit. Mus. Suppl.*, No. 639) contains anonymous *manāḳib* of Aḥmad (27 fol.); cf. also *Berlin Cat.*, ix. 466, 10064, 7 (3 fol.).

A later publication concerning Aḥmad is one by

Ḥasan Rās̲h̲id al-Mas̲h̲hadī al-K̲h̲afād̲j̲ī: *al-Nafaḥāt al-aḥmadīya wa'l-d̲j̲awāhir al-ṣamadānīya* (Cairo 1321, 4°, 316 pp.). Aḥmad is often treated of along with the other *aḳṭāb*, for instance by Muḥammad b. Ḥasan al-ʿAd̲j̲lūnī (c. 899/1494), cf. *Berlin Cat.*, i. 60, 163; and by Aḥmad b. ʿUt̲h̲mān al-S̲h̲arnūbī (c. 950/1543), cf. *ibid.*, iii. 226, 3371. A short poem on Aḥmad is found *ibid.*, v. 29, 5432; vii. 197, 8115, 3 (of the year 1175). Later accounts, such as ʿAlī Mubārak, xiii. 48—51, borrow mostly from al-S̲h̲aʿrāwī and ʿAbd al-Ṣamad. Cf. also E. W. Lane, *Modern Egyptians*; Brockelmann, *GAL*, i. 450; *Suppl.* i. 808.

AḤMADĪYA is the name of the adherents of Mirzā G̲h̲ulām Aḥmad Ḳādiānī (of Ḳādiān, district of Gurdaspur in the Pand̲j̲āb. In 1900 they were with their own approval entered under that name on the official census lists of the Indian Government, as a separate modern Mohammedan sect. The Aḥmadīs are especially numerous in the Pand̲j̲āb, but also in other provinces of the Presidency of Bombay and elsewhere in India and Pakistan. They are found besides in other Mohammedan countries such as Afg̲h̲ānistān, Persia, Arabia, Egypt etc. Their number is gradually increasing in consequence of zealous propagandism. Their principal organ is the *Review of Religions*, written in English, which since 1902 has been published regularly once a month at Ḳādiān. But they also make use of various other papers in Indian languages, weeklies, monthlies and quarterlies. They have also separate extensive writings, amongst which *Barāhīn-i Aḥmedīya* (*The Arguments of the Aḥmedīya*), written by the founder Mīrzā Aḥmad, is the most important. The first volume of this work appeared in 1880, and in it the author claimed the dignity of a Mahdī, though not until March 4th 1889 did he demand the homage of his adherents.

The doctrines of the Aḥmadīya agree on the whole with those generally taught by the Islām. The most striking differences concern only the Christology, the vocation of the Mahdī and the *d̲j̲ihād* (the holy war). As to the first mentioned doctrine, they assume that Jesus did not die on the cross, but after his apparent death and resurrection migrated to India, strictly speaking to Kas̲h̲mīr, in order to preach the gospel in that country. There he is said to have died at the age of 120 years; his tomb at Srinagar is still known, but is mistaken for that of a prophet called Yuz Asaf (which according to the Aḥmadīs must not be explained as a corruption of Bodhisatwa!). At the instigation of a certain Mawlā Muḥammed Ḥusain a *fatwā* against Mīrzā Aḥmad was published in India, purporting that this doctrine disagreed with the Ḳurʾān and therefore had to be looked upon as heresy. Regarding the vocation of the Mahdī and the *d̲j̲ihād* the Aḥmadīya teach that the task of the former is one of peace, and that the *d̲j̲ihād* against the unfaithful must be conducted with peaceful means instead of instruments of war; under all circumstances sincere obedience must be given to the Government. The Mahdī himself must be considered an incarnation both of Jesus and Muḥammad and at the same time an avatar of Krishna. To believe in him as the Second or the Promised Messiah is an article of faith, because first of all his coming early in the 14th century of the Hid̲j̲ra was predicted by Muḥammad, and secondly because he proved his divine vocation by his prophetic gift. On various occasions this gift has manifested itself: not only the terrible destructions caused by pestilence and earthquake during the last decades but also the death of certain people are said to have been prophesied by him. When one of his last mentioned predictions came true through the murder of an inhabitant of Lahore, Mīrzā Aḥmad was accused of the crime by three Christian missionaires, but acquitted in court.

After the Mahdī had resigned his leadership because of old age, the affairs of the Aḥmadīya were conducted by the Ṣadr And̲j̲uman-i Aḥmadīya.

Mīrzā G̲h̲ulām Aḥmad died in 1908 and was succeeded by the k̲h̲alīfa Nūr al-Dīn. When the latter died in 1914 and the founder's son Mīrzā Bas̲h̲īr al-Dīn Maḥmūd Aḥmad was chosen as second k̲h̲alīfa, a group, headed by K̲h̲wād̲j̲a Kamāl al-Dīn and Maulvi Muḥammad ʿAlī, seceded and formed the Lahore Party, the original group being called the Ḳādiān Party. The difference between both parties is that, while the Ḳādiān Party regarded Mīrzā G̲h̲ulām Aḥmad as a prophet (*nabī*), the Lahore Party considered him merely as a reformer (*mud̲j̲addid*). The Lahore Party organized itself as *Aḥmadīya Andjuman-i-Is̲h̲āʿat-i-Islām*. This section has already practised an extensive missionary propaganda throughout India and in foreign countries, notably in England — where the mosque of Woking is their centre — and Germany. Maulvi Muḥammad ʿAlī, who is president of the Lahore organisation, has published an English translation of the Ḳurʾān with a critical commentary (*The Holy Qur-ân*, 2nd ed. Lahore 1920) and, besides other works, a voluminous treatise on "*The Religion of Islam*" (Lahore 1936). Both the latter work and the Ḳurʾān translation have already been translated into different other languages. They are remarkable for many new and untraditional interpretations of the Ḳurʾānic text (such as *islām* by "entering into peace"), in accordance with the on the whole untraditional attitude of the Aḥmadīya.

After the Lahore group the Ḳādiān section has also begun an extensive missionary activity among non-Muslims; they also have a mosque in London. Mīrzā Bas̲h̲īr al-Dīn, the present leader, wrote a treatise in Urdu, which was translated into English under the Title *Ahmadiyya or the True Islam* and published in Ḳādiān in 1924. A later publication is called *8500 Precious Gems from World's best Literature*, 3rd ed. Secunderabad 1943; it contains quotations from ancient and modern, Islamic and non-Islamic, religious and litterary works on religious and moral subjects, alphabetically arranged. The Ḳādiān missionaries likewise spread their own Ḳurʾān translations.

In 1947 the Aḥmadīya community in Ḳādiān had much to suffer from the troubles that arose in connection with the demarcation of the new frontier between Pakistan and India. They have now transferred their centre to Rabwa in Pākistān.

In 1930 the number of Aḥmadiya followers was estimated at about half a million, of whom perhaps 60.000 in India itself (Titus).

Bibliography: H. A. Walker, *The Ahmadiyah Movement*, Calcutta 1918; L. Bouvat in *JA*. ccxiii (1928) p. 159 *sq.*; Murray T. Titus, *The religious Quest of Indian Islam*, Oxford 1930, p. 217 *sq.*; H. A. R. Gibb, *Modern Trends in Islam*, Chicago 1947, p. 61 *sqq.*

AḤMAD K̲H̲ĀN, the son of Saiyid Muḥammad Muttaḳī K̲h̲ān, was born at Delhi, on 17th October 1817. His ancestors came from Arabia to Herāt, and thence to India during the reign of Akbar S̲h̲āh. When Saiyid Aḥmad was 19 years of age, his father died, and the year following (1837) he entered the service of the British Government as record-keeper in the Criminal Department at Dehli. In 1841 he was appointed *munṣif*, or Subordinate Judge, at Fatehpur Sikri in the District of Āgra. During the mutiny of 1857 he was *munṣif* at Bijnaur, and saved the lives of the European residents by sending them safely to Meerut. For his unswerving loyalty to the British Government, and his conspicuous courage, he was rewarded by the grant of a pension, and subsequently by the title of a Companion of the Star of India. When 52 years of age (1869) he visited England, taking his two sons with him in order to give them the advantages of a Western education. He took the greatest interest in the welfare and education of his co-religionists, and, on his return to India, he founded a college at G͟hāzipur. Subsequently, on his transfer to Aligarh, he founded a Literary and Scientific Society, and finally succeeded in inaugurating the Muḥammadan Anglo-Oriental College at Aligarh, despite much opposition from many who regarded the introduction of a system of Western education as being subversive of the orthodox faith of Islām. The college was opened in May 1875, and the foundation-stone of the present college building was laid by Lord Lytton in January 1877. An account of this institution is given by the late Theodore Beck, formerly principal of the college, in an appendix to Lieut.-Colonel G. Graham's *Life and work of Syed Aḥmed K͟han* (London, 1885). He retired from service in 1876, becan e a Member of the Legislative Council from 1878 to 1882, and was made a Knight Commander of the Star of India in 1888. The rest of his life, till his death in 1898, was devoted to literary pursuits, and to the advancement of the interests of the college.

The life work of Saiyid Aḥmad K͟hān or, as he is often called, Sir Saiyid, was his social and educational work among the Muslims of India, pursued in a spirit of reconciliation towards the representatives of Western civilisation, on which he modelled his own ideas. This brought him the bitter enmity of other Islamic groups, such as the movement headed by D̲j̲amāl al-Dīn al-Afg͟hānī; the latter, who had heard of him while he was exiled in India (1879), attacked him violently in his periodical *al-ʿUrwa al-Wut͟hḳā*, accusing him of being a *dahrī*. Also the S͟hīʿa and later the Aḥmadīya belonged to his opponents.

In the beginning of his career, Saiyid Aḥmad K͟hān wrote, beside some theological treatises, historical works, of which the best known is *Āt͟hār al-Ṣanādīd* (1847), a kind of historical-archeological description of Indian towns. Of his many writings of a later period should be named his *Essays on the Life of Mohammed* (1870), which appeared soon afterwards in Urdu, and a Ḳurʾān commentary in Urdu called *Tafsīr al-Ḳurʾān* (1880—1895), which goes as far as Sūra xvii (cf. Goldziher, *Richtungen*, p. 319). In 1862 he had written a Bible Commentary under the title *Tabyīn al-Kalām*, remarkable for being the first of its kind and for its mild views.

Bibliography: H. A. R. Gibb, *Whither Islam*, 1932, p. 192 sqq.; H. K. Sherwani, *The Political Thought of Sir Syed Ahmad Khan* in *Islamic Culture* 1944; J. M. S. Baljon, *The Reforms and religious ideas of Sir Sayyid Ahmad Khân*, Leiden 1949, in which more bibliographical references are given.

ʿĀʾIS͟HA bint Abī Bakr, the favourite wife of Muḥammad, was born at Mecca 8 or 9 years before the Hid̲j̲ra (613—4). Her mother was called Umm Rūmān bint ʿUmair b. ʿĀmir, and her own *kunya* was Umm ʿAbd Allāh, after the name of her nephew ʿAbd Allāh b. al-Zubair. After the death of K͟hadīd̲j̲a Muḥammad was inconsolable. One day K͟hawla bint Ḥakīm, the wife of ʿUt͟hmān b. Maẓʿūn, suggested to him the idea of marrying either ʿĀʾis͟ha, who was still a child, or Sawda bint Zamʿa, a widow of mature age. Muḥammad asked Abū Bakr for the hand of ʿĀʾis͟ha. At first Abū Bakr made some objections but finally complied with his wishes, and dissolved her existing betrothal to D̲j̲ubair b. Muṭʿim, after which she was married to Muḥammad, two or three years before the Hid̲j̲ra, when she was only six or seven years old. But the marriage was not consummated until six or seven months after Muḥammad's departure to Madīna (April-June 623). Her dowry from Muḥammad amounted to 50, or according to Ibn His͟hām (p. 1001), 400 dirhams. She brought her toys with her to the home of her elderly husband, and soon succeeded in winning the affection of Muḥammad, who sometimes joined in her games. But an unfortunate accident afterwards endangered ʿĀʾis͟ha's power over her husband. It happened when Muḥammad was on his way back from his expedition against the Banū Muṣṭaliḳ in the year 6/628. The historians do not agree in regard to certain details, although all found their accounts on ʿĀʾis͟ha's own statement. The majority of them assert that ʿĀʾis͟ha was her husband's sole companion in that campaign. She travelled in a litter carried by a camel. During one of the stops, not far from Madīna, ʿĀʾis͟ha withdrew from the camp in order to perform her ablutions. When she came back to her litter she discovered that she had forgotten her necklace of Yemen shells, and went back to fetch it, leaving the curtains of the chair closed. In her absence Muḥammad gave the signal for the departure, and ʿĀʾis͟ha's retinue loaded the litter on the camel and started on their journey. ʿĀʾis͟ha finding on her return that she had been left behind, sat down on the ground and waited until some one should come to fetch her. Then Ṣafwān b. al-Muʿaṭṭal happened to find her there. He mounted her on his camel and led the animal by the rein. The sight of ʿĀʾis͟ha arriving alone in the company of a young man gave rise to grave accusations. The principal accuser was ʿAbd Allāh b. Ubaiy and many influential persons were scandalized. The Prophet consulted ʿAlī and Usāma b. Zaid as to what he should do. ʿAlī advised him to repudiate ʿĀʾis͟ha (hence the hatred of the latter against ʿAlī); but Usāma did his utmost to prove the innocence of the young wife to Muḥammad. Finally the Prophet exculpated her as the result of a revelation (Ḳurʾān xxiv. 10 *sqq.*), which states that no charge of adultery is valid, unless it is supported by four witnesses, and that those who accuse but cannot bring forward four witnesses shall be punished with stripes.

At the time of Muḥammad's death ʿĀʾis͟ha was 18 years old. She has always remained a sacred personage to the majority of the Muslims. She opposed ʿUt͟hmān and declared that he must do penance or resign, and she doubtless had a hand in the insurrection against that Caliph. But when ʿUt͟hmān was besieged in his palace ("the day of the house"), ʿĀʾis͟ha was not at Madīna but had prudently gone on a pilgrimage to Mecca. When afterwards ʿAlī, her mortal enemy, was elected Caliph, she did her utmost to raise the Muslims against him, under the pretext of wanting only to avenge the murder of ʿUt͟hmān. She joined Ṭalḥa and al-Zubair, who assembled a great army and provisions and started for Baṣra. The Tamīmite Yaʿlā b. Munya, who contributed largely to this expedition, bought for ʿĀʾis͟ha a thorough-bred camel, called ʿAskar, for which he gave 200 dīnārs. The armies of ʿAlī and of Ṭalḥa and al-Zubair met in battle on 10th Djumādā II 36/Dec. 4, 656. Victory was on the side of ʿAlī. ʿĀʾisha on her camel was in the thick of the fight; seventy men of the Banū Ḍabba, seeking to defend her, fell one after the other, until the camel was killed (hence its designation as the "Battle of the Camel"). ʿAlī gave orders to conduct ʿĀʾisha to the house of Ṣafīya bint al-Ḥārith b. Ṭalḥa al-ʿAbdī, and supplied her subsequently with everything she wanted for her return to Madīna. Seeing how much stronger ʿAlī's party was, ʿĀʾisha suggested to him that she should stay with him and be his companion on subsequent expeditions against his enemies. But ʿAlī declined this offer and intimated that she had to depart. Once again she appeared on the scene at the death of al-Ḥasan b. ʿAlī. It was suggested that he should be buried at the side of the Prophet, but ʿĀʾisha opposed this plan, arguing that the tomb was her property. That day she was again mounted on a camel; the people of Madīna began to murmur against her, but finally gave way to her wishes. The date of her death is generally assumed to be 17th Ramaḍān (or 19th Ramaḍān) 58, but the years 56 and 57 are also given. But as the day of the week is stated to have been Tuesday, only the first mentioned date (17th Ramaḍān 58/July 13, 678) appears to be exact. Her last wish was to be buried that same night, and she was interred in al-Baḳīʿ (the cemetery of Madīna).

ʿĀʾisha occupies a prominent place amongst the most distinguished traditionists. 1,210 traditions are recorded as having been reported by her direct from the mouth of the Prophet. She was often consulted on theological and juridical subjects. She is praised for her talents. She had learnt to read, and knew several poems by heart. Some writers assert that she possessed a special copy of the Ḳurʾān.

Bibliography: Ibn Hishām p. 163, 731, 966, 1000 *sqq.*; Ibn Saʿd, viii. 39 *sqq.*; Ibn Ḥadjar, *Iṣāba*, iv. 691 *sqq.*; Ṭabarī, see index; Masʿūdī, *Murūdj*, iv.; Ibn al-Athīr (ed. Tornb.), ii., iii.; do., *Usd al-ghāba*, v. 501 *sqq.*; Nawawī, p. 848 *sqq.*; Sprenger, *Das Leben und die Lehre des Mohammad*, i. 409, 416—417; iii. 62 *sqq.*; Muir, *The Life of Mahomet*; A. Müller, *Der Islam im Morgen- und Abendland*, i. 133, 312 *sq.*; F. Buhl, *Das Leben Muhammeds*, p. 281, 352.

AIYŪB, the Job of the Bible, is mentioned in the Ḳurʾān amongst the other just men. He is called there "the servant of God", and represented as the patient man. It is related briefly in the Ḳurʾān that God put Job to the test, that the latter afterwards addressed prayers to God, that he was restored to his former state and that God returned to him all his family and possessions (sūra xxi. 83—84; xxxviii. 41—44). The Muslim writers however tell a great many stories about Job, which they derived mainly from the Book of Job and the Jewish Haggadah. Job is generally represented as a "Rūmī", a descendant of Esau (see *Testament of Job*, ed. James, i.). He was the son of Amos (Amūs; the spelling, however, is not quite fixed), and of a daughter of Lot. But according to one authority quoted by Ṭabarī, he was the son of "him who believed in Abraham". The majority of the Muslim writers call the wife of Job Raḥma, daughter of Ephraim, son of Joseph. But one isolated authority states her name to have been Machir (Mākhīr), daughter of Manasseh (Mīshā), whose son was mistaken for a daughter. Finally his wife is also referred to by the name of Leah (Līyā), daughter of Jacob (cf. Baiḍāwī on the Ḳurʾān, *l.c.*). This last statement was evidently occasioned by a confusion of the names of Leah, the wife of Jacob, and of Dina, his daughter, who in the Haggadah is said to be the wife of Job (*Baba Batra*, p. 15b; *Bereshīt Rabba*, lvii; *Targum* on Job ii. 9), and also in the *Testament of Job* (*l.c.*). The traditionists, amongst others Kaʿb al-Aḥbār, have even described Job's appearance: a tall man with a big head, crisp hair, beautiful eyes, short neck and long limbs. His riches are described according to the Book of Job, with some exaggeration of course. A certain author ascribes to him twelve sons and twelve daughters. Job was very pious and very generous; the was a kind guardian to orphans and a protector of widows. He was a prophet and God had sent him to preach monotheism to the people of his country, which, according to some, was the Ḥawrān, and according to others Bathanīya. Every evening all those who believed in his word assembled in his mosque and recited with him the same prayers (cf. *Baba Batra*, *l.c.*; *Sēder ʿŌlam Rabba*, xxi.; *Berēshīt Rabba*, xxx. 9; *Abōt R. Natan*, ed. Schechter, p. 33—34, 164). The Muslim traditionists have reproduced almost literally that part of the Book of Job (i. 6—ii. 7), where it is narrated how Job was put to the test, and they add that Iblīs was driven by envy to strike Job. When finally God had given him full power over the body of Job (except over his tongue, his heart and his intellect), Iblīs blew into his nostrils, causing thereby an inflammation of the body and filling it with worms. His body began to smell so horribly that he was forced to leave the town and make his lair on a dunghill (cf. *Abōt R. Natan*, p. 164; *Testament of Job*, v.). The wife of Job had to seek work wherewith to earn food for herself and her unfortunate husband. Although Iblīs saw that in afflicting Job he had missed his aim, he never ceased to contrive new and artful means of torturing him still more. All these means having failed, Iblīs declared himself vanquished. The majority of the Muslim authors are of opinion that Job was 70 years old when he was afflicted by Iblīs (see *Berēshīt Rabba*, lviii. 3; lxi. 4; *Testament of Job*, xii.; cf. however Baiḍāwī on sūra xxi. 83). The duration of his affliction is differently estimated by various authors. The Ḳurʾān (sūra xxxviii. 43) only says briefly that Job caused a well to spring up from the ground by stamping on it at God's command, after which he bathed himself and drank from the water. The Muslim legend however puts this command in the mouth of the angel Gabriel. The obscure passage in the Ḳurʾān (xxxviii. 44): "Take a bundle, beat with it, and do not forswear thyself", is explained by the commentators as referring to Job's wife, whom he was commanded by God to beat, because he had sworn to give her a hundred blows. The narrators do not agree in their statements regarding the children which were born to Job after his recovery. According to some they were the same children which had perished and had been called back to life, but others assert that his wife became young again and bore him other children, their number varying up to 26. Some authors fix the life of Job at 93 years, asserting that he lived 20 years after his recovery; but others affirm that he lived the same lenght of time after as before his affliction. Masʿūdī testifies that the mosque of Job, together with the spring in which he bathed himself, was still celebrated in his time, and that they were to be found at a short distance from Nawā in the province of Urdunn (cf. Yāḳūt, *Muʿdjam*, ii.

640 s.v. *Dair Aiyūb*). Still at the present day one is shown there the *ḥammām Aiyūb* ("bath of Job") and in its neighbourhood the *maḳām Shaikh Saʿd*, formerly called *maḳām Aiyūb*. The famous "stone of Job" (*ṣakhrat Aiyūb*) must also be mentioned. It is actually an Egyptian monument of Ramses II, as is sufficiently well known. It is interesting to note that En-rogel, mentioned in the Bible (Joshua xvii. 7 and elsewhere), is now called *Biʾr Aiyūb* ("the well of Job"; cf. Mudjīr al-Dīn, *Hist. de Jérusalem*, publ. in the *Fundgruben des Orients*, ii. 130).

Bibliography: Ṭabarī, i. 361—364; do., Persian version, transl. by Zotenberg, i. 255 *sqq.*; Thaʿlabī, *al-ʿArāʾis*, p. 134 *sqq.*; Kisāʾī, *Ḳiṣaṣ al-anbiyāʾ*, ed. Eisenberg, p. 179 *sqq.*; Masʿūdī, *Murūdj*, i. 91 *sqq.*; Sale, *Koran*, ii. 138; Grünbaum, *Neue Beiträge zur semitischen Sagenkunde*, Leiden 1893, p. 262 *sq.*; J. Horovitz, *Koranische Untersuchungen*, Berlin 1926, p. 100 *sq.*

AKBAR Abu'l-Fatḥ Djalāl al-Dīn Muḥammad, third Tīmūrid Emperor of Hindūstān, was born at Umarkot in Sind on the 15th October 1542, was crowned at Kalānūr in the Pandjāb, on the 14th Febr. 1556 and died in Āgra on the 16th October 1605, leaving his throne to his son Salīm (Djahāngīr). He traced his descent to Amīr Tīmūr Barlās (1336—1405); he was Bābur's grandson and the son of Humāyūn and Ḥamīda Bānū, a daughter of a Persian scholar in the service of Hindāl, Bābur's youngest surviving son.

Akbar was born in exile in one of the greatest centuries of history and in it he was the greatest ruler. Not Europe only was in mental ferment; a leaven worked also in Hindūstān, as indications of the presence of which there may be named the Kabīr Panthī, the Rawshānīs and the ṣūfism of which Shaikh Mubārak Nāgōrī was the exponent in closest touch with Akbar.

It is a well-attested statement that through his long life of intellectual activity he did not master the arts of reading and writing. This is in him the more singular as he came of a family of traditional culture and as he lived not only amongst men of education but was closely associated with at least two women accomplished in letters, his wife, Salīma Sulṭān, and his aunt, Gulbadan. His lack of instruction in childhood may well have been owing to his father's unsettled position and procrastinating character, but in adult life, only his own deliberate choice will explain it. A keen observer, avid of knowledge, a student of at least one branch of knowledge, Religion, his dependence on the ear is a fact of great interest which falls into place only when one recalls blind men who have been distinguished. It seems as though Akbar learnt best by the living word.

The long story of his military success does not lend itself to summary and it will suffice here to set in apposition his territory at accession and at death. He had gone with his father to Hindūstān in January 1555 from Kābul and had been present at the decisive battle of Sirhind over Sikandar Sūr on the 22th June 1555, which gave Āgra and Dehlī again to the Tīmūrids. When his father died (24th January 1556), he was with his begata, Bairām Khān Bahārlū, pursuing Sikandar in the Pandjāb. On that day the only land he owned was a small part of the Pandjāb; Āgra had been taken by Hemū, Dehlī had been evacuated by his general; Ḥaram Begam and Sulaimān Badakhshī had seized Kābul. He was then fourteen years old. When in 1605 he laid aside the cares of empire, he left to Salīm a stable heritage of the whole of Upper India, Kābul, Kāshmīr, Bihār, Bengal, Orissa and a great part of the Dekkan.

Great as he was as a soldier, it is as an administrator that he has gained highest fame. His revenue reforms with which the Hindū, Todar Mall, is closely associated were pushed through all opposition and pursued untiringly; so too was the safe-guarding of lowly people; he had the genius of taking pains and the open-mindedness which is symbolized by his favourite motto, "Peace with all". Changing perennial Muḥammadan practice in Hindūstān, he ruled for the Hindū majority of his subjects, and set these free from insulting and oppressive enactments. In return they provided him splendid and faithful servants.

Perhaps what rivets attention to Akbar more than his genius as a sovereign, is his own pursuit of truth. It is well-known that he broke away from orthodox Islām and promulgated an eclectic *tawḥīd-i ilāhī*, a Divine Faith. This appears to have been pure Theism, the common element of all the creeds he sought into. If men craved for a symbol, as in truth his own researches must have convinced him they did crave, he recommended for this the Sun or its earthly counterpart, fire. He allowed of no priesthood and inculcated purity and plainness of living.

What adherence the *tawḥīd-i ilāhī* obtained outside the inner Court circle cannot now be said; eighteen names are recorded as those of members of the Faith. Most of those inscribed are literary men, poets; one great emīr only is there, ʿAzīz Kūka, whom extortion in Mecca had driven from orthodoxy. There are men to whose ṣūfī influence Akbar's perversion from Islām was ascribed, Shaikh Mubārak Nāgōrī and his sons. Akbar's earliest interest was with the sects within Islām itself and he became disgusted by the rancour of orthodox disputants; he married a Rādjpūtnī, the mother of Salīm, and he studied Brāhmanism from learned priests and through Hindū Scriptures which he had translated for himself; ṣūfī thinking was strong round him and Persians were of his home circle; he acquired special sympathy for the Sunworship of the Parsīs, a sympathy not likely to be less that Rādjpūts claim to be the children of that luminary. To none of the Eastern creeds, however, did he give such close and admiring attention as to Roman Catholic Christianity. Shaikh Nūr al-Ḥaḳḳ who writes without the bias of either Abu 'l-Faḍl or ʿAbd al-Ḳādir Badāʾūnī, says that the Emperor tried to take the good from all differing opinions and this with one sole object, the ascertaining of truth. What he finally accepted was but the basal fact of all creeds, man's first tenet, and to this he added a plain rule of conduct.

Bibliography: Abu'l-Faḍl ʿAllāmī, *Akbarnāme*; ʿAbd al-Ḳādir Badāʾūnī, *Muntakhab al-tawārīkh*; Shaikh Nūr al-Ḥaḳḳ, *Zubdat al-tawārīkh*; *Dabistān al-madhāhib*; Shams al-ʿUlamāʾ Mawlawī Muḥammad Ḥusain, *Darbār-i akbarī* (Lahore 1898); Blochmann, *Āīn-i-akbarī*; Count von Noer, *Kaiser Akbar* (Leipzig), French and (revised) English translations; Elphinstone, *History of India*; Father Goldie, *Missions to the Great Mogul* (Dublin 1897); H. Beveridge, *Notes on General Maclagan's papers* (*Journ. of the As. Soc. Bengal*, 1896); Malleson, *Akbar* (*Rulers of India Series*); Tennyson, *Akbar's Dream*; R. Grousset, *Figures de Proue*, Paris 1948.

ʿAḲĪDA (A.), creed, as distinct from the confession of faith (*shahāda*; q.v.) and from the confession of Allāh's unity (*tawḥīd*; q.v.). The earliest creed extant in Muḥammadan literature is the *Fiḳh Akbar* I. It is ascribed to Abū Ḥanīfa [q.v.] and it may be said that its main contents go back to him. The ten sentences of which it consists are chiefly refutations of the sectarian views of the Khāridjites, the Ḳadarites, the Shīʿa and the Djahmites. This means that this creed is not an exposition of the chief dogmas confessed by the orthodox community; articles on Allāh and on Muḥammad are lacking. The wording is very brief; some sentences are also found in canonical *ḥadīth*. The translation of this text is as follows:

Art. 1. We do not consider any one to be an infidel on account of sin; nor do we deny his faith. — Art. 2. We enjoin what is just and prohibit what is evil. — Art. 3. What reaches you could not possibly have missed you; and what misses you could not possibly have reached you. — Art. 4. We disavow none of the Companions of the Apostle of Allāh; nor do we adhere to any of them exclusively. — Art. 5. We leave the question of ʿUthmān and ʿAlī to Allāh, who knoweth the secret and hidden things. — Art. 6. Insight in matters of religion is better than insight in matters of knowledge and law. — Art. 7. Difference of opinion in the community is a token of divine mercy. — Art. 8. Whoso believeth all that he is bound to believe, except that he says, I do not know whether Moses and Jesus (peace be upon them) do or do not belong to the Apostles, is an infidel. — Art. 9. Whoso sayeth, I do not know whether Allāh is in Heaven or on the earth, is an infidel. — Art. 10. Whoso sayeth, I do not know the punishment in the tomb, belongeth to the sect of the Djahmites, which goeth to perdition.

The next creed in date of composition is the so-called "Testament of Abū Ḥanīfa", which certainly does not go back to the imām, but is based rather on the views of Aḥmad b. Ḥanbal (d. 241 = 855). It consists of 27 articles, many of which are fairly elaborate. It equally reflects the questions that were uppermost at the time of its genesis, such as the nature of faith, its relation to works, *ḳadar*, anthropomorphism, the nature of the Ḳurʾān as opposed to the views of the Muʿtazila, some ritual questions and eschatological representations.

This creed is put into the mouth of the community, many articles opening with the words "We confess that.....". Like the *Fiḳh Akbar* of Abū Ḥanīfa, the Testament cannot be said to represent the *summa* of orthodox belief, articles on Muḥammad and Allāh still being lacking.

The so-called *Fiḳh Akbar* II, often commented upon, is the first complete and systematically composed creed. It reflects the debates with the Muʿtazila, dwelling largely upon Allāh's essence and His eternal qualities. The latter are defined by means of formulas which tradition ascribes to al-Ashʿarī [q.v.]. In the question of anthropomorphism the Ḥanbalite formula *bi-lā kaifa* is retained (art. 4); new is the introduction of *tanzīh* (q.v.; art. 3), although the term is not used. Predestination is maintained in a mitigated form (the Ashʿarite *kasb* [q.v.]; art. 6). The impeccability of the Prophets, especially of Muḥammad, is mentioned for the first time (artt. 8, 9); together with the signs of the Prophets, the miracles of the saints are called a reality (art. 16). Although this creed cannot with certainty be ascribed to al-Ashʿarī it may be said to express the views ascribed to this theologian. Its origin may therefore be sought in the first half of the tenth century A.D.

The Testament of Abū Ḥanīfa and on a larger scale the *Fiḳh Akbar* II reflect the earlier phase of the scholastic discussions, chiefly in connection with Allāh's being and qualities as well as with the nature of the Ḳurʾān. In the tenth and eleventh centuries A. D. dogmatics are founded on a new basis, that of philosophy. The Aristotelic categories of *wādjib*, *mumkin* or *djāʾiz* and *mustaḥīl*, as well as the doctrine of essence and accident, had already made their entrance into Muslim thought. Now, however, the creed opens with a compendium of the theory of knowledge, upon which is based the proof of the existence of Allāh.

This development of dogmatics was prepared for by such theologians as al-Baghdādī [q.v.; d. 418/1027], Ibn Ḥazm [q.v.; d. 456/1064] and al-Ghazzālī [q.v.; d. 505/1111], as well as by the philosophers such as al-Fārābī [d. 339/950] and Ibn Sīnā [d. 428/1037]. In the creed it is found for the first time in a concise form in the catechism of Abū Ḥafṣ ʿUmar al-Nasafī [cf. AL-NASAFĪ, d. 537/1142]. A very complete specimen of this type of creed is the *Fiḳh Akbar* ascribed to the imām al-Shāfiʿī (*Fiḳh Akbar* III); it may date from the same epoch as Nasafī's *ʿaḳīda*.

The introduction of the Aristotelian elements just mentioned — the doctrine of knowledge, the proof of the existence of God and the logical triad *wādjib*, *mumkin* and *mustaḥīl* — completes the systematisation of the creed; perhaps the purest specimen of this type of ʿaḳīda is al-Sanūsī's [q.v.; d. 895/1490] *Umm al-barāhīn*, which deduces the quintessence of Islām from the Aristotelian triad.

Apart from numerous catechisms in prose and verse, large works on dogmatics were written, such as the *Mawāḳif* of al-Īdjī [q. v.; d. 756/1355] in which the scholastic method was applied to the whole as well as to the details of the creed, so as to resemble a huge Gothic cathedral in which every detail is representative of the style of the whole.

The intellectualisation of the faith as inaugurated by al-Ashʿarī found a powerful opponent in al-Ghazzālī, whose *Iḳtiṣād fi'l-iʿtiḳād*, written before his conversion, still represents the Ashʿarite method. After his conversion he protested against the amalgamation of religion with jurisprudence and with scholasticism (*kalām*). His protests, however, were not able to banish the scholastic method; yet it may be said that his works greatly promoted the development of the "religion of the heart", as he himself called it.

Bibliography: *Fiḳh Akbar* I, printed Ḥaidarābād 1321, with a (spurious) commentary by al-Māturīdī; *Waṣīyat Abī Ḥanīfa* in the same collection, with a commentary by Mollā Ḥusain b. Iskandar al-Ḥanafī; *Fiḳh Akbar* II, in the same collection, with a commentary by Abu'l-Muntahā; with a commentary by ʿAlī al-Ḳārī, Cairo 1327; al-Shāfiʿī, *al-Fiḳh al-Akbar* III (see *GAL., Suppl.* i. 305); al-Samarḳandī (Isḥāḳ b. Muḥammad b. Ismāʿīl Abu'l-Ḳāsim), *al-Sawād al-aʿẓam* (Būlāḳ 1253); al-Samarḳandī (Abu'l-Laith Naṣr b. Muḥammad), *ʿAḳīda*, ed. A. W. Th. Juynboll, in *TTLV*, 4th ser., vol. v. (1881), p. 215—231, 267—274; ʿAbd al-Ḳāhir al-Baghdādī, *Uṣūl al-dīn* (Stambul 1928); al-Ashʿarī, *Kitāb al ibāna ʿan uṣūl al-diyāna*, Ḥaidarābād 1321; al-Ṭaḥāwī, *Bayān al-sunna wa'l-djamāʿa*, Ḥalab 1344; with an explicit commentary Mecca 1349; German translation by J. Hell, *Von Mohammed bis Gha-*

zali, Jena 1915, p. 39 *sqq.*; al-Ghazzālī, *Iḥyā' ʿulūm al-dīn*, Book i., ch. ii.: *Ḳawāʿid al-ʿaḳā'id*; German translation by H. Bauer, *Die Dogmatik Al Ghazali's nach dem II. Buche seines Hauptwerkes* (Halle a/d. Saale 1912); Abū Ḥafṣ ʿUmar al-Nasafī, *ʿAḳā'id*, ed. Cureton, *The Pillar of the Creed* (London 1843, No. 2); with the commentary of al-Taftazānī, Cairo 1335; French translation in d'Ohsson, *Tableau de l'Empire othoman*, i. 21 *sqq.*; Abu'l-Barakāt ʿAbd Allāh al-Nasafī, *al-ʿUmda*, ed. Cureton, *The Pillar of the Creed*, No. 1; al-Īdjī, *Mawāḳif*, ed. Soerensen, Leipzig 1848; Constantinople 1242; al-Sanūsī, *Umm al-barāhīn*, ed. and transl. M. Wolff, Leipzig 1848; al-Faḍālī, *Risāla fī lā ilāha illā'llāh* (Cairo 1320); English translation by D. B. Macdonald; German translation by M. Horten, in *Kleine Texte für Vorlesungen und Übungen*, No. 139 (Bonn); D. B. Macdonald, *Development of Muslim Theology, Jurisprudence and Constitutional Theory* (New York 1903); E. Sell, *The Faith of Islam* (London and Madras 1880); A. J. Wensinck, *The Muslim Creed* (Cambridge 1932).

ʿAḲĪḲA (A.) is the name of the sacrifice on the seventh day after the birth of a child. According to religious law it is recommendable (*mustaḥabb* or *sunna*) on that day to give a name to the new-born child, to shave off its hair and to kill a victim (for a boy two rams or two he-goats; for a girl one of these suffices). If the offering of the ʿaḳīḳa has been neglected on the seventh day, it can be done afterwards, even by the child itself when it has come of age. The greater part of the flesh of the sacrifice is distributed amongst the poor and indigent.

Some of the older scholars (amongst other Dāwūd al-Ẓāhirī) have looked upon the offering of the ʿaḳīḳa as a duty. Abū Ḥanīfa on the contrary regarded it as only allowed by the law.

The shorn hair of the child is also called ʿaḳīḳa, and the law recommends to the faithful to spend not anything less than the weight of this hair in silver (or gold) in almsgiving.

The ʿaḳīḳa sacrifice was doubtless derived from old Arabian heathenism. The Prophet is said to have observed: "When some one wishes to offer a sacrifice for his new-born child, he may do so". In heathenish times it was the custom to wet the child's head with the blood of the animal. According to a tradition Muḥammad had allowed the Muslims to do the same. But the jurisconsults maintain that this custom is not desirable (*sunna*).

According to Doughty (*Travels in Arabia Deserta*, i. 452) the ʿaḳīḳa is one of the most frequent sacrificial ceremonies in the Arabian desert, but there it is only performed at the birth of a boy, never when a girl is born. In Mecca on the seventh day after the birth of a child a wether is usually killed, but it does not occur to the Meccan people that this custom has anything to do with the ʿaḳīḳa ceremony (cf. Snouck Hungronje, *Mekka*, ii. 137).

Bibliography: Bukhārī, *Ṣaḥīḥ* (ed. Krehl), iii. 5q2 *sqq.* and the other collections of traditions; Bādjūrī (Cairo 1307), ii. 311 *sqq.* and the other fiḳh-books; Dimishḳī, *Raḥmat al-umma fi 'khtilāf al-a'imma* (Būlāḳ 1300), p. 61; J. Wellhausen, *Reste arabischen Heidentums* (2nd ed), p. 174; do., *Die Ehe bei den Arabern* in *N. G. W. Gött.*, 1893. p. 459; W. Robertson Smith, *Kinship and marriage in early Arabia*, p. 152 *sqq.*; Th. Nöldeke, in *ZDMG*, xl. 184; Freytag, *Einleitung in das Studium der arab. Sprache*, p. 212. — Concerning the origin of this custom in general cf. G. A. Wilken, *Über das Haaropfer* etc., p. 92 (*Revue coloniale internationale*, 1887, i. 381). — Concerning the ʿaḳīḳa in Indonesia cf. C. Snouck Hurgronje, *De Atjèhers*, i. 423 (= *The Achehnese*, i. 384); van Hasselt, *Midden-Sumatra* p. 269 *sqq.*; Matthes, *Bijdragen tot de ethnologie van Zuid-Celebes*, p. 67.

ʿĀḲIL (A.) = "in the full possession of one's mental faculties", in the Muslim law-books often combined with the adjective *bāligh*, i.e. "grown up", "of age". Such a person is capable of acting with a purpose in view and deliberately. That is why the jurisconsults briefly describe the *ʿāḳil-bāligh* as *mukallaf*, i.e. "one who is obliged to fulfil the precepts of the law", to whom the commandments and prohibitions of the religious law refer in general.

Amongst the Druses and a few other sects the name *ʿāḳil* (plur. *ʿuḳḳāl*) is used to denote one who is an adept in the doctrines of the sect, as contrasted with the *djuhhāl* (sing. *djāhil*), who form the majority. [See the art. DRUSES].

ʿĀḲILA (A.) is the name of a man's male relatives who according to the religious law have to pay the bloodwit (*ʿaḳl*) for him, when unintentionally he has caused the death of a Muslim. This precept is based on a verdict of the Prophet. One day in a quarrel between two women of the Hudhail tribe, one of them, who was with child, was killed by the other with a stone, which hit her in the womb. When, soon after, the other woman also died, the Prophet decided, that her kin (*ʿāḳila*, or, according to a different reading, her *ʿaṣaba*, i.e. agnates), in accordance with an old custom, had to pay the bloodwit to the relatives of the woman who had been killed.

The original custom in Arabia was that the whole tribe was obliged to pay the wergild (Robertson Smith, *Kinship and Marriage in early Arabia*, p. 53; O. Procksch, *Über die Blutrache bei den vorislamischen Arabern*, p. 56 *sqq.*). It made no difference whether the author of the deed had acted premeditatedly or not. According to the Muslim law however, the penalty can only be claimed from the kinsmen in case of manslaughter, because according to the generally accepted version of the above-mentioned tradition the Hudhailian woman had slain her adversary unintentionally. The majority of the jurisconsults agree that the author of the deed himself should not be obliged to pay the penalty. Only the Ḥanafites and a few Mālikite scholars maintain that he should be treated in the same manner as the other members of the family and therefore should contribute his share to the amount.

There are moreover various contradictory opinions regarding most of the special problems which refer to this matter. For example the majority of the Muslim scholars consider only the male relatives of the author of the deed as ʿāḳila. But the Ḥanafites maintain that in consequence of the altered political and social conditions not only the members of the family, but rather all persons who are obliged to help one another (such as the members of the guild to which the perpetrator belongs, his neighbours, or the inhabitants of the same part of the town etc.) should be compelled to share in the payment. They defend this theory with an appeal to the example given by the second Caliph, who had commanded that in the various districts, lists (*dīwāns*) of Muslim brothers-in-arms should be drawn up. The persons whose names were contained in those *dīwāns* owed one another mutual assistance and had to contribute to the payment of the bloodwit for manslaughter committed by one of their community.

The kinsmen (the ʿāḳila) have to pay the money within three years' time. The full amount, precisely fixed by the law, is a so-called "light" penalty [cf. the article DIYA]. The question as to the amount of the share which each separate person has to contribute, is solved again in different ways. According to the Ḥanafites no one need give more than three or, at the highest, four dirhams, i.e. only one (resp. $1^1/_3$) dirham a year. According to the Shāfiʿites $^1/_2$ dīnār or 6 dirhams may be claimed from well-to-do people, and according to the Mālikites and Ḥanbalites each person is liable to pay as much as he is able. Muslim tradition makes the Prophet proclaim emphatically, that neither will the children have to atone for the sins of their fathers, nor the fathers to answer for the sins of their children. This statement implies, according to many jurisconsults, that neither ascendants nor descendents are obliged to pay the penalty. Consequently they consider as bound to pay: first the brothers of the perpetrator, next the sons of these, then the uncles, then the uncles' sons etc. If the author of the deed has no kindred at all, the penalty must be paid out of public funds.

Bibliography: Bukhārī, *Ṣaḥīḥ*, iv. (Leyden 1908), 324—325; Ḳasṭallānī, x. 77 *sqq.*; Shawkānī, *Nail al-awṭār*, vi. 369—376. See further, besides the other collections of traditions and the fiḳh-books of the various schools: Māwardī (ed. Enger), p. 393—394; Dimishḳī, *Raḥmat al-umma fi 'khtilāf al-aʾimma* (Būlāḳ 1300), p. 134; J. Krcsmárik, in *ZDMG*, lviii. 551—556; Freytag, *Einleitung in das Studium der arab. Sprache*, p. 192; E. Sachau, *Muhamm. Recht nach schafiit. Lehre*, p. 761, 771—773; M. B. Vincent, *Études sur la loi Musulmane* (*Rite de Malek*). *Législation criminelle*, p. 83, 114 *sqq.*; Th. W. Juynboll, *Handleiding*, 3rd ed. p. 302, 321.

ʿAḲL. [See ʿĀḲILA].

ALEXANDER. [See DHU'L-ḲARNAIN].

ʿALĪ B. ABĪ ṬĀLIB was a cousin and the son-in-law of Muḥammad and the fourth orthodox caliph. His father, Abū Ṭālib, whose *kunya* concealed the heathen name ʿAbd Manāf, was the son of ʿAbd al-Muṭṭalib b. Hāshim; his mother was called Fāṭima bint Asad b. Hāshim. ʿAlī received the surname Abū Turāb from Muḥammed, whose daughter Fāṭima he married. Concerning his descendants cf. the art. ʿALIDS. He embraced Islām at an age which cannot be ascertained with exactitude, and, after Khadīdja, was the first Muslim (Buraida b. al-Ḥuṣaib, according to Abū Dharr, al-Miḳdād, Abū Saʿīd al-Khudrī etc.), or the second (after Abū Bekr; Masʿūdī, *Tanbīh*, ed. de Goeje, p. 231; transl. by Carra de Vaux, p. 306). He was one of the ten to whom Paradise was expressly promised by the Prophet, and one of the six electors appointed by ʿUmar [q. v.] on his death-bed. He had a dark brown complexion and big protruding eyes; he was corpulent, bald, and rather short than tall; he wore a thick, long, white beard, which he dyed sometimes; his face was handsome; he showed his teeth when he smiled (*Tanbīh*, p. 297; transl., p. 388; Nawawī, p. 441).

History. When Muḥammad had decided to emigrate to Yathrib and suddenly disappeared from Mecca, his escape was facilitated by ʿAlī, who made people believe that he was still in the house he had occupied. He also stayed behind a few days in order to return to the owners the deposits which had been entrusted to the Prophet. ʿAlī accompanied Muḥammad in the battles of Badr, Uḥud, al-Khandaḳ ("the ditch"), and in nearly all his expeditions, except that of Tabūk, during which he had the command at Madīna in the absence of Muḥammad; he himself conducted an expedition to Fadak against the Jewish tribe of Saʿd (6/628). He received sixteen wounds at Uḥud, and on the day when Khaibar was stormed he carried the banner. The Prophet sent him to Minā (9/630) to read in public several verses from the ninth Sūra (*al-Barāʾa*), which had been revealed to him shortly before and, at the same time, to proclaim four decisions with regard to the prohibition of polytheists from the pilgrimage; to the circumambulation of the Kaʿba, which no one was to make naked; to the entrance of the Muslims into Paradise; and to the observation of the time granted for their conversion. In the year 10/631—2, he conducted an expedition to Yemen, in consequence of which the Hamdānids were converted.

It was ʿAlī who advised ʿUmar to adopt the *hidjra* or the emigration of the Prophet as the starting-point of the Muḥammadan calendar. He was entrusted with the task of making representations to ʿUthmān on account of the complaints which came from the provinces; when ʿUthmān began to feel uneasy about his safety, ʿAlī was the intermediary between him and the discontented, in the name of whom he accepted the three days' delay demanded by the caliph; during the siege of ʿUthmān's house (*waḳʿat al-dār*), he showed himself favourable to him and inclined to support him. At first he modestly refused to take the power into his own hands, but five days later he accepted it, and on Friday 25th Dhu 'l-Ḥidjdja 35/June 24, 656 allegiance was paid to him as khalīfa in the Mosque of the Prophet at Madīna; he was the first to ascend the pulpit for this ceremony. In the year 36/656 he left Madīna never to enter it again; he marched against Baṣra where ʿĀʾisha, Ṭalḥa and Zubair refused to acknowledge him and defeated them in the "battle of the camel" which took place at Khuraiba, outside Baṣra on 10th Djumādā II/Dec. 4, 656. He bewailed the fallen, had them honourably buried, and waited three days before entering the town. He sent ʿĀʾisha back to Madīna, escorted by a train of attendants amongst whom were forty women of distinction. He distributed amongst the inhabitants the money which he found in the treasury, and promised the same amount to them for the projected campaign in Syria. A month later he entered Kūfa, where his faithful lieutenant al-Ashtar had prepared the way for him. From thence he went to Ctesiphon (al-Madāʾin), crossed the Euphrates at Raḳḳa, and, in the plain of Ṣiffīn, gave battle to Muʿāwiya in a series of combats which lasted from Dhu 'l-Ḥidjdja 36 till Ṣafar 37/June-July 657. ʿAlī had almost gained the final victory, owing to the bravery of al-Ashtar, when ʿAmr b. al-ʿĀṣī thought of advising Muʿāwiya to have recourse to a stratagem which proved successful. The Syrian troops fastened leaves of the Ḳurʾān to their lances, to indicate that they appealed to the judgment of the book of God. This stratagem beguiled the troops of ʿIrāḳ to demand the submission of the issue to God's word. ʿAlī, therefore, yielded to the urgency of his companions in arms and accepted the arbitrament proposed by Muʿāwiya. The latter appointed ʿAmr b. al-ʿĀṣī his arbiter; ʿAlī was urged, against his will, to choose Abū Mūsā al-Ashʿarī. The two arbiters met in Ramaḍān 37/Febr. 658 or, according to Wellhausen, 38/Febr. 659, furnished with a written document (*ṣaḥīfa*) giving them full power. Abū Mūsā, who wished to see his son-in-law ʿAbd Allāh b. ʿUmar become caliph, let himself be outwitted by ʿAmr, who made him admit that Muʿāwiya was fully entitled to avenge the murder of ʿUthmān, of which, it was falsely rumoured, ʿAlī had been an accomplice. So Abū Mūsā deposed ʿAlī (Ṭabarī, i. 3359; Masʿūdī, *Murūdj*, iv. 397 adds: "by taking off his turban", which detail seems to have been inserted afterwards). ʿAmr followed his example, after which he proclaimed Muʿāwiya caliph, in spite of the protests of the Prophet's old companion, whom he had deceived (variants in Masʿūdī, *ibid.*, p. 399, 402).

The Khāridjites, i.e. the old-Muslim party that refused to negotiate with the rebels, forsook ʿAlī after he had submitted to the arbitration (*taḥkīm*), rose in arms against him to the number of 4,000 under the leadership of ʿAbd Allāh b. Wahb al-Rāsibī, with shouts of *lā ḥukma illā li 'llāh* ("to God alone belongs the decision"). They conquered Ctesiphon and committed all sorts of atrocities there. ʿAlī was persuaded to march against them. He advanced to Nahrawān, where he defeated and exterminated the Khāridjites, of whom only ten escaped (9th Ṣafar 38/17th July 658). This battle is known in history by the name of *waḳʿat al-nahr* (Brünnow, *Die Charidschiten*, p. 19 *sq.*; Ṭabarī, i. 3386; Masʿūdī, *Murūdj*, iv. 418; al-Mubarrad, *Kāmil*, p. 528 *sq*)..

ʿAlī, forsaken by part of his troops, withdrew to Kūfa, while Muʿāwiya despatched one expedition after another to make the best of his opportunity. At Kūfa ʿAlī was assassinated by the Khāridjite ʿAbd al-Raḥmān b. Muldjam al-Ṣārimī, who, with two of his fellow-believers, had concerted a plan to murder ʿAlī, Muʿāwiya and ʿAmr b. al-ʿĀṣī on the same day, in order to revenge the slaughter of their relatives at Nahrawān. Ibn Muldjam, accompanied by two accomplices, waited for the caliph in a narrow passage and struck him on the forehead with a poisoned sabre that penetrated to the brain (17th Ramaḍān 40/Jan. 24, 661; cf. Abū Maʿshar and Wāḳidī in Ṭabarī, i. 3456; other dates *ibid.*; Masʿūdī, *Tanbīh*, p. 387 gives the 21st, which seems more probable, that day being nearer to the 22nd, which was a Friday). ʿAlī died three days afterwards and was interred at Kūfa, according to the usual tradition (other traditions in Masʿūdī, *Murūdj*, iv. 189; *Tanbīh*, p. 387), close by the dike which protected the town against the inundations of the Euphrates, on the spot where afterwards the town of Nadjaf (Yāḳūt. *Muʿdjam*, iv. 760), the present Mashhad ʿAlī, arose. He was either 58 years old, according to his son al-Ḥasan, or 63, as is affirmed by his other son Muḥammad b. al-Ḥanafīya.

Sunnite doctrine. — ʿAlī is said to have transmitted 586 *ḥadīth*, twenty of which were accepted unanimously by Bukhārī and Muslim; nine others were also acknowledged by Bukhārī alone, and fifteen by Muslim only. They have been transmitted by his three sons al-Ḥasan, al-Ḥusain and Muḥammed b. al-Ḥanafīya, and further by Ibn Masʿūd, Ibn ʿUmar, Ibn ʿAbbās, Abū Mūsā al-Ashʿarī, ʿAbd Allāh b. Djaʿfar, ʿAbd Allāh b. al-Zubair, etc. At Madīna his opinions had authority, so that he was consulted upon difficult questions. He was very pious, inflicting mortifications on himself, such as burdening his stomach with a heavy stone in order to diminish the pains of hunger, and giving away all his possessions in alms (Aḥmad b. Ḥanbal, *Musnad*). He despised the world and used to say: "The world is carrion; whoever wants a part of it, must be satisfied to live with dogs". He also said: "Blessed are those who have renounced this world and only aspire to the life to come!" When he died he only left 600 dirhams.

Shīʿite doctrine. By the Shīʿites, ʿAlī is styled the *walī Allāh*, "the friend of God", the man who is attached to the divinity by the mystical tie of the *wilāya*, "proximity, friendship", a sense of the word which soon developed into that of "sanctity". ʿAlī is pre-eminently the saint of Islām, by which quality he is clearly distinguished from Muḥammad, who is only the *nabī*, "the prophet of God". All Shīʿism, with its numberless sects, is based on this conception. The Shīʿites are also unanimous in attributing to ʿAlī the threefold character of *imām*, of warrior and of saint. According to them, the investiture of ʿAlī as imām goes back as far as the sermon near the pool of Khumm, when Muḥammad, on his return from his farewell pilgrimage, said to the people: "I shall soon be called back to Heaven; I leave amongst you two important things, the first more important than the other: the Ḳurʾān and my family". Already on his return from the expedition to al-Ḥudaibiya (18th Dju 'l-Ḥidjdja 6/April 29, 628; Masʿūdī, *Tanbīh*, p. 338; Goldziher, *Muh. Stud.*, ii. 116), Muḥammad had said: "He, whose master I am, has also ʿAlī for his master". One day, the Prophet assembled ʿAlī, Fāṭima, al-Ḥasan and al-Ḥusain, covered them with a mantle (*kisāʾ*) which he used to put on when he went to sleep, and pronounced a prayer which gave rise to the revelation of Sūra xxxiii. 33; hence the expression *aṣḥāb al-kisāʾ* to denote the family of the Prophet (cf. St. Guyard, *Fetwa d'Ibn Taïmiyyah*, p. 24, note 1 = *JA*, 1871, and *Fragments*, p. 217). ʿAbd Allāh b. Sabaʾ, a Jew from Yemen, is said to have been the first to attribute divine honour to ʿAlī: "Thou art God", he is reported to have said to him, in allusion, perhaps, to *ʿalī* as one of the epithets of God (Sūra iv. 34; xlii. 51; Hirschfeld, *JRAS*, 1904, p. 151). The Shīʿites have never been able to understand how the caliphate, which implied the status of imām (the right to lead the *ṣalāt*), could be conferred by election; that accounts for the fact that their adherents were especially recruited from amongst the Persians, the inveterate champions of divine right. The following titles and surnames are most frequently employed by the Shīʿites: *Murtaḍā* (he in whom God is well pleased), *Ḥaidar* (the lion), *Ḥaidar-i karrār* (the impetuous lion), *Asad Allāh al-ghālib* (the lion of God, the Victorious), *Shīr-i Yazdān* (the lion of God), *Shāh-i wilāyat* (the king of sanctity) or *Shāh-i awliyāʾ* (the king of saints). There are a great many others, a detailed list of which is found in the *Djannāt al-khulūd*, tab. vii.

Legends. — The legends, which, especially amongst the Shīʿites, have gathered round the name of ʿAlī, had their root in his twofold character of warrior and saint. Their early development is visible in Masʿūdī (*Murūdj*, iv. 376), where, in the account of the battle of Ṣiffīn, the author tells us that ʿAlī, with his own hand, killed 523 men in one day. Afterwards extraordinary feats were told of him, how he had severed heads from their bodies and had hewn bodies in two with his sabre Dhu 'l-Faḳār (mod. Arab. Fiḳār), the upper part rolling on the ground while the lower part of the body remained on horseback. He is represented as waiting unmoved for the attack of the enemy, and knocking down 33 assailants by simply extending his arm. But however great he may be as a warrior, he is incomparable as a saint; he works miracles (*karāmāt*) which his adherents do not hesitate to compare to the miracles of the prophets (*muʿdjizāt*). Already in Yaʿḳūbī, ii. 39, God is represented as giving orders to the archangels Michael and Gabriel to descend to Mecca and protect ʿAlī while he occupied the place of Muḥammad on the night of the hidjra. But afterwards other feats, much more miraculous, are mentioned, including the raising of a man from the dead. The Persians of the present day speak of more than a thousand of ʿAlī's miracles, but sixty only have been placed upon record. (*Djannāt al-khulūd*, tab. vii.). His judgments deserve to be compared to those of David and Solomon; his maxims and aphorisms have always been celebrated all through the Muḥammadan East; a hundred were collected by the Persian poet Rashīd al-Dīn Waṭwāṭ (*Maṭlūb kull ṭālib*, ed. and transl. by Fleischer, *Ali's hundert Sprüche*, Leipzig 1837), and some of them, at the command of Fakhr al-Dawla ʿAlī b. Ḥusain, the minister of the Seldjūḳide of Rūm, Ghiyāth al-Dīn Kāi-Khusraw III, were graven, in 670/1271—2, on the walls of the Gök-Medrese at Sīwās (Cl. Huart, *Epigr. ar. d'Asie-Mineure*, p. 91 *sq.*). Some Arabian poems, a forgery of Shīʿite origin of uncertain date, have erroneously been attributed to ʿAlī (Brockelmann, *GAL*, i. 43; Goldziher, *Abhandl. zur arab. Philol.*, i. 126; *Transactions of the IXth Congr. of Orient.*, London 1893, ii. 115).

Incarnation of the divinity in the person of ʿAlī. The Shīʿites who are called *ghāliya*, *ghulāt* ("ultras") have even gone to the length of believing that God had become incarnate in the person of the Prophet's son-in-law by "indwelling" (*ḥulūl*; cf. Shahrastānī, p. 132 = Haarbrücker, i 199). The best known of these sects is that of the Nuṣairī, who regard ʿAlī as the first of the three persons of the Trinity (R. Dussaud, *Histoire et religion des Nosairîs*, p. 45, 52, 55, 65; Sulaimān, *Bākūra*, p. 3; Huart, in *JA*, ser. 7, xiv. 260); this sect is still known in Persia by the name of ʿAlī-ilāhī (Gobineau, *Trois ans en Asie*, p. 338); see also the art. AHL-I ḤAḲḲ.

Bibliography: The historical works of Ṭabarī, Masʿūdī, Dīnawarī, Yaʿḳūbī; Ibn Saʿd iii/i, 11 *sqq.*; Naṣr b. Muzāḥim, *Waḳʿat Ṣiffīn* (Cairo 1365); al-Sharīf al-Murtaḍā, *Nahdj al-balāgha* (Beirut 1885, etc.); Nawawī, p. 437 *sqq.*; Madjdī, *Zīnat al-madjālis*, fol. 27ᵇ *sqq,*; Shahrastānī, p. 122 (Haarbrücker i, 185); Caetani, *Annali dell' Islam*, esp. voll. ix, x (Rome 1926); G. Levi della Vida, 'Il Califfato di ʿAli secondo il *Kitāb Ansāb al-Ašrāf* di al-Balāḏurī' (*RSO* vi, 1913, 427—507); Wellhausen, *Die religiös-politischen Oppositionsparteien im alten Islam* (*Abh. G. W. Gött.*, N. S., v. 2); do., *Das arabische Reich und sein Sturz*, Chap. ii; W. Sarasin, *Das Bild Alis bei den Historikern der Sunna* (Basle 1907): F. Buhl, *Das Leben Muhammeds*, p. 150, 192, 282, 337, D. M. Donaldson, *The Shīʿite Religion*, London 1933, p. 27-53; see also KHĀRIDJITES.

ʿALĪ MUḤAMMAD [See BĀB].

ʿALIDS, descendants of ʿAlī b. Abī Ṭālib, who had fourteen sons and at least seventeen daughters, namely: 1. by Fāṭima, daughter of Muḥammad, his only lawful wife while she lived: al-Ḥasan, al-Ḥusain, Muḥassin (Muḥsin among the Persian Shīʿites) who died in infancy, Zainab the elder, Umm Kulthūm the elder; 2. by Umm al-Banīn bint Ḥizām: al-ʿAbbās, Djaʿfar, ʿAbd Allāh, ʿUthmān (all killed at Karbalāʾ, without issue, save the first); 3. by Lailā bint Masʿūd b. Khālid: ʿUbaid Allāh, Abū Bakr; 4. by Asmāʾ bint ʿUmais al-Khathʿamīya: Yaḥyā, Muḥammad the youngest (according to Hishām b. Muḥammad) or Yaḥyā, ʿAwn (according to Wāḳidī, Muḥammad the youngest being the son of a slave); 5. by Umm Ḥabīb bint Rabīʿa, surnamed al-Ṣahbāʾ, a slave captured by Khālid b. al-Walīd at ʿAin al-Tamr: ʿUmar, Ruḳaiya; 6. by Umāma bint Abi'l-ʿĀṣī b. al-Rabīʿ, whose mother was Zainab, daughter of the Prophet: Muḥammad the second; 7. by Khawla bint Djaʿfar: Muḥammad the eldest, surnamed Ibn al-Ḥanafīya; 8. by Umm-Saʿīd bint ʿUrwa b. Masʿūd al-Thaḳafī: Umm al-Ḥasan, Ramla the elder; 9. by Maḥyāt bint Imruʾ al-Ḳais b. ʿAdī: a daughter who died in infancy; 10. by different mothers whose names are not known: Umm Hāniʾ, Maimūna, Zainab the younger, Ramla the younger, Umm Kulthūm the younger, Fāṭima, Umāma, Khadīdja, Umm al-Kirām, Umm Salama, Umm Djaʿfar, Djumāna, Nafīsa (Ṭabarī, i. 3471 *sq.*).

Five of these sons left issue, namely: al-Ḥasan, al-Ḥusain, Muḥammad b. al-Ḥanafīya, ʿUmar and ʿAbbās (Wāḳidī in Ṭabarī, i. 3473; Masʿūdī, *Murūdj*, v. 149; do., *Tanbīh*, transl. Carra de Vaux, p. 388). The most celebrated line is that of al-Ḥusain; the last nine of the "twelve Imāms" of the Shīʿa are directly descended from it: ʿAlī Zain al-ʿĀbidīn, Muḥammad al-Bāḳir, Djaʿfar al-Ṣādiḳ, Mūsā al-Kāẓim, ʿAlī al-Riḍā, Muḥammad al-Djawād, ʿAlī al-Hādī, Ḥasan al-ʿAskarī, Muḥammad al-Mahdī.

The descendants of ʿAlī b. Abī Ṭālib were, for the most part, unfortunate; and their misfortunes fill the pages of Muslim history. The ʿAlids were persecuted by the Umaiyads (Ibrāhīm the imām at Ḥarrān, Zaid b. Zain al-ʿĀbidīn at Kūfa); and they were outwitted by the ʿAbbāsids, who diverted to their own advantage the sympathies of the Persian adherents to the Shīʿa cause. Many, it is said, died by poison, as al-Ḥasan and Djaʿfar al-Ṣādiḳ at Madīna; Mūsā al-Kāẓim at Baghdād; ʿAlī al-Riḍā at Ṭūs; Muḥammad al-Djawād at Baghdād; others revolted against the authority of the caliphs, and died fighting or at the hands of the executioner. Above all the branch of al-Ḥasan has furnished a large number of unsuccessful pretenders: Muḥammad al-Nafs al-Zakīya (brother of the Idrīs who founded a dynasty in the Maghrib) at Madīna in 145/762—3; a brother of his, Ibrāhīm, at Baṣra; Husain b. ʿAlī at Mecca in 169/785—6; Muḥammad b. Ṭabāṭabā in the ʿIrāḳ 199/814—5; Muḥammad b. Sulaimān at Madīna; ʿAlī b. Muḥammad at Baṣra (at the same time as Zaid b. Mūsā al-Kāẓim); Ibrāhīm b. Mūsā in Yemen; al-Ḥasan b. Zaid in Ṭabaristān (250/864); al-Ḥusain at Kūfa; Ismāʿīl b. Yūsuf at Mecca; Muḥammad b. Zaid in Ṭabaristān (281—287/894—900); Aḥmad b. Muḥammad in Upper Egypt; Ḥasan b. ʿAlī in Ṭabaristān (301/913—4); etc. The branch of al-Ḥusain, which was distinguished for its piety, its holiness, and the purity of its morals, has furnished fewer insurgents; yet in addition to Zaid b. Mūsā, who is mentioned above, Muḥammad b. Djaʿfar al-Ṣādiḳ, who revolted at Mecca in 200/815—6, may be cited; as also al-Ḥusain al-Afṭas, at Madīna; Muhammad b. Ḳāsim in Khurāsān (219/834); al-Ḥasan al-Karkī at Ḳazwīn (250/864), Muḥassin (Muḥsin) b. Djaʿfar, surnamed Ibn Riḍā, at Damascus. The Idrīsids are certainly ʿAlids (al-Ḥasan's branch); the case of the Fāṭimids and the Almohads (al-Muwaḥḥidūn) is less certain. A list of the ʿAlids who died a violent death may be found in Masʿūdī, *Murūdj*, vii. 404. Among the Umaiyads, ʿUmar II b. ʿAbd al-ʿAzīz was the only one who felt qualms of conscience on account of the fact that the family of the Prophet had been deprived of its rights; he distributed ten thousand dīnārs among the descendants of ʿAlī by

Fāṭima who resided at Madīna (*Murūdj*, v. 421); among the ʿAbbāsids, al-Maʾmūn proclaimed the above-mentioned 8th imām ʿAlī al-Riḍā as his successor; but the persecutions began again with al-Mutawakkil, who broke open and ransacked the tomb of al-Ḥusain at Karbalāʾ, and lasted until the time of al-Muntaṣir.

At the present day the descendants of the Prophet are very numerous and are diffused throughout all Muslim countries; they are distinguished from the other Muslims by the title of *saiyid* or *sharīf*, and the right to wear the green turban. Their descent is established more or less authentically by a certificate or genealogical tree (*shadjara, silsile-nāme*). In the Ottoman Empire, they were subjected to the supervision and the authority of the *naḳīb al-ashrāf* (inspector of the ʿAlids) whose office was re-established by Sulṭān Bāyazīd II; there was one in every large city; he controlled the certificates, gave them to those who had proved their descent, and punished offenders who made use of the rank of *sharīf* [cf. also SHARĪF].

ʿAlid Dynasties. Branch of al-Ḥasan: 1. Idrīsids, descendants of Idrīs b. Idrīs b. ʿAbd Allāh b. Ḥasan II in the Maghrib until 296/908; 2. Sulaimānids, descendants of Sulaimān b. Dāwūd b. Ḥasan II, at Mecca, then in Yemen (al-Suwaidī, *Sabāʾik al-dhahab*, p. 77); 3. Sulaimānids, descendants of Sulaimān, brother of Idrīs b. ʿAbd Allāh b. Ḥasan II, in the Maghrib (al-Suwaidī, *l.c.*); 4. Banū Ukhaiḍir, descendants of Mūsā al-Djawn, brother of Muḥammad al-Nafs al-Zakīya, at Mecca and in Yemen from 251 till 350 (865—961; cf. Munadjdjim Bāshī, ii. 429); 5. Banū Ṭabāṭabā in Yemen, 288/901; 6. the Hawāshim (Banū Falīta), descendants of Abū Hāshim b. Muḥammad, of the branch of ʿAbd Allāh b. Ḥasan II, emīrs of Mecca, from 460 till 598 (1067—1202): 7. Banū Ṣāliḥ, descendants of Ṣāliḥ b. ʿAbd Allāh b. Mūsā, of the same branch, at Ghāna in the Sūdān; 8. the Ḥasanids of Āmul, from 250 till 300 (864—913); 9. the Banū Ḳatāda, emīrs of Mecca, from 598/1201—2 to 1343/1924; 10. the Saʿdid sharīfs in Morocco, from 957/1550 till 1070/1659; 11. the Filālī sharīfs in Morocco, from 1075/1664 until the present; 12. and 13. the Wazzānī and Kittānī sharīfs in Morocco, up to the present time.

Branch of al-Ḥusain: 1. the Fāṭimids or ʿUbaidids, descendants of Djaʿfar al-Ṣādiḳ; 2. the Ḥusainids of Ṭabaristān and of Dailam, from 301 to 318 (913—930); 3. other branches in Djurdjān, from 304 to 356 (916—967); 4. Banū al-Muhannā at Madīna, since before 601/1204 (cf. Munadjdjim Bāshī, ii. 665); 5. Rassids, descendants of Ḳāsim Rassī, who died in 246/860, of the branch of Zaid b. ʿAlī b. al-Ḥusain, at Saʿda in Yemen, until 680/1281; 6. Zaidids of Ṭabaristān, from 250 to 316 (864—928); 7. Zaidids of Ṣanʿāʾ, descendants of Ḳāsim b. Muḥammad.

Uncertain descent: 1. Banū Mūsā at Mecca and at Madīna, from 350 to 453 (961—1061); 2. Banū Ḥammūd at Cordova and Malaga, from 407 to 449 (1016—1057).

ALLĀH, the Supreme Being of the Muslims:

I. Before Islām. That the Arabs, before the time of Muḥammad, accepted and worshipped, after a fashion, a supreme god called Allāh — "the *ilāh*" or the god, if the form is of genuine Arabic origin; if of Aramaic, from *alāhā*, "the god" — seems absolutely certain. Whether he was an abstraction or a development from some individual god, such as Hubal, need not here be considered. For the archaeological and non-Arabic evidence see Wellhausen, *Reste arabischen Heidentums*, 2nd ed., p. 117 *sq.*; Nöldeke's article on Arabs (ancient) in Hasting's *Dictionary of Religion and Ethics*, i. 662 and Brockelmann in *Archiv für Religions-wissenschaft*, xx. 99–121. Here it will suffice to give the evidence of the Ḳurʾān. There, the Meccans admit that Allāh is creator and supreme provider (xiii. 16; xxix. 61, 63; xxxi. 25; xxxix. 38; xliii. 9, 87; it is surely a strain on xiii. 18 and xxix. 63 to make them prove that Allāh was a rain-god); they call upon him in times of special peril (x. 22; xvi. 53; xxix. 65; xxxi. 32; but these passages hang together and hardly have independent weight); they recognize him by swearing solemnly and specially by him (vi. 109; xvi. 38; xxxv. 42); they assign him a separate portion, distinct from that of all other deities (vi. 136); they urge that he had never forbidden them to worship other gods with him (vi. 148; xxxvii. 168). But they also recognized and tended to worship more fervently and directly other strictly subordinate gods. Here it is not always easy to distinguish between their views and the interpretation of their views adopted by Muḥammad, especially between their vocabulary and that of Muḥammad. It is certain that they regarded particular deities (mentioned in sūra liii. 19—20 are al-ʿUzzā, Manāt or Manāh, al-Lāt [?]; some have interpreted vii. 180 as a reference to a perversion of Allāh to Allāt) as daughters of Allāh (vi. 100; xvi. 57; xxxvii. 149; liii. 21); they also asserted that he had sons (vi. 100). But whether the Meccans used of these the term *shurakāʾ* we cannot tell; perhaps less probable is that they spoke of them as *malāʾika*. On all ordinary occasions they worshipped these rather than Allāh; their offerings were made by preference to them, and Allāh was defrauded (vi. 136 *sq.*); at least these would intercede with Allāh (liii. 26); yet the Meccans were uncertain as to whether these were creators (xiii. 16 *sq.*) and in all extremities they came back to Allāh; as to him there was no doubt. Certain also is that they asserted a "kinship" (*nasab*) between Allāh and the *djinn* (xxxvii. 158; cf. for Ḳurʾānic use of the word xxv. 54; xxiii. 101) and made them partners of Allāh (vi. 100); made offerings to them (vi. 128); sought aid of them (lxxii. 6). Whether they had the idea of angels and asserted their "partnership" is not so certain; that may be Muḥammad's interpretation (vi. 100; lii. 28). As for Muḥammad, his attitude in these matters is also clear. Besides Allāh, there existed angels and *djinn* with Satan, and the Satans in some relationship to the two latter. These, in reality, are the beings on whom the Meccans call; but they can do nothing for them (xvii. 56); making them feminine and giving them names is unwarranted invention. It will be seen, then, that whatever may have been the earlier case in Mecca and whatever the case in the rest of Arabia, and whatever may have been the origin of the names applied, the religion of Mecca in Muḥammad's time was far from simple idolatry. It resembled much more a form of the Christian faith, in which saints and angels have come to stand between the worshippers and God. And Muḥammad naturally regarded himself as a reformer who was preaching an earlier and simpler faith and putting angels and *djinn* back into their true places.

II. Muḥammed's Doctrine of Allāh. His attitude is stated most simply in the first article of the essential Muslim creed: *Lā ilāhᵃ illa ʾillāhᵘ*, "There is no god save Allāh". This meant, for Muḥammad and the Meccans, that of all the gods whom they worshipped, Allāh was the only real deity. It took no account of the nature of God in the abstract, only of the personal position of Allāh. "Allāh", therefore, was and is the proper name of God among Muslims. It corresponds to Yahwe among the Hebrews, not to Elōhīm. No plural can be formed from it. To express "gods", the Muslim must fall back upon the plural of *ilāh*, the common noun from which Allāh is probably derived; this Muḥammad does frequently when speaking of the "other gods" (e.g. *ālihat*[an] *ukhrā*: vi. 19) which the Meccans joined to Allāh, and Islām has followed him, with, however, a preference to use instead the more distinctive *aṣnām* or *awthān*, "idols". Cf. article *Allāh* in Hasting's *Dictionary of Religion and Ethics*.

But, though the name was the same for the Meccans and for Muḥammad, their conceptions of the nature of the bearer of the name must have differed widely. The Meccans, evidently, had in general no fear of him; the fear of Allāh was an essential element in Muḥammad's creed. Allāh lay in very shadowy remoteness from Meccan life; he was very terribly near to Muḥammad at every moment — nearer than the neck-artery (l. 16). The Meccans did not hesitate to disregard him and to cultivate the minor gods; Muḥammad knew him as a jealous and vindictive sovereign, who would assuredly judge and condemn in the end. A vague abstraction had become an overwhelming personality.

We must now analyze that personality, as Muḥammad conceived it. Fortunately, the exigencies of the *sadj*ᶜ rhyme led him to characterize Allāh by a number of epithets, and later Islām, in gathering up these "Most Beautiful Names" (*al-asmā*ʾ *al-ḥusnā*) — the phrase itself occurs several times in the Ḳurʾān (vii. 180; xvii. 110; xx. 8; lix. 24) and shows Muḥammad's own relish for such descriptions — and using them devotionally, has followed a sound instinct. They express the concrete directness of Muḥammad's God far better than the lists of qualities (*ṣifāt*) of the scholastic dogmaticians, and may be used safely as an aid in correlating and stating Muḥammad's too often spasmodic and contradictory utterances. Cf. on them the article by Redhouse, in *J R A S*, 1880, xii. 1—69.

First, Allāh in and by himself. The descriptions are at first sight a strange combination of anthropomorphics and metaphysics. Yet when Muḥammad speaks of Allāh's two hands (v. 64; xxxviii. 75) or of his grasp (xxxix, 67) or of his eyes (liv. 14) or of his face (ii. 115, 278; vi. 52; xviii. 28 and often) or describes him as settling himself upon his throne (xx. 5 and often) we are not to regard that as due to an anthropomorphic theology but rather as the still plastic metaphor of a poet. To speak technically, we have here only *madjāz*; *tadjsīm* and *tashbīh* lay with the future exegetes. Similarly in the case of the metaphysics. The fire of Muḥammad's imagination expressing itself with concrete directness could call Allāh the First (*al-awwal*) and the Last (*al-ākhir*), the External (*al-ẓāhir*) and the Internal (*al-bāṭin*; all lvii. 3), and even the Self-Subsisting (*al-ḳaiyūm*: ii. 255; iii. 2) — the poets had already developed in Arabic a vivid power of wielding descriptive epithets; but the Existing (*al-wādjid*) does not occur in the Ḳurʾān, though it easily might, and the Necessarily Existing (*wādjib al-wudjūd*) belonged to the future scholasticism. Allāh, then, is the One (*al-wāḥid*, often), the Living (*al-ḥaiy*: ii. 255; iii. 2 etc.), the Exalted in and through himself (*al-mutaᶜāl*: xiii. 9 only), the Exalted (*al-ᶜalī*, often), the Comprehensive (*al-wāsi*ᶜ: ii. 247 etc.), the Powerful (*al-ḳadīr*: ii. 20, etc.), the Self-Sufficing (*al-ghanī*: ii. 263 etc.), the Absolute Originator (*al-badī*ᶜ: ii. 117; vi. 101 only), the Enduring (*al-bāḳī*; as an epithet this does not occur in the Ḳurʾān; but the verb is very frequent of Allāh; see below), the Eternal (*al-ṣamad*: cxii. 2 only; but the exact meaning and origin of this ἅπαξ λεγόμενον were uncertain to the earliest commentators; cf. Ṭabarī, *ad loc.*), the Mighty (*al-ᶜazīz*, often), the Grand (*al-ᶜaẓīm*, often), the Dominant (*al-ḳahhār*: xii. 39, etc.), the Haughty (*al-mutakabbir*: lix. 23 only; an epithet of dispraise when used of any one but Allāh), the Great (*al-kabīr*, often), the Laudable (*al-ḥamīd*, often), the Glorious (*al-madjīd*: xi. 73; lxxxv. 15 only; otherwise of the Ḳurʾān itself; another of the Names, "*al-mādjid*", does not occur in the Ḳurʾān), the Generous (*al-karīm*, often; in Arabic it means strictly *generosus*), He of Majesty and Generosity (*dhu 'l-djalāl wa 'l-ikrām*: lv. 78), the Majestic (*al-djalīl*; as epithet not in the Ḳurʾān but the idea in other forms is very frequent), the Strong (*al-ḳawī*, often), the Firm (*al-matīn*: li. 58 only), the Knower (*al-ᶜalīm*, often), the Subtle (*al-laṭīf*: vi. 103 etc.), the Aware (*al-khabīr*, often), the Wise (*al-ḥakīm*, often), the Hearer (*al-samī*ᶜ, often), the Seer (*al-baṣīr*, often), the Holy King (*al-malik al-ḳuddūs*: lix. 23; lxii. 1 only; *ḳuddūs* alone is reckoned as one of the Names; but it occurs only in combination with King; what idea Muḥammad associated with it is quite obscure, perhaps only of separateness; elsewhere the root is used only of the Holy Spirit, Gabriel; of the Holy Land; of the Holy Wādī in which Allāh met Moses; of the angels sanctifying Allāh; the commentators explain it, of course, as a term of *tanzīh*), the Peace (?; *al-salām*: lix. 23 only; again the idea is quite obscure but is almost certainly not "peace"; the commentators explain it as *salāma* = "immunity from lack or defect", which is not at all impossible. It may be only a reminiscence of some phrase of a Christian religious service caught up by Muḥammad), Justice (?; *al-ᶜadl*: occurs in tradition only but is worth adding, as no other of the Names represents the same idea; nearest comes the Best of Judges = *khair al-ḥākimīn*: vii. 87; x. 109; xii. 80 only; but *ᶜadl* in the Ḳurʾān is used differently), the Benefactor (*al-barr*: lii. 28 only), the L ght of the heavens and the earth (*al-nūr*: xxiv. 33 only; the context seems to point to worship in Christian churches and monasteries, and in that case the picture is derived from the lighted altar, and the Ḳurʾānic phrases in the context recall "the Light of the World" in the Gospel and "Light of Light" in the Nicene Creed), the Real, or Reality (*al-ḥaḳḳ*; most frequently in the Ḳurʾān of the content of the message of Muḥammad, *al-ḥaḳḳ min rabbika*, but also of Allāh in xx. 114; xxii. 6, 62; xxiv. 25; xxxi. 30 in phrases "the real king", "he is the reality").

These epithets state for us a Being who is self-sufficing, all-powerful, all-knowing, all-encompassing, eternal; who is the only Reality. His few ideal qualities are rarely and obscurely stated. What "holiness", "peace", "light" meant for Muḥammad, in regard to Allāh, we can hardly guess. That he would have thought fit to call him "just" may be doubted. The epithet frequently translated "truth" means, rather, "reality".

Next, Allāh in relation to others, that is, in relation to his creation; for nothing exists save him and that which he has made. He is the Creator (*al-khāliḳ*: lxix. 24 etc.; *al-bāri*ʾ: ii. 54; lix. 24 only; the last was evidently taken over by Muḥammad from the Hebrew, and is used without especial meaning), the Shaper (*al-muṣawwir*: liii. 24 only), the Beginner (*al-mubdiʾ*), the Restorer (*al-muʿīd*; these two not as epithets in the Ḳurʾān, but the idea frequently, e.g. xxix. 19; lxxxv. 13), the Giver of Life (*al-muḥyī*: xli. 39 only, but the idea often), the Giver of Death (*al-mumīt* not as epithet in the Ḳurʾān, but the idea frequently, e.g. xv. 23), the Heir (*al-wāri<u>th</u>*: xv. 3) of all when all save him are dead, the Reckoner and Recorder of all things in a book (*al-muḥṣī*: not as epithet, but idea frequently, cf. xxxvi. 12; lxxviii. 29), the Sender of the dead from the graves (*al-bāʿi<u>th</u>*: not as epithet in the Ḳurʾān, but idea very frequently), the Assembler of all, again, at the last (*al-<u>dj</u>āmiʿ*: iii. 9; iv. 140), the Strengthener (*al-muḳīt*: iv. 85 only), the Guardian (*al-ḥāfiẓ*: lxxxvi. 4 only), the King (*al-malik*, often), the Lord of Kingship (*mālik al-mulk*: iii. 26 only), the Governor (*al-wālī*: xiii. 11 only), the Prevailer (*al-muḳtadir*: xviii. 45 etc.), the Tyrant (*al-<u>dj</u>abbār*: lix. 23 only, the word elsewhere, 9 times, is used of men and in a bad sense only, coupled with *ʿanīd*, *<u>sh</u>aḳī*, *ʿaṣī*, *mutakabbir*; cf. the last as applied to Allāh).

Allāh is thus the absolute Creator, Sustainer, Ruler, Destroyer, Restorer, Recorder; there is no power nor strength save in him. Expressions can be used of him in his absoluteness, which would mean evil, if used of men, who have no such primal right. He is the Exalter (*al-rāfiʿ*) and the Honourer (*al-muʿizz*), and he is the Abaser (*al-mu<u>dh</u>ill*). He is the Withholder (*al-māniʿ*) and he is the Advantager (*al-nāfiʿ*); he is the Deferrer (*al-muʾa<u>kh</u><u>kh</u>ir*) and he is the Advancer (*al-muḳaddim*). He is the Contractor (*al-ḳābiḍ*) and he is the Spreader (*al-bāsiṭ*); he is the Distresser (*al-ḍārr*). It is true that these last do not occur as epithets in the Ḳurʾān; but their roots are common as used of Allāh. Curiously enough, the epithet form of the last, the Distresser, is used in the Ḳurʾān of Satan (lviii. 10).

Next, Allāh in relation to mankind. He is the Compassionate Compassionator (*al-raḥmān al-raḥīm*) or the Compassionate *Raḥmān*, according to the degree of nominality which we assign to *Raḥmān*. These are the most frequent of the epithets, and stand at the head of all the Sūras but one. Also *al-Raḥmān* was at one time used by Muḥammad as a proper name, equivalent to Allāh, and the Meccans regarded this as one of his innovations. Compare the story of the treaty of Ḥudaibiya where they rejected the formula containing it and insisted on the old Meccan form "In thy name, O Allāh!" (Baiḍāwī, in Sūra xlviii. 26; Ibn Hi<u>sh</u>ām, i. 747).

That Muḥammad derived the formula from South Arabia seems proved; see a paper by Mordtmann and Müller, in *WZKM*, x. 285 *sq.* But it was no mere formula. Man's standing naked, defenseless and excuseless in God's presence was one of Muḥammad's most dominant ideas, and is expressed in these Names more frequently than any other. From the root meaning "to forgive" comes a crescendo of three: the Forgiver (*al-<u>gh</u>āfir*: vii. 155; xl. 3 only), the Much Forgiver (*al-<u>gh</u>afūr*, often), the Forgiver *par métier* (*al-<u>gh</u>affār*: xx. 82 etc.). He is also the Pardoner (*al-ʿafūww*: iv. 43 etc.), the Clement (*al-ḥalīm*, often), the Repenter (*al-tawwāb*: ii. 37 etc.; used also of man), the Grateful (*al-<u>sh</u>akūr*: xxxv. 30 etc.; used also of man, and explained by commentators as meaning in the case of Allāh, "the acknowledger of thanksgiving"), the Very Patient (*al-ṣabūr*: not as epithet in the Ḳurʾān, but idea frequently). Two more intimate Names of the same class are the Kind (*al-raʾūf*: ii. 143 etc.) and the Loving (*al-wadūd*: xi. 89; lxxxv. 14 only). But he is also the Watcher (*al-raḳīb*: iv. 1 etc.), the Reckoner (*al-ḥasīb*, iv. 86; xxxiii. 39 only), the Witness (*al-<u>sh</u>ahīd*: often). Again, on man's behalf, he is the Faithful (*al-muʾmin*; of man it means "the believing"), the Protector (*al-muhaimin*: lix. 23 only), the Guide (*al-hādī*, often), the Guardian (*al-wakīl*, often), the Patron (*al-walī*, often). The last word is used of man also, and is the basis of the doctrine of saints in Islām. It means, literally, one who is near, a comrade or companion, and thus can be either the aiding patron or the dependent client. That there is a special class of the latter, the *walīs* or saints, the proof text is Sūra x. 62: "Ho! the *walīs* of Allāh, there is no fear upon them, and they sorrow not". Naturally, then, he is the Avenger (*al-muntaḳim*: not as epithet in the Ḳurʾān; but cf. v. 95), and the final Opener (*al-fattāḥ*: xxxiv. 26, and in other forms) who judges and distinguishes and divides between men — used also to indicate the "opener" of gain and victory. And as all things are in his hands, so all comes from him. He is the Giver (*al-wahhāb*: iii. 8 etc.), the Provider (*al-razzāḳ*: li. 58 only as epithet; but the idea of the dependence of all creation upon *rizḳ* from Allāh is very frequent), the Answerer of prayer (*al-mu<u>dj</u>īb*: xi. 61 only; but the conception of prayer and petition is frequent); the Giver (*al-muʿṭī*) and the Sufficer (*al-mu<u>gh</u>nī*), taken later in the sense of the Enricher, do not occur as epithets in the Ḳurʾān, but their ideas are fundamental; cf. e.g. xx. 50 and iv. 130.

Man's relation to Allāh, then, is that of dependence. He needs Allāh's forgiveness and patience. Allāh is a watcher and reckoner over him; but he is also a faithful protector and guide. From him comes all "sustenance" in the widest sense. He does everything directly — hence these epithets — and, logically, no angels or intermediaries are needed in the scheme. They must be in Islām, because Muḥammad found them in the fundamental religion of his day and had to accept them. And all is by his will: "he leadeth astray whom he wills, and guideth aright whom he wills" (xiii. 27; xvi. 93; lxxiv. 31). Each one can but hope that Allāh will guide him aright, submit himself to Allāh in absolute fear, and trust that Allāh will not cause him to forget and be of the losers in the Fire (lix. 19, 20). Antinomies had no terrors for Muḥammad. He, evidently, never thought about predestination and free-will, whatever later traditions may have put into his mouth; he expressed each side as he saw it at the moment, and as the need of the moment stood. So Allāh is kind, loving, patient [see above] on one side, and on another he says: "I created not the *<u>dj</u>inn* and mankind save that they should worship me. I seek not from them any sustenance, and I seek not that they should feed me". Allāh is the Sustainer, He of strength, the Firm! (li. 56—58). Again he is the Haughty (*al-mutakabbir*), the Tyrant (*al-<u>dj</u>abbār*); if he aids, he also distresses (*ḍarr*). Again: "Whom Allāh guideth aright, he allows himself to be guided aright, and whom he leads astray, they are the losers" (vii. 178). And so frequently Allāh is said to lead astray (*ḍall*). And whenever the root *ṭ b ʿ* occurs (iv. 155; vii. 100 *sq.*; ix. 87, 93; x. 74; xvi. 108; xxx. 59; xl. 35; xlvii. 16; lxiii. 3) it expresses the fundamental fact that Allāh "seals" the hearts of the unbelievers that they may not believe. These aspects of Allāh may not be contradictory; but their separate statement thus and the emphasis upon the last were full of meaning for the future theological development.

Muḥammad's position, then, was theistic in the highest degree, and his theology was theocentric. Yet it might rather be said that he was God-intoxicated, than that he had a theology. Certain ideas and phrases dominated him, and he neither thought nor cared whither they might lead. Thus Allāh was for him the Reality (al-ḥaḳḳ); but he never asked what that meant. He would have said, without hesitation, that time was when there was nothing but Allāh. Whether he would have gone on to say that time would be when there would be nothing but Allāh — as did some later sects — is uncertain. If put in a rhetorical form, he would probably have accepted it as an exalting of Allāh over his creatures. In fact, he pushed in certain phrases the absolute existence of Allāh so far that the later, pantheistic development is amply conditioned and explained. This occurs especially in connection with the phrase "the Face of Allāh", a phrase of unknown origin, but which for some reason seems to have impressed him deeply. The word "face" (waḏjh) in the Ḳurʾān is used frequently with the meaning "self" (nafs, ḏhāt) in connection with men (e.g. ii. 112; iii. 20; iv. 125; vi. 79; x. 105; xxx. 30, 43; xxxi. 22; xxxix. 24; perhaps the origin of the idiom), but when used of Allāh, more colour and flavour of the original metaphor seem to remain, though the ultimate meaning is undoubtedly "self". Thus, men act out of desire for the Face of Allāh (ii. 278; xiii. 22; xcii. 20); they "desire" or "make for (yurīdūna) the Face of Allāh" (vi. 52; xviii. 28; xxx. 38 sq.); they "act for the sake of the Face of Allāh" (lxxvi. 9). Then come the great texts. "Allāh's are the East and the West; wherever ye turn, there is the Face of Allāh" (ii. 115); "Everything goes to destruction (hālik) except his Face" (xxviii. 88); "Whoever is upon it (the earth) is fleeting (fānī); and the Face of the Lord abides, He of Majesty and Generosity" (lv. 26—27). In each case, "Allāh Himself" could be substituted with no essential loss; but Muḥammad, undoubtedly, felt the picturesqueness of the phrase, and later Ṣūfism built thereon its theories. With the commentators, the explanation is that all things besides Allāh are only "possible of existence" (mumkin), while he is "necessary of existence" (wāḏjib al-wudjūd); they may, therefore, be described according to their essential definition as "non-existent" (maʿdūm); i.e. because they may go to destruction, they are going to destruction. It may be doubted whether such a distinction, or, in fact, any clear thought was in Muḥammad's mind.

He left, then, this problem for the future Islām. It had to reconcile the intense personality and clear separateness of Allāh from the world with a direct working in the world, which amounts to immanence. The problem was further complicated by diverse phrases which suggested the essential non-existence of everything except Allāh. It may be said here, in short, that the scholastic theologians followed the idea of personality, and separated Allāh from his creation to a point where it was hard for them to explain how he could affect the world; in doing this they developed the doctrines of tanzīh (removal) and muḵẖālafa (difference), i.e. removal from Allāh of all qualities of impermanence, and assertion of the essential difference of his qualities and the similarly named qualities of human beings. The history of the development of Ṣūfism, on the other hand, is that of a gradual merging of the world in Allāh until it could be asserted that Allāh was All. The Aristotelian-Neoplatonic philosophers followed a third line. Working essentially in independence of

the exegesis of the Ḳurʾān, but seeking, for protection at least, to adapt themselves to its statements, they reached the other pantheistic position that All, i.e. the Aristotelian World, was Allāh. It was the life work of al-Ghazzālī to mediate, and to state a position which orthodox Islām has not yet passed.

It should now be in place to take up the position of Muḥammad as developed in the traditions. But to attempt to find in them anything that can be assigned to him with historic certainty is a perfectly hopeless task. A large element, it is quite plain. cannot be due to him; and what nucleus really came from his lips we probably never shall know. Goldziher has taught us that the traditions are really a record of the first centuries of dogmatic strife, that therein is their true historical value. But that record is so confused, misdated, indirect, misleading, that it can be used only to illustrate and supplement other more direct sources. Any consideration, therefore, of the traditions, either with reference to the views of Muḥammad or to those of the early Muslim Church, must now be brief. Even where the traditions have points of similarity with the Ḳurʾān, these are deceptive. Thus, in the Ḳurʾān, Muḥammad develops quite naïvely two separate views of Allāh's working, one rigidly predestinarian and the other leaving scope for free-will. This was due to a real duality in his own mind. But the similar phenomenon in the traditions had a different origin. There it was due to the contradictory traditions having originated in opposing schools, who freely forged and fathered them on the Prophet in support, each, of their own views. There are traditions which state very clearly that Muḥammad objected to all such discussions, while there are others, in which he enters on the subject at length. But the first of these are equally suspicious with the second; they are probably due to that party which objected for long to the use of reason (ʿaḳl) in theology, and contented itself with repeating the formulae which tradition brought to them (naḳl). In the traditions, then, come the following expansions and differences. There is a marked mythological increase. The figure of Allāh becomes more picturesque, and his relations to the angels and devils more detailed. The doctrine of the latter is more developed, and the simplicity of Allāh's working obscured (frequent in al-Buḵẖārī's Ṣaḥīḥ; see specially Kitāb al-tawḥīd and Badʾ al-ḵẖalḳ). The Face of Allāh recurs, and also his throne (ʿarsh); the cosmography of the heavens and the earth is worked out. He descends to the lowest heaven (al-samāʾ al-dunyā) and cries: "Is there a suppliant? Is there a seeker of forgiveness"? (Kitāb al-tawḥīd in Ṣaḥīḥ of al-Buḵẖārī, ed. Cairo 1312, iv. 179). Then there is the story of the man who will be last in Paradise, and of how he will make Allāh laugh (ibid., iv. 172, 173). At last, Allāh will take the earth on one of his fingers and the heavens on another, and cry aloud: "I am the King, where are the kings of the earth"? (ib., iv. 167, 181). He will press his foot down in hell, so as to make room there (ib., iv. 167, 175). His eyes, mentioned in the singular and the plural in the Ḳurʾān (sing. in xx. 39), are opposed to the one eye of al-Daḏjḏjāl (ib., iv. 169). Secondly, His qualities become still more flatly contradictory. A saying recurs frequently: "My mercy overcomes or precedes my wrath" (e.g. ib., iv. 169, 175), and, on the other hand, there is the monstrous tradition: "These to heaven, and I care not; these to hell, and I care not" (cf. Iḥyāʾ of al-Ghazzālī, ed. with commentary of Saiyid Murtaḍā, vol. vii., p. 308). It is significant that it is precisely on such questions of salvation that the most glaring contradictions appear. At one point, the recital of the first half of the creed and a minimum of works is judged enough, and at another, 999 men out of 1,000 shall go to the Fire. It is true that this is turned to a jest; the 999 are to be made up out of the people of Yād̲j̲ūd̲j̲ and Mād̲j̲ūd̲j̲ (*ib.*, iii. 143). Evidently, we have here echoes of later controversy. Still clearer is this when it is said that the saved remnant of the people will be in Syria (*ib.*, iv. 176), an unmistakable reference to the Umaiyads. Again, there is the absurd explanation of the uncovering of the leg at the Last Day (sūra lxviii. 42), an explanation that Muḥammad would never have dreamt of, but which has become fixed in Muslim exegesis (*Ṣaḥīḥ*, p. 173; cf. *Durra* of al-G̲h̲azzālī, ed. Gauthier, p. 69). A similar attempt is made to exegete the strange name of Allāh, *al-salām* (al-Buk̲h̲ārī, *loc. cit.*, iv. 167). There are long traditions, too, on free-will etc. (p. 176), on the doctrine of intercession (p. 169, 181); others of Murd̲j̲iʾite tendency (p. 175, 180); that Allāh can be called a "thing" (*s̲h̲aiʾ*: p. 170); that Allāh was and there was nothing before him (*kān Allāh wa-lam yakun s̲h̲aiʾ ḳablahu*: p. 170). With the last, we fairly reach Muʿtazilite metaphysics. The traditions, plainly, are no historic stage by themselves.

III. The Doctrine of the Person of Allāh as developed in the Muslim Church. The theocentric nature of Muḥammad's religious ideas and the influences which were active in the later development, especially that of the theology of the Greek Church, with its great emphasis on the person of God — as opposed to the Latin Church with its doctrine of sin, and the Reformed Churches with their doctrine of Scripture — made this doctrine (*al-tawḥīd*, "the unifying") cover the greater part of the field of Muslim theological thought. Similarly, the expressions of Muḥammad, partly concretely poetical and partly crudely metaphysical, went to condition future controversies. With only a little ingenuity in one-sidedness an absolutely anthropomorphic deity could be put together, or a practically pantheistic, or a coldly and aloofly rationalistic. The only impossiblity, as the Muʿtazilites found in the end, was a *fainéant* God, a stripped, abstract idea.

It is obviously impossible within the limits of an article to trace this development *qua* development. The most that can be attempted is to give the different tendencies, with the influences bearing upon them and the results to which they came. For details and a more precise working out of historical relationships, see the general works on Muslim theology.

The first steps towards resolving Muḥammad's brilliant contradictions seem to have been forced by the early civil wars. Men were compelled to ask themselves what really constituted a Muslim — what was of faith as to Islām. What view of Allāh must be held; of man's responsibility and of Allāh's supreme control? Naturally, some would damn all who did not hold and profess in every particular with themselves, while political necessities would lead others to some simple external test, leaving the rest to Allāh, who alone knew the hearts of men. So the Murd̲j̲iʾite [s. MURD̲J̲IʾA] sect arose with its doctrine of *ird̲j̲āʾ*, postponing such questions to the Last Day. Similarly on free-will, the usual extremists appeared with the usual attempts at mediation. Such and such political opponents could or could not help what they did. So the Ḳadarites and D̲j̲abrites arose.

But very soon other clarifying, if complicating, influences came to bear from without. The elaborate doctrine of God in the Greek Church, especially as formulated by John of Damascus, led men on from the simple Names of Allāh to questionings as to his Qualities (*ṣifāt*). Muḥammad could call him this and that, but what was meant thereby? they were forced to ask. They found that some explained the persons in the Christian Trinity as hypostatized qualities. Evidently they must run no risk of nine and ninety persons in Allāh. Yet the very nominality in Muḥammad's statement of these qualities raised dangers. There was growing, also, a belief that one of Allāh's qualities — although not expressed in a Name — must be Speech (*kalām*). This, especially, must be guarded against hypostatizing into a Logos. At all points there was need of careful definition.

Another influence was Greek philosophy. The students of it in Islām were going to the roots of all things, and, with it as guide, they attacked the problem of the nature of Allāh. Unity (*tawḥīd*), religiously and philosophically, they had to preserve; but, in preserving it, the nature of Allāh himself was gradually reduced to a bare, undefinable something, described in negatives. For example, Allāh for Muḥammad was the Knower (*al-ʿalīm*). Therefore, he must have the quality *ʿilm*, "knowledge". But of what was his knowledge, of something within himself or without? If the first, there was a duality in himself; if the second, his knowledge depended upon something outside of himself and was not absolute; therefore he himself, the possessor of this quality, was not absolute. Evidently, if Allāh's unity and independence were to be preserved, he could not be given any positive description.

In this development three tendencies persistently appear. There is traditionalism (*naḳl*), the acceptance of a doctrine because it was accepted and taught in the past. Its followers were called the people of tradition (*ahl al-ḥadīt̲h̲*); they followed proofs which they had heard (*adilla samʿīya*), derived from the Ḳurʾān, the *sunna* (usage of the Prophet as expressed in *ḥadīt̲h̲s*) and the agreement (*id̲j̲māʿ*) of the Muslim people. For them reason must not be applied either to criticise or to expand; the statement must be taken just as it stands. For example, in the Ḳurʾān we read that Allāh has settled himself firmly upon his throne (e.g. sūra xx. 5). That must be believed; we must not argue about it; we must not ask how he so sits; we must not go on to compare his sitting with that of a man; we must stay by the recorded word. This has developed into the phrase *bi-lā kaifa wa-lā tas̲h̲bīh*, "without enquiring how and without making comparison". But it is obvious that this is not a permanent position. And so, two further steps were taken, one by the general body of Muslims, the other by certain more rigidly logical. There developed the doctrine of *muk̲h̲ālafa*, "difference"; everything in Allāh is different from the similarly named thing in men; we must not think of it as like. This is also called *tanzīh*, "removing", that is removing Allāh from any danger of confusion or association with his creatures. In general, this process stopped at a point where it was still possible to form a conception of Allāh. He was different, it was conceded; but still, Allāh must be thinkable, and these names and phrases gave a thought of him not essentially wrong; we could not get from them what he was, but something like what he was. Others, however, went further and argued that from these expressions we could gain no conception of Allāh's real nature. That nature must always be a mystery to us, and we need not think that even the Names gave any light. The Ḳur'ān calls Allāh "the Most Merciful of them that show mercy" (vii. 151; xii. 64, 92; xxi. 83); but that cannot mean for us that he has the human quality of mercy, of or anything in any way similar. The course of things in the world disproves that. He has only given himself that Name, and what the Name means we cannot know and should not enquire. The great division here lies in admitting or rejecting the possibility of any discovering of the nature of Allāh other than purely negative — he is not this, he is not that. But, naturally, there have been many subdivisions, varying from simple exhortation to hold the faith of the Fathers (*al-salaf*) and not enquire too closely into the sacred mysteries to a sweeping application of the thesis that the absolute is the unknowable. Only, in Islām the latter position does not lead to agnosticism, but back to a dependence on authority. The main tendency now seems to be towards that latter position, and though the work of earlier theologians is accepted because of familiarity and antiquity, formal theology at the present day is more and more *tanzīh*. In Cairo, at present, the rhyme is current: *Kull^u mā khaṭar bi-bālik, fa-huwa hālik, wa'llāh bi-khilāf dhālik*, "Everything that comes into your mind is perishing, and Allāh is different from that". That is, Allāh is different from any thought we can possibly have, for our thoughts are of transitory things.

The second tendency is rationalism. All would recognize the necessity of the use of reason (*ʿaḳl*), but would differ as to its being a normal source of theological truth. We have already seen the beginnings of this in the study of Greek philosophy. The Muʿtazilites [q.v.] continued that development, and frankly reasoned out their religious position, creating their theology by means of reason. On the doctrine of Allāh, they, as we have seen, especially objected to his qualities. These were contrary to his unity; at least they must be described as being his essence, not as in his essence. But they tended to reject them altogether, and to reduce Allāh to a vague unity. They further objected to absolute predestinarianism as contrary to Allāh's justice (*ʿadl*). Their rejection of the possibility of the Beatific Vision of Allāh in Paradise was part of their jealousy for his spirituality. These three points, then, unity, justice, spirituality, are their position in brief, which they founded on and maintained by dialectic. This, of course, drove in time the traditional party to similar weapons. But with them dialectic was purely defensive; the doctrines were already given and accepted. Yet reconstruction could not fail to go on, if only in form of statement.

It was in the early part of the fourth century of the Hidjra, and especially at the hands of al-Ashʿarī [q.v.] that the use of dialectic (*kalām*; q.v.) was finally and fully accepted by orthodox Islām. Thereafter, only extreme traditionalists objected to it; scholastic theology was founded. The final system of al-Ashʿarī himself followed strictly orthodox lines. It was simply the phrase: "without enquiring how, and without making comparison". The first element was directed against the Muʿtazilites, and the second against anthropomorphism (*tadjsīm*). On free-will, he took a middle course and taught a doctrine, the puzzle of Islām ever since. It is that there is in the creature a certain power of "acquiring" (*iktisāb*) his actions, which, though they are strictly produced by Allāh, makes them also his own.

The school of al-Ashʿarī followed him closely in its creed, but developed his metaphysical ideas into a system which was finally formulated by al-Bāḳillānī (d. 403/1012—3) and thereafter won its way to being the ultimate Muslim conception of the nature and relationship of Allāh and his world. It has been stated thus (Macdonald, *Development of Muslim Theology*, p. 201 *sq.*):

"First, as to ontology. The object of the Ashʿarites was that of Kant, to fix the relation of knowledge to the thing in itself. Thus, al-Baḳillānī defined knowledge (*ʿilm*) as cognition (*maʿrifa*) of a thing as it is in itself. But in reaching that "thing in itself" they were much more thorough than Kant. Only two of the Aristotelian categories survived their attack, substance and quality. The others, quantity, place, time and the rest, were only relationships *iʿtibār*) existing subjectively in the mind of the knower, and not things. But a relationship, they argued, if real, must exist in something and a quality cannot exist in another quality, only in a substance. Yet it could not exist in either of the two things which it brought together; for example, in the cause or the effect. It must be in a third thing. But to bring this third thing and the first two together, other relationships would be needed and other things for these relationships to exist in. Thus we would be led back in an infinite sequence, and they had taken over from Aristotle the position that such an infinite series backwards (*tasalsul*) is inadmissible. Relationships, then, had no real existence but were mere phantoms, subjective non-entities. Further, the Aristotelian view of matter was now impossible for them. All the categories had gone except substance and quality; and among them, passion. Matter, then, could not have the possibility of suffering the impress of form. A possibility is neither an entity, nor a non-entity, but a subjectivity purely. But with the suffering matter, the active form and all causes must also go. They, too, are mere subjectivities. Again, qualities, for these thinkers, became mere accidents. The fleeting character of appearances drove them to the conclusion that there was no such thing as a quality planted in the nature of a thing; that the idea "nature" did not exist. Then this drove them further. Substances exist only with qualities, i.e. accidents. These qualities may be positive or they may be negative; the ascription of negative qualities to things is one of their most fruitful conceptions. When, then, the qualities fall out of existence, the substances themselves must also cease to exist. Substance as well as quality is fleeting, has only a moment's duration.

"But when they rejected the Aristotelian view of matter as the possibility of receiving form, their path, of necessity, led them straight to the atomists. So atomists they became, and, as always, after their own fashion. Their atoms were not of space only, but also of time. The basis of all the manifestation, mental and physical, of the world in place and time, is a multitude of monads. Each has certain qualities; but has extension neither in space nor time. They have simply position, not bulk, and do not touch one another. Between them is absolute void. Similarly as to time. The time-atoms, if the expression may be permitted, are equally unextended and have, also, absolute void — of time — between them. Just as space is only in a series of atoms, so time is only in a succession of untouching moments, and leaps across the void from one to the other with the jerk of the hand of a clock. Time, in this view, is in grains, and can exist only in connection with change. The monads differ from those of Leibnitz in having no nature in themselves, no possibility of development along certain lines. The Muslim monads are, and again are not; all change and action in the world are produced by their entering into existence and dropping out again, not by any change in themselves.

"But this most simple view of the world left its holders in precisely the same difficulty, only in a far higher degree, as that of Leibnitz. He was compelled to fall back on a pre-established harmony to bring his monads into orderly relations with each other; the Muslim theologians, on their side, fell back upon God and found in His will the ground of all things.

"We here pass from their ontology to their theology; and as they were thorough-going metaphysicians, so now they are thorough-going theologians. Being was all in the one case; now it is God that is all. In truth, their philosophy is in its essence a scepticism which destroys the possibility of a philosophy, in order to drive men back to God and His revelations and compel them to see in Him the one grand fact of the universe. From their ontology they derived an argument for the necessity of a God. That their monads came so and not otherwise must have a cause; without it there could be no harmony nor connection between them. And this cause must be one, with no cause behind it; otherwise we would have the endless chain. This cause, then, they found in the absolutely freewill of God, working without any matter beside it and unaffected by any laws or necessities. It creates and annihilates the atoms and their qualities and, by that means, brings to pass all the motion and change of the world. These, in our sense, do not exist. When a thing seems to us to be moved, that really means that God has annihilated — or permitted to drop out of existence, by not continuing to uphold, as another view held — the atoms making up that thing in its original position, and has created them again and again along the line over which it moves. Similarly of what we regard as cause and effect. A man writes with a pen and a piece of paper. God creates in his mind the will to write; at the same moment he gives him the power to write and brings about the apparent motion of the hand, of the pen and the appearance on the paper. No one of these is the cause of the other. God has brought about, by creation and annihilation of atoms, the requisite combination to produce these appearances. Thus we see that free-will, for the Muslim scholastics, is simply the presence, in the mind of man, of this choice created there by God. Further, it will be observed, how completely this annihilates the machinery of the universe. There is no such thing as law, and the world is sustained by a constant, ever-repeated miracle. Miracles and what we regard as the ordinary operations of nature are on the same level. The world and the things in it could have been quite different. The only limitation upon God is that He cannot produce a contradiction. A thing cannot be and not be at the same time. There is no such thing as a secondary cause; when there is the appearance of such, it is only illusional. God is producing it, as well as the ultimate appearance of effect. There is no nature belonging to things. Fire does not burn and a knife does not cut. God creates in a substance a being burned when fire touches it and a being cut when the knife approaches it.

"In this scheme there are, certainly great difficulties, philosophical and ethical. It establishes a relationship between God and the atoms. But we have already seen that relationships are subjective illusions. That, however, was in the case of things of the world, perceived by the senses — contingent being, as they would put it. It does not hold of necessary being. God possesses a quality called Difference from originated things (*al-mukh̲ālafa li'l-ḥawādith̲*). He is not a natural cause, but a free cause; and the existence of a free cause they were compelled by their principles to admit. The ethical difficulty is perhaps greater. If there is no order of nature and no certainty, or nexus, as to causes and effects, if there is no regular development in the life, mental, moral and physical, of a man — only a series of isolated moments, how can there be any responsibility, any moral claim or duty? This difficulty seems to have been recognized more clearly than the philosophical one. It was met, formally, by the assertion of a certain order and regularity in the will of God. He sees to it that a man's life is a unity, and as for details, that the will to act and the action always coincide". See further in Heinrich Ritter's paper, *Über unsere Kenntniss der arabischen Philosophie*, Göttingen 1844.

But all this was strictly defensive of positions already taken up; and such a scheme as this, while it took in a way the place of the study of philosophy in Islām, was concealed from the masses, and was viewed with more or less dislike by the pious. The study of it was permitted only in defence of the Faith against heretics and unbelievers. Therein was the difference between the orthodox theologians and the Muʿtazilites. The latter had believed that by reason they could reach ultimate truth; Islām assured itself that reason could never grasp the nature of Allāh, he is unknowable to human powers, and we must accept and believe what we are taught by him.

And so the third tendency is mysticism (*kas̲h̲f*, unveiling; Ṣūfism, *taṣawwuf*; q.v.). There must be a supernatural basis for our own knowledge of Allāh, and, therefore, Islām early came to the position that in the individual human soul there resided a power of reaching and knowing God directly, a personal supplementation of the truth taught to mankind by his messengers, the prophets. That this was in the mind of Muḥammad himself, jealous as he was of the prophetic office, seems clear, and it has appeared through the whole history of his Church, in degrees and forms varying from simple, devout meditation to high ecstasy, union with God and essential pantheism. In the earlier centuries of Islām, this doctrine struggled as a private opinion, held generally by the great majority, approved explicitly by many outstanding theologians, leading from time to time to extreme antinomian and pantheistic positions, denounced by some few authorities because of these wanderings; but still unassimilated to the general body of Muslim truth. In its forms it was partly ascetic and partly speculative; it sought Allāh by exercises of devotion or by flights of devout imagination, assisted by plain hypnotism, auto and otherwise. In its development it was affected by Neoplatonism, by Christian mysticism, by Buddhism and by the primitive monism, which is the basis of all oriental thought. Its ultimate tendency, therefore, however denounced and avoided, was to find in Allāh the One Existent (*wāḥid al-wud̲j̲ūd*) rather than the Necessarily Existent (*wād̲j̲ib al-wud̲j̲ūd*).

It was the work of al-G̲h̲azzālī (d. 505/1111) to construct a mystical system, in which this pantheistic element was restrained if not destroyed and to weave into the fabric of the theology of Islām the thread of the unveiling of the Ṣūfī, beside those of tradition and reason. Reason he used to destroy itself and to demonstrate that with it we can reach no absolute knowledge. Tradition he used to discipline, guide and restrain the devout imagination of the mystic. On the facts of the religious consciousness, so given, developed and guided, he built his theology.

Yet, in his view of Allāh, he followed closely the conception of Muḥammad. For him, Allāh was Will; he saw everywhere around him the touch and working of Allāh. And man was kin to Allāh, especially in this fact of Will. There he passed beyond the *tanzīh* of the ordinary theologian. *Volo ergo sum* was the basis of al-Ghazzālī's psychology. Allāh had breathed into man of his spirit (sūra xv. 29; xxxviii. 72). The soul of man, therefore, is different from everything else in the world; is a *djawhar rūḥānī*, a spiritual substance; created but unshaped; not subject to dimension or locality. From its exile here, it seeks the divine, and, therefore, our souls yearn back to Allāh. In a tradition, too, it is recorded that Allāh created Adam in his own form (*ṣūra*). That, for al-Ghazzālī, meant that there is a likeness between the spirit of man and that of Allāh in essence, quality and actions. So, just as man rules his body, Allāh rules the world (*al-Maḍnūn al-ṣaghīr*, p. 2 *sq.*).

In spite of all pantheistic dangers in these views, there is no question that they are very close to the mind of Muḥammad. And so, for the Church of Islām, al-Ghazzālī soon became and still remains her greatest doctor, with the standing of Augustine or Aquinas in Christendom. When a Muslim theologian now disagrees with him, he prefers to describe the rejected doctrine as a misunderstanding of al-Ghazzālī's true position. In consequence, alongside of the ossified system of the traditionalists, al-Ghazzālī's *Iḥyā'* is earnestly studied; and in that study, without doubt, is the hope for the future in Islām.

As, then, these three tendencies ran together in al-Ghazzālī, and as any statement by him of Muslim faith is received with respect, at the present day, by all Muslims except such extreme traditionalists and anthropomorphists as the Wahhābites and the followers of Ibn Taimīya [q.v.], one should consult his *Risāla ḳudsīya*, written at Jerusalem and thereafter incorporated in his *Iḥyā'* (ii. 86 *sq.* of the Cairo edition with commentary by the Saiyid Murtaḍā al-Ḥusainī). It states very fairly the orthodox Muslim position on the person of Allāh. Space does not permit the insertion of a translation here. Reference, therefore, may be made to a very full analysis of it in Asin Palacios' *Algazel* (Saragossa 1901), i. 233—283, to a shorter statement in de Vaux' *Gazali* (Paris 1902), p. 97 *sq.* and to a translation by H. Bauer, *Die Dogmatik. Al Ghazālī's nach dem II. Buche seines Hauptwerkes* (Halle a/d. Saale 1912). Reference may be made, also, to translations of several other creeds in D. B. Macdonald's *Development of Muslim Theology*, p. 293—351.

The statement given in the *Risāla ḳudsīya* is specifically Ash'arite. But al-Ash'arī's close contemporary, al-Māturīdī (d. 333/944—5), founded also a school, still existent and regarded as equally orthodox. It followed the line of thought of Abū Ḥanīfa (d. 150/767), and it is, in consequence, often called Ḥanafite. It is followed largely by Turks, and in Macdonald's *Development of Muslim Theology*, p. 308 *sq.* will be found a Māturīdite creed in full, that of al-Nasafī. None of the points of difference between al-Māturīdī and al-Ash'arī are regarded as involving either unbelief (*kufr*) or heresy (*bid'a*, innovation) and those bearing on the nature of Allāh can be summed up as follows:

1. To the eternal qualities of Allāh al-Māturīdī added "Making to be" (*takwīn*). Other names for this quality are Creating (*khalḳ*), Bringing to Life (*iḥyā'*), Sustaining (*razḳ*), Bringing to Death (*imāta*). These are called active qualities (*ṣifāt al-af'āl*) and are originated according to the Ash'arites; but — because the same as *takwīn* — eternal according to the Māturīdites. This is evidently an attempt to surmount the barrier between the unchanging Allāh and the changing world. 2. Instead of al-Ash'arī's *iktisāb* — which appears to be nothing but an attempt to explain how we feel that we are free; that is, God creates in us that feeling — al-Māturīdī simply says that we have "actions of choice" (*ikhtiyār*) for which we are rewarded or punished, and leaves the question there. 3. Yet all actions are by the will of Allāh; only, good actions are by his good pleasure (*riḍā*) as well; and bad actions are not by his good pleasure. 4. When Allāh requires anything of a creature, he gives him the ability (*istiṭā'a*) thereto; that is the basis of the validity of the imposition of the task. 5. Allāh's qualities are unchanging; but changes come in creatures of happiness to misery and *vice versa*. This is by change in happiness and misery, and not by change in making-happy or making-miserable. Again, the unchanging Allāh and the changing world. 6. A Māturīdite remarked that there was nothing logically in the Ash'arite position to prevent all the believers being eternally in the Fire, and all the unbelievers eternally in the Garden; but that what we were taught was distinctly the opposite. So while the Mu'tazilites held that it was incumbent upon Allāh to reward and punish according to justice, the Māturīdites only said that Allāh is exalted in and through himself from any injustice, for it would be unbecoming to his wisdom.

Of the differences between al-Ghazzālī's statement and the views of the Mu'tazilites, it is unnecessary to say more. Al-Ghazzālī in this *Risāla* is writing specifically against them; and makes clear their positions which consisted in negating the Qualities, in asserting incumbency upon Allāh, especially that he must do what is most advantageous to his creatures and in denying his Speech and the Vision of him in Paradise. His argument that the world is created, and must, therefore, have a creator is directed against the Aristotelian-Neoplatonic philosophers, who taught the eternity of the world. He himself did not regard that argument as valid. That the world was created he knew, because he, personally and immediately, knew Allāh, the Creator. See his description of his religious experiences, in his *Munḳidh*. His treatment of the anthropomorphists is more gentle. Yet he marvels once at the mystery of Allāh's so keeping some of his creatures in the dark that they cannot understand the difference, even, between relative and absolute priority (section on Allāh's Speech). Thrice, he comments caustically upon their insisting on a wrong use of words, although their ideas were correct enough. The Karrāmites [q.v.] used "substance" (*djawhar*) of Allāh, thinking that substance meant "an existing being not in a place", but "existing in itself". The Ḥanbalites [q.v.] and Karrāmites both used "body" (*djism*) of Allāh in the sense simply of "an existing being" or "one existing in himself". The anthropomorphists, generally, clung to the expression that Allāh had direction, as indeed their exegesis of his *istiwāʾ* on his throne required. But, finally, in Base I, Source VI, there is a most absolute statement that any resemblance is impossible between Creator and creature, which is hard to bring into agreement with the later sections of his book, where the mystical basis of faith is taught and with his exegesis of the Ḳurʾānic passage, where Allāh breathes into man of his Spirit (*rūḥ*: xv. 29; xxxviii. 72) and of the tradition that Allāh created Adam in his own form (*ṣūra*). See reference above to the *Maḍnūn al-ṣag͟hīr*, p. 2 *sq.* But in the same book he takes up this very problem. Do not such views, it is asked, with regard to the soul of man destroy Allāh's "difference", and constitute *tas͟hbīh*, making a resemblance? Al-G͟hazzālī replies (*loc. cit.*, p. 9) that *tas͟hbīh* applies only to Allāh's most peculiar quality (*akhaṣṣ waṣfihi*), that he is *ḳaiyūm* (self-subsisting), subsisting in himself, while everything else subsists in him, not through its own essence. "Nay, things through their own essence have nothing but non-existence, and existence comes to them only from something else, by way of loan. But the existence of Allāh is essential, unborrowed. This reality of self-subsistence belongs to Allāh alone".

This, then, is the esoteric explanation of the prohibition of *tas͟hbīh*. It rules out the materialistic *tas͟hbīh* of the anthropomorphists; but practically leaves free scope on the mystical and spiritualizing side. In another of his books (*Ildjām al-ʿawāmm ʿan ʿilm al-kalām*, p. 47 *sq.*) al-G͟hazzālī discusses the double danger of, on the one hand, too much *tanzīh* in describing Allāh leading the masses to atheism and on the other, the use of ambiguous and pictorial terms leading them to *tas͟hbīh*. The danger from *tanzīh* he considers much the greater, and advises that the people should be addressed in language and figures that they can understand. An economy of teaching should also be exercised; which does not mean that they should be taught anything positively that is not so; only that certain subjects need not be considered with them.

We have, then, to regard what is given in his statement of the As͟hʿarite position as one side only. It is complete from the point of view of the dogmatic theologian, and it is as a dogmatic theologian that he here writes. Yet it cannot but excite surprise that so de-humanized a system should have obtained such a control that a man like al-G͟hazzālī had to cast his dogmatics into its mould. He, certainly, believed greatly in the fear of Allāh, and the thought of the Fire had been a powerful influence in his own conversion; but it is plain from his writings elsewhere that his own Allāh was by no means the unattractive Force here depicted. To produce this personification of the irresponsible, non-moral and uncontrollable working of nature, the Muslim theologians must have passed through a stage of defending their faith by showing its agreement with the facts of life and thus made Allāh so emphatically the God of things as they are. With this object, they took from Muḥammad's representation the elements which suited them.

In consequence, the already narrow character of the Allāh of the Ḳurʾān is still further impoverished. Another weighty influence in the same direction was the dialectic necessity of representing Allāh as unconditioned Being. They had, therefore, to eliminate from him, so far as possible, the elements entailing relationship and all human attributes.

For al-G͟hazzālī, therefore, as a mystic, it became necessary to supplement this system; and so gave it its essential basis in the subsequent chapters of his work, especially where he deals with "the secrets of the heart", and describes how the heart sees and knows God. "He who knows his own heart, knows his Lord", says the tradition; and on that teaching the mystical life is founded. But here we pass from theology to religion, and from the doctrine of the person of Allāh to the psychology of belief (see D. B. Macdonald, *The religious Attitude and Life in Islām*). For the doctrine itself it may be said broadly that it is still unchanged and that there exist the same different aspects of *tanzīh*, *tas͟hbīh* and the mystical vision in varying proportions in the faith of every Muslim of the present day. The use of reason has gone, except to demonstrate the possibility of a doctrine; tradition has become the tradition of the later systematizers, rather than the words of Muḥammad and the Fathers; mysticism has heired the dead Aristotelian-Neoplatonic philosophy, and so far as a Muslim, now, is a thinker he is a mystic. For the later plainly pantheistic development in Persian and Turkish Ṣūfism, see TAṢAWWUF. The views of the philosophers do not come within the scope of this article; but reference may be made to the essays of Averroes on what may be called the theology of an educated man, which were published at Munich by M. J. Müller, in Arabic in 1859, and in a German translation, after Müller's death, in 1875. They are an attempt to render it possible for a thinking man to remain in connection with the Muslim Church, are largely directed against al-G͟hazzālī, and, as they have been reprinted in the East, may be of importance for the future development of the doctrine of Allāh. A Muslim who did not know Averroes' real philosophical position could study them, agree with them and still remain in his Faith.

Bibliography: Besides the above-mentioned works: A. v. Kremer, *Gesch. der herrsch. Ideen des Islams* (Leipzig 1868); M. Th. Houtsma, *De strijd over het Dogma in den Islam tot op al-Aschʿari* (Leyden 1875); Goldziher, *Muhammedanische Studien* (Halle a. S. 1889—1890); *Die Ẓâhiriten* (Leipzig 1884); *Materialien zur Kenntniss der Almohadenbewegung in Nordafrica* (*Z D M G*, xli. 30 *sq.*); *Die Bekenntnissformeln der Almohaden* (*Z D M G*, xliv. 168 *sq.*); *Le livre d'Ibn Toumert* (Algiers 1903); Krehl, *Beiträge zur muhammedanischen Dogmatik* (*Sitzungsber. d. K. Sächs Ges. d. Wiss., Phil.-hist. Classe*, xxxvii., Leipzig 1885); *Beiträge zur Charakteristik der Lehre vom Glauben im Islam* (Leipzig 1877); A. de Vlieger, *Kitāb al-Qadr* (Leyden 1903); Edward Sell, *The Faith of Islam* (London 1896); Th. Haarbrücker, *Asch-Schahrastâni's Religionspartheien und Philosophen-Schulen übersetzt und erklärt* (Halle 1850—1851); H. Steiner, *Muʿtaziliten* (Leipzig 1865); T. W. Arnold, *The Muʿtazila* (Leipzig 1902); Shaikh Muhammad Iqbal, *The Development of Metaphysics in Persia* (London 1908); G. van Vloten, *Irdjâ* (*Z D M G*, xlv. 181 *sq.*); W. Spitta, *Zur Geschichte Abu 'l-Hasan al-Ashʿarī's* (Leipzig 1876); M. Schreiner, *Zur Geschichte des Ashʿaritenthums* (*Actes du VIIIe Congr. Intern. des Oriental.*, i. 1, Leyden 1891, p. 77 *sq.*); *Beiträge zur Geschichte der theologischen Bewegungen im Islam* (*Z D M G*, lii. 463 *sq.*, 513 *sq.*; liii. 51 *sq.*); Grimme, *Mohammed, II. Teil, Einleitung in den Koran*, etc. (Münster i. W. 1895); C. de Vaux, *Avicenne* (Paris 1900); S. M. Zwemer, *The Moslem Doctrine of God* (Edinburgh 1905); Tj. de Boer, *Die Entwicklung der Gottesvorstellung im Islam*, in *Die Geisteswissenschaften*, i., 1913/14,

p. 228 *sqq.*; A. J. Wensinck, *The Muslim Creed*, (Cambridge) 1932. L. Gardet et M. N. Anawati, *Introduction à la théologie Musulmane*, Paris 1948.

AMĪR AL-MUʾMINĪN, i.e. commander of the faithful. ʿUmar was the first to bear this title. In the East the Umaiyad and ʿAbbāsid caliphs followed his example, as did those of their opponents who thought themselves entitled to claim the Caliphate (ʿAlids, Ḳarmaṭīs, Fāṭimids). It was not till the fall of Baghdād (656/1258) that the smaller rulers in the East also styled themselves Amīr al-Muʾminīn.

In the West the title occurs more frequently: it was borne by the Rustamids, Aghlabids, Zīrids, Ḥammādids, the Umaiyads after 316/928 and some of the petty Spanish kings. On the other hand those dynasties which recognized the supremacy of the ʿAbbāsids contented themselves with the title *amīr al-muslimīn*, e.g. the Almoravids. Their opponents, the Almohades, founded again the independent African Caliphate and called themselves "commanders of the faithful", as also in part the Ḥafṣids, Marīnids and Zaiyānids. At present the Sharīfs of Morocco are still styled Amīr al-Muʾminīn. — It may be added that as early as the year 2 of the Hidjra ʿAbd Allāh b. Djaḥsh bore this title during the expedition to Nakhla.

Bibliography: M. van Berchem, *Titres califiens d'Occident* (*JA*, series x., xi. 245—335), where complete bibliographical references are given.

ʿAMR B. AL-ʿĀṢ (al-ʿĀṣī) AL-SAHMĪ, a contemporary of Muḥammad of Kuraishite birth. The part which he played in Islāmic history begins with his conversion in the year 8/629—30. At that time he must already have been of middle age, for at his death which took place ca. 42/663 he was over ninety years old. He passed for one of the most wily politicians of his time, and we must endorse this verdict. The more clear-sighted inhabitants of Mecca already foresaw shortly after the unsuccessful siege of Madīna that this fact was the turning-point in Muḥammad's career. It is not strange therefore that men like Khālid b. al-Walīd, ʿUthmān b. Ṭalḥa and ʿAmr b. al-ʿĀṣ went over to Islām even before the capture of Mecca. Not much importance is to be attached to the story of their conversion. That of ʿAmr is said to have taken place in Abyssinia under the influence of the Christian Negus. — Muḥammad at once made use of his newly-gained assistance: after a few small expeditions he sent ʿAmr to ʿUmān, where he entered into negotiations with the two brothers who ruled there, Djaifar and ʿAbbād b. Djulandā, and they accepted Islām. He was not to see the Prophet again. The news of the latter's death reached him in ʿUmān, and occasioned his return to Madīna. But he did not remain there long. Probably in the year 12/633 Abū Bakr sent him with an army into Palestine. The accounts of the conquest of this country are known to be somewhat confused (cf. also Caetani, *Annali dell' Islām*, A. H. 12); but so much is certain, that in this undertaking ʿAmr played a most prominent part. The subjection of the country west of the Jordan especially was his achievement, and he was also present at the battles of Adjnādain and the Yarmūk as at the capture of Damascus.

Yet his real fame is due to his conquest of Egypt. According to some sources, he betook himself there with his troops on his own responsibility. It is more probable, however, that ʿUmar was informed of the matter (cf. Wellhausen, *Skizzen und Vorarbeiten*, vi. 93) or even that it was undertaken at his order. It is certain that reinforcements were soon sent out to him, under al-Zubair. In the summer of 19/640 the Greeks were defeated at Heliopolis. In 20/641 Babylon was occupied by the Arabs, in 21/642 Alexandria lay in their power. He founded Fusṭāṭ, which was later called Miṣr and in the 4th (10th) century al-Ḳāhira. Up to this day the mosque of Old Cairo bears his name.

We can understand that ʿAmr felt himself wronged when the Caliph ʿUthmān recalled him in favour of ʿAbd Allāh b. Saʿd, shortly after his accession to the throne. When circumstances became threatening for ʿUthmān, ʿAmr was wise enough not to commit himself openly on the side of his enemies; but he secretly incited ʿAlī, Ṭalḥa and al-Zubair against him. Yet it was not till after the Battle of the Camel, when only the two opponents ʿAlī and Muʿāwiya survived, that he once more came to the front, associating himself with Muʿāwiya. At the battle of Ṣiffīn he commanded the Syrian cavalry. When the battle turned in favour of ʿAlī, he conceived the clever device of placing leaves of the Ḳurʾān on the lances. The ruse was successful and the battle remained undecided. A court of arbitration was agreed upon, which was to consist of Abū Mūsā al-Ashʿarī and ʿAmr b. al-ʿĀṣ. Before the day appointed came, ʿAmr rendered Muʿāwiya the important service of occupying Egypt for him. It was an easy task to dispose of the youthful ʿAlid governor, Muḥammad b. Abī Bakr: he defeated him (early in 38/658) and put him to death.

In the same year (Shaʿban) ʿAmr proceeded to Adhruḥ to the court of arbitration (according to al-Wāḳidī's chronology in Ṭabarī, i. 3407). He succeeded in conducting matters so far that Abū Mūsā declared both ʿAlī and Muʿāwiya unworthy of the highest office. ʿAlī lost thereby his title of Caliph, Muʿāwiya however, who had only fought for "Uthmān's blood", lost nothing. Until his death [see above] 'Amr remained Governor of Egypt. On the 15th Ramaḍān 40/January 22, 661 he escaped by mere chance assassination at the hands of Zādawaih, one of the three Khāridjites, who had chosen out the three leaders of Islām ʿAlī, Muʿāwiya and ʿAmr as the victims of their fanaticism. ʿAmr felt unwell on that day and left the leadership of the *ṣalāt* to Khāridja b. Ḥudhāfa. So the latter was mortally wounded. "I meant ʿAmr, but God meant Khāridja", the assassin is reported to have said after accomplishing his deed.

Bibliography: Ibn Ḥadjar, *Iṣāba*, ii. 1 *sq.*; Ibn al-Athīr, *Usd al-ghāba* (Cairo 1286), iv. 115; Nawawī, p. 478 *sq.*; Balādhurī, see Index; Ṭabarī, see Index; Ibn Saʿd, iiia. 21; Wüstenfeld, *Die Statthalter von Ägypten* (*Abh. G. W. Gött.*, xx.); Wellhausen, *Skizzen und Vorarbeiten*, vi. 51 *sq.*, 89 *sq.*; Yaʿḳūbī, see Index; Caetani, *Annali dell' Islām*; Butler, *The Arab Conquest of Egypt* (London 1902); S. Lane Poole, *A History of Egypt* (London 1901), vi; Ibn Ḳutaiba, *Maʿārif* (ed. Wüstenf.), p. 145; G. Wiet, *L'Egypte arabe* (Paris 1937).

ʿAMR B. ʿUBAID ABŪ ʿUTHMĀN, one of the earliest Muʿtazilites [q.v.]. Originally a follower of the ascetic school of Ḥasan al-Baṣrī, he adopted the opinion of Wāṣil b. ʿAṭāʾ on the question as to the status of the Muslim who has fallen into sin. We have no information about his literary activity, but it is known that he was distinguished among his contemporaries by his moral earnestness and piety. It is in keeping with this character that he joined the party of Yazīd III who claimed the throne as a rival of the frivolous Walīd II. Later on ʿAmr was on very friendly terms with the ᶜAbbāsid caliph al-Manṣūr. He died in 145/762 at Marrān on his return from the pilgrimage to Mecca.

Bibliography: Ibn Ḳutaiba, *Maᶜārif* (ed. Wüstenf.), p. 244; Ibn Khallikān, No. 514; Arnold, *al-Muᶜtazilah*, p. 22 *sq.*; Masᶜūdī, *Murūdj*, vi. 211; Houtsma, *De strijd over het dogma*, p. 51 *sq.*

AMRAM. [See ᶜIMRĀN.]

ANAS B. MĀLIK ABŪ ḤAMZA, one of the most prolific traditionists. After the Hidjra his mother gave him to the Prophet as servant; according to his own statement he was then ten years of age. He was present at Badr, but took no part in the battle, and is therefore not counted among the combatants. He remained in Muḥammad's service up to the time of the latter's death, later he took part in the wars of conquest. He also played small parts in the civil wars. In the year 65/684 he officiated as imām of the *ṣalāt* at Baṣra, acting on behalf of the rival caliph ᶜAbd Allāh b. al-Zubair. At the insurrection of ᶜAbd al-Raḥmān b. al-Ashᶜath he was reproached by al-Ḥadjdjādj with being a partisan of the rebels just as he had formerly taken the part of the enemies of the Umaiyads, ᶜAlī and Ibn al-Zubair; and although he was highly respected as a companion of the Prophet, al-Ḥadjdjādj had no scruples in putting round his neck a cord with his seal (72/691). It is said however that the caliph ᶜAbd al-Malik asked his pardon for al-Ḥadjdjādj's disrespectful act. Anas died at Baṣra at a very advanced age, which is variously given at from 97 to 107 years (the dates most frequently found are 91—93/709—711). — His reputation as a traditionist is none of the highest. Abū Ḥanīfa, it is said, refused to acknowledge his authority in matters of tradition; a version of the *miᶜrādj* (Muḥammad's ascension to heaven) goes back to him. A large collection of his traditions is contained in the *Musnad* of Aḥmad b. Ḥanbal.

Bibliography: Aḥmad Ibn Ḥanbal, *Musnad*, iii. 92 *sq.*; Balādhurī, p. 381; Ṭabarī, i. 2409, 2559, 2960; ii. 465, 855; Ibn Ḳutaiba, *Maᶜārif* (ed. Wüstenf.), p. 157; Nawawī, p. 166; Ibn al-Athīr, *Usd al-ghāba* (Cairo 1286), i. 127 *sq.*; Ibn Ḥadjar, *Iṣāba*, i. 138; Ibn Khallikān, transl. by de Slane, ii. 588; Damīrī, *Ḥayāt al-ḥayawān*, p. 350 quoted by Caetani, *Annali dell' Islām* (Introd., § 26, note 1).

AL-**ANṢĀR** (A.), 'the helpers', title of the believers of Madīna who received and assisted the Prophet after his flight from Mecca. They are sometimes called more explicitly Anṣār al-Nabī, 'the helpers of the Prophet'. The word is probably the plural of *naṣīr* which however does not occur in the sense of the religious term in question. To express the singular the patronymic form *Anṣārī* was derived from the plural *anṣār*; this form however is also used as a patronymic in the sense of 'descending from one of the Anṣār' and as an adjective 'belonging to the Anṣār', and forms the plural *anṣārīyūn*. In making Jesus call the disciples helpers of God (Sūra iii. 52; lxi. 14) Muḥammad seems to play on the resemblance of the word with *Naṣārā*, the name of the Christians; the idea that the believers should be helpers of Allāh is several times expressed by Muḥammad. He mentions the Anṣār with special distinction together with the *Muhādjirūn* [q.v.] as those who led the way, and who are followed by the other believers (Sūra ix. 100); besides Sūra ix. 117 this is the only passage in the Ḳur'ān in which the word is directly applied to the faithful of Madīna.

After the Hidjra the first followers of Muḥammad were chiefly members of the Madīnite tribe of Khazradj [q.v.], and the name Anṣār must be understood as referring to them; the tribe of Aws kept back in the beginning, and was partly even hostile to the Prophet; within the ranks of the Anṣār themselves not a few made a distinction between the assistance which they were prepared to render to Muḥammad as prophet and as statesman. The community of believers at Madīna is thus divided into Muhādjirūn and Anṣār, and the two constituent parts remained distinctly separate, although the Prophet strove from the very beginning to knit them together as closely as possible by establishing the bond of brotherhood between individual Muhādjirūn and Anṣār. The most intimate companions of the Prophet always belonged to the circle of Meccan companions of the Hidjra; and within the Anṣār themselves there remained certain pre-Islāmic tribal contrasts, which however never again became as acute as before. The want of enthusiasm shown at first by the Anṣār in the fulfilment of the military duty was a source of much anxiety for the Prophet. Gradually the helpers became his subjects. While expected to advance his cause they were also prohibited from rendering any form of assistance to his enemies; they were commanded e.g. to lay information with Muḥammad against their pagan relatives. At the same time they preserved up to a certain point the right of criticism, and demanded respect for their persons, which Muḥammad was ready to accord. — After passing through the critical period the community of the Anṣār soon began to flourish; rich spoils of war flowed into the town, and trade improved. After the taking of Mecca many Anṣār feared that Muḥammad might transfer the seat of government to that town, but he allayed their fears by saying that he wished to live where they lived and to die where they died [cf. further the article MUḤAMMAD].

The Anṣār never succeeded in securing the dignity of caliph for one of their number, but it was only due to the influence of ᶜUmar that, after the Prophet's death, the choice did not fall on the Khazradjite Saᶜd b. ᶜUbāda. Afterwards the Anṣār remained for ever excluded from the succession. Many of them, however, joined the victorious armies of Islām and came to prominence. They were on the whole strong supporters of the Umaiyads. In Spain most of the Arab chiefs were descendants of ᶜAbd Allāh b. Rawāḥa, who, like Ḥassān b. Thābit, belonged to the Khazradj and praised the Prophet in his poems.

On the other hand they became the classical types of Muslim piety, devoted to the memory of Muḥammad and pre-eminent in the science of tradition. This distinction was their answer to the pride of the Meccans, which occasionally found expression in venomous words; they could also appeal to the fact that they alone had rendered assistance to the persecuted believers in their direct need, and the recognition which their conduct had received from the Prophet. Like the Ḳuraish they traced back their excellence to the character of their noble ancestors and opposed the confident pride of the Ḳuraish in their ancestral nobility by an embellished version, probably invented at that time and for this purpose, of their own early history, which told of a glorious past in South Arabia, their traditional home; it is probable that the famous contrast between Northern and Southern Arabs established by the genealogists, had its chief source in the jealous imagination of the Anṣār (see Goldziher, *Muhammedanische Studien*, i. 93 *sq.*).

The genealogists state that the Khazradj, together with the Aws and the Ghassānids had migrated from South-Arabia after the bursting of the dam at Maʾrib. The genealogy of the divisions of each tribe is fairly well established, as they were registered under ʿUmar b. al-Khaṭṭāb in the second category of those entitled to pensions. Both the Khazradj and the Aws were divided into a number of clans at the time of the Prophet.

Ancient historical tradition tells of the settling of the two tribes in Yathrib and their struggle with the Jews whom they found established there. They were helped by the Ghassānids or other Yamanites, but afterwards they fell out among themselves. In the fight of Buʿāth, shortly before the Hidjra, the Khazradj, who were originally stronger in force, were defeated by the Aws and their allies, including some of the Jews. Afterwards a kind of equilibrium was reached, but only after the arrival of Muḥammad the internal struggle ceased. We get a fair estimate of the number of fighting men in each of the two tribes by the list of participants in the battle of Badr, for Ibn Saʿd, in his *Ṭabaḳāt* (vol. II/ii) gives the names of 63 members of the tribe of Aws and 175 names of those drawn from the Khazradj.

Bibliography: al-Samhūdī, *Khulāṣat al-wafāʾ* and Wüstenfeld's translation *Geschichte der Stadt Medina* in *Abh. G. W. Gött.*, vol. ix; Wellhausen, *Medina vor dem Islam* (*Skizzen und Vorarbeiten*, iv, 3—64); A. J. Wensinck, *Mohammed en de Joden te Medina*, Leiden 1908; H. Lammens, *La Mecque à la veille de l'Hégire*, Bairut 1924; Caetani, *Annali*; Buhl, *Das Leben Muhammeds*, p. 205 *sqq.* and the other works dealing with the life of the Prophet.

AL-**AʿRĀF**. [See DJAHANNAM].

ʿARAFA or ʿARAFĀT, a hill famous as a place of pilgrimage with the adjoining plain of the same name, 6 hours to the East of Mecca. It is a granite hill of moderate dimensions reaching a relative height of 150—200 feet. On the East broad steps of stone lead to the top; on the 60th step there is a platform containing the pulpit from which a *khuṭba* (sermon) is annually delivered on the afternoon of the 9th Dhu 'l-Ḥidjdja (the day of ʿArafa). On the top there stood formerly a *ḳubba* named after Umm Salima (thus Ibn Djubair, ed. Wright-de Goeje, p. 173) which was destroyed by the Wahhābīs. According to ʿAlī Bey pious Muslims may not penetrate beyond the platform. The hill is usually called Djabal al-Raḥma (Hill of Mercy). Another name is said to have been Ilāl, but it is doubtful whether this appellation really referred to the hill; Wellhausen regards it as the name of a shrine or perhaps of the deity worshipped on the spot in the pre-Islāmic period. Pictures of the hill are found in ʿAlī Bey and Burton [see *Bibliography*]. — The plain of ʿArafāt spreads southwards from the hill of ʿArafāt and is bounded on the East by the lofty mountainchain of Ṭāʾif. It is covered by a low growth of mimosa plants, and is filled with life only on one day of the year (9th Dhu 'l-Ḥidjdja) when the pilgrims pitch their camp for the celebration of the prescribed *wuḳūf*. Cf. the pictures in Burckhardt and especially in Snouck Hurgronje, *Bilder aus Mekka*, xiii.—xvi. The *wuḳūf* or festival assembly takes place on the afternoon of the day mentioned and lasts until after sunset. The pilgrims present express their religious fervour by loud shouts of *labbaika*, by prayers and recitation of the Ḳurʾān.

The origin of the name ʿArafa is unknown. The legendary explanation is that Adam and Eve who had been separated from each other after their expulsion from Paradise, met again at this spot and recognised one another (*taʿārafa*); Arabic authors also mention other etymologies of a similar nature.

Bibliography: Wüstenfeld, *Die Chroniken der Stadt Mekka*, i. 418—419; ii. 89 etc.; Yāḳūt, *Muʿdjam*, iii. 645—646; Ibn Djubair (ed. Wright-de Goeje), p. 168—169; Ibn Baṭṭūṭa (ed. Paris), i. 397—398; Burckhardt, *Travels in Arabia*; ʿAlī Bey, *Travels*, i. 67 *sq.*; Burton, *Pilgrimage to el-Medinah and Meccah* (2nd ed.), ii. 214 *sq.*; Snouck Hurgronje, *Het Mekkaansche feest*, p. 141 *sq.*; al-Batanūnī, *al-Riḥla al-Ḥidjāzīya*, p. 186 *sqq.*

ʿĀRĪYA (A.), gratuitous loan (commodatum). In Muslim law this is defined as a contract by which a person relinquishes a thing belonging to him — the use or employment of which is permitted by law and does not immediately destroy the object in question — to another person for the latter's use without demanding payment, but under the condition that the recipient should restore the object lent after using it.

Bibliography: E. Sachau, *Muhamm. Recht nach schafiitischer Lehre*, p. 457—471; L. W. C. van den Berg, *Principes du droit musulman selon les rites d'Abou Ḥanîfah et de Chafiʾî* (Algiers, 1896), p. 105; G. Bergsträsser. *Grundzüge d. Islam. Recht*, p. 96; and the chapter on 'Baiʿ and other legal transactions' in the Muslim manuals of Fiḳh.

AL-**ARḲAM**, a companion of Muḥammad. His name was al-Arḳam (= Abū ʿAbd Allāh) b. Abi 'l-Arḳam (= ʿAbd Manāf) b. Asad (= Abū Djundub) b. ʿAbd Allāh. He belonged to the Makhzūm, one of the wealthiest and most respected families of Mecca. His mother Umaima came from the tribe of Khuzāʿa. He accepted Islām as a young man and was one of the earliest believers. Although the Makhzūm were bitterly opposed to the Prophet, al-Arḳam became his devoted adherent and during the time of persecution put his house at the disposal of Muḥammad to serve as a place of assembly for the community. Soon after ʿUmar's conversion Muḥammad left the house of al-Arḳam. The date and duration of his stay there are not definitely given, but may be placed in the years 615—617. Ibn Hishām does not give any account of the house of al-Arḳam, but may very well have known the story; Ṭabarī similarly knows it and even uses it for chronological purposes, yet does not relate it in his biography of the Prophet. Al-Arḳam took part in the emigration to Madīna, where he inhabited a house in the quarter of the Banū Zuraiḳ which was also known as 'the house of al-Arḳam'. Like many *muhādjirūn* he seems to have preserved a reverent affection for his Meccan family; and when the Faithful in the battle of Badr gained possession of the sword al-Marzubān, an heirloom of the Makhzūmite Banū ʿĀʾidh, he recognised it and asked the Prophet for it. At Madīna he took part in all the important battles of the believers, but does not appear to have played any further part in the history of Muḥammad. Saʿd b. Abī Waḳḳāṣ seems to have been a particularly intimate friend of his; at any rate he ordained that Saʿd should perform the prayer for the dead at his bier. He died in 54 or 55/674—675 over 80 years old. From a slave-girl he had a son ʿUthmān, the ancestor of a widely diffused family, a branch of which lived in Syria.

For Muslim chronology the period during which Muḥammad taught in the house of al-Arḳam became important in cases where it was desired to determine the order of the early conversions and the high place of honour in Islām which depended on it. Among the later believers not only the person of al-Arḳam, but also his house situated on the hill Ṣafā was an object of great veneration. It is frequently mentioned as 'house of al-Arḳam' or 'house of Islām', and down to the time of the caliph Manṣūr it remained in the possession of the descendants of al-Arḳam who had turned it into a kind of family foundation. Manṣūr forced the Arḳamids to sell it to him for his own family; it was inhabited for a time by al-Khaizurān, the mother of Hārūn al-Rashīd, whence it is also called 'house of al-Khaizurān'. The building which is regarded as the house of al-Arḳam has been restored or rebuilt on several occasions, a fact which is alluded to in inscriptions found there. It is still or was visited by Mecca pilgrims.

Bibliography: Sprenger, *Das Leben und die Lehre des Mohammad*; Caetani, *Annali dell' Islam*, Index s.v.; Ali Bey Bahgat, in *Bull. de l'Inst. égypt.*, series 5, vol. ii., p. 68—81; Buhl, *Das Leben Muhammads*, p. 169.

AṢḤĀB [See ṢAḤĀBA].

AṢḤĀB AL-KAHF, "the people of the cave". This is the term used in the Ḳur'ān to denote the youths who in the West are commonly called "the Seven Sleepers of Ephesus". This is the story almost as Muḥammad tells it (Sūra xviii. 9 *sq.*): Some youths in a pagan town are loyal to the one God; they conceal themselves in a cave, whose entrance is on the north side. There God puts them and their dog to sleep. "And if you had come upon them you would have fled thence and been filled with terror". After 309 years the sleepers awake and send one of their number into the town to buy bread. — The Ḳur'ān has no more to relate; there is only added that their number is variously given as 3, 5 or 7 and that the story is intended to confirm faith in the resurrection.

The historians and commentators have more to tell. Of the various traditions which al-Ṭabarī (i. 775 *sq.*; *Tafsīr*, fasc. xv. 123 *sq.*) communicates the majority are of the following type: In a town of Rūm (i.e. in Greece or Asia Minor) some youths, who have gone over to Christianity, refuse to worship the idols. They flee from the town and with a dog which would not be chased away conceal themselves in a cave, where they go to sleep. The pagan king Dāḳyūs (Dāḳīnūs, Dāḳyānūs) soon appears on the scene with his servants to seize the persons of the young men. But no one is able to enter the cave, and so the only thing possible for him to do is to build up the entrance that those shut in may die of hunger and thirst. This he does. Afterwards the thing is forgotten. One day an owner of herds sends workmen to remove the wall at the entrance, and causes a sheepfold to be constructed there. The workmen however do not observe the sleepers. In God's good time the latter awake. Filled with anxiety they send, observing all caution, one of their number into the town to buy bread. The baker does not recognise the coin which is given in exchange and brings the young man before the king, when everything is explained: the men have slept for 309 years; in the meantime the pagan has given place to a Christian generation. The king is much rejoiced, for the presence of this youth is proof that the body is raised with the spirit, a thing which some had doubted. As soon as the young man enters the cave again he goes to sleep beside his companions. A church is then built at the spot.

This account must suffice. Only one differing version need be mentioned which originates from Wahb b. Munabbih (Ṭabarī, i. 778 *sq.*; Ibn al-Athīr, i. 254 *sq.*): One of the apostles went to the abovementioned town; at the gate he found that an idol had been set up before which every one who entered had to prostrate himself. In consequence he remained outside the town and hired himself out as an attendant at the baths. There he carried on his propaganda and won the youths for Christianity. One day as the son of the king was about to enter the baths in company with a female the apostle admonished him. This time he was prevailed upon to forego his intention, but not the next time. Then the divine punishment fell on them both, and they died in the bath. As soon as this reached the King's ears he issued a warrant of arrest on the person of the apostle. But he and the young men were carried off for safety to a cave by an acquaintance; there was also a dog with them.

The pagan king is named Dāḳyūs, i.e. Decius (249—251), who persecuted the Christians, and the Christian is Theodosius II (408—450). This however does not agree with the Ḳur'ānic account, that the sleep lasted 309 years, nor with others, according to which it lasted 372. — The question as to which town is the scene of the story is important. The western sources all name Ephesus; some of the oriental, Afsūs. The Arabs know of two places called Afsūs: the one is the well-known town; the other is the old Arabissus in Cappadocia, which is called also Absūs (now Yarpuz). De Goeje has adduced proofs out of the literature in favour of the view that the latter place is the scene where the original story was laid.

Another important question is connected with the meaning of the last word in the Ḳur'ānic "men of the cave and (of) al-Raḳīm". Many take it to be the name of the dog, or to be the tablet which contains the story of the youths. The Arab geographers regard it as a geographical name; Ibn Khurdādhbeh (pp. 106, 110) e.g., calls the cave near Arabissus in which 13 male corpses were preserved by the name of al-Raḳīm; he lays the scene of the story of the youths at Ephesus. Al-Muḳaddasī on the other hand, while regarding the 13 men discovered in this cave as the Aṣḥāb al-Kahf, knows of a place al-Raḳīm in the country to the East of the Jordan not far from ʿAmmān. There a wonderful incident occurred with 3 men who are therefore called Aṣḥāb al-Raḳīm. Clermont Ganneau visited the cave there and considered it to be the one described in the Ḳur'ān.

The oldest mention of the legend in the east we find made by Dionysius of Tell Mahra in a Syrian work of the vth cent. A.D.; in the west by Theodosius in his book on the Holy Land. In these versions the names of the youths are Greek. Opinions differ on the question whether the version found in Dionysius was translated from the Greek or was originally composed in Syriac. — The legend is widely spread in the literatures of east and west. On this point see the work by John Koch, who has attempted to give it a mythological interpretation.

Bibliography: *Dionysii Telmaharensis Chronici Liber primus* (ed. Tullberg, p. 161 and 133); Guidi, *Testi orientali inediti sopra i sette dormienti di Efeso* (*Acad. dei Lincei*, 1884—1885); Land, *Anecdota syriaca*, i. 38; iii. 87; Ṭabarī i. 775 *sq.*; also *Tafsīr*, xv. 123 *sq.*; de Goeje, *BGA*, Indices, s.v. al-Raḳīm, Absūs, Afsūs, Ṭarsūs; Yāḳūt, *Muʿdjam*, s. iisdem vocc.; Ibn al-Athīr, i. 254 *sqq.*;

al-Bīrūnī, *Chronology* (ed. Sachau), p. 290; al-Ḳazwīnī (ed. Wüstenf.), i. 161 *sq.*; Maḳrīzī, *Hist. des sultans mamlouks* (transl. of Quatremère), vol. i. part 2, p. 142; Nöldeke, in *GGA.*, 1886, p. 453; de Goeje, *De legende der zevenslapers van Efeze* (*Versl. en Meded. Akad. Amsterdam, Letterk.*, Reeds 4, Deel iv.), p. 9 *sq.*; John Koch, *Die Siebenschläferlegende, ihr Ursprung und ihre Verbreitung* (1883); Theodosius, *De situ terrae sanctae* (ed. Gildemeister), p. 27; Damīrī, *Ḥayāt al-ḥayawān*, s.v. *kalb*; T͟haʿlabī, *Ḳiṣaṣ al-anbiyāʾ* (Cairo 1297), p. 394 *sq.*; Clermont Ganneau, *Etudes d'Archéologie orientale*, iii. 295; W. Tomaschek, *Historisch-topographisches vom oberen Euphrat und aus Ost-Kappadokien* (in *Kiepert-Festschrift*, Berlin 1898); G. le Strange, *Palestine under the Moslems*, p. 274—286; cf. also Brockelmann, in *MSOS.*, iv. 228 und B. Heller, in *Revue des Etudes juives*, xlix. 190 *sq.*; Huber, *Beitrag zur Siebenschläferlegende*, Leipzig 1903-04; do., *Die Wanderlegende von den Siebenschläfern* (Leipzig 1910); W. Weyh, *Zur Gesch. der Siebenschläferlegende, ZDMG*, lxv. 289 *sqq.*; P. Peeters, *Le texte original de la passion des Sept Dormants* in *Anal. Bollandiana*, xli. 369 *sqq.*; C. C. Torrey, in *Oriental Studies Browne*, Cambridge 1922, p. 457 *sqq.*; J. Horovitz, *Koranische Untersuchungen*, Berlin 1926, p. 95, 98 *sq.*; L. Massignon, *Recherche sur la valeur eschatologique des Sept Dormants*, in *Actes du* XXe *congrès des Orientalistes*, Louvain 1940, p. 302-303.

AṢḤĀB AL-**UKHDŪD**, "the people of the ditch", mentioned in Sūra lxxxv. 4 *sq.* The Muslim historians relate as follows in regard to this passage:

King D͟hū Nuwās of Yemen was a devotee of Judaism and intolerant of the Christians. He bade them choose between Judaism and death. The Christians preferred martyrdom. Thereupon the king caused a long ditch to be constructed in which they were burned alive.

This story is partly confirmed by Christian sources and enlarged upon. When the Kūs͟hites were unable, since winter had set in, to send a viceroy to Yemen, D͟hū Nuwās (he is variously named), who was a convert to Judaism, usurped the authority and persecuted the Christians. Moreover he laid siege to Nad͟jrān, and breaking his word on the capture of the town destroyed the steadfast Christians with fire and sword. Of a real ditch however, there is no mention. — Almost the same as this is the account given by Simeon of Bēt Ars͟hām and by the anonymous writer in Boissonade. The account of these events was written in the spring of 524 A.D. in Syria; they happened therefore towards the end of 523. According to Axel Moberg, it is very doubtful whether the verses of the Ḳurʾān regarding the aṣḥāb al-ukhdūd have anything to do with the story of the martyrs of Nad͟jrān; cf. his *The Book of the Himyarites*, Lund 1924.

Other explanations are also given, e.g. that the "people of the ditch" were Daniel and his companions (Ṭabarī, *Tafsīr*, *l.c.*), a view which Geiger (*Was hat Mohammed* etc., p. 192) and Loth (*ZDMG*, xxxv. 121) regard as probable. — According to a tradition in T͟haʿlabī, the "people of the ditch" were Antiochus in Syria, Nebuchadnezzar in Persia, and D͟hū Nuwās in Yemen. H. Grimme (*Mohammed*, ii. 77), who is followed by J. Horovitz (*Koranische Untersuchungen*, p. 12, 92 *sq*)., thinks that *aṣḥāb al-ukhdūd* only means the sinners in hell-fire, synonymously with *aṣḥāb al-d͟jaḥīm*.

Bibliography: Ibn His͟hām, p. 24 *sq.*; Ṭabarī, i. 925; the Ḳurʾānic commentaries on Sūra lxxxv. 4 *sq.*; Masʿūdī, *Murūd͟j*, i. 129 *sq.*; Caussin de Perceval, *Essai sur l'histoire des Arabes*, i. 128 *sq.*; Nöldeke, *Geschichte der Araber und Perser zur Zeit der Sasaniden* (Leyden 1879), p. 185 *sq.*; Assemannus, *Bibliotheca orientalis*, i. 364 *sq.*; Guidi, *La lettera di Simeone vescovo di Bêth-Arsam sopra i martiri omeriti* (*Memorie dell' Accademia dei Lincei*, 1881, p. 471 *sq.*); Boissonade, *Anecdota graeca*, v. 1 *sq.*; Fell, in *ZDMG*, xxxv. 1 *sq.*; Duval, *Littérature syriaque*, p. 136 *sq.*; T͟haʿlabī, *Ḳiṣaṣ al-anbiyāʾ* (Cairo 1297), p. 421 *sq.*

AL-ʿ**AS͟HARA** ʾL-**MUBAS͟HS͟HARA**, the ten to whom Paradise was promised. The term does not occur in canonical *ḥadīt͟h*, to which, however, the conception goes back. The traditions in question have usually the form: "Ten will be in Paradise", whereupon the names are enumerated. There are differences in the lists. Those who appear in the various forms extant are: Abū Bakr, ʿUmar, ʿUt͟hmān, ʿAlī, Ṭalḥa, Zubair, ʿAbd al-Raḥmān b. ʿAwf, Saʿd b. Abī Waḳḳāṣ, Saʿīd b. Zaid. In some traditions Muḥammad himself is put before these nine (Abū Dāwūd, *Sunna*, bāb 8; Aḥmad b. Ḥanbal, i. 187, 188 *bis*). In others Muḥammad is absent and the tenth place is taken by Abū ʿUbaida b. al-D͟jarrāḥ (Tirmid͟hī, *Manāḳib*, bāb 25; Ibn Saʿd, III/i. 279; Aḥmad b. Ḥanbal, i. 193). Conceptions of this kind owe their origin to the hierarchic tendencies that were prominent in the Muslim community, and which found expression even in the earliest creeds.

AL-**AS͟HʿARĪ**, ABU ʾL-ḤASAN ʿALĪ, famous theologian, born at Baṣra in the year 260/873—4, a descendant of the undermentioned. The complete genealogy is: ʿAlī b. Ismāʿīl b. Isḥāḳ b. Sālim b. Ismāʿīl b. ʿAbd Allāh b. Mūsā b. Bilāl b. Abī Burda. Until his 40th year he was a zealous pupil of the Muʿtazilite theologian al-D͟jubbāʾī, then on the occasion of a dispute with his teacher on the propriety of God's predetermination disagreed with him and went his own way. But Spitta has shown that we have to do here with a biassed legend and that probably the study of the traditions elucidated for him the contradiction between the Muʿtazilite views and the spirit of Islām. However that may be, he henceforth championed the orthodox views against the Muʿtazilites and composed a large number of works of a dogmatic and polemic nature. For the rest he belonged to the *mad͟hhab* of the S͟hāfiʿites. He spent the closing years of his life in Bag͟hdād and died there in the year 324/935.

The number of al-As͟hʿarī's books amounted, according to Ibn Fūrak to about 300. Ibn ʿAsākir gives the titles of 99 of them. The work *al-Ibāna ʿan uṣūl al-diyāna* was printed with three supplements at Ḥaidarābād in 1321 (1903) and translated by W. C. Klein (New Haven 1940); also his *Risāla fī istiḥsān al-khawḍ fī ʾl-kalām* (Ḥaidarābād, 1323).

The most remarkable of his printed works is *Maḳālāt al-islāmīyīn* (ed. H. Ritter, i.—ii., Istanbul 1929—1930, in *Bibliotheca Islamica*, Ia., *b.*). This work consists of three parts: *a.* (p. 1—289) a survey of the Muslim sects and dissensions (S͟hīʿa, K͟hawārid͟j, Murd͟jiʾa, Muʿtazila, Mud͟jassima, D͟jahmīya, Ḍirārīya, Nad͟jd͟jārīya, Bakrīya, Nussāk); *b.* (p. 290—300) the creed of the orthodox community (*aṣḥāb al-ḥadīt͟h wa-ahl al-sunna*) and the slight deviations of al-Ḳaṭṭān, Zuhair al-At͟harī, Abū Muʿād͟h al-Tawmanī; *c.* (p. 301—610) a survey of the different opinions on the concepts of *kalām*. So the work appears to be composed of the same parts as John of Damascus' *Fons Scientiae*, where the sequence is the following: *a. Dialectica*, the philosophical basis; *b. De Haeresibus*; *c. De Fide Orthodoxa.*

The *Maḳālāt* is the first work of the kind in Muslim literature. It goes into the views of the sects in detail; the author possesses firsthand data concerning them. It is free from any schematising tendency as well as from any bias. This implies a serious defect of style; it is hardly more than a *catalogue raisonné*, a phenomenon quite unexpected in the passionate author of the *Ibāna*. On this ground it has been conjectured that the *Maḳālāt* was composed by its author at an age when the conversion and its consequences were no longer recent events. In the preface he declares that what led him to the composition of the book was the fact that an objective exposition of Muslim haeresiology was lacking. Possibly it was also the desire to be objective that withheld him from mentioning any of the special dogmatical views which tradition ascribes to him. In this connection the difficulty of making a clear distinction between the man and his school must be remembered. The third part of the book may prove valuable for the history of Muslim scholastics.

Al-Ashʿari enjoys the credit of having overcome the antipathy of the older Muslim scholars to dialectic in articles of faith by his successful utilisation of it to combat the Muʿtazilites and the chiefs of other sects who were suspected of heresy. He is, therefore, the founder of orthodox scholasticism (*kalām*), since the few orthodox teachers who had ventured on it before him had too little culture to be able to avoid giving offence by certain of their expressions. His method in consequence found acceptance especially with the Shāfiʿites, and he gathered round him a circle of pupils from whose midst there went forth various famous theologians who developed and spread his dogmas. The best-known of these older Ashʿarites are al-Bāḳillānī, Ibn Fūrak, al-Isfarāʾīnī, al-Ḳushairī, al-Djuwainī (Imām al-Ḥaramain) and especially al-Ghazzālī. Outside the *madhhab* of al-Shāfiʿī the opinions of al-Ashʿarī met with less recognition. The Ḥanafites preferred the doctrine of his contemporary al-Māturīdī, who however differed from him only in subordinate controversial points; the Ḥanbalites kept to the old point of view and remained opponents of the Ashʿarite school. In Spain Ibn Ḥazm [q.v.] opposed the doctrine of al-Ashʿarī. Under the first Saldjūḳ, Toghrul-Beg, the distinguished Ashʿarite teachers were even persecuted at the instance of the wazīr al-Kundurī; however, his successor, Niẓām al-Mulk, soon put an end to this treatment of them. They gained more and more influence generally, especially through the writings of the famous al-Ghazzālī. In the Maghrib they found an ardent champion in Ibn Tūmart, the founder of the empire of the Almohades. The eventual result was that the Ashʿarite *kalām* was everywhere taught in the schools of the Sunnīs and the initial opposition became silent.

Bibliography: Ibn Khallikān, No. 440; *Fihrist* (ed. Flügel), i. 181; Shahrastānī, p. 65 *sq.*; Spitta, *Zur Geschichte Abu 'l-Ḥasan al-Asʿarī's*; Mehren, *Exposé de la Réforme de l'Islamisme* etc., in *Travaux de la 3ème Session du Congrès des Orientalistes* (St. Petersburg), p. 167 *sq.*; Schreiner, *Zur Geschichte des Asʿaritentums*, in *Actes du 8ème Congrès intern. des Orient.*, sect. Iª, p. 79 *sq.*; Macdonald, *Development of Muslim Theology* etc., p. 187 *sq.*; I. Goldziher, *Beiträge zur Literaturgeschichte der Šiʿa* in *Sitz. Ber. Wien*, vol. lxxviii, p. 473 sq.; R. Strothmann, in *Isl.*, xix. 193 *sqq.*; A. J. Wensinck, *The Muslim Creed*, Cambridge 1932; A. S. Tritton, *Muslim Theology*, London 1947; Brockelmann, *GAL* ² i. 207 *sq.*, *Suppl.* i 345 *sq.*

AL-ASHʿARĪ, Abū Mūsā ʿAbd Allāh b. Ḳais, governor. Abū Mūsā came from Yaman and early accepted Islām. According to the usual tradition, after his conversion in Mecca he joined the emigration to Abyssinia and only returned on the conquest of Khaibar. Thereupon he was appointed governor of a district by Muḥammad. In the year 17/638 ʿUmar conferred on him the governorship of Baṣra on the deposition of al-Mughīra b. Shuʿba. When the inhabitants of Kūfa were dissatisfied with their governors the caliph acquiesced in their desires, and since they declared they would like best of all to have Abū Mūsā, he was transferred to Kūfa in the year 22/642—3. But soon it proved that the new governor also was unable to satisfy the capricious people of Kūfa, and he was recalled after a year and given back his post in Baṣra. Soon after he was sued before the caliph who, however, accepted his excuses, and even after ʿUmar's death Abū Mūsā, who had distinguished himself as a commander on the field, filled the governorship of Baṣra. But some years after ʿUthmān's accession he was deposed and ʿAbd Allāh b. ʿĀmir nominated his successor, whereupon Abū Mūsā settled in Kūfa. In the year 34/654—5 ʿUthmān appointed him governor of Kūfa; but when on the murder of the caliph this town joined the cause of ʿAlī, Abū Mūsā was forced aside and had to flee. Once again he appears in the history of Islām, for, when hostilities were interrupted in the Battle of Ṣiffīn in the month of Ṣafar 37/July 657, and the combatants agreed to leave the decision as to the matters in dispute between ʿAlī and Muʿāwiya to two impartial arbiters, Abū Mūsā and ʿAmr b. al-ʿĀṣ were entrusted with the commission. When the two arbiters met in Adhruḥ, Abū Mūsā was outwitted, and declaring both ʿAlī and Muʿāwiya unworthy of the caliphate left the choice of a successor to the Islamic community. ʿAmr then stepped forward and agreed with him in regard to ʿAlī, but according to the usual tradition, he confirmed Muʿāwiya's possession of the dignity. This was the end of Abū Mūsā's political activity. Equally unpopular with both parties he only with difficulty managed to save himself and escape to Mecca. But here also he felt insecure, and later betook himself to Kūfa. The year of his death is variously given. According to the oldest tradition, he died in Kūfa in the year 42/662—3 or in 52.

Bibliography: Ibn Saʿd, iv./i. 78 *sq.*; vi. 9; Yaʿḳūbī, ii. 136 *sq.*; Balādhurī, p. 55 *sq.*; Ṭabarī, see Index; Ibn al-Athīr, i. 9 *sq.*; Nawawī, p. 758; Masʿūdī, *Murūdj*, iv., v. *passim*; *Kitāb al-Aghānī*, see Guidi, *Tables alphabétiques*; Müller, *Der Islam im Morgen- und Abendland*, i. 243 *sq.*; Muir, *The Caliphate, its Rise, Decline, and Fall* (new edition by Weir), p. 179 *sq.*; Wellhausen, *Das arabische Reich*, p. 56 *sqq.*; Caetani, *Annali dell' Islām*, passim.

ʿĀSHŪRĀʾ, name of a voluntary fast-day which is observed on the 10th Muḥarram. When Muḥammad came to Madīna he adopted from the Jews amongst other days the ʿĀshūrāʾ. The name is obviously the Hebraic עָשׂוֹר with the Aramaic determinative ending; in Lev. xvi. 29 it is used of the great Day of Atonement. Muḥammad retained the Jewish custom in the rite, that is, the fast was observed on this day from sunset to sunset, and not as in other fasts only during the day. When in the year 2 Muḥammad's relations with the Jews became strained, Ramaḍān was chosen as the fast month, and the ʿĀshūrāʾ-fast was no longer a religious duty but was left to the option of the individual. — On which day of the Arabian year the fast was originally observed cannot now be ascertained owing to our defective knowledge of the calender of the period; naturally its observance coincided with the Jewish on the 10th Tishri, and so fell in the autumn. The 10th Muḥarram finds early mention as the ʿĀshūrāʾ; probably the tenth day of the first Muslim month was selected to harmonise with the tenth day of the first Jewish month. From the calculations which have already been made, it does not seem possible that it could have been originally celebrated on the 10th Muḥarram (see Caetani, *Annali*, i. 431 *sq.*).

Presumably for the sake of distinguishing themselves from the Jews some fixed the 9th Muḥarram either along with or in place of the tenth as a fast day with the name *Tāsūʿāʾ*.

The Jewish origin of the day is obvious; the well-known tendency of tradition to trace all Islāmic customs back to the ancient Arabs, and particularly to Abraham, states that the Meccans of olden time fasted on the ʿĀshūrāʾ. It is not impossible that the tenth, as also the first nine days of Muḥarram, did possess a certain holiness among the ancient Arabs; but this has nothing to do with the ʿĀshūrāʾ.

The fast of the ʿĀshūrāʾ was later and is still regarded by Muslims as commendable; the day is kept by the devout of the entire Sunnī world; it is holy also on "historical" grounds: on it Noah left the ark, etc. In Mecca the door of the Kaʿba is opened on the day of the ʿĀshūrāʾ for visitors (see Snouck Hurgronje, *Mekka*, ii. 51). In lands which are Shīʿite or come under Shīʿite influence quite different usages have become associated with the 10th Muḥarram; in this connection see MUḤARRAM.

Bibliography: The Chapter *Ṣawm ʿAshūrāʾ* in the Collections of Traditions, and the appropriate sections in the Fiḳh-books; Goldziher, *Usages juifs d'après la littérature des musulmans*, in *Rev. des Etudes juives*, xxviii., p. 82—84; A. J. Wensinck, *Mohammed en de Joden te Medina*, p. 121—125; Th. W. Juynboll, *Handbuch des islamischen Gesetzes*, p. 115 *sq.*; Nöldeke-Schwally, *Geschichte des Qorāns*, i. 179, note; Sprenger, *Das Leben und die Lehre des Moḥammad*, iii. 53, note; Buhl, *Das Leben Muhammeds*, p. 214, 226; Lane, *Modern Egyptians*, Ch. xxiv.; Doutté, *Marrâkech* (Paris 1905), p. 371—2; Boulifa, *Textes berbères de l'Atlas marocain* (Paris 1909), p. 116—167.

ʿAṢR (A.), time, particularly the afternoon, hence *Ṣalāt al-ʿAṣr* = Afternoon-prayer (see Th. W. Juynboll, *Handbuch des islām. Gesetzes*, Index); *Sūrat al-ʿAṣr* is the title of Sūra ciii.

ASRĀFĪL. [See ISRĀFĪL].

ASSASSINS is the name given to those Ismāʿīlīs, who at the time of the Crusades occupied various hill-fortresses in Syria and other Muslim countries, and were wont to rid themselves of their opponents by assassination. The term Assassin goes back to the rendering in the French chroniclers on the Crusades since the xiith century of the Arabic word *ḥashīshī*, denoting a consumer of *ḥashīsh*. *Ḥashīsh* is a preparation of hemp (Cannabis indica), which oriental mystics sometimes consumed in order to induce the ecstatic state and to become intoxicated. It is said that those who were selected, the so-called Fidāʾīs, by the spiritual leaders of the Assassins to carry out any important mission, e.g. an assassination, were urged to its use in order that they might be ready for any deed. From the Fidāʾīs Ibn Khaldūn calls the Assassins in general also Fidāwīya; but in the oriental sources, when they are not simply called Ismāʿīlīs, they are often named Malāḥida (heretics) or Nizārīs. The appellation *ḥashīshīyūn* is seldom found except in Syrian texts of the xiith century.

It has become customary to apply the term Assassins to the followers of the Nizārī branch of the Ismāʿīlīya [q.v.], who were originally headed and organized by Ḥasan b. Ṣabbāḥ [q.v.] after his return from Egypt, shortly before 483/1090. Under his rule the Nizārī's occupied also strongholds in Syria.

In so far as the Assassins are a branch of the Ismāʿīlīs, the principles which they hold in common with all Ismāʿīlīs will be referred to in the article on the latter. What specially distinguishes them is less a doctrine differing from the other Ismāʿīlīs than their political organisation into a secret league whose members owed blind obedience to the spiritual head; and also the fact that they availed themselves of murder to get rid of their foes was no new phenomenon in Islām. Abū Manṣūr al-ʿIdjlī and Mughīra b. Saʿīd, whose followers were called "Stranglers" (*khannāḳ*), had previously resorted to it and magnified assassination for political ends as a religious and meritorious act. For the rest, the theological tenets of the Assassins, so far as they are not contained in the Ismāʿīlī writings, are insufficiently known to us.

The history of the Assassins commences with the conquest of the hill-fortress of Alamūt by Ḥasan b. Ṣabbāḥ in the year 483/1090—1; he removed his residence there and from this place of difficult access carried on his propaganda. This consisted first in his followers obtaining possession of a large number of hill-fortresses in all parts of Persia, and getting rid of the most dangerous of their opponents by assassination. One of the first victims was the famous wazīr Niẓām al-Mulk (485/1092). The death of Sulṭān Malik-Shāh which occurred soon after, and the resulting disputes for the succession among the various pretenders, and the appearance soon after of the Crusaders in the lands of Islām threw the Muslim world into a disorder which assured great success to the Assassins. Their strength consequently became very considerable in a few years, until the Saldjūḳ Sulṭān Muḥammad I. ascended the throne and strained every nerve to combat the Assassins. The fortress of Dizkūh, called Shāh-Diz after Malik-Shāh, in the vicinity of Iṣpahān, was at that time in the hands of a distinguished leader of the Assassins of the name of Ibn ʿAṭṭāsh, who had counted Ḥasan b. Ṣabbāḥ among his pupils. It was captured after a courageous resistance (500/1107; cf. the official account of this in Ibn al-Ḳalānisī, ed. Amedroz, p. 152 *sqq.*). The Turkish Emīr Anushtegīn Shīrgīr was then entrusted with the conduct of the war against the Assassins, and he after several successes was on the point of taking the fortress of Alamūt itself when the death of Muḥammad (511/1118) forced him to raise the siege. Ḥasan survived this danger almost 7 years; he died in 518/1124 leaving the leadership of the Assassins to Kiaya Buzurg Ummīd Rūdbārī, who bequeathed the conduct of affairs to his descendants. The following were the rulers of Alamūt:

Ḥasan b. Ṣabbāḥ	483—518 (1090—1124)
Buzurg Ummīd Rūdbārī.	518—532 (1124—1138)
Muḥammad b. Buzurg Ummīd	532—557 (1138—1162)
Ḥasan b. Muḥammad ...	557—561 (1162—1166)
Nūr al-Dīn Muḥammad..	561—607 (1166—1210)
Djalāl al-Dīn Ḥasan b. Muḥammad	607—618 (1210—1220)
ʿAlāʾ al-Dīn Muḥammad.	618—653 (1220—1255)
Rukn al-Dīn b. Muḥammad	653—654 (1255—1256)

During the rule of these Grand-Masters the Assassins had more than once to endure sore persecution, but neither the Caliphs nor the Saldjūḳ Sulṭāns succeeded in breaking their power and destroying their nests of brigandage. They skilfully rid themselves of their most implacable enemies by assassination and zealously carried on their propaganda. Especially did they succeed in gaining firm foot in Syria, where the Saldjūḳ of Ḥalab, Riḍwān, availed himself of their aid. A certain Abū Ṭāhir, apparently a goldsmith by profession and hence called al-Ṣāʾigh, was sent to Syria as emissary and won many followers, particularly in Ḥalab. In 499/1105—6 he managed by treachery to clear the governor of Apamea out of the way, but was disappointed in his hopes of becoming himself master of the town since the Crusaders soon after took possession of it. The bloody persecution of the Assassins in Ḥalab after the death of Riḍwān in 507/1113 did not prevent another Persian emissary named Bahrām some years later from obtaining a large following and even gaining possession (520/1126) of the town of Bāniyās, which was surrendered three years later to the Crusaders. The Assassins often entered into friendly relations with the Christians, and contrived to strengthen their position by cleverly availing themselves of the political conditions. In 535/1140—1 they conquered the hill-fortress of Ḥiṣn al-Maṣyād (Masayāf) and other fortresses situated in North-Syria, e.g. Kahf, Ḳadmus, ʿUllaiḳa, al-Khawābī, etc. The contemporary chief of these Syrian Assassins was usually called *shaikh al-djabal* (translated by the Christians as "the Old Man of the Mountain", "le Vieux de la Montagne"), so that this term does not denote, as is sometimes stated, the Persian Grand-Master, the universal chief of the Assassins. One of the most famous of the Syrian rulers is Rashīd al-Dīn Sinān.

The Mongols who effected such great changes in the political conditions of Asia accomplished also the downfall of the Assassins. The last Grand Master Rukn al-Dīn had just entered upon his dignity when Hulagu marched his forces on Alamūt. Resistance was impossible; Rukn al-Dīn had to submit (654/1256), and was to be brought before the Great-Khān, but was executed on the way thither. The strongholds held by the Assassins were taken and some of them razed to the ground. The hill-fortresses of Syria, e.g. Maṣyād, fell in 658/1260 for the time being under the power of the Mongols, but it was reserved for the Mamlūk Sulṭān Baibars to give the Assassins the finishing blow (671/1272). This ended for ever the political power of the dreaded sect, but there were and are to the present day in the mountains of the Nuṣairīs Ismāʿīlīs descended from the Assassins, as also in Persia and India. [Cf. the arts. ISMĀʿĪLIYA and KHODJA].

Bibliography: The history of the Assassins is contained in the Universal Histories of Ibn al-Athīr, Ibn Khaldūn, Abu 'l-Fidāʾ etc. Cf. also the appropriate section in Djuwainī, *Taʾrīkh-i djihān gushā*, Part iii, Leiden 1937 (*GMS* XVI, 3), in Mīrkhond's History, separately edited in *Notices et Extraits*, ix. 194 *sqq.* and in *Taʾrīkh-i guzīda*, translated in *JA*, 1848; de Sacy, *Mémoire sur la dynastie des Assassins*; Quatrèmere, *Notice historique sur les Ismailiens* (*Mines de l'Orient*, iv.); von Hammer, *Geschichte der Assassinen aus morgenländischen Quellen*; Defrémery, *Nouvelles recherches sur les Ismaéliens*, in *JA*, series 4, xiii.; series 5, ii. iii. v. viii. xi.; St. Guyard, *Fragments relatifs à la doctrine des Ismaélis* (*Notices et Extraits*, xxii[a]); do., *Un grand-maître des Assassins*, in *JA*, series 7, ix. (1877), p. 324—489; van Berchem, *Epigraphie des Assassins de Syrie* (*ibid.*, 1897); Browne, *A Literary History of Persia*, ii. 193 *sq.*; W. Ivanow, *A guide to Ismaili Literature*, London 1933; Gaudefroy-Demombynes, *La Syrie à l'époque des Mamelouks*, p. 114-116.

AL-ASWAD, epithet of ʿAihala (according to some, ʿAbhala) b. Kaʿb of the Madhḥidjite tribe ʿAns. He had another epithet Dhu'l-Khimār, "the veiled" (not Dhu'l-Ḥimār, as printed in Balādhurī, p. 105). Shortly before the death of Muḥammad he assumed the lead of a national revolt in South Arabia which soon overthrew the Persian officials and with them the suzerainty of the Prophet. He set out from Kahf Khabbān, conquered Nadjrān, defeated and put to death Shahr, son of the former Persian governor Bādhān, and took possession of the capital Ṣanʿāʾ, so that the whole of South-West Arabia came under his sway in rather less than a month. The majority of Muḥammad's officials in the country fled to Madīna or to Ḥaḍramawt. To legitimise his claims he married the widow of the murdered Shahr. But his power was of short duration. A member of another Madhḥidjite tribe, Ḳais b. Hubaira al-Makshūḥ, with whose aid he had conquered the country, allied himself with the overthrown Persians, at whose head stood Fērōz and Dādhawaih, and obtained effective support from the widow of Shahr, who had wed the usurper much against her will. With her help they made their way into the fort and, according to tradition, killed al-Aswad as he lay on his couch a few days before the death of Muḥammad. The fall of al-Aswad had however no importance for the Muslims, since Ḳais soon afterwards arrogated to himself the authority and separated from the Persians who had given him their help. The accounts about al-Aswad are of special interest from the fact that they represent him as possessing prophetic aspirations, a statement which undoubtedly has an historical basis. According to Balādhurī he was a *kāhin* or prophet and styled himself Raḥmān of Yemen (i.e. he who speaks in the name of Raḥmān), just as Musailima had come forward as Raḥmān of Yamāma.

Bibliography: Balādhurī, p. 105—107; Ṭabarī, i. 1795—1798, 1853—1868 (where 1856—1864 contains a parallel account with what follows); Wellhausen, *Skizzen und Vorarbeiten*, vi. 31—37; Caetani, *Annali dell' Islām*. Register s.v.

AWḲĀF. [See WAḲF].

AL-AWS, [See ANṢĀR].

AWTĀD (A., sing. *watad*), lit. "pegs", the third category in the hierarchy of the *ridjāl al-ghaib*, containing four holy beings; they are also called *al-ʿumud*, the pillars [see BADAL]. Each of them is entrusted with the supervision and care of one of the four quarters of the heavens, in the centres of which they have their dwelling-place.

ĀYA. [See ḲURʾĀN].

ĀZAR, in the Ḳurʾān (Sūra vi. 73) the name of

Abraham's father. There appears to be some confusion here as the name is nowhere else given to Abraham's father. That he was called Tāraḥ (Tāra<u>kh</u>) is also related by Muslim commentators and historians; to reconcile these two statements the usual artifices are resorted to, but these have no value. According to Maracci (*Prodromi*, iv. 90), the form Āzar is due to a false reading 'Αθαρ in Eusebius' Ecclesiastical History. Neither Maracci, nor any of those who cite him later, has given a more exact reference to the passage. Eusebius regularly writes Θαρρα in other places. But in any case it seems very improbable. J. Horovitz, *Koranische Untersuchungen*, p. 85 *sq.* explains the name as a corruption of Eliezer, the name of Abrahams servant.

For the life of Āzar and his son Ibrāhīm the reader is referred to the latter article where the bibliography is also given.

AZHAR (<u>Dj</u>āmiʿ al-Azhar, from *al-<u>Dj</u>āmiʿ al-azhar*), mosque and college in Cairo.

Buildings and endowments. The mosque was built by <u>Dj</u>awhar al-Kātib al-Ṣiḳillī (alias al-Ṣaḳlabī) general of Abū Tamīm Maʿadd, a year after the occupation of Egypt by the Fāṭimids, and immediately after the foundation of the new capital (al-Ḳāhira: <u>Dj</u>umādā I 359 — Ramaḍān 361). It was consecrated and opened for services in Ramaḍān 361 (June—July 972). It was situated not far from the "great castle" then in existence between the Dailam quarter (N.) and the Turkish quarter (S.) in the southeast of the city. <u>Dj</u>awhar placed an inscription on the dome, dated 360 A. H., the text of which has been preserved to us by al-Maḳrīzī (*<u>Kh</u>iṭaṭ*, ii., 273, 24-26; van Berchem, *Corp. Inscr. Arab.*, i, 43, No. 20); it has since disappeared. Several other Fāṭimid rulers built additions to the mosque and endowed it with grants and foundations; al-ʿAzīz Nizār (365—386/976—996) for example made it an academy and erected an almshouse in it for 35 men.

A *ṭilasm* (τέλεσμα, talisman) is mentioned as a curiosity on the first building; figures of birds were placed on the tops of three columns which prevented these birds from nesting or breeding in the mosque. Further additions were made to the building under al-Ḥākim (386—411/996—1020) and endowments and gifts were bestowed on the Azhar and other mosques. A document relating to these of the year 400 has been handed down to us by al-Maḳrīzī, (ii. 273 *sqq.*). In the year 519/1125 al-ʿĀmir built a prayer niche (*miḥrāb*) with carvings in wood, the inscription on which is still preserved in the Arab Museum in Cairo (Ravaisse, *Sur trois miḥrābs*, p. 10; van Berchem, *Corp. Inscr. Arab.*, i., No. 455). Its name also may be explained from the Fāṭimid origin of the mosque, it being rightly interpreted as an allusion to al-Zahrā', a title of Fāṭima; a *maḳṣūra* of the mosque also took its name from her (Maḳrīzī, ii. 275, 16). Smaller additions are also due to the caliphs al-Mustanṣir and al-Ḥāfiẓ.

With the Aiyūbid rule a reaction set in, since they as ardent Sunnīs sought to destroy every trace of the <u>Sh</u>īʿite Fāṭimids. Saladin took from the mosque the right of the *<u>kh</u>uṭba* and deprived it of several of al-Ḥākim's endowments. Nearly a century passed before the favour of the rulers and nobles was again bestowed on it. Al-Malik al-Ẓāhir Baibars made new additions to it, made provision for academic instruction and restored to it the privilege of the *<u>kh</u>uṭba* (665/1266—7: *<u>dj</u>awāz al-<u>dj</u>umʿa*; cf. van Berchem, *Corp. Inscr. Arab.*, i., No. 128 v.). Several emīrs followed his example. From this period dates the prosperity of the Azhar as a mosque and educational institute. Apart from the attention bestowed on it at home it was further benefitted by the fact that the ravages of the Mongols in the East and the decline of Islām in the West destroyed or weakened so many of the old, flourishing *madrasas*. When in 702/1302—3 the mosque was damaged by an earthquake, the Emīr Salār (Sallār) rebuilt it. From the year 725/1325 date the new buildings by Muḥammad b. Ḥusain al-Isʿirdī (from Seʿirt in Armenia), the *muḥtasib* of Cairo; about the same time colleges (*madāris*) were built by emīrs near the mosque: in 709/1309—10 by Ṭaibars, in 740 /1339—40) by Aḳbu<u>gh</u>ā ʿAbd al-Wāḥid (cf. van Berchem, *Corp. Inscr. Arab.*, i., No. 110, 125, 126, 127). These were later brought under the Azhar and still belong to it. Various additions and repairs were made by the eunuch Basīr al-<u>Dj</u>āmdār al-Nāṣirī (about 761/1360). He also presented a Ḳur'ān, endowed a reader for it, refitted the kitchen for the poor and founded a chair of Ḥanafī Law. In the year 800/1397—8 a minaret fell in, but was at once rebuilt from Sulṭān Barḳūḳ's privy purse. This catastrophe was twice repeated (817/1414—5 and 827/1423—4) but the damage was always made good. About the same time a cistern was dug, a *sabīl* built and a basin for ablutions (*mīḍa'a*) erected. A school just beside the mosque was also built by the eunuch <u>Dj</u>awhar al-Ḳanḳabā'ī (died 844/1440—1). Further information regarding this school (al-<u>Dj</u>awharīya) will be found in ʿAlī Mubārak, *al-<u>Kh</u>iṭaṭ al-<u>dj</u>adīda*, iv. 19 *sq.* The greatest benefactor of the mosque in the ixth century was Ḳā'it Beg. His extensive additions were finished in 900/1494—5, just shortly before his death. Besides these, many foundations for the poor as well as for the learned were due to him. We also know of his buildings from inscriptions (van Berchem, *Corp. Inscr. Arab.*, i., No. 21—25). Ibn Iyās (ii. 167, 22 *sqq.*) relates a remarkable habit of this ruler: he used to go to the mosque of al-Azhar disguised as a Ma<u>gh</u>ribī, pray there and listen to what the people said about him. We are not told the sequel. The last great Mamlūk ruler, Ḳānṣūh al-<u>Gh</u>ūrī (906—922/1500—1516), built the double-towered minaret; on the inscriptions see van Berchem, *Corp. Inscrip. Arab.*, i., No. 26, 27.

In the Ottoman period the splendour of the mosque naturally paled a little. At the same time many acts of attention have to be noted. The conqueror Selīm <u>Sh</u>āh often visited and prayed there, ordered the Ḳur'ān to be read in it, and bestowed gifts on poor students (Ibn Iyās, *Chronicle*, iii. 116, 132, 246, 309, 313). The style of the buildings of the Ottoman period shows a marked deterioration from those of earlier periods. In regard to cultural development, the hall for the blind is worthy of mention (*zāwiyat al-ʿumyān*) which was built by ʿU<u>th</u>mān Ket<u>kh</u>odā al-Ḳazdo<u>gh</u>lī (Ḳāṣid O<u>gh</u>lu) in 1148/1735—6 (cf. also J. Hirschberg, *Ägypten*, 1890, p. 101). Among the greatest benefactors of the mosque must be reckoned ʿAbd al-Raḥmān Ket<u>kh</u>odā or Kiḥya (died 1190/1776), a relative, it appears, of the above mentioned ʿU<u>th</u>mān al-Ḳazdo<u>gh</u>lī. He built a large and richly furnished *maḳṣūra* (a sanctuary screened by lattice work), a prayer-niche, a pulpit, an elementary school for orphans, a cistern, and a tomb for himself in which he was afterwards buried. The above-mentioned *madrasas* of al-Ṭaibarsīya (Ṭabarsīya) and Aḳbu<u>gh</u>āwīya (whose name was later corrupted to Ibti<u>gh</u>āwīya) were connected with one another by new buildings. Beside making other smaller alterations in the buildings he made provision for the supply of food and clothing to poor students. It is significant that al-Djabartī says that in his time, about 1220/1805, a generation after their founder, most of these pious foundations had fallen into neglect. Soon afterwards the French expedition came, which inflicted much hardship on the Azharites, though not undeservedly. The national restoration under Muḥammad ʿAlī was at first not favourable to the Azhar; but the later Khedives did their best to keep up the fame of the revered building. ʿAlī Mubārak gives an exact description of the present building, not of course from the standpoint of the archaeologist but from that of the educated Muslim (*al-Khiṭaṭ al-djadīda*, iv. 14—26), detailing the extent, doors, sanctuaries, prayer-niches, closets, lavatories, court-yards, minārets, sundials, both the above-mentioned *madrasas*, the loggias (*arwiḳa*), living-rooms (*ḥārāt*), cisterns, lamps, mats and carpets. Several parts of interest to the archaeologist, e.g. the gateway of Ḳāʾit Beg and the prayer-niche of the *madrasa* al-Ṭaibarsīya, are reproduced in Franz Pascha's *Kairo* (1903), p. 21 *sqq.* with plan; cf. also Baedeker's *Egypt.*

Even in the middle ages the students, as at the present day, seem to have lived partly in and partly outside the Azhar. The internal students were divided into territorial groups, most of which had and still have their own *ḥāra* and their *riwāḳ*. By the *ḥārāt* (for the word cf. *ZDMG*, xxxii. 753; xlii. 314) are to be understood the living-rooms where the students kept their furniture though they frequently slept outside in the court, or in the loggias, where the libraries were kept etc. The loggia (*riwāḳ*, pl. *arwiḳa*) is strictly speaking the space between two pillars; it was here that in former days instruction was given to many little groups, here the *dhikr* is celebrated, discussions and conversation take place. In the last century there were 38 *riwāḳs* and 15 *ḥāras*. These were: 1. al-Ṣaʿāʾida, for students from upper Egypt, large and important, chief residence of the Mālikīs; 2. al-Ḥaramain, Mecca and Madīna; 3. al-Dakārina (Dakārna), for the Takārīr, people of Takrūr, from Sennār, Dārfūr, Wadai etc. [cf. 8]; 4. al-Shawām, Syrians; 5. al-Djāwā, Javanese and others from Indonesia and surrounding countries; 6. al-Sulaimānīya, from Afghānistān and Khurāsān; 7. al-Maghāriba, from North-West Africa, large and influential; 8. al-Sennārīya, instituted by Muḥammad ʿAlī [cf. 3]; 9. al-Atrāk, Turks; 10. al-Birnīya, from Bornu and the neighbourhood; 11. al-Djabartīya, from the Somali coast; 12. al-Yamanīya, from South Arabia; 13. al-Akrād, Kurds; 14. al-Humūd, Indians; 15. al-Baghdādīya (Bughdādīya), from ʿIrāḳ; 16. al-Beḥeira, from the North-west of the Nile Delta; 17. al-Faiyūmīya (Fayama), from the Faiyūm-Oasis; 18. al-Aḳbughāwīya (Ibtighāwīya), belonging to the above-mentioned *madrasa*; 19. al-Shanawānīya (al-Adjāhira, al-Wāṭīya), from the Southern Delta; 20. al-Ḥanafīya, of the Ḥanafī sect; 21. al-Feshnīya, from Central Egypt; 22. Ibn Muʿammar, a private foundation open to all nationalities; 23. al-Barābira (Barābra), Nubians; 24. Dakārnat Ṣelēḥ, from the country round Lake Chad; 25. al-Sharḳāwiya, from the North East Delta, in honour of ʿAbd Allāh al-Sharḳāwī, recently instituted; 26. al-Ḥanābila (Ḥanābla), the sect of Ibn Ḥanbal, very small.

The inter-Islāmic importance of the mosque can be seen from nothing better than from this list of names of students from countries outside of Egypt. Political and economic affairs of course often regulate the attendance, hence there are great variations in the statistics; the improvement of methods of communication exercises its influence here as at the great *ḥadjdj*. The division into *riwāḳs* is, as can easily be seen, partly according to nationality, partly according to sects and rarely according to special foundations.

The students are called from their close connection with the mosque, *mudjāwir* (plur. *-ūn*), as learners *ṭālib* (plur. *ṭalabat*) *al-ʿilm* "seekers after knowledge". The teachers or professors are officially known as *mudarris*, and collectively as *mashāyikh*. In the Ottoman period an academic head or Rector (*shaikh ʿumūm* or *shaikh mashāyikh al-Azhar*, now generally called *al-shaikh al-akbar*) replaced the former Inspector (*nāẓir*), who had been chosen from among the higher officers of State. The Rectors belonged to either the Mālikī or Shāfiʿī *madhhab* down to 1870, since when the office has been held by Ḥanafīs. Apart from maintaining internal discipline, their duty has been to represent the mosque in its dealings with the government.

Until recent times the curriculum followed the general lines of instruction in the *madrasa*, devoting most attention to theology, jurisprudence, and *ḥadīth*, as well as the disciplines of philology and rhetoric, but other branches of learning were cultivated also, though to a diminishing degree (see generally the article MADRASA; for a detailed account of studies in the eighteenth century, J. Heyworth-Dunne, *Introduction to the History of Education in Egypt*, 36 sqq., and for the early nineteenth century E. W. Lane, *Modern Egyptians*, ch. ix). From 1872 onwards the government began to interest itself in measures of reform. In 1895 an Administrative Committee was set up, which reorganized the curricula and examinations, mainly owing to the efforts of Shaikh Muḥammad ʿAbduh [q.v.], and placed the stipends of the teachers on a more regular footing by means of a government subsidy. Affiliated institutes (*maʿāhid*) were established in the chief provincial cities. But the growth of competition with newer institutions — *Dār al-ʿUlūm* (founded 1873), the Muslim Law School (1907), finally the Fuʾād I University (1927) — forced the authorities of al-Azhar into more radical measures. In 1930 the higher studies were divided into three Faculties, those of Theology, of Islamic Law, and Arabic Language; and the teaching activities were gradually transferred from the old mosque to modern college buildings.

The general plan of religious education was eventually stabilized by Law no. 26 of 1936, under Shaikh Muḥammad Muṣṭafā al-Marāghī, as follows: Students enter one or other of the Faculties after four years in the primary section, and five years in the secondary section of the Institutes, and obtaining a secondary education certificate. On completion of a course extending over four years they qualify for a Higher Certificate; a further course of two years is required for the Diploma, which carries the grade of *ʿālim*. The study of one or more foreign languages is an optional subject in most of these courses. Students holding the *ʿālimīya* diploma may proceed to the Specialization Section (*ḳism al-takhaṣṣuṣ*) in *Fiḳh*, *Tawḥīd*, *Ḳurʾān* and *Ḥadīth*, History of Islām, or Philology. By the same law, the old designation of the madrasa as *al-djāmiʿ al-azhar* was replaced by the term *al-djāmiʿa al-azharīya*, i.e. the University of al-Azhar.

Bibliography: Works mentioned in the article — Further: al-Maḳrīzī, *Khiṭaṭ*, ii. 273—277;

al-Suyūṭī, *Ḥusn al-muḥāḍara* (1299), ii. 183 *sq.*; al-Djabartī's *Chronicle* and ʿAlī Mubārak's *al-Khiṭaṭ al-djadīda*, iv. 19—44; Muṣṭafā Bairam, *Risāla fī taʾrīkh al-Azhar* (1321/1903); Sulaimān Raṣad al-Ḥanafī al-Zaiyātī, *Kanz al-djawhar fī taʾrīkh al-Azhar* (1322/1904); I. Goldziher in G. Ebers, *Aegypten*, ii. 71—90; A. v. Kremer, *Aegypten*, ii. 50 *sqq.*; E. Dor, *L'Instruction publique en Egypte* (1872), p. 373—378; Yacoub Artin, *L'Instruction publique en Egypte* (1889); p. 34 *sqq.*, 205 *sq.*; P. Arminjon, *L'enseignement, la doctrine et la vie dans les Universités musulmanes d'Egypte* (Paris 1907); J. Pedersen, *Al-Azhar* (Copenhagen 1922); A. Sékaly, *L'Université d'el-Azhar et ses Transformations*, in *REI*, i, ii; see also MADRASA.

B

BĀB, an Arabic word signifying "gate", early received among the Ṣūfīs the meaning of "gate by which one enters, means of communication with that which is within" and was applied to prominent Shaikhs (Hudjwīrī, *Kashf al-maḥdjūb*, transl. Nicholson, p. 234). Among the Ismāʿīlīs, this word is used symbolically for the Shaikh or spiritual leader, who initiates into the mysteries of religion, the *asās* (Guyard, *Fragments*, p. 106); among the Nuṣairīs, Salmān al-Fārisī, who was entrusted with the propaganda, is the Bāb (R. Dussaud, *Noṣairīs*, p. 62, n. 4). The Druses call by this name the first spiritual minister, who embodies universal reason (*mawlāya ʿaḳl* "Monseigneur l'esprit"; cf. Sacy, *Druzes*, ii. 59). The name has been made famous by the Saiyid ʿAlī Muḥammad of Shīrāz who called himself Bāb, when he declared himself to be the gateway to knowledge of divine truth (5th Djumādā II 1260 /June 11, 1844). Born on the 1st Muḥarram 1236 (March 26, 1821), the son of a merchant, he became an orphan and was placed under the guardianship of his maternal uncle; he continued his father's business but at the same time occupied himself with religious questions. He then made the pilgrimage to Karbalāʾ and there received instruction from the Shaikhīs. Returning to Shīrāz he proclaimed himself a reformer and delivered a series of sermons, in the Mosque of the Smiths, interspersed with denunciations of the official clergy. A Shaikhī, Ḥusain of Bushrūye, who was seeking a successor to the Saiyid Kāẓim of Resht, who had just died, chose ʿAlī Muḥammad and became his first disciple. The latter thereupon set out for Mecca via Būshīr and Masḳaṭ and took advantage of the pilgrimage to write various treatises which were considered divine revelations. On his return he published a confession of faith in which he added to the Shīʿī formula the declaration that "ʿAlī before Nebīl (i.e. ʿAlī Muḥammad, the prophet being surnamed Nebīl by the Bābīs) is the mirror of the breath of God". A rising followed and the governor had the missionaries of the Bāb imprisoned. Saiyid Yaḥyā of Dārāb, who was sent to investigate the doctrine, became a convert to it. Meanwhile cholera had broken out and all who could quitted Shīrāz. At Iṣfahān ʿAlī Muḥammad enjoyed the protection of Manūčihr-Khān Muʿtamad al-Dawla, governor of the city, but on his death, his successor received orders to place the Bāb in the fortress of Mākū in Ādharbāidjān where he was detained.

Meanwhile Ḥusain of Bushrūye continued his preaching and converted two brothers in Ṭeherān, Mīrzā Yaḥyā Nūrī (later called Ṣubḥ-i Azal) and Mīrzā Ḥusain ʿAlī Nūrī (who became Bahāʾ Allāh). At Ḳazwīn, a young woman, Zarrīn Tādj, surnamed Ḳurrat al-ʿAin, daughter of Mullā Ṣāliḥ Barakānī. of rare beauty and superior intelligence, declared herself a follower of the new religion in consequence of a correspondence with the Bāb. Being forced to quit the town after the murder of her uncle Muḥammad Taḳī, a fanatical *mudjtahid*, in which she was accused of being implicated, she fled by night and sought refuge in Bedesht in Khurāsān where the first assembly of the disciples of the reformer took place.

After a long stay in Mākū, ʿAlī Muḥammad in consequence of the troubles which had broken out in Shaikh Ṭabarsī and in Zendjān [see BĀBĪ] was transferred to Čehrīk and from there taken to Tabriz. He was condemned and his execution entrusted to the Christian regiment of Bahādurān who shot him with his disciple Muḥammad ʿAlī of Yezd. At the first volley the bullets only severed the cords which bound him so that it was necessary to fire again (27th Shaʿbān 1266/July 8, 1850). After the execution, his body was thrown into the town ditch but was taken up by his devoted disciples, and carried to Ṭeherān, where it lay buried for 29 years when it was taken out of its place of concealment by order of Bahāʾ Allāh and, according to an oral tradition, carried to St. Jean d'Acre (ʿAkkā).

His Doctrine. Under an apparent reform of Islām the Bāb founded a new religion with its own beliefs, dogmas and its own conceptions of a new state of society. God is one and ʿAlī Muḥammad is the mirror in which He is reflected and in which every one can regard Him. "You ought to make mirrors of yourselves and your deeds so that you shall only see in these mirrors the sun which you love", says the Arabic *Bayān* (transl. by Nicolas, p. 133). God created the world by means of seven attributes called the Letters of Truth, which are Predestination, Predetermination, Will, Volition, Permission, Doom and Revelation (*ḳadar, ḳaḍāʾ, irāda, mashīya, idhn, adjal, kitāb*). Cabbalistic counting plays an important role: the number 19 is sacred. It is found in the numerical value of the letters composing the word *wāḥid* and *wudjūd*, existence; the year is divided into 19 months (*Bayān*, p. 146), the months into 19 days (= 361 days in a year). A council of 19 members is to regulate the affairs of the community; into its hands is paid the tax of one fifth of the value of property which is levied each year on the capital, provided the latter has not diminished meanwhile (p. 188); the believer is pledged to pay it, but neither the spiritual nor temporal authorities may employ force to make him pay it. All penalties are abolished except fines and the interdiction of cohabitation between married people for longer or shorter periods. The absolute freedom of trading and contract is recognised (p. 155); payment of interest is allowed on goods sold on credit.

Every year there is a fast of one month (19 days) from the rising of the sun to its setting, compulsory from the age of eleven to forty-two. Ablutions are merely recommended without being formally prescribed. There should be a bath in each locality. All women may be seen unveiled and are allowed to be spoken to without restriction by any one, but not obtruded upon; it is advisable, however, to limit the number of words exchanged to 28 (p. 182).

Journeys are not as a rule advisable except those for purposes of trade; sea-voyages are forbidden except to pilgrims and merchants. Prayer is no longer to be offered up in common except at funerals (p. 200), although preaching in mosques is recommended.

ʿAlī Muḥammad was the author of several works, all in manuscript: the two *Bayān* (Arabic and Persian), *Kitāb bain al-ḥaramain* and of a commentary on the Sūrat Yūsuf.

Bibliography: Cte de Gobineau, *Les Religions et les Philosophies dans l'Asie centrale*, (Paris 1865), p. 141—172; Mīrzā Kāẓim-beg, *Bab et les Babis*, in *JA*, series vi., vol. vii., p. 129 *sqq.*; Cl. Huart, *La Religion de Bab* (Paris 1889); E. G. Browne, *A Traveller's Narrative*, p. 1—45, 226 *sqq.*; do., *A Year amongst the Persians*, p. 58, 320 *sqq.*; A. L. M. Nicolas, *Seyyéd Ali Mohammed dit le Bâb* (Paris 1905, with portrait); *Le Béyân arabe*, transl. Nicolas (Paris 1905). Further bibliography is indicated in Geiger and Kuhn's *Grundr. der iran. Philol.*, ii. 367, 602 *sq.*

BĀBĪ, the designation of the followers of the Bāb [q.v.] who however prefer to call themselves *ahl-i bayān*. The preaching of the doctrine began with the sending of missionaries into various Persian provinces; their teaching, which aroused the protestations of the Shīʿa population, brought about persecutions which the Bābīs resisted; in consequence the sect, at first of a purely religious character, became a political party. After a counsel held at Bedesht, Mullā Ḥusain of Bushrūye set out for Barfurūsh at the head of a little troop which could no longer defend themselves in the town and entrenched himself in the sanctuary of Shaikh Ṭabarsī which he turned into a fortress; when besieged by the Royal troops he made several successful sorties but fell in the final encounter. Under pressure of famine the Bābīs signed a capitulation in spite of which they were all massacred in 1265 (July—August 1849). In Zandjān, the chief town of the province of Khamsa, the Bābīs barricaded the town and seized the citadel of ʿAlī Merdān Khān but after various vicissitudes were dislodged from their position and overpowered (May 1849—February 1850). Saiyid Yaḥyā Dārābī whom the inhabitants of Nairīz, discontented with the agents of the central authority called upon to lead them, shut himself up in the ancient fortress there and held out for several days (January 1850). Nāṣir al-Dīn Shāh having been wounded by an attempt directed against him by the Bābīs (28th Shawwāl 1268/16th August 1852), this was the signal for a general persecution of the Bābīs which extended throughout the Empire. Mīrzā Yaḥyā Nūrī surnamed Ṣubḥ-i Azal, who had declared himself the successor of the Bāb, left Persia and retired to Baghdād from which town he was brought to Cyprus by the Turkish government and detained in Famagusta. His half-brother Mīrzā Ḥusain ʿAlī surnamed Bahāʾ Allāh, arrested, then acquitted after an enquiry, obtained permission to go on pilgrimage to Karbalāʾ, and stopped in Baghdād [see BAHĀʾ ALLĀH]. A certain number of Bābīs took refuge at ʿAshkābād in Russian territory where they were allowed to build a mosque. The schism between Ṣubḥ-i Azal and Bahāʾ Allāh divided the Bābīs into two sects, the Azalīs and the Bahāʾīs; the former, who represent the pure doctrine of the master, are now but few in number; the latter, who look upon the Bāb merely as the forerunner of Bahāʾ Allāh, are spread throughout the world and besides Persians have made some converts among Europeans and Americans.

Bibliography: Cte de Gobineau, *Les Religions et les Philosophies dans l'Asie centrale*, p. 175—307; Mirza Kazem-beg, *Bab et les Babis*, in *JA*, VI/vii.; E. G. Browne, *A Traveller's Narrative*, p. 64 *sq.*; do., *The Babis of Persia*, in *JRAS* 1889, p. 485—526; 881—1009; do., *A Year amongst the Persians*, p. 58 *sq.*, 514, 562; Andreas, *Die Bābī in Persien* (Leipzig and Berlin 1896); *Grundriss der iran. Philol.*, ii. 602 *sq.*; H. Roemer, *Die Bābī-Behāʾī's, die jüngste Mohammedanische Sekte*, Potsdamm 1912.

BADĀʾ (A.), appearance; in the dogmatic sense: the intervention of new circumstances which bring about the alteration of an earlier divine determination (Dozy, *Essai sur l'histoire de l'Islamisme*, p. 223, gives the term too wide a signification translating it "mutabilité de Dieu"). Three sorts of badāʾ are distinguished (Shahrastānī, p. 110) according as the word refers to the knowledge, the will, or the command of God (*badāʾ fi 'l-ʿilm, fi 'l-irāda, fi 'l-amr*). The possibility of badāʾ is, in opposition to the very divergent orthodox Sunnī doctrine, always dealt with in the chapter on divine knowledge (*ʿilm*) in the text-books of Shīʿī dogmatics, in which however it has found no uniform statement. In its widest conception, which includes the hypothesis of the mutability of the divine will, it is taught only in the ultra-Shīʿī sects (*badāʾīya*); the moderate Imāmīya-school are careful to exclude the mutability of divine knowledge or at least to give it very moderate expression [see below]. The former could quote the doctrine of the Shīʿī *mutakallim* Hishām b. al-Ḥakam according to which God's knowledge only appears on the realisation of the object; that which does not yet exist (*al-maʿdūm*) could not be an object of his knowledge; this follows on a nescience of things as soon as they become phenomena (al-Baghdādī, p. 49), subtleties which are also treated of in modern times in the religious philosophy of the Shīʿī Shaikhī sect (cf. *RMM*, xi. [1910], 435—438). This conception leaves room for the admission of God's knowledge being in correspondence with new experiences and of His changing a fixed resolution. The Islāmic historians of the sect agree that the doctrine of badāʾ was first propounded by Mukhtār and then became the thesis of the Shīʿī faction of the Kaisanīya (al-Baghdādī, p. 36; cf. Aḥmad b. Yaḥyā b. al-Murtaḍā, in M. Horten, *Die philos. Probleme der spekulat. Theologie im Islam*, Bonn 1910, p. 124). ʿAbd Allāh b. Nawf is occasionally said to be the originator of this doctrine (cf. Wellhausen, *Die religiös-politischen Oppositions-parteien im alten Islām*, p. 88). When Mukhtār had to defend himself in the battle, which was to decide the fate of his enterprise, against the superior forces of Muṣʿab b. al-Zubair, he (or ʿAbd Allāh b. Nawf) announced that God had revealed to him that he was assured of victory. When the alleged oracle was proved false by his defeat, Mukhtār (or ʿAbd Allāh) said referring to Sūra xiii. 39 that something had intervened (*badaʾa lahu*) which had caused God to alter his determination. After the defeat of the Shīʿī community this view had to be accepted as a convenient explanation of the failure of the hopes and prophecies of victory for the defeated Imām. It has been God's determination that the deliverance (*faradj*) and victory of the lawful Imāmate should take place at a certain moment. He had however, meanwhile, altered his determination on grounds of expediency. This principle also serves the Shīʿīs to explain the alteration which took place in the legitimate succession of the Imāms which had been appointed by God from all time, when in place of the predestined Ismāʿīl, his brother Mūsā al-Kāẓim succeeded Djaʿfar al-Ṣādiḳ as the seventh bearer of this theocratic dignity. They ascribe to Djaʿfar the saying "God has never been so led by a new consideration (to alter his determination) as in the case of my son Ismāʿīl (*mā badaʾa li 'illāhi kamā badaʾa fī Ismāʿīl ibnī*)". To many Shīʿī theologians this crass application of the principle of badāʾ might have appeared discreditable; so the speech of Djaʿfar has been made tolerable by the alteration of the word *ibnī* to *abī*. God's change of mind is by this reading referred not to the son but to the ancestor of the Imām, Ismāʿīl the son of Abraham, the predetermined *dhabīḥ* whom God originally ordered Abraham to sacrifice but later freed from this obligation. (Dildār ʿAlī, I, 111).

The most important arguments adduced by the Shīʿīs in support of the doctrine of badāʾ are *a.* firstly the passages in the Ḳurʾān: Sūra xiii. 39; xiv. 10 at the end (these are the strongest proofs); lv. 29^b; the assurance frequently repeated that God in consequence of the repentance of sinners will change his determination to punish them: vii. 153; particular narratives in the Ḳurʾān in support of this are especially the sparing of the people of Yūnus devoted to destruction: x. 98; the rescinding of the command to Abraham to offer up his son: xxxvii. 102—107; the lengthening of the period allowed Moses for his intercourse with God from 30 to 40 nights: vii. 142; *b.* Traditions according to which by the exercise of certain virtues (honouring one's parents), the span of life originally allotted may be lengthened, by doing good an appointed destiny (*al-ḳaḍāʾ al-mubram*) may be altered; the prayer of ʿUmar that "God might strike his name out of the Book of the Damned and write it in that of the Blessed" (Ibn Ḳutaiba, *Kitāb taʾwīl mukhtalif al-ḥadīth*, Cairo 1326, p. 7); *c.* a series of pious legends from which it is evident that misfortunes predetermined to individuals may be averted by acts pleasing to God; *d.* the doctrine of the abrogation of divine laws (*naskh*) which is also a tenet of the Sunnī doctrine.

As Shīʿī dogmatics in general are influenced by Muʿtazilī speculation so also in the case of badāʾ the Muʿtazilī foundation is closely connected with the principle of *aṣlaḥ*, that God is determined in his operations with regard to men by the motives of expediency and the general good. Accordingly it comprehends badāʾ under the point of view "that (divine) determinations on things may alter with changes in the requirements of well-being" (*taḳdīrāt al-umūr tatabaddal bi-tabaddul al-maṣāliḥ*). The moderate Shīʿī dogmatists had to exercise much ingenuity to reconcile the theological antinomies which this conception implies, in order to reconcile the assumptions of the appearance of new determining moments in God's knowledge as implied in the word badāʾ with the belief in the absolute omniscience of God, in the eternity of His knowledge identical with His being as is specially required by the Muʿtazilī doctrine in general; to meet the objection of the orthodox dogmatists to the assumption of the possibility of God's ignorance of the end of things (*ʿawāḳib al-umūr*) which implies the admission of badāʾ (cf. Djurdjānī, to Īdjī, *Mawāḳif*, ed. Soerensen, Leipzig 1848, p. 348, $_6$). The effort to meet the objections from this point of view led them, in spite of all protests against the Jewish and Sunnī deniers of badāʾ, to prepare formulae by which these objections might be combatted and to accuse their Sunnī opponents of crediting them with a false definition of badāʾ invented by the Sunnīs. Their next contention is that the term badāʾ is not to be understood in its literal dictionary meaning but metaphorically (*madjāzan*). They reject the view that badāʾ, according to its literal meaning, implies an alteration in the divine knowledge. In fine the distinction of the Imāmī dogmatist with respect to the Sunnī *kalām* ends in a profitless war of words for the former also explain the fact of a badāʾ intervening in the future as included in the eternal foresight of God which includes all particulars (*ʿalā wadjh al-tafṣīl*). A very remarkable way of reconciling badāʾ with the idea of the *lawḥ maḥfūẓ* required by the Ḳurʾān is the assumption of two tables of fate, the *lawḥ maḥfūẓ* on which the definite unalterable decrees of fate are set out and a *lawḥ al-maḥw wa 'l-ithbāt* (according to Sūra xiii. 39) which contains the decrees which may be altered in consequence of the intervention of new causes (Dildār ʿAlī, i. 114 below), a view which has also penetrated into Sunnī circles and has given rise to esoteric mystic subtleties (*kalimāt ʿadjība wa-asrār ghāmiḍa*) (Fakhr al-Dīn al-Rāzī, *Mafātīḥ al-ghaib*, v. 310). According to this, two kinds of divine knowledge must be distinguished: *ʿilm maḥtūm*, the unalterable knowledge the objects of which God announces to the prophets and angels, and *ʿilm makhzūn*, the knowledge entrusted by God to no one, which concerns matters in suspense (*umūr mawḳūfa ʿind Allāh*; cf. Kulīnī, p. 85).

While the Shīʿa lay the greatest stress on the preservation of the conception of badāʾ for the reasons given above (they allowed one of their Imāms to say: "one can serve God by nothing better than recognising badāʾ", since repentance, prayer and humility before God to procure forgiveness of sins or the alteration of one's fate can only have meaning if the proposition of badāʾ is granted), this doctrine is a constant point of attack with the opponents of the Shīʿa. Even Sulaimān b. Djarīr, an adherent of the Zaidī Shīʿa sect, reproached the Imāmīs with embracing two erroneous conceptions: the principle of *taḳīya* [q.v.] and the proposition of badāʾ (Shahrastānī, p. 119 ult.). The bitterest opponents of the latter doctrine were the Jews who base their rejection of the abrogation of divine law (*naskh al-sharīʿa*) on the fact that this proposition implies the recognition of badāʾ, as was shown by the Jewish theologian Yaḥyā b. Zakarīyāʾ al-Kātib al-Ṭabarānī in Palestine in his controversy with al-Masʿūdī (*Kitāb al-tanbīh wa 'l-ishrāf*, ed. de Goeje, in *BGA*, viii. 113, $_{15}$; for اعبك reading البداء). In the third (ninth) century, the question of badāʾ seems on account of difficulties connected with it which could only be explained by subtle arguments, to have belonged to those questions by which keen intellect and originality could be tested. This may be inferred from Djāḥiẓ, *Tria Opuscula*, ed. van Vloten, p. 113, 7 (correcting النداء to البداء).

Bibliography: Abū Djaʿfar Muḥammad al-Kulīnī, *al-Uṣūl min al-djāmiʿ al-kāfī* (Bombay 1302), p. 84—86; Dildār ʿAlī, *Mirʾāt al-ʿuḳūl fī ʿilm al-uṣūl* (Lucknow 1318—1319), i. 110—121 (the utterances and definitions of the most moderate Shīʿī authorities on badāʾ are here quoted in full); I. Friedländer, *The Heterodoxies of the Shiites according to Ibn Ḥazm* (New Haven 1909 = *JAOS*, xxix. 72).

BADAL (A.), substitute. The terms *abdāl* (pl. of *badal*; in Persian and Turkish the plural *abdāl* is often used as a singular) and *budalāʾ* (pl. of *badīl*) are connected with a Ṣūfī doctrine, which goes back to the iiird (ixth) century, that the cosmic order is preserved by a fixed number of saints, so that when a holy man dies his place is immediately filled by a "substitute". Some writers explain *badal* as "one who, when he departs from a place, has the power to leave his 'double' (*shakhṣ rūḥānī*) behind him", or "one who has experienced a spiritual transformation". There is great discrepancy in the accounts given of the number of *abdāl* and their position in the saintly hierarchy headed by the *ḳuṭb* or "pole". The *Musnad* of Ibn Ḥanbal mentions 40 whom God created in Syria (i. 112) and also states that there are 30 in Muḥammad's community (v. 322). Al-Makkī refers to 300 *abdāl*, comprising *ṣiddīḳūn*, *shuhadāʾ* and *ṣāliḥūn* (*Ḳūt al-ḳulūb*, ii. 78; cf. Sūra iv. 69). According to Hudjwīrī, they are 40 in number and occupy the fourth grade, being subordinate to 7 *abrār*, 4 *awtād*, and 3 *nuḳabāʾ* (*Kashf al-maḥdjūb*, ed. Schukovski, p. 269; transl. Nicholson, p. 214). Ibn al-ʿArabī (*Futūḥāt*, ii. 9) limits their number to 7, ranks them under the *awtād* (so Ibn al-Fāriḍ, *Tāʾiyat al-kubrā*, v. 501) and above the *nuḳabāʾ*, associates each of them with a particular prophet (Abraham, Moses, Aaron, Idrīs, Joseph, Jesus and Adam), and represents each as exercising sway over one of the seven climes into which the world is divided.

Bibliography: *Lisān al-ʿArab*, s.v.; M. ʿAlāʾ al-Tahānawī, *Kashshāf*, p. 145; E. Blochet, *Études sur l'ésoterisme musulman*, in *JA*, xix. (1902), p. 528 *sqq.* and xx. (1902), p. 49 *sqq.*; L. Massignon, *Passion*, p. 754, and *Essai sur les origines du lexique de la mystique musulmane*, p. 112 *sqq.*; D. Haneberg, *Ali Abulhasan Schadheli*, in *ZDMG*, vii. 21 *sqq.*; G. Flügel, *Schaʿrânî und sein Werk über die muhammedanische Glaubenslehre*, in *ZDMG*, xx. 37 *sqq.*

AL-**BADAWĪYA**. [See AḤMAD AL-BADAWĪ].

AL-**BAGHDĀDĪ**, ABŪ MANṢŪR ʿABD AL-ḲĀHIR B. ṬĀHIR, Muḥammadan theologian, came with his father to Nishāpūr and studied various sciences there. Later in life he made himself famous by his skill in arithmetic, on which he wrote a work, but it was theological studies that attracted him most; Abū Isḥāḳ al-Isfarāʾinī was his teacher in these subjects. After the latter's death in 418/1027 he succeeded him until the revolt of the Turkomans forced him to leave the town in 429/1037. He then betook himself to Isfarāʾin where he died soon after. His work on the Muslim sects entitled *Kitāb al-farḳ bain 'l-firaḳ* was published at Cairo in 1328 (1910). (English translation by K. C. Seelye, New York 1919, and A. S. Halkin, Tel-Aviv 1935), and vol. i of his *Uṣūl al-dīn* at Istanbul in 1928.

Bibliography: Ibn Khallikān, No. 365; Wüstenfeld, *Die Schâfiʿiten*, No. 345; Brockelmann, *GAL*, *Suppl.*, I, 666 *sq.*; Friedländer, in *JAOS*, xxviii. 26 *sq.*

BAHĀʾ ALLĀH ("splendour of God"), surname of MĪRZĀ ḤUSAIN ʿALĪ NŪRĪ, born at Nūr in Māzandarān on the 12th November 1817, halfbrother of Mīrzā Yaḥyā surnamed Ṣubḥ-i Azal, was almost thirty years of age when he became a convert to the new doctrine preached by the Bāb [see BĀBĪ]. Without having ever seen him he became one of the Bāb's chief disciples and was recognised as his successor by the greater part of the Bābīs. After the attempt on the life of the Shāh he was imprisoned in Ṭihrān; he was then exiled and settled in Baghdād in 1852. It was there that he declared himself to be the person announced by the Bāb in the mysterious words: *man yuẓhiruhu 'llāh*: "He whom God will manifest". He lived the life of a hermit outside Sulaimānīya, where he drew up the main scheme of his work, which was to make the religion of the Bāb, somewhat modified, a universal religion; he was interned in Adrianople (1864), then at Acre (August 1868) where he died on the 29th May 1892, leaving his spiritual authority to his eldest son, ʿAbbās Efendi, surnamed ʿAbd al-Bahāʾ (d. Nov. 1920).

His Doctrine. Right living consists in doing harm to no one, in loving one another, in bearing injustice without rebellion, only regarding the good, being humble and devoting oneself to healing the sick; such are the principles adopted by Bahāʾ, an obvious echo of Christianity. The ultimate aim is universal peace which is to be brought about by the adoption of this religion, which possesses neither clergy nor ceremonial. Every town is to institute a place of assembly for a managing committee, consisting of nine members which is called *bait al-ʿadl*, their chief resources are to consist of bequests to the treasury, recepts from fines and a tax of one nineteenth on capital to be paid once and for all. Austerities are forbidden; man was created for happiness.

The principal works of Bahāʾ are the *Kitāb al-aḳdas* (ed. Bombay and St. Petersburg), the *Kitāb al-īḳān* (transl. by H. Dreyfus and Ḥabīb Ullāh Shīrāzī, Paris 1904), *Ṭarāzāt*, *Kalimāt-i Firdawsīya*, *Ishrāḳāt*, *Tadjalliyāt* (transl. in the *Préceptes du Béhaisme*, Paris 1906), *Kalimāt-i maknūne* (Hidden Words, Paris 1905). The lessons of Acre have been collected by Mrs. Clifford Barney (*An-Nūru 'l-Abhā*, London 1908) and translated from the Persian text by H. Dreyfus (Paris 1908); his last words have been edited by Toumanski (St. Petersburg 1892).

Bibliography: H. Dreyfus, *Essai sur le Béhaisme, son histoire, sa portée sociale*, Paris 1909; Edw. G. Browne, *A Year amongst the Persians*, p. 60, 300 *sq.*; do., in Hasting's *Encyclopaedia of Religions and Ethics*, ii. 299—308; do. *Literary History of Persia*, iv. 198—220; H. Roemer, *Die Bābī-Behāʾis*, Potsdam 1912.

BAḤĪRĀ, the name of a Christian monk. It is related that in his twelfth year Muḥammad was taken by his uncle Abū Ṭālib on a caravan journey to Syria. When the travellers were near or in Buṣrā, a monk who lived there in his cell noticed that one of them was accompanied by a cloud and that the branches of the tree, under which he sat, sprouted to give him shade. The monk whose name was Baḥīrā thereupon invited the whole company to eat with him. They went, but left Muḥammad behind to guard the caravan. Baḥīrā missed among his guests him, whose features were described in his books as those of the last prophet, and asked if they were really all. On learning that one had been left he insisted on the boy's coming too. When the latter was sent for and entered, he gazed fixedly at him and asked him by al-Lāt and al-ʿUzzā to answer his questions. After Muḥammad had taken the opportunity to show his aversion to heathen deities, he convinced him by his answers that he was the promised one. The monk thereupon warned Abū Ṭālib to protect the youth from the Jews.

This is the version of the legend given by Ibn Hishām (p. 155 *sq.*); according to others Abū Bakr was present at this meeting and was even then prepared for future events. Masʿūdī (*Murūdj*, i. 146) tells us that the name of the monk was Sergius and that he belonged to the ʿAbd al-Ḳais; according to Ḥalabī (i. 157) his name was Georgius or Sergius.

Besides this story is an account of a similar meeting, which happened 12 years later. Muḥammad was then travelling to Syria in the service of Khadīdja in the company of her servant Maisara. In Buṣrā he met a monk Nestor who recognised the future prophet by certain signs. We are also told of some men of Rūm who arrived at one of these meetings to seek the future prophet.

In the oldest versions the name of the monk is lacking (Ibn Hishām, p. 119 *sq.*). In the later Muslim and Christian sources he is called Sergius; Baḥīrā (the Aramaic *beḥīrā* "chosen") is interpreted as an epithet.

On the authenticity of such legends little can be said when, as here, all clues are lacking. In the cycle of legends which have gathered round Muḥammad, they form a class of which numerous examples appear which all show the same type, namely the tendency to prove by an apparent accident that "the people of the book" had learned beforehand from their books that Muḥammad was to be a prophet (cf. A. J. Wensinck, *Mohammed en de Joden te Medina*, p. 54—60).

The figure of Baḥīrā is, under the name Sergius, mentioned quite early in Byzantine literature in a connection which agrees with isolated Muslim traditions (cf. Sprenger, *Das Leben und die Lehre des Moḥammad*, ii. 384 *sq.*).

Thus Theophanes (ed. Classen, i. 513) and Georgius Phrantzes (ed. Bekker, p. 295 *sq.*), relate that after the first appearance of Gabriel and Muḥammad's epileptic fit, Khadīdja betook herself in great anxiety to Sergius, a heretical banished monk; he comforted her with the assurance that the angel was sent to all prophets.

The Muslim Baḥīrā traditions have been preserved in a much expanded form in the Baḥīrā-Apocalypse, a Christian production, which in its present form perhaps dates from the xi[th] or xii[th] century and has been preserved to us in several recensions in Syriac and Arabic (cf. Gottheil, *A Christian Bahira Legend*, in *ZA*, vol. xiii. *sq.*).

This book which is said to have been composed by one Ishōʿyab falls into three parts: 1) the stories referring to the Muḥammadan dynasties which Sergius Beḥīrā saw on Mount Sinai; 2) his conversations with the young Muḥammad in the desert of Yathrib; 3) the prophecies of Sergius, partly a repetition of 1. In the second part it is told how Sergius communicated to Muḥammad his doctrine and laws and parts of the Ḳurʾān with a view to making the Arabs acquainted with the one God. The object of this part of the work is clearly to expose Muḥammad as an impostor who received his pretended revelations from a heretical monk.

Sergius is also mentioned in the literature of the middle ages.

Bibliography: Ibn Hishām, p. 115 *sq.*, 119 *sq.*; Ibn Saʿd, I[a], p. 76, 82 *sq.*; Ṭabarī, i. 1123 *sq.*; al-Ḥalabī, *al-Sīra al-Ḥalabīya* (Cairo 1292), i. 156 *sq.*, 177 *sq.*; Tirmidhī (Cairo 1292), p. 282; al-Diyārbakrī, *Taʾrīkh al-Khamīs* (Cairo 1283), i. 257 *sq.*, 262 *sq.*; *Fihrist* (ed. Flügel), p. 22; Nöldeke, in *ZDMG*, xii. 699 *sq.*; Sprenger, *ibid.*, p. 238 *sq.*, also *ibid.*, iii. 454; iv 188 *sq.*; vi. 457 *sq.*; vii. 413 *sq.*, 580; viii. 557 *sq.*; ix. 779 *sq.*; x. 807; Sprenger, *Leben und Lehre des Moḥammad*, i. 178 *sq.*; Ibn Ḥadjar, *Iṣāba*, i. 357 *sq.*; Buhl, *Das Leben Muhammeds*, p. 118.

BAIʿ (A.), Two roots are used in Arabic to describe the contract of sale: *b-y-ʿ* and *sh-r-y*; in the first verbal form both usually mean to sell, but also to buy, in the eighth form to sell exclusively; this use to express both sides of a mutual arrangement is shared by these two words with a number of other old legal terms. *Baiʿ* originally means the clasping of hands as the indication of the conclusion of an agreement, *sh-r-y* perhaps the busy activity of the market. For selling we usually find *bāʿa* and for buying *ishtarā*; the usual term for the contract of sale is *baiʿ*, infinitive of *bāʿa*. The frequent use of *sharā* for a profitable and of *ishtarā* for an unprofitable transaction (in the metaphorical sense) in the Ḳurʾān may only be due to the parallel train of ideas in the separate particular passages.

Commercial law must have been already at a high level of development in pre-Muḥammadan Mecca; the trade on which alone the existence of the town depended, occupied such a predominant position there that the Ḳurʾān not only shows an interest in it throughout but uses a series of terms of the language of commerce to reproduce religious ideas [cf. above]. There cannot fail to have been elements of foreign origin in this old Arab commercial law; definitely belonging to it in particular are the *ribā* contracts rejected by Islāmic law (their names however are Islāmic) and certain dealings in credit exchange and speculation; to all appearance the legal conception of the contract as mutual agreements based on offer and acceptance as well as a part of the terminology (besides *b-y-ʿ* and *sh-r-y* especially sale with a time-limit *salam* and offer *īdjāb* [q.v.]; — a term which in turn reveals another unilateral juridical conception — and acceptance *ḳabūl*) go back to this pre-Islāmic stratum; besides the general injunction to give full measure and weight and in particular to fulfil agreements as well as the special demand that agreements with a time-limit should be in writing (Sūra ii. 282 *sq.*; in the system of evidence of the fiḳh this injunction has been deprived of its binding character), the two prohibitions of the Ḳurʾān which forbid the taking of interest (*ribā*) and games of chance (*maisir*) (Sūra ii. 275 *sq.*; v. 90 *sq.*) directly affect commercial law; they have been developed to the utmost limit in fiḳh. Tradition contains a certain number of teachings regarding commerce in general and the duties of the good and the punishment of the wicked merchant and the prohibitions of certain transactions (generally the taking of interest and speculation). As legal principles which now appear for the first time may be mentioned: the recognition of the right of withdrawal (*khiyār*) unconditional during the negotiations and under certain conditions either agreed or fixed by law after the agreement has been made; the legal maxim *al-kharādj bi'l-ḍamān* ("profit goes where the responsibility lies"); the rule that the profits in existence at the moment of sale belong to the vendor, unless the contrary is stipulated; the prohibition of a sale in which there is an inherent risk, because its object cannot be exactly defined (e.g. in the sale of ripe fruits on the tree etc., the consensus of tradition is satisfied with an estimate); the prohibition of further sale of provisions or of goods in general before possession has been completed (as a consequence of the prohibition of *ribā*) or in general of the sale of things which are not already the property of the vendor; the exclusion of certain things from commerce, ritually impure or forbidden as well as things which, like surplus water, are common property. A certain probability of going back to the Prophet himself may be claimed at least by the special treatment, diverging from the general law, of the case in which the vendor of the udder of a milkcow in order to suggest a greater yield does not milk it before the sale. How far the resulting Islāmic commercial law was influenced by the law and economic life of peoples incorporated in the Muslim empire cannot be decided with certainty.

The contract of sale forms the basis of the Muslim law of contract (the following details follow the Ḥanafī school). Its categories are evolved in every detail from the sale contract, and other business dealings are interpreted as in the nature of sales, although not actually dealt with as contracts of sale (e.g. hire [*idjāra*] and even marriage [*nikāḥ*; q.v.]). A sale is defined as an exchange of commodities, so that it includes exchange.

Things which are not included among commodities (*māl*) cannot therefore form the subject of a contract of sale (although servitudes on estates can), i.e. 1. things which are completely excluded from legal traffic, e.g. animals not ritually slaughtered (*maita*; q.v.), blood; 2. things in which there is no ownership, e.g. endowments (*waḳf*; q.v.) or which are public property or constituents in which no separate private property exists; 3. slaves in whom there is only restricted ownership, particularly the *umm al-walad* [q.v.]; 4. things on the disposal of which there are restrictions, e.g. things which are ritually impure, like wine and the pig and other things without market value (*māl ghair mutaḳawwim*) which are not rigorously defined; 5. things in which there is no ownership such as things lost or seized and runaway slaves: here the power to dispose of the property is refused, to exclude the risk. A bargain made concerning an object of this kind is not valid (*ghair ṣaḥīḥ* or *ghair djāʾiz*); the Ḥanafīs however do not regard all contracts of this nature as void (*bāṭil*; q.v.; this always in cases 1, 2, 3), but in certain circumstances as *fāsid* only (something like assailable: in the other schools synonymous with *bāṭil*); a bargain of this kind even if the exchange has been completely effected creates simply a "bad ownership" (*milk khabīth*) and is liable to cancellation (*faskh*) until a more definite pronouncement. An impost in favour of or against one of the parties is invalid and makes the contract *fāsid*. A time-limit and stipulations are not allowed in this agreement. An adult (*bāligh*) in full possession of his faculties (*ʿāḳil*; q.v.) is qualified to conclude a bargain; freemen (*ḥurr*) and also, with the approval of the guardian or master, the minor (*ṣabī*; only according to the Ḥanafīs and Ḥanbalīs and only under certain conditions) and the slave; the latter can be given permission to trade either in the particular or the general case. Representation (*wakāla*) is also possible: in this case the representative is regarded as the main contracting party with corresponding rights and obligations, but the rights of ownership go direct to the principal. The conclusion of the bargain (*ṣafḳa*, lit. "handclasp") is made in sales and similar business by offer and acceptance which must take place at the same transaction (*madjlis*), the transfer of ownership thus takes place (*milk*). The transfer of ownership however is only completed when possession is taken (surrender: *taslīm*; appropriation: *ḳabḍ*) but this is not gone through in the case of real estate; on the other hand, the existence of the right of withdrawal (*khiyār*) restricts the transfer of ownership even in the case where possession has been taken. The withdrawal of the offer is among the Ḥanafīs and Mālikīs (deviating from the literal sense of a tradition) only possible before acceptance, among the Shāfiʿīs and Ḥanbalīs also after, in the course of the *madjlis* (the so-called *khiyār al-madjlis*); there is further in favour of the purchaser in law the *khiyār al-ruʾya*, the right of withdrawal at the time when he sees the goods and the *khiyār al-ʿaib* the right of withdrawal on account of a defect. Lastly the right of withdrawal may be reserved in general in favour of a party to a contract or two or a third (*khiyār al-sharṭ*) and according to the Ḥanafīs and Mālikīs for at most three days. The vendor is also responsible to the amount of the price paid in the case of a claim if the ownership is not complete (*istiḥḳāḳ*, the so-called *darak*). — On the prohibition of *ribā* see that article. — The prohibition of risk (*gharar*) affirms that the obligations of the parties must be definite (*maʿlūm*), in particular the object of the sale, the price and the term. The first demand is particularly strict in the case of objects liable to the prohibition of *ribā* so that here no indefinite amount (*djuzāf*) is permissible even with the price per unit mentioned. — In the special sense of purchase as distinct from exchange, one talks of goods and price (*thamān*) or value (*ḳīma*). When the price is not fixed for each thing (in contrast to a separately priced article) its use is permitted without charge even in the case when the bargain is later rescinded and continued even before possession is taken. A special kind of purchase is that with time-limit (*salam* or *salaf*; q.v.) when the price is paid at once for goods to be delivered later; the expression *raʾs al-māl* ("capital") for the price shows the economic meaning of the transaction: the financing of the enterprise of the vendor.

In view of its contact with the subject of the prohibition of usury, *salam* is very carefully treated and is the subject of numerous detailed regulations. The postponement of payment for goods delivered immediately is also possible but this kind of sale plays a minor part in Muslim law; the term purchase on credit (*baiʿ al-ʿīna*) is given *a potiori* to an evasion of the prohibition of *ribā* based on this transaction. Exchange of goods (*muḳāyaḍa*) is hardly distinguished from sale; on account of the prohibition of usury money changing (*ṣarf*) is important, which is interpreted as the sale of price for price.

The actual practice of commerce in the Muslim middle ages was not controlled by these theoretical rules but by a system of use and wont which adhered to the main principles of the *sharīʿa* such as the recognition of the prohibition of *ribā* but showed a greater flexibility. On the content of this customary law very few details are so far available; a unique source for conditions in Islām about 400/1000 is the younger recension of the *Kitāb al-ḥiyal waʾl-makhāridj* of (Pseudo-) al-Khaṣṣāf.

Bibliography: Torrey, *The Commercial-Theological Terms in the Koran*; Wensinck, *Handbook*, s.v. BARTER; Juynboll, *Handleiding tot de kennis van de Mohammedaansche wet* (3rd ed.), p. 265 *sqq.*; Bergsträsser, *Grundzüge des islamischen Rechts*, p. 47 *sqq.*, 60 *sqq.*, 69 *sqq.*; Schacht, *The origins of Muhammadan jurisprudence*, see Index.

AL-**BAIḌĀWĪ**, ᶜABD ALLĀH B. ᶜUMAR, one of the most renowned commentators on the Ḳur'ān, was a son of the chief justice of Fārs under the atabeg Abū Bakr b. Saᶜd (613—658/1226—1260), held himself the post of a judge in Shīrāz and finally settled in Tabrīz where he died according to Ṣafadī in 685/1282, according to Subkī in 691/1291; cf. Suyūṭī, *Bughyat al-wuᶜāt*, p. 286), but perhaps not till 716/1316 (cf. Rieu, *Suppl. to the Cat. of Arab MSS. in the British Museum*, no. 116). His chief work, the *Anwār al-tanzīl wa-asrār al-ta'wīl*, a commentary on the Ḳur'ān, based on the *Kashshāf* of Zamakhsharī but considerably amplified from other sources, is regarded by the Sunnīs as the best and almost as a holy book; but he is too inaccurate and not complete on any one of the branches with which he occupies himself: historical exegesis, lexicography, grammar, dialectic, various readings etc. (cf. Nöldeke-Schwally, *Gesch. des Qorāns*, ii, 176). This work was edited by H. O. Fleischer (Leipzig, 1846—1848, 2 vols; with *Indices* by W. Fell), and has also often been printed in the East; it was used as a text-book in the Islāmic schools and therefore many scholars wrote super-commentaries on it for the benefit of their pupils; of these the most re-nowned is that of Muḥammad b. Muṣṭafā al-Ḳūdjawī Shaikhzāde (d. 950/1543), printed in 4 vols. Stambul 1283. Besides some smaller grammatical and juridical works Baiḍāwī wrote the *Minhādj al-wuṣūl ilā ᶜilm al-uṣūl*, printed Cairo 1326, on the principles of jurisprudence, based on the *Kitāb al-ḥāṣil* of al-Urmawī (d. 656/1258), an abridgment of Fakhr al-Dīn al-Rāzī's (d. 606/1209) *Kitāb al-maḥṣūl*. His account of Metaphysics was also much used: *Ṭawāliᶜ al-anwār min maṭāliᶜ al-anẓār*. Finally he wrote in Persian a history of the world from the time of Adam to 674/1275, called *Niẓām al-tawārīkh* (cf. de Sacy, in *Notices et extraits*, iv., p. 672—695; Rieu, *MSS. Brit. Mus.*, ii. 823; printed Hyderabad 1930). As in the Hamburg MS. Orient. No. 187 — cf. *Katalog der orient. HSS. der Stadt-Bibliothek zu Hamburg mit Ausschluss der hebr.*, pt. i. by C. Brockelmann, No. 231 — the beginning of this work is followed by the history of China from Rashīd al-Dīn's History of the World, this has been printed under the erroneous title of Abdallae Beidavaei *Historia Sinensis* persice e gemino manuscripto ed. lat. quoque reddita ab Andrea Mullero Greifenhagio, Jenae 1689.

Bibliography: Subkī, *Ṭabaḳāt al-shāfiᶜiya*, Cairo 1324, v. 19; Suyūṭī, *Bughyat al-wuᶜāt*, Cairo 1320, p. 286; Khwāndamīr, *Ḥabīb al-siyar*, Bombay 1857, iii. 77; Elliot, *History of India*, ii. 252 *sq.*; Brockelmann, *GAL*², i. 530; *Suppl.*, i. 738; C. A. Storey, *Persian Lit.*, sect. ii, fasc. I, 70-71.

BAIRAM, an Osmanli-Turkish word which denotes the two great Muslim festivals: *küčük-bairam*, "the little festival", also called *sheker-bairam*, "feast of sweets", on account of the custom of making presents of sweetmeats then, is the festival on the breaking of the fast (*ᶜīd al-fiṭr*; q.v.) which lasts three days. The *büyük-bairam*, "the great festival", usually called *ḳurbān-bairam*, "feast of the sacrifice", is the *ᶜīd al-aḍḥā* [q.v.] which lasts four days beginning 10 Dhu'l-Ḥidjdja. A *rikᶜāb-i humāyūn*, "official reception", was held at the Imperial Palace on each of these two festivals.

BAIRAMĪYA, an order of Derwīshes, founded by Ḥādjdjī Bairam of Angora. The founder died there in 833/1429—30. His grave adjoins the ruins of the temple of Roma and Augustus, the walls of which bear the famous inscription, the Monumentum Ancyranum. The Bairamī order is a branch of the Naḳshbandīs. In Constantinople it had settlements in Stambul, Eiyūb, Skutarī and Ḳāsim-Pasha.

Bibliography: Gibb, *Ottoman poetry*, i. 299, remark; Depont and Coppolani, *Confréries religieuses*, p. 532; Ḥādjdjī Khalīfa, *Djihān-numā*, p. 643; J. P. Brown, *The Darvishes*, v. Index.

BAIYŪMĪYA, a religious order, founded by Sīdī ᶜAlī b. al-Ḥidjāzī b. Muḥammad, born at Baiyūm in Egypt in 1108/1696. The order belongs to the Ḳādirīya. Its founder, *muḳaddam* of the Khalwatīya, renewed the ritual of the Badawīya, to which he gave a more stimulating character and made stricter by more stringent exercises. There are (or were) settlements of this order in Arabia (Djidda and Mecca) in the Euphrates and Indus valleys; the mother-*zāwiya* is in a village near Cairo. The *dhikr* of the order consists in calling out *yā Allāh*! with an inclination of the head and crossing of the hands on the breast, followed by raising the head and clapping the hands.

Bibliography: Depont and Coppolani, *Confréries religieuses*, p. 336; Lane, *Modern Egyptians*, i. 332; ii. 208.

BAḲĪᶜ AL-**GHARḲAD** (also briefly called *al-Baḳīᶜ*), the cemetery of Madīna. The name denotes a field which was originally covered with a kind of high growing bramble; there were several such Baḳīᶜ's in Madīna. The place was and is situated at the southeast end of the town, outside the modern town-wall, through which a gate, Bāb al-Baḳīᶜ, gives admittance to the cemetery (see the map of Madīna in Caetani, *Annali*, II, i. p. 73, and Rutter, *Holy Cities* p. 208). The first to be buried in al-Baḳīᶜ was ᶜUthmān b. Maẓᶜūn, the ascetic companion of the Prophet; the latter's daughters, the little Ibrāhīm, and his wives were also buried here. It gradually became an honour to be granted a last resting-place here among the relations of Muḥammad, the Imāms and Saints. The graves of the famous dead had memorials and domes built over them by their descendents; the dome of Ḥasan b. ᶜAlī for example rose to a considerable height as Ibn Djubair informs us. When Burckhardt visited the place after the invasion of the Wahhabites, he found it the most wretched of all the cemeteries of the East, and Rutter, who saw it shortly after the second Wahhabite occupation, in 1926, compares it with the broken remains of a town which had been demolished by an earth-quake. Like the grave of Ḥamza at Uḥud and Ḳubā', al-Baḳīᶜ is one of the *ziyāra* places of Madīna, where the pilgrims were accustomed to pray.

Bibliography: Ibn Djubair (ed. de Goeje), p. 195 *sq.*; Burckhardt, *Travels* (London 1829), ii, 222—226; Burton, *Pilgrimage to al-Medinah and Meccah* (London 1857), ii, 31 *sqq.*; Wüstenfeld, *Geschichte der Stadt Medina* (Göttingen 1860), p. 140 *sqq.*; al-Batānūnī, *al-Riḥla al-Ḥidjāziya*, p. 256; A. J. Wensinck, *Mohammed en de Joden te Medina*, Leiden, 1908, p. 15; Eldon Rutter, *The Holy Cities of Arabia*, London and New York 1928, ii, 256 *sqq.*

BAḲLĪYA, a Ḳarmaṭian sect, which arose in the Sawād of Wāsiṭ in 295/908 under the leadership of a certain Abū Ḥātim. He is said to have forbidden his people to eat garlic, leeks and turnips, but otherwise to be vegetarians for he forbade the slaying of animals. This is probably the explanation of the name Baḳlīya. He abolished religious observances, and gave other prescriptions, which we do not exactly know. When the Baḳlīya, allied with the Beduins of the neighbourhood under Masʿūd b. Ḥuraith and others began to plunder, the caliph sent Hārūn b. Gharīb with troops against them; he scattered them and slew numbers of them in 316/928.

Bibliography: Masʿūdī, *Tanbīh* (ed. de Goeje), p. 391; ʿArīb (ed. de Goeje), p. 137; Ibn al-Athīr (ed. Tornberg), viii. 136; de Sacy, *Exposé de la religion des Druzes, Introduction*, p. 210; Friedländer, in *JAOS*, xxix. 110 *sq.*

BĀLIGH. [See ʿAḲIL, TAKLĪF].

BĀRĀ WAFĀT is the Indian name for the 12th day of the month Rabīʿ al-Awwal. It is a compound word of *bārā*, "twelve", and *wafāt*, "death". It is observed as a holy day in commemoration of the death of the prophet Muḥammad. His life and teachings are on that day generally recited in private houses and mosques throughout India, and is a great day of rejoicing for the Muslims of the whole world, who consider it at the same time as the day of his birth. For more details see the art. MAWLID.

Bibliography: Herklots, *Qanoon-e-Islam* (ed. 1832), p. 233 *sq.*; Garcin de Tassy, *L'Islamisme* (3rd ed.), p. 336 *sq.*; Sell, *The Faith of Islam* (2nd ed.), p. 313 *sq.*

BARṢĪṢĀ, name of a devotee. The story of Barṣīṣā is always connected with Ḳurʾān, Sūra lix. 16: ... "like the devil when he said to the man [*or* to man]: 'Disbelieve', then, when he had disbelieved, he said, "Lo, I am clear of thee, lo, I fear Allāh, the Lord of the Worlds". This is explained by the commentators in three ways: of man in general; of the story of how the devil misled Abū Djahl at the battle of Badr (cf. Sūra, viii. 48 and Ibn Hishām, p. 474); of a certain monk or devotee. The older exegetical tradition prefers the third explanation, which is some form, shorter or longer, of the following story. There was a devotee (*rāhib*, *ʿābid*, *ḳass*, of the children of Israel or otherwise) living in his cell, who had long (sixty years, etc.) withstood Satan. At length he falls with a woman who is brought or comes to him (she is a shepherdess, a neighbour's daughter, a princess, sister of four or three brothers, ill, possessed, left in his charge). She becomes pregnant, and, to conceal his sin, he kills and buries her in his house or under a tree. The stories vary as to how far back the machinations of Satan extend. Some tell that he possesses the woman that she may be brought to be healed. Others, that he tempts the devotee to sin with her after she has been brought. Others, that he only points out the escape by killing her. Then Satan reveals the crime, in a dream or otherwise; this is verified by finding the body and its condition; the devotee is taken and led away to death; Satan reveals himself to the devotee as his temptor and offers deliverance if he will worship him. The devotee does so, and Satan retires, uttering the words of the Ḳurʾān. Four versions of this are given by Ṭabarī (*Tafsīr*, xxviii. 31 *sq.*) going back to ʿAlī, to Ibn Masʿūd, to Ibn ʿAbbās and to Ṭāʾūs. By far the fullest form is in the *Sirādj al-munīr* of Shirbīnī (Būlāḳ 1299, iv. 243 *sq.*) which professes to be derived, through a certain ʿAṭāʾ, from Ibn ʿAbbās but is quite different from the form ascribed to Ibn ʿAbbās in Ṭabarī. It is very close to the longer narrative given by Goldziher-Landberg from the *Forty Vezirs* (ed. Stambul 1303, p. 120—126) in which collection the legend had found a permanent resting place in 850/1446. In that edition of the *Forty Vezirs* the story is different and much fuller than in the texts translated by Petis de la Croix and by Gibb. Through different forms of the *Forty Vezirs* the story passed into Europe and became eventually the source of M. G. Lewis' *Ambrosio or the Monk*. But the pre-Muslim source of the story is still unknown. It is told all over the Muslim world. Landberg found it in Ḥadramawt; Hartmann (*Der islamische Orient*, i. 23 *sq.*) found it localized in the province of Aleppo; Ibn Baṭṭūṭa (i. 26) found a *ḳaṣr* of Barṣīṣ the *ʿābid* east of Alexandria, on the road from Tripoli. For further references see Chauvin, *Bibliographie arabe*, viii. 128 *sq.*

BARZAKH, a Persian and Arabic word meaning "obstacle", "hindrance", "separation" (perhaps identical with Persian *farsakh*, measure of distance). It is found three times in the Ḳurʾān (xxiii. 100; xxv. 53 and lv. 20) and is interpreted sometimes in a moral and sometimes in a concrete sense. In verse 100 of Sūra xxiii. the godless beg to be allowed to return to earth to accomplish the good they have left undone during their lives; but there is a barzakh in front of them barring the way. Zamakhsharī here explains the word by *ḥāʾil*, an obstacle, and interprets it in a moral sense: a prohibition by God. Other commentators take the word more in a physical sense; the barzakh is a barrier between hell and paradise or else the grave which lies between this life and the next. In the two other passages of the Ḳurʾān it is a question of two seas, or great stretches of water, one fresh, the other salt, between which there is a barzakh which prevents their being mixed. The same thing is mentioned in verse 61 of Sūra xxvii. and in this passage the word *ḥādjiz* or hindrance takes the place of barzakh. The commentators say that there is here an allusion to the fresh waters of the Shaṭṭ al-ʿArab which flow a great distance out into the salt sea without mixing with it; the impediment here is the effect of a law of nature established by God.

In eschatology, the word barzakh is used to describe the boundary of the world of human beings which consist of the heavens, the earth and the nether regions and its separation from the world of pure spirits and God. See the pictures representing this conception in the *Maʿrifatnāme* of Ibrāhīm Ḥaḳḳī (Būlāḳ 1251, 1255); cf. also Carra de Vaux, *Fragments d'eschatologie musulmane*.

According to ʿAbd al-Razzāḳ, the Ṣūfīs use this term in the sense of space between the material world and that of the pure spirits; hence several shades of meaning; cf. C. E. Wilson, in *The Masnavī*, book ii., vol. ii., note 20.

The same expression is also found in the philosophy known as "illuminating" (*al-ḥikma al-mashriḳīya*). It there denotes the dark substances, i.e. bodies: the barzakh or the body is dark by nature and only becomes light on receiving the light of the spirit. The celestial spheres are "animated" or "living" barzakh, inanimate bodies on the other hand are "dead" barzakh (cf. C. de Vaux, *La Philosophie illuminative d'après Suhrawardi Meqtoul*, in *JA*, Jan.-Febr. 1902). The term barzakh is sometimes rendered by Purgatory, in parallelism with the Christian representation of the Purgatory, but incorrectly. It is also used in the sense of limbo. See further Tahānawī, *Dict. of Technical Terms*, s.v.

BASMALA. The formula *bism*ⁱ *'llāh*ⁱ *'l-raḥmān*ⁱ *'l-raḥīm*ⁱ, usually translated "in the name of God, the merciful and compassionate", is called the *basmala* or *tasmiya*. The readers and jurists of Madīna, Baṣra and Syria, as Zamakhsharī tells us, do not consider it a verse at the beginning of the *fātiḥa* or other Sūras. They hold that it is only placed there to separate the Sūras and as a benediction. This is also the opinion of Abū Ḥanīfa and this is why those who follow him do not pronounce these words in a loud voice in prayer. On the other hand, the readers and jurists of Mecca and Kūfa consider the basmala a verse at the beginning of the *fātiḥa* and other Sūras and utter it with a loud voice. This is Shāfiʿī's opinion and is based on the fact that these words were written on the leaves in which the Ḳur'ānic texts were collected, while the word *āmīn* was not written.

The custom of beginning every important business by invoking the name of God is found everywhere. It is particularly noted that the ancient Arabs prefaced invitations to weddings with the words: *bi 'l-rifā' wa 'l-banīna*, or also: *bi 'l-yumn*; and Zamakhsharī supposes that in pagan times they said: "in the name of al-Lāt", or: "in the name of al-ʿUzzā". In Sūra xi. verse 41 of the Ḳur'ān we have an example of the basmala: "in the name of God", said Noah, "be its setting forth and casting anchor!"

The basmala has great virtues in the eyes of pious men and magicians; the latter use it in talismans; they believe that it was written on Adam's side, on Gabriel's wing, Salomon's seal and the tongue of Jesus (cf. Doutté, *Magie et Religion dans l'Afrique du Nord*, p. 211). This formula is a decorative *motif* much employed in manuscripts and architectural ornamentation.

BASṬ (A.), a technical term of the Ṣūfīs, explained as applying to a spiritual state (*ḥāl*) corresponding with the station (*maḳām*) of hope (*radjā'*): it is contrasted with *ḳabḍ* [q.v.]. The Ḳur'ānic authority generally quoted for these terms is: "And God contracts (*yaḳbiḍ*) and expands (*yabsuṭ*)" (ii. 245). As *basṭ* is a *ḥāl*, it bears no relation to personal mental or spiritual processes, but is a sense of joy and exaltation vouchsafed to the mystic by God. For this reason many Ṣūfīs accounted it to be inferior to *ḳabḍ*, on the ground that, until God is finally attained and the human individuality is lost in Him, any feeling other than that of desolation is inappropriate. The following saying of al-Djunaid illustrates this point: "The fear of God contracts me, and the hope for Him expands me... When He contracts me through fear, He causes me to pass away from self, but when He expands me through hope, He restores me to myself" (Ḳushairī, *Risāla*, p. 43). These lines of Ibn al-Fāriḍ (*al-Tā'iya al-kubrā*, ii. 646—7) summarise the Ṣūfī theory excellently: "in the mercy of expansion the whole of me is a wish whereby the hopes of all the world are expanded, and in the terror of contraction the whole of me is an awe and over whatsoever I let mine eye range, it reveres me" (tr. Nicholson, in *Studies in Islamic Mysticism*, p. 256). Hudjwīrī writes (tr. Nicholson, p. 374); "*Ḳabḍ* denotes the contraction of the heart in the state of being veiled, and *basṭ* denotes the expansion of the heart in the state of revelation". The mood of *basṭ* appears to be similar to that in which Pascal cries: "The world hath not known Thee, but I have known Thee. Joy! Joy! Joy! Tears of joy!"

BĀṬIL (A.), futile, vain. In the religious language of the Ḳur'ān and orthodoxy, it denotes the vain and unreal as opposed against *ḥaḳḳ* [q.v.]. in the sense of the real (cf. S. xxii, 62; xxxi, 30; xxxiv, 49; etc.); those who pursue ungodly aims are therefore called *mubṭilūna*. In the logical sense it means: false, wrong [cf. KHAṬA']; in the juridical sense: null and void, without legal effect, the lowest degree in the scale of legality in Muḥammadan law [cf. SHARĪʿA]. This scale is further developed in its details among the Ḥanafīs than among the other schools: the latter simply contrast *bāṭil* and *ṣaḥīḥ* (valid). The Ḥanafīs on the other hand distinguish according to the degree of legality among others: 1. *ṣaḥīḥ*, if both substance (*aṣl*) and attributes (*waṣf*) of the transaction are in keeping with the law (*mashrūʿ*); 2. *fāsid*, imperfect, if the *aṣl* is in keeping with the law but the *waṣf* is not; 3. *bāṭil*, if neither are in keeping with the law. In the former case the full legal effects take place, e.g. in a purchase the right of property (*milk*) arises; in the second case, according to the nature of the business, there is a restricted legal effect; e.g. in the case of a purchase a so-called "bad right of property" (*milk khabīth*) only arises when possession is taken (*ḳabḍ*), and the rescinding (*faskh*) of the agreement is possible until a further sale; an imperfect *muḍāraba* (something like joint partnership) works as a hire; in the third case there is no legal effect at all, the declarations made being regarded as ineffective (*laghw*). *Fāsid* thus is practically the same as voidable. In the field of obligations connected with worship (*ʿibādāt*), *fāsid* and *bāṭil* are synonymous with the Ḥanafīs too, as the legal obligation is not fulfilled in either case. The conception *fāsid* was originally brought into use for commercial law in order to prevent a series of further transactions being invalidated as the result of a single, perhaps slight deviation from the demands of the law. It is perhaps out of considerations of public interest that it was introduced also into the law of marriage. But even among the Ḥanafīs no strict distinction between the two conceptions was ever reached: there is no exact definition of *aṣl* and *waṣf*, and *bāṭil* and *fāsid* are frequently used without any recognisable distinction.

Bibliography: Bergsträsser, *Grundzüge des islamischen Rechts*, p. 32; Chafik Chehata, *Essai d'une théorie générale de l'obligation en droit musulman*, vol. i., p. 132 *sq.*; Hooper, *The Civil Law of Palestina and Trans-Jordan*, vol. ii., p. 140 *sq.*

BĀṬINĪYA, a name applied to a number of Muslim sects. As its derivation from *bāṭin*, "inner", indicates, the term means *those who seek the inner or spiritual meaning of the Ḳur'ān*, as against the exoteric or material meaning, and who adopt the method of allegorical interpretation called *ta'wīl* (see TAFSĪR). Sunnī writers use the name as a term of reproach for a variety of sects, several of which, such as the Khurramīya [q.v.], have probably no connection with the movements properly so-called, namely the Ḳarmaṭians [q.v.] and Ismāʿīlīya [q.v.]. The extremer Shīʿite groups which composed these movements differed in their allegiance, but generally agreed upon the principle of *ta'wīl* and the doctrine of "Prophetic" (*nāṭiḳ*) imāms, in whom the Divine Light is incarnated, and whose teaching is maintained in the intervals by "Silent" (*ṣāmit*) imāms, a doctrine introduced by Abu'l-Khaṭṭāb (executed 138/755), a discredited follower of the sixth shīʿite Imām, Djaʿfar aṣ-Ṣādiḳ [q.v.]. They were characteized also by secret propaganda, the details of which, owing to the multiplicity of the groups and the fact that they are known to us mostly from hostile Sunnī sources, are often obscure. In later times Bāṭinī doctrines were considerably influenced by philosophical speculations, which have been summarized by al-Shahrastānī (pp. 147—153). The epithet Bāṭinī was also applied at times to certain Ṣūfīs.

Bibliography: see the works cited under KARMAṬIANS and ISMĀʿĪLĪYA.

BEKTĀSHĪYA. Derwīsh order in Turkey. The patron of the order is Ḥādjdjī Bektāsh Walī, whose biography as given in the order's traditional writings, (the first version of which remounts to about the beginning of the XVᵗʰ century) is purely legendary, its purpose being manifestly to bring together the saint with famous religious personalities and to account for the later political importance of the Bektāshīya by insisting on the activity of its alleged founder. It is completely excluded that Bektāsh was ever in relation with ʿOthmān and Orkhān and that he was the founder of the Janissary corps (established for the first time under Murād I), as is maintained by the Bektāshī tradition and by some historical sources written under its influence.

We may take it, however, as sure that there appeared in the XIIᵗʰ century, among the Anatolian derwīshes, a certain Ḥādjdjī Bektāsh from Khurāsān. It remains uncertain whether he was a disciple of Bābā Isḥāḳ, whose rebellion took place in 1239, for the authority for this fact, though dated as early as 1353, issues from the aristocratic surroundings of the rival Mawlawīya order. It is not certain either whether the order originated from the circle of his disciples or whether it was linked only at a later time to the already legendary saint. For in the *Maḳālāt* of Ḥādjdjī Bektāsh, originally written in Arabic, and versified in Turkish in 1490 by Khaṭīb Oghlu and afterwards also rendered into Turkish prose, the characteristic secret doctrines and rites of the Bektāshīya are not particularly stressed. The order, whose immediate predecessors seem to have been the Abdalān-i Rūm, existed at least already in the beginning of the XVᵗʰ century; it was a century later that the grandmaster Bālim Sulṭān, the "second Pīr", gave it its definite form.

The Turkish derwīsh institutions had received their characteristic features in W. Turkestan from Aḥmad Yasawī (d. in 1166); they had acquired an ever increasing expansion in Anatolia, but at the same time they had adopted heretical tendencies. The Bektāshīya was able to conserve a good deal of pre-Islamic and hermetical elements. In those regions where the order absorbed Moslem as well as Christian sects it came to include a large part of the population, as for instance in Southern Anatolia and particularly in Albania, where there arose a kind of mixed religion, composed of Islamic and Christian elements. Also other communities with closely related dogmas and rites, and especially the groups comprised under the denomination of Kīzīlbash, stood in certain relations to it.

The attitude of the Bektāshī's towards Islām is marked both by the general features of popular mysticism, and by their farreaching disregard for Moslem cult duties, even including the *ṣalāt*. In their secret doctrines they are Shīʿites, acknowledging the twelve imāms and holding particularly Djaʿfar al-Ṣādiḳ in high esteem. The centre of their worship is ʿAlī; they unite ʿAlī with Allāh and Muḥammad into a trinity. From 1 till 10 Muḥarram they celebrate the mourning nights (*mātem gedjeleri*); also the other ʿAlid martyrs and especially the *maʿṣūm-i pāk* (those who have perished in an infantile age) are highly venerated by them. In the XVᵗʰ century the cabbalistic number speculations of the Ḥurūfī's spred among them, while the *Djāwīdān* of Faḍlullāh Ḥurūfī in its Persian redaction, and the Turkish version of this work, written by Ferishteoghlu under the title ʿAshḳnāma, have canonical authority with them. Furthermore they believe in the migration of souls.

The Christian elements may already partly have belonged to the Anatolian predecessors of the Bektāshīya; other parts were perhaps taken over from Christian groups who joined them later. On the occasion of the reception of new members there is a distribution of wine, bread and cheese, which is probably a survival of the Holy Communion as practised by the Artorytes. Moreover the Bektāshī's make a confession of sins before their spiritual chiefs, who grant them absolution. Women take part in their rites without veiling their faces. A narrower group vow themselves to celibacy, the celibates wearing earrings as a distinctive mark. It is not yet made clear whether celibacy existed already in the early times of the Bektāshīya or whether it was introduced for the first time by Bālim Sulṭān.

The Bektāshī's not seldom settled in famous places of pilgrimage, explaining the sanctity of the latter in conformity with their own traditions, for instance in Seiyid Ghāzī and in several places in Albania. The miracles described in the legends of their saints have often conserved shamanistic features.

The entire order was governed by the Čelebi, who resided in the mother-monastery (*pīr ewi*) at Ḥādjdjī Bektāsh, constructed over the saint's tomb (between Kīrshehir and Ḳaisarīye). This office used to pass in the XVIIIᵗʰ and XIXᵗʰ centuries from father to son; it was not, however, always hereditary. The celibates have their own grandmaster or *dede*. The head of one single monastery (*tekkiye*) is called *baba*; the fully initiated member *derwīsh*, the member who has only taken the first vow *muḥibb*, the not yet initiated adherent *ʿāshiḳ*. The discipline is chiefly governed by the relation of the *murshid* to his disciples and novices.

The Bektāshīya wear a white cap, consisting of four or twelve foldings. The number four symbolises the "four gates": *sharīʿa*, *ṭariḳa*, *maʿrifa*, *ḥaḳīḳa*, and the four corresponding classes of people: *ʿābid*, *zāhid*, *ʿārif*, *muḥibb*; the number twelve points to the number of the imām's. Particularly characteristic are further the twelve-fluted *taslīm tashi*, which is worn round the neck, and the *teber* (double-ax). Illustrations are to be found in the work of J. K. Birge (see bibliography).

The big *tekkiye's* comprise the following parts: *maidān ewi*, the proper monastery with the cult room; *ekmek ewi*, the bake-house and the women's quarters; *ash ewi*, the kitchen department; *mihmān ewi*; the guest house.

Among the many earlier settlements of the order the following are to be mentioned. In Rumelia: Dimetoka and Ḳalḳandelen; in Anatolia: ʿOthmāndjīḳ and Elmali in Lycia; near Cairo firstly at Ḳaṣr al-ʿAin and soon afterwards also on the Muḳaṭṭam slope (already as early as the XVᵗʰ century); further in Baghdād and at Kerbelāʾ.

The Bektāshī form of the derwīsh religion deeply influenced the pious attitude of the Turkish people. Next to the proper mystical writings of the order there florished also a rich and fervent lyric poetry of Bektāshī poets.

The order's political importance was due to its connection with the Janissaries; the latter had been from the beginning, in the same way as all other early political institutions of the Ottomans, under the influence of religious corporations. In the second half of the XVth century at the latest the Bektāshīya acquired exclusive authority amongst them. The receptivity of the Janissaries may be explained as well by their Christian origin. Their connection with this strictly organised order gave the Janissary corps the character of a close corporation. The Bektāshī's also took part in several derwīsh rebellions against the Ottoman power, e.g. the revolt of Ḳalender Oghlu (1526—1527). The annihilation of the Janissaries in 1826 by Maḥmūd II affected also the order to which they were linked; many monasteries were destroyed at the time. Towards the middle of the XIXth century began the renewal of the order and the rebuilding of the monasteries; the Bektāshīya experienced a revival which found ex pression in its literary activity at the end of the XIXth century and even after 1908.

In the autumn of 1925 the Bektāshīya, like all derwīsh-orders in Turkey, was dissolved; it was, however, precisely the Bektāshīya who had cleared the way for many measures inaugurated by the Turkish republic (relation to Islamic orthodoxy; position of women). To-day the Bektāshīya continue their existence in the Balkan peninsula, particularly in Albania where their chief monastery is in Tirana. On the Muḳaṭṭam near Cairo there is still in existence the famous Tekkiye of Kaighusuz Abdāl.

Bibliography: Pioneer works in critical research are the studies of G. Jacob and Köprülüzade Mehmed Fuad and his school. These writings and the remaining bibliography are mentioned in: John Kingsley Birge, *The Bektashi Order of Derwishes*, London and Hartford (Conn.) 1937. Further H. H. Schaeder in *OLZ* 31 (1928), 1038—1057; H. Jansky in *OLZ* 29 (1926), 553—559; F. Babinger, *Das Bektashikloster Demir Baba*, in *MSOS As.* XXXIV (1931); Else Kohn, *Vorislamisches in einigen vorderasiatischen Sekten und Derwischorden*, in *Ethn. Studien* i., 295—345, und *Kleine Beiträge zur Kenntnis islamischer Sekten und Orden auf der Balkanhalbinsel*, in *Mitteilungsb. der Ges. für Völkerkunde* 1931.

BIDʿA is the exact opposite of *sunna* [q. v.], and means some view, thing or mode of action the like of which has not formerly existed or been practised, an innovation or novelty. The word became important theologically in the revolt against the precise following of the *sunna* of the Prophet, and came thus to indicate all the unrest of new ideas and usages which grew up naturally in the Muslim church, covering dogmatic innovations not in accordance with the traditional sources (*uṣūl*) of the Faith, and ways of life different from those of the Prophet. The word, therefore, came to suggest individual dissent and independence, going to the point of heresy although not of actual unbelief (*kufr*).

In this development two broad parties showed themselves. One, conservative, in the past mostly Ḥanbalī and now practically Wahhābī only, taught that the duty of the believer was "following" (*ittibāʿ*) — the *sunna* understood — and not "innovating" (*ibtidāʿ*). The other accepted the facts of change of environment and condition, and taught, in varying degrees and ways, that there were good and even necessary innovations. According to al-Shāfiʿī, anything that is new and contradicts Ḳurʾān, *sunna*, Agreement or Traditions (*āthār*) is a bidʿa which leads astray. But a good novelty which does not so contradict is a praiseworthy bidʿa. A more elaborate classification divides innovations under the five rules (*aḥkām*) of canon law. Innovations which are also duties incumbent on the Muslim community (*farḍ kifāya*) are study of Arabic philology in order to understand the Ḳurʾān etc.; accepting and rejecting legal witnesses (*ʿādil*), distinguishing sound from corrupt traditions; codifying canon law (*fiḳh*); confuting heretics. Forbidden are all heretical systems (*madhāhib*) opposed to orthodox Islām. Recommended (*mandūb*) are such things as the founding of religious houses for devotees (*ribāṭāt*) and schools. Disliked (*makrūh*) is such as the decorating of mosques and Ḳurʾāns. Permitted (*mubāḥ*) is such as expenditure in eating, drinking etc.

Finally, the distinction between *bidʿa*, heresy, and *kufr*, unbelief, is said to lie on the origin of *bidʿa* being only a confusion (*shubha*) as to a sound proof, while that of *kufr* is obstinate opposition (*muʿānada*).

Bibliography: The classical history of the development is by Goldziher, in his *Muh. Studien*, ii. 22 *sqq.* See, too his *Vorlesungen über den Islam*, and Macdonald, *Development of Muslim Theology*, index s.v. *bidʿa* and *mubtadiʿ*.

BILĀL b. Rabāḥ, the first muʾadhdhin, a slave of Abyssinian origin, who belonged to a man of the tribe of Djumaḥ b. ʿAmr, was early attracted by Muḥammad's preaching and joined his little band of followers. For this he was persecuted by the Prophet's enemies, but remained steadfast in his belief in the one God, which induced Abū Bakr to purchase him and give him his freedom. He fled with Muḥammad to Madīna where he immediately found a welcome from Saʿd b. Khaithama. He afterwards lived in the house of Abū Bakr, where he like the other members of the household was attacked by the fever then raging in Madīna. According to Ibn Isḥāḳ, Muḥammad established a bond of brotherhood between him and the Khathʿamī Abū Ruwaiḥa, so that he — one of the five non-Arabs to whom grants were assigned by ʿUmar — appears in the lists of names along with Abū Ruwaiḥa; according to others this bond was made with ʿUbaida b. al-Ḥārith b. al-Muṭṭalib. When the Prophet after some hesitation introduced the call to prayer [see the article adhān] he appointed Bilāl his *muʾadhdhin*. He was also entrusted with the office of carrying the prayer-spear *ʿanaza* before the Prophet at public prayer on the great festivals. He accompanied Muḥammad on all his campaigns and is said to have had Umaiya b. Khalaf put to death at Badr in revenge for Umaiya's ill-treatment of him in the past. After the occupation of Mecca he had the triumph of calling to prayer from the roof of the Kaʿba. In several narratives he is mentioned as the man whose duty it was to look after the food supply on journeys and Abū Hadjar calls him the Prophet's steward (*khāzin*).

After the death of Muḥammad he was filled with a longing to take part in the holy war, which was granted him, not however, as one version has it, by Abū Bakr but only in the time of ʿUmar. He accompanied Abū ʿUbaida on the campaign into Syria and when ʿUmar visited the conquered land, he is said to have been once more asked to call to prayer, which he did amidst the sobs of all present. He died in 20 (641; according to others in 21 or 28 A.H.) about the age of 60, in Damascus and was buried there or in the adjacent Dārīyā (according to others in Aleppo). He is described as tall and thin with a stooping gait; his complexion was dark, his face thin and his thick hair strongly tinged with gray.

Bibliography: Ibn Hishām, p. 205, 345—347, 414, 448; Wāḳidī (transl. by Wellhausen), p. 401 etc.; Ṭabarī, i. 1326, 2525, 2594; Balādhurī, 11, 455; Ibn Saʿd, III/i., p. 165—170; Ibn Ḥadjar, *al-Iṣāba*, i. 336 *sq.*; Nawawī, p. 176—178; F. Buhl, *Das Leben Muhammeds*, p. 216.

BILḲĪS is the name among Muslims for the Queen of Sheba. The story, given in I Kings x. 1—10, 13, of how the Queen of Sheba (Saba) came to Solomon to prove him with hard questions, early gave rise to the formation of further legends.

In the Ḳurʾān, Sūra xxvii. 20—45, it is related that the heathen Queen of Sheba, who worshipped the sun, received a letter, borne by a hoopoe, from Solomon demanding that she should worship the true God. The Queen in terror sent presents to Solomon which were not well received. When she herself came to Solomon, the latter had her throne taken away by an ʿIfrīt to see if she would recognise it again. He afterwards led her to a room paved with glass. As Solomon expected — according to the commentators he wished to see if she really had goats' feet — she took the glittering floor for water and raised her garments. Finally she became converted.

The name Bilḳīs is not found in the Ḳurʾān. It has been variously explained: as the Greek παλλακίς, which would point to the story of the marriage of Solomon and the Queen of Sheba, which was widespread among the Jews at quite an early period, or as a corruption — quite comprehensible in the Arabic script — of Naukalis, as Josephus calls his Queen of Sheba, whom he regards as ruler of Egypt and Ethiopia. The later Muslim legend, the development of which is not yet quite clear, places Bilḳīs in the dynastic lists of Southern Arabia. The elaborate narrative given by Hammer-Purgstall in *Rosenöl* and G. Weil, *Biblische Legenden der Musulmänner*, p. 247 *sq.*, could only have attained its final form under Indian and Persian influences. The story appears elsewhere in different forms. The Persian extract from Ṭabarī (transl. by Zotenberg, i. 443 *sq.*) for example, contains a pretty tale of the birth of Bilḳīs, according to which she was the daughter of a Chinese king Abū Sharḥ and a Peri, while according to Zamakhsharī she belonged to the family of the Ḥimyarī Tubbaʿ, son of Shurāḥīl and lived in the palace of Maʾrib. At any rate it appears that the Muslims were long aware of the fact that she did not properly belong to Islām; we therefore have occasional polemics against individual portions of the story such as her supernatural origin.

In Christian Abyssinia the legend of the Queen of Sheba has become naturalised in a form which traces the descent of the ruling house from the marriage of Solomon and the Queen of Sheba who is here called Mākedā.

Bibliography: Grünbaum, *Neue Beiträge zur semitischen Sagenkunde*, p. 211—221; Salzberger, *Die Salomosage* (diss., 1907); for the Abyssinian Legend see Praetorius, *Fabula de regina Sabaea apud Aethiopes*; E. Littmann, *The Legend of the Queen of Sheba in the tradition of Axum* (*Bibliotheca Abessinica*, i.); J. Horovitz, *Koranische Untersuchungen*, p. 102; Jones and Monroe, *Histoire de l'Abyssinie*, French transl., Paris 1935, p. 31.

BIRGEWĪ or BIRGĪLĪ, Muḥammad b. PĪR ʿALĪ, a Turkish theologian, born in Bālikesrī 928/1522 received his earlier education in his native town and afterwards studied in Constantinople, where he attached himself to the Bairamīya order [q.v.]. After spending some time in Edirne, he wished to retire from public life but was appointed *mudarris* at the *madrasa* in Birge by ʿAṭāʾ Allāh Efendi. He worked here until his death in 981/1573. Numerous works and schoolbooks, mostly composed in Arabic, testify to his literary activity. The majority of these deal with theology in its widest sense, the art of reading the Ḳurʾān, dogmatics, homiletics, legal questions, e.g. on the conditions of *waḳf*-foundations, on which he had a controversy with this contemporary, the chief *muftī* Abu 'l-Suʿūd; others of his works deal with Arabic grammar. A list of these writings is given by Brockelmann, *GAL*², ii. 583 *sq.*, *Suppl.* ii., 654 *sq.* He is particularly known by his Turkish catechism, which is usually briefly known as *Risāla-i Birgewī*, also called the *Waṣīyat-nāma*, and has been repeatedly printed and translated. Cf. thereon Zenker, *Bibliotheca orientalis*, i., No. 1463 *sq.*; ii., No. 1192 *sq.*; *JA*, 1843, ii. 32, 55; 1859, i. 524; Dieterici, *Chrestomathie Ottomane*, p. 38 *sq.*; of the translations, the French one by Garcin de Tassy in his *L'Islamisme d'après le Coran* etc., 3rd ed. (1874), may be particularly mentioned here.

Bibliography: In addition to the works above mentioned: ʿAlī b. Bālī, *al-ʿIḳd al-manẓūm fī dhikr afāḍil al-Rūm*, p. 430 *sq.* (on the margin of edition of Ibn Khallikān of Cairo 1310).

AL-**BISṬĀMĪ**, ABŪ YAZĪD (BĀYAZĪD) ṬAIFŪR B. ʿĪSĀ B. SURŪSHĀN (not to be confused with the homonymous ascetic Abū Yazīd Ṭaifūr al-Bisṭāmī al-Aṣghar), a native of Bisṭām in the province of Ḳūmis, was one of the most celebrated Ṣūfīs of the iiird century A.H. His grandfather Surūshān, as the name indicates, was a Zoroastrian convert to Islām. Concerning the life of Bāyazīd hardly anything is known: the ancient biographers give few details, while the additional circumstances related by such writers as ʿAṭṭār belong, for the chief part if not entirely, to the domain of legend. Before embracing *taṣawwuf* he studied Ḥanafite law, the elements of which he taught to Abū ʿAlī al-Sindī, from whom in turn he received instruction in the highest truths of mysticism (*al-tawḥīd wa 'l-ḥaḳāʾiḳ*) and the theory of *fanāʾ*. Except for short periods, when the hostility of orthodox theologians forced him to go into exile, he passed his life at Bisṭām as a solitary recluse. Another century elapsed ere his followers, the Ṭaifūrīs, formed a school, which according to the account given in the *Kashf al-maḥdjūb* of Hudjwīrī (ed. Schukovski, p. 228, *penult. et sqq.* = transl. Nicholson, p. 184 *sqq.*) was opposed to that of Djunaid in preferring mystical "intoxication" (*sukr*) to mystical "sobriety" (*ṣaḥw*). Bāyazīd died in 260/874. His tomb in the centre of the town attracted many notable visitors, including Hudjwīrī, Nāṣir-i Khusraw and Yāḳūt; in 713/1313, a cupola was erected over it by order of the Mongol Sulṭān Ūldjāitū Muḥammad Khudābanda, whose spiritual director, Shaikh Sharaf al-Dīn, was, or claimed to be, a descendant of the saint (*Safarnāma*, transl. Schefer, p. 7, note 3).

Bāyazīd left no written work, and though fragments from early collections of his *shaṭaḥāt* (ecstatic utterances) have come down to us, the sayings ascribed to him in later compilations lack authenticity. He combined strict asceticism and reverence for the religious law with an extraordinary power of intellectual and imaginative speculation. A monistic tendency, perhaps exaggerated by ʿAṭṭār and other Persian mystics, is apparent even in the oldest sources available (e.g. *Lumaʿ*, p. 380—393) on which Massignon's brilliant analysis of his doctrine is based (*Essai sur les origines du lexique technique de la mystique musulmane*, p. 245—256). His attempt to reach absolute unity by a negative process of abstraction (*tadjrīd, fanāʾ bi 'l-tawḥīd*) is pursued relentlessly to a point where, having denuded himself of personality, like a snake which casts off its skin, he assumes divine attributes and cries *Subḥānī*, "Glory to Me! How great is My majesty!" etc. The following passages may be quoted in illustration. "If I could say sincerely, 'There is no god but Allāh', I should not care about anything after that" (*Ḥilyat al-awliyāʾ*, Leyden MS., ii. 220). "Twelve years I was the smith (*ḥaddād*) of my 'self' (*nafs*), and five years the mirror of my heart (*ḳalb*). Then, for a year, I considered between my 'self' and my heart; and lo, on my waist I saw an outward girdle (of infidelity). Twelve years I laboured to cut it; then I looked and saw a girdle within me. Five years I laboured, considering how I should cut it; and it was loosed. I looked on God's creatures and perceived them to be dead and pronounced four *takbīrs* over them" (Ḳushairī, *Risāla*, Cairo 1318, p. 57, l. 23 *sqq.*; cf. ʿAṭṭār, *Tadhkirat al-awliyāʾ*, i. 139, l. 5 *sqq.* and *JRAS*, 1906, p. 327 *sq.*). "As soon as I attained to oneness (*waḥdānīya*) I became a bird with a body of unity (*aḥadīya*) and wings of everlastingness; and I continued flying in the air of quality (*kaifīya*) for ten years, until I reached an atmosphere a hundred million times as large (as that of quality); and I flew on until I arrived in the field of eternity (*azalīya*), and there I saw the tree of unity". Then, after describing its soil, roots, branches, foliage and fruit, he said, "I looked, and I knew that all this was a cheat" (*Lumaʿ*, p. 384, l. 12 *sqq.*). The last words, I think, are no more than a recognition of the fact that every description of reality is deceptive. The view that they are a confession of failure and disillusionment (Massignon, *Essai*, p. 248) seems to me psychologically improbable; this would surely be a lame and impotent conclusion to the supreme mystical experience, which in Bāyazīd's case is depicted as a *miʿrādj* in imitation of the Prophet (see *Lumaʿ*, p. 382—387; *Islamica*, vol. 2, fasc. 3, p. 402 *sqq.*, a ivth century Arabic version ed. and transl. by R. A. Nicholson; and ʿAṭṭār, *Tadhkirat al-awliyāʾ*, i. 172—176). On the other hand, it is quite natural that Djunaid, who wrote a commentary on the *shaṭaḥāt*, should have criticised the imperfections of his predecessor (*Lumaʿ*, *loc. cit.*). While ʿAbd Allāh al-Anṣārī of Herāt (d. 481) reckons the *miʿrādj* as one of the many fictions which have been fathered on him (*Nafaḥāt al-uns*, ed. Nassau Lees, p. 63, l. 1 *sqq.*), in the later Persian Ṣūfī literature Bāyazīd, like Ḥallādj, typifies the pantheistic enthusiasm so congenial to the race. If we acquit him of conscious pantheism, there are grounds for believing that his countrymen have not altogether mistaken his character or misunderstood the drift of his doctrine.

Bibliography: This is given in the article and, fully, by Massignon, *Essai*, p. 243 *sqq.*

BOHORAS (from Gudjrātī *vohorvun*, to trade), the name of the Indian Ismāʿīlīs, belonging to the Mustaʿlian branch of the sect [see ISMĀʿĪLĪYA], originally converts from Hinduism. In Western India a small number of Hindu Bohoras is still found; there are also a few Sunnī Bohoras. The majority, Ismāʿīlī Bohoras, according to the latest Census figures exceed 200,000. They are almost exclusively traders, residents in towns; a number of them may be found practically in every town in India. Many of them live in East Africa, Mauritius, etc. The chief mass lives in Gudjrāt (Sūrāt, Aḥmadābād, Siddhpūr), in Karachī, Udjdjain, Burhānpūr, and especially Bombay, where their religious head, the High Priest or Mullā-djī Ṣāḥib, or Dāʿī Muṭlaḳ, resides. Their original caste sense and caste organisation is now replaced by the sense of religious unity. Instances of intermarriage with their Arab co-religionists from the Yaman (extremely rare, in fact) are not condemned.

As is known, Ḳarmaṭian and Ismāʿīlī propaganda gained great numbers of followers in Sindh, and generally Western India, long before the triumph of the Fāṭimids in Northern Africa. By the time of al-Muʿizz their community in Sindh was quite large. The Bohora tradition, however, preserves no memory of this early period, and their story begins with certain missionaries Aḥmad, ʿAbd Allāh, etc., whose tombs are still revered in Cambay. Most probably their activities belong to the end of the vth (xith) century, when they preached in favour of the Mustaʿlian school, to which the community belongs.

The sect apparently was not molested by the local Hindu rādjās, and attained considerable importance by the time of the Muslim conquest of Gudjrāt, when towards the end of the xvith century the Gudjrātī community completely eclipsed the original community in the Yaman. This circumstance forced their religious heads, the *dāʿīs*, to transfer their residence to India. It may be noted that after the assassination of the Fāṭimid caliph al-Āmir in 524/1131, his alleged infant successor Ṭaiyib soon became "concealed". The religious authority became entrusted to the successive *dāʿīs*, the first being Dhuʾaib b. Mūsā. This supreme authority was handed by each *dāʿī* to his successor, until in 999/1591, on the death of the 26th *dāʿī*, Dāwūd b. ʿAdjab Shāh, the community split apart: the Indians supported Dāwūd b. Ḳuṭb Shāh (therefore becoming known as *Dāwūdīs*), while the majority of the Yamanites (*Sulaimānīs*) sided with Sulaimān b. Ḥasan. Both parties still exist in India and the Yaman. The Sulaimānīs are in majority in the Yaman, but in India form only an insignificant minority.

In the long evolution of the sect there were many instances of splits, and occasional conversion to Sunnism, as in the case of the Djaʿfarīs (first half of the xvth century, under the Muslim kings of Gudjrāt). There are still to be found a few real subsects, numerically quite insignificant, such as the ʿAliyās (who seceded in 1624); Nāgūshīs, i.e. vegetarians, of Baroda (since 1789); Hibatīs, or Hiptīyās of Udjdjain (end of the xviiith c.); Mahdībāgh-wāllās of Nagpur (since 1897), etc.

A new split is in process of formation amongst the Dāwūdīs at present, dividing them into the "pro-Mullā-djī" and "anti-Mullā-djī" parties. The former party may be described as conservatives, including a great proportion of persons who adopt a rather indifferent attitude. The other party may be called progressists in so far as they insist on various concessions to the modern spirit in the domain of education, style of life, etc. It may be noted that no religious or dogmatic questions are involved, except the question of the succession of the *dāʿīs*. The opponents of the Mullā-djī take the succession of the 47th Dāwūdī *dāʿī*, Nadjm al-Dīn, in 1840, as irregular, and declare him, and all his successors, as not true *dāʿīs*. They demand strict control of communal funds, changes in the policy of education, etc. So far the modernists have not brought the matter to an open secession, but their movement is remarkably popular, and many of those who in appearance remain loyal to the Mullādjī in reality assist the opponents, and finance the incessant litigation. The chief weapon of the High Priest, excommunication, formerly so much dreaded, is considerably blunted now, with the general decay of the survivals of the caste spirit and organisation amongst Indian Muslims.

The Bohoras are organised on strictly theocratical lines, and everything that is not controlled by the general laws of the Indian Government, or custom, is regulated by the authority of the Mullā-djī, and his accredited representatives, *ʿāmils*. Their functions are not only those connected with religious ceremonies, but also those of the justice of peace, of the collection of the fees, donations, etc.

The history of the community in India is not yet written, and there are apparently only very inadequate materials for this. For a list of the names of the *dāʿīs* in both the Sulaimānī and the Dāwūdī branches see A. A. A. Fyzee, *A Chronological List of the Imams and Daʿis of the Mustaʿlian Ismailis* (*JBBRAS*, 1934, p. 8—16). For the religious doctrine of the sect see the art. ISMAʿĪLĪYA. A general review of their literature is given in W. Ivanow, *A Guide to Ismaili Literature* (London 1933).

The Sulaimānīs do not differ from the Dāwūdīs except in recognising a different line of the *dāʿīs* after the 26th *dāʿī*. Up till recently their *dāʿīs* resided in the Yaman, and were all Arabs. But since the end of 1936, following the death of the 45th *dāʿī*, ʿAlī b. Muḥsin, his Indian successor, Ghulām Ḥusain, has remained in Bombay.

Bibliography: In addition to the works referred to above, and mentioned in the article ISMAʿĪLĪYA, see also the *Gazetteer of the Bombay Presidency*, vol. ix., part ii., p. 24 *sq.*; also D. Menant, *Les Bohoras du Guzarate* (*RMM*, x., p. 465 *sq.*); H. F. Hamdani, *The history of the Ismāʿīlī Daʿwat and its literature* etc., in *JRAS*, 1932, p. 126 *sqq.*; do., *Some unknown Ismāʿīlī authors*, in *JRAS*, 1933, p. 359 *sqq.*

AL-**BUKHĀRĪ**, MUḤAMMAD B. ISMĀʿĪL ABŪ ʿABD ALLĀH AL-DJUʿFĪ, Arab traditionist, born 13th Shawwāl 194/21st July 810 at Būkhārā, the grandson of a Persian, named Bardīzbah. He began the study of the Traditions at the early age of eleven and in his sixteenth year made the pilgrimage and attended the lectures of the most famous teachers of Tradition in Mecca and Madīna. He then went to Egypt in search of Tradition and continued it for the next sixteen years, of which five were spent in Baṣra, in wandering through all Asia. He then returned to his native town where he died on the 30th Ramaḍān 256/31st August 870; he is buried in Khartanak, two parasangs from Samarḳand. His collection on Tradition *al-Djāmiʿ al-ṣaḥīḥ* established his reputation. After his return to Bukhārā he began to sift the enormous material brought together in his travels; only a very small part of it he dared to use as authentic teaching of the Prophet. His work is divided according to the chapters of the *fiḳh*, for which he had planned a complete scheme, although he did not succeed in preparing the necessary material of Tradition for all chapters. In his selection of *ḥadīths* he showed the greatest critical ability and in editing the texts sought to obtain the most scrupulous accuracy. Yet he does not hesitate to explain the material by brief notes, quite distinct from the text. The transmission of the *Ṣaḥīḥ* texts was from the beginning most carefully done but it was impossible wholly to prevent the appearance of variants, which are given us by the commentaries. The Vulgate at present in use was edited by ʿAlī b. Muḥammad al-Yūnīnī (died 701/1302) with the help of the famous philologist Ibn Mālik (died 672/1273). The only complete translation is *El Bokhari, Les traditions islamiques*, transl. of the Arabic text with notes and index by O. Houdas and W. Marcais, (4 vols., Paris 1903). Of the numerous commentaries on the *Ṣaḥīḥ* the most renowned is *Irshād al-sārī fī sharḥ al-Bukhārī* by Aḥmad b. Muḥammad b. Abī Bakr al-Ḳasṭallānī (died 923/1517), together with the *Tuḥfat al-bārīʾ* of Zakarīyā al-Anṣārī (died 926/1520). In later times al-Bukhārī's *Ṣaḥīḥ* gained the reputation of a sacred book, little inferior to the Ḳurʾān. As a preliminary to his *Ṣaḥīḥ*, Bukhārī had prepared, on his first pilgrimage in Madīna, a work on the lives of the transmitters entitled *al-Taʾrīkh al-kabīr*. Besides some smaller works there is also ascribed to him a *Tanwīr al-ʿainain bi-rafʿ al-yadain fi ʾl-ṣalāt*, Calcutta 1256 (with Urdu translation), identical with *Ḳurrat al-ʿainain* on the edge of the *Khair al-kalām fi ʾl-ḳirāʾa khalf al-imām*, Cairo 1320, also ascribed to him.

Bibliography: Goldziher, *Muhammedanische Studien*, p. 234—245; Brockelmann, *GAL*², i. 163—166; *Suppl.*, i. 260—5.

BURĀḲ. This name, which is connected with *barḳ*, "lightning" (on its etymology cf. Horn, *Grundriss der neupersischen Etym.*, Strassburg 1893, p. 36 *sq.*) is applied by tradition to the fabulous animal which the Prophet mounted on the night of his ascension (*miʿrādj*, q.v.). Allusion is made in the Ḳurʾān (Sūra xvii. 1, 60; liii. 1—18) to a vision which the Prophet had in which he seemed to be borne from Mecca to Jerusalem and thence to heaven. The animal which carried him is neither described nor mentioned by name in the Ḳurʾān; but the commentators say that on this night Muḥammad was in the *ḥidjr* of the Holy House, that is, in the precincts of the Kaʿba, and that the Archangel Gabriel brought Burāḳ to him.

This legend has been considerably embellished and has become a favourite motif with poets and miniaturists. There are long descriptions of Burāḳ, who is represented as a mare with a woman's head and peacock's tail. For its representation in pictorial art see T. W. Arnold, *Painting in Islam* (Oxford 1928), pp. 117—122 and plates liii—lvi. Burāḳ was also used by Ibrāhīm on the visits he paid to his son Ismāʿīl, banished to Mecca (cf. Ṭabarī, *Persian Chronicle*, transl. Zotenberg, i. 165). In the mosque al-Ṣakhra in Jerusalem a stone of a quaint shape is shown to the pilgrims as being the saddle of Burāḳ; cf. Gerardy-Saintine, *Trois ans en Judée*, Paris 1860. The "stable of Burāḳ" (near the S.W. wall of the *ḥaram*) played a considerable part in the controversies between Jews and Muslims in Palestina.

Biliography: Thorning, *Beiträge z. Kenntnis d. isl. Vereinswesens* (Berlin 1913), p. 25, note 2; Blochet, in *RHR*, XL. 203 *sqq.*, Arnold, *loc. cit.*; see also the article MIʿRĀDJ.

C

ČISHTĪ, MUʿĪN AL-DĪN MUḤAMMAD, founder of a Ṣūfī brotherhood [cf. ČISHTĪYA], widely disseminated throughout India and one of the greatest of the saints of India, as the name Aftāb-i Mulk-i Hind (sun of the kingdom of Hind), which is given him, shows. Muʿīn al-Dīn belonged to Sīstān and was born in 537/1142; when he was fifteen years of age, his father Ghiyāth al-Dīn Ḥasan died; he then lived in various towns in Khurāsān and finally came to Baghdād. During this period he made the acquaintance of the most famous Ṣūfis of the time, including Nadjm al-Dīn Kubrā, Shihāb al-Dīn al-Suhrawardī, and Awḥad al-Dīn Kirmānī. In 589/1193 he came to Dihlī, but almost immediately moved to Adjmīr where he died in 633/1236; his tomb there became a very popular place of pilgrimage; the great Emperor Akbar made a pilgrimage to it on foot. A splendid mausoleum (*dargāh*) was erected which is much visited to this day.

He is not, however, the only Indian saint, who bears the name Čishtī; we need only mention Salīm Čishtī, the contemporary of Akbar, whose *dargāh* at Fatḥpūr Sikri is likewise held in great reverence. Other individuals who bore the *nisba* Čishtī are cited under their names.

Bibliography: Abu 'l-Fazl, *Akbar-nāma*, ed. Calcutta, ii. 154 *sq.*; *Āʾīn-i Akbarī*, transl. Jarrett, iii. 361; *Taʾrīkh-i Firishta*, ii. 711 *sq.*

ČISHTĪYA, Indian Order or Caste of faḳīrs, founded according to some by one Abū Isḥāḳ, descended in the ninth generation from ʿAlī, who migrating from Asia Minor, settled at Čisht, a village of Khurāsān, or, in another account, settled in Syria and was buried at Acre; according to others by Banda Nawāz, who is buried at Kalbarga; according to others by Khwādjā Aḥmad Abdāl of Čisht (d. 355/965—6) brought to India by Muʿīn al-Dīn Čishtī [q.v.]. His *khalīfa* was Khwādjā Ḳuṭb al-Dīn Bakhtiyār Kākī (d. 633/1235—6), buried near the Ḳuṭb Manār in Dehli, and his *khalīfa* Bābā Barīd Shakargandj (d. 668/1268—9), whose shrine is at Pak Pattan in Montgomery (Pandjāb). "The descendants of his relations and children, whether carnal or spiritual, have developed into a caste which is found in the lower Satluj and chiefly in the Montgomery district" (Ibbetson, *Panjab Castes*, 1916, p. 224).

Bābā Farīd had two disciples, ʿAlī Aḥmad Ṣābir, whose shrine is at Piran Kaliar near Rurki, and whose followers are known as Ṣābir Čishtī; the other Niẓām al-Dīn Awliyāʾ (636—725/1238—1324), whose followers are called Niẓāmī. His tomb at Dehli is described in the Urdu work *Āthār Dehli* (Dehli 1911).

The ancestors of the Montgomery Čishtīs are supposed to have come from Kābul to Lahore in the thirteenth century, and then to have moved to Montgomery; they were till lately nomad and claimed Ḳurashī origin. They intermarry with Radjput women. Ibbetson quotes a saying (of which he does not know the origin); "you can tell a Čishti by his squint eye".

Practices of the Order. They lay special stress on the words *illa 'llāhᵘ*, use vocal music in their religious services, and wear coloured clothes, dyed with ochre or the bark of the acacia tree. The *murīd* (neophyte) after a prayer of two *rakʿas* is given certain instructions, e.g. that he should observe the sense of the word *faḳīr*, *fāḳa* (poverty), *ḳanāʿa* (content), *yād Allāh* (mention of Allāh), *riyāḍa* (austerity). Presently some *ism* (divine name) is disclosed to him, and he is told to go to a shrine and there fast forty days, called *čilla kashi*; finally the spiritual pedigree of the order is communicated to him; after this he should see visions.

Drugs such as *bang*, *čaras*, tobacco, and liquors are strictly forbidden.

History of the Order. According to Crooke (iv. 302; see below), it produced a personage of importance and fresh founder in the Shaikh Salīm, by whose intercession a son of the same name was born to the emperor Akbar; but the *Akbar nāma* (transl. Beveridge, ii. 502). which dilates on this event, does not call this Shaikh Čishtī, nor does its author mention him in his list of Čishtī saints (*Āʾīn-i Akbarī*, transl. Jarrett, iii. 361). It at one time displayed great vitality in Bahawalpur (N. Radjputana), where a village Čishtian was founded by descendants of Tādj al-Dīn Čishtī, grandson of Shakar-gandj. After the movement had become moribund it was revived by Khwādjā Nūr Muḥammad. Ḳibla-i ʿĀlam, a Punwar Radjput of the Karral tribe. Five suborders are enumerated: Zaidī (named after Khwādjā ʿAbd al-Aḥad b. Zaid), Iyāḍī (after Khwādjā Fuḍail b. Iyāḍ), Adhamī (after Ibrāhīm b. Adham), Hubairī and Čishtī (simply).

Literature of the Order. They are said to have a number of songs (*ḳāfiya*), which are considered "the food of the soul". Their chief poets are said to be Budha Shāh, Ghulām Shāh and Khwādjā Ghulām Farīd.

A list of their shrines is given in *Glossary of the Tribes and Castes of the Panjab and N. W. Frontier Province*, Lahore 1919, i. 530, 531; an important Ṣābirī shrine is at Thaska Mirandj, in Karnal district, founded 1131/1718—9 by Nawwāb Roshan al-Dawla, minister of Muḥammad Shāh. A list of their saints is given *ibid.*, i. 531—538. A distribution table of their communities is given by Crooke, *Tribes and Castes of N. W. Provinces and Oudh.*, iv. 302. From these works the information given above is mainly derived.

Lists of Čishtī saints are to be found in the works *Siyar al-awliyāʾ* by Muḥammad Mubārak Kirmānī, and *Khazīnat al-aṣfiyāʾ* by Muftī Ghulām Sarwar Lāhorī.

D

AL-**DADJDJĀL** or AL-MASĪḤ AL-DADJDJĀL (rarely *al-Kadhdhāb*: Bukhārī, *Fitan*, bāb 26 and *Masīḥ al-ḍalāla*: Ṭayālisī, No. 2532), the Muslim Antichrist. The word is not found in the Ḳur'ān; it is probably an Aramaic loan-word. In Syriac it is found as an epithet of the Antichrist, e.g. in Matthew xxiv. 24 where the Peshitta translates ψευδόχριστον by *meshīḥē daggālē*. We also find in Syriac *nebīyā daggālā* "pseudo-prophet", *shāhedā daggālā* "false witness" etc. On the other hand, the existence in Arabic of the verb *dadjala* with the meaning "to deceive", given in the lexicons without further references, seems to be doubtful: this verb is not found in the Ḳur'ān nor in Tradition.

As M. Bousset has shown, the figure of the Antichrist in early Christian literature is made up of several elements: the principal — and this also applies to the Muslim conceptions — are the following: *a.* that of Satan as the eschatological enemy of God; b. that of the eschatological king who will reunite the peoples against Israel; *c.* that of the antagonist of Christ, the tempter, who is followed mainly by the Jews; *d.* that of the tyrant belonging to the tribe of Dan who will found a kingdom in Jerusalem, where he and his forces will be destroyed by Christ.

These features occur again, often corrupted, in canonical Tradition: *a.* the connection between al-Dadjdjāl and Satan, or rather their identity, is found in a well-known tradition: the Muslim armies, about to divide the booty of Constantinople, retire in haste warned by a false alarm raised by Satan suggesting to them that al-Djadjdjāl has attacked their families in their absence. When they reach Syria the "enemy of God" appears, but faced with Christ he disappears like salt in water (Muslim, *Fitan*, trad. 34; Ibn Mādja, *Fitan*, trad. 33). — In the second place the connection between the Antichrist and Satan is apparent in the description of al-Dadjdjāl's appearance.

He is reddish (Bukhārī, *Ru'yā*, bāb 33) with frizzy hair (Bukhārī, *Libās*, bāb 68), corpulent (Bukhārī, *Libās*, bāb 33), he has a wide throat (Ṭayālisī, No. 2532), he is one-eyed (Bukhārī, *Anbiyā'*, bāb 3; *Ru'yā*, bāb 11). His one eye in his broad forehead (Ṭayālisī, No. 2532) is like a floating grape (Bukhārī, *Maghāzī*, bāb 77). On his forehead is written *kāfir* ("unbeliever": Bukhārī, *Ḥadjdj*, bāb 30; *Anbiyā'*, bāb 8). Or else one of his eyes is as if made of green glass (Ṭayālisī, No. 544), in the other is a hard nail (Ṭayālisī, No. 1106). His relations also are described as monsters (Ṭayālisī, No. 865).

b. Al-Dadjdjāl is also an eschatological type appended to the *malāḥim* (Ibn Mādja, *Fitan*, bāb 35) who, like the eschatological tyrant of the Old Testament, will come from a remote region, not the north, but from some region in the east (Ibn Mādja, *Fitan*, bāb 33), from Khurāsān (Ibn Ḥanbal, i. 4, 7) or (Iṣbahān (Ibn Ḥanbal, iii. 224; 75), — Times of great hardship will precede his appearance (Ibn Ḥanbal, vi. 125, 453 *sqq.*) which is the subject of detailed descripti ns (Muslim, *Fitan*, trad. 110 which also deal with his connection with Yādjūdj and Mādjūdj, the eschatological peoples of the north in the Old Testament, trad. 111—117; Abū Dāwūd, *Malāḥim*, bāb 14; Tirmidhī, *Fitan*, bāb 57—59 etc.).

c. He is the great tempter, which is explained by his resemblance to Christ (Antichristos in the sense of counterpart of Christ; cf. the fact that he rides an ass — a Messianic feature [Ibn Ḥanbal, iii. 367] and that his eyes sleep but not his heart — a prophetic feature [Ṭayālisī, No. 856]). His followers will be unbelievers and *munāfiḳ* (q.v.; Ibn Ḥanbal, iii. 238), women (*ibid.*, ii. 67) and Jews (Muslim, *Fitan*, trad. 124; Ibn Mādja, *Fitan*, bāb 33; Ibn Ḥanbal, iii. 224, 292; vi. 75). Every prophet has warned his community against this tempter (Bukhārī, *Tawḥīd*, bāb 17; Abū Dāwūd, *Malāḥim*, bāb 14; Ibn Ḥanbal, i. 195; ii. 135; iii. 79, 103, 173, etc.). Like the Gospel (Matthew, xxiv. 24; Mark, xiii. 22), Ḥadīth emphasises the large number of pseudo-messiahs (Bukhārī, *Fitan*, bāb 25; Muslim, *Fitan*, trad. 83—85).

d. He will appear bringing supplies of food, water and fire (Muslim, *Fitan*, trad. 106—108; Ibn Mādja, *Fitan*, trad. 33 etc.) conquering the earth, except Mecca and Madīna, and will perish in Syria and Palestine at the hands of Christ or the Mahdī (q.v.; Muslim, *Ḥadjdj*, trad. 486; Ibn Mādja, *Fitan*, bāb 33; Ibn Ḥanbal, ii. 397—398, 407—408 etc.) after having exercised power for 40 days or 40 years (Abū Dāwūd, *Malāḥim*, bāb 14; Ibn Mādja, *Fitan*, bāb 33; Ibn Ḥanbal, ii. 166; iv. 181 etc.).

According to later legend, he dwells in one of the islands of the empire of the Mahārādj or the Zābadj (Java). The sailors of Sīrāf and of ʿUmān say that, in passing near this island, beautiful music is heard, produced on the lute, the oboe, the tambourine and other instruments, accompanied by dancing and the clapping of hands. This story is widely diffused; it is found in Ibn Khurradādhbih, al-Bīrūnī, Ḳazwīnī, Dimishḳī, Djurdjānī, Ibn Iyās, Masʿūdī (*Murūdj*, i. 343 and *al-Tanbīh*, p. 62), the *ʿAdjā'ib al-Hind*, etc. It appears also in the story of Sindbād the Sailor. Ibn Khurradādhbih (p. 68 [transl. p. 48]) calls this island Braṭā'īl; the *Abrégé des Merveilles* (p. 38 and 57) gives it the same name and adds that cloves are brought there; commerce is carried on without the inhabitants being seen; they place their goods on the shore and the merchants take what they want, leaving an equivalent for them. According to the same work (p. 150), the Dadjdjāl is tied to a rock in an island in the sea and demons bring him his food. He is said to have been visited by Tamīm al-Dārī, a contemporary of the Prophet (cf. Masʿūdī, *Murūdj*, iv. 28).

Bibliography: The statements in Tradition, especially the story of Tamīm al-Dārī regarding al-Dadjdjāl as a demon of the sea, are cited in Wensinck, *Handbook*, s.v. Dadjdjāl. See also Ṭabarī, Persian synopsis ed. Zotenberg, i., 67 *sq.* For the story of the meeting of Muḥammad with the alleged Dadjdjāl Ibn Ṣayād (Ṣā'id), see Wensinck, *Handbook*, s.v.; D. A. Attema, *De Mohammedaansche opvattingen omtrent het tijdstip van den jongsten dag*, Amsterdam, 1942.

DAHRĪYA (A.), a name applied with reference to Ḳur'ān xlv. 24 (where it is said of the unbelievers: And they say: "There is no other than our present life; we die and we live and nothing but the course of time [*al-dahr*] destroyeth us") to those people who, not content with repudiating the belief in one God, the creation of the world by Him and His Providence, and denying the postulates of any positive religion (divine laws, a future life, retribution), teach the eternity of time and of matter and ascribe all that happens in the world merely to the operation of natural laws (or the movement of the spheres). As the most characteristic principle of their teaching on which all the others depend, stress is laid on their doctrine that time is without beginning (*Mafātīḥ al-ʿulūm*, ed. van Vloten, p. 35 penult., 40, $_{1}$). It would be difficult to give a satisfactory translation of the term *dahrīya* in the sense in which it is used in Islāmic literature, for (as is also the case with the application of the term *zindīḳ*; q.v.) its connotation is not rigidly defined and it is easier to define it in negative than in positive terms. Discrepancies are by no means absent in theological literature as regards the details of their teaching. S̲h̲ahrastānī in one passage (p. 201 l. 7) says of them that they deny the existence of intelligible entities (*maʿḳūlāt*) and only allow those which can be perceived by the senses (*maḥsūsāt*) and in another he contradicts this by saying that they also allow *intelligibilia* (p. 202, l. 13). We even find a definition of the Dahrīya according to which they grant the existence of God but explain the origin of the world from the random concurrence of atoms whirling about in space: Atomists (D̲j̲amāl al-Dīn al-Ḳazwīnī, *Mufīd al-ʿulūm wa-mubīd al-humūm* [Cairo 1310], p. 37). One comes nearest the meaning of the name Dahrīya by translating it Materialists or Naturalists; the meaning Fatalists, formerly much in vogue, is quite wide of the mark. — The oldest definition of the meaning of *dahrīya*, which we have in the main followed above, is to be found in D̲j̲āḥiẓ's *Kitāb al-ḥayawān* (Cairo 1325, vii. 5) where (with reference to Sūra xlv. 23: "he who taketh his desires for his God") they are credited with a hedonistic view of life in addition to Atheism and Naturalism using the terms in their most general sense: "he (the *dahrī*) knows no distinction between man and beast, only what stands in the way of his desires is evil in his sight; everything with him turns upon the question of pleasure and pain; that alone is right which is to his advantage, though it should cost a thousand men their lives". It follows from their general doctrines that they deny popular superstitions and scoff at the existence of demons and angels, the interpretation of dreams and the efficacy of magic (D̲j̲āḥiẓ, *ibid.*, ii. 50, $_{4}$ *sq.*); on the other hand many of them are said to grant the possibility of the metamorphosis of men into animals (*mask̲h̲*) on rationalistic grounds (*ibid.*, iv. 24, $_{5}$ *sq.*). As do the *mutakallimūn* generally, the Jewish Arabic theologian Sāʿadyah (died 942) also repeatedly combats the *dahrīya*; first in the introduction to his commentary on the *Sēfer Jeṣīrah* (ed. Lambert, Paris 1891), afterwards in the first book of his *Kitāb al-amānāt wa 'l-iʿtiḳādāt* (ed. Landauer, Leyden 1880, p. 63—65) in connection with his refutation of those who deny the origin of the world within time, and in the latter place he devotes particular attention to contradicting their limitation of the perceptible to that which is perceptible by the senses. In his translation of Job, he refers characteristically xxii. 15 to the Dahrīya and translates the *ōrach ʿōlām* of the text by *mad̲h̲āhib al-dahrīyīn*; cf. also several passages in his commentary on Proverbs (B. Heller, in *REJ*, xxxvii. 229).

The origin of the Dahrīya is traced to the Greek schools of philosophy; they are distinguished by G̲h̲azzālī (*al-Munḳid̲h̲ min al-ḍalāl*, Cairo 1309, composite vol., No. 8) from the *ṭabīʿīyūn* (φυσικοί) who while granting the existence of a creating and controlling Deity, deny the substantiality of the soul and in consequence its immortality, and from the *ilāhīyūn* (θεολόγοι, Socrates, Plato, Aristotle). — With the penetration of European natural science and Darwinism among oriental scholars (translation of Büchner's *Kraft und Stoff* into Arabic by S̲h̲iblī S̲h̲umail al-Lubnānī, Alexandria 1884, and the pamphlet *al-Ḥaḳīḳa*, by the latter, Cairo n.d.) the principles of the materialist philosophy and the Indian school of Naturism were identified with those of the *dahrīya* and combatted by the Afg̲h̲ān scholar and agitator D̲j̲amāl al-Dīn al-Afg̲h̲ānī [q.v.] in a pamphlet, which originally appeared in Persian (Bombay 1298, lith.), was afterwards translated into Urdu (Calcutta 1883) and into Arabic (by Muḥammad ʿAbduh) and in the latter form was printed first in Bairūt (1303) and again in a new edition at Cairo (1312) under the title *Risālat fī ibṭāl madhhab al-dahrīyīn wa-bayān mafāsidihim wa-it̲h̲bāt anna 'l-dīn asās al-madanīya wa'l-kufr fasād al-ʿumrān* and has been widely disseminated in Muslim circles. To this literature also belongs *al-Durra al-sanīya fī 'l-radd ʿala 'l-māddīya wa-it̲h̲bāt al-nawāmīs al-s̲h̲arʿīya bi 'l-adillat al-ʿaḳlīya* by ʿAbd Allāh ʿAlā al-Dīn al-Bag̲h̲dādī al-Dihlawī (Cairo 1313). It is clear then that in this connection *māddīya* (materialists) and ***dahrīya*** are used as synonymous. Philologists allow that the latter word may also be pronounced *duhrīya* according to a vowel change common in *nisbas* (Sībawaihi, ed. Derenbourg, ii. 64, $_{19-21}$).

Bibliography: *Rasāʾil Ik̲h̲wān al-ṣafā* (Bombay 1306), iii. 39; D̲j̲āḥiẓ, *loc. cit.*; Sāʿadyah, *loc. cit.*; S̲h̲ahrastānī, *loc. cit.*; *Dictionary of Technical Terms* etc. (*Bibl. Ind.*), s.v., p. 480; Ed. Pococke, *Notae miscellaneae philolog. Bibl.*, p. 251 (Leipzig 1705, p. 239); cf. W. L. Schramaier, *Über den Fatalismus der vorislamischen Araber* (Bonn 1881), p. 12—22; M. Horten, *Die philosophischen Systeme der spekulativen Theologen im Islam* (Bonn 1912), Index, s.v. Dahriten.

DĀʿĪ, literally "he who summons [sc. men to the good or to the Faith]", the nomen agentis of the verb *daʿā*, which is frequently used in the Ḳurʾān in such contexts. This term acquired a special significance in those S̲h̲īʿite sects which were engaged in secret propaganda, particularly the ʿAbbāsid mission during the latter years of the Umayyad Caliphate, and the Ismāʿīlīs, Ḳarmatians and Drūzes later on (see these articles); it was the name given to their missionaries, and more especially to the organizers of the mission in distant regions, such as Abū ʿAbd Allāh, the founder of the Fāṭimid empire in the Mag̲h̲rib. Under the Fāṭimid Caliphate the missionary organization became one of the principal departments of state, headed by the Chief Dāʿī (*Dāʿī al-duʿāt*), who ranked next after the wazīr and the Chief Ḳāḍī. In later times, his office and that of the Chief Ḳāḍī were frequently combined. In the system of the Drūzes, the *dāʿī* is the principal officer of the lower order of ministers.

Bibliography: See the articles cited above.

DĀR AL-ḤARB. In Muslim constitutional law the world is divided into *dār al-ḥarb* and *dār al-Islām*. "Abode of Islām" is that which is already under Muslim rule; "Abode of War" is that which is not, but which, actually or potentially, is a seat of war for Muslims until by conquest it is turned into "Abode of Islām". For an anomalous and disputed exception, see DĀR AL-ṢULḤ. Thus to turn *dār al-ḥarb* into *dār al-Islām* is the object of *dji̱hād* [q.v.], and, theoretically, the Muslim state is in a constant state of warfare with the non-Muslim world. But practically that is now impossible. The rulers of Islām are not in a position to keep up a constant warfare *contra mundum*. To meet this situation the early and logical position has had to yield. Land once Abode of Islām does not become Abode of War, except on three conditions: (i.) that the legal decisions of unbelievers are regarded and those of Islām are not; (ii.) that the country immediately adjoins an Abode of War, no Muslim country coming between; (iii.) that there is no longer protection for Muslims and their non-Muslim *dh̲immīs* [see DH̲IMMA]. Of these, the first is the most important, and some have even held that so long as a single legal decision (*ḥukm*) of Islām is observed and maintained, a country cannot become *dār al-ḥarb*. The *Dictionary of Technical Terms* (p. 466), having a regard for the situation in India, sums up: "This country is an abode of Islām and of Muslims although it belongs to the accursed ones and the authority externally belongs to these Satans". Practically, of course, no rebellion under such circumstances would be legal unless it has a good prospect of success and were led by a Muslim sovereign. These conditions being fulfilled, unbelieving control of an Abode of Islām is an illegal absurdity. When a Muslim country does become a *dār al-ḥarb*, it is the duty of all Muslims to withdraw from it, and a wife who refuses to accompany her husband in this, is *ipso facto* divorced.

Bibliography: Juynboll, *Handbuch des islamischen Gesetzes*, p. 343; Snouck Hurgronje, *Politique Musulmane de la Hollande*, p. 14 (= *Verspr. Geschr.* IV/ii., 232); Hughes, *Dictionary of Islam*, p. 69 *sq.*; W. W. Hunter, *Indian Musulmans*; the last two on the Indian situation.

DĀR AL-ISLĀM. An "abode of Islam" is a country where the ordinances of Islām are established and which is under the rule of a Muslim sovereign. Its inhabitants are Muslims and also non-Muslims who have submitted to Muslim control and who, under certain restrictions and without the possibility of full citizenship, are guaranteed their lives and property by the Muslim state [see DH̲IMMA]. They must belong to a People of Scripture (*ahl al-kitāb* and may not be idolaters. See, also, DĀR AL-ḤARB and DĀR AL-ṢULḤ and the *Bibliographies* given there.

DĀR AL-ṢULḤ. Besides *dār al-ḥarb* and *dār al-Islām* [q.v.] some schools of canon law recognize the existence of a third division, *dār al-ṣulḥ*, or *al-ʿahd*, which is not under Muslim rule, yet is in tributary relationship to Islām — *ṣulḥ^{an}*, "by agreement", being generally used in canon law as the opposite of *ʿanwat^{an}* "by force". The two historical examples of such a status, and the origin, apparently, of the whole conception, are Nadjrān and Nubia. With the Christian population of Nadjrān Muḥammad himself entered on treaty relationships, guaranteeing their safety and laying on them a certain tribute, regarded by some afterwards as *k̲h̲arādj* [q.v.] and by others as *djizya* [q.v.] (cf. on the whole story Balādh̲urī, *Futūḥ*, ed. de Goeje p. 63 *sq.*; Sprenger, *Leben Mohammads*, iii. 502 *sq.*). In the course of events, and because of their position within Arabia, this protection for the people of Nadjrān amounted to very little. The case of Nubia was somewhat different. By their skill with the bow the Nubians were able to hold off the Muslim attack and to maintain their independence for centuries. In consequence, ʿAbd Allāh b. Saʿd entered into treaty (*ʿahd*) with them, not requiring the head-tax (*djizya*) but only a certain tribute in slaves. Others, however, evidently disliking the implication that there could be any territory in a status of neither Islām nor war, and therefore outside of Muslim conquest, maintained that this was not really a *ṣulḥ* or *ʿahd* but only a truce (*hudna*) and an arrangement for an exchange of commodities (Balādh̲urī, *Futūḥ*, ed. de Goeje, p. 236 *sq.*; Weil, *Gesch. d. Chalifen*, i. 16 *sq.*; Lane-Poole [following Maḳrīzī], *Hist. of Egypt*, p. 21 *sq.*; Torrey [transl. from Ibn ʿAbd al-Ḥakam], in *Yale Bibl. and Sem. Studies*, p. 307 *sq.*). This conception in some vague form was probably also the basis on which treaty relations with Christian states were accepted as possible; the presents sent by such states would then be regarded as *k̲h̲arādj*. The constitutional situation on the matter is thus formally laid down by Māwardī. All territories, into the control of which, in different degrees of directness, Muslims come, fall into three divisions: (i.) those taken by force of arms; (ii.) those taken without fighting after the flight of their previous owners; (iii). those taken by treaty (*ṣulḥ*). The last divides again into two, according as the title to the soil is (a) vested in the Muslim people as a *waḳf*, or (b) remains with the original owners. In the first case the original owners can remain in actual possession, becoming *dh̲immīs* [q.v.], and paying *k̲h̲arādj* and *djizya* and the land becoming *dār al-Islām* [q.v.]. In the second case, (b), the terms of the treaty are that the owners retain their lands and pay a *k̲h̲arādj* from their produce; that this *k̲h̲arādj* is regarded as a *djizya* which falls away when they embrace Islām; that their country is neither *dār al-Islām* nor *dār al-ḥarb* [q.v.] but *dār al-ṣulḥ* (otherwise called *dār al-ʿahd*); and that their lands are absolutely their own to sell or pledge. When these pass to a Muslim, *k̲h̲arādj* can no longer be collected. This condition of the owners holds so long as they observe the requirements of the treaty, and the *djizya* cannot be collected from them as they are not in a *dār al-Islām*. Abū Ḥanīfa, however, held that by the treaty their country had become a *dār al-Islām* and they were *dh̲immīs* and should pay the *djizya*. As to what was the situation if they broke the treaty after entering into it, there was dispute between the schools. Al-S̲h̲āfiʿī held that if their territory was then conquered, it came into the category (i. above) of territory taken by force; and if it was not conquered, it became a *dār al-ḥarb*. Abū Ḥanīfa, however, held that if there was a Muslim in their territory, or if a Muslim country came between their territory and a *dār al-ḥarb*, then their territory was a *dār al-Islām* and they were rebels (*bug̲h̲āt*). If neither of these conditions held, then it was a *dār al-ḥarb*. But others maintained that it was a *dār al-ḥarb* in both cases (Māwardī, *Aḥkām al-sulṭānīya*, ed. Cairo 1298, p. 131 *sq.*). But that this situation was anomalous and ambiguous, appears plainly. Māwardī himself, when reckoning the lands of Islām (*bilād al-Islām*), includes among them this *dār al-ṣulḥ* (*ibid.*, p. 150 and 164), and Balādh̲urī, when dealing with the rules of *k̲h̲arādj*, makes no mention of this distinction.

Bibliography: References are given in the article. The subject has been little treated by western scholars. See, however, Juynboll, *Handbuch des islamischen Gesetzes*, p. 340 and 348 and the authors cited there p. 344—345. Further: Yaḥyā b. Ādam, *Kitāb al-k̲h̲arādj* (ed. Juynboll),

p. 35 *sq.*; al-Ṭabarī, *K. I*<u>*kh*</u>*tilāf al-fuḳahā'*, ed. Schacht, Leiden 1933, p. 14 *sqq.*

DARAZĪ was one of the founders of the religion of the Druzes [q.v.], not the most important who seems to have been Ḥamza, but the one who has given his name to the sect. Several historians, both Muḥammadan and Christian, have written about him and he is also referred to in the books of the Druzes; unfortunately these different sources do not at all agree with one another.

It seems certain that Darazī began as a Bāṭinī missionary or *dā'ī* [q.v.]. According to the Christian historians John of Antioch and al-Makīn, the first of whom was contemporary with him, he was called Muḥammad b. Ismā'īl and was of Persian origin; according to the books of the Druzes he bore the praenomen Ne<u>sh</u>tegīn which is Turkish. The vocalisation *Darazī* is given in the books of the Druzes.

He came to Egypt in 408/1017. He had recognized Ḥamza as Imām in the preceding year (407/1016), for the latter says in his epistles that Darazī had been won over to the unitarian religion by the *ma'*<u>*dh*</u>*ūn* (a missionary of low rank) 'Alī b. Aḥmad Ḥabbāl.

In Cairo he entered the service of the caliph al-Ḥākim bi-Amr[1] 'llāh and at first enjoyed his favour. He then tried to supplant Ḥamza; by 409/1018 he had around him partisans called after him Darazites whom Ḥamza persecuted; the most important of them was Bar<u>dh</u>ā'īl. There still exist writings of Ḥamza in which he speaks of Darazī's undertakings; he calls him, "the insolent one, the Satan" and describes him as opposed to the Imām, i.e. himself; he also complains that he has "gone from beneath the cloak of the Imām" and taken the title *saif al-īmān* or "Sword of the Faith" (409/1018).

Darazī was the first publicly to recognize the divinity of the caliph Ḥākim; according to him, universal reason became incarnate in Adam at the beginning of the world and passed from him into the Prophets, then into 'Alī and thence into his descendants, the Fāṭimid caliphs. Darazī wrote a book to develop this doctrine, which was only an application of that of the previous Bāṭinī system. He read this book in the principal Mosque in Cairo, and, although Ḥākim did not protest, this doctrine caused a scandal. It is also said that he allowed wine, the forbidden marriages and taught metempsychosis.

According to Abu 'l-Maḥāsin, Darazī, in consequence of the scandal which arose, had to retire to Syria; there he preached his doctrine to the mountaineers, especially in the valley of Taim-Allāh and the Bāniyās territory. He came into conflict with the Turks and fell in a battle against them.

John of Antioch and, following him, al-Makīn do not give this account of his end; according to them he was killed by the Turkish pages, on account of the scandal which his teaching caused in Cairo, while actually in Ḥākim's carriage. After his death his house was pillaged, and there was a riot for three days in the city, the gates of which had to be closed. The Turk who had slain him was arrested and put to death on another pretext. The Druze sources would lead one to believe that it was at Ḥamza's instigation that he was assassinated; several of his followers, including Bar<u>dh</u>ā'īl, shared his fate (410/1019).

Bibliography: S. de Sacy, *Exposé de la Religion des Druzes*, vol. i., Introduction, p. ccclxxxiii.—ccclxxxiv.; vol. ii., p. 157 *sq.*, 170, 190; John of Antioch, *Chronique*, ed. Cheikho, Carra de Vaux and Zayāt.

AL-**DĀRIMĪ**, ABŪ MUḤAMMAD 'ABD ALLĀH B. 'ABD AL-RAḤMĀN B. AL-FAḌL B. BAHRĀM B. 'ABD AL-ṢAMAD AL-TAMĪMĪ, traditionist, was born in 181/797—8 at Samarḳand where he died on the 8th or 9th <u>Dh</u>u 'l-Ḥi<u>dj</u><u>dj</u>a 255/18th—19th November 869.

In his search for Islāmic traditions he travelled through <u>Kh</u>urāsān, Syria, 'Irāḳ, Egypt and the Ḥi<u>dj</u>āz, and studied under Abu 'l-Yamān al-Ḥakam b. Nāfi', Yaḥyā b. Ḥassān, Muḥammad b. 'Abd Allāh al-Raḳā<u>sh</u>ī, Muḥammad b. al-Mubārak, Ḥibbān b. Hilāl, Zaid b. Yaḥyā b. 'Ubaid al-Dimi<u>sh</u>ḳī, Wahb b. <u>Dj</u>arīr, etc. Among his pupils were Muslim, Abū Dā'ūd, al-Tirmi<u>dh</u>ī, al-Nasā'ī (except in his *Sunan*), 'Abd Allāh b. Aḥmad b. Ḥanbal, 'Īsā b. 'Umar al-Samarḳandī, etc.

Appointed ḳāḍī of Samarḳand, he only judged one case and resigned. He was pious, fervent, of keen intellect and poor.

He is the author of the following works:

1°. *al-Musnad*, a collection of *ḥadī*<u>*th*</u>, edited for practical use: the traditions are classified in chapters following the order in the law-books. Though not one of the six canonical collections, it enjoyed a good reputation and is reproduced in the *CTM*.

2°. *al-Tafsīr* and 3°. *Kitāb al-*<u>*Dj*</u>*āmi'* considered lost.

Bibliography: al-<u>Dh</u>ahabī, *Ta*<u>*dh*</u>*kirat al-ḥuffāẓ* (Ḥaidarābād n.d.), ii. 115; Ibn al-Ḳaisarānī, *al-*<u>*Dj*</u>*am' baina kitābai Abī Naṣr al-Kalābā*<u>*dh*</u>*ī wa-Abī Bakr al-Iṣbahānī* (Ḥaidarābād 1323), i. 270; Ibn al-A<u>th</u>īr, *al-Kāmil* (Cairo 1303), vii. 71; al-Diyārbakrī, *Ta'rī*<u>*kh*</u> *al-*<u>*kh*</u>*amīs* (Cairo 1283), ii. 341; Abu 'l-Fidā', *Ta'rī*<u>*kh*</u> (Constantinople 1286), ii. 49; Brockelmann, *GAL*, i. 163 (2nd ed. i. 172) and *Suppl.*, i. 270; I. Goldziher, *Muh. Studien* ii. pp. 258—260.

DASŪḲĪ or **DUSŪḲĪ**, IBRĀHĪM B. ABI 'L-MA<u>DJ</u>D 'ABD AL-'AZĪZ (or 'Abd al-Ma<u>dj</u>īd) (633—676/1235—1278), native of Dusūḳ, a village of Lower Egypt in the <u>Gh</u>arbīya District; founder of the Dusūḳī Order. According to the commentator on his *ḥizb* (Ḥasan <u>Sh</u>amma, *Masarrat al-'ainain bi-*<u>*sh*</u>*arḥ ḥizb Abi 'l-'Ainain*, Cairo n.d.), his father came from a village Mrḳs (Marcus?) on the opposite bank of the Nile, and was himself a *walī*; his mother was daughter of another *walī* Abu 'l-Fatḥ al-Wāsiṭī. He is said to have studied <u>Sh</u>āfi'ī jurisprudence before he followed the Ṣūfīs, to have stayed ten years in his <u>*kh*</u>*alwa* at Dusūḳ, and composed many books. Autobiographical details are quoted from some of these (called *al-Ḥaḳā'iḳ*, *al-*<u>*Dj*</u>*awāhir*, *al-*<u>*Dj*</u>*awhara*), given most fully in *Ṭabaḳāt al-*<u>*shaikh*</u> *Aḥmad al-*<u>*Sh*</u>*arnūbī* by Muḥammad al-Bulḳīnī (Cairo 1280), but these are of almost unparalleled extravagance: at the age of one he could catch angels, and at the age of two taught the <u>*dj*</u>*inn* the Ḳur'ān, etc. In a poem preserved in the British Museum (MS. Rich. 7596) he asserts that the sulṭān of Egypt came against him with his armies; various saints came to his assistance and he became sulṭān of Egypt and 'Irāḳ with authority over men and <u>*dj*</u>*inn*. <u>Sh</u>a'rānī in his *Lawāḳiḥ al-anwār* (Cairo 1299, i. 221—245, the sole biography of him used by 'Alī Pa<u>sh</u>a Mubārak, *al-*<u>*Kh*</u>*iṭaṭ al-*<u>*dj*</u>*adīda al-tawfīḳīya*, Būlāḳ 1305, xi. 7) cites and apologizes for some of his pretensions, e.g. that he was commanded to invest all saints with the <u>*kh*</u>*irḳa*, which he did, and that he gave orders to the angels which they obeyed; they are more severely handled in Ṣāliḥ b. Mahdī's *al-ʿAlam al-s͟hāmik͟h* (Cairo 1328, p. 476). His reputation appears to have spread far, since the author of the *Tād͟j al-ʿarūs* calls him one of the four *aḳṭāb* (the other three being ʿAbd al-Ḳādir al-Gīlānī, al-Rifāʿī and Aḥmad al-Badawī), and states that he visited his tomb twice. In a Leyden MS. containing some of his sermons he is called *burhān al-milla wa 'l-dīn* (*Catal.*, iv. 333). Ḥasan S͟hamma mentions two festivals celebrated at Dusūḳ in his honour, and ʿAlī Pas͟ha Mubārak three, in the Coptic months Barmudah, Tubah, and Misra respectively; the last of these continues for eight days and is the occasion of a crowded fair, at which goods of all sorts are sold. The location of these festivals in Coptic months suggests that Ibrāhīm had accorded to him honours which had belonged to some earlier cult or cults.

Some further information about him is furnished by A. le Châtelier (*Les Confréries Musulmanes du Hedjaz*, Paris 1887, p. 190), who, however, misdates him by a century; in S͟haʿrānī's quotations he repeatedly declares that he is in the vii[th] (xiii[th]) century. The homiletic matter in these consists in injunctions to strict morality and Sunnī orthodoxy. His *ḥizb* (mentioned above) is partly magical in character, and since he claims to have mastered the *ṭalāsim* of all the Sūras, probably he owes his fame to miracle-working. Since in an interview which he professes to have had with the Prophet Muḥammad, his "brother" ʿAbd al-Ḳādir al-Gīlānī was behind him and al-Rifāʿī behind ʿAbd al-Ḳādir, his system is likely to have been based on theirs, though he claims superiority over all other saints even more emphatically than ʿAbd al-Ḳādir, and went somewhat beyond al-Ḥallād͟j in identifying himself with Allāh, whereas al-Ḥallād͟j had called himself *al-ḥaḳḳ*.

DAVID. [See Dāwūd].

DAʿWĀ, means accusation or arraignment in civil and criminal law. It should be noted that according to Muḥammadan law, prosecution in penal proceedings is still partly a private affair in as much as the aggrieved person himself or his heir (and not the authorities) has the right either to pardon the culprit or to demand his punishment. The law however distinguishes between the private right of a human being (*ḥaḳḳ ādamī*) and the right of Allāh (*ḥaḳḳ Allāh*). There is for example a human claim for justice when any one has to demand the blood-money (*diya*) in atonement for a murder or the price of a thing sold by him or the return of something stolen from him by a thief. If on the other hand no human being has been affected in his rights, but it is solely a divine commandment that has been transgressed, the punishment of the guilty one is regarded as a right of God. In the latter case every believer has the right to bring the sinner to judgment *Dei causa*, so that the judge may pass sentence on him (*taʿzīr*). Such an accusation is called *daʿwa 'l-ḥisba*, and the office of *muḥtasib*, who supervises commercial transactions in the markets and bazars and when necessary has to act as public prosecutor, has arisen out of this right to arraign those who trespass divine commands. But a *daʿwa 'l-ḥisba* is not alllowed when it is a question of a crime which requires a *ḥadd* punishment. In this case the judge, if suspicion falls on any one for any reason, must himself go into the matter and order punishment to be executed on the guilty individual in accordance with the strict letter of the law, if his guilt is conclusively and legally demonstrated. Yet, according to religious law it is meritorious (even for the judge also) to avert punishment from the guilty one as far as possible, if it is purely a question of a *ḥaḳḳ Allāh* [cf. ʿAd͟hāb].

As regards impeachment on a question of the private right of a human being, the following is in the procedure to be observed. After the accuser (*al-muddaʿī*) has duly preferred his charge and explained it, the judge hears the reply of the accused (*al-muddaʿā ʿalaihi*). If the latter concedes the justice of the accusation it requires no further proof. If, on the other hand, the accused disputes the justice of the charge, the judge must as a rule not pass sentence until the prosecutor has brought forward evidence in support of his statements. The judge is however allowed in certain circumstances, if he is personally acquainted with the facts of the case, to give a verdict from his own knowledge without further evidence being brought by either party, and he is never required to give a verdict, based on evidence formally valid adduced by the parties, but contrary to his own better knowledge. Valid evidence in a law-suit is mainly the testimony of free adult believers, who are known as *ʿadl*; written documents are not legally valid evidence unless their contents are confirmed by reliable witnesses. If the prosecutor cannot bring any proof he is nonsuited if the accused swears that the charge is unfounded. If the accused declines to take this oath, the accuser is held to be in the right if he will testify on oath to the justice of the charge. The judge also can make one of the parties take an oath in order to make the testimony of a witness quite conclusive. Finally it is to be noted that the judge must dismiss a charge if it appears that the prosecutor has, without valid grounds, neglected during an unusually long time to claim to his rights, for this can only be interpreted as meaning that his demand is unfounded. The period of limitation is however not definitely fixed. According to some *faḳīhs* it is 15 years, while others say it is 30 or somewhat more.

Bibliography: In addition to the chapter on the administration of justice in the collections on tradition and the *fiḳh* books and in Juynboll's *Handbuch des islāmischen Gesetzes*; Sachau, *Muhamm. Recht nach schafiit. Lehre*, p. 683 *sq.*; C. Snouck Hurgronje, in *ZDMG*, liii. (1899), 163—166 and in *TBGKW*, xxxix. (1897), 431—457 (= *Verspreide Geschriften*, ii. 410—413 and 327—348); Bergsträsser, *Grundzüge des islamischen Rechts* (Berlin-Leipzig 1935), p. 108 *sq.*; J. Wellhausen, *Reste arab. Heidentums* (2nd ed.), p. 186—195.

DAWSA. The *dōsa*, literally "trampling", was a ceremony performed at Cairo by the s͟haik͟h of the Saʿdī fraternity of derwīs͟hes on the *mōlids*, or birthday celebrations, of the Prophet, of al-S͟hāfiʿī, of Sulṭān Ḥanafī (a celebrated saint of Cairo who died in 847/1443: ʿAlī Pas͟ha Mubārak, *al-K͟hiṭaṭ al-d͟jadīda*, iii. 93; iv. 100), of s͟haik͟h Das͟htūtī (or Ṭas͟htūs͟hī, another saint; see Lane, *Modern Egyptians*, chap. xxv. and *K͟hiṭ. d͟jad.*, iii. 72, 133; iv. 111) and of s͟haik͟h Yūnus (see below). These took place by day; a similar ceremony was performed by the S͟haik͟h al-Bakrī on the *mōlid* of Das͟htūtī, but by night. This ceremony has been described at length by Lane (*loc. cit.*), but it, in short, consisted in about three hundred derwīs͟hes of that order laying themselves down with their faces to the ground and the s͟haik͟h riding over them on horseback. By a special *karāma* [q.v.], inherent in the order, none was ever injured, and by such physical contact the blessing (*baraka*) belonging to the s͟haik͟h was communicated to his followers. The same ceremony is performed elsewhere. Lady Burton found it at Barze near Damascus (*Inner Life of Syria*, chap. x). Dozy, *Supplément* (s.v.) refers also to *Voyage au Ouaday* (trad. par Perron, p. 700). In other orders, also, benediction has been ascribed to rubbing with the feet of the shaikh and even to the dust on which he has trodden. The use of a horse by the Saʿdīs has been associated with the rank of their founder as a descendant from the Prophet. The origin of the Cairo dōsa is obscure, but the legend told of it is that when shaikh Yūnus, the son of Saʿd al-Dīn al-Djibāwī, the founder of the Saʿdī *ṭarīḳa*, came to Cairo, the Saʿdī derwīshes there asked him to establish for their usage a *bidʿa ḥasana* (good innovation) which would be a *karāma* in proof of his walī-ship and of the sacred origin of their order. He directed them to lay round glass vessels in rows on the ground, and he then rode over those on horseback without breaking them. This his successor could not do, and prostrate derwīshes were substituted for the more fragile glass (Goldziher in *ZDMG*, xxxvi. 647 *sq.*; Muḥammad ʿAbduh, *Taʾrīkh*, Cairo 1324, ii. 147 *sq.*). This shaikh Yūnus is said by some (e.g. Goldziher's authority) to be buried in the Bāb al-Naṣr, and by others, outside of that gate on the way to ʿAbbāsīya (*Khiṭ. djad.*, ii. 72). The dates are quite uncertain apparently because of the quarrel as to origin between the Saʿdī and the Rifāʿī derwīshes. Perhaps, also, there has been confusion with the *madjdhūb* shaikh Yūnus al-Shaibānī (Maḳrīzī, *Khiṭaṭ*, 1st ed., ii. 435 = iind ed., iv. 304 *sq.*), the founder of the Yūnusī order. Saʿd al-Dīn is commonly assigned to the second half of the viith (xiiith) century. The dōsa was finally abolished by the Khedīwe Muḥammad Tewfīḳ in 1881, on the basis of a *fatwā* from the chief *muftī* of Egypt. It was judged to be a *bidʿa ḳabīḥa* (evil innovation), as involving contemptuous treatment of Muslims. The Saʿdīs petitioned that they might be permitted to hold it at least on the *mōlid* of shaikh Yūnus himself, but even that was forbidden. At present all that is left is that on the morning of those *mōlids* their shaikh finds before his door a number of derwīshes lying on the ground and walks over them (A. Le Chatelier, *Confréries musulmanes*, p. 225).

Bibliography: Add to references above: ʿAlī Pasha Mubārak, *al-Khiṭaṭ al-djadīda al-tawfīḳiya*, iv., p. 112; Depont et Coppolani, *Confrèries religieuses musulmanes*, p. 329 *sq.*

DĀWŪD, the Biblical David. The Ḳurʾān has several passages in which reference is made to the legend of the kingly prophet David, the *khalīfa* of Allāh (Sūra xxxviii. 26). Like the legends of the other prophets, it shows signs of Rabbinical influence. Muḥammad knew that David slew Goliath (Djālūt) (Sūra ii. 249 *sq.*) and that he received the Psalms from God. The Psalms (*zabūr*) is one of the four Scriptures with which Muḥammad was acquainted. David shares with Solomon the gift of wisdom (ii. 251; xxvii. 15); together on one occasion they delivered a remarkable judgment in a case concerning the damage done by some sheep in a field (xxi. 78 *sq.*). The commentators say that in this case, Solomon, though only 11 years of age, showed his wisdom by improving on the sentence passed by his father. In another passage, the case of two suitors is referred to, who came to David to reproach him with his fault in the guise of asking him to deliver judgment (xxxviii. 21—26). Mention is made of the repentance of David in Sūra xxxviii. 17. The royal prophet is thought to be the inventor of coats-of-mail, that is to say he replaced by them the cuirasses of plates of metal. Iron seemed to become ductile in his hands (xxi. 80 and xxxiv. 10); he had the gift of song; the mountains and the birds alternated with him in his songs (xxi. 79; xxxiv. 10; xxxviii. 18 *sq*); this is evidently only the literal interpretation of verses in which the Psalmist invites the hills and beasts of the field to praise the Lord. Lastly by combining verses v. 78 *sq.* and ii. 65 of the Ḳurʾān we learn that David punished Sabbath-breakers by changing them into monkeys.

The brief references to David are considerably developed in the commentators and agree in the main points with the Bible. The following are the main points in Ṭabarī: Djālūt (Goliath), a descendant of the ʿĀdites and Thamūdites, having attacked Ṭālūt (Saul), David slays him with his sling; he marries the daughter of Ṭālūt and shares his authority. Ṭālūt becomes jealous and tries to kill him; David flees and hides in a cave across the entrance to which a spider weaves its web, thus protecting David from Saul. Ṭabarī gives David's genealogy, tells the story of Bathsheba, wife of Uriah, David's repentance and the plan of building the temple; he also adds a few anecdotes.

Masʿūdī knew the *miḥrāb Dāwūd*, built by this king in Jerusalem and still standing in this historian's time; it is, he says, the highest building in the city; from it one can see the Dead Sea and the Jordan. It is apparently the Citadel or Tower of David.

Down to the viiith (xivth) century the Muslims like the Christians before them located the tomb of David in Bethlehem although other traditions regarding its site were known to them. In the Crusading period a tomb alleged to be David's was found on the southwest hill of Jerusalem. In the ixth (xvth) century it was taken over by the Muslims who still regard it as particularly sacred (cf. *al-Mashriḳ*, xii. 898—902; Kahle, in *Palästina-Jahrbuch*, vi. 74 and 86).

In Kurdistān there still exists a small sect of followers of David (Dāwūdīs); they live in the mountainous district of Kirnid, near Khāniḳīn, and at Mandala, north of Baghdād; to them David is the most important of the Prophets (cf. le Père Anastase, *La Secte des Davidiens*, in *Mashriḳ*, 1903, No. 2, p. 60—67).

Bibliography: In addition to the Ḳurʾān and the works dealing with the lives of the Prophets: Masʿūdī, *Murūdj*, i. 106—112; al-Hudjwīrī, *Kashf al-mahdjūb*, transl. Nicholson (*GMS*, 1911) p. 197, 402 *sq*,; al-Kisāʾī, *Ḳiṣaṣ al-anbiyāʾ*, ed. Eisenberg, p. 250 *sqq.*; Thaʿlabī, *Ḳiṣaṣ al-anbiyāʾ* (Cairo 1325), p. 170—180; Weil, *Biblische Legenden der Muselmänner*; Grünbaum, *Neue Beiträge zur semitischen Sagenkunde*, p. 189 *sq.*; J. Horovitz, *Koranische Untersuchungen*, p. 109 *sq.*

DĀWŪD B. **KHALAF**. [See ẒĀHIRĪYA].

DERḲĀWĀ (plural of the ethnic DERḲĀWĪ), a name collectively applied to the members of the *ṭarīḳa* or Muḥammadan religious brotherhood, composed of the followers of Mūlāy ʾl-ʿArbī al-Derḳāwī, the area of whose influence extends over Northwest Africa, particularly Morocco and Algeria. An individual member is called *Derḳāwī* while the plural is *Derḳāwā*. They are also called Shādhilīya-Derḳāwā, their brotherhood being an offshoot of the much older *ṭarīḳa* of the Shādhilīya, founded by the Maghribī Ṣūfī Abu ʾl-Ḥasan ʿAlī al-Shādhilī.

Origin of the Derḳāwā: The doctrine of the Derḳāwā was first preached by an Idrīsid Sharīf called ʿAlī b. ʿAbd al-Raḥmān al-Djamāl. He studied

Ṣūfism at Fās under the direction of Abū ʿAbd Allāh Djassūs and afterwards joined the brotherhood of Abu 'l-Maḥāmid Sidi 'l-ʿArbī b. Aḥmad b. ʿAbd Allāh Maʿan al-Andalusī, who taught the doctrines of Shādhilī. On the death of the latter he succeeded him and built a *zāwiya* at Fās in the place called Humat al-Ramīla. He had passed his hundred and fifth year when he died in 1193 A.H. according to some, in 1194 according to others (1779—1780 A.D.). Many disciples had gathered around him, of whom the most famous was his successor Mūlāy 'l-ʿArbī al-Derḳāwī who was destined to give his name to the brotherhood.

The latter, Abū Ḥāmid Mūlāy 'l-ʿArbī b. Aḥmad b. al-Ḥusain b. Muḥammad b. Yūsuf b. Aḥmad was an Idrīsid Sharīf, belonging to that section of the Derḳāwā Sharīfs settled among the Moroccan tribe of Banū Zarwal. These Sharīfs were so called after their ancestor Yūsuf b. Djannūn surnamed Abū Derḳā (the man with the leather buckler). Born after 1150/1737 Mūlāy 'l-ʿArbī died among the Banū Zar- wal, in his Zāwiya of Bū Barīḥ, in 1239/1823.

ʿAlī b. ʿAbd al-Raḥmān al-Djamāl, Mūlāy 'l-ʿArbī's Shaikh, had preached the renunciation of the things of this world, contempt for riches and power, return to the pure sources of Ṣūfism, more especially to the doctrine of Shādhilī. Mūlāy 'l-ʿArbī al-Derḳāwī proved himself as strict as his master and followed, moreover, the practices of certain "enlightened ones". One day he met in a street of Fās, standing before a shop, the illustrious enlightened Sidi 'l-ʿArbī al-Baḳḳāl. The latter was in a state of mystic intoxication, much excited, surrounded by a crowd which he was haranguing. Mūlāy 'l-ʿArbī al-Derḳāwī came to his side. The enlightened saint called him, took hold of him, pressed him to his bosom, and put his tongue into Mūlāy 'l-ʿArbī's mouth saying "suck, suck, suck". He added prophetically: "I give thee (power over) the East and the West". Mūlāy 'l-ʿArbī went on and the "enlightened" saint died two days later. This form of initiation was afterwards revived by several Derḳāwā groups (notably the Habrīya) and the leader of the rising of Margueritte.

Now at the head of his brotherhood, Mūlāy 'l-ʿArbī at once organised it on a solid basis, considerably increased the number of his followers and gave them in his *rasāʾil* (letters) suitable rules of conduct, a kind of law which assured unity of doctrine among them. The *khwān* or "brothers" of the guild who were henceforth known by the name of Derḳāwā (i.e. followers of Derḳāwī) multiplied on all sides. They may be recognised by the staff on which they lean in imitation of the prophet Moses; by the necklet of large wooden beads, which they wear in imitation of Abū Huraira, the companion of the prophet Muḥammad; by the beard generally worn long, and by their garments of rags (among the more fanatical) in imitation of Abū Bakr and of ʿUmar b. al-Khaṭṭāb which has earned them the soubriquet of *Abū Derbala* (wearers of rags). Some, especially in Southern Morocco, have adopted the green turban. Their Shaikh had further recommended them to celebrate the praises of God in dancing (*raḳṣ*), to pray alone or in the desert, to walk with bare feet or with simple shoes, to endure hunger, to mortify themselves frequently by fasting, to avoid the society of those in authority and only to consort with men of piety.

Besides these ascetic practices the actual initiation is simple. The Shaikh takes the initiate by the right hand and reads the following verse of the Ḳurʾān (Sūra xvi. 91): "Be faithful to your covenant with God which ye have concluded with him; and violate not the oaths which ye have solemnly taken. You have taken God as a witness and he knows what ye do". The Shaikh then orders him to recite a hundred times in the morning and in the evening the prayer called *istighfār*, as follows: "I testify that there is no god but God, the One only, who has no associate, to Him be the dominion and the praise; He is powerful above all". The initiate has to conclude his prayer by saying a hundred times: "There is no god but God etc.". Such is the *dhikr* [q.v.] or prayer peculiar to the order and compulsory. After initiation, the brothers present unite in *ḥaḍra*, a pious assembly in honour of the new *Derḳāwī* interspersed with songs and *raḳṣ* (dances), a kind of rhythmic march.

The brotherhood of the Derḳāwā, under the influence of several large tribes which adopted its tenets, later divided into several branches, some of which played a political rôle in opposition firstly to the Turks and afterwards to the French. It has also, with some modifications, has given rise to certain religious groups in Morocco, which are even more strict. Such are the Kittānīyūn (disciples of Sidi Muḥammad al-Kittānī, author of the *Ṣalawāt al-anfās*), the Ḥarrāḳīyūn, veritable anarchists (disciples of Sidi Muḥammad al-Ḥarrāḳ, 3rd successor of Mūlāy 'l-ʿArbī al-Derḳāwī) etc. The influence of these groups hardly extends beyond Fās and its environs.

Bibliography: R. Basset, *Recherches sur les Sources de la Salouat al-Anfās* (Algiers 1905), p. 1 *sq.*; Abū Ḥāmid Muḥammad al-ʿArbī al-Fāsī, *Mirʾāt al-maḥāsin* (Fās 1323), passim; Mūlāy 'l-ʿArbī Derḳāwī, *Rasāʾil* (Fās 1318), passim; al-Salāwī, *Kitāb al-istiḳṣā* (Cairo 1312), iv. 140 *sq.*; al-Kittānī, *Ṣalawāt al-anfās* (Fās 1316), passim, particularly i. 176, 267, 358; A. Cour, *Etablissement des dynasties des Cherifs* (Paris 1904), p. 227 *sq.*; Depont et Coppolani, *Les Confréries Musulmanes* (Algiers 1897), p. 503 *sq.*; E. Doutté, *L'Islām en 1900* (Algiers 1901), passim; Feraud, *Hist. de Gigelli* (Constantine 1870), passim; De Grammont, *Hist. d'Alger* (Paris 1887), p. 349 *sq.*; Lacroix, *Les Derkaoua d'Hier et d'Aujourd'hui* (Algiers 1902); Montet, *De l'Etat Présent et de l'Avenir de l'Islām* (Paris 1910), p. 96 *sq.*; do., *Les Confréries Religieuses de l'Islām Marocain*, in *RHR*, 1902, vol. xlv., p. 16 *sq.*; Nehlil, *Notice sur la Zaouiya de Zegzel* (Algiers 1910); Rinn, *Marabouts et Khouan* (Algiers 1884), p. 233 *sq.*; Rousseau, *Chronique du Beylik d'Oran* (Algiers 1854), passim; Delpech, *Résumé Historique sur le Soulèvement des Derk'-aoua de la Province d'Oran, in Revue Africaine*, vol. xviii., p. 39 *sq.*; L. Voindt, *Confréries et Zawiya au Maroc*, in *Bulletin de la Soc. d. Géogr. d'Oran*, fasc. 204—206.

DERWĪSH (DARWĒSH) is commonly explained as derived from Persian, and meaning "seeking doors", i.e. a mendicant (Vullers, *Lexicon*, i., p. 839^{a}, 845^{b}; *Grundr. der iran. Phil.*, I/i., p. 260; ii., p. 43, 45). But the variant form, *daryōsh*, is against this, and the real etymology appears to be unknown. Broadly through Islām it is used in the sense of a member of a religious fraternity, but in Persian and Turkish more narrowly for a religious mendicant called in Arabic a *faḳīr*. In Morocco and Algeria for derwīshes, in the broadest sense, the word most used is *ikhwān*, "brethren", pronounced *khouān*. These fraternities (*ṭuruḳ*, plural of *ṭariḳa*, "path", i.e. method of instruction, initiation and religious exercise) form the organized expression of religious life in Islām. For centuries that religious life [cf. TAṢAWWUF] was on an individual basis. Beyond the single soul seeking its own salvation by ascetic practices or soaring meditations, there was found at most a teacher gathering round himself a circle of disciples. Such a circle might even persist for a generation or two after his death, led by some prominent pupil, but for long there was nothing of the nature of a perpetual corporation, preserving an identity of organization and worship under a fixed name. Only in the vi^th^ (xii^th^) century — the troubled times of the Saldjūḳ break-up — did continuous corporations began to appear. The Ḳādirīs, founded by ʿAbd al-Ḳādir al-Djīlānī (q.v.; d. 561/1166), seem to have been the first still existing fraternity of definitely historical origin. Thereafter, we find these organizations appearing in bewildering profusion, founded either by independent saints or by split and secession from older bodies. Such historical origins must, however, be sharply distinguished from the legends told by each as to the source of their peculiar ritual and devotional phrases. As the origin of Ṣūfism is pushed back to the Prophet himself, and its orthodoxy is thus protected, so these are traced down from the Prophet (or rather from Allāh-Gabriel-Prophet) through a series of well-known saints to the historic founder. This is called the *silsila* or "chain" of the order, and another similar *silsila* or apostolic succession of heads extends from the founder to the present day. Every derwīsh must know the *silsila* which binds him up to Allāh himself, and must believe that the faith taught by his order is the esoteric essence of Islām, and that the ritual of his order is of as high a validity as the *ṣalāt*. His relationship to the *silsila* is through his individual teacher (*shaikh, murshid, ustādh, pīr*) who introduces him into the fraternity. That takes place through an *ʿahd*, "covenant", consisting of religious professions and vows which vary in the different bodies. Previously the neophyte (*murīd*, "willer", "intender") has been put through a longer or shorter process of initiation, in some forms of which it is plain that he is brought under hypnotic control by his instructor and put into rapport with him. The theology is always some form of Ṣūfism, but varies in the different *ṭarīḳas* from ascetic quietism to pantheistic antinomianism. This goes so far that in Persia derwīshes are divided into those *bā-sharʿ* "with law", that is, following the law of Islām, and those *bī-sharʿ* "without law", that is, rejecting not only the ritual but the moral law. In general the Persians and the Turks have diverged farther from Islām than the Syrians, Arabs or Africans, and the same *ṭarīḳa* in different countries may assume different forms. The ritual always lays stress on the emotional religious life, and tends to produce hypnotic phenomena (auto and otherwise) and fits of ecstasy. One order, the Khalwatī, is distinguished by its requiring from all its members an annual period of retreat in solitude, with fasting to the utmost possible limit and endless repetitions of religious formulae. The effect on the nervous system and imagination is very marked. The religious service common to all fraternities is called a *dhikr* [q.v.], a "remembering", that is, of Allāh (Sūra xxxiii. 41 is the basal text), and its object is to bring home to the worshipper the thought of the unseen world and of his dependence upon it. Further, it is plain that a *dhikr* brings with it a certain heightened religious exaltation and a pleasant dreaminess. But there go also with the hypnosis, either as excitants or consequents, certain physical states and phenomena which have earned for derwīshes the various descriptions in the west of barking, howling, dancing, etc. The Mawlawīs [q.v.], founded by Djalāl al-Dīn al-Rūmī (d. at Ḳonya in 672/1273), stimulate their ecstasies by a whirling dance. The Saʿdīs used to have the *dawsa* [q.v.] and still in their monasteries use the beating of little drums, called *bāz*. The use of these is now forbidden in the Egyptian mosques as an innovation (*bidʿa*; Muḥammad ʿAbduh, *Taʾrīkh*, ii. 144 *sq.*). The Saʿdīs, Rifāʿīs and Aḥmadīs have particular feats, peculiar to each *ṭarīḳa*, of eating glowing embers and live serpents or scorpions and glass, of passing needles through their bodies and spikes into their eyes. But besides such exhibitions, which may in part be tricks and in part rendered possible by a hypnotic state, there appear amongst derwīshes automatic phenomena of clairaudience and clairvoyance and even of levitation, which deserve more attention than they have yet received. These, however, appear only in the case of accepted saints (*walīs*; q.v.), and are explained as *karāmāt* (q.v.; χαρίσματα), wrought by Allāh for them. But besides the small number of full members of the orders, who reside in the monasteries (*khānḳāh, ribāṭ, zāwiya, takīya* or *takya*) or wander as mendicant friars (the Ḳalanderīs, an order related to the Bektāshīs, must wander continually), there is a vast number of lay members, like Franciscan and Dominican tertiaries, who live in the world and have only a duty of certain daily prayers and of attending *dhikrs* from time to time in the monasteries. At one time the number of regular derwīshes must have been much larger than now. Especially in Egypt under the Mamlūks, their convents were very numerous and were richly endowed. Their standing then was much higher than it is now, when derwishes are looked down upon by the canon lawyers and professed theologians (*ʿulamāʾ*) in the essential contest of intuitionists on the one hand and traditionists and rationalists on the other. For this division see further the art. TAṢAWWUF. Now their numbers are drawn mostly from the lower orders of society, and for them the fraternity house is in part like a church and in part like a club. Their relation to it is much more personal than to a mosque, and the fraternities, in consequence, have come to have the position and importance of the separate church organizations in Protestant Christendom. As a consequence, in more recent times, the governments have assumed a certain indirect control of them. This, in Egypt, is exercised by the Shaikh al-Bakrī, who is head of all the derwīsh fraternities there (see p. 279 *sq.* of *Kitāb bait al-ṣiddīḳ*). Elsewhere there is a similar head for each city. The Sanūsīs [q.v.] alone, by retiring into the deserts of Arabia and North Africa and especially by keeping their organization inaccessible in the depths of the Sahara, have maintained their freedom from this control. Their membership is also of a distinctly higher social order than that of the other fraternities. As women in Islām have generally the same religious, though not legal, status as men, so there are women derwīshes. These are received into the order by the shaikh, but are often instructed and trained by women, and almost always hold their *dhikrs* by themselves. In mediaeval Islām such female derwīshes often led a cloistered life, and there were separate foundations and convents for them with superiors of their own sex. Now, they seem to be all tertiaries. For a complete list of fraternities see the art. ṬARĪḲA.

Bibliography: The bibliography on this subject is very large, and the following is only a selection: Depont et Coppolani, *Les confréries religieuses musulmanes* (Algiers 1897); A. Le Chatelier, *Les confréries musulmanes du Hedjaz* (Paris 1887); Goldziher, *Vorlesungen*, p. 168 *sq.*, 195 *sq.*; Lane, *Modern Egyptians*, chapt. x., xx., xxiv., xxv; J. P. Browne, *The Derwishes, or Oriental Spiritualism* (London 1868); Hughes, *Dictionary of Islam*, s.v. *Faqīr*; D'Ohsson, *Tableau général de l'Empire Othoman*, ii. (Paris 1790); Sir Charles N. E. Eliot, *Turkey in Europe* (London 1900); E. G. Browne, *A Year among the Persians* (London 1893); T. H. Weir, *Shaikhs of Morocco* (Edinburgh 1904); B. Meakin, *The Moors* (London 1902), chap. xix.; H. Vambéry, *Travels in Central Asia* (London 1864) and all Vambéry's books of travel and history; W. H. T. Gardner, *The "Way" of a Mohammadan Mystic* (in *Moslem World* for April 1912 *sq.*); Macdonald's article *Dervish* in *Encyclopaedia Britannica*, xi[th] ed., but to correct by above,; do., *Religious Attitude and Life in Islām* (Chicago 1909) and *Aspects of Islām* (New York 1911), both by index.

AL-DHAMMĪYA, i.e. "the Blamers", a Shīʿī sect who accused Muḥammad of having claimed for himself the honour due to ʿAlī, because in their opinion Muḥammad ought rather to be regarded as the messenger of the divine ʿAlī. They are followers of a certain ʿIlbā (the form is not certain) b. Dhirāʿ al-Sadūsī, of whom nothing further in known. In another connection the followers of Abū Hāshim Djubbāʾī, according to al-Baghdādī (ed. Muḥ. Badr., p. 169), are called Dhammīya.

Bibliography: Shahrastāni, p. 134; Friedländer in *JAOS*, xxix. 102.

DHIKR in the mind (*bi'l-ḳalb*) means "remembrance", and with the tongue (*bi'l-lisān*), "mentioning", "relating", then, as a religious technical term (pronounced *zikr*), the glorifying of Allāh with certain fixed phrases, repeated in a ritual order, either aloud or in the mind, with peculiar breathings and physical movements. When these are pronounced aloud, it is a *dhikr djalī*, when inwardly, a *dhikr khafī*. There is much dispute as to which is of the higher value. This practice is based ultimately on Sūra xxxiii. 41: "O ye who believe, remember (or glorify) Allāh with much remembering (or glorifying)". A tradition from Muḥammad is also frequently quoted: "There sits not a company remembering (or glorifying) Allāh, but the angels surround them and the (divine) mercy covers them, and Allāh Most High remembers (or glorifies) them among those who are with him." For the early development of the practice, individually and in company, of such *dhikrs* see Goldziher in *WZKM*, xiii. 35 *sq.* When, then, the later derwīsh fraternities arose and their ritual became fixed, an essential part of each *ṭariḳa* was its dhikr. These consist of the repetition a great number of times of such phrases as *lā ilāh*[a] *illa 'llāh*, *subḥān*[a]*-'llāh*, *al-ḥamd*[u] *li'llāh*, *Allāh*[u] *akbar*, *astaghfir*[u] *'llāh* and the different names of Allāh. Spiritual songs, often indistinguishable from love songs, may be introduced, as also dancing and playing on different kinds of drums and pipes. At the regular Friday service (*ḥadra*) in the *takīya* or *zāwiya*, which all derwīshes are expected to attend, the ritual consists especially of the formula *lā ilāh*[a] *illa 'llāh*, called the *dhikr al-djalāla*, and of the *ḥizb* [q.v.], or "office" in the technical sense, of the order, which is made up of extended selections from the Ḳurʾān and of other prayers. A simpler dhikr is that of *awḳāt* ("hours" in the technical sense), formulae to be repeated after each regular *ṣalāt*, or at least twice daily. Another term used in this connection is *wird*, explained by Ṣūfīs as meaning "access", "arrival" (with Allāh), and applied to a short invocation, drawn up by a founder of a fraternity, the recitation of which is now a pious work. Both *ḥizb* and *wird* are otherwise used to signify portions of the Ḳurʾān or of prayer recited at particular times (Lane, *Lexicon*, s.v. *ḥizb* and *wird*). Each fraternity has a dhikr, or ritual, of its own, constructed and imposed by its founder, but these can be modified freely by the *shaikh* or *muḳaddam*. They are given under the separate fraternities. For 18 usages of the word dhikr which theologians have found in the Ḳurʾān, and for further description of its meaning and value with followers of the mystical path (*sālikūn*) see *Dict. of techn. Terms*, i. 512 *sq.* For descriptions of actual dhikrs see Lane's *Modern Egyptians* by index and Macdonald's *Aspects of Islam*, p. 159 *sq.* For an attempt to clear the dhikr of superstitious elements, see *Kitāb al-taʿlīm wa 'l-irshād*, p. 63 *sq.*, the manual for derwīsh shaikhs and their pupils drawn up under the direction of the Shaikh al-Bakrī.

Bibliography: A. le Chatelier, *Les Confréries musulmanes du Hedjaz* (Paris 1887); Depont et Coppolani, *Les Confréries religieuses musulmanes* (Algiers 1897); Goldziher, *Vorlesungen*, by index s.v. *Dhikr*; J. P. Browne, *The Derwishes or Oriental Spiritualism* (London 1868); Hughes, *Dictionary of Islam*, s.v. *Zikr*; D. B. Macdonald, *Religious Attitude and Life in Islām* (Chicago 1909), by index s.v. *Darwīsh* and *Dhikr*.

DHIMMA. According to Muslim canon law on the conquest of a non-Muslim country by Muslims, the population which does not embrace Islām and which is not enslaved is guaranteed life, liberty and, in a modified sense, property. They are, therefore, called *ahl al-dhimma*, "People of the covenant or obligation", or simply *al-dhimma* or *dhimmīs* — the *dhimma* involving temporal rights from Muslims and duties towards Muslims. If, however, they have been captured in arms, they may be killed or enslaved or ransomed or exchanged or simply set free. The wives and children of combatants in any case must become slaves. But such a dhimma is, in strictness, open only to a "People of Scripture" (*ahl al-kitāb*), i.e. to Jews, Christians and Sabaeans, which has been interpreted to cover Zoroastrians. All others, classed roughly as *dahrīs*, or materialists, and as idolaters, must be killed or enslaved. But practically this distinction has fallen to the ground, and Muslim states have found themselves compelled to tolerate other than "People of Scripture". Each adult, male, free, sane *dhimmī* must pay a poll-tax (*djizya*; q.v.) of an amount which is fixed in the agreement. His real estate either becomes a *waḳf* for the whole body of Muslims, but of which he continues to have the use, or he holds it still as his own. In either event he pays on it and its crops a land-tax (*kharādj*; q.v.) which, in the first case, inheres in the land and must be paid even though the land comes into the possession of a Muslim; but, in the second case, on the owner's becoming a Muslim, falls. He is liable also to other exactions for the maintenance of the Muslim armies. He must distinguish himself from believers by dress, not riding on horseback or carrying weapons, and by a generally respectful attitude towards Muslims. He is also under certain legal disabilities with regard to testimony in law-courts, protection under criminal law and in marriage. Of course all these points have been and are enforced with very varying degrees of rigour. On the other hand, the Muslims guarantee them security to life and property, protection in the exercise of their religion and defence against others. They may repair and even rebuild existing churches, but not erect new ones on new sites. Nor in the exercise of their worship may they use an offensive publicity. Their life, public and private, must be of a quiet, inoffensive nature. And they are not citizens of the Muslim state. Rather, each non-Muslim community governs itself under its responsible head — rabbi, bishop, etc. — who is its link of connection with the Muslim government.

Bibliography: Juynboll, *Handb. des isla-mischen Gesetzes*, p. 350 *sq.* and references there; Hughes, *Dict. of Islām*, p. 710 *sq.*, a good statement of the legal situation as to marriage, inheritance, bequests etc.; R. J. H. Gottheil, *Dhimmis and Moslems in Egypt* (in *Old Testament and Semitic Studies in memory of William Rainer Harper*, vol. ii., Chicago 1908); Māwardī, *Aḥkām al-sulṭānīya* (Cairo 1298), p. 121 *sq.*; Balādhurī, *Futūḥ*, p. 447 *sq.* on *kharādj*; Tritton, *Islam and the protected religions*, *JRAS*, 1928, 1929, 1931.

DHU 'L-ḲARNAIN, the "two-horned", a name always given to the individuals cited below, more particularly to the third. The two horns go back to an old mythological idea. Naram-Sin was for example represented as Adad with 2 horns (on the stele of Susa; cf. *Fouilles à Suse*, i., pl. x.). The two horns of Jupiter Ammon are well known; and Alexander the Great appears on coins as Jupiter Ammon incarnate. In Arabic, the name Dhu 'l-Ḳarnain, the true meaning of which was not known to the Arabs and which they therefore interpreted in the most varied fashion, is borne by the following persons:

1. al-Mundhir al-Akbar b. Māʾ al-Samāʾ, the grandfather of al-Nuʿmān b. al-Mundhir. He is said to have worn two long curled locks on his forehead and therefore to have received the name Dhu 'l-Ḳarnain. According to Ibn Duraid's explanation he is the Dhu 'l-Ḳarnain who is referred to in verse lx. 3 of Imruʾl-Ḳais (Ahlwardt, *Six Divans*, p. 158):

aṣadda nashāṣa dhi 'l-Ḳarnaini ḥattā
tawallā ʿāriḍu 'l-maliki 'l-humāmi

Winckler sees a thunder-god in this Dhu 'l-Ḳarnain.

2. The South Arabian king Tubbaʿ al-Akran or Dhu 'l-Ḳarnain. According to the South Arabian interpretation he is the Dhu 'l-Ḳarnain mentioned in the Ḳurʾān (cf. under 3).

3. Alexander the Great is by far the most frequently referred to as Dhu 'l-Ḳarnain. He is mentioned by this name even in the Ḳurʾān (Sūra xviii. 83 *sq.*), after the original in the Syriac legend which arose in the viᵗʰ century A.D., in which Alexander says to God: "I know that thou hast caused horns to grow upon my head, so that I may crush the kingdoms of the world with them". The Syriac legend is, as Nöldeke has shown, the source of the "Two-Horned" in the Ḳurʾān. For the details of this story and the accounts of Alexander the Great in the rest of Arabic literature see the article AL-ISKANDAR.

4. ʿAlī b. Abī Ṭālib more rarely bears the name Dhu 'l-Ḳarnain.

Bibliography: 1. *Lisān al-ʿArab*, xvii. 211; Winckler, *Arabisch-Semitisch-Orientalisch* (*MVAG*, 1901, No. 4), p. 138 *sq.*

2. A. v. Kremer, *Über die südarabische Sage* (Leipzig 1866), p. 70 *sq.*

3. Nöldeke, *Beiträge zur Geschichte des Alexanderromans* (*Denkschriften der Kais. Akademie der Wissenschaften*, phil.-hist. Klasse, vol. 38, Vienna 1890, Abh. 5), p. 27 and 32; *Lisān al-ʿArab*, xvii. 210 *sq.*; Thaʿlabī, *Ḳiṣaṣ al-anbiyāʾ* (Cairo 1310), p. 226; Masʿūdī, *Murūdj*, ii. 248—249; J. Horovitz, *Koranische. Untersuchungen* p. 111 *sqq.*

4. *Ḳāmūs*, s.v. *ḳ-r-n*.

DHU 'L-KIFL is an individual mentioned in the Ḳurʾān, Sūra xxi. 85; xxxviii. 48, in connection with a series of prophets, whose identity is wrapped in uncertainty. The Muslim commentators hesitatingly identify him with various people, chiefly Biblical personages like Joshua, Elijah, Zachariah, or Ezekiel. The view is more definitely advanced (Ṭabarī, *Annales*, i. 364; Mudjīr al-Dīn, *al-Uns al-djalīl*, p. 68), that Dhu 'l-Kifl is an epithet of Bishr (according to some, e.g. *TA*: Bashīr), a son of Aiyūb, whom God chose as a prophet to convert a heathen people (or King Kinʿān) in Shām, where he spent his whole life and died at the age of 75. The accepted collections of *ḥadīths* make not the slightest mention of Dhu 'l-Kifl, a proof that *ḥadīth* criticism places no value on the manifold legends about this individual. The *ḳuṣṣāṣ* have therefore been all the more industrious in finding motives for the name of this figure, which is quite colourless in tradition, by etymological inventions, all of which are connected with various meanings of the word *kifl* and the verbal stem *k-f-l*. First with the meaning "pledge" or "security" of the word *kifl*; Dhu 'l-Kifl is said to have pledged himself to the Prophet Elisha (whose cousin, *ibn ʿamm*, he was according to some — Baiḍāwī), to whom he proposed himself as successor in leadership of the people of Israel, to fulfil three conditions: to fast by day, to spend the night in pious devotions and never to fall into a passion. In spite of the temptations of Satan he fulfilled these conditions. In the legends of Bashīr he gives the heathen king Kinʿān a written guarantee that the king will attain Paradise if he becomes converted. Other legends are connected with the meaning of *kifl* as "double". Dhu 'l-Kifl enjoyed a double measure of God's rewards because he had done a double share of pious works. The name is connected with *takaffala* in the meaning of "to attend to the maintenance of any one", in a legend according to which its bearer maintained 70 (or 100) Israelites (or prophets) who were persecuted by a cruel king; in this story A. Geiger (*Was hat Moh. aus dem Judent. aufgenommen?*, 2ⁿᵈ ed., Leipzig 1902, p. 192) has rightly recognised an echo of the story of Obadiah (I Kings, xviii. 4). *Kifl* is also the name of a garment (connected with the meaning of "doubled") a cloak of double thickness: the prophet wore a garment of this kind which it has been sought to connect with II Kings, ii. 8 (Elijah, *wayyiglōm*) (*Ein muhammedanischer Katechismus*, by Meḥmed Mesʿūd, ed. by F. C. Andreas, Potsdam 1910).

Besides this Dhu 'l-Kifl a different saint of the same name is mentioned (Ibn al-Athīr, *Muraṣṣaʿ*, ed. C. F. Seybold, p. 190, l. 4 from the foot, *sq.*), whose legend is however connected by Thaʿlabī with the prophet Dhu 'l-Kifl. This Dhu 'l-Kifl was originally a sinful man, who took advantage of the indigent position of a certain virtuous woman to tempt her to sin, but was restrained from actual sinning by her apparent compliance and converted to a virtuous life. He therefore was doubly (*kifl*) rewarded by God on the principle that a converted sinner is of more value in the eyes of God than a pious man who never sins (*al-tā'ib ʿind Allāh aḥsan min al-ʿābid*).

It is clear from the stories quoted here that the Muslims are not at all agreed on the character of Dhu 'l-Kifl: whether he was a prophet or merely a pious servant of God (*ʿabd ṣāliḥ*). The champions of the first view rely solely on the circumstance that Dhu 'l-Kifl has received a place in Sūra xxi. (*sūrat al-anbiyā'*).

Muslim local tradition has located tombs and holy places of Dhu 'l-Kifl at various places in Muḥammadan territory from Palestine to Balkh (cf. the references to these places in R. Basset, *Nédromah* [*et les Traras* Paris 1901] and Goldziher's notes in *RHR*, xlv. [1902], p. 219). To two of these places in particular the memory of Dhu 'l-Kifl is more seriously attached by Muḥammadan tradition. One, the erst-while association of which has now, according to Clermont Ganneau's account (*Archaeological Researches in Palestine*, ii. 308), been quite forgotten, is a *ḳubba* of *nebī Kafil* in Kafil Ḥāris (from Kafr Ḥāris; the name is also used in the earlier form in Mudjīr al-Dīn, *al-Uns al-djalīl*, p. 68, 7 and *Tādj al-ʿarūs*, viii. 99, 15) near Nablus, in the district of which the graves of many prophets are located (cf. *ZDPV*, ii. 15). In this case the identification of Dhu 'l-Kifl with Bishr, the son of Aiyūb (see above), was proposed; the Samaritans ascribe it to Kālēb, the companion of Joshua, son of Nūn. Of greater importance down to recent times was the tomb of Dhu 'l-Kifl in Kafil (Massignon prefers the pronunciation Kifil) formerly Ber (Bīr) Mallāḥa, on the left bank of the Hindīya Canal, south of Ḥilla in Mesopotamia, in which districts the tombs of many saints were located and honoured, without a doubt first by the Jews (Yāḳūt, ii. 594).

Bibliography: *a*. The legend: See the commentaries on the passages from the Ḳur'ān referred to above, more particularly: Ṭabarī, *Tafsir*, xvii. 52—54; Zamakhsharī, *Kashshāf* (Cairo 1307), ii. 53; Fakhr al-Dīn al-Rāzī, *Mafātīḥ al-ghaib* (Būlāḳ 1289), vi. 185; Ṭabarī, i. 364; Thaʿlabī, *ʿArā'is* (Cairo 1312), p. 154—155; Ibn Iyās, *Badā'iʿ al-zuhūr fī waḳā'iʿ al-duhūr* (Cairo 1295), p. 96; *TA*, viii. 99, s.v. *k-f-l*; Muṭahhar b. Ṭāhir al-Muḳaddasī (Pseudo-Balkhī) collected the various accounts of Dhu 'l-Kifl in his lost *Kitāb al-maʿānī* (*Livre de la création et de l'histoire*, ed. Cl. Huart, iii. 100, l. 3 from the foot).

b. The Tomb: Niebuhr, *Reisebeschreibung nach Arabien* etc. (Copenhagen 1778), ii. 264—266; Layard, *Niniveh and Babylon* (London 1853), p. 500—501; Jules Oppert, *Expédition scientifique en Mésopotamie*, i. (Paris 1863), 243—246; P. Anastase, in *Mashriḳ*, ii. 61—66; L. Massignon, *Mission en Mésopotamie* (Cairo 1910, in *MIFAO*, xxviii.), p. 53; A. Nöldeke, *Erlebnisse eines türkischen Deserteurs*, in *Beiträge zur Kenntnis d. Orients*, ed. by H. Grothe, vii. 53—54 (where a photograph of the Chefil is given).

DHU 'L-NŪN Abu 'l-Faiḍ (or Faiyāḍ) Thawbān b. Ibrāhīm al-Miṣrī, a celebrated Ṣūfī, son of a Nubian, was born at Ikhmīm in Upper Egypt about the year 180/796. His life is shrowded in obscurity, but certainly he lived at Cairo, and travelled extensively. He was arrested for supporting the anti-Muʿtazilite thesis that the Ḳur'ān is uncreated, and was transported to Baghdād, where, however, after a term of imprisonment he was released, returning to die at Djīza near Cairo in 245/859. His tombstone, which is still extant — its authenticity is apparently not questioned — gives this date (*CIA*, No. 562; Massignon, *Recueil de textes*, p. 15). The Ṣūfī biographers regard him as the father of mystical theory, and after their fashion attribute to him the formulation of the doctrine of gnosis (*maʿrifa*) and the classification of the mystical states and stations (*tartīb al-aḥwāl wa'l-maḳāmāt*). He is also claimed by the writers on magic as a prime authority, and Ibn al-Ḳifṭī (*Ta'rīkh al-ḥukamā'*, ed. Lippert, p. 185) states that he belonged to the school (*ṭabaḳa*) of Djābir b Ḥaiyān; and indeed the *Fihrist* (ed. Flügel, p. 358) mentions as his *al-Rukn al-akbar* and *Kitāb al-thiḳa*; neither of these books has however survived and this ascription seems to be no more credible than the report that he knew the secrets of the hieroglyphs. It is also improbable that the surviving opuscules attributed to him (listed in Brockelmann, *GAL. Suppl.*, i., 353) are really genuine. Many of his "sayings" are quoted by later compilers, and of particular interest is the account of the lengthy disquistition on the pious life said to have been delivered by him to the Caliph al-Mutawakkil on the occasion of his examination for heresy, and related by al-Khaṭīb (*Ta'rīkh Baghdād* (viii., p. 393—4) on the authority of Yūsuf b. al-Ḥusain (i.e. al-Rāzī). His sayings display the same intensity of style and rich imagery which characterize other such Ṣūfīs as Djunaid and Abū Yazīd al-Bisṭāmī (examples are given by Massignon, *Essai sur les origines*, p. 187—191). His skill in epigram is illustrated by the saying, "Make thyself dead during the days of thy lifetime, that thoug mayest live among the dead when thou art gone" (Ibn ʿAsākir, *Ta'rīkh Dimashḳ*, v., p. 283). A number of his verses are cited by all authorities, while Sarrādj preserves passages from his letters, including the following, to a sick man who had solicited his prayers: "My brother, thou askest me to petition God that He may make thy blessings to cease. Know, my brother, that sickness and disease are a means of intimacy for the pure in heart... Wherefore let there be in thee a shame of God, to prevent thee from complaining" (*Kitāb al-lumaʿ*, p. 235). Detailed biographies by late authors are extant, including *al-Sirr al-maknūn fī manāḳib Dhi 'l-Nūn* by Suyūṭī: but much that is related of him is doubtless legendary, as witness the picturesque account of his death in Hudjwīrī (transl. Nicholson, p. 100), and it is hazardous, in our present state of knowledge, to attempt a precise elucidation of his particular contribution to Ṣūfī doctrine.

Bibliography: Hudjwīrī, *Kashf al-maḥdjūb* (transl. Nicholson), p. 100—103; Djalāl al-Dīn Rūmī, *Mathnawī* (transl. C. E. Wilson, London, 1910), ii. 121—128; further the works dealing with the history of Ṣūfism, as the *Nafaḥāt* of Djāmī, and the biography of the Saints (*Tedhkerāt-i-ewliyā*) of Ferīd al-Dīn ʿAṭṭār.

DĪN. Behind the chaos of meanings given by the Arabic lexicographers under the form *dīn* (see, e.g. Lane, *Lexicon*, p. 944) lie three separate words. There is (i.) an Aramaic-Hebrew loanword meaning "judgment"; (ii.) a genuine Arabic word meaning "custom", "usage" which is cognate to (i.), being related as the Hebrew *mishpāṭ* to *shāphaṭ*; (iii.) an entirely distinct Persian word meaning "religion" (cf. Nöldeke, in *ZDMG*, xxxvii., p. 534, note 2, and for the Persian word, derived from *daēnā*: *Grundr. d. iran. Phil.*, i/1, p. 107, 270; i./2, p. 26, 170; ii., p. 644). Vollers contested the existence of *dīn* as a genuine Arabic word and, showing that the Persian *dīn*, "religion", was already in use in Arabic in pre-Islāmic times, held that the meaning "custom", "usage" was derived from it (*ZA*, xiv. 351). This confusion naturally involved the Muslim exegetes of the Ḳur'ān in endless difficulties. Thus, for example, in *malik' yawm' 'l-dīn* (Sūra i. 4; cf. Baiḍāwī, Rāzī and Ṭabarī, i., p. 51), they mostly recognized a necessary meaning of "reckoning", "recompense", yet were in great doubt how to reach it. But under one or other of these three meanings all the Ḳur'ānic passages can be brought. Theologically, dīn is defined as a divine institution (*waḍ' ilāhī*) which guides rational beings, by their choosing it, to salvation here and hereafter, and which covers both articles of belief and actions (*Dict. of Tech. Terms*, p. 503). It thus means "religion" in the broadest sense and is so vague that it was felt necessary to define its difference from *milla* [q.v.] "religious community", *madhhab* "school of canon law" and *sharī'a* [q.v.] "system of divine law". It may mean any religion, but is used peculiarly for Islām, "the religion with Allāh" (Sūra iii. 19). It covers three things: *islām* in its five elements: witnessing to the unity of Allāh and to the prophetship of Muḥammad, worship, poor-rate, fasting, pilgrimage; *īmān*, faith; *iḥsān*, rightdoing. These three make up the dīn of Muslims; see the tradition of how Muḥammad answered Gabriel's questions (Shahrastānī, p. 27). Similarly, all religious, as opposed to intellectual knowledge, meaning what is gained by prophets through major inspiration (*waḥy*) and by saints through minor inspiration (*ilhām*) and received by others on authority from them, can be called *al-'ulūm al-dīnīya*.

Bibliography: Besides the references above, Juynboll, *Handb. des islamischen Gesetzes*, p. 40, 58.

DIYA or 'AḲL is the bloodwit or compensation paid by one who has committed homicide or has wounded another. In the Djāhilīya [q.v.] the price paid by the homicide is said to have been ten she-camels. 'Abd al-Muṭṭalib redeemed his son 'Abd Allāh by the sacrifice of ten she-camels, but, as he had to repeat the sacrifice ten times, a hundred she-camels was henceforth considered the equivalent of a life; and this is the amount laid down in a letter written by Muḥammad to 'Amr b. Ḥazm. The same letter fixed the compensation for a blow penetrating the brain or abdomen at one third of that amount, for the loss of an eye or hand or foot at half, for a tooth or for a wound exposing the bone at five camels. 'Umar put the money equivalent of a hundred camels at 1,000 dīnārs or 12,000 dirhams — the former payable by the 'people of gold' (the people of Egypt and Syria) and the latter by the 'people of silver' (the people of 'Irāḳ), payment being spread over three or four years. Camels were not accepted as payment from these 'people of the towns'; gold was not accepted from the 'people of silver', nor silver from the people of gold, and neither gold nor silver from the tent-dwellers, who paid the she-camels. These camels must be of a definite age and condition, twenty-five she-camels one year old, twenty-five two years old, twenty-five three years old and twenty-five four years old — this for intentional homicide: for unintentional homicide twenty she-camels one year old, twenty two years old, twenty he-camels two years old, twenty she-camels three years old, and twenty she-camels four years old.

A woman receives the same compensation as a man up to one third of the diya of 100 camels: if above one third, then she receives half of what a man does. This is in the system of Mālik: in that of Shāfi'ī she receives in certain cases half a man's diya, *e.g.* five camels for the loss of a finger instead of ten (cf. Lane, s.v. *'aḳala*). A minor or an insane person is not personally liable to give compensation in ordinary circumstances. The diya for the latter is paid by the state. If a minor and a person of age together kill a Muslim intentionally, the latter is put to death, the former paying half the diya. Similarly if a slave and freeman kill a slave intentionally, the former is put to death, the latter paying half the value of the murdered slave.

The diya for wounding a slave so as to expose the bone is a twentieth of his value, for a wound penetrating the brain or abdomen one third, and so on in proportion to the loss in his market value. The law of retaliation holds between slaves as between free persons. If one slave kill another, the owner of the latter may demand the life of the former, or the value of his own slave, or the owner of the former may surrender his slave in compensation. If a Muslim slave wound a Jew or a Christian his master must pay compensation, even if he have to sell the slave, but may not hand over his Muslim slave to these.

If a Christian or a Jew be killed, his bloodwit is half that of a free Muslim. A Muslim may not be put to death for an unbeliever unless he have killed him treacherously. The bloodwit of a Magian is 800 dirhams. The compensation due to these three classes for minor injuries is in the same proportion.

In cases of homicide or wounding unintentionally the perpetrator alone is liable to fine, and, if he cannot pay, the fine remains a debt against him, but his kin may pay it if they wish, for the sake of peace. In this respect, his nearest kin are his brothers on his father's side, then all the male descendants of his father's father, and so on.

A murderer or homicide cannot inherit the diya of his victim, nor can the former inherit his property, since that might have been his motive in killing him.

The diya is of two kinds: *diyat al-'amd*, compensation for an intentional injury, and *diyat al-khaṭa'*, compensation for an unintentional. The diya in full is paid not only for a life, but also for the destruction of the lips, of the eye of a one-eyed person, of the tongue and of the two ears if the hearing be destroyed. If the sight of one eye be destroyed the diya is a hundred dīnārs, and that for a deep wound in the face is more than for one in another part of the head.

Women and children are not liable to pay diya. Employers are liable for injury to minor employees. In the case of a riot between two parties the injured or killed should receive *'aḳl* from the other side. Owners are responsible for their animals, and those who cause them for accidents. There are many injuries for which no diya is named and these cases must be referred to the *mudjtahid*.

Bibliography: The *Muwaṭṭa'* of Mālik b. Anas, section on *'uḳūl*; Bukhārī, section on *diyāt*; al-Marghīnānī, *Hidāya*, English transl. by C. Hamilton (London 1870), Book L; Th. W. Juynboll, *Handbuch des islāmischen Gesetzes*, p. 294—300.

DJABARŪT, a technical term used by the neo-Platonic philosophers and more particularly by those mystics who are devoted to the illuminative philosophy (*al-ishrāḳ*). The form of the word is not Arabic; it is analogous to that of the word *malakūt* which is similarly employed and is Hebrew. *Djabarūt* has the same meaning as the Hebrew *g^e^būrah*, power. The world of djabarūt (*ʿālam al-djabarūt*) is that of divine omnipotence; it is like the world of *malakūt* (*ʿālam al-malakūt*) or divine authority a region above that of earthly things and also above that of real individual things, which corresponds to some extent with the Platonic world of Ideas. The meaning of the word however varies according to the authors who employ it. The world of djabarūt (*ʿālam al-djabarūt*) has been defined by several authors as the "middle world", i.e. the world intermediate between that of Divine Being (*al-lāhūt*) which is above and that of Authority (*al-malakūt*) which is below; cf. the glossary entitled *Iṣṭilāḥāt al-ṣūfīya al-wārida fi 'l-Futūḥāt al-Makkīya*, printed at the end of Djurdjānī's *Taʿrīfāt*.

In Suhrawardī Maḳtūl, a neo-Platonic philosopher put to death for his heterodox opinions in 587/1191, the World of Power (*djabarūt*) is that which the sages see in their ecstasies. "It is possible", he says "that they shall see the Light expanding throughout the world of Power, as well as the beings of the world of Authority whom Hermes and Plato saw".

In the Turkish dictionary entitled *Maʿrifet-nāme*, there is a diagram illustrating the totality of the worlds. In it the world of djabarūt lies between the divine throne (*kursī*) which is below and the Tabernacle (*ʿarsh*) which is above it. Below the throne lies the world of authority (*malakūt*); these two worlds have below them the mortal worlds including Paradise.

According to the opinion of the Ṣūfī ʿAbd al-Razzāḳ al-Ḳāshānī (died 730/1329—30), to whom we owe an interesting treatise on Fate, the world of djabarūt is the place of *ḳaḍāʾ* [q.v.], i.e. of divine determination. It is the world of pure spirit which is above the world of soul. The author here gives the word djabarūt the meaning of "compulsion". The general forms of things existing in that world in a certain measure impose upon the individual realizations in the lower world a part of their perfections. This idea of a constraining force is also found in the illuminative philosophy, where it is stated that the "victorious light" conquers darkness. Ibn Gebirol's philosophy is similar (see S. Karppe, *Etude sur les origines et la Nature du Zohar*, Paris 1911, p. 177—179).

Bibliography: Carra de Vaux, *La Philosophie illuminative d'après Suhrawerdi Meqtoul*, in *JA*, 1902, p. 16 [78]; do., *Fragments d'eschatologie musulmane* (Brussels 1895), p. 27 *sq.*, with an explanation of the diagram in the *Maʿrifet-nāme*; ʿAbd el-Razzāḳ al-Kāshānī, *Risāla fi'l-ḳaḍāʾ wa'l-ḳadar*, ed. Guyard, 1879, p. 3; A. J. Wensinck, *On the Relation between Ghazālī's Cosmology and his Mysticism*, in *Med. Kon. Ak. Wetensch. Amst.*, vol. 75, ser. A., No. 6.

DJABRĀʾĪL, or Djibrīl, Gabriel, is the best known figure among the angels of Islām. He is one of the four archangels, favoured by or "brought near" God, (*muḳarrabūn*) and one of the divine messengers. His duty is to bear the orders of God to mortal prophets and to reveal his mysteries to them. The name as well as the function have been taken over from Jewish and Christian religious tradition (cf. J. Horovitz, *Koranische Untersuchungen*, p. 107; cf. also the art. MALĀʾIKA).

Gabriel plays an important part in the Ḳurʾān; Muḥammad applied the legend of this celestial messenger holding converse with the prophets to himself and believed that he had received his mission and the subject of his preaching from him. Gabriel's name only appears three times in the Ḳurʾān; but in other and important passages, a certain personage is designated by titles or epithets such as "the Spirit", "the Terrible" or even quite indirectly, and the commentators unanimously recognise Gabriel in this personage. This identification is quite justified by a comparison of the different passages.

It is possible that Muḥammad did not at once give a name to the spirit with which he felt himself possessed, as the three passages in which Gabriel's name appears are late (ii, 97 *sq.*; lxvi, 4). In Sūra xcvi., which in all probability is connected with the first revelation of the spirit and the crisis in which he received his mission, the angel is not designated by any name or title; the account, which is quite brief and perhaps mutilated, is impersonal; there it is said: "Recite, in the name of thy Lord who has created; ... recite, for thy Lord is the most beneficent". According to tradition, this first revelation took place on Mount Ḥirāʾ near Mecca, whither Muḥammad had retired, and the voice is said to have added: "O Muḥammad, thou art the apostle of God, and I am Gabriel". But this may be only a later development, inspired by i. 19 of the Gospel of St. Luke, where the angel says to Zacharias: "I am Gabriel, that stand in the presence of God; and I am sent to speak unto thee, and to shew thee these glad tidings".

It appears that as a rule Muḥammad heard the spirit but did not see him. Indeed there are verses in Sūra liii. (1—18) written with great vigour and a deep feeling of sincerity from which it is clear that he only saw him on two occasions: "It is one Mighty in power that has taught him; it is the Vigorous One; he hovered in the loftiest sphere, then he came down and remained suspended in the air. He was at a distance of two bows' length or nearer still; and he revealed to the servant of God, what he had to reveal to him ... he had already seen him in another vision near the lote tree that marks the boundary ... the lote tree was all covered". The minuteness of the details leave no room to doubt the sincerity of the visionary. Tradition adds that after this vision, Gabriel brought to the Prophet the mare or chimaera Burāḳ [q.v.].

The legend of the Archangel Gabriel is highly developed among the Muslims; this is soon noticed if one looks through works rich in legends, like the *Mukhtaṣar al-ʿadjāʾib* (*Abrégé des Merveilles*, transl. Carra de Vaux) or the first volume of Ṭabarī's Persian *Chronicle* (transl. Zotenberg). There is scarcely a prophet to whom this celestial envoy has not brought help or revelations. Gabriel consoled Adam after the Fall and revealed to him twenty-one leaves; he taught him the cultivation of wheat, the working of iron and the letters of the alphabet; he took him to the site of Mecca where he taught him the rites of pilgrimage. It was Gabriel also who showed Noah how to build the Ark; he saved Abraham from the flames (cf. Sūra xxi. 69) and had many further relations with this patriarch. He helped Moses to fight against the magicians of Egypt; at the Exodus he appeared on a horse with white feet to decide the Egyptians to enter the Red Sea which was to swallow them up. He appeared to Samuel, and to David to whom he taught the art of making coats-of-mail; he comforted this prophet and brought him leaves with ten riddles which Solomon solved. As in the Gospel, he came to Zacharias to announce the birth of St. John.

In the preparation of charms and talismans, Gabriel also plays an important part; his name frequently appears on the sides of magic squares, for example, along with those of the other Archangels, Mīkāʾīl, Azrāʾīl and Isrāfīl.

DJABRĪYA is the name given in the history of the sects to those, who in opposition to the Ḳadarīya deny the freedom of the will, and on this point make no distinction between man and inanimate nature, in as much as his actions are subordinate to the compulsion (*djabr*) of God. The most prominent champion of this view is Djahm b. Ṣafwān [q.v.]; the Nadjdjārīya, Ḍirārīya, Kullābīya and Bakrīya are also considered Djabrīya. Muʿtazilī writers however also charge the orthodox Ashʿarīya with being Djabrīya, which, as Shahrastānī rightly points out, is not strictly correct as, although they deny the freedom of the will, they allow that man has some influence on action (*kasb*, appropriation; q.v.).

Bibliography: Shahrastānī, p. 59 *sq.*; Horten, *Die philosophischen Systeme der spekulativen Theol. im Islam*, p. 54 *sq.*

DJAʿFAR b. Muḥammad also called al-Ṣādiḳ ("the Trustworthy"), the sixth of the twelve Imāms. Djaʿfar was born in 80/699—700 or 83/702—3 and succeeded his father Muḥammad al-Bāḳir as Imām. He played no part in politics. On the other hand he was celebrated for his thorough knowledge of Tradition and is said also to have occupied himself with astrology, alchemy, and other secret sciences; but the works which bear his name are later forgeries. He died in Madīna in 148/756. The members of the Imāmīya sect are agreed upon the succession to the Imāmate down to his time; but they do not agree as to his rightful successor, for he had several sons and no fewer than four of them, Muḥammad, ʿAbd Allāh, Mūsā, and Ismāʿīl, claimed the Imāmate. His son Mūsā al-Kāẓim is however recognised by most as the seventh Imām.

Bibliography: Ṭabarī, iii. 2509 *sq.*; Ibn Khallikān, No. 128 (de Slane's translation, i. 300 *sq.*); Shahrastānī, p. 16, 124 (Haarbrücker, p. 24, 187); Nawbakhtī, *Firaḳ al-Shīʿa, (Bibl. Isl.* 4), index; *GAL Suppl.*, i, 104.

DJAFR. There developed very early in Shīʿī Islām a belief that the descendants of ʿAlī were in possession of a secret tradition, a body of religious and political esoteric knowledge covering all things to the end of the world. The general Muslim reverence for the family of the Prophet had grown in the Shīʿa to a belief that the Imāms could neither sin nor err. Thus, a book was ascribed to ʿAlī giving the inner meaning of the Ḳurʾān (Ibn Saʿd, ii., p. 101, l. 19), in intelligible enough opposition to the Sunnī exegesis of Ibn ʿAbbās. Even the Khāridjīs made a jest of the secret knowledge professed by the ʿAlids (*Aghānī*, xx., p. 107, ll. 16 *sq.*), and in the third (ninth) century, Bishr b. al-Muʿtamir, the Muʿtazilī, names a book by which they are deceived as the *Djafr* (Djāḥiẓ, *Ḥayawān*, vi., p. 94, l. 1). Ibn Ḳutaiba (d. 276/889) also refers to this book. In a quotation by Damīrī in his *Kitāb al-ḥayawān* (s.v. *djafr*, vol. i., p. 171, ed. of 1313) from Ibn Ḳutaiba's *Adab al-kātib* the *Djafr* is said to be a book by Djaʿfar b. Muḥammad al-Ṣādiḳ (the sixth Imām, d. 148/765), written on the skin of a *djafr*, a just weaned kid or lamb, for the information of the House of the Prophet, containing all that they needed to know and all that was to happen until the Last Day. This passage does not seem to be in Grünert's text, and Damīrī may have mistaken his book. For Ibn Ḳutaiba, according to Ibn Khallikān, has a passage to the same effect in his *Mukhtalif al-ḥadīth* and adds there some lines by Hārūn b. Saʿd (or Saʿīd) al-Idjlī, head of the Zaidīs, ridiculing this pretension (Ibn Khallikān, de Slane's text, p. 432; de Slane's transl., ii., p. 184; Wüstenfeld's text, No. 419; Goldziher, in *ZDMG*, xli., p. 123; Friedländer, in *JAOS*, xxix., p. 106). Ibn Ḳutaiba's etymology is more than dubious; there seems no trace of *djafr* being used in the sense "vellum" or "parchment". Van Vloten (*Chiitisme*, p. 56, note 6) suggested a connection with γραφή and Goldziher (*Beitr. z. Liter. der Shīʿa*, p. 20, note 5) with Djaʿfar. But more singular still is the fact that while the *Fihrist* has many references to Djaʿfar al-Ṣādiḳ (p. 178, l. 13; p. 198, l. 7; p. 224, ll. 20 *sq.*; p. 317, l. 26; p. 355, ll. 1 *sq.*) and does not hesitate to bring him into connection with Djābir b. Ḥaiyān the alchemist (p. 355) and questions, though to reject, his asserted authorship of a medical book on myrobalan (p. 317, l. 26), it has no scrap of mention of this *Djafr*. A *Kitāb al-malāḥim* by ʿAlī b. Yaḳtīn is referred back to his authority (p. 224, l. 24), and it is plain that such books were current in his environment; cf. another *Kitāb al-malāḥim* (p. 223, l. 20) and a *Kitāb al-kashf* (p. 222, l. 17). Yet the *Djafr* would certainly fall within the class of *malāḥim* books. The existence, however, of this unseen, infallible book was universally asserted by Shīʿīs. When a Shīʿī author tells how Maʾmūn appointed the ʿAlid Imām, ʿAlī b. Mūsā al-Riḍā (eighth Imām of the Twelvers; d. 202/817) as his successor, he always adds that ʿAlī in accepting, wrote to Maʾmūn "although the *Djafr* and *Djāmiʿa* indicate the opposite of this" (e.g. *al-Fakhrī*, ed. Cairo, p. 198). The *Djāmiʿa* is another similar book often mentioned in this connection (for it see Goldziher, *Beitr. z. Liter. d. Shīʿa*, p. 55 and note, and for an interesting hypothesis of its origin, bringing it together with the *Rasāʾil* of the Ikhwān al-Ṣafāʾ: Casanova, in *JA*, series 9, vol. xi., p. 151 *sq.*). Yet another such book is the *Maṣḥaf Fāṭima* (Goldziher, *l.c.*). Another historical occasion with which it is always connected is the appearance in the Maghrib of Ibn Tūmart. It was the Muwaḥḥid tradition that their Mahdī had been a favourite pupil of al-Ghazzālī, the custodian at the time of the *Djafr*, that al-Ghazzālī had learned from the *Djafr* the high destiny of Ibn Tūmart, and that at his death the book had passed into the custody of Ibn Tūmart (see Macdonald, *Life of al-Ghazzālī*, in *JAOS*, vol. xx., p. 113, and especially *Ḳarṭās*, p. 116 *sq.*; add the pseudograph *Sirr al-ʿalamain*, ed. Bombay 1314, p. 2). But the opinion of the saner and more sceptical public may be gathered from al-Bīrūnī and Ibn Khaldūn, Al-Bīrūnī (d. 440/1048) speaks (*Chronology*, transl. Sachau, p. 76, 182) with the greatest reverence of al-Ṣādiḳ, but has no patience with the decisions on the calendar falsely ascribed to him. He does not mention the *Djafr*. Ibn Khaldūn treats the *Djafr* in connection with the books of *malāḥim* (Quatremère's text, ii., p. 184, 191; ed. Būlāḳ 1274, p. 162, 164; de Slane's transl., ii., p. 214, 224). He believes that the House of Muḥammad had, like all the *walīs*, the *karāma* of prophecy. Such a book, therefore, might have been produced by Djaʿfar al-Ṣādiḳ, but he finds no proof of such connection. The fragments in currency may, he thinks, be related to a book called *al-Djafr* which Hārūn b. Saʿīd al-Idjlī possessed and which he said had come to him from Djaʿfar al-Ṣādiḳ. But of that descent there was no proof (but see above as to this Hārūn). There was trace also, said Ibn Khaldūn, of another book called

Djafr. It was by Ya'kūb b. Isḥāḳ al-Kindī, astronomer to Hārūn al-Rashīd; it treated astrologically of the fates of the Muslim empire and was based on astronomical conjunctions. But it had been completely lost. So far, the connection of the *Djafr* has been with prophetic traditions and astrological calculations (cf. de Goeje's *Mémoire sur les Carmathes*, p. 115 *sq.*). But in time there arose a belief that in it meanings were cabalistically expressed by separate letters, and *'ilm al-djafr* came to mean *'ilm al-ḥurūf*, the method of prediction by assigning (by *abdjad*) numerical values to letters (Ḥādjdjī Khalīfa, ii. 603 *sq.*). To this science (*al-sīmiyā'*) Ibn Khaldūn devotes a section (Quatremère, iii., p. 137 *sq.*; de Slane, iii., p. 188 *sq.*; Būlāḳ ed., p. 245 *sq.*), but makes no allusion to Dja'far or the *Djafr*. In his exposition *sīmiyā'* reads like a reductio ad absurdum of nominalism, and, certainly, the idea that letters in themselves represent real things, combined with a recognition that Arabic is sacred in itself as the vehicle of the Muslim message, seems to have led to this transition (*Dict. of Techn. Terms*, i., p. 202 *sq.*; also on p. 127—131, s.v. *basṭ*, on *djafr* as *'ilm al-ḥurūf*). This has come to be the ruling association with the word *djafr*. For further details, references and instances of existing treatises and fragments bearing this name, see Brockelmann, *GAL* i. 44, l. 11; p. 220, note; p. 446 (Ibn 'Arabī, No. 77, 78, 80); p. 464 (No. 5, 6); *Suppl.* i, 75, 798, 839; Murādī, *Silk al-durar*, i., p. 51 (a translation into Turkish of *Djafr al-Aḳyādjī* [?] still said to be preserved in the library of the Serai at Constantinople); Ahlwardt, *Berlin Cat.*, iii., p. 551 *sq.*; Rieu, *Suppl. to the Cat. of Arab. MSS in Brit. Mus.*, No. 828. For use in popular literature, see the Story of 'Aṭṭāf in Burton's *Arabian Nights*, Library ed., vol. xii., p. 114 *sq.*: the book is in the library of Hārūn al-Rashīd and is consulted by him.

Bibliography: Goldziher, *Vorlesungen* [1], p. 224 *sq.*, 263 *sq.* (important); Ed. Doutté, *Magie et Religion*, p. 117 *sq.* (on *'ilm al-ḥurūf*); Reinaud, *Monuments musulmans*, i., p. 346 *sq.*, 370 *sq.*

DJAHANNAM, the Muslim name of Hell. The word is derived from the Hebrew *gēhinnōm* or valley of *ḥinnōm* (Joshua, xv. 8); it was a valley near Jerusalem in which sacrifices were offered to Moloch, in the days of impiety. The form with the long vowel (*djahannām*) means a deep well.

The word *djahannam* and the idea of hell frequently appear in the Ḳur'ān, whether because Muḥammad himself had been much struck with the idea or because he thought it useful to insist on it to work upon the feelings of his hearers. He does not however seem to have had a very definite picture before him; in fact, in certain passages, he speaks of it as if it were something portable: "Bring hell" God shall say on the last judgment (Sūra lxxxix. 22—3); the angels will then form their ranks "and hell shall be brought nigh". In this passage it would appear that Muḥammad represented hell as a kind of gigantic monster, with gaping, glowing jaws, ready to devour the damned; western artists of the middle ages have sometimes similarly depicted the purgatory of St. Brandan. This explains how in another passage Muḥammad says: "hell shall almost burst for fury" (Sūra lxvii. 8).

Al-Ghazzālī, in his curious eschatological treatise entitled *al-Durra al-fākhira*, has discussed these laconic texts. Hell begins to tremble when God commands that it shall be brought in. The angels having told it that God does not wish to punish it but to punish guilty men with it, it allows itself to be led. It walks on four legs, each of which is bound by 70,000 rings; on each of them are 70,000 demons each of which is strong enough to rend mountains to pieces. In moving, hell gives forth a buzzing, groaning and rattling noise; sparks and smoke are sent out from it and the horizon is filled with darkness. At the moment when it is still separated from mortals by a space of a thousand years. it escapes the hands of the demons and throws itself with a terrible noise on the crowd of men assembled at the place of judgment.

But the conception of hell as an animal is not the dominant one in the Ḳur'ān; beside it there is the well-known architectural conception of a hell composed of concentric circles arranged in the form of a crater. This representation has its prototypes in antiquity, in the infernal rivers of the Greeks, in the Assyrian hell with seven gates in the legends of Ishtar. It is the conception which took hold of the popular imagination in the middle ages, in the east as well as in the west, and which we find expressed with so much power in Dante's work.

Muḥammad had only a generalized notion of the structure of hell; he speaks of its gates, specifying that there are seven (Sūra xxxix. 71; xv. 43—44). A plan of hell is given in the Turkish work, the *Ma'rifet-nāme*. It is situated under the pedestal of the world, above the Bull and the fish (corresponding to the Behemoth and Leviathan of the Bible) who support the earth. It is composed of seven stories forming a vast crater. Above is a bridge thrown the whole length across it; this bridge, as narrow as the edge of a sword, has to be crossed by the souls in order to enter Paradise; the souls of saints cross it in a moment; those of ordinary righteous people take a longer or shorter time to cross it, while those of the unrighteous do not reach Paradise but fall into the gulf.

At the lowest stage of hell is a tree called *Zaḳḳūm* which has for flowers the heads of demons (cf. Sūra xxxvii. 60—64), a cauldron of boiling and stinking pitch and a well which reaches to the bottom of all things.

The punishments in the Muslim hell are varied and graduated according to the kind and importance of the sins, as in Dante's Inferno; the Ḳur'ān hardly mentions them; but they are described by some authors, notably Suyūṭī (died 911/1505).

These very materialistic representations of the structure of hell and its punishments have not satisfied all spirits in Islām; even the pious and believing Ghazzālī allows himself to explain away a little on this point. Thus the road or bridge thrown across hell has for him only a moral meaning; it is merely the "straight path", by which God conducts the faithful and symbolises the just mean between opposite faults; it is the boundary between excess and failure, in which perfection lies (see the end of his *Maḍnūn*, ed. Bombay, p. 126). According to Avicenna, the pains of hell chiefly consist in sinful souls retaining their sensual inclinations after death; but thus they suffer horribly as they have no bodies wherewith to satisfy them.

The Ḳur'ān appears to hesitate a little on the question of the eternity of punishment in hell; the passages which refer to this point do not quite agree. Perhaps this uncertainty is due merely to the fact that Muḥammad, who was not a speculative philosopher, was not able to clarify a question into which there entered such an abstract conception as eternity.

"They for whom the balance shall be light",

it is said in one passage (Sūra xxiii. 103) "are those who have destroyed themselves in hell and shall dwell there for ever (*khālidūn*)". But elsewhere (xi. 106—7) Muḥammad says: "The damned shall be cast into the fire ... they shall dwell there so long as the heavens and the earth shall last, unless God wills otherwise".

Al-Ashʿarī has reproached the Muʿtazilīs and the Ḳadarīs with making men despair of the mercy of God, by teaching that sinners are condemned to eternal fire. This, according to him, is contrary to the words of the Ḳurʾān (Sūra iv. 116): "he will pardon all else except idolatry to whom he will" and to this traditional saying of the Prophet: "he shall make men come out of hell after they have been burned and reduced to cinders". This Imām's view is that which has prevailed in Islām.

Bibliography: Carra de Vaux, *La Doctrine de l'Islām* (Paris 1909), chap. ii.; do., *Fragments d'Eschatologie Musulmane* (Brussels 1895); Léon Gautier, *La Perle Précieuse de Ghazālī* (ed. and transl. 1878); A. F. Mehren, *Abou 'l-Hasan Ali al-Ashari*, in *Travaux de la 3e session du Congrès Intern. des Orientalistes*, 1876, p. 47; Miguel Asín Palacios, *La escatologia Musulmana en la Divina Comedia*, Madrid 1919; Wensinck, *The Muslim Creed*, Index, s.v. Hell; E. Cerulli, *Il "Libro della Scala"*, Vat. City, 1949.

DJĀHILĪYA is the name given to the state of things which obtained in Arabia before the promulgation of Islām, or in a narrower sense the period when there was no prophet, between Jesus and Muḥammad. It is the collective noun from *djāhilī*, a pagan Arab, especially a poet of the earliest of the four chronological classes, of which the second is *mukhadram*, denoting one who was born in pagan times, but who died under Islām.

As to the exact meaning of the term Djāhilīya the usual opinion is that of J. D. Michaelis (1781) and others, that it is "the time of Ignorance", as the period before Christianity is named in Acts xvii. 30, Islām being regarded as the period of enlightenment and knowledge. *Djahila* 'to be ignorant' is the antonym of *ʿalima* 'to know' frequently in the old language and oftener in more recent times. Thus ʿAntara, *Muʿallaḳa*, l. 43: *in kunti djāhilat^{an} bi-mā lam taʿlamī*. But Goldziher points out that this sense of *djahila* is really secondary and that in its primary sense it is opposed not to *ʿalima* but to *ḥaluma*, to be clement, forbearing, grave, and so means to be rude or rough or boorish, and he cites a number of verses in which derivatives from these two roots stand together by way of contrast, e.g. al-Shanfarā, *Lāmīyat al-Arab*, v. 53: *wa-lā tazdahi 'l-adjhālu ḥilmī*. Hence he renders al-Djāhilīya "Barbarei" (*Muhammedanische Studien*, i. 219 *sq*).. The word occurs in the Ḳurʾān Sūra iii. 154; v. 50; xxxiii. 33; xlviii. 26.

Goldziher draws a sharp distinction between the Arabs of the South and those of Central Arabia. The former were of a distinctly religious turn of mind, the latter had practically no religion. But this statement has to be modified by the consideration that so many southern Arabs migrated to the north. This was especially the case with Yathrib. Moreover, as D. S. Margoliouth has remarked, inscriptions may yet be found which will throw light on the religious ideas of the Central Arabian tribes, as has been done in the case of the southern and northern. But, so far as we know at present, the people of Central Arabia, to judge from the poetical and other remains, were indifferent to religious ideas. The utmost they could attain to was a vague deism or belief in Fate (*manāyā, manūn*). The descriptions of idolaters in the Ḳurʾān refer largely to times long past and very little at all to Muḥammad's contemporaries, whose treatment of Muḥammad shows that their reverence for their idols was not very deep.

What was of very much more importance to the pagan Arab than religion was his tribal connection. The clan was the unit from which all the society he had was built up. Even Islām was powerless to displace his attachment to his tribe. and tribal feuds were carried on after the time of Muḥammad as before, if not to the same extent. The great rivalry of North and South was still being fought out in Khurāsān in the iind (viiith) century (Masʿūdī, vi. 36 *sq*.) and even at the present day the population of a district will keep up the distinction of Ḳaisī and Yamanī (Finn, *Stirring Times*, i. 226 *sq*.). Much of the old poetry consists of panegyric of the poet's tribe and satire of those to which he does not belong; and the tribe is sometimes a very wide term.

The pagan Arab's idea of morality is expressed by the word *muruwwa*, that is, manliness, virtus. This consists mainly in courage and generosity. His courage is shown by the number of enemies he kills, by his defending his own clan, but also by chivalrous treatment of his foes very much akin to that of the mediaeval knight. His generosity appears in his being always more ready to join in the fray than to share in the spoil, in his readiness to slaughter his camels for behoof of the guest and of the poor and helpless, and in his being generally more willing to give than to receive.

Arab hospitality no doubt often led to excesses in both eating and drinking, such as were common in Europe a century ago, and it cost them a hard struggle to give up the use of wine on turning Muslims. It was considered with some a point of honour to remain in a tavern until the wine-merchant was compelled to take down his sign, the wine being spent. At the same time the sot or habitual drunkard was not tolerated. Barrāḍ b. Ḳais was expelled from more than one tribe on account of his vicious habits in this respect. Wine-songs continued to be composed long after Islām had forbidden the drinking of wine, poetry and religion presenting in this respect a curious contrast. But so strong was the Arab liking for wine that its use was permitted during the Umaiyad period, though forbidden again under the ʿAbbāsids.

The position of women among the pagan Arabs was in some respects freer than under Islām. Marriage with two sisters and the *nikāḥ al-maḳt* (marriage with the mother-in-law) were permitted, but on the other hand the institution of the veil was unknown. Divorce was not more easy than it is under the Muslim code and women had the right to it as well as men. Indeed, the relations of the sexes before the time of Muḥammad were in some respects quite good. In any case they were capable of being improved, whereas after the law of Islām had once come into force, alteration was not to be thought of. The worst feature of the Islāmic marriage code — that of the *mustaḥill* — was unknown.

The produce of the soil of Arabia has always been insufficient to support its inhabitants. In certain favoured spots such as the Yemen, and in the oases food was to be had in plenty. The people of Mecca made their living as carriers between the Yemen and Syria, to which fell to be added the profit they made out of the pilgrims who annually thronged their town. But the desert population of Arabia has always been in a state of chronic starvation. Partly for this reason they had recourse to the practice of burying female infants at their birth. The flesh and milk of their camels was supplemented by constant raids upon neighbouring tribes. These raids did not increase the total amount of supplies available, but they helped to keep down the number of mouths to feed.

For the purposes of trade and commerce, as well as in order to enable tribes living at a distance to visit the national shrines and attend the fairs, four months in each year were set apart as sacred months in which raids could not be undertaken. By far the most important of the sacred places to which pilgrimages were made annually was Mecca, and the most famous of the fairs was that of ʿUkāẓ. During these months caravans could pass almost unarmed throughout the country. Muḥammad's first success in arms was due to a breach of this "truce of God", and when he made the Arab year purely lunar he ruined the annual fairs; but the habit of pilgrimage to sacred places was too deeply rooted in the Arab nature for him to put a stop to it. The utmost he could do was to abolish all the shrines save one, and make that the house of the One God.

Bibliography: Ṭabarī, i. 1073 *sq.*; Ibn ʿAbd Rabbihi, *al-ʿIḳd al-farīd* (Cairo 1304), i. 34, 81; iii. 48 *sq.*; Masʿūdī, iii. 78 *sq.*; Ibs̲h̲īhī, *Mustaṭraf* (Būlāḳ 1268), chapter 59; Caussin de Perceval, *Essai sur l'histoire des Arabes* (Paris 1847—1848); Goldziher, *Muhammedanische Studien* (Halle a. S. 1888—1890), i., 219 *sq.*; W. R. Smith, *Kinship and marriage in early Arabia* (3th ed., London, 1885); J. Wellhausen, *Reste arabischen Heidentums*, (2th ed. Berlin 1897); G. Jacob, *Altarabisches Beduinenleben* (2d ed. Berlin 1897); H. Lammens, *Le berceau de l'Islam* (Rome 1914); do. in *MFOB* (1922, 1924, 1926); I. Guidi, *L'Arabie antéislamique* (Paris 1921); B. Farès, *L'Honneur chez les Arabes avant l'Islam* (Paris 1932).

DJAHM B. ṢAFWĀN ABŪ MUḤRIZ, a client of the Banū Rāsib, called AL-TIRMIDHĪ by some and AL-SAMARḲANDĪ by others, a Muḥammadan theologian, who attached himself to Ḥārit̲h̲ b. Suraid̲j̲, the "man with the black banner", during the risings in K̲h̲urāsān towards the end of the Umaiyad period and was therefore put to death in 128/745—6 by Salm b. Aḥwaz. As a theologian he occupies an independent position in as much as he agreed with the Murd̲j̲iʾīs on the one hand in teaching that belief is an affair of the heart and with the Muʿtazilīs in denying all anthropomorphic attributes of God, but on the other hand he was one of the strongest defenders of *d̲j̲abr* [cf. the article DJABRĪYA]. He only allowed that God is all-powerful and the Creator because these are things which cannot be predicated of any created being. He further denied the eternity of Paradise and Hell. His followers, called *D̲j̲ahmīya* after him, survived down to the vth (xith) century around Tirmid̲h̲ but then adopted the doctrines of the As̲h̲ʿarīs.

Bibliography: Ṭabarī, ii. 1918 *sq.*; al-S̲h̲ahrastānī, p. 60 *sq.*; Horten, *Die philosophischen Systeme der spekulativen Theologen im Islām*, p. 135 (with further Bibliography); al-Ashʿarī, *Maḳālāt al-Islāmīyīn* (ed. Ritter, Istanbul-Leipzig 1929) i., 279 *sq.*; W. M. Watt, *Free will and predestination in early Islam*, London 1948, p. 99—104; A. Subhan, *Al-Jahm bin Safwan and his philosophy*, in *Isl. Culture*, xi. 221—27.

DJĀʾIZ is commonly reckoned as one of the Five Orders (*al-aḥkām al-k̲h̲amsa*; best in Goldziher, *Ẓâhiriten*, p. 66 *sq.*; cf. also *Dict. of Techn. Terms*, i. 379 *sq.*; T. W. Juynboll, *Handbuch*, p. 59 *sq.*) and as synonymous with *mubāḥ* "permitted", an action legally indifferent, neither forbidden nor commanded nor recommended, the doing of which will not be rewarded, nor the omission punished. But *d̲j̲āʾiz* is much wider, and from its meaning of "current", "allowable", covers not only *mubāḥ* but anything not legally hindered, thus *wād̲j̲id*, *mandūb* and *makrūh*. Further, it can be taken intellectually as well as legally and mean what is not unthinkable, whether necessary, probable, improbable or possible (*Dict. of Techn. Terms*, i. 207 *sq.*).

DJALĀL AL-DĪN RŪMĪ, one of the great mystic poets of Islām, was born at Bal̲k̲h̲ in 604/1207. His family claimed descent from Abū Bakr and was connected by marriage with the royal family of K̲h̲ʷārizm. When three years of age (607/1210), he was taken by his father to Nīs̲h̲āpūr and presented to the aged ʿAṭṭār. The latter, according to the legend, predicted his future greatness and gave him his *Book of Secrets*. His father Bahāʾ al-Dīn Walad had to leave Bal̲k̲h̲ at this time, because he had incurred the wrath of the ruler Muḥammad Ḳuṭb al-Dīn K̲h̲ʷārizms̲h̲āh. He took the young D̲j̲alāl al-Dīn with him and after visiting Bag̲h̲dād, Mecca, Damascus, Malaṭya, Arzand̲j̲ān and Laranda, finally settled in Ḳōnya about 623 or 625 (1226 or 1227) where he found a protector in the person of the Sald̲j̲ūḳ prince ʿAlāʾ al-Dīn Kaiḳubād. He was appointed professor there and on his death in 628/1230—1, D̲j̲alāl al-Dīn succeeded him in the chair; he never again left Ḳōnya except for a short journey.

The event which had the greatest effect on his intellectual and moral life was his meeting with the Ṣūfī S̲h̲ams al-Dīn Tibrīzī. The latter in the course of his wanderings came to Ḳōnya; there he saw D̲j̲alāl al-Dīn, on whom he exercised a powerful influence. Rūmī acknowledged what he owed to his master by dedicating a great part of his works to him. As a result of this meeting, he abandoned the study of sciences in order to devote himself entirely to mysticism. He founded the order of Mawlawīs or "dancing derwīs̲h̲es"; contrary to the general Muslim practice he gave a considerable place to music in the ceremonies of the order. He died at Ḳōnya in 672/1273.

His tomb is in the monastery founded by him. The architecture of this *tekke* is of remarkable delicacy and beauty; the mosque is adorned with carved candelabra, valuable tapestries, embroideries and beautifully engraved inscriptions. His successors are interred near D̲j̲alāl al-Dīn. The order has always had at its head one of his descendants who lives in Ḳōnya; he is called the Čelebi. D̲j̲alāl al-Dīn is often invoked under the title *mawlānā*.

Al-Rūmī's principal work is the *Mat̲h̲nawī*, a vast Persian poem in six books, a mixture of fables, anecdotes, symbols and reflections intended to illustrate and explain Ṣūfī doctrines; he undertook it at the instigation of his secretary and first successor Ḥusām al-Dīn; he took fourteen years to compose it. He also wrote a *Dīwān* and a prose treatise entitled *Fīhi mā fīhi* "what is within is within"; this last work, which is unknown in Persia, is to be found in several Istanbul libraries. D̲j̲alāl al-Dīn is a poet of the first rank; he possesses the most diverse qualities: variety and originality of imagery, dignity and picturesqueness, learning and familiar charm, depth of feeling and of thought. The composition of the *Mat̲h̲nawī* is, it must be granted, very disjointed; the stories follow one another in no order; the examples suggest reflections which in their turn suggest other examples so that the narrative is often interrupted by long digressions; but this want of order seems to be a result of the lyrical inspiration, which carries the poet along as if by leaps and bounds, and if the reader yields to it, the effect is by no means displeasing.

As a philosopher, al-Rūmī is less original than as a poet. His teaching is that of Ṣūfism, expressed with glowing enthusiasm; it is not systematically expounded and the thought is sometimes carried away by the lyrical fervour; to reconstruct this philosophy, it would be necessary to collect the elements, which are scattered throughout the book, and fix some points.

As amongst other Ṣūfī writers, many Neo-Platonic ideas are found in Rūmī; others are closely allied to those of Christian mystics; some are very boldly expressed, which may be excused on account of the poetic form. As an example of the last we note this thought, bold enough in theodicy, that even evil contributes to the glory of God, that it makes part of his perfection; a painter who wishes to represent the ugly, shows skill if he renders it in a hideous fashion: "The ugly says: O King, Creator of the ugly, you are as powerful in the beautiful as in the ugly which is despised". — Another very bold idea is that of an old S̲h̲aik̲h̲ who says to the Ṣūfī Bāyazīd, when he was going on a pilgrimage: Go around me; that will be equivalent to going round the Kaʿba; "although the Kaʿba is the house of God, destined by him for the accomplishment of religious rites, my being is superior to it as the house of his secrets". — The episode of Moses and the herdsman has often been quoted, in which the author appears to teach that the manner of expressing one's religious feeling is of no importance, that rites and formulae are nothing and that the feeling is everything: "What can words do for me"? says God to Moses, "it is a glowing heart that I want; inflame the hearts with love and pay no heed to thought or expression".

Another well known passage is one that contains a kind of doctrine of transmigration: "I die as a stone and become a plant; I die as a plant and am raised to the rank of an animal; I die as an animal and am reborn man ... dying as man, I shall come to life again an angel ... I shall even transcend the angel to become something no man has seen, and then I shall be the Nothing, the Nothing". And lastly this apparently pantheistic fragment, in which the poet identifies himself with all nature: "I am the mote in the sunbeam; I am the ball of the sun; I am the glow of morning; I am the breath of evening, etc.".

The *Mat̲h̲nawī* has been often commented upon, in Turkish by al-Anḳarawī, in Persian by Baḥr al-ʿUlūm, in Arabic and even in Urdu; there exists a Turkish translation in verse.

The dance of the whirling derwīs̲h̲es, which goes back to D̲j̲alāl al-Dīn, seems to be an attempt to express the Neoplatonic idea of the perfection and the harmony of the movement of the heavenly bodies. The same idea is to be found in Ibn Ṭufail's philosophical romance *Ḥaiy b. Yaḳẓān.*

Bibliography: *Mat̲h̲nawī*, text with Turkish verse translation by Sulaimān Naḥīfī (Būlāḳ 1268); *Mat̲h̲nawī*, with the Turkish commentary of Anḳarawī, in 6 volumes (Imprimerie ʿĀmire 1289); G. Rosen, *Mesnewi oder Doppelverse des Scheich Mewlānā Dschelāl-ed-Dīn Rūmī* (Leipzig 1849) (transl. of Book i.); transl. of Bk. i. by Sir James Redhouse (London 1881) in verse; an abridged transl. of the whole poem by E. H. Whinfield, London 1887 and 1898; edition and translation by R. A. Nicholson, in *GMS*, 1925—37, 6 vols.; von Rosenzweig, *Auswahl aus den Divanen des grössten mystischen Dichters Persiens* (Vienna 1838); Rückert, *Aus dem Dīwān* (1819; *Ges. Werke, herausgeg. von* Laistner, iii., p. 246—258); Tholuck, *Blütensammlung*, p. 53—191; *Moïse et le Chevrier apologue persan*, transl. by F. Baudry, in *Magasin Pittoresque*, 1857, p. 242; *The Maṣnavī*, Book ii., by E. H. Wilson (London 1901), 2 vol. (vol. i. transl., vol. ii. commentaries); *Mat̲h̲nawi 'l-aṭfāl* ("Mat̲h̲nawī for Children"), a volume of selections with illustrations, printed in Persia 1309; E. G. Browne, *A Literary History of Persia*, ii. 515 *sq.*; P. Horn, *Geschichte der persischen Litteratur* (Leipzig 1901), p. 161—168; Carra de Vaux, *Gazali* (Paris 1902), p. 291—306; do., *Les Penseurs de l'Islam*, iv. (Paris 1923), p. 317—328; Clement Huart, *Koniah, la ville des Derviches Tourneurs*; Farīdūn b. Aḥmad Sipahsālār, *Aḥwāl-i Mawlānā D̲j̲alāl al-Dīn Mawlawī*, ed. Saʿīd Nafīsī, Tihrān 1325 (1946).

D̲J̲ĀLŪT, the Goliath of the Bible. Muslim tradition has somewhat increased his importance, for in addition to the well known story of David's fight with him, several other episodes from various chapters of the Bible, relating to the wars of the Israelites with the Midianites and Philistines, are connected with his name.

The Ḳur'ān briefly narrates how D̲j̲ālūt attacked Ṭālūt (Saul) and how he was killed by David (ii. 249—251). It places in this campaign the story of the soldiers who were tested by their manner of drinking at the crossing of a river, an episode which really refers to an expedition of Gideon against the Midianites (*Judges*, vii); cf. also Horovitz, *Koranische Untersuchungen*, p. 106.

According to Masʿūdī (iii. 241) Palestine was originally inhabited by Berbers and D̲j̲ālūt was the name borne by the Berber Kings down to the the one who was killed by David. This last king was, according to Masʿūdī, a son of Mālūd, son of Dabāl, son of Ḥattān, son of Fāris; he invaded the lands of the Israelites with several Berber tribes. The same author gives the episode of the crossing of the river as in the Ḳur'ān and adds that David slew Goliath "with his sling", which is not stated in the Ḳur'ān. This incident took place at Baisān in the G̲h̲ōr or lower valley of the Jordan. Near Baisān are a spring and a valley, which are actually called Goliath's spring and valley (*ʿAin D̲j̲ālūt*) to this day.

In the *Muk̲h̲taṣar al-ʿad̲j̲ā'ib* (*Abrégé des Merveilles*, transl. Carra de Vaux, p. 101), Goliath is classed among the Canaanites, the descendants of Kanaʿān son of Ham, and the verse (v. 22) in the Ḳur'ān: "In this land there is a people or giants", is referred to them. According to Ṭabarī's *Chronicle* (Persian synopsis, transl. Zotenberg) Goliath was a descendant of the ʿĀdites and the T̲h̲amūdites; he was 500 *mann* high and reigned over the Israelites for a period before Samuel, and oppressed them; this appears to correspond to the period preceding Gideon, during which the Jews were oppressed by the Midianites (*Judges*, ch. vi.). D̲j̲ālūt afterwards slew the sons of Eli and carried off the ark; here he is the personification of the Philistines (I *Samuel*, iv.);

the account, which follows, of Saul's campaign against the Philistines, the challenging of the Israelites by Goliath, David's selection as their champion and the fight, is substantially the same as that in the Bible (I *Samuel*, xvii.).

DJAMĀL AL-DĪN AL-AFGHĀNĪ, AL-SAIYID MUḤAMMAD B. ṢAFDAR, one of the most remarkable figures in the Muslim world in the xix[th] century. He was — in the opinion of E. G. Browne — at once philosopher, author, orator and journalist, but above all he was a politician regarded by his opponents as a dangerous agitator. He exercised great influence on the liberationist and constitutional movements which have arisen in Muḥammadan countries in the last few decades. He agitated for their liberation from European influence and exploitation, for their independent internal development by the introduction of liberal institutions, for the union of all the Islāmic states (including Shīʿite Persia) under a single caliphate and the creation of a powerful Muslim Empire capable of resisting European intervention.

Djamāl al-Dīn was one of the most convinced champions of the pan-Islāmic idea with tongue and pen. His family traced its descent through the famous traditionist ʿAlī al-Tirmidhī from Ḥusain b. ʿAlī, which entitled them to bear the title Saiyid. According to his own account, he was born at Asʿadābād near Kanar in the district of Kābul in Afghānistān in 1254/1838—9 in a family following the Ḥanafī law; but others say it was at Asadābād near Hamadān in Persia that he first saw the light. Djamāl al-Dīn, according to them, wished to escape Persian despotism by claiming to be an Afghān subject. In any case Afghānistān was the scene in which his earliest childhood and youth were spent. In Kābul he studied all the higher branches of Muḥammadan learning till his 18th year, at the same time devoting attention to the study of philosophy and exact sciences in the traditional fashion of the Muslim East. He next spent over a year in India, made the pilgrimage to Mecca (1273/1857) and, on his return from the *ḥadjdj* to Afghānistān, entered the service of the Amīr Dōst Muḥammad Khān whom he accompanied on his campaign against Herāt. After the death of the Amīr, by his adherence to Muḥammad Aʿẓam, brother of the Amīr Shīr ʿAlī who had succeeded to the throne, he became involved in the dynastic civil wars and after the fall of his patron, whom he had served as minister during his brief rule, resolved to leave Afghānistān. Under a pretext of again undertaking the pilgrimage (1285/1869), after a brief stay in India and Cairo, where during a fortnight's stay he came in contact with the Azhar circles and held private lectures in his dwelling, he reached Constantinople (1287/1871). As a great reputation had preceded him, a very hearty welcome awaited him at the hands of the leaders of society in the Turkish capital. He was soon appointed to the council of education and invited to deliver public lectures in the Aya Sofia and the Aḥmadīya Mosque. A lecture for students delivered by him in the *Dār al-funūn* before a distinguished audience, on the value of the arts, in which he mentioned the gift of prophecy among the various social activities, gave Ḥasan Fahmī, the Shaikh al-Islām, who was jealous of his growing influence, an opportunity to charge him with revolutionary views; he had classed prophecy among the arts. On account of the intrigues of his opponents against him he had therefore to make up his mind to leave Constantinople and go to Cairo, where he was very kindly received by the authorities and educated classes. The government granted him an annual allowance of 12,000 Egyptian piastres without binding him to any definite official duties. He was free to instruct the young men eager for knowledge who gathered round him at his house and in unrestricted intercourse in the higher branches of philosophy and theology and at the same time pointed out to them the way to literary activity. In politics also he influenced those around him in the direction of a nationalist revival and liberal constitutional institutions; his activity was not without influence on the nationalist movement which came to a head in 1882 and led to the bombardment of Alexandria, the battle of Tell el-Kebīr and the English occupation. Shortly before this, in 1879, the inflammatory agitator, whose political activities were as inconvenient to the English representative as his regeneration of philosophical studies had been irritating to conservative circles at the Azhar, was at the instigation of the former deported and detained in India (Ḥaidarābād, and later Calcutta) until, after the suppression of ʿArābī's rising, he was allowed to leave India. During his stay in Ḥaidarābād he composed his *"Refutation of materialism"* (cf. thereon the article DAHRĪYA). From a memorandum by W. S. Blunt who was interested in Egyptian politics (in Browne, p. 401) we learn what is not mentioned by other biographers, that Djamāl al-Dīn went from India to America, where he spent some months in order to obtain naturalisation as an American citizen without however carrying out this intention. In 1883 we find him for a brief period in London, soon afterwards along with his friend and devoted pupil, afterwards the Egyptian Muftī Muḥammad ʿAbduh, in Paris where he devoted his literary activities to giving vent to his disapproval of English intervention in the affairs of Muḥammadan peoples. The most prominent and influential newspapers opened their columns to his essays, to which much attention was paid by competent authorities, on the Oriental policy of Russia and England, conditions in Turkey and Egypt, and the meaning of the Mahdī movement which had meanwhile arisen in the Sūdān. To this period also belongs his polemic with Ernest Renan arising out of the latter's Sorbonne lecture on "Islām and Science" in which he stated that Islām did not favour scientific activity; Djamāl al-Dīn sought to refute this in an article which first appeared in the *Journal des Débats* (also in German; cf. *Bibl.*). It may be mentioned in passing that, soon afterwards, Renan's lecture was translated into Arabic by Ḥasan Efendi ʿĀṣim and lithographed in Cairo (n.d.) along with a refutation (*radd*). The greater part of Djamāl al-Dīn's literary and political activities in Paris were however devoted to an Arabic newspaper published at the expense of a number of Indian Muḥammadans in conjunction with Muḥammad ʿAbduh (as actual editor), entitled *al-ʿUrwat al-wuthḳā* ("Le Lien Indissoluble") which unsparingly criticised English policy in Muḥammadan countries (particularly India and Egypt); the newspaper, the first number of which appeared on the 15th Djumādā I 1301/13th March 1884, was suppressed by the English authorities in the East, its introduction to Egypt and India prevented, and it was only possible by sending it under covered post for it to reach those whom it was intended to influence (information supplied by Djamāl al-Dīn himself). Although as a result of these obstacles it was destined to but a brief existence (Djamāl al-Dīn and Muḥammad ʿAbduh brought out 18 numbers in 8 months, the last appearing on the 26th Dhu 'l-Ḥidjdja 1301/17th October 1884), it exercised great influence on the awakening of liberationist anti-English views in Muslim circles and may be considered the first literary harbinger of the nationalist movements in the Muḥammadan territories of England, which were gradally strengthened by it. That its authority is not lessened at the present day may be concluded from the fact that, even after the lapse of more than half a century, new editions of the *ʿUrwa al-Wuthḳā* still continue to appear from the Arabic presses of the East. — In spite of his frankly acknowledged Anglophobe agitation, the leading statesmen of England, through the intervention of W. S. Blunt, entered into personal relations with Djamāl al-Dīn with the object of putting down the Mahdī movement in the Sūdān but no practical result was attained. Soon afterwards (1886) Djamāl al-Dīn, whose agitation for the awakening of Islāmic peoples was penetrating far and wide, received a telegraphic invitation to the court of Shāh Nāṣir al-Dīn in Teheran, where he had a most distinguished reception and was shown great honour and granted high political offices. But this did not last long as the Shāh, soon becoming suspicious, became tired of the increasing influence and growing popularity of his guest and Djamāl al-Dīn had to leave Persia under pretext of considerations of health. From there he went to Russia where he again entered into important political negotiations and remained till on the occasion of his visit to the Paris Exhibition of 1889 he met the Shāh, who was then in Europe, at Munich and was induced by him to accompany him to Persia. During his second stay in Persia he experienced the fickleness of the Oriental ruler's favour in a still more marked fashion. At first he enjoyed the Shāh's full favour and confidence, but the intrigues of the Grand Vizier Mīrzā ʿAlī Aṣghar Khān, Amīn al-Sulṭān, who had a grudge against Djamāl al-Dīn and felt he had a rival in the learned and popular stranger, succeeded in arousing the Shāh's mistrust, to which the reform in the administration of justice proposed by Djamāl al-Dīn largely contributed. Recognising the danger of his position, he now retired to the sanctuary of Shāh ʿAbd al-ʿAẓīm near Teheran, which was considered an inviolable asylum, where he remained for seven months, surrounded by a body of admirers listening to his views of the reform of the down-trodden country, until the Shāh incited by the Grand Vizier, disregarding the undisputed inviolability of the sanctuary, had him seized (about the beginning of 1891) by 500 armed cavalry and in spite of his invalid state carried in chains in the middle of winter to the town of Khāniḳīn on the Turco-Persian frontier. From here, after a brief stay in Baṣra, he went to England again, where he conducted a great agitation in lectures and articles against the reign of terror in Persia. Djamāl al-Dīn's cruel expulsion from Persia was a signal in the country itself for a rally of the reform party and its open activity, which was continually encouraged by Djamāl al-Dīn himself in letters, which he sent to influential individuals after his deportation. A special incitement to action was given by the Tobacco Concession granted in March 1890 by the Persian government to an English financial group, whereby the state renounced an important source of revenue in favour of foreign speculators. This gave Djamāl al-Dīn an opportunity to write an impassioned letter from Baṣra to Mīrzā Ḥasan-i Shīrāzī, the first *mudjtahid* of Samarrā, in which he called attention to the squandering of the properties of the state on the "enemies of Islām", as the economic supremacy of the Europeans had already been brought about by important concessions and now the tobacco monopoly in Persia was further to be handed over to them. He also referred to the misrule and cruelty of the government, particularly of ʿAlī Aṣghar Khān, in order, by repeatedly emphasising religious motives, to arouse this high ecclesiastical dignitary and his colleagues to active intervention in the name of religion (this letter may be found in Arabic in *Manār*, x. 820 *sq.*, and in English in Browne, *op. cit.*, p. 15—21). The immediate result of this step was a *fatwā* from the *mudjtahid*, forbidding the enjoyment of tobacco to every believer, as long as the government did not annul the concession agreement. It was thus forced to do this on paying a substantial indemnity to the concessionaires, as a result of the resistance of the people. The reform movement which soon afterwards assumed great dimensions and was supported by religious circles in Persia, is also connected with Djamāl al-Dīn's agitation, another result of which was the murder of the Shāh by Mīrzā Muḥammad Rizā, a disciple of Djamāl al-Dīn (11th March 1896). During his brief stay in London (1892), during which he was most active politically, he received through the Turkish ambassador Rustam Pasha in London ʿAbd al-Ḥamīd's written invitation to settle permanently in Constantinople as the Sulṭān's guest. He accepted the Sulṭān's offer not without reluctance. Besides a monthly allowance of £ 75 Turkish, a beautiful house on the Nishāntāsh hill near the Imperial Yildiz palace was allotted him, where he was able to live in princely comfort and meet people who sought his inspiring conversation. Here he spent the last five years of his life "tossed between the proofs of ʿAbd al-Ḥamīd's favour and the innumerable hostile machinations which have been set in operation against him from the Sulṭān's entourage, and although he has repeatedly sought permission to depart, he is always refused and lives in the beautiful house allotted him as in a kind of gilded cage".

Thus a German visitor describes his position in Nishāntāsh in June 1896. The kind of intrigues indulged in by his enemies may be judged from Djamāl al-Dīn's statement to another German interviewer. "The young Khedīve ʿAbbās Pasha had come to Constantinople for the first time. He wished to make my acquaintance. They sought to prevent this. I do not know who told the Khedīve that I was then in the habit of going every afternoon to the Sweet Waters. The Khedīve came there as if by accident, came up to me and introduced himself. We spoke for a quarter of an hour. This was told to the Sulṭān, the accidental meeting represented as pre-arranged and it was added that I had declared in the conversation that the Khedīve was the true *khalīfa*. However the Sulṭān was not then to be influenced by intrigue". His situation became more and more unpleasant, particularly after the murder of the Shāh, as his enemies in Persia charged him openly with conducting the conspiracy against the Shāh from Istanbul and instigating the murderer, one of his devoted followers, to the deed. Although the Sulṭān would not consent to his extradition, the insinuations of his enemies became more and more effective. Amongst his most dangerous opponents was the notorious Abu 'l-Hudā, the most influential ecclesiastic at the Sulṭān's court, who had the sovereign's ear. When Djamāl al-Dīn died on the 9th

Pilgrims throw stones on the Djamrat al-Wusṭā at Minā

Art. Djamra

March 1897 of a cancer, which began in his chin and gradually spread, it was freely suspected that this mortal illness was due to poisoning at the instigation of Abu 'l-Hudā. Djamāl al-Dīn found his last resting place in the cemetery at Nishāntāsh.

In spite of his scholarly command of Muslim theology and philosophy, Djamāl al-Dīn wrote very little in these fields. His tractate against materialistic philosophy [cf. DAHRĪYA] which appeared in three languages may be mentioned; he also wrote a short sketch of Afghān history entitled *Tatimmat al-bayān* (lith. Cairo n.d., 45 pp.) and the article on the Bābīs in Buṭrus al-Bustānī's *Dā'irat al-ma'ārif*. His activities were mainly devoted to publishing inflammatory political articles. In addition to *al-'Urwat al-wuthkā* he was (1892) joint-founder and an industrious contributor to the bilingual (Arabic and English) monthly *Ḍiyā' al-khāfiḳaini* ("Splendour of the Two Hemispheres") in which under the name "al-Saiyid" or "al-Saiyid al-Ḥusainī" he directed the fiercest attacks on the Shāh, whose deposition he always urged, his ministers and their abuse of their powers.

Bibliography: E. G. Browne, *The Persian Revolution of* 1905—1909 (Cambridge 1910) contains a detailed and authoritative biography and appreciation of Djamāl al-Dīn with full references and a portrait (frontispiece); a biography is also incorporated in the first volume of Muḥammad Rashīd Riḍā's monograph on Muḥammad 'Abduh (*Ta'rīkh al-ustādh ad-imām*, Cairo 1325/1907); Vollers, in *ZDMG*, xliii. 108; L. Massignon, in *RMM*, xii. (1910), p. 561 *sq.*; Ernest Renan, *L'Islamisme et la science*, in *Discours et conférences* 6th ed. p. 375. Criticism on this conference by Djamāl al-Dīn in *Journal des Débats*, 18 May 1883. Two lectures by Djamāl al-Dīn (on education and craftmanship) are given in the Arabic periodical *Miṣr* (Alexandria, 5th Djumādā I 1296); two essays on absolute governments (*Fi 'l-ḥukūmāt al-istibdādīya*) in *Manār*, vol. iii. Much material for his biography is also contained in the accounts in periodicals of meetings and conversations with Djamāl al-Dīn; of descriptions of him in German we may particularly mention the articles in the *Berliner Tageblatt* of the 23rd June 1896 (evening edition) and in the *Beilage zur Allgemeinen Zeitung* (Munich, 24th June 1896) from which some of the above quotations are taken; Charles C. Adams, *Islam and Modernism in Egypt* (London 1933), p. 4—17.

DJĀMI'. [See MASDJID].

AL-**DJAMRA**, originally a pebble, is particularly used of the heaps of stones in the valley of Minā which have been formed by the stones thrown by the pilgrims returning from the festival at 'Arafāt. There are three heaps which are a bowshot from one another: *al-djamra al-ūlā* (or *al-dunyā*) to the east near the Mosque of al-Khaif, *al-djamra al-wusṭā* in the centre and *djamrat* (*dhāt*) *al-'Akaba* at the western exit of the valley. The first two are bounded by thick stone pillars and the third by a wall. *Al-Muḥaṣṣab* is also used for al-Djamra but it is also the name of a plain between Mecca and Minā. On the third or western heap pilgrims throw seven stones immediately before the sacrifice on the 10th Dhu l'-Ḥidjdja; after visiting Mecca they again return to Minā and on each of the three Tashrīḳ days at sunset throw seven stones on each of the three heaps. At each throw they say: "In the name of God; God is great". The pilgrims ought to provide themselves with stones beforehand but, according to Burckhardt's account, they do not trouble to do this and take the stones thrown by others. Among the erotic poets of the Umaiyad period, the ceremony of stone-throwing was a favourite *motif*, as women when performing it, lifted their veils a little (e.g. *Kitāb al-aghānī*, vi. 30.; Yāḳūt, iv. 427; Mubarrad, *Kāmil*, ed. Wright, p. 166, 13; cf. p. 370, 8 *sq.*).

This peculiar custom, which is not directly prescribed in the Ḳur'ān, but is mentioned in the biographies of Muḥammad and in the *ḥadīth* (e.g. Ibn Hishām, p. 970; Wāḳidī, transl. Wellhausen, p. 417, 428 *sq.*; Ibn Sa'd, ii./l, p. 125; viii. 224 *sq.*) was taken over by Islām from paganism. In heathen times, there were, according to Ibn Hishām, p. 534, 17 (where one should read *maghrī* with Wellhausen) blood-stained sacrificial stones near the heaps of stones; cf. also the stones which were worshipped at al-Muḥaṣṣab in a poem by al-Farazdaḳ (ed. Boucher, p. 30). As to the meaning of the ceremony, Burckhardt's observation, that the Muslims wish thereby to protect themselves from the Devil, is certainly correct in so far as the stone-throwing was originally here as elsewhere a cursing ceremony.

But what was to become accursed thereby is not clear. Van Vloten suggested the *shaiṭān* of the place, thinking of the story in Ibn Hishām, p. 300, 8. Houtsma on the other hand, following his view that the *ḥadjdj* was originally an autumn festival, sees in the being who is cursed and banished the sun, which was occasionally called *al-shaiṭān* by the Arabs (Goldziher, *Abhandlungen z. arab. Philol.*, i. 113). The question of course can only be settled in connection with a discussion of the whole *ḥadjdj* [q.v.]. The fact that at the principal festival stones are cast only on the 'Aḳaba heap, while it is not till the final celebrations that they are cast on the other two, suggests that the two latter are of quite secondary importance, for which idea one might also adduce the description of Abū Bakr's pilgrimage in Wāḳidī (Wellhausen, p. 417). But we must not overlook the fact that not only does the above-mentioned verse in Ibn Hishām speak of several other heaps beside the sacrificial stones but Ḥassān b. Thābit in a lament on the Prophet (Ibn Hishām p. 1023, 17) calls the 'Aḳaba heap *al-djamra al-kubrā*, which seems to suggest the existence of other heaps.

Bibliography: Lane, *Arab. Lex.*, i. 453e; Muḳaddasī, in *BGA*, iii. 76; Bakrī, *Mu'djam* (ed. Wüstenfeld), p. 245; Yāḳūt, *Mu'djam* (ed. Wüstenfeld), iv. 426 *sq.*, 508; Bukhārī, *Kitāb al-Ḥadjdj*, chap. *Ramy al-djimār*; Tirmidhī, *Djāmi'* (Dehli 1315), i. 109 *sq.*; Azraḳī (ed. Wüstenfeld: *Chroniken der Stadt Mekka*, i.), p. 402—405; Burckhardt, *Reisen in Arabien*, p. 414 *sq.*; Burton *Pilgrimage*, ch. xxviii.; Snouck Hurgronje, *Het Mekkaansche Feest*, p. 159—161, 171 *sq.*; van Vloten, in *Feestbundel aan de Goeje* (1891), p. 33 *sq.* and in *WZKM*, vii. 176; Houtsma, in *Versl. Med. Ak. Amst.*, 1904, Afd. Letterkunde, Reeks 4, vi. 154 *sq.*; Wellhausen, *Reste arab. Heidentums*, 2nd ed., p. 111; Juynboll, *Handbuch des islāmischen Gesetzes* (Leyden 1910), p. 155—157.

DJANĀBA is the so-called "major" ritual impurity. One who is in this unclean state is called *djunub* and can only become "clean" again by a so-called major ritual ablution (*ghusl*). On the other hand, the law prescribes for a Muslim in a state of so-called "minor" impurity only a *wuḍū'* (minor ritual ablution). The distinction is based on the different beginnings of verse 6 of Sūra v. of the Ḳur'ān. Djanāba is the unclean condition described there: "When ye have had marital intercourse with your wives, purify yourselves". The law further prescribes that any effusio seminis shall be considered the same as marital intercourse.

The *djunub* cannot legally perform a valid *ṣalāt*. Neither can he make a *ṭawāf* round the Kaʿba nor stay in a mosque — except in cases of necessity. The *djunub* is further forbidden to touch copies of the Ḳurʾān or quote verses from it during his unclean condition.

Djanāba is also called "the major *ḥadath*" in opposition to minor ritual impurity.

Bibliography: The chapter on purity in the collections on tradition and the *fiḳh* books; I. Goldziher, *Die Ẓâhiriten* (Leipzig 1884), p. 48—52.

DJANNA, "Garden" is the name most frequently given in the Ḳurʾān and Tradition to Paradise, the abode of the blessed. It is only once referred to in the Ḳurʾān by the Persian name *firdaws* alone and a second time by the two words together *djannat al-firdaws*. It is fairly often called *djannāt ʿadn*, the gardens of Eden; cf. the Biblical name *gan ʿēden* (*Genesis*, ii. 15).

Muḥammad's description of Paradise is well known to be expressed in materialistic terms; it is found in several Sūras, which belong to the first period of his preaching: e.g. Sūra xlvii. 15: "this is the description of the Paradise that has been promised to the pious; rivers whose water never becomes tainted, and rivers of milk whose taste changes not; and rivers of wine the delight of those that drink of them; and rivers of pure honey, all kinds of fruits, and pardon for sins". Sūra lv. 54: The elect "shall repose on couches the linings of which shall be of brocade .... there are young virgins with modest looks who have never been deflowered by man nor spirit". Sūra lvi. 15—22: "They shall repose on couches adorned with gold and precious stones, reclining opposite to one another thereon. Youths eternally young shall go round about them to attend them with goblets and beakers and cups of flowing wine, and with fruits which they shall choose to their taste and the flesh of those birds they most desire". *Ibid.*, 28—34: "They shall abide among lotus trees without thorns and of laden banana trees, under a shade far-spreading, near a copiously-flowing water... they shall repose on lofty beds". *Ibid.*, 35—36: "We have created the women of Paradise by a special creation, we have preserved their virginity". Sūra lv. 72: [these houris] "are secluded in pavilions".

All these descriptions are quite clearly drawn pictures and seem to be inspired by the art of painting. Muḥammad or his unknown teacher must have seen Christian miniatures or mosaics representing the gardens of Paradise and have interpreted the figures of angels as being those of young men or young women.

In Sūra lv., a sūra which is composed in the very unusual form of a hymn with a refrain, Muḥammad speaks of two gardens given to the elect, each of them filled with shady trees, watered by flowing streams and containing two kinds of fruit. In the same Sūra, verses 16—19, he also mentions two easts, two wests and two seas. This dualism, except perhaps the two seas, is not at all easy to explain; see on this Nöldeke-Schwally, i. 106—7, and R. Blachère, *Le Coran*, i. 74.

To sum up then, his Paradise is essentially a garden in which there are beautiful women, couches covered with rich brocades, flowing cups and luscious fruits.

At a later period Paradise was represented as a pyramid or cone in eight stories; it was given one storey more than Hell as it was believed the elect would be greater in number than the damned. The different stories are built of materials of increasing value and each has a gate. At the top grows the lote-tree of the boundary, mentioned in Sūra liii. 16, whose branches shade the whole pyramid.

The books in which are written the deeds of men are kept in Paradise along with a prototype of the Ḳurʾān; this is what Muḥammad calls the "perspicuous book" (x. 61), the "guarded tablet" (lxxxv. 22) or the "mother of the Book" (xiii. 39). Beside it is the *ḳalam* or reed-pen which writes on the tablet; there is also a prototype of the Kaʿba in Paradise, called the "frequented house" and objects which are to be used at the last judgment like the balance for weighing the deeds of men, seats for the prophets, and standards. The standard of the prophet Muḥammad, or rather its heavenly prototype, is planted on a mountain called the mountain of glory which rises on the flank of the pyramid of Paradise.

Paradise with all its contents is placed above the astronomical heavens in which the planets revolve, and rests on a number of "seas" having abstract names like "the sea of divided substance, the sea of grace, the sea of the Lord". Above the pyramid lie the worlds of dominion (*malakūt*) and power (*djabarūt*), the Throne and the Tabernacle of God.

Orthodox Muslim theology, as represented especially by Ghazzālī and Ashʿarī, has admitted sensual pleasures into Paradise, though pointing out that they will only begin after the Resurrection. The pleasures of imagination and of intelligence are also admitted. According to al-Ghazzālī, the object of delight imagined by the elect will be realised at once although not quite in an objective manner, at least as regards sight and the other senses so that the blessed shall live in a perpetual hallucination. Paradise will be like a great market in which images will be bought. The pleasures of intelligence shall accompany those of the senses, they shall consist in the joy of knowledge, of possession, of dominion, and in the contemplation of the glory of the righteous. But the greatest happiness of the elect will be the sight of God.

The beatific vision or sight of God is allowed by orthodox Muslim theology and was one of the doctrines most vigorously defended against Muʿtazilite objections. As to the nature of the beatific vision, there were differences of opinion in orthodox circles, ranging from anthropomorphic literalism to the view of Ghazzālī that God will be seen without being and without form. According to a tradition given in the *Mukhtaṣar al-ʿadjāʾib* (*Abrégé des Merveilles*, transl. Carra de Vaux, p. 9) the prophet asked the archangel Gabriel "Hast thou ever seen thy Lord?" The archangel was troubled and replied "O Muḥammad, between Him and me there are seventy thousand veils of light; if I approached a single one of these veils, I should be consumed".

God does not appear in the Ḳurʾānic descriptions of Paradise. He is however present at the last judgment which is described in the Ḳurʾān in a fashion similar to that of Christian traditions and imagery.

The words *djanna*, *firdaws* and *ʿadn* are also employed to designate the earthly Paradise [cf. ĀDAM].

Bibliography: Wensinck, *CTM* vol. I; do., *Handbook*, s.v. *Paradise*; and general works on Muslim theology; Ibrāhīm Ḥaḳḳī, *Maʿrifet-Nāme*, Būlāḳ 1251, 1255 (cf. Carra de Vaux. *Fragments d'Eschatologie musulmane*, Brussels 1895); E. Cerulli, *Il "Libro della Scala"*, Vatican City 1949.

DJIHĀD (A.), holy war. The spread of Islām by arms is a religious duty upon Muslims in general. It narrowly escaped being a sixth *rukn*, or fundamental duty, and is indeed still so regarded by the descendants of the Khāridjīs. This position was reached gradually but quickly. In the Meccan Sūras of the Ḳur'ān patience under attack is taught; no other attitude was possible. But at Madīna the right to repel attack appears, and gradually it became a prescribed duty to fight against and subdue the hostile Meccans. Whether Muḥammad himself recognized that his position implied steady and unprovoked war against the unbelieving world until it was subdued to Islām may be in doubt. Traditions are explicit on the point; but the Ḳur'ānic passages speak always of the unbelievers who are to be subdued as dangerous or faithless. Still, the story of his writing to the powers around him shows that such a universal position was implicit in his mind, and it certainly developed immediately after his death, when the Muslim armies advanced out of Arabia. It is now a *farḍ ʿala 'l-kifāya*, a duty in general on all male, free, adult Muslims, sane in mind and body and having means enough to reach the Muslim army, yet not a duty necessarily incumbent on every individual but sufficiently performed when done by a certain number. So it must continue to be done until the whole world is under the rule of Islām. It must be controlled or headed by a Muslim sovereign or Imām. As the Imām of the Shīʿīs is now invisible, they cannot have a djihād until he reappears. Further, the requirement will be met if such a sovereign makes an expedition once a year, or, even, in the later view, if he makes annual preparation for one. The people against whom the djihād is directed must first be invited to embrace Islām. On refusal they have another choice. They may submit to Muslim rule, become *dhimmīs* [q.v.] and pay *djizya* and *kharādj* [q.v.] or fight. In the first case, their lives, families and property are assured to them, but they have a definitely inferior status, with no technical citizenship. and a standing only as protected wards. If they fight, they and their families may be enslaved and all their property seized as booty, four-fifths of which goes to the conquering army. If they embrace Islām, and it is open to them to do so even when the armies are face to face, they become part of the Muslim community with all its rights and duties. Apostates must be put to death. But if a Muslim country is invaded by unbelievers, the Imām may issue a general summons calling all Muslims there to arms, and as the danger grows so may the width of the summons until the whole Muslim world is involved. A Muslim who dies fighting in the Path of Allāh (*fī sabīl Allāh*) is a martyr (*shahīd*) and is assured of Paradise and of peculiar privileges there. Such a death was, in the early generations, regarded as the peculiar crown of a pious life. It is still, on occasions, a strong incitement, but when Islām ceased to conquer it lost its supreme value. Even yet, however, any war between Muslims and non-Muslims must be a djihād with its incitements and rewards. Of course, such modern movements as the so-called Muʿtazilī in India and the Young Turk in Turkey reject this and endeavour to explain away its basis; but the Muslim masses still follow the unanimous voice of the canon lawyers. Islām must be completely made over before the doctrine of djihād can be eliminated. See also the art. DĀR AL-ḤARB, DĀR AL-ISLĀM and DĀR AL-ṢULḤ. The latter seems to be a mediating position which failed.

Bibliography: Juynboll, *Handb. d. islām. Gesetzes*, p. 57, 336 *sq.*, especially for division of booty; Hughes, *Dictionary of Islam*, p. 243 *sq.*, full on Ḳur'ān, traditions and details of Ḥanafī law; Wensinck, *Concordance de la Tradition Musulmane*, s.v.; do., *Handbook*, s.v.; Snouck Hurgronje, *Politique musulmane de la Hollande*, p. 16 *sq.*, (*Verspr. Geschriften* IV, ii, p. 233 *sqq.*) especially for the permanent character of djihād in Islām; Māwardī, *al-Aḥkām al-sulṭānīya* (ed. Cairo 1298), p. 54 *sq.*; al-Ḳudūrī, *Institutiones iuris mohamm. circa bellum*..., in Rosenmüller, *Analecta arabica*, i., Leipzig 1826; al-Ṭabarī, *Ikhtilāf al-fuḳahā'*, ed. Schacht, Leiden 1933, p. 1 *sqq.*

DJINĀZA (or djanāza, from a root dj-n-z = to cover) means 1) a stretcher, 2) the corpse thereon, 3) the funeral. According to some Arabic scholars, it is a Nabataean word (*LA*, vii, 189). It is especially in the third sense that djināza is of importance in Islām, as far as it concerns the rites to be observed at a funeral.

The Ḳur'ān does not contain anything about funerals. The fiḳh-books on the other hand deal very minutely with it; their prescriptions mostly reach back, by the intermediary of Tradition, to pre-Islāmic times (cf. Wellhausen, *Reste*, p. 177—186).

As soon as a Muslim is dead, he is laid on a stretcher, the head in the direction of the ḳibla; then begins the ritual washing (*ghusl*), for which the intention (*nīya*) is not necessary. The *ghusl* [q.v.] is very precisely dealt with (e.g. the beard of the deceased is washed with an extract of lotus), and takes place an odd number of times (Bukhārī, *Djanā'iz*, b. 8 and 9). Then the body is enveloped in shrouds. Here there is difference of opinion; Goldziher (in *Bemerkungen zur arabischen Trauerpoesie*, *WZKM* xvi. 338) says that it appears from Arabic poetry that the dead is covered only by two garments; Juynboll remarks (*Handl.* p. 163) that the shrouds must be odd in number. The last opinion is also that of the fiḳh; it is also in accordance with the general predilection for the odd number (cf. the odd number of washings, and the prescription that the hair of a dead woman must be divided into three [odd] parts). The Muslim practice, however, shows two shrouds (Lane, *Manners*, p. 518); as practice often has a tenacious life, it is possible that here also it is older than the prescriptions of the fiḳh and a remnant of pre-islāmic times (cf. also the dress of a *muḥrim* which consists of two pieces of cloth). In Tradition there are indications for one, two, or three shrouds (Bukhārī, *Djanā'iz*, b. 20, 27, 94). The fiḳh says that a man is to be enveloped in three or (less preferable) five shrouds, a woman in five. About the sort of shrouds there is also divergence of opinion among the Arabic scholars; the tradition in Muslim, *Djanā'iz*, tr. 45, which runs: "the Prophet was enveloped in three white cloths from Saḥūl (a town in Yemen), among which were neither a *ḳamīṣ* nor an *ʿimāma*", was interpreted by the Mālikī's as if the exclusion of the two named garments was here an exception to the rule (see the commentary of Nawawī on the passage quoted). Al-Shāfiʿī, though not recommending this practice, did allow it. The *ḳamīṣ*, a shirt, and the *ʿimāma*, a turban, were a modern dress, and therefore not allowed as mourning-dress; there are found also other tendencies against luxurious garments in the ḥadīth, e.g. Mālik, *Djanā'iz*, tr. 6, from Abū Bakr: "a living person needs new clothes more than one dead".

The best shroud is the *ḥulla*, consisting of a *ridā'* (wrapped round the shoulders), and an *izār* (round the loins); further the *lifāfa*, not a garment in the strict sense but only a tie or a cloth wrapped round the body. A woman is shrouded in a *dirʿ* (a sort of shirt), an *izār*, *a khimār* (a veil) and a *lifāfa*.

According to the Ḥanafī's, in case of need, one cloth suffices. The shrouds must be white, but other colours are found: black (*LA* i, 455), green and black (Snouck Hurgronje, *Mekka* ii, 194). When a person dies in the state of *iḥrām*, the shrouds may not be sewn, and the head not covered (Bukhārī, *Djanāʾiz*, b. 27), in accordance with the clothing-prescriptions of the *iḥrām*.

When this has been done, the ṣalāt for the dead is performed; this ṣalāt is equal to the ordinary ṣalāt, except for the addition of a prayer for the deceased, the formula of which is minutely described in the fiḳh-books. This *ṣalāt al-djināza* takes place in the house of mourning or in the mosque (see further ṢALĀT IV).

It is forbidden to perform the ṣalāt for an unbeliever (sūra ix, 84), nor may he be washed, but he must be buried. A martyr is not to be washed, in order not to wash out the trails of blood which are witnesses to his martyrdom, nor is it necessary to say a prayer for his soul.

To keep watch over a dead body is not prescribed in the fiḳh; it occurs however in Egypt (Lane, *Manners*, p. 57). The burning of a light by the side of a dead person is an old Semitic custom (e.g. *Pesaḥīm*, iv, 14), but Tradition disapproves of it (Nasāʾī, *Djanāʾiz*, b. 104).

After all this has been done, the funeral-procession begins. The stretcher is borne to the burialplace by male persons, even when the deceased is a woman; this work is to be done carefully. The corpse of a woman must be hidden from the eyes of the public. Whether the bystanders have to stand up at a funeral-procession is disputed; there are traditions (Muslim, *Djanāʾiz*, tr. 73) that Muḥammad rose to his feet at a funeral (with two different additions: 1) for the angels of death who go before the procession, 2) out of respect for the deceased). Another tradition, however, says that this custom was abrogated since the Jews followed the same practice. Mālik, Abū Ḥanīfa and Shāfiʿī declare in favour of the latter view, Aḥmad b. Ḥanbal leaves it free.

It is very recommendable to follow a funeral procession (Bukhārī, *Īmān*, b. 35; *Djanāʾiz*, b. 2); it is forbidden to do this on horseback, since the angels of death go on foot.

The burial itself is done by an odd number of men; the body is laid down in the grave with the head in the direction of the ḳibla, after which the bystanders each cast three handfuls of earth on the grave. On this occasion the confession of faith is prompted in the deceased's ear (*talḳīn*), provided this has not yet been done on the deathbed, in order that the may give the right answer when the Angels Munkar and Nakīr [q.v.] interrogate him in his grave.

The Mālikī's disapprove of the *talḳīn*. Sometimes also the *Fātiḥa* and the *Muʿawwidhatān* (the last two sūra's) are recited (al-Ḳummī, p. 32).

The grave of a woman is covered with a garment, according to al-Shāfiʿī also that of a man.

The ornamenting of graves, even by an inscription, is disapproved of by the fiḳh; only the place where the head rests may be marked by a stone or a piece of wood. The often greatly embellished tombs, however, especially those on the graves of saints, play, in spite of all fiḳh, a great part in popular veneration. The visiting of graves was also forbidden at first. but later permitted (Muslim, *Djanāʾiz*, tr. 105, 108).

Before and after the burial visits of condolence are paid; the fiḳh gives detailed prescriptions on this subject, what one should say, etc. [cf. TAʿZIYA]. The holding of a banquet (*walīma*) after the burial, is also recommended, except on the day of the burial itself; on that occasion passages from the Ḳurʾān are recited, with which good work the deceased is credited.

Bibliography: The fiḳh-books on the chapter *ṣalāt al-maiyit* or *ṣalāt al-djināza*; in the Tradition works especially the *kitāb al-djanāʾiz*; A. J. Wensinck, *Handbook*, s.v. Biers; do., *Some Semitic Rites of Mourning and Religion*, in *Verh. KAW*, New Series xviii, no. i.; on modern practice: Lane, *Manners and Customs of the modern Egyptians*, p. 317—344; M. Galal, *Les rites funéraires en Egypte actuelle*, in *REI* 1937; Paul Kahle, *Die Totenklage im heutigen Ägypten* in *Festschrift H. Gunkel*, Göttingen 1923; J. L. Burckhardt, *Notes on the Bedouins and Wahabys*, p. 280; Snouck Hurgronje, *Mekka* ii. p. 188—198; d'Ohsson, *Tableau de l'Empire Othoman* i, p. 235—252; A. Jaussen, *Coutumes Palestiniennes* (i., Nablus), p. 333—345; do., *Coutumes des Arabes du pays de Moab*, p. 95—105; S. G. Wilson, *Persian Life and Customs*, p. 209—212; A. Musil, *The Manners and Customs of the Rwala Bedouins*, p. 670; Snouck Hurgronje, *The Achenese* i, p. 418—430; do., *Verspr. Geschr.* iv./1 p. 241—245 (Java); E. Westermarck, *Ritual and Belief in Morocco*, vol. ii.

DJINN. The djinn for Muslims are airy or fiery bodies (*adjsām*), intelligent, imperceptible, capable of appearing under different forms and of carrying out heavy labours (Baiḍāwī on Sūra lxxii. 1; Damīrī, *Hayawān*, s.v.). They were created of smokeless flame (Sūra lv. 15), while mankind and the angels, the other two classes of intelligent beings, were created of clay and light. They are salvable; Muḥammad was sent to them as well as to mankind; some will enter the Garden and some will be cast into the Fire. Their relation to Iblīs [q.v.] the Shaiṭān, and to the *shaiṭāns* in general, is obscure. In Sūra xviii. 50, Iblīs is said to be of the djinn; but Sūra ii. 34 implies that he is of the angels. In consequence there is much confusion, and many legends and hypotheses have grown up (cf. the latter passage in Baiḍāwī and in Rāzī's *Mafātīḥ*, ed. Cairo 1307, i. 288 *sq.*). The Arab lexicographers tend to explain the name *djinn* from *idjtinān*, "becoming concealed, hidden" (cf. Lane, s.v. and Baiḍāwī on Sūra ii. 8; Fleischer's ed., i. 22, l. 13). But this etymology is very difficult, and derivation as a loan-word from *genius* is not quite excluded. "Naturalem deum uniuscuiusque loci" (Serv. Verg. G. i. 302) exactly expresses the strong localization of the djinn (cf. e.g. Nöldeke, *Moʿallaḳāt*, i., p. 64, 78 and ii., p. 65, 89) and their quasi-standing as deities in old Arabia (Robertson Smith, *Rel. of Semites* ², p. 121). An individual is a *djinnī*; *djānn* is used synonomously with *djinn* (but see Lane, *Lexicon*, p. 492ᶜ); *ghūl*, *ʿifrīt*, *siʿlāt* are classes of the djinn. For an Ethiopic point of contact with *djānn* see Nöldeke, *Neue Beiträge*, p. 63.

Consideration of them divides naturally under three heads, though these necessarily shade into one another.

I. The djinn in pre-Islāmic Arabia were the nymphs and satyrs of the desert, the side of the life of nature still unsubdued and hostile to man. For this aspect, see Robertson Smith, *loc. cit.*; Nöldeke on ancient Arabs, in Hastings' *Encycl. of Rel. and Ethics*, i., p. 669 *sq.*; Wellhausen, *Reste*; van Vloten,

Dämonen ... bei d. alt. Arabern, in *WZKM*, vols. vii. and viii., uses materials in Djāḥiẓ, *Ḥayawān*. But in the time of Muḥammad they were passing over into vague, impersonal gods. The Meccans asserted a kinship (*nasab*) between them and Allāh (Sūra xxxvii. 158), made them partners of Allāh (vi. 100), made offerings to them (vi. 128), sought aid of them (lxxii. 6). See further the art. ALLAH.

II. In official Islām the existence of the djinn was completely accepted, as it is to this day, and the consequences were worked out to the end. Their legal status in all respects was discussed and fixed, and the possible relations between them and mankind, such as in marriage and property, were examined. Stories of the loves of djinn and mankind were evidently of perennial interest. The *Fihrist* gives titles of sixteen of these (p. 308) and they appear in all the collections of short tales (e.g. Dāwūd al-Anṭākī, *Tazyīn al-aswāḳ*, ed. Cairo 1308, p. 181 *sq.*; al-Sarrādj, *Maṣāriʿ al-ʿushshāḳ*, ed. Constantinople 1302, p. 286 *sq.*). There are many stories, too, of relations between saints and the djinn; see Macdonald's *Religious Attitude and Life in Islām*, p. 144 *sq.* A good compilation on all this is the *Ākām al-mardjān fī aḥkām al-djānn* by Badr al-Dīn al-Shiblī (d. 769/1368; Cairo 1326); see, too, Nöldeke's review, in *ZDMG*, lxiv., p. 439 *sq.* Few, even of the Muʿtazilī's, ventured to doubt their existence and only constructed different theories of their nature and working on material things. The earlier philosophers, even al-Fārābī, tried to avoid the question by dubious definitions. But Ibn Sīnā, in defining the word, asserted flatly that there was no reality behind it. The later believing philosophers used subterfuges, partly exegetical and partly metaphysical. Ibn Khaldūn, for example, reckoned all references to the djinn among the *mutashābih* passages of the Ḳurʾān, the knowledge of which Allāh has reserved to himself (Sūra ii. 6). These different attitudes are excellently treated in the *Dict. of Techn. Terms*, i. 261 *sq.*; cf. also Rāzī, *Mafātīḥ*, on Sūra lxxii.

III. The djinn in folk-lore. The transition to this division comes most naturally through the use of the djinn in magic. Muslim theology has always admitted the fact of such a use, though judging varyingly its legality. The *Fihrist* traces both the approved and the disapproved kinds back to ancient times, and gives Greek, Ḥarrānian, Chaldean and Indian sources. At the present day, books treating of the binding of djinn to talismanic service are an important part of the literature of the people. All know and read them, and the professional magician has no secrets left. In popular stories, also, as opposed to the tales of the professed littérateur, the djinn play a large part. So throughout the *Arabian Nights*, but especially in that class of popular religious novels of which Weil published two in his translation of the *Nights*, the second version of "Djūdar the Fisherman" and "Alī and Ẓāhir of Damascus". Still nearer to the ideas of the masses are the Märchen collected orally by Artin, Oestrup, Spitta, Stumme etc. In these the folklore elements of the different races overcome the common Muslim atmosphere. The spirits appearing in them are more North African, Egyptian, Syrian, Persian and Turkish than Arabian or Muslim. Besides this there are the popular beliefs and usages, so far very incompletely gathered. All through these, also, there are points of contact with the official Islāmic view. Thus, in Egyptian popular belief, a man who dies by violence becomes an *ʿifrīt*, and haunts the place of his death (Willmore, *Spoken Arabic of Egypt*², p. 371, 374), while in the Islām of the schools a man who dies in deadly sin may be transformed into a *djinnī* in the world of al-Barzakh (*Dict. of Techn. Terms*, i., 265). Willmore has other details on the djinn in Egypt. For South Arabia see "Abdullah Mansûr", *The Land of Uz*, p. 22, 26, 203, 316—320. See too, R. C. Thomson, in *Proc. of Soc. of Bibl. Arch.*, xxviii. 83 *sq.*; Sayce, in *Folklore*, 1900, ii. 388 *sq.*; Lydia Einszler, in *ZDPV*, x. 170 *sq.*; Mrs. H. H. Spoer, in *Folklore*, xviii. 54 *sq.*; D. B. Macdonald, *Aspects of Islam*, p. 326 *sq.*

Bibliography: *CTM* s.v.; Damīrī, *Ḥayawān*, s.v. *djinn*, *siʿlāt*, *ʿifrīt*, *ghūl*; also in Jayakar's translation, London and Bombay 1906—1908; Ḳazwīnī, *ʿAdjāʾib*, p. 368 *sq.* of Wüstenfeld's ed.; Lane, *Modern Egyptians*, index s.v. *Ginn*; Lane, *Arabian Nights*, Introduction, note 21, chap. i., notes 15 and 24; Goldziher, *Arabische Philologie*, i., index; do., *Vorlesungen*, p. 68, 78 *sq.*; Doutté, *Magie et Religion*, throughout; Macdonald, *Religious Attitude and Life in Islam*, chap. v. and. x and index; A. J. Wensinck, *The etymology of djinn*, in *Versl. Med. Ak. Amst.* Ser. V, vol. 4.

DJIZYA (A.), "tribute, poll-tax", the name given in Muḥammadan law to the indulgence-taxes levied on the *ahl al-dhimma*.

1. The Theory of the djizya in the Fiḳh. In the Fiḳh-books, the djizya is discussed in connection with the holy war (*djihād*; q.v.). While pagans have the choice only between Islām or death, the possessors of a scripture (*ahl al-kitāb*) may obtain security and protection for themselves, their families and goods by paying the djizya. This dogma is founded on Sūra ix. 29, where it is laid down: "Fight them, that believe not in God and the last day and who hold not as forbidden what God and his apostle have forbidden, and do not profess the true religion, those that have a scripture, until they pay the djizya in person in subjection" Relying on this passage the fiḳh regards the djizya as an individual poll-tax, by payment of which Christians, Jews, Magians, Sabeans or Samaritans make a contract with the Islāmic community, so that they are henceforth not only tolerated but even have a claim for protection. Certain Christian groups, like the Banū Taghlib and the Christians of Nadjrān occupy a special position and do not pay djizya. Only adult males in the full possession of their physical and mental faculties and having the means to pay are liable to the tax. Women, children and old men are exempted, as war is not waged on them. Blind men and cripples only pay when they are wealthy; poor men and beggars are not expected to pay. Monks are exempted, if they are poor. But if their monasteries are wealthy, the superiors have to pay the tax. Slaves also are exempted. Alongside of this mild treatment of the poor and weak, there is a corresponding strictness with the wealthy and care is to be taken that no one who ought to pay escapes. Collectors are therefore particularly warned not to levy round sums on communities on a basis of their numbers alone. How to deal with the tax in the case of a *dhimmī* who becomes a convert to Islām, or one who dies in the current exchequer-year is a question of *ikhtilāf*.

The djizya should be paid in money but it may be paid in kind, e.g. in garments, cattle or even needles, but wine, and cattle that have died a natural death (*maita*), are not legal payment; the proceeds of their sale may however be taken. The normal tax at first was 1 dīnār. This later became the minimum. In countries where the standard was a silver one, it was the equivalent, 12 dirhams. For *dhimmīs* in better circumstances the tax was next placed at 2 dīnārs or 24 dirhams, and for the rich 4 dīnārs or 48 dirhams. According to Abū Yūsuf, from whom most of these facts are taken, money-changers, dealers in cloths, landowners, merchants and physicians were considered rich, while artisans such as tailors, dyers, cobblers and shoemakers were counted poor; he gives no details of the middle class. If a man could not pay his djizya, he was not to be forced to do so by corporal punishment (flogging, exposure in the sun, soaking with oil) but only by imprisonment. According to the verse which introduced it, the djizya was to be paid "in submission" (*wahum ṣāghirūn*), which al-Shāfiʿī, no doubt correctly, explained as referring to the dominion (*ḥukm*) of Islām, which the *dhimmīs* were under. Others, on the authority of this passage, demanded a very humiliating method of paying it and it is most probable that the degrading prescriptions regarding dress etc. are only interpretations of this passage. The income from the djizya was paid into the state treasury (*bait al-māl*) and with the *kharādj* [q.v.], the land-tax, formed the revenue from the *fai'* [q.v.] which belonged to the whole community.

2. The History of the conception of Djizya in Practice.

Djizya originally meant the collective tribute levied on conquered lands. The Arabs everywhere left the administrative conditions which they found unchanged and regarded the revenues of the provinces as their djizya. The distinction which later became usual between djizya as a poll-tax and *kharādj* as a land-tax did not at first exist, for our authorities frequently speak of a *kharādj* from a poll-tax and a djizya from land. The revenue from the *fai'* is even quite generally called djizya in allusion to the passage quoted from the Ḳur'ān. For example, in the Egyptian papyri of the first (seventh) century besides the djizya (δημόσια) as the principal tax in gold, only the payment in kind is mentioned, which cannot be discussed here. According to the Arab view, this djizya was a poll-tax; for on the conclusion of treaties of occupation, a hypothetical number of inhabitants and not the area of arable land was taken as the basis for estimating the tribute. Now a poll-tax existed before the conquest in the conquered lands, Sāsānian and Byzantine (ἐπικεφάλιον, ἀνδρισμός), but the main source of revenue and hence of the tribute was the land-tax, which bore the Aramaic name of *kharāgā*. This term was identified with the Arabic *khardj* or *kharādj* (Sūra xviii. 94: xxiii. 72) and from the ʿAbbāsid period was in general use in the non-Aramaic provinces also. *Kharādj* as "revenue", "income from land-tax" is interchangeable with djizya, even in the oldest literature that has survived to us. If it was the income from the tribute that was emphasised, it was called *kharādj*, but if one were thinking more of the tribute paid by those who had been conquered by Islām, the Ḳur'ānic expression djizya was used. With the consolidation of Arab power *kharādj* gradually became the term applied to the land-tax, which with the gradual conversion to Islām of the subjected peoples came to be levied on Muslims also, and thus lost its tribute (djizya) character. The Ḳur'ānic djizya was replaced by the individual poll-tax which Islām found already in existence and which was of course levied on non-Muslims only. In the early literature and in Egyptian receipts for the payment of the poll-tax the term *djāliya* (plur. *djawālī*) was used, which became synonymous with *djizya*. This *djāliya* or djizya was counted *li-kharādj* of this or that year, because the total income from the *fai'* was also called *kharādj* [cf. KHARĀDJ]. Thus in the course of a century and a half arose the terminology of *kharādj* and djizya, although the fiḳh treats them as having existed from the beginning.

On the practice in ancient times we have satisfactory information only as to the custom in Egypt. After payment one was given a lead-seal round the neck, but the Caliph Hishām introduced regular receipts called *barā'a*'s. Numbers of these have survived but they have not yet been thoroughly investigated. Egypt is said to have had levied on it at the conquest a tax of 2 dīnārs a head and as a matter of fact, according to the Greek taxation-rolls of the end of the first century, the totals give this as an average; but much smaller amounts are found. For later centuries it is evident from the receipts that in practice the minimum of 1 dīnār, prescribed by the fiḳh, was often very much smaller. In the first century however many persons were entirely exempt from taxation, though we do not know why; there is still much to be explained on the whole subject. The monks were strictly compelled to pay djizya in Egypt from the time of ʿAbd al-ʿAzīz, the brother of ʿAbd al-Malik, although they had apparently been previously exempted.

With the gradual adoption of Islām, the djizya as purely a poll-tax gradually declined and by Saladin's time the revenue in Egypt from this source was only 130,000 dīnārs (Maḳrīzī, *Khiṭaṭ*, i. 107, 23; 108, 27). Nevertheless this tax, levied as a sign of their subjection on the non-Muslim citizens of the second class, remained a permanent institution. We have exact details only for Turkey; these have been collected by Heidborn, *Les Finances Ottomanes* (Vienna-Leipzig 1912), p. 23 *sq.* from v. Hammer and other sources (there is a reproduction of a Turkish receipt for *djizya* in Karabacek, *Führer durch die Ausstellung der Papyri Erzherzog Rainer*, p. 176). Djizya existed in Turkey down to the time of the Crimean War. By the law of 10th May 1855 (F. Bamberg, *Geschichte der oriental. Angelegenheit*, p. 263), the djizya as a tax on the free exercise of religion was replaced by a tax for exemption from military service. The last trace of it only disappeared after the Revolution in Turkey since when Christians also do military service.

Bibliography: All the *fiḳh*-books under *djihād*; cf. more particularly Abū Yūsuf, *Kitāb al-kharādj*, p. 69 *sq.*; al-Shāfiʿī, *Kitāb al-umm*, iv. 82 *sq.*; Māwardī, *al-Aḥkām al-sulṭāniya*, passim; al-Ṭabarī, *K. Ikhtilāf al-fuḳahā'*, ed. Schacht, Leiden 1933, p. 199 *sqq.*; d'Ohsson, *Tableau Général de l'Empire Othoman*, iii. 9 *sq.*; Wellhausen, *Das arabische Reich*, p. 172 *sq.*; Becker, *Beiträge*, p. 81; *Papyri Schott-Reinhardt*, i. 37 *sq.*; H. I. Bell, *Greek Papyri in the British Museum, Catalogue*, vol. iv., p. xxv. *sq.*; 166 *sq.*; Caetani, *Annali dell' Islam*, iv., H. 21, § 235 *sq.*; v., H. 23, § 562 *sq.*; Løkkegaard, *Islamic taxation in the classic period*, Copenhagen 1950.

DJUMʿA, i.e. the day of "general assembly", is Friday, because it is a religious obligation on Muslims to attend on this weekly holy day the divine service, which takes the place of the daily midday ṣalāt (*ṣalāt al-ẓuhr*). The Friday ṣalāt itself is also called *djumʿa*. In the Ḳur'ān, in a sūra revealed at Madīna (Sūra lxii. 9) it is expressly ordained: "When ye are called to the Friday ṣalāt, hasten to the praise of Allāh and leave off your business". It is by reason of this verse in the Ḳurʾān that attendance at the Djumʿa is regarded as a duty binding on every male, adult, free Muslim, at least as far as he is legally considered "resident in the locality" (*muḳīm*). Apart from this the weekly holy day of Islām is not a day of rest and thus essentially different from the Jewish Sabbath or the Christian Sunday.

The Friday service consists of a ṣalāt of two rakʿa's in the mosque and a sermon, which is delivered by a *khaṭīb* before this ṣalāt. But it is considered meritorious and is the usual practice to perform another ṣalāt of two rakʿa's before the khuṭba also. For a djumʿa to be valid, there must, according to the Shāfiʿī school, be at least 40 Muslims present in the mosque, who are legally entitled to take part in the worship of God. The Ḥanafīs and Mālikīs do not however adhere to the number 40; they say that the service should only be held in a town or community of some size. According to the Shāfiʿīs and most of the other Faḳīhs it is further illegal to hold the Friday service in more than one mosque in the same place, except in cases of necessity when it is impossible for all the inhabitants to meet in one building.

It may be presumed that Muḥammad used to hold a communal ṣalāt with a sermon, after the Jewish fashion, in the court of his house in Madīna on Fridays, and that he used to begin with the ṣalāt which was followed by the address, just as in other assemblies of the same kind in older times the ṣalāt preceded the other business. At the Friday service in the great military camps of the Muslims after the death of Muḥammad, the Umaiyads and their governors used to conduct the service appearing with all symbols of their rank. The individual tribes in these camps used at that time to meet in a masdjid of their own, but the Umaiyads endeavoured to unite them in one common mosque. It is probably from this period, that the commandment against holding the djumʿa in more than one mosque in the same town or holding it outside the town dates.

In the later Umaiyad period the ceremonies at the Friday service became more and more influenced by the Christian service. Thus the ceremonial adhān (which is held on Friday once more in the mosque, after the faithful are gathered there, before the sermon) and the peculiar form of the khuṭba, in two sections before the Friday Ṣalāt, seem to have arisen under influence of the Christian mass. The professional preacher gradually came to take the place of the Caliph or his governor as conductor of the service.

Bibliography: Besides the chapters on the *Ṣalāt* in the collections on Tradition and the Fiḳh books: Dimishḳī, *Raḥmat al-umma fi 'khtilāf al-aʾimma* (Būlāḳ 1300), p. 29 *sq.*; C. H. Becker, *Zur Geschichte des islāmischen Kultus* (*Isl.*, iii., 1912), p. 374 *sq.*; do., *Die Kanzel im Kultus des alten Islām* (*Nöldeke-Festschrift*); I. Goldziher, *Die Sabbathinstitution im Islam* (*Gedenkbuch für David Kaufmann*), p. 86—105; do., *Islamisme et Parsisme* (*RHR*, xliii., 1901), p. 27 *sq.*; do., *Muḥamm. Studien*, ii. 40—44; do., in *ZDMG*, 1895, xlix. 315; C. Snouck Hurgronje, *Islām und Phonograph*, p. 9—12 (*Verspr. Geschr.* ii., 419-448); E. W. Lane, *An Account of the Manners and Customs of the Modern Egyptians*, chapt. iii.; A. J. Wensinck, *Mohammed en de Joden te Medina* (Leyden 1908), p. 110 *sq.*

AL-**DJUNAID**, ABU 'L-ḲĀSIM B. MUḤAMMAD B. AL-DJUNAID AL-KHAZZĀZ AL-ḲAWĀRĪRĪ AL-NIHĀWANDĪ, the celebrated Ṣūfī, nephew and disciple of Sarī al-Saḳaṭī, a native of Baghdād, studied law under Abū Thawr, and associated with Ḥārith al-Muḥāsibī [q.v.], with whom indeed he is said to have discussed during walks all kinds of questions relating to mysticism, Muḥāsibī giving his replies extempore and later writing them up in the form of books (Abū Nuʿaim, *Ḥilyat al-awliyāʾ*, Leyden MS, fol. 284*a*). He died in 298/910. With Muḥāsibī he is to be accounted the greatest orthodox exponent of the "sober" type of Ṣūfism, and the titles which later writers bestowed on him — *saiyid al-ṭāʾifa* ("Lord of the Sect"), *ṭāʾūs al-fuḳarāʾ* ("Peacock of the Dervishes"), *shaikh al-mashāʾikh* ("Director of the Directors") — indicate in what esteem he was held. The *Fihrist* (ed. Flügel, p. 186) mentions his *Rasāʾil*, which have in large measure survived, in a unique but fragmentary MS (see Brockelmann, *GAL*, *Suppl.*, i., p. 354—5). These consist of letters to private persons (examples are quoted by Sarrādj, *Kitāb al-lumaʿ*, p. 239—243), and short tractates on mystical themes: some of the latter are cast in the form of commentaries on Ḳurʾānic passages. His style is involved to the point of obscurity, and his influence on Ḥallādj [q.v.] is manifest. He mentions in one of his letters that a former communication of his had been opened and read in the course of transit: doubtless by some zealot desirous of finding cause for impugning his orthodoxy; and to this ever-present danger must in part be attributed the deliberate preciosity which marks the writings of all the mystics of Djunaid's period. Djunaid reiterates the theme, first clearly reasoned by him, that since all things have their origin in God they must finally return, after their dispersion (*tafrīḳ*), to live again in Him (*djamʿ*): and this the mystic achieves in the state of passing-away (*fanāʾ*). Of the mystic union he writes, "For at that time thou wilt be addressed, thyself addressing; questioned concerning thy tidings, thyself questioning; with abundant flow of benefits, and interchange of attestations; with constant increase of faith, and uninterrupted favours" (*Rasāʾil*, fol. 3*a*—*b*). Of his own mystical experience he says, "This that I say comes from the continuance of calamity and the consequence of misery, from a heart that is stirred from its foundations, and is tormented with its ceaseless conflagrations, by itself within itself: admitting no perception, no speech, no sense, no feeling, no repose, no effort, no familiar image; but constant in the calamity of its ceaseless torment, unimaginable, indescribable, unlimited, unbearable in its fierce onslaughts" (fol. 1*a*). Eschewing those extravagances of language which on the lips of such inebriates as Abū Yazīd al-Bisṭāmī and Ḥallādj alarmed and alienated the orthodox, Djunaid by his clear perception and absolute self-control laid the foundations on which the later systems of Ṣūfism were built.

AL-**DJUWAINĪ**, ABU 'L-MAʿĀLĪ ʿABD AL-MALIK, celebrated by the honorary name of IMĀM AL-ḤARAMAIN, a renowned author on the principles of Jurisprudence, according to the Shāfiʿī school. Born on the 18th Muḥarram 419/12th Febr. 1028 in Bushtanikān, a village near Nīsābūr, he succeeded to his father's post on his death, though not yet 20 years old. In dogmatics he adopted the teaching of al-Ashʿarī. When ʿAmīd al-Mulk al-Kundurī, the vizier of the Saldjūḳ Tughrilbeg, took steps against these dogmatic innovations and had their protagonists like the Rawāfiḍ cursed from the pulpits, he left his native town with Abu 'l-Ḳāsim al-Ḳus̲h̲airī, went first to Bag̲h̲dād and thence in 450/1058 to the Ḥid̲j̲āz, where he taught for four years in Mecca and Madīna, whence his honorary name. When the vizier Niẓām al-Mulk had risen to power in the Sald̲j̲ūḳ empire, he favoured the As̲h̲ʿarīs and requested the refugees to return. Al-D̲j̲uwainī was among those who returned to Nīsābūr and Niẓām al-Mulk even founded a madrasa specially for him, which, like its sister-institution in Bag̲h̲dād, was called Niẓāmīya. Al-D̲j̲uwainī taught there till his death. He died in his birthplace, to which he had gone in the hope of recovering from an illness, on the 25th Rabīʿ II 478/20th Aug. 1085. His literary activity was so great that Subkī, *Ṭabaḳāt*, ii. 77, 20, thinks one could only comprehend his works by a miracle. But in spite of the esteem which he enjoyed, none of his works ever became very popular. His *Kitāb al-burhān fī uṣūl al-fiḳh* which has not survived, was planned on quite a new scheme and contained so many difficulties that Subkī, *Ṭab.*, iii. 264 proposed to call it *Lag̲h̲z al-umma*. His *K. al-irs̲h̲ād fī uṣūl al-iʿtiḳād* was edited and translated by J. D. Luciani (Paris 1938). His greatest work *Kitāb al-waraḳāt fī uṣūl al-fiḳh* was commented on down to the xith century A.H., and printed in *Mad̲j̲mūʿ mutūn uṣūlīya li-as̲h̲har mas̲h̲āhīr ʿulamāʾ al-mad̲h̲āhib al-arbaʿa*, Damascus, n.d., and on the margin of Aḥmad b. Idrīs al-Karāfī, *Tahāfut al-fuṣūl fī 'l-uṣūl*, Cairo 1306.

Bibliography: Brockelmann, *GAL* ², i. 486—8 and *Suppl.*, i. 671—3; Ibn K̲h̲allikān, no. 331; Subkī, *Ṭabaḳāt*, iii. 249—83; Ibn al-At̲h̲īr x., 77 (anno 485); Wüstenfeld, *Die Akademien der Araber*, no. 38; Schreiner in *Grätz' Monatsschrift*, xxv., 314 *sq.*; Gardet en Anawati, *Introduction à la Théologie musulmane* (Paris 1948), index.

DRUZES. The Druzes are a community living in the Lebanon and Anti-Lebanon, around Damascus and in the mountains of Ḥawrān. They have their own religion and held a special position in the administrative arrangements of the Ottoman empire.

Their name is derived from that of Darazī [q.v.]. Their ethnographical origin is obscure. It is probable that they already had distinct racial features before the founding of their religion and that they were never quite converted to Islām. They may be the remnants of some ancient peoples, who sought refuge in the mountains in times of invasion and always retained a certain amount of independence in those places so easy to defend. They have sometimes been regarded as the descendants of Persian colonists. In the xviith century they were regarded as the survivors of the Latin Christians, who escaped the massacre at Acre when al-As̲h̲raf, Sulṭān of Egypt took this town in 1291 and destroyed the last remnants of Frankish power in the Holy Land; this last tradition is clearly worthless, as it would place the date of the origin of the Druzes much too late; it is however interesting in as much as it is connected with the claim put forward by the Druze chiefs of the xviith century to be descended from Godfrey de Bouillon.

The Druzes, who have an *amīr* or a *ḥakam* at their head, have had two very celebrated Emīrs in the course of their history: the Emīr Fak̲h̲r al-Dīn, popularly called Fakardin, in the xviith century, and the Emīr Bas̲h̲īr al-S̲h̲ihābī in the xixth. The descendants of Fak̲h̲r al-Dīn, of the family of Maʿn, continued to rule the Druzes till the beginning of the xviiith century when the power passed from the family of Maʿn to that of S̲h̲ihāb.

Religion. What is called the Druze religion is a learned system which is not known to all the people. Those who know it, are called *ʿuḳḳāl* (the learned); the others are the *d̲j̲uhhāl* (the ignorant). The *ʿuḳḳāl* alone take part in the religious meetings which are held in the night from Thursday to Friday; the place of meeting is called *k̲h̲alwa* (retirement). The most meritorious of the *ʿuḳḳāl*, in the proportion of one in 50, become *ad̲j̲āwid* (perfect). These are the religious chiefs; the highest in degree resides at Ḳanawāt in the Ḥawrān.

Belief in metempsychosis is widespread among the people; the good are born again in infants, but the wicked return in the bodies of dogs. Polygamy is allowed and it is said that the marriage of brother and sister is sometimes practised; but the law forbids this (cf. de Sacy, ii. 700).

The religion of the Druzes, in its learned form, belongs to the Bāṭinī [q.v.] system. It was founded in the time of the Fāṭimid Caliph Ḥākim (386—411/996—1021) by Ḥamza [q.v.] and Darazī [q. v.]. It is known to us from over a hundred works to be found in European libraries. These scriptures, some of which go back to Ḥamza, are professions of faith, expositions of doctrine, works dealing with the organisation of the sect, diplomas for the installation of different ministers, letters, fragments of polemics against the Nuṣairīs and the Mutawālī, neighbours of the Druzes, against the Ismāʿīlīs, from whom they separated, and against several ministers and missionaries who had corrupted the doctrine from the beginning. These dissenters are accused of preaching licentious doctrines and favouring the worship of the calf. The figure of a calf actually appears in the ceremonies of the Druzes and some authors say they worship it; but it is probable that in the true religion the calf is the symbol for the demon and only appears as an object of execration.

The Ismāʿīlī doctrine was based on the idea that God became incarnate in man in all ages; and God himself, or at least the creative force, was conceived as composed of several principles which proceeded one from the other. Each of these principles became incarnate in a man. Druze theology retained this system. According to it the Caliph Ḥākim represented God in his unity; this is why Ḥamza called his religion "Unitarian". Ḥākim is worshipped and is called "Our Lord". His eccentricities and his cruelties are explained symbolically. He was the last incarnation of God; they do not admit that he is dead; he is only hidden, in a state of "occultation" and will re-appear one day, according to the Mahdist idea. Below Ḥākim there are five superior ministers who are incarnations of principles that have come forth from God. The first is the incarnation of universal intelligence (*ʿaḳl*), the second of universal soul (*nafs*). The conceptions of universal soul and universal intelligence are derived from philosophy. The third minister is the incarnation of the Word (*kalima*) which is produced from the soul by the Intelligence; the fourth is called the Right Wing or the Preceder; the fifth the Left Wing or the Follower. Together they are called *ḥudūd*, i.e. bounds or precepts, and they have other symbolic names also. At the foundation of the sect these ministers were respectively: Ḥamza, the founder; Ismāʿīl b. Muḥammad al-Tamīmī, one of the writers of the sect; Muḥammad b. Wahb; Salāma b. ʿAbd al-Wahhāb al-Samurrī; Abu 'l-Ḥasan ʿAlī b. Aḥmad al-Samūkī.

Below these superior ministers are those of lower rank, divided into three classes. These are not incarnations of eternal principles, they are functionaries, preachers and heads of communities. They are called in the order of the classes, *dāʿī* [q.v.] or missionary; *maʾdhūn* or he who has received permission; the *mukassir*, destroyer, also called *naḳīb*. The *dāʿī* is also called "industry"; the *maʾdhūn*, "the opening", he who opens the door to the aspirant; and the *mukassir*, the "phantom", the apparition in the night of error. The Bāṭinīs employ the same terms in a somewhat different order.

The knowledge of the nature of God, of his attributes, his manifestations in the series of principles which are incarnate in the ministers, constitutes the dogmatics of this religion. Its moral system is summed up in seven precepts which take the place of those of Islām viz., to love truth (but only between believers); the adepts are pledged to watch over one another's safety; to renounce the religion to which one formerly belonged; to cut one's self off from the demon and those that are living in error; to recognise the existence in all ages of the principle of divine unity in humanity; to be satisfied with the works of "Our Lord" (Ḥākim), whatever they are; to be absolutely resigned to his will — it seems to be understood: in as far as it is manifested through his ministers. — These precepts are binding on both sexes.

Bibliography: Many travellers have written on the Druzes: Bon I. Taylor, *La Syrie, la Palestine et la Judée* (Paris 1855), p. 76—83, 35—40; Lamartine, *Voyage en Orient* (1832—1833), chapters on the Emīr Bashīr and on the Druzes; Mrs. Charles Roundell, *Lady Hester Stanhope* (London 1909), p. 54, 91, 216; Cte F. van den Steen de Jehay, *De la Situation légale des Sujets Ottomans non-Musulmans* (Brussels 1906), chapter on the Druzes; C. H. Churchill, *Mount Lebanon* 1842—1852 (London 1853); *The Druzes and the Maronites under Turkish rule, from* 1840 to 1860 (London 1862); F. Tournebize, *Les Druzes*, in *Études des Pères de la Cie de Jésus*, 5 Oct. 1897; Max Freiherr von Oppenheim, *Vom Mittelmeer zum Persischen Golf*; *Magasin Pittoresque*, 1841, p. 367 (costumes), and 1861, p. 226; François Lenormant, *L'Histoire des Massacres de Syrie en* 1860; A. de la Jonquière, *Histoire de l'Empire Ottoman* (Paris 1881), p. 491—505, and p. 521—525. — On the literature and religion of the Druzes, cf. Silvestre de Sacy, *Exposé de la Religion des Druzes* (2 vol., Paris 1838); Regnault, *Catéchisme à l'usage des Druses djahels* (ignorants, païens) *qui veulent être initiés*, in *Bulletin de la Société de Géographie*, vii. 22—30; C. F. Seybold, *Die Drusenschrift Kitāb al-Noqaṭ wal-Dawāʾir* (Tübingen 1902); Philip K. Hitti, *The Origins of the Druze People and Religion* (New York 1928); N. Bouron, *Les Druzes* (Paris 1930); M. Sprengling, *The Berlin Druze Lexicon*, *AJSL*, lvi. (1939) p. 388 *sq*.

DUʿĀʾ (A.) "blessing", "prayer", in the same sense as the Hebrew *berākā*, hence comes also to mean "curse", not to be confused with *ṣalāt*, which is often also translated prayer, but really means the whole service.

As the first Sūra of the Ḳurʾān forms the usual Muslim prayer, it is commonly called *Sūrat al-duʿāʾ*. There are of course quite a number of other forms of prayer for different occasions, which are given in the catalogues under the name *duʿāʾ* or *ḥizb*. The *ḥizb al-baḥr* of al-Shādhilī [q.v.] is for example very popular, as is al-Djazūlī's (d. 870/1465) collection of prayers. Belief in the magic power of the word is very general. — Cf. the articles DHIKR, ḤIZB, ṢALĀT, WIRD.

ḌUḤĀ. [See ṢALĀT].

E

ELIAS. [See ILYĀS].

EZRA. [See ʿUZAIR].

F

AL-**FAḌĀLĪ**, MUḤAMMAD B. SHĀFIʿĪ AL-SHĀFIʿĪ, a Cairene Shaikh born at Munyat Faḍāla near Samannud in the Delta (*Khiṭaṭ djadīda*, ix. 2; xvi. 80; Bādjūrī, *Taḥḳīḳ al-maḳām ʿalā kifāyat al-ʿawāmm*, p. 9 of ed. of Cairo, 1316) who died in 1236/1821 (*Cat. of Khediv. Library*, ii., p. 39). He appears to be known only as the author of the theological treatise *Kifāyat al-ʿawāmm min ʿilm al-kalām* and the teacher of the more fertile Bādjūrī who added the gloss, mentioned above, to his master's work. Text and *ḥāshiya* seem always to go together in the Mss. and editions. A translation of the text is given in D. B. Macdonald's *Development of Muslim Theology etc.*, p. 315—351.

Bibliography: *GAL*, ii. 489, *Suppl.* ii. 744; Ahlwardt's Berlin Cat., iv., p. 459, No. 5148; *Die Katechismen des Fudali und Sanusi. Muh. Glaubenslehre*, übers. u. erl. von M. Horten, Berlin 1916; Ellis, *Cat. of Ar. Printed Books in British Museum*, under *Muḥammad ibn Shāfiʿī al-Faḍḍālī*; but the *nisba* according to the *Khiṭ.djad*. is as above.

FAIʾ. By this word Muslim scholars in general understand all things taken from the unbelievers "without fighting" and further very often the lands in conquered territories. The name *faiʾ* may be explained from the peculiar expression in the Ḳurʾān, Sūra lix. 6 and 7: "What God has made to return to his apostle" (*mā afāʾa ʾllāhu ʿalā rasūlihi*). The possessions of the unbelievers which are "returned" to the Muslims form the *faiʾ*.

Sūra lix., 6 and 8—10 of the Ḳurʾān was revealed,

according to Muslim tradition, when Muḥammad had resolved not to divide the fields and orchards left by the Banu 'l-Naḍīr, who had been driven out of the country, as booty of war among those who had taken part in the siege, but to give them to the Muhādjirs exclusively. He justified this action by arguing that these were really obtained not by fighting but in a peaceful fashion, by surrender.

After the conquest of Khaibar and Fadak also the lands of the Jews there were not wholly divided among the troops as booty but in part placed at the Prophet's disposal. It was probably on this occasion that Sūra lix. 7 was revealed: "What God hath granted his apostle as *faiʾ* from the people of the towns, belongs to God — to his apostle, to his family, to the orphan, to the poor and to the traveller —; what the apostle of God gives you, accept, but what he forbids you, abstain from!" What could not properly be regarded as booty, was to be managed by the Prophet himself as state property and the proceeds therefrom were to be applied to the general good, like the fifth of the *ghanīma* [q.v.].

At a later period ʿUmar I in consonance with the view of his advisers of the *ṣaḥāba* thought that this principle should be applied to the newly conquered territories also. He ordered that only movable property captured should be divided among the Arab conquerors but not the land. The land was to be applied not only for the advantage of the generation then living but as *faiʾ* belonging for all time to the whole community for the benefit of all future generations of Muslims also. It was also feared at that time that if the Arabs devoted themselves to agriculture they would become less capable fighters. As a rule therefore, only the native population was to till the ground and deliver a certain portion of the yield as tribute to the Muslim treasury. This payment (*kharādj*) was to be bound up with the possession of the land for all time. It was therefore decreed that the inhabitants who cultivated *faiʾ* estates, even if they adopted Islām, should continue to be bound to pay the *kharādj*. As the payment of *kharādj* was regarded as a sign of subjection, the Arabs at first felt themselves prevented from acquiring land that belonged to the *faiʾ*; for they would thus have put themselves in a position where they would have to pay *kharādj* themselves. The only exception was those districts whose inhabitants had voluntarily surrendered on the approach of the Arab army on condition that they were allowed to retain possession of their lands. In such districts (the so-called *dār al-ṣulḥ*; q.v.] the land did not belong to the *faiʾ*.

When in the course of the first century the people of the conquered lands adopted Islām, they began, in spite of all measures of the Muslim authorities, to avoid the payment of *kharādj* and only gave the *zakāt* of the yield of their fields like the Arab Muslims. The land in the conquered provinces thus gradually ceased to be regarded as *faiʾ*.

The views of later Muslim scholars on this point differ; the lands and estates in provinces conquered at a later period are, according to the Shāfiʿīs, always to be divided among the conquerors as *ghanīma*, according to the Mālikīs on the other hand, they are to be considered the property of all Muslims, i.e. as *faiʾ*, while the Ḥanafīs would place them at the *imām*'s disposal so that he may administer them either as *faiʾ* for the common good or divide them as *ghanīma* among the troops according as the cause of Islām may be best advanced.

Besides the land, the *kharādj*, the *djizya* and all other tribute to be paid by unbelievers, as for example the duties they have to pay on their goods in order to be allowed to trade in Muslim countries, are included in *faiʾ*. According to Shāfiʿī teaching a fifth part of the *faiʾ* must be set aside and applied in five equal portions to the same five purposes as the fifth part of the *ghanīma*; the other four fifths of the *faiʾ* are, according to the same school, to be used for the payment of the regular troops, the maintenance of mosques, roads and bridges and for other objects of general utility to Muslims. On the other hand the other Fiḳh schools hold that the *imām* should always apply the *faiʾ* in its entirety for the good of the Muslim community as circumstances require it.

Bibliography: In addition to the chapter on *djihād* in the *fiḳh* books: the works on *kharādj* by Abū Yūsuf and Yaḥyā b. Ādam; Māwardī, *al-Aḥkām al-sulṭāniya* (ed. M. Enger, Bonn 1853), p. 217 *sq.*, 237 *sq.*, 293 *sq.*; Dimishḳī, *Raḥmat al-umma fi 'khtilāf al-aʾimma* (Būlāḳ 1300), p. 151 *sq.*; and the literature cited in Th. W. Juynboll, *Handbuch des Islām. Gesetzes* (Leyden 1910), p. 352 *sq.*

FAIḌ (A.), effusion, emanation, is much used in the Arabic tradition of Neo-Platonism, as a name for the gradual but steadily descending creative development of the world out of God and its maintenance through his providence. No definition (*ḥadd*) can be given of God's essence and of its creative activity, but it is possible to describe it in other words (*rasm*), e.g. to say: He is the existent one from whom all else emanates (*yafīḍ*). For this the philosophers primarily use the expressions of the Ḳurʾān and Tradition (*khalḳ*, *ibdāʿ* etc.) interpreted in a spiritual sense (*taʾwīl*). At the same time however, they find it necessary to use a language based on that of the Neo-Platonists with the knowledge that this language too requires an allegorical interpretation (clearly expressed for example by Fārābī, "Abhandlungen", ed. Dieterici, p. 30 and 51).

Before we outline the Arab tradition concerning *faiḍ*, it is necessary in order to understand it, to elucidate the position of this doctrine in the *Enneads* of Plotinus. There are, as already in Plato, in Plotinian thought two motives, often contradictory associated with one another: 1. the necessity for a philosophical cosmology: the way has to be described which leads from the most perfect being (God) through the spheres of heaven to the less perfect earthly world, i.e. everything comes from God and is, although in a diminishing degree, good in itself and has its definite function, the soul, for example, as organising principle forms and guides its body; 2. a religious motive: the fate of the soul on its journey through the world. From this point of view the soul has fallen from the world of spirits and feels itself in the world of bodies as in a cave, a prison, a tomb, and longingly seeks release from its body by reflecting on the higher world. In Plotinus both views are intimately connected but the second predominates, the cosmological theory is appreciated more in the religious than in the philosophical sense.

Speculation regarding *faiḍ* is of a cosmological, or, if preferred, of a cosmogonic nature, whether it is considered from the religious point of view or not. This article is confined to this aspect.

The Neo-Platonists, particularly Plotinus, used, to describe the origin of the world out of God, many words with the meaning of emerging or issuing and sought to make this metaphysical process more intelligible by metaphors borrowed from the world of the senses. For example, the origin of the world was compared with the radiation of the light of the sun (e.g. *Enn.*, v. 1, 6), with the gushing forth or overflow of water (iii. 8, 10) or with procreation (v. 4, 1). As Allāh does not procreate, the latter image could not be adopted by orthodox Islām; the two other comparisons however found wide circulation, not only among gnostics but also among philosophers and mystic theologians. In these, *faiḍ*, originally used of the flowing or overflowing of water, was also applied to the radiation of light.

The dissemination of the doctrine of emanation can be traced mainly to the *Theology of Aristotle* and to the *Liber de causis*. According to the *Theology*, a series of spiritual beings (the *ʿaḳl*, through whose intermediary the soul, through the latter nature) emanates from God and there flows from him not only the strength for their existence but also for their preservation. Creation and preservation are not distinguished. Nor is there any distinction made between substantialism and energism. Energism, i.e. the doctrine that powers emanate from God (*ḳuwwa*: here not in the sense of a receptive power but in the real sense of deed = *fiʿl*), predominates. Therefore this doctrine of emanation may be called a dynamic or energetic pantheism.

The evolution of the world out of God is indicated in the *Theology* in general as a *k͟hurūd͟j* or a *ẓuhūr* i.e. phenomenon of the inner (*bāṭin*) in the outer (*ẓāhir*); cf. Dieterici's edition, p. 49 *sq.*, 111, 136. *Faiḍ* is used, but more frequently, with the same meaning; also *inbid͟jās* (p. 136) which is generally used of the flowing of water. In any case it is clear (in connection with the doctrine of *insān awwal* = *insān ʿaḳlī* or *insān kāmil*, p. 51, 150) that *faiḍ* and *is͟hrāḳ* (radiation of the light of the sun) are used synonymously. It may be further noted that *faiḍ* is used for the activities both of God and of the lower spiritual beings and of the first man, of course with reference to God's activity in the highest sense.

In the *Liber de causis faiḍ* has become rather vague; its use may be compared to that of the word "influence". In general the doctrine is the same as in the *Theology*; it is also connected with the speculation on the *nūr* but everything is more systematised. It is not Plotinus but Proclos who is speaking here. The *Theology* starts out from the soul, the *Liber de causis* from God as the originator of the world. The soul here appears as a cosmological quantity, a member in the series of emanations, its function is to form and guide the world of bodies. As in the *Theology*, God is called the first cause of the world. His influence (*faiḍ*) however is not only the first cause, but in spite of repeated transmission is always for all that exists the strongest and nearest cause i.e. God is not far from us. Everything comes from him; to be more definite: the good simply, being or existence as well as all perfection. In particular, knowledge is transmitted through the *ʿaḳl* and life through the soul. The whole emanation is described as in the *Theology* as a gift or communication from God.

In the *Liber de causis* it is particularly emphasised (ed. Bardenhewer, § 17) that God's activity is in the nature of *ibdāʿ* (absolute creation), the activity of the spirits below him is in the nature of shaping. This is however not in the Greek original.

Among the Ik͟hwān al-Ṣafāʾ everything revolves round the fate of the soul, and the doctrine of emanation of the Neo-Platonists with many neo-Pythagorean and gnostic additions is also used for edifying purposes. The series of emanations is given a double name and in place of the Neo-Platonic triad we have the Pythagorean quaternad. According to the abstract series, there emanate from God: being (*wud͟jūd*), existence (*baḳāʾ*), completion (*tamām*) and perfection (*kamāl*); according to the concrete series come the *ʿaḳl* (direct from God, further transmitted), the world soul (nature, third in the Neo-Platonic series, is called one of the powers of the soul), first matter and absolute body, which is also called second matter. Everything comes from God just as the series of numbers comes from one (cf. esp. the *Rasāʾil*, No. 29, 32, 35). The Ik͟hwān al-Ṣafāʾ also used the above mentioned comparisons. Among the synonyms of *faiḍ* are *sarayān* and *ṣudūr*, the latter already found in Fārābī, and general in the later philosophic usage.

Fārābī, Ibn Sīnā and Ibn Rus͟hd added nothing essential to the emanation theory. There are only little differences of schematisation and use of terms. Fārābī and Ibn Sīnā use *faiḍ* and *ṣudūr* synonymously; this may be here observed because, as it appears, later mystics have posited a distinction between the two terms (cf. Horten, *Die Philosophie des Islām*, 1924, p. 162).

Fārābī lays stress (*Abhandlungen*, ed. Dieterici, p. 58) on the world's emanating (*ṣudūr*, *ḥuṣūl*) from God as not arising from natural necessity, but with knowledge and approval, neither arbitrarily nor for an extra-divine purpose, i.e. it lies in the essential goodness of God (cf. Plato's *Timaios*) that he creates from his superabundance. Ibn Sīnā lays stress on this also when he puts forward the doctrine that the creation of the world is an eternal necessity on God's part.

Against this G͟hazzālī raises his protest in the *Tahāfut* (ed. Bouyges, p. 90 *sq.*, 214 *sqq.*). In his opinion the philosophers, although they deny it, are in this way lowering God's activity to the causality of nature. God is however not an impersonal 'first cause' but a *fāʿil* i.e. one who makes the world with knowledge and free will, when and how he wills. This does not prevent him using the philosophical vocabulary: *faiḍ* (for this also, as already in Ibn Sīnā, *Nad͟jāt*, p. 76, the impressive *fayaḍān*) and *ṣudūr* etc. Cf. e.g. *Maḍnūn ṣag͟hīr*, p. 90 *sq.*, where he compares God's blowing (*nafk͟h*) the soul (*rūḥ*) into man, not to the pouring of water from a vessel, nor with the blowing of breath (water and air are too near to earth) but only with the *fayaḍān* of the sunlight.

Ibn Rus͟hd (cf. v. d. Bergh, *Epitome*, p. 131 *sqq.*) adopts in the main the theory of emanation from Fārābī and Ibn Sīnā and defends it against G͟hazzālī (*Tahāfut al-tahāfut*, ed. Bouyges, p. 438 *sqq.*) with the observation that God's will is above the antagonisms of necessity and free will. Besides, the theory of emanation in its connection with the Ptolemaic system is not capable of exact proof but is a probable hypothesis.

The Neo-Platonists were interested almost entirely in the genealogy of spiritual beings (from God to nature) but the Muslim Aristotelians from Fārābī onwards (cf. his *Abhandlungen*, ed. Dieterici, p. 39 *sqq.*, and *Musterstaat*, p. 19) also sought to define the relation of the pure spirits (*ʿuḳūl*) to the separate souls and bodies of the spheres. Along with the above outlined series of emanations in three or four stages a ten- or elevenfold series was also laid down, corresponding to the Aristotelian and Ptolemaic conception of the world. The systematic exposition of this theory is found in Ibn Sīnā (see M. Horten, *Die Metaphysik Avicennas*, p. 595 *sqq.*)

in the following way. From God the absolute one, in whom thinking, thought and idea coincide, can — a Neo-Platonic dogma! — only a simple incorporeal being (νοῦς, *ʿaḳl*) proceed, a superworldly spirit. This is in its origin simple but as a caused being it has plurality, more exactly the triad, in it. When it thinks of its cause (God), a second spirit flows out of it; when it thinks of itself and regards itself as a contingent being, the soul and the body of the surrounding sphere proceed from it. From this second spirit flows a third, as well as the soul and the body of the sphere of the fixed stars. And so it flows further through the spheres of the seven planets from Saturn to the Moon. The last spirit in this series of emanations, proceeding from the spirit of the Moon (or is it identical with the spirit of the moon?, cf. Ghazzālī, *Tahāfut*, ed. Bouyges, p. 114 *sq.*) is called *ʿaḳl faʿʿāl*, active spirit, because from it or through its intermediary all forms of the earthly world flow. This whole process is said to take place timelessly like the radiation of light.

Ibn Rushd was not enthusiastic for this presentation of the theory. Ibn Sīnā's first *ʿaḳl* is in his view superfluous and the soul of the planets is not to be distinguished from their thinking spirit. The Neo-Platonic principle of unity from unity and the idea of contingency do not please him either (cf. S. v. d. Bergh, *Die Epitome des Averroes*, p. 116, 132 *sqq.*).

Bibliography: On Neo-Platonism cf. W. R. Inge, *The Philosophy of Plotinus*, 2 vol., London 1918; E. Bréhier, *La philosophie de Plotin*, Paris 1928; see the artt. ḲARMAṬIANS, KHALḲ, NAFS, NŪR, TAṢAWWUF.

FAKHR AL-**DĪN** AL-RĀZĪ. [SEE AL-RĀZĪ].

FAḲĪH. A *faḳīh* is, in the first instance, one who possesses knowledge of or understanding about a thing (syn. *ʿālim, fāhim*). Then as *fiḳh* [q.v.] passed from being synonymous with *ʿilm* (as in *fiḳh al-lugha*) and became limited to religious knowledge (*ʿilm al-dīn*) then to the religious law (*al-sharīʿa*) and finally to the derivative details of the last (*al-furūʿ*), so *faḳīh* passed from meaning an intelligent, understanding person to meaning a theologian, then a canon lawyer and finally a casuist (*Lisān al-ʿArab*, xvii. 418). The book ascribed to Abū Ḥanifa, *al-Fiḳh al-akbar* ("The Greater Fiḳh", i.e. *ʿilm al-kalām*) is on the border line of the development, and in it (ed. Allāhābād, p. 2) *faḳīh* is used in a purely general sense. This restriction of meaning was gradually brought about by the employment of the word to translate the (*juris*) *prudens* of Roman law (cf. FIḲH and Goldziher in *Kultur der Gegenwart*, i. 3, p. 102). On the distinction between *faḳīh* and *mudjtahid* see the latter and *Dict. of tech. Terms*, p. 30 *sq.*, 198 *sq.*, 1157. In Egypt the word, in the corrupted form *fiḳī*, has come to mean a schoolmaster or a professional reciter of the Ḳurʾān just as *khaṭīb* in Syria now means a schoolmaster (Lane, *Modern Egyptians*, chap. ii).

Bibliography: under FIḲH.

FAḲĪR. One who is in need, either physical or spiritual. Thus opposed to *ghanī*, one who is independent, rich; and commonly contrasted with *miskīn*, one who is in a miserable state. A beggar is *sāʾil*, an asker. Thus in Sūra xxxv. 15: "Ye are the needers (*fuḳarāʾ*) of Allāh; but Allāh is the Self-sufficient (*ghanī*)". Faḳīr has in consequence come to indicate need in relation to Allāh and dependence (*tawakkul*) of every kind upon Allāh, and is used in Arabic-speaking countries for a mendicant derwīsh (q.v.; cf. also Goldziher, *Vorlesungen*, p. 154). The saying ascribed to Muḥammad, *al-faḳr fakhrī*, "Poverty is my pride", has assisted this. In western languages the term has been extended to cover Indian ascetics and yogis. The coincidence with the English *faker* is curious and sometimes misleading.

FANĀʾ (A.), an important technical term of Ṣūfism meaning "annihilation, dissolution". The Ṣūfī who attains perfection must be in a kind of state of annihilation.

The authors of treatises on Muslim mysticism have often compared the "annihilation" of Ṣūfism with the Buddhist nirvāna; but according to others this comparison is entirely inadequate, as the Buddhist idea of annihilation is independent of the idea of God and includes the idea of the transmigration of souls, to which nirvāna puts an end. In Muslim mysticism on the other hand there is no question of metempsychosis and the notion of a personal and allpresent God is throughout predominant.

The origin of the Muslim conception of *fanāʾ* has rather to be sought in Christianity from which it seems to be borrowed. This conception simply means the annihilation of the individual human will before the will of God, an idea which forms the centre of all Christian mysticism.

The oldest systematic exposition of pantheistic Ṣūfism, the *Kashf al-maḥdjūb* ("Revelation of concealed Matters") of al-Hudjwīrī gives all the explanation that could be desired of *fanāʾ*.

The virtue of poverty understood in the mystic sense consists "in averting the gaze from all created things; in that general annihilation, seeing only the All-One, the *ṣūfī* hastens towards the fullness of eternal life" (p. 20 of Nicholson's transl.). — Mystic poverty, we are further told, consists in the annihilation of the human attributes (*ṣifāt*), which dwell in the Ego, so that one is now only rich in God and through God. — "The Ṣūfī is he that has nothing in his possession nor is himself possessed by anything. This denotes the essence of annihilation (*fanāʾ*)". — When this feeling has attained its perfection it is called *fanāʾ-i kullī* "absolute annihilation".

The expression *fanāʾ* is often interchanged with *ṣafāʾ* "purity"; this word means that the Ṣūfī should keep his soul pure from all attachment to any creature. *Fanāʾ* is further often associated with *baḳāʾ* "subsistence": the man, who has destroyed his own will, henceforth lives in God; the human will is transitory while God's will is eternal.

The author of the *Kashf al-maḥdjūb* expressly states (p. 243) that *fanāʾ* does not mean loss of essence and destruction of personality as some ignorant Ṣūfīs think. It is not the essence but the human attributes, which are a danger to the perfection of being, that are destroyed (p. 28). "In India", says the author, "I had a dispute with a man who claimed to be versed in Ḳurʾānic exegesis and theology. When I examined his pretensions, I found that he knew nothing of annihilation" (p. 243); i.e. he had understood the word *fanāʾ* in a metaphysical sense.

Bibliography: al-Hudjwīrī, *Kashf al-maḥdjūb*, (transl. by Nicholson, London 1911); Carra de Vaux, *Gazali* (Paris 1902), s. Index s.v. "anéantissement"; cf. also the *Kitāb al-taʿrīfāt* of Djurdjānī.; R. A. Nicholson, *The Mystics of Islam*, pp. 17—19; the same, *The Idea of Personality in Ṣūfism*, p. 14; I. Goldziher, *Vorlesungen über den Islam*, 2nd ed. p. 162; L. Massignon, *Essai sur les origines du lexique...*, Paris 1922, by Index.

FARĀʾIḌ is the name given to the fixed shares in an estate ($^1/_2$, $^1/_4$, $^1/_8$, $^2/_3$, $^1/_3$ and $^1/_6$) expressly mentioned in the verses dealing with the laws of inheritance in the Ḳurʾān (iv. 11—12 and 176) which fall to the twelve so-called "people of fixed shares" (*dhawu ʾl-farāʾiḍ* or *aṣḥāb al-farāʾiḍ*). As the accurate knowledge of these fixed shares was considered as very important the whole science of the laws of inheritance was called *ʿilm al-farāʾiḍ*.

Although the Ḳurʾān only recognises fixed portions for the daughter, the two parents, the husband and wife, and the brothers and sisters, Muslim scholars have extended the laws applicable to the daughters of a deceased person to the daughters of his son and in the same way those applicable to his parents to the grand-parents; a distinction has further been made in sisters between full and half-sister on the father's side and on the mother's. The total number of these so-called "Ḳurʾānic" heirs has thus been raised to twelve, viz., in descending order: 1. the daughters of the deceased and those of his sons; 2. in ascending order: father, mother and grandfather on the father's side, grandmother on both sides (and further all other female relatives of the deceased, in ascending line, in so far as they are not related to him through a male relative in ascending line who is not legally qualified to inherit); 3. in the collateral line: the full sister, the half-sister on the father's side and the half-brother and half-sister on the mother's side; 4. widower and widow.

The daughter of the deceased is entitled to half his estate; if there are two or more daughters, they receive together $^2/_3$ of the estate. The son's daughters, full sisters and half-sisters on the father's side are subject to the same rules (Ḳurʾān, iv. 11 and 176). Each of the heirs in ascending line may claim $^1/_6$ of the estate; the mother, however, only receives this share if there are children, son's children, or two or more brothers or sisters of the deceased; otherwise she gets $^1/_3$ of the estate (Ḳurʾān, iv. 11). Each of the half-sisters and half-brothers on the mother's side also gets $^1/_6$ of the estate; if two or more inherit together, they receive $^1/_6$ in all. The widower receives $^1/_2$ of the estate except when a child or son's child inherits with him in which case his share is only $^1/_4$. The widow has (Ḳurʾān, iv. 12) only a claim to half of what a widower would receive in the same circumstances, i.e. $^1/_4$ or $^1/_8$ of the estate, according as she inherits with children (or son's children) or not.

If there are several *dhawu ʾl-farāʾiḍ* either together or with other relatives of the deceased, they are in many cases excluded from their fixed shares. They then according to circumstances either receive nothing at all or the residue of the estate, after the other heirs have received what they are entitled to. The *dhawu lʾ-farāʾiḍ* can never all inherit at the same time.

Bibliography: Besides the chapter on inheritance in the collections on Tradition and the Fiḳh books, the literature quoted in Th. W. Juynboll, *Handbuch des islāmischen Gesetzes* (Leyden 1910), p. 237 and 356 *sq.*; E. Sachau, in *Sitzungsberichte der Berliner Akademie der Wissenschaften*, 1894, i. 159—210; L. W. C. van den Berg, in *Bijdragen tot de Taal-, Land- en Volkenkunde van Nederl.-Indië*, series 5, vii. 500 *sq.*; Bergsträsser, *Grundzüge des islamischen Rechts* (Berlin-Leipzig, 1935), p. 91 *sqq.*; F. Peltier and G. H. Bousquet *Les Successions agnatiques mitigées*, Paris 1935. See also MĪRĀTH.

FARĀʾIḌĪYA. This sect was founded in Eastern Bengal about the year 1804 by Ḥādjdjī Sharīʿat Allāh, born of obscure parents, who resided in a village, Bahādurpūr, in the district of Farīdpūr. When eighteen years of age he went on a pilgrimage to Mecca, but instead of returning, as usual, he remained a disciple of al-Shaikh Ṭāhir al-Sunbul al-Makkī, the head of the Shāfiʿī school there in those days. About 1802, after an absence of twenty years, he came back to India, a skilful disputer, and a good Arabic scholar. On his way home he fell into the hands of Dacoits (banded robbers) who plundered him of everything, including many relics of his residence in Arabia. Finding life insupportable without books or relics, he joined the gang, and shared their many wanderings. The simplicity of his character and the sincerity of his religious convictions struck these wicked men, who ultimately became his most zealous followers. Such is the story told at the present day of the first step taken towards proselytism by this remarkable man. For several years Sharīʿat Allāh quietly promulgated his newly framed doctrines in the villages of his native districts, encountering much opposition and abuse, but attracting a band of devoted adherents, he by degrees acquired the reputation of a holy man.

The chief innovation introduced by him was the non-observance of the Friday prayers and of the two great *ʿīds*, on the ground that India under British rule was *dār al-ḥarb* [q.v.]. He also ordered that the titles of *ustādh* (teacher) and *shāgird* (pupil), terms which did not imply complete submission, should in future be used in the place of *pīr* (master) and *murīd* (disciple), which had for ages been the representative designations of the religious preceptor and his pupil. He further prohibited the usual ceremony of joining hands, which was customary at the initiation of a disciple, but required from every one of his would-be disciples *tawba*, or repentance for past sins, and a solemn determination to lead a more righteous and godly life in future. It is a curious fact that none of these ideas excited much opposition, but on his promulgating a dogma that to allow a mid-wife to cut the navel cord of a new born babe was a deadly sin borrowed from the Hindus, and his insisting that it was the duty of the father to do this, he roused a spirit of opposition which caused many of his adherents to fall away. The zamīndārs (landlords) were alarmed at the spread of the new creed, which bound the Muḥammadan peasantry together as one man. Disputes and quarrels soon arose, and Sharīʿat Allāh was driven away from Navābārī, in the Dhākā district, where he had settled, and was compelled to return to his birthplace. There he resumed his holy office as a minister of the faith, and in a short time enlisted the sympathies and support of a vast majority of the uneducated and the most excitable classes of the Muḥammadan population. His influence became unbounded, and no one hesitated to carry out his orders. He acted with great prudence and caution, rarely assuming any other character than that of a religious reformer. The movement set on foot by this man attracted little attention during his lifetime, and his name is rarely met with in the annals of those days. On looking back, however, at his career there is much which amply repays an inquiry.

A very different person was his son, Muḥammad Muḥsin, better known as Dūdhū Mīyān, who, though of ordinary abilities, exerted an influence far surpassing that of his father. His name is a household word throughout the districts of Farīdpūr, Pubna,

Bāķirgandj, Dhākā and Noakhali, and the number of his followers at the present day testifies to the thoroughness of the method with which he and his father fulfilled their mission.

Dūdhū Mīyān was born in 1819, and, while still young, visited Mecca, where, as he asserted and made his followers believe, visions and revelations of a nature tending to his future greatness, were vouchsafed to him. On his return he devoted himself to the spread of his father's doctrines, as well as many more which he himself introduced afresh.

The most remarkable advance made during Dūdhū Mīyān's lifetime was the organisation of the society. Following the example of the *vaishnavas*, he divided Eastern Bengal into circles, and appointed a khalīfa, or agent, to each, with power to collect contributions for the furtherance of the objects of the central association. They further kept Dūdhū Mīyān, usually styled the Pīr, or simply Maulwī, acquainted with everything occurring within their jurisdiction, and whenever a zamīndār tried to enforce his legal rights against any one member of the sect, funds were provided to sue him in the court, or, if it could be safely done, men with clubs were sent to plunder his property and to thrash his servants. During his father's lifetime the sect was never opposed to, nor collided with, the law of the land; but the measures adopted by the son united the zamīndārs and the indigo planters against him.

It was among the cultivators and village workman that Dūdhū Mīyān made the largest number of converts. He asserted the equality of mankind, and taught that the welfare of the lowly and poor was as much an object of interest as that of the high and the rich.

Dūdhū Mīyān and the ḥādjdjīs, as his followers were originally called, became objects of dread to the Hindus, old Muḥammadans, and European landholders. Evidence to convict a prisoner could not be got. It was, however, against the levying of illegal cesses by landlords that Dūdhū Mīyān made his most determined stand. In this he was certainly right, as the only apology for their continuance was their antiquity, and adaptation to the feelings of the people. But, he advanced a step further when he proclaimed that the earth is God's, and that no one has a right to occupy it as an inheritance, or levy taxes upon it. The peasantry were, therefore, persuaded to settle on Khāṣṣ Maḥall lands, managed directly by the Government, and thus escape the payment of any taxes but that of the land revenue, claimed by the State. His rapid success, however, excited the jealousy of the contemporary landlords and many false suits were brought against him. In 1838 he was charged with abetting the plunder of several houses; in 1841 he was committed to the sessions on a charge of murder but was acquitted; on several occasions he was tried for different reasons, but each time he was acquitted for lack of evidence. At Bahādurpūr, where he generally resided, every Muḥammadan stranger was fed, while Eastern Bengal was frequented by his spies, and the interests of the whole neighbourhood were in his keeping. He settled disputes, administered summary justice, and punished any Hindu, Muḥammadan or Christian who without first referring matters to him dared to bring suits, as for recovery of debt, in the adjoining munṣif's court. Emissaries carried his orders to distant villages, and his letters, signed *Aḥmad nām nā maʿlūm*, (Aḥmad of unknown name) often had the ordinary Hindu superscription to allay suspicion. He taught that there was no sin in persecuting those who refused to embrace his doctrines, or who appealed to Government courts against the orders of the society and its acknowledged leaders. Dūdhū Mīyān is described as having been a tall handsome man, with a dark flowing beard, and a large turban wound round his head. He died at Bahādurpū 24th September, 1860, and was buried there.

His three surviving sons did not prove able to prevent the sect from diminishing in number after his death.

The sect of which he was the leader is generally known as the Farāʾiḍī Sect; and those who profess his doctrines have been enjoined to say the *ẓuhr* (mid-day) *farḍ* (compulsory) prayer on Fridays instead of the usual *djumʿa* or Friday prayer, which is customary with the majority of the Muḥammadans.

FARḌ means that which is strictly prescribed and obligatory, the omission of which will be punished while the execution will be rewarded. According to the Ḥanafī school *farḍ* means that which is regarded as duty on the basis of cogent arguments; *wādjib* (i.e. necessary) on the other hand is that which is considered a duty by the faķīhs on grounds of probability only. According to the Shāfiʿīs and other *fiķh* schools *farḍ* and *wādjib* are synonyms. The law distinguishes *farḍ al-ʿain*, to which every one is bound, and *farḍ al-kifāya* (or: *ʿala 'l-kifāya*), if it is only demanded that a sufficient number of Muslims should fulfil the religious duty concerned (as, for example, the performance of the *ṣalāt* in the mosque and the waging of the holy war).

Bibliography: *A Dictionary of the Technical Terms used in the Sciences of the Musalmans*, ed. by Mawlawies Mohammed Wajih, Abd al-Hakk and Gholam Kadir, p. 1125 *sq.*; E. W. Lane, *Arab.-Engl. Lexicon*, s.v.; I. Goldziher, *Die Ẓahiriten* (Leipzig 1884), p. 66.

FĀSIĶ (i.e. sinner) means not only one who has committed a great sin but also one who has been guilty of everyday trifling offences against the law. In the latter respect, in the unanimous opinion of the *faķīhs* almost every Muslim is to be considered a *fāsiķ*.

The testimony of a *fāsiķ* has no legal weight; only the irreproachable Muslim (*ʿadl*) is a credible witness. This is the origin of the custom of having certain persons of good reputation to act as professional witnesses at the conclusion of contracts (especially of marriage-contracts). Such persons are often called *ʿadl* or *shāhid*; cf. the literature quoted by Dozy, *Supplément aux Dict. Arab.*, s.v. *ʿadl*; E. W. Lane, *The Manners and Customs of the Modern Egyptians*, Chap. IV (government); Ph. Vassel, *Über marokkanische Processpraxis* (*MSOS*, v., part 2, p. 170 *sq.*).

Marriage is also invalid, according to the Shāfiʿīs (and some Ḥanbalīs), if the nearest relative (*walī*), who gives the bride in marriage, is *fāsiķ* at the conclusion of the marriage contract; it is therefore the custom in some Shāfiʿī countries that the conclusion of this contract is preceded by the "conversion" of the *walī* of the bride; for one who is converted from his sins to a better way of life is again considered *ʿadl*. Cf. C. Snouck Hurgronje, *Verspreide Geschriften*, ii. 182.

FASKH. [See ṬALĀĶ].

FĀTIḤA, the first and most popular Sūra in the Ķurʾān. Its name means the "opener" (i.e. of the Ķurʾān). This short Sūra which only contains seven verses has a certain number of peculiar features; it is at the beginning of the book, while all the other short Sūras are at the end; it is in the form of a prayer while the others are in the form of a sermon or lecture; in reciting it the word *amīn* (amen) is added to it, which is not done in any of the others.

In Sūra xv. 87 there is possibly an allusion to the *fātiḥa* under the name of the seven (i.e. verses) which ought to be constantly repeated (= *sabʿan min al-mat͟hānī*; cf. AL-MAT͟HĀNĪ); and these seven verses occupy a special position with reference to the portion of the Ḳurʾān revealed at that time. "We have already given thee the seven verses which ought to be constantly repeated as well as the great Ḳurʾān". At the period then, when Sūra xv., which is Meccan, was revealed, the *fātiḥa* may already have been the favourite prayer of the little community of believers.

It has been said that this Sūra is the oldest or one of the oldest in the Ḳurʾān. Nöldeke has urged against this view that it contains expressions which are not found in the Sūras of the first period; notably certain epithets of Allāh, "the merciful, the compassionate, *al-raḥmān, al-raḥīm*", appear there for the first time. Nevertheless the *fātiḥa* is relatively old and should be placed at the end of the first Meccan period. It is, as we have just mentioned, quoted in Sūra xv. which belongs to the second period; and its first verse "glory be to God, the lord of the worlds" is repeated at the end of Sūra xxxvii. (verse 182) which also belongs to the second period. Al-Baiḍāwī's commentary (ed. Fleischer p. 3) mentions an opinion according to which this Sūra was revealed twice, once in Mecca and again in Madīna.

The words *al-mag͟hḍūb ʿalaihim* "those against whom God is enraged", and *al-ḍāllīn*, "twose who err", in verse 7 of the *fātiḥa*, are said to refer respectively to the Jews and Christians.

The *fātiḥa* forms part of the ṣalāt; its recitation is a divine order according to S͟hāfiʿī, while Abū Ḥanīfa says it is only obligatory by canon. Various pious scholars have written on the virtues of this Sūra.

Bibliography: Th. Nöldeke-Schwally, *Geschichte des Qorâns*, i. p. 110 *sq.*; d'Ohsson, *Tableau général de l'Empire Othoman*, ii. 79, 88; the annotated translations of and commentaries on the Ḳurʾān.

FĀṬIMA, daughter of Muḥammad and his first wife K͟hadīd͟ja, born at Mecca probably about the year 605 A.D. The early Arabic sources give conflicting statements as to her age; these have been examined (though in a far from objective spirit) by H. Lammens in his monograph *Fātima et les filles de Mahomet* (Rome 1912). She was brought to Madīna after the Hid͟jra by ʿAlī or Zaid b. Ḥārit͟ha, and married to ʿAlī after the battle of Badr (or in some accounts after the battle of Uḥud). Her sons Ḥasan and Ḥusain [q.v.] were most probably born in A.H. 4 and 5 respectively; according to S͟hīʿite tradition, a third son, Muḥassin, died in infancy. There were also two daughters of the marriage. Zainab and Umm Kult͟hūm, the latter born in the last year of Fāṭima's life. Apart from these facts, the historical details for her life are scanty. After Muḥammad's conquest of the rich oases of Northern Hid͟jāz, he allotted to Fāṭima, as to each of this wives, an annual allowance of 85 loads of wheat. She is said to have accompanied him on the expedition in which Mecca surrendered (A.H. 8) and on the "Farewell Pilgrimage" (A.H. 10), and was present at his death. After Abū Bakr was elected as Muḥammad's *K͟halīfa* she remained implacably hostile to him, either because of her feud with ʿĀʾis͟ha (see below), or because ʿAlī had been passed over, or because Abū Bakr refused to allow her claim to inherit the oasis of Fadak, on the plea that it was the private property of her father. But before the close of the same year (11/633) she died. She appears to have suffered from poor health during the greater part of her life.

It may appear surprising that the earliest sources contain so little information about her, and that too so confused. Even among the traditionists she is rarely cited; in Ibn Ḥanbal's compilation, her *musnad* occupies only one page against the 250 devoted to ʿĀʾis͟ha. For the other daughters of Muḥammad, however, there is even less; while, in contrast to them, a considerable biographical literature grew up around her at a later date. The explanation of these facts is largely to be sought in the sectarian disputes of the first and second centuries of the Hid͟jra.

On the one hand, the ancient orthodox school paid little attention to the Prophet's daughters in general, and showed far greater interest in his wives, especially in ʿĀʾis͟ha, between whom and Fāṭima there was bitter hostility. Conscious opposition to S͟hīʿite claims may later have contributed to the overshadowing of Fāṭima, especially in the interests of the ʿAbbāsids. On the other hand, the early S͟hīʿites themselves were divided between supporters of the Fāṭimid line and supporters of the non-Fāṭimid descendants of ʿAlī (Kaisānīya, Hās͟himīya, etc.). It is possible that the beginnings of the exaltation of Fāṭima are to be ascribed to the controversy between the latter, and that they were subsequently taken up into general S͟hīʿī polemics. With this object, numerous incidents were either invented or (more probably) elaborated in order to portray Muḥammad's special care and fondness for Fāṭima. The most famous of these is the celebrated scene of the *aṣḥāb al-kisāʾ* ("privileged ones of the cloak"), when Muḥammad, having taken ʿAlī, Fāṭima, and the "two Ḥasans" under his cloak, is said to have exclaimed "These are the members of my family".

In the eyes of the S͟hīʿa, Fāṭima represents "the embodiment of all that is divine in womanhood, — the noblest ideal of human conception" (Syed Ameer Ali). Her birth was miraculous, her union with ʿAlī decided by divine decree. Having been the person most dear to the Prophet, she was carried off by grief for his death. Later Sunnī literature also, following its general tendency, has been influenced by these S͟hīʿī traditions, and without going to the same lengths, has progressively enhanced the position of Fāṭima in the Prophet's household. The Sunnīs do not reject the ḥadīt͟hs in which she is declared to be "queen of the women of Paradise next Maryam, daughter of ʿImrān"; they give her the enigmatic epithet *batūl*, "virgin", and the further we come down the collections of Tradition, the longer grows the lists of her *faḍāʾil* (virtues) and *k͟haṣāʾiṣ* (privileges).

Bibliography: Yaʿḳūbī, ii.; Ṭabarī, i., iii.; *Ag͟hānī*, xi. 67; xiv. 164; xviii. 204; Masʿūdī, *Murūd͟j* iv. 146, 157, 161—162, 190, 450; v. 148; vi. 55—56; do., *Tanbīh*; Ibn ʿAbd al-Barr, *Istīʿāb* (Hyderabad), p. 770—773, 795; Ibn His͟hām, p. 121, 776; Ibn Saʿd, iii/1, 11, 12, 13—16; viii. 11—19; Ibn Ḳutaiba, *Maʿārif* (ed. Wüstenfeld), p. 70, 106; Nawawī, p. 850—851; Ibn al-At͟hīr, *Usd al-g͟hāba*, v. 519—521; do., *Kāmil* (ed. Tornberg), ii.; Ibn Ḥad͟jar, *Iṣāba* (Calcutta), iv. 723—730; Diyārbakrī, *Taʾrīk͟h al-k͟hamīs* (Cairo 1302), i. 307, 308, 310, 313, 407—409, 462—464,

471; Ibn Ḥanbal, *Musnad*, i. 79; ii. 21, 182—183, 263; iii. 150—152; iv. 107, 326; v. 26; vi. (the *Musnad* of ʿĀʾis̲h̲a, passim) 29—282, 339, 340, 390—391; Wāḳidī (ed. Kremer), p. 245—246, 283, 303; Abu 'l-Farad̲j̲, *Maḳātil al-ṭālibīyīn*, p. 18, 19; Balād̲h̲urī, *Futūḥ*; do., *Ansāb al-as̲h̲rāf* (ms. Paris), 258—260, 340—341, 384, 397—399, 431, 439—442, 591—592; H. Lammens, *Études sur le règne du calife omaiyade Moʿāwia Ier*, index; do., *Le califat de Yazīd Ier*, p. 132—133; *do.*, *Fātima et les filles de Mahomet*; *notes critiques pour l'étude de la Sīra*, Rome 1912; do., *Le triumvirat Abou Bakr, ʿOmar et Abou ʿObaida*, in *Mél. Fac. Orientale de Beyrouth*, iv. 113—144; Sprenger, *Moḥammed*, i. 199, 203; Caetani, *Annali*, i. 173—174, 460; ii. 137, 687—689; F. Buhl, *Das Leben Muhammads*, (Leipzig 1930), 250, 282, 294; G. H. Stern, *Marriage in Early Islam* (London 1939).

FATWĀ (A.). A *fatwā* is a formal legal opinion given by a *muftī* or canon lawyer of standing, in answer to a question submitted to him either by a judge or by a private individual. On the basis of such an "opinion" a judge may decide a case, or an individual may regulate his personal life. It must be rendered in precise accordance with fixed precedent; a muftī cannot now follow his own judgment. But inasmuch as these opinions deal with actual cases, as opposed to the abstractions of text-books of canon law, published collections of them, which are numerous, are valuable as exhibitions of real situations. In the ideal Muslim state, where canon law would rule absolutely, all these decisions would be equally backed by state authority, and would be the law of the land. But as the case is, in practically all Muslim states, a distinction has arisen, and the canon law expressed in these *fatwā*'s rules only in such matters as marriage, inheritance and divorce. All other legal questions are decided by other codes or by the will of the sovereign. And *fatwā*'s on the side of canon law which regulates the details of the personal religious life, have validity only for the pious. Further, there is a tendency in some Muslim states to favour some one or other of the four legal schools. Thus Turkey everywhere upheld the Ḥanafī school and appointed Ḥanafī judges only. It might appoint muftī's of all four schools; but only the fatwā's of Ḥanafī muftīs were admitted in the law courts. The others were purely for the private convenience of the followers of the other schools.

Bibliography: Juynboll, *Handbuch d. islāmischen Gesetzes*, p. 54 *sq.*, 320, 339; Lane, *Modern Egyptians*, chap. iv.; Snouck Hurgronje, *Verspr. Geschr.* ii., 378 *sq.*; Macdonald, *Development of Muslim Theology etc.*, p. 115 *sq.*, 227 *sq.*

FIDĀʾĪ (in vulgar Arabic *fidāwī*), he who offers up his life, a name given to the Ismāʿīlīs, particurlarly to the Assassins [q.v.] appointed to murder their victims (Ibn Baṭṭūṭa, i. 167; v. Hammer, *Fundgruben des Orients*, iii. 204; do., *Assassinen*, p. 88); but the word has frequently also a good sense, "paladin, knightly, courageous, brave, undaunted" (Quatremère, *Mongols*, p. 124a; cf. v. Oppenheim, *Vom Mittelmeer zum Persischen Golf*, ii. 100). In Algeria *fidāwī* means a narrator of heroic deeds and *fidāwīya*, a tale or song of heroic deeds. During the Persian revolution *fidāwī* was applied in the first place to the adherents of the republican party and then to the defenders of liberal ideas and the constitution.

Bibliography: Ibn K̲h̲aldūn, *Prolégomènes*, transl. of de Slane, i. 122, 5; Lane, *Modern Egyptians*, ii. 147; H. d'Allemagne, *Du Khorassan au pays des Backhtiaris* (Paris 1911), iv. 304 (*photogr.*, p. 294, 299); E.G. Browne, *Literary Hist. of Persia*, ii. 206 *sq.*; do., *Persian Revolution*, p. 127, 151; *RMM*, i. 49; iv. 176; v. 361; xii. 217.

FIDYA (A.), "ransom". Sūra ii. 184, 196, demands a *fidya* on the omission of certain religious duties (fast, pilgrimage). The same passage indicates of what it should consist and further details are given in the commentaries. Cf. Juynboll, *Handbuch des islām. Gesetzes*, p. 122; on the *padya* (= *fidya*) in Java and Sumatra, for ṣalāts omitted in a lifetime, cf. Snouck Hurgronje, *The Atchehnese*, i. 435 *sq.* — See also the article KAFFĀRA.

The people of Syria and the country east of Jordan give the name *fidya* or *fedū* to a bloody sacrifice, by which it is hoped to protect children or property (house or cattle) from misfortune or destruction, or which is offered for (to) the dead, cf. S. I. Curtis, *Ursemitische Religion*, Index, s.v. *fedu*, *fidje*; Jaussen, *Coutumes des Arabes*, p. 357 *sq.* and 361 *sq.*; do., *Mission arch. en Arabie*, i. 472.

In Morocco *fedya* is the name of a peculiar ceremony, also performed in several parts of Algeria under the name *fedwa*, at which a man, in the hope of securing freedom from punishment in the next world, has all the preparations for his burial made, after which a number of *ṭolba* recite the sections of the Ḳurʾān used at burials; cf. W. Marçais, *Textes arabes de Tanger*, p. 409 (glossary).

FIḲH ("intelligence, knowledge") is the name given to jurisprudence in Islām. It is, like the *jurisprudentia* of the Romans, *rerum divinarum atque humanarum notitia* and in its widest sense covers all aspects of religious, political and civil life. In addition to the laws regulating ritual and religious observances (*ʿibādāt*), as far as concerns performance and abstinence, it includes the whole field of family law, the law of inheritance, of property and of contract, in a word provisions for all the legal questions that arise in social life (*muʿāmalāt*); it also includes criminal law and procedure and finally constitutional law and laws regulating the administration of the state and the conduct of war.

All aspects of public and private life and business should be regulated by laws recognised by religion; the science of these laws is *fiḳh*.

In older theological language the word had not this comprehensive meaning; it was rather used in opposition to *ʿilm*. While the latter denotes, besides the Ḳurʾān and its exposition, the accurate knowledge of the legal decisions handed down from the Prophet and his companions (Ibn Saʿd, II./ii. 127, $_{16}$: *al-riwāyāt wa 'l-ʿilm*, synonymously), the term *fiḳh* is applied to the independent exercise of the intelligence, the decision of legal points by one's own judgment in the absence or ignorance of tradition bearing on the case in question. The result of such independent consideration is *raʾy* (opinion, *opinio prudentium*), with which it is also sometimes used synonymously. In this sense *ʿilm* and *fiḳh* are regarded as distinct qualities of the theologian (Nawawī, p. 703, $_{8}$); *fiḳh wa-riwāya* (Ibn Saʿd, v (7ʿ23^{10}). The sum total of all wisdom is defined by Mud̲j̲āhid (in explanation of Sūra ii. 269: *man yuʾta 'l-ḥikma*) as composed of the following elements: *al-Ḳurʾān wa 'l-ʿilm wa 'l-fiḳh* (Ṭabarī, *Tafsīr*, iii. 56, $_{3}$). [Even the Jewish Karaitic expositor of the Bible, Jepheth b. ʿAlī (910—980 A.D.), has adopted this distinction for he translates *tiftāyē* in Daniel, iii. 2 (ed. D. S. Margoliouth, *Anecdota Oxoniensa*, 1889, p. 33, $_{7}$) by:

ahl al-ʿilm wa 'l-fikh]. Hārūn al-Rashīd instructs his governor Harthama to consult the *ulī al-fikh fī dīn Allāh* and the *ulī al-ʿilm bi-kitāb Allāh* in doubtful cases (Ṭabarī, iii. 717, $_{10}$). Further passages are quoted in Goldziher's *Muh. Stud.*, ii. 176, note 6.

In this sense the *ʿālim* (plur. *ʿulamāʾ*) is distinguished from the *faḳīh* (plur. *fuḳahāʾ*) or the combination of both sciences in one individual is expressed by the combination of these two ephitets or their synonyms. Ibn ʿUmar was *djaiyid al-ḥadīth* but not *djaiyid al-fiḳh* (Ibn Saʿd, II./ii. 125, $_{5}$); on the other hand Ibn ʿAbbās was *aʿlamu* with reference to decisions handed down by Tradition and at the same time *afḳahu* (or *athḳafu raʾy^{in}*) in new cases that arose, for which no precedent could be found in Tradition and in which it was necessary to use one's own judgment (*ibid.*, p., 122; 124); the same is true of Zaid b. Thābit (*ibid.*, p. 116); cf. *faḳīh fi 'l-dīn ʿālim fi 'l-sunna* (*ibid.*, III./i. 110). Saʿīd b. al-Muṣaiyab is *faḳīh al-fuḳahāʾ* on the one hand and *ʿālim al-ʿulamāʾ* (*ibid.*, II./ii. 129; 130; v. 90) on the other. Among the *tābiʿūn* there were *fuḳahāʾ wa-ʿulamāʾ* i.e. those who were authorities on the chain of evidence of *ḥadīth* and *āthār* as well as on *fiḳh* and were competent to give (independent) decisions, *fatwā* (*ibid.*, II./ii. 128). Abū Thawr was *aḥad aʾimmat al-dunyā fiḳh^{an} wa-ʿilm^{an}* (in Dhahabī, *Ṭabaḳāt al-ḥuffāẓ*, viii. 106).

In the oldest period of the development of Islām the authorities entrusted with the administration of justice and the conduct of the religious life had in most cases to fall back on the exercise of their own *raʾy* owing to the scarcity of legislative material in the Ḳurʾān and the dearth of ancient precedents. This was regarded as a matter of course by every one, although they were naturally very pleased, if the verdict could as far as possible be based on *ʿilm*. When ʿAṭāʾ b. Abī Rabāḥ (died 114/732) was giving a judgment, he was asked: "Is this *ʿilm* or *raʾy*"? If it was founded on a precedent (*athar*), he said it was *ʿilm* (Ibn Saʿd, v. 345). The *raʾy* was not, however, thereby discredited. It was considered an equally legitimate factor in the decision of a point of law and was destined in the near future to be regarded as the undoubted opinion of old authorities and in later times to be actually considered an element of the *ʿilm*. From the very beginning one could have recourse to it as soon as *ʿilm* failed. According to an old story which certainly reflects the conditions of the Umaiyad period, although it does not actually date from the time in which its scene is laid Muʿāwiya finally applied to Zaid b. Thābit on a legal question, on which neither he nor other companions to whom he propounded it, could quote any ancient evidence (*falam yūdjad ʿindahu* — or *ʿindahum* — *fiha ʿilm^{un}*); the latter gave a verdict based on this own independent *raʾy* (Ṭabarī, *Tafsīr*, ii. 250 *ult.* on 2, 228). The ḳāḍī of Egypt asked the advice of the Caliph ʿUmar II on a point not provided for in Tradition; the latter wrote to him: Nothing has reached me on this matter, therefore I leave the verdict to you to be given according to your opinion (*bi-raʾyika*) (Kindī, *Governors and Judges of Egypt*, ed. Guest, p. 334 = Gottheil's ed., p. 29) [cf. the article IDJTIHĀD].

Corresponding to this recognition of *raʾy* as an approved source of law are the instructions ascribed to the Prophet and the early Caliphs, which they gave to the officials sent to administer justice in the conquered provinces, and which contain the principles to which they gave their approval, in so far as they were actually propounded by the judges sent (Goldziher, *Ẓâhiriten*, p. 8 *sq.*, cf. Ibn al-Athīr, *Usd al-ghāba*, i. 314; Mubarrad, *Kāmil*, p. 9 *sq.*; Ibn Ḳutaiba, *ʿUyūn al-akhbār*, p. 87). In the digests which were developed from these simple origins we find deduction from decisions in allied cases expressly mentioned (*al-ashbāh, al-naẓāʾir*, cf. *ʿUyūn al-akhbār*, p. 72) i.e. the application of analogy (*ḳiyās*) as a methodical adjustement or *raʾy* (equity). In the investigation of the *ʿillat al-sharʿ*, the motive of law (*ratio legis*) and the resulting reduction of doubtful cases to a rational point of view, we find this principle given systematic validity. We thus have — there is evidence of it at a very early period — a kind of popular element adopted among the constitutive sources for the eduction of laws: the conception of *idjmāʿ* (consensus) i.e. the general usage of the community which has been established by agreement in the larger circles of believers independent of the written, traditional or inferred law. As in Roman law, the principle was applied, that: *consuetudinem aut rerum perpetuo similiter judicatarum auctoritatem vim legis obtineri deberi*; also: *nam diuturni mores consensu utentium comprobati legem imitantur.*

It was quite natural from the changed conditions after the conquests that the formation of the law, not only in its special provisions, but particularly in the point of view they adopted in their method of deductive operation (*Muh. Stud.*, ii. 75) as laid down in fiḳh, was greatly influenced by what the authorities on the development of law in Syria and Mesopotamia were able to learn of Roman law, sometimes of the special laws for the particular provinces. It was obvious that a quite uncultured people coming from a land in a primitive stage of social development into countries with an ancient civilisation, where they established themselves as rulers, would adopt from among their new surroundings as much of the customary law of the conquered lands as could be fitted in with the conditions created by the conquest and be compatible with the demands of new religious ideas. The detailed investigation of this fact in the history of law, which, although emphasised and established in its main outlines long ago, has only been sporadically investigated within a limited field, is one of the most attractive problems of this branch of the study of Islām. Santillana has collected much material for the investigation of this subject in his plan for a *Code Civil et Commercial Tunisien* (Tunis 1899). The comparative study of one chapter of private law has yielded the most conclusive proofs of the thoroughgoing adoption of Roman law by the jurists of Islām (Franz Frederik Schmidt, *Die Occupatio im islamischen Recht* [reprint from *Isl.*, i.], Strassburg 1910). I. Goldziher had previously in this connection made the suggestion that even the names of legal speculation (*fiḳh* = intelligence) and of its students *fuḳahāʾ* (intelligent) have been influenced by the Latin terms (*juris*) *prudentia* and (*juris*) *prudentes* in their special application to the study of law and teachers of law. An analogous example in support of the influence of Roman Law is the use of the words *chokhmā* and *chakhāmīm* among the Jews of Palestine (*Kultur d. Gegenw.*, vol. i., part. iii., 1st half, p. 103; *ZDMG*, li. 318).

Roman Law, however, does not exhaust the sources drawn upon in the development of Muslim Law. The receptive character that marks the formation and development of Islām also found expression, naturally first of all in matters of ritual (Wensinck, in *Isl.*, i. 101), in borrowings from Jewish Law (cf. *REJ*, xxviii. 78; xliii. 4; E. Mittwoch, *Zur Entstehungsgeschichte des islamischen Gebets u. Kultus* [*Abhandl. der Kön. Preuss. Akad. der Wissenschaften*], Berlin 1913). According to Kremer (*Culturgesch. d. Orients*, i. 535) even many of the provisions of Roman Law that have been adopted by Islām only found a place in *fiḳh* through the intermediary of the Jews. — It still remains to be investigated, however, if and in what degree Persian influence can be traced in the development of many details of Muslim Law.

We thus have four "roots" in operation for the deduction of laws, as methodical principles from which legal prescriptions may be legitimately laid down, viz.: 1. *Ḳur'ān*, 2. *Sunna*, 3. *Ḳiyās*, 4. *Idjmā'*. With the gradual recognition of the sources of legal knowledge the terms *fiḳh* and *fuḳahā'* gradually lost their original limitation to deductions not based on tradition. *Fiḳh* next became the science which co-ordinated and included all the branches of knowledge derived from the four roots; similarly those who are masters of this science were called *fuḳahā'* i.e. jurists. — *Fiḳh* was also used as the result of deduction from the positive sources of law, the sum total of the deductions derived from them, e.g. *wa-fī hādha 'l-ḥadīth ḍurūb min al-fiḳh* (Mubarrad, *Kāmil*, p. 529, cf. *WZKM*, iii. 84). In a still wider generalisation *fiḳh* was used for religious science in general (*al-Ḳur'ān wa 'l-fiḳh* in opposition to the study of poetry, *Aghānī*, vii. 55, 22; *laisa bihim raghbatun fi 'l-dīn wa-lā raghbatun fi 'l-fiḳh*: *Musnad* of Aḥmad b. Ḥanbal, i. 155). *Fuḳahā'* likewise was applied to students of religion, theologians (not only students of law) e.g. Ṭabarī, *Tafsīr*, xii. 73, 13: *fuḳahā'una wa-mashā'ikhunā*; *ibid.*, p. 112, 8, where Abū 'Ubaid al-Ḳāsim b. Sallām says with reference to an explanation by Abū 'Ubaida Ma'mar of a word in the Ḳur'ān contradictory to the traditional explanation: *al-fuḳahā' a'lam bi 'l-ta'wīl minhu*, the *fuḳahā'* are more conversant with exegesis than he" (who is not a theologian but only a philologist); cf. also *Ẓāhiriten*, p. 19. In eastern and western dialects of spoken Arabic the word *fiḳi*, *fḳē*, *fgī* (all from *faḳīh*) has come to mean an elementary schoolteacher of the lowest rank (W. Marçais, *Textes arabes de Tanger* [Paris 1911], p. 415, where further references are given).

The sporadic attempts that were made during the Umaiyad period in the field of Law did not lead to a systematic codification of the material in existence. It was only with the rise of the 'Abbāsid caliphate that this attempt was made, favoured and indeed even furthered by the pronounced religious character of the government. From the very beginning of this process of codification it was always these four "roots" that were recognised as authoritative by the theologians who made the first endeavour in the beginning of the second century A.H. in Madīna, Syria and the 'Irāḳ, to evolve a finished system of Muslim law. According as they made a limited or free use of one or other of the "roots" or selected one in preference to another of the contradictory traditions, they attained different results on particular points of law. Only names have survived to us from the literature created by these early efforts. We learn a good deal in the Arabic sources about theologians who arranged the *'ilm* or *sunan* in chapters and thence deduced the *fiḳh* inferences (*Muh. Stud.*, ii. 211; cf. also 'Abd Allāh b. al-Mubārak: *dawwana al-'ilm fi 'l-abwāb wa 'l-fiḳh* [Dhahabī, *Tadhkirat al-ḥuffāẓ*, i. 250], Abū Thawr: *ṣannafa al-kutub wa-farra'a 'ala 'l-sunan* [*ibid.*, ii. 95]). Little value can be attached to the statement ascribed to Hishām b. 'Urwa that many *kutub fiḳh* of his father's perished in the flames on the day of Ḥarra (*Biographien*, ed. Aug. Fischer, p. 41). At that ancient period ('Urwa died in 94/712, the so-called Fuḳahā' year — the year of the death of many fuḳahā' — Ibn Sa'd, vi. 135) there could be no real *kutub* in existence; the reference must therefore be to rough notes only. We might also mention the statement that Zuhrī's *Fatāwī* were collected in three, Ḥasan al-Baṣrī's in seven books (*asfār*) arranged in the order of the *abwāb al-fiḳh* (Ibn Ḳaiyim al-Djawzīya, *I'lām* [Cairo 1325], i. 26). E. Griffini has published, from among the South Arabian treasures of the Ambrosian library in Milan, a compendium of fiḳh attributed to the founder of the Shī'ī sect of the Zaidīya entitled the *Madjmū'a of Zaid b. 'Alī* (died 122/740), under the title of *Corpus Juris di Zaid ibn 'Alī*, Milan 1919, partial translation by G.-H. Bousquet and J. Berque, *Recueil de la Loi Musulmane de Zaïd ben 'Ali*, Alger 1941. This would be the oldest attempt at a codification of Muslim law in existence; in any case it is to be reckoned with in the literature of the older fiḳh. If it should be a direct product of the circle of Zaid b. 'Alī himself, we should have to recognise the priority of the Shī'ī (Zaidī) branch of Islām in fiḳh literature among the works that have survived.

The oldest *corpus juris* of the Sunnī branch of Islām that has survived from the early period of fiḳh is the *Muwaṭṭa'* ("paved path") of the Madīna teacher Mālik b. Anas (97—179/715—795) [q.v.], who easily surpassed all his contemporaries with this work (*Muh. Stud.*, ii. 213 *sq.*) and created an organic synthesis of the four roots of jurisprudence in the chapters on private law. His work represents a codification of the fiḳh as it developed in the Ḥidjāz in its theological centre Madīna. Almost at the same time the fiḳh was being methodically systematised in other lands of the Muslim empire also. In Syria 'Abd al-Raḥmān al-Awzā'ī (died 157/774) was teaching a system of fiḳh which remained in force, even among the Muslims of Spain (al-Ḍabbī, ed. Codera, No. 751), till the Madīna system was introduced there by disciples of Mālik and became supreme. The most vigorous efforts to create a code of law were made in the 'Irāḳ, where about the same time studies in other branches (philology, philosophy, exact sciences and dogmatics) were being industriously pursued. Although the Ḥidjāz school recognised the validity of *ra'y* without restriction and made free use of it in establishing legal principles, the 'Irāḳ school went far beyond them in their use of this source of law. Ḥammād b. Abī Sulaimān (died c. 120/738) may here be mentioned as the pioneer who was the first to gather a circle of scholars around him, to whom he taught a system of fiḳh in which *ra'y* had a predominant influence. To his school belonged Abū Ḥanīfa [q.v.] who is regarded as the patriarch of the 'Irāḳ school of fiḳh, which was placed on a firmer footing by his two great pupils Abū Yūsuf (died 182/795) and Muḥammad b. al-Ḥasan al-Shaibānī (died 189/804), who also distinguished themselves by monographs on important chapters of constitutional law (C. Brockelmann, *GAL* 2, i. 176 *sqq.*, *Suppl.* i. 284 *sqq.*). The name of the former of these scholars is also associated with the recognition of canon law in the government of the state. At the request of the Caliph Hārūn al-Rashīd, Abū Yūsuf compiled his *Kitāb al-kharādj*, which, however, covers much wider ground than is indicated in its title, for it includes the whole field of administration in consonance with canon law, and was imitated by writers in later reigns. The Caliph al-Muhtadī (255-6/869-70.) entrusted the jurist al-Khaṣṣāf with the compilation of a similar work. The administration of the state was, theoretically at least, to be brought into absolute harmony with canon law. The starting-point was naturally always the *sunna*; but in spite of a most generous recognition of aprocryphal traditions there was of necessity ample scope left for the use of *ra'y*. The school of Abū Ḥanīfa placed little restraint on the use of *ra'y*. A certain amount of freedom was even allowed to individual opinion in face of methodical analogy (*ḳiyās*) by allowing practical considerations also to be taken into account. This is expressed in the term *istiḥsān* (holding for better). The legal authority is justified in deviating from a ruling suggested by the *ḳiyās*, if due consideration showed him that another procedure was more suitable to the conditions in question. (Early examples of *istiḥsān* are given in Abū Yūsuf, *Kitāb al-kharādj* [Būlāḳ 1302], p. 109, 112, 117: *wa 'l-ḳiyās kāna ... illā annī istaḥsantu ...*; Shaibānī, *al-Djāmiʿ al-saghīr* [printed on the margin of the *Kharādj*], p. 17: *adjza'ahum fī 'l-ḳiyās walā yudjzi'uhum fi 'l-istiḥsān*, p. 72; Bukhārī, *Kitāb al-ikrāh*, No. 7, ed. Juynboll, p. 338). In the school of Mālik also a similar subjective element in *ra'y* has been recognised as legitimate; in is called *istiṣlāḥ* (consideration of what if beneficial or expedient — *maṣlaḥa*) or *murāʿāt al-aṣlaḥ*. This right to set aside the ruling based on methodical analogy in favour of the judgment of a competent jurist, when considerations of expediency justify it reminds one of the Roman *corrigere jus propter utilitatem publicam* (in the Talmudic law: *mippenē tiḳḳūn hā-ʿōlām*).

The ʿIrāḳ school of fiḳh had another important teacher in the Baṣrī theologian Sufyān al-Thawrī (died 161/778), whose system remained for long authoritative even among the Muslims of the Maghrib (Ibn Taghrībirdī, ed. Popper, p. 120); his system has, however, like that of the above mentioned Awzāʿī, not survived in its entirety but is only known in its application to isolated cases, particularly in points where it differed from other schools (*ikhtilāfāt*).

Although the foundations of Muslim jurisprudence as outlined above met with the approval of authoritative circles in the Muslim world, from the very beginning of its development it was opposed by a hostile minority who refused to recognise *ra'y* as a proper basis for the deduction of laws. This opposition was largely due to the subtle casuistries (*taʿannut Abī Yūsuf wa-Muḥammad*, Ḳazwīnī, ed. Wüstenfeld, ii. 151—153; 211 at the foot) which the ʿIrāḳ jurists exercised in a most sophistical fashion in their use of *ra'y* (cf. Goldziher, *Vorlesungen über den Islām*, p. 67 *sq.*). *Ara'aita*... "what do you think (i.e. of a case propounded in a sophistical fashion)"? is the formula with which such tests of ingenuity were introduced (early examples in the *Kitāb al-kharādj*, p. 36; *Muwaṭṭa'*, ii. 37, 330; iii. 19) and therefore the wrath of those who regarded this legal skill as idle abuse of the law was vented against this formula (s. *Ẓâhiriten*, p. 17; cf. Ibn Saʿd, vi. 68, 12 [*lā tuḳāʿid aṣḥāb ara'aita ara'aita*] and a host of traditions on the point in the *Sunan* of al-Dārimī, p. 37; Abū Dāwūd, i. 17). Although the Ḥidjāz school did not entirely reject the use of *ra'y* it made a moderate use of it in comparison with the ʿIrāḳ school, from which it differs in many ways in its results, and the Ḥidjāz school had many objections to the application of ḥadīth by the jurists of ʿIrāḳ (cf. *Muh. Studien*, ii. 78—83). This distinction is antedated to a time when it did not yet exist, to the prejudice of the ʿIrāḳ school; even the Caliph ʿAbd al-Malik is made to fulminate against the eastern school in favour of Madīna (Ibn Saʿd, v. 160, 173 *sq.*).

There were also individuals who would not agree to recognise the opinion of any mortal (unless of the Prophet himself) as a deciding factor in legislation. It was not conceivable, they said, that God and his Prophet had not provided legislation for all contingencies that might arise. "We have omitted nothing in the scripture" (Sūra, vi. 38) and if a point is not expressly provided for in the Ḳur'ān, Muḥammad has certainly expounded it in a ḥadīth by God's command. They quoted in this connection the combination *al-kitāb wa 'l-ḥikma* (cf. *ZDMG*, lxi. 869 *sq.*), which appear in so many passages in the Ḳur'ān, which the adherents of this view explained as referring to the Ḳur'ān and Sunna (in Ṭabarī, *Tafsīr*, ii. 275; xxii. 7). With the vast number of ḥadīths that had been forged, it was quite easy to quote a ḥadīth on any point and thus readily to dispense with *ra'y* and *ḳiyās*. To be able to give a ruling from ḥadīths on all cases that arose, one had, however, to refrain from the exercise of strict criticism and be ready to use badly authenticated, interrupted and isolated traditions. To be correct, in form at least, an opinion, which was honestly admitted to be *ra'y*, was clothed in the form of a ḥadīth, given a pompous *isnād* and traced back to the Prophet.

Thus arose the distinction between *aṣḥāb al-ḥadīth* and *aṣḥāb al-ra'y*; a mediator between the two extremes now appeared in the person of Muḥammad b. Idrīs al-Shāfiʿī (died 204/820) [q.v.]. His great claim to fame is that he systematised the method for the deduction of laws from the sources of law (*uṣūl al-fiḳh*) and laid down the exact limits within which each might be used. In his *Risāla* (latest edition by A. M. Shākir, Cairo 1938) he created the science of the use which could be made of speculative deduction without lessening the undisputed prerogatives of Scripture and Tradition; he regulated their application and limited their arbitrary use by strict rules. For example, he did not approve the subjective *istiḥsān* (ed. Shākir, p. 134); on the other hand, with the principle of *istiṣḥāb* [q.v.], he opened up a fruitful source for juristic presumption. His school might be said to belong to the *aṣḥāb al-ra'y* as readily as to the *aṣḥāb al-ḥadīth*, but out of it, through preponderating attachment to the latter, there again developed a tendency to overemphasise *fiḳh* which was based on traditional sources, first of all in the school of Aḥmad b. Ḥanbal (died 241/855); and this tendency was even more marked in the Ẓāhirīya school founded by Dāwūd b. ʿAlī al-Iṣfahānī (died 270/883), which set aside speculative elements and carried the limitations for the deduction of law from traditional sources to extremes, but had soon to confess that it would soon be at a standstill without a moderate use of *ḳiyās*.

Among the opponents of *ḳiyās* at this time is mentioned Yaḥyā b. Aktham (died 242/856), an older contemporary of Dāwūd and celebrated Shāfiʿī and Ḳāḍī of Baghdād under Ma'mūn; he wrote a work (*Kitāb al-tanbīh*), which is wholly devoted to an attack on the ʿIrāḳ school; he constantly exchanged ideas with Dāwūd b. ʿAlī (Ibn Khallikān, No. 803). Such attacks, however, were only of theoretical importance; they were quite without influence on the practical administration of law.

Down to the beginning of the third century then, the historical development of the study of law had produced two divisions of the science of fiḳh, viz.: 1. the science of the *uṣūl al-fiḳh*, i.e. the doctrine of the "roots", the sources of law and the methodology of their application; 2. that of the *furūʿ al-fiḳh*, the doctrine of the branches, i.e. applied fiḳh, the systematic elaboration of positive law under its separate heads. The latter can show authoritative works even from the period of the founders of the schools; its important furūʿ works were published by immediate pupils or edited and handed down by them as lectures of their teachers.

At the present day fiḳh has developed in four directions within orthodox Sunnī Islām, each of which goes back to codifications of the law, differing in little details, by the independently developing schools of the above mentioned founders of the second and third centuries A.H., and which in course of time were considerably developed along these lines. These four schools (*madhāhib*, sing. *madhhab*; only utter ignorance can call them sects) which have survived to the present day and prevail in different parts of the Muḥammadan world are called after the Imāms on whose teachings they are founded: 1. the Ḥanafī, which is followed in by far the greater part of the Muslim world (the Turkish empire, Central Asia and the Indian mainland); 2. the Shāfiʿī (Egypt, South Arabia, Indonesia, East Africa and Syria after it had supplanted the Awzāʿī *madhhab* there in 284/897; cf. Subkī, *Ṭabaḳāt al-Shāfiʿīya*, ii. 174 at the foot, 214 and the extremely important data given *ibid.*, v. 134 *sq.*); 3. the Mālikī (the Maghrib, to a great extent in Upper Egypt also, West Africa) and 4. the Ḥanbalī, strongly represented (down to the viii^th^ = xiv^th^ century) in the ʿIrāḳ, Egypt, Syria and Palestine (cf. the article AḤMAD B. ḤANBAL), now limited to Arabia (cf. the article WAHHABĪS). The Ḥanafī madhhab became the only authoritative code of law in the public life and official administration of justice in all the provinces of the Ottoman empire. All the other once prominent schools of fiḳh have disappeared from the field after a brief existence; for example, at a very early period the school of Awzāʿī (see above), that of Sufyān al-Thawrī (in 405/1014 the last muftī taught according to this madhhab; cf. Ibn Taghrībirdī, ed. Popper, p. 120), that of the Ẓāhirīs already mentioned and the school founded by the celebrated historian Ṭabarī [q.v.] called Djarīrīya, which this scholar expounded in numerous works which no longer exist (*WZKM*, ix. 364). The teachings of these obsolete schools are not taken account of in the *idjmāʿ* of Sunnī Islām; the four madhāhib above mentioned are considered equally orthodox elements of it; they differ from one another only in details of *furūʿ* which according to the orthodox conception do not form fundamental differences. In the Azhar mosque [q.v.], the most important Muslim university of the present day, all four schools are still represented by teachers and pupils just as before the coming of Ottoman supremacy, whereby the Ḥanafī *madhhab* became supreme; all four systems were represented in the great centres of Islām by judicial functionaries, who gave their decisions in important cases at a joint conference. Each of these four *madhāhib* has produced an enormous literature of codices, compendiums and commentaries in the schools of the lands in which its adherents are found.

Cases not provided for in such codices, as well as new points of law that crop up, are decided by professional jurists in *fatwā*'s (decisions), of which considerable collections have been and are still being made. Since various European countries have extended their authority over Muslims, in their possessions and protectorates in the east, handbooks of fiḳh of the *madhāhib* prevailing in the respective countries have been published in western languages also, and in this connection editions and translations of the best known works on fiḳh have been prepared by European scholars.

The dissenting sects of the Khāridjīs and Shīʿīs have also developed the legal system along lines parallel to the fiḳh of the Sunnīs. The most fundamental differences between these systems and that of the Sunnīs are naturally to be found in questions of constitutional law (*khilāfa*). The Shīʿīs also show differences in their law of marriage (*mutʿa*; marriage with women of the *ahl al-kitāb*) and are more rigid in their laws regulating intercourse with unbelievers. In their liturgy (*adhān*) trifling deviations from the usage of the Sunnīs may also be noted; in their calender of feasts also there are certain feast days peculiar to them. Otherwise the differences in law between these sects and the Sunnīs are scarcely more considerable than those of the different orthodox *madhāhib* within Sunnī Islam from one another (cf. *Vorlesungen über den Islām*, p. 237—239). Among the Shīʿīs, besides the Imāmī "Twelvers", the sect of Zaidīs (particularly strong in South Arabia) has developed a very rich fiḳh literature, of which R. Strothmann has given a very thorough account; cf. *Isl.*, i. 354—368; ii. 49—78; *Das Staatsrecht der Zaiditen* (Strassburg 1912); *Der Kultus der Zaiditen* (ibid. 1912).

In giving an appreciation of fiḳh one must not forget to mention the fact that the codifications from a very early period for the most part represent an academic code of law, a system given ideal validity, a doctrine of duties, as Snouck Hurgronje, the creator of the historical criticism of fiḳh, so admirably described it, which the theologians represent as alone corresponding to the ideal demands of religion. History teaches us that, as is the case at the present day, even so in the oldest period of Islām, the actual practice assumed in many instances a different form from that required by the demands of canon law (*sharīʿa*). Certain parts of fiḳh have been quite obsolete for centuries; on the other hand in many districts customary law (*ʿurf*, *ʿāda*), which for the most part can be traced back to pre-Islamic times, has retained its validity [cf. the articles ʿADA and ADAT LAW]. Modern conditions have also produced many reforms of legal practice in Muslim countries and have produced a system of civil law different from the religious law (*sharīʿa*) alongside of the latter. This dualism in the administration of justice can be traced back to an earlier period in which it also existed (*Ẓâhiriten*, p. 205, note 4, an example from Egypt, x^th^ century A.H.; Ibn Ḳaiyim al-Djawzīya, *al-Ṭuruḳ al-ḥikmīya fi 'l-siyāsa al-sharʿīya* [Cairo 1317], p, 218, dual system of law in Syria; Massignon, *Mission en Mésopotamie*, ii. [Cairo 1912], p. 30, the *Ḳaḍāyā yarghūdjīya* were in operation in the ʿIrāḳ under Mongol rule alongside of the *Ḳaḍāyā sharʿīya*; Ibn Baṭṭūṭa [Paris], iii. 11, from Khʷārizm).

On attempts at a codification of Muslim Law after modern legal methods cf. Snouck Hurgronje, *Politique musulmane de la Hollande*, (*Verspr. Geschr.*, iv/ii, p. 253 *sq.*); C. H. Becker, in *AR*, xv. (1912),

p. 549; H. Bruno, *Le Régime des Eaux en Droit musulman* (Paris 1913), p. 183 *sq.*

Bibliography: Mirza Kazem Beg, *Notice sur la marche et le progrès de la Jurisprudence parmi les sectes orthodoxes muselmanes*, in *JA*, 1850 (in part obsolete); Ed. Sachau, *Zur ältesten Geschichte des muhammedanischen Rechtes*, in *Sitzungsber. K. Ak. d. Wiss. zu Wien, phil.-hist. Kl.*, Vol. 65 (1870); A. von Kremer, *Culturgeschichte des Orients unter den Chalifen*, i. (Vienna 1875), p. 470 *sq.*; C. Snouck Hurgronje, *Nieuwe Bijdragen tot de kennis van den Islam* and other important articles and critical reviews in *Verspr. Geschr.* ii.; do., *Mekka*, ii. (The Hague 1889), 200 *sq.*; I. Goldziher, *Die Ẓâhiriten* (Leipzig 1884); do., *Muhammedanische Studien*, ii. (Halle 1890), p. 66—87; do., *Muhammedanisches Recht in Theorie und Wirklichkeit*, in *Zeitschr. für vergleichende Rechtswissenschaft*, vii. (1888); Th. W. Juynboll, *Handbuch des islāmischen Gesetzes* (Leyden 1910) 4th ed. (Dutch) Leiden 1930; G. Bergsträsser, *Grundzüge des islamischen Rechtes* (Berlin-Leipzig 1935); J. Schacht, *The origins of Muhammedan Jurisprudence* (Oxford 1950); N. P. Aghnides, *Mohammedan Law and Finance*, (New York 1916), Introduction and Bibliography.

Islāmic literature on fiḳh according to the different Ma<u>dh</u>āhib and the European editions see Juynboll, *l.c.*, p. 350—363 and the pertinent sections in Brockelmann, *GAL* and *Suppl.*

FIRʿAWN (plur. Farāʿina), Pharaoh. The word is explained by the commentaries on Sūra ii. 49 of the Ḳurʾān as a *laḳab* or *ʿalam* of the Amalakite kings, like Kisrā and Ḳaiṣar of the Kings of the Persians and Romans. The verb *tafarʿana* means "to be arrogant and tyrannous", hence the Ḳurʾānic Firʿawn is called *al-<u>dj</u>abbār* "the tyrant" by al-Yaʿḳūbī (ed. Houtsma), i. 31. A number of Firʿawns are mentioned in Arabic literature; their number is very differently given. In the Ḳurʾān, however, Firʿawn is always the king with whom Mūsā and Hārūn had to deal; the word is here clearly understood as a proper name.

The Ḳurʾānic data concerning Firʿawn are on some points fuller than the Biblical. The most important are the following. In place of his daughter his wife, Āsiya, is mentioned; a certain Hāmān [q.v.] is also mentioned who (Sūra xxviii. 38, xl. 36) is commissioned to build a tower (*ṣarḥ*), which shall reach to heaven, by which Firʿawn will ascend to Mūsā's God. There are obviously several confusions here; Hāmān is an echo of the vizier of this name in the Book of Esther; the tower and its description recall the Tower of Babel. It is probably the Biblical account of the building of the "treasure cities, Raamses and Pitom", that has given rise to the confusion last mentioned.

Another member of Firʿawn's suite who defends Mūsā when Fir ʿawn wants to kill him is not mentioned by name in the Ḳurʾān (xl. 28, 29).

Firʿawn is twice called "he of the pegs" in the Ḳurʾān (*<u>dh</u>u 'l-awtād*, Sūra xxxviii. 11, lxxxix. 10). This expression is variously explained by the commentators; some say that it means that this dynasty is firmly established as by tent pegs, while others say that his armies are meant by the pegs. Others again say that he bound people to be punished hand and foot to pegs driven into the ground.

A further addition to the Biblical narrative is the statement that the magicians were threatened with dreadful punishment by Firʿawn when they became converts (Sūra vii. 117 *sq.*; xxvi. 45 *sq.*). Finally Firʿawn himself is said to have become converted the moment he was being drowned; but God did not accept his conversion and caused his body to be cast upon land as an example for others (Sūra x. 90 *sq.*). These verses are, however, open to different explanations; cf. L. Massignon, *Kitâb al-Ṭawâsîn*, p. 172 *sq.* For Ṣūfic views regarding Firʿawn, cf. the same work, p. x., 6, 93, 94, 170, 172, 173.

It is said of him that he had himself worshipped as a God (Sūra xxviii. 38). On the day of resurrection he will go into Hell at the head of his people (Sūra xi. 98). The Ḳurʾān makes no distinction between the Pharaoh of the Bondage and of the Exodus. This is clear from the fact that when Mūsā and Hārūn come to him Firʿawn recognises the former (Sūra xxvi. 18).

Muslim Tradition gives a fuller account of the Firʿawns. In contrast to the Ḳurʾānic account, Firʿawns are mentioned as early as the stories of Abraham and Joseph and some even tell us that Joseph's first Firʿawn was called al-Raiyān b. al-Walīd and his successor Ḳābūs b. Muṣʿab. According to others Joseph was the vizier of al-Walīd (or Dārim) b. al-Raiyān (Ṭabarī's *Tafsīr* and Baiḍāwī on Sūra ii. 46 [49]; Ṭabarī [ed. de Goeje], i. 443 *sq.*).

Ibn Isḥāḳ in Ṭabarī (ed. de Goeje), i. 444 *sq.*, closely follows Exodus, i. 8; when Joseph and his Pharaoh, al-Raiyān b. al-Walīd, had died the throne was occupied by Amalekite Firʿawns to the time when al-Walīd b. Muṣʿab ascended it; Mūsā was sent to him; he was the most arrogant and cruel of all and reigned for the longest period. Cf. also Yaʿḳūbī i. 211, Masʿūdī ii. 397 and Zamak<u>hsh</u>arī's *Ka<u>shsh</u>āf* on Sūra vii. 103.

The other Egyptian kings who are mentioned in connection with the history of the kings of Israel are also called Firʿawn in Tradition, often with an attribute like *al-Aʿra<u>dj</u>* etc.

The Ḳurʾānic accounts of Firʿawn assume the following form in Tradition. Firʾawn had enslaved the Israelites and instituted forced labour. When his astrologers or priests one day told him or, as others say, when he had dreamed that an Israelite would be born who was destined to rob him of his power, he commanded that every new-born Israelite boy should henceforth be slain. When a want of servants thus began to be felt, he altered the edict so that they were preserved in alternate years. This explains how Hārūn, who was older than Mūsā, was saved.

Concerning the member of his suite who, according to the Ḳurʾān, was a convert, we are told that he was called <u>Kh</u>irḳīl, <u>Sh</u>imʿān or Ḥabīb. According to some he was a nephew of Firʿawn, according to others his treasurer, or an Israelite carpenter who had made the box for Mūsā's mother in which the child was exposed. He is said to have been slain by Firʿawn with the magicians, along with his wife, the princesses' maid, who shared the beliefs of her husband; but it is also said that he was present at the passage of the Red Sea.

Tradition also gives further details of the building of the tower. The object of building it was to strengthen Firʿawn's position because he feared that his subjects would follow Mūsā. He also wished to reach the God of Mūsā. The tower was the highest that had ever been built. When the sun was rising its shadow darkened the west and when it was setting, the east. When it was finished Firʿawn climbed up and shot an arrow upwards to strike Mūsā's God. Then God tested him; he caused the arrow to fall down bloodred. Firʿawn then thought he had achieved his purpose. But Gabriel came and broke the tower into three pieces with his wings; one of them fell in India, one into the Ocean and a third in the Maghrib, so high was the tower. According to Zamakhsharī on Sūra xxviii. 38, a piece fell on Firʿawn's army and slew many of his soldiers.

At the passage of the Red Sea Hāmān commanded Firʿawn's vanguard. When no one dared enter the sea, Gabriel rode in front on a mare; attracted by the mare the stallions of the Egyptians could not be restrained and the whole host rode in and was drowned. When Firʿawn uttered the words professing conversion given in the Ḳurʾān, Gabriel descended and closed his mouth with a piece of mud so that he might not be able to obtain the mercy of God by repeating the words. God then caused Firʿawn's body to be cast up so that the Israelites might believe that he was really dead. — Cf. also the article MŪSĀ.

Bibliography: The Ḳurʾān commentaries on the various passages where Firʿawn is mentioned; Ṭabarī, i. 378 *sq.*, 442 *sq.*; Yaʿḳūbī, i. 30 *sq.*, 211 *sq.*; Masʿūdī, *Murūdj*, i. 92 *sq.*; ii. 368 *sq.*, 397 *sq.*, 410—414; iii. 273; al-Kisāʾī, *Ḳiṣaṣ al-anbiyāʾ*, ed. Eisenberg, p. 195 *sqq.*; Thaʿlabī, *Ḳiṣaṣ al-anbiyāʾ* (Cairo 1290), p. 146 *sq.*; Abu 'l-Fidāʾ (ed. Fleischer), p. 98 *sq.*; Maḳrīzī, *Khiṭaṭ*, i. 142, 30 *sq.*; ii. 465, 466; Grünbaum, *Neue Beiträge z. sem. Sagenkunde*, p. 152 *sq.*; G. Weil, *Bibl. Legenden der Muselmänner*, p. 126 *sq.*; Wüstenfeld, *Die älteste aeg. Gesch. nach den Zauber- u. Wundererzähl. d. Araber*, in *Orient u. Occident*, i. (1862), p. 336 *sq.*; J. Horovitz, *Koranische Untersuchungen*, p. 130 *sq.*

FIRDAWS is an artificially formed singular to *farādīs* which was taken by the Arabs from παράδεισος and understood by them as a plural (G. Hoffmann, in *ZDMG*, xxxii. 761). The rare measure *fiʿlaul* (Lumsden, *Arabic Grammar*, p. 365, 368) was probably chosen to distinguish it from a form (perhaps *furdūs*) derived from the genuinely Arabic root *fardasa* (*LA*, viii. 45; Lane, *s.v.*). *Firdaws* occurs in old Arabian poetry in the sense of a fertile hollow of land (Bakrī, *Geogr. Wörterb.*, ed. Wüstenfeld, p. 514; Yāḳūt, iii. 870 *sq.*) and twice in the Ḳurʾān (xviii. 107; xxiii. 11) and was evidently for Muḥammad a synonym for *djanna* in the ordinary sense, "garden". Farādīs occurs as a proper name at Damascus and Aleppo (Yāḳūt, iii. 862 *sq.*). It is curious that the fundamental sense of the Zend *pairidaēza*, "a place walled in" survives even in the remotely derivative Arabic, and a *firdaws* is defined by the lexicons more narrowly as *ḥadīḳa*. It also suggests grape-vines and palm-trees (Baiḍāwī on Sūra xviii. 107). In Ṭabarī (*Tafsīr* xvi. 25—27) are given the guesses of the earliest expositors, only two points having any basis — that it is a *rūmī* word and indicates a vineyard. Otherwise they say that it is the lordliest, finest, widest and loftiest part of the Garden, the abode of those who in life commanded kindness and forbade disliked actions. To Muḥammad himself tales are traced back that it is the uppermost story of the Garden, that from it the four rivers of Paradise divide, etc. On this last see more details in the abbreviation by al-Shaʿrānī of the *Tadhkira* of al-Ḳurṭubī (ed. Cairo 1324), p. 83, and on *al-firdaws* generally on p. 84 and 86. But the Saiyid Murtaḍā in his commentary on the *Iḥyāʾ* (vol. x., p. 525) says that it is the second story of Paradise below the *ʿarsh* of Allāh, and that above it comes the *djannat ʿAdn*. Others, again, held that *ʿIllīyūn* was the loftiest; see a long discussion, involving the doctrine of the vision of Allāh and the presence of Muḥammad with his people in the Garden, in the *Ibrīz* of Aḥmad b. al-Mubārak (ed. Cairo, 1316), p. 277 *sq.*

FIṬRA is a "noun of kind" (Wright[3], i. 123[a]) to the infinitive *faṭr* and means (an Ethiopic loan-meaning: Schwally in *ZDMG*, liii. 199 *sq.*; Nöldeke, *Neue Beiträge*, p. 49), "a kind or way of creating or of being created". It occurs in Sūra xxx. 30 (*khilḳa*, Baiḍāwī) and other forms of its verb in the same meaning occur 14 times. But though Muḥammad uses derived forms freely, it was obscure to his hearers. Ibn ʿAbbās did not understand it until he heard a Bedawī use it of digging a well, and then the Bedawī probably meant the genuinely Arab sense of *shaḳḳ* (*Lisān*, vi., p. 362, l. 20). Its theologically important usage is in the saying of Muḥammad, "Every infant is born according to the *fiṭra* (*ʿala 'l-fiṭra*; i.e. Allāh's kind or way of creating; "on God's plan", cf. Macdonald, *Religious Attitude in Islam*, p. 243); then his parents make him a Jew or a Christian or a Magian". This is one of several contradictory traditions on the salvability of the infants of unbelievers. On the whole question the theologians were uncertain and in disagreement. This text evidently means that every child is born naturally a Muslim; but is perverted after birth by his environment. But in this interpretation — that of the Muʿtazilī (cf. *Kashshāf*, ed. Lees, ii., p. 1094) — there were found serious theological and legal difficulties. (i.). It interferes with the sovereign will (*mashīʾa*) and guidance (*hidāya*) of Allāh. Orthodox Islām, therefore, holds that the parents could be only a secondary cause (*sabab*) and that the guiding aright and leading astray must come from Allāh himself. (ii.). This view, and indeed almost any view of the tradition, would involve that such an infant, if his parents died before he reached years of discretion, could not inherit from them, and that if he died before the years of discretion, his parents could not inherit from him. For this presupposes that he is a Muslim up to years of discretion, and canon law lays down that a Muslim cannot inherit from a non-Muslim or vice versa (*ḥāshiya* of al-Bādjūrī on the *sharḥ* of Ibn Ḳāsim on the *matn* of Abū Shudjāʿ, ed. Cairo 1307, vol. ii., p. 74 *sq.* and Sachau, *Muhammedanisches Recht*, p. 186, 204, 206 — a favourite subject for hair-splitting). Two attempts have been made to escape this. (i.). This statement of Muḥammad is to be regarded as a decision (*hukm*) and was abrogated by the later decision as to inheritance. But it is pointed out that it is not really a decision, but a narrative (*khabar*) and that narratives are not abrogated. (ii.). The being made a Jew, Christian or Magian is to be regarded as not actual, but figurative, and takes place in this figurative sense from the point of birth; the legal religion of the infant is automatically that of his parents, although he comes actually to embrace that religion only with maturity of mind. Another view was that being created according to the *fiṭra* meant only being created in a healthy condition, like a sound animal, with a capacity of either belief or unbelief when the time should come. Another was that *fiṭra* meant only "beginning" (*badʾa*). Still another was that it referred to Allāh's creating man with a capacity of either belief or unbelief and then laying on them the covenant of the "Day of *Alastu*" (Sūra, vii. 172). Finally that it was that to which Allāh turns round the hearts of men.

Bibliography: Mālik b. Anas, *Muwaṭṭaʾ* (ed. Cairo 1279—1280 with Zurḳānī), ii. 35; *Dict. of tech. Terms*, p. 1117 *sq.*; *LA*, vi. 362 *sq.*; *Risāla* on *īmān* by Abū Manṣūr Muḥammad al-Samarḳandī prefixed to the Hyderabad ed. of the *Fiḳh al-akbar* of Abū Ḥanīfa, p. 25 *sq.*; *Miṣbāḥ* of al-Faiyūmī, *s.v.*; Krehl, *Beiträge z. muh. Dogm.*, p. 235; Hughes, *Dict. of Islam*, under *Infants*; Wensinck, *The Muslim Creed*, General Index, *s.v.*; Rāzī, *Mafātīḥ al-ghaib*, (Cairo 1308) iv. 16; vi. 480; Ṭabarī, *Tafsīr*, xxi., p. 24.

FURḲĀN (A.), discrimination, revelation, salvation. The word is found in Arabic literature as an original Arabic word and also as one borrowed from the Aramaic. The meaning of the word in various passages in the Ḳurʾān cannot always be exactly determined.

Muḥammad made much use of it; he was fond of words with a long vowel in the last syllable on account of their solemn sound.

1. The Arabic word means separation, distinction, proof. Probably, however, this meaning is not found in the Ḳurʾān, although the commentators constantly expound it as having the theological shade of meaning of "discrimination between true and false". It is not impossible that Muḥammad came by this means to use it in the meaning of

2. Revelation, as this meaning of the word is not found in Aramaic. Thus it is applied in the Ḳurʾān to pre-Muhammadan revelations, e.g. Sūra xxi. 48, iii. 4, where, according to Zamakhsharī, it is a name for the whole class of heavenly books. But it is used of the Ḳurʾān in Sūra xxv. 1, where it is said: "Blessed is he that hath sent down the *furḳān* to his servant, that he might be a warner to the creatures"; and among later writers it has become a synonym for Ḳurʾān.

3. In the meaning "salvation" the word is certainly an Aramaic loanword. Thus in Sūra viii. 41 ". . . . and what we have revealed to our servant on the day of the *furḳān*, on the day when the two hosts met". Here the battle of Badr is called the "day of the *furḳān*". Some of the commentators on this passage give the meaning *al-naṣr* "victory". But this is the Aramaic *furḳānā*, synonymous with the Hebrew *yēshaʿ* "salvation". (Cf. also viii, 29).

Bibliography: A. Geiger, *Was hat Mohammed aus dem Judenthume aufgenommen?* p. 55 *sq.*; Schwally, *ZDMG*, lii. 134 *sq.*; Nöldeke-Schwally, *Geschichte des Qorāns*, i. 34; Nöldeke, *Neue Beiträge zur semitischen Sprachwissenschaft*, p. 23 *sq.*; J. Horovitz, *Koranische Untersuchungen*, p. 76 *sq.*; cf. *A Dictionary of Technical Terms* (*Bibliotheca Indica*), ii. 1130.

FURŪʿ. [See FIḲH, UṢŪL].

FUTUWWA. In common use this word denotes the whole of praiseworthy qualities, which are significant for the chivalrous young man (*fatā*), especially liberality (*karam, sakhāʾ*). In the Ḳurʾān *fatā* means both a youth (S. xviii, 9; xxi, 60) and a slave (S. xii, 30, 36, 62; xviii. 60, 62). In a tradition quoted in the *Lisān al-ʿArab* (xx, 4) and attributed to the Prophet it is said: "Do not say my *ʿabd*, but say my *fatā*" (cf. Bukhārī, *ʿItḳ*, B. 17; Muslim, *Alfāẓ*, trad. 13—15).

Availing themselves of an alleged saying of the Prophet: *Lā fatā illā ʿAlī walā saif illā Dhu'l-Faḳār* (cf. *Chronique de Tabari*, ed. Zotenberg, iii. 27; according to another tradition it was called from heaven by an angel, cf. Muḥibb al-Dīn al-Ṭabarī, *al-Riyāḍ al-naḍira*, Cairo 1327, or it was an exclamation by an unknown person in the battle of Uḥud, cf. Ibn Hishām, *Sīra*, Cairo 1346, ii, 89. On the use made of this saying in general cf. Reinaud, *Monumens*, ii, 153, 307; *Tijdschr. voor Ned.-Indië*, 1873, ii, 333 *sqq.*) the members of the Prophet's family considered themselves as the true representatives of the *futuwwa*, which was derived from their ancestor, while it acquired in course of time the meaning of chilvalry, knighthood. It is reported notably that the caliph al-Nāṣir li-Dīn Allāh (575—622/1180—1225), who, according to the *K. al-Fakhrī* was an Imāmite, accorded the *futuwwa*-rank to several princes and dignitaries, while combining with this rank the privilege of *ramy al-bunduḳ*. The reception into this dignity was effected by the ceremonial investment with a pair of trousers, called *sarāwīl al-futuwwa* or *libās al-futuwwa*, and by drinking the cup of knighthood (*kaʾs al-futuwwa*). The knight, whose dignity was hereditary, was entitled to use on his escutcheon the figure of the cup or the trousers or both. According to the *K. ʿumdat al-ṭālib* the ʿAlid family Āl Muʿaiya was since al-Nāṣir entitled to accord the *futuwwa*. The naḳīb Tādj al-Dīn Muḥammad, belonging to this family, accorded also the *khirkat-al-taṣawwuf*.

Ibn Djubair (edition of 1907, p. 280, where the MS. reading *yaḥzimūnahu* is to be maintained) speaks of a society in Syria, whose members practised the *futuwwa* by a ruthless persecution of the Rāfiḍites. The oaths they swore by the futuwwa were unconditionally respected.

Ibn Baṭṭūṭa found in Asia Minor fraternal corporations, whose members (*fityān*) for the greater part plied the same trade and lived together, under the supervision of a chief (*akhī*) in a convent (*zāwiya*), from what they earned by their external labour. After the common meal they used to pass the evening with singing and dancing. Their clothing consisted of a cloak (*ḳabāʾ*), a white woollen cap (*ḳalansūwa*) on the upper part of which there was fastened a ribbon of an ell's length, and shoes (*akhfāf*); in their belt they wore a knife of two ells. They were hospitable towards travellers and proceeded ruthlessly against tyrannical potentates and their companions (ed. Paris, ii, 260 *sq.*). This author stayed in Ḳonya in the *zāwiya* of Ḳāḍī Ibn Ḳalam Shāh, where the inmates (*fityān*) wore *sarāwīl* and traced back their *futuwwa*-regulations to ʿAlī. They were conspicuous for their hospitality (o.c. ii, 281 sq.). Ibn Baṭṭūṭa found lodging in many similar convents of *fityān* (o.c. ii, 270—368 passim).

In the Ṣūfī vocabulary *futuwwa* stands for a state of mind which is active in several directions and therefore cannot be rendered by one single word. Generally *futuwwa* is described as "placing other people above one's self" (*īthār ʿalā nafsihi*), which, according to al-Ghazzālī, is the highest degree of *sakhāʾ*. This state of mind is made manifest by liberality, altruism, self-denial, immunity against disappointment, indulgence for other people's short-comings, etc. Al-Ḳushairī, by a series of paraphrases and anecdotes, conveys to some extent the scope of this meaning. Besides there is a relation between the *futuwwa* and the *makārim al-akhlāḳ* (the prominent virtues), which constitute a component part of the mystical *futuwwa* (cf. al-Sulamī, *K. al-Futuwwa*, Ms. Aya Sofia No. 2049, fol. 80). Al-Tustarī, the dogmatic moralist, on the other hand restricts the *futuwwa* to the *makārim al-akhlāḳ* (cf. MS. *Dār al-Kutub*, Cairo, *Taṣawwuf wa-akhlāḳ dīniya*, No. 994, fol. 9).

Finally the *futuwwa* is one of the essential elements in the Islamic guild institutions, which, from this point of view, have taken over many elements from the mystic fraternities.

Bibliography: Hammer-Purgstall, *JA* 1849, p. 5—14; 1855, p. 282—290; Quatremère, *Histoire des sultans mamlouks*, i., 58, N. 83 (the quotations from the *ʿUmdat al-ṭālib* are to be found in the edition Bombay 1318, p. 150); Dozy, *Suppl.* sub voce; al-Ḳushairī, *Risāla*, Cairo 1318, p. 122 *sqq.*; al-Djurdjānī, *Taʿrīfāt*, ed. Flügel, p. 171; *Dict. of Techn. Terms*, ed. Sprenger, ii, 1156; *Tādj al-ʿarūs*, 2d ed. x, 376 *sqq.*; B. Faris, *L'honneur chez les Arabes avant l'Islam*, Paris 1932; F. Taeschner, *Die islamischen Futuwwabünde*, in *ZDMG*, lxxxvii (1933). On the *futuwwa* in the sense of knighthood: Goldziher, in *ZDMG*, lxxiii (1919), 127—8; J. Schacht in *Festschrift Jacob*, Leipzig 1932, p. 277 *sqq.*; Ibn al-Sāʿī, *al-Djāmiʿ al-mukhtaṣar*, ed. M. Djawad and p. Anastase, Bagdad 1934, ix, 221—6; P. Kahle, in *Arch. für Orientforschung*, Berlin 1933, p. 52—58; F. Taeschner, in *Beiträge zur Arabistik etc.*, Leipzig 1944, p. 340—385. On the mystical futuwwa: Suhrawardī, *K. ʿAwārif al-maʿārif*, Cairo 1384, iii, 31—2; F. Taeschner in *Isl.* xxiv (1937); L. Massignon, *Salmān Pāk*, Paris 1933, p. 28—9. On the *futuwwa* in the guild institutions: H. Thorning, *Beiträge zur Kenntnis des islamischen Vereinwesens*, Berlin 1913 (*Türk. Bibl.* Vol. 16).

G

GABRIEL. [See DJABRĀʾĪL].

GHAIBA is used as the infinitive from its root, *ghaib* having come to equal *ghāʾib*. It thus means "absence", often "absence of mind". This latter force was developed by Ṣūfīs into absence of the heart from all except Allāh, expressed, on the other side, by *ḥuḍūr*, "presence" with Allāh. It is a stage on the passage to *fanāʾ* [q.v.], complete "ceasing" or passing away of the self. For details of the development of this idea see Nicholson's translation of the *Kashf al-maḥdjūb* of al-Hudjwīrī, p. 248 *sq.*, and index; also the *Risāla* of al-Ḳushairī with the commentaries of Zakarīyā al-Anṣārī and al-ʿArūsī, ed. Būlāḳ 1290, vol. i., p. 66 *sq.*, and the Saiyid al-Murtaḍā's commentary on the *Iḥyāʾ* of al-Ghazzālī, vii. 248 and Macdonald, *Religious Attitude and Life in Islam*, p. 260, 262.

Another common use of the word is to describe the condition of any one who has been withdrawn by Allāh from the eyes of men and whose life during that period (called his *ghaiba*) has been miraculously prolonged. Of this the outstanding example is the Hidden Imām, or Mahdī, of the Shīʿī Twelvers. He, though thus kept generally invisible, still lives on earth (cf. AL-KHADIR), has from time to time been seen by some and been in correspondence with others and maintains a control over the fortunes of his people (Goldziher, *Vorlesungen*, p. 232 *sq.*, 269 *sq.*; do., *Arabische Philologie* ii., p. lxii. *sq.*); cf. the treatise of Ibn Bābūya *Fī ithbāt al-ghaiba*, ed. Möller (*Beitr. zur Mahdilehre des Islam*, I).

GHĀLĪ (A.), plur. *ghulāt*, "one who exaggerates or goes beyond all bounds", particularly in reverence for certain individuals, notably ʿAlī and the ʿAlids, and considers them incarnations of the Deity. What heads of sects are to be called *ghulāt* depends on the point of the view of the writer, but as a rule those who have adopted such notions, originally foreign to Islām as incarnation (*ḥulūl*), metempsychosis (*tanāsukh*) etc., are considered to be *ghulāt*. Cf. Friedländer, in *JAOS*, xxix. 12.

GHANĪMA, spoils of war. By *ghanīma* Muslim scholars mean the weapons, horses and all other movable possessions taken in battle from unbelievers (cf. FAIʾ). Fourfifths of the booty are to be divided among the troops who have been present at the battle, whether they have actually fought in it or not. Horsemen can claim a share three times as large (according to Abū Ḥanīfa's view only twice) as that of a foot-soldier; one who has slain an enemy in battle also receives his equipment (*salab*).

The remaining fifth belongs to Allāh: "Know that a fifth of what ye have won belongs to Allāh — to his apostle, his family, to the orphan, the needy, and the traveller — if ye believe in Allāh". This verse in the Ḳurʾān (Sūra viii. 41) was revealed shortly after the battle of Badr. From ancient times Arab chiefs had been accustomed to receive a certain portion of the booty and it was thus nothing new when the Prophet had one fifth of the *ghanīma* granted him in God's name in this verse of the Ḳurʾān to defray the expenses of the state.

After Muḥammad's death the Imām was at first considered qualified to apply the fifth of the spoils in the way that seemed to him best to further the general interest of the Muslims. This was also the teaching of Mālik b. Anas. But most of the later Muslim scholars have interpreted Ḳurʾān viii. 41 literally. In their view the fifth allotted to Allāh must be divided into five equal portions among the five categories expressly mentioned in Ḳurʾān viii. 41 (in Abū Ḥanīfa's view however only among three of these categories: the orphan, the needy and the traveller); the portion originally allotted to the Prophet himself is, according to the Shāfiʿī school, to be applied to the general good of the Muslim community.

Prisoners of war are also included in the *ghanīma*. Unbelievers, who are taken prisoners of war by Muslims — women and children as well as men — are divided as slaves among the troops who are entitled to the booty. The Imām may, however, dispose of freeborn, male, adult prisoners of war in other ways. He can, as the interest of the Muslims demands it, also set them free on payment of a ransom (or even without such payment), exchange them for captured Muslims or on the other hand he may put them to death; according to Abū Ḥanīfa, however, he may not set them free.

The rules regulating the divison of *ghanīma*, in the view of most Muslim scholars, do not apply to the division of lands in the conquered countries (cf. FAIʾ).

Bibliography: The commentaries on Sūra viii. 41 and the chapter on *djihād* in the collections on Tradition and the *fikh* books; Māwardī, *al-Aḥkām al-sulṭānīya* (ed. M. Enger, Bonn 1853), p. 217, 226 *sq.*; al-Ṭabarī, *K. Ikhtilāf al-fuḳahāʾ*,

ed. Schacht, Leiden 1933, p. 68 *sqq.*; F. F. Schmidt, *Die Occupatio im islamischen Recht* (*Isl.*, i. 300 *sq.*); and the bibliography given on p. 345 *sq.* of Th. W. Juynboll's *Handbuch des islām. Gesetzes* (Leyden 1910), 4th ed. (Dutch), Leiden 1930, p. 344 *sq.*

GHAWTH ("succour", "deliverance") is an epithet of the ḳuṭb, the head of the Ṣūfī hierarchy of saints. It is used of him only when he is thought of as one whose help is sought; but that, from the nature of the ḳuṭb, is practically always. Thus it is a normal sequent to ḳuṭb. Others say that the ghawth is immediately below the ḳuṭb in the hierarchy.

Bibliography: Djurdjānī, *Taʿrīfāt* (ed. Cairo 1321), p. 109; *Dict. of Techn. Terms*, p. 141, 1091, 1167; Lane's *Lexicon* s.v., p. 2306a; Hughes, *Dict. of Islam*, p. 139a; Hudjwīrī, *Kashf al-maḥdjūb*, transl. Nicholson, p. 214; A. v. Kremer, *Gesch. der herrschenden Ideen des Islams* (1868), p. 172 *sq.*

AL-**GHAZZĀLĪ**, ABŪ ḤĀMID MUḤAMMAD B. MUḤAMMAD AL-ṬŪSĪ AL-SHĀFIʿĪ (for the evidence at present available on his name see *JRAS*, 1902, p. 18—22 and *OM*, XV, p. 58), was the most original thinker that Islām has produced and its greatest theologian.

1. Life. He was born at Ṭūs in 450/1058 and was educated there and at Naisābūr, especially under al-Djuwainī, the Imām al-Ḥaramain, with whom he remained until the Imām's death in 478/1085. A sceptical attitude showed itself in him from the first. Although in a Ṣūfī environment and practising the Ṣūfī exercises, no impression was made on him by these, and he preferred rather to investigate theological and legal subtleties. This began when he was under twenty; with *taḳlīd* [q.v.] he had broken from his earliest youth. From Naisābūr he went to the court of Niẓām al-Mulk, the Seldjūḳ wazīr, and formed part of his retinue of canonists and theologians until 484/1091 when he was appointed to teach in the Niẓāmīya madrasa at Baghdād. During this time he became an absolute sceptic, not only as to religion but also as to the possibility of any certain knowledge. Scepticism he never overcame so far as philosophy was concerned. At Baghdād he taught and wrote on canon law; he wrote also controversial books against the Taʿlīmīs (Bāṭinīya, Imāmīya, Ismāʿīlīya; Niẓām al-Mulk and Malik Shāh were assassinated by them in 485/1092). For himself he laboured to recover a possible intellectual and theological position and from 483 to 487 (1090—1094) studied diligently the different schools of thought around him, especially philosophy. Finally he turned seriously to Ṣūfism. Intellectualism had failed him; what of religious experience? He had returned to belief in God, prophecy and the last judgment — or, as he put it, God had restored to him these beliefs — and fear of that Day of Wrath seized him. From Radjab to Dhu 'l-Ḳaʿda 488/1095, he was in the throes of a conversion wrought by terror, and under it he collapsed physically and mentally. Finally, in Dhu 'l-Ḳaʿda he put behind him his brilliant position and worldly ambitions and fled from Baghdād as a wandering derwīsh. By giving himself to the ascetic and contemplative life he sought peace for his soul and certainty for his mind. And these he gained. From that time his position was pragmatic and he taught that the intellect should only be used to destroy trust in itself and that the only trustworthy knowledge was that gained through experience. A purely philosophical structure could have no base. On that his dialectic was inexorable as that of Hume. Even the systems of the speculative theologians had no intellectual certainty, although their doctrines were correct. By speculative methods they could not be proved; but only by the direct knowledge with which God floods the heart of the believer. By that personal experience (*maʿrifa*) the fact of prophetic revelation is established and the truth of the theological structure assured. Yet there can be no question that his thinking had been indefinitely clarified by his philosophical studies and that with him the forms of Greek dialectic made their final entry into Muslim thought. What al-Ashʿarī half consciously began, al-Ghazzālī wittingly finished. Further, that he used the forms of Greek dialectic to found a pragmatic system in his originality and distinction. The later theologians did not always understand or follow him in this. That the account which he himself gives of all this in the *Munḳidh min al-ḍalāl* is true cannot be doubted; the philosophical necessity, both for al-Ghazzālī as an individual and for the development of Muslim thought, both of which had got into a *cul-de-sac*, is plain. As in al-Ashʿarī's case only a great emotional experience could break the fetters of tradition and give the personal force needed to turn the current of the age. Political complications may have helped to bring on his nervous breakdown.

Barkiyārūḳ became Great Seldjūḳ in 488/1095 and killed his uncle Tutush immediately before the flight of al-Ghazzālī and the Khalīfa at whose court al-Ghazzālī held an important place declared for Tutush. Similarly his return to active life in 499/1105 followed the death of Barkiyārūḳ in 498/1104. About two years he passed in strict retirement in Syria, finally pilgrimaging at the end of 490/1097. Then came nine years of retreat in different places, with, from time to time, periods of return to his family and the world. The *Iḥyāʾ* and other books were written, and he preached at Baghdād and taught the *Iḥyāʾ* there and at Damascus. Finally "the Sulṭān of the time" (*Munḳidh*, ed. of 1303, p. 42) compelled him to become a teacher in the Niẓāmīya madrasa at Naisābūr, and he consented in Dhu 'l-Ḳaʿda 499/1105. The times called for some strong reforming influence. That he had himself recognized and also that there was need of a powerful and religious-minded ruler who would crush heresy and unbelief. Such a ruler was apparently found in Muḥammad, the brother of Barkiyārūḳ, who became Great Seldjūḳ in 498/1104, and to whom he addressed the original Persian form of his *Tibr al-masbūk*, a manual of ethical guidance for kings. The immediate influence in his recall was, however, Fakhr al-Mulk, the son of his old patron, Niẓām al-Mulk, who was wazīr at Naisābūr to Sandjar, the governor of Khurāsān. But he did not long stay in public life. His yearnings to quiet and contemplation continually drew him and there are stories, too, of friction. He returned to Ṭūs and lived there in retirement with some personal disciples, having charge of a madrasa and a khānḳāh or Ṣūfī monastery. There he died on the 14th of Djumādā II 505/Dec. 19th 1111.

2. Doctrine and influence. Although a formative canon lawyer of a rank short only of the first, he yet deposed fiḳh from the position it had usurped, lashed its casuistry and refused it a place as a part of religion. He dealt similarly with *kalām* and especially denounced the tendency to make the faith of the masses a structure of logically demon-

strated articles (*ʿaḳāʾid*). In this he followed the founder of his *madhhab*, al-Shāfiʿī. He opposed the Mutakallims also in the intolerance which they had developed. All, he taught, who agreed in the broad principles of Islām were believers. This he lays down in his *Tafriḳa*; but he taught also in the *Ildjām* (ed. of 1303, p. 31, 32, 51, 62) and the *Munḳidh* (ed. of 1303, p. 42) that the religion of the unlearned should be protected by the secular arm of the state. These reforms his high rank as a scholar and popularity as a preacher carried through. They have been accepted by the Agreement of the Muslim people (*al-idjmāʿ*) and he himself is reckoned as not only the *mudjaddid* (renewer) of his century, but as the great restorer of the faith. Of course both canon lawyers and speculative theologians continued and still continue to spin their systems and to try to enforce them. He also brought philosophy into the open and dissipated the glamour of mystery which had surrounded it. It was simply "thinking", and the philosophers and their systems could be understood by any intelligent man. Further, by philosophy the ultimate and unconditioned could not be reached; there could be no metaphysics on a basis of pure thought. This agnosticism was a development into more perfect form of the system of the later Ashʿarīs. On the positive side he continued the work of al-Ḳushairī and gave Ṣūfism a firm standing in Muslim orthodoxy. In this al-Ghazzālī marked the second great epoch of development as al-Ashʿarī with his applying of logical argument to the defence of orthodoxy had marked the first. Thus for al-Ghazzālī the basis of all religious certainty was ecstatic experience. By it he and all *ʿārifs* (those who have direct experiential knowledge, perhaps a translation of "gnostic"; cf. Bauer, *Dogmatik al-Ghazālī's*, p. 35) learn that the theological positions of the Fathers (*al-salaf*) are true, and how these should be interpreted. To that age of simple faith he looked back with longing. This led him to what might be called a Biblical theology-study of the Ḳurʾān and of the record of the teachings of Muḥammad. Practically he endeavoured to arouse men to religion and lead them back to the old ways by preaching the Wrath to come at the Judgment. His own conversion had been under the pressure of fear. Strongly contrasted and forming the paradox of his position is the emphasis which he laid on the love of Allāh. It is part of the contrast between the emotional life of the saints with Allāh which he had known and the dogmatism of the theological system which he felt compelled to accept. In spite of the curiously intolerant passage as to the faith of the masses referred to above, his influence has been and is for charity, the stimulation of free enquiry and intellectual life. His indirect influence on European thought, even the most modern, has also been marked. It flowed through the *Pugio Fidei* of Ramón Martin and affected, first, Thomas Aquinas and, later, Pascal. For his alleged relationship to the ʿAlids and to the book *Djafr*, see DJAFR and references there and for his real relationship to magic, see *Descr. of Ar. and Turk. MSS. in Newberry Library, Chicago*, p. 6 *sq.*

3. Sincerity. Even by his contemporaries the reality of his conversion was doubted; the change, it was felt, was so great from the pugnacious, sceptial canonist to the ecstatic saint with his sermons on the fear of God. Later, the philosophers, hard hit by his dialectic, and unable to believe that a man who knew philosophy so well should not be, at least secretly, a philosopher, sought in his writings proofs of an esoteric teaching. Two things aided them in that. 1. He had openly preached an economy of teaching and had written a book with that publicly as its title, *al-Madnūn bihi ʿalā ghair ahlihi* — "That which is to be concealed from those who are not worthy of it" — a book, however, in which there is no heretical doctrine. In his *Imlāʾ*, an answer to attacks on his *Iḥyāʾ*, he formally defends by the example of the Prophet and the Companions, the practice of keeping certain theological reasonings and developments secret from those who are not in a position to understand them and who might thereby be led astray either in faith or in practice (ed. on margin of *Itḥāf al-sāda*, Cairo 1311, pp. 45, 159—164, 225 *et seq.*, 247 *et seq.*). There are other references to the same practice in the *Arbaʿīn* (ed. of 1328, pp. 25 *et seq.*); the *Djawāhir* (ed. of 1329, pp. 25 *et seq.*, esp. 30 *et seq.*), all very important passages on the order in which his books were written; the *Mishkāt* (ed. of 1322, pp. 54 *et seq.*) and the *Mīzān al-ʿamal* (ed. of 1328, pp. 212 *et seq.*) on *madhhab*'s and what a man has a right to keep to himself. And this had really been the practice of Islām from the beginning. Even al-Shāfiʿī, while denouncing kalām, had admitted that some should study it for the defence of the faith. The position of Ibn Khaldūn, at the extreme end of the development, was similar, only in his day the need had passed (ed. Quatr., iii. 43; de Slane, iii. 63). It was always a *farḍ kifāya* and not a *farḍ ʿain* and had a similar origin with the *bilā kaifa* of al-Ashʿarī. Thus the advanced doctrine did not contradict, but only developed, based and deepened the simpler faith, and knowledge of it was open to all who would fit themselves for it. In the end, this led most ironically to the Averroistic doctrine of the two-fold truth. That was only a special case of the multiform truth which Islām has always admitted. 2. Those direct perceptions of religious truths which al-Ghazzālī had reached in ecstasy he was compelled to express in language by means of metaphor and symbol. He teaches consistently that there are ideas which language cannot render in exact terms and the contents of which can be suggested only by pictures. When, then, such expressions were examined and held to account as intellectually exact statements, misunderstanding was certain to follow. Thus Ibn Rushd was led by the metaphor of the sun in the *Mishkāt* (p. 55) to believe that al-Ghazzālī was there teaching the Neoplatonic doctrine of emanation (*ṣudūr*). But the context is in the teeth of such an explanation, and the metaphor is one frequently used by al-Ghazzālī to suggest the relationship between God and the world. On this point and on the *Mishkāt* generally see W. H. T. Gairdner's translation of this book.

The view put forth by J. Obermann, that al-Ghazzālī is in his thinking unbiassed by his Islamic environment, mainly based on the *Munḳidh*, has been refuted by A. Th. van Leeuwen, who, following the suggestions made by H. Kraemer, and by an analysis of the *ʿAḳāʾid* and the *Tahāfut*, concludes that al-Ghazzālī never strayed from the fundamental conceptions of Islām (see *Bibliography*).

4. Works. Our knowledge of al-Ghazzālī's works is still incomplete both as to extent and relative order (cf. Bouyges in the introduction to his ed. of *Tahāfut* and Massignon, *Recueil de textes*, p. 93), not to speak of dating. For approximately complete lists reference can be made to the introduction by the Saiyid al-Murtaḍā (based on al-Subkī) prefixed to his *Itḥāf al-sāda*, a commentary on the *Iḥyāʾ* (ed. Cairo

1311, vol. i. pp. 41—44) and to Brockelmann, *GAL*², i. 535 *sqq.*; *Suppl.*, i. 744 *sqq.* The *Iḥyā' ʿulūm al-dīn* (the title expresses al-Ghazzālī's consciousness of the part the book was to play, cf. Bauer in *Der Islam*, iv. 159 *et seq.*) as a compendium of his whole system stands by itself, although it does not go into the ultimate details, either on philosophy, *kalām* or Ṣūfism. On its date see above. It divides into two parts, each consisting of two quarters (*rubʿ*); the first is on external acts of devotion and religious usage, the second upon the inner side of life, the heart and its workings, good and evil. The four quarters are *Rubʿ al-ʿibādat* (Acts of a creature towards his Lord); *Rubʿ al-ʿādāt* (Usages of life); *Rubʿ al-muhlikāt* (Destructive matters in life); *Rubʿ al-mundjiyāt* (Saving matters). Each contains ten Books; the first of the forty is on *ʿilm*, the second on *kalām* and the last on eschatology. Otherwise all is experiential, traditional and practical. D. B. Macdonald has translated Book viii. in *Rubʿ* ii. on the relation of music and singing (*samāʿ*) to the Ṣūfī ecstasy, in *JRAS*, 1901—1902; he has analyzed with extracts Book ii. of *Rubʿ* iii. on the marvels of the human heart, in Lectures vii.—x. of his *Religious Attitude*, and Book vi. of *Rubʿ* iv. on the love of Allāh, in Hasting's *Dict. of Religions*, vol. ii., pp. 677—680. A great part of the *Iḥyā'* is also analyzed by Miguel Asín in his *Algazel*; and H. Bauer has translated some chapters. Another short introduction to *ʿilm* in general is his *Fātiḥat al-ʿulūm*; it resembles the first book of the *Iḥyā'*. His remaining printed works may be classified as follows: 1. Canon law: *Kitāb al-wadjīz*, the smallest of his general treatises on fiḳh; *al-Mustaṣfā min ʿilm al-uṣūl*, written after his return (ed. of 1322, i., pp. 3 *et seq.*). 2. Logic and books against the philosophers: *Miʿyār al-ʿilm*, an elaborate treatise on logic; *Miḥakk al-naẓar*, a smaller book; *Maḳāṣid al-falāsifa*, statement of their teachings on all subjects save the absolutely demonstrable, professes to be a *ḥikāya* (ed. Cairo, 1331); *Tahāfut al-falāsifa*, demonstration that they could not by reason prove their system (cf. de Boer, *Widersprüche der Philosophie*; there are translations also in Asín's *Algazel*, pp. 735—880; also a translation begun by Carra de Vaux in *Muséon*, vol. xviii.); ed. with introduction and analysis by P. Bouyges (Bairūt 1927). 3. Contra Bāṭinīya: *al-Ḳusṭās al-mustaḳīm*; Goldziher, *Streitschrift des Gazālī gegen die Bāṭinijja-Sekte* (Leyden 1916); *Die Streitschrift des Gazali gegen die Ibāḥīya in pers. Text*, herausgeg. und übers. von O. Pretzl, München 1933. 4. Speculative theology: *al-Risāla al-Ḳudsīya*, incorporated in the *Iḥyā'* as *Ḳawā'id al-ʿaḳā'id* (an abridged translation of it in H. Bauer, *Die Dogmatik al-Ghazālī's*, Halle 1912); *al-Iḳtiṣād fi 'l-iʿtiḳād*, an expansion of the preceding and his most elaborate treatment of kalām (M. Asín Palacios, *El justo medio en la creencia*, Madrid 1929). 5. Books to be kept from those unfitted for them: *al-Maḍnūn bihi ʿalā ghair ahlihi*, on Allāh and his creation — on angels, djinn etc. — on prophets and miracles — on eschatology; *al-Maḍnūn al-ṣaghīr*, otherwise called *al-Adjwiba al-ghazzālīya fi 'l-masā'il al-ukhrawīya* (analyses and translations from these in Asín's *Algazel*, pp. 609—733); *Mishkāt al-anwār*, on the mystical meaning of Allāh as Light and on the guidance of the Inner Light to Allāh — a book of the end of his life (transl. by W. H. T. Gairdner, London, 1924). 6. Expositions of the Faith of the Fathers on the basis of the Ḳur'ān and tradition: *Djawāhir al-Ḳur'ān*; *Kitāb al-arbaʿīn*, a second part of the preceding; *al-Maḳṣad al-asnā fī asmā' Allāh al-ḥusna* (exhortation to imitation of the divine qualities); *al-Ḥikma fī makhlūḳāt Allāh*, evidence of creation for the wisdom of Allāh; *al-Durra al-fākhira*, eschatology (text and transl. by L. Gautier); *al-Kashf wa'l-tabyīn fī ghurūr al-khalḳ adjmaʿīn*, how all mankind have strayed from obedience; *Ildjām al-ʿawāmm ʿan ʿilm al-kalām*, see above; *Risalā fi 'l-waʿẓ wa'l-iʿtiḳād*, another *Ildjām*. 7. Books of religious experience and edification, personal and systematized: *al-Risāla al-ladunīya*, on knowledge which is gained immediately from Allāh (transl. by Marg. Smith, *JRAS*, 1938); *Kīmiyā' al-saʿāda*, original in Persian, an abbreviation of the *Iḥyā'* (transl. by Ch. Field; partially by H. Ritter, Jena 1923); *Aiyuha 'l-walad*, on the need of works besides knowledge (text and translation by G. H. Scherer, Beirut, 1936); *Mukāshafat al-ḳulūb*, the ed. of Būlāḳ 1300 is a *mukhtaṣar*; *Bidāyat al-hidāya*; *Mīzān al-ʿamal* (Hebr. transl. of Abraham bar Chasdai, ed. J. Goldenthal, Leipzig, 1839), on saving works; *Khulāṣat al-taṣānīf fi 'l-taṣawwuf*, what is worth while in religion — from the Persian and, if genuine, of the very end of his life; *Minhādj al-ʿābidīn*, his last book, dictated (the prologue is translated by Asín in his *Algazel*, pp. 881—899). 8. Defences of himself: *al-Imlā' ʿan ishkālāt al-iḥyā'*, in the margin of *Itḥāf al-sāda*, vol. i., pp. 41—252; *al-Tafriḳa bain al-Islām wa'l-zandaḳa*; *al-Munḳidh min al-ḍalāl*, written after 500 (transl. by Barbier de Meynard in *JA*, vii., vol. ix.). 9 Miscellaneous: *al-Tibr al-masbūk*, an ethical Mirror for Princes, see above; *Sirr al-ʿālamain wa-kashf mā fi 'l-dārain*, a manual for kings to worldly success, assertedly after his return, but almost certainly apocryphal; *Antworten auf Fragen, die an ihn gerichtet wurden*, ed. from Hebrew version in 1896 by Heinrich Malter, but certainly apocryphal; *al-Taḥbīr fī ʿilm al-taʿbīr*, on principles of dream interpretation; *al-Radd al-djamīl li-Ilāhīyāt ʿĪsā bi-Ṣarīḥ al-Indjīl*, ed. and transl. by R. Chidiac, Paris, 1939; on a ḳaṣīda of al-Ghazzālī cf. Mart. Schreiner in *ZDMG*, xlviii. 43 *sq.*, also Steinschneider, *Die hebr. Übers.*, i. 347; *Maʿāridj al-ḳuds*, Cairo 1346.

Bibliography: It is very large and the following is a selection only of the more recent books. The period of Schmoelders and Gosche is past, and the popular articles, based upon these, in encyclopaedias and histories of philosophy are untrustworthy. The principal sources for the life are the *Munḳidh* and the materials in the introduction of the Saiyid Murtaḍā to his *Itḥāf*, vol. i., pp. 2—53. These can be controlled by al-Subkī, *Ṭabaḳāt*, iv., pp. 101—182 and by the extracts from Ibn ʿAsākir in Mehren's *Exposé*, (*Trans. of iii*rd. *Congress of Orientalists*, vol. ii.). For the order and dating of the works there are numerous references scattered through them (see above for some), but these are not yet sufficiently collected and examined. Formal biographies, in order of date, are: D. B. Macdonald, *Life of al-Ghazzālī with special reference to his religious experiences and opinions*: *JAOS* for 1899, vol. xx., p. 71—132 (cf. also Chap. iv. of the same writer's *Development of Muslim Theology*, 1903); Miguel Asín Palacios, *Algazel, dogmática, moral, ascética*, Zaragoza 1901; do., *La espiritualidad de Algazal y su sentido cristiano*, Madrid-Granada 1934—41, 4 vols.; Carra de Vaux, *Gazali*, Paris 1902; H. Frick, *Ghazali's Selbstbiographie*, Leipzig 1911; W. H. T. Gairdner, *An account of Ghazzali's Life and Works*, Madras 1919; S. M. Zwemer, *A Moslim*

Seeker after God, London 1920; J. Obermann, *Der philosophische Subjektivismus des Ghazālī*, Vienna 1921; E. F. Tscheuschner, *Mönchsideale des Islams*, Gütersloh 1933; H. Kræmer, *Enkele grepen uit de moderne apologie van de Islam* (*Tijdschr. Bat. Gen. K. en W.* 1935); A. J. Wensinck, *La pensée de Ghazzālī*, Paris 1940; A. Th. van Leeuwen, *Ghazālī als apologeet van de Islam*, Leiden 1947. Goldziher has a luminous treatment in his *Vorlesungen über den Islam*, by index, and especially, pp. 117 *sq.* Al-Ghazzālī's place in the history of philosophy De Boer has treated in his *Geschichte der Philosophie im Islam*, p. 138—150 and by index (English trans., p. 154—168). Cf. also Goldziher in *Kultur der Gegenwart*, i. 5, p. 62 *sq.* and, for his logic, Prantl, *Geschichte der Logik*, ii. 361 *sq.* (based on a mediaeval Latin translation of the *Maķāṣid*). — On his place in history cf. Nicholson, *Literary History of the Arabs*, pp. 338 *sq.*, 380 *sq.* and by index; Browne, *A Literary History of Persia*, by index; *Jewish Enc.*, v., 649 *sq.* Horten has not treated him systematically; but see (by index) many suggestive remarks in his *Philos. Systeme d. specul. Theologen im Islam*; cf. also *Die Hauptlehren des Averroes nach seiner Schrift: die Widerlegung des Ghazālī*, p. 323—328 of the same author. — For Ghazzālī's attitude towards Christianity, cf. L. Massignon, in *REI*, 1933. For Muslim criticism of al-Ghazzālī see Asín, *Un Faqîh Siciliano, contradictor de al-Gazzālī*, in *Centenario di Michele Amari*, vol. ii., p. 216—244 and Muḥ. Zakī Mubārak ʿAbd al-Salām, *al-Akhlāķ ʿinda 'l-Ghazzālī*, Cairo 1924 (cf. Snouck Hurgronje in *Verspr. Geschr.*, vi. 206 *sqq.*). — For his cosmology: A. J. Wensinck in *Med. Kon. Ak. Wet. Amst.*, vol. 75, Series A, No. 6.

GHŪL. For the ancient Arabs the *ghūl* (fem., pl. *ghīlān* and *aghwāl*) was a peculiarly bestial, diabolic and hostile variety of the mārids of the djinn which allured men from their path by assuming different forms, then fell upon them unawares, destroyed and devoured them. In the root seem to lie two ideas: 1. changing into different appearances and 2. treacherously assailing and destroying. There are many references to them in the early poets. According to the *Aghānī* (vol. xviii. 209 *sq.*) Taʾabbaṭa-Sharran spoke frequently in his verses of them; see especially his description of one (*ibid.*, p. 212 foot) and his boasting of comradeship with them as a wanderer of deserts (*ibid.*, p. 210 top). It was said to be the same as the *siʿlāt* (pl. *saʿālī*) which had a similar power of transforming itself and which was called on that account the sorceress (*sāḥira*) of the djinn. The masculine of the ghūl was said to be the *ķuṭrub*. It is plain that the word ghūl is a descriptive, for it can be used, and not apparently as a metaphor, of any destruction which comes upon a man; so even of spiritual things (*Taʿrīfāt* of al-Djurdjānī, *sub voce*, and Horten, *Theologie des Islām*, p. 335). Otherwise a man could hardly have been called Abu 'l-Ghūl (*Ḥamāsa*, ed. Freytag, p. 12) and Kaʿb b. Zuhair in his Burda-poem could not have compared Suʿād, even in her changeableness, to a ghūl. For some reason Muḥammad disliked the word, and only one derivative from the root occurs in the Ķurʾān (xxxvii. 47) *ghawl*, "insidious destruction", used of the effects of wine (cf. *Mufradāt* of al-Rāghib, p. 375). In a tradition, also, he declares that there is no such thing as a ghūl (*LA*, xix., p. 21, ll. 10 *sq.*). This has justified Muslims, especially Muʿtazilīs, in denying the existence of the ghūl altogether, e.g. **Zamakhsharī** om Sūra xxxvii. 47 (ed. Calcutta, p. 1205). But others held that it was only the changing of appearance (*taghawwul*) which the Prophet denied, and they quoted traditions from him telling how to drive away the ghūl by reciting the *adhān*. For the mediaeval system in which the ghūl is fully accepted, see Damīrī *sub voce*, also under *siʿlāt* and *ķuṭrub* (Jayakar's transl., vol. ii. 47 *sq.*). Ķazwīnī classifies the ghūl among the diabolic (*mutashaiṭina*) djinn (ed. Wüstenfeld, i. 370) and that is overwhelmingly the later attitude. In the popular mind ghūl (also *ghūla*; similarly *ķuṭruba*) was an ordinary word for cannibal, whether human or demonic, and thus became equivalent to the European ogre, and the standard 'Märchen' told elsewhere of ogres are connected with them. For Persia see Sir John Malcolm's *Sketches of Persia*, chap. xvi.; for Egypt, Spitta's *Contes arabes*, index, s.v. ghūl; for North Africa, Stumme, *Märchen aus Tripolis*, passim; for Turkey, Kúnos, *Türkische Volksmärchen*, by index under *Dew* and *Dschinn* and passim. See also in *Arabian Nights*, Sindbad, voyage iv., Story of Saif al-Mulūk, Story of the envious Wazīr, all with Lane's notes. On ghūls haunting graves and feeding on dead bodies see Lane, *Modern Egyptians*, chap. x.; *Arabian Nights*, end of note 21 to Introduction and addition by editor, with reference to a passage in Maķrīzī's *Khiṭaṭ*, to note 39, chap. x. For ghūl as a demon producing hydrophobia (al-Madīna) see Burton's *Pilgrimage*, chap. xviii. — *Ṣaidāna*, a kind of ghūl, is an Ethiopic loanword; see Nöldeke, *Neue Beiträge*, p. 50.

Bibliography: Besides the above references, *LA*, s.v. and especially, p. 21 *sq.*; al-Djāḥiẓ *Kitāb al-ḥayawān* (Cairo 1325), vi. 48; cf. van Vloten, *WZKM*, vii. 178; Wellhausen, *Reste*, p. 137 *sq.*; *Ḥamāsa*, p. 12; Nöldeke, in Hasting's *Encycl. of Religion*, i. 670.

GHULĀT. [See GHĀLĪ].

GHUSL is the so-called "major" ritual ablution, which the law ordains for a *djunub*, i.e. a man who is in a state of major ritual impurity (cf. the article DJANĀBA). The *ghusl* consists in washing the whole body. The formulation, previously, of the *nīya* (intention) is indispensable for this and the believer has to be careful that not only is every impurity removed from his body but also that the water moistens every part of his body and his hair.

Bibliography: The chapter on purity (*ṭahāra*) in the collections on Tradition and the Fiķh books; R. Strothmann, *Kultus der Zaiditen* (Strassburg 1912), p. 21 *sq.*; A. J. Wensinck, in *Isl.*, i. 101 *sq.*; iv. 219 *sq.*; Th. W. Juynboll, *Handbuch des Islamischen Rechts*, Leiden 1910, p. 56 *sq.* 165 *sq.*

H

ḤABĪB AL-NADJDJĀR (the carpenter), the saint of Anṭākiya, after whom Mount Silpius is called by the Arabs, because of a much visited tomb, alleged to be his. This Muslim saint is no other than the Agabus mentioned in *Acts* xi. 27—30 and xxi. 10 *sq.*, and his legend, which is related in Sūra xxxvi. 13 *sq.*, although his name is not mentioned, is consequently of Christian origin. When Allāh, as is there related, sent two apostles and afterwards a third (their names are variously given by the commentators) to convert the inhabitants and the latter threatened them with death if they did not give up preaching, a man came running from the most distant part of the town, who warned his fellow-citizens to believe the messengers and proclaimed himself a believer. The wrath of the people was thereupon turned against him and, when they were putting him to death, they cried in scoffing tones to him "Enter thou into paradise", but he rejoiced that he was worthy of the high honour of martyrdom. Allāh thereupon put all the blasphemers to death and without sending an army against them: a single cry (a voice from heaven) was heard and all were dead.

That man, say the expositors of the Ḳur'ān, was Ḥabīb al-Nadjdjār, a carpenter who made idols but had become a convert, when he saw the miracles performed by the apostles. As it appears from the Ḳur'ānic account as if Ḥabīb had prided himself on his martyr's death after he had suffered it, we find in al-Dimashḳī, *Nukhbat al-dahr* (ed. Mehren, p. 206) the fantastic story, that Ḥabīb took his decapitated head in his left hand and placed it in his right and walked for three days and nights through the city in this fashion, while the head cried with a loud voice out the verses mentioned in the Ḳur'ān.

Bibliography: The commentaries on Ḳur'ān, Sūra xxxvi.; Ṭabarī, i. 790 *sqq.*; Thaʿlabī, *ʿArā'is al-madjālis*, (Cairo 1312), p. 239.

HĀBĪL and **ḲĀBĪL**, the names given by Muhammadans to the two sons of Adam, mentioned, but not by name, in the Ḳur'ān, who brought an offering to God. Jealous that his sacrifice was rejected the one slew his brother. A raven sent by God, which scratched upon the ground, showed him how he could dispose of the body (Sūra v. 27—32). As this account in the Ḳur'ān, following the Bible narrative, appears bald and uninteresting, Ḳur'ānic exegesis, like the Biblical, endeavours to discover the psychological motives underlying the affair. According to it, the sons of Adam were all born with twin sisters; Ḳābīl's (also sometimes called Ḳain, Ḳā'in and Ḳāyin) was called Aḳlīma, Hābīl's, who was two years younger, Labūdā (the names are given in varying forms). According to one tradition which is traced back to scholars *bi 'l-kitāb al-awwal* (presumably the book of Genesis is meant), Ḳābīl first saw the light in Paradise and Hābīl was born on earth, as also *Pirke de R. Elieser*, 21. Adam demanded that each should marry the other's twin sister; but Ḳābīl wished to marry his own twin sister who was the fairer. It was to be decided by a sacrifice to which of the two the fairer sister was to go (so also *Jebamoth*, 62; *Gen. R.*, 22 etc.). According to another tradition, to which the marriage with a sister was abhorrent, Hābīl was to have married a houri of Paradise, while Ḳābīl had to marry a woman of the Djinns, with which he did not agree. Enraged at the rejection of his sacrifice (according to Ṭabarī, i. 144 *infra*, he had sacrificed fruits of the field of little value, while Hābīl slew his favourite sheep), Ḳābīl slew his twenty year old brother, according to one account following the example of Iblīs, who appeared with a bird in his hand and struck off its head (a similar story is given in *Sanhedrin*, 30). As Hābīl was the first man that had died, the murderer did not know what to do with the corpse; he therefore carried it for a year on his back in a sack to protect him from the birds and wild beasts. He then noticed a raven fighting with another kill his opponent and bury him by scratching the earth over him. Ḳābīl did the same with his brother (similarly in *Pirke de R. Elieser*, 21, while according to *Gen. R.*, 22, the birds and beasts buried Abel). When God said to him: "The voice of thy brother's blood crieth unto Me from the ground. Wherefore hast thou slain him?", Cain replied: "Where is his blood, if I have slain him?"; thereupon God forbade the earth ever again to drink human blood.

Bibliography: Ṭabarī, i. 137 *sq.*; Ibn al-Athīr, p. 30 *sq.*; al-Yaʿḳūbī, i. 4; al-Thaʿlabī, *Ḳiṣaṣ al-anbiyā'* (ed. Cairo 1325), p. 34—37; al-Kisā'ī, *Ḳiṣaṣ al-anbiyā'*, ed. Eisenberg, p. 70—75; Grünbaum, *Neue Beiträge* etc., p. 68; Weil, *Legenden* etc., p. 38—40.

ḤADATH (A.), ritual impurity. The law recognises two conditions of ritual impurity which are distinguished from one another as "major" and "minor" *ḥadath*. A Muslim in a condition of *ḥadath* can only regain his ritual purity (*ṭahāra*) by the prescribed ritual ablutions (*ghusl* or *wuḍū'* respectively); cf. DJANĀBA, GHUSL and WUḌŪ'. Not only is a *muḥdith* (a person in a condition of "minor" *ḥadath*) forbidden to perform the *ṣalāt*, but also he is not allowed to make the *ṭawāf* around the Kaʿba nor to touch a copy of the Ḳur'ān; further the *ṣalāt* and *ṭawāf* of a *muḥdith* are legally invalid. The same regulations apply to a case of "major" *ḥadath*; but there are a few additional rules applicable to the latter. Th. W. Juynboll, *Handleiding*, ed. 1930, p. 167 *sq.*

ḤADD (A., plural *ḥudūd*), boundary, limit, stipulation, also barrier, obstacle. As a scientific term the word is used in several senses.

In the Ḳur'ān, where it is always found in the plural, it means the "limits" laid down by God, i.e. the provisions of the Law, whether commands or prohibitions. It appears in this sense at the end of several verses which contain legal provisions, e.g. Sūra ii. 187, where it is said after the exposition of the rules regarding fasts: "These are God's *ḥudūd* (the bounds prescribed by God), come not too near them" (lest ye be in danger of crossing them). Cf. also Sūra ii. 229 *sq.*, where the law of divorce is laid down, and other passages. According to Kazimirski (note to Sūra ii. 187) the expression recalls the *sepes legis*, the hedge drawn round the Mosaic law.

In Muslim criminal law *ḥadd* means an unalterable punishment prescribed by canon law, which is considered a "right of God" (*ḥaḳḳ Allāh*). (cf. the article ʿADHĀB). These punishments are 1. stoning or scourging for illicit intercourse (*zinā*ʾ, q.v.); 2. scourging for falsely accusing (*ḳadhf*, q.v.) a married woman of adultery; 3. the same punishment for the drinking of wine and other intoxicating liquors; 4. cutting off the hands for theft; 5. various punishments for robbery which differ according to circumstances, cf. Sūra, v. 33 *sq*. — Although the above mentioned breaches of the law are considered very serious, the criminal can nevertheless hope for the mercy of God, because he has offended against Him. If he denies the deed and refutes the accusations brought against him, the judges are recommended not to press him further, but to give him every possible opportunity to clear himself; for further details see Th. W. Juynboll, *Handbuch des islāmischen Gesetzes*, p. 300 *sqq*. and the 4th (Dutch) edition, Leiden 1930, p. 307 *sq*.

In philosophy *ḥadd* means definition; according to the *Taʿrīfāt* of al-Djurdjānī it is the qualities that differentiate an object. The definition is perfect when it gives the genus proximum and the differentia specifica, e.g. man is an *animal rationale*. There is a kind of definition, which places the object to be defined between two limits so that it is the end of one and the beginning of the other.

Ḥudūd is also the name given to the definitions which stand at the beginning of various sciences, e.g. at the beginning of Euclid's geometry; the postulates are called *muṣādarāt* (*Codex Leidensis* 399, 1. *Euclidis Elementa*, ed. Besthorn and Heiberg, 1893).

In astronomy *ḥadd* means certain areas under each sign of the zodiac, which are each allotted to one of the five planets.

Among the mystics *ḥadd* and particularly the participle *maḥdūd* means the finiteness of creatures in contrast to the infiniteness of God; man is limited and bounded (*maḥdūd*) in space and time.

ḤADĪTH (A.), Tradition. The word *ḥadīth* means primarily a communication or narrative in general whether religious or profane, then it has the particular meaning of a record of actions or sayings of the Prophet and his companions. In the latter sense the whole body of the sacred Tradition of the Muḥammadans is called "the *ḥadīth*" and its science *ʿilm al-ḥadīth*.

I. Subject-matter and Character of Ḥadīth. Even among the heathen Arabs (see I. Goldziher, *Muhamm. Stud.*, i. 41, note 8) it was considered a virtue to follow the "*sunna*" of one's forefathers (*sunna* is properly the way one is accustomed to go, i.e. use and wont, ancient tradition). But in Islām the *sunna* could no longer consist in following the customs and usages of heathen ancestors. The Muslim community had to hold up a new *sunna*. Every believer had now to take the conduct of the Prophet and his companions as a model for himself in all the affairs of life and every endeavour was made to preserve information regarding it.

At first the *ṣaḥābī's* (i.e. people who had lived in the society of the Prophet) were the best authority for a knowledge of the *sunna* of Muḥammad. They had themselves listened to the Prophet and witnessed his actions with their own eyes. Later the Muslims had to be content with the communications of the *tābiʿūn* (i.e. "successors", people of the first generation after Muḥammad), who had received their information from the *ṣaḥābī's* and then, in following generations, with the accounts of the so-called "successors of the successors" (*tābiʿū al-tābiʿīn* i.e. people of he second generation after Muḥammad, who had consorted with the successors), and so on.

The traditions retained the form of personal statements for several generations; every perfect *ḥadīth* therefore consists of two parts. The first contains the names of the persons who have handed on the substance of the tradition to one another; this part is called the *isnād* (or also *sanad*) i.e. the "support", i.e. for the trustworthiness of the statement. He who communicates the tradition (A) says "I have heard from B. (or "B has told me") on the authority of C", and so on, whereupon the whole chain of transmission should follow, beginning with A, the last authority, and ending with the original authority. The second part is the *matn* or text, the real substance of the report. For details see Goldziher, *op. cit.*, ii. 6—8.

After Muḥammad's death the original religious ideas and usages which had prevailed in the original community could not remain permanently unaltered. A new period of development set in. The learned began systematically to develop the doctrine of duties and dogmatics in accordance with the new conditions. After the great conquests Islām covered an enormous area, new ideas and institutions were borrowed from the peoples conquered, and not only Christianity and Judaism, but Hellenism, Zoroastrianism and Buddhism also influenced the life and thought of the Muslims of the day in many respects.

Nevertheless the principle was steadfastly adhered to, that in Islām only the *sunna* of the Prophet and the original Muslim community could supply a rule of conduct for believers. This of necessity soon led to deliberate forgery of Tradition. The transmitters brought the words and actions of the Prophet into agreement with the views of the later period. Thus numerous interested traditions were put into circulation, in which Muḥammad was made to say or do something which was at that time considered the proper view. Christian texts, sayings from the Apostles and the Apocrypha, Jewish views, doctrines of Greek philosophers, etc. which had found favour in certain Muslim circles, appear in the *ḥadīth* simply as sayings of Muḥammad (Goldziher, *op. cit.*, ii., 382 *sqq.*; do. *Neutestamentliche Elemente in der Traditionslitteratur des Islam*, in *Oriens Christianus*, 1902, p. 390 *sq.*). No scruples were felt in making the Prophet expand in this form the legends or stories only briefly outlined in the Ḳurʾān, or proclaim new doctrines and dogmas, etc. A very large portion of these sayings ascribed to the Prophet deals with the *aḥkām* (legal provisions), religious obligations, *ḥalāl* and *ḥarām* (i.e. what is "allowed" and "forbidden"), with ritual purity, laws regarding food, criminal and civil law, and also with courtesy and good manners; further they deal with dogma, retribution at the last judgment, Hell and Paradise, angels, creation, revelation, the earlier prophets, and in a word with everything that concerns the relations between God and man; many traditions also contain edifying sayings and moral teachings in the name of the Prophet.

In course of time the records of Muḥammad's

words and deeds increased more and more innu mber and copiousness. In the early centuries after Muḥammad's death there reigned great diversity of opinion in the Muslim community on many questions of the most diverse nature. Each party therefore endeavoured to support its views as far as possible with sayings and decision sof the Prophet. He who could base his view on these was certainly right and thus arose the numerous utterly contradictory traditions on the *sunna* of the Prophet. In the great partisan struggles also, both sides used to make an appeal to Muḥammad (Goldziher, *Muhamm. Stud.*, ii. 88 *sq.*). Thus for example the Prophet was said to have prophesied the foundation of their dominion to the ʿAbbāsids. In general not only the course of later political events and religious movements but also the new social conditions, that first arose out of the great conquests (the increasing luxury etc.), were made to have been prophesied in apocalyptic-prophetic form to justify them in the eyes of the community. A special branch of these prophetic traditions is formed by the sayings ascribed to Muḥammad regarding the merits of various places and districts in the lands which were only at a later period to be conquered by the Muslims (Goldziher, *op. cit.*, ii. 128 *sq.*).

The majority of traditions then cannot be regarded as really reliable historical accounts of the *sunna* of the Prophet. On the contrary, they express opinions which had come to be held in authoritative circles in the early centuries after Muḥammad's death and were only then ascribed to the Prophet. Scholarship is deeply indebted to I. Goldziher (see his *Muhamm. Stud.*, Halle 1890 and other works) and C. Snouck Hurgronje (cf. his *Verspreide Geschriften* vol. ii., in which his writings on Muḥammadan Law have been collected) for having first clearly demonstrated the true character and historical importance of the *ḥadīth* in this respect.

Although the invention and wanton dissemination of false traditions was condemned by Muslims, alleviating elements were recognised in certain circumstances, particularly when it was a question of edifying sayings and moral teachings in the name of the Prophet. For details see Goldziher *op. cit.*, ii. 131 *sq.*, 153 *sq.*; do., in *ZDMG*, lxi. 860.

The *ḥadīth* is held in great reverence next to the Ḳurʾān throughout the whole Muḥammadan world and the scruples which were originally raised in certain circles against the dissemination and recording in writing of Muḥammad's words (cf. Goldziher, *Kämpfe um die Stellung des Ḥadīth im Islam*, in *ZDMG*, lxi. 860 *sq.*), were soon overcome. In some cases it is even believed that the actual "word of God" is to be found in the *ḥadīth* as well as in the Ḳurʾān. Such traditions, usually beginning with the words "God said" are designated *ḥadīth ḳudsī* (or also *ilāhī*, i.e. "holy" or "divine" *ḥadīth*) by Muslim scholars in opposition to the ordinary *ḥadīth nabawī* (*ḥadīth* of the Prophet). A list of such holy traditions is given in Ibn ʿArabī, *Mishkāt al-anwār*, Ḥalab 1346.

II. Muslim criticism of Tradition. According to the Muslim view, a tradition can only be considered credible when its *isnād* offers an unbroken series of reliable authorities. The critical investigation of *isnād*'s has caused the Muslim scholars to make thorough researches. They endeavoured not only to ascertain the names and circumstances of the authorities (*ridjāl*) in order to investigate when and where they lived, and which of them had been personally acquainted with the other, but also to test their reliability, truthfulness and accuracy in transmitting the texts, to make certain which of them were "reliable" (*thiḳa*). This criticism of the authorities was called *al-djarḥ wa'l-taʿdīl* (wounding and authentication) (Goldziher, *Muhamm. Stud.*, ii. 143 *sq.*). The so-called "knowledge of the men" (*maʿrifat al-ridjāl*) was considered indispensable for every student of *ḥadīth*; all the commentaries on the collections of Tradition therefore contain more or less copious details concerning the authorities. Special works are also devoted to this subject, among them many of the so-called *ṭabaḳāt* works (i.e. biographies arranged in "classes" of various scholars, transmitters of Tradition and other persons, cf. O. Loth, *Ursprung und Bedeutung der Ṭabaḳāt*, in *ZDMG*, xxiii. 593—614), for example the famous "class book" of Ibn Saʿd (died 230/844) and the *Ṭabaḳāt al-ḥuffāẓ* of al-Dhahabī (died 748/1347). To this class also belong the works on those "weak" in transmitting, e.g. Nasāʾī's *Kitāb al-ḍuʿafāʾ* (Goldziher, ii. 141 *sq.*) and the biographies of the *ṣaḥābī's*, e.g. *al-Iṣāba fī tamyīz al-ṣaḥāba* of Ibn Ḥadjar al-ʿAsḳalānī (died 852/1448) and *Usd al-ghāba fī maʿrifat al-ṣaḥāba* of Ibn al-Athīr (died 630/1232).

Now opinions on the reliability of the authorities might differ very considerably. The same person, whose communications might be absolutely trusted in the view of one party, was sometimes considered by others exceedingly "weak" in transmission or even as a liar. Originally even the authority of many highly respected contemporaries of Muḥammad was not generally recognised; for example the truthfulness of Abū Huraira was hotly disputed by very many. The verdict usually differed with the standpoint of the party, and this often gave rise to bitter quarrels. We must, however, remember in this connection that the substance of the transmitted statements was really always the main thing. If the truthfulness of the authorities was disputed, it was in reality almost always the bias of their substance that aroused opposition. The ultimate decision then rested not on the reputation of the authorities but rather on the substance of the accounts transmitted by them.

But at a later period, after the ritual, dogma and the most important political and social institutions had taken definite shape in the second and third centuries, there arose a certain *communis opinio* regarding the reliability of most transmitters of Tradition and the value of their statements. All the main principles of doctrine had already been established in the writings of Mālik b. Anas, al-Shāfiʿī and other scholars, regarded as authoritative in different circles, and mainly on the authority of traditional sayings of Muḥammad. In the long run no one dared to doubt the truth of these traditions; nor was it any longer possible to regard men like Abū Huraira, who had put these accounts into circulation, as liars. Even traditions which contained the most obvious anachronisms were generally considered reliable. Only such traditions were rejected as could not be brought into agreement with what had been long regarded by the majority as well established. But on the whole the inclination was to give credence to such traditions also, at least when it was possible to explain them in a conciliatory spirit. The old quarrels had now in course of time lost all practical interest for the younger generations and it was found that the majority of the traditions connected with them, although sharply opposed to one another, could very often be reconciled to one another by skilful interpretation of the contents. The rejection of a tradition thus came to be considered an extreme measure, only to be resorted to in desperation. The many contradictory traditions on the same subject, which have been adopted side by side as reliable in the great collections of Tradition, thus often form priceless evidence to the historian of the internal development of Islām. The traditions were not, however, all considered of equal value by Muslim scholars, but divided into categories distinguished by definite technical terms according to the completeness of their *isnād's*, the reliability of their transmitters etc.

III. The classification of Tradition. *a.* In the first place the three following categories are distinguished: 1. *ṣaḥīḥ* (sound); this name is given to the utterly faultless tradition in whose *isnād* there is no *ʿilla* (weakness) and whose tendency does not contradict any generally prevalent belief. 2. If a tradition is not absolutely faultless, e.g. because its *isnād* is not quite complete, or because there is no perfect agreement regarding the reliability of the authorities for it, it is called *ḥasan* (beautiful). 3. On the other hand, every tradition is considered *ḍaʿīf* (weak), against which serious doubts can be raised, e.g. by reason of its contents or because one or more of its transmitters is considered unreliable or not quite orthodox.

b. Further it may happen that the value of a statement is uncertain because some remarks by a transmitter have been interpolated among the words of the Prophet and it is impossible accurately to separate these two components of the text; such a tradition is called *mudradj*. — If a tradition is transmitted by only one informant, whose authority besides is considered weak, it is called *matrūk* ("abandoned", "no longer considered"). — If a tradition is considered absolutely false, it is called *mawḍūʿ* ("invented").

c. All traditions do not deal with sayings or doings of the Prophet; we also find in the *ḥadīth* information regarding the *ṣaḥābī's* and Successors. In this connection a distinction is made between: 1. *marfūʿ* a tradition which contains a statement about the Prophet; 2. *mawḳūf*, a tradition that refers only to sayings or doings of the *ṣaḥābī's*; 3. *maḳṭūʿ*, a tradition which does not at most go farther back than the first generation after Muḥammad and deals only with sayings or doings of the *tābiʿūn*.

d. The following distinctions are made according to the completeness of the *isnād*. If a tradition can be traced through an unbroken chain of trustworthy authorities to a companion of the Prophet, it is usually called *musnad* ("supported"). If it also contains special observations regarding all the authorities (e.g. if it is expressly mentioned that all the authorities swore an oath as they handed on the tradition, or that they all gave one another the hand), the tradition is called *musalsal* (in the first case *musalsal al-ḥalf*, in the second *musalsal al-yad*, etc.). Cf. W. Ahlwardt, *Katal. der arab. HSS. der Kgl Bibliothek zu Berlin*, ii. 267—273.

If the *isnād*, although complete, is comparatively very short because the last authority only received the statement from the original authority through the intermediary of few persons, the tradition is called *ʿālī*. This is considered a great advantage, because the possibility that errors have crept into the tradition is very small in this case. On long-lived transmitters of tradition cf. Goldziher, *op. cit.*, ii. 170, 174.

If the chain of transmitters is unbroken and complete, it is called *muttaṣil*, in the opposite case *munḳaṭiʿ* (in the general sense), but as a rule *munḳaṭiʿ* (in the particular sense) means a tradition in whose *isnād* the authority in the second generation (the *tābiʿī*) is wanting. — *Mursal* is the name given to a tradition handed down by a *tābiʿī* about the Prophet, when it is not known from what *ṣaḥābī* he received his statement. The question whether such traditions are valid was answered in different ways; the older teachers such as Abū Ḥanīfa and Mālik b. Anas answered in the affirmative but the later ones in the negative (cf. e.g., *ZDMG*, xxiii. 595, note 3). — If two or more transmitters are lacking anywhere in the *isnād* (or, according to some other scholars, if they fail consecutively), the tradition is called *muʿḍal*. — If the authorities in the *isnād* are only connected by the preposition *ʿan* (e.g. A *ʿan* B, i.e. A from B), it is possible that they were not personally acquainted with one another, but only heard the statement through the intermediary of other persons not mentioned in the *isnād*. In this case the tradition is called *muʿanʿan* (for further information cf. Goldziher, *Muhamm. Stud.*, ii. 248). — *Mubham* is the name of a tradition in which one of the authorities is only indicated in the *isnād* as "a man", without mention of his name.

e. The following categories are distinguished according to the *ṭuruḳ* ("ways" i.e. according to the different chains of transmitters): 1. *mutawātir* is a communication handed down on many sides, which was generally known from very early times and to which objections have never been raised; 2. *mashhūr* is a statement, which is handed down by at least three different reliable authorities, or, according to another view, a statement which, although widely disseminated later, was originally only transmitted by one person in the first generation; 3. *ʿazīz* is the name of a statement which is transmitted by at least two persons and was not so generally disseminated as those traditions which are called *mutawātir* or *mashhūr*; 4. *āḥād* are traditions given by only one authority; 5. *gharīb* is in general a rare tradition; with reference to the *isnād*, *gharīb muṭlaḳ* means a tradition which is transmitted in the second generation only by one *tābiʿī*; if a tradition is transmitted by only one definite person of later generations, it is called *gharīb* "in reference to that person" (*gharīb bi 'l-nisbat ilā shakhṣ muʿaiyan*). A tradition which contains foreign or rare expressions in the text is also called *gharīb* (with reference to the contents).

These technical terms were not originally understood in the same sense by all Muslim scholars. For example it is expressly mentioned that the Imām al-Shāfiʿī made no distinction between *maḳṭūʿ* and *munḳaṭiʿ*; in later works also there is no absolute agreement concerning all these definitions. For details see F. Risch, *Commentar des ʿIzz al-Dīn Abū ʿAbd Allāh über die Kunstausdrücke der Traditionswissenschaft nebst Erläuterungen*, Leipzig (dissertation) 1895; cf. Djurdjānī, *Kitāb al-taʿrīfāt* (ed. G. Flügel) and: *A Dictionary of Technical Terms* (ed. A. Sprenger and others). The division of traditions into different categories is also discussed in the general introductory works on the principles of *ʿilm al-riwāya* (i.e. science of transmission). Such introductory works are amongst others the three following: 1. *ʿUlūm al-ḥadīth* of Ibn al-Ṣalāḥ (died 643/1245); cf. Goldziher, *op. cit.*, ii. 187 *sq.*; Brockelmann, *GAL*²,

i. 440, *Suppl.* i. 610 *sq.*; 2. *al-Taḳrīb wa 'l-taysīr* of al-Nawawī (died 676/1277), with its commentary the *Tadrīb al-rāwī* of al-Suyūṭī (died 911/1505); 3. *Nukhbat al-fikr* of Ibn Ḥadjar (died 852/1448) with a commentary by the author himself, published by N. Lees in the *Bibl. Indica*, No. 37 of the second series, Calcutta 1862.

IV. The Collections of Tradition. Numerous collections of traditions have been prepared by different scholars. Some of these works have obtained almost canonical standing among later Muslims. An official codification of Tradition, which would be exclusively valid, has however never been made.

At first traditions were not arranged according to their contents but only according to their transmitters (*ʿala 'l-ridjāl*). Such a collection was called *musnad* after the traditions with complete *isnād*'s incorporated in it. This name was thus transferred from the single tradition to the whole collection. The best known of these works is the *Musnad* of Aḥmad b. Ḥanbal (died 241/855). For further details on this collection see Goldziher, *Neue Materialien zur Litteratur des Überlieferungswesens bei den Muḥammedanern*, in *ZDMG*, l. 465—506.

Such *musnad*'s were also formed at a later period; some scholars, for example, arranged the traditions contained in the great collections for greater convenience in alphabetical order, others incorporated the traditions which were mentioned in the *Muwaṭṭaʾ* of Mālik b. Anas or other similar works not planned as proper collections of Tradition in separate collections etc. (see Goldziher, *Muhamm. Stud.*, ii. 226 *sqq.*).

But as a rule the later collections of tradition were almost all arranged according to the contents of the traditions. Such a collection arranged "according to chapters" (*ʿala 'l-abwāb*) is called *muṣannaf* (i.e. arranged). Six of these *muṣannaf* works were in course of time generally recognised by the orthodox Muslim world as authoritative; they all arose in the third century A.H.; they are the collections by 1. al-Bukhārī (died 256/870), 2. Muslim (died 261/875), 3. Abū Dāwūd (died 275/888), 4. al-Tirmidhī (died 279/892), 5. al-Nasāʾī (died 303/915) and 6. Ibn Mādjā (died 273/886). These works are usually called briefly the "six books" (*al-kutub al-sitta*) or also "the six *ṣaḥīḥ's*" i.e. the "sound" (i.e. the correct, reliable collections). They were, so to speak, looked upon as sacred books of second rank next to the Ḳurʾān, God's own word. The collections by al-Bukhārī and Muslim were held in particularly high esteem. They are known as the "two *ṣaḥīḥ*'s" (*al-ṣaḥīḥān*) i.e. the two collections particularly recognised as authoritative. Only traditions which are recognised as absolutely *ṣaḥīḥ* are included in these works. In this respect, however, the *shurūṭ* (i.e. the "stipulations") of Bukhārī were not the same as those of Muslim (Goldziher, *op. cit.*, ii. 247). Al-Bukhārī has besides often added fairly copious notes to the headings of his chapters, which are quite lacking in Muslim's *Ṣaḥīḥ*. Both trace the traditions where possible to different *ṭuruḳ* and both collections contain not only traditions relating to "canon law" and to the "permitted" and "forbidden", but also many historical, ethical and dogmatic traditions (for details, see Goldziher, *op. cit.*, ii. 234—248).

On the other hand the traditions included in the works of the four other compilers deal almost exclusively with the *sunna*'s, i.e. use and wont. Hence their collections are usually put together as "the four *sunan* works". They further contain not only the traditions which are considered *ṣaḥīḥ*, but also the "beautiful" ones and in general all traditions on which the learned have relied in their deductions of the law even if doubts can be raised against their *isnād*. When the collectors think that one of the traditions given by them should be rejected they usually call the reader's attention to the fact. Cf. Goldziher, *op. cit.*, ii. 248 *sq.*

The prestige enjoyed by these six books in Islām is readily explained. In the third century circumstances were peculiarly favourable for the work of the collector of traditions. A certain unanimity had been attained on all questions of law and doctrine and a definite opinion regarding the value of most traditions had been formed by the majority of Muslim scholars. It was thus now possible to proceed to collect all that was recognised as reliable. The merit of al-Bukhārī and the compilers of the other *ṣaḥīḥ*'s therefore lay not so much in the fact that (as is often wrongly stated) they decided for the first time which of the numerous traditions in circulation were genuine and which false, — for the personal opinion of the compilers would have had scarcely any appreciable influence on the prevailing opinion — but rather in the fact that they brought together everything that was recognised as genuine in orthodox circles in their time, (cf. Snouck Hurgronje, *Verspr. Geschr.* ii., p. 295).

Although other famous collections arose in the third century, e.g. the *Sunan* of ʿAbd Allāh al-Dārimī (died 255/868), these works were never permanently able to attain such great prestige in the Muslim world as the six *ṣaḥīḥ*'s. Even the general recognition of the latter works themselves was only attained very gradually; Ibn Mādja's collection in particular was for long viewed with suspicion on account of the many "weak" traditions in it. Besides, in spite of the great authority of the "six books", it was not considered improper to criticise freely traditions, which, although included in the great collections, were not universally recognised as *ṣaḥīḥ*. ʿAlī al-Dāraḳuṭnī (died 385/995) for example compiled a work in which he proved the weakness of 200 traditions given in al-Bukhārī and Muslim (cf. Goldziher, *op. cit.*, ii. 257).

Even at a later period new collections were made by many scholars. The work of these late collectors of tradition was limited chiefly, however, to the preparation of more or less comprehensive compilations in which they exerpted the contents of the "six books" (and sometimes at the same time of other famous collections like that of Ibn Ḥanbal) and arranged them in different ways. One of these is Baghawī's (died 510/1116) collection called *Maṣābīḥ al-sunna* (i.e. the lamps of the *sunna*), which, on account of its fullness and convenience, has always been popular among Muḥammadans. It contains a selection of traditions which are taken from older collections with the *isnād*'s omitted. The recension of this collection by Walī al-Dīn al-Tibrīzī is particularly well-known; it bears the title *Mishkāt al-maṣābīḥ* (the name is taken from Ḳurʾān, xxiv. 35 and is usually interpreted the "niche of the lamps"). Among large collections of the later period we may mention al-Suyūṭī's (died 911/1505) two works entitled *Djamʿ al-djawāmiʿ* and *al-Djāmiʿ al-ṣaghīr*. Suyūṭī's main object was to give a comprehensive compilation of extant collections (for details see W. Ahlwardt, *Katalog der arab. HSS. der Kgl. Bibliothek zu Berlin*, ii. 155 *sq.*). Other compilers confined themselves to a definite section of the traditions contained in the larger collections (e.g. to the "moral"), or to a definite number of important traditions. Thus arose, for example, the numerous so-called "*Arbaʿīn*" works (i.e. collections which contain 40 important traditions).

As the substance of the *ḥadīth* was in many respects no longer intelligible to the later generations of believers, many scholars felt compelled to prepare commentaries on the collections of Tradition. Obsolete words and expressions required explanation; in particular many contradictions had to be explained, or rendered harmless by artificial "explanation". Most commentators further dealt with the prescriptions to be deduced from the traditions and the divergent opinions which had been championed by different scholars in this connexion. Among the best known copious commentaries we may mention those of Ibn Ḥadjar (died 852/1448) and al-Ḳasṭallānī (died 932/1517) on the *Ṣaḥīḥ* of al-Bukhārī and of al-Nawawī (died 676/1277) on the *Ṣaḥīḥ* of Muslim (cf. C. Brockelmann, *GAL*², i. 163 *sq.*, *Suppl.* i. 255 *sqq.*).

The Shīʿīs judged *ḥadīth* from their own standpoint and only considered such traditions reliable as were based on the authority of ʿAlī and his adherents. They have therefore their own works on this subject and hold the following five works in particularly high esteem: 1. *al-Kāfī* of Muḥammad b. Yaʿḳūb al-Kulīnī (died 328/939); 2. *Man lā yastaḥḍiruhu 'l-faḳīh* of Muḥammad b. ʿAlī b. Bābūya al-Ḳummī (died 381/991); 3. *Tahdhīb al-aḥkām* and 4. *al-Istibṣār fī-ma 'khtalafa fīhi 'l-akhbār* (extract from the preceding) of Muḥammad al-Ṭūsī (died 459/1067); and 5. *Nahdj al-balāgha* (alleged sayings of ʿAlī) of ʿAlī b. Ṭāhir al-Sharīf al-Murtaḍā (died 436/1044) or of his brother Rāḍī al-Dīn al-Baghdādī; cf. C. Brockelmann *GAL*², i. 199, 510 *sq.*, *Suppl.* i. 321, 704 *sq.*; E. Sell, *The Faith of Islām* London 1880, p. 69, note 2; Goldziher, *op. cit.*, ii. 148, note 4; do., *Beiträge zur Literaturgesch. der Shīʿa*, in *Sitz.-Ber. Wiener Akad.*, *phil.-hist. Cl.*, lxxviii. (1874), p. 508.

V. The Transmission of Tradition. The general view of Muslims that a knowledge of sacred learning could only be obtained through oral instruction from a teacher, who had himself acquired his knowledge in this way (cf. C. Snouck Hurgronje, in *ZDMG*, l. 145), was from ancient times held to be particularly applicable to Tradition. The traditions had to be "heard" and students even used to take long journeys to attend the lectures of such persons as were famous as reliable authorities (*ḥamala*, i.e. properly "bearers") of Tradition. In many sayings of the Prophet, travel "*fī ṭalab al-ʿilm*" (i.e. to search for knowledge) is recommended as work pleasing to God. For further information regarding those *ṭalab* journeys and their degeneration (how, for example, vain scholars prided themselves on having travelled through far distant lands to "hear" a few almost unknown traditions) see Goldziher, *op. cit.*, ii. 175—193.

In transmission, the traditions were delivered orally by the teacher. It was also very usual for one of the students to read out a copy while the others listened and the teacher when necessary improved what was read and gave explanatory notes. In this case also it was the custom to say of traditions learned in this way: N.N. (the teacher) told me (*ḥaddathanī* or *akhbaranī* namely *ḳirāʾatan ʿalaihi*, i.e. while the tradition was read in his presence). One who had heard traditions in this way under the direction of a teacher, could now in his turn again communicate them to others and often received from his teacher a so-called *idjāza* (i.e. sanction, permit, namely for further transmission of these traditions) for this purpose. The old method of transmitting traditions, however, was not always held in respect. The copying and collation of written texts often became the main object and oral transmission fell quite into disuse. The traditions were then simply copied and permission was obtained to transmit them with the usual formula *ḥaddathanī* (i.e. "N.N. told me"), just as if the contents had been acquired by direct oral intercourse from the teacher. For details of the *idjāza* custom and its degeneration in Islām cf. Goldziher, *op. cit.*, ii. 188—193; A. Sprenger, in *ZDMG*, x. 9 *sq.*; W. Ahlwardt, *Katal. der arab. HSS. der Kgl. Bibliothek zu Berlin*, i. 54—95.

In certain circles the copying of traditions (*kitābat al-ḥadīth*) was originally regarded as actually forbidden. Credence was only given to those traditions which had been preserved in the memories of reliable men and orally transmitted by them, but not to texts copied often without sufficient care or from unreliable records; cf. Ibn ʿAsākir's warning: "Strive eagerly to obtain traditions and get them from the men themselves, not from written records, lest they be affected by the disease of corruption of the text" (Goldziher, *op. cit.*, ii. 200). Nevertheless, scholars who utterly abstained from paper and books are always quoted as the exceptions only, and the recording in writing of Tradition seems to have been the general custom even in the most ancient times. At the same time it could of course be acknowledged in this connexion that the writing only served to aid the memory and that the knowledge was really to be preserved "by heart" and not on the paper. For details on the writing down of *ḥadīth* and the objections to it, see Goldziher, *op. cit.*, ii. 194—202; do., in *ZDMG*, l. 475, 489; lxi. 862; A. Sprenger, *loc. cit.*, x. 1 *sq.*; do., in *JASB*, xxv. 303—329.

Bibliography: Besides the books and treatises mentioned: El-Bokhari, *Les traditions islamiques*, trad. de l'arabe avec notes et index par O. Houdas et W. Marçais (*Public. de l'Ecole des Langues or. viv.*, series iv., vol. vi. *sq.*), i.—iv., Paris 1903—1914; F. Peltier, *Le livre des testaments du Çahîh d'el Bokhâri*, trad. avec éclaircissements et commentaire, Paris 1909; do., *Le livre des ventes du Çahîh d'El-Bokhâri*, trad. avec éclairc. et comm., Paris 1910; do., *Le livre des ventes du Mouwattâ de Mâlik ben Anas*, trad. avec éclairc., Algiers 1911; W. Marçais, *Le taqrîb de En-Nawawi*, traduit et annoté (*Journ. Asiat.*, 9th Series, xvi, xvii, xviii), also separately, Paris 1901; A. N. Matthews, *Mishcât ul-masābīh or a Collection of the most authentic Traditions regarding the Actions and Sayings of Muḥammed*, Calcutta 1809—1810; J. Schacht, *Der Islām*, in *Religionsgeschichtliches Lesebuch*, 16, Tübingen 1931, p. 1—24; Th. Nöldeke, *Zur tendenziösen Gestaltung der Urgeschichte des Islām*'s, in *ZDMG*, lii. 16—33; I. Goldziher, *Die Religion des Islam* (*Kultur der Gegenwart*, T. I, Abt. III, 1. Hälfte, p. 99 *sq.*); do., *Vorlesungen über den Islam*, Heidelberg 1910, p. 40 *sq.*; A. Guillaume, *The Traditions of Islam*, Oxford 1924; H. A. R. Gibb, *Mohammedanism*, London 1949, p. 72—87; M. Muhammad Ali, *A Manual of Hadith* (Lahore s.d.); J. Schacht, *The Origins of Muhammadan Jurisprudence*, Oxford 1950; A. J. Wensinck, *A handbook of early Mu-*

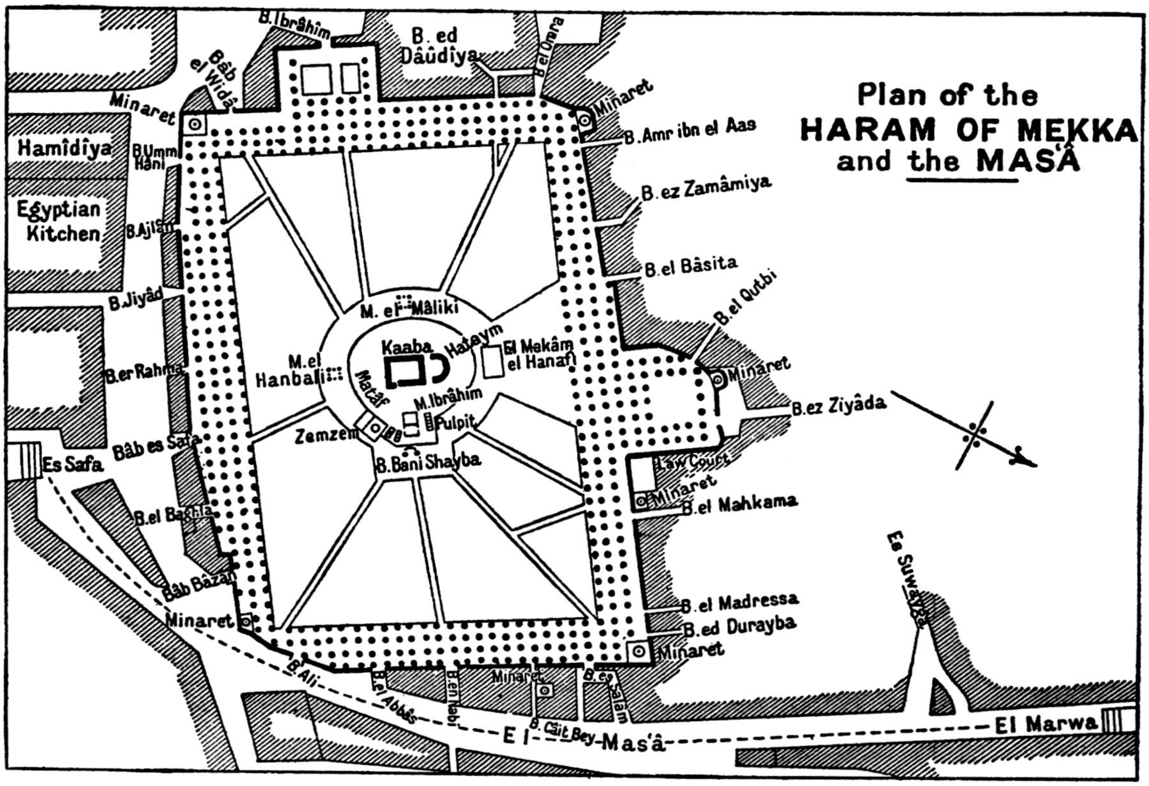

Art. ḤADJDJ

from: E. Rutter, The Holy Cities of Arabia

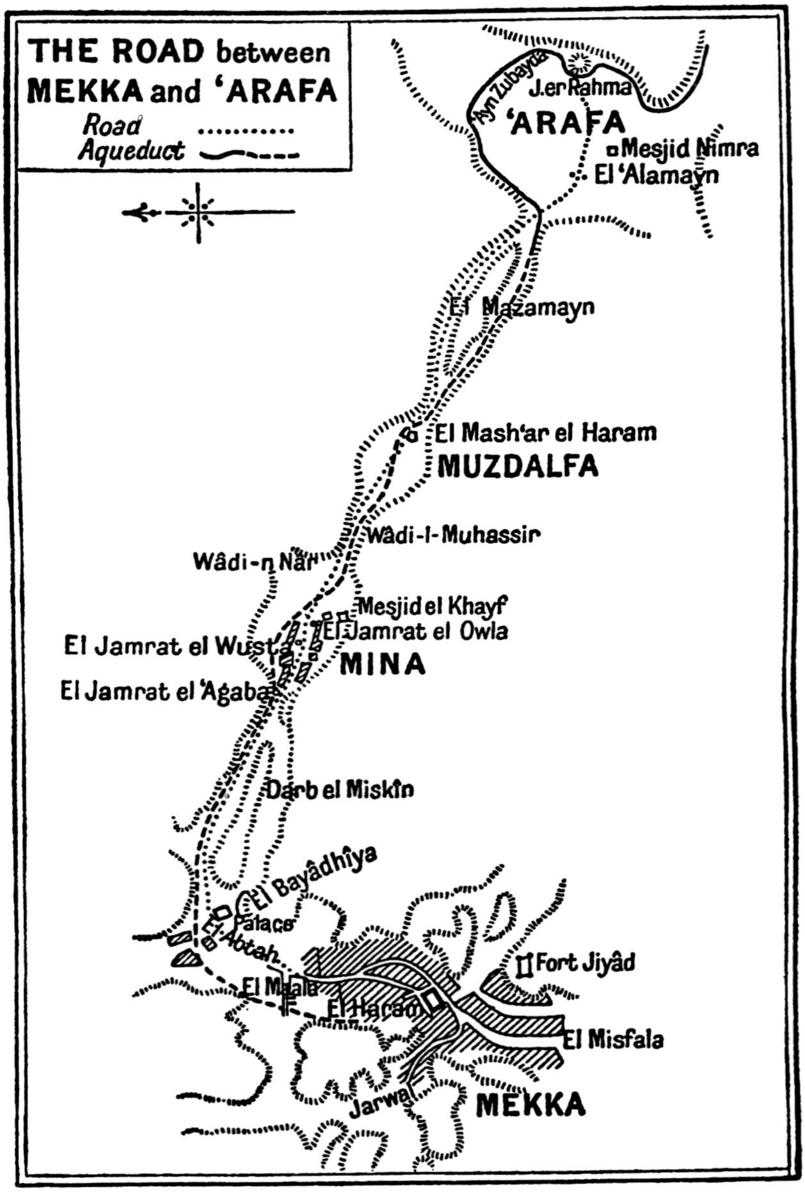

Art. ḤADJDJ — from: E. Rutter, The Holy Cities of Arabia

hammadan tradition, alphabetically arranged, Leyden 1927; do., *Concordance et indices de la tradition musulmane*; *les six livres, le Musnad d'al-Dārimī, le Muwaṭṭa' de Mālik, le Musnad de Aḥmad ibn Ḥanbal*, vol. I, II, Leyden 1933—1936—1943 (continued by J. P. M. Mensing); see also the biliography in Goldziher, *Muhamm. Stud.*, ii. 6.

ḤADJDJ (A.), the pilgrimage to Mecca, ʿArafāt and Minā, the fifth of the five "pillars" of Islām.

I. The islāmic Ḥadjdj.

a. The journey to Mecca. — According to the law every adult Muslim, of either sex, has to perform the Ḥadjdj at least once in the course of his life, provided he is able to do so (cf. Sūra iii. 97). The fulfilment of the last proviso depends on various circumstances. Lunatics and slaves are exempted from the obligation; likewise women who have not a husband or a relative (*dhū maḥram*) to accompany them. The want of the necessary means of subsistence, the inability to provide beasts of burden, the precariousness of the journey, are circumstances which relieve one of the obligation to perform the pilgrimage. The Shāfiʿī school further allows its followers to postpone the pilgrimage beyond the grave provided a deputy is hired out of the estate of the deceased. This explains how the majority of Muslims die without ever having seen Mecca. Even among Caliphs and Sulṭāns many have remained at home all their lives while others have made the pilgrimage several times; even some who were not Muslims have taken part in the Ḥadjdj; their works are invaluable sources for our knowledge of this subject.

Since Muḥammad instituted an absolute lunar year, the Ḥadjdj runs in time through all seasons as it is fixed for certain days in the first half of the month Dhu 'l-Ḥidjdja. When it falls in summer the toils of the journey prove fatal to many a pilgrim. Muḥammad is therefore said to have said: "The pilgrimage is a sort of punishment" (Ibn Mādja, *Sunan, Bāb al-khurūdj ila 'l-Ḥadjdj*). Those pilgrims suffer most who have to come from their homes to Mecca by land either on foot or on horseback. The modern means of conveyance, however, have considerably diminished their number. The pilgrim-caravans only survive out of religious conservatism.

The Syrian caravan followed the ancient trade-route from Damascus through the trans-Jordan territory, the ancient Moabitis, via Maʿān, Madā'in Ṣāliḥ and al-Madīna. It was the largest of the caravans (in 1876, according to C. M. Doughty's estimate, it contained about 6,000 persons) and was accompanied by a *maḥmal* [q.v.]. Blockhouses were built at the stations where food was kept ready and facilities for refreshment provided. According to Burckhardt (*Travels*, ii. 3), the journey from Damascus to al-Madīna took 30 days.

The Egyptian caravan was likewise accompanied by a *maḥmal*; in it was the new *kiswa* for the Kaʿba. According to Lane (*Manners and Customs*, London 1899, p. 493), it usually left Cairo in the last week of Shawwāl and reached Mecca in 37 days, following the route along the sea-coast. (A favourite route for pilgrims from Egypt and the Maghrib used to be from Cairo or somewhere else in the north to one of the harbours on the Red Sea opposite Djidda; cf. Ibn Djubair's journey and al-Batanūnī, *al-Riḥla al-Ḥidjāzīya* [2], p. 27 *sq*.).

A caravan from the ʿIrāḳ made its way across Arabia. Burckhardt, in Appendices I and II to his *Travels*, gives the stations of the caravan from Yemen as well as further geographical notes.

The Saʿūdī Government has not failed to bestow great care on the caravan roads, on providing the pilgrims with water and accomodation and on their hygiene.

The caravans were composed of the most diverse elements; princes, beggars, traders with their wares, Beduins, travellers on foot and on horseback found their place there, which was usually settled by their place of origin, so that people from the same town travelled together. Most pilgrims made an arrangement with a *muḳawwim* who for a definite sum provided for all the necessities of the journey.

The danger of attack by Beduins has always been an unpleasant feature of the pilgrimage; if the pilgrims submitted to being plundered, they usually escaped with their lives, but otherwise not always. The Meccan authorities were finally forced to conclude agreements with the chiefs through whose lands the caravans came, whereby the pilgrims were allowed to travel freely. The authorities had to pay a fixed sum (called *ṣurra*) for this privilege. In the history of the Ḥadjdj there have been many other powers obstructing the pilgrims, e.g. the Ḳarmaṭians, the Egyptian authorities, pirates and the Wahhābīs. Nowadays, however, the Saʿūdī Government has been able to bring about a state of perfect safety.

The arrival of the Syrian and Egyptian caravans with the two *maḥmal*'s was always a great event for the Meccans. Both were received with ceremony; they encamped on certain spots outside the town proper (see the plan of the town in C. Snouck Hurgronje, *Mekka*, i); but in recent years the importance of the *maḥmal* has been much diminished.

The numbers of the pilgrims are fairly well known. We find that in the years before the second World War the number has varied from 36,000 to 108,000 and averages 70,000. Only during the years of economic depression was even the minimum not reached. If Burckhardt could now accompany the pilgrimage again, he would not be able to repeat his observations (*Travels*, ii. 1) made in 1814 on the number of the pilgrims and the pious zeal of the Muslims.

Most pilgrims arrive shortly before the time of the Ḥadjdj; a considerable number, however, even spend the month of Ramaḍān of the year in Mecca, which is considered particularly meritorious. Many ḥādjdjīs also remain in Mecca after they have completed the Ḥadjdj, either to pursue sacred studies or to die in the holy city. The number of pilgrims is usually particularly large when it is expected that the principal day of the Ḥadjdj, the 9th Dhu 'l-Ḥidjdja, will fall on a Friday (*ḥadjdj akbar*). It may further be noted that the Shīʿīs also take part in the pilgrimage; but travellers report that the adherents of ʿAlī do not always have a peaceful time in the holy city. Interesting data on the Ḥadjdj of the Shīʿīs are given in Kazem Zadeh, *Relation d'un pèlerinage à la Mecque*, in *RMM*, xix., 1912, p. 144 *sq*. (also published separately).

b. Arrival in Mecca. The holy ceremonies are performed in a state correspondingly holy; the law therefore recommends the pilgrim as soon as he sets out from home to assume the *iḥrām* [q.v.]. But as in most cases this is not convenient, they generally enter the holy condition when they approach the holy territory. One should enter Mecca as a *muḥrim* and then perform the *ʿumra* [q.v.]. Almost every pilgrim does this as well as the other sacred duties, accompanied by a guide (*shaikh, dalīl, muṭawwif*), who on each occasion pronounces the prescribed formulae, which are then repeated by his protégés. These guides further do all sorts of business for the pilgrims who in their ignorance of the language, of local customs etc., would be for the most part quite helpless without them.

When the sevenfold circumambulation (*ṭawāf*, q.v.) of the Kaʿba and the sevenfold running (*saʿy*, q.v.) between Ṣafā and Marwa has been performed the pilgrim may cut his hair and come out of the *iḥrām*, till the Ḥadjdj proper begins. But if the *iḥrām* has been assumed for *ʿumra* and *ḥadjdj* (*kirān*), this is not allowed [on these and related questions cf. the article IḤRĀM].

c. The Ceremonies of the Ḥadjdj. On the 7th Dhu 'l-Ḥidjdja there is usually preaching in the mosque of the Kaʿba, by which the pilgrims are prepared for the holy ceremonies. In the evening of the same day or in the morning of the next the pilgrims leave Mecca. The 8th is called *yawm al-tarwiya* ("day of moistening"), because (according to an improbable explanation) on this day the pilgrims provide themselves with water for the following days. The two *maḥmal*'s united formerly outside the town and led the way; then followed the variegated seething mass of representatives of different races, on foot and in litters, on asses and horses, perpetually pushing and struggling. The plain of ʿArafāt, where a halt is to be made (*wuḳūf*), is reached via Minā (now usually pronounced Munā) and Mudzalifa (also called Djamʿ and al-Mashʿar al-Ḥarām). Here the representative of the caliph used to plant a standard.

The description of the thickly covered plain by the nineteenth-century travellers agrees in its main features with those of the old Arab annual markets in the classical authors. Tents and booths (see C. Snouck Hurgronje, *Bilder aus Mekka*, No. 13—16, cf. also 10—12) are everywhere, in the latter the numerous traders expose their wares as in the bazaar; jugglers and fakirs entertain the crowd with their skill. Many pilgrims ascend the sacred mountain (*Djabal al-Raḥma*), and repeat the prescribed formulae after their shaikh at the proper places; loud cries of *labbaika* [see TALBIYA] are heard everywhere. Thus the time is passed till the evening, at which brilliant illuminations take place. Pious pilgrims spend the night in the repetition of prayers, others amuse themselves in worldly fashion.

The *wuḳūf* proper takes place on the 9th and lasts from the time when the sun has crossed the meridian to its setting. Almost the whole period is filled by two *khuṭba*'s, celebrated as a rule by the ḳāḍī of the holy city. The latter rides up to the platform on the holy hill, from which he reads pious commonplaces out of a book, which are not audible to the greater part of those present, or, if heard, could not be understood by them. But this does not prevent them being much moved and continually calling *labbaika* loudly, waving the holy garments in the air and weeping and sobbing. But as soon as the sun disappears behind the western hills, the *ifāḍa* (or *dafʿ*, *nafr*), i.e. the running to Muzdalifa begins. Amid the greatest confusion as the horses are spurred through the rushing crowd, amid continual shooting and din, accompanied by military music, every one rushes to Muzdalifa. The *ʿalamain*, which mark the boundary of the *ḥaram* [q.v.] are passed; the evening darkness soon falls and torches are kindled; fireworks are discharged and the soldiers keep firing off their guns. In this fashion, rarely without accidents, Muzdalifa is reached, where the Maghrib and ʿIshā ṣalāt's are celebrated together and the night is spent. The mosque here is illuminated. On the morning of the 10th (*yawm al-naḥr*) *wuḳūf* is again held at the mosque before sunrise and the ḳāḍī of Mecca again preaches a *khuṭba*. After the completion of the morning service the crowd goes to Minā.

Here quite different duties have to be performed. Each pilgrim has on this day to throw seven small stones at one of the three so-called *djamra*'s here [q.v.], the *Djamrat al-ʿAḳaba*. For this purpose he has previously gathered the stones in Muzdalifa. Amid a tremendous crush a rush is made for this Djamra, which stands at the west end of the valley of Minā. A picture of it is given in Kazem Zadeh, *op. cit.*, opposite p. 222. Only the stoning of this Djamra is prescribed for this day in the law and the turn of the other djamra's does not come till the following days. The accounts in ʿAlī Bey and Burton agree very well with this prescription. It should, however, be noted that Burckhardt (*Travels*, ii. 578) and Keane (*Six Months in Meccah*, p. 161) expressly state that the pilgrims on the 10th Dhu 'l-Ḥidjdja throw seven stones, which they have brought from Muzdalifa, first at the eastern Djamra (*Djamrat al-ūlā, al-ṣughrā*), then at the middle one (*al-wusṭā*) and finally at the western (*al-suflā, al-aḳṣā, al-ʿAḳaba*); perhaps however this is an error of the two last-named travellers.

According to the Muslim explanation, this stoning is really a stoning of Satan, who is said to have appeared here to the patriarch Ibrāhīm and to have been driven away by him in this fashion. After the stoning the crying of *labbaika* ceases and the Ḥadjdj proper is at an end; various ceremonies, however, have still to follow, first that of the sacrifice, which has given this day its name. Thousands of sacrificial victims, chiefly sheep and goats, are kept ready in Minā by the Beduins and merchants and sold at high prices. Only people of high rank slaughter camels. The pilgrim who does not care to kill the animal himself may get a butcher to do it for him. Although there is no place specially prescribed by the law in Minā for the sacrifice, a rock at the west end of the valley near the ʿAḳaba is preferably used for this purpose (Burckhardt, *Travels*, ii. 59; Burton, *A Pilgrimage*, ii. 240). It is considered meritorious to give the flesh of the animals sacrificed to the poor as *ṣadaḳa*; what they do not use is left lying. The sacrifice, which is celebrated on this day throughout the whole Muslim world, is *sunna* (see the article ʿĪD AL-AḌḤĀ). Its omission may be made good by fasting.

It is usual to have the head shaved after the sacrifice; for this purpose there are a number of barbers' booths in Minā. Both the barber and the pilgrim observe certain rules during the process, such as turning towards the *ḳibla* etc. Thereafter the *iḥrām* may be discarded and a return made to a secular condition (*iḥlāl*); but the pilgrim is not yet allowed to transact all the business of everyday life. The series above described, stone-throwing, sacrifice, shaving, is described in the law as *sunna* (*Minhādj*, i. 331); but it should be noted that there is no time legally prescribed for the sacrifice and the two other ceremonies are only limited as to time in so far that they must be performed on the 10th day.

It is usual to return to Mecca on the same day

to perform a *ṭawāf* there, on which occasion the Kaʿba is seen for the first time with its new covering. Ordinary garments are donned if this has not been done in Minā already; the pilgrim bathes and washes, which is usually very desirable after being in the previous "holy state". It is usual also to drink from the holy Zamzam water or to have oneself sprinkled with it; but this may as well be done on any other day.

The following days, 11—13th Dhu 'l-Ḥidjdja, the so-called *aiyām al-tashrīḳ* (on the explanation of this name see below) called by Muḥammad "days of eating, drinking and sensual pleasure", are spent in Minā; seven stones are to be thrown at each of the three Djamra's each day, after midday. It is also the custom to sacrifice at a granite block on the slope of mount Thabīr (cf. Burckhardt, *Travels*, ii. 65; al-Batanūnī, *al-Riḥla*, p. 696). Abraham is said to have prepared his son for the sacrifice here. The law itself (cf. Sūra ii. 203) permits departure from Minā even on the 12th Dhu 'l-Ḥidjdja. It seems from the works of the travellers that this permission is usually taken and the pilgrims return to Mecca on this day. It is the custom to throw stones at the alleged grave of Abū Lahab in the vicinity of the town. Finally the *ʿumrat al-wadāʾ* (farewell *ʿumra*) has to be performed. For this purpose the pilgrim goes to Tanʿīm, again to assume the *iḥrām*. Modern travellers thus often call Tanʿīm also "al-ʿUmra". With the performance of *ṭawāf* and *saʿy* the Ḥadjdj is at an end. Some days later the caravans leave Mecca and go to Madīna to honour the tomb of the Prophet with a visit.

From what has been said above it is clear that the law divides the ceremonies of the Ḥadjdj into various categories; but is should be noted that the various schools differ from one another in almost all details. A good survey is given in the table on p. 178 of al-Batanūnī's work.

II. The origin of the islāmic Ḥadjdj

Muḥammad's attitude to the Ḥadjdj was not always the same; in his youth he must have often taken part in the ceremonies. After his "call" he paid little attention at first to the festival: in the oldest sūras it is not mentioned and it does not appear from other sources that he had adopted any definite attitude to this originally heathen custom. If many obviously polytheistic practices had been usual at it, he would hardly have been so silent about it and Tradition would probably have preserved expressions of opinion from which we could ascertain more or less clearly the ancient practices.

Muḥammad's interest in the Ḥadjdj was first aroused in al-Madīna. Several causes contributed to this, as Snouck Hurgronje has shown in his *Mekkaansche Feest*. The brilliant success of the battle of Badr had aroused in him thoughts of a conquest of Mecca. The preparations for such a step would naturally be more successful if the secular as well as the religious interests of his companions were aroused. Muḥammad had been deceived in his expectations regarding the Jewish community in Madīna and the disagreements with the Jews had made a religious breach with them inevitable. To this period belongs the origin of the doctrine of the religion of Abraham, the alleged original type of Judaism and Islām. The Kaʿba now gradually advances into the centre of religious worship; the father of monotheism built it with his son Ismāʿīl and it was to be a "place of assembly for mankind". The ceremonies performed there are traced to the divine command (Sūra ii. 125 *sq.*). In this period also the Kaʿba was made a *ḳibla* (cf. Sūra ii. 142—150) and the Ḥadjdj is called a duty of man to Allāh (iii. 97). This is the position of affairs in the year 2 of the Hidjra. It was only after the unsuccessful siege of al-Madīna by the Meccans in the year 5 that Muḥammad was able to attempt to carry out his plans. The first effort was made in the expedition to Ḥudaibiya, which, although it did not bring him to Mecca, by the treaty with the Ḳuraish brought an *ʿumra* into prospect for next year. In the year 7 Muḥammad instituted the ceremonies at the Kaʿba; but it was only after the conquest of Mecca in 8 that the opportunity was afforded of publicly celebrating the festival. But he did not take advantage of this occasion himself, for in the year 9 he sent Abū Bakr in his stead as leader of the pilgrim caravan to Mecca. While the latter was on the way, he was overtaken by ʿAlī b. Abī Ṭālib, who had been commissioned to read out to the pilgrims the *barāʾa* (Sūra ix. 1 *sq.*) which had been revealed in the meanwhile; in these verses the performance of the pilgrimage was forbidden to unbelievers except those with whom the Prophet had made special treaties.

In the year 10 Muḥammad himself led the Ḥadjdj. Tradition has much to tell on the subject of this so-called farewell-pilgrimage (*ḥadjdjat al-wadāʿ*). These accounts of the ceremonies performed by Muḥammad agree essentially with the later practice. The arrangements which he made on this occasion are of importance, however, for the history of the Ḥadjdj, notably the abolition of the "intercalation" (*nasīʾ*) and the introduction of the purely lunar year which is mentioned in the Ḳurʾān with the words: "Verily the number of months with God is twelve months in God's book, on the day when he created the heavens and the earth; of these four are sacred; that is the true religion. In these shall ye do no injustice to one another. But fight the unbelievers, as they fight you, one and all, and know that God is with the righteous. The intercalation is but an increase of the unbelief, in which the unbelievers err, for they make it (i.e. the time in which it falls or should fall) lawful one year and unlawful the next" (Sūra ix. 36 *sq.*). On other ordinances of Muḥammad on this occasion see below.

III. The pre-islāmic Ḥadjdj.

The investigation of the original meaning of the root *ḥ-dj* goes no further than hypotheses of varying probability. The Arabic lexicographers give the meaning "to betake oneself to"; this would agree with our "pilgrimage". But this meaning is as clearly denominative as that of the Hebrew verb. Probably the root חוג, which in North as well as South Semitic languages means "to go around, to go in a circle", is connected with it. With this we are not much farther forward however; for we do not even know whether religious circumambulations formed part of the original Ḥadjdj. We do know that in the pre-Muslim period two annual markets were held in the month of Dhu 'l-Ḳaʿda, in ʿUkāẓ and Madjanna. These were followed in the early days of Dhu 'l-Ḥidjdja by that of Dhu 'l-Madjāz and thence the people went direct to ʿArafāt. The Muslim practice of going out from Mecca to ʿArafāt is therefore probably an innovation; and Islām knows nothing of religious circumambulations in ʿArafāt and we as little.

This Ḥadjdj in ʿArafāt was not a local peculiarity;

pilgrimage to a sanctuary is an old Semitic custom, which is prescribed even in the older parts of the Pentateuch as an indispensable duty. "Three times a year shall you celebrate for me a *ḥag*" is written in Exodus xxiii. 14, and "three times a year all thy males shall appear before the Lord Jahwe" (*ibid.*, 17 and xxxiv. 23). But in Arabia also there were probably several places of pilgrimage where festivals like that of the Ḥadjdj of ʿArafāt were celebrated. The month of Aggathalbaeith mentioned by Epiphanius seems to presuppose a sanctuary in the north.

The Ḥadjdj of ʿArafāt took place on the 9th Dhu 'l-Ḥidjdja; the most diverse Arab tribes took part in it, but this was only possible when peace reigned in the land. The consecutive months Dhu 'l-Ḳaʿda, Dhu 'l-Ḥidjdja and Muḥarram thus formed a sacred period during which tribal feuds were at rest; weapons were laid aside in the holy territory.

It may be regarded as certain that in Muḥammad's time the sacred festival fell in the spring. Wellhausen has, however, made it appear probable that the original time of the Ḥadjdj was the autumn. If, as is probable, the above mentioned intercalary month had for its object to maintain this time of the year, the intercalation did not effect its purpose; from what cause we do not know. If the Ḥadjdj originally fell in the autumn, it is natural when inquiring into its original significance to compare it with the North Semitic autumnal festival, the "feast of booths" (or day of atonement), a proceeding which finds further support in the fact that the feast of booths in the Old Testament is often called briefly the *ḥag* (e.g. Judges, xxi. 19; 1 Kings, viii, 2, 65). We will actually find several features in agreement.

Great fairs were from early times associated with the Ḥadjdj which was celebrated on the conclusion of the date-harvest. These fairs were probably the main thing to Muḥammad's contemporaries, as they still are to many Muslims. For the significance of the religious ceremonies had even then lost its meaning for the people. The following may be stated. A main part of the ceremony was the *wuḳūf* "the halt" in the plain of ʿArafāt; in Islām the Ḥadjdj without *wuḳūf* is invalid. This can only be explained as the survival of a pre-Muslim notion. Houtsma has compared the *wuḳūf* with the stay of the Israelites on Mount Sinai. The latter had to prepare themselves for this by refraining from sexual intercourse (Ex. xix. 15) and the washing of their garments (Exod. xix. 10, 14). Thus they waited upon their God (נכונים, 11, 15). In the same way the Muslims refrain from sexual intercourse, wear holy clothing and stand before the deity (*w-ḳ-f* = כון = stand) at the foot of a holy mountain.

On Sinai, the deity appeared as a thunder- and lightning-god. We know nothing of the god of ʿArafāt; but he probably existed. Muḥammad is related to have said at the farewell pilgrimage: "The whole of ʿArafāt is a place for standing (*mawḳif*), the whole of Muzdalifa is a place of standing, the whole of Minā a place of sacrifice". Snouck Hurgronje has explained these words to mean that at the particular places where heathen ceremonies were performed these were to lose their importance through these words. A little is known of thesen heathen places in Muzdalifa and Minā (see below).

It is uncertain whether the day of ʿArafāt was a fast-day or not. In Tradition it is several times expressly stated that Muḥammad's companions did not know what was his view on this question. He was therefore invited to drink and he drank. The ascetic character of the Ḥadjdj days is clear from the *iḥrām* prohibitions. That these were once extended to include food and drink is clear from Muḥammad's explanation. "The Tashrīḳ days (11th—13th Dhu 'l-Ḥidjdja) are days of eating, drinking and sensual pleasure". In early Islām ascetically disposed persons therefore chose the Ḥadjdj as the special time for their self-denials (cf. Goldziher, in *RHR*, xxxvii. 318, 320 *sq.*).

The *wuḳūf* lasts in Islām from the moment after midday till sunset. Tradition records that Muḥammad ordered that ʿArafāt should not be left till after sunset, while it had previously been usual to begin the *ifāḍa* even before sunset. But the Prophet is said not only to have shifted the time, but even to have suppressed the whole rite by forbidding the running to Muzdalifa and to have ordered that it should be slowly approached. But how tenacious the old custom is, is clear from the above description of the *ifāḍa*. Snouck Hurgronje sees a solar rite in the latter, a view which has been more definitely formulated by Houtsma in connection with the character of the Ḥadjdj (see below), viz. that it was originally considered a persecution of the dying sun.

The god of Muzdalifa was Ḳuzaḥ, the thunder-god. A fire was kindled on the sacred hill also called Ḳuzaḥ. Here a halt was made and this *wuḳūf* has a still greater similarity to that on Sinai, as in both cases the thunder-god is revealed in fire. It may further be presumed that the traditional custom of making as much noise as possible and of shooting was originally a sympathetic charm to call forth the thunder.

As soon as the sun was visible, the *ifāḍa* to Minā used to begin in pre-Islāmic times. Muḥammad therefore ordained that this should begin before sunrise; here again we have the attempt to destroy a solar rite. In ancient times they are said to have sung during the *ifāḍa*: *ashriḳ thabīr kaimā nughīr*. The explanation of these words is uncertain; it is sometimes translated: "Enter into the light of morning, Thabīr, so that we may hasten".

When they arrived in Minā, it seems that the first thing they did was to sacrifice; the 10th Dhu 'l-Ḥidjdja is still called *yawm al-aḍāḥī*, "day of the morning sacrifices". In ancient times the camels to be sacrificed were distinguished by special marks (*taḳlīd*) even on the journey to the *ḥaram*; for example two sandals were hung around their necks. Mention is also made of the *ishʿār*, the custom of making an incision in the side of the hump and letting blood flow from it; or wounds were made in the animal's skin. It is frequently mentioned also that a special covering was laid on the animals.

According to a statement in Ibn Hishām, (p. 76 *sq.*), the stone throwing only began after the sun had crossed the meridian. Houtsma has made it probable that the stoning was originally directed at the sun-demon; this view would be further supported if it is the fact that the Ḥadjdj originally coincided with the autumnal equinox; similar customs are found all over the world at the beginning of the four seasons. With the expulsion of the sun-demon, whose harsh rule comes to an end with summer, worship of the thunder-god who brings fertility and his invocation may easily be connected, as we have seen above at the festival in Muzdalifa. The name *tarwiya* "moistening", also may be explained in this connection as a sympathetic rain-charm, traces of which survive in the libation

The Djabal al-Raḥma at ʿArafāt, occupied by pilgrims

Art. Hadjdj

of Zamzam water. These are again parallels to the feast of booths (or day of atonement): the goat, which was thrown from a cliff for ʿAzazel, is not difficult to identify as the type of the sun-demon; and the libation of water from the holy well of Siloah was also a rain-charm, for the connection between the feast of booths and rain is expressly emphasised (Zach. xiv. 17). Further we may call attention to the illumination of the temple on the feast of booths, which has its counterpart in the illumination of the mosques in ʿArafāt and Muzdalifa, as well as the important part which music plays at both feasts.

Quite other explanations of the stone throwing are given by van Vloten (*Feestbundel.... aan Prof. M. J. de Goeje aangeboden*, 1891, p. 33 *sq.*) and Chauvin (*Annales de 'l Acad. Royale d'Arch. de Belgique*, 5th Ser., Vol. iv., p. 272 *sq.*). The former connects the stoning of Satan and the Ḳur'ānic expression *al-S̲h̲aiṭān al-radj̲īm* with a snake, which was indigenous to the ʿAḳaba. The latter finds in it an example of scopelism: the object of covering the Ḥadj̲dj̲ ground with stones thrown on it was to prevent the cultivation of it by the Meccans. Both these theories have been satisfactorily refuted by Houtsma. Cf. also Doutté, *Magie et Religion*, p. 430 *sq.* — On the significance of the shaving in connection with the history of religions, cf. the article IḤRĀM.

On the *Tas̲h̲rīḳ* days some of the pilgrims dry the flesh of the animals sacrificed in the sun to take it with them on the return journey. This custom agrees with the meaning of the word *tas̲h̲rīḳ*, given by the Arab lexicographers, i.e. "to dry strips of meat in the sun"; but it may be doubted whether this is the original meaning of the word. A satisfactory explanation has not yet been given. Cf. however Th. W. Juynboll, *Über die Bedeutung des Wortes Taschrīḳ* (*ZA*, xxvii. 1 *sq.*). It must also be noted that Dozy in his book *De Israëlieten te Mekka*, traces the words *tas̲h̲rīḳ* and *tarwiya* as well as the whole Ḥadj̲dj̲ to a Jewish origin; but his thesis may be considered definitely refuted by Snouck Hurgronje's *Het Mekkaansche Feest.*

Bibliography: On the whole subject: C. Snouck Hurgronje, *Het Mekkaansche Feest* (Leyden 1880); the pertinent sections in the monographs and standard works on Islām; F. Wüstenfeld, *Die Chroniken der Stadt Mekka*, passim.

On I: C. M. Doughty, *Travels in Arabia Deserta* (Cambridge 1888), vol. i.; *Travels of Ali Bey* (London 1816), vol. ii.; J. L. Burckhardt, *Travels in Arabia* (London 1829); R. F. Burton, *Personal Narrative of a Pilgrimage to el-Medinah and Meccah* (London 1857), vol. ii.; T. F. Keane, *Six Months in Meccah* (London 1881); H. v. Maltzan, *Meine Wallfahrt nach Mekka* (Leipzig 1865); C. Snouck Hurgronje, *Mekka* (The Hague 1888), passim; do., *Verspreide Geschriften* IV², p. 173 *sqq.*; 307 *sqq.*; Hagikhan and W. Sparroy, *With the Pilgrims to Mecca*, London and New York 1905; Lady Evelyn Cobbold, *Pilgrimage to Mecca*, London, no year; E. Rutter, *The Holy Cities of Arabia*, 2 vols., London and New York, 1928, 1930; J. Eisenberger, *Indië en de bedevaart naar Mekka*, Leyden 1928; Abdoel Patah, *De medische zijde van de bedevaart naar Mekka*, Leyden 1935; Muḥammad Labīb al-Batanūnī, *al-Riḥla al-Ḥidj̲āzīya*² (Cairo 1329), an interesting and remarkable book; Rif'at Pasha, *Mir'āt al-Ḥaramain* (Cairo 1349); Ibn Dj̲ubair, *Travels* (ed. M. J. de Goeje); the various Fiḳh books, as well as the handbooks for pilgrims known as *Manāsik*. On the Ḥadj̲dj̲ of the S̲h̲īʿa s. Kazem Zadeh, in *RMM*, xix. (1912), 144 *sq.*

On II: The biographies of Muḥammad and the works on Tradition.

On III: R. Dozy, *De Israëlieten te Mekka* (also in German); J. Wellhausen, *Reste arab. Heidentums*², p. 68 *sq.*; M. Th. Houtsma, *Het skopelisme en het steenwerpen te Mina* (*Versl. en Meded. der Kon. Akad. v. Wetenschappen*, Amsterdam, Afd. Letterkunde, Ser. iv., Part. vi, p. 185 *sq.*); H. Winckler, *Altorient. Forschungen*, Ser. ii., Vol. ii., p. 324—350; also the articles by v. Vloten and Chauvin quoted in the text; Gaudefroy-Demombynes, *Le pèlerinage à la Mekke* (*Annales du Musée Guimet*, vol. xxxiii.), Paris 1923.

ḤĀDJDJ, ḤĀDJDJĪ, one who has performed the pilgrimage to Mecca. [See ḤADJDJ].

ḤAḌRA, "presence", is used broadly by mystics as synonym of *ḥuḍūr*, "being in the presence [of Allāh]". Its correlative is *g̲h̲aiba* (q.v. with its references), "absence" from all except Allāh. On the controversy as to whether in expressing this relation to Allāh *ḥaḍra* or *g̲h̲aiba* is to be preferred — that is, which is the more perfect, final element — see especially *Kas̲h̲f al-maḥdj̲ūb* (transl. Nicholson), p. 248 *sqq.* The term was later extended by Ibn ʿArabī, in working out his monistic scheme, to "The Five Divine *ḥaḍarāt*, stages or orders of Being in the Neoplatonic chain [see DJABARŪT]. There is a short statement of these in the *Taʿrīfāt* of Dj̲urdj̲ānī, p. 6 (Cairo 1321), which has been translated by Horten in his *Theologie des Islams*, p. 294 *sq.*, where, and on p. 151, he also gives some minor uses of the term. See, too, al-Ḥallādj̲, *Kitāb al-Ṭawāsīn*, (ed. Massignon), p. 183 with a reference to Ibn ʿArabī's *Fuṣūṣ al-ḥikam*, and Hughes, *Dict. of Islam*, p. 169. In consequence, the Plotinian scheme of dynamic emanation was called in Islām *madh̲hab al-ḥaḍarāt* (Ibn K̲h̲aldūn, *Muḳaddima*, ed. Quatremère iii., p. 69; De Slane, iii., p. 100). Derwishes call their regular Friday service *ḥaḍra*. The use of *ḥaḍra* (*ḥaḍrat*) as a title of respect for the Deity, saints, prophets, any educated man, belongs to the Lexicon.

ḤAFṢA, daughter of the Caliph ʿUmar and wife of the Prophet. She had first married the Ḳurais̲h̲ī K̲h̲unais b. Ḥud̲h̲āfa, who had died childless in Madīna soon after the battle of Badr. She must then have been about 20 years of age. Muḥammad, who wished to secure ʿUmar's co-operation, married her after the "day" of Uḥud. She was once repudiated, it is not known on what grounds, but was restored to favour by divine command in consideration of her Muslim virtues, i.e. her devotion to prayer and fasting. In Muḥammad's ḥarīm Ḥafṣa took the side of ʿĀ'is̲h̲a against his other wives and threw her whole influence into the service of the "triumvirate" i.e. the party, which was endeavouring to secure the succession to Muḥammad for Abū Bakr and ʿUmar. Like the other wives she received her share in the booty of K̲h̲aibar and on Muḥammad's death an annual revenue which was entered in the Dīwān and amounted to about 10,000 dirhams. On the whole, even in her father's Caliphate, she played a very modest part in striking contrast to ʿĀ'is̲h̲a. On the occasion of the *ḥukūma*, of the "judgment" of Ad̲h̲ruḥ Ḥafṣa induced her brother ʿAbd Allāh to appear as a claimant to the Caliphate. There is general agreement that she died in 45 aged about 60. On the part played by Ḥafṣa in connection with the collection of the Ḳur'ān, see this article. Her marriage with Muḥammad was a childless one.

Bibliography: Ibn Saʿd, iii./i. 285—286; viii. 56—60; Ibn Ḥadjar, *Iṣāba*, iv. 273—274; H. Lammens, *Le triumvirat Abū Bakr, ʿOmar et Abū ʿObaida* (extract from the *MFOB*, iii. 120); Ibn Hishām, p. 321, 1001; H. Lammens, *Fāṭima et les filles de Mahomet*, p. 15, 23, 46, 56, **86**; Ibn Ḥanbal, *Musnad*, vi. 283—288; Sprenger, *Das Leben des Mohammad*², iii. 74 *sq.*; Buhl, *Das Leben Muhammeds*, p. 261.

ḤAIḌ (A.), menstruation. Even in pre-Muḥammadan times the menstruating (*ḥāʾiḍ*, other terms in Wellhausen, *Reste arab. Heidentums*, p. 170, note 6) could not take part in feasts and sacrifices and this remained the case in Islām. During this period a woman is ritually impure, may not perform the *ṣalāt* nor the *ṭawāf*, nor fast, nor touch a Ḳurʾān, nor repeat a verse from it nor enter a mosque (cf. Juynboll, *Handbuch des Islām. Gesetzes*, p. 174 *sq.*). She only becomes ritually pure again on the completion of her courses after a major ablution (*ghusl*, q.v.). According to Sūra ii. 222, sexual intercourse with her during this period is forbidden, but it does not, like the Jewish law (Lev. xv. 19 *sq.*), prescribe seven days' separation.

ḤAḲĪḲA (A., pl. *ḥaḳāʾiḳ*) is (*a*) an abstract noun meaning "reality", so a thing which has no reality, *lā ḥaḳīḳa lahu*, then "the reality of a thing", meaning that by which the thing is what it is with regard to its reality (distinguish *huwīya* "individuality" and *māhīya* "quidditas") or, broadly, what distinguishes it from other things; this is called also its *dhātīya*. Then (*b*) "a reality" in the sense of a thing which certainly exists; using the verb you say: *ḥaḳḳa 'l-shaiʾ*, "the thing certainly exists". Hence *ahl al-ḥaḳīḳa* are the mystics who know the real nature of God, as opposed to *ahl al-ḥaḳḳ*, the orthodox followers of the Sunna, and *al-ḥaḳīḳa* is the last thing reached at the end of the derwīsh *ṭarīḳa* (W. H. T. Gairdner, *The way of a Moh. mystic*, p. 19 and 23). Also *ḥaḳīḳat al-ḥaḳāʾiḳ* is Allāh as the stage of unity which embraces all realities, otherwise called the *ḥaḍrat al-djamʿ*, "Presence of joining", and *ḥaḍrat al-wudjūd*, "Presence of Being" (see art. ḤAḌRA). The *ḥaḳīḳa* of Allāh is distinguished by Ṣūfīs from his *ḥaḳḳ*; it indicates his Qualities (*ṣifāt*) while *ḥaḳḳ* indicates his *dhāt* (*Dict. of techn. terms*, p. 333 *sq.*). With this apparently connect the following definitions belonging to the system of Ibn ʿArabī, but formative for all later mysticism in Islām (*Fuṣūṣ al-ḥikam* of Ibn ʿArabī, ed. of Cairo 1309 with comm. of ʿAbd al-Razzāḳ al-Ḳāshānī *passim*, and Djurdjānī, p. 62). The *ḥaḳāʾiḳ* of the Names of Allāh are individualizings of his essence and are its relationships to the things of the world; by relationship to these things, which are called also the Qualities (*ṣifāt*) and which are infinite in number, the primal unity is broken up. Also the *ḥaḳīḳa al-muḥammadīya* is the divine essence taken along with the first of these individualizings (i.e. Muḥammad); it is also the Most Great Name (*al-ism al-aʿẓam*; *Fuṣūṣ*, p. 428, l. 4). Ḥaḳīḳa also indicates (*c*) a descriptive noun or phrase used in a primary or real sense as opposed to a metaphor (*madjāz*). When, however, the metaphor has been used so often as to have become conventional, the word or phrase may be called *ḥaḳīḳa ʿurfīya* (Mehren, *Rhetorik*, p. 31, 78).

See also ḤAḲḲ.

Bibliography: Djurdjānī, *Taʿrīfāt*, Cairo 1321, p. 6 *sq.*; *Dict. of techn. terms*, p. 330 *sq.*; al-Rāghib al-Iṣfahānī, *Mufradāt*, p. 125; Lane, *Lexicon*, p. 609; Horten, *Theologie des Islam*, p. 152 *sq.*, 295 *q.*; Hudjwīrī, *Kashf al-mahdjūb*, transl. Nicholson, index; Ḳushairī, *Risāla* with comm. of ʿArūsī and Zakarīyā, ii. 92 *sqq.*

ḤAḲḲ. The original meaning of the root *ḥ-ḳ-ḳ* has become obscured in Arabic but can be recovered by reference to the corresponding root in Hebrew with its meanings of "cut in" or "on", thence "prescribe", "fix by decree" (Brown-Driver-Briggs, *Hebrew Lexicon*, p. 349 *sq.*). We have thus in Arabic to begin with the primary idea of permanence, fixity (*thubūt*) and not with that of correspondence, suitableness (*muṭābaḳa, muwāfaḳa*) which is essentially secondary and a discovery of the rhetoricians (*ahl al-maʿānī*; Djurdjānī, *Taʿrīfāt*, p. 61, *sqq.* cf ed. of Cairo 1321). This point is unfortunately confused in Lane (s.v., p. 605 *sqq.*), following some of the Arab lexicons. *Al-ḥaḳḳ*, then, means that which is fixed, permanent, real, and is regularly paraphrased in the commentaries on the Ḳurʾān as *al-thābit*. Thus Baiḍāwī explains al-Ḥaḳḳ, meaning Allāh, as *al-thābitu rubūbīyatuhu*, "he whose lordship is fixed, real" (Sūra x. 32; Baiḍāwī, ed. Fleischer, i. 414, l. 8); similarly *al-thābitu ilāhīyatuhu*, "whose divinity is fixed," contrasted with that of false gods which is *bāṭil*, "vain", "unreal" (Sūra xxxi. 30; Baiḍawī ii. 116, ll. 10 *sq.*); in Sūra xx. 114 he is *thābit* in his essence and qualities (Baiḍ., i. 607, l. 4); further, on Sūra xxii. 6, Baiḍ. explains (i. 628, l. 6) "because he is the *thābit* in himself by whom things became realities", *bihi tataḥaḳḳaḳu 'l-ashyāʾu*. On this last passage, Rāzī explains (*Mafātīḥ*, vi. 144, l. 3 of ed. of 1308) "he is *al-mawdjūd al-thābit*". The *Ṣaḥāḥ* contents itself with defining *ḥaḳḳ* as the opposite of *bāṭil*, and that is the fixed usage in the Ḳurʾān and elsewhere. This is pre-Islāmic as in the well known verse of Labīd (Huber, *Diwan des Lebīd*, xli., verse 9): *Alā kullu shaiʾin mā khalā 'llāha bāṭilu*, "Lo, everything is vain except Allāh alone". In Semitic psychology it connects also with Hebrew conceptions of nothingness, vanity, unreality contrasted with that which is sure, real and trustworthy. So *bāṭil* stands in Arabic over against *ḥaḳḳ*, and *al-ḥaḳḳ* is most suitably a name for Allāh, the absolutely real, even as *neʾemān*, "trustworthy" is said of Yahwé (cf. *al-muʾmin* of Allāh in Sūra lix 23). Allāh is real of himself and of necessity (Baiḍāwī on Sūra xxii. 62, i. 638, l. 15), while other beings depend for their reality on him (see Baiḍāwī above on Sūra xxii. 6). "The Real", or "The Reality" is therefore the nearest rendering of the word when used as one of the Names (*asmāʾ*, see art. ALLĀH) of Allāh, and "the Truth", as it is often translated, is misleading. All the Muslim authorities distinguish carefully between *ḥaḳḳ* and *ṣidḳ* with its opposite *kidhb*, and lay down the rule that *ḥaḳḳ* is equivalent to *ṣidḳ* only when used of a judgement (*ḥukm*). Thus when an event (*wāḳiʿa*) really took place, so it is *ḥaḳḳ*; but a judgment or statement about it is *ṣidḳ*, though the statement may also be called in this sense a *ḥaḳḳ*. Used as one of the Names, *al-ḥaḳḳ* is frequently explained as Creator, but for this the only basis seems to be its constant contrast with *al-khalḳ* "creation", e. g. in *Itḥāf al-sāda*, vol. x., p. 556, l. 20, *alsinat al-khalḳ aḳlām al-ḥaḳḳ*: "Vox populi, vox dei!". Yet see another explanation suggested in al-Ḥallādj, *Kitāb al-Ṭawāsīn*, (ed. Massignon) p. 174. Besides the above meanings of "reality" — used absolutely of Allāh and derivatively of his creation — and "truth" used of a statement corresponding to reality, *ḥaḳḳ* means also "right", "duty", going back to the idea of prescription. Thus, *ḥaḳḳ lī*, "a right due to me", and *ḥaḳḳ ʿalaiya*, "a right obligatory on me". From this comes the *ḥaḳḳ Allāh* — as distinguished from the *ḥaḳḳ ādamī, ḥaḳḳ al-nās* — the punishment for trespasses against Allāh by which no man is injured in his rights (see Juynboll, *Handbuch des islām. Ges.*, p. 292 and index). Again, just as *al-ḥaḳīḳa* [q..v.] is the last thing reached by the Ṣūfī on his journey, after even *maʿrifa* is passed, so *ḥaḳḳ al-yaḳīn* is that real certainty which comes with the passing away (*fanāʾ*) of the creature in his *ḥāl* in the Reality after he has had visual certainty (*ʿainu 'l-yaḳīn*) and scientific certainty (*ʿilmu 'l-yaḳīn*). On this see *Kashf al-mahdjūb*, transl. p. 381 *sq.*; Ḳushairī, *Risalā* with commentaries of ʿArūsī and Zakarīyāʾ, ii. 99 *sqq.* and Djurdjānī, *loc. cit.*, the phrase is derived from Sūra lvi. 95. Among Ṣūfīs the *ḥuḳūḳ al-nafs* are such things as are necessary for the support and continuance of life as opposed to the *ḥuẓūẓ*, things desired by the *nafs* but not necessary to its existence (*Dict. of techn. terms*, p. 311, 330 and 417, ll. 10 *sqq*).

Bibliography: *Dict. of tech. terms*, p. 329 *sq.*; Hudjwīrī, *Kashf al-mahdjūb*, transl. Nicholson, index; al-Ḥallādj, *Kitāb al-Ṭawāsīn*, ed. Massignon, index; Rāghib, *Mufradāt*, p. 124 *sq.*; Horten, *Theologie des Islam*, p. 152 *sq.*, 295 *sq.*; also references given above.

ḤĀL, also Ḥāla (pl. *aḥwāl, ḥālāt*), means a "state", normally regarded as present, transitory and changeable. On its use in grammar see Wright³, ii. 112 *sqq.*; *Mufaṣṣal*, ed. Broch², p. 27 *sqq.*; *Alfīya*, ed. Dieterici, p. 170 *sqq.*; Fleischer, *Kl. Schr.*, i., index. In rhetoric (*ʿilm al-maʿānī*) it means the situation or subject to be dealt with, and it is the object of rhetoric to show how to find verbal expression corresponding to "the requirement of the situation" (*muḳtaḍa 'l-ḥāl*, see preface to *Talkhīṣ* of Ḳazwīnī; Mehren, *Rhetorik*, p. 3, 47). Compare with this *lisān al-ḥāl*, what the situation itself says. In philosophy the *kaifīyāt al-nafsānīya*, "modalities of the *nafs*" are *ḥālāt*, so long as they are transitory. When they become permanent faculties in the mind they are *malakāt* (*Dict. of techn. terms*, p. 1257; Djurdjānī, *Taʿrīfāt*, p. 127). In systematic theology (*kalām*) a *ḥāl* — for those who accept that view — is a quality (*ṣifa*) belonging to an existent thing (*mawdjūd*), but itself being neither existent nor non-existent. Things, then, are four: entities, nonentities, states and relationships (*iʿtibārāt*) (Baidjūrī's comm. to the *Kifāyat al-ʿawāmm* of Faḍālī, p. 59 of ed. of Cairo 1315 and Macdonald, *Muslim Theology* etc., p. 159 *sq.*, 201 *sq.*, 241 *sq.*). Thus the *aḥwāl* are a kind of universals, and include the genera and differentiae; such *aḥwāl* exist in the essence of Allāh and are his qualities of "being a knower" (*ʿālimīya*), "being powerfull" (*ḳādirīya*) etc. (Ibn Khaldūn, *Proleg.*, ed. Quatremère, iii. 114; de Slane's transl., iii. 157 *sq.*). See on the whole doctrine of *aḥwāl* as opposed to *ṣifāt*: Horten, who calls them *modi*, in *ZDMG*, lxiii. 308 *sqq.*, and in his *Philos. Systeme*, p. 412 *sqq.* and also *passim*. In the science of *uṣūl* (Foundations) *ḥāl* means a legal status, which according to the principle of *istiṣḥāb* (Juynboll, *Handbuch des islam. Gesetzes*, p. 53 *sq.*; Goldziher, in *WZKM*, i. 228 *sqq.*) is juridically assumed to remain unchanged so long as there is no evidence to the contrary (*Dict. of techn. terms*, p. 809). In medicine there are three *aḥwāl*: health, disease and an intermediate state; a lengthy scholastic discussion of this by Ibn Sīnā and others in *Dict. of techn. terms*, p. 813 *sq.* under *ṣiḥḥa*.

In mysticism a *ḥāl* is a mental condition, given immediately and momentarily by divine grace, not to be gained by application or effort, consisting of joy, sorrow, depression, exaltation etc. It passes when the powers of the *nafs* get the upper hand, but may be followed immediately by another *ḥāl*. Djurdjānī teaches (*Taʿrīfāt*, p. 56) that it may continue, apparently by the effort of the *murīd* on whom it falls, and then becomes a possession (*milk*) and is called a *maḳām*. But usually the *maḳāmāt* are sharply distinguished from the *aḥwāl* as gains by human effort from divine gifts and are the stages in the progress of the *murīd* to repose in the Divine (*tamkīn*). They are reached by his intention and exertion and have a certain fixed order *Kashf*, transl. Nicholson, p. 180, 370). There is much controversy as to the possibility of the continuance (*dawām*) of *aḥwāl*. To be distinguished also from the ḥāl is the *waḳt*. It is that "Now" of the present, with its content of presence with or absence from God, and with it alone the Ṣūfī should be occupied. It belongs to the *murīd* and is his religious experience under the effect of an ever renewed Now, while the *ḥāl* comes from God and enters that Now "like a soul in a body" *Kashf*, transl. p. 367 *sq.*; Ḳushairī, *Risāla*, ii. p. 21 *sqq.*).

Bibliography: References as above and also *Dict. of techn. terms*, p. 359 *sqq.*; Horten, *Theologie des Islam*, p. 156, 298; Macdonald, *Emotional Religion in Islam*, in *JRAS*, 1901—1902, *passim*; E. Blochet, *L'Esotérisme musulman*, p. 181 *sqq.*; Macdonald, *Religious Attitude*, p. 182, 188 *sqq.*; Fr. Meier, *Vom Wesen der islamischen Mystik*, Basel 1943, p. 10 *sq.*

al-**ḤALABĪ**, Nūr al-Dīn b. Burhān al-Dīn ʿAlī b. Ibrāhīm b. Aḥmad b. ʿAlī b. ʿUmar al-Ḳāhirī al-Shāfiʿī, an Arab author, born in 975/1567 in Cairo, was a professor in the Madrasa al-Ṣalāḥīya there and died on the 30th Shaʿbān 1044/17th Febr. 1634. He wrote many commentaries, supercommentaries and textbooks current in his time but the best known of his numerous works is the biography of the Prophet, entitled *Insān al-ʿuyūn fī sīrat al-amīn al-maʾmūn*, usually called *al-Sīra al-Ḥalabīya*, an excerpt from *al-Sīra al-Shaʾmīya* of Shams al-Dīn al-Ṣāliḥī al-Shaʾmī (died 942/1536), considerably expanded by numerous additions, completed in 1043/1633.

Bibliography: Muḥibbī, *Khulāṣat al-athar*, iii. 122 *sq.*; Wüstenfeld, *Die Geschichtschreiber der Araber*, No. 560; Brockelmann, *GAL*², ii. 395, *Suppl.* ii. 418.

al-**ḤALLĀDJ** ("the carder") Abu l-Mughīth al-Ḥusain b. Manṣūr b. Maḥammā al-Baiḍāwī, a Persian mystic and theologian who wrote in Arabic. He was born about 244/858 at al-Ṭūr near al-Baiḍā (Fārs), the grandson of a fireworshipper, or descendant, it is said, of the Ṣaḥābī Abū Aiyūb. From 260/873 to 284/897 he lived in retirement (*khalwa*) with Ṣūfī teachers (Tustarī, ʿAmr Makkī, Djunaid). Then he broke with them and went out into the world to preach (*daʿwā*) asceticism and mysticism, resembling the mission of a Ḳarmaṭian *dāʿī*, in Khurāsān (Ṭālikān), Ahwāz, Fārs, India (Gudjarāt) and Turkistān. On his return from Mecca to Baghdād in 296/908 disciples (Ḥallādjīya) rapidly gathered round him. He was then accused of being a charlatan by the Muʿtazila, excommunicated by a *tawḳīʿ* of the Imāmīya and a *fatwā* of the Ẓāhirīya, and twice arrested by the ʿAbbāsid police. Brought before the vizier Ibn ʿĪsā and put on the pillory in 301/913, he spent eight years in prison in Baghdād. The patronage of Shaghab, mother of al-Muḳtadir, and of the *ḥādjib* Naṣr brought upon him the hatred of the vizier Ḥāmid, who had him executed after a seven months' trial on a *fatwā* approved by the Mālikī Ḳāḍī Abū ʿUmar. On Tuesday 24th Dhū'l-Ḳaʿda 309/26th March 922, on the esplanade of the new prison of Baghdād (on the right bank of the river) opposite the Bāb al-Ṭāḳ, al-Ḥallādj was flogged, mutilated, exposed on a gibbet (*maṣlūb*) and finally decapitated and burned. This "crucifixion" gave rise, as in the case of Christ, to legends of substitution (cf. *RHR*, lxii., 195—207). His persecuted disciples gathered round Abū ʿUmāra al-Hāshimī in al-Ahwāz, and Fāris al-Dīnawarī in Khurāsān. It was from this last group that the mystic revival of Persian poetry originated with Abū Saʿīd and of Turkish with Aḥmed Yesewī and Nesīmī.

Madhhab (doctrines) of the Ḥallādjīya:

a. in *Fiḳh*, the five *farā'iḍ*, even the Ḥadjdj, may be replaced by other works (= *isḳāṭ al-wasā'iṭ*).

b. in *Kalām*, God's transcendence (*tanzīh*) above the limits of creation (*ṭūl*, *ʿarḍ*); the existence of an uncreated Divine spirit (*rūḥ nāṭiḳa*) which becomes united with the created *rūḥ* (spirit) of the ascetic (*ḥulūl al-lāhūt fi l-nāsūt*); the saint (*walī*) becomes the living and personal witness of God (*huwa huwa*), whence the saying: *Anā 'l-Ḥaḳḳ*, "I am Creative Truth" (cf. *Ṭawāsīn*, vi, 32).

c. in *Taṣawwuf*, perfect union with the divine will (*ʿain al-djamʿ*) through desire of and submission to suffering, The *dhikr* given them by Shaikh Sanūsī is modern.

Few men in Islām have been so much discussed; in spite of the *idjmāʿ* of the judges who condemned him, popular devotion has canonised him. The following are the principal doctors who have taken part in this cause célèbre: (*k* = *takfīr*, *w* = *wilāya*, *t* = *tawaḳḳuf*).

A. Fuḳahā': Ẓāhirīya (*k*: Ibn Dā'ūd, Ibn Ḥazm); Imāmīya (*k*: Ibn Bābūya, Ṭūsī, Ḥillī, *w*: Shūshtarī, ʿĀmilī); Mālikīya (*k*: Ṭurṭūshī, ʿIyād, Ibn Khaldūn, *w*: ʿAbdarī, Dulundjāwī); Ḥanābila (*k*: Ibn Taimīya, *w*: Ibn ʿAḳīl [retracted], Ṭawfī); Ḥanafīya (*t*: Ibn Buhlūl, *w*: Nābulusī); Shāfiʿīya (*t*: Ibn Suraidj, Ibn Ḥadjar, Suyūṭī, ʿUrḍī, *k*: Djuwainī, Dhahabī, *w*: Maḳdisī, Yāfiʿī, Shaʿrāwī, Haitamī, Ibn ʿAḳīla, Saiyid Murtaḍā).

B. Mutakallimūn: Muʿtazila (*k*: Djubbā'ī, Ḳazwīnī); Imāmīya (*k*: Mufīd, *w*: Naṣīr Ṭūsī, Maibūdhī, Amīr Dāmād); Ashāʿira (*k*: Bāḳillānī, *w*: Ibn Khafīf, Ghazzālī, Fakhr Rāzī); Sālimīya (*w*); Māturīdīya (*k*: Ibn Kamālpāshā; *w*: Ḳārī).

C. Ḥukamā': *w*: Ibn Ṭufail, Suhrawardī Ḥalabī.

D. Ṣūfīya: *k*: ʿAmr Makkī and most early writers except (*w*) Ibn ʿAṭā', Shiblī, Fāris, Kalābādhī, Naṣrābādhī, Sulamī, and (*t*): Ḥuṣrī, Daḳḳāḳ, Ḳushairī; then *w*: Ṣaidalānī, Hudjwīrī, Abū Saʿīd, Harawī, Fārmadhī, ʿAbd al-Ḳādir Gīlanī, Baḳlī, ʿAṭṭār, Ibn al-ʿArabī, Rūmī, and most later ṣūfīs except (*t*:) Aḥmad Rifāʿī, ʿAbd al-Karīm Djīlī.

Among European scholars different verdicts have been passed upon him. A. Müller and d'Herbelot think him to have been secretly a Christian; Reiske accuses him of blasphemy, Tholuck of paradox; Kremer makes him a monist, Kazanski a neuropath and Browne "a dangerous and able intriguer". Al-Ḥallādj, a dialectician and extatic (cf. Lullius, Swedenborg), endeavoured to bring dogma into harmony with Greek philosophy on a basis of mystic experience; he was in this a precursor of Ghazzālī; and although he would have repudiated their cautious esoterism, the Ṣūfīs have made him their "martyr" par excellence. — Of his works (cf. *Kitāb al-Fihrist* i, 192) there remain the *Kitāb al-Ṭawāsīn* (ed. Massignon, Paris, 1913), 27 *Riwāyāt* of the year 290/902; 400 fragments in prose and 150 in verse of rare beauty.

Bibliography: L. Massignon, *La Passion d'al-Hallâj, martyr mystique de l'Islam*, Paris 1922. This work, based on all the available literary sources (enumerated in Chap. xv, *Bibliographie Hallâjienne*) has now replaced all earlier expositions of the mystic's life and times; cf. also *RMM*, lviii (1924), 261—267. Preparatory studies were the edition of the *Kitāb al-Ṭawāsīn*, mentioned in the text, and *Quatre textes inédits relatifs à la biographie d'al-Hallâj*, publ. par L. Massignon, Paris 1914, cf. also Massignon in *Isl.* iii. (1912), 248-9 and Goldziher in *Isl.* iv. (1913), 165-9. Later additional publications are: *Dîwân d'al-Hallâj*, ed. Massignon in *JA*, 1931 (i), p. 1-58; *Akhbār al-Ḥallādj*, ed. Massignon and Kraus, Paris 1936; articles by Massignon in *REI*, 1941—46.

ḤĀM, the son of Noah, known from the Bible. The Ḳur'ān mentions none of Noah's three sons by name but alludes to Ḥām: — one of Nūḥ's sons, in spite of his appeal, remains away from the ark saying the mountain would protect him; in spite of Nūḥ's intercession he is drowned in the Deluge (xi. 42—47). It is evident that Muḥammad was here thinking of Ḥām, the son of Nūḥ branded in the Bible and Haggada. In the Bible for his lack of reverence he is cursed that he shall become the slave of his brothers (Gen. ix. 22—25); Haggada credits him with further sins (Ginzberg, *Legends of the Jews*, i, 168, v. 60, 191).

As Muḥammad had made one son of Nūḥ perish in the Deluge, and the Ḳur'ān exegists knew Sām, Ḥām and Yāfith as the three sons of Nūḥ who were saved and all mankind was descended from them, Islāmic tradition had to invent a fourth son. Ṭabarī i. 199) already makes Kanʿān, Ḥām's son in the Bible, the fourth son of Nūḥ and adds that the Arabs call him Yām (so also Ṭabarī, i. 192; Ibn al-Athīr, i. 50). Al-Kisā'ī frankly reads Kanʿān into the Ḳur'ānic text (ed. Eisenberg, p. 96).

Islāmic legend further develops the Biblical and Haggada story: exhausted by the hardships in the ark, Nūḥ falls asleep on Sām's bosom: A breeze reveals his nakedness, Sām and Yāfith cover him up, but Ḥām laughs at him (al-Kisā'ī, p. 98).

The earth is divided among Nūḥ's sons; Ḥām receives the Sūdān, Nubia, Ethiopia and Zandj, according to some also Hind-Sind. His children are born black and increase through the marriage of brothers and sisters (al-Ḳisa'ī, p. 101); of his descendants the most famous is Namrūd b. Kūsh b. Ḥām. Of the 72 languages which arose in Babel, 36 fell to Yāfith, 18 to Sām and 18 to Ḥām. At the request of the Apostles, Ḥām was awakened by Jesus from the dead simply to tell about the ark and the Flood (Ṭabarī, i. 187).

ḤAMĀ'IL (A.), talismans. The use of amulets is very widespread in the lands of Islām. In North Africa they are called *ḥurz*, among the Arabs in the East *ḥamāya* or *ḥāfiẓ*, *ʿūdha* or *maʿādha*, and in Turkey *yafta*, *nuskha* or *ḥamā'il*. They are often carried in little bags, lockets or purses, which are worn round the neck or fastened to the arm or turban. Among rich people they are of gold or silver. Children are given these amulets as soon as they are forty days old; the crudest articles may be used as amulets, such as a shell, a piece of bone, sewn into leather and fastened under the left arm (see Emily Ruete, *Memoirs of an Arabian Princess*, transl. by L. Strachey, New York 1904, p. 68). Bedouin girls have an amulet which they call *ḥurz* and prize highly; it is a book of prayers 7 cm. long and 4—5 broad enclosed in a gold or silver box and is worn as a brooch.

The prayers, signs and figures on these talismans are of very different origin and their investigation offers great difficulties. We find on them divine names, names of angels, verses from the Ḳurʾān, astrological symbols, Kabbalistic letters, magic squares, signs of geomancy, figures of animals and men. The divine names (Doutté, *Magie et Religion dans l'Afrique du Nord*, p. 200; see also Redhouse, in *JRAS*, 1880) may be used as one pleases or arranged according to the numerical value of the letters composing them. Besides these, God has a name not to be spoken, which men do not know, but which is revealed only to prophets and saints.

The names of the angels are also numerous. The best known are those of the four archangels Mīkhāʾīl, Djabrāʾīl, ʿAzrāʾīl and Isrāfīl, which are found on many amulets. Besides these there is a host of others, which are given in the angelologies. There are several works of this kind in Arabic which are ascribed to suppositious authors like Andrūn or Andahriush; they contain a doctrine which is derived from the notion of the gnostic aeons. There are angels who preside over the planets; others preside over the months or the days of the week. Seven are given for each day; their names, barbaric in their sound, frequently appear in pairs e.g. Ṭalīkh and Ilīkh, Ḳaiṭar and Maiṭar, Ḳinṭash and Yāḳinṭash. An angel very prominent in the world of magic, who presides sometimes over the planet Jupiter and sometimes over Mercury, and whom the Arabs seem sometimes to have confused with Mīkhāʾīl, is Meṭaṭron. He is one of the great figures in Kabbalistic literature (cf. Renan, *Vie de Jésus*, p. 247, note 4; *Les Apôtres*, p. 270; Schwab, *Vocabulaire de l'angélologie*, p. 170). — Two other angels, who have a history of their own, also mentioned in the Ḳurʾān, likewise appear on talismans, namely Hārūt and Mārūt [q.v.]. — Besides the angels, several mythical beings are also invoked, notably the seven sleepers (*aṣḥāb al-kahf*, q.v.).

Of the verses of the Ḳurʾān the most efficacious as amulets are the short sūras cxiii. and cxiv. These two sūras are called *al-muʿawwidhatān* ("the two who preserve"). In the first the evil women are mentioned "who blow upon knots"; it is believed that it is particularly efficacious against the ills of the flesh; the other is credited with more power against psychic afflictions. Besides these the Sūra *Yā-sīn* is highly esteemed by pious Muslims. This is also true of the *Fātiḥa*, the *Āyat al-kursī* (Sūra ii. 255) and the throne-verse, *Āyat al-ʿarsh* (Sūra ix. 129). Other verses than these are also used in special circumstances.

The astrological signs, the signs of the planets and of the zodiac are well-known; they are naturally used for talismans. We often find quite peculiar signs which may be traced to different Kabbalistic alphabets; these frequently turn out to be transformations or corruptions of Hebrew or Kūfic letters. Kabbalistic alphabets are given by Ibn al-Waḥshīya in his *Kitāb shawḳ al-mustahām*. Small circles, or rings or ornaments are often found behind the Hebrew letters; these scrolls are called "little moons" or "crowns". According to the *Sefer yeṣīrā*, every letter in a talisman ought to have its crown (*Sepher yeṣira*, transl. by Mayer Lambert, p. 114).

Geomantic figures formed by points arranged in different groups are also sometimes used. Geomancy, Arabic *ʿilm al-ramal*, is divination from points formed in sand. Four lines are drawn in the sand, points marked at regular intervals and some of them wiped out at random. The remainder form definite figures to which names and different meanings have been given. These figures are used on talismans.

Magic squares (*wafḳ, wifḳ*) are also often met with. They consist of 9 or 16 compartments. Usually the same number is added to each of the 9 or 16 numbers of which they consist. This gives the thing a more learned look. Thus they begin with 9 instead of 1 and run from 9 to 24 instead of 1 to 16. Instead of numbers, letters are often written in the squares, e.g. the four letters of the name Allāh, *allh*, four times in different order. The problem of magic squares was thoroughly studied by the Arabs, for we see from the Ikhwān al-Ṣafāʾ that squares of 9 columns were known. There exists even a very good general solution of this problem in a pamphlet by al-Būnī, *Sharḥ ism Allāh al-aʿẓam* (Cairo, n.d.), a solution which is not due to al-Būnī himself, for it contains Persian terms.

Forms of men and animals are rarely found in North Africa on talismans; but in the East we find them on amulets and charms, which have been produced under the influence of Persian art. Lookingglasses, cups and seals to which magic power is ascribed, are often adorned with them. For this purpose figures of angels or animals, particularly griffins with human heads or the signs of the zodiac are used. Several other examples are given in Herklots, *The Customs of the Musulmans of India*, p. 339 *sq.*

The human hand is a very popular symbol among Muslims. It is carried around the neck, cut out of gold or silver or engraved on a medallion; it is said to avert the evil eye. This charm is usually called "the hand of Fāṭima". The Shīʿīs interpret the five fingers as the five saints: Muḥammad, ʿAlī, Fāṭima, Ḥasan and Ḥusain.

To sum up, it may be said that the subjects used, except the verses from the Ḳurʾān, may for the most part be traced back to Gnostic or Talmudic sources. According to Arab tradition, Adam himself discovered or rather revealed the talisman. According to the *Abrégé des Merveilles* (transl. Carra de Vaux, p. 142), ʿAnāḳ, the daughter of Adam, stole from Eve, while she slept, the charms she used to conjure spirits; but she made a bad use of them. Solomon was a great magician, according to Muslim belief; his ring plays a great part in Talmudic legends and Arabian tales. The djinnī, who appears in the story of the fisherman in the "Arabian Nights", was confined in a vase, which had been sealed with Solomon's ring. The talisman, still known as Solomon's seal and worn by Muslims and Jews alike, represents a six pointed star.

In Arabic literature, there are various treatises on the science of talismans. The most celebrated writers on this subject are Maslama al-Madjrīṭī (died 398/1007), who brought the writings of the Ikhwān al-Ṣafāʾ to Spain, the "forger" Ibn al-Waḥshīya, the author of *al-Filāḥa al-Nabaṭīya*, and al-Būnī. The use of talismans is denounced in Ch. IV Section 4 of the *Muḳaddima* of Ibn Khaldūn.

Muslim theology, which prohibits sorcery [see SIḤR], tolerates the use of amulets. They are usually prepared by dervishes, who belong to various brotherhoods, and are only of value when they are received from their hands.

Bibliography: Reinaud, *Monumens arabes, persans et turcs du Cabinet du Duc de Blacas*, 2 vol., Paris 1828; E. Doutté, *Magie et religion dans l'Afrique du Nord*, Algiers 1909; Ismael Hamet, *Les Amulettes en Algérie*, in *Bulletin des séances de la société philologique*, 1905; *Magasin pittoresque*, reproductions of talismans, 1872, p. 64 and 272; Depont and Coppolani, *Confréries religieuses*, p. 140; Abdes Selam b. Choʿaib, *Notes sur les amulettes chez les indigènes algériens* (Tlemcen 1905); Westermarck, *Ritual and Belief in Morocco*, i. 208 *sqq.*; E. W. Lane, *Modern Egyptians*; M. Massé, *Croyances et coutumes persanes*, Paris 1938, p. 325 *sq.* — On magic squares: Paul Tannery, *Le Traité manuel de Moschopoulos sur les carrés magiques*, Greek text and translation, Paris 1886; on Kabbalistic alphabets: Gottheil, in *JA*, 1907; on the processes of incantation: Carra de Vaux, in *JA*, 1907. See also SIḤR.

HĀMĀN, the Persian minister hostile to the Jews in the book of Esther, according to the Ḳurʾān (xl. 24) acted with Ḳārūn (Ḳoraḥ) on Firʿawn's council and filledt he office of grand vizier. These two learned of the approaching birth of Mūsā and advised that the boys should be slain and the girls allowed to live. When Mūsā appeared as a prophet of God, they called him a liar. Firʿawn said: "O Hāmān, build me a tower, on which I shall reach the paths, the paths to heaven and ascend to the god of Mūsā" (Sūra xl. 36 *sq.*, cf. xxviii. 38). That Muḥammad places Hāmān in this period betrays his confused knowledge of history, of which many other examples may be found in the Ḳurʾān. Indeed the Talmud (*Sanh.* 106) and Midrash (*Exodus R.* 18) contain a similar anachronism when they make Balaam, Job and Jethro all members of Pharaoh's great council which advised that Moses should be disposed of. The commentary on the above passages (xl. 24, xxviii. 38 and xi. 36) is interesting for the account it gives of the building of the tower by Hāmān. In any case it is remarkable that neither Ḳurʾān nor commentary nor the Arab historians know anything of the true Hāmān of the book of Esther. It must be presumed nevertheless that the story of Hāmān was not quite unknown in Arabia.

Bibliography: The Commentaries of Zamakhsharī and Baiḍāwī; Thaʿlabī, *Ḳiṣaṣ al-anbiyāʾ*, Cairo 1213, p. 110—111; al-Kisāʾī, *Ḳiṣaṣ al-anbiyāʾ*, ed. Eisenberg, p. 212—2141 Horowitz, *Koranische Unters.*, p. 149.

ḤAMDALA means the saying of the formula *al-ḥamdu li 'llāh* (for the different vocalizations — *du, di, da* — see *LA*, iv. 133, ll. 7 *sq.*): "Praise (in its whole genus and of every species) belongs to Allāh"; for from him all praiseworthiness proceeds and to him it returns. *Ḥamd* is the opposite of *dhamm*, being praise for something dependent on the will of him who is praised and it differs in this from *madḥ* which is not so limited; it is thus different from, although it may be an expression of *shukr*, "gratitude", the opposite of which is *kufrān*; *thanā*, often rendered "praise", more exactly "taking account of", is used both of praise and dispraise. The phrase is formally *ikhbārī* or *khabarī*, "narrative" but in its use it is *inshāʾī*, "assertive", for the speaker makes it an expression of the praise which he at the moment directs towards God (Muḥammad ʿAbdūh in *Tafsīr al-Fātiḥa*, Cairo 1323, p. 28; see, too, the elaborate discussion by Baidjūrī in his *Ḥāshiya* on the *Kifāyat al-ʿawāmm* of Faḍālī, p. 3 *sq.* of ed. of Cairo, 1315). In Lane's translation, "Praise be" (*Lexicon*, p. 638) he means an emphatic affirmation, not a *duʿāʾ*; this is plain from his letter to Fleischer on the translation of *tabāraka* etc. in *ZDMG*, xx., p. 187. But this use of "be" is misleading and hardly defensible as English. Perhaps the *inshāʾī* force could be indicated by a mark of exclamation as Palmer does in his translation of the Ḳurʾān. As the phrase occurs twenty-four times in the Ḳurʾān, besides other forms such as *lahu 'l-ḥamd*, it naturally became frequent in Muslim usage. All things come from Allāh, and for all things, pleasant or grievous, he is to be praised. Yet the verb *ḥamdala* does not seem to belong to the classical language and is thus later than *basmala*, which may even be pre-Islamic. In the *Ṣaḥāḥ* and the *Lisān* it does not occur, though *basmala* is in both, in the latter fortified with a verse from ʿUmar b. Abī Rabīʿa (Schwarz, *Dīwān*, No. 413, ii. 241; the evidence for the line and the usage is fullest in the *TA*, s.v.). In the *Miṣbāḥ* (finished A.H. 784) *ḥamdala* is mentioned, but only under *basmala*; it has no entry of its own. Finally, it is entered in its place in the *Ḳāmūs*; so slowly did it win recognition as a word. Besides its broad, devout usage the phrase is statedly a part of the *ṣalāt* and of the supplemental *tasbīḥ*, being repeated thirty-three times in the latter (Lane, *Modern Egyptians*, chap. iii.; *Lexicon*, p. 1290^b^). Further, as one of the seven *mathānī*, in the sense of the verses of the *Fātiḥa*, it has part with the *Fātiḥa* in various mystical and magical usages and meanings. Thus it is the *mathnā* assigned to the first of the seven stages of the Rifāʿī *ṭarīḳa* (W. H. T. Gairdner, *Way of a Mohammedam Mystic*, p. 12, 23). Even in orthodox tradition the *Fātiḥa* has begun to have magical value; cf. in Bukhārī (*Kitāb al-tafsīr, Bāb fātiḥat 'l-kitāb*) the story of the man who used it as a charm (*ruḳya*) against gnat-bites, and the Prophet approved. For later elaborate developments in magic, see al-Būnī, *Shams al-maʿārif*, faṣl x., and Aḥmad al-Zarḳāwī, the modern Egyptian magician, *Mafātīḥ al-ghaib*, p. 175. But the *ḥamdala* does not seem to be used by itself in magic as is the *basmala*. Again, the tendency to use the phrase as an introductory formula soon expressed itself as a tradition from the Prophet: "Whatever speech (or thing of importance) is not begun with praise of Allāh is maimed" (cf. BASMALA). Thus the *ḥamdala* became one of the three required things at the beginning of any formal writing. But this requirement was distinctly later, for, while the use of the *basmala* in this way held from the earliest times, we do not find the *ḥamdala* prefixed to the *Sīra* of Ibn Hishām nor to the *Kitāb al-aghānī* nor even to the *Fihrist*. See on this usage and the traditions supporting it, the commentary of the Saiyid Murtaḍā on the *Iḥyāʾ*, i. 53 *sq.* On the praiseworthiness of this exclamation see especially *ibid.*, v. 13 *sq.* (*Kitāb al-adhkār*).

Bibliography: References as above and also Baiḍāwī, ed. Fleischer, i. 5, ll. 26 *sq.*; Ṭabarī, *Tafṣīr*, i. 45 *sq.*; Rāzī, *Mafātīḥ*, i. 115 *sq.* (Cairo 1307).

ḤAMDĀN ḲARMAṬ B. AL-ASHʿATH, an Ismāʿīlī missionary, the founder of the Ḳarmaṭian sect, was a peasant in the neighbourhood of Kūfa; his nickname *karmīthā*, which belongs to the Aramaic dialect spoken in that district, seems to mean "man with red or fiery eyes" (Ṭabarī, iii. 2125). He settled in Kalwādhā near Baghdād, from which he could easily keep in touch with the mission in Khurāsān and with the Grand Master, who resided in ʿAskar-Mukram (261/875); near Kūfa he built himself an official residence called *Dār al-hidjra* (place of refuge); this became a centre around which his followers settled and from which they undertook their raids (277/890). Later he went to Syria, where he died soon after. His brother-in-law ʿAbdān who composed most of the sacred books of the sect was murdered soon afterwards by Zikrawaih, one of Aḥmad's followers. To obtain funds Ḳarmaṭ had introduced a series of taxes, each heavier than the preceding, first the *fiṭr*, a silver piece per head, then the *hiḏjra*, one gold piece per head, which was changed to the *bulgha* or seven gold pieces; finally he demanded *ulfa* or community of wives and property.

Bibliography: See the article KARMAṬIANS.

ḤAMZA, zon of ʿAbd al-Muṭṭalib, uncle of the Prophet, and his fosterbrother, as Tradition adds in the effort to glorify this hero of the earliest days of Islām, otherwise so little known. Panegyrists make him at the same time take part in the Fiḏjār wars, but this statement is a fiction, according to the author of the *Kitāb al-aghānī*. At first, like the other Hāshimīs, he adopted a hostile attitude to the new creed. But revolting against the extravagant attitude of Abū Djahl, he is said to have attached himself to the Prophet two (according to others, six) years after the first revelation. He migrated with him to Madīna.

Ḥamza is described to us as a valiant soldier. This quality won him the title of "Lion of God and his Prophet", which soon found a place in poetry. Muḥammad made use of his services by sending him at the head of a small column to hold up a Ḳuraish caravan. His fame as a soldier is particularly associated with the battle of Badr, where he and ʿAlī shared the honours. He also took part in the siege of the Madīna Jewish clan of Ḳainuḳāʿ. He met his fate at the battle of Uḥud where he wrought wonders of valour. The negro Waḥshī pierced him with a javelin, tore his breast open and brought his still beating heart to Hind, the mother of Muʿāwīya, who buried her teeth in it. So at least says one story hostile to the Umaiyads and without much support. Ḥamza is said to have been about 57—59 years old. None of Ḥamza's children left issue.

Bibliography: Ibn Saʿd, iii./i. 3-11; Ibn Ḥadjar, *Iṣāba* (Egyptian edition), i. 353—354; H. Lammens, *Fāṭima et les filles de Mahomet*, p. 23, 25, 30, 45, 46, 138; Ibn Hishām, p. 69, 120, 184, 232, 322, 344, 419, 433, 442, 485, 516, 563, 657; Ibn Ḳais al-Ruḳaiyāt, *Dīwān* (ed. Rhodokanakis), No. xxxiv. 20; *Aghānī*, iv. 25; xiv. 15, 22; xix. 81—82; Sprenger, *Das Leben des Moḥammad* [2], ii. 69, 81, 88; iii. 100, 120, 172, 180; H. Lammens, *L'âge de Mahomet et la chronologie de la Sīra* (*JA*, 1911 [1], p. 209—250); Buhl, *Das Leben Muhammeds*, p. 115, 257.

ḤAMZA B. ʿALĪ B. AḤMAD, founder of the theological system of the Druses and author of several treatises, which have obtained a place among the sacred books of the Druses. Little is known of his life with certainty. According to al-Nuwairī, he was a native of Zawzan (Zūzan) in Persia and was by trade a maker of felt (*labbād*). In 410/1019 he is said to have first publicly put forward his doctrines, but, according to Ḥamza's own statements, this took place two years earlier in 408/1017, from which year the Druses date the manifestation of the divine incarnation in the person of the Fāṭimid caliph al-Ḥākim bi-Amr Allāh and the beginning of the Druse era. It is not certain when he came to Egypt, possibly in 405 or 406. But after he publicly proclaimed his doctrines in a mosque in Cairo, a riot broke out and Ḥamza had to remain in concealment for a time under the Caliph's protection. What became of him after the latter's disappearance (411/1020) is unknown. He plays a still greater rôle in the religious system of the Druses as *ḳāʾim al-zamān* or last incarnation of the universal intelligence (*ʿaḳl*). According to al-Makīn and other authors, he was usually called *al-Hādī* i.e. *Hādi 'l-mustadjībīn*, leader of those who obey (the divine call).

Bibliography: De Sacy, *Exposé de la religion des Druzes, Introduction*, p. 387 *sq.*; *Texte*, i. 98 *sq.*; ii. 2 *sq.*; Blochet, *Le Messianisme*, p. 94 *sq.*; see also art. DRUZES.

ḤANAFITES, the *madhhab* named after the Imām Abū Ḥanīfa [q.v.]. Abū Yūsuf Yaʿḳūb (d. 182/798) and Muḥ. b. al-Ḥasan al-Shaibānī (d. 189/805) are regarded as the pupils of Abū Ḥanīfa; the former left the *Kitāb al-kharādj* (French transl. by E. Fagnan, Paris 1921), a treatise on taxation and constitutional questions, the latter was responsible for the frequently commented standard works of the school: *Kitāb al-aṣl* or *al-Mabsūt*, *al-Djāmiʿ al-ṣaghīr* and *al-Djāmiʿ al-kabīr*. These two pupils are more authoritative for the development of the teachings of the school than even Abū Ḥanīfa himself; there is often even a controversy between these three authorities. Thus a uniform school-character has found much less expression in the Ḥanafī *madhhab* than in the other schools. The Ḥanafites are unjustly reproached for distinguishing themselves from the other schools by applying subjective opinion (*raʾy*). The Ḥanafī school originated in ʿIrāḳ and was in the time of the ʿAbbāsids the prevailing official doctrine. It spread to the East and flourished particularly in Khurāsān and Transoxania. Numerous famous jurists of this school came from there. From the fifth century till well into the time of the Mongols the family Ibn Māza wielded even the political power in Bukhārā as hereditary *raʾīs* (chief) of the Ḥanafites of the town, with the title of *ṣadr*. In Khurāsān they developed from the third century an irrigation law of their own, adapted to the canalsystem there (cf. Gardīzī, *Zain al-akhbār*, p. 8). But also in the Maghrib they had their adherents alongside the Mālikites until the fifth century; in Sicily they even predominated (Maḳdisī, p. 236 sqq.). With the decline of the ʿAbbāsid caliphate the Ḥanafī school also declined in power, but with the rise of the Ottoman Empire they revived. Under the Ottomans the judgment-seats were occupied by Ḥanafites sent from Constantinople, even in countries where the population followed another madhhab. Even nowadays the Ḥanafī school prevails in the former Ottoman countries; in Tunisia for instance it is equal to the Mālikī rite and also in Egypt it is the officially recognised law-school. Further it is predominant in Central Asia (Afghānistān, Turkestan, Bukhārā, Samarḳand) and in India.

Of older jurists of the school should be mentioned: al-Khaṣṣāf (d. 261/847) specially famous for his book on legal artifices (*ḥiyal*; cf. Schacht, *Die arab. ḥiyal-Literatur*, in *Isl.* xv. p. 211—32), al-Ṭaḥāwī (d. 321/933), al-Ḥākim (d. 334/945), Abu 'l-Laith al-Samarḳandī (d. 375/985) and notably al-Ḳudūrī (d. 428/1036), upon whose *Mukhtaṣar* later works draw a good deal. Then come Shams al-Aʾimma al-Sarakhsī (d. 483/1090) with his comprehensive *Mabsūṭ*, which shows a certain independence, a commentary on al-Ḥākim's synopsis of Shaibānī's *Mabsūṭ*, and al-Kāsānī's (d. 587/1191) *Badāʾiʿ al-ṣanāʾiʿ* which has a strictly systematic arrangement. These older works were however ousted by later works and their commentaries. One of the most important is the *Hidāya* of al-Marghīnānī (d. 593/1197; Engl. transl. by C. Hamilton, London 1870), the principal commentaries on which are: al-Sighnāḳī's *Nihāya* (compiled in 700/1300), al-Bābartī's (d. 786/1384) *ʿInāya* and al-Kurlānī's (8th century) *Kifāya*. A synopsis of the *Hidāya* was prepared by Maḥmūd b. Ṣadr al-Sharīʿa al-Awwal (7th century) entitled *Wiḳāya*, on which a commentary was written by Ṣadr al-Sharīʿa al-Thānī (d. 747/1346), who also made a synopsis entitled *Nuḳāya*. A supercommentary on the *Nuḳāya* was written by al-Kūhistānī (d. 950/1543) entitled *Djāmiʿ al-rumūz*. The second important later work is the *Kanz al-daḳāʾiḳ* of al-Nasafī (d. 710/1310), a synopsis of the same author's *Wāfī*. The most important commentaries are: *a) Tabyīn al-ḥaḳāʾiḳ* by al-Zailaʿī (d. 743/1342); *b) Ramz al-ḥaḳāʾiḳ* by al-ʿAinī (d. 855/1451); *c) Tabyīn al-ḥaḳāʾiḳ* by Mullā Miskīn al-Harawī (written 811/1408); *d) Tawfīḳ al-Raḥmān* by al-Ṭāʾī (d. 1192/1778); *e)* the most important, *al-Baḥr al-rāʾiḳ* by Ibn Nudjaim (d. 970/1562). In the Ottoman Empire the *Durar al-ḥukkām* by Mullā Khusrew (d. 885/1480) obtained a particular authority; a commentary was made thereon by al-Wānḳūlī (d. 1000/1591) and numerous glosses; further the *Multaḳā al-abḥur* by al-Ḥalabī (d. 956/1549; French transl. by H. Sauvaire, Marseille 1882) with the commentary *Madjmaʿ al-anhur* by Shaikhzāde (d. 1078/1667) and the *Tanwīr al-abṣār* by Timurtashī (d. 1004/1595) with the commentary *al-Durr al-mukhtār* by al-Ḥaṣkafī (d. 1088/1677) and a super-commentary by Ibn ʿĀbidīn (d. 1252/1836). Finally there should be mentioned the *Medjelle*, compiled in the Tanẓīmāt-period by a special commission under the leadership of Aḥmed Djewdet Pasha (French transl. in Young, *Corps de droit ottoman*, Oxford 1906, vi. 169 sqq.), with its Turkish commentary *Durar al-ḥukkām* by ʿAlī Ḥaidar (ed. 1912); and also the codification of personal law edited by the Egyptian Minister of Justice Muḥ. Ḳadrī Pasha in 1875: *al-Aḥkām al-sharʿīya fi 'l-aḥwāl al-shakhṣīya* (with an official French, Italian and Engl. transl., the latter by W. Sterry and N. Abcarius under the title of *Code of Moh. Personal Law*, London 1914); both are, however, not "codes" in the usual sense but they are destined to serve for the easier information of the judge on the teachings of the *sharīʿa* (on the question of codification cf. Snouck Hurgronje, *Verspr. Geschr.*, iv./ii., 260 *sqq.*).

The most important fatwā-compilations are: *Dhakhīrat al-burhānīya* by Burhān al-Dīn Ibn Māza (d. about 570/1174), *al-Khānīya* by Ḳādīkhān (d. 592/1196), *al-Sirādjīya* by Sirādj al-Dīn al-Sadjāwandī (end of the 6th century), *al-Tātārkhānīya* by Ibn ʿAlāʾ al-Dīn (d. ca. 800/1397), *al-Bazzāzīya* by al-Bazzāzī (d. 827/1424), *al-Zainīya* by Ibn Nudjaim (d. 970/1563), *al-Ḥāmidīya* by Ḥāmid Effendi al-Ḳonawī (d. 985/1577), *al-Khairīya* by Khair al-Dīn al-Fārūḳī (d. 1081/1670), by the Shaikh al-Islām Abū Suʿūd (d. 982/1574), by the Shaikh al-Islām al-Anḳarawī (d. 1098/1687), by the Shaikh al-Islām ʿAlī Efendi (d. 1103/1691), and the compilation made by order of the Mughal Emperor Awrangzēb ʿĀlamgīr (1069—1118/1659—1707): *al-Fatāwā al-ʿĀlamgīrīya*. Famous uṣūl-works are: *Kanz al-wuṣūl* by al-Pazdawī (d. 482/1089), *Manār al-anwār* by al-Nasafī (d. 710/1310), *Tawḍīḥ* by al-Maḥbūbī (d. 747/1346), with the commentary *Talwīḥ* by the Shāfiʿī al-Taftāzānī (d. 792/1398), *Taḥrīr* by Ibn al-Humām (d. 861/1457), with the commentary *Taḳrīr* by Ibn Amīr al-Ḥādjdj (d. 879/1474).

In spite of their importance little attention has been paid in Europe to the teachings of the Ḥanafī school. There exist only the following expositions: L. Blasi, *Instituzioni di diritto musulmano*, Città di Castello 1914, and the excellent book of G. Bergsträsser, *Grundzüge des islamischen Rechts*, ed. by J. Schacht, Berlin 1935 (both with exclusion of the ritual prescriptions); a description of the real legal status in Turkey is given by M. d'Ohsson in his *Tableau de l'Empire Othoman*, Paris 1787—1820, while the numerous English works are intended for the English courts in India, so among others N. B. E. Baillie, *A digest of moohammadan law*, London 1865 (sec. ed. 1887); Abdur Rahman, *Institutes of mussulman law*, Calcutta 1907; A. C. Gosha, *The principles of Anglo-Moh. law*, Calcutta 1917; Ameer Ali, *Mahommedan law*, 2 vols., Calcutta 1911—1929; R. K. Wilson, *Anglo-Muh. law*, London 1930.

Bibliography: On the spread of the Ḥanafītes: Ibn Khaldūn, *Muḳaddima*, Cairo 1327, p. 500 (transl. de Slane, in *NE*, xx./i. p. 10); A. Mez, *Die Renaissance des Islam*, Heidelberg 1922, p. 202—6; Aḥmad Taimūr, *Naẓra taʾrīkhīya fi ḥudūth al-madhāhib al-arbaʿa*, Cairo 1344, p. 8 *sqq.*

ḤANBALITES. [See Aḥmad b. Muḥammad b. Ḥanbal].

ḤANĪF (a.) (pl. *ḥunafaʾ*) appears repeatedly in the Ḳurʾān as the name of those who possess the real and true religion; e.g. in Sūra, x. 105; xxii. 31; xxx. 30; xcviii. 4 etc. It is used particularly of Abraham as the representative of the pure worship of God. As a rule it contrasts him with the idolaters as in iii. 95; vi. 79, 161; x. 105; xvi. 120, 123; xxii. 31; but in one or two passages it at the same time describes him as one who was neither a Jew nor a Christian; e.g. ii. 135: they (the *ahl al-kitāb*) say, become Jews or Christians that ye may be rightly guided! But thou shalt say: the religion of Abraham as a ḥanīf; he was not one of the polytheists, and iii. 67: Abraham was neither Jew nor Christian, but *ḥanīf muslim* and was not one of the polytheists. The simple collocation of ḥanīf and *muslim* found in this passage is sufficient to show that for Muḥammad the word was not the name of a particular religious body, whch is still clearer from the phrase *ḥunafāʾ li 'llāhi*, xxii. 31, so that the existence of Ḥanīfism as an organised body as insisted particularly by Sprenger has no support in the Kurʾān itself. Sūra xxx. 30 is of special importance for the understanding of the Ḳurʾān meaning of the word, where is said: "Turn thy face towards religion as ḥanīf, (namely) Allāh's creation (*fiṭra*) according to which he has created man; there is no change in the work of Allāh"; cf. also vi. 79; x. 105. It is clear here that the word means the original, innate, primitive religion in contrast to the particular religions which arose later, polytheism on the one hand and the in part corrupt religions of the possessors of scriptures. As to the period of composition of the passages quoted, they may be mainly ascribed with certainty to Madīna, only in vi. 79, x. 105, xcviii. 4, is it doubtful.

The later Islāmic application of the word depends on the linguistic usage of the Ḳurʾān. The Ḥanīfīya (very rarely Ḥanafīya) means the religion of Abraham, e.g. Ibn Hishām, p. 143, 147, 822. But as Muḥammad renovated the pure religion of Abraham, *ḥanīf* is frequently used in the sense of *muslim* (Muḥammadan), e.g. Ibn Hishām, p. 982, 995, cf. also p. 871, where *ḥanīf* is used of religion itself in the sense of "pure, orthodox" as well as the obscene verse of Farazdaḳ,

Naḳā'iḍ, i. 378, where the variant offers a different reading.

In various traditions the Prophet describes the religion proclaimed by him as *al-ḥanīfīya al-samḥa*, the mild or liberal Ḥanīfism, in opposition to ascetic movements, e.g. Ibn Saʿd, i/i. 128; iii/i. 287. The verb *taḥannuf* sometimes means the purer exercise of religion in the pagan period (Wellhausen, *Skizzen und Vorarbeiten*, iv. 156), sometimes it is practically the equivalent of "to adopt Islām", *Kāmil*, p. 526 (a poem by Djarīr); *LA*, x. 404. It is the same with the verb *taḥannuth*, which Hirschfeld and Lyall, as previously E. Deutsch, wish to derive from the Hebrew *teḥinnōth*, but it perhaps rather derived from *taḥannuf* (cf. Nöldeke, *Neue Beiträge zur semit. Sprachwissenschaft*, p. 72); for the latter is explained by Ibn Hishām p. 152, and Ṭabārī, i. 1149, by *tabarrur*, to practise piety, but means also, to become Muḥammadan: Ṭabarī, i. 2827.

The above mentioned passage also (Sūra xxx. 30) where the word means the innate religion is again found in later Arabic authors; e.g., *Kāmil*, p. 244: What is a *ḥanīf ʿala 'l-fiṭra*...? or Diyārbakrī, ii. 177: If I die *ʿalā fiṭrati 'llāhi*. Connected with this, but at the same time remarkably modified, is the use of the word by some authors as the designation not of the pure primitive religion but of the ancient paganism, which preceded the later separate religions. Thus Yaʿḳūbī calls the Philistines, who fought against Saul and David, *ḥunafā'* and adds that they worshipped the stars; and particularly Masʿūdī in his *Tanbīh* uses the word as identical with *ṣābi'ūn* [see AL-ṢĀBI'A] of the people of Persia and the Roman empire, before they adopted Mazdaism and Christianity respectively, and distinguishes this step in religious development as the first *ḥanīfīya* from the pure *ḥanīf* religion. At the same time he says that the word is an arabicised form of the Syriac *ḥanīfu*, in which connection it should be remembered that the Syriac *ḥanfē* is actually used particularly of the Ṣābians (e.g. Barhebraeus, *Chronic.*, p. 176).

As to the origin and earliest history of the word *ḥanīf*, scholars have arrived at utterly different results, e.g. Wellhausen thinks that ḥanīf originally meant a Christian ascetic, de Goeje explains the word by "heathen", and D. S. Margoliouth thinks the word everywhere means Muslim. This last meaning undoubtedly best fits an oft quoted verse of the first century A.H. (Yāḳūt, ii. 51; *Kitāb al-aghānī*, xvi. 45 etc.), where the ḥanīf is distinguished from the Christian priest and the Jewish rabbi. On the other hand, it is doubtful if this meaning is also found in the story of the death of the Bakrī Christian Bisṭām, the scene of which is laid in north-east Arabia (*Kāmil*, p. 131; *Naḳā'iḍ*, ed. Bevan, i. 314). In Ṣakhr's verse (*Hudhailiten*, ed. Kosegarten, xviii 11), where the wine-drinking Christians are making a noise around a *ḥanīf*, one of the scholiasts suggests *muslim*; but the passage would equally fit an ascetic who refrained from wine. The same holds of the *ḥanīf* in the verse of Dhū Rumma, *LA*, xiii. 206, who turns to the west when praying, unlike the Christians; cf. the commentary. The Hudhailī verse, *LA*, vi. 133, where there is a reference to a stay for worship made by a *ḥanīf* is quite colourless. Greater value might, on the other hand, be attached to some verses where the verb *taḥannuf* appears in the above mentioned sense of performing acts of worship. One is by a heathen poet Djirān al-ʿAwd of the Hawāzin tribe of Numair in Nadjd (*LA*, x. 404; cf. *Khizānat*, iv. 198) and mentions *al-ʿābid al-mutaḥannif*, who observes his prayers (*ṣalāt*), by which he can only mean an Arab ascetic; Djarīr (*Naḳā'iḍ*, ii. 595) must also be thinking of such a one when he says of a tribe, that they have allied themselves with shame as the Christians with the religion of him who *yataḥannafu*. Of uncertain value are the verses placed in the mouth of the Awsī opponent of the Prophet, Abū Ḳais b. al-Aslat, in which he calls for the foundation of a *dīn ḥanīf*, a pure faith (Ibn Hishām, p. 180, 2), and contrasts this primitive religion to Christianity and Judaism (*ibid.*, p. 293). The genuineness of the poem of Umaiya b. Abi 'l-Ṣalt, which speaks of the *dīn al-ḥanīfīya* as the only religion which will survive the resurrection (see Schulthess, *BA*, viii. 3), is, to say the least, very doubtful. It seems quite certain that Muḥammad in his use of this word was simply following a recognised usage. That it was connected with the religious movements of South Arabia, as modern scholars suppose, is possible, but by no means certain, as the most reliable of the verses quoted belong to the north.

As to the etymology of the word, as has already been mentioned, even Masʿūdī had seen in it an Aramaic loanword and his opinion has also a number of champions in modern times, who derive the word from the Canaanite-Aramaic *ḥanef* "hypocrite, godless, heathen, heretic". The word would then be a foreign name for heretic, which those to whom it was applied, had somehow adopted in Arabia in a good sense. In any case, we should have to be content with this derivation from the Aramaic, as the corresponding Ethiopic word to which H. Winckler proposes to trace it, is a foreign loanword only found in literature. Schulthess has, it is true, rightly pointed out that the Aramaic *ḥanef*, *ḥanfā* cannot become the Arabic *ḥanīf*, but this probably only shows that we must presuppose an intermediate form, and this is supported by the form of the word in Mandaean, cf. the Syriac abstract noun *ḥanīfū*, mentioned by Masʿūdī. Besides we might, if forced, attain the meaning "secessionist" from the Arabic *ḥanafa* "to break off" which would give a similar development of meaning.

Bibliography: *LA*, x. 402—405; Yaʿḳūbī, i. 51 *sq.*; Masʿūdī, *Tanbīh*, viii. 6, 90 *sq.*, 122 *sq.*, 136 (cf. the Glossary, *s.v.*); Sprenger, *Leben Muḥammads*, i. 46 *sq.*; Kuenen, *National Religions and Universal Religions* (Hibbert Lectures), 1882, p. 19 *sq.*; Wellhausen, *Reste arab. Heidentums* 2, p. 238 *sq.*; Nöldeke, in *ZDMG*, xli. 721; do., *Neue Beiträge z. semit. Sprachwissensch.*, p. 30; H. Winckler, *Arabisch-Semitisch-Orientalisch*, p. 79; H. Grimme, *Mohammed*, i. 13; ii. 59 *sq.*; D. S. Margoliouth, in *JRAS*, 1903, p. 467—493; Lyall, *ibid.*, p. 771—781; Schulthess, *Orient. Studien* (*Festschrift Nöldeke*), i. 86—88; do., in *BA*, viii. 3, 5; J. Horovitz, *Koranische Untersuchungen*, p. 56 *sq.*; R. Bell, *Origin of Islam in its Christian Environment* (London 1926); A. Jeffery, *Foreign vocabulary of the Qur'ān*, p. 112—5.

ḤARAM (A.), forbidden, sacred; *ḥaram* is the name of the sacred area of the two cities of Mecca and al-Madīna (often in the dual *al-ḥaramān*), as well as of that of Jerusalem; then it is also used for the female apartments inaccessible to strangers and their occupants (harem), in this sense = *ḥarīm*.

ḤARĀM, forbidden by the Sacred Law. One of the five categories in the scale of religious appreciations according to the theory of the fiḳh [q.v.]. From another point of view anything that is not forbidden is called *ḥalāl*. Within the sphere of *ḥarām* itself there are gradations depending on the legal validity of the forbidden action, which may be either void (*bāṭil*), deficient (*fāsid*) or even fully valid (*ṣaḥīḥ*).

ḤARĪM (A.), forbidden, particularly the women's apartments and their occupants (harem). — Certain pieces of ground, which are withdrawn from cultivation or building without the owner's consent, are likewise called *ḥarīm*, such as the *Ḥarīm Dār al-Khilāfa* and the *Ḥarīm al-Ṭāhirī* in Baghdād, which included whole stretches of the town.

ḤARRĀN, a very old town situated in the Djazīra province of Mesopotamia, near the sources of the Balīkh river, between Edessa and Ra'়s ʿAin. It is familiar as the home of Abraham and Laban, but is especially famous as the chief seat of the Ṣābians and of their religion. To the Greeks it was known as Χαῤῥάν, to the Romans as Carrhae, to some Church Fathers as Hellenopolis ('heathen city'), to the Muḥammadans as Ḥarrān or Arrān. In its long history Chwolsohn distinguishes five periods; the Biblical, the Greek, the Roman, the Christian and the Muḥammadan. The form of the name found on the cuneiform inscriptions, Ḥarrānu, that is 'route', points to the importance of the place as a trading emporium; but it is chiefly famous all down its history as the seat of the worship of the moon-god Sin, whose temple was adorned by more than one of the Assyrian kings. From the time of Alexander a large Macedonian population settled in northern Mesopotamia, which became known as Mygdonia, and the deities worshipped in Ḥarrān received Greek names. About the beginning of the Christian era the indigenous Syrian population of northern Mesopotamia was largely mixed with Macedonians and Greeks, as well as Armenians and Arabs. As a frontier town Ḥarrān was treated with indulgence by the earlier Emperors, and it was not until Christianity became the religion of the state that efforts were made to suppress the cult of which Ḥarrān was the chief seat. These attempts were not carried to extremes, no doubt owing to the fact that in Ḥarrān, as in other places, the people depended for their livelihood upon the temple. Hence the Church Fathers speak of Ḥarrān as a heathen city, and, although bishops of Ḥarrān were appointed, the place continued a seat of idolatry, even after the country had become a province of the Caliphate. The same commercial necessity may account for the existence here from the beginning of the sixth century of a Monophysite community with a bishop at their head. The majority of the people, however, continued heathen.

Ḥarrān capitulated to ʿIyāḍ b. Ghanm in the year 639 A.D., at which time it was the chief town of Diyār Muḍar. It was the favourite residence of Marwān, the last Umaiyad Caliph (744—750), and here Ibrāhīm the ʿAbbāsid was imprisoned and put to death. The people, however, appear to have been allowed to continue the practice of their religion, but under Rashīd a violent persecution arose, from which the Ḥarrānians sought to free themselves by means of bribes. It was in 830 A.D. that Ma'mūn offered the Ḥarrānians the choice between Islām, the adoption of one of the tolerated religions, and extermination. They claimed that they were Ṣābians; and by this device they saved themselves from extinction [see AL-ṢĀBI'A]. At the present day the site is marked by a village of sugarloaf cottages and ruins of ancient buildings of basalt.

The fame of Ḥarrān will always rest on the long line of philosophers and men of science who flourished there, of whom Thābit b. Ḳurra, and his sons and grandsons, and al-Battānī are the best. known.

Bibliography: Chwolsohn, *Die Ssabier und der Ssabismus* i., cap. x.; Ibn Djubair (ed. de Goeje), p. 244 *sq.*; Chesney, *Expedition to Euphrates and Tigris*, vol. i., p. 112 *sq.*; Sachau, *Reise in Syrien und Mesopotamien*, p. 417 *sq.* G. Le Strange, *The Lands of the Eastern Califate*, p. 103.

HĀRŪN B. ʿIMRĀN, the Aaron of the Bible, born 3 years before Mūsā, when Firʿawn's command to slay the male children was given (Thaʿlabī, p. 100; Ṭabarī, i. 448). When Mūsā received the command of God to effect the deliverance of the Israelites out of Egypt from Firʿawn, he asked for a companion of his own kin (Sūra xx. 29—33). Hārūn, who sat on Firʿawn's council (al-Kisā'ī, p. 211, and *Tanchuma Exodus*), was entrusted with this position. He served Mūsā as spokesman as he had an eloquent tongue (Sūra xxviii. 34—35). He took the greatest share in the erection of the golden calf (Sūra vii. 148 *sqq.*; xx. 87—94 and *Exodus*, xxxiii. 1—7). According to the Talmud (*Sanh.* 77) he had been forced to do this by fear of the Israelites who would have slain him. But other legends show that the Israelites were particularly attached to Hārūn. For example al-Kisā'ī, p. 238, Thaʿlabī, p. 146 and Ṭabarī, i. 502 give the following story in almost identical words: Mūsā and Hārūn once noticed a cave from which light streamed. They went in and found there a golden throne with the inscription "destined for him whom it fits". As Mūsā proved too small, Hārūn sat upon it. The angel of death at once appeared and received his soul; he was 127 years old. When Mūsā had returned to the Israelites, they asked where Hārūn was. "He is dead", said Mūsā. "Thou hast slain him", they answered. Angels then at once appeared with Hārūn's bier and cried: "Do not suspect Mūsā of such a crime". According to another tradition (Thaʿlabī, *ibid.*; Ṭabarī, i. 505), Mūsā led the Israelites to Hārūn's tomb, where he called him back to life, and Hārūn confirmed the story of his death. Midrasch *Jelamdenu*, *Yalḳut*, 764; *Aboth dᵉ R. Nathan*, 32; *Pirke dᵉ R. El.*, 12 also give this Arabic legend.

Bibliography: Ṭabarī, i. 448, 471—493, 502; Thaʿlabī, *Ḳiṣaṣ al-anbiyā'*, Cairo 1312, p. 100, 123—125, 146; al-isKā'ī, *Ḳiṣaṣ al-anbiyā'*, p. 222 *sq.* and 238; Eisenberg, *Moses in der arabischen Legende* (1910), p. 48; J. Horovitz, *Koranische Untersuchungen*, p. 148 sq.

HĀRŪT and **MĀRŪT**, two angels who are mentioned in the Ḳur'ān (Sūra ii. 102) in the words "and it was not Sulaimān that was an unbeliever but the devils, who taught men sorcery and that which had been revealed to the two angels in Bābil, Hārūt and Mārūt; but they taught no one without saying "we are but a temptation, therefore be not unbelieving". People learn from them means by which they may separate man and wife" etc. A number of stories are attached to this passage, the main outlines being as follows. When the angels in heaven saw the sinful children of men, they spoke contemptuously of them before Allāh. But He said: "If you had been in the same position you would not have done any better". They did not agree to this and received permission to send two of their number to earth as an experiment. The two chosen were Hārūt and Mārūt, who were ordered to abstain from grievous sins such as idolatry, whoredom, murder and the drinking of wine. But when they saw a wonderfully beautiful woman they were soon led astray and, when they were discovered, they slew the man who had discovered them. Then Allāh asked the angels to look down at their brethren on the earth; then they said: "In truth, Thou wast right". The pair were given the choice between punishment in this world or the next. They chose the former and were incarcerated in Bābil, where they have since suffered grievous torments.

A. Geiger has already noted that these elements are in the main also found in a Jewish midrash; and it can now be added that many are found as early as the New Testament (2 *Petr.*, ii. 4; *Jude*, v. 6) and the Book of Enoch, in connection with *Genesis* vi. This is clear from the following.

The incident is said to have taken place, according to a Muslim version, "when men were multiplying and sinning". In the same circumstances the sons of God descend to earth in *Genesis* vi.: "and they took to themselves wives". The two angels are called Shamḥazai and ʿAzael in the midrash. These names are found in a corrupt form even in the book of Enoch. Thaʿlabī gives the following story: Three angels descended, Hārūt or ʿAzā, Mārūt or ʿAzābā, and Azriyāʾīl. The latter on the very first day felt himself too weak for earthly temptations and was at his own request taken up to heaven again. According to one version, Hārūt and Mārūt are said to have flown up to heaven at the end of each day; but when they had sinned their wings were disabled. A connected motif is found in the *Schatzhöhle* (ed. Bezold, p. 68—69), where the sons of Seth are no longer allowed to climb the holy mountain after their sin. It is also stated that the disabled ones begged their contemporary Idrīs to intercede with Allāh for them. According to Ḳazwīnī (ed. Wüstenfeld, i. 61), the scoffing at men by Hārūt and Mārūt took place while Adam was still alive. Hārūt and Mārūt remained in Bābīl and taught sorcery (cf. Enoch, Chap. viii. 8; ix. 7). It is also related that they were kept imprisoned in a well in Demāwend. Their tortures are painted in vivid colours; they are kept in chains, as is already related of the fallen angels in the Book of Enoch (Chap. xiv. 5; lxix. 28) and in the Jubilees (v. 6) (cf. also the Syriac Apokalypse of Baruch, ed. Ceriani, p. 152, col. a., ult. = Chap. 56, v. 13).

In a legendary history of Egypt, translated by Wüstenfeld in *Orient und Occident* (i. 329) it is related that Hārūt and Mārūt lived in the time of the Egyptian king ʿAryāḳ.

The names Hārūt and Mārūt are connected by de Lagarde with Haurvātāti and Ameretāti. But it is remarkable that the pair of names shows a strong analogy to other such pairs, found in the Ḳurʾān, such as Yādjūdj and Mādjūdj, Ṭālūt and Djālūt. One of each of these pairs may be traced to pre-Muslim tradition, the other was formed by Muḥammad by altering the first consonant of the former. Mārūt is quite a common Syriac word for power, it possibly contains a remembrance of עזאל.

On the use of the two names in magic cf. Doutté, *Magie et Religion*, p. 391.

In Persian *hārūt* has become a word for magician.

Bibliography: The commentaries on Sūra ii. 102; Thaʿlabī, *Ḳiṣaṣ al-anbiyāʾ* (1282), p. 52 *sqq.*; al-Kisāʾī, *Ḳiṣaṣ al-anbiyāʾ*, ed. Eisenberg, p. 45 *sqq.*; Geiger, *Was hat Mohammed aus dem Judenthume aufgenommen* ², p. 104—106; Grünbaum, in *ZDMG*, xxxi. 224 *sqq.*; de Lagarde, *Gesammelte Abhandlungen*, p. 14 *sqq.*; Abu ʾl-Fidāʾ (ed. Fleischer), p. 232; E. W. Lane, *The 1001 Nights*, Chapter iii., note 14; Littmann, in *Festschrift f. Andreas*, 1916; J. Horovitz, *Koranische Untersuchungen*, p. 146 *sqq.*

AL-ḤASAN B. ʿALĪ B. ABĪ ṬĀLIB, the eldest son of ʿAlī and Fāṭima, the daughter of the Prophet. The exact date of his birth (the year 3 or 4?) depends on the date still to be settled of the marriage of his parents. The *Sīra* represents him as a particular favourite of his grandfather. An abundant apocryphal literature has grown up around this subject, taken from the domestic life of Muḥammad. After the premature death of Fāṭima, he was not on particularly good terms with his father and brothers. He spent the best part of his youth in making and unmaking marriages; about a hundred are enumerated. These easy morals earned him the title *miṭlāḳ* "the divorcer" and involved ʿAlī in serious enmities. He was present at the battle of Ṣiffīn, without taking an active part in it, and took no further interest in public affairs during the lifetime of his father.

After the assassination of ʿAlī, Ḥasan was proclaimed Caliph in the ʿIrāḳ. His partisans tried to persuade him to renew the war against the Syrians. Their importunities, however, led to a rupture between himself and the ʿIrāḳīs. The latter ended by severely wounding their nominal sovereign. From this time on, Ḥasan's one idea was to come to an arrangement with the Umaiyads. Muʿāwiya left to him the task of fixing his own price for the renunciation of the Caliphate. Besides a pension of two million dirhems for his brother Ḥusain, Ḥasan asked for himself a sum of five millions and the revenues of a district in Persia during his lifetime. At a meeting at Adhruḥ Muʿāwiya induced him to renew publicly his renunciation of power. Henceforth Muʿāwiya ceased to trouble about him. Dissension continued to reign among the ʿAlids however. Ḥasan was not on good terms with Ḥusain while both were in league against Ibn al-Ḥanafīya and the other children of ʿAlī.

Ḥasan died at Madīna of consumption. An attempt has been made to throw the responsibility for his end on Muʿāwiya; in addition to the stain which would thus be thrown upon the Umaiyads the object of this charge was to justify the title *shahīd* (martyr) and "*saiyid* of the martyrs" given in compliment to Fāṭima's son. Only Shīʿī writers, or those particularly favourable to the ʿAlids, dare openly voice such a grave accusation. It at the same time gave an opportunity to implicate the family of Ashʿath b. Ḳais, detested by the Shīʿīs on account of his share in the coup of Ṣiffīn. Muʿāwiya was not the man to commit an unnecessary crime and Ḥasan had long become quite inoffensive. He probably died in 49 A.H. at the age of about 45. By his death his brother Ḥusain became head of the ʿAlids. In the later history of this faction we generally find that the numerous descendants of Ḥasan have to give way to the more enterprising Ḥusainids.

Bibliography: Ibn Ḥadjar, *Iṣāba* (Egypt. ed.), i. 328—331; *Aghānī*, xi. 56, 57; xv. 47; Yaʿḳūbī, ii. 254—256; Ṭabarī, ii. 1—10; Dīnawarī, *al-Akhbār al-ṭiwāl* (ed. Guirgass), p. 153, 154, 163, 194, 209; Nawbakhtī, *Firaḳ al-Shīʿa* (1931), index, and other works on Shīʿī history and sects; Ibn Saʿd, iii[a], 26; [al-Balādhurī] *Il Califfo Muʿāwiya I secondo il "Kitāb Ansāb al-Ašrāf"*, trans. O. Pinto and G. Levi della Vida (Rome 1933), index; further references in H. Lammens, *Etudes sur le règne du calife omaiyade Moʿāwia Ier*, p. 127, 140—154, 443; do., *Fāṭima et les filles de Mahomet*, index; do., *Le Berceau de l'islam*; do., *L'Arabie occidentale à la veille de l'Hégire*, i. 98; D. M. Donaldson, *The Shiʾite Religion*, London 1933, p. 66 *sqq.*

AL-ḤASAN B. ABI 'L-ḤASAN AL-BAṢRĪ, a prominent figure in the first century of the Hidjra. During the wars of conquest his father was carried off as a slave from Maisān and brought to Madīna. There he became a client of the celebrated Zaid b. Thābit and married a client of Umm Salama named Khaira. Ḥasan was born of this marriage in 21/642. Brought up in Wādi 'l-Ḳurā, he afterwards settled in Baṣra. There he won a great reputation for strength of character, piety, learning and eloquence. While other men who where held in great esteem, such as Ibn Sīrīn and al-Shaʿbī, being questioned on Yazīd's succession, did not dare voice their opinion, Ḥasan frankly expressed his disapproval. He showed the same freedom of speech in his letters to ʿAbd al-Malik and al-Ḥadjdjādj, so that later authors, like al-Shahrastānī, who thought they detected a leaning towards the doctrine of free will in them, preferred to ascribe them to Wāṣil b. ʿAṭā' [q.v.]. He was considered the equal of his contemporary al-Ḥadjdjādj as an orator; he was highly esteemed as a transmitter of tradition, because he was believed to have been personally acquainted with 70 of those who took part in the battle of Badr, although his chief authority was Anas b. Mālik [q.v.]. He exercised a lasting influence on the development of Ṣūfism, by his ascetic piety, which shone all the more by contrast, as by this time a worldly spirit had penetrated all classes in Islām. Numerous pious sayings are placed on his lips and the Ṣūfīs see in him a predecessor, whom they quote as often as do the orthodox Sunnīs. But the Muʿtazila also openly reckon him one of themselves, not only because the first representatives of their doctrine, ʿAmr b. ʿUbaid and Wāṣil b. ʿAṭā', were among his pupils, but because he himself like them inclined to the doctrine of free wil. That Wāṣil b. ʿAṭā' afterwards separated from him does not alter the case. In this way almost all religious movements within Islām go back to Ḥasan and we cannot be surprised when we are told that, when he died full of honour on the 1st Radjab 110/10th Oct. 728, the whole city of Baṣra attended his obsequies.

Bibliography: Ibn Saʿd, vii. 133 *sqq.*; *Fihrist*, p. 183; Ibn Khallikān, No. 155; Aḥmad b. Yaḥyā, *al-Muʿtazila*, ed. Arnold, p. 12 *sqq.*; Shahrastānī, p. 32; al-Hudjwīrī, transl. Nicholson (in *GMS*, vol. xvii.), p. 86 *sq.*; Farīd al-Dīn ʿAṭṭār, *Tadhkirat al-awliyā'*, ed. Nicholson, i. 24 *sqq.*; v. Kremer, *Geschichte der herrschenden Ideen des Islam*, p. 22 *sq.*, 56 *sq.*; Horten, *Die philosophischen Systeme*, etc., p. 120 *sq.*; Massignon, *Essai sur les origines* etc., p. 152 *sqq.*; H. H. Schaeder, in *Isl.*, xiv. 1 *sqq.*; H. Ritter, *ibid.*, xxi. 1 *sqq.*

AL-ḤASAN B. AL-ṢABBĀḤ, founder of the order of Assassins. According to passages in the *Djāmiʿ al-tawārīkh*, the *Ta'rīkh-i guzīda* and in Mīrkhwānd, based on the *Sargudhasht-i Saiyidnā* his genealogy was Ḥasan b. ʿAlī b. Muḥammad b. Djaʿfar b. al-Ḥusain b. al-Ṣabbāḥ al-Ḥimyarī. Ḥasan claimed to be descended from the ancient Ḥimyarite kings, but Mirkhwānd quotes on this point a statement of Niẓām al-Mulk that the people of Ṭūs alleged the contrary and said that his ancestors had been peasants in their country. While Ḥasan is said to have further alleged that his father migrated from Kūfa to Ḳum, we find him simply called Rāzī, i.e. native of Raiy, in Ibn al-Athīr. The date of his birth is unknown, but he was still a young man when he was won over for the Fāṭimid propaganda. The chief *dāʿī* in Persia was then Ibn ʿAṭṭāsh; the latter commissioned him in 464/1072 to go to Cairo to the Fāṭimid Caliph al-Mustanṣir. In 471/1078 (Ibn al-Athīr, ix. 304, gives the date as 479) he arrived there after first travelling through Persia, Mesopotamia and Syria. In the struggle as to who was to succeed the aged ruler, he took the side of Nizār, while others preferred another of Mustanṣir's sons, who actually occupied the Egyptian throne on his father's death under the name al-Mustaʿlī. He then returned to the east and eagerly advocated Nizār's cause in different places. Finally, in 483/1090—1), he gained possession of the strong mountain fortress of Alamūt, although the stories in the *Sargudhasht-i Saiyidnā* (also in the *Ta'rīkh-i guzīda*) on this point are legendary. According to Ibn al-Athīr, x. 216, he was able to win the confidence of the commander, an ʿAlid, and then had him seized by his men and taken to Dāmaghān. The same thing happened, although by different means, with other fortresses, probably by Ibn ʿAṭṭāsh's orders, whose son, likewise usually called Ibn ʿAṭṭāsh, himself resided in the fortress of Shāhdiz near Iṣpahān. As long as the latter lived, Ḥasan played no prominent part, although the famous Saldjūḳ vizier Niẓām al-Mulk had already long suspected him on account of his frequent meetings with Egyptian missionaries. The well-known story of the early friendschip of these two men, in which ʿUmar-i Khaiyām appears as a third, even if, as Browne has shown, it is accepted by Rashīd al-Dīn also, is however a fable (cf. Houtsma, *Recueil de textes rel. à l'histoire des Seldjoucides*, ii., Introduction, p. 14, note). To make this dangerous opponent harmless, the Assassins resorted to assassination, a means they were so often to use in the years following. Niẓām al-Mulk was to be first to fall, being murdered in 485/1092. It is probably also in this period that the organisation of the Assassins into a secret society falls; on their organisation and aims, cf. the article ASSASSINS. It has also been pointed out there that conditions were then favourable to them, and that it was only after the death of Barkiyārūḳ that Sulṭān Muḥammad could seriously think of putting an end to the Assassins' reign of terror. After Shāhdiz had been taken in 500/1107 and Ibn ʿAṭṭāsh executed, the other robbers' nests fell one by one, but during the siege of Alamūt, Muḥammad died (511/1118) and his troops as a result dispersed; Ḥasan, who after the death of Ibn ʿAṭṭāsh had presumably been recognised as Grand Master of the Assassins, was saved. Seven years later (518/1124). he died after arranging that K'aya Buzurg Ummīd Rūdbārī should succeed him.

If Ḥasan is considered the founder of the Assassins, it must not be supposed that the main object of his life was to secure his personal power by planning assassinations; it is not even proved that he recommended or used this detestable means. Assassination had, as is pointed out in the article ASSASSINS, already for long before Ḥasan's time been commended as a religious duty by the leaders of certain sects, and shortly before Ḥasan's public appearance it had been practised wholesale, notably in Iṣpahān (cf. also Ibn al-Athīr, x. 214). Ḥasan's importance lies much rather in the fact that he gave the Assassins' power a central stronghold in Alamūt, so that it maintained itself there even after his death also. He also devoted his activities to authorship and composed several works in Persian, which were all unfortunately destroyed at the capture of Alamūt by the Mongols. The quotations from them given by Shahrastānī and others go no farther than well-known Shīʿī doctrines; the fact expressly emphasised by the authorities that he did not publicly proclaim his teaching to the people, also agrees entirely with the Shīʿī principle of *taḳīya*. He only differed from other Shīʿīs in that he recognized Nizār, son of al-Mustanṣir, as Imām even after the had been incarcerated by al-Mustaʿlī in 488/1095. How far he was responsible for the organisation of the sect as a secret society cannot be ascertained from the lack of exact details. That he was held in great reverence by his followers is proved by the title *saiyidnā*, "our lord", by which he was called by them.

Bibliography: In addition to works quoted in the article ASSASSINS: Shahrastānī, p. 150 *sqq.*; Schefer, *Siasset Nameh, Supplém.*, p. 48 *sqq.*; Müller, *Der Islam*, ii. 97 *sqq.*; Blochet, *Le Messianisme dans l'hétérodoxie musulm.*, p. 105 *sqq.*; Browne, *A Literary History of Persia*, i. 201 *sqq.*; Djuwainī, *Taʾrīkh-i Djihān-gushā*, iii. (*GMS*, old ser. xvi, 3) p. 186 *sqq.*

ḤASANIDS. [See SAIYID, SHARĪF].

ḤASHWĪYA, also ḤASHAWĪYA or AHL AL-ḤASHW, a contemptuous term for those among the men of Tradition (*aṣḥāb al-ḥadīth*,), who recognised the coarsely anthropomorphic traditions as genuine, without criticism and even with a kind of preference, and interpreted them literally. A few names of individuals who made themselves notorious in this way and who belonged neither to the Karrāmiya nor to those Shīʿīs who did the same, are mentioned by al-Shahrastānī, p. 77. The Sālimīya also (cf. Goldziher, in *ZDMG*, lxi. 79) are among them. The Muʿtazila scorned the whole of the *aṣḥāb al-ḥadīth* as Ḥashwīya because they tolerated anthropomorphic expressions, although without the lack of good taste of the Ḥashwīya proper and often with reservation as to the "how" (*bilā kaifa*).

Bibliography: Van Vloten, in *Actes du 11e Congrès internation. des Oriental.*, 3e Session, p. 99 *sq.*; M. Th. Houtsma, in *ZA*, xxvi. 196 *sqq.* (where further references are given); A. S. Halkin, *The Hashwiyya*, *JAOS* liv. 128.

ḤAWĀLA (A.), literally "turn"; in Muslim law the transference of a debt from one person to another. The *ḥawāla* is an agreement by which a debtor is freed from a debt by another becoming responsible for it (N. Seignette, *Code Musulman par Khalīl*, p. 173). This transference of the obligation is the angle around which this legal mechanism "turns".

The word *ḥawāla* then comes to denote the document by which the transference of the debt is completed and next receives the meaning of cheque, or order to pay, on a public chest also.

Bibliography: N. de Tornauw, *Das muslimische Recht aus den Quellen dargestellt*, Leipzig 1855, p. 139 *sqq.*; A. Querry, *Droit Musulman* (Shīʿī), i. 480; G. Bergsträsser, *Grundzüge des Islamischen Rechts*, p. 66 *sq.*, 78 *sq.*

ḤAWĀRĪ, apostle. The word is borrowed from the Ethiopic, where *ḥawārī* has the same meaning (see Nöldeke, *Beiträge zur sem. Sprachwiss.*, p. 48). The derivations from the Arabic "he who wears white clothes" etc. are erroneous. Tradition delights to give foreign epithets which were current among the "people of the scripture", to the earliest missionaries of Islām. Abū Bakr is called *al-Ṣiddīḳ*, ʿUmar *al-Fārūḳ*, al-Zubair Ibn al-ʿAwwām *al-Ḥawārī.*

At the same time we find the collective name al-Ḥawārīyūn for twelve individuals, who are said to have been appointed *naḳībs* of the Madīnese at the "second ʿAḳaba" by Muḥammad (or by those present) as "surety for their people just as the apostles were sureties for ʿĪsā b. Maryam and I (Muḥammad) am for my people". Christian influence is also found elsewhere in the account of the "second ʿAḳaba", the total number of those present being usually given as 70 or 72, apparently on the analogy of the Evangelical accounts of the 70 or 72 apostles (St. Luke, x. 1, 17). Of these twelve Ḥawārīyūn 9 are said to have belonged to the Khazradj and 3 to the Aws.

According to another account however, the Ḥawārīyūn belonged exclusively to the tribe of Ḳuraish (cf. Thaʿlabī, *Ḳiṣaṣ al-anbiyāʾ*, Cairo 1290, p. 425). From these accounts it is again clear how the rivalry between Anṣār and Muhādjirūn has influenced Tradition.

The tradition regarding these twelve Muslim apostles has perhaps, like so many traditions, arisen as a deduction from a statement in the Ḳurʾān. In Sūra iii. 52, lxi. 14, Jesus says: "Who are My Anṣār for God ('s cause)?" and the Ḥawārīyūn answered: "We are the Anṣār of God".

The parallel with Muḥammad's own position is here clear enough and it is obvious that Muslim Ḥawārīyūn were found to be a necessity alongside of the Muslim Anṣār.

There are statements in several Muslim writers regarding the disciples of Jesus, which for the most part go back to passages in the Apostles. Cf. also the article ʿĪSĀ.

ḤAWḌ, the basin at which on the day of the resurrection Muḥammad will meet his community. This idea is not found in the Ḳurʾān, but in Tradition, which supplies a great variety of details of which the following are the more important.

Muḥammad is called the precursor (*faraṭ*) of his community. On the day of the resurrection the latter, the poor in the first place, who have not known the pleasures of life, will join him near the basin. So far as one can judge, the question is one of admittance. Muḥammad pleads with God for his Companions, but he is told: Thou dost not know what they have done since thy death. Some have gone back on their steps (Bukhārī, *Djanāʾiz*, bāb 73; *Musāḳāt*, bāb 10; *Riḳāḳ*, bāb 52; Aḥmad b. Ḥanbal, ii. 132; al-Ṭayālisī, No. 995).

The descriptions of the basin raise questions of cosmological topography. Its dimensions equal the distance between Djarbāʾ and Adhruḥ (variants: Aila-Ṣanʿāʾ; ʿAden-ʿUmān; al-Madīna-Ṣanʿāʾ etc.) and its jars are numberless as the stars. Its waters are white as milk and sweet as honey. It is filled by two spouts from Paradise, one gold, the other silver. Some traditions connect the basin with the river of Paradise, al-Kawthar [q.v,]. but these associations are secondary, Kawthar only having become a proper name of a river of Paradise at a later date. The representation of the throne of Muḥammad as being above the basin is also part of the topography of Paradise ("a garden of Paradise"). Details taken from the Bible are fairly numerous, like the very common tradition that he who drinks of the waters of the reservoir will never thirst (cf. St. John's Gospel, iv. 14).

It is hardly possible to assign a definite place to the reservoir among the eschatological sites. According to a canonical tradition (Tirmidhī, *Ḳiyāma*, bāb 9; Aḥmad b. Ḥanbal, iii. 178). Muḥammad said that if he is not found near the *ṣirāṭ* he should be sought near the *mīzān* or rather near the basin. In the creed known as *Fiḳh Akbar II* the basin comes immediately after the balance (art. 21). — Neither Ghazzālī, in *al-Durra al-fākhira*, nor the author of the *Kitāb aḥwāl al-ḳiyāma* mention the basin. In the *Iḥyā'* it comes between the intercession and the descriptions of Hell and Paradise, without there being any connection with the one or the other. This uncertainty which connects the basin sometimes with Paradise sometimes with the trials at the last judgment, has given rise to the idea of two basins.

Bibliography: The statements in the collections of canonical tradition in Wensinck, *Handbook*, s.v. *Basin*; Ṭabarī, *Tafsīr*, xxx. 176 *sqq.*; the articles of the creeds in Wensinck, *The Muslim Creed*, index, s.v. *Basin*; al-Ghazzālī, *Iḥyā'*, Cairo 1302, iv. 478.

ḤAWWĀ, the wife of Adam, created in Paradise out of a left rib from her sleeping husband, which operation caused him no pain. Otherwise no man would cleave to his wife (Thaʿlabī, p. 18; Kisā'ī, p. 31). As she was formed from a living being, he called her Ḥawwā (*ibid.*, also Ṭabarī, i. 109; Ibn al-Athīr, i. 24, cf. *Genesis* 2, 23). As Adam was created out of dust and Ḥawwā out of a bone, man becomes more beautiful with increasing years but woman more ugly (Thaʿlabī, *ibid.*, agreeing with *Deut. R.*, 6, *Genesis R.*, 14 and 17). Ḥawwā, whose name does not occur in the Ḳur'ān, (Sūra vii. 19 *sq.*) bore the main guilt of the first sin, as, tempted by Iblīs, she ate of the tree of evil. Tradition relates that Ḥawwā offered her husband first wine, than the forbidden fruit and so became the cause of original sin (Thaʿlabī and *Gen. R.*, ibid.). Wine is therefore considered the source of all evil. Another tradition says that this meal plunged mankind into eternal grief (Thaʿlabī und the Midrash, *ibid.*). Ten punishments, including menstruation, pregnancy and travail, remind the daughters of Eve of their mother's trespass. To console her, Ḥawwā received the assurance that every pious woman, devoted to her husband, would share Paradise in recompense for the mortal agonies of travail. If she died in child-bed, she would be enrolled in the body of martyrs and united with her husband in Paradise. Jewish and Arab sources mention in almost the same words the marriage of Adam and Ḥawwā at which God, Gabriel and the other angels were present (*Baba B.*, 75; *Sanh.*, 8; *Erubin*, 11; *Gen. R.*, 11, 17; *Levit. R.*, 20; *Ḳoheleth R.*, 8 and Kisā'ī, p. 35). After the expulsion from Paradise Adam and Ḥawwā made the pilgrimage to Mecca, observed several ceremonies and Ḥawwā had her first menstruation. Then Adam stamped on the ground and the well of Zamzam burst forth and she used it for a bath of purification. Ḥawwā died two years after Adam and was buried beside him.

Bibliography: Ṭabarī, i. 109 *sqq.*; Ibn al-Athīr, i. 24—26; Thaʿlabī, *Ḳiṣaṣ al-anbiyā'* ed. Cairo 1312, p. 18—29; Kisā'ī, *Ḳiṣaṣ al-anbiyā'*, p. 30—78; Grünbaum, *Beiträge*, p. 64 *sqq.*; Weil, *Bibl. Legenden* etc., p. 17—30.

ḤIDJĀB (A.), any partition which separates two things. In the Ḳur'ān it has the sense of "curtain, veil", e.g. one should speak with women from behind a curtain (Sūra xxxiii. 53); in the next world the elect and the damned will be separated by a curtain (vii. 46); the term here seems to be synonymous with *al-aʿrāf* and was therefore early explained as "wall" (Ṭabarī, *Tafsīr*, viii. 126; Baiḍāwī, ii. 326) in allusion to Ḳur'ān lvii. 13. The unbelievers said to the Prophet: "There is a ḥidjāb between thee and us" (xli. 5). It is not possible for a man to hear God speaking unless by a revelation or from behind a curtain (xlii. 51), as was the case with Moses (Asbāṭ, according to al-Suddī; Ṭabarī, *Tafsīr*, xxv. 25). Among the mystics ḥidjāb, meaning "all that veils the end", signifies the impression produced on the heart by the phenomena constituting the visible world, which prevents it admitting the revelation of truth (Djurdjānī, *Taʿrīfāt*, p. 86; ʿAbd al-Razzāḳ al-Ḳāshānī, *Technical Terms*, ed. Sprenger, p. 35, No. 116). The passions (*nafs*) are the main cause of the obscurity; but each limb has a special passion that gives rise to a particular veil; substances, accidents, elements, bodies, forms, and qualities are so many veils which conceal divine secrets. The higher truth is hidden from all men except saints (*walī*) alone. The opposite of ḥidjāb is *kashf*; the condition of soul in the former case is called *ḳabḍ* (contraction) in the second *basṭ* (expansion). Mystic love (*wadjd*) is aroused on account of the obstacle opposed to it in the first case (occultation), and satisfied by contemplation in the second (revelation). These expressions are borrowed from the Gnostics (*Pistis Sophia* in E. de Faye, *Gnostiques et gnosticisme*, 1913, p. 269).

Bibliography: ʿAlī b. ʿUthmān al-Djullābī al-Hudjwīrī, *Kashf al-maḥdjūb*, transl. Nicholson (in *GMS*), p. 48, 149, 325, 374, 414; Hirschfeld, *New Researches into the Exegesis of The Qoran*, p. 43.

AL-ḤIDJR (HADJER, HADSCHER, HÖDSCHER, AL-HHEGR in Ritter), a town in Arabia, a day's journey from Wādi 'l-Ḳurā south of Taimā', identical with the ancient commercial town of "Εγρα in Ptolemy and Egra in Pliny. The town no longer exists. At present the name al-Ḥidjr is given by the Bedouins to the flat valley between Mabrak al-Nāḳa (Mazḥam) and Bīr al-Ghanam which stretches for several miles and has a fertile soil with many wells at which numerous Bedouins encamp with their herds. Two roads lead from al-Ḥidjr to Mecca, the Nadjd road, the modern pilgrim route, and the Marw road,, which was in ancient times the road followed by the pilgrims to Mecca. To the west of al-Ḥidjr is a mountain of five isolated sandstone cliffs, called Athālith (in Doughty, *Travels*, always written Ethlib), on which are carved a large number of artistic monuments. Ch. M. Doughty, the first European to visit Ḥidjr (1876—1877) and to examine closely the cliffs with their carvings, found the latter to be almost exclusively tombs (family vaults) with niches and remains of human bodies. Pilgrims going to Mecca rest on Mount Athālith for a day and offer up prayers here.

The verses 80—84 of Sūra xv, called *al-Ḥidjr*, speak about a godless and arrogant cave-dwelling people who lieved in this place and who in other places in the revelation are called Thamūd [q.v.]. It is related of them that they hewed their houses out of rock. To convert them God sent a kinsman of theirs, the prophet Ṣāliḥ [q.v.], to them, who made a camel and her young one arise out a cleft in the rock as evidence of his divine mission. But when they continued in their idolatry and slew the camel which Ṣāliḥ begged them to spare, God sent an earthquake which destroyed them. The sandstone cliffs of al-Ḥidjr with the monuments carved in them are also called *Madā'in Ṣāliḥ* "Ṣāliḥ's towns" after Ṣāliḥ.

Al-Ḥidjr also finds a place in the history of the Prophet. When Muḥammad was going through Tabūk towards Damascus in the year 9/631 he came with his army into the neighbourhood of al-Ḥidjr. The troops wanted to rest here to refresh themselves at the wells but the Prophet would not allow them to enter this place that had been visited by the wrath of God. In modern times the Wahhābī chief Saʿūd wished to build a town here but the scheme fell through on account of the vehement objections of the ʿulamāʾ to rebuilding on a site cursed by God.

For the *ḥidjr* adjacent to the Kaʿba of Mecca, where Ismāʿīl is said to have been buried, see the art. KAʿBA.

Bibliography: Ṭabarī, i. 215, 217, 244—251, 278—279, 352; Ibn Hishām, i. 898—899; Hamdānī, *Djazīra* (ed. Müller), p. 131, 14-15; Yāḳūt, *Muʿdjam* ii. 208; K. Ritter, *Erdkunde*, xii. 154—157; 162, xiii. 265—266, 418, 436, 440—442; Caussin de Perceval, *Essai sur l'histoire des Arabes avant l'islamisme* (Paris 1847—1848), i. 24—25, 212; iii. 285; W. Muir, *The Life of Mahomet* (London 1858), i. 138 note; A. Sprenger, *Die alte Geographie Arabiens*, Index s.v.; Jaussen and Savignac, *Mission archéol. en Arabie*, i. 107 *sqq.*, 144; J. Euting, *Tagebuch einer Reise in Inner-Arabien*, ii. 215 *sqq.*; E. Renan, *Documents épigraphiques recueillis dans le nord de l'Arabie par M. Charles Doughty*, Paris 1884 (in a special volume of the *Académie des Inscr. et Belles Lettres*); Doughty, *Travels in Arabia Deserta*, i. 23, 81—83, 93—96, 102—123, 133—136, 180—188 and Index, s.v. el-Héjr and Medain Ṣāliḥ.

HIDJRA (HEGIRA), the migration of the Prophet from Mecca to Madīna, the starting point of the Muḥammadan era.

The Prophet, not having succeeded in overcoming the resistance of the Ḳuraish and on the other hand having already won friends among the people around Madīna (then called Yathrib), resolved to remove to the latter town. The Arabic word *hidjra* should not be translated "flight", for the idea of fleeing is not properly expressed by the verb *hadjara*. This verb means "to break off relations, to abandon one's tribe, to emigrate". For the events connected with Muḥammad's migration to Madīna, cf. the articles MUḤAMMAD and AL-MUHĀDJIRŪN.

Authorities are not agreed on the exact date of the Hidjra. According to the most usual account it took place on the 8th Rabīʿ I (20th Sept. 622). But this would not be the date of the departure from Mecca but of the arrival in Madīna. According to other versions, it was the 2nd or the 12th Rabīʿ I. Al-Bīrūnī says that the Jews were just celebrating the ʿĀshūrāʾ festival (Day of Atonement) when the Muslims arrived in Madīna (cf. also TAʾRĪKH).

The 8th was preferred as it was a Monday. According to a tradition, the Prophet is said to have answered when asked why he observed Monday especially: "on this day was I born, on this day I received my prophetic mission and on this day I migrated".

The fixing of the Hidjra as the beginning of the Muḥammadan era dates from the Caliph ʿUmar. The traditions which try to trace it to the Prophet himself are devoid of all probability. According to another tradition, Yaʿlā b. Umaiya, Abū Bakr's governor in the Yemen, was the first to use it, but the view that it dates from ʿUmar is by far the most prevalent.

It is related in various forms that ʿUmar after having regulated the administration of finance and made up the register and the levies of taxes found himself embarrassed about the dating, or rather he was reproached for not dating at all. According to a tradition quoted by al-Bīrūnī, Abū Mūsā al-Ashʿarī wrote to him saying: "Thou art sending us letters undated". The Caliph discussed the matter with his officers and after investigating the customs of the Greeks and Persians, it was decided to establish an era. Some proposed to date from the birth of the Prophet, but this date was not certain. ʿAlī is then said to have proposed to take the Hidjra as the beginning of the era, as it marked the date when the Prophet began to assume sovereign power. This decision was come to in the year 17 or 18, some however say 16, but the general view is the year 17.

Before fixing this date the Muslims gave their years names such as "year of the permission", "year of the earthquake", "year of the farewell" etc. (cf. al-Bīrūnī, *Chronology*, p. 35). When Muḥammad began his preaching, the Arabs were reckoning from the "year of the elephant".

The year of the Hidjra was then chosen as the year 1; but as the calendar was already fixed by the Ḳurʾān, the months were retained and Muḥarram was retained as the first month because business is resumed then after the pilgrimage. The era thus began, not with the day of the Hidjra but with the 1st day of the month of Muḥarram of the Hidjra year. This first day fell on a Friday and corresponded to the 16th Tammūz (July) 933 of the Seleucid era, and 622 of the Julian calendar.

Bibliography: L. Lacoine, *Table de concordance des dates des calendriers*, Paris 1891; Ideler, *Handbuch der mathematischen und technischen Chronologie*, Berlin 1826; Ulysse Bouchet, *Hémérologie*, Paris 1868; Ginzel, *Handbuch der math. und techn. Wissenschaften*, Leipzig 1906, i. 258 *sqq.*; E. Mahler, *Vergleichungstabellen der muhammedanischen und christlichen Zeitrechnung*, Leipzig 2th. ed. 1926.

ḤIZB. A word of Ethiopic or South-Arabian origin meaning people or tribe, applied in the Ḳurʾān also to a religious party or sect (Jeffery, *Foreign Vocabulary of the Qurʾān*, 108). At an early date the word acquired the meaning of "a part, a section" and came to be used in much the same sense as *wird*, i.e. a special part of the Ḳurʾān or other prayer-formula which one proposes to recite. This practice has led in some Muslim countries (as in Egypt, cf. Lane, *Modern Egyptians*, chap. xxvii) to a division of the Ḳurʾān into 60 *aḥzāb*, by the side of the other division into 30 *adjzāʾ*. But this did not or does not obtain, as it appears, everywhere; al-Ghazzālī in his *Iḥyāʾ* (first quarter, book 8, bab 2), speaks of the 30 *adjzāʾ*; he uses *ḥizb*, however, in a very undefined way. With the rise of the derwīsh-brotherhoods, the word got a particular meaning in those circles. In Egypt every brotherhood is a *ḥizb* (Lane *o.c.* xviii); but *ḥizb* means also the "office" of the brotherhood, which was recited in the regular Friday-service (*ḥadra*) in the *zāwiya* or *takīya*, and consisted of long passages of the Ḳurʾān and other prayers (see DHIKR). From here seems to have started the use of the word in a narrower sense, namely its application to prayer-formulas (*duʿāʾ*), originating from famous saints and recited either regularly or at special occasions. Judging from the titles of books enumerated by Brockelmann (*GAL*, index, s. v. ḥizb) and Ḥādjdjī Khalīfa (ii., 56—60), the word was not applied to such prayers earlier than the vith century. The most famous of all these prayers is the *ḥizb al-baḥr* of al-Shādhilī (d. 656/1258; see SHĀDHILĪYA), also named *al-ḥizb al-ṣaghīr*. It is in high esteem with travellers, in particular at sea; the complete text is to be found in Ibn Baṭṭūṭa (i, 40 *sqq.*; cf. also *ZDMG* vii, 25).

ḤIZ̲K̲ĪL (EZEKIEL) B. BŪRĪ, whose mother when advanced in years prayed to God for offspring and had her prayer granted, was the successor of Kālib. He is not mentioned by name in the Ḳurʾān but in Sūra ii. 243 ("Didst thou not see those ones who abandoned their dwellings in their thousands from fear of death? and God said "Die!" Then he restored them to life") an allusion to Ezekiel xxxvii. 1—10 is generally recognised.

Of the various traditions in T̲h̲aʿlabī, p. 148 and Ṭabarī, i. 530, 538, the following, which are of Talmudic origin, may here be mentioned. In the days of Ḥizḳīl a plague carried off numerous Israelites. Many corpses could not be buried and became food for birds and beasts. By God's command Ḥizḳīl proclaimed: "Ye dead bones, God commands you to assume again the flesh that covered you!" At once the bones clothed themselves with flesh and once more had skin, blood, veins, and arteries. Ḥizḳīl continued: "O breath of life, make these bodies live again". They were breathed upon by the spirit of life and rose in their dead clothes. They returned to their people again, founded families and multiplied (Sanh., 92; Gen.. R., 14; Cant. R, 7).

According to T̲h̲aʿlabī, p. 101, one of the members of Firʿawn's council in Egypt was likewise called Ḥizḳīl, while Kisāʾī calls him Ḥirbil. He was originally a carpenter. Mūsā's mother applied to him to make a small box in which to place her new born son and throw him into the sea; but he hurried to the royal police to tell them of it. His tongue then became paralysed and he lost the power of speech. He only regained it after swearing that he would betray nothing. Henceforward he honoured Mūsā in secret and protected him from all danger (cf. Sūra xl. 28).

Bibliography: Ṭabarī, ii. 530—538; T̲h̲aʿlabī, Ḳiṣaṣ al-anbiyāʾ, ed. Cairo 1312, p. 101 and 148; al-Kisāʾī, Ḳiṣaṣ al-anbiyāʾ, p. 202; Eisenberg, Moses in der arab. Legende, 1910, p. 20.

HUBAL, the name of an idol, which was worshipped at Mecca in the Kaʿba but otherwise is known only from a Nabataean inscription (Corp. Inscr. Semit., ii., No. 189 = Jaussen and Savignac, Mission Archéol. en Arabie, i. 169, 170) where it is mentioned along with Dūs̲h̲arā and Manūtu. It is thus probable that the tradition according to which ʿAmr b. Luḥaiy brought the idol with him from Moab or Mesopotamia, is correct in retaining a memory of the foreign, to be more accurate Aramaic, origin of Hubal, although the substance of the tradition is otherwise quite legendary. The name cannot be explained from the Arabic for the etymologies in Yāḳūt etc. condemn themselves, but Pocock's supposition that Hubal is equivalent to הַבַּעַל, although defended by Dozy, is hardly better founded. Another tradition indeed relates that Hubal was an idol of the Banū Kināna, worshipped also by the Ḳurais̲h̲, and had been placed in the Kaʿba by K̲h̲uzaima b. Mudrika wherefore it used to be called Hubal K̲h̲uzaima. It is further related that the idol was of red carnelian in the form of a man; the Ḳurais̲h̲ replaced the right hand which was broken, by a golden one; it was the custom to consult the idol by divination with arrows; this was done for example by ʿAbd al-Muṭṭalib with reference to his son ʿAbd Allāh, etc. We learn nothing further about the cult of this idol and the legends are quite worthless for the comprehension of the real nature of the deity. After the conquest of Mecca Hubal shared the lot of all other idols and the image was removed from the Kaʿba and destroyed.

Bibliography: Ibn His̲h̲ām, i. 50 sq.; Wüstenfeld, Die Chroniken der Stadt Mekka, i. 58, 73, 107, 133; Yāḳūt, Muʿd̲j̲am, iv. 949 sq.; Yaʿḳūbī, i. 295; Ṭabarī, i. 1075 sqq.; Pocock, Spec. Hist. Arab., ed. White, p. 98; Krehl, Über die Religion der vorisl. Araber, p. 90; Osiander, in ZDMG, vii. 493; Caussin de Perceval, Essai sur l'hist. des Arabes avant l'islamisme, i. 215 sqq.; Wellhausen, Reste arab. Heidentums[2], p. 75, 221.

HŪD, the prophet who, according to the Ḳurʾān, appeared among the ʿĀd [q.v.]. His story is told in Sūras vii, xi, xxvi, xlvi and xlix and his name is found in the first three of these. Sūra xi even bears his name, where the verses 50-60 deal with him. He is represented as one of the kinsmen (ak̲h̲) of ʿĀd and his genealogy (which is transmitted in various forms) therefore coincides in part with that of their founder ʿĀd. He is also identified with ʿĀbir (the Biblical ʿEber, the ancestor of the Hebrews); in another reference he is called the son of ʿĀbir. His figure is even more shadowy than the picture of his people and like every warner he is represented in the same position as Muḥammad in Mecca, i.e. he found only infidelity and pride among the people and his followers were few. God therefore punished the ʿĀd with a three years' drought, as the later legend tells us. A deputation was sent to Mecca to pray for rain there. God made three clouds appear in the sky, one white, one red and one black. One of the deputation, called Ḳail, was given the choice of one of the three by a voice from heaven. He chose the black one with the result that a terrible storm broke over the ʿĀd and destroyed the whole people with the exception of Hūd and his followers. Hūd is said to have lived 150 years. There are various traditions regarding his grave; there is a Ḳabr Hūd not far from Biʾr Barahūt in Ḥaḍramaut which has been visited by van der Meulen and v. Wissmann. In Ibn Baṭṭūṭa (ed. Paris, i. 205; ii. 203) it is mentioned that the grave of Hūd is in the great mosque at Damascus; according to other traditions he rests near the Kaʿba with 98 other prophets.

In the article ʿĀD attention has already been called to the fact that the existence of a tribe of ʿĀd is problematic. This is still truer of Hūd. The word Hūd in the Ḳurʾān is a name for the Jews as a body (Sūra ii. 111, 135, 140), and the root h-w-d means to profess Judaism (ii. 62; iv. 46 etc.). The proper name looks as if it had been derived from the verb and the noun; the traditional identification of Hūd with the ancestor of the Hebrews probably points in the same direction. Hirschfeld is perhaps correct when he calls Hūd an allegorical figure (Beiträge zur Erklärung des Ḳorân, Leipzig 1886, p. 17, note 4). Von Kremer's suggestion (Über die südarabische Sage p. 21 sq.), that the crater of Barahūt was the immediate cause of the rise of the Hūd legend is worthy of note.

Bibliography: Besides the works mentioned in the text and in the articles ʿĀD: the commentaries on the Ḳurʾān; T̲h̲aʿlabī, Ḳiṣaṣ al-anbiyāʾ (1290), p. 63 sqq.; Sale, The Koran, Preliminary Discourse, p. 8; Maracci, Refutationes (Patavii 1698), p. 282 and the older literature there given; Geiger, Was hat Muhammad aus dem Judenthume aufgenommen[2], p. 111 sqq.; v. d. Meulen and von Wissmann, Ḥaḍramaut, p. 158 sqq.; J. Horovitz, Koranische Untersuchungen, p. 149.

ḤUKM (A.), plural aḥkām, primarily the infinitive of ḥakama, and so "a restraining" like ḥikma. All ḥikma is, in the classical language, ḥukm, but the latter denotes also: 1. a judgment or legal decision

(Ḳurʾān xxi. 78), especially of God (xiii. 41); 2. a logical judgment expressed in a *djumla*; in this respect it sometimes must be rendered by "relation" (*isnād amr ʿalā ākhir*, cf. Lane's *Lexicon* s.v. and also Baidjūrī's *Ḥāshiya* ed. Cairo 1326, ii 93); 3. the exercise of administrative authority, rule or dominion (similarly *ḥukūma*); 4. an ordinance or decree, synonymous with *ḳaḍāʾ* (Ḳurʾān xviii. 26); 5. a rule in grammar, and then a rule generally (see further in Dozy, *Supplément*). On the five *aḥkam* of the law, cf. the art. SHARĪʿA.

Bibliography: Lees' *Dictionary of Technical Terms*, Pt. i., p. 372 *sqq.*; Juynboll, *Handbuch des isl. Gesetzes*, p. 54, 59; L. Gauthier, *La racine arabe ḥ-k-m- et ses dérivés* (*Homenaje a D. Francisco Codera*, Saragossa 1904, p. 435—454).

ḤULŪL, a philosophical term, derived from *ḥalla* "to loosen, unfold, alight, settle in a place (*maḥall*)", whence its classical acceptations in Muslim theology, the relation between a body and its place, an accident and its substance. *Ḥulūl* has also been applied to the substantial union 1. of the body and the soul, *ḥulūl al-rūḥ fi'l-badan*, 2. of a divine spirit with man, *ḥulūl al-ʿaḳl al-faʿʿāl fi 'l-insān* (Fārābī, *Ārāʾ ahl al-madīna al-fāḍila*, ed. Cairo, 1906, p. 86). *ḥulūl al-lāhūt fi 'l-nāsūt* (cf. AL-ḤALLĀDJ). The Aristotelian doctrine of hylomorphism, like the Christian doctrine of the incarnation, proposed the union to matter of a spiritual substance as its specific form; it may be compared to a force in its sphere of action. Almost all Muslim theologians (*mutakallimūn*) reject it; followers of atomism, with al-Ashʿarī, admitted *ḥulūl* in case 1., for they saw in the *rūḥ* a subtle body, even in the angels and demons, but they rejected it in case 2. as submitting the divine essence to a partition (*tadjazzuʾ*), and to transmigration (*tanāsukh*), whence the excommunication both by Sunna and Shīʿa of the following sects as *ḥulūlīya* on the same grounds as the Christians: (*a*) the extreme Shīʿa (*ghulāt*): Sabāʾīya, Bayānīya, Djanāḥīya, Khaṭṭābīya, Namīrīya (Nuṣairīya), Muḳannaʿīya, Rizāmīya, Bāṭinīya, ʿAzāḳira, Druses. *b*. Sunnī Ṣūfīya: Ḥulmānīya, Fārisīya (cf. AL-ḤALLĀDJ), Shabbāsīya. *c*. Monists: Ittiḥādīya (Ibn Taimīya calls "*ḥulūl muṭlaḳ*" their "*waḥdat al-wudjūd*", cf. *tadjassud al-aʿmāl*" according to Farghānī, *Muntaha 'l-madārik*, (ed. Cairo 1293, ii. 84—86; cf. IBN AL-ʿARABĪ).

Bibliography: al-Sulamī, *Ghalaṭāt al-Ṣūfīya*, MS. Cairo, *Fihr.*, vii. no. 178 *sqq.*, 77—79; al-Hudjwīrī, *Kashf al-maḥdjūb*, transl. Nicholson, p. 260—4; Ghazzālī, *al-Maḳṣad al-asnā*, Cairo 1324, p. 76; Ibn al-Dāʿī, *Tabṣira*, lith. Teheran, p. 406, 419; Ibn Taimīya, *Kawākib*, Ms. Damascus xxvi, (extr. printed in Alūsī, *Djalā*, p. 54—61); al-Haitamī, *Fatāwā ḥadīthīya*, p. 238—9; Ḳāḍī ʿIyāḍ, *al-Shifaʾ*, chap. iv. 3, n. 5. with the commentaries of al-Daladjī and al-Khafādjī; al-Tahānawī, *Kashshāf iṣṭilāḥāt al-funūn*, ed. Sprenger, p. 349—352; Friedländer, in *JAOS*, xxviii. 34, 36, 65—72; xxix, 13, 52, 90, 96.

ḤŪR (A.), plural of *ḥawrāʾ*, fem. of *aḥwar*, literally "the white ones", i.e. the maidens in Paradise, the black iris of whose eyes is in strong contrast to the clear white around it. The nomen unitatis in Persian is *ḥūrī* (also *ḥūrī-bihishtī*), Arabic *ḥūrīya*. The explanation of the word found in Arabic works "those at whom the spectator is astounded (*ḥār*[a])" is of course false and is therefore rejected even by other Arab philologists.

These maidens of Paradise are described in various passages in the Ḳurʾān. In Sūra ii. 25, iii. 15, iv. 57, they are called "purified wives"; according to the commentators, this means that they are free alike from bodily impurity and defects of character. In Sūra lv. 56, it is said that their glances are retiring i.e. they look only upon their husbands. "Neither man nor djinn has even touched them"; this is interpreted to mean that there are two classes of them, one like man and the other like the djinn. They are enclosed in pavilions (lv. 72). They are compared to jacinths and pearls (lv. 58).

Later literature is able to give many more details of their physical beauty; they are created of saffron, musk, amber and camphor, and have four colours, white, green, yellow, and red. They are so transparent that the marrow of their bones is visible through seventy silken garments. If they expectorate into the world, their spittle becomes musk. Two names are written on their breasts, one of the names of Allāh and the name of their husband. They wear many jewels and ornaments etc. on their hands and feet. They dwell in splendid palaces surrounded by female attendants and all possible luxury etc.

When the believer enters Paradise, he is welcomed by one of these beings; a large number of them are at his disposal; he cohabits with each of them as often as he has fasted days in Ramaḍān and as often as he has performed good works besides. Yet they remain always virgins (cf. Sūra lvi. 36). They are equal in age to their husbands (*ibid.* 37), namely 33 years (al-Baiḍāwī).

These are all very sensual ideas; but there are also others of a different kind. In discussing the Ḳurʾānic term "wives" (ii. 25), al-Baiḍāwī asks what can be the object of cohabitation in Paradise as there can be no question of its purpose in the world, the preservation of the race. The solution of this difficulty is found by saying that, although heavenly food, women etc., have the name in common with their earthly equivalents, it is only "by way of metaphorical indication and comparison, without actual identity, so that what holds good for one may hold for the other also". In another passage (on Sūra xliv. 54) al-Baiḍāwī observes that it is not agreed whether the *ḥūrī*'s are earthly women or not. Likewise Ṣūfī authors have spiritualised the *ḥūrīs* (see especially Berthels, *loc. cit.*).

Sale (*The Koran*, London 1821, *Preliminary Discourse*, p. 134) and others (see Berthels, *l.c.*, p. 287) think that Muḥammad owed the idea of the maidens of Paradise to the Parsis. In the article DJANNA it is suggested that Muḥammad misunderstood Christian pictures of Paradise and that the angels in them are the originals of the youths and maidens of the Ḳurʾān.

Bibliography: The Ḳurʾān commentaries on the passages mentioned; Bukhārī, *Ṣaḥīḥ*, *Kitāb badʾ al-khalḳ*, *Bāb fī ṣifat al-djanna*; Ghazzālī, *Iḥyāʾ* (Cairo 1282), iv. 464; *Kitāb aḥwāl al-ḳiyāma* (ed. M. Wolff), p. 111 *sqq.* (German ed., p. 199 *sqq.*); the European works on Islām; T. Andrae, *Der Ursprung des Islams und das Christentum*, p. 82; E. Berthels. *Die paradiesischen Jungfrauen (Ḥūrīs) im Islam*, in *Islamica*, i. 263 ff.

ḤURŪFĪ, a Shīʿī sect founded by Faḍl Allāh of Astarābād at the end of the viii[th] (xiv[th]) century, introduced into the Ottoman empire by one of his disciples, ʿAlī al-Aʿlā, and adopted by the Bektāshī dervishes. Their creed, which is epitomised in the *Maḥram-nāme*, composed in 828/1425, is based on the idea that the universe is eternal and moves with an unceasing rotation, which is the cause of the changes observed in it. These changes are divided into cycles, the beginning and end of which are marked by similar phenomena, the appearance of an Adam at the beginning and a last judgment at the end. God is manifest in the person of man, particularly his face, for man was made in the image of God.

This manifestation is produced under the successive forms of the prophet, saint and God; Muḥammad was the last of the prophets, then came the saints, from ʿAlī to Ḥasan ʿAskarī, the eleventh Imām; Faḍl Allāh, the last of the saints, is also the first of the divine series, he is God incarnate. The distinguishing feature of man is speech or language which is written with the 28 characters of the Arabic alphabet; calculations derived from the numerical value of the letters borrowed from the Ismāʿīlīya (St. Guyard, *Fragments Ismaélis*, p. 108 *sqq.*) play a great part in their doctrines, but they also make use of groupings of the alphabet by letters composed of one, two, three or four written characters. The lines in the features number seven (four eyelashes, two eyebrows, and the hair, or else two halves of the mustache, two whiskers, the beard divided into two, and tuft on the lower lip), multiplied by the number of the elements, we get 28, the number of letters in the Arabic alphabet. Their chief books are the six *Djāwidān* (one written by Faḍl Allāh himself, the others by his disciples), the *Ḥaḳīḳat-nāme, Istiwā-nāme, Hidāyāt-nāme* and *Maḥram-nāme*, some in Persian mingled with passages in the Astarābād dialect, others in Ottoman Turkish. Unlike other dervishes, they have no *wird* or *dhikr*; every morning they meet in the house of their spiritual chief, called *bābā*, and he gives each one, by the hands of a servant, a glass of wine, a slice of bread and a piece of cheese; those present make a great noise; the superior takes the glass of wine and gives it to each one present who takes it respectfully, touches his face and eyes with it and drinks it. They have a kind of confession to the *bābā*.

Bibliography: Isḥāḳ Efendi, *Kās͟hf al-asrār* (in Turkish); G. Jacob, *Beiträge zur Kenntnis der Bektaschis*; C. Huart, *Textes persans relatifs à la secte des Houroûfîs* (*GMS*, vol. ix.), and Dr. Riḍā Tewfīḳ (Feylesouf Riẓā), *Étude*, in continuation of the preceding.

AL-**ḤUSAIN**, the second son of ʿAlī and Fāṭima, born in Madīna in the fourth or fifth year A.H. As in the case of his brother al-Ḥasan [q.v.] — the two are known together as *al-Ḥasanān*, the 'two Ḥasans' — tradition pictures the young Ḥusain overwhelmed with marks of tenderness by his maternal grandfather. During the troubled caliphate of ʿAlī, Ḥusain remained in obscurity. After ʿAlī's death he followed his elder brother into retirement in Madīna and during Muʿāwiya's reign, particularly after Ḥasan's death made him head of the Shīʿa, he resisted the sollicitations of his partisans in the ʿIrāḳ and maintained a more dignified attitude to the Umaiyads than Ḥasan. The accession of Yazīd altered his views and Ḥusain decided to listen to the appeal once more made by his ʿIrāḳ partisans. But before doing anything he resolved to test how matters stood through his cousin Muslim b. ʿAḳīl. On the latter's arrival thousands of Shīʿīs rushed to swear fidelity to Ḥusain. Muslim wrote to the son of ʿAlī to persuade him to come to take charge of the movement. In the meanwhile ʿUbaid Allāh b. Ziyād, appointed governor of the ʿIrāḳ, had succeeded in capturing Muslim and executed him. Leaving Mecca, where he had sought refuge after refusing to swear fealty to Yazīd, Ḥusain took the road to Kūfa, according to Muslim's instructions. A few stages from this town he learned of the tragic end of his emissary. ʿUbaid Allāh had established outposts on all the roads leading from the Ḥidjāz to the ʿIrāḳ and parties of cavalry were patrolling the roads. The weak escort of relatives and devoted followers attached to Ḥusain came in contact with one of these detachments. On their refusal to halt ʿUbaid Allāh's horsemen accompanied them at a short distance. In this fashion they reached Karbalāʾ destined to be ten days later the scene of Ḥusain's death. The circle of steel formed by the soldiers sent by ʿUbaid Allāh closed in around him. The Umaiyad governor wished to persuade or force him to surrender. He cut off all access to the Euphrates, hoping to reduce him by thirst. Ḥusain hoped for a revulsion of feeling in his favour among the soldiers of Kūfa, who had been secretly won over to the Shīʿa but had been terrorised by the execution of Muslim.

The 10th Muḥarram 61 A.H./10th October 680 dawned. ʿUmar b. Saʿd b. Abī Waḳḳāṣ had taken command of the 4,000 men assembled at Karbalāʾ. Ḥusain was summoned to surrender at discretion. The ultimatum being unanswered, ʿUmar executed a turning movement to envelop the son of ʿAlī. His partisans tried to resist. Ḥusain did not stir. An engagement resulted in which Ḥusain fell wounded in many places. His tents were pillaged. At first merely a police operation, the scheme degenerated into a general mêlée. "It did not last long; just time to slay a camel or to take a nap". Thus a verbal report delivered to Yazīd describes it. The Caliph deplored this ending; he had neither desired nor ordered it. His instructions were to secure the person of Ḥusain, to prevent him prolonging a dangerous agitation. He treated the ʿAlids who survived the catastrophe of Karbalāʾ with honour, provided generously for their needs and gave them an escort to Madīna. Ḥusain's descendants lived there in obscurity, at variance with their relatives, the Ḥasanids. They usually left to their cousins the right of enforcing the political privileges of ʿAlī's family in Arabia.

On the significance of the death of Ḥusain in the faith of the Shīʿīs see this article and the article MUḤARRAM.

Bibliography: The standard historical works; H. Lammens, *Etudes sur le règne de Moʿāwia Ier*, p. 132—183, and particularly, do., *Le califat de Yazīd Ier*, p. 138—182, where a detailed bibliography is given; Wellhausen, *Das arabische Reich und sein Sturz*, p. 89, 91—92; Snouck Hurgronje, *Mekka*, i. 32 *sqq.*; D. M. Donaldson, *The Shi'ite Religion*, London 1933, p. 79 *sqq.*

I

ʿIBĀDĀT (A., pl. of *ʿibāda*), the ordinances of divine worship. The term *ʿibāda* is already found in the Ḳurʾān in this sense (e.g. Sūrā x. 29; xviii. 110; xix. 65 and *passim*) but is only very rarely applied also to the worship of idols (e.g. Sūra xix. 83; xlvi. 6). — Under this general head is comprised the first part of the works on law in Islām: *ṭahāra, ṣalāt, zakāt, ṣawm, ḥadjdj* and sometimes also *djihād* According to al-ʿAbbādī (*al-Djawhara al-naiyira*, Constantinople 1323, i. 146) the *mashrūʿāt* are divided into five groups: 1. the articles of the creed; 2. the *ʿibādāt*; 3. the *muʿāmalāt* which include contracts (*muʿāwaḍāt*) between two parties relating to things (*māl*), the laws regulating marriage (*munākaḥāt*), onesided contracts (*amānāt*) based on confidence, and inheritances; 4. punishments (*ʿuḳūbāt*); 5. expiations (*kaffārāt*). Instead of the last group however, Ibn Nudjaim (*al-Baḥr al-rāʾiḳ*, i. 7) and Ibn ʿĀbidīn (*Radd al-mukhtār*, i. 58) have the *ādāb*, prescriptions of a moral or ethical nature, which, like the articles of faith in general, are not dealt with in the Fiḳh books but in the works on Tradition. The arrangement in the lawbooks however does not agree with this theoretical division. The groups *ʿibādāt, muʿāmalāt, munākaḥāt, djināyāt, ḥudūd*, and *ḥukūmāt* are, from at latest the fifth century, fixed terms for definite parts of the lawbooks which are however differently arranged in the various *madhhabs*. Down to the third century these terms were subject to great variations of meaning. Thus in Ḥadīth prayer (*duʿāʾ*) is described as "the best *ʿibāda*" or "the" *ʿibāda* (Tirmidhī, *Daʿawāt*, bāb 1) and in older works *ṣawm* and *ḥadjdj*, which were later added to them, are inserted among other legal matters (for example in al-Shaibānī, *al-Djāmi al-kabīr* and in the works on Tradition by Abū Dāwūd and Ibn Mādja). The term *muʿāmalāt* has also a very limited meaning in Ḥadīth and refers only to buying and selling (Nasāʾī, *Aimān*, bāb 46, 47). For all details, especially on the influence of Jewish models on the lawbooks among the Ḥanafīs and Hellenistic conceptions among the Shāfiʿīs, cf. Heffening, *Zum Aufbau der islamischen Rechtswerke*, in *Festschrift P. Kahle*, Leiden 1935, p. 101—118.

IBĀḌIYA. One of the main branches of the Khāridjīya (q.v.); they are to be found to-day in ʿUmān, East Africa, Tripolitania and Southern Algeria.

The name is derived from one of their presumed founders, ʿAbd Allāh b. Ibāḍ al-Murrī al-Tamīmī. The usual form of the name is Abāḍiya, though the contemporary Ibāḍite authors often use the form Ibāḍīya as the more correct one. Of other denominations of the sect that of Shurāt is especially known.

The beginnings of the Ibāḍīya seem to be older than the year 65, when, according to tradition, ʿAbd Allāh b. Ibāḍ dissociated himself from the extreme Khāridjites. The earlier history of the sect is probably to be connected with those groups of Khāridjite *ḳaʿada* (quietists), who in the middle of the first century originated in Baṣra round Abū Bilāl Mirdās b. Udaiya al-Tamīmī and from which also the Khāridjite Ṣufrīya arose. After the death of Abū Bilāl, ʿAbd Allāh b. Ibāḍ became the leader of the moderates, since in the year 65 he parted from the Azraḳīya. When the latter, in their *khurūdj* against the Umaiyads, left Baṣra, Ibn Ibāḍ remained there with his adherents. The first epoch of the history of the Ibāḍīya, beginning with this event, could be called that of the *kitmān*. The sources often give to Ibn Ibāḍ the name of *imām al-taḥḳīḳ*, or *imām al-muslimīn*; perhaps one may see in this title an allusion to his function as leader in a secret theocratic government, the so-called *djamāʿat al-muslimīn*. There must, however, have been friendly relations between Ibn Ibāḍ and the caliph ʿAbd al-Malik. The year of his death is unknown.

The policy of Ibn Ibāḍ towards the Umaiyads was continued by his successor Abū 'l-Shuʿthāʾ Djābir b. Zaid al-Azdī, the chief scholar of the Ibāḍīya, who came from Nazwā in ʿUmān and died about 100. This Djābir was highly esteemed by all Muslims of his time and is probably the author of the oldest collection of traditions. It was he who established the definite form of the Ibāḍite doctrine and is called therefore *ʿumdat al-Ibāḍīya* or *aṣl al-madhhab*. Likewise the proper organisation of the sect is probably due to him. He succeeded in entering into friendly relations with al-Ḥadjdjādj, at the very time when the latter combated the extreme Khāridjites.

Towards the end of the first century the Ibāḍīya of Baṣra — who also maintained relations with the Muhallabids — became more radical and this caused a rupture with the governor. Most of the leaders, among them Djābir himself, were banished to ʿUmān. His disciple and successor Abū ʿUbaida Muslim b. Abī Karīma al-Tamīmī was imprisoned, but after the death of al-Hadjdjādj (95 H) he was charged with the leadership of the Ibāḍīya. Abū ʿUbaīda was an eminent scholar and wrote a compilation of traditions; the Ibāḍites of all Muslim countries came to seek instruction from him. After the death of ʿUmar II the favourable conditions for the Ibāḍīya came to an end; revolutionary tendencies begin to be perceived at this time. At first Abū ʿUbaida was opposed to direct action, but, fearing a schism, he changed his attitude. He would not, however, leave the town as the Azraḳīya had done before, but planned revolts in the different provinces, in order to build upon the ruins of the Umaiyad caliphate a universal imāmate of the Ibāḍīya. In Baṣra he established a centre of study, where the pupils, coming from all parts, were trained to be missionaries. The different groups of these *ḥamalat al-ʿilm* were to propagate their ideas, and, after they had won a certain number of adherents, to proclaim the state of *ẓuhūr* (public revolt). The action of Abū ʿUbaida had an enormous success; after only a few years Ibāḍite insurrections broke out in several Muslim countries.

After the death of Abū ʿUbaida (still under the caliphate of al-Manṣūr) begins the decline of the Ibāḍite community of Baṣra.

The Ibāḍīya communities outside Baṣra.

In ʿIrāḳ (particularly Kūfa) and Mesopotamia (particularly al-Mawṣil) Ibāḍite communities continued to exist for a considerable time.

Also in Mekka and Medīna and in Central Arabia there were communities in the second century. In Southern Arabia an Ibāḍite revolt broke out in 128/9, which not only wrested Ḥaḍramaut and Ṣanʿāʾ from the Umaiyads, but spread also to Mekka and Medīna for a certain time. In the year 130 the Ibāḍites were finally defeated near Wādī' l'-Ḳurā.

The earlier history of the Ibāḍīya in ʿUmān seems to be closely connected with the activity of the pre-Ibāḍite group of Abū Bilāl. In the first half of the second century however there began a more serious propaganda. In the year 132 a revolt broke out, at the head of which a descendant of the former ruler of the country, al-Djulandā b. Masʿūd, was elected imām. After the collapse of this imāmate a few years later, in consequence of an ʿAbbāsid expedition, a new activity developed about the second half of the second century with the town of Nazwā as centre; it was in this place that shortly afterwards also the *mashāʾikh* of Baṣra established themselves, so that this region became the spiritual centre of the Ibāḍīya. Until 280 the Ibāḍīya of ʿUmān were independent; in that year the ʿAbbāsids reconquered the country. After 400 the ʿAbbāsid power came to an end. To-day the Ibāḍīya is the religion of the main branches of the Ghāfirī and Hināwī clans in ʿUmān.

In East Africa most of the Ibāḍītes live now in Zanzibar. Also in Persia (the island of Ḳishm and Khurāsān) the sect was spread in the Middle Ages. From ʿUmān the Ibāḍīya also exercised influence in Sind at that time.

For some time the North African Ibaḍīya played the chief part in the history of the sect. Towards the beginning of the second century Salāma b. Saʿīd from Baṣra was active as a missionary in Ḳairawān. Soon afterwards there was formed in Tripolitania an Ibāḍite state, which collapsed about 132, though the population remained Ibāḍīte. Intensive connections continued to exist between these Berbers and Baṣra, and owing to the activity of a group of missionaries, formed by Abū ʿUbaida, in 140 a new Imām was elected in Tripolitania in the person of Abu 'l-Khaṭṭāb. The Berber tribes Hawwāra, Nafūsa and others which stood under his command, conquered the whole country and seized Ḳairawān from the Ṣufrite Warfadjūma in 141. The imāmate of Abu 'l-Khaṭṭāb extended over a great territory, but was destroyed in 144 by an ʿAbbāsid army, in consequence of a defeat near Tāwargha. Gradually there arose subsequently new centres of opposition against the ʿAbbāsids. Thus the former Ibāḍīte governor of Ḳairawān, ʿAbd al-Raḥmān b. Rustam, founded a principality in Sūf Adjdjādj and afterwards in Tāhert, where several Ibāḍite Berber tribes gathered round him. As a result of the activity of the different leaders a rebellion broke out in the year 151 in North Africa, in which also the Ṣufrites took part; Abū Ḥātim stood at the head of the movement, with the title of *imām al-difāʿ* (see below); finally he was worsted in 155 by an ʿAbbāsid army. After this defeat the town of Tāhert, whose ruler, ʿAbd al-Raḥmān b. Rustam, was chosen imām in the year 160 (or 161), became the main centre of the North African Ibāḍīya. ʿAbd al-Wahhāb, the successor of Ibn Rustam succeeded towards the end of the second century in uniting all the Ibāḍite regions and tribes of Ifrīkīya and the Maghrib under his power. The Ibāḍite groups of Baṣra and of the entire Orient recognised likewise the authority of the Rustamids. Political schisms and the successes of the Aghlabids then resulted in the second half of the third century in the decline of the imāmate of Tāhert. After the definite suppression by the Fāṭimids of attempted risings in the first half of the fourth century, the Ibāḍīya reverted to the state of *kitmān*. In different parts of the Maghrib and Ifrīḳīya small Ibāḍite-Wahbite organisations were formed. The best known is the Djabal Nafūsa group, which had since the second half of the third century its own leaders. Afterwards there grew up here the theocratic form of government composed of councillors, *ʿazzāba* by name, under the leadership of a *shaikh*. After the invasion of the Banū Hilāl (443), the Ibāḍīya of North Africa were reduced little by little to their present-day conditions. The Ibāḍite settlements in the Sahara were in the 7th century for the greater part annihilated by Ibn Ghanīya. The most important groups which remained are those of the Djabal Nafūsa, the isle of Djarba, Bilād al-Djarīd, the oases of Righ and Wardjlān and Mzāb. There have, however, always been relations between the Ibāḍite scholars of Africa and the Orient.

In the Eastern Sūdān also the Ibāḍite doctrine obtained a foothold, at first in Awdaghasht, where it was introduced by merchants. It held out there for several clenturies. There were Ibāḍite colonies also on the Northern frontier of the Central Sūdān. The existence of Ibāḍite colonies in Spain and Sicily in the fifth century is known from literary sources.

Doctrine. With the Ṣufrīya the Ibāḍīya constitute the moderate branch of the Khāridjites. They do not consider the non-Khāridjites as *kuffār* or *mushrikūn* and reject therefore *istiʿrāḍ* (political murder). Marriage with non-Ibāḍites is allowed. In political matters they do not hold, in accordance with the Muḥakkima (early Khāridjites), the existence of an imāmate to be an unconditional necessity. The imāmless state is called *kitmān*, and the doctrine opposes it to the *ẓuhūr*, i.e. the proclamation of the imāmate. A normally elected imām is called *imām al-baiʿa*, an imām who is elected by the *ahl al-kitmān* is called *imām al-difāʿ*.

The imām was elected secretly by a council of prominent laymen or by shaikhs, and then proclaimed in public. Often the elegibility is limited to a single tribe or even a family. The imām is required to rule in accordance with the Ḳurʾān, the sunna of the Prophet and the example of the first imāms. Anyone who tries to restrict his power by *sharṭ*, is taken for a heretic; in this way the schism of the Nukkār came into existence. The imām can be dismissed when he does not observe the dogmas. The simultaneous existence of several imāms in several countries seems, according to the facts, to be considered as allowed; nevertheless there exists in the Ibāḍite world the tendency to the forming of a universal imāmate. From historical statements it might be concluded that there could also be a sort of condominium, which would mean, however, an annulment of the Khāridjite principles. In general the dogmatics and the political-religious theories of the Ibāḍīya approach in some main points those of the Sunnites. They differ from the Mālikites only in a few points, among them their thesis of the creation of the Ḳurʾān at the time of the Prophet (cf.

Smogorzewski, *Un poème abāḍite sur certaines divergences entre les Mālikites et les Abāḍites*, in *RO*, ii, 260—268). Attention has also been drawn to the close relationship between Ibāḍite dogmatics and those of the Muʿtazila (Goldziher, *Vorlesungen*, p. 207 and 259). Al-Bakrī calls the sect of the Ibāḍīya *al-Wāṣilīya-Ibāḍiya*.

Ibāḍite sects. The schismatic divisions were at first, during the epoch of *kitmān*, merely dogmatic in nature; later on others were added as a result of political crises. Two political causes seem to have a particular importance; the question of the condominium and the s̲h̲arṭ (see above).

The Wahbīya was the greatest and most important of all the Ibāḍite subsects; it is almost the only K̲h̲āridjite sect that has continued to exist down to our days. The name is derived sometimes from the Rustamid imām ʿAbd al-Wahhāb, but it is connected with more probability with the K̲h̲āridjite imām ʿAbd Allāh b. Wahb al-Rāsibī. Besides the Wahbīya the only K̲h̲āridjites known to exist at present are the small groups of the Nukkārites, the Nafāt̲h̲ites and the K̲h̲alafites, which count only a few adherents. The beginning of the Nukkārīya reaches back to the beginning of the second century, when its adherents refused to acknowledge the second imām of Tāhert, ʿAbd al-Wahhāb. As well as in North Africa they are found also in ʿUmān and Southern Arabia. The Nafāt̲h̲īya originated in the Bilād al-Djarīd in the beginning of the third century. Their founder Nafāt̲h̲ reproached the Rustamid imām with neglect of the war against the *muswadda* (the Ag̲h̲labids). Towards the end of his life Nafāt̲h̲ retired to the Djabal Nafūsa. The K̲h̲alafīya are adherents of K̲h̲alaf b. al-Samaḥ, who, at the end of the second century, proclaimed himself imām in Tripolitania. They are found to-day still in G̲h̲ariyān and Djabal Nafūsa. Further there have existed in history at least 12 other different schismatic groups; they are enumerated by the Ibāḍite authors and partly also in the work of al-S̲h̲ahrastānī.

Bibliography: Historical Ibāḍite sources: al-S̲h̲ammāk̲h̲ī, *Kitāb al-siyar*, Cairo 1301 (cf. Lewicki, *Une chronique ibāḍite*, in *REI* 1934, p. 72); al-Sālimī, *K. al-lumaʿ al-muḍīʾa*, Cairo 1326; al-Barrādī, *K. al-djawāhir*, Cairo 1306; do. *Siyar al-ʿUmānīya*, *MS* in Lwów; Abū Zakarīya, *Chronique*, ed. E. Masqueray, Algiers-Paris 1878; al-Bārūnī, *Risālat sullam al-ʿāmma*, Cairo 1324; *Chronique d'Ibn Ṣaghir sur les Imams Rustamides de Tahert*, par A. de Motylinksi (*Actes xiv^th congrès des Or.* iii B 3—132); Muḥ. b. Yūsuf Aṭfiyāsh al-Mīzābī, *Risāla s̲h̲āfiya fi baʿd al-tawārīk̲h̲*, Algiers 1299; al-Dardjīnī, *K. ṭabaḳāt al-mas̲h̲āʾik̲h̲*, MS in Lwów; al-Sālimī, *Tuḥfat al-aʿyān bi-sīrat ahl ʿUmān*, 2 vols., Cairo 1347. Further: A. de Motylinski, *Bibliogr. du Mzab. Les livres de la secte abadhite*, in *Bull. de Correspondance Africaine* iii, Algiers 1885; Smogorzewski, *Zrédia ibadyckie do historii Islāmu*, Lwów 1926; Badger, *History of the imāms and seyyids of Omān by Salīl-ibn-Razīk*, London 1871; Brünnow, *Die charidschiten unter den ersten Omayyaden*, Leyden 1884; Wellhausen, *Die rel. pol. Oppositionsparteien*, Berlin 1901; further the standard historical works, e.g. Ṭabarī and in particular Ibn K̲h̲aldūn. Concerning the doctrine of the Ibāḍīya: al-S̲h̲ammāk̲h̲ī, *K. al-īḍāḥ*, lith. 1309; al-Djaiṭalī, *Ḳanāṭir al-k̲h̲airāt*, lith. Cairo 1307; al-Sadrātī, *Ḳ. al-dalīl wa 'l-burhān*; lith. Cairo 1306; ʿAbd al-ʿAzīz al-Isgenī, *Ḳ. al-Nīl*, lith. Cairo 1305 (cf. Aṭfiyāsh, *S̲h̲arḥ K. al-Nīl*); Zeys, *Législation Mozabite*, Algiers 1886; Sachau, *Muhamm. Erbrecht nach der Lehre der ibaditischen Araber*, in *SBPrAk* 1894; Motylinski, *Les livres sacrés de la secte abadhite*, Algiers 1889; do., *L'Aqida des Abadhites* in *Rec. xiv^th Congr. des Or.*; M. Mercier, *Etude sur le waqf abadhite*, Algiers 1927. Also the general Muslim works on the sects, such as al-S̲h̲ahrastanī and al-Bag̲h̲dādī (cf. Hitti, *Bag̲h̲dadi's characteristics of Muslim Sects*, Cairo 1924).

IBĀḤĪYA. [See Taṣawwuf].

IBLĪS, the personal name of the Devil. The word is probably a corruption of διάβολος; a different etymology has been proposed by D. Künstlinger, in *Rocznik Orjentalistyczny*, vi. 76 *sqq.*; the Arab philologists derive it from the root *b-l-s* "because Iblīs has nothing to expect (*ublisa*) from the mercy of God". He is also called *al-S̲h̲aiṭān* (Satan), *ʿaduww Allāh* (enemy of God) or *al-ʿaduww*. *Al-S̲h̲aiṭān* however is not a proper name. In the Ḳurʾān he appears mainly in the early history of the world (ii. 34; vii. 11; xv. 31 *sq.*; xvii. 62; xviii. 50; xx. 116; xxxviii. 73 *sq.*) as rebellious at the creation of Adam and as the tempter of Eve in Paradise. After Allāh had formed Adam [q.v.] out of earth and breathed the breath of life into him, he issued an order to the angels to bow down before him. The only one who refused to do so was Iblīs, because he, being created of fire, thought it beneath his dignity to pay homage to a being made of earth. He was therefore banished and cursed; but he begged postponement of his punishment till the Day of Judgment; he was granted this as well as power to lead astray all those who are not true servants of God. When Adam and Eve were in Paradise, he tempted them to eat of the fruit of the tree. Muḥammad has here combined two independent stories, the creation of Adam and the temptation of Eve in Paradise. It is to be noted that in the story of the creation, the devil is always called Iblīs; in the story of Paradise, however, al-S̲h̲aiṭān, at least when not denoted by a pronoun. The story of Iblīs is based on Christian tradition. In the *Life of Adam and Eve*, 15 (Kautzsch, *Aprokryphen*) it is related that Michael had commanded the angels to worship Adam. The Devil objected that Adam was less important and younger than they; he and his hosts refused and were cast down upon the earth. According to the *Schatzhöhle* (ed. Bezold, p. 15 *sq.* of the Syriac-Arabic text), God gave Adam power over all creatures. The angels thereupon reverenced him, except the Devil, who had become jealous and said: He ought to worship me, who am light and air, while he is only earth. He was therefore cast out of heaven with his hosts; then he was called Satan, Daemon, etc.

Muslim tradition has adorned the Ḳurʾānic account with various features, some well known. The difficulty had first to be overcome that in the Ḳurʾān Iblīs is numbered among the *djinn* [q.v.] as well as among the angels, and these are usually considered two different classes of beings. Zamak̲h̲s̲h̲arī says that Iblīs is only a *djinnī* and that the name angel in the Ḳurʾān applies to both classes (*Kas̲h̲s̲h̲āf* on Sūra xx. 116). But it is also said that Iblīs was an archangel. Others say that the djinn were a division of the angels, who had to guard Paradise (*al-djanna*); hence their name (Ṭabarī, i. 80). These djinn were created of the fire of *samūm* (Sūra xv. 27) while the angels are created of light (Ṭabarī, p. 81). In the beginning the djinn inhabited the earth. But they quarrelled with one another and finally blood was shed. Allāh then sent Iblīs who, at that time, bore the name of ʿAzāzīl or al-Ḥārith, with a troop of angels against the brawlers who were driven back into the mountains. According to other accounts however, Iblīs was one of the earthly djinn and was brought back a prisoner to heaven by the angels sent by Allāh to punish the unruly djinn; he was still quite young at this time (*ibid.*, p. 84). The name al-Ḥakam is also given to Iblīs before his fall, as Allāh had appointed him judge over the djinn; he filled this office for 1000 years. He then became vain of the name and created unrest among the djinn, which lasted another 1000 years. Allāh then sent fire which consumed them; but Iblīs took refuge in heaven and remained a faithful servant of Allāh till the creation of Adam (*ibid.*, p. 85; Masʿūdī, i. 50 *sqq.*).

But there are other traditions about the pride of Iblīs. Ṭabarī (p. 83) relates that he felt himself superior to the other angels, whereupon Allāh said: "I will create a *khalīfa* on earth" (Sūrā ii. 30); Ṭabarī (p. 79 *sq.*) further says that Iblīs was one of the archangels and ruled over the djinn on earth and in the lowest heaven. He then became rebellious and was called *shaiṭān radjīm* by Allāh. For Iblīs' *tawḥīd*, cf. Massignon, *Kitāb al-Ṭawâsîn*, p. 42 and the index, s.v.

In the end Iblīs will be thrown into hell-fire with his hosts and the damned among men. "Then shall they (the idols) be thrown into it (i.e. into hell) as well as those who have been seduced and the hosts of Iblīs" (Sūra xxvi. 94 *sq.*). The phraseology of this verse recalls Matthew, xxv. 41: "Then shall he say also unto them on the left hand: Depart from me, ye cursed, into everlasting fire prepared for the devil and his angels".

But in the meanwhile he plays many a trick on men, and leads them astray, except the believers (Sūra xxxiv. 20). The *hātif* so frequently mentioned in Arabic literature is often simply the voice of Iblīs. For example, he is said to have warned ʿAlī in this way not to wash the Prophet's corpse; another *hātif* then brought the Prophet's son-in-law into the right course again (Thaʿlabī, *Ḳiṣaṣ*, p. 44).

Bibliography: In addition to the sources mentioned in the text, the commentaries on the passages quoted from the Ḳurʾān; Weil, *Biblische Legenden der Muselmänner*, p. 12 *sqq.*; Grünbaum, *Neue Beiträge zur semitischen Sagenkunde*, p. 60 *sqq.*; al-Diyārbakrī, *al-Khamīs* (Cairo 1283), i. 31 *sqq.*; Bukhārī, *Ṣaḥīḥ*, *Bāb ṣifat Iblīs wa-djunūdihi.*

IBN ʿABBĀS. [See ʿABD ALLĀH B. ʿABBĀS].

IBN (AL-)**ʿARABĪ**, ABŪ BAKR MUḤAMMAD B. ʿALĪ MUḤYI 'L-DĪN AL-ḤĀTIMĪ AL-ṬĀʾĪ (as a descendant of Ḥātim al-Ṭāʾī) AL-ANDALUSĪ, a celebrated mystic of pantheistic doctrine, styled by his followers al-Shaikh al-Akbar; in Spain he was also called Ibn Surāḳa but in the East generally Ibn ʿArabī, without the article, to distinguish him from the Ḳāḍī Abū Bakr Ibn al-ʿArabī. He was born on the 17th Ramaḍān 560/28th July 1165 at Murcia. In 568/1172—3 he removed to Seville which he made his home for nearly thirty years. There and also at Ceuta he studied *ḥadīth* and *fiḳh*. He had visited Tunis in 590/1194, and in 598/1201—2 he set out for the East, from which he did not return. In the same year (598) he reached Mecca; in 601 he spent twelve days in Baghdād, to which he returned in 608/1211—2, and he was back in Mecca in 611/1214—5. Here he stayed for some months, but the beginning of the following year finds him in Aleppo. He visited also Mōṣul and Asia Minor. His fame went with him everywhere and he was the recipient of pensions from persons of means, which he bestowed in charity. When in Asia Minor he received from the Christian governor the gift of a house, but he presented it to a beggar. Finally he settled in Damascus and died there in Rabīʿ II 638/Oct. 1240; he was buried at the foot of Djabal Ḳāsiyūn, where his two sons were later buried.

As to ritual, Ibn ʿArabī belonged nominally to the Ẓāhirī school of his compatriot Ibn Ḥazm (q.v.; cf. Goldziher, *Die Ẓâhiriten*, p. 185 *sq.*), but he rejected *taḳlīd* (recognition of authority in doctrinal matters) and in matters of belief he passed for a *bāṭinī* (esoteric). Although conforming to the practice of the Muslim faith and professing its beliefs, Ibn ʿArabī's sole guide was the inner light with which he believed himself illumined in a special way. He held that all Being is essentially one, as it all is a manifestation of the divine substance. The different religions were thus to his opinion equivalent. He believed that he had seen the beatified Muḥammad, that he knew the Greatest Name of Allāh, and that he had acquired a knowledge of alchemy, not by his own labour, but by revelation. He was denounced as a *zindīḳ*, and in Egypt there was a movement to assassinate him.

His principal work, *al-Futūḥāt al-Makkīya*, which was later epitomised by al-Shaʿrānī (d. 973), gives a complete system of mystic knowledge, in 560 chapters, of which chapter 559 contains a summary of the whole. His contemporary Ibn al-Fāriḍ (d. 632), being asked by Ibn ʿArabī for a commentary on his *Tāʾīya*, replied that the best commentary was his own *Futūḥāt*. This work was printed in Būlāḳ in 1274, Cairo 1329. Next to the *Futūḥāt* comes the *Fuṣūṣ al-ḥikam*, begun in Damascus in the beginning of 627/1229, printed with Turkish commentary, Būlāḳ 1252, and lithographed with the commentary of ʿAbd al-Razzāḳ al-Ḳāshānī, Cairo 1309, 1321.

In 598/1201—2, on his arrival at Mecca, Ibn ʿArabī had made the acquaintance of a learned lady of that town, and, on his return thither in 611/1214—5, he wrote a small collection of love-poems celebrating her learning and loveliness and their mutual friendship, but in the following year he found it advisable to write a commentary on these, explaining them in a mystical sense. These poems with an English translation of both poems and commentary have been published by R. A. Nicholson (*The Tarjumán al-Ashwáq, a Collection of Mystical Odes*, in *Or. Transl. Fund*, New Ser., vol. xx. [London 1911]). This is the only one of Ibn ʿArabī's numerous works which has appeared in a European edition with the exception of a small glossary of Ṣūfī terms appended to the *Taʿrīfāt* of Djurdjānī, edited by Flügel in 1845, a short treatise, ascribed to him in a Glasgow MS., called the *Kitāb al-adjwiba*, of which an English translation appeared in the *JRAS* for 1901, and the collection edited by H. S. Nyberg (*Kleinere Schriften des Ibn ʿArabī*, Leyden 1919).

Altogether some 150 of his writings are known to exist, and this is said to be only half of what he actually composed.

Various theologians took exception to the contents of his writings and charged him with heretical doctrines such as *ḥulūl* [q.v.] and *ittiḥād* [q.v.]. Still he found many followers and zealous defenders. Whilst Ibn Taimīya, al-Taftazānī and Ibrāhīm b. ʿUmar al-Biḳāʿī denounced him as a heretic, amongst his defenders were found ʿAbd al-Razzāḳ al-Ḳāshānī, al-Fīrūzābādī (cf. Ḥabīb al-Zaiyāt, *Khazāʾin al-kutub fī Dimashḳ*, etc., p. 50, No. 20, 2) and al-Suyūṭī,

Bibliography: Sibṭ b. al-Djawzī, *Mir'āt* (ed. Jewett), p. 487; al-Shaʿrānī, *al-Yawāḳīt wa'l-djawāhir*, Cairo 1306, p. 6—14; al-Maḳḳarī, ed. Dozy etc., i. 567—583; *Khātimat al-Futūḥāt*, ed. Būlāḳ 1274, iv.; Ḥādjdjī Khalīfa, index (vii. 1171); Hammer-Purgstall, *Literaturgeschichte d. Araber*, vii. 422 *sqq.*; von Kremer, *Gesch. der herrsch. Ideen des Islams*, p. 102 *sqq.*; R. A. Nicholson, *The Lives of ʿUmar Ibnu 'l-Farid and Ibnu 'l-ʿArabi*, in *JRAS*, 1906, p. 797 *sqq.*; do., *A Literary History of the Arabs*, p. 399 *sqq.*; do., *The Tarjumán al-Ashwáq*, London 1911; do., *The Mystics of Islam*, London 1914, s. index; M. Schreiner, *Beitr. z. Gesch. d. theol. Bewegungen im Islam*, in *ZDMG*, lii. 516—525 (also published separately, p. 52 *sqq.*); Asín Palacios, *La psicologia segun Mohidin Abenarabi*, in *Actes du xvie Congrès intern. des Orient.*, Algiers 1905, iii. 79—150; do., *El mistico murciano Abenarabi*, Madrid 1925—28; do., *El Islam cristianizado*, Madrid 1931; A. E. Affifi, *The Mystical Philosophy of Muḥyid-dīn Ibnul ʿArabi*, Cambridge 1939; Goldziher, *Vorlesungen*, p. 171 *sqq.* and index; Macdonald, *Muslim Theology*, p. 261 *sqq.*; Brockelmann, *GAL*² i. 571 *sqq.* and *Suppl.*, i. 790 *sqq.*, and the bibliography given there.

IBN ʿAṬĀʾ ALLĀH, AḤMAD B. MUḤAMMAD ABU 'L-FAḌL TĀDJ AL-DĪN AL-ISKANDARĪ AL-SHĀDHILĪ, an Arab mystic and one of the most vigorous opponents of Ibn Taimīya [q.v.], died on the 16th Djumādā II 709/21st Nov. 1309 in the Madrasa al-Manṣūrīya in Cairo. Of his numerous works on theosophy and ascetics the most renowned is his collection of mystical sayings *al-Ḥikam al-ʿAṭāʾīya*, still read not only in Arabic but also in Turkish and Malay lands and often commented upon; with the commentary of the Spanish mystic Muḥammad b. Ibrāhīm al-Rondī (died 796/1394), printed at Cairo 1306, it is still the standard textbook of mystic study in the Djāmiʿ al-Zaitūna in Tunis (*REI*, iv., 1930, p. 433).

Bibliography: Subkī, *Ṭabaḳāt al-Shāfiʿīya al-kubrā*, v. 176; Suyūṭī, *Ḥusn al-muḥadara*, i. 301; ʿAlī Bāshā Mubārak, *al-Khiṭaṭ al-djadīda*, vii. 70; Wüstenfeld, *Die Geschichtsschreiber der Araber*, no. 382; *GAL*² ii. 143 *sq. Suppl.* ii. 145 *sqq.*

IBN AL-FĀRIḌ. ʿUMAR B. ʿALĪ (SHARAF AL-DĪN) AL-MIṢRĪ AL-SAʿDĪ, known as IBN AL-FĀRIḌ — that is, "son of the notary" — was a celebrated Ṣūfī poet. His father was a native of Ḥamāt, but removed to Cairo, where the son was born on 4th Dhu 'l-Ḳaʿda 577/12th March 1182. After the usual studies of *fiḳh* and *ḥadīth*, he experienced the conversion to Ṣūfism, and lived among the Muḳaṭṭam hills. He visited Mecca and remained there some time, but returned to die at Cairo in 632/1235. He is buried at the foot of the Muḳaṭṭam range, in a quiet garden overlooking the great city. His *Dīwān*, though not voluminous, is justly esteemed by both Oriental and European scholars, and has in particular been studied by Von Hammer (*Das arabische hohe Lied der Liebe*, Vienna 1854), Nallino (*RSO*, viii. 1—106, 501—526, reviewing Di Matteo's *Il gran poema mistico*, Rome 1917) and Nicholson (*Studies in Islamic Mysticism*, Cambridge 1921, p. 199—266); these studies relate in the main to the *ḳaṣīda* called *Naẓm al-sulūk*, better known as *al-Tāʾīyat al-kubrā*, which, in 756 rhymes, depicts the whole of the poet's mystical experience. This is Ibn al-Fāriḍ's greatest poem, and innumerable commentaries have been written upon it in a variety of oriental languages. Another poem which has attained celebrity in the west is the *Khamrīya*, rhyming in *mīm*, of which there are versions in English and French. To this day the odes of Ibn al-Fāriḍ are known by heart to the Ṣūfīs of Egypt.

IBN ḤADJAR AL-HAITAMĪ. AḤMAD B. MUḤAMMAD B. ʿALĪ IBN ḤADJAR SHIHĀB AL-DĪN ABU 'L-ʿABBĀS AL-HAITAMĪ AL-SAʿDĪ a famous Arabic jurist of the Shāfiʿite school, was born towards the end (or in Radjab) of the year 909/1504 at Maḥallat Abiʾl-Haitam in the Gharbīya province in Egypt. After losing his father in infancy, the Shaikhs Shams al-Dīn Ibn Abi'l-Ḥamāʾil (d. 932), a well-known mystic, and Shams al-Dīn Muḥammad al-Shanāwī, a disciple of the latter, took hs education in hand. Al-Shanāwī brought him to the Maḳām of Saiyid Aḥmad al-Badawī, and from 924 he continued his studies at the Azhar. Notwithstanding his youth he attended the lectures of the scholars of the time, among others those of Zakariyā al-Anṣārī (d. 926); ʿAbd al-Ḥaḳḳ al-Sunbāṭī (d. 931), Shihāb al-Dīn Aḥmad al-Ramlī (d. 958), Nāṣir al-Dīn al-Ṭablāwī (d. 966), Abu'l-Ḥasan al-Bakrī (d. 952), Shihāb al-Dīn Ibn al-Nadjdjār al-Ḥanbalī (d. 949). Owing to his proficiency in the theological-juridical sciences, he obtained, though barely 20 years old, permission to give fatwā's, and to teach. After marrying, at the instance of al-Shanāwī, in 932 the niece of the latter, he went in 933 on a pilgrimage to Mecca, where he remained also the next year. He continued his activity as a juridical author, which he began in that town, after his return to Egypt, until in 937 he made with his family a pilgrimage, and again made a stay at Mecca. After a third pilgrimage in the year 944 he made his permanent residence in the Holy City, where from far and near people came to get fatwā's from him. With the Shāfiʿite Muftī of Zabīd, Ibn Ziyād (d. 975), he had a heated polemic (cf. Snouck Hurgronje, *Verspr. Geschr.* ii. p. 423—5). He died 25th Radjab 974/3rd Febr. 1567 in Mecca and was buried at the Maʿlāt.

The commentary of Ibn Ḥadjar on the *Minhādj al-ṭālibīn* of al-Nawawī, *Tuḥfat al-muḥtādj li-sharḥ al-minhādj*, became, next to the *Nihāya* of al-Ramlī, the authoritative code of law of the Shāfiʿite madhhab. After the Ḥadjarīyūn (mainly in Ḥaḍramaut, Yaman and Ḥidjāz) and the Ramlīyūn (in Egypt and Syria) had at first put up a vigorous fight against each other, they ended by considering both Ibn Ḥadjar and al-Ramlī as the decisive authorities on the right Shāfiʿite point of view (Snouck Hurgronje, *o.c.* and *ZDMG*, liii. 142 *sq.*). Among his further writings *al-Fatāwā al-kubrā al-fiḳhīya* (Cairo 1308) deserves special mention.

Bibliography: Bibliographical notices in the preface of *al-Fatāwā al-kubrā* (Cairo 1308), i. 3—5; *Manāḳib* to *Tuḥfat al-muḥtādj* (Cairo 1308); ʿAbd al-Ḳādir b. Shaikh al-ʿAidarūsī, *al-Nūr al-sāfir ʿan akhbār al-ḳarn al-ʿāshir* (Cairo 1353) p. 287—92; Ibn al-ʿImād, *Shadharāt al-dhahab fī akhbār man dhahab* (Cairo 1350), viii. 370—72; al-Shawkānī, *al-Badr al-ṭāliʿ bi-maḥāsin man baʿd al-ḳarn al-sābiʿ* (Cairo 1348), i. 109; Brockelmann, *GAL*² ii. 508 *sqq.*, *Suppl.* ii. 527—9; Sarkīs, *Muʿdjam al-maṭbūʿāt* (Cairo 1346), Col. 81—4.

IBN ḤAZM, ABŪ MUḤAMMAD ʿALĪ B. AḤMAD B. SAʿĪD, a versatile Spanish-Arabic scholar, famous theologian, and prominent poet, was born on the last day of Ramaḍān 384/7 Nov. 994 in Cordoba. His family originated from the village of Manta Līsham in the district of Niebla (cf. *Irshād al-arīb* v. 88) and his great-grandfather was the first of his ancestors to be converted to Islām. His father, who had risen to the rank of a vizier of the majordomo al-Manṣūr and his son al-Muẓaffar, assumed a genealogy going back to a Persian client of Yazīd b. Abī Sufyān. As the son of a high official, Ibn Ḥazm had an excellent education; the court-circles in which he spent his youth did not prevent his active mind striving to develop in all directions. As his master in various branches of knowledge he mentions in the *Ṭauḳ al-ḥamāma.* — which gives us many data for his biography — ʿAbd al-Raḥmān b. Abī Yazīd al-Azdī. Before 400 he attended already the lectures of Aḥmad b. al-Djasūr and, in the midst of the political turmoils, we find him a student of ḥadīth in Cordoba.

After the revolution which brought Hishām II on the throne again (400/1010), he had, like his father, to endure many mortifications; towards the end of Dhu 'l-Ḳaʿda 402 his father died. In Muḥarram 404 he left the town of Cordoba, which had been sorely tried by the civil war and where the beautiful palace of his family at Balāṭ Mughīth was destroyed by the Berbers. He lived then rather quietly in Almeria, until ʿAlī b. Ḥammūd, in alliance with the ruler of Almeria, Khairān, overthrew the Umaiyad Sulaimān (Muḥarram 407). Khairān, induced to suspect him of intriguing in favour of the Umaiyads, imprisoned him for some months with his friend Muḥ. b. Isḥāḳ and then banished them. The two friends went to Hiṣn al-Ḳaṣr, whose ruler received them kindly. On learning that ʿAbd al-Raḥmān IV al-Murtaḍā had been proclaimed caliph in Valencia, they left their host after a few months and travelled by sea to this town, where Ibn Ḥazm met also other acquaintances. In the army of al-Murtaḍā, whose vizier he was, he fought at Granada; he was taken prisoner, but was released after some time. In Shawwāl 409 he returned to Cordoba, where al-Ḳāsim b. Ḥammūd was now caliph. After the latter's expulsion, the intellectual ʿAbd al-Raḥmān V al-Mustaẓhir was chosen caliph (414/1024); the latter chose his friend Ibn Ḥazm as vizier, but already after some months (Dhu 'l-Kaʿda 414) ʿAbd al-Raḥmān was murdered and Ibn Ḥazm found himself once more in prison. How long he was in prison, cannot be definitely ascertained; it is certain, however, that he lived in Jativa about 418/1027. According to al-Djaiyānī (in Yāḳūt) he filled the office of vizier again under Hishām al-Muʿtadd. Only scanty notices of his later life are available.

One of his earliest works — already made known by Dozy — was *Ṭauḳ al-ḥamāma fi 'l-ulfa wa 'l-ullāf* (ed. by D. K. Petroff, Leiden 1914; Engl. transl. by A. R. Nykl, *A book containing the Risala known as the Dove's Neckring about Love and Lovers*, Paris 1931; ed. with French trans. by L. Bercher, Algiers 1949; German translation by M. Weisweiler, *Halsband der Taube*, Leiden 1941), which he wrote in Játiva about 418 (Nykl in his *Introduction* places the date of composition in 412—3/1022). In this treatise Ibn Ḥazm shows himself a keen observer, a brilliant stylist and a charming poet. Probably about the same time he wrote the treatise known as *Risāla fī faḍl al-Andalus*, dedicated to his friend Abū Bakr Muḥ. b. Isḥāḳ, which is given in al-Maḳḳarī (ed. Dozy, ii. 109—121). He wrote also some historical works (cf. Brockelmann, *GAL, Suppl.* i. 694—5).

But it was particularly as a traditionist and theologian that Ibn Ḥazm displayed great literary activity. As first he was an ardent follower of the Shāfiʿite school; to the works written in this period belongs the *K. al-muḥallā bi 'l-āthār fī sharḥ al-mudjallā bi 'l-iḳtiṣār* (Cairo 1347—52). Later on he went over to the opinions of the Ẓāhirīya [q.v.] of which he became a devoted advocate. This change had apparently been completed by the time he wrote the above mentioned *Risāla.* Possibly the teaching of his master Abu 'l-Khiyār, i.e. Masʿūd b. Sulaimān, had not been without influence upon him. He defended with vigour his position that the details of legal deduction not resting on tradition and revelation must be rejected, in his treatise *Ibṭāl al-ḳiyās wa 'l-istiḥsān wa 'l-taḳlid wa 'l-taʿlīl* (Ms. Gotha, (Pertsch, *Verz.* no. 640), which Goldziher first thoroughly studied in *Die Ẓāhiriten.*

Ibn Ḥazm was original in the application of the Ẓāhirite tenets to dogmatics. Here also the primary meaning of the written word and the established tradition was to be decisive. From this point of view he sharply criticised religious groups in Islām in his most famous work *Kitāb al-faṣl fī 'l-milal wa 'l-ahwāʾ wa 'l-niḥal* (ed. Cairo 1317—21 and 1929) and particularly attacked the Ashʿarites, notably their views on the divine attributes. With regard to the anthropomorphic expressions in the Ḳurʾān however, Ibn Ḥazm found himself forced to put aside his own method in order to bring these into conformity with a spiritual interpretation. An analytical edition and partial translation has been given by Asín Palacios in *Abenházam de Cordoba y su historia critica de las ideas religiosas*, 5 vols. Madrid 1927—35; before him Goldziher had touched upon the main points in *Die Ẓāhiriten.* In this work Ibn Ḥazm also criticises non-Islamic creeds, especially those of the Jews and Christians, and endeavours to find out contradictions in their writings (cf. Goldziher, *Jeschurun, Ztschr. für die Wiss. des Judenthums*, viii. (1872), p. 76 *sqq.* and in *ZDMG*, xxxii. p. 363 *sqq.*). The logical arrangement of the *K. al-faṣl* has been interrupted by the incorporation in it of writings originally separate (cf. I. Friedländer in *Or. Stud. Th. Nöldeke gewidmet*, i. 267 *sqq.*), One chapter of the book was translated by E. Bergdolt in *ZS*, ix. (1933), p. 139—146).

In the domain of logic Ibn Ḥazm wrote *K. al-taḳrīb fī ḥudād al-manṭik*, which has not survived. He seems to refer to it in some passages of the *K. al-faṣl.* His work on this science departed, however, from the usual treatment of this subject and met with little approval. The fruits of his mature years and many bitter life-experiences was his ethical treatise *K. al-akhlāḳ wa'l-siyar fī mudāwat al-nufūs*, the editions of which diverge from each other. It was studied by Asín Palacios and translated into Spanish in *Los caracteres y la conducta. Tratado de moral practica por Abenhazam de Cordoba* (Madrid 1916). Cf. also Nykl in *AJSL*, xl. (1923/4), 30—36.

Ibn Ḥazm was a doughty opponent; "whoever resisted him, rebounded from him as from a stone" (Ibn Ḥaiyān in Yāḳūt). According to a proverbial saying the pen of Ibn Ḥazm was like the sword of al-Ḥadjdjādj in sharpness. Yet he always endeavoured to do his opponents justice. He succeeded only to a modest extent in gaining a hearing for his views. Under the patronage of Aḥmad b. Rashīḳ, Mudjāhid's Wālī of Majorca, he succeeded, in the years after 430, in winning adherents on the island. After 440, however, he was obliged to leave Majorca again. His charge of heresy against the great orthodox authorities, such as al-Ashʿarī, Abū Ḥanīfa, Mālik, brought upon him the wrath of the theologians, who warned their disciples against his false doctrines and made him suspected by the rulers. His strong sympathies for the Umaiyads was a further reason why he appeared dangerous. This constant baiting obliged him to retire to his family estate in Manta Lī<u>sh</u>am. His writings were publicly burned in Seville. Ibn Ḥazm derided the stupidity of this proceeding in sarcastic epigrams. According to the statement of his son the number of his writings amounted to 400, containing 80000 folios, but "the majority did not cross the threshold of his district" (Ibn Ḥaiyān). Ibn Ḥazm died in his village on 28th <u>Sh</u>aʿbān 456/ 15th Aug. 1064. The Almohad al-Manṣūr is alleged to have remarked on one occasion at his tomb: "All scholars have to apply to Ibn Ḥazm when in difficulty".

Ibn Ḥazm's teachings were particularly attacked in writings after his death. The Ḳāḍī Ibn al-ʿArabī wrote about 500 in refutation of his heresy the *K. al-ḳawāsim wa 'l-ʿawāṣim* (Algiers 1346). About a century later the Mālikite theologian ʿAbd al-Ḥaḳḳ b. ʿAbd Allāh wrote a *K. al-muʿallā*, directed against the *K. al-muḥallā*. But he had also adherents in later times, among whom was the mystic Ibn ʿArabī.

Bibliography: Yāḳūt, *Ir<u>sh</u>ād*, v. 86 *sqq.*; Ibn <u>Kh</u>allikān, ed. Wüstenfeld no. 459; Ibn al-Ḳifṭī, *Taʾrī<u>kh</u> al-ḥukamāʾ*, ed. Lippert, p. 232; Ibn Ba<u>sh</u>kuwāl, *al-Ṣila*, no. 888 and no. 40; al-Ḍabbī, *Bu<u>gh</u>yat al-multamis*, no. 1204 and 412; ʿAbd al-Wāḥid al-Marrāku<u>sh</u>ī, *al-Muʿdjib*, ed. Dozy², *Ind.*; Ibn <u>Kh</u>āḳān, *Maṭmaḥ*, Const. 1302, p. 55 *sq.*; al-Yāfiʿī, *Mirʾāt al-<u>dj</u>anān*, Ḥaidarabad 1337—40, iii., 79—81; al-<u>Dh</u>ahabī, *Ta<u>dh</u>kirat al-ḥuffāẓ*, ed. Ḥaidarabad, iii. 341 *sqq.*; al-Maḳḳarī, ed. Dozy a.o., i. 511; Saʿīd b. Aḥmad al-Andalusī, *Ṭabaḳāt al-umam*, ed. Cheikho, Bairūt 1912, p. 75—7 (transl. by R. Blachère, Paris 1935, p. 139—141); Ibn <u>Kh</u>aldūn, *Muḳaddima*, ed. Paris, iii. 4; Dozy, *Script. Ar. de Abbadidis loci*, ii. 75, 130 *sq.*; do., *al-Bayān al-mu<u>gh</u>rib*, *Introd.*, p. 64 *sqq.*; do., *Hist. des Musulm. d'Espagne*, nouv. ed. Leiden 1932, ii. 326—32; al-Nuwairī, *Historia de los Musulmanos de España y Africa*, ed. and transl. by Remiro, Granada 1917; Schreiner, *Beitr. zur Gesch. der theologischen Bewegungen im Islam*, p. 3 *sqq.*; Macdonald, *Development of Muslim Theology*, p. 209 *sqq.*, 245 *sqq.*; Friedländer, *The Heterodoxies*, *Introd.*; Horten, *Die philos. Systeme der spekul. Theologen*, p. 564 *sqq.*; Brockelmann, *GAL²*, i., 505 *sq.*; 534; *Suppl.* i., 692—7; Pons Boigues, *Ensayo bio-bibliográfico* no. 103, p. 130 *sqq.*; G. Palencia, *Historia de la literatura arabigo-española*, Barcelona 1928, p. 140—157; E. Algermissen, *Die Pentateuchzitate Ibn Hazm*'s, Münster, 1933.

IBN HI<u>SH</u>ĀM. [See IBN ISḤĀḲ].

IBN ISḤĀḲ, ABŪ ʿABD ALLĀH MUḤAMMAD, an Arab author and authority on Tradition, was the grandson of Yasār, client of the tribe of ʿAbd Allāh b. Ḳais in Madīna. Muḥammad also grew up there; he devoted his attention to the collection of stories and legends of the life of the Prophet and thus soon came into conflict with the representatives of religious and legal tradition which dominated public opinion in the town, notably with Mālik b. Anas who decried him as being a <u>Sh</u>īʿī and as being the inventor of many legends and poems transmitted by him. He therefore left his native land and went first of all to Egypt and then to the ʿIrāḳ. The Caliph al-Manṣūr induced him to come to Ba<u>gh</u>dād, where he died in 150/767, or 151 or even 152. He seems to have gathered the materials for the Prophet's biography in three volumes: 1. the *Kitāb al-mubtadaʾ* (*Fihrist*, p. 92) or *Mubtadaʾ al-<u>kh</u>alḳ* (Ibn ʿAdī in Ibn Hi<u>sh</u>ām, ed. Wüstenfeld, ii., p. viii., l. 18) or *Kitāb al-mabdaʾ wa-ḳiṣaṣ al-anbiyāʾ* (al-Ḥalabī, *al-Sīra*, ii. 235), 2. the history of the Prophet to the Hi<u>dj</u>ra, and 3. the *Kitāb al-ma<u>gh</u>āzī*. His work is preserved in comprehensive extracts in Ṭabarī and others, but independently only in the version of Ibn Hi<u>sh</u>ām (d. 218/834), who knew the book through a pupil of Ibn Isḥāḳ, the Kūfī Ziyād b. ʿAbd Allāh al-Bakkāʾī. He took from the first part only the history of Muḥammad's ancestors since Ibrāhīm and combined the two independent parts with occasional considerable abridgments into the *Kitāb sīrat Rasūl Allāh*.

Bibliography: J. Fück, *Muḥammad b. Isḥāq*, Frankfurt a.M. 1925; Ibn Ḳutaiba, *K. al-maʿārif*, (ed. Wüstenfeld), p. 247; Ṭabarī, *<u>Dh</u>ail al-mu<u>dh</u>aiyal*, under the year 150, iii. 4, p. 2512; Ibn <u>Kh</u>allikān, ed. Wüstenfeld, No. 623, ed. Cairo 1299, i. 611; Yāḳūt, *Ir<u>sh</u>ād al-arīb*, vi. 399—401; Sprenger, in *ZDMG*, xiv. 288—290; do., *Leben Mohammads*, iii., lxx.; Nöldeke—Schwally, *Geschichte des Qorâns*, ii. 129 *sqq.*; Wellhausen, *Mohammed in Medina*, p. xi.; Ranke, *Weltgeschichte*, v. 2, 252; Wüstenfeld, *Geschichtschreiber der Araber*, No. 28; M. Hartmann, *Der islamische Orient*, i. 32 *sqq.*; A. Fischer, *Biographien von Gewährsmännern des Ibn Isḥāq, hauptsächlich aus aḍ-Ḍahabī*, Leyden 1890, cf. *ZDMG*, xlvi. 148 *sqq.*; *Das Leben Muhammed's nach Muhammed Ibn Ishâk bearbeitet von Abd al-Malik Ibn Hischâm*, ed. by F. Wüstenfeld, Göttingen 1858—1860, anastat. reprint Leipzig 1899, reprinted Būlāḳ 1295; new editions Cairo 1356/1937 and 1357/1938; P. Brönnle, *Die Commentatoren des Ibn Isḥāq und ihre Scholien*, Diss. Halle 1895; *Die Kommentare des Suhailī und des Abū Ḏarr zu den Uḥud-Gedichten in der Sīra des Ibn Hišām* (ed. Wüst., *I*, 611—638) *nach den Hdss. zu Berlin, Strassburg, Paris und Leipzig*, ed. by A. Schaade, Diss. Leipzig 1908 (*Leipz. Sem. Stud.*, iii. 2); *Commentary on Ibn Hisham*'s *Biography of Muhammad according to Abu Dzarr's Mss. in Berlin, Constantinople and the Escorial*, ed. by Paul Brönnle (*Monuments of Arabic Philology*, i., ii.), Cairo 1911; see also the art. SĪRA.

IBN ḲAIYIM AL-<u>DJ</u>AWZĪYA, i.e. the son of the director of the Madrasa al-<u>Dj</u>awzīya at Damascus. His real name was <u>SH</u>AMS AL-DĪN ABŪ ʿABD ALLĀH MUḤAMMAD B. ABĪ BAKR, a Ḥanbalī theologian and disciple of the celebrated Ibn Taimīya [q.v.]. He was born in Damascus in 691/1292 and died there in 751/1350. "He was in every respect a faithful disciple of his teacher and he adopted the latter's literary mode. Even during the lifetime of Ibn Taimīya he was persecuted and as he condemned the pilgrimage to Hebron, he was thrown into prison. Like his teacher he combats the philosophers, the Christians, and the Jews; he holds up the doctrine of the eternity of rewards and of the finiteness of the punishments of hell" (Schreiner, in *ZDMG*, liii. 56). For his numerous writings see Brockelmann, *GAL²* ii. 128; *Suppl.* ii. 126 *sqq.*; also de Vlieger, *Kitāb al-Qadr, Matériaux pour servir à l'étude de la doctrine de la prédestination dans la théologie musulmane*, Leiden 1903; A. Laoust, *La Traité de Droit Public d'Ibn Taimīya* (Beyrouth 1943), Introd. p. xl.

IBN AL-ḲĀSIM, ABŪ ʿABD ALLĀH ʿABD AL-RAḤMĀN B. AL-ḲĀSIM AL-ʿUTAḲĪ, was the Imām Mālik's most prominent pupil. He studied under him for 20 years and after Mālik's death was regarded as the greatest Mālikī teacher. Through him Mālikī teaching was disseminated in the Maghrib, where it is still predominant. He died in Cairo in 191/806.

One of the chief works of the Mālikīs, the so-called *Mudawwana*, is usually ascribed to Ibn al-Ḳāsim. It was originally put together by Asad b. al-Furāt and consists of the answers of Ibn al-Ḳāsim to Asad's questions on the doctrine of Mālik b. Anas. Saḥnūn Abū Saʿīd al-Tanūkhī (died 240/854), the ḳāḍī of Ḳairawān, copied the work. When he went to see Ibn al-Ḳāsim in 188 = 804, the latter gave him many emendations, and after his death Saḥnūn arranged the whole book. In Ibn al-Ḳāsim's *Mudawwana* we therefore have an account of the doctrines of Mālik b. Anas in Saḥnūn's recension. The work was printed in 20 vol. at Cairo in 1323 (1905). Various Mālikī scholars have written commentaries on the *Mudawwana*.

Bibliography: Ibn Khallikān, No. 370; Ibn Khallikān's *Biographical Dictionary*, translated by M. G. de Slane, Paris 1843, ii. 86 *sqq.*; Ibn al-Nādjī, biography of Asad Ibn al-Furāt in *Maʿālim al-īmān* (Tunis 1320, ii. 2—17), ed. and transl. by O. Houdas and R. Basset, *Mission de Tunisie*, 2nd part, p. 104—143; M. B. Vincent, *Etudes sur la loi musulmane* (*Rite de Malek*), Paris 1842, p. 38 *sqq.*; C. Brockelmann, *GAL*², i. 186, *Suppl.* i, 299.

IBN MĀDJA, Abū ʿAbd Allāh Muḥammad b. Yazīd al-Ḳazwīnī, compiled one of the six canonical collections of traditions (*Sunan*, Dihlī 1282, 1289; Cairo 1313). He was born in 209/824, travelled in ʿIrāḳ, Arabia, Syria, and Egypt to collect traditions and died in 273/886. According to Ibn Khallikān, he also wrote a commentary on the Ḳurʾān and a chronicle (*taʾrīkh*).

Bibliography: Ibn Khallikān, No. 625; Brockelmann, *GAL*², i. 171, *Suppl.* i. 270.

IBN MASʿŪD, ʿAbd Allāh b. Ghāfil b. Ḥabīb b. Shamkh b. Faʾr b. Makhzūm b. Ṣāhila b. Kāhil b. al-Ḥārith b. Tamīm b. Saʿd b. Hudhail, a Companion of the Prophet. Like many of Muḥammad's first adherents he belonged to the lower stratum of Meccan society. As a young man he herded cattle for ʿUḳba b. Abī Muʿait; Saʿd b. Abī Waḳḳāṣ at a later date in a polemic calls him a Hudhailī slave (Ṭabarī, i. 2812). He is usually described as a client (*ḥalīf*) of the Banū Zuhra; his father is also so described. Nothing more is known of the latter; ʿAbd Allāh's brother ʿUḳba and his mother Umm ʿAbd bint ʿAbd Wudd b. Sawāʾ belong to the older Ṣaḥāba so that he is called by al-Nawawī (ed. Wüstenfeld, p. 370) Ṣaḥābī b. Ṣaḥābīya. His conversion is represented as due to a miracle. When Muḥammad and Abū Bakr were fleeing before the heathens (on what occasion is not stated), they met ʿAbd Allāh who was herding sheep. Their request for some milk was refused out of conscientiousness. Muḥammad then took a ewe lamb and stroked its udder which swelled and yielded an abundant flow of milk; he then made it resume its former size.

ʿAbd Allāh is regarded rightly as one of the first converts; he was fond of calling himself the "sixth of six" (Muslims); according to other traditions, he was converted before Muḥammad entered the house of Arḳam, or even before ʿUmar. He is said to have been the first to recite the Ḳurʾān openly in Mecca, although his friends found him unfit for the task, as he did not have his clan with him for protection; he was therefore harshly treated. Of course he went to Abyssinia, according to some traditions twice.

In Madīna he lived behind the great mosque; he used to be so often seen entering Muḥammad's house with his mother that strangers thought they were members of the family. But ʿAbd Allāh was only the faithful servant "of the slippers, the cushion, and the dung hill". He imitated his master in externals, but was often mocked for his thin legs. He wore his red hair, which he did not dye, very long; this peculiarity as well as his white garments and his constant use of scent are probably to be attributed to religious views. He laid great value on the *ṣalāt* and fasted relatively little to preserve his strength for the divine service.

He took part in all the *mashāhid*; at Badr he cut off the head of the severely wounded Abū Djahl and carried it in triumph to his master. He was also one of those to whom Paradise was promised by the Prophet. When Abū Bakr during the *ridda* thought it necessary to make Madīna capable of defence, ʿAbd Allāh was one of the men chosen to guard the weak points of the town. He was also present at the battle of the Yarmūk.

He was naturally as little fitted to rule as any other representative of the pious of Madīna. ʿUmar sent him to Kūfa as administrator of the public treasury and as a teacher of religion. He was much consulted on account of his knowledge of the Ḳurʾān and Sunna; he is said to be the authority for 848 traditions; it was a peculiar feature of his that in giving information about the Prophet, he trembled, the sweat even broke out on his forehead and he used to express himself with great caution, less he should say anything incorrect. His authority is relied upon for a mild interpretation of the interdiction of wine (Goldziher, *Vorlesungen*, p. 65, and *ʿUyūn al-akhbār*, ed. Brockelmann, p. 373).

The accounts of his end are contradictory. It is said that ʿUthmān deprived him of his office in Kūfa. When the news came, the people wished however to keep him. He then said: "Leave me; if there must be offences (*fitan*), I will not be the instigator of them" (cf. Matthew, xviii. 7). He is said to have returned to Madīna and to have died there in 32 or 33 A.H. over 60 and to have been buried by night in the Baḳīʿ al-Gharḳad.

When ʿUthmān visited him on his deathbed and solicitously asked how he was and what were his desires he is said to have given answers which are typical of ancient piety. He appointed al-Zubair his executor and expressed a desire to be buried in a *ḥulla* with 200 dirhams.

According to others, however, he died in Kūfa and was not dismissed from office in 26 along with Saʿd b. Abī Waḳḳāṣ by ʿUthmān.

Ibn Masʿūd is best known as a traditionist and authority on the Ḳurʾān. He belonged to those Ṣaḥābī's who had a Ḳurʾānic text of their own, which was different from the redaction of ʿUthmān; the codex propagated by him in Kūfa was often copied and maintained itself for a long time alongside of the official recension; it was particularly esteemed in Shīʿite circles. This codex did not contain the Sūra's i, cxiii. cxiv and had a divergent order of the Sūra's (cf. A. Jeffery, *Materials for the History of the text of the Qurʾan*, Leiden 1937, p. 20 *sqq.*). Ibn Masʿūd's traditions are collected in Aḥmad b. Ḥanbal, i. 374—466.

Bibliography: Sachau in the introduction to the third volume of Ibn Saʿd, p. xv. *sq.*; Ṭabarī, s. Indices s.v.; Ibn Hishām, Index s.v.; Ibn al-Athīr, *Usd al-ghāba*, s.v.; Ibn Ḥadjar, *Iṣāba*, s.v.; Nawawī, s.v.; Ibn Saʿd, ed. Sachau, iii. 105 *sqq.*; Caetani, *Annali*, Indices s.v.

IBN SAʿD, Abū ʿAbd Allāh Muḥammad b. Saʿd b. Manīʿ al-Baṣrī al-Zuhrī, a client of the Banū Hāshim known as kātib al-Wāḳidī (secretary to al-Wāḳidī). He was born in 168/764—5, as appears from Ibn Saʿd, vii./ii., 99, where it is said that he died in 230/845 at the age of 62. He studied tradition under Hushaim, Sufyān b. ʿUyaina, Ibn ʿUlaiya, al-Walīd b. Muslim, and notably with Muḥammad b. ʿUmar al-Wāḳidī. Abū Bakr b. Abi 'l-Dunyā and other traditioners derived traditions from him. His great work, the *Kitāb al-ṭabaḳāt*, i.e. the book of the classes, is famous and gives the history of the Prophet, the Companions and Successors down to his own time. Besides the larger work, Ibn Khallikān and Ḥādjdjī Khalīfa mention his smaller book of classes. When the author of the *Fihrist* speaks of a *Kitāb akhbār al-nabī* of Ibn Saʿd, this is probably not a separate work but the first part of the book of classes, which deals with the *sīra* of the Prophet. The whole work has been published under the title: *Ibn Saad, Biographien Muhammeds, seiner Gefährten und der späteren Träger des Islams bis zum Jahre* 230 *der Flucht*, im Verein mit C. Brockelmann, J. Horovitz, J. Lippert, B. Meissner, E. Mittwoch, F. Schwally und K. Zetterstéen, herausgegeben von Ed. Sachau, Leyden 1904—1928 (vol. i.—viii., 1904—1917; vol. ix. [indices], 1921, 1928, 1940).

Bibliography: *Fihrist*, p. 99; Dhahabī, *Tadhkira*, Ṭab. viii., No. 14 (= vol. ii. 13); Ibn Khallikān, No. 656; Wüstenfeld, *Geschichtschreiber*, No. 53; Brockelmann, *GAL*², i. 142 *sq.*; Loth, *Das Classenbuch des Ibn Saʿd*, Habilitationsschrift, Leipzig 1869; cf. Wüstenfeld, in *ZDMG*, iv. (1850), p. 187, and Loth, *ibid.*, xxiii. (1869), p. 593; Sachau, *Einleitung zu Ibn Saad*, vol. iii./i.

IBN TAIMĪYA, Taḳī al-Dīn Abu 'l-ʿAbbās Aḥmad b. ʿAbd al-Ḥalīm b. ʿAbd al-Salām b. ʿAbd Allāh b. Muḥammad b. Taimīya al-Ḥarrānī al-Ḥanbalī, Arab theologian and jurist, was born on Monday 10th Rabīʿ I 661/22 January 1263 at Ḥarrān. Fleeing from the exactions of the Mongols, his father took refuge at Damascus with all his family, in the middle of the year 667/1268. In the capital of Syria, the young Aḥmad devoted himself to the study of Muslim sciences and followed his father's lectures and those of Zain al-Dīn Aḥmad b. ʿAbd al-Dā'im al-Muḳaddasī, Nadjm al-Dīn b. ʿAsākir, Zainab bint Makkī, etc.

He was not yet 20 when he completed his studies, and on the death of his father in 681/1282 he succeeded him as professor of Ḥanbalī law. Each Friday he expounded the Ḳur'ān *ex cathedra.* Well versed in the Ḳur'ānic sciences, Ḥadīth, law, theology etc., he defended the sound tradition of the earlier Muslims by arguments which, although taken from the Ḳur'ān and Ḥadīth, had hitherto been unknown; but the freedom of his polemics made him many enemies among the scholars of the other orthodox schools. In 691/1292 he made the pilgrimage to Mecca. In Rabīʿ I 699/1299 or 698 at Cairo he gave to a question sent from Ḥamāh on the attributes of God, a "response" which displeased the Shāfiʿī doctors, aroused public opinion against him, and cost him his post of professor. Nevertheless he was appointed in the same year to preach the Holy War against the Mongols and for this purpose went next year to Cairo. He was present in this capacity at the victory over the Mongols at Shaḳḥab, near Damascus. After having in 704/1305 fought againxt the people of Djabal Kasrawān in Syria, including Ismāʿīlīs, Nuṣairīs, Ḥākimīs, who believed in the infallibility of ʿAlī b. Abī Ṭālib and considered the Companions unbelievers, who neither prayed nor fasted, ate pork etc. (Marʿī, *Kawākib*, p. 165), he went in 705/1306-7 to Cairo along with the Shāfiʿī ḳāḍī, where, after five sittings of the council of judges and notables in the audiencehall of the Sulṭān who had accused him of anthropomorphism, he was condemned to be interned with his two brothers in the dungeon (*djubb*) of the citadel where he remained for a year and a half. In Shawwāl 707/1308, he was examined regarding a work which he had written against the Ittiḥādīya [cf. ittiḥād] but the evidence he gave disarmed his enemies at once. Released to return to Damascus, he was forced back to Cairo after one stage of the journey and for political reasons was imprisoned in the ḳāḍī's prison for a year and a half, which he spent in teaching the principles of Islām to those under confinement. After a few more days of liberty he was shut up in the fortress (*burdj*) of Alexandria for eight months. He then returned to Cairo where, although he refused Sulṭān al-Nāṣir a *fatwā* allowing him to revenge himself on his enemies, he obtained the post of professor in the school founded by this prince.

In Dhu 'l-Ḳaʿda 712/Febr. 1313, he was authorised to accompany the army departing for Syria, and after going through Jerusalem he reentered Damascus after an absence of seven years and seven weeks. He then resumed his duties as professor, but in Djumādā II 718/August 1318, he was forbidden by the Sulṭān to give *fatwā*'s on the oath of repudiation (to swear to repudiate a wife for example if something is done or not done), a question on which he had allowed himself several concessions not admitted by the jurists of the other three orthodox schools (Ibn al-Wardī, *Ta'rīkh*, ii. 267) who hold that he who takes such an oath, although he is bound to fulfil his contract, is liable to a discretionary punishment.

Refusing to obey this order he was condemned to imprisonment in the citadel of Damascus in Radjab 720/August 1320. After 5 months and 18 days he was again set at liberty. He resumed his old activities till his enemies, on account of a *fatwā* regarding the visitation of tombs of saints and prophets, which he had issued in 710/1310, had him interned by the Sulṭān's order in Shaʿbān 726/July 1326 in the citadel of Damascus. He was allotted a room, in which he devoted himself to writing with his brother's assistance a commentary on the Ḳur'ān, pamphlets against his detractors and entire volumes on the questions which had resulted in his imprisonment. But when these works came to the knowledge of his enemies, he was deprived of his books, paper and ink. This was a terrible blow to him, and although he sought relief in prayer and the recitation of the Ḳur'ān, he fell ill and died after twenty days in the night of Sunday-Monday 20th Dhu 'l-Ḳaʿda 728/26—27 Sept. 1328. The people of Damascus, who held him in great honour, gave him a splendid funeral and it was estimated that 200,000 men and 15,000 women attended his obsequies at the Ṣūfī cemetery. Ibn al-Wardī composed his funeral elegy.

Although belonging to the Ḥanbalī school, Ibn Taimīya did not follow all its opinions blindly but considered himself a *mudjtahid fi 'l-madhhab* [s. mudjtahid]. His biographer Marʿī in *Kawākib* (p. 184 *sqq.*) gives a certain number of points on which Ibn Taimīya rejected *taḳlīd* [q.v.] and even *idjmāʿ* (consensus) [q.v.]. In the majority of his works he claims to follow the letter of the Ḳur'ān and the Ḥadīth but he does not think it wrong to employ *ḳiyās*, reasoning by analogy in his polemics (notably *Madjmūʿat al-rasā'il al-kubrā*, i. 207); indeed he devoted a whole *risāla* (*op. cit.*, ii. 217) to this method of reasoning.

A bitter enemy of innovations (*bidʿa*), he attacked the cult of saints and pilgrimages to tombs: did not the Prophet say: "One should only journey to three mosques: the sacred mosque of Mecca, that of Jerusalem, and mine" (*op. cit.*, ii. 93). Even a journey solely undertaken to visit the tomb of the Prophet is an act of disobedience (*maʿṣiya*) (Ibn Ḥadjar al-Haitamī, *Fatāwī*, p. 87). On the other hand, following the opinion of al-Shaʿbī and Ibrāhīm al-Nakhaʿī, he considered a visit paid to the tomb of a Muslim as not lawful only if it necessitated a journey and if it had to take place on a fixed day. With these restrictions he considered it as even a traditional duty (Ṣafī al-Dīn al-Ḥanafī, *al-Ḳawl al-djalī*, p. 119 *sqq.*).

An inveterate anthropomorphist, Ibn Taimīya interpreted literally all the passages in the Ḳur'ān and tradition referring to the Deity. He was so imbued with this belief that, according to Ibn Baṭṭūṭa, he said one day from the pulpit in the mosque of Damascus: "God comes down from heaven to earth, just as I am coming down now", and he came down one of the steps of the pulpit staircase (cf. especially *Madjmūʿat al-rasā'il al-kubrā*, i. 387 *sq.*).

Both by word and pen he combatted all the Muslim sects, Khāridjī, Murdji'ī, Rāfiḍī, Ḳadarī, Muʿtazilī, Djahmī, Karrāmī, Ashʿarī, etc. (*Risālat al-furḳān*, passim, in the *Madjmūʿa* quoted, i., p. 2). Al-Ashʿarī's dogmatics, he said, is only a fusion of the opinions of the Djahmīs, Nadjdjārīs, Ḍirārīs etc. He particularly objected to Ashʿarī's explanation of predestination (*ḳadar*), the divine attributes (*asmā'*) and judgments (*aḥkām*), execution of the threat (*infādh al-waʿīd*), etc. (*op. cit.*, i. 77, 445 *sqq.*).

In many cases he disagreed with the opinion of the principal jurists. For example: 1. He rejected the practice of *taḥlīl* by which a woman definitively divorced by triple repudiation (*ṭalāḳ*) could be married again by her husband after having contracted an intermediate marriage with a man who had agreed to repudiate her immediately afterwards (*muḥallil*, he who makes permissible). 2. Repudiation pronounced during a menstrual period is void. 3. The taxes which are not prescribed by divine order are admissible and if one pays them he is freed from *zakāt*. 4. To hold an opinion contrary to *idjmāʿ* is neither infidelity nor impiety.

He also attacked the reputation of men whose authority is recognised in Islām: ʿUmar b. al-Khaṭṭāb made many mistakes, he said in the pulpit of the mosque of al-Djabal in al-Ṣāliḥīya. ʿAlī b. Abī Ṭālib made three hundred mistakes, was another of his statements. He also violently attacked al-Ghazzālī, Muḥyi 'l-Dīn Ibn ʿArabī, ʿUmar b. al-Fāriḍ and the Ṣūfīs in general. As to the first, he attacked the philosophical views laid down in his *Munḳidh min al-ḍalāl* and even in his *Iḥyā'*, which contains a large number of apocryphal ḥadīths. "The Ṣūfīs and the *mutukallimūn* are from the same valley" (*min wādⁱⁿ wāḥid*)", he declared. Greek philosophy and its Muslim representatives, notably Ibn Sīnā and Ibn Sabʿīn, were attacked with the greatest vigour by Ibn Taimīya. "Does not philosophy lead to unbelief? Is it not for a great part the cause of the different schisms which have been produced in the bosom of Islām?"

Islām being sent to replace Judaism and Christianity, Ibn Taimīya naturally attacked these both religions. As well as accusing the Jews and Christians of changing the meaning of a certain number of words in their sacred books, he wrote pamphlets against the maintenance or building of synagogues and particularly of churches.

Muslim scholars are not agreed on the orthodoxy of Ibn Taimīya. Among those who consider him at the very least an heretic we may mention: Ibn Baṭṭūṭa, Ibn Ḥadjar al-Haitamī, Taḳī al-Dīn al-Subkī and his son ʿAbd al-Wahhāb, ʿIzz al-Dīn Ibn Djamāʿa, Abū Ḥaiyān al-Ẓāhirī al-Andalusī, etc. However, those who praise are perhaps more numerous than his detractors: his disciple Ibn Ḳaiyim al-Djawzīya, al-Dhahabī, Ibn Ḳudāma, al-Ṣarṣarī al-Ṣūfī, Ibn al-Wardī, Ibrāhīm al-Kūrānī, ʿAlī al-Ḳārī al-Harawī, Maḥmūd al-Ālūsī, etc. This divergence of opinion on Ibn Taimīya exists to this day: Yūsuf al-Nabhānī does not spare him in his *Shawāhid al-ḥaḳḳ fi 'l-istighātha bi-saiyid al-khalḳ* (Cairo 1323), which was refuted by Abu 'l-Maʿālī al-Shāfiʿī al-Salāmī in his *Ghāyat al-amānī fi 'l-radd ʿala 'l-Nabhānī* (Cairo 1325?).

We know that the founder of the Wahhābīs was connected with the Ḥanbalī scholars of Damascus and naturally made use of their works and particularly of those of Ibn Taimīya and of his pupil Ibn Ḳaiyim al-Djawzīya [q.v.]. The principles of the new doctrine are those for which the great Ḥanbalī theologian struggled all his life [cf. WAHHĀBĪS]. Also in the Egyptian reform-party of Muḥ. ʿAbduh the works of Ibn Taimīya are held in high esteem.

Bibliography: Besides the works already mentioned: al-Dhahabī, *Tadhkirat al-ḥuffāẓ*, Ḥaidarābād n.d., iv. 288; Ibn Shākir al-Kutubī, *Fawāt al-wafayāt*, Būlāḳ 1299, i. 35 (biogr. extr. from the *Tadhkirat al-ḥuffāẓ* of Ibn ʿAbd al-Hādī), i., 42; al-Subkī, *Ṭabaḳāt*, Cairo 1324, v. 181—212; Ibn al-Wardī, *Ta'rīkh*, Cairo 1285, ii. 254, 267, 270, 271, 279, 284—289; Ibn Ḥadjar al-Haitamī, *al-Fatāwā al-ḥadīthīya*, Cairo 1307, p. 86 *sqq.*; al-Suyūṭī, *Ṭabaḳāt al-ḥuffāẓ*, xxi., 7; al-Ālūsī, *Djalā' al-ʿainain fī muḥākamat al-Aḥmadain*, and on the margin: Ṣafī al-Dīn al-Ḥanafī, *al-Ḳawl al-djalī fī tardjamat al-Shaikh Taḳī al-Dīn Ibn Taimīya al-Ḥanbalī*, Būlāḳ 1298; Muḥammad b. Abī Bakr b. Nāṣir al-Dīn al-Shāfiʿī, *al-Radd al-wāfir ʿalā man zaʿama anna man sammā Ibn Taimīya Shaikh al-Islām kāfir*; Marʿī b. Yūsuf al-Karmī, *al-Kawākib al-durrīya fī manāḳib Ibn Taimīya* etc., publ. in a collection, Cairo 1329; Ibn Baṭṭūṭa, ed. Paris, i. 215—218; Wüstenfeld, *Die Geschichtschreiber der Araber*, S. 197, No. 393; Goldziher, *Die Ẓâhiriten* (Leipzig 1884), p. 188—192; do., in *ZDMG*, liii. 156—157; lxii. 25 *sqq.*; do., *Vorlesungen über den Islām*, cf. Ind.; Schreiner, in *ZDMG*, lxii. 540 *sqq.*; liii. 51 *sqq.*, and *REJ*, xxxi. (1896), p. 214 *sqq.*; D. B. Macdonald, *Development of Muslim Theology* etc., p. 270—278, 283—285; Brockelmann, *GAL²*, ii. 125 *sqq.*, *Suppl.* ii. 119 *sqq.*; H. Laoust, *Quelques opinions sur la théodicée d'Ibn Taimiya* (*MIFAO*, lxviii. 431 *sqq.*); do., *Essai sur les doctrines sociales et politiques d'Ibn Taimīya*, Cairo 1939; do., *La biographie d'Ibn Taimīya* (BEO, Damas 1943); do., *Le Traité de droit public d'Ibn Taimīya*, Beyrouth 1948.

IBN TŪMART, a celebrated Muslim reformer in Morocco, known as the Mahdī of the Almohads. His real name was, according to Ibn Khaldūn, *Amghār* which in Berber means "chief". Ibn Tūmart in this language means "son of ʿUmar the little". This was his father's name who was also called ʿAbd Allāh. The names of his ancestors also are Berber. The date of his birth is unknown but it must have been between 470/1077—8 and 480 /1087—8. He was born at Idjli-en-Warghān, a village of Sūs. His family belonged to the Iserghīn, a branch of the Hintāta, one of the most important tribes of the Atlas. Ibn Khaldūn tells us that it was distinguished for piety and that Ibn Tūmart was very fond of learning and industriously visited mosques where he burned so many candles that he was called *Asafīr* (fire-brand). His journey to the east was probably dictated only by the desire for knowledge, for it can hardly be assumed that he had already conceived the plan which he afterwards carried out, and which rather owes its origin to the doctrines he learned there.

The Almoravid dynasty which ruled in the Maghrib and part of Spain had then begun to decline. Moral decay had followed in the footsteps of conquest and the shallowness of intellectual life is shown by the studies which were prosecuted. The doctrine of Mālik b. Anas, one of the narrowest in Islām, was the prevailing one. Study was confined to the handbooks of the *furūʿ* which had taken the place of the Ḳurʾān and Ḥadīth. In the east al-Ghazzālī had taken up a vigorous attitude against this in the first book (*Kitāb al-ʿilm*) of his *Iḥyāʾ ʿulūm al-dīn*. This book therefore attracted the hatred of such *fuḳahāʾ* as the Ḳāḍī ʿIyāḍ and even of the Ashʿarīs like al-Ṭurṭūshī who tolerated no independent minds in their school. Al-Ghazzālī's works were therefore burned by order of the Almoravid Emīrs. The coarsest anthropomorphism (*tadjsīm*) was also in vogue; the allegorical expressions of the Ḳurʾān were taken literally and God was given a corporeal form.

Ibn Tūmart began his travels in Spain and it was there that his views began to be affected by the writings of Ibn Ḥazm. He then went to the east but the chronology of his travels is not certain. If, contrary to al-Marrākushī's statement, he attended on his first visit to Alexandria the lectures of Abū Bakr al-Ṭurṭūshī, who in spite of his Ashʿarī tenets was an opponent of al-Ghazzālī, they must have made a lasting impression on him. He then made the pilgrimage to Mecca and studied in Baghdād and perhaps in Damascus also. He there absorbed al-Ghazzālī's ideas and later writers represent this influence symbolically as if Ibn Tūmart had resolved at al-Ghazzālī's instigation to reform the beliefs of his country. In reality the two never met.

These years of study and travel had utterly transformed the Maghribī *ṭālib*. He had formed his plan, if not in detail at least in its main outlines. On the ship on which he returned he preached to the sailors and passengers, who began to recite the Ḳurʾān at his admonition and to offer prayers; it was afterwards related that a miracle recounted by al-Marrākushī confirmed this report. He continued his preaching in which he championed Ashʿarite doctrines in Tripolis and al-Mahdīya, where the reigning Sulṭān, Yaḥyā b. Tamīm, showed him great honour when he had heard him defend his case, and then in Monastir and finally in Bougie. He there set up as an inexorable critic of morals, literally following the ancient commandment: "Whoso among you sees anything blameworthy shall alter it with the hand (i.e. by force); if he cannot do this, he shall do it with the tongue (i.e. by preaching); if he cannot do this, he shall do it at heart, this is the least that religion demands". The Ḥammūdī ruler was enraged at this encroachment on his authority and the people also rose against the reformer; the latter fled to the Banū Uriagal, a Berber tribe of the neighbourhood, who took him under their protection. Here it was (contrary to the view of the *Rawḍ al-ḳirṭās*, in which Tādjera is given as the place of meeting) that he met the man who was to continue his work, ʿAbd al-Muʾmin, a poor *ṭālib* of Tādjera, north of Nedroma who like himself was going to the east to study. The legend which credits Ibn Tūmart with secret knowledge acquired in the east relates that he recognised in this young man by certain signs the person he sought, just as al-Ghazzālī had recognised himself as the future reformer. We only know that he had a conversation with ʿAbd al-Muʾmin, in which he questioned him very closely and that he finally persuaded him to abandon his journey to the east and follow him. He then came back to the Maghrib via Warsenis (Wānsherīsh) and Tlemcen, from which he was banished by the governor, then to Fās and Miknāsa where the people returned his admonitions with blows; finally he arrived in Marrākush where more than ever he became an inexorable reformer of doctrines and morals. The women of the Lamṭūna went unveiled as those of the Tuareg and Kabyles still do. Ibn Tūmart insulted them on this account and even threw Sūra, the sister of the Almoravid Emīr ʿAlī, from her horse; the latter, more patient and tolerant than the reformer, did not inflict on him the chastisement he merited but contented himself with summoning a meeting in which Ibn Tūmart was set to dispute with Almoravid jurists. They disputed on such questions as the following: "Are the ways to knowledge limited or not in number? The principles of true and false are four in number: knowledge, ignorance, doubt, and supposition". It was not difficult for Ibn Tūmart to get the better of them although there was a clever Spaniard among them, who was no less intolerant than he, called Mālik b. Wuhaib, who is said to have to no purpose advised ʿAlī to put him to death. The Emīr spared him however and Ibn Tūmart fled to Aghmāt where he had other disputations, and thence to Agabin, where he began his apostolate in a methodical fashion. He first appeared as merely a reformer of customs as far as these were contrary to the Ḳurʾān or Tradition; after he had won a certain influence over his circle, he proceeded to expound his own doctrines; he vigorously attacked the dynasty, who followed "lying doctrines", and declared every one an infidel who differed from him. This meant preaching a holy war, not only against heathens and polytheists but also against other Muslims. He chose ten companions, including ʿAbd al-Muʾmin and after he had paved the way by describing the characteristics of the Mahdī, he had himself recognised as such and fabricated a genealogy, in which he traced his origin from ʿAlī b. Abī Ṭālib. His doctrine was already no longer purely Ashʿarite but was mixed with Shīʿī ideas. The historians report all kinds of cunning tricks by which he endeavoured to justify his claims. He collected around himself the tribe of the Hergha and a great part of the Maṣmūda, who had always been hostile to the Lamṭūna, indeed Yūsuf b. Tāshfīn had founded Marrākush for the purpose of keeping them in check. Ibn Tūmart had prepared for them various treatises in the Berber language, which he spoke remarkably well; one of these, the *Tawḥīd*, is preserved in an Arabic translation, published at Algiers in 1903. The ignorance of Arabic was such that, in order to teach the *Fātiḥa* to the barbarous Maṣmūda, he called individuals of them by a word or a sentence from this Sūra: the first was called *al-Ḥamdu li 'llāhi* (Praise be to God), the second *Rabbi* (the Lord) and the third *al-ʿĀlamīna* (of the Worlds). He told them to give their names in the order in which he placed them till he succeeded in getting them to repeat the first Sūra of the Ḳurʾān. He regularly organised his followers and divided them into different categories; the first consisted of the ten who had first recognised him; they were the *d̲j̲amāʿa* (community). The second consisted of 50 devoted followers. He called them all "believers", *muʾminūn*, or "Unitarians" (*muwaḥḥidūn*, whence the name "Almohads"). His authority was however not recognised everywhere, at least not among the people of Tīnmāl (or Tīnmelal); he penetrated into the town by stratagem, massacred 15,000 men and made the women slaves, dividing the houses and estates among his followers, and also built a fortress. Either voluntarily or as a result of pressure, the neighbouring tribes became converted and in 517 A.H. he sent an army commanded by ʿAbd al-Muʾmin against the Almoravids. He suffered a fearful defeat and found himself besieged in Tīnmāl. Some of his followers thought of surrendering, but Ibn Tūmart with the aid of ʿAbd Allāh al-Wāns̲h̲erīs̲h̲ī whom he had brought from Warsenis had recourse to some trickery, and after his prestige was restored he had those he was not certain of put to death. According to Ibn al-At̲h̲īr, 10,000 men were thus put to death, a number which is obviously exaggerated. The Almohad cause gained in strength in proportion as the Almoravid power became daily weaker in Spain and Africa. When in 524/1130 (according to others 522/1128) the Mahdī died, ʿAbd al-Muʾmin, whom he had destined as his successor, was ready to take up the struggle again. Ibn Tūmart's grave still exists in Tīnmāl, but his name and history is utterly forgotten. According to the *Rawḍ al-ḳirṭās*, Ibn Tūmart was a fine looking man, of a light dull brown colour, with separated eye brows, an eagle nose, deep eyes, a scanty beard, and a black mole on the hand. He was a clever and able man, burdened by few scruples and did not shrink from bloodshed. He knew the traditions of the Prophet by heart, was learned in religious questions and a perfect master of the art of disputation.

Bibliography: Ibn al-At̲h̲īr, x., 400—407; ʿAbd al-Wāḥid al-Marrākus̲h̲ī, *al-Muʿd̲j̲ib* (*History of the Almohades*), ed. Dozy², p. 128—139; Ibn K̲h̲allikān, No. 699; Anonymous, *al-Ḥulal al-maws̲h̲īya* (Tunis 1329), p. 78—88; Ibn K̲h̲aldūn, *Kitab al-ʿibar* (Būlāḳ 1284), vi. 225—229; Ibn Abī Zarʿ, *Rawḍ al-ḳirṭās* (ed. Tornberg), i. 110—119; Ibn al-K̲h̲aṭīb, *Raḳm al-ḥulal* (Tunis 1314), p. 56—58; al-Zarkas̲h̲ī, *Taʾrīk̲h̲ al-dawlatain* (Tunis 1259), p. 1—5; Ibn Abī Dīnār, *al-Muʾnis fī ak̲h̲bār Ifrīḳiya* (Tunis 1286), p. 107—109; al-Salāwī, *Kitāb al-istiḳṣāʾ* (Cairo 1312), i. 130—139; *Le livre de Mohammed ibn Toumert*, ed. Luciani (Algiers 1903), with a valuable introduction by I. Goldziher; do., *Materialien zur Kenntniss der Almohadenbewegung*, in *ZDMG*, xli. (1887), p. 30—140; Bel, *Les Almoravides et les Almohades* (Oran 1910), p. 9—16; Gaudefroy-Demombynes, *Introduction* to his transl. of *Masālik al-abṣār* of al-ʿUmarī, Paris 1927, p. X *sqq.*; *Documents inédits d'histoire almohade*, ed. E. Lévi-Provençal, Paris 1928; H. Terrasse, *Histoire du Maroc*, i. 261—81, Casablanca 1949; Brockelmann, *GAL*², i. 506 *sq.*, *Suppl.* i. 697.

IBN ʿUMAR. [See ʿAbd Allāh b. ʿUmar].

IBRĀHĪM, the Biblical Abraham, was, according to the Ḳurʾān (Sūra vi. 74), the son of Āzar, which name is apparently to be derived from Elazar, the name of his servant (cf. S. Fraenkel, in *ZDMG*, lvi. 72). The Biblical names of Abraham's ancestors: Tārik̲h̲ b. Nāḥūr b. Sārūg̲h̲ b. Arg̲h̲ū b. Fālig̲h̲ b ʿĀbir b. S̲h̲ālik̲h̲ b. Ḳainān b. Arfak̲h̲s̲h̲ad b. Sām b. Nūḥ are found in al-T̲h̲aʿlabī, p. 44, and Ibn al-At̲h̲īr, i. 67, and this genealogy agrees perfectly with *Genesis* xi. 10—27 and 1 *Chronicles* i. 17—27. Ḳainān alone seems to have been inserted from *Genesis* v. 12. Born in 1263 after the Deluge or 3337 after the creation (al-T̲h̲aʿlabī, *l.c.*) he at once undertook his mission of preaching a holy war against King Namrūd. His mother Ūs̲h̲ā had to take refuge in a cave at Kūt̲h̲ā where he first saw the light of the world (al-T̲h̲aʿlabī, *l.c.*; Ṭabarī, i. 256; Zamak̲h̲s̲h̲arī, i. 172; Baiḍāwī, i. 133; Ibn al-At̲h̲īr, i. 96; Yāḳūt, s.v. Kūt̲h̲ā; al-Bakrī, p. 485; al-Muḳaddasī, p. 86; *Bābā bāt̲h̲rā*, 91 ; Maimonides, *Dalālat al-ḥāʾirīn*, chap. 29). For bad dreams had induced Namrūd to have pregnant women watched and their newborn sons killed. The slayers visited Ibrāhīm's mother to examine her before the pains of childbirth had come upon her. They examined her body on the right and the child hid on the left; they sought it on the left and it fled to the right so that they had to depart after doing nothing (al-Kisāʾī, p. 115—120). The story in the *Sefer hayyās̲h̲ār* (section *Noah*) that Terach was ordered to hand over Abraham to be executed and in his place delivered up the son of a handmaid has its origin in Muslim tradition. While still quite a child (*Talmud, Nedārīm*, 32) an experience gave him the knowledge of Allāh which is mentioned in the Ḳurʾān vi. 75—79. When he had left the cave and was coming to his father's house, night fell upon him and he saw a star. He said: "That is my Lord!" But when it set, he said: "I do not love those that set!" He saw the moon rise and said: "That is my Lord!" As it also disappeared, he said: "Verily, if my Lord does not guide me, I shall become one of those that go astray!" When he saw the sun rise, he said: "That is my Lord, he is the greatest!" When it also set, he said: "O my people, I am free from your idolatry. See, I turn my face to the creator of Heaven and Earth!" etc. Of the various legends (in al-T̲h̲aʿlabī, p. 45—47, and al-Kisāʾī, p. 125—140) which describe Ibrāhīm's wars with Namrūd and which also found a way into later Rabbinical literature (Jellinek, *Bēth hammidr.*, i. 25—34; *Sefer hayyās̲h̲ār* [*Noah*]; *Sefer Eliyāhū zōṭā*, ch. 25, and *Pirḳē de R. El.*, ch. 32) the following may find a place here, which are based on Ḳurʾān xxi. 58—67, as well as on *Genesis Rabbā*, section 38. One day his fellow tribesmen left the town to offer sacrifices to their Gods. Ibrāhīm pretended to be unwell and remained in the town. Armed with an axe he went to the temple of the gods where tables were laid with food. He said: "Why do ye not eat?" and struck off the hand of one, the foot of another and the head of a third. He put the axe into the hand of the biggest and placed various dishes before him. When the people of the town saw this on their return, they accused Ibrāhīm of the deed. He answered: "Verily, the biggest of them has done this; ask them, if they can speak". They said: "You surely know that they cannot speak". He said: "Do you, disregarding Allāh, worship what can neither help nor harm you? Fie upon you and your worship of idols!" Thrown into a limekiln as a punishment he left it unharmed after being three or seven days in it (al-T̲h̲aʿlabī and al-Kisāʾī, *l.c.*). Namrūd was completely defeated and Ibrāhīm with his followers set out for Palestine, being now called *K̲h̲alīl Allāh*, "the friend of God" (al-Kisā'ī and al-Thaᶜlabī following *Isaiah*, xli. 8; *Shabbāth* 137; *Menāhōth* 53). In Egypt his beautiful wife Sāra was taken before Firᶜawn (*Genesis* xii. 10—20; al-Thaᶜlabī, p. 44; Ṭabarī, i. 225; Ibn al-Athīr, i. 72). She said he was her brother so that he might not be slain on her account. She was not telling a lie, as he was her brother in the faith. When Firᶜawn tried to touch her, his hand was paralyzed and restored again when he had sent her back. In Sabaᶜ in Palestine he dug a well of fresh clear water. Being molested by the inhabitants he had to go away whereupon the water dried up (*Genesis* xxi. 25—30; al-Thaᶜlabī and Ibn al-Athīr, *l.c.*). The people hurried after him to beg him to return. But he refused and gave them seven goats (*Genesis* xxi. 27 *sqq.*) with instruction to place them at the well; the water would flow then again. When a menstruating woman had drunk from the well, the water entirely disappeared. In his 120th year he circumcised himself (al-Thaᶜlabī, p. 59). He died at the age of 175 and was buried in the family tomb at Khabrūn. On the day of the Resurrection, he will, clothed in white, take his place at the left hand of Allāh and guide the pious into Paradise (al-Thaᶜlabī, p. 60; cf. *Genesis R.*, par. 48).

Sprenger (*Leben und Lehre des Moḥammad*, ii. 276 *sqq.*) was the first to point out that the figure of Ibrāhīm in the Ḳur'ān has a history before he finally develops into the founder of the Kaᶜba. This thesis was further expounded by Snouck Hurgronje as follows (*Het Mekkaansche Feest*, p. 20 *sqq.*): In the older revelations (Sūra li. 24 *sqq.*, xv. 5 *sqq.*, xxxvii. 83 *sqq.*, vi. 76 *sqq.*, xi, 69, xix. 41 *sqq.*, xxi. 52 *sqq.*, xxix. 18 *sqq.*) he is an apostle of God, who has to admonish his people, like other prophets. Ismāᶜīl is not yet connected with him. At the same time it is emphasised that Allāh had not yet sent an admonisher to the Arabs (xxxii. 1; xxxiv. 44; xxxvi. 6); Ibrāhīm never appears as the founder of the Kaᶜba and the first Muslim.

In the Madīna Sūras on the other hand, Ibrāhīm is called *ḥanīf* [q.v.] *muslim*, the founder of the "religion of Ibrāhīm", whose palladium, the Kaᶜba, he founded along with Ismāᶜīl (ii. 124 *sqq.*; iii. 67, 90 etc.). This change is explained as follows. Muḥammad had appealed to the Jews in Mecca; in Madīna it was soon shown that they seceded from him. Muḥammad was therefore forced to find other support; he therefore ingeniously created the new role of the patriarch; he could now be independent of contemporary Judaism by appealing to the Judaism of Ibrāhīm, which was also the precursor of Islām. When Mecca again became prominent in his ideas, Ibrāhīm at the same time became the founder of the sanctuary there.

Bibliography: al-Thaᶜlabī, *Ḳiṣaṣ al-anbiyā'*, Cairo 1312, p. 43—47, 59 *sq.*; al-Kisā'ī, *Ḳiṣaṣ al-anbiyā'*, p. 128—145, 153; Ṭabarī, i. 220—225; Ibn al-Athīr, i. 67—98; Grünbaum, *Beiträge*, p. 122—130; Eisenberg, *Abraham in der arab. Legende*, 1912; Weiss, *Leben Abrahams*, Berlin 1913 [contains a fragment from al-Kisā'ī, which seems to be of very late origin and differs in many respects from the original.]; J. Horovitz, *Koranische Untersuchungen*, p. 86 *sq.*

IBRĀHĪM B. ADHAM B. MANṢŪR B. YAZĪD B. DJĀBIR (ABŪ ISḤĀḲ) AL-TAMĪMĪ AL-ᶜIDJLĪ, the famous ascetic, was a native of Balkh. The dates given for his death, which is said to have occurred while he was taking part in a naval expedition against the Greeks (*Ḥilyat al-awliyā'*, vii. 388), range between 160 and 166 (776—783). Some verses composed on this occasion by the poet Muḥammad b. Kunāsa of Kūfa (died 207/822), whose mother was the sister of Ibrāhīm b. Adham, praise his ascetism, the nobility of his character, and his personal courage and refer to "the Western tomb", *al-djadath al-gharbī*, in which he was buried (*Aghāni*, xii. 113, *sqq.*). According to one account, he was buried at Sūḳīn, a fortress in Rūm (Yāḳūt, ed. Wüstenfeld, iii. 196). The fact that after his conversion to Ṣūfism he migrated to Syria, where he worked and lived by his labour until his death, is established by many anecdotes related in the *Ḥilyat al-awliyā'*. He is reported to have said to ᶜAbd Allāh b. Mubārak, who asked him why he had left Khurāsān: "I find no joy in life except in Syria, where I flee with my religion from peak to peak and from hill to hill, and those who see me think I am a madman or a camel-driver".

The Ṣūfī legend of Ibrāhīm b. Adham is evidently modelled upon the story of Buddha (see Goldziher, *A Buddhismus hatása az Islámra*, summarised by T. Duka in *JRAS*, 1904, p. 132 sqq.). Here Ibrāhīm appears as a prince of Balkh who, while hunting, was warned by an unseen voice that he was not created for the purpose of chasing hares or foxes; whereupon he dismounted, clad himself in the woollen garment of one of his father's shepherds, to whom he gave his horse and all that he had with him, and "abandoned the path of worldly pomp for the path of asceticism and piety" (for other accounts of his conversion, see Goldziher, *loc. cit.*, and *Fawāt al-wafayāt*, Būlāḳ, 1283, i. 3). In later centuries this gave rise to a number of romances on the subject of the renunciation of the world by "the Sulṭān Ibrāhīm", which are found also in Turkish, Indian, and Malay versions.

The anecdotes and sayings of Ibrāhīm, as recorded by his earliest biographers, show that he was essentially an ascetic and quietist of a practical type; we look in vain for any traces of the speculative mysticism which developed in the following century. Like many of the ancient Ṣūfīs, he took every precaution that his food should be 'lawful' in the religious sense of the word. He did not carry the doctrine of *tawakkul* to the point of refusing to earn his livelihood; on the contrary, he supported himself by gardening, reaping, grinding wheat, etc. While he approved of begging, in so far as it incites men to give alms and thereby increases their chance of salvation, he condemned it as a means of livelihood. He said: "There are two kinds of begging. A man may beg at people's doors, or he may say, 'I frequent the mosque and pray and fast and worship God and accept whatever is given me'. This is the worse of the two kinds. Such a person is an importunate beggar". A trait far more characteristic of Indian and Syrian than of Moslem asceticism appears in the story that one of the three occasions on which Ibrāhīm felt joy was when he looked at the fur garment that he was wearing, and could not distinguish the fur from the lice, because there were so many of the latter (al-Ḳushairī, *Risāla*, Cairo 1318, p. 83 *sqq.*). As examples of his mystical sayings the following may be quoted: "Poverty is a treasure which God keeps in heaven and does not bestow except on these whom He loves"; "This is the sign of him that knows God, that his chief care is goodness and devotion, and his words are mostly words of praise and glorification". In answer to Abū Yazīd al-Djudhāmī, who declared that Paradise is the utmost that devotees hope to obtain from God hereafter, Ibrāhīm said: "By God, I deem that the greatest matter, as they consider it, is that God should not withdraw from them His gracious countenance". Although such ideas mark the transition from asceticism to mysticism, we cannot regard Ibrāhīm b. Adham as one who had crossed the border-line. The keynotes of his religion are renunciation of the world and self-mortification, and in these he finds the fullest peace and joy, not in the ecstasy of contemplation or the enthus iasm of self-abandonment.

Bibliography: in addition to the references given in the article: al-Sulamī, *Ṭabaḳāt al-Ṣūfiya*, Brit. Mus. MS., f. 4a; Abū Nuʿaim al-Iṣfahānī, *Ḥilyat al-awliyāʾ*, vii. 367—viii. 58; al-Ḳushairī, *Risāla*, Cairo 1318, p. 9; al-Hudjwīrī, *Kashf al-maḥdjūb*, transl. Nicholson, p. 103 *sqq.*; ʿAṭṭār, *Tadhkirat al-awliyāʾ*, ed. Nicholson, i., 85—106; Djāmī, *Nafaḥāt al-uns*, ed. Lees, no. 14; al-Shaʿranī, *al-Ṭabaḳāt al-kubrā*, i., 91; Ibn Khallikān, *Wafayāt al-aʿyān*, ed. Wüstenfeld, add. p. 18 *sqq.*; al-Kutubī, *Fawāt al-wafayāt*, i. 3; A. von Kremer, *Gesch. der herrschenden Ideen des Islams*, p. 57 *sqq.*; Nicholson, *Ibrāhīm b. Adham*, in *ZA*, xxvi, 215—220; Goldziher, *Vorlesungen*, p. 163; E. G. Browne, *A literary History of Persia*, i., 425. Concerning the pictorial representation of an incident in the legend of Ibr. b. Adham, see *JRAS* 1909, p. 751, and 1910, p. 167.

ʿĪD, festival. The word is derived by the Arab lexicographers from the root *ʿ-w-d* and explained as "the (periodically) returning". But it is really one of those Aramic loanwords, which are particularly numerous in the domain of religion: cf. or example the Syriac *ʿīdā, ʿēḏā, ʿīḏō* "festival, holiday". The term occurs in Sūra v. 114, where ʿĪsā prays that a table may come down from heaven (reminiscence of the Eucharist?).

The Muslim year has two canonical festivals, the *ʿīd al-aḍḥā* or "sacrificial festival" on the 10th Dhu 'l-Ḥidjdja and the *ʿīd al-fiṭr* "festival of breaking the fast" on the 1st Shawwāl. The special legal regulations for these are dealt with in the following articles. Common to both festivals is the *ṣalāt al-ʿīd(ain)*, festival of public prayer of the whole community, which is considered sunna. In many ways it has preserved older forms of the *ṣalāt* than the daily or even the Friday *ṣalāt* (although in other points it has come to resemble the latter) and in its general style much resembles the *ṣalāt* for drought and eclipses. It consists only of two *rakʿa*'s [see art. ṢALĀT II] and contains several *takbīr*'s more than the ordinary *ṣalāt*. After it a *khuṭba* [q.v.] in two parts is held. It has no *adhān* [q.v.] and no *iḳāma* [q.v.]; as in the oldest times the only summons to it is the words *al-ṣalāt djāmiʿatan*. It should be celebrated in the open air on the *muṣallā* [q.v.], which is still often done, though mosques are frequently now preferred. The time for its performance is between sunrise and the moment when the sun has reached its zenith.

At both festivals, which last three or four days in practice, the Muslim puts on new or at least his best clothes; people visit, congratulate, and bestow presents on one another. The cemeteries are visited, and people stay in them for hours, sometimes the whole night in tents. These more popular practices are more usual at the *ʿīd al-fiṭr* than at the *ʿīd al-aḍḥā*; the festival of breaking the fast is much more joyfully celebrated because the hardships of Ramaḍān are over, so that at the present day the "minor festival" has in practice become of much greater importance than the "major festival".

Bibliography: The Fiḳh books in the chapter *ṣalāt al-ʿīdain*; Juynboll, *Handbuch des islāmischen Gesetzes*, p. 126 *sqq.*; Mittwoch, *Zur Entstehungsgeschichte des islamischen Gebets und Kultus* (*Abhandl. d. K. Pr. Akad. d. Wiss., phil.-hist. Kl.*, 1913, No. 2), p. 19, 27 *sqq.*, 40—41; E. W. Lane, *Manners and Customs of the Modern Egyptians*; M. d'Ohsson, *Tableau général de l'Empire Othoman* (Paris 1788), ii. 222—31 and 423—36; Sell, *The Faith of Islam*, 2nd ed. (London 1896), p. 318—26; Garcin de Tassy, *Mémoire sur les particularités de la religion musulmane dans l'Inde*, 2nd ed. (Paris 1869), p. 69—71; Herklots, *Qanoon-e-Islam*, London 1832, p. 261—269; Snouck Hurgronje, *Het Mekkaansche Feest*, p. 159 *sqq.*; do., *Mekka*, ii. 91—97; do., *The Atchehnese*, i. 237—244; do., *Het Gajōland* (Batavia 1903), p. 325 *sq.*; Doutté, *Magie et Religion*, chap. x.

ʿĪD AL-AḌḤĀ (also called *ʿīd al-ḳurbān* or *ʿīd al-naḥr*) "sacrificial feast" or *ʿīd al-kabīr*, "the major festival", in India *baḳar ʿīd* (*baḳra ʿīd*), in Turkey *büyük-bairam* or *ḳurbān-bairam*. It is celebrated on the 10th Dhu 'l-Ḥidjdja, the day on which the pilgrims sacrifice in the valley of Minā (cf. ḤADJDJ) and the three following days, the *aiyām al-tashrīḳ* [cf. TASHRĪḲ]. The old Arab custom of sacrificing on this day in Minā was adopted by Islām not only for pilgrims but also for all Muslims as sunna. It is a necessary duty [*wādjib*] only by reason of a vow [*nadhr*].

This *sunna* (*muʾakkada ʿala 'l-kifāya*) is obligatory on every free Muslim who can afford to buy a sacrificial victim. Sheep (one for each person) or camels or cattle (one for one to seven persons) are sacrified. The animals must be of a fixed age and be free from certain physical defects (one-eyed, lame etc.). The period of the sacrifice begins with the *ṣalāt al-ʿīd* and ends with sunset on the third of the three *aiyām al-tashrīḳ*. The following practices are recommended to the sacrificers: 1. the *tasmiya*, i.e. the saying of the *basmala* [q.v.]; 2. the *ṣalāt ʿala 'l-nabī*, the blessing on the Prophet; 3. the turning towards the *ḳibla*; 4. the three-fold *takbīr* before and after the *tasmiya*; 5. a request for the kindly acceptance of the sacrifice. If the latter is offered on account of a vow, the sacrificer must eat none of it but must give it all for pious purposes. If the sacrifice, as is usually the case, is made voluntarily, the sacrificer enjoys a portion (a third) of the animal and gives the rest away.

On the public prayer and the usages at the festival on this holiday see ʿĪD.

Bibliography: In addition to the works mentioned at the art. ʿĪD the *fiḳh* books in the chapter on *Uḍḥiya*.

ʿĪD AL-FIṬR, "festival of the breaking off the fast" or *al-ʿīd al-ṣaghīr* "the minor festival", Turkish *küčük-bairam* or *sheker-bairam*, is the festival celebrated on the 1st Shawwāl and the following days. If the Muslim has not paid the *zakāt al-fiṭr* [cf. ZAKĀT] before the end of the period of fasting, he is legally bound to do this on the 1st Shawwāl at latest and is recommended to do it before the communal *ṣalāt* which is celebrated on this day [cf. ʿĪD].

As the festival marks the end of the difficult period of fasting, it is, although called the "minor", celebrated with much more festivity and rejoicing than the "major festival"; cf. ʿĪD.

Bibliography: The *fiḳh* books in the section *zakāt al-fiṭr* and the bibliography to the article ʿĪD.

ʿIDDA (A.) is the prescribed period of waiting, during which widows and divorced women cannot contract a new marriage after the dissolution of the previous one. The ʿidda prescribed for widows is legally 4 months and 10 days (cf. Sūra ii. 234). Among the ancient Arabs a longer period of mourning was prescribed. Then it was the custom for a widow after the death of her husband to withdraw to a small tent, where she spent a whole year during which she was not allowed to cleanse herself (cf. J. Wellhausen, *Die Ehe bei den Arabern*, in *Nachrichten der Kgl. Gesellsch. der Wissensch. zu Göttingen*, 1893, p. 454 *sqq.*). ʿIdda after divorce was unknown to the ancient Arabs. Whoever married a divorced woman who was pregnant, was considered the father of the child born after the marriage even though the previous husband was really the father. In Islām, however, the actual father was considered the father of the child and no woman was allowed to remarry within a definite period (ʿidda) after the dissolution of the first marriage. If she bore a child during this period only the previous husband could be considered its father. This ʿidda after divorce lasts, according to Muslim law, for three menstrual periods (*ḳurūʾ*) or for non-menstruating women three months; if a divorced woman is pregnant she must not contract a new marriage in any circumstance for 40 days after the birth of the child (cf. Sūra ii. 228; lxv. 4). An ʿidda is also prescribed for slave women, but in place of an ʿidda of four months and 10 days, it only lasts two months and 5 days, and in place of an ʿidda of three *ḳurūʾ*, one of two *ḳurūʾ* and in place of an ʿidda of three months, one of one and a half months.

ĪDJĀB (A.), i.e. offer (in contracts), really the solemn declaration that the offer is irrevocable (cf. the Arabic expression *ḳad wadjaba al-baiʿ*, i.e. the contract of sale is binding and irrevocable). In all legal transactions including marriage the observation of the prescribed legal form is most necessary and the mutual declarations, known in the *fiḳh* books as *īdjāb* and *ḳabūl* (i.e. offer and acceptance), are as a rule indispensable. Nevertheless in detailed books on law the question is discussed how far contracts are legal without such an *īdjāb* or *ḳabūl*. For example, in cases where it is the local custom for parties to exchange goods for their price without further formalities, can a valid transfer of the property take place without *īdjāb* and *ḳabūl*? Many scholars reply in the affirmative, but others hold such an "exchange" without the legally prescribed declarations to be valid only in cases of things of very little value.

Bibliography: The chapter on *baiʿ* in the *fiḳh* books and C. Snouck Hurgronje, *De Atjèhers*, ii. 353 (*The Achehnese*, ii. 320); cf. *Indische Gids*, 1884, i. 745, 753—55.

AL-**ĪDJĪ**, ʿAḌUD AL-DĪN ʿABD AL-RAḤMĀN B. AḤMAD, theologian and philosopher, author of various handbooks which were often annotated by later authors. His principal work is *al-Mawāḳif fī ʿilm al-kalām*, a philosophical and theological treatise, and a brief catechism known as *al-ʿAḳāʾid al-ʿAḍudīya*, on which many commentaries have been written. Other works are given by Brockelmann, *GAL*², ii. 267 *sqq.*; *Suppl.* ii. 287 *sq.* Very little is known of al-Īdjī's life. We only know that he was native of Īg, a fortress in Fārs, held the office of ḳāḍī and mudarris at Shīrāz (see Ḥāfiẓ, *Dīwān*, ed. Rosenzweig, iii. 242) and died in the year 756/1355.

IDJMĀʿ (literally "agreeing upon") is one of the four *uṣūl* from which the Muslim faith is derived and is defined as the agreement of the *mudjtahid*'s of the people (i.e. those who have a right, in virtue of knowledge, to form a judgment of their own: see IDJTIHĀD) after the death of Muḥammad, in any age, on any matter of the faith. As this agreement is not fixed by council or synod but is reached instinctively and automatically, its existence on any point is perceived only on looking back and seeing that such an agreement has actually been attained; it is then consciously accepted and called an *idjmāʿ*. Thus the agreement gradually fixed points which had been in dispute; and each point, when thus fixed, became an essential part of the faith, and disbelief in it an act of unbelief (*kufr*); cf., however, Goldziher, *Über iǧmāʿ*, in *Nachr. K. Ges. d. Wiss. Göttingen*, phil.-hist. Kl., 1916, p. 81 *sqq.* Each agreement, that is, became a *ḥudjdja* for its own and all succeeding periods. It could be expressed in speech (*idjmāʿ al-ḳawl*) or in action (*idjmāʿ al-fiʿl*) or by silence regarded as assent (*idjmāʿ al-sukūt* or *al-taḳrīr*); cf. the similar classification as to the *sunna* of the Prophet. It is especially excluded that it means the agreement of the masses (*al-ʿawāmm*), and in al-Shāfiʿī's earlier view, before he went to Egypt, a statement by a single Companion was binding on the following generations. But later he gave up this opinion and it has now been generally abandoned.

A general principle of agreement was held in different forms from an early period. The legal system of Mālik b. Anas was built largely on the agreement of al-Madīna, the city of the Prophet; this agreement was local. The agreement of the two camp-cities (*amṣār*) of Kūfa and al-Baṣra, with their masses of veterans of the early wars, had great weight. For later generations the agreement of the Companions was naturally decisive. But it was al-Shāfiʿī who developed this general principle into a definite *aṣl*, and ranged it with the other three. Further, from deciding points left uncertain by the other *uṣūl* it has come to be regarded as stamping with assurance points decided by another *aṣl*. This is in virtue of a divine protection against error (*ʿiṣma*) which inheres in the Muslim people. In Shāfiʿī books of *fiḳh* the statement is normal: — "such and such a passage (Ḳurʾān or Sunna), before the Agreement (*ḳabl al-idjmāʿ*), is the basis for such and such a rule". At present the Wahhābīs (following the vanished Ẓāhirīs) reject the universality of this principle and limit agreement to that of the Companions. And such specific sects as the Shīʿa and the Ibāḍīya are, of course, quite outside of the *idjmāʿ* of the Sunnīs.

The statement of the principle, which is given formally by the canonists, is as above. But the real working has been even wider. The basal tradition from Muḥammad runs (Ibn Mādjā, *Fitan*, b. 8): "My people will never agree in an error"; — and there are also Ḳurʾānic texts: iv. 115, denouncing those who follow other than the way of the believers (*ghaira sabīli 'l-muʾminīn*), and ii. 143: "We have made you a normal people" (*ummatan wasaṭan*; cf. Baiḍāwī). In consequence there is in the thought and working of the people as a whole a power to create doctrine and law, and not simply to stamp with approval that which has otherwise been reached. By means of *idjmāʿ* what was at first an innovation (*bidʿa*, the opposite of *sunna*), and as such heretical, has been accepted and has overridden the earlier *sunna*. Thus the cult of saints has become practically part of the *sunna* of Islām and, strangest of all, in the doctrine of the infallibility and sinlessness

(*ʿiṣma*) of Muḥammad, the *idjmāʿ* has overcome clear statements of the Ḳurʾān. In this, *idjmāʿ* has not simply fixed unsettled points, but has changed settled doctrines of the greatest importance. It is thus regarded by many, at present, both within and without Islām, as a powerful instrument of reform; the Muslim people, they assert, can make Islām whatever they, as a whole, please, although on this point there is grave divergence of opinion.

Bibliography: al-Shāfiʿī, *Risāla*, ed. Cairo, 1312, p. 125 *sqq.*; al-Ḳarāfī, *Sharḥ tanḳīḥ al-fuṣūl fi 'l-uṣūl*, ed. Cairo 1306, p. 140 *sqq.*, also, on its margin, *Sharḥ* of Aḥmad b. Ḳāsim on *Sharḥ* of Maḥallī on *Waraḳāt* of Djuwainī, p. 156 *sqq.*; *Dict. of Techn. Terms*, p. 238 *sqq.*; Goldziher, *Ẓâhiriten*, p. 32 *sqq.*; do., *Muh. Studien*, ii. 85, 139, 214, 284; do., *Vorlesungen*, by index; Snouck Hurgronje, *Le Droit Musulman*, in *RHR*, xxxvii. 15 *sqq.*, 174 *sqq.* (= *Verspr. Geschr.* ii. 296 *sqq.*; 303 *sqq.*); Juynboll, *Handb. des islām. Gesetzes*, p. 46—49; Bergsträsser, *Grundzüge des isl. Rechts*, Index; ʿAlī ʿAbd al-Rāziḳ, *al-Idjmāʿ fi 'l-sharīʿa al-islāmīya*, Cairo 1947.

IDJTIHĀD means the exerting of one's self to the utmost degree to attain an object and is used technically for so exerting one's self to form an opinion (*ẓann*) in a case (*ḳaḍīya*) or as to a rule (*ḥukm*) of law (*Dict. of techn. Terms*, p. 198; *Lisān*, iv. 109, ll. 19 *sqq.*). This is done by applying analogy (*ḳiyās*) to the Ḳurʾān and the Sunna. Thus in the earliest usage *idjtihād* was formally equated with *ḳiyās*, as by al-Shāfiʿī in his *Risāla* (ed. Cairo 1312, p. 127 *sqq.*, *Bāb al-idjmāʿ*). In his section on *idjtihād* he quotes first as a proof Sūra ii. 150 and demonstrates that it involves that each must follow his own judgment as to the direction of the *ḳibla*. It was therefore for al-Shāfiʿī practically the same as *raʾy*, "opinion" and the *mudjtahid* was one who by his own exertions formed his own opinion, being thus exactly opposed to the *muḳallid*, "imitator", who, as Subkī in his *Djamʿ al-djawāmiʿ* says, "takes the saying of another without knowledge of its basis (*dalīl*)". For thus applying himself he would, according to a tradition from the Prophet, receive a reward even though his decision were wrong; while, if it was right, he received a double reward (Goldziher, in *ZDMG*, liii. 649). The duty and right of *idjtihād* thus did not involve inerrancy. Its result was always *ẓann*, fallible opinion. Only the combined *idjtihād* of the whole Muslim people led to *idjmāʿ*, agreement, and was inerrant. On the controversy as to the possibility of error in *mudjtahids* see Taftāzānī on the *ʿAḳāʾid* of Nasafī, ed. Cairo 1321, p. 145 *sqq.* But this broad *idjtihād* soon passed into the special *idjtihād* of those who had a peculiar right to form judgments and whose judgments should be followed by others. At this point, and from the nature of the case, a difference entered between theology (*kalām*) and law (*fiḳh*). Even to the present day many theologians assert that *taḳlīd* does not furnish a saving faith; see, for example, the *Kifāyat al-ʿawāmm* of Faḍālī, *passim*, and the translation in D. B. Macdonald's *Development of Muslim Theology*, p. 315—351. But all canon lawyers for centuries have admittedly been *muḳallids* of one degree or another. When later Islām looked back to the founding of the four legal schools (*madhāhib*), it assigned to the founders and to some of their contemporaries an *idjtihād* of the first rank. These had possessed a right to work out all questions from the very foundation, using Ḳurʾān, *sunna*, *ḳiyās*, *istiḥsān*, *istiṣlāḥ*, *istiṣḥāb* etc., and were *mudjtahid's* absolutely (*muṭlaḳ*). Later came those who played the same part within the school (*fi 'l-madhhab*), determining the *furūʿ* as the master had settled the broad principles (*uṣūl*) of *fiḳh* and had laid down fundamental texts (*nuṣūṣ*). If the view so stated was found implicitly in a *naṣṣ* of the founder of the *madhhab*, it was called a *wadjh*. Still later and inferior were those who had a right only by their knowledge of previous decisions to answer specific questions submitted to them; these were called *mudjtahidūn bi'l-fatwā*, "by legal opinion". All *mudjtahid's* had been in a sense *muftī's*, givers of *fatwā's*; but these were *muftī's* only. Such was the formal and generally accepted position. But from time to time individuals appeared who, moved either by ambition or by objection to fixed positions, returned to the earliest meaning of *idjtihād* and claimed for themselves the right to form their own opinion from first principles. One of these was Ibn Taimīya [q.v.] (d. 728), a Ḥanbalite (Goldziher, *Die Ẓâhiriten*, p. 188 *sqq.*). Another was Suyūṭī (d. 911), in whom the claim to *idjtihād* unites with one to be the *mudjaddid*, or renewer of religion, in his century. At every time there must exist at least one *mudjtahid*, was his contention (Goldziher, *Characteristik... as-Sujûṭî's*, p. 19 *sqq.*), just as in every century there must come a *mudjaddid*. Another, but a very heretical one, was the Emperor Akbar (Goldziher, *Vorlesungen*, p. 311). In Shīʿī Islām there are still absolute *mudjtahid's*. This is because they are regarded as the spokesmen of the Hidden Imām. Their position is thus quite different from that of the *ʿulamāʾ* among Sunnīs. They freely critizice and even control the actions of the Shāh, who is merely a *locum tenens* and preserver of order during the absence of the Hidden Imām, the ruler *de iure divino*. But the Sunnī *ʿulamāʾ* are regarded universally as the subservient creatures of the government (Goldziher, *Vorlesungen*, p. 215—218, 233, 285).

Bibliography: Ḳarāfī, *Sharḥ tanḳīḥ al-fuṣūl fi 'l-uṣūl*, ed. Cairo 1306, p. 18 *sqq.*, also, on its margin, *Sharḥ* of Aḥmad b. Ḳāsim on *Sharḥ* of Maḥallī on *Waraḳāt* of Djuwainī, p. 194 *sqq.*; Snouck Hurgronje, *Le droit musulman*, in *RHR*, xxxvii., *passim*; review of Sachau's *Mohammedanisches Recht*, in *ZDMG*, liii. 139 *sqq.* (*Versp. Geschr.* ii. 369); Juynboll, *Handb. d. islām. Ges.*, p. 32 *sqq.*

IDRĪS, the name of a man who is twice mentioned in the Ḳurʾān. Sūra xix. 56 *sq.*: "Mention Idrīs in the book. Verily he was an upright man, a prophet and we raised him to a high place". And Sūra xxi. 85 mentions him along with Ismāʿīl and Dhu 'l-Kifl as one of the patient (*ṣābirūn*) ones. These passages are not calculated to give any explanation of this character. Even the name was for long a puzzle to orientalists till Nöldeke pointed out that it probably concealed the name Andreas (*ZA*, xvii. 84 *sq.*). That this Andreas who was raised to a high place, is Alexander's cook who obtained immortality, has been suggested, probably rightly, by R. Hartmann (*ibid.*, xxiv. 314). The post-Ḳurʾānic Muslim writers unanimously insist that Idrīs is the Biblical Enoch who also obtained immortality or, as Jewish literature says, was taken alive into Paradise.

The information given by those Arab writers regarding Idrīs is mainly derived from Apocryphal and later Jewish sources. The Biblical Enoch has three striking features which are repeated in the Muslim legends from Jewish models (Genesis v. 23 *sq.*): 1. he is a pious man; 2. he lives 365 years on earth, which suggests a solar hero; 3. God takes him to himself. The name Enoch, the consonants of which suggest the meaning "initiated" has probably also affected the formation of this legend.

As to the last point, Idrīs appears also in Muslim literature as 'initiated' in sciences and arts. He was the first to use pens (*ḳalam*), to sew garments and wear them; previously people had been content with skins. He is therefore the patron saint of tailors, one of the seven patrons in the guild system. He was also the first astronomer and chronologist and was skilled in medicine (*ṭibb*).

Idrīs is also identified with Ilyās and al-Khaḍir [q.v.], The Greeks are said to know him under the name Hurmuz, or as Bar Hebraeus says (*Hist. Dynast.*, ed. Pocock, p. 9) Hermes Trismegistes. For further information see Ibn al-Ḳifṭī, *l.c.* In agreement with passages of the apocalypse of Enoch Muslim legends also tell that he went through Hell.

On the relation of the Ḥarrānīs to Idrīs-Hermes see Chwolsohn, *Die Ssabier und der Ssabismus*, Index, s.v.

Bibliography: The commentaries on the passages in the Ḳurʾān mentioned; Ṭabarī, i. 172 *sqq.*; Yaʿḳūbī i. 8 *sq.*, 166; Masʿūdī, i. 73; Ibn al-Athīr, i. 44; al-Kisāʾī, *Ḳiṣaṣ al-anbiyāʾ*, ed. Eisenberg, p. 81 *sqq.*; Thaʿlabī, *Ḳiṣaṣ al-anbiyāʾ* (Cairo 1290), p. 43 *sqq.*; Ibn al-Ḳifṭī (ed. Lippert), p. 1 *sqq.*; Diyārbakrī, *Taʾrīkh al-khamīs* (Cairo 1283), p. 66 *sq.*; Abū Zaid, *Kitāb al-badʾ wa 'l-taʾrīkh* (ed. Huart), iii. 11 *sqq.*; Weil, *Biblische Legenden der Muselmänner*, p. 62 *sqq.*; I. Friedländer, *Die Chadhirlegende und der Alexanderroman* (Leipzig 1913), Index s.v. Henoch and Idrīs; Thorning, *Beitr. z. Kenntnis des islam. Vereinswesens* etc. p. 94, 96, 268 *sqq.*

IFRĀD. [See IḤRĀM].

ʿIFRĪT, according to the usual explanations, is one who overcomes his antagonist and rolls him in the dust (*ʿafar*); who successfully carries matters through (*mubāligh*); who is, therefore, powerful in a hostile sense, evil, crafty (Zamakhsharī and Baiḍāwī on Sūra xxvii. 39; *LA*, vi. 263, l. 1 *sqq.*, l. 14 *sqq.*; De Sacy, *Ḥarīrī* [2], p. 355). The classical and only Ḳurʾānic occurrence is in Sūra xxvii. 39: "an ʿifrīt of the *djinn*". Hence it has come to be used peculiarly of the *djinn*; but in the first instance it was plainly a general epithet, and thus the Ḳurʾānic passage might be translated: "a powerful *djinnī*". So, too, "an ʿifrīt of the *djinn*" occurs in two traditions from Muḥammad in Damīrī's *Ḥayawān* (ed. Cairo 1313, i. 179, l. 15 *sqq.*; ii. 104, l. 22 *sqq.*, under *djinn* and *ʿifrīt*). But soon the word became identified with the *djinn* and especially with the more satanic and malignant element among them. So Rāghib, in his *Mufradāt* (p. 393), speaks of its application to human beings as metaphorical, and even Ṭabarī, *Tafsīr*, xix. 93, seems to limit the word to the *djinn*. But it was not understood as meaning a specific class of these as e.g. *ghūl* [q.v.]; contrast the classification (*aṣnāf*) in al-Munadjdjim, *Ākām al-mardjān*, p. 17 *sq.*; and in the *Fihrist* (p. 309, l. 2) *ʿafārīt* is used as a general name for both *djinn* and *shaiṭān*'s. Even the distinctive meaning of hostility seems often to have been lost. In *The 1001 Nights* (Galland MS. of xiv[th] cent. A.D.; Story of Second Shaikh, Night vii.) it is said of a benevolent Muslima, *ṣārat ʿifrīta djinnīya*, "she turned into an *ʿifrīta*, a *djinnīya*". In Egypt the word has come to mean also the ghost of a murdered man, or of one who has died a violent death (Lane, *Modern Egyptians*, chap. x.; Willmore, *Spoken Arabic of Egypt* [2], p. 371 *sqq.*; "Niya Salima", *Harems et Musulmanes d'Egypte*, chap. xiv.; St. John, *Two years residence in a Levantine family*, chap. xx.). It also survives in the original sense of a strong man of violence, e.g. the *ḥārat al-ʿifrīt* in Cairo which is explained as the one-time abode of a *ḥarāmī*. But the most normal modern usage is of a powerful, evil, clever *djinnī*.

Bibliography: has been given above. Add: Dozy, *Suppl.* ii. 143, and Fleischer, *Kleinere Schr.*, ii. 640.

IḤRĀM (A.), infinitive iv[th] from the root *ḥ-r-m*, which has the meaning of "warding off" (*manʿ*), as the *LA*, xv. 9 says: "to declare a thing *ḥarām*" or "to make *ḥaram*" (the opposite is *iḥlāl* "to declare permitted"). The word *iḥram* has however become a technical term for "sacred state"; one who is in this state is called *muḥrim*. For example, a person fasting may be called *muḥrim*. The word iḥrām, however, is only used for two states: the sacred state in which one performs the *ʿumra* and *ḥadjdj*, and the state of consecration during the *ṣalāt*. Thirdly the word can be used of the dress in which the *ḥadjdj* and *ʿumra* are made.

1. The iḥrām in the major or minor pilgrimage. The law declares it meritorious for the pilgrim to assume the iḥrām at the very beginning of his journey to Mecca. But as this is very inconvenient, it is usually only done when the pilgrim approaches the sacred territory (*ḥaram*, q.v.). Pilgrims who make the journey by steamer often however assume the iḥrām as soon as they arrive in Djidda. The law has prescribed several stations (*mawāḳīt*, plur. of *mīḳāt*) where this is usually done namely: Dhu 'l-Ḥulaifa for the pilgrims from al-Madīna; al-Djuḥfa for those from Syria and Egypt; Ḳarn al-Manāzil for those from Nadjd; Yalamlam for those from Yemen; Dhāt ʿIrḳ for those from ʿIrāḳ. Any one who assumes the iḥrām too late has later to sacrifice an animal in atonement. These *mawāḳīt* are also called *mahall* i.e. the place where the *ihlāl* begins. The latter means "loud calling" i.e. the calling of *labbaika* [q.v.]. *Ihlāl* is thus used in the same sense as iḥrām and one says for example, *ahalla bi 'l-ḥadjdj* in the sense of *aḥrama bi 'l-ḥadjdj* i.e., to assume the iḥrām for the *ḥadjdj*. The law further ordains that people who live within the area bounded by these villages shall assume the iḥrām in their dwellings (*Tanbīh*, ed. A. W. T. Juynboll, p. 72), when it is a question of performing the *ḥadjdj*. For an *ʿumra* they must go to one of the boundary places of the *ḥill*; usually Tanʿīm is chosen for this purpose, and is thus erroneously also called al-ʿUmra by modern travellers.

As one can only enter a state of consecration after casting off all that is ritually impure, one must first of all perform the ceremonies necessary for this. The *ghusl* is usually performed; the pilgrim dyes his nails and perfumes himself, all of them ceremonies which were connected with exorcism. Frequently also the pilgrim has himself shaved, his beard trimmed and his nails cut (Burton, *A Pilgrimage*, London 1857, ii. 133, 377; al-Batanūnī, *al-Riḥla al-Ḥidjāzīya* [2], p. 172). On the significance of shaving, see below.

A particular dress has to be worn in which no seams are allowed. This dress consists of two pieces: a sheet that reaches from the navel to the knees (*izār*) and another thrown round the body, which partly covers the left shoulder, back, and breast and is knotted on the right side. This latter is called *ridā'* and from the manner in which it is knotted *wishāḥ*. Both garments are ordained by law to be white, but red stripes are also found (see the illustration in Burton, ii. facing p. 58). On this dress we may remark that it is probably the old Semitic sacred dress. The upper garment of the High Priest in the Old Testament was according to Josephus (*Antiq.*, iii. 7, 4) also made without a seam. The Jewish priests wear the ephod around the hips and the Meʿīl around the shoulders. In Islām itself there are analogies at the *ṣalāt* and the burial service [see DJINĀZA]. The old Arabs also, when consulting an oracle, as well as the later ascetics, wore two garments (Goldziher, in *WZKM*, xvi. 138, 338; Wellhausen, *Reste* [2], p. 122). White is also the sacred colour in many religions; at first the mourning colour (cf. Wilken, *Verspreide Geschriften*, ed. van Ossenbruggen, ii. 416—422) it was next adopted as a sign of a consecrated state: the ephod of the priests as well as the robes of ascetics are white.

The iḥrām dress is thus very old and does not owe its origin to Islām. The wearing of shoes is also forbidden. The most that may be allowed is sandals. This custom is also an old Semitic one. Among the Jews mourners as well as the officiating priests went barefooted. In the consecrated state also it is forbidden to cover the head; perhaps this is also an old mourning custom (cf. Ezekiel, xxiv. 17).

Women need not wear any particular dress. But they usually wrap themselves in a long robe which reaches from the head to the feet, while the face, which really ought to be uncovered, is concealed by a kind of mask (cf. the picture in Burton, *op. cit.*, ii. 58).

A *ṣalāt* of two *rakʿa*'s is offered and the *nīya* [q.v.] is pronounced. The latter be can done in three ways. The iḥrām can be assumed:

a. either for the *ḥadjdj* or for the *ʿumra*. This method is called *ifrād* (separation).

b. for the *ʿumra*, although the *ḥadjdj* is to be made at the same time. This is called *tamattuʿ* (*bi 'l-ʿumra ilā 'l-ḥadjdj*), i.e. the utilisation of the *ʿumra* for the *ḥadjdj*.

c. for both *ʿumra* and *ḥadjdj*. This is called *ḳirān* i.e. combination. On the origin and estimation of these three kinds of *nīya* a good deal has been written in Muslim literature. The four schools of law have different views on the order of importance of the various *nīya*'s, as regards the merit acquired by them. The kind called *tamattuʿ* owes its name to an expression in the Ḳur'ān (Sūra ii. 196), which later became a technical term. According to Snouck Hurgronje's suggestion (*Het Mekkaansche Feest*, p. 86 *sqq.*), the restrictions which were imposed by the iḥrām became too severe for Muḥammad, so that during his stay in Mecca before the *ḥadjdj* he conducted himself in a secular fashion. As his followers looked askance at him for this, the revelation in Sūra ii. 196 is said to have been given: "Any one who avails himself of the *ʿumra* until the *ḥadjdj* (shall offer) as many animals as is convenient for him; any one who is not in a position to do this shall fast for three days during the *ḥadjdj* and seven days after his return". What therefore appeared to the Prophet and his contemporaries as an omission which could be atoned for by a punishment, was considered by later generations as a thing permitted. Pilgrims who arrive in Mecca long before the *ḥadjdj* secure themselves by the *tamattuʿ* from a painful abstinence. As soon as they have performed the *ʿumra*, they put off the iḥrām and only assume it again when the time of the *ḥadjdj* aproaches. But the *tamattuʿ* is forbidden to those who have sacrificial animals with them (Sūra ii. 196). Originally the *ʿumra* took place in the month of Radjab and, according to some traditions, an *ʿumra* during the *ḥadjdj* period was an unheard of thing in pre-Islāmic times.

When one has formulated the *nīya*, the *labbaika* calling begins, which is to be repeated as often as possible and only ceases after the shaving on the 10th Dhu 'l-Ḥidjdja.

The state of consecration imposes certain pledges of abstinence: sexual intercourse, care for one's toilet, the shedding of blood, hunting and the uprooting of plants are forbidden. With regard to this the following remark may be made. In other cases in other Semitic religions a state of consecration excludes sexual intercourse, at least in the monotheistic ones. The neglect of the body is a well known feature of a sanctified condition among the Semitic peoples. The old Arab mourning women who were in a sanctified state of mourning are described as being dirty and having dishevelled hair (*shuʿth*: al-Khansā', *Dīwān*, ed. Cheikho, Bairūt 1896, p. 28, v. 4).

During mourning the Jews are forbidden to bathe or clip their nails. It is reported of the pre-Islāmic pilgrims and of Muḥammad that when in the state of iḥrām they smeared something on their hair to make its filthy condition more endurable (Bukhārī, *Ṣaḥīḥ*, *Kit. al-ḥadjdj*, bāb 126; Muslim, with Nawawī's comm., Cairo 1283, iii. 205; cf. *LA*, iv. 391). In a tradition given by Ibn Mādja (*Bāb mā yūdjib al-ḥadjdj*) Muḥammad in answer to the question: "What is the *ḥādjdj* (pilgrim)?" said: "He whose hair is dishevelled and whose mouth smells (*al-ashʿath al-tafil*)". The idea underlying all these customs, including the shaving at the beginning of the period of consecration is perhaps that everything that grows on the body during the period of consecration is devoted to the object of the sanctified condition. At the end of the period in most cases an offering of hair may have been made. The endeavour to make oneself unrecognisable may also have played a part.

The *muḥrim* is not ordered to fast. But there are numerous traditions which answer this question, some in the negative and some in the affirmative. It may be that in ancient times this ascetic custom was associated with the others.

When one arrives in Mecca from his *mīḳāt*, he performs the *ṭawāf* and *saʿy* [q.v.], sometimes also drinks water from Zamzam, and has his hair cut if the iḥrām was only assumed for an *ʿumra*. But if it was assumed for a *ḥadjdj*, the shaving and hair cutting is not performed till the 10th Dhu 'l-Ḥidjdja in Minā, after the ceremonies of the *ḥadjdj* proper are over. The pilgrim can now assume his ordinary dress again. But it is usual to put on new clothes (Burckhardt, *Travels*, London 1829, ii. 60). The law however prescribes another *ṭawāf* in Mecca and many pilgrims put on their ordinary dress only after this ceremony. Finally on leaving the holy city a farewell *ʿumra* has to be performed. For this purpose the pilgrim goes to Tanʿīm, performs a *ṣalāt* of two *rakʿa*'s, returns to Mecca to perform the *ṭawāf* and *saʿy* there. He then definitely puts off the iḥrām.

2. The consecrated state during the *ṣalāt*. This state also can only be entered when one is ritually pure and dressed in a prescribed fashion and

has taken one's stand behind a *sutra* [q.v.]. This state is announced by the *takbīr* [q.v.] which is also called *takbīr al-iḥrām*. The ceremonies of the *ṣalāt* proper begin then and can only take place during this consecrated state. One has to avoid everything which might destroy the latter, that is: every superfluous act and every superfluous word. The jurists specially mention greeting, sneezing, coughing, laughing, all that is connected with sexual life or the process of digestion. These are all actions which were orginally ascribed to demoniac or animistic influences. We frequently find the idea that angels are present during the iḥram (cf. the commentaries on Sūra xvii. 78).

The consecrated state is ended by the two *taslīma*'s, that is the formulas of greeting pronounced while turning the head first to right and then to left. According to some jurists, the object of the first is to leave the consecrated state as well as to greet those present; the latter is only a greeting for those present. Who those are is a question which is answered in various ways: according to some, it is the angels who are summoned by the *takbīrat al-iḥrām* and are now dismissed by the *taslīmat al-iḥlāl* (the formula by which one returns to the secular state).

The transition from the sanctified to the secular state is dreaded for demoniacal influences. These are averted by the so-called *ḳunūt* (q.v.). (cf. Goldziher, in *Orient. Studien Theol. Nöldeke gewidmet*, i. 323 *sq.*).

Bibliography: On 1: Wellhausen, *Reste arabischen Heidentums* [2], p. 122 *sqq.*; Snouck Hurgronje, *Het Mekkaansche Feest*, p. 68 *sqq.*; Juynboll, *Handb. des islām. Gesetzes*, p. 143 *sqq.*; W. Robertson Smith, *Lectures on the religion of the Semites* [2], p. 481 *sqq.*; Gaudefroy-Demombynes, *Le pèlerinage à la Mecque*, Paris 1923, p. 168 *sqq.*; the *fiḳh*- and *ḥadīth*-books s.v. *ḥadjdj*; the travels of Burckhardt, Burton, v. Maltzan, Keane; H. Kazem Zadeh, in *RMM*, xix. 198 *sqq.*; A. J. Wensinck, *Some Semitic Rites of Mourning and Religion*, in *Verhandl. der Kon. Akad. van Wetensch.*, Nieuwe Reeks, Dl. xviii., No. 1, *passim*. — On 2: The *fiḳh*-books s.v. *ṣalāt*; Juynboll, *o.c.*, p. 79 *sq.*; A. J. Wensinck, in *Isl.*, iv. 229—232.

IḲĀMA (A.) is the second call to the *ṣalāt* which is pronounced by the *mu'adhdhin* in the mosque before each of the five prescribed daily *ṣalāt*'s as well as before the *ṣalāt* at the Friday service. This second call gives the moment at which the *ṣalāt* begins. The formulae of the iḳāma are the same as those of the *adhān* [q.v.]. According to the Ḥanafīs, they are repeated as often as in the *adhān*; according to the other *fiḳh* schools, they are pronounced only once with the exception of the words "God is great", which are repeated twice at the beginning as well as at the end of the iḳāma. Moreover after the formula "come unto blessedness", twice in succession there are repeated the words "*ḳad ḳāmat al-ṣalāt*" (now begins the *ṣalāt*). In the lawbooks the calling of the iḳāma is recommended as *sunna* also to every believer who is performing the *ṣalāt* alone.

According to E. Mittwoch (*Zur Entstehungsgeschichte des islamischen Gebets und Kultus*, in *Abh. d. Kgl. preuss. Akad. d. Wissensch.*, 1913, phil.-hist. Kl., No. 2, p. 24) the calling of the *iḳāma* was borrowed by the Muslims originally from the benedictions in Jewish prayer. According to C. H. Becker (*Zur Geschichte des islamischen Kultus*, in *Isl.*, iii. 389) on the other hand, this Muslim custom developed out of the original *adhān* in the mosque, which was modelled on the Christian mass (see however al-Maḳrīzī, *Khiṭaṭ*, Būlāḳ 1270, ii. 271, l. 14—15).

Iḳāma denotes the action of the *mu'adhdhin* (the calling of the prescribed formulae) by which he causes the *ṣalāt* to begin. On this linguistic usage see C. Brockelmann, *Iqāmat aṣ-Ṣalāt* (*Festschr. E. Sachau*, 1915, p. 314—320) and J. Weiss, in *Isl.*, vii. (1916), 131—136; cf. the expressions: *aḳāma 'l-ṣalāt* and *uḳīmat al-ṣalāt* (gloss. to Shīrāzī, *Tanbīh*, ed. A. W. T. Juynboll, s.v.; Bukhārī, *Ṣaḥīḥ*, *Adhān*, No. 23—24). In the *fiḳh*-books however iḳāma is also explained as the call which is intended to summon the believers to rise for the *ṣalāt*. See Bādjūrī (Būlāḳ 1307), i. 167, l. 12.

Bibliography: In addition to the collections on tradition and the *fiḳh*-books see also: Dimashḳī, *Raḥmat al-umma fi'khtilāf al-a'imma* (Būlāḳ 1300), p. 14 *sqq.*

IKHLĀṢ (A.), to keep (or make) clear and pellucid, to keep free from admixture. In connection with the Ḳur'ānic use of the expression *ikhlāṣ al-dīn lillāh* (cf. iv. 146, vii. 29, x. 23, xxxix, 11, 14, etc.), i.e. to honour and serve Allāh exclusively, *ikhlāṣ* by itself received the meaning (cf. Ḳur'ān, ii. 139) of "absolute devotion to Allāh" and came to be used in opposition to *ishrāk*, *shirk*, "associating divine beings with Allāh". Sūra cxii. which emphasises the unity and uniqueness of God and denies that he has any associates was called *Sūrat al-Ikhlāṣ* (also *Sūrat al-Tawḥīd*); this Sūra is frequently recited in the *ṣalāt*.

With the development of the conception of *shirk*, which covers "every kind of worship of God which is not an aim in itself" and also the cherishing of interested motives in religious practice (cf. Goldziher, *Vorlesungen*, p. 46), the development of *ikhlāṣ* is somewhat parallel. According to al-Ghazzālī, *ikhlāṣ*, apart from the above technical sense, properly means only that one's action should be dictated by a single motive, so that for example it can be ascribed to one who gives alms only with the intention of being seen to do so. In the language of religious ethics as developed especially by the Ṣūfīs, *ikhlāṣ* particularly refers to the effort to come nearer to God and means the keeping free of this ideal from all subsidiary thoughts. In this sense it is often opposed to *riyā'*, the wish to be seen. *Ikhlāṣ* demands selflessness with regard to one's own religious practice and the abolition of the selfish element which mars devotion to God. At the highest stage of *ikhlāṣ* even the consciousness of *ikhlāṣ* itself must disappear and all thought of divine reward in this world or the next be put aside. Cf al-Ḳushairī, *al-Risāla fī ʿilm al-taṣawwuf*, Cairo 1318, p. 111—4; al-Harawī, *Manāzil al-sāʾirīn*, Cairo 1326, p. 16 *sq.*; al-Ghazzālī, *Iḥyā'*, Cairo 1282, iv. 323—332; ed. with comm. of al-Murtaḍā, Cairo 1311, x. 42 *sqq.*; transl. by H. Bauer, *Islamische Ethik*, I. *Über Intention, reine Absicht u. Wahrhaftigkeit* etc., Halle a. S. 1916, p. 45 *sqq.*; R. Hartmann, *al-Ḳuschairīs Darstellung des Ṣûfîtums* (*Türk. Bibl.*, Vol. xviii.), p. 15 *sqq.*, 59, 60.

IKHTILĀF (A.), difference of opinion; in contrast to *idjmāʿ* [q.v.], the difference of views among the authorities on Muslim law and dogmatics on details of legal practice and doctrine which do not affect great principles, particularly of the former, as it appears in the diversities between the *madhāhib* [q.v.] and also in those within each one of them. In opposition to contrary views urging unity of practice, and in face of the reality of the existence of this difference of opinions, the conviction has arisen in Muslim orthodoxy that they are of equal value and this view finds expression in an authoritative form in the saying attributed originally to various caliphs and latterly to the Prophet himself: "Difference of opinion in the Muslim community is a sign of (divine) favour". The registering of these differences has produced a considerable literature in Islām since the foundation of the study of *fiḳh*. Among the earliest existing works on ikhtilāf are the treatises of Abū Yūsuf on the differences between Abū Ḥanīfa and al-Awzāʿī and between Abū Ḥanīfa and Ibn Abū Lailā (Cairo 1357; also in Shāfiʿī, *Umm* vii. 303 *sqq.* and 87 *sqq.*); the *K. al-Ḥudjadj* of al-Shaibānī on those between the *fuḳahā*ʾ of ʿIrāḳ and Medīna (Lucknow 1888; cf. *Umm* vii. 277 *sqq.*); *K. Ikhtilāf Mālik wa'l-Shāfiʿī* (*Umm* vii. 177 *sqq.*). Shāfiʿī's *K. Ikhtilāf ʿAlī wa-ʿAbdallāh b. Masʿūd* (*Umm* vii, 151 *sqq.*) treats of the points on which the Iraḳians diverge from traditions of ʿAlī and Ibn Masʿūd.

Bibliography: Snouck Hurgronje, in *RHR*, xxxvii. 178 *sqq.* (= *Verspr. Geschr.* ii. 306 *sqq.*); Goldziher, *Die Ẓâhiriten*, p. 94—102; do., *Vorlesungen über den Islam*, p. 51—53; do., in *Beiträge zur Religionswiss.*, by the Society for the Study of Religions in Stockholm, i. (1913/1914), p. 115—142; F. Kern, in *ZDMG.*, lv. 61—73, and his Introduction (Arabic) to his edition of Ṭabarī, *Ikhtilāf al-fuḳahā*ʾ (Cairo 1902); J. Schacht, *Das Konstantinopler Fragment des Kitāb Ihtilāf al-Fuqahā*ʾ *des Abū Gaʿfar Muḥ. b. Garīr aṭ-Ṭabarī*, Leyden 1933; do., *The origins of Muhammadan Jurisprudence* (Oxford 1950); A. J. Wensinck, *The Muslim Creed*, Cambridge 1932, index.

IḲRĀR (A.), confession. If the accused in the case before the *ḳāḍī* confesses that the prosecutor is right, no further proof is needed according to Muslim law. The judge can at once give his verdict. An iḳrār however can only be considered valid when it is made by a person of age in full possession of his faculties and without any pressure by the ḳāḍī. Measures to extort a confession are absolutely forbidden. Even an iḳrār made by some one perhaps from fear of a flogging is invalid. If the case concerns the law of property or contracts, the one who acknowledges the demand must be capable of independent action (*rashīd*). If the justice of an accusation is once recognised in a case, a later repudiation of the iḳrār is invalid, except when the accused has confessed a crime which is liable to be punished as a *ḥaḳḳ Allāh* (see ʿADHĀB).

Recognition of children who are not born in wedlock is of no value according to Muslim law. If, however, the paternity of a legitimate child is uncertain and the husband expressly acknowledges his paternity, then no further proof is required. The paternity of the child is then established by the iḳrār. The declaration however must be contrary neither to the actual circumstances nor to the law.

In other cases also a person's genealogy can be established beyond all doubt by iḳrār without further proof in certain circumstances, for example, if a male Muslim who has attained his majority declares that any one is his father, brother or uncle. If however relationship is claimed with some one still living, the latter must confirm the iḳrār, if he is not incapable of doing so on account of youth or mental deficiency. If the iḳrār refers to more distant degrees of relationship, (e.g. brother or uncle), the men through whom the alleged relationship has arisen (e.g. father, grandfather) must be already dead.

Bibliography: The chapter on *iḳrār* in the *fiḳh* books; C. Snouck Hurgronje, *Rechtstoestand van kinderen buiten huwelijk geboren uit Inlandsche vrouwen die den Mohammedaanschen godsdienst belijden*, (*Verspr. Geschr.* ii. 349—362); Th. W. Juynboll, *Handb. d. islām. Gesetzes*, S. 192 *sqq.*, 314.

ĪLĀ. [See TALĀḲ].

ILĀH is undoubtedly the same as אֱלוֹהַּ and has the same problem of ultimate derivation (*Encyclopaedia Biblica*, iii., col. 3323 *sqq.*; Brown-Driver-Briggs, *Hebrew Lexicon*, p. 42 *sqq.*; Fleischer, *Kleinere Schr.*, i. 154 *sqq.*; Fischer, in *Islamica*, i. 390 *sqq.*). Here only the Arabic use is considered. The pre-Muslim Meccans regarded *Allāh* as a proper name (*ism ʿalam*) and this view is practically universal in Islām; for the arguments of the few who held that it was a descriptive noun (*ṣifa*) see Rāzī, *Mafātīḥ*, ed. Cairo 1307, i. 83, 24 *sqq.* But, according to Rāzī (*loc. cit.*), al-Khalīl, Sībawaihi and most of the formulators of the Muslim fundamentals (*al-uṣūlīyūn*) held that it had no derivation, was *murtadjal*. This Rāzī supports with various *a priori* arguments. Others, according to Rāzī, held that *Allāh* was of Syriac or Hebrew origin; others, of the school of al-Kūfa, that it was from *al-ilāh*; and others, of the school of al-Baṣra, that it was from *al-lāh*, the infinitive of *l-y-h*, "to be high", or "to be veiled". Of course, as to *al-ilāh*, "the Deity", Rāzī had no doubt that it had a derivation, although its usage had come to be practically as a proper name and equal to *Allāh*. Later Islām has decided that, while *Allāh* is a proper name, it is also derived (*mushtaḳḳ, manḳūl*) and most probably from *al-ilāh*, in some one or other of its meanings. *Al-ilāh*, then, would mean: i. "the god already mentioned", the article being *li'l-ʿahd*, ii. "the Deity", iii. it was softened to *Allāh* by frequency of usage and in that form came to be a proper name. But *ilāh*, "a god", still survived in the construct and undefined, as also *ālihat*un, "gods", in the plural. Apparently *al-ilāh* does not occur in the Ḳurʾān as a form; but there are cases where *Allāh* has the same meaning. So in Sūra vi. 3: *wa-huwa 'llāhu fi 'l-samawāti*, "and he is the deity in the heavens" (cf. Zamakhsharī, *Kashshāf*, ed. Lees, p. 394), and in Sūra xxviii. 70: *huwa 'llāhu 'lladhī lā ilāha illā huwa*, "he is the deity than whom there is no deity" (cf. *Kashshāf*, p. 1064). Then later *al-ilāh* came back in the two senses noted above and was used and is still used by theological writers much as is our "the Deity". Eight derivations have been suggested for *ilāh* (Rāzī, i. 84—86; Baiḍāwī, ed. Fleischer, i. 4) but they practically come down to the following: 1. *alaha*, "worship", but, as Zamakhsharī points out (*Kashshāf*, p. 8), this with the vth and xth stems are derived from the noun. 2. *aliha*, "be perplexed, confounded" — for the mind is confounded in the experience of knowing Allāh; *waliha* has the same meaning. 3. *aliha ilā*, "turn to for protection, or to seek peace, or in longing", again *waliha* has the same meaning. For Allāh the school of al-Baṣra preferred the derivation from *lāha* in either of its two meanings, "to be veiled" or "to be lofty". Zamakhsharī mentions only 1 and 2, the latter being his choice; in 2 and 3 *waliha* may easily be more original; for the interchange cf. *Mufaṣṣal*, ed. Broch, p. 172, l. 20.

Bibliography: Add to above: Ṭabarī, *Tafsīr*, i. 40; on margin, p. 53, 63: *Gharāʾib* of Naisābūrī (d. ca. 710; follows Rāzī closely but corrects him); on margin of Rāzī, p. 18, 19: *Tafsīr* of Abu 'l-

Suʿūd (d. 982); *LA*, xvii. 358; article ALLĀH above and in Hastings, *Dict. of Religion and Ethics*.

ILHĀM, (A.), inspiration, means literally "to cause to swallow or gulp down" (*LA*, xvi. 29, especially last two lines). In the Ḳurʾān it occurs only in xci. 8 — a celebrated but difficult passage — *fa-alhamahā fudjūrahā wa-taḳwāhā*, then he (Allāh) made her (a *nafs*) swallow down her sins and her godly fear". The oldest exegetical tradition (Ṭabarī, *Tafsīr*, xxx. 115 *sq.*) gives two explanations: i. Allāh explained these to the *nafs*; ii. Allāh created these in the *nafs*. The Muʿtazilīs chose the first (Zamakhsharī, *Kashshāf*, ed. Lees, p. 1612) but orthodox Islām generally chose the second, the almost certainly correct view. Thus Rāzī (*Mafātīḥ*, ed. Cairo 1308, viii. 438) and Naisabūrī (margin of Ṭabarī, xxxv. p. 100). But Baiḍāwī (ed. Fleischer, ii. 405) follows Zamakhsharī and Abu 'l-Suʿūd (margin of Rāzī, p. 273) follows Baiḍāwī.

But by far the most important use of ilhām is in connection with the doctrine of saints. Allāh reveals himself in two ways: to men individually by knowledge cast into their minds, and to men generally by messages sent through the prophets. The first, individual, revelation is ilhām; the second, and general, is *waḥy*. Saints, especially, are the recipients of this ilhām, because their hearts are purified and prepared for it. It differs from intellectual knowledge (*ʿilm ʿaḳlī*) in that it cannot be gained by meditation and deduction; but is suddenly communicated while the recipient cannot tell how, whence or why. It is a pure gift from the generosity (*faiḍ*) of Allāh. It differs from *waḥy* only in that the angel messenger who brings *waḥy* may be seen by the prophet and that *waḥy* brings a message to be communicated to mankind, while ilhām is for the instruction of the recipient. From *waswās* or satanic whispering in the heart, it differs in respect of the causer — an angel as opposed to a devil; and in the things to which it incites — good as opposed to evil (Ghazzālī, *Iḥyāʾ*, ed. with comm. of Saiyid Murtaḍā, vii. 244 *sqq.*, 264 *sqq.*; D. B. Macdonald, *Religious Attitude and Life in Islam*, p. 252 *sqq.*, 275 *sqq.*). But while the fact of *ilhām* was universally admitted, even Ṣūfīs raised the question of the certainty of the knowledge given by it. So Hudjwīrī (*Kashf al-maḥdjūb*, transl. Nicholson, p. 271) contends that ilhām cannot give assured knowledge (*maʿrifa*) of Allāh; but Ghazzālī would probably have said that Hudjwīrī was using ilhām in the sense of an idea which one found in his mind, and not of the flashing out of the divine light on the soul which, once experienced, can never be mistaken. Others taught that, while it was sufficient for the recipient, it could not be used to convince others or reckoned as a source of knowledge for men in general. This appears to have been Nasafī's position; see his *ʿAḳāʾid* with commentaries of Taftzāānī and others, ed. Cairo 1321, p. 40 *sq*. A very curious use is by Ibn Khaldūn in the sense of "instinct" (*Muḳaddima*, ed. Quatremère, ii. 331; transl. de Slane, ii. 384) but this, though a natural development, does not seem to have been taken up by others. Yet Ibn Ḥazm speaks of ilhām as a *ṭabīʿa* and refers as an illustration to Sūra xvi. 68 on the instinct of bees (*Milal*, v. 17).

Bibliography: Add to references above: *Dict. of Techn. Terms*, p. 1308; Djurdjānī, *Taʿrīfāt*, ed. Cairo 1321, p. 22 foot; al-Rāghib al-Iṣfahānī, *Mufradāt*, p. 471; Massignon, *Ṭawāsīn*, p. 125—128.

ʿILM is the broadest word in Arabic for "knowledge". In the lexicons it is often equated with *maʿrifa* and *shuʿūr* (Lane, p. 2138*c*), but there are marked distinctions in usage. The verb governs one or two accusatives as it indicates knowledge of a thing or of a proposition (German *kennen* and *wissen*). But *maʿrifa* is "coming to know by experience or reflection", and implies preceding ignorance. It thus cannot, unmodified, be used of Allāh's knowledge. Yet some contested this on the basis of actual occurrences of the word used of Allāh (al-Faḍālī, *Kifāyat al-ʿawāmm*, ed. Cairo 1315, p. 11). *Shuʿūr* is "perception" especially of details, the *shāʿir* is the "perceiver", "feeler", and thence "poet". Another early distinction has already been pointed out by Goldziher in his article on FIḲH [cf. above]. ʿIlm, in its early usage, was knowledge of definite things (*Ḳurʾān, tafsīr, aḥkām*) but *fiḳh* was the independent exercise of the intelligence. So *faḳīh* (pl. *fuḳahāʾ*) was one who was thus intelligent, but that word has come now to indicate a minor canon lawyer or casuist, while *ʿālim* (pl. *ʿulamāʾ*), following a broadening of the meaning of ʿilm to "science" and of *al-ʿulūm* to "the sciences", has come to mean a scholar in a wide sense and especially one using intellectual processes. Against this change of meaning there is a vigorous protest by Ghazzālī, in his *Iḥyāʾ*, book i., *bāb* 3, who denounces especially that the praise given in the Ḳurʾān to the *ʿālim* in respect of Allāh, should be applied to these dialecticians and canon lawyers. Further, this brought the *ʿālim* into sharp distinction on another side from the *ʿārif*, who is the mystical knower by immediate experience and vision, almost, but not quite the same as gnostic. For this distinction of ʿilm and *maʿrifa* in Ṣūfī theology see Ḳushairī's *Risāla*, ed. Cairo 1290, with comm. of Zakarīyāʾ al-Anṣārī, iv. 60 *sqq.* But when ʿilm became philosophical it had to submit itself to the system of the scholastic theologians (*mutakallimūn*). They gave it a place in the scheme of Aristotelian predicaments (*al-maʿḳūlāt*). There it is an *ʿaraḍ* ("accident", in the sense of the older logicians), one of those characterized by life (*mukhtaṣṣ bi'l-ḥayāt*), coming (along with will, power etc.) in the class of the modalities (*kaifīyāt*) of the *nafs*, the lower or appetitive soul (*Mawāḳif* of Īdjī with comm. of Djurdjānī, ed. Būlāḳ 1266, p. 272 *sqq.*; *Dict. of Techn. Terms*, p. 1061, cf. p. 1055—1066). It is divided into eternal (*ḳadīm*) and originated (*ḥādith*, *muḥdath*), according as it exists in God or in a creature, and there is no resemblance (*shabah*) between these two. Originated knowledge is of three kinds: intuitional (*badīhī*); necessary (*ḍarūrī*), by the evidence of the senses and by unanimous assertion (*khabar mutawātir*), deductive (*istidlālī*; cf. the *ʿAḳāʾid* of Nasafī with the commentary of Taftāzānī and others, ed. Cairo 1321, p. 19 *sqq.*, and for a number of short definitions of ʿilm see the *Taʿrīfāt* of Djurdjānī, *sub voce*). Those scholastic theologians who distinguished between ʿilm and *maʿrifa* used ʿilm of compounds and universals and *maʿrifa* of simple things (*basāʾiṭ*; see *basīṭ* in Djurdjānī's *Taʿrīfāt*) and particulars (Taftāzānī on Nasafī, p. 40). Another distinction enters in the relation of ʿilm to *ʿamal*, "works" in the theological sense. There is *ʿilm naẓarī*, such as knowledge of things; when you know them you have done every thing. But opposed to it is *ʿilm ʿamalī*, knowledge of religious duties (*al-ʿibādāt*); your knowledge is not complete until you have acted upon it (Rāghib, *Mufradāt*, p. 348). This is put rather differently in the *Tanḳīḥ* of Ḳarāfī (ed. Cairo 1306, p. 193). It is the duty of every Muslim to seek knowledge; therefore he who knows and acts on his knowledge has two acts of obedience to his credit; if he neither knows nor acts, he has disobeyed twice; if he knows and does not act, he has obeyed once and disobeyed once. This in the end joins the question as to what is saving faith (*īmān*).

For a descriptive classification of al the arts and sciences which have been reduced to writing (*al-ʿulūm al-mudawwana*) see *Dict. of Techn. Terms*, p. 2—53. Ibn Khaldūn in his *Muḳaddima* (*faṣl* v., vi.) deals with these more historically and philosophically in their development and their relation to the essential facts of life (De Slane's transl., ii. 319 *sqq.*; Quatremère's text, ii. 272 *sqq.*). But with regard to all sciences there is a fundamental distinction. They are divided into those praiseworthy and those blameworthy (*al-maḥmūda wa 'l-madhmūma*), and among the blameworthy are reckoned those which are not useful for this world or for that to come. The basis is the frequently quoted tradition: "It is of the beauty of a man's Islām that he leaves alone what does not concern him" (*mā lā yaʿnīhi*). The religious Muslim should therefore avoid such sciences as are not demonstrably useful for this life or for his eternal salvation (Ghazzālī, *Iḥyā*ʾ, book I, *bāb* 2; Ibn Khaldūn, *Muḳaddima*, ed. Quatremère, iii. 136; Goldziher, *Muh. Studien*, ii. 157, and review in *ZDMG*, lxvii. 532; Hudjwīrī, *Kashf al-maḥdjūb*, transl. Nicholson, p. 11).

ILYĀS, the Biblical prophet Elias, is twice mentioned in the Ḳurʾān. In Sūra vi. 85 he is mentioned with Zakarīyāʾ, Yaḥyā, and ʿĪsā as one of the *ṣāliḥūn* without further details. In Sūra xxxvii. 123—130 his history is related in the fashion which is stereotyped for all stories of prophets in the Ḳurʾān. That Muḥammad however knew something more of him is clear from the mention of the Baʿl, which is differently interpreted by the commentators, sometimes as lord, sometimes as an idol who has given his name to the town of Baalbek, sometimes as a woman whom the Israelites served. Verse 130 calls him Ilyāsīn which has given rise to much conjecture; it is however clear from the context that this name was only formed by Muḥammad with his usual freedom to get a rhyme in *-īn*. The commentaries on Sūra xxxvii. 123 *sqq.*, as well as the universal historians and the collectors of legends of the prophets give the following about Ilyās. He lived in the reign of king Aḥāb (Lādjab in al-Thaʿlabī) and his wife Izabal (variously written). Aḥāb used to follow Ilyās but the Israelites were worshippers of the Baʿl. One day, however, Aḥāb cast him off saying that the kings who served gods had as much success as he had. Astonished at this Ilyās prayed God to give him power over the rain. Thereupon a drought arose which lasted three years; Ilyās concealed himself during this period but was provided with food. He cured Alīsaʿ, the son of a widow, who became his disciple. At the end of the three dry years God reproached him with causing the deaths of many innocent persons by his severity. Thereupon Ilyās proposed to the Israelites that they should appeal to their gods for help and, if they did not hear, they should return to God. The gods could not hear their worshippers and at Ilyās' prayer the desired rain fell. The Israelites however were not converted. Enraged at this obduracy, Ilyās begged God to take him up. When he came out with his disciples Alīsaʿ, a fiery horse appeared. Then Ilyās ascended amid the cries of Alīsaʿ. God transformed him; he became a feathered being of light exalted above all human passions, half angel and half man, of earth and heaven at the same time. This is the version of al-Ṭabarī.

Al-Thaʿlabī is much more detailed. According to him, Queen Arbīl (Jezebel), the representative of Lādjab, is the incarnation of all wickedness. Her chancellor however is a pious man, who conceals his faith. As in the Bible, here also, the story of Naboth (Naboth is called Mazdakī, obviously an echo of Mordechai) is the cause of Ilyās' exhortation and the king's wrath. Ilyās conceals himself for seven years in ravines. Thereupon Lādjab's most beloved son falls ill. Four hundred priests of Baal set out to slay Ilyās, the alleged cause of his illness. The latter, however, instils them with such respect that they return full of awe. Lādjab then sends 50 soldiers who call out to Ilyās that they have been converted. The latter prays God to consume them with fire, if they are lying. This happens and a second body of soldiers meets the same fate. Finally, Lādjab sends the believing chancellor ot the queen with a free conduct and with a treacherous troop. At God's advice Ilyās goes with him to save the chancellor. On the arrival in the palace the child dies, so that the king forgets Ilyās and the latter is able to depart unnoticed. As he wearies of his stay in the mountains he enters the house of the mother of the prophet Jonah who, being then a child, was raised from the dead by Ilyās. He then goes back to the mountains and begs God to give him power over the rain for seven years. He is only granted it for three years during which he himself is fed by the birds. The whole of Israel has now to suffer famine, only one widow is supplied in a miraculous fashion by Ilyās with meal and oil. The rest of the story of Ilyās, the healing of Alīsaʿ, etc., is practically the same as that of al-Ṭabarī. Here also Ilyās is described as half mortal and half heavenly, appearing to men on earth. Al-Thaʿlabī tells of a man who met Ilyās in Palestine; after talking to him he went away on his camel.

There is another Elias story in the Ḳurʾān, although the name is not mentioned and the person who here takes the place of Elias is not identified by tradition with him, but with al-Khaḍir. In Sūra xviii. 65 *sqq.* it is related how Mūsā and his servant while fishing met a servant of God whom Mūsā wished to follow. The unknown one however replied that Mūsā had not the necessary self-control. While travelling together the servant of God performed several apparently ungrateful and cruel deeds. Mūsā reproached him each time, so that the guide finally separated from him after showing him that each of his supposed wicked deeds was justified. Jewish legend relates a journey of Elias with Joshua ben Levi on which Elias did similar things to those of the unnamed servant of God in the Ḳurʾān. Here also Joshua ben Levi, apparently rightly indignant at them, is shown by Elias to be wrong in his premature judgment. The similarity between the two stories is so great that it cannot be doubted that the Ḳurʾānic one goes back to the Jewish. The unnamed servant of God in the Ḳurʾān is usually identified with al-Khaḍir. It should be noted, however, that al-Baiḍāwī for example says on Sūra xviii. 65: "it is also said that he is Alīsaʿ or that he is Ilyās". This confusion of Ilyās and al-Khaḍir is significant and further cases may be mentioned. The reason is that in view of the Biblical story of Elias' s being taken up to heaven, the latter like al-Khaḍir is numbered among the immortals. Perhaps al-Khaḍir's name shows this. Al-Khaḍir "the green" is only an epithet of the man who was called B-l-y-ā or, according to another reading, Y-l-y-a, i.e. Ilyās. But elsewhere they are twins, not genealogically, but in their work and common activity. They go together to the fountain of life and drink from it, a trait which was originally only in the Alexander legend, but which again guarantees Ilyās's immortality, as his name shows, which is interpreted as *al-Ās*, "the myrtle", the symbol of immortality. Ilyās and al-Khaḍir having survived to the first revelation to Muḥammad are said to have wished to die. But Muḥammad is said to have replied to them: "O Khaḍir, it is your duty to aid my community in the desert and you, O Ilyās, must aid them at sea". Usually however al-Khaḍir-Glaukos is the sea daemon, while Ilyās is the patron on land. The two spend Ramaḍān each year in Jerusalem, observing the fast. They then make the pilgrimage to Mecca, without any one recognising them, unless God grants this favour. Their food is pond-weed (*karafs*) and truffles (*kamʾa*). After the pilgrimage they clip one another's hair and separate with eulogies. Any one who repeats these formulas three times at morning and evening is immune against theft, fire, and drowning (*sarḳ*, *ḥarḳ*, *gharḳ*), as well as against higher powers, Satan, snakes, and scorpions. Al-Khaḍir and Ilyās meet every night at Alexander's Dam where they fly in the air. In the Jewish legend he also flies about giving help everywhere. (See also the article AL-KHAḌIR).

Besides al-Khaḍir Muslim legend also knows the immortal Enoch-Idrīs [q.v.]. Ilyās is therefore some times also identified with the latter. In various genealogies of Ilyās he is said to be really Idrīs. Usually however his genealogy is traced to Aaron: Aaron-Eleazar-Pinehas. The latter is described as his grandfather. The name of this father has become, perhaps from Tisbī, N-s-b-y, Y-s-y, and finally Yāsīn.

It may further be noted that Ilyās, like al-Khaḍir, is often identified with St. George probably because the latter is also a patron saint.

Bibliography: The Ḳurʾān commentaries on Sūra vi. 85, xxxvii. 123—130, xviii. 65; Ṭabarī, 415, 540 *sqq.*; Diyārbakrī, *Taʾrīkh al-khamīs*, i. 107; Thaʿlabī, *Ḳiṣaṣ al-anbiyāʾ* (Cairo 1290), p. 221 *sqq.*; al-Kisāʾī, *Ḳiṣaṣ al-anbiyāʾ*, ed. Eisenberg, p. 243 *sqq.*; Ṭabarī (ed. Zotenberg), i. 409—411, 373; Friedländer, *Die Chadhirlegende und der Alexanderroman* (Leipzig-Berlin 1913), Register s.v. Elias; Geiger, *Was hat Mohammed aus dem Judenthume aufgenommen?* (Leipzig 1902), p. 187 *sqq.*; J. Horovitz, *Koranische Untersuchungen*, p. 99. — The Jewish Elias legend: Jellinek, *Beth ha-Midrasch*, v. 133-135.

IMĀM (A., plur. *aʾimma*). The term is used seven times in the sing., and five times in the plur. in the Ḳurʾān, where it means: sign, indication, model, pattern, leader, etc. In ordinary life it is technically used in three different senses:

1. Imām = leader of the congregational prayer (*ṣalāt*; q.v.). Any respectable Muslim, sufficiently versed in the technique of the *ṣalāt*, can act as an imām. If no previous arrangements are made, the honour of leading is offered to the most learned or important member of the assembly. But usually the community owning a mosque engage, for remuneration, a special man, possessing the neccessary theological education, whose duty is to act as an imām at all prayers. Imāmship, *imāma*, is neither a profession, nor a qualification: the imām is an *imām* only so long as he is actually engaged in leading the prayer. Persians use the term *pīshnamāz*.

2. The Sunnīs apply the term imām to the Caliphs, as leaders of the Community, and also, in an honorific sense, to the eminent doctors of Islām, such as the founders of the orthodox schools, etc., e.g. Imām Abū Ḥanīfa, al-Shāfiʿī, al-Ghazzālī, etc.

3. The implications of the term imām, as used by the Shīʿīs, are so numerous and varied that it is impossible to review all of them here. The evolution of the idea of imām was very long and complex. Here only its principal phases may be indicated. The nucleus of the idea, in which all Shīʿī sects agree, is only that of a descendant of ʿAlī b. Abī Ṭālib as the supreme ruler of the world of Islām. Everything beyond this was the subject of long and acute controversies.

The earliest phase of the idea of imām, still preserved almost intact in the Zaidī [q.v.] sect, demands from the candidate to imāma, first of all, reproachless genealogy, showing his direct descent either from Ḥasan or Ḥusain, sons of ʿAlī. He must not be a minor, must be sound in mind and body, possess sound theological knowledge, and general capability to be a ruler. He may either be elected to the throne by his followers, or seize it by force of arms. The Zaidīs, probably against all other Shīʿīs, believe that there may be several rightful imāms at one and the same time; or that there may be a period of time in which there is no imām at all.

The next phase, which reflects early Ithnā-ʿasharī and Ismāʿīlī ideas, still treats the term imām mostly as a synonym of the term *khalīfa* [q.v.], i.e. caliph, and applies it not only to the earliest caliphs, but also to the impious Umaiyads and the ʿAbbāsids, qualifying them, however, as false imāms. But the authority of the real imām is at this stage already regarded as a divine institution, intended for the continuation of the mission of the Prophet, and the guidance of the human race after him. Therefore there can only be one rightful imām at a time, a direct descendant of ʿAlī and the Prophet, through the latter's daughter Fāṭima. He thus is a legitimate successor of ʿAlī and the earlier imāms. His authority can only be hereditary, received from his own father, by the latter's special nomination (*naṣṣ*). He is not only the possessor of the exclusive right to be the secular ruler of the whole Islamic world, but also the only supreme pontiff of Islām. This latter dignity belongs to him as only he knows the esoteric side of the religion of Islām which the Prophet, finding his followers unable to understand it, revealed only to ʿAlī b. Abī Ṭālib, his closest associate, relative and friend, whom he always treated as his brother. The real imām inherits this secret knowledge from his forefathers, and therefore he possesses exclusive authority to give final and binding interpretations of the Ḳurʾān and *ḥadīths*, on which the legal system of Islām is based. In this he relies on the miraculous guidance (*taʾyīd*) of God, and therefore is infallible (*maʿṣūm*), though occasionally his actions may appear wrong, because ordinary mortals are ignorant of the higher motives by which he acts.

This phase may be regarded as the incipient "orthodox" Shīʿī idea. Its early development had to force its way amongst a multitude of heterodox Shīʿī ideologies which sprang from different combinations of early Islām with remnants of pre-Islāmic beliefs, chiefly doctrines of various gnostic sects, of Manichaeism, Mazdeism, etc. These sects [*ghulāt*; see GHĀLĪ] usually held extremist opinions, deifying this or that ʿAlid whom they regarded as the rightful imām of the time. Though these ideas left more lasting traces in the Shīʿa than one would expect, especially in the popular forms of the religion, yet the sects themselves were rather mushroom formations, rarely surviving one or two generations.

The original moderate, or "orthodox" theory of the imām was continually undergoing substantial modifications, and receiving additional dogmas owing to various historical circumstances, happenings in the family of the imāms, splits amongst their followers, evolution of Messianistic expectations, etc. Thus the extinction of the different lines of the imāms gave rise to the speculations about the religious significance of the number of the imāms in the line, about the theory of *satr* (occultation), or disappearance (*ghaiba*), or discontinuation (*waḳf*), etc. The hidden imām became the expected Messiah, Mahdī (the divinely guided one), or *ḳā'im*, "one who arises" at the end of the world, etc. All such theories, introduced by different branches of the movement, took an enormous amount of time and labour for their elaboration, systematisation, and founding on the appropriate quotations from the Ḳur'ān and *ḥadīths*, with the help of the system of *ta'wīl*, i.e. authoritative allegorical interpretation.

The next important phase of the doctrine began with the all-Islāmic movement of the adaptation of the ancient Greek philosophy and its methods to the needs of the evolving Muslim theology, approximately towards the end of the ivth (xth) century. While less intellectual circles made use only of such auxiliary disciplines as logic, etc., those more advanced undertook a complete adjustment of the dogma of Islām to the ideas of the philosophy of the day, i.e. a later and rather eclectic form of Neo-Platonism. In these theories the belief in prophets and imāms rapidly developed into the ideas of cosmic principles or forces. If — as the late Greek schools thought — man is the crown of the creation, then the Prophet, who is the perfect man (*al-insān al-kāmil* [q.v.]), is the quintessence of the cosmos. He is a kind of channel through which the divine organising and regulating energy flows to mankind, and thus to the world. As in the ancient philosophy such primal formative force was world-reason (*ʿaḳl al-kull*), the Prophet thus had to be regarded as the human hypostasis of it. Further on, in the same system, the *ʿaḳl al-kull* was supplemented in its work by its emanation, the world-soul (*nafs al-kull*). This surely could only be hypostasized in the imām, the spiritual guide of mankind. Again tremendous work was done to set strictly Islāmic theology on the lines of early scholastic philosophy and cosmogony, making it a symbolic replica of the cosmos, centring around the principle of divine revelation, and its bearers, prophets and imāms.

Fāṭimid theologians were first to achieve a complete success in such remodelling. Their theories, which could only be followed by persons of good education, were treated as esoteric doctrine intended for intellectuals only. The leading minds of other Shīʿī sects all moved in the same direction, but at a slower pace; at certain periods they were even left behind by the Sunnīs, the Ṣūfīs and, in some respects, al-Ghazzālī. Each sect developed its own terminology, but the ideas were remarkably alike.

The latest important phase of the theory of *imāma* came with the triumph of the Shīʿī Ṣafawī dynasty in Persia. It may be regarded as a sign of reaction and decadence, or concession to the lower classes of the population in their craving for the miraculous. The extremist tone of the doctrine was apparently caused by the fact that all the elaborate technique of the symbolism of Persian Ṣūfic poetry was mobilised for the glorification of the imāms, who, apart from what they were in the religious sphere, were also regarded as the ancestors of the ruling kings. Therefore by glorifying the imāms in the most stilted, hyperbolic and quasi-ecstatic terms, the poet would indirectly glorify the king, thus advertising his loyalty and political zeal. All restraint and the sober-mindedness of responsible and learned theologians were cast aside, and only fantastic speculations in Ṣūfic ecstatic style were admired.

In this new version of the theory of *imāma* (or, in Persian pronunciation, *imāmat*), the most important cosmic force is the divine light of guidance, pre-eternal, the real instrument of the creation. Its bearers, the imāms, follow each other in an uninterrupted and uninterruptible chain. One of them always is present in the world; the latter will perish at once if the imām disappears from it even for a moment. The part of the imām in the universe is the same as that of the *pīr*, or *murshid*, in a Ṣūfic community; only with the help of his guidance can one attain the knowledge of truth, i.e. salvation. With the light of *imāmat* continually flowing into the world, the institute of prophetship, or apostleship, occupied only an auxiliary position, as a series of periodical "missionary campaigns" of the deity, launched for the preaching of eternal religion to the backward and disobedient majority of the human race.

The first *pīr*, in this sense, in the Islāmic period was really ʿAlī, though in appearance he was only a disciple of the Prophet. The relation between the imām and God is in this theory approximately the same as that between Jesus Christ and the Deity in Christian theology, and is the subject of many mystical allegories. This phase may be called Shīʿī neo-gnosticism. Though it never received the assent of learned theologians, it nevertheless became the ideology of the wide Shīʿī masses, and strongly influenced not only Persian Ṣūfīs, but also the Ismāʿīlīs, Persian and Indian.

These principal stages of the evolution of the idea must not be understood as gradual and uniform in all branches of the Shīʿīs. In fact, different phases co-existed not only in different sects, but also within one and the same sect, the more advanced view being treated as esoteric doctrine. The general practice of the principle of *taḳīya*[q.v.] greatly facilitated this state of things.

Of all the very numerous features of the theory of *imāma* in the different Shīʿī sects two in particular were often misunderstood. One is the supposed belief in the transmigration of the soul of the imām, his rebirths, incarnations, etc. All such things are rarely found in the ideas of very backward and primitive sects, and also the great majority of the Shīʿīs have nothing to do with it. The simile best suited to explain this may be taken from modern life: the beam from the projector of the "divine light" is continuously trained on the head of the imām, who otherwise is an ordinary mortal. As soon as he dies, it is instantly diverted upon the head of his successor. The soul and the body, the personality of the imām have quite an independent existence from the eternal divine light of *imāma*.

Another question is that of the imām's power to work miracles. Popular belief was always particularly unyielding on this point, demanding miracles from the imāms, as a proof of their divine mission, or voluntarily attributing them the power to work these. For obvious reasons such ideas were rigorously opposed by the imāms and the leading circles of the community. The favorite final argument usually is the famous verse of the Ḳur'ān (Sūra xvii. 110): "I am a man like yourselves".

IMĀM-BĀRĀ ("enclosure of the Imāms"), a building in which the Muḥarram festival in India is celebrated, and the *taʿziyas* [q.v.] are kept when they are not being carried in procession; it sometimes serves also as the mausoleum of the founder and his family; the best-known examples are those in Lucknow and Murshidābād.

Bibliography: Mrs. Meer Hassan Ali, *Observations on the Mussulmans of India* (Oxford 1917), i., 33; H. G. Keene, *Handbook of Lucknow* (Calcutta 1875), p. 102—103; J. H. T. Walsh, *History of the Murshidabad District* (London 1902), p. 76—77.

IMĀM AL-ḤARAMAIN. [See AL-DJUWAINĪ].

IMĀM-SHĀH, i.e. Imām al-Dīn ʿAbd al-Raḥīm b. Kabīr al-Dīn Ḥasan b. Ṣadr al-Dīn, a missionary of the Nizārī Ismāʿīlīs of Persia [cf. under ISMĀʿĪLĪYA], who, according to tradition, converted a large number of Hindus in Gudjrāt, at the end of the fifteenth century.

Very little authentic information is available about him. He is believed to be a descendant of the first Nizārī Ismāʿīlī missionary who came to India in the fourteenth century, *pīr* Shams al-Dīn, or "Shamsī Tabrīz", — not to be confounded with the Shamsī Tabrīz who was an associate of Djalāl al-Dīn Rūmī [q.v.]. This *pīr* is buried in Multan. He was succeeded by his son Naṣīr al-Dīn, and grandson Shihāb al-Dīn. The son of the latter, *pīr* Ṣadr al-Dīn, converted to Ismāʿīlism many Hindus of the Lohana caste in Lower Sindh and Kachh; later on they became known under the name of Khodjas [q.v.]. His son and successor, Kabīr al-Dīn Ḥasan, also was a famous saint and missionary. On his death, most probably about 853/1449, he was succeeded by his brother, Tādj al-Dīn (d. ca. 872/1467). Imām Shāh visited Persia, and, after the death of his father, went to preach in Gudjrāt, apparently in the reign of Shāh Maḥmūdi Bēgrā (1458—1511). He settled in Pīrāna, ten miles from Aḥmadābād, where he died in the first quarter of the xth (xvith) century. As far as it is possible to ascertain, he cannot be regarded as the founder of a new sect, as he remained loyal to the Imām of his time. But his son and successor, Nūr, or Nar Muḥammad Shāh, later on proclaimed himself the Imām, thus causing a split in the community. The followers of Nar Muḥammad and of his successors are called Satpanthīs. The sect is still numerous in Gudjrāt, Baroda, and Eastern Khāndesh, and is subdivided into several subsects.

Imām Shāh was the author of many works in archaic Sindhī and Gudjrātī. Nine of them are preserved.

Bibliography: W. Ivanow, *The Sect of Imam Shah in Gujrat* (*Journal of the Bombay Branch of the Royal Asiatic Society*, 1936, p. 19—70), where earlier bibliography is given.

ĪMĀN (A.), faith. The basal idea in the root *ʾ-m-n* is rest of mind and security from fear (Rāghib, *Mufradāt*, p. 24; *LA*, xvi. 160, l. 6 *sqq.*). In consequence the fourth stem can mean both "to render secure" and "to put one's trust in" something or some one. Hence in theology al-īmān means: 1) the putting of one's trust, the having faith, in Allāh and his prophet and his message, and 2) the content of that message. A consideration of the first of these uses divides roughly into three; cf. the discussion in al-Ghazzālī's *Iḥyāʾ*, book ii., chap. iv.

I. The Ḳurʾān sometimes distinguishes and sometimes confuses īmān and *islām* and is ambiguous as to their relationship to good works. Theological controversy followed, which is mirrored in the traditions, and the technical use of īmān in *fiḳh* and *kalām* is, in consequence, very contradictory. A tradition, assertedly from Muḥammad, says that whoever has in his heart the weight of a grain of faith (īmān) will come forth from the Fire. But what here is īmān? Some taught that it is simply a holding fast in the mind (*ʿaḳd bi'l-ḳalb*), others added a testifying with the tongue (*shahāda bi'l-lisān*); others added a third element, works according to the fundamentals of the faith (*ʿamal bi'l-arkān*). The first has been the position of most Ashʿarites and Māturīdites; the second of the Ḥanafites and the third of the Khāridjites. The Karrāmites held that faith was simply acceptance with the tongue (*taṣdīḳ bi'l-lisān*), i.e. confession (*iḳrār*), equivalent to Islām in the narrower sense; others, such as the Djahmites, a sect of Djabrites, that it was only knowledge (*maʿrifa*) of Allāh gained by reason (*ʿaḳl*) and of the messages of the prophets gained by revelation. Orthodox Islām has come to the conclusion, which it, as usually, states as having been the position of the Fathers (*al-salaf*), that faith consists of acceptance in the mind of and firm adherence to a belief (*taṣdīḳ, iʿtiḳād*; q.v.), statement with the tongue of this acceptance (*iḳrār, ḳawl*) and good works. The second is Islām in the narrower sense. He who has all three will enter the Garden. But in the case of one who possesses *taṣdīḳ* and *islām* and dies with a single mortal sin (*kabīra*) unrepented of, the Muʿtazilites held that he was neither a believer (*muʾmin*) nor an unbeliever (*kāfir*) but a *fāsiḳ*, a "reprobate", and that he would remain eternally in the Fire. In the last point the Khāridjites agreed; but they held also that all sins were mortal. Orthodox Islām applies the same name to such a one but holds that eventually he will enter the Garden; for sinful believers the Fire is Purgatory and not Hell, and good works are not of the essence of belief but are additions. At the opposite extreme were the Murdjiʾites, the "postponers". Historically they arose in early Islām from the difficulty which the pious found in treating as Muslims those who professed to be Muslims but were yet notoriously evil-doers. The Khāridjites said roundly that such were unbelievers; the Murdjiʾites preferred to "postpone" decision until Allāh revealed all secrets. In the meantime they treated as a Muslim him who claimed to be a Muslim. In one form or another and to one degree or another Islām has accepted this position. All who worship towards the *ḳibla* are to be accepted as Muslims, with no questions asked. But the later Murdjiʾites developed this into antinomian heresy. It is faith that saves, they taught, and evil works do not hinder the effectiveness of faith, even as obedience in good works cannot save one who is an unbeliever (Van Vloten, *Irdja*, in *ZDMG*, xlv. 161 *sqq.*; Goldziher, *Vorlesungen*, index s.v. *Murdschiʾa*). Lastly there is the case of one who professes Islām and acts as a Muslim, that is, goes through the ritual and external observance of Islām, but has no internal faith. He is a hypocrite (*munāfiḳ*) and an unbeliever. In this connection it is to be remembered that "obedience" (*ṭāʿa*) and "good works" (*ʿamal ṣāliḥ*) in Islām primarily and ordinarily mean obedience to the ritual law (*al-ʿibādāt*).

II. Does faith increase and decrease? In the Ḳurʾān increase of faith is frequently mentioned and the Fathers (*al-salaf*) held that it increased with acts of obedience and decreased with acts of disobedience. By this, so later Islām taught, they meant that the mental acceptance (*taṣdīḳ*) remained and that the good works were not to be regarded as parts of it or essentially affecting it but as additions to it by which it was increased in amount. Conversely with acts of disobedience its amount diminished but it itself essentially remained. So the Prophet could speak of faith to the amount of a grain, showing that its amount could vary; and al-Ghazzālī shows with great psychological truth and beauty how good deeds go to nourish faith. But the question remained as a subject for verbal dialectic. Those who held that faith (īmān) meant acceptance (*taṣdīḳ*) and good works (*ʿamal*) taught that it increased and diminished, and those who held that faith was simply *taṣdīḳ* taught that there could be no question of quantity in it.

III. There appears to have been an early disinclination to say: "I am a believer" (*anā muʾmin*) without the qualification, *in shaʾ Allāh*, "if it be the will of Allāh", and still more with the addition *ḥaḳḳ^an*, "in verity", or "really", or *ʿinda ʾllāh^i*, "in the sight of Allāh." Examples are quotes in al-Ghazzālī's *Iḥyāʾ*, book ii., chap. iv., *masʾala* iii.; cf. the commentary of the Saiyid al-Murtaḍā. Hence the Ashʿarites with the mass of Shāfiʿites, Mālikites and Ḥanbalites insisted on adding *in shāʾ Allāh*, while the Māturīdites and Ḥanafites prohibited it and permitted the addition of *ḥaḳḳ^an*. They urged that to say "If it be the will of Allāh" implied doubt (*shakk*) and doubt in such a connection meant unbelief (*kufr*). In reply the Ashʿarites argued that the formula was used not to imply doubt of the reality of the absolute acceptance in the mind, but *a*) to guard against a making of one's self out to be pure (*tazkiyat al-nafs*; cf. Sūra iv. 49; liii. 32); *b*) out of courtesy (*taʾaddub*) and to gain a blessing (*tabarruk*) by submitting all things to the will of Allāh; *c*) to express a doubt as to the perfectness of the faith in question though not as to its reality, or if works are reckoned a part of faith, a doubt as to whether there will be works; and *d*) to express a doubt as to whether Allāh will permit the believer in question to die in the faith, for all things must be judged by their ends (*khawātim*). For the Ashʿarite side see al-Ghazzālī, reference above, and for the Māturīdite, al-Taftāzānī's commentary on the *ʿAḳāʾid* of al-Nasafī, Cairo 1321, p. 127 *sqq*.

Bibliography: Add to references above: al-Īdjī, *Mawāḳif*, ed. Soerensen, p. 274—290, ed. Būlāḳ, 1266, p. 594—600; *Dict. of Techn. Terms*, p. 94—98; al-Bukhārī, *Ṣaḥīḥ*, *Kitāb al-īmān*; Krehl, *Zur Lehre vom Glauben im Islam* (Leipzig 1877); A. J. Wensinck, *The Muslim Creed*, Cambridge 1932, index, s.v. *īmān* and Faith.

ʿIMRĀN, the Biblical ʿAmrām, was the son of Yiṣhar b. Ḳāhith b. Lāwī, and married Yukhābid, who bore him Mūsā in his seventieth year. He lived 137 years (Ibn al-Athīr, i. 119; al-Thaʿlabī, p. 99; al-Kisāʾī, p. 201; and Ṭabarī, i. 443). This account differs from the Biblical in so far as, according to Exodus, vi. 20, Amram was son of Kehat and brother of Yizhar, and reached the age of 137. ʿImrān was appointed grand-vizier of Egypt and had to keep watch every night by Firʿawn's bed (al-Kisāʾī, p. 201). One night he saw a bird in Firʿawn's apartments, carrying his wife upon its wings. He was at once enflamed with love for her and had intercourse with her. The bird then took her back home, without the thousand watchers outside the royal palace noticing. Next morning the astrologers announced to the king that the conception of his future enemy had just taken place and also that his star was in the ascendant and brilliant. Firʿawn ordered the midwives of Egypt to seek out and register the pregnant women from house to house. They did not however dare to examine ʿImrān's wife, as they knew that ʿImrān did not leave Firʿawn's side. Mūsā thus escaped certain death (al-Kisāʾī, *ibid.*). The Talmud likewise describes Amram as the most prominent man in Egypt (Sōṭā 12; Baba B. 120; Exodus R. i. 13). The ʿImrān mentioned in the Ḳurʾān (Sūra iii. 35), whose wife dedicated the fruit of her womb to Allāh, is not identical with the Biblical ʿAmrām or ʿImrān. Thaʿlabī (p. 220) expressly mentions this, with the note that there was an interval of 1800 years between the two bearers of this name.

Bibliography: The commentaries on the Ḳurʾān by Zamakhsharī, Baiḍāwī, etc.; Thaʿlabī, *Ḳiṣaṣ al-anbiyāʾ*, Cairo 1312, p. 91—92 and 220; al-Kisāʾī, *Ḳiṣaṣ al-anbiyāʾ*, p. 193—195; Ṭabarī, i. 443—445; Ibn al-Athīr, i, 119—120; Weil, *Bibl. Legenden*, p. 131; Eisenberg, *Moses in der arab. Legende*, Cracow 1910, p. 16; J. Horovitz, *Koranische Untersuchungen*, p. 12.

INDJĪL, Gospel, derived indirectly from εὐαγγέλιον through Ethiopian *wăngēl* (Nöldeke, *Neue Beiträge*, p. 47; Grimme in *Festsch. Goldziher*, p. 164; Jeffery, *Foreign Vocabulary of the Qurʾān*, p. 71—72); the variant *andjīl* may possibly be influenced by Persian or Mesopotamian usage. The *Indjīl* is represented in the Ḳurʾān (v. 46; lvii. 27, etc.) as a book revealed to Jesus; it is also, however, the scripture possessed and read by the contemporary Christians (v. 47; vii. 157), i.e. the four Gospels, often extended in general usage to the whole of the New Testament. The confusion to which this gave rise in later controversial disputes was frequently resolved on the Muslim side by the charge that the Christians had corrupted the orginal Indjīl (see e.g. Mingana, *Woodbrooke Studies*, ii. (1928), 35-6). Nevertheless, it is clear that many Muslims had a certain knowledge of the Gospels, though it if often difficult to define positively and not merely by way of induction how this knowledge was obtained. Some of it was certainly obtained orally in controversies or friendly conversations between Christians and Muslims, but his method of transmission for the most part lacks historical record. There were also reminiscences of Christianity brought in by Christians converted to Islām. A similar Christian influence made itself felt on the rise of Ṣūfism, in the teachings of which traces of Christianity can be clearly seen. Finally, one may certainly assume that, besides polemical writers such as Ibn Ḥazm (q.v.) and al-Ghazzālī (see below), there were Muslim seekers after knowledge who read Arabic translations of the Gospels made by Arabic-speaking Christians. We therefore give here a brief survey of the early translations, followed by some examples of materials from the New Testament in the Ḳurʾān and later Arabic literature.

The Gospels were translated into Arabic from the Greek, Syriac and Coptic versions. Although Barhebraeus speaks of a translation made between 631 and 640 by the Monophysite Johannes by order of an Arab prince, ʿAmr b. Saʿd, the oldest known MSS and fragments of translations from the Greek (Vatican, arab. 13, Borgiana, arab. 95, and other fragments) are most probably of the early ninth century. The oldest surviving translation from the Syriac (Leipzig, or. 1075) is of the same period. That passages from the Gospels were put into Arabic at a much earlier date cannot be doubted. George, bishop of the Arab tribes of Mesopotamia, a friend and contemporary of James of Edessa (d. 578), wrote scholia on the scriptures. Sprenger (*Das Leben des Mohammad*, i, 131 *sq.*) even thought a passage in Muḥammad b. Isḥāḳ's *Sīra* (Ibn Hishām, ed. Wüstenfeld, 149—150) could be regarded as a fragment of a pre-Islamic translation. In this translation of John xv, 23—27, the word by which παράκλητος is rendered, namely *al-m-n-ḥ-mna*, is neither Arabic nor Syriac, but Palestinian and rather old. The passages from the Gospels quoted in the history of the Patriarchs of Egypt by Severus ibn al-Muḳaffaʿ (tenth cent.) are based upon a Coptic version, possibly in the form of lectionaries. The same or a similar version from the Coptic appears also to have been utilized by al-Ghazzālī in his polemical work *al-Radd al-djamīl* (see R. Chidiac, *Réfutation excellente de la divinité de Jésus-Christ*, Paris 1939). In addition to the canonical Gospels, there are early Arabic versions of many of the New Testament apocrypha, such as the Protevangelion of James, Gospel of the Infancy, Apocalypse of Paul, and the apocryphal Acts of the Apostles.

The spread of Christian ideas in Arabia, together with narratives from the Gospels and the apocryphal books, before the rise of Islām was, however, largely if not entirely effected by oral teaching and communication. In Yaman there existed an organized Christian community, in active rivalry with the Jews and in close relations with the Ethiopians, whose occupation of Yaman about A.D. 525 certainly strengthened its position. In the north-east, the influence of the Nestorian church was spread from al-Ḥīra, whence it was carried not only by monks and possibly by preachers but also, though more superficially, by the poets who frequented the court of the Lakhmid princes. The Christian or christianized poets of the Ḥidjāz, on the other hand (Zaid b. ʿAmr b. Nufail and Waraḳa b. Naufal of Mecca, and Umaiya b. Abi 'l-Ṣalt of Ṭāʾif, are represented as being in relation with the Christians of Yaman and of Syria, where the Ghassānid princes and the tribes under their influence had also adopted the Monophysite doctrine. It is even asserted (*Aghānī* iii, 14) that Waraḳa, who wse a cousin of Muḥammad's wife Khadīdja, made written versions or copies of the Indjīl.

The passages in the Ḳurʾān which reflect the canonical and apocryphal gospels can therefore be most probably assumed to be derived from the same Christian communities, an assumption which is to some extent borne out by the high proportion of Ethiopic and southern Arabic terms which they contain (e.g. sūra v. 112—115). The great majority of these passages are narratives relating to the birth of Jesus, Mary and John the Baptist, and the mission, miracles and ascension of Jesus (see ʿĪSĀ, MARYAM, YAḤYĀ). There are also allusions to several of the parables, e.g. of the sower (xlviii. 29) and of the virgins (lvii. 13), to the supposed prophecy of the coming of another Apostle (vii. 157), and to many single phrases. More surprisingly, yet not intrinsecally improbable in view of the rivalry between Jews and Christians in Yaman, there are also echoes of the arguments directed against the Jews in the Gospels and Epistles, which, as pointed out by Andrae and Ahrens (see *Bibl.*), are sometimes employed in the Ḳurʾān against Christians as well as Jews.

The New Testament had an important influence on Tradition (*ḥadīth*; q.v.). Various miracles, sayings, and ideas which are attributed to Muḥammad or his followers have been traced to the Gospels. Numerous traditions regarding the high position of the poor and the difficulty of the rich in entering heaven, again reflect the doctrine of the Gospel and are in contrast to the views of the heathen Arabs. As Goldziher has shown, an Arab traditionist, Abū Dāwūd, even puts a version of the Lord's prayer into the mouth of Muḥammad. The parable of the labourers of the eleventh hour (Matt. xx. 1—16) is applied to the Jews, Christians and Muslims in Mālik's *Muwaṭṭaʾ* (*riwāya* of al-Shaibānī, *bāb al-tafsīr*). Likewise on the legends of the Mahdī and on Muslim eschatology Christian apocalyptic literature had a considerable influence.

In several Muslim historians we find a rather extensive knowledge of the Gospels. Al-Yaʿḳūbī, one of the fathers of Arab history, gives a synopsis of them. Such an inquiring spirit as al-Masʿūdī does not conceal his relations with the Christians. In Nazareth, as he tells us, he visited a church highly venerated by Christians and received a large number of Gospel stories from them. He knows of the birth of Jesus in Bethlehem, his childhood in Nazareth, the saying of God in Matthew iii. 17: "This is My beloved Son", which he gives with slight alterations. He had also heard the story of the Magi who visited the infant Messiah, according to the Gospel and other sources. He gives the story of the summoning of the Apostles accurately. He also names the Four Evangelists and speaks of the "book of the Gospel", of which he gives a summary, as if he had seen it. On the other hand, he shows a certain distrust of this book, in contrast to the great reverence with which the Ḳurʾān speaks of it. Al-Masʿūdī is comparatively well informed about the lives of the Apostles. He twice speaks of the martyrdom of the apostles Peter and Paul, but ascribes to the latter the same kind of martyrdom as, according to tradition, was the fate of Peter only. He knows Thomas as the apostle of India. On the whole, Thomas seems to be the apostle best known to the Muslims next to Peter, and even Paul is less known than Peter.

Al-Bīrūnī is still better informed than al-Masʿūdī. In order to write his *Chronology*, he had to consult Nestorian Christians. He knows various parts of the Gospels and also the commentary of Dādīshōʿ (Jesudad; cf. Duval, *Litt. syriaque*, 2nd ed., p. 64) and discusses it with a certain spirit of criticism. The four Evangelists to him are four recensions, which he compares with the three copies of the Bible, the Jewish, Christian, and Samaritan. He notices, however, that these recensions differ considerably from one another. Al-Bīrūnī gives the genealogies of Joseph in full from Matthew and Luke, and tells in a very interesting passage how the Christians explain this difference. He speaks of other gospels which the Marcionites, Bardesanites, and Manichaeans possessed, the two first of which differed, according to him, "in some parts" from the Christian Gospels, while the others were contradictory. In view of all these different recensions he concludes that one cannot rely very much on the prophetical value of the Gospels.

The Persian version of Tabarī's *Chronicle* (French ed. by Zotenberg) contains New Testament legends which are more detailed than in the Arabic original and correspond with those found in the stories of the Prophets (*ḳiṣaṣ al-anbiyāʾ*). Certain details from the Passion for example are given, such as the repudiation by "Simeon", the betrayal by one of the Apostles, who is not mentioned by name, and the story of Mary under the Cross. For the rest the author holds the Muslim view that another person, whom he calls Josua, was substituted for Jesus. As to the history of the Apostles he gives the tradition which makes John come to Edessa.

In the mystic literature, one finds numerous allusions to the Gospel, and there are even traces of some knowledge of the exposition of some passages in scripture by the Fathers of the Church. On the sayings attributed to Jesus in the writings of the Muslim mystics see the article ʿĪSĀ, at the end. We find also in al-Suhrawardī an accurate and complete version of the parable of the sower. The *Rasāʾil Ikhwān al-Ṣafāʾ* contain remarkable passages about the crucifixion of Jesus, the actuality of which they assume, about the Resurrection, the assembling of the Apostles at the last supper and their scattering over the face of the earth. The *Acts of the Apostles* (*Afʿāl al-ḥawārīya*) is expressly quoted there (Dieterici, p. 605). For other features cf. Massignon's *Ḥallâj*; there is a miniature representing Ḥallādj on the cross, with Christ's face; and the beautiful epic romance of Ḥamza (*Sīrat al-amīr Ḥamza*, Cairo n.d., iii, 822 *sqq.*).

The philosophic literature also shows a large number of controversies between Christians and Muslims, beginning in all probability from the time of John of Damascus, whose father, Sergius b. Manṣūr, was secretary to four Umaiyad Caliphs. Among the celebrated polemicists we need only mention here Abū ʿAlī ʿĪsā b. Zurʿa, who in 387 composed a reply to Abu 'l-Ḳāsim ʿAbd Allāh b. Aḥmad al-Balkhī, and Yaḥyā b. ʿAdī, a Christian scholar and pupil of al-Fārābī. The latter produced an apology for Christianity, which he dedicated to Shaikh Abū ʿĪsā Muḥammad b. al-Warrāḳ. He also replied to strictures by al-Kindī on the Trinity. [See also the articles ʿĪSĀ and AL-MAHDĪ].

Bibliography: On the Christian Arabic translations see: Guidi, *Le traduzioni degli Evangelii in arabo* etc., in *Atti della R. Acc. dei Lincei*, Scienze mor. e fil., Ser. iv., Vol. iv., 1888; G. Graf, *Gesch. der christlichen arabischen Lit.*, i (Vatican 1944), 142 *sqq.*, 224 *sqq.*; H. Goussen, *Beitr. zur christl.-arab. Literaturgesch.*, Part iv.: *Die christl.-arab. Lit. der Mozaraber*, Leipzig 1909; Seb. Euringer, *Die Überlieferung der arab. Übers. des Diatessarons*, in *Biblische Studien*, xvii., 2nd Number, Freiburg i. Br. 1912; K. Vollers and E. von Dobschütz, *Ein spanisch-arab. Evangelienfragment*, in *ZDMG*, lvi. 633 *sqq.*; I. Gildemeister, *De Evangeliis in arabicum et Simplici Syriaca translatis commentatio academica*, Bonn 1865; C. Peters, in *Biblica*, vol. 21 (1940), p. 138 *sqq.*; do. in *AO*, vol. 17 (1940), p. 124 *sqq.* — On controversies: van den Ham, *Disputatio pro religione Mohammedanorum adversus Christianos*, Leyden 1890; Goldziher, *Über muhammedanische Polemik gegen Ahl al-Kitāb*, in *ZDMG*, xxxii. 341; ʿAlī b. Rabban al-Ṭabarī, *K. al-dīn wa 'l-daula*, transl. by A. Mingana, Manchester 1922, p. 140 *sqq.*; A. Jeffery, *Ghevond's Text of the Correspondence between ʿUmar II and Leo III*, in *Harvard Theol. Rev.* xxxvii, 1944, 269—332. — On the influence of the New Testament on Tradition: Goldziher, *Muhammedanische Studien*, ii. 382 *sqq.*: *Ḥadîth und Neues Testament*; do., *Neutestamentl. Elemente in der Traditionslit. des Islam*, in *OC*, 1902, p. 390 *sqq.* — On the Apocrypha: *Indjīl al-ṭufūlīya, Evang. Infantiae*, ed. H. Sike, Utrecht 1697; Thilo, *Codex Apocr. Novi Test.*, Leipzig 1832; R. Duval, *Lit. syriaque*, 2e ed., Paris 1900; P. Dib, in *ROC*, 1905, p. 418—423, quotes Arabic translations of the New Testament from the Coptic and Syriac. — On the Poets: L. Cheikho, *Poètes arabes chrétiens*, Bairūt 1890—1891; Lammens, *Le Chantre des Omiades*, in *JA*, 9 sér., iv., 1894; Cl. Huart, *Une nouvelle source du Qorân*, in *JA*, 10e sér., iv., 1904; Power, *Umaiya ibn Abī-ṣ-Ṣalt*, in *MFOB*, 1906; Louis Massignon, *Al-Ḥallâj, martyr mystique de l'Islam*, Paris 1922, ii. 771; do., *Essai sur les origines du lexique technique de la Mystique musulmane*, Paris 1922, pp. 51—55; J. Horovitz, *Koranische Untersuchungen*, p. 71; Tor Andrae, *Der Ursprung des Islams und das Christentum*, Uppsala-Stockholm 1926; K. Ahrens, *Christliches in Qoran*, in *ZDMG*, N.F., 9, 15—69, 143—190, Leipzig 1930; H. Lammens, *Les Chrétiens à la Mecque*, in *L'Arabie Occidentale*, Beyrouth 1928, 1 *sqq.*

Arabic authors quoted: al-Yaʿḳūbī, i 74—89 (cf. thereon Klamroth, *Der Auszug aus den Evangelien bei dem arab. Historiker Jaʿqûbî*, in *Festschr. z. Einweihung des Wilhelm-Gymnasium*, Hamburg 1885, and G. Smit, "*Bijbel en Legende*" *bij den Arabischen schrijver Ja'qubi*, Leyden 1907); al-Masʿūdī, *Murūdj al-dhahab*, ed. Paris; al-Bīrūnī, *Chronology*, transl. by Sachau; *Chronique de Tabari*, transl. by H. Zotenberg, 1867—1874; al-Suhrawardī, *ʿAwārif al-maʿārif*, on the margin of the *Iḥyāʾ* of al-Ghazzālī, Cairo 1312 (the parable of the Sower is given in i., 78—79); *Die Abhandlungen der Ichwan Es-Safā*, ed. Dieterici, Berlin 1886, p. 594 *sqq.*

AL-INSĀN AL-KĀMIL. This expression, which means literally "The Perfect Man", is used by Muḥammadan mystics to denote the highest type of humanity, i.e. the theosophist who has realised his essential oneness with God. Abū Yazīd al-Bisṭāmī (d. 261/874), quoted in the *Risāla* of al-Ḳushairī (Cairo 1315, p. 140, l. 12 *sqq.*; cf. R. Hartmann, *Al-Ḳuschairîs Darstellung des Ṣûfîtum*, in *Türkische Bibliothek*, vol. xviii., p. 168 *infra sq.*), speaks of the mystic who after having been invested with certain divine names, passes away (*faniya*; cf. FANĀʾ) from them and becomes "the perfect and complete" (*al-kāmil al-tāmm*). We may identify the person so described with *al-insān al-kāmil*, a phrase which occurs, perhaps for the first time, in the writings of Ibn al-ʿArabī (cf. *Fuṣūṣ al-ḥikam*, chap. 1) and forms the title of a well-known work, *al-Insān al-kāmil fī maʿrifat al-awākhir wa 'l-awāʾil*, by ʿAbd al-Karīm al-Djīlī [q.v.] who died about 820/1417. These authors base their theory of the Perfect Man on a pantheistic monism which regards the Creator (*al-ḥaḳḳ*) and the creature (*al-khalḳ*) as complementary aspects of Absolute Being. A similar but by no means identical doctrine had already been set forth by al-Ḥallādj (see *Kitāb al-ṭawāsīn*, ed. Massignon, p. 129 *sqq.*) "Man", says Ibn al-ʿArabī, "unites in himself both the form of God and the form of the universe. He alone manifests the divine Essence together with all its names and attributes. He is the mirror by which God is revealed to Himself, and therefore the final cause of creation. We ourselves are the attributes by which we describe God; our existence is merely an objectification of His existence. While God is necessary to us in order that we may exist, we are necessary to Him in order that He may be manifested to Himself".

Al-Djīlī, who differs from Ibn al-ʿArabī in certain details, gives a full and systematic exposition of the theory (see R. A. Nicholson, *Studies in Islamic Mysticism*, p. 77—142). His argument runs somewhat as follows:

Essence (*dhāt*) is that to which names and attributes are attached, although in reality there is no distinction between the Essence and its attributes. It may be either existent or non-existent. The existent is either Pure Being (God) or Being joined to not-being (created things). Absolute or Pure Being is the simple Essence, without manifestation of names, attributes, and relations. The process of manifestation involves a descent from simplicity, which has three stages: (1) *aḥadīya*, (2) *huwīya*, (3) *anīya*. At this point appear the names and attributes whereby the Essence is made known. They are communicated by means of mystical illumination (*tadjallī*). The Perfect Man, who typifies the emanation of Absolute Being from itself and its return into itself, moves upward through a series of illuminations until he ultimately becomes merged in the Essence. In the first degree, called the Illumination of the Names, "he is destroyed under the radiance of the name by which God reveals Himself, so that if you invoke God by that name, the man answers you, because the name has taken possession of him". The second degree is called the Illumination of the Attributes. These are received by the mystic in proportion to his capacity, the abundance of his knowledge, and the strength of his resolution. To some men God reveals Himself by the attribute of life, to others by the attribute of knowledge, to others by the attribute of power, and so on. Moreover, the same attribute is manifested in different ways. For example, some hear the divine speech (*kalām*) with their whole being, some hear it from human lips but recognise it as the voice of God, some are informed by it concerning future events. The final degree, which is the Illumination of the Essence, sets the seal of deification upon the Perfect Man. He now becomes the Pole (*ḳuṭb*) of the universe and the medium through which it is preserved; he is omnipotent, nothing is hidden from him; it is right that mankind should bow down in adoration before him, since he is the vicegerent (*khalīfa*) of God in the world (cf. Sūra ii. 30). Thus, being divine as well as human, he forms a connecting link between God and created things. His universal nature (*djamʿīya*) gives him a unique and supreme position in the order of existence. Al-Djīlī divides the attributes of God into four classes: attributes of the Essence (Oneness, Eternity, Creativeness, and the like), attributes of beauty (*djamāl*), attributes of majesty (*djalāl*), and attributes of perfection (*kamāl*). While the attributes of beauty, majesty, and perfection are manifested both in this world and the next — Paradise und Hell, for instance, being respectively absolute manifestations of beauty and majesty — the Perfect Man alone displays the whole sum of divine attributes and possesses the divine life in all its fullness. This microcosmic function, according to the Ṣūfistic interpretation of Sūra xxxiii 72, he freely accepted as a trust from the hands of his Maker. He contains the types of every spiritual and material thing. His heart corresponds to the Throne of God (*ʿarsh*), his reason to the Pen (*ḳalam*), his soul to the Tablet (*al-lawḥ al-maḥfūẓ*), his nature to the elements (*ʿanāṣir*). He is the copy of God (*nuskhat al-ḥaḳḳ*); cf. the tradition that God created Adam in His own image.

This theory shows the influence upon Ṣūfism of Gnostic ideas (cf. Bousset, *Hauptprobleme der Gnosis*, p. 150 *sqq.*). The Insān al-Kāmil is the *Insān al-ḳadīm* of the Manichaeans, the *Ādām ḳadmōn* of the Ḳabbālā. It was inevitable that on Islāmic ground the representative Superman should be the Prophet Muḥammad, the dogma of whose pre-existence established itself, even in orthodox circles, at an early date (see Goldziher, *Neuplatonische und gnostische Elemente im Hadīt*, in *ZA*, xxii. 234 *sqq.*). Many Ṣūfīs, adopting the Plotinian doctrine of emanation, identify Muḥammad, the Perfect Man, with Universal Reason or the Logos. Al-Djīlī takes care to state that Muḥammad is the Most Perfect Man (*akmal*), to whom the saints and the rest of the prophets are subordinate. He holds that in every age Muḥammad assumes the form of a living saint and in that guise makes himself known to mystics (cf. Goldziher, *loc. cit.*, concerning the doctrine of the transmission of the *nūr muḥammadī*; *q.v.*). We find a further concession to Islām in the principle that the Perfect Man must continue to obey the religious law. "Perception of the sublime Essence", al-Djīlī says, "consists in thy knowing, by way of mystical revelation (*kashf*), that thou art He and that He is thou, and that this is not *ḥulūl* [q.v.] nor *ittiḥād* [.qv.], and that the slave is a slave and the Lord a lord, and that the slave does not become a lord nor the Lord a slave".

Bibliography: In addition to the references given in the article, *Gulshan-i rāz* of Maḥmūd Shabistarī, ed. Whinfield, ii., p. 312—561; Tholuck, *Ssufismus*, chap. 4; Palmer, *Oriental Mysticism*, chap. 3; Shaikh Muḥammad Iḳbāl, *The Development of Metaphysics in Persia*, p. 150—174; Nicholson, *The Mystics of Islam*, chap. 5; H. H. Schaeder in *Isl.* xiv. (1924).

IRAM, the name of an individual or tribe which occupies the same position in Muslim genealogy as Aram in Biblical, as may be seen from a comparison of the Muslim series ʿŪṣ b. Iram b. Sām b. Nūḥ with the Biblical ʿŪṣ b. Aram b. Shem b. Noah (*Gen.* X, 23; 1 *Chron.* I, 17). The Muslim line probably, like many others, entered historiography under Jewish influence and therefore gives us no new information regarding the dissemination of Aramaeans in Arabia. The name is identified with that of the Iram dhāt al-ʿImād discussed below, the vocalisation of which was established. Perhaps this explains why the Muslims say Iram instead of Aram.

Tradition has still further developed the connection with the Aramaeans. The people ʿĀd [q.v.] were called Iram; when the ʿĀdīs were destroyed, the name Iram was transferred to Thamūd whose descendants were thought to be the Nabataeans of the Sawād. It was also known to Muslim scholars that Damascus in ancient times was called Iram, i.e. Aram.

Bibliography: see the next article.

IRAM DHĀT AL-ʿIMĀD occurs in the Ḳurʾān only in Sūra lxxxix. 7: "(6) Hast thou not seen how thy Lord dealt with ʿĀd, (7) Iram dhāt al-ʿImād, the like whereof hath not been created in the lands". — The connection between ʿĀd and Iram in these verses may be interpreted in various ways, as the commentaries explain at length. If Iram is taken in contrast to ʿĀd, it is intelligible why Iram also has been taken as a tribal name; ʿimād could then be taken in the sense of "tent-pole". According to others, the poles are a description of the giant figure of the Iram, which is thus particularly emphasised. If Iram stands in *iḍāfa* to ʿĀd, it is more probable that Iram dhāt al-ʿImād is a geographical term: "Iram with the pillars". This is the prevailing opinion among Muslims. What is exactly referred to, however, is a point on which opinions differ widely both in east and west. According to Yāḳūt, the view most frequently held is that which considers Dhāt al-ʿImād an epithet of Damascus. Djairūn b. Saʿd b. ʿĀd is said to have settled here and have built a town adorned with marble columns. Loth has used this tradition in support of his view that only Aramaic traditions are associated with the name Iram.

Iram, however, is frequently referred by Muslims to South Arabia to which ʿĀd also belonged. ʿĀd had two sons, S̲h̲addād and S̲h̲adīd. After the death of the latter, S̲h̲addād subdued the kings of the world; when he heard of Paradise he had a town built on the steppes of Aden which was to be an imitation of Paradise. Its stones were of gold and silver and its walls studded with jewels, etc. When S̲h̲addād, after neglecting the warning of Hūd [q.v.], wished to see the town, he was destroyed by a tornado with his whole retinue a day's journey from Iram and the whole town buried in sand.

In a tradition given by al-Masʿūdī (ii. 421) the story does not have a tragic ending. After S̲h̲addād had built Iram, he wished to erect a duplicate of the town on the site of Alexandria. When Alexander the Great came to found Alexandria, he discovered traces of a great building with many columns of marble. On one of these was an inscription of S̲h̲addād b. ʿĀd b. S̲h̲addād b. ʿĀd in which he related that he had had this town built on the model of Iram d̲h̲āt al-ʿImād; but God put an end to his life: no one should be tempted to undertake too great a thing. — It is easy to see that this tradition is connected with the romance of Alexander in which it is related (Pseudo-Callisthenes, ed. C. Müller, i. 33) that at the building of Alexandria a temple with obelisks was found which had an inscription of King Sesonchis who ruled the world. The warning mentioned in al-Masʿūdī's inscription is also quite in the tenor of the Alexander legend. We therefore must not expect here a tradition concerning the site of Iram. It must be noted, however, that Ṭabarī also in his commentary on the Ḳurʾān gives the view that Iram was identical with Alexandria.

It is further related that a certain ʿAbd Allāh b. Ḳilāba while seeking two lost camels came by chance on the buried town, from the ruins of which he brought musk, camphor, and pearls to Muʿāwiya. All these however became dust when exposed to the air. Muʿāwiya summoned Kaʿb al-Aḥbār to him and asked him about the town. The latter at once replied: "It must be Iram of the pillars, which was to be found in thy caliphate by a man whose appearance is as follows". The description fitted ʿAbd Allāh exactly. The hardly concealed tone of mockery with which al-Masʿūdī relates all this (*Murūd̲j̲*, iv. 88) is worth noting.

According to Muslim scholars, this Iram d̲h̲āt al-ʿImād lay near ʿAden or between Ṣanʿāʾ and Ḥaḍramawt or between ʿUmān and Ḥaḍramawt. It should be noted that the form of the name Iram is South Arabian: Hamdānī mentions a hill and a well of the name Iram in South Arabia. This fact is a refutation of the opinion of Loth, who considers Aramaic references exclusively.

It is likewise clear that we have not to accept the connection between the tribe Iram = Aram and Iram d̲h̲āt al-ʿImād which is assumed by Muslim tradition. — The story of the finding of the family tomb of ʿĀd b. Iram is found in D. H. Müller, *Südarabische Studien* (*Sitzber. Akad. Wien*, phil.-hist. Klasse, lxxxvi. 134 *sqq.*).

Bibliography: Commentaries on Sūra lxxxix. 7; Masʿūdī, ii. 421; iii. 271; iv. 88; Ṭabarī, i. 214, 220, 231, 748; Ḳazwīnī, *Āt̲h̲ār al-bilād* (ed. Wüstenfeld), p. 9 *sq.*; Yāḳūt, *Muʿd̲j̲am*, s.v.; Diyārbakrī, *K̲h̲amīs* (Cairo 1283), i. 76; T̲h̲aʿlabī, *Ḳiṣaṣ al-anbiyāʾ*, (Cairo 1290), p. 125—130; Hamdānī (ed. Müller), Index s.v.; D. H. Müller, *Die Burgen u. Schlösser*, p. 418; Caussin de Perceval, *Histoire*, i. 14; Sprenger, *Leben und Lehre Moḥammads*, i. 505—518; Loth, in *ZDMG*, xxxv. 625 *sqq.*; J. Horovitz, *Koranische .Untersuchungen*, p. 89 *sq.*

IRMIYĀ, Jeremiah, the prophet. His name is vocalised in Arabic also ARMIYĀ or ŪRMIYĀ (see *TA*, x. 157) and these forms are occasionally given with *madd* also (*Irmiyāʾ*).

Wahb b. Munabbih gives an account of him which turns upon the main points of the Old Testament story of Jeremiah: his call to be a prophet, his mission to the king of Judah, his mission to the people and his reluctance, the announcement of a foreign tyrant who is to rule over Judah. Jeremiah then rends his garments and curses the day on which he was born; he would rather die than live to see this. God then gives him the promise that Jerusalem shall not be destroyed except at Jeremiah's own request.

Buk̲h̲t Naṣṣar then attacks the city on account of the increasing sinfulness of the people. God sent an angel in the form of an ordinary Israelite to Jeremiah to find out his opinion on the fall of Jerusalem. He twice sent the angel away to enquire how the people were behaving. The latter returned with the worst reports and communicated them to Jeremiah who was sitting on the wall; the prophet called out: "O Lord, if they are on the right path, let them live, but if they are on the path of evil, destroy them!" Hardly had he spoken these words than God sent a thunderbolt (*ṣāʿiḳa*) from heaven which laid the altar and part of the city in ruins. In despair Jeremiah rent his garments, but God said: "You yourself gave the word". He then realised that his companion was an angel in disguise. He fled into the desert (Ṭabarī, i. 658 *sqq.*). — The second episode in the Muslim legend of Jeremiah refers to his meeting with Buk̲h̲t Naṣṣar. The king found the prophet in prison in Jerusalem, where he had been interned on account of his prophesies of ill fortune. Buk̲h̲t Naṣṣar at once released him and showed him honour. He thereafter remained in Jerusalem with the miserable remnants of the population. When the latter besought Jeremiah to implore God to accept their repentance, God said to the Prophet: "Tell them only that they are to remain here". They refused to do this and took Jeremiah with them into Egypt (Ṭabarī, i. 646 *sq.*). According to Yaʿḳūbī, Jeremiah had hidden the ark in a cave before Nebuchadnezzar's entry into the city. — The third episode runs as follows. When Jerusalem was destroyed and the army had retired, Jeremiah came back riding on an ass. In his hand he carried a bowl of grape-juice and a basket of figs. When he stopped at the ruins of Īliyā (Aelia), he became irresolute and said: "How can God call all this to life again?" God thereupon deprived him and his ass of life. After a hundred years had passed, God awakened him and said: "How long hast thou slept?" He replied: "A day". God then told him what had happened and brought his ass to life again before his eyes; the grape-juice and the figs had remained fresh. God then granted him long life; he appeared to men in the city and in the desert (Ṭabarī, i. 666).

Of the first two episodes one can say that they are a development of Biblical statements. The third however is based on an misunderstanding connected with Sūra ii. 259: ... "like him who passed by a city which had been laid in ruins; then he said: How could God revive this after its death? Then God caused him to die for a hundred years; He then wakened him and said: "How long wast thou dead?" He said: "A day or so". He replied, "Nay, a hundred years; look on thy food and thy drink; they are not corrupted; and look on thine ass: we will make thee a sign unto men: And look on the bones, how we will join them together, then clothe them with flesh".

The commentaries on the Ḳurʾān identify this doubting man with various Old Testament figures, including Jeremiah. But we know that the story in Oriental legend was associated with ʿEbed Melek, who appears in the story of Jeremiah (Jeremiah, xxxix. 16 *sqq.*; cf. *The Paraleipomena of Jeremiah the Prophet*, ed. Rendel Harris). The confusion of Jeremiah with ʿEbed Melek has apparently given rise to another one. ʿEbed Melek, according to the Jewish view, is one of the immortals who never saw death. In Muslim legend al-Khaḍir is one of the immortals. This is probably why Wahb b. Munabbih explains al-Khaḍir, "the green", as an epithet of the prophet Jeremiah. This also explains the emphasis laid on his retirement to the desert where, as in the towns, he sometimes meets men; for this is a statement which elsewhere refers to al-Khaḍir in contrast to Ilyās [q.v.] who is the patron saint on the sea.

Bibliography: The Ḳurʾān commentaries on Sūra ii. 259; Mudjīr al-Dīn al-Ḥanbalī, *al-Uns al-djalīl* (Cairo 1283), i. 138 *sqq.*; (Muṭahhar b. Ṭāhir al-Maḳdisī), *Kitāb al-badʾ waʾl-taʾrīkh* (ed. Huart), iii. 114; Thaʿlabī, *Ḳiṣaṣ al-anbiyāʾ* (Cairo 1290), p. 292 *sqq.*; Yaʿḳūbī, i. 70; I. Friedländer, *Die Chadhirlegende und der Alexanderroman*, p. 269 *sq.*

ʿĪSĀ, the proper name of Jesus, in the Ḳurʾān, and thence in Islām, is explained by some western scholars (Maracci, ii. 39; Landauer and Nöldeke, in *ZDMG*, xli. 720) as a form imposed upon Muḥammad by the Jews and used by him in good faith. They called Jesus Esau (עֵשָׂו) in hatred and said that the soul of Esau had been transferred to him (cf. Lammens, in al-Mashriḳ, i. 334). Others (J. Derenbourg, in *REJ*, xviii. 126; Fränkel, in *WZKM*, iv. 334; Vollers, in *ZDMG*, xlv. 352; Nestle, *Dict. of Christ and the Gospels*, i. 861) hold that the name originated naturally by phonetic change from the Syriac Yeshūʿ (ܝܫܘܥ) combined with imitation of Mūsā. For the Muslim explanation of the name see al-Baiḍāwī on Sūra iii. 45 (ed. Fleischer, i. 156, l. 2). Titles and descriptions applied to Jesus in the Ḳurʾān and of importance for his position in the theological system of Islām are: "Son of Maryam" (e.g. iii. 45; iv. 171; xix. 34, and often); he was born of Mary, a virgin, by the direct creative act of Allāh; — "a Word (*kalima*) from Allāh" and "his (Allāh's) Word" (iii. 45; iv. 171); this is the creative word "Be" (*kun*) which Allāh cast (*alḳā*) into Mary; the creation of Jesus is thus compared (iii. 59) to that of Adam; — *al-Masīḥ* (iii. 45; iv. 171 and often) evidently from the Hebrew *māshīaḥ*, but how understood by Muḥammad is quite uncertain; for Muslim explanations see al-Baiḍāwī, i. 156, *sqq.*; — "a Spirit from Allāh" (iv. 171), so the angels are called spirits and he was a spirit directly from Allāh, so, too, Allāh formed Adam and breathed into him of his spirit (*min rūḥī*, xv. 29; xxxviii. 72); later Islām called him *al-rūḥ* (*LA*, iii. 290, l. 15) and even *rūḥ Allāh* (*al-Kashshāf* of al-Zamakhsharī, ed. Lees, i. 338); — *ʿabd Allāh* (xix. 30); "he is nought but an *ʿabd*" (xliii. 59); "he will never disdain to be an *ʿabd* of Allāh" (iv. 172); *ʿabd*, literally "slave", is best rendered theologically by our "creature"; man, for Islām, is the property of Allāh and not simply his servant; cf. *ʿébhedh* in the O.T. and δοῦλος in the N.T. and especially of Jesus in Philippians, ii. 7; — "One of those brought near" (to Allāh, *min al-muḳarrabīn*, iii. 45), again the angelic association; later Islām sometimes explains this of his state after his ascension (*ṣuʿūd, rafʿ*), when he was a semi-angel flying round the throne (*ʿarsh*) of Allāh (*insī malakī*: *Ḳiṣaṣ* of al-Thaʿlabī, ed. Cairo 1314, p. 227); but Muḥammad in his *miʿrādj* found him in the second heaven (*Ṣaḥīḥ* of al-Bukhārī, v. 53, ed. Cairo 1315); — *wadjīh*, "worthy of regard in this world and in that to come" (iii. 45); al-Baiḍāwī explains: "as prophet in the one and as interceder in the other"; — *mubārak*, "blessed wherever I am" (xix. 31); but al-Baiḍāwī explains the word here and elsewhere as "possessing much profit for others", apparently possessing a *baraka*; — *ḳawl al-ḥaḳḳ*, "the sure saying", in xix. 34 is obscure and may be not a title but apply to the statement made — see al-Baiḍāwī, i. 580, l. 25. He is a *nabī*, "prophet" (xix. 30), and *rasūl*, "messenger" (iv. 157, 171; v. 75), and he has a "book" (*kitāb*, xix. 30), which is the *Indjīl* (v. 46; lvii. 27). The sending of him is a "sign" (*āya*) and "mercy" (*raḥma*, xix. 21); he and his mother are a "sign" (xxiii. 50); he is made an "example", "parable" (*mathal*, xliii. 57, 59). He brought "proofs" (*baiyināt*) and "wisdom" (*ḥikma*, xliii. 63; v. 110), and was aided by Allāh with the *rūḥ al-ḳudus* (ii. 87; v. 110), obscure like all mentions of *rūḥ* in the Ḳurʾān but explained by later Islām as Djibrīl; so al-Baiḍāwī (*in loco*) and *LA*, iii. 290, l. 15. Allāh taught him (iii. 46; v. 110) and he possessed peculiar miraculous powers of raising the dead, healing the sick and making clay birds and, by the permission of Allāh, breathing life into them (iii. 47 *sqq.*; v. 110 *sqq.*).

On the death of Jesus the statements of the Ḳurʾān are contradictory. It is certain that Muḥammad rejected the crucifixion and accepted the ascension, apparently in an earthly body and not in a glorified body; the crucifixion was prevented by a change of resemblance (*shubbiha lahu*, iv. 157), again an obscure phrase explained later by the commentators that his likeness was put upon another and the other crucified in his place. But his death is referred to: — "before his death" (iv. 159); "on the day I die and on the day I am raised, alive" (xix. 33), yet this verse may have been a mistaken repetition of verse 15. In iii. 55 Allāh says to him: "I am about to take thee to myself (*mutawaffīka*) and lift thee up (*rāfiʿuka*) unto me". The first expression is commonly used of a blessed death, but that is not necessarily its meaning here, for it is also used in the Ḳurʾān (vi. 60) of Allāh's taking to himself the souls of sleepers during sleep, to be returned when they awake; cf. Fränkel in *ZDMG*, lvi. 77. For his second coming the only Ḳurʾānic authority is xliii. 61, a very obscure verse, the reading even of which is in doubt. Some read: "And he is verily a knowledge (*la-ʿilm^{un}*) of the Hour", i.e. by (the descent of) whom the approach of the Hour known. But others read: "a sign (*la-ʿalam^{un}*) of the Hour", and even: "a reminder (*la-dhikr^{un}*)". Others, again, refer the pronoun in *wa-innahu* to the Ḳurʾān, "it is". His second coming being taken as established, his death is put after it and the references in iv. 159 and xix. 33 are thus explained; as also the descriptive *kahl^{an}* in iii. 46, because he was taken up by Allāh as a "youth" (*shābb*) before he attained *kuhūla*, "middle age" (cf. al-Baiḍāwī on these passages). The later doctrine of his return is given soberly by al-Baiḍāwī on xliii. 61: that he will descend in the Holy Land at a place called Afīḳ with a spear in his hand; that he will kill with it al-Dadjdjāl and come to Jerusalem at the time of the *ṣalāt* of the morning (*ṣubḥ*); that the imām will seek to yield place to him but that he will refuse and will worship behind him according to the *sharīʿa* of Muḥammad; thereafter he will kill the swine and break the cross and lay in ruins the synagogues and churches and kill all Christians (Naṣārā) who do not believe in him (ed. Fleischer, ii. 241). To this last point reference is supposed to be made in iv. 159: "there is none of the People of Scripture but will verily believe in him (or: in it) before his death". One of the explanations of this in al-Baiḍāwī (i. 241, l. 4) is that after he has killed the false Messiah (*al-Masīḥ al-dadjdjāl*) not one of the People of Scripture will be left who does not believe in him, so that the community (*milla*) will become one, the community of Islām. Then will come universal security of man and beast and Jesus will remain for forty years; thereafter he will die and the Muslims will hold funeral service for him and bury him [at Madīna, it is universally accepted, beside Muḥammad, in a vacant space between Abū Bakr and ʿUmar]. But others interpret: "before he — the believer — dies", even though it is thus a useless belief, he being at the point of death.

So little can be gathered from the Ḳurʾān. The oldest traditions have but little more, as in the *Ṣaḥīḥ* of al-Buḵẖārī where ʿĪsā is merely mentioned in connection with Dadjdjāl in *Kitāb al-fitan*, b. 26. Muḥammad had been interested in the idea of Anti-Christ as the story of Ibn Ṣaiyād (the Anti-Christ) shows (Macdonald, *Religious Attitude in Islam*, p. 34 *sqq.*), but the early Muslims, for political and theological reasons, developed elaborately in forged traditions the doctrine of the Last Things, and especially of the Mahdī and Jesus. Thus the *Maṣābīḥ* has much more, see ed. Cairo, 1316, ii. 136 *sqq.*, 140 *sq.* (chaps. on Signs of the Hour and on the Descent of ʿĪsā). See, too, al-Thaʿlabī, *Ḳiṣaṣ*, p. 22 *sqq.*; the full account of ʿĪsā, the most complete of all, covers p. 215—229; Ṭabarī, i. 713 *sqq.*, and Ibn Wāḍiḥ, *Historiae*, ed. Houtsma, i. 74 *sq.*, give extracts from the Gospels. But in this development the rôles assigned to Jesus and to the Mahdī came to be confusingly alike, and one party tried to cut the knot with a tradition from Muḥammad: "There is no Mahdī save ʿĪsā b. Maryam". For this and also for their respective roles when they were distinguished, see al-Shaʿrānī, *muḵẖtaṣar* of the *Tadhkira* of al-Ḳurṭubī, p. 118 *sqq.* (ed. Cairo 1324). Ibn Ḵẖaldūn in his *Muḳaddima* (ed. Quatremère, ii. 142—176 = De Slane's transl., ii. 158—205) gives a philosophical examination of the whole subject, showing the untrustworthiness of the different traditions and tracing the development of the idea of a restorer of Islām before the end, as it was influenced by Shīʿites of different degrees, by Fāṭimids and by Ṣūfīs. An explanation given by him of the tradition quoted above is: "None has spoken in the cradle (*mahd*; cf. Sūra xix. 29) save ʿĪsā" (ed. Quatremère, ii. 163); for another see al-Ḳurṭubī, p. 118. On the whole subject Goldziher in his *Vorlesungen*, p. 230 *sqq.* and notes thereon, has a few luminous pages. See the same, p. 313 *sq.*, for the modern Aḥmadīya sect in India which teaches that Jesus escaped from Jerusalem, wandered to the East, settled at Srinagar in Kaṣẖmīr and died there, where his tomb is still shown. Ḡẖulām Aḥmad, the founder of the sect, professed to be both Jesus returned and also the Mahdī [see AḤMADĪYA]. Finally, Goldziher has well remarked that for Sunnī Islām, as opposed to Shīʿism and other outlying sects, the expectation of a future restorer of faith and life has never

become fixed as a dogma but is only the mythological embellishment of an ideal representation of the future. This may well be due to lack of Ḳurʾānic basis.

From the above it is evident that Muḥammad had learned a definite story of Jesus from some heretical Christian teacher, in defense of whose position he polemizes vigorously in the Ḳurʾān. He knows more about him, in his particular way, than about any other of the religious figures of the past. But it is evident, too, that he omits something. For the appearance on earth of this unique figure, a second Adam, a semi-angel, a Logos much like that of Philo but with a difference, we are given no reason. It is not explained how he is a "sign", a "mercy", and an "example" or "parable" (xix. 21; xxiii. 50; xliii. 57, 59). At his birth he — as had been the case with his mother — was guarded from the touch of Satan, who seeks by touching every newly born infant to implant a tendency to sin (iii. 33 and al-Baiḍāwī, *in loco*). Some even say that he and his mother, in consequence of this, never committed sin (*Ḳiṣaṣ*, p. 210). But it should be noticed that the same is said, even more absolutely, of John the Baptist because he it called *ḥaṣūr*, "chaste" in Sūra iii. 36; cf. al-Baiḍāwī and *Ḳiṣaṣ*, p. 211 *sqq.* But all the Ḳurʾān has is that Mary's mother exclaimed (iii. 33): "Verily, I put her and her seed in thy (Allāh's) care from the stoned Shaiṭān". How much or how little of the later view was in the mind of Muḥammad or was a legitimate development of his position it is impossible to say. He left something untold and classed ʿĪsā with all the other prophets, although so essentially different. The story of the table with food sent down from heaven (v. 112 *sqq.*) which is to be to them a festival (*ʿīd*) and a sign to all generations seems a genuine confusion on the part of Muḥammad himself in regard to the eucharist. It is significant that the commentators (al-Baiḍāwī, i. 280) most commonly say that the food was a large fish, thus suggesting the ἰχθύς symbol.

Later Islām has pictured ʿĪsā as separated from all human ties except to his mother, as constantly wandering, barefoot and without abiding place, passing the night in worship wherever he might be when the sun sets, living from day to day for nothing but devotion and miracles of benevolence (*Ḳiṣaṣ*, p. 218). At the Judgment he will be the example of absolute poverty (*faḳr*; al-Ḡẖazzālī, *Durra*, p. 90 *sqq.*). At the *mawḳif* on that day men will ask him to intercede for them with Allāh and he will refuse, not for any sin of his own, as in the case of the other prophets, but because his followers have taken him and his mother as gods along with Allāh (*Durra*, p. 62 *sqq.*); cf. many other forms of this tradition in the *Iḥyāʾ*, ed. with comment. of Saiyid Murtaḍā, x. 489 *sqq.* Margoliouth has gathered a valuable catena of his sayings and doings from the *Iḥyāʾ*, in the *Expository Times*, vol. v., 1893—94, p. 59, 107, 177, 503, 561; a fuller collection containing 233 sayings and narratives was published by M. Asín y Palacios (*Logia et Agrapha Domini Jesu*) in *Patrologia Orientalis*, vols. xiii and xix.

Bibliography: S. D. Margoliouth, *Christ in Moh. Liter.*, in *Dict. of Christ and the Gospels*, ii. 882 *sqq.*; S. M. Zwemer, *Moslem Christ*, Edinburgh 1902; Ed. Sayous, *Jésus Christ d'après Mahomet*, Paris 1880; C. F. Gerock, *Versuch* etc., Hamburg-Gotha 1839; G. Weil, *Bibl. Legenden der Muselmänner*, Frankfort o.M. 1845, p. 280 *sqq.*; Manneval, *La Christologie du Koran*, Toulouse 1887; H. P. Smith, *Bible and Islam*; Hughes, *Dict. of Islam*,

p. 229 *sqq.*; J. Horovitz, *Koranische Untersuchungen* p. 128 *sqq.*; J. Robson, *Christ in Islam*, London 1929.

ISḤĀḲ, the Biblical Isaac, whose birth, according to the Talmud (*Rōsh hash-shānā*, p. 11), took place at the feast of Passah and, according to Muslim tradition, in the night of ʿĀshūrāʾ (al-Thaʿlabī, p. 60 and al-Kisāʾī, p. 150), was promised to his father Ibrāhīm a year previously by Allāh (also in *Gen. R.* 45). Ibrāhīm was in the habit of eating only when the poor and hungry shared his meals. On one occasion fifteen (al-Thaʿlabī, p. 48) or three (al-Kisāʾī, p. 146) days happened to pass without a guest appearing. Three strangers then appeared before whom he set a roasted calf. But they did not touch it (Sūra xi. 70). They said: "We eat nothing without paying its price". He said: "The price is that you should utter a blessing before and after the meal" (al-Thaʿlabī, *l.c.*; *Gen. R.* 54). They then foretold to him the birth of a son. Sāra laughed at this, as she was 90 and Ibrāhīm 120 years old. The latter said: "Then he shall be sacrificed as an offering to God!" (These features probably have their origin in the accounts in the Midrash [*Gen. R.* 55; *Tanchuma Gen.* 40]). When seven years old, Isḥāḳ visited the sacred place. Ibrāhīm then received in a dream the order to make a sacrifice to God. In the morning he sacrificed a bullock and divided its flesh among the poor. In the night the voice again said to him: "God demands a more valuable offering". He killed a camel. In the following night the voice said: "God demands thy son as an offering". Ibrāhīm awoke in horror and said: "O my son, I saw in a dream that I must sacrifice thee" (Sura xxxvii. 102). The latter replied: "Father, do what was ordered thee. Thou wilt find me a patient person, if God will" (102). Taking a knife and a rope they went together to the mount. Isḥāḳ said: "Father, take my shirt from my body, lest my dear mother find blood upon it and weep for me. Bind me firmly, so that I do not move, and look away while sacrificing me, lest thou lose thy courage" (al-Kisāʾī and al-Thaʿlabī, *l.c.*, following *Gen. R.* 56; cf. also *Sefer hayyāshār*, *Wayyērā* and *Pirḳē de R. El.* 31). "May God comfort thee for my loss! Give my mother my shirt that it may comfort her and do not tell her how thou didst sacrifice me. Never look at boys of my age, lest grief overwhelm thee!" Ibrāhīm directed the knife against the throat of his son but three times it slipped and glanced aside. Then a voice called to him: "Ibrāhīm, Thou hast fulfilled the vision" (Sūra xxxvii. 105). Then a ram appeared, which said it had been the offering of Hābīl and had hitherto been in Paradise; it was offered as a sacrifice (*Aboth* v.; *Pirḳē de R. El.* 32, and al-Kisāʾī). When a rumour arose that Isḥāḳ was a foundling adopted by Ibrāhīm, God gave father and son the same figure so that they were very like one another. But Ibrāhīm was grey (*Baba M.* 87; *Gen. R.* 53; al-Kisāʾī, p. 152).

As the Ḳurʾān verse above quoted does not state which son was to have been sacrificed, many Muslim theologians refer the intended sacrifice to Ismāʿīl (*al-dhabīḥ*; al-Zamakhsharī and al-Baiḍāwī on the passage; al-Ṭabarī, i. 291; Ibn al-Athīr, i. 88; al-Thaʿlabī, p. 55—56; al-Kisāʾī, p. 150). But it may be said that the oldest tradition — al-Thaʿlabī expressly emphasises the *aṣḥāb* and *tābiʿūn*, i.e. the Companions of the Prophet and their successors from ʿUmar b. al-Khaṭṭāb to Kaʿb al-Aḥbār — did not differ from the Bible on this question.

Bibliography: al-Zamakhsharī, i. 234; al-Baiḍāwī, i. 233; al-Thaʿlabī, *Ḳiṣaṣ al-anbiyāʾ* (Cairo 1312), p. 48—60; al-Kisāʾī, *Ḳiṣaṣ al-anbiyāʾ*, p. 136—140; al-Ṭabarī, i. 272—292; Ibn al-Athīr, i. 87—89; Grünbaum, *Beiträge*, p. 110—120; Eisenberg, *Abraham in der arab. Legende*, 1912, p. 30—31; *Encyclop. Hebrew*, New-York, v. 18, s.v. Isak; I. Goldziher, *Die Richtungen der isl. Koranauslegung*, Leiden 1920, p. 79 *sqq.*; J. Horovitz, *Koranische Untersuchungen*, p. 90 *sq.*; see also the art. ISMĀʿĪL.

AL-**ISKANDAR**, Alexander the Great (the Arab authors usually see the Arabic article in the first two letters of the name). In the Muḥammadan accounts of the world-conqueror there are here and there echoes of genuine historical tradition but as a rule we have to deal with legendary tales, which originate in the romance of Alexander and were considerably extended and embellished by later writers. We confine ourselves here to giving in its broad outlines what the older Arab historians relate on the subject. In the first place it should be noted that Alexander's genealogy is artificially made up in various ways, as may be seen from Friedländer's *Die Chadhirlegende und der Alexanderroman*, p. 294 *sqq.* As a rule, however, the name of his father Philip is correctly given, frequently in the form Fīleḳūs, Failaḳūs or otherwise corrupted, as well as that of his mother Olympias (also almost always in a corrupt form); some authorities even give the name of his grandfather Āminta or Āmintās. Even in the earliest historians however we find also the view, which owes its origin to Persian national pride, that Alexander was not the son of Philip, but of Dārāb (Dārā al-Akbar) so that he was the half-brother of Dārā (Dārā al-Aṣghar), the last Persian king. It is said that, when Philip was conquered by Dārāb and had to pay a yearly tribute in golden eggs, his daughter, who is given the name of Halai (otherwise in Firdawsī) to get a fantastic etymology for the name Alexander, was married by Dārāb but on account of her repulsive odour was at once repudiated by him and sent back to her father. They endeavoured in vain to cure her defect by a medicine called *sandarūs*; when the princess bore a son, he was called Alexandros after the name of his mother and that of the medicine. The boy was brought up at the court of his grandfather; his tutor was Aristotle, and after Philip's death he succeeded him. Alexander soon omitted to pay the tribute, and, when his half-brother, who had in the meantime become king of Persia, demanded it, Alexander sent the messenger home with the answer that he had killed and eaten the hen which laid the golden eggs. We omit here the story of the symbolic gifts which Dārā sent to Alexander and Alexander's reply, although it is found as early as al-Ṭabarī, i. 699. Alexander then prepared for war, collected a great army and went first of all to Egypt, where he founded buildings. In the meanwhile Dārā also had assembled his troops and Alexander advanced against him, until the two armies met on the Euphrates where a sanguinary battle took place (its site is also placed elsewhere), in which Alexander was victorious. Dārā fled, but was treacherously wounded to death by two of his own people who sought thereby to gain the favour of Alexander. According to some accounts, several encounters took place between Alexander and Dārā but in the end the result was the same and Alexander met his dying foe. The latter recommended his wife to his care and asked him to see to the punishment of the murderers and to other matters; in particular he expressed the wish that Alexander should marry his daughter Rushang (Roxana). Alexander promised to fulfil his requests and ordered Dārā's obsequies to be carried out in regal fashion. As a result of his marriage with Rushang he now acted as the legitimate ruler of Persia, ordered the affairs of the government, and advanced on India to conquer Fūr (Porus), who was allied with Dārā. He had a fierce battle with Porus and only succeeded in disposing of him by rendering his elephants innocuous by stratagem and finally overcoming his opponent in single combat. Another Indian king, named Kaid, submitted to him voluntarily and sent him four valuable gifts (a virgin of wondrous beauty, a vessel which never became empty, a physician and a philosopher who could answer every question). He then took an interest in the Brahmans (gymnosophists) and had a conference with them in which he put various questions which they answered. After thus becoming acquainted with India he began his expeditions throughout the whole world, which are however usually but briefly mentioned by the historians. After India, came China and Tibet (Dīnawarī mentions the meeting with Candace) and finally he went to the Land of Darkness and met Khiḍr (Khaḍir). The historians apparently knew a great deal about all this, but they omit to narrate it, either because they thought that it was not the contemporary of Dārā but an older Dhu 'l-Ḳarnain who was the real hero of these incidents, or for other reasons. We shall deal with this question below; here it is sufficient to say that Alexander finally died on his return to Persia at Shahrzūr or in Bābil, according to al-Dīnawarī in Jerusalem, at the age of 36, after reigning 13 or 14 years (many other figures are also given). According to some accounts, he died from poison and having a presentiment of his approaching end, sent a letter of consolation to his mother in Alexandria. The corpse was placed in a golden sarcophagus, over which the philosophers spoke in turn and in brief speeches emphasised the vanity of earthly greatness. The sarcophagus was taken to Alexandria and buried there in a tomb, which, according to al-Masʿūdī, still existed in 332/943.

Among Orientals, Alexander is not only the world-conqueror and founder of cities — he is said to have founded 12, all called Iskandarīya —, but the hero who reached the ends of the earth (cf. i. Macc. i. 3). It was not lust of conquest but the thirst for knowledge that was his motive. Philosophers therefore accompanied him everywhere and the wonders of nature and enigmatical problems attracted his special interest. Mubashshir b. Fātik and al-Shahrazūrī, quoted by Mirkhwānd, therefore deal with Alexander in their biographies of Greek philosophers (cf. Meissner, in *ZDMG*, xlix. 583 *sqq.*). At the same time he appears as the champion of the true faith, because his epithet, Dhu 'l-Ḳarnain, which is variously interpreted, led to his being identified with the prophet of the same name mentioned in Sūra xviii. 83 *sqq.* This is however not approved of by all expositors; the majority distinquish an earlier and a later Dhu 'l-Ḳarnain; the later is then identical with Alexander. For further details and the peculiar confusion with Mūsā in Sūra xviii. 60 *sqq.* see the articles DHU 'L-ḲARNAIN, KHAḌIR and YĀDJŪDJ WA-MĀDJŪDJ. The connection indicated by Lidzbarski, Meissner and others of these stories with very ancient Oriental ideas and myths (Gilgamish epic) will there be dealt with.

Bibliography: All universal histories deal with Alexander so that we need here only mention the older Arab historians: al-Yaʿḳūbī, i. 96, 161 *sqq.*; al-Dīnawarī, ed. Girgas, p. 31 *sqq.*; Al-Ṭabarī, i. 693 *sqq.*; al-Masʿūdī, ii. 250 *sqq.*; Eutychius, ed. Pocock, p. 281 *sqq.*; al-Thaʿlabī, *ʿArāʾis*, ed. Cairo 1314, p. 203 *sqq.*, etc.

ISLĀM, as a technical term to denote the system of beliefs and rituals based on the Ḳurʾān, is derived from the recurrent use of the verb *aslama* ("submit", *sc.* oneself) in the Ḳurʾān to denote the characteristic attitude of the true believer in relation to God (cf., however, Lidzbarski, "Islām und Salām", *ZS*, i., 85 *sqq.*, and D. Künstlinger in *Roczn. Or.* xi. (1936), 128 *sqq.*). The infinitive *Islām* occurs in eight passages, in some of which it may already by employed in this technical sense, e.g. sūra iii. 19: "The [true] religion with God is al-Islām", and v. 3: "This day have I perfected for you your religion and completed My favour towards you, and approved al-Islām for you as a religion", although some early Muslim commentators interpret the word even in these contexts in the more general sense (cf. Ṭabarī *ad loc.*).

The early disputes on the primacy of faith or works, initiated by the Khāridjites [q.v.], produced a tendency to distinguish between *īmān*, "faith", and *islām*, based on sūra xlix. 14: "Say *aslamnā*, for *īmān* hath not yet entered your hearts"; see further the article ĪMĀN. But the established theology of Islām finally declared faith to be one of the five "pillars of Islām", together with *ṣalāt*, *zakāt*, the fast of Ramaḍān, and the Pilgrimage (*ḥadjdj*) — see these articles — thus asserting that Islām consists of both faith and works. For the further dispute as to *djihād*, see the article.

Similar attempts to narrow down the signification of Islām in a sectarian sense, in such a way as to exclude dissident groups, were also rejected by the Sunnīs, in contrast to the Khāridjites and some of the Shīʿa [q.v.]. A tradition, which is frequently quoted, was made to assert that 73 sects would arise within Islam, of which only one would lead to salvation (*al-firḳa al-nādjiya*). Nevertheless, adherents of the different sects were still regarded as Muslims (a point of practical importance in view of the mutual exclusion of Muslims and unbelievers from inheritance, see MĪRĀTH); and another form of the tradition asserted that all but one of the sects would end in Paradise. Numerous attempts were made in theological works to define these sects and to draw a dividing line between Muslim and pervert, but the only group on whose exclusion there is general agreement is that of the Zindīḳs [q.v.].

The wider signification given to the term Islām as a cultural complex, embracing specific political structures and legal and social traditions, which is current in modern Muslim usage, may be due partly to the adoption of European terminology, but also underlies the tradititional concept of the *Dār al-Islām* [q.v.], as opposed to non-Muslim communities.

Various estimates of the total number of Muḥammadans in the world have been made, differing as widely as from 300 to 400 millions; but there is a large element of uncertainty about any estimate, as in several countries where Muḥammadans are to be found in large numbers, no religious census has ever been taken, and accurate statistics are accordingly wanting. This is particularly the case in the land in which Islām had its origin, and any estimate of the total Arab population must be conjectural only. Before 1939 Saʿūdi Arabia was credited with 4.500.000, Yaman 3.500.000, and ʿUmān 500.000 inhabitants. Some reliance may be placed on the figures given for the districts under European control, as 60.331 (1931) for Aden and the neighbouring islands, Perim, Sokotra, etc. and 120.000 (1931) for the Baḥrain Islands; estimates of the population in such parts of Arabia as Nadjd, Ḥaḍramawt, etc. can be tentative only. The Arabs are not however confined to the limits of the country that bears their name; as early as the third century of the Christian era commenced those scattered migrations of Arabs to the north which gradually led to the formation of settlements in Palestine, Syria, and Mesopotamia; as time went on, advantage was taken of the conflicts between the Byzantine and Persian empires, and larger numbers of nomad Arabs settled in the more fertile countries bordering on the arid land of their origin. This migratory movement culminated in the vast expansion of the Arab race, rendered possible by the conquests of the seventh century, when the Arabs despoiled the Byzantine empire of some of its fairest provinces and subjugated the whole of the territories of the Persian king. The fact that the Arab language was gradually adopted throughout the greater part of Syria, Egypt and North Africa is some evidence of the interpenetration of Arab blood in the population of these countries, and a steady, though intermittent, stream of migration from Arabia into Africa set in across the Red Sea. Another stream moved eastward across the Indian Ocean and by the middle of the eighth century Arab traders had made their way as far as China and were present in large numbers in Canton. Arab trading settlements are found scattered throughout the Malay Archipelago, and at different historical periods small groups have established themselves on the coasts of India, and individual Arabs have made their way to most parts of the Muḥammadan world, especially those accessible by sea. But no attempt has ever been made to estimate the total number of these Arabs living outside the limits of the Arabian Peninsula, as separate groups in the Muslim populations of which they form a part.

For some countries of Asia formerly or actually under European rule, we have accurate statistics. In India, where varieties of religious belief are carefully noted, the Muḥammadans, according to the Census of 1931, numbered 77.677.545, out of a total population of rather more than 338 millions, and that of 1941 92.058.096 out of 388 millions. About 60 millions of these have since 1947 been included in Pakistan. Among the chief causes assigned for the rapid growth of the Muslim community are that their social customs are more favourable to a higher birth-rate than those of the Hindus; they have fewer marriage restrictions, and widows frequently remarry. Conversions to other religions are not frequent, but Christian converts from Islām are numbered by thousands in Northern India, especially in the Pandjāb (*The Mohammedan World of To-day*, pp. 170, 294), and a certain number of Muḥammedans of Hindu origin have been re-absorbed into Hinduism through the missionary activity of the Āriya Samādj. In Ceylon, in spite of the intimate trade relations with Arabia, Islām has not achieved any great extension among the inhabitants and there were in 1931 only 350.000 Muḥammadans, out of a population of over 5 millions.

For the Malay Peninsula and Archipelago, complete statistics are wanting. Officially, the Muḥammadan population of the Federated Malay States and the Straits Settlements consisted in 1921 of 2.025.000 Muslims (48% of the total). Introduced into Malacca from India, Islām spread along the great trade route to Java and the other islands of the Archipelago. The Muslim population of Indonesia in 1905 was 35.034.025, including 29.605.653 in Java, and was said to be rapidly increasing as the result of conversions to Islām from among the sections of the populations that still remain heathen; according to the census of 1930 the number of Muslims had reached 55 millions (90%). On the other hand Christian missionaries had some success in winning converts from Islām in Java, and in 1906 there were living 18.000 Christians who had been converted from Islām (*The Mohammedan World of To-day*, p. 237); in Sumatra also there were several active missionary societies. In relation to the estimated increase in the population since 1930, the same proportion (90 %) would give about 70.000.000 Muslims in 1950.

In Siam, Islām has never succeeded in exercising much influence; converts have been won in the north through contact with the neighbouring Malay States, and in the coast towns as the result of intercourse with the Malay Archipelago; but the total number of Muḥammadans is probably not more than 630,000 (1937).

The figures given for Indo-China showed 240.000 Muḥammadans out of a population of 23 millions; in the Asiatic possessions (including the south of the Caucasus) of the USSR 16 million (1933) Muḥammadans out of a population of nearly 25 millions; and in the Philippine Islands, 680.000 (1948) out of 19 million inhabitants.

But when we pass to countries in which accurate census returns after the European method are entirely wanting, there is still more uncertainty as to the figures. In Persia, an estimate made by Christian missionaries assigns to Islām all but 500.000 out of the fifteen to seventeen millions of inhabitants. In Afghānistān it is conjectured that there are about twelve million Muḥammadans.

The first serious attempts to ascertain the number of the Chinese Muslims were made by Broomhall and d'Ollone; the former suggests 8.421.000 (*Islam in China*, p. 215), the latter (*Recherches sur les Musulmans Chinois*, p. 430), 4.000.000 only. The *Chinese Year Book* for 1936 gives between 15 and 20 millions. In Tibet there are believed to be 30.000 Muslims only, most of them settlers from China and Kashmīr, with a few converts, and descendants of converts. Islām has succeeded in gaining few adherents and building mosques in Japan, and these in quite recent years; there are probably not more than 5000 Muslims in Japan itself, but about the same number in Formosa; in Manchuria and in Mongolia again the same number.

In regard to some of the oldest parts of the Muḥammadan world the following estimates are given: Syria and Lebanon 3.100.000, Palestine 825.000 (1935), Transjordan 350.000, Irak 4.600.000, Turkey 19.000.000.

Next to Asia, Africa is the continent that contains the largest number of Muslims, but materials for an exact judgment are so wanting that estimates given by different investigators vary considerably. Approximate figures are: Morocco 7.800.000, Tunisia 2.920.000 (1946), Algeria 7.650.000 (1948), Libya about 1.000.000, Egypt about 18.000.000, East Africa 4 million, Anglo-Egyptian Sudan 6.500.000, French W. Africa 5 million, Nigeria 8 million, French Equat. Africa 1.300.000 and about 1.300.000 for the other West-African colonies.

Among the Bantus, Islām is very slowly progressing: in Usoga (Uganda), Kenya, Tanganyika (including Zanzibar), and Nyasaland a little more than two millions. In South Africa, Indian Muslims. In the Comores and Madagascar 850.000.

In Europe, on the contrary, the influence of Islām continues to decline. What the population of Muslim Spain may have been in the days of its widest extent, it is impossible even to conjecture, but in 1492 the Jewish and Muslim community together numbered over two millions, and when Philip III expelled the last remnants of the Moriscos in 1609—1615, the number of those who left the country was probably about 500.000 (H. C. Lea, *The Moriscos of Spain*, London 1901, p. 359).

At the present time, the Muḥammadans in Europe are almost entirely confined to Russia and those countries that formed part of the Turkish dominations at the beginning of the 19th century. In the USSR there are nearly 4 millions, 2.000.000 in Tataristan, 800.000 in Bashkiria, 200.000 in the Crimea, 1.500.000 in Ciscaucasia. In Finland 1000, in Lithuania 1200, in Poland 11.000. In the Balkans, the Turkish elements returned after 1923 to Asia, leaving 105.000 Muslims in Greece, 700.000 in Bulgaria, 200.000 in Rumania, 1.400.000 in Yugoslavia, and 700.000 in Albania (majority).

In France, since the war, 70.000 Muslims (North-African workmen), 5000 in Belgium and Luxemburg. Elsewhere in Europe there are only a few scattered converts, a great many of whom must be put to the account of the Aḥmadīya movement.

In America: USA 30.000, Mexico 1000, Brazil 30.000, the Argentine 30.000, Surinam 30.000, Trinidad 20.000, Jamaica 5000. Elsewhere some few hundreds.

In Oceania: Australia 4000, Fiji 3000.

Bibliography: The number of general works on Islām is very large; see G. Pfannmüller, *Handbuch der Islam-literature*, 1923. Among works published since the beginning of this century are D. B. Macdonald, *Development of Muslim Theology* 1903; E. Sell, *The Faith of Islam*, 3rd. ed., 1907; D. S. Margoliouth, *Early Development of Mohammedanism*, 1914; C. Snouck Hurgronje, *Mohammedanism*, 1916; I. Goldziher, *Vorlesungen über den Islam*, 2nd ed., 1925 (French translation, *Le Dogme et la Loi dans l'Islam*, 1920); Syed Ameer Ali, *The Spirit of Islam*, revised ed., 1922; H. Massé, *L'Islam*, 1930; A. J. Wensinck, *The Muslim Creed*, 1932; R. Levy, *Introduction to the Sociology of Islam*, 1933; H. Lammens, *L'Islam, Croyances et Institutions*, 2nd ed., 1941; G. E. von Grunebaum, *Medieval Islam*, 1946; H. A. R. Gibb, *Mohammedanism*, 1949. Illustrative texts are translated in J. Schacht, *Der Islam mit Ausschluss des Qorʾans*, 1931.

Bibliography of the expansion of Islām, with statistical sources, in T. W. Arnold, *The Preaching of Islam*, 2nd ed., 1913. Religious statistics are given in *The Statesman's Year Book*, published annually in London, and *Annuaire du Monde Musulman*, third ed. by L. Massignon, 1929 (a revised ed. is in preparation). All earlier statistical studies (e.g. in the *Revue du Monde Musulman*, see the *Index Général*, 1926) are now out of date. More recent detailed figures and estimates of Muslim population are given in *Atlas of Islamic History* (Princeton 1951), pp. 3, 4, 5, 34, 40.

ʿIṢMA (A.), in dogmatics, immunity from error and sin, such as is ascribed in Sunnī Islām to the prophets and in the Shīʿa to the imāms also. As to the extent of their immunity, the orthodox theologians differ in opinion as regards the prophets except Muḥammad (on such points as whether it also exists before or only after their prophetic calling or whether it includes immunity from all kinds of sin or only applies to minor slips). It is applied in unlimited fashion to Muḥammad only, in opposition to his own conviction. Among Sunnī authorities Fakhr al-Dīn al-Rāzī in particular extends the ʿiṣma to all prophets in the greatest degree. According to the Shīʿa teaching, ʿiṣma is inherent in the imāms to a higher degree than in the prophets on account of their exalted qualities of substance. Abū Zaid al-Balkhī (d. 322/934) wrote a *Kitāb ʿiṣmat al-anbiyāʾ* (Yāḳūt, *Irshād*, i. 142, 5 *a fine*), as did Fakhr al-Dīn al-Rāzī (Brockelmann, *GAL*², i. 668, No. 14). Every work on Muslim dogmatics contains a chapter on these questions and the different views in regard to them (e.g. Ibn Ḥazm, *Milal*, ed. Cairo 1321, iv. 1—31; *Mawāḳif*, ed. Soerensen, p. 220 *sqq.*); a mystic definition of ʿiṣma is given by al-Ghazzālī, *Mīzān al-ʿamal* (Cairo 1328), p. 116.

Bibliography: C. Snouck Hurgronje, *Nieuwe Bijdragen tot de Kennis van den Islam* (*Bijdragen tot de Taal-, Land- en Volkenkunde v. Ned.-Indië*, 4th Ser., Vol. vi., p. 41 = *Verspr. Geschr.*, ii. 37 *sq.*); Goldziher, *Vorlesungen über den Islam*, p. 220—223; do., in *Isl.*, iii. 238—245; *Manār*, v. 12—21, 87—93; Tor Andrae, *Die Person Muhammeds* (Upsala 1917), p. 124—174.

ISMĀʿĪL, the son of the patriarch Ibrāhim, is mentioned several times in the Ḳurʾān. In Sūra ii. 136 (= iii. 84) and iv. 163 it is said of him that he received revelations. In xix. 54 he is called a messenger and prophet, who summoned his people to *ṣalāt* and *zakāt*. These references fit in very well with Muḥammad's account of the religion of Ibrāhīm. In Sūra ii. 133, he is called one of the fathers of Jacob, along with Ibrāhīm and Isḥāḳ; and in ii. 125, he, along with Ibrāhīm, is commanded to purify the Holy House at Mecca.

Tradition knows nothing of Ismāʿīl as a messenger nor of his revelations nor has it explained his relations to the spread of the religion of Ibrāhīm. It knows that his mother Hādjar bore him to Ibrāhīm as his first-born and that a feud arose between Hādjar and Sara. With the intention of disfiguring Hādjar, Sara even pierced her ears; so this then became the fashion with women. Ismāʿīl and Isḥāḳ are also said to have fought with one another occasionally. In the end, Sara's jealousy induced Ibrāhīm to decide to travel to Arabia with Hādjar and Ismāʿīl. The party was guided by the *sakīna* or, according to others, by Gabriel (on the form of the *sakīna*, cf. A. J. Wensinck *The Navel of the Earth*, in *Verh. Kon. Akad. v. Wetenschappen*, Afd. Letterkunde, Nieuwe Reeks, xvii., No. 1, p. 60 *sqq.*).

When Ibrāhīm and Ismāʿīl had dug the foundations of the Holy House Ismāʿīl helped his father in the building of the temple. When this work was completed Ibrāhīm abandoned the boy with his mother in the barren country, afflicted by thirst. In her need Hādjar stood on the hills al-Ṣafā and al-Marwa and looked for water and ran hither and thither between them, the origin of the *saʿy* q.v.]. Gabriel then called: "Who art thou? To whom did Ibrāhīm entrust thee?" The boy then impatiently thrust his foot (or finger) into the sand and a spring arose; if Hādjar had not hurriedly scooped up the moisture in her jug, the Zanzam would have become a bubbling spring. It is also said that Gabriel pushed his heel into the ground and the Zamzam burst forth beneath it.

In those days the Djurhum lived near the sanctuary; after Hādjar's death, Ismāʿīl married one of their daughters. In his absence Ibrāhīm visited his wife but did not find a very hospitable reception; when the woman afterwards repeated to her husband some words which Ibrāhīm had said, he understood that the latter was suggesting he should divorce his wife. He did this; afterwards he married another woman of the Djurhum. Ibrāhīm visited her also and in the same allusive fashion gave his approval to the new choice.

Ibrāhīm and Hādjar, according to Muslim tradition are buried in the *ḥidjr* of the Holy House, a distinction which they share with most of the prophets: the prophet belongs to the home of the prophets.

Muslim tradition also knows the story given in Genesis xxii. But there are several theologians who say it was not Isḥāḳ but Ismāʿīl that was the *dhabīḥ*. For this reason people called Ismāʿil may have the *kunya* of Abu 'l-Fidāʾ. For this view the sayings of ʿAbd Allāh b. ʿUmar, Ibn ʿAbbās, al-Shaʿbī, Mudjāhid, etc. are quoted. It is related, for example, that ʿUmar b. ʿAbd al-ʿAzīz asked a Jew converted to Islām about this difference of opinion and he answered: "The *dhabīḥ* is Ismāʿīl; the Jews know this also, but as they are jealous of you, they say it was Isḥāḳ".

Ismāʿīl is also considered the ancestor of the North Arabian tribes. In the Arab genealogies, the Arabs are divided into three groups: *al-bāʾida* (those who have disappeared), *al-ʿāriba* (the indigenous) and *al-mustaʿriba* (the arabicised). Ismāʿīl is considered the progenitor of the last group, whose ancestor is called ʿAdnān. The chain between Ismāʿīl and ʿAdnān is given in very divergent forms, sometimes in partial agreement with the list in Genesis xxv.

Bibliography: The commentaries on the passages quoted from the Ḳurʾān; Ṭabarī, i. 275 *sqq.* and Index, s.v.; Muṭahhar b. Ṭāhir, *Kitāb al-badʾ wa'l-taʾrīkh*, ed. Huart, iii. 60 sqq.; Thaʿlabī, *Ḳiṣaṣ al-anbiyāʾ* (Cairo 1290), p. 69 *sqq.*, 88—90; Abu 'l-Fidāʾ, ed. Fleischer, p. 192; Ibn Ḳutaiba, ed. Wüstenfeld, p. 18, 30; *Die Chroniken der Stadt Mekka*, ed. Wüstenfeld, *passim*; *Sīrat ʿAntar*, Cairo 1306, i. 35—38; Weil, *Bibl. Legenden der Muselmänner*, p. 82 *sqq.*; Grünbaum, *Neue Beiträge z. sem. Sagenkunde*, p. 102 *sqq.*; Goldziher, *Die Richtungen der islamischen Koranauslegung*, p. 79 *sqq.*; J. Horovitz, *Koranische Untersuchungen*, p. 91 *sq*.

ISMĀʿĪLĪYA, a sect of Islām, a branch of the Shīʿīs [q.v.], is subdivided into several subsects, some of which differ widely one from the other in their tenets. Their names are explained further on.

1. History. Officially the Ismāʿīlīya comes into existence as a sect of the Shīʿīs on the death of Ismāʿīl, son of Imām Djaʿfar al-Ṣādiḳ [q.v.], not long before 148/765. Instead of the new nominee, the brother of Ismāʿīl, Mūsā al-Kāẓim, they recognized as their Imām the son of the former, Muḥammad, and his successors. The names of these before ʿUbaid Allāh, al-Mahdī, the founder of the Fāṭimid dynasty, and their sequence, are doubtful. The Fāṭimid version is: ʿAbd Allāh, Aḥmad, Ḥusain. Persian Nizārī: Aḥmad, Muḥammad, Aḥmad. Indian Nizārī: Aḥmad, Muḥammad, ʿAbd Allāh. Druze version: Ismāʿīl II, Muḥammad, Aḥmad, ʿAbd Allāh, Muḥammad, Ḥusain, and Aḥmad (seven instead of three)

As it is possible to infer, a split occurred after the death of Imām Muḥammad b. Ismāʿīl. A branch of the sect accepted the belief that he was the final, the Seventh Imām, who was to return on the Last Day. The sect became known as *Sabʿīya* [q.v.], i.e. "Seveners". Later on, towards the close of the iii^rd^ (ix^th^) century, they came to be called, after their leader, Ḥamdān Ḳarmat, Ḳarāmiṭa, or Ḳarmaṭians [q.v.]. As the latter by their depredations and atrocities made their name hateful to all Muslims, the enemies of the Fāṭimids always tried to prove that both are the same, and applied the name of Ḳarāmiṭa to the other branch also.

The Fāṭimid line of the Ismāʿīlīya accepted one of the sons of Muḥammad b. Ismāʿīl as their Imām, as also later on his appointed successors. As the Imāms lived in strict disguise, and even their names were concealed, there was not much difference between both the branches, which were rapidly increasing in Khuzistān and Southern Mesopotamia. The split became complete about 280/893, probably owing to the desire of the Imāms to advance to the realisation of their aspirations. The Ḳarmaṭians remained faithful to their early doctrine, did not recognize the Imāms, and remained for ever hostile towards the Fāṭimid branch. They continued for about two centuries, and ultimately disappeared.

The story that the sect was founded by ʿAbd Allāh b. Maimūn al-Ḳaddāḥ (d. ca. 210/825) obviously is a legend, and the doctrine is most probably a spontaneous development of the early Shīʿī esoterism. Both these sects, Ismāʿīlīs and Ḳarmaṭians, were also called Bāṭinīya [q.v.], or Taʿlīmīya. Genuine Ismāʿīlī literature preserves almost no memory of ʿAbd Allāh b. Maimūn.

By the end of the iiird (ixth) century the movement had a large number of followers in Khuzistān, Southern Mesopotamia, Syria, Egypt, the Yemen, and was rapidly spreading in the Maghrib. After an abortive attempt to conquer Syria for al-Mahdī, on the part of Yaḥyā and Ḥusain, sons of Zikrūya, in 289—291/902—904, the Imām ʿUbaid Allāh fled to the Maghrib, and headed the victorious movement there. Intense propaganda was carried on through the ivth (xth) century, and by the middle of the vth (xith) century Ismāʿīlism was strong from the Atlantic to the remote Eastern corners of the Islāmic world, Transoxiana, Badakhshān and India. It was especially strong in Persia, which produced the leading Ismāʿīlī philosophers, the real founders of the Fāṭimid doctrine, such as Abū Yaʿḳūb Sidjistānī and Abū Ḥātim Rāzī (both d. ca. 331), Ḥamīd al-Dīn Kirmānī (d. ca. 410), al-Muʾaiyad Shīrāzī (d. 470); add also Nāṣir-i Khusraw and Ḥasan b. Ṣabbāḥ.

Outside the Fāṭimid empire Ismāʿīlism was persecuted as a dangerous political movement; but the chief causes of its rapid decline after an astounding success were the same as those which undermined the Shīʿa in general, i.e. splits and rivalries amongst their leaders. The first serious split was that of the Ḥākimīya, i.e. Druzes [q.v.], who did not believe in the death of al-Ḥākim, in 411/1021, and expected his return. The split on the death of al-Mustanṣir in 487/1094 was a great catastrophe. His eldest son and original nominee, Nizār, was dispossessed of the throne by the party of his brother al-Mustaʿlī, under the commander-in-chief. The Egyptians remained rather apathetic, Nizār had no sufficient support, was captured and murdered in prison (together with his son), by the order of his brother. The news created indignation in Syria and all over the East, and a great majority seceded, preserving their allegiance to the first *naṣṣ*.

Similar indifference reigned amongst the Ismāʿīlīs of Egypt, the Mustaʿlians, when the line of the Fāṭimid Imāms of Egypt became extinct, when al-Āmir was assassinated in 524/1130, and his infant son and heir, al-Ṭaiyib (whose existence is much doubted by historians), was "taken into concealment". The last four Fāṭimid caliphs of Egypt were not regarded as Imāms even by themselves, and the *khuṭba* was read in the name of al-Ḳāʾim, the promised Imām who will come on the Last Day. The followers of the Fāṭimid tradition, the Mustaʿlians, still believe that the Imāms, successors of al-Ṭaiyib, are living in great secrecy somewhere, and are going to manifest themselves when the time comes.

After this the sect remains split to this day into two principal branches: the Mustaʿlians, who on the whole preserve intact the doctrine as it was under the later Fāṭimids, and the Nizārīs, i.e. the partisans of Nizār and of his successors, who later on introduced some reforms into the Fāṭimid doctrine.

a. Mustaʿlians. Their religious centre was transferred to the Yaman, where the community was ruled by "popes" (*al-dāʿi 'l-muṭlaḳ*). In Egypt and the Maghrib Ismāʿīlism disappeared very soon, but in the Yaman it remained in obscurity for about 500 years. Its propaganda had great success in India and the religious centre was transferred to Gudjrāt early in the xith (xviith) century. This was accompanied by another split: after the death of the 26th *dāʿī*, Dāʾūd b. ʿAdjab-Shāh (999/1591), in Aḥmadābād, the majority (Dāʾūdīs) followed Dāʾūd b. Ḳuṭb-Shāh, whom they regarded as their 27th *dāʿī*, while the Yamanite party stuck to Sulaimān b. Ḥasan (= Sulaimānīs). The present Sulaimānī *dāʿī*, Ghulām Ḥusain, residing in Yaman, is the 46th, and the Dāʾūdī *dāʿī*, Ṭāhir b. Muḥammad, residing in Bombay the 51st. (For the names of the *dāʿīs* of both branches see: Asaf A. A. Fyzee, *A Chronological List of the Imams and Daʿis of the Mustaʿlian Ismailis*, in *JBRAS*, 1934, p. 45—56). There are are no real dogmatic differences between the Daʾūdīs and the Sulaimānīs.

b. Nizārīs. According to the Nizārī tradition, which seems to be substantially correct, the son of Nizār, al-Hādī, was murdered together with his father in prison. But his infant son and heir, al-Muhtadī, was brought by trusted servants to Persia, (Alamūt), and was there brought up by Ḥasan b. Ṣabbāḥ in great secrecy. When he died in 557/1162, his son, al-Ḳāhir bi-Aḥkām Allāh Ḥasan (the traditional genealogy of the Nizārīs at present gives instead of him two Imāms, Ḳāhir and Ḥasan), openly ascended the throne, and on the 17th Ramaḍān 559 /Aug. 8, 1164 proclaimed the great Resurrection, the *ḳiyāmat al-ḳiyāmāt*. He prescribed to his followers spiritual worship, reducing the importance of the *ẓāhir*, as is suitable to those who are saved and have entered the spiritual Paradise. This Paradisial state of the faithful most probably is the real basis of the well-known legend about the garden planted by Ḥasan b. Ṣabbāḥ on the barren rocks of Alamūt to imitate Paradise, and to dupe his followers.

The history of other four *khudāwands* of Alamūt i.e. ʿAlāʾ al-Dīn (or Ḍiyāʾ al-Dīn), Djalāl al-Dīn, ʿAlāʾ al-Dīn II and Rukn al-Dīn Khūrshāh, is to some extent known (the best summary is found in E. G. Browne's *Literary History of Persia*, ii. 453—460).

The son of Rukn al-Dīn Khūrshāh, Shams al-Dīn Muḥammad, was carefully hidden when still a child. He and his successors had either to live in complete concealment, or, probably, pose as Ṣūfī shaikhs, of whom at that time there was a great number. Many of them, according to the tradition, occupied a prominent position, were governors of some provinces, intermarried with the Ṣafawī shāhs, etc. Unfortunately very few details and dates are so far available.

After Shams al-Dīn a split arose in the house of the Nizārī Imāms; one line, the Ḳāsim-Shāhīs, still exists and is represented by the present Imām of the Nizārīs, Sulṭān Muḥammad Shāh, well known to the public as the Aga Khan.

The other line, the Muḥammad-Shāhīs, apparently became extinct at the end of the xith (xviith) century. For this little known subsect of the Ismāʿīlīs see W. Ivanow, *A forgotten sect of the Ismailis*, in *JRAS*, 1937. The followers of this branch of the Imāms were numerous in Badakhshān, Persia and India; all Syrian Nizārīs belonged to this branch, but about sixty years ago the majority joined the Ḳāsim-Shāhī line, and now only about 4,000 of the Muḥammad-Shāhīs, locally known as the Suwaidanīya, are living in Maṣyāf and Ḳādmūs.

Nizārīs in Syria mostly had a history quite independent of that of the Persian community. Their most prominent leader, Sinān Rāshid al-Dīn (whom the Muḥammad-Shāhīs believe to be Imām ʿAlāʾ al-Dīn Muḥammad) (557—588/1162—1192), played a considerable role in the wars against the Crusaders on the side of Saladin (cf. Stan. Guyard, *Un Grand Maître des Assassins*, in *JA*, 1877, p. 324—489). Formerly the Ismāʿīlīs (Muḥammad-Shāhīs) were very numerous in Syria, where they inhabited a broad stretch of land on the coast near Ṭarṭūs and Baniās, the hills of Ḳādmūs and Maṣyāf, the districts of Ḥamā, Salamīya, Maʿarrat al-Nuʿmān, etc. According to the census of 1936, their total number is now just over 22.000, out of which four thousand only are Muḥammad-Shāhīs. The last war with their ancient enemies, the Nuṣairīs, in 1919, caused them enormous losses in land and in property, inclusing almost all their religious books.

Nizārīs in India. Ismāʿīlī propaganda in India (in Sindh and Multān) was already started in the iiird (ixth) century, and was energetically continued during the rule of the Fāṭimids; a large number of Hindus were converted. The "Ḳarmaṭians" (i.e. Ismāʿīlīs) held Multān in the vth (xith) century, and were still strong two centuries later in Delhi. With the disappearance of the Fāṭimid Imāms, local communities apparently were left without proper guidance, and either partly joined Sunnī schools, or partly relapsed into Hinduism. Yemenite Mustaʿlians later on successfully carried on propaganda in the South (Gudjrāt), while Nizārī missionaries came from Persia in the xivth century to the North (Pandjāb, Upper Sindh, and Kashmīr). Their doctrine, generously mixed with Ṣūfism, absorbed much of the Hinduistic doctrine which probably in the course of centuries was incorporated into local Ismāʿīlism. They accepted Hinduistic terminology and style in their works, and their sect became known under the name of *Satpanth*, i.e. "true Path". Later it spread further South, where its followers became known under their present name of Khodjas [q.v.]. In the beginning of the xvith century Muḥammad Shāh, the son of Imām Shāh [q.v.], proclaimed himself an Imām, and initiated another split. His sect substantially relapsed into Hinduism, and became split into different branches. Its centre is near Aḥmadābād in Gudjrāt (for details see: W. Ivanow, *The Sect of Imam Shah in Gujrat*, in *JBRAS*, 1936, p. 19—70). The Khodjas preserved relations with their Imāms in Persia, and, under their guidance, succeeded later on in getting rid of many of their Hinduistic beliefs.

2. The present distribution of the Ismāʿīlīs. The Nizārīs are found in Syria, — Salamīya and district of Ṭarṭūs (Khawābī); in Persia, — in the provinces of Khurāsān and Kirmān; in Afghānistān, — North of Djalālābād and in Badakhshān; in Russian and Chinese Turkestan, — Upper Oxus districts, Yarkand, etc.; in Northern India, —Chitral, Gilgit, Hunza, etc.; and in Western India, — Sindh, Gudjrāt, Bombay, etc. Their colonies are found all over India, in Eastern Africa, etc. The total number of Nizārīs may be about 250.000.

The Bohoras, or Indian Mustaʿlians, live chiefly in Gudjrāt, Central India, and Bombay. According to the last Census of India there are 212.000 of them. There are many colonies of them in Eastern Africa. Only a few hundreds are Sulaimānīs, all others are Dāʾūdīs. In the Yaman there are still a few thousands of Ismāʿīlīs, the majority being Sulaimānīs.

3. Doctrine. The information which has so far been the basis of our knowledge about the doctrine of the Ismāʿīlīs, derived from different works by the orthodox historians and heresiologists, appears to be of very little value when compared with the original genuine Ismāʿīlī works. The facts appear to be so confused, distorted and perverted, either intentionally or not, that it will take a long time before the truth can be sifted from the untruth. The best appears to be to leave it for the present, and to give here the most salient facts derived from the original works, and from the sectarian tradition.

Apparently very few pre-Fāṭimid works are now preserved, and as little authentic information about early Ismāʿīlī doctrine is available as generally about the early Shīʿa. But it is beyond doubt that, except in a few esoteric principles and the theory of Imāmate, early Ismāʿīlism differed very little from the Ithnā-ʿasharī dogmas and practice. It was divided into two interdependent branches, the *ẓāhir*, or all that is concerned with outward piety and righteous life, and the *bāṭin*, the theory of the esoteric meaning of religious commandments, beliefs, of the Sacred Book, etc. Fāṭimid Ismāʿīlism rigidly insisted on the principle that "there is no *ẓāhir* without its corresponding *bāṭin*, just as there is no *bāṭin* without its own *ẓāhir*".

a. The exoteric doctrine, the *ẓāhir*, was a conservative form of Islām, resembling in many respects the practice of the Twelvers, but in some points coming nearer to Sunnism. The prayers, fasts, and generally all the prescriptions of the *sharīʿa*, were obligatory upon all, even those in possession of the highest esoteric knowledge (the point which is deliberately disregarded by all heresiologists). For a complete exposition of the official Fāṭimid religion see W. Ivanow, *A Creed of the Fatimids* (Bombay 1936).

b. The esoteric doctrine, or *bāṭin*, consists of two main parts. One is the *taʾwīl* of the Ḳurʾān and of the *sharīʿa*, in which Ḳāḍī Nuʿmān and Djaʿfar b. Manṣūr al-Yamanī excelled. The second, by far more interesting, are the *ḥaḳāʾiḳ* (plur. of *ḥaḳīḳa*, the truth), or the Ismāʿīlī system of philosophy and science, co-ordinated with the religion and serving as a revelation of its inner content as also of the religious prescriptions, and intended to prove the divine origin of the institution of the Imāmate and the exclusive rights of the Fāṭimids to it. The ideal of Ismāʿīlism always was the form of religion which is adapted to the level of education and the intelligence of the believer. As it was obviously unwise to communicate difficult philosophical and theological theories to the people who were not prepared to understand them, the study could only be gradual. But it appears that all the stories about the "degrees of initiation", similar to masonic degrees, etc., are pure fiction, — genuine Ismāʿīlī literature preserves no trace of them.

The student impressed by the usual stories about the great impiety and the anti-Islāmic tendencies of the secret Ismāʿīlī doctrine, will be bitterly disappointed on reading the most secret amongst the Ismāʿīlī books, such as, for instance, the *Rāḥat al-ʿaḳl* by Ḥamīd al-Dīn Kirmānī, some esoteric *Madjālis* of al-Muʾaiyad Shīrāzī, the *Kanz al-walad* by Ibrāhīm al-Ḥāmidī, the *Dhakhīra* by ʿAlī b. Muḥammad b. al-Walīd, the *Zahr al-maʿānī* by ʿImād al-Dīn Idrīs, etc. These works prove beyond any doubt that the fundamental principles of the highest esoteric doctrine were the basic points of Islām: the unshakeable belief in the Unity of God, the divine mission of Muḥammad, the divine revelation of the Ḳurʾān, etc. There is also no doubt that the only aim of the authors was to develop and to refine the primitive principles of Islām, making them acceptable and attractive to the critical and sophisticated mind of a cultured man, who had gone a long way from the crude mentality of the Arabs of the first century.The system is a typical production of the Muslim mind of the ivth (xth) or vth (xith) century, and in many points resembles the philosophy of al-Fārābī and al-Ghazzālī [q.v.].

The most prominent element of this system is Neo-Platonic philosophy, derived not directly from the Enneads of Plotinus, or his early commentators, but from some later versions, considerably adulterated, and mixed up with heterogeneous matters. Ismāʿīlism (just like some Christian and Jewish systems) tried to find in the Plotinian philosophy the synthesis between the monotheistic idea and the plurality of the visible world. The system of ancient Greek science, on which Plotinus could build his system, had changed greatly by the xth century. Many theories were forgotten, many Greek works remained unknown to Muslims, and many forgeries were in general use. Thus the natural philosophy of Ismāʿīlism, with its ideas of the organic and inorganic world, psychology, biology, etc., is to some extent based on Aristotle, and partly on Neo-Pythagorean and other early speculations. There are, however, no references to these original Greek works, and only a vague mention of "Greek philosophers", *al-ḥukamāʾ al-yūnānīya*, may be found, very rarely. Much is added from the debased science of the later periods, in the form of crude astrological, alchemical and cabalistic beliefs, speculations about the mystical and magical force of numbers, letters, etc. All this, indeed, is familiar to every student of early mediaeval culture. Traces of Manichaeism are very faint. Christianity is more strongly felt; Ismāʿīlī authors, when citing Christian Scriptures, usually are remarkably accurate, showing that they consulted the real books, and not simply their own fantasy, like the majority of the orthodox Muslim authors.

Anyone who wishes to form a first hand idea of the early *ḥaḳāʾiḳ*, can with advantage peruse the well-known Encyclopaedia of the *Ikhwān al-Ṣafāʾ*,

many times printed, and partly studied and translated by the late Dieterici. The work is regarded by the Musta'lians as a compilation by the second of the concealed Imāms, Aḥmad; quotations from it are common in the *ḥaḳā'iḳ* books.

Thus, as we can see, there is very little original or unknown in this system. The only original thing about it is the way in which all this heterogeneous material was combined and amalgamated with Islām. But even in this respect the *ḥaḳā'iḳ* completely resemble the Ṣūfī speculations, which differ from them only in terminology and in the fact that Ṣūfism emphatically accepts the Plotinian doctrine of ecstasy while Ismā'īlism completely ignores it.

We may note that the Musta'lians firmly believe that all this was revealed by their Imāms, that nobody except themselves possesses this knowledge, and even that it would be unintelligible to outsiders. Even now the Bohoras intentionally keep aloof from modern science which they regard as heretical.

Outlines of the system. The *ḥaḳā'iḳ* emphasize very strongly the parallelism between the Macrocosmos and Microcosmos. The Islāmic *tawḥīd* is here carried to the last limit, and no attributes derived from the experience of the senses are given to God (*al-ghaib ta'ālā*). By an act of pre-eternal volition the One produces the first (*sābiḳ*) emanation (*munba'ath*); in accordance with the Plotinian system, it is the *'aḳl al-kull*, or the all-pervading conscious formative principle, the *de facto* first "Initiator" of the world (*mubdi'*). The second emanation, which appears from the preceding, is the conscious life-giving principle, *nafs al-kull*, the third member of the original Plotinian triad. Here appears a new development, obviously produced by an effort to reconcile this idea with the system of Ptolemy. A few more *'aḳls* are inserted. They are "logical" moving principles of the different spheres, *falak*, i.e. of the spheres of fixed stars and Zodiacal constellations, of the five planets, the sun and the moon. The latter is the *'aḳl* in charge of the earth, *al-'aḳl al-fa''āl*, the actual creator of the "forms" (*ṣūra*), and called the "second *mubdi'*". To him are transferred all functions which in the Plotinian system belong to the *nafs al-kull*. The forms which, by working upon the substratum of matter, the *haiyūlā* (ὕλη), produce the visible world, have their perfect prototypes, after which they are created. This is obviously a version of Plato's theory of ideas, which is wrongly understood. Here it forms the bridge between philosophy and religion. If there is to be a perfect prototype of humanity, Perfect Man, it must exist here, in this world, as otherwise humanity could not exist. But who can this Perfect Man be except the Chosen one, the last and the greatest Messenger of God, His Prophet Muḥammad? As man is the crown of creation, and the Perfect Man is the crown of humanity, he, the Prophet, corresponds with what in the cosmic world is *'aḳl al-kull*. The hypostasis of the *nafs al-kull* cannot be any one else than the *waṣī*, or the executor of the Prophet's will, 'Alī. The Imāms, who are permanently in charge of this world, are the hypostasis of the final *'aḳl*. The soul, being the "form" of the human being, belongs to the higher, spiritual world, but is entangled in the impure world of "becoming and decaying" (*kawn wa-fasād*). By associating itself with the nearest higher substance, the Imām, the soul can "ascend", and return to the Original Source, attaining to ultimate salvation. The method of this association is *al-'ibāda al-'ilmīya*, i.e. acquisition of the knowledge revealed by the Imāms, and obedience to their command. "Who dies without having recognised the Imām of his time, dies as a *kāfir*".

This system remains fossilized in the Musta'lian tradition, but the Nizārīs have slightly altered it. The Fāṭimids did not encourage extremist ideas, and in the early literature *imām* was almost the same as *khalīfa*, caliph. The Fāṭimids claimed to be the lieutenants of the Founder of the religion, the Prophet. The Nizārīs, probably under the strong influence of Ṣūfī ideas, emphasized the spiritual life, reduced the *ẓāhir*, and made the "light" of the Imāma the Supreme Principle. They regard the principle of Imāma, or divine guidance, as eternal, starting before the creation. The world never is without an Imām, otherwise it will perish instantly. The imām is the hypostasis of the Primal Volition, *amr*, or "word", logos, *kalima*, the Ḳur'ānic primordial "be". This substance rests in the Imām, who otherwise is a mortal man, and is transferred from the father to the son only, by *naṣṣ*. There are no smaller and no greater Imāms (contrary to Fāṭimid belief), all are one and the same substance. The Imām is not "incarnated", there is no *ḥulūl* or *tanāsukh* in Ismā'īlism. The first Imām at the beginning of the period (*dawr*) of Muḥammad was 'Alī, and his progeny, *dhurrīya*, are his successors. Ḥasan, who is regarded as the first Imām by the Musta'lians, is struck off the list, as he was merely acting on behalf of his brother. The Prophet remains the *'aḳl al-kull*, but the *nafs al-kull* is hypostasized by the *ḥudjdja* (in the Fāṭimid time one of the twelve or twenty-four "bishops"). He is usually a close relative of the Imām, sometimes even a woman, or a child. The *ḥudjdja* possesses an innate miraculous knowledge of the Imām, and teaches the faithful.

The hierarchy of religious dignitaries (*ḥudūd al-dīn*) corresponded with the "degrees of initiation" probably only at the earliest period when learning was exclusively confined to missionaries. The number of the *ḥudūd* was often changed, and the names of the different ranks altered. The fundamental always were: *mustadjīb*, or "initiated"; *ma'dhūn*, or "licenced to teach"; *dā'ī*, or "preacher"; and *ḥudjdja*, or "commissioner of a see" (*djazīra*).

The system of *fiḳh*, founded by Ḳāḍī Nu'mān, and preserved by the Musta'lians, never received further development. The calendar of the Musta'lians differs from the general Muslim one, being ahead of it by a day or two, because the beginning of the lunar months is calculated astronomically, and does not depend on the visibility of the moon.

Astrological beliefs, superstitious ideas about the mystical meaning of numbers and letters, play a great part in their speculations, especially the number seven. The history of the world was divided into seven periods (*dawr*) each initiated by one of the great prophets: Adam, Noah, Abraham, Moses, Jesus and Muḥammad; the seventh, Ḳā'im, is expected to come at the end of the world. Each of these great prophets has a *waṣī*, who is succeeded by Imāms.

Bibliography: Much has been written about Ismā'īlism, but very little is based on genuine sources. The best bibliography up to 1922 is given by L. Massignon, *Esquisse d'une bibliographie Qarmaṭe*, 1922 (*Or. Studies presented to Prof. E. G. Browne*). This bibliography is continued and supplemented in two papers by A. A. A. Fyzee, in *JBRAS*, 1935 (p. 59—65) and 1936 (p. 107—109) — A summary of historical information only: O'Leary, *A Short History of the Fatimid Khalifate*, London 1923; B. Lewis, *The origins of Ismāʿīlism*, Cambridge 1940; S. M. Stern, *The succession of the Fatimid Imām al-Āmir etc.*, in *Oriens* iv. 193—255; — About Ismāʿīlī works referred to in this note see W. Ivanow, *A Guide to Ismaili Literature*, London 1933. — On Nizārī doctrine: W. Ivanow, *An Ismailitic Work by Nasiru 'd-din Tusi*, in *JRAS*, 1931, p. 527—564. — On Ismāʿīlī *fiḳh*: Asaf A. A. Fyzee, *Ismaili Law of Wills*, Bombay 1933.

ISNĀD (A.), the chain of traditionists. See ḤADĪTH, (sections ii. and iii.) and cf. on the connection with Jewish tradition: J. Horovitz, *Alter und Ursprung des Isnād*, in *Isl.*, viii. (1917), 39—47.

ISRĀʾ. The term *isrāʾ* is taken from the Ḳurʾān, Sūra xvii. 1: "Glory to Him who caused His servant to journey by night (*asrā bi ʿabdihi lailan*) from the sacred place of worship to the further place of worship, which We have encircled with blessings, in order that We might show him some of our signs! Verily He (i.e.God) is the Hearer and the Beholder". — We do not know whether this verse originally formed part of chap. xvii. or was first promulgated in some other context, nor need we enquire what may have been the real sense of the verse. In any case it is noticeable that the tradition gives but three explanations.

1°. The older one, which disappears from the more recent commentaries, detects in this verse an allusion to Muḥammad's Ascension to Heaven. This is the more interesting, as these traditions (Bukhārī, ed. Cairo 1278, ii. 185, *Bāb kāna 'l-nabīyu tanāmu ʿainuhu walā yanāmu ḳalbuha*, no. 2; Muslim, ed. Būlāḳ, 1290, i. 59; Ṭabarī, *Tafsir*, xv. 3, cf. *Der Islam*, vi. 12, 14) retain also the original signification of the story of the Ascension which has been shown to be the initiation to the prophetic career (Bevan, *Mohammed's Ascension to Heaven*, p. 56; Schrieke, *Der Islam*, vi. 1 *sqq.*; see the art. MIʿRĀDJ). This explanation interprets the expression *al-masdjid al-aḳṣā*, "the further place of worship" in the sense of "Heaven" and, in fact, in the older tradition *isrāʾ* is often used as synonymous with *miʿrādj* (*Der Islam*, vi. 14).

2°. The second explanation, the only one given in all the more modern commentaries, interpretes *al-masdjid al-aḳṣā* as "Jerusalem" and this for no very apparent reason. It seems to have been an Umaiyad device intended to further the glorification of Jerusalem as against that of the holy territory (cf. Goldziher, *Muh. Stud.*, ii. 55 *sqq.*; *Der Islam*, vi. 13 *sqq.*), then ruled by ʿAbd Allāh b. Zubair. Ṭabarī seems to reject it. He does not mention it in his "History" and seems rather to adopt the first explanation (see *Der Islam*, vi. 2, 5, 6, 12, 14; Ṭabarī, i. 1157 *sqq.*, a passage which appears to represent the historian's final verdict formed on full consideration of the evidence before him, cf. Bevan, *op. cit.*, p. 57).

Explanations 1° and 2° concur in interpreting *ʿabd* in xvii. 1 by Muḥammad and this seems to be right (*Der Islam*, vi. 13, note 6). The *idjmāʿ* admitted both interpretations and, when the Umaiyad version had arisen, harmonised the two by assigning to *isrāʾ* the special sense of night journey to Jerusalem. The Ascension, having lost its original meaning, was altered in date, being made to fall at a later period (see art. MIʿRĀDJ) and it became possible to combine both stories as appears, in fact, to have been done previously by Ibn Isḥāḳ in the oldest extant biography of Muḥammad (Bevan, *op. cit.* p. 54).

The story of the night journey to Jerusalem runs as follows.

One night as Muḥammad was sleeping in the neighbourhood of the Kaʿba at Mecca (or in the house of Umm Hāniʾ, *Der Islam*, vi. 11) he was awakened by the angel Gabriel who conducted him to a winged animal, called Burāḳ (Bevan, *op. cit.*, p. 55, 57, 59; *Der Islam*, vi. 12 *sq.*, with the literature quoted there and the art. BURĀḲ), and with Muḥammad mounted on this animal they journeyed together to Jerusalem. On the way thither they encounter several good and several wicked powers (*Mishkāt al-maṣābīḥ*, ed. Dihlī 1268, p. 521 *sq.*; Baghawī, *Maṣābīḥ al-sunna*, ed. Cairo 1294, ii. 179, with a harmonising interpolation) and visit Hebron and Bethlehem (Nasāʾī, *Sunan*, ed. Cairo 1312, i. 77 *sq.*; Nuwairī, *Nihāyat al-arab*, i. 338). At Jerusalem they meet Abraham, Moses, and Jesus, of whom a description is given (e.g. Bukhārī, ed. Cairo 1278, ii. 147). The ṣalāt is performed, Muḥammad acting as imām and thereby taking precedence of all the other prophets there assembled. This meeting with the prophets at Jerusalem resembles and may well have been modelled on the transfiguration of Jesus on Mount Tabor (Matth. xvii, 1; Mark ix. 1; Luke ix. 28), cf. *Der Islam*, vi. 15.

3°. The third interpretation of Sūra xvii. 1 is based on xvii. 60, where *ruʾyā* "vision" is explained as *isrāʾ*. This implies that the night journey was not a real journey but a vision. Standing at the *ḥidjr* Muḥammad saw Jerusalem and described it to the unbelieving Ḳuraishites (Bukhārī, ii. 221, iii. 102; Muslim, i. 62; Ṭabarī, *Tafsīr*, xv. 5, l. 14 a. f., etc.). The story is woven into a connected whole as follows: Muḥammad journeys by night to Jerusalem, returns and at Mecca describes his adventures; the Ḳuraishites disbelieve him and Muslims apostasize; Muḥammad seeks to defend the truth of his story, but he has forgotten the particulars; whereupon Allāh causes him to actually behold Jerusalem (see *Der Islam*, vi. 15 *sq.*).

In the more modern and longer narratives the story is further amplified (see e.g. A. Müller, *Der Islam in Morgen- und Abendland*, i. 86 *sq.*). The Prophet is said to have held 70.000 conversations with Allāh, although the whole journey proceeded so quickly that, when he returned, his bed was still warm and the watercup which he had overthrown with his foot at his hurried departure, was not yet empty. By Muslim theologians the question has been discussed, whether the *isrāʾ* happened while Muḥammed was asleep or awake and whether it was his spirit or his body which journeyed. The orthodox opinion is that the journey was performed by Muḥammad with his body and awake. Ṭabarī in his commentary (xv. 13) very decidedly supports this meaning for the following reasons: 1) If the Prophet had not been carried away in a corporeal sense the event would afford no proof of his divine mission and those who disbelieved the story could not be accused of infidelity. 2) It is stated in the Ḳurʾān that God caused his servant to journey, not that He caused his servant's spirit to journey. 3) If the Prophet had been carried away in spirit only, the services of Burāḳ would not have been required, since animals are used for carrying bodies, not for carrying spirits (Bevan, *op. cit.*, p. 60; Schrieke, *Der Islam*, vi., 13; Ṭabarī, Baiḍāwī, and Baghawī, *Tafsīr*, ad xvii. 1). Mystics and philosophers often favour an allegorical interpretation (Goldziher, *Geschichte der Philosophie im Mittelalter* in *Kultur der Gegenwart*, i.v., p. 319).

Bibliography: Bevan, *Mohammed's Ascension to Heaven*, in *Beihefte zur Zeitschr. für die Alttestam.*

Wissensch., vol. xxvii. p. 51 *sqq.*; Schrieke, *Die Himmelsreise Muhammed's*, in *Der Islam*, vi., 13 *sqq.*, with the literature there quoted; E. Cerulli, *Il „Libro della Scala"*, Vatican City 1949.

ISRĀFĪL, the name of an archangel, which is probably to be traced to the Hebrew *Serāfim* as is indicated by the variants *Sarāfīl* and *Sarāfīn* (*TA*, vii. 375). The change of liquids is not unusual in such endings. His size is astounding; while his feet are under the seventh earth, his head reaches up to the pillars of the divine throne. He has four wings: one in the west, one in the east, one with which he covers his body and one as a protection against the majesty of God. He is covered with hair, mouths and tongues. He is considered to be the angel who reads out the divine decisions from the well-kept Tablet and transmits them to the Archangel to whose department they belong. Three times by day and three times by night he looks down into Hell and is convulsed with grief and weeps so violently that the earth might be inundated by his tears.

For three years he was the companion of the Prophet, whom he initiated into the work of a prophet. Gabriel then took over this task and began the communication of the Ḳurʾān.

Alexander is said to have met him before his arrival in the land of darkness; there he stood upon a hill and blew the trumpet, tears in his eyes. If he is called Lord of the Trumpet, it is mainly because he continually holds the trumpet to his mouth in order to be able to blow at once as soon as God gives the order for the blast which is to arouse men from their graves. It is however also said that Isrāfīl will be first aroused on the day of the Resurrection. He will then take his stand upon the holy rock in Jerusalem and give the signal which will bring the dead back to life.

In modern Egypt it is said that his music will refresh the inhabitants of Paradise.

Bibliography: Kisāʾī, *ʿAdjāʾib al-malakūt*, Ms. Leyden, 538 Warner, fol. 4 *sq.*; Ḳazwīnī, *ʿAdjāʾib al-makhlūḳāt*, ed. Wüstenfeld, p. 56 *sq.*; Ṭabarī, i. 1248 *sq.*, 1255; Ghazzālī, *al-Durra al-fākhira*, ed. Gautier, p. 42; M. Wolff, *Muhammed. Eschatologie*, p. 9, 49; Sale, *The Koran, Prelimi- nary Discourse*, p. 94; Friedländer, *Die Chadhirlegende und der Alexanderroman*, p. 171, 208; Lane, *Manners and Customs* (London 1889), p. 80.

ISRĀʾĪL, the name of the patriarch of Israel, appears only once in the Ḳurʾān, apart from the frequent name, Banū Isrāʾīl, for the people of Israel. In Sūra iii. 93 it is said: "All foods were permitted to the Israelites except that which Israel declared forbidden for himself before the Tora was revealed". According to the commentators, this means that the restrictions on food were only revealed as a result of the wickedness of the Israelites. Their ancestor himself only refrained from eating camel flesh or drinking camel milk: according to some, because he was afflicted with the disease called *ʿirḳ al-nasā*, which kept him awake by night and left him during the day. He therefore made a vow to abstain from his favourite food, if he should be cured. According to others, he did not eat the *ʿirḳ al-nasā* (*nervus ischiadicus*) by the advice of his physicians; or he abstained from all sinews (*ʿirḳ*). The word is a translation of the Hebrew *gīd* and *al-nasā* is a transcription of the Hebrew *nāshè*. This points to *Genesis* xxxii., the well known story of the dislocation of Jacob's thigh by the angel as an explanation of the fact that the Israelites "to this very day" do not eat the *nervus ischiadicus*.

The question remains how Jacob's private abstinence could be obligatory for the Israelites. According to some, a prophet, as Jacob was, is by nature qualified to decide questions of law (Arabic *mudjtahid*). According to others, Jacob received God's permission to make this regulation.

The rest that is told of Isrāʾīl in the Ḳurʾān is found under the name Yaʿḳūb [q.v.]. At first Muḥammad seems to have regarded Yaʿḳūb as a son of Ibrāhīm. In the prophecy made to Sara, he says: "Then we promised her Isḥāḳ and afterwards Yaʿḳūb" (xi. 71; cf. Snouck Hurgronje, *Het Mekkaansche Feest*, p. 32). The commentaries hasten to explain that according to the Arabic usage "afterwards" must refer to the grandson.

It is further stated in the Ḳurʾān that Yaʿḳūb on his death-bed warned his sons to be steadfast in the faith of Ibrāhīm (ii. 132 *sqq.*); like most of the patriarchs he received revelations (ii. 136 etc.).

Muslim legend is acquainted with the main points of Jacob's history. Only divergent and non-Biblical features will be noted here. Yaʿḳūb was actually older than his twin brother Esau. When he was going to be born earlier than the latter, Esau was angry and the two brothers quarrelled even in the mother's womb. Esau then said: "Wa'llāh, if thou wishest to be born first, I shall close up my mother's womb and kill her". Yaʿḳūb then yielded and Esau was the first born. — This story is also found in Jewish literature. — After winning the firstborn's blessing by trickery, Yaʿḳūb fled to his uncle. From fear of Esau he concealed himself by day and travelled by night (*yasrī* or *yasīr fi'l-lail*), hence the name Isrāʾīl. The Muslim legend therefore does not know of the change of name at Penuel. — As to his marriage with two sisters, it is said that Moses was the first to forbid this. But it is also said that Yaʿḳūb did not marry Rāḥīl until after Līyā's death.

Bibliography: The commentaries to the passages quoted from the Ḳurʾān; Ṭabarī, i. 353 *sqq.*; Yaʿḳūbī, i. 26 *sqq.*; Thaʿlabī, *Ḳiṣaṣ al-anbiyāʾ* (Cairo 1290), p. 88 *sqq.*; J. Horovitz, *Koranische Untersuchungen*, p. 91.

ISTIḤSĀN and **ISTIṢLĀḤ**, two methods of reasoning much discussed in the books on the *uṣūl al-fiḳh* [q.v.] in connection with the doctrine of *ḳiyās* [q.v.]. The two conceptions as a result of their close relationship are sometimes confused. No one ever seems to have reached a clear and lucid definition of their mutual relationship.

I. The authorities for istiḥsān which the followers of this method quote from the Ḳurʾān (xxxix. 18, 55), Ḥadīth (*mā raʾāhu 'l-muslimūn ḥasanan fa-huwa ʿinda 'llāhi ḥasanun*) and *idjmāʿ* (going to the bath without previous arrangement about payment etc.), are easily deprived of weight by the opposition, and therefore need not be further discussed. On the other hand, it is interesting to note that istiḥsān already leaves its literary impress in ḥadīth (e.g. Bukhārī, *Waṣāyā*, bāb 8), thus going back to the first half of the viiith century A.D. (see Wensinck, *The Muslim Creed*, p. 59). Half a century later, Mālik (d. 795) uses the expression in connection with legal decisions for which he cannot find authority in tradition (Ibn al-Ḳāsim, *Mudawwana*, Cairo 1323, xvi. 217). About the same time Abū Yūsuf (d. 798) says: "according to the *ḳiyās* this and that would be prescribed but I have decided according to my opinion (*istaḥsantu*)" (*Kitāb al-kharādj*, Būlāḳ 1302, p. 117). Istiḥsān is thus contrasted even more distinctly with the usual method of deducing legislation (*ḳiyās*). The term, in later centuries also, means a method of finding the law which for any reason is contradictory to the usual ḳiyās.

It is noteworthy that S̲h̲āfiʿī (d. 820), the founder of the science of the *uṣūl al-fiḳh*, fundamentally rejected istiḥsān, because he feared that in this way by going beyond the methodically secure and generally recognised principles of legal interpretation, a loophole would be made for arbitrary decision. "God has not permitted any man since His Messenger to present views unless from knowledge that was complete before him" (*Risāla*, Būlāḳ 1321, p. 70). If any one in spite of this uses istiḥsān he is botching the work of God, the highest legislator.

The supporters of the doctrine of istiḥsān — they belong for the most part to the Ḥanafī *madhhab* (Pazdawī [d. 1089], Saraḳhsī [1090], Nasafī [1310] etc. down to Baḥr al-ʿUlūm [1810]) — make every effort to deprive these objections of their force. Their principle of diverging in certain cases from ḳiyās and using istiḥsān is — they say — not decided by personal inclinations or by a lack of methodical thinking but on the contrary by purely material considerations provided for in the law. It is a "concealed ḳiyās" (*ḳiyās k̲h̲afī*), a divergence from an externally obvious ḳiyās to an inner and self-conditioned decision. It is not true that istiḥsān can be traced back to the principle of *tak̲h̲ṣīṣ* and thus be brought within the sphere of ḳiyās proper. It really lies outside of this narrow sphere and must therefore be recognized as a special form of deduction. For the rest, if we investigate more carefully, we can assert that the form of istiḥsān represented by the Ḥanafites is also used by representatives of other *madhhabs*. It is in practice the common property of all legists.

If we consider the very minute work of systematisation which the later Ḥanafites (e.g. Ibn al-Humām (d. 1457) — Ibn Amīr al-Ḥād̲j̲d̲j̲ī (1474) and Bihārī (1708) — Baḥr al-ʿUlūm (1810)) have done on istiḥsān, we may actually agree with this last deduction. This method of reasoning, which originally aroused such misgiving because it was undefined, is given a place in the casuistic step-ladder of the *ʿilm uṣūl al-fiḳh*, and its possibility of application thus limited to a few accurately definable cases. If nevertheless discussion continued on whether it is justified or not this can only be explained by the fact that the followers of the S̲h̲āfiʿī school felt themselves bound from a certain traditional principle not to drop the polemic against istiḥsān which had long ago been originated by their master — under different conditions and with more right.

II. Istiṣlāḥ is, as regards its negative side, closely connected with istiḥsān; here we have again a question of a principle by which the otherwise usual method of deduction is to be excluded in the preparation of legal decisions. The difference from istiḥsān is seen only when we enquire into the guiding ideas which forms the positive foundation for this principle which is negative in its effects. We then see that istiṣlāḥ is more limited and more closely defined in content than istiḥsān in so far as it replaces the, in itself only formal, "finding-good" of the latter by the material principle of *maṣlaḥa*. It argues with the demands of human welfare in the widest sense. It might therefore be contrasted with the more comprehensive and more indefinite general conception of istiḥsān as a more exactly defined or subordinated species, as indeed al-Is̲h̲bīlī (Mālikī, d. 1151) already pointed out. It is just through this greater definiteness that istiṣlāḥ

gains in force compared with istiḥsān. For it is evident that such an illuminating idea as that of anxiety for human welfare carries much more conviction in the derivation of legal principles and can be more readily established than the formal and empty criterion of istiḥsān. In this way is probably to be explained why the principle of istiṣlāḥ was on the whole not so strongly disputed as that of istiḥsān and why it occasionally, going beyond the denial of the usual ḳiyās, even questioned the validity of legal principles emanating directly from the Ḳurʾān, Sunna and *id̲j̲māʿ*.

The history of the origin and development of istiṣlāḥ cannot be traced so far back as that of istiḥsān. It is true that it is asserted by different authorities that Mālik (d. 795) was the first to use istiṣlāḥ, and indeed there is some ground for this, as for example when he declares it permitted in special cases to sell fresh dates not yet pulled for ripened dates — against the usual regulation that fresh fruits cannot be sold for dried (*Mudawwana*, x. 90 *sqq.*). But it should be remembered that the term *maṣlaḥa* or istiṣlāḥ is not mentioned at all in this connection; and it should also be noted that S̲h̲āfiʿī (d. 820) in his famous *Risāla* confines the discussion to istiḥsān. From this it is probably safe to deduce that the problem of istiṣlāḥ was not yet ripe for discussion in his time — unless it was then still regarded as a subdivision of istiḥsān and therefore not particularly emphasised. The assertion that Mālik was the first to use istiṣlāḥ is therefore in all probability a later antedating of the fact that the Mālikites made the most frequent use of this principle.

Nor in the period following Mālik and his generation is it possible yet to demonstrate clearly the development of istiṣlāḥ. The names which are quoted as authorities in the later works in discussion of the principle — apart from Mālik and S̲h̲āfiʿī — belong at earliest to the xi[th] century. Perhaps the gap could be filled to some extent if the old and still unpublished *uṣūl* works, especially the writings of Muʿtazilite or S̲h̲īʿite authors were systematically studied.

Imām al-Ḥaramain al-D̲j̲uwainī (d. 1085, S̲h̲āfiʿīite) is the first of those who are mentioned as followers of the principle of istiṣlāḥ. The imām G̲h̲azzālī (d. 1111), also quoted as an authority, takes us into the very heart of the discussion (*Mustaṣfā*, Būlāḳ 1322, i. 284—315). He defines the legal term *maṣlaḥa* as "consideration for what is aimed at for mankind in the law". By this he means five things: maintenance of religion, of life, of reason, of descendants and property. The consideration of *maṣlaḥa* and its counterpart, the averting of corruption (*dafʿ al-mafsada*), is, according to G̲h̲azzālī, generally given by the legal text and therefore coincides with the usual ḳiyās. In the cases in which it cannot be deduced by the usual process it is only decisive when there are cogent and unequivocally defined considerations affecting the whole community (*ḍarūrī, ḳaṭʿī, kullī*). Otherwise it is not allowed to use istiṣlāḥ.

After G̲h̲azzālī, other S̲h̲āfiʿīite legal theorists express themselves on the problem of istiṣlāḥ, e.g. Baiḍāwī (d. 1282 or later) — Isnawī (1370) and Subkī (1370) — Maḥallī (1460) — Bannānī (1784). They discuss at considerable length the views of their predecessors, especially G̲h̲azzālī, but contribute very little that is new. On the other hand, the tendency to systematization of the different cases of istiṣlāḥ increases. This tendency to systematization however only reaches its height in the later Ḥanafite works on *uṣūl* by Ṣadr al-S̲h̲arīʿa Maḥbūbī (d. 1346)

— Taftāzānī (1390 or later) — Fanarī (c. 1500) and especially Ibn al-Humām (1457) — Ibn Amīr al-Ḥādjdj (1474) and Bihārī (1708) — Baḥr al-ʿUlūm (1810). Here we cannot go into the details of their explanations which are often difficult to follow.

In the foregoing it has already been mentioned that the Mālikites are regarded as the principal champions of istiṣlāḥ. But too much stress should not be laid on this general opinion. It is of course true that Mālikite legal theorists like Shāṭibī (d. 1194) and Ḳarāfī (1285) took up the discussion and carried it further. But on the other hand, Ibn al-Ḥādjib (1249), who was also a Mālikite, is reckoned one of the opponents of the principle. On the other hand, the circle of those who recognise the principle of istiṣlāḥ in practice extends far beyond the limits of the Mālikite school. Ḳarāfī even points out that "if one looks more carefully, it is in general use in the *madhhabs*" (*Sharḥ Tanḳīḥ al-fuṣūl*, Cairo 1306, p. 170). Shāfiʿites and Ḥanafites — although with certain limitations and in part under other names — have adopted it and developed it further. From amongst the Ḥanbalites Ibn Ḳaiyim al-Djawzīya (d. 1350) deserves to be mentioned in this connection, and — last not least — Nadjm al-Dīn al-Ṭawfī (1316), the most radical of all upholders of istiṣlāḥ. His bold *Risāla fi 'l-maṣāliḥ al-mursala* has been published twice: in the *Madjmūʿ rasāʾil fī uṣūl al-fiḳh* (Bairūt 1324), and in vol. x. of Rashīd Riḍā's (d. 1935) well known periodical *al-Manār*. This shows, that even for modern Muslims the problem of istiṣlāḥ is still of some importance and interest.

Bibliography: I. Istiḥsān: Shāfiʿī, *Risāla* (at the beginning of *Kitāb al-umm*, Būlāḳ 1321), p. 69 *sq.*; Ghāzzālī, *al-Mustaṣfā* (2 vols., Būlāḳ 1322—1324), i. 274—283; Baiḍāwī, *Minhādj al-wuṣūl*, with commentary *Nihāyat al-suʾūl* by Djamāl al-Dīn al-Isnawī (on the margin of the *al-Taḳrīr wa 'l-taḥbīr* of Ibn Amīr al-Ḥādjdj, 3 vols., Būlāḳ 1316—1317), iii. 140—147; Tādj al-Dīn al-Subkī, *Djamʿ al-djawāmiʿ*, with the commentary of Djalāl al-Dīn al-Maḥallī and glosses of Bannānī (2 vols., Cairo 1297), ii. 288; Pazdawī, *Kanz al-wuṣūl*, with commentary (*Kashf al-asrār*) of ʿAbd al-ʿAzīz al-Bukhārī (4 vols., Stambul 1307—1308), iv. 2—14, 40, 83; Abu 'l-Barakāt al-Nasafī, *Kashf al-asrār* (*Sharḥ manār al-anwār*), with commentary by Mullā Djīwan and glosses by Muḥammad ʿAbd al-Ḥalīm al-Luknawī (2 vols., Būlāḳ 1316), ii. 164—168; Ṣadr al-Sharīʿa al-Maḥbūbī, *Sharḥ al-tawḍīḥ ʿala 'l-tanḳīḥ*, with commentary (*al-Talwīḥ*) by Taftāzānī and glosses by Fanarī and Mullā Khusraw (3 vols., Cairo 1322), iii. 2—10; Ibn al-Humām, *al-Taḥrīr*, with commentary (*al-Taḳrīr wa 'l-taḥbīr*) by Ibn Amīr al-Ḥādjdj (3 vols., Būlāḳ 1316 *sq.*), iii. 221—238; [Mullā Khusraw], *Mirḳāt al-wuṣūl ilā ʿilm al-uṣūl*, (Stambul 1307), p. 23 *sq.*; Muḥibb Allāh b. ʿAbd al-Shukūr (Bihārī), *Musallam al-thubūt*, with commentary (*Fawātiḥ al-raḥamūt*) by Muḥammad ʿAbd al-ʿAlī Niẓām al-Dīn (Baḥr al-ʿUlūm), printed along with Ghazzālī's *al-Mastaṣfā* (2 vols., Būlāḳ 1322—1324), ii. 230—234; Ibn Taimīya, *Madjmūʿat al-rasāʾil wa 'l-masāʾil* (5 vols., Cairo 1341—1349), v. 22 *sq.*; Shāṭibī, al-*Muwāfaḳāt* (4 vols., Cairo 1341), iv. 116—118; al-Shaikh Muḥammad al-Khiḍrī Bey, *Uṣūl al-fiḳh* (2nd ed., Cairo 1352/1933), p. 413—416; ʿAbd al-Raḥīm, *I Principi della Giurisprudenza Musulmana*, transl. Guido Cimino (Rome 1922), p. 181—184; D. Santillana, *Istituzioni di Ditítto Musulmano Malichita*, i., Rome 1926, p. 56 *sq.* — II. On Istiṣlāḥ: Ghazzālī, *op. cit.*, i. 284—315; Baiḍāwī-Isnawī, *op. cit.*, iii. 134—139; Subkī-Maḥallī-Bannānī, *op. cit.*, ii. 229—234; Maḥbūbī-Taftāzānī-Fanarī, *op. cit.*, ii. 374 *sqq.*, esp. p. 391—396; Ibn al-Humām-Ibn Amīr al-Ḥādjdj, *op. cit.*, iii. 141—167, esp. 150 *sqq.*; Bihārī-Baḥr al-ʿUlūm, *op. cit.*, ii. 260 *sqq.*, esp. p. 266 *sq.* and 301; Ibn Taimīya, *op. cit.*, v. 22 *sqq.*; Shāṭibī, *op. cit.*, iv. 110 *sqq.*, esp. p. 116—118; Ḳarāfī, *Sharḥ Tanḳīḥ al-fuṣūl*, Cairo 1306, p. 170 *sq.*; Nadjm al-Dīn al-Ṭawfī, *Risāla fi 'l-maṣāliḥ al-mursala* (*Madjmūʿ rasāʾil fī uṣūl al-fiḳh*, Bairūt 1324, p. 37—70); the same work publ. in Rashīd Riḍā's periodical *al-Manār*, vol. x., p. 745—770 (according to *Tafsīr al-Manār*, v., Cairo 1328, p. 212); Muḥammad al-Khiḍrī, *op. cit.*, p. 381—392; ʿAbdu 'r-Raḥīm, *op. cit.*, p. 175, 184; Santillana, *op. cit.*, p. 55 *sq.*

ISTIKHĀRA (A.), the prayer (*duʿāʾ*) of a man who has not yet made up his mind, in order to be inspired with a salutary decision regarding an intended enterprise, a journey, etc. This term is connected with the first conjugation of the verb *khāra*; especially in its use in phrases like *Allāhumma khir li-rasūlika* (Ṭabarī, i. 1832, $_{6}$); *khir lahu* (Ibn Saʿd, II/ii., 73, $_{11}$, 75, $_{2}$); *khāra 'llāhu lī* (*ibid.*, viii. 92, $_{25}$). The proverb *istakhir allāha fi 'l-samāʾi yakhir laka biʿilmihi fi 'l-ḳaḍāʾi* (Ibn Saʿd, viii. 171, $_{18}$; Ḳālī, *Amālī*, ii. 106 *paen.*) is even given from the pre-Islāmic period, but it is hardly to be believed that such an aphorism could date from that time. In Islām the formality of the religious istikhāra consists of a form or prayer of some length, traced back to the Prophet in Bukhārī, *Tawḥīd*, b. 10, *Daʿawāt*, b. 48 (ed. Krehl-Juynboll, iv. 202, 450), Ibn Mādja (Dihlī 1282, p. 99 *infra*) — the authenticity of which however is doubted even by Muslim critics, in Ibn Ḥadjar al-Haitamī, *Fatāwī ḥadīthīya*, Cairo 1307, p. 210 —, whereas Tirmidhī (Būlāḳ 1397), ii. 266, gives only the brief formula: *Allāhumma khir lī wa'khtir lī* (cf. Dhahabī, *Mīzān al-iʿtidāl*, ed. Lucknow 1884, i. 315, $_{4}$) only as a *ḥadīth* of doubtful authenticity. It is introduced by two *rakʿa*'s (*ṣallā rakʿatai al-istikhāra*: Subkī, *Ṭabaḳāt al-Shāfiʿīya*, vi. 175, $_{6}$ *infra*). Directions are also given regarding the verses of the Ḳurʾān to be recited within the two *rakʿa*'s (Nawawī, *Adhkār*, p. 56). In ʿAwfī, *Lubb al-albāb* (ed. Browne), i. 210, $_{12}$, people go to the mosque to perform the *namāz-i istikhāra*; but this is not obligatory. It is the rule that the istikhāra appeal should be made from case to case before a definite purpose, and not in a summary fashion (e.g. in the morning for all cases which may crop up in the course of the day) ʿ(Abdarī, *Madkhal*, iii. 240 *infra*).

In keeping with the above mentioned traditional saying, Muslim practice shows the istikhāra in use from the earliest times. The oldest example, propably quite independent of that *ḥadīth*, seems to be *Aghānī*, xix. 92, $_{3}$ *sqq.* The poet ʿAdjdjādj (*Dīwān*, No. 12, $_{83}$; *Arādjīz al-ʿarab*, p. 120) praises Ḥadjdjādj, because he undertakes nothing without securing God's approval (*illā rabbahu istakhāra*). And when ʿAbd Allāh b. Ṭāhir enters on his office of prefect of the ʿIrāḳ, his father impresses upon him repeatedly in a letter of advice he sends him, to observe the istikhāra in all official business (Ṭaifūr, *Kitāb Baghdād*, p. 49, $_{7}$, 52, $_{3}$ *infra*, 53, $_{4}$). In this way literature gives numerous examples of the custom that the Muslim before important as well as unimportant resolutions, in private as well as public enterprises, also conquerors before their expeditions, thought to secure the divine approval by istikhāra. This habit indeed is sometimes fictitiously credited to them, as for example when Muʿāwiya is made to observe the istikhāra before designating Yazīd as his successor (*Aghānī*, xviii. 72, 6). The Caliph Sulaimān tears up the patent of succession drawn up in favour of his son Aiyūb, when he feels that the salutariness of his decision was not suggested to him by istikhāra (Ibn Saʿd, v. 247, 6). Ma'mūn observes istikhāra for a month before appointing ʿAbd Allāh b. Ṭāhir (Ṭaifūr, *op. cit.*, p. 34, 6). Cf. the loud istikhāra prayer of al-Muḳtadir on his accession (with four *rakʿa*'s!, ʿArīb, ed. de Goeje, p. 22, 14). In the 1001 *Nights* in the tale of Uns al-Wudjūd and Ward fī 'l-Akmām the latter's mother performs a "*ṣalāt al-istikhāra* of two *rakʿa*'s" in order to obtain an effectual indication in regard to her daughter's love affair (373th Night, Būlāķ 1279, ii. 269). The choice of a baby's name seems occasionally to be made after an istikhāra by the namer (Snouck Hurgronje, *Mekka*, ii. 139, 1). There is no lack of examples to show that in deciding thorny theological questions the learned arguments were strengthened by istikhāra (e.g. Nawawī, *Tahdhīb*, ed. Wüstenfeld, p. 237, 3 *infra*). Authors in the introductions to their books very frequently mention istikhāra as the motive or excuse for the publication (cf. Dhahabī, *Tadhkirat al-ḥuffāẓ*, ii. 288, 1). A story, of course quite unhistorical, makes ʿUmar II only allow the publication of a work of Ahran b. Aʿyun which he had in his library, after he had exposed it for 40 days with an istikhāra at his place of prayer (Ibn Abī Uṣaibiʿa, i. 163 *infra*).

The form of the istikhāra laid down by religious usage (*istikhāra sharʿīya*) is usually in actual practice accompanied by all kinds of forms not sanctioned in the *ḥadīth*, for example the expectation of receiving the divine inspiration in a dream (ἐγκοίμησις) after a prayer (Snouck Hurgronje, *Mekka*, ii. 16, note 3; Doutté, *Magie et religion dans l'Afrique du Nord*, p. 413) or strengthening the istikhāra formula by an oracular casting of lots, in which the alternatives are written on cards (Ṭabarsī, *Makārim al-akhlāķ*, Cairo 1303, p. 100). Such additions are strongly condemned by fervid Sunnī orthodoxy (ʿAbdarī, *op. cit.*, iii. 91 *sqq.*). There is also the istikhāra by opening the Ķur'ān (*al-ḍarb ... fi 'l-maṣḥaf ... wa-taķdīm istikhārat*[in], in Ibn Bashkuwāl, p. 243 ult., cf. *Faradj baʿd al-shidda*, i. 44; an anecdote on the subject is given by Ķazwīnī, ed. Wüstenfeld, ii. 113, 18 *sqq.*); other works (see Suyūṭī, *Bughyat al-wuʿāt*, p. 10, 17), as in the case of the *Sortes Virgilianae*, are employed for the purpose by the Persians, especially the *Dīwān* of Ḥāfiẓ, or the *Mathnawī* of Djalāl al-Dīn Rūmī (cf. *Bankipore Catalogue*, i., No. 151). This use of the Ķur'ān is likewise rigorously forbidden by most Sunnī authorities (cf. Damīrī, s.v. *ṭair*, ii. 119, 8 *sqq.*, ed. Būlāķ 1284; Murtaḍā, *Itḥāf al-sāda al-muttaķīn*, Cairo 1311, ii. 285 *infra*); this custom in connection with the istikhāra has led among the people to an excessive use of *fa'l* magic with the Ķur'ān of which a full account is given in Lane, *Manners and Customs* [5], chap. xi., i. 328. — There is a proverb *mā khāba man istakhāra wa-lā nadima man istashāra* (as *ḥadīth* in Ṭabarānī, *Muʿdjam ṣaghīr*, Dihlī, p. 204 *infra*). Abū ʿAbd Allāh al-Zubairī in the beginning of the ivth (xth) century wrote a *Kitāb al-istishāra wa 'l-istikhāra* (Nawawī, *Tahdhīb*, p. 744, 3).

Bibliography: The above mentioned *ḥadīth* passages; Ghazzālī, *Iḥyā' ʿulūm al-dīn* (Būlāķ 1289), i. 197; Murtaḍā, *Itḥāf*, iii. 467—469, and the pertinent sections of the *fiķh* books. — Cf. *JA*, 1861, i. 201, note 2; 1866, i. 447; Phillott, *Bibliomancy, Divination, Superstitions among the Persians*, in *JASB*, 1906, ii. 399 *sqq.*; *Bulletin de la Société de Géographie d'Oran* (1908), xxviii. Number 1.

ISTINDJĀ' (A.) means a purification fully described in the *fiķh* books in the chapter on ritual purity. It is a religious duty (according to Abū Ḥanīfa, however, only a recommended action) for every Muslim who has attended to the call of nature. A Muslim is in general allowed to delay this purification until he is about to perform the *ṣalāt*, or has to be in a state of ritual purity for some other reason.

Bibliography: al-Dimashķī, *Raḥmat al-umma fi 'khtilāf al-a'imma* (Būlāķ 1300), p. 7; A. J. Wensinck, in *Isl.*, i. 101 *sq.*

ISTINSHĀĶ (A.), the inhaling of water through the nose, is considered by most faķīhs as a *sunna* (i.e. a commendable act, according to Aḥmad b. Ḥanbal, however, as a religious duty) both at the *ghusl* [q.v.] and the *wuḍū'* (i.e. the major and minor ritual purification).

Bibliography: al-Dimashķī, *Raḥmat al-umma fi 'khtilāf al-a'imma* (Būlāķ 1300), p. 8; al-Khwārizmī, *Mafātīḥ al-ʿulūm* (ed. van Vloten), p. 10, 6.

ISTIṢḤĀB (A.), i.e., the seeking for a link (i.e., to something which is known and certain). This is the name of a process of settling *fiķh* rules by argument, which was especially used in the Shāfiʿī school and with certain limitations among the Ḥanafīs also. This seeking for a link means the endeavour to link up a later set of circumstances with an earlier, and is based on the assumption that the *fiķh* rules applicable to certain conditions remain valid so long as it is not certain that these conditions have altered. If for example on account of the long absence of some one it is doubtful whether he is alive or dead, then by *istiṣḥāb* all rules must remain in force which would hold if one knew for certain that he was still alive. The Ḥanafīs only recognise *istiṣḥāb* in so far as it concerns the retention of rights already granted, the Shāfiʿīs on the other hand even when it is a question of assigning new rights. An absent man for example would not be recognised by the Ḥanafīs as legitimate heir to an inheritance falling due while he was away, but he would be according to the Shāfiʿīs, as the latter assume that even during his absence he can obtain new rights.

Bibliography: I. Goldziher, *Das Prinzip des Istiṣḥâb in der Muhammedan. Gesetzwissenschaft*, in *WZKM*, i. 128—236.

ISTISĶĀ' (A.), prayer for rain. The treatises on canon law expound in what circumstances the ḥadīth prescribes the *istisķā'* prayer as an obligatory act or leaves it to individual discretion. They also give details of the special ritual to be observed in this prayer. This ritual comprises 1. a prayer of two *rakʿa*'s performed in the morning outside the town; 2. the faithful ought to put on ordinary dress, without elaboration or luxury; 3. the prayer is followed by two *khuṭba*'s, of which the first is accompanied by a turning of the cloak (a sympathetic rite to produce a change in the weather); 4. the *duʿā'* which follows the prayer is a supplication for rain; 5. the usual *takbīr* is replaced by an invocation intended to implore God's pardon (*istighfār*). This prayer ought to be completed by a series of pious works recommended to the faithful (fasting, almsgiving). Prayers for rain by non-Muslims according to their religions. (Jewish or Christian) are admitted and even recommended in orthodox Islām.

Rites and ceremonies to obtain rain are as ancient as man himself and vary not only according to different religious beliefs, but even among the different groups of human beings belonging to the same religion, as shown by A. Bel in *Quelques rites pour obtenir la pluie en temps de sécheresse chez les musulmans maghribins*, dans *Recueil de Mémoires et de Textes publié en l'honneur du XIVe Congrès des Orientalistes, par les professeurs de l'Ecole supérieure des Lettres et des Médersas*, Alger 1905, p. 49—98. The ceremonies and rites, rather varied for the Muslim countries and all, even in the orthodox ritual, much impregnated with animism and magic, may however be grouped under several rubrics: adaptation to the cult of saints; physical and moral sufferings which the faithful impose upon themselves: formulas, songs and hymns; rites relating to a kind of divinity of rain, named *g͟handj͟a* or an analogous name in Barbary; sacrifices of victims and communal meals; sympathetic and symbolic acts.

In the article referred to, there will be found, in addition to useful bibliographical notes, references to analogous ceremonies in non-Muslim countries. There it will also be seen that for the Mag͟hrib these religious services have rather the character of agrarian festivals and that they take place at a fixed period of the year, but not in every season.

Bibliography: Cf. also Goldziher in *RHR*, lii. (1905), p. 226—9; do., in *Oriental. Studien Th. Nöldeke ... gewidmet*, i. 208—212, and in *Der Islam*, vi. 304; Narbeshuber, *Aus dem Leben der arabischen Bevölkerung in Sfax*, Leipzig 1907, p. 26—29; A. J. Wensinck, *Mohammed en de Joden te Medina*, diss. Leiden 1908, p. 140 *sqq.*; Juynboll, *Handb. des Islām. Gesetzes*, p. 93; Biarnay, *Etude sur le Dialecte des Beṭṭioua* (Alger 1911), p. 241—243; do., *Notes d'ethnographie et de linguistique nord-africaines*; Doutté, *Magie et Religion dans l'Afrique du Nord* (Alger 1909), p. 582—588; Lammens, *Le berceau de l'Islam*, i. 20 (note 3) and 106; do., *Les sanctuaires préislamites*, p. 24; Ibn al-ʿArabī, *Risāla* (in *Vidas de Santones andaluces*, transl. M. Asín Palacios, Madrid 1933, p. 56—57;) Bargès, *Vie du célebre marabout Cidi Abou Medien*, Paris 1884, p. 107—116; al-Kittānī, *Salwat al-anfās*, Fez (lith. 1316), i. 29; W. Marçais and A. Guiga, *Textes arabes de Takrouna*, i. 197 *sqq.*, note p. 205—8 and 224; Probst-Biraben, *Les rites d'obtention de la pluie dans la province de Constantine*, in *Journal des Africanistes*, ii. part. 1, p. 95—102; Joleaud, *op. cit.* iii., parts 1 and 4; M. Gaudry, *La femme chaouïa de l'Aures*, p. 263; for the *sacra* to obtain rain, sec *RHR* cviii. 1938, 144 *sqq.*; *Rev. de Folklore fr. et de folkl. colonial*, 1929, nr. 2, p. 80 *sqq.*; for the procession see *op. cit.* vi. nr. 1, p. 39; for the gods of the Phoenicians, *RHR*, 1931, ii. 367; 1932, i. 299.

ISTIṢLĀḤ. [See ISTIḤSĀN].

ITHNĀ ʿAS͟HARĪYA (Arabic *it͟hnā ʿas͟hara*, twelve), "the Twelvers", a name given in contrast to the Sabʿīya [q. v.], the partisans of the seven imāms, to those S͟hīʿīs who allow the series of twelve imāms and say that the imāmate passed from ʿAlī al-Riḍā to his son Muḥammad al-Taḳī, to the latter's son ʿAlī al-Naḳī, then to his son al-Ḥasan al-ʿAskarī al-Zakī, and finally to Muḥammad al-Mahdī, who disappeared and will come again at the end of time to announce the last judgment and to fill the earth with justice. The series of twelve imāms is made up as follows: 1. ʿAlī al-Murtaḍā; 2. al-Ḥasan al-Mud͟jtabā; 3. al-Ḥusain al-S͟hahīd; 4. ʿAlī Zain al-ʿĀbidīn al-Sad͟jd͟jād; 5. Muḥammad al-Bāḳir; 6. D͟jaʿfar al-Ṣādiḳ; 7. Mūsā al-Kāẓim; 8. ʿAlī al-Riḍā; 9. Muḥammad al-Taḳī; 10. ʿAlī al-Naḳī; 11. al-Ḥasan al-ʿAskarī al-Zakī; 12. Muḥammad al-Mahdī al-Ḥud͟jd͟ja.

Such has been the succession which has been definitely admitted since the vth (xi[th]) century; but this sect has not always been in agreement with itself, and at one time numbered no less than eleven parties, without special names but distinguished from one another as follows: 1. al-Ḥasan al-ʿAskarī is not dead, he is only absent; 2. al-Ḥasan died without children, but he will return from the dead; 3. al-Ḥasan nominated his brother D͟jaʿfar by will; 4. the latter died without leaving heirs; 5. Muḥammad son of ʿAlī is the imām; 6. al-Ḥasan had a son, two years before his death, who was called Muḥammad; 7. there was indeed a son, but he was born eight months after his father's death; 8. al-Ḥasan died without children and the world is without an imām on account of the sins of men; 9. al-Ḥasan had a son, but he is not known; 10. an imām is necessary, but it is not known if he is descended from al-Ḥasan or not; 11. a stop is made at ʿAlī al-Riḍā and the coming of the last imām is awaited, whence the name Wāḳifīya given to this party, i.e. those who suspend their judgment regarding the imām's death.

The It͟hnā ʿas͟harīya were at first called Ḳaṭʿīya (Ḳiṭṭiʿīya), because, unlike the Wāḳifīya, they admitted the reality of the imām's death or, according to others, because they interrupted the line of the imāms at Mūsā al-Kāẓim, son of D͟jaʿfar, in order to keep it exclusively in the line of his descendants. Others admitted after Mūsā the imāmate of his son Aḥmad, excluding ʿAlī al-Riḍā; it is also said that Muḥammad, the latter's son, being very young at the time of his father's death, had not been able to receive from him the training for the imāmate; others admitted his quality of imām, but asked which of his sons Mūsā or ʿAlī should succeed him. After ʿAlī the same question arose between D͟jaʿfar and al-Ḥasan. Those who admitted the imāmate of al-Ḥasan al-ʿAskarī were called by objectors al-Ḥimārīya because they described the chosen imām as an ignoramus. After the death of al-Ḥasan, some adopted D͟jaʿfar, the pretended son of a concubine, al-Ḥasan according to them not having left any children.

The Ṣafawids, who claimed descent from Mūsā al-Kāẓim, made the S͟hīʿa and more particularly the doctrine of the It͟hnā ʿas͟harīya the state religion of Persia, as it still is. After his accession S͟hāh Ismāʿīl (906/1500) gave formal orders to the preachers of Ād͟harbāid͟jān to preach the sermon in the name of the twelve imāms, and to the muʾad͟hd͟hins to add the S͟hīʿa formula: "I testify that ʿAlī is the *walī* of God". The troops were ordered to put to death any objector.

The cult of the twelve imāms has attained an extraordinary importance among the Persians; hypostases of the Divinity, they direct the destinies of the world, and preserve it and guide it. With them all is salvation; without them all is perdition (Gobineau, *Religions et philosophies*, p. 60). Their ministry, their intercession (*tawassul*) are indispensable. Prayers with special formula are reserved for them; Sunday is sacred to ʿAlī and Fāṭima; the second hour of each day to al-Ḥasan, the third to al-Ḥusain, the fourth to Zain al-ʿĀbidīn and so on. Pilgrimage to their tombs (*ziyāra*) procures special rewards (Muḥammad Riḍā, *D͟jannā al-k͟hulūd*, passim).

Bibliography: al-Baghdādī, *al-Farḳ*, p. 47; Ibn Ḥazm, *al-Faṣl*, cf. I. Friedlaender, *The Heterodoxies of the Shiites*, Index; al-Shahrastānī, p. 17, 128 *sqq.* (transl. Haarbrücker, p. 25, 193 *sqq.*); Abu 'l-Maʿālī, *Bayān al-adyān*, ed. ʿAbbās Eghbāl, Teheran 1312; al-Diyārbakrī, *al-Khamīs*, ii. 286—8; Muṭahhar b. Ṭāhir al-Maḳdisī (pseudo-Balkhī), *Kitāb al-badʾ*, ed. and transl. Cl. Huart, v. (1916), p. 132 *sqq.*; Ibn Bābūye al-Ḳummī, *Kitāb kamāl al-dīn* etc., partly ed. by Möller (*Beitr. z. Mahdilehre des Islams*, Heidelberg 1901); al-Ḥillī, *al-Bāb al-Ḥādī-ʿashar*, transl. W. M. Miller (London 1928); Goldziher, *Vorlesungen*, Index, s.v. "Zwölfer"; D. M. Donaldson, *The Shiʾite Religion*, London 1933; R. Strothmann, *Die Zwölfer Schiʿa*, 1916.

IʿTIḲĀD is belief that a thing is so. It may be only in the sense of the English "thinking", the German "Glauben", or it may be a feeling perfectly assured, and so the word is used especially of belief in religious dogmas (Lane; Dozy, *Supplément*). It is then exactly equivalent to *taṣdīḳ*, firm acceptance in the mind of a thing as true, and is distinguished from *īmān*, "faith" in that some held *īmān* to cover works (*ʿamal*) and confession (*iḳrār*). Al-Taftāzānī, in his commentary on the *ʿAḳāʾid* of al-Nasafī (ed. Cairo 1321, p. 7) explains that some of the revealed prescripts (*aḥkām sharʿīya*) connect with manner of action and are called *farʿīya*, "derivative", and *ʿamalīya*, while others connect with belief (*al-iʿtiḳād*) and are called *aṣlīya* "basal" and *iʿtiḳādīya* (cf. al-Bādjūrī, *Ḥāshiya ʿalā sharḥ Ibn Ḳāsim*, Cairo 1321, i. 20; *Ḥāshiya ʿalā matn al-Sanūsīya*, Cairo 1283, p. 11 *sq.*; Luciani, *Les prolégomènes théol. de Senoussi*, p. 4 *sqq.*;. *Dict. of Techn. Terms*, s.v. *ḥukm*). In consequence *al-iʿtiḳādāt* is used much in the sense of *al-ʿaḳāʾid*, the doctrines of the faith. The exact scholastic definition of the word evidently gave difficulty. In the *Dict. of Techn. Terms* (p. 954) two uses are distinguished: one generally known, "firm belief", and a rare, "conviction, certainty". The first is a mental judgment, absolute (*djāzim*), but susceptible of doubt (*yaḳbal al-tashkīk*); the second is a mental judgment, absolute or preponderant (*rādjiḥ*) and includes *ʿilm*, "knowledge", which is a mental judgment incompatible with doubt or belief or opinion (*ẓann*). The second is sometimes called "certain knowledge" (*al-ʿilm al-yaḳīn*) and excludes "compound ignorance" (*al-djahl al-murakkab*), the ignorance that does not know that it is ignorance. Others distinguished the first iʿtiḳād into two; that which corresponds to fact and that which does not. [See also ĪMĀN].

IʿTIKĀF (A.), is the name of a religious custom of which the main feature is that the believer retires for a time from the world in a mosque. The iʿtikāf is always considered meritorious (*sunna*) and is numbered among those good works which are recommended in the law-books to be performed during the last ten days of Ramaḍān, in order to participate in the blessings of the holy *ḳadar* night. According to the Muslim tradition, the Prophet also used to spend the last third of the month in the mosque in Madīna. On the *lailat al-ḳadar* (Night of the Divine Decree) see Sūra xliv. 3; xcvii. 1—5; cf. ii. 185. The question what night is to be considered the *ḳadar* night is not settled. According to the view of most Muslim scholars, it must be assumed that one of the last nights of the month of fasting (especially one of the five odd nights, i. e. 21, 23, 25, 27 or 29 Ramaḍān) is meant. According to others — and this was Abū Ḥanīfa's view —, there are no indications that the *ḳadar* night belonged to this period of the year. [See also RAMAḌĀN].

Bibliography: The chapter on the month of fasting and the iʿtikāf in the collections of Traditions and the *fiḳh* books; al-Dimashḳī, *Raḥmat al-umma fī 'khtilāf al-aʾimma* (Būlāḳ 1300), p. 50; Th. W. Juynboll, *Handbuch des islām. Gesetzes*, p. 125; A. J. Wensinck, *Arabic New-year*, in *Verhand. d. Kon. Akad. v. Wetensch. te Amsterdam*, Afd. Letterk., Nieuwe Reeks, xxv (1925), N⁰. 2.

ʿITḲ [See ʿABD; UMM AL-WALAD].

ITTIḤĀD (A.), becoming one. Muslim scholastics distinguish two kinds of ittiḥād: 1) 'real' (*ḥaḳīḳī*); 2) 'metaphorical' (*madjāzī*). The former class has two subdivisions, according as the term is applied *a*) to two things which become one, *e. g.*, ʿAmr becomes Zaid, or Zaid becomes ʿAmr; *b*) to one thing which becomes another thing that was not existent before, *e. g.*, Zaid becomes some individual who did not previously exist. Ittiḥād in this 'real' sense is necessarily impossible; hence the saying: *al-ithnān lā yattaḥidān*. The 'metaphorical' class has three subdivisions, according as the term denotes *a*) one thing's becoming another thing by instantaneous or gradual transformation, *e. g.*, water becomes air (in which case the real nature of water is destroyed by the removal of its specific form from its substance, and to this substance the specific form of air is added), or black becomes white (in which case one attribute of an object disappears and is replaced by another attribute); *b*) one thing's becoming another thing by means of composition, so that a third thing results, *e. g.*, earth becomes clay by the addition of water; *c*) the appearance of one person in the form of another, *e. g.*, of an angel in the form of a human being. All these three species of 'metaphorical' ittiḥād actually occur. In the technical language of the Ṣūfīs, the name ittiḥād is given to the mystical union by which the creature is made one with the Creator, or to the theory that such a union is possible. This conception of the unitive state, like the parallel doctrine of *ḥulūl*, i. e. the doctrine that the Creator becomes incarnate in the creature, is generally regarded by the Ṣūfīs as heretical, on the ground that it involves homogeneity and is therefore inconsistent with the true notion of divine unity (*tawḥīd*), which admits no real existence except that of God. Ittiḥād, thus understood, presupposes the existence of two beings which are made one, whereas, according to the more orthodox mystics, human individuality is only a phenomenon that passes away in the One Eternal Reality (*fanāʾ fi 'l-ḥaḳḳ*). Sometimes the term ittiḥād is employed like the Ṣūfistic *waḥdat* or *tawḥīd*, in reference to the doctrine that all things are non-existent in themselves, but derive their existence from God and, in this respect, are one with God (ʿAbd al-Razzāḳ al-Kāshānī, *al-Iṣṭilāḥāt al-ṣūfīya*, ed. Sprenger, p. 5). According to ʿAlī b. Wafā (quoted by Shaʿrānī in *al-Yawāḳīt wa 'l-djawāhir*, Būlāḳ 1277, p. 80, l. 18 *sqq.*), the meaning of ittiḥād in the terminology of the Ṣūfīs is "the passing away of that which is willed by the creature in that which is willed by God".

Bibliography: *Dictionary of the Technical Terms used in the Sciences of the Mussalmans*, ed. Sprenger, p. 1468; Djurdjānī, *Taʿrīfāt*, ed. Fluegel, p. 6; Hudjwīrī. *Kashf al-maḥ djūb*, translated by Nicholson, p. 254; Maḥmūd Shabistarī, *Gulshan-i rāz*, ed. by Whinfield, p. 452—455; Tholuck, *Ssufismus*, p. 141 *sqq.*; Macdonald, *The religious Attitude and Life in Islam*, p. 258.

ʿIZRĀʾĪL (in European literature one also finds ʿAzrāʾīl), the name of the angel of death, one of the four archangels (next to Djibrīl, Mīkhāʾīl, Isrāfīl). The name is perhaps a corruption of עסריאל, which is given by Eisenmenger, *Entdecktes Judenthum*, ii. 333, as the name of the prince of Hell. Like Isrāfīl, whose office of trumpet-blower at the last judgment is sometimes given to him, he is of cosmic magnitude; if the water of all the seas and rivers were poured on his head, not a drop would reach the earth. He has a seat (*sarīr*) of light in the fourth or seventh heaven, on which one of his feet rests; the other stands on the bridge between paradise and hell. He is however also said to have 70,000 feet.

The description of his appearance agrees almost exactly with that in Jewish literature: he has 4,000 wings and his whole body consists of eyes and tongues, the number of which corresponds with that of the living. He, however, is also said to have four faces.

At first he was an angel like others. When Allāh wanted to create man, he ordered Djibrīl to snatch from the earth for this purpose a handful of its main constituents. The earth, however, stirred up by Iblīs, offered resistance, so that neither Djibrīl, nor Mīkhāʾīl nor Isrāfīl could carry out the commission. But ʿIzrāʾīl managed to do it. On account of his hard-heartedness (*ḳillat al-raḥma*) Allāh then appointed him angel of death.

On account of his strength he is also master of death. When Allāh had created Death, he summoned the angels to look at him. When they saw his astonishing strength, they fell down unconscious and remained prostrate for a thousand years. Then they awakened and said: "Death is the most powerful of creatures". But Allāh said: "I have appointed ʿIzrāʾīl to be lord over him".

Several angels of death are mentioned, as in Jewish literature; and it is said that ʿIzrāʾīl deals with the souls of the prophets while the souls of ordinary men are under his *khalīfa*. Special stress is laid on the beginning of Sūra lxxix. as authority for a number of angels of death: "By those who tear forth and by those who draw forth" etc. The former are said to be those angels who drag the souls of the unbelievers by force from their bodies, while by the latter are meant those who have to separate the souls of the believers from their bodies. The explanation of the verse however is not certain. In Sūra xxxii. 11 mention is made of the angel of death (in the singular).

ʿIzrāʾīl keeps a roll of mankind. But he does not know the date of death of the individuals. Whether one belongs to the blessed or the damned, he sees from the fact that the names in the first category are surrounded by a bright and those in the second by a dark circle.

When the day of a man's death approaches, Allāh causes to fall from the tree below his throne the leaf on which the man's name is written. ʿIzrāʾīl reads the name and has to separate the person's soul from his body after 40 days.

But there are some people who strive against the separation, and object that the angel of death is acting arbitrarily. The latter then goes back to Allāh and tells him his experience. Allāh then gives him as a credential an apple from Paradise on which the *basmala* [q. v.] is written; when the man sees this, he yields.

Man also has other means of making it difficult for the angel of death to carry out his task. If the latter wants to creep into his throat to fetch out his spirit, the dying man recites a *dhikr* [q. v.] and thus closes the entrance. The angel then returns to Allāh, who advises him to try it with the dying man's hand. If the latter however is just making a *ṣadaḳa* [q. v.], the angel's entrance is again impossible. Finally however ʿIzrāʾīl writes the name of God on the man's hand. Then the bitter feeling of separation disappears and the angel can enter to fetch the spirit. — On the other hand, it is also said that he pierces men with a poisoned lance. Another account is as follows: When a believer is on his death-bed, the angel of death stands at his head and draws his soul out as gently as water runs out of a skin. He hands it to his assistants who carry it through the seven heavens up to the highest and then place it with the body in the grave (the soul's journey to heaven; cf. Bousset, in *AR*, iv.).

But if an unbeliever dies, the angel of death tears the soul out of his body in the roughest fashion. The gate of heaven closes before the soul, as it is carried up, and it is thrown down to earth again.

Idrīs, Ilyās, ʿĪsā and al-Khaḍir [q. v.], as is well known, were not subject to death. As regards Moses the same thing could not be asserted; but the Bible throws a veil over his death. Muslim tradition accordingly says that Moses defended himself against the angel of death, who came with the fatal message to him, and bruised his eye. Allāh said to the angel when he came back: "If he places his hand on a cow, as many years are to be granted him as his hand covers hairs". "And then?", asked Moses. "Death", said Allāh. — It is also related that the angel of death came to Moses with an apple from Paradise; when he had smelled this, he died.

On an experience of Solomon's with the angel of death, see al-Baiḍāwī on Sūra xxxi. 34; on his visit of Idrīs, see that article.

Bibliography: The commentaries on Sūra ii. 30; xxxii. 11 and lxxix. 1; M. Wolff, *Muhammedanische Eschatologie*, p. 11 *sqq.*; al-Ghazzālī, *al-Durra al-fākhira*, ed. L. Gautier, p. 7 *sqq.*; al-Kisāʾī, *ʿAdjāʾib al-malakūt*, Leiden MS. 538 Warn., f. 26 *sq.*; al-Ṭabarī, i. 87; al-Masʿūdī, i. 51; Ibn al-Athīr, i. 20; al- Diyārbakrī, *Taʾrīkh al-khamīs* (Cairo 1283), i. 36; al-Thaʿlabī, *Ḳiṣaṣ al-anbiyāʾ* (Cairo 1290), p. 23, 216 *sq.*; Mudjīr al-Dīn al-Ḥanbalī, *Kitāb al-uns al-djalīl* (Cairo 1283), i. 16 *sq.*; al-Bukhārī, *Djanāʾiz*, bāb 69; (Muṭahhar b. Ṭāhir al-Maḳdisī), *Kitāb al-badʾ waʾ l-taʾrīkh*, ed. Huart, i. 175, ii. 214; al-Khaṭīb al-Tibrīzī. *Mishkāt al-maṣābīḥ*, transl. by A. N. Matthews, i. 365 *sqq.*; Bodenschatz, *Kirchliche Verfassung der heutigen Juden* (Erlangen 1748), iii. 93; Eisenmenger, *Entdecktes Judenthum* (Königsberg 1711), i., chap. xix, ii. 333.

J

JACOB. [See Isrāʾīl, Yaʿḳūb].
JAPHET. [See Yāfīth].
JEREMIAH. [See Irmiyāʾ].
JERUSALEM. [See al-Ḳuds].
JESUS. [See ʿĪsā, Masīḥ].

JETHRO. [See Shuʿaib].
JOB. [See Aiyūb].
JONAH. [See Yūnus].
JOSEPH. [See Yūsuf].
JOSHUA. [See Yūshaʿ].

K

KAʿB b. MĀLIK, ʿAbū Allāh, a native of Madīna of the Khazradjī tribe of Salima. After taking an active part in the sanguinary tribal battles in Madīna, he was won over to Islām even before the Hidjra and took part in the momentous second meeting at the ʿAḳaba. He was a poet and along with Ḥassān b. Thābit and ʿAbd Allāh b. Rawāḥa was employed by Muḥammad to glorify his military exploits and answer the polemical poems of the enemies. He did not fight at Badr but was in most of the other battles. At Uḥud, wounded himself, he found the wounded Prophet, who was thought to be slain. On the other hand, he was one of the few followers of Muḥammad who, in spite of their devotion to him, could not bring themselves to take part in the difficult campaign against Tabūk. But he later regretted it and after severe penance received the forgiveness of the Prophet (cf. Sūra ix. 102, 106, 117 *sq.*). It is noteworthy that he, who was fond of emphasising the connection of his tribe with the Ghassānids, was at that time summoned by a Ghassānī chief to abandon Madīna and Muḥammad. In the caliphate of ʿUthmān we again hear of him when he with Ḥassān and Zaid b. Thābit vigorously championed the Caliph, when he was assailed; after ʿUthmān's death he wrote an elegy on him and declined to pay homage to ʿAlī. He died blind in 53/673; according to others, as early as 50 A. H. His poems have a somewhat nobler tone than those of Ḥassān and show a real enthusiasm for the religion of Muḥammad besides a strong local patriotism.

Bibliography: Ibn Hishām, p. 294—301, 310, 574, 896, 907—13 (the poems, p. 520—871 *passim*; cf. al-Mubarrad, *al-Kāmil*, p. 66, and on the other side Ibn Ḳutaiba, *Kitāb al-shiʿr*, ed. de Goeje, p. 180); al-Ṭabarī, i. 1217—1225, 1406, 1695, 1705, 2937, 3049, 3062, 3070; al-Wāḳidī, transl. by Wellhausen, p. 113, 123, 136, 169, 326, 393, 411—4; *al-Aghānī*, xv. 26—32; al-Nawawī, p. 23 *sq.*; *BGA*, vii. 224; F. Buhl, *Das Leben Muhammeds*, p. 187, 326.

KAʿBA, the palladium of Islām, situated almost in the centre of the great mosque in Mecca.

I. The Kaʿba and its immediate neighbourhood

The name, not originally a proper name, is connected with the cube-like appearance of the building. The wall facing northeast, in which the door is (the front of the Kaʿba) and the opposite wall (back) are 40 feet long; the two other are about 35 feet long. The height is 50 feet.

The Kaʿba is built of layers of the grey stone produced by the hills surrounding Mecca. It stands on a marble base 10 inches high, projecting about a foot (*shādharwān*). Four lines drawn from the centre through the four corners (*rukn*, pl. *arkān*) would roughly indicate the four points of the compass. The north corner is called *al-rukn al-ʿirāḳī*, the western *al-rukn al-shaʾmī*, the southern *al-rukn al-yamānī*, and the eastern *al-rukn al-aswad* (after the Black Stone).

The four walls of the Kaʿba are covered with a black curtain (*kiswa*) which reaches to the ground and is fastened there with copper rings, which are fixed in the *shādharwān*. Gaps are left only for the water-spout and the door. The *kiswa* is prepared in Egypt every year and brought to Mecca by the pilgrim caravan. The old covering is taken down on the 25th (or according to al-Batanūnī, the 28th) Dhu 'l-Ḳaʿda, and the Kaʿba temporarily covered with a white covering which hangs down to within 6 feet of the ground; the Kaʿba is then said to have put on the *iḥrām* [q. v.]. At the end of the Ḥadjdj it is covered with the new cloth. The door is covered by a separate covering also of Egyptian manufacture, which in Egypt is called *al-burḳuʿ* (the veil).

The *kiswa* consists of black brocade, into which the *shahāda* is woven (see Snouck Hurgronje, *Bilderatlas zu Mekka*, N⁰. xvii). At two-thirds of its height a gold embroidered band (*ḥizām*) runs round, which is covered with verses from the Ḳurʾān in fine calligraphy. Every inch of the garment, which is taken down each year, is of course regarded as a relic and small pieces are sold by the Banū Shaiba, the door-keepers of the Kaʿba, as amulets.

In the north-east wall, about 7 feet from the

ground, is the door, parts of which have mountings of silver-gilt. In Burckhardt's and Ali Bey's times the threshold was lit up every night by a row of candles. When the Kaʿba is opened, a wooden staircase (*daradj̲*, *madradj̲*) running on wheels is pushed up to the door; when not in use, it is kept between the Zamzam building and the Gate of the Banū S̲h̲aiba (see Snouck Hurgronje, *Bilderatlas zu Mekka*, Nº. ii.). For a picture of the staircase, see Ali Bey, *Travels*, ii. 80.

In the interior of the Kaʿba are three wooden pillars, which support the roof, to which a ladder leads up. The only furnishing is the numerous golden and silver lamps suspended. On the inner walls there are many building inscriptions. The floor is covered with slabs of marble.

In the eastern corner, about 5 feet above ground, not far from the door, the Black Stone (*al-ḥadj̲ar al-aswad*) is built into the wall; it now consists of three large pieces and several small fragments stuck together and surrounded by a ring of stone, which in turn is held together by a silver band. The stone is sometimes described as lava and sometimes as basalt; its real nature is difficult to determine, because its visible surface is worn smooth by hand touching and kissing. Ali Bey (ii. 76) gives a profile sketch of it which clearly shows the surface hollowed out in undulations. Its diameter is estimated by al-Batanūnī (p. 105) at 12 inches. The colour is reddish black with red and yellow particles.

The part of the wall between the Black Stone and the door is called *al-multazam*, because the visitors press their breasts against it while praying fervently.

In the west corner too, about five feet above the ground, another stone (*al-ḥadj̲ar al-asʿad*), the "lucky", is built into the wall. It is only touched and not kissed during the perambulation.

Outside the buildings there is still to be mentioned the gilt water-spout (*mīzāb*), which juts out below the top of the north-west wall, and has an appendage which is called the "beard of the *mīzāb*". The spout is called *mīzāb al-raḥma*, "spout of mercy" (on it cf. Ben Chérif, *Aux Villes Saintes de l'Islam*, p. 75); the part between it and the west corner is the exact *ḳibla* [q. v.]. The rain water falls through the spout on the pavement below which here is inlaid with designs in mosaic. The ground all round the Kaʿba is covered with marble slabs.

Opposite the north-west wall, but not connected with it, is a semi-circular wall (*al-ḥaṭīm*) of white marble. It is three feet high and about five feet thick; its ends are almost six feet from the north and west corners of the Kaʿba. The semi-circular space between the *ḥaṭīm* and the Kaʿba enjoys an especial consideration, because for a time it belonged to the Kaʿba [see ii.]; in the perambulation therefore it is not entered; the *ṭawāf* goes as close as possible along the outer side of the *ḥaṭīm*. The space bears the name *al-ḥidj̲r* or *ḥidj̲r Ismāʿīl*. Here are said to be the graves of the patriarch and his mother Hagar. The pavement on which the *ṭawāf* is performed is called *maṭāf*; a depression in it just opposite the door has still to be mentioned; it is called *al-miʿdj̲an* "the trough"; according to legend, Ibrāhīm and Ismāʿīl [q. v.] here mixed the morter used in building the Kaʿba.

Around the *maṭāf*, and a little higher than it, runs a paved border, a few paces broad, on which stand 31 or 32 slender pillars. Between every two pillars hang seven lamps, which are lit every evening — to make the darkness visible, as Burton says. Nowadays the sanctuary is lighted by electric

power. The row of columns is closed by the Bāb Banī S̲h̲aiba, an arch which stands opposite the north-west wall of the Kaʿba and affords an entrance to the *maṭāf*. Between this archway and the Kaʿba is a little building, a kind of pagoda, with a small dome, the *maḳām Ibrāhīm*. In it is kept a stone, on which Ibrāhīm is said to have stood at the building of the Kaʿba. Admission is granted to visitors on payment; Europeans have however not been able to see the stone. Burton says that the five dollars asked was too high for his finances. According to Oriental travellers and historians, it is a soft stone on which the footprints of Ibrāhīm can still be seen. During al-Mahdī's caliphate it was provided with a gilt band holding it together. Beside the *maḳām Ibrāhīm*, also opposite the north-east wall of the Kaʿba and within the row of pillars, but farther north of the Maḳām, is the pulpit (*minbar*) of white marble. It consists of the usual staircase, shut at the foot by a door, and above the staircase are four short pillars supporting a spire like that of a Gothic church tower.

The pavement on which the row of pillars stands is somewhat lower than that which runs round them, to which eight paved paths from the colonnades round the mosque give access. On this outer paved part are four small buildings. Close beside the Bāb Banī S̲h̲aiba, on the left of the entrance and just opposite the Black Stone, stands the *ḳubba* built over the Zamzam well. In the room on the ground floor is the well, which is walled in; its water is drawn up in buckets, fastened to a pulley. On one part of the flat roof is a small chapel partly open, which has a roof with a small dome.

In d'Ohsson's as well as in Ali Bey's plan of the sacred mosque we find two further buildings north-east of the Zamzam building, at the edge of the outer paving, which are called *al-ḳubba-tain*, "the two Ḳubba's", by him, Burckhardt and Burton. They are not marked in Snouck Hurgronje's pictures because they were demolished in the eighties and removed entirely. One held various objects, such as chronometers, jars for Zamzam water; the other, books.

The three other small buildings on the outer pavement are the so-called *maḳām*'s, the standing-places of the imāms of the various ritual schools during the *ṣalāt*. The *maḳām* or *muṣalla 'l-Ḥanbalī* stands south of the Zamzam building, opposite the south-east wall of the Kaʿba. It consists of a roof tapering to a point and supported by slender marble culumns. The *maḳām al-Mālikī* is of the same form and is opposite the south-west wall of the Kaʿba. The *maḳām al-Ḥanafī* looks out on the *ḥaṭīm* and the north-west wall of the Kaʿba; it has two roofs, one above the other. — The S̲h̲āfiʿīs have no *maḳām* of their own; during the *ṣalāt* they stand under the *ḳubba* on the roof of the Zamzam well or at the Maḳām Ibrāhīm. — The Wahhābī regime, however, has abolished the existence of the *madhhab*'s within the precinct of the sacred mosque.

Finally we may mention receptacles placed here and there beside the pavements, in which various articles are kept (see Snouck Hurgronje, *Bilderatlas*, Nº. 1., ii.; *Bilder aus Mekka*, Nº. 1., iii.).

II. History

The Arabs possess no historical or semi-historical records of the origin of the Kaʿba, and we as little. According to Snouck Hurgronje's supposition, the Zamzam spring in a waterless valley may have been the cause of the rise of a sacred place. It is to be noted that Ptolemy (*Geography*, vi. 7) in place of Mecca mentions Macoraba, which is probably to be interpreted, as does Glaser (*Skizze der Gesch. u. Geogr. Arabiens*, Berlin 1890, ii. 235), as the South Arabian or Ethiopic *mikrāb*, "temple". From this one may conclude that the Kaʿba already existed in the second century A. D. The accounts of Abraha's campaign, which has been elaborated with legendary features, also suggest the existence and worship of the Kaʿba in the sixth century but tell us nothing of its appearance or equipment. The Tubbaʿ Asʿad Abū Karib al-Ḥimyarī, who came to Mecca, is said to have for the first time provided the building with a *kiswa* and with a door with a lock. The information available regarding the distribution of the offices [see below iii.] among the sons of Ḳuṣaiy shows that the worship of the sanctuary had developed into a carefully regulated cult several generations before Muḥammad.

The historical references begin only with Muḥammad. When Muḥammad had reached man's estate, the fire of a woman incensing the Kaʿba is said to have caught the building and laid it waste. It happened that a Byzantine ship was thrown ashore at Dji̱dda and the Meccans brought its wood hither and used it for the new building. The old Kaʿba is said to have only been of the height of a man and to have had no roof. The threshold is said to have been on the level of the ground so that the water had an easy entrance in the frequent floods (*sail*). The Kaʿba was then built of alternate layers of stone and wood, its height was doubled and a roof covered it. The door was placed above the level of the ground so that whoever wished to enter had to use a ladder. Unwelcome visitors were tumbled down from the high threshold. When the Black Stone was to be put in its place, the Meccans quarrelled among themselves as to who should have the honour. They had just decided that the first comer should be given the task, when Muḥammad (who had been engaged in helping to carry the stones) came past. With superior wisdom he is said to have placed the precious object in a cloth — or in his cloak — and to have ordered the heads of tribes each to take an end. He himself then took out the stone and placed it in position.

At the conquest of Mecca in 8 A. H. [see iii. below], Muḥammad left the Kaʿba as a building unaltered. But according to tradition, he later said that only the very recent conversion of the Meccans prevented him from instituting all kinds of innovations. These real or alleged intentions of Muḥammad were brought to realization in 64/683 by ʿAbd Allāh b. al-Zubair. As anti-Caliph he was besieged by al-Ḥusain b. Numair in Mecca. Catapults were erected on the hills round Mecca, which hurled a hail of stones on the town and sanctuary and so damaged the house of Allāh that it finally looked "like the torn bosoms of mourning women". ʿAbd Allāh and his helpers pitched their tents beside the sanctuary (he henceforth called himself *al-ʿāʾidh bi 'l-bait*, "he who took refuge at the temple") and again a conflagration did its best to complete the destruction. In the fire the Black Stone was split in three pieces.

When the Umaiyad army was withdrawn, ʿAbd Allāh discussed with the Meccan authorities the demolition and rebuilding of the Kaʿba. When he had made his decision and the ruins had to be cleared away, no one dared to begin the work. The bulk of the populace, with Ibn ʿAbbās at their head, had left the town because they feared a punishment from heaven. But ʿAbd Allāh climbed up himself, axe in hand, and began the grim task. When his people saw that he remained unharmed, they took courage and assisted.

During the building a covered scaffolding was left on the spot to mark the *ḳibla* and the *maṭāf* at least. The masons are said to have worked behind the covering. ʿAbd Allāh guarded the Black Stone, wrapped in a piece of brocade, in the council hall (*dār al-nadwa*). When put back into its place it, or rather the three pieces, into which it was broken, was bound with a band of silver.

The Kaʿba was then built entirely out of Meccan stone and Yaman mortar and built to a height of 27 ells. According to the tradition of the Prophet, the *ḥidjr* was included in the building and two doors were made on the level of the ground, the eastern as an entrance and the western as an exit. In the *ṭawāf* the four corners were kissed.

These alterations lasted only a short period. In 74/693 al-Ḥadjdjādj b. Yūsuf conquered Mecca and killed ʿAbd Allāh b. al-Zubair. In agreement with the Caliph ʿAbd al-Malik he again separated the *ḥidjr* from the Kaʿba and walled up the west door. The building, in keeping with the wish of the Umaiyads, thus practically received its pre-Islāmic form again and this form has survived to the present day. The piety of the populace has always resisted any considerable innovations. Only to an unimportant degree have the authorities now and then made improvements. As was the case in the heathen period, floods have continued to be a danger to the building. When in 1611 it threatened to collapse, a girdle of copper was used to avert the disaster. But a new *sail* made this support also insufficient, so that in 1630 renovations were decided upon. But the old stones were used as much as possible for the rebuilding.

The Kaʿba successfully withstood the Ḳarmaṭian invasion of 317/929; only the Black Stone was carried off. After an absence of some twenty years it was sent back to Mecca (cf. de Goeje, *Mém. sur les Carmathes* etc. [2], p. 104—111, 145—8).

The custom of covering the Kaʿba is said to have been introduced by the Tubbaʿ. The annual re-covering of the Kaʿba only became an established custom in modern times; for the oldest Muslim period, the ʿĀshūrāʾ day is mentioned as the day of covering, but in Radjab also and in other months the building has changed its covering. The *kiswa* consisted sometimes of Yaman and sometimes of Egyptian or other cloth; during ʿUmar's Caliphate the building threatened to collapse on account of the many coverings hung on it. All sorts of colours are mentioned also. The Wahhābīs even covered the Kaʿba with a red *kiswa*.

The *maḳām*'s around the Kaʿba are mentioned as early as the ʿAbbāsid period; sometimes under the name *ẓulla* ("a shade"). The present buildings are said to date from 1074/1663. A dome over the Zamzam well is mentioned at an equally early period; the present one was built in 1072.

The Kaʿba had offerings dedicated to it in the heathen as well as the Muslim period. Al-Azraḳī devotes a detailed chapter to this subject (ed. Wüstenfeld, p. 155 *sqq.*). Many a worldly ruler has used these treasures for political purposes. Tradition reports that ʿUmar said: "I will leave neither gold nor silver in the Kaʿba but distribute its treasures". To this, however, ʿAlī is said to have raised vigorous objections so that ʿUmar desisted from his plan.

III. The Kaʿba and Islām

We do not know the personal feelings of the youthful Muḥammad towards the Kaʿba and the Meccan cult, but they were presumably of a conventional nature. The Meccan revelations tell us nothing about these relations during this important period in the life of the Prophet. In any case he felt no enthusiasm for the Meccan sanctuary.

During the first period after the Hidjra Muḥammad was busy with very different problems. But when the expected good relations with Judaism and the Jews did not come about, a change set in. Henceforth — about a year and a half after the Hidjra — the Kaʿba and the Ḥadjdj are mentioned in the revelations.

The change of attitude was first shown in the *ḳibla* edict: the faithful were no longer to turn towards Jerusalem in the *ṣalāt* but to the Kaʿba (Sūra ii. 144). From the dogmatic point of view this volte-face was justified by an appeal to the "religion of Abraham" (Sūra ii. 135; iii. 95 etc.); cf. Snouck Hurgronje in his *Mekkaansche Feest*. This religion of Abraham, the prototype of Judaism and Islām, is said to have been obscured by the Jews and to have been brought to light again by Muḥammad. The Meccan cult was now drawn into it. Ibrāhīm and Ismāʿīl laid the foundations of the Kaʿba (Sūra ii. 127). The Maḳām Ibrāhīm is described as a place suitable for the *ṣalāt* (ii. 125). Ibrāhīm prescribed the pilgrimage to mankind at Allāh's behest (xxii. 27); and the Kaʿba is said to be the first sanctuary that was founded on earth (iii. 96); it is now called the Holy House (v. 97), or the Ancient House (xxii. 29, 33).

In this way there was created for the reception of the old heathen cult into Islām a basis in religious history, which was at the same time a political programme; henceforth the eyes of the faithful were turned towards Mecca.

In the year 6 A. H. a prospect of taking part in the Meccan cult was held out to the Muslims by the pact of al-Ḥudaibīya; in connection with it, the *ʿumrat al-ḳaḍāʾ* took place in the year 7. Muḥammad's political endeavours culminated in the conquest of Mecca in the year 8. All the accumulation of heathendom, which had gathered round the Kaʿba, was now thrust aside. 360 idols are said to have stood around the building. When touched with the Prophet's rod they all fell to the ground. The statue of Hubal which ʿAmr b. Luḥaiy is said to have erected over the pit inside the Kaʿba was removed as well as the representations of the prophets. When they began to wash the latter with Zamzam water, Muḥammad is said to have placed his hands on the pictures of Jesus and Mary and said: "Wash out all except what is below my hands". He then withdrew his hands. A wooden dove also which was in the Kaʿba is said to have been shattered by Muḥammad's orders. The two horns of Abraham's ram did not crumble to dust until the rebuilding of the Kaʿba by ʿAbd Allāh b. al-Zubair.

At the capture of Mecca, Muḥammad made arrangements regarding the religious and secular offices which had been filled in Mecca from ancient times. The historians say that in the old heathen period Ḳuṣaiy after a fierce struggle with the tribe of Khuzāʿa became master of the Kaʿba and held all the important offices, religious and secular: the administration of the *dār al-nadwa* and the tying of the standard, the provision of the pilgrims with food (*rifāda*) and with drink (*siḳāya*) as well as the supervision of the Kaʿba (*sidāna* and *ḥidjāba*). His descendants

ʿAbd Manāf — Hāshim — ʿAbd al-Muṭṭalib — ʿAbbās, Abū Ṭālib

ʿAbd al-Dār — ʿUthmān — ʿAbd al-ʿUzza — Abū Ṭalḥa, ʿAbd Allāh

administered the offices after his death, ʿAbd Manāf and his descendants getting the *rifāda* and *siḳāya* etc., while ʿAbd al-Dār and his descendants saw to the *sidāna* and *ḥidjāba* etc.

When Muḥammad conquered Mecca his uncle ʿAbbās [q. v.] or, according to another tradition, ʿAlī asked for the administration of these offices. But Muḥammad said that they must all be crushed beneath his feet except the *siḳāya* and the guardianship of the Kaʿba. The former remained in the hands of ʿAbbās; the latter he gave to ʿUthmān b. Ṭalḥa who appointed his cousin Shaiba b. Abī Ṭalḥa [q. v.] his deputy. The Banū Shaiba are the doorkeepers at the Kaʿba to this day. The *rifāda*, which was in the hands of Abū Ṭālib, was taken over by Abū Bakr in the year 9; after his death the caliphs looked after the feeding of the pilgrims.

Muḥammad's control over Mecca and the Meccan cult was first clearly marked at the *ḥadjdj* of the year 9. As plenipotentiary of the Prophet, who did not participate in the pilgrimage, Abū Bakr announced to the assembled pilgrims the latest arrangements, which were expressed in a revelation. They are contained in Sūra ix., which from them is often called the Sūra of Immunity (*barāʾa*) (v. 1—12, 28, 36 *sq.*). According to it, idolators are henceforth forbidden to participate in the Meccan festival as they are impure (*nadjas*). Moreover, they are declared outlaws. A period of four months is given them during which they can go freely about the country; but after that "kill them wherever ye find them". Excepted are those with whom an alliance has been made in so far as they have punctiliously observed its terms and helped no one against the Muslims.

In the year 10 A. H. Muḥammad himself led the pilgrimage, at which therefore according to tradition not a single idolator was present: the Kaʿba had become an exclusively Muslim sanctuary, and Mecca was and is for Islām what Rome is to the Roman Catholic and Jerusalem to the Jew. At every *ṣalāt* the Muslims throughout the world turn towards Mecca and at the ceremonies of the pilgrimage the Kaʿba forms the beginning and the end of the holy rites.

Two special ceremonies concerning the Kaʿba may here be mentioned, the opening and the washing of the building. The opening takes place on definite days and men are first admitted, then the women. On this occasion the above mentioned staircase is pushed up to the building. It is considered particularly meritorious to perform the *ṣalāt* in the Kaʿba.

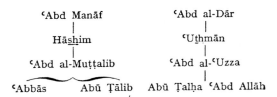

After the Ḥadjdj is completed, at the end of the month Dhu 'l-Ḥidjdja, the Kaʿba is washed, a ceremony in which the authorities as well as a number of pilgrims take part. The first to enter was the Sharīf, who after a *ṣalāt* of two *rakʿa*'s, himself washed the ground with Zamzam water which poured away through a hole in the threshold. The walls were washed with a kind of broom made of palm leaves. The Sharīf then sprinkled everything again with rose water and finally the building was fumigated with all manner of perfumes (cf. *al-Ḳibla*, N°. 409, p. 1). The Sharīf threw the broom away among the crowd of pilgrims who fought among themselves for possession of it. Al-Batanūnī says (p. 109) that the Zamzamīs and the Muṭawwifs sell the pilgrims similar brooms for a minimum of half a real.

As is evident from this example, the veneration for the sacred building extends to all that comes in contact with it: Black Stone, water-spout, Zamzam water. It is however said — cf. Wensinck, *A Handbook of Early Muh. Tradition*, s. v. Stone — that ʿUmar thus expressed himself on the Black Stone: "I know that thou art a stone, that neither helps nor hurts, and if the messenger of Allāh had not kissed thee, I would not kiss thee". But then he kissed the stone. And hardly a single pilgrim will think of ʿUmar's words during the *ṭawāf*. The *ṣalāt* under the water-spout is described as particularly efficacious: "Anyone who performs the *ṣalāt* under the *mathʿab* becomes as pure as on the day when his mother bore him" (al-Azraḳī, p. 224). The Zamzam water, which the pilgrim has poured over him again and again, is useful for every purpose for which it is drunk (*māʾ Zamzam li-mā shuriba lahu*: Ḳuṭb al-Dīn, ed. Wüstenfeld, p. 34).

There is abundant testimony in Muslim as well as European literature to the intensification of devotional feeling which the sight of the Kaʿba produces in the pilgrims. We may here quote al-Batanūnī's description of the *ṣalāt* at the Kaʿba as particularly characteristic (p. 26): "The whole assembly stood there in the greatest reverence before this highest majesty and most powerful inspirer of awe, before which the greatest souls become so little as to be nothing. And if we had not been witness of the movements of the body during the *ṣalāt* and the raising of the hands during the prayers, and the murmuring of the expressions of humility and if we had not heard the beating of the hearts before this immeasurable grandeur, we would have thought ourselves transferred to another life. And truly we were at that hour in another world: we were in the house of God and in God's immediate presence, and with us were only the lowered head and the humble tongue and the voices raised in prayer and weeping eyes and the fearful heart and pure thoughts of intercession" (cf. also Macdonald, *The Religious Attitude and Life in Islam*, Chicago 1909, p. 216 *sqq.*; Ben Chérif, *Aux Villes Saintes de l'Islam*, p. ii. *sq.*, 45 *sq.*, 68).

Even the Shīʿīs and the Wahhābīs have left the Kaʿba its place in Islām. For the Ḳarmaṭians alone has an exception to be made, as can be well understood.

As to the mystics, their attitude to the Kaʿba depends on their position regarding the law. For the, so to speak, nomistic mystics like al-Ghazzālī, the Kaʿba is, it is true, the sacred building which one has to go round in the *ṭawāf*. The *ṭawāf* and its object however only receive their value for men when they give them an inducement to rise to a higher spiritual level. Ibn al-ʿArabī goes a step further when he says that the true Kaʿba is nothing other than our own being (*al-Futūḥāt al-Makkīya*, i. 733); the Kaʿba however also plays a part in his mystic experiences. Hudjwīrī further quotes some sayings of mystics, who no longer require the Kaʿba as an inducement to rise, and even reject it. Muḥammad b. al-Faḍl says: "I wonder at those who seek His temple in this world: why do they not seek contemplation of Him in their hearts? The temple they sometimes attain and sometimes miss, but contemplation they might enjoy always. If they are bound to visit a stone, which is looked at only once a year, surely they are more bound to visit the temple of the heart, where He may be seen three hundred and sixty times in a day and night. But the mystic's every step is a symbol of the journey to Mecca, and when he reaches the sanctuary he wins a robe of honour for every step". Abū Yazīd (al-Bisṭāmī) says: "If anyone's recompense for worshipping God is deferred until to-morrow he has not worshipped God aright to-day", for the recompense of every moment of worship and mortification is immediate. And Abū Yazīd also says: "On my first pilgrimage I saw only the temple; the second time, I saw both the temple and the Lord of the temple; and the third time I saw the Lord alone". In short, where mortification is, there is no sanctuary: the sanctuary is where contemplation is. Unless the whole universe is a man's trysting-place where he comes nigh unto God and a retired chamber where he enjoys intimacy with God, he is still a stranger to Divine love; but when he has vision the whole universe is his sanctuary. "The darkest thing in the world is the Beloved's house without the Beloved". Accordingly, what is truly valuable is not the Kaʿba, but contemplation and annihilation in the abode of friendship, of which things the sight of the Kaʿba is an indirect cause (Hudjwīrī, transl. Nicholson, p. 327). On the meaning of the Kaʿba in the mystical symbolism of Ibn al-ʿArabī's *Futūḥāt* see Fritz Meier, *Das Mysterium der Kaʿba*, in *Eranos-Jahrbuch* 1944, Zürich 1945, p. 187 *sqq.*

IV. The Kaʿba in Legend and Popular Belief

The association with Abraham supplied a basis for the esteem in which the Muslims held the Kaʿba. Legend attached itself to the Ḳurʾānic statements and spun them out. There was, it is true, a local tradition, but it consists of semi-historical reminiscences of the last few centuries before Islām. But all that tradition relates regarding the origin of the Kaʿba and its connection with Biblical personages, belongs to Islāmic legend.

The latter first of all attached itself to the statement that Ibrāhīm and Ismāʿīl raised (*rafaʿa*) the foundations of the Kaʿba (ii. 127). God's command to Ibrāhīm to build the Kaʿba is by some placed before the episode of Hagar and by others after it. The patriarch came to Arabia led by the *sakīna*, which had the shape of a stormy wind with two heads; it is also described as having a snake's head. When it reached the site of the Kaʿba it wound itself round its foundation [see below] and said "Build on me". According to others, Ibrāhīm built on its shadow. He was helped by Ismāʿīl in this; the stones were taken from five (or seven) hills: Ḥirāʾ, Thabīr, Lebanon, Mount of Olives and the Djabal al-Aḥmar near Mecca (other names are also given). When the building had risen to some height, he stood at his work on the stone which still shows the impress of his feet, the *maḳām Ibrāhīm.* The Black Stone, which was still white in those days and only received its present colour as a result of contact with the impurity and sin of the pagan period, was brought to him by Gabriel after having been kept in Abū Ḳubais since the Deluge. Within the building (which was not high and had no roof) Ibrāhīm dug the hole which afterwards served as a treasury. When the work of building was completed, he took his stand on the *maḳām*, which now rose high above the mountains, and proclaimed the pilgrimage to all men. From all sides they answered: *Labbaika, Allāhumma! Labbaika!*

On the other hand, Muslim legend has developed the passage Sūra iii. 96: "Truly, the first temple that was founded for men is that in Bakka; a blessed house and a guidance for (all) creatures". The ambiguous expression according to which Ibrāhīm and Ismāʿīl "raised" the foundations of the Kaʿba left room for the view that the foundations already existed on which he erected the building. Al-Ṭabarī in his commentary on Sūra ii. 127 (i. 408 *sq.*), however, recognises that there are two views: according to the one, Adam, according to the other, Ibrāhīm laid the foundations. Legend relates the following regarding the foundation by Adam. When after the Fall Adam was hurled out of Paradise to the earth, he came to Mecca. Gabriel with his wing uncovered a foundation, which had been laid in the seventh earth, and the angels threw blocks on it from Lebanon, the Mount of Olives, Djabal Djūdī and Ḥirāʾ until the hole was filled level with the earth. God then sent from Paradise a tent of red jacinth in which Adam lived; what was afterwards the black stone, then a white jacinth from Paradise, served as a seat. When God made his covenant with men, the latter acknowledged God's suzerainty; the document on which their acknowledgment was written was given by God to be swallowed by the Black Stone. At the Last Day it will be given a tongue, to bear witness against men; according to others, because it was originally an angel.

There was a particular reason for sending down the prototype of the latter Kaʿba. Originally Adam's stature was so great that he could hear the song of the heavenly hosts around God's throne. As a result of the Fall, however, his stature was shortened; he then lamented to God that the higher spheres were now closed to him. God then sent down the tent around which Adam now performed the *ṭawāf*, following the example of the angels. But Mecca was without inhabitants and the sanctuary without worshippers. When he gave vent to his regrets on this point, he was promised by God that in time this place would be the site of a cult; that the sanctuary would enjoy a particular *karāma*; that it would be a *ḥaram* [q. v.] whose *ḥurma* would extend above, below and around, and to which men would make pilgrimage with dishevelled hair and covered with dust, breaking out of every cleft with weeping and *takbīr* [q. v.] and *talbiya* [q. v.].

After Adam's death his descendants (Shīth is specially mentioned) built the Kaʿba. But the Deluge washed the building away while the sacred stone was concealed by the angels in Abū Ḳubais. According to others, however, the flood did not touch the Kaʿba and Noah performed the *ṭawāf* round the holy house. According to the first tradition, only a red mound was left of the Kaʿba, which Abraham afterwards found.

But the legends also extend to the period after Abraham. The hole in the Kaʿba, which is called *al-akhsaf* or *al-akhshaf*, is said to have been several times plundered under the Djurhum. Therefore at God's command a snake took up its abode there and guarded the treasures. When the Ḳuraishites wanted to pull down the Kaʿba, the monster opposed this plan, until God sent a bird which carried it off to one of the surrounding hills. — Every renovation of the Kaʿba is said to have been carried out amid terrible portents, such as lightning-flashes. It is also said that on such occasions the foundation of the Kaʿba was brought to light and it looked like the necks of camels intertwined.

This legendary story of the origin of the Kaʿba was easily brought into conformity with the cosmological views current among Christians and Jews in the East, the central point of which was the sanctuary itself. Muslim tradition at first adopted this cosmology completely, as is evident from the statements which are still wholly under the influence of the predominance of Jerusalem. They were however not content with this and transferred a considerable part of these sayings to Mecca. These traditions are grouped round the navel theory, the main ideas of which are as follows. The earth has a navel, whose functions are parallel to those of the human navel. It forms the part of the earth which was created before the rest of it and around which the rest stretches. It is also the highest point, the place which provides the whole world with its nourishment; and it forms the place of communication with the upper and under world.

This navel was at first Jerusalem and later Mecca. But not all the properties of the navel are attached in equal degree to Mecca. They may be briefly summed up as follows. About 40, according to others, 2,000 years before the creation of the world, the sanctuary was an agglomeration (*ghuthāʾ*) in the world ocean. The beginning of the creation consisted in the stretching out of the earth around this point as centre, in the following order: after the substance of the earth (which coincides with the navel) heaven was formed and lastly the earth itself. In agreement with this theory is the fact that in the Ḳurʾān Mecca is called the mother of cities (*umm al-ḳurā*) (vi. 92; xlii. 7) and in popular literature the navel of the earth (Yāḳūt, *Muʿdjam*, iv. 278; Diyārbakrī, *al-Khamīs*, i. 37; al-Ḥalabī, *Sīra*, i. 195, etc.).

That the sanctuary is the highest point in the world cannot be scientifically maintained. The popular traditions however like to move in this direction. Thus, in the story of the creation, it is said that the earth is extended below the sanctuary. The semi-scientific cosmography says that the position of the Kaʿba corresponds to the Pole Star; as the latter is the highest point in the heavens, so the Kaʿba is the highest point on earth (al-Kisāʾī, *ʿAdjāʾib al-malakūt*, MS. Leyden, f. 15^b). This view is probably connected with the conception of heaven and earth as domes or tents put one upon the other, which can be shown to exist in Muslim literature.

The view that the sanctuary connects on the one side with heaven and on the other with the lower world is not so clearly stated with regard to Mecca as to Juresalem. But it is said that no place on earth is nearer heaven than Mecca; and in the pagan period men are said to have gone up on to Abū Ḳubais to offer particularly urgent prayers. Whether the pit in the Kaʿba was really regarded as the entrance to the underworld, like the corresponding arrangements in Jerusalem and Hierapolis, is uncertain.

One typical characteristic of the lower world is certainly possessed by Mecca. It is described as a tomb. Not only Ismāʿīl, but a whole series of prophets, numbering hundreds, is said to have been buried round the Kaʿba. Every prophet belongs to Mecca. This is his essential starting point and termination of his career. Muḥammad therefore also belongs to Mecca and Mecca is his real grave, as theoreticians say (al-Ḥalabī, i. 197), in opposition to the fact that he is buried in Madīna.

Traditions which emphasise Mecca's importance for the nourishment of the world are hardly represented at all.

These theories had to be brought into consonance with the later cosmology of Islām, which regards the universe as a series of storeys of seven heavens and seven earths. The Kaʿba is now not only placed in the centre of the earth (according to the navel theory) but it forms the central point of the whole universe. Its foundations as well as those of Abū Ḳubais lie in the seventh earth and form a kind of axis which runs through all these worlds.

The storeys of the universe resemble one another in plan. Every one has a sanctuary in the centre so that if the top one fell down, it would fall exactly on the lowest in the seventh world. The highest of the sanctuaries is the throne of God. Of those which lie between the throne and the Kaʿba two are mentioned by name: the *Bait maʿmūr*, the name of which is taken from the Ḳurʾān (lii. 4), and *al-Ḍurāḥ*. Jewish literature was already acquainted with a heavenly sanctuary in which the angels act as priests. In Islām these priestly functions are usually replaced by the *ṭawāf*.

V. Comparative History of the Cult.

From the fact that Ptolemy calls Mecca Macoraba (i. e. *mikrāb*, temple) we may conclude that in his time the Kaʿba was regarded as the dwelling of one or more deities. According to a statement of Epiphanius (*Haereses*, v., following the text in *Philologus*, 1860, p. 355), Dhu 'l-Sharā had his χααβου in Petra, in which word Kaʿba is also probably concealed. It is however not clear from Epiphanius, whether the term applied to the temple in Petra or the quadrangular black stone, which represented Dhu 'l-Sharā. Al-Bakrī (*Muʿdjam*, ed. Wüstenfeld, p. 46) relates that the tribe of Bakr Wāʾil as well as the main body of the tribe of Iyād had their centre of worship in Sindād in the region of Kūfa, and that their holy tent (or temple, *bait*) here was called Dhāt al-Kaʿabāt (cf. however al-Hamdānī, *Ṣifat djazīrat al-ʿArab*, p. 171, 230). According to Wellhausen, the Kaʿba owed its sanctity to the Black Stone; this may be right, for the religion of the ancient Arabs was essentially stone-worship.

The form of the building may be compared with the apse of the Jerusalem temple, which was twenty ells in each direction.

It is not related that the Black Stone was connected with any special god. In the Kaʿba was the statue of the god Hubal who might be called the god of Mecca and of the Kaʿba. Caetani gives great prominence to the connection between the Kaʿba and Hubal. Besides him, however, al-Lāt, al-ʿUzzā, and al-Manāt were worshipped and are mentioned in the Ḳurʾān; Hubal is never mentioned there. What position Allāh held beside these is not exactly known. The Islāmic tradition has certainly emphasized him at the expense of other deities.

It may be considered certain that the Black Stone was not the only idol in or at the Kaʿba. The Maḳām Ibrāhim was of course a sacred stone from very early times, but its name has not been handed down. Beside it several idols are mentioned, among them the 360 statues.

The Kaʿba possessed in a high degree the usual characters of a Semitic sanctuary. First of all it made the whole surrounding area into consecrated ground. Around the town lies the sacred zone (*ḥaram*) marked by stones, which imposes certain restrictions on each one who enters it [see IḤRĀM]. Moreover, the sanctity of the area is seen in the following points. In the *ḥaram* the truce of God reigns. When the Arab tribes made a pilgrimage to the Kaʿba, all feuds were dormant. It was forbidden to carry arms. Next, the *ḥaram* — and the Kaʿba especially — is a place of refuge. Here the unintentional manslayer was safe just as in the Jewich cities of refuge. On the Kaʿba there was a kind of handle to which the fugitives clung (al-Azraḳī, p. 111), an arrangement which recalls the purport of the horns on the Jewish altar.

Blood was not allowed to flow in the *ḥaram*. It is therefore reported that those condemned to death were led outside the *ḥaram* to execution. The idea of peace extended even to the flora and fauna. Animals — except a few injurious or dangerous sorts — are not to be scared away; hence the many tame doves in the mosque. Trees and bushes were not cut down except the *idhkhir* shrub, which was used for building houses and in goldsmiths' work. These regulations were confirmed by Islām and are in force to this day.

As to the rites, it is said that in the heathen period victims were slain at the Kaʿba. Among the ancient Arabs the idol of stone replaced the altar; on it they smeared the blood of the sacrificial animals. In Islām the killing takes place in Minā.

It is a question whether and how far the Kaʿba was connected with the *ḥadjdj* in the pre-Islāmic period. Wellhausen (*Reste arab. Heidentums*, 2nd ed., p. 79) defends the view that originally only the *ʿumra* [q. v.] was concerned with the Kaʿba while the scene of the *ḥadjdj* was ʿArafāt, Muzdalifa and Minā. The connecting of pilgrimage and *ʿumra* is regarded by him as a rather clumsy correction made by Islām. It must be conceded that Wellhausen with justice points to the fact that the *ʿumra* far down into Islām was closely connected with the month of Radjab. Moreover, the *ḥadjdj* is called simply *ḥadjdj ʿArafāt* and, according to the Shāfiʿī school, the *wuḳūf* in ʿArafāt is the main ceremony of the *ḥadjdj*. On the other hand, it should be remarked that in the Ḳurʾān (iii. 97) pilgrimage is connected with the Kaʿba (*ḥadjdj al-bait*) and that tradition nowhere gives us the slightest hint of this being an innovation. The facts emphasised by Wellhausen may however be interpreted otherwise. He himself has pointed out that the ancient Arabs were fond of connecting sacred places situated close to one another by ceremonial rites. It is therefore more probable that the "rather clumsy" alteration had taken place by the pre-Islāmic period and is to be regarded as the result of a connection of the cult of ʿArafāt with that of Mecca.

As was said above, the Tubbaʿ is regarded as the first who covered the Kaʿba. Whether this tradition is historically correct is beyond our knowledge. It is noteworthy that the coloured cloths are mentioned which were placed over the building, a rite which one has to consider in connection with similar rites used in other cases. The Jewish tabernacle, the high places of Canaan (Ezekiel xvi. 16), the throne of Solomon, the throne of the bishops, the *maḥmal*, and sacred tents in ancient Arabia as well as the *sidrat al-muntahā* in Paradise are all covered with coloured cloths. It is misleading to give a general explanation of all such things. But the idea of a connection with the sun shining in the heavens suggests itself here; particularly for the *sidra* this notion can be traced further. The question might even be asked whether and how far the Kaʿba was regarded as an astral symbol. For the affirmative there is the fact that the Kaʿba is the object of the *ṭawāf* and that *ṭawāf* and Kaʿba are represented by Muslim tradition itself as connected with the host of spirits round the throne of God. The throne of God is, as is well known, a cosmic magnitude, and the Kaʿba and the Black Stone are described as the throne of God's *k͟halīfa* on earth, Adam. The dance of the heavenly spirits can easily be interpreted as a dance of the planets. Moreover, golden suns and moons are repeatedly mentioned among the votive gifts (al-Azraḳī, p. 155 *sqq.*). According to al-Masʿūdī (*Murūd͟j*, iv. 47), certain people regarded the Kaʿba as a temple dedicated to the sun, the moon and the five planets. The 360 idols placed round the Kaʿba also point in this direction. It can therefore hardly be denied that traces exist of an astral symbolism. At the same time one can safely say that there can be no question of any general conception on these lines. The cult at the Kaʿba was in the heathen period syncretic, as is usual in heathenism. How far also North Semitic cults were represented in Mecca cannot be exactly ascertained. It is not excluded that Allāh was of Aramaic origin. The dove of aloes wood which Muḥammad found in the Kaʿba may have been devoted to the Semitic Venus.

Bibliography: On the whole article Wüstenfeld, *Die Chroniken der Stadt Mekka* (Leipzig 1857—1861, 4 vols.).

On i. and ii.: J. L. Burckhardt, *Travels in Arabia* (London 1829, 2 vols.); Ali Bey, *Travels* (London 1816, 2 vols.); R. Burton, *Personal Narrative of a Pilgrimage to el-Medinah and Maccah* (London 1857, 2 vols.); A. Müller, *Der Islam im Morgen- und Abendland* (Berlin 1885, 2 vols.); C. Snouck Hurgronje, *Mekka* (The Hague 1888—89, 2 vols.), with *Bilderatlas*; do., *Bilder aus Mekka* (Leyden 1889); Caïd Ben Chérif, *Aux villes saintes de l'Islam* (Paris 1919); al-Batanūnī, *al-Riḥla al-Ḥid͟jāzīya*² (Cairo 1329); E. Rutter, *The Holy Cities of Arabia*, 2 vols., London 1928; Ibrāhīm Rifʿat, *Mirʾāt al-Ḥaramain*, vol. i (Cairo 1925; fully illustrated); Gaudefroy-Demombynes, *Le pélérinage à la Mekke* (Paris 1923); al-Azraḳī, p. 86 *sqq.*; al-Fākihī, p. 18 *sqq.*; al-Ṭabarī, i. 901 *sqq.*, 936 *sqq.*, 1130 *sqq.*; Ibn ʿAbd Rabbihi, *ʿIḳd*, ed. 1321, iii. 297 *sqq.* (transl. by Muh. S͟hafīʿ in *Memorial Vol. E. G. Browne*, Cambridge 1922, p. 423 *sqq.*); al-Masʿūdī, i. 133; iv. 115 *sqq.*; v. 165—167, 193; *Bibl. Geogr. Arab.*, i. (al-Iṣṭak͟hrī), 15 *sq.*; ii. (Ibn Ḥawḳal), 23 *sq.*; iii.² (al-Muḳaddasī), 71 *sqq.*; v. (Ibn al-Faḳīh), 16—22; vii. (Ibn Rosteh), 24—54; Yāḳūt, *Muʿd͟jam* (ed. Wüstenfeld), iv. 278 *sqq.*; Ibn D͟jubair, *Riḥla* (*GMS*, v.), p. 81 *sqq.*; al-Buk͟hārī, *Ṣaḥīḥ*, *Kitāb al-ʿilm*, bāb 48; Gaudefroy-Demombynes, *Notes sur la Mekke et Médine* (*RHR*, lxxvii. 316 *sqq.*).

On iii.: C. Snouck Hurgronje, *Het Mekkaansche Feest* (Leyden 1880); the Eastern and Western biographies of Muḥammad; commentaries on the Ḳurʾān on the passages mentioned.

On iv.: al-Azraḳī, p. 1 *sqq.*; al-Ṭabarī, i. 130 *sqq.*, 274 *sqq.*; al-T͟haʿlabī, *Ḳiṣaṣ al-anbiyāʾ* (Cairo 1290), p. 69 *sqq.*; al-Diyārbakrī, *Taʾrīk͟h al-K͟hamīs* (Cairo 1283, 2 vols.); Caussin de Perceval, *Essai sur l'hist. des Arabes* (Paris 1847—48); A. J. Wensinck, *The Navel of the Earth* (*Verh. Kon. Akad. v. Wetensch.*, Dl. xvii., N⁰. 1); J. L. Palache, *Het Heiligdom in de voorstelling der semietische volken* (Leyden 1920); L. Caetani, *Annali dell' Islam*, Introduzione, §§ 62 *sqq.*; J. Wellhausen, *Reste arab. Heidentums*² (Berlin 1897), p. 73 *sqq.*; H. Grimme, *Mohammed* (Munich 1904), p. 45 *sq.*

ḲABḌ (A.), a technical term of the Ṣūfīs, meaning literally „contraction" and hence contrasted with *basṭ* or „expansion" [q.v.], is applied to a spiritual state or *ḥāl* corresponding with the station (*maḳām*) of fear (*k͟hawf*). God is the agent, and seizes on and contracts the heart of the mystic, inducing in him a sense of desolation, which is well illustrated by the saying of al-D͟junaid quoted s.v. *basṭ*. In this saying it appears that the author has in mind the other meaning of the verb *ḳabaḍa* as applied to God, namely, „to cause to die", for he says, „When He contracts me through fear, He causes me to pass away from self", hinting at the state of *fanāʾ* (q.v.] in which the mystic is dead unto self. Sarrād͟j's definition (*Kitāb al-lumaʿ*, ed. Nicholson, p. 342) is excellent: „*Ḳabḍ* and *basṭ* are two noble spiritual states belonging to gnostics. When God contracts them, He causes them to shrink from partaking of subsistence and permitted things, of eating, drinking and talking; when He expands them, He restores them to these things, undertaking to protect them therein. *Ḳabḍ* is the state of a gnostic who has no room left (*faḍl*) for anything but the gnosis of God". The corresponding term in mediaeval Christian mysticism is *desolatio* or „spiritual dryness".

KABĪR, an Indian mystic, of the xvᵗʰ century, who was claimed both by the Hindus and Muslims as belonging to their faith. A large collection of Hindī verses is attributed to him, but their authenticity is doubtful, and a like uncertainty attaches to his biography, which is obscured by legends. He is said to have been the son, or adopted son, of a Muḥammadan weaver, and to have become the disciple of Rāmānanda, the Vaishnav reformer, at whose feet he sat in Benares, joining in the theological and philosophical arguments that this master held with Brahmans and Ṣūfīs. He appears to have earned his living as a weaver, and to have been a married man, the father of a family, and to have been as contemptuous of the professional asceticism of the Yōgī as he was disregardful of the doctrines and ordinances of orthodoxy, whether Hindu or Muslim. The boldness with which he sang his mystical doctrine of the divine unity exposed him to persecution, and he is said to have been driven from Benares in 1495, when he was about 60 years of age, and to have died at Maghar, in the district of Bastī, in 1518. Legend says that his Hindu and Muslim disciples disputed as to the disposal of his body, which the former wished to burn and the latter to bury; when they lifted the cloth that covered the body, they found in place of the corpse only a heap of flowers; of these the Hindus burnt half in Benares, while the Muslims buried the rest at Maghar, where the shrine is still in the charge of Muḥammadan Kabīr-Panthīs. Modern scholars, like Kabīr's contemporaries, claim him for one or other of the rival creeds: H. H. Wilson (*op. cit.*, p. 69, 74) and R. G. Bhandarkar (*op. cit.*, p. 69) maintain that he was a Hindu; G. H. Westcott that he was a Muslim (*op. cit.*, p. 29 *sqq.*); G. A. Grierson's theory (*JRAS*, 1907, p. 325, 492) that he derived his opinions from Christian sources, may be dismissed as a pious fiction. A study of his poems makes it clear that he had no desire to attach himself to any organised religion: "Let me make self-reflection my saddle, And put my foot in the stirrup of divine love.... Saith Kabīr, they are good riders Who keep themselves aloof from the Vedas and the Ḳurʾān"; nor did he attempt to formulate any religious or philosophical system of his own, but he popularised the current Vaishnav teaching of his age, without however connecting it with any particular incarnation, and he spoke of God indifferently as Rām, Hari, ʿAlī or Allāh. He rejected the outward signs of Hinduism, e.g. the sacred thread, the distinctions of caste, the ritual observances of temple worship, etc., and his references to Muslim authorities and institutions (e.g. the Ḳurʾān, circumcision, pilgrimage, the Mullā, the Ḳāḍī etc.) are accompanied with a denial of their validity. He represented God as the omnipresent reality, but maintained the separate individuality of the human soul which could attain union with God through love, not by knowledge or by ceremonial observances. Through his homely illustrations and his close contact with daily life, he presented his doctrines in a form readily acceptable to unlettered persons, who appear to form the majority of his followers.

Bibliography: *Dabistān-i-madhāhib*, (Calcutta 1809), p. 246—248, transl. Shea and Troyer, (Paris 1843) ii. 186—191; H. H. Wilson, *Essays on the Religion of the Hindus*, (London 1862) i. 68 *sqq.*; *Gli scritti de Padre Marco Della Tomba*, racolti ... da A. de Gubernatis, (Florence 1878) p. 191 *sqq.*, 205 *sqq.*; E. Trumpp, *Bemerkungen über den indischen Reformator Kabīr*, in *Atti del iv. Congresso internat. degli Orientalisti*, (Florence 1880—81) ii. 159 *sqq.*; *Kabīr-charitra*, edited by Pandit Wālji Bèchar (Surat 1881); G. H. Westcott, *Kabir and the Kabir Panth* (Cawnpore 1907); M. A. Macauliffe, *The Sikh Religion*, (Oxford 1909) vi. 122 *sqq.*; *One Hundred Poems of Kabir* translated by Rabindranath Tagore assisted by Evelyn Underhill (London 1914); Ram Chandra Bose, *Hindu Heterodoxy*, (Calcutta 1887) chap. x.; Sir R. G. Bhandarkar, *Vaiṣnavism, Śaivism, and minor religious systems* (*Encyclopaedia of Indo-Aryan Research*, Vol. iii., Part 6), p. 67—73; *The Bijak of Kabīr*, translated by the Rev. Aḥmad Shāh (Hamīrpur 1917); G. N. Farquhar, *An Outline of the Religious Literature of India*, p. 331—5 (Oxford 1920). No critical edition of the works attributed to Kabīr has yet appeared; for a list of these see Westcott, *op. cit.*, p. 73—4, 169—172.

ḲAḌĀʾ means literally "deciding" (*ḥukm, faṣl, ḳaṭʿ, tartīb*; cf. Ibn Ḥazm, *Milal*, iii. 51) but the root is developed in many diverging senses already in the Ḳurʾān, "commanding", "judging", "making so as to be fixed", "informing", "substituting", "discharging (obligation)" etc.; cf. al-Iṣfahānī, *Mufradāt*, p. 416, and *LA*, xx. 47 *sqq.* Technically it indicates *a*) the office and functioning of a judge (*ḳāḍī*); *b*) the discharging of a previously neglected religious obligation, e. g. of the daily worship or of fasting in Ramaḍān; thus opposed to *adāʾ*, the performance of the duty at the appointed time (Juynboll, *Handb. des islām. Gesetzes*, p. 68, note; Lane, *Lexicon*, p. 38b); *c*) the eternal, universal decision of Allāh as to all existent things as they are continuously, very nearly the "eternal decree" of Calvinism. The point in doubt in the last use is the relation of the term to *ḳadar* (*ḳadr*), "measuring or estimating an amount", "assigning something by measure"; to *ʿināya*, "providence"; and to the will (*irāda*) and knowledge (*ʿilm*) of Allāh; further whether ḳaḍāʾ is one of the "essential qualities" (*al-ṣifāt al-dhātīya*) of Allāh or of His "qualities of action" (*al-ṣifāt al-fiʿlīya*); is eternal (*ḳadīm*) or originated (*ḥādith*). For orthodox Ashʿarites ḳaḍāʾ is the will of Allāh (al-Baiḍāwī on Sūra ii. 117 [111]) and its eternal connection (*taʿalluḳ*), while *ḳadar* is His bringing things into existence in accordance with His will. Or it is His eternal knowledge and its connection with the thing known, while *ḳadar* is His bringing the thing into existence in accordance with His knowledge. Ḳaḍāʾ, therefore, is eternal as one of the eternal qualities and *ḳadar* is originated because one of the "connections" of Allāh's quality of power. But others taught that ḳaḍāʾ is the bringing forth (*ibrāz*) of transitory things (*al-kāʾināt*) in accordance with the knowledge of Allāh, while *ḳadar* is the eternal defining of each thing with what of good and bad, advantage and disadvantage, it is to have when it exists. Ḳaḍāʾ, then, is originated and *ḳadar* is eternal. Further, ḳaḍāʾ, if it equals Allāh's will or knowledge, is one of the essential qualities, but if it is this "bringing forth" it is only one of the connections of Allāh's power, and these, according to the Ashʿarites, are originated. But the Māturīdites called these "active qualities" and held that they were eternal because they were names for the Māturīdite quality *takwīn* (making to become) which the Ashʿarites did not admit as a quality (al-Faḍālī with commentary of al-Bādjūrī, Cairo 1315, p. 55, 61; al-Nasafī's *ʿAḳāʾid* with commentary of al-Taftāzānī etc., Cairo 1321, p. 95). But the overwhelmingly accepted position makes ḳaḍāʾ the universal, general and eternal decree, and *ḳadar* the individual development or application of that in time. A phrase quoted in the *Ṣaḥāḥ* under *ḳ-d-r* is significant: *Mā yuḳaddiruhu 'llāh min al-ḳaḍāʾ*, "That which Allāh measures out of ḳaḍāʾ". Al-Rāzī on Sūra xxxiii. 37, 38 (*Mafātīḥ*, Cairo 1308, vi. 527) even applies the distinction to the problem of evil and of human responsibility. That which is by *ḳadar* comes in incidentally, almost accidentally, and the disadvantages (*ḍarar*) of the world are through it, while the good (*khair*) is by ḳaḍāʾ. Man was created by Allāh subject to lust and anger in order that, striving against these under the guidance of reason and religion, he might be rewarded. That leads in some to sin, but Allāh did not produce this consequential sin in them by intention, although it was by His *ḳadar*. Again, that which is by ḳāḍaʾ being universal is always perfectly intelligible — we see it happening all the time; but some of weak understanding may ask the reason for a thing which is by *ḳadar*. Yet it must not be thought that these latter things are necessary consequences following of themselves according to be Muʿtazilite doctrine of *tawlīd* or the philosophical teaching that there is a nature in things (*ṭabʿ*). Everything is by the choice (*ikhtiyār*) of Allāh and He admits only a certain custom (*ʿāda*) in things. Among philosophers the tendency is to equate ḳaḍāʾ with Allāh's knowledge or with His eternal providence (*ʿināya*) or even to say that it is an expression for the existence of all existent things, taken as a whole, in the world of reason, while *ḳadar* is their external existence, separated, one after another (*Dict. of Techn. Terms*, p. 1234 *sq.*). [See, too, ḲADAR].

ḲADAR (A.), decree. The contradictory statements of the Ḳurʾān on free will and predestination show that Muḥammad was a preacher and politician and not a systematic theologian. It has been demonstrated (Grimme, *Einleitung in den Koran*, vol. ii.) that his predestinarian position steadily hardened towards the close of his life, and the earliest conscious Muslim attitude on the subject seems to have been of an uncompromising fatalism. *ḳ-d-r* was the root used most generally to express it [see, too, ḲAḌĀʾ] and appears to mean primarily "to measure, estimate" and then "to assign specifically by measure" as though Allāh "measured out" his decrees. On the early opposition to this, which showed itself apparently before A. D. 700 and under Christian influences, see ḲADARĪYA. In the course of the conflict two extreme views and two mediating views developed, the mediating views becoming those possible in orthodox Islām. All could appeal to Ḳurʾānic texts and to traditions. The traditions are, of course, in great part shadows thrown back from the later controversies. They may be found in al-Bukhārī, *Kitāb al-ḳadar* and also in part of the *Kitāb al-ṭibb*; see, too, al-Ashʿarī, *Kitāb al-ibāna*, Ḥaidarābād, p. 84 *sqq.* (*Bāb al-riwāyat fi 'l-ḳadar*). The Djabrīya [q. v.] were absolute predestinarians; man had no part at all in the actions which apparently proceeded from him. This became an heretical position in Islām. The other extreme, that man produced his own actions, was that of the Ḳadarites who eventually merged in the Muʿtazilites. At first they did not venture to use the word "create" (*khalḳ*) — Allāh alone was *khāliḳ* — of this producing, but employed supposedly safer terms, such as *īdjād*, *ikhtirāʿ*, but eventually they came to speak of man "creating" his actions. The intermediate, orthodox, parties were the Ashʿarites and the Māturīdites. Of these the Ashʿarites had thought out their position most logically, while the Māturīdites stated simply the evident facts in the case. The basis of the upholders of free will seems to have been ethical; the justice (*ʿadl*) of Allāh requires man's freedom. But orthodox Islām in general cared little for that, although some, as al-Taftāzānī and al-Rāzī, spend dialectic on the point. It maintained the Pauline parallel of the potter and the vessels; Allāh could do what he pleased with his own. The orthodox difficulty was rather man's consciousness of freedom. This the Māturīdites met by admitting that man did possess "free-choice actions (*afʿāl ikhtiyārīya*) for which he is rewarded or punished" (al-Nasafī, *ʿAḳāʾid*, ed. with commentary of al-Taftāzānī, Cairo 1321, p. 97). Man knows the difference between a voluntary grasping and an involuntary trembling, but the contradiction of this with the absoluteness of Allāh's creative power is left unsolved. Al-Ashʿarī introduced the idea of *iktisāb* [see KASB] "accepting for one's self": man accepts for himself the action of Allāh and this accepting is man's consciousness of free will. Apparently al-Ashʿarī meant that this consciousness was only another part of Allāh's creative action. Man is still an automaton, although part of his machinery is that he believes himself free. Between the two wide scope was left even in orthodox Islām for discussion. The ultimate, scholastic, Ashʿarite statement, denying that man possesses any action at all — which must not, however, be taken for the only possible one in Islām — will be conveniently found in al-Faḍālī's *Kifāyat al-ʿawāmm* with al-Bādjūrī's commentary, and in Luciani, *Prolégomènes théologiques de Senoussi*. This attitude struck so deep that even al-Ghazzālī, and that even at the end of the wonderful psychological analysis of the book of the *Iḥyāʾ* on "the marvels of the heart", could quote with approval the tradition: "These to Heaven and I care not, and these to Hell and I care not" (ed. with commentary of al-Saiyid al-Murtaḍā, vii. 308); (cf. Macdonald, *Religious Attitude in Islam*, p. 301).

Bibliography: von Kremer, *Gesch. d. herrsch. Ideen des Islams*, Leipzig 1868, p. 29 *sqq.*; Houtsma, *De strijd over het dogma*, etc., Leyden 1875, p. 42 *sqq.*; Goldziher, *Vorlesungen über den Islam*, p. 95 *sqq.*; A. de Vlieger, *Kitāb al-ḳadr*, especially for traditions; cf. also Goldziher's review in *ZDMG*, lvii. 392 *sqq.*; Krehl, *Über die koranische Lehre von der Prädestination*, etc., in *Bericht. über die Verhandl. der Kgl. Sächs. Gesellsch. der Wiss. zu Leipzig*, phil.-hist. Kl., xxii. (Leipzig 1870); Salisbury, *Muhammadan Doctrine of Predestination and Free Will*, in *JAOS*, viii. 152; *Dict. of Techn. Terms*, p. 1179 *sqq.*; al-Rāzī, *Mafātīḥ*, Cairo 1308, on Sūra liv. 49, part vii. 571 *sqq.*; Wensinck, *The Muslim Creed*, index, s.v. predestination; L. Gardet et M. Anawati, *Introduction à la Théologie Musulmane*, Paris 1948, p. 37, 151; W. M. Watt, *Free will and predestination in early Islam*, London 1948.

ḲADARĪYA, the name of a sect which is given regularly as a descriptive or surname (*laḳab*) of the Muʿtazila, but it points back to a pre-Muʿtazilite time when the Muslims were beginning to ask theological questions and when, the first apparently among these questioners, there were doubters of the harsh predestinarianism of Muḥammad's last period. The later Muʿtazilites resented the name and held that it applied better to those who maintained Allāh's *ḳadar* of all things, good and bad, than to themselves who held that man has a certain power (*ḳudra*) over his actions. This, the orthodox said, was because they wished to avoid the saying of the Prophet: "The Ḳadarites are the Madjūs (Zoroastrians, Dualists) of this People", which meant that they made man a *khāliḳ al-afʿāl*, "creator of actions", thus giving Allāh a partner in creating. But this saying was certainly later than the rise of the Ḳadarites and the name may well have been first invented and applied to themselves by those who claimed a *ḳadar* over their own actions. Another saying ascribed to Muḥammad in this connection is: "They are the opponents of Allāh in *ḳadar*", i. e. they profess to have a rival *ḳadar* to that of Allāh. Al-Taftāzānī (on al-Nasafī, p. 96) has a pointed story of how a certain Madjūsī silenced (*alzama*) ʿAmr b. ʿUbaid on both these points. The name which the Muʿtazilites preferred for themselves in regard to this doctrine was "the People of Justice" (*ʿadl*); Allāh's justice required that man must be free if he were to be rewarded or punished.

Bibliography: See that of ḲADAR and add al-Īdjī, *Mawāḳif*, Būlāḳ 1266, p. 620; al-Shahrastānī, *Milal*, i. 54 on margin of *Milal* of Ibn Ḥazm; Nallino, *Sul nome di Qadariti*, in *RSO*, vii. 461 *sqq*; A. S. Tritton, *Muslim Theology*, London 1947, p. 54.

ḲADHF (A.) is slander in a special sense. If anyone accuses a respectable person (*muḥṣan*) of incontinence, without being able to bring four witnesses to support him, he is liable by law to a definite punishment (*ḥadd*) of 80 lashes for ḳadhf. The regulations on this subject in the law-books are based mainly on Sūra xxiv. 4. In a case of ḳadhf, all male and female persons are considered *muḥṣan* who have never been guilty of incontinence and who, in addition, are believers, freemen, of age, and in possession of their mental faculties. The right to demand the punishment of the guilty one is in the view of most *faḳīh*'s a private right of the person slandered (i. e. a. *ḥaḳḳ ādamī*) so that the latter (or his heir) may also voluntarily refrain from exercising it. In the view of the Ḥanafī school, however, the *ḥadd* punishment for ḳadhf is a right of God (*ḥaḳḳ Allāh*), and neither the person slandered nor his heir can avert this punishment from the guilty one. If a husband has accused his wife of unfaithfulness without being able to prove the charge in the prescribed manner, he can secure exemption from punishment by pronouncing the *liʿān* formula [see under ṬALĀḲ]. Punishment, moreover, may not be inflicted on the father, mother or more distant ascendants of the insulted party, nor on minors and lunatics. For a slave the punishment is only 40 lashes.

Bibliography: The chapter on *ḥadd* in the collections on Tradition and the *fiḳh* books; al-Bādjūrī, *Ḥāshiya ʿalā sharḥ Ibn Ḳāsim al-Ghazzī*, (Būlāḳ 1307) ii. 241 *sqq*.; Ṣadr al-Sharīʿa al-thānī, *Mukhtaṣar al-wiḳāya* (Ḳazān 1296), p. 167 *sq*.; al-Dimashḳī, *Raḥmat al-umma fi 'khtilāf al-aʾimma* (Būlāḳ 1300), p. 142 *sq*.; E. Sachau, *Muhamm. Recht nach schafiitischer Lehre*, p. 810, 826 *sqq*.; Th. W. Juynboll, *Handb. des islām. Gesetzes*, p. 303 *sq*.; Bergsträsser, *Grundzüge des islamischen Rechts* (Berlin-Leipzig 1935), p. 99 *sq*.

ḲĀḌĪ (A.) is the judge, who, according to the theory of Muslim law, has to decide all cases involving questions of civil and criminal law. In practice, however, there has been from quite an early period throughout the Muslim east a twofold method of administration of law, which we can distinguish one from the other, with a certain amount of correctness, as "religious" and "secular". Only such questions as are popularly felt to be closely connected with religion (e. g. disputes on points of family law or inheritance, legal questions concerning pious foundations, etc.) are brought to be decided, in conformity to canon law, before the ḳāḍī, the "religious" judge; all other questions, according to the popular view current in the east, come within the province of the secular authorities, and they as laymen usually decide them by other standards.

The ḳāḍī must, according to the law, be a Muslim scholar of blameless life (*ʿadl*), thoroughly conversant with the prescriptions of the sacred law. Originally the theory of most *madhhab*'s even demanded that the ḳāḍī should be able to derive the laws to be applied in his verdicts independently as a *mudjtahid* [see IDJTIHĀD] from the sacred sources. Later, however, no one was any longer considered qualified to give his own interpretation of the law; the judges could only be *muḳallid*'s, who were tied down to the decisions of earlier authoritative scholars. The ḳāḍī therefore in giving his decisions has to adhere strictly to the rules which he finds laid down in the *fiḳh* books of his *madhhab*.

The administration of justice is considered a religious duty for the Muslim community. In each district the competent authority must appoint a suitable person as ḳāḍī. If there is only one, who can be considered legally qualified for the office of judge, he is bound to accept the office if appointed and even bound to seek the office if the authorities should neglect to give it to him.

The ḳāḍī has to conduct his court exactly in accordance with the procedure laid down by the law. He has to treat the parties, if they are both believers, as equals in every respect. If the defendant admits that the plaintiff is in the right, no further proof is necessary. If the defendant, on the other hand, does not acknowledge any justification for the charge, the plaintiff must support his assertions by proofs. The judgement of the ḳāḍī is decisive for the parties; there is no appeal from it.

To secure the independance of the judge, the law forbids the ḳāḍī to take presents from people who are appearing in his court. He also should avoid engaging in trade, either personally or through the intermediary of persons known to be his agents, as people might then attempt to win him to their side by offering special advantages in business.

In spite of these and many other regulations to secure as faultless an administration of justice as possible "the bad ḳāḍī's" have at all times given cause for complaint in Islām. Many judges were ignorant and corrupt. If upright men filled the office, they frequently found themselves forced to bend the law to suit the will of authority. In religious circles then there soon arose a strong disinclination to fill the office of judge. Traditions were put into currency in which the Prophet was made to utter grave warnings against accepting the position of ḳāḍī. Pious *faḳīh*'s, e. g. Abū Ḥanīfa declined to fill the office of judge (see also A. J. Wensinck, *The refused Dignity*, in the *E. G. Browne Memorial Volume*, Cambridge 1922, p. 497 *sqq*.).

For many centuries past no Muslim judge has any longer come up to the original theoretical requirements of the law; therefore any existing ḳāḍī is regarded by Muslim scholars only as *ḳāḍī 'l-ḍarūra*, i. e. as an emergency ḳāḍī, to whom one must go, in default of a better.

On the history of the office of ḳāḍī and of the ḳāḍī's see: R. J. H. Gottheil, *The Cadi, the History of this Institution*, in *Revue des Études ethnographiques et sociologiques*, i. (1908), p. 385—393; E. Tyan, *Histoire de l'Organisation judiciaire en pays d'Islam*, 2 vol. Paris 1938—1943; *The History of the Egyptian Cadis as compiled by Abu Omar Muhammed al-Kindi*, ed. by R. J. H. Gottheil, New York 1908 (with an introduction); cf. *The Governors and Judges of Egypt of el-Kindi*, ed. by R. Guest (*GMS*, xix.), 1912; and also the important remarks on the office of ḳāḍī in Cordova by Ribera in the introduction to his edition of al-Khushanī, *Kitāb al-ḳuḍāt bi-Ḳurtuba* (*Hist. de los Jueces de Córdoba por Aljoxani*, Madrid 1914; cf. Ḥādjdjī Khalīfa, ii. 141, N⁰. 2279).

The office of ḳāḍī in Islām was taken over from governmental institutions in the conquered Byzantine and Persian countries, the preislamic Arabs having no other way of settling their disputes than the appointing of an arbitrator (*ḥakam*) for each special case (cf. Tyan, Ch. i). The Prophet and the early Caliphs often decided disputes in person, as did their governors and prefects in the various provinces. Justice was always administered in Muslim lands to a great extent by local authorities, notably the police officials. This was sometimes called *naẓar fi 'l-maẓālim* (al-Māwardī, ed. Enger, p. 128 *sqq.*; H. F. Amedroz, *The Mazalim Jurisdiction in the Ahkam Sultaniyya of Mawardi*, *JRAS*, in 1911, p. 635 *sqq.*; Tyan, vol. ii, 141—288).

ʿUmar and ʿUthmān and their successors had also appointed special officers as judges (*ḳāḍī*). These ḳāḍī's, who usually belonged to the *faḳīh* class, never obtained an independent position in Islām. They were often dismissed — soon after their appointment — and always remained subject to the caprice of the ruler. Cf. for example *Autobiographie d'Ibn Khaldoun*, transl. M. de Slane, Paris 1844, p. 103—110 (*JA*, 4th Ser., iii. 328 *sqq.*).

The ḳāḍī's had not only to decide cases but they had also to administer pious foundations (*waḳf*) and the estates of orphans, imbeciles and other persons. They had often to draw up contracts of marriage for women without male relations, etc. The chief ḳāḍī in the capital was one of the high officials (al-Maḳrīzī, *al-Khiṭaṭ*, Būlāḳ 1270, i. 403). In eastern countries he was called *ḳāḍi 'l-ḳuḍāt*, in the western *ḳāḍi 'l-djamāʿa* (Dozy, *Suppl. aux Dict. Arab.*, ii. 363b). In later times the *ḳāḍi 'l-ʿaskar* was also a high official (cf. al-Ḳalḳashandī, *Ṣubḥ al-aʿshā*, iv. 36; *Autobiogr. d'Ibn Khaldoun*, p. 102; Tyan, vol. ii, 289—306; J. v. Hammer, *Des Osmanischen Reichs Staatsverfassung*, ii. 378 *sqq.*). Some ḳāḍī's were military leaders.

In the large cities, where numerous adherents of the different *fiḳh* schools lived together, a ḳāḍī was appointed, if necessary, for each *madhhab*. For example, there were in later times four ḳāḍī's in Cairo (Quatremère, *Hist. des sultans mamlouks*, i. 1, p. 98, note; Gaudefroy-Demombynes, *La Syrie à l'époque des Mamelouks*, Paris 1923).

Bibliography: In addition to the chapter on the administration of law in the *fiḳh* books: al-Khaṣṣāf, *Adab al-ḳāḍī* (Cod. 550 Warn., *Cat. Cod. Or. Bibl. Lugd.-Bat.*, iv. 106); D. S. Margoliouth, *Omar's Instructions to the Kadi* (*JRAS*, 1910, i. 307—326); al-Māwardī (ed. Enger), p. 107 *sqq.* (French transl. by E. Fagnan, Algiers 1915, p. 131 *sqq.*); al-Shawkānī, *Nail al-awṭār* (Būlāḳ 1297), viii. 495 *sqq.*; al-Dimashḳī, *Raḥmat al-umma fi 'khtilāf al-aʾimma* (Būlāḳ 1300), p. 108 *sqq.*; al-Shaʿrānī, *al-Mīzān al-kubrā* (Cairo 1279), ii. 211 *sqq.*; Ibn Khaldūn, *al-Muḳaddima*, § iii, ch. 31, transl. by de Slane (*NE*, xix. 448 *sqq.*); C. Snouck Hurgronje, *Mekka*, i. 182 *sqq.*; do., *Anzeige von Sachau's Muhamm. Recht*, in *ZDMG*, liii. (1899), p. 138, 154 *sqq.*, = *Versp. Geschr.*, ii. 369 *sqq.*; do., *Mohammedanism*, New York 1916, p. 110 *sqq.*; do., *The Achehnese*, i. 94 *sqq.*; I. Goldziher, *Muhamm. Studien*, ii. 39 *sq.*; A. von Kremer, *Culturgesch. des Orients* (Vienna 1875), i. 415—419; H. F. Amedroz, *The Office of Kadi in the Ahkam Sultaniyya of Mawardi*, in *JRAS*, 1910, p. 761—796; cf. 1909, p. 1138—1146; Th. W. Juynboll, *Handb. des islāmischen Gesetzes*, p. 309 *sqq.*; Bergsträsser, *Grundzüge des islamischen Rechts* (Berlin-Leipzig 1935), p. 108 *sqq.*; E. Sachau, *Muhamm. Recht nach schafiitischer Lehre*, p. ix—xi., 696 *sqq.*; E. Lane, *The Manners and Customs of the Modern Egyptians*, Chapt. on Government; Ph. Vassel, *Über Marokkanische Processpraxis*, in *MSOS*, 1902, v., 2nd sect., p. 170 *sqq.*; M. d'Ohsson, *Tableau général de l'empire othoman*, ii. (Paris 1790), 267—283; J. v. Hammer, *Des Osmanischen Reichs Staatsverfassung und Staatsverwaltung* (Vienna 1815), ii. 372 *sqq.*

ḲĀDIRĪYA, Order (*ṭarīḳa*) of dervishes called after ʿAbd al-Ḳādir al-Djīlānī (or al-Djīlī) [q.v.].

1. Origin. ʿAbd al-Ḳādir al-Djīlī (d. 561/1166) was the principal of a school (*madrasa*) of Ḥanbalite Law and a *ribāṭ* in Baghdād. His sermons (collected in *al-Fatḥ al-rabbānī*) were delivered sometimes in the one, sometimes in the other; both were notable institutions in the time of Ibn al-Athīr, and Yāḳūt (*Irshād al-arīb*, v. 274) records a bequest of books made to the former by a man who died in 572/1176-7. Both appear to have come to an end at the sack of Baghdād in 656/1258, till when it is probable that their headship remained in the family of ʿAbd al-Ḳādir, which was numerous and distinguished. In the *Bahdjat al-asrār*, where an accurate account of his descendants is given (p. 113—117), it is stated that ʿAbd al-Ḳādir was succeeded in the *madrasa* by his son ʿAbd al-Wahhāb (552—593/1157—1196), who was followed by his son ʿAbd al-Salām (d. 611/1214). Another son, ʿAbd al-Razzāḳ (528—603/1134—1206-7), was a notable ascetic. Several members of the family perished during the sack of Baghdād, when it would appear that both these institutions came to an end.

A *ribāṭ* was at this time distinguished from a *zāwiya*, the former being a *coenobium*, the latter a place where an ascetic lived in solitude (al-Suhrawardī, *ʿAwārif al-maʿārif*, margin of the *Iḥyāʾ*, Cairo 1306, i. 217). In the time of Ibn Baṭṭūṭa *zāwiya* had come to be used in the former sense also, and his description of the religious exercises practised at the *zāwiya* (i. 71) would probably suit what went on at ʿAbd al-Ḳādir's *ribāṭ*. The body of rules and doctrines which had his authority was sufficient to constitute a system (*madhhab*; *Bahdja*, p. 101), and by accepting the *khirḳa* [q.v.] from the shaikh the *murīd* signified that he subordinated his will to that of the former (al-Suhrawardī, i. 192). A long list is given in the *Bahdja* of men who attained various degrees of distinction who had received the *khirḳa* from ʿAbd al-Ḳādir, two of them at the age of seven and one at the age of one. These persons were said to "ascribe themselves" (*intasaba or intamā* or even *tasammā*) to ʿAbd al-Ḳādir, and could bestow the *khirḳa* on others as from him; in doing so they would stipulate that the *murīd* was to regard ʿAbd al-Ḳādir as his shaikh and director after the Prophet. In a tradition which is likely to be apocryphal (*Bahdja*, p. 101), dated 592/1196, ʿAbd al-Ḳādir declared that assumption of his *khirka* was not absolutely necessary for entry into his order; personal attachment to himself was sufficient. It would appear that during his lifetime several persons carried on propaganda in favour of his system; one ʿAlī b. al-Ḥaddād obtained proselytes in Yaman, and one Muḥammad al-Baṭāʾiḥī, resident in Baalbek, did likewise in Syria; one Taḳī al-Dīn Muḥammad al-Yūnīnī, also of Baalbek, was another propagandist, and one Muḥammad b. ʿAbd al-Ṣamad in Egypt "ascribed himself to ʿAbd al-Ḳādir and in treading the Path relied on him after God and His Apostle" (*Bahdja*, p. 109, 110). Since all who ascribed themselves to him were promised Paradise, the order is likely to have been popular; and even in recent times missionaries in Africa appear to have little difficulty in obtaining fresh adherents to it (cf. O. Lenz, *Timbuktu*, ii. 33).

That ʿAbd al-Ḳādir's sons had some share in spreading the order is likely, though Ibn Taimīya (d. 728/1328) mentions that he had associated with one of his descendants who was an ordinary Muslim and not a member of it, and so did not agree with those who held fanatical views about him (*Bughyat al-murtād*, p. 124). The *Bahdja* however does not bear out Le Chatelier's assertion (*Confréries musulmanes du Hedjaz*, p. 35) that in ʿAbd al-Ḳādir's life-time some of his sons had been preaching his doctrine in Morocco, Egypt, Arabia, Turkestan and India. It says much of ʿAbd al-Razzāḳ, but nothing of the "mosque now in ruins, whose seven gilded domes have often served as the subject of description by Arabic historians", which this son is supposed to have built. Indeed this mosque appears to be later than Ḥamd Allāh Mustawfī (740/1339—40), the first author later than the *Bahdja*, who mentions ʿAbd al-Ḳādir's tomb (*Nuzhat al-ḳulūb*, transl. Le Strange, p. 42). Nor does it confirm the statement that this ʿAbd al-Razzāḳ introduced the use of music in the ritual, and indeed the employment of this was earlier than ʿAbd al-Ḳādir's time, and is discussed by al-Suhrawardī (ii. 116) withhout allusion to ʿAbd al-Razzāḳ. E. Mercier (*Histoire de l'Afrique Septentrionale*, iii. 14) asserts that the Order of Ḳādirīya existed in Berbery in the xii[th] century A. D., and was closely connected with the Fāṭimids (whose rule terminated 567/1171), but he gives no authority for these statements.

Al-Suhrawardī holds that the exercises of each *murīd* should be determined by his shaikh in accordance with his individual needs, whence it is unlikely that ʿAbd al-Ḳādir instituted any rigid system of *dhikr*, *wird* and *ḥizb*, and indeed those in use among different Ḳādirī communities differ (Rinn, *Marabouts et Khouan*, p. 183 *sqq.*). The initiation ceremonies given on Turkish authority by J. P. Brown (*The Dervishes*, p. 98) are quite different from those furnished by Rinn on North African authority. In one of these latter there is a tendency to set ʿAlī above Muḥammad and to insist on the importance of Ḥasan and Ḥusain, which cannot well represent the views of the Ḥanbalite ʿAbd al-Ḳādir. The *wird* of ʿAbd al-Ḳādir in *al-Fuyūḍāt al-rabbānīya* is given on the authority of one ʿAbd Allāh b. Muḥammad al-ʿAdjamī, who lived 185 years (536—721), and may be regarded as mythical.

2. Development. Ḳādirism seems from an early period to have developed on different lines according as ʿAbd al-Ḳādir was regarded as the founder of a system involving rites and practices, or as a worker of miracles. In the latter direction it meant the deification of ʿAbd al-Ḳādir, the extremists holding that he was Lord of Creation after God, absolutely, whereas the more moderate supposed that he was so only in his own age (*Bughyat al-murtād, l.c.*). The latter was the view of Ibn ʿArabī, who takes him as an example of a *khalīfa* who showed himself and practised sovereignty (*taṣarruf*; *al-Futūḥāt al-Makkīya*, ii. 407); such a *khalīfa* in his system is independent of the revelation to Muḥammad (*Fuṣūṣ al-ḥikam*, § 16). But there was also a theory that ʿAbd al-Ḳādir practised in his grave all the activities (*taṣarruf*) of the living (Ibn al-Wardī [d. 749], *Taʾrīkh*, ii. 70); and Ibn Taimīya (*al-Djawāb al-ṣaḥīḥ*, i. 323) mentions him among saints who in his time still appeared to people, being in reality impersonated by demons. In the initiation ceremonies recorded by J. P. Brown, *l. c.*, the candidate for admission to the Order sees ʿAbd al-Ḳādir in dreams; in one case so often and so clearly that without having seen ʿAbd al-Ḳādir's portrait he could recognize him among a thousand. The form of Ḳādirism which means the worship of ʿAbd al-Ḳādir seems to prevail in North Africa, where it is called Djīlālīya (for Djīlānīya) and whole communities are called Djīlāla. Their system has been described as the application of Ṣūfic mysticism to beliefs that are certainly pre-Islāmic, and the materialization of that mysticism under the form of a cult of hidden subterranean powers (E. Michaux-Bellaire, in *Archives Marocaines*, xx. 235). Here the word *khalwa* is used for a heap of stones where women attach rags to reeds planted between the stones and where they burn benzoin and styrax in potsherds (*ibid.*, xvii. 60). Such *khalwa's* are to be found in all the Arab villages. Similarly "in the province of Oran on all the roads and on the summits of the chief mountains *qubbah*'s are to be found in the name of ʿAbd al-Ḳādir Jilali" (E. de Neveu, *Ordres religieux chez les musulmans d'Algérie*, p. 30). The society of the Genāwah or Negroes of Guinea has placed itself entirely under the protection of Mawlāy ʿAbd al-Ḳādir with all his array of male and female demons; wherein M. Michaux-Bellaire finds traces of the powers which, according to the Ḳurʾān (and even earlier authorities), belonged to Solomon. The cult of ʿAbd al-Ḳādir is most ardently practised by the women in the Khloṭ and Ṭlīḳ, who come to the *khalwa* for every sort of object, and to satisfy their loves and hates in all the acts of their existence. The men, on the other hand, chiefly go to the *khalwa* when they are ill (*Arch. Maroc.*, vi. 329).

That this development is inconsistent with Islāmic orthodoxy is evident, and it is attacked by such authorities as Ibn Taimīya and Ibrāhīm al-Shāṭibī (*Iʿtiṣām*, i. 348 *sqq.*). The system to which the name Ḳādirīya is more ordinarily applied differs from other orders mainly in ritual, although, through circumstances connected with its origin, "it has not that homogeneity of statutes which is to be found in other congregations, which seem to form small exclusive churches outside which there is no salvation" (Rinn, p. 186). Though the founder was a Ḥanbalite, membership is by no means confined to that school, and the order is theoretically both tolerant and charitable.

3. Geographical Distribution. Since historical and geographical works rarely distinguish between the different *ṭuruḳ* in their accounts of religious buildings, little can be said with cer-

tainty of the date at which the first Ḳādirī *zāwiya* or *khānḳāh* was established in any country save ʿIrāḳ. The order is said to have been introduced into Fez by the posterity of two of ʿAbd al-Ḳādir's sons, Ibrāhīm (d. 592/1196 in Wāsiṭ) and ʿAbd al-ʿAzīz (who died in Djiyāl, a village of Sindjar); they had migrated to Spain and shortly before the fall of Granada (897/1492) their descendants fled to Morocco. The full genealogy of the Shurafāʾ Djīlāla of Fez is given in *Arch. Maroc.*, iii. 106—114, on the authority of *al-Durr al-sanī* of Ibn al-Ṭaiyib al-Ḳādirī (1090/1679), who claims to have used a series of authentic documents. The *khalwa* of ʿAbd al-Ḳādir in Fez is mentioned as early as 1104/1692-3 (*ibid.*, xi. 319). The order was introduced into Asia Minor and Constantinople by Ismāʿīl Rūmī, founder of the *khānḳāh* known as the Ḳādirīkhānah at the Top-khānah. This personage (d. 1041/1631), who is called *pīr-i thānī*, "Second Shaikh", is said to have founded some 40 *tekiye*'s in these regions (*Ḳāmūs al-aʿlām*). A Ḳādirī *ribāṭ* in Mecca is mentioned by Ṣāliḥ b. Mahdī in *al-ʿAlam al-shāmikh*, p. 381, about 1180/1669-70, but the assertion that a branch was established there during the lifetime of ʿAbd al-Ḳādir (Le Chatelier, *o. c.*, p. 44) is not improbable, since Mecca has a natural attraction for the Ṣūfīs. In the *Aʾīn-i akbarī* (about 1600; transl. Jarrett, iii. 357) the Ḳādirīya order is mentioned as one that is highly respected but is not included among those recognized in India; nor does there appear to be any allusion to it in the list of Indian Ṣūfīs in the *Maʾāthir-i kirām* (1752), though some other orders are noticed, and ʿAbd al-Ḳādir himself is mentioned. Yet see Khāfī Khān, *Muntakhab al-lubāb*, ii. 604.

Some statistics (to be received with caution) of the Ḳādirīs and their *zāwiya*'s are given by Depont et Coppolani (*Confréries religieuses musulmanes*, p. 301—318). Much of its development is admittedly recent, and may be due to the fame won by the namesake of ʿAbd al-Ḳādir who for so many years resisted the French occupation of North Africa. It is doubtless represented in all Islāmic countries, though it would appear that certain derived *ṭuruḳ* enjoy greater popularity in many places. Thus the Ḳādirīya of Touba in Guinea, which has become a distinct sign whereby the Diakanke tribe can be recognized, is derived through the Sidia from the Ḳādirīya of the Kounta of Timbuctu (P. Marty, in *RMM*, xxxvi. 183). These Kounta however form a branch of the Ḳādirīya, and some of them prefer to call themselves Shādhilīya (*ibid.*, xxxi. 414).

4. O r g a n i z a t i o n. The Ḳādirī community acknowledges nominal allegiance to the keeper of ʿAbd al-Ḳādir's tomb in Baghdād, and the deeds of investiture published by Rinn, p. 179 and in *RMM*, ii. 513 and ix. 290, are from this source. It would seem however that the actual authority of this personage is chiefly recognized in Mesopotamia and India. The Indian Ḳādirīs periodically send gifts which form the main source of the revenues of his establishment; the members of this family find it worth while to learn Urdu. The Meccan *zāwiya*'s are subject to the *shaikh al-ṭuruḳ*, who has the right to nominate their *muḳaddam*. The Egyptian branch is under the control of the Saiyid al-Bakrī, who is also *shaikh al-ṭuruḳ*; ʿAlī Pasha Mubārak (iii. 129; see also P. Kahle, in *Isl.*, vi. 154) reckons the order as one of the four which go back to a *ḳuṭb*, but asserts that it has neither

furūʿ nor *buyūt*. In Africa, according to Rinn, each *muḳaddam* names his successor; in the event of one dying without having nominated, an election is made by the *ikhwān* at a *ḥaḍra*. The approval of the head of the order in Baghdād is then solicited, and has never been refused. The organization of the order in North Africa is described somewhat fully by Rinn and Depont et Coppolani, in the works cited. The system appears to be in general congregational, i.e. the *zāwiya*'s are independent, and the relation between them and the central institution in Baghdād is very loose. The principle whereby the headship of a *zāwiya* is hereditary is generally recognized.

5. S y m b o l s a n d R i t e s. The sign of the Turkish Ḳādirīs is said to be a rose which is green, having been adopted by Ismāʿīl Rūmī. The candidate for admission to the order after a year brings an *ʿaraḳīya* or small felt cap, to which if the candidate be accepted the Shaikh attaches a rose of 18 sections, with Solomon's Seal in the centre. This cap is called by them *tādj*. The symbolism of this is explained by J. P. Brown, *The Dervishes*, p. 98 sqq. (copied by Wilberforce Clarke, transl. of *ʿAwārif al-maʿārif*, p. 159; the Urdu translation *Kashf asrār al-mashāyikh* adds nothing to Brown's information). According to him, they prefer the colour green, though they allow others; in Lane's time the turbans and banners of the Ḳādirīs in Egypt were white; most members of the order were fishermen, and they in religious processions carried upon poles nets of various colours (*Modern Egyptians*, 1871, i. 306). In India there are festivities in honour of ʿAbd al-Ḳādir on 11 Rabīʿ II, and pilgrimages are made in many places in Algeria and Morocco to the *zāwiya*'s and shrines of the saint (Rinn, p. 177). The *mawsim* of the Djīlāla at Salé is described at length by L. Mercier, in *Arch. Maroc.*, viii. 137—139; it commences the seventh day of the *mūlud* (*mawlid*), i. e. the Feast of the Prophet's Birthday, and lasts four days, 17—20 Rabīʿ I. Sheep and oxen are presented to the descendants of ʿAbd al-Ḳādir. M. Michaux-Bellaire distinguishes in Morocco between the ceremonies of the Ḳādirīya, who recite the *ḥizb*, and the Djīlāla, who recite the *dhikr* to the accompaniment of instruments; and again between the Djīlāla of the country, whose instruments are the *bender* (a short of big tambourine without bells) and *ʿawāda*, and those of the town, whose instruments are the *ṭebila*, *ṭabal* and *ghaiṭa* (*Arch. Maroc.*, vi. 330 and xvii. 60). A description of the *ḥaḍrat al-mallūk*, a performance executed with these last instruments, which leads to ecstasy, is given by him in the first passage cited. He further records some special ceremonies connected with the Awlād Khalīfa in the Gharb (*ibid.*, xx. 287). All the Hilālī of the Gharb are Djīlāla, and in all the *ḥaḍra*'s (services) of the Djīlāla the presence of at least one Khalīfī is necessary for the direction of ceremonies, and when no actual Khalīfī is present, some one there takes the name in order to perform the priestly duty. The origin of the name Awlād Khalīfa is obscure (p. 284); it may be noticed that the *Bahdja* mentions one Khalīfa b. Mūsā al-Nahrmalikī as having played a leading part in the propagation of ʿAbd al-Ḳādir's system. "The *ḥaḍra* of the Djīlāla of the country contains neither the *ḥizb* nor the *dhikr* instituted by the Shaikh, but a plain *dhikr* of improvised words in the ceremonial rhythm of the *banādir* (plur. of *bender*). These improvi-

sations always terminate with the words: "Thus spake Mawlāy ʿAbd al-Ḳādir" or "O Mawlāy ʿAbd al-Ḳādir!" " (Michaux-Bellaire, p. 288).

Various collections of rituals supposed to have been recommended by ʿAbd al-Ḳādir have been published in Egypt, Turkey and India. In *al-Fuyūḍāt al-rabbānīya* he who is about to enter upon *khalwa* (retreat) is advised to fast in the day and keep vigil at night. The *khalwa* lasts forty days. "If a figure reveal itself to him saying "I am God", he should say "nay rather thou art in God", and if it be for probation, it will vanish; but if it remain, then it will be a genuine revelation (*tadjallī*)" (Dihlī 1330, p. 60). Reduction of food during the 40 days should be gradual till for the last three fasting is complete. At the end he returns by degrees to his former diet. Some practices peculiar to the Djīlāla of Tangier are recorded by G. Salmon (*Arch. Maroc.*, ii. 108).

The first time that the Ḳādirīs appear to have played a political part was during the French conquest of Algeria, when the chief of the Ḳādirīya Muḥyi 'l-Dīn, having been offered the leadership in the war against the infidel, permitted his son ʿAbd al-Ḳādir to accept it. This person was able to utilize the religious organization of his order in order to establish the sovereignty which the French had accorded him, and when his sovereignty was threatened could fall back on his rank as *muḳaddam* of his order to win fresh recruits (H. Garrot, *Histoire générale de l'Algérie*, Algiers 1910, p. 800, 863 etc.). Since the fall and exile of this personage it would appear that the Ḳādirīs in Africa have lent their support to the French government. (Ismaël Hamet, *Les Muselmans Français du Nord de l'Afrique*, Paris 1906, p. 276). — In the Ottoman revolution of 1908 it is said that their sympathies were with the revolutionists, but that for fear of being outdone in religious zeal by the rival Rifāʿī order they joined in Baghdād in the "pogrom" against the Jews (L. Massignon, in *RMM*, vi. 461).

Bibliography: Oriental editions cited: ʿAlī b. Yūsuf al-Shaṭṭanawfī, *Bahdjat al-asrār*, Cairo 1304; *al-Fatḥ al-rabbānī*, Cairo 1302; Ṣāliḥ b. Mahdī, *al-ʿAlam al-shāmikh fī īthār al-ḥaḳḳ ʿala 'l-ābāʾ wa'l-mashāʾikh*, Cairo 1328; *Kashf asrār al-mashāʾikh*, Lucknow 1891; Khāfī Khān, *Muntakhab al-lubāb*, in *Bibl. Ind.*, 1869—74; *Bughyat al-murtād*, Cairo 1329.

KAFĀLA (A.), the pledge given by any one (the *kafīl*) to a creditor (the *makfūl lahu*) to secure that the debtor (the *makfūl bihi*) will be present at a definite place, e. g. to pay his debt or fine or, in case of retaliation, to undergo punishment.

If the *makfūl bihi* is not there at the time arranged, the guarantor can be kept prisoner till the debtor comes or until it is proved that he cannot come (e. g. because he is dead).

As to the question whether the guarantor is bound to pay for the *makfūl bihi* or to suffer his punishment, the opinions of the different *madhhab*'s vary. According to the Shāfiʿī school, he is not bound to do so, not even if he has expressly bound himself to do so.

Bibliography: al-Bādjūrī, *Ḥāshiya ʿalā sharḥ Ibn Ḳāsim al-Ghazzī* (Būlāḳ 1307), i. 395 *sq.*; E. Sachau, *Muhammedan. Recht nach schafiitischer Lehre*, p. 405 *sqq.*; Bergsträsser, *Grundzüge des islamischen Rechts*, p. 77 *sq.*; al-Dimashḳī, *Raḥmat al-umma fi 'khtilāf al-aʾimma* (Būlāḳ 1300), p. 81; A. Querry, *Droit musulman*, i. 483—486.

KAFFĀRA (A.), atonement, expiation, literally, what "covers" the sin. The kaffāra has usually to consist in releasing a Muslim slave or — for those who are not sufficiently well off — in a three days' (and in some cases even two months') fast or as a substitute — for those who are not able to fast — in bestowing food or clothes on a definite number of poor people (from 10 to 60).

In some cases the Ḳurʾān has already prescribed a definite kaffāra for the sinner, e. g. Sūra iv. 92, after killing by accident or by design, Sūra v. 89, to avert the evil consequence of breaking an oath, Sūra lviii. 3 *sq.*, if a man by pronouncing the old Arab *ẓihār* formula has sworn to refrain from all sexual intercourse with his wife.

These and many other cases (e. g. the breaking of the fast prescribed in the month of Ramaḍān by fornication or marital intercourse during the day) were afterwards more precisely defined by the *faḳīh*'s and fully described in the *fiḳh* books of the different *madhhab*'s.

Bibliography: Ibn Ḳāsim al-Ghazzī, *Fatḥ al-ḳarīb*, ed. L. W. C. van den Berg, p. 262, 266, 500, 568, 662; Th. W. Juynboll, *Handb. des islāmischen Gesetzes*, p. 122, 225, 267, 298. See also ḲASAM.

KĀFIR (A.), originally "obliterating, covering", then, "concealing benefits received" = "ungrateful"; this meaning is found even in the old Arab poetry and in the Ḳurʾān, Sūra xxvi. 19. In the Ḳurʾān the word is used with reference to God: "concealing God's blessings" = "ungrateful to God", see Sūra xvi. 55 and xxx. 33: "That they are ungrateful for our gifts"; cf. also Sūra, xvi. 83. The next development — probably under the influence of the Syriac and Aramaic where the corresponding development took place earlier — is the more general meaning of "infidel" which is first found in Sūra lxxiv. 10 and is thereafter very common; plural *kāfirūn* or *kuffār*, once (Sūra lxxx. 42) *kafara*. The term is first applied to the unbelieving Meccans, who endeavour to refute and revile the Prophet: Sūra l. 2 and elsewhere. The subject of incredulity is sometimes more nearly defined with added *bi-*, e. g. Sūra xxxiv. 34: "We do not believe in your mission"; Sūra vi. 89. In the early Meccan period a waiting attitude towards the unbelievers is still recommended (Sūra lxxxvi. 17; lxxiii. 10 *sq.*; see also Sūra cix. entitled *al-Kāfirūn*), but later the Muslims are ordered to keep apart from them (Sūra iii. 118, also 28), to defend themselves from their attacks and even to take the offensive against them (Sūra ii. 190 and elsewhere). In most passages the reference is to unbelievers in general, who are threatened with God's punishment and Hell [cf. the article DJAHANNAM].

In the literature of Tradition also the ḥadīths — with minute elaboration in details — deal partly with the fate of the kāfir on the day of judgment and his punishment in Hell, and partly with the believer's attitude towards him. For the rest they reflect the great controversy in early Islām on the question whether a Muslim should be considered a kāfir for committing a "major sin" (cf. al-Bukhārī, *Kitāb al-īmān*, bāb 22). Thus we find ḥadīths such as: "If a Muslim charges a fellow Muslim with *kufr*, he is himself a kāfir, if the accusation should prove untrue"; or "The reproach of *kufr* is equivalent to murder" etc. Nevertheless, kāfir in theological polemics is a fairly frequent term for the Muslim protagonist of the opposite view.

Eternal damnation for the kāfir has remained an established dogma in Islām. In the dogmatic controversies of the early centuries the reasons were discussed for which a Muslim could be equated with a kāfir and so have to suffer eternal punishment (see ĪMĀN).

According to the *LA*, vi. 459 *sq.*, the following kinds of unbelief are distinguished: 1) *kufr al-inkār* — neither recognising nor acknowledging God; 2) *kufr al-djuḥūd* — recognising God, but not acknowledging Him with words, that is remaining an unbeliever in spite of one's better knowledge; 3) *kufr al-muʿānada* — recognising God and acknowledging Him with words but remaining an unbeliever (obdurate) out of envy or hatred; 4) *kufr al-nifāḳ* — outwardly acknowledging, but at heart not recognising God and thus remaining an unbeliever, that is being an hypocrite [cf. MUNĀFIḲŪN].

In the systematic Fiḳh books the *kuffār* are discussed in the following passages: 1) in the *Kitāb al-ṭahāra*. For the opinion deduced from Sūra ix. 28 that the unbeliever is unclean, we find all views represented, form the strictest to the most tolerant. The *ahl al-kitāb* [q.v.] are usually regarded more leniently than other *kuffār*; for their benefit for example the questions of the *dhabāʾiḥ* and of *munākaḥa* with Muslims are discussed. — 2) In the *Kitāb al-djihād* (*wa 'l-siyar*). The *djihād* [q.v.] against the unbelieving habitants of the *dār al-ḥarb* [q.v.] is a *farḍ ʿala 'l-kifāya*. The *ahl al-kitāb* again occupy a special position as by paying *djizya* and *kharādj* [q.v.] they become *dhimmī*'s [see DHIMMA] and can receive *amān*. These categories of unbelievers in the *dār al-islām* called *dhimmī* and *mustaʾmin* have a legal claim to protection. Another class also distinguished from the mass of the *kāfirūn* are the renegades [see MURTADD] for whom the law prescribes death, with the opportunity first of obeying a demand to return to Islām. — 3) In several further points the law discriminates between *kuffār* and believers; the very strict interpretation of the law is however in practice only held by a small minority.

To understand the historical development in the attitude of Islām to the unbeliever, it should be observed that it was settled in the early centuries not so much by religious as by political and social conditions. Even down to the time of the Crusades there prevailed in Islām a tolerance towards the unbeliever, especially the *ahl al-kitāb*, such as is impossible to imagine in contemporary Christendom. We find for example Christians in the highest official positions. In this early period there is no question of any religious fanaticism towards unbelievers. It was only aroused and nourished by the repeated wars with unbelievers (Crusades, wars with the Turks). War-psychology, on the other hand, at the time of the wars between Persia and Turkey could even bring it about that the Persians were called *kuffār* in Turkish *fetwās* etc. (see Pečewī, i. 311, 319), a term applied to the Turks themselves in the proclamations of the Mahdī of the Sūdān.

Since the historical trend of affairs has apparently been quite in the opposite direction, and Muslims have been more and more impeded in carrying out measures against the *kuffār* by the political decline of Islām and the rise of unbelieving nations (pressure of the Powers, capitulations, etc.), the very feeling of impotence in face of these facts may have contributed not a little to the strengthening of hatred and to periodical manifestations of it (in massacres etc.). This also explains the grotesque caricature of the kāfir, which one sometimes finds in the popular imagination at the present day (see Snouck Hurgronje *Mekka*, ii. 48 *sq.*) and which is connected with the ideas of the Arch-Kāfir, Dadjdjāl [q.v.], who bears *k-f-r* on his forehead (cf. Goldziher, in *Isl.*, xi. 178).

It may also be due to the hatred of the Franks (and to dogmatic squabbles) that kāfir developed into a term of abuse, frequent in the Turkish form *gʿawr* (the Persian *geber* is said to be the same), although in theory it is (*ZDMG*, lviii. 562) affirmed that the Muslim commits a punishable offence if he says to the Christian or Jew: "Thou unbeliever". From the Turkish the word kāfir has entered into most Slavonic languages. The Spanish *cafre* and the French *cafard* also go back to kāfir or *kuffār*. In two cases kāfir has actually become a proper name, the name of a people, the kaffirs, and of a country Kāfiristān.

Kāfir and *kufr* underwent a special development of meaning in the terminology of mysticism. Compare, for example, the well-known verse of Abū Saʿīd: "So long as belief and unbelief are not perfectly equal, no man can be a true Muslim", with the various explanations given in Muḥammad Aʿlā, *Dict. of Technical Terms* (ed. Sprenger, etc.), s.v., according to one of which *kufr* is just the equivalent of *īmān-i ḥaḳīḳī*.

Bibliography: In addition to the sources already quoted above, see for the old Arab poetry; *ZDMG*, xliv. 544. — Tradition: Wensinck, *Handbook*, s.v. Kāfir, Kufr. — Dogmatic: al-Māturīdī, *Sharḥ al-Fiḳh al-akbar* (Ḥaidarābād 1321), p. 2 *sq.*, 9 and *passim*; Ibn Ḥazm, *al-Faṣl fi 'l-milal wa 'l-niḥal* (Cairo 1320), iii. 142 *sqq.*; Muḥammad b. Djaʿfar al-Kattānī, *Shifāʾ al-asḳām* (Fās. 1321); Houtsma, *De strijd over het dogma in den Islâm tot op el-Ash'ari*, p. 16 *sqq.*; Goldziher, *Vorlesungen*, p. 101, 182 *sq.*, 202, 205; Snouck Hurgronje, *Mekkanische Sprichwörter und Redensarten*, p. 60, note. — For other classifications of *kuffār* s. Muḥ. Aʿlā, *Dict. of Techn. Terms*, s.v. cf. also al-Djurdjānī, *al-Taʿrīfāt* ed. Flügel, s.v. *īmān*. — For *kuffār* in fiḳh: Goldziher, *Die Ẓāhiriten*, p. 59 *sqq.*; do., *Vorlesungen*, p. 182; Juynboll, *Handb. d. islām. Gesetzes*, p. 173. — Historical: Goldziher, *Vorlesungen*, p. 183 *sq.*; Becker, *Christentum und Islam*, p. 15 *sqq.*; Mez., *Die Renaissance des Islāms* (Heidelberg 1922), p. 28 *sqq.*, especially p. 47 *sqq.* On the so called *Kuffār al-Turk*, of whom Barhebraeus also speaks (*Chronicon*, ed. Bruns and Kirsch, Leipzig 1789, p. 324), cf. Steinschneider, *Polem. u. apologet. Literatur in arabischer Sprache*, p. 296. On the Mystics: Massignon, *Essai sur les origines du lexique technique de la mystique musulmane* (Paris 1922), p. 23, and do., *La passion d'al-Hosayn-ibn-Mansour al-Hallaj* (Paris 1922), p. 99* of the Index.

KĀHIN (A., plur. *kuhhān* or *kahana*; fem. *kāhina*, plur. *kawāhin*, abstract of profession *kihāna*) is the name of the seer or soothsayer among the pagan Arabs. It corresponds to the Hebrew *kōhēn*, Aramaic *kāhen*, *kāhnā* (priest); it is not an arabicised form of this however, but belongs to the original stock of the old Arabic language (otherwise Nöldeke, *Neue Beiträge zur semitischen Sprachwissenschaft*, p. 36, note 6), for the Jewish kōhen, kāhen is entirely different in character from the Arab kāhin: the former, although in all probability at one time also a soothsayer, later appears only as a dealer in oracles and particularly as sacrificer and teacher of the Tora, while it cannot be shown that the latter, who is never a priest (in contradiction to von Kremer — see below in the *Bibliography* — p. 74 *sqq.*, and also to Wellhausen, p. 134 and elsewhere), ever held these functions, neither was he permanently connected at all with worship and places of worship, but seems to have been quite unrestricted in the exercise of his activities.

The kāhins of course have their origin in the shamans, medicine-men, and fetish-priests, but in the form in which we first meet them in the old Arabic tales, in the Ḥadīth and, much more rarely, in the pre-Islāmic poetry, they have already passed beyond the ruder forms of shamanism. Their mantic knowledge is based on ecstatic inspiration. They have also, it is true, visions by night which reveal to them future and other events and things hidden from the ordinary mortal (al-Masʿūdī, iii. 379, 394 *sq.*; Sprenger i. 176 *sq.* etc.), but they are not really visionaries. Their inspiration is of demoniacal origin: a *djinnī* or *shaiṭān* "demon" (δαιμόνιον) who is called their *tābiʿ* "companion", *ṣāḥib* "comrade", *mawlā* or *walī*, "friend" ("familiar spirit"), not infrequently also their *raʾī* or *riʾī* (probably "seer"), speaks out of them. This personification of their ecstasy, which at once stamps them as connected with the old fashioned *shāʿir* "bard" (literally "knower"), also endowed by djinns with supernatural, magic knowledge (cf. *vates* = *poeta*), is conceived as being so substantial that the *daimonion* regularly appears as the I — his *alter ego*, the kāhin, on the other hand, appears as the "thou" of the prophetic utterance, that the latter clearly notices the approach of the spirit, feels himself struck by his foot, hears his voice from a distance etc. (Sprenger, *loc. cit.*; Hölscher p. 85), that indeed, these demons even have their own names (like the familiar spirits of the poets, see Yāḳūt, *Muʿdjam*, ed. Wüstenfeld, iv. 914 *sq.* and al-Djāḥiẓ, *Ḥayawān* vi. 69 = van Vloten, *WZKM* viii. 65). The kāhins give their utterances in the form of the *sadjʿ*, short sentences in rhythmic prose, with single or more rarely alternating rhyme, such as had been usual in Arabia from early times for all utterance in the higher and lower branches of divination and magic, etc. (Only very rarely is regular verse also used, e.g. *Aghānī*, xi. 161). Besides the *sadjʿ*, the *zamzama* is characteristic of the kāhin's utterance, the mysterious "humming" with which it was delivered (Ibn Hishām, i. 171, and thereon ii. 58). The word *sadjʿ* may in this sense have originally meant nothing more than the "purring" or "chirping" or such like of an alleged demon's voice: the verb *sadjaʿa* is also used in other connections of "purring" or "chirping" of the djinns, and more regularly of the "cooing" of pigeons and also of the "groaning" of camels; cf. in the O.T. e.g. *Isaiah*, xxix. 4. The kāhins, the majority of whom are to be considered frauds, of course often express themselves in very obscure and ambiguous language. They give greater emphasis to their utterance by striking oaths, swearing by the earth and sky, sun, moon and stars, light and darkness, evening and morning, plants and animals of all kinds etc. (For kāhins' utterances, see e.g. Hölscher, p. 87 *sq.*, 95 *sqq.*; al-Masʿūdī, iii. 387 *sqq.*; al-Ibshīhī, Ch. 60; *Aghānī*, xi. 161, *ff sqq.*).

Kāhins play an extremely important part in public as well as private life. They are interrogated on all important tribal and state occasions — especially before warlike enterprises, razzias, etc., in which they take part themselves as a rule; indeed, they sometimes lead them in person (cf. Deborah in the O.T.). Kings and queens therefore keep their prophet or prophetess (D. H. Müller, *Die Burgen und Schlösser Südarabiens nach dem Iklîl des Hamdânî*, i. 74, and al-Ṭabarī, i. 762, *f*), and the tribes have a kāhin or kāhina as well as a *shāʿir* "poet" and *khaṭīb* "orator". In private life the kāhins especially act as judges in disputes and points of law of all kinds, so that the conception of *kāhin* is closely connected with that of *ḥakam* "judge" (al-Ḥuṭaiʾa, no. xvii. 7; al-Ibshīhī, Cairo 1321, ii. 73, *f*). Their decision is considered as a kind of divine judgment against which there is no appeal. At the same time they interpret dreams, find lost camels, establish adulteries, clear up other crimes and misdemeanours, particularly thefts and murders etc. In these proceedings they descend to a somewhat lower scale of divination, viz. to that of the *ʿarrāf* or *muʿarrif* cf. Ibn al-Athīr, *al-Nihāya*, iv. 40, al-Djāḥiẓ, *Ḥayawān*, vi. 62, *infra*, and al-Masʿūdī, iii. 352). For such work they received an honorarium — forbidden in the Ḥadīth — (*ḥulwān*; al-Bukhārī, ed. Krehl-Juynboll, ii. 43, 55 *et passim*). Of course, people liked to test their mantic abilities before paying them.

The influence of these men and women was naturally great and often stretched far beyond the bounds of their tribes. They were not by any means recruited solely from the lower strata of society, but sometimes belonged to most distinguished families, occasionally even the *saiyid* or chief of a tribe was also its *kāhin* (Lammens, p. 204, 257: al-Djāḥiẓ, vi. 62 = van Vloten, *WZKM* vii. 184; also Wellhausen, p. 134 who, however, says wrongly that such aristocratic kāhins had inherited their office). They were in any case among the leaders or the intellectual aristocracy of their tribe (cf. the chapter *Asmāʾ al-kuhhān wa 'l-ḥukkām wa 'l-khuṭabāʾ wa 'l-ʿulamāʾ min Ḳaḥṭān* "The names of the seers, judges, orators and learned men of Ḳaḥṭān" in al-Djāḥiẓ, *al-Bayān*, i. 136 *infra*, cf. also 113, *sqq.*, ed. Cairo, 1333, i. 192, cf. 159).

The prophet Muḥammad disclaimed being a *kāhin* (Sūra lii. 29, lxix. 42; also passages like lxxxi. 22 *sqq.*). But his earliest appearance as a prophet reminds us strongly of the manner of these soothsayers. He was an ecstatic and had "true dreams" like them; his *daimonion* (*ṣāḥib*) was the (holy) spirit, whose place was later taken by the angel Gabriel. His revelations are, like the utterance of the *kāhin*, comprised in *sadjʿ* and sometimes begin with the usual abstruse oaths; even the forms which he was still using for administering justice and settling disputes in Madīna during the early years of his stay there correspond in their main features to those of the pagan kāhin and ḥakam.

Islām with its monotheism, its doctrine of the cessation of all revelation with Muḥammad and its regulation of all social customs through the fiḳh, wiped out the old soothsayers, only gradually, it is true, for we still hear in 132 A.H. of a kāhin (al-Ṭabarī, iii. 21; on *kahana* in modern Arabia, see Landberg, *La langue arabe et ses dialectes*, p. 70; on woman seers in Muslim N. W. Africa, see Doutté, p. 32 *sqq.*). Muḥammad himself probably never doubted the supernatural nature of the kāhin's utterance. But when he declared the knowledge possessed by the demons, whom he at the same time degraded to devils, to have been stolen from heaven and to be falsified and confused (Sūra lxxii. 8 *sqq.*, xxxiv. 14, vi. 112; Ibn Hishām, *Sīra*, i. 131 *sq.*), he brought their prophecies into great disrepute, and thus those traditions arose which warned believers against utilising the services of a kāhin (al-Suyūṭī, *al-Djāmiʿ aṣ-ṣaghīr*, sub *man atā kāhinan*; al-Bukhārī, ii. 43, 55 *et passim*; cf. also the remark of Ibn ʿAbbās *iyākum wa 'l-kihāna* etc. in al-Zamakhsharī's *Kashshāf*, on Sūra xxxi. 34).

Bibliography: Wellhausen, *Reste arabischen Heidentums*, p. 134 *sqq.*, 143, 206 *sqq.*; Sprenger, *Das Leben und die Lehre des Moḥammad*², i., especially p. 255 *sqq.*; von Kremer, *Studien zur vergleichenden Culturgeschichte, vorzüglich nach arabischen Quellen*, iii. and iv. (*Sitzungsb. der phil.-hist. Kl. der Wiener Akademie*, cxx. no. 8), p. 73 *sqq.*; van Vloten, *Dämonen, Geister und Zauber bei den alten Arabern. Mitteilungen aus Djâhitz' Kitâb al-haiwân*, in *WZKM*, vii. 169 *sqq.*, 233 *sqq.*, viii. 59 *sqq.*; Goldziher, *Abhandl. zur arab. Philologie*, i. 18 *sqq.*, 69, 107 *sqq.*; Lagrange, *Études sur les religions sémitiques*², p. 218 *sq.*; Doutté, *Magie et Religion dans l'Afrique du Nord*, p. 28 *sqq.*; D. B. Macdonald, *The Religious Life and Attitude in Islam*, p. 25—33 *et passim*; Hölscher, *Die Profeten. Untersuchungen zur Religionsgeschichte Israels*, p. 79 *sqq.*; Lammens, *Le berceau de l'Islam*, i. 204 *sq.*, 257; Schrieke, *Die Himmelsreise Muhammeds*, in *Der Islam*, vi. 22 *sqq.*; al-Djāḥiẓ, *Kit. al-ḥayawān*, *passim* (cf. v. Vloten); Johs. Pedersen, *The rôle played by inspired persons among the Israelites and the Arabs*, in *Studies in Old Testament Prophecy presented to Th. H. Robinson*, Edinburgh 1950, p. 126-142; A. Guillaume, *Prophecy and Divination among the Semites*, London 1950; al-Masʿūdī, *Murūdj*, ii. 347 *sqq.*; al-Ḳazwīnī, *ʿAdjāʾib al-makhlūḳāt*, ed. Wüstenfeld, p. 318 *sqq.*; Ibn Khaldūn, *Muḳaddima*, ed. Quatremère, *Not. et Extr.*, xvi. 181 *sqq.*; transl. de Slane, xix. 206 *sqq.* (ed. Cairo 1327, p. 112 *sqq.*); al Ibshīhī, *al-Mustaṭraf*, Ch. lx.

KAIN. [See Hābīl].

ḲAINUḲĀʿ (Banū), one of the three Jewish tribes of Yathrib. The name differs from the usual forms of Arabic proper names but at the same time has nothing Hebrew about its type. Nothing certain is known regarding their immigration into Yathrib. They possessed no land there but lived by trading. That their personal names known to us are for the most part Arabic says as little regarding their origin as the occurrence of Biblical names among them. But there seem to be no valid reasons for doubting their Jewish origin.

In Yathrib they lived in the south-west part of the town, near the *muṣallā* and close to the bridge over the Wādī Buṭhān, where they occupied two of the castles (*āṭām*), characteristic of Yathrib. They practised the goldsmith's art among other trades; al-Bukhārī (*Farḍ al-khums*, bāb i), incidentally mentions a goldsmith of the Ḳainuḳāʿ. On their expulsion they left behind them arms and tools, which were divided among the Muslims after Muḥammad had received his fifth share. The number of their fully equipped fighting men varies in the references to it between 400 and 750.

After the dominating power in the old Yathrib had passed from the Jews to the Banū Ḳaila the Ḳainuḳāʿ were in alliance with the Khazradj. In Muḥammad's settlement of the relations of believers and other sections of the community (Ibn Hishām, p. 341 *sqq.*) they are not mentioned by the name of their tribe any more than the Naḍīr [q.v.] and Ḳuraiẓa [q.v.] but are described as "Jews of the Nadjdjār, Ḥārith, Sāʿida and Djusham" (articles 26—29), i.e. as allies of different subdividions of the Khazradj.

After the battle of Badr (Ramaḍān 2 H./March 624) Muḥammad's relations with the Jews of Madīna became troubled. The Ḳainuḳāʿ, as they lived in the city itself, were those he wished to be rid of first. With this description of the situation, his attack on the Ḳainuḳāʿ (in all probability as early as Shawwāl 2 H./April 624) is sufficiently explained. What the Muslim writers give as special reasons for the attack has hardly more than anecdotal value. Sometimes it is said to have been a jest that a Muslim made to a Jewish woman, sometimes the Ḳainuḳāʿ are said to have behaved with particular arrogance. Sūra iii. 12 *sqq.* and viii. 60 *sqq.* are said to refer to these incidents. Sūra iii. 13 refers to the victory at Badr as an example and warning, and viii. 58 speaks of vengeance against people from whom treachery is feared.

After a fourteen days' siege, the Ḳainuḳāʿ surrendered without striking a blow; the men were bound and seemed to have to fear the worst. The energetic intervention of ʿAbd Allāh b. Ubaiy, chief of the Khazradj and leader of the Munāfiḳūn, however, effected an amelioration of their lot. They departed first to the Jewish colonies in the Wādi 'l-Ḳurā, north of Madīna, and from there they went to Adhriʿāt in Syria.

Bibliography: Ibn Hishām, p. 383 *sqq.*, 545 *sqq.*; al-Wāḳidī, *al-Maghāzī*, ed. v. Kremer, p. 177 *sqq.* (= abbrev. transl. by Wellhausen entitled *Muhammed in Medina*, p. 92 *sqq.*); al-Ṭabarī, i. 1359 *sqq.*; al-Diyārbakrī, *Taʾrīkh al-khamīs* (Cairo 1283), p. 408 *sqq.*; al-Ḥalabī, *Sīra* (Cairo 1292), ii. 273 *sqq.*; the European biographies of Muḥammad; L. Caetani, *Annali dell' Islam*, i. 520 *sqq.*; A. J. Wensinck, *Mohammed en de Joden te Medina* (Leyden 1908), p. 39, 146—151; R. Leszynsky, *Die Juden in Arabien zur Zeit Mohammeds* (Berlin 1910), p. 60 *sqq.*; Müller, *Der Islam im Morgen- und Abendland*, i. 96—119.

KAISĀNĪYA was a name first applied to the Kūfa group of Shīʿites, the mawālī, represented by Kaisān Abū ʿAmra, whose interests were championed by al-Mukhtār. The name was then extended to those who held the views which had considerable currency among the Shīʿites led by al-Mukhtār, and continued to be influential even later. When the little-known Kaisān came in time to be practically forgotten, his name was often explained as a *laḳab* of al-Mukhtār. Mukhtārīya thus became another name for the older stratum of the Kaisānīya. The latter name, however, is also derived from a certain Kaisān, a mawlā of ʿAlī, who fell at Ṣiffīn (al-Ṭabarī, i. 3293), from whom al-Mukhtār is said to have derived his views. The Kaisānīya were also called Khashabīya from the wooden clubs which the mawālī carried as a weapon. These clubs are called *kāfirkūbāt* (unbeliever-clubs), a name found later also with the adherents of Abū Muslim.

The contemporary Kaisānīs ascribed special knowledge to al-Mukhtār and to some extent regarded him as a prophet. There must also have been among them an echo of a cult, followed especially by some Yaman clans and described as Sabaʾī, the worship of an alleged chair of ʿAlī's, which was compared with the Ark of the Covenant and also used as an oracle. Their Imām in succession to al-Ḥusain was Muḥammad b. al-Ḥanafīya, whom al-Mukhtār put forward as a mere figure-head. As al-Shahrastānī tells us, the Kaisānīs held the view that he was master of all knowledge and had obtained from the two Saiyids (i.e. al-Ḥasan and al-Ḥusain) all mystical, allegorical and esoteric knowledge as well as knowledge of the celestial spheres and of the souls. In time there came to be Kaisānīs who regarded Ibn al-Ḥanafīya as the Imām in immediate succession to his father and thus excluded al-Ḥasan and al-Ḥusain. In proof of this they pointed to the tradition that ʿAlī in the Battle of the Camel had entrusted the standard to Muḥammad b. al-Ḥanafīya. This view probably arose in opposition to those held by the Imāmīs and Zaidīs.

Ibn al-Ḥanafīya's death, probably in 81/700, resulted in a split in the Kaisānīya. Apart from those who raised his son ʿAlī to be Imām, a section of them transferred the Imāmate to his son Abū Hāshim, who was regarded as heir to the secret knowledge of his father. They were called Hā<u>sh</u>imīyā; but after the death of Abū Hā<u>sh</u>im (98/716—7 or 99/717—8) they broke up into various branches on the question of succession. The ʿAbbāsids now spread the idea that Abū Hā<u>sh</u>im before his death had transferred his rights to the Imāmate to Muḥammad b. ʿAlī b. ʿAbd Allāh b. ʿAbbās.

A group of the Kaisānīya, however, did not believe in the death of Muḥammad b. al Ḥanafīya. According to them, he lived in concealment in a ravine in the mountains of Raḍwā out of which he would one day emerge at the head of his followers as Mahdī [q.v.] in order to fill the earth with righteousness. His stay there is described with Messianic features by the Kaisānī poets al-Ku<u>th</u>aiyir (d. 105/723) and al-Saiyid al-Ḥimyarī (d. 173/789). These views of the concealment (*ghaiba*, q.v.) and return (*rad<u>j</u>ʿa*) are attributed to a certain Abū Karib (Kuraib), whose followers were therefore distinguished as Karibīya (Kuraibīya).

According to al-<u>Sh</u>ahrastānī, all Kaisānīs held the view that religion consisted in obedience to a man; by means of allegorical interpretation (*taʾwīl*) the prescriptions of law were transferred to such men. — Among the Kaisānīs also arose the view that "the intervention of new circumstances can produce the alteration of a divine decision already made" (*badāʾ*, q.v.). Besides the doctrine of the return of the hidden Imām, metempsychosis (*tanāsu<u>kh</u>*, q. v.) had also followers among them.

The Kaisānīs were unable to survive alongside of the Imāmīya and the Zaidīya [q.v.]. For Ibn Ḥazm the Kaisānīya was an extinct sect. — To Kaisānī influences should probably be ascribed the fact that concealment and return were attributed to ʿAlids whom the Zaidīs had championed. — A remarkable document, which is said to contain Ḳarmaṭian doctrines (see ḲARMAṬIANS) may also emanate from Kaisānī circles. In it a certain Aḥmad b. Muḥammad b. al-Ḥanafīya appears as Mahdī and Prophet (al-Ṭab., iii. 2128 *sq.*; Ibn al-A<u>th</u>īr, vii. 311, *sqq.*; de Sacy, *Exposé de la religion des Druzes*, Paris 1838, i. Introd. p. clxxvii. *sqq.* An Aḥmad is, however, not known among the sons of Muḥammad b. al-Ḥanafīya (cf. Ibn Saʿd, v. 67; Aḥmad b. ʿAlī al-Dāʾūdī al-Ḥasanī, *ʿUmdat al-ṭālib fī ansāb āl Abī Ṭālib*, Bombay 1318, p. 319 *sqq.*).

Bibliography: al-Tabarī, ii. 598 *sqq.*; al-Dīnawarī, *al-A<u>kh</u>bār al-ṭiwāl* (Leiden 1888), p. 298 *sqq.*; al-Masʿūdī, v. 180 *sqq.*, 226, 227, 268, 475, vi. 58, vii. 117; Ibn Ḳutaiba, *Kitāb al-maʿārif* (ed. Wüstenfeld), p. 300; *al-A<u>gh</u>ānī* vii. 3 *sqq.*, viii. 32, *sqq.*; al-<u>Kh</u>ʷārizmī, *Mafātīḥ al-ʿulūm* (Leiden 1895), p. 29 *sq.*; ʿAbd al-Ḳāhir al-Ba<u>gh</u>dādī, *al-Farḳ* p. 16 *sqq.*, 27—38, 53; Ibn Ḥazm, *al-Faṣl fi 'l-milal* (Cairo 1317—21), iv. 94, 179, 180 *sqq.*; Abu 'l-Maʿāli, *Bayān al-adyān* (Teheran 1315); al-Nawba<u>kh</u>tī, *Firaḳ al-<u>Sh</u>īʿa* (Bibl. Isl. 4, Istanbul 1931), index s.v.; al-<u>Sh</u>ahrastānī, p. 109 *sqq.*; H. D. van Gelder, *Mo<u>h</u>tar de valsche Profeet* (Leiden 1888), p. 82 *sqq.*; G. van Vloten, *Recherches sur la Domination arabe, le Chiitisme* etc. (*Verh. Kon. Ak.* Amst., Afd. Letterkunde, i. no. 3, Amsterdam 1894), p. 41 *sqq.*; Isr. Friedlaender, *The Heterodoxies of the Shiites according to Ibn Ḥazm* (*JAOS* xxviii., xxix.), see Ind. under *Keisan*; H. Banning, *Muḥammad ibn al-Ḥanafīja*, Diss. Erlangen 1909, p. 46—53; F. Buhl, *Alidern s Stilling til de shiʿitiske Bevaegelser under Umajjaderne* (*Oversigt over det Kgl. Danske Videnskabernes Selskabs Forhandlinger*, 1910, no. 5), p. 364 *sqq.*; C. van Arendonk, *De opkomst van het Zaidietische Imamaat in Yemen* (Leiden 1919), p. 11—13; A. S. Tritton, *Muslim Theology*, London 1947 s.v. <u>Kh</u>a<u>sh</u>abī, p. 21 *sqq.*

ḲAIṢAR (A.), the usual name in Arabic for the Byzantine Emperor. The word represents the Greek Καῖσαρ and came to the Arabs through the intermediary of the Aramaic (cf. Fraenkel, *Die aramäischen Fremdwörter im Arabischen*, Leiden 1886, p. 278 *sq.*). The word does not occur in the Ḳurʾān but is quite frequent in the biography of Muḥammad and especially in Tradition, where Ḳaiṣar — always, we may note, without the article like a proper name — is usually mentioned in the first place among contemporary secular rulers; next to him come the king of the Persians and the Negus of Abyssinia (that the Persian Hurmuzān in al-Bu<u>kh</u>ārī, *Ṣaḥīḥ, <u>Dj</u>izya*, bāb 1 = ed. Krehl-Juynboll, ii. 292 gives a different opinion is, of course, not to be wondered at). In the narratives mentioned a great part is played by the epistle said to have been sent by Muḥammad through Diḥya to the governor of Boṣrā and through him to the Emperor Heraclius, who thereupon interrogated Abū Sufyān, who happened to be within reach, regarding the new prophet. Here as well as in the story of the embassy of the Prophet to the <u>Gh</u>assānid al-Ḥāri<u>th</u> b. Abī <u>Sh</u>amir (of doubtful authenticity; cf. Nöldeke, *Die Ghassanischen Fürsten* etc., in *Abhandl. d. Kgl. Preuss. Akad. d. Wiss. zu Berlin*, 1887, phil.-hist. Klasse, p. 53 *sqq.* of the reprint), Heraclius (in contrast to Kisrā) appears as a man, at heart inclined to Islām, whom only fear of his subjects prevents from openly professing the new religion. His attitude is described differently and — by a lucky accident — more in conformity with historical truth in a later popular legend, where Heraclius is represented from the beginning as an exasperated enemy of Muḥammad (cf. Martin Abel, *Die arabische Vorlage des Suaheli-Epos Chuo cha Herkal*, Hamburg 1937). — The traditions further record all sorts of sayings and prophesies of Muḥammad regarding Ḳaiṣar, which can at once be recognised as later views thrown back into the past. In al-Bu<u>kh</u>ārī, *Tafsīr* to Sūra lxvi., bāb 2 (Kr.-J., iii. 360 middle of page) Muḥammad comforts ʿUmar, who is lamenting the neediness of his existence, contrasted with the splendid court of Kisrā and Ḳaiṣar, with the words: "Art thou not content that this world belongs to them and the next to us?" In *<u>Dj</u>ihād*, bāb 93 (Kr.-J., ii. 229 below) we read: "To the first army of my community that plunders the city of Ḳaiṣar (Constantinople) its sins are forgiven". In *Aimān*, bāb 3 (Kr.-J., iv. 259, 9) the Prophet foretells the final decline of the power of the East Roman Empire as well as that of the Persian kingdom.

Bibliography: Abu 'l-Fidāʾ, *Mu<u>kh</u>taṣar taʾrī<u>kh</u> al-ba<u>sh</u>ar*, partly ed. and transl. by Fleischer as *Abulfedae Historia anteislamica*, p. 132 at end;

Imru᾽ al-Ḳais, *Dīwān*, ed. Ahlwardt, No. 13, No.
20; Ibn Hi<u>sh</u>ām, p. 971; Ibn Saʿd, i/ii. 16; al-
Bu<u>kh</u>ārī, *al-Ṣaḥīḥ*, <u>Sh</u>urūṭ, bāb 15 (ed. Krehl-
Juynboll, ii. 179); ibid., *Ma<u>gh</u>āzī*, b. 82 heading
(Kr.-J., iii. 183, ₁₆); ibid., *D̲j̲ihād*, b. 99 (Kr.-J.,
ii. 232), b. 102 (Kr.-J., ii. 233 *sqq.*); ibid.,
Tafsīr on Sūra iii., b. 4 (Kr.-J., iii. 214 — 216)
and *passim*; Muslim, *Ṣaḥīḥ* (Cairo 1327), ii. 79
below — 81; al-Tirmi<u>dh</u>ī, *Sunan* (Cairo 1292), ii.
119 — 120; Wellhausen, *Skizzen u. Vorarb.*, iv.
98; Caetani, *Annali*, year 6 A.H., § 50.

AL-KALĀBĀ<u>DH</u>Ī, ABŪ BAKR MUḤAMMAD B.
IS<u>H</u>ĀḲ, a well-known authority on early
Ṣūfism, died at Bu<u>kh</u>ārā, probably in the year
385/995. Details of his biography are lacking, but
he is included by ʿAbd al-Ḥaiy al-La<u>kh</u>nawī in his
list of Ḥanafī lawyers, and he is stated to have studied
fiḳh under one Muḥammad b. Faḍl. His *nisba* refers
to Kalābā<u>dh</u>, a quarter of Bu<u>kh</u>ārā. He was the
author of two extant works, *viz.* (1) *Kitāb al-Taʿ-
arruf li-ma<u>dh</u>hab ahl al-taṣawwuf*, a manual in 75
chapters describing the tenets and spiritual experiences of the Ṣūfīs, on which surviving commentaries
were written by ʿAlā᾽ al-Dīn al-Ḳōnawī (d. 729/
1329), and al-Mustamlī, published before 710/1310
and lithographed at Lucknow in 1912, the latter
in Persian, as well as a third anonymous commentary
erroneously ascribed to al-Suhrawardī al-Maḳtūl;
this text has been published (Cairo 1934) and translated (Cambridge 1935) by A. J. Arberry; (2)
Baḥr al-fawā᾽id, a commentary, Ṣūfī in colouring,
on 222 selected traditions; in the latter, many verses
and sayings preserved in the former work are again
cited (see also *GAL*², i. 217, *Suppl.* i. 360). The source
on which al-Kalābā<u>dh</u>ī largely draws as a primary
authority is Fāris, and this lends great interest to
his quotations from al-Ḥallād̲j̲ [q.v.], to whom he
generally refers, with great caution, simply as "one
of the great Ṣūfīs". His purpose in writing the
Taʿarruf was to bridge the chasm between orthodox
theology and Ṣūfism, which the execution of al-
Ḥallād̲j̲ had greatly widened; and this explains why,
in his chapters treating with the doctrinal beliefs
of the Ṣūfīs, he quotes verbally from the "creed"
called *al-Fiḳh al-akbar* (II), falsely ascribed to Abū
Ḥanīfa. As a first-hand source for the history of
early Ṣūfism, al-Kalābā<u>dh</u>ī may rank with al-Sar-
rād̲j̲, Abū Ṭālib al-Makkī, al-Sulamī and al-Ḳushairī.

KALĀM (A.), speech, scholastic theology.

I. It is defined by the grammarians as such utterance (*lafẓ*) with the voice as is compound (*murak-
kab*), not single words, and which conveys a meaning
by convention, not nature (*waḍʿ*, not *ṭabʿ*, as in ex-
clamations; θέσει not φύσει). The *Dictionary of
Techn. Terms* (p. 1268—1270) gives a thoroughly
scholastic discussion of kalām and its parts, pho-
netically, grammatically, lexicographically, rheto-
rically. See, also, De Sacy in *Anthol. Gramm.*, Arabic
text, p. 73 and 93 and notes. In lexicography kalām
is a generic noun for speech, little or much (al-
D̲j̲awharī in *Ṣaḥāḥ* and *LA*, xv. 428), applying to
every kind of talk, *li-kulli mā yutakallamu bihi* (Ibn
ʿAḳīl), or an expression for successive sounds (*aṣwāt*)
giving an intelligible meaning (al-Faiyūmī, *al-
Miṣbāḥ*). This is the actual usage of the root in the
language. Thus *bi-kalāmī*, said by Allāh to Mūsā
(Sūra vii. 144) is paraphrased by al-Baiḍāwī (ed.
Fleischer, i. 343 *infra*) *bi-taklīmī iyāka*, "by my
speaking to thee", and on Sūra xlviii. 15, al-Baiḍāwī says that kalām is an *ism* for *taklīm* (ii. 268).
In the remaining two occurrences, *kalām Allāh*, Sūra
ii. 75, is ambiguous and may mean either Allāh's

actual speaking to Mūsā or the Law, while in Sūra
ix. 6, it seems to mean clearly the content of Islām.
The 2ⁿᵈ stem of the verb is used frequently in the
Ḳur᾽ān in the sense "to speak to" some one with
the accusative of the person addressed (al-A<u>sh</u>ʿarī,
al-Ibāna, ed. Ḥaidarābād, p. 27, says that *taklīm*
means *al-mu<u>sh</u>āfaha bi᾽l-kalām*) and the 5ᵗʰ stem
occurs four times (xi. 105, xxiv. 16, xxx. 35, lxxviii.
38) in the neuter sense "to speak, talk, discuss"
with a *bi* of the subject discussed; in xxiv. 16 appears
a shade of contemptuous reference, mere "talking
with the mouth" (cf. Dozy, *Suppl.*, ii. 486ᵃ). In
the later development kalām came to mean the
statement of an intellectual position or an argument
upholding such a statement, and a *mutakallim* was
a person making use of such kalām's; so *passim* in
the *Fihrist*. By al-Masʿūdī (viii. 161) *takallam* is
used of the "patter" of a public story-teller and
mimic by the roadside.

II. The first technical use of kalām seems to have
been in the phrase *kalām Allāh*, meaning either the
Ḳur᾽ān or Allāh's quality (*ṣifa*) called Speech. For
these applications the way was prepared in the
Ḳur᾽ān passages already quoted. But the order in
which they came and the influences which produced
them are still, like all the beginnings of Muslim
theology, exceedingly obscure, and we are not yet
in a position, in spite of Horten's collection of materials in *Die philosophischen Systeme der spekulativen
Theologen im Islam* (Bonn 1912) even to sketch their
development. It seems clear that the Muslim thinkers
were affected (1) broadly by the conceptions, classifications and dialectic of Greek philosophy; (ii)
much more minutely by personal intercourse and
discussion with the theologians of the Oriental
Christian Church and (iii), perhaps, by some ideas
of the Indian philosophical schools. The last influence has been suggested tentatively by Horten,
especially at several points in his *Systeme*; but he
has not supported it by any detailed references or
translations from Indian literature; it remains, therefore, a bare, although very possible suggestion; cf.
further on it Massignon's review in *Isl.*, iii. 408.
The idea of representing the problem of the personality of Allāh as a combination of a *dhāt* or essence
with *ṣifāt*, or "qualities", seems partly due to the
methods of Greek theories of personality, partly to
the Ḳur᾽ānic rhetoric which, following the fashion
of the old poetry, describes Allāh by means of
epithets, and partly to Christian explanations of
the relation of the persons in the Trinity. The problem, however, remained of the relation between
these qualities and the essence, and was eventually
given up by orthodox Islām which took refuge in
the statement: "they are not He (i.e. Allāh himself),
nor are they other than He"; this was an admission
that the relationship was a theological mystery,
ungraspable by human thought. These qualities,
further, were uncreated and eternal; the personality
of Allāh was unthinkable without them. But rationalistic Islām, later the Muʿtazilites, could not admit such a mystery and tended to reject the qualities
as having necessary relationship to the essence. In
these discussions the quality "Speech" was evidently
prominent, and on it the influence of the Christian
theologians was peculiarly felt. It is never represented
by an epithet in the Ḳur᾽ān, i.e. Allāh is never a
Speaker, *mutakallim* or *kalīm*, although the later theologians used *mutakallim* frequently of him, and there
is only one certain use of kalām for the actual Speech
of Allāh (Sūra ii. 144); but Allāh is represented again
and again by means of verbs as "speaking", and al-

Ash<u>̲</u>ʿarī (*al-Ibāna*, p. 23 *sqq.*) quotes over ten passages, using different expressions, as bases for the doctrine that both the Speech of Allāh, as a quality inherent in Him, and the Ḳurʾān as a manifestation of that quality are uncreated. These passages, it may be said, give distinctly the impression that the doctrine was historically reached through other means, or arose by other causes, and that these proof-texts were then sought as a Ḳurʾānic basis. The rationalistic theologians, on the other hand, denied the possibility of a material, yet uncreated, manifestation of the eternal quality of Speech. Thus when Allāh spoke to Mūsā (Sūra iv. 164; vii. 143 *sqq.*; xx. 9 *sqq.*; xxviii. 30) from the tree (*shadjara*) they held that the sound of the words was created in the tree as a *maḥall*, and was therefore a state (*ḥāl*) in it (cf. Goldziher on Fakhr al-Dīn al-Rāzī, in *Isl.*, iii. 245 *sqq.*). This the later Ashʿarites met by explaining that Mūsā did not hear this Speech as an ordinary act of hearing, but spiritually and as coming from every direction and perceived by every one of his organs. It was thus received in his sensorium by the *ḥiss al-mushtarak*, the Aristotelian "common sense" (al-Baiḍāwī on Sūra vii. 143, xx. 12; ed. Fleischer, i. 343, 593). Further, it was recognized at least as early as al-Ashʿarī (*al-Ibāna*, p. 25) that this Speech must go on without ceasing, for the quality is perfect and silence would be an imperfection in it. The Ḳurʾān (xviii. 109; xxxi. 27) and traditions (*al-Ibāna*, p. 25) speak also in violent metaphors of the *kalimāt*, separate words of Allāh, as being numberless; from all eternity Allāh has been speaking. But al-Ashʿarī protests (*op. cit.*, p. 41) against the application of the term *lafẓ*, verbal utterance, to the Ḳurʾān; that is not seemly even in the case of our recital of it. Similarly the *LA* (xv. 427) says that you must not call the Ḳurʾān *ḳawl Allāh*. Al-Ashʿarī does not seem himself to have reached the position of the later Ashʿarites that the Speech of Allāh is thinking, at least "ideas in the mind", kalām or *ḥadīth nafsī*, and therefore can go on without letters or words. Al-Ashʿarī's desire was only to protect the Ḳurʾān arbitrarily from any approximation to the transitory and created, and he had not thought out what his position meant. The numberless *kalimāt* of Allāh are still speech but not like our utterance with the mouth. In part they are His creative acts, as He created by the single word, *kun*, "come into being!"

For the later orthodox theologians the proof of the kalām of Allāh was simplified down to an *idjmāʿ* [q.v.] of all peoples that Allāh has spoken to the prophets and must therefore be a speaker, possess a quality of Speech; see, e.g., al-Taftāzānī's commentary on the *ʿAḳāʾid* of al-Nasafī, Cairo 1321, p. 75 *sq.* Its nature has been indicated above. But the relation of this quality to the *kalām Allāh* of the Ḳurʾān was still to be defined. The Ḥanbalites continued to avoid any closer definition as al-Ashʿarī had done; it was the uncreated, eternal Speech of Allāh, and that was an end of it. Some even tried to transfer its uncreated character to the very material on which it was written. For the Muʿtazilites it was simply created, like the words which reached the ears of Mūsā. The Māturīdites followed their normal method in dealing with theological mysteries of putting the two elements flatly side by side and attempting no solution. Al-Nasafī (*ʿAḳāʾid*, p. 79) says: "The Ḳurʾān, the Speech of Allāh, is created and it is written in our copies, preserved in our hearts, recited by our tongues and heard by our ears. Yet it does not reside (*ḥāll*) in these". Al-Taftāzānī, as an Ashʿarite, suggests as an explanation that the word "fire" written on a piece of paper does not have in it the burning quality of fire and consume the paper.

The later Ashʿarite view of this relation may be given in the words of al-Faḍālī (d. 1236/1820; see AL-FAḌĀLĪ) in his *Kifāya* (ed. 1315 with al-Baidjūrī's commentary, p. 50). "These Glorious Expressions [the words of the Ḳurʾān] are not a guide to the eternal quality in the sense that the eternal quality can be understood from them. But what is understood from the expressions equals (*musāwī*) what would be understood from the eternal quality if the veil were removed from us and we were to hear it"; apparently the distinction between ὁμοούσιος and ὁμοιούσιος. Thus the wording of the Ḳurʾān is created, and al-Faḍālī has even a shade of doubt whether that wording goes back to the Preserved Tablet, that is to Allāh, or is due to Djibrīl or even to Muḥammad. Similarly Ibn Ḥazm [q.v.] reports (*Milal*, Cairo 1317, p. 211 *infra*) that this was the Ashʿarite doctrine even in his time and especially of al-Bāḳillānī (d. 403/1013) and that their formula was that the Ḳurʾān was the kalām of Allāh only in the sense that it was an *ʿibāra*, an "expression" for the kalām of Allāh. Similarly in *al-Fiḳh al-akbar*, ascribed to Abū Ḥanīfa (d. 150) with a commentary by al-Māturīdī (d. 333), the word for this relation is already *ʿibāra* and also *ḥikāya*, "reproduction" (Ḥaidarābād 1321, p. 23). There is a very complete analytical and objective, but not historical, statement of the different positions in the *Mawāḳif* of al-Īdjī with commentary of al-Djurdjānī, Būlāḳ 1266, p. 495.

In this the influence of Christian theologians seems plain. The parallel between the uncreated but creating Logos, the reason and word of God, with its earthly manifestation in Jesus and this kalām, as eternal quality, as creative agency and as revelation in time is very close. The position of the Ashʿarite school that the quality is practically the thinking of Allāh, althought they carefully guard against confusion with our "thoughts" which originate in time (al-Faḍālī, p. 52), suggests the rational side of the Logos, the Hebrew *ḥokhmā*, the divine σοφία. But it is not allowable to ascribe *ʿaḳl*, νοῦς, to Allāh because of philosophical and etymological implications; cf. *Mawāḳif*, ed. Cairo, p. 541, ed. Sörensen, p. 161, and al-Baiḍāwī on Sūra ii. 44, ed. Fleischer, i. 57. The Christian theologians naturally translated their Syriac *mellᵉthā*, ὁ λόγος, with *al-kalām*. On Christian influence in Muslim theology see further Graf, *Die arabischen Schriften des Theodor Abu Kurra* and the various articles cited by Horten in his *Philos. Systeme*, p. 626; especially C. H. Becker, *Christliche Polemik u. islamische Dogmenbildung*, in *ZA*, xxvi. 175 *sqq.*

III. It is not an overhazardous conjecture that similar influence worked in developing the use of kalām = theology and of *mutakallim* = theologian. The Syriac *mallel* (= *takallama*) and its derivatives were parallel to λέγω and λόγος on both sides of their meanings of reason and speech. Thus *mᵉmallel allāhāyāthā* meant θεολόγος and *mᵉlīla*, λογικός. Starting, therefore, with kalām = speech, the development was easy to intellectual argument, especially as applied to theology. How much in the dark Muslims were on the origin of this use is evident from the eight explanations which al-Taftāzānī gives (commentary on al-Nasafī, p. 10 *sqq.*); (i) Theologians begin: "The kalām (statement, argument) on such and such a doctrine is ..." (ii) Deals most with doctrine of speech of Allāh. (iii) Gives same weight to speech in theology as philosophers give to *manṭiḳ*, logic. (iv) Most essential of sciences taught by speech. (v) Speech between opponents is necessary to it rather than consideration or reading. (vi) The most disputatious of the sciences taught by speech. (vii) For its weightiness it is *the* "statement" as opposed to other sciences. (viii) The cutting, impressive science, from *kalm* = *d̲j̲arḥ*. Ibn K̲h̲aldūn, (see below) gives only two explanations: (i) That the science deals with speech only and not with action (*ʿamal*). (ii) The same as (ii) above; cf. further Haarbrücker's translation of al-S̲h̲ahrastānī's *Milal*, i. 26, and remarks, ii. 388—393. The connection between kalām and λόγος has been combated by Wensinck, *The Muslim Creed*, p. 79, who endeavours to show that kalām in the sense of scholastic theology has its origin in Arabic itself.

But kalām came only slowly to be the name for theology. At first, *fiḳh*, "intelligence", was used for the whole speculative side of theology and canon law, as opposed to *ʿilm* for the traditional side [see FIḲH]. Then theology came to be called "the greater *fiḳh*", *al-fiḳh al-akbar*, as in the book ascribed to Abū Ḥanīfa and al-Māturīdī, referred to above. There, p. 6, it is said: "*al-fiḳh fi'l-dīn afḍal min al-fiḳh fi'l-ʿilm*", which would have been expressed later: "kalām is more excellent than *fiḳh*". Kalām, in that book, is not used technically except for the Speech of Allāh, *ḳawl* generally taking its place; in the *Ibāna* of al-As̲h̲ʿarī [q.v.] kalām occurs, similarly, only in titles to sections. But in the *Fihrist* (c. 377—400) kalām is used normally in the sense of "statement" and also technically, with *takallam* and *mutakallim*, of theology; while *fiḳh* is used, as regularly thereafter, of canon law. But there followed speedily a further development; *ʿilm al-kalām* came to mean not simply theology, but scholastic theology of an atomistic type, going back most strangely to Democritus and Epicurus, and a *mutakallim* came to mean a theologian, first Muʿtazilite and later orthodox, behind whose theology lay the atomistic system which was Islām's most original contribution to philosophy. The importance of this conception of the matter of the universe, as being of a grained structure and not infinitely divisable and continuous can hardly be over-emphasized. In Europe, until the xvii[th] century, it was eclipsed by the authority of Aristotle; but it re-appeared then, first in a qualitative form (Boyle and Newton) and later quantitative (John Dalton). It would be curious to contrast the experimental researches of these with the a priori speculations of Islām. A *mutakallim*, then, was thus distinguished, although calling himself an As̲h̲ʿarite, from the Ḥanbalite conservative traditionalists among whom al-As̲h̲ʿarī had reckoned himself, from the mystics who found their basis in religious experience (*maʿrifa*; *k̲h̲aṭarāt* and *wasāwis* in *Fihrist*, p. 183) rather than in *ʿilm* and dialectic, and from the philosophers (*ḥukamāʾ*) who based upon a blend of Aristotelian and Neoplatonic philosophy; although all these might profess to hold the same doctrines of the Sunnite faith. This leaves out of account, of course, the S̲h̲īʿite system, a structure of Muʿtazilite rationalism erected on the doctrine of *taʿlīm*, i.e. that the ultimate basis of our knowledge is not reason but authoritative instruction by an inerrant guide, always in the world, whom man must seek and obey (cf. e.g. al-G̲h̲azzālī's *Munḳid̲h̲*, ed. 1203, p. 21 *sqq.* and Goldziher's *Streitschrift des Gazālī gegen die Bāṭinijja-Sekte*, *passim*) and the pantheistic side of Ṣūfism which is not really Muslim at all, except in vocabulary and imagery.

It is a great misfortune that the beginning of the vth *maḳāla* of the *Fihrist*, which deals with kalām in this sense, is lost, and with it the account of the origin of this science, and that the first *fann*, especially, has reached us in so hopeless a condition (Houtsma, in *WZKM*, iv. 217—235, essentially supplementing Flügel's ed.). Yet it is clear that the author divided the *mutakallim*'s of his day (end of iv[th]/x[th] century) into five: (i) Muʿtazilites; (ii) S̲h̲īʿites, both Imāmites and Zaidites; (iii) Predestinarians and Anthropomorphists; (iv) K̲h̲ārid̲j̲ites; (v) ascetic Ṣūfīs. This arrangement may be due to the S̲h̲īʿism and, therefore, Muʿtazilism of the author; but the Muʿtazilites were certainly the first *mutakallim*'s. He places al-As̲h̲ʿarī in the third class and has evidently no idea of the importance of his school — he seems to have been a joke (p. 181); yet he died c. 330. Nor is there any mention of al-Māturīdī who had died 333. Al-Bāḳillānī died 403, four years after the last date in our MSS. of the *Fihrist* (Flügel's preface, p. xii.). Certainly the author of the *Fihrist* grievously misread the future, for in his third class lay orthodox Sunnite Islām. Of his fourth class only the Ibāḍites [q.v.] continued to have any importance. Nor does he show any idea of the speculative possibilities in his fifth class.

We cannot, as yet, write a connected history of the atomic theory of Islām, the essential *differentia* of the system of the *mutakallim*'s, but reference may now be made to the work of Sal. Pines, *Beiträge zur islamischen Atomlehre*, Berlin 1936. We have only references to and short quotations from the earlier disputants upon that system. Even the extant writings of al-As̲h̲ʿarī do not give us any help, and those of al-Bāḳillānī, which probably would, have still to be studied. Fortunately Horten has gathered up and untangled, with great diligence, in his *Philosophische Systeme* the later references and quotations, and from these it would appear that the Muʿtazilite Abu 'l-Hud̲h̲ail al-ʿAllāf (d. 235 or 226; cf. Horten, p. 246 *sqq.*) was the founder of the atomic school and was opposed in it by two other Muʿtazilites, His̲h̲ām b. al-Ḥakam (d. 231 [?]; cf. Horten, p. 170 *sqq.*) and al-Naẓẓām (q.v.; d. 230; Horten, p. 189 *sqq.*). It thus arose among the Muʿtazilites, however it may have reached them; but we cannot be sure to what extent their system was exactly that which lies behind all the reasonings of the later *mutakallim*'s. It is unnecessary to describe the system here, as it has already been given in the art. ALLĀH. It may, however, be worth while to give the following references to Horten where he deals especially with it: p. 22 *sqq.*, 42 *sqq.*, 178, 191, 246 *sqq.*, 263 *sqq.*, 526, 551. P. 195, 235, 236 make it plain that the division of time into atoms, which could not be further divided, i.e., that time is not endlessly divisable, goes back to Zeno's paradox of Achilles and the tortoise; it was a solution of that paradox and made motion possible; cf. William James, *A Pluralistic Universe*, p. 228—231. Ibn Ḥazm in his *Milal*, because of his very hostility, has given us particularly full accounts, e.g.v. 92 *sqq.* But in the nature of the case it is not probable that the earlier disputants put their discussions into permanent written form, and still less permitted copies to be freely made and spread abroad. We have the classic case of al-D̲j̲unaid (q.v.; d. 297/909), a very great theologian and ascetic Ṣūfī, on whom no shadow of real suspicion of heresy ever fell, but who openly said that the seeker of the divine Reality might expect to be called a heretic

(Goldziher, *Vorlesungen*, p. 175; see, further, al-Ḳushairī, *Risāla*, Būlāḳ 1290, p. 139 *sqq*.). When he discussed questions of *tawḥīd*, that is the doctrine of the person of Allāh, with his students, it was behind closed doors. We can hardly imagine that these discussions were concerned with such questions as those in al-Ghazzālī's *al-Risāla al-Ḳudsīya* or *al-Iḳtiṣād*, or even al-Taftazānī on al-Nasafī; they must have cut much deeper and have been like those which Ibn Ḥazm has exposed to us with malicious indignation, dragging those godless *mutakallim*'s from behind their closed doors. In reply the *mutakallim*'s would have protested that he was not playing the game and did not understand their object. The Muʿtazilites preceded the orthodox theologians in open publication. We still have the *Masāʾil* of Abū Rashīd, a Muʿtazilite, who wrote about 400/1009 (Horten, *Philosophie des Abu Raschid*; Arthur Biram, *Atomistische Substanzenlehre*). Al-Ghazzālī, at a somewhat later day, actually did put such discussions into writing in his two *al-Maḍnūn*; but it was on the basis of Neoplatonic philosophy and not of atomism [see below].

In the *Muḳaddima* of Ibn Khaldūn (d. 808/1406) we get another view of this development, about four centuries later than the *Fihrist* (ed. Quatremère, iii. 27—43; Būlāk 1274, p. 223—228; transl. De Slane, ii. 40—64). In Quatremère's text (p. 44—59; transl. De Slane, p. 64—85) there follows a section on the *mutashābih* passages in the Ḳurʾān which is not found in some of the MSS., nor in the Būlāḳ editions. Ibn Khaldūn evidently added it later from a perception (i) that his view of these passages was essential to his general position and (ii) that he had not dealt fully enough with some of the theological matters of controversy. He traced, in fact, the origin in great part, of the science of kalām, viewed as defensive scholasticism, to these ambiguous and obscure passages; it sprang, thus, more from exegetical than from philosophical pressure. There is certainly truth in this; but it seems also certain that the early Muslim theologians, under the influence of outside ideas which were pressing in upon them, made use of the obscure verses to secure a possible footing in Islām for these outside ideas. In this they were greatly aided by Muḥammad's own way of thinking, and also by a certain largeness of conception and width and freedom of ideas which belonged to his greatness; he had not been a metaphysician, but a keen psychologist. But it is especially characteristic of Ibn Khaldūn's position, and in striking contrast to his otherwise openmindedness and genuinely scientific spirit, that he rejected all *taʾwīl*, or elucidation, of these passages as absolutely as Aḥmad b. Ḥanbal or al-Ashʿarī themselves. He interpreted Sūra iii. 7 (cf. al-Baiḍāwī, ed. Fleischer, i. 146) as meaning that only Allāh knew their meaning and that man should abstain from useless speculation. He thus secured a method of practically throwing out all the passages of the Ḳurʾān which did not suit his view of the universe, e.g. those speaking of the *djinn* [q.v.], and also, which was worse, set up a limit to man's investigation of the world.

Kalām having thus arisen from these difficulties, or impossibilities, of exegesis, the different sects developed according as the anthropomorphic Ḳurʾānic expressions bearing on the essence (*dhāt*) of Allāh or on his qualities (*ṣifāt*) were treated literally (*tashbīh*, *tadjsīm*) or as having a meaning different in his case from the literal and unknown to us (*tanzīh*) or according as *tanzīh* was applied also to the other descriptives of Allāh, the meanings of which were quite plain and possible in the literal sense becaeus they all expressed ideas apart from the concrete. This last was the position of the Muʿtazilites, between whom and the first sect, the anthropomorphists, stood the sect which professed to follow the doctrines of "the Fathers" (*al-salaf*). So the orthodox party was driven to the use of rational proofs (*adilla ʿaḳlīya*) and there arose al-Ashʿarī who combined *ʿaḳl* and *naḳl*, denied *tashbīh*, establishing "the qualities consisting of ideas" (knowledge, power, will, life), and limited *tanzīh* as the *salaf* had done. He also established "hearing" and "sight" and "the speech which exists in the mind" (*al-ḳāʾim biʾl-nafs*). He also discussed (*takallama*) with the Muʿtazilites their ethical position (*aṣlaḥ*, *taḥsīn*, *taḳbīḥ*) and eschatology and future rewards and punishments. He discussed with the Imāmīya the principle of government, and demonstrated that it was not a part of the Faith, but a convenience upon which the people had agreed. With all this compare and contrast Goldziher in *Vorlesungen*, p. 119 *sqq*. The next great name given is that of al-Bāḳillānī (d. 403). He reduced the whole to a system and established the intellectual basis and arranged the arguments. Thus he established the atom (*al-djawhar al-fard*) and the void (*al-khalāʾ*) — it is to be noticed that *djawhar* with the Aristotelian Neoplatonists means "substance" in the philosophical sense, and that *al-khalāʾ* is exactly the Lucretian *inane*; that an accident (*ʿaraḍ*) cannot subsist in an accident and that it cannot continue through two atoms of time (see also, Ibn Khaldūn, ed. Quatremère, p. 114; De Slane, p. 157). So he made these principles only secondary in importance to the articles of the Faith, because he held that the nullity of an argument meant logically the nullity of the thing which it proved, and the converse. These principles were arguments for the Faith; the Faith was true, therefore these principles must be true. It is evident that formal logic was not the strong point of those who built up this system, however ingenious it might be; and that is what Ibn Khaldūn remarks. And it is further evident that with al-Bāḳillānī the historical value of Ibn Khaldūn's outline begins. He makes no mention of Ibn Ḥazm [q.v.], a theological free lance, who died in 456; but he gives the titles of two of the books of the Imām al-Ḥaramain (al-Djuwainī [q.v.], d. 478), a teacher of al-Ghazzālī, apparently because of his reputation, although no distinctive development is attached to his name. Immediately after him the science of formal logic was taken up by the theologians who had discovered that it was only a tool for thinking and not a part of philosophy. But this led to an examination of their foundations and to the rejection of a great part of them; so that they no longer argued, as al-Bāḳillānī had done, from the nullity of the proof to the nullity of the thing proven. Their new proofs were derived, to a considerable extent, from the physics and metaphysics of the philosophers, and thus they entered upon a new method which was called *ṭarīḳat al-mutaʾakhkhirīn*; yet they also introduced into it a considerable amount of opposition to the philosophical positions because these seemed to be the same as their own earlier heresies. Leaders in this new school were al-Ghazzālī (d. 505) and al-Rāzī (d. 606; see on him especially Goldziher, in *Isl.*, iii. 213—247) and to their books Ibn Khaldūn would still send the student of theology who wished guidance in his criticism of the philosophers, although there was in them some amount of opposition to the older method. It is to be remembered, too, that al-Rāzī was a systematic user of *ta'wīl* (Goldziher, p. 227), of which Ibn Khaldūn disapproved. But such students as wished simply to follow the path of the *salaf* in theology should take the old method of the *mutakallim*'s — only there could true *ʿilm al-kalām* be found — and especially should study the *Irshād* of the Imām al-Ḥaramain. This apparently means that with al-Ghazzālī there came a sharp abandonment of the method of the atomists and a going to school instead with the Aristotelian Neoplatonists. Such, too, is certainly the evidence of al-Ghazzālī's writings. After al-Ghazzālī and al-Rāzī came still deeper confusion between theology and philosophy, until the subject matter of the two was regarded as one. Yet the *mutakallim*'s had distinguished sharply the physics and metaphysics of the philosophers from their own theocentric position, using an intellectualist system in defence of dogmas laid down by divine authority. He gives as an example of this confusion the *Ṭawāliʿ* of al-Baiḍāwī (d. 685/1286) and every user of al-Baiḍāwī's Ḳur'ān commentary will recognize what he means. The learned of Persia (al-ʿAdjam) who followed al-Baiḍāwī had used the same method in all their works. Of the kind of kalām that was left in his own day Ibn Khaldūn had no good opinion; its ambiguities (*īhāmāt*) and generalities (*iṭlāḳāt*) were a profanation of the Creator rather than a defence. And no kalām was longer needed; it had been a defence against the *Mulḥida* (heretics) and the *Mubtadiʿa* (innovators) and they were extinct. But it was rather disgraceful for one who knew the Sunna by heart not to be able to give a reason for the faith that was in him.

Yet kalām had still a long course to run, and the commentary of al-Baidjūrī on the short treatise of al-Faḍālī, already referred to, gives a good idea of the development of the system of the *mutakallim*'s. Text and comment are quite modern — al-Faḍālī died in A.D. 1821 and al-Baidjūrī in A.D. 1844; they are finished scholasticism and the title *Kifāyat al-ʿawāmm fī ʿilm al-kalām*, "The Sufficiency of the Commonalty in the Science of kalām", with reiterated statements in the text that only so much is given as is necessary for salvation, shows a purely intellectual view of religion. The commentary is based throughout on atomistic reasonings; the physics and the metaphysics are atomic. The text suggests an intentional counterblast to the treatise of al-Ghazzālī with a similar title, *Ildjām al-ʿawāmm ʿan ʿilm al-kalām*, "Reining back of the Commonalty from the Science of Kalām", yet the intention is nowhere expressed. In it al-Ghazzālī had denounced the corrupting of the simple faith of the multitude with intellectualist arguments and had advocated very subtly what we would now call psychological methods — startingly, for modern ideas, backed by the secular arm of the state. But al-Ghazzālī had opposed the *mutakallim* system and method from the beginning. On the one hand he knew, as a fact of psychology, that being convinced against one's will left one of the same opinion, and on the other, he did not approve of atomism as philosophy. He appears to make no specific reference to it in his works, and where he does give an abstract of theology, as a formal science (e.g. in *al-Risāla al-Ḳudsīya*, and in *al-Iḳtiṣād*) he stops short of absolutely philosophical bottoming. That, for him, was intellectually impossible; but such an outline of concatenated dogmatics, as in the two books mentioned, was justifiable (*Arbaʿīn*, ed. 1328, p. 25 *sqq.*). The only real philosopy for him was, apparently, the Aristotelian-Neoplatonic amalgam, and with it he had dealt in his books which have reached us in a sceptical but respectful spirit. Probably following the economy of teaching, which he himself professed, and which he and all Islām practised, he dealt thoroughly and destructively in other books with the atomic system, and this may explain the mysterious allusions which have been called "the secret" of al-Ghazzālī (e.g. W. H. T. Gairdner on the *Mishkāt* in *Isl.*, v. 121—153). For his attitude towards the *mutakallim*'s see further AL-GHAZZĀLĪ; *al-Munḳidh*, p. 8 *sqq.*, and *Mishkāt al-anwār*, Cairo 1322, p. 47 *sqq.*

It is significant that reform movements in Islām at the present time seem to have cut loose from the atomic philosophy, and to have gone back for leadership to Ibn Sīnā, Ibn Rushd and the Aristotelians generally. Djamāl al-Dīn al-Afghānī (q.v.; cf. E. G. Browne, *The Persian Revolution of* 1905—1906, Cambridge 1910, chap. i.; Goldziher, *Die Richtungen der islamischen Koranauslegung*, Leiden 1920, p. 322 *sqq.*) and his friend and pupil Muḥammad ʿAbduh [q.v.] were the protagonists of this renaissance and continued the long interrupted method of al-Ghazzālī, even on the side of the economy of teaching. The atomic system had crystallized and had become identified with the stiffest orthodoxy. In its origin, also, it had been, even with the Muʿtazilites, a weapon for the defence of accepted views and not an instrument of free investigation. Modern Islām, therefore, could have nothing to do with it, although it is possible that modern western atomic speculation may galvanize it into a semblance of life. Yet it should never be forgotten that this theory is the most original contribution which Muslim thinkers have made to the history of philosophy.

Bibliography: It has mostly been given above, and almost all the bibliography under ALLĀH applies. There may be added: M. Th. Houtsma, *De strijd over het dogma in den Islam tot op el-Ashʿari*, Leiden 1875; Goldziher, *Vorlesungen über den Islam* (Heidelberg 1910) *passim*, but especially chap. iii.; do., *Islamische Philosophie des Mittelalters*, in *Kultur der Gegenwart*, i. 5, p. 302 *sqq.*; T. J. De Boer, *Geschichte der Philosophie im Islam* (Stuttgart 1901), p. 56 *sqq.*; Wensinck, *The Muslim Creed*, index, s.v.; A. S. Tritton, *Muslim Theology*, London 1947; L. Gardet et M.-M. Anawati, *Introduction à la théologie musulmane*, Paris 1948; Maimonides, *Le Guide des Egarés*, ed. and transl. by S. Munk (Paris 1856—66); S. Horovitz, *Über den Einfluss der griech. Philosophie auf die Entwicklung des Kalam*, Breslau 1909 (*Jahres-Ber. des jüd.-theol. Sem. Fraenckel'scher Stiftung*, 1909); al-Bāḳillānī, *Kitāb al-Tamhīd*, ed. by al-Khaḍīrī and Abū Rīda, Cairo 1322/1947; K. Lasswitz, *Geschichte der Atomistik*, Hamburg—Leipzig 1890, i. 143—152; S. Pines, *Beiträge zur islamischen Atomenlehre*, Berlin 1936.

ḲALANDARĪYA. According to all the information available regarding the early history of the Ḳalandar dervishes, it is more than probable that we have not here to do with a body similar to the other dervish orders introduced from Eastern Persia, but rather with a kind of wandering monks, who followed in their mental and physical mode of life the ideal which al-Maḳrīzī, *al-Khiṭaṭ* (Būlāḳ 1270), ii. 432 *sq.* attributes to them, à propos of his description of the Ḳalandarī monastery in Cairo (cf. thereon de Sacy, *Chrest. arabe*², Paris 1826, i. 263—275). According to this and to descriptions which e.g. al-Suhrawardī (in Silvestre de Sacy, in *NE*, xii., Paris 1831, p. 341) or Djāmī, *Nafaḥāt al-uns*, ed. W. Nassau Lees (Calcutta 1859) as well as Saʿdī himself (cf. *Gulistān*, transl. by K. H. Graf, *Moslicheddin Saʿdi's Rosengarten*, Leipzig 1846, p. 294 *sq.*) give of the Ḳalandar dervishes of the time, we have to deal with wandering dervishes, Malāmatī's (cf. al-Maḳrīzī, *al-Khiṭaṭ*, ii. 432; but on the other hand see the *Burhān-i ḳāṭiʿ* under *ḳalandar*, where a rigid distinction is made between *ḳalandar*, *malāmatī* and *ṣūfī*), without fixed abode and without fixed rules for their order and with an utter neglect of thelaws of religion or of the forms of society. To Abū Saʿīd b. Abi 'l-Khair is ascribed a quatrain on them, which gives a clear idea of the real ḳalandar of his time (cf. *Sitzungsber. der Kgl. Bayr. Akad. der Wissensch.*, phil.-hist. Kl., 1875, ii. 157; Ign. Goldziher, *Vorlesungen über den Islam*, Heidelberg 1911, p. 172; F. Babinger, in *Isl.*, xi., 1911, p. 66 *sq.*). One then who is usually called the founder of a so-called order of ḳalandars, is apparently nothing more than some important protagonist of these views. This is certainly true of Yūsuf, said to have been a Spanish Arab, who is often represented as the founder of the Ḳalandarīya, as well as of Shaikh Djamāl al-Dīn of Sāwa in Persia, who, Ibn Baṭṭūṭa says (i. 61 *sq.*), settled in Damietta and ended his days there. The expression *ḳudwa* in Ibn Baṭṭūṭa here obviously means nothing more than "pattern, model". The ḳalandars seem to have originated in Central Asia and to have been strongly influenced by Indian ideas, and it seems quite possible that the word *ḳalendar* is of Indian origin (see however, J. P. Brown, *The Dervishes* [London 1868], where the presumably not Persian origin of the word *ḳalender*, *ḳarendal* etc. is also discussed [cf. besides Dozy, *Supplément*, ii. 340, also *Der Islam*, xi. 94, note]). According to al-Maḳrīzī (d. 1442), they came about 400 years before his time into Arab lands. About 610 (1213) the first of them appeared in Damascus (*al-Khiṭaṭ*, ii. 433). Here there died in 722/1322 the Persian Shaikh Ḥasan of the Djawāliḳī sect, who flourished under Sulṭān al-Malik al-ʿĀdil Ketbogha and founded a monastery of ḳalandars not far from Cairo (Seryākūs = Kyriakos?; Maḳrīzī, *loc. cit.*, also *Sulūk*, vol. ii., Cairo 1941, p. 239). The Ḳalandarīs may have been most numerous in Persia and the great bulk of them, still in the xvii[th] century at least, seems to have been concentrated in Ardabīl, the stronghold of the Ṣafawīya (cf. Adam Olearius, *Persianische Reisebeschreibung*, 1656, p. 685: the *Kalenderan*). In Anatolia also and even in Rumelia in the early Ottoman period down to the xvi[th] dentury, they several times played a dangerous part by attacks on the authority of the state and serious risings (cf. F. Babinger, in *Isl.*, xi. 14; Pečewī, *Taʾrīkh*, Stambul 1283, i. 120). Even in the Saldjūḳ period similar risings seem to have been led by Ḳalandarīs. There are also various indications of connections between Ḳalandarīs and Bektāshīs. On the *ḳalenderlik* in the Ottoman Empire a thorough investigation is still lacking. It seems that the ḳalenderī's found their way hither from Eastern Turkestan, as may be induced from the fact that a certain Ḥādjdjī Ḳalender is found in a *silsile* of the Selmānī-order (MS. Arundel Or. 8, Brit. Mus.; cf. Rieu, *Turk. Mss.*, p. 239) between Ustādh Ḥāfiẓ Khwārizmī and Ustādh Khurram Sabzawārī.

In nearly all accounts of the Levant from the XVIth century the ḳalenderī's are mentioned in some way, generally by corrupted names; see e.g. Leunclavius, *Annales*, p. 371: *fibulatus calender*; Spanduni (Spandugino), Florence edition, p. 192 *sq.* (ed. Schefer, p. 291 *sq.*): *calendieri*; Schweigger, *Tage-Buch*, p. 195; F. Sansovino, *Cose de Turchi*, p. 31[a]: *carandolo*; illustration in Nicolas de Nicolay, *Navigations*.

Ḳalandarī has also become the name of a certain tune in Turkish.

Bibliography: cf., besides the works quoted above, also F. Babinger, in *Isl.*, xi. 94 and the references given here; also d'Herbelot, *Bibliothèque Orientale* (Paris 1697), p. 244; do., (Maestricht 1776), p. 224 s.v. *Calender*; Adam Olearius, *Persianischer Rosenthal*, Book viii., § 67; *Burhān-i ḳāṭiʿ*, ed. Th. Roebuck (Calcutta 1818), s.v.; J. P. Brown, *The Dervishes*. Cf. also Dozy, *Supplément*, ii. 340 and *Isl.* xi. 94 note.

KALB, the dog, is also in Islām one of the "unclean beasts" (hence *kalb* as an abusive word, specially to unbelievers), primarily because its flesh may not be eaten (al-Nawawī, *Minhādj al-ṭālibin*, ed. v. d. Berg, iii. 312); and further because, according to the Ḥadīth, there are several special regulations regarding it. For example dogs render food which they lick impure and render unavailable water intended for ritual purifications (al-Bukhārī, *Wuḍūʾ*, bāb 33). Vessels, likewise, which have been licked by dogs, require to be cleaned several times, including once with sand. In a certain way they render impure the whole room in which they are; for angels do not enter a house in which there is a dog and Muḥammad had first to sprinkle the place on which a young dog had lain concealed with purificatory water before Djibrīl would appear to him (Muslim, *Libās*, trad. 81 *sqq.*). — Dogs "cut off the ṣalāt", i.e. they make the ṣalāt worthless when they come into the immediate vicinity of the man at prayer (Ibn Mādja, *Iḳāma*, bāb 30), and one is all the more inclined to attribute this rule to the impurity of the dog, as it also holds for menstruating women. The Arab commentators, however, explain it by saying that the dog frightens the worshipper and distracts him from his devotions (al-Sindī, commentary on Ibn Mādja as cited above). This is especially true of the black dog, for "he is Satan". This saying is either to be interpreted literally as meaning that Satan occasionally appears in the form of a black dog (cf. Faust) or it only means that black dogs in general are considered particularly dangerous. Dogs in general are considered noxious and should therefore be exterminated (al-Nasāʾī, *Ṣaid wa 'l-dhabāʾiḥ*, bāb 9—14), but as "Allah does not create anything in which there is not a trace of His wisdom" (al-Sindī, commentary on this passage), this rule is applied only to black dogs.

It is only permitted to keep dogs for hunting, for herding and for watching (al-Nasāʾī, *op. cit.*); whoever keeps a forbidden dog has to forfeit a portion of his possessions daily (cf. *Babylon. Talmud*, *Shabbāth*, fol. 63[a]: "whoever possesses a dangerous dog keeps good fortune away from his house"). Dealing in dogs on the other hand is strictly forbidden (al-Bukhārī, *Buyūʿ*, bāb 25).

But in spite of its impurity and dangerousness the Arabs are able to appreciate the good qualities and services of the dog. Muḥammad himself promises a woman a divine reward for a kindness which she had done a thirsty dog (al-Bukhārī, *Wuḍūʾ*, bāb 33), and al-Ḳazwīnī (p. 403) characterises the dog as "a particularly intelligent, very useful animal, patient in hunger and on the watch, whose cleverness and fidelity are shown in many ways". A large part of Djāḥiẓ's *Kitāb al-ḥayawān* is occupied by a dialogue on the virtues and defects of dogs and cocks.

For the dog of the seven sleepers cf. AṢḤĀB AL-KAHF; ḲIṬMĪR.

Bibliography: Wensinck, *Handbook*, s.v. Dogs; al-Ḳazwīnī, *ʿAdjāʾib al-makhlūḳāt* (ed. Wüstenfeld), p. 403 *sq.*; al-Damīrī, *Kitāb ḥayāt al-ḥayawān al-kubrā* (Cairo 1275), ii. 320—360; (1315), ii. 230—259; Ibn al-Marzubān, *Kitāb faḍl al-kilāb ʿalā kathīr mimman labisa al-thiyāb* (Cairo 1341). — Travellers in the East, e.g. Ch. M. Doughty, *Travels in Arabia Deserta* (Cambridge 1888), s. Index; A. Musil, *Arabia Petraea*, iii. (Vienna 1908), s. Index; Julius Euting, *Tagbuch einer Reise in Inner-Arabien*, ii. 53 on dog's names. On dogs in Oriental towns cf. von Oppenheim, *Vom Mittelmeer zum Persischen Golf* (Berlin 1899—1900), i. 69—71.

KANʿĀN, the biblical K^{e}naʿan, is a personality, regarding whom the traditions, in spite of their sparsity, agree in hardly a single point. Al-Baiḍāwī (ed. Fleischer, i. 513) mentions him as the father of the famous Namrūd; he is also regarded as the ancestor of the Kanʿāniyūn (*LA*, x. 191) and of the Berbers (al-Dimashḳī, *Nukhbat al-dahr*, ed. Mehren, p. 266 and Ibn Khaldūn, *al-ʿIbar*, vi. 93, *sqq.*, 97 *sqq.*). — Very little is known about him. Many refer to him the story in Sūra xi. 42 *sq.*, that a son of Nūḥ in spite of his pressing appeal refused to take refuge in the Ark with him and thus perished in the Flood with the unbelievers (al-Baiḍāwī, ad locum and al-Thaʿlabī, *Ḳiṣaṣ al-anbiyāʾ*, Cairo 1324, p. 36 below). — Al-Ṭabarī (i. 199) also knows of a son of Nūḥ called Kanʿān, who lost his life at the Flood, but refers the Ḳurʾān verse in question to Yām b. Nūḥ (see *Tafsīr*, ad Sūra xi. 42 *sq.*), whom, however, he identifies with Kanʿān in i. 199.

KANĪSA (plural *kanāʾis*), synagogue, church, the arabicised form of the Aramaic k^{e}*nīshtā* "meeting (place), school, synagogue" (cf. J. Levy, *Neuhebr. und Chald. Wörterbuch*, ii. 359 *sq.*). The *Lisān al-ʿArab*, viii. 83, $_2$ *sq.* is nearly right in so far as it derives *kanīsa* from *kunisht*; al-Khafādjī (*Shifaʾ al-ghalīl*, Cairo 1282, p. 195), however, rejects this view and expresses the opinion that the word denotes an especially Christian institution and goes back to *kalīsa*, an abbreviated form of *kalīsiya* (ἐκκλησία). Al-Bustānī also considers the word as being the arabicised ἐκκλησία (*Muḥīṭ al-muḥīṭ*, Beyrouth 1286, p. 1847).

In Arabic *kanīsa* denotes the Jewish as well as the Christian place of worship; this appears also from the various statements of the lexica; some refer to churches, other to synagogues exclusively (cf. al-Djawharī, *Ṣaḥāḥ*, Būlāḳ 1282, i. 473 *ult.*; al-Zamakhsharī, *Asās al-balāgha*, Cairo 1299, ii. 212; *Lisān al-ʿArab*, *loc. cit.*; Yāḳūt, *Muʿdjam*, ed. Wüstenfeld, iv. 314, $_7$). According to al-Fīrūzābādī, *al-Ḳāmūs*, Būlāḳ 1272, i. 549 $_1$, *kanīsa* denotes the place of worship (*mutaʿabbad*) of the Jews, the Christians or the Kāfir's; cf. also *Tādj al-ʿArūs*, iv. 235 *infra*.

In early literature *kanīsa* is often found in the meaning of "church". Two documents on papyrus of the year 88/707 mention the church of a monastery called (*Munyat*) *Kanīsat Mārya* in Egypt (*Papyri Schott-Reinhardt*, i., ed. C. H. Becker, Heidelberg 1906, p. 111, g. line 4, p. 112, i., line 4). In a satyrical verse Djarīr speaks of the churches of Taghlib (al-Mubarrad, *al-Kāmil*, ed. Wright, p. 485). The treaties which ʿUmar or his generals are said to have concluded with the inhabitants of several towns usually contain stipulations concerning the *kanāʾis* (al-Balādhurī, *Futūḥ al-buldān*, ed. de Goeje, p. 173; al-Yaʿḳūbī, ii. 167; al-Ṭabarī, i. 2405 *sq.*, 2588; Eutychius, ed. Cheikho, ii. 17; Ibn ʿAsākir, *al-Taʾrīkh al-kabīr*, Damascus 1329 *sqq.*, i. 178; cf. also Abū Yūsūf, *Kit. al-kharādj*, Būlāḳ 1302, p. 80). In the Ḥadīth it is related how Umm Ḥabība and Umm Salama told the Prophet of a church in Abyssinia adorned with images (al-Bukhārī, *Ṣalāt*, bāb 48, 54; *Djanāʾiz*, bāb 70; *Manāḳib al-Anṣār*, bāb 37).

Kanīsa further occurs very often with a following noun in the genitive as a local appellation in Egypt and Syria e.g. Kanīsat Ḥanas (in Alexandria, Yāḳūt, *op. cit.*, i. 257).

Al-Maḳrīzī denotes synagogues as well as churches by the word *kanīsa* (*al-Khiṭaṭ*, Būlāḳ 1270, ii. 464 *sqq.*, 510 *sqq.*).

In Spain and in the Maghrib the Form *kanīsiya* (perhaps influenced by *iglesia*) was in use; it is still current in Morocco and Tunisia (vgl. Dozy, *Supplément*, ii. 493).

In the modern language *kanīsa* denotes a church, *kanīs* a synagogue (al-Bustānī, *loc. cit.*). For the Egyptian dialect cf. S. Spiro Bey, *Arabic-English Dictionary*, 2nd ed., Cairo 1923, s.v.).

On the rules for churches laid down by the Muslims cf. the art. NAṢĀRĀ.

KARĀMA is strictly the infinitive of *karuma* (to be *karīm* "generous" in the widest sense); but in usage it is a noun of similar meaning to *ikrām* and *takrīm*, to show one's self *karīm* to any one (*Lisān*, xv. 456 *sqq.*). It does not occur in the Ḳurʾān although *karīm* is very frequently used of Allāh and his workings (al-Rāghib al-Iṣfahānī, *al-Mufradāt*, s.v.). It has come, therefore, in the devotional language of Islām, to mean the exhibition by Allāh of his generosity, favour, protection, help towards any one, e.g. al-Baiḍāwī on sūra. x. 62 (ed. Fleischer, i. 419, *ult.*), a *locus classicus* on the *walīs*; and *karāmāt* mean individual cases of this generosity. In a special sense, the *karāmāt* then come to mean the miraculous gifts and graces with which Allāh surrounds, protects and aids his Saints (*al-awliyāʾ*). A Ḳurʾānic basis for these was sought in the story (sūra iii. 37) of the food which came miraculously to Maryam in the locked *miḥrāb* and in the transporting in a moment from Yaman of the throne of Bilḳīs by a unnamed companion of Solomon (sūra xxvii. 40). As neither Maryam nor the unnamed companion was a prophet these could not be evidentiary miracles (*muʿdjizāt*). See the whole discussion in al-Taftāzānī on al-Nasafī's *ʿAḳāʾid*, Cairo 1321, pp. 134 *sqq.* But the real basis lay in the innumerable narratives of *karāmāt* in the lives of the *walīs*, exaggerated and distorted reflections of indubitable facts in the ecstatic religious life. The fact of these all orthodox Islām admits, even so philosophical an historian as Ibn Khaldūn (ed. Quatremère, i. 169, 199; transl. de Slane, i. 190, 277) and a peripatetic philosopher like Ibn Sīnā (*Ishārāt*, ed. Forget, pp. 209, 219, 221 *sqq.*). These were evidently driven by the pressure of facts to fall back on the hypothesis of still unsolved mysteries in nature; cf. Goldziher, *Die Richtungen der islamischen Koranauslegung*, Leiden 1920, p. 139, note 3. Only the Muʿtazilites, who were certain that nature held no mysteries for them and that they need only apply reason to their theological positions, protested and found, even in the Ḳurʾān, basis for their protest. See al-Zamakhsharī on sūra lxxii. 26, 27 (*al-Kashshāf*, ed. Nassau Lees, ii. 1539) and on the whole development Goldziher, *op. cit.*, pp. 144 *sqq.* The coincidence in sound, in derivation and in meaning between these *karāmāt* and the χαρίσματα of the early Christian Church (I Cor. xii.) is most striking and can hardly be accidental. The religious phenomena behind both are the same; but the verbal link is not clear; the Syriac Church called the χαρίσματα simply "gifts", *mauhᵉbhāthā*, in Arabic *mawāhib*, which indeed occurs in this sense; it is possible that the Greek word taken over into Syriac may have suggested to users of Arabic their own *karāmāt*. Technically, such a *karāma* is one of the *khawāriḳ al-ʿāda*, "the breakers of usage"; for there is no Nature in orthodox Islām, only, and at best, a custom which Allāh has established (Goldziher, *Vorlesungen*, p. 130). It differs from the *muʿdjiza* or "evidentiary miracle" in that it is not worked by Allāh for a prophet in proof of his mission and is not accompanied by a *daʿwā nubūwa* or a *taḥaddī*, a claim of prophetship or a challenge to the unbeliever. It differs from the *maʿūna*, "help", in that while the recipient of the *maʿūna* is a Muslim he has had not special religious experience; and from the *irhāṣ*, an anticipatory miracle worked for a prophet before his call. It differs from the *istidrādj* and *ihāna* as these are wrought at the instance of unbelievers to lead them astray and bring them to shame (*Dict. of Techn. Terms*, i. 144 *sqq.*; al-Nasafī, *ʿAḳāʾid*, *loc. cit.* with accomp. commentaries). A *walī* should conceal his wonders, while a prophet must display them; a *walī* may not know about them, while a prophet cannot help knowing. Yet the *karāma* of a *walī* may be regarded as a *muʿdjiza* for the prophet whose follower he is. Finally, a *walī* should disregard them as much as possible and should look on them as tests rather than as privileges.

Bibliography: al-Ḳushairī, *al-Risāla*, Būlāḳ 1290, with commentaries, iv. 146 *sqq.* (cf. Richard Hartmann, *Al-Ḳuschairi's Darstellung des Sufitums*); Goldziher, *Muhammed. Studien*, ii. 372 *sqq.*; al-Īdjī, *Mawāḳif*, Būlāḳ 1266, with comm. of al-Djurdjānī, pp. 578 *sqq.*, pp. 547 *sqq.*; al-Hudjwīrī, *Kashf al-maḥdjūb*, transl. by R. A. Nicholson, by index; al-Shaʿrānī, *al-Ṭabaḳāt al-kubrā*, passim; Yūsuf al-Nabahānī, *Djāmiʿ karāmāt al-awliyāʾ*, Cairo 1329 (a great thesaurus of legend); Ibn Baṭṭūṭa, *Tuḥfat al-nuẓẓār*, passim; D. B. Macdonald, *Religious Attitude and Life in Islam*, Lectures 3—7, 9.

KARĀMAT ʿALĪ, Indian reformer, born (date uncertain, early in the xixᵗʰ century?) at Djawnpūr, of a Shaikh family, which had held the office of *khaṭīb* under Muḥammadan rule; his father was *sarishtadār* in the Djawnpūr Collectorate. He studied theology and other Muslim sciences under various celebrated teachers of the time, esp. Shāh ʿAbd al-ʿAzīz, *muḥaddith* of Dihlī, who was also the teacher and afterwards follower of Saiyid Aḥmad of Barēlī. Between 1820 and 1824, Saiyid Aḥmad made a tour through Bengal and Northern India, collecting a band of disciples, and Karāmat ʿAlī was one of the most devoted of the younger men who followed him, but he does not appear to have taken part in the *djihād* which Saiyid Aḥmad waged against the Sikhs, or to have ever been in the Afghān borderland, where Saiyid Aḥmad was slain in battle in 1831. The Saiyid's old master, Shāh ʿAbd al-ʿAzīz, now became his khalīfa, and an active propaganda for the revival of Islām was organised in Bihār and Bengal. With this peaceful propaganda Karāmat ʿAlī was identified, and he may be regarded as its most successful apostle, as he was certainly its most brilliant exponent. During the early decades of the xixᵗʰ century, there were several minor reform movements in Eastern Bengal, led by men with more zeal than learning, notably by Ḥādjdjī Sharīʿat Allāh [cf. the art. FARĀʾIḌĪYA], who in 1252/1836—7 met Karāmat ʿAlī in Calcutta. By 1855 the two schools had made some progress towards a rapprochement, and in the meeting then held at Barisal, Karāmat ʿAlī was able to agree on several points with the representative of the other movement, Mawlawī ʿAbd al-Djabbār, though on the question of the lawfulness of *djumʿa* and *ʿīd* prayers in India, he could not overcome the stubborn opposition of ʿAbd al-Djabbār, and he had to appeal to the humour of ʿAbd al-Djabbār's followers by pointing out that their leader mistook grasshoppers (which were unlawful food) for locusts (which were lawful: *Ḥudjdjat-i ḳāṭiʿa*, p. 29—32).

Karāmat ʿAlī's life was a double struggle: first, he combated the Hindu customs and superstitions which had crept into the practice of Islām in Eastern Bengal, against which he wrote a book, entitled *Radd al-bidʿa*, besides inveighing against them throughout his writings; and secondly, he tried to bring back into the fold of orthodoxy the new heterodox schools against which he waged a successful war; to this subject, also, he devoted a special book, *Hidāyat al-rāfiḍīn*, besides constant references to "the ignorant" in his voluminous writings. He kept in touch with the Muslims of Bengal, and distributed to the needy all the presents that he received. He was a trained *ḳāriʾ* and an expert calligraphist.

He died on the 3ʳᵈ of Rabīʿ II, 1290/30ᵗʰ May, 1873 and was buried in Rangpūr (*Tadjallī-i nūr*, ii. 136), in the province in which he had laboured for the regeneration of Islām all his life. He was succeeded in his work by his son, Mawlawī Ḥāfiẓ Aḥmad (d. 1898), and his nephew, Muḥammad Muḥsin. His following was so large that there was hardly a Bengal village without his disciples and he still exerts a living influence in certain districts of that province.

He wrote chiefly in Urdū. Raḥmān ʿAlī (*op. cit.*, p. 171—2) gives a list of 46 of his works, without claiming that it is exhaustive. One of his works, *Miftāḥ al-djannat*, has run through numerous editions and is accepted in India as a correct statement of Islāmic principles. His writings may be divided into four classes: 1) general works, like *Miftāḥ al-djannat*; 2) works on the reading and verbal interpretation of the Ḳurʾān, and formal prayers and ablutions; 3) works on the doctrine of spiritual preceptorship (*pīrī murīdī*), the cornerstone of orthodox Islām in India; in accepting this doctrine, Karāmat ʿAlī stands in sharp opposition to the Wahhābī sect and merges insensibly in the *taṣawwuf* schools, which he brings into relation with the traditional religious orders; 4) polemics against Sharīʿat Allāh, Dūda Miyān, the Wahhābīs, etc.

The common conception that Karāmat ʿAlī was a Wahhābī is refuted by the detailed exposition of his own views as set forth in his *Mukāshafāt-i raḥmat*; he had not seen any Wahhābī books, but had made verbal enquiries and found that they were so fanatical (*ḍiddī*) that they called all who did not agree with them *mushrik* (p. 38-9); he and his school carefully distinguished between *shirk*, which was the negation of Islām, and *bidʿa*, which was only an error in doctrine (p. 39). In his *Ḥudjdjat-i ḳāṭiʿa* he draws a clear distinction between a *fāsiḳ* (sinner) and a *kāfir* (infidel) and inveighs against those who would deny funeral prayers to those who did not pray but repeated the *kalima* (p. 21); if non-Muslims conquer Muslim lands, the *djumʿa* prayer and the two *ʿīd* [q.v.] prayers were not only lawful but obligatory (p. 13 *bis*). He laid great stress on authority, successively handed down by living teachers, and based his doctrine on the orthodox Sunnī books of the Ḥanafī school (*Mukās̲h̲afāt-i raḥmat*, p. 37). He accepted the six orthodox books of tradition (*Ṣiḥaḥ sitta*), the commentaries (*tafāsīr*), the principles of ceremonial law as interpreted by the masters (*uṣūl-i fiḳh*), and the doctrines of *taṣawwuf* and *pīrī murīdī* (p. 38, 35), even basing the mission of Saiyid Aḥmad on the ḥadīt̲h̲ (p. 32): "In every century a teacher is born to revivify the faith": Saiyid Aḥmad was such a teacher for the xiii[th] century and should be followed until another teacher arise for the xiv[th] cent. (p. 34).

Bibliography: Sir W. W. Hunter, *The Indian Muselmans*, p. 114; C. E. Buckland, *Dictionary of Indian Biography*, p. 229; *Census of India*, 1901, vol. vi., part i. (Bengal, p. 174; Calcutta 1902); *JAS of Bengal*, vol. lxiii., part iii., p. 54-6 (Calcutta 1894); Garcin de Tassy, *Hist. de la littérature hindoustanie*, ii. 162 (Paris 1870) Saiyid Nūr al-Dīn Zaidī, *Tad̲j̲allī-i nūr* (biographies of the famous men of D̲j̲awnpūr), p. 135-6 (D̲j̲awnpūr 1900).

A correct appreciation of Karāmat ʿAlī's doctrines can only be gained by a study of his own writings, the most important of which are the following: *Miftāḥ al-d̲j̲annat* (Calcutta 1243) (frequently reprinted); *Kawkab-i durrī* (Calcutta 1253) (translates passages from the Ḳurʾān for the benefit of those who know only a little Arabic); *Baiʿat-i tawba* (Calcutta 1254) (defends the legality of repentance at the hands of a *pīr*, and other practices of the religious orders); *Zīnāt al-ḳāriʾ* (Calcutta 1264) (on the correct principles for the reading aloud of the Ḳurʾān); *Faiḍ-i ʿāmm* (Calcutta 1282) (a tract on speculative theology, expounding the doctrines of S̲h̲aik̲h̲ Aḥmad Sarhindī); *Ḥud̲j̲d̲j̲at-i ḳāṭiʿa* (Calcutta 1282) (a polemical tract against the school of S̲h̲arīʿat Allāh and his son Dūda Miyān); *Nūr al-hudā* (Calcutta 1286) (on the doctrines of *taṣawwuf*, of the *mud̲j̲addidīya* school, apparently the new school of Saiyid Aḥmad of Barēlī); *Mukās̲h̲afāt-i raḥmat* (Calcutta 1286) (gives an account of the life and work of Saiyid Aḥmad of Barēlī, and discusses and disowns the Wahhābīs); *Zīnāt al-muṣallī* (Calcutta 1259) (instructions for ablutions and prayers, etc.); *Zād al-taḳwā* (Calcutta 1287, reprint) (treats of the beliefs and practices of Islām, and *taṣawwuf*; accepts the Naḳs̲h̲bandīya teaching). A list (not complete) of Karāmat ʿAlī's works is given in Raḥmān ʿAlī's *Tad̲h̲kira-i ʿulamaʾ-i Hind*, p. 171 (Lucknow 1894): 46 separate works are mentioned.

KARBALĀʾ. [See MES̲H̲HED ḤUSAIN].

ḲARMAṬIANS (ḲARMAṬĪ, plur. ḲARĀMIṬA: Carmathians). In the strict application of the word, the name was given to the rebel federations of Arabs and "Nabataeans", which were organised in Lower Mesopotamia after the servile war of the Zand̲j̲ from 264/877 and based on a system of communism into which initiation was necessary; active propaganda extended this secret society among the masses, peasants and artisans; — in al-Aḥsā, where they founded a state independent of the Caliph of Bag̲h̲dād; — in K̲h̲urāsān, in Syria and in Yaman, where they formed lasting hotbeds of discontent.

In the broader sense, the name Ḳarmaṭian means the great movement for social reform and justice based on equality, which swept through the Muslim world from the ninth to the twelfth centuries of our era; this movement, captured and controlled by an ambitious family, the Ismāʿīlī dynasty [cf. ISMĀʿĪLĪYA, SABʿĪYA], who founded the Fāṭimid anti-caliphate in 297/910, became abortive and finally succumbed with this dynasty before the counter-stroke of the Crusades.

The movement was characterised, from the point of view of language-history, by the adaptation of the Arabic language to certain technical achievements of foreign origin, especially Hellenistic (Neo-Platonic, pseudo-Hermetic and "Sabaean" writings); from the political point of view, by the exploitation of the ʿAlid legitimist tradition on behalf of a conspiracy, carried on in a strict secrecy, in which the name of the supreme leader was never pronounced; from the point of view of worship, by the use of an allegorical and methodical catechism, Ḳurʾānic in origin, adapted to all creeds, to all races and all castes. The movement was based on reason, tolerance and equality, with a system of graduated initiation and the ritual of a gild which — encouraging the rise of the trade gild movement and universities — seems to have reached the West and to have influenced the formation of European gilds and freemasonry.

I. Etymology and early history.

The etymology of the word *ḳarmaṭ* (not *ḳirmiṭ*) is disputed. It appears as a descriptive adjective in the name of the first leader of the insurrection, Ḥamdān Ḳarmaṭ (cf. ʿAlī b. Ḳarmaṭ, a heretic quoted by the Nuṣairī author Maimūn al-Ṭabarānī). Vollers has connected it with the Greek γράμματα, but it is more probable that we should see in it a borrowing from the local Aramaic dialect of Wāsiṭ, where *ḳurmaṭā* to this day means *mudallis* (Arabo-Aramaic dialect of the Mīdān, cf. Anastase, in *Machriq*, x. 1907, p. 857). From the year 255/868 we find mentioned in the same region, along with the Furātīya, a corps of Ḳurmāṭīya among the rebellious troops of the Zand̲j̲ (al-Ṭabarī, iii. 1757; cf. iii. 1749: Rās̲h̲id Ḳurmāṭī).

The name *ḳarmaṭ* in palaeography means a particular kind of *nask̲h̲ī*; in addition there is a special secret Ḳarmaṭian alphabet used in the Yemenī texts recently studied by Griffini.

The Ḳarmaṭian insurrection was begun by Ḥamdān in the neighbourhood of Wāsiṭ; in 277/890 he founded a *dār al-hid̲j̲ra* (an entrenched place of retreat) east of Kūfa for his partisans, whose various voluntary contributions supported the common chest: these contributions were alms at breaking the fast (*zakāt al-fiṭr*), dues for the use of the place of refuge, a fifth of all income (*k̲h̲ums*), dues for participation in the agapes (*bulg̲h̲a*; cf. the art. NUṢAIRĪ); community of all objects of general utility (*ulfa*) was prescribed. These details, which we know from Sunnī sources, are perhaps accurate; at the agapes they ate "bread of Paradise"; this detail which we find in the contemporary trial of al-Ḥallād̲j̲ is perhaps simply a transference of the consecrated bread (*pehta*) used among the Mandaeans of Wāsiṭ (*mug̲h̲tasila* = *nāṣōrāyā*; cf. al-Ṭabarī, year 278 on the Ḳarmaṭian Farad̲j̲ b. ʿUt̲h̲mān of Naṣrāna; or to be pointed Naṣurāya).

We find along with Ḥamdān his brother-in-law ʿAbdān (d. 286/899), author of a manual of initiation for the seven degrees (*balāg̲h̲āt sabʿa*). Both seem to have been dependent on leaders whose identity remained a secret, living outside of Sawād, the *ṣāḥib al-ẓuhūr*, who is said to have invested Ḥamdān, and the *ṣāḥib al-nāḳa*, who had dismissed ʿAbdān and put in his place D̲h̲ikrawaih al-Dindānī. D̲h̲ikrawaih in 288/900 gave the signal in the desert of Syria among the Banū ʿUlaiṣ for the general Ḳarmaṭian rising — so long prepared (expected in Khurāsān for the year 290/902) — and proclaimed as leader the *ṣāḥib al-nāḳa*, under the Ismāʿīlī regnal name Abū ʿAbd Allāh Muḥammad, with the dynastic name of "Fāṭimid". The latter was killed in 289/901 at the siege of Damascus and his place was taken by his, brother, the *ṣāḥib al-khāl*, who as ruler took the name Abū ʿAbd Allāh Aḥmad, and who was captured and executed at Baghdād in 291/903. The Ḳarmaṭian movement in Lower Mesopotamia, drowned in blood, ceased to be an active factor in politics in 294/906 with the death of Dhikrawaih.

In time the movement regained strength in al-Aḥsā, where the *ṣāḥib al-naḳa* had sent as his representative Abū Saʿīd Ḥasan b. Bahrām al-Djannābī in 281/894; with the support of the Rabīʿī tribe of the ʿAbd al-Ḳais, al-Djannābī seized the whole of al-Aḥsā (286/899) and made it an independent state, the bulwark of Ḳarmaṭian power and the terror of the Caliphate of Baghdād. His son and successor Abū Ṭāhir Sulaimān (301—332/914—943) began to lay waste Lower Mesopotamia, cut the pilgrim routes and finally seized Mekka (on the 8th of Dhu 'l-Ḥidjdja 317/Jan. 12, 930), from which he carried off the Black Stone six days later to take it to al-Aḥsā. Abū Ṭāhir, like his father, was only the emissary of a secret organisation, its "commissary for foreign affairs" for al-Aḥsā; while waiting the opportunity to enthrone the expected Imām there, he appointed a representative council over it, the *sāda* (i.e. the elders of the tribe), for the political administration of home affairs. This organisation was still in existence in 422/1030 after the decline of the military power of the Ḳarmaṭians; it seems to have maintained local autonomy down to the xviiith century, when the revival of propaganda took the form of a new Ismāʿīlī dynasty (Makramīs). The capital was al-Muʾminīya (new name given to Hadjar; on the site of the present Hufūf).

In Yaman, Ḳarmaṭian propaganda, directed from 266/879 by Manṣūr al-Yaman (title of Ibn Ḥawshab) with the *dār al-hidjra* near ʿAdnalāʿa, failed against the resistance of the local Zaidī chiefs and could only found some little principalities, the Ṣulaiḥīs of Ṣanʿāʾ and the Makramīs of Nadjrān (cf. van Arendonk, *De opkomst v.h. Zaidietische Imamaat in Yemen*, Leiden 1919, p. 108 sqq. and the texts studied by Griffini).

In Khurāsān the movement began in 260/873 at Raiy with Khalaf; then it spread to Marw al-Rūdh and Ṭālaḳān in Djūzdjān, where the Amīr became a Ḳarmaṭian adept. Later it was active in Dailam, which was to become a bulwark of the Ismāʿīlī dynasty [see the art. ASSASSINS], finally Muḥammad al-Nasafī al-Baradhaʿī (d. 331/942) undertook the conversion of the Sāmānid rulers. His execution destroyed the political hopes of the party; the small Ḳarmaṭian centres of eastern Khurāsān — if we except the works of Nāṣir-i Khusraw — only produced a moderate literary activity (texts studied by Ivanow).

In Syria the centre seems to have been Salamīya; but, except for some biassed Sunnī records, we do not know what happened there after the insurrection of 288/901, nor the part played in it by the future ʿUbaid Allāh, the first Fāṭimid Caliph. Syrian Ḳarmaṭianism is still dormant, without showing any signs of activity nor of contact with the Druzes, who are its distant brethren.

The small local bodies, among which Ḳarmaṭian manuscripts have survived down to our days, have not been the scene of any serious doctrinal activity apart from the writings of the Syrian Rashīd al-Dīn Sinān (xivth) cent.), the *Dabistān* of the Indian Maḥmūd Fānī (Mobed Shāh) (xviith cent.) and the Turkish and Persian texts of the Ḥurūfīs (xvth—xviith cent.).

II. The position of the Ḳarmaṭians relative to the Fāṭimids.

The general tendency of Ḳarmaṭian doctrine was to consider ʿAlid legitimism as a means rather than an end. The Imāmate, the supreme authority, is not a hereditary monopoly transmitted in a dynasty; it is an intellectual characteristic, a divine investiture, an imperative mandate ((*ṣūrat al-amr*) conferred (*tafwīḍ*) on the new holder of the title from among the initiates by a sudden illumination of his intellect, which makes him "substituted" or "spiritual son" of his predecessor. Such is the justification, given in the formula of initiation in the Druze books, for these alleged "usurpations" of genealogy, which are the rule in the annals of the Ḳarmaṭians from ʿAbd Allāh b. Maimūn down to Ḥasan ʿalā dhikrihi 'l-salām. And this is the meaning of the definitions of the imāmate given by adepts like Ibn Masarra, Ruʿīnī, Ibn Hānī and the Ikhwān al-Ṣafāʾ. Indeed, when the *ṣāḥib al-nāḳa* in 288/900, and ʿUbaid Allāh in 297/909 had assumed a Fāṭimid dynastic title, neither the one nor the other plainly indicated their genealogical connection with the ʿAlid Ismāʿīlī line (cf. al-Maḳrīzī, *Ittiʿāẓ*, ed. Bunz. p. 7—11). And if this claim was of importance with respect to the public, in the opinion of their enemies, it seems that it hardly interested those initiated into the true doctrine, who expected above all else a chief, possessing a special divine appointment, of the "intellectual order", whether he was ʿAlid or not.

The official version of the ancestry of the family of ʿUbaid Allāh compiled by his Ḳāḍī, the Mālikī al-Nuʿmān b. Abī Ḥanīfa al-Tamīmī (259—363/873—974), is a laudatory and lying composition specially written in reply to a Buwaihid attack. The versions of two Sunnī anti-Ḳarmaṭian pamphlets by Muḥammad b. Rizām al-Ṭāʾī, president of the "Maẓālim" in Baghdād in 329 A.H., and by Muḥammad Ākh Muḥassin Ibn al-ʿĀbid, an ʿAlid of Damascus, who died about 375 A.H., are hardly of any more value. S. de Sacy, Guyard and de Goeje thought they could rely on them as Ibn al-Nadīm, al-Nuwairī and al-Maḳrīzī had done. But a comparison with the statements contained in the biographical collections (*ṭabaḳāt*) of orthodox Imāmī *muḥaddithūn*, in which the early Ḳarmaṭian propagandists have a prominent place, shows that there are serious errors in the exposé by these two opponents. Maimūn al-Ḳaddāḥ (d. about 180 A.H. at latest) was not a "Bardesanian"; he was a client of the Makhzūmī clan (Ḳuraish), a native of Mekka, a well-known theologian, the official *rāwī* of the fifth and sixth Imāms, al-Bāḳir and al-Ṣādiḳ. His son ʿAbd Allāh, who was official *rāwī* of al-Ṣādiḳ (which provoked the irony of the poet Abu 'l-ʿAlāʾ al-Maʿarrī), did not die in 250 A.H. but in 210 at latest, "in prison in Kūfa under al-Maʾmūn"; Ḍindān (and not Zaidān) is the sobriquet of a known Imāmī author, Aḥmad b. al-Ḥusain al-Ahwāzī, who died about 250—270 A.H., etc. In these circumstances the statements made in the two Sunnī sources mentioned regarding the assassination of ʿAbdān, the illegitimacy of ʿUbaid Allāh and the usurpation of

the soi-disant "son" of D̲h̲ikrawaih in 288—291
A.H. have to be received with caution.

After the proclamation of the Fāṭimid Caliphate
in the Mag̲h̲rib the general attitude of the Ḳarmaṭians
in al-Aḥsā as in Yaman and in K̲h̲urāsān was
one of expectancy, which the assassination of the
ṣāḥib al-bad̲h̲r (297/909) by ʿUbaid Allāh amply
justified. Let us take al-Aḥsā for example: Abū Saʿīd
had from the first paid the fifth to the ṣāḥib al-
nāḳa; after various evasions, which the intrigues
of the court of Bag̲h̲dād do not quite explain, Abū
Ṭāhir sent it to al-Ḳāʾim; but with so little conviction
of his legitimacy, that he welcomed and enthroned
in 319/913 as the expected Imām a madman, Abu
'l-Faḍl al-Zakarī al-Tamīmī (a kind of Heliogabalus,
soon put to death). The Black Stone was restored to
the Meccans in 340/951 by order of the Fāṭimid Cali-
liph al-Manṣūr; but in 360/970 the Ḳarmaṭian chief
Ḥasan b. Aḥmad thought it no breach of his oath
of initiation to give his Buwaihid allies a document,
which was solemnly read at Damascus, testifying
that the first Fāṭimid Caliph had forged his creden-
tials. In 422/1030 the Druze writer Muktanaʿ in
vain urged the Ḳarmaṭian sāda of al-Aḥsā to adopt
the cult of the Fāṭimid al-Ḥākim.

On the other hand there are abundant proofs of
the adoption of Ḳarmaṭian doctrine by the Fāṭimid
dynasty. It was to the dār al-hid̲j̲ra of the Mag̲h̲rib,
Īkid̲j̲d̲j̲ān (or Guedjal) founded by the Ḳarmaṭian
ṣāḥib al-bad̲h̲r, that ʿUbaid Allāh fled before his
proclamation as Caliph. The oraisons of Muʿizz (publ.
by Guyard) are pure Ḳarmaṭian in style as well
as the ritual of the lodge of initiation (maḥwil;
the present masonic term is maḥfil) which he founded in Cairo. The Druze religion is simply a Ḳarmaṭian heresy. The introduction by ʿUbaid Allāh
of the ṣalāt ʿala 'l-Nabī at the end of the ad̲h̲ān
(Ibn Ḥammād, in JA., 1855, p. 542) is to be traced
to the part of nāṭiḳ, recognised in the Prophet by
the Ḳarmaṭians.

III. The Ḳarmaṭian Doctrine.

It is no longer possible to rely, as used to be done,
on the accounts of Ḳarmaṭian doctrine given by
the Sunnī anti-Ḳarmaṭian writers on heresies; al-
Masʿūdī has judiciously said of the latter that they
contradict one another and that the Ḳarmaṭians
themselves recognise nothing of their doctrines in
them. Except for a few lines that are accurate in
the Tanbīh of al-Malaṭī (d. 377/987) we have
to come down to the xiith century of our era to find
a conscientious author, al-S̲h̲ahrastānī, able to give
us authentic Ḳarmaṭian fragments, some quite old
(of Maimūn al-Ḳaddāḥ and Aḥmad al-Kaiyāl) from
original sources, which he does not mention, but
which Fak̲h̲r al-Dīn al-Rāzī (Masāʾil ʿas̲h̲r) has
identified with the Fuṣūl arbaʿa of Ḥasan al-Ṣabbāḥ
(on Sabaeism: ii. 47—155 of the Cairo edition of
1317) and the Ṣunwān al-ḥikma of Abū D̲j̲aʿfar Sid̲j̲zī
b. Būya (d. 370/980) (on Hellenism: ii. 155—193,
of the Cairo edition of 1317).

To define the problem more precisely one must
search the polemical literature of the Imāmīs and
particularly the apologetic treatises in which the
various extremist sects endeavour to convert one
another, starting from their common technical terms.
Lastly the encyclopaedic collection of the Ik̲h̲wān
al-ṣafāʾ, which has not yet been thoroughly studied
since Dieterici, is invaluble for the synthetic understanding of Ḳarmaṭian thought.

According to them, the world is a sum total of
phenomena which repeat themselves in cycles, playing
and replaying the same drama to us time after time:
— this spectacle, presented to intelligences (invariable in number) so that they may be illuminated,
is the gradual disappearance of the material veil,
perceptible by our senses, a multiform and transitory
mirage; then the intelligences are born (k̲h̲alḳ
t̲h̲ānī) by gaining consciousness of a pure intellectual
distinctiveness of a unique and impersonal thought,
which is divinity itself.

The divine being, in fact, outside of which nothing
exists, is only the distinction of a single idea, an
authentication of indifferentiated intelligibility and
devoid of all content; the via remotionis (tanzīh) of
the Ḳarmaṭians, still more rigorous than the taʿṭīl
of the D̲j̲ahmīya, denies all divine attributes and
postulates an absolute monism of fundamental intellectualism.

True religion consists in knowing how to recognize
— as the result of a graduated initiation — what
have been the stages of the creative evolution of
the universe outside of God; this leads the initiated
by a process of gnostic involution in the reverse
direction to forget these stages and to become
absorbed in God.

a) Creative evolution: — the divine essence
or supreme light (nūr ʿulwī), alone in the beginning
and in the end, gives forth first of all the nūr s̲h̲aʿ-
s̲h̲aʿānī, "glistening" and "victorious (ḳāhir) light"
which then engenders the universal intelligence
(ʿaḳl kullī) and the soul of the world (nafs); the latter
under various modes produce human intelligences
(those of the prophets, imāms and elect; the others
are only phantoms of nothingness). The nūr s̲h̲aʿ-
s̲h̲aʿānī in the second degree gives forth the nūr
ẓulāmī "tenebrous light"; that is matter, passive,
"vincible" (maḳhūr), destined to disappear; it appears
in various modes as stars at the skies (aflāk), as
perishable bodies on earth.

b) Gnostic involution: — the intelligences
of the prophets, imāms and their adepts are sparks
of "glistening light" suddenly illuminated in the
midst of the tenebrous light of blind and unreal
matter like reflections in mirrors, following the cyclic
intermittances of the initiatory illumination; these
sparks then shine out, on becoming conscious of their
divine identity in a liberating intuition, so that, losing
all individuation, they are "delivered from the
five tyrants": — the sky, which makes day alternate with night, nature, which gives desires and
regrets, law, which commands and forbids, the
state, which controls and punishes, necessity,
which forces one to daily labour.

c) The immaterial succession of initiatory
investitures (nuḳla, tafwīḍ). Initiatory illumination
brings the separated intelligences, divine sparks in-
dividualised for a moment, into cohesion, following
two convergent hierarchic series: decreasing, of the
initiators (nāṭiḳ, ṣāmit, bāb); and increasing, of
the initiated (dāʿī, ḥud̲j̲d̲j̲a, imām). Historically the
list of their titulars was classed in cycles of limited
number; the intelligences, in invariable number,
"transmigrate" from cycle to cycle (without "finding"
again "their" personality, since they have only the
appearance of individuality).

d) Planetary denominations of the cycles
of transmigration (akwār, adwār, ḳirānāt). The
cycles just mentioned are named from their material
veils, i.e. from the planetary revolutions, periods
and conjunctions. This is a very fine point which
must be appreciated. The Ḳarmaṭians are nominal-
ists; they do not believe that the name determines

the thing and they unanimously assert that the planetary bodies have no directing influence on the intelligences; but the divine volition (*kun*) which regulates the intermittances of the initiatory illumination makes them coincide fatefully with astral periods which form the imprint or shadow cast by these cycles of illumination, and provide the horoscope of the intelligences which pertain to them (change of cults, *milal*, every 960 years, of empires every 240 years, of sovereigns every 20 years, of epidemics every year, of genethliac dispositions every month and every day). When the moment comes for the final cessation of every action (*bīkār = daidjūr* of the Ḥadīth, *ṣaihūr*) cycles and periods will cease together.

e) The degrees of individual initiation. Initiatory illumination is transmitted to the adept by degrees as in the ancient initiations (Greek, Manichaean) and in modern freemasonries. It emanates from the divine volition in accordance with a mode of irrefutable and infallible authority (*taʿlīm*, whence the name *taʿlīmiya* given by al-Ghazzālī to the Karmaṭians). The adept submits himself to it (in the fourth degree) by a declaration — a solemn contract with a clause (*ṭalāḳ muʿallaḳ*) of triple repudiation of his favourite wife if he should reveal the secrets (*ifshāʾ al-sirr*, which constitutes Karmaṭian adultery, *zinā*). Its formula has been studied by Goldziher. We find it first used during the revolt of the Zandj (al-Ṭabarī, iii. 1750) and Usāma alludes to it in his *Memoirs*. The Sunnī heresiographers record 3, 5, 7 (ʿAbdān and Ibn Ḥamdān) or 9 degrees; but the names which ʿAbd al-Ḳāhir al-Baghdādī gives them are doubtful: *tafarrus*, diagnostic of the future adept, described as "fertile" or "sterile" earth, *taʾnīs* (taming), *tashkīk* (apprenticeship to methodic doubt), *taʿlīḳ* (taking of the oath), *rabṭ*, *tadlīs*, *taʾsīs*, *khalʿ* and *salkh*. The programme for the five highest (secret) grades is little known. The "letter of ʿUbaid Allāh to Abū Ṭāhir", an apocryphal curiosity (recalling certain modern anti-masonic productions), analysed by al-Baghdādī, puts in various maxims of cynical impiety, among others the mediaeval parable *De Tribus Impostoribus* (the earliest reference to it; cf. *RHR*, 1920). Al-Maḳrīzī's reference to the *maḥwil* of Cairo (transl. by de Sacy and Casanova) shows that initiation simply amounted to showing that the exterior rites (*ẓāhir*) of all the revealed cults conceal under equivalent and inadequate allegories the same hidden meaning (*bāṭin* whence the name *Bāṭinīya* of the Karmaṭians), purely negative and without mystery; initiations being reduced to teaching of the use of wholly speculative philosophical reasoning, which propounds without practical differentiation the antithesis, opposite conceptions like "law" and "breach of law", *tawḥīd* and *talḥīd* [cf. DRUZES]. But this is only, as we have seen, one aspect of the fundamental intellectual monism of the Karmaṭians.

IV. Its Imāmī technical vocabulary; its criticism of the other extremist Shīʿī sects (*ghulāt*).

Terrified by the wide and rapid spread of Karmaṭian doctrines in the most cultivated centres of the Muslim world, the Sunnī heresiographers strove to discover and denounce an anti-Muslim offensive in it, originating in a foreign religion — Mazdeism, Mazdakism (*Khurramīya*), Manichaeism —, in racial hatred, setting Iranian against Arab, the tribe of Rabīʿa against that of Muḍar (*shuʿūbīya*). They also quoted parallels which are not very convincing.

The hypothesis of the Ṣabian origin of the Karmaṭians, which is also found among them, is more seductive. It seems to have been put forward by the Karmaṭians themselves with a view to gaining citizenship in the Sunnī Muslim state, presenting their syncretism as the Abrahamic (*khalīlīya*) heir of those mysterious "Ṣabians" mentioned by the Ḳurʾān. Such is probably the leading idea in the Ṣabian tale developed among others by al-Shahrastānī in some pages borrowed without acknowledgment from the Karmaṭian Ḥasan b. al-Ṣabbāḥ. The documents hardly permit us to connect effectively the Karmaṭians with the pseudo-"Ṣabians" of Ḥarrān or Wāsiṭ.

In reality an examination of the Karmaṭian technical terms shows that this doctrine was formed before the end of the second century A.H. in the Imāmī circles of Kūfa. The Karmaṭians retained, embedded in their system, various series of Imāmī special terms, which we find again among other extremist sects, Isḥāḳīya, Sharīʿīya, Namīrīya (Nuṣairīya), Khasakīya, Ḥallādjīya; e.g.: *nūrānī, nafsānī, rūḥānī, djismānī, shaʿshaʿānī, waḥdānī*; *nāmūs, lāhūt, nāsūt, djabrūt*; *faiḍ, ḥulūl, ẓuhūr, djawlān*; *takwīn, lalwīḥ, taʾyīd*; the mystic sense of the 28 letters according to the *djafr* [q.v.].. The last orthodox Imāmī Muḥaddithūn received into the Karmaṭian *isnād*'s are Mufaḍḍal b. ʿUmar and Muḥammad b. Sinān al-Ẓāhirī (also admitted by the Nuṣairīs).

The first clearly Karmaṭian author is Abu 'l-Khaṭṭāb Muḥammad b. Abī Zainab al-Asadī al-Kāhilī (d. 145—7/762—4 at Kūfa); he substituted in place of the "personifying" Ḳurʾānic exegesis of the early Shīʿīs an abstract allegorical exegesis; in cosmogony he replaced the use of letters (cf. Mughīra) by their corresponding numerical values (mystic meanings of *djafr*); it was he also who seems to have invented the pledge guaranteeing the secret of initiation: for the Khaṭṭābīya, his adepts, are the only Imāmī sect whom al-Shāfiʿī (*Kitāb al-shahadāt*) will not allow to take the oath, on the ground that they make of the *taḳīya* (negative practice of secrecy) a positive precept justifying false testimony (to keep a secret).

After him, Abū Shākir Maimūn al-Ḳaddāḥ al-Makhzūmī (d. towards 180/796) gave definite dogmatic form to the Karmaṭian doctrine of emanation; he substituted the abstract first principles for the five *aitām* (deified historical personages), demiurges of the first *ghulāt*. He denies that the divine essence has any attributes and defines the "eternal Ḳurʾān" as a pure divine illumination in intelligences.

If one compares Karmaṭian dogma with the preceding Imāmī systems, their naively "materialising" (*tadjsīm*) and "personifying" (*tashakhkhuṣ*) doctrines and their idolatry of ʿAlī and his descendants, we see that, though related, there is a transposition: here they are intellectualised, objectified in abstractions. Finally the Karmaṭians, considering only rank and the external role played, restore to Muḥammad priority over ʿAlī. Not that they in turn deify Muḥammad — it is simply his predestined role of pre-eternally foreseen messenger or herald (*nāṭiḳ*) that they look at. They are (to use the exact term) not *Muḥammadīya* but *Mīmīya* (the letter *mīm* means in *djafr* the name, *ism*: that is to say the mission of onomaturge, *nāṭiḳ*, devolved on the prophet), in opposition to the *ʿAinīya* (the letter *ʿain* in *djafr* means the original sense, *maʿnā*, whence: the hidden meaning, the "silent" [*ṣāmit*] role of "tacitly designated" chief, devolved on ʿAlī), like al-Dūsī and al-Nakhaʿī.

During the polemics that went on in Kūfa between Imāmī writers down to the third century A.H. the

Ḳarmaṭian authors, Abu 'l-Khaṭṭāb, al-Faiyāḍ and al-Nahīkī, were "Mīmīya"; they place Muḥammad (*nāṭiḳ* = *ʿaḳl* = *ḳāʾim* = *nabī*) above ʿAlī (*ṣāmit* = *nafs* = *walī* = *waṣī*). The Nuṣairī al-Khaṣībī, modifying the doctrine of the ʿAinīya to suit the exigencies of controversy, maintains ʿAlī (*maʿnā* = *imām*) above Muḥammad (*ḥidjāb* = *ḥudjdja*) and Salmān (*ism* = *bāb*). To the Nuṣairī arguments that Muḥammad is the "veil" uncovering the divine appearance called ʿAlī, the Druzes reply with good Ḳarmaṭian logic that a "veil" only covers and that Muḥammad has given more perfect evidence of God by his words than ʿAlī by his silence. Inner sanctity is set aside in favour of the gift of prophecy and sinlessness must yield precedence to infallibility.

It is the same polemical attitude which dictates to Maimūn al-Ḳaddāḥ the order in which he associates his two first principles (followed in that by al-Kaiyāl, al-Baradhaʿī, the Druzes and Ḥasan b. al-Ṣabbāḥ): first the intellect (*ʿaḳl* = *nafs nāṭiḳa* = *awwal* = *sābiḳ*) and secondly the soul (*nafs* = *nafs ḥayawānīya* = *thānī* = *tālī* = *lāḥiḳ*). Then comes the "fiat" (*kun djadd*), the central sign of divine intervention; before the second pair of principles, there is a simple reduplication of the first among the Druzes (*ʿaḳl* and *nafs*) and in Ḥasan b. al-Ṣabbāḥ (*fatḥ* and *khayāl*). The identification of the five Ḳarmaṭian first principles with those of the Hellenistic philosophers like the physician Rāzī (intellect, soul, matter, space and time) does not seem to be primitive and represents a later effort at syncretic conciliation.

In psychology the Ḳarmaṭians deprive each human individuality of all definitive reality; the body being eliminated *a priori* as an unreal veil, there only remains a momentary principle of individuation to which they refuse any name implying internal finality, like *rūḥ*, *nūr*, *maʿnā* (employed by the early Imāmīs); they substitute for it the term *ʿaḳl* "intelligence", indicating a simple causation "ab extra", God playing the role of an observer who takes no actual part in what he sees.

They criticise the gross materialism of the first *ghulāt* (and of the Nuṣairīs) who believe that souls are former stellar bodies, fallen from the higher heaven (of which the sun or the moon is the threshold) and destined to return there by that same predestined attraction which caused them to adore the divine apparitions imperfectly seen in the course of the cycles of bodily transmigration (*tanāsukh*). For the Ḳarmaṭians there is no corporeal transmigration, not even for the damned (they have only been phantoms) into bodies of animals; and we cannot even speak of true spritual "transmigration" for the elect, since the immortality of the intelligence is only impersonal whether it assumes modes as "sparks" or not.

Contrary to the Nuṣairīs, who refuse initiation (and immortality) to women, the Ḳarmaṭians admit them (*risālat al-nisāʾ* in the Druze canon).

The Ḳarmaṭians profess an integral nominalism; the letters of the alphabet are only intellectual symbols; the name is the mask of the thing, not its manifestation (Nuṣairī view); each symbol has to be *destroyed* to permit access (*taḥṣīl*) to the pure Idea. The obligatory duties of religion etc. are only supererogatory counsels leaving free play to all human faculties (*ibāḥa*).

V. Its connections with Hellenistic philosophy.

Ḳarmaṭianism preserved from its place of origin an old stock of primitive Islāmic terms, Ḳurʾānic and others, in which it retained the archaic special meanings they had before the third century A.H. (e.g. *amr*, *ṭūl*, *ʿarḍ*, *kun*, *samʿ*, *shāhid*, *balāgh*, *ghāya*, *yaḳīn*, *istiḳāma*, *ikhlāṣ*, *riḍā*, *taslīm*). From the same period it retained an ignorance of certain problems, which were only put forward later, among the Imāmīs after Ibn al-Ḥakam, among the Sunnīs after al-Naẓẓām, such as the perception of sensation, the conceptual process, the modality of a harmony between the movements of the limbs and the intentions of the heart which accompany them. The Ḳarmaṭians on these three points profess a kind of fatalism, a blind occasionalism, something like that of the Djahmīya.

They, however, like the Muʿtazilīs in another field, marked the very first awakening of Muslim philosophic reflection at its contact with Hellenistic science: by the systematic employment of the word *ʿaḳl*, intelligence, to designate the principle of individuation which constitutes man. This brought them not only to the abstract allegorical exegesis analysed above, in which dialectic gives place to logic, but also to the direct acceptance of scientific bases, of natural constants — viz. consideration of arithmetical properties (numbers 3, 5, 7, 9, etc.), permitting the calculation of the astronomical calendar (new-moon festivals: against the Sunnīs), of the four elements and the "humours" (*ṭabāʾiʿ*), specific remedies (*ʿaḳāḳīr*), the foundation of medicine.

Without going further or assimilating the whole corpus of Hellenistic philosophy, as the *Ikhwān al-ṣafāʾ* attempted to do, Ḳarmaṭianism prepared many minds to understand it; it presented to them as divine prophets the ancient philosophers of Greece: Pythagoras, Empedocles and Plato, the masters of hermetism (Agathodaemon, etc.), stimulating in consequence its adepts to read works coming from these foreigners as freely as the Ḳurʾān.

The same licence was to a less degree allowed for certain Persian sources (books of Djāmāsp; the "amshaspands", being regarded as prophets) and much later for Hindu sources also.

VI. The role of Ḳarmaṭianism in the evolution of the Islām.

The influence of Ḳarmaṭian authors, especially of the encyclopaedia of the "Faithful Friends" (*Rasāʾil ikhwān al-ṣafāʾ*), on diverse Muslim thinkers belonging to the Sunna or to orthodox Imāmism has been considerable.

In philosophy, it inspired the political theory of idealistic imāmism (*istiʿdād li'l-nubuwwa*) of al-Fārābī and Ibn Sīnā (al-Rāzī had polemics on this subject with al-Kaiyāl), and the emanation theory of the ten *ʿuḳūl* (Ibn Sīnā). The famous parable of the self-taught (Ḥaiy b. Yaḳẓān) would also be of Ḳarmaṭian origin [cf. the art. DRUZES].

There were in the same way various infiltrations into dogmatic theology: abstract allegorical exegesis of the Ḳurʾān, *tanāsukh* of Ibn Ḥāʾiṭ and Ibn Yanūsh, and the *nūr Muḥammadī*.

In mysticism, it is still clearer from Sahl al-Tustarī [q.v.] to al-Suhrawardī of Aleppo (*nūr ḳāhir*). The mystics who attack Ḳarmaṭianism use its vocabulary (al-Ḥallādj, al-Tawḥīdī, al-Ghazzālī [q.v.]). Ibn Taimīya rightly pointed out the adoption of Ḳarmaṭian theses in works of the Andalusian school of Sunnī mystics, Ibn Barradjān, Ibn Ḳasyī, even of their pupil, the great mystic Ibn al-ʿArabī [q.v.]. When he defined the five phases of creative evolution and of gnostic involution (same number in al-Farghānī; three phases in ʿAbd al-Karīm al-Djīlī) and when he identified the spirit (*rūḥ*) with the intellect (*ʿaḳl*) in his monist descriptions of the fundamental unity of being (*waḥdat al-wud̲j̲ūd*) in reference to the Ḳurʾānic themes of the covenant (*mīt̲h̲āḳ*) and the Nocturnal Ascension (*ḳāb ḳawsain*), — Ibn al-ʿArabī only took up Ḳarmaṭian exegesis again in a more moderate form.

The remarkable organisation of trades and Muslim also gilds goes back to the Ḳarmaṭians.

Bibliography: On the sources in general see L. Massignon, in *Oriental Studies presented to E. G. Browne*, Cambridge 1922, p. 329—38, and in particular: *Rasāʾil Ik̲h̲wān al-ṣafāʾ*, Bombay 1303, ii. 60—62, 83—91; iv. 182—217 etc.; Ḥamza al-Durzī, *Risāla mustaḳīma*; do., *Risāla dāmig̲h̲a* (in the Druze canon); Muḳtanaʿ al-Durzī, *Risālat al-sifr ila 'l-sāda* (in the Druze canon); Niẓām al-Mulk, *Siyāsat-nāma*, transl. and ed. by Schefer, 1893, ch. xlvii.; al-G̲h̲azzālī, *al-Mustaẓhirī* (= *Streitschrift gegen die Bâṭinijja-Sekte*, ed. Goldziher, 1916); do., *al-Ḳusṭās al-mustaḳīm*, Cairo n.d.; S. de Sacy, *Essai sur les Druzes*, Paris 1838; S. Guyard, in *NE*, xxii. 1, Paris 1874; E. Griffini, *Die jüngste ambrosianische Sammlung*, in *ZMDG*, 1915, lxix. 80—88; W. Ivanow, in *JRAS*, 1919, 1924; de Goeje, *Mémoire sur les Carmathes* (1st ed., 1862; 2nd ed., 1880); do., *Fin des Carmathes de Bahrayn*, in *JA*, 1895; I. Friedländer, in *JAOS*, 1907; Asín Palacios, *Abenmasarra y su escuela*, Madrid 1913.

KARRĀMĪYA, sect, called after Abū ʿAbd Allāh Muḥammad b. Karrām (or Karām, Kirām or Kirrām; see *Mīzān al-iʿtidāl*, iii. 127, and for further ancestors Ibn al-At̲h̲īr, vii. 149; for the pronunciation Kirrāmīya cf. *Dict. techn. Terms*, p. 1266). Of this person, who is called al-Sid̲j̲istānī, a fairly full biography is given by al-Samʿānī, *Ansāb*, fol. 476b, 447a. According to this, he was of the Banū Nizār, was born in a village of Zarand̲j̲, was brought up in Sid̲j̲istān, and afterwards went to K̲h̲urāsān, where he attended the courses of Aḥmad b. Ḥarb, the ascetic (d. 234); at Balk̲h̲ he heard Ibrāhīm b. Yūsuf al-Mākiyānī (d. 257), in Merw ʿAlī b. Had̲j̲ar (d. 244), and in Herāt ʿAbd Allāh b. Mālik b. Sulaimān; and he recited many traditions on the authority of Aḥmad b. ʿAbd Allāh D̲j̲awbārī (d. 247) and Muḥammad b. Tamīm Faryānānī: "had he known these two, he would have left them alone", both being notorious fabricators. After spending five years in Mekka he returned to Sid̲j̲istān, where he sold all his possessions. He proceeded to Naysābūr, where he was imprisoned by the governor Muḥammad b. Ṭāhir b. ʿAbd Allāh (according to the *TA*, on two occasions); after his release in 251 he left Naysābūr and proceeded to Jerusalem, where he ended his days in 255. The sanctuary of his followers there, dalled K̲h̲āniḳāh, is mentioned by Muṭahhar b. Ṭāhir (*Livre de la création*, ed. Huart, v. 149) a hundred years later, as also by al-Muḳaddasī.

2. Doctrines. The opinions of this person were set forth in a work called *ʿAd̲h̲āb al-ḳabr*, "The Torment of the Tomb", of which some citations are given in ʿAbd al-Ḳāhir al-Bag̲h̲dādī's *Farḳ bain al-firaḳ*, (ed. Cairo 1328) p. 202—214, where there is the fullest account of the sect, with some of whose members the author held debates. His chief theological doctrine, which caused the inclusion of his sect among the Mus̲h̲abbiha, was that the Divine Being is a Substance (*d̲j̲awhar*), for which some of his followers substituted Body (*d̲j̲ism*), though without human members, and in contact (*mumāssa*, for which the euphemism *mulāḳāt* was substituted) with the Throne, which is located in space. This was apparently a deduction from the Ḳurʾānic *ʿala 'l-ʿars̲h̲i 'stawā* (vii. 55; x. 3; xiii. 2; xx. 5; etc.), and, indeed, the rest of his theology would seen to have been an endeavour to work the Ḳurʾānic texts into certain parts of the Aristotelian philosophy, notably the distinction between Substance and Accident, and that between *dynamis* and *energeia*. Thus his followers could maintain that God was "speaking" before He spoke, and could be worshipped before there were any worshippers. The doctrine of the eternity of the world was reconciled with the Ḳurʾānic creation by some subtle expedients: God, he held, was subject to certain Accidents, such as willing, perceiving, speaking, coming in contact; over such accidents He has power, but not over the world and the objects therein, which were created not by His will, but by the word *kun*. Thus, it would seem, the tense in *kun fa-yakūnu* could have its proper meaning.

Another doctrine to which allusion is often made in *kalām* works is that faith (*īmān*) is constituted by a single utterance of the two *s̲h̲ahāda*'s, and involves neither conviction nor works. This view, though similar to the chief thesis of the Murd̲j̲iʾa, is said to have been held by no one before him (Ibn Taimīya, *Kitāb al-īmān*, Cairo 1325, p. 57, who refutes it at length). The rest of his opinions, as recorded in the *Farḳ*, seem to have been in the direction of moderation. Thus the infallibility of prophets was confined within certain limits, and a reason was found (somewhat in the style of Ibn Ṭufail) why those whom no prophetic message had reached ought to believe in prophetic missions; he held that there might be two *imām*'s simultaneously, and that each would have a right to his followers' allegiance, even when the two were at variance. His innovations in the *furūʿ* were such as to render the law more flexible.

3. History of the Sect. It would seem that the Karrāmī doctrine spread chiefly in K̲h̲urāsān, and in 370 the author of the *Farḳ* debated with a member of the sect in the presence of the Sāmānid commander Muḥammad b. Ibrāhīm b. Sīmd̲j̲ūr. It was favoured by Sabuktakīn of G̲h̲azna out of respect for the asceticism of Abū Bakr Isḥāḳ b. Maḥmas̲h̲ād̲h̲ (d. 383), the chief of the Karrāmīs in his time, who is said to have converted some 5,000 *d̲h̲immīs*. This person's son Muḥammad encouraged Maḥmūd b. Sabuktakīn in a violent persecution of the Bāṭinīs; of this there seems to be an echo in the Life of the Ṣūfī Abū Saʿīd (357—440; ed Zhukovsky, 1899, i. 84—91), where Isḥāḳ b. Maḥmas̲h̲ād̲h̲ makes common cause with the ḳāḍī Ṣāʿid (a Ḥanafite) against the saint; the numbers of the Karrāmīs in Naysābūr at the time are given as 20,000. In 403, however, this ḳāḍī, who had made the pilgrimage, and been favoured by the Caliph al-Ḳādir, complained of the Karrāmī heresy before Maḥmūd of G̲h̲azna; Muḥammad b. Isḥāḳ thereupon repudiated the doctrine, while those who openly adhered to it were penalized. Many, however, continued to hold it at Naysābūr; Ibn al-At̲h̲īr in 488 records a civil war in that city between the Karrāmīs and the joint forces of the Ḥanafīs and S̲h̲āfiʿīs, the leaders of the first and second of these being descendants of the leaders in Maḥmūd's time. Yāḳūt (s.v. Bid̲j̲istān) mentions a Karrāmī preacher who acquired popularity at Naysābūr in the middle of the sixth century; and ʿAbd al-Ḳādir D̲j̲īlānī (d. 561; *G̲h̲unya*, Cairo 1288, i. 81) speaks of them as still numerous in K̲h̲urāsān. Fak̲h̲r al-Dīn al-Rāzī (d. 606; *Asās al-taḳdīs*, Cairo 1328, p. 96—98) apparently thinks of them as still existing; his biography describes the Karrāmīya as his most embittered opponents [see AL-RĀZĪ]. It

is probable, however, that the sect was practically exterminated when the lieutenants of Čingh̲iz Kh̲ān massacred the inhabitants of Kh̲urāsān; and when writers of a later time allude to its doctrines (e.g. Ibn Taimīya and the author of the *Mawāķif*) they probably derive their knowledge from earlier works. J. Ribera (*Disertaciones y opúsculos*, Madrid 1928, i. 380 *sq.*) credits them with encouraging the monastic life and founding *madrasa*'s.

4. Literature of the Sect. In the *Farķ* it is stated that the sect was subdivided into three minor sects, which however, were mutually tolerant; these were called Ḥaķķākīya (?), Ṭarā'iķīya (?) and Isḥāķīya. Sh̲ahrastānī mentions twelve minor sects, of which he enumerates six: Isḥāķīya (as above), ʿĀbidīya, Nūnīya, Zarībīya, Wāḥidīya, and Haiṣamīya. Of these the first was doubtless named after that Isḥāķ who was mentioned above; whereas the last was named after one Muḥammad b. al-Haiṣam, who is called their *mutakallim* in the *Mīzān*. The works wherein the founders of these minor sects put forth their views seem to have obtained little notoriety; the author of the *Bayān al-adyān* (485; Schefer, *Chrestomathie persane*, i. 152 text), though living at Gh̲azna, just knows the name of the main sect; and ʿAbd al-Ķādir (*loc. cit.*) in giving the names of Karrāmī authorities is in error in each case. The work of the founder *ʿAdh̲āb al-ķabr* seems to be known only from the citations in the *Farķ*.

Bibliography: besides the works quoted above see also al-ʿUtbī's *Ta'rīkh̲ Yamīnī*, Delhi 1847, p. 429 *sqq.*; Cairo 1386, ii. 315 *sqq.*; Maķrīzī, *Kh̲iṭaṭ*, ii. 357; van Vloten, in *Actes du 11e Congrès int. d. Orientalistes*, Paris 1899, 3th sect., p. 114; Horten, *Die philos. Systeme*, p. 340 *sqq.*; Barthold, *Turkestan*, p. 306.

ĶĀRŪN occurs in Sūra xxviii. 76—82; xxix. 39; xl. 24. In the second and third passages he, with Hāmān, is an unbelieving minister of Firʿawn in oppressing the Israelites; he behaves proudly towards Mūsā and says that he is an enchanter and a liar. In Sūra xxviii. he is the Biblical Ķoraḥ (Num. xvi.) and he behaves proudly towards the people of Mūsā, but on the ground of his immense wealth which he believes to have been given to him on account of his knowledge (*ʿalā ʿilmin ʿindī*). He makes a great public display of his wealth and is swallowed up by the earth with his palace (*dār*). He is thus an example of those who prefer the fleeting wealth of this world to gaining by alms and humility and righteousness the abiding riches given by Allāh in the world to come. This is apparently a moralized echo of a story heard and remembered vaguely by Muḥammad. To this the commentators and the compilers of prophetic *ķiṣaṣ* have added a long and involved legend derived in whole or in part from rabbinic literature. For this, on the rabbinic side, see the *Jewish Encyclopaedia*, vii. 556 *sqq.* and, on the Muslim side, the notes in Sale's translation of the Ķur'ān and al-Th̲aʿlabī, *Ķiṣaṣ*, Cairo 1314, p. 120 *sqq.* It is plain that Hāmān has become a minister of Pharaoh because he is bracketed with Ķoraḥ in rabbinic literature for rapacious wealth. The legend of Ķārūn has had two special developments: 1. From his wealth and knowledge (above and Sūra xxviii. 78) he has become one of the founders of alchemy. See the preliminary statement of the *Fihrist* on alchemy (p. 352, l. 1); and al-Masʿūdī alludes to this (*Murūdj̲ al-dh̲ahab*, viii. 177). 2. He is associated in Egypt with lakes. Thus what is left of Lake Moeris in the Faiyūm bears his name (Baedeker, *Ägypten*6, p. 184; Joanne, *L'Egypte*, p. 611; Herodotus, ii. 149). Also, beside the Birkat al-Fil to the south of Cairo, near the Mosque of Ibn Ṭūlūn, there was formerly a Birkat Ķārūn which had evidently associations of supernatural legend. Al-Maķrīzī describes it (*al-Kh̲iṭaṭ*, ed. 1325, iii. 261 *sq.*) and relates that Kāfūr who built beside it was said to have been driven from his house by *dj̲inn*. It figures also in the Story of Dj̲udar the Fisherman in Zotenberg's (cf. *NE.*, xxviii., i. 167 *sqq.*) Egyptian Recension of "The 1001 Nights" (Nights 606—624) as a place where spirits take refuge from magicians. Von Hammer suggested in a note to his transl. of this story (*Der Tausend und Einen Nacht noch nicht übersetzte Märchen*, etc., transl. Zinserling, ii. 32; transl. Trébutien, i. 291) that Ķārūn had here become combined with the Egyptian Charon.

Bibliography: Ṭabarī, *Tafsīr*, xx. 62 *sqq.*; do., *Ta'rīkh̲*, ed. de Goeje, i. 517—28; Rāzī, *Mafātīḥ al-gh̲aib*, ed. Cairo 1308, vi. 421 *sqq.*; Ibn al-Ath̲īr, *al-Kāmil*, Cairo 1301, i. 87 *sq.*; A. Geiger, *Was hat Mohammed aus dem Judenthume aufgenommen?*, 2nd ed., Leipzig 1902, p. 153; J. Horovitz, *Koranische Untersuchungen*, p. 231.

ĶASAM (A.) (verb *aķsama*) is with *yamīn* the general term for oath. As *ķasama* means "to divide", we seem to have here the usual transition between the meanings "to cut" and "to decide" so that *ķasam* would be the deciding, strong word (cf. Hebrew *ķesem*), while *ḥilf* (verb *ḥalafa*), which also means swearing, would properly be used in special circumstances.

The oath plays a great part in the social life of the Arabs and is mentioned by Zuhair (*Dīwān*, i. 40) as the principal means of ascertaining the truth, along with arbitration and absolute clearness. The oath is the word into which the person taking it puts his whole strength. As the tribe forms a moral unit with joint responsibility, the oath in important matters becomes a tribal oath. This, called *ķasāma*, consists in 50 men of the tribe swearing to their being right; this may be the oath of an accuser or an oath of purgation. Those participating swear not as witnesses — on the contrary, they need not have been present at the deed — but as responsible persons. That the swearer stakes his whole soul on his word is often expressly stated in the wording of the oath. He swears upon his soul or upon his life (*bi-nafsī, bi-ḥayātī, la-ʿamrī* or simply (*ʿamrī*), upon his honour and strength or upon particular things with which honour is associated, for example the forelock or the lance; this oath is exactly the same as that by the tribe or by kinship or the very common oath by the fathers (*wa-abī, wa-dj̲addika* etc.) and by the god who supports the life of the swearer, in the Ḥidj̲āz especially by Manāt, al-ʿUzzā and al-Lāt; among Muslims one also swears by the faith. The man taking the oath puts all that he values on his word. It is assumed that falsehood and injustice are negative forces so that a false oath imperils the soul and all that is precious to it. The oath is a pledge to God (*ʿahdu 'llāhi, mīth̲āķu 'llāhi, dh̲immatu 'llāhi*) and if the person taking it lies or does not keep his promise (*wafā'*) he imperils his own soul and offends the divine being. The oath therefore has often the form of a hypothetical surrender (*barā'a*) of the things the swearer values most, e.g. *anā barī'un min ḥawli 'llāhi wa-ķuwwatihi in faʿaltu kadh̲ā*, "I am exempt from the strength and force of God, if I do so". Formulae of this kind are common in the official oath taken by officials of different confessions in the Mamlūk empire (al-

ʿUmarī, *al-Taʿrīf bi 'l-muṣṭalaḥ al-sharīf*, Cairo 1312, p. 146—164; al-Ḳalḳashandī, *Ṣubḥ al-aʿshā*, xiii., Cairo 1337 [1918], p. 205 *sqq*.). The *barāʾa* oath is of the same kind as another oath, invoking a curse upon oneself in certain contingencies, e.g.: "May Allāh slay me if I do not kill thee"; "I will eat blood if I do not do such and such a thing". This form of oath is used in the *liʿān* ceremony when married people take oaths in giving evidence against one another in cases of alleged adultery (Sūra xxiv. 6—9; cf. Juynboll, *Handbuch des islāmischen Gesetzes*, p. 192). A curse can also have a positive value and be used to strengthen an assertion, as in *ḳatalahu 'llāhu mā ashdjaʿahu*, i.e. "May Allāh slay him, how brave he is". The curse is here used *li-'l-taʿadjdjub*, as in Sūra lxxiv. 19, 20 (see al-Baiḍāwī on the passage).

The taking of a vow as an oath comes near to this hypothetical cursing oneself. It is especially common as an oath of vengeance among the Arabs, generally as an oath before war [cf. NADHR]. The man concerned dedicates himself thereby and takes an increased obligation (*ʿahd*) upon himself. Vice versa, one may give force to one's word by taking a special obligation upon oneself in case of breaking it. This pledge, of course, must be inviolable in character and usually takes one of three forms: giving of camels to be sacrificed, releasing of slaves (male and female) or divorce from a wife. These pledges may be made more or less severe; thus one can promise to divorce or release present and future wives and slaves, a kind of oath which was banned by al-Shāfiʿī but nevertheless often occurs.

In taking the oath one must endeavour to remember its character as a serious, sacred expression. It is best to swear at sacred places, in ancient times at the holy stone or idol (*Aghānī*, ix. 10, 12). In pre-Islāmic days and later the Kaʿba was a particularly favourite place for taking an oath (Ibn Hishām, p. 317; Ibn al-Kalbī, p. 19; al-Ṭabarī, iii. 861), especially by *al-Ḥaṭīm* (al-Ṭabarī, i. 3464); this oath is still considered a very strong one (Snouck Hurgronje, *Mekka*, ii. 306; al-Batanūnī, *al-Riḥla al-Ḥidjāzīya*, Cairo 1329, p. 127). One swears by the tombs of saints at the same time laying a hand on the tomb (see e.g. Jaussen, *Coutumes des Arabes au pays de Moab*, p. 311; Musil, *Arabia Petraea*, iii. 338, 342). Oaths are taken in the mosque, especially on the *minbar* (e.g. al-Ṭabarī, ii. 92). Special seasons make the oath more serious, notably the period after the *ṣalāt al-ʿaṣr* (see Goldziher, in *Archiv für Religionswiss.*, ix. 297 *sqq*.). There is evidence of oaths in connection with sacrifice from the pre-Islāmic period (Zuhair, i. 50; *Ḥamāsa*, p. 423, $_{10}$). Swearing by the sacrificial animals is common, still more frequent by the lord of the sacrificial animals (e.g. *Ḥamāsa*, p. 715, verse 6). Among the traditional forms of oath is the *hūla*. According to al-Djawharī, *Ṣiḥāḥ*, s.v., it consists in taking the oath by the fire of the tribe into which salt is thrown. This ceremony, referred to by al-Kumait etc. (*al-Hāshimīyāt*, ed. Horovitz, No. 4, verse 36; Djāḥiẓ, *Bayān* [Cairo 1927], iii. 3 *sq*.), still survives (Landberg, *Arabica*, v. 133 *sq*.).

The magic circle is often used at the present day; this, which is sometimes divided by lines at right angles, often has something put in it, such as dung, ashes or a piece of cloth. One solemn oath consists in sticking a sword in the ground in the centre of the circle and placing ants beside it; this is the *shemle wa-nemle* oath. Sometimes one takes a piece of wood in the hand and swears "by the life of this wood"; this is the *dīn al-ʿūd*. Other popular customs could be mentioned, such as laying a hand on the tent-pole, taking bread and coffee in the hand, turning towards the *ḳibla* etc. (see the works of Musil, Jaussen, Landberg, Burckhardt and Doughty). Increasing the gravity of the oath by various procedures is acknowledged in official Islām and called *taghlīẓ al-yamīn* or *taʿẓīm al-yamīn*; for example, the Ḳurʾān or al-Bukhārī's *Ṣaḥīḥ* is placed in the bosom while the oath is being taken (cf. Goldziher, *Die Ẓāhiriten*, p. 115; Lane, *Manners and Customs*, 3rd ed., i. 168, 470). Great oaths are called *aimān bāligha* (Sūra lxviii. 39; cf. *djahd aimānihim*: Sūra v. 53; vi. 109 xvi. 38). In later times very solemn oaths were called *aimān al-baiʿa*, "oaths of allegiance", cf. Ibn Ḥawḳal, 2nd ed. i. 52, ii. 341; al-Tanūkhī, *Faradj*, ed. Cairo, i. 158; see also Ḳalḳashandī ix. 280, xiii. 211.

The oath formulae give the substance of the oath. Apart from special kinds of oaths such as those connected with curse and vow, the usual formula is for that by which one swears to be introduced by a particle. The most common particles in this connection are *bi*, *ta* and *wa*, which are all used in solemn oaths (*wa-llāhi wa-bi-'llāhi wa-ta-'llāhi*); the two last mentioned are not so freely used as *bi*. The particle *bi* is the common preposition "in combination with"; *ta* is probably the termination as in *amānata* or *ḥayāta*; *wa* is an intensive particle like *la*, which is used particularly in the formula *la-ʿamrī*, *la-ʿamruka* "by my (thy) life", etc. Other demonstrative particles occur in oaths.

Just as an oath is taken at a holy place or at a sacrifice, so we find oaths taken by the place or by the sacrifice (or by its lord). The Kaʿba and all that belongs to it as well as the pilgrimage are used in oaths in continually changing phrases. The old Arabs swore specially by their gods and fathers. The *kāhin*'s often swore by natural phenomena (Ibn Hishām, p. 11). It is in keeping with the character of the oath that in Islām swearing by Allāh is alone permitted, but that, on the other hand, swearing by fathers, saints and especially by the Prophet is found in everyday life. Swearing by one's father was particularly forbidden by the Prophet but it is sometimes used by ʿUmar and Abū Bakr and even by the Prophet himself (Muslim, commentary of al-Nawawī, iv. 99). It is a good Muslim oath to swear "by the Lord of my father" or "by the Lord of the Kaʿba, of the sacrificial animals" etc. The formula may call God to witness, as, for example, "God knows that I am not lying", "God is witness that I am saying this", etc. God is often referred to by some descriptive phrase; for example, "by Him Who sent Muḥammad with truth", while a Jew says "Mūsā" for "Muḥammad". The oath can also be adapted to particular situations; many have their favourite oaths; the Prophet, for example: "by Him in Whose hand my soul is", etc. The oath is intensified by repeating the formula three or more times.

One is freed from an oath to fulfil a vow, when one has performed it (*abarra* or *ḥallala yamīnan*). The man, to whom someone has vowed to do something, may, however, release the latter from his oath. The latter is allowed to disregard his oath if higher considerations demand it. There is evidence from the Muslim as well as the pre-Muslim period that such a solemn statement was accompanied by the taking off or rending of certain articles of clothing (al-Wāḳidī, transl. by Wellhausen, p. 197; al-Ṭabarī, iii. 862). Release from a vow is obtained among the modern Beduins by a sacrifice. One may bind others with an oath if one conjures them. The formula is often of this kind: "I call (*nas͟hada*) God to thee" or "I mention (*d͟hakkara*) God to thee". But it is an oath of the speaker and it depends upon the relation between the latter and the person adjured whether the latter will fulfil the vow; in such forms of oath appeal is often made to mutual friendship or relationship. One can also conjure God. "A servant of God is one whose oath God redeems when he conjures him" (al-Buk͟hārī, *Kitāb al-ṣulḥ*, b. 8; *al-D̲j̲ihād*,, b. 12). God is more pressingly conjured, if the appeal is made through one of His favourites, like the Prophet (*tawassul bi 'l-nabi*).

Between the popular use of the oath among the ancient Arabs and in Islām there is no essential difference, as is clear from what we have already said. But there are special rules regarding the oath in Islām. In the Ḳur'ān, especially in the older Sūras, the oaths known from the kāhins by natural phenomena are usual (Sūra lvi. 75; lxxxi. 15—18; lxxxvi. 1; lxxxix. 1—3; xci. 1—7 etc.); we also have instances of swearing by the Ḳur'ān (xxxvi. 1; xxxviii. 11; xliv. 1; l. 1), by the angels (xxxvii. 1, lxxvii. 1) etc. Two passages in the Ḳur'ān are of special importance for the use of the oath. In Sūra v. 89 and ii. 224 *sq.* it is said that inconsidered expressions (*lag͟hw*) in oaths can be (broken and) expiated. The context in both passages makes it probable that the references are to vows of abstention, sometimes from food, sometimes from women. Vows of the last mentioned kind, called *īlā'*, are limited to four months (ii. 226), in connection with Sūra ii. 224 *sq.*, after which time they must be expiated or the man must divorce the wife. A particular vow of this kind (*ẓihār*) in which the husband says "Thou art henceforth as the back of my mother to me (*ka-ẓahri ummī*)" is especially condemned in Sūra xxxiii. 4; lviii. 2, 4 *sq.* (see Juynboll, *Handbuch des islāmischen Gesetzes*, Leyden and Leipzig 1910, p. 224 *sqq.*; Sachau, *Muh. Recht*, 1897, p. 13, 68 *sqq.*).

The practice of atonement for such oaths after repenting of having taken them seems to be taken from the Jews (cf. *Mis͟hna*, *N^edarīm*, and *Lev.*, v. 4 *sq.*). In Sūra lxvi. 2 we read "God hath prescribed for you the dissolution of your oaths" and this prescription is applied to a case in which the Prophet had sworn to his wife Ḥafṣa not to touch the slave-girl Māriya, which he later regretted (cf. al-Ṭabarī, *Tafsīr*, xxviii. 90 *sqq.*).

Among ḥadīt͟hs first place must be given to a saying of the Prophet: "I never take a vow without being prepared to expiate it, if I see that another is better, and adopting the better". In this and similar sayings, which are collected by al-Buk͟hārī, Muslim and other traditionists (see *Kitāb al-aimān wa 'l-nud͟hūr*), the expiation of vows is recommended in cases other than vows of abstention. On the other hand, it is insisted in Ḳur'ān and Ḥadīt͟h that one should keep one's oath. But an oath must always give way to a higher consideration. It is therefore recommended not to take an oath without adding the *istit͟hnā'* (the formula "if God so will").

These statements in the Ḳur'ān and in the *sunna* form the foundation of the *fiḳh* system on the subject. According to this, the person taking the oath must be *mukallaf*, he must be acting deliberately as a free agent and intend the oath. He must not take an oath to commit a sin; views are divided on the question whether such an oath is valid at all. One can only swear by God, either by His essence or by one of His names or attributes. The oath by the Prophet is recognised by some Ḥanbalīs but in general is not considered a binding oath. The *barā'a* oath already mentioned is not recognised by the *fiḳh*. The breaking of a vow (*ḥint͟h*) is considered a duty in certain cases, when one has sworn to commit a sin. The *īlā'* already referred to must be broken within four months if the man does not divorce his wife; after the *ẓihār* the wife must at once be divorced or the vow must be expiated.

Expiation (*kaffāra*) consists, according to Sūra v. 89, in setting free a slave, feeding ten poor men or clothing the same number; for those who cannot afford this, three day's fasting is equivalent. The things to be done are described in detail in the *fiḳh* books. In the *īlā'* the expiation is the same as in other oaths while in the *ẓihār* it consists in releasing a slave who is a believer or fasting for two months or feeding 60 poor people (Sūra lviii. 3—4). The Muslim law recognises the oath of affirmation as well as the vow to perform. In lawsuits only the former occurs. A special case is formed by the *ḳasāma* already mentioned which was taken over from the ancient Arabs. It is limited in Islām to trial for murder and consists of 50 oaths which can be sworn by one or more individuals. The oath is imposed on the accuser but only in connection with certain indications (*lawt͟h*) which must be regularly ascertained. If the accuser refuses to take the oath, the 50 oaths are applied to the accused; if he refuses they apply again to the accuser. In other cases the principle in Islām is that the onus of proof is on the accuser and the accused has to take the oath. Witnesses as a rule do not take an oath; witnesses to the will of a testator who has died in a foreign country are an exception (Sūra v. 106). If the plaintiff has only one of the two necessary witnesses, the oath of one of the parties may take the place of the second witness. When the plaintiff has not valid proofs, the oath is put to the defendant; if he declines to take it, it is put to the plaintiff (*yamīn al-radd*). Perjury on account of some accomplished fact is called *yamīn g͟hamūs* by Muslim scholars, an expression which originally meant a peculiarly binding oath. Such oaths can be expiated in the above fashion according to the S͟hāfi'ī school, according to other views they cannot. The latter hold that expiation only applies to promissory oaths.

The formalism of the legal system opens the way for all kinds of artifices by which an oath can be broken, yet formally kept. There thus arose a whole literature regarding such subterfuges; the best known work is al-K͟haṣṣāf's *Kitāb al-ḥiyal wa 'l-mak͟hārid̲j̲* (ed. by Joseph Schacht, Hannover 1923 [autogr.]; printed Cairo 1314); al-Ḳazwīnī, *Kitāb al-ḥiyal fi 'l-fiḳh*, ed. J. Schacht, Hannover 1924; cf. *Der Islam*, xv, 211 *sq.*

Bibliography: Johs. Pedersen, *Der Eid bei den Semiten*, 1914; J. Wellhausen, *Reste arabischen Heidentums*², 1897, p. 128 *sq.*, 186 *sqq.*; I Goldziher, *Abhandlungen zur arabischen Philologie*, 1896, i. 1—120; G. Jacob, *Altarabisches Beduinenleben*², 1897, p. 174, 219; Th. W. Juynboll, *Handbuch des islāmischen Gesetzes*, 1910, p. 192, 225 *sq.*, 266—270, 315 *sq.*; E. Sachau, *Muhammedanisches Recht*, 1897, Index.

KASB. The root occurs a large number of times in the Ḳur'ān with the meanings: "seek", "attain", "earn", "work" (good and evil); see C.C. Torrey, *The Commercial Theological Terms in the Koran* (Leyden 1892), p. 27 *sqq.* and Nöldeke's note there. Stems i. and viii. are used synonymously, although al-Baiḍāwī on Sūra ii. 286 (Fleischer's ed., i. 143), following al-Zamakhsharī on the same passages, tries to show that there is more personal, reflexive force (*iʿtimāl*) in viii. Hence *kasb* and *iktisāb* mean much the same. There are two technical usages: I. It is equivalent to the *iktisāb* of the Ashʿarites. "The action of a creature is created, originated, produced by Allāh but it is 'acquired' (*maksūb*) by the creature, by which is meant its being brought into connection with his power and will without there resulting any effect from him in it or any introduction to its existence, only that he is a locus (*maḥall*) for it" (al-Djurdjānī on *al-Mawāḳif* of al-Īdjī, Būlāḳ 1266, p. 515). Al-Ghazzālī, perhaps desiring to emphasize the personal acceptance, apparently preferred *iktisāb*; see his statement in the *Iḥyā*ʾ (ed. with commentary of al-Murtaḍā al-Zabīdī, ii. 165 *sqq.*) and the elaborate commentaries thereon. Al-Rāzī on Sūra ii. 286 (ed. Cairo 1308, ii. 388) states the different views as to the two terms. Al-Sanūsī in his *Muḳaddima* (ed. Luciani, p. 68 *sqq.*, also note p. 237) uses *iktisāb* only twice and evidently in the same sense as *kasb*; his statement is an extension of that of al-Djurdjānī. This is the most subtle question in all Muslim *kalām* (*adaḳḳ min kasb al-Ashʿarī*) but it may be guessed that al-Ashʿarī wished only to explain our consciousness of freedom to choose and that his explanation was that this consciousness is a separate creation by Allāh in the mind; man for him was an automaton with consciousness as part of the machinery. The later mutakallims, especially under the influence of the more ethical Māturīdite system, turned it otherwise; cf. e.g. al-Taftāzānī in his commentary on the *ʿAḳāʾid* of al-Nasafī (a Māturīdite), Cairo 1321, p. 98 *sqq.* II. *Kasbī* and *iktisābī* are applied to that knowledge (*ʿilm*) which belongs to created things and is attained by the voluntary (*ikhtiyārī*) application of secondary causes (*asbāb*), (*a*) like reason and consideration of premises in deduction and (*b*) like listening and turning the eye in sense perception. They are thus wider than *istidlālī* which applies only to reasoning. *Ḍarūrī*, "necessary", is sometimes opposed to *iktisābī* and sometimes to *istidlālī*. Others arrange thus: knowledge in a created being is of two kinds: (*a*) *ḍarūrī* and (*b*) *iktisābī*; in the acquisition of (*b*) the *asbāb* are of three kinds: the healthy senses, reliable narrative, rational consideration (*naẓar*); *naẓar* is of two kinds: immediate intuition (*badīha*) and *istidlāl*, deduction (al-Taftāzānī on the *ʿAḳāʾid* of al-Nasafī, p. 39 *sq.*; also al-Djurdjānī on *al-Mawāḳif*, p 16, 21).

Bibliography: Is given above; add for both uses: *Dict. of Techn. Terms*, p. 1243 *sq.*; further F. L. Bakker, *De verhouding tusschen de almacht Gods en de zedelijke verantwoordelijkheid v. d. mensch in de Islam*, Amsterdam 1922; A. J. Wensinck, *The Muslim Creed*, see Index.

KASHF, "uncover", in the emotional religious life (*taṣawwuf*), is the broadest term for the unveiling of the mystic. When this is analyzed more carefully it is commonly divided into three: (i.) *muḥāḍara* in which reason (*ʿaḳl*) is the means by proof (*burhān*); (ii.) *mukāshafa* in which taught knowledge (*ʿilm*) is the means by explanation (*bayān*); (iii.) *mushāhada* by means of immediate, personal experience (*maʿrifa*). By (i.) *ʿilm al-yaḳīn* is reached by the *aṣḥāb al-ʿuḳūl*: this is still in the realm of reason and is not really *kashf*. By (ii.) *ʿain al-yaḳīn* is reached by the *aṣḥāb al-ʿulūm* and by (iii.) *ḥaḳḳ al-yaḳīn* is reached by the *aṣḥāb al-maʿārif*; the last is the immediate Vision of God and is sometimes called *muʿāyana* (al-Ḳushairī, *al-Risāla*, ed. with commentaries of Zakarīyā al-Anṣārī and al-ʿArūsī, Būlāḳ 1290, ii. p. 79 *sqq.*); on this cf. R. Hartmann, *al-Kuschairîs Darstellung des Ṣûfîtums* (*Türk. Bibl.*, xviii.), p. 72 *sqq.*; Hudjwīrī, *Kashf al-maḥdjūb*, transl. Nicholson, p. 373 *sqq.* and by index.

Bibliography: Is given above; add for both uses: *Dict. of Techn. Terms*, ii. 1254.

AL-ḲASṬALLĀNĪ, Abu 'l-ʿAbbās Aḥmad b. Muḥammad b. Abī Bakr al-Khaṭīb Shihāb al-Dīn al-Shāfiʿī, an authority on tradition and theologian, born on Dhu 'l-Ḳaʿda 12, 851/January 20, 1448 in Cairo, where he spent his life as a preacher — apart from two stays of some duration in Mecca — and died on Friday, Muḥarram 7, 923/January 31, 1517. He owes his literary fame mainly to his exhaustive commentary on the *Ṣaḥīḥ* of al-Bukhārī entitled *Irshād al-sārī fī sharḥ al-Bukhārī*, which exists in numerous MSS. and printed copies; of these latter the earliest may be that of Būlāḳ of 1267 and next the Lucknow edition of 1869 (others in Brockelmann, *GAL*², i. 165; *Suppl.* i. 262). The Cairo edition of 1325/6 gives the glosses of Yaḥyā al-Anṣārī and the Cairo edition of 1279 those of Ḥasan al-ʿIdwī (d. 1203/1887). Great popularity is enjoyed in the Muslim world by his history of the Prophet entitled *al-Mawāhib al-ladunīya fi 'l-minaḥ al-Muḥammadīya*, which he completed on Shaʿbān 15, 899/May 22, 1494 and which caused him to be accused of plagiarism by al-Suyūṭī. It exists in numerous MSS. and has also been printed several times, e.g. Cairo 1281, several times commented on, e.g. by al-Zurḳānī (d. 1122/1710), printed in 8 vols. Būlāḳ 1278, 1291, and translated by ʿAbd al-Bāḳī, the renowned poet, into Turkish, printed Stambul 1261. Al-Nabhānī, the President of the Court of Justice in Bairūt, prepared a synopsis of it entitled *al-Anwār al-Muḥammadīya min al-Mawāhib al-ladunīya*, Bairūt 1310—1312. Besides he wrote some smaller works on tradition, the readings of the Ḳurʾān, on mysticism and kindred objects.

Bibliography: al-Sakhāwī, *al-Ḍawʾ al-lāmiʿ*, ii. 103; Wüstenfeld, *Die Geschichtsschreiber der Araber*, No. 509; Brockelmann, *GAL*², ii. 87; *Suppl.*, ii. 78.

ḲATL (a.), killing, putting to death.

I. Ḳatl as a crime

1) In the Ḳurʾān unlawful slaying is forbidden in a series of verses, which date from the second Mekkan period to nearly the end of the Madīna period: xvii. 31 (second Meccan period): "Kill not your children for fear of being brought to want; ... verily the killing them is a great sin ... (33). And kill not the soul which God hath forbidden (to kill), except for just cause; but whosoever is killed unjustly, We have given his next of kin (*walī*) authority (to demand satisfaction), yet let him not exceed in killing; verily he is helped"; xxv. 68 *sqq.* (second Meccan period): "(And the servants of the Merciful are those) who kill not the soul, which God hath forbidden (to be killed) unless for a just cause ...; (69) doubled for him will be the punishment on the day of Resurrection and he will remain in it for ever despised; (70) except him who repents and believes and does righteous works" ... (here killing and unbelief are considered together so that the question, what happens to a believer who kills unlawfully, is left quite out of the question); vi. 151 (third Meccan period; similar to xvii. 31, 33); iv. 92 *sq.* (about the years 3—5): "It is not for a believer to kill a believer unless by mistake (*khaṭaʾ*); but if anyone kill a believer by mistake, a believing slave shall be set free

and a *diya* paid to his people, unless they remit it; but if he be from a tribe hostile to you, but a believer, a believing slave shall be set free; but if he be from a tribe betwixt whom and you there is a treaty, a *diya* shall be paid to his people and a believing slave set free; if anyone cannot find the means, he must fast for two successive months so that Allāh may turn to him again..., (93) but if anyone kill a believer deliberately (with *ʿamd*), his reward is hell in which he shall remain for ever and Allāh will be wrath with him and curse him and prepare for him a great punishment" (the true interpretation is undoubtedly this, that every Muslim who kills another Muslim with *ʿamd* is condemned to eternal hell-fire and that Allāh will not accept his repentance, a view which is ascribed, amongst others, to al-Ḍaḥḥāk; the view that the verse refers to the particular case of a *murtadd* who has killed a believer is not to be accepted; this is already a transition to the interpretation that has finally prevailed, which tones down the literal wording of the passage, either by adding with Mud̲j̲āhid "unless he repents" or by holding, as has become usual, that Allāh will not leave a Muslim eternally in hell, and can even remit entirely the threatened punishment of hell-fire; but this is only the result of speculation and combination with other passages in the Ḳurʾān [e.g. xi. 106—108; xxxix. 55]); iv. 29 *sq.* (from about the same time; similar to iv. 93); lx. 12 (probably dates from soon after the treaty of al-Ḥudaibīya; similar to xvii. 31); ii. 84 *sqq.* and v. 32 it is asserted that the same prohibition existed already for the Jews.

There are also a number of verses in which killing is more or less strongly deprecated and represented as a mark of the unbeliever, just as committing no murder is a sign of the believer.

2) In the so-called ordinance of the community, which dates from the first Madīna period, the Prophet decrees that no believer may kill a believer on account of an unbeliever; further on, he says: "If anyone murders a believer and is convicted, then vengeance takes place, unless the *walī* of the slain waive it"; in all probability Muḥammad had in mind here as the murderer a non-Muslim member of the community. In the *baiʿa*, the initiation into the community, the initiate had to pledge himself, among other things, not to commit an unlawful act of slaying (cf. Sūra lv. 13). Once Muḥammad cursed a murderer [cf. ḲIṢAṢ]. In the so-called first temple-speech (of the year 630), the genuineness of which, however, seems doubtful on this point, there appears the by no means exactly defined conception of *ḳatl s̲h̲abah ʿamd* (see below, sub 5*c*); the Prophet is also said to have declared there that all blood-guilt attached to a Muslim dating from the period of paganism was to be cast off.

3) Also in the traditions (*ḥadīt̲h̲*) which represent the views of the authoritative circles in the older period, the slaying of a Muslim is strictly forbidden; by the adoption of Islām life and property become protected. All blood-guilt from an earlier period is thus wiped out by the adoption of Islām, even if the crime was committed just before conversion. Only if a Muslim commits a crime worthy of death, can he be slain. Killing with *ʿamd* is one of the deadliest sins (*kabāʾir*); it is usually considered the gravest sin, along with the *s̲h̲irk* (polytheism). Murder is punished in the next world as well as on earth. As to the punishment itself, a whole stratum of *ḥadīt̲h̲* reflects the already mentioned view regarding the eternalness of punishment in hell for slaying with *ʿamd*; e.g. "whosoever sheds blood in an unlawful way, for him there exists no way of escape"; "whosoever contributes though only by a word to the slaying of a Muslim must despair of the mercy of Allāh". In several passages the deliberate murder of a Muslim is considered equivalent to unbelief. Such *ḥadīt̲h̲* were naturally rendered harmless by "interpretation" by the representatives of the other, prevailing view, if they were not entirely suppressed. Thus the description of deliberate murder as unbelief is sometimes taken as a reference to the refusal of the protection of Islāmic law, which occurs in both cases, to the life of the slayer or of the unbeliever. This was not found sufficient, however, and traditions were put into currency to prove the contrary, namely that Allāh would accept the repentance of a murderer, even if he had committed several murders; one of these traditions is provided with a grotesque story as corroboration. It is even asserted in public controversy against the views of the other side that after the Day of Judgment no Muslim will go to hell and that, on the contrary, all sins will be forgiven them. — The prohibition of suicide, which we do not find laid down in the Ḳurʾān, is given in the *ḥadīt̲h̲* and the suicide is threatened with eternal punishment in the next world.

4) The controversy regarding the punishment of murder in the next world centres round a passage in the Ḳurʾān (iv. 93), which in itself has a direct bearing on the question, and is therefore in part at least independent and original. This controversy is, however, very closely connected with the disputes aroused by the K̲h̲ārid̲j̲īs, Ḳadarīs and Muʿtazilīs; for details see these articles; here it is sufficient to recall the following questions: "Is the committing of deadly sins unbelief?" "Does man create his own actions himself, or do they happen through *ḳadar*?" "Can man by his intervention interfere with Allāh's decision, for example by killing another shorten the period predestined for the latter's life?" We have more than one example of these questions being cited in connection with ḳatl. The Muʿtazilī view of the eternalness of hell-punishment for him who commits a deadly sin and does not repent, is specially important in this connection; al-Zamak̲h̲s̲h̲arī gives an explanation of the verse of the Ḳurʾān in question from this point of view. Finally the consensus of orthodox opinion agreed that the deliberate killing of a Muslim is certainly a deadly sin, but the slayer, if he repents and voluntarily submits to the punishment prescribed, will not be further punished in the next world and, even if he does not repent, will in no case remain in hell eternally.

5) A statement of the prevailing Ḥanafī views on killing. Ḳatl may be qualified by any of the five "legal categories"; it is permitted (*mubāḥ*), e.g. in self-defence, i.e. in defending oneself against an illegal attack on one's life, person or property, if the attack cannot otherwise be averted; on further questions there is difference of opinion, also on the question whether a man who surprises another in adultery with his wife and kills him, is acting legitimately or not; a tradition on the subject is interpreted in different ways.

Illegal killing, which is regarded as forbidden (*ḥarām*), may take place in five ways:

a) as *ʿamd*, i.e. someone wilfully makes another the direct object of an action in general fatal so that the other dies as a result; the intention of killing is always presumed in the case of any act generally fatal in its result, which is illegally inflicted on another; this killing is a sin (*ma'tham*) and may be punished by *ḳiṣāṣ*, or else the slayer is bound to pay the heavier *diya*; he loses, moreover, any claim to the inheritance from the deceased;

b) as *khaṭa'* [q.v.], i.e. there is no intention of committing an act illegally on the other, while the action itself is premeditated; e.g. someone supposes another to be a wild beast, kills him (here the *khaṭa'* is in the intention, *fi 'l-ḳaṣd*), or someone hits another unluckily, while shooting at a target so that he dies (here the *khaṭa'* is in the action, *fi 'l-fiʿl*); this killing is not sin but brings with it (without *ḳiṣāṣ*) the obligation upon the *ʿāḳila* of the slayer to pay the smaller *diya* and makes the slayer lose any claim to the inheritance; besides, he has to perform the *kaffāra*;

c) as *shabah* (or *shibh*) *ʿamd*, "similar to *ʿamd*", i.e. someone intentionally makes another the direct object of some action, not always but sometimes fatal, and death results. Actions which experience has shown not to be fatal at all are thus excluded; if anyone dies as a result of such an action as this, it is an unfortunate accident, which is not followed by any penal consequences. This killing is a sin and brings with it (without *ḳiṣāṣ*) the obligation upon the *ʿāḳila* of the slayer to pay the heavier *diya* and makes the slayer lose any claim to the inheritance; besides, he has to perform the *kaffāra*.

d) as *djārī madjra 'l-khaṭa'* "equivalent to *khaṭa'*," i.e. the factor of deliberation is lacking in the action in the circumstance of *b*) and *c*), e.g. someone falls upon another from a roof and kills him; the legal consequences are the same as in *b*);

e) as *ḳatl bi-sabab* "indirect killing", i.e. someone brings about the death of another without doing anything directly against him; e.g. he digs a well and someone falls into it and dies as the result; it is a matter of indifference, whether this act is deliberate or not, intentional or unintentional; even if the action has been planned against another person with the intention of causing his death, it does not alter the situation. The legal consequences are in any case limited to the obligation upon the *ʿāḳila* of the slayer to pay the lighter *diya*.

Two cases are especially dealt with, namely the causing of an abortion and killing through giving false evidence.

6) We may add the following differences of opinion among the schools.

Abū Ḥanīfa limits *ʿamd* to the use of a weapon or of a thing which can be used like a weapon to cut off limbs; deliberate killing, for example with a large unsharpened stone, or a big stick, which in the oridinary way would kill, is therefore considered by Abū Yūsuf and al-Shaibānī, as well as by the authorities of the other *madhāhib*, as *ʿamd*, but by Abū Ḥanīfa as *shabah ʿamd*, and this view was later considered the better by the Ḥanafīs. In the Mālikī and Ḥanafī view no *kaffāra* is to be performed for *ʿamd*; al-Shāfiʿī, on the other hand, demands it if the *ḳiṣāṣ* is not executed and both views are given on the authority of Ibn Ḥanbal. Except in the Ḥanafī madhhab, categories *d*) and *e*) are not distinguished from *khaṭa'*, which also was the earliest Ḥanafī view; we thus have three kinds of ḳatl: *ʿamd*, *shabah ʿamd* and *khaṭa'*, of which *shabah ʿamd* is considered to be composed of *ʿamd* and *khaṭa'*. Mālik allows *ḳiṣāṣ* in *shabah ʿamd*. In the case of *ḳatl bi-sabab*, Mālik, al-Shāfiʿī and Ibn Ḥanbal demand *kaffāra* in addition, if the occasioning of the cause of the death was illegal.

II. Ḳatl as punishment.

The punishment of death may be described quite generally as ḳatl; in constrast to *radjm* and *ṣalb* (cf. below) ḳatl is also used in the narrower sense of execution with the sword.

1) In the cases of illegal killing described in detail above, the nearest relative of the dead man, who in this capacity is called *walī al-dam*, is entitled to kill the culprit in retribution if certain definite conditions are fulfilled. This punishment is called *ḳiṣāṣ* or *ḳawad*; for further information see the article ḲIṢĀṢ.

2) There are special regulations regarding sorcerers (*sāḥir*), about whom there are also various traditions.

3) The punishment of death by stoning (*radjm*) — in certain circumstances also by the sword (ḳatl) — occurs as *ḥadd* in certain cases of immorality; on this see the article ZINĀ'

4) Highway robbery (*ḳaṭʿ al-ṭarīḳ*) is in certain circumstances to be punished with death. The authority for this is Sūra v. 33 *sq.* (from about the year 6 or 7, before the capture of Khaibar): "The reward of those who make war against Allāh and His apostle and create corruption upon the earth is that they shall be slain or crucified or their hands and feet cut off on alternate sides or be banished from the land; that is a disgrace for them in this world and in the next world there is for them a great punishment, (34) except those who repent before ye have them in your power." It can be asserted with certainty that this refers to the unbelievers, very probably to the Jews; ruthless war is to be waged on them and their repentance is the adoption of Islām. There are still traces of this interpretation in the commentaries. But in general this passage is brought into connection with the attitude of the Prophet to certain *murtadd*'s which will be dealt with in section 5); this cannot be correct, if only because the procedure there practised does not entirely conform to these rules, so that harmony had to be restored in different fashions. Those *murtadd*'s were considered as highway robbers from the point of view of the later definition, and only in this way could a law for the punishment of highway robbers be found in the Ḳur'ān.

The more important prescriptions of the developed system of law are the following. Mālik gives the imām absolute freedom in the choice of punishment, even in a cumulative application, whatever form the crime may have taken; but if the person concerned has killed someone, he must at least be executed with the sword. The three other Imāms grade the punishment to fit the different forms of highway robbery: according to Abū Ḥanīfa, the criminal is executed with the sword if he has killed a victim; if he has also robbed him, he may be further punished by cutting off his hands and feet on alternate sides and/or with crucifixion (instead of simple execution); if he has only committed robbery, there is only the cutting off of hands and feet on alternate sides; al-Shāfiʿī and Ibn Ḥanbal have him executed and crucified afterwards, if he has killed and committed robbery, and agree with Abū Ḥanīfa in the other cases; if he has only made the neighbourhood unsafe, then according to Abū Ḥanīfa, al-Shāfiʿī and Ibn Ḥanbal, he is put in prison. For Abū Ḥanīfa and Mālik crucifixion consists in the criminal being tied alive to a cross or a tree and his body ripped up with a spear so that he dies, and this is certainly the more original form; according to al-Shāfiʿī and Ibn

Ḥanbal, he is first killed with a sword and then his corpse is ignominiously exposed on a tree or cross. All these punishments are *ḥadd* and a "right of Allāh"; therefore any renunciation by the *walī al-dam* of the *ḳiṣāṣ* is of no avail. If the criminal repents before he falls into the hands of the authorities these *ḥadd* punishments are dropped; but claims by individuals to *ḳiṣāṣ* etc. can still be enforced against him.

5) The *murtadd*, that is the renegade from Islām, is liable to the death-penalty. If we leave out the passages dealing with the *munāfiḳ*'s [q. v.] whose execution is prescribed under certain conditions in Sūra iv. 89, there is no such law in the Ḳur'ān referring specially to the *murtadd*. Among the traditions we find in various forms the story that Muḥammad mercilessly mutilated and killed some *murtadd*'s who had killed one or more of his herdsmen and driven away the camels; this may be genuine, just because it is not in conformity with the later system. Two *murtadd*'s, each of whom had killed a Muslim, were executed by the Prophet's orders after the capture of Mekka; a third man, against whom there was nothing but his apostasy, was granted security (*amān*) on the instances of his foster-brother ʿU̲th̲mān. There is also a saying of Muḥammad's: "Slay anyone who changes his religion", and others similar, and a story that Muʿād̲h̲ b. D̲j̲abal killed a *murtadd* because Allāh and His Prophet had so ordained; but all this can hardly be genuine. There are also the traditions regarding the *ahl al-ridda* [cf. RIDDA] who refuses the *zakāt* and were treated as apostates by Abū Bakr.

According to the later system, only an adult in full possession of his faculties and not acting under compulsion can become an apostate from Islām. There is difference of opinion regarding an attempt at conversion, previous to execution, and the granting of a period, usually fixed at three days, for reflection. If the *murtadd* does not repent, he is to be beheaded with the sword; torture and cruel methods of execution are forbidden. According to al-S̲h̲āfiʿī, his punishment is left to his owner, if he is a slave. Abū Ḥanīfa and his school limit the punishment of death to male apostates; a woman is to be imprisoned and beaten till she repents; according to Abū Ḥanīfa (contrary to Abū Yūsuf and al-S̲h̲aibānī), she may also be made a slave and this is recognised as right by the school.

Similar to the punishment of the *murtadd* is that of the *zindīḳ*, i. e. anyone who, professing to be a Muslim, is really an unbeliever or anyone who belongs to no religion. The conversion of a non-Muslim to another non-Muslim religion is similarly dealt with; he can only escape punishment by adopting Islām.

For further information see the article MURTADD.

6) There is no law in the Ḳur'ān for dealing with a man who omits the *ṣalāt* (*tārik al-ṣalāt*), and no unequivocal ḥadīt̲h̲ on the subject can be found. The system of the *s̲h̲arīʿa* lays down the law as follows: Anyone who does not perform the obligatory *ṣalāt* without denying its obligatoriness (anyone who does this is *murtadd*) and has no — even invalid — excuse for this, according to the Mālikīs, the S̲h̲āfiʿīs and the Ḥanbalīs, if he does not repent, is to be executed with the sword. According to the Ḥanafīs, the culprit is imprisoned till he again performs the *ṣalāt*. Another view attributed to Aḥmad b. Ḥanbal deals with him entirely as a *murtadd*; but even the former regulations are modelled on those for apostasy.

There are two more cases in which the fighting (*ḳitāl*) of the enemies of orthodox Islām is prescribed; killing, of course, there plays the main part.

7) Firstly, the fighting of the *bug̲h̲āt* is prescribed. It is said in Sūra xlix. 9 (late Madīna period): "If two parties of the believers quarrel make peace between them; but if one of the twain oppresses the other (*bag̲h̲at* — from which *bug̲h̲āt* is the plural of the participle) fight the party which oppresses until it return to Allāh's command; and if it return, make peace between them with equity and act with justice" (this refers to a quarrel among the *anṣār*). The Prophet at any rate did not know the later conception of *bug̲h̲āt*. The system of the *s̲h̲arīʿa* understands by *bug̲h̲āt* sectarianising Muslims who reject the authority of the *imām*, are able to offer resistance, and justify their attitude, although erroneously, with their dogmatic conviction. If they do not attack the orthodox community, they need not be fought; otherwise their suppression is a duty of the *imām* and a *farḍ al-kifāya* for the Muslims [cf. FARD]. In general the rule is that only participants in the actual battle can be killed during the fighting.

8) Regarding the *d̲j̲ihād* see that article. If the unbelievers in question are not among those from whom the *d̲j̲izya* can be taken, the men are killed if they do not adopt Islām. If, in the contrary case, they refuse Islām and will not pay the *d̲j̲izya*, they are to be fought. All able-bodied men can be killed so long as they are not taken prisoners. The free, able-bodied prisoners may be (*a*) executed with the sword if they will not now adopt Islām; (*b*) made slaves; (*c*) exchanged for Muslim prisoners; (*d*) ransomed; (*e*) or set free without a ransom being paid (at the discretion of the *imām*).

Every unbeliever who does not pay the *d̲j̲izya* or does not belong to a people which has a treaty with the Muslim community or is not a *musta'min*, is *ḥalāl al-dam* (to be killed with impunity) and may at any time be killed by any Muslim without his being liable to *ḳiṣāṣ* or to pay any *diya* or perform *kaffāra*. This enactment is only the natural consequence of the *d̲j̲ihād* law and the Prophet himself not infrequently made use of it.

9) The infliction and execution of the death penalty was in practice very often, if not mostly, in strong contradiction to the regulations laid down in the *s̲h̲arīʿa* [cf. ʿAD̲H̲ĀB]. The historians afford many examples for the actual practice and so do the accounts of travellers. On the conditions in the empire of the caliphs in the tenth century cf. Mez, *Die Renaissance des Islâms*, p. 347 *sqq.*; do., *El Renacimiento del Islam*, p. 400 *sqq.* (further, Massignon, *al-Hallâj*, vol. i. especially p. 200 *sqq.*, 292 *sqq.*), on those in Egypt during the first half of the nineteenth century, Lane, *Manners and Customs of the Modern Egyptians*, at the end of the chapter on *Religion and Laws*, on those in Persia at the same period, Polak, *Persien*, i. 328 *sq.*, on those in the Ottoman empire of the eighteenth century, Mouradgea d'Ohsson, *Tableau général de l'empire othoman*, especially vi. (1824), 244 *sqq.*; autonomous laws for capital punishment, long before the introduction of penal codes on European lines into most Muslim countries, are incorporated in the Ottoman *ḳānūn-nāme*'s (cf. *Mitteilungen zur osmanischen Geschichte*, i. 13 *sqq.*, and among the texts cited there, Digeon, ii. 245, 262; Hammer, *Staatsverfassung*, i. 125, 133, 143—150; *TOEM*, vol. iii. [1328], supplement i. 27 *sq.*; ii. 1—4, 7, 9; *MTM*, i/ii. 341 *sq.*).

Bibliography: Wensinck, *Handbook*, s.v. Murder, Punishment; Juynboll, *Handleiding tot de kennis van de mohammedaansche wet* (3rd ed.), p. 291 *sqq.*, and the works cited there; Bergsträsser, *Grundzüge des islamischen Rechts*, p. 96 *sqq.*; art. Murder and Execution in T. P. Hughes, *Dictionary of Islam.*

KAWTHAR, a word used in Sūra cviii. 1 after which this Sūra is called *Sūrat al-kawthar*. Kawthar is a *faw*ʿ*al* form from *kathara*, of which other examples occur in Arabic (e.g. *nawfal*; further examples in Brockelmann, *Grundriss der vergleichenden Grammatik*, i. 344). The word, which also occurs in the old poetry (e. g. the examples in Ibn Hishām, ed. Wüstenfeld, p. 261, and Nöldeke-Schwally, *Geschichte des Qorāns*, i. 92), means "abundance" and a whole series of Muslim authorities therefore explain al-Kawthar in Sūra cviii. 1 as *al-khair al-kathīr* (see Ibn Hishām, *op. cit.*; al-Ṭabarī, *Tafsīr*, xxx. 180 *sq.*). But this quite correct explanation has not been able to prevail in the *tafsīr*. It has been thrust into the background by traditions according to which the Prophet himself explained Kawthar to be a river in Paradise (see already Ibn Hishām, p. 261 below, and notably al-Ṭabarī, *Tafsīr*, xxx. 179) or Muḥammad says that it was a pool (cf. ḤAWḌ) intended for him personally and shown to him on his ascension to Paradise (al-Ṭabarī, *Tafsīr*, xxx. 180), which latter view al-Ṭabarī considers the most authentic. Even the earliest Sūras (lxxvii. 41; lxxxviii. 12 etc.) know of rivers that flow through Paradise, but it is not till the Madīna period that they are more minutely described, notably in Sūra xlvii. 15: "there are rivers of water which does not smell foul; rivers of milk the taste whereof does not change; and rivers of wine, a pleasure for those that drink, and rivers of clarified honey". These rivers correspond to the rivers of oil, milk, wine and honey, which had already been placed in Paradise by Jewish and Christian eschatology; the only difference is that Muḥammad replaced oil by water; in Arabia pure water was not to be taken for granted and besides it was necessary to mix with the wine of Paradise (see Horovitz, *Das koranische Paradies*, p. 9). When, after the Prophet's death, eschatological explanations of the "abundance" of Sūra cviii. 1 began to be made, al-Kawthar was identified as one of the rivers of Paradise and when we find in one of the versions quoted in al-Ṭabarī's *Tafsīr* that "its water is whiter than snow and sweeter than honey" or "and its water is wine", etc. we have obviously an echo of Sūra xlvii. 15. But they did not stop at simply transferring these Ḳurʾānic descriptions to the Kawthar but the imagination of later writers gave the river of Paradise a bed of pearls and rubies and golden banks and all sorts of similar embellishments. According to a later view (see *Aḥwāl al-ḳiyāma*, ed. Wolff, p. 107), all the rivers of Paradise flow into the *ḥawḍ al-kawthar* which is also called *nahr Muḥammad*, because, as we have seen above, it is the Prophet's own.

KĀZARŪNĪ, SHAIKH ABŪ ISḤĀḲ IBRĀHĪM B. SHAHRIYĀR, founder of a darwīsh order called after him Isḥāḳīya or Kāzarūnīya, lived 352—426/963—1033 in Kāzarūn (province of Shīrāz), where he is buried in his monastery. Although he came of a family of fire-worshippers — his father was the first of the family to be converted to Islām (Djāmī, *Nafaḥāt al-uns*, Turk. transl. of Lāmiʿi, Istanbul, n. d., p. 297) — he was an ardent missionary and is said to have converted no less than 24,000 fire-worshippers and Jews to Islām (Farīd al-Dīn ʿAṭṭār, *Tadhkirat al-awliyāʾ*, ed. Nicholson, ii. 296). His order remained a militantly missionary one which preached and organised *djihād* and *ghazāʾ* against the infidels. The Isḥāḳīya spread through Persia to India and China where it had settlements, particularly in the seaports (e. g. Kalikut and Zaitūn; cf. Ibn Baṭṭūṭa, ed. Defrémery and Sanguinetti, ii. 64, 88—92; iii. 244—248; iv. 103), and to Anatolia to which the founder in his lifetime is said to have sent his disciples to war for the faith but where the existence of the order can only be proved from the xivth century (W. Caskel, in *Isl.*, xix, 284 *sq.*). The Isḥāḳīya must have played a considerable part in the Ottoman empire of the xvth century owing to its militant missionary spirit. It is mentioned as one of the four great orders in a tractate by Spandugino (beginning of the xvith century) (in Sansovino, Venice 1654, p. 129). It naturally spread also into Rumelia (its *tekke* in Adrianople is mentioned in Ewliyāʾ Čelebi, iii. 454). The order reached Aleppo (Caskel, *op. cit.*) from Anatolia where it had establishments in Brussa, Ḳonya and Erzerum (Abū-Isḥāḳ-Khāne). It must have been very well organised in the xivth century, for its management used to draw cheques upon people who had to fulfil a vow for Kāzarūnī. The earth from the tomb of the founder was considered to have miraculous effects, particularly with sailors and merchants. In Turkey in the xviith century the Isḥāḳiya became merged in younger orders but reverence for Kāzarūnī was still found occasionally among the people.

Bibliography: L. Massignon, *La passion d'al-Ḥallādj*, i. 410 *sq.*; Köprülüzāde Meḥmed Fuʾād in *Isl.*, xix. 18 *sqq.*, with references to some still unutilised *manāḳib-nāme*'s. An edition of a Persian version of al-Kāzarūnī's biography *Firdaws al-Murshidīya fi Asrār al-Ṣamadīya* by Maḥmūd b. ʿUthmān, was published by Fr. Meier, Leipzig 1948 (*Bibliotheca Islamica* 14); cf. A. J. Arberry, *The Biography of Shaikh Abū Isḥāq al-Kāzarūnī* in *Oriens* Vol. iii (1950), p. 163 *sqq.*

KARBALĀʾ. [See MASHHAD ḤUSAIN].

KHADĪDJA, Muḥammad's first wife, was a daughter of Khuwailid of the Ḳuraish family of ʿAbd al-ʿUzzā. The authorities are unanimous in saying that when she made Muḥammad's acquaintance and took him into her service she was a well-to-do merchant's widow who was carrying on business independently. She had been twice married previously and had children of both marriages. The one husband was a Makhzūmī, the other a Tamīmī, Abū Hāla, whose real name is variously given; but this Abū Hāla is also mentioned by others among the followers of Muḥammad, which — if both stories are true — would make Khadīdja a divorced woman. When she discovered the brilliant qualities of her young employee — the story of this is adorned with all sorts of legendary features — she proposed marriage to him; according to the generally accepted story, her father was dead by this time, according to another, still alive and opposed to the marriage, so that she only obtained his consent after making him intoxicated — a favourite motif in fiction. Most authorities make Muḥammad twenty-five at this time and Khadīdja forty. We do not need to doubt the essential accuracy of the tradition, for the alteration in Muḥammad's circumstances has witness borne to it in the Ḳurʾān (xciii. 6 *sq.*) and the fact that he was content with one wife so long as Khadīdja lived may be related to her superior social position. Her wealth must have been a great help to him during his struggle and her death (which is said to have taken place three years before the Hidjra), after she had probably suffered considerable losses through the hostility of the great merchants, contributed to make his position still less endurable. But her personality seems to have been of even greater weight with her husband; in any case tradition draws a very attractive picture of the moral support which she afforded him during the excitement and agitation of the first revelation. That Waraḳa b. Nawfal [q. v.] was her cousin must have he ped to make her sympathetic to Muḥammad's aims.

Bibliography: Ibn Saᶜd, viii. 7—11; Ibn Hishām, p. 119—122, 153—156, 232—277, 1001; al-Ṭabarī, i. 1127—1130, Ibn Ḥadjar, *al-Iṣāba*, ed. Sprenger, iii. 1130; al-Azraḳī, ed. Wüstenfeld, p. 463; Sprenger, *Das Leben . . . des Mohammad*, i. 194 *sqq.*; Caetani, *Annali dell' Islām*, i. 138—144, 166—172; Robertson Smith, *Kinship and Marriage in early Arabia*, p. 273 *sqq.*; Lammens, *Fāṭima*, p. 12 *sqq.*; F. Buhl, *Das Leben Muhammeds*, p. 118 *sqq.*; G. A. Stern, *Marriage in Early Islam* (London 1939), index.

AL-**KHAḌIR** (AL-KHIḌR), the name of a popular figure, who plays a prominent part in legend and story. Al-Khaḍir is properly an epithet ("the green man"); this was in time forgotten, hence the secondary form Khiḍr (meaning perhaps "the green"), which in many places has displaced the primary form.

Legends and stories regarding al-Khaḍir are primarily associated with the Ḳur'ānic story in Sūra xviii. 60—82, the outline of which is as follows. Mūsā goes on a journey with his servant (*fatā*), the goal of which is the *madjmaᶜ al-baḥrain*. But when they reach this place, they find that as a result of the influence of Satan they have forgotten the fish which they were taking with them. The fish had found its way into the water and had swum away. While looking for the fish the two travellers meet a servant of God. Mūsā says that he will follow him if he will teach him the right path (*rushd*). They come to an arrangement but the servant of God tells Mūsā at the beginning that he will not understand his doings, that he must not ask for explanations and as a result will not be able to bear with him. They set out on the journey, however, during which the servant of God does a number of apparently outrageous things, which causes Mūsā to lose patience so that he cannot refrain from asking for an explanation, whereupon the servant of God replies: "Did I not tell you that you would be lacking in patience with me?" He finally leaves Mūsā and on departing gives him the explanation of his actions, which had their good reasons.

This servant of God is called al-Khaḍir by the majority of the commentators. Others, however, identify him with Mūsā's servant (see below). Both interpretations have their roots in Oriental legends. The Ḳur'ānic story may be traced back to three main sources: the Gilgamesh epic, the Alexander romance (cf. C. Hunnius, *Das syrische Alexanderlied*, in *ZDMG*. lx. 169 *sqq.*, 188 *sqq.*), and the Jewish legend of Elijah and Rabbi Joshua ben Levi (printed in Jellinek, *Bet ha-midrash*, v. 133—135). The two first are, of course, again closely related to one another; at the same time it should be noted that the fish episode is lacking in the epic and is only found in the romance (cf. R. Hartmann, in *ZA*, xxiv. 307 *sqq.*).

The chief figure in the Ḳur'ānic story is called Mūsā. Some commentators doubt his identity with the great prophet (see below). There is not, however, the slightest hint of another Mūsā anywhere in the Ḳur'ān. On the other hand, we have no legends of Moses, which make him, like Gilgamesh and Alexander, go on the great journey. We might suggest the following explanation of the difficulty. The figure of Joshua ben Levi, with which Muḥammad first became acquainted through the Jews and which does not again appear in Muslim legend, was identified, as we shall see, with Joshua b. Nūn. This identification may have resulted in a confusion of his master Elijah with Joshua b. Nūn's master Moses. Mūsā thus represents Gilgamesh and Alexander in the first part of the Ḳur'ānic story and Elijah in the second.

The figure of the travelling-companion is not connected with the Gilgamesh epic, where it is not found, but with the Alexander romance and the Jewish legend. It probably comes in the first place from the romance. This is suggested by the fact that the companion is called *fatā* (here practically "servant"), a term that points to Alexander's cook rather than to Rabbi Joshua; the fish episode, which also is only found in the Alexander romance, points in the same direction.

The Madjmaᶜ al-baḥrain is given as the goal of the journey. The expression has no direct original either in the epic or the romance, although there are points of contact in both. Utnapishtim lives *ina pi narati*, i.e. at the mouth of the rivers. It is not quite certain what this expression means, but it is probable that the place in the extreme west is meant where the sources of all running water are. This, however, still leaves the dual in the Ḳur'ānic expression unexplained. This is still the case, if we attempt to trace it to the Alexander romance where (i. e. in the Syriac Alexander legend; see Budge, *op. cit.*, p. 259) Alexander with his army crosses a strip of land between the eleven bright seas and the ocean. It is also possible that the expression goes back to none of these but to another story unknown to us, which perhaps never found its way into literature, in which there was mention of the meeting-place of two seas. According to western Semitic cosmology, this in the end of the world where the oceans of earth and heaven meet.

We can likewise only guess at the origin of the rock (verse 63). It also belongs to cosmology (see A. J. Wensinck, *The Ocean in the Literature of the Western Semites*, in *Verh. Ak. Amst.*, xix., N°. 2, p. 26 *sqq.*). It is found neither in the epic nor in the romance, again an indication that the Ḳur'ānic story borrowed from other sources also.

The servant of God at the Madjmaᶜ recalls Utnapishtim-Khasisatra in the Gilgamesh epic. He is called (verse 64) one to whom God's mercy had been shown, to whom divine wisdom had been granted. This sounds almost like a translation of the name Khasisatra and the granting of divine favour is perhaps an echo of Utnapishtim's immortality.

The test of patience to which he subjects the newcomer comes from the Jewish legend only; the servant of God in this respect thus represents Elijah.

II

The commentators, Ḥadīth, and historians have collected a mass of statements around the Ḳur'ānic story, additions which, like the story itself, came for the most part from the three sources already mentioned.

The first question discussed is whether the principal character is Mūsā b. ʿImrān or Mūsā b. Mīshā (= Manasseh) b. Yūsuf b. Yaʿḳūb, i. e. a descendant of the patriarch Jacob (al-Rāzī, *Mafātīḥ al-ghaib*, iv. 333; al-Zamakhsharī, *Kashshāf*, on verse 59). Commentators are almost unanimous in favour of the former alternative and base their opinion on the following legend, which is transmitted in several forms. When Mūsā, the famous prophet, was one day preaching to the children of Israel he was asked if there was any man wiser than he. When he replied in the negative, Allāh revealed to him that his pious servant al-Khaḍir was wiser than he. He thereupon decided to visit this wise man. The story comes from Jewish legend; it is found in a considerable number of Arabic sources (al-Bukhāri, *ʿIlm*, bāb 16, 19, 44; *Anbiyā'*, bāb 27; *Tafsīr*, Sūra xviii., bāb 2—4; Muslim, *Faḍā'il*, trad. 170—174; al-Tirmidhī, *Tafsīr*, Sūra xviii., bāb 1; al-Ṭabarī, ed. de Goeje, i. 417; *Tafsīr*, xv. 165 *sq.*; Fakhr al-Dīn al-Rāzī, *op. cit.*, iv. 333).

The (salted) fish serves as a guide to the route; the place where it is lost or revived by contact with water is the spring of life where al-Khaḍir lives (al-Ṭabarī, i. 417). A further indication of the spring of life is that it is marked by the rock, for it rises at its foot (al-Ṭabarī, *Tafsīr*, xv. 167; al-Bukhārī, *Tafsīr*, Sūra xviii., bāb 4). The rock is also located before the river of oil or the river of the wolf (al-Baiḍāwī and al-Zamakhsharī on Sūra xviii. 62; al-Ṭabarī, *Tafsīr*, xv. 164). Some connection between a river of oil and the spring of life is in itself not impossible. According to many statements, oil is a feature of Paradise rivers. Then *dhi'b* would be an error in writing *zait* which could easily arise. Vollers considers the reverse probable; he thinks that "river of the wolf" is a translation of the name Loukos, which is not uncommon in classical literature as a river-name. If this hypothesis is correct, one might think of the Lukkos in Morocco or the Lycus on the Syrian coast, two regions with which the idea of extreme west is associated, as we shall see directly.

The Madjmaʿ al-baḥrain is explained in various ways. Some regard it as "the place where the Persian Ocean unites with the Roman Sea, to the east" (al-Baiḍāwī on Sūra xviii. 60; al-Ṭabarī, *Tafsīr*, xv. 163). This points to the Isthmus of Suez and is an echo of the idea that the coast of Syria was the extreme west (see A. J. Wensinck, *Bird and Tree as Cosmological Symbols in Western Asia*, in *Verh. Ak. Amsterdam*, 1921, p. 17 *sqq.*). Others say that it is the junction of the Roman Sea with the Ocean (Ṭandja, Ifrīḳiya; al-Ṭabarī, *Tafsīr*, xv. 163, and al-Zamakhsharī on the passage). This view reflects a later cosmological standpoint which regarded the Straits of Gibraltar as the extreme west. A far-fetched explanation is that the union of the two seas means the meeting of Mūsā and al-Khaḍir, the two seas of wisdom (e. g. al-Damīrī, *Ḥayāt al-ḥayawān*, i. 318).

When Mūsā first sees Khaḍir he is wrapped up in his cloak, as the Ḳur'ān says; "because he was sleeping", says al-Ṭabarī (ed. de Goeje, i. 418). When he sees a bird drinking out of the sea he says to Mūsā: "Your wisdom is as insignificant compared with that of God as the amount the bird drinks is compared with the sea" (al-Ṭabarī, ed. de Goeje, i. 418; al-Bukhārī, *Tafsīr*, Sūra xviii., bāb 3; al-Rāzī, *Mafātīḥ al-ghaib*, iv. 333 *sq.*). Al-Khaḍir lives on an island (al-Ṭabarī, ed. de Goeje, i. 422), or on a green carpet (*ṭinfisa*) in the heart of the sea (*ʿalā kabid al-baḥr*; al-Bukhārī, *Tafsīr*, Sūra xviii., bāb 3).

The test of patience is embellished by the commentators with a wealth of detail. It would take up too much space to go into them here; cf. the commentaries on Sūra xviii. 60 *sqq.*, and the works on history and tradition mentioned in the *Bibliography*.

As may be expected from what we have said above, another branch of tradition lays particular emphasis on the connection between al-Khaḍir and Alexander's search for the spring of life. Friedländer, however, goes much too far when he says (*Die Chadhirlegende*, p. 108 *sq.*) "that originally Chadhir had nothing at all to do with the puzzling servant in verse 65 — who belongs to quite a different cycle of stories — but with the servant of Moses (Alexander) who has charge of the fish in verse 60 *sqq.*, in other words he is identical with Alexander's cook whom we know so well from Pseudokallisthenes and the Syriac homily". For Khaḍir is, as we have seen and will see further, connected with Utnapishtim as well as with Alexander's companion.

There is no translation of the Alexander romance in the Arabic literature known to us (cf. Weymann, see *Bibliography*). On the other hand, there are a number of, in part unedited, versions of the Alexander saga, which have been examined by Friedländer. It would take us too far to go into the differences between these versions with regard to our subject. These sources show their independence of the Ḳur'ān not only by the fact that they make Khaḍir the companion of Dhu 'l-Ḳarnain, but also by the complete absence of any reference to the *fatā* of the Ḳur'ān. Al-Khaḍir usually appears as the commander of Alexander's vanguard on his march to the spring of life. In al-Ṣūrī's version he is called the king's vizier and has become the principal character, throwing the king himself into the background; in ʿUmāra he is Alexander's cousin, conceived and born in similar circumstances to him and at the same time. The usual account of the journey to the spring of life makes Alexander and al-Khaḍir go their ways separately; in some versions, the latter has the fish with him and discovers the miraculous well through the fish's becoming alive when it touches the water; in other stories, on the other hand, there is no mention of the fish and al-Khaḍir recognises the spring by other signs; in others again he dives into it without knowing its virtues (e. g. al-Ṭabarī, i. 414). In one version in Niẓāmī, al-Khaḍir does not go with Alexander but with Elijah to the spring, out of which both drink and both become immortal.

III

The descriptive character of the name al-Khaḍir is so obvious from its meaning that tradition could not but give the hero's real name, as well as his genealogy and date. We find him most frequently called Balyā b. Malkān. In al-Mas'ūdī (*Murūḏj̱*, iii. 144) the latter is called a brother of Ḳaḥṭān and thus given a place in the South Arabian genealogy. This makes it probable that Malkān is identical with Malkam (I Chronicles, viii. 9), who is also included among the South Arabian patriarchs. This genealogy is next traced back to Shem through Fālagh (Phaleg) and 'Ābir (Eber) (e. g. al-Ṭabarī, ed. de Goeje, i. 415; al-Mas'ūdī, *Murūḏj̱*, i. 92; al-Nawawī, on Muslim's *Ṣaḥīḥ*, v. 135). Is this Balyā perhaps not a corruption of Elia which is identical with the Syriac form of the name Elijah? On the other hand, Elijah is also given in the Muslim form Ilyās as al-Khaḍir's proper name and also Elisha, Jeremiah (cf. God's words in *Iṣāba*, p. 887), Khaḍrūn (al-Ṭabarī, ed. de Goeje, i. 415; al-Diyārbakrī, *Ta'rīkh al-khamīs*, i. 106, and Friedländer's *Chadhirlegende*, p. 333, under Chadhir).

Ibn Ḥaḏj̱ar also gives the following g e n e a l - o g i e s (*Iṣāba*, p. 883 *sq.*): (1) He is a son of Adam (weak *isnād*); with this is connected the story (*Iṣāba*, p. 887 *sq.*; Abū Ḥātim al-Siḏj̱istānī, *Kitāb al-mu'ammarīn*, p. 1) that al-Khaḍir took care of Adam's body and finally buried it after the flood; (2) He is a son of Ḳābil called Khaḍrūn; (3) He is al-Mu'ammar (the Long-lived) b. Mālik b. 'Abd Allāh b. Naṣr b. al-Azd; (4) He is Ibn 'Amā'il b. al-Nūr b. al-'Īṣ b. Isḥāḳ; (5) He is the son of Pharaoh's daughter; (6) He is a Persian, or his father was a Persian, his mother a Greek or vice versa; it is also said that he was born in a cave, fed there on the milk of wild beasts and finally entered the service of a king (al-Damīrī, i. 318; Ibn Ḥaḏj̱ar, p. 891 *sq.*); cf. also his meeting "on the market-place of the Banū Isrā'īl" with the man who asks him for alms *bi-waḏj̱h Allāh* (*Iṣāba*, p. 894 *sq.*).

This does not, however, exhaust the traditions about his names and genealogy. We shall only quote here the following from Maracci, *Prodromi* to Sūra xviii. 58: Alchedrus, quem fabulantur Moslemi eundem fuisse ac Phineas filium Eleazari, filii Aaron; cujus anima per metempsychosin emigravit primo in Eliam, deinde ex Elia in S. Gregorium, quem propterea Mahumetani omnes summo honore prosequuntur. — The latter identification is probably due to a confusion with St. George, with whom al-Khaḍir has certain points of resemblance; cf. thereon Clermont-Ganneau, in *Revue archéologique*, vol. xxxii. *sq.*, and Friedländer, *op. cit.*, p. 275. Clermont-Ganneau further pointed out the relationship between the consonants *kh-ḍ-r* and the North Semitic group *ḥ-ṣ-r*. The name has also been taken as a corruption of Khasisatra (Guyard, in *RHR*, i. 344 *sq.*) or connected with Ahasuerus, the wandering Jew (Lidzbarski, in *ZA*, vii. 116).

Very varying dates are given for al-Khaḍir's period. Sometimes he is called a contemporary of Abraham, who left Babel with him (al-Ṭabarī, ed. de Goeje, i. 415); sometimes he is put in the period of Afrīdūn; he is a contemporary of Alexander and lived down to the time of Mūsā (Ibn Ḥaḏj̱ar, *Iṣāba*, p. 886); according to others, he was born in the period of Nāṣhiyā b. Amūṣ (i. e. Isaiah b. Amos) (al-Ṭabarī, *op. cit.*, p. 415 *sq.*). The divergence in these statements is partly connected with his immortality [see below].

More important are the e x p l a n a t i o n s of t h e n a m e given in the Oriental sources. He is said to have become green through diving into the spring of life and thus got his name (Ethiopic Alexander romance; cf. Friedländer, *op. cit.*, p. 235 *sq.*). As already mentioned, he lives on an island (al-Damīrī, *op. cit.*, p. 317); he is also said to worship God on the islands (al-Ṣūrī, see Friedländer, *op. cit.*, p. 183; al-Tha'labī, p. 197). This may point to al-Khaḍir's having originally been a marine being. The following circumstances point in the same direction: he is frequently called the patron of seafaring people (e. g. *Ta'rīkh al-khamīs*, i. 107); he is said to be appealed to on the Syrian coast by sailors in stormy weather. In India he has become a regular river-god under the name Khwāḏj̱a Khiḍr [q. v.], who is represented sitting on a fish. Clermont-Ganneau and Friedländer sought the origin of the figure mainly in this direction, the latter on the assumption that the Greek Glaukos legend reached the Muslims through a Syriac intermediary (*op. cit.*, p. 107 *sqq.*). But apart from the fact that we know nothing of any such intermediary, a connection between al-Khaḍir and Glaukos would only explain one aspect of the former; nor would it tell us anything about the origin of the figure, indeed one may doubt whether it is right to seek for the origin of a figure so complicated as al-Khaḍir, who has characteristics in common with Utnapishtim, with Alexander's cook and other figures.

There are other things to be considered. In a number of Arabic explanations of the name, al-Khaḍir is conceived not as belonging to the sea but to the vegetable kingdom. "He sat on a white skin and it became green" (e. g. al-Nawawī on Muslim's *Ṣaḥīḥ*, v. 135; cf. al-Ṭabarī, *Tafsīr*, xv. 168). "The skin", adds al-Nawawī, "is the earth". Al-Diyārbakrī (i. 106) is still more definite. "The skin is the earth when it puts forth shoots and becomes green after having been bare". According to 'Umāra, al-Khaḍir is told at the spring of life: "Thou art Chadhir and where thy feet touch it, the earth will become green" (Friedländer, *op. cit.*, p. 145). Wherever he stands or performs the *ṣalāt*, it will become green (al-Nawawī, *op. cit.*; al-Rāzī, *Mafātīḥ al-ghaib*, iv. 336). These are statements (especially the last) which remind us of a Messianic passage in the Old Testament: "Behold the man whose name is the branch and he shall grow up out of his place" (Zechariah, vi. 12). Al-Khaḍir is really connected with two Messianic figures — with Elijah [cf. the art. ILYĀS] and with Jesus; these three form with Idrīs [q. v.] the quartette of those who have not tasted death (*Ta'rīkh al-khamīs*, i. 107).

The variations in the character of al-Khaḍir result in different views regarding his n a t u r e. If he is a p r o p h e t (see *Iṣāba*, p. 882 *sqq.*) it remains doubtful whether he is to be included among the Apostles (al-Nawawī, *op. cit.*, p. 135). He is, however, also human, angelic, mundane and celestial (al-Ṭabarī, ed. de Goeje, i. 544, 798). Popular piety as well as Ṣūfī circles readily regard him as a saint (*walī*). According to one Ṣūfī view, every age has its Khaḍir, in so far as the *naḳīb al-awliyā'* for the time being is al-Khaḍir (*Iṣāba*, p. 891). As *walī*, if three times appealed to, he protects men against theft, drowning, burning, kings and devils, snakes and scorpions (*Ta'rīkh al-khamīs*, i. 107; *Iṣāba*, p. 903). Sky and sea and all quarters of the earth obey his sway; he is God's *khalīfa* on the sea and his *wakīl* on land; he can make himself invisible at will ('Umāra in Friedländer, *op. cit.*, p. 145). He flies through the air, meets Elijah on the dam of Alexander and makes the pilgrimage to Mekka with him every year (cf. *Iṣāba*, p. 904 *sqq.*). Every Friday he drinks from the Zamzam well and Solomon's pool and washes in the well of Siloa (*Ta'rīkh al-khamīs*, i. 107; Friedländer, *op. cit.*, p. 148 *sq.*, 151); he can find water below the ground and talks the languages af all peoples (al-Ṣūrī in Friedländer, p. 184.)

His immortality is particularly emphasised (cf. Rückert's poem "Chidher"; ʿUmāra in Friedländer, *op. cit.*, p. 145; Abū Ḥātim al-Sidjistānī, *Kitāb al-muʿammarīn*, p. 1; *Iṣāba*, p. 887 *sqq.*, 892, 895). According to the *Iṣāba*, p. 882, he was given immortality after a conversation with his friend, the angel Rafā'īl, in order to establish the true worship of God on the earth and maintain it. Ibn Ḥadjar describes a meeting between al-Khaḍir and Muḥammad in various versions (*Iṣāba*, p. 899 *sqq.*). On meetings with individuals who lived at a later date see *ibid.*, p. 908 *sqq.*; on the table which was let down to him from heaven see *ibid.*, p. 919; on his presence at the battle of Ḳādisīya see *Murūdj al-dhahab*, iv. 216.

He lives in Jerusalem and performs his *ṣalāt* every Friday in the mosques of Mekka, Madīna, Jerusalem, Ḳubā' and on the Mount of Olives; his food is *kam'a* and water-parsley (*Ta'rīkh al-khamīs*, i. 107; *Iṣāba*, p. 889 *sq.*, 904).

On his marriages we have as early as classical Ḥadīth (Ibn Mādja, *Zuhd*, bāb 23) a legend also mentioned by al-Thaʿlabī, *Ḳiṣaṣ*, p. 193 *sqq.*, which in its main features must have come from Christian sources. It is the motif of the pious youth who, married by his parents against his will, persuades his young wife to preserve her virginity (cf. the Syriac Acts of Thomas, 2nd Praxis). The story links up with that of Pharaoh's daughter's handmaid.

Bibliography: The commentaries on the Ḳur'ān, Sūra xviii. 60—82; ii. 259; xi. 85; xxvii. 40; and the works on Ḥadīth and history quoted above: al-Thaʿlabī, *Ḳiṣaṣ al-anbiyā'*, Cairo 1290, p. 125, 190 *sqq.*; al-Diyārbakrī, *Ta'rīkh al-khamīs*, Cairo 1283, i. 106 *sq.*; Ibn Ḥadjar, *Iṣāba*, Calcutta 1856—93, p. 882 *sqq.*; al-Damīrī, *Ḥayāt al-ḥayawān*, Cairo 1274, i. 317 *sqq.*; al-Nawawī, *Tahdhīb al-asmā'*, ed. Wüstenfeld, p. 228 *sqq.*; Abū Ḥātim al-Sidjistānī, *Kitāb al-muʿammarīn*, ed. Goldziher, in *Abh. zur arab. Philologie*, ii. 1; al-Masʿūdī, *Murūdj al-dhahab*, ed. Paris, iv. 216; Firdawsī, *Shāhnāme*, ed. Mohl, v. 216 *sq.*; ed. Macan, iii. 1340; Niẓāmī, *Sikendernāme*, in the poem on Alexander's search for the water of life; Fr. Spiegel, *Die Alexandersage bei den Orientalen*, Leipzig 1851; Ethé, *Alexanders Zug zum Lebensquell*, in *S. B. Bayr. Ak. Wiss.*, 1871, p. 343—405; Clermont-Ganneau, *Horus et Saint Georges d'après un bas-relief inédit du Louvre*, in *Revue d'archéologie*, vol. xxxii.—xxxiv.; S. I. Curtiss, *Ursemit. Religion im Volksleben des heut. Orients*, Leipzig 1903, register, s. v. Chidr; Dyroff, *Wer ist Chadhir?*, in *ZA*, 1892, vii. 319—327; I. Friedländer, *Zur Geschichte der Chadhirlegende*, in *AR*, 1910, xiii. 92 *sqq.*; do., *Alexanders Zug nach dem Lebensquell und die Chadhirlegende*, in *AR*, xiii. 161 *sqq.*; do., *Die Chadhirlegende und der Alexanderroman*, Leipzig 1913; M. Lidzbarski, *Wer ist Chadhir?*, in *ZA*, 1892, vii. 104—116; Nöldeke, *Beiträge zur Geschichte des Alexanderromans* (*Denkschr. Ak. Wien*, xxxviii., N°. 5); K. Vollers, *Chidher*, in *AR*, 1909, xii. 234—284; G. Zart, *Chidher in Sage und Dichtung* (Sammlung gemeinverst. wiss. Vorträge, N°. 280, 1897); Weymann, *Die äthiopische und arabische Übersetzung des Pseudokallisthenes*, Kirchhain 1901; R. Paret, *Sīrat Saif ibn Dhī Jazan*, Hanover 1924, Index I, s. v.; G. W. I. Drewes, *Drie Javaansche Goeroes*, Leyden Diss. 1925, p. 56 *sq.*, 195 *sq.*

KHWĀDJA KHIḌR (or Khizr in India), the well known Muslim saint [cf. AL-KHAḌIR] is in many parts of India identified with a rivergod or spirit of wells and streams. He is mentioned in the *Sikandar-nāma* as the saint who presided over the well of immortality. The name was naturalized in India, and Hindūs as well as Muslims reverence him; it is sometimes converted by Hindūs into Rādja Kidār. On the Indus the saint is often identified with the river, and he is sometimes to be seen as an old man clothed in green. A man who escapes drowning is spoken of as evading Khwādja Khizr (Temple, *Legends of the Pandjāb*, i. 221). In a poem by a Balōč regarding a fight on the Indus a boat is unloosed "to float on the Khwādja's waves", and it is asserted "the Khwādja himself will remember that battle" (*Popular Poetry of the Baloches*, i. 74), and by one poet his name is substituted for that of Mīkā'īl as one of the archangels. His principal shrine is on an island of the Indus near Bakhar, which is resorted to by devotees of both creeds (*Sind Revisited*, ii. 226). Manucci who was present at the siege of Bakhar in 1658, alludes to this shrine under the name of Coia Quitan. Burnes also mentions it in his *Travels into Bokhara*.

The saint is believed to ride upon a fish, which was adopted as a crest by the Kings of Oudh, and appears on their coins. Possibly in this case there is also a survival of the fish-avatār of Vishnu. Muslims offer prayers to Khwādja Khiḍr at the first shaving of a boy, and a little boat is launched at the same time; also at the close of the rainy season. — See further KHAḌIR.

Bibliography: Crooke, *Popular Religion and Folklore of N. India*, London 1896; Burton, *Sind Revisited*, London 1877; Temple, *Legends of the Panjāb*, i., Bombay 1884; Longworth Dames, *Popular Poetry of the Baloches*, London 1907; W. Irvine, *Storia de Mogor* (*Manucci*), London 1907; A. Burnes, *Travels into Bokhara*, London 1834; J. Wise, *Muhammadans of Eastern Bengal*, in *Journ. As. Soc. Bengal*, 1894, lxiii., part iii., p. 38 *sqq.*

KHĀLID B. AL-WALĪD B. AL-MUGHĪRA AL-MAKHZŪMĪ, a contemporary of Muḥammad and a Muslim general. In the battle of Uḥud, where Khālid commanded the right wing of the Mekkan forces, and by his intervention at the right moment decided the battle in favour of the enemies of the Prophet, he first displayed that brilliant talent for leadership to which in later days Islām owed so many successes. After Khālid had gone over to Islām with ʿAmr b. al-ʿĀṣ at the beginning of the year 8/629 he took part in the unsuccessful campaign against the Byzantines, and after the defeat at Mu'ta he succeeded with great difficulty in bringing back the defeated army to Madīna. As a reward the Prophet gave him the title of honour "Sword of God", and in the same year he took part in the entry of the Muslims into Mekka. After the capitulation of the town he is said to have destroyed the sanctuary of the heathen goddess al-ʿUzzā by order of Muḥammad. He was soon afterwards sent as ambassador to the Banū

Djadhīma and in Radjab of the next year (Oct./Nov., 630) he undertook an expedition against Ukaidir, the Christian king of Dūmat al-Djandal. At the beginning of the year 10 (summer of 631) Muḥammad sent him to Nadjrān to convert the Banu 'l-Ḥārith b. Kaʿb to Islām, which was also done without bloodshed. In the following year he was sent by Abū Bakr against Ṭulaiḥa b. Khuwailid and defeated him at Buzākha and next led his forces against the Banū Tamīm who dwelled in the vicinity. One clan, which was under Mālik b. Nuwaira, was at feud with the others. When the latter submitted, Mālik also laid down his arms but was nevertheless taken prisoner and put to death and Khālid then married his widow. When an accusation was laid before the Caliph against Khālid he is said to have excused himself by saying that the incident was due to a misunderstanding. In consequence of dialect differences the Beduins had got a wrong idea of his order. In any case Abū Bakr was satisfied with administering a reprimand to him and kept him in office in spite of vigorous protests from ʿUmar. Soon afterwards Khālid took the field against the false prophet Musailima. At ʿAkrabāʾ, on the frontier of al-Yamāma, the latter was defeated and killed, whereupon his followers submitted (12/633). Khālid was then sent against the Persians, conquered al-Ḥīra and soon afterwards occupied the whole Euphrates area. Finally the Byzantines are said to have crossed the Euphrates and to have been defeated at al-Firāḍ (Dhu 'l-Ḳaʿda, 12/Jan., 634), whereupon Khālid set out on his campaign against Syria. In Djumādā I or II 13 (= summer of 634) the Byzantines were completely defeated at Adjnādain and retired to Damascus. Defeated again by Khālid, they were surrounded and besieged and in Radjab, 14/Aug.-Sept., 635, Damascus had finally to surrender. About the same time Khālid was deprived of the supreme command and replaced by Abū ʿUbaida b. al-Djarrāḥ but continued to take part in the military operations in Syria. In the battle of the Yarmūk on Radjab 12, 15/Aug. 20, 636, he commanded the cavalry and contributed largely to the victory of the Muslims. Ḥimṣ was recaptured soon afterwards. Khālid then advanced against Ḳinnasrīn and after he defeated a Byzantine army under Mīnās the town had to surrender and Khālid took up his quarters here for the time. He was for a time governor of a part of Syria but was later dismissed. He died in Ḥimṣ or Madīna in the year 21/641—2.

Bibliography: Ibn Hishām, p. 273 *sqq.*; al-Wāḳidī, *al-Maghāzī*, ed. Wellhausen, p. 77 *sqq.*; Ibn Saʿd, iv./ii. 1 *sq.*; Ibn Ḳutaiba, *al-Maʿārif*, ed. Wüstenfeld, p. 136; al-Balādhurī, p. 38 *sqq.*; al-Yaʿḳūbī, ii. 48—180; al-Ṭabarī, i., *passim*; glossary, p. ccxli.; al-Masʿūdī, i. 216—222; iv. 211; *al-Aghānī*, Index; Ibn al-Athīr, *al-Kāmil*, ii., *passim*; do., *Usd al-ghāba*, ii. 101—104; Ibn Ḥadjar, *al-Iṣāba*, i., N°. 2190; Weil, *Gesch. der Chalifen*, i. 18 *sqq.*; Müller, *Der Islam im Morgen- und Abendland*, i. 124, 145, 150 *sqq.*, 165, 177 *sqq.*, 226—237, 250—257; Muir, *The Caliphate, its Rise, Decline, and Fall* (new ed. by Weir), p. 16 *sqq.*; Wellhausen, *Reste arabischen Heidentums* ², p. 36 *sqq.*; do., *Skizzen und Vorarbeiten*, vi. 9 *sqq.*, 37—65; Caetani, *Annali dell' Islām*, i.—iv., see Indices; Huart, *Histoire des Arabes*, i. 30 *sqq.*

KHALĪFA, "successor, vicegerent", title of the supreme head of the Muslim community, the *imām* [q. v.], as successor or vicegerent of the Prophet (*khalīfat rasūl Allāh*).

I. The word appears frequently, both in the singular and the plural (*khalāʾif*, *khulafāʾ*), in the Ḳurʾān; in the latter case, the persons referred to are called "successors" as entering into the blessings enjoyed by their forefathers (e. g. vi. 165; xxiv. 55; xxvii. 62, used of the righteous; vii. 69, 74, of the idolatrous tribes of ʿĀd and Thamūd); the singular is used of Adam (ii. 30), either as successor of the angels who lived on earth before him, or as representative of God, and of David (xxxviii. 26): "We have made thee a khalīfa in the land; then judge between men with the truth, and follow not thy desires, lest they cause thee to err from the path of God." In none of these verses is there any clear indication that the word was intended to serve as the title of the successor of Muḥammad. Muslim historians commonly assert that it was first so used by Abū Bakr; it is doubtful, however, whether he ever assumed it as a title (Caetani, *Annali dell' Islām*, 11 A. H., § 63, n. 1). But from the reign of ʿUmar, it has been the common designation of the *amīr al-muʾminīn*. The designation *khalīfat rasūl Allāh*, "successor of the apostle of God", implies assumption of the activities and privileges exercised by Muḥammad, — with the exception of the prophetic function, which was believed to have ceased with him; the later phrase, *khalīfat Allāh*, "vicegerent of God", implies a bolder claim, and is said to have excited the indignation of Abū Bakr, but it was used as early as 35 A. H. by Ḥassān b. Thābit in an elegy he wrote on the Khalīfa ʿUthmān (ed. H. Hirschfeld, xx. 1. 9), and it became quite common under the ʿAbbāsids and later princes (Goldziher, *Muhammedanische Studien*, ii. 61).

In the course of Muslim history, however, the term khalīfa has not been confined to such exalted reference. As early as the first century of the Hidjra, it was used in the Aphrodito papyri for the ἀποκρισιάριος or agent at the capital through whom the local official of the finance department made payments of taxes (*Greek Papyri of the British Museum*, vol. iv., p. xxv., 35; C. H. Becker, *Islamstudien*, i., p. 257). It had frequently been used as a personal name (see Index to Ṭabarī, etc.). In the religious orders, especially among the Ḳādirīya, the Khalīfa is the delegate of the Shaikh of the order and is invested with a certain amount of his powers and represents him in countries remote from the parent *zāwiya*. Among the Tidjānīya, the Khalīfa is the inheritor of the spiritual power (*baraka*) of the founder of the order, to whom alone the title Shaikh is applied (O. Depont and X. Coppolani, *Les confréries religieuses musulmanes*, Algiers 1897, p. 194—195; L. Rinn, *Marabouts et Khouan*, Algiers 1884, p. 78).

In the Mahdist movements, the Khalīfa is the successor of the Mahdī; Mīr Dilāwar was thus Khalīfa of Saiyid Muḥammad Mahdī (d. 910 A. H.), the founder of the Mahdawīs; ʿAbd Allāh was the Khalīfa of Muḥammad Aḥmad, the Mahdī of the Sūdān; and the son and second successor of Ghulām Aḥmad Ḳādiyānī (see AḤMADĪYA) is so described by his followers at the present day. Humbler persons have also received this designation, e. g. in the household of the Emperor Bābūr, khalīfa denoted a woman who exercised surveillance over other women-servants (Gul-badan Begam, *Humāyūn-nāma*, translated by A. S. Beveridge, p. 136). In more modern times, the word khalīfa was commonly applied in Turkey to any junior clerk in a public office (C. M. d'Ohsson, *Tablau général de l'Empire*

Othoman ², vii. 271), and is still a title of respect for an assistant teacher in a school. In Morocco it indicates the deputy of the governor of a city (B. Meakin, *The Moorish Empire*, p. 224). In modern India it is used even of such insignificant persons as a working tailor, a barber, a fencing master or a cook (H. A. Rose, *Glossary of the Tribes and Castes of the Punjab*, ii., p. 490. Lahore 1911). In Togo and neighbouring parts of W. Africa, alfa (= khalīfa) denotes a Muslim teacher or even Muḥammadans generally (*Die Welt des Islams*, ii., p. 200).

Bibliography: In addition to the works already quoted, see Goldziher, *Du sens propre des expressions Ombre de Dieu, pour désigner les chefs dans l'Islam* (*R H R*, xxxv., 1897); D. S. Margoliouth, *The sense of the title Khalīfah* (*A Volume of Oriental Studies presented to Edward G. Browne*, p. 322—328).

II. As a distinction can be drawn between the history of the Khilāfa or of the political institution of which the Khalīfa was the head, and the theories connected with it, and as the former was chronologically prior, it is proposed here to deal with it first.

1. History. The immense wealth and power acquired by the early successors of Muḥammad, through the conquest of such provinces of the Roman Empire as Syria and Egypt, together with the dominions of the Persian king, raised them to a status and a dignity which gave to the humble title they bore a new significance; so even before the Arab conquests had reached their limit, the Khalīfa had become one of the most powerful and wealthy monarchs in the world. As *amīr al-mu'minīn* he was commander of these conquering armies and so he described himself on his coins; as *imām* [q. v.], he took the foremost place in public worship and delivered the *khuṭba* [q. v.] in the mosque; as Khalīfa he claimed from his Muslim subjects some of the reverence that had previously been paid to the founder of their faith. The civil war that broke out in the reign of ʿAlī b. Abī Ṭālib laid the foundation for those rival theories as to the qualifications of the Khalīfa, which took definite shape in political and sectarian doctrines. Under the Umaiyads the religious associations of the office of the Khalīfa were not emphasised, though many of them kept up the practice of leading the public worship, for (with the exception of ʿUmar b. ʿAbd al-ʿAzīz) religious considerations appear to have had little weight with them, and it was mainly in Madīna that the foundations of Muslim dogma and the systematisation of the *sharīʿa* [q. v.] were laid, with little encouragement from the Khalīfa in Damascus. The claim of the descendants of ʿAlī to the leadership of the Muslim world found expression in the formation of the Shīʿa party [q. v.], but for some generations their efforts met with no political success. The ʿAbbāsids [q. v.] came into power largely through their pretended support of ʿAlid claims, and largely too through their professions of religious zeal. In Baghdād the Khilāfa took on a new character; the Khalīfa became a generous patron of the ʿulamā' and laid emphasis upon his function as protector of the religion of Islām, and under his fostering care the capital took the place of Madīna as the chief centre of theological activity, and the great schools of law [cf. FIKH] received definite shape. The Khalīfa was no longer regarded as a mere secular monarch, as many of the Umaiyads had appeared to be in the eyes of devout Muslims, and the awe with which he was regarded was enhanced by the elaboration of court etiquette and ceremonial. The Umaiyads, especially in their early days, had generally been readily accessible to their subjects; Muʿāwiya had preserved in a great measure the frank, familiar manners of an Arab chief of pre-Islāmic times, and moved among other Arab chiefs as *primus inter pares*. But in the new capital, the traditions of the Persian monarchy reasserted themselves, the ʿAbbāsid sat on his throne in solemn majesty, surrounded by his guards, the executioner with drawn sword by his side. At the same time he emphasised the religious aspect of his office by wearing the mantle of the Prophet, and his relationship to the Prophet was reiterated in official documents and in the lucubrations of eulogists and court flatterers.

From the ixᵗʰ century onwards, the direct control of the Khalīfa over the administration weakened in consequence of the increasing delegation of power to the wazīr [q. v.] and the growing elaboration and efficiency of the government offices. About the same period began the decline of the temporal power of the Khalīfa, in consequence of the break-up of the empire and the rise of independent principalities in the various provinces, until at last his authority hardly extended beyond the precincts of the city of Baghdād. Concurrently with this decline of his temporal power, increasing stress was laid on his position in the religious order, as *imām* [q. v.] and as the defender of religion, and the persecution of heretics and of the adherents of non-Muslim faiths increased. By the year 946 all effective power had passed out of the hands of the Khalīfa, and there were to be seen in Baghdād three personages who had held this high office, but now deposed and blinded were dependent for their livelihood upon charity. From this period until c. 1180 the Khalīfa for the time being was but a puppet in the hands of the Būyids and the Saldjūḳs successively. But in spite of his entire lack of administrative authority, men could not forget the great position once held by his ancestors, and the impotent Khalīfa was still regarded by theorists as the source of all authority and power in the Muslim world. Accordingly, there were to be found independent rulers who sought from him titles and diplomas of appointment, e. g. Maḥmūd of Ghazna when he renounced his allegiance to the Sāmānid prince in 997, received from the Khalīfa recognition of his independent position, together with the titles Yamīn al-Dawla, Amīn al-Milla; and about a century later, Yūsuf b. Tāshfīn, the founder of the Almoravid dynasty, received the title of Amīr al-Muslimīn from the Khalīfa al-Muḳtadī. When in 1175 Saladin assumed the sovereignty of Egypt and Syria, he was confirmed in this rank by the Khalīfa al-Mustaḍī, who sent him a diploma of investiture and robes of honour. The founder of the Rasūlid dynasty in the Yaman, Nūr al-Dīn ʿUmar, likewise asked the Khalīfa for the title of Sulṭān and a diploma of investiture as his lieutenant, and Mustanṣir in 1235 sent a special envoy with the required document. This same Khalīfa had in 1229 responded to the request of Iltutmish, the Turkish ruler of Northern India, for the title of Sulṭān and for confirmation in the possession of his dominion; and succeeding kings of Dilhī continued to put the name of Mustaʿṣim, the last Khalīfa of Baghdād, upon their coins for more than thirty years after this unfortunate prince had been put to death by the Mongols.

In contrast to this recognition of the Khalīfa in Baghdād as the legitimate source of authority, is the establishment of two rival Khilāfats; in 928 ʿAbd al-Raḥmān III of Spain assumed the title of Khalīfa which continued to be borne by his descendants; these Umaiyads of Spain, like their predecessors in Damascus, were Sunnīs; but the Fāṭimids of Egypt, whose founder styled himself Khalīfa first in Mahdīya in 909, were Shīʿīs, and were serious rivals to the ʿAbbāsids in Baghdād until the destruction of their dynasty by Saladin in 1171.

In 1258 Hūlāgū captured Baghdād and put to death the Khalīfa Mustaʿṣim, who perished leaving behind him no heir. The catastrophe was without parallel in the history of Islam, and for the first time the Muslim world found itself without a theoretical head whose name could be mentioned in the *khuṭba* in the mosques on Fridays. Two members of the ʿAbbāsid family, who had escaped the massacre in Baghdād, took refuge one after the other with the Mamlūk Sulṭān of Egypt; the first, an uncle of Mustaʿṣim, was invited by Baibars to Cairo, and was there installed with great pomp as Khalīfa in 1261. Baibars is said to have conceived the idea of re-establishing the ʿAbbāsid dynasty in Baghdād and left Cairo with a large army, but after he had reached Damascus he provided the Khalīfa with only a small body of troops, which was destroyed by the Mongols on its way through the desert, and nothing more was ever heard of the Khalīfa. The second claimant arrived in Cairo in 1262 and was similarly installed as Khalīfa, but no attempt was made to repeat the rash experiment of regaining Baghdād, and the Khalīfa was kept a virtual prisoner in Cairo, though treated with outward marks of respect. For more than two centuries and a half, his descendants one after another continued to hold this shadowy office in Cairo, dependent on the bounty of the Mamlūk Sulṭān, who found the Khalīfa useful as lending a show of legitimacy to his rule. Each new Sulṭān was ceremoniously installed by the Khalīfa, to whom he in his turn paid allegiance. But not a single one of them (with the exception of Mustaʿīn, who was made the plaything of rival political factions in 1412 and for six months was styled Sulṭān) ever exercised any function of government or enjoyed any political power. Maḳrīzī describes the Khalīfa as spending his time among the nobles and officials, paying them visits to thank them for the dinners and entertainments to which they had invited him (*Histoire d'Egypte*, ed. E. Blochet, p. 76).

The rest of the Muslim world outside Egypt for the most part ignored the existence of the ʿAbbāsid Khalīfa in Cairo. From the xiii^th^ century there had been a Sunnī Khalīfa in the Maghrib, and from time to time various princes in the eastern lands of the Muḥammadan world assumed this title, Saljūḳs, Tīmūrids, Turkomans, Uzbegs and Ottomans.

But a small number of independent princes, desiring to legitimize their claim to the obedience of their subjects, asked for formal recognition of their position and a grant of titles from the Khalīfa, e. g. the first two princes of the Muẓaffarid dynasty in southern Persia (1313—1384); Muḥammad b. Tughlaḳ (1325—1351) and his successor on the throne of Dilhī, Fīrūz Shāh (1351—1388); even Bāyazīd I is said to have applied in 1394 to the ʿAbbāsid Khalīfa in Cairo for a formal grant of the title of Sulṭān (v. Hammer, *Gesch. d. Osman. Reiches* [2], i. 195), but doubt has been cast upon the accuracy of this report. For, from the latter part of the xiv^th^ century, when after the conquest of Adrianople, Philippopolis etc. his father, Murād I, was styled "the chosen Khalīfa of God" (Ferīdūn, i. 93, l. 22), it became common for the Ottoman Sulṭāns, as for other contemporary Muḥammadan potentates, to claim for themselves the Khilāfa and to find this claim recognised by their subjects and their correspondents in other lands. The qualification of belonging to the tribe of Ḳuraish was ignored and sanction was sought for the usage in such verses of the Ḳurʾān as xxxviii. 26: "We have made thee a Khalīfa on the earth", and this and similar verses (e. g. vi. 165; xxv. 35) are constantly quoted in the diplomatic correspondence of the period. So when Selīm made his victorious entry into Cairo in January, 1517, and made an end of the ʿAbbāsid Khilāfa, by transporting the last representative of it, Mutawakkil, to Constantinople, he had already been accustomed to the use of the title Khalīfa as applied to himself, and to his ancestors for a century and a half. The legend that Mutawakkil made a formal transfer of his dignity to Selīm was first published by Constantine Mouradgea d'Ohsson in 1788 (*Tableau général de l'Empire Othoman*, i. 269—270, ed. 8vo., Paris 1788—1824). None of the contemporary authorities who record the conquest of Egypt makes any mention of such a transference of the office, and after the death of Selīm, Mutawakkil was allowed to return to Egypt and was Khalīfa there until his death in 1543. For the next two centuries, there were only two Muḥammadan potentates whose extent of territory and power could add dignity to the title of Khalīfa (in contrast to the indiscriminate use of it by insignificant princes) namely, the Ottoman Sulṭān and the Mughal Emperor in India. With the fall of the Mughal empire in the xviiith century, the Ottoman Sulṭān became manifestly the greatest figure in the Muslim world; but even his power was being threatened by his aggressive neighbour on the north, and after the war with Russia (1768—1774) he was obliged to surrender territories on the north shore of the Black Sea and recognize the independence of the Tartars of the Crimea. Catherine II claimed to be the patroness of the Christians of the Orthodox Church dwelling in Ottoman territories, and the Ottoman plenipotentiaries who negotiated the treaty of Küčük Kainardji in 1774 took advantage of the title of Khalīfa, to make a similar claim for asserting the religious authority of the Khalīfa over the Tartars who had ceased to owe him allegiance as a temporal sovereign. From this period onwards, it became a common error in Christian Europe to regard the Khalīfa as the spiritual head of all Muslims (just as the Pope is the spiritual head of all Catholics), and to credit him with the possession of spiritual authority over his co-religionists, though they might not owe him civil obedience as Sulṭān of Turkey. There is reason to believe that this widespread error in Christian Europe reacted upon opinion in Turkey itself. Particularly in the reign of Sulṭān ʿAbd al-Ḥamīd II (1876—1909), emphasis was laid on his position as Khalīfa, and in the Constitution promulgated at the beginning of his reign it was affirmed that "H.M. the Sulṭān, as Khalīfa, is the protector of the Muslim religion". He appears to have sent emissaries to different parts of the Muḥammadan world to encourage reverence for his own person as Khalīfa, and his efforts met with a certain response, since thoughtful Muḥammadans (and especially those whose minds were disturbed by the growing control of European Powers over the affairs of the Muḥammadan world) recognised that Turkey was the only independent Muslim power left which was of any account in the civilised world. But the despotic and reactionary character of ʿAbd al-Ḥamīd's government, his cruel suppression of all liberal movements and all efforts for constitutional reform, alienated the more enlightened sections of his own subjects, and when he was deposed in 1909, the affairs of Turkey passed under the control of a body of men who had little sympathy with the Islāmic spirit and realised the impossibility of reconciling an autocracy that claimed to be based on divine revelation with modern constitutional methods of government. In November, 1922, Turkey became a republic and abolished the Sulṭānate, leaving the Khalīfa shorn of all temporal power; but it had not become clear what were to be the functions of the new Khalīfa before, in March, 1924, his office was abolished altogether.

The events of the war 1914—1918 did not fail to cause repercussions in the Islamic world. In India there was formed as early as in 1919 the All India Khilafat Conference, an association which regularly organized meetings and had put at first their hopes in the policy of Muṣṭafā Kemāl in Turkey. After having seen their hopes destroyed by the events of March 1924 they began to look on Ibn Saʿūd as a possible candidate for the Caliphate, but without success. Meanwhile, already before the abolition of the Ottoman Caliphate, King Ḥusain of the Ḥidjāz had been induced, seemingly against his will, to accept the title of *Amīr al-Muʾminīn*. This pretension was nearly immediately rejected by Ibn Saʿūd and the abdication of Ḥusain (Oct. 1924) made away with his caliphate at the same time. In Egypt the sollicitude for a better political organisation of Islām had been voiced by the moderate modernist writer Rashīd Riḍā, pupil of Muḥammad ʿAbduh, in his treatise *al-Khilāfa aw al-imāma al-ʿuẓmā*, which appeared in 1922 (French trans. by H. Laoust, Beirut 1938), but his views had met with little sympathy in the conservative circles of the Azhar University. The Egyption ʿulamāʾ, however, took immediately action after the abolition of the Ottoman Caliphate and began to prepare a Caliphate Congress. This congress met from 13 till 19 May 1926 in Cairo under the presidency of the Rector of al-Azhar. It was attended by representatives from the Muslims of many countries. But the representative of India attended in a private capacity and Turkey, Persia, Afghanistan and also Ibn Saʿūd were not represented at all. The resolutions of this first Caliphate Congress were in the main negative. Although it was recognized that the Islamic Caliphate is capable of realisation, nothing more was decided than an appeal to all the Muslims of the world to work together for the establishment of the Caliphate. As such a cooperation came never to be realized, the matter has remained unsolved since then, for which on the whole the nationalistic tendencies in the Islamic countries may be held responsible. Even such a powerful ruler as Ibn Saʿūd has never shown aspirations to assume the highest dignity in Islam and an occasional attempt to proclaim the King of Egypt as Caliph met with no response.

In the above account, attention has been confined to the historic Sunnī Khilāfa which has played the most important part in Muḥammadan history. The two other Sunnī Khilāfats, that of Spain and that of the Maghrib and Egypt, have been only of local importance, and did not inspire loyalty in any other parts of the Muḥammadan world; nor has the assumption of the title Khalīfa by some of the princes of Java been recognized except by their own subjects.

Among the Shīʿīs, the attempts made from time to time to secure for the ʿAlids a position of power and independence met with but scant success, and the Fāṭimids of Egypt represent the only Shīʿī Khilāfa of any importance. In Persia the establishment of the Ṣafawid dynasty in 1502 did not succeed in making Shīʿism the State religion in Persia until long after the doctrine of the hidden *imām* had become a cardinal doctrine of the Shīʿa faith in that country.

Bibliography: An enumeration of the sources for the history of the Khilāfa would comprise the major part of the historical literature of the whole of the Muḥammadan era. For the Arabic sources F. Wüstenfeld, *Die Geschichtschreiber der Araber und ihre Werke*, and C. Brockelmann, *GAL* may be consulted. Among the more important sources may be mentioned: Ṭabarī, *Annales*; Ibn al-Athīr, *Chronicon*; al-Suyūṭī, *Taʾrīkh al-khulafāʾ* and *Ḥusn al-muḥāḍara*; al-Maḳrīzī, *al-Sulūk li-maʿrifat duwal al-mulūk* (partly translated by Quatremère in *Histoire des Sultans Mamlouks*); al-Maḳḳarī, *Nafḥ al-ṭīb*; *Chroniken der Stadt Mekka*, ed. F. Wüstenfeld; Rashīd al-Dīn, *Djāmiʿ al-tawārīkh*; Aḥmad Ferīdūn Bey, *Munshaʾāt al-salāṭīn*; Muṣṭafā Ṣabrī al-Tūḳārī, *al-Nakīr ʿalā munkiri ʾl-niʿmati min al-dīni wa ʾl-khilāfati wa ʾl-umma*, Bairūt 1924. Among European writers: Caetani, *Annali dell' Islām* (Milano, 1905 —); G. Weil, *Geschichte der Chalifen*, 5 vols. (1846—1862); A. Müller, *Der Islam im Morgen- und Abendland* (1885, 1887); W. Muir, *The Caliphate*; J. von Hammer, *Geschichte des Osmanischen Reiches*; A. de la Jonquière, *Hist. de l'empire ottoman*, 2nd ed., Paris 1914; *Oriente Moderno* (Rome 1921 —); C. A. Nallino, *La fine del così detto Califfato ottomano* (*Oriente Moderno*, iv. 137 *sqq.*); R. Hartmann, *Wesen u. Ende des osm. Chalifats*, Leipzig 1924; H. Ritter, *Die Abschaffung des Kalifats* (*Arch. f. Politik und Geschichte*, ii. 343 *sqq.*, Berlin 1934); A. J. Toynbee, *Survey of International Affairs* 1925, Vol. i, *The Islamic World since the Peace Settlement*, Oxford-London 1927, pp. 25—91.

2. Political Theory. As stated above, the theory of the Khilāfa was largely an outgrowth from the political circumstances of early Muḥammadan history, but speculation has elaborated many forms of the doctrine that have failed to secure for themselves expression in actual historical facts. Al-Shahrastānī (ed. Cureton, p. 12) says that no article of faith has given rise to such bloodshed and contention in every period of Muslim history as this.

(*a*) The orthodox Sunnī doctrine first found expression in the *ḥadīth*, which emphasised pre-eminently two essential characteristics of the Khalīfa: one, that he must be of the tribe of the Ḳuraish (*Kanz al-ʿummāl*, iii., N°. 2983; vi., N°. 3452, 3469), and the other, that he must receive unhesitating obedience, for whosoever rebels against the Khalīfa, rebels against God (*ibid.*, iii., 2580, 2999, 3008). This claim on obedience to the despotic power of the Khalīfa as a religious duty was impressed upon the faithful by the designations that were applied to him from an early date, — Khalīfa of God, and Shadow of God upon earth. The first systematic exposition of the generally accepted doctrine is found in Māwardī's *al-Aḥkām al-sulṭānīya* (ed. R. Enger, Bonn 1853; Cairo 1298, 1327; transl. E. Fagnan, Algiers 1915). Māwardī insists upon the following qualifications in a Khalīfa: — membership of the tribe of Ḳuraish, male sex, full age, good character, freedom from physical or mental defects, competency in legal knowledge, administrative ability, and courage and energy in the defence of Muslim territory. In spite of the fact that the office became hereditary in two families successively, the Umaiyad and the ʿAbbāsid, Māwardī maintained that it was elective, and was at pains to reconcile the doctrine of election with the historic fact that from the reign of Muʿāwiya (661—680) almost every Khalīfa had nominated his successor. The fiction of election was preserved in the practice of *baiʿa*, the taking of the oath of allegiance, first by the nobles of the court and then by the general assembly before whom the new Khalīfa was proclaimed. The functions of the Khalīfa were defined by Māwardī as follows: the defence and maintenance of religion, the decision of legal disputes, the protection of the territory of Islām, the punishment of wrongdoers, the provision of troops for guarding the frontiers, the waging of *djihād* against those who refused to accept Islām or submit to Muslim rule, the organisation and collection of taxes, the payment of salaries and the administration of public funds, the appointment of competent officials, and lastly, personal attention to the details of government. About three centuries later Ibn Khaldūn approached the subject in a more critical spirit and discussed the institution of the Khilāfa in his *Muḳaddima* (chap. 25—8; transl. by de Slane, i. 384—468), written between 1375 and 1379; he faced the facts of history and recognized that with the disappearance of the Arab supremacy there was nothing left of the Khilāfa but the name. His account of the origin and purpose of the institution agrees with that given by Māwardī; the Khalīfa is the representative (*nāʾib*) of the Prophet, the exponent of the divinely-inspired law (*sharīʿa*), and his functions are the protection of religion and the government of the world; he must belong to the tribe of the Ḳuraish, and possess the other personal qualifications laid down by Māwardī. But there were other legists who frankly faced the fact that force had taken the place of theory in the Muslim world, and worked out a constitutional theory accordingly; of such writers Badr al-Dīn Ibn Djamāʿa (d. 733/1333) is a typical example; in his *Taḥrīr al-aḥkām fī tadbīr millat al-Islām* (ed. Kofler, *Islca*, vi. p. 349—414), he lays it down that the *imām* may obtain his office either by election or by force; in the latter case allegiance must be paid to an *imām* who by force of arms seizes the office, and such usurpation is justified in consideration of the general advantage and unity of the Muslim community gained thereby (ibid. 357). Another school of legists abandoned all such attempts to justify the fluctuating course of Muslim history and based their doctrine on the *ḥadīth* that the Khilāfa endured for only thirty years, i. e. up to the death of ʿAlī (*Kanz*, iii., N⁰. 3152); this was the view of al-Nasafī [q. v.] (d. 537/1142; see *al-ʿAḳāʾid*, ed. Cureton, London 1843, p. 4), and it was adopted by the great Turkish jurist, Ibrāhīm Ḥalabī (d. 956/1549), whose *Multaḳa 'l-abḥur* became the authoritative code of Ottoman law.

(*b*) The Shīʿī theologians made the doctrine of the Imāmate a cardinal principle of faith; they laid stress on legitimacy and confined the office of the Khalīfa not merely to the Ḳuraish but still further to the family of ʿAlī; with the exception of the Zaidīya [q. v.], they rejected the doctrine of election, and held that ʿAlī was directly nominated by Muḥammad as his successor and that ʿAlī's qualifications were inherited by his descendants, who were pre-ordained by God for this high office. Muḥammad is said to have communicated to ʿAlī certain secret knowledge, which was in turn handed on to his son and was thus carried on from generation to generation; each *imām* possesses superhuman qualities which raise him above the level of the rest of mankind, and he guides the faithful with infallible wisdom, and his decisions are absolute and final. According to some, ʿAlī owed this superiority to a difference in his substance, for from the creation of Adam a divine light passed into the substance of one chosen descendant in each generation and has been present in ʿAlī and in each one of the *imām*'s that succeeded him. The sectarian development of Shīʿa doctrine was considerable, see the art. ITHNĀ ʿASHARĪYA, ISMĀʿĪLĪYA, SABʿĪYA, ZAIDĪYA. (*Bibliography*: al-Shahrastānī, *Kitāb al-milal wa 'l-niḥal*, p. 108 *sqq.*; Ibn Khaldūn, *Prolégomènes*, i., p. 400 *sqq.*).

(*c*) The antithesis of Shīʿī doctrine was taught by the Khawāridj [see KHĀRIDJITES], who so far from confining the office of Khalīfa or *imām* to one tribe or family, held that any believer was eligible, even though he were a non-Arab or even a slave; they further separated themselves from other Muslims in maintaining that the existence of an *imām* is not a matter of religious obligation and that at any particular time the community can fulfil all the obligations imposed upon them by their religion, and have an entirely legitimate form of civil administration, without any *imām* being in existence at all; when, under special circumstances, it may be found convenient or necessary to have an *imām*, then one may be elected, and if he is found to be in any way unsatisfactory, he may be deposed or put to death (al-Shahrastānī, *op. cit.*, i., p. 85 *sqq.*).

All the above classes of political theory found expression in some form or other of actual political organisation, but there were also statements of the doctrine of the Khilāfa that never emerged out of the sphere of speculation, especially those elaborated by thinkers of the Muʿtazila school e. g. that the office of *imām* should not be filled during periods of civil war but only in times of peace; that no one could be *imām* except with the unanimous consensus of the whole Muslim community (al-Shahrastānī, *op. cit.*, p. 51; Goldziher, *Hellenistischer Einfluss auf muʿtazilitische Chalifatstheorien*, in *Isl.*, vi. 173—7).

Bibliography: The *ḥadīth* can be most conveniently studied in al-Suyūṭī's *Kanz al-ʿummāl*, Haidarābād 1312—1314. Muslim expositions: Māwardī (see above); ʿAḍud al-Dīn al-Īdjī, *al-Mawāḳif fī ʿilm al-kalām* (Constantinople 1239); Ibn Ḥazm, *Kitāb al-faṣl fi 'l-milal wa 'l-ahwāʾ wa 'l-niḥal*, iv. 87 *sqq.*, Cairo 1320; al-Shahrastānī, *Kitāb al-milal wa 'l-niḥal*, ed. W. Cureton, London 1842, 1846; Ibn Khaldūn, *al-Muḳaddima*, ed. Quatremère, Paris 1858; transl. MacGuckin de Slane, Paris 1862—8; ʿAbd al-ʿAzīz Shawīsh, *al-Khilāfatu 'l-islāmīya*, Berlin (?) 1915; Mirza Djevad Khan Kasi, *Das Kalifat nach islamischem Staatsrecht* (*Die Welt des Islams*, v. 189 *sqq.*, 1918); Abu 'l-Kalām, *Khilāfat wa-Djazīrat-i ʿArab*, Calcutta 1920; Muḥammad Rashīd Riḍā, *al-Khilāfa*, Cairo 1923; ʿAlī ʿAbd al-Rāziḳ, *al-Islām wa-uṣūl al-ḥukm*, Cairo 1925. European writers: A. von Kremer, *Geschichte der herrschenden Ideen des Islams*, Leipzig 1868, and *Culturgeschichte des Orients unter den Chalifen*, Vienna 1875—7; J. W. Redhouse, *A vindication of the Ottoman Sultan's title of "Caliph", showing the antiquity, validity, and universal acceptance*, London 1877; Martin Hartmann, *Die islamische Verfassung und Verwaltung* (*Die Kultur der Gegenwart*, Teil II, Abteilung II, 1); C. Snouck Hurgronje, *Verspreide Geschriften*, iii., iv.; C. H. Becker, *Islamstudien*, i.; I. Goldziher, *Muhammedanische Studien*, ii. 55 *sqq.*; W. Barthold, *Khalif i Sultan* (in *Mir Islama*, i. 203 *sqq.*, 345 *sqq.*, St. Petersburg 1912; partly translated in *Der Islam*, vi. 350 *sqq.*, 1915); J. Greenfield, *Kalifat und Imamat* (*Blätter für vergleichende Rechtswissenschaft und Volkswirtschaftslehre*, xi., 1915); Th. W. Juynboll, *Handbuch des islamischen Gesetzes*, Leyden 1910; C. A. Nallino, *Appunti sulla natura del 'Califfato' in genere e sul presunto 'Califfato Ottomano'*, Rome 1917; L. Massignon, *Introduction à l'étude des revendications islamiques* (*RMM*, xxxix. 1 *sqq.*); T. W. Arnold, *The Caliphate*, London 1924; D. Santillana, *Il concetto di Califfato e di sovranità nel diritto musulmano* (*Oriente Moderno*, iv. 339 *sqq.*, 1924); C. Snouck Hurgronje, *Islam and Turkish Nationalism* (*Foreign Affairs*, vol. iii., Nº. 1, p. 61 *sqq.*, New York 1924 = *Verspr. Geschr.* vi. 435—452); *Etudes sur la notion islamique de souveraineté*, in *RMM*, 1925; Henri Laoust, *Le Califat dans la doctrine de Rašīd Riḍā*, Beyrouth 1938.

KHALḲ (A.) is the term applied in the Ḳurʾān (Sūra ii. 164; xl. 57; lxvii. 3) to God's creative activity, which includes not only the original creation *ex nihilo* but also the making of the world and of man and all that is and happens. The verbal forms *khalaḳa* and *khalaḳnā* are of the most frequent occurrence.

Among the most beautiful names of Allāh in the Ḳurʾān (cf. Sūra lix. 24) are *al-khāliḳ* (Sūra vi. 102, et passim), *al-khallāḳ* (Sūra xv. 86; xxxvi. 81), *al-bāriʾ* (besides Sūra lix. 24 only ii. 54) and *al-muṣawwir*. Epithets like the Almighty, the All-knowing etc. are also applied to the Creator. Their meaning is as a rule clear. The only obscure expressions are (cf. H. Grimme, *Mohammed*, ii. 44, 47) "Allāh created *bi 'l-ḥaḳḳ*" (Sūra xvi. 3; xxxix. 2, 5; xliv. 39; xlvi. 3) or as "*al-Ḥaḳḳ*" (Sūra xxii. 5 *sq.*). If we are justified in supposing gnostic speculations in the Ḳurʾān it may be recalled that in the Gnosis objectified or personified truth coalesces with higher reality (cf. St. John's Gospel, xiv. 6; also S. v. d. Bergh, *Die Epitome der Metaphysik des Averroes*, p. 218 *sq.*).

Allāh is the Creator of all things (Sūra vi. 101 *sq.*, et passim). He creates what He will (Sūra xxxvi. 82, et passim) but the Ḳurʾān describes at greatest length the creation of man from dust, earth or clay, drops of semen and congealed blood (Sūra xxii. 5; xxiii. 14 *sq.*, et passim) and the resurrection of the dead on the day of judgment, a new creation not more wonderful than the first creation (Sūra ii. 28, et passim). How important the creation of man is, is evident from Muḥammad's coming forward (in Sūra xcvi. 1, generally regarded as the earliest revelation) in the name of his Lord "Who created, created man from congealed blood". Everything on earth was created for man (Sūra ii. 29, et passim), especially the animals (Sūra xvi. 5). The same thing is shown in the stages of the creation; it is regarded as taking place from the lowest upwards. In six days the world was completed, the earth first in two days, all that is in it in two more days and in the last two days the world of the seven heavens. Allāh is only formally called the Creator of heaven and earth (Sūra vi. 101, et passim) and it is announced as a secret (Sūra xl. 57) that the creation of heaven and earth is greater than the creation of man, i. e., according to the usual explanation, heaven and earth were created out of absolutely nothing but man was made from dust.

There is no creator but God. He is the One (Sūra xiii. 16, et passim; Sūra xxiii. 14 is no exception). He has begotten no children, only created things and beings, none of whom are like Him (Sūra cxii.). But passages like Sūra xv. 29, xxxviii. 72, where it is said that Allāh, after forming man, breathed of His spirit (*rūḥ*) into him, make the difference between the Creator and creature appear less rigidly marked.

The creation of man is above all a mark of divine power or, in so far as that which has been created is useful to man, of divine goodness. Reference to the harmony of the heavens (Sūra lxvii. 3) and the beauty of the human form (Sūra lxiv. 3) are rare. Finally we may mention that God created all things after one *ḳadar* (Sūra liv. 49 *sq.*; *ḳadar* is here perhaps a synonym for *amr*?) and heaven and earth "for a definite period" (Sūra xlvi. 3) i. e. probably to the last day.

The earlier traditions added very little to this. Before the creation Allāh was in the clouds (al-Tirmidhī, *Tafsīr*, Sūra xi., bāb 1) and He created in darkness (do., *Īmān*, bāb 18; cf. Sūra xxxix. 6). He wrote a *kitāb* before the creation (al-Bukhārī, *Tawḥīd*, bāb 55). The *ḳalam* was the first thing created (al-Tirmidhī, *Ḳadar*, bāb 17). Allāh created man after his own image (Muslim, *Birr*, trad. 115; cf. Sūra lxiv. 3; lxxxii. 8).

In the later traditions the process of creation is elaborated with speculations regarding God's throne, primeval water etc. and influenced by ideas of Hellenistic and Oriental origin regarding the manifestation or emanation of God in the world. The Neoplatonic expression put in Allāh's mouth is often quoted: "I was a hidden treasure but wished to be known and therefore I created the world". Knowledge (*ʿilm*) or intelligence (*ʿaḳl*) is therefore said to have been the first creation.

Just as God's superiority over man and the world is particularly apparent from the Ḳurʾān, so we find throughout the theology of Sunnī Islām the distance between the Creator and the creature emphasised. In general it is concluded from the transitory character of this world that its Creator is eternal. To emphasize of God's omnipotence causality in Nature (cf. *Atomic Theory*, in Hastings' *Encyclopaedia of Religions and Ethics*) and freedom of action on the part of man, if not absolutely denied, are suppressed as much as possible. Djahm, one of the first Djabrīs [cf. DJABRĪYA], wished to define God simply as the omnipotent Creator. Ibn Ḥazm (*Kitāb al-faṣl*, i. 39; ii. 161 *sq.*) asserts that one can only show with regard to God that He is the Eternal, the Unique, the True, the Creator (*al-awwal, al-wāḥid, al-ḥaḳḳ, al-khāliḳ*), for only by these qualities is He absolutely distinguished from this world.

But misgivings against this sharp distinction were raised, particularly under the influence of Christian dogmatics and philosophical speculation, from three sides i. e. by the Muʿtazilīs, the mystics and the philosophers. The Muʿtazilīs emphasised the wisdom of God in His creation much more than His omnipotence and His will. According to their teaching, God only creates what is good and man is the creator of his own actions. Naẓẓām said that God could only create what is good and His creating is thought i. e. not an act of volition in the proper sense. According to others, like Abu 'l-Hudhail and Muʿammar, God's will is a kind of intermediary between the Creator and the created world. Al-Djāḥiẓ teaches that God cannot destroy the created world (arguing on Platonic lines, like Philo etc.).

In contrast to this estimation of the world and of human activity, mysticism appears as a depreciation of all that is worldly — but only of the material world. While the mystics regarded this world simply as a ladder to God, they could intensify their spiritual life of the soul up to the feeling of godlike creative activity (cf. L. Massignon, *La Passion d'al-Hallāj*, p. 513 *sq.*).

Two schools may be distinguished among the philosophers: one older, more neo-Platonic (e. g. the *ikhwān al-ṣafā'*), according to which the emanation of a series of spirits precedes the creation of a temporal material world, and a second, more Aristotelian school (notably Ibn Sīnā and Ibn Rushd) which makes the development of the intellectual and material world proceed by stages, but without beginning and parallel, after the first *ʿaḳl* has emanated from the divine being. Both schools regard God only as the first cause between Whose activity and this world there are many intermediaries.

The attitude of orthodox Islām to these tendencies developed in very different ways in course of time. The Muʿtazilī doctrine of the *khalḳ al-afʿāl* could only be accepted in a modified form; a *kasb* (Ashʿarīs) or an *ikhtiyār* (according to al-Māturīdī) was ascribed to man instead of *khalḳ*. The philosophic assumption of a world without beginning was decisively rejected, but the theory of the spheres connected with it was adopted while the spirits of the stars were interpreted as angels of heaven. It was very easy to make common cause with mysticism, which, of course, always insisted that there was no creator except Allāh. The creation of man in God's image and the breathing of the divine spirit into him were of more importance to the mystic than the creation of the physical world and of human activities [see the art. ḲAḌĀ' and ḲADAR] (cf. Massignon, *op. cit.*, p. 599 *sqq.*).

In the struggle then against the Muʿtazila and philosophy, the Sunnī doctrine developed — in part in alliance with mysticism — and with the greatest success in the Ashʿarī school. According to the latter, Allāh is the Omnipotent from eternity, Who can create if and when and what He will but does not need to create, Who with the creation of the material world at the same time places limits of time and space to it and every moment creates the world anew. Allāh is also the eternally Speaking as regards the word of creation, especially the word of creation in the Ḳur'ān. If the eternalness of the word is taught contrary to the Muʿtazilī view, there is hesitation, as regards the activity of creation, in calling God the eternally creating, and therefore, the so-called *ṣifāt al-fiʿl* (*khalḳ, razḳ*, etc.), which are regarded as temporal relations, are distinguished from the eternal qualities of His nature. In this respect the system of al-Māturīdī differs from the teaching of the Ashʿarī school: he assumes as an eternal quality in the divine being *takwīn*, creative production. This means an approximation to the teaching of the philosophers that, because there is no cause without effect, God as the first cause created the world from eternity, and thus is really an eternal Creator, Whose being and actions are alike unalterable. Some philosophers and certainly many mystics got over the difficulty of this doctrine by the assumption that before the manifestation of His creation "the eternal Creator" was concealed in God (cf. Massignon, *op. cit.*, p. 657).

We find the bond between orthodox Ashʿarī beliefs and gnostic-mystic speculation in al-Ghazzālī. On the one hand he teaches quite definitely the temporal creation of the world as an act of divine freedom. After eternal but free deliberation out of pure goodness He created this world and He is creating it down to the last day. He is also the originator of human activities; man has only a *kasb*. On the other hand, however, al-Ghazzālī is fond of adopting mystic theories of intermediation. God and man are not simply to one another in the relation of Creator and creature. The world is divided (e.g. in *al-Maḍnūn al-ṣaghīr*, on Sūra xvii. 85; cf. Sūra vii. 74) into the *ʿālam al-khalḳ*, i.e. the material spatial world, and the *ʿālam al-amr*, the non-spatial world of the angels and the human spirits (the former in the *Iḥyā'*, iv. 20 *sqq.*, is also called *ʿālam al-mulk wa 'l-shahāda*, the latter *ʿālam al-ghair wa 'l-malakūt*). As a member of the world of spirits (*al-Maḍnūn al-ṣaghīr*, on the tradition that Allāh or *al-Raḥmān* created Adam in his own image), man in his being, qualities and actions shows similarity to God. The human will acts in his body (microcosm) like the Creator in the macrocosm. Besides the above-mentioned division into sensible and supersensual world, al-Ghazzālī also gives the threefold division (*al-Durra al-fākhira*, p. 2 *sqq.*; cf. Sūra v. 17 etc., where there is mention of the "kingdom of the heavens and of the earth and what is between"): *ʿālam dunyawī* (= *al-mulk*), *ʿālam malakūtī* and *ʿālam djabarūtī* [cf. DJABARŪT]. Man thus appears as a citizen of three worlds, corresponding to the old triad: body, soul, spirit, as it was developed by gnosticism in the system of the heavenly hierachy. On *mulk, malakūt* and *djabarūt* cf. κυριότητες, ἀρχαί, ἐξουσίαι in St. Paul, Ep. to Col., i. 16. According to al-Ghazzālī, the human spirit, related to God, will survive not only this material world and the spiritual world of the angels and *djinn* but also the spiritual world of the highest angels.

In spite of the authority of this "father of the church in Islām", the development of the idea was not yet finished. Ibn Rushd then advanced against him (*Tahāfut al-tahāfut*) the doctrine that the world had no beginning; many theologians (from al-Rāzī [d. 605/1209] onwards) followed more closely the conceptions of the so-called Aristotelians, and extreme mystics, like Ibn al-ʿArabī, let the distinction between *al-ḥaḳḳ* (the Creator) and *al-khalḳ* (the creature) disappear in the absolute primeval being [cf. AL-INSĀN AL KĀMIL]. In conclusion, stressing the differences, we can say: four answers are given to the problem of creation. God created the world by His powerful will, says the traditionalist; by His good wisdom, the Muʿtazilite; by His overflowing love, the mystic; by an intellectual act, the philosopher (cf. Tj. de Boer, *The Moslem Doctrines of Creation*, in *Proceed. of the 6th Internat. Congr. of Philosophy*, New York 1927, p. 597 *sqq*.).

Bibliography: Besides books mentioned in the text: M. Worms, *Die Lehre von der Anfangslosigkeit der Welt bei den mittelalterlichen arabischen Philosophen des Orients und ihre Bekämpfung durch die arabischen Theologen* (*Beitr. z. Gesch. der Philos. des Mittelalters*, iii. 4); A. Rohner, *Das Schöpfungsproblem bei Moses Maimonides, Albertus Magnus und Thomas von Aquin*, ibid., xi. 5, Münster 1913; Tj. de Boer, *Die Widersprüche der Philosophie nach al-Gazzālī und ihr Ausgleich durch Ibn Rošd*, Strassburg 1894; do., *De Wijsbegeerte in den Islam*, Haarlem 1921; A. J. Wensinck, *The Muslim Creed*, Index s.v. *Creation*. — See also the articles ALLĀH and ṢIFA.

KHAMR (A.), wine. The word, although very common in early Arabic poetry, is probably a loanword from Aramaic. The Hebrew *yain* has in Arabic (*wain*) the meaning of black grapes. The question has been fully treated by I. Guidi in his *Della sede primitiva dei popoli semitici*, in *Memorie della R. Acad. dei Lincei*, series iii., vol. iii., p. 603 *sqq.*

In the days of Muḥammad the people of Mekka and Madīna used to indulge in drinking wine as often as an occasion offered itself, so that drunkenness often became a cause of scandal and of indulgence in a second vice, gambling, which together with wine, incurred Muḥammad's condemnation. Tradition has not refrained from describing how Ḥamza b. ʿAbd al-Muṭṭalib, Muḥammad's uncle, in a fit of drunkenness mutilated ʿAlī's camels. And the commentaries on the Ḳurʾān relate how Muḥammad's companions held drinking-parties which caused them to commit faults in ritual prayer (see al-Ṭabarī, *Tafsīr* ad Sūra xiv. 43; Muslim, *Faḍāʾil al-ṣaḥāba*, trad. 44, cf. 45; Aḥmad b. Ḥanbal, i. 185 *sq.*).

The prohibition of wine was not on Muḥammad's programme from the beginning. In Sūra xvi. 67 we even find it praised as one of the signs of Allāh's grace unto mankind: "And of the fruit of palmtrees, and of grapes, ye obtain an inebriating liquor, and also good nourishment". But the consequences of drunkenness manifesting themselves in the way just mentioned are said to have commoved Muḥammad to change his attitude. The first revelation giving vent to these feelings was Sūra ii. 219: "They will ask thee concerning wine and gambling (*maisir*). Answer, in both there is great sin and also some things of use unto men: but their sinfulness is greater than their use". This revelation, however, was not considered as a prohibition. As people did not change their customs and the order of prayer happened to be disturbed in consequence thereof, a new revelation was issued, viz. Sūra iv. 43: "O true believers! come not to prayers when ye are drunk, until ye understand what ye say" etc. But neither was this revelation considered as a general prohibition of wine, until Sūra v. 90 made an end to drinking: "O true believers! surely wine and *maisir* and stone pillars and divining arrows are an abomination, of the work of Satan; therefore avoid them, that ye may prosper".

This sequence of revelations regarding wine is the accepted one among the traditionists and commentators of the Ḳurʾān (see Aḥmad b. Ḥanbal, *Musnad*, ii. 351 *sq.*; Ṭabarī, *Tafsīr*, v. 58 ad Sūra iv. 43).

The prohibition of wine may, however, also be looked upon from a wider aspect, as Islām is not the only monotheistic religion which has taken a negative attitude towards wine. It is well known that, according to the Old Testament (Numbers vi. 3 *sq.*), the Nazarite who had wholly devoted himself to Yahwe, had to abstain from wine and spirits, just as the priests before administering the sacred rites (Lev. x. 9). The Nabataeans, according to Diodorus Siculus (xix. 94, 3), likewise abstained from wine, and one of their gods is called in their inscriptions "the good god who drinks no wine". Likewise, the abstention from wine belonged to the rule of many Christian monks.

The prohibition of the Ḳurʾān has been taken over by the doctors of the law; all *madhhab*'s, and also the Shīʿa, call wine *ḥarām* and the wine-trade is forbidden. For an exposition of the Shāfiʿī view, see al-Nawawī, *Minhādj*, ed. v. d. Berg. iii. 241; for that of the Ḥanafīs, *Fātāwā ʿĀlamgīrī*, vi. (Calcutta 1835), 604 *sqq.*; for that of the Mālikīs, Zurḳānī in his commentary on the *Muwaṭṭaʾ* (Cairo 1280), iv. 26; for that of the Shīʿa, al-Ḥillī, *Sharāʾiʿ al-Islām* (Calcutta 1839), p. 404. Theology reckons the drinking of wine among the gravest sins (*kabāʾir*).

Ḥadīth has many utterances regarding this theme. Wine is the key of all evil (Aḥmad b. Ḥanbal, *Musnad*, v. 238; Ibn Mādja, *Ashriba*, bāb 1). Who drinks wine in this world without repenting it, shall not drink it in the other world (Bukhārī, *Ashriba*, bāb 1; Muslim, *Ashriba*, trad. 73, 76—78 etc.). Cursed is he who drinks, buys, sells wine or causes others to drink it (Abū Dāwūd, *Ashriba*, bāb 2; Ibn Mādja, *Ashriba*, bāb 6; Aḥmad b. Ḥanbal, i. 316; ii. 25, 69, 71, 97, 128 etc.). Who drinks a draught of wine on purpose shall have to drink pus on Doomsday (Ṭayālisī, No. 1134). Prayer of him who drinks wine is not accepted by Allāh (Nasāʾī, *Ashriba*, bāb 43; Dārimī, *Ashriba*, bāb 3), and faith is incompatible with drinking it (Bukhārī, *Ashriba*, bāb 1; Nasāʾī, *Ashriba*, bāb 42, 44). It is even inadvisable to use it as medicine (Muslim, *Ashriba*, trad. 12; Aḥmad b. Ḥanbal, iv. 311, 317 bis etc.); and it is prohibited to use wine for manufacturing vinegar (Tirmidhī, *Buyūʿ*, bāb 59; Aḥmad b. Ḥanbal, iii. 119, 260 bis). But times will become ever worse and there will be people who declare wine allowed (Bukhārī, *Ashriba*, bāb 6; Nasāʾī, *Ashriba*, bāb 41 etc.) and so it will be drunk by the generation of the last days (Bukhārī, *Ashriba*, bāb 1; Aḥmad b. Ḥanbal, iii. 176, 202, 213 *sq.*).

The prohibition of wine, although unanimously accepted, gave rise to dissensions between the juridical schools, dissensions which are reflected in ḥadīth, in a historical disguise. The discussions start from the question: what is wine? Anas b. Mālik (Bukhārī, *Ashriba*, bāb 2) says that there was scarcely any wine from grapes in Madīna, when the prohibition was revealed; people used wine from *busr* and *tamr* (two kinds of dates). In another tradition (*ib.*, bāb 3) wine from *faḍīkh* and *zahw* (two other kinds of dates) is mentioned. ʿUmar is represented delivering a *khuṭba* which was meant to settle the question; according to his son ʿAbd Allāh he said: Wine has been prohibited by the Ḳurʾān; it comes from five kinds of fruits: from grapes, from dates, from honey, from wheat and from barley; wine is what obscures the intellect (*wa 'l-khamr mā khāmara al-ʿaḳl*; Bukhārī, *Ashriba*, bāb 2). The question remained, whether beverages prepared from grapes in a different way were prohibited. There was e.g. a kind of syrup. "When ʿUmar visited Syria, the population complained of its unhealthy and heavy climate and they added: This drink alone will heal us. Then ʿUmar allowed them to drink honey. Then they said: Honey cannot heal us. Thereupon one of the natives of Syria said to him: May we not prepare something of this drink for you? It has no inebriating power. He said: Well. Then they cooked it till two thirds were evaporated and one third of it remained. They brought it ʿUmar, who put his finger into it and licked it. Then he said: This is *ṭilāʾ* like camels' *ṭilāʾ* (viz. the pitch with which they smeared their skins). Then he allowed them to drink it" (Mālik, *Ashriba*, bāb 14). According to the first chapter of the same *kitāb*, however, ʿUmar punished a man who had become drunk on *ṭilāʾ*. Juice from grapes, prepared by pressing them only, is considered as wine. Ṭāriḳ b. Suwaid al-Ḥaḍramī said to the Prophet: We have in our country grapes which we press. May we drink the juice? He said: No. This negative answer is given three times and when Ṭāriḳ asks whether the juice may be given the sick to drink, Muḥammad answers: It is no medicine, it is sickness (Aḥmad b. Ḥanbal, v. 292 *sq.*). And not only those who drink and sell wine are cursed by Muḥammad, but also those who press grapes and have them pressed in order to drink the juice (Ibn Mādja, *Ashriba*, bāb 6).

Another question of importance arose in connection with spirits: Had they to be considered as wine or not? All the *madhhab*'s, except the Ḥanafīs, have answered the question in the affirmative sense. They have consequently extended the prohibition of wine, in accordance with the intention underlying it. Tradition, which is the best source for the history of the origin of several institutions, shows that the question belongs to the much debated ones. The standard ḥadīth which is found very frequently in the classical collections runs as follows (I pick out Muslim's version, *Īmān*, trad. 26, because it contains important details): "Some men of ʿAbd al-Ḳais went to the Apostle of Allāh and said to him: O Prophet of Allāh, we are a tribe belonging to Rabīʿa; between us and yourself dwell the infidels of Muḍar, so that we can only reach you in the sacred month. Tell us therefore what we have to tell our tribespeople which will open Paradise for us if we cling to it. The Apostle of Allāh answered: I order four things and I forbid four things. Serve Allāh without associating anything with him. Perform *ṣalāt*, deliver *zakāt*, fast the month of Ramaḍān and deliver the fifth part of booty. And I forbid four things: *dubbāʾ*, *ḥantam*, *muzaffat* and *naḳīr*. They asked: O Apostle of Allāh, how do you know what the *naḳīr* is? He said: Well, it is a palmtrunk which you hollow out; then you pour small dates into it and upon them water. When the process of fermentation has finished, you drink it with the effect that a man hits his cousin with the sword. — Now among these men there was someone who had received a blow of the sword in this way. He says: I had concealed it out of shame before the Apostle of Allāh. Then I said: But from what vessels should we drink then, O Apostle of Allāh? He answered: From leather skins, the mouthpieces of which are smeared with pitch. They answered: O Prophet of Allāh, our country teems with mice so that no single skin can be kept whole. Then the Prophet of Allāh answered: Even though the mice should eat them, even though the mice should eat them, even though the mice should eat them".

This tradition did not meet with general approval. It is said that the Anṣār or other people complained of their difficulty in finding the skins necessary for preserving drinks without their becoming fermented. Thereupon the Prophet is said to have withdrawn his prohibition, wholly or partly (Bukhārī, *Ashriba*, bāb 8; Muslim, *Ashriba*, trad. 63-66 etc.) In some versions of this tradition there occurs the restriction, that all fermented inebriating drinks remain prohibited. Innumerable are the traditions which only contain the rule: All drinks which may cause drunkenness are prohibited in any quantity (*kull muskir ḥarām kathīruhu wa-ḳalīluhu*) and this rule has passed into many books of fiḳh (Bukhārī, *Maghāzī*, bāb 60; Muslim, *Ashriba*, trad. 67—75; Aḥmad b. Ḥanbal, i. 145; ii. 16 bis; iii. 38; iv. 87; v. 25 *sq.*; vi. 36 etc.). Of special traditions prohibiting fermented drinks may be mentioned the following. It is forbidden or disapproved of to sell raisins if they are to be used for preparing *nabīdh* (Nasāʾī, *Ashriba*, bāb 51, 52). It is prohibited to mix together different kinds of fruits so that the mixture should become intoxicating. This tradition occurs frequently.

It can easily be seen that the difficulty in this matter was caused by two circumstances. People were accustomed to prepare from all kinds of dates, from raisins and other fruits, drinks which only became inebriating if they were preserved a long time and probably also if they were prepared after special methods. Where was the line of demarcation between the allowed and the prohibited kind? Several collections of traditions went so far as to mention *nabīdh* among the drinks prepared by Muḥammad's wives and drunk by him. Abū Dāwūd (*Ashriba*, bāb 10) and Ibn Mādja (*Ashriba*, bāb 12) have preserved a tradition on this subject which is instructive. I translate Ibn Mādja's version: Says ʿĀʾisha: "We used to prepare *nabīdh* for the Apostle of Allāh in a skin; we took a handful of dates or a handful of raisins, cast it into the skin and poured water upon it. The *nabīdh* we prepared in this way in the morning, was drunk by him in the evening; and when we prepared it in the evening he drank it the next morning". In another tradition of the same bāb Ibn ʿAbbās says that the Prophet used to drink this *nabīdh* even on the third day; but what was left then, was poured out.

All this could, however, not persuade the majority of the *faḳīh*'s to declare *nabīdh* allowed; three of the *madhhab*'s as well as the Shīʿa prohibit the use of *nabīdh*. The Ḥanafī school, on the other hand, allows it, when used with moderation, for medicinal purposes etc.

Allowed according to the *idjmāʿ* is every non-fermented, sweet drink.

Prohibited (*ḥarām*), according to the *idjmāʿ*, are wine and *sakar* of every kind. As to wine there are six cases: to drink it in any quantity or to make use of it is *ḥarām*; to deny this is *kufr*; to buy, sell, present it etc. is *ḥarām*; no responsibility (*ḍamān*) rests on him who spoils or destroys wine (*mutlifhā*); whether wine is a possession (*māl*) is an unsettled point; it is *nadjis* just as blood and urine; who drinks any quantity of it is liable to punishment.

Several kinds of products prepared by means of grapes (*bādhiḳ*, *munaṣṣaf*, etc.) are prohibited according to the majority (*ʿāmma*) of the *faḳīh*'s.

Allowed, according to the majority of the *faḳīh*'s, are *ṭilāʾ* [vide supra] or *muthallath* and *nabīdh* from dates with the restrictions mentioned above. So is juice from grapes when the process of cooking has made two thirds to evaporate. Muḥammad al-Shaibānī [q.v.] has a deviating opinion on this point.

As to the punishment of him who drinks wine, ḥadīth tells us that Muḥammad and Abū Bakr were wont to inflict forty blows by means of palmbranches or sandals (Bukhārī, *Ḥudūd*, bāb 2—4; Muslim, *Ḥudūd*, trad. 35—37). Under ʿUmar's caliphate, however, Khālid b. al-Walīd reported to him that people were indulging in prohibited drinks. Thereupon ʿUmar consulted the *ṣaḥāba* who advised him to fix the number of blows at eighty, a number suggested by the Ḳurʾān which prescribes that those who accuse *muḥṣanāt* of *zināʾ*, without being able to prove their accusation by the aid of four witnesses, shall be punished with eighty blows (Sūra xxiv. 4).

The different *madhhab*'s have adopted ʿUmar's view; drinking wine is punished with eighty blows; if the transgressor is a slave this number is however reduced to forty, because in the Ḳurʾān the punishment of the handmaid's *zināʾ* is fixed at half the amount of blows with which the free woman is punished (Sūra iv. 35). The Shāfiʿites however cling to the practice ascribed to Muḥammad and Abū Bakr; with them the number of blows is consequently forty, resp. twenty (see Zurḳānī, iv. 42; Nawawī on Muslim, iv. 156).

The prohibition of wine and (according to three of the four *madhhab*'s) spirits is one of the distinctive marks of the Muslim world; its consequences can hardly be overrated. This is not seriously affected by the fact that transgressors have been numerous, according to literary evidence. The praise of wine, not uncommon in pre-Islāmic poetry, remained one of the favourite topics also of Muslim poets (cf. the wine-songs by Ibn al-Muʿtazz, Abū Nuwās etc.) and at the court of the Caliphs wine was drunk at revelling parties as if no prohibition existed at all (see e.g. The 1001 Nights, *passim*). Even the common people could not always and everywhere refrain from their national drink, datewine of several kinds; the caliph ʿUmar b. ʿAbd al-ʿAzīz deemed it necessary to promulgate a special edict in order to abolish this custom (see v. Kremer, *Culturgeschichtliche Streifzüge*, Leipzig 1873, p. 68 *sq.*).

Wine has a special place in the literary products of the mystics, where it is one of the symbols of ecstasy. In this point they only took over the language of their Christian and non-Christian predecessors. As early as Philo of Alexandria ecstasy is compared with intoxication (see especially his *De Vita Contemplativa*). Among the Ibāḥīya, language may have been a reflex of practice; but this cannot be said of Ṣūfī's in general, who, on the contrary, clung to the ascetic methods of the via purgativa. As to Ḥāfiẓ' wine- and love-songs, it is an unsettled point whether they are merely metaphorical or not.

Bibliography: Freytag, *Einleitung in das Studium der arabischen Sprache* (Bonn 1861), p. 272 *sq.*; G. Jacob, *Studien in vorislamischen Dichtern*, iii., 2nd ed., Berlin 1897, p. 96 *sqq.*; A. v. Kremer, *Culturgeschichte des Orients*, Vienna 1875—1877, i. 149; ii. 204 *sqq.*; A. Mez, *Die Renaissance des Islams*, Heidelberg 1922, index; I. Goldziher, *Muhammedanische Studien*, i. 19—33; do., in *ZDMG*, xii. (1887), 40, 95 *sq.*; do., *Muh. Recht in Theorie und Wirklichkeit*, in *Zeitschr. f. vergl. Rechtswiss.*, viii. (1889), 408; Nöldeke-Schwally, *Geschichte des Qorāns*, i. 182, 3; 199, note 1, 3; Snouck Hurgronje, *Verspreide Geschriften*, gen. index, s.v. WIJN; Th. W. Juynboll, *Handbuch des isl. Gesetzes*, p. 178 *sqq.*, 304; 3rd ed., in Dutch, p. 172 *sq.*, 308.

KHARĀDJ (A.). The word kharādj, in contradiction to earlier views (see P. Schwarz, *Die Herkunft von arabisch ḫarāǧ, Grundsteuer*, in *Isl.* vi, 97 *sqq.*), is derived, through the Persian, from Aramaic *halāk* as used in the Persian empire (cf. Henning, in *Orientalia* iv, 291 *sqq.*). It originally meant the tribute in a general sense (just as did *djizya*) to which unbelievers in Muslim lands were liable. In the later *fiḳh*-works the word kharādj sometimes still has this general meaning (see e.g. *Fatḥ al-ḳarīb*, ed. van den Berg, p. 620). But by the first century A.H. kharādj — probably because it was taken to be an original Arabic word in the sense of "yield of the fields" — came to mean particularly the tax paid on landed property as opposed to the *djizya*, which was now used exclusively in the sense of "poll-tax".

When at the time of the great conquests the inhabitants of the newly acquired territory were left in undisturbed possession of their fields, it was, however, ordained that the soil should be liable to taxation. Henceforth the inhabitants were to pay a definite part of the harvest as a tribute to the Muslim treasury and remained bound to pay this kharādj for all time, even if they became converts to Islām [see the art. FAIʾ].

They had been previously accustomed to a tax of this kind in these regions under Byzantine and Persian rule and the old methods of administering it were retained by the Arabs in many details. The tribute was paid mainly in kind. Definite contributions of corn or other foodstuffs were levied on villages or in some cases on districts. The Muslim officials turned these into money. Very considerable revenues reached the Muslim treasury in this way, especially in the first century A.H.

At the beginning of the ʿAbbāsid period we find different scholars (e.g. Abū Yūsuf, al-Khaṣṣāf and Yaḥyā b. Ādam) still endeavouring to collect the traditions and legal enactments on the kharādj and arranging them in special chapters in their books. The regulations regarding the collection of the kharādj in these days were still a very important subject. But after the peoples of the conquered territories had generally adopted Islām they began gradually to drop payment of the kharādj. It was thought that with the payment of the tithe of the yield of one's fields [see ʿUSHR] enough had been done and the kharādj in the end fell everywhere into desuetude. In the later *fiḳh*-books we therefore only find the regulations regarding the poll-tax still given in detail, while those for the kharādj are only dealt with cursorily or even not at all. Only in al-Māwardī's special work on the Muslim system of administration do we find the regulations for the kharādj still dealt with in considerable detail.

Bibliography: In addition to works mentioned in the article FAIʾ see: A. von Kremer, *Culturgeschichte des Orients*, i. 75 *sqq.*, 175 *sqq.*; M. van Berchem, *La propriété territoriale et l'impôt foncier, étude sur l'impôt du kharâǵ*, Diss. Leipzig 1886; J. Wellhausen, *Das arabische Reich und sein Sturz*, Berlin 1902, p. 18 *sqq.*, 168 *sqq.*; C. H. Becker, *Beiträge z. Gesch. Agyptens*, ii. 83 *sqq.*, 124 *sqq.*; do., *Die Entstehung von ʿUšr- und Ḫarāǧ-Land in Ägypten*, in *ZA*, 1904/1905, xviii. 301—319; do., *Papyri Schott-Reinhardt*, i., Heidelberg 1906, p. 37 *sqq.*; E. Fagnan, *Abou Yousof Yaʿkoub, Le livre de l'impôt foncier*, Paris 1921; Fr. Løkkegaard, *Islamic Taxation in the classic Period*, Copenhagen 1950.

AL-**KHARGŪSHĪ**, ABŪ SAʿD (or Saʿīd) ʿABD AL-MALIK B. MUḤAMMAD, a celebrated preacher (and therefore nicknamed al-Wāʿiẓ) and ascetic, was born in the Khargūsh street of Nīshāpūr: the arabicized form of his name is al-Kharkūshī. He went to Baghdād in the year 393/1002 on his way to perform the pilgrimage, and thereafter resided at Mecca for a while, returning to Nīshāpūr to die there in 406/1015 or 407/1016. Three works are ascribed to him (Brockelmann, *GAL*², i. 218, *Suppl.* i. 361). The first is a biography of Muḥammad, or rather a classified collection of traditions relating to him, in 8 volumes, variously entitled *Sharaf al-Nabī* (*al-Muṣṭafā, al-nubuwwa*) or *Dalāʾil al-nubuwwa*; a Persian translation of this, by Maḥmūd b. Muḥammad al-Rāwandī, is extant (Storey, *Persian Literature*, p. 175—6). The second is a treatise on oneiromancy entitled *al-Bishāra wa 'l-nidhāra fī taʿbīr al-ruʾyā*, a pietistic compilation. The third, and most important work, is a systematic account of Ṣūfism in 70 chapters, *Tahdhīb al-asrār*, which has survived in a single manuscript (Berlin, No. 2819). This last work derives not directly from al-Khargūshī himself, but from the recital of Abū ʿAbd Allāh al-Shīrāzī, a notorious charlatan who led a rising against the governor of Ādharbāidjān and died in 439/1047. For this and other reasons the value of the book cannot be rated very high, and it has been shown (cf. A. J. Arberry in *BSOS*, 1938, p. 345—9) that it is not entirely original, but plagiarizes to a considerable extent the *Kitāb al-lumaʿ* of Abū Naṣr al-Sarrādj. Nevertheless it contains material for the history of Ṣūfism not extant elsewhere, and cannot therefore be entirely disregarded.

KHĀRIDJITES (A., *Khawāridj*, sing. *Khāridjī*), the members of the earliest of the religious sects of Islām, whose importance lies particularly, from the point of view of the development of dogma, in the formulation of questions relative to the theory of the Caliphate and to justification by faith or by works, while from the point of view of political history the principal part they played was disturbing by means of continual insurrections, which often ended in the temporary conquest of entire provinces, the peace of the eastern part of the Muslim empire during the last two years of the Caliphate of ʿAlī and during the Umaiyad period, and involuntarily facilitating first Muʿāwiya's victory over ʿAlī, then that of the ʿAbbāsids over the Umaiyads.

I. The Origins of the Khāridjī movement.

The occasion for the schism was given by the proposal presented to ʿAlī by Muʿāwiya during the battle of Ṣiffīn (Ṣafar, 37 / July, 657; cf. the art. ʿALĪ) to settle the differences arising out of the murder of ʿUthmān, which had provoked the war, by referring it to two arbitrators who would pronounce judgment "according to the Ḳurʾān". While the majority of ʿAlī's army readily adopted this proposal, either because they were tired of war or because the *ḳurrāʾ* or "Ḳurʾān-readers" hoped there would emerge from this Ḳurʾānic judgment the justification of the furious campaign they had conducted against ʿUthmān which had ended in the latter's assassination, one group of warriors, mainly of the tribe of Tamīm, vigorously protested against the setting up of a human tribunal above the divine word. Loudly protesting that "judgment belongs to God alone" ("*lā ḥukma illā li-llāhi*") they left the army, and withdrawing to the village of Ḥarūrāʾ, not far from Kūfa, they elected as their chief an obscure soldier, ʿAbd Allāh b. Wahb al-Rāsibī [q.v.]. These first dissenters took the name *al-Ḥarūrīya* or *al-Muḥakkima* (i.e. those who repeat the above phrase; cf. *RSO*, viii. 789, note 1), which is often applied by an extension of meaning to the later Khawāridj also. This little group gradually increased on account of successive defections, especially when the arbitration ended in a verdict quite contrary to what the *ḳurrāʾ* expected (probably in Ramaḍān or Shawwāl, 37 / Febr.—March, 658); on this occasion a large number of partisans of ʿAlī, including a number of *ḳurrāʾ* "went out" (*kharadja*) secretly from Kūfa (to which the army had gone during the truce) to join the camp of Ibn Wahb, who in the meantime had gone to the Djūkhā country on the left bank of the Tigris, to a place which commanded the exits of the roads from Fārs and the bridge-head, at which in those days stood the little village of Baghdādh, which later was to become the capital of the empire. The rebel camp lay along the Nahrawān canal. It is to this episode of the exodus from Kūfa that the sect of the Khawāridj owes its name ("those who went out"), more probably than to a general epithet describing them as having gone out of the community of the faithful, as it was later interpreted, probably at quite an early period. Another name given to those first Khawāridj (which has also been extended to their successors and seems to be the one which they gave themselves) is *al-Shurāt* (plural of *Shārī*), the "vendors" i.e. those who have sold their soul for the cause of God (this idea is found in several contemporary verses).

The tense fanaticism of the Khawāridj at once manifested itself in a series of extremist proclamations and terrorist actions: they proclaimed the nullity of ʿAlī's claims to the Caliphate but equally condemned ʿUthmān's conduct and disclaimed any intention of avenging his murder; they went farther and began to brand everyone infidel and outside the law who did not accept their point of view and disown ʿAlī as well as ʿUthmān. They then committed many murders, not even sparing women. Little by little the strength of the Khāridjī army grew by the accession of other fanatical and turbulent elements, including a number of non-Arabs, attracted by the principle of equality of races in the faith that the Khawāridj proclaimed. ʿAlī, who had so far tried to avoid dealing with the rebels, in order to avoid a war in his rear so long as he had to face the army of Muʿāwiya after the rupture of the preliminaries of peace, was obliged to take steps to avert the growing danger. He attacked the Khawāridj in their camp and inflicted a terrible defeat on them in which Ibn Wahb and the majority of his followers were slain (battle of Nahrawān, Ṣafar 9, 38 / July 17, 658). But the victory cost ʿAlī dear. Not only was the rebellion, so far from being suppressed, prolonged in a series of local risings in 39 and 40, but ʿAlī himself perished by the dagger of the Khāridjī ʿAbd al-Raḥmān b. Muldjam al-Murādī, the husband of a woman whose family had lost most of its members at Nahrawān. The tradition that a conspiracy of Khawāridj had aimed at killing simultaneously ʿAlī, Muʿāwiya and the governor of Egypt, ʿAmr b. al-ʿĀs, is almost certainly aprocryphal.

It should be noted that the narratives of Arab historians on the origin of the Khāridjī movement are very confused and contradictory, and seem to have lost sight of the real connection between it and the arbitration; on the other hand the nature and date of the latter are quite uncertain. The reconstruction which is given above is in contradiction to the view of Wellhausen (followed by Lammens and Caetani), who thinks that the Khāridjī rebellion and the arbitration are independent of one another and even dates the battle of Nahrawān before the verdict of the arbiters.

II. The Wars of the Khawāridj under the Umaiyads.

The wise and energetic administration of Muʿāwiya succeeding the feeble and vacillating rule of ʿAlī prevented the agitation of the Khāridjīs from breaking out, but did not succeed in extinguishing it any more than it succeeded in suppressing the feelings and aspirations of the Shīʿa. Our sources mention several risings that broke out in Kūfa and Baṣra during the twenty years of Muʿāwiya's reign (40—60/660—680), but they were promptly put down and only served to increase the roll of martyrs, reverence and vengeance for whom became one of the features of the Khāridjī movement. It is at Baṣra in particular, under the governors Ziyād b. Abīhi and his son ʿUbaid Allāh, that we find most risings and suppressions of risings. These insurrections, of which the most formidable was that of Mirdās b. Udaiya al-Tamīmī Abū Bilāl, settled the tactics of the Khawāridj, whose raids henceforth took the form of guerilla warfare and owed their successes mainly to the rapidity — which soon became legendary — of their cavalry (the names of some of their horses are preserved in Arabic works on hippology). They mobilised unexpectedly, swept through the country, surprised undefended towns and then retired rapidly to escape the pursuit of the government troops. The centres of concentration of the Khawāridj were the marshy country of the Baṭāʾiḥ around Baṣra and around Djūkhā, on the left bank of the Tigris, where their movement had originated, from which they could, if defeated, rapidly gain the mountainous lands of the Irānian plateaus.

It was only with the great civil war that broke out after the death of Yazīd I, that in the midst of the general disorder the Khāridjī movement assumed serious dimensions and contributed more than anything else to render precarious the pretender ʿAbd Allāh b. al-Zubair's hold on the territory that he had at first been able to subdue. After the fall of Ibn Zubair, it was the Umaiyad governors who had to wage a hard struggle with these indomitable rebels, enemies alike of victors and vanquished. It is at this time that we begin to distinguish among the Khawāridj half political and half theological subdivisions the origin of which is not at all clear, for the tradition which makes them appear at the same time quite suddenly at Baṣra on the death of Yazīd has probably altered the real succession of events. In any case we henceforth find the Khawāridj breaking out throughout the eastern part of the empire (Syria was always free from them and Africa only knew them under the ʿAbbāsids) into serious rebellions at the head of which they placed individuals who have given their names to the *Azāriḳa* or *Azraḳīs*, the *Abāḍīya* or (better) *Ibāḍīya* [see IBĀḌĪYA] and to the *Ṣufrīya*. Of all these movements the most dangerous to the unity of the Muslim Empire and the most terrible on account of its ferociously uncompromising character was without doubt that led by Nāfiʿ b. al-Azraḳ which gave the Khawāridj temporary control of Kirmān, Fārs and other eastern provinces, constituted a permanent threat to the security of Baṣra and surrounding country, and which al-Muhallab b. Abī Ṣufra at first, and later al-Ḥadjdjādj b. Yūsuf only overcame — in 78 or 79 (698 or 699) — after long years of effort which ended in the defeat and death of the last and most remarkable of the Azraḳī leaders, the valiant Ḳaṭarī b. al-Fudjāʾa. Less serious and less extensive and prolonged but quite as stubborn as the Azraḳī movement was the insurrection which was called after Shabīb b. Yazīd al-Shaibānī (76—77/696—697), although he did not begin it but was only its most distinguished leader; it began in the high Tigris country between Mārdīn and Niṣībīn and its object was the conquest and devastation of Kūfa. The partisans of Shabīb, who advanced only in little bands of several hundred horsemen, but who often gathered round them large bands of malcontents, sowed terror throughout the ʿIrāḳ, and having several times defeated al-Ḥadjdjādj's troops were only destroyed by the help of an army of picked troops summoned from Syria. Shabīb himself perished, drowned in the Dudjail, while trying to reach the mountains of Kirmān; his successors caused a certain amount of trouble to the governors of Yazid II and Hishām but never again were a serious danger.

Arabia was another field of Khāridjī activity, where during the government of Ibn al-Zubair between the years 65/684—5 and 72/691—2 their leaders Abū Ṭālūt, Nadjda b. ʿĀmir and Abū Fudaik captured in succession Yamāma, Ḥaḍramawt, Yaman and the town of al-Ṭāʾif, and were only restrained by religious scruples from taking the holy cities. They were only destroyed after the intervention of al-Ḥadjdjādj, but they left the seeds of future movements, especially in the eastern part of the peninsula.

Owing mainly to the energy of al-Ḥadjdjādj, Khāridjism seemed definitely quelled. Another factor contributed considerably to its failure, namely the fanaticism and intolerance of the rebels, whose religious disputes ended in splitting their ranks and sometimes resulted in the removal of their ablest leaders on the charge of having on some or other occasion failed to carry out their principles to the last iota. Another cause of weakness may be recognized in the eternal feud between the Arab element and that of the *mawālī* which brought fatal consequences along with it, especially among the remnants of the Azraḳīs after the death of Ḳaṭarī b. al-Fudjāʾa. But under the last Umaiyads in the midst of the irreparable collapse of the central government, the Khawāridj again raised their heads, and resumed their exploits, this time not in little bands but in large bodies. While the two most serious risings of this period, those of al-Ḍaḥḥāk b. Ḳais al-Shaibānī in the Djazīra and the ʿIrāḳ and that of ʿAbd Allāh b. Yaḥyā, surnamed *Ṭālib al-Ḥaḳḳ*, and of Abū Ḥamza in Arabia (in the course of which Madīna itself was occupied), ended in defeat, it is nevertheless true that the anarchy which they provoked destroyed the eastern rampart of Umaiyad power and enabled the ʿAbbāsid insurrection to penetrate more easily to the heart of the empire.

Under the ʿAbbāsid Caliphs, the Khāridjī movement continued to express itself in sporadic risings (see L. Veccia Vaglieri in *RSO*, xxiv. 31—44), but except in Mesopotamia it no longer presented any serious danger and only survived as a religious sect, without, however, any remarkable vitality or wide dissemination. In Eastern Arabia, on the other hand, in North Africa and later on the eastern coast of Africa, one of the principal branches of the Khawāridj, that of the Ibāḍīya (Abāḍīya), played an important part in politics, and even after this role was ended it continued to be of importance from the religious point of view. It survives in our day with its dogmas, its rites and its special laws [cf. IBĀḌĪYA].

III. The political and religious theories of the Khawāridj.

The Khawāridj, who, as we have seen, never had any true unity of military and political action. did not have either a uniform body of doctrines. Their teachings seem to us like the particular views of a number of independent sub-sects (the collections of *milal* number not less than a score including principal and subsidiary together), some of which represent theological schools as well as political movements of a collectivist character, while others confine themselves to expressing differences of individual opinions among the theorists of the sect. One article is common to all: it is that which treats of the question of the Caliphate, a question which has been the starting point of all the religious divisions in Islām. On this question the Khawāridj are opposed equally to the legitimism of the Shīʿa and the quietism of the Murdjiʾa. On the one hand they assert what Wellhausen aptly calls their "nonconformity" i.e. the obligation on believers to proclaim illegitimate and ipso facto deposed the *imām* who has gone off the right path (this is how they justify their abandonment of ʿAlī after his acceptance of the arbitration); on the other hand they declare every believer who is morally and religiously irreproachable to be capable of being raised by the vote of the community to the supreme dignity of the imāmate "even if he were a black slave". The result is that each of their leaders was recognised by them as *Amīr al-Muʾminīn* although none of them had, among other things, the qualification of Ḳuraishī birth. Consequently the only other caliphs besides their own that they recognise as legitimate are Abū Bakr and ʿUmar (the latter is particularly venerated by them); ʿUthmān only during the first six years of his reign and ʿAlī till the battle of Ṣiffīn.

Another capital article of Khāridjī heterodoxy is the absolute rejection of the doctrine of justification by faith without works. They push their moral strictness to the point of refusing the title of believer to anyone who has committed a mortal sin and regarding him as a *murtadd* (apostate); and their extreme wing, represented by the Azraḳī's, says that he who has become an infidel in this way can never re-enter the faith and should be killed for his apostasy along with his wives and children. Of course all non-Khāridjī Muslims are regarded as apostates. Here we have the principle of *istiʿrāḍ* (religious murder) which we find applied from the beginning of the Khāridjī movement, even before it had been formulated in theory, and which found its completest application during the war of the Azraḳī's. This ferocious principle forms a strange but not illogical contrast with the spirit of tolerance shown by the Khawāridj to non-Muslims and which in some of their schools goes so far as to recognise as equal to Muslims in every way those Jews or Christians who will pronounce the *shahāda* with the modification: "Muḥammad is the Apostle of God to the Arabs but not to us." The tendency to the levelling of the Arabs and the *mawālī* (which was already a result of their attitude to the problem of the imāmate) was pushed so far by one of the theorists of Khāridjī doctrine, Yazīd b. Abī Anīsa (founder of the *Yazīdīya*), that he says that God will reveal a new Ḳurʾān to a prophet among the Persians and that he will found a new religion for them, divine in the same sense as Judaism, Christianity and Islām, which will be no other than that of the Ṣābiʾūn mentioned in the Ḳurʾān.

The same Puritanism which characterises Khāridjism in its conception of the state and of faith is found in its ethical principles: it demands purity of conscience as an indispensable complement to bodily purity for the validity of acts of worship; one of their sects goes so far as to remove Sūra xii. (*Sūrat Yūsuf*) from the Ḳurʾān because its contents are worldly and frivolous and make it unworthy to be the Word of God. If, on the other hand, they seem to be less strict than the orthodox in the punishment they inflict on adulterers, for whom they do not allow stoning, this is due simply to the fact that they do not recognize the authenticity of the famous verse (*āyat al-radjm*) said to be added by ʿUmar to the primitive text of the Ḳurʾān (cf. Nöldeke-Schwally, *Gesch. d. Qorāns*, i. 248—252).

Outside of general principles and a few particular cases, the law and dogmatics of the Khawāridj are not known to us in their totality except for the Ibāḍīya, whose survival to the present day has preserved in its integrity their religious tradition. The Ibāḍīya represents (as does the Ṣufrīya on the other side) a comparatively moderate school and their present views, in dogma as well as law, have been to some degree influenced by other Muslim schools. Attention has recently been drawn (C. A. Nallino, *RSO*, vii. 455—460) to the very close connection between the dogmatics of the Ibāḍīya and of the Muʿtazila. It may also be supposed that it was the latter which, in certain points at least, received a stimulus from Khāridjism. What seems beyond doubt is that, as Wellhausen points out, Khāridjism played a very important part in the development of Muslim theology either directly or by the impetus which it gave to reflection on the problems of the faith.

Although Khāridjism seems to us an essentially popular movement in its origins, we must be careful not to think of it as devoid of intellectualism. On the contrary, the very radicalism of its theories must have exercised an attraction on many cultivated minds, much as similar doctrines have done in other times and countries. It is particularly at the time of the early ʿAbbāsids, under the influence of and at the same time in opposition to the refined and sceptic culture of the period, that we find many scholars and men of letters who were thought to cherish Khāridjī views, without this preventing their frequenting high society and enjoying the favour of the court. The best known of these Khawāridj *sub rosa* was the famous philosopher Abū ʿUbaida Maʿmar b. al-Muthannā, regarding whose fanaticism, in conversation at least, a rather piquant anecdote is recorded by Ibn Khallikān (i. 107 of the 1310 edition; the poetic quotation should be corrected from the *Amālī* of al-Murtaḍā, iii. 88—89). Poetry and eloquence were also cultivated among the Khawāridj, which is explained by the fact that the majority of their leaders, especially in the early days, belonged to the Beduin element in the military camps of Kūfa and Baṣra. Collections were compiled of the _khuṭab_ pronounced by the Khāridjī leaders, and what survives of them, besides giving an excellent idea of their views, gives us a fairly high opinion of their oratorical talent. We also possess numerous fragments of their poetry (which had also been collected in particular _dīwān_'s), especially of those of ʿImrān b. Ḥiṭṭān (who is at the same time considered one of the founders of the Khāridjī fiḳh). A long list of Khāridjī orators, poets and jurists was prepared by Djāḥiẓ, _Bayān_, Cairo 1313, i. 131—133, ii. 126—127.

The wars of the Khāridjī's had been recorded from the beginning of Arabic historiography in several works which have not come down to us in their entirety; we know, however, the substance of the more important among them, those of Abū Mikhnaf, Abū ʿUbaida and al-Madāʾinī, from the extracts which have been preserved in the historical sources given below, and from later ʿIbāḍī writings.

Bibliography: Sections I—II: al-Mubarrad, _al-Kāmil_, ed. Wright, _passim_ (translated by O. Rescher, _Die Kharidschitenkapitel aus dem Kāmil_, Stuttgart 1922); al-Ṭabarī, i. 3341 _sqq._, ii. _passim_; al-Balādhurī, _Ansāb al-ashrāf_, RSO, vi. 488—497 (résumé and specimens of the text for the period of the caliphate of ʿAlī; errata: _ibid._, p. 925); do., ed. Ahlwardt, p. 78—96, 125—151 (for the period of the caliphate of ʿAbd al-Malik); al-Masʿūdī, vols. iv.—vi., _passim_; L. Caetani, _Annali dell' Islām_, ix. 541—55ʻ, x. 76—151, 168—195, and _passim_ (translation by Levi della Vida of the historical texts for the period of the caliphate of ʿAlī and of other material relating to the Khawāridj, taken from the collections of Ḥadīth, etc.); do., _Chronographia Islamica_, i.; R. E. Brünnow, _Die Charidschiten unter den ersten Omayyaden_, Leiden 1884; J. Wellhausen, _Die religiös-politischen Oppositionsparteien im alten Islam_, i. _Die Chavārig_ (_Abh. G. W. Gött._, New Series, 1901, v. 2); H. Lammens, _Le caliphat de Moʿāvia I^er_ (reprint from the _MFOB_), p. 125—140; G. Levi della Vida _RSO_, 1913, vi. 474—488; L. Veccia Vaglieri, _Il conflitto ʿAlī-Muʿāwiya e la secessione khārigita_ in _Annali dell' Istituto Universitario Orientale di Napoli_, iv. 1—94 (1952). Section II: al-Shahrastānī, p. 85—103 (transl. Haarbrücker, _Religionsparteien und Philosophenschulen_, p. 128—156); Ibn Ḥazm, iv. 188—192; ʿAbd al-Ḳāhir al-Baghdādī, p. 54—92 and 263—265 (translation by K. Ch. Seelye, _Moslem Schisms and Sects, Columbia University Oriental Series_, vol. xv., New-York 1919, i. 74—115); I. Goldziher, _Vorlesungen über den Islam²_, Heidelberg 1925, p. 191—196 (first ed., p. 204—208; French transl. by F. Arin, p. 159—164). Section III: M. Th. Houtsma, _De strijd over het Dogma in den Islam tot op al-Ashʿari_, Leiden 1875; I. Goldziher, _Vorlesungen über den Islam_, Heidelberg 1910, Index; W. Thomson, _Khārijitism and the Khārijites_, in _Macdonald Presentation Volume_; A. J. Wensinck, _The Muslim Creed_, see Index; A. S. Tritton, _Muslim Theology_, London 1947; L. Gardet and M.-M. Anawati, _Introduction à la Théologie Musulmane_, Paris 1948.; W. N. Watt, _Free will and predestination in early Islam_, p. 32—35.

KHASHSHĀBĪYA. [see KAISĀNĪYA].

KHAṬAʾ (A.), a mistake which is made in thought (speech) or action; hence: error; failure; from the last meaning develops that of a wrong which is committed, of a transgression, even of a deliberate sin.

1. As a technical term, khaṭaʾ means an unintentional action (opposite _ʿamd_); this use comes from Sūra iv. 92 _sq._ [cf. ḲATL]; it may be more accurately defined as an act contrary to law, in which the intention of committing an illegal act is lacking, while the action itself may be deliberate; the degree of negligence is left quite out of the question in the juridical appreciation. The Muʿtazila asserted that one could not be punished by Allāh for it, for punishment is only conceivable for a deliberate illegal act; orthodoxy, on the contrary, teaches that, while khaṭaʾ is not a sin (_ithm_), any negligence, however, is something deliberate, and the khaṭaʾ, as its result, is liable to be punished; but Allāh in his mercy will overlook the punishment in the next world; the khaṭaʾ is thus considered as an ameliorating — often even exonerating — circumstance (_shubha_) in the infliction of punishment in this world: it cannot be punished by _ḥadd_. But not all of Allāh's rights are dropped: anyone who, contrary to the prohibition, kills an animal in the _ḥaram_, the sacred territory of Mekka, whether with _ʿamd_ (deliberately) or from khaṭaʾ (unintentionally), has to make the prescribed atonement; Dāwūd al-Ẓāhirī alone in this case also considers khaṭaʾ as an excuse. In the case of khaṭaʾ there also is a full liability for any injury done to another; here _ḳiṣāṣ_ [q.v.] is a special case: its application is excluded when khaṭaʾ is present; instead the _diya_ is to be paid and the _kaffāra_ to be performed. For further details see the article ḲATL.

2. Another technical sense of khaṭaʾ is that of error in logic (opposite _ṣawāb_), synonymous with _bāṭil_, the "wrong" (opposite _ḥaḳḳ_, the "right"). The works which deal with the _uṣūl al-fiḳh_ [see the art. UṢŪL] discuss the question whether the _mudjtahid muṭlaḳ_ [cf. IDJTIHĀD] can err. In the orthodox community the opinion has prevailed that the _mudjtahid_ can err and in cases of difference of opinion only one can be right at a time, and a tradition is even cited on this point; the Muʿtazila asserted that every _mudjtahid_ is right, and even celebrated orthodox teachers held this view, e.g. Abū Yūsuf, Muḥammad b. al-Ḥasan al-Shaibānī, Ibn Suraidj, al-Muzanī, al-Ashʿarī and his school, al-Bāḳillānī, al-Ghazzālī; Abū Ḥanīfa adopts a middle view. The champions of the orthodox view believe, in keeping with this, that Allāh has already come to a definite decision before every _idjtihād_ and that the correctness or otherwise of the decision of the _mudjtahid_ results from its agreement or not with that of Allāh; those of the Muʿtazila assume either different decisions by Allāh which coincide with those of the individual _mudjtahid_'s and are valid for them and their _mukallid_'s [cf. TAḲLĪD], so that all differing decisions of the _mudjtahid_'s are equally justified, or they consider one decision more justified than the others and believe that Allāh has taken no decision in such cases but "if He did do so", would express a definite one; those which differ from it are considered in the right with respect to the basis, the _idjtihād_ (_ibtidāʾan idjtihādan_) as the _mudjtahid_ has endeavoured with all his power to find the decision, in the wrong with respect to the result, the decision itself (_intihāʾan ḥukman_). The representatives of the orthodox view, who are essentially in close agreement with this form of the Muʿtazilī view, make the same distinction. But this difference only exists in questions of the derivation of legal rules from the _uṣūl al-fiḳh_ (_fi 'l-sharʿīyāt_) and only in the case when no clear decision is given in the _uṣūl_; if there is one, but it has not been regarded by the _mudjtahid_, he is, of course,

wrong. In the domain of the *uṣūl al-dīn*, of *kalām* [q.v.], particularly in reasoned deductions (*fi 'l-ʿaḳlīyāt*), according to the general consensus, only one view can be right. Only a few Muʿtazilīs, as whose representatives Abu 'l-Ḥasan ʿAbd Allāh al-ʿAnbārī and al-Djāḥiẓ are cited, asserted that also in dogmatics every *mudjtahid* (the word is used in a wider sense, meaning everyone who does all in his power to solve a problem) is right; while al-ʿAnbārī adds so long as he can be still described as a Muslim, and al-Djāḥiẓ without this exception. In the Muʿtazilī doctrine, however, the other meanings of khaṭa' come into consideration so that it is doubtless correctly explained that by "being right" is only meant that the *mudjtahid* has duly fulfilled the task imposed on him. That, taken purely logically, several differing views could be right at the same time has never been asserted. — The *mudjtahid* in the wrong is not punished for his error and is not considered as being in a religious error (*ḍalāl*), but is regarded as excused and is rewarded as he has done everything that is demanded of him if he has really used all his energy for the derivation of the legal rule. The Shīʿīs follow the Muʿtazilī view and regard their *mudjtahid*'s as infallible.

Bibliography: Lane, *Arab.-engl. Lexicon*, part 2, p. 761; for the technical uses in general see *Dictionary of the Technical Terms used in the Sciences of the Musalmans* (Bibliotheca Indica, Old Series), vol. i., p. 401 *sq.*; Djurdjānī, *Taʿrīfāt*, ed. G. Flügel, p. 104; for particulars, the works on *uṣūl* and the treatises on *fiḳh* are indispensable.

KHAṬĪ'A (A., plur. *khaṭāyā* and *khaṭī'āt*), sin, synonymous with *dhanb*. The root *kh-ṭ-'* has the meaning of stumbling (in Hebrew: *Proverbs*, xix. 2), committing an error (*akhṭa'a* is said e.g. of the bowman whose arrow misses the aim); see the art. KHAṬA'. The definition of *khaṭī'a* is "a sin committed on purpose"; that of *khiṭ'* (see Sūra xvii. 31) simply "a sin", whereas *ithm* is applied to heavy sins. It is only in accord with the general character of the Ḳur'ān that this book does not contain an elaborate theory of sin; frequent are, however, the passages in which the consequences and forgiveness of sins is spoken of. Allāh, *al-Raḥmān al-Raḥīm*, through the preaching of His Apostles and Prophets, calls men for the forgiveness of their sins (Sūra xiv. 10; xlvi. 31; lxxi. 4, 7). Who avoids heavy sins and immoral deeds will find plenteous forgiveness with his Lord (Sūra liii. 32), who forgiveth sin and accepteth re pentance (Sūra xl. 3); He is the best of forgivers (Sūra vii. 155); He forgiveth sins totally (*djamīʿan*; Sūra xxxix. 53).

This is the general exposition of forgiveness of sins in the Ḳur'ān. Further details are also given. When Mūsā says: "O my Lord, I have wronged myself (*ẓalamtu nafsī*), forgive me", Allāh forgives him (Sūra xxviii. 16; cf. Sūra xxxviii. 24—5 [Dāwūd], etc.). But he who dies as an infidel or as a polytheist will not find forgiveness (Sūra iv. 48, 137; xlvii. 34); *kufr* [q.v.] is forgiven, however, when it is done away with (Sūra viii. 38). But he who "is enveloped" by his sin will remain in Hell for ever (Sūra ii. 81).

This is a mild view; it agrees, on the whole, with the position of Judaism and Catholicism on this point. But it is not to be forgotten that Allāh remains free: "He spareth whomsoever He pleaseth and punisheth whomsoever He pleaseth" (Sūra iii. 129).

The mild attitude regarding sinners taken by the Ḳur'ān is retained by Islām. Yet the doctrine of sin, the distinction of light and heavy sins as well as their punishment, were the object of serious controversy in early Islām.

The distinction between light (*ṣaghā'ir*) and heavy (*kabā'ir*) sins could be maintained in accordance with passages from the Ḳur'ān such as Sūra xlii. 37, where the term *kabā'ir* is already used. Christian dogmatics have certainly exercised an influence, as may be seen from the doctrine of the (seven) capital sins which occurs in Ḥadīth: "The Apostle of Allāh said: Avoid the seven capital sins (*mūbiḳāt*). When he was asked what they are, he answered: Polytheism, sorcery, killing those who may not be killed except for a lawful reason, spoiling the possessions of orphans, usury, fleeing from battle against the enemy, and abusing helpless, faithful *muḥṣanāt*" (Muslim, *Īmān*, trad. 144; al-Bukhārī, *Waṣāyā*, bāb 23). In other enumerations of the capital sins there are deviations from this scheme; theology and ethics maintain the view that there are sins heavier than those enumerated in the tradition just mentioned (cf. the commentary of al-Nawawī, i. 170).

The theory concerning light and heavy sins and their forgiveness, which may be called representative of the views of orthodox Islām, was not shared by two sects of widely divergent tendencies, the Khāridjīs [q.v.] and the Muʿtazilīs [q.v.]. Both hold the position that the consequence of heavy sins will be eternal punishment. This position is connected with the question concerning the relation existing between faith and works. While orthodox Islām, theoretically at least, emphasises the value of faith, these sects lay stress upon works as the criterion of a man being faithful or not; their most consequent opponents in this respect were the Murdji'īs [q.v.]. The line of distinction which orthodox Islām draws between Muslims and Kāfirs was removed to the right by the Khawāridj and the Muʿtazila, so as to add to the damned also the Muslims who were guilty of heavy sins. The echo of the fervent debates between the parties is still heard in the commentaries on the Ḳur'ān. Al-Baiḍāwī comments upon Sūra ii. 81 (75) (see above): The "envelopment" mentioned here can only refer to Kāfirs; consequently those who have committed heavy sins do not fall under the verdict of this verse.

Verses like Sūra xxxix. 53: "Allāh forgiveth sins in their totality" and Sūra ii. 284: "He forgiveth whomsoever He pleaseth and He punisheth whomsoever He pleaseth", prove that punishment of sins is not necessary and that heavy sins are also pardoned (Fakhr al-Dīn al-Rāzī, *Mafātīḥ al-ghaib*, ii. 82). Al-Baiḍāwī (see also Fakhr al-Dīn al-Rāzī, v. 455): "It is not true that for the forgiveness of sins *tawba* [q.v.] is necessary; this is only required for *shirk*" [q.v.]. Still, however strong this assertion may be, Fakhr al-Dīn al-Rāzī does not fail to declare in his commentary on Sūra xxxix. 53: "Perhaps He will pardon sins in general, but perhaps He will punish in Hell for a time and pardon afterwards".

Al-Zamakhsharī, who was a moderate Muʿtazilī, combats such views. Commenting upon the words "He pardoneth whomsoever He pleaseth" (Sūra iii. 129) he remarks: "On account of *tawba*, for He is not disposed to grant forgiveness except to those who repent". And he fulminates against the interpretation of the verse which is put into the mouth of Ibn ʿAbbās: "He forgiveth heavy sins to whomsoever He pleaseth and He punisheth whomsoever

He pleaseth on account of light sins"; words, indeed, to bring a Muʿtazilite to despair.

As is to be expected, the orthodox view of heavy sins being pardonable is also to be found in Ḥadīth. All this is elaborately treated in the traditions on intercession [see the article SHAFĀʿA] where it is stated anew that Muḥammad intercedes also on behalf of grave sinners and that through his intercession they are allowed to leave Hell.

Innumerable are the traditions in which Muḥammad mentions forgiveness of sins on account of good works of every kind. In some of these traditions the qualification occurs: "except heavy ones"; this clausula represents the common orthodox view (see above) that light sins are repaired by good works of every kind, that heavy ones require *istighfār* and that *shirk* requires *tawba* [q.v.]. *Shirk*, polytheism, is consequently the heaviest sin; the lightest is the so-called *ḥadīth al-nafs*, i.e. sinful thoughts which do not issue into reality; it is even said that no account of these thoughts is taken in the computation of sins on the Day of Resurrection. The idea is expressed in the following tradition: "The Apostle of Allāh said: Allāh does not take into account what the members of my community think as long as they do not pronounce it or carry it out" (Muslim, *Īmān*, trad. 201—208). This tradition, which also occurs in other forms, is another proof of the mild attitude taken by orthodox Islām towards sin, an attitude which forms a counterbalance against the severe doctrine of *ḳadar* [q.v.]. The tradition just mentioned and the attitude from which it arises are the more remarkable because Muslim theology is very strict in matters regarding the intention [cf. NĪYA]. On the other hand, scrupulousness regarding sinful thoughts is highly praised (Muslim, *Īmān*, trad. 209). In this connection also the following *ḥadīth* may be mentioned. "Anas said: Verily, you do things which, in your eyes, are more insignificant than a hair is thick; but in Muḥammad's lifetime we considered them as capital sins" (al-Bukhārī, *Riḳāḳ*, bāb 32). Finally one tradition must be mentioned which could be called a step in the direction of the attitude of Khāridjīs and Muʿtazilīs regarding heavy sins. "The Apostle of Allāh said: Who commits fornication is not a believer at the same time, nor is he who steals or drinks wine" (Muslim, *Īmān*, trad. 100; cf. trad. 101—105; cf. al-Bukhārī, *Ḥudūd*, bāb 1, 6, 20 etc.). Al-Nawawī in his commentary is anxious to prove that the words "is not a believer" do not imply a total, but only a partial lack of faith. Cf. also A. S. Tritton, *Muslim Theology*, London 1947, by index.

In ethical and mystical literature we find a more systematic and elaborate classification of sins; cf. Abū Ṭālib al-Makkī, *Ḳūt al-ḳulūb*, i. 85 *sq.*; al-Ghazzālī, *Iḥyāʾ*, vol. iv., book i. (on repentance). Abū Ṭālib recognises four classes of sins, a division which was borrowed from him by al-Ghazzālī. Those of the first kind are called *rubūbīya*, sins such as haughtiness and pride, boasting, arrogance, love of praise, love of life, ambition, despotism; those of the second class are called satanic (*shaiṭānīya*); it comprises such sins as envy and deceit; those of the third class bear the epithet of "animal" sins (*bahīmīya*); these are avidity, covetousness, rage and lust; the fourth class comprises those sins which remind of the nature of the beasts of prey (*sabuʿīya*), such as wrath, fighting and murder.

Al-Ghazzālī rejects the view of those who do not recognise a practical difference between light and heavy sins. He mentions the enumerations of heavy sins, varying between four and eleven, and cites Abū Ṭālib al-Makkī's view that "there are 17 heavy sins, four in the heart, to wit: polytheism, persevering in sin, despair of Allāh's compassion, and false security; four in the tongue, to wit: false witness, abusing the *muḥṣan*, false oath, and sorcery; three in the belly: drinking wine and intoxicating drinks, spoiling the goods of orphans, and usury; two in the genitals: fornication and pederasty; two in the hands: murder and theft; one in the feet: fleeing from battle; one in the whole body: disobedience to one's parents.

The mystics, notwithstanding such classifications, see sin in a more general light. It is man as such who is a sinner. It is necessary for him to know Allāh in His highness and to know himself in his baseness. For the soul is like a mirror disfigured by rust, which has to be cleaned and polished, so as to be able to reflect the higher world. This polishing process dominates the life of the mystic and gives rise e.g. to the *muḥāsaba*, the daily examination of one's self with a view to sins committed and to the means to avoid them in future (*Iḥyāʾ*, vol. iv., book viii.; cf. Asín Palacios, *La Mystique d'al-Ghazzālī*, in *MFOB*, vii. 90 *sq.*). It is this consciousness of sinfulness which lies at the root of the mournful attitude of the mystics and which has inspired so many sayings expressing their fear to appear before Allāh after death (cf. R. Hartmann, *Al-Ḳuschairī's Darstellung des Ṣûfîtums*, p. 11 *sq.*).

Two deviating attitudes regarding sin taken by the mystics have still to be mentioned: that of the *Ibāḥīya* and that of the *Malāmatīya*. The former have turned their back on the *via purgativa* of the mystic and maintain that the fetters of law and morals have no longer to be borne by him who participates in true mystic life. For a full description see the art. TAṢAWWUF — The *Malāmatīya*, on the other hand, start from the conception that the mystic has to avoid all that may confer on him the praise of mankind and their admiration. They therefore do not shun actions which expose them to general reproval or disdain, actions which in their case are not the outcome of their indulging in sinful inclinations and which, without the purpose of incurring blame, would lose nothing of their sinful character.

KHAṬĪB (A.), plur. *khuṭabāʾ*, was, among the ancient Arabs, the name for the spokesman of the tribe. The khaṭīb is therefore often mentioned along with the *shāʿir*, the poet, and, like the *kāhin* and the *saiyid*, was one of the leaders of the tribe. The character and significance of his office is clearly explained by Djāḥiẓ, *Kitāb al-bayān wa 'l-tabyīn*, Cairo 1332, vols. 1—3. The distinction between khaṭīb and *shāʿir* is not absolutely definite but practically is that the *shāʿir* uses the poetic form while the khaṭīb expresses himself in prose, often, however, also in *sadjʿ* (cf. Djāḥiẓ, *op. cit.*, i. 159). According to Djāḥiẓ, only few *khuṭabāʾ* were also *shuʿarāʾ* (i. 27). In the *djāhilīya* the *shāʿir* is said to have been more highly esteemed than the khaṭīb but when the number of poets gradually increased and they sank to the level of beggars, the khaṭīb obtained more prestige (i. 136; iii. 227); the office was sometimes hereditary in the same family. The *khuṭabāʾ* did not form a gild or caste; they were the men who had the ability to be spokesmen. They appear not only at the head of a *wafd* to negotiate as representatives of their tribe, as we know from the *sīra*, but, like the poets, they were also the leaders in the war of wits with the enemy (*mufākhara*). The *khaṭīb* had to be able to extol the glorious deeds and the noble qualities of his tribe and to narrate them in perfect language and to be able likewise to expose the weaknesses of his opponents. Lampoons give the following characteristics of a poor khaṭīb: his pronunciation is bad, he turns to and fro, stammers, coughs, strokes his beard, twists his fingers, a sign of cowardice (*Ḥamāsa*, ed. Freytag, p. 650, verse 5; *Kāmil*, ed. Wright, p. 20 *sq.*). It is in keeping with the character of the ancient Arab khaṭīb that he is included among the fighting knights and nobles (al-Ḳuṭāmī, *Dīwān*, xiv. 20; Djāḥiẓ, i. 134 *sq.*, 172), indeed, khaṭīb itself is used as a name for a brave warrior (Djāḥiẓ, i. 129). When the khaṭīb makes a public appearance his insignia are lance, staff or bow (*al-makhāṣir*), just as a man taking an oath carries tokens of masculine honour; he often strikes the earth with it (cf. al-Ḳuṭāmī, xxvii. 6; Labīd, *Dīwān*, ed. al-Khālidī, 7 [p. 27], 9 [p. 45]; Djāḥiẓ, i. 197 *sq.*; iii. 3 *sqq.*, 61 *sq.*).

In the earliest days of Islām the khaṭīb retained much of his old character. "The prophet came forward as a khaṭīb" after the conquest of Mekka (Ibn Hishām, p. 823) speaking publicly with ceremony and authority. But the *khuṭba* now became solely an address to the Muslims, not a part of the war against the enemy, and *mufākhara* was no longer part of the activities of the Muslim khaṭīb. But it is quite in keeping with the nature of early Islām and with that of the Arab khaṭīb that the ruler himself was spokesman and that he as khaṭīb not only made edifying speeches from the *minbar* but also issued orders, made decisions and pronounced his views on political questions and other questions of general interest. This was the case under the first four caliphs and the Umaiyads (cf. Djāḥiẓ, i. 190), and the governors appointed by them also acted as *khuṭabā'* (e.g. al-Yaʿḳūbī, ii. 318; Djāḥiẓ, i. 179 middle, etc.); the local governors appointed by the latter were also entrusted with the control of the *minbar* and of the *ṣalāt* (al-Ṭabarī, ii. 929). Diatribes against and curses on the enemy were part of their *minbar* speeches, e.g. the curses on ʿAlī and occasionally on Ṭalḥa and al-Zubair (Djāḥiẓ, i. 165). Khaṭīb was therefore still synonymous with "leader". An inheritance from the ancient Arab spokesman is the staff or lance which the Muslim khaṭīb holds in his right hand during the *khuṭba*, a custom which provoked the scorn of the Persians (Djāḥiẓ, iii. 3). But the close connection between the *khuṭba* and divine service gave the Muslim khaṭīb a specifically religious character. After the conclusion of the wars of the first generations, this element became more predominant and in the time of the ʿAbbāsids, as early as Hārūn al-Rashīd, the caliph left it to the ḳāḍīs to deliver the sermon at the service while he himself was simply a listener (Djāḥiẓ, i. 161). But in theory the leaders of divine service in the great mosques are representatives of the caliph (cf. Ibn Khaldūn, *Muḳaddima*, Cairo 1322, p. 173), and the Egyptian Fāṭimids still occasionally preached themselves. By and by special *khuṭabā'* were everywhere appointed. The khaṭīb usually was also the conductor (*imām*) of the Friday *ṣalāt* at which he preached and, according to Abū Ḥanīfa and a tradition of Mālik, he must actually do so unless there were special reasons for a deviation from the rule. The daily *ṣalāt*'s are as a rule conducted by other *imām*'s (al-Māwardī, *al-Aḥkām al-sulṭānīya*, ed. Enger, p. 181). According to al-Shāfiʿī and Mālik, the Friday service with *khuṭba* can only be held in one mosque in each town, if the size of the town does not make it impossible, while Abū Ḥanīfa has no such rule. Abū Ḥanīfa, on the other hand, allows divine service in which a khaṭīb takes part only in a large town (*miṣr*), in which the ruler or his deputy is present in person. The other schools are less rigorous on the point. But the *imām*-khaṭīb of the Friday service is, according to the other schools also, in theory the representative of "the highest *imām*". The document confirming the appointment of the khaṭīb under the Mamlūks is evidence of the khaṭīb's dignity (cf. al-Ḳalḳashandī, *Ṣubḥ al-aʿshā*, Cairo, ii. 222—225; iv. 39; al-ʿUmarī, *Kitāb al-taʿrīf* Cairo 1312, p. 126 *sq.*). He is the natural authority to whom new converts announce their conversion to Islām (Ibn al-Ḥādjdj, *Kitāb al-madkhal*, p. 76); the people touch his robe *li 'l-tabarruk*, etc. (al-Shaʿrānī, *Kitāb al-mīzān*, i. 169). According to al-Māwardī (p. 185), the khaṭīb ought preferably to wear black clothes, according to al-Ghazzālī, white, while the first mentioned would be *bidʿa* (*Iḥyā'*, Cairo 1322, p. 131). His insignia are *al-ʿūdāni*, the "two things of wood", i.e. the *minbar* and the staff or wooden sword which he has to hold in his hand during the sermon, according to the *fiḳh* books also. According to the law of 1911 applied to al-Azhar, art. 59, every one who has passed through the second of the three divisions of the institute (in the law No. 49 of 1930: "the section of specialisation") can become a khaṭīb. In larger mosques several *khuṭabā'* can be appointed. Thus there were in 1909 in the mosque of the Prophet in Madīna 46, in Mekka 122 *khuṭabā'*, besides their deputies. They enjoy certain foundations and the office is on the whole hereditary (al-Batanūnī, *al-Riḥla al-Ḥidjāzīya* [2], Cairo 1329, p. 101, 242).

Beside the official khaṭīb, the *wāʿiẓ* and the *ḳāṣṣ* exercised the function of an edifying preacher, without set forms (cf. A. Mez, *Die Renaissance des Islāms*, 1922, p. 318 *sqq.*; Djāḥiẓ, *Bayān*, i. 167 *sq.*).

Bibliography: I. Goldziher, *Der Chaṭîb bei den alten Arabern*, in *WZKM*, 1892, vi. 97—102; C. Snouck Hurgronje, *Islam und Phonograph* (*Verspreide Geschriften*, 1923, ii. 426 *sqq.*); C. H. Becker, *Die Kanzel im Kultus des alten Islam*, in *Islamstudien*, 1924, i. 450—471; do., *Zur Gesch. d. islamischen Kultus*, in *Islamstudien*, i. 472—500; T. W. Juynboll, *Handbuch des islāmischen Gesetzes*, 1910, p. 87—89; E. W. Lane, *Manners and Customs of the Modern Egyptians* (Every Man's Library), p. 84; the *fiḳh*-books under *Ṣalāt al-djumʿa* and al-Shaʿrānī, *Kitāb al-mīzān*, Cairo 1329, i. 164—171; Ibn ʿAbd Rabbihi, *al-ʿIḳd al-farīd*, Cairo 1321, ii. 128 *sqq.*

KHATM (A.) or KHATMA, the technical name for the recitation of the whole of the Ḳur'ān from beginning to end. It is an infinitive from *khatama*, which is derived with the meaning "to end, to conclude" from the foreign word *khātam*, "seal, seal-ring" (Fränkel, *Die aramäischen Fremdwörter im Arabischen*, p. 252), because the seal was affixed at the end of a document. The complete recitation of the Ḳur'ān is, especially if it is done within a short time, a meritorious achievement, e.g. in 8 nights, as Ubaiy b. Kaʿb is said to have done (Ibn Saʿd, iii./ii. 60; cf. on ʿUthmān, *ibid.*, iii./i. 53). It is related of Sulaimān al-Aʿmash (in Lane) that he accomplished the *khatma* sometimes after ʿUthmān's edition and sometimes after that of Ibn Masʿūd. For a dead man the reciters were asked to recite the *ḳirā'at al-khatamāt* (e.g. in the 1001 Nights in the story of the merchant Aiyūb and his son). In Egypt the *khatma* was used as an entertainment for guests. In modern Mekka the so-called *iḳlāba* is celebrated when a boy has read through the whole of the sacred book (the ceremony after the half or one third is called *iṣrāfa*). In South Arabia a *khātam* is presented to one who has recited the whole book for the first time.

Bibliography: Snouck Hurgronje, *Mekka*, ii. 146, 272; Landberg, *Arabica*, v. 126 *sqq.*; Lane, *Arabian Nights*, i. 382; Goldziher, in *Isl.*, vi. (1915), 214, on *Khatm al-Bukhārī*.

KHAṬṬĀBĪYA, name of a sect reckoned among the Shīʿite extremists (*ghulāt*), called after Abu'l-Khaṭṭāb Muḥammad b. Abī Zainab al-Asadī al-Adjdaʿ, who is said to have asserted the immanence (*ḥulūl*) of the deity in the Imām Djaʿfar al-Ṣādiḳ (83—148/702—765) and afterwards in himself. He obtained a following in al-Kūfa, where he was attacked by ʿĪsā b. Mūsā, who was governor for some years till 147/764—5; he armed his followers with stones, reeds and knives, assuring them that these would prevail against the enemy's swords and lances. This promise proved deceptive; his followers to the number of seventy were slaughtered, and he himself was captured in Dār al-Rizḳ on the bank of the Euphrates, impaled, his trunk afterwards burned and his head sent to Baghdād (138/755—6). This disaster did not terminate the existence of the sect, some of whom maintained that neither Abu 'l-Khaṭṭāb nor his followers had been really killed, the appearance having been delusive. Their numbers are computed by the best informed writer about 300 A.H. at 100,000, their location being the Sawād of al-Kūfa and Yaman; they had, however, no power or force. There is a brief allusion to their doctrine in Ibn Ḳutaiba's *Maʿārif*, which is somewhat earlier, and in the work of al-Muṭahhar b. al-Ṭāhir, who is some fifty years later, but they seem to have done nothing which attracted the attention of the historians. After Abu 'l-Khaṭṭāb's death his followers are said to have transferred the imāmate to Muḥammad b. Ismāʿīl b. Djaʿfar al-Ṣādiḳ, and are thus to be reckoned among the Ismāʿīlīs.

The statements about their specific doctrines are scanty and to be accepted with caution. They held, it is asserted, that Muḥammad transferred the prophetic office from himself to ʿAlī on the Day of the Pond; and it would seem that Abu 'l-Khaṭṭāb must have asserted that similar transference had taken place from Djaʿfar to himself. Both Sunnī and Shīʿī writers maintain emphatically that Djaʿfar repudiated the claims made for him by Abu 'l-Khaṭṭāb, whose relation to him seems to have been similar to that of al-Mukhtār b. Abī ʿUbaid to Ibn al-Ḥanafīya.

The Khaṭṭābīya seem to have repudiated the idea that the ʿAlids were predestined in themselves for the imāmate, but maintained that only spiritual adoption counted, for which their example was the spiritual adoption of Salmān al-Fārisī [q.v.] by Muḥammad. Abū 'l-Khaṭṭāb pretended to have been adopted by Djaʿfar and considered himself as the spiritual successor of Salmān in the role of *Sīn* in the terminology of the Shīʿite extremists (see the art. KARMAṬIANS). The origin of the two sects of the Ismāʿīlīya and the Nuṣairīs can both be traced back to Abū 'l-Khaṭṭāb.

Of his other doctrines the best attested is that he taught absolute ruthlessness in dealing with opponents. Men, women and children were all to be massacred, his argument being the same as was employed by the Azāriḳa. False witness was lawful in dealing with them. Al-Muṭahhar asserts that in consequence the evidence of members of this sect was not accepted in the courts.

The later heresiologues know far more about the sect than do the earlier. With al-Muṭahhar the Bāzighīya are a separate sect, but al-Shahrastānī makes them a subdivision of the Khaṭṭābīya. The latter writer makes another subdivision, the ʿUmairīya, who figure in Baghdādī's work as a subdivision of the Djanāḥīya. Al-Shahrastānī also treats the Muʿammarīya as a branch of the Khaṭṭābīya, but Ibn Ḥazm evidently regarded them as independent. By the time of al-Maḳrīzī the number of subdivisions had reached fifty, and Abu 'l-Khaṭṭāb's father's *kunya* was variously given as Abū Thawr and Abū Yazīd, probably through misreadings of the name Zainab. The sect is charged with repudiating the whole of the moral law as well as the whole ritual of Islām. Transmigration also appears among their supposed tenets.

Bibliography: I. Friedländer, *The heterodoxies of the Shiites*, *JAOS*, xxvii and xxix (translation with notes of Ibn Ḥazm, *Faṣl*, v. 187 *sqq.*); al-Shahrastānī, transl. Haarbrücker, i., 206; al-Baghdādī, p. 242; al-Nawbakhtī, *Madhāhib firaḳ ahl al-imāma*, ed. Ritter, Istanbul 1931; al-Kashshī, *Maʿrifat akhbār al-ridjāl*, Bombay 1317; Maḳrīzī, *Khiṭaṭ*, ii., 352; al-Īdjī, *Mawāḳif*, ed. Sörensen, p. 346; other sources are mentioned in W. Ivanow, *Notes sur l'Ummu 'l-Kitāb des Ismaëliens de l'Asie Centrale*, in *REI*, 1932, p. 419—482; L. Massignon, *Salmân Pâk*, Paris 1934, pp. 19, 38, 44; the same in his note on the Banū 'l-Furāt in *Mélanges Maspéro*, Cairo 1938, vol. ii; A. S. Tritton, *Muslim Theology*, London 1947, pp. 26, 28, 53, 206.

AL-**KHAZRADJ** [see ANṢĀR].

KHIDHLĀN (A.), nomen actionis from the root *kh-dh-l*, "to leave in the lurch", a technical term in Muḥammadan theology. applied exclusively to Allāh when He withdraws His grace or help from man. The disputes regarding it first appear in connection with the quarrel over *ḳadar* [q.v.]. A starting point is found in Sūra iii. 160: "but if He abandon you to yourselves (*yakhdhulkum*), who will help you after Him? Let the faithful therefore trust in God". On this al-Rāzī observes: "The Companions deduce from this verse that belief is exclusively a result of Allāh's help (cf. John, vi. 65), while unbelief is a result of His khidhlān. This is obvious as the verse points out that the matter is entirely in God's hands".

A more detailed exposition is given by Ibn Ḥazm (iii. 50 *sq.*) "Right guidance and assistance consist in God's preparing (*taisīr*) the believer for the good for which He has created him; while khidhlān consists in His preparing the *fāsiḳ* for the evil for which He has created him. Linguistic usage, the Ḳurʾān, the force of logic, and the attitude of the faḳīhs and those in the past who handed down traditions and of the companions and successors as well as of those who came after them and of the whole body of Muslims with the exception of those whom God has led astray as regards their intelligence, namely such as belong to the followers of slanderers and outcasts, like al-Naẓẓām, Thumāma, al-ʿAllāf and al-Djāḥiẓ, are all unanimous". Then follows this reasoning: Allāh has given man two forces, hostile and opposed to one another, *tamyīz* (power of discrimination) and *hawā* (passion, desire). When Allāh protects the soul, *tamyīz* prevails by His help and power. But when He leaves the soul to itself (*khadhala*), He strengthens the *hawā* with a strength which amounts to leading astray (*iḍlāl*).

Khidhlān is therefore, according to Ibn Ḥazm,

the opposite of *hudā* and *tawfīḳ* and the conception approaches that of *iḍlāl*. The Muʿtazilīs (as already indicated by Ibn Ḥazm's words) see in it a contradiction to Allāh's justness: according to them, Allāh does not urge a man to evil. In their terminology *khidhlān* therefore means the refusal of divine grace (*manʿ al-luṭf*), while, according to the Ashʿarīs, khidhlān is "the creation of the ability to disobey".

Bibliography: Fakhr al-Dīn al-Rāzī, *Mafātīḥ al-ghaib*, ii. 296; *Dictionary of Technical Terms*, ed. Sprenger and Nassau Lees, Calcutta 1862, p. 449; M. Th. Houtsma, *De strijd over het dogma in den Islam*, Leyden 1875, p. 58; Wensinck, *The Muslim Creed*, p. 213.

KHIḌR, KHIZR. [See Khaḍir, Khwādja Khiḍr].

KHIRḲA (A.,) "rag", hence a mystic's coarse woollen robe, because it was originally made up of pieces (synonym *muraḳḳaʿa*). "It is the inner flame (*ḥarḳa*) which makes the Ṣūfī" said al-Hudjwīrī "not the religious dress" (*khirḳa*). This dress was the outward sign of the vow of poverty taken by the Ṣūfī; it was originally as a rule blue, the colour of mourning. Certain mystics, however, refused to wear a special costume, saying that if a distinctive mark of this kind was adopted for God's sake, it was useless, for God knows best what is under the robe; and if it is for men, one cannot escape from this dilemma — either the vocation of the dervish is true and then it is pure ostentation, or it is pretended and it is hypocrisy. Nevertheless the distinctive dress was generally adopted. It could not be obtained by the novice until the expiry of the three years necessary for his novitiate. The investiture of the *murīd* with the *khirḳa* by his tutor (*shaikh*, *pīr*) had a ceremonial character. "The donning of the robe", says Suhrawardī in the *ʿAwārif al-maʿārif*, "is the tangible sign that the man is entering upon the way of truth, the symbol of his entrance upon the mystic path, the sign that he is abandoning himself and putting himself entirely in the hands of the shaikh". There are two kinds of robe: *khirḳat al-irāda* (robe of good-will), which one asks from the shaikh, being fully conscious of the duties which this investiture imposes on one and of the passive obedience to which one condemns oneself in accepting it; and *khirḳat al-tabarruk* (robe of benediction) given ex officio by the shaikh to persons whom he thinks qualified to enter upon the mystic path, without their fully realising the significance of the investiture. The first is naturally much superior to the second and distinguishes the true Ṣūfīs from those "who only resemble them in external appearance" (E. Blochet, *Études sur l'ésotérisme musulman*, in *Muséon*, X, 1909, p. 176 *sqq*.).

The Prophet's mantle, under the name of *Khirḳa-i Sharīf* was formerly claimed to be kept in custody in the imperial harem of the Ottoman sultans.

Bibliography: al-Hudjwīrī, *Kashf al-maḥdjūb*, transl. Nicholson, p. 45 *sqq*.; H. Thorning, *Beiträge zur Kenntnis des islam. Vereinswesens* (*Türkische Bibliothek*, xvi.), index; S. de Sacy, *Pendnameh*, p. lxiii. in *NE*, xii. 305; Cl. Huart, *Konia, la ville des derviches tourneurs*, p. 204.

KHITĀN (A.), circumcision. According to the *LA*, s.v. *kh-t-n*, the term is exclusively used in connection with the circumcision of males, whereas in the case of females *khafḍ* is the proper word. If this statement should be exact, the expression *al-khitānāni* "the two circumcised parts" (viz. that of the male and that of the female) would be a dual *a potiori*. This expression occurs in the tradition: "If the two circumcised parts have been in touch with one another, *ghusl* is necessary" (Bukhārī, *Ghusl*, bāb 28; Muslim, *Ḥaiḍ*, trad. 88; Abū Dāwūd, *Ṭahāra*, bāb 81, 83).

Some words connected with the root *kh-t-n* denote the father-in-law, the son-in-law, the daughter-in-law (*khatan*, *khatana*), or marrying (*khutūna*). The root must have belonged to the primitive Semitic language, as they occur also in the same or cognate forms in North-Semitic languages.

Circumcision must have been a common practice in early Arabia. It is mentioned, not in the Ḳurʾān, but in old poetry (e.o. in the *Dīwān* of the Hudhalī's, Farazdaḳ and other poets) and in *ḥadīth*. The early language has also a special word for "uncircumcised" (*aghral*, Hebrew *ʿārēl*).

In *ḥadīth* it is said that Ibrāhīm was circumcised in his 80th year (Bukhārī, *Anbiyāʾ*, bāb 8; Muslim, *Faḍāʾil*, trad. 151). This tradition is based on the Biblical report. Ibn Saʿd has preserved a tradition according to which the patriarch was already circumcised at the age of 13 (*Ṭabaḳāt*, 1/i. 24).

This tradition is apparently a reflex of the practice of circumcision in the first centuries of Islām. We may confront it with the statements concerning Ibn ʿAbbās' circumcision in *ḥadīth*.

Circumcision is mentioned in *ḥadīth* in the story of the Emperor Heraclius' horoscope (Bukhārī, *Badʾ al-waḥy*, bāb 6). Heraclius read in the stars the message of "the king of the circumcised". Thereupon an envoy of the king of Ghassān arrived who reported the news of Muḥammad's preaching of Islām. This envoy appeared to be circumcised himself and he informed the Emperor of the fact that circumcision was a custom prevalent among the Arabs.

It is further recognized in *ḥadīth* that circumcision belongs to the pre-islāmic institututions. In the traditions which enumerate the features of natural religion (*al-fiṭra*), circumcision is mentioned together with the clipping of nails, the use of the toothpick, the cutting of moustaches, the more profuse length of the beard etc. (Bukhārī, *Libās*, bāb 63; Muslim, *Ṭahāra*, trad. 49, 50; Tirmidhī, *Adab*, bāb 14 etc.). Perhaps circumcision of females is implicitly understood here. In a tradition preserved by Aḥmad b. Ḥanbal (v. 75) circumcision is called *sunna* for males, honourable for females.

There are differences between the several *madhhab*'s concerning rules for circumcision. Instead of giving a survey of the different views it may be sufficient to translate the passage al-Nawawī in his commentary on Muslim, *Ṭahāra*, trad. 50 (ed. Cairo 1283, i. 328) has devoted to the subject, also because it contains a description of the operation.

"Circumcision is obligatory (*wādjib*) according to al-Shāfiʿī and many of the doctors, *sunna* according to Mālik and the majority of them. It is further, according to al-Shāfiʿī, equally obligatory for males and females. As regards males it is obligatory to cut off the whole skin which covers the *glans*, so that this latter is wholly denudated. As regards females, it is obligatory to cut off a small part of the skin in the highest part of the genitals. The sound (*ṣaḥīḥ*) view within the limits of our school, which is shared by the large majority of our friends, is that circumcision is allowed, but not obligatory in a youthful age, and one of the special views is that the *walī* is obliged to have the child circumcised before it reaches the adult age. Another special view is, that it is prohibited to circumcise a child before its tenth year. The sound view according to us, is that circumcision on the seventh day after birth is *mustaḥabb* (recommendable). Further there are two views regarding the question whether in the "seventh day" the birthday is included or not".

The treatment of circumcision has not a prominent place in the books of law. More important, however, is the value attached to it in popular estimation. "To the uneducated mass of Muslims", says Snouck Hurgronje, "as well as to the great mass of non-Muslims, both of whom pay the greatest attention to formalities, abstention from pork together with circumcision have even become to a certain extent the criterium of Islām. The exaggerated estimation of the two precepts finds no support in the law, for here they are on the same level with numerous other precepts, to which the mass attaches less importance" (*De Islam*, in *Verspr. Geschriften*, i. 402; cf. IV/i. 377). In many Islāmic countries the rite is simply colled *sunna* or *sunnat*.

In Atchin circumcision of infidels only is considered as the ceremony of reception into Islam (Snouck Hurgronje, *The Achehnese*, i. 398). The importance attached to circumcision appears also from the tradition according to which Muḥammad was born circumcised (Ibn Saʿd, *Ṭabaḳāt*, I/i. 64). In North Africa a child born with a short foreskin is considered as a blessing (Douté, *Merrâkech*, Paris 1905, p. 353).

At Mecca, where the rite is called *ṭahār*, children are circumcised at an age of 3—7 years, girls without festivities, boys with great pomp. On the day preceding that on which the rite will be performed, the boy who is clad in heavy, costly garments, is paraded through the streets on horseback, several footmen walking on both sides in order to prevent him from falling and to refresh him by means of a perfumed handkerchief. He is preceded by men with drums and duffs who accompany the *dhikr*'s sung by others. Nearest to the boy goes an elderly black handmaid of his father's, bearing on her head a brazier burning with charcoal, resine and salt. The second part of the procession is formed by the boy's poorer comrades, equally on horseback. The procession passes through the main streets during the time of *ʿaṣr* and comes back to its starting-point a little before sunset. The female members of the family pass the evening with their friends; the party is enlivened by female singers.

Next morning, at sunrise, the barber performs the operation. The foreskin is pressed together by means of a thong, the boy lying on his back, while his mother tries to divert his attention by sweets. A plaster is applied to the wound which usually is healed in a week. The operation is followed by a breakfast for the nearest relatives. It is to be observed that Ḥaḍramites who still cling to their native customs, circumcise their children on the 40th day after birth (Snouck Hurgronje, *Mekka*, ii. 141 *sqq.*).

In Egypt boys are (or were) circumcised at the age of about five or six years. Before the operation the boy is paraded through the streets. Often the train is combined with a bridal procession in order to lessen expenses; in this case the boy and his attendants lead the procession. He is dressed as a girl, in a gorgeous manner. (Lane, *Manners and Customs of the Modern Egyptians*, Chapter on Infancy and Education).

D'Ohsson in his *Tableau de l'empire othoman*, Paris 1787, i. 231 *sqq.*, describes circumcision as practised in Turkey under the heading "Circoncision, *sunneth*", a designation which is also reflected in the word *sünnetdji* for the barber who performs the operation. It took place in the presence of the imām of a mosque who accompanied the ceremony with prayers for the preservation of the child, who was usually 7 years old when he was circumcised. The circumcision of the imperial princes used to give occasion for a display of great pomp.

In North Africa children are circumcised at ages varying between the 7th day after birth and 13 years, by the barber who makes use of a knife or a pair of scissors. According to Dan, as cited by Doutté, *Merrâkech*, p. 351, at Algiers a stone knife was used for the operation. Nowadays this custom seems to be no longer known. In North Africa as well as in Egypt often several boys are circumcised together, the father of the richest bearing the expenses of the ceremony.

On Java circumcision of boys is often combined with the *khatm*- or *kataman*-ceremony. On the different designations of circumcision used in this part of the Archipelago cf. Snouck Hurgronje, *Verspreide Geschriften*, IV/i. 205. *sqq.* The age at which boys are circumcised varies in the different parts of Java; among the conservative populations it is higher (14—15 years) than in circles which are in closer touch with Muslim law (10 years or younger).

In Atchin boys are usually circumcised by the *mudém* (probable = *muʾadhdhin*) at the age of 9 or 10 years, immediately after finishing their Ḳurʾān study. The operation (for details see Snouck Hurgronje, *The Achehnese*, i. 399 *sqq.*) consists in a complete circumcision; in some parts of Java it is rather an incision.

KHIYĀR (A.), option, is the right to withdraw a declaration (e.g. one made under compulsion) in general, and in particular the right to the unilateral cancellation (*faskh*) or ratification (*imḍāʾ*, *idjāza*) of a contract; this right can be conferred by law automatically or agreed upon by the contracting parties.

An option by law exists in the case of a sale (and a hire) in favour of the purchaser (or hirer) at the time at which he sees the object (*khiyār al-ruʾya*); also in the case of a defect (*khiyār al-ʿaib*), or lack of a stipulated quality, or inducement into error (*khiyār al-taghrīr al-fiʿlī*), or deceit (*khiyār al-ghabn*). There are special regulations regarding the option for execution contrary to the agreement in the case of the hire of an artisan. In general the tendency is clear to allow withdrawal from contracts for defects or nonfulfilment, although this is not always called by the term *khiyār*; the demand of *faskh* of a marriage is regarded actually as the exercise of a *khiyār*. According to Ḥanafī teaching, a woman who was married without her consent by another than her ascendant as a minor, on reaching her majority, has the right to withdraw from the marriage (*khiyār al-bulūgh*) [cf. NIKĀḤ]. There is also a legal option with regard to the acts of an unauthorised agent (*fuḍūlī*).

By agreement of the contracting parties there can be conferred at sales and hires on one of them or on both or on a third party the general right of option (*khiyār al-sharṭ*) within a period of time, mostly a strictly limited one; further in the case of a sale on the buyer the right of choosing from among several objects (*khiyār al-taʿyīn*); also, on the seller, an option as to payment by a certain time (*khiyār al-naḳd*).

Finally *khiyār* is the name given to the decision (option) of a woman who has been granted authority by her husband, if she wishes, to pronounce a divorce (*tafwīḍ al-ṭalāḳ*).

Bibliography: Dimitroff, *Asch-Schaibānī*, in *MSOS*, vol. xii., 2nd section, p. 60 *sqq.*; Hooper, *The Civil Law of Palestine and Trans-Jordan*, vol. ii., p. 113 *sq.*; *Dictionary of the Technical Terms Used in the Sciences of the Musulmans* (Bibliotheca Indica), vol. i., p. 421; G. Bergsträsser, *Grundzüge des Islamischen Rechts*, Berlin und Leipzig 1935, see Index. Cf. also the art. BAIʿ.

KHODJA, name of an Indian Muslim caste. According to their own tradition they originally were members of the Lohana caste of Hindus, in Lower Sindh, Kachh and Gudjrāt. The original Hindu caste is still numerous in the same provinces, and also in many other places in Western India. The Khodjas were converted in the fourteenth century by the Persian Ismāʿīlī missionary, *pīr* Ṣadr al-Dīn. Their present name, as they believe, was given by the *pīr* himself. It is a Persian word *khwādja*, which was introduced to replace the original Hindu term *thakur* or *thakkar*, also meaning "lord, master"; it is still used in addressing Lohanas and Khodjas, amongst themselves, because the Lohanas are regarded as Kshatrias.

Ismāʿīlism, as is known, was usually persecuted, and new converts either had to remain in appearance Hindus, or to practice strict *taḳiya* [q.v.], pretending to be Sunnīs, or Ithnā-ʿasharīs (the latter being the only tolerated Shīʿī sect under the Muslim rulers of India). Very often, in the case of small communities, there were no qualified members to perform religious ceremonies, and Sunnī mullas were invited to officiate at weddings, burials, etc. A great majority of the Khodjas remained faithful to the religion to which they were originally converted; but a certain number of isolated families, in the course of time, became so much accustomed to the schools of Islām which they used originally for disguise, that they turned into genuine Sunnīs or Ithnā-ʿasharīs. For this reason there are at present three varieties of Khodjas: the great majority are Nizārī Ismāʿīlīs (further they will be called simply Khodjas because they are the Khodjas of the official documents and general press); they are the followers of H. H. the Agha Khān. Secondly, there are Sunnī Khodjas, chiefly in Bombay; their number is insignificant. And thirdly, there are a few thousand of Ithnā-ʿasharī Khodjas, chiefly in Bombay and Zanzibar. The latter two groups are not the followers of H. H. the Agha Khān.

The Khodjas belonging to each of these three schools of Islām differ from their non-Khodja coreligionists only in so far as they stick to their caste ideas, inherited from their Hindu ancestors, and preserved for a long time due to the necessity of posing as Hindus. These customs are chiefly connected with the rules concerning inheritance and marriage. These are recognised by the courts of law in India. It must be clearly realised that these caste practices have nothing to do with religion; there is no such thing as "Khodjaism", or "religion of Khodjas", other than the Indian Nizārī school of Ismāʿīlism [cf. under ISMĀʿĪLĪYA]. A convert to their religion who is not a Khodja by caste, does not become a Khodja, — he becomes a Nizārī Ismāʿīlī. A Khodja is a Khodja only by the right of birth. If he embraces any religion other than Ismāʿīlism, or generally Islām, he ceases to be an Ismāʿīlī, or Muslim, but does not cease to be a Khodja. If a Khodja marries a woman who does not come from a Khodja family, she does not become through this a Khodja, even if she is an Ismāʿīlī, but the children from such a union are recognized as Khodjas.

Great confusion is introduced through the application of the name Khodja to all the followers of H. H. the Agha Khān. This is completely erroneous: not only are all his non-Indian followers not Khodjas, but also in India there are different groups of Nizārī Ismāʿīlīs, who do not differ in their beliefs, practices, and even language from the Khodjas, but who, nevertheless, are not Khodjas. Such are the Momnas of Siddhpur, the Guptis (= Kunbis) of Gudjrāt, the Shamsīs of the Pandjāb, etc. The Nizārī Ismāʿīlīs in Persia, Central Asia, Afghānistān, Syria, etc., not only have nothing to do with the Indian caste of Khodjas, but even do not know their religious literature, which is in Sindhī and Gudjrātī.

It is extremely difficult to find the correct number of the Ismāʿīlī Khodjas, because official statistics are utterly unreliable. The figures given in the Census of India Reports, etc., are quite fantastic. The chief places in which the Khodjas reside are: Bombay, Kachh, Kathyawar, Lower Sindh, Gudjrāt, Zanzibar, and East Africa; also in many large trading centres, such as Calcutta, Madras, Rangoon, and in many other large and small cities and towns of India. It is probable that the total number of the Ismāʿīlī Khodjas considerably exceeds 200 thousand persons.

Formerly the caste ties were strong amongst the different varieties of the Khodjas, and intermarriage was common. Now instances of this have become rare.

The Khodjas, as a wealthy trading community, are far ahead of other Nizārī Ismāʿīlīs, — culturally, and in organisation. Every province in which a considerable number of Khodjas reside, has a supreme Ismāʿīlī council which generally looks after the welfare and education of the community, and performs the duty of the "justice of peace" in cases in which only members of the Khodja community are concerned. Local communities in the districts have their district councils, which are represented in the Supreme Provincial Councils, under whom they are. Every small community, or "parish", centring around a *djamāʿat-khāna*, or praying-hall, which is also used as a mosque, are cared for by a *mukhī*, a kind of a religious leader, and a *kamaḍiyā* (pronounced *kamriyā*), an account-keeper. These dignitaries are selected and proposed by the parishioners, and finally appointed by the district councils, or directly by H. H. the Agha Khān.

Formerly the Khodjas, just as generally all persecuted religious minorities, kept their beliefs and religious literature as a strictly guarded secret. Now, with changed times, this policy is abandoned, and many of their religious works in Gudjrātī and Sindhī are printed, and sold to any one. Almost every province has its own periodicals. The largest is the Bombay weekly (in Gudjrātī, with an English section) — the "Ismaili". There are also other publications in Bombay, such as the "Ismaili Aftab", "Fidai", etc. (all in Gudjrātī). There are several newspapers in English published in East Africa ("Ismaili Voice", etc.).

Aga Khan, or Agha Khān, i.e. Āḳā Khān, ordinarily is a title which was occasionally bestowed on different noblemen by the early Ḳādjār Shāhs of Persia. The person who at present is known all over the world under this surname is His Highness Sir Sulṭān Muḥammad, whom the Nizārī Ismāʿīlīs [cf. under ISMĀʿĪLĪYA] in India, Persia, Central Asia, Syria, etc., regard as their 48th Imām. For his genealogy see the article Ismāʿīlīya. The title was originally bestowed on his grand-father, Ḥasan-ʿAlī Shāh, at that time quite a young man, by Fatḥ-ʿAlī Shāh Ḳādjār, not long before the latter's death in 1834. The Shāh also married one of his daughters to the young Āḳā Khān, and appointed him the governor of the province of Kirmān. Under the successor of Fatḥ-ʿAlī, the weak Muḥammad Shāh, intrigues started by the notorious Ḥādjdjī Āḳā-sī, the prime minister, caused the young Āḳā Khān to lose the governorship. He went to live on his estate in Maḥallāt, North from Iṣfahān, but even there intrigue did not leave him in peace. Finding the situation precarious, he decided to go to Mecca. His move was interpreted as a rebellion, and he had to fight his way all through Persia to Afghānistān, through which he ultimately came to India, Sindh, in 1842. After touring round the country, he ultimately settled in Bombay, where he died in 1881. He was succeeded by his son, ʿAlī Shāh, and the latter, on his death on the 17th April 1885, was succeeded by his eight year old son, the present Agha Khān, Sulṭān Muḥammad (born on the 2nd Nov. 1877). He was brought up by his mother, Lady ʿAlī Shāh (Shams al-Mulūk Khānum, a grand-daughter of Fatḥ-ʿAlī Shāh Ḳādjār). In 1898 he went for the first time to Europe. Spending some time in India and Africa after his return, he again went to Europe, where he now normally resides, visiting India almost every winter. He has two sons, ʿAlī Shāh and Ṣadr al-Dīn. He is the author of several works of which the best known is "*India in Transition*" (London 1918).

KHUBAIB B. ʿADĪ AL-ANṢĀRĪ, one of the first martyrs of Islām. The main features of his history common to all versions are as follows: Some time after the battle of Uḥud a small body of ten of the Prophet's followers was spied out and surrounded between Mecca and ʿUsfān by 100 (or 200) Liḥyānīs who belonged to the Hudhail. The leader of the hard-pressed little band, ʿĀṣim b. Thābit al-Anṣārī (according to others the leader was al-Marthad), proudly refused to yield. He and six others were killed, whereupon Khubaib, Zaid b. al-Dathina and a third surrendered; the latter fell a victim to his stubbornness and the two former were taken to Mecca and sold. Khubaib fell into the hands of the Banu 'l-Ḥārith b. ʿĀmir b. Nawfal b. ʿAbd Manāf who on the expire of the sacred period took him out of the Ḥaram to al-Tanʿīm, bound him to a stake and killed him with lances (*ṣabran*) in revenge for al-Ḥārith whom Khubaib had killed in the battle of Badr. Before he was tied to the stake, Khubaib asked for time to perform two rakʿa's which was a *sunna* for martyrs, comparable to the last prayer of Christian martyrs. Khubaib is said to have recited two verses at the stake to the effect that he as a Muslim martyr cared nothing about the treatment of his body as Allāh was able to bestow his blessing even upon his severed members. *Ḳunūt* formulae uttered by him besides these verses have also been handed down in which he appealed to Allāh for vengeance on his enemies. Those present are said to have shown great trepidation at this curse of the dying man; it is related that Abū Sufyān hurriedly pressed the little Muʿāwiya to the ground to protect him from the consequences of the ill-omened words; and Saʿīd b. ʿĀmir used to fall into long swoons whenever he thought of the scene.

The figure of the protomartyr Khubaib lent itself readily to embellishment. The daughter of al-Ḥārith (according to others of Māwiya, a client of Hudjair b. Abī Ihāb) in whose house he was kept a prisoner, saw him one day eating grapes, although these could not be found elsewhere in Mecca. — When his martyrdom approached, he asked for a knife with which to remove the hair on his privy parts (as was usual in such cases); the woman sent her little boy with it to him, but became terrified at the thought of possible revenge; when Khubaib noticed her terror, he calmed her with the assurance that no such cruelty need be feared from him. — The verses above mentioned, which he is said to have uttered at the stake have grown in Ibn Hishām to a whole poem. The same author (p. 644 *sqq.*) gives the laments for him. For how his corpse was taken from the Ḳuraish and swallowed up by the earth, see Ṭabarī, i. 1436 *sq.* = *Iṣāba*, i. 862.

Bibliography: al-Zuhrī's or Abū Huraira's tradition in Aḥmad b. Ḥanbal, *Musnad*, ii. 294 *sq.*, 310 *sq.* and in al-Bukhārī, *Djihād*, b. 170; Ibn Isḥāḳ's version, (Ibn Hishām, p. 638 *sqq.*), goes back to ʿĀṣim b. ʿUmar b. Ḳatāda; al-Wāḳidī, transl. Wellhausen, p. 156 *sqq.* (cf. 226 *sq.*) compiled the whole story from various sources; Ibn Saʿd, ii/i. 39 *sq.* iii/ii. 33 *sq.*; al-Diyārbakrī, *Taʾrīkh al-khamīs*, Cairo 1203, i. 454 *sqq.*; Ibn Ḥadjar, *Iṣāba*, i. 860 *sqq.*; Ibn al-Athīr, *Usd al-ghāba*, ii. 111 *sqq.*; Caetani, *Annali dell' Islām*, Anno 4, § 7, 8; Anno 6, § 2; Ṭabarī, i. 1431 *sqq.*, who gives the two main versions; Wensinck, *Handbook*, s.v.

KHULʿ. [See TALĀḲ].

KHURRAMĪYA, a sect whose name is derived by Samʿānī from the Persian word *khurram* "agreeable", on the ground that they regarded everything that was agreeable as lawful; but it is more likely to be derived from Khurram, a district of Ardabīl, where the sect may have arisen. According to Masʿūdī, *Murūdj*, vi. 186, they came into prominence after the execution of Abū Muslim of Khurāsān in 137/755, but while some of them denied that he was dead and foretold his return "to spread justice in the world", others maintained the imāmate of his daughter Fāṭima, whence they got the names *Muslimīya* and *Fāṭimīya*. One Sanbādh started a rebellion in Khurāsān, demanding vengeance for Abū Muslim, but this was suppressed within seventy days. They are next heard of in the reign of Maʾmūn, when Bābak the Khurramī rebelled against the Muslim government and entrenched himself in Badhdh (sometimes Badhdhān), "a village between Ādharbāidjān and Arrān"; he maintained himself from 201 till 223, when his fortress was taken by Afshīn, an officer of Muʿtaṣim; he was himself captured and sent to Sāmarrā, where he was tortured to death, displaying marvellous fortitude under torture (al-Tanūkhī, *Nishwār al-muḥāḍara*, p. 75). His daughter was taken into Muʿtaṣim's ḥarem (Yāḳūt, *Irshād al-arīb*, i. 369). Many odes of both Abū Tammām and Buḥturī are devoted to eulogizing the conquerors, who are said to have served the cause of Islām. In Masʿūdī's time (332), members of the sect were to be found in Raiy, Iṣpahān, Ādharbāidjān, Karadj, Burdj, and in Māsabādhān. Shortly before Masʿūdī wrote, some fortresses held by them were stormed by ʿAlī b. Buwaihi (Miskawaihi, i. 278); and about 40 years later they were in possession of some fortresses in the neighbourhood of Tīz and Mukrān, which they surrendered to ʿAḍud al-Dawla's agent, ʿĀbid b. ʿAlī (*ibid.*, ii. 321).

The best account of their doctrines seems to be that furnished by Muṭahhar b. Ṭāhir, who states that he had met members of the community in their homes, Māsabādhān and Mirhirdjān-ḳadhaḳ. It is as follows (*Livre de la création*, ed. Huart v. 30):

"They are divided into various sects and sorts, but all agree on "return" (i.e. transmigration), asserting, however, that names and bodies are changed. They maintain that all the Apostles, though their codes and religious systems differ, are inspired by one spirit; that revelation never ceases; and in their opinion every adherent of a religion is in the right, so long as he hopes for reward and fears punishment. They do not approve of defaming such a person or harming him, provided he shows no desire to injure their own community or attack their system. They strenuously avoid bloodshed except when they are in open rebellion. They highly esteem Abū Muslim and curse al-Manṣūr for having put him to death. They frequently implore the divine favour for Mahdī b. Fīrūz owing to his being a descendant of Abū Muslim's daughter Fāṭima. They have *imām*'s to whom they have recourse in legal matters, and Apostles who go on circuit among them, and whom they call by the Persian name *firishtah* (Angel). Wine and liquors are in their opinion more fortune-bringing than all other things. The basis of their system is Light and Darkness. Those whom we have met in their homes in Māsabādhān and Mihirdjān-ḳadhaḳ were found by us to be most scrupulous about cleanliness and purity, and most anxious to win people's favour by spontaneous acts of kindness. Some of them, we found, permit promiscuity where the women consent, and indeed the enjoyment of anything craved by the natural mind, provided no injury results to any one therefrom".

Iṣṭakhrī (p. 203) somewhat similarly says of them: "They have mosques in their villages, and they read the Ḳur'ān, only it is asserted that secretly they hold no religious dogma but lawlessness" (*ibāḥa*). Probably then they differed from the Sunnī Muslims in their theory of the imāmate, which they supposed to be inherent in the family of Abū Muslim, whereas their practice of promiscuity (if true) was similar to the Shīʿī *mutʿa*; further in believing in the continued existence of Abū Muslim and in supposing his daughter to inherit his rights they resembled various Shīʿī groups.

Since the member of the sect who attracted most attention was Bābak, we should have expected to learn something of his doctrine, and indeed a special history of this person by Wāḳid b. ʿAmr al-Tamīmī is quoted in the *Fihrist*; it is a string of fables, translated by Flügel in *ZDMG*, xxiii. 351 *sq.* This writer agrees with Ṭabarī in assigning him a predecessor named Djāwīdān. Al-Baghdādī (*al-Farḳ bain al-firaḳ*, p. 252) asserts that the followers of Bābak make the founder of their religion a prince of theirs who lived in pre-Islāmic times, called Sharwīn, whose father was of the Zandj, whereas his mother was the daughter of a Persian king. This would seem to be another form of a story told by Ibn Isfandiyār (transl. E. C. Browne, p. 237) that one Sharwīn of the house of Bāw (called by Ṭabarī, iii. 1295,5 : Sharwīn b. Surkhāb b. Bāb) was the first person who took the title "King of the Mountains". He adds that they have a feast on their mountains which is marked by gross licentiousness; but for all that they ostensibly maintain the ceremonies of Islām. The attempts made to connect them with the old Persian Mazdakites are probably without historical basis.

KHUṬBA (A.), sermon, address by the *khaṭīb* [q.v.]. The khuṭba has a fixed place in Muḥammadan ritual, viz. in the Friday-service, in the celebration of the two festivals, in services held at particular occasions such as an eclipse or excessive drought. In the Friday service it precedes the *ṣalāt*, in all the other services the *ṣalāt* comes first. A short description of the rules for the khuṭba according to al-Shīrāzī (*Tanbīh*, ed. Juynboll, p. 40), one of the early Shāfiʿī doctors, may be given here:

a. One of the conditions for the validity of the Friday-service is that it must be preceded by two sermons. The conditions for the validity of these sermons are the following; the *khaṭīb* must be in a state of ritual purity; his dress must be in accord with the prescriptions; he must pronounce the two khuṭba's standing and sit down between them; the number of auditors required for a valid *djumʿa* must be present. Regarding the sermon itself are obligatory: the *ḥamdala*, the *ṣalāt* on the Prophet, admonitions to piety in both khuṭba's, prayer (*duʿā'*) in behalf of the faithful, recitation of a part of the Ḳur'ān in the first khuṭba or, according to some doctors, in both. It is commendable (*sunna*) for the khaṭīb to be on a pulpit or an elevated place; to salute the audience when directing himself towards them; to sit down till the *adhān* is pronounced by the *mu'adhdhin*; to lean on a bow, a sword or a staff; to direct himself straightway to his audience; to pray on behalf of the Muslims; to make his khuṭba short.

b. Regarding the khuṭba's on the days of festival the same author says (p. 42) that they are like those of the Friday-service, except in the following points: the *khaṭīb* must open the first with nine *takbīr*'s, the second with seven. On the *ʿīd al-fiṭr* he must instruct his audience in the rules for the *zakāt al-fiṭr*, on the *ʿīd al-aḍḥā* in the rules for the sacrifice of this day. It is allowed to him to pronounce the sermon sitting. Regarding the khuṭba's of the service during an eclipse, al-Shīrāzī (p. 43) remarks that the preacher must admonish his audience to fear Allāh, and in the service in times of drought he must ask Allāh's pardon, in the opening of the first khuṭba nine times, in the second seven times; further he must repeat several times the *ṣalāt* on Muḥammad as well as *istighfār*, recite Sūra lxvi. 9, elevate his hands and say Muḥammad's *duʿā'* (which is communicated by al-Shīrāzī in full). Further he must direct himself towards the *ḳibla* [q.v.] in the middle of the second khuṭba and change his mantle, putting the right side to the left, the left to the right, the upper part beneath and keep it on till he puts off all his other garments.

C. H. Becker was the first to point to the relation between the Muḥammadan pulpit and the judge's seat in early Arabia. This explains why the *khaṭīb* must sit down between the two khuṭba's; it explains also why he must lean on a staff, sword or bow; for these were the attributes of the old Arabian judge. It is not easy to see why the khuṭba precedes the services on Friday, whereas on the days of festival and the other special occasions *ṣalāt* comes first. *Ḥadīth* tells us that Marwān b. al-Ḥakam was the first to change this order of things by pronouncing the khuṭba before the performance of the *ṣalāt* on the days of festival (e.g. Bukhārī, *ʿĪdain*, bāb 6 and especially the emotional picture in Muslim, *ʿĪdain*, trad. 9).

It is also said that Marwān was the first to hold the *khuṭba* on these days on a pulpit, the old custom being a service without *minbar* or *adhān*. According to other authorities (cf. Muslim, *Īmān*, trad. 78, 79 and al-Nawawī's commentary), the khuṭba before the *ṣalāt* was an institution going back to ʿUthmān or even to ʿUmar. The common opinion of traditionists is, however, that it was an innovation due to the general tendency of the Umaiyads to favour their own dynastic interests rather than those of religion. If this opinion should be right, the innovation as well as the holding of the khuṭba in a sitting attitude may be looked upon as an endeavour to go back to the pre-Islāmic judicial usages concerning *minbar* and khuṭba.

Regarding the prayer on behalf of the faithful (*duʿāʾ li ʾl-muʾminīn*) it must be observed that in this prayer before the Friday-*ṣalāt* it has become customary to mention the ruling sovereign. The history of Islām is full of examples of the importance which was attached to this custom, especially in times of political troubles, the name mentioned in this *duʿāʾ* betraying the *imām*'s political opinion or position. Though it is not prescribed by law to mention the ruler's name the suppression of the name at this occasion exposed the *khaṭīb* to suspicion on the part of the ruler. In countries where Muslims live under non-Muslim rule, even a prayer for the worldly prosperity of the ruler may expose the *khaṭīb* to suspicion on the part of his fellow-Muslims (cf. Snouck Hurgronje, *Islam und Phonograph*, in *Verspr. Geschr.*, ii. 430 *sq.*; do., *Mr. L. W. C. van den Berg's beoefening van het mohammedaansche recht*, in *Verspr. Geschriften*, ii. 214 *sq.*). The custom of mentioning the ruler in prayer is found as early as the fifth century B.C. in the Aramaic papyri of Elephantine (Pap. i., line 26; cf. also Harnack, *Mission und Ausbreitung des Christentums*, i. 286).

Several of the characteristics of the khuṭba prescribed by the doctors of the law occur also in *ḥadīth*. The khuṭba's of Muḥammad usually begin with the formula *ammā baʿdu* (Bukhārī, *Djumʿa*, bāb 29). Side by side with the *ḥamdala* (Muslim, *Djumʿa*, trad. 44, 45) the *shahāda* occurs (Aḥmad b. Ḥanbal, ii. 302, 343: "A khuṭba without the *shahāda* is like a mutilated hand"). In a large number of traditions it is stated that Muḥammad used to recite passages from the Ḳurʾān (e.g. Muslim, *Djumʿa*, trad. 49—52; Aḥmad b. Ḥanbal, v. 86 *sq.*, 88, 93 etc.). The khuṭba must be short, in accord with Muḥammad's saying: "Make your *ṣalāt* long and your khuṭba short" (Muslim, *Djumʿa* trad. 47). Just like the *ṣalāt* the khuṭba must be right to the purpose (*ḳaṣd^{an}*: Muslim, *Djumʿa*, trad. 41). The audience must be silent and quiet ("who says to his neighbour "listen", has spoken a superfluous word": Bukhārī, *Djumʿa*, bāb 36). The two khuṭba's pronounced by the standing *khaṭīb*, who sits between them, are based on Muḥammad's example (Bukhārī, *Djumʿa*, bāb 27; Muslim, *Djumʿa*, trad. 33—35; Aḥmad b. Ḥanbal, ii. 35, 91, 98). During the *adhān* Muḥammad used to sit on the *minbar*; the *iḳāma* was spoken when he had descended (in order to hold the khuṭba standing); this order was observed by Abū Bakr and ʿUmar (Aḥmad b. Ḥanbal, iii. 449 bis).

Neither the term khuṭba nor the verb *khaṭaba* in their technical meaning occur in the Ḳurʾān. Even in the passage containing an admonition not to abandon the Friday-service for worldly profit, it is only the *ṣalāt* which is mentioned (Sūra lxii. 9—11). It would be wrong to conclude from this silence that the khuṭba did not yet form a constituent part of worship in Muḥammad's time. Still, it is not probable that the different kinds of service were precisely regulated from the beginning. *Ḥadīth* has preserved descriptions showing that Muḥammad's khuṭba often did not have much to do with the regular sermon of later times (cf. Abū Dāwūd, *K. al-Diyāt*, bāb 13; Aḥmad b. Ḥanbal, iii. 56 *sqq.*; Muslim, *ʿĪdain*, trad. 9; do., *Djumʿa*, tr. 54—60).

However uncertain the value of these traditions may be, it seems not out of place to suppose that a fixed order of service on Friday and the days of festival arose only after Muḥammad's lifetime. This order reposes on three elements: the early-Arabian khuṭba, Muḥammad's *sunna* and the example of Jews and Christians.

In his study *Zur Geschichte des islāmischen Kultus* C. H. Becker endeavoured to establish a close connection between the services on Friday and the days of festival on the one hand, and the Mass on the other. The main features of his position are the following: The ceremonies preceding the first khuṭba correspond to the first part of the Mass ("Vormesse"). *Adhān*, and the khuṭba also in part, recall the responses between the deacon and the priest who administers the Mass. The first khuṭba with the obligatory recitation of the Ḳurʾān corresponds to the recitation of the Scripture. The second khuṭba corresponds to the sermon and the general prayer. The *ṣalāt* corresponds to the eucharistic part of the Mass. Concerning the two khuṭba's he states that this duality is a matter of *ikhtilāf* on the part of the *faḳīh*'s; it has found its way into the service on the days of festival from the Friday-service.

This view was combated by Mittwoch who found in the Jewish liturgy features corresponding to *adhān* and *iḳāma*, to the *ḥamdala*, the recitation of the *Tora* (first khuṭba) and the recitation from the Prophets (second khuṭba). It is perhaps impossible to decide the question; probably the example of the Jewish as well as that of the Christian liturgy exercised an influence on the final constitution of the Muḥammadan service.

Muḥammad's first and second khuṭba in Madīna are textually given in Ibn Isḥāḳ's *Sīra* (ed. Wüstenfeld, p. 340) but are hardly genuine. His last sermon is communicated in Bukhārī's collection, *Djumʿa*, bāb 29; his emotion when he preached is described in Muslim, *Djumʿa*, trad. 43. An accurate description of the Friday-service with a translation of two khuṭba's in Lane, *Manners and Customs*, ch. iii, 'Religion and laws'.

A collection of sermons ascribed to ʿAlī is in the Staatsbibliothek in Berlin; among them is a khuṭba without the letter *alif*.

As the office of the khaṭīb became a regular function, the khuṭba became to the khaṭīb what a calligraphed document is to the professional scribe: the one displayed his art in flourished initials, the other in rhymed prose. Collections of sermons are often arranged following the calendar, viz. four sermons for every month and additional ones for the days of festival, the Prophet's birthday, and his Ascension; see Ahlwardt, *Verzeichnis der arab. Hss.*, iii., p. 437.

It is customary to hold the khuṭba in Arabic. This rule has often been broken in Turkey and after the great reform in that country Turkish took the place of Arabic in the sermon.

Bibliography: Juynboll, *Handleiding tot de kennis van de Moh. Wet*, Leiden 1925, p. 71 *sq.*, 109 *sq.*; Shaikh Niẓām, *al-Fatāwī al-ʿĀlamgīrīya*, Calcutta 1828 *sqq.*, i. 205 *sq.*; 210 *sq.*, 214 *sq.*; al-Muḥaḳḳiḳ Abu ʾl-Ḳāsim al-Ḥillī, *Kitāb sharāʾiʿ al-Islām*, Calcutta 1893, i. 44, 48; C. H. Becker, *Islamstudien*, i, 450 *sqq.*, 472 *sqq*; E. Mittwoch, *Zur Entstehungsgeschichte des islamischen Gebets und Kultus*, in *Abh. Pr. Ak. W.*, 1913, No. 2; Brockelmann, *GAL*, i. 92; *Suppl.* i. 149; Abū ʾl-Ṭaiyib Ṣadīḳ al-Bukhārī, *al-Mawʿiẓa al-ḥasana bimā yukhṭab fī shuhūr al-sana*, Bhopal 1295.

ĶIBLA, the direction of Mecca (to be exact of the Kaʿba or the place between the water-spout [*mīzāb*] and the western corner), which has to be observed during the *ṣalāt*.

From very early times the direction at prayer and divine service was not a matter of choice among the Semitic peoples. There is already an allusion to this in I Kings, viii. 44 and it is recorded of Daniel (Dan., vi. 11) that he offered prayer three times a day in the direction of Jerusalem (which has remained the Jewish *ķibla* to this day). As is evident from the names of the quarters of the heavens, the whole life of the Semitic peoples was turned eastwards. The Essenes prayed in the direction of the rising sun and the Syriac Christians also turned eastwards at prayer (*Ancient Syriac Documents*, ed. Cureton, p. 24, 60; *Acta Martyrum occid.*, ed. Assemani, ii. ii. 125). It may therefore very well be assumed in agreement with the tradition that Muḥammad appointed a *ķibla* at the same time as he instituted the *ṣalāt*. It is certain that in the period immediately following the Hid̲j̲ra the direction taken by the Jews was also used by the Muslims. Tradition dates the alteration in the *ķibla* to 16 or 17 months after the Hid̲j̲ra, in Rad̲j̲ab or S̲h̲aʿbān of the year 2, probably rightly, for at this period we have the important change in Muḥammad's attitude to the Jews. The Kaʿba was brought into prominence as a religious centre and the Ḥad̲j̲d̲j̲ began to be treated as a Muslim rite. The alteration in the ķibla is a not unimportant fact in this series of events and this train of thought. The Ķurʾān verses, ii. 142 *sqq.*, refer to this: "The fools among the people will say: What has induced them to abandon their former ķibla? Say: To Allāh belongs the east and the west. He guides whomsoever he pleaseth unto the right path. Thus have we made you an intermediate community, so that ye may be witnesses for mankind while the Prophet is a witness for you. We only appointed your previous ķibla to distinguish him who follows the Prophet from him who turns back on his heels. Verily this is a grievous sin from which he is free who is guided by Allāh, but Allāh will not allow your faith to be of no avail, for He is gracious and kindly to man. We see how thy face turns to all the quarters of the heavens so we will cause thee to turn to a ķibla pleasing to thee. Turn then thy face toward the holy *masd̲j̲id*; turn your faces to it wherever you are. Whatever signs thou wert to give to the people of scripture, they will not follow thy ķibla" etc.

The importance placed by Muḥammad himself upon the change is clear from these words. It is not necessary to assume with the tradition that it was brought about by scornful remarks of the Jews regarding Muḥammad's dependence on the prescriptions of their religion (so Ṭabarī, ed. de Goeje, i. 1280). In other traditions, the new ķibla is represented as that of Ibrāhīm (Ṭabarī, *Tafsīr*, i. 378, ii. 13). Here we have a glimmering of the real truth of the matter, namely the connection with Muḥammad's new politico-religious attitude. According to one tradition (Buk̲h̲ārī, *Ṣalāt*, bāb 32; *Tafsīr*, Sūra 2, bāb 14), the revelation of the above quoted verses from the Ķurʾān was communicated to the believers in the morning ṣalāt in Ķubāʾ; according to another story, Muḥammad had with a portion of the community performed two rakʿa's of the *ẓuhr*-ṣalāt in a mosque of the Banū Salima, when he turned round to the direction of Mecca (Baiḍāwī, on Sūra ii. 144 (139[1]). The mosque received the name of *Masd̲j̲id al-ķiblatain*, "the mosque of the two ķibla's".

If it may then be considered established that Muḥammad and his community turned towards Jerusalem at the ṣalāt during the first period of the Hid̲j̲ra, the question still remains what was his ķibla before the Hid̲j̲ra. In Tradition two answers are given to this question and a third deduced by harmonising the other two. According to one, Muḥammad in Mecca observed the ķibla to the Kaʿba (Ṭabarī, *Tafsīr*, ii. 4; Baiḍāwī, on Sūra ii. 138); according to the other story, the ķibla had always been Jerusalem (Ṭabarī, *Tafsīr*, ii. 3, 8; ed. de Goeje, i. 1280; Balād̲h̲urī, *Futūḥ*, p. 2); according to the third (Ibn His̲h̲ām, p. 190, 228), Muḥammad in Mecca was careful to have the Kaʿba and Jerusalem in a straight line in front of him at the *ṣalāt*. The first view is influenced by the theory of the "religion of Ibrāhīm" for al-Tibrīzī also represents ʿAbd al-Muṭṭalib as knowing that Ibrāhīm appointed the Kaʿba as ķibla (*Ḥamāsa*, i. 125). If the second opinion had not an historical basis, one does not quite understand how it could have arisen, for Tradition does not like to acknowledge Muḥammad's dependence on Jewish practice. This view is therefore, in my opinion, the most probable. It is further mentioned as a distinguishing peculiarity of Barāʾ b. Maʿrūr that even in the period before the Hid̲j̲ra he would not turn his back on the Kaʿba (Ibn His̲h̲ām, p. 294); this tradition would lose its point if the old ķibla had been in the direction of the Kaʿba. Besides these traditional views, others have been put forward in recent years. According to Tor Andrae, *Der Ursprung des Islams und das Christentum*, Uppsala and Stockholm 1926, p. 4 (cf. Buhl, *Das Leben Muhammad's*, p. 216 *sqq.*), the original ķibla was to the east. Andrae bases his view not on the material of Tradition but on the general agreement between early Muslim and Christian religious usages. Schwally held that the Jerusalem ķibla was introduced in Mecca, it is true, but not as a specifically Jewish institution, perhaps a Jewish-Christian one (*Geschichte des Qorans*, i. 175, note k.).

The direction of the ķibla was, or is, not assumed at the ṣalāt only and with the points of the toes (Buk̲h̲ārī, *Ṣalāt*, bāb 28; *Ad̲h̲ān*, bāb 131; Nasāʾī, *Sahw*, Bāb 25; *Taṭbīķ*, bāb 96), but also at the *duʿāʾ* (Buk̲h̲ārī, *Daʿawāt*, bāb 24), at the *iḥlāl* or *iḥrām* (Buk̲h̲ārī, *Ḥad̲j̲d̲j̲*, bāb 29) and after the stone-throwing at the central D̲j̲amra (Buk̲h̲ārī, *Ḥad̲j̲d̲j̲*, bāb 140—142); the head of an animal to be slaughtered is turned to the ķibla and the dead are buried with the face towards Mecca (Lane, *Manners and Customs*, chap. xxviii; Snouck Hurgronje, *Verspr. Geschr.* iv./i. 243; v. 409).

In the *ḥadīt̲h̲* it is forbidden to turn towards Mecca when relieving nature (Buk̲h̲ārī, *Wuḍūʾ*, bāb 11; Muslim, *Ṭahāra*, trad. 61; Nasāʾī, *Ṭahāra*, bāb 18—20). On the question whether it is allowable in doing this to turn one's back to Mecca and thus in some parts of Arabia be facing Jerusalem no unanimity prevails (cf. Buk̲h̲ārī, *Wuḍūʾ*, bāb 14; *K̲h̲ums*, bāb 4; *Ṣalāt*, bāb 29; Muslim, *Ṭahāra*, trad. 59, 71 *sq.*; Abū Dāwūd, *Ṭahāra*, bāb 4); one should not expectorate in the direction of Mecca (Buk̲h̲ārī, *Ṣalāt*, bāb 33).

The observance of the ķibla is given in old traditions along with the performance of the *ṣalāt* and ritual slaughter as a criterion of the Muslim (Buk̲h̲ārī, *Ṣalāt*, bāb 28; cf. *Aḍāḥī*, bāb 12). One of the terms for the orthodox community is *ahl al-ķibla wa 'l-d̲j̲amāʿa*. In many Muslim lands the word has become the name of a point of the compass, according to the direction in which Mecca lies; thus ķibla (pronounced *ibla*) means in Egypt and Palestine, south, in the Mag̲h̲rib, east.

In the mosques the direction of the ṣalāt is indicated by the *miḥrāb* [q.v.]; in classical *ḥadīth* this word does not occur and ḳibla is used to mean the wall of the mosque towards which one turns. At a ṣalāt outside a mosque, a *sutra* [q.v.] marks the direction. In Egypt, small compasses specially made for this purpose are used to ascertain the ḳibla (Lane, *op. cit.*, p. 228). — It should be noted that many mosques are not accurately but only approximately orientated (according to the *djiha*). It sometimes happens that this error has been later corrected by the drawing of lines or the stretching of threads. For an important discussion of this matter see Maḳrīzī, *Khiṭaṭ*, ii. p. 246 *sqq.*

The laws relating to the ḳibla are here given very briefly only and according to the Shāfiʿī school as laid down in al Shīrāzī's *Kitāb al-tanbīh* (ed. Juynboll, p. 20). The adoption of a ḳibla is a necessary condition for the validity of a *ṣalāt*. Only in great danger and in a voluntary *ṣalāt* on a journey can it be neglected. But if one is on foot or can turn his steed round, it should be observed at the *iḥrām, rukūʿ* and *sudjūd*. One should turn exactly in the direction of the ḳibla, and one who is near it can do so with certainty, and one who is remote as nearly as he can judge. According to others in the latter case only the general direction (*djiha*) is obligatory. Outside of Mecca one turns towards the *miḥrāb* within a mosque; when not in a mosque one follows the direction of reliable people; only a man who is in a deserted region is allowed to ascertain the direction for himself by means of certain indications. For details of the laws see the *Bibliography*.

Bibliography: The Ḳurʾān commentators on Sūra ii. 142 *sqq.*; A. J. Wensinck, *Mohammed en de Joden te Medina*, Leiden 1908, p. 108—110, 133—135; Caetani, *Annali dell' Islām*, iii., index; Th. W. Juynboll, *Handleiding tot de kennis van de Mohammedaansche Wet*, Leiden 1925, p. 67, note 5; al-Nawawī, *Minhādj al-ṭālibīn*, ed. van den Berg, i. 69—73; *al-Fatāwā al-ʿĀlamgīrīya*, Calcutta 1828, i. 86—89; al-Muḥaḳḳiḳ Abu 'l-Ḳāsim, *Sharāʾiʿ al-islām*, Calcutta 1255, p. 28—30 (transl. Querry, *Droit Musulman*, Paris 1871, i. 56 *sqq.*); al-Khalīl, *Mukhtaṣar*, Paris 1900, p. 16 *sq.*

ḲIRĀʾA, the method of recitation, punctuation and vocalisation of the text of the Ḳurʾān. Al-Suyūṭī has classified according to Ibn al-Djazarī the various readings of the Ḳurʾān into three series:

1. The ḳirāʾa accepted authentically, which possess the *idjmāʿ al-ṣaḥāba* and the *tawātur*, that is the seven canonical readings of the ʿUthmānic text, attributed to Abū ʿAmr b. al-ʿAlāʾ, Ḥamza, ʿĀṣim, Ibn ʿĀmir, Ibn Kathīr, Nāfiʿ and al-Ḳisāʾī, which Ibn Mudjāhid (d. 324/936) published (*al-ḳirāʾāt al-sabʿa*; cf. ḲURʾĀN, § 18). To these are sometimes added Yaʿḳūb, Khalaf, Abū ʿUbaid, in order to arrive at the figure ten. 2. The *ḳirāʾa shādhdha* which are authentic, but have only *idjmāʿ* without *tawātur*; they are the *maṣḥaf* of Ibn Masʿūd and Ubaiy; it is forbidden since the condemnation of Ibn Shannabūdh in 323/935 to make use of them. 3. The *ḳirāʾa shādhdha* which are pure innovations, grammatical corrections proposed by critics such as Khalaf, Abū ʿUbaid and Ibn Saʿdān, exercising the right of *ikhtiyār*, an anti-traditional claim condemned from 322/934 onwards (ḳirāʾa of Ibn Muḳsim al-ʿAṭṭār condemned).

Bibliography: Nöldeke, *Geschichte des Qorāns*, (2. ed.), iii.; A. Jeffery, *Materials for the History of the Text of the Qurʾān*, Leyden 1937; Suyūṭī, *Itḳān*, Cairo 1278, i. 96; ʿAbd al-Masīḥ al-Kindī, *Risāla*, p. 79—83; Yāḳūt, *Irshād*, ed. Margoliouth, vi. 300 *sq.*, 499 *sq.*

ḲIRĀN. [See IḤRĀM].

ḲIṢĀṢ (A.), synonymous with *ḳawad*, retaliation, as well for killing (*ḳiṣāṣ fi 'l-nafs*, bloodvengeance) as for wounds which are not fatal (*ḳiṣāṣ fī-mā dūn al-nafs*).

1. The Ḳurʾān takes it for granted that the blood-vengeance of Arab paganism — in which in contrast to the unlimited blood feud, definite retaliation, although not always on the person of the culprit himself, forms the essential feature — is a divine ordinance, with the obvious limitation that only the culprit himself can be slain: Sūra xvii. 33; xxv. 68; vi. 151 (cf. ḲATL, i. 1; already in xvii. 33 the avenger of blood is forbidden to kill any one other than the culprit); ii. 178 *sq.* (before Ramaḍān of the year 2): "O ye who believe, the ḳiṣāṣ is prescribed to you for the killed, the free for the free, the slave for the slave, the female for the female; but if anyone is pardoned anything by his brother he shall be asked (to pay) with kindness and pay him with goodwill. This is an alleviation from your Lord and a mercy ..... (179) For you in ḳiṣāṣ is there life". This passage means that a freeman can only be slain for a freeman, and for a slave and a woman only a slave and a woman respectively; it is to be deduced that a slave or a woman can be slain for a freeman; in the other cases the payment of compensation (*diya*) has to take place. The treatment of the freeman in relation to the slave is a matter of course according to old Arab views, but that of the woman, which cannot be completely explained from there, represents a new decision. The commentators had difficulty in reconciling the passage with later developments; one explanation, later completely abandoned, interprets the verse correctly, but makes it abrogated by v. 45 (after the first encounter with the Madīna Jews but before the outbreak of open hostilities): "and we have prescribed for them (the Jews) in it (the Torah): a life for a life, an eye for an eye, a nose for a nose, an ear for an ear, a tooth for a tooth, and for wounds ḳiṣāṣ; but if anyone remits it, it is an expiation for him (i.e. for his sins)". In the years 3—5 with iv. 92 *sq.* there came the distinction between deliberate and accidental killing [of ḲATL, i. 1]: in this the application of ḳiṣāṣ is excluded.

2. The facts gathered from the records of the life of the Prophet are in agreement with this. In the so-called ordinance of the community which belongs to the early Madīna period it is laid down that if any one slays a believer and is convicted, talion takes place unless the avenger of the blood of the slain man desists; all believers must be against the murderer and can only take sides against him. Here the ḳiṣāṣ is brought from the sphere of tribal life into that of the religious-political community (*umma*), but is still recognised as a personal vengeance; it is also laid down for the Madīna Jews that no one is to be prevented from avenging a wound. A limitation of ḳiṣāṣ, logical from the standpoint of the *umma*, lies in the fact that the believer is forbidden to kill a Muslim on account of an unbeliever. On two occasions when Muslims had killed heathens who had however treaties with Muḥammad, he did not allow ḳiṣāṣ to be made "because they were heathen", but paid the compensation himself. On two occasions, for political reasons, he insisted on the acceptance of compensation when

the avenger of blood undoubtedly had the claim to ḳiṣāṣ, but in one case he cursed the murderer. After the capture of Mecca the Prophet is said to have laid down the principle that any blood-guilt attaching to a Muslim dating from the period of heathendom was to be disregarded [cf. ḲATL, i. 2]. But he also intensified the operation of ḳiṣāṣ and on two occasions had the murderer executed, when there were aggravating circumstances, without offering the avenger of blood the choice between ḳiṣāṣ and compensation; the proscription and execution of murderers who were also *murtadd*'s [cf. ḲATL, ii. 5] is however to be interpreted differently. From everything it is clear that the Prophet supervised the carrying out of ḳiṣāṣ.

3. Among the traditions that one may be genuine according to which Muḥammad had a Jew, who had smashed the head of a Muslim *d̲j̲āriya* (slave girl) with a stone, killed in the same way. Later, when Sūra ii. 178 (cf. above § 1) was interpreted in a new way, the attempt was made to see in it evidence that a man might be put to death for a woman. That Ḳur'ānic prescription was very early interpreted to the contrary of its evident meaning; it is true that ʿUmar b. ʿAbd al-Aʿzīz, al-Ḥasan al-Baṣrī, ʿAṭā' and ʿIkrima are quoted as representatives of the view that a man cannot be put to death for a woman, but Saʿīd b. al-Musaiyab, al-S̲h̲aʿbī, Ibrāhīm al-Nak̲h̲aʿī and Ḳatāda held the opposite view and this prevails in the *mad̲h̲hab*'s without any opposition; it is remarkable that traditions expressing the rejected view are hardly to be found.

4. The *ḳiṣāṣ fi 'l-nafs* according to the system of the *s̲h̲arīʿa*. In the cases of illegal slaying noted in the article ḲATL, i., § 5 and 6, ḳiṣāṣ comes into operation, i.e. the next-of-kin of the slain person, who in this capacity is called *walī al-dam* (avenger of blood), has the right to kill the culprit under certain conditions. This punishment still partakes for the most part of the character of personal vengeance, and only occasionally the idea of punishment by public prosecution on behalf of the authority crops up.

For the application of ḳiṣāṣ the fulfilment of the following conditions is necessary: 1) The life of the person slain must be permanently secured by the *s̲h̲arīʿa*; this is the case with a Muslim, *d̲h̲immī* and *muʿāhad*, at least so long as they are in the *dār al-islām* [q.v.] and the *dār al-ṣulḥ* [q.v.] in contrast to the *musta'min*, *murtadd* and *ḥarbī*. This point of view is to be distinguished from that of the illegality of the slaying, although the two ideas have a certain amount in common: the killing of a *musta'min* is illegal but there is no ḳiṣāṣ. 2) The slain person must not be a descendant of the slayer, nor his slave or the slave of one of his descendants. 3) It needs no comment that the slayer when he committed the deed must be of years of discretion and be in full possession of his faculties. 4) Further conditions are disputed (cf. below). — The adoption of Islām wipes out all previous blood guilt and supervening lunacy in the culprit prevents the execution of ḳiṣāṣ. If one of several persons who have slain someone jointly cannot be put to death for one reason or the other, the others also escape ḳiṣāṣ. If the slayer dies before ḳiṣāṣ is carried out, all claim by the avenger of blood ceases according to Abū Ḥanīfa and Mālik; according to al-S̲h̲āfiʿī and Ibn Ḥanbal compensation can still be claimed.

Mālik, al-S̲h̲āfiʿī, and Ibn Ḥanbal demand, before ḳiṣāṣ can be allowed, in addition to the conditions mentioned, that the slain person is at least the equal of the slayer as regards Islām and liberty, while the Ḥanafīs take no account of this. According to Mālik the slayer may be put to death, if he has deliberately "slaughtered" his descendant and this view is also admitted in the S̲h̲āfiʿī school. Several may be put to death for the killing of one, according to Abū Ḥanīfa, Mālik and al-S̲h̲āfiʿī, if they have done the deed together, provided the part taken by each was such that if he had acted alone, death would have resulted likewise.

Ḳiṣāṣ can only be applied after definite proof of guilt is brought. The procedure of proof in a murder trial is essentially the same as in any other case; in *ḳiṣāṣ fi 'l-nafs* there is however also the old Arab institution of the *ḳasāma* [cf. ḲASAM] which Islām allowed to survive (cf. § 3 above); according to Mālik, Ibn Ḥanbal and al-S̲h̲āfiʿī's earlier opinion, ḳiṣāṣ can be inflicted on the accused (but according to Mālik on one only) if the *ḳasāma* is performed and the other conditions are fulfilled; according to Abū Ḥanīfa and the later view of al-S̲h̲āfiʿī, which became predominant in his school, he has only to pay compensation.

The execution of ḳiṣāṣ is open to the avenger of blood and according to Abū Ḥanīfa consists in beheading with the sword or a similar weapon; according to Mālik and al-S̲h̲āfiʿī, the culprit with certain limitations is killed in the same way as he killed his victim; both views are related from Ibn Ḥanbal.

Ḳiṣāṣ as a rule takes place only when the next of kin (*walī*) of the slain person or his owner, if he was a slave, demands it; if there are several (equally nearly related) avengers of blood all must express this desire; if one of them remits ḳiṣāṣ, the refusal affects all.

5. *Ḳiṣāṣ fī-mā dūn al-nafs* according to the system of the *s̲h̲arīʿa*. If any one deliberately (with *ʿamd*; cf. ḲATL, i. 5) and illegally has inflicted an injury, not fatal, which could be inflicted on the doer's person in an exactly similar way he is liable to ḳiṣāṣ on the part of the wounded man (except that Mālik makes it to be carried out by an expert), if the conditions necessary for the *ḳiṣāṣ fi 'l-nafs* are present with the following modifications: according to Abū Ḥanīfa, *ḳiṣaṣ fī-mā dūn al-nafs* is not applied between man and woman or between slaves, but it is according to Mālik, al-S̲h̲āfiʿī and Aḥmad b. Ḥanbal; Abū Ḥanīfa and Mālik further allow no *ḳiṣāṣ fī-mā dūn al-nafs* between freemen and slaves; according to Mālik, al-S̲h̲āfiʿī and Aḥmad b. Ḥanbal this ḳiṣāṣ is inflicted for one on several, but not according to Abū Ḥanīfa.

6. If ḳiṣāṣ is not permitted or if the person entitled to it voluntarily remits his claim, compensation may nevertheless be demanded; for an unlawful slaying, the blood money (*diya*; q.v.) is to be paid to the slain person's inheritance, for an unlawful wounding which is not fatal, according to the particular case, either the full *diya* or a definite part of it or an amount defined by the law (*ars̲h̲*) or a percentage of the *diya* laid down by the judge (the so-called *ḥukūma*) to the injured person; all this on the supposition that the slain or wounded person is a freeman. If he is a slave his value must be made good. If the culprit is a slave, his owner has to pay these contributions for him; he can however escape by handing over the slave.

7. Of the regulations of the S͟hīʿa, which are essentially the same as the Sunnī, we need only mention that according to the Twelver Imāmīs, if a man has killed a woman, ḳiṣāṣ can be carried out if the *walī* of the woman pays the relatives of the man the difference between the two respective *diya*'s.

Bibliography: Wellhausen, *Reste arabischen Heidentums*, p. 186 sqq.; Procksch, *Über die Blutrache bei den vorislamischen Arabern und Mohammads Stellung zu ihr*; *Zum ältesten Strafrecht der Kulturvölker, Fragen zur Rechtsvergleichung*, gestellt von Th. Mommsen, section v.—vii.; Lammens, *L'Arabie occidentale avant l'hégire*, p. 181 sqq. — Wensinck, *Handbook* s.v. — Juynboll, *Handleiding tot de kennis van de mohammedaansche wet* (3rd ed.), p. 299 sqq.; G. Bergsträsser, *Grundzüge des Isl. Rechts*, 1935; J. Schacht, *Origins of Muh. jurisprudence*, passim.

KISWA. [See KAʿBA].

ḲIṬFĪR is the name in Muḥammadan legend of the Biblical Potiphar. Ḳiṭfīr is corrupted from Fiṭfīr like Bilḳīs, queen of Saba, from Nikaulis (in Josephus, *Ant.* viii., vi., 2, 157) or as in the Yūsuf legend we have ʿAinam or Ḥainam from Muppīm, Ḥuppim. Ḳiṭfīr was then further corrupted to Iṭfīr (so generally in Ṭabarī and Thaʿlabī), Iṭfīn (Maḳrīzī), only fortuitously resembling Potiphar's name Puṭinun in *Gen. R.* lxxxvi., and almost unrecognisably to Ḳiṭṭīn (Ṭabarī, i. 377) and Ḳiṭṭifīn (Ṭabarī, *Tafsīr*, xii. 98). On the other hand al-Kisāʾī always has Ḳūṭifar (probably a slip of the pen for Fūṭifar), a direct borrowing from Potiphar.

The Egyptian who buys Yūsuf is not mentioned by name in the Ḳurʾān, but only indicated as buyer (xii. 21), or as master of the house (xii. 23). When he however is called al-ʿAzīz (xii. 30, 51), this is to be taken as a common noun frequently recurring in the Ḳurʾān with the meaning of „a mighty man, a ruler" — in the same way as Yūsuf, after his elevation, is addressed as al-ʿAzīz by his brothers (xii. 78, 88). Yūsuf succeeded indeed to Ḳiṭfīr as Treasurer of Egypt, according to some in Ḳiṭfīr's lifetime after his dismissal from office, according to others only after his death, when Yūsuf inherited his office and his wife. In course of time al-ʿAzīz became a personal name as related e.g. by Abu 'l-Fidāʾ (ed. Fleischer p. 28): the Treasurer of Egypt whose name was al-ʿAzīz, bought him. Thus he is called also in Firdawsī's epic "*Yūsuf and Zulaika*", in S͟hāhin's Genesis-book which follows Firdawsī (Bacher, *Zwei jüdisch-persische Dichter, Schahin und Imrāni*, p. 120), and in the legend of the Moriscos (Grünbaum, *Gesamm. Aufsätze*, p. 574). Post-Ḳurʾānic legend knows also Ḳiṭfīr's father Ruhaib or Rahīb (Thaʿlabī), places Ḳiṭfīr in a favourable light, and counts him — along with Jethro's daughter who offered hospitality to Moses, and Abū Bakr who magnanimously appointed ʿUmar his successor — among the three *afras*, those humans who acted in the most noble and most chivalrous way.

Bibliography: Ṭabarī, i. 378, 381, 382, 391, 392; the commentaries on Sūra xii.; Thaʿlabī, *Ḳiṣaṣ al-anbiyāʾ*, Cairo 1325, p. 74, 75, 76, 80; al-Kisāʾī, ed. Eisenberg, p. 161, 162, 164, 168.

KITMĀN. [See TAḲĪYA].

ḲIṬMĪR is the name of the dog which accompanied the Seven Sleepers (see AṢḤĀB AL-KAHF). This name is not found in the Ḳurʾān text; here the word only occurs in the meaning of the skin (*lifāf*) of a date-stone (Sūra xxxv, 13; cf. Baiḍāwī's commentary). Ḳiṭmīr as name of the dog goes back to a tradition of Ibn ʿAbbās; several other names also are reported, some of which have a certain resemblance with it (Ḳitmār, Ḳanṭūr, Ḳatmūn, Ḥamrān, Nasīf, etc.). The tradition rests on the same sources as the other names of the Seven Sleepers, which seem to betray a Greek origin. The dog Ḳiṭmīr has gained a great importance in the popular fantasy of several Muḥammadan peoples. In Persia, for instance, if somebody is afraid of a dog, he should recite Sūra xviii, 18: "And their dog stretched forth his fore legs in the mouth of the cave" (Massé, *Croyances et Coutumes persanes*, Paris 1938, p. 205). The name Ḳiṭmīr provides also a *baraka* or magical protection. For this reason the Tatars in Russia and the Muḥammadans in the Caucasus write the word Ḳiṭmīr on a letter which they intend to safeguard against loss; this amounts to its being a registered letter (cf. Weyh in *ZDMG*, lxv, p. 289). This same use is found in Indonesia.

Bibliography: al-Thaʿlabī, *ʿArāʾis*, Cairo 1282, p. 462; al-Damīrī, *Ḥayāt al-ḥayawān*, Cairo 1275 s.v. *Kalb*, p. 320.

AL-ḲIYĀMA (A.), the arising (of men at the Resurrection), and *al-sāʿa*, "the Hour" (or Day of Judgement), come for theologians under the general term *al-maʿād*, "the returning", i.e. the return to life after death; and they rank them among *al-samʿiyāt*, i.e. things based on Ḳurʾān or Tradition (*Mawāḳif* of al-Īdjī, Būlāḳ 1266, p. 544 *sq.*).

A schematic statement of the order of events in Muslim eschatology. I. The signs which will announce the coming of the end, especially the appearance of the Antichrist, al-Dadjdjāl [q.v.], who will lead almost all men astray, followed by the descent of ʿĪsā, or the Mahdī [q.v.] (or ʿĪsā is both), who will kill al-Dadjdjāl. A period of faith will follow. II. The first blast of the trumpet; all living things will die. The interval. The second blast of the trumpet, bringing all living things to life again and uniting them at the place of gathering (*al-maḥshar*). The long standing there (*al-mawḳif*) in the presence of Allāh and the sweat (*al-ʿaraḳ*). III. The Judgment begins. The questioning of each individual directly by Allāh. The books of record. The weighing of the deeds of those as to whom there might be doubt. Adjustment of enmities and requital of wrongs between man and man, and man and beast. IV. The bridge over Hell into Paradise (*al-ṣirāṭ*). The Intercession [see S͟HAFĀʿA]. The tank of Muḥammad [see ḤAWḌ]. V. The fire (hell and purgatory; see DJAHANNAM); the garden (paradise; see DJANNA); a limbo (according to some theologians). — *Iḥyāʾ* of al-G͟hazzālī, Cairo 1334, iv. 436—453; *Itḥāf*, commentary on *Iḥyāʾ*, x. 447—530.

For Muḥammad, a revivalist preacher seeking to strike terror in his hearers, the doctrines of the resurrection and of the judgement were of the first importance, and the Ḳurʾān, in consequence, is full of references to them. The word *maʿād* occurs once only (Sūra xxviii. 85) and evidently has not this application there: it may mean the place of Muḥammad's resurrection or Mecca to which he will return from exile (Baiḍāwī in loc.). But the verb is used very frequently; in Sūra x. 4, 34; xxi. 104; xxx. 11, 27; lxxxv. 13, of Allāh's bringing men back at the resurrection, in contrast to his first production of them (*abdaʾa*); in contrast to his *anbata* in Sūra lxxi. 17, 18; in contrast to his *faṭara* in Sūra xvii. 51. The same verb is used of the repeated processes of creative power in the earth in Sūra xxvii. 64; xxix. 19 and of man being brought back to the earth at death and burial, Sūra xx. 55. Al-Ḳiyāma, only in the phrase *yawm al-ḳiyāma*, occurs 70 times, e.g. ii. 85, 113, 174, 212; iii. 55, 77, 149; lxviii. 39; lxxv. 1, 6 (last occurrences). On the meaning of ḳiyāma (*ḳiyām* with the feminine termination of emphasis) see *Mufradāt* of Rāghib al-Iṣbahānī, p. 429, ll. 2 *sq*. *Al-sāʿa* occurs 40 times, generally in fixed phrases and always, when with the article, of the Hour; e.g. vi. 31, 40; vii. 187; xii. 107; xv. 85; xlvii. 18; liv. 1, 46; lxxix. 42 (last occurrences). In the *Iḥyāʾ* of al-Ghazzālī (iv. 440 *sq*.; *Itḥāf*, x. 462—465) there is a long list of names of the Hour which occur in the Ḳurʾān or can be formed from Ḳurʾānic phrases. The following may be mentioned: *al-ḳāriʿa*, "the striker", Sūra xiii. 31; lxix. 4; ci. 1, 2; *al-ghāshiya*, "the coverer", Sūra xii. 107; lxxxviii. 1 only; *al-ṣākhkha*, "the deafener", Sūra lxxx. 33 only; *yawm al-faṣl*, "day of dividing", xxxvii. 21; xliv. 40; lxxvii. 13, 14, 38; lxxviii. 17 only; *al-wāḳiʿa*, "the event", lvi. 1; lxix. 15 only; *al-ḥāḳḳa*, "the certainty", lxix. 1, 2, 3 only; *yawm al-ḥisāb*, "day of reckoning", xxxviii. 16, 26, 53; xl. 27; *yawm al-baʿth*, "day of arousing", xxx. 56 only (*al-baʿth* alone xxii. 5 only); *yawm muḥīt*, "an encompassing day", xi. 84 only; *yawm al-dīn*, "day of judgement", i. 4; lxxxiii. 11 and very often; also *al-dīn* alone in meaning "the judgement" very often; for meanings of *dīn* in the Ḳurʾān see the art. DĪN.

In the overwhelmingly theocentric theology of Muḥammad the doctrine of the resurrection and judgement was second only to that of Allāh's creation of the world, was a necessary consequence to it and could be proved by it. Allāh as Creator meant Allāh as ruler and Allāh as judge. But a judgement meant a resurrection and all the analogies of what we call nature pointed to the possibility of such a return and repetition of life, if under other conditions. So Muḥammad was primarily a preacher of this wrath to come and of the need of repentance and self-surrender to Allāh before it should come. For the Arabs of his time the resurrection was, if anything, a harder doctrine than the creation. Muḥammad proved the one by the other. He had possibly a foothold for this in the primitive Arab conception that the dead had a continued and conscious existence of a kind in their graves; cf. among the Hebrews: Job, xiv. 20—22. Through Muḥammad this belief passed into Islām and is the basis in Islām of the doctrine of the two judgements (see below), of punishment in the grave (*ʿadhāb al-ḳabr*; see MUNKAR and NAKĪR), and of bliss in the grave, i.e. that the grave for each individual is a preliminary hell or paradise. This doctrine does not seem to have any sure Ḳurʾānic basis although texts from the Ḳurʾān (vi. 93; ix. 107; xiv. 27; xl. 11, 46; lxxi. 25) are used by the theologians in support of it (*Mawāḳif* of al-Īdjī, p. 591; al-Taftāzānī on *ʿAḳāʾid* of al-Nasafī, Cairo 1321, p. 109; al-Bukhārī in heading to *Djanāʾiz*, b. 87). It is possible that there may be a reference to it in Sūra xxxv. 22 where Muḥammad seems to be warned not to preach to the dead in their graves, as (e.g.) he preached to the *djinn*. But that it was taught by Muḥammad seems certain from the mass of traditions on the subject (Muslim, *Djanna*, trad. 63 *sqq*.; al-Bukhārī, *Djanāʾiz*, b. 87 *sqq*.). In consequence of all this the Ḳurʾān from beginning to end is full of lurid descriptions of the Day with picturesque details of its certainty, its nearness and its overwhelming terrors — passing into descriptions of the fire and, in contrast, of the garden. In the Ḳurʾān it is a judgement of individuals and not of peoples or of religious bodies in masses; this, as Wellhausen pointed out, shows the Christian, as opposed to Jewish, theological influence upon Muḥammad. Later traditions and still more the theologians were going to change all that in accordance with the "agreement" (*idjmāʿ*) of Islām. As examples of these multitudinous, longer or shorter descriptions, reference will suffice to Sūra vi. 22—31; xix. 66—73; xxii. 1—2; xxiii. 99—end; xxxix. 68—end; lxix.; lxxv.; lxxxi.—lxxxiv.; xcix.—ci. Naturally the most picturesque details are in the earlier and more poetical Sūras. The descriptions of the garden changed also with Muḥammad's changing circumstances and age; cf. Josef Horovitz, *Das Koranische Paradies*, Jerusalem 1923.

In these descriptions there are certain references and allusions which (i) tradition has developed more precisely and elaborately, of which (ii) the systematic theologians have made chary use in their short eschatological statements, but which (iii) the writers for religious edification have expanded in intolerable and contradictory detail. Thus (1) the *ṣirāṭ* is only once in the Ḳurʾān (xxxvii. 23) *ṣirāṭ al-djaḥīm* — a mere allusion to "the road to hell". This has become in tradition "the bridge", elaborately described, "over the back of hell" (for reference, cf. Wensinck, *Handbook*, s.v. Bridge). (2) The noun *mawḳif* does not occur in the Ḳurʾān, but four times (vi. 27, 30; xxxiv. 31; xxxvii. 24) there are allusions to man standing in the presence of Allāh on the Day. This has become the awful scene which al-Ghazzālī develops so fully in his *Durra* (ed. Gautier, 1878, p. 58, transl. p. 50 *sq*.). (3) Sūra lxviii. 42: "on the day when a shank (*sāḳ*) shall be uncovered" means, according to the commentators (e.g. Baiḍāwī, Fleischer's ed., ii., p. 350, l. 10), a day of stress and trouble when skirts will be tucked up for flight. In the traditions (Muslim, *Īmān*, trad. 302; *Fitan*, trad. 116; Bukhārī, *Kitāb al-tawḥīd*, b. 24) the *sāḳ* is that of Allāh and the uncovering of it is a sign between him and the true believers. (4) On the resurrection trumpet there is much more in the Ḳurʾān. The Ḳurʾānic formula is *nufikha fi 'l-ṣūr* (vi. 73; xviii. 99; xx. 102; xxiii. 101; xxvii. 87; xxxvi. 51; xxxix. 68; l. 20; lxix. 13; lxxviii. 18), except in lxxiv. 8, where it is *nuḳira fi 'l-nāḳūr*. In lxix. 13 a single blast, *nafkha wāḥida*, is enough, but in xxxix. 68 there are two blasts; at the first all in heaven and earth, save whom Allāh wills, swoon (*ṣaʿiḳa*); at the second they are restored and stand up. This whole passage has evidently been of the first importance in the forming of the later picture of the Day. In tradition the first blast of the trumpet is reckoned among the signs of the Day (Muslim, *Kitāb al-fitan wa-ashrāṭ al-sāʿa*, trad. 108 *sqq*., 133). (5) The word for "balances" when used in the singular in the Ḳurʾān expresses the general idea of justice (xlii. 17; lv. 7-9; lvii. 25 and Baiḍāwī on these passages) but the plural, *mawāzīn* (vii. 8, 9; xxi. 47; xxiii. 102, 103; ci. 6-9), is used only, in fixed phrases, of weighing men's good and bad deeds in the eschatological Balances on the Day. (6) There is a personal account between Allāh and every man (*ḥisāb* and other terms; cf. C. C. Torrey, *Commercial-theological terms in the Koran*, Leyden 1892, p. 9 *sq*.) and there are books written by recording angels (*safara*, *kātibūn*; lxxx. 11—15; lxxxii. 10—12; lxxxiii. 7, 18). Each man has a book of his own deeds or there is simply the book (x. 61; xvii. 13, 14; xviii. 49; lxix. 19, 20, 25—7; lxxxiv) 7—12); Allāh himself is a witness (*shahīd*, often.

or he is watching in a lurking place, like a hunter waiting for game (lxxxix. 14, *la-bi'l-mirṣād*); or *dj̲ahannam*, personified, is such a *mirṣād* (lxxviii. 21), a dubious phrase which gives the commentators much trouble. (7) Again, *dj̲ahannam* (occurs 77 times) is brought as though it were moveable (lxxxix. 23) and there is a description of it (lxvii. 7, 8) as braying and boiling and almost bursting with rage as though it were a wild animal. What this became in tradition is seen in the *Ṣaḥīḥ* of Muslim, *Djanna*, tr. 30 *sq.*; *Maṣābīḥ al-sunna*, Cairo 1318, ii. 154—156; *Mis̲h̲kāt al-maṣābīḥ*, Dihli 1327, p. 428—430. Al-G̲h̲azzālī develops the idea still further, for pious edification, in his *Durra*, p. 66, transl. p. 56 *sq.* (8) In Sūra xliv. 10 there is a very obscure expression: "Then look for the day when the heaven shall bring plain smoke" (*duk̲h̲ān mubīn*). Baiḍāwī (Fleischer's ed., ii., p. 245, ll. 22 *sq.*) gives as a possible interpretation a reference to smoke as one of the signs of the Day; for the traditions on this see *CTM*, s.v. (9) For a supposed Ḳur'ānic allusion to the descent (*nuzūl*) of ʿĪsā as one of the signs of the Day see above ʿĪSĀ and add to the references there *Ṣaḥīḥ* of Muslim, *Īmān*, tr. 242 *sq.*, 273; *Fitan*, tr. 34 *sqq.* (10) Another of the signs to which allusion is made in the Ḳur'ān (xxvii. 82) is the beast of the earth (*dābbatan min al-arḍ*; cf. *CTM*, s.v.). Baiḍāwī (*in loc.*) identifies it with *al-dj̲assāsa*, "the searcher out", described in a tradition in the *Ṣaḥīḥ* of Muslim (*CTM*, s.v.) as in attendance, according to Tamīm al-Dārī, on the Masīḥ al-Dad̲j̲d̲j̲āl in a certain island; see, also, *LA*, vii. 337; Damīrī, *Ḥayāt al-ḥayawān*, Cairo 1313, ii. 170. (11) On al-Dad̲j̲d̲j̲āl, who is not in the Ḳur'ān at all, see DAD̲J̲D̲J̲ĀL. (12) The tank (*ḥawḍ*) of Muḥammad also plays an obscure part in the picture of the Day, although it does not occur in the Ḳur'ān [see ḤAWḌ]. (13) In the story of D̲h̲u 'l-Ḳarnain in the Ḳur'ān (xviii. 83—98) he builds a great wall to keep back Yād̲j̲ūd̲j̲ and Mād̲j̲ūd̲j̲. But that will hold them only until the Day; then it will be made as dust (verse 98) and they will come out (Sūra xxi. 96). For this, among the signs, in tradition see *Ṣaḥīḥ* of Buk̲h̲ārī, *Fitan*, bāb 4; *Ṣaḥīḥ* of Muslim, *Fitan*, tr. 1—3, and often.

There is thus very little in the Ḳur'ān as to the signs preceding the last day; but such picturesque and accidental references as there are have proved useful in the later development. The systematic theologians have been by far the most cautious in this. Nasafī in his *ʿAḳā'id* gives only five: the appearance of al-Dad̲j̲d̲j̲āl; the beast of the earth; Yād̲j̲ūd̲j̲ and Mād̲j̲ūd̲j̲; the descent of ʿĪsā; the rising of the sun in the west. Taftāzānī in his commentary on this passage (p. 145) gives ten: the smoke; Dad̲j̲d̲j̲āl; the beast; the rising of the sun in the west; ʿĪsā; Yād̲j̲ūd̲j̲ and Mād̲j̲ūd̲j̲; three eclipses, in west, in east and in Arabia; a fire which will break out in al-Yaman and drive men to the place of gathering; cf. a similar list in the *Ṣaḥīḥ* of Muslim, *Fitan*, tr. 39. But the traditionalists have luxuriated in tendencious details. A chapter in the tradition works is devoted to *al-fitan wa-as̲h̲rāṭ* or *āyāt al-sāʿa*, "trials and signs of the Hour"; *Maṣābīḥ*, ii. 128—42; *Mis̲h̲kāt*, p. 392—410. To give any full analysis of these would be impossible here. Reference may be made for this and for details on the resurrection and judgement to Wensinck, *The Muslim Creed*, index, and especially D. S. Attema, *De Mohammedaansche opvattingen omtrent het tijdstip van den Jongsten Dag en zijn voortekenen*, Amsterdam 1942. Even among mystics in Islām religious conversion has normally been wrought by fear of the wrath of Allāh; in consequence their books are full of pictures of the horrors of death, the resurrection and the judgement. This is the whole bearing of the last Book of al-G̲h̲azzālī's *Iḥyā'* (iv. 361—469) on "Taking thought of death and that which comes after it" (*D̲h̲ikr al-mawt wa-mā baʿdahu*), until it ends in a few pages on the beatific vision in Paradise and the wideness of Allāh's mercy, for luck! (*ʿalā sabīl al-tafā'ul*). His smaller treatise, *al-Durra al-fāk̲h̲ira*, on the same subject, goes still further in this direction.

Yet in this mass of traditions certain drifts of influence and development show themselves, theological and historical. Reference has already been made to the development of the doctrine of two judgements, a lesser on the death and burial of the individual and the greater on the Day itself. It is difficult to say whether this was in the mind of Muḥammad, but it was a natural development of the doctrine of the punishment of the grave which is so strongly represented in traditions. The doctrine, also, that the fire itself will be a temporary place of purgation for "certain rebellious ones of the believers" would naturally grow out of this. It, too, is represented in tradition and has become fixed in theology (Taftāzānī on Nasafī, p. 114—19). On the whole question, see *Immortality in Mohammedanism* by D. B. Macdonald in E. H. Sneath's *Religion and the Future Life*, New York 1922, p. 311 *sq.* Cf. also A. S. Tritton, *Muslim Theology*, London 1947, Index s.v. *Grave*. This leads naturally to the relation of faith and works and of sins, greater and lesser, and that involves a classification of different ranks even among the saved believers. On the whole question, see ĪMĀN. Some believers will enter Paradise without any punishment or even reckoning (*ḥisāb*); there will be 70,000 of these (Muslim, *Īmān*, tr. 370 *sqq.*). Then there are the *s̲h̲uhadā'*, whose spirits (*arwāḥ*) seem already to be in Paradise (Muslim, vi. 38) and a man who is killed in defence of his property is a *s̲h̲ahīd* [q.v.] and his slayer is in the fire (Muslim, *Īmān*, tr. 225). But the theological question which seems to have weighed most heavily in the Muslim world when traditions were being formed was that of intercession (*s̲h̲afāʿa*; q.v.).

The historical influences are equally plain in these traditions. Some may go back to Muḥammad himself, full of forebodings as to the future of his people; the times must be evil before they are better. Such are those which tell that the Hour will not come until no one in the world says, "Allāh! Allāh!" — i.e. there is no faith left (Muslim, *Īmān*, tr. 230 *sqq*). But others seem clearly connected with the later civil strife. The traditions prophesying the murder of ʿUt̲h̲mān run into prophecies of the Hour (Muslim, *Fitan*, tr. 14 *sqq.*) and show the deep feeling of despair produced among the pious by the civil wars and the growing unbelief. Again, when the dream of the speedy conquest of Constantinople faded, the belief rose that that conquest would be one of the signs of the end. As soon as the cry of Muslim triumph was heard in that city their armies would be recalled to face Antichrist, al-Dad̲j̲d̲j̲āl (Muslim, *Fitan*, tr. 37 *sq.*). Then ʿĪsā would descend. So some traditions see the whole world plunged in unbelief before the end, and others make the crowning conquest of Islām introduce the end.

The theologians have seen quite clearly that it was impossible to construct out of these materials a consistent narrative of what would take place on the Day. So they have abandoned the attempt and contented themselves with saying that such and such things — the *ṣirāṭ*, the weighing, the tank, etc. — are realities (*ḥaḳḳ*) and leave generally untouched what kind of reality is meant. Philosophically, they knew very well, there are different kinds of reality (Nasafī and Taftāzānī, p. 110 *sq.*; Īdjī, p. 592). They thus abandon picturing the Day to such religious writers as have edification for their object, not fact. Apparently the distinction was quite clear in their minds, and it goes back to the fundamental principle in Islām of the economy of teaching ("Speak to the people according to their understanding" — a saying ascribed both to ʿAlī and to the Prophet) which was the ultimate source of the mediaeval doctrine of the two-fold truth. The situation may be illustrated by al-Ghazzālī's method which was at least threefold. In the last book of the *Iḥyāʾ* and, still more, in the *Durra* his frank object is to strike terror; these are all realities — very dreadful realities! Yet his philosophical conscience troubles him and even in the *Iḥyāʾ* (book of *al-tawba*, "Repentance", iv. 20 *sq.*) he teaches that words applied to concrete things in this world can be used of things in the world to come only by metaphor, as *amthāl*; and he defends this by Sūra xxix. 43. But in his *Iḳtiṣād* (Cairo 1320, p. 96—98) he is a sober scholastic — the *mīzān* and the *ṣirāṭ* are *ḥaḳḳ* by revelation and the reason cannot deny them; in his *Maḍnūn* (Cairo 1303, intended for theological specialists) he develops to a certain extent the philosophical bottoming of these ideas — the intercession (p. 28), the reckoning and the *ṣirāṭ* (p. 36), the pleasures of paradise (p. 38 *sq.*) which will be sensuous, imaginative, rational (*ḥissī*, *khayālī*, *ʿaḳlī*). The feeling left in the mind is that there are still more distinctions, explanations and refinements behind the two *Maḍnūn*'s, and that feeling is strengthened by his *Mishkāt al-anwār* (see the translation of this by W. H. T. Gairdner in *Asiatic Society Monographs*, vol. xix.). Further, al-Ghazzālī developed the doctrine of a limbo for those who, by reason of youth, mental affliction, historical and geographical situation and environment, had not been able to become Muslims and, therefore, had no works of obedience, in the technical sense, to their credit. There was nothing against them and punishing them in the fire would be unjust: but there was nothing also for which they could be rewarded. He found a place for them, therefore, in the Ḳurʾānic *al-Aʿrāf* (vii. 45—47) which he explained as "Heights" whence those in the limbo look down on both heaven and hell and their inhabitants. Such a conception was beyond doubt very far from Muḥammad's mind, but as a theological fiction it was sufficient for al-Ghazzālī's purpose. For the fourfold classification of man which thus resulted see his *Iḥyāʾ*, iv., p. 20—28; *Itḥāf*, viii., p. 548—570; for this particular class see his *Faiṣal al-tafriḳa*, ed. Cairo 1319, p. 75 *sq.* and *Iḥyāʾ*, iv. 27 *sq.*; the *Itḥāf*, viii., p. 564—568 gives different views on the subject and there is an attack on al-Ghazzālī's position in *Les Prolégomènes théologiques de Senoussi* by J. D. Luciani (Algiers 1908), p. 106 *sq.* On the whole subject see Miguel Asín, *La Escatologia musulmana en la Divina Comedia*, Madrid 1919, p. 99 *sq.* The treatment of eschatology by al-Īdjī in his *Mawāḳif* is of the dryest scholasticism, in startling contrast to the picturesqueness of the materials which he uses. Like al-Ghazzālī he makes no use of the signs; they were history, apparently, and not philosophical theology. He begins with the possibility of a return to existence of a nonentity (*maʿdūm*) and fights that out with the different unbelieving philosophical schools: the different elements that follow suggest to him only dogmas to be demonstrated, and even the doctrine of the intercession of Muḥammad interests him only by its connection with the Muʿtazilite heresies. For eschatological ideas as developed among the mystics see Louis Massignon, *La Passion d'al-Hallâj*, Paris 1922, ii. 644—698.

ḲIYĀS (A.), infinitive III of *ḳāsa*, deduction by analogy. The term is used with a multitude of meanings; cf. the lexicons, especially Dozy, *Supplément*, s.v. Here we shall confine ourselves to ḳiyās as one of the "roots" of the *fiḳh*, i.e. the deduction of legal prescriptions from the Ḳurʾān and the *sunna* by reasoning by analogy. — The death of Muḥammad deprived the community of the means of obtaining revelations and at the same time of its guide in matters political and religious. At first they relied on the book of Allāh and the example of the Prophet. The Ḳurʾān and the *sunna* naturally became the guides of the community. The expansion under the first Caliphs, the growing interest in theological and juridical speculation, the whole new world, intellectual and material, raised questions previously unknown, the answers to which could not be found in the Ḳurʾān nor in the *sunna*. Men thus found themselves forced to take decisions or to regulate their conduct from their own opinion. The beginnings of this process were certainly not theoretical in character.

In the second half of the first century A. H. *fiḳh* began to develop at the same time as *ḥadīth*. This parallelism gave rise to a rivalry between the "historical" and "rationalist" schools, the *ahl al-ḥadīth* or *ahl al-ʿilm* and the *ahl al-raʾy*. The earliest founders of *madhhab*'s compiled their manuals of law, either by oral communication like Abū Ḥanīfa (d. 150/767) or in writing like Mālik b. Anas (d. 179/795) without much worrying about questions of general principle. Al-Shāfiʿī (150—204/767—820) was probably the first to give an outline of the "roots" (*uṣūl-al fiḳh*), of the value and function of the Ḳurʾān, *sunna*, *idjmāʿ* and ḳiyās in the theological and judicial system of Islām. "Ḳiyās", he says, "is used in the cases which are not dealt with by the Ḳurʾān nor *sunna* nor *idjmāʿ*" (*Risāla*, p. 65). For him, "ḳiyās and *idjtihād* [q. v.] are two terms for the same idea" (*op. cit.*, p. 66). It might be added that there are other terms, more or less synonymous. We have already mentioned *raʾy*, a word which is often used as a synonym of ḳiyās, but which assumed the meaning of "pure reasoning", whereas ḳiyās has always a more limited meaning in as much as it is applied to a particular method of reasoning, which otherwise ought to be applied to the other roots of *fiḳh* also. As more or less synonymous terms, we may mention *istiḥsān*, *istiṣlāḥ* [q. v.], *mafhūm* (see below), *tamthīl* (see below).

The attitude defended by al-Shāfiʿī was not long in arousing fervent discussions. Among its opponents may be mentioned in the first place Dāwūd al-Ẓāhirī, who, although rejecting the employment of ḳiyās, approached the method of analogy when he relied on the *mafhūm* of the sacred texts.

Al-Bukhārī, himself a Shāfiʿī, included in his collection of traditions a chapter entitled "That one must adhere to the Ḳurʾān and to the Sunna". The *tardjama* of bāb 7 begins thus: "Traditions relative to the disapproval of *raʾy* and to the practice of ḳiyās". Equally significant is the *tardjama* to the ninth *bāb*: "How the Prophet taught his community what Allāh had taught him, without *raʾy* or *tamthīl*".

This last term is explained by ḳiyās in the commentary of al-Ḳasṭallānī.

Al-Dārimī collected in his *Sunan* a number of traditions disapproving of the use of *ra'y* and ḳiyās in cases in which neither the Ḳur'ān nor *sunna* settle the problem (*Introduction*, bāb 16, 21). Among traditions we may mention that which traces the origin of the use of ḳiyās to Iblīs (cf. Sūra vii. 12).

On the other side, the supporters of ḳiyās rely on the ḥadīth which tells how Muḥammad when he sent Mu'ādh b. Djabal to the Yemen as ḳāḍī, asked him "How will you decide when a question arises"? He replied: "According to the Book of Allāh". — "And if you do not find the answer in the Book of Allāh?" — "Then according to the *sunna* of the Messenger of Allāh". — And if you do not find the answer neither in the *sunna* nor in the Book?" — "Then I shall come to a decision according to my own opinion (*adjtahidu ra'yī*) without hesitation". Then the Messenger of Allāh slapped Mu'ādh on the chest with his hand saying: "Praise be to Allāh who has led the messenger of the Messenger of Allāh to an answer that pleased him" (Abū Dāwūd, *Aḳḍiya*, b. 11; Tirmidhī, *Aḥkām*, b. 3; Dārimī, *Introduction*, b. 19).

In spite of the opposition already mentioned, ḳiyās has found its place among the *uṣūl al-fiḳh*. In some traditions (Nasā'ī, *Ādāb al-ḳuḍāt*, b. 11) there is mention not only of the Ḳur'ān and *sunna*, but also of the "usage of pious individuals" (*al-ṣāliḥūn*) taking precedence of ḳiyās among the *uṣūl*. "The usage of pious individuals" has taken the place usually accorded to *idjmā'* [q.v.] which is the third "root", ḳiyās occupying the last place.

Although it is admitted, ḳiyās is nevertheless surrounded by restrictions. Here are some examples. The opponents of ḳiyās quote Sūra iv. 59: "and if there are differences of opinion between you and your chiefs, try to settle them, relying on Allāh and his Messenger". "Allāh and his Messenger", according to them, means Ḳur'ān and *sunna*. The verse therefore passes over ḳiyās in silence. Baiḍāwī replies to this objection: "Settling the differences by referring them to the texts is done by *tamthīl* (see above) and by deduction", i.e. by ḳiyās.

This verse has given rise to a full exposition of the limitations of ḳiyās on the part of the commentator Fakhr al-Dīn al-Rāzī, who lays down the rule that Ḳur'ān and *sunna* have precedence absolutely over ḳiyās. Only when it is impossible to use these "roots", the use of ḳiyās is permissible, cf. the tradition about Mu'ādh (translated above) and the example of Iblis, who argued instead of obeying the commandment of Allāh (see above). The text of the Ḳur'ān is established by *tawātur*, while ḳiyās is only *maẓnūn* and following one's *ẓann* (individual opinion) is what the *kuffār* do (cf. Sūra x. 66). If traditions require to be verified by the sacred text, ḳiyās does still more so. The Ḳur'ān is the word of Allāh, while ḳiyās is the work of the feeble intelligence of man.

See also the articles FIḲH, SHARĪ'A and UṢŪL.

Bibliography: Mawlawī Muḥammad A'la b. 'Alī, *Dictionary of the Techn. Terms used in the Sciences of the Musulmans*, Calcutta 1862, ii. 1189 *sqq.*; al-Shāfi'ī, *Risāla fī uṣūl al-fiḳh*, Būlāḳ 1321, p. 65—66; Fakhr al-Dīn al-Rāzī, *Mafātīḥ al-ghaib*, Būlāḳ 1289, ii. 465; E. Sachau, *Zur ält. Gesch. des muh. Rechts*, in *S. B. Ak. Wien*, vol. 65 (1870), p. 699 *sqq.*; C. Snouck Hurgronje, *Nieuwe bijdragen tot de kennis van den Islam*, in *Verspr. Geschr.*, ii. 50—56; do., review of *Die Ẓâhiriten* by Goldziher, in *Verspr. Geschr.*, vi. 23; I. Goldziher, *Die Ẓâhiriten*, p. 11 *sqq.*; D. B. Macdonald, *Development of Muslim Theology, Jurisprudence and Constitutional Theory*, London 1903, p. 106 *sqq.*; Th. W. Juynboll, *Handl. tot de kennis v. d. Moh. Wet*, Leyden 1925, p. 41—44; G. Bergsträsser, *Anfänge und Charakter des jurist. Denkens im Islam*, in *Isl.*, xiv., 1924, p. 79; D. Santillana, *Istituzioni di diritto musulmano malichita*, Rome 1926, i. 36—37; H. Laoust, *Essai sur les doctrines sociales et politiques de Takî-d-Dîn Aḥmad b. Taimîya*, Le Caire 1939, p. 113—216; Schacht, *The origins of Muhammadan jurisprudence*, p. 98 *sqq.*

KORAH. [See ḲĀRŪN].

KORAN. [See ḲUR'ĀN].

ḲUBBAT AL-ṢAKHRA, the Dome of the Rock, in Jerusalem, often erroneously designated the Mosque of 'Umar. In the first place, it is not a mosque but a shrine or oratory erected above the sacred rock (*ṣakhra*) and similar to the other domed edifices scattered over the *ḥaram* area; in the second place, it was not built by 'Umar but by the fifth Umaiyad Caliph, 'Abd al-Malik b. Marwān. Jew, Christian and Muslim alike revere the sacred rock which they regard as the *omphalos* of the world. It is even said to be 18 miles nearer heaven than any other spot. Muslims set it next to the Ka'ba in order of sanctity.

Although there is no specific mention of the Ṣakhra in the O.T. it is nevertheless referred to in the Talmud and Targums. But Muḥammadan tradition has greatly magnified all this legendary material. Angels visited the Rock 2,000 years before Adam was created, and Noah's ark rested here after the Deluge. It is said to be acually one of the rocks of Paradise, and that here on the Resurrection Day the Angel of Death, Isrāfīl, will blow the last trumpet. Previous to this the Ka'ba will come from Mekka as a bride unto the Ṣakhra. They assert that it rests on a palm-tree beneath whose shade Āsiya, Pharaoh's wife, and Maryam, Moses' sister, will give the faithful a cooling draught from one of the rivers of the Garden. All the sweet waters on the earth are believed to originate somewhere beneath it. The Rock itself is, by others, reported to be miraculously hung between heaven and earth, but since this wonder was too remarkable for human eyes to behold, it has been purposely hidden by the surrounding building. Beneath the Rock is a cave (*maghāra*) the floor of which when stamped upon by the foot emits a hollow sound pointing to the presence of a cavern beneath, perhaps a well, the so-called "Well of the Spirits" (*bi'r al-arwāḥ*) where the souls of the departed are believed to assemble twice weekly. This hollowness of walls and floor has no doubt given rise to the legend of its being suspended in mid-air. Tradition states that all the prophets of God up to the time of Muḥammad have come to pray here at the Rock which is daily surrounded by a bodyguard of 70,000 angels (Ali Bey, *Travels*, ii. 220). God is said to have ordered Moses to institute the Ṣakhra as the ḳibla [q.v.], and Muḥammad intended doing likewise; only he was told by God to take the Ka'ba at Mekka as the ḳibla. The change took place in Radjab A.H. 2.

When 'Umar conquered Jerusalem he (guided by Ka'b al-Aḥbār, the converted Jew) found the Ṣakhra scandalously covered with filth. This he ordered to be removed by the Nabataeans, and after three showers of heavy rain had cleansed the Rock, he instituted prayers there (Le Strange, *Palestine under the Muslims*, p. 139 *sqq*.). In the years 69—72/688—691, ʿAbd al-Malik b. Marwān built the Dome of the Rock. The political situation at the time was the immediate cause of this undertaking. The rival claimant to the Caliphate, ʿAbd Allāh b. al-Zubair, was favoured by the inhabitants of the Ḥaramain (Mecca and Madīna). Fearing lest his Palestinian subjects who visited the Kaʿba on pilgrimage should return infected with the spirit of revolt, ʿAbd al-Malik determined on a plan to divert the Meccan pilgrims from the seditious area and lead them instead to Jerusalem. After sending out feelers in the shape of circulars stating his intentions, and after receiving warm support, he proceeded with his project, the embellishment of Jerusalem (de Vogüé, *Le Temple de Jérusalem*, p. 75). Then he declared to his people: "This Rock (Ṣak͟hra) shall be unto you in the place of the Kaʿba" (Yaʿḳūbī, ii., p. 311). For the expenses of the building he is said to have set apart a sum equal to the revenue from Egypt for seven years, and as a treasure-house for this money he commanded to be built after his own design the edifice in the neighbourhood that is now known as the *Ḳubbat al-silsila* (Dome of the Chain). This building is said to have pleased him so much that he ordered the Dome of the Rock to be modelled after it. The Ṣak͟hra was surrounded by a latticed screen of ebony and curtains of brocade. At this time also a precious pearl, the horn of Abraham's ram, and the crown of K͟husraw were suspended to the chain which hung in the centre of the Dome, but with the coming of the ʿAbbāsids these were transferred to the Kaʿba (Palmer, *Jerusalem*, p. 86). In those days the building was so full of incense that a person who had been there was known at once by the odour which clung to him. Another reason why ʿAbd al-Malik built the Ḳubbat al-Ṣak͟hra is given by al-Muḳaddasī, who says that the Caliph "noting the greatness of the Dome of the Ḳumāma [the Christian Church of the Anastasis (*ḳiyāma* corrupted to *ḳumāma*, ordure)] and its magnificence, was moved lest it should dazzle the minds of the Muslims, and hence erected, above the Rock, the Dome which now is seen there" (Le Strange, *Pal. Expl. Fund's Q.*, 1887, viii., p. 103). For long, controversy has been waged regarding the true founder and builder of the Ḳubbat al-Ṣak͟hra. It seemed too wonderful an achievement for the Arabs. Ferguson argued that it was the work of Byzantine architects under Constantine and that it marked the site of the Holy Sepulchre. Conder was the chief opponent of this view. No doubt ʿAbd al-Malik employed Greek architects in the construction, and there was abundance of Greek columns and capitals at hand among the ruins of the churches destroyed by the Persians, which could easily be incorporated into the structure. Ferguson's argument, besides being fallacious, is contrary to the evidence of Arab historians.

That the Ḳubbat al-Ṣak͟hra was erected by ʿAbd al-Malik is indicated by the famous Kūfic inscription in yellow and blue mosaics above the cornice round the base of the Dome: "Hath built this dome the servant of Allāh, ʿAbd al-Malik, commander of the Faithful, in the year two and seventy — Allāh accept him". When the ʿAbbāsid Caliph al-Maʾmūn repaired the place in 831 A.D. and built the octagonal wall, some of the tiles were removed and others containing this Caliph's name inserted in place of ʿAbd al-Malik's. But the forgery is easily detected, the mosaics are of a darker blue while the letters of the name are closer together (a chromo-lithographic facsimile is to be found in de Vogüé, *ibid.*, p. xxi.)

The history of the Ḳubbat al-Ṣak͟hra is fairly well known by historical literature; it had to be restored several times in the following centuries. In 1099 the Crusaders entered Jerusalem and the building, endowed by Baldwin II, became the *Templum Domini*, the Church of the Knights Templars. It was redecorated inside and outside with Christian paintings and images of the saints. A marble altar was set up on the Ṣak͟hra, and a large golden cross on the summit of the dome. A large iron screen of French workmanship with four gates was erected between the pillars of the inner ring. The cave beneath was transformed into a Chapel. They believed it to be the Holy of Holies, and called it the Confessio (Joannes Phocas, *PPTS*, p. 20). The building thus became the type of "Temple" Churches built in Europe. The dome was the symbol of the order and appeared on the Grand Master's seal. A polygonal type of building reminiscent of the Dome of the Rock appears in Raphael's *Marriage of the Virgin* as the Jewish Temple (de Vogüé, *ibid.*, p. 78, note).

In 1187 Saladin captured the Holy City and removed all Christian additions from the Dome. Inside the cupola there is the inscription set up by Saladin to record his restoration (text in de Vogüé, *ibid.*, p. 91 *sq.*). There have been other restorations since.

The building is in the shape of a regular octagon, with side 66 feet in length. The diameter within is 152 feet; that of the dome at its base being 66 feet. The dome, 99 feet high, is wooden, covered outside with lead, and inside with stucco, beautifully gilded and richly ornamented. Ḳurʾānic passages wonderfully inscribed in interwoven characters form a frieze round the building. In the interior four massive piers and twelve columns surround the Ṣak͟hra in the centre. The dome rests on these.

The Rock, about 56 feet long by 42 feet wide, is almost semicircular in form, the curved sloping side lying to the East, and the higher straight side to the West. Geologically it forms a portion of one of the harder grey beds of the Jerusalem plateau, and has been left practically in its rough unhewn state throughout the ages. In visiting this sacred spot the devout pilgrim has to be careful to keep the Ṣak͟hra on his right hand, so that he performs the circumambulation of the holy relic in the opposite direction from the circuit of the Kaʿba. Ibn ʿAbd Rabbihi (in his *ʿIḳd al-farīd*, transl. in part by Le Strange in *Pal. Quart. Stat.*, 1887, p. 99) states: "Now when thou enterest the Ṣak͟hra make thy prayer in the three corners thereof, and also pray on the slab which rivals the Rock itself in its glory for it lies over a gate of the gates of Paradise". This slab is a portion of the marble pavement near by the Bāb al-D̲j̲anna and is supposed by some to mark the place where the prophet Elias knelt in prayer. Others believe it covers the Tomb of Solomon (*ḳabr Sulaimān*). All, however, assert that it was originally part of Paradise, and is generally termed the Flagstone of Paradise (*balāṭat al-d̲j̲anna*). A tradition has it that Muḥammad drove into this slab nineteen golden nails which are destined to drop out periodically. When all have fallen through, the end of the world has come. The Devil almost succeeded in removing them but the angel Gabriel intervened in the nick of time. Nowadays three nails remain in place, while one has sunk a little. It is with humble step and slow, therefore, that the pious pilgrim treads this holy place lest by dislodging one of the nails he should hasten the day of judgment.

The temple square with the Dome of the Rock at Jerusalem

Art. ḲUBBAT AL-ṢAKHRA

On a detached piece of a marble column on the S.W. of the Ṣak͟hra, covered by a rude shrine which also contains hairs from the Prophet's beard, is to seen the *ḳadam Muḥammad* (or Footprint) which he left behind him on the night of his ascension to heaven on his steed al-Burāḳ [q.v.]. During the Crusades when the Christians occupied the Ḳubbat al-Ṣak͟hra this was known as the Footprint of Jesus. The round hole in the middle of the Rock was where the Prophet's body pierced its way upwards. And near by is shown the very Saddle of al-Burāḳ in the shape of several marble fragments. There is also pointed out on the West side of the Rock the impression of the Handprint of Gabriel (*kaff sayidnā D͟jibrīl*) where he held down the Rock when it was about to rise with Muḥammad. Directly opposite are preserved the banners of Muḥammad and ʿUmar, and the buckler of Ḥamza. The cases containing these relics are dust-covered. Once a year this dust is carefully gathered and sold in minute quantities as a panacea of miraculous power. A slight depression in the pavement on the East side of the Rock is pointed out as the Footprint of Idrīs. In the N.E. corner is the recess known as the Prophets' Ḳibla (*ḳiblat al-anbiyāʾ*). There are also several ancient Ḳurʾāns and a dwarf screen known as Taḳlīd Saif ʿAlī (the imitation of the sword of ʿAlī).

The entrance to the cavern beneath is by means of the Bāb al-Mag͟hāra, at the S.E. corner of the Rock, the pilgrim humbly descending the eleven steps with the following prayer on his lips, known as the "Prayer of Solomon": "O God, pardon the sinners who come here, and relieve the injured". The average height of the cave is six feet, and on the roof may be seen the impress of Muḥammad's head. The floor is paved with marble and the sides are whitewashed. It is said to be able to hold 62 persons (Ibn al-Faḳīh, in *BGA*, v. 100). A projecting piece of rock known as the Tongue of the Rock (*lisān al-ṣak͟hra*) is so-called because it greeted ʿUmar on one occasion. There is also to be seen the slender column supposed to uphold the Rock. The guide points out on the right the *miḥrāb Sulaimān* (Solomon's prayer-niche); on the left, the *maḳām al-K͟halīl* (Abraham); on the N. corner, the *maḳām al-K͟hiḍr* with the *miḥrāb Dāwūd* opposite.

On the S.E. of the Ṣak͟hra a staircase leads upwards to the gallery of the dome whence the crescent on the summit may be reached. The eulogy pronounced on it by Muḳaddasī (*BGA* iii. 170) still holds good at the present day: "At dawn when the light of the sun first strikes on the Cupola, and the Drum catches the rays, then is this edifice a marvellous sight to behold, and one such that in all Islām I have never seen its equal".

Bibliography: The fullest description is by K. A. C. Creswell, *Early Muslim Architecture*, vol. i., Oxford 1932, pp. 42—94, with a *Contribution on the Mosaics of the Dome of the Rock* by Marguérite van Berchem, pp. 147—228. See also R. Hartmann, *Der Felsendom in Jerusalem*, Strassburg 1909; al-Yaʿḳūbī, *Taʾrīk͟h*, ed. Houtsma, ii. 311; H. Sauvaire, *Histoire de Jérusalem et d'Hébron*, Paris 1876 (part translation of Mud͟jīr al-Dīn, *Ins al-d͟jalīl*); Idrīsī, ed. J. Gildemeister, in *ZDPV* 1885, viii. 7; Guyard, *Géographie d'Aboulfeda*, ii. 3 *sqq.*; Ibn Baṭṭūṭa, i. 120 *sqq.*; Ibn K͟hallikān, *Biogr. Dict.*, transl. de Slane, iv. 521; K. A. C. Creswell, *The Origin of the plan of the Dome of the Rock*, British School of Archaeology in Jerusalem, suppl. papers, No. 2, London 1924; E. T. Richmond, *The Dome of the Rock*, Oxford 1924; Gaudefroy-Demombynes, *La Syrie à l'époque des Mamelouks*, p. 60 *sqq.*; Mariti, *Histoire de l'Etat présent de Jérusalem*, Paris 1853, p. 249 *sqq.*; Nāṣir-i K͟husraw, *Sefer Namah*, ed. Schefer, p. 89 *sqq.*; Muḥammad al-Batanūnī, *al-Riḥla al-Ḥid͟jāzīya*, Cairo 1329, p. 162 *sqq.*; van Berchem, *CIA*, p. iii., v. 267, 754; *ZDPV*, xliv. 34 *sqq.*; C. D. Matthews, *Palestine — Mohammedan holy land*, New Haven 1949, p. 2 *sqq.*; Strzygowsky, *Felsendom und Aksamoschee*, in *Isl.*, ii. 79 *sqq.*; Herzfeld, *Die Qubbat al-Sak͟hra, ein Denkmal früh-islamischer Baukunst*, in *Isl.*, ii. 235; H. Schmidt, *Der heilige Fels in Jerusalem*, Tübingen 1933; T. Canaan, *Mohammedan Saints and Sanctuaries*, London 1927, p. 80—83, 213—14; G. Wiet, *Répertoire chronologique d'épigraphie arabe*, Cairo, i. 7—11, 165—67.

AL-ḲUDS, the usual Arabic name for Jerusalem in later times. The older writers call it commonly Bait al-Maḳdis (according to some: *Muḳaddas*; cf. Gildemeister, in *ZDMG*, xxxvi. 387 *sq.*; Fischer, *ibid.*, lx. 404 *sqq.*) which really meant the Temple (of Solomon), a translation of the Hebrew Bēt-hammiḳdas͟h (e.g. Ibn His͟hām, ed. Wüstenfeld, p. 263, 2), but it became applied to the whole town. They also frequently used the name Īliyāʾ, from Colonia Aelia Capitolina, the Roman name given it after 135 A.D. They likewise knew the old name Jerusalem, which they reproduce as Uris͟halim (or -am) (variants in Yāḳūt, ed. Wüstenfeld, i. 402). The name al-Balaṭ also occurs in Muḳaddasī, a word of uncertain meaning derived from *palatium*, but which probably means "royal residence". For other names of rarer occurrence see Gildemeister, *op. cit.*

Although Jerusalem lay outside the regular orbit of the Prophet's interests it became of real significance for him in the period when, following the example of the Jews, he turned at prayer in the direction of the holy city [cf. ḲIBLA]. According to the usual explanation, moreover, Sūra xvii. 1 with the expression *al-masd͟jid al-aḳṣā* indicates Jerusalem as the goal of the Prophet's nocturnal journey, not however the later mosque of the name but the site of the old Temple of Solomon. The correctness of this interpretation is however not certain for there is a certain amount of support for Horowitz's (*Isl.*, ix. 159; following Schrieke, *ibid.*, vi. 1 *sqq.*) suggestion that Muḥammad was rather thinking of a place in heaven in this phrase [see ISRĀʾ]. But the traditional view, which must have arisen very early, gained the greatest importance for Jerusalem, for on it is based the classing of the sanctuary at Jerusalem among the three most holy places of prayer in the world; indeed it is sometimes even given the preference over the other two.

Two different accounts of the taking of Jerusalem by the Arabs have been handed down. According to the most usual version, the Arab general Abū ʿUbaida in 17/638 asked the Caliph ʿUmar to come to his head-quarters at D͟jābiya, as the people of Jerusalem would only capitulate on condition that ʿUmar himself concluded the treaty with them. According to the other story, which de Goeje, *Mémoire sur la conquête de la Syrie*, 1864, p. 110 *sqq.*, rightly prefers, the Caliph came to D͟jābiya of his own accord to arrange the affairs of the conquered regions and from there (according to Balād͟hurī, p. 139) he sent K͟hālid b. T͟hābit to Jerusalem to besiege the town and the terms made by the latter for the surrender were then approved by ʿUmar. These terms, which are preserved in several versions (e.g. Ṭabarī, i. 2404 *sq.*; cf. Balādhurī, p. 139; Yaʿḳūbī, ii. 167; cf. de Goeje, *op. cit.*, p. 122 *sqq.*) were quite mild. The Christian inhabitants were granted security for their lives, property, churches and crucifixes, while the Jews were not to live among them; the churches were not to be used as dwellings, and not to be torn down or reduced in size, and the Christians retained their religious liberty; in return they were to pay the *djizya* and assist in warding off the Byzantine troops and raiders. The statements on the date of the taking of Jerusalem also vary; Ṭabarī for example gives Rabīʿ II of the year 16 (i. 2408).

Further details of ʿUmar's conduct at the capture of Jerusalem are given by various Christian and Muslim authors. Theophanes (ed. de Boor, i. 339) who wrote towards the end of the viiith century, records under the year 637 that the Caliph on the conclusion of the treaty, so favourable to the Christians, entered the holy city wearing soiled robes — according to this author a sign of his devilish hypocrisy — and demanded to be led to the site of the Temple which he then made a place of pagan worship. Writing in the tenth century, the Egyptian Christian Eutychius (*Annales*, ed. Pococke, ii. 285 *sqq.* and in Vincent and Abel, *Jérusalem*, ii. 243) tells somewhat more fully how ʿUmar refused to perform his *ṣalāt* in the basilica of the Church of the Resurrection and instead said his prayers on the steps at the entrance in order, as he explained, to prevent the Muslims from using the authority of his example to turn the church into a mosque and that he gave the Patriarch Sophronius a document confirming this. At his request, Sophronius then pointed out the "Rock" covered with debris on the site of the Temple as a suitable site for his masdjid. The Caliph at once began to clear off the rubble and as the Muslims followed his example the rock soon came into sight. At the same time he gave instructions that the masdjid should be so planned that the worshippers had the rock behind and not in front of them. It is apparent that the story is intended to confirm the inalienable right of the Christians to their churches by the authority of the great Caliph. There is naturally no such tendency in the Muslim historians — the earliest is al-Musharraf in the tenth century with whom Shihāb al-Dīn al-Maḳdisī, Shams al-Dīn al-Suyūṭī and Mudjīr al-Dīn (see below) are in substantial agreement — who on the contrary show the Christians in a less favourable light. According to them the Patricius, who appears here more correctly in the place of the Patriarch, at first tried to deceive ʿUmar when he demanded to be taken to David's *masdjid*, by showing him the Church of the Holy Sepulchre and the Church of Sion. But the Caliphs saw through the deception, as the Prophet had described to him the place as he had seen it on his nocturnal journey; he was ultimately taken to the site of the Temple, which he recognised as the right place, but it had first of all to be cleared of debris. Another story is given by Ṭabarī, i. 2408.

If we examine these traditions more closely, we see that they all agree that ʿUmar had a Muslim place of worship erected on the deserted Temple area. That we are on firm historical ground here is corroborated by Biship Arculfus about 670 (*Itinera Hierosolymitana*, ed. P. Geyer, 1898, p. 226 *sq.*; cf. Arculf, transl. by Mickley, 1917, p. 19 *sq.*) who describes this masdjid as a very simple building (*Saraceni quadrangulam orationis domum quam subrectis tabulis et magnis trabibus super quasdam ruinarum reliquias construentes vili fabricati sunt opere ipsi frequentant*), but it could hold 3,000 men. In reality this was a very practical settlement of the situation that had arisen from the conquest of Jerusalem; the Caliph acquired a site long held sacred, without coming into conflict with the privileges granted to the Christians, as they would not build a church on the site of the Temple. It is further clear that what Eutychius tells us about ʿUmar's praying on the steps of the basilica of the Sepulchre is an unhistorical invention intended to avert any enchroachments by the Muslims. But this bias of the story only becomes evident from a further story of Eutychius, according to which the Muslims "of our day" (i.e. the first half of the tenth century) overrode ʿUmar's regulations, when they took possession of the half of the forecourt on the steps to the Constantinian Basilica and built a masdjid there, which they called the Masdjid ʿUmar, because ʿUmar had prayed there. Schmalz (*Mater Ecclesiarum*, p. 361) thinks a few remains of columns from this mosque can still be seen.

Under the Umaiyads the political conditions contributed in a peculiar way to increase the prestige of Jerusalem. Their interest in Muḥammad's dispositions was not considerable so that it was not difficult for them to abandon the holy cities in Arabia when the prescribed visits to them met with difficulty for any reason, and Jerusalem in particular, the holiness of which the Prophet, according to the usual exposition of Sūra xvii. 1, had recognised, formed a welcome substitute, all the more so as it was much easier to reach from Damascus than Mecca or Madīna. Evidence of the esteem in which Jerusalem was held was early shown by Muʿāwiya, who had himself proclaimed Caliph here. A Syriac source published by Nöldeke, in *ZDMG*, xxix. 90, records that in July 971, Seleuc. (660 A.D. = Ṣafar-Rabīʿ A.H. 40) many Arabs assembled in Jerusalem to make him king and that he ascended to Golgotha and prayed there and next went through Gethsemane to the Tomb of Mary, where he again prayed. Arabic sources (Ṭabarī, ii. 4; Masʿūdī, *Murūdj*, v. 14; Ibn al-Athīr, iii. 388) say that homage was paid to him in Jerusalem in the year 40, and this must have happened only after ʿAlī's assassination on 17th Ramaḍān, which is less probable than the Syriac story. ʿAbd al-Malik (65—86/685—705) took a further step in this direction. When the anti-caliph Ibn Zubair had become master of Mecca, ʿAbd al-Malik feared, not without reason, that the Syrians who made the pilgrimage thither, might be persuaded or forced to join him. He therefore forbade them to go there and when the people appealed to the definite command of the Prophet, he ordered them to go on pilgrimage to the holy Rock in Jerusalem and referred them to a tradition recorded by the famous traditionist al-Zuhrī, according to which Muḥammad classed Mecca, Madīna and Jerusalem as places of pilgrimage of equal value, nay, from what is apparently the original form of the ḥadīth, the last town was to be placed above the other sanctuaries (cf. Yaʿḳūbī, ii. 167; Balādhurī, p. 143; Yāḳūt, ed. Wüstenfeld, ii. 818; Ibn al-Athīr, ed. Tornberg, ii. 390; Goldziher, *Muhammedanische Studien*, ii. 35 *sq.*). To express this esteem for the town in fitting and splendid form, the Caliph had a cupola built on the Rock upon which the Prophet had placed his foot on his journey to heaven, the Ḳubbat al-Ṣakhra [q.v.] around which the *ṭawāf* was to be performed. That (Muḳaddasī, in *BGA*, iii. 159) the Caliph in building it intended to surpass the beautiful cupola of the Church of the Sepulchre is probably quite in keeping with his general aims. Others make Walīd I the builder of the Ḳubbat al-Ṣakhra, but this is at once contradicted by an inscription that survives, in which however the name of ʿAbd al-Malik has been altered to that of the ʿAbbāsid Caliph al-Maʾmūn but in such a way that not only does the difference in colour betray the alteration but the date 72 (691) has fortunately remained intact. According to later writers (Ibn Taghribirdī, ʿUlaimī, etc.), ʿAbd al-Malik also built the Aḳṣā Mosque, which was given its name from Sūra xvii. 1; but if the mosque was built out of the Church of Justinian, this can only mean that the Caliph in converting the church into a mosque committed a direct breach of the promise made by ʿUmar.

In the course of the following centuries Jerusalem had much the same history as the other towns in Palestine and Syria, while its original significance for the religion of Islam fell to the background. After the Umaiyad period it belonged to the ʿAbbāsids, 878—904 to the Ṭūlūnids and after 974 to the Fāṭimids. In 1009 the Church of the Holy Sepulchre was destroyed by order of al-Ḥākim, but rebuilt by the Byzantine Emperor by treaty after 1038. The Fāṭimids lost it to the Seldjūḳids in 1070; after a revolt in 1076 its population was massacred; its recapture in 1096 by the Fāṭimid caliph al-Mustaʿlī was followed in 1099 (July 15) by the victorious entry of the Crusaders and further massacres. The latter took over the mosques and turned them into Christian churches.

After Saladin had recaptured Jerusalem in 1187, the town lost its Christian character and the traces of the Christian occupation were removed. Great care was bestowed by Saladin on the restoration of the Aḳṣā Mosque. Many Christians, however, were allowed to remain. From 1229 till 1244 Christians had again possession of Jerusalem — with exception of the Muslim sacred places on the Ḥaram — in consequence of the treaty concluded by the emperor Frederick II with the Aiyūbid al-Kāmil. In 1244 it again fell into Aiyūbid hands, soon after which it became, together with the whole of Syria and Palestine, part of the domain of the Mamlūks.

After 1516 Jerusalem belonged to the Ottoman Empire and had a rather uneventful history, interrupted only by the Egyptian occupation 1831—1840 under Muḥammad ʿAlī. In the course of the xixth century Christian influence gradually became greater and after the Crimean war the prohibition to non-Muslims to enter the site of the Temple was abolished. From 1881 there was a considerable immigration of Jews.

By the events of the first world war Jerusalem became the capital of the British mandated territory of Palestine. In the struggle that followed between the Arabs and the Jewish immigration during the Palestinian mandate and afterwards nationalist feeling strongly reinforced the traditional Muslim attachment to the Jerusalem sanctuary. Even after the constitution of the state of Israel in 1948 the ultimate status of Jerusalem has still remained undecided.

Bibliography: Among the works dealing with Jerusalem as a place consecrated by pious Islamic tradition there may be mentioned the *Kitāb Faḍāʾil Bait al-Maḳdis wa ʾl-Shaʾm* by al-Musharraf (d. 1099, cf. *GAL, Suppl.* i. 576, 876) and the *K. al-Djāmiʿ al-mustaḳṣā fī faḍāʾil al-Masdjid al-Aḳṣā* by Ibn ʿAsākir (d. 1203, cf. *GAL, Suppl.* i. 567 *sq.*). Both these books are used in the *K. bāʿith al-nufūs ilā ziyārat al-Ḳuds al-Maḥrūs* by Ibn Firḳāh (d. 1329, cf. *GAL, Suppl.* ii. 130), which was edited by C. D. Matthews in the *JPOS*, Vol. xiv and xv (1934-5) and translated by the same in *Palestine — Mohammadan Holy Land*, New Haven 1949. — Futher the anonymous Turkish treatise *Taʾrīkh we-faḍāʾil-i-Ḳuds-i Sherīf*, Constantinople 1265; G. Le Strange, *Palestine under the Moslems*, 1890; Gildemeister, *Die arabischen Nachrichten zur Geschichte der Harambauten*, in *ZDPV* xiii, 1 sqq.; R. Hartmann, *Geschichte der Aksamoschee*, in *ZDPV*, xxxii, 185 *sqq.* and the bibliography of the article ḲUBBAT AL-ṢAKHRA.

KUFR. [See KĀFIR].

ḲUNŪT, a religious technical term, with various meanings, regarding the fundamental signification of which there is no unanimity among the lexicographers. "Refraining from speaking", "the prayer during the *ṣalāt*", "humility and recognition that one's relation to Allāh is that of a creature to his creator", "standing" — these are the usual dictionary definitions, which are also found in the commentaries on different verses of the Ḳurʾān where ḳunūt or derivatives from the root *ḳ-n-t* occur. There is hardly one of these for which the context provides a rigid definition of the meaning (cf. Sūra ii. 116, 238; iii. 17, 43; iv. 34; xvi. 120; xxx. 26; xxxiii. 31, 35; xxxix. 19; lxvi. 5, 12).

The Ḥadīth gives more definite contexts. "The best *ṣalāt* is a long ḳunūt" (e.g. Muslim, *Ṣalāt al-musāfirīn*, trad. 164, 165, *Bāb afḍal al-ṣalāt ṭūl al-ḳunūt*; Tirmidhī, *Ṣalāt*, bāb 168). Here in the unanimous opinion of all the commentators (see Nawawī on the passage) *ḳunūt* means "standing". In the well known *ḥadīth*: equal to the fighter on the path of Allāh is he who fasts, who stands, who *ḳānit bi-āyāt Allāh*" (Muslim, *Imāra*, trad. 110), *ḳānit* has obviously the meaning of "to recite standing" (cf. Abū Dāwūd, *Shahr Ramaḍān*, bāb 9: "and he who recites 100 verses of the Ḳurʾān standing, is enrolled among the *ḳānitūn*"). Ḳunūt, however, usually seems to be connected in meaning with *duʿāʾ*, e.g. in the often quoted tradition which tells how Muḥammad in the *ṣalāt al-ṣubḥ* appealed to Allāh for a month against the tribe of Riʿl and Dhakwān, as they had slain the *ḳurrāʾ* at Biʾr Maʿūna (Bukhārī, *Witr*, bāb 7); in this case the meaning is certain from the explanation *yadʿū ʿalā* (Bukhārī, *Witr*, bāb 7; *Djihād*, bāb 184). In the parallel tradition, Bukhārī, *Maghāzī*, bāb 28, trad. 3 there is added "and till then we were wont to perform the ḳunūt". Some sources (see Goldziher, *loc. cit.*, p. 323) add that this was in the month of Ramaḍān.

The rite also appears in parallel traditions in a more precise form; it is said that the ḳunūt took place in the *ṣalāt al-fadjr* (Bukhārī, *Daʿawāt*, bāb 59) after the *rukūʿ* (Bukhārī, *Witr*, bāb 7). It is still more precisely defined in a *ḥadīth* in al-Nasāʾī, *Taṭbīḳ*, bāb 32: "...that he heard how the Prophet when he raised his head after the first *rakʿa* at the *ṣalāt al-ṣubḥ*, said: "O Allāh, curse this and that man" (i.e. some of the *munāfiḳūn*); thereupon Allāh revealed: "It does not concern thee whether He turns to them with favour or punishes them" (Sūra, iii. 128). The following is another example of ḳunūt: "When the messenger of Allāh lifted his head after the second *rakʿa* at the *ṣalāt al-ṣubḥ*, he said: "O Allāh, save Walīd b. Abī Walīd and Salima b. Hishām and ʿAiyāsh b. Abī Rabīʿa and the weak ones in Mecca. O Allāh, tread heavily on Muḍar and send them years of famine, like the years of Joseph" (al-Nasāʾī, *Taṭbīḳ*, bāb 28). According to another tradition, which also goes back to Abū Huraira (Bukhārī, *Adhān*, bāb 126), the ḳunūt consisted of prayers and blessings for the Muslims and curses upon the unbelievers.

We are also told that the ḳunūt was regularly performed at the morning and evening *ṣalāt* (*ṣubḥ* and *maghrib*; Tirmidhī, *Ṣalāt*, bāb 177; al-Nasāʾī, *Taṭbīḳ*, bāb 30). Tirmidhī gives the following note on this tradition: "The learned differ in their views about the ḳunūt at the *ṣalāt al-fadjr*. Some of the scholars of the *ṣaḥāba* and later generations advocate this ḳunūt, such as Mālik and al-Shāfiʿī". Aḥmad (b. Ḥanbal) and Isḥāḳ say: "There is no ḳunūt uttered at the *ṣalāt al-fadjr* except in a calamity, which affects the Muslims as a body". In such a case the Imām has to pray for the Muslim armies. *Ẓuhr* and *ʿishāʾ* are also mentioned as *ṣalāt*'s into which the ḳunūt was inserted (Bukhārī, *Adhān*, bāb 126: Nasāʾī, *Taṭbīḳ*, bāb 29).

There is further a difference of opinion as to where in the *ṣalāt* the ḳunūt should be inserted. ʿĀṣim is said to have asked Anas b. Mālik about the ḳunūt. Anas replied: "The ḳunūt took place..." I asked: "Before or after the *rukūʿ*?" He replied: "Before the *rukūʿ*". I said: "But I have been told on your authority: after the *rukūʿ*". Anas replied: "Then they lied. The apostle of Allāh only uttered the ḳunūt prayer after the *rukūʿ* for a month. I think, after he, etc. etc." (here follows the story of Biʾr Maʿūna, see above; Bukhārī, *Witr*, bāb 7). It is even said that the ḳunūt is a *bidʿa*. Abū Mālik al-Ashdjaʿ records a tradition on the authority of his father, that the latter had performed the *ṣalāt* under the direction of Muḥammad, Abū Bakr, ʿUmar, ʿUthmān and ʿAlī and that none of these uttered the ḳunūt prayer. He adds "it is therefore a *bidʿa*, my son" (al-Nasāʾī, *Taṭbīḳ*, bāb 33).

Nevertheless it continued to be known as the name of the prayer (*duʿāʾ*) at the *ṣalāt*. In the books of tradition a formula is given for the *ḳunūt al-witr* (it occurs often and in different forms, though it is not always called ḳunūt but is given names like *duʿāʾ* etc.): "O Allāh, lead me amongst those whom Thou guidest, and pardon me among those whom Thou pardonest, and care for me among those for whom Thou carest and bless me with what Thou distributest, and protect me from the evil that Thou hast decreed: for Thou decidest and none decides about Thee. Disgrace will never come upon him for whom Thou carest. Thou art blessed and exalted, O our Lord" (Tirmidhī, *Witr*, bāb 10). The same formula is found as an element in the *ṣalāt* in Nawawī, *Minhādj*, ed. van den Berg, i. 83, 455 *sq.*; Lane, *Lexicon*, s.v. *ḳ-n-t*, who gives another.

Bibliography: I. Goldziher, *Zauberelemente im islamischen Gebet*, in *Orient. Studien, Theod. Nöldeke ... gewidmet*, Giessen 1906, i., p. 323 *sq.* and the references given there; Wensinck, *Handbook*, s.v.

ḲURAISH. [See Mekka, I.].

ḲURAIẒA, Banū, one of the three Jewish tribes of Yathrib, related to the Banu ʾl-Naḍīr. The two tribes together bore the name of Banū Darīh, and were said to have settled in Yathrib much later than the other Jews. In what proportion their original Palestinian stock had intermixed with the Arabs, is not possible to say, but al-Yaʿḳūbī's statement that both tribes were only hebraized Djudhām (Ḳuḍāʿa), is not credible.

The Banū Ḳuraiẓa consisted of two branches: Banū Kaʿb and Banū ʿAmr; they resided outside the city on the southern side, along the Wādī Mahzūr, with the sister-tribe of Hadal, having the Aws Allāh on the N.W., the Banū ʿĀbd al-Ashhal on the N.E. and the Ḥara on the E. Landowners and cultivators, the Ḳuraiẓa had brought agriculture to a high degree of development, and lived prosperously on the produits of the soil and their commerce. At the time of Muḥammad's arrival in Madīna, they had 750 warriors, and possessed large stores of arms and armour.

Allied, like the Naḍīr, to the Banū Aws, they had fought on their side in the battle of Buʿāth, which took place on their territory a few years before the Hidjra.

In Muḥammad's communal constitution they, like the other Jewish tribes, are not mentioned by name, but appear only as allies of different sections of the Aws (art. 25, 30, 31 and 47).

Their attitude towards the Prophet was hostile from the first, like that of the other Jews (see above the article Kainuḳāʿ, and in Ibn Hishām, p. 352, a list of Muḥammad's Ḳuraiẓī enemies), but no definite break took place until the siege of Madīna (Dhu ʾl-Ḳaʿda, 5 a.h.), when the Ḳuraiẓa, who in the beginning had contributed spades and baskets to the digging of the trench, withdrew their support. According to tradition Ḥuyaiy b. Akhṭab, sent by Abū Sufyān, had succeeded in gaining the support of their chief, Kaʿb b. Asad, despite a written treaty of alliance with Muḥammad. The Prophet sent Saʿd b. Muʿādh, Saʿd b. ʿUbāda and two others to ascertain their attitude: they returned after a stormy interview, confirming the Ḳuraiẓa's defection.

The latter seem to have planned an attack on Madīna, together with the Ḳuraish and Ghaṭafān; it was not executed through lack of mutual confidence and their only exploit was an unsuccessful night-expedition of eleven men. Having failed to reach an agreement with the Ḳuraish, who refused to give them hostages in exchange for military support, the Ḳuraiẓa finally abandoned the campaign, thus hastening its end.

This traditional version is open to many doubts: the existence of a particular treaty with Muḥammad does not seem plausible, as his relations with the Ḳuraiẓa were already defined by the communal constitution; it was probably invented to justify the action taken against them. Their support of the Ḳuraish appears to have been purely negative; on the other hand, it is easy to see how the important position they occupied on the side of the town not defended by the trench practically put Madīna at their mercy. One of the fortresses incorporated in the line of defence, Rātidj, belonged to Jews (tribe unknown), and formed a dangerously weak point in the Muslims' position. All these circumstances caused much anxiety and hatred of the Jews during the siege, suggesting immediate action against them: on the very day of the Ḳuraish's departure Muḥammad was ordered by Gabriel not to lay down arms until he had punished the Ḳuraiẓa; the siege of their fortresses began the same evening (23rd Dhu ʾl-Ḳaʿda) and lasted 15 or 25 days, with an active exchange of arrows, stones and strong language, but no casualties.

Having at last decided to surrender, the Ḳuraiẓa asked for the same conditions obtained by the Banu ʾl-Naḍīr, but were told they must yield without condition, giving up all they possessed. They turned to their ally and protector Abū Lubāba b. ʿAbd al-

Mun<u>dh</u>ir, hoping through his intercession to emigrate, but he gave them to understand that the situation was desperate, and that inevitable surrender would be followed by destruction.

Having surrendered without attempting any resistance, the Ḳuraiẓa were separated from their women and children, and put under custody. The Aws interceded on their behalf, and obtained that their fate should be decided by their own chief, Saʿd b. Muʿā<u>dh</u>; the latter, however, decreed that all males who had reached puberty should be slain, and the women and children sold as slaves. On the morrow, in the market-place, from 600 to 900 men were beheaded, the execution lasting all day. It is worthy of note that only four chose to save their lives by conversion.

The women and children were sold at auction, mostly in Madīna, the remainder in Syria and Na<u>dj</u>d, and the price divided in the usual way of spoils. Their land was partitioned into five portions: one went to Muḥammad, and the various families, divided into four groups, drew lots for the rest. Among the captives Muḥammad chose for himself Raiḥāna bint Zaid al-Naḍarīya.

Several passages in the Ḳur'ān are referred to the Ḳuraiẓa; see especially viii. 58 and xxxiii. 26—27.

Bibliography: Ibn Hi<u>sh</u>ām, p. 13, 352, 674—675; al-Ṭabarī, i. 1485—1498; al-Wāḳidī, *Kitāb al-ma<u>gh</u>āzī*, transl. Wellhausen under the title *Muhammed in Medina*, p. 196—224; Wellhausen, *Skizzen und Vorarbeiten*, iv.; Wensinck, *Mohammed en de Joden te Medina*, Leiden 1908; Caetani, *Annali dell' Islām*, i.; Lammens, *Les Juifs à la Mecque à la veille de l'Hégire*, in *L'Arabie Occidentale*, Beyrouth 1928, 51—99; R. Leszynsky, *Die Juden in Arabien zur Zeit Mohammeds*, Berlin 1910; F. Buhl, *Das Leben Muhammeds*, p. 273 *sqq*; W. M. Watt, in *Muslim World*, 1952, 160—171; Wensinck, *Handbook*.

AL-ḲUR'ĀN (A.), the sacred book of the Muḥammadans, contains the collected revelations of Muḥammad in definitive written form.

1. Even among Muslims there is no unanimity regarding the pronunciation, derivation and meaning of the word. Some pronounced it Ḳurān without hamza and saw in it a proper noun not occurring elsewhere, like *tawrāt* and *in<u>dj</u>īl*, or they derived it from *ḳarana*, to tie together. Others rightly began with *ḳur'ān* with hamza and explained it either as an infinitive in the sense of a past participle or as an adjective from *ḳara'a*, to collect. It is really very easy to see an infinitive in it as it occurs as such in Sūra lxxv. 17 (cf. Ṭabarī, ed. de Goeje, gloss. s.v.). The exact meaning must be sought in the usage of the Ḳur'ān itself where the verb *ḳara'a* frequently occurs. In Sūra xvii. 93 it certainly stands for "to read", but the most frequent meaning is rather "to recite, to discourse", which does not necessarily pre-suppose a written text. Thus Allāh says, lxxv. 16, 17: "Move not thy tongue too quickly with it for it behoves us to collect and recite it". Similarly the word is used of Muḥammad who recites the revelations made to him (vii. 204; xvi. 98; xvii. 45; lxxxiv. 21; cf. the 4th form in lxxxvii. 6) or of the beliefers when they recite the revelations at prayer (lxxiii. 20). Cf. also: "If thou mentionest thy Lord, the unique, in reading aloud" (*fi 'l-ḳur'ān*, xvii. 46). We thus come to the meaning discourse, what is uttered, i.e. what Muḥammad heard from Allāh and repeated ("follow our recital of it", lxxv. 18; "We enable thee to repeat so that thou mayest not forget", lxxxvii. 6), and then later uttered before men. Schwally, Wellhausen, in *ZDMG*, lxvii. 634, and Horovitz, in *Isl.*, xiii. 67, on the other hand, see in it a Syriac or Hebrew loanword *ḳeryānā, ḳiryānā* (lectio, reading, or what is read) and they rightly insist that *ḳara'a* is not genuine Arabic with the meaning "to read". We should have to imagine that Allāh actually read to the Prophet out of the heavenly book, but even then the further use of the word is no easier explained.

The word is not found in the Ḳur'ān itself in the above sense of "collected revelations in written form" because they were only collected after the death of the Prophet. It is used either for the separate revelations which were made one by one to the Prophet (e.g. x. 15; xii. 3; lxxii. 1; cf. ii. 185, the Ḳur'ān sent down in Ramaḍān) or as an general term for the divine revelation which was sent down piece by piece (xvii. 108; xx. 1; lxxvi. 23; cf. xxv. 32; lix. 21) which he received from Allāh (xxvii. 6) so that he could communicate it to men (xxviii. 85).

The term *al-kitāb* (the scripture or the book) is used as an alternative of Ḳur'ān. They often appear to be synonymous. The "scripture" is also sent down (e.g. xl. 2; xlv. 2; in "a blessed night", xliv. 2, i.e. like the Ḳur'ān of a single revelation). It is said in xv. 1, "these are the miraculous tokens (*āyāt*) of the scripture and of a perspicuous scripture", and in xxvii. 1, "these are the miraculous tokens of the Ḳur'ān and of a perspicuous scripture". On further consideration however there is a distinction between the two expressions. When we read xii. 1, "These are the miraculous tokens of the perspicuous scripture and we have sent them down as the Arabic Ḳur'ān", cf. xx. 113, or "we have made the perspicuous scripture into an Arabic Ḳur'ān", xliii. 2 *sq.*, or, when the Ḳur'ān is called (x. 37) an exposition of the scripture of the Lord of Heaven, it is evident that *al-kitāb* is the more comprehensive term and that it is "Ḳur'ān" in so far as its contents are revealed in a way intelligible to man.

From its contents the Ḳur'ān is frequently called *<u>dh</u>ikr*, a word of several meanings, which in this case means admonition, warning, xxi. 24, 42; xxxviii. 87 etc. The *<u>dh</u>ikr* also is sent down, xv. 6; xxi. 50; xxxviii. 8 and is called "a noble scripture" in xli. 41; cf.: "This is an admonition and a perspicuous Ḳur'ān", xxxvi. 69. How the conceptions flowed into one another is seen in xxi. 7, where the "people of a scripture" (*ahl al-kitāb*) are called on one occasion *ahl al-<u>dh</u>ikr*. *Al-ḥikma*, the wisdom, may be mentioned here as it is not only associated with the scripture in ii. 129, 151; iii. 164; lxii. 2, but in ii. 231; iv. 113, there is a reference to its being sent down and in xxxiii. 34 to its recitation. On the loanword *furḳān* see that article. A term peculiar to the Ḳur'ān, the origin and original meaning of which is still obscure, is *sūra*. It is used only for the separate revelations, while Ḳur'ān has sometimes a more comprehensive sense, and is found in the Mecca as well as the Madīna sections; for further details see the article SŪRA.

Smaller sections of the sūras were called *āya*, plural *āyāt*. It means properly, like the related Hebrew word *ōt*, token, token of belief (ii. 248; iii. 41; xxvi. 197); and especially a token of Allāh's existence and controlling power, xii. 105 xxxvi. 33, etc., hence often "miracle" (iii. 48; xliii. 46 *sqq.*), and gives a very instructive glimpse into Muḥammad's ideas and consciousness. In Mecca the demand of his opponents that he should give proof by some miracle of his credibility as a messenger of Allāh caused him serious difficulties. The gift of performing miracles, possessed for example by Jesus, was denied him but the revelations offered him a valid substitute, of the divine origin of which he was firmly convinced (vi. 158; vii. 203; xx. 133; xxix. 50 *sq.*). They were the only convincing miracles and thus received the name *āyāt*. They were sent down from heaven (ii. 99; xxviii. 87) to the Prophet of Allāh (ii. 254; iii. 58; xlv. 5) and proclaimed by him to men (ii. 151; iii. 164; lxv. 11) as in former times by the Prophets (xxviii. 59): "Allāh expounds his *āyāt*" (ii. 187); "the believers recite them in the night" (iii. 113); "the unbelievers dispute them" (xxix. 47, etc.). The only noteworthy point is that Muḥammad when he expresses himself more definitely does not use the word like *sūra* of the revelations but only of the smaller parts of which they consist; e.g. "a Sūra which we have sent down with perspicuous *āyāt*" (xxiv. 1), "a scripture which we have sent down so that they may reflect on its *āyāt*" (xxxviii. 29); "these are the *āyāt* of the wise scripture" (x. 1; xii. 1; xiii. 1; xxvi. 1; xxxi. 1); "these are the *āyāt* of the Ḳur'ān and of a perspicuous scripture" (xxviii. 1; cf. xxvi. 1); "a scripture the *āyāt* of which are firmly linked together" (xi. 1; xli. 3) and especially: "in the scripture are unambiguous *āyāt* and others which have several meanings" (iii. 7); and "if we abrogate an *āya* or consign it to oblivion, we put a better or a similar one in its place" (ii. 106); "if we exchange one *āya* for another", etc. (xvi. 101). Unfortunately one cannot see from such passages how large or small these component parts of the revelations were. Later scholars took them to be verses in the technical sense but this does not agree with xxx. 58 and other passages where the reference is clearly to divisions required by the sense without it being possible to define their length more exactly.

2. From what has already been said we can see how Muḥammad regarded the origin of his revelations. They came from heaven and were taken from a well-guarded tablet (lxxxv. 22), a concealed book only to be touched by the pure (lvi. 79), the "mother of the scripture" (the original scripture, xliii. 4; otherwise iii. 7). The book is called "an admonition on noble, lofty, pure leaves through the hands of noble scribes" (lxxx. 11 *sqq.*; cf. lii. 2, where Muḥammad swears by a scripture written on unrolled parchment, and lxi. 2-4: "by the reed-pen and what it writes", xcvi. 4 *sq.*: "with the reed-pen he taught men what they did not know"). The Prophet did not become acquainted with the whole of this book but only with isolated sections of it, which were given to him in Arabic dress: "Proclaim", it is said in xviii. 27, "what is communicated to thee of Allāh's scripture; no one may alter its words", and in iv. 164; xl. 78, he says expressly that Allāh told him of some of the Prophets but not of all. Nevertheless, we can obtain from the revelations given by Muḥammad an idea of the heavenly scripture from which they are taken, for it is apparent that it contained a similar mixture of instruction dealing with the being of Allāh, the creation of the world and especially of man, good and evil spirits, the coming judgment, paradise and hell and the experiences of the older prophets, and in addition all sorts of regulations regarding the worship of Allāh, and the life of the community, including quite special laws (iv. 103, 127, 138; xxxiii. 6). The field of cosmology is touched on in the reference to the twelve months (ix. 36), the temptation of man by Satan in xxii. 4. But further perspectives are opened up when it is said that the heavenly book comprises all that has happened in the universe and will happen (x. 61; xxii. 70; xxvii. 75; xxxiv. 3; vi. 38, 59; xi. 6; cf. xx. 51 *sq.*; lv. 57; xxxv. 11; xvii. 58, etc.); even if the Muslims had remained in their houses at the battle of Uḥud, those who were destined to die would have gone forth to the places where they were to fall (iii. 154); (cf. F. Buhl in *Oriental Studies dedicated to Paul Haupt*, 1926, p. 34). The Ḳur'ān contains only a few and very obscure hints regarding the process of communication of the revelations; it is wrapped in a secrecy which Muḥammad either could not or would not illuminate. It is not from the Ḳur'ān but from reliable ḥadīths that we learn something about the half-abnormal ecstatic conditions with which he was overcome [cf. the article MUḤAMMAD]; the wrapping in lxxiii. 1, lxxiv. 1, at most might contain only a slight reference to them. The main thing was however, as already observed, not what he saw but what he heard, which is also emphasised in the descriptions of the visions (liii. 10; lxxxi. 19); that he had visions is evident from liii. 5 *sqq.*; lxxxi. 23 *sqq.* It was the voice of Allāh that with a few exceptions talked to him in the stereotyped "we" and stamped even what the Prophet had to say by a prefixed *ḳul* "say!" as a divine utterance. But he did not hear this divine voice directly — for this his conception of Allāh's superiority was too great — but through the intermediary of the "spirit" or of an angel, according to the later passage ii. 97, Gabriel. "The trustworthy spirit brought the revelation down into the heart of Muḥammad" (xxvi. 192 *sq.*); "the spirit of holiness brought it down from Muḥammad's Lord with truth" (xvi. 102); "Allāh sends the angel down with the spirit of (? *min*) his word to whom He will" (xvi. 2); "The Lord of the throne sends the spirit of his word to whom he will of his servants so that he may admonish" (xl. 15); "We have revealed to thee a spirit of our word" (xlii. 52), — all somewhat obscure expressions, which are not made any clearer by the fact that the spirit is in other passages (lxx. 4; lxxviii. 38; xcvii. 4) associated with the angels, but which at least show that the Prophet had formed some idea for himself of the "How?" of the revelation. It is also certain that one particular revelation must have had decisive importance for him, without doubt the one by which a prophetic mission was imposed upon him. Ramaḍān was later chosen as the month of the fast because the Ḳur'ān was sent down in it (ii. 185); "the perspicuous scripture was sent down in a blessed night" (xliv. 3 *sqq.*), namely in the "night of all-power" in which the angels and the spirit at their Lord's command descended on account of every matter (to be settled) (xcvii. 1 *sqq.*; Schaade proposes to read *tunazzilū* — they bring down commands of all kinds) — apparently a late offshoot of the old Babylonian idea of a day on which the events of the year were settled. That Muḥammad was able to distinguish the words heard by him from his own thoughts is evident from xx. 114; lxxv. 16 *sqq.*; lxix. 44 *sqq.*; x. 15 *sq.*; vii. 203, just as it is in general certain that he was firmly convinced of the reality and truth of his revelations [see MUḤAMMAD]. Like the earlier prophets (xx. 49) he had to fight with the whisperings of Satan (vii. 200, xxiii. 97; xli. 36) and that these sometimes endeavoured to mingle with the revelations seems to be indicated by xvi. 98. To protect himself from these he sought protection with Allāh, but a reliable tradition reports that at least once he allowed himself to be tempted by Satan to recognize the Meccan

goddesses al-Lāt, al-ʿUzzā and al-Manāt to some extent. But he afterwards discovered his error, whereupon the revelation is said to have received the form now found in liii. 19 *sqq*.

It would certainly be wrong to identify those inspirations received under these mysterious conditions with what we now read in the Ḳur'ān. Even the oldest short Sūras which might have been heard by him in their underlying form may have received their present form with rhymes etc., in a later recasting. At any rate this is evident in the later long sections, like the histories of the prophets or the reproductions of dialogues between Muḥammad and his opponents, where of course only his answers can be based on inspirations. An exact distinction between the auditions of the Prophet and their later formalisation is however an impossibility.

3. A special feature of the revelations which much occupied Muḥammad himself and his opponents, was that they were communicated piecemeal, although they existed complete in the heavenly book (xvii. 106; lxxvi. 23): "The unbelievers say, why was the Ḳur'ān not sent down to him as a whole? We wished to strengthen thy heart thereby and we arranged it (in this way)" (xxv. 32). That the breaking up of the Ḳur'ān into small parts was in reality connected with the fact that the separate revelations were provoked in Mecca by the attacks of the opponents, in Madīna by political and other conditions, was a fact Muḥammad did not clearly realise and yet this circumstance had a decisive influence on the form and contents of the Ḳur'ān. Its striking incompleteness is connected with this. Nowhere do we find an exhaustive treatment of the principles of belief or of laws but the Prophet as a rule goes quickly from one subject to another according as conditions demand. In the Ḳur'ān we thus find for example only a few scattered indications regarding the great pilgrimage so that it would not be possible to reconstruct the whole ceremony from the Ḳur'ān without the help of ḥadīths. In such cases one must always consider the possibility that ḥadīths antedate all sorts of later customs; and that this actually happened we see from the instructive example of the settling of the times of daily prayers. According to tradition, the angel Gabriel taught them to the Prophet but the Ḳur'ān mentions only two obligatory periods of prayer, to which ii. 238 adds the afternoon prayer [cf. ṢALĀT]; when there is mention of the five times of prayer in Muḥammad's letter to ʿAmr b. Ḥazm (Ibn Hishām, p. 962), this is probably an indication of a later recasting of the text (cf. thereon Ibn Saʿd, iv/i. 159) .That Muḥammad knew quite well that the full contents of the heavenly book had not been communicated to him is evident from the passages mentioned above, according to which Allāh had told him of some of the prophets but not of others.

Of special significance for Muḥammad's own conception of the revelations is the distinction which he makes between them. Thus it is said in iii. 7 of the Ḳur'ān: "In it are unambiguous *āyāt* which are the mother of the scripture (its firm foundation, otherwise in xliii. 4) and others which are ambiguous; those in whose hearts there is a tendency to err adhere to the ambiguous because they seek discord and (arbitrary) exposition; yet no one knows the exposition except Allāh; but those who are strengthened in knowledge say: we believe in it; everything comes from our Lord". The obscure passages which to the pain of the Prophet produced criticism and quarrelling, are ascribed to divine inspiration equally with the clear passages. But there are cases where the divine revelation not only abrogated principles of the earlier religions of revelation but even regulations which Muḥammad himself had proclaimed. How he reconciled this with the idea of an original scripture in heaven, the contents of which were revealed to him, is not easy to see, if he ever really reflected on the point at all; but in any case the idea itself that Allāh revoked and altered the announcements of His will caused him no difficulty. This is the doctrine, later thoroughly discussed by the theologians, of *nāsikh* and *mansūkh*, the abrogating and abrogated (cf. A. Haqq, *Abrogations in the Koran*, Lucknow). There were special works on the subject, e.g. by Abu 'l-Ḳāsim Hibat Allāh b. Salāma (d. 410/1019) and ʿAbd al-Ḳāhir b. Ṭāhir (d. 429/1038). The terminology goes back to ii. 106, where it is said with reference to the alteration of the direction at prayer: "if we abrogate an *āya* or consign it to oblivion, we offer something better than it or something of equal value"; cf. also xvi. 107: "if we put one *āya* in the place of another — and Allāh surely knows best what He sends down — they say "thou art simply romancing", but this verse may also refer to unintentional variations in the repetition of earlier pronouncements.

If Muḥammad did not have quite a clear conception of these points of view, he was all the more sensitive when the Meccans pointed out that his wisdom was communicated to him by mortal teachers, some of them foreigners (xvi. 103; xxv. 4 *sq*.; xliv. 14). His defence on this points is very weak and he really concedes the justice of the charge. What he learned in this way was probably transformed into indubitable divine words when it re-echoed in his trance-like moments of mental absorption.

4. Among the most engrossing of Muḥammad's conceptions is the idea that not only his mission but also the revelations of the earlier prophets and the holy scriptures of the Jews and Christians were based on the original heavenly scripture, so that they coincided in part with what he himself taught. The Ḳur'ān "was sent down in perspicuous Arabic language and it is in the scriptures of the ancients; is it not a sign that the learned men of the Jews know it?" (xxvi. 195 *sq*.). The Ḳur'ān thus confirms what was earlier revealed (iii. 81; vi. 92; xxxv. 31; xlvi. 12 etc.). The Law was given to Moses, the Gospel to Jesus, and in addition there is the Psalter which David received (iv. 163; xvii. 55). They all came out of the heavenly book and therefore the Jews and Christians are called *ahl al-kitāb*, the people of the (original) scripture. From such statements alone it can be seen that Muḥammad had no idea of the real contents of these books and that he can never have read them, so that it is labour lost to try to ascertain what is meant by the "leaves of Abraham", which are mentioned alongside of the leaves of Moses (liii. 36 *sqq*.; lxxxvii. 18 *sq*.), or the books which the Prophets brought according to xxxv. 25. The Ḳur'ān expressly confirms this position of the Prophet by the word *ummī* (from *umma*, like *laikos*, from *laos*; according to Wensinck, in *Acta Orientalia*, ii. 191, rather *ethnikos*; cf. however, Sūra ii. 78), i.e. a layman, who could not read the holy scriptures of the earlier religions of a revelation (ii. 78; iii. 20, 75; see further UMMĪ). "Allāh has sent amongst the uninstructed a messenger from their midst, who proclaims his *āyāt* to them and teaches them the scripture and

wisdom" (lxii. 2); "Thou didst not know what scripture or belief was" (xlii. 52; cf. xxi. 48). This idea of the essential identity of his teaching with the earlier books of revelation is found all through the Meccan period, and in Madīna also he still adheres to it although with some modifications. He now regards the older religions in a more critical spirit and emphasises their differences from his own. The Jews received only a part of the "scripture" (iii. 23; iv. 44) and, what is more important, there are in their laws regulations which have only a limited validity like the observance of the Sabbath which is binding only on them (ii. 65; iv. 47, 154) or the forbidden foods which were intended as a punishment for the Jews (iv. 160; vi. 147; no doubt an interpolation of the Madīna period; otherwise in v. 5). The main point however is that he defends himself against Jewish criticism by the assertion that in their scripture the Jews had forgotten (v. 13) or concealed (ii. 174), or actually corrupted all sorts of things. "They have perverted the words from their places" (iv. 46; v. 16, 43), and a similar charge is raised against the Christians because they worship Jesus as God and have introduced monasticism.

5. Although Muḥammad owed not only his general religious and moral ideas but certainly also the idea of God's revelation through prophets sent by Him to contact with Jews and Christians, or probably more correctly with the numerous sectarian offshoots of these religions settled in Arabia — his series of prophets, strange to Judaism proper, in which the regular prophets of the scriptures are lacking, recalls somewhat the Clementine writings for example — his teaching developed in the early period, not according to Biblical models but in the style of the pagan Arab soothsayers (vide KĀHIN) with their oracles, formulae for blessings and curses, etc. In the introductions to the oldest sūras, he swears by the most remarkable things, by the fig- and olive-tree and by Mount Sinai (xcv. 1), by the heavens and the signs of the Zodiac, by the dawn and by the ten nights, by the double and the single (lxxxix. 1 *sq.*) etc. He also uses a form found with these soothsayers which gives the older parts of the Ḳur'ān a distinctive character. While he rejects with indignation the assertion of his opponents that he is a poet (xxi. 5; xxxvii. 36; lii. 30; lxix. 41; cf. also the judgement on the poets: xxvi. 224 *sqq.*) and his discourses really have nothing in common with the productions of Arabic poetry of the time, highly developed as regards language and rhythm, he used, after the fashion of the soothsayers, rhymed prose, *sadj*ᶜ, which consists in two or more short sections of the utterance being linked together by a rhyme. In view of the constant suffix forms and endings and wealth of the vocabulary of Arabic, such sentences can be formed without much trouble especially as the finer rules of the rhymes of poetry do not apply to *sadj*ᶜ. Muḥammad also used the *sadj*ᶜ form with great freedom, frequently repeated the same rhyming word and used "false" rhymes. In his later revelations he became still more negligent in their application (cf. the material collected by Vollers, *Volkssprache und Schriftsprache im alten Arabien*, 1905, p. 15 *sqq.*; Nöldeke-Schwally, *Geschichte des Qorāns*, i. 36 *sqq.*) so that Muslim scholars assert, not quite without justice, that the Ḳur'ān is not composed in proper *sadj*ᶜ. Nevertheless this form may be used with caution for critical excisions (e.g. lxxiv. 31; lxxxv. 10 *sq.*) or emendations (e.g. lxxiv. 42; *djaḥīm* for *saḳar*). Rhymed prose was of importance for the style of the Ḳur'ān, as it enabled Muḥammad to use peculiar (e.g. xxxvii. 130; xcv. 2) or rare words (e.g. lxxxiii. 18 *sq.*) or even had a definite influence on the contents (e.g. the nineteen angels, lxxiv. 30; the eight, lxix. 17; the dual form, lv. 46 *sqq.* etc.). Among other artifices Muḥammad occasionally used the refrain (e.g. Sūra liv. and especially lv.) without however actually reaching a regular strophe formation. Among the rhetorical artifices may also be mentioned the frequent similes, as Muḥammad atributed a special value to them and reflects on Allāh's use of them (xiv. 25; xxiv. 35; xxix. 43; lix. 21; and notably ii. 26). The *amthāl* are as a rule simple comparisons which are not infrequently very effective and much to the point (e.g. xiii. 14, 17; xxiv. 39). In so far as they are taken from nature, it is made to appear in vii. 58; xiii. 17, as if Allāh had so formed the processes of nature as to express a moral lesson. In other cases the *amthāl* are taken from history, as warnings or incitements (xiv. 48, xliii. 57; lxvi. 10 *sq.*); a remarkable simile is found in the "Light-Verse" (xxiv. 35), which is practically isolated in its strongly mystical colouring. On one occasion a simile is spun out into a regular parable (xviii. 32 *sqq.*), but it is rather spoiled by the confusion of the picture and the truth to be illustrated by it. That Muḥammad at any rate later heard something of the parables in the Gospels is shown by xlviii. 29, from which however it can once more be seen that he possessed no real knowledge of the New Testament.

6. The language in which Muḥammad delivered his revelations was, according to the most natural assumption, the Ḥidjāz dialect of the people of Mecca. The view put forward by Vollers that it was a purely popular speech, distinct from literary Arabic with its strict grammatical rules, so that the present text only came into existence as the result of a later revision, has been rightly refuted by R. Geyer and Nöldeke, as there is no support for it either in the oldest traditions nor in the evidence of language, although the inadequate reproduction in an alphabet of consonants does not exclude the possibility that the pronunciation on the lips of the Prophet may have offered all sorts of shades of variation. The style is quite different in the earlier and later parts of the Ḳur'ān, although it bears everywhere undeniably the stamp of the same individual. To Muslims the absolute perfection of the language of the Ḳur'ān is an impregnable dogma, the acknowledgment of which is not however easy to a reader with some stylistic training and a certain amount of taste. In the earliest revelations one is carried away by the wild fancy and rhapsodic presentation, sometimes also by a warmer feeling, so that it would be pedantic to lay much weight on points of language or logic. In the later sections also higher flights are not lacking, for example when the Prophet expresses his admiration for the wonders of creation and of life; but as a rule his imagination soon exhausted itself and gave place to passages of prose, which, with their switches in reasoning, a comprehensive catalogue of which has been made by Nöldeke, *Neue Beiträge zur semitischen Sprachwissenschaft*, p. 5 *sqq.*, make a wearisome impression. The Prophet now often indulges in repetitions of long stories (cf. for example, "the most beautiful tale": Sūra xii.) or psychological explanations, or polemics which prove little to those who do not share his premisses. As an example, the naive argumentation iii. 44 may be quoted in which he sees in the fact that he was not present when the events narrated took place, a proof that it must have been communicated to

him by revelation. See also *Der Sprachstil des Koran*, aus dem Nachlass von G. Richter, herausgeg. von O. Spies, Leipzig 1940 and T. Sabbagh, *Le métaphore dans le Coran*, Paris 1943. We should however not forget that the really effective element in his preaching lay not in his speeches but in the unusually suggestive power of his personality and also that many weaknesses in his style may be explained by the fact that (like the Alexandrine translators of the Old Testament) he had first to create a language for ideas new and remote to his countrymen.

7. What was the exact state of the Ḳur'ān at the death of Muḥammad is a question that cannot be answered with absolute certainty. One thing only is certain and is openly recognised by tradition (al-Suyūṭī, *Itḳān*, i. 71) namely, that there was not in existence any collection of revelations in final form, because, so long as he was alive, new revelations were continually being added to the earlier ones. But, on the other hand, everything points to the fact that even then much of the later Ḳur'ān must have already been written down. In the early period of his mission his discourses were probably preserved as a rule in the memories of his hearers, after he had repeatedly delivered them, and, as the lasting importance of his words probably only gradually dawned on them, we must probably consider the possibility that a good deal has been lost, of the earliest revelations in particular. Passages like lxxxvii. 6 *sq.*: "We will enable thee to discourse and thou shalt forget only what Allāh wishes", or ii. 106: "If we make thee forget an *āya*" (the reading *nansa'uhā* is of course a dogmatic correction), clearly suggest that the discourses in question were not written down. But it cannot have been long before they felt obliged to secure the revelations from Allāh by writing them down, and it is easy to understand that the material readiest to hand, like shoulder-blades, palm-leaves, stones, etc. were used, as we are told in the stories of the later collection of the Ḳur'ān. What we are told of the knowledge of the art of writing in Mecca and Madīna (al-Balā̲dh̲urī, ed. de Goeje, p. 471, 473; cf. Goldziher, *Muh. Stud.*, i. 110), is not of much value, although the story is not without interest that among the wives of the Prophet, Ḥafṣa and Umm Kul̲th̲ūm could write and ʿĀ'is̲h̲a and Umm Salama could read but not write. There can be however no doubt that in a commercial city of the importance of Mecca with its international connections not a few were able to write more or less well — according to al-Azraḳī, *Ta'rīk̲h̲ Makka*, ed. Wüstenfeld, p. 102, etc., documents and bills were prepared there before Islām — and there were certainly not lacking either there or later in Madīna people who wrote down Muḥammad's revelations. Whether the Prophet himself could read or write is therefore of minor importance, however eagerly this question has been discussed by Muslims, but only from dogmatic points of view and as a rule with an erroneous application of the term *ummī* already mentioned. From the Meccan passage xxix. 48, it might be concluded that he only learned late in life, but the expression is obscure and probably refers only to the reading of sacred texts. All the more important therefore is the passage xxv. 5, where his opponents say: "These are nothing but old fables which he writes down (or causes to be written down?) and they are dictated to him morning and evening". But such remarks refer rather to the matter collected by the Prophet than directly to his discourses themselves. But when Muḥammad (xi. 13) challenges his opponents to produce ten sūras like his own, this undoubtedly presupposes that sūras were available for comparison in writing. This is still more clearly shown by the already mentioned formal abrogation of earlier utterances, which would not have been necessary if these had only been orally transmitted. In the story of ʿUmar's conversion (Ibn His̲h̲ām, ed. Wüstenfeld, p. 226 *sq.*) there is a reference to a page of writing, but not much stress can be laid on such details in tradition. As ruler in Madīna, Muḥammad had drawn up by various followers a number of documents, several of which were preserved with a note of the writer (cf. also Wāḳidī, transl. by Wellhausen, p. 35, on the Nak̲h̲la letter), and it is obvious that the same was the case with the later revelations, especially with such as refer to legal regulations. The traditions (Balā̲dh̲urī, p. 472 *sq.*; al-Ṭabarī, ed. de Goeje, i. 1782) give the names of Meccans and Anṣār who helped him as secretaries, including two in particular, Ubaiy b. Kaʿb and Zaid b. T̲h̲ābit. According to a curious story, ʿUt̲h̲mān's foster-brother, ʿAbd Allāh b. Abī Sarḥ, often acted as Ḳur'ān-writer to him and he had the honour of having an enthusiastic exclamation of his on listening to the dictation of Sūra xxiii. adopted in it (Balā̲dh̲ūrī, p. 473 and the commentators). According to other stories (cf. Wāḳidī, transl. by Wellhausen, p. 55), he boasted before the Ḳurais̲h̲ that he had often induced the Prophet to alter the wording of the revelations whence it ultimately came to be said that he had falsified the Ḳur'ān (Goldziher, *Die Richtungen der islamischen Koranauslegung*, p. 35). Finally we may call attention to important evidence in a poem by Muḥammad's laureate Ḥassān b. T̲h̲ābit after the battle of Badr (*Dīwān*, ed. Hirschfeld, p. 15), in which he speaks of a *k̲h̲aṭṭ al-waḥy* on smooth page, which here must almost certainly mean the writing of a revelation (see Nöldeke, in *S. B. Ak. Wien*, 1900 on Labīd, *Muʿallaḳa*, verse 2). What was officially written down in this way formed with the earlier private notes and what people had retained in their memories the Ḳur'ān in an embryonic state. The conflict of this state of affairs with some traditions (principal, Ibn Saʿd, II/ii. 113 *sqq.*) according to which various people already collected the Ḳur'ān in Muḥammad's life-time is only apparent. The explanation is that *d̲j̲amaʿa* here, as usual elsewhere (e.g. *Fragm. Hist. Arab.*, ed. de Goeje, p. 275; cf. *Itḳān*, i. 72), means "to learn by heart and know". The same is true of a tradition, later popular among the S̲h̲īʿīs, to the effect that ʿAlī wished to avoid paying homage to Abū Bakr until he *d̲j̲amaʿa* the Ḳur'ān (Ibn Saʿd, II/ii. 101 *sqq.*; *al-ʿIḳd al-farīd*, ii. 176) which originally meant simply "had learned by heart", but was later misunderstood. Lastly a passage may be mentioned which would be of the greatest importance for the history of the Ḳur'ān in the time of Muḥammad if it could be trusted. In the Prophet's letter of instruction to ʿAmr b. Ḥazm (Ibn His̲h̲ām, p. 961; cf. Sperber, *Die Schreiben Muḥammeds an die Stämme Arabiens*, in *MSOS*, vol. xix. 2, 83) it is laid down among other things that no one may touch the Ḳur'ān except in a state of purification; but Caetani, *Annali dell' Islām*, ii. 1, p. 319, note 1, is undoubtedly right in thinking that the regulations laid down in this document were in many cases formulated from a point of view of later date.

8. With the death of the Prophet the position was radically altered. The source of revelations ceased

to flow, and the believers in cases of doubt had no one whom they might consult, as no one had inherited Muḥammad's prophetic gift. The discourses left by him thus acquired increased importance, for in them spoke the Prophet or rather God through him to his community, if they were able to interpret his words correctly. The task therefore naturally presented itself of collecting his valuable legacy in as complete and accurate a form as possible and preserving it from destruction. This obvious development is also confirmed by the traditions but unfortunately in a way which leaves much obscure. The most popular view (see Nöldeke-Schwally, ii. 11 *sq.*) finds the stimulus to the first collection of revelations in the circumstance that many who knew the Ḳur'ān (*ḳurrā'*, reciters; on the later meaning "pious ascetics", see Goldziher, *Vorlesungen über den Islam*, p. 189) had perished in the battle with the false prophet Musailima. This aroused in ʿUmar the fear that all knowledge of the revelations might be lost wherefore he, although with some difficulty, induced the caliph Abū Bakr to begin the collection of the scattered discourses. The work was entrusted to the already mentioned secretary of Muḥammad, Zaid b. Thābit. He collected everything that was written on different, often primitive (cf. above), materials, and what people retained in their breasts (i.e. memories) and wrote it on separate leaves (*ṣuḥuf*, pl. of *ṣaḥīfa*, written leaf), which he gave to Abū Bakr. After the latter's death, this book passed into the possession of ʿUmar, who bequeathed it to his daughter Ḥafṣa, the widow of Muḥammad. In this story the first thing that strikes one is that there is no reference to the official transcripts made by order of the Prophet himself, although they would at any rate have reduced the danger threatened by the death of the *ḳurrā'*. Caetani moreover (*Annali dell' Islām*, II/i., p. 713 infra) has called attention to the fact that those who fell in the battle with Musailima were, according to the lists, which have been handed down, mainly new converts, none of whom could be expected to have an extensive knowledge of the Ḳur'ān. If the whole story is thereby rendered uncertain, it becomes more important to note that there are other traditions, according to which it was ʿUmar himself who ordered and supervised the collection (*Itḳān*, i. 73) and indeed we are even told (Ibn Saʿd, III/i. 212) that ʿUmar died before the task was completed. As it is easier to understand how such a pious work could have been antedated than that it could have been transferred from Abū Bakr to his successor, the second story is perhaps somewhat more probable, although the mechanical way in which ʿUmar is said to have tested the genuineness of the separate parts (if they were known to two authorities) does not sound very trustworthy. Zaid's participation in the work remains the one thing certain in the stories and on the other hand the realistic feature that the *ṣuḥuf* came into the possession of Ḥafṣa. But this very point raises other difficulties. If the *ṣuḥuf* was to be an authorized standard codex it is difficult to understand why it was given to a woman. G. Weil thinks that Ḥafṣa was to take care of it but this could have been more safely done in other ways; and if it was to be a standard MS. from which copies could be made, it was quite inconvenient to leave it with Ḥafṣa, as not every one had access to the widow of the Prophet. There is never any reference to any authorization at all. The whole business was handled with great freedom, as we hear of several variant versions of the Ḳur'ān from the pre-ʿUthmānic period. The only solution of the difficulty may be in the hypothesis suggested in the next section, that a distinction should be made between the simple material collection of the *ṣuḥuf* and a regular arrangement and editing by Zaid of the sūras contained in them. If this is so, the "leaves" would lose any real importance and it is not difficult to believe that they might be given to ʿUmar's daughter as a gift of honour.

9. The men to whom particular editions are ascribed were the already mentioned Ubaiy b. Kaʿb (Ibn Saʿd, II/ii. 103; III/ii. 59—62), ʿAbd Allāh b. Masʿūd [see IBN MASʿŪD], Abū Mūsā ʿAbd Allāh al-Ashʿarī [see AL-ASHʿARĪ] who became famous in the story of ʿAlī, and Miḳdād b. ʿAmr (see Ibn Saʿd, III/i. 114—116). All these recensions gradually disappeared after the authorisation of ʿUthmān's Ḳur'ān; but several very valuable items of information regarding the first two are given in the *Fihrist*, ed. Flügel, p. 26 *sq.* and in *al-Itḳān*, i. 80—82, which throw some light on the oldest phase of the history of the Ḳur'ān. They had the same sūras as ʿUthmān's Ḳur'ān but in a somewhat different order and with the important difference that Ubaiy had two additional sūras (prayers recalling Sūra i.), while in Ibn Masʿūd Sūra cxiii. and cxiv. and probably also Sūra i. were not given. Besides these recensions there was a further one, on which ʿUthmān's edition was later based, and which is associated with the Zaid already mentioned. If, as Schwally does, we tried to identify Zaid's edition with the *ṣuḥuf*, it would be difficult to understand the divergencies of the other recensions in view of the former's prestige. Besides, the name "the leaves" suggests rather a loose collection of separate leaves, and not a definite arrangement of the portions. This is definitely expressed in another tradition, according to which Zaid collected the sūras with much difficulty in no particular order (Nöldeke-Schwally, *Geschichte des Qorāns*, ii. p. 11 *sqq.*). These difficulties are most easily disposed of by the assumption that Zaid after collecting the *ṣuḥuf* prepared an edition of his own with a definite order of the sūras, which added a fifth to the already mentioned four editions, one by which the others did not feel themselves bound. The sūras in it were, as in Ibn Masʿūd and Ubaiy, arranged on the principle of decreasing length; but it was only a general principle (taken from Jewish examples?) the details of which were left to the individual. Zaid's version later received authoritative importance, when it was used as the basis for ʿUthmān's Ḳur'ān. A further light might be thrown by a phenomenon which, although in itself exceedingly obscure, seems to permit some significant deductions. We refer to the mysterious letters, discussed more fully below, which are found at the beginning of about a quarter of the sūras. In this connection Nöldeke and following him H. Hirschfeld and more recently especially H. Bauer, in *ZDMG*, lxxv. 1 *sqq.*, have called attention to the fact that some of these letters are repeated before several sūras and that these sūras form little consecutive series. Thus *ḥ—m* is found before xl.—xlvi. (according to Bauer originally before xxxix. also; before xlii. with following *ʿ—s—ḳ*), *'—l—r* before x.—xv. (before xiii. *'—l—m—r*), *ṭ—s—m* before xxvi.—xxviii. (before xxvii. however without *m*), *'—l—m* seems to be an exception, as it is found not only before xxix.—xxx. but also before ii.—iii.; but we can easily see that the reason is that the order in this case is upset by the principle of decreasing length, by which the sūras already mentioned are placed at the head of the collection while the others

being shorter are placed later. This remarkable phenomenon can have only one explanation, namely that these groups formed little separate collections, which Zaid found already formed and would not break up. Bauer has also called attention to the interesting fact that Ibn Masʿūd did not feel himself bound by them but inserted the separate components approximately where they belonged from their length, with the exception however of the *h—m* group which he left together, although in a different order. It seems therefore to have had a particular significance for him, which is also indicated by the fact that he called this group *dībādj al-Ḳur'ān* (see *Itḳān*, i. 71; cf. the article *dībādj* in Lane, s.v.); Ubaiy on the other hand paid no attention to the small series but arranged all the sūras according to their length, although in a very inexact fashion. We see then that there were links between the separate scattered sūras and the *ṣuḥuf*, small collections probably of a purely private character. This gives us definite evidence that the collection in its present form cannot go back to the Prophet himself.

10. On the other hand, it is a very difficult question whether the sūras which Zaid found were given the form in which we know them by the Prophet himself or whether other hands intervened. That the oldest, quite short, revelations are original units is generally recognized. This is also true of several longer ones, especially xii. which forms a connected story, or of Sūra lv. with its refrains. Nöldeke moreover rightly utters a warning against assuming that whenever the thread of continuity appears to break, we have the work of a later hand, as abruptness and lack of coordination is really characteristic of Muḥammad's style. There are also certainly small pieces of later periods which the Prophet himself may have inserted for some reason in older pieces. In other cases, however, we have the impression that various accidents, which we can no longer know of, may have played their part in the shaping of the sūras, among them perhaps the circumstance that several short discourses might have been written on the same piece of material, which would simply explain, for example, the transitions from xcvi. 5 to 6, or from lxxiv. 10 to 11. The most difficult thing is undoubtedly to suppose that Muḥammad himself composed the unusually long second Sūra in which we find in the middle of speeches of the second year A.H., without any explanation, pieces from the Meccan period (21—39, 163—171) and also of the later Madīna period. That the beginnings of the sūras (with perhaps the exception of xlviii., lxxi., xcvii., cviii. which begin with *innā*) regularly coincide with the actual beginnings of the revelations is proved by the introductory conjurations or formulae like "These are the *āyāt* of the Book" or "This is the Book", or "See, a Sūra, which we have sent down, etc.". But the next question is whether such exordiums refer to the whole Sūra or only to what immediately follows, to which the rest may have been later joined; cf. e.g. the introduction xix. 2, which only fits the story of Zakarīyā' and Mary, while, on the other hand, the formula in verse 16 is adopted in 41, 51, 54 and 56. In brief we are here unfortunately usually confronted with questions which cannot be answered with certainty, however important the correct answer would be for an understanding of the Ḳur'ān.

11. With the reign of ʿUthmān we enter upon more solid ground. According to a statement of Ibn al-Athīr (ed. Tornberg, iii. 86), the four recensions mentioned above found acceptance, each in a particular region: Ubaiy's in Damascus, Miḳdād's in Ḥimṣ, Ibn Masʿūd's in Kūfa and al-Ashʿarī's in Baṣra; support is given to this statement by the fact that the two last named held offices in the provinces mentioned. That the existence of several divergent versions would produce uncertainty is easily understood. We are told in a widely disseminated tradition that the general Ḥudhaifa thought that the quarrels among his followers about the correct form of the sacred book, while on a campaign in Armenia and Ādharbāidjān, were dangerous and asked the Caliph ʿUthmān to try to abolish this unfortunate state of affairs, so that believers might not quarrel like Jews and Christians over their scriptures. The Caliph recognised the justice of the request and asked Ḥafṣa to let him have the *ṣuḥuf* for a time so that copies might be made of them (*nasakhūhā fi 'l-maṣāḥif*). Ḥafṣa agreed and the Caliph entrusted the task to a commission consisting of Zaid, already mentioned, ʿAbd Allāh b. Zubair [q.v.], Saʿīd b. al-ʿĀṣ (Ibn Saʿd, v. 19—24) and ʿAbd al-Raḥmān b. al-Ḥārith (*ibid.*, v. 1 *sqq.*). Other individuals are also named but the usual tradition appears the most reliable and in any case it may be considered practically certain that Zaid, on account of his previous services, shared in the work. From the attitude which ʿAbd Allāh and his father al-Zubair soon afterwards took up towards the Caliph, one might perhaps suppose that the members were chosen, not so much by the Caliph in person, as by a wider circle. Besides it is not easy to see clearly what their work really was. If they had only to make copies of a standard text, reliable scribes would have sufficed so that the men named would at most exercise some sort of supervision over the work. According to the tradition, they were to retain the Ḳuraishī dialect in cases of doubt, but this probably only reflects a later notion of the dialect of the Ḳur'ān. Further they could not have made clear fine distinctions of pronunciation with the imperfect Arabic alphabet. At any rate the most important point is that the version of ʿUthmān was based on the *ṣuḥuf* or as just explained on Zaid's edition of them so that we can in this way gain some idea of the contents and form of this basic manuscript. We are next told that, of the copies then made, one was kept in Madīna, while three were sent as standard texts to Kūfa, Baṣra and Damascus, that is practically to the regions in which the four differing versions above mentioned were current. Mecca however is added and other authorities give a larger number (cf. Nöldeke-Schwally, ii. 112 *sq.*). The authorised edition was readily accepted everywhere; the people of Kūfa alone are said to have refused to give up their Ibn Masʿūd. Against the accuracy of the whole story, it might perhaps be urged that a knowledge of the Ḳur'ān and interest in its correct form must really have been much too slight among Muslim soldiers in this period of the great wars of conquest to give rise to dissensions in the army. But on the other hand, it may be recalled that in the fighting which soon afterwards broke out between ʿAlī and Muʿāwiya, there is mention of Ḳur'ān readers (*ḳurrā'*) not only among ʿAlī's troops but also among the Syrians (al-Dīnawarī, ed. Guirgass, p. 175, 204); the very fact that there were different versions of the Ḳur'ān in Syria and in al-ʿIrāḳ must have given rise to comparisons and disputes. Whether the Caliph, as we are told in the different traditions, had the extant differing versions burned, torn up or obliterated, has been doubted by Schwally and not without reason, especially as such steps would

have been quite ineffectual against the Ḳur'ān-reciters who carried the sacred texts in their memories. In any case the alleged destruction cannot have been completely carried out, for according to al-Muṭarrizī (in Lane, s.v.), Sulaimān al-Aʿmash could recite the whole of the Ḳur'ān [cf. KHATM] according to both ʿUthmān's and Ibn Masʿūd's versions and the author of the *Fihrist* even asserts that he had seen a two hundred year old copy of the Ḳur'ān according to Ibn Masʿūd (cf. the obscure statements in Nöldeke, *Gesch. d. Qorāns*, 1st ed., p. 276 *sq.*). Even without any such drastic measures, the new version must have gradually driven out the variants because of its official authority and the general desire for uniformity. It was in this way that there came into being the authorised Ḳur'ān, which has remained generally authoritative to the present day and in spite of all vicissitudes has formed, with the Sunna, the solid foundation for Muslim life and thought. It differed from Ubaiy's Ḳur'ān by the omission of the two sūras only found in his version, while it was a little larger than Ibn Masʿūd's Ḳur'ān, which omitted Sūra cxiii. and cxiv. and probably also Sūra i. (see Nöldeke-Schwally, ii. 39 *sqq.*). While its order generally, with the already mentioned exceptions, was based on the principle of decreasing length, the first Sūra, the celebrated *fātiḥa*, stands outside of this arrangement, apparently because it was intended to serve as an introductory benediction and prayer. It is specially noteworthy because of its lack of any distinctively Muslim thought and the presence of Jewish and Christian terminology. Sūra cxiii. and cxiv. are not the shortest and are thus not in their proper place, but it is hardly necessary to lay much stress on this point. Although they are made into utterances of Allāh by the prefixed *ḳul*, these formulae for protection against evil powers (cf. xvi. 98; xli. 36) are very different in character from the rest of the Ḳur'ān. In these circumstances the omission of the three sūras in Ibn Masʿūd becomes significant and the question arises whether they do not represent a secondary arrangement of the sūras about the origin of which nothing definite can be said, whether the work of the Prophet himself or others.

12. This leads to a further and very important question, whether all the revelations in the authorised Ḳur'ān come from Muḥammad himself or whether foreign matter has been added or passages forged for propagandist purposes. As a matter of fact, there has been no lack of such assertions, in the Muslim world and by modern scholars. The arguments brought forward on this point, within Islām, are however of no real importances as they are based on purely dogmatic premisses. For example, some of the puritanically-minded Khāridjīs are said to have rejected Sūra xii. as a love-story unworthy of the Ḳur'ān (al-Shahrastānī, *Kitāb al-milal wa'l-niḥal*, ed. Cureton, p. 95 *sq.*). But it so undeniably bears the stamp of the Prophet's style that the forger must have had an astonishing power of imitation: forgery is all the more improbable as the Sūra was found in Ibn Masʿūd and in Ubaiy and must therefore have been very old. The fact, that some reject as false passages those in which Muḥammad curses his opponents is due to the more refined religious ideas of the Muʿtazila and perhaps to Christian influence. But in general it is the Shīʿīs who have pronounced against the integrity of the ʿUthmānic Ḳur'ān. This however was only a result of the fact that they missed very much in it pronouncements on the prominent position of ʿAlī and his family and their claims to sovereignty and to the coming forth of the hidden Imām at the end of the world; and they roundly insisted that all this had been most maliciously suppressed by the godless ʿUthmān. In support of this assertion, they very cleverly point to the undeniable lack of coherence in several sūras, but the situation is not improved by filling the gaps with references to ʿAlī. But not only are odd verses said to have been suppressed but whole sūras, which glorified ʿAlī, only two of which have been published, the sūras *al-nūrain* and *al-walāya* (see Nöldeke-Schwally, ii. 102 *sq.*; Goldziher, *Die Richtungen der islamischen Koranauslegung*, p. 271; Casanova, i. 17, 24). As there is no agreement among the Shīʿīs themselves regarding the genuine form of the book of revelations, the attempts made by them to produce the complete text have regularly failed, and they have therefore retired to the safe position, that the authentic form is secretly transmitted by each imām to his successor, to be communicated with the true exposition to the believers ultimately on the coming forth of the hidden imām. Till then, faute de mieux, they use the ʿUthmānic Ḳur'ān and make shift with an exegesis which gives unrestricted freedom to interpretation and arbitrary alterations in the text, which however they refrain from in all liturgical uses.

Several modern scholars have endeavoured in a different fashion to prove the occurrence of passages in the Ḳur'ān which are not genuine. Thus de Sacy (*Journ. des Savants*, 1832, p. 535) suggested that ʿUmar's doubt about the death of Muḥammad would have been impossible if the verse quoted against it (iii. 144) by Abū Bakr were genuine, so that it must have originated with Abū Bakr. G. Weil agrees but, as a logical result, he rejects a series of verses of similar content (iii. 185; xxi. 34 *sq.*; xxix. 57; xxxix. 30 *sq.*). But it is just this increase in the number of passages attacked (which even yet is not sufficient, cf. e.g. vi. 162 and notably xxxiii. 53) which makes criticism unreliable and what is to be deleted is in perfect keeping with what Muḥammad says out of his purely human nature. The question is usually attacked from the wrong side, for the fault is not in the Ḳur'ān but in the tendencious tradition, which in reality is attacking the belief that crops up in a disappearance and return of the Prophet; cf. especially the antitheses between the worship of Allāh and of Muḥammad. Weil's doubt regarding xvii. 1 and xlvi. 15 is no better founded, nor are H. Hirschfeld's objections to v. 69, 101; lxi. 6 and all passages in which the name of Muḥammad occurs. When Weil in particular asserted that ʿUthmān falsified the Ḳur'ān by all sorts of omissions, this is refuted, like the Shīʿa charges before mentioned, by the simple fact that nowhere in the oldest records is there any hint of such a thing although his opponents collected a long list of charges against him.

13. Another question is raised by the additional sūras in Ubaiy's recension, which, according to *Itḳān*, i. 82, are also found in Abū Mūsā's version and in the Ḳur'ān of Ibn ʿAbbās: do we really have in the authorised Ḳur'ān all the revelations in existence at the death of Muḥammad? Although by the completion of the collection, the utterances that came from the heavenly book and Muḥammad's own words were sharply delimited, there are references in the traditions to several utterances which really belonged to the Ḳur'ān but were not included for various reasons, including some that are said to have been in the Ḳur'āns of Ubaiy and Abū

Mūsā; cf. Nöldeke-Schwally, i. 234—261; ii. 44 *sq.* and thereon al-Ṭabarī, ed. de Goeje, i. 1627, and the glossary under *ṭ-l-ʿ*. We need not reject this statement offhand. It would really not be surprising if the difference between the two kinds of pronouncements was at first not rigid, especially in so far as they were only preserved by memory. But nowhere is the genuineness of the revelations said not to have been accepted conclusively proved; of some the falsity is much more probable and it must be further remembered that they would not contribute any real addition to the Ḳur'ān. The best known is the so-called "verse of the stoning" (*āyat al-radjm*) according to which incontinence in women not virgins can be punished by stoning. As regards matter it might well belong to Sūra xxiv.; but it is in direct contradiction to its second verse and on the other hand it cannot be included among those abrogated, as, according to the traditions, ʿUmar punished this crime in this drastic fashion. It seems therefore to be a secondary verse intended to authorise the more severe punishment.

If a critical examination of the Ḳur'ān on these lines leads to a satisfactory result, it must not be taken to mean that the canonical Ḳur'ān gives an absolutely true and faultless reproduction of the utterances of the Prophet. On the contrary it undoubtedly contains not a few explanatory additions (cf. e.g. the probably secondary *kabīr*: ii. 219) and harmless interpolations (cf. e.g. A. Fischer, in *Nöldeke-Festschrift*, 1906, p. 33 *sqq.* whose arguments however are hardly cogent). Transferences of sentences may also have taken place, cf. the striking example quoted by Goldziher (*Vorlesungen*, p. 33 *sq.*), xxiv. 61*a*, which breaks up the context. But this is something quite different from a deliberate and tendencious falsification of the revelations, against which protests would certainly have been raised at once.

In contrast to the view above given and generally held of the origin of the authorised Ḳur'ān, A. Mingana (*The Transmission of the Ḳur'ān* reprinted from the *Journal of the Manchester Egyptian and Oriental Society*, 1915—1916 and *An ancient Translation of the Ḳur'ān* reprinted from the *Bulletin of the John Rylands Library*, vol. ix., Jan. 1925, following Casanova in *Mohammad et la fin du monde*) claims to prove that the authorised version of the Ḳur'ān and the preparation of a uniform text was brought about by al-Ḥadjdjādj in the reign of the Umaiyad caliph ʿAbd al-Malik (685—705). He bases his argument partly on the silence of earlier Christian writers regarding a sacred book of the Muḥammadans and partly on direct statements in Barhebraeus, Maḳrīzī and particularly al-Kindī regarding the steps taken by the two men above mentioned for the introduction of an authorised and uniform Ḳur'ān. In the Ḳur'āns of Ubaiy, Ibn Masʿūd, ʿUthmān and others, he sees only independent products of an anxiety which arose after the death of the Prophet in several of his followers to record the available utterances of the Prophet not in the form of books but on loose leaves. ʿUthmān's collection only attained greater importance from the fact that he became caliph, but it was only with the efforts of ʿAbd al-Malik assisted by al-Ḥadjdjādj that there came into existence an officially recognized version in book form, which Muslims were bound to use. Against this view however, we have the above mentioned references to older recensions, especially to Ibn Masʿūd's Ḳur'ān, of which copies existed for a considerable time. From these references, it is evident that these were not loose collections of material, but contained essentially the same matter and only differed in the order of the earlier sūras, i.e. they were regular books and not loose leaves. This is also true of ʿUthmān's recension and there is absolutely no reason for doubting what has been handed down regarding the authorised version. What these writers say about Ḥadjdjādj probably only means that the authorized Ḳur'ān still met with opposition in some districts in his time and he tried to put an end to this opposition.

Of greater interest is what Mingana says in his second article about a work found by him of the Syrian bishop Dionysios bar Ṣalībī (d. 1171; cf. Baumstark, *Gesch. der syr. Lit.*, 1922, p. 295—298) which, in a refutation of Muḥammadanism, contains a number of verses and pieces of the Ḳur'ān in Syriac translation. In this translation which Mingana, no doubt rightly, attributes to an earlier period we find readings differing from the *textus receptus* and verses which do not occur in the authorised Ḳur'ān, including some which are known from other sources as non-canonical.

14. The Sūras were originally separated from one another by the *basmala* ("in the name of God, the Merciful, the Compassionate") placed at the beginning of each (see the art. BASMALA). It is only lacking in Sūra ix., probably because Sūra viii. was originally joined to it. In the text itself, the formula is found in xxvii. 30 at the head of a letter from Solomon to the queen of Saba', a proof that the Prophet regarded it as a regular form of introduction. In keeping with this is the fact that it often occurs in his despatches (Ibn Saʿd, II/i. 23—37 *passim*) and according to Ibn Hishām, ed. Wüstenfeld, i. 341, at the beginning of the ordinance of the community. But he also used the older formula: "in Thy name, *Allāhumma*" (Ibn Saʿd, II/i. 19; cf. Ibn Hishām, p. 747 on the treaty of Ḥudaibīya). It therefore doubtless opened the sūras which the Prophet himself had caused to be written down and was then placed at the beginning of all the sūras. The order of the sūras in ʿUthmān's Ḳur'ān was probably already the present one. That there were variations however is evident from the story of the revolution against ʿUthmān (al-Ṭabarī, ed. de Goeje, i. 2963) in which we find the tenth Sūra quoted as the seventh, which agreed with the order in Ibn Masʿūd and Ubaiy. According to the *Itḳān*, i. 79, Ibn ʿAbbās also described the tenth Sūra as the last of the seven "long ones", but this perhaps refers not to its position in the Ḳur'ān but in relation to the actual lengths. In any case al-Ṭabarī in *Tafsīr*, i. 33 (see *ZDMG*, xxxv. 598) quotes a tradition going back to the Prophet himself, according to which the Ḳur'ān was divided as follows: the seven longest sūras, ii.—vii. and x., the *mi'ūna* (sūras of about 100 verses), the *mathānī* and *al-mufaṣṣal*, the short sūras which begin with xlix. The name *al-mathānī* apparently goes back to the very variously explained "seven *mathānī*" of xv. 87 in which Geiger and Nöldeke see the Aramaic *matnītā*, Hebrew *mishnā*.

15. Immediately following the *basmala* we have in 29 sūras the mysterious letters already mentioned (*al-fawātiḥ*) which have challenged the ingenuity of Muslim and modern European scholars alike. The sūras in which they occur belong with the exception of sūras ii. and iii. to the later Meccan period. There are 14 letters in all that occur, sometimes singly, sometimes from 2 to 5 together, some occur only once, others are repeated before two, five or six sūras. All recollection of their real sig-

nificance had been lost, as the great variety of explanations proffered shows (see *Itḳān*, ii. 10 *sqq.*; *ZDMG*, xxxv. 603 *sqq.*). Some Muslims see in them simply letters of the alphabet, intended to call the Prophet's attention to the approach of a revelation, while others tried to explain them from the old numerical value of the letters; or they were read with the names of the letters *yā*, *sīn*, *ḳāf*, etc., and all kinds of mystical names were found. The most popular explanation was that they were abbreviations which had to be expanded, thus for example *khyʿṣ* would stand for *karīm*, *hādī*, *yaḳīn*, *ʿalīm* and *ṣadīḳ*. But this offered such a wealth of possibilities that the attempts to solve the problem degenerated into a kind of game, which became all the more varied when some proposed to place the letters from different sūras together and read for example: *ʾlr*, *ḥm* and *n* as *al-Raḥmān*. It is no wonder then that in the end some, like al-Suyūṭī, saw in the letters a mystery, the solution of which Allāh kept a secret to himself. Modern scholars have in part repeated these old suggestions. Nöldeke, abandoning his earlier view, suggested that the Prophet attached no special significance to the letters but only intended to give a mystic reference to the heavenly original text. But in this case they should have been found before all the revelations and not only before a smaller part of them. The most popular theory more recently has been that of abbreviation, but this has developed into the same kind of guesswork as among the Muslims, and rarely convinces anyone except the ingenious inventor. H. Bauer in the essay already mentioned has sought a safer basis for interpretation, starting from the fact that some sūras take their name from the introductory letters, *viz.* xx., xxxvi., xxxviii., l., xlii. and lxviii., the two latter however with variants. Now as the names of the sūras are catchwords taken from the sūras concerned (see below), he supposes that these letters are something similar. But this conclusion is by no means certain and his ingenious attempts to find the passages concerned in the sūras are, as a rule, not very convincing, and it should be remembered also that he cannot apply this explanation to the letters that occur before several sūras, but has to be content with seeking an internal or external relation between these sūras and the letters. The same may be said against Gossen's attempt in *Der Islām*, xiii. 191 *sqq.* H. Hirschfeld revived Nöldeke's earlier explanation that the letters were originally marks put on by the owners of some of the manuscript copies made by Zaid to show they were their own property, except that he regards the group of letters not as single names (e.g. *ṭh* for Ṭalḥa) but names of several owners (e.g. *ṭh* for Ṭalḥa and Abū Huraira). In comparison with earlier suggestions, this strikes one as very moderate and unfanciful. Nor is it refuted by Nöldeke's argument that such abbreviations are not to be expected in the beginnings of written Arabic literature; for it is not at all improbable that the people of Mecca with their highly developed trade may have marked, e.g. in the annual trading-caravans, the goods of individual citizens taking part in them in some such way, and that his custom was adopted in another branch of life, where it was necessary to guarantee the genuineness of a document or some such thing. It might also be possible that there was an imitation of the Jewish practice; cf. the article "abbreviations" in the *Jewish Encyclopaedia*. In any case this hypothesis would agree very well with the above discussed connection of the letters with small private collections of copies of the revelations. But even this view does not lead to any final result, as the expansion of the letters to names offers so many possibilities.

16. Among the secondary elements in the Ḳurʾān are the names of the sūras. These are catchwords which refer either to the beginning of the sūras (e.g. lxxiii.—cxi.) or to some subject dealt with in them (e.g. "The Cow" in ii. 67 *sqq.*; "The House of ʿImrān" in iii. 33; "Hūd" in xi. 50 etc.). That they were generally known in the first half of the eight century is certain, as some of them are mentioned by John of Damascus (in Migne, *Patrol. Graeca*, xciv. 769, 772); viz: "the Cow" (Sūra ii.), "the Women" (Sūra iv.), "the Table" (Sūra v.) and in addition a name no longer found, "the Camel", which might refer to vii. 73—77, xi. 64 *sq.* or xxvi. 155 *sqq.* This however does not prove that they were already adopted in the manuscripts at this time; and that they do not all come from Muḥammad himself, as John says, is evident from their varying (Sūra ix. for example is also called *al-Tawba*: cf. *Itḳān*, i. 66 *sq.* and the above notes on Sūra xlii. and lxviii.). Besides, they originally ran "the sūra in which the cow is mentioned" etc. and appeared in the manuscripts not as super- but as subscriptions (Nöldeke, *Geschichte des Qorāns*, p. 320). The two non-canonical sūras of Ubaiy had similar names: *sūrat al-khāl* and *sūrat al-ḥafd.*

The sūras were divided into "verses", which were called *āyāt*, following the linguistic practice of the Ḳurʾān already mentioned. They are generally arranged according to the rhymes, but as the divisions were originally not marked in the manuscript, there is a difference of opinion about their divisions and numbering (see *Itḳān*, i. 83 *sq.*; Nöldeke, *Gesch. des Qorāns*, p. 300).

17. Although the ʿUthmānic Ḳurʾān prevailed over its rivals, it did not provide for the Muslim word a real *textus receptus*, and yet one would think that, if ever one were necessary, it would be for such a book as the Ḳurʾān, as Allāh speaks in it everywhere. Even ʿUthmān himself, according to one story (al-Ṭabarī, *Tafsīr*, iv. 24), did not adhere to the text authorized by him, but read Sūra iii. 104 with an addition not now found in it; and if this is correct, it is no wonder that others took still greater liberties. Various circumstances contributed to the continual variations in the form of the text. First there was the carelessness of the few trained copyists; even the copies of the Madīna standard codex (*al-imām*) sent to the provinces are said not always to have been identical with it, and lists are given of Madīna, Damascus, Baṣra and Kūfa readings, to which a few from Mecca are added. These refer however only to minor points, which are of interest for the history of the language and orthography, but not for the matter. The second cause of variation in the text was of greater importance, namely the different readings which the *ḳurrāʾ* retained in their memories and would not always abandon, even when they had a written Ḳurʾān before them. These are primarily readings which were found in the rival versions and had thus gained currency. Finally there was a third factor, the deficiencies of the Arabic script. It lacked not only signs for the short and to some extent for the long vowels, the pronunciation of which was left to the reader (which meant, for example, also the choice between active and passive) and for double consonants, but different consonantal sounds were expressed by one character, e.g. *d* and *dh*, *ḥ* and *kh*, etc. and in the degenerate Arabic

script, very different letters had come to assume the same form, so that for example *r* and *z*, *b*, *t* and *th*, and at the beginning or in the middle of a word *n* and *y* also, were indistinguishable. In any case however the sense was little affected by such possibilities, e.g. xxxii. 10, where it was a matter of indifference whether one read *ṣalilnā* or *ḍalilhā*; but in other cases a different pronunciation was a matter of moment, e.g., v. 6, where the alteration of a case-ending modifies the rule about ablution before prayer. Such possibilities afforded a means by which perplexed spirits could explain away various passages that troubled them, e.g. xii. 110 where in place of the offending *kadhabū*, *kudhibū* or *kudhdhibū* could be read. In this way there arose a perplexing confusion of readings and, in place of the striving for uniformity that one would have expected, people became accustomed to unlimited liberty in these matters, so that they did not hesitate to substitute for particular words their synonyms or to insert short explanatory additions. This freedom was all the more unbridled in its development, as the Umaiyad caliphs had little feeling on such questions and preferred to take care that passions were not aroused by state interference in such matters.

18. Gradually however, the situation came to arouse misgivings. As by this time the state of affairs just described had developed to such an extent that the preparation of a canonical text was not to be thought of, and there was, besides, no authority who could enforce the adoption of one, the endeavour was made to eliminate the worst defects by more general principles. Not every variant was allowed, but only those which were based on recognized authorities, preferably such men as had received their reading from the successors of the companions of the Prophet. At the same time the overwhelming mass of small details led the art of reading the Ḳur'ān, hitherto transmitted orally, to be replaced by critical writings. The first book of this kind is said to have been written by a Jewish convert to Islām, Hārūn b. Mūsā (d.c. 184/800). Of later works dealing with variant readings, special mention may be made of that of Abū ʿUbaid al-Ḳāsim (d. 223/837; Brockelmann, *GAL*², i. 105, *Suppl.* i. 166) and of the celebrated Ṭabarī's *al-Djāmiʿ*. In the fourth Islamic century there were written three books bearing each the title *Kitāb al-maṣāḥif*, one by Ibn al-Anbārī (d. 328/940), one by Ibn Ashta (d. 360/970) and one by Ibn Abī Dāwūd al-Sidjistānī (d. 316/928). The latter is extant and was published by A. Jeffery in his *Materials for the History of the text of the Qur'an*, Leiden 1937. These reservations were however too indefinite to be really effective and the attempt was therefore made to limit the number of authorities, for example by emphasising the importance of ten recognized teachers. The number seven was especially popular in this connection and support was found for it in an alleged saying of the Prophet regarding the seven *aḥruf* in which the Ḳur'ān is revealed and which all possess divine authority. Although "seven" in this tradition is probably only a round number meaning "several" and it was quite uncertain what the word *aḥruf* really meant, the number was taken literally and *aḥruf* was given the unauthorized meaning of variant readings. The complete historical inaccuracy of this assertion was sharply criticized by several scholars, but it found wide acceptance, especially after Abū Bakr b. Mudjāhid (d. 324/936) had chosen seven from among well known teachers and declared them authoritative Ḳur'ān-readers, and with each of them two men were associated as transmitters (*rāwī*, pl. *ruwāt*). The seven were Nāfiʿ, Ibn Kathīr, Abū ʿAmr al-ʿAlā', Ibn ʿĀmir, Abū Bakr ʿĀṣim, Ḥamza and the famous philologist al-Kisā'ī. The selection was quite an arbitrary one, but the method used elsewhere by Muslims, e.g. in the four *madhāhib*, of declaring several rivals authoritative and equally trustworthy had decided practical advantages as it averted endless and passionate disputes. There was of course no lack of protest by prominent scholars who rightly objected to the unjustifiable exclusion of other equally authoritative teachers. In the xi[th] century A.D. however, the exclusive authority of the seven canonical teachers began to prevail and their readings were specially dealt with by several authors, among them Abū ʿAmr ʿUthmān al-Dānī (d. 444/1053) whose *Kitāb al-taisīr* displaced Ibn Mudjāhid's work, in Abu 'l-Ḳāsim Ḳāsim al-Shāṭibī's (d. 590/1194) versification. But a number of scholars with critical ability did not hesitate to take into consideration readings of other readers not included among the celebrated seven, especially those of Yaʿḳūb al-Ḥaḍramī. What degree of liberty in selecting readings was claimed by the abler critics is seen from the rule laid down by Muḥammad al-Djazarī (d. 833/1429; cf. Brockelmann, *GAL*², ii. 257) who is followed by al-Suyūṭī (*Itḳān*, i. 94): "Every reading which is in consonance with the Arabic language — although only in some respect — and with the ʿUthmānic manuscripts of the Ḳur'ān — although only as a possibility — and whose chain of tradition is faultless, is considered a correct reading and must not be rejected but belongs to the seven *aḥruf*, in which the Ḳur'ān is revealed, whether it comes from the seven or the ten or from other recognised Imāms; but if it does not fulfil one of these three conditions it is to be branded as weak, arbitrary or false, whether it comes from the seven or from any one who is older than they". But this freedom was only exercised in learned works; in all public readings before the people the readings of the seven canonical readers were observed. At the present day only two methods of reading are in general use, that of Ḥafṣ, *rāwī* of ʿĀṣim, and in Africa, except Egypt, that of Nāfiʿ. This is the extent to which Muslim textual criticism has prevailed. A proper critical edition of the Ḳur'ān making use of all available material is a task which still awaits modern scholarship. The Egyptian standard edition of the Ḳur'ān (Cairo 1342) is said to represent the reading of Ḥafṣ.

19. This work on the text was considerably facilitated by the introduction of different means of restricting the ambiguity of the old script. Diacritical points were introduced to distinguish letters of the same form, marks indicating the pronunciation of the vowels, nunation, the feminine ending *-at*, the consonantal pronunciation of *alif*, and the sign for the doubling of a consonant. As is usual in such cases all recollection of the period of their introduction had been lost among the Arabs. It is certain that they are based on an imitation of the Syrian practice and recent finds of coins, inscriptions and particularly of papyri have thrown some light on the question. These show that at the beginning of the viii[th] century the diacritical points were in use, at any rate to some extent; but they were certainly older and had perhaps been already introduced in the pre-Muḥammadan period. The vowel signs were originally dots in varying positions and were only replaced after the middle of the viii[th] century by the signs now in use, modelled on the semivowels, ',

w and *y* (Nöldeke, *Gesch. d. Qorāns*, iii. 264 *sqq.*). In some the use of these signs in the manuscripts of the Ḳur'ān aroused misgivings. According to the *Itḳān*, ii. 202, the Madīnese Mālik b. Anas (d. 179/795), for example, permitted their use only in copies intended for students and did not permit them in the large manuscripts used in public worship. Others, on the other hand, permitted their use without hesitation, as the signs from their form could not be regarded as a component part of the sacred book. To make the distinction clear, the vowel signs were originally distinguished by another colour, while the diacritical points were written in black as parts of the letters. On the incorporation of the names of sūras into the manuscripts, see above; on the different marks for separating the verses, especially for every 5 and 10 verses, see Nöldeke, *Gesch. d. Qorāns*, iii. 258; see *ibid.* on the *sadjda*, the mark for the passages in the text where one should prostrate oneself.

20. In editing the Ḳur'ān, no attention at all was, as we have seen, paid to chronological order, a result of the composite character of many sūras, which also made an arrangement according to their contents impossible. Instead, the sūras were arranged, although only approximately, according to their length, which however only led to the inconvenient result that the very earliest sūras, being the shortest, were put at the end. But as chronological arrangement is of fundamental importance for the understanding of the text, the commentators were faced with a task, the necessity of which had already been recognised by the Muslims. The main thing was to establish whether the sūras were of the Mecca or Madīna period, or whether they were composed of pieces from both periods. This problem has on the whole been solved, although views differed on many points of detail (cf. *Itḳān*, i. 15 *sqq.*). In practice this question can be satisfactorily answered in most cases, if a series of criteria are used, some of which may be outlined here.

When Muḥammad disputes with this countrymen about the resurrection of the dead or the oneness of God, when he refutes the assertion that he is a magician, a poet or one possessed, when he inveighs against the custom of burying newly born girls alive, we know that we are in Mecca. The difficulties only begin when we try to arrange the separate pieces of this group in their chronological order, for there is an entire lack of distinct references to definite events; and even if there were any, it would help very little as the chronological statements in the old traditions of Muḥammad's life in the Meccan period are quite unreliable. A rare exception is formed by Sūra xxx. with the mention of the defeat of the Byzantines by the Persians, probably in the year 614 A.D. More uncertain, although not improbable is the connecting of Sūra liii. with the emigration of some of the Prophet's followers to Abyssinia. There is the further difficulty that Muḥammad, not unintentionally, delivered his orations in a kind of chiaroscuro and it is exceedingly rarely that personal names are mentioned (cxi. 1; xxxiii. 37). The traditions however are everywhere able to tell us exactly who the anonymous individuals that appear in the Ḳur'ān were, but these identifications are certainly due to horror of a vacuum and are often definitely wrong. We have therefore to rely essentially on internal criteria. G. Weil laid the foundations for a classification of the Meccan sūras by dividing them into three classes. He was followed by Nöldeke, who in turn is followed by H. Grimme, although with certain variations in the order which are not of great importance, and show that generally accepted results are not to be obtained in this field. The most certainly recognizable is the first group, a series of short addresses full of excited passion, glowing imagination and no little poetic power. These are such distinct features that it is certainly a mistake when Lammens, *Fâṭima*, p. 64, wants to transfer Sūras xciii. and xciv. to the latest Madīna period. Characteristic of the group are also the already mentioned conjuration formulae; and the peculiar phrase occurring thirteen times *mā adrāka*, "thou surely knowest not"; *mā yudrīka*, xlii. 17, lxxx. 3, also belongs here, in which case xxxiii. 63 is perhaps a verse that has been separated from its context. Snouck Hurgronje (*Verspr. Geschr.*, i., 203, 272) called attention to the very important point that Muḥammad did not from the very first proclaim strict monotheism as the principal thing but the approach of the Last Judgment, from which he was to save his countrymen. The assertion that there is no god but Allāh appears sporadically from lxxiii. 9 onwards: and it must certainly have taken some time before there was a definite breach with the idolators (Sūra cix.) and before he met them with the declaration of the oneness of God (Sūra cxii.). It is not till the second group that everything centres round monotheism and for this reason the polemical passages lii. 39 *sqq.* and liii. 19 *sqq.* directed against the daughters of Allāh are probably a little later than the adjacent verses. Starting with the assumption that the Ḳur'ān gives a complete picture of Muḥammad's preaching, the Muslims have discussed the question which Sūra is the oldest, presumably containing his call to be a Prophet (see above). The majority decided for Sūra xcvi. 1—5 (see *Itḳān*, i. 29) and many modern critics have followed them in this. Properly understood, the passage really does fit this view very well; but it is not absolutely certain and, as already mentioned, we must allow for the possibility that it is just of the earliest revelations that much may have been lost before people began to learn them by heart or record them in writing.

Of the next two classes, the third is probably the easiest to define. It is the weakest part of the Ḳur'ān in which Muḥammad's imagination apparently became exhausted, and he was content with tiresome repetitions of his earlier ideas and especially with the tales of the prophets. The form becomes discursive and more prosaic, in which respects this group resembles the following ones. The transition to this group is formed by the second. The opening enthusiasm gives place to calm and the Prophet's aim is to influence his hearers by proofs, such as descriptions of phenomena of nature and in the life of man, in which occasionally we have a flash of the old poetic fire. Considerable space is occupied by the stories of the experiences of earlier prophets, which were intended to warn his enemies and to encourage himself, because he constructed them with great daring on the model of his own experiences. The introductory conjuration formulae become rarer and rarer and completely disappear in the third group. To the second group belongs the remarkable episode in which Muḥammad frequently uses for Allāh the name al-Raḥmān, unknown to the Meccans. In the sūras of the first group it is found once only, in Sūra lv. 1, rarely in the third and nowhere in the Madīna sections.

Instead of this simple grouping, which excellently characterises the Meccan sūras, H. Hirschfeld has proposed another, quite artificial, system, in which the sūras following xcvi. 1—5 are arranged under the following heads: declamatory, narrative, descriptive and legislative. The result is not so very different from Nöldeke's, but the system is mechanical and often arbitrary in its application, e.g. when xciii. 9 *sqq.*, where the change of rhyme alone proves nothing, is cut off and added to the legislative series.

21. In the revelations of the Madīna period, the question is much easier to settle. Everywhere that we find Muḥammad attacking the Jews or the *munāfiḳūn* [q.v.], that he summons to the holy war ("on the path of Allāh") or where he lays down criminal or civil legislation, we are in Madīna, whether we are dealing with whole sūras or small sections or single verses, e.g. viii 47 *sqq.*; xxiv. 1—10; xxxiii. 31—34*a*. The references to events known to us from the *sīra* in the Madīna period, the battles in Muḥammad's wars, his treaties etc., afford us a particularly safe means of arranging the sūras chronologically. There are also all kinds of details in which an investigation of the pertinent passages reveals at least their relative order, e.g. his opinions on wine and his varying utterances on the attitude to other religions and on the holy war. Such details are very suitable for the subjects of special studies and may often yield very important results. Snouck Hurgronje put forward an argument of far-reaching importance in *Het Mekkaansche Feest*, p. 33 *sqq.* In the Meccan sūras it is often said that no prophetic admonisher had been sent to the Arabs before Muḥammad, as to other peoples (xxxii. 3; xxxiv. 44; xxxvi. 6). Abraham occupies a prominent position among the prophets (xix. 41); he is however only a prophet like the others and has nothing to do with the Arabs. When he is called *ḥanīf* [q.v.], this is in contrast to the polytheists (vi. 79; xvi. 120; cf. x. 105), just as Muḥammad himself is called a *ḥanīf*; and when there is a reference to the *millat Ibrāhīm* (vi. 162; xvi. 123), it may also be understood of monotheism; cf. the words of Joseph in xii. 38. Abraham on the other hand gains quite another significance in Madīna, after the definite breach with the Jews had been made. In direct contrast to the previous neglect of the Arabs, we are now told that Abraham lived in Mecca and founded the sanctuary of the Black Stone with his son Ishmael: ii. 125—129; iii. 95—97, a legend (invented by Arabian Jews?) which is never referred to in Mecca (xxviii. 57; xxix. 67). When Abraham is now called a *ḥanīf*, the word is used not only in contrast to the polytheists but also to the Jews and Christians: iii. 67; iv. 125; cf. ii. 135; and the *millat Ibrāhīm* is now the original pure religion, which Muḥammad is now reinstating (ii. 130, 135; iii. 95; iv. 125), for Torah and Gospel were only sent down after Abraham (iii. 65) and the Jews and Christians corrupted the original religion (see above). This would show that passages like xiv. 28—37; xxii. 26, 78, could not have arisen in Mecca, but only later in Madīna, which may perhaps also be true of vi. 161, and xvi. 123 above mentioned. Less convincing is another criterion of criticism pointed out by the same scholar (*Verspr. Geschr.*, i., 221). He sees in Muḥammad's polemics against the Christians a result of the breach with the Jews and therefore thinks that all passages in which they occur must be Madīnese. In the great majority of cases this dating is certainly right, but there is at least one such passage which can only be Meccan. In one of the frequent verbal duels between the Prophet and his polytheistic countrymen, xliii. 57 *sqq.*, the latter endeavour to involve him in the difficulty that Jesus, whom he himself takes as a model, is actually worshipped as God by the Christians; and Muḥammad sharply repudiates this view for "Jesus was and only professed to be a man". Muḥammad was however in the Meccan period always convinced of the full agreement of his teaching with that of the Jews and Christians; but we must remember that, as already mentioned, the main thing with him at first was not monotheism but the proclamation of the imminent judgment, an idea which he certainly adopted from the Christians; what they thought about Christ was quite subordinate to this and it is also possible that the very Christians with whom he was in contact at this time had heretical views with regard to ecclesiastical Christology. He would soon learn that there were differences on various questions among the "peoples of a scripture" (xxiii. 53; xxvii. 47; xlii. 14), and as strict monotheism had become to him the central element in religion, he had at once to reject orthodox Christology as a degeneration of pure Christianity. Passages like xix. 34 *sqq.* may thus have already originated in Mecca.

Just as the first revelation received by Muḥammad was sought among the Meccan sūras, so also Muslims sought the last among the Madīnese, especially as this question was of some importance for possible abrogations. But the Muslim statements vary considerably: cf. *Itḳān*, i. 33 *sq.* Sūra v. or ix. or cx. is given as the last sūra; ii. 278, or 281 or iv. 174 as the last verse, while others say v. 3*b* or ix. 128 *sq.* The last is connected with a tradition which says that Zaid in collecting the Ḳur'ān found these two verses last. Much more plausible is the view that v. 3*b* is the last, which is probably rightly connected with the farewell pilgrimage (cf. the emphasised "to-day"); as regards content, it would be very suitable as a final verse, although the meaning is not that Muḥammads' mission was completed but that Allāh's cause had been victorious.

22. For the Muḥammadans, the Ḳur'ān is not the sacred book in the usual sense but something of much greater significance. It is, as already mentioned, the faithful reproduction of the original scripture in heaven. This sounds rather strange, when we remember that this heavenly book, according to the passages above quoted only became by Allāh's grace an "Arabic" Ḳur'ān, intelligible to Muḥammad and his people, as the scriptures of the *ahl al-kitāb* were closed to them; but this distinction gradually disappeared for the religious consciousness. After the conception of eternity and the uncreatedness of the word of God had become known to Muslim theologians through the polemics of Christian theologians (cf. C. H. Becker, *Islamstudien*; Leipzig 1924, 443 *sqq.*), it was applied by them to the copy in heaven and then finally by the strictly orthodox school to the Arabic copies of the Ḳur'ān and expressed epigrammatically in the sentence: "What lies between the two covers is the word of God". The Muʿtazilīs and the more free-thinking theologians raised a protest, it is true, but after al-As͟hʿarī himself, in the last version of his dogmatics, had championed the view that the written or recited Ḳur'ān is identical in being and reality with the uncreated and eternal word of God, the victory was won by the orthodox school.

Bibliography: Text edition by G. Flügel, *Corani textus arabicus*, Leipzig 1834 and reprints; many oriental editions, especially Cairo 1342; G. Flügel, *Concordantiae Corani Arabicae*, Leipzig 1869 and 1898. — On the variants A. Jeffery,

Materials for the History of the Text of the Qur'an, Leiden 1937. — Translations: On the first Latin translation of the Ḳur'ān by Robert of Chester cf. U. Monneret de Villard, *Lo Studio dell' Islam in Europa nel XII e nel XIII secolo*, Rome 1944, p. 5, 11 *sqq.*; the most famous Latin translation, together with the Arabic text and commentary is that by Lud. Maracci, *Alcorani textus universus*, Padua 1698. — English: G. Sale, 1734 (and frequently since); I. M. Rodwell, 1876 (and afterwards; chronologically arranged); E. H. Palmer, *The Qur'an*, in *Sacred Books of the East*, 1880, and reprints; M. Pickthall, *The Meaning of the Glorious Koran*, London 1930; Mirza Abul Fazl, Allahabad 1900 (chronologically arranged); R. Bell, *The Qur'ân, translated with a critical re-arrangement of the surahs*, Edinburgh 1937-39; A. Yūsuf ʿAlī, *The Holy Quran*, Lahore 1934. — Danish by Fr. Buhl (1921, a selection chronologically arranged) — French: Kasimirsky, Paris 1840 (and often afterwards); E. Montet, Paris 1925, 1929; O. Pesle et A. Tidjani, 1936; R. Blachère, Paris 1947 *sqq.* — German: L. Ullmann, 1862 (and afterwards); F. Rückert, *Der Koran im Auszuge*, 1888; M. Henning, Leipzig (Reclam) 1901; Klamroth, *Die fünfzig ältesten Suren des Korans in gereimter deutscher Uebersetzung*, 1890; partial translation by L. Goldschmidt, 1916, 1923. — Italian: A. Fracassi, Milan 1914; L. Bonelli, Milan 1929. — Swedish: Zetterstéen, 1917. See further A. Fischer, *Der Wert der vorhandenen Koran-übersetzungen*, in *Berichte... Sächs. Ak.* 1937.

Introductions: Djalāl al-Dīn al-Suyūṭī, *Kitāb al-itḳān fī ʿulūm al-Ḳur'ān*, Calcutta 1852—1854, here quoted from the Cairo edition, 1871; G. Sale, *Preliminary Discourse*, etc. (with his transl.; cf. above); L. Maracci, *Refutatio Alcorani*, 1698; G. Weil, *Historisch-kritische Einleitung in den Koran*, 2nd ed., 1878; Nöldeke, *Geschichte des Qorāns*, 1860; 2nd ed., by Schwally, i., 1909; ii., 1919; Bergsträsser-Pretzl, iii. 1926—35; E. Sell, *The Historical Development of the Koran*, Madras 1898; cf. Schwally, in *Sachau-Festschrift*, 1915, p. 321 *sqq.*; Nöldeke, *Orientalische Skizzen*, 1892, p. 21 *sqq.*; H. Hirschfeld, *New Researches in the Composition and Exegesis of the Qoran*, 1902; W. St. Cl. Tisdall, *Original Sources of the Quran*, London 1905; Ahmed Shah, *Studies in the Quran*, I, Cawnpore 1905; H. U. W. Stanton, *The Teaching of the Qur'an*, London 1919 (with subject index and comparative verse numberings); R. Blachère, *Introduction au Coran* (Introduction to his translation), Paris 1947. See also MUḤAMMAD, *Bibliography*.

Commentaries: al-Ṭabarī, *Tafsīr al-Ḳur'ān*, 30 vols., Cairo 1321; al-Zamakhsharī, *al-Kashshāf*, ed. Lees, Calcutta 1856, Cairo 1318; al-Baiḍāwī, ed. Fleischer, 1846—1848; *Tafsīr al-Djalālain*, Cairo 1305 and often; Fakhr al-Dīn al-Rāzī, *Mafātīḥ al-Ghaib*, Cairo 1307; and many others. — J. Barth, *Studien zur Kritik und Exegese des Qorans*, 1915 (*Isl.* vi. 1916, p. 113 *sqq.*); I. Goldziher, *Die Richtungen der islamischen Koranauslegung*, 1920. The following monographs may be mentioned: A. Geiger, *Was hat Muhammed aus dem Judentum aufgenommen?*, 1833, 2nd ed., 1902; H. Hirschfeld, *Beiträge zur Erklärung des Ḳorân*, 1886; Schapiro, *Die Haggadischen Elemente im erzählenden Teil des Korans*, 1907 (Heft i. only); C. F. Gerock, *Versuch einer Darstellung der Christologie des Korans*, 1839; E. Sayous, *Jésus Christ d'après Mahomet*, 1880; O. Pautz, *Mohammeds Lehre von der Offenbarung*, Leipzig 1898; C. Torrey, *The Commercial-Theological Terms in the Koran* (Diss. Strassburg 1892); J. Horovitz, *Koranische Untersuchungen*, 1926; J. Walker, *Bible Characters in the Koran*, Paisley 1931; D. Sidersky, *Les origines des légendes musulmanes dans le Coran et dans les vies des prophètes*, Paris 1932; K. Ahrens, *Christliches im Qoran*, in *ZDMG*, 84 (1930), 15—68, 148—190; S. Fränkel, *De vocabulis in ... Corano peregrinis*, Leiden 1880; A. Jeffery, *The foreign vocabulary of the Qur'an*, Baroda 1938.

ḲURBĀN, sacrifice. The word goes back to the Hebrew *ḳorbān*, perhaps through the intermediary of the Aramaic (cf. Mingana, *Syriac Influence on the Ḳur'ân*, in *Bulletin of the John Rylands Library*, vol. xi., No. 1, p. 85; S. Fränkel, *De vocabulis in ... Corano peregrinis*, p. 20). The language of the Ḳur'ān, as is well known, shows a preference for religious technical terms ending in *-ān* and some of them are not always used with their original significations. This is true of ḳurbān, which occurs three times in the Ḳur'ān. In Sūra iii. 183 and v. 27 it obviously means sacrifice. In Sūra xlvi. 28, however, we read: "Did those help them, whom they had taken for ḳurbān as gods to the exclusion of Allāh!" Here the word must be more or less synonymous with "gods". Probably it has a meaning which is connected with the Arabic *ḳ-r-b* (see below); the commentators take the same view and the word is explained as "mediators" [cf. SHAFĀʿA].

The word occurs in canonical *ḥadīth* in two places only, both of them bearing an apologetic character. "The *ṣalāt* is ḳurbān" (Aḥmad b. Ḥanbal, *Musnad*, iii. 321, 399); and "He who attends to the Friday service is equal to him who offers a ḳurbān" (*ibid.*, ii. 499). The *LA* mentions two traditions which are striking enough: "The characteristic of this community (i.e. the Muslims) lies in the fact that their ḳurbān is their blood", i.e. that instead of sacrifice they have offered the blood of their martyrs. And the other: "The *ṣalāt* is the sacrifice of every pious man". We may suppose there are apologetic tendencies in both traditions.

The term also came to be applied in Muslim ritual to the killing of an animal on the 10th Dhu 'l-Ḥidjdja, and the whole celebration on this and the following *tashrīḳ* days is called *ʿīd al-ḳurbān* [cf. ʿĪD AL-AḌḤĀ], in Turkish speaking countries *ḳurbān-bairam* [cf. BAIRAM].

In Christian-Arabic the word means the eucharist. — In conclusion it should be pointed out that there seems to be a genuine Arabic word *ḳurbān*, plur. *ḳarābīn*, which means the courtiers and councillors in immediate attendance on a king; the word probably comes directly from *ḳ-r-b-* "to be near" (see above).

KURSĪ, an Arabic loan-word from the Aramaic *kurseyā* (Hebrew: *kissē*; S. Fraenkel, *De vocabulis peregrinis*, p. 22; Jeffery, *Foreign vocabulary*, p. 249), throne. It is found only twice in the Ḳur'ān (ii. 255; xxxviii. 34); its occurrence in the first of these has given the verse the name of the Throne Verse (*āyat al-kursī*); the reference is to the throne of God, which is large enough to embrace the heavens and the earth. In the second passage the reference is to the throne of Solomon. The use of two different words, *ʿarsh* and *kursī*, for the throne of God, very early troubled the exegists; some have seen in the second the stool placed in front of a throne on which a sovereign rests his feet, while others took it to be only a synonym of *ʿarsh*, and one school interpreted it allegorically, saying that the kursī of God is simply his knowledge (Ṭabarī, *Tafsīr*. iii. 7). The use of this word in the second passage for "a throne on which one sits" shows clearly that it is a synonym of *ʿarsh*.

Through neoplatonic influences the terms *ʿarsh* and kursī were also applied in the cosmology. — In Muslim theology it is especially the former that has played a rôle in the question of the interpretation of the anthropomorphic expressions in the Ḳurʾān (cf. Wensinck, *The Muslim Creed*, index, s.v. Throne).

AL-**ḲUSHAIRĪ**, ABU 'L-ḲĀSIM ʿABD AL-KARĪM B. HAWĀZIN B. ʿABD AL-MALIK B. ṬALḤA B. MUḤAMMAD, born in 376/986, died in 465/1074, was in dogmatic theology the pupil of the Ashʿarī Abū Bakr b. Fūrak and in mysticism a follower of al-Sulamī and Abū ʿAlī al-Daḳḳāḳ, whose daughter Fāṭima (d. 480/1087) he married. He was persecuted, with the other Ashʿarīs, by Ḥanbalī jurists and the Saldjūḳ officials from 440—55/1048—63. His best known works are the two manifestos, the *Risāla ilā djamāʿat al-ṣūfīya bi-buldān al-Islām*, written in 438/1046 to adapt Ṣūfism to Ashʿarī metaphysics, and the *Shakāya ilā ahl al-sunna bi-ḥikāyat mā nālahum min al-miḥna* written in 446/1054 to clear the memory of al-Ashʿarī from the charge of heterodoxy laid against his atomist metaphysics (publ. in Subkī, *Ṭabaḳāt*, first ed. Cairo, 1324, ii. 276—288). We also have from Ḳushairī's pen a mystical commentary on the Ḳurʾān entitled *Laṭāʾif al-ishārāt* and a manual of mystic paths, *Tartīb al-sulūk*, the esotericism of which is deliberately obscure. The *Risāla*, a classical manual of Muslim mysticism, was criticized from the Imāmī point of view by Ibn al-Dāʿī (*Tabṣira*, lith. Teherān 1312, p. 405—409) and published with the *sharḥ* of al-Anṣārī at Cairo in 1290 in 4 volumes. — This is the only useful edition; the little editions in one volume (1318 A.H., etc.) are swarming with typographical mistakes.

Bibliography: Subkī, *Ṭabaḳāt al-Shāfiʿīya*, first ed. Cairo, 1324, iii. 243—248; Brockelmann, *GAL* ², i. 556, *Suppl.* i. 770—2; R. Hartmann, *Al Ḳuschairîs Darstellung des Ṣûfîtums*, Berlin 1914.

ḲUṬB. [See BADAL; TAṢAWWUF].

L

LABBAIKA. [See TALBIYA].

LAILAT AL-**BARĀʾA**. [See RAMAḌĀN, SHAʿBĀN].

LAILAT AL-**ḲADAR**. [See RAMAḌĀN].

AL-**LĀT**, an old Arabian goddess. The name (from *al-ilāhat*) means "the goddess" but was the proper name of a definite deity, according to the Arabs themselves (e.g. Ibn Yaʿīsh, ed. Jahn, p. 44) the sun. She is found as early as the Nabataean and Palmyran inscriptions and was later worshipped by various Beduin tribes (e.g. the Hawāzin; Ibn Hishām, p. 849). An oath by al-Lāt is frequently found in the poets, e.g. Abū Saʿd in Ibn Hishām, p. 567; Mutalammis, ed. Vollers, p. 2; Aws b. Ḥadjar, ed. Geyer, p. 11, and even in al-Akhṭal, *Kitāb al-Aghānī*, vii. 173. She had her principal sanctuary in the valley of Wadjdj near Ṭāʾif, where the Muʿattib (ʿAttab) b. Mālik b. Kaʿb were her priests and a white stone hung with all kinds of decorations was her symbol. She is fequently mentioned along with al-ʿUzzā (Ibn Hishām, p. 145, 206, 871, where Wudd also is mentioned; Aws b. Ḥadjar, p. 11), and among the Ḳuraish, she, along with this goddess and Manāt, was held in such high esteem, that Muḥammad once went so far as to recognize these three goddesses as intercessors with Allāh but soon afterwards withdrew this (Sūra liii. 19 *sqq*.). According to Ṭabarī, i. 1395 Abū Sufyān carried al-Lāt and al-ʿUzzā with him into the battle of Uḥud. After the capture of Mecca, al-Lāt was destroyed with her sanctuary in Ṭāʾif by al-Mughīra, who was related to her priests. But she was not forgotten, for, according to Doughty, there were still in Ṭāʾif blocks of stone which the people called al-ʿUzzā, Hubal and al-Lāt, and at which they secretly sought help in cases of illness.

Bibliography: Yāḳūt, *Muʿdjam*, ed. Wüstenfeld, iii. 665 *sqq*.; iv. 336 *sqq*.; Azraḳī, ed. Wüstenfeld, p. 79; Ibn Hishām, p. 55, 914 *sqq*.; Ṭabarī, i. 1192 *sqq*.; Wāḳidī, transl. by Wellhausen, p. 384 *sq*.; Ibn Saʿd, 1/i. 137 *sq*.; Lidzbarski, *Handbuch der nordsemitischen Epigraphik*, p. 219; Baethgen, *Beiträge zur semitischen Religionsgeschichte*, p. 97 *sq*., 128; Lagrange, *Etudes sur les Religions sémitiques* ², p. 76, 135; Wellhausen, *Reste arabischen Heidentums*, p. 29—34, 61; Lammens, in *MFOB*, viii. 202 *sq*.; Doughty, *Travels in Arabia Deserta*, ii. 511, 515 *sq*.

LAWḤ (A.), board, tablet; the first meaning is found in the Ḳurʾān, Sūra liv. 13, where Noah's ark is called *dhāt alwāḥ*. The second meaning is that of lawḥ as writing material, e.g. the tablets of the Law (Sūra vii. 145, 150, 154, where the plural *alwāḥ* is used; see *LA*, iii. 421). *Al-dawāt wa 'l-lawḥ* (Bukhārī, *Tafsīr al-Ḳurʾān*, Sūra iv., bāb 18) corresponds to our "paper and ink". The expression *mā baina 'l-lawḥain* "what lies between the two boards" is found in Ḥadīth, to describe the whole Ḳurʾān (Bukhārī, *Tafsīr*, Sūra lix., bāb 4; *Libās*, bāb 84); cf. *mā baina 'l-daffatain* (Bukhārī, *Faḍāʾil al-Ḳurʾān*, bāb 16).

Al-lawḥ also means the tablet kept in heaven which in Sūra, lxxxv. 22 is called *lawḥ maḥfūẓ* (cf. the art. AL-ḲURʾĀN, § 2). According to this passage it is usually described as the "safely preserved" tablet. But it is not certain whether the words in this passage are really syntactically connected. If we read *maḥfūẓ^{un}*, the word does not go with *lawḥ^{in}* but with the preceding *Ḳurʾān^{un}* and the translation is: "Verily it is a Ḳurʾān, famous, preserved on a tablet" (see the commentaries); "preserved" i.e. against alteration.

In the commentaries on Sūra xcvii. 1, the tablet is again mentioned: "We sent it down (the Ḳurʾān) in the night of the decree"; this refers either to the first revelation made to Muḥammad or to the descent of the Ḳurʾān from that tablet which is above the seventh heaven, to the lowest.

The tablet as the original copy of the Ḳurʾān is thus identical with *umm al-kitāb*.

The decisions of the divine will are also written on the *lawḥ* with the pen, *ḳalam*. We have therefore to distinguish two quite different conceptions:

a. The tablet as the original copy of the Ḳur᾿ān. This idea is found in the pseudepigraphical literature. In the *Book of Jubilees*, iii. 10, it is said that the laws relating to the purification of women after childbed (Leviticus xii.) are written on tablets in heaven. Jub., xii. 28 *sq*., says the same of the law regarding the "feast of booths" (Lev., xxiii. 40—43) and Jub., xxxii. 15 of the law of tithes (Lev. xxvii.).

b. The tablet as the record of the decisions of the divine will is also found in the *Book of Jubilees*. In Jub., v. 13 it is said that the divine judgement on all that exists on earth is written on the tablets in heaven. Enoch prophecies the future from the contents of these tablets (Book of Enoch, xciii. 2; cf. lxxxi.; ciii. 2; cvi. 19).

For other passages, cf. the Index to Charles, *The Apocrypha and Pseudepigrapha of the Old Testament*, s.v. "Tablets"; it cannot always be said definitely to which of these two conceptions a particular statement belongs.

In mystical and philosophical literature *lawḥ* is given a place in the cosmic system and sometimes explained as *ʿaḳl faʿʿāl* and sometimes as *nafs kullī* or *umm al-hūlī*.

In Ghazzālī's cosmology the *lawḥ maḥfūẓ* is the centre of the eternally active ideas (cf. Wensinck, *On the Relation between Ghazālī's Cosmology and his Mysticism*, in *Med. Ak. Amst.*, part 15, ser. A, No. 6).

Bibliography: The Ḳur᾿ān commentaries on the passages quoted; J. Horovitz, *Koranische Untersuchungen*, Berlin-Leipzig 1926, p. 65 *sq*.; *Dict. of the Technical Terms*, ii. 1291—1293.

LAZARUS is the name in the Gospels of 1) the poor man who finds compensation in Abraham's bosom for the misery of this world (Luke xvi. 19—31); 2) the dead man whom Jesus raises to life (John xi, xii.). The Ḳur᾿ān mentions neither the one nor the other. But the scene of the poor Lazarus in Paradise is partly reproduced in Sūra vii. 46—50; the rich who are condemned to Hell long for some drops of water to be provided by the poor in Paradise, but they are separated from them by an abyss (*al-aʿrāf*).

Nor does the Ḳur᾿ān mention the Lazarus who was raised to new life. But it is also to him that Jesus' miracles may be applied, namely that he forms birds from loam and blows life into them, that he heals the blind and the lepers and that he raises from the dead (iii. 49). It is especially the raising from the dead which made an impression on Muḥammad. Also the covenant by means of thepieces of flesh (Gen. xv) is interpreted by him in this sense, that the dismembered animals are restored to life (ii, 260). On Allāh as one who raises the dead cf. Speyer, *Die bibl. Erzählung im Qoran*, p. 163.

The post-Ḳur᾿ānic legend reveres Jesus as reviver of the dead. According to Ṭabarī, Jesus restored Ḥām b. Nūḥ to life, at the request of the apostles, so that he might give information on the Flood and the Ark (*Annales* i. 187). Thaʿlabī (Cairo 1325, p. 248) relates, closely following St. John's Gospel: "Alʿāzar died, his sister sent to inform Jesus, Jesus came 3 (in the Gospel 4) days after his death, went with his sister to the tomb in the rock and caused Alʿāzar to arise; children were born to him". Thaʿlabī still writes al-ʿĀzar. In Abu 'l-Fidā᾿ (ed. Fleischer, p. 58), he is called simply ʿĀzar, the *al-* being taken for the article and then dropped. The same form is found in Ibn al-Athīr (ed. Būlāḳ, i. 124), who has more to say about Jesus' raising of the dead: while the 10 years old Jesus is playing with other boys, one of his comrades is killed; the murderer denies; Jesus raises the murdered one, who then indicates the murderer (*l.c.* p. 123). Al-Kisā᾿ī finally makes Jesus revive the following persons: ʿĀzar who had been dead 3 days; a dead woman, who brings up children after the event; Sām, the son of Nūḥ, who had been dead by then already 4000 years; ʿUzair (Ezra, perhaps because of the resemblance of his name to ʿĀzar); and also Yaḥyā b. Zakarīyā, St. John the Baptist.

Bibliography: Ṭabarī, i. 187, 731, 739; Ibn al-Athīr, i. 122, 123; Thaʿlabī, *Ḳiṣaṣ al-anbiyā᾿*, Cairo 1325, p. 307; al-Kisā᾿ī, *Ḳiṣaṣ al-anbiyā᾿*, ed. Eisenberg, p. 307. On the name Elʿazar, Eliezer, ʿĀzar, see S. Fraenkel, in *ZDMG*, 1902, lvi. 71—73; J. Horovitz, *Hebrew Union College Annual*, 1925, ii., p. 157, 161; do., *Koranische Untersuchungen*, 1926, p. 12, 85, 86.

LIʿĀN. [See ṬALĀḲ].

LOTH. [See LŪṬ].

LUĶAṬA (A.), an article found (more precisely: "picked up"). The leading principle in the Muslim law regarding articles lost and found may be said to be protection of the owner from the finder, sometimes mingled with social considerations. The picking up of articles found is generally permitted, although it is sometimes said to be more meritorious to leave them. The finder is bound to advertise the article which he has found (and taken) for a whole year unless it is of quite insignificant value or perishable. After the termination of the period, the finder, according to Mālik and al-Shāfiʿī, has the right to take possession of the article and do what he pleases with it, according to Abū Ḥanīfa, only if he is "poor"; but its use as religious alms (*ṣadaḳa*) even before the expiry of a year, is permitted in a preferential clause by Abū Ḥanīfa and Mālik. If the owner appears before the expiry of the period he receives the object back, as he does after the expiry of the period if it is still with the finder; if the finder has disposed of it in keeping with the law, he is liable to the owner for its value; Dāwūd al-Ẓāhirī alone recognized no further claim by the loser in this case. The establishment of ownership is facilitated, compared with the ordinary process, according to Mālik and Ibn Ḥanbal. As regards the finding of domestic animals in the desert, there are special regulations which are more onerous for the finder if they are safe from danger, and less onerous in the contrary case. Al-Shāfiʿī and Ibn Ḥanbal have some still more strict regulations for articles found in the *ḥaram*, the sacred territory in Mecca, which at bottom go back to the old idea of a special right of ownership by Allāh in the *ḥaram* and all it contains.

These prescriptions of the *fiḳh* are based on certain *ḥadīth*'s which have been handed down with several variants. It may be mentioned that in a very old stratum, later worked over, there is mention of a two or three year period. In the conception of the primitive jurists the article found is sometimes described as deposited (*wadīʿa*); further, out of special religious scruples, one is careful not to pick up found dates and eat them, as they might belong to the *zakāt*; finally there is a *ḥadīth* which forbids the Mecca pilgrims (*ḥādjdj*) to pick up articles found at all.

Bibliography: Wensinck, *Handbook*, s. v. LUKṬA; Juynboll, *Handleiding tot de kennis van de mohammedaansche wet* (3rd ed.), p. 386; Santillana, *Istituzioni di Diritto Musulmano Malichita*, vol. i., p. 328 *sq.*; G. Bergsträsser, *Grundzüge*, index s. v. *Luqta*; J. Schacht, *Origins of Muh. jurisprudence*, p. 161.

LUKMĀN, a legendary figure of the period of Arab paganism, who was adopted into the Ḳur'ān and later legend and poetry. The story of Luḳmān shows three main stages of development: I. The pre-Ḳur'ānic: Luḳmān al-Muʿammarī, the long-lived hero of the Djāhilīya; II. The Ḳur'ānic: Luḳmān, the wise author of proverbs; III. The post-Ḳur'ānic: Luḳmān, the writer of fables.

I. Luḳmān in the old Arab tradition.

Even the earlier legends already show Luḳmān in several aspects: 1. as Muʿammar; 2. as a hero; 3. as a sage. — He is offered a long life. He chooses the duration of the lives of seven vultures; he brings up a vulture; when it dies, he keeps a second one and so on, for six vultures, which he survives, but he dies at the same time as the seventh, Lubad (cf. Damīrī, *Ḥayāt al-ḥayawān*, s. v. *nasr* and *lubad*). The vulture was by far the most popular emblem of longevity among the Arabs (Ps. ciii. 4; Goldziher, *Abh. zur arabisch. Phil.*, ii., p. li. *sqq.*); R. Basset (*Loqmân Berbère*, p. xxvii.—xxix.) finds a remarkable parallel in the interpretation given by Sidonius Apollinarius, for example, of Romulus' watching for birds: Romulus sees twelve vultures, which means the twelve periods through which Rome will endure. The *Kitāb al-muʿammarin* of Abū Ḥātim al-Sidjistānī gives Luḳmān second place for longevity, after Khaḍir. — R. Basset, *Loqmân Berbère*, Paris 1890, p. xxx.—xxxiv., has investigated the traces of Luḳmān in the poets of the Djāhilīya, Horovitz, *Koranische Untersuchungen*, 1926, p. 133—138 among the poets of the early Muslim period. Al-Aʿshā knows of the 7 vultures, Labīd of his longevity. Imru' al-Ḳais and Labīd call him the son of ʿĀd. In later tradition the old Arab legend is fused with the Ḳur'ānic. Luḳmān belongs to the people of Hūd (Ṭabarī, i. 235—240). The old legend knows Luḳmān as a hero, Ṭarafa even as a player at *maisir*. Luḳmān is also said to have been the first to punish adultery by stoning (he himself kills his unfaithful wife and her paramour in this way) and robbery by cutting off the hand. Later legend (Ṭabarī, Abu 'l-Fidā') even makes him king of Yemen. In pre-Islāmic legend as in the poets of the Djāhilīya, e.g. al-Aʿshā, Labīd, Luḳmān is primarily a wise man; Muḥammad also knew him as such.

II. Luḳmān, the author of proverbs.

In Sūra xxxi. of the Ḳur'ān, called the *Sūrat Luḳmān*, Muḥammad introduces Luḳmān as a sage who utters various pious admonitions. These latter do not bear the stamp of Luḳmān nor of Muḥammad but belong to the common stock of proverbial sayings. A characteristic example is the following: "If all the trees in the earth were pens, and if God where to swell the sea into seven seas of ink, the words of God would not be exhausted" (Sūra xxxi. 27). This powerful hyperbole is found in hundreds of variants. It is recorded that this saying arose out of a dispute with the *aḥbār* of the Jews. The *aḥbār* claimed to possess all knowledge through the Torah, and the saying is directed against them. In the admonition of Luḳmān: "Moderate thy pace, lower thy voice, for of all voices, that of the ass is most hateful" (Sūra xxxi. 19), Rendel Harris has found the model in Akhiḳar: "Lower thy head, speak quietly, and look down! For if a house could be built by a loud voice, the ass would build two houses in a day".

Once Muḥammad had consecrated Luḳmān as the wise utterer of proverbs, everything that was thought pious or sensible could be attributed to him. Wahb b. Munabbih is credited with saying that he had read 10,000 chapters of Luḳmān's wisdom. The Arabic collections of proverbs (notably Maidānī) attribute much to Luḳmān (see R. Basset, *op. cit.*, xliv.—liv.). Thaʿlabī devotes a chapter of his *Madjālis* to the wisdom of Luḳmān. Many sayings seem to link up with the Sūra of Luḳmān. Sūra xxxi. 14 *sq.* advises reverence for parents but warns against being led astray by parents to worship false gods. Thaʿlabī's authority makes Luḳmān say: "Be amenable to your friends but never so far as to act against God's laws". There is much that recalls Akhiḳar. Luḳmān teaches that the rod benefits the child like water the seed. In Akhiḳar we have: "Spare not thy son, for strokes of the rod are to a boy like dung to the garden", etc. In Maidānī's Arabic proverbs Luḳmān is credited with the following admonition: "My son, consult the physician before thou fallest ill!" This corresponds to the first saying in Ben Sira's alphabet: "Honour the physician before thou requirest him".

Muslim legend is fond of making the sages and wise men of the past into prophets. But since Muḥammad quotes Luḳmān as a sage, the story was told that God offered Luḳmān the choice between becoming a prophet or a sage. Luḳmān chose wisdom and became vizier to King David, who called him fortunate: "Hail to thee, thine the wisdom, ours the pain!" Luḳmān lived down to the time of the prophet Yūnus (Jonah). He is also called judge of the Jews. Muslim legend sometimes also, although very rarely, makes Luḳmān a prophet and even gives him the "Madjalla" (*megilla*), the roll of wisdom (Ṭabarī, i. 1208). The *Dhikr Luḳmān* distinguishes the *nabī'* from the *rasūl*, *mursal*; Luḳmān, like Daniel and Dhu 'l-Ḳarnain, was *nabī'*, but not charged with a mission to a nation.

III. Luḳmān the writer of fables.

Luḳmān was honoured by Muḥammad and after him as an author of proverbs. A few centuries later he became a writer of fables also perhaps because *amthāl* meant both proverbs and fables. Luḳmān thus became the Aesop of the Arabs. Much was transferred to Luḳmān that was told in Europe of Aesop. The tendencies to this can be traced quite early. While the very earliest legend saw in Luḳmān the hero and Muslim legend makes him a sage, judge, vizier, or even a prophet, the later Oriental legend delights in describing him as a carpenter, a shepherd, a tailor, a deformed slave, an Egyptian, Nubian or Ethiopian slave, a feature which is obviously modelled on the story of Aesop.

The older Arabic literature does not know fables of Luḳmān. They first appear in the late middle ages. The Paris manuscript published by Jos. Derenbourg belongs to the year 1299 and contains 41 fables. These fables have often been published and thoroughly discussed in scholarly fashion especially by Derenbourg, R. Basset and Chauvin. Out of the 41 fables, No. 22 alone has no parallels: the thornbush begs the gardener to tend it so that kings may delight in its flowers and fruits; the gardener waters it twice a day and the thornbush overruns the whole garden. R. Basset recalls the fable of Jotham of the thornbush which destroys everything (*Judges*, ix.). All the others with the exception of the thirteenth (the midge and the bull) are found in the Syriac fables of Sophos (= Aesopus) published by Landsberg. All are found in Aesop, except No. 9 (the gazelle in the well), No. 22 (thornbush), No. 24 (wasp and bee), No. 40 (the man and the snakes). It has been further observed that in these fables the very animals indigenous among the Arabs, the ostrich, the hyena, the jackal and the camel, play no part. As these fables first appear in the late middle ages there can now be no doubt that we have to deal with a selection of Aesop's fables translated into Arabic.

IV. Related legendary figures.

Luḳmān is a manysided figure: he is *muʿammar*, hero, sage, maker of proverbs, and writer of fables. It is no wonder then that he has often been compared and identified with other legendary heroes, Prometheus, Alkmaion, Lucian and Solomon. Abu 'l-Faraḏj makes Luḳmān the teacher of Empedocles. Three of these equations deserve closer examination: 1) with Balʿam, 2) with Aḵhiḳar and 3) with Aesop. The identification with Balʿam is old. Arabic legend gives the following genealogy: Luḳmān b. Baʿūr b. Nāḥūr b. Tāriḵh (= Āzar, father of Ibrāhīm). It is evident that the Ḳurʾān exegists sought for something corresponding to Luḳmān in the Bible. They found this in Balʿam, as the roots *balaʿ* and *laḳama* both mean the same: "to swallow". This then became a Muslim tradition, which entered the Hebrew *Miṣhle Sindbad* where Luḳmān is one of the seven wise teachers of the king's son (ed. Cassel, p. 220 sq.) and also the *Disciplina clericalis* of Petrus Alphonsus, where the correct text is: "Balaam qui lingua arabica vocatur Lucaman" (ed. Hilka-Söderhjelm, p. 3). The Ḳurʾān exegists had no doubt about this identity. The question arises however: did Muḥammad see Balʿam in Luḳmān? — and next: is Luḳmān really Balʿam? Derenbourg, Basset and Eduard Meyer (*Die Israeliten und ihre Nachbarstämme*, p. 378) answer in the affirmative. But it is quite incredible. In no other instance did Muḥammad translate a biblical name into Arabic. The pre-Ḳurʾānic tradition about Luḳmān, the Sūra which shows deep reverence for Luḳmān, have no single feature of the hated Balʿam of the Bible and the Haggada. This identification was only made later by Ḳurʾānic exegists, who wished to connect Luḳmān with the Bible at any cost, and made him the son of Beʿor, i.e. Balʿam, just as they sometimes made him the nephew or cousin of Job.

Luḳmān's similarity to Aḵhiḳar was also noticed long ago, but it is only quite recently that the identification has found a vigorous champion in Rendel Harris, who devotes chap. vii. of his *Story of Aḥiḳar* to it. He bases his identification on the agreement of Sūra xxxi. 19 with Aḵhiḳar's warning about the voice of the ass, and on Arab hypotheses which compare Luḳmān with other figures in legend and history, notably to the relationship of Luḳmān, Aḵhiḳar and Aesop. The story of Aesop shows originally a close relationship to that of Aḵhiḳar. The later legend of Luḳmān has borrowed much of the story of Aesop and thus becomes like the Aḵhiḳar story but in reality Luḳmān is not directly connected with Aḵhiḳar but with Aesop.

Bibliography: The Ḳurʾān commentaries on Sūra xxxi., esp. Ṭabarī's *Tafsīr*, Cairo 1321, xxi. 39—50; Ṯhaʿlabī, *Ḳiṣaṣ al-anbiyāʾ*, Cairo 1325, p. 220—222. Many other sources in René Basset's *Loqman Berbère*, Paris 1890, (important both for old traditions and for comparative folklore) where also the *Ḏhikr Luḳmān b. ʿĀd* is published, p. LXXI—LXXX. — See also C. H. Toy, *The Lokman-legend*, in *JAOS*, xiii., 1889, p. CLXXII—CLXXVII; Jos. Horovitz, *Koranische Untersuchungen*, Berlin-Leipzig 1926, devotes a very full section to Luḳmān, p. 132—136. — On the fables of Luḳmān, their editions and their many relationships see Chauvin, *Bibliographie des ouvrages arabes*, iii. 1—82. — On Luḳmān-Balʿam see Jos. Derenbourg, *Fables de Loqmân le Sage*, Berlin-London 1850, p. 5—50. — On Aḵhiḳar-Aesop see Nöldeke, *Untersuchungen zum Achiqar-Roman*, Berlin 1913, p. 61—63. — On Luḳmān-Aḵhiḳar see Conybeare, Rendel Harris, Agnes Smith Lewis, *The Story of Aḥiḳar*, Cambridge 1913[2], p. LXXIX—LXXXIII.

LŪṬ, the Lot of the Bible attains in Islām, even as early as the Ḳurʾān, an importance which he does not have in the Bible and Haggada or even in the Church. Künstlinger (*Christliche Herkunft der kurʾānischen Lot-Legende*, in *RO*, 1930, vii. 281—295) sees Christian influence in this. But there is perhaps a simpler explanation. In the sharp contrast between Lūṭ and the people of Sodom Muḥammad saw the counterpart of the differences between him and the unbelievers. Lūṭ became like Nūḥ, Hūd, Ṣāliḥ, Ibrāhīm, Mūsā, a predecessor of Muḥammad as a prophet of punishment. If Muḥammad is called a liar, Nūḥ's people, ʿĀd and Thamūd, Ibrāhīm's and Lūṭ's people had called their prophets liars (Sūra xxii. 42). "Lūṭ's people" (*ḳawm Lūṭ*; once, l. 13, *iḵhwān Lūṭ*), generally found in the Ḳurʾān between Thamūd and Madyan, stands for Sodom (in later legend Sadūm). Speyer (*Die bibl. Erzählungen im Qoran*, p. 110, 176) observes that *salām* was promised to Nūḥ, Ibrāhīm, Mūsā, Hārūn and Ilyās but not to Lūṭ and Yūnus; this however may be ascribed to chance or cursoriness. Lūṭ is expressly numbered among the *mursalūn* (xxvi. 160; xxxvii. 133), as *rasūl amīn*, 'trustworthy prophet' (xxvi. 162), participator in *ḥukm* and *ʿilm*, judgment and knowledge.

When Ibrāhīm warns his people, Lūṭ believes him (xxix. 26). When Ibrāhīm flees from his native land, Lūṭ becomes a *muhāḏjir* (xxix. 26); they go into the blessed land (xxi. 71). Lūṭ's people prohibit hospitality (xv. 70); they are highway robbers: they are the first to practice sodomy. God sends his angels to punish them. Ibrāhīm intercedes in vain for them (xi. 79, 80). He appeals to the fact that Lūṭ lives among them (xxix. 32). The angels calm him by promising to save Lūṭ and his family except his wife. The angels come to Lūṭ. His people demand his guests for sinful purposes. In vain he offers his daughters instead. The angels reassure him saying: "We shall save thee but let no one turn round, thy wife will do it". In the morning the angels destroy the town completely. It rains *siḏjḏjīl*-stones (xv. 74) which bear the mark of God (xi. 83).

The Ḳurʾān mentions no other name in the history of Lūṭ. The destroyed city is called *al-muʾtafika* (liii. 53) of which the plural is *al-muʾtafikāt* (ix. 70; lxix. 9) corresponding to the Hebrew *mahpeka*, which is used in the Bible of Sodom.

The Ḳurʾān commentators and the authors of histories of the prophets (Ṯhaʿlabī, Kisāʾī) also know the Biblical story quite accurately (Ṭabarī, i. 346, 347). They are able to fill all the gaps and give all names. The Muslim legend explains everything. Lūṭ takes his name from *lāṭa*, "to attach oneself", because Ibrāhīm's heart was affectionately attached to Lūṭ (Ṯhaʿlabī). Lūṭ's wife is called Halsaḳaʿ or Wāʾila, his older daughter Rīth(?), the younger Rariya(?) (Ṭabarī), Zug͟har (Yāḳūt), or Rawāya(?) (al-Kisāʾī). Not only is Sadūm mentioned, but also four other towns, in whose names may be recognised the Biblical ʿAmōra, Admah, Ṣebaʿim and Ṣoʿar. Of Ṣoʿar, T͟haʿlabī says it was saved (Gen. xix. 20—22), "because it believed in Lūṭ". Abu 'l-Fidāʾ, (ed. Fleischer, p. 24) knows also the name Bāʾlaʿ, the Belāʿ of the Bible, the former name of Ṣoʿar (Gen. xiv. 2, 8). The Dead Sea is still called *Baḥr Lūṭ*.

The Muslim legend has little in common with the old Haggada (*Genesis rabba*, xlix., I.; *Sanhedrin*, 109 *sq.*). The reason why Luṭ's wife became a pillar of salt is noteworthy. The old Jewish Haggada says it was because she refused her guests salt (*Genesis rabba*, l. 4; li. 5). Muslim legend elaborates this: When the guests arrive she runs to the neighbours, borrows salt from them ostentatiously in order to call their attention to the fact that Lūṭ is entertaining forbidden guests (T͟haʿlabī, Cairo 1325, p. 66). This Muslim elaboration found its way into the late *Midras͟h haggadol* (ed. Schechter, p. 288, 289) and in the Targum Pseudo-Jonathan is already connected with Gen. xix. 26: an interesting example of the circulation of a legend.

Bibliography: Ibn al-At͟hīr, i. 46—48; T͟haʿlabī, *Ḳiṣaṣ al-anbiyāʾ*, Cairo 1325, p. 65—67; al-Kisāʾī, *Ḳiṣaṣ al-anbiyāʾ*, ed. Eisenberg, i. 145—149; Geiger, *Was hat Muhammed...?*, 1902², p. 109, 124, 129—131; M. Grünbaum, *Neue Beiträge*, p. 132—141; Horovitz, *Hebrew Union College Annual*, 1925, ii., p. 152, 187; do., *Koranische Untersuchungen*, 1926, p. 21, 26, 45, 49, 50 *sq.*, 54, 136; Speyer, *Die biblische Erzählungen im Qoran*, p. 151—158; J. Walker, *Note on the Koranic word "Sijjil"*, *Islamic Culture* 1935, p. 635—637; D. Künstlinger, *Christliche Herkunft der Ḳurānischen Lōṭ-Legende*, *RO* 1930.

M

AL-MADĪNA, a town in Arabia, the residence of Muḥammad after the Hid͟jra, and capital of the Arab empire under the first caliphs. The real Arabic name of the town was Yat͟hrib, Yathrippa (this is the correct reading) in Ptolemy and Stephan Byzantinus, Yt͟hrib in Minaean inscriptions (M. Hartmann, *Die arabische Frage*, p. 253 *sq.*). Al-Madīna, on the other hand, is a descriptive word "the town" and is taken from the Aramaic, in which *medīnta* means strictly "area of jurisdiction" and hence town (of some size). In the Meccan sections of the Ḳurʾān it is found as an appellative with the plural *al-madāʾin*, while in the Madīna sūras al-Madīna is used as a proper name for the new residence of the Prophet (ix. 101, 120; xxxiii. 60; lxiii. 8). The old name Yat͟hrib on the other hand is found only once (xxxiii. 13). It is evident from these references that the usual explanation of the name as "the town" (of the Prophet) is a later one. It is rather to be supposed that it was a result of the existence of a strong Jewish element in Yat͟hrib that the Aramaic loan-word became the regular name of the town. It is analogous to the originally South Arabian *had͟jar* "town", which is applied to the capital in Baḥrain. Of the Madinese poets, Ḳais b. al-K͟haṭīm uses the name Yat͟hrib exclusively, while Ḥassān b. T͟hābit and Kaʿb b. Mālik use both names, which is also the case with Muḥammad's ordinance of the community (Ibn His͟hām, p. 341 *sqq.*).

Madīna is situated in the Ḥid͟jāz on a plain sloping very gently towards the north, the boundaries of which are marked in the north and northwest by the hills of Uḥud and ʿAir about four miles from the town, two outer spurs of the range which forms the boundary between the Arabian highlands and the low lying coastlands (Tihāma). West and east the plain is bounded by the Ḥarras or Lābas, barren areas covered with black basalt, but the eastern Ḥarras lie at a greater distance and leave between them and the town room for more fertile patches so that the eastern frontier of the plain is really formed by a row of low black hills. In the south the plain stretches away farther than the eye can reach. Its noteworthy feature is a richness in water unusual in Arabia. All the water-courses come from the south or from the Ḥarras and flow to the north, where they combine at Zag͟hāba and then take a westerly course to the coast in the wādī Iḍam. As a rule they contain water only after rain but they keep the level of the subterranean water fairly high so that there are a considerable number of wells and springs. After heavy rains the open square of al-Munāk͟ha (see below) forms a lake and considerable inundations are not rare and may even be dangerous to the buildings in the southern part of the town. One such flood was particularly threatening in the reign of the Caliph ʿUt͟hmān so that he had a dam built as a protection against it (Balād͟hurī, p. 11) and even worse were those of the years 660 and 734 A.H., when the wall created by the great volcanic outburst was broken through by the water (Samhūdī-Wüstenfeld, p. 23). The water is in places salt and unpalatable, and different governors of the town have made aqueducts to bring to the town good water from wells of sweet water farther to the south. The water courses have different names: in the west al-ʿAḳīḳ with wādī Buṭḥān and Ranūnā, in the east wādī Ḳanāt with Mahzūr and Mud͟hānib (or -nīb). The soil is of salty sand, lime and loamy clay and is everywhere very fertile, particularly in the south. Date-palms flourish exceedingly, also oranges, lemons, pomegranates, bananas, peaches, apricots, figs and grapes. The winters are cool and wet, the summers hot but rarely sultry. Modern travellers say the air is pleasant but not very healthy and fevers are and always have been a plague, especially for newcomers as Muḥammad's followers had frequently to learn (Balād͟hurī, p. 11; Farazdaḳ, ed. Boucher, p. 9; Burckhardt, *Reisen in Arabien*, p. 482 *sqq.*, 605; Burton, *A Pilgrimage*, p. 176 *sq.*; Wensinck, *Mohammed en de Joden*, p. 31; H. Lammens, *Fāṭima*, p. 54; Goldziher, *Muhammedanische Studien*, ii. 243). The Umaiyads called the town "the filthy" in contrast to the honorific *al-ṭaiyiba* which the Prophet is said to have given it (Goldziher, *op. cit.*, ii. 37).

The way in which Madīna is favoured by nature forms a striking contrast to Mecca which lies in a rocky valley where corn does not grow (Sūra xiv. 37). From the very beginning it was not a regular town but a collection of houses and cottages which were surrounded by gardens and cultivated fields, the inhabitants of which were devoted to agriculture and therefore contemptuously called "Nabataeans" by the Beduins. These scattered settlements only gradually became consolidated to a townlike agglomeration, which however lay farther north than the later town, as the name Yat͟hrib, according to Samhūdī (Wüstenfeld, *Geschichte der Stadt Medina*, p. 37), was especially associated with a place west of the tomb of Ḥamza where the Banū Ḥārit͟ha settled. The town which arose in this way was not surrounded by a wall so that its defences were the thick groves of palms and the orchards which surrounded the houses. As they were less thick on the north and west sides, these were most exposed to hostile attacks. The little forts (*ʾuṭum*, plur. *āṭām*, or *ud͟jum*, plur. *ād͟jām*) which were built in considerable numbers formed a substitute for a wall and the inhabitants could retire into them in times of trouble.

There were in later times no reliable traditions regarding the origin and earliest history of Madīna and the historians endeavoured to fill the gap themselves and as elsewhere made the D͟jurhum (see Krauss, in *ZDMG*, lxx. 352) and the quite unhistorical ʿAmalekites play a part in it (cf. also Ḥassān b. T͟hābit, ed. Hirschfeld, No. 9, verse 6). It is only with the coming of Jews to Madīna that we are on surer ground, but the historians know so little of the exact period of these settlements that they connect them sometimes with Moses, sometimes with the deportation of the Jews under Nebuchadnezzar, and sometimes with the conquest of Palestine by the Greeks or by the Romans. According to various references in the Talmud, there were Jews in Arabia in the early centuries of the Christian era and this certainly means North Arabia in the main (see Hirschfeld, *Beiträge zur Erklärung des Koran*, p. 49 *sq.*) and that they were numerous is evident from the existence of Jewish communities in Ṭaimāʾ, Ḥid͟jr (Jaussen and Savignac, *Mission*, p. 150, 242), K͟haibar, Wādi ʾl-Ḳurā, Fadak and Maḳnā, with which that in Madīna was connected. Everywhere in these oases they took over and developed the cultivation of the soil, and it was probably due to them that these scattered settlements developed into a kind of town; evidence of this is found in the Aramaic name Madīna for Yat͟hrib. According to the definite statement of Ḥassān b. T͟hābit (No. 9, verse 8 in Hirschfeld), they built a number of small forts in this town; but from the fact that they were not the first to do this it may probably be concluded that the earliest inhabitants were not pure Beduins (according to Lammens, *Ṭāʾif*, p. 72, these forts were built after the model of those of the Yemen). The Jewish tribe of Ḳainuḳāʿ played a prominent part in the immigration, as at a later period one of the principal markets in the western part of the town was called after it. But gradually the tribes of Ḳuraiẓa and Naḍīr came to be the leading ones in Madīna Jewry. The former dwelled with the Bahdal on the wādī Mahzūr, the Naḍīr on the wādī Buṭhān (*Kitāb al-ag͟hānī*, xix. 95, where the Jewish tribes and the judaized Arab tribes are detailed). While in this passage, as usual, the Ḳuraiẓa and the Naḍīr are numbered among the pure Jews, according to a notable statement in the historian Yaʿḳūbī (ed. Houtsma, ii. 49, 52), they were not pure Jews but judaized clans of the Arabic tribe of D͟jud͟hām, which Nöldeke has repeatedly emphasized as a genuine tradition. Now it is historically certain that at that time there were many Jewish proselytes (cf. Ibn Ḳutaiba, *Kitāb al-maʿārif*, p. 299) but in spite of this there are decisive reasons for believing that the Jewish element in Madīna did not arise in this way. It is of special significance that the Ḳuraiẓa and Naḍīr are frequently called the *Kāhināni*, the "two (tribes of) priests", which shows that the Jews knew their genealogy and laid stress upon their descent (cf. e.g. Ibn His͟hām, p. 660: "thou revilest the pure of the two tribes of priests"). The same thing is seen from the fact that the Naḍīrite Ṣafīya married by Muḥammad is described as belonging to the family of Aaron (Ibn Saʿd, viii. 86). But the decisive fact is the way in which the Prophet speaks in the Madīna sūras to the Jews there. He apostrophises them as sons of Israel and reminds them that God has raised them above all men (ii. 47, 122); he brackets them with the ancient Israelites as if they had taken part in the Exodus from Egypt (ii. 49 *sq.*); Allāh gave Moses the scriptures so that they might be rightly guided (ii. 53); they break the laws which he bound them to observe at the treaty of alliance (ii. 83 *sqq.*) etc. Such expressions suggest as clearly as possible that he regarded them as true descendants of the ancient Israelites. There must therefore have been in addition to the judaized Arabs a stock of true Jews, and indeed it is obvious that without such there could have been no proselytes. Wellhausen moreover has aptly pointed out that the Arabian Jews by their language, their knowledge of the scriptures, their manner of life, their fondness for malicious mockery, secret arts, poison, magic, and cursing, and their fear of death, make an unusual impression which cannot be explained simply by the judaizing of pure Arabs. But on the other hand, it must not be forgotten that the Jews in Arabia were very much influenced by their surroundings and had assumed a character of their own. For example we find among them the division into tribes and families, characteristic of the Arabs, with the obligations associated with this. The names of these tribes cannot be traced to old Jewish names but are thoroughly Arabic in appearance, which is also true of their personal names among which true Jewish names like Samawʾal and Sāra are rare. The arabicisation of the Jews is particularly notable in the poems which are ascribed to Jews, most of which might have been equally well written by Beduins (see Nöldeke, *Beiträge zur Kenntniss der Poesie der alten Araber*, p. 52 *sqq.*).

While the Jews were supreme in other places like K͟haibar, al-Fadak etc., the position was changed in Madīna as a result of a new immigration which the Arabs associate with the bursting of the dam at Maʾrib and the migrations of South Arabian tribes produced by it. In this way the two so-called Ḳaila tribes, Aws and K͟hazrad͟j [vide ANṢĀR], came to Madīna. No particulars of their coming are recorded, but from an interesting verse in Ibn K͟hurdād͟hbih (*BGA*, vi. 128) and Yāḳūt, iv. 460, it is evident that they were for a long time subject and tributary to the Jews and that this part of Northern Arabia was at this time under Persian rule, in keeping with the usual Jewish policy of maintaining friendly relations with Persia. Later the Ḳaila Arabs however succeeded in casting off the Jewish yoke and bringing the Jews under their rule. According to tradition, the occasion of this was that a powerful Jewish king named Fityawn, who exercised the jus primae noctis, was murdered by a Khazradjī Mālik b. al-ʿAdjlān to save his threatened sister. As to later events there are two different traditions: some make Mālik after his deed seek the help of a Ghassānid ruler, Abū Djubaila (cf. the name Djabula among the Ghassānids), others of a South Arabian Tubbaʿ, Asʿad Abikārib (c. 430; M. Hartmann, *Die arabische Frage*, p. 482, 497).

The new lords of Yathrib took over the forts occupied by the Jews and built several more (Samhūdī, p. 37). They also learned "Nabataean" arts from them and began to cultivate palms and pursue agriculture. The Khazradjīs, whose principal family was Nadjdjār (or Taim al-Lāt), as the most powerful tribe assumed the leadership and occupied the centre of the town where the modern Madīna lies. West and south of them lived other Khazradjī tribes while the territory of the Ḥārith ran to the east. The Awsīs, who also comprised several families, settled south and east of their brethren, the Nabīt in the northeast being separated by the Ḥārith from their kinsmen. The two principal Jewish tribes Naḍīr and Ḳuraiẓa preserved a certain amount of independence and retained their lands under the Awsīs while the Ḳainuḳāʿ retained their lands in the southwest although their main industry was practising the goldsmith's art. Further details of the parts occupied by the tribes and families are given in Samhūdī (Wüstenfeld, p. 29 *sq.*, 37 *sq.*) but these can only now be partly identified. Besides there were in Madīna, in addition to the Jews and the immigrant Ḳaila tribes, several Arab tribes, some of which were already there when the former came. They were closely connected with the Jews and were partly judaized. The settlement of affairs reached in this way gave the town a period of peace, which was however gradually broken as an increasing enmity arose between the two Ḳaila tribes, as was not infrequently the case with Arab brother-tribes. At first it was individual families that fought one another but the conflagration gradually spread until the existence of the whole town was threatened. The quarrel began with the feud of Sumair, so-called after an Awsī named Sumair. This was settled by an arbitrator but it was not long till renewed friction led to renewed hostilities, of which the so-called feud of Ḥātib was the most serious. We are introduced to this second period by the poems of Ḳais b. al-Khaṭīm of the Awsī family of al-Nabīt. The fighting throughout ended unfavourably for the Awsīs and the Nabīt were finally driven from their possessions. In their need the Awsīs appealed for help to the two principal Jewish tribes. They at first refused it; but when the Khazradjīs had foolishly slain some Jewish hostages, they concluded an alliance with the Awsīs and declared themselves ready to assist them. It was no longer a fight between a few families but a struggle between the two great rival tribes in their full strength, and the other inhabitants of Yathrib, even the Beduins of the country round, also took sides. At Buʿāth after long preparations a decisive battle was finally fought. It at first looked as if the Awsīs were again to be defeated. The tables were turned and the Khazradjīs suffered a severe reverse. It is interesting to note that ʿAbd Allāh b. Ubaiy of the Khazradjīs on this occasion displayed the same irresolution that he did later in his opposition to Muḥammad; he took the field with the others but did not enter the battle. On the day of al-Sarāra he actually ran away. The battle of Buʿāth restored the equilibrium between the principal tribes, but the continual fighting had sapped the strength of the town and the bitter feeling which continually revealed itself made the lives of the inhabitants more and more unendurable. Then a momentous change took place when the people of Madīna, who required a leader with a strong hand, and Muḥammad, who had only to a slight extent succeeded in winning over the Meccans to his religious views, came into contact with one another.

The Ḳaila tribes at the time of their immigration to Yathrib had been heathens like the great majority of the Arabs. The principal deity they worshipped was Manāt, after whom the Aws Allāh were originally named, but they also reverenced among others al-Lāt (cf. the name Taim al-Lāt already mentioned). Through living alongside of Jews they became influenced by their religious and moral ideas, but unfortunately we know very little of their spiritual outlook before the coming of the Prophet. The poet Ḳais deals in the Beduin style mainly with the quarrels between the tribes and families and rarely refers to religious matters. He nowhere mentions the local deities but refers to Allāh (No. 6, verse 22) whom he calls the creator (5, 6; cf. Goldziher, in *ZDMG*, lvii. 398), which is in itself sufficient to prove Jewish or Christian influence. Of him he says in No. 11, verse 8: "Allāh will only what he will"; verse 13, 12: "Praise be to Allāh, the lord, the lord of the building" refers to the Kaʿba in Mecca, the *masdjid* covered with carpets (5, 14). The three days in Minā are mentioned in 4,4 which shows that they then, as later according to the Muslim poets, gave the young men an opportunity for love-affairs with women of other tribes. In rejecting a life after death, 6, 22, he is quite on a level with the pagan Meccans. Alongside of such representatives of a mixed religion there were others whose conceptions had developed farther through contact with Jews or Christians, so that they were reckoned *ḥanīfs* [q.v.] as they definitely rejected the popular deities and had assumed a tendency to asceticism. Abu 'l-Haitham and Asʿad b. Zurāra for example professed monotheism before they became acquainted with Muḥammad (ʿIbn Saʿd, III/ii. 22, 139). One result of living alongside of Jews in Madīna was that the art of writing was quite well known there (cf. Ibn Ḳutaiba, *Kitāb al-maʿārif*, p. 132 *sq.*, 166; Balādhurī, p. 473 *sq.*; Ibn Saʿd, III/ii., *passim*).

The spiritual influence of the Jews on the Arab inhabitants of Madīna became an important factor in the relations between them and Muḥammad, for it made them receptive to his religious ideas with which they became acquainted by visits to Mecca and in other ways. How finally a treaty was concluded between him and several representatives of the Madīnese, by which the latter pledged themselves to take him into their community and to defend him as if he were one of themselves, and how he and those of his followers who were still faithful to him thereupon migrated to Madīna is related in the article MUḤAMMAD. After a brief stay in the southern suburb of Ḳubāʾ he entered the town and took up his abode with a Khazradjī, Abū Aiyūb Khālid b. Zaid, with whom he lived till a dwelling was arranged for him. Hardly anything ever showed so clearly his gift, based on his unshakeable belief in his prophetic call, of leading men to follow his will, as the fact that he succeeded in a very short time in bringing some kind of order into Madīna, hopelessly split up by feuds, and making a kind of unity out of the heterogeneous elements in the town, the earlier Arab inhabitants of Yathrib, the later immigrants, now predominant Ḳaila tribes, the Muhād̲j̲irūn from Mecca and the Jews or judaized Arabs. We get a glimpse of the first step towards this goal from the ordinance of the community preserved in Ibn His̲h̲ām, p. 341 *sqq.* ("Book of the weregeldes"; cf. Ṭabarī, Glossary, s.v. ʿ-*ḳ-l*) which Wellhausen, *Skizzen und Vorarbeiten*, iv. 67 *sqq.* and following him Caetani, *Annali dell' Islam*, i. 395 *sqq.* and Wensinck, *Mohammed en de Joden te Medina*, p. 78 *sqq.* have discussed. In it Muḥammad calls himself the messenger of Allāh, but there is no reference to his divine inspiration. His object is to form a unified *umma* out of the inhabitants of Madīna and this is defined from the religious side as the community of believers from Mecca and Yat̲h̲rib. But the non-believers are not excluded, for the *umma* coincides rather with the town of Madīna which included also Jews and heathens, of whom it is not demanded that they should adopt Islām. The tribes retain their autonomy as regards blood-vengeance and ransoming of prisoners, but against the rest of the world generally the affording of protection was obligatory on every member of the community without exception and no one could conclude peace separately with the enemies of the community (particularly the Ḳurais̲h̲). All important matters, out of which misfortune might befall the community, were to be brought before Allāh and Muḥammad. The Valley of Yat̲h̲rib was to be *ḥaram* (or *ḥarām*) for all who were bound by this ordinance. The provisions of this document were soon rendered obsolete by the rapid progress of events, certainly not against the wish of Muḥammad whose plans went far beyond what was laid down in it. The main cause of its loss of importance was the breach which soon occurred between Muḥammad and the Jews, and which the latter provoked by their scornful criticism of Muḥammad's revelations, especially of the divergent points in his reproduction of stories from the Old Testament. This meant a serious threat to his authority and in addition the Jews endeavoured to destroy the agreement reached in Madīna by attempting to revive the old hostility between the two Ḳaila tribes (Ibn His̲h̲ām, p. 385 *sqq.*; cf. Sūra iii. 118 *sqq.*). To meet these difficulties, which of course were very welcome to his enemies in the town, Muḥammad worked hard to unite his followers for a common object, the war with the Meccans, by which he could at the same time avenge the resistance offered him there. It was at first difficult for him to arouse enthusiasm for this war among the Muhād̲j̲irūn and even more the Anṣār but finally, when a fortunate accident occurred to help him, he succeeded in bringing about a war with the Meccans which led to the momentous victory at Badr. On the further fighting of this campaign, the battle of Uḥud and the war of the ditch, cf. the article MUḤAMMAD. The latter campaign gets its name from the ditch (*k̲h̲andaḳ*) which Muḥammad on the advice of a Persian (Salmān) had dug around the unprotected parts of the town and which, in spite of its modest dimensions (it is said to have been a fathom broad), formed a serious obstacle to the enemy. Ibn D̲j̲ubair in the xii^th^ century still saw traces of it, an arrowshot west of the town. On its further course cf. Wensinck, *Mohammed en de Joden*, p. 26, 31. The Meccans themselves in this fighting gave him every material assistance by their lack of warlike ability and energy, and the war contributed to consolidate his position in Madīna, aided not a little by the lack of resolution among the Munāfiḳūn who never managed to seize opportunities favourable to them. He was thus not only in a position to continue the war against his native city but also to repay the Jews in ruthless fashion for all the annoyance they had caused him. After the battle of Badr, the Ḳainuḳāʿ were driven out of the town and after the battle of Uḥud, which went against the Prophet, the same fate was meted out to a Kāhin tribe, the Naḍīr. But the worst lot was that of the Ḳuraiẓa, who, in spite of the intercession of the Awsīs, were massacred. These events however do not show the Jewish tribes in a favourable light as they made no attempt to help one another but left each other in the lurch. The Ḳuraiẓa alone at the massacre showed a courage which to some extent atones for their previous attitude. In this way Muḥammad succeeded in disposing of the danger that threatened him from the Jews, for the Jews who were left in Madīna were of no importance and caused him no serious difficulties.

With the treaty of Ḥudaibīya in the year 6 A.H. [cf. MUḤAMMAD] the war with the Ḳurais̲h̲ was practically finished, for in it his genius for diplomacy succeeded in bringing them to recognise Madīna as a power equal in importance to Mecca. The official conclusion of the struggle was the bloodless occupation of his native city in 8 A.H. However great a triumph this was for the Prophet, it produced a new tension which was to prove fateful for Islām after the death of Muḥammad. Even before the decisive turn in the struggle with Mecca, in the campaign against the Banū Muṣṭaliḳ, the ill-feeling between the emigrants and a section of the people of Madīna came to a head in an ominous fashion and ʿAbd Allāh b. Ubaiy delivered several boastful speeches threatening to expel the troublesome intruders (cf. Sūra lxiii. 8), which he naturally denied when the Prophet later took him to task. But when Muḥammad had entered Mecca, his faithful followers in Madīna became anxious, as they feared he would now abandon their town and return to his native place. He calmed them however and declared that he would live and die with them (Ibn His̲h̲ām, p. 824). But when he began to treat the Meccans with great clemency and after the battle at Ḥunain was striving to win them over to his religion by rich gifts, the Anṣār with justice felt themselves slighted and once again feared that he would abandon them. But he delivered them a speech in which he reminded them how he had united them when they were living in hostility to one another and declared his gratitude for all that they had done for him, and when he concluded by asking them to be satisfied if others went home with captured herds but they with the messenger of Allāh, they burst into tears and withdrew satisfied (Ibn His̲h̲ām, p. 885 *sq.*). While in such stories there may be an echo of the later antagonism between the Anṣār and the Ḳurais̲h̲, they undoubtedly give a not inaccurate idea of the feelings which found expression at this time. It is all the more remarkable that according to various indications there must have been an opposition to Muḥammad at the time of the Tabūk campaign in Madīna. His orations against the Munāfiḳūn in the ninth Sūra sound unusually excited and recall those of the Meccan period with their threats of punishment. There is also the notable, but unfortunately not quite clear story of the Mas-d̲j̲id al-Ḍirār (cf. also Lammens) which some men had built south of the town in the land of the ʿAmr b. ʿAwf and which he sanctioned until he saw that its object was to provoke dissension among the believers for the benefit of his former enemies (Sūra ix. 108 *sqq.*), wherefore he had it destroyed.

Faithful to his promise, the Prophet remained in Madīna till his death on June 8, 632. The unity created by his strong hand at once fell apart; the Anṣār assembled and chose the Khazradjī Saʿd b. ʿUbāda as their chief, while others proposed that the government should be shared between the Anṣār and the Muhādjirūn. ʿUmar's rapid and vigorous intervention however succeeded in thwarting these plans so threatening to Islām and carrying through the election of Abū Bakr as Caliph. He and his two successors resided in Madīna which thus became the capital of the rapidly growing empire. Abū Bakr and ʿUmar, like the Prophet, were buried under the house of ʿĀʾisha, while ʿUthmān's body was brought in the darkness on a door to the Jewish cemetery amidst objurgations and stone-throwing. In this period no one thought of strengthening the defences of the capital, not even during the *ridda* after the Prophet's death and still less later when the holy wars were waged exclusively in foreign lands. ʿUthmān had the forts taken down, but remains of them could be seen as late as the tenth century (Masʿūdī, *Tanbīh*, in *BGA*, viii. 206).

ʿAlī's reign brought a complete change for Madīna. When the great civil war broke out between him and his rivals and the decisive battles were fought in the provinces, the Caliph recognised that the vast empire could not possibly be governed from the remote corner of the world in which Madīna lay. While the earlier caliphs had remained in the capital and sent out armies of conquest from it, ʿAlī placed himself at the head of his troops and set out from Madīna in 36/656, never again to see it. He made Kūfa his capital and after Muʿāwiya's victory Damascus took its place. Madīna now sank, like its old rival Mecca, to the rank of a provincial town, unaffected by the current of the world's events. What pious old folks thought of this change is reflected in a characteristic tradition (Dīnawarī, p. 152 *sq.*) according to which several prominent Anṣār tried to induce ʿAlī to abandon his plan of leaving Madīna: "What thou dost lose in the form of prayers in the mosque of the Prophet and the course between his tomb and his pulpit is of more value than what thou expectest to find in the ʿIrāḳ; reflect how ʿUmar used to send his generals to war; there are still just as capable men amongst us as then!" But the Caliph replied: "The wealth of the state and the armies are in the ʿIrāḳ and attacks threaten from the Syrians, and I must be near them".

Madīna with its venerable associations and the tomb of the Prophet could not of course become quite unimportant; on the contrary, its sanctity increased in the eyes of Muslims, the more the figure of Muḥammad became important in their conceptions; but the life of the town became more and more remote from the real world in which actual history was being unfolded. Hither retired all who wished to keep aloof from the turmoil of political happenings, like ʿAlī's son Ḥasan, after he had abandoned all his claims (Ṭabarī, ii. 9; Dīnawarī, p. 223). Ḥusain also went there from Kūfa, but left it again to make his desperate attempt to gain his rights, and it is significant that none of the Madīnese Anṣār went with him (Wellhausen, *Die Oppositionsparteien*, p. 69). When he was slain, his wives and son were brought to Madīna, where they lived in peace and took no further part in the fighting. ʿAlī's son, Muḥammad b. al-Ḥanafīya, resided in Madīna (Dīnawarī, p. 308). It was not, however, only relatives and ardent followers of the Prophet, who preferred to live here in his city, but several of his former enemies, the Umaiyads, also felt attracted thither by the quiet and easy life and would not go to Damascus (Lammens, *Études sur le règne de Moʿâwia*, p. 35). In this way Madīna gradually became the home of a new population, consisting of people who wished to enjoy undisturbed the great wealth which the wars of conquest had brought them. Life there became more and more luxurious until finally the holy city became so notorious (*Kitāb al-aghānī*, xxi. 197), that during a rising in the year 127/745 the last Umaiyad Caliph Marwān II could ask one of the participants in it how it was that the wines and singing-girls of Madīna had not held him back from taking part in it (Ṭabarī, ii. 1910). Such stories remind us of Doughty's description of the present inhabitants of Madīna (*Travels in Arabia*, 3rd ed., p. 151: "carding, playing, tippling in arak, brutish hemp smoking, ribald living"). This was the golden period of Madīna about the glories of which the poets sang. Flourishing, well-watered gardens and meadows surrounded the town, and there were a number of splendid palaces built by wealthy Ḳuraish, especially in the Wādi 'l-ʿAḳīḳ of which traces can still be found (cf. Batanūnī, *Riḥla*, p. 261 *sq.*; Lammens, *Moʿâwia*, p. 228).

Anther section of the people of Madīna was attracted thither by the quiet life, although for other reasons. Their object was not worldly enjoyments but they devoted themselves to the memories in the town of its sacred past, by collecting and studying the legal and ritual enactments dating from the Prophet, in so far as they were based on the *sunna* of Madīna and the *idjmāʿ* there. The most distinguished representative of this group was Mālik b. Anas (d. 179/795), the author of the *Muwaṭṭaʾ*, who as founder of the Mālikī school gathered many pupils around him (Goldziher, *Muhammedanische Studien*, ii. 213 *sqq.*). One of them, Ibn Zabāla, composed the first history of the town of Madīna (199/814) but it has not survived.

Madīna was now ruled by governors appointed by the Caliph, lists of whom are given by Ṭabarī and Ibn al-Athīr. The town was however not entirely unaffected by the wars of the first centuries after Muḥammad. In the reign of Yazīd, feeling in Madīna, even among the Umaiyads, was more or less hostile to the Caliph and many took the side of his rival ʿAbd Allāh b. Zubair in Mecca. The expedition of the governor ʿAmr b. Saʿīd, which Yazīd ordered, was a failure. In 63/682-3 the Madīnese rebelled openly, appointing ʿAbd Allāh b. Ḥanẓala as their leader and building a wall with a ditch to defend the town on the north. The Caliph sent an army under the leadership of Muslim b. ʿUḳba which took up its quarters on the Ḥarra N.E. of the town and fought the battle of the Ḥarra, which ended in the defeat of the Madīnese — according to the usual story, a result of the treachery of the Banū Ḥāritha. That the inhabitants were abandoned to the ill-treatment of the Syrian troops is probably a malicious libel (Wellhausen, *Das arabische Reich*, p. 98 *sq.*). Towards the end of Umaiyad rule, in the year 130/747-8, the Khāridjīs under Abū Ḥamza defeated the Madīnese at Kubaid; but he was surprised by Marwān's troops and slain (Ṭabarī, ii. 200 *sqq.*; *BGA*, viii. 327). When the ʿAbbāsids became supreme, two ʿAlid brothers, Muḥammad and Ibrāhīm, sons of ʿAbd Allāh, made an attempt to fight for their rights. Muḥammad who called himself al-Mahdī appeared in Madīna in 145/762-3 where he found not a few adherents, among them Mālik b. Anas and Abū Ḥanīfa. He endeavoured in various ways to imitate the example of the Prophet, used his sword, had the ditch dug by him round the town restored (see above) etc. The Caliph sent his relative ʿĪsā b. Mūsā with 4,000 men against him and when he bridged the ditch by throwing a couple of doors over it and entered the town, most of al-Mahdī's followers lost heart, as was usual with the supporters of the ʿAlids, and when he renewed the hopeless struggle, he was mortally wounded. About 20 years later (169/786), another ʿAlid, Ḥusain b. ʿAlī, arose against the ʿAbbāsids. After ravaging Madīna he was driven out and slain at Fakhkh near Mecca. In spite of the harm he did to the town of the Prophet, he was celebrated by the ʿAlid party as a martyr (Ṭabarī, iii. 551 *sqq.*; Ibn al-Athīr, vi. 60 *sqq.*). In the caliphate of Wāthiḳ, Madīna suffered severely from the attacks of the Sulaim and the Banū Hilāl. Boghā the elder came to their assistance in 230/844-5 and imprisoned the Beduins. When he left the town again, the latter succeeded in breaking out of prison; the Madīnese however discovered their escape and put them to death (Ibn al-Athīr, vii. 12). Their love for Wāthiḳ was shown by their lamenting him every night after his death (*ibid.*, vii. 21).

In the centuries that followed, Madīna is only rarely mentioned by the historians, and what they tell us about it is of little interest as a rule. When the Fāṭimids became lords of Egypt and were threatening the holy cities in the Ḥidjāz, a wall was at last built round Madīna. This was erected in 364/974-975 by the Būyid ʿAḍud al-Dawla but enclosed only the central part of the town. It was restored in 540/1145-1146 by a vizier of the sons of Zangī. But as a considerable proportion of the inhabitants lived outside the wall without protection from the attacks of the Beduins, the Atābeg of Syria, Nūr al-Dīn Maḥmūd b. Zangī, in 557/1162 built a second wall of greater extent with towers and gateways. The present wall, 35—40 feet high, was built by the Ottoman Sulṭān Sulaimān b. Salīm the Magnificent (1520—1566) of basalt and granite (Samhūdī-Wüstenfeld, p. 126). A trench was dug around it. The same Sulṭān brought a covered aqueduct from the south into the town. Finally the wall was raised to a height of 80 feet by Sulṭān ʿAbd al-ʿAzīz, which height it has retained.

Under the rule of the Turks Madīna continued to lead a quiet life, little heeded by the outside world, and it is rarely mentioned, a circumstance much facilitated by the fact the holy city could not be entered by non-Muslims. Radical changes only came about in the xixth century. In 1804, the Wahhābīs took the town, plundered its treasures and prevented pilgrimages to the Tomb of Muḥammad. An attempt to destroy the dome over the tomb failed, but the great treasures in pearls, jewels, etc., presented by pious visitors to the mosque were carried off. It was not till 1813 that Muḥammad ʿAlī's son Ṭusūn succeeded in retaking the town and at the treaty of peace in 1815 ʿAbd Allāh b. Saʿūd recognised Turkish suzerainty over the holy places in the Ḥidjāz. This restoration of Turkish rule brought at least one important innovation: the building of the Ḥidjāz railway from Damascus to Madīna in 1908. It was primarily intended for pilgrims but was also of military importance and therefore suffered severely in the first world wai. After the peace which ended the world war, the Turkish troops evacuated Madīna in 1918. In the meanwhile a stronger opponent to Ḥusain had arisen in ʿAbd al-ʿAzīz b. Saʿūd, who had once more raised the Wahhābīs to a position of supremacy. Ḥusain's bold move in assuming the title of caliph found no support among the Arab chiefs, and the people of the Ḥidjāz forced him to abdicate. Ibn Saʿūd seized this opportunity, entered Mecca in October 1924 and forced Ḥusain's son ʿAlī to leave the town. The two holy cities fell therefore both into the hands of the Wahhābis and belong since 1932 to the Saʿūdī Kingdom. In course of time the Wahhābīs became more tolerant and permit visits to the Mosque of the Tomb and other holy places and only forbid actual worship there.

In spite of the inaccessibility of Madīna to all non-Muslims the reports of various modern travellers enable us to form a fairly clear picture of it, which can only be briefly outlined heie. In keeping with the configuration of the ground, the plain on which Madīna lies is divided into an upper southern part and a lower northern part, *al-ʿāliya* and *al-sāfila*, names found even in the earliest writers. Al-ʿāliya is reckoned to run to the above mentioned village of Ḳubāʾ, 3 miles away, al-sāfila to the hill of Uḥud. The older wall encloses the town proper; the already mentioned later wall which is now partly in ruins encloses the western rather large suburb of al-ʿAnbarīya and the "camp of the camels", ***barr al-munākha***, 400 yards broad lying between it and the town. Here is pointed out the traditional site of the ***muṣallā*** [q.v.], a tradition probably worthy of credence, as otherwise it would have been natural to locate it in the great mosque mentioned below. Along the south side of the wall runs the road of the funeral processions, *darb al-djanāza*, which leads to the old general burial-place, *baḳīʿ al-gharḳad* [q. v.] in the east of the town. Among the thousands who are buried here are the little son of the Prophet, Ibrāhīm, his wives (whether also his daughter Fāṭima is disputed; see below), many of his companions, al-ʿAbbās, Muḥammad al-Bāḳir, Djaʿfar al-Ṣādiḳ, the already mentioned jurist, Mālik b. Anas, and many others. At the north-west corner of the town stands the castle built on to the town wall. There are several gates in the walls, including the Bāb al-Djumʿa in the east, and the Bāb al-ʿAnbarīya in the west. From a spring of fresh water in the village of Ḳubāʾ an aqueduct runs into the town, first laid by Marwān when governor of Madīna. It frequently fell into disrepair and was restored for example by several Ottoman sultāns, on the last occasion by ʿAbd al-Ḥamīd after the Wahhābīs had destroyed it. The damage not infrequently done by floods has already been mentioned. In 734 the Madīnese were prevented for six months by an inundation from visiting the grave of Ḥamza. The streets of Madīna are clean but narrow and only the main streets are paved. The houses are well built of stone and a number have two stories. Several of them are surrounded by gardens, but the houses with gardens are mainly found outside the north and south wall, especially towards the south where vegetable gardens and orchards alternate with palmgroves and cornfields. The dates of which there are 70 varieties are, as in ancient times, one of the principal products. The pilgrim traffic is however the most important source of revenue for the inhabitants, who let their dwellings to the strangers and guide them to the sacred places and instruct them about ritual duties. The ***muzawwirūn*** here play the same role as the ***muṭawwifūn*** in Mecca. Burton (ii. 189) gives the number of inhabitants as 16,000—18,000, in addition to 400 men in the garrison. Wavell (p. 63) in 1908 put it at 30,000, excluding soldiers and pilgrims, while Batanūnī gave 60,000 including many foreign visitors. The population used to increase gradually by visitors settling often permanently in the sacred city. Of descendants of the old Anṣār there are very few left in Madīna; according to Burckhardt there were only ten families in his time. There are a number of Shīʿīs in the suburbs.

Madīna possessess no sanctuary venerated from remote times like the Kaʿba; on the other hand it possesses compensation for this of inestimable value in Muslim eyes in the mosque which encloses Muḥammad's grave and is the goal of countless pilgrims. Some teachers even put this sanctuary higher than the Meccan one, but this view is not general, and the visiting of this mosque is not obligatory like the pilgrimage to Mecca and also may be undertaken at any time. According to unanimous tradition the Prophet was buried under ʿĀʾisha's house, where also the two first caliphs found their last resting-place. Further, all the earlier stories agree that Muḥammad soon after his arrival in Madīna had a mosque built, which he enlarged after the taking of Khaibar, and they are also agreed that the dwellings of his wives were close by so that ʿĀʾisha's house with the grave could easily have been taken into the mosque. That there is nothing improbable in itself in a mosque having been built in the time of the Prophet is shown by the mention of a rival mosque, Sūra ix. 107 *sqq.*; cf. xxiv. 36. But Caetani, *Annali*, i. 432 *sqq.*, has disputed with important arguments the correctness of the tradition and from various statements drawn the conclusion that originally on the site of the later mosque there was more probably only the *dār* of Muḥammad with a courtyard and various dwellings. If this is right, it is not known who built the mosque; but probably it was erected not long after Muḥammad's death, for the rapidly increasing reverence for the Prophet must very soon have aroused the desire to bring his resting-place into touch with his religion. To this mosque, early built, can then be referred what tradition tells us of Muḥammad's mosque: — a simple building of brick with pillars of palm stems and a roof of branches. According to the same tradition, ʿUmar had it extended and after him ʿUthmān who replaced it by a building of stone and mortar with a roof of teak. When Marwān was governor of Madīna, he had a *maḳṣūra* of coʾoured stones erected; but no important advance was made till the reign of Walīd, who commissioned the then governor, afterwards caliph, ʿUmar b. ʿAbd al-ʿAzīz, in 87/706 to adorn the building in greater splendour. For this ʿUmar used Greek and Coptic builders, and the Byzantine emperor is said to have contributed 1,000 *mithḳāl* of gold and large quantity of mosaic stones towards it. On this occasion four minarets were placed at the corners of the sanctuary and the roofs covered with plates of lead. The mosque remained unaltered till the reign of al-Mahdī. After this Caliph had visited Madīna, it was rebuilt and extended in 162/778-9 and its length was now 300 and its breadth 200 ells. In the following century another restoration was necessary and was carried through by al-Mutawakkil in the year 247/861-2.

Of the mosque which thus came into existence there are very full descriptions by Ibn ʿAbd Rabbihi (d. 328/940), Muḳaddasī (375/985), Ibn Djubair who travelled in the east in the years 578—581/1182—1186, and also Yāḳūt. Of the many details given by these authors only a few can be quoted here. As is quite evident from several of these descriptions, the mosque had the form, always retained later, of an open court-yard covered with sand or gravel, *ṣaḥn*, which was surrounded on all four sides by rows of pillars. In the eastern part of the southern pillared hall was the holy of holies, the tomb of the Prophet, with the tombs of Abū Bakr and of ʿUmar. It is described by Yāḳūt (iv. 458) as a high building, separated at the top only by a space from the roof of the pillared hall. Regarding the relative positions of the three graves there were in his time different views. North of them, according to some traditions, was the tomb of Fāṭima while according to others this was in the general burying ground. The part of the pillared hall lying west of the graves bore the name *al-Rawḍa*, the garden, from an alleged utterance of the Prophet. The total number of pillars is said to have been 290; those in the southern part were stuccoed, with gilded capitals, the others were of marble. The walls were adorned with marble, gold, and mosaic. Along the southern border of the *Rawḍa* ran a barrier, with which several highly venerated relics were associated: — the remains of the trunk of a tree, on which Muḥammad used to lean, and especially his *minbar* or pulpit. According to tradition Muʿāwiya wished to remove this; but immediately a vigorous earthquake began and he abandoned the idea and instead raised it by an upper structure five steps higher. Al-Mahdī later wished to remove this addition, but he was dissuaded from doing this as the nails had been driven into the old *minbar* (Yaʿḳūbī, ed. Houtsma, ii. 283; Ṭabarī, iii. 483; Muhaddasī, ed. de Goeje, p. 82). According to the descriptions it had 8 steps and there was a slab of ebony over the seat which visitors might touch. The remnants of the tree-trunk were kissed and stroked with the hands, an interesting imitation of ancient Arabian religious customs. Among the various treasures of the mosque was the Madīna standard manuscript of the canonical text of the Ḳurʾān prepared by ʿUthmān. The mosque had 19 doors of which only four, two in the east and two in the west, were opened. There were three minarets, two at the corners of the north side and one at the southern corner.

While the Mosque of the Tomb escaped a volcanic eruption in the year 654/1256 it suffered in the same year from a fire due to the carelessness of a caretaker, which destroyed a part of it. An appeal to the caliph of Baghdād for assistance to rebuild it remained unanswered as the ʿAbbāsid dynasty was then tottering before its fall, which was to take place two years later. Only the roof was repaired in the year after the fire in makeshift fashion; the rubble was not even cleared away from the tombs but remained there for over two centuries. Several of the Mamlūk Sulṭāns showed some interest in the sanctuary, among them Baibars I, who, according to Mudjīr al-Dīn (Cairo 1283, p. 434), placed a railing round the tomb of the Prophet and had its roof gilt, while others sent workmen and materials, and notably al-Mansūr Ḳalāʾūn in 678/1279 to mark the site of the tomb built a dome over it covered with plates of lead. Ashraf Saif al-Dīn Ḳāʾit Bey (873—890/1468—1495) was however the first to deal with the mosque in really energetic fashion and he had the minaret at the southeast corner, al-Rāʾisīya, taken down and rebuilt. A great calamity then fell upon the mosque for, in a terrible thunderstorm in 886/1481, it was struck by lightning and partly destroyed, and the library with its valuable manuscripts of the Ḳur'ān perished. Samhūdī, who lost his own library on this occasion, gives an account of the conflagration. The indefatigable Sulṭān however sent a large number of workmen with tools and materials, and in 889/1484 the building was restored and among other alterations the dome over the tomb was enlarged; he also presented the brass railing which surrounds the *maḳṣūra*. On this occasion, the Sulṭān also presented to the town baths and a hypocaust for them, an aqueduct and a water mill, as well as a large number of valuable books to replace those destroyed. Its misfortunes however were not at an end for in 898/1492 it was again struck by lightning; the Rā'isīya at the southeast corner was destroyed and had to be rebuilt. The mosque received its present form by an extension to the north, made by ʿAbd al-Madjīd in 1270/1853—4 which Burton saw before its completion. The many inscriptions which cover the walls, include various Sūras and formulae and the mystical poem *al-Burda*.

The immediate vicinity of the city of the Prophet is of course very rich in places with which are associated anecdotes and traditions of him. The most important of these is the hill of Uḥud with the graves of those who fell for the faith there. It is rivalled by the village of Ḳubā' where Muḥammad on his arrival in his new home stayed from Monday till Thursday (Ibn Hishām, p. 335). The village, which was at that time occupied by the ʿAmr b. ʿAwf, is according to the Arab geographers 2 miles, according to Burckhardt, 3/4 hours from Madīna; to be accurate it is about 3 miles. Tradition marks the spot where the Prophet's camel knelt (*al-mabrak*) and here also was the mosque mentioned in Sūra, ix. 108 built out of piety, as well as its counterpart, the *masdjid al-ḍirār*, destroyed by Muḥammad's orders (cf. Wāḳidī—Wellhausen, p. 411; Ibn Saʿd, iii/i. 32, and above). The mosque of Ḳubā' with its simple minaret was in ruins in Burckhardt's time but has since been replaced by a stone structure.

Bibliography: Samhūdī, *Wafā' al-wafā'*, extr. transl. in Wüstenfeld's *Geschichte der Stadt Medina* (*Abh. Ges. Wiss. Gött.*, vol. ix. [1860]); do., *Khulāṣat al-wafā'*, Būlāḳ 1285; Balādhurī, ed. de Goeje, p. 5 *sqq.*; *BGA*, ed. de Goeje, i. 18; ii. 26; iiii. 80—82; Yāḳūt, *Muʿdjam*, ed. Wüstenfeld, iv. 458—68; Ibn Djubair, ed. de Goeje, p. 189 *sqq.*; Ibn Baṭṭūṭa, *Tuḥfat al-nuẓẓār*, ed. Defremery and Sanguinetti 1853—1858; Eijub Ṣabrī, *Mir'āt-i Medine*. Der-i Seʿādat 1305. — On the Mosque of the Tomb: Ibn ʿAbd Rabbihi, *al-ʿIḳd*, Cairo 1331, iv. 272 *sqq.*; Burckhardt, *Reisen in Arabien*, p. 480—607; Burton, *A Pilgrimage to El-Medinah and Meccah*, ii. (1855), 1 *sqq.*; Wavell, *A modern Pilgrim in Mecca*, 1912, p. 72 *sqq.*; al-Batanūnī, *al-Riḥla al-Ḥidjāzīya*, Cairo 2nd ed. 1329, p. 236 *sqq.*; Ibrāhīm Rifʿat Pāshā, *Mir'āt al-Ḥaramain*, Cairo 1925, vol. i. 383 *sqq.*; K. A. C. Creswell, *Early Muslim Architecture*, vol. i. (Oxford 1932); J. Sauvaget, *La Mosquée Omeyyade de Médine*, Paris 1947 (fundamental). — On Ḳubā' cf. *BGA*, i. 28; iii. 83; Yāḳūt, *Muʿdjam*, iv. 23 *sq.*; Burckhardt, *Reisen in Arabien*, p. 54, 558—561; Burton, *A Pilgrimage*, ii. 195—223. — J. F. Keane, *My Journey to Medinah*, London 1881; E. Rutter, *The Holy Cities of Arabia*, London and New York 1928, 1930, ii. 189 *sqq.*; Lady Evelyn Cobbold, *Pilgrimage to Mecca*, London, n.d., p. 31 *sqq.*; Wellhausen, *Skizzen und Vorarbeiten*, iv. 1 *sqq.* (*Medina vor dem Islam, Die Gemeindeordnung Muhammeds*); Wensinck, *Mohammed en de Joden te Medinah*, 1908, p. 9 *sqq.*; Hirschfeld, *Essai sur l'histoire des Juifs de Médine*, in *REJ*, vii. 167—193; x. 10—31; D. S. Margoliouth, *The Relations between Arabs and Israelites prior to the Rise of Islam*, 1924, p. 57 *sqq.* — On the most recent history of the town, cf. Musil, *Zur Zeitgeschichte von Arabien*, 1918; R. Hartmann, *Die Wahhābiten*, in *ZDPV*, N.S., iii. 176 *sqq.*

MADJŪS (A.), the Zoroastrians. The Greek word μάγος (which itself renders an Īrānian word; cf. old-Persian *magush*, new-Persian *mugh*) passed into Arabic through an Aramaic medium. According to the Arabic lexicographers, Madjūs is a collective like *Yāhūd*; in the singular Madjūsī is to be used; the religion of the Madjūs is called *al-madjūsīya*. The lexicographers cite from the root *m-dj-s* a iind form (*madjdjasa*) and a vth (*tamadjdjasa*). In a poem, cited in the *Lisān* and the *Tādj al-ʿArūs*, the phrase *nār madjūsa* is found; if we only could be sure that this poem is really (as is asserted in the *Lisān*) a composition of Imru 'l-Ḳais and al-Taw'ām al-Yashkurī conjointly, the word would already occur in the oldest Arabic literature extant.

In the Ḳur'ān the word Madjūs occurs once (xxii. 17); with this verse, ii. 62 and v. 69 are to be compared. In these three places the *ahl al-kitāb* [q.v.] are mentioned, but it is only in xxii. 17 that the name Madjūs is also found. In this same verse, however, the *mushrik*'s also are mentioned, who, of course, can by no means be included in the term *ahl al-kitāb*. Now, in Muslim law, the Zoroastrians are, it will be seen, treated as if they belonged to the *ahl al-kitāb*, but this conception cannot be based on the Ḳur'ānic verse xxii. 17. Also the commentators (al-Baiḍāwī, ed. Fleischer, p. 629; al-Zamakhsharī, *Kashshāf*, p. 901; al-Rāzī, *Mafātīḥ al-ghaib*, iv. 554; al-Naisābūrī in marg. al-Ṭabarī, *Tafsīr*, ed. Cairo, xvii. 74 etc.) give nothing that can point to the fact of the Madjūs being, theoretically, *ahl al-kitāb*. The words of al-Rāzī, who states that the Madjūs are those who do not follow a real prophet, but only a *mutanabbi'*, might suggest that he takes Madjūs to be a sect intermediate between the real *ahl al-kitāb* and the *mushrik*'s, the heathen. Al-Naisābūrī also says that the prophet of the Madjūs — who, moreover, are dualists — is no real prophet but a *mutanabbi'*; the *mushrik*'s, on the other hand, have no prophet at all, nor a sacred scripture. In Arabic historical literature the Zoroastrian Persians are themselves occasionally called *mushrik*, e.g. al-Balādhurī, p. 302, 303, 380, 387 (*mushrik*); p. 407 (*kuffār*). Finally it must be added that the Ḳur'ān-verse xxii. 17 seems to be a later addition to this Sūra (cf. Nöldeke-Schwally, *Gesch. des Qorāns*, i. 214: the verse must be Madīnan).

In the *ḥadīth*, which represents the theory of Muslim law, there is not very much to be found on the Madjūs in particular (cf. A. J. Wensinck, *Handbook* s.v. *Madjūs*). The substance of the *ḥadīth* concerning the Magians is that they are to be treated like the *ahl al-kitāb*, and, in consequence, are bound to pay the *djizya*. Practically, the rising Muslim state power could not follow any other way. The subjection of Īrān would have become impossible, had the Arabs considered the Zoroastrians as mere heathens, who were to be given the choice either of Islām or the sword. And, even before that time, to deal with the Zoroastrians of Baḥrain in this rigorous way would have been a grave political fault. Thus tradition, though it also hands down an account of how the Prophet gave the Zoroastrians of Baḥrain the choice of either Islām or death, reports that

ʿAbd al-Raḥmān b. ʿAwf stated that the Prophet had accepted the *djizya* from these Madjūs. This tradition was regarded as authoritative afterwards, and the other, stating that the Prophet refused to consider Madjūs otherwise than as *mushrik*'s, was abandoned (cf. Abū Dāwūd, *Kharādj*, b. 29). ʿAbd al-Raḥmān b. ʿAwf is said to have delilivered his statement on an occasion when the caliph ʿUmar felt doubtful whether he should accept the *djizya* from the Īrānians, or not (cf. al-Balādhurī, p. 267: the Prophet, according to ʿAbd al-Raḥmān, had said: *sunnū bihim sunnat ahl al-kitāb*). There is a tradition relating that ʿUmar, a year before his death, wrote to Djazʿ b. Muʿāwiya regarding the Madjūs, instructing him to put to death every sorcerer (*sāḥir*), to separate each Madjūsī from his wife and children, and to forbid the practice of *zamzama* (the muttering of Zoroastrian prayers, new-Persian *bādj* or *bāž*). Djazʿ began to execute these rigid orders, and ʿUmar refused to accept the *djizya* from the Madjūs, until ʿAbd al-Raḥmān b. ʿAwf asserted that the Prophet had accepted it from the Madjūs of Baḥrain (Abū Dāwūd, *loc. cit.*; Aḥmad b. Ḥanbal, *Musnad*, i. 190, 194; al-Bukhārī, *Ṣaḥīḥ*, *Djizya*, bāb 1). Al-Bukhārī, moreover (ii. 145), cites the following answer given to a Persian ambassador: "Our Prophet has commanded us to fight you, until you serve God, and Him alone, or until you pay the *djizya*". So here likewise the Madjūs are put on the same level as the *ahl al-kitāb*. The determination of the position of the Zoroastrians in respect of the Muslim state, is the main point of the *ḥadīth* concerning them. Moreover, there is a tradition in al-Dārimī, *Farāʾiḍ*, bāb 42, regulating the hereditary portion of Zoroastrians (not altogether clear, however). Other, not very important traditional matter respecting the Madjūs is cited: *Lisān*, viii. 99; Lane, *Lexicon*, s.v. *fiṭra*; cf. the article ḲADARĪYA.

The traditions of the Muslims about Zoroaster are in accordance with their idea of the Zoroastrians being a kind of inferior *ahl al-kitāb*. Al-Ṭabarī relates that Zarādusht b. Isfīmān (Isfīmān is an adaptation of the Avestic Spitama, the name of the ancestor of the family to which Zoroaster belonged) laid claim to the title of a prophet after three years of the reign of king Bishtāsb (the Avestic Wīshtāspa) had elapsed (i. 675 *sq.*); the same historian reports, on the authority of Hishām b. Muḥammad al-Kalbī, that Zarādusht, who by the Madjūs is said to be their prophet, was, according to the learned men of the *ahl al-kitāb*, an inhabitant of Palestine, and a servant of one of the disciples of the prophet Jeremiah. He committed a fraud against his master, who cursed him, so that he became leprous. Zarādusht then went to Ādharbāidjān and began to promulgate the religion called Madjūsīya; afterwards he proceeded to Balkh, where Bishtāsb resided. This king became a convert to the religion of Zarādusht, and compelled his subjects to embrace that religion also (i. 648; cf. al-Thaʿālibī, *Histoire des rois des Perses*, ed. Zotenberg, p. 256).

Another tradition, likewise preserved in al-Ṭabarī's work, brings Zarādusht together with a Jewish prophet *s-m-y* (vocalisation uncertain), who was sent to Bishtāsb, and at his court met with Zarādusht and the sage Djāmāsb (Avestic Djāmāspa, the minister of Wīshtāspa and son-in-law of Zoroaster). Zarādusht is said to have noted down in Persian the teachings which the Jew delivered in Hebrew. Bishtāsb and his father Luhrāsb (Avestic Aurwaṭaspa) had been Ṣābians before *s-m-y* and Zarādusht proclaimed their religion (Ṭabarī, i. 681, 683). These traditions aim at bringing the Zoroastrian faith into a certain connection with the Jewish religion: in the one, Zoroaster is an apostate Jew, in the other, he acts in agreement with a Hebrew prophet. In the *ḥadīth* there is a saying of Ibn ʿAbbās: "When the prophet of the Persians had died, Iblīs wrote for them the lore of the Madjūs" (Abū Dāwūd, *Kharādj*, bāb 29). This isolated tradition might perhaps in some way be connected with the reports about *s-m-y*.

Some Arabic authors, of course, had a better knowledge of Zoroaster and his religion, cf. for instance al-Balādhurī, p. 331, where it is stated that according to the Madjūs, Zarādusht came from Urmiya, and, especially, al-Shahrastānī *Kitāb al-milal* (ed. Cureton, p. 182 *sqq.*), whose scientific treatise, however, contributes nothing to the knowledge of the ideas about Zoroastrianism prevalent among the *faḳīh*'s. It is enough to say, that al-Shahrastānī, whose information goes back to Īrānian sources, gives a succinct, but in general correct account of Zoroaster and the Madjūs, whom he subdivides into three principal sects: the Kayūmarthīya, the Zarwānīya and the Zarādushtīya, the latter, according to him, properly the followers of Zoroaster. The Madjūs are, he rightly remarks, not *ahl al-kitāb*, but, like the dualists, only possessing something like an inspired scripture (*shubhatu kitāb*: p. 179); before the rise of the Madjūsīya, the Persians professed the religion of Ibrāhīm (p. 180).

It appears from historical sources (esp. al-Balādhurī) that, during the Islamic conquest of Arabia, the Zoroastrians living in al-Yaman, ʿUmān and Baḥrain were allowed to pay the *djizya*, as far as they did not adopt Islam spontaneously. Likewise in Armenia the Madjūs were treated on the same foot as the Jews and the Christians.

In Iran the regular treatment of the places which surrendered themselves is the imposition of the *djizya* and the *kharādj*. In some Persian places, however, only a restricted number of men were comprised in the *amān* accorded by treaty. In the following centuries the Zoroastrians remained numerous (cf. al-Masʿūdī, iv. 86) and were left in the free exercise of their religion, although, already at the period of the conquest, there occurred many conversions to Islam (cf. T. W. Arnold, *The Preaching of Islam*, p. 177 *sqq.*) Some instances are given where converts to Islam had to exchange their original name for an Arab one (al-Balādhurī, p. 339, 344).

Although, at least in the first centuries of Islam, the Muslims took a largely tolerant attitude, the emigration of Zoroastrians to India began as early as the viii^th^ century; the first group is said to have left Khurāsān about 750 and to have arrived in 766 at Diu in the Golf of Cambay.

The position of the Zoroastrians in Iran became worse in course of time. Their number seems to have greatly diminished by the disturbances which ensued after the death of Nādir Shāh (1160/1747), when the Afghans destroyed the Zoroastrian quarter at Kirmān, and by the war between Agha Muḥammad Khān Ḳadjar and Luṭf ʿAlī Khān. In modern times the number of Zoroastrians in Persia is estimated by v. Houtum-Schindler (1879) at 8.400 at all; by Browne (1887-8) at 7.000—8.000 for Kirmān and Yazd and environs alone. The statements for the xix^th^ century are however very divergent (cf. Karaka, *History of the Parsis*, 1884, i. 55); in *The Middle East* 1948 p. 217 the total number of Zoroastrians in Persia is given as 10.000.

In some places, notably at Yazd, their situation was not too good in the xix[th] century. But in 1882 the Indian Parsis obtained the abolition of the *djizya* of the Zoroastrians in Yazd and Kirmān by means of the "Persian Zoroastrian Amelioration Fund". In the xx[th] century tolerance has become more and more spread in Iran under the influence of the revised appreciation of the Iranian past. The name of *gabar*, which had a contemptuous flavour, fell into disuse.

The Zoroastrians who had emigrated to India, the Parsis, have developed into a properous community; in the course of the xviii[th] century Bombay became their chief centre. Their history and peregrinations have been described in the *Ḳiṣṣa-i Sandjān* by Bahman Kai Kabad from Nawsārī (1600) and the *Ḳiṣṣa-i Zartushtiyān-i Hindūstān* by Dastūr Shapurdji Manockdji Sandjana (1735—1805; cf. J. J. Modi in *Journal of the K. R. Cama Oriental Institute*, xvii (1930), xix (1931), xxv (1938).

The name Madjūs has also been extended to peoples who had nothing to do with Zoroastrianism, but who, being neither Jews, nor Christians, nor Muslim converts, had to be treated, for practical purposes, as *dhimmīs* paying the *djizya*. This was done in North Africa and Spain by the Madhhab of al-Awzāʿī and by the Mālikites and the Ḥanafites on the strength of the tradition that the Prophet had accepted the *djizya* from the Madjūs in Baḥrain. So the Berbers were considered as Madjūs, and so also were the Scandinavians who raided the Spanish coast since 844 and with whom occasional peace treaties were concluded (cf. R. Brunschvig in *Annales de l'Institut d'Etudes Orientales*, Alger, t. vi. 1942—47, p. 112; Dozy, *Recherches*, ii. 250 sqq.; *Rerum Normannicarum fontes Arabici*..... collegit et ed. A. Seippel, i, Christiania 1896).

MAḌMŪN is 1. in the legal institution of the *ḍamān* "surety", a term which occurs in the following connections: *maḍmūn ʿanhu* "debtor", *maḍmūn lahu* or *ʿalaihi* "creditor", *maḍmūn* (*bihi*) "pawn". For the parties to the agreement and the article in question in a bond, the rules hold which apply to all other contracts.

2. In the chapters of the Fiḳh books which deal with the law of obligations, *maḍmūn* is used for the thing for which one is liable or responsible, i.e. is bound to replace. In this way *ḍamān* comes to mean in the wider sense, "liability, obligation to restore" in contracts. This liability consists either in the producing of something identical (*mithl*) i.e. of a thing of the same quality and quantity (*ṣifat wa-wazn[an]*), e.g. in edible things (*mithliyāt*) which are measured by quality, weight, or number (*mawzūn wa-makīl wa-maʿdūd*) or in the value of the thing (*ḳima*) e.g. in nonedible things (*muḳawwamāt*) which have a special individuality, and are therefore *ʿain* = species.

Bibliography: For details cf. the pertinent chapters in the Fiḳh books and Sachau, *Muhammed. Recht*, p. 385 *sqq.*; Khalīl, *Mukhtaṣar*, transl. Santillana, ii. 249 *sqq.*; Tornauw, *Moslem. Recht*, p. 139 *sqq.*; Juynboll, *Handleiding*[4], p. 384: Bersträsser, *Grundzüge*, p. 64.

MADRASA. Name of an institution where the Islāmic sciences are studied. In the following the different educational institutions of Islām will be treated.

I. Children's Schools.

These were older than Islāmic science, since at the very beginning of Islām reading and writing were taught in Arabia. In Madīna the teachers were often Jews (see Balādhurī, p. 473 *infra*; cf. the name *rabbānī* for the teacher: Sūra, iii. 79; v. 44, 63; Bukhārī, *ʿIlm*, bāb 10; Yaʿḳūbī, ii. 243); but ability to write was not so common here as in Mecca. After the battle of Badr, several captured Meccans were released to teach writing in Madīna (*Kāmil*, ed. Wright, p. 171). A contemporary of ʿUmar's, Djubair b. Ḥaiya, who was later an official and governor, was a teacher (*muʿallim kuttāb*) in a school in Ṭā'if (Ibn Ḥadjar, *Iṣāba*, Cairo 1323, i. 235). Muʿāwiya, who had acted as the Prophet's amanuensis, took a great interest in the education of the young. They learned reading, writing, counting, swimming and a little of the Ḳur'ān and the necessary observances of religion. Famous men like al-Ḥadjdjādj and the poets Kumait and Ṭirimmāh are said to have been schoolmasters (Lammens, *Moʿâwia*, p. 329 *sqq.*, 360 *sqq.*). The main subject taught was *adab*, so that the schools of the children were called *madjālis al-adab* (*Aghānī*, xviii., 2nd Cairo ed., p. 101), and the teacher was called *mu'addib*, also *muʿallim* or *mukattib* (al-Makkī, *Ḳūt al-ḳulūb*, i. 158, 8), in modern times *fiḳīh* (s. Lane, *Manners and Customs*, p. 61). The teacher was as a rule held in little esteem, perhaps a relic of the times when he was a slave, but we also find distinguished scholars teaching in schools; thus Daḥḥāk b. Muzāḥim, the exegist, traditionist and grammarian, who died in 105 or 106 (723 or 724), had a school in Kūfa, said to have been attended by 3,000 children, where he used to ride up and down among his pupils on an ass (Yāḳūt, *Udabā'*, iv. 272 *sq.*). As language was of the utmost importance, we find a Beduin being appointed and paid as a teacher of the youth in Baṣra (*ibid.*, ii. 239). Schools spread during the Umaiyad period, and instruction was also given at home in the houses (see Haneberg, *Schul- und Lehrwesen*, p. 4 *sq.*). Under the Fāṭimids, there was a boys' school in the palace where the youth of the upper classes was prepared for the Caliph's service (Maḳrīzī, ii. 209—211). It is natural to find a children's school also attached to the mosque as education became more and more centred round the Ḳur'ān. In the Mosque of the Umaiyads children were taught (Ibn Djubair, p. 272; Ibn Baṭṭūṭa, i. 213) and the teachers had special rooms at the north door of the mosque (Ibn Djubair, p. 271). In Palermo Ibn Ḥawḳal counted 300 *katātib*, the teachers of which were held in high esteem (*BGA*, ii. 87; see however 2nd ed. p. 126).

In the sixth century there were also many independent schools. In Cairo, Ibn Djubair found a large number of schools mainly for orphans and poor children and the teachers and pupils were maintained by the Sulṭān (p. 52) and in Damascus he saw a similar large institution (p. 272). In Jerusalem Ṣalāḥ al-Dīn built a school (v. Berchem, *Corpus*, 11/i., 108 *sq.*). As a rule the school was placed close to the mosque and beside a drinking fountain. During the Mamlūk period, nearly every founder of a madrasa built in connection with it a similar institution for orphans and poor children, who received free instruction and sometimes also maintenance in it (see Maḳrīzī, s.v. *madāris*, *passim*). The object of one such school beside the mosque of Ibn Ṭūlūn is thus defined by Lādjīn as "to teach the orphans of the Muslims to recite the Book of God, the Exalted, and also for other works pleasing to

God and the various kinds of piety" (Maḳrīzī, iv. 41). Elsewhere it is often said to be "to teach them the Ḳur'ān". In the Maghrib also, the children only learned the Ḳur'ān, i.e. to recite it, while in Andalus they also learned reading and writing (*kitāb*), poems and a little grammar. In Ifrīḳiya they learned, beside the Ḳur'ān, some Ḥadīth and a little of other sciences (Ibn Khaldūn, *Muḳaddima, faṣl* vi., 32).

The children's school is called *maktab* or *kuttāb*; those founded for poor children *kuttāb sabīl* or *maktab sabīl*. The word *sabīl* characterizes the school as a public benevolent institution. Cf. on elementary education: Goldziher, art. *Education*, in Hastings, *Encycl. of Rel. and Ethics*; Mez, *Renaissance*, p. 177 *sq.*; Lane, *Manners and Customs*; Snouck Hurgronje, *Mekka*, ii. 144 *sqq.*

II. Islāmic studies in the Mosque to the end of the Fāṭimid period.

The new studies stimulated by Islām were from their nature associated with the mosque. The learning by heart and the understanding of the Ḳur'ān formed the starting-point and next came the study of Ḥadīth, by which the proper conduct for a Muslim had to be ascertained. The Prophet was often questioned on matters of belief and conduct, in or outside the mosque (Bukhārī, *ʿIlm*, bāb 6, 52; 23, 24, 26, 46). After the death of the Prophet, his Companions were consulted in the same way and scientific study began with the collection and arrangements of ḥadīths. This process is reflected in the ḥadīths themselves. According to them, even the Prophet in his lifetime was asked about ḥadīths (*ibid.*, bāb 4, 14, 33, 50, 51, 53); the Prophet sits in a mosque surrounded by a *ḥalḳa* and instructs this hearers; the latter repeat the ḥadīths three times until they have learned them (*ibid.*, bāb 8, 30, 35, 42). The Prophet sent teachers of the Ḳur'ān to the tribes, and so did ʿUmar in the year 17 (*ibid.*, bāb 25). The necessity of *ʿilm* is strongly emphasized. Jewish influence is perhaps to be recognized when learning is compared with the drinking of water (Bukhārī, *ʿIlm*, bāb 20; cf. *Proverbs*, xviii. 4.; *Pirḳē Abōth*, i. 4, 11) and the teachers are called *rabbāniyūn* (Bukhārī, *ʿIlm*, bāb 10). A special class of students, *ahl al-ʿilm*, was formed who spread the knowledge of traditions throughout Muslim lands (*ibid.*, bāb 7, 12). They collected people around them to instruct them in the most necessary principles of the demands of Islām. In this simple form of instruction which was indistinguishable from edifying admonitions lay the germ of Islāmic studies. The knowledge imparted is *ʿilm* or *ḥikma* (*ibid.*, bāb 15). The typical scholar, in addition to the *ḳāri'*, was the *muḥaddith* (*ibid.*, bāb 29), although new branches of study were soon added as a result of contact with lands with older cultures, notably linguistic studies and in this connection the study of the old poetry, philosophical and speculative studies, logic, etc. The learned man of the old period was also called *faḳīh* (Ṭabarī, ii. 1183, 1266; *Aghānī*, 2nd ed. viii. 89; Ibn Saʿd, v. 167). Even after the new branches of learning were added to the older studies, the mosque remained the chief centre of instruction, just as in Christian countries studies were prosecuted in connection with monasteries and churches.

We hear of a madjlis for studies in the Madīna mosque in the first century A.H. (*Aghānī*, i. 48; iv. 162 *sq.*). Yazīd b. Abī Ḥabīb, sent by ʿUmar b. ʿAbd al-ʿAzīz as muftī to Egypt, is said to have been the first to teach in Egypt (Suyūṭī, *Ḥusn al-muḥāḍara*, i. 131); he is mentioned along with another as teacher of al-Laith (Kindī, *Wulāt*, p. 89) and the latter, upon whose pronouncements fatwā's were issued, had his *ḥalḳa* in the mosque (*Ḥusn*, i. 134). ʿUmar II had before this sent al-Nāfiʿ, the mawlā of Ibn ʿUmar, to Egypt to bring them the *sunan* (*ibid.*, p. 130). He also sent an able reciter of the Ḳur'ān to the Maghrib as ḳāḍī to teach the people *ḳirā'a* (*ibid.*, p. 131). Education was arranged for by the government by allowing suitable people to give instruction in addition to their regular office. The first teachers in the mosques were the *ḳuṣṣāṣ*, as a rule ḳāḍīs, whose discourses dealt with the interpretation of the Ḳur'ān and the proper conduct of divine service. Their *mawʿiẓa* was the direct continuation of the moral instruction given by the old Companions (cf. Bukhārī, *ʿIlm*, bāb 12). The instruction started in the mosque of ʿAmr was continued for centuries. In the third century A.H., al-Shāfiʿī taught various subjects here every morning till his death (204/820) (Suyūṭī, *Ḥusn al-muḥāḍara*, i. 134; Yāḳūt, *Udabā'*, vi. 383). It was after his time that the study of fiḳh came markedly to the front and the great teachers used at the same time to give fatwās (cf. *Ḥusn*, i. 182 *sq.*).

Arabic philological studies were ardently prosecuted in the mosques. The interest of the early Arabs in rhetoric survived under Islām; the faḳīh Saʿīd b. al-Musaiyab (d. 95/713-4; cf. Ṭabarī, ii. 1266) discussed Arabic poetry in his madjlis in the mosque in Madīna; but it was still thought remarkable that poems should be dealt with in a mosque (*Aghānī*, i. 48; iv. 162 *sq.*). In the year 256/870, al-Ṭabarī by request dictated the poems of al-Ṭirimmāḥ beside the Bait al-Māl in the Mosque of ʿAmr (Yāḳūt, *Udabā'*, vi. 432). In the chief mosque of Baṣra, the *aṣḥāb al-ʿarabīya* sat together (*ibid.*, iv. 135). In Baghdād al-Kisā'ī gave his lectures in the mosque which bears his name. At quite an early date we read of special apartments (which were certainly also lecture-rooms) for authorities on the Ḳur'ān, for, according to al-Wāḳidī, ʿAbd Allāh b. Umm Maktūm lived in Madīna in the *dār al-ḳurrā'* (*Ḥusn al-muḥāḍara*, ii. 142).

As is evident from the examples quoted, studies were not only prosecuted in the chief mosques but also in other mosques. In Egypt, not only the Mosque of ʿAmr but also the chief mosques of later date were important centres of study. As soon as the Mosque of Ibn Ṭūlūn was founded, a pupil of al-Shāfiʿī began to lecture in it on Ḥadīth (*Ḥusn al-muḥāḍara*, ii. 139). During the Fāṭimid period this was continued. In the year 361/972, the Azhar Mosque was finished. Soon afterwards, the new Shīʿī ḳāḍī, ʿAlī b. al-Nuʿmān, lectured in it on Fiḳh according to his school; in 378/988 al-ʿAzīz and his vizier Yaʿḳūb b. Killis founded 35 lectureships, and in addition to their salaries the lecturers were given quarters in a large house built beside the mosque (Maḳrīzī, iv. 49; Sulaimān Raṣad al-Ḥanafī, *Kanz al-djawhar fī ta'rīkh al-Azhar*, p. 32 *sqq.*).

III. Special Institutions for Studies.

In the descriptions of the larger mosques the libraries are often mentioned. These collections were gradually brought together from gifts and bequests, and it was a common thing for a scholar to give his books for the use of the *muslimīn* or *ahl al-ʿilm* (e.g. al-Khaṭīb al-Baghdādī: Yāḳūt, *Udabā'*, i. 252; cf. iv. 287). Many other libraries were semi-public. These often supplemented the libraries of the mosques, because they contained books in which the mosques were not much interested, notably on logic, falsafa, geometry, astronomy, music, medicine and alchemy; the latter were called *al-ʿulūm al-ḳadīma* or *ʿulūm al-awāʾil* (cf. Goldziher, in *Abh. Pr. Ak. W.*, 1915, phil. hist. kl. no. 8, Berlin 1916). The academy, *bait al-ḥikma*, founded by al-Maʾmūn (198—218/813—833) in Baghdād, deserves first mention. It recalls the older academy founded in Gundeshāpūr to which Manṣūr had invited Georgios b. Gabrīʾēl as head of the hospital; he also translated works from the Greek (Ibn Abī Uṣaibiʿa, i. 123 *sq.*). In the new academy there was a large library, and it was extended by the translations which were made by men qualified in the above-mentioned fields; there was also an astronomical observatory attached to the institution, in which there were also apartments for the scholars attached to it (*Fihrist*, ed. Flügel, p. 243; cf. Ibn al-Ḳifṭī, *Taʾrīkh al-ḥukamāʾ*, p. 98). When the caliph al-Muʿtaḍid (279—289/892—902) built himself a new palace, he had apartments and lecture-rooms in an adjoining building for men learned in every science, who received salaries to teach others (Maḳrīzī, iv. 192 ₂, *sqq.*; *Ḥusn al-muḥāḍara*, ii. 142).

Private individuals of wealth continued benefactions on these lines. ʿAlī b. Yaḥyā, who died in 275/888 and was known as al-Munadjdjim, had a palace with a library, which was visited by those in search of knowledge from all lands; they were able to study all branches of learning in this institution, called *khizānat al-ḥikma*, without fee; astronomy was especially cultivated (Yāḳūt, *Udabāʾ*, v. 467). In Mawṣil, Djaʿfar b. Muḥammad al-Mawṣilī (d. 323/935) founded a *dār al-ʿilm* with a library in which students worked daily at all branches of knowledge and were even supplied with free paper. The founder lectured on poetry in it (*ibid.*, ii. 420). In the fourth century al-Maḳdisī visited in Shīrāz a large library founded by ʿAḍud al-Dawla (367—372/977—983) to which people of standing had access. The books were arranged in cases and listed in catalogues and the library (*khizānat al-kutub*) was administered by a director (*wakīl*), an assistant (*khāzin*) and an inspector (*mushrif*) (*BGA*, iii. 449). Similar institutions are known in Baṣra, Rām-Hurmuz, Raiy and Karkh (*ibid.*, p. 413; Yāḳūt, *Udabāʾ*, ii. 315; Ibn Taghrībirdī, ed. Popper, ii. p. 51 *sq.*).

In Cairo they are well known under the Fāṭimids. In their palace, they had a library which was said to be the largest in Islām. It had about 40 rooms full of books and all branches of knowledge were represented; they had for example 1,200 copies of al-Ṭabarī's History and 18,000 books on the "old learning" (Maḳrīzī, ii. 253—255). The vizier Yaʿḳūb b. Killis founded an academy with stipends for scholars and spent 1,000 dīnārs a month on it (Yaḥyā b. Saʿīd, ed. Tallquist, fol. 108ᵃ; Ibn Khallikān, *Wafayāt*, Cairo 1310, ii. 334; cf. Maḳrīzī, iv. 192). It was overshadowed by the "House of Knowledge" (*dār al-ʿilm* or *dār al-ḥikma*) founded by al-Ḥākim in 395/1005. It contained a library and reading-room as well as rooms for meetings and for classes. Librarians, assistants, with their servants administered it and scholars were given allowances to study there; all branches of learning were represented — astronomy, medicine etc. in addition to the specifically Islāmic subjects. Al-Ḥākim built similar institutions in al-Fusṭāṭ (Maḳrīzī, ii. 334 *sqq.*). The whole institution was closely associated with Shīʿa propaganda, which is obvious from the fact that it was administered by the *dāʿi 'l-duʿāt* who held conferences with the learned men there every Monday and Thursday (Maḳrīzī, iv. 226; Ḳalḳashandī, *Ṣubḥ al-aʿshāʾ*, iii. 487). A similar missionary institute (*dār al-daʿwa*) was built in Ḥalab in 507/1113—4 by the emīr Fakhr al-Mulk (Ibn Taghrībirdī, ed. Popper, ii. p. 360). We may assume that these buildings were also arranged for the performance of the ṣalāt.

With the *dār al-ḥikma*, Islām was undoubtedly continuing Hellenistic traditions. Al-Maḳrīzī mentions a *dār al-ḥikma* of the pre-Islāmic period, where the learned men of Egypt used to work (iv. 377); Ibn Abī Uṣaibiʿa also mentions pre-Islāmic seminaries in Egypt where Hellenistic learning was cultivated (*dār al-ʿilm*, i. 104) and the similarity with the Alexandrine *Museion*, which was imitated in Pergamon and Antioch, for example, is apparent (John W. H. Walden, *The Universities of Ancient Greece*, New York 1919, p. 48—50). Al-Ḥākim's institution was finally closed with the end of the Fāṭimid dynasty (567/1171). Ṣalāḥ al-Dīn had all the treasures of the palace, including the books, sold over a period of ten years. Many were burned, thrown into the Nile, or thrown into a great heap, which was covered with sand so that a regular "hill of books" was formed. The number of books said to have disposed of varies from 120,000 to 2,000,000 but many were saved for new libraries (Maḳrīzī, ii. 253—255; Abū Shāma, *Kitāb al-rawḍatain*, Cairo 1287, i. 200, 268).

Bibliography: A. Mez, *Die Renaissance des Islāms*, 1922; M. Meyerhof, in *SB Pr. Ak. W. ph.-hist. Kl.*, xxiii., 1930, p. 388—429; do. in *BIE*, xv., 1933, p. 109—23; do., in *The legacy of Islam*, 1931, p. 311—55; J. Schacht and N. Meyerhof, *The medicophilosophical controversy between Ibn Butlan of Baghdad and Ibn Ridwan of Cairo*, [Egyptian University] 1937; Olga Pinto, *Le biblioteche degli Arabi nell' età degl' Abbasidi*, Florence, 1928.

IV. Origin and spread of the Madrasa.

While the institutions called the *dār al-ʿilm* devel oped in Fāṭimid countries into centres of Shīʿa propaganda, the madrasa grew up in the east out of similar Sunnī institutions. It is interesting to note that in 395/1005 al-Ḥākim built a Sunnī *dār al-ʿilm* in Cairo (Ibn Taghrībirdī, ed. Popper, ii., p. 64, 105, 106). But after three years, this institution was abolished and its two learned teachers executed. With the growing strength of the Sunna, especially in the Shāfiʿī and Ḥanafī form, many educational institutions arose in the east which had a pronounced Sunnī character (*BGA*, iii. 232, 365, 415). Many teachers built houses of their own, where they dictated ḥadīths and held lectures on fiḳh, e.g. a teacher who died in Merw in 420/1029 (Wüstenfeld, *Imâm Schâfiʿi*, 232). Abū Ḥātim al-Bustī born in 277/890, founded in his native town a school with a library with apartments and allowances for the maintenance of foreign students (*ibid.*, p. 163; cf. 204, 245).

In Naisābūr especially, where studies were vigorously prosecuted in the mosque (e.g. Wüstenfeld, *Schâfiʿi*, 236), many such institutions arose. Thus a special school was built for the Shāfiʿī fiḳh-scholar al-Ṣāʾigh al-Naisābūrī (d. 349/960; *ibid.*, 156; cf. 160). Abū ʿAlī al-Ḥusainī (d. 393/1003) himself founded a school in which to teach ḥadīth and it was attended by 1,000 scholars (*ibid.*, p. 203). Ibn Fūrak (d. 406/1015—6; *ibid.*, p. 216) did the same, likewise Abu 'l-Ḳāsim al-Ḳushairī in 437/1045—6 (*ibid.*, 284); and for Rukn al-Dīn al-Isfarāʾinī (d. 418/1027) a school was built which surpassed all others (*ibid.*, 229). As early as the fourth century, we find al-Maḳdisī praising the very fine *madāris* of Īrān*sh*ahr (*BGA*, iii. 315). In the first half of the fifth century, there were four especially famous madāris in Naisābūr: al-Madrasa al-Baihaḳīya, founded by al-Baihaḳī (d. 458/1066), when he became a teacher in Naisābūr in 441/1049—50 (Wüstenfeld, *Schâfiʿi*, iii. 270), al-Saʿīdīya founded by the emīr Naṣr b. Subuktakīn (governor of Naisābūr in 389/999), one built by Abū Saʿd Ismāʿīl al-Astarābādī and another built for the teacher Abū Isḥāḳ al-Isfarāʾinī. A Niẓāmīya was also built here by Niẓām al-Mulk for the Imām al-Ḥaramain al-Djuwainī (Maḳrīzī, iv. 192; *Ḥusn al-muḥāḍara*, ii. 141 *sq.*). It was an event of great importance when Niẓām al-Mulk (456—485/1064—1092 vizier of the Saldjūḳ sulṭāns Alp Arslān and Malik Shāh) founded the celebrated Niẓāmīya Madrasa in Baghdād; the building was begun in 457/1065 and on the 10th Dhu 'l-Ḳaʿda 459/ Sept. 1067 it was consecrated. It was founded for the Shāfiʿī teacher Abū Isḥāḳ al-Shīrāzī.

The Muslim historians are in some doubt about the history of the madrasa. Niẓām al-Mulk is given the credit of having founded it, but al-Maḳrīzī and al-Suyūṭī point out that *madāris* were already in existence before him and mention the four above named, but, as we have seen, even they were not innovations. Al-Subkī thinks (says al-Suyūṭī) the new feature was that Niẓām al-Mulk endowed scholarships for the students. This again however was nothing new. But the enthusiasm and energy of Niẓām al-Mulk meant the beginning of a new period of brilliance for the Madrasa. The Sulṭān and men of high rank were now interested in it and the type evolved by Niẓām al-Mulk, a school in which the students were boarded, became the prevailing one after his time. We may presume that the older schools also had a place for prayer in them, i.e. they were a kind of mosques. The type of school known to us is built as a complete mosque. Since even the older mosques contained living-rooms which were frequently used by students, there is no difference in principle between the school and the ordinary mosque; only the schools were especially arranged for study and the maintenance of students. This character is expressed by the name *madrasa*, plural *madāris*; it is a genuine Arabic formation from the word *darasa*, "to read", "to study", taken from Hebrew or Aramaic.

In the time of Niẓām al-Mulk and immediately afterwards, the madrasa spread in the ʿIrāḳ, Khurāsān, al-Djazīra etc. He was not content with the two he founded in Naisābūr and Baghdād. There was also a *Madrasa Niẓāmīya* in Balkh (Wüstenfeld, *Schâfiʿi*, 240), in Mawṣil (*ibid.*, p. 319), in Herāt to which al-Shāshī (d. 485/1092) was called from Ghazna (*ibid.*, p. 310) and in Merw (Yāḳūt, iv. 509). The great vizier's rival Tādj al-Mulk (d. 486/1093) founded a *Madrasa Tādjīya* in Baghdād (*ibid.*, p. 311). In Naisābūr, other madrasas were founded at the same time, for example one by al-Manīʿī (d. 463/1070—1; *ibid.*, p. 277) and a Shaṭibīya (*ibid.*, p. 327).

The prosperity of the madāris stimulated by Niẓām al-Mulk in the fifth century survived for a long time in the east. In the sixth century Ibn Djubair (580/1184) mentions some thirty madāris in Baghdād, all in the eastern part of the town, the most notable being the Niẓāmīya, renovated in 504/1110—1 (*Riḥla*, p. 229). In 631/1234, the caliph al-Mustanṣir founded the magnificent Mustanṣirīya as a school for the four rites, each with a teacher and seventy-five students and a teacher for Ḳurʾān and one for Ḥadīth, as well as a physician. Attached to it were a library, baths, hospital and kitchens; there was a clock at the entrance; beside it was a garden where the caliph had a pavilion (*manẓara*) from which he could survey the whole building (cf. Le Strange, *Baghdad*, p. 266 *sq.*; Wüstenfeld, *Akademien der Araber*, p. iv. and 29).

The Niẓāmīya and the Mustanṣirīya survived the destruction of Baghdād by Hūlāgū and both are mentioned at the beginning of the xiiith century by Ibn Baṭṭūṭa (ii. 108 *sq.*) and the building of the latter still exists. Ten others are known of the viiith—ixth century, which were founded for Shāfiʿīs, Ḥanafīs and for the study of Ḳurʾān and Ḥadīth (L. Massignon, *Les Medresehs de Bagdâd*, in *BIFAO*, vii., 1909, p. 77—86; the inscriptions, do., in *MIFAO*, xxxi., 1912). Although the Tatars in 699/1300 destroyed many madāris (Quatremère, *Hist. des Sult. Maml.*, ii/ii. 163 *sq.*), Ibn Baṭṭūṭa shows that in the eighth century there were still flourishing schools in the east. The Mongols also built madāris; Hūlāgū's mother built two madrasas in Bukhārā where 1,000 students studied daily in each (*JA*, ser. 4, xx. 389; Quatremère, *Hist. Sult. Maml.*, 1/i., 56). The period of greatest prosperity of the madāris in Central Asia was under the Tīmūrids, notably in Samarḳand, where Tīmūr built a djāmiʿ "in the Indian style", and his wife a madrasa (Ibn ʿArabshāh, *Vita Timuri*, ed. Manger, 1767, p. 444 *sqq.*; see also Diez, *Kunst der islam. Völker*, p. 99 *sq.*).

In the towns of Mesopotamia and Syria the movement spread from the fifth century onwards.

In Damascus the two rulers Nūr al-Dīn b. Zangī (541—569/1146—1163) and Ṣalāḥ al-Dīn (570—589/ 1174—1193) displayed a munificent activity in this direction as did their emīrs and relatives. This activity was continued into the seventh to ninth centuries so that al-Nuʿaimī (d. 927/1521; s. *JA*, ser. 9, iii.—vii.) can give the following totals: seven *dār al-Ḳurʾān*, sixteen *dār al-hadīth*, three for both Ḳurʾān and Ḥadīth, sixty Shāfiʿī, fifty-two Ḥanafī, four Mālikī and ten Ḥanbalī madāris, also three *madāris al-ṭibb*, all of which belong to the seventh century. The founders were mainly rulers and emīrs, but also included merchants and quite a number of men of learning, and a few women also.

Ṣalāḥ al-Dīn introduced the madrasa into Jerusalem. According to Mudjīr al-Dīn (d. 927/1521), there were thirty-one madāris and monasteries (which were in part used in the same ways as madāris) in direct connection with the Ḥaram area, 29 near it, and sixteen at some distance. Of these some forty are especially called *madrasa*, one a *dār al-Ḳurʾān* and one a *dār al-ḥadīth* (Sauvaire, *Hist. Jérus. et Hébr.*, 1876, p. 139 *sqq.*; v. Berchem, *Corpus*, ii. 1; cf. for Ṣalāḥ al-Dīn: Ibn Khallikān, *Wafayāt*, ii., Cairo 1310, p. 402 *sq.*).

Next to Niẓām al-Mulk, Ṣalāḥ al-Dīn has the greatest reputation as a builder of madrasas. He owes this mainly to the fact that his great activity as a builder lay in countries which became of great importance in the Muslim world, Syria with Palestine, and Egypt. Even before the fall of the Fāṭimids, in the year 566/1171 he had founded in Cairo the Nāṣirīya for Shāfiʿīs and the Ḳamḥīya for Mālikīs; for Shāfiʿīs also the Sharīfīya and notably the great Ṣalāḥīya or Nāṣirīya (for the identity of the two cf. Maḳrīzī, iv. 251, with *Ḥusn al-muḥāḍara*, ii. 142 *sq.*) beside al-Shāfiʿī's mausoleum (*Ḥusn al-muḥāḍara*, ii. 141 *sq.*; Maḳrīzī, iv. 192 *ssqq.*; Ibn Khallikān, ii. 402 *q.*). Those around him emulated this activity.

During the period of the Aiyūbids and Mamlūks the number of madāris increased to an extraordinary degree. In the street called Bain al-Ḳaṣrain there were two long rows of madāris on the site of the old Fāṭimid palace in Cairo (cf. P. Ravaisse, in *MMAF*, i., 1889, p. 409 *sqq.*, pl. 3). Al-Maḳrīzī (d. 845/1442) mentions 73 madāris, fourteen for Shāfiʿīs, four for Mālikīs, ten for Ḥanafīs, three for Shāfiʿīs and Mālikīs, six for Shāfiʿīs and Ḥanafīs, one for Mālikīs and Ḥanafīs, four for all four rites, two exclusively used as *dār al-ḥadīth*, while the rite of twenty-five is not mentioned and four remained unfinished. Of these madāris, according to him, about thirteen were founded before 600, twenty in the seventh century, twenty-nine in the eight century and two after 800.

In Ṣalāḥ al-Dīn's time, the madrasa was also introduced into the Ḥidjāz. In the year 579/1183—4 the governor of ʿAden built in Mecca a madrasa for the Ḥanafīs and in the following year a Shāfiʿī madrasa was also founded there (*Chron. Mekka*, ii. 104). Up to the beginning of the ninth century, eleven madāris are mentioned (*ibid.*, p. 104—107) but others were added (*ibid.*, iii. 177 *sq.*, 211 *sq.*, 225 *sq.*, 351 *sqq.*, 417). In the xviii^th^ century A.D. they ceased entirely to be used for their original purpose (see Snouck Hurgronje, *Mekka*, ii. 229 *sqq.*). Madāris were also built in Madīna (Wüstenfeld, *Medina*, p. 58, 98, 112).

In Asia Minor, madrasas spread under the Saldjūḳs; the oldest known date from the seventh century (Cl. Huart, *Konia*, 1897; Fr. Sarre, *Reise in Kleinasien*, 1896; R. Hartmann, *Im neuen Anatolien*, 1928, p. 106 *sqq.*).

In Tunis, many madāris were erected under the Ḥafṣids (625—941/1228—1534), the oldest being the Madrasat al-Maʿraḍ about 650/1252. In the Chronicle of Tunis (Zarkashī, *Chronique des Almohades et des Hafçides*, transl. E. Fagnan, in *Rec. Not. et Mém. Soc. Arch. Const.*, xxi., 1895, see index) eleven are mentioned. The first madrasa in the Maghrib was, according to Ibn Marzūḳ's *Musnad*, the Madrasa al-Ṣaffārīn built by the Marīnid Abū Yūsuf Yaʿḳūb b. ʿAbd al-Ḥaḳḳ (656—685/1258—1286) in Fās in 684 [also called al-Ḥalfāʾīyīn; see the edition by Levi-Provençal in *Hespéris*, v., 1925, p. 34 (Arabic) = p. 44 (French)]. Other Marīnids and their successors continued the building of madāris in Fās, Tilimsān and other cities (cf. Bel, *Inscriptions de Fés*, in *JA*, ser. 11, x., 1917; xii., 1918; G. Marçais, *Manuel d'Art Musulman*, ii., 1927, p. 465 *sqq.*).

In Spain, according to Ibn Saʿīd (vii^th^ = xiii^th^ century), there were no madrasas; instruction was given in the mosques (al-Maḳḳarī, ed. Dozy, i. 136); in the following century, however, a large madrasa was founded in Granada by the Naṣrid Yūsuf Abu 'l-Ḥadjdjādj in 750/1349 (Almagro Cardenas, in *Boletin de la Real Acad. de la Hist.*, xxvii. 490; Marçais, *op. cit.*, p. 516 *sq.*).

Ibn Khaldūn (808/1406) testifies to the spread of madrasas in Tunis and the Maghrib but laments the decline in education. In al-Andalus, Muslim culture was dying out and after the decline of Ḳurṭuba and Ḳairawān, education in the Maghrib was on a low level; while the old schools in the ʿIrāḳ were no longer of importance, Cairo was a centre of learning to which all made their way, and studies also flourished in Persia (*Muḳaddima*, *faṣl* 6, No. 2). This decline in interest in learning soon became general. The learning of the time lacked vitality and international scholarship was affected by political conditions. In 1517 A.D., Leo Africanus says that the lecture-rooms in Cairo were large and pleasant but the numbers who attended them were small. Some still studied fiḳh, but very few the arts (*Descr. de l'Afr.*, iii. 372, in *Rec. de Voy. et de Doc.*, ed. Schefer, Paris 1896—1898).

V. Madrasa and Mosque.

There was, as already mentioned, no difference in principle between the madrasa and other mosques. Even after the introduction of madāris, the regular mosques remained schools as before. Ibn Baṭṭūṭa, who travelled in the eighth century, in the period when madāris flourished most, attended lectures on Ḥadīth in the Djāmiʿ of Shīrāz and in the Djāmiʿ Manṣūr in Baghdād (ii. 83, 110). In Damascus in 580/1184, Ibn Djubair refers to rooms in the Mosque the Umaiyads, which were used for Shāfiʿī and Mālikī students, who received considerable stipends (*idjrāʾ*, *maʿlūm*) (*Riḥla*, p. 272 supra). In Egypt in the time of al-Maḳrīzī (ninth century), there were 8 rooms for fiḳh studies in the Mosque of ʿAmr (Maḳrīzī, iv. 20, 21). In al-Azhar in the seventh century and later after the earthquake of 702 many lecture-rooms with paid teachers were built (*ibid.*, p. 52), likewise in the Mosque of Ḥākim (*ibid.*, p. 57).

When a particular room was set apart for teaching purposes in a mosque, this was often called a madrasa; for example 6 of the Damascus madāris were in the Mosque of the Umaiyads (*JA*, ser. 9, iii. 410, 432, 437; iv. 262, 270, 481; others: vii. 230). The madrasas were often also built close beside the large mosques so that they practically belonged to them. This was the case in Mecca (*Chron. Mekka*, ii. 104 *sqq.*; cf. Ibn Baṭṭūṭa, i. 324).

Though the madrasa was an independent institution the distinction between madrasa and ordinary mosque was very slight, all the less as sermons were also preached in the madrasa. In the Niẓāmīya in Naisābūr, services were held as soon as it was finished (by ʿAbd al-Raḥīm: Wüstenfeld, *Schâfiʿi*, iii. 285) and the Niẓāmīya in Baghdād had a minbar (Ibn Djubair, p. 219). In Egypt from 569 to 665 there was only one Friday khuṭba, but after this time there was usually a minbar in the larger madrasas.

It was only natural that the *madrasa* should also be called *masdjid* (cf. Ibn Djubair, p. 48). Ibn al-Ḥādjdj in the viii^th^ century still wants to distinguish between *masdjid* and *madrasa* and to give more importance to the former (*Madkhal*, ii. 3, 48). The distinction remained however quite an artificial one and this is also true of the distinction between *madrasa* and *djāmiʿ*. The name madrasa was decided by the main object of the institution and the special style of the building. The name djāmiʿ was only given if the Friday service was held in it.

The connection between mausoleum and mosque was also found with the madrasa. The tomb of the founder was placed in Nūr al-Dīn's madrasa in Damascus (Ibn Djubair, p. 284, *sq.*) and during the Mamlūk period it was the regular custom for the founder of a madrasa to be buried under a ḳubba in it.

On education and the madrasa in general cf. also F. Wüstenfeld, *Die Akademien der Araber und ihre Lehrer*, Göttingen 1837; Kremer, *Culturgeschichte*, 1877, ii. 479 *sqq.*; Haneberg, *Abhandlung über das Schul- und Lehrwesen der Muhammedaner im Mittelalter*, 1850; v. Berchem, *Corpus Inscr. Arab.*, i. 252—269; G. Gabrieli, *Manuale di Bibliografia Musulmana*, i. 1916, p. 109 *sqq.*; Johs. Pedersen, in *Islamic Culture*, iii., 1929, p. 525—37; A. Talas, *La Madrasa Nizamiyya et son histoire*, Paris 1939.

VI. Monasteries.

It was quite a common thing for devout men to live permanently in the mosque, e.g. in the minaret or somewhere else on the roof or in subsidiary buildings or in a cell in the mosque. Such a cell which can be used for study or for meditation is called *zāwiya*, lit. corner (Ibn Djubair, p. 240, 245, 266; Maḳrīzī, iv. 20; cf. Greek γωνία; see Dozy, *Supplément*, s.v.). Pious ascetics however had retained from the older religion the custom of living in special monasteries e.g. in Djawlān in the fourth century (*BGA*, iii. 188); Muslim historians trace these back to the time of the Companions (Maḳrīzī, iv. 272 *sq.*). In the fourth century ascetics and Ṣūfīs, especially the Karrāmīya [q.v.] or Kirrāmīya (cf. Mez, *Renaissance*, p. 273), had quite a number of monasteries (*khawāniḳ*, also *khuwāniḳ*, sing. *khānaḳāh*) in Farghāna, Marw al-Rūdh, Samarḳand, Djurdjān, Ṭabaristān etc. (*BGA*, iii. 323, 365); in Jerusalem and in Egypt also the Kirrāmīya had their monasteries in which they held *dhikr* (*ibid.*, p. 179, 182, 202).

Another term for monastery, *ribāt* (plur. *rubuṭ*) [q.v.], designated properly speaking a dwelling for men who waged the *djihād* on the frontier, but the word was also used in the meaning of Khānaḳāh by Ṣūfīs, who waged a spiritual *djihād* (cf. Maḳrīzī, iv. 292 *sq.*). When Ibn Marzūḳ says that they had only two *rubuṭ* of the eastern kind (in Safī and Salā: *Hespéris*, v. 36, 71), it is doubtful whether he means an establishment of Ṣūfīs or of ghāzīs. Rubuṭ, probably of a military character, are frequently mentioned in the East in the fourth century (*BGA*, iii. 303, 354, 415), but the *ribāṭ* had its greatest development in the West [cf. RIBĀṬ]. The original distinction between *khānaḳāh* and *ribāṭ* is never quite forgotten; as late as the beginning of the eighth century we find *ribāṭ* used of a barracks (Maḳrīzī, iv. 276). Ibn Baṭṭūṭa shows that the word *khānaḳāh* had not reached the west; here the old Arabic term *zāwiya* was used (Ibn Baṭṭūṭa, i. 71; *khānaḳāh* however in Ibn Marzūḳ, *Hespéris*, v. 35 *sq.*). But usually we find the three terms used without any definite distinction being made between them (*ṣawmaʿa* also seems to be used in the *Rawḍ al-ḳirṭās* of a Muslim monastery; ed. Tornberg, p. 18, 143); for all three names are applied to Ṣūfī monasteries, which also take in strangers, i.e. are used as hospices.

Ibn Baṭṭūṭa mentions many monasteries in the ʿIrāḳ and Persia. Beside the tomb of al-Rifāʿī, not far from Wāsiṭ, was a ribāṭ, which he calls *riwāḳ*, where "thousands of poor men", i.e. Ṣūfīs, lived (ii. 4). In al-Lūr especially, he found a vast number of monasteries; the sulṭān there built 460 *zawāyā* and spent one third of his revenues on them and on the madāris (ii. 31).

For Syria, Ibn Djubair testifies to the flourishing monasteries which were often regular palaces and he says that the names *khānaḳāh* and *ribāṭ* are used indiscriminately (p. 243, 271, 284); the word *khānaḳāh* sounded strange to him as a westerner, as to Ibn Baṭṭūṭa (p. 284). Nevertheless al-Nuʿaimī distinguishes the three terms and mentions 29 khawāniḳ, 23 rubuṭ and 26 zawāyā. The oldest khānaḳāh mentioned by him (Duwaira) was founded for a learned man who died in 401 (Sauvaire, in *JA*, ser. 9, v. 269, 377, 387 *sqq.*).

It was similar with Egypt. The first khānaḳāh was built by Ṣalāḥ al-Dīn in 569 in Cairo (al-Ṣāliḥīya, originally called Dār Saʿīd al-Suʿadā: Maḳrīzi, iv. 273), the next in the seventh century by Baibars al-Bunduḳdārī, who also founded many monasteries in Syria (*ibid.*, p. 282, 298). Of *khawāniḳ*, al-Maḳrīzī mentions 22 (Ibn Duḳmāḳ only one); of the sixth century: one, seventh: one, eighth: 18, ninth: one. Of rubuṭ 12 (Ibn Duḳmāḳ 8); of the seventh century: 9, of the eighth: one, besides 5 on al-Ḳarāfa. Of zawāyā 26 (Ibn Duḳmāḳ 9); these were mainly outside the town and were obviously quite small, often being simply the house, later the tomb of some devout man. The oldest dated from the sixth century. In Jerusalem also Ṣalāḥ al-Dīn built a *khānaḳāh* (v. Berchem, *Corpus*, ii., 1, p. 87 *sqq.*). Among the khawāniḳ, zawāyā and rubuṭ in this city the last named seem to have been specially intended as hostels for pilgrims (*ibid.*, p. 197 *sqq.*; see also Sauvaire, *Jérus. et Hébron*, index). In Mecca 50 rubuṭ are mentioned; the oldest dated before 400 (*Chron. Mekka*, ii. 108—115). At places of pilgrimage, the monasteries played an important part as hostels but even in other places they also gave accommodation to strangers. Ibn Baṭṭūṭa on his travels usually stayed in them (he calls them *zawāyā*) but he also lodged in *madāris*, which were generally used as hospices (cf. Quatremère, *Hist. Sult. Maml.*, II/ii. 35, note). Some of these institutions were convents for single women (Maḳrīzī, iv. 293 *sq.*).

The main object of monasteries, however, was to afford Ṣūfīs a home and place for their devotional exercises. In the khānaḳāh of Baibars founded in 706, 400 Ṣūfīs were maintained (Maḳrīzī, iv. 276 *infra*) and in the khānaḳāh Siryāḳūs 100 (*ibid.*, p. 285). They were given lodging, food, clothing and money; there were often baths attached to them. The building was arranged for *dhikr* exercises, and also for ṣalāts. A ribāṭ may be called a masdjid (Maḳrīzī, iv. 294; cf. *khānaḳāh* and *masdjid*, p. 282). The monastery founded by Ṣalāḥ al-Dīn was actually given a minaret in 780 (*miʾdhana*) and it is recorded that people used to wear sandals to walk in the *ṣaḥn* (Maḳrīzī, iv. 275 *infra*). There might therefore be an imām on the staff of the khānaḳāh (*ibid.*, p. 287). We also sometimes find a khānaḳāh built close to a large mosque like the khānaḳāh of Āḳbughā beside the Azhar Mosque (*ibid.*, p. 292; cf. p. 289: Ḳūsūn), or the founder built a masdjid for the Friday ṣalāt beside the monastery (Siryāḳūs, *ibid.*, p. 285). At a later date, we find the monasteries with a minbar for the Friday and festival khuṭbas (*ibid.*, p. 297) and al-Muʾaiyad made a house, that had been begun before he came to the throne, into a *djāmiʿ wa-khānaḳāh* (*ibid.*, p. 234 *infra*). Baibars al-Bunduḳdārī was buried in his khānaḳāh and the monasteries had as a rule tombs, either of the founder, or of devout men wo had lived in them.

The development of the monastery is analogous to that of the madrasa, because learning and manifestation of piety are inseparable in Islām. Learning was also cultivated in the monasteries. ʿAbd al-Laṭīf (d. 629/1231) lectured in a ribaṭ in Baghdād on *uṣūl*, *ḥadīth*, etc. (Ibn Abī Uṣaibiʿa, ii. 203) and a Ribāṭ al-Khātūnī is mentioned here, which had a library (Ibn al-Ḳifṭī, ed. Lippert, p. 269). There are other references to libraries in monasteries (see for Marw: Yāḳūt, iv. 509). In the Khānaḳāh Shaikhū founded in 756, an extensive course of lectures, Fiḳh according to all four Madhāhib, Ḥadīth and Iḳrāʾ (Maḳrīzī, iv. 283), was given. In the Ribāṭ al-Āthār in the eighth century, instruction was given in Shāfiʿī Fiḳh (*ibid.*, p. 296); the Ḥanafī madrasa al-Djamālīya (730) was also a khānaḳāh (*ibid.*, p. 238 *supra*); they had a common director.

In the eighth and ninth century this combination of the two institutions became quite frequent, for example in the Niẓāmīya in Cairo of the year 757 (v. Berchem, *Corpus*, i. 242 *sqq.*), in the mausoleums of Barsbāi, 835 (*ibid.*, p. 365 *sq.*; cf. Ibn Iyās, ii. 21, 22, 41), of al-Malik al-Ashraf Ināl, 855—860 (*ibid.*, No. 271 *sqq.*) and of Ḳā'it Bāi, 879 (*ibid.*, p. 431 *sqq.*). In the east, Ibn Baṭṭūṭa found the same relationship, for example in Shīrāz and in Kerbelā' (ii. 78 *sq.*, 88, 99) and this is what he means when he says the Persians call the zāwiya madrasa (ii. 30, 32). In the west, he lauds his own sovereign, who had built a splendid zāwiya in Fās (i. 84); here also learning and Ṣūfism were associated (see the quotation in Dozy, *Supplément*, s.v. *zāwiya*) and the zāwiya still plays an important part in North Africa [cf. ZĀWIYA]. — Cf. on the monasteries: v. Berchem, *Corpus*, i. 163 *sqq.*, 174 *sq.*; A. Mez, *Die Renaissance des Islāms*, 1922, Index, s.v. Klöster.

VII. The subjects taught and the methods of instruction.

As already explained, in the earliest period the principal subjects studied in the mosque were Ḳur'ān and Ḥadīth to which was added the study of the Arabic language. In Bukhārī (*Kitāb al-ʿIlm*) *ʿilm* still means Ḥadīth but, with the development of the systems of law and theology, these were also taught in the mosques. In the mosque of al-Manṣūr in Baṣra, al-Ashʿarī heard al-Djubbā'ī expound the Muʿtazila *kalām* (Wüstenfeld, *Schâfiʿî*, p. 131); closely connected with this was methodology (*al-mudhākara wa 'l-naẓar*: cf. Yāḳūt, *Udaba'*, vi. 383). But many different subjects could also be taught. Al-Khaṭīb al-Baghdādī, who taught in Manṣūr's Djāmiʿ in Baghdād, lectured on his history of Baghdād (Yāḳūt, *Udabā'*, i. 246 *sq.*). Philosophy proper however disappeared from the mosques. In Spain, we are told, *falsafa* and *tandjīm* were only cultivated in secret, as those who studied them were branded as zindīḳ, even stoned or burned (Maḳḳarī, ed. Dozy, i. 136). The madāris were mainly established to teach the systems of fiḳh and originally each school was intended to represent only one madhhab. Where the four madhāhib are represented in one school, one can speak of four madāris, e.g. *al-Madāris al-ṣāliḥīya* (Maḳrīzī, iv. 209, 282).

The ordinary madāris however included other subjects beside the study of fiḳh alone. Special mention is made of *naḥw* (al-Ṣāḥibīya: Maḳrīzī, iv. 205). In the Niẓāmīya in Baghdād and in other madāris in the east, philological studies were prosecuted (cf. Yāḳūt, *Udabā'*, v. 423 *sq.*; vi. 409). The custom, often occurring before Niẓām al-Mulk's time, of founding a *dār al-ḥadīth* was continued after him, e.g. in Cairo and Damascus. In 604/1207 al-Malik al-Muʿaẓẓam built beside the Ṣakhra mosque a *Madrasa naḥwiya*, exclusively for Arabic linguistic studies (Sauvaire, *Hist. Jér. et Hébr.*, p. 86, 140) and schools for special subjects were not rare (cf. Subkī, *Muʿīd*, ed. Myhrmann, p. 153). Al-Subkī mentions, in addition to the special Ḥadīth schools, also *madāris al-tafsīr* and *madāris al-naḥw*.

In his *Muḳaddima* (*faṣl* 6, No. 4 *sqq.*), Ibn Khaldūn gives a survey of the divisions of Islāmic studies. They are divided into *ʿulūm ṭabīʿīya* and *naḳlīya*. The former are based on observation by the senses and deduction and are therefore also called *falsafīya* or *ʿaḳlīya*, the latter are dependent on revelation by the lawgiver (*al-wāḍiʿ al-sharʿī*), and are therefore based on special transmission. The *ʿulūm naḳlīya* therefore comprise all branches of knowledge which owe their existence to Islām, namely *Ḳur'ān*, i.e. *tafsīr* and the seven *ḳirā'āt* (No. 5), *ḥadīth* with the sciences auxiliary to it, including *al-nāsikh wa 'l-mansūkh*, *muṣṭalaḥ al-ḥadīth* (No. 6), *al-fiḳh* with special emphasis on *al-farā'iḍ*, the law of inheritance (No. 7—8), *uṣūl al-fiḳh* with the principles of law including methods of deduction and the differences between the madhāhib (No. 9), *al-kalām*, theology, which is *naḳlīya* in as much as it is really a further development of *īmān* which comes under the head of religious duties, but is *ʿaḳlīya* in its nature since it is entirely based on abstract proofs (No. 10), *al-taṣawwuf*, something like practical theology (No. 11), *taʿbīr al-ru'yā*, interpretations of visions (No. 12).

Linguistic sciences are related to the study of Ḳur'ān and Ḥadīth (cf. No. 4, 37 beginning), which are divided into 4 parts: *al-naḥw*, *al-lugha*, *al-bayān*, *al-adab* (No. 37), and in the last named category comes the whole study of Arabic literature.

The *ʿulūm ʿaḳlīya* are variously classified, usually into 7 main sections (No. 13), and are *al-manṭiḳ*, logic, which is the foundation of all others (No. 17), *al-arithmāṭīḳī*, arithmetic, including *ḥisāb* etc. (No. 14), *al-handasa*, geometry (No. 15), *al-hai'a*, astronomy (No. 16), *al-mūsīḳī*, the theory of tones and their definition by number etc. (see No. 13); then there is *al-ṭabīʿīyāt*, the theory of bodies at rest and in motion, — heavenly, human, animal, plant and mineral; among its subdivisions, special mention is made of *al-ṭibb*, medicine, and *al-falāḥa*, agriculture (No. 18—20; cf. No. 29). The seventh main head is *ʿilm al-ilāhīyāt*, metaphysics (No. 21). Magic, talismans, mysterious properties of numbers etc. also form branches of Muslim learning (No. 22 *sqq.*).

Medicine was not only taught in special schools but also in the mosques and the madāris; about 600 A.H., ʿAbd al-Laṭīf lectured in the Azhar Mosque but it is not quite clear whether his instruction in *ṭibb* was also given there (Ibn Abī Uṣaibiʿa, ii. 207) and in any case the "philosophical sciences" were cultivated outside the mosques.

Another system divides the sciences into principal sciences (*maḳāṣid*) and instrumental sciences (*ālāt* or *wasā'il*). To the former belong *kalām*, *al-akhlāḳ al-dīnīya* (ethics, practically the same as *taṣawwuf*), *fiḳh*, *uṣūl al-fiḳh*, *Ḳur'ān* (*tadjwīd* and *tafsīr*), *ḥadīth*. The latter comprise linguistics, (*ṣarf*, *maʿānī*, *bayān*, *badīʿ*) and in addition metrics and prosody (*ʿarūḍ*, *ḳāfiya*), logic (*manṭiḳ*) including the theory of proof (*ādāb al-baḥth*), probably the same as the older *mudhākara* and *naẓar*, mathematics (*ḥisāb* and *djabr*), *muṣṭalaḥ al-ḥadīth* (cf. Muṣṭafā Bairam, *Risāla*, Cairo 1902, p. 20; Snouck Hurgronje, *Mekka*, ii. 200 *sqq.*).

The method of teaching was by lecturing and learning by heart (*talḳīn*). The first task was to learn the Ḳur'ān by heart and then acquire as many traditions as possible. The ḥadīth was repeated three times so that the student could remember it (Bukharī, *ʿIlm*, p. 30). Lecturing soon became dictation (*imlā'*), when the student wrote down what was said, except in the case of the Ḳur'ān (approved: Bukhārī, *ʿIlm*, bāb 34, 36). The method was the same for linguistic or literary subjects as for Ḥadīth, Tafsīr, etc. The philologists not only used to dictate their grammatical works, as for example Ibn Duraid (Wüstenfeld, *Schâfiʿî*, p. 127) or Muḥammad b. ʿAbd al-Wāḥid (d. 345/957) who dictated from memory 30,000 folios on *lugha* (Yāḳūt, *Udabā'*, vii. 26), but also the text of the poets, like al-Ṭabarī, who lectured on al-Ṭirimmāḥ in the Mosque of ʿAmr in 256/870 (*ibid.*, vi. 432). Dictation was specially important in the case of Ḥadīth, as the exact establishment of the text was the first necessity. It is therefore always said "he dictated Ḥadīth" (*Ḥusn al-muḥāḍara*, ii. 139; Yāḳūt, *Udabā'*, i. 246). The class of a teacher is therefore *madjlis al-imlā'* (*ibid.*, ii. 243; vii. 74), and his famulus among the students is *al-mustamlī* (cf. *ibid.*, vi. 282; vii. 74). Problems of fiḳh were also dictated (so Abū Yūsuf, Ibn Ḳuṭlūbughā, ed. Flügel, No. 249).

The class (*dars*) began with the recitation of the Ḳur'ān by a *ḳāri'*, with blessings on the Prophet, and other religious formulae (*Madkhal*, i. 56; cf. Mez, *Renaissance des Islams*, p. 172 *sq.*). At the present day, the teacher as a rule simply pronounces the *basmala* himself. Dictation alone was not everywhere the custom. In time, there came to be so many copies of the chief texts that the students were able to get copies for themselves. The text was in this case read aloud and the teacher gave his comments and emendations on the text (Yāḳūt, *Udabā'*, i. 255). It was only natural that the dictation of texts was first abandoned in philology; it is said to have been dropped as early as the fourth (tenth) century (Mez, *Renaissance*, p. 171). This does not mean that dictation was completely abandoned, for the teacher still made his pupils write down his comments; for example Muḥammad b. ʿAbd al-Raḥmān (d. 584/1188) dictated his lessons (Yāḳūt, *Udabā'*, vii. 20), and the method of having a text read aloud, while the lecturer explained only any remarkable phrases, was used as early as by the teacher of Ḥadīth, Ibn Kaisān (d. 299/912; *ibid.*, vi. 282).

Ibn Khaldūn laments that so few teachers in his time understand the correct methods of teaching (*ṭuruḳ al-taʿlīm*). They put difficult questions at once to the pupil instead of arranging the *talḳīn* so that it is always combined with explanations, and it is a fundamental principle that the pupil should not mix the different subjects. They laid too much stress on learning by heart (*ḥifẓ*) (*Muḳaddima*, *faṣl* 6, No. 2, 29, 30; cf. Subkī, *Muʿīd al-niʿam*, ed. Myhrmann, p. 151 *sq.*). Mechanical learning by heart is recognized for the Ḳur'ān. When the above mentioned Ibn Kaisān expounded ḥadīths, he also asked his hearers about their meaning. Vice versa, the class was at liberty to ask questions of the teacher. Al-Shāfiʿī used to sit in his great ḥalḳa in Mecca and say: "Ask me what you want and I will then give you information on the Ḳur'ān and *sunna*" (*ibid.*, vi. 391; cf. *BGA*, iii. 379). The teacher was sometimes overwhelmed with questions (Yāḳūt, *Udabā'*, v. 272). Ibn Djubair saw written questions being handed to a teacher in the Niẓāmīya in Baghdād (p. 219 *sq.*). Both practices are still in vogue and even in large classes the student may interrupt with questions.

VIII. The Teachers

The name for a teacher is *mudarris*; *ustādh* is a kind of honorary title (see Yāḳūt, *Udabā'*, i. 113, 209; ii. 271; v. 353, 354, 358, 448); it is still in use and applied also to students. There were a very large number of teachers in the great mosques. In the madrasa at first only one was appointed. A madrasa frequently took its name from a distinguished teacher (e.g. the Ghaznawīya in Cairo: Maḳrīzī, iv. 235; the Sharīfīya, originally the Nāṣirīya: *ibid.*, p. 193; cf. Masdjid al-Kisā'ī in Baghdād). In the larger madāris, however, several teachers were appointed; Ṣalāḥ al-Dīn appointed 4 lecturers to the Ḳamḥīya in Cairo (*ibid.*, p. 193 *sq.*); in this case a definite number (20) of students was allotted to each teacher (cf. *Chron. Mekka*, ii. 105 *sq.*).

It is easily understood that the conditions in the older mosques, where every one could come and go, were freer than in the madāris, which were built for particular teachers and students. There was probably as a rule no official recognition of the teachers in the earliest period. After textbooks had come into use, the certificate of qualification was the *idjāza*, and so it has remained to modern times. Any one who had studied with a teacher could get permission from him to teach from the book, which he had copied out and studied from his dictation; the teacher wrote this permission (*idjāza*) in the book (e.g. Yāḳūt, *Udabā'*, i. 253; ii. 272). A teacher could also give an *idjāza ʿāmma*, which permitted the individual concerned to teach from all his works (Ibn Baṭṭūṭa, i. 251). It was the usual thing for a travelling scholar to collect numerous *idjāzāt*; thus ʿAbd al-Laṭīf had certificates of this kind from teachers in Baghdād, Khurāsān, Egypt and Syria (Ibn Abī Uṣaibiʿa, ii. 202). There were special formulae for the *idjāza* for *tadrīs* and *futyā* (al-Ḳalḳashāndī, *Ṣubḥ al-aʿshā'*, xiv. 322 *sqq.*). Some scholars only gave occasional lectures, and others only dealt with a very limited subject; thus one was appointed to the Niẓāmīya to lecture on Bukhārī's *Ṣaḥīḥ* because he had attended lectures on this from a celebrated teacher. There were however many learned men who devoted themselves mainly to teaching and taught several subjects; often they taught many hours every day (e.g. Yāḳūt, *Udabā'*, vi. 282, 383; vii. 176), and pious teachers even spent the night in the mosque in prayer (Wüstenfeld, *Schafiʿi*, p. 258). Sometimes a young teacher began by dictating ḥadīth and later received a post with a wider scope in a mosque (*ibid.*, p. 239).

The distinction between teacher and taught was not absolute; any one could have an *idjāza* in one subject, while he was still a student in others and even men of ripe scholarship attended the lectures of notable teachers. This led students to travel from one seat of learning to another, just as they used to travel in early days to collect ḥadīths (Bukhārī, *ʿIlm*, p. 7, 19, 26). All the biographies of learned men give examples of this; the old Hellenistic custom was thus continued (cf. J. W. H. Walden, *The Universities of Ancient Greece*, New York 1910) and royal courts still played the same part; at them learned guests received donations, which enabled them to appear as teachers in the mosques (e.g. Ibn Baṭṭūṭa, ii. 75 *sqq.*; Ibn Khaldūn, *Kitāb al-ʿIbar*, Būlāḳ 1284, vii. 452; Ibn Abī Uṣaibiʿa, ii. 205; cf. Mommsen, *Römische Geschichte*, v. 589). Distinguished scholars were of course much visited by lovers of learning; of one of the latter, it is said *ruḥila ilaihi* or *ilaihi kānat al-riḥla* "they used to travel to him" (Yāḳūt, *Udabā'*, vii. 174; *Ḥusn al-muḥāḍara*, i. 207; cf. p. 141). As in the Christian universities of Europe, public disputations were held in the mosques, in which considerable feeling might be displayed, e.g. in the disputations in the Ruṣāfa mosque in Baghdād between Ibn Suraidj (d. 306/918) and the son of Dāwūd al-Ẓāhirī in which the former was victorious (Wüstenfeld, *Schâfiʿi*, p. 110 *sq.*). The learned constituted the class of "the turban-wearers" (*muʿammam*, *mutaʿammim*, *arbāb al-ʿimāma*, *aṣḥāb al-ʿimāma*; see Maḳrīzī, ii. 246; Quatremère, *Hist. Sult. Maml.*, 1/i. 244 *sq.*; 11/ii. 266; Dozy, *Supplément*, ii. 169[a]).

In spite of all flexibility a certain stability developed in the teaching staff of the mosques. This was connected with the question of pay. It was for long in dispute whether it was permitted to accept payment for giving instruction. In the collections of Ḥadīth the practice is both supported and condemned and it is said that the teacher may accept money, but not demand it, and avaricious teachers are strongly condemned. There are continual references to people who gave lecturers without payment (Bukhārī, *Idjāza*, bāb 16; Abū Dāwūd, *Buyūʿ*, bāb 36; Ibn Mādja, *Tidjārāt*, bāb 8). The custom of the older Jewish scholars of exercising a handicraft was not common among the Muslims but was found occasionally. Among men of learning we find shoemakers, locksmiths, sandal-makers (Wüstenfeld, *Schâfiʿi*, p. 227, 231, 267; cf. also Mez, *Renaissance des Islam*, p. 179). It was the rule however for the teacher to be paid for his work. This might be a wholly personal donation from a prince or other rich man, for example al-Ṭabarī was given a sum of money when he taught in the Mosque of ʿAmr (Yāḳūt, *Udabāʾ*, vi. 428; cf. the remarks above on wandering scholars); it was as a rule however a regular salary which was paid out of endowment, so that the position was a regular professorial chair; this was especially the case in the madāris. The salaries of the teachers (*maʿlūm*, also *djawāmik*, sg. *djamakīya*; see Dozy, *Supplément*, s.v.) varied considerably, according to the endowment. According to al-Maḳrīzī, learned men might have 50 dīnārs a month in all in addition to allowances in kind (iii. 364). On ceremonial occasions, they often were given special marks of distinction, such as gifts in money and robes of honour.

The men of learning were organized in a guild. How the organisation worked in detail is not known. At the end of the third century we find the institution of the *riʾāsa* established in Egypt, but even earlier the title *raʾīs* appears among scholars. There is also evidence of the *riyāsa* within the special subjects, e.g. *shaikh al-ḳurrāʾ bi-Miṣr* (*Ḥusn*, i. 230), *riyāsat al-ḥadīth bi-Miṣr* (*ibid.*, i. 163: al-Rashīd), *riyāsat al-fatwā* (Quatremère, *Hist. Sult. Maml.*, II/ii. 27), *riyāsat al-iḳrāʾ wa 'l-iftāʾ* in Alexandria (*Ḥusn*, i. 210). The physicians of a district had their *raʾīs al-aṭibbāʾ* (Maḳrīzī, iv. 237; Ibn Abī Uṣaibiʿa, ii. 86, 247). *Shaikh al-islām* is found as a title of honour for a scholar, e.g. in the viith, viiith, ixth century (*Ḥusn*, i. 143, 205; Quatremère, *op. cit.*, II/i. 68, note; II/ii. 270, 280: Ibn Taimīya), probably also used earlier (Mez, *Renaissance*, p. 179), while *shaikh al-shuyūkh* means the most distinguished leader of the Ṣūfīs (Maḳrīzī, iv. 285).

It is not clear what real importance the organisation of teachers had in the earlier period. In different districts there was a principal director of the organisations, a *raʾīs al-ʿulamāʾ*, in Madīna (Ibn Djubair, p. 200, $_{6}$), in Baghdād (*ibid.*, p. 220, $_{12}$), in Cairo and Upper Egypt (*Ḥusn*, i. 141, 143, 191), also called *raʾīs al-ruʾasāʾ* (Ibn Abī Uṣaibiʿa, ii. 204; Yāḳūt, *Udabāʾ*, i. 248). Every madhhab had its *raʾīs* for the district (*Ḥusn*, i. 148, $_{21}$; Yāḳūt, iv. 512). The chief raʾīs could interfere in the activities, for example, of the teachers of Ḥadīth (Yāḳūt, *Udabāʾ*, *loc. cit.*). He is probably identical with the *naḳīb al-nuḳabāʾ*, without whose permission the caliph would not admit a teacher to the Mosque of al-Manṣūr in 451 (*ibid.*, i. 246 *sq.*). Whether appointments were made after an examination we do not know. The right of lecturing was in any case limited in this way in practice, but a systematic set of regulations hardly existed.

The teacher had his particular place in the mosque, often beside a pillar: this was his *madjlis*, which was inherited by his successors (*Ḥusn al-muḥāḍara*, i. 135; cf. 181 infra, 182; Maḳrīzī, iv. 5; Yāḳūt, *Udabāʾ*, iv. 135; Wüstenfeld, *Schâfiʿi*, p. 239). The outward appearance of the class did not alter through the centuries. His hearers sit in a circle (*ḥalḳa*: the listeners *taḥallaḳū*: Maḳrīzī, iv. 49, $_{17}$ *sq.*; cf. on the word Quatremère, *Hist., Sult. Maml.*, I/ii. 197 *sqq.*) on the ground before the lecturer. The teacher sits on a carpet (*sadjdjāda*; cf. Yāḳūt, *Udabāʾ*, i. 254) or skin (*farwa*). This was described as a symbol of his dignity in his *waṣīya* (al-ʿUmarī, *Taʿrīf*, p. 134). We often find in large audiences that the teacher has a raised seat (for the older period see Ibn Baṭṭūṭa, i. 212).

It was not the custom for teachers to live in the mosque. Of course a teacher, like any other pious individual, could stay in the mosque and even have a room there; al-Ghazzālī for example lived in the mosque of the Umaiyads, where Ibn Djubair saw his room. But these were exceptions; al-ʿAzīz built a dwellinghouse for the teachers in the Azhar near the mosque (Maḳrīzī, iv. 49). The earlier madāris founded by Niẓām al-Mulk had often lodgings for the teacher, especially as the teacher sometimes made his lodging his classroom and this is also found later. Thus in the Ṣalāḥīya the head of the college had his home within the buildings (Ibn Djubair, p. 48).

Of the teachers many were also ḳāḍīs (as in their day were the ḳuṣṣāṣ, who were in a way the predecessors of the teachers). The ḳāḍīs frequently were able to accumulate a considerable number of offices. The chief ḳāḍī Ibn Bint al-Aʿazz (c. 700) had 17 offices (Quatremère, *Hist. Sult. Maml.*, II/i. 137 *sq.*). The teacher could also be a muftī (e.g. Yāḳūt, *Udabāʾ*, iv. 136).

Alongside of the teacher proper, a repeater (*muʿīd*) was often appointed, usually two for each teacher. His duty was to read over with the students the lecture after the class and explain it to the less gited students. The celebrated faḳīh al-Bulḳīnī began as a repeater with his father-in-law in the Kharrūbīya (Maḳrīzī, iv. 202); it was also possible to be an independent teacher in one school and a repeater in another (al-Naṣīr, d. 669; *Ḥusn al-muḥāḍara*, i. 189). The Ṣalāḥīya, which ought to have had 4 teachers with 2 repeaters, was run for 30 years by 10 repeaters and no teachers (Maḳrīzī, iv. 251; cf. also p. 210; Subkī, *Muʿīd al-niʿam*, p. 154 *sq.*; Ḳalḳashandī, *Ṣubḥ al-aʿshāʾ*, v. 464 and Haneberg, *Schul- und Lehrwesen der Muhammedaner*, p. 25; Wüstenfeld, *Die Akademien der Araber und ihre Lehrer*, 1837).

IX. The Students

Every one was absolutely free to join a *ḥalḳa* in the mosques in order to hear a teacher. Al-Maḳdisī for example tells us that the learned men of al-Fārs used to sit from early morning till midday and from *ʿaṣr* to *maghrib* for the common people (*li 'l-ʿawāmm*) (*BGA*, iii. 439). But as soon as the teachers developed into a regular class of society, the students (*ṭalaba*, *ṭullāb*, sg. *ṭālib*) who were systematically training in the Muslim sciences also became a recognized section of the community. Together with the teachers, they formed the guild of the educated, *aṣḥāb al-ʿimāma* (now *ahl al-ʿimme* in Egypt). They were able to select their teachers as they pleased; the most celebrated teachers had therefore large numbers of students. Many never finished studying for they could always find new teachers to study under up to their old age, even if they themselves also taught. The ambitious would only study under (*darasa ʿalā*) great teachers and therefore travelled about the Muslim world a great deal (cf. *BGA*, iii. 237). This travelling, partly as teacher and partly as student, for the sake of *ṭalab al-ʿilm* was long kept up in Islām.

When the student had completed his teacher's course, the teacher declared his knowledge mature in the particular subject and the student was able to regard himself as perfect in it (*takharradja ʿalaihi*). The relation of student to teacher is patriarchal and the student kisses his hands. This does not prevent quarrels breaking out and in such cases the teachers might be treated very disrespectfully (cf. Sulaimān Raṣad, *Kanz al-djawhar*, p. 141 *sqq.*, 192 *sqq.*).

The madāris introduced an innovation into the relationship of teacher to student, when a definite number of students (as a rule twenty) was allotted to a particular teacher. Instruction was thus organized on more systematic lines. But even then irregular students were also admitted. It is only in quite modern times that the instruction has been really properly organized.

We hear exceptionally of women students; one was a member of al-Shāfiʿī's madjlis (*Ḥusn al-muḥāḍara*, i. 181, *infra*). In the early centuries it cannot have been unusual; for it is several times mentioned in ḥadīths, which reserve special days for women (Bukhārī, *ʿIlm*, bāb 32, 36, 50).

In the *madāris* and some mosques, students were offered lodging and certain allowances in addition, food, bread (*djarāya*) and money.

A student living in a mosque is called *mudjāwir* (Maḳrīzī, iv. 54), a word which is also applied to Meccan pilgrims (Ibn Djubair, p. 122) and to anyone living in a mosque. The students' apartments are divided into *arwiḳa*, usually according to nations, a word which is derived from the fact that they originally lived in the colonnades. Each *riwāḳ* is under a shaikh. Many students live in khānaḳāh's, other in private houses.

X. Recent Reforms in Education

When intercourse between the Muslim world and Europe became active, the decline in Islāmic studies was already far advanced. On the one hand it resulted in the planning of new educational institutions on the European model, on the other in the reformation of the old system of education in the mosques.

In India in the xviii[th] century education was given in the mosques as in other Muslim countries, except that Persian played a considerable part alongside of Arabic (cf. *Report on the State of Education in Bengal*, Calcutta 1835, *Second Report* etc., 1836). In 1782 Warren Hastings founded the Calcutta Madrasah with a reformed system of education in order to train officials; it was imitated by other madāris. When in 1837 Persian was abolished as the language of the law courts, the madāris only retained significance mainly as religious institutions. Other institutions arose of more markedly English character, like the Anglo-Oriental College in Aligarh in 1875 (cf. Th. Morison, *The History of the Muhammadan Anglo-Oriental College Aligarh*, Allāhābād 1909; *RMM*, ii., 1907, p. 380 *sqq.*) and the Islamic College in Lahore etc. This led to new reforms in the madāris. In the Calcutta Madrasah an Anglo-Persian Department was instituted. Conferences were held in 1907—1908, 1909—1910 and 1912, and on July 31, 1914 the *Reformed Madrassah Scheme* was promulgated. English was to be learned in the reformed madāris and Muslim studies to be based on modern text-books; only the Calcutta Madrasah retained a department, the Arabic department, where the old Islāmic education, although somewhat modernized, was still given. The education in the madrasas is linked up with the new universities in Calcutta and elsewhere (*Calcutta University Commission*, 1917—1919, *Report*, Calcutta 1919, i/i. 143—187; v/ii. 60—70). In 1922 there were already 14 universities of which five were founded after 1919 (*Oriente Moderno*, ii., 1922, p. 60; on earlier discussions on the foundation of a university see *RMM*, xxi., 1912, p. 268 *sqq.*). The older universities, founded on the model of that of London, are those of Calcutta 1857, Madras and Bombay 1857, Lahore 1882, Allāhābād 1887 (*RMM*, vi. 4; on Chief's Colleges, *ibid.*, p. 1—51; ix. 44—81). The essential feature of the reforms is the new method of instruction, the systematic organization of the courses, which are concluded by examinations and the creation of a qualified body of competent teachers.

Inspired by the same spirit, if not so thorough, were the reforms which were carried through at the capital of Islāmic studies, the Azhar in Cairo, without the assistance of a European power. In 1872 an examination for those beginning teaching was instituted and new regulations were introduced in 1885, 1888 and 1895. The Rector could however appoint teachers without examination. The students had to be registered so that unworthy persons should not share the stipends. On June 4, 1895, a council of five members was appointed to prepare reforms. They dealt with the finance and organization. In 1896 the mosque-schools in Ṭanṭā, Damietta, and Dassūḳ and in 1903 those of Alexandria were put under the Azhar. On July 1, 1896 (supplemented in 1897 and 1898) examinations for students were arranged; history, geography and mathematics were introduced as voluntary subjects and it was forbidden to read glosses and supercommentaries in the first four years. The driving power in the council was one of its members, Muḥammad ʿAbduh, but he retired in 1905. The Khedive ʿAbbās II Ḥilmī in 1908 and in 1911, after several commissions had been working at the subject, promulgated a new law. The administration of the Azhar Mosque and the institutions connected with it (particularly other mosques and the Ḳāḍī School) were reorganized. New subjects were instituted, such as *akhlāḳ* in combination with the *sīra*, history, especially Muslim, geography, natural history, chemistry, mathematics, drawing, hygiene, education. By new laws of 1921, 1923 and 1924, the examinations were reformed and the relationship to the Ḳāḍī School, Dār al-ʿUlūm and other educational institutions reorganised, so that in the Azhar a *ḳism al-takhaṣṣuṣ* for *fiḳh*, *tafsīr*, *ḥadīth*, *tawḥīd*, *manṭiḳ*, *waḍʿ*, *bayān*, *akhlāḳ*, Islāmic history and practical courses in teaching and court practice were instituted. When by the law of Aug. 26, 1927, a university was founded with faculties of arts, law, science, and medicine (cf. *OM*, v., 1925, p. 110 *sq.*, 434—436; vii., 1927, p. 672 *sqq.*), the question of education in the mosque again came up and a new commission Nov. 27, 1927 was charged to consider new proposals (for the reforms of Egyptian institutions see P. Arminjon, *L'enseignement, la doctrine et la vie dans les universités musulmanes d'Égypte*, 1907; Muṣṭafā Bairam, *Risāla*, 1902; Sulaiman Raṣad al-Zaiyātī, *Kanz al-djawhar fī taʾrīkh al-Azhar*, 1320, p. 147 *sqq.*; *Aʿmāl madjlis idārat al-Azhar*, Cairo 1323, anonymous, but by ʿAbd al-Karīm Salmān, cf. *al-Manār*, xxv., 1324, p. 703; *Commission de la*

Réforme de l'Université d'El Azhar. Project de Réforme présenté par Muh. Pacha Said, Cairo 1911, and the official regulations; Johs. Pedersen, *al-Azhar*, Copenhagen 1922, p. 65 *sqq.*; A. Sékaly, in *REI*, i., 1927, p. 95 *sqq.*, 465 *sq.*; ii., 1928, p. 47 *sqq.* etc.; *OM*, v., 1925, p. 113 *sq.*; vii., 1927, p. 634). As a result a new ordinance was issued in 1933. According to it (cf. *REI*, v., p. 241 *sqq.*) al-Azhar is a school of Islāmic religion and Arabic language, divided into four sections (see further AZHAR). — In Morocco the ruler in 1844 introduced European subjects into the Madrasa in Fās D̲j̲adīd (whence its name *Madrasat al-muhandisīn*); these innovations did not become permanent, but in 1916 the madāris in Fās and Rabaṭ were reformed (Bell, in *JA*, ser. 11, x. 152; Péretié, in *Arch. Maroc.*, xviii., 1912, p. 257 *sqq.*; see for Tunis: *RMM*, iii. 385; *REI*, iv. p. 441 *sqq.*; for the ʿIrāḳ, *ibid.*, vi., p. 231 *sqq.*).

Since the First World War, throughout the world of Islām, particularly in Turkey, very far-reaching reforms in education have been introduced, the results of which cannot yet be surveyed.

AL-MAHDĪ (A.), means literally "the guided one", and, as all guidance (*hudā*) is from Allāh, it has come to mean the divinely guided one, guided, that is, in a peculiar and individual way. For Allāh, in the intense and immediate theism of Islām, is guiding every one and everything in the world, whether by the human reason or by the instincts of the lower animals, to a knowledge of Himself and to what is needed for their existence and continuance (*LA*, xx. 228, foot). One of His names is *al-hādī*, "the Guide" (Sūra xxii. 54; xxv. 31), and the idea of His guidance is reiterated in the Ḳurʾān. For a statement of its different kinds see Baiḍāwī on Sūra i. 6 (Fleischer's ed., i. 8, ll. 21 *sqq.*); *Mufradāt* of al-Rāg̲h̲ib al-Iṣfahānī, p. 560 of ed. Cairo 1324; *al-Maḳṣad al-asnā* of al-G̲h̲azzālī, p. 80 of ed. Cairo 1324. But it is singular that the word *mahdī* (the passive participle of the I stem) never occurs in the Ḳurʾān and that the passive of that stem occurs only four times. In the usage of the Ḳurʾān the VIII stem, *ihtadā*, strictly "he accepted guidance for himself", is used as a quasi or reflexive passive. Thus the man whom Allāh guides is not simply "guided" but reacts himself to the divine guidance.

There seems to be no original authority for the vocalisation *al-muhdī* which Edward Pococke gave as No. xvi. of the Signs in his *Porta Mosis*, ii. 263 of ed. 1655, with the meaning "director"; cf. Lane's note in the *Supplement* to his lexicon, p. 3042c. Margoliouth suggests that it may mean "the giver" and refers to traditions (see below) of the Mahdī bestowing uncounted wealth; but there does not seem to be any oriental authority for this epithet. Also, the verb used in these traditions is *aʿṭā*.

But one who is *mahdī*, or *al-mahdī*, is in a different position; he is absolutely guided. It is used of certain individuals in the past and of an eschatological individual in the future. Thus the *Lisān* (xx. 229, l. 9 from below) quotes from a tradition "the usage of the k̲h̲alīfas who followed the right way and were guided" (*sunnatu 'l-k̲h̲ulafāʾ al-rās̲h̲idīn al-mahdīyīn*), meaning the first four k̲h̲alīfas, and goes on to state that it is applied especially, as a name, to the Mahdī of whom the Prophet gave good tidings that he would come in the End of Time. There are many other instances of the non-eschatological application of the term *mahdī* to historical personages. Goldziher (*Vorlesungen*, p. 267, v., note 12, ₁) has gathered a number of such cases: thus D̲j̲arīr (*Naḳāʾiḍ*, ed.

Bevan, No. 104, v. 29) applies it to Abraham and Ḥassān b. T̲h̲ābit (*Dīwān*, ed. Tunis, p. 24, ₄) to Muḥammad (see, too, Ibn Saʿd, xi. 94, ₉). It is often applied by Sunnites to ʿAlī, in distinction even to the other three k̲h̲alīfas; thus in *Usd al-g̲h̲āba* (iv. 31, ₃) he is *hādiyan mahdīyan*, and Sulaimān b. Ṣurad calls Ḥusain, after his death, "Mahdī son of the Mahdī" (Ṭabarī, ii., p. 546, ₁₁). Farazdaḳ and D̲j̲arīr applied it as an honorific even to the Umaiyad k̲h̲alīfas. As applied by the pious to ʿUmar II, the Umaiyad (Ibn Saʿd, v. 245, ₅), it seems to have been more than an honorific; he was regarded as a real *mud̲j̲addid* and under peculiar divine guidance. In the view of later Islām he was the first of these "renewers" of the Faith and the eighth and last of these would be either the Mahdī, a descendant of the Prophet, or ʿĪsā (*al-masīḥ al-muhtadī*), according to the two positions [cf. the article ʿĪsĀ]. See on the whole question of the *mud̲j̲addid* and his relation to the Mahdī: Goldziher, *Zur Charakteristik ... us-Suyūṭī's*, in *S.B. Ak. Wien*, lxxx., p. 10 *sqq.* It is characteristic of Islām to take a very pessimistic view of human nature; men always fall away from the faith and have to be brought back. This will be so especially towards the end of the world. Men will become thoroughly secular and Allāh will leave them to themselves. The Kaʿba will vanish, and the copies of the Ḳurʾān will become blank paper, and its words will vanish, also, from the memories of men. They will think only of poems and songs. Then the end will come.

In a similar heightened sense the term Mahdī was applied by Ibn al-Taʿāwīd̲h̲ī (*Dīwān*, ed. Margoliouth, p. 103, ₅, ₆) to the ʿAbbāsid k̲h̲alīfa al-Nāṣir (575—622/1180—1225); he is the Mahdī and no other eschatological Mahdī need be looked for. In a narrower but more true etymological sense it came to be applied to converts to Islām; Allāh had guided these to the right Way. For such, Turks use the more Ḳurʾānic term *muhtadī*; see above for the distinction. Goldziher (p. 268) gives cases. In a heightened sense, also, the term was applied very early (A.H. 66) to Muḥammad b. al-Ḥanafīya, a son of ʿAlī by another wife than Fāṭima. After the death of Ḥusain at Karbalāʾ, Muk̲h̲tār b. Abī ʿUbaid put forward this Muḥammad as a claimant of the k̲h̲alīfate and called him "the Mahdī, son of the legatee (*al-waṣī*)", a term applied to ʿAlī by those who asserted that the Prophet had bequeathed the headship of the people to him (Ṭabarī, ii. 534). This was after the deaths of Ḥasan and Ḥusain, the two sons of ʿAlī by Fāṭima, the daughter of the Prophet, and shows a different drift as to the inheritance of the imāmate from that of the S̲h̲īʿite legitimists. This Muḥammad was heir as the son of ʿAlī and not as possessing the blood of the Prophet. He seems himself to have declined the dignity thus thrust upon him but, *malgré lui*, he became the founder of the Kaisānīya [q.v.] sect which looked for his return from his grave in Mount Raḍwā, where he remains undying. This was maintained by the poet Kut̲h̲aiyir (d. 105/723) and by the Saiyid al-Ḥimyarī (d. 173/789; *Ag̲h̲ānī*, viii. 32; cf. Masʿūdī, *Murūd̲j̲*, v. 180 *sqq.*). Muḥammad thus became an "expected Mahdī", *mahdī muntaẓar*, like the Hidden Imām of the Twelver S̲h̲īʿites. For the position of the Kaisānīya see S̲h̲ahrastānī's *Milal wa-niḥal*, ed. on margin of Ibn Ḥazm, i. 196; Muk̲h̲tār, disgusted with Muḥammad, eventually founded the Muk̲h̲tārīya sect which was strict S̲h̲īʿite and upheld Ḥusain b. ʿAlī (S̲h̲ahrastānī, p. 197). The whole episode is interesting as showing the extreme fluidity of the religio-political parties at the time. It also shows very clearly how the term *mahdī* gradually hardened from being a general honorific into a special designation, and even a proper name, for a restorer of the Faith in the last days.

The Hidden Imām of the Twelver Shīʿites, whose return (*radjʿa*) is awaited, is also called, by the Shīʿa, al-Mahdī. But his status is entirely different from that of the future restorer looked for by the Sunnites. The very essence of Sunnite Islām is that the Muslim people shall itself rule and can attain truth and certainty by its own exertions. When, at any time, its qualified scholars (*mudjtahid*'s) have applied the three *uṣūl* — Ḳurʾān, *sunna, ḳiyās* — to any point of Islām and have come to an agreement (*idjmāʿ*) on it, that point is assured and the acceptance of it as of faith is binding on all Muslims. The idea of an absolute Mahdī, therefore, as an infallible guide, suggests too much that *taḳlīd* [q.v.], which the later Sunnite theologians rejected. Sunnite Islām, as Goldziher has taught us, is a recoil against against the idea of blind submission to any human teacher. Even ʿĪsā, as restorer, is called *muhtadī*, which is much less emphatic in its suggestion of infallibility. Yet the masses demanded an absolute restorer and it was among the masses that the belief in a Mahdī was, and is, strong. To return — the Mahdī, or ʿĪsā when he comes as a restorer and ruler, will restore and apply that Consensus of Islām which has been reached by the successive generations of *mudjtahid*'s. Thus the Muslim people not only rules itself but is also the ultimate and infallible interpreter of the revelation through the Prophet. The Shīʿites, on the other hand, admit no such authority either in the Muslim people or in their own *mudjtahid*'s; by Ḳurʾān, *sunna, ḳiyās* and *idjmāʿ* no certainty can be reached. Certainty can only be gained from the instruction (*taʿlīm*; cf. Goldziher's *Streitschrift des Gazālī gegen die Bāṭinīya-Secte*, passim) of the hidden *Imām* who is divinely protected (*maʿṣūm*) against all error and sin and whose function it is to interpret Islām to men. The *mudjtahid*'s of the Shīʿa are his intermediaries with men; but they in their intermediation may err. When the Hidden *imām* returns he will rule personally by divine right. He is called a Mahdī, but it is in a different sense from any Sunnite use of that term. The idea of protection against error and sin (*ʿiṣma*; q.v.) seems to have been introduced into Sunnite Islām from the Muʿtazilite system by Fakhr al-Dīn al-Rāzī (d. 606/1209; see, further, Goldziher in *Isl.*, iii. 238—245), but there it has been limited strictly to prophets. No "successor" (*khalīfa*) can enjoy it and the Madhī, for those Sunnites who expect him, is strictly an ultimate khalīfa of the Prophet. For those Sunnites who look to ʿĪsā to play the part of the Mahdī he will not return as a prophet in his own right. It will not be a return (*radjʿa*) in his case but simply a "descent" (*nuzūl*) and he will rule according to the law (*sharīʿa*) of Muḥammad; see the article ʿĪSĀ. As all Shīʿite sects agree on this status of their *imām* it is unnecessary to go into further details on them; see in general, the article SHĪʿA.

Another important point of difference between Shīʿites and Sunnites as to the Mahdī is that he is an essential part of the Shīʿite creed but not of the Sunnite. That there will be a final restorer of the faith all Sunnite Islām believes as a part of its eschatology, but not that he will be called Mahdī. There is no mention of the Mahdī in either of the two *Ṣaḥīḥ*'s, of Muslim or of Bukhārī. Similarly Sunnite systematic theologians do not deal with him. The *Mawāḳif* of al-Īdjī has nothing on him; nor, indeed, on any of the Signs of the Hour (*ashrāṭ al-sāʿa*; cf. the article ḲIYĀMA). Nasafī in his *ʿAḳāʾid* has, of these, only al-Dadjdjāl and the descent of ʿĪsā; Taftazānī, in his commentary, gives ten Signs but not the Mahdī. Even al-Ghazzālī, a popularizing theologian, has nothing on the Signs in the last Book of his *Iḥyāʾ*, that on eschatology, and has only a slight allusion in the Book dealing with the *ḥadjdj* (ed. 1334, i. 218; *Itḥāf*, the commentary of the Saiyid Murtaḍā, iv. 279) to the coming of al-Dadjdjāl, the descent of ʿĪsā and his slaying of al-Dadjdjāl: there is no mention of the Mahdī either in the text or in the commentary. Al-Ghazzālī's whole point in this passage is to stress the final falling away from the faith of all men to which reference has been made above.

It was, then, in the hearts of the Muslim multitude that the faith in the Mahdī found its resting-place and support. In the midst of growing darkness and uncertainty — political, social, moral, theological — they clung to the idea of a future deliverer and restorer and of a short millennium before the end. This belief is, therefore, expressed in a multitude of later traditions, often expansions and expositions of better authenticated and older traditions, and often linking themselves to old stories of inter-tribal and inter-dynastic conflicts in the civil wars after the murder of ʿUthmān. We, therefore, find among them references to historical movements and sects which had failed in their time but had left remains, if only a name, to add to the confusion of this eschatological picture. These are gathered up in the later edifying collections, such as the *Tadhkira* of Abū ʿAbd Allāh al-Ḳurṭubī (d. 671/1273; Brockelmann, *GAL*², i. 529) which we have in a *mukhtaṣar* by al-Shaʿrānī (d. 973/1565; Brockelmann, *GAL*², ii. 441; ed. Cairo 1324) and the *Mashāriḳ al-anwār* of a modern writer, Ḥasan al-ʿIdwī al-Ḥamzāwī (d. 1303/1886; Brockelmann, *GAL*², ii. 638; many editions).

But the clearest presentation of the alleged basis for this belief is given by Ibn Khaldūn (d. 808/1406) in his *Muḳaddima* (ed. Quatremère, ii. 142 *sqq.*; transl. by De Slane, ii. 158 *sqq.*): "A section on the descendant of Fāṭima and what the people hold as to him and on clearing up the obscurity as to that. It has been commonly accepted (*mashhūr*) among the masses (*al-kāffa*) of the people of Islām, as the ages have passed, that there must needs appear in the End of Time a man of the family of Muḥammad (*min ahl al-bait*) who will aid the Faith (*dīn*) and make justice triumph; that the Muslims will follow him and that he will reign over the Muslim kingdoms and be called al-Mahdī. The appearance of al-Dadjdjāl and of the other Signs of the Last Day (*ashrāṭ al-sāʿa*), which are established in sound tradition (*al-ṣaḥīḥ*) will come after him. ʿĪsā will descend after his appearance and will kill al-Dadjdjāl or will descend along with him and aid him in that killing; and in worship ʿĪsā will follow the Mahdī as his *imām*. In support of this position traditions are used which some authorities on tradition have alleged and which others have disputed and often opposed with other narrations. The later Ṣūfīs have followed another course and method of proof in the case of this descendant of Fāṭima and often seek support, as to that, in the mystical "unveiling" (*kashf*) which is the basis of their method".

This is a very careful statement of the strictly

popular drift in Ibn Khaldūn's time, a drift with which he evidently had no sympathy. He goes on to give formally 24 traditions bearing upon this restorer and adds six variants, criticizing the authenticity of them all. In only 14 of these is this restorer named Mahdī. For references to traditions on the Mahdī in Aḥmad b. Ḥanbal's *Musnad*, Abū Dāwūd's *Sunan*, Tirmidhī's *Ṣaḥīḥ* and Ibn Mādja's *Sunan*, see Wensinck's *Handbook* under MAHDĪ; in the *Maṣābīḥ al-sunna* of al-Baghawī, see ii. 134 of ed. Cairo 1318 and in the *Mishkāt al-maṣābīḥ*, see p. 399—401 of ed. Dihlī 1327. All these, however, have only a certain number of the mass of traditions quoted by Ibn Khaldūn. In the *Tadhkira* of al-Ḳurṭubī, on the other hand, there is (p. 117—121 of ed. Cairo 1324) a further mass of luxuriant detail which Ibn Khaldūn had evidently disdained to incorporate; cf. his later reference to the town Māssa, p. 173, l. 7. In the *Tadhkira* the Prophet, for example, foretells the future conquest and re-conquest of Spain by name. Al-Ḳurṭubī died in 617/1272 in the first years of the Naṣrids of Granada when Granada was the only part of Spain left to the Muslims. He and those around him felt grievously the need of such a restorer and Mahdī, and detailed traditions sprang up as to his coming. The situation called for a mightier and more and more specific champion of Islām than ʿĪsā whose business strictly was to kill al-Dadjdjāl. Devotion, also, to the blood of the Prophet, of whom the Mahdī was to come, and which was so strong even in the Sunnite Maghrib, may have helped this. Al-Ḳurṭubī's Mahdī was to come from the Maghrib as opposed to the earlier ones who were to come from Syria or Khurāsān. He will come from a place in the Djabal of the Maghrib, on the shore of the sea, called Māssa; they will swear allegiance to him there and again, a second time, at Mecca. Here the tradition joins and attempts to explain an earlier one, given by Abū Dāwūd and quoted by Ibn Khaldūn (p. 148; see, also, below), telling of an expedition against Kalb and of the booty of Kalb, thus linking up with the earliest inter-tribal conflicts. This western Mahdī will also kill al-Sufyānī who is supported by Kalb. This is not the place to enter upon the story how the Marwānid branch of the Umaiyads supplanted their cousins, the Sufyānids. But from the mystery connected with the voluntary abdication and speedy death of Muʿāwiya II, the succession of Marwān b. al-Ḥakam and the sudden death or assassination of Walīd b. ʿUtba b. Abī Sufyān (*ṭuʿina wa-saḳaṭa maiyitan*: Masʿūdī, *Murūdj*, v. 170) at the burial of Muʿāwiya II, there seems to have sprung an Imāmite party among the Umaiyads (*ḳawl al-Umawīya min al-Imāmīya*: al-Ghazzālī in Goldziher's *Streitschirft*, p. 14 of the Arabic text); yet this Walīd appears later alive in Ṭabarī's narrative. In the account of Khālid b. Yazīd in the *Aghānī* (xvi. 88) there is a story that he was the first to start this (*waḍaʿa khabar al-Sufyānī wa-kabbarahu wa-arāda an yakūna li 'l-nās fīhi ṭaʿaman*), although that is also denied and a more general and earlier origin is asserted. In the civil war at the rise of the ʿAbbāsids one of the "white", i.e. Umaiyad, revolts was in support of the claims of "the Sufyānid of whom there used to be mention" (*wa-ḳālū hādha 'l-Sufyānī 'lladhī kāna yudhkaru*: Ṭabarī, iii. 53; Ibn al-Athīr, vi. 172). Apparently the Sufyānids continued to assert their claims in the under-ground Imāmite fashion against the Marwānids and, later, the ʿAbbāsids, supporting themselves with traditions, as all the parties did. The details are exceedingly obscure for this was one of the lost causes of Islām and has left only a name and that name underlies the general opprobrium which fell upon the Umaiyads in all later Islām, Sunnite and Shīʿite. An earlier stage in this appears in a tradition quoted by Ṭabarī in his commentary on Sūra xxxiv. 51 (part xxii., p. 63 foot). The Prophet mentioned a dissension (*fitna*) which would arise between the East and the West. Then there would come forth al-Sufyānī from the Dry Wādī (*al-wādī 'l-yābis*; otherwise unknown; in Yāḳūt, iv. 1000: "the Wādī of Yābis: from a man; it is said that al-Sufyānī will come from it in the End of Time") "in that outburst of his", or "when his time comes" (*fī fawrihi dhālik*). Much is said of the armies he will send out and the destruction he will spread, slaying 300 chiefs of the Banu 'l-ʿAbbās until Djibrīl is sent against him and destroys him. His appearance, thus, for Ṭabarī, is not eschatological and there is nothing about the Mahdī and the End of Time. But in an apocalypse incorporated by Muḥyi 'l-Dīn Ibn al-ʿArabī in his *Muḥāḍarat al-abrār* and studied in detail historically and astrologically, by Richard Hartmann in his *Islamische Apokalypse aus der Kreuzzugszeit* and dated by him about 576/1180, this tradition is used, expanded and brought into the eschatological picture, and al-Sufyānī is finally killed by the Mahdī. A hundred years later al-Ḳurṭubī expands it still further and calls al-Sufyānī Muḥammad b. ʿUrwa. For other references on al-Sufyānī see Goldziher, *Streitschrift*, p. 52, note 1; Snouck Hurgronje, *Der Mahdi*, in *Verspreide Geschriften*, i. 155; De Goeje, *Frag. hist. ar.*, ii. 526; Van Vloten, *Recherches sur la domin. ar.*, p. 61; Lammens, *Le califat de Yazîd*, i. 17; do., *Moʿâwiya II ou le dernier des Sofiânides*, p. 43.

It is obviously impossible to give in detail the traditions bearing on this restorer, but their types can be indicated and some recurrent characteristics. The great majority are put directly in the mouth of the Prophet, a very few go back to ʿAlī. If there remain of the world a single day Allāh will lengthen it until he sends this restorer; the world shall not pass away; the Hour shall not come until then. He will be of the People of my House (*min ahl baitī*); of my kindred (*min ʿitratī*); of my nation (*min ummatī*); of the offspring of Fāṭima (*min walad Fāṭima*); his name will be my name and his father's name my father's name. He will resemble the Prophet in disposition (*khulḳ*) but not in appearance (*khalḳ*); this is put in the mouth of ʿAlī. He will be bald of the forehead, hook-nosed, high-nosed. He will find the world full of evil and ungodliness; if a man say: "Allāh! Allāh!" he will be killed. He will fill the world with equity and justice; he will beat men until they return to Allāh (*al-ḥaḳḳ*). The Muslims will enjoy under him a prosperity the like of which has never been heard of; the earth will bring forth its fruits and the heavens will pour down its rain; money in that day will be like that which is trodden under foot and will be uncounted; a man will stand up and say: "O Mahdī, give to me", and he will say: "Take!" and he will pour into his robe as much as he can carry. It is suggested that this is a *tafsīr*, legitimate or illegitimate, of a tradition in the *Ṣaḥīḥ* of Muslim: "There will come in the end of my nation a khalīfa who will scatter wealth, not counting it". See many references for this munificent khalīfa and the abundance of money in the last days in Wensinck, *Handbook*, p. 100*b*, foot. But in this tradition, as in all Muslim and Bukhārī, there is no mention of the Mahdī.

Again: the Mahdī is of us, the People of the House. Allāh will bring him suddenly and unexpectedly (? *yuṣliḥuhu 'llāhu fī lailatin*). He will rule five, seven, nine years. There are frequent allusions to his coming in a time of dissensions (*fitan*). These will be such that it will take a voice from heaven to still them, saying: "Your Amīr is so-and-so" (Ibn Khaldūn, p. 162). This is very like an ironical comment, but it is cited as a simple foretelling. In these earlier traditions he will come from the East (al-Mashriḳ; Khurāsān), from beyond the River (Oxus); in later times (e.g. Ḳurṭubī and Ibn Khaldūn, p. 171—176) he was to come from the wide, unknown, lands of the Maghrib. The original Black Banners (*rāyāt sūd*) tradition about the ʿAbbāsids, apparently forged to lead them to support the ʿAlids, does not mention the Mahdī (Ibn Khaldūn, p. 153), but in an evidently later form there is added, "for he is the khalīfa of Allāh, the Mahdī" (Ibn Khaldūn, p. 159). One long tradition (Ibn Khaldūn, p. 148) may be given entire as an illustration of a type and because of the later expansion and use of it by Ḳurṭubī: "There will arise a difference at the death of a khalīfa and a man of the people of al-Madīna will go forth, fleeing to Mecca. Then some of the people of Mecca will come to him and make him go out (apparently rise in insurrection) against his will and they will swear allegiance to him between the *rukn* and the *maḳām*. And an army will be sent against (or "to", *ilā*) him from Syria but will be swallowed up in the earth in the desert (*al-baidāʾ*) between Mecca and al-Madīna. Whenever the people see that, the *abdāl* ("Substitutes" or "Nobles") of Syria and the *ʿaṣāʾib* ("Companions" or "Sectaries"; see Lane, p. 2059*b*) of al-ʿIrāḳ will come to him and they will swear allegiance to him. Thereafter there will arise a man of Ḳuraish with maternal grandfathers of Kalb. So he will send against them an army and it will overcome them and that will be the expedition (*baʿth*) of Kalb. And oh! the disappointment of those who will not have part in the booty of Kalb! He will divide the wealth and rule over the people according to the *sunna* of their Prophet and he will subject himself to the support of Islām. He will remain seven or nine years and then die and the Muslims will pray over him". This is evidently an echo of the conflicts with Yazīd and is not eschatological nor does it mention the Mahdī. But its motifs of the *abdāl* and of the earth swallowing up in the desert (*al-baidāʾ*) re-appear in other traditions which are concerned with the End of Time (p. 156, 161) and it is worked into al-Ḳurṭubī's tradition of the Mahdī from the Maghrib. Again, in a tradition evidently eirenic between the ʿAbbāsids and the ʿAlids, the Muslims are exhorted to "turn to the youth of the tribe of Tamīm (*ʿalaikum bi 'l-fatā 'l-Tamīmī*) for he will come from the East and will be the standard-bearer of the Mahdī" (Ibn Khaldūn, p. 162). But it is plain, too, that the doctrine of the Mahdī arose late and was not generally received. Thus the doctrine of al-Dadjdjāl is fixed in all Muslim eschatology, official and popular, but a tradition tries to assert that belief in the Mahdī is more of Faith than belief in him: "Whoever denies the Mahdī is an unbeliever but whoever denies al-Dadjdjāl is only a denier" (Ibn Khaldūn, p. 144). On the other hand, a tradition asserts that there is no Mahdī but ʿĪsā. The upholders of the Mahdī tried to turn this by saying that it means that no one ever spoke in the cradle (*mahd*; Sūra iii. 46) except ʿĪsā (Ibn Khaldūn, p. 163; Ḳurṭubī, p. 118). For al-Ḳaḥṭānī, another restorer who is not mentioned in any of the collections of traditions used above, see Snouck Hurgronje's article *Der Mahdi*, p. 12 (*Verspr. Geschr.*, i. 156).

The later, therefore, we go and the more popular are our sources the more fixed do we find the belief in the eschatological Mahdī. The more, too, the Muslim masses have felt themselves oppressed and humiliated, either by their own rulers or by non-Muslims, the more fervent has been their longing for this ultimate restorer of the true Islām and conqueror of the whole world for Islām. And as the need for a Mahdī has been felt, the Mahdīs have always appeared and Islām has risen, sword in hand, under their banner. It is impossible here to give the history of these risings. See for details upon them the article *Mahdī* by Margoliouth in Hasting's *Encyclopaedia of Religion and Ethics*, viii. 336—340 and Goldziher, *Vorlesungen*, p. 231, 268, 291. For the Sūdānese Mahdī, see especially Snouck Hurgronje's article *Der Mahdi*, reprinted in *Verspr. Geschr.*, i., p. 147—181. This contains, also, a fundamental discussion of the origin and history of the idea of a restorer in Islām; see also beneath, s.v. MUḤAMMAD AḤMAD.

Bibliography: has been given in the course of the article. The three important treatments of the subject are undoubtedly those by Snouck Hurgronje, Goldziher and Margoliouth.

MAḤMAL (or more correctly: MAḤMIL, A.), the name of the splendidly decorated empty litters, which since the viith/xiiith century have been sent by Muḥammadan princes on the Ḥadjdj to Mecca, to display their independence and claims to a place of honour at the ceremony. The camel which bears the maḥmal is not ridden but led by the bridle. It goes at the head of the caravan and is regarded as its sanctifying element. What extravagance the rivalry of princes led to is shown by the mention of a maḥmal adorned with much gold, pearls and jewels, which was sent in 721/1321 from the ʿIrāḳ to Mecca (*Die Chroniken der Stadt Mekka*, ed. F. Wüstenfeld, ii., 1859, p. 278). The maḥmal which was most esteemed, that which accompanied the pilgrim caravan from Cairo, is described by Lane as a square wooden framework, with a pyramid at top and covered with black brocade richly worked with inscriptions and ornamental embroidery in gold, in some parts upon a ground of green or red silk; it is bordered with a fringe of silk and silver balls are fixed to the corners and to the top of the pyramid. On the front of the pyramidal roof is a view of the Kaʿba embroidered in gold. In the brief description given by Burckhardt of the Egyptian maḥmal it is added that it was decorated with ostrich feathers. According to him there was only a prayer-book in the empty interior, which on its return was exhibited in Cairo and kissed by the people; according to Lane on the other hand, there were two silver receptacles in the maḥmal which contained two Ḳurʾāns, one in a scroll, the other in book form. The maḥmal was carried by a fine tall camel, which after the pilgrimage was spared any further work. On their arrival in Mecca the maḥmals were hailed with joy and led through the crowded streets in a solemn procession after which they went with the pilgrims to ʿArafāt where they occupied a position reserved for them. It used to be generally supposed that the covering of the Egyptian maḥmal was used to cover the tomb of Muḥammad or the Kaʿba but this is wrong; the *kiswa* is of course taken to Mecca with the great pilgrim caravan but it has nothing to do with the maḥmal.

According to Maḳrīzī the custom of sending a maḥmal to Mecca was first introduced in 670/1271—2 by the Mamlūk Sulṭān Baibars but others attribute it to the Sharīf Abū Numaiy; it is also said that it was a princess going on the pilgrimage in a splendid litter that gave Baibars the idea of sending one with the pilgrim caravan. This is however only a story and it is a much more important question whether the custom did not arise at an earlier date and whether it did not originally have a direct religious significance. It is natural to recall the portable sanctuaries of the Arabs and the maḥmal particularly reminds one of the description which Musil (*Die Kultur*, 1910, p. 8 *sq.*) gives of the "Abū Ẓhur al-Markab" of the Ruwāla tribe: a framework of thin pieces of wood adorned with ostrich feathers which is fastened on to the saddle of a pack-camel and is the visible centre of the tribe. This would at any rate lead us to the practical significance of the later maḥmal, a visible sign of independence and claim to suzerainty of the various Muslim states. It is just this significance which gives the maḥmals a certain historical inteiest as political changes and rivalries are reflected in them in course of time. There have occasionally been rulers who by sending maḥmals gave expression to their endeavour to obtain recognition as sovereigns and protectors of the sharīfs, only to be soon driven from power again by others. That the Egyptian maḥmal came to obtain a place of honour, that from Syria being the only other at all comparable to it, was a result of the political influence of the Mamlūk Sulṭāns. It is noteworthy that Ottoman rule made no alteration in this respect and an attempt to send a maḥmal from Constantinople met with no success. In 1807 an interruption was caused by the conquest of Mecca by the Wahhābīs who forbade this empty pomp so hateful to them; but this ceased when they were driven out and Muḥammad ʿAlī's rule again gave the Egyptian maḥmal pride of place.

After the first World War the sending of a maḥmal from Syria stopped. Difficulties arose between the Egyptian government and King Ḥusain (1915—1924) regarding the powers of the heads of a field-hospital which was to accompany the maḥmal as well as regarding the ceremony of its reception, which twice resulted in the maḥmal not being sent.

When Ibn Saʿūd had become king of the Ḥidjāz, long negotiations took place over the maḥmal. The Wahhābī ruler insisted on the music which usually accompanied the maḥmal being omitted and all sort of superstitious customs being dropped; he also protested against the armed escort as a denial of his sovereignty. The attempt made in 1926 to harmonize the demands of the two sides came to nothing: a fight broke out between the Ikhwān of Ibn Saʿūd and the Egyptian soldiers which was only stopped by the personal intervention of Ibn Saʿūd. For some years the Egyptian government sent neither a maḥmal nor a *kiswa*, but in 1929, following on an agreement with Ibn Saʿūd, the annual expedition of the maḥmal was reinstated.

Bibliography: Burckhardt, *Reisen in Arabien*, p. 394, 396, 407 *sq.*: Burton, *A Pilgrimage to el-Medinah and Mecca*, 1856, iii., p. 12, 267; Wavell, *A modern Pilgrim in Mecca*, 1912, p. 152, 155 *sq.*; Lane, *Manners and Customs of the Modern Egyptians*, 1836, ii., p. 180—186, 245 *sqq.* (with a picture of the Eygptian maḥmal); Snouck Hurgronje, *Mekka*, i. 29, 83 *sq.*, 152, 157 (with a photography in the *Atlas*, Pl. v.); Juynboll, *Handbuch des islāmischen Gesetzes*, p. 151 *sq.*

MAHR (A.), Hebrew *mohar*, Syriac *mahrā*, "bridal gift", originally "purchase-money", synonymous with *ṣadāḳ* which properly means "friendship", then "present", a gift given voluntarily and not as a result of a contract, is in Muslim law the gift which the bridegroom has to give the bride when the contract of marriage is made and which becomes the property of the wife.

1. Among the pagan Arabs the *mahr* was an essential condition for a legal marriage and only when a mahr had been given did a proper legal relationship arise. A marriage without a mahr was regarded as shameful and looked upon as concubinage. In the romance of ʿAntar the Arab women, who are being forced to marry without a mahr, indignantly reject such a marriage as a disgrace. Victors alone married the daughters of the conquered without giving them a mahr.

In the pre-Islāmic period, the mahr was handed over to the *walī*, i.e. the father, or brother or relative in whose guardianship (*walāʾ*) the girl was. Here the original character of the marriage by purchase is more apparent. In earlier times the bride received none of the mahr. What was ususally given the woman at the betrothal is the *ṣadāḳ*; the mahr, being the purchase price of the bride, is given to the walī.

But in the period shortly before Muḥammad, the mahr, or at least a part of it, seems already to be given to the woman. According to the Ḳurʾān, this is already the prevailing custom. By this amalgamation of mahr and ṣadāḳ the original significance of the mahr as the purchase price was weakened and became quite lost in the natural course of events. There can be no doubt that the mahr was originally the purchase price. But the transaction of purchasing in course of long development had become a mere form. The remains, however, as they survived in the law of marriage in Islām, still bear clear traces of a former marriage by purchase.

2. Muḥammad took over the old Arab patriarchal ceremony of marriage as it stood and developed it in several points. The Ḳurʾān no longer contains the conception of the purchase of the wife and the mahr as the price, but the mahr is in a way a reward, a legitimate compensation which the woman has to claim in all cases. The Ḳurʾān thus demands a bridal gift for a legal marriage: "And give them whom ye have enjoyed their reward as a wedding-gift" (lit. *farīḍa* "allotment of property", Sūra, iv. 24) and again: "And give the women their dowries voluntarily" (Sūra, iv. 3); cf. also Sūra, iv. 25, 34; v. 5; lx. 10.

The bridal gift is the property of the wife; it therefore remains her own if the marriage is dissolved. "And if ye wish to exchange one wife for another and have given one a talent, take nothing of it back" (iv. 20). Even if the man divorces the wife before he has cohabited with her he must leave half the mahr with her (Sūra ii. 236-237).

Down into the Muslim period the wife was considered after the death of the husband as part of his estate; the heir simply continued the marriage of the deceased. Such levirate marriages are found in the Old Testament also. Muḥammad abolished this custom, which still remained in his time, by Sūra iv. 19; "O ye who are believers, it is not permitted to you to inherit women against their will".

3. There was an ample store of traditions about the mahr and these pave the way for the theories laid down by the jurists in the fiḳh-books. From all the traditions, it is clear that the mahr

was an essential part of the contract of marriage. According to a tradition in Bukhāri the mahr is an essential condition for the legality of the marriage "every marriage without mahr is null and void". Even if this tradition, so brief and to the point, is not genuine, a number of traditions point to the fact that the mahr was necessary for the marriage, even if it only consisted of some trifling thing. Thus in Ibn Mādja and Bukhārī traditions are given, according to which the Prophet permitted a marriage with only a pair of shoes as mahr and approved of a poor man, who did not even possess an iron ring, giving his wife instruction in the Ḳur'ān as mahr.

A few ḥadīths endeavour to show that the mahr must be neither too high nor too low. From the traditions we also learn what mahr was given in particular cases in the Prophet's time: for example, the bridal gift of ʿAbd al-Raḥmān b. ʿAwf was an ounce of gold, that of Abū Huraira 10 ūḳīya and a dish, that of Shahal b. Saʿd an iron ring.

In the ḥadīths we again frequently find the Ḳur'ānic regulation that in a divorce after cohabitation the woman has the right to the whole mahr.

4. According to Muslim fiḳh-books, marriage is a contract (*ʿaḳd*) made between the bridegroom and the *walī* of the bride. An essential element in it is the mahr or *ṣadāḳ*, which the bridegroom binds himself to give to the bride. The marriage is null without a mahr. The jurists themselves are not quite agreed as to the nature of the mahr. Some regard it practically as purchase-money (e.g. Khalīl: "the mahr is like the purchase-money") or as an equivalent (*ʿiwaḍ*) for the possession of the woman and the right over her, so that it is like the price paid in a contract of sale, while other jurists see in the mahr a symbol, a mark of honour or a proper legal security of property for the woman.

All things can be given as mahr that are things (*māl*) in the legal sense and therefore are possible to deal in, that is can be the object of an agreement. The mahr may also — but opinions differ on the point — consist in a pledge to do something or in doing something, e.g. instructing the woman in the Ḳur'ān or allowing her to make the pilgrimage. The whole of the mahr can either be given at or shortly after the marriage or it may be paid in instalments. When the latter is the case it is recommended to give the woman a half or two-thirds before cohabitation and the rest afterwards. The woman may refuse to allow consummation of the marriage before a part is given.

Two kinds of mahr are distinguished:

a. Mahr musammā, "definite mahr", the amount of which is exactly laid down in the wedding contract.

b. Mahr al-mithl in which the amount is not exactly laid down, but the bridegroom gives a bridal gift befitting the wealth, family and qualities of the bride. This *mahr al-mithl* is also applied in all cases in which nothing definite about the mahr was agreed upon in the contract.

The mahr becomes the property of the wife and she has full right to dispose of it as she likes. In the case of any dispute afterwards as to whether certain things belong to the mahr or not, the man is put upon oath.

The Sharīʿa lays down no maximum or minimum for the amount of the mahr; but limitations were introduced by the various law-schools; the Ḥanafīs and Shāfiʿīs insist upon 10 dirhams as a minimum and the Mālikīs three dirhams. The difference in the amount fixed depends on the economic conditions in the different countries where the madhhabs in question prevail.

If the man pronounces a divorce, the mahr must be paid in every case if cohabitation has taken place; but the bridegroom may withdraw from the marriage before it is consummated; in this case he is bound to give the woman half the mahr.

Bibliography: W. Robertson Smith, *Kinship and Marriage in early Arabia*, Cambridge 1885 (cf. thereon Th. Nöldeke, in *ZDMG*, xl. [1886], 148 *sq.*); Wellhausen, *Die Ehe bei den Arabern*, *N. G. W. Gött.*, 1893, p. 431 *sqq.*; G. Jacob, *Altarabisches Beduinenleben*, Berlin 1897; Gertrude H. Stern, *Marriage in early Islam*, London 1939. — For the ḥadīths cf. Wensinck, *Handbook*, p. 145 *sq.* — The chapters *Nikāḥ* and *Ṣadāḳ* resp. *Mahr* in the Fiḳh-books. Further: Juynboll, *Handbuch des islam. Gesetzes*, p. 181 *sqq.*; Sachau, *Muham. Recht*, p. 34 *sqq.*; Santillana, *Istituzioni di diritto Musulmana Malichita*, Rome 1926, p. 168 *sqq.*; van den Berg, *Principes du droit musulman* (transl. France de Tersant), Algiers 1896, p. 75; Khalīl, *Mukhtaṣar*, transl. Santillana, Milan 1919, ii. 39 *sqq.*; Tornauw, *Moslem. Recht*, Leipzig 1855, p. 74 *sqq.*; Bergsträsser, *Grundzüge*, by index; Schacht, *Origins*, p. 107, 226.

MAIMŪNA, the last wife that Muḥammad married. She was the daughter of al-Ḥārith of the Hawāzin tribe of Ṣaʿṣaʿa and a sister-in-law of ʿAbbās. After she had divorced her first husband, a Thaḳīfī, and her second, the Ḳuraishī Abū Rukm, had died, she lived as a widow in Mecca, where the Prophet wooed her, primarily no doubt for political reasons, on the *ʿumra* allowed him in the year 7. His wish to marry her in Mecca was refused by the Meccans in order not to prolong his stay there; the marriage therefore took place in Sarif, a village north of Mecca. Her brother-in-law ʿAbbās acted as her *walī* at the ceremony. The question whether the Prophet on this occasion was still in the *iḥrām* or not is a much disputed and variously answered question. The bridal gift is said to have been 500 dirhams. Maimūna survived the other wives of the Prophet and died in 61/681 in Sarif, where she is said to have been buried on the spot where she was married.

Bibliography: Ibn Hishām, p. 790 *sq.*; Ibn Saʿd, viii. 94—100; Ṭabarī, i. 1595 *sq.*; al-Bakrī, ed. Wüstenfeld, p. 772 *sq.*; Caetani, *Annali dell' Islām*, ii. 66 *sq.*; F. Buhl, *Das Leben Muhammeds*, p. 299.

MAISIR, casting lots by arrows, a method by which a head of cattle was divided. This was the custom of the Arabs before Islām. The word seems almost to mean lucky chance, easy success, from *yasira*, to be easy, *yassara*, to succeed; cf. *maisara*, comfort, riches. A group of ten Arabs used to buy a young camel, which was cut into ten portions and the *yāsir* presiding distributed the portions among his companions by means of arrows on which he had written their names and which he drew at random out of a bag. In another system 28 portions were made of the animal; there was one part for the first arrow, 2 for the second and 3 for the third and so on up to 7; the three last got nothing. These arrows, each of which bore a special name, were deposited with the guardians of the temple in Mecca.

The game was considered a pagan practice and the Ḳur'ān (ii. 219 and v. 93) forbade it along with wine and idols as a major sin.

Arrows were also consulted before undertaking a journey or an affair. They were drawn before an idol, one bearing the inscription "yes", the other "no"; or they were three in number, which answered: order, prohibition or suspense. This procedure was called *istiḳsām*; Doutté compares it with rhabdomancy.

The word *maisir* has acquired a wider sense among the commentators and in certain traditions. Zamakhsharī gives it the same sense as *ḳimār*. According to a tradition of the Prophet, *maisir* is applied also to dice: "these accursed dice are the *maisir* of Persia (*maisir al-ʿadjam*)"; according to a tradition attributed to ʿAlī it is also to be extended to backgammon and chess (presumably in so far as dice were used in these games) and according to Ibn Sīrīn to every practice in which there is an element of chance.

Cf. the Dictionaries; Zamakhsharī, *Kashshāf*, ed. Nassau Lees, i. 380; al-Yaʿḳūbī, ed. Houtsma, i. 300 *sqq.*; A. Huber, *Über das Maisir genannte Spiel*, Leipzig 1883; Freytag, *Einleitung in das Studium der arab. Sprache*, p. 170 *sqq.*; E. Doutté, *Magie et religion dans l'Afrique du Nord*, Algier 1909, p. 373 *sqq.*

MAITA (A.), feminine of *mait*, dead; as a substantive it means an animal that has died in any way other than by slaughter. In later terminology the word means firstly an animal that has not been slain in the ritually prescribed fashion, the flesh of which therefore cannot be eaten, and secondly all parts of animals whose flesh cannot be eaten, whether because not properly slaughtered or as a result of a general prohibition against eating them.

In the Ḳurʾān, maita (in its main substantive meaning) occurs in the following passages: xvi. 115 (of the third Meccan period, previous to vi., 145 which is of similar wording); vi. 139, 145: "They have said: What is in the womb of these cattle is lawful to the males, but forbidden to our wives; but if it is maita (still born), (all) are partners therein ... (145) Say: I find in what has been revealed to me nothing forbidden, which must not be tasted, unless it be maita or blood that has been shed or pork — for that is filth — or an abomination at which another than Allāh has been invoked, but if anyone is forced (to eat it) neither revolting nor transgressing, thy Lord is forgiving and merciful" (of the third Meccan period); ii. 173 (of the year 2 of the hidjra, before the battle of Badr, again in the wording similar to vi. 145); v. 3: "Forbidden to you is maita, blood, pork, that at which another than Allāh has been invoked, the strangled, knocked down or killed by a fall, the gored, and that which wild beasts have eaten — except what you make pure — and that which has been sacrificed on stones set up (i.e. to idols) .... But if anyone in (his) hunger is forced to eat of them without wishing to commit a sin, Allāh is forgiving and merciful" (in all probability revealed after the valedictory pilgrimage of the year 10).

It is quite evident from Sūra vi. 139 that the maita was of some significance for the Meccans in the many laws about food with which Arab paganism was acquainted. Although it is no longer possible to define exactly the part it played (even the statements recorded by Ṭabarī from the earliest interpreters reveal the complete disappearance of any reliable tradition), it may be assumed without misgiving that the Ḳurʾānic prohibition carries on a corresponding pre-Islāmic prohibition, although perhaps modifying it. Both continue the old Semitic religious reluctance to consume the blood of animals, and indeed in all the Ḳurʾān passages quoted, blood is mentioned alongside of maita. It is unnecessary to assume that Muḥammad was influenced by Judaism on this point and the suggestion is to be rejected especially as the prohibition in its stereotyped wording occurs in Sūra ii. 173 just at the time of vigorous reaction against Judaism, and Sūra vi. 146 (Madīnese, a later insertion) contrasts the prohibition of maita etc. with the Jewish laws relating to food. Sūra v. 3 tells us in detail what is to be understood by maita: the second half of the verse enumerates the principal kinds of maita (with the exception of the animal that dies of disease, as this obviously enters into the plain sense of the word), which itself has already been mentioned before; thus the commentators could come to interpret the single cases wrongly as different from the maita proper. The "purification" (in the Ḳurʾān mentioned only in this passage) must mean ritual slaughter, by which, even if done at the last moment, the animal does not become maita but can be eaten.

These prescriptions of the Ḳurʾān are further developed in the Traditions. According to the latter it is forbidden to trade in *maita* or more accurately its edible parts; some traditions (mainly on the authority of Ibn Ḥanbal) even forbid any use being made of all that comes from *maita*; others again expressly permit the use of hides of *maita*. An exception from the prohibition of *maita* is made in the cases of fish and locusts; "the two kinds of *maita* that are permitted" without ritual slaughter (because they have no "blood"). While some tradition, extending this permission by the earliest *ḳiyās*, say that all creatures of the sea, not only fishes, can be eaten without ritual slaughter, including even seafowl, others limit the permission to those animals and fishes which the sea casts up on the land or the tide leaves behind, in contrast to those which swim about on the water, but there is also quoted an alleged saying of Abū Bakr expressly declaring what swims on the surface to be permitted. In this connection we have the story af a monster cast up by the sea (sometimes described as a fish) which fed a Muslim army under the leadership of Abū ʿUbaida when they were in dire straits; but in this tradition and in the interpretation that has been given it (that they only ate of it out of hunger) is clearly reflected the uncertainty that prevailed about such questions as were on the border line. In the Traditions, we find it first laid down that portions cut out of living animals are also considered *maita*. The way is at least paved for the declaration that all forbidden animal-dishes are *maita*. The question whether the embryo of a slaughtered dam requires a special "purification" is raised in one tradition and decided in the affirmative.

The most important regulations of the fully developed system of the *sharīʿa* about *maita* are as follows: It is unanimously agreed that *maita* is ritually impure and "forbidden" (*ḥarām*), and also that fish are exceptions to this; the Mālikīs and Ḥanbalīs also except the majority of creatures of the sea, and according to the more correct Shāfiʿī view, this applies to all marine creatures; as regards these the Hanafīs make a distinction, according to their being "thrown up" or "swimming the surface" and, later on "killed by an external cause" or "died of itself". The edible parts of *maita* are also *maita*, as are the bones, hair etc. among the Shāfiʿīs, but not the Hanafīs, and only the bones among the Mālikīs; the hide, when tanned, is in general considered pure and may be used. Emergency slaughter (*dhakāt* or *tadhkiya*; ritual slaughter in general is *dhabḥ* or *naḥr*) is according to the Ḥanafīs and the better known view of the Shāfiʿīs permitted, even if the animal will certainly die, provided it still shows signs of life at the moment of slaughter; according to the view predominant among the Mālikīs, the emergency slaughter in such a case is not valid and the animal becomes *maita* (in contrast to Mālik's own view). The question of the embryo is answered in the affirmative by the Ḥanafīs, following Abū Ḥanīfa himself (al-Shaibānī held the same view as the Mālikīs) but in the negative by the Mālikīs and Shāfiʿīs (in this case it is said that "the ritual slaughter of the dam is also the ritual slaughter of the embryo"), except that the Mālikīs make it a condition that the embryo should be fully developed. That anyone who is forced to eat *maita* may do so, is the unaminous opinion; only on the questions whether one is bound to eat *maita* to save his life, whether he should satisfy his hunger completely, or only eat the minimum to keep himself alive etc., there is a difference of opinion; the Shāfiʿīs and Ḥanbalīs further demand that one should not have been brought to these straits though illegal action (a narrow interpretation of the wording of the Ḳurʾān).

A clear definition of *maita* and its distinction from other kinds of forbidden animal foods was never reached. Sometimes it is separated from its own subdivisions given in Sūra v. 3, sometimes it is made to cover extensive allied fields. This terminological uncertainty has not infrequently caused confusion in the discussion of differences of opinion.

Bibliography: Lane, *Ar.-Engl. Lexicon*, part 7, p. 2742; Wensinck, *Handbook*, s.v.; Juynboll, *Handleiding tot de kennis van de mohammedaansche wet* (3rd ed. p. 169 *sq.*

MAKRŪH. [See ḤUKM; SHARĪʿA].

MAKS, toll, customs duty, is a loan-word in Arabic and goes back to the Aramaic *maksā*, cf. Hebrew *mekes* and Assyr. *miksu*; from it is formed a verb *m-k-s* I, II, III and *makkās*, the collector of customs. According to the Arabic tradition preserved in Ibn Sīda even in the Djāhilīya there were market-dues called maks, so that the word must have entered Arabic very early. It is found in Arabic papyri towards the end of the first century A.H.

Becker has dealt with the history of the maks, especially in Egypt, and we follow him here. The old law books use maks in the sense of *ʿushr*, the tenth levied on the merchants, more properly the equivalent of an excise duty than of a custom. They still show some opposition to the maks, then give it due legal force, but the word continued to have unpleasant associations, cf. the ḥadīth: *inna ṣāḥiba 'l-maksi fi 'l-nār*: "the tax-collector will go to hell": Goldziher has suggested that the Jewish view of the publican may have had some influence here.

The institution of the customs duty was adopted by Islām about the beginning of the Umaiyad period or shortly before it. While theological theory demanded a single customs area in Islām, the old frontiers remained in existence by land and water, and Egypt, Syria and Mesopotamia were separate customs areas. The amount of the duty in the canon law was settled not so much by the value of the goods as by the person, i.e. the religion of the individual paying it; but in practice, attention was paid to the article and there were preferential duties and no attention was paid to the position of the owner in regard to Islām. The laws of taxation were very complicated and graduated; the duties rose in course of time from the tenth (*ʿushr*) to the fifth (*khums*).

The Egyptian maks was levied on the frontier at al-ʿArīsh and in the ports (*sawāḥil*) ʿAidhāb, al-Ḳuṣair, al-Ṭūr and al-Suwais but there was also an octroi to be paid in al-Fusṭāṭ at a place called Maks. This name is said to have replaced an old Umm Dunain and then became identified with the Maks = custom-house of Cairo. All grain had to pass through here before it could be sold and two dirhams per *artaba* and a few minor charges (*lawāḥiḳ*) had to be paid on it. Further details of the administration of the maks in the earliest period are not known but there are references towards the end of the first century A.H. to a *ṣāḥib maks Miṣr* in papyri and in literature also.

The conception of the maks was extended in the Fāṭimid period when all kinds of small dues and taxes became known as *mukūs*, especially — emphasising the already mentioned unpleasant associations of the word — the unpopular ones which the people regarded as unjust. Such occasional taxes had been levied from time to time in the early centuries of Islām. The first to make them systematic was the dreaded financial secretary and noted opponent of Aḥmad b. Ṭūlūn, Aḥmad b. al-Mudabbir. The latter introduced not only an increase in the ground-tax and the three great monopolies of osiers, fisheries and soda (in connection with which, it is interesting to note, a reversion was made to old Roman taxes), but also a large number of smaller taxes which were called *maʿāwin* and *marāfiḳ* and included among the *hilālī*, the taxes to be paid according to lunar years. Such artifices (known as *mukūs* from the Fāṭimid period and later as *maẓālim*, *ḥimāyāt*, *rimāyāt* or *mustaʾdjarāt*) were destined to develop in time into the main form of oppressing the people and to become one of the principals causes of the economic decline of Egypt, until under the Mamlūks a limit was reached where hardly anything was left untaxed and *mukūs* were even granted as fiefs and "misfortune became general" (*wa-ʿammat al-balwā*). These small taxes however (but not the monopolies) were repeatedly abolished by reforming rulers, indeed *ibṭāl al-mukūs* (other terms are *radd*, *musāmaḥa*, *isḳāṭ*, *waḍʿ*, *rafʿ al-mukūs*) even formed part of the style and title of such rulers. Thus it is recorded of Aḥmad b. Ṭūlūn that he abolished some duties, and later of Saladin, Baibars, Ḳalāʾūn and his sons Khalīl and Nāṣir Muḥammad, of Ashraf Shaʿbān, Barḳūḳ and Djaḳmaḳ. Maḳrīzī gives a long list of *mukūs* abolished by Saladin and Ḳalḳashandī gives copies of the texts of *musāmaḥāt*, which are decrees of the Mamlūk Sulṭāns abolishing taxes or granting exemption from dues which were sent to the governors and read from the minbars and sometimes contain very full details, while shorter decrees were probably carved on stone and are given among the fragments published by van Berchem. It would of course be wrong to deduce from such abolitions of taxes that the government was a particularly good one, while on the other hand the continually recurring extortion of the same taxes shows that the abuses had been restored in the interval. Maḳrīzī, i. 111 concludes with the well known jibe at the Copts: "even now there are *mukūs*, which are in the control of the vizier, but bring nothing to the state but only to the Copts, who do exactly as they like with them to their great advantage".

Among the great variety of dues which were of course not all levied at the same place and at the same time were the following: *hilālī*-taxes on houses, baths, ovens, walls and gardens; harbour-dues in Gizeh, in Cairo at "the corn-quay" (*sāḥil al-ghalla*) and at the arsenal (*ṣināʿa*), also levied separately on each passenger; market-dues for goods and caravans (*baḍāʾiʿ wa-ḳawāfil*) especially for horses, camels, mules, cattle, sheep, poultry and slaves; meat, fish, salt, sugar, pepper, oil, vinegar, turnips, wool, silk, linen and cotton; wood, earthenware, coal, halfa grass, straw and henna; wine and oil-presses, tanned goods; brokerage (*samsara*) charges on the sale of sheep, dates and linen. Taxes on markets, drinking-houses and brothels which were euphemistically called *rusūm al-wilāya*. Warders deprive prisoners of everything they have; indeed this right is sold to the highest bidder; officers consume the fiefs of their soldiers; peasants pay their lords forced labour and give them presents (*barāṭīl, hadāyā*) and many officials (*s̲h̲ādd, muḥtasib, mubās̲h̲irūn, wulāt*) also accept them; when a campaign is begun the merchants pay a special war-tax and a third of inheritances falls to the state; when news of victories is received and when the Nile rises, levies are made; the d̲h̲immīs, in addition to paying the poll-tax, have to contribute to the maintenance of the army; pilgrims to the Holy Sepulchre pay a tax in Jerusalem; separate special taxes are levied to maintain the embankments, the Nilometer etc.

Outside of Egypt we occasionally hear of the maks as toll or market-due, e.g. in D̲j̲idda, in North Africa (cf. Dozy, *Suppl.*, ii. 606). Ibn al-Ḥād̲j̲d̲j̲, iii. 67 mentions a *musāmaḥat maẓālim*, but does not use the word *mukūs* in this sense.

Bibliography: Ibn Mammātī, *Ḳawānīn al-dawāwīn*, p. 10—26; Maḳrīzī, i. 88 *sqq.*, 104—111; ii. 267; Ḳalḳas̲h̲andī, iii. 468 *sqq.* (= Wüstenfeld, p. 169 *sqq.*); xiii. 20 *sqq.*, 117; Becker, *Papyri Schott-Reinhardt*, p. 51 *sqq.*; do., *Beiträge zur Geschichte Agyptens*, p. 140—148; do., *Islamstudien*, i. 177, 267, 273 *sq.*; van Berchem, *Matériaux pour un Corpus Inscriptionum Arabicarum*, i. 59, 560; ii. 297, 332 *sqq.*, 374, 377[1], 384; Mez, *Renaissance*, p. 111 *sqq.*, 117; Heffening, *Fremdenrecht*, p. 53 *sqq.*, 117; Bowen, *ʿAlī b. ʿĪsā*, p. 124; Wensinck, *Handbook*, p. 228; Fagnan, *Additions*, p. 165; Yāḳūt, *Muʿd̲j̲am*, iv. 606 on Maks; Ibn Faḍl Allāh al-ʿUmarī, *Masālik al-abṣār*, i. transl. Gaudefroy-Demombynes (Paris 1927), p. 170.

MAḲṢŪRA. [See MASD̲J̲ID I, D, 2b).

MALĀʾIKA, angels, is the Arabic broken plural of an early Semitic (Canaanite?) word *malʾak*, meaning "messenger". The evidence would suggest that it is a loan-word, coming into Arabic from Hebrew; the verb *l-ʾ-k* occurs in Ethiopic, in the sense of "to send". The singular in Arabic is normally *malak* without *hamza*, and so always in the Ḳurʾān; although the *Lisān* in two places (xii. 274, 371) quotes the same verse as a proof that *malʾak* does occur, but as an exceptional form (*s̲h̲ād̲h̲d̲h̲*). Both singular and plural in Arabic are used only in the sense "angel". In the Ḳurʾān it occurs twice in the dual (*malakain*, ii. 102, vii. 20), of the two angels Hārūt and Mārūt [q.v.], and of Adam and Eve being tempted in the Garden to believe that they may become angels. The plural occurs very often in the Ḳurʾān (in Flügel's *Concordance* under *l-ʾ-k*, p. 271) but the singular only 12 times (Flügel under *m-l-k*, p. 183). These are of the people demanding revelation by an angel rather than a human being (*bas̲h̲ar*, vi. 8, 9, 50; xi. 12, 31; xvii. 95; xxv. 7); women think Joseph an angel for his beauty rather than a human being (xii. 31); an angel's intercession (*s̲h̲afāʿa*, liii. 26) does not avail; twice as collective for angels, beside the *ʿars̲h̲* (lxix. 17), and in rows and rows (lxxxix. 22).

In xxxii. 11 "the angel of death" (*malak al-mawt*) occurs but not by name; see article ʿIZRĀʾĪL, and references in tradition in Wensinck, *Handbook*, p. 22*b*. D̲j̲ibrīl, the angel of revelation, is named three times (ii. 97, 98; lxvi. 4); cf. traditions on him in Muslim, *Īmān*, tr. 280 *sqq.*, and other references in Wensinck, p. 59. In Sūra xxvi. 193—195, D̲j̲ibrīl, unnamed, is called "the Faithful Spirit" (*al-rūḥ al-amīn*); he brings down the revelation to the *ḳalb* of Muḥammad in a clear Arabic tongue. There are other descriptions of him, still unnamed, in Sūra liii. 5—18 and lxxxi. 19—25, as appearing plainly to Muḥammad in revelation. He, as "our Spirit" (*rūḥanā*), was sent to Maryam (xix. 17). He is called "the Holy Spirit" (*rūḥ al-ḳudus*) in xvi. 102 and Allāh aided ʿĪsā with the same (ii. 90, 159; v. 110). Mīkāʾīl [q.v.] (variant Mīkāl) is named (ii. 98) as an angel of the same rank as D̲j̲ibrīl; see a long and apparently true story of how his naming came about in Baiḍāwī (Fleischer's ed., i. 74 *sqq.*); in traditions he, with D̲j̲ibrīl, appears to Muḥammad and instructs him; he does not laugh (Wensinck, p. 152); Muḥammad called the two his wazīrs of the angels. To Isrāfīl [q.v.], the angel with the trumpet of resurrection, there is no reference either in the Ḳurʾān or in canonical traditions but very much in eschatological legend. In Sūra xliii. 77, the tortured in hell call to the keeper of hell, "O Mālik!" and in xcvi. 18, the guards of hell are called al-Zabānīya, an otherwise unused word, meaning apparently, "violent thrusters" (*Lisān*, xvii. 55); the number of these, Sūra lxxiv. 30, is nineteen and they are asserted specifically to be angels, apparently to guard against the idea that they are devils; they are called "rough, violent" (*g̲h̲ilāẓ, s̲h̲idād*). Another class of angels are those "Brought Near" (to Allāh), *al-muḳarrabūn* (iv. 172); these praise Allāh day and night without ceasing (xxi. 20); Baiḍāwī calls them also *al-ʿalawīyūn* (on Sūra ii. 30; Fleischer's ed., i. 47) and *al-karrūbīyūn* (כרובים) (on Sūra iv. 172; Fleischer's ed., i. 243) as those that are around the *ʿars̲h̲*. The same term, *muḳarrab*, is used of ʿĪsā (Sūra iii. 43) as he is in the company of the angels nearest Allāh; cf. article ʿĪSĀ, above, for his semi-angelic character. At the beginning of the Sūra of the Angels (Sūra xxxv.) there is a significant description: "making the angels messengers (*rusulan*), with wings two and three and four; He increases in the creation what He wills"; this has had much effect on later descriptions and pictures. They are guardians (*ḥāfiẓīn*) over mankind, cognizant of what man does and writing it down (*kātibīn*; Sūra lxxxii. 10—12). In xxi. 94 the writing down is ascribed to Allāh himself. In lxx. 4; lxxviii. 38; xcvii. 4, there occurs the very puzzling phrase "the angels and *al-rūḥ*". Baiḍāwī on the first two passages shows how perplexing the distinction was found (Fleischer's ed., ii. 356, [5]; p. 383, [4]): "the *rūḥ* is an angel set over the spirits (*al-arwāḥ*); or he is the whole genus of spirits; or D̲j̲ibrīl; or a creation (*k̲h̲alḳ*) mightier than the angels"; cf. too, Ḳazwīnī's *ʿAd̲j̲āʾib*, ed. Wüstenfeld, p. 56. For spirits and the conception "spirit" in Islām see the article RŪḤ. In the Ḳurʾān there is no reference to the two angels, Munkar and Nakīr, who visit the dead man in his grave, on the night after his burial, and catechize him as to his faith. Thereafter, if he is an unbeliever, his grave becomes a preliminary hell, and if he is a believer, it becomes a preliminary purgatory from which he may pass at the Last Day into paradise; it may even, if he is a saint, be a preliminary paradise. This is called technically the Questioning (*suʾāl*) of

Munkar and Nakīr and, also, the Punishment of the grave (*ʿadhāb al-ḳabr*). This doctrine, similar to the Lesser Judgement of Christian theology, is one of the *samʿīyāt* (testimony based on revelation, i.e. Ḳurʾān or *sunna*) and is based on the implicit meaning of Ḳurʾānic passages (xiv. 27; xl. 11, 46; lxxi. 25) and upon explicit traditions (Taftazānī's commentary on Nasafī's *ʿAḳāʾid*, ed. Cairo 1321, p. 109; *Mawāḳif* of al-Īdjī with commentary of al-Djurdjānī, ed. Būlāḳ 1266, p. 590 *sqq.*). There is a still fuller account and discussion by the Ḥanbalite theologian Ibn Ḳaiyim al-Djawzīya in his *Kitāb al-Rūḥ*, ed. Ḥaidarābād 1324, p. 62—144, §§ vi.—xiv.

The angels are, also, called the heavenly host, or multitude (*al-malaʾ al-aʿlā*, xxxvii. 8; xxxviii. 69) and guard the walls of heaven against the "listening" of the *djinn* and *shaiṭān*'s. Cf. SIḤR.

The Ḳurʾān lays stress on the absolute submission and obedience of the angels to Allāh. "To Him belong those who are in the heavens and in the earth and those who are with Him (*ʿindahu*) are not too proud for His service (*ʿibāda*) and they do not become tired. They praise, night and day, without intermission" (xxi. 19, 20). "They do not anticipate Him in speech and they labour in His command" (xxi. 27). At the creation of Adam they are distinguished in this respect from him and his future race: "while we praise Thee and sanctify Thee" (ii. 30). Over the Fire there are set certain terrible and powerful angels, "they do not rebel against Allāh as to what He commands them and they do what they are commanded" (lxvi. 6). But does this absolute obedience extend to impeccability (*ʿiṣma*; q.v.)? The Ḳurʾān is emphatic as to their obedience, but is in contradiction as to their created nature and as to their relationship in that respect to the *djinn* and to the *shaiṭān*'s. Thus, in several passages in the Ḳurʾān, the story is told of the creation of man out of clay and that the angels were bidden by Allāh to prostrate themselves to him. This they all did "except Iblīs" (*illā Iblīs*; Sūra ii. 34; vii. 11; xv. 31; xviii. 50; xxxviii. 74). Iblīs, therefore, must have been an angel; as Baiḍāwī says, "If not, the command to them did not apply to him and his being excepted from them was illegitimate" (Fleischer's ed., i. 51, $_{21}$). This would mean that the angels were not impeccable. But, again, in Sūra xviii. 50 the statement is expanded, "except Iblīs; he was of the *djinn*; so he departed from the command of his Lord" (*fasaḳa ʿan amr^{i} rabbihi*). Further, in Sūra vii. 12; xxxviii. 76, Iblīs pleads in justification that man was created of clay (*ṭīn*) but he of fire (*nār*); and the *djinn* are acceptedly created of fire: "fire of the *samūm*" in Sūra xv. 27, "of a *māridj* of fire" in Sūra lv. 15. The meaning of *māridj* is unknown; the *Lisān* (iii. 189, $_{18-19}$) gives a number of contradictory explanations, but it is probably an unidentified loan-word. Iblīs and the *djinn*, then, were created of fire; but there is no statement in the Ḳurʾān as to the material out of which the angels were formed. A tradition traced back to ʿĀʾisha is the foundation of the accepted position that the angels were formed of light: "The Prophet said, 'The angels were formed of light (*khuliḳat min nūr*) and the *djānn* were formed of a *māridj* of fire and Adam of that which was described to you" (Muslim, *Zuhd*, tr. 60; Baiḍāwī, i. 52, $_{4}$). Another difficulty in the doctrine of the impeccability of the angels is the Ḳurʾānic statement as to Hārūt and Mārūt referred to above. These two angels are supposed to have yielded to sexual temptation, to be confined in a pit near Bābil and there to teach magic to men. But, it is answered, (i.) the Ḳurʾān says nothing of their fall; (ii.) teaching magic is not practising magic; (iii.) they always first warn those who come to them: "We are only a temptation (*fitna*); so do not disbelieve" (Sūra ii. 102); cf. further, Taftazānī on the *ʿAḳāʾid* of Nasafī, ed. Cairo 1321, p. 133.

In Baiḍāwī on Sūra ii. 34, there is a long discussion of the angelic nature (ed. Fleischer, i. 51, $_{20}$ to p. 52, $_{8}$) which, however, runs out in the despairing statement that knowledge on the point is with Allāh alone (*al-ʿilm ʿinda ʾllāhi*). Perhaps Iblīs was of the *djinn* as to his actions (*fiʿl^{an}*) but of the angels as to species (*nawʿ*). Also, Ibn ʿAbbās has a tradition that there was a variety (*ḍarb*) of the angels who propagated their kind (this has always been regarded as an essential characteristic of the *djinn* and of the *shaiṭān*'s as opposed to the angels) and who were called *al-djinn*; and Iblīs was of these. Or, that he was a *djinnī* brought up among the angels and identified with them. Or, that the *djinn* were among those commanded to prostrate themselves to Adam. Or, that some of the angels were not impeccable, although that was their characteristic in general, just as some men, e.g. the prophets, are guarded against sin but most are not. Further, perhaps a variety of the angels are not essentially different from the *shaiṭān*'s but differ only in accidents and qualities as men are virtuous or evil, while the *djinn* unite both, and Iblīs was of this variety. The tradition from ʿĀʾishā is no answer to this explanation, for light and fire in it are not to be taken too precisely; they are used as in a proverb, and light is of the nature of fire and fire of light, they pass into another; fire can be purified into light and light obscured to fire. So al-Baiḍāwī.

With this should be compared the scholastic discussion in the *Mawāḳif* of al-Īdjī, with the commentary of al-Djurdjānī (ed. Būlāḳ 1266, p. 576). In it the objector to the *ʿiṣma* of the angels has two grounds: (i.) their urging upon Allāh that he should not create Adam showed defects (slander, pride, malice, finding fault with Allāh) in their moral character; (ii.) that Iblīs was rebellious, as above. These grounds are then answered scholastically. Then various Ḳurʾānic texts, as above, on the submission and obedience of the angels are quoted. But it is pointed out that these texts cannot prove that all of them, at all times, are kept free from all sins. The point, therefore, cannot be absolutely decided. Individual exceptions under varying circumstances may have occurred, just as, while the *shaiṭān*'s as a class were created for evil (*khuliḳū li'l-sharr*), there is a definite tradition (*Sharḥ* ascribed to al-Māturīdī on *al-Fiḳh al-akbar* ascribed to Abū Ḥanīfa, ed. Ḥaidarābād 1321, p. 25) of one Muslim *shaiṭān*, a great-grandson of Iblīs, who appeared to Muḥammad and was taught by him certain sūras of the Ḳurʾān.

The story of Hārūt and Mārūt suggests that the angels possess sex, although they may not propagate their kind. But "they are not to be described with either masculinity or femininity" (*ʿAḳāʾid* of Nasafī, ed. Cairo 1321, p. 133). Taftazānī and the other commentators in this edition explain that there is no authority (*naḳl*) on this point and no proof by reason (*ʿaḳl*); it should, therefore, be left unconsidered and that, apparently, was the course followed by al-Īdjī and al-Djurdjānī. They may have sex and not use it. In that respect man who has in him the possibility of sin and must himself rule his appetites of lust (*shahwa*) and of anger (*ghaḍab*) has a higher potentiality of excellency than the angels (Baiḍāwī on Sūra ii. 30, ed. Fleischer, i. 48, $_{28}$ *sqq.*).

This leads to the second question as to the angels which scholastic theology has considered, the relative excellency of angels and men, and, especially, of angels and prophets. This is stated shortly by Nasafī (p. 147 of ed. cited above): (i.) "The Messengers (*rusul*) of mankind (*al-bas͟har*) are more excellent than the Messengers of the angels and (ii.) the Messengers of the angels are more excellent than the generality of mankind and (iii.) the generality of mankind are more excellent than the generality of the angels". Taftazānī develops that there is general and indeed necessary agreement on the excellency of the messengers of the angels over mankind in general, but that the other two statements (i. and iii.) will bear argument. He urges (i.) the prostrating of the angels to Adam; (ii.) that Adam was taught all the names of things (Sūra ii. 31); (iii.) that Allāh "chose" (*iṣṭafā*) Adam and Nūḥ and the family of Ibrāhīm and the family of ʿImrān over all created things (*ʿala 'l-ʿālamīn*; Sūra iii. 33); (iv.) that mankind achieves excellencies and perfections of knowledge and action in spite of the hindrances of lust and anger. But the Muʿtazilites and the "philosophers" (*al-falāsifa*) and some As͟hʿarites held the superior excellency of the angels. They urged (i.) that they were spirits, stripped of materiality (*arwāḥ mud͟jarrada*), complete actually, free of even the beginnings of evils and defects, like lust and anger, and from the obscurities of form and matter (*ẓulumāt al-hāyūlā wa 'l-ṣūra*), capable of doing wonderful things, knowing events (*kawāʾin*), past and to come, without error. The answer is that this description is based on philosophical and not Muslim principles. (ii.) That the prophets learn from the angels, as in Sūra xxvi. 193; liii. 5. The answer is that the prophets learn from Allāh and that the angels are only intermediaries. (iii.) That there are multiplied cases both in Ḳurʾān and in tradition where mention of the angels precedes that of the prophets. The answer is that precedence is because of their precedence in existence or because their existence is more concealed (*ak͟hfā*) and, therefore, faith in them must be emphasized. (iv.) In Sūra iv. 172, "*al-masīḥ* does not disdain to be an *ʿabd* to Allāh and of the angels" must mean, because of linguistic usage, that the angels are more excellent than ʿĪsā. The answer is that the point is not simple excellency but to combat the Christian position that ʿĪsā is not an *ʿabd* but a son to Allāh. In the *Mawāḳif* (p. 572—578) there is a similar but much fuller discussion which involves a philosophical consideration of the endowment — mental, physical, spiritual — of all living creatures from immaterial spirits to the lower animals (*al-bahīma*).

In the *ʿAd͟jāʾib al-mak͟hlūḳāt* of al-Ḳazwīnī (ed. Wüstenfeld, p. 55—63) there is an objective description of the angels in all their classes, in which the statements of Ḳurʾān and Sunna are adjusted to the Aristotelian-Neoplatonic universe with its spheres (*al-aflāk*,) in accordance with al- Ḳazwīnī's general aim to give a picture of the created universe in its details and wonders. Yet, apparently, while the angels possess the quality "life" (*ḥayā*) and are the inhabitants of the heavens and of the heavenly spheres (*sukkān al-samawāt*) they are not to be reckoned among the animals (*al-ḥayawān*). Al-Damīrī includes mankind and the *d͟jinn*, even the diabolic (*mutas͟haiṭina*) *d͟jinn*, such as the *g͟hūl*, in his *Ḥayāt al-ḥayawān* but not the angels. Equally acute and scholastic with the discussion in the *Mawāḳif*, and more spiritual than that by Ḳazwīnī, is al-G͟hazzālī's treatment of the mystery of the angelic nature in some of his specialistic smaller treatises. For him it is part of the general question of the nature of spirit to which his smaller *Maḍnūn* is devoted. See, too, the larger *Maḍnūn* (ed. Cairo 1303) in *Rukn* ii., p. 23 *sqq.*, and the translation by W. H. T. Gairdner of his *Mis͟hkāt al-anwār* (London, *Royal Asiatic Society*, 1924), *passim*.

The above is a statement of Muslim ideas as to the angels. But Muslim literature also takes account of non-Muslim ideas on them, as those of "philosophers", Christians, dualists, idolaters. These will be found given shortly by Baiḍāwī on Sūra ii. 30 (ed. Fleischer, i. 47, 18 *sqq.*) and in more detail in *Dict. of techn. Terms*, p. 1337 *sqq.*

Bibliography: Besides the references above: Walter Eickmann, *Angelologie u. Dämonologie des Korans*, New York and Leipzig 1908; Josef Horovitz, *Koranische Untersuchungen*, Berlin 1926; do., *Jewish proper names in the Koran*, in *Hebrew Union College Annual*, vol. 2; do., *Muhammeds Himmelfahrt*, in *Isl.*, ix. 159 *sqq.*; E. W. Lane, *Thousand and One Nights*, notes 1 and 12 to Introduction; note 15 to chap. i.; P. A. Eichler, *Die Dschinn, Teufel und Engel im Koran*.

MALAK. [See MALĀʾIKA].

MALAKŪT. [See D͟JABARŪT].

MĀLIK b. ANAS, Muslim jurist, the *imām* of the *mad͟hhab* of the Mālikīs, which is named after him, and frequently called briefly the *imām* of Madīna.

I. The sources for Mālik's biography

The oldest authority of any length for Mālik, the account of Ibn Saʿd (d. 230/845) based on al-Wāḳidī (d. 207/823) in the sixth class of the Madīna "successors" of his *Ṭabaḳāt*, is lost as there is a hiatus in the manuscript of the work, but it is possible to reconstruct the bulk of it from the quotations preserved, mainly in al-Ṭabarī, in the *Kitāb al-ʿuyūn* (*Fragm. hist. arab.*, i. 297 *sq.*), in Ibn K͟hallikān and al-Suyūṭī (*Tazyīn*, Cairo 1325, p. 3, 6 *sq.*, 12 *sq.*, 41, 46). From this it is evident that the brief biographical notes in Ibn Ḳutaiba (d. 276/889) and the somewhat more full ones in the *Fihrist* (compiled in 377/987) are based on Ibn Saʿd. The article on Mālik in al-Ṭabarī, iii. 2519 *sq.* is essentially dependent on the same source, while a few other short references there and in his history are based on other authorities. The long article on Mālik in Abū Nuʿaim, *Ḥilya*, Cairo 1936, vi. 316 is in its first part a mosaic of notices, sayings and anecdotes drawn from different sources and often of doubtful authenticity whereas its second part consists of a collection of traditions related by Mālik, most of which are not to be found in the *Muwaṭṭaʾ*. The chapter in Ibn ʿAbd al-Barr, *al-Intiḳāʾ*, is on the whole of the same kind as that first part; the collection of sayings of other authorities on Mālik is remarkable. Al-Samʿānī (p. 41) with the minimum of bare facts gives only the legendary version of an otherwise quite well established incident, while in Ibn K͟hallikān (no. 560), particularly in al-Nawawī (p. 530 *sqq.*) and also in al-D͟hahabī (i. 193 *sqq.*) the legendary features are still more pronounced although isolated facts of importance are also preserved by them. Al-Suyūṭī gives a detailed compilation from Ibn Saʿd and other works, most of which are now no longer accessible but are for the most part of later date and unreliable, like the *Musnad ḥadīth al-Muwaṭṭaʾ* of al-Fāfiḳī, the *Kitāb al-muttafaḳ wa 'l-muk͟htalaf* of al-K͟haṭīb al-Bag͟hdādī, the *Kitāb tartīb al-madārik* of al-Ḳāḍī ʿIyāḍ, the *Faḍāʾil Mālik* of Abu ʾl-Ḥasan Fihr. The bulk of the Mālikite *ṭabaḳāt* and of the later *manāḳib*, for example those of al-Zawāwī, is of no independent value.

II. Mālik's Life

Mālik's full name was Abū ʿAbd Allāh Mālik b. Anas b. Mālik b. Abī ʿĀmir b. ʿAmr b. al-Ḥārith b. Ghaimān b. Khuthail b. ʿAmr b. al-Ḥārith al-Aṣbaḥī; he descended from the Ḥimyar, his family had joined the Banū Taim b. Murra (Taim Ḳuraish).

The date of his birth is not known; the dates given, varying between 90 and 97, are hypotheses, which are presumably approximately correct. As early as Ibn Saʿd we find the statement that he spent three years in his mother's womb (over two, according to Ibn Ḳutaiba, p. 290), a legend, the origin of which in a wrong interpretation of an alleged statement by Mālik on the possible duration of pregnancy is still evident in the text of Ibn Saʿd. According to a tradition preserved by al-Tirmidhī, the Prophet himself is said to have foretold his coming as well as that of Abū Ḥanifa and al-Shāfiʿī. His grandfather and his uncle on the father's side are mentioned by al-Samʿānī as traditionists, so that there is nothing unusual in his also being a student. According to the *Kitāb al-Aghānī*, he is said to have first wanted to become a singer, and only exchanged his career for the study of *fiḳh* on his mother's advice on account of his ugliness (cf. Goldziher, *Muh. Studien*, ii. 79, note 2); but such anecdotes are little more than evidence that some one did not particularly admire him. Very little reliable is known about his studies, but the story that he studied *fiḳh* with the celebrated Rabīʿa b. Farrūkh (d. 132 or 133 or 143) who cultivated *raʾy* in Madīna, whence he is called Rabīʿat al-Raʾy, and from whom Mālik has taken over traditions, can hardly be an invention, although it is only found in somewhat later sources. Later legends increase the number of his teachers to incredible figures: 900, including 300 *tābiʿūn*, are mentioned. In the *ḳirāʾa* he followed Nāfiʿ. He transmitted traditions from al-Zuhrī, Nāfiʿ the Mawlā of Ibn ʿUmar, Abu ʾl-Zinād, Hāshim b. ʿUrwa, Yaḥyā b. Saʿīd, ʿAbd Allāh b. Dīnār, Muḥammad b. al-Munkadir, Abu ʾl-Zubair and others, but the *isnāds* of course are not sufficient evidence that he studied with the authorities in question; a list of 95 *shuyūkh* is given by al-Suyūṭī, p. 48 *sqq.*

A fixed chronological point of his life, most of which he spent in Madīna, is his being involved in the rising of the ʿAlid pretender Muḥammad b. ʿAbd Allāh in 145/762 (on the other hand the story of Mālik's alleged dealings with Ibn Hurmuz in the same year appears to be quite apocryphal). As early as 144/761 the caliph al-Manṣūr sent to the Ḥasanids of Mecca through him a demand that the two brothers Muḥammad and Ibrāhīm b. ʿAbd Allāh suspected of being pretenders should be handed over to him; this shows that Mālik must have already attained a position of general esteem and one at least not openly hostile to the government; he was even given a salary out of the proceeds of the confiscated property of the captured ʿAbd Allāh, father of the two brothers above named. This mission met with no success. When Muḥammad in 145/762 by a coup made himself master of Madīna, Mālik declared in a *fatwā* that the homage paid to al-Manṣūr was not binding, because it was given under compulsion, whereupon many who would otherwise have held back joined Muḥammad. Mālik took no active part in the rising but stayed at home. On the failure of the rebellion he was punished by flogging by Djaʿfar b. Sulaimān, the governor of Madīna, when he suffered a dislocation of the shoulder, but this is said to have still further increased his prestige and there is no doubt that the stories of Abū Ḥanīfa's ill-treatment in prison are based on this episode in the life of Mālik (there is a tendentious notice going back to al-Ṭabarī which gives as the reason for Mālik's ill-treatment his opinion on a question of *fiḳh*). He must have later made his peace with the government: in 160/776—7 the caliph al-Mahdī consulted him on structural alterations in the Meccan sanctuary, and in the year of his death (179/795) the caliph al-Rashīd visited him on the occasion of his pilgrimage. While this fact may be considered certain, the details in the *Kitāb al-ʿuyūn* are already somewhat legendary, and in Abū Nuʿaim quite fantastic. Quite fictitious again is the story that the caliph wanted to make the *Muwaṭṭaʾ* canonical and only abandoned his intention on the representations of Mālik; this is related of al-Manṣūr as early as in Ibn Saʿd, of al-Mahdī, in a parallel *riwāya* in al-Ṭabarī, and of al-Rashīd, with fantastic detail, in Abū Nuʿaim.

Mālik died, at the age of about 85 after a short illness, in the year 179/795 in Madīna and was buried in al-Baḳīʿ. The governor ʿAbd Allāh b. Zainab conducted his funeral service. An elegy on him by Djaʿfar b. Aḥmad al-Sarrādj is given in Ibn Khallikān. The *ḳubba* over his grave has been destroyed by the Wahhābīs; pictures of its latest state are given in al-Batanūnī, *al-Riḥla al-Ḥidjāzīya* [2], opposite p. 256, and in Ibrāhīm Rifʿat Pasha, *Mirʿāt al-Ḥaramain*, vol. i., opposite p. 426.

As early as Ibn Saʿd (certainly going back to al-Wāḳidī) we have a fairly full description of Mālik's personal appearance, his habits and manner of life, which however cannot claim to be authentic, nor can the sayings attributed to him, which became more and more numerous as time went on. The few certain facts about him have been buried under a mass of legends; the most important facts have already been noted and the others will be found in al-Suyūṭī and al-Zawāwī.

On the transmitters of Mālik's *Muwaṭṭaʾ* and the earliest members of his *madhhab* see sect. III. and V.; here we will only mention the most important scholars who handed on traditions from him. These were ʿAbd Allāh b. al-Mubārak, al-Awzāʿī, Ibn Djuraidj, Ḥammād b. Zaid, al-Laith b. Saʿd, Ibn Salama, al-Shāfiʿī, Shuʿba, al-Thawrī, Ibn ʿUlaiya, Ibn ʿUyaina, Yazīd b. ʿAbd Allāh and his *shaikhs* al-Zuhrī and Yaḥyā b. Saʿīd; al-Suyūṭī, p. 18 *sqq.* gives a long list of transmitters but most of them are not corroborated. We may just mention the apocryphal story of Mālik's meeting with the young al-Shāfiʿī (*Fragm. hist. ar.*, i. 359; Wüstenfeld, in *Gött. Abh.*, 1890, p. 34 and 1891, p. 1 *sqq.*), which is simply an expression of the view that was held of the relation between the two Imāms.

III. Mālik's Works

Further sources for his teachings

1. Mālik's great work is the *Kitāb al-Muwaṭṭaʾ*, which, if we except the *Corpus juris* of Zaid b. ʿAlī (of which the authenticity, however, is very improbable), is the earliest surviving Muslim law-book. Its object is to give a survey of law and justice, ritual and practice of religion according to the *idjmāʿ*

of Islām in Madīna, according to the *sunna* usual in Mādina and to create a theoretical standard for matters which were not settled from the point of view of *idjmā*ʿ and *sunna*. In a period of recognition and appreciation of the canon law under the early ʿAbbāsids, there was a practical interest in pointing out a "smoothed path" (this is practically what *al-muwaṭṭa*ʾ means) through the far-reaching differences of opinion even on the most elementary questions. Mālik wished to help this interest on the basis of the practice in the Ḥidjāz and to codify and systematise the customary law of Madīna. Tradition, which he interprets from the point of view of practice, is with him not an end but a means; the older jurists are therefore hardly ever quoted except as authorities for Mālik himself. As he was only concerned with the documentation of the *sunna* and not with criticism of its form, he is exceedingly careless in his treatment of traditions from the formal point of view. The *Muwaṭṭa*ʾ thus represents the earliest stage of literary development which was common to both *fiḳh* and *ḥadīth*.

Mālik was not alone among his contemporaries in the composition of the *Muwaṭṭa*ʾ; al-Mādjashūn (d. 164/763) is said to have dealt with the consensus of the scholars of Madīna without quoting the pertinent traditions, and works quite in the style of the *Muwaṭṭa*ʾ are recorded by several Madīna scholars of the same time (cf. Goldziher, *op. cit.*, p. 219 *sq.*), but nothing of them has survived to us. The success of the *Muwaṭṭa*ʾ is due to the fact that it always takes an average view on disputed points.

In transmitting the *Muwaṭṭa*ʾ, Mālik did not make a definitive text, either oral or by *munāwala*, to be disseminated; on the contrary, the different *riwāya*'s (recensions) of his work in places differ very much. The reason for this, besides the fact that in those days very little stress was laid on accurate literal repetition of such texts and great liberty was taken by the transmitters, lies probably in the fact that Mālik did not always give exactly the same form to the same lectures in different "classes". But the name *Muwaṭṭa*ʾ, which almost certainly goes back to Mālik himself and is found in all recensions, is a guarantee that Mālik wanted to create a "work" in the later sense of the term, although of course the stories which make Mālik talk of his writings reflect the conditions of a later period. In later times the *Muwaṭṭa*ʾ was regarded by many as canonical (cf. Goldziher, *op. cit.*, p. 213, 265 *sq.*; al-Suyūṭī, p. 47) and numerous legends deal with its origin (al-Suyūṭī, p. 42 *sqq.*).

Fifteen recensions in all of the *Muwaṭṭa*ʾ are known, only two of which still survive in their entirety, while some five were studied in the iii^th^–iv^th^ centuries A.H. in Spain and twelve were still available to al-Rūdānī (d. 1094/1683) (Heffening, *Fremdenrecht*, p. 155, note 1):

a. the vulgate of the work transmitted by Yaḥyā b. Yaḥyā al-Maṣmūdī (d. 234/848), often printed, e.g. Delhi 1216, 1296 (without *isnāds*, with Hindustānī translation and commentary), Cairo 1279—1280 (with the commentary of Muḥammad b. ʿAbd al-Bāḳī al-Zurḳānī, d. 1122/1710), Tunis 1280; numerous commentaries, recastings and extracts; cf. Brockelmann, *GAL*², i. 185; *Suppl.*, i. 297; Ahlwardt, *Katalog Berlin*, No. 1145; al-Suyūṭī, *Tazyīn*, p. 58 (chief passage); the same, *Isʿāf al-mubaṭṭaʾ bi-ridjāl al-Muwaṭṭa*ʾ, Delhi 1320; Muḥammad b. Ṭāhir al-Patnī, *Madjmaʿ biḥār al-anwār*, Lucknow 1283;

b. the recension of Muḥammad b. al-Ḥasan al-Shaibānī (d. 189/904) which is also a recasting and critical development of Mālik's work, as al-Shaibānī at the end of most chapters gives his own views and those of Abū Ḥanīfa on the questions discussed, sometimes with very full reasonings; often printed, e.g. Lahore 1211—1213 (with Hindustānī translation and notes), Ludhiana 1293, Lucknow 1297 (with valuable introduction, also to the vulgate recension, and commentary by Muḥammad ʿAbd al-Ḥaiy al-Lakhnawī), Kasan 1910 (do.); several commentaries; cf. Brockelmann, *op. cit.*; and the works quoted under *a*.

On the relation of these *riwāya's* to one another cf. Goldziher, *op. cit.*, p. 223 *sqq.*

c. The quotations from the recension of ʿAbd Allāh b. Wahb (d. 197/812) which are preserved in the two fragments of al-Ṭabarī's *Kitāb Ikhtilāf al-fuḳahā*ʾ (ed. Kern, Cairo 1902, and Schacht, Leiden 1933) are fairly extensive; this *riwāya* follows that of Yaḥyā b. Yaḥyā rather closely.

Quite appreciable fragments of Mālik's doctrines in a form diverging slightly more from the vulgate, as transmitted by Ashhab (d. 204/819–20) have been preserved in the same work. Although a *riwāya* of the *Muwaṭṭa*ʾ itself by this disciple is not otherwise known to exist, this may very well be the case, our information about its transmission not being necesssrily complete.

The other attested recensions of the *Muwaṭṭa*ʾ are given by al-Lakhnawī; further lists of transmitters of the *Muwaṭṭa*ʾ are given in al-Suyūṭī, p. 48, 51 and in al-Nawawī.

2. Whether Mālik composed other works besides the *Muwaṭṭa*ʾ is doubtful (the statement in the *Fihrist*, p. 199, *sq.*, which speaks of a number of writings by Mālik is quite vague and uncertain). The books ascribed to him fall into two groups: legal and otherwise. Among the legal we read of a *Kitāb al-sunan* or *al-Sunna* (*Fihrist*, p. 199,) transmitted by Ibn Wahb or by ʿAbd Allāh b. ʿAbd al-Ḥakam al-Miṣrī, a *Kitāb al-manāsik* (al-Suyūṭī, p. 40), a *Kitāb al-mudjālasāt*, transmitted by Ibn Wahb (*ibid.*), a *Risāla fi 'l-aḳḍiya*, transmitted by ʿAbd Allāh b. ʿAbd al-Djalīl (*ibid.*, p. 41) and a *Risāla fi 'l-fatwā*, transmitted by Khālid b. Nizār and Muḥammad b. Muṭarrif (*ibid.*). The genuineness of all these is, however, uncertain and even if they go back to Mālik's immediate pupils (sometimes they are actually attributed to the latter; cf. al-Lakhnawī) Mālik's own share in them would be still uncertain. A book (Gotha, No. 1143) said to have been transmitted by ʿAbd Allāh b. ʿAbd al-Ḥakam al-Miṣrī (d. 214/829) and heard by him along with Ibn Wahb and Ibn al-Ḳāsim is certainly apocryphal and besides does not pretend to give any utterances of Mālik himself. The same author's *Sīrat ʿUmar b. ʿAbd al-ʿAzīz* (Cairo 1327, 1346; cf. Brockelmann, *Suppl.*, i. 228) contains traditions from Mālik.

Of other titles are mentioned a *Tafsīr*, a *Risāla fi 'l-ḳadar wa 'l-radd ʿala 'l-ḳadarīya* (cf. section IV, end), a *Kitāb al-nudjūm* and a *Kitāb al-sirr* (al-Suyūṭī, p. 40 *sq*). which remain within the usual sphere of apocryphal literature. The suspicion of falsity is also strcng in the case of the *Risāla* containing advice to the caliph al-Rashīd, mentioned as early as the *Fihrist* alongside of the *Muwaṭṭa*ʾ (printed Būlāḳ 1311) which looks like a Mālikī counterpart of the *Kitāb al-kharādj* of Abū Yūsuf; already al-Suyūṭī mentions doubts on its genuineness, although for reasons which are not convincing to us.

3. There are two other main sources for Mālik's teaching (setting aside the later accounts of the doctrine of the Mālikī *madhhab*):

The more important is the *al-Mudawwana al-kubrā* of Saḥnūn (d. 240/854) which contains replies by Ibn Ḳāsim (d. 191/806) according to the doctrine of Mālik or according to his own *ra'y* to questions of Saḥnūn as well as traditions and opinions of Ibn Wahb (d. 197/812).

Further, al Ṭabarī, who in his *Kitāb ikhtilāf al-fuḳahā'* has preserved fragments of the *Muwaṭṭa'* (cf. above), also quotes frequently traditions and opinions of Mālik in his commentary on the Ḳur'ān on the "legal" verses.

IV. Mālik's position in the history of *fiḳh*

Mālik represents, in time, a stage in the development of *fiḳh* in which the reasoning is not yet thorough and fundamental but only occasional and for a special purpose, in which the legal thought of Islām has not yet become jurisprudence and, in place, Madīna where the decisive foundations of Muslim law were laid down. One of the main objects in the juristic thought that appears in the *Muwaṭṭa'* is the permeation of the whole legal life by religious and moral ideas. This characteristic of the formation of legal ideas in early Islām is very clear, not only in the method of putting questions but in the structure of the legal material itself. The legal material, having in itself no connection with religion, but that has to be permeated by religious and moral points of view, is the customary law of Madīna, by no means primitive but adapted to the demands of a highly developed trading community, which for us is the principal representative of old Arabian customary law: it appears in Mālik sometimes as *sunna* "use and wont", sometimes it is concealed under the Madīna *idjmā'* which he ascertains with great care; broadly speaking this only means that objections on religious grounds have not been raised by anyone against a principle etc. of customary law. Besides this, there appears another main object of the older jurisprudence: the formation of a system which sets out from principles of a more general character, aiming at the formation of legal conceptions in contrast to the prevailing casuistry, and is to some extent rounded off in a codification, if still a loose one, of the whole legal material.

While the islamisation of the law had been already concluded in its essential principles before Mālik, many generations had still to work at its systematisation; therefore Mālik's own legal achievement can only have consisted in the development of the formation of a system. How great his share in it was cannot be ascertained with certainty from the lack of material for comparison. The surprising success achieved by the *Muwaṭṭa'* of Mālik out of a number of similar works would in any case be completely explained by the fact that it recorded the usual consensus of opinion in Madīna without any special contribution of the author's own, and came to be regarded as authoritative as the expression of compromise (just as the works on Tradition came to be regarded as canonical). The *Muwaṭṭa'* would in this case have to be regarded less as evidence of Mālik's individual activity than as evidence of the stage reached in the general development of law in his time. It may be said that this average character was just what Mālik aimed at (cf. sect. III. 1).

The high estimation in which Mālik is held is grounded in the older sources by his strict criticism of *ḥadīth* and not by his activity for the *fiḳh* (al-Ṭabarī, iii. 2484, 2492; al-Sam'ānī; al-Nawawī; Goldziher, *op. cit.*, p. 147, 168; do., *Ẓâhiriten*, p. 230); even this only shows that with his *ḥadīths* he kept within the later consensus. That al-Shāfi'ī devoted special attention to him out of all the Madīna scholars (cf. his *Kitāb ikhtilāf Mālik wa 'l-Shāfi'ī*) is explained by the fact that he was a disciple of his.

As to the style of legal reasoning found in the *Muwaṭṭa'*, *ḥadīth* is not by any means the highest or only court of appeal for Mālik; on the one hand he gives the *'amal*, the actual undoubted practice in Madīna, the preference over traditions, when both differ (cf. al-Ṭabarī, iii. 2505 *sq.*) and on the other hand in cases where neither Madīna tradition nor Madīna *idjmā'* existed, he laid down the law independently; in other words he exercises *ra'y*, and to such an extent that he is occasionally reproached with *ta'arruḳ*, agreement with the 'Irāḳīs (cf. Goldziher, *Muh. Studien*, ii. 217; do., *Ẓâhiriten*, p. 4 *sq.*, 20, note 1). According to a later anti-*ra'y* legend, he is said to have repented of it on his deathbed (Ibn Khallikān). It is scarcely to be supposed that he had diverged seriously from his Madīna contemporaries in the results of his *ra'y*.

In the field of dogmatics, Mālik opposed the historian and traditionalist Ibn Isḥāḳ (d. 150/767 or 151/768) on account of the latter's inclining towards the Ḳadarites (cf. Fück, *Muḥammad ibn Isḥāq*, 1925).

V. The Mālikī *madhhab*

In the strict sense Mālik no more formed a school than did Abū Ḥanīfa; evidence of this is found in the oldest names *ahl al-Ḥidjāz* and *ahl al-'Irāḳ* resp., compared for example with *aṣḥāb al-Shāfi'ī*. These names at once indicate the probable origin of the Mālikī *madhhab*; after a regular Shāfi'ī school had been formed, which in view of al-Shāfi'ī's personal achievement for the development of *fiḳh* is quite intelligible, it became necessary for the two older great schools of *fiḳh*, whose difference was probably originally the result of geographical conditions in the main, also to combine to form regular schools, when a typical representative of the average views like Mālik or Abū Ḥanīfa was regarded as head. In the case of Mālik the high personal esteem, which he must have enjoyed even in this life-time (cf. sect. II), no doubt contributed to this also. But it is to his pupils that his elevation to the head of a school is mainly due. Traces of this process are still to be found in the varving classification of old jurists as of the Ḥidjāz school as Mālikīs or as independent *mudjtahids* (cf. also *Fihrist*, p. 199, 22).

The Mālikī doctrine spread mainly in the west of the Muslim world; after it had succeeded in driving out the *madhhab* of al-Awzā'ī and the Ẓāhirī school, it prevailed not only in the Maghrib (Tunis, Algeria, Morocco, including Muslim Spain) but almost in all the rest of Africa, so far as it has adopted Islām. The Mālikī school has many followers in Egypt: in Upper Egypt it occupies about the same position as the Shāfi'ī in Lower Egypt. This geographical distribution seems to go back to corresponding conditions existing before the formation of the *madhhabs*. Particularly ardent and successful disseminators of Mālik's teaching were 'Abd al-Malik b. Ḥabīb al-Sulamī (d. 238/853 or 239/854) and Ismā'īl b. Isḥāḳ (d. 282/895; *Fihrist*, p. 200, 8); but there are also mentioned earlier scholars for whose time the existence of a regular school is doubtful.

Bibliography: On Mālik's life: Ibn Ḳutaiba, *Kitāb al-maʿārif*, ed. Wüstenfeld, p. 250, 290; al-Ṭabarī, Index, s.v.; *Kitāb al-Fihrist*, ed. Flügel, p. 198; Abū Nuʿaim, *Ḥilyat al-awliyāʾ*, vol. vi. (Cairo 1936), p. 316 *sqq.*; Ibn ʿAbd al-Barr, *al-Intiḳāʾ fi faḍāʾil al-thalātha al-aʾimma al-fuḳahāʾ* (Cairo 1350); al-Samʿānī, *Kitāb al-ansāb*, in *GMS*, xx., fol. 41a; Ibn Khallikān, ed. Wüstenfeld, No. 560; al-Nawawī, p. 530; al-Dhahabī, *Tadhkirat al-ḥuffāẓ*, i. 193 *sqq.* (more in detail in the 18th class of his *Taʾrīkh* which has not yet been printed); de Goeje, *Fragmenta historicorum arabicorum*, Index, s.v.; al-Suyūṭī, *Tazyīn al-mamālik*, in Ibn al-Ḳāsim, *al-Mudawwana*, vol. i., Cairo 1314 (also printed separately); ʿĪsā b. Masʿūd al-Zawāwī, *Manāḳib saiyidinā al-imām Mālik*, ibid.; the further *manāḳib* and Mālikī *ṭabaḳāt*-literature; a modern list by Muḥammad ʿAbd al-Ḥaiy al-Lakhnawī in the introduction to his edition of the *Muwaṭṭaʾ* of al-Shaibānī (cf. above III., 1b).

On Mālik's writings: Brockelmann, *GAL*², i. 185; *Suppl.*, i. 297 *sq.*; Goldziher, *Muhammedanische Studien*, ii. 213 *sqq.*; al-Lakhnawī, *op. cit.*

On Mālik's position in the history of *fiḳh*: Bergsträsser, in *Isl.*, xiv. 76 *sqq.*; Goldziher, *op. cit.*; J. Schacht, *The origins of Muhammadan Jurisprudence*, Oxford 1950.

The older Mālikīs are given in *Fihrist*, p. 199 *sqq.* Of the Mālikī *ṭabaḳāt*-works there have been printed e.g. *al-Dībādj* of Ibn Farḥūn (d. 799) along with the *Takmīl al-Dībādj* of Aḥmad Bābā (d. 1032), Fez 1898; *Nail al-ibtihādj bi-taṭrīz al-Dībādj* of the same Aḥmad Bābā, Fez 1317 (cf. Fagnan, in *Homenaje Codera*, p. 105); Muḥammad b. Muḥammad Makhlūf, *Shadjarat al-nūr al-zakīya fi ṭabaḳāt al-Mālikīya*, and *Tatimma*, Cairo, 1349/50. On the spread of the Mālikīs: Aḥmad Pasha Taimūr, *Naẓara taʾrīkhīya fi hudūth al-madhāhib al-arbaʿa*, Cairo 1344; Juynboll, *Handleiding*³, p. 21; Ibn Farḥūn, *op. cit.*, p. 17; Bergsträsser, in *ZDMG*, 1914, p. 410 *sq.*; López Ortiz, *La recepción de la escuela malequi en España*, Madrid 1931.

Discussion of the Mālikī teaching in European languages (some further references): Perron, *Précis de jurisprudence musulmane* (transl. of the *Mukhtaṣar* with extracts from the commentaries), 1848; Sautayra-Cherbonneau, *Du statut personnel et des successions* (drawn from the *Mukhtaṣar*; the commentary considers the modern decisions), 1873; ʿAbd al-Raḥīm, *The Principles of Mohammedan Jurisprudence*, 1911 (Italian transl. by Cimino, 1922); al-Ḳairawānī, *Risāla*, transl. by Fagnan, 1914; the same, ed. and transl. by L. Bercher, Alger 1945; Ruxton, *Mâliki Law* (extracts from French translations of the *Mukhtaṣar*), 1916; Khalīl b. Isḥāḳ, *Mukhtaṣar*, transl. and explained by Guidi and Santillana (Italian), 1919; Santillana, *Istituzioni di diritto musulmano malichita*, i. 1926, ii. 1943; Russell-Suhrawardy, *A Manual of the Law of Marriage*, from the *Mukhtaṣar*; as well as other French treatises on single chapters of the law (cf. the bibliography in Juynboll, *Handleiding*³).

MĀLIKĪS. The school of law called after the Imām Mālik b. Anas (*madhhab Mālik*). On the origin and development of this school see the article MĀLIK B. ANAS, sect. V., where, in the *Bibliography*, the European expositions of this system are given (to be added are Marcel Morand, *Etudes de Droit Musulman Algérien*, Algiers 1910; do., *Introduction à l'Etude du Droit Musulman et du Droit Coutumier berbère*, Algiers 1931; Manuel del Nido y Torres, *Derecho Musulman*, 2nd ed., Tetuan 1927 [for practical use by judges in Spanish Morocco]; G. H. Bousquet, *Précis Elémentaire de Droit Musulman*, Paris 1936, and the excellent short survey by I. López Ortiz, *Derecho Musulmán*, Barcelona 1932). The following were regarded as standard works in the earliest period: 1. *al-Mudawwana al-kubrā* by Saḥnūn (d. 240/854). 2. *al-Wāḍiḥa* by Ibn Ḥabīb al-Sulamī (d. 238/852). 3. *al-ʿUtbīya* by al-ʿUtbī (d. 255/869) with the commentary *al-Bayān* (d. 520/1126) by Ibn Rushd, grandfather of Averroes. 4. *al-Mawāzīya* by Ibn Mawāz (d. 281/894). These works were however driven from the field by a synopsis of the *Mudawwana*, the *Tahdhīb* of Abū Saʿīd al-Barādhiʿī (second half of the ivth [xth] century), while in Spain the *ʿUtbīya* with its commentaries prevailed. An earlier and much esteemed compendium was the *Risāla* of Ibn Abī Zaid al-Ḳairawānī (d. 386/996) translated by L. Bercher (Alger 1945). A strictly systematic account of the system is given by Averroes (Ibn Rushd, d. 595/1189) in his *Bidāyat al-mudjtahid.* At a later date the authority was the *Mukhtaṣar* of Khalīl (d. 776/1374), French translation by A. Perron, *Précis de Jurisprudence musulmane*, 6 vols., Paris 1848—51: 2nd edition 1877; Italian translation by I. Guidi and D. Santillana, *Sommario del Diritto Malechita*, 2 vols., Milan 1919. The most important commentaries on it are those of al-Khirshī (d. 1101/1689) with the glosses of al-ʿAdawī (d. 1189/1775), al-Dardīr (d. 1201/1786) with the glosses of al-Dāsūḳī (d. 1230/1815) and al-Zurḳānī (compiled 1090/1678) with the glosses of al-Bannānī (1173/1759); al-Dardīr's synopsis *Aḳrab al-masālik* should also be mentioned.

A celebrated compendium in verse is the *Tuḥfat al-ḥukkām* of Ibn ʿĀṣim (d. 829/1426), translated by O. Houdas and F. Martel, *Traité de droit musulman*, Algiers 1893. The most important comprehensive collection of *fatwās* is that of al-Wansharīsī (d. 914/1508) *al-Miʿyār al-mughrib.* (Selections transl. by E. Amar, *La Pierre de touche des Fetwas*, 2 vols., Paris 1908-9).

Bibliography: Ibn Khaldūn, *Muḳaddima*, Cairo 1327, p. 501 *sqq.*; transl. de Slane, in *NE*, xxi/1 (1868), p. 13 *sqq.*; M. Morand, *Introduction à l étude du droit musulman*, Algiers 1921, p. 72 *sqq.*; Pröbster, in *Islamica*, iii. (1927), 352 *sqq.*; I. López Ortiz, *La recepción de la escuela malequi en España*, in *Anuario de Historia del Derecho español*, vii. (1931), 1—169; Aḥmad Taimūr, *Naẓra taʾrīkhīya fi hudūth al-madhāhib al-arbaʿa*, Cairo 1344, p. 19 *sqq.*

MAMLŪK (A., plural *mamlūkūn* and *mamālīk*), participle passive I of *malaka* "to possess", denotes the slave as his master's possession. The term owes its origin probably to the current phrase of the Ḳurʾān *mā malakat aimānukum* "what your right hands possess", a general designation of slaves without specialisation of gender. Mamlūk occurs once only in the Ḳurʾān (Sūra xvi. 75), in the expression *ʿabd mamlūk* "a slave in the possession of his master", mamlūk alone not yet being a technical term for slave, to all appearance. In *ḥadīth*, *ʿabd mamlūk* occurs likewise (Dārimī, *Siyar*, b. 34), but throughout the literature of *ḥadīth* mamlūk alone is already a technical term synonymous with *ʿabd.* — The distinction between a born slave and a slave born from free parents must be made by the addition of a genitive to *ʿabd*, in the former case *ḳinn* (*ʿabd*ᵘ *ḳinn*^{in}), in the latter *mamlaka* (*ʿabd*^{u} *mamlakat*^{in}),

It may be remarked that neither in *ḥadīth*, nor, to all probability, in Arabic literature, has the term mamlūk ever received the religious meaning of devotee, as is the case with *ʿabd*.

The Ḳurʾān enjoins the master to be humane towards "what his right hand possesses" (Sūra iv. 36). *Ḥadīth* is copious on this point. It assures us that Muḥammad on his death-bed did not cease repeating "(I recommend to you) *ṣalāt* and what your hands possess" (Aḥmad b. Ḥanbal, *Musnad*, iii. 117; cf. i. 78). "Whosoever does not treat his mamlūk as he ought to do, shall not enter Paradise" (Aḥmad b. Ḥanbal, i. 12). "When the mamlūk performs *ṣalāt*, he is thy brother" (Ibn Mādja, *Adab*, b. 10). "The mamlūk may claim his food and raiment" (Muslim, *Aimān*, trad. 41). "The Apostle of Allāh used ... to protect the mamlūk who appealed to his help" (Ibn Mādja, *Zuhd*, b. 16). "The mamlūk who acquits himself of his obligations towards Allāh and towards his master, will receive double wages" (Bukhārī, *ʿIlm*, b. 31) and one is bound to pardon his mamlūk even unto seventy times a day (Aḥmad b. Ḥanbal, ii. 111).

For the legal position of slaves see ʿABD.

It may be finally remarked that in certain circles mamlūk had the special meaning of white slave. See Fagnan, *Additions aux lexiques arabes*, s.v.

MANĀRA, tower, minaret. [See art. MASDJID, D. 2].

MANĀT, an old Arabian goddess. Her character can only be deduced from her name, which may safely be connected as a plural (for *manawāt*) with the Aramaic *m*^{e}*nāta*, plur. *m*^{e}*nāwātā*, portion, lot, Hebrew *mānā*, plur. *mānōt* and also with the god of fate *m*^{e}*ni*, Is. lxv. 11 (cf. lxx.). In Arabic we have corresponding to it, *manīya*, plur. *manāya*, "the allotted, fate, especially of death". She was therefore a goddess of fate, especially of death. Her main sanctuary was a black stone among the Hudhailīs in Ḳudaid, not far from Mecca on the road to Madīna near a hill called Mushallal. She was however worshipped by many Arab tribes, primarily by the Aws and Khazradj in Yathrib. In Mecca she was very popular along with the goddess al-Lāt and al-ʿUzzā [q.v.]; the three (according to the Ḳurʾān) were regarded as Allāh's daughters, and for a moment Muḥammad declared their worship permitted (cf. Sūra liii. 19 *sqq.*). The obscure expression "Manāt, the third, the other" is probably due simply to the rhyme. According to Ibn al-Kalbī, she was the oldest deity, whose worship gave rise to that of the others, because names compounded with Manāt occur earlier than other theophoric names. Another view is found in the poem of Ibn Hishām, p. 145, where "the two daughters of ʿUzzā" are Manāt and al-Lāt. As an independent deity, we find her in the Nabataean inscriptions of al-Ḥidjr, where מנותו (the Aramaic plural form; cf. above) is often found along with Dushāra and others. Manāt is connected in a peculiar way by some writers with the great *ḥadjdj* [q.v.], for we are told that several tribes including the Aws and Khazradj assumed the *iḥrām* at the sanctuary of Manāt and on the conclusion of the rites cut their hair there and dropped the *iḥrām* [q.v.]. Wellhausen sees in this an erroneous confusion of an independent pilgrimage to Manāt with the great *ḥadjdj*, as later writers acknowledge none but the latter; it is however possible that some such confusion may really have taken place in pagan times.

That Manāt was also a domestic deity is evident from the story in Ibn Hishām, p. 350 (cf. Wāḳidī, ed. Wellhausen, p. 350). The destruction of the great sanctuary in Ḳudaid after the capture of Mecca is attributed by some to Abū Sufyān, by others to ʿAlī, according to Wāḳidī, *op. cit.*, Ibn Saʿd, III/ii. 15, 25, to the Awsī Saʿd b. Zaid.

Bibliography: Yāḳūt, *Muʿdjam*, iv. 652—654; Wellhausen, *Reste arabischen Heidentums* ², p. 25—29; Ibn Hishām, p. 55; Ṭabarī, i. 1649; Azraḳī, ed. Wüstenfeld, *Chron. d. Stadt Mekka*, i. 76, 82, 154; commentaries on Sūra liii. 19; Nöldeke, in *ZDMG*, xli. 709; Bukhārī, *Tafsīr al-Ḳurʾān*, Sūra 53, Bāb. 3 (ed. Krehl, iii. 340); Jaussen and Savignac, *Mission archéologique*, i. 491 (Index); Caskel, *Das Schicksal in der altarabischen Poesie* (*Morgenl. Texte und Forschungen*, ed. by A. Fischer, I/5).

MANDŪB. [See ḤUKM; SHARĪʿA].

MANSŪKH. [See ḲURʾĀN].

MARABOUT, is the name given, especially in North-Africa, to a Muslim saint or to his descendants. This term, which is derived from the Arabic *murābiṭ* through the Portuguese *marabuto* (Spanish *morabito*), appears under its present form already in 1651 in the narrative of a traveller; for him the marabout is a "Muslim who devotes himself to the practice and the teaching of religion" (O. Bloch, *Dict. étymol. de la langue française*, Paris 1932, s.v.). In the whole Maghrib, the classical *murābiṭ* has given way to the dialectic form *mrābeṭ* (fem. *mrābṭa*; plur. *mrābṭīn*).

In the Muslim society of the middle ages, in particular in the West, the *murābiṭ* was a man who went into the state of *ribāṭ*, a sort of conventual retreat coupled with ascetic practices and, occasionally, with military exercises which formed a training for the holy war. These retreats were mostly practised in fortifications named themselves *ribāṭ* or *rābiṭa* (cf. for details the art. RIBĀṬ; G. Marcais, *Note sur les ribāṭs en Berbérie*, in *Mélanges René Basset*, Paris 1925, ii., 395—430; J. Oliver Asín, *Origen árabe de rebato, arrobda y sus homónimos*, Madrid 1928; E. Lévy-Provençal, *L'Espagne musulmane au X*^{e} *siecle*, Paris 1932, p. 138—139). One knows the extraordinary success of one group of these *murābiṭūn*, gathered round ʿAbd Allāh b. Yāsīn among the Ṣinhādja of Mauritania by the middle of the vth/xith century in a settlement of this kind: their propagation of Islām among the populations of the extreme south of Morocco soon became so active that it was transformed into a real political domination. That was the origin of the North African dynasty of the Murābiṭūn, commonly called the Almoravids, who were able to maintain themselves in Morocco, in the rest of North Africa and in Spain for nearly three quarters of a century. The institution of the *ribāṭ* has little by little fallen into disuse in modern times; but the corresponding name *murābiṭ* has survived, changing a little its original sense. This term is nowadays used only for Muslim saints, or, in certain cases, for their descendants. The current name in Algeria for a saint is *mrābeṭ*; in Morocco however, it is less used than its equivalents *ṣāliḥ*, *walī* and particularly *saiyid*; here *mrābeṭ* is only applied to a member of a marabout family or clan, descendants of an eponymous saint, from whom he has inherited a part of his miraculous power (*baraka*).

The cult of saints, already developed in the Maghrib before the introduction of Islām, spread in that country remarkably, especially since the end of the middle ages; concurrently with Sharīfism (see the art. SHARĪF), Maraboutism began to play a very active part in social life, and of course also in religious life. But there are very diverse categories of marabouts, from the venerated patron of a capital or a region to the modest anonymous local saint, whose tomb is mostly only recognisable by a little circular wall (*ḥawsh*) round it. The frequency of the whitewashed domes (*ḳubba*) which are spread all over the country (becoming more and more numerous as one goes from East to West), is a well-known feature of the worship of saints in North Africa. When a certain marabout enjoyed in the region where he was buried a greater esteem than other local saints, his mausoleum became the centre of a real agglomeration, or at least of a *zāwiya* [q.v.]; this *zāwiya* forms as a rule a sacred territory (*ḥurm*) and thus an inviolable asylum; it has sometimes important revenues, supplied either from voluntary gifts of the people who make a pious visitation (*ziyāra*) to it, or from lands belonging to it and let on lease. At its head is the most direct descendant of the saint, the *muḳaddam*, who administers the revenues and shares them with the other members of the marabout family, who also live, sometimes exclusively, by the hallowed reputation of their ancestor and on his alleged power to transfer his *baraka* to those who keep his cult.

The marabouts, men or women, have come by their sanctity in every possible way; some during their life-time for their knowledge, their devotion, their ascetism, their power to work miracles, sometimes even for their more or less mystic madness (*madjdhub*); others have come into prominence by miracles and apparitions after their death. The warrior for the faith (*mudjāhid*), who meets with death in an encounter with the infidels, is often sanctified; he is, in the proper sense of the word, a *murābiṭ*. It is not necessary that a marabout belongs to an Arabic speaking population; there are marabouts in regions where only Berber is spoken; they are called *agurram*. The name of the marabout is always preceded by the title *sīdī* (*saiyidī*); sometimes also, especially in Morocco, by that of *mūlāi* (*mawlāya*); names of sainted women are always preceded by the Berber title of *lālla*. In the Abāḍite enclaves of the Maghrib, where too saints are to be found, the title of the marabout is *ʿammī*.

Many sainted persons of the Maghrib, who enjoy even at this time a marabout cult, have been authenticated by history; biographical collections have been dedicated to them for different epochs, especially in Morocco, where hagiographical literature flourished greatly down from the xvi^th^ century (for this question cf. notably E. Lévi-Provençal, *Les historiens des Chorfa*, Paris 1922). Among the most famous marabouts in Morocco may be mentioned, besides Idrīs II, the great founder and patron of Fās, Mūlāi ʿAbd al-Salām b. Mashīsh, the patron of the Djebāla, buried on the Djabal al-ʿĀlam; Mūlāi Bū-Salhām (Abū Salhām, "the man with the burnous"), in the Gharb; Mūlāi Bū-Shtā (Abū 'l-Shitāʾ, "the rain-maker"), north of Fās; Sīdī Muḥammad b. ʿĪsā, patron of Meknes and founder of the brotherhood of the ʿĪsāwa (Aïssaoua); Mūlāi Bū-Shʿīb (Abū Shuʿaib), in Azemmour; Mūlāi Bū-ʿAzzā (Abū Yaʿazzā), in the Tādlā; Sīdī Bel-ʿAbbās (Abū 'l-ʿAbbās) al-Sabtī, born in Ceuta and patron of Marrakech. In Algeria the saints of far-spread reputation are rather few in number, in view of the multitude of marabouts in the country; there may be mentioned however the patron of Tlemcen, Sīdī Bū-Madyan (Abū Madyan al-Ghawth); the patron of Algiers, Sīdī ʿAbd al-Raḥmān al-Thaʿālibī; the saint of Miliana, Sīdī Aḥmad b. Yūsuf, famous for his satiric verdicts. In Tunisia, there may be mentioned, among others, the saint of Ḳairawān, Sīdī 'l-Ṣāḥeb, a companion (*ṣāḥib*) of the Prophet, and the female saint of Tunis, Lālla ʿĀʾisha al-Mannūbīya.

Attention must also be drawn to the fervent veneration tributed to ʿAbd al-Ḳādir al-Djīlānī (d. 561/1166), the great saint and eponymous of the brotherhood (*ṭarīḳa*) of the Ḳādirīya [q.v.], who is venerated all over the Muslim world. A great number of sanctuaries spread over all North Africa give witness of the devotion paid to him; he is called al-Djilālī and surnamed *ṭair al-marāḳib*, "the bird of the observatories", as the chapels dedicated to him often dominate the surroundings.

Besides these categories of historical saints a special place should be given to the numerous sanctified persons in the Maghrib whose real existence seems often doubtful. Indeed their sanctuaries are in general of very modest construction; sometimes it is not more than a little rampart of bricks (*ḥawiṭa*). These saints are mostly anonymous; when they have a name, it may mean that one has to do with an old animistic cult from pre-Islamic times. Very common names in North Africa are such as Sīdī 'l-Mukhfī ("the hidden lord"), a sort of *sancti ignoti*; and Sīdī Ḳāḍī 'l-Ḥādja ("the lord who fulfills the vows"). Even among the historically known saints some are concealed under names which indicate their wonder-working (e.g. Mūlāi Bū-Shtā). There are saints who have a double tomb: such a one is then called Sīdī Bū-Ḳabrain. It is to be noticed finally that certain Muslim marabouts in North Africa are venerated by the Jews, sometimes even by certain elements of the European population; on the other hand it happens that Muslims venerate Jewish saints (examples in Morocco and Tunisia).

The social standing of the marabout families was still very important in the Maghrib in the end of the xix^th^ century. Their members often acted as arbiters, protected travellers, settled differences between tribes or ethnic groups. This influence is declining nowadays in Algeria, as well as in North Morocco, where the attachment of the mass to the worship of saints is severely condemned and sometimes even actively combated by both the progressive elements and the adherents of strict orthodoxy.

Bibliography: There exists an abundant literature about the marabouts of North Africa. The work of E. Doutté, *Notes sur l'Islam maghribin*, is obsolete but still useful. Further: L. Rinn, *Marabouts et Khouan*, Algiers 1884; E. Montet, *Le culte des saints en Afrique du Nord*, Genève 1909; A. Bel, *Coup d'oeil sur l'Islam en Berbérie*, Paris 1920; E. Westermarck, *Ritual and belief in Morocco*, 2 vols., London 1926.

MĀRISTĀN, hospital. We commonly find, e.g. in Ibn Djubair and al-Maḳrīzī, the hospital, *bīmāristān*, *māristān*, *mūristān*, mentioned in close connection with the madrasa, probably because it was administered by learned men and as a rule also contained a medical school. Al-Walīd is said to have been the first in Islām to build a hospital, in the year 88/707 (Maḳrīzī, iv. 285 *sq.*; *BGA*, v. 106). The name, however, points to Persian origin, probably in connection with the medical schools in Gundīshāpūr; cf. Abu 'l-Faradj, *Taʾrīkh al-duwal*, p. 214. In Cairo in 259 or 261 (i.e. before the mosque) Ibn Ṭūlūn built a hospital for the poor. At the same time he installed a dispensary behind the mosque and a physician used to sit here to be consulted every Friday. According to al-Maḳrīzī, his māristān (called in Ibn Duḳmāḳ, p. 99 the "upper") was the first in Egypt; this probably means the first free public hospital; it is improbable that this Hellenistic institution did not already exist in Egypt (Maḳrīzī, iv. 38, 39, 258; Suyūṭī, *Ḥusn*, ii. 139). Al-Maḳrīzī (iv. 259 *sqq.*) mentions in addition to this hospital in Cairo the *māristān* Kāfūr (in 346, perhaps identical with that called the "lower" by Ibn Duḳmāḳ, p. 99), al-Maghāfir (232—247), al-Manṣūrī (683) al-Mu'aiyadī (823). To these must be added the two which Ṣalāḥ al-Dīn maintained in Miṣr and Ḳāhira (Ibn Djubair, p. 51, 52; cf. Ibn Khallikān, ed. Wüstenfeld, xii. 85). In Damascus Ibn Djubair found two hospitals, one of them the *bīmāristān al-Nūrī* (p. 283 *sq.*; cf. Ibn Khallikān, xii. p. 86). He also mentioned one in Naṣībīn (p. 240), in Ḥarrān 2 (p. 247), in Ḥalab 1 (p. 253), in Ḥamā 1 (p. 257); in Baghdād he refers to a number without particularising them but we know of hospitals here from the third century and in 304 Sinān b. Thābit was director of the 5 hospitals of Baghdād; he was responsible for the foundation of three more (Ibn al-Ḳifṭī, ed. Lippert, p. 193; cf. Hilāl al-Ṣābī, *Kitāb al-wuzarā'*, ed. Amedroz, p. 21 and on the whole question: Mez, *Renaissance*, p. 326 *sq.*). There was a hospital attached to the great Mustanṣirīya madrasa (Le Strange, *Baghdad*, p. 268).

As regards the teaching of medicine, Ibn Abī Uṣaibiʿa shows (i. 103 *sqq.*) that it was continued without interruption in Islām: for example, he mentions ʿAbd al-Malik b. Abdjar, who was in charge of the medical school in Alexandria and after the conquest adopted Islām. At a later date the chief medical schools were in Anṭākiya and Ḥarrān, among other places (i. 116 *infra*). For a long period most of the physicians were Christians (cf. also al-Maḳdisī, *BGA* iii. 183). Teaching was usually given in connection with the hospitals. The head physician collected the students around him whom he trained (*kharradja*) and they assisted him (e.g. the Georgios summoned from Gundēshāpūr to Baghdād by Manṣūr: Ibn Abī Uṣaibiʿa, i. 124). Ḳalā'ūn had a lecture-room installed in his hospital, the Manṣūrī, where the *ra'īs al-aṭibbā'* lectured on medical science (Maḳrīzī, iv. 260); instruction was also given in the great al-Bīmāristān al-Nūrī in Damascus (Ibn Abī Uṣaibiʿa, ii. 192). Lectures on medicine (*ṭibb*) were sometimes given in the mosques also but in this case it was for the most part a theoretical science closely connected with philosophy. Ibn al-Haitham (d. c. 430/1039) lectured on *ṭibb* in the reign of al-Ḥākim in the Azhar (*ibid.* ii. 90) and when Lādjīn restored the mosque of Ibn Ṭūlūn he also endowed lectureships on this subject (Maḳrīzī, iv. 41; which shows that *ṭibb* should be read in Quatremère, *Hist. Sult. Maml.* II/ii. 47). *Ṭibb* could also be studied in a madrasa; for example al-Djīlī who died in 641/1244 lectured on it in the ʿAdhrāwīya in Damascus (Ibn Abī Uṣaibiʿa, ii. 171). At the same time there were special *madāris al-ṭibb*; thus in the seventh century three were built in Damascus (*JA*, ser. 9, iv. 497—499; Fleischer *Kl. Schr.* iii. 329). The teachers in them could also be physicians at the hospitals (Ibn Abī Uṣaibiʿa, ii. 266).

MAʿRŪF AL-KARKHĪ, Abū Maḥfūẓ b. Fīrūz or Fīrūzān, who died in 200/815—6, was a celebrated ascetic and mystic of the Baghdād school. The *nisba* al-Karkhī probably refers to Karkh Bādjaddā, a township in eastern ʿIrāḳ (Samʿānī, *Ansāb*, p. 478*v*, l. 10; cf. Yāḳūt, *Mushtarik*, ed. Wüstenfeld, p. 369, l. 8 *sqq.*), though some authorities connect him with the Karkh quarter of Baghdād. His parents are generally said to have been Christians; according to Ibn Taghrībirdī (ed. Juynboll and Matthes, i. 575), they were Ṣābi'ans belonging to the districts of Wāsiṭ. Bakr b. Khunais al-Kūfī and Farḳad al-Sabakhī, also of Kūfa, are named as his teachers in Ṣūfism (Abū Ṭālib al-Makkī, *Ḳūt al-ḳulūb*, i. 9; *Fihrist*, p. 183). Of those whom he taught or influenced the most famous was Sarī al-Saḳaṭī, who in his turn became the master of al-Djunaid [q.v.]. The story that Maʿrūf was a client of the Shīʿī *imām*, ʿAlī b. Mūsā al-Riḍā, before whom he made profession of Islām and induced his parents to do the same, deserves no credence. Among the sayings attributed to him are the following: "Love is not to be learned from men; it is a gift of God and comes of His grace". "The saints are known by three signs: their cares are for God, their business is in God, and their flight is unto God". "Ṣūfism consists in grasping the realities (*ḥaḳā'iḳ*) and renouncing that which is in the hands of created beings". Maʿrūf was venerated as a saint, and his tomb at Baghdād on the west bank of the Tigris is still a great resort for pilgrims. Ḳushairī relates that the people used to go there in order to pray for rain, saying: "The tomb of Maʿrūf is an approved remedy (*tiryāḳ mudjarrab*)".

Bibliography: Ḳushairī, *Risāla*, Cairo 1318, p. 11; Hudjwīrī, *Kashf al-maḥdjūb*, ed. Schukovski, Leningrad 1926, p. 141 = p. 113 in Nicholson's translation; ʿAṭṭār, *Tadhkirat al-awliyā'*, ed. Nicholson, i. 269 *sqq.*; Ibn Khallikān, *Wafayāt al-aʿyān*, No. 371; transl. de Slane, *Biographical Dictionary*, ii. 88; Djāmī, *Nafaḥāt al-uns*, ed. Lees, p. 42; Massignon, *Essai sur les origines du lexique technique de la mystique musulmane*, p. 207; Nicholson, *The origin and development of Ṣufism*, in *JRAS*, 1906, p. 306.

MARWA. [See saʿy; ʿumra].

MARYAM, Mary. The Arabic form of the name is identical with Syriac Maryam and Greek μαριάμ which are used in the Syriac and in the Greek Bible. in the New as well as in the Old Testament. In the latter it corresponds to the Hebrew מִרְיָם. This name, like other ones with the same suffix, such as ʿAmram, Bilʿam, points to the region between Palestine and Northwestern Arabia as its home. According to Muslim interpretation the name means "the pious" (*al-ʿābida*; cf. the commentaries on Sūra iii. 36). It occurs frequently in the Ḳur'ān in the combination [ʿĪsā] Ibn Maryam "[Jesus]] the son of Mary" (ii. 87, 253; iii. 36 *sqq.*; iv. 157, 171; v. 17, 46, 72, 78, 110, 112, 114, 116; ix. 31; xix. 34; xxiii. 50; xxxiii. 7; xliii. 57; lvii. 27; lxi. 6, 14), no father being mentioned, because, according to Muslim tradition also, ʿĪsā had no earthly father. In the majority of these passages ʿĪsā is clearly regarded as the higher of the two. Yet Maryam's place is important from a dogmatical as well as from a historical point of view.

Maryam is mentioned in the Ḳur'ān throughout, from the oldest parts down to the later Madīnese Sūras. To the first Makkan period belongs Sūra xxiii. 50: "And we made the son of Maryam and his mother a sign; and we made them abide in an elevated place, full of quiet and watered with springs". Here is possibly the first allusion in the Ḳur'ān to the virgin birth. This idea is emphasized in Sūra xix. 20, where Maryam gives to the spirit (i.e. the angel) who announces to her the birth of a male child, this reply: "How should I have a male child, no human

man having touched me?" (cf. Luke i. 34 *sq.*: Then said Mary unto the angel, How shall this be, seeing I know not a man? And the angel answered and said unto her: The Holy Ghost shall come upon thee, and the power of the Highest shall overshadow thee).

The virgin birth is also mentioned in Sūra lxvi. 12 (Madīnian): "And Maryam bint ʿImrān who kept her body pure. Then we breathed into it from our spirit. She acknowledged the truth of the words of her Lord and of his book and she belonged to the obedient".

A third mention of the annunciation and the virgin birth is in Sūra iii. 42: "When the angels said, O Maryam, verily Allāh has elected and purified thee and elected thee above the women of all created beings. O Maryam, be obedient unto thy Lord and prostrate thyself and bow down with those who bow down" (cf. Luke i. 28). Maryam is indeed reckoned as one of the four best women that ever existed, together with ʿĀʾisha [q.v.], Khadīdja [q.v.] and Fāṭima [q.v.] (Aḥmad b. Ḥanbal, *Musnad*, iii. 135), and the chief of the women of Paradise (Ibn Ḥanbal, iii. 64, 80).

According to tradition the annunciation took place in the following way: Djibrīl appeared to Mary in the shape of a beardless youth with a shining face and curling hair, announcing to her the birth of a male child. She expressed her amazement, but, on the angel's reassuring answer, she complied with the will of God.

Thereupon the angel blew his breath into the fold of her shirt, which she had put off. When the angel had withdrawn, she put on the shirt and became pregnant. The annunciation took place in the cavern of the well of Silwān, whither Maryam had gone, as usual, to fill her pitcher; she was then 10 or 13 years of age; and it was the longest day of the year. In Christian tradition also the voice of the angel was heard by Maryam for the first time when she had gone to fill her pitcher. According to a different tradition ʿĪsā's spirit entered Maryam through her mouth (Ṭabarī, *Tafsīr*, vi. 22).

A second important dogmatical feature is that Maryam belongs to the Trinity according to the Ḳurʾān. A glimpse of this conception is given in Sūra v. 75: "al-Masīḥ, the son of Maryam, is an Apostle only, who was preceded by other Apostles, and his mother an upright woman; and both were wont to take food". This verse is apparently meant as a refutation of the Christians who venerated ʿĪsā and his mother as divine persons, elevated above human needs. With this verse may be compared Sūra iv. 171: "O people of the book, beware of exaggeration in your religion and say of Allāh nothing but the truth. ʿĪsā b. Maryam is only the Apostle of Allāh and His word, which He conveyed unto Maryam, and a spirit that came forth from Him. Believe, therefore, in Allāh and his Apostles and say not 'three'. Beware of this, this will be better for you. Allāh is but one God" etc.

Clearer is Sūra v. 116: "And when Allāh said, O ʿĪsā b. Maryam, hast thou said to the people, Take me and my mother as two Gods besides Allāh? He answered: Far be it, that I should say that to which I am not entitled. If I should have said it, Thou wouldst know it" etc.

The commentaries also describe the Trinity as consisting of Allāh, ʿĪsā and Maryam. Al-Baiḍāwī, however, admits that in Sūra iv. 171 there could be an allusion to the Christian doctrine of one God in three hypostases: Father, Son and Holy Ghost.

The question how Muḥammad had come to conceive of Maryam as one of the persons of the Trinity has often been asked. Maracci has a reference to Epiphanius, *Adv. Haereses*, Haeres. lxxviii., § 23, where this author speaks of women in Arabia who venerated Mary as God, and offered to her cakes, from which the heresy is often called that of the Collyridians. Sale, in his *Preliminary Discourse*, p. 45, mentions the Mariamites, who worshipped a Trinity consisting of God, Christ and Mary, referring to a passage in the work of al-Makīn. It may, however, be that Muḥammad's conception was not influenced by any sect, but by the veneration of which Mary was the object in the Church itself. Or it may be an inference due to the identification of ʿĪsā with the Holy Ghost (cf. Sūra iv. 171 as translated above), which made a vacant place in the Trinity, which Mary seemed entitled to occupy. A different explanation is attempted by Sayous, *l.c.*, p. 61 (see *Bibliography*).

A comparatively large place is occupied in the Ḳurʾān by the story of Maryam and ʿĪsā. Many of the features narrated agree, partly or wholy, with narratives in the apocryphal Gospels. Sūra xxiii. 50 (see above) mentions the elevated place that was prepared for ʿĪsā and his mother. It is not clear which tradition is here alluded to. According to St. Luke i. 39, Mary went to the mountains to visit Elisabeth. In the *Protevangelium Jacobi* (chap. xxii; Syriac text, p. 20) it is Elisabeth who flees together with John to a mountain, which opens to protect them against their persecutors. The Muslim commentators mention Jerusalem, Damascus, Ramla, Egypt as being possibly meant by the "elevated place". Maracci thinks of Paradise.

In two passages of the Ḳurʾān there is a fuller narrative of ʿĪsā's birth and what is connected with it, viz. in Sūra xix. (which bears the title of Maryam), vs. 1—34, and in Sūra iii. 35—47.

Sūra xix. opens with the story of Zakarīyāʾ and Yaḥyā (vs. 1—15); on this follows the story of Maryam and ʿĪsā (vs. 16—33). Sūra iii. 35—47 contains *a.* the birth of Maryam; *b.* the annunciation of Yaḥyā (vs. 38—41); *c.* the annunciation of ʿĪsā (vs. 42—46). The comparison of Sūra xix. with Sūra iii. makes it probably that Muḥammad became acquainted with the story of the birth of Maryam later than with that of Yaḥyā and ʿĪsā.

a. The birth of Maryam. This story goes back to a Christian tradition corresponding closely with that contained in the *Protevangelium Jacobi* and *De nativitate Mariae*. Mary's father is called ʿImrān in the Ḳurʾān, Ioachim in Christian tradition; Ibn Khaldūn (*ʿIbar*, ii. 144) is also acquainted with the name Ioachim. It has been supposed that the name of ʿImrān, which apparently corresponds with the Biblical ʿAmram, the father of Moses, as well as the fact that Maryam is called a sister of Hārūn (Sūra xix. 28), is due to a confusion between the two Biblical Maryam's. Sale, Gerock and others think such a confusion improbable. At any rate Muslim tradition assures us that there is a distance of 1,800 years between the Biblical ʿAmram and the father of Mary.

ʿImrān's wife, ʿĪsā's grandmother, is not mentioned by name in the Ḳurʾān. In Christian as well as in Muslim tradition she is called Ḥanna. It is only in Muslim tradition that her genealogy is worked out. She is a daughter of Fāḳūdh and a sister of Ishbāʿ, the Biblical Elisabeth.

Fāḳūdh

Ḥanna married ʿImrān — Ishbāʿ married Zakarīyāʾ

Maryam — Yaḥyā

ʿĪsā

According to a different genealogy Ishbāʿ and Maryam were sisters, daughters of ʿImrān and Ḥanna (Masʿūdī, *Murūdj*, i. 120 *sq.*; Ṭabarī, *Tafsīr*, iii. 144):

ʿImrān

Ishbāʿ — Maryam

Yaḥyā — ʿĪsā

ʿImrān and Ḥanna were old and childless. One day the sight of a bird in a tree, which was feeding her young, aroused Ḥanna's desire for a child. She prays God to fulfil her desire and vows, if her prayer should he heard, the child to the temple. She had however forgotten that, according to the Jewish law, it would be impossible to accomplish her vow, if she should give birth to a female child (cf. *Protev. Jacobi*, chapters iii., iv.; Syriac text, p. 4). Compare with this Sūra iii. 35—36: "How the wife of ʿImrān said: O my Lord, I have vowed to Thee what is in my womb. Now accept [this vow] from me, Thou art the hearing, the knowing. And when she had given birth to the child, she said: O my Lord, I have given birth to a female child.... and I have called her Maryam".

Then the Ḳurʾān relates how she invoked on behalf of Maryam and her posterity Allah's protection from Satan. On this verse is based the well-known *ḥadīth*: "Every child that is born, is touched (or stung) by Satan and this touch makes it cry, except Maryam and her son" (Bukhārī, *Anbiyāʾ*, bāb 44; *Tafsīr*, Sūra 3, b. 2; Muslim, *Faḍāʾil*, trad. 146, 147; Aḥmad b. Ḥanbal, *Musnad*, ii. 233, 274 *sq.*, 288, 292, 319, 368, 523). This tradition is used in support of the impeccability (*ʿiṣma*) of ʿĪsā, Maryam and the Prophets in general (cf. al-Nawawī on Muslim, *l.c.* and al-Baiḍāwī on Sūra iii. 35).

The Ḳurʾān further relates (iii. 37) that the child grows up in a chamber in the temple (*miḥrāb*; cf. the κοιτῶν in *Protev. Jac.*, vi.; Syr. text, p. 5 *sq.*) under the divine grace and under Zakarīyāʾ's care. According to Muslim tradition, ʿImrān had died before the birth of Maryam, and Zakarīyāʾ claimed authority over her on account of his being her uncle; the rabbis did not recognize his claim; his right was proved by an ordeal, consisting in the parties throwing their pens or arrows in a river; the only one that floated was that of Zakarīyāʾ. Sūra iii. 44 refers to this. Christian tradition knows of an ordeal only in the case of Joseph, who, because a dove comes forth from his staff, is recognized as Maryam's guardian.

As often as Zakarīyāʾ enters Maryam's *miḥrāb*, he finds her being provided with food in a miraculous way (iii. 37). This feature also belongs to Christian tradition (*Protev. Jacobi*, chap. viii.; Syr. text, p. 7). The person of Joseph is not mentioned in the Ḳurʾān. In Muslim tradition he takes care of Maryam, his cousin, because Zakarīyāʾ is no longer able to do so, on account of old age. Maryam stays however in the temple, which she leaves during her monthy period only. According to Christian tradition, Joseph takes her into his house when she attains to womanhood, lest she should defile the temple.

b. The annunciation of Yaḥyā. See the articles YAḤYĀ and ZAKARĪYĀʾ.

c. The annunciation and birth of ʿĪsā. The more detailed narrative is that of Sūra xix. 16 *sqq.* Maryam retires to "a place situated eastward", were she hides herself behind a curtain. The commentaries do not know whether a place to the east of Jerusalem is meant, or the eastern part of her house, to which she retires every month. It is said that this is the origin of the *ḳibla* of the Christians.

In vs. 17—21 the story of the annunciation is given (cf. above), followed by that of ʿĪsā's birth, which, according to some Muslim traditions, followed the conception either immediately or very soon. The pains of childbirth came upon Maryam when she was near the trunk of a palm. "She said: would to God I had died before this, and had become a thing forgotten, and lost in oblivion. And he who was beneath her [i.e. the child, or Djibrīl, or the palm] called to her, saying: Be not grieved; God has provided a rivulet under thee; and shake the trunk of the palm and it shall let fall ripe dates upon thee, ready gathered. And eat and drink and calm thy mind". This story may, perhaps, be considered as a parallel to the Christian tradition in which it is related that, during the flight to Egypt, the babe Jesus ordered a palm in the desert to bow down in order to refresh Mary by its dates; thereupon the palm obeyed and stayed with its head at Mary's feet, till the child ordered it to stand upright again and to open a vein between its roots in order to quench the thirst of the holy family (Apocryphal Gospel of Matthew, chap. xx.). The Ḳurʾān goes on (vs. 26): "And when thou seest any man, say: I have vowed a fast unto the Merciful; so I may not speak to any man to-day". The commentaries say, this was meant to avoid importunate questions. This feature is not in Christian tradition; yet in the *Protevangelium Jacobi* it is said (chap. xii.; Syr. text, p. 11) that Mary, who was then 16 years of age, hid herself from the Israelites. According to Muslim tradition, she stayed in a cavern during forty days. "Then she brought him", continues the Ḳurʾān (xix. 27), "to her people, carrying him. They said: O Maryam, now thou hast done a strange thing. O sister of Hārūn, thy father was not a bad man, neither was thy mother a harlot. Then she pointed to the child". Then the child begins to speak, one of the wellknown miracles ascribed to ʿĪsā. The "very shameful calummy" which the Israelites brought forth against Maryam, is also mentioned in Sūra iv. 156.

As to the words "O sister of Hārūn" (cf. above), it may be added that, according to the commentaries, this Hārūn was not Moses' brother, but one of Maryam's contemporaries, who was either a wicked man, with whom she is compared in this respect, or her pious brother.

A legend about loaves of bread which Maryam gave to the Magi, is mentioned by al-Masʿūdī, iv. 79 *sq.*

The flight to Egypt is not mentioned in the Ḳurʾān, unless the "elevated place" (Sūra xxiii. 50; cf. above) should be an allusion to it. According to Muslim tradition which is acquainted with it, their stay lasts 12 years. After the death of Herod the holy family returns to Nāṣira.

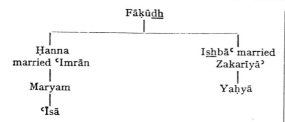

After his alleged death ʿĪsā consoles his mother from heaven. According to others it was Mary Magdalene. The stories of the *Transitus Mariae* have not obtained a place in Muslim tradition. Instead of these, there is a narrative of how Maryam went to Rome in order to preach before Mārūt (Nero), accompanied by John (the disciple) and Shimʿūn, the coppersmith. When Shimʿūn and Tadāwus (Thaddaeus?) were crucified with their heads downward, Maryam fled with John. When they were persecuted the earth opened and withdrew them from their persecutors. This miracle was the cause of Mārūt's conversion.

Bibliography: Ibn Hishām, p. 407; al-Ṭabarī, i. p. 711 *sqq.*; do., *Tafsīr*, iii. 144 *sqq.*; vi. 21, 179; vii. 82; xvi. 28 *sqq.*; xviii. 17; al-Yaʿḳūbī, i. 74 *sqq.*; al-Masʿūdī, i. 120 *sqq.*; ii. 145; iv. 79 *sq.*; al-Kisāʾī, *Ḳiṣaṣ al-anbiyāʾ*, ed. Eisenberg, p. 301, *sqq.*; Ibn al-Athīr, i. 211; al-Thaʿlabī, *ʿArāʾis al-madjālis*, Cairo 1290, p. 326 *sqq.*; the commentaries on the Ḳurʾān; Maracci, *Prodromi*, Padua 1698, iv. 85—87, 104 *sq.*, 178 *sqq.* and the notes to his translation of the Ḳurʾān; C. F. Gerock, *Versuch einer Darstellung der Christologie des Korans*, Hamburg and Gotha 1839, p. 22 *sqq.*, 72 *sqq.*; G. Weil, *Biblische Legenden der Muselmänner*, Francfort 1845, p. 280 *sqq.*; E. Sayous, *Jésus-Christ d'après Mahomet*, Paris-Leipzig 1880; G. Smit, *Bijbel en legende bij den arab. schrijver Jaqubi*, Leyden 1907, p. 86 *sqq.*; J. Horovitz, *Koranische Untersuchungen*, Berlin and Leipzig 1926, p. 138 *sqq.*; A Pieters, *Circumstantial Evidence of the Virgin Birth*, in *MW*, xiv. (1929), 350 *sqq.*; *Evangelia apocrypha*, rec. C. de Tischendorf, second ed., Leipzig 1876; *Apocrypha syriaca, the Protevangelium Jacobi and Transitus Mariae* ...., ed. and transl. A Smith Lewis, (*Studia Sinaitica*, xi.), London 1902.

MASDJID (A.), Mosque

A. Origin
B. Foundation of mosques after Muḥammad's death
C. The mosque as a religious centre
D. The building and its equipment
E. The mosque as a state institution
F. Administration
G. The staff

A. Origin of the Mosque

The word *msgdʾ* (from *s-g-d* "to prostrate oneself") is found in Aramaic, meaning in Nabataean a stele, a sacred pillar, or perhaps "place of worship" (Cooke, *North Semitic Inscriptions*, p. 238), as already in the Jewish Elephantine Papyri (ed. Sachau, pl. 32). Arabic *masdjid* is taken over from Aramaic or formed independently from *sadjada* "prostrate oneself", which comes from Aramaic, like Ethiopic *mĕsgād* "temple, church".

1. The Meccan period

The word is used in the Ḳurʾān especially of the Meccan sanctuary (*al-masdjid al-ḥarām*, Sūra ii. 144, 149; v. 2; viii. 34; xvii. 1 etc. According to tradition the term *al-masdjid al-aḳṣā* (Sura xvii. 1) means the Jerusalem sanctuary but the reference is rather to a place of prayer in heaven. The word is also applied to non-Islāmic sanctuaries. "If God had not taken men under his protection, then monasteries, churches and places of prayer (*ṣalawāt*) and *masādjid* would have been destroyed" (Sūra xxii. 40, cf. xviii. 21). The word is also used in a *ḥadīth* of an Abyssinian church and in another of Jewish and Christian tomb-sanctuaries. Even Ibn Khaldūn still uses the word in the general meaning of a temple or place of worship of any religion.

To the Prophet the Meccan sanctuary always remained the principal mosque, known as *Bait Allāh* even before the time of the Prophet. It was therefore the goal of the Prophet to conquer it from the Ḳuraish who drove the believers out of it (cf. Sūra ii., 144, 217 et al.), and afterwards it was revealed in the year 9: "It is not right for polytheists to frequent the mosques of God" (Sūra ix. 17 *sq.*) and the opponents of the new religion were excluded from the sanctuary. According to the *sīra*, Muḥammad and his followers like other Meccans regularly made the *ṭawāf* around the Kaʿba and kissed the Black Stone; it is frequently stated that he used to sit in the masdjid like his fellow-citizens, alone or with a follower or disputing with an opponent. Muḥammad took part in the traditional rites there before the Hidjra (Sūra cviii., 2); in the year 1, one of his followers, Saʿd b. Muʿādh, took part in the pilgrimage ceremonies and in the year 2 he himself sacrificed on the 10th Dhu 'l-Ḥidjdja on the muṣallā of the Banū Salima. Here as elsewhere, he retained ancient customs where his new teaching did not directly exclude them. But when an independent religion developed out of his preaching, a new type of divine service had to be evolved.

In Mecca, the original Muslim community had no special place of worship. The Prophet used to perform the ṣalāt in secret in the narrow alleys of Mecca with his first male follower ʿAlī and with the other earliest Companions also. References are made to the solitary ṣalāt of the Prophet, sometimes beside the Kaʿba, sometimes in his own house. The believers prayed together in a house. Occasionally also ʿUmar is said to have conducted the ritual prayer with others beside the Kaʿba (Ibn Hishām, p. 224) because ʿUmar was able to defy the Ḳuraish.

In the dogma taught by Muḥammad a sanctuary was not a fundamental necessity. Every place was the same to God, and humility in the presence of God, of which the ritual prayer was the expression, could be shown anywhere; hence the saying of the Prophet that he had been given the whole world as a masdjid, while earlier prophets could only pray in churches and synagogues and also the saying: "Wherever the hour of prayer overtakes thee, thou shalt perform the ṣalāt and that is a *masdjid*" (Muslim, *Masādjid*, tr. 1). That he nevertheless remained firmly attached to the traditional sanctuary of the Kaʿba, produced a confusion of thought which is very marked in Sūra ii. 142 *sqq.* When in Madīna he was able to do as he pleased, it must have been natural for him to create a place where he could be undisturbed with his followers and where they could perform the ritual *ṣalāt* together.

2. The Foundation of the Mosque in Madīna

According to tradition the Prophet bought the ground for the mosque in Madīna from two orphans, in one tradition on the spot where his camel stopped when he entered the town. The site was covered with graves, ruins and palm-trees and was used as a place for keeping camels. The site was cleared, the palms cut down and the walls built. The building material was bricks baked in the sun (*labin*); the mosque was a courtyard surrounded by a brick wall on a stone foundation with three entrances: the gateposts were of stone. On the *ḳibla* side (i.e. the north wall) stems of palmtrees were soon set up as columns and a roof was put over them of palm-leaves and clay. On the east side two huts of similar materials were built for the Prophet's wives Sawda and ʿĀʾis̲h̲a; their entrances opened on to the court and were covered with carpets: they were later increased so that there were nine little houses for the Prophet's wives. When the *ḳibla* was moved to the south, the arbour at the north wall remained; under this arbour called *ṣuffa* or *ẓulla* the homeless Companions found shelter. On the south side, later the *ḳibla* side, an arbour was probably built also, for the Prophet used to preach leaning against a palmtrunk and this must have been on the *ḳibla* side. How large the arbours were cannot be ascertained. The mosque was the courtyard of the Prophet's house and at the same time the meeting-place for the believers and the place for common prayer.

According to the sources, it was the Prophet's intention from the very first to build a mosque at once in Madīna; according to a later tradition Gabriel commanded him in the name of God to build a house for God; but this story is coloured by later conditions. It was been made quite clear that the earliest masd̲j̲id had nothing of the character of a sacred edifice. Much can be quoted for this view from *ḥadīt̲h̲* and *sīra*. Believers and unbelievers went freely about in the mosque, tents and huts were put up there, disputes took place in it, often it had the outlook of the headquarters of an army.

The mosque was the place where believers assembled for prayer around the Prophet, where he delivered his adresses, which contained not only appeals for obedience to God but regulations affecting the social life of the community (cf. Buk̲h̲ārī, *Ṣalāt*, bāb 70, 71); from here he controlled the religious and political community of Islām. Even at the real old sanctuaries of Arabia, there were no restrictions on what one could do; what distinguished the mosque from the Christian church or the Meccan temple was that in it there was no specially dedicated ritual object. At the Kaʿba also people used to gather to discuss everyday affairs and also for important assemblies, if we may believe the *Sīra*. Beside the Kaʿba was the *dār al-nadwa*, where important matters were discussed and justice administered. From the Madīna mosque was developed the general type of the Muslim mosque. It depended on circumstances whether the aspect of the mosque as a social centre or as a place of prayer was more or less emphasized.

3. Other Mosques in the time of the Prophet

According to tradition another mosque was founded before the mosque of Madīna, viz. that of Ḳubāʾ. It is said that Muḥammad found it there on his Hid̲j̲ra, or that he founded it himself on that occasion. That other mosques existed at the lifetime of the Prophet appears from the Ḳurʾān: "in houses which God hath permitted to be built that his name might be praised in them, in them there praise Him, morning and evening, men whom neither business nor trade distracts from praising God and performing the *ṣalāt* and the giving of alms", etc. (Sūra xxiv. 36 *sq.*). As this revelation dates from the Madīna period, it cannot refer to Jews and Christians. Another passage speaks of dwelling in the mosques (Sūra ii. 187). The separate tribes had public places of prayer at a very early date. The Ḳurʾān strongly condemns an "opposition mosque" (*masd̲j̲id al-ḍirār*), because it was not founded on piety, but for division among the believers (Sūra ix. 108 *sq.*). This dates from the Prophet's march to Tabūk and refers to a mosque built by the Banū Sālim.

B. Foundation of Mosques after the time of the Prophet

1. Chief Mosques

What importance the Madīna mosque had attained as the centre of administration and worship of the Muslims is best seen from the fact that the first thought of the Muslim generals after their conquests was to found a mosque as a centre around which to gather.

Conditions differed somewhat as between newly-founded cities and already existing towns. Important examples of the first kind are Baṣra, Kūfa and al-Fusṭāṭ. Baṣra was founded by ʿUtba b. G̲h̲azwān as winter-quarters for the army in the year 14/635 (or 16 or 17). The mosque was placed in the centre with the *dār al-imāra*, the dwelling of the commander-in-chief with a prison and *dīwān*, in front of it. Prayer was at first offered on the open space which was fenced round; later the whole was built of reeds and when the men went off to war the reeds were pulled up and laid away. Abū Mūsā al-As̲h̲ʿarī, who later became ʿUmar's wālī, built the edifice of clay and bricks baked in the sun (*labin*) and used grass for the roof. It was similar in Kūfa which was founded in 17/638 by Saʿd b. Abī Waḳḳāṣ. In the centre was the mosque and beside it the *dār al-imāra* was laid out. The mosque at first was simply an open quadrangle, *ṣaḥn*, marked off by a trench round it. It seems that reeds were also used for building the walls here and later Saʿd used *labin*. On the south side (and only here) there was an arbour, *ẓulla*, built. The *dār al-imāra* beside the mosque was later by ʿUmar's orders combined with the mosque. The plan was therefore an exact reproduction of that of the mosque in Madīna; the importance of the mosque was also expressed in its position and the commander lived close beside it. There was no difference in al-Fusṭāṭ, which, although there was already an older town here, was laid out as an entirely new camp. In the year 21/642, after the conquest of Alexandria, the mosque was laid out in a garden where ʿAmr had planted his standard. The court was quite simple, surrounded by a wall and had trees growing in it; a simple roof is mentioned; it must be identical with the above mentioned *ẓulla* or *ṣuffa*. ʿAmr b. al-ʿĀṣī lived just beside the mosque and around it the *ahl al-rāya*. Like the house of the Prophet, the general's house lay on the east side with only a road between them. There were two doors in each wall except the southern one. We find similar arrangements made in al-Mawṣil in the year 20/641.

In other cases the Muslims established themselves in old towns either conquered or surrendered by treaty; by the treaty they received a site for their mosque. But the distinction between towns which were conquered and those which were surrendered soon disappeared and the position is as a rule not clear. Examples of old towns in which the Muslims established themselves are al-Madāʾin, Damascus and Jerusalem. — In al-Madāʾin Saʿd b. Abī Waḳḳāṣ after the conquest in 16/637 made Kisrā's *īwān* into a mosque, after he had conducted the *ṣalāt al-fatḥ* in it. In Damascus which was occupied in 14 or 15 by capitulation, the Church of St. John was, according to tradition, divided so that the eastern half became Muslim, from which Muslim tradition created the legend that the city was taken partly by conquest and partly by agreement. As a matter of fact however, the Muslims seem to have laid out their own mosque here just beside the church and close beside it again was the Khaḍrā', the commander-in-chief's palace, from which a direct entrance to the *maḳṣūra* was later made. Conditions here were therefore once again the same as in Madīna. But the possibility of an arrangement such as is recorded by tradition cannot be rejected, for there is good evidence of it elsewhere; in Ḥimṣ for example, the Muslims and Christians shared a building in common as a mosque and church, and it is evident from al-Iṣṭakhrī and Ibn Ḥawḳal that this was still the case in the time of their common authority, al-Balkhī (309/921), and a similar arrangement is recorded for Dabīl in Armenia.

There were special conditions in Jerusalem. The Muslims recognised the sanctuary there, as is evident from the earlier *ḳibla* and from Sūra xvii. 1 (in the traditional interpretation). It must therefore have been natural for the conquerors, when the town capitulated, to seek out the recognized holy place. Indeed we are told that ʿUmar in the year 17/638 built a mosque in Jerusalem on the site of the temple of Solomon. That the *ḳubbat al-ṣakhra* [q.v.] which replaced the Mosque of ʿUmar, stands on the old site of the Temple is undoubted. How he found the site is variously recorded [cf. AL-ḲUDS]. The building was, like other mosques of the time of ʿUmar, very simple. Arculf who visited Jerusalem about 670, says: "The Saracens attend a quadrangular house of prayer (*domus orationis*, e.i. *masdjid*) which they have built with little art with boards and large beams on the remains of some ruins, on the famous site where the Temple was once built in all its splendour" (*Itinera Hierosolymitana*, ed. P. Geyer, 1898, p. 226 *sq.*). It is of interest to note that this simple mosque, like the others, was in the form of a rectangle; in spite of its simple character it could hold 3,000 people, according to Arculf.

As late as the reign of Muʿāwiya we find a new town, Ḳairawān, being laid out on the old plan as a military camp with a mosque and *dār al-imāra* in the centre. The Muslim conquerors even at a later date always built a mosque in the centre of a newly conquered town, at first a simple one in each town, and it was a direct reproduction of the simple mosque of the Prophet in Madīna. It was the exception to adapt already existing buildings in towns. But soon many additional mosques were added.

2. Tribal mosques and Sectarian mosques

Probably even before Islām the tribes had, like the Meccans, their *madjlis* or *nādī* or *dār al-shūrā*, where they discussed matters of general importance, therefore it was natural that tribal mosques should come into existence.

The tribal mosque was a sign that the independence of the tribe was still retained under Islām. The mosque of Ḳubā', mentioned above, was the mosque of ʿAmr b. ʿAwf. Indeed we hear everywhere of tribal mosques, for example around Madīna that of the Banū Ḳuraiẓa, of the Banū Ḥāritha, of the Banū Ẓafar, of the Banū Wā'il, of the Banū Ḥarām, of the Banū Zuraiḳ, said to have been the first in which the Ḳur'ān was publicly read, that of the Banū Salima etc.; the "mosque of the two Ḳiblas" belonged to the Banū Sawād b. Ghanm b. Kaʿb b. Salima. This then was the position in Madīna: the tribes had usually their own mosques and one mosque was the chief mosque. This was probably the position within the Prophet's lifetime; for in the earliest campaigns of conquest, mosques were built on this principle. ʿUmar is said to have written to Abū Mūsā in Baṣra to that effect. Similarly he wrote to Saʿd b. Abī Waḳḳās in Kūfa and to ʿAmr b. al-ʿĀṣī in Miṣr. On the other hand in Syria, where they had settled in old towns, they were not to build tribal mosques. It is actually recorded that the tribes in each *khiṭṭa* had their own mosques around the mosque of ʿAmr in al-Fusṭāṭ and even much later a tribal mosque like that of the Rāshida was still in existence. Even in the chief mosque, the tribes had their own places. We have similar evidence from the towns of ʿIrāḳ.

During the wars these tribal mosques were the natural rallying points for the various tribes; the mosque was a madjlis, where councils were held and the people were taught from its minbar; battles often centred for this reason round these mosques. Gradually, as new sects arose, they naturally had mosques of their own, just as Musailima before them is said to have had his own mosque. Thus we read later of the mosque of the Ḥanbalīs in Baghdād, in which there was continual riot and confusion. In particular the Sunnīs and Shīʿīs as a rule had separate mosques. It sometimes even happened that Ḥanafīs and Shāfiʿīs had separate mosques. These special mosques were a great source of disruption in Islām and we can understand that a time came when the learned discussed whether such mosques should be permitted at all.

3. Adaptation to Islām of Older Sanctuaries; Memorial Mosques

According to the early historians, the towns which made treaties with the Muslims received permission to retain their churches, while in the conquered towns the churches fell to the Muslims without any preamble (Balādhurī, p. 120 *sq.*; Ṭabarī, i. 2405, 2407). Sometimes also it is recorded that a certain number of churches were received from the Christians, e.g. fifteen in Damascus according to one tradition. It is rather doubtful whether the process was such a regular one; in any case the Muslims in course of time appropriated many churches to themselves. With the mass-conversions to Islām, this was a natural result. The churches taken over by the Muslims were occasionally used as dwellings; at a later date it also happened that they were used as government offices, as in Egypt in 146/763 (Maḳrīzī, iv. 35; cf. for Kūfa, Balādhurī, p. 286). The obvious thing, however, was to transform the churches taken into mosques. A saying regarding churches and synagogues, "Perform thy ṣalāt in them; it will not harm thee" (*Corpus iuris di Zaid b. ʿAlī*, ed. Griffini, No. 364) is intended to remove any misgivings about the use of captured churches and synagogues as mosques. The most important example of this kind was in Damascus where al-Walīd b. ʿAbd al-Malik in 86/705 took the church of St. John from the Christians and had it rebuilt; he is said to have offered the Christians another church in its stead. He is said to have transformed into mosques ten churches in all in Damascus. It must have been particularly in the villages, with the gradual conversion of the people to Islām, that the churches were turned into mosques. In the Egyptian villages there were no mosques in the earlier generations of Islām. But when al-Maʾmūn was fighting the Copts, many churches were turned into mosques (Maḳrīzī, iv. 28 *sq.*, 30). It is also recorded of mosques in Cairo that they were converted synagogues or churches.

We hear about mosques that were successors of ancient temples, near Kerbelāʾ, in Maṣīṣa, in Dihlī (Balādhurī, p. 165 *sq.*; Ibn Baṭṭūṭa, iii. 151; Goldziher, *Muh. Stud.*, ii. 331 *sq.*), especially "fire-temples" as related by Masʿūdī. Thus in Islām also the old rule holds that sacred places survive changes of religion. It was especially easy in cases where Christian sanctuaries were associated with Biblical personalities who were also recognized by Islām: e.g., the Church of St. John in Damascus and many holy places in Palestine. One example is the mosque of Job in Shēkh Saʿd, associated with Sūra xxi. 83, xxxviii. 39; here in Silvia's time (fourth century) there was a church of Job (Masʿūdī, i. 91).

But Islām itself had created historical associations which were bound soon to lead to the building of new mosques. Even in the lifetime of the Prophet, the Banū Sālim are said to have asked him to perform the ṣalāt in their masdjid to give it his authority. After the death of the Prophet, his memory became so precious that the places where he had prayed obtained a special importance and his followers, who liked to imitate him in everything, preferred to perform their ṣalāt in such places. But this tendency was only an intensification of what had existed in his lifetime; and so it is not easy to decide how far stories about prayer-places initiated by him reflect later conditions. Mosques very quickly arose on the road between Mecca and Madīna at places where, according to the testimony of his Companions, the Prophet had prayed; the same was the case with the road which the Prophet had taken to Tabūk in the year 9 (Ibn Hishām, p. 907; Wāḳidī-Wellhausen, p. 394, 421 *sqq.*). Mosques were built on such places in Faḍīkh in Khaibar, outside Ṭāʾif etc.

Mosques arose in and around Madīna, "because Muḥammad prayed here" (Wüstenfeld, *Gesch. d. Stadt Medina*, p. 31, 38, 132 *sqq.*). It is obvious that in most of these cases later conditions are put back to the time of the Prophet; in connection with the "war of the Ditch" we are told that: "he prayed everywhere where mosques now stand" (Wāḳidī-Wellhausen p. 208). Since, for example, the Masdjid al-Faḍīkh is also called Masdjid al-Shams (Wüstenfeld, *Medina*, p. 132) we have perhaps here actually an ancient sanctuary.

Mosques became associated with the Prophet in many ways. In Madīna, for example, there was the Masdjid al-Baghla where footprints of the Prophet's mule were shown in a stone, the Masdjid al-Idjāba where the Prophet's appeal was answered, the Masdjid al-Fatḥ which recalls the victory over the Meccans, etc. (see Wüstenfeld, *Medina*, p. 136 *sqq.*). Al-Ghazzālī says that in Madīna 30 such places are visited (*Iḥyāʾ*, i. 183). In Mecca there was naturally a large number of places sacred through associations with the Prophet and therefore used as places of prayer. So the house of Khadīdja, the Prophet's birthplace, the house where his first meetings were held, the place where he used to pray outside the town, where the Djinn overheard his revelation etc. Further places referred to his Companions, such as Ḥamza, ʿUmar and ʿAlī, his son Ibrāhīm, ʿĀʾisha, his slave Māriya; these places are mentioned in *Chron. Mekka.*

In al-Ḥidjāz the Muslims thus acquired a series of mosques which became important from their association with the Prophet, his family and his Companions, and made Muslim history live. On the other hand, in lands formerly Christian, they took over sanctuaries which were associated with the Biblical history which they had assimilated (see Le Strange, *Palestine*, passim). Other mosques soon became associated with Biblical and Muslim history. The mosque founded by ʿUmar on the site of the Temple in Jerusalem was identified as *al-masdjid al-aḳṣā* mentioned in Sūra xvii. 1 and therefore connected with the Prophet's night journey and the journey to Paradise. The rock is said to have greeted the Prophet on this occasion and marks in a stone covering a hole are explained as Muḥammad's footprints, sometimes also as those of Idrīs; cf. Le Strange, *Palestine*, p. 136. The name al-Masdjid al-Aḳṣā was used throughout the early period for the whole Ḥaram area in Jerusalem, later partly for it, and partly for the building in its southern part (cf. *op. cit.*, p. 96 *sq.*). Then there were the mosques which had specifically Muslim associations, like the Masdjid of ʿUmar on the Mount of Olives where he encamped at the conquest (*BGA*, iii. 172).

In Egypt the Mosque of Ibn Ṭūlūn, we are also told, was built where Mūsā talked with his Lord (Maḳrīzī, iv. 36); according to al-Ḳuḍāʿī there were in Egypt four Masādjid of Mūsā (Ibn Duḳmāḳ, ed. Vollers, p. 92); there was a Masdjid Yaʿḳūb wa-Yūsuf (*BGA.*, iii. 200) and a Joseph's prison, certainly dating from the Christian period (Maḳrīzī, iv. 315). There was also a Mosque of Abraham in Munyat Ibn al-Khaṣīb (Ibn Djubair, p. 58). The chief mosque of Ṣanʿāʾ was built by Shem, son of Noah (*BGA*, vii. 110). The old temple near Iṣṭakhr. converted into a mosque, was connected with Sulaimān (Masʿūdī, *Murūdj*, iv. 77; Yāḳūt, i. 299). In the mosque of Kūfa not only Ibrāhīm but one thousand other prophets and one thousand saints, described as *waṣī*, are said to have offered their prayers; here was the tree Yaḳṭīn (Sūra xxxvii. 146); here died Yaghūth and Yaʿūḳ, etc., and in this mosque there was a chapel of Abraham, Noah and Idrīs (Yāḳūt, iv. 325; also Ibn Djubair, p. 211 *sq.*). A large number of mosques were associated with Companions of the Prophet. What emphasis was laid on such an association is seen, for example, from the story according to which ʿUmar declined to perform the *ṣalāt* in the Church of the Resurrection in Jerusalem, lest the Church should afterwards be claimed as a mosque.

4. Tomb Mosques

A special class of memorial mosques consisted of those which were associated with a tomb. The graves of ancestors and of saints had been sanctuaries from ancient times and they were gradually adopted into Islām. In addition there were the saints of Islām itself. The general tendency to distinguish places associated with the founders of Islām naturally concentrated itself round the graves in which they rested. In the Ḳurʾān, a tomb-masdjid is mentioned in connection with the Seven Sleepers (Sūra xviii. 21) but it is not clear if it was recognized. The Prophet is said to have visited regularly at al-Baḳīʿ in Madīna the tombs of the martyrs who fell at Uḥud and paid reverence to them. Whatever the exact amount of truth in the story is, the general trend of development stimulated an interest in graves which led to the erection of sanctuaries at them. The progress of this tendency is more marked in al-Wāḳidī, who died in 207/823, than in Ibn Isḥāk who died in 151/768.

The collections of Ḥadīth made in the third century contain discussions on this fact which show that the problem was whether the tombs could be used as places of worship and in this connection whether mosques could be built over the tombs. The ḥadīths answer both questions in the negative, which certainly was in the spirit of the Prophet. It is said that "Ṣalāt at the graves (*fi 'l-maḳābir*) is *makrūh*" (Bukhārī, *Ṣalāt*, bāb 52); "sit not upon graves and perform not ṣalāt towards them" (Muslim, *Djanā'iz*, tr. 97 *sq.*); "hold the ṣalāt in your houses, but do not use them as tombs" (Muslim, *Ṣalāt al-musāfirīn*, tr. 208 *sq.*). On the other hand it is acknowledged that Anas performed the *ṣalāt* at the cemetery (Bukhārī, *Ṣalāt*, bāb 48). We are also told that tombs cannot be used as *masādjid* (Bukhārī, *Ṣalāt*, bāb 48; *Djanā'iz*, bāb 62). On his deathbed the Prophet is said to have cursed the Jews and the Christians because they used the tombs of their prophets as *masādjid* (Bukhārī, *Ṣalāt*, bāb 48, 54). The Ḥadīth finds in this the explanation for the fact that the tomb of the Prophet was not at first accessible (Bukhārī, *Ṣalāt*, bāb 48, 55; *Djanā'iz*, bāb 62; *Anbiyā'*, bāb 50; Muslim, *Masādjid*, tr. 19 *sqq.*); as a matter of fact its precise location was not exactly known (*Djanā'iz*, bāb 96). Although this view of tomb-mosques is still held in certain limited circles (cf. Ibn Taimīya, the Wahhābīs), the old pre-Islāmic custom soon alo became a Muslim one. The expositors of Ḥadīth like al-Nawawī (on Muslim, *Masādjid*, tr. 3, lith. Dihlī 1319, i. 201) and al-ʿAskalānī (Cairo 1329, i. 354), explain the above passages to mean that only an exaggerated reverence of the dead is forbidden so that tombs should not be used as a ḳibla; otherwise it is quite commendable to spend time in a mosque in proximity to a devout man.

The name given a tomb-mosque is often *ḳubba*, a word which is used of a tent (Bukhārī, *Djanā'iz*, bāb 62 et al.; Ṭarafa, *Dīwān*, vii. 1), but later came to mean the dome which usually covers tombs and thus became the general name for the sanctuary of a saint. *Maḳām* also means a little chapel and a saint's tomb. The custom of making a *ḳubba* at the tomb of a saint was firmly rooted in Byzantine territory, where sepulchral churches always had a dome (Herzog-Hauch, *Realenzyclopädie* [3], x. 784). The usual name however for a tomb-sanctuary was *mashhad*; this is applied to places where saints are worshipped, among Muslim tombs particularly to those of the family and relations of the Prophet (v. Berchem, *Corpus Inscr. Arab.*, i., No. 32, 63, 457, 544; Makrīzī, iv., p. 265, 309 *sqq.*) but also to tombs of other recognized saints, e.g. Mashhad Djirdjīs in Mawṣil (Ibn Djubair, *Riḥla*, p. 236) etc.

The transformation of the tombs of the Prophet and his near relatives into sanctuaries seems to have been a gradual process. Muḥammad, Abū Bakr and ʿUmar are said to have been buried in the house of ʿĀ'isha; close to it were the houses of the Prophet's other wives. Al-Walīd acquired the houses, had them torn down and erected new buildings. The tombs were enclosed by a pentagonal wall; the whole area was called *al-Rawḍa* "the garden"; it was not till later that a dome was built over it (Wüstenfeld, *Medina*, p. 66 *sqq.*, 72 *sq.*, 78 *sqq.*, 89). In the cemetery of Madīna, al-Baḳīʿ, a whole series of *mashāhid* came to be built where tombs of the family and of the Companions of the Prophet were located (*ibid.*, p. 140 *sqq.*; Ibn Djubair, *Riḥla*, p. 195 *sqq.*). They were regarded as sacred and were visited *li 'l-baraka*. The name al-Rawḍa given to the Prophet's tomb became later applied to other tomb-sanctuaries. Separate limbs were revered in some mosques, like the head of al-Ḥusain in Cairo, which was brought there in 548/1153—4 from ʿAsḳalān (ʿAlī Pāshā Mubārak, *al-Khiṭaṭ al-djadīda*, iv. 91 *sqq.*; cf. Sauvaire, *Hist. Jérus. Hébr.*, p. 16); his head was also revered for some time in the *mashhad al-ra's* in Damascus (according to Ibn Shākir, *JA.*, 9th ser., vii. 385).

Gradually a vast number of Muslim tombs of saints came into existence; and to these were added all the pre-Islāmic sanctuaries which were adopted by Islām. No distinction can therefore be drawn between tomb-mosques and other memorial mosques. It was often impossible to prove that the tomb in question ever really existed and several saints had more than one tomb; ʿAlī e.g. in Mashhad ʿAlī, in Kūfa, in Damascus and elsewhere (Ibn Djubair, *Riḥla*, p. 212, 267; *BGA*, ii. 46, iii., 163 et al.), Abū Huraira in Madīna, Djīza and various places in Palestine, the prophet Jonah in Niniveh and in Palestine. There are examples of names being confused. Wherever Shīʿīs ruled, there arose numerous tomb-mosques of the *ahl al-bait*. In Egypt Ibn Djubair gives a list of 14 men and five women of the Prophet's family, who were honoured there (*Riḥla*, p. 46 *sq.*). Islām was always creating new tombs of saints who had been distinguished for learning or asceticism or miracle-working, e.g. the tomb of al-Shāfiʿī in Cairo and Aḥmad al-Badawī in Ṭanṭā. In and around Damascus were a number of mosques which were built on the tombs of prophets and unnamed saints (Ibn Djubair, *Riḥla*, p. 273 *sqq.*).

Like the sanctuaries of persons mentioned in the Bible there were those of people mentioned in the Ḳur'ān. For example, outside the Djāmiʿ in ʿAkkā was shown the tomb-mosque of the prophet Ṣāliḥ (Nāṣir-i Khusraw, *Sefer-nāme*, ed. Schefer, p. 15_1 = 49), and in Syria that of his son (Ibn Djubair, p. 46); that of Hūd was also shown near ʿAkkā (*Sefer-nāme*, p. 16_5 = 52), farther east that of Shuʿaib and of his daughter (*ibid.*, p. 16_{12} = 63); the tomb of Hūd was also pointed out in Damascus and in Ḥaḍramawt (Yāḳūt, ii. 596_{16}); along with there we have peculiarly Muslim saints like Dhu 'l-Kifl, the son of Job (*ibid.*, p. 16_4 = 52). Then there are the sanctuaries of saints who are only superficially Muslim but really have their origins in old popular beliefs, like al-Khaḍir who had a *mashhad* in Damascus (Yāḳūt, ii. 596_9), or a saint like ʿAkk, founder of the town of ʿAkkā, whose tomb Nāṣir-i Khusraw visited outside the town (*Sefer-nāme*, p. 15_6 from below = 51). Such tombs were much visited by pious travellers and are therefore frequently mentioned in literature (on Mashāhid of the kinds mentioned here in the ʿIrāḳ, see *BGA*, iii. 130; for Mawṣil etc., *ibid.*, p. 146).

Just as the ḳubba under which the saint lay and the mosque adjoining it was sanctified by him so vice-versa a ḳubba and a mosque could cause a deceased person to become considered a saint. It was therefore the custom for the mighty not only to give this distinction to their fathers but also to prepare such buildings for themselves even in their own lifetime. This was particularly the custom of the Mamlūk sulṭāns, perhaps stimulated by the fact that they did not found dynasties in which power passed from father to son. Such buildings are called *ḳubba* (van Berchem, *CIA*, i., No. 82 *sqq.*, 95, 96,

126, 138 etc.), exceptionally *zāwiya* (*ibid.*, No. 98), frequently *turba* (*ibid.*, No. 58, 66, 88, 106, 107, 116, etc.); the latter word acquired the same meaning as masdjid, partly saint's grave and partly sacred site (cf. Ibn Djubair, *Riḥla*, p. 114, 196); but this word does not seem to be used of ordinary tomb-mosques, although the distinction between these and mosques in honour of saints often disappeared. In these ḳubbas the regular recitation of the Ḳur'ān was often arranged and the tomb was provided with a *kiswa*. The mausoleum might be built in connection with a great mosque and be separated from it by a grille.

5. Mosques as pious foundations

In the early period the building of mosques was a social obligation on the ruler as representative of the community and on the tribes. As Islām spread, the governors built mosques in the provinces. A governor of Media about 391/1000 is said to have endowed 3000 mosques and hostels (Mez, *Renaissance des Islāms*, p. 24). Very soon a number of mosques came into existence, endowed by individuals. In addition to tribal and sectarian mosques prominent leaders built mosques which were the centres of their activity, for example the Masdjid ʿAdī b. Ḥātim (Ṭabarī, ii. 130) etc. As old sanctuaries entered Islām, the mosque received more of the character of a sanctuary and the building of a mosque became a pious work; there arose a ḥadīth, according to which the Prophet said: "for him who builds a mosque, God will build a home in Paradise"; some add "if he thereby aims at the face of God" (*Corpus juris di Zaid b. ʿAlī*, ed. Griffini, No. 276; Bukhārī, *Ṣalāt*, bāb 65; Muslim, *Masādjid*, tr. 4 etc.). Like other sanctuaries, mosques were sometimes built as a result of a revelation in a dream. A mosque may also be built out of gratitude for seeing the Prophet (Maḳrīzī, iv. 209). The collections of inscriptions, as well as the geographical and topographical works, reveal how the number of mosques increased in this way.

In Egypt, al-Ḥākim in the year 403/1012–3 had a census taken of the mosques of Cairo and there were eight hundred (Maḳrīzī, iv. 264); Ibn Djubair (p. 43) was told that there were 12.000 or 8000 mosques in Alexandria. The fantastic figure of 30.000 for Baghdād is found as early as Yaʿḳūbī (*BGA*, vii. 250). In Baṣra where Ziyād built 7 mosques (*BGA*, v. 191), the number also increased rapidly, but here again an exaggerated figure (7.000) is given (*BGA*, vii. 361). In Damascus, Ibn ʿAsākir (d. 571/1176) counted 241 within and 148 outside the city (*JA*, Ser. 9, vii. 383). In Palermo Ibn Ḥawḳal counted over 300 and in a village above it 200 mosques; everyone wanted to build a mosque for himself (Yāḳūt, i. 719; iii. 409, 410). As a matter of fact, one can almost say that things tended this way; Yaʿḳūbī mentions in Baghdād a mosque for the Anbārī officials of the tax office (*BGA*, vii. 245) and several distinguished scholars practically had their own mosques. The mosques thus founded were very often called after their founders, and memorial and tomb-mosques after the person to be commemorated. Sometimes a mosque is called after some devout man who lived in it (Makrīzī, iv. 97, 265 *sqq.*) and a madrasa might be called after its head or a teacher (*ibid.*, iv. 235; Yāḳūt, *Udabā'*, vii. 82). Lastly a mosque might take its name from its situation or from some feature of the building.

C. The Mosque as the Centre for Divine Service

1. Sanctity of the Mosque

The history of the mosque in the early centuries of Islām shows an increase in its sanctity, which was intensified by the adoption of the traditions of the church and especially by the permeation of the cult of saints. The sanctity already associated with tombs taken over by Islām was naturally very soon tranferred to the larger and more imposing mosques. The expression *bait Allāh* "house of God", which at first was only used of the Kaʿba, came now to be applied to any mosque.

In the house of God the miḥrāb and the minbar (see below) enjoyed particular sanctity, as did the tomb, especially in Madīna. The visitors sought *baraka*, partly by touching the tomb or the railing round it, partly by praying in its vicinity; at such places "prayer is heard" (*Chron. Mekka*, iii. 441, 442). There were often places of particular sanctity in mosques. In the mosques at Ḳubā' and Madīna, the spots where the Prophet used to stand at prayer were held to be particularly blessed (Balādhurī, p. 5; Bukhārī, *Ṣalāt*, bāb 91; Wüstenfeld, *Medina*, p. 65, cf. 82, 109). In other mosques, places where a saint had sat or where a divine phenomenon had taken place, e.g. in the Mosque of ʿAmr and in the Azhar Mosque (Maḳrīzī, iv. 19, 52) or the Mosque in Jerusalem (Maḳdisī, *BGA*, iii. 170), were specially visited. Pious visitors made *ṭawāf* [q.v.] between such places in the mosque.

This increase in sanctity had as a natural result that one could no longer enter a mosque at random as had been the case in the time of the Prophet. In the early Umaiyad period, Christians were still allowed to enter the mosque without molestation (cf. Lammens, *Moʿâwia*, p. 12 *sq.*). At a later date entrance was forbidden to Christians and this regulation is credited to ʿUmar.

According to some traditions, a person in a state of ritual impurity could not enter the mosque and in any case only the pure could acquire merit by visiting the mosque, and in a later period it is specially mentioned that the *wuḍū'* cannot be undertaken in the mosque itself nor could shaving.

It is always necessary to be careful not to spit in a mosque, although some traditions which are obviously closer to the old state of affairs say, "not in the direction of the ḳibla, only to the left!" (Bukhārī, *Ṣalāt*, bāb 33 *sq.*). The custom of taking off one's sandals in the mosque is put back to the time of ʿUmar (Ṭabarī, i. 2408). That it is based on an old custom observed in sanctuaries is obvious (cf. Exod. iii. 5). The custom however seems not to have been always observed. The visitor on entering should place his right foot first and utter certain prayers with blessings on the Prophet and his family (which Muḥammad is said to have done!) and when he is inside perform two rakʿa's (Bukhārī, *Ṣalāt*, bāb 47 et al.). Certain regulations for decent conduct came into being, the object of which was to preserve the dignity of the house of divine service. Public announcements about strayed animals were not to be made, as the Beduins did in their houses of assembly, and one should not call out aloud and thereby disturb the meditations of the worshippers (Bukhārī, *Ṣalāt*, bāb 83 et al.). One should put on fine clothes for the Friday service, rub oneself with oil and perfume oneself (Bukhārī, *Djumʿa*, bāb 3, 6, 7, 19).

A question which interested the teachers of morality was that of the admission of women to the mosques. That many did not desire their presence is evident from the ḥadīth that one should not prevent them if there is no *fitna* connected with it, but they must not be perfumed (Muslim, *Ṣalāt*, bāb 29; Bukhārī, *Djumʿa*, bāb 13). Other ḥadīths say they should leave the mosque before the men (al-Nasāʾī, *Sahw*, bāb 77; cf. Abū Dāwūd, *Ṣalāt*, bāb 14, 48). Sometimes a special part of the mosque was railed off for them. According to some, women must not enter the mosque during their menstruation (Abū Dāwūd, *Ṭahāra*, bāb 92, 103 et al.).

Although the mosque became sacred it could not quite cast off its old character as a place of public assembly and in consequence the mosque was visited for many other purposes than that of divine service. Not only in the time of the Umaiyads was considerable business done in the mosques (Ṭabarī, ii. 1118; cf. Lammens, *Ziād*, p. 98), which is quite in keeping with the ḥadīth which actually found it necessary to forbid the sale of wine in the mosque, but a writer in the viiith century, Ibn al-Ḥādjdj, records with disapproval that business was done in the mosques. The list given by this author gives one the impression of a regular market-place (*Madkhal*, ii. 54). Strangers could always sit down in a mosque and talk with one another, and they had the right to spend the night in the mosque (see below D. 2^{b}). It naturally came about that people also ate in the mosque; this was quite common, and regular banquets were even given in them (e.g. Maḳrīzī, iv. 67, 121 *sq.*; cf. in Ḥadīth: Ibn Mādja, *Aṭʿima*, bāb 24, 29; Aḥmad b. Ḥanbal, ii. 106, $_{10}$ from below). It is even mentioned as a sign of the special piety of al-Shīrāzī (d. 476/1083) that he often brought food into the mosque and consumed it there with his pupils (Wüstenfeld, *Der Imâm Schafiʿī*, iii. 298). Gradually the mosques acquired also large numbers of residents (see D. 2^{b}).

2. The Mosque as a Place of Prayer Friday Mosques

As places for divine service, the mosques are primarily "houses of which God has permitted that they be erected and that His name be mentioned in them" (Sūra xxiv. 36), i.e. for His service demanded by the law, for ceremonies of worship (*manāsik*), for assemblies for prayer (*djamāʿāt*) and other religious duties (cf. *Chron. Mekka*, iv. 164). The mosques were *maʿābid* (Maḳrīzī, iv. 117, 140). In Madīna after a journey, the Prophet went at once to the mosque and performed two rakʿa's, a custom which was imitated by others and became the rule (Bukhārī, *Ṣalāt*, bāb 59 *sq.* et al.). In this respect, the mosque played a part in public worship similar to that of the Kaʿba in Mecca at an earlier date and the Rabba sanctuary in Ṭāʾif. The daily ṣalāts, which in themselves could be performed anywhere, became especially meritorious when they were performed in mosques because they expressed adherence to the community. A *ṣalāt al-djamāʿa*, we are told, is twenty or twenty-five times as meritorious as the ṣalāt of an individual at home or in his shop (Muslim, *Masādjid*, tr. 245; Bukhārī, *Ṣalāt*, bāb 87; *Buyūʿ*, bāb 49). There are even ḥadīths which condemn private ṣalāts: "Those who perform the *ṣalāt* in their houses abandon the *sunna* of their Prophet" (Muslim, *Masādjid*, tr. 257; but cf. Bukhārī, *Ṣalāt*, bāb 52). It is therefore very meritorious to go to the mosque; for every step one advances into the mosque, he receives forgiveness of sins, God protects him at the last judgment and the angels also assist him (Muslim, *Masādjid*, tr. 49—51; Bukhārī, *Ṣalāt*, bāb 87 et al.).

This holds especially of the Friday ṣalāt (*ṣalāt al-djumʿa*) which can only be performed in the mosque and is obligatory upon every free male Muslim who has reached years of discretion (cf. Juynboll, *Handbuch*, p. 86; Guidi, *Sommario del Diritto Malechita*, i. 125 *sq.*). The origin of this divine service, referred to in Sūra lxii. 9, is obscure. The assemblies of the Jews and Christians on a particular day must have formed the model (cf. Bukhārī, *Djumʿa*, bāb 1). Its importance in the earlier period lay in the fact that all elements of the Muslim camp, who usually went to the tribal and particular mosques, assembled for it in the chief mosque under the leadership of the general. The chief mosque, which for this reason was particularly large, was given a significant name. It is called *al-masdjid al-aʿẓam*, *al-masdjid al-akbar*, *al-masdjid al-kabīr*, *masdjid al-djamāʿa*, *masdjid li 'l-djamāʿa*, *masdjid djāmiʿ*, then *masdjid al-djāmiʿ*, and as an abbrevation we find also *al-djamāʿa* and especially *djāmiʿ*. As the *khuṭba* was the distinguishing feature, we also find *masdjid al-khuṭba*, *djāmiʿ al-khuṭba* or *masdjid al-minbar*.

Linguistic usage varied somewhat in course of time with changing conditions. In the time of ʿUmar there was properly in every town only one Masdjid Djāmiʿ for the Friday service. But when the community became no longer a military camp and Islām replaced the previous religion of the people, a need for a number of mosques for the Friday service was bound to arise. This demanded mosques for the Friday service in the villages on the one hand and several Friday mosques in the towns on the other. This meant in both cases an innovation compared with old conditions, and thus there arose some degree of uncertainty. The Friday service had to be conducted by the ruler of the community, but there was only one governor in each province; on the other hand, the demands of the time could hardly be resisted and, besides, the Christians converts to Islām had been used to a solemn weekly service.

As to the villages (*al-ḳurā*), ʿAmr b. al-ʿĀṣī in Egypt forbade their inhabitants to celebrate the Friday service for the reason just mentioned (Maḳrīzī, iv. 7). At a later period the khuṭba was delivered exceptionally, without minbar and only with staff, until Marwān in 132/749—50 introduced the minbar into the Egyptian *ḳurā* also (*ibid.*, p. 8) and a village with a minbar is called *ḳarya djāmiʿa* (Bukhārī, *Djumʿa*, bāb 15), an idea which was regarded by Bukhārī (d. 256/870) as quite obvious. In introducing minbars into the Egyptian villages, Marwān was apparently following the example of other regions. In the fourth century, Ibn Ḥawḳal mentions a number of *manābir* in the district of Iṣṭakhr (*BGA*, ii. 182 *sqq.*) and a few in the vicinity of Marw (*ibid.*, p. 316) and in Transoxania (*ibid.*, p. 378; cf. p. 384), and al-Maḳdisī does the same for other districts of Persia (*BGA*, iii. 309, 317) and he definitely says that the *ḳurā* of Palestine are *dhāt manābir* (*ibid.*, p. 176; cf. i. 58); Balādhurī (p. 331) also uses the name minbar for a village mosque built in 239; in general when speaking of the *ḳurā*, one talks of *manābir* and not of *djawāmiʿ* (cf. *BGA*, i. 63). Later however the term Masdjid Djāmiʿ is also used for a village mosque (Ibn Djubair, p. 217). The conditions of primitive Islām are reflected in the teaching of the Ḥanafīs, who only permit the Friday service in large towns (cf. al-Māwardī, *al-Aḥkām al-sulṭānīya*, ed. Enger, p. 177).

The ʿAmr-mosque at al-Fusṭāṭ

Art. MASDJID

The Sīdī ʿUḳba-mosque at Ḳairawān

Art. MASDJID

As to the towns, the S͟hāfiʿīs on the other hand have retained the oɪiginal conditions, since they permit the Friday service in only one mosque in each town (cf. D͟JUMʿA and al-Māwardī, p. 178 *sq.*), but with the reservation that the mosque is able to hold the community. The distinction between the two rites was of importance in Egypt. When in 569/1174 Ṣalāḥ al-Dīn became supreme in Egypt, he appointed a S͟hāfiʿī chief ḳāḍī and the Friday service was therefore held only in the Ḥākim mosque, as the largest; but in 665/1266 al-Malik al-Ẓāhir Baibars gave the Ḥanafīs preference and many mosques were therefore used as Friday mosques (Maḳrīzī, iv. 52 *sq.*; al-Suyūṭī, *Ḥusn al-muḥāḍara*, ii. 140; Quatremère, *Hist. Sult. Maml.*, ɪ/ii. 39 *sqq.*). During the Umaiyad period and to some extent in the ʿAbbāsid period, the number of d͟jawāmiʿ in the towns was still very small. The geographers of the third and fourth centuries in their descriptions of towns as a rule mention only "the d͟jāmiʿ". In keeping with the oldest scheme of town planning, it was very often in the middle of the town, surrounded by the business quarters, and the *dār al-imāra* was still frequently in the immediate vicinity of the chief mosque (*BGA*, ii. 298, 314; iii. 426).

But in Baṣra al-Maḳdisī (375/985) mentions 3 d͟jawāmiʿ (*BGA*, iii. 117). In Bag͟hdād, Yaʿḳūbī (278/891) mentions only one d͟jāmiʿ for the eastern town and one for the western. After 280/893 there was added the d͟jāmiʿ of the eastern palace of the caliph (Mez, *Renaissance*, p. 388). Al-K͟haṭīb al-Bag͟hdādī in 460/1058 gives 4 for west Bag͟hdād, 2 for the east town. Ibn D͟jubair in 581/1185 gives in the east town 3, and 11 d͟jawāmiʿ for the whole of Bag͟h-dād. For Cairo, Iṣṭak͟hrī gives two d͟jāmiʿ: the ʿAmr and Ṭūlūn mosques (*BGA*, i. 49) besides that in al-Ḳarāfa, which was regarded as a separate town. Al-Maḳdisī, who writes (375/985) shortly after the Fāṭimid conquest, mentions the ʿAmr and Ṭūlūn mosques, the new mosque in al-Ḳāhira (al-Azhar), also one in al-D͟jazīra, in D͟jīza and in al-Ḳarāfa (*BGA*, iii. 190—200, 209). As these places were all originally separate towns, the principle was not abandoned that each town had only one d͟jāmiʿ. The Fāṭimids however extended the use of Friday mosques and, in addition to those already mentioned, used the D͟jāmiʿ al-Ḥākim, al-Maḳs and Rās͟hida (Maḳrīzī, iv. 2 *sq.*). Nāṣir-i K͟husɪaw in 439/1047 mentions in one passage the four d͟jawāmiʿ of Cairo, in another seven for Miṣr and fifteen in all (ed. Schefer, p. 134 *sq.*, 147). This was altered in 569/1174 by Ṣalāḥ al-Dīn (see above) but the quarters, being still regarded as separate towns, retained their own Friday mosques.

After the Friday service in Egypt and Syria was freed from restriction, the number of d͟jawāmiʿ increased very much. Ibn Duḳmāḳ (about 800/1398) gives a list of only eight d͟jawāmiʿ in Cairo, but this list is apparently only a fragment (in all he mentions something over twenty in the part of his book that has survived); al-Maḳrīzī (d. 845/1442) gives 130 d͟jawāmiʿ (v. 2 *sqq.*). In Damascus, where Ibn D͟jubair still spoke of "the d͟jāmiʿ", al-Nuʿaimī (d. 927/1521) gives twenty d͟jawāmiʿ (*JA*, ser. 9, vii. 231 *sqq.*), and accoɪding to Ibn Baṭṭūṭa, there were in all the villages in the region of Damascus *masād͟jid d͟jāmiʿa* (i. 236). The word d͟jāmiʿ in Maḳrīzī always means a mosque in which the Friday service was held (vi. 76, 115 *sqq.*) but by his time this meant any mosque of some size. He himself criticizes the fact that since 799 the *ṣalāt al-d͟jumʿa* was performed in al-Akmar, although another d͟jāmiʿ stood close beside it (iv. 76; cf. also 86).

The great spread of Friday mosques was reflected in the language. While inscriptions of the viii[th] century still call quite large mosques *masd͟jid*, in the ninth most of them are called d͟jāmiʿ (cf. on the whole question, van Berchem, *Corpus*, i. 173 *sq.*); and while now the madrasa begins to predominate and is occasionally also called d͟jāmiʿ, the use of the word *masd͟jid* becomes limited. Though, generally speaking, it can mean any mosque, it is more especially used of the smaller unimportant mosques. While Ibn Duḳmāḳ gives 472 *masād͟jid* in addition to the d͟jawāmiʿ, madāris, etc., al-Maḳrīzī gives only nineteen, not counting al-Ḳarāfa, which probably only means that they were of little interest to him. D͟jāmiʿ is now on the way to become the regular name for a mosque of any size, in agreement with modern usage, in Egypt at least. Among the many Friday mosques one was usually distinguished as the chief mosque; we therefore find the expression *al-d͟jāmiʿ al-aʿẓam* (Ibn Baṭṭūṭa, ii. 54, 94; cf. the older *al-masd͟jid al-aʿẓam, ibid.*, p. 53).

3. Other religious activities in the Mosque

"The mentioning of the name of God" in the mosques was not confined only to the official ritual ceremonies. The recitation of the Ḳurʾān must have come to be considered an edifying and pious work at an early date. Al-Maḳdisī tells of recitation circles in the mosques of Naisābūr and of Cairo (*BGA*, iii. 205, 328), and so does Ibn D͟jubair for Damascus. Beside the recitation of the Ḳurʾān there were praises of God etc., all that is classed as *d͟hikr*, and the activities particularly cultivated by Ṣūfism. This form of worship also took place in the mosque (al-Makkī, *Ḳūt al-ḳulūb*, i. 152). In the Mosque of the Umaiyads and other mosques of Damascus, *d͟hikr* was held during the morning on Friday (Maḳrīzī, iv. 49). In Egypt, Aḥmad b. Ṭūlūn and K͟humārawaih allowed twelve men to quarter in a chamber near the minaret to praise God, and during the night four of them took turns to praise God with recitatious of the Ḳurʾān and with pious *ḳaṣīdas*. From the time of Ṣalāḥ al-Dīn an orthodox *ʿaḳīda* was recited by the muʾad͟hd͟hins in the night (*ibid.*, iv. 48). Mosques and particularly mausoleums had as a rule regularly appointed reciters of the Ḳurʾān. In addition there was, e.g. in Hebɪon and in a mosque in Damascus, a s͟haik͟h who had to read Buk͟hārī (or also Muslim) for three months (Sauvaire, *Hist. Jérus. Hébr.*, p. 17; *JA*, ser. 9, iii. 261).

Sermons weɪe not only delivered at the *ṣalāt al-d͟jumʿa*. In the ʿIrāḳ, even in aɪ-Maḳdisī's time, one was preached every morning, according to the *sunna* of Ibn ʿAbbās (*BGA*, iii. 130), it was said. Ibn D͟jubair, in the Niẓāmīya in Bag͟hdād, heard the S͟hāfiʿī *raʾīs* preach on Friday after the ʿaṣr on the minbar. His sermon was accompanied by the skilled recitation of the *ḳurrāʾ* who sat on chairs; they were oveɪ twenty in number (Ibn D͟jubair, p. 219—222). The unofficial sermons, which moreover were not delivered in mosques alone, were usually delivered by a special class, the *ḳuṣṣāṣ* (plur. of *ḳāṣṣ*) (on these cf. Goldziher, *Muh. Stud.*, ii. 161 *sqq.*; Mea, *Die Renaissance des Islāms*, p. 314 *sqq.*). The ḳuṣṣāṣ, who delivered edifying addresses and told popular stories, were early admitted to the mosques.

Tamīm al-Dārī is said to have been the first who in Madīna used to deliver such adresses during the caliphate of ʿUmar, before the ɔaliph entered for the Friday prayer, and under ʿUthmān he was allowed to preach twice a week in the mosque. In the Mosque of ʿAmr in Cairo by the year 38 or 39 (658—660), a *ḳāṣṣ* was appointed, who was also ḳāḍī (Kindī, *Wulāt Miṣr*, ed. Guest, p. 303 *sq.*). There are other instances of the combination of the two offices, which shows that the office of ḳāṣṣ was quite an official one. Under the Fāṭimids also, ḳuṣṣāṣ were appointed to the mosques (Maḳrīzī, iv. 18 infra). There is also evidence of the employment of ḳuṣṣāṣ in the mosques of the ʿIrāḳ in the ʿAbbāsid period (Yāḳūt, *Udabā*ʾ, iv. 268; v. 446). The ḳāṣṣ read from the Ḳurʾān standing and then sat down to deliver an explanatory and edifying discourse, the object of which was to instil the fear of God into the people (Maḳrīzī, iv. 18). The ḳuṣṣāṣ were called *aṣḥāb al-karāsī*, because they delivered their discourses on the *kursī* (al-Makkī, *Ḳūt al-ḳulūb*, i. 152; ii. 288; Ibn al-Ḥādjdj, *Madkhal*, i. 159; cf. Maḳrīzī, iv. 121). Their discourse was called *dhikr* or *waʿẓ* or *mawʿiẓa*, whence the ḳāṣṣ was also called *mudhakkir* (*BGA*, iii. 205) or *wāʿiẓ*. Specimens of their discourses are given by Ibn ʿAbd Rabbihi (*al-ʿIḳd al-farīd*, Cairo 1321, i., p. 294 *sqq.*). It was not only those officially appointed who delivered such discourses in the mosque. Ascetics made public appearances in various mosques and collected interested hearers around them (cf. e.g. Maḳrīzī, iv. 135).

The *ḳaṣaṣ* was thus completely taken over by popular Ṣūfism and later writers would hardly reckon, as al-Makkī does, the "story-tellers" among the *mutukallimūn* (*Ḳūt al-ḳulūb*, i. 152). The whole system degenerated to trickery and charlatanry of all kinds, as may be seen in the Maḳāma literature (cf. thereon Yāḳūt, *Udabā*ʾ, vi. 167 *sq.* and see also Mez and Goldziher, *op. cit.*). Al-Maḳrīzī therefore distinguishes between *al-ḳaṣaṣ al-khāṣṣa*, the regular and edifying discourse in the mosque, and *al-ḳaṣaṣ al-ʿāmma*, which consisted in the people gathering round all kinds of speakers, which is *makrūh* (Maḳrīzī, iv. 17, cf. al-Ghazzālī, *Iḥyā*ʾ, i. 26, 134). Others also have recorded their objections to the *ḳuṣṣāṣ* and attempted to forbid their activities in the mosque completely. As late as 580/1184—5 the *wuʿʿāẓ* still flourished in the mosques of Baghdād, as is evident from the *Riḥla* of Ibn Djubair (p. 219 *sqq.*, 224), and in the ninth century there were in the Azhar mosque *madjālis al-waʿẓ* as well as *ḥalaḳ al-dhikr* (Maḳrīzī, iv. 54). See further J. Pedersen, *The Islamic Preacher*, in *Goldziher Memorial Volume* i. Budapest 1948, pp. 226 *sqq.*

Iʿtikāf [q.v.], retirement to a mosque for a period, was adopted into Islām from the older religions. The word *ʿakf* means in the Ḳurʾān the ceremonial worship of the object of the cult (Sūra vii. 133; xx. 91, 97; xxi. 52; xxvi. 71; cf. al-Kumait, *Hāshimīyāt*, ed. Horovitz, p. 86, 18) and also the ritual stay in the sanctuary, which was done for example in the Meccan temple (Sūra ii. 125; xxii. 25). In this connection it is laid down in the Ḳurʾān that in the month of Ramaḍān believers must not touch their wives "while ye pass the time in the mosques" (*ʿākifūn fi ʾl-masādjid*, Sūra ii. 187), an expression which shows, firstly that there were already a number of mosques in the lifetime of the Prophet, and secondly that these had already to some extent taken over the character of the temple. The Prophet, according to the ḥadīth, used to spend ten days of the month of Ramaḍān in *iʿtikāf* in the mosque of Madīna (Bukhārī, *Iʿtikāf*, bāb 1; *Faḍl Lailat al-Ḳadar*, bāb 3), and in the year in which he died as many as twenty days (*id.*, *Iʿtikāf*, bāb 17). During this period the mosque was full of booths of palm branches and leaves in which the *ʿākifūn* lived (*ibid.*, bāb 13; cf. 6, 7). The Prophet only went to his house for some very special reason (*ibid.*, bāb 3). According to Zaid b. ʿAlī, the *iʿtikāf* can only be observed in a chief mosque (*djāmiʿ*) (*Corpus iuris di Zaid b. ʿAlī*, No. 447). The custom persisted and has always been an important one among ascetics. There were pious people, who spent certain periods or even their whole time in a mosque (*aḳāmū fīhi*, Maḳrīzī, iv. 87, 97). Nocturnal vigils in the mosque very early became an established practice in Islām. According to Ḥadīth, the Prophet frequently held nocturnal ṣalāts in the mosque with the believers (Bukhārī, *Djumʿa*, bāb 29) and by his orders ʿAbd Allāh b. Unais al-Anṣārī came from the desert for twenty-three successive nights to pass the night in his mosque in rites of worship (Ibn Ḳutaiba, *Maʿārif*, ed. Wüstenfeld, p. 142*sq.*). Ou t of this developed the *tahadjdjud* [q.v.] ṣalāt, particularly recommended in the law, and notably the *tarāwīḥ* ṣalāts [q.v.].

During the nights of the month of Ramaḍān there were festivals in the mosques and on other occasions also, such as the New Year, sometimes at the new moon, and in the middle of the month. The mosque on these occasions was illuminated; there was eating and drinking; incense was burned and *dhikr* and *ḳirāʾa* performed.

The Friday Ṣalāt was particularly solemn in Ramaḍān, and in the Fāṭimid period the caliph himself delivered the khuṭba (see Maḳrīzī, ii. 345 *sqq.*; Ibn Taghrībirdī, II/i., ed. Juynboll, p. 482—486 and II/ii., ed. Popper, p. 331—333). The mosques associated with a saint had and still have their special festivals on his *mawlid* [q.v.]; they also are celebrated with *dhikr*, *ḳirāʾa*, etc. (cf. Lane, *Manners and Customs*, ch. xxiv. *sqq.*).

The mosque thus on the whole took over the role of the temple. The rulers from ʿUmar onwards dedicated gifts to the Kaʿba (*BGA*, v. 20 *sq.* and *Gl.*, x.v. *Shamsa*), and as in other sanctuaries we find women vowing children to the service of the mosque (Bukhārī, *Ṣalāt*, bāb 74; Maḳrīzī, iv. 20). *Ṭawāf* was performed, as at the Kaʿba, in mosques with saints' tombs, as is still done. Especially important business was done here. In times of trouble the people go to the mosque to pray for help, for example during drought, for which there is a special ṣalāt (which however usually takes place on the *muṣallā*), in misfortunes of all kinds (e.g. Wüstenfeld, *Medina*, p. 19—20; Maḳrīzī, iv. 57); in time of plague and pestilence, processions, weeping and praying with Ḳurʾāns uplifted, were held in the mosques or on the *muṣallā*, in which even Jews and Christians sometimes took part (Ibn Taghrībirdī, II/ii., ed. Popper, p. 67; Ibn Baṭṭūṭa, i. 243 *sq.*; cf. Quatremère, *Hist. Sult. Maml.*, II/i. 35, 40; II/ii. 199) or for a period a sacred book like Bukhārī's *Ṣaḥīḥ* was recited (Quatremère, *op. cit.*, II/ii. 35; al-Djabartī, *ʿAdjāʾib al-āthār*, French transl., vi. 13). Certain mosques were visited by barren women (Wüstenfeld, *Medina*, p. 133). An oath is particularly binding if it is taken in a mosque; this is particularly true of the Kaʿba, where written covenants were also drawn up to make them more binding. The contract of matrimony (*ʿaḳd al-nikāḥ*) also is often concluded in a mosque (Khalīl, *Mukhtaṣar*, trans. Santillana, ii. 548; *Madkhal*, ii. 72 infra; Snouck Hurgronje, *Mekka*, ii. 163 *sq.*), and the particular form of divorce which is effected by the *liʿān* [see ṬALĀḲ] takes place in the mosque (Bukhārī, *Ṣalāt*, bāb 44; cf. Joh. Pedersen, *Der Eid etc.*, p. 114).

It is disputed whether a corpse may be brought into the mosque and the *ṣalāt al-djināza* performed there. ʿĀʾisha pointed out that the Prophet had done this with the body of Suhail b. Baiḍāʾ (Muslim, *Djanāʾiz*, tr. 99; cf. also Ibn Saʿd, I/i. 14 *sq.*). In theory it is permitted by al-Shāfiʿī, while the others forbid it (see Juynboll, *Handbuch*, p. 170; Khalīl, *Mukhtaṣar*, trans. Guidi, i. 151). The matter does not seem to be quite clear, for Ḳuṭb al-Dīn says that only Abū Ḥanīfa forbids it, but he himself thought that it might be allowable on the authority of a statement by Abū Yūsuf (*Chron. Mekka*, iii. 208—210). That later scholars often neglected the prohibition is easy to understand, for it is in accordance with the ever increasing tendency to found mosques at tombs. Even Ibn al-Ḥādjdj, who was anxious to maintain the prohibition, is not quite sure and realy only forbids the loud calling of the *ḳurrāʾ*, *dhākirīn*, *mukabbirīn* and *murīdīn* on such occasions (*Madkhal*, ii. 50 *sq.*, 64, 81).

4. Mosques as Objects of Pilgrimage

Especially the memorial mosques associated with the Prophet and other saints became the object of pious visits. Among them three soon became special objects of pilgrimage. In a ḥadīth the Prophet says: "One should only mount into the saddle to visit three mosques: al-Masdjid al-Ḥarām, the Mosque of the Prophet and al-Masdjid al-Aḳṣā" (Bukhārī, *Faḍl al-ṣalāt fī masdjid Makka wa 'l-Madīna*, bāb 1, 6 et al.). This ḥadīth reflects a practice which only became established at the end of the Umaiyad period. The pilgrimage to Mecca had been made a duty by the prescription of the Ḥadjdj in the Ḳurʾān. The pilgrimage to Jerusalem was a Christian custom which could very easily be continued, on account of the significance of al-Masdjid al-Aḳṣā in the Ḳurʾān. This custom became particularly important when ʿAbd al-Malik made it a substitute for the pilgrimage to Mecca (Yaʿḳūbī, ed. Houtsma, ii. 311). Although this competition did not last long, the significance of Jerusalem was thereby greatly increased. Pilgrimage to Madīna developed out of the increasing veneration for the Prophet. In the year 140/757—8 Abū Djaʿfar Manṣūr on his ḥadjdj visited the three sanctuaries (Ṭabarī, iii. 129) and this became a very frequent custom. Mecca and Madīna however still held the preference. Although those of Mecca and Jerusalem were recognized as the two oldest (the one is said to be 40 years older than the other; Muslim, *Masādjid*, tr. 1; *Chron. Mekka*, i. 301; *JAOS*, xv. 52), the Prophet however is reputed to have said "A ṣalāt in this mosque of mine is more meritorious than 1,000 ṣalāts in others except *al-masdjid al-ḥarām*" (*Chron. Mekka*, i. 303 etc.). This ḥadīth is said by some to have been pronounced because someone had commended performing the ṣalāt in Jerusalem, which the Prophet was against (Wāḳidī-Wellhausen, p. 349). This belongs to the discussions of the Umaiyad period. The three mosques however retained their pride of place (Ibn Khaldūn, *Muḳaddima*, faṣl 4, 6).

Although these three mosques officially hold a special position, others also are highly recommended e.g. the mosque in Ḳubāʾ [see AL-MADĪNA]. Attempts were also made to raise the mosque of Kūfa to the level of the three. ʿAlī is said to have told some one who wanted to make a pilgrimage from Kūfa to Jerusalem that he should stick by the mosque of his native town, it was "one of the four mosques" and two rakʿa's in it were equal to ten in others (*BGA*, v. 173 *sq.*; Yāḳūt, *Muʿdjam*, iv. 325). The Meccan sanctuary, however, always retained first place by reason of the Ḥadjdj. It was imitated by al-Mutawakkil in Sāmarrāʾ: he built a Kaʿba there as well as a Minā and an ʿArafa and made his amīrs perform their ḥadjdj there (*BGA*, iii. 122).

D. Equipment of the Mosque

1. The Development of the Edifice

Except in the case of Mecca the earliest mosques, as described above (B. 1), were at first simply open spaces with a *ẓulla*. The space was sometimes, as in al-Fusṭāṭ, planted with trees and usually covered with pebbles. These conditions could only last so long as the Arabs retained their ancient customs as a closed corporation in their simple camps. The utilisation of churches and the assimilation with older cultures called forth a change.

ʿUmar made alterations in the mosques both in Madīna and in Mecca. He extended their areas and surrounded them with walls of *labin* to the height of a man; the Kaʿba was thus given its *fināʾ* or open court like the mosque in Madīna (Balādhurī, p. 46; *Chron. Mekka*, i. 306 *sq.*; Wüstenfeld, *Medina*, p. 68 *sq.*). ʿUthmān also extended these two mosques but introduced an important innovation in using hewn stone and plaster (*djaṣṣ*) for the walls and pillars. For the roof the used teak (*sādj*). The booths, which had been extended by ʿUmar, were replaced by him by pillared halls (*arwiḳa*, sing. *riwāḳ*) and the walls were covered with plaster (Bukhārī, *Ṣalāt*, bāb 62; Balādhurī, p. 46; Wüstenfeld, *Medina*, p. 70 *sq.*). Saʿd b. Abī Waḳḳāṣ is said to have already taken similar steps to relieve the old simplicity of the barely equipped mosque in Kūfa.

By ʿUmar's orders he extended the mosque so that it became joined up with the *dār al-imāra*. The Persian architect used bricks (*ādjurr*) for the building, which he brought from Persian buildings, and in the mosque he used pillars which had been taken from churches in the region of Ḥīra belonging to the Persian kings; these columns were not erected at the sides but only against the Ḳibla wall. The original plan of the mosque was therefore still retained, although the pillared hall, which is identical with the original *ẓulla* (200 *dhirāʿ* broad), replaced the simple booth and the materials were better in every way (Ṭabarī, i. 2498 *sq.*, 2494). Already under the early Caliphs we can therefore note the beginning of the adoption of a more advanced architecture.

These tendencies were strongly developed under the Umaiyads. Even as early as the reign of Muʿāwiya, the mosque of Kūfa was rebuilt by his governor Ziyād. He commissioned a pagan architect, who had worked for Kisrā, to do the work. The latter had pillars brought from al-Ahwāz, bound them together with lead and iron clamps to a height of 30 *dhirāʿ* and put a roof on them. Similar halls, built of columns (*ṣuffa* and *ẓulla*, pl. *ẓilāl*) were added by him on the north, east and western wall (Ṭabarī, i. 2492, $_6$ *sqq.*, cf. 2494, $_7$; Yāḳūt, *Muʿdjam*, iv. 324, $_1$ *sqq.*; Balādhurī, p. 276). Al-Ḥadjdjādj also added to the mosque (Yāḳūt, iv. 325 *sq.*). Ziyād carried out similar works in Baṣra. He erected the Dār al-Imāra close to the ḳibla side. This was taken down by al-Ḥadjdjādj, rebuilt by others, and finally taken into the mosque by Hārūn al-Rashīd (Balādhurī, p. 347 *sqq.*; Yāḳūt, i. 643 *sq.*). In Mecca also in the same period similar work was done. Ibn al-Zubair and al-Ḥadjdjādj both extended the mosque, and Ibn al-Zubair was the first to put a roof on the walls; the columns were gilt by

ʿAbd al-Malik and he made a roof of teak (*Chron. Mekka*, i. 307, 309). The Mosque of ʿAmr was extended in 53/673 whith Muʿāwiya's permission by his governor Maslama b. Mukhallad to the east and north; the walls were covered with plaster (*nūra*) and the roofs decorated; it is evident from this that here also the original booth of the south side was altered to a covered hall during the early Umaiyad period. A further extension was made in 79 in the reign of ʿAbd al-Malik (Maḳrīzī, iv. 7, 8; Ibn Duḳmāḳ, iv. 62). Thus we find that during the early Umaiyad period and in part even earlier the original simple and primitive mosques were some extended, some altered. The alteration consisted in the old simple booth of the Mosque of the Prophet being gradually enlarged and transformed into a pillared hall with the assistance of the arts of countries possessing a higher degree of civilisation. In this way what had originally been an open place of assembly developed imperceptibly into a court, surrounded by pillared halls. Very soon a fountain was put in the centre of the court and we now have the usual type of mosque. The same plan is found in the peristyle of the houses and in the aithrion of a basilica like that of Tyre (Herzog-Hauch, *Realencyclopädie*[3], x. 780).

The great builders of the Umaiyads, ʿAbd al-Malik and his son al-Walīd I, made even more radical progress. The former entirely removed the original mosque in Jerusalem and his Byzantine architects erected the Dome of the Rock as a Byzantine building (cf. Sauvaire, *Jérus. et Hébron*, p. 48 *sqq.*) Al-Walīd likewise paid equally little attention to the oldest form of mosque, when, in Damascus, he had the church of St. John transformed by Byzantine architects into the Mosque of the Umaiyads. As al-Maḳdisī distinctly states, they wanted to rival the splendours of the Christian churches (*BGA*, iii. 159). The new mosques, which were founded in this period, were therefore not only no longer simple, but they were built with the help of Christians and other trained craftsmen with the use of material already existing in older buildings Columns from churches were now used quite regularly (e.g. in Damascus: Masʿūdī, *Murūdj*, iii. 408; Ramla: *BGA*, iii. 165; cf. Balādhurī, p. 143 *sqq.*; for Egypt see Maḳrīzī, iv. 36, 124 *sq.*). The building activities of al-Walīd extended to al-Fusṭāṭ, Mecca and Madīna (cf. *BGA*, v. 106 *sq.*) where no fundamental alterations were made, but complete renovations were carried out. With these rulers the structure of the mosques reaches the level of the older architecture and gains a place in the history of art. There is also literary evidence for the transfer of a style from one region to another. In Iṣṭakhr, for example, there was a djāmiʿ in the style of the Syrian mosques with round columns, on which was a *baḳara* (*BGA*, iii. 436 *sq.*; cf. for Shīrāz, p. 430). Al-Walīd also rebuilt the Mosque of the Prophet in part in the Damascus style (*BGA*, iii. 80; Ḳazwīnī, ed. Wüstenfeld, ii. 71).

This revolution naturally did not take place without opposition, any more than the other innovations which Islām adopted in the countries with a higher culture which it conquered. After the Mosque of the Prophet had been beautified by Christian architects with marble, mosaics, shells, gold, etc. and al-Walīd in 93 was inspecting the work, an old man said: "We used to build in the style of Mosques; you build in the style of churches" (Wüstenfeld, *Medina*, p. 74). The discussions on this point are reflected in ḥadīths. When ʿUmar enlarged the Mosque of the Prophet, he is reported to have said: "Give the people shelter from the rain, but take care to make them red or yellow lest you lead the people astray", while Ibn ʿAbbās said: "You shall adorn them with gold as the Jews and Christian do" (Bukhārī, *Ṣalāt*, bāb 62). Ibn ʿAbbās here takes up the Umaiyad attitude and ʿUmar that of old-fashioned people, according to whom any extension or improvement of the *ẓulla* was only permissible for strictly practical reasons. The conservative point of view is naturally predominant in Ḥadīth. It is said that extravagant adornment of the mosques is a sign of the end of the world; the works of al-Walīd were only tolerated from fear of the *fitna* (Ibn Ḥanbal, *Musnad*, iii. 134, 145, 152, 230, 283; al-Nasāʾī, *Masādjid*, bāb 2; Ibn Mādja, *Masādjid*, bāb 2; cf. al-Ghazzālī, *Iḥyāʾ*, i. 61; ii. 64 et al.). The lack of confidence of pious conservatives in the great mosques finds expression in a ḥadīth, according to which the Prophet (according to Anas) said: "A time will come upon my *umma* when they will vie with one another in the beauty of their mosques; then they will visit them but little" (al-ʿAsḳalānī, *Fatḥ al-bārī*, i. 362). In the Fiḳh, we even find divergence from the oldest quadrangular form of the mosque condemned (Khalīl, *Mukhtaṣar*, trans. Guidi, i. 71). Among the types which arose later was the "suspended" (*muʿallaḳ*) i.e. a mosque situated in an upper story e.g. in Damascus, (*JA*, ser. ix., vol. v. 409, 415, 422, 424, 427, 430). See also J. Sauvaget, *La Mosquée omeyyade de Médine* (Paris 1947).

2. Details of the Equipment of the Mosque

a. The Minaret

The earliest primitive mosques had no minaret. When the *adhān* call was introduced, Bilāl is said to have summoned the faithful in Madīna to the early ṣalāt from the roof of the highest house in the vicinity of the mosque (Ibn Hishām, p. 348; Wüstenfeld, *Medina*, p. 75); on the day of the conquest of Mecca, the Prophet instructed Bilāl to utter the call to prayer from the Kaʿba; according to al-Azraḳī, from the roof (*Chron. Mekka*, i. 193; cf. Ibn Hishām, p. 822). During the early days of Islām, the muʾadhdhin did not, however, utter his summons from an elevated position (cf. below G 4). It is doubtful when the minaret was introduced and whether it was adopted into Islam expressly for the call to prayer.

The Umaiyad caliph al-Walīd (86—96/705—15) undoubtedly had considerable importance for the history of the minaret, although even before his reign Sīdī ʿUḳba in Kairawān had been built by Ḥassān b. Nuʿmān in 84/703 with a minaret (so according to Bakrī: H. Saladin, *La Mosquée de Sidi Okba*, 1899, p. 7, 19). There was also a minaret in the Umaiyad mosque in Damascus. At the present day, the mosque has 3 minarets as was the case in the time of Ibn Djubair, (*Riḥla*, p. 266) and Ibn Baṭṭūṭa (i. 203). One of the earliest authorities, Ibn al-Faḳīh (d. 289/902), however mentions only one minaret (*miʾdhana*) and says that in the days of the Greeks it had been a watch-tower (*nāṭūr*), which belonged to the church of St. John and was left standing by al-Walīd (*BGA*, v. 108 [5]; different traditions by al-Maḳdisī, *BGA*, iii. 159. Yāḳūt, *Muʿdjam*, ii. 596 and Ibn Baṭṭūṭa, i. 203 *sq.*; cf. Le Strange, *Palestine under the Moslems*, p. 229). In Mecca also, al-Walīd built crests (*shurrāfāt*; *Chron. Mekka*, i. 310), and some minarets (as is evident from *ibid.*, p. 310, 311). They were later increased so that

Ḳuṭb al-Dīn mentions 7 minarets (*ibid.*, iii. 424—426). While al-Samhūdī says that there were no minarets in Madīna before al-Walīd, he asserts on the other hand that ʿUmar had already built towers in the four corners of the mosque (Wüstenfeld, *Medina*, p. 75; cf. Ibn Baṭṭūṭa, i. 272). In the time of Ibn Djubair (in 580) there were still only 3 minarets there (*Riḥla*, p. 195). It was not until 706/1306—7 that Muḥammad b. Ḳalāʾūn rebuilt the fourth minaret (Wüstenfeld, *op. cit.*, p. 76).

After the time of al-Walīd, minarets became more and more numerous and it is probable that he was the first to introduce the minaret into Syria and the Ḥidjāz. That he introduced it into Islām itself (cf. Schwally, in *ZDMG*, liii. 1898, p. 143 *sqq.*) is however not certain. According to Balādhurī (d. 279/892), Ziyād in Baṣra, where he was governor in 45/665—6, built the minaret of stone, when he built the mosque of brick (p. 348). This seems to suggest that there was a minaret there even before. According to the Egyptian historians, Maslama b. Mukhallad in al-Fusṭāṭ by Muʿāwiya's orders in 53/673 built a tower (*ṣawmaʿa*) at each corner of the mosque of ʿAmr, which had not been done before (Maḳrīzī, iv. 7 *sq.*, 44; Ibn Taghrībirdī, i. 77). The staircase leading up to the minaret was originally outside the mosque, but was later put inside it. Maslama is said to have introduced the minaret into other mosques also in al-Fusṭāṭ (i.e. in all except those of Tudjīb and Khawlān; cf. Maḳrīzī, iv. 44; Ibn Taghrībirdī, *loc. cit.*).

There are three names in common use for the minaret. *Maʾdhana* or *miʾdhana*, "place of the *adhān* call", which is in general use in Egypt and Syria at the present day, is frequently found in literature and inscriptions. *Ṣawmaʿa*, especially used in North Africa (Marçais, *Les Monuments arabes de Tlemcen*, 1903, p. 45), means also cloister or cell and in the older literature is used as the equivalent of *dair* (Sūra xxii. 40 et al.). *Manāra* is the most usual word in literature. It has the same meaning as Syr. *mᵉnārtā* but is probably an analogous, independant formation. The word means candlestick, stand in which a light is put, also lighthouse. *Manār(a)* also means a boundary stone or a signpost (*ʿalam*), or a watch-tower; the boundary stones of the *ḥaram* area, for example, are called *manār al-ḥaram* and Abraham was called *dhu 'l-manār*, because he put up signposts; obelisks are also called *manāra*. The derivation of the last named *manār* from *miliarion* (Fraenkel, *Fremdwörter*, p. 283) is little likely and still less probable is a derivation from a Persian building for fire-worship (c. Berchem in E. Diez, *Churasanische Baudenkmäler*, i. [1908], 113 *sqq.*). Probably the signposts received their name from the watch-tower. There are a number of references to the existence on the coasts of a series of *manāʾir* and each *manāra* gave warning by light-signals of the movements of the enemy (*BGA*, iii. 177). According to al-Balādhurī (p. 128: *manāẓir*), this was already the custom in ʿUmar's time and was in all probability an inheritance from the Byzantines. Similar watch-towers (*sēmantērion*) were used inland in the Byzantine period, e.g. in the eastern Ḥawrān, and the Persians had similar towers on their frontiers (Ṭabarī, i. 864, 878; cf. for the ʿIrāḳ Ibn Djubair, p. 210; *BGA*, v. 167; for the Maghrib: *JA*, ser. 4, xx. [1852], 99, 144). That these towers used fire-signals is very probable and Musil gives evidence of this custom for the Edom territory (*Arabia Petraea* ii. 2, 232). In the viii[th]/xvi[th] century again al-ʿUmarī (*Taʿrīf bi 'l-muṣṭalaḥ al-sharīf*, Cairo 1312, p. 199 *sq.*) refers to the use of a series of heights and towers for light-signals, including the *maʾdhanat al-ʿarūs*, one of the minarets of the Umaiyad mosque of Damascus (on the whole question see R. Hartmann, in *ZDMG*, lxx., 1916, p. 486, 505; *Memnon*, iii. 221; *Isl.*, i. 388 *sq.*). It is obvious that the tower of the mosque was given the name *manāra* from its resemblance to similar watch-towers and it is possible that its use for fire-signals was more general in earlier times. In Fās the hours of prayer were indicated by lamps from the minarets (*JA.*, ser. 11, xii. 1918, p. 341).

According to Ibn al-Faḳīh and others, the minaret was incorporated in the Mosque of the Umaiyads, simply because it was already there as a part of the church (cf. above); this agrees with de Vogüé's observation that the use of towers in churches and the larger public buildings in Syria in the iv[th] and v[th] century was common (*La Syrie centrale*, i. 57) and the tower in the mosque of Boṣrā is thought to be an original church-tower (cf. Diez, *Die Kunst der islamischen Völker*, p. 19 *sq.*). This indicates that the minaret in Syria became part of the mosque in a purely architectural way. But after its introduction it was soon used as a place in which the muʾadhdhin could stand, which must have been an obvious thing to do. This did not happen at once however. From Ṭabarī and others we can see that the call to prayer at a much later date could still be uttered in the street, and al-Farazdaḳ (d. about 110/728) who refers to the existence of *manār al-masādjid* (*Kāmil*, p. 481; *Aghānī*, 2nd ed. Cairo, xix. 18), also speaks of muʾadhdhins on the city wall (Ṭabarī, ii. 1302; *Naḳāʾid*, p. 365; see J. Horovitz, in *Isl.*, xvi., 1927, p. 253, 255) with which we may compare the tradition that the Prophet considered whether he ought to permit the call to prayer to be uttered on the fortifications of Madīna (cf. Ibn Saʿd, i. 7).

It is however by no means impossible that the minaret may have arisen elsewhere in a different way. If we can trust the account by al-Maḳrīzī and others (see above), the minaret was introduced into Egypt by Muʿāwiya's orders as a corner tower. Here it was at once used in a way which recalls the dwelling-towers of ascetics. It was used for the adhān, but not only for the five calls to prayer but also for vigils, in which the muʾadhdhins repeated litanies (Maḳrīzī, iv. 44 middle) and its architect, Maslama b. Mukhallad, used it for the *iʿtikāf* (*ibid.*, p. 44). This suggests the meaning of minaret expressed by the word *ṣawmaʿa* as a saint's cell. This use of the minaret was kept up during the golden age of Islām (cf. Ibn Djubair, *Riḥla*, p. 266; Yāḳūt, *Muʿdjam*, ii. 596 et al.).

If the minaret did not have a single origin, it is improbable that a single type of tower served as the model for it. Ziyād is said to have built the minaret in Baṣra of stone. The quadrangular Syrian Umaiyad type (*BGA*, iii. 182), which was taken over from the church-tower, was also of stone. In Egypt, on the other hand, according to al-Maḳrīzī, minarets for many centuries were only built of brick and the earliest stone minarets in this country were not built till shortly before 700 in al-Manṣūrīya and al-Āḳbughāwīya (Maḳrīzī, iv. 224). In North Africa where the Umaiyad-Syrian type was introduced a round minaret of brick in 7 stories with pillars was built in ʿAbbāsīya south of Ḳairawān in 184/800 (Yāḳūt, *Muʿdjam*, iv. 119).

In Indonesia the type of mosque (here called *mēsigit*) differs fundamentally from the mosques in other countries. There are as a rule no minarets, or very low ones, although some of the oldest mosques (xvi[th] century) possess rather massive towers; modern mosques again have minarets. Where the minaret is lacking, the *adhān* is called from the roof. These roofs traditionally consist of several stories, like a pagoda, and end in a point which is crowned by a peculiar ornament (cf. G. F. Pijper, *The Minaret in Java* in *India Antiqua*, Leiden 1947).

b. The Chambers

The old mosque consisted of the courtyard and the open halls running along the walls: these were called *al-mughaṭṭā* (*BGA*, iii. 82, 158, 165, 182), because they were roofed over. The halls were particularly extensive on the *ḳibla* side because the congregations gathered here. The space between two rows of pillars was called *riwāḳ*, pl. *arwiḳa* or *riwāḳāt* (*BGA*,. iii. 158, 159; Maḳrīzī, iv. 10, 11, 12, 49). Extension often took the form of increasing the number of the *arwiḳa*. In some districts a sail-cloth was spread over the open space as a protection from the sun at the time of the service (*BGA*, iii. 205, 430).

The courtyard was called *ṣaḥn*. The open space around the Kaʿba is called *finā' al-Kaʿba. Finā'* is also the name given to the open space around the mosque (Maḳrīzī, iv. 6). Trees were often planted in the courtyard: e.g. in the mosque of ʿAmr. In Madīna, at the present day there are still trees in the *rawḍa* (Batanūnī, *Riḥla*, p. 240), as in Ibn Djubair's time. In other cases the court was covered with pebbles (see above D 1); but this was altered with a more refined style of architecture. Frequently, as in Ramla, the halls were covered with marble and the courtyard with flat stone (*ibid.*, p. 165). In the halls also the ground was originally bare or covered with little stones; for example in the mosque of ʿAmr until Maslama b. Mukhallad covered it with mats. The floor of the Mosque of ʿAmr was entirely covered with marble in the Mamlūk period (Maḳrīzī, iv. 13 *sq.*; cf. in Shīrāz: Ibn Baṭṭūṭa, ii. 53). But in the mosque of Mecca, the *ṣaḥn* is still covered with little stones (Batanūnī, *Riḥla*, p. 99 below; cf. *Chron. Mekka*, ii. 10 *sq.*). In Madīna also little pebbles were used (Ibn Djubair, p. 190; Ibn Baṭṭūṭa, i. 263).

There were not at first enclosed chambers in the halls. A change in this respect came with the introduction of the *maḳṣūra* (on this word cf. Quatremère, *Hist. Sult. Maml.*, I/i., p. 164, note 46), a box or compartment for the ruler built near the miḥrāb. Al-Samhūdī gives the history of the maḳṣūra in Madīna (Wüstenfeld, *Medīna*, p. 71 *sq.*, 89 *sq.*). The traditions all agree that the maḳṣūra was introduced to protect the ruler from hostile attacks, by ʿUthmān or by Muʿāwiya or by Marwān. This much seems to be certain, that the maḳṣūra was at any rate introduced at the beginning of the Umaiyad period and it was an arrangement so much in keeping with the increasing dignity of the ruler that, as Ibn Khaldūn says, it spread throughout all the lands of Islām (*Muḳaddima*, faṣl 37). The governors built themselves compartments in the principal mosques of the provinces, e.g. Ziyād in Kūfa and Baṣra (Balādhurī, p. 277, 348) and probably Ḳurra b. Sharīk in al-Fusṭāṭ (Maḳrīzī, iv. 12). In 161/777—8, al-Mahdī prohibited the *maḳāṣīr* of the provinces and al-Ma'mūn even wanted to clear all the boxes out of the *masādjid djāmiʿa*, because their use was a *sunna* introduced by Muʿāwiya (Maḳrīzī, iv. 12; Yaʿḳūbī, ed. Houtsma ii. 571). But this attempt did not succeed. On the contrary, their numbers rapidly increased. According to Ibn Khaldūn, the *maḳṣūra* was an innovation of Islām's own. The question must however be left open, whether in its introduction and development there may not be some connection with the boxes of the Byzantine court, at least, for example, when the Turks in the Yeshil Djāmiʿ in Brussa put the Sulṭān's box over the door (R. Hartmann, *Im neuen Anatolien*, p. 27).

A special room, *maḳṣūra* or *zāwiya*, might also be introduced for other purposes, e.g. for the *ḳurrā'* or the students or the lawyers, being either cut off in the great hall or built in subsidiary buildings. Thus in the halls of the Mosque of ʿAmr there were several compartments for teaching, which are called maḳṣūra and zāwiya, in which studies were prosecuted (Maḳrīzī, iv. 20, $_{16, 25}$). In the Azhar Mosque a *maḳṣūrat Fāṭima* was made in the time of the Fāṭimids, where she had appeared, and the emīrs in the following period made a large number of such *maḳāṣīr* (*ibid.*, p. 52, 53). In the Aḳṣā Mosque about 300/912, there were three maḳṣūras for women (*BGA*, v. 100). These divisions might be a nuisance at the great Friday assemblies and this is why al-Mahdī wanted to remove them in 161/778 from the masādjid al-djamāʿāt (Ṭabarī, iii. 486).

The mu'adhdhins lived not only in the minarets, where, at any rate in the Ṭūlūnid period, they held vigils (Maḳrīzī, iv. 48). They had rooms (*ghuraf*, sg. *ghurfa*) on the roof and these rooms in time came to be numerous (*ibid.*, p. 13, 14). All kinds of rooms were put in subsidiary buildings for the khaṭīb (*ibid.*, p. 13), for judges, for studies etc. In addition there were dwelling-houses, not only for the staff but also for others. As already mentioned, devout men used to take up their residence in the mosque for a considerable period for *iʿtikāf* and any one at any time could take up his quarters in the mosque; he could sleep there and make himself at home. It therefore came quite natural to the devout to reside permanently in the mosque. Ascetics often lived in the minaret (see above), others made themselves cells in the mosque, or they lived in the side rooms of the mosque, as was the case, for example, in the Mosque of the Umaiyads (Ibn Djubair, p. 269; Ibn Baṭṭūṭa, i. 206). In particularly holy mosques like that in Hebron, houses for *al-muʿtakifūn* were built around the sacred place (Sauvaire, *Hist. Jérus. et Hébron*, p. 11 *sq.*). Kitchens were therefore erected with the necessary mills and ovens, and cooked food (*djashīsha*) and 14—15,000 loaves (*raghīf*) were daily distributed to those who stayed there and to visitors (Sauvaire, p. 20 *sq.*; cf. Quatremère, *Hist. Sult. Maml.*, 1/i., 231). Those who lived in and beside the mosque were called *mudjāwirūn* (cf. *BGA*, iii. 146); they were organized under a *ḳaddīm*, like the North Africans under an *amīn* in Damascus (Ibn Djubair, p. 277 *sq.*). They were pious ascetics, students, and sometimes travellers. The students generally found accommodation in the madāris but large mosques like that of the Umaiyads or al-Azhar had always many students who lived in them. The name of the halls *riwāḳ*, plur. *arwiḳa*, was later used for these students' lodgings (cf. v. Berchem, *Corpus*, i. 43, note 1; perhaps Maḳrīzī, iv. 54, $_{23}$). In smaller towns it was the natural thing for the traveller to spend the night in the mosque and to get food there (Yāḳūt, iii. 385; Ibn al-Ḳifṭī, *Ta'rīkh al-ḥukamā'*, ed. Lippert, p. 252). Travellers like Nāṣir-i Khusraw, Ibn Djubair, Ibn Baṭṭūṭa, al-ʿAbdarī (*JA*, ser. 5, iv., 1854, p. 174) were able to travel throughout the whole Muslim world from one mosque (or *madrasa* or *ribāṭ*) to the other. Large endowments were created for those who lived in the mosques (Ibn

Djubair, *op. cit.*; Ibn Taghrībirdī, II/ii., 105 *sq.*).

The very varied uses to which the mosques were put resulted in their becoming storehouses for all sorts of things. In 668/1269—70, the Mosque of the Umaiyads was cleared of all such things; in the courtyard there were for example stores for machines of war and the zāwiya of Zain al-ʿĀbidīn was a regular khān (*JA*, ser. 9, vol. vii. 225 *sq.*).

c. Miḥrāb

Whether the Prophet considered it necessary to erect an indicator of the direction of prayer in Madīna may be considered doubtful.

In al-Fusṭāṭ ʿAmr is said to have ascertained the ḳibla very carefully with the help of many others (Maḳrīzī, iv. 6 supra; *BGA*, viii. 359; Ibn Taghrībirdī, i. 75 *sq.*). But we are not told how it was indicated, probably by a pole or something of the kind. At first they were probably content with the direction, roughly correct, in keeping with a ḥadīth of Abū Huraira, according to which the ḳibla in general lies between east and west (Tirmidhī, *Mawāḳīt al-ṣalāt*, b. 139; Maḳrīzī, iv. 24). But later the problem was tackled seriously. Maḳrīzī mentions the different solutions of it in Egypt (iv. 21—33). The direction was ascertained from the stars. In the transformation of churches into mosques, frequent under al-Maʾmūn, their orientation from east to west was decisive. The door on the east side as a rule was made the miḥrāb (Maḳrīzī, iv. 30).

The word *miḥrāb* before and after the beginning of Islām meant in the first place a palace or a part of one, secondly a niche wehre a bust stood, especially a niche with an image of a Christian saint (ʿUmar b. Rabīʿa, p. 262, $_9$). Perhaps the part of the palace, called miḥrāb, is simply a niche with a throne in it (cf. esp. *Mufaḍḍalīyāt*, p. 21, $_{13}$). The same use of the word is found in the Ḳurʾān. In Sūra xxxviii. 21, it means the part of the palace where the king is; xxxiv. 13, most probably a place where images are put and iii. 37 *sq.*; xix. 11, a temple or rather a cell in a temple where one prays. *Miḥrāb* has been derived from *ḥarba* "spear" and from South Arabic *mikrāb*, Ethiop. *mekʷrāb* "temple" but the etymology is not certain (see on the whole question; J. Horovitz, in *Isl.*, xvi., 1927, p. 260 *sqq.*).

The use of the word miḥrāb to denote the niche placed in the mosque in the direction of prayer, connects quite well with the usual usage of the word. All are agreed that the miḥrāb did not originally belong to the mosque, and that it was taken over from the church finds confirmation in Muslim literature (see Lammens, *Ziād*, p. 33, note 7; 94, note 1) and it is evident that the innovation found its way into the mosque by a purely architectural way. The miḥrāb became the place where the imām stood during the ṣalāt. It may therefore be assumed that it was one of the principal niches in the church, which was taken over into the mosque; it may have contained the bishop's throne or the image or picture of an important saint.

There is no unanimity as to the date when the miḥrāb was introduced into the mosque. Muʿāwiya is occasionally mentioned (*BGA*, v. 109, $_2$); as a rule, however, and probably with greater right, al-Walīd. His governor Ḳurra b. Sharīk (90—96/709—14) is recorded to have introduced the prayer niche (*miḥrāb mudjawwaf*) into Egypt (Maḳrīzī, iv. 6, $_{14}$, 9, $_9$ et al). Only occasionally is Muʿāwiya's governor Maslama b. Mukhallad (47—62/667—82), or ʿAbd al-ʿAzīz b. Marwān (65—85/685—704) mentioned as having introduced this innovation (Maḳrīzī, iv. 6) The miḥrāb is however said not yet to have come into general use in the second century (see Lammens, *Ziād*, p. 94, note 1); on the other hand, Ṭabarī presupposes a *miḥrāb* in the Muslim sense as early as David (Ṭabarī, i. 2408, $_{7, 12}$; *BGA*, ii. 112, *sq.*; other prophets also had their miḥrābs in Jerusalem: *ibid*).

In the larger mosques there were usually several miḥrābs, used by the different madhāhib. They might be of wood, but as a rule they were built of masonry and adorned with pillars. They were often highly ornamented. A Fāṭimid adorned a miḥrāb in the mosque of ʿAmr and one in the Azhar mosque with a silver girdle which weighed 5,000 dirhams (Maḳrīzī, iv. 52).

The general objections to adorning mosques were also applied to the miḥrāb. A ḥadīth is said to have forbidden this as an inheritance from the churches; it is compared with the altars (see Lammens, *Ziād*, p. 33, note 7), but even a puritan like Ibn al-Ḥādjdj does not reject the miḥrāb in principle; he only condemns its adornment (*Madkhal*, ii. 48). In fact the miḥrāb was held in special respect as the most important part of the mosque which found expression in the erection of a ḳubba over it (e.g. Maḳrīzī, iv. 91; cf. v. Berchem, *Corpus*, i., No. 79). We hear of holy men sitting "in their *miḥrāb*" (al-Ghazzālī, *Iḥyāʾ*, ii. 247). The special importance of the miḥrāb is shown from the fact that its position was occasionally revealed in dreams, e.g. in Ḳairawān (Yāḳūt, iv. 213) and in the Mosque of Ibn Ṭūlūn (Maḳrīzī, iv. 39). In the principal mosque of Ṣanʿāʾ there was a prophet's tomb under the miḥrāb (*BGA*, vii. 110), which recalls Christian altars. As the most sacred part of the mosque, the miḥrāb is compared not only with Christian altars, but the word is used of the sacred place of prayer in any sanctuary, e.g. in the pre-Christian temple, whih stood on the site of the later mosque of the Umaiyads (*JA*, ser. 9, vii. 371). In Palestine, in keeping with this idea, very many miḥrābs are said to have been the miḥrābs of Biblical personalities (see Sauvaire, *Hist. Jér. et Hébr.*, p. 42, 76, 96 *sq.*, 102; Le Strange, *Palestine*, Index).

d. Minbar

In contrast to the miḥrāb, the *minbar* was introduced in the time of the Prophet himself. The word, often pronounced *mimbar*, comes from the root *n-b-r* "high"; it could be derived from the Arabic quite easily with the meaning "elevation, stand", but is more probably a loanword from the Ethiopic (Nöldeke, *Neue Beiträge z. sem. Sprachw.*, 1910, p. 49). Its case is therefore somewhat similar to that of masdjid. It means "seat, chair" and is used, for example, for a saddle and of a litter. It is therefore identical with *madjlis*, with *sarīr*, *takht* or *kursī*. The use of the word for the pulpit derives from its history.

When the *khaṭīb* [q.v.] spoke among the Arabs, he usually did so standing, frequently beating the ground with bow and lance; or he sat on his mount as did e.g. Ḳuss b. Sāʿida (al-Djāḥiẓ, *Bayān*, i. 25, 31; ii. 141). The Prophet did both of these things. In ʿArafa he sat on his camel during his *khuṭba* and on other occasions, when addressing the community during the early period, even as late as the day of the capture of Mecca, he stood (cf. Sūra lxii. 11). The people sat on the ground around him (Bukhārī, *Djumʿa*, B. 28; *ʿĪdain*, B. 6). In the mosque in Madīna he had a particular place beside one one of the palm-tree trunks used as pillars in the mosque. For "beside" (usually *ḳāma ilā*; Bukhārī,

Buyūʿ, B. 32: *ʿinda*) "upon" (*ḳāma ʿalā*; already in Bukhārī, *Djumʿa*, B. 26) is sometimes found later, and the column or trunk is replaced by a stump on which he stood.

Various passages record how the minbar was introduced, (s. Wensinck, *Handbook*, s.v. *Pulpit*; *Usd al-ghāba*, i. 43 infra, 214; Wüstenfeld, *Medina*, p. 62 *sq.*; Diyārbakrī, *Khamīs*, i. 129; ii. 75 *sq.* and *Sīrat al-Ḥalabī*, ii. 146 *sqq.*). The details are variously given. The maker was a Byzantine or a Copt and was called Bāḳūm or Bāḳūl, but the name Ibrāhīm and others are also given. He was a carpenter, but a slave of the wife of one of the Anṣār or (Bukhārī, *Hiba*, B. 3) of the Muhādjirūn. Most narratives take it for granted that the minbar was primarily intended for the *khuṭba*; in some it is added that the object was to enable the large assembly to hear him (Ibn Saʿd, I/i. 10, 11). We are told also that the Prophet performed the ṣalāt on it and, during the *sudjūd*, he came down from it. He also took care that the people could see his *ṣalāt* and follow him (Bukhārī, *Ṣalāt*, B. 18; *Djumʿa*, B. 26). This last tradition however presupposes the later custom of standing upon the minbar.

According to a tradition in Ibn al-Athīr the Companions asked the Prophet to take up a raised position as many *wufūd* were coming (*Usd al-ghāba*, i. 43). This agrees with another tradition that the Prophet, when he was visited by a man named Tamīm, sat on a *kursī* and addressed him from it (*ibid.*, p. 214). Here we have a seat of honour on which the ruler sits. This is undoubtedly in keeping with the character of the minbar; while the raised seat was in general use among the northern Semites the Arabs usually sat on the ground, often leaning against a saddle. The raised seat was the special mark of the ruler or, what is the same thing, of the judge. Al-Ḥadjdjādj, for example, when he addressed the people (hardly in the mosque) sat on a chair which belonged to him (*kursī lahu*: Ṭabarī, ii. 959) and when he tried and condemned his enemies, a *sarīr* was erected for him (*ibid.*, p. 1119); in the same way a *kursī* was placed for Yazīd when he issued his orders for a battle (*ibid.*, p. 1107; see also Becker, *Islamstudien*, i. 450 *sqq.*).

If tradition usually suggests that the minbar was introduced exclusively for the khuṭba, this seems to be a somewhat one-sided view. The minbar was primarily, as Becker was the first to point out, the the throne of the mighty Prophet in his capacity as a ruler. In keeping with this is the tradition that it was introduced in the year 7, 8 or 9 (Ṭabarī, i. 1591; *Khamīs*, ii. 75; *Usd al-ghāba*, i. 23). The Prophet used it for the publication of important announcements, for example, the prohibition of wine. That he should also make his public speeches to the community from the new seat was only natural.

The Prophet's minbar is often called *aʿwād* from its material. It consisted of two steps and a seat. After the time of the Prophet, it was used in the same way by Abū Bakr, ʿUmar and ʿUthmān. Its significance as a throne is seen from the fact that in the year 50/670 Muʿāwiya wanted to take it to Syria with him; he was not allowed to do so but he raised it by 6 steps.

That the Umaiyads should have a minbar of their own was natural. Muʿāwiya took it with him on his journey to Mecca (*Chron. Mekka*, i. 333): it was thus still portable and indispendable for the sovereign, when he wished to make a public appearance as such.

The minbar taken to Mecca by Muʿāwiya remained there till the time of al-Rashīd; when the latter visited Mecca on his ḥadjdj in the year 170 or 174 a *minbar manḳūsh* with 9 steps was presented to him by the *ʿāmil* of Egypt and the old one was put up in ʿArafa (*Chron. Mekka*, i. 333; iii. 114). The Meccan minbar was a movable one. It usually stood beside the *maḳām* but was put beside the Kaʿba during the khuṭba (Ibn Djubair, p. 95, 97; cf. *Chron. Mekka*, iii. 429). According to al-Batanūnī, this custom was kept up until Sulṭān Sulaimān I (926—974/1520—66) built a marble minbar, north of the *maḳām* (*al-Riḥla al-Ḥidjāzīya*, p. 100).

It seems at first to have been doubtful whether *manābir* should be put up in the provinces or not. According to al-Ḳuḍāʿī, ʿAmr had a minbar made in al-Fusṭāṭ but ʿUmar ordered him to take it away: he was not to raise himself above the Muslims so that they would have to sit below his heels (Maḳrīzī, iv. 6 *sq.*; Ibn Taghrībirdī, i. 76; Suyūṭī, *Ḥusn al-muḥāḍara*, i. 63; ii. 135). The idea obviously was that the throne belonged to the caliph alone. After ʿUmar's death however, ʿAmr is said to have used a minbar (Maḳrīzī, iv. 8, 27). A large new minbar was placed in the mosque of ʿAmr in 405/1014 by al-Ḥākim (Maḳrīzī, iv. 8; Ibn Taghrībirdī, i. 78 *sq.*).

We hear of no objections in other places to the manābir in the amṣār. The minbar was the symbol of rule, and the governor sat on it as the representative of the ruler. It formed a feature of the Masdjid al-Djamāʿa, where the community was officially addressed. In the year 64/683—4 therefore, there were minbars in all the provinces. In this year homage was paid to Marwān b. al-Ḥakam not only in the capital but in the other manābir in the Ḥidjāz, Miṣr, Shaʾm, Djazīra, ʿIrāḳ, Khurāsān, and other amṣār. (*BGA*, viii. 307).

In the first century and beginning of the second, we still find the walī in the smaller towns delivering the *khuṭba* standing, with the staff only. But in 132/749—50 the governor ʿAbd al-Malik b. Marwān had *manābir* put up in the ḳurā of Egypt (Maḳrīzī, iv. 8, 17 *sqq.*; Ibn Taghrībirdī, i. 350 *sq.*). When the khuṭba became purely a divine service and the ruler was no longer the khaṭīb [q.v.], the minbar became the pulpit of the spiritual spreacher and every mosque in which the Friday service was celebrated was given a minbar. At the same time, i.e. after al-Rashīd, the change was completed and the preacher spoke, standing on the pulpit. Ḥadīths therefore came into existence, according to which the Prophet used to deliver two khuṭbas on Friday, standing "just as is done to-day" (Bukhārī, *Djumʿa* b. 27, 30; and ʿUmar, *ibid.*, b. 2).

The minbar was thus now quite analogous to the Christian pulpit. It is very probable that this latter also influenced its form. A minbar in the mosque of ʿAmr was said to be of Christian origin. (Maḳrīzī, iv. 8). The same thing came to be said of the Prophet's minbar (Wüstenfeld, *Medina*, p. 63). The oldest minbars were all of wood. A minbar of iron was made as early as the Umaiyad period (Ibn Taghrībirdī, i. 78, 8: *al-minbar al-ḥadīd*, cf. 79, 4) and also of stone (Goldziher, *Muh. Stud.*, ii. 42 note 5); later they were also built of bricks (Wüstenfeld, *Medina*, p. 64, 96). As a rule the minbar stood against the ḳibla wall beside the miḥrāb. Al-Mahdī had tried to reduce the *manābir* to their original small size (Ṭabarī, iii. 486, 12; Maḳrīzī, iv. 12, 13 *sqq.*), but he could not arrest the development. In the larger mosques several *manābir* were even built.

The importance which the minbar already had in the time of the Prophet caused special reverence to be paid to it and the sanctity of the mosque was concentrated round this and around the miḥrāb. The minbar was stroken for the *baraka*, and oaths were particularly taken on or beside the minbar. A false oath taken on or beside the minbar of the Prophet led to hell absolutely (Ibn Saʿd, I/i. 10, *sq.* 12, 19 *sq.*; Ibn Ḥanbal, *Musnad*, ii. 329; cf. Johs. Pedersen, *Der Eid*, p. 144, 147). Legends grew up which represented the Prophet seeing into the future from the minbar (Bukhārī, *Djumʿa*, bāb 29) and being able to follow the battle of Muʾta from it (cf. Wāḳidī—Wellhausen, p. 311; Ibn Hishām, p. 796) and also how his prayers on the minbar were specially efficacious.

Just as the Kaʿba was covered (*kasā*) so a covering was soon put over the minbar. ʿUthmān is said to have been the first to cover the minbar of the Prophet with a *ḳaṭīfa* (*Khamīs*, ii. 75, 1 from below). Muʿāwiya did the same thing when he had to give up his attempt to carry it off (*ibid.*, p. 76, 4; Ṭabarī, ii. 92, 4). Under the ʿAbbāsids a new *kiswa* was sent every year for the minbar of the Prophet from Baghdād; the Sulṭāns later renewed it less frequently (Wüstenfeld, *Medina*, p. 64). We find other references to the covering of the minbar on special occasions (Ibn Djubair, p. 149, 16).

e. Dakka

In the larger mosques there is usually found near the minbar a platform to which a staircase leads up. This platform (*dakka*, popularly often *dikka*) is used as a seat for the muʾadhdhins when pronouncing the call to prayer in the mosque at the Friday service. This part of the equipment of a mosque is connected with the development of the service (cf. below under G 4 and C. H. Becker, *Zur Geschichte des islamischen Kultus*, in *Islamstudien*, i. 472—500; E. Mittwoch, *Zur Entstehungsgeschichte des islamischen Gebets und Kultus*, in *Abh. Pr. Ak. W.*, 1913, phil.-hist. Kl., No. 2). The first adhān-call is pronounced from the minaret, the second (when the khaṭīb mounts the minbar) and the third (before the ṣalāt, *iḳāma*) in the mosque itself. These calls were at first pronounced by the muʾadhdhin standing in the mosque. At a later date raised seats were made for him.

Al-Ḥalabī records that Maslama, Muʿāwiya's governor in Egypt, was the first to build platforms (here called *manābir*) for the calls to prayer in the mosques (*Sīra Ḥalabīya*, ii. 111 below). This story however, given without any reference to older authorities, is not at all reliable. It seems that a uniform practice did not come into existence at once. In Mecca the muʾadhdhins for a time uttered the second call (when the preacher mounted the minbar) from the roof (*Chron. Mekka*, i. 332 *sq.*). The position in the mosque of ʿAmr in Cairo was similar. Here also the adhān was uttered in a chamber (*ghurfa*) on the roof and in 336/947—8 there is a reference to its enlargement. In the Mosque of Ibn Ṭūlūn the adhān was pronounced from the cupola in the centre of the *ṣaḥn* (Maḳrīzī, iv. 11, 40). Al-Maḳdisī records in the fourth century as a notable thing about Khurāsān that the muʾadhdhins there pronounced the adhān on a *sarīr* placed in front of the minbar (*BGA*, iii. 372).

In the viii[th] century, Ibn al-Ḥādjdj mentions the dakka as a *bidʿa* in general use, which should be condemned as it unnecessarily prevents freedom of movement within the mosque (*Madkhal*, ii. 45 above). The dakkas mentioned in inscriptions from Cairo all date from the period before and after 900 A.H.

f. Kursī, Ḳurʾāns and Relics

In the mosques there is usually a kursī, that is a wooden stand with a seat and a desk. The desk is for the Ḳurʾān, the seat for the *ḳāṣṣ*, or reader, *ḳāriʾ*. The ḳuṣṣāṣ are therefore called by al-Makkī *aṣḥāb al-karāsī* (*Ḳūt al-ḳulūb*, i. 152, quoted *K. al-Madkhal*, i. 159). Several karāsī are often mentioned in one mosque (cf. for the Mosque of ʿAmr Maḳrīzī, iv. 19). Whether the karāsī mentioned for the earlier period always had a desk cannot be definitely ascertained. The karāsī with dated inscriptions given by van Berchem in his *Corpus* all belong to the ix[th]/xv[th] century (No. 264, 302, 338, 359bis, 491).

The mosques had many copies of the Kurʾān beside the one kept on the *kursī*. Some mosques claimed to possess copies from ʿUthmān (cf. Nöldeke, *Gesch. d. Qorāns*[2], iii. 8, note 1). Valuable Ḳurʾāns had the character of relics and belonged to the *khizāna* of the mosque. They were often kept in a chest, *ṣandūḳ*. Ibn al-Faḳīh mentions 16 chests with Ḳurʾāns in the Jerusalem mosque (*BGA*, v. 100). In the mosque there were also *ṣanādīḳ* for other things, such as lamps (Maḳrīzī, iv. 53; Wüstenfeld, *Medina*, p. 82 = Ibn Djubair, p. 194), a *tābūt* for alms (*K. al-Madkhal*, ii. 44, *infra*), for the *bait al-māl* or the property of the mosque (see below). There were also chests for rosaries (*Madkhal*, ii. 50) which were in charge of a special officer.

The Ḳurʾāns were not the only relics to be kept in the mosques. Bodies or parts of the bodies of saints and other *āthār* were kept and revered in mosques: the rod of Moses, the Prophet's sandals, his cloak, hair from his beard and many other things (see Goldziher, *Muh. Stud.*, ii. 358 *sqq.*; Mez, *Renaissance d. Islams*, p. 325 *sq.*). These relics were often kept in valuable reliquaries. The head of Ḥusain was buried in a silver *tābūt* in his mosque in Cairo (Ibn Djubair, p. 45).

On the other hand, pictures and images were excluded from the mosques, in deliberate contrast to the crucifixes and images of saints in churches, as is evident from Ḥadīth (Bukhārī, *Ṣalāt*, bāb 48, 54 et al.; cf. on the question Becker, *Islāmstudien*, i. 445 *sqq.*). In some circles the opposition to pictures extended to other relics also. Ibn Taimīya condemned the reverence paid to the Prophet's footprint, which was shown in Jerusalem, and in a Damascus mosque also (Quatremère, *Hist. Maml.* II/ii. 246).s

g. Carpets

Carpets were used to improve the appearance of the mosques. The custom of performing the ṣalāt upon a carpet is ascribed by Ḥadīth to the Prophet himself. As a rule, he used a mat woven of palm leaves, *khumra* (Bukhārī, *Ṣalāt*, bāb 19, 20, 21, et al.). In any case, it is clear from Balādhurī (p. 277, 348) that the ṣalāt was at first performed in the mosque simply in the dust and then on pebbles. Later, when the halls were extended, the ground, or the paving, was covered with matting.

The first to cover the ground in the Mosque of ʿAmr with *ḥuṣur* instead of *ḥaṣbāʾ* was Muʿāwiya's governor Maslama b. Mukhallad (Maḳrīzī, iv. 8; *Ḥusn al-muḥāḍara*, ii. 136; Ibn Taghrībirdī, i. 77). The different groups which frequented the mosque had their places on particular mats (al-Kindī, *Wulāt*, p. 469). Later the chief mosques had the floor covered with a great number of sumptuous carpets, and on feast-days they were adorned with carpets in a particularly luxurious fashion (see Ibn Taghrībirdī, ed. Juynboll, ii. 483). The puritans rejected all this as *bid'a* and preferred the bare ground (*Madkhal*, ii. 46, 49, 72, 74, 76) as the Wahhābīs still do.

h. Lighting

Where evening meetings and vigils were of regular occurrence, artificial lighting became necessary. Al-Azraḳī gives the history of the lighting of the Meccan Mosque. The first to illuminate the Ka'ba was 'Uḳba b. al-Azraḳ, who placed a large lamp (*miṣbāḥ*) in his house next to the mosque. But later lanterns with oil lamps were put up around the Ka'ba (*Chron. Mekka*, i. 200 *sqq.*, cf. 458 *sq.*). According to Ibn al-Faḳīh (before 300), 1,600 lamps were lit every evening in Jerusalem (*BGA*, v. 100) and in the next century al-Maḳdisī says that the people of Palestine always burn *ḳanādīl* in their mosques, which were hung from chains as in Mecca (*BGA*, iii. 182).

This great interest in the lighting of the mosque was not entirely based on practical considerations. Light had a significance in the divine service and Islām here, as elsewhere, was taking over something from the Church. When, in 227/842, the caliph al-Mu'taṣim was on his deathbed, he asked that the ṣalāt should be performed over him with candles and incense (*bi 'l-sham' wa 'l-bukhūr*) exactly after the fashion of the Christians (Ibn Abī Uṣaibi'a, i. 165; cf. ii. 89). A light was used particularly in the miḥrāb, because it represented the holy cell, to which light belongs (cf. Sūra xxiv. 35). Then, in Mecca, lamps were placed before the imāms in the miḥrābs and there were considerable endowments for such miḥrāb lamps (Ibn Djubair, *Riḥla*, p. 103, 144). Light, as was everywhere the custom in ancient times, was necessary in mausoleums, and the documents of endowment show that a large number of oil-lamps were used in this way (cf. e.g. the document for al-Malik al-Ashraf's mausoleum, v. Berchem, *Corpus*, i., No. 252).

On ceremonial occasions a great illumination was absolutely necessary. In the month of Ramaḍān, says Ibn Djubair, the carpets were renewed and the candles and lamps increased in number, so that the whole mosque was a blaze of light (*Riḥla*, p. 143); on certain evenings trees of light were made with vast numbers of lamps and candles and the minarets were illuminated (*ibid.*, p. 149—151, 154, 155).

i. Incense

According to some traditions, even the Prophet had incense burned in the mosque (Tirmidhī, i. 116; see Lammens, *Mo'âwia*, p. 367, note 8) and in the time of 'Umar, his client 'Abd Allāh is said to have perfumed the mosque by burning incense while he sat on the minbar. The same client is said to have carried the censer (*midjmar*: cf. Lammens, *loc. cit.*) brought by 'Umar from Syria before 'Umar when he went to the ṣalāt in the month of Ramaḍān (A. Fischer, *Biographie von Gewährsmännern* etc., p. 55, note). According to this tradition, the use of incense was adopted into Islām very early as a palpable imitation of the custom of the Church.

Under the Umaiyads, incense was one of the regular requirements of the mosque (*ṭīb al-masdjid*: Ṭabarī, ii. 1234). Mu'āwiya is named as the first to perfume the Ka'ba with perfume (*khalūḳ*) and censer (*midjmar*: *BGA*, v. 20, $_{12}$). It became the custom to anoint the Ka'ba as well as the sacred tombs with musk and *ṭīb* (*Chron. Mekka*, i. 150, $_{10}$; Ibn Djubair, *Riḥla*, p. 191, $_{9}$). Incense, as well as candles, was used at burials (cf. de Goeje, *ZDMG*, 1905, p. 403 *sq.*; Lammens, *Mo'âwia*, p. 436, note 9). The consumption of incense in the mosques gradually became very large, especially at festivals (see for the Fāṭimids: Ibn Taghrībirdī, II/i., 484, $_{12}$; II/ii., ed. Popper, p. 106, $_{3}$; Maḳrīzī, iv. 51). On vessels for holding incense see the Bibliography in *Isl.*, xvii., 1928, p. 217 *sq.*).

j. Water-Supply

In the early days of Islām the Zemzem water in Mecca was used for drinking purposes and for ablutions. But under the Umaiyads Khālid al-Ḳasrī led water from other wells to the mosque and planned arrangements for ablutions at the entrance and a basin with a running fountain in the *ṣaḥn* (*Chron. Mekka* i. 299, 339 *sq.*). This arrangement seemes to have been a typically Umaiyad one and to have been introduced from the north.

The usual name for the basin, *fisḳīya* (in Egypt now *fasḳīya*) is *piscina*, which in the *Mishna* and in Syriac takes the form *piskīn*. At the same time, however, *birka* or *siḳāya* or *ṣihrīdj* which probably comes from the Persian, or the old Arabic *ḥawḍ* are also used. The running fountain is called *fawwāra*, the arrangements for ablutions *maṭāhir* or *mayāḍi'u*, sing. *mīḍa'a* (now usually *mēḍa*), "place for *wuḍū'*".

In Damascus, where every house, as is still the case, was amply supplied with water, Yāḳūt (d. 626/1229) found no mosque, madrasa or khānaḳāh which did not have water flowing into a *birka* in the *ṣaḥn* (Yāḳūt, ii. 590). Ibn Djubair (p. 267 *sqq.*) describes the arrangements in the Mosque of the Umaiyads. In the *ṣaḥn*, as is still the case, there were three ḳubbas. The centre one rested on four marble columns, and below it was a basin with a spring of drinking-water surrounded by an iron grille. This was called *ḳafaṣ al-mā'* "water-cage". There was also running water in an adjoining *mashhad*, in the khānaḳāh and madrasa, and in a hall beside the living apartments there was again a ḳubba with a basin (*ḥawḍ*) and spring water. There were also *siḳāyāt* against the four outer walls of the mosque, whole houses fitted up with lavatories and closets; a century earlier, we are told that at each entrance to the mosque there was a *mīḍa'a* (*BGA*, iii. 159). The whole arrangements correspond exactly to those made by Khālid al-Ḳasrī in Mecca in the Umaiyad period. It was the same in other Syrian and Mesopotamian towns e.g. Sāmarrā', Kūfa, Ḥalab, Naṣībīn, Mawṣil, Ḥarrān etc.

In Egypt the Mosque of Ibn Ṭūlūn was apparently the first to be arranged similarly to the Syrian mosques. In the centre of the ṣaḥn there was a gilt dome, supported by sixteen marble columns and surrounded by a railing. This upper story was supported by nineteen marble columns and below was a marble basin (*ḳaṣ'a*) with a running fountain (*fawwāra*); the *adhān* was called from the dome (Maḳrīzī, iv. 37; the description is not quite clear). A *mīḍa'a* with an apothecary's shop was made at the request of the people behind the mosque (*ibid.*, p. 38, 39; *Ḥusn al-muḥāḍara*, ii. 139; Ibn Taghrībirdī, II/i. 10).

The importance of the birka of the mosque as a drinking-place diminished as piousf ounders erected drinking fountains everywhere (cf. for Mecca: *Chron. Mekka*, ii. 116—118; also *BGA*, iv. 211, s.v. *ḥubb*; p. 258, s.v. *sabīl*) and especially when it became the custom to build a sabīl with a boy's school in part of the mosque. A *ḥawḍ* for watering animals was also sometimes built in the vicinity of the mosque (Maḳrīzī, iv. 76). The custom of using the water supply of the ṣaḥn for *wuḍū'* survived in many places in Egypt. There were therefore usually called *mīḍa'a* or rather *mēḍā* (which is not found in the inscriptions). If they had taps, they were called *ḥanafīya*; according to Lane's suggestion because the Ḥanafīs permitted ablutions only with running water or from a cistern 10 ells broad and deep (*Lexicon*, s.v.; cf. *Manners and Customs*, Everyman's Library, p. 69; cf. on the question: Max Herz, *Observations critiques sur les bassins dans les Ṣaḥns des Mosquées, BIE* iii./7, 1896, p. 47—51). Ibn al-Ḥādjdj condemns bringing water into the mosque, because the only object is for ablutions and ablutions in the mosque are forbidden by "our learned men" (*Madkhal*, ii. 47 *sq.*, 49); like shaving, ablutions should be performed outside the mosque in keeping with the Prophet's saying.

E. The Mosque as a State Institution

1. The Mosque as a political centre. Its relation to the Ruler

It was inherent in the character of Islām, that religion and politics could not be separated. The same individual was ruler and chief administrator in the two fields, and the same building, the mosque, was the centre of gravity for both politics and religion. This relationship found expression in the fact that the mosque was placed in the centre of the camp, while the ruler's abode was built immediately adjacent to it, as in Madīna (and in al-Fusṭāṭ, Damascus, Baṣra, Kūfa). We can trace how this *dār al-imāra* or *ḳaṣr* with the growth of the mosque gradually became incorporated in it in al-Fusṭāṭ and al-Baṣra and was replaced by a new building. The tradition remained so strong that in Cairo, when the new chief mosque Djāmiʿ al-ʿAskar was being planned in 169/785—6, a *dār umarāʾ Miṣr* was built beside it with direct access to the mosque (Maḳrīzī, iv. 33 *sq.*), and when Ibn Ṭūlūn built his mosque, a building called the *dār al-imāra* was erected on its south side, where the ruler, who now lived in another new palace, had rooms for changing his dress, etc., from which he could go straight into the maḳṣūra (*ibid.*, p. 42).

The ʿAbbāsids at the foundation of Baghdād introduced a characteristic innovation, when they made the palace the centre of the city; the case was similar with Fāṭimid Cairo. Later rulers who no longer lived just beside the mosque, had special balconies or something similar built for themselves in or beside the mosque. Ṣalāḥ al-Dīn built for himself a *manẓara* under the great minaret of the mosque of ʿAmr (Maḳrīzī, iv. 13; *Ḥusn al-muḥāḍara*, ii. 137) and just to the south of the Azhar mosque the Fāṭimids had a *manẓara* from which they could overlook the mosque (Maḳrīzī, ii. 345).

The caliph was the appointed leader of the ṣalāt and the khaṭīb of the Muslim community. The significance of the mosque for the state is therefore embodied in the minbar. The installation of the caliph consisted in his seating himself upon this, the seat of the Prophet in his sovereign capacity. When homage was first paid to Abū Bakr by those who had decided the choice of the Prophet's successor, he sat on the minbar. He delivered an address, the people paid homage to him and he delivered a khuṭba, by which he assumed the leadership (Ibn Hishām, p. 1017; Ṭabarī, i. 1828 *sq.*; *K. al-khamīs*, ii. 75; Yaʿḳūbī, ii. 142); it was the same with the following caliphs. Even at a much later date, when spontaneous acclamation by the population was no longer of any importance, the ceremonial installation on the minbar was still important (Maḳrīzī, iv. 94).

The caliph spoke chiefly from the minbar of the capital, but when he made the pilgrimage he also spoke from the *manābir* in Mecca and Madīna (cf. e.g. Ṭabarī, ii. 1234; Yaʿḳūbī, ii. 341, 501; *Chron. Mekka* i. 160). Otherwise, in the provinces, the governor stood in the same relation to the mosques as the caliph in the capital. He was appointed "over ṣalāt and sword" or he administered "justice among the people" and the ṣalāt (Ṭabarī, iii. 860). Speaking from the minbar was a right which the caliph had delegated to him and it was done in the name of the caliph. ʿAmr b. al-ʿĀṣī therefore refused to allow people in the country to hold *djumʿa* except under the direction of the commander (Maḳrīzī, iv. 7). This point of view was never quite abandoned. The khuṭba was delivered "in the name of" the caliph (*ibid.*, p. 94) or "for" him (*li*: *ibid.*, p. 66, 74, 198; Ibn Taghrībirdī, II/i. 85 *infra*; *BGA*, iii. 485 *supra*) and in the same way an emīr delivered a khuṭba "for" a sulṭān (Maḳrīzī, iv. 213, 214). The sulṭān did not have the "secular" and the caliph the "spiritual" power, but the sulṭān exercised as a Muslim ruler the actual power which the caliph possessed as the legitimate sovereign and had formally entrusted to him.

Like the caliph, the governor also made his formal entry into office by ascending the minbar and delivering a khuṭba; this was the symbol of his authority (e.g. Ṭabarī, ii. 91, 238, 242; *Chron. Mekka*, ii. 173; cf. *Ḥamāsa*, p. 660, v. 2—3; Djāḥiẓ, *Bayān*, iii. 135). After glorifying God and the Prophet he announced his appointment or read the letter from the caliph. The khuṭba was not inseparably connected with the Friday service. The commander-in-chief could at any time issue a summons to the *ṣalāt* and deliver his khuṭba with admonitions and orders (see Ṭabarī, ii. as above and p. 260, 297 *sq.*, 298, 300, 863, 1179).

Since war was inseparably associated with early Islām and the mosque was the public meeting place of ruler and people, it often became the scene of warlike incidents. While the governor in his khuṭba was issuing orders and admonitions relating to the fighting, cheers and counter-cheers could be uttered (*ibid.*, p. 238) and councils of war were held in the mosque (Ṭabarī, i. 3415; ii. 284; Balādhurī, p. 267). Rowdy scenes occasionally took place in mosques (Kindī, *Wulāt*, p. 18); Ziyād was stoned on the minbar (Ṭabarī, ii. 88); one could ride right into the mosque and shout to the governor sitting on the minbar (*ibid.*, p. 682); fighting often took place in and beside the mosque (*ibid.*, p. 960, 1701 *sqq.*; Wüstenfeld, *Medina*, p. 13 *sq.*).

It thus came to be the custom for the enemies of the ruler and his party to be cursed in the mosques, as was done between the Umaiyads and the ʿAlids. This custom continued the old Arab custom of regular campaigns of objurgation between two tribes but can also be paralleled by the Byzantine ecclesiastical anathematisation of heretics (cf. Becker, *Islāmstudien*, i. 485).

It was very natural to mention with a blessing upon him the ruler in whose name the Friday khuṭba was delivered. Ibn ʿAbbās, when governor of Baṣra, is said to have been the first to pronounce such a *duʿāʾ* over ʿAlī (Ibn Khaldūn, *Muḳaddima*, *faṣl* 37, end); it is not improbable that the custom arose out of the reciprocal objurgations of ʿAlids and Umaiyads; the *ḳuṣṣāṣ*, who had to curse the ʿAlids in the mosques, used to pray for the Umaiyads (Maḳrīzī, iv. 17). Under the ʿAbbāsids, the custom became the usual form of expressing loyalty to the ruler (Ibn

Taghrībirdī, II/i. 151). After the caliph, the name of the local ruler or governor was mentioned (*ibid.*, p. 156, 161).

In general, the mosque, and particularly the minbar, was the place where official proclamations were made, of course as early as the time of the Prophet (Bukhārī, *Ṣalāt*, bāb 70, 71). Al-Walīd announced from the minbar the deaths of two distinguished governors (Ibn Taghrībirdī, i. 242); the results of battles were announced in khuṭbas (Yāḳūt, i. 647; *al-ʿIḳd al-ʿfarīd*, ii., Cairo 1321, p. 149 *sq.*). In the Fāṭimid and ʿAbbāsid periods also proclamations, orders, edicts about taxation etc. by the ruler were announced in the principal mosque (Ṭabarī, ii. 40; iii. 2165; Ibn Taghrībirdī, II/ii. 68; Maḳrīzī, *Ittiʿāẓ*, ed. Bunz, p. 87 *supra*; Quatremère, *Hist. Maml.*, I/ii. 89; II/ii. 44, 151); documents appointing the more important officers were also read upon the minbar (Kindī, *Wulāt*, p. 589, 599, 603, 804, etc. *pass.*; Maḳrīzī, ii. 246; iv. 43, 88); frequently the people trooped into the mosque to hear an official announcement (Kindī, *Wulāt*, p. 14; cf. Dozy, *Histoire des musulmans d'Espagne*, Leiden 1932, ii. 286).

2. The Mosque and public administration

The actual work of government was very early transferred from the mosque into a special *dīwān* or *madjlis* (see Ṭabarī, *Gloss.*, s.v.) and negotiations were carried on and business frequently done in the *ḳaṣr al-imāra* (cf. Ṭabarī, ii. 230 *sq.*). But when financial business had to be transacted at public meetings, the mosque was used; of this there is particular evidence from Egypt. Here the director of finance used to sit in the Mosque of ʿAmr and auction the farming out of the domains, with a crier and several financial officers to assist him (Maḳrīzī, i. 131 *sq.*).

The connection with the administration was also seen in the fact that the treasure-chest, the *bait al-māl*, was kept in the mosque. In al-Fusṭāṭ Usāma b. Zaid, the director of finance, in 97/715—6 or 99/717—8 built in the Mosque of ʿAmr a *ḳubba* on pillars in front of the minbar for the *bait al-māl* of Egypt. A drawbridge was placed between it and the roof. In the time of Ibn Rósta (c. 300/912) it was still possible to move about freely below the ḳubba but in 378—379/988—90 al-ʿAzīz put up a running fountain below it (*BGA*, vii. 116; Maḳrīzī, iv. 9, 11, 13; *Ḥusn al-muḥāḍara*, ii. 136; Yāḳūt, iii. 899).

In Kūfa, the *buyūt al-amwāl*, at least during the early period, were in the dār al-imāra (Ṭabarī i. 2489, 2491 *sq.*); in the year 38/658—9 during the fighting, it was saved from Baṣra and taken with the minbar to the Mosque of al-Ḥuddān (*ibid.*, p. 3414 *sq.*). In Palestine, in the chief mosque of each town, there was a similar arrangement to that in the Mosque of ʿAmr (*BGA*, iii. 182). In Damascus the *bait al-māl* was in the most western of the three ḳubba's in the court of the Mosque of the Umaiyads; it was of lead and rested on 8 columns (*BGA*, iii. 157; Ibn Djubair, p. 264, 267; Ibn Baṭṭūṭa, i. 200 *sq.*); similar arrangements were introduced in the eastern countries.

3. The Mosque as a court of justice

That the Prophet used to settle legal questions in his mosque was natural (see Bukhārī, *Aḥkām*, bāb 19, 29 etc.; cf. *Ṣalāt*, bāb 71; *Khuṣūmāt*, bāb 4); but he could also deliver judgments in other places (*ibid.*, pass). In Ḥadīth it is recorded that some ḳāḍīs of the earlier period (Shuraiḥ, al-Shaʿbī, Yaḥyā b. Yaʿmar, Marwān) sat in judgment beside the minbar, others (al-Ḥasan, Zurāʿa b. Awfā) on the open square beside the mosque (Bukhāri, *Aḥkām*, bāb 18). The custom had all the better chance of survival, as churches were used in the same way (Joshua Stylites, ed. Wright, ch. 29; Mez, cf. *Renaissance*, p. 223). Sitting in judgment was primarily the business of the ruler but he had to have assistants; ʿUmar is already called Abū Bakr's ḳāḍī (Ṭabarī, i. 2135) and a number of judges appointed by ʿUmar are mentioned (*BGA*, vii. 227). In Baṣra, we are told that al-Aswad b. Sarīʿ al-Tamīm immediately after the building of the mosque (i.e. in the year 14/635) acted in it as ḳāḍī (Balādhurī, p. 364). Even the Christian poet al-Akhṭal was allowed to act as arbiter in the mosque of Kūfa (see Lammens, *Muʿâwia*, p. 435 *sq.*).

In al-Fusṭāṭ, as early as 23/644 or 24/645 by command of ʿUmar, ʿAmr b. al-ʿĀṣī appointed a ḳāḍī named Ḳais (*Ḥusn al-muḥāḍara*, ii. 86; Kindī, *Wulāt*, p. 300 *sq.*). The ḳāḍī held his sessions in the Mosque of ʿAmr but not exclusively there. The ḳāḍī Khair b. Nuʿaim (120—127/738—745) held his sessions sometimes before his house, sometimes in the mosque, and for Christians on the steps leading up to the mosque (Kindī, *Wulāt*, p. 351 *sq.*). A successor of his (177—184/793—800) invited Christians who had lawsuits into the mosque to be heard (*ibid.*, p. 391); of another judge (205—211/820—826) it is recorded that he was not allowed to sit in the mosque (*ibid.*, p. 428). It seems that the ḳāḍī could himself choose where he would sit. During the Fāṭimid period, the subsidiary building on the north east of the Mosque of ʿAmr was reserved for the judge. This judge, called from the year 376/986—7 onwards *ḳāḍī 'l-ḳuḍāt* (cf. *Ḥusn al-muḥāḍara*, ii. 91; Kindī, *Wulāt*, p. 590), sat on Tuesday and Saturday in the mosque and laid down the law (Maḳrīzī, ii. 246; iv. 16, 22; cf. Kindī, *Wulāt*, p. 587, 589; cf. *Sefer-nāme*, transl. Schefer, p. 149).

In Yaʿḳūbī's time in Baghdād, the judge of the east city used to sit in its chief mosque (*BGA*, vii. 245), in Damascus the vice-ḳāḍī in the fourth century had a special riwāḳ in the Mosque of the Umaiyads (*BGA*, iii. 158) and the notaries (*al-shurūṭiyūn*) also sat in the Mosque of the Umaiyads at the Bāb al-Sāʿāt (*ibid.*, p. 17). In course of time the judge was given a *madjlis al-ḥukm* of his own (cf. *Ḥusn*, ii. 96). But the administration of justice did not at once lose all connection with the mosque, which still continued to be the centre of law studies [s. MADRASA].

F. The Administration of the Mosque

1. Finances

The earliest mosques were built by the rulers of the various communities and the members of the community did all the work neccessary in connection with the primitive mosques. The later mosques as a rule were erected by rulers, emīrs, high officials or other wealthy men and maintained by them. The erection of the mosque of Ibn Ṭūlūn cost its builder 120,000 dīnārs, the Mosque of Muʾaiyad 110,000 (Maḳrīzī, iv. 32, 137, 138). The upkeep of the mosque was provided for by estates made over as endowments (*waḳf*, *ḥabs*). In the third century we thus hear of houses which belonged to the mosques and were let by them (*Papyrus Erzherzog Rainer, Führer*, No. 773, 837) and Ibn Ṭūlūn constituted a large number of houses as an endowment for his mosque and hospital (Maḳrīzī, iv. 83). This custom was taken over from the Christians by the Muslims (see Becker, in *Isl.*, ii. 404).

The estates were often at a considerable distance: the mosques in Egypt often had estates in Syria (v. Berchem, *CIA*, i., No. 247; Maḳrīzī, vi. 107, 137). Not only were mosques built and endowed but already existing ones were given endowments for new rooms for teachers, minbars, stipends for Ḳur'ān reciters, teachers etc. There were often special endowments for the salaries of the imām and the mu'adhdhins, for the support of visitors, for blankets, food etc. (see Ibn Djubair, p. 227). The endowments and the purpose for which they might be used was precisely laid down in the grant and the document attested in the court of justice by the ḳāḍī and the witnesses (cf. Maḳrīzī, iv. 50, 76, 81, 196 *infra*). The text was also often inscribed on the wall of the mosque. Certain conditions might be laid down, e.g. in a madrasa that no Persian should be appointed there (Maḳrīzī, iv. 202 *infra*) or that the teacher could not be dismissed or some such condition (v. Berchem, *CIA*, i., No. 201), that no women could enter (*JA*, ser. 9, iii. 389), that no Christian, Jew or Ḥanbalī could enter the building (*ibid.*, p. 405), etc. Endowments were often made with stipulations for the family of the founder or other purposes. That mosques could also be burdened with expenses is evident from an inscription in Edfū of the year 797/1395 (v. Berchem, *CIA*, i. No. 539). If a mosque was founded without sufficient endowment, it decayed (e.g. Maḳrīzī, iv. 115, 201, 203) or the stipends were reduced (*ibid.*, p. 251), but in the larger mosques as a rule the rulers provided new endowments. According to al-Māwardī, there were also special "Sulṭān-mosques" which were directly under the patronage of the caliph and their officials paid from the Bait al-Māl (*al-Aḥkām al-sulṭānīya*, ed. Enger, p. 172 *supra*, 176 *supra*).

Just as the Bait al-Māl of the state was kept in the mosque, so was the mosque's own property kept in it: e.g. the *kanz* or *khizānat al-Kaʿba*, which is mentioned in ʿUmar's time and may be presumed to have existed under his predecessors (Balādhurī, p. 43 *supra*; *Chron. Mekka*, i. 307, ii. 14). The *bait māl al-djāmiʿ* in Damascus was in a ḳubba in the ṣaḥn (*BGA*, iii. 157; Ibn Djubair, p. 267; Ibn Baṭṭūṭa, i. 201; cf. for Madīna: Wüstenfeld, *Medina*, p. 86).

2. Administration

As Imām of the Muslim community, the caliph had the mosques under his charge. This was also the case with the sulṭān, governor or other ruler who represented the caliph in every respect. The administration of the mosques could however not be directly controlled by the usual government offices. By its endowment the mosque became an object *sui generis* and was withdrawn from the usual state or private purposes. Their particular association with religion gave the ḳāḍīs special influence and on the other hand the will of the testator continued to prevail. These three factors determined the administration of the mosque but the relation between them was not always clear.

a. Administration of the separate mosques

The mosque was usually in charge of a *nāẓir* or *walī* who looked after its affairs. The founder was often himself the *nāẓir* or he chose another, and after his death his descendants took charge or whoever was appointed by him in the foundation charter. Even in the case of chief mosques the descendants of the founder could maintain a claim on the mosque, if we may believe Nāṣir-i Khusraw, according to whom al-Ḥākim paid the descendants of Ibn Ṭūlūn 30,000 dīnars for the mosque and 5,000 for the minaret and similarly to the descendants of ʿAmr b. al-ʿĀṣī 100,000 dīnārs for the Mosque of ʿAmr (*Sefer-nāme*, ed. Schefer, p. 39, and 146, 40 and 148). In the case of mosques and madāris founded during the Mamlūk period, it is often expressly mentioned that the administration is to remain in the hands of the descendants of the founder (Maḳrīzī, iv. 66, 89, 205, 232; cf. v. Berchem, *CIA*, II/i. 129). Sometimes an emīr or official was administrator e.g. in the Mu'aiyad (Maḳrīzī, iv. 140). It might be the *kātib al-sirr* or the *khāzindār*, but it was more frequently a ḳāḍī; for example in the mosque of Baibars, the Ḥanafī ḳāḍī was to take charge after the descendants (Maḳrīzī, iv. 89); in the Āḳbughawīya, the Shāfiʿī ḳāḍī was appointed, but his descendants were expressly excluded (*ibid.*, p. 225). In Cairo we find during the Mamlūk period that emīrs and ḳāḍīs alternately acted as nāẓirs in the large mosques (e.g. the Mosque of Ibn Ṭūlūn: Maḳrīzī, iv. 42). Cases are also found however in which descendants of the founder unsuccessfully claimed the office of nāẓir (Maḳrīzī, iv. 218, 255). This was the result of the increasing importance of the ḳāḍīs. In the madāris the nāẓir was often also the headmaster (*ibid.*, p. 204, 238 *supra*).

The nāẓir managed the finances and other business of the mosque. Sometimes he had a fixed salary (v. Berchem, *CIA*, i., No. 252). His control of the funds of the mosque was often limited by the central commission for endowments. The nāẓir might also see to any necessary increase of the endowments. He appointed the staff and he fixed their pay (cf. e.g. Maḳrīzī, iv. 41). Generally speaking the nāẓir's powers were considerable. In Mecca, according to Ḳuṭb al-Dīn, the *nāẓir al-ḥaram* was in charge of the great festival of the mawlid of the Prophet (12th Rabīʿ I) and distributed robes of honour in the mosque on this occasion (*Chron. Mekka*, iii. 439). In the Azhar, no nāẓir was appointed after about 1100 but a learned man was appointed Shaikh al-Azhar, principal and administrator of the mosque (Sulaimān Raṣad al-Zaiyātī, *Kanz al-djawhar fī ta'rīkh al-Azhar*, p. 123 *sqq.*). Conditions are similar in Mecca (Snouck Hurgronje, *Mekka*, ii. 235 *sqq.*, 252 *sq.*).

As we have seen, ḳāḍīs were often nāẓirs of mosques. This was especially the case in the madāris, where the ḳāḍīs were often teachers (cf. Maḳrīzī, iv. 209, 219, 222, 238, etc.); the ḳāḍīs were particularly anxious to get the principal offices in the large schools (cf. Ḳalḳashandī, xi. 235). Their influence was however further increased by the fact that, if a nāẓir qualified by the terms of the founder's will no longer existed, the ḳāḍī of the madhhab in question stepped into his place (cf. *ZDMG*, xlv., 1897, p. 552). By this rule, which often gave rise to quarrels between the different ḳāḍīs (e.g. Maḳrīzī, iv. 218: the Ẓāhirīya), a ḳāḍī could accumulate a large number of offices and "milk the endowments" (*ibid.*, iii. 364). Sometimes their management was so ruthless, that the schools soon declined (e.g. the Ṣāḥibīya and the Djamālīya: Maḳrīzī, iv. 204 *sq.*, 238).

b. Central Administration of the Mosques

The large mosques occupied a special position in the Muslim empire, because the caliph was particularly interested in them; especially those of Mecca and Madīna where the rulers and their governors built extensions and executed renovations (cf. *Chron. Mekka*, i. 145; iii. 83 *sqq.*). These works were carried out by the governors or the chief ḳāḍīs in the capital and in the holy cities.

The importance of the ḳāḍī was based primarily on his special competence in the field of religion. A zealous ḳāḍī could order the management of the mosque (Kindī, *Wulāt*, p. 469). After the building of the Ṭūlūnid mosque, a commission was appointed under the ḳāḍī 'l-ḳuḍāt to settle the ḳibla of the mosque (Maḳrīzī, iv. 21 *sq.*). But at a quite early date they also obtained a say in the management of the funds. The first ḳāḍī to lay his hands on the *aḥbās* was Tawba b. Namir al-Ḥaḍramī; while hitherto every endowment had been administered by the children of the testator or some one appointed by him, in 118/736 Tawba brought about the centralisation of all endowments and a large dīwān was created for the purpose (Kindī, *Wulāt*, p. 346). How this system of centralisation worked is not clear at first, but it was carried through under the Fāṭimids.

Al-Muʿizz created a special *dīwān al-aḥbās* and made the chief ḳāḍī head of it as well as of the *dja-wāmiʿ wa 'l-mashāhid* (Maḳrīzī, iv. 83 and 75; cf. Kindī, *Wulāt*, p. 585, 587, 589), and a special *bait al-māl* was instituted for it in 363/973—4; a yearly revenue of 1,500,000 dirhams was guaranteed; anything left over went to form a capital fund. All payments were made through this office after being certified by the managers of the separate mosques (Maḳrīzī, iv. 83 *sq.*). The mosques were thus administered by the ḳāḍīs, directly under the caliph. The *dīwān al-birr wa 'l-ṣadaḳa* in Baghdād (Mex, *Renaissance*, p. 72) perhaps served similar purposes.

Al-Ḥākim reformed the administration of the mosques. In 403/1012–3 he had an investigation made and when it proved that 800 (or 830) had no income (*ghalla*), he made provision for them by a payment of 9,220 dirhams monthly from the Bait al-Māl; he also made 405 new endowments for the officials of the mosque (Maḳrīzī, iv. 84, 264). Under the Fāṭimids, the ḳāḍīs used to inspect all the mosques and mashāhid in and around Cairo at the end of Ramaḍān and compare them with their inventories (*ibid.*, p. 84).

The same conditions continued under the Aiyūbids and for a time under the Mamlūks. From the middle of the seventh century, we often find emīrs as administrators of the chief mosques. The ḳāḍī had however obtained so much authority that he was conceded "a general supervision of all matters affecting the endowments of his madhhab" (al-ʿUmarī, *Taʿrīf bi 'l-muṣṭalaḥ al-sharīf*, p. 117; cf. *ZDMG*, xlv., p. 559); according to this theory the ḳāḍī could intervene to stop abuses.

Sulṭān Baibars reformed the endowments, which were now administered in three departments, and the control of these was soon taken over by the Emīrs, who often used them for personal purposes (Maḳrīzī, iv. 83—86). In modern times, as a rule, endowments in Muslim lands have been combined under a special ministry.

To be distinguished from the administrators of the mosque is the *nāẓir* who is only concerned with the supervision of the structure of the mosques. Any one could be entrusted with the building of a mosque (e.g. Maḳrīzī, iv. 92). Under the Mamlūks there was also a clerk of works, *mutawallī shadd al-ʿamāʾir* or *nāẓir al-ʿimāra*: he was the overseer of the builders (*ibid.*, p. 102; see Khalīl al-Ẓāhirī, *Zubdat kashf al-mamālik*, ed. Ravaisse, p. 115, cf. p. 109; v. Berchem, *CIA*, i. 742 *sq.*, 751).

The caliph or the ruler of the country was in this, as in other matters, supreme. He intervened in the administration and directed it as he wished. He was also able to interfere in the internal affairs of the mosque, if necessary through his usual officers. The adhān formulae for instance were laid down in edicts by the ruler (Maḳrīzī, iv. 44, 45). The importance of the sovereign in connection with the mosque depended on his personality. As a rule he recognized the authority of the regular officials. When for example al-Khaṭīb al-Baghdādī asked the Caliph al-Ḳāʾim for authority to read Ḥadīth in the mosque of al-Manṣūr, the latter referred the question to the *naḳīb al-nuḳabāʾ* (Yāḳūt, *Udabāʾ*, i. 246 *sq.*; cf. Wüstenfeld, *Schâfiʿi*, iii. 280).

Indonesian mosques, especially in Java, are hierarchally organised, in so far as the director of the mosque of the capital of a regency, called *pang(h)ulu*, has also the supervision of the mosques in the smaller towns, the directors of which are his deputies. The mosques here are generally considered to be *waḳf* (*wakap*), even where this is not legally the case. Their revenues consist in *waḳf*-donations and in contributions of *zakāt* (*djakat*). These are collected in a mosque fund, which is likewise administered by the panghulu. The panghulus have still many other functions connected with Islamic Law, such as jurisdiction and the control of marriages. In the villages there are very simple houses of prayer (called *langgar* in Java), which also serve for other purposes of general interest. Their upkeep is an affair of the community as represented by the religious official of the village.

G. The Personnel of the Mosque

1. The Imām

From the earliest days of Islām the ruler was the leader of the ṣalāt; he was *imām* as leader in war, head of the government and leader of the common ṣalāt. The governors of provinces thus became leaders of the *ṣalāt* and heads of the *kharādj*, and when a special financial official took over the fiscal side, the governor was appointed *ʿala 'l-ṣalāt wa 'l-ḥarb*. He had to conduct ritual prayer, especially the Friday ṣalāt, on which occasion he also delivered the khuṭba. If he was prevented, the chief of police, *ṣāḥib al-shurṭa*, was his khalīfa (cf. Maḳrīzī, iv. 83). This was altered under the ʿAbbāsids. The caliph no longer regularly conducted the ṣalāts (Maḳrīzī, iv. 45), and ʿAnbasa b. Isḥāḳ, the last Arab governor of Egypt (238—242/852—56), was also the last emīr to conduct the ṣalāt in the djāmiʿ. An imām, paid out of the *bait al-māl*, was now appointed (*ibid.*, p. 83), but the governor still continued to be formally appointed *ʿala 'l-ṣalāt*.

The imām appointed was chosen from among those learned in religious matters; he might at the same time be a ḳāḍī or his nāʾib (see Kindī, *Wulāt*, p. 575, 589; Ibn Baṭṭūṭa, i. 276 *sq.*). During the ṣalāt he stood at the miḥrāb; he could also stand on an elevated position; on one occasion Abū Huraira conducted the *ṣalāt* in the Meccan mosque from the roof (Bukhārī, *Ṣalāt*, bāb 17). In Mecca, in Ibn Djubair's time, each of the four recognized madhāhib (with the Zaidīs in addition) had an imām; they conducted the ṣalāt one after the other, each in his place (*Riḥla*, p. 101, 102, 143 *sq.*). This continued down to recent times. (Snouck Hurgronje, *Mekka*, ii. 79 *sq.*).

When the imām no longer represented a political office, each mosque regularly had one. He had to maintain order and was in general charge of the divine services in the mosque. It was his duty to conduct every ṣalāt which is only valid *fī djamāʿa*. He must conform to the standards laid down in the law; but it is disputed whether the ṣalāt is invalid in the opposite case. According to some, the leader of the Friday ṣalāt should be a different man from the leader of the five daily ṣalāts (Māwardī, *al-Aḥkām al-sulṭānīya*, ed. Enger, p. 171 *sqq.*; Ibn al-Ḥādjdj, *K. al-Madkhal*, ii. 41, 43 *sqq.*, 50, 73 *sqq.*; al-Subkī, *Muʿīd al-niʿam*, ed. Myhrman, p. 163 *sq.*; for ḥadīths s. Wensinck, *Handbook*, p. 109 *sq.*).

2. The Khaṭīb

The development of this office is analogous to that of imām. When the ʿAbbāsid caliph no longer delivered khuṭbas regularly, a man learned in religious matters was appointed to the office of khaṭīb [see E 1 and the article KHAṬĪB]. As the khaṭīb in theory represented the ruler, he uttered a blessing on the caliph and his heir and the king of the country. When the caliph himself preached, he also pronounced a prayer for himself (Yāḳūt, *Udabāʾ*, ii. 349 *sq.*) and the Fāṭimids mentioned their fathers. The sermons gradually became quite stereotyped; Ibn Baṭṭūṭa (i. 348) praises the khaṭīb in Mecca, because he gave a new sermon every Friday. A ḳāḍī was frequently chosen as khaṭīb, or he could be a "witness" (Hilāl al-Ṣābi, *Kitāb al-wuzarāʾ* ed. Amedroz, p. 421) or hold another office like that of *kātib al-sirr* (Maḳrīzī, iv. 137, 138, 139, 140); in the last-mentioned case the office was hereditary, which we also find elsewhere. The khaṭīb had frequently a khalīfa. Later we find in the larger mosques a number of khuṭabāʾ being appointed who relieve one another.

Very frequently the khaṭīb and the imām were one individual, especially in the smaller mosques, but sometimes also in larger ones (Yāḳūt, *Udabāʾ*, vii. 174, 179; Maḳrīzī, iv. 124).

In the smaller mosques of Indonesia the chief superindentent is generally called *kĕtip* (from *khaṭīb*); this official has many duties besides delivering the *khuṭba*.

3. Ḳāṣṣ (wāʿiẓ) and Ḳāriʾ

On these see C 3. The *ḳurrāʾ* are also frequently appointed to madrasas and particularly to mausoleums (Maḳrīzī, iv. 223; Yāḳūt, iv. 509; Subkī, *Muʿīd*, p. 162; v. Berchem, *CIA*, i., No. 252).

4. The Muʾadhdhin

According to most traditions, the office of muʾadhdhin was instituted in the year 1, according to others only after the *isrāʾ*, in the year 2, according to some weak traditions while Muḥammad was still in Mecca. At first the people came to the ṣalāt without being summoned. According to a tradition he consulted his companions about this. They proposed the use of trumpets (*būḳ*) or rattles (*nāḳūs*) or fires after the custom of Jews, Christians and Mādjūs, but ʿAbd Allāh b. Zaid learned the adhān formula in a dream and it was approved by the Prophet and when Bilāl proclaimed it, it was found that ʿUmar had also learned the same procedure in a dream (Ibn Hishām, p. 357 *sq.*; *Khamīs*, i. 404 *sq.*; Bukhārī, *Adhān*, bāb 1; Zurḳānī, i. 121 *sqq.*). There are also variants of the story, among the suggestions made is mentioned the hoisting of a flag (*Sīra Ḥalabīya*, ii. 100 *sqq.*). Noteworthy is a tradition which goes back to Ibn Saʿd, according to which at ʿUmar's suggestion at first a *munādī*, Bilāl, was sent out who called in the streets: *al-ṣalātᵘ djāmiʿatᵃⁿ*. Later the other possibilities were discussed, but the method already in use was confirmed by the dream, only with another formula, the one later used (*Khamīs*, i. 404; *Sīra Ḥalabīya*, ii. 100 *sq.*). According to this account, the consideration of other methods would be a secondary episode and probably the tradition in general represents a later attitude to the practices of other religions. But in Islām other methods were certainly used. In Fās, a flag was hung out in the minarets and a lamp at night (*JA*, ser. 11, xxii. 341).

The public crier was a well-known institution among the Arabs. Among the tribes and in the towns important proclamations and invitations to general assemblies were made by criers. This crier was called *munādī* or *muʾadhdhin* (*Sīra Ḥalabīya*, ii. 170; Lammens, *La Mecque*, p. 62 *sqq.*, 146; do., *Berceau*, i. 229 note; do., *Moʿâwia*, p. 150). *Adhān* therefore means proclamation, Sūra ix. 3, and *adhdhana*, *muʾadhdhin*, Sūra xii. 70 "to proclaim" and "crier". *Munādī* (Bukhārī, *Farḍ al-khums*, bāb 15) and *muʾadhdhin* (*ibid.*, *Ṣawm*, bāb 69; *Ṣalāt*, bāb 10 = *Djizya*, bāb 16; *Sīra Ḥalabīya*, ii. 270) are names given to a crier used by the Prophet or Abū Bakr for such purposes. Sadjāḥ and Musailima used a muʾadhdhin to summon the people to their prayers (Ṭabarī, i. 1919, 1932; cf. *Annali dell' Islam*, i. 410 *sq.*, 638 *sq.*). It therefore was a very natural thing for Muḥammad to assemble the believers to common prayer through a crier (*nādā li'l* or *ila 'l-ṣalāt*, Sūra v. 58; lxii. 9); the summons is called *nidāʾ* and *adhān*, the crier *munādī* (Bukhārī, *Wuḍūʾ*, bāb 5; *Adhān*, bāb 7) and *muʾadhdhin*; the two names are used quite indiscriminately.

In these conditions, it was very natural for the crier in the earliest period to be regarded as an assistant and servant of the ruler. Al-Ḥusain had his *munādī* with him and the latter summoned to the *ṣalāt* on al-Ḥusain's instructions (Ṭabarī, ii. 297, 298). During the earliest period the muʾadhdhin probably issued his summons in the streets and the call was very short: *al-ṣalātᵘ djāmiʿatᵃⁿ* (Ibn Saʿd, i. 7, 7; *Chron. Mekka*, i. 340; Ṭabarī iii. 861, here still in the year 196/812; *Sīra Ḥalabīya*, ii. 101; *Khamīs*, i. 404 *sq.*). This brief summons was, according to Ibn Saʿd, also used later on irregular occasions. Perhaps also the summons was issued from a particular place even at a quite early date (see D 2a). After the public summons the muʾadhdhin went to the Prophet, greeted him and called him to prayer; the same procedure was later used with his successors: when he had come, the muʾadhdhin announced the beginning of the ṣalāt (*aḳāma 'l-ṣalāt*). The activity of the muʾadhdhin thus fell into three sections: the asssembling of the community, the summoning of the imām and the announcement of the beginning of the ṣalāt. With time changes were made in all three stages.

The assembling of the community by crying aloud was not yet at all regular in the older period, but the public call to prayer had to be organised lest confusion arose, and the custom of calling from a raised position became general after the introduction of the minaret. While previously the call to prayer had only been preparatory and the *iḳāma* was the final summons, the public call (*adhān*) and the *iḳāma* now formed two distinct phases of the call to prayer. Tradition tells us that ʿUthmān introduced a third adhān, a call in al-Zawrāʾ, which was made before the call from the minaret: this call however was transferred by Hishām b. ʿAbd al-Malik to the minaret (Bukhārī, *Djumʿa*, bāb 22, 25; *Sīra Ḥalabīya*, ii.

110; Ibn al-Ḥādjdj, *Madkhal*, ii. 45). This may be evidence of the gradual cessation of the custom of summoning the community by going through the streets. Ibn Baṭṭūṭa tells us that the muʾadhdhin in Khwārizm still fetched the people from their houses and those who did not come were whipped (iii. 4 *sq.*), which recalls Wahhābī measures. When exactly the Sunnī, and in distinction to it the Shīʿī formula, finally developed can hardly be ascertained [see ADHĀN]. The call *ḥaiya ʿala 'l-falāḥ* is known from the time of ʿAbd al-Malik (65—86/685—705), (al-Akhṭal, ed. Ṣalḥānī, p. 154; see Horovitz, in *Isl.*, xvi., 1927, p. 254; on *takbīr* see *ibid.*; on *adhān* formulae see further *Sīra Ḥalabīya*, ii. 105 *sq.*). At first the call was only made at the chief mosque, as was the case in Madīna and Miṣr (Maḳrīzī, iv. 43 *infra*), but very quickly other mosques also were given muʾadhdhins.

The summoning of the imām, at first associated with the ruler's mosque, was observed not only in Madīna but was also usual under the Umaiyads. The formula was: *al-salām ʿalaika aiyuha 'l-amīr wa-raḥmatu 'llāh wa-barakātuhu, ḥaiya ʿala 'l-ṣalāt, ḥaiya ʿala 'l-falāḥ al-ṣalāt, yarḥamuka 'llāh* (Maḳrīzī, iv. 45; *Sīra Ḥalabīya*, ii. 105). After the alteration in the adhān and the greater distance of the ruler from the mosque, to summon him was no longer the natural conclusion to the assembling of the community, and it was given up.

The *iḳāma* always remained the real prelude to the service and is therefore regarded as the original adhān (Bukhārī, *Djumʿa*, bāb 24 *sq.*). In the earliest period, as it was fixed by the arrival of the ruler, it might happen that a considerable interval elapsed between the summoning of the people and the *iḳāma* (cf. Ṭabarī, ii. 260, 297 *sq.*). The times were later more accurately defined; one should be able to perform 1—3 ṣalāts between the two calls (Bukhārī, *Adhān*, bāb 14, 16). Some are said to have introduced the practice of the muʾadhdhin calling *ḥaiya ʿala 'l-ṣalāt* at the door of the mosque between the two calls (*Sīra Ḥalabīya*, ii. 105). From the nature of the case the *iḳāma* was always called in the mosque; at the Friday service, it was done when the imām mounted the minbar (Bukhārī, *Djumʿa*, bāb 22, 25; *Sīra Ḥalabīya*, ii. 110; Makrīzī, iv. 43) while the muʾadhdhin stood in front of him. A similarity to the responses in the Christian service is found in the fact that the call of the muʾadhdhin, which contains a confession of faith, is to be repeated or at least answered by every one who hears it (Bukhārī, *Djumʿa*, bāb 23). It is possible that we should recognise in this as well as in the development of the formulae the influence of Christians converted to Islām (cf. Becker, *Islamstudien*, i. 472 *sqq.* and Mittwoch, in *Abh. Gr. A. W.*, 1913, phil.-hist. Kl. 2).

The muʾadhdhin thus obtained a new importance. His work was not only to summon the people to divine service, but was in itself a kind of religious service. His sphere of activity was further developed. In Egypt we are told that Maslama b. Mukhallad (47—62/667—82) introduced the *tasbīḥ*. This consisted in praises of God which were uttered by the muʾadhdhins all through the night until *fadjr*. This is explained as a polemical imitation of the Christians, for the governor was disturbed by the use of the *nawāḳīs* at night and forbade it during the adhān (Maḳrīzī, iv. 48). In the time of Aḥmad b. Ṭūlūn and Khumārawaih, the muʾadhdhins recited religious texts throughout the night in a special room. Ṣalāḥ al-Dīn ordered them to recite an *ʿaḳīda* in the night adhan and after 700/1301 *dhikr* was performed on Friday morning on the minarets (*ibid.*, p. 48 *sq.*; *Sīra Ḥalabīya*, ii. 111). In Mecca also the muʾadhdhins performed dhikr throughout the night of the first Shawwāl on the roof of the ḳubba of the Zemzem well (Ibn Djubair, p. 155, 156; cf. for Damascus: Maḳrīzī, iv. 49). Similar litanies are kept up in modern times as well as a special call about an hour before dawn (*ebed, tarḥīm*: see Lane, *Manners and Customs* [Everyman's Library], p. 75 *sq.*; cf. p. 86; Snouck Hurgronje, *Mekka*, ii. 84 *sqq.*).

The original call of the muʾadhdhin thus developed into a melodious chant like the recitation of the Ḳurʾān. Al-Maḳdisī tells us that in the fourth century in Egypt during the last third of the night, the adhān was recited like a dirge (*BGA*, iii. 205). The solemn effect was increased by the large number of voices. In large mosques, like that of Mecca, the chief muʾadhdhin called first from one minaret, then the others came in turn (*Chron. Mekka*, iii. 424 *sq.*; Ibn Djubair, p. 145 *sqq.*; cf. *BGA*, vii. 111, 1 *sqq.*, et *supra*). But in the mosque itself the *iḳāma* was pronounced by the muʾadhdhins in chorus on the dakka (see D. 2 e) erected for this purpose. In the third and fourth centuries we hear of these melodious recitations (*taṭrīb*) of the muʾadhdhins on a raised *podium* in widely separated parts of the Muslim world.

The new demands made on the muʾadhdhins necessitated an increase in their number, especially in the large mosques. The Prophet in Madīna had two muʾadhdhins, Bilāl b. Ribāḥ, Abū Bakr's *mawlā* and Ibn Umm Maktūm, who officiated alternately. It is therefore regarded as commendable to have two muʾadhdhins at a mosque (Muslim, *Ṣalāt*, tr. 4; cf. Subkī, *Muʿīd*, p. 165).

The office of muʾadhdhin was sometimes hereditary. The descendants of Bilāl were for example muʾadhdhins in al-Rawḍa of the Madīna Mosque (Ibn Djubair, p. 194); and we find parallel conditions in other mosques; it is however possible that this was really the result of a system of guilds of muʾadhdhins. ʿUthmān is said to have been the first to give payment to the muʾadhdhins (Maḳrīzī, iv. 44). and Aḥmad b. Ṭūlūn gave them large sums (*ibid.*, p. 48). They regularly received their share in the endowments, often by special provisions in the documents establishing the foundations.

The muʾadhdhins were organised under chiefs (*ruʾasāʾ*; Maḳrīzī, iv. 14). In Mecca the *raʾīs al-muʾadhdhinīn* was identical with the *muʾadhdhin al-zamzamī* who had charge of the singing in the upper story of the Zemzem building (*Chron. Mekka*, iii. 424 *sq.*; Ibn Djubair, p. 145; cf. Snouck Hurgronje, *Mekka*, ii. 322). The raʾīs was next to the Imām but subordinate to him.

Closely associated with the muʾadhdhin is the *muwaḳḳit*, the astronomer, whose task it was to ascertain the ḳibla and the times of prayer (Subkī, *Muʿīd*, p. 165 *sq.*); sometimes the chief muʾadhdhin did this (Snouck Hurgronje, *Mekka*, ii. 322).

In Java the *muʾadhdhin* is generally called *modin*; in many parts of Indonesia also *bilal.*

5. Servants

According to Abū Huraira, the Mosque of the Prophet was swept by a negro (Bukhārī, *Ṣalāt*, bāb 72, cf. 74). The larger mosques gradually acquired a large staff of servants (*khuddām*), notably *bawwāb*, *farrāsh*, and water-carriers (cf. e.g. v. Berchem, *CIA*, i., No. 252). In Mecca there have always been special appointments, such as supervisor of the Zemzem and guardian of the Kaʿba (*sādin*, pl. *sadana* also used of the officials of the mosque: Maḳrīzī, iv. 76; cf. Ibn Djubair, p. 278). In Ibn Baṭṭūṭa's time the servants (*khuddām*) of the Mosque of the Prophet were eunuchs, particularly Abyssinian; their chief (*shaikh al-khuddām*) was like a great emīr and paid by the Egyptian-Syrian government (i. 278, 348). In the Mosque of Jerusalem about 300/912—3, there were no less than 140 servants (*khādim*: *BGA*., v. 100); others give the figure 230 (Le Strange, *Palestine*, p. 163) and according to Mudjīr al-Dīn, ʿAbd al-Malik appointed a guard of three hundred black slaves here, while the actual menial work was done by certain Jewish and Christian families (Sauvaire, *Hist. Jér. et Hébr.*, p. 56 *sq.*).

In other mosques superintendents (*ḳaiyim*, pl. *ḳawama*) are mentioned, a vague title which covered a multitude of duties: thus the Madrasa al-Madjdīya had a ḳaiyim who looked after the cleaning, the staff, the lighting and water-supply (Maḳrīzī, iv. 251), the Azhar Mosque had one for the mīḍaʾa, who was paid twelve dīnārs (*ibid.*, p. 51) and also 4 ḳawama, who were paid like muʾadhdhins (two dīnārs a month) and are mentioned between them and the imāms, probably supervisors of the staff (*ibid.*, p. 51). In other cases a *ḳaiyim al-djāmiʿ*, sometimes a ḳāḍī, is mentioned, who is apparently the same as the imām, the khaṭīb or some similar individual of standing (*ibid.*, p. 75, 121, cf. 122; cf. Ibn Djubair, p. 51).

AL-**MASDJID** AL-**AḲṢĀ**, the mosque built on the Temple area in Jerusalem. The name means "the remotest sanctuary" and is first found in the Ḳurʾān, Sūra xvii. 1: "Praise Him who made his servant journey in the night from the holy place to the remotest sanctuary, which we have surrounded with blessings to show him of our signs".

As is explained in the article MIʿRĀDJ, the older exegesis refers this verse to the journey to heaven and sees in the name al-Masdjid al-Aḳṣā a reference to some heavenly place (cf. *Sidrat al-muntahā*, Sūra liii. 14).

This explanation had however in time to give way to another, according to which the expression is a name of Jerusalem. This explanation is connected with Muḥammad's "journey in the night" (*isrāʾ*). The combination of the *isrāʾ* and *miʿrādj* thus gives the story of the Prophet's journey by night to the Masdjid al-Aḳṣā (Jerusalem) and his journey following it from Jerusalem to the heavens.

The question arises how Jerusalem gained this distinction among the exegists of the Ḳurʾān. According to Schrieke [cf. MIʿRĀDJ] it is a result of the Umaiyad tendency to glorify Jerusalem at the expense of the holy land of Islām. Horovitz has challenged this explanation (in *Isl.*; cf. the *Bibl.*). In any case, Jerusalem was from very early times regarded in Islām as a sacred place, the original Ḳibla, which, although abandoned in favour of Mecca, still retained its sanctity, as may be seen, for example, from the fact that ʿUmar had a Masdjid built on the site of the Temple [see AL-ḲUDS].

The name al-Masdjid al-Aḳṣā is now particularly attached to the mosque in the south of the Temple area, which according to some was originally a church built by Justinian [cf. AL-ḲUDS]. According to late Arab writers the mosque was built by the caliph ʿAbd al-Malik (65—86/685—705), a statement which might simply mean that Justinian's church was rebuilt. On this compare AL-ḲUDS where the further history of the mosque is given.

For a picture of the site and the mosque see de Vogüé, *Le temple de Jérusalem*, Paris 1864; plan and description of the interior in *Travels* of Ali Bey, London 1816, ii. 214 *sqq.*; Baedeker, *Palästina und Syrien* ⁷, p. 54 *sqq.*

Bibliography: *Bibl.* to the art. MIʿRĀDJ and AL-ḲUDS; *BGA*, iii. 168—171; Mudjīr al-Dīn, *al-Ins al-djalīl*, Cairo 1283, i. 201—203, 238 *sqq.*, 248 *sqq.*, 365 *sqq.*; R. Hartmann, *Geschichte der Aḳṣāmoschee*, in *ZDPV*, xxxii. 185 *sqq.*; Caetani, *Annali*, A.H. 21, § 87 *sq.*; a picture, *ibid.*, vol. iv., p. 504; J. Horovitz, *Koranische Untersuchungen*, Berlin and Leipzig 1926, p. 140; do., in *Isl.*, ix. 161 *sqq.*; A. J. Wensinck, *Tree and Bird as Cosmological Symbols*, in *Verh. Ak. Amst.*, 1921, p. 31; F. Buhl, *Das Leben Muhammeds*, Leipzig 1930, p. 190, note 159.

AL-**MASDJID** AL-**ḤARĀM**, the name of the Mosque of Mecca. The name is already found in the pre-Muḥammadan period (Horovitz, *Koranische Studien*, p. 140 *sq.*) in Ḳais b. al-Khaṭīm, ed. Kowalski, v. 14: "By Allāh, the Lord of the Holy Masdjid and of that which is covered with Yemen stuffs, which are embroidered with hempen thread"(?). It would be very improbable if a Madīna poet by these references meant anything other than the Meccan sanctuary. The expression is also fairly frequent in the Ḳurʾān after the second Meccan period (Horovitz, *op. cit.*) and in various connections: it is a grave sin on the part of the polytheists that they prohibit access to the Masdjid Ḥarām to the "people" (Sūra ii. 217; cf. v. 2; viii. 34; xxii. 25; xlviii. 25); the Masdjid Ḥarām is the pole of the new ḳibla (Sūra ii. 134, 149); contracts are sealed at it (Sūra ix. 7).

In these passages *masdjid ḥarām* does not as in later times mean a building but simply Mecca as a holy place, just as in Sūra xvii. 1 al-Masdjid al-Aḳṣā [q.v.] "the remotest sanctuary" does not mean a particular building.

According to tradition, a ṣalāt performed in the Masdjid al-Ḥarām is particularly meritorious (Bukhārī, *al-Ṣalāt fi masdjid Makka*, bāb 1). This masdjid is the oldest, being forty years older than that of Jerusalem (Bukhārī, *Anbiyāʾ*, bāb 10, 40).

This Meccan sanctuary included the Kaʿba [q.v.], the Zamzam [q.v.] and the Maḳām Ibrāhīm [see KAʿBA], all three on a small open space. In the year 8, Muḥammad made this place a mosque for worship. Soon however it became too small and under ʿUmar and ʿUthmān adjoining houses were taken down and a wall built. Under ʿAbd Allāh Ibn al-Zubair, the Umaiyad and ʿAbbāsid caliphs, successive enlargements and embellishments were made. Ibn al-Zubair put a simple roof above the wall. Al-Mahdī had colonnades built around, which were covered by a roof of teak. The number of minarets in time rose to seven. Little columns were put up around the Kaʿba for lighting purposes. The mosque was also given a feature which we only find paralleled in a few isolated instances: this was the putting up of small wooden buildings, or rather shelters for use during the ṣalāt by the imām, one for each of the four orthodox rites. The fact that one of these maḳāms might be more or less elaborate than another occasionally gave rise to jealousies between the Ḥanafīs and the Shāfiʿīs. Ultimately the ground under the colonnades, originally covered with gravel, was paved with marble slabs, also in the maṭāf around the Kaʿba as well as on the different paths approaching the maṭāf.

The mosque was given its final form in the years 1572—1577, in the reign of the Sulṭān Selīm II, who, in addition to making a number of minor improvements in the building, had the flat roof replaced by a number of small whitewashed cone-shaped domes.

A person entering the mosque from the masʿā or the eastern quarters of the town, has to descend a few steps. The site of the mosque, as far as possible, was always left unaltered, while the level of the ground around — as usual in oriental towns and especially in Mecca on account of the sēl — gradually rose automatically in course of centuries (cf. Snouck Hurgronje, *Mekka*, i. 18—20).

The dimensions of the Ḥaram (interior) are given as follows (al-Batanūnī, *Riḥla*, p. 96): N. W. side 545, S. E. side 553 feet, N. E. side 360, S.W. side 364 feet; the corners are not right angles, so that the whole roughly represents a parallelogram.

Entering the maṭāf from the eastern side, one enters first the Bāb Banī S͟hēba, which marks an old boundary of the masd͟jid. Entering through the door, the Maḳām Ibrāhīm is on the right, which is also the Maḳām al-S͟hāfiʿī, and to the right of it is the minbar. On the left is the Zamzam building. As late as the beginning of the xixth century, there stood in front of the latter, in the direction of the northeast of the mosque, two domed buildings (*al-ḳubbatain*) which were used as store-houses (*Chron. d. Stadt Mekka*, ii. 337 *sq.*). These ḳubbas were cleared away (cf. already Burckhardt, i. 265); they are not given in recent plans.

Around the Kaʿba are the maḳāms for the imāms of the mad͟hhabs, between the Kaʿba and the south-east of the mosque, the maḳām (or muṣallā) al-Ḥanbalī, to the south-west the maḳām al-Mālikī, to the north-west the maḳām al-Ḥanafī. The latter has two stories; the upper one was used by the muʾad͟hd͟hin and the muballig͟h, the lower by the imām and his assistants. Since Wahhābī rule has been established, the Ḥanbalī imām has been given the place of honour; it is also reported that the *ṣalāt* is conducted by turns by the imāms of the four rites (*Or. Mod.*, vii. 25). The maḳām al-Ḥanafī stands on the site of the old Meccan council-chamber (*dār al-nadwa*) which in the course of centuries was several times rebuilt and used for different purposes. The maṭāf is marked by a row of thin brass columns connected by a wire. The lamps for lighting are fixed to this wire and in the collonnades. Recently the mosque has been provided with an installation for electric light (*OM*, xvi. 34; xviii. 39).

The mosque has for centuries been the centre of the intellectual life of the metropolis of Islām. This fact has resulted in the building of madrasas and riwāḳs for students in or near the mosque, for example the madrasa of Ḳāʾit Bey on the left as one enters through the Bāb al-Salām. Many of these waḳfs have however in course of time become devoted to other purposes (Burckhardt, i. 282; Snouck Hurgronje, *Mekka*, i. 17). For the staff of the mosque cf. SHAIBA (BANŪ); Burckhardt, i. 287—291.

Bibliography: F. Wüstenfeld, *Die Chroniken der Stadt Mekka*, ii. 10 *sq.*, 13—16, 337 *sqq.*; i. 301—333, 339—345; iii. 73 *sqq.*; iv. 121, 139, 159, 159, 165, 190, 203, 205, 227 *sq.*, 268 *sq.*, 313 *sq.*; Ibn D͟jubair, *Riḥla*, in *GMS*, v. 81 *sqq.*; Ibn Baṭṭūṭa, ed. and transl. Defrémery and Sanguinetti, i. 305 *sqq.*; Yāḳūt, *Muʿd͟jam*, ed. Wüstenfeld, iv. 525 *sq.*; *BGA*, i. 15 *sq.*; v. 18—21; index to vol. vii. and viii., s.v.,; Ibn ʿAbd Rabbihi as translated by Muḥ. S͟hafīʿ in *Browne Memorial Volume*, p. 423 *sqq.*; Muḥammad Labīb al-Batanūnī, *al-Riḥla al-ḥid͟jāzīya*, Cairo 1329, p. 94 *sqq.*; *Travels of Ali Bey*, London 1816, ii. 74—93 and pl. liii., liv.; J. L. Burckhardt, *Travels in Arabia*, London 1829, p. 243—295; A. F. Burton, *Personal Narrative of a Pilgrimage to Mecca and Medina*, Leipzig 1873, iii. 1—37; C. Snouck Hurgronje, *Mekka*, Hague 1888—1889, i., chap. i.; ii. 230 *sqq.*; *Bilder-atlas*, No. i., ii., iii.; do., *Bilder aus Mekka*, Leyden 1889, No. 1 and 3; P. F. Keane, *Six months in Mecca*, London 1881, p. 24 *sqq.* Eldon Rutter, *The Holy Cities of Arabia*, London 1928.

MAS͟HHAD. [See MASD͟JID, B. 4].

MAS͟HHAD, capital of the Persian province of K͟hurāsān, the greatest place of pilgrimage for the S͟hīʿīs in Persia. It lies 3,000 feet above sea level in 59° 35′ E. Long (Greenw.) and 16° 17′ N. Lat. in the valley from 10 to 25 milles broad of the Kes͟hef-Rūd, which runs from N. W. to S. E. This river, also called Āb-i Mas͟hhad (the "river of Mas͟hhad"), rises about 12 miles N. W. of the ruins of Ṭūs in the little lake of Čes͟hme-i Gīlās (cf. Fraser, *op. cit.*, p. 350; Khanikoff, *op. cit.*, p. 110; Yate, *op. cit.*, p. 315) and joins the Herī (Harī)-Rūd (cf. Le Strange, *op. cit.*, p. 407 *sq.*) about 100 miles S. E. of Mas͟hhad on the Russo-Persian frontier. Mas͟hhad lies about 4 miles south of the bank of the Kes͟hef-Rūd. The hills which run along the valley rise to 8,000 or 9,000 feet at Mas͟hhad.

In consequence of its high situation and proximity to the mountains, the climate of Mas͟hhad is in the winter rather severe, in the summer, however, often tropically hot; it is regarded as healthy.

Mas͟hhad may in a way be regarded as the successor of the older pre-Muḥammadan Ṭūs, and it has not infrequently been erroneously confounded with it.

When Hārūn al-Ras͟hīd was preparing to take the field in K͟hurāsān, he was stricken mortally ill in a country house at Sanābād͟h where he had stopped, and died in a few days (193/809). The caliph, we are told (Ṭabarī, iii. 737), realising he was about to die, had his grave dug in the garden of this country mansion and consecrated by Ḳurʾān-readers.

About 10 years after the death of Hārūn, the caliph al-Maʾmūn on his way from Merw spent a few days in this palace. Along with him was his son-in-law ʿAlī al-Riḍā b. Mūsā, the caliph designate, the eighth imām of the Twelvers. The latter died suddenly here in 203/818; the actual day is uncertain (cf. Strothmann, *Die Zwölfer-S͟hīʿa*, Leipzig 1926, p. 171).

It was not the tomb of the caliph but that of a highly venerated imām which made Sanābād͟h (Nūḳān) celebrated throughout the S͟hīʿa world, and the great town which grew up in course of time out of the little village actually came to be called *al-Mas͟hhad* (Mes͟hhed) which means "sepulchral chapel" (primarily of a martyr belonging to the family of the Prophet). Ibn Ḥawḳal (p. 313) calls our sanctuary simply Mas͟hhad, Yāḳūt (iii. 153) more accurately al-Mas͟hhad al-Riḍāwī = the tomb-chapel of al-Riḍā; we also find the Persian name *Mas͟hhad-i muḳaddas* = "the sanctified chapel" (e.g. in Ḥamd Allāh al-Mustawfī, p. 157). As a place-name Mas͟hhad first appears in al-Maḳdisī (p. 352), i.e. in the last third of the ivth/tenth century. About the middle of the viiith/xivth century the traveller Ibn Baṭṭūṭa (iii. 77) uses the expression "town of Mas͟hhad al-Riḍā". Towards the end of the middle ages the name Nūḳān, which is still found on coins in the first half of the viiith/xivth century under the Īlk͟hāns (cf. Codrington, *A Manual of Musalman Numismatics*, London 1904, p. 189), seems to have been gradually ousted by al-

The mosque in the Sanctuary of the Imām Riḍā at Mas_h_had

Art. Mas_h_had

Mas͟hhad or Mas͟hhad. At the present day Mas͟hhad is often more precisely known as Mas͟hhad-i Riḍā, Mas͟hhad-i Muḳaddas, Mas͟hhad-i Ṭūs (so already in Ibn Baṭṭūṭa, iii. 66). Not infrequently in literature, especially in poetry, we find only Ṭūs mentioned, i.e. New Ṭūs in contrast to Old Ṭūs or the proper town of this name; cf. e.g. Muḥammad Mahdī al-ʿAlawī, *Taʾrīk͟h Ṭūs aw al-Mas͟hhad al-Riḍāwī*, Bag͟hdād 1927, p. 3.

The history of Mas͟hhad is very fully dealt with in the work of Muḥammad Ḥasan K͟hān Ṣanīʿ al-Dawla entitled *Maṭlaʿ al-s͟hams* (3 vols., Ṭeherān 1301—1303). The second volume is exclusively devoted to the history and topography of Mas͟hhad; for the period from 428/1036 to 1302/1885 he gives valuable historical material. On this work cf. Yate, *op. cit.*, p. 313—314 and E. G. Browne, *A History of Pers. Lit.*, Cambridge 1924, iv., p. 455—456.

The importance of Sanābād͟h-Mas͟hhad continually increased with the growing fame of its sanctuary and the decline of Ṭūs, which received its death blow in 791/1389 from Mīrāns͟hāh, a son of Tīmūr. When the Mongol noble who governed the place rebelled and attempted to make himself independent, Mīrāns͟hāh was sent against him by his father. Ṭūs was stormed after a siege of several months, sacked and left a heap of ruins; 10,000 inhabitants were massacred. Those who escaped the holocaust settled in the shelter of the ʿAlid sanctuary. Ṭūs was henceforth abandoned and Mas͟hhad took its place as the capital of the district.

The sacred area divides the principal street into two parts: the Bālā (= Upper) K͟hiyābān in the N. W. and the Pāʾīn (= Lower) K͟hiyābān in the S. E., of which the former is about 3 times as long as the latter.The sacred area covered by the sanctuary of the Imām al-Riḍā is usually called Bast. The name Ḥaram-i S͟harīf or Ḥaram-i Muḳaddas or Ḥaram-i al-Riḍāwī (al-Riḍā's Ḥaram) is often also applied to it; frequently it is called simply "Imām", as in Persia as in the ʿIrāḳ this title is applied also to a building or piece of ground sacred to an Imām. The Bast, a rectangle 900 feet × 700 feet in area, is in the lower half of the K͟hiyābān. With its courts, mosques, sanctuaries, madrasas, caravanserais, bazaars, dwellinghouses etc. it forms a town by itself; a wall around it cuts it off completely from the rest of Mas͟hhad. The main entrances from the K͟hiyābān are two great doors on north and south, but they are barred by chains so that no vehicle or riding-beast can enter; for the ground of the Bast is holy and may only be trodden on foot. Animals which get in by accident become the property of the administration of the Imām. The Bast also has the right of asylum (whence the name *bast*). Debtors who take refuge in it are safe from their creditors; criminals can only be handed over by order of the Mutawallī-Bās͟hī, which is now usually done after three days. In the whole of the sacred area strict discipline is maintained by its own police; there is a special prison for thieves (see the plan in Yate, p. 332, No. 75).

Entrance to the Bast is strictly forbidden to all non-Muslims. In earlier times the rule does not seem to have been so strict, for Clavijo in 1404 was able to visit the sepulchral chapel of the Imām al-Riḍā. In the xixth century Fraser (1822, 1833), Conolly (1830), Burnes (1832), Ferrier (1845), Eastwick (1862), Vámbéry (1863), Colonel Dolmage (in the sixties) and Massy (1893) visited the sacred area. Only Fraser, Conolly, Dolmage and Massy actually entered the sepulchral chapel itself. Vámbéry and Massy were dressed as Muslims while the others retained their European dress. Except Dolmage, all these travellers have given more or less full descriptions of the sacred area. The full and accurate description given by Sykes in *JRAS*, 1910, p. 1130—1148 and in the *Glory of the Shia World* is based on information supplied by the attaché to the British Consulate, K͟hān Bahādur Aḥmad Dīn-K͟hān.

The most detailed plan of the Bast is in the already mentioned *Maṭlaʿ al-s͟hams* of Ṣanīʿ al-Dawla (1885), also given in Yate, *op. cit.*, p. 332. A plan on a somewhat smaller scale was prepared by the Persian architect Muʿāwin-i Ṣanāʾiʿ and was published by Sykes in *JRAS*, 1910, p. 1128 and in *Glory of the Shia World*, p. 100. The latter differs in details not inconsiderably from Ṣanīʿ al-Dawla's plan; which is right we have not the means of telling.

In spite of the number of times which the ʿAlid sanctuary has been plundered in course of time, it still has countless treasures within its buildings and puts in the shade, as regards this wealth and the extent of its buildings and courts, all the other great Muḥammadan sanctuaries, except perhaps Mecca, but including the much admired Nad͟jaf and Kerbelāʾ.

A detailed and accurate description of the Ḥaram and an account of its architectural history based on its present state cannot be given because the strict prohibition of admission to members of other faiths has prevented non-Muslim scholars from examining thoroughly and reproducing the buildings. Relying on descriptions of the sacred area prepared by Europeans and Orientals and on the valuable data contained in inscriptions (the latter were first noted by Khanikoff, p. 103—104; the more important were published by Sykes assisted by K͟hān Bahādur Aḥmad Dīn, in *JRAS*, 1910, p. 1131 *sq.*), we can assume with considerable probability that, except the tomb proper, which in its present form (excluding the later dome) according to the inscription (512/1118), dates from the beginning of the vith/xiith century, only insignificant remains of the earlier mediaeval period have survived. The Ḥaram in its present form is in the main a creation of the last 500 years.

The dome of the tomb with its various annexes rises in the centre of the sacred area and is bounded on the north and east by two great rectangular courts, the Ṣaḥn-i Kuhna and the Ṣaḥn-i Naw, while in the south it is adjoined by the extensive buildings of the D͟jawhar S͟hād͟h mosque.

The most popular entrance to the Bast and the one preferred by pilgrims is the gateway in the Bālā-K͟hiyābān barred by a chain. The road runs for 250 yards through this street filled with shops and ends at a great gateway through which the Ṣaḥn-i Kuhna, the "old court", is entered. Its northern part dates from the time of S͟hāh ʿAbbās I, while the southern is as old as the second half of the ixth/xvth century (reign of Sulṭān Ḥusain Bāiḳarā) but was completely restored by Nādir S͟hāh. Four great towers with niche-like halls (hence called *aiwān*) admit to the court. The simplest are the west and east towers built by ʿAbbās I; the former has the clock tower, while the platform of the latter is used as *naḳḳāra-k͟hāne*, i.e. "music-house", where, according to an old Persian custom, found in other royal cities, sunrise and sunset are greeted with music. From the east gate one reaches the eastern exit of the Bast through the Bazar of the Pāʾīn-K͟hiyābān. Much more impressive from the architectural point of view are the northern gateway built by ʿAbbās II and especially the southern gateway of the court, "Nādir's Golden Gate", Nādir Shāh's most splendid achievement and the most imposing building of the whole Ḥaram. At each of the two great gates stands a minaret 100 feet high, the upper part of which is covered with gold; the builder of the northern gate was Ṭahmāsp I and of the southern Nādir Shāh. Nādir built in the centre the famous octagon of "Nādir's Well" covered by a gilt baldachin (*Saḳḳā-Khāne-i Nādiri* = "Nādir's water carrier-house"); it was hewn out of a huge block of white marble which the Shāh had brought at great expense from Herāt. The walls of the court are pierced by two rows of alcoves, the lower of which is occupied by artisans, schools and dwellings of the servants of the mosque, while the higher officials of the Imām occupy the upper storey. The whole courtyard which has a length of about 100 yards and a breadth of 70, is paved with dark Mashhad stones which are also to some extent tombstones. For pictures of the Ṣaḥn-i Kuhna with clock tower and Nādir's Well see Yate, p. 340, 346; Sykes, *Glory of the Shia World*, p. 241; picture of Nādir's Golden Gate in Yate, p. 328 and Sykes, *op. cit.*, p. 245.

Nādir's golden gateway leads southwards into the area of the holy tomb, the sepulchral chamber with the halls and rooms surrounding it. Strictly speaking, it is only this nucleus of the whole sacred area that should be called *Ḥaram* or *Ḥaram-i muḳaddas* or *Ḥaram-i mubārak*, terms often extended to the whole Bast. The names *al-Rawḍa al-muṭahhara* and *Āsitāne* = the (holy) threshold, are also used. After passing through the Golden Gate one enters the *Dār al-siyāda*, built by Djawhar Shādh, the finest hall in the sacred quarter. Hung on a wall here is a round dish said to be that on which the poisoned grapes were offered to ʿAlī al-Riḍā. The pilgrim can see into the sepulchral chamber through a silver grille from the Dār al-Siyāda. Turning to the south-east one enters a smaller, more simply decorated chamber, the *Dār al-ḥuffāẓ*.

Adjoining the Dār al-Ḥuffāẓ in the north is the dome of the Mausoleum of the Imām. The interior of the sepulchral chamber (see the picture in Sykes, *op. cit.*, p. 251), an almost square area, 30 × 27 feet, is, as there are no proper windows, lit by the dim light from golden lamps and chandeliers and furnished with the greatest splendour. The tomb itself is in the N. E. corner and surrounded by three beautiful grilles, one of which, dated 1747, is said to come from the mausoleum of Nādir Shāh now destroyed. ʿAbbās I gave the top of the tomb with its gold covering. In a projection at the foot of the tomb, Fatḥ ʿAlī Shāh placed a false door of gold inlaid with jewels (picture in Sykes, *op. cit.*, p. 255). In niches in the wall behind glass are kept very valuable votive offerings (jewelled arms, etc., mainly gifts of the ruling house). On the wall are the two inscriptions already mentioned of 512/1118 and 612/1215 of which the first is the earliest known example of the so-called round hand (*thulth*) in Arabic epigraphy. These enable us to place the building of the present chamber in the beginning of the vith/xiith century, while the dome 65 feet high covered with sheets of gilt copper was built only in 1607 by ʿAbbās I and renovated in 1675 by Sulaimān I, according to inscriptions on its outside. As the thread of tradition regarding the site of the Imām's grave can hardly have been broken, it may be assumed practically with certainty that the present dome is built on the true site. There is no longer any trace of Hārūn's grave; it probably was in the centre of the mausoleum, whence the tomb of the ʿAlid who died later was put in a corner of the same place.

Of the other chambers and isolated buildings belonging to the system of the Ḥaram proper, we shall only mention here the *gumbad* (domed tomb) of Allāh Wardī Khān, which lies to the N. E. and takes its name from its builder, a famous general of ʿAbbās I.

Leaving the sacred chamber by the eastern door one reaches, after traversing two adjoining rooms, the "Golden Gate" of Nāṣir al-Dīn, which leads into the New Court (*Ṣaḥn-i naw*, a modest imitation of the Ṣaḥn-i Kuhna; its northside is bounded by the Pāʾīn Khiyābān); Fatḥ ʿAlī Shāh began this court in 1818. His two successors continued the building, which was completed in 1855.

If one turns southwards from the Dār al-Siyāda already mentioned, one soon enters the area of the charming mosque endowed by Sulṭāna Djawhar Shādh and bearing her name. Like the Ṣaḥn-i Kuhna this older court, an oblong running N. to S. about 100 yards long and 90 broad, is broken in the middle of each of its four sides by an arched hall (*aiwān*), while the unbroken parts of the walls have rows of alcoves fitted up as dwellings. The largest and finest of these four aiwāns of the mosque the Aiwān-i Maḳṣūra in the south, is used for prayers; in it is a wooden pulpit in which the Mahdī will one day show himself to the faithful. The entrance hall is covered by a blue dome which surpasses that on the tomb of the Imām in height and width, and is flanked by two high minarets covered with blue glass tiles. The centre of the court is occupied by the *Masdjid-i pīr-i zan* = "Mosque of the Old Woman", (about this name cf. the legend in Massy, *op. cit.*, p. 1001 and Sykes, *The Glory ....*, p. 261) a square unroofed area surrounded by a wooden balustrade around which runs water in a deep stone channel.

The Djawhar Shādh mosque is the noblest and finest building in the sacred area.

Of the various small sanctuaries which the pilgrims visit in the Ḥaram, only two need be mentioned here, the Ziyārat-i Ḳadam-i Mubārak or Sharīf = "the place of pilgrimage of the blessed or excellent foot" also called *Djā-i sang-i čahār-pā* = "place of the foot-stone" (see the plan in Yate, p. 332, No. 16), a circular space covered by a dome (east of the north aiwān of the Djawhar Shādh mosque), in which reverence is paid to a dark grey oval-shaped stone said to contain an impression of ʿAlī al-Riḍā's foot. The second noteworthy feature of the Bast is a tall stone-pillar, out of which a water basin has been roughly hewn. It is said to have fallen into the Bast as a shapeless block from heaven.

Inside of the sacred area are the richest and busiest bazars of the town, the most richly endowed madrasas, the most profitable caravanserais and the most popular baths. These are all, like the dwelling houses there, the absolute property of the Imām, the ʿAlid buried here, i.e. of the ecclesiastical authorities who administer the sanctuary on his behalf. The whole Bast belongs exclusively to them. This dead hand however has still more possessions in land, buildings, canals (*ḳanāt*), in all the provinces of Persia, especially in the immediate and more distant vicinity of Mashhad. To the vast sums which these properties yield in produce and rents, are to be added the considerable payments for funerals and tombs, the gifts of pilgrims etc. There is also considerable expenditure, the payment of a considerable number of higher officials and of a large number of lower officials and servants, the maintenance of many pilgrims, the cost of repairs, lighting, decoration of the sanctuaries etc.

At the head of the administration of the Ḥaram there has been from early times a Mutawallī-Bās͟hī, who must be a layman. In view of the very influential position which this official occupies in his capacity as head of the greatest Persian sanctuary and treasurer of a very considerable estate, it is only natural that an appointment to such a position of trust is regarded as a veiy special honour. As it was not uncommon for disputes about the limits of their respective spheres of autority or other matters to arise between the holder of this office, the representative of ecclesiastical power, and the governor of K͟hurāsān, the clerical element has since the middle of the xix^th^ century been subordinated to the civil power by giving the office of Mutawallī-Bās͟hī to the governor of the time (see Yate, p. 322, 344). This very lucrative double office — the Mutawallī-Bās͟hī gets 10% of the revenues of the Ḥaram — is as a rule only held for a few years by the same individual.

The Mutawallī-Bās͟hī is assisted by a staff of higher officials (*mutawallīs*). He has further at his command the varied hieraichy of the sacred area, among whom the *mud͟jtahids*, who have a thorough knowledge of religious law and are men of great prestige and influence, occupy the first place. Next comes a regular army of lower clerics (*mullās*) who conduct the services, teach in the schools and guide the rites of the pilgrims; not a few of them make a living by supplying official documents sealed with the seal of the Imām (see the picture in Sykes, *Glory of the Shia World*, p. 278), which deal among other matters with the answering of petitions made by the pilgrims at the sacred tomb.

As we know from mediaeval Arabic sources, pilgrimage to the tomb of ʿAlī al-Riḍā began at an early date. We occasionally hear also of royal visits from the vth/xi^th^ century onwards.

As to the number of pilgrims who visit Mas͟hhad annually we have different estimates for the xix^th^ century. While Yate (p. 334) gives the annual number for the last decade of the xix^th^ century at 30,000, earlier travellers, except Marsh (1872 : 20—30,000) give much higher figures e.g. Bellew (1872) : 40—50,000; Ferrier (1845) : 50,000; Khanikoff (1859) and Eastwick (1862) : over 50,000, Curzon (1889) even gives 100,000, but this is certainly too high. The numbers go up considerably when special religious ceremonials are going on e.g. at the anniversary of ʿAlī al-Riḍā's death (cf. the pictures in Diez, *Persien* etc., p. 46) and during the first third of the month of Muḥarram at the *taʿziya* [q.v.] in memory of the tragedy of Kerbelāʾ. We have a full description of the Muḥarram festival of the year 1830 from Conolly and a shorter one of 1894 by Yate; cf. also the illustrations in Yate, p. 146 and the drawing by the painter ʿAlī Riḍā ʿAbbāsī of a Mas͟hhad pilgrim at the time of the Muḥarram festival in Sarre and Mittwoch, *Zeichnungen des Riza Abbasi* (Munich 1914), plate I (thereon p. 23, 49 and *Isl.*, ii. 216 *sq.*).

Every pilgrim who arrives has a right to free maintenance for three (according to Vámbéry: six) days. In the sacred quarter, south of the Bālā K͟hiyābān, there is a special kitchen used exclusively for pilgrims, which supplies 5—600 free meals every day.

On the ceremonies which the pilgrims have to perform at their visit to the tomb of ʿAlī al-Riḍā we have accounts by Massy, *op. cit.*, and the notes supplied by K͟hān Bahādur Aḥmad al-Dīn K͟hān in Sykes, *JRAS*, 1910, p. 144—45 and in the *Glory of the Shia World*, p. 240 *sq.* Special mention may be made of the three circumambulations (*ṭawāf* [q.v.]) of the tomb and the cursing of all enemies of the imām three times, especially the Caliphs Hārūn and Maʾmūn.

Every pilgrim who has performed the pilgrimage to ʿAlī al-Riḍā's grave in the prescribed fashion is entitled to call himself *mas͟hhadī*.

Mas͟hhad occupies first place among all the places of pilgrimage in Persia. Among the great sanctuaries of the Muslim world, Mas͟hhad stands seventh in the view of S͟hīʿa theologians, coming after not only Mecca and Madīna, but also the four specifically S͟hīʿa sanctuaries of the ʿIrāḳ, Nad͟jaf, Karbalāʾ, Sāmarrā and Kāẓimain, in this order (cf. Sykes, *The Glory of the Shia World*, p. xiii). According to a version current in S͟hīʿa circles which Curzon (i. 150) gives, Mas͟hhad is entitled to the sixth place, coming between Kāẓimain as fifth and Sāmarrā which is put seventh.

The longing of every S͟hīʿī to find a last resting place in the shadow of one of the beloved Imāms caused extensive cemeteries to be laid out at an early date at the great centres of pilgrimage. Thousands of corpses are brought every year to Mas͟hhad, mainly of course from Persia, but also from all the S͟hīʿa lands, particularly India, aiso Afg͟hānistān and Turkestān. As the ground of the cemeteries must be used over and over again, the graves change their occupants every few years. Fine solid tombstones are not used, but simply rough blocks of granite or soapstone from the quarries of the neighbourhood. Graves within the sacred quarter itself are naturally most desired. Every available space there is used for the purpose; the pavingstones in the courtyards are often tombstones for the dead below. The fees for graves within the Bast, which vary with the distance from the Mausoleum of ʿAlī al-Riḍā, bring a not inconsiderable revenue to the authorities.

Of the large cemeteries (*maḳbaras*) outside the Bast the most important is the Maḳbara-i Ḳatl Gāh ("place of the killing") lying north of the sacred area. East of it is that of Saiyid Aḥmad in which three children of the seventh Imām, Mūsā al-Kāẓim, are buried (cf. Mahdī al-ʿAlawī, p. 8). In the Pāʾīn K͟hiyābān quarter is the Maḳbara-i Pīr-i Pālāndūz. S.E. of the citadel is the cemeteiy of Gumbad-i Sabz ("Green dome") which takes its name from a half ruined mausoleum there, now inhabited by dervishes.

In the Nūḳān quarter is the Maḳbara-i S͟hāh-zāde Muḥammad. We may also mention that outside the Nūḳān gate on the site of the old town of Nūḳān (see above), are visible the remains of a gigantic cemetery on which according to Sykes (*JRAS*, 1910, p. 1116), there may be found stone sarcophagi with inscriptions carved upon them dating from 760 to 1099 (1359—1688).

Outside of Mas͟hhad, a good half hour's journey to the south, on rocky ground is the cemetery of Mīrzā Ibrāhīm al-Riḍawī (see Mahdī, *op. cit.*, p. 8) and still further from the town, 3 miles north of it, that of K͟hʷād͟ja Rabīʿ (cf. Sykes, *op. cit.*, p. 1124 and Ibn Saʿd, vi. 127 *sq.*). According to the popular view, he was a Sunnī in spite of his relations with ʿAlī and is therefore in a way regarded as the patron of the Sunnīs in K͟hurāsān, of whom those who live in Mas͟hhad are usually buried neai his tomb. Rabīʿs mausoleum is one of the most interesting in the whole of Khurāsān: it is a large octagonal building crowned by a dome but now it is in a half ruined condition.

Mashhad is the centre of Muslim theological and legal studies in Persia. A number of colleges (*madrasas*) there are devoted to teaching these subjects. Lists of them with dates are given by Fraser (p. 456—460) who mentions 14 of the present 16 madrasas, also by Khanikoff (p. 107) who gives 13, and by Mahdī al-ʿAlawī (p. 9—12). The latter observes that there were 20 older colleges, of which he gives 15, and a number of more modern ones. Fraser also gives brief notes on the possessions of the various madrasas and the clerics (*mullās*) attached to them. Yate (p. 329—330) simply mentions six of the best known. From these lists, which supplement one another in welcome fashion, we get the names of 20 colleges. From the dates of foundation we find that the oldest of the madrasas still standing in Mashhad is the Madrasa Dūdar, which was built in 823/1420 by the Tīmūrid Sulṭān Shāh Rukh and restored by Sulaimān I. Under the same ruler was built the Parīzād Madrasa which was completely remodelled by Sulaimān I. From the time of ʿAbbās II date the two almost contemporary colleges Khairāt Khān (1058/1649) and Mīrzā Djaʿfar (1059/1650). The majority of the older colleges, no fewer than nine in number, date from the time of Sulaimān I, who also restored some buildings (1666—1694). As to the Ḳādjārs, one was founded in the reign of Fatḥ ʿAlī Shāh and two in that of Nāṣir al-Dīn, who also restored two that had fallen into ruins.

From the artistic point of view, the finest is the Madrasa of Mīrzā Djaʿfar which was built and richly endowed in 1059/1650 by a Persian of this name who had made a fortune in India. It is generally regarded as the third finest building in Mashhad, next to the Mausoleum of ʿAlī al-Riḍā and the Djawhar Shādh Mosque. In its plan, with vaulted halls and courtyard with niches, and its rich decoration, it follows the style of the courts and mosques of the sacred area above described, typical of the ecclesiastical architecture of Persia. Not only the Madrasa of Mīrzā Djaʿfar but also other richly endowed colleges, like that of Pāʾīn-Pā (both of the time of Sulaimān I), owe their origin to Persians who had made fortunes in India. The most esteemed colleges are in the Bast, namely the three already mentioned as the oldest, Dūdar, Parīzād and Khairāt-Khān, also Bālāsar and ʿAlī Naḳī Mīrzā. Others, like the above mentioned Mīrzā Djaʿfar Madrasa and the Mustashār Madrasa have doors communicating with the Ṣaḥn-i Kuhna of the Ḥaram quarter.

Students also live in the madrasas, their maintenance being provided for by pious endowments. While in Khanikoff's time (1858) there were no outstanding teachers there and the number of students was small, the reputation of the Mashhad colleges went up again in the second half of the xix[th] century so that Sykes (*The Glory* etc., p. 267 *sq.*) in 1910 puts the attendance at 1,200 students, who came from Persia, India and other Shīʿa regions. The student who wishes to take a higher theological training after the nine years' course at Mashhad must go to Mashhad ʿAlī (Nadjaf; q.v.) and attend the lectures of the teachers there, who are the first authorities on Shīʿa theology.

Several of the Mashhad colleges have considerable libraries. The library of the administration of the Ḥaram was founded in the first half of the xv[th] century by Shāh Rukh; these treasures were for the most part lost when Mashhad was sacked by the Özbegs under ʿAbd al-Muʾmin Khān (1589). Since 1926 there has begun to appear a catalogue of the Mashhad manuscripts under the title *Fihrist-i Kutubkhāna-i Mubāraka-i Āsitāna-i Ḳuds-i Riḍawī*, the first three volumes of which appeared in 1305 (solar year = 1345 Hidjra), the fourth volume being published in 1325/1946.

In this connection we may mention the activity of the Mashhad printing presses (newspapers etc.), which began with the last decade of the xix[th] century; see thereon Browne, *The Press and Poetry of Modern Persia* (Cambridge 1914), p. 348 (Index, s.v. Meshed); Browne, *Literary History of Persia*, iv., Cambridge 1928, p. 223, 489; Mahdī al-ʿAlawī, p. 12.

Mashhad is remarkably rich in mosques which are built in the sacred area, at cemeteries and at separate tombs, and are connected with madrasas and other buildings of a religious character.

Here we may also mention the Muṣallā which stands outside the town, $^1/_2$ mile from the Pāʾīn Khiyābān gate on the Herāt road. It is a hall (*aiwān*) about 30 feet high which opens into a gigantic arch about 60 feet high.

As to the population of Mashhad — the permanent residents, excluding the many pilgrims — it was at its highest in the reign of Nādir Shāh, who frequently held his court here and in every way contributed to the prosperity of the town. At that date Mashhad had not less than 60,000 inhabitants. But the half century of turmoil which followed the reign of Nādir Shāh brought about a great decline in the town so that only 3,000 houses were reckoned there in 1796 (cf. Yate, p. 330). In the xix[th] century began a slow but steady rise. Truilhier in 1807 estimated the number of houses at 4,000; Fraser in 1822 at 7,700 with 25—30,000 inhabitants. Conolly (1830) and Burnes (1832) estimate 40,000 inhabitants; Ferrier (1845) and Khanikoff (1858) at 60,000. In 1874 Khurāsān suffered a terrible famine and 24,000 in Mashhad alone died of starvation (see Goldsmid, i. 361). Baker is too high in putting the figure at 80,000 in 1873 and Curzon too low at 45,000 for 1889. Mashhad at the present day is said to have 100,000 inhabitants (see Mahdī al-ʿAlawī, p. 4); it is in any case the third largest town in Persia.

For the housing of the numerous pilgrims and other strangers who come to Mashhad, a considerable number of caravanserais are available. In Fraser's time (1822), there were at least 25—30 such places in use, apart from some that had been abandoned and fallen into ruins (see Fraser, *Narrative*, p. 460). Khanikoff (p. 107—108) gives 16, four of which, intended for pilgrims only, were inside the Bast; of these latter the oldest is the Sulṭān Caravanserai, built by Ṭahmāsp I; others date from Sulaimān I.

Bibliography: In addition to references already given: *BGA* (ed. de Goeje), i. 257; ii. 313; iii. 25, 50, 319, 333; vi. 24; vii. 171, 278; Yāḳūt, *Muʿdjam* (ed. Wüstenfeld), iii. 113, 486, 560 *sq.*; iv. 824; Ḳazwīnī, *Āthār al-bilād* (ed. Wüstenfeld), p. 262, 275; Abu 'l-Fidāʾ, *Taḳwīm al-buldān* (ed. Paris), p. 450, 452; Ḥamd Allāh Mustawfī, *Nuzhat al-ḳulūb*, (= *GMS*, xxiii), p. 150 *sq.*; Ibn Baṭṭūṭa (ed. Paris), ii. 79; ʿAbd al-Karīm (1741), *Bayān-i wāḳiʿa*, or the French transl. of this Persian work entitled *Voyage de l'Inde à la Mekke par Abdoul-Kérym* by Langlès, Paris 1797, p. 69—74; Nāṣir al-Dīn Shāh's *Reise nach Khorāsān* (1866) Pers. text, Teheran 1286/1869, p. 180—225; Ibrāhīm

Beg, *Siyāḥet-nāme* (ed. Istanbul), or in the transl. by W. Schultz, *Zustände des heutigen Persiens, wie sie das Reisetagebuch Ibrahim Beys enthüllt*, Leipzig 1903, p. 40—49; Muḥammad Mahdī al-ʿAlawī, *Taʾrīkh Ṭūs aw al-Mashhad al-Riḍawī*, Baghdād 1346/1927. Cf. also the manuscript diary of a pilgrimate to Meshhed in 1819—1820 by Ḥusain Khān b. Djaʿfar al-Mūsawī in the Berlin State Library, s. Pertsch, *Verzeichniss der persisch. Hdschr. ... zu Berlin*, Berlin 1888, No. 360, p. 378—379. On the *Maṭlaʿ al-shams* of Ṣanīʿ al-Dawla s. above.

As to descriptions of Mashhad by Europeans we owe the first full description to Fraser (1822); Conolly (i. 260) and Burnes (ii. 78) both say it is thoroughly reliable. Valuable notes on the town are given by Conolly, Ferrier, Khanikoff, East wick, MacGregor, Bassett, O'Donovan, Curzon, Massy, E. Diez, and especially by C. E. Yate and Sykes, each of whom spent several years (1893—1897 and 1905—1912 resp.) in Mashhad as British Consul-General for Khurāsān. — Ruy Gonzalez de Clavijo (1404), *Embassy to the Court of Timur*, ed. C. R. Markham (Hakluyt Society, vol. xxvi., London 1859), p. 109—110; Truilhier (1807), in *Bulletin de la Société de Géogr.*, vol ix., Paris 1838, p. 272—282; J. B. Fraser (1822), *Narrative of a Journey into Khorasan in the years 1821—1822*, London 1825, p. 436—548; A. Conolly (1830), *Journey to the North of India*, London 1834, i. 255—289, 296—368; A. Burnes (1832), *Travels into Bokhara*, London 1834, ii. 76—87; J. B. Fraser (1833), *A Winter's Journey from Constantinople to Teheran*, London 1838, i. 213—255; J. P. Ferrier (1845), *Caravan Journeys and Wanderings in Persia* [2], London 1857, p. 111—133; N. de Khanikoff (1858), *Mémoire sur la partie méridionale de l'Asie centrale*, Paris 1861, p. 95—111; N. de Khanikoff, *Méched, la ville sainte et son territoire*, in *Le Tour du Monde*, Paris 1861, No. 95—96; Eastwick (1862), *Journal of a diplomat's three years residence in Persia*, London 1864, ii. 190—194; H. Vámbéry (1863), *Reise in Mittelasien* [2], Leipzig 1865 (1873), p. 248—258, identical with H. Vámbéry, *Meine Wanderungen und Erlebnisse in Persien*, Pesth 1867, p. 313—327; H. W. Bellew (1872), *From the Indus to the Tigris*, London 1874, p. 358—368; Fr. John Goldsmid (and Evan Smith, 1872), *Eastern Persia*, London 1876, i. 356—366; C. M. MacGregor (1875), *Narrative of a Journey through the province of Khorasan*, London 1879, i. 277—309, ii. 4; J. Bassett (1878), *Persia, the Land of the Imams*, London 1887, p. 219—247; E. O'Donovan (1880), *The Merw Oasis*, London 1882, i. 478—502, ii. 1—24; G. Curzon (1889), *Persia and the Persian Question*, London 1892, i. 148—176; H. St. Massy (1893), *An Englishman in the shrine of Imam Reza in Mashad*, in *The Nineteenth Century and after*, London 1913, lxxiii[b], 990—1007; C. E. Yate (1885, 1893—1897), *Khurasan and Sistan*, Edinburgh 1900; P. Sykes (1893, 1902, 1905—1912), *Ten Thousand Miles in Persia*, London 1902; do., *Historical notes on Khurasan*, in *JRAS*, 1910; do. (and Khān Bahādur Aḥmad Dīn Khān), *The Glory of the Shia World*, London 1910, p. 227—269 (with pictures); Ella C. Sykes, *Persia and its people*, London 1910, p. 88—105; H. R. Allemagne (1907), *Du Khorassan au pays des Bakhtiaris*, Paris 1911, iii. (with very fine illustrations); W. Jackson (1907), *From Constantinople to the Home of Omar Khayyam*, New York 1911; O. von Niedermayer, *Unter der Glutsonne Irans*, Dachau 1925, p. 207; D. M. Donaldson, *The Shiʿite Religion*, London 1933, p. 170 *sqq*.

For the importance of the Mashhad sanctuary for the history of art cf. E. Diez, *Churasanische Baudenkmäler*, vol. i. Berlin 1918; do. *Persien: Islamische Baukunst in Churasan*, Hagen i. W. 1923; A. U. Pope, *A Survey of Persian* Art, London and New York, ii. (1939), v. (1938).

MASHHAD ʿALĪ. [See NADJAF].

MASHHAD ḤUSAIN (KARBALĀʾ), a place of pilgrimage west of the Euphrates about 60 miles S.S.W. of Baghdād on the edge of the desert (Yāḳūt, *Muʿdjam*, ed. Wüstenfeld, iv. 249). It lay opposite Ḳaṣr Ibn Hubaira (al-Iṣṭakhrī, in *BGA*, i. 85; cf. al-Balādhurī, *Futūḥ*, ed. de Goeje, p. 287; al-Maḳdisī, *BGA*, iii. 121).

The name Karbalāʾ is probably connected with Aram. *karbelā* (Daniel 3, 21) and Assyr. *karballatu* (a kind of headdress; cf. G. Jacob, in *Türkische Bibliothek*, xi. 35, note 2). It is not mentioned in the pre-Arab period.

After the taking of al-Ḥīra, Khālid b. al-Walīd is said to have encamped in Karbalāʾ (Yāḳūt, iv. 250). On the Āshūrāʾ day (10th Muḥarram) 61 (Oct. 10, 680) the Imām Ḥusain b. ʿAlī (q.v.) on the march from Mecca to the ʿIrāḳ, where he intended to enforce his claims to the caliphate, fell in the plain of Karbalāʾ in the district of Nīnawā (al-Ṭabarī, iii. 2190; Yāḳūt, iv. 870; now according to Massignon: Khaimat Ḳāʿa; according to Musil: Ishān Nainwa) in a battle with the troops of the governor of al-Kūfa and was buried in al-Ḥāʾir (Yāḳūt, ii. 188 *sq.*; al-Ṭabarī, iii. 752).

The place where the decapitated body of the Prophet's grandson was interred (on the fate of the head which was cut off and sent to Damascus to Yazīd I, cf. van Berchem, *Festschrift Ed. Sachau gewidm.*, Berlin 1915, p. 298—310), called Ḳabr al-Ḥusain, soon became a celebrated place of pilgrimage for the Shīʿīs [cf. art. SHĪʿA].

As early as 65/684—685 we find Sulaimān b. Ṣurad going with his followers to Ḥusain's grave, where he spent a day and a night (al-Ṭabarī, ed. de Goeje, ii. 545 *sq.*). Ibn al-Athīr (*Kāmil*, ed. Tornberg, v. 184; ix. 358) mentions further pilgrimages in the years 122/739–740 and 436/1044–1045. The religious officials of Mashhad Ḥusain at quite an early date were endowed by the pious benefactions of Umm Mūsā, mother of the caliph al-Mahdī (al-Ṭabarī, iii. 752).

The caliph al-Mutawakkil in 236/850—851 destroyed the tomb and its annexes and had the ground levelled and sown; he prohibited under threat of heavy penalties visiting the holy places (al-Ṭabarī, iii. 1407; Ḥamd Allāh al-Mustawfī, *Nuzhat al-ḳulūb*, ed. Le Strange, p. 32). Ibn Ḥawḳal (ed. de Goeje, p. 166), however, mentions about 367/977 a large *mashhad* with a domed chamber, entered by a door on each side, over the tomb of Ḥusain, which in his time was already much visited by pilgrims. Ḍabba b. Muḥammad al-Asadī of ʿAin al-Tamr, supreme chief of a number of tribes, devastated Mashhad al-Ḥāʾir (Karbalāʾ) along with other sanctuaries, for which a punitive expedition was sent against ʿAin al-Tamr in 369/979—980 before which he fled into the desert (Ibn Miskawaih, *Tadjārib al-umam*, ed. Amedroz, in *The Eclipse of the Abbasid Caliphate*, ii. 338, 414). In the same year, the Shīʿī Būyid ʿAḍud al-Dawla took the two sanctuaries of Mashhad ʿAlī (= al-Nadjaf) and Mashhad al-Ḥusain (M. Ḥairī) under his special protection

(Ibn al-Athīr, viii. 518; Ḥamd Allāh al-Mustawfī, *loc. cit.*).

Ḥasan b. al-Faḍl, who died in 414/1023—1024, built a wall round the holy tomb at Mashhad al-Ḥusain (Ibn Taghrībirdī, *Nudjūm*, ed. Popper, ii. 123, 141), as he also did at Mashhad ʿAlī (Ibn al-Athīr, ix. 154).

In Rabīʿ al-awwal 407/Aug.-Sept. 1016, a great conflagration broke out caused by the upsetting of two wax candles, which reduced the main building (*al-ḳubba*) and the open halls (*al-arwiḳa*) to ashes (Ibn al-Athīr, ix. 209).

When the Saldjūḳ Sulṭān Malik Shāh came to Baghdād in 479/1086—1087 he did not neglect to visit the two Mashhads of ʿAlī and al-Ḥusain (Ibn al-Athīr, x. 103). The two sanctuaries at this time were known as al-Mashhadān (al-Bundārī al-Iṣfahānī, *Tawārīkh āl-Saldjūḳ*, ed. Houtsma, in *Recueil de textes*..., ii. 77) on the analogy of the duals al-ʿIrāḳān, al-Baṣratān, al-Ḥīratān, al-Miṣrān etc.

The Īlkhān Ghāzān in 703/1303 visited Karbalāʾ and gave lavish gifts to the sanctuary. He or his father Arghūn is credited with bringing water to the district by leading a canal from the Furāt (the modern Nahr al-Ḥusainīya) (A. Nöldeke, *Das Heiligtum al-Ḥusains zu Kerbelāʾ*, Berlin 1909, p. 40).

Ibn Baṭṭūṭa (ed. Defrémery and Sanguinetti, ii. 99) visited Karbalāʾ in 727/1326—1327 from al-Ḥilla and describes it as a small town which lies among palm groves and gets its water from the Furāt. In the centre was the sacred tomb; beside it was a large madrasa and the famous hostel (*al-zāwiya*) in which the pilgrims were entertained. Admission to the tomb could only be obtained by permission of the gate-keeper. The pilgrims kissed the dilver sarcophagus, above which hung gold and silver lamps. The doors were hung with silken curtains. The inhabitants were divided into the Awlād Rakhīk and Awlād Fāyiz, whose continual feuds were detrimental to the town, although they were all Shīʿīs.

About the same date, Ḥamd Allāh al-Mustawfī (*op. cit.*) gives the circumference of the town as 2,400 paces; he mentions there also the tomb of Ḥurr Riyā (b. Yazīd), who was the first to fall fighting for Ḥusain at Karbalāʾ.

The Ṣafawid Shāh Ismāʿīl I (d. 930/1524) made a pilgrimage to al-Nadjaf and Mashhad Ḥusain.

Sulṭān Sulaimān the Magnificent visited the two sanctuaries in 941/1534—1535, repaired the canal at Mashhad al-Ḥusain (al-Ḥusainīya) and transformed the fields which had been buried in sand into gardens again. The Manārat al-ʿAbd (see below), formerly called Engusht-i Yār, was built in 982/1574—1575. Murād III in 991/1583 ordered the wālī of Baghdād, ʿAlī Pasha b. Alwand, to build or more correctly restore a sanctuary over the grave of Ḥusain. Soon after the capture of Baghdād in 1623, ʿAbbās the Great won the Mashhads for the Persian empire. Nādir Shāh visited Karbalāʾ in 1743; while he is credited with gilding the dome in Mashhad ʿAlī, he is also said to have confiscated endowments intended for the imāms of Karbalāʾ.

The great prosperity of the place of pilgrimage and its large number of inhabitants is emphasized on the occasion of the pilgrimage of ʿAbd al-Karīm, a favourite of Nādir Shāh. Raḍīya Sulṭān Begum, a daughter of Shāh Ḥusain (1694—1722), presented 20,000 nādirīs for improvements at the mosque of Ḥusain.

The founder of the Ḳādjār dynasty, Agha Muḥammad Khān, towards the end of the xviiith century, presented the gold covering for the dome and the manāra of the sanctuary of Ḥusain (Jacob in A. Nöldeke, *op. cit.* p. 65, note 4).

In April 1802 in the absence of the pilgrims who had gone to al-Nadjaf, 12,000 Wahhābīs under Shaikh Saʿūd entered Karbalāʾ, slew over 3,000 inhabitants there and looted the houses and bazaars. In particular they carried off the gilt copper plates and other treasures of the sanctuary and destroyed the shrine. But after this catastrophe contributions poured in for the sanctuary from the whole Shīʿī world.

After a temporary occupation of Karbalāʾ by the Persians, Nadjīb Pasha in 1843 succeeded by force of arms in enforcing the recognition of Turkish suzerainty over the town; the walls of the present old town were now for the most part destroyed. The governor Midḥat Pasha in 1871 began the building of government offices, which remained incomplete, and extended the adjoining marketplace (references for the history of Mashhad Ḥusain are given in A. Nöldeke, *op. cit.*, p. 35—50).

At the present day with over 50,000 inhabitants, Karbalāʾ is the second largest and perhaps the richest town of the ʿIrāḳ. It owes its prosperity not only to the great number of pilgrims who visit the tomb of Ḥusain, but also to the fact that it is the most important starting point for the Persian pilgrim caravans to al-Nadjaf and Mecca, and through its situation on the edge of the alluvial plain it is an important "desert port" for trade with the interior of Arabia.

The old town with its tortuous streets is surrounded by modern suburbs. About half to three quarters of the citizens are Persians, the remainder Shīʿī Arabs. The most important tribes among them are the Banī Saʿd, Salālme, al-Wuzūm, al-Tahāmze and al-Nāṣirīye. The Dede family is the richest: for constructing the Nahr al-Ḥusainīya it was rewarded with extensive estates by Sulṭān Selīm.

The name Karbalāʾ strictly speaking only applies to the eastern part of the palm gardens which surround the town in a semi-circle on its east side (Musil, *The Middle Euphrates*, p. 41). The town itself is called al-Mashhad or Mashhad al-Ḥusain.

The sanctuary of the third Imām lies in a courtyard (*ṣaḥn*) 354 × 270 feet in area, which is surrounded by *līwāns* and cells. Its walls are decorated with a continuous ornamental band which is said to contain the whole Ḳurʾān written in white on a blue ground. The building itself is 156 × 138 feet in area. The rectangular main building entered by the "golden outer hall" (picture in Grothe, *Geogr. Charakterbilder*, pl. lxxviii., fig. 136) is surrounded by a vaulted corridor (now called *djāmiʿ*; A. Nöldeke, *op. cit.*, p. 20) in which the pilgrims go round the sanctuary (*ṭawāf*) (Wellhausen, *Reste arab. Heidentums* ^{2}, p. 109—112). In the middle of the central domed chamber is the shrine (*ṣandūḳa*) of Ḥusain about 6 feet high and 12 long surrounded by silver *mashrabīya* work, at the foot of which stands a second smaller shrine, that of his son and companion-in-arms ʿAlī Akbar (Masʿūdī, *Tanbīh*, ed. de Goeje, in *BGA*, viii. 303).

"The general impression made by the interior must be called fairy like, when in the dusk — even in the daytime it is dim inside — the light of innumerable lamps and candles around the silver shrine, reflected a thousand and again a thousand times from the innumerable small crystal facets, produces a charming effect beyond the dreams of imagination. In the roof of the dome the light loses its strength; only here and there a few crystal surfaces gleam like the stars in the sky" (A. Nöldeke, *op. cit.*, p. 25 *sq.*).

The sanctuary is adorned on the Ḳibla face with magnificent and costly ornamentation. Two manāras flank the entrance. A third, the Manārat al-ʿAbd, rises before the buildings on the east side of the *ṣaḥn*; south of it the face of the buildings surrounding the court recedes about 50 feet; on this spot is a Sunnī mosque. Adjoining the *ṣaḥn* on the north side is a large madrasa the courtyard of which measures about 85 feet square with a mosque of its own and several *miḥrābs* (on the present condition of the sanctuary cf. A. Nöldeke, *op. cit.*, p. 5—26. on its history p. 35—50 and on its architectural history, p. 51—66).

About 600 yards N.E. of the sanctuary of Ḥusain is the mausoleum of his half-brother ʿAbbās. On the road which runs westward out of the town is the site of the tent of Ḥusain (*khaimagāh*). The building erected there (plan in Nöldeke, pl. vii.; photograph in Grothe, pl. lxxxiv., fig. 145) has the plan of a tent and on both sides of the entrance there are stone copies of camel saddles.

On the desert plateau (*ḥammād*) west of the town stretch the graves of the devout Shīʿīs. North of the gardens of Karbalāʾ lie the suburbs, gardens and fields of al-Bḳēre, N.W. those of Ḳurra, S. those of al-Ghādhirīya (Yāḳūt, iii. 768). Among places in the vicinity, Yāḳūt mentions al-ʿAḳr (iii. 695) and al-Nawāyiḥ (iv. 816).

A branch line diverging north of al-Ḥilla connects Karbalāʾ with the Baghdād—Baṣra railway. Caravan roads lead to al-Ḥilla and Nadjaf. The sanctuary of Ḥusain still has the reputation of securing entrance to Paradise for those buried there, wherefore many aged pilgrims and those in failing health go there to die on the holy spot.

Bibliography: al-Ṭabarī, ed. de Goeje, Indices; Ibn al-Athīr, *al-Kāmil*, ed. Tornberg, Indices; al-Iṣṭakhrī, in *BGA*, i. 85; Ibn Ḥawḳal, *BGA*, ii. 166; al-Maḳdisī, *BGA*, iii. 130; al-Idrīsī, *Nuzha*, iv. 6, transl. Jaubert, ii. 158; Yāḳūt, *Muʿdjam*, ed. Wüstenfeld, ii. 189, iii. 695, iv. 249 *sq.*; al-Masʿūdī, *Kitāb al-Tanbīh*, *BGA*, viii. 303; al-Bakrī, *Muʿdjam*, ed. Wüstenfeld, p. 162, 456, 471; al-Zamakhsharī, *Lexicon geogr.*, ed. de Grave, p. 139; Ḥamd Allāh al-Mustawfī al-Ḳazwīnī, *Nuzhat al-ḳulūb*, ed. Le Strange, p. 32, transl. p. 39; Ibn Baṭṭūṭa, *Tuḥfa*, ed. Defrémery-Sanguinetti, ii. 99 *sq.*; O. Dapper, *Umbständliche und eigentliche Beschreibung von Asia*, Nürnberg 1681, p. 137; Carsten Niebuhr, *Reisebeschreibung nach Arabien u.a. umliegenden Ländern*, ii., Copenhagen 1778, p. 254 *sq.*; J. B. L. J. Rousseau, *Description du pachalik de Bagdad*, Paris 1809, p. 71 *sqq.*; C. J. Rich, in: *Fundgruben des Orients*, iii., Vienna 1813, p. 200; J. L. Burckhardt, *Bemerkungen über die Beduinen und Wahaby*, Weimar 1831; M. v. Thielmann, *Streifzüge im Kaukasus, in Persien und in der Asiatischen Türkei*, Leipzig 1875, p. 398—401; Nolde, *Reise nach Innerarabien*, Braunschweig 1895, p. 113 *sq.*; M. v. Oppenheim, *Vom Mittelmeer zum Persischen Golf*, ii., Berlin 1900; G. Le Strange, *The Lands of the Eastern Caliphate*, Cambridge 1905 [reprint 1930], p. 78 *sq.*; A. Nöldeke, *Das Heiligtum al-Husains zu Kerbelâ*, Berlin 1909 (= *Türkische Bibliothek*, ed. by G. Jacob, xi.; p. 30—34 further references); H. Grothe, *Geographische Charakterbilder aus der asiatischen Türkei*, Leipzig 1909; L. Massignon, *Mission en Mésopotamie* (1907—1908), i., Cairo 1910, p. 48 *sq.* (= *MIFAO*, xxvii.); Lamberto Vannutelli, *Anatolia meridionale e Mesopotamia*, Rome 1911, p. 361—363; G. L. Bell, *Amurath to Amurath*, London 1911, p. 159—116; Stephen Hemsley Longgrigg, *Four Centuries of Modern Iraq*, Oxford 1925, Index; A. Musil, *The Middle Euphrates*, New York 1927 (= *American Geographical Society, Oriental Explorations and Studies*, No. 3); D. M. Donaldson, *The Shiʾite Religion*, London 1933, p. 88 *sqq.*

AL-MASIḤ, the Messiah; in Arabic (where the root *m-s-ḥ* has the meanings of "to measure" and "stroke") it is a loanword from the Aramaic where Mᵉshīḥā was used as a name of the Redeemer. Horovitz (*Koranische Untersuchungen*, p. 129) considers the possibility that it was taken over from the Ethiopic (*masīḥ*). Muḥammad of course got the word from the Christian Arabs. In Arab writers we find the view mentioned that the word is a loanword from Hebrew or Syriac. Ṭabarī (*Tafsīr* on Sūra iii. 45: vol. iii., p. 169) gives only purely Arabic etymologies, either with the meaning "purified" (from sins) or "filled with blessing". Horovitz, *op. cit.* calls attention to the occurrence of the word in inscriptions, proper names and in the old poetry.

In the Ḳurʾān the word is first found in the Madīnan sūras, *a.* alone: Sūra iv. 172; ix. 30; *b.* with Ibn Maryam: Sūra v. 17, 72, 75; ix. 31; *c.* with ʿĪsā b. Maryam: Sūra iii. 45; iv. 157. None of these passages make it clear what Muḥammad understood by the word. From Sūra iii. 45: "O Maryam, see, Allāh promises thee a word from Him, whose name is al-Masīḥ, ʿĪsā b. Maryam" one might suppose that al-Masīḥ was here to be taken as a proper name. Against this view however is the fact that the article is not found with non-Arabic proper names in the Ḳurʾān.

In canonical Ḥadīth, al-Masīḥ is found in three main connections: *a.* in Muḥammad's dream, in which he relates how he saw at the Kaʿba a very handsome brown-complexioned man with beautiful locks, dripping with water, who walked supported by two men; to his question who this was the reply was given: al-Masīḥ b. Maryam (Bukhārī, *Libās*, bāb 68; *Taʿbīr*, bāb 11; Muslim, *Īmān*, trad. 302); *b.* in the descriptions of the return of ʿĪsā [q.v.]; *c.* at the Last Judgment the Christians will be told: "What have you worshipped?" They will reply: "We have worshipped al-Masīḥ, the Son of God". For this they shall wallow in Hell (Bukhārī, *Tafsīr*, Sūra iv., bāb 8; *Tawḥīd*, bāb 24; Muslim, *Īmān*, trad. 302).

In Ḥadīth also we frequently find references to al-Masīḥ al-Kadhdhāb and al-Masīḥ al-Dadjdjāl; see the article AL-DADJDJĀL.

AL-MATHĀNĪ, a term of uncertain meaning which occurs twice in the Ḳurʾān, namely in Sūra xv. 87: "and we have brought thee seven of the mathānī and the noble Ḳurʾān", and Sūra xxxix. 23: "Allāh sent down the most beautiful recital, a book which is in harmony with itself, mathānī, at which the skin of those who fear their Lord creeps".

The interpretation of the word is made more difficult by the fact that in the latter passage it seems to mean the Ḳurʾān itself, in the former, on the other hand, something similar to the Ḳurʾān.

In Ṭabarī (*Tafsīr*, xiv. 32 *sqq.*; cf. xxiii. 124 *sq.*) we find the following opinions.

a. Mūsā was given six out of the seven mathānī: two were lost when he broke the tablets. The seven mathānī are like seven long sūras, i.e. ii.—vii. and a seventh, on the identity of which there is a difference of opinion; it is either Sūra x. or viii. and ix. combined.

b. The seven mat͟hānī mean the *fātiḥa* which contains six verses. These with the *basmala* in the beginning make seven. It is called the *mat͟hānī*, i.e. repetitions, because it is repeated in the ṣalāt's at each *rakʿa*. This explanation is supported by quoting the term *mutas͟hābih* ("in harmony with itself") which immediately precedes the word *mat͟hānī* in Sūra xxxix. 23.

c. The mat͟hānī means the Ḳurʾān in general. Ḥadīt͟h hesitates among these interpretations *a*. (Tirmid͟hī, *Tafsīr*, Sūra ix., trad. 1; cf. Buk͟hārī, *Ad͟hān*, bāb 106) and *b*. (Buk͟hārī, *Tafsīr*, Sūra i., bāb 1; Sūra xv., bāb 3; *Faḍāʾil al-Ḳurʾān*, bāb 9; Tirmid͟hī, *Tafsīr*, Sūra xv., trad. 3, 4; Nasāʾī, *Iftitāḥ*, bāb 26).

Nor is there any unanimity in explaining the form mat͟hānī. Baiḍāwī on Sūra xxxix. 23 (24) gives as the singular *mut͟hannan*, *mut͟hnan* or *mut͟hnin*. Zamak͟hs͟harī gives *mat͟hnā*. The latter form is found in the Ḳurʾān (Sūra iv. 3; xxxiv. 46; xxxv. 1) and in Ḥadīt͟h (Buk͟hārī, *Ṣalāt*, bāb 84; *Witr*, bāb i.; *Tahad͟djud*, bāb 10; Muslim, *Musāfirīn*, trad. 145—148; *Tirmid͟hī*, *Ṣalāt*, bāb 206 etc.) as a distributive, meaning "occurring in pairs". This meaning however would not be at all suitable for *mat͟hānī*.

Geiger (*Was hat Mohammed aus dem Judenthume aufgenommen?*, p. 57 *sq*.) has already compared the Hebrew *mis͟hnā* (Aram.: *mat͟hnīt͟hā*). According to him then mathānī would mean the Ḳurʾān itself as a whole. His suggestion is approved by Nöldeke-Schwally (*Geschichte des Qorāns*, i. p. 114 *sq*.). Attention might further be called to the fact that *mis͟hnā* means a single law as well as the whole codex and from this could be derived the double meaning of mat͟hānī (separate verses and the whole Ḳurʾān), a derivation which could be supported by the parallel double meaning of the word Ḳurʾān (single revelation and all revelation as a whole).

Sprenger (*Das Leben und die Lehre des Moḥammad*, Berlin 1861, i. 463 *sq*.) explains the word from the Hebrew *s͟hānā* "to repeat" and the conception from Sūra xxxix. 23, from which it would appear that the mat͟hānī are part of the stories of punishment. This view has been adopted by D. H. Müller, *Die Propheten in ihrer ursprünglichen Form*, i. 43, 46, note 2; H. Grimme, *Mohammed*, ii. 77; N. Rhodokanakis, in *WZKM*, xxv. 66 *sq*.; J. Horovitz, *Kor. Unters*., p. 26 *sq*. This would imply that, at least when Sūra xv. 87 was revealed, there were seven of these legends of punishment.

Early evidence of the use of the word outside of the Ḳurʾān is found in a poem of Abu 'l-Aswad al-Duʾalī (text and transl. by Nöldeke, in *ZDMG*, xviii. 236 *sq*.; cf. thereon Bevan, in *JRAS*, 1921, p. 584 *sq*.; Horovitz, *op. cit*.). Here the mat͟hānī are mentioned along with the *miʾūna*, "the seven versed" along with the "hundred versed" sūras of the Ḳurʾān. The exact content of these groups is unknown.

In conclusion it may be mentioned that Goldziher (*ZDMG*, lxi. 866 *sqq*.) has called attention to a term *mat͟hnāt*, which occurs in non-canonical tradition and is obviously a new formation modelled on the Hebrew *mis͟hnā*.

Bibliography: In addition to the references in the article: Th. Nöldeke, *Neue Beiträge z. sem. Sprachwissenschaft*, p. 26; Fak͟hr al-Dīn al-Rāzī, *Mafātīḥ al-g͟haib*, iv. 110—112; al-Suyūṭī, *Itḳān*, p. 124; *Lisān al-ʿArab*, xviii. 127 *sqq*.; Lane, *Lexicon*, s.v. *mat͟hnan*.

AL-MĀTURĪDĪ, Abū Manṣūr Muḥammad b. Muḥammad b. Maḥmūd al-Ḥanafī al-Mutakallim al-Māturīdī al-Samarḳandī is the titular head of the Māturīdite School of theology which, with the As͟hʿarite School, form orthodox Sunnite Islām. The two Schools are equally orthodox, but there has always been a tendency to suppress al-Māturīdī's name and to put al-As͟hʿarī forward as the champion of Islām against all heretics except in Transoxiana (Mā warāʾ al-Nahr) where his School has been, and is, the dominant, representing the views of *ahl al-sunna wa 'l-d͟jamāʿa*. Next to nothing is known of al-Māturīdī's life, but he died at Samarḳand in 333/944, a contemporary of al-As͟hʿarī who died a little earlier about 330/941, while al-Ṭaḥāwī, another contemporary, died in Egypt in 321/933. All three represented the movement, which must have been very widely spread, to defend orthodox Islām by the same weapons of logical argument with which the Muʿtazilites had attacked it. Māturīd or Māturīt is a locality (*maḥall*, *ḳarya*) in Samarḳand. Its geographical reality and the identity of Abū Manṣūr al-Māturīdī are assured by the article Māturītī in the *Ansāb* of al-Samʿānī (fol. 498ᵇ, 1. 4; cf. also Barthold, *Turkestan down to the Mongol Invasion*, in *GMS*, p. 90, notes 9 and 10; p. 267, note 5, and the Russian references there). The books of Ḥanafite *Ṭabaḳāt* give the names of his teachers, but to us they are names only (see Ibn Ḳutlūbug͟hā, ed. Flügel, No. 173, and Flügel's *Hanefiten*, p. 274, 293, 295, 298, 313). The Saiyid Murtaḍā in his little treatise on Māturīdī, inserted in his commentary on the *Iḥyāʾ* (ii. 5—14), complains that he has found only two biographies and that both are short (*ʿala 'l-ik͟htiṣār*). Even Yaḳūt in his *Muʿd͟jam* has no mention either of him or of Māturīd. Ibn K͟haldūn in his sketch of the origin and history of *kalām* (*Muḳaddima*, transl. de Slane, iii. 55 *sqq*.; ed. Quatremère, iii. 38 *sqq*.) has no place for him and speaks only of As͟hʿarī and the As͟hʿarites. For Ibn Ḥazm (d. 456/1064; *Faṣl*, ii. 111) the orthodox opponent of al-As͟hʿarī is Abū Ḥanīfa and he has no mention of al-Māturīdī. Similarly S͟hahrastānī (d. 548/1153) gives the views of Abū Ḥanīfa but does not mention Māturīdī. Abū Ḥanīfa, he says, inclined to the Murd͟jiʾites and his followers were even called the Murd͟jiʾites of the Sunna (i. 105; trans. Haarbrücker, i. 159), meaning, apparently, a form of Murd͟jiʾism consistent with orthodoxy. Similarly the Saiyid Murtaḍā (*loc. cit*., p. 13 foot) says that the Muʿtazilites claimed Abū Ḥanīfa for themselves and rejected his authorship of one book because it was too flatly against their positions. The truth evidently was that Abū Ḥanīfa (d. 150/767) was the first to adopt the methods of the Muʿtazilites and apply their arguments to the foundation of the Faith. Also, from the beginning, his standing was so high that it was simply impossible to call him a heretic. This status continued in the Māturīdite School.

All this goes back to the time before *kalām* had become a technical term and when *fiḳh* meant both theology and canon law, with the difference that theology was called "the greater *fiḳh*" (*al-fiḳh al-akbar*; see the article kalām). That was the title of one of Abū Ḥanīfa's [q.v.] books and we have a commentary on it dubiously ascribed to Māturīdī (Ḥaidarābād 1321), the only writing assertedly by him in print. This does not occur in the two exactly similar lists which we have of his books (Saiyid Murtaḍā, p. 5; Ibn Ḳulṭūbug͟hā, p. 43). 1. *Kitāb al-Tawḥīd*; 2. *Kitāb al-Maḳālāt*; 3. *Kitāb*

Radd awā'il al-adilla li 'l-Ka'bī; 4. *Kitāb Bayān wahm al-Mu'tazila*; 5. *Kitāb Ta'wīlāt al-Ḳur'ān*. (Brockelmann, *GAL*², i. 209; S. i. 346). The *Ta'wīlāt al-Ḳur'ān* is highly praised by the biographers. The others suggest only anti-Mu'tazilite polemic (for al-Ka'bī see Horten, *Philosophische Systeme*, by index). As a matter of fact it is only in one MS. of the commentary on the *Fiḳh Akbar* that this work is ascribed to al-Māturīdī.

How the theological school of Abū Ḥanīfa came to be known as that of al-Māturīdī we do not know. The epithet *al-mutakallim*, applied to al-Māturīdī, may mean that he was the theologian of the school of Abū Ḥanīfa as opposed to those who were canon lawyers (*fuḳahā'*). But the two tendencies to accept him and to suppress him still continue. The *'Aḳā'id* of one of his followers, al-Nasafī, fortified with the commentary of al-Taftāzānī, an As͟h'arite, is the theological text-book of the last two years of the Azhar course and is a final authority in Egypt. Yet when Muḥammad 'Abduh [q.v.], the late Chief Muftī of Egypt, a regenerator and reformer of Islām, put his views of the development of Muslim theology and of its final position into a course of lectures at Bairūt (*Risālat al-tawḥīd*; French trans. by B. Michel and Moustapha 'Abdel Razik, Paris 1925) he showed himself a Māturīdite with no mention of al-Māturīdī.

The differences between the two Schools are commonly reckoned as thirteen in number; six, a difference in idea (*ma'nawī*) and seven in expression (*lafẓī*) (for them in detail see the Saiyid Murtaḍā, p. 8 *sqq.* and Abū 'Ud͟hba, *al-Rawḍa al-bahīya*, Ḥaidarābād 1904). They have been studied by Goldziher in his *Vorlesungen*, p. 110 *sqq.*, and by Horten in his *Philosophische Systeme*, p. 531 *sqq.* It is frequently said that these points of difference are slight, but that is not so. The normal position of Abū Ḥanīfa is as plain in them as in his canon law. Al-As͟h'arī was concerned only to maintain the absoluteness of Allāh's will; that he could do anything; and that a thing was "good" because he willed it. Future rewards and punishments, therefore, had no "moral" basis. But Abū Ḥanīfa, and after him al-Māturīdī and his School, recognizes that man possesses free-will (*ik͟htiyārī*) actions for which he is rewarded and punished. No explanation is attempted of this fundamental antinomy of predestination and free-will; they are stated side by side as equal, if contradictory, facts. Similarly, while Abū Ḥanīfa admits that evil deeds are by the will (*irāda*) of Allāh — otherwise they could not happen — he cannot bring himself to say that they are by the "good pleasure" (*riḍwān*) of Allāh. Further, the Māturīdite School admits the doctrine of "assurance of salvation" and the As͟h'arite does not. A Māturīdite may say, "I am a believer, assuredly" (*ḥaḳḳ^an^*), but an As͟h'arite must say, "I am a believer if Allāh wills", Because, then, of this essential difference in human and moral feeling the School of al-Māturīdī has steadily penetrated the School of al-As͟h'arī and even the professed As͟h'arite at the present time is, to a greater or less extent, a Māturīdite. See also the art. KALĀM and A. S. Tritton, *Muslim Theology*, London 1947, p. 274 *sqq.*

MAWLĀ (A.), a term with different meanings (cf. *Lisān al-'Arab*, xx. 289 *sqq.*) of which the following may be mentioned:

a. Tutor, trustee, helper. In this sense the word is used in the Ḳur'ān, Sūra xlvii. 11: "God is the mawlā of the faithful, the unbelievers have no mawlā" (cf. Sūra iii. 150; vi. 62; viii. 40; ix. 51; xxii. 78; lxvi. 2). In the same sense mawlā is used in the S͟hī'ite tradition, in which Muḥammad calls 'Alī the mawlā of those whose mawlā he is himself. According to the author of the *Lisān*, mawlā has the sense of *walī* in this tradition, which is connected with G͟hadīr al-K͟humm (cf. C. van Arendonk, *De opkomst van het Zaidietische imamaat*, p. 18, 19). It may be observed that it occurs also in the *Musnad* of Aḥmad b. Ḥanbal (i. 84, 118, 119, 152, 330 *sq.*; iv. 281 etc.).

b. Lord. In the Ḳur'ān it is in this sense (which is synonymous with that of *saiyid*) applied to Allāh (Sūra ii. 286; cf. vi. 62; x. 30), who is often called *mawlānā* "our Lord" in Arabic literature. Precisely for this reason in Tradition the slave is prohibited from calling his lord mawlā (Buk͟hārī, *D͟jihād*, bāb 165; Muslim, *Alfāẓ*, trad. 15, 16).

It is not in contradiction to this prohibition that Tradition frequently uses mawlā in the sense of "lord of a slave", e.g. in the well known *ḥadīt͟h*: "Three categories of people will receive twofold reward...and the slave who fulfils his duty in regard to Allāh as well as to his lord" (Buk͟hārī, *'Ilm*, bāb 31; Muslim, *Aimān*, trad. 45).

Compositions of mawlā and suffixes are frequently used as titles in several parts of the Muslim world, e.g. *mawlāy(a)* (*mūlāy*), "my Lord" (especially in North Africa and in connection with saints); *mawlawī* (*mollā*), "Lordship" (especially in India and in connection with scholars or saints).

The term mawlā is also applied to the former lord (patron) in his relation to his freeman, e.g. in the tradition: "Who clings to a (new) patron without the permission of his (legal) mawlā, on him rests the curse of Allāh" (Buk͟hārī, *D͟jizya*, bāb 17; Muslim, *'Itḳ*, trad. 18, 19).

c. Freed slave, e.g. in the tradition "the mawlā counts as the people to whom he belongs" (Buk͟hārī, *Farā'iḍ*, bāb 24, etc.). In this sense mawlā, or rather the plural *mawālī*, is frequently used in Arabic literature. The evolution of the idea as well as the position and the aspirations of the *mawālī* have been expounded by von Kremer (*Culturgeschichte des Orients unter den Chalifen*, ii. 154) and by Goldziher (*Muhammedanische Studien* i. 104 *sqq.*), by the latter especially in connection with the *s͟hu'ūbīya*. On the position of the *mawālī* in the law of inheritance cf. the art. MĪRĀT͟H.

Bibliography: in the article; also Doutté in *RHR*, xli. 30 *sqq.*; Littmann, in *NGW*, 1916, p. 102.

MAWLAWĪYA (Turkish pronunciation Mewlewīya), Order of Derwishes called by Europeans Dancing or Whirling Derwishes.

1. Origin of the Order. Its name is derived from *mawlānā* ("our master"), a title given *par excellence* to D͟jalāl al-Dīn al-Rūmī (e.g. by the Turkish writers Sa'd al-Dīn and Pečewī, cited below), of which the Persian equivalent was according to the *Manāḳib al-'ārifīn* (translated by Huart as *Les Saints des Derviches Tourneurs*, Paris 1918—1922) bestowed on D͟jalāl al-Dīn [q.v.] by his father, with whom this hagiography commences. According to the same authority (i. 162), his adherents adopted the name *Mewlewī*, and indeed copyists of the *Mat͟hnawī* of the years 687 and 706 A.H. thus designate themselves (Nicholson's ed., i. 7 and iii. 11); yet Ibn Baṭṭūṭa, who visited Ḳonya after the latter date, asserts that they were styled D͟jalālīya,

and the word Mawlawī seems to be used occasionally in the *Manāḳib* in the sense of "scholar", which it it ordinarily had in India. This work asserts that one Badr al-Dīn Guharṭās̲h̲ (a historical personage, since he is mentioned in Ibn Bībī's chronicle of the Seldjūḳs of Asia Minor) built a college at Ḳonya for the children of D̲j̲alāl al-Dīn's father, which was inherited by D̲j̲alāl al-Dīn. The *Manāḳib* (by S̲h̲ams al-Dīn Aḥmad al-Aflākī, d. 761/1360), however, so teems with anachronisms and extravagances that its statements must be used with great caution.

The European name is taken from the ritual of the *d̲h̲ikr*, in which the derwishes revolve, using the right foot as a pivot, to the tune of various instruments. D̲j̲alāl al-Dīn is said to have claimed that he had elevated the practice, but denied that it was an innovation (*Manāḳib*, ii. 79). Certainly "dancing" (*raḳṣ*) is mentioned as a Ṣūfī practice in works earlier by some centuries than D̲j̲alāl al-Dīn's time, often with severe condemnation. The historian Sak̲h̲āwī (*al-Tibr al-masbūk*, p. 220) in recording an edict issued in 852/1448 against the practice in Egypt cites verses by one of "the earliest Saiyids" in which the Ṣūfīs who perform it are compared to apes and are bitterly reproached.

Dancing is indeed a natural accompaniment of music (*Ag̲h̲ānī*, x. 121) or poetry (*Irs̲h̲ād al-arīb*, v. 131), but the whirling of the derwishes would seem to have for its purpose the production of vertigo rather than the presentation of an idea in rhythm. Of the various reasons which have been assigned for it the most interesting is that recorded in the *Manāḳib* (i. 190) as the excuse of D̲j̲alāl al-Dīn, viz. that it was a concession to the pleasure-loving inhabitants of Asia Minor, who might thereby be drawn to the true faith. The theory that the whirling was a reproduction of the motions of the celestial bodies is found in his *Mat̲h̲nawī* (ed. Nicholson, iv. 734), and the same view is offered in the much earlier *Risāla* of Ibn Ṭufail (Cairo 1922, p. 75), where its hypnotic effect is emphasized. The saints in the *Manāḳib* are represented as able to maintain the exercise for many days and nights continuously, but the actual *d̲h̲ikr* lasts only about an hour, with some intermission.

2. Relations with other Orders. Although the earlier mystics, such as D̲j̲unaid, Bisṭāmī and Ḥallād̲j̲ are mentioned in the *Manāḳib* with profound reverence, the treatment of founders of orders who came near D̲j̲alāl al-Dīn's time is very different. ʿAbd al-Ḳādir of D̲j̲īlān is ignored, Ibn ʿArabī mentioned with contempt and Rifāʿī with severe condemnation. Ḥād̲j̲d̲j̲ī Bekṭās̲h̲ is represented as having sent a messenger to inquire into the proceedings of D̲j̲alāl al-Dīn, and to have acknowledged the supremacy of the latter. At a later period the rivalry of the Mawlawī with the Bekṭās̲h̲ī Order became acute.

It has been shown by F. W. Hasluck (*Christianity and Islam under the Sultans*, Oxford 1929, ii. 370 *sqq.*) that the environment wherein the Mawlawī Order originated was favourable to Christians, and that throughout its history it has shown itself tolerant and inclined to regard all religions as reconcilable on a philosophic basis. He suggests that the veneration of the Muslims of Ḳonya for the supposed burial-place of Plato (in a mosque which was once the church of St. Amphilochius) may have been intentionally favoured by the Mawlāwī derwished, or possibly their founder, as providing a cult which Muslim and Christian might share on equal terms. In three other sanctuaries of Ḳonya, one of them

the mausoleum of D̲j̲alāl al-Dīn himself, he found evidence of a desire to provide an object of veneration to the adherents of both systems. It is not, however, easy to accept his inference that some sort of religious compromise on a philosophic basis was devised between the Seldjūḳ Sulṭān ʿAlā al-Dīn, D̲j̲alāl al-Dīn, and the local Christian clergy. It appears from the *Manāḳib* that the Order was frequently exposed to persecution from the *fuḳahāʾ* in consequence of the music and dancing; and they found an analogy in Christian services to the employment of the former. They are credited in recent times with having impeded the massacres of Armenians.

3. Spread of the Order. The *Manāḳib* attributes its progagation outside Ḳonya to D̲j̲alāl al-Dīn's son and second successor, Sulṭān Bahāʾ al-Dīn Walad who "filled Asia Minor with his lieutenants" (ii. 262). It would however appear from Ibn Baṭṭūṭa's narrative (ii. 282) that its following was not in his time extensive outside Ḳonya, and was confined to Asia Minor. The story told after Saʿd al-Dīn by v. Hammer (*GOR*, i. 147) and others, that as early as 759/1357 Sulaimān son of Ork̲h̲ān received a cap from a Mawlawī derwish at Bulair, has been shown by Hasluck (ii. 613) to be a fiction. The historians make no allusion to any importance attaching to the Mawlawī chief when Murād I took Ḳonya in 1386; but when the city was taken by Murād II in 1435, peace was negotiated, according to Saʿd al-Dīn (i. 358), by Mawlānā Ḥamza, but according to Nes̲h̲rī (quoted *ibid.*) by a descendant of Mawlānā D̲j̲alāl al-Dīn al-Rūmī, ʿĀrif Čelebi, "who united all the glories of worth and pedigree and possessed mystic attainments"; the rebellious vassal supposed that a holy man of the family of the Mawlā would inspire more confidence. The same person performed a similar service in 1442 (Saʿd al-Dīn, i. 371). According to V. Cuinet (*La Turquie d'Asie*, i. 829) Selīm I when passing through Ḳonya in 922/1516 in pursuit of the Persians (?) ordered the destruction of the Mawlawīk̲h̲āna, at the instance of the S̲h̲aik̲h̲ al-Islām; and though this command was repealed, the moral and religious authority of the head of the Order was gravely compromised. That the saints of Ḳonya were highly reverenced in the Ottoman Empire later in the sixteenth century appears from the list of graves visited by Saiyid ʿAlī Ḳapūdān in 1554, which commences with those of D̲j̲alāl al-Dīn, his father and his son (Pečewī's History, 1283, i. 371). In 1634 Murād IV assigned the *k̲h̲arād̲j̲* of Ḳonya to the Čelebi. Yet the first reference to "dancing" derwishes in Constantinople which Hasluck produces, is from the time of the Sulṭān Ibrāhīm (1640—1648). Cuinet mentions three Mawlawīk̲h̲āna of the first rank and one Tekye of the second in Constantinople and the neighbourhood; he gives the names of the saints whose tombs they contain, without dates. He mentions seven other Mawlawīk̲h̲āna of the first rank, at Ḳonya, Manissa, Ḳarahiṣār, Bahariya, Egypt (Cairo?), Gallipoli and Brusa; and as the more celebrated of the second rank that of S̲h̲amsī Tabrīzī at Ḳonya, and those in Madīna, Damascus and Jerusalem. To these Hasluck adds Tekyes at Canea (Crete), founded about 1880, Ḳaramān, Ramla, Tatar (in Thessaly), and possibly Tempe (for one in Smyrna see *MW*, 1922, p. 161; for one in Salonica see the work of Garnett, and for one in Cyprus that of Lukach cited below). It would seem then that the Order was confined to the limits of the Ottoman Empire, and indeed to its European and Asiatic territories.

By a decree of Sept. 4, 1925 all the Tekyes in Turkey were closed, and the library of the Mawlawīkhāna of Ḳonya was transferred to the Museum of the city (*Oriente Moderno*, 1925, p. 455; 1926, p. 584).

4. Political importance of the Order. Reference may be made to Hasluck's work (ii. 604 *sq.*) for refutation of the stories uncritically reproduced by Cuinet and some less authoritative writers. In these "the Shaikh of the Mawlawī becomes first the legitimate successor by blood of the Seldjūḳ dynasty, and finally the real Caliph!" Hasluck supposes these tales to be based on the supposed "traditional right" of the Mawlawī Shaikh to gird the new Sulṭān with a sword. This right cannot be traced earlier than 1648 and appears to have obtained recognition in the nineteenth century (*Isl.* xix, 184). It would seem that reforming Sulṭāns used the Mawlawī Order as a make-weight against the Bektāshīs, who supported the Janissaries, and then against the ʿUlamāʾ, who supported the treatment of the Muslim community as a privileged community against the *dhimmīs*. In recent times the Sulṭāns ʿAbd al-ʿAzīz and Meḥmed Reshād were members of the Order.

5. The ritual of the Order has been described by numerous travellers, e.g. J. P. Brown, *The Dervishes*, 1868, p. 198—206; 1927, p. 250—258; V. Cuinet, *loc. cit.*, p. 832; Garnett and Lukach in the works cited; M. Hartmann, *Der islamische Orient*, 1910, iii. 12; S. Anderson, in *MW*, 1923. The attire consisted of a cap called *sikke*, a long sleeveless skirt called *tennūre*, a jacket with sleeves called *deste-gul*, a waistband called *elif-lām-end*, and a cloak with sleves called *khirḳe*, thrown over the shoulders (in Lukach's description [Cyprus] "a violet gown worn over a dark green cassock"). The instruments employed according to the last writer (dealing with Ḳonya) are six: reed-flute, zither, rebeck, drum, tambourine, and one other. Cuinet enumerates four, of which three agree with the above, the last being *halīle*, vulgarly *zil*, a sort of small cymbal. Brown enumerates three: flute, violin, and kettle-drum. Those mentioned in the *Manāḳib* are rendered by Huart: *flûte violin* and *tambour de basque*. The service in Ḳonya according to Lukach was held twice a month after the Friday prayer; in Constantinople, where there were several *tekyes*, they were held more frequently, to enable the members of different *tekyes* to join in.

6. Administration of the Order. The head of the Order, resident at Ḳonya, had the titles *Mullā Khunkʿār*, *Ḥaḍret-i Pīr*, *Čelebi Mullā*, and *ʿAzīz Efendi*. A list of persons who have held the office is given by Hartmann (*loc. cit.*, p. 193) after the *Ḥaḳāʾiḳ-i adhkār-i mawlānā*, making 26 in all down to 1910; this list appears to be imperfect, and the Čelebi whom Lukach found in Ḳonya was uncertain whether he was the 39th or the 40th. The head of the establishment at Manissa counted as second in authority. Cuinet enumerates seven officials subordinate to the Čelebi at Ḳonya, but the names of several seem seriously mutilated. Others mention a secretary (*wekīl*). An account of the discipline which those who would enter the Order had had to endure is given by Huart (*Konia, la Ville des Derviches Tourneurs*, Paris 1897). They had to perform menial service for 1001 days, divided into periods of 40; when this was over, they were clothed in the uniform of the *tekye*, assigned cells, and instructed in the exercises of the Order; and they had to remain thus occupied till they believed themselves able to enter into relation with the Deity by means of whirling, meditation and music.

Bibliography: see especially the works of Brown, Cuinet, Hartmann, and Hasluck, cited above; Lucy M. Garnett, *Mysticism and Magic in Modern Turkey*, London 1912; H. C. Lukach, *The City of Dancing Derwishes*, London 1914; S. Anderson, in *MW*, 1923, p. 188—191; J. H. Mordtmann, *Um das Mausoleum des Molla Hunkiar in Konia*, in *Jahrbuch der asiat. Kunst*, ii (1925), p. 197; H. Ritter, in *Isl.* xxvi. (1942), p. 116 *sqq.*

MAWLID (A.) or Mawlūd (pl. *mawālīd*), time, place and celebration of the birth of any one, particularly of the Prophet Muḥammad (*mawlid al-nabī*). From the moment when Islām in its attitude to Muḥammad abandoned the lines laid down in the Ḳurʾānic view of him and began to bring his personality within the sphere of the supernatural, the scenes among which his earthly life had been passed naturally began to assume a higher sanctity in the eyes of his followers. Among these, the house in which he was born, the *mawlid al-nabī*, in the modern Sūḳ al-Lail in Mecca, the history of which is preserved principally in the chronicles of the town (ed. Wüstenfeld, i. 422), does not seem at first to have played a part of any note. It was al-Khaizurān (d. 173/789—90), the mother of Hārūn al-Rashīd, who first transformed it from a humble dwelling-house to a place of prayer. As they did to the tomb of the Prophet in Madīna, the pious now made pilgrimages also to his mawlid to show their reference for it and to receive a share of its blessings (*li 'l-tabarruk*). In time also the reverence in which the house was held found expression in its development in a fitting architectural fashion (Ibn Djubair, p. 114, 163; al-Batanūnī, p. 34; on the recent state of the house: Snouck Hurgronje, *Mekka*, i. 106; ii. 27).

Records of the observation of the birthday of the Prophet as a holy day only begin at a late date; according to the generally accepted view, the day was Monday the 12th Rabīʿ I. The story which Wüstenfeld originated, according to which the pious Shāfiʿī Karadjī (d. 343/944–5) observed this day by breaking his fast upon it, which he only did on one other occasion, the *ʿīd al-fiṭr* (*Abh. GWG*, xxxvii., No. 126), does not seem to find any confirmation in the sources and is in contradiction to the general custom of fasting on Monday, as this day plays a special part in the life of Muḥammad as the day of his birth, of his Hidjra and of his death (Ghazzālī, *Iḥyāʾ* [Būlāḳ], i. 363 and *pass.* On the Jewish origin of fasting on Monday, see Wensinck, *Mohammed en de Joden*, p. 126). But that on this day a special celebration was arranged, as distinct from private observation, one first learns for Mecca, where one would expect it earliest from the local traditions, from Ibn Djubair (d. 614/1217; p. 114—115), who however is obviously referring to a custom which had already been a considerable time in existence. The essential feature of the celebration is however only a somewhat considerable increase in the number of visitors to the Mawlid house which was exceptionally open the whole day for this purpose. This visit and the ceremonies associated with it (*masḥ* etc.) are carried through entirely in forms which are characteristic of the older Muslim cult of saints.

But just as the later cult of the Prophet cannot be put on a level with the reverence shown to other holy men, so new and special forms developed for his birthday celebrations, which in spite of minor differences in time and place show the same general features everywhere and are comprised under the name *lailat al-mawlid* or briefly *mawlid al-nabī*. An anticipation of the Mawlid celebration is found in Egypt as early as the middle and later Fāṭimid period. During the period of office of the vizier al-Afḍal (487–515/1095—1121), we hear that the "four Mawālid" were abolished but a little later revived in all their old glory (Maḳrīzī, *al-Ḵẖiṭaṭ*, i. 466; for the description of the festival: i. 433 *sqq.*). The celebration still took place in broad daylight and participation was practically limited to the official and religious circles of the city. There were not yet any preliminary celebrations; but we already have a solemn procession of all the dignitaries to the palace of the caliph, in whose presence — he sits, covered with a veil on one of the balconies of the palace — the three *ḵẖuṭabāʾ* of Cairo (cf. the art. KHAṬĪB) in succession deliver a religious address, during which a special ceremonial is observed. As to the matter of the discourses, we only know that they were like those delivered on the nights of the illumination so that they presumably dealt mainly with the occasion of the celebration. It is interesting to note that the mawlid ceremonies here are not confined to that of the Prophet but the mawlids of ʿAlī, Fāṭima and even that of the reigning Caliph, the *imām al-ḥāḍir*, are similarly observed. As in the fundamental idea of these celebrations (*mawlid al-imām al-ḥāḍir*), Shīʿa influence can also be traced in separate elements of it. It has not yet come to be a festival of the common people in the time of the Fāṭimids. This no doubt explains why — except in Maḳrīzī and Ḳalḳashandī — there is hardly any reference to these celebrations in the literature emanating from Sunnī circles, not even when writers like ʿAlī Pasha Mubārak are dealing with features peculiar to Cairo and deal very fully with the history of the Mawlid festival.

The memory of these Fāṭimid mawālid seems to have almost completely disappeared before the festivals in which Muslim authors unanimously find the origin of the Mawlid, the Mawlid which we find first celebrated in Arbalāʾ in 604/1207 by al-Malik Muẓaffar al-Dīn Kökbūrī, a brother-in-law of Saladin. The fullest account is given by a somewhat later contemporary, Ibn Ḵẖallikān (d. 681/1282), on whom later writers continually base their statements (e.g. al-Suyūṭī, *Ḥusn al-maḳṣid fī ʿamal al-mawlid* [Brockelmann, *GAL²*, ii. 202] and others). The personality of this ruler, his period so disturbed by the turmoil of the Crusades, and his milieu to which Ibn Ḵẖallikān calls special attention, lead us to suggest marked Christian influence in the development of this celebration; his close relations with the Ṣūfī movement on the other hand suggest the possibility of influence of quite a different nature. This is clear from the description of the celebrations. Preparations are begun long before and people come in from remote districts. The prince takes special care that the visitors are housed in splendid wooden ḳubbas specially built and they are entertained with music, singing and all kinds of amusements (shadow-plays, jugglers etc.).. The streets of the town were for weeks as busy as on the occasion of an annual fair. On the eve of the Mawlid night a torchlight procession took place from the citadel of the town to the ḵẖānḳah, led by the prince after the maghrib ṣalàt. Next morning the whole populace assembled in front of the ḵẖānḳah, where a wooden tower had been erected for the ruler and a pulpit for the *wāʿiẓ*. From this tower the prince surveyed not only the crowd as-

sembled to hear the address but also the troops summoned to be reviewed on the adjoining maidān. We are told nothing of the substance of the address. On its conclusion the prince summoned the distinguished guests up to the tower to give them robes of honour. The people were then feasted at the prince's expense in the maidān, while the notables were entertained in the ḵẖānḳah. The following night was spent by the prince with many others in the midst of the Ṣūfīs in *samāʿ* (Ibn Ḵẖallikān, ed. Wüstenfeld, vi. 66).

In contrast to the Fāṭimid celebrations, what is specially striking here is the large share taken in the festival by the Ṣūfīs and the common people, a circumstance which is all the more notable, as it is probably in this association with Ṣūfism that we have the reasons for the later great popularity of the mawlid. At the same time the torchlight procession, really foreign to Muslim sentiment, and borrowed from contemporary Christian customs at festivals, deserves our attention; it is not found at the celebration in Cairo which was purely a day ceremony, while the lavish entertainment of all present, especially with sweets, and the addresses are found in both cases. In this remarkable ceremonial, we seem really to have the foundation of all Mawlid celebrations. With the great political and religious movement, which we may call Saldjūḳ reaction, the Mawlid reached Egypt in Saladin's time, where it is significant that Ṣūfism very quickly took deep roots, thus preparing the way for an observance like the Mawlid, which is essentially kept up by popular religious sentiment.

The observance of the festival spread sooner or later from here to Mecca where its old form was transformed. Its further progress was along the coast of North Africa to Ceuta, Tlemcen and Fās to Spain but it also went eastwards to India, so that ultimately the whole Muslim world is united on this day in a ceremonial, frequently of unprecedented splendour, but alike everywhere in its main features. We have innumerable descriptions of the festival from all parts of the Muslim world, most fully for Mecca (*Chroniken*, ed. Wüstenfeld, iii. 438 *sq.*; Ibn Ḥadjar al-Haitamī, *Mawlid* [Brockelmann, *GAL²*, ii. 510]; for modern times: Snouck Hurgronje, *Mekka*, ii. 57 *sqq.*), where the celebrations have always been famous, for Egypt (J. W. Mc Pherson, *The Moulids of Egypt* [Cairo 1941]; Lane, *Manners and Customs⁵* [1871], ii. 166 *sqq.*) and the Indies (Snouck Hurgronje, *Achehnese*, i. 207; do., *Verspreide Geschriften*, ii. 8 *sqq.*; Herklots, *Qanoon e Islam* [1832], p. 233 *sq.*; Goldziher, *Culte des saints* [1880], p. 13; here it is frequently not the birth but the death of the Prophet that is commemorated). The Turkish element in Islām also has not resisted the advance of the celebration of the Mawlid (Turk.: *mewlūd*). Since Sulṭān Murād III introduced it in 996/1588 into the Ottoman empire, it has enjoyed increasing popularity. Since 1910 it has been celebrated as a national festival. Accurate descriptions of the festival as celebrated in the older period of the court of Constantinople (Mouradgea d'Ohsson, *Tableau général*, Paris 1787, i. 255 *sqq.*; *GOR*, viii. 441) clearly reveal its relationship with the festivals of a more popular nature in other lands of Islām.

One element in particular is very prominent, and that is the most characteristic one of the later celebrations, namely the recital of *mawlid*'s i.e. panegyrical poems of a very legendary character, which start with the birth of Muḥammad and praise his life and virtues in the most laudatory fashion. The origin of these addresses is already to be found in the religious addresses in Fāṭimid Cairo and in Arbela and perhaps in part at least goes back to the sermon usual at Christian festivals. The *Kitāb al-Tanwīr fī mawlid al-sirāḏj̲*, which Ibn Diḥya composed during his stay in Arbela at the suggestion of Kökbūrī was already famous as a *mawlid* at this period (Brockelmann, *GAL²*, i. 380). It was not till later times however that mawlids became a predominant element in the celebration, along with torchlight processions, feasting and the fairs in the street, ever increasing in size. In Mecca, for example, at the present day they form the main feature of the celebration in the mosque; among the pious they are the most popular evening entertainment for days before the celebration and teachers interrupt their lectures in order to deliver mawlids to the students and the people on the streets and in the coffee houses find edification and entertainment in listening to them. The number of such mawlids is quite considerable. Beside the famous but not very popular *Bānat Suʿād* of Kaʿb b. Zuhair of the older period, the *Burda* and the *Hamzīya* of al-Buṣīrī and their numerous imitations, there are a whole series of regular mawlids, some of which are intended to instruct like that of Ibn Ḥadjar al-Haitamī, others purely edifying like a shorter version of it, and notably that of Ibn al-Ḏj̲awzī (*GAL²*, i. 662) and al-Barzandj̲ī (*GAL²*, ii. 503). In addition to those in Arabic, there are a great many mawlids in Turkish (Irmg. Engelke, *Süleymān Tschelebi's Lobgedicht*, 1926). It is significant of the part played by these poems that they have passed from the mawlid celebrations to other festivals, so that the word has actually become a name for "festival" and particularly "feast" (*ʿaẓima*; cf. Snouck Hurgronje, *Mekka*, ii. 147, 154 and *pass.*; Becker, in *Isl.*, ii. 1911, p. 26 *sqq.*). Quite apart from any festivals, the recitation of mawlids is popular, in Palestine for example in fulfilment of a religious vow (T. Canaan, in *Journ. of the Pal. Or. Soc.*, vi., 1926, p. 55 *sqq.*; cf. also the introductory anecdote in the mawlid alleged to be by Ibn al-ʿArabī [*GAL²*, i. 582]). Like the substance of these mawlids, the form is also very regular. Prose and poetry alternate, interrupted frequently by appeals to utter blessings on the Prophet. Ḏh̲ikrs are usually added at the end.

The Mawlid as the finest expression of reverence for Muḥammad has found almost general recognition in Islām, as fulfilling a religious need of the people and as a result of the strength of the Ṣūfī movement. This must not however blind us to the fact that at all times there has also been vigorous opposition to it. This is found as early as the festival of Arbela (al-Suyūṭī, *Ḥusn al-maḳṣid*). The celebration is a *bidʿa*, a religious innovation, which is in sharp contradiction to tradition. Even ardent advocates of the festival confess this and the strictly orthodox, who adhere to the sunna, reject it most emphatically. But, as in so many other things, practice has here proved stronger than dogmatic theory. Once the festival had been thoroughly established in the religious life of the people, it was bound in time to find approval as an element of the *idj̲māʿ*. Its supporters found it easy to get this *bidʿa* legitimated, in theory at least, as a *bidʿa ḥasana*. When the festival had been accepted by the consensus of the community, the essential thing had been done and legitimate ground for opposition had been removed. While the opposition thus finds itself reduced to

combating the outer forms of the festival and its developments, its supporters are never tired of calling attention to the merit that lies in feeding the poor, in the more frequent reading of the Ḳurʾān and mawlids, and in expressions of joy over the birth of the Prophet and all that the day brings with it. It is significant of the character of the opposition that the opponents object to those very forms which show the influence of Ṣūfism (dancing, *samāʿ*, ecstatic phenomena etc.) or Christianity (processions with lights etc.). The most interesting document of this feud is a *fatwā* by al-Suyūṭī (*Ḥusn al-maḳṣid*) which gives a brief survey of the history of the festival, then discusses the pros and cons very fully and concludes that the festival deserves approval as a *bidʿa ḥasana*, provided that all abuses are avoided. Ibn Ḥadjar al-Haitamī in his *Mawlid* and Ḳuṭb al-Dīn (*Chroniken der Stadt Mekka*, ii. 439 *sq.*) take the same view, while Ibn al-Ḥādj̲idj̲ (d. 737/1336) as a more strict Mālikī condemns it most vehemently (*Kitāb al-Madk̲h̲al* [1320], i. 153 *sqq.*).

Although the height of this struggle was apparently reached in the eighth-ninth century, it did not completely die down in later years; indeed it received new life with the coming of the Wahhābīs. The cult of the Prophet is in such contradiction with their fundamental principle, the restoration of the ideal purified primitive Islām, that we can understand that they should completely disapprove of this, the most popular and most splendid expression of it. In doing this, they are only putting into action the protests of the extreme Ḥanbalī Ibn Taimīya (d. 728/1328), the famous precursor of their movement, against innovations which are contrary to the sunna (Ibn Taimīya against the holding of *k̲h̲atmas* in the Mawlid night: *Fatāwā* [Cairo 1326], i. 312). Similar ideas are still found to-day even when Wahhābism is rejected, notably in the school which Goldziher calls "Kulturwahhābismus", founded by the celebrated Muḥammad ʿAbduh (q.v.; d. 1905), who in connection with the worship of saints condemns the Mawlid also, in the periodical *al-Manār* (Goldziher, *Richtungen der islam. Koranauslegung*, p. 369 *sqq.*).

In the reverence shown to other Muslim saints, the Mawlids also play a great part. Although the success of an appeal to a saint does not depend on particular days, yet certain days and birthdays in particular are regarded as especially favourable. These celebrations are often connected with places to which a certain sanctity had been attached from pre-Islāmic times (the Mawlid of Shaik̲h̲ Ḥasan al-Badawī in Ṭanṭa: Goldziher, *Muh. Stud.*, ii. 338 *sq.*). There are also Mawlids of nameless saints. In the derwish orders, next to that of the Prophet, the Mawlid of the founder is held in particular popularity. ʿAlī Pas̲h̲a Mubārak (*K̲h̲iṭaṭ dj̲adīda*, i. 90; iii. 129 *sqq.*) mentions a large number of such festivities in modern Cairo, the characteristic features of which, he says, are the brilliant illumination of the town, the ceremonial procession (*maḥfil*; at the mawlid al-nabī: *mawkab*; cf. P. Kahle, in *Isl.*, vi., 1916, p. 155 *sq.*) and the great feasts. One cannot now imagine the popular religion of Egypt without these feasts.

Bibliography: Besides the works already mentioned: Muḥ. Tawfīḳ al-Bakrī, *Bait al-ṣiddīḳ*, Cairo 1323, p. 404 *sqq.*; al-Sak̲h̲āwī, *al-Tibr al-masbūk*, Būlāḳ 1896, p. 13 *sq.*; numerous Mawlid texts are given in the *Verzeichn. der arab. Hs. der Kgl. Bibl. zu Berlin*. Of special value is the Mawlid of Abu 'l-ʿAbbās b. ʿAbd Allāh al-Lak̲h̲mī of Ceuta (Brockelmann, *GAL²*, i. 452); J.-J. L .

Bargès, *Complément de l'histoire des Beni-Zeiyān*, 1887, p. 47 *sqq*; *Description de l'Egypte*, Paris 1826, xiv. 196 *sqq.*; A. Mez, *Renaissance d. Islāms*, 1922, p. 403; Goldziher, *Vorlesungen über den Islam*², 1925, p. 257.

MECCA.

I

On the eve of the Hid̲j̲ra.

It is with the birth of Muḥammad — between 570—580 A.D. — that Mecca suddenly emerges from the shadows of the past and thrusts itself upon the attention of the historians. The geographer Ptolemy seems to know it under the name Macoraba; but it must have been in existence long before his time. Mecca was probably one of the stations on the "incense route", the road by which the produce of East, especially valuable perfumes, came to the Mediterranean world. It owes its importance to its position at the intersection of great commercial routes. The town that had grown up around the well of Zamzam and the sanctuary of the Kaʿba was advantageously placed at the extreme ends of the Asia of the whites and the Africa of the blacks, near a breach in the chain of the Sarāt, close to a junction of roads leading from Babylonia and Syria to the plateaus of the Yemen, to the shores of the Indian Ocean and the Red Sea. By the latter it was in communication with the mysterious African continent.

At an early date we see the Meccans opening negotiations with the states adjoining Arabia. They obtained from them safe conducts and capitulations, permitting the free passage of their caravans. This is what their chronicles call the "guarantee of Caesar and of Chosroes". They also concluded agreements with the Negus of Abyssinia, with the principal s̲h̲aik̲h̲s of Nad̲j̲d, the *ḳail*'s of the Yemen, with the phylarchs of G̲h̲assān and of Ḥīra. In the negotiations with the Greeks and Persians the principal of the "open door" was not admitted. Commercial transactions were carried through at posts on the frontier or in towns specially designated for the purpose. In Palestine these were the ports of Aila and G̲h̲azza and perhaps also Jerusalem. In Syria, Boṣrā was their principal outlet, their great market.

Sūra cvi. 2 mentions as a permanent institution "the double caravan of winter and summer". The *nassāba*, genealogists, record the names of the Ḳurais̲h̲ chiefs who had succeeded in obtaining by negotiation permits to trade. The countries open to commerce in this way were called *wad̲j̲h*, direction, *matd̲j̲ar*, region of trade. There were innumerable restrictions, limiting the extension of the privilege. Eastern governments did not permit free trade. Distrustful of merchants even when her own subjects, Byzantium showed herself still more suspicious of foreigners, especially Bedouins. The latter had therefore to make heavy sacrifices, to pay onerous taxes, to pay continual customs-dues and tolls or to hand over hostages before negotiations could be begun. Mecca was not inspired by principles any more broad-minded; she took care to recompense herself from foreign traders and to levy various charges upon them, tithes, charges for permits to stay in the country, to travel about and to trade. Tithes had to be paid before entering Mecca. There was also, as at Palmyra, a "departure" tax or tax on exportation. In short, foreign merchants were entangled in a very intricate fiscal system, whether they settled in Mecca or only passed through it, especially those who did not obtain the *d̲j̲iwār* or guarantee of a local clan or notability.

The population. About the time of the Hid̲j̲ra, the people of Mecca claimed descent from a common ancestor. They called him Ḳurais̲h̲ or Fihr, sometimes also al-Naḍr surnamed Ḳurais̲h̲. The origins of the Ḳurais̲h̲ were humble and little is known of them. They formed one of the less wealthy branches of those who went back to the main stock of the Kināna. At first they led a miserable existence in the wild mountains around the sacred territory of Mecca. A condottiere from the northern Ḥid̲j̲āz, Ḳuṣaiy, is said to have installed them by force of arms in Mecca, which he took from the control of the tribe of K̲h̲uzāʿa. Some ten main clans can be distinguished among them: Hās̲h̲im, Umaiya, Nawfal, Zuhra, Asad, Taim, Mak̲h̲zūm, ʿAdī, D̲j̲umaḥ and Sahm. These occupied mainly the centre of the town, the bottom of the valley, al-Baṭḥāʾ, where the water of the well of Zamzam accumulated, the hollow where the Kaʿba stood. Their living in this neighbourhood earned them the epithet of *Abṭaḥī*, *Biṭāḥī* or *Ḳurais̲h̲ al-Biṭāḥ*. This central quarter of the town was regarded as that of the aristocracy and of the oldest Ḳurais̲h̲ families. Among these ten groups some owe to Islām a renown hitherto denied them. Such were the Taim and the ʿAdī rendered illustrious by the caliphs Abū Bakr and ʿUmar. Other clans more vaguely connected with the eponymous ancestor were thrust towards the outskirts of Mecca, on the lower slopes or in the gorges (*s̲h̲iʿb*) of the hills which dominate the town. They were called the "Ḳurais̲h̲ of the outskirts" (*Ḳurais̲h̲ al-Ẓawāhir*). Held in less consideration than their fellow-tribesmen of the Baṭḥāʾ, these suburbans had the advantage of being distinguished from them by their bravery. They supplied the Ḳurais̲h̲ community with its best soldiers and never failed to cast this up to the Meccans "of the centre".

Government and Administration. It is not easy to discover definite indications of this. There must however have been a rudimentary system of archives in which to preserve treaties of alliance and commerce, and later the equivalent of an office to take charge of the collection of taxes on foreign traders. Nowhere do we find any explicit allusion to the working of such administrative organisations. A tradition records the existence of purely honorary offices with no jurisdiction. But it does not agree either upon the number (ten or six) nor upon the functions of these offices. The only allusion to it is in the verses of a Madīnese poet, Ḥassān b. T̲h̲ābit. The office of "pavilion and reins" has nothing to do — as has been supposed — with the art of war. This dignity, which was an ancient one and no longer understood, was a memory of the ritual processions held in pagan Arabia. The *ḳubba* was simply the pavilion or portable tabernacle, containing the fetish of the tribe and solemnly carried on the back of a camel. The chiefs and notables took turns at holding the reins of the animal bearing this precious burden. It is taking nothing from the glory of K̲h̲ālid b. al-Walīd to say that he had not a monopoly of this privilege. Behind the legend of the Meccan dignities, we perceive the intention of glorifying the cradle of the Prophet. In giving it administrative institutions, an attempt was made to conceal the modest beginnings of the Hās̲h̲imīs and no less those of Abū Bakr and ʿUmar. The onerous office of *is̲h̲nāḳ*, which had to pay compensation for murder and injury, was far beyond the financial resources of a modest citizen like Abū Bakr. The entrusting to ʿUmar of the *safāra* or diplomatic missions cannot be reconciled with his extreme youth.

Lammens, for lack of a better term, called Mecca "a merchant republic". If Abū Sufyān is called "Shaikh and chief of the Ḳuraish", several of his contemporaries are given equally high sounding titles. There is not the slightest reason to think that he was a kind of Ḳuraish doge. The manner in which the events of the first eight years of the Hidjra are recorded produces the fallacious impression that he held the power in Mecca in his hands. In reality he was only the ablest and most intelligent of his peers, the chiefs of the Ḳuraish clans. As al-Fāsī pertinently observes, all were equal: "no one exercised authority unless delegated or freely permitted to do so by them". Did these chiefs constitute a regular official body? Yes, says tradition. Mecca is even said to have had a kind of Senate or Grand Council, the *dār al-nadwa.* It met only in extraordinary circumstances. Usually however, we find that it is in the *madjlis*, family groups or clubs, the *nādī ḳawm* opening on the square of the Kaʿba — the forum and bourse of the town — that affairs of general interest were dealt with.

The Ḳurʾān cannot conceive of authority without a council of notables, without the *malaʾ*. This institution is so frequently mentioned in the Ḳurʾān that the Prophet must have seen it working before his eyes. We think then that Mecca was ruled by the oligarchy of the *malaʾ*, the equivalent in the town of the *madjlis* of the nomad tribe. This was an assembly of the chiefs of the wealthiest and most influential families. This is why Umaiyads and Makhzūmīs are most usually mentioned as composing the *malaʾ*. Neither election nor birth could necessarily open the way to a seat on it, but rather the fame of services rendered, the prestige of ability and wealth. Thus it welcomed to its counsels the very wealthy Ibn Djudʿān, a member of the humble clan of Taim. An assembly of elders or if you like of senators, in conformity with the principle of seniority among the Arabs; its authority, purely moral, was limited to advising, studying, looking ahead and giving to the merchant community the benefit of the experience of its conscript fathers. In the absence of any coercive powers, persuasion was the only force it had to make its wishes obeyed. Hence the importance of eloquence in a milieu like this, where every family and every clan claimed autonomy. The cause of peace was in continual conflict with their claims. Without infringing their prerogatives, the *malaʾ* was able to exert moral pressure when the general good required it. The system recalls, though remotely, the organisation of Palmyra and of Venice.

Site and climate. In the form of an elongated crescent with its points turned towards the flanks of the Ḳuʿaiḳiʿān, the town was hemmed in by a double range of bare and steep hills. The centre of this ill-ventilated couloir coincided with a depression in the soil. The early town occupied the bottom of this; this was the *wādī*, the valley, the *baṭn Makka*, the hollow of Mecca. The centre, the lowest part of this depression, was called al-Baṭḥāʾ (cf. above). Some buildings in this quarter were so close to the Kaʿba that in the morning and in the evening their shadows were merged in that of the sacred edifice. Between these houses and the Kaʿba [q.v.] a narrow esplanade (*fināʾ*) lay below the level of the surrounding soil. This open area formed the primitive *masdjid*, a sanctuary open to the heavens. The pre-Islāmic Baṭḥāʾ knew no other. The ends of the little streets opening on this open space were called the "gates of the ḥaram or of the masdjid". The so-called gates or openings took their names from the clans settled around the Kaʿba. Thus one regularly spoke of the "gate of the Banū Djumaḥ". The walls of their houses served to mark the boundaries of the masdjid. It was on the ground floor of the buildings facing the sides of the Kaʿba that the *madjlis* or *nādī* of the chief families met, those that formed the *malaʾ* (cf. above).

In the suburbs (*ẓawāhir*), and at a later date in the ravines (*shiʿb*) which had been dug by erosion out of the flanks of the hills, was a confusion of poor houses, low and ramshackle hovels. The unpleasant features of a town of this kind are obvious. The geographer Maḳdisī has summed these up strikingly: "suffocating heat, deadly winds, clouds of flies". The continual difficulty was the dearth of water. The population was dependent on the variable output of the Zamzam. There were other wells, mainly outside the town. Those inside had a doubtful reputation. The scarcity of drinking-water is evident from the amount of precaution taken when some thousands of pilgrims had to be supplied. In such deplorable conditions one can imagine what suffering the long days brought, *ramḍāʾ Makka* "the burning heat of Mecca"; why the great families preferred to send their children to be brought up in the desert; why the *sīra* only incidentally mentions the plague of Mecca (*wabāʾ Makka*). Smallpox is mentioned only in connection with the enemies of the Prophet.

Rains are few and far between. Droughts sometimes last for four years. But when the winter season is wet, the rains may sometimes attain an unheard-of degree of violence. To the east of Mecca a rocky wall raises its steep barrier, a succession of strata and summits merging into the chain of the Sarāt. These jagged hills collect on their flanks the surplus rains of the monsoon which brings fertility to the Yemen. All along these slopes, where no shrub interrupts the fall — at the bottom of each a *sail* is formed — the cataracts augmented by all these tributaries fall into the hollow of Mecca, *baṭn Makka*, of which the Kaʿba occupies the bottom. The waters rush to this depression, they force a passage through the "gates of the masdjid" and flow over the area around the sanctuary. They fill it and rise to attack the Kaʿba. Before the Hidjra, the Ḳuraish syndicate seems to have paid no heed to the flooding or said they were powerless to prevent it. Efforts made by the caliphs yielded "only mediocre results".

This is why destructions by the *sail* fill the annals of Mecca. On several occasions their violence has overthrown the Kaʿba and turned the court of the great mosque into a lake. As a result of the floods, epidemics broke out. The deposit of filth brought by the waters polluted the wells: bodies left unburied formed centres of epidemic infection. The annalists avoid dwelling on this, troubled by the Tradition which says that the plague never reaches Mecca. The absolute sterility of the soil brought another scourge, that of famine. The slightest irregularity in the convoys of grain from Syria or the Sarāt was enough to cause it. It continues to figure along with the ravages of flood and plague in the annals of the town.

Economic life and finance. On examining closely the picturesque literature of the *sīra* and *ḥadīth*, one receives the impression of an intense business activity bursting out of the narrow and sterile valley of Mecca. The Ḳur'ān only strengthens this impression. All his life the Prophet retained the impress of his Ḳuraish education and training. This fundamentally mercantile character is revealed at every turn.

Writing and arithmetic! One is amazed at their importance in the economic life of the town. Relying on the Ḳur'ānic epithet *ummī*, i.e. pagan, gentile, and on biassed writers like al-Balādhurī, it has been held that, except for some fifteen individuals mentioned by name, all the pre-Hidjran Ḳuraish were illiterate. Alongside of the "book" of accounts, the scales always figure in the Meccan shops: not so much to weigh goods as to verify and check payments of all kinds including cash. Now, coins were not plentiful on the Meccan market; they were supplemented by the precious metals, ingots of gold and silver, by *tibr*, gold dust. Only the scales could determine the value. In the more delicate cases, recourse was had to the services of a *wazzān* or professional weigher.

It would be difficult to imagine a society in which capital enjoyed a more active circulation. The *tādjir*, business man, was not only engaged in hoarding, in gathering wealth into his strong boxes. He had a blind faith in the unlimited productivity of capital, in the virtue of credit. Brokers and agents, the bulk of the population lived on credit. The sleeping partnership (*muḍāraba*) was much in favour, especially the "partnership for the half", which supposes 50% participation in the profits by the sleeping partners. Thanks to the development of these institutions the humblest sums could be invested, down to a gold dinār or even a *nashsh* or half dīnār. Such a flexible organisation stimulated even the humblest to take his share in commercial enterprises.

The coins brought to Mecca were of very different kinds: the *denarius aureus* of the Byzantines and the silver drachm of the Sāsānids and Ḥimyar. These pieces often worn, rudely engraved, very unequal in weight and format, came from the most varied mints. Only the money-changer had the requisite flair, the eye sufficiently trained to deal with the confusion of currencies, to determine accurately the standards, values, and the kinds in circulation. In addition there were the complications caused by the difference of standard and the oscillations of exchange. The Byzantine provinces, Syria and Egypt, were among the *ahl al-dhahab* or countries with a gold standard. Babylonia was *ahl al-wariḳ*, a land with a silver, the Sāsānian, standard. On the eve of the departure of the caravans for Syria, there were regular battues in search of dīnārs. The Meccan *tādjir* was not distinct from the financier. His first article of trade was money. When occasion arose, he invested his capital in business, in the organisation of large caravans. To the leaders of the caravan, to the traders and to the factors, he advanced the funds necessary for their operations.

Primarily a clearing house, a banking town, Mecca had customs and institutions peculiar to this kind of transaction and to finance. Sometimes it is *ribā*, usury, in all its ugliness: dīnar for dīnār, dirham for dirham, i.e. 100% interest. To the condemnation of *ribā* in the Ḳur'ān, the Ḳuraish objected that they saw in it only "a kind of sale" (sūra ii. 275), of letting out capital for a rent. Speculation too was rampant, on the rates of exchange, the load of a caravan which one tried to buy up, the yield of the harvests and of the flocks and lastly the provisioning of the town. Fictitious associations were formed and sales were made on which loans were borrowed. "Every Arab", says Strabo, "is either a trader or a broker". In Mecca, says the ḥadīth, "he who was not a merchant counted for nothing". In setting out on a military expedition the citizens always took merchandise along with them. This is what they did when going to relieve the Badr caravan. The first thing the Meccan *muhādjirūn* did on arriving in Madīna was to ask the way to the market-place. The women shared these commercial instincts: Abū Djahl's mother ran a perfumery business. The activities of the *tādjira* Khadīdja are well known. Hind, the wife of Abū Sufyān, sold her merchandise among the Kalbīs of Syria. Like their husbands the Meccan women had financial interests in the caravans. On the return of the convoys they gathered round Abū Sufyān to know what their money and their contributions had earned and to get their share of the profits.

The caravans. The organisation of a caravan was the subject of interminable discussions in the *nādī* around the Kaʿba. Its departure and return were events of public interest. The whole population was associated with it. En route it remained in continual communication with the metropolis through Beduins met on the journey or special couriers. Abū Sufyān sent one of these messengers to describe the critical position of the Badr caravan. It cost him 20 dīnārs, an enormous sum, but one proportionate to the value of the convoy in which Mecca had 50,000 dīnārs invested. The Meccan caravans were of considerable size. Neither horses nor mules appeared in them. The number of camels on occasion rose to 2,500. The men (merchants, guides [*dalīl*] and guards) varied from 100 to 300. The escort was strengthened on approaching areas infested by bandits (*ṣaʿlūk*) or when traversing the territory of hostile tribes. The Badr caravan may be taken as typical. We do not know of another in which the capital invested attained such an amount. The greater part was supplied by the important Umaiyad firm of Abū Uḥaiḥa, i.e. the family of Saʿīd b. al-ʿĀṣ. This firm had formed a company of the family, adding to their own considerable reserves the contributions of its sleeping partners. To their 30,000 dīnārs the other Umaiyad houses added 10,000. Four-fifths of the capital of the Badr caravan was therefore of Umaiyad origin. We can understand why the direction and supreme control of the convoy was entrusted to Abū Sufyān, who was personally interested in the enterprise.

In the first place a caravan from Mecca carried skins and leather, sometimes also the *zabīb* of Ṭā'if, a kind of currant; then ingots of gold and silver partly from the mines of the Banū Sulaim and *tibr*, gold dust from Africa. The texts frequently call it *laṭīma*, i.e. a convoy laden with perfume and rare spices. Of the perfumes, the most esteemed came not from the Ḥidjāz, but from southern Arabia, the "land of frankincense", or even from India and Africa. To these might be added aromatic gums and medicinal drugs, like the senna of Mecca, all objects of small bulk and purchased at higher prices by the luxury of the civilized countries.

From the Yemen the Meccan caravans brought back the products of India, the silks of China, the rich *ʿadanī* cloths, so called from ʿAden. Besides gold dust, the main exports of Africa were slaves and ivory. From Africa Mecca recruited her labourers and her mercenary soldiers, the Aḥābīsh or Abyssinians. In Egypt and in Syria, the Ḳuraish traders bought luxury articles, products of the industry of the Mediterranean, mainly cotton, linen or silk stuffs and cloths dyed in vivid purple. From Boṣrā and the Sharāt (Syria) came arms, cereals and oil, much appreciated by the Beduins. The pace of the caravan was slow but the articles transported, leather, metals, scented woods, feared neither damage nor the delays of long journeys. The expenses were confined to the hire of the animals, the payment of the escort, the tolls and presents to the chiefs of the tribes. With such an economical organisation, the profits of 100% attested by our authors were quite usual. This was the case with the caravan of Badr "each dīnār having brought back a dīnār". Two years after this brilliant affair, the Companions of the Prophet who had sought refuge in Madīna were able to carry out as profitable a transaction in the same field "since each of their dirhams gained a second dirham", that is to say a profit of 100% again.

Fortunes in Mecca. We can now imagine how money had gradually accumulated in the chests of the Meccan financiers, who where naturally of a saving disposition. This explains Pliny the Elder's ill-humour when he recalls "the millions of sesterces which the Arabs take annually from the Roman Empire giving nothing in return (*nihil invicem redimentibus*"; *Hist. Natur.*, vi. 28). This last statement is an exaggeration, but it should be remembered that the Meccan caravan carried only articles of high value, and that with regard to the Empire the Arabs were mainly importers, so that the trade balance was always very much in their favour. The 30,000 dīnārs invested by the one house of Abū Uḥaiḥa in the Badr caravan suggests that H. Winckler is quite right when he tells us to think of the Palmyra of Zenobia if we wish to get an idea of the financial capacity of Mecca. The fortunes of the Makhzūmīs were no less than those of their Umaiyad rivals. The Taimī ʿAbd Allāh b. Djudʿān must have been a millionaire if the poet thought of comparing him to Caesar. The principal organisers of the Badr caravan were also millionaires. The thousands of dīnārs subscribed by them did not even represent all their fortune. Other portions of their capital were out at interest or put in other speculations. Among other millionaires we may mention the Makhzūmīs Walīd b. al-Mughīra and ʿAbd Allāh, father of the poet ʿUmar b. Abī Rabīʿa.

Next to these representatives of high finance come the well-to-do Meccans, like ʿAbd al-Raḥmān b. ʿAwf who had a capital of 8,000 dīnārs and al-Ḥārith b. ʿĀmir and Umaiya b. Khalaf. Of the latter two, the first had 1,000 and the second 2,000 dīnārs in the Badr caravan. Lastly there were the small traders, brokers and shopkeepers who formed the petite bourgeoisie of the town. To their commerce a number added the supervision of some industry like ironwork or carpentry. The most typical representative of this class is given us by the future caliph Abū Bakr, a *bazzāz*, retailer of cloth. He belonged like Abū Djudʿān to the plebeian clan of Taim, rich in men and women of initiative, like ʿĀʾisha, daughter of Abū Bakr. He seems to have had a capital of 40,000 dirhams. ʿAbbās, the uncle of the Prophet, is also mentioned among the rich bankers of Mecca, but we have no details about him. The other Hāshimīs lived in circumstances bordering on poverty. Those Meccans most certainly must have been wealthy who paid without a murmur the enormous ransoms demanded for their relatives after the defeat of Badr. After this sacrifice — it cost them not less than 200,000 dirhams — the Meccan chiefs gave up their share of the profits in the Badr enterprise — some 25,000 dīnārs — to prepare for the revenge. They did this *ṭaiyibu 'l-anfus* "with a good heart", with the easy grace of opulent financiers, used to running the risks of speculations on a large scale. One touching detail is recorded. They refused to touch the modest shares of the small contributors. This example shows how at Mecca, "the strong", *ahl al-ḳuwwa* (Wāḳidī), i.e. the patricians, were able in critical circumstances to realise a spirit of solidarity and of sound democracy.

Mecca before the Hidjra had neither ships nor a port. It was only exceptionally that foreign ships cast anchor in the little bay of Shuʿaiba off a desert shore. It was here that the Byzantine ship was wrecked, the wood of which went to the rebuilding of the Kaʿba. It was to Shuʿaiba that the first Muslim emigrants for Abyssinia went, no doubt on hearing that two merchant ships had touched there. More rarely sailings took place from the desolate shore of Djidda, which was nearer Mecca. From the time of ʿUthmān, Djidda took the place of Shuʿaiba and became the port of the Ḳuraish metropolis. When Muḥammad settled in Madīna and cut their communications with Syria, the Meccan leaders never thought of taking to the sea but resigned themselves to the enormous detour through al-Nadjd. The creation of an Arab navy was the work of the caliph Muʿāwiya.

2. After the Hidjra. We need not rehearse the events of the first eight years of the Hidjra. They are summed up in the struggle with the Prophet. This struggle and the eventual surrender of Mecca, were fatal to its economic prosperity. One after the other, the great families migrated to Madīna, now the capital of Islām. This tendency increased under the first three caliphs, who made their headquarters among the Anṣār. ʿAlī definitely left Arabia to settle in Kūfa. Richly endowed by the state, the leading Ḳuraish, becoming generals and governors of provinces, lost interest in commerce. No more is heard about caravans or fairs in the Ḥidjāz. It was only at the period of the pilgrimage that Mecca became alive again and saw the caliphs reappear at the head of the pilgrims. The conquest of the ʿIrāḳ dealt the last blow to the economic decline of western Arabia. The Indian trade resumed its old route by the Persian Gulf and the valley of the Euphrates. Direct communication was established by land with the markets of the middle east.

Umaiyad period. The situation improved with the coming of the Umaiyad dynasty. Muʿāwiya took an active interest in his native town. He erected buildings there and developed agriculture in the environs, dug wells and built dams to store up the water. Under his successors, especially the Marwānids, Mecca became a city of pleasure and ease, the rendezvous of poets and musicians, attracted by the brilliant society formed by the sons of the Companions of the Prophet. Many people returned to live in Mecca after making their fortunes in the government of conquered provinces. Contact with foreign civilisations had made them refined and fastidious. They had become accustomed to baths, a luxury which presupposes an abundant water-supply. Water had to be procured from the hills of the Sarāt. Khālid al-Ḳasrī's name is associated with this undertaking which changed the aspect of the town. To meet the scourge of flood, the caliphs ʿUmar and ʿUthmān had called in the aid of Christian engineers, who built barrages in the high-lying quarters. They also secured the area round the Kaʿba by making dykes and embankments. The Umaiyad caliphs continued and completed these works. They dug a new bed along the course of the *sail* and endeavoured to break its violence by barriers built at different levels. Their great anxiety was to protect the depression of the Baṭḥāʾ where the Kaʿba stood. The skill of the engineers of the period did not succeed in overcoming the topographical difficulties nor in averting the ravages of the winter rains, regular cloudbursts. They were frustrated by the steep slope of the ground, still further aggravated by the unusual shape of the Baṭḥāʾ, a basin with no outlet. The houses on the bank of the *sail* were taken down and the alleys adjoining the Kaʿba removed. Each modification of the old plan meant the sacrifice of more buildings. These clearances in time changed the traditional aspect of Mecca, where the *sail* continued to sow destruction.

Along with these precautions against flooding an endeavour was made to enlarge the exiguous court around the Kaʿba. Islām aspired to possess a temple in keeping with its worldwide claims. Successive expropriations begun by ʿUmar and finished by Walīd I prepared an esplanade. The plan of the great mosque [cf. AL-MASDJID AL-ḤARĀM] with its galleries, a vast courtyard with the Kaʿba in the centre, is the work of the Umaiyad caliph. He had the assistance of Christian architects from Syria and Egypt to carry it out. The important governorship of the Ḥidjāz with its three cities, Madīna, Mecca and Ṭāʾif, could in principle be given only to a member of the ruling family. Among the most celebrated of these Umaiyads may be mentioned Saʿīd b. al-ʿĀs and the two future caliphs Marwān b. al-Ḥakam and ʿUmar b. ʿAbd al-ʿAzīz. When no Umaiyad was available the choice fell upon an official of tried capacity like Ḥadjdjādj and Khālid al-Ḳasrī. At first they were given Ṭāʾif and then transferred to Mecca. It was only after this probation that the three towns were entrusted to them. But even then the centre of government remained in Madīna, which under the Umaiyads eclipsed Mecca by its political importance and by the fact that it was the home of the new Muslim aristocracy.

Under Yazīd I, the rising of ʿAbd Allāh b. al-Zubair [q.v.] brought Syrian troops to Mecca. The rebel had made his headquarters in the court of the great mosque. A scaffold of wood, covered with straw, protected the Kaʿba. The carelessness of a Meccan soldier set it on fire. Ibn al-Zubair rebuilt the edifice and included the Ḥidjr within it [see KAʿBA]. When Ḥadjdjādj had overthrown the Zubairid anti-caliph, he restored the Kaʿba to its former dimensions which have since remained unaltered. In 129/747 a Khāridjī rebel from the Yemen seized Mecca without meeting opposition. He was soon defeated and slain by the troops of the caliph Marwān II. In 132/750, Mecca passed with the rest of the caliphate under the rule of the ʿAbbāsids.

II

1. Mecca under the ʿAbbāsids down to the foundation of the Sharīfate (132—350/750—961).

Although the political centre of gravity in Islām now lay in Baghdād, this period at first presents the same picture as under Umaiyad rule. The *Ḥaramān* are as a rule governed by ʿAbbāsid princes or individuals closely connected with them (*Die Chroniken der Stadt Mekka*, ed. Wüstenfeld, ii. 181 *sqq.*). Sometimes Mecca and Ṭāʾif were under one ruler, who was at the same time leader of the Ḥadjdj, while Madīna had a separate governor of its own.

Arabia had however from the first century A.H. contained a number of ʿAlid groups, who, as was their wont, fished in troubled waters, lay in wait as brigands to plunder the Ḥadjdj caravans and from time to time hoisted their flags when they were not restrained either by the superior strength or by the bribes of the caliphs. We find al-Manṣūr (136—156/754—774) already having trouble in Western Arabia. Towards the end of the reign of al-Mahdī (156—169/774—785) a Ḥasanid, Ḥusain b. ʿAlī, led a raid on Madīna, which he ravaged; at Fakhkh near Mecca, he was cut down with many of his followers by the ʿAbbāsid leader of the Ḥadjdj. The place where he was buried is now called al-Shuhadāʾ. It is significant that he is regarded as the "martyr of Fakhkh" (Ṭabarī, iii. 551 *sqq.*; *Chron. Mekka*, i. 435, 501 *sq.*).

Hārūn al-Rashīd on his nine pilgrimages expended vast sums in Mecca. He was not the only ʿAbbāsid to scatter wealth in the holy land. This had a bad effect on the character of the Meccans. There were hardly any descendants left of the old distinguished families and the population grew accustomed to living at the expense of others and were ready to give vent to any dissatisfaction in rioting. This attitude was all too frequently stimulated by political conditions.

In the reign of al-Maʾmūn (198—218/813—833) it was again ʿAlids, Ḥusain al-Afṭas and Ibrāhīm b. Mūsā, who extended their rule over Madīna, Mecca and the Yemen (Ṭabarī, iii. 981 *sqq.*; *Chron. Mecca*, ii. 328), ravaged Western Arabia and plundered the treasures of the Kaʿba. How strong ʿAlid influence already was at this time is evident from the fact that Maʾmūn appointed two ʿAlids as governors of Mecca (Ṭabarī, iii. 1039; *Chron. Mecca*, ii. 191 *sqq.*).

With the decline of the ʿAbbāsid caliphate after the death of Maʾmūn, a period of anarchy began in the holy land of Islām, which was frequently accompanied by scarcity or famine. It became the regular custom for a number of rulers to be represented at the Ḥadjdj in the plain of ʿArafāt and to have their flags unfurled; the holy city was rarely spared fighting on these occasions. The safety of the pilgrim caravans was considerably affected; it was very often ʿAlids who distinguished themselves in plundering the pilgrims.

The ʿAlid cause received an important reinforcement at this time by the foundation of a Ḥasanid dynasty in Ṭabaristān (Ṭabarī, iii. 1523—1533, 1583 *sq.*, 1682—1685, 1693 *sq.*, 1840, 1880, 1884 *sq.*, 1940). In Mecca the repercussion of this event was felt in the appearance of two Ḥasanids (*Chron. Mekka*, i. 343; ii. 10, 195, 239 *sq.*), Ismāʿīl b. Yūsuf and his brother Muḥammad, who also ravaged Madīna and Djidda in the way that had now become usual (251/865—866).

The appearance of the Ḳarmaṭians [q.v.] brought still further misery to the country in the last fifty years before the foundation of the sharīfate (Ṭabarī, iii. 2124—2130). Hard pressed themselves at the heart of the empire, the caliphs were hardly able even to think of giving active support to the holy land, and, besides, their representatives had not the necessary forces at their disposal. From 304/916 onwards the Ḳarmaṭians barred the way to the pilgrim caravans. In 317/930, 1500 Ḳarmaṭian warriors raided Mecca, massacred the inhabitants by the thousand and carried off the Black Stone to Baḥrain. It was only when they realised that such deeds were bringing them no nearer their goal — the destruction of official Islām — that their zeal began to relax and in 338/950 they even brought the Stone back again. Mecca was relieved of serious danger from the Ḳarmaṭians. The following years bear witness to the increasing influence of the ʿAlids in western Arabia in connection with the advance of Fāṭimid rule to the east and with Būyid rule in Baghdād. From this time the Meccan ʿAlids are called by the title of Sharīf which they have retained ever since.

2. From the foundation of the Sharīfate to Ḳatāda (c. 350—598/960—1200).

a. The Mūsāwīs. The sources do not agree as to the year in which Djaʿfar took Mecca. 966, 967, 968 and the period between 951 and 961 are mentioned (*Chron. Mekka*, ii. 205 *sqq.*). ʿAlids had already ruled before him in the holy land. It is with him however that the reign of the Ḥasanids in Mecca begins, who are known collectively as sharīfs, while in Madīna this title is given to the reigning Ḥusainids.

The rise and continuance of the sharīfate indicates the relative independence of Western Arabia in face of the rest of the Islāmic world from a political and religious point of view. Since the foundation of the sharīfate, Mecca takes the precedence possessed by Madīna hitherto.

How strongly the Meccan sharīfate endeavoured to assert its independence, is evident in this period from two facts. In 365/976 Mecca refused homage to the Fāṭimid caliph. Soon afterwards the Caliph began to besiege the town and cut off all imports from Egypt. The Meccans were soon forced to give in, for the Ḥidjāz was dependent on Egypt for its food supplies (Ibn al-Athīr, *Kāmil*, viii. 491; *Chron. Mekka*, ii. 246).

The second sign of the Sharīfs' feeling of independence is Abu 'l-Futūḥ's (384—432/994—1039) setting himself up as caliph in 402/1011 (*Chron. Mekka*, ii. 207; Ibn al-Athīr, *Kāmil*, ix. 233, 317). He was probably induced to do this by al-Ḥākim's heretical innovations in Egypt. The latter however was soon able to reduce the new caliph's sphere of influence so much that he had hurriedly to return to Mecca where in the meanwhile one of his relatives had usurped the power. He was forced to make terms with al-Ḥākim in order to be able to expel his relative.

With his son Shukr (432—453/1039—1061) the dynasty of the Mūsāwīs, i.e. the descendants of Mūsā b. ʿAbd Allāh b. Mūsā b. ʿAbd Allāh b. Ḥasan b. Ḥasan b. ʿAlī b. Abī Ṭālib came to an end. He died without leaving male heirs, which caused a struggle within the family of the Ḥasanids with the usual evil results for Mecca. When the family of the Banū Shaiba (q.v.; the Shēbīs) went so far as to confiscate for their private use all precious metals in the house of Allāh, the ruler of Yaman, al-Ṣulaiḥī (*Chron. Mekka*, ii. 208, 210 *sqq.*; Ibn al-Athīr, *Kāmil*, ix. 422; x. 19, 38), intervened and restored order and security in the town. This intervention by an outsider appeared more intolerable to the Ḥasanids than fighting among themselves. They therefore proposed to al-Ṣulaiḥī that he should instal one of their number as ruler and leave the town.

He therefore appointed Abū Hāshim Muḥammad (455—487/1063—1094) as Grand Sharīf. With him begins the dynasty of the

b. Hawāshim (455—598/1063—1200), which takes its name from Abū Hāshim Muḥammad, a brother of the first Sharīf Djaʿfar; the two brothers were descendants in the fourth generation from Mūsā II, the ancestor of the Mūsāwīs.

Duing the early years of his reign, Abū Hāshim had to wage a continual struggle with the Sulaimānī branch, who thought themselves humiliated by his appointment. These Sulaimānīs were descended from Sulaimān, a brother of the Mūsā II above mentioned.

The reign of Abū Hāshim is further noteworthy for the shameless way in which he offered the suzerainty, i.e. the mention in the *khuṭba* as well as the change of official rite which is indicated by the wording of the *adhān*, to the highest bidder i.e. the Fāṭimid caliph or the Saldjūḳ sulṭān (*Chron. Mekka*, 253; Ibn al-Athīr, x. 67). It was very unwelcome to the Meccans that imports from Egypt stopped as soon as the official mention of the Fāṭimid in the khuṭba gave way to that of the caliph. The change was repeated several times with the result that the Saldjūḳ, tired of this comedy, sent several bodies of Turkomans to Mecca.

The ill-feeling between Sulṭān and Sharīf also inflicted great misery on pilgrims coming from the ʿIrāḳ. As the leadership of the pilgrim caravans from this country had gradually been transferred from the ʿAlids to Turkish officials and soldiers, Abū Hāshim did not hesitate occasionally to fall upon the pilgrims and plunder them (*Chron. Mekka*, ii. 254; Ibn al-Athīr, x. 153).

The reign of his successor is also marked by covetousness and plundering. The Spanish pilgrim Ibn Djubair, who visited Mecca in 579/1183 and 58.'1185, gives hair-raising examples of this. Even then however the Hawāshim were no longer absolutely their own masters, as over ten years before, the Aiyūbid dynasty had not only succeeded to the Fāṭimids in Egypt but was trying to get the whole of nearer Asia into their power.

Saladin's brother, who passed through Mecca on his way to South Arabia, abandoned his intention of abolishing the sharīfs, but the place of honour on the Ḥadjdj belonged to the Aiyūbids and their names were mentioned in the khuṭba after those of the ʿAbbāsid caliph and the sharīf (Ibn Djubair, p. 75, 95). The same Aiyūbid in 581/1186 also did away with the Shīʿī (here Zaidī, for the Sharīfs had hitherto been Zaidīs) form of the *adhān* (*Chron. Mekka*, ii. 214), had coins struck in Saladin's name and put the fear of the law into the hearts of the sharīf's bodyguard, who had not shrunk from crimes of robbery and murder, by severely punishing their misdeeds. — A further result of Aiyūbid suzerainty was that the Shāfiʿī rite became the predominant one.

But even the mighty Saladin could only make improvements in Mecca. He could abolish or check the worst abuses but the general state of affairs remained as before.

3. The rule of Ḳatāda and his descendants down to the Wahhābī period (c. 1200—1788).

In the meanwhile a revolution was being prepared which was destined to have more far-reaching consequences than any of its predecessors. Ḳatāda, a descendant of the Mūsā (see above) from whom the Mūsāwīs and the Hawāshim were descended, had gradually extended his estates as well as his influence from Yanbuʿ to Mecca and thad gathered a considerable following in the town. According to some sources, his son Ḥanẓala made all preparations for the decisive blow on the holy city; according to others, Ḳatāda seized the town on the 27th Radjab when the whole population was away performing a lesser *ʿumra* in memory of the completion of the building of the Kaʿba by ʿAbd Allāh b. al-Zubair, which was celebrated on this day along with the festival of Muḥammad's ascension to heaven. However it came about, Ḳatāda's seizure of the town meant the coming of an able and strongwilled ruler, the ancestor of all later sharīfs. He steadfastly followed his one ambition to make his territory an independent principality. Everything was in his favour; that he did not achieve his aim was a result of the fact that the Ḥidjāz was once again at the intersection of many rival lines of political interest.

Ḳatāda began by ruining his chances with the great powers; he ill-treated the son of the Aiyūbid al-Malik al-ʿĀdil (540—615/1145—1218) in brutal fashion (*Chron. Mekka*, ii. 263). He roused the ire of the caliph by his attitude to pilgrims from the ʿIrāḳ. He was able however to appease the latter and the embassy he sent to Baghdād returned with gifts from the caliph. The caliph also invited him to visit Baghdād. According to some historians, however, the sharīf turned home again before he actually reached Baghdād. On this occasion, he is said to have expressed his policy of the "splendid isolation" of the Ḥidjāz in verse, as he did in his will in prose (see Snouck Hurgronje, *Qatâdah's Policy of Splendid Isolation* etc. in *Verspr. Geschr.* iii. 355 *sqq.*).

On the other hand, Ḳatāda is said to have vigorously supported an imām of Ḥasanid descent in founding a kingdom in the Yemen. After the reconquest of this region by a grandson of al-ʿĀdil, the Aiyūbids of Egypt, Syria, and South Arabia were mentioned in the khuṭba in Mecca along with the Caliph and the Sharīf.

Ḳatāda's life ended in a massacre which his son Ḥasan carried out in his family to rid himself of possible rivals (*Chron. Mekka*, ii. 215, 263 *sqq.*; Ibn al-Athīr, *Kāmil*, xii. 262 *sqq.*). The Aiyūbid prince Masʿūd however soon put a limit to his ambition and had Mecca governed by his generals. On his death however power again passed into the hands of the sharīfs, whose territory was allowed a certain degree of independence by the rulers of the Yaman as a bulwark against Egypt.

About the middle of the xiiith century the world of Islām assumes a new aspect as the result of the advent of persons and happenings of great importance. In 1258 the taking of Baghdād by Hūlāgū put an end to the caliphate. The pilgrim caravan from the ʿIrāḳ was no longer of any political significance. In Egypt power passed from the Aiyūbids to the Mamlūks; Sulṭān Baibars (658—676/1260—1277) was soon the most powerful ruler in the lands of Islām. He was able to leave the government of Mecca in the hands of the Sharīf, because the latter, Abū Numaiy, was an energetic individual who ruled with firmness during the second half of the xiiith century (1254—1301). His long reign firmly established the power of the descendants of Ḳatāda.

Nevertheless the first half century after his death was almost entirely filled with fighting between different claimants to the throne. ʿAdjlān's reign also (1346—1375) was filled with political unrest, so much so that the Mamlūk Sulṭān is said on one occasion to have sworn to exterminate all the sharīfs. ʿAdjlān introduced a political innovation by appointing his son and future successor Aḥmad co-regent in 1361 by which step he hoped to avoid a fratricidal struggle before or after his death.

A second measure of ʿAdjlān's also deserves mention, namely the harsh treatment of the *muʾadhdhin* and imām of the Zaidīs; this shows that the reigning sharīfs had gone over to the predominant rite of al-Shāfiʿī and forsaken the Zaidī creed of their forefathers.

Among the sons and successors of ʿAdjlān special mention may be made of Ḥasan (1396—1426) because he endeavoured to extend his sway over the whole of the Ḥidjāz and to guard his own financial interests carefully, at the same time being able to avoid giving his Egyptian suzerain cause to interfere.

But from 1425 he and his successors had to submit to a regular system of control as regards the allotment of the customs.

From the time of Ḥasan, in addition to the bodyguard of personal servants and freedmen, we find a regular army of mercenaries mentioned which was passed from one ruler to another. But the mode of the sharīfs, unlike that of other Oriental rulers, remained simple and in harmony with their Arabian surroundings. As a vassal of the Egyptian Sulṭān the sharīf received from him every year his *tawḳīʿ* and a robe of honour. On the ceremonies associated with the accession of the sharīfs see Snouck Hurgronje, *Mekka*, i. 97 *sq.*

Of the three sons of Ḥasan who disputed the position in their father's lifetime, Barakāt (I) was chosen by the sulṭān as co-regent; twenty years later, he succeeded his father and was able with slight interruptions to hold sway till his death in 1455. He had to submit to the sulṭān sending a permanent garrison of 50 Turkish horsemen under an emīr to Mecca. This emīr may be regarded as the precursor of the later governors, who sometimes attained positions of considerable influence under Turkish suzerainty.

Mecca enjoyed a period of prosperity under Barakāt's son Muḥammad (*Chron. Mekka*, ii. 341 *sqq.*; iii. 230 *sqq.*), whose reign (1455—1497) coincided with that of Ḳāʾit Bey in Egypt. The latter has left a fine memorial in the many buildings he erected in Mecca.

Under Muḥammad's son Barakāt II (1497—1525) who displayed great ability and bravery in the usual struggle with his relatives, without getting the support he desired from Egypt (*Chron. Mekka*, ii. 342 *sqq.*; iii. 244 *sqq.*), the political situation in Islām was fundamentally altered by the Ottoman Sulṭān Selīm's conquest of Egypt in 1517.

Although henceforth Constantinople had the importance for Mecca that Baghdād once had and there was little real understanding between Turks and Arabs, Mecca at first experienced a period of peace under the sharīfs Muḥammad Abū Numaiy (1525—1566) and Ḥasan (1566—1601). Under Ottoman protection the territory of the sharīfs was extended as far as Khaibar in the north, to Ḥalī in the south and in the east into Nadjd. Dependence on Egypt still existed at the same time; when the government in Constantinople was a strong one, it was less perceptible, and vice versa. This dependence was not only political but had also a material and religious side. The Ḥidjāz was dependent for its food supply on corn from Egypt. The foundations of a religious and educational nature now found powerful patrons in the Sulṭāns of Turkey.

A darker side of the Ottoman suzerainty was its intervention in the administration of justice. Since the sharīfs had adopted the Shāfiʿī madhhab, the Shāfiʿī ḳāḍī was the chief judge; this office had also remained for centuries in one family. Now the highest bidder for the office was sent every year from Constantinople to Mecca; the Meccans of course had to pay the price with interest.

With Ḥasan's death a new period of confusion and civil war began for Mecca. In the language of the historians, this circumstance makes itself apparent in the increasing use of the term *Dhawī*... for different groups of the descendants of Abū Numaiy who dispute the supremacy, often having their own territory, sometimes asserting a certain degree of independence from the Grand Sharīf, while preserving a system of reciprocal protection which saved the whole family from disaster (Snouck Hurgronje, *Mekka*, i. 112 *sqq.*).

The struggle for supremacy, interspersed with disputes with the officials of the suzerain, centred in the xvii^th^ century mainly around the ʿAbādila, the Dhawī Zaid and the Dhawī Barakāt.

Zaid (1631—1666) was an energetic individual who would not tolerate everything the Turkish officials did. But he was unable to oppose successfully a measure which deserves mention on account of its general importance. The ill-feeling between the Sunnī Turks and the Shīʿī Persians had been extended to Mecca as a result of an order by Sulṭān Murād to expel all Persians from the holy city and not to permit them to make the pilgrimage in future. Neither the Sharīfs nor the upper classes in Mecca had any reason to be pleased with this measure; it only served the mob as a pretext to plunder well-to-do Persians. As soon as the Turkish governor had ordered them to go, the Sharīfs however gave permission as before to the Shīʿīs to take part in the pilgrimage and to remain in the town. The Sharīfs likewise favoured the Zaidīs, who had also been frequently forbidden Mecca by the Turks.

The further history of Mecca down to the coming of the Wahhābīs is a rather monotonous struggle of the Sharīfan families among themselves (Dhawī Zaid, Dhawī Barakāt, Dhawī Masʿūd) and with the Ottoman officials in the town itself or in Djidda.

4. The Sharīfate from the Wahhābī period to its end. The Kingdom.

Although the Wahhābīs [q.v.] had already made their influence perceptible under his predecessors, it was Ghālib (1788—1813) who was the first to see the movement sweeping towards his territory like a flood; but he left no stone unturned to avert the danger. He sent his armies north, east and south; his brothers and brothers-in-law all took the field; the leaders of the Syrian and Egyptian pilgrim caravans were appealed to at every pilgrimage for help, but without success. In 1799 Ghālib made a treaty with the emīr of Darʿīya, by which the boundaries of their territories were laid down, with the stipulation that the Wahhābīs should be allowed access to the holy territory. Misunderstandings proved inevitable however and in 1803 the army of the amīr Saʿūd approached the holy city. After Ghālib had withdrawn to Djidda, in April Saʿūd entered Mecca, the inhabitants of which had announced their conversion. All ḳubbas were destroyed, all tobacco pipes and musical instruments burned, and the *adhān* purged of praises of the Prophet.

In July, Ghālib returned to Mecca but gradually he became shut in there by enemies as with a wall. In August the actual siege began and with it a period of famine and plague. In February of the following year, Ghālib had to submit to acknowledging Wahhābī suzerainty while retaining his own position.

The Sublime Porte had during all these happenings displayed no sign of life. It was only after the Wahhābīs had in 1807 sent back the pilgrim caravans from Syria and Egypt with their maḥmals, that Muḥammad ʿAlī was given instructions to deal with the Ḥidjāz as soon as he was finished with Egypt. It was not till 1813 that he took Mecca and there met Ghālib who made cautious advances to him. Ghālib however soon fell into the trap set for him by Muḥammad ʿAlī and his son Tusun. He was sent to Salonica, where he lived till his death in 1816.

In the meanwhile Muḥammad ʿAlī had installed Ghālib's nephew Yaḥyā b. Sarūr (1813—1827) as sharīf. Thus ended the first period of Wahhābī rule over Mecca, and the Ḥidjāz once more became dependent on Egypt. In Mecca, Muḥammad ʿAlī was honourably remembered because he restored the pious foundations which had fallen into ruins, revived the consignments of corn, and allotted stipends to those who had distinguished themselves in sacred lore or in other ways.

In 1827 Muḥammad ʿAlī had again to interfere in the domestic affairs of the sharīfs. When Yaḥyā had made his position untenable by the vengeance he took on one of his relatives, the viceroy deposed the Dhawī Zaid and installed one of the ʿAbādila, Muḥammad, usually called Muḥammad b. ʿAwn (1827—1851). He had first of all to go through the traditional struggle with his relatives. Trouble between him and Muḥammad ʿAlī's deputy resulted in both being removed to Cairo in 1836.

Here the sharīf remained till 1840 when by the treaty between Muḥammad ʿAlī and the Porte the Ḥidjāz was again placed directly under the Porte. Muḥammad b. ʿAwn returned to his home and rank. Ottoman suzerainty was now incorporated in the person of the wālī of Djidda. Friction was inevitable between him and Muḥammad b. ʿAwn; the latter's friendship with Muḥammad ʿAlī now proved of use to him. He earned the gratitude of the Turks for his expeditions against the Wahhābī chief Faiṣal in al-Riyāḍ and against the ʿAsīr tribes. His raids on the territory of Yaman also prepared the way for Ottoman rule over it.

In the meanwhile the head of the Dhawī Zaid, ʿAbd al-Muṭṭalib (1851—1856), had made good use of his friendship with the grand vizier and brought about the deposition of the ʿAbādila in favour of the Dhawī Zaid. ʿAbd al-Muṭṭalib however did not succeed in keeping on good terms with one of the two pashas with whom he had successively to deal. In 1855 it was decided in Constantinople to cancel his appointment and to recall Muḥammad b. ʿAwn. ʿAbd al-Muṭṭalib at first refused to recognize the genuineness of the order; and he was supported by the Turkophobe feeling just provoked by the prohibition of slavery. Finally however, he had to give way to Muḥammad b. ʿAwn, who in 1856 entered upon the sharīfate for the second time; this reign lasted barely two years. Between his death in March 1858 and the arrival of his successor ʿAbd Allāh in October of the same year took place the murder of the Christians in Djidda (June 15) and the atonement for it (cf. DJIDDA, in *EI* and Snouck Hurgronje, *Een rector der Mekkaansche Universiteit*, in *Verspr. Geschr.*, iii. 65 *sqq.*

The rule of ʿAbd Allāh (1858—1877) who was much liked by his subjects, was marked by peace at home and events of far-reaching importance abroad. The opening of the Suez Canal (1869) meant on the one hand the liberation of the Ḥidjāz from Egypt, on the other however more direct connection with Constantinople. The installation of telegraphic connections between the Ḥidjāz and the rest of the world had a similar importance. The reconquest of Yaman by the Turks was calculated to strengthen the impression that Arabia was now Turkish territory for ever.

The brief reign of his popular elder brother Ḥusain (1877—1880) ended with the assassination of the sharīf by an Afghān. The fact that the aged ʿAbd al-Muṭṭalib (see above) was sent by the Dhawī Zaid from Constantinople as his successor (1880—1882) gave rise to an obvious supposition.

Although the plebs saw something of a saint in this old man, his rule was soon felt to be so oppressive that the notables petitioned for his deposition (Snouck Hurgronje, *Mekka*, i. 204 *sqq.*). As a result, in 1881 the energetic ʿUthmān Nūrī Pasha was sent with troops to the Ḥidjāz as commander of the garrison with the task of preparing for the restoration of the ʿAbādila. ʿAbd al-Muṭṭalib was outwitted and taken prisoner; he was kept under guard in one of his own houses in Mecca till his death in 1886.

ʿUthmān Pasha, who was appointed wālī in July 1882, hoped to see his friend ʿAbdilāh, one of the ʿAbādila, installed as Grand Sharīf alongside of him. ʿAwn al-Rafīḳ (1882—1905) was however appointed (portrait in Snouck Hurgronje, *Bilder aus Mekka*). As the wālī was an individual of great energy, who had ever done much for the public good, and ʿAwn, although very retiring, was by no means insignificant, nay even tyrannical, trouble between them was inevitable, especially as they had the same powers on many points, e.g. the administration of justice and supervision of the safety of the pilgrim routes. After a good deal of friction ʿUthmān was dismissed in 1886. His successor was Djamāl Pasha, who only held office for a short period and was succeeded by Ṣafwat Pasha. Only Aḥmad Rātib could keep his place alongside of ʿAwn and that by shutting his eyes to many things and being satisfied with certain material advantages. After ʿAwn's death ʿAbdilāh was chosen as his successor. He died however before he could start on the journey from Constantinople to Mecca. ʿAwn's actual successor was therefore his nephew ʿAlī (1905—1908). In 1908 he and Aḥmad Rātib both lost their positions with the Turkish Revolution.

With Ḥusain (1908—1916—1924), also a nephew of ʿAwn's, the last sharīf came to power. But for the Great War his sharīfate would probably have run the usual course. The fact that Turkey was now completely involved in the war induced him to declare himself independent in 1916. He endeavoured to extend his power as far as possible, first as liberator (*munḳidh*) of the Arabs, then (June 22, 1916) as king of the Ḥidjāz or king of Arabia and finally as caliph. Very soon however, it became apparent that the Sulṭān of Nadjd, ʿAbd al-ʿAzīz Āl Saʿūd, like his Wahhābī forefathers, was destined to have a powerful say in the affairs of Arabia. In Sept. 1924 his troops took Ṭāʾif and in October Mecca. King Ḥusain fled first to ʿAḳaba and from there in May 1925 to Cyprus. His son ʿAlī retired to Djidda. Ibn Saʿūd besieged this town and Madīna for a year, avoiding bloodshed and complications with European powers. Both towns surrendered in December 1925.

Since January 1926, Ibn Saʿūd has been king of the Ḥidjāz; the official title of his kingdom, at first Ḥidjāz, Nadjd and dependencies, is now kingdom of Saʿūdī Arabia. A political unit has thus been formed which covers a larger area than the sharīfs ever ruled and possesses greater internal strength than has been seen in Arabia since the end of ʿAbbāsid power.

By the organisation of the Nadjd warriors (*ikhwān*) as agriculturists also, by the maintenance of a strict discipline among the Beduins, by the creation of a military police, which is held in awe, a security was created such as Arabia has perhaps never known and secure foundations laid for traffic, especially of the pilgrims.

With the representatives of foreign government in Djidda the king maintains friendly relations. Several states have raised their consulates there to the rank of an embassy. Treaties have been concluded with a number of states.

The religious and economic life of the city has from the earliest times centred round the pilgrimage [cf. the article ḤADJDJ] and the Mosque [cf. AL-MASDJID AL-ḤARĀM]. The character of Mecca as the metropolis of Islām is reflected in the great variety of its population. Besides the original Meccan nucleus we have numerous Arab elements — among which the Ḥaḍramīs are particularly prominent on account of their energy — and colonies of foreigners from all parts of the Muslim world who have out of worldly or religious motives taken up their abode permanently in the capital. Among these, special mention must be made of those from the Malay Archipelago who are known collectively as Djāwa; with them it is exclusively religious motives that have caused them to take up permanent residence in Mecca.

Even at the present day slaves, mainly African, form an important element in Meccan society. Abyssinian slave girls have always been highly esteemed as concubines. The slave-market however is no longer of the importance it once was. Freedmen rise from the slave caste and their dwellings, huts put together of every conceivable material, are on the outskirts of the city.

Artisans are, or at least down to the end of the xixth century were, organised in gilds. Among these gilds that of the pilgrim guides (*muṭawwif*; q.v.), who have agents in Djidda and outside Arabia, is the most important; it lives entirely on the pilgrim traffic.

This is true in a way of the whole population, which has arranged to let houses to the pilgrims for a considerable portion of the year. By the eighth month, tens of thousands of these visitors are in the town. Their number increases till the twelfth. In Muḥarram, Mecca resumes its usual appearance.

During the last few hundred years — except for the first Wahhābī period — the cult of saints in Mecca has steadily increased. Numerous places have sacred memories of Muḥammad and his family, the most prominent *muhādjirūn* and later saints; numerous ḳubbas were built over their graves and ḥawls and mawlids were celebrated in their honour. The Wahhābīs have done away with a great deal of this since their occupation of the city.

Mecca is the seat of the government, although the king's residence is in Riyāḍ. The official gazette *Umm al-Ḳurā* appears weekly. There are also printing presses, which mainly print Wahhābī or Ḥanbalī literature.

Bibliography: al-Azraḳī and al-Fāsī in *Die Chroniken der Stadt Mekka*, ed. Wüstenfeld; al-Yaʿḳūbī, vol. ii; al-Wāḳidī, *K. al-Maghāzī*, ed. Kremer; al-Ṭabarī; Ibn al-Athīr, *al-Kāmil*; Aḥmad b. Zainī Daḥlān, *Khulāṣat al-Kalām fī umarāʾ al-balad al-ḥarām*, Cairo 1305; al-Maḳdisī, *Aḥsan al-taḳāsīm*, *BGA* iii, and the other geographers; al-Mas'ūdī, *Murūdj al-dhahab*, iii; Ibn 'Abd Rabbihi, *al-'Iḳd al-farīd*, vol. ii; Ibn Djubair, *Riḥla*; J. L. Burckhardt, *Travels in Arabia*, London, 1829; C. Snouck Hurgronje, *Mekka*, 2 vols., The Hague 1889 (English translation by J. H. Monahan, Leiden 1931 under the title *Mecca in the latter part of the 19th century*); Gaudefroy-Demombynes, *Le pèlerinage à la Mekke*, Paris 1923.

For part i.: The Tradition collections of Bukhārī, Muslim, Ibn Ḥanbal, Abū Dāwūd, Nasā'ī, Ibn Mādja, and the *Maṣābīḥ al-sunna* by al-Baghawī; Ḥassān b. Thābit, *Dīwān*, ed. Hirschfeld; Ibn Hishām, *Sīra*, ed. Wüstenfeld, and other oriental and western biographies of the Prophet; al-Balādhurī, *Futūḥ al-buldān*, ed. de Goeje; Ibn Duraid, *K. al-Ishtiḳāḳ*, ed. Wüstenfeld; Ibn Sa'd, *Ṭabaḳāt*, ed. Sachau; al-Djāḥiẓ, *Tria opuscula*, ed. van Vloten, p. 61 *sqq.*; H. Lammens: a. *La Mecque à la veille de l'Hégire* (*Mél. Univ. St. Joseph*, Beyrouth, ix, 3); b. *Etudes sur le règne du calife omaiyade Mo'āwiya* I (*MFOB*, i-iii); c. *Le califat de Yazīd* I (*MFOB*, v-vii); d. *Les chrétiens à la Mecque à la veille de l'Hégire* (*BIFAO* xix); e. *Les juifs à la Mecque à la veille de l'Hégire* (*Recherches de science religieuse*, viii); f. *Fatima et les filles de Mahomet*, Rome 1912; g. *Les Aḥābiš et l'organisation militaire de la Mecque au siècle de l'Hégire* (*JA* 1916,; h. *Les culte des bétyles et les processions religieuses chez les Arabes préislamites* (BIFAO, xvii); i. *Le berceau de l'Islam; l'Arabie occidentale à la veille de l'Hégire*, Rome 1914; k. *La cité arabe de Taif à la veille de l'Hégire* (*Mél. Univ. St. Joseph*, Beyrouth, viii); l. *La république marchande de la Mecque vers l'an* 600 *de notre ère* (*BIE* 1910); A. Sprenger, *Die alte Geographie Arabiens*; Wellhausen, *Reste arabischen Heidentums*; Caetani, *Annali dell 'Islam*.

For part ii.: Wüstenfeld, *Die Scherife von Mekka im XI.* (*XVII*). *Jahrhundert* (*Abh. G. W. Gött.* xxxii, 1885); Ali Bey, *Travels*, London 1816; R. Burton, *Personal Narrative of a Pilgrimage to al-Medinah and Meccah*; T. F. Keane, *Six months in Mecca*, London 1881; Hadji Khan and W. Sparroy, *With the Pilgrims to Mecca*, London and New York 1905; Ibrāhīm Rif'at Bāshā, *Mir'āt al-ḥaramayn*, vol. i, Cairo 1925; E. Rutter, *The Holy Cities of Arabia*, London and New York 1928, 1930; Amīn al-Raiḥānī, *Ta'rīkh Nadjd*, Beyrouth 1928; do., *Mulūk al-'Arab*, Beyrouth 1924; H. St. J. B. Philby, *The Heart of Arabia*, London 1922; do., *Arabia*, London and New-York 1930; C. Snouck Hurgronje, *The Revolt in Arabia* (*Verspr. Geschr.* iii, 311 *sqq.*; do. *Prins Faisal bin Abdal-Aziz al-Saoed* (*Verspr. Geschr.* vi, 465 *sqq.*); *Oriente Moderno*, passim.

The geographical position of Mecca was found to be roughly 39° 60′ E. Long. (Greenw.) and 21° 25′ N. Lat. by N. Scheltema (*Determination of the geographical latitude and longitude of Mecca and Jidda, executed in* 1910—1911, in *Verh. Ak. Amst.* 1912).

METAWILA. [See MUTAWĀLĪ].

MIḤNA (A.), noun derived from the root *m-ḥ-n*, appearing in the Arabic verb *maḥana*, "to smooth", and in some Ethiopic derivations: trial (e.g. the trials to which the prophets and especially the family of Muḥammad, the 'Alids, are exposed in this world; cf. Goldziher, *Vorlesungen*, p. 212 *sq.*, 261), inquisition. In the latter sense it is usually applied to the Mu'tazilite inquisition and persecution extending from 218—234/833—848. On the viiith form of the verb, *imtaḥana*, "to torture", cf. especially Quatremère, *Histoire des Sultans Mamlouks*, 1/ii., p. 81, note 101.

The first Mu'tazilite inquisition was instituted towards the end of his reign by the 'Abbāsid caliph al-Ma'mūn (198—218/813—833), who was a Mu'tazilite by conviction, especially with regard to the creation of the Ḳur'ān [cf. the articles AL-ḲUR'ĀN and AL-MU'TAZILA]. He sent a letter to the governor of Baghdād, Isḥāḳ b. Ibrāhīm, ordering him to cite before him the ḳāḍīs under his jurisdiction in order to test them with regard to their opinion on the Ḳur'ān (Ṭabarī, iii. 1112 *sqq.*, transl. by Patton, *op. cit.*, p. 57—61; *Kitāb Baghdād*, p. 338 *sqq.*; cf. Ibn Taghrībirdī, i. 636 *sqq.*; *Fragmenta hist. arab.*, p. 465). Those who declared their opinion in conformity with that of the caliph, should cite the legal witnesses under their jurisdiction and institute a similar inquisition.

This letter was sent to the provinces. In Egypt little was done. At Kūfa the general feeling was against yielding to the order of the caliph. In Damascus, the latter, probably on his way to Asia Minor, personally conducted the testing of the doctors of the town.

In a second letter he ordered Isḥāḳ b. Ibrāhīm to send to him seven of the leading theological authorities of Baghdād, that he might test them himself. The name of the chief champion of the orthodox view, Aḥmad b. Muḥammad b. Ḥanbal [q.v.], which was at first in the list, was cancelled at the instance of the chief ḳāḍī Aḥmad b. Abī Du'ād, the most vigorous advocate of the miḥna under al-Ma'mūn and his successors. Among the seven who were summoned to the court was Muḥammad b. Sa'd, the secretary of al-Wāḳidī, and author of the *Kitāb al-Ṭabaḳāt*. All of them gave way to the pressure, assented to the view forced upon them and were sent back to Baghdād, where Isḥāḳ b. Ibrāhīm had them repeat their confession before the theologians (Ṭabarī, iii. 1116 *sq.*; *Kitāb Baghdād*, p. 343 *sqq.*). The success of the caliph moved him to cling to the method inaugurated by him. In a third letter which is interwoven with theological arguments (Ṭabarī, iii. 1117 *sqq.*; Patton, *op. cit.*, p. 65 *sqq.*), he enjoined Isḥāḳ b. Ibrāhīm to test all the ḳāḍīs under his jurisdiction, who in their turn should test all witnesses and assistants in matters of law. Isḥāḳ b. Ibrāhīm cited before him a number of the most notable doctors of Baghdād (Ṭabarī, iii. 1121 *sqq.*; Patton, *op. cit.*, p. 69 *sqq.*), among them Aḥmad b. Ḥanbal. The result of the test was that some of them yielded and others remained steadfast; Aḥmad b. Ḥanbal belonged to the group of the latter.

In a fourth letter to Isḥāḳ b. Ibrāhīm (Ṭabarī, iii. 1125 *sqq.*; Patton, *op. cit.*, p. 74 *sqq.*), the caliph discussed the attitude of each of the doctors in connection with his character and way of life, and ordered those who had given unsatisfactory answers to be sent to his camp in Ṭarsūs. After a further examination by Isḥāḳ b. Ibrāhīm two of them only remained steadfast, Aḥmad b. Ḥanbal and Muḥammad b. Nūḥ. They were sent to Ṭarsūs as prisoners. On the way thither the report of the caliph's death reached them. They were sent back to Baghdād; Muḥammad b. Nūḥ died before he had reached the capital.

Aḥmad b. Ḥanbal remained in prison. Although he was urged to make use of *taḳīya* [q.v.] as others had done, he stuck to his attitude. Cited before al-Ma'mūn's brother and successor al-Mu'taṣim (218—

227/833—842), there originated lively debates on the nature of the Ḳur'ān and other theological subjects between him, the caliph, Aḥmad b. Abī Du'ād and others, which lasted three days. No change, however, being brought about in Aḥmad's attitude, he was scourged at the order of the caliph, and afterwards, from fear of an insurrection (for Aḥmad was very popular), set free. Little more is heard of the miḥna under al-Muʿtaṣim (Ibn Taghrībirdī, i. 649; Patton, p. 113), who had neither the interest nor the training of his predecessor in theological matters.

His son al-Wāthiḳ bi'llāh (227—232/842—847) who succeeded him, returned to the methods of al-Ma'mūn (Ibn Taghrībirdī, i. 683; Patton, p. 115 *sqq.*), although it is said that he had restrained his father from prosecuting the miḥna any farther. He ordered the governors of the provinces to test the notables under their jurisdiction. Little is known of the consequences of this order. Aḥmad b. Ḥanbal in the meanwhile had become a favourite teacher; when, however, he heard of the renewed activity of Aḥmad b. Abī Du'ād he refrained of his own will from teaching, and was henceforth left alone.

Al-Wāthiḳ personally intervened in the trial of one person of note, the theologian Aḥmad b. Naṣr b. Mālik al-Khuzāʿī who had moreover taken part in a conspiracy (Weil, ii. 341; Patton, p. 116 *sq.*; cf. Ṭabarī, iii. 1343 *sqq.*; de Goeje, *Fragmenta hist. arab.*, p. 529 *sqq.*). Questioned about the Ḳur'ān, al-Khuzāʿī replied that he believed it to be the word of God. The trial had not proceeded much farther, when the caliph put an end to it and personally made an attempt to behead his victim, in which he did not succeed without the assistance of some one more skilled than himself (Shaʿbān 231/846).

Other persons of note who remained steadfast under al-Wāthiḳ were Nuʿaim b. Ḥammād and the well known Abū Yaʿḳūb Yūsuf b. Yaḥya 'l-Buwaiṭī, the pupil of al-Shāfiʿī and editor of some of his works (Patton, p. 119). Both died in prison. As an instance of the fanaticism of Aḥmad b. Abī Du'ād it is related that, when in 231/846 it was proposed to ransom 4,600 Muslim prisoners from the Byzantines, he proposed to abandon those who would not admit the creation of the Ḳur'ān; this was actually done (Ṭabarī, iii. 1351 *sqq.*; *Fragm. hist. arab.*, ii. 532; Ibn Taghrībirdī, i. 684; Patton, p. 120). It is said that al-Wāthiḳ gave up his Muʿtazilite views before his death. The miḥna continued to exist during the first years of the reign of his successor al-Mutawakkil (232—247/847—861), but in 234 this caliph stopped its application and forbade the profession of the creation of the Ḳur'ān on pain of death.

Bibliography: al-Yaʿḳūbī, *Ta'rīkh*, ed. Houtsma, ii. 491, 500—509, 521, 528, 575, 582: al-Ṭabarī, ed. de Goeje, iii., as cited in the article; al-Masʿūdī, *Murūdj*, Paris ed., vi. 283 *sqq.*; vii. 101; viii. 300 *sqq.*; x. 45, 51, 70; *Fragmenta historicum arabicorum*, ii., ed. de Goeje, Leyden 1871, as cited in the article; Aḥmad b. Abī Ṭāhir Ṭaifūr, *Kitāb Baghdād*, ed. Keller, Leipzig 1908; Ibn al-Athīr, *al-Kāmil*, ed. Tornberg, vi. 297—301, 314; vii. 14 *sq.*; Abu 'l-Fidā', *Ta'rīkh*, Constantinople 1286, ii. 31 *sqq.*; Abu 'l-Maḥāsin b. Taghrībirdī, *al-Nudjūm al-zāhira*, ed. T. G. J. Juynboll, as cited in the article; Tādj al-Dīn ʿAbd al-Wahhāb al-Subkī, *Ṭabaḳāt al-Shāfiʿīya*, Cairo 1324, i. 205 *sqq.*; W. M. Patton, *Aḥmed b. Ḥanbal and the Miḥna*, Leyden 1897; A. von Kremer, *Geschichte der herrschenden Ideen des Islams*, Leipzig 1868, p. 233 *sqq.*; M. Th. Houtsma, *De strijd over het dogma in den Islam tot op el-Ash'ari*, Leyden 1875, p. 107 *sqq.*; G. Weil, *Geschichte der Chalifen*, ii. 262 *sqq.*, 297 *sq.*, 340 *sqq.*; A. Müller, *Der Islam im Morgen- und Abendland*, i., II/iv. 451 *sqq.*, 523 *sq.*; W. Muir, *The Caliphate* [3], ed. T. H. Weir, Edinburgh 1924, p. 507, 512, 520 *sq.*, 525; Goldziher, *Vorlesungen über den Islam*, Heidelberg 1910, as cited in the article; do., in *ZDMG*, lii. 155 *sqq.*

MIḤRĀB. [See MASDJID D, 2c. and ḲIBLA].

MĪKĀ'ĪL. [See MĪKĀL].

MĪKĀL, the archangel Michael [cf. MALĀ'IKA], whose name occurs once in the Ḳur'ān, viz. in Sūra ii. 98: "Whosoever is an enemy to Allāh, or his angels, or his apostles, or to Gabriel or to Michael, verily Allāh is an enemy to the unbelievers". In explanation of this verse two stories are told. According to the first, the Jews, wishing to test the veracity of the mission of Muḥammad, asked him several questions, on all of which he gave the true answer. Finally they asked him who transmitted the revelations to him. When he answered Gabriel, the Jews declared that this angel was their enemy and the angel of destruction and penury, in opposition to Michael whom they said to be their protector and the angel of fertility and salvation (Ṭabarī, *Tafsīr*, i. 324 *sqq.*). — According to the second story, ʿUmar once entered the synagogue (*midrās*) of Madīna and asked the Jews questions concerning Gabriel. They gave of that angel as well as of Michael an account similar to the one mentioned above, whereupon ʿUmar asked: What is the position of those two angels with Allāh? They replied: Gabriel is to His right and Michael to His left, and there is enmity between the two. Whereupon ʿUmar answered: If they have that position with Allāh, there can be no enmity between them. But you are unbelievers more than asses are, and whosoever is an enemy to one of the two, is an enemy to Allāh. Thereupon ʿUmar went to meet Muḥammad, who received him with the words: Gabriel has anticipated you by the revelation of: "Whosoever is an enemy" etc. (Sūra ii. 98; Ṭabarī, *Tafsīr*, i. 327; Zamakhsharī, p. 92; Baiḍāwī ad Sūra ii. 98(2)).

We do not know of any Jewish traditions which ascribe to Gabriel a hostile attitude towards the Jews. For the statements regarding Michael as communicated above, there is sufficient literary evidence. In Daniel xii. 1 Michael is called the great prince, the protector of the people of Israel; cf. *Targum Canticum*, viii. 9: "Michael, the lord of Israel"; Daniel x. 13, 21, where Michael is said to have protected the Jews against the kings of Persia and Greece; further 1 Enoch xx. 5, where he is called the protector of the best part of mankind; *Testamentum Levi*, xv. 6; *Test. Dan*, vi. 2.

In *Vita Adae et Evae*, chap. xii. *sqq.*, it is Michael who orders Satan and the other angels to worship Adam. Although the story is mentioned several times in the Ḳur'ān [cf. IBLĪS], there is no trace in Muslim literature of the role ascribed to Michael in *Vita Adae et Evae*; the only mention of Michael in the Muslim legend is that he and Gabriel were the first to worship Adam, in opposition to Iblīs who refused to do so (al-Kisā'ī, p. 27).

Neither does Muslim literature seem to have preserved other features ascribed to Michael in Jewish Apocrypha (mediator between God and mankind, 1 Enoch xl. 9; *Test. Dan*, vi. 2: 3 Baruch, xl. 2), or in the New Testament (Ep. Jude, vs. 9: Michael disputing with the devil about the body of Moses; Revelation xii. 7 *sqq.*; Michael and his angels fighting against the dragon and the final disconfiture of the latter). Perhaps a faint recollection of Michael as the protector of mankind (the Jews, the Christians) may be found in the tradition according to which Michael has never laughed since the creation of Hell (Aḥmad b. Ḥanbal, iii. 224). Further, however, Michael is rarely mentioned in *ḥadīth* (Bukhārī, *Badʾ al-khalḳ*, b. 7, where he, together with Mālik, the guardian of Hell, and Gabriel, appears to Muḥammad in a dream; Nasāʾī, *Iftitāḥ*, b. 37 where Michael incites Gabriel to urge Muḥammad to recite the Ḳurʾān according to the seven *aḥruf*).

Al-Yaʿḳūbī mentions a story of which we have no counterpart in Jewish or Christian literature either, which is not amazing, the story bearing an outspoken Shīʿite tendency. One day Allāh announced to Gabriel and Michael that one of them must die. Neither however was willing to sacrifice himself on behalf of his partner, whereupon Allāh said to them: Take ʿAlī as an example, who was willing to give his life on behalf of Muḥammad (the night before the *hidjra*; Yaʿḳūbī, ii. 39).

Michael is further mentioned by name as one of the angels who opened the breast of Muḥammad before his night journey (Ṭabarī, i, 1157—59; Ibn al-Athīr, ii. 36 *sq.*), and as one of those who came to the aid of the Muslims in the battle of Badr (Ibn Saʿd, II/i. 9).

In the text of the Ḳurʾān as well as in a verse cited by Ṭabarī (ed. de Goeje, i. 329), the form of the name is Mīkāl as if it were a *mifʿāl* form from *wakala* (Horovitz). A direct reminiscence of the Greek, probably also of the Hebrew and Aramaic forms of the name is to be found in the tradition preserved by al-Kisāʾī (p. 12), which calls Mīkhāʾīl the attendant of the second heaven, in contra-distinction to Mīkāʾīl, who is the guardian of the sea in the seventh heaven (p. 15). Other forms of the name are Mikaʾil, Mīkāʾil, Mīkaʾīl, Mīkāʾīn and Mīkāʾill. It is hardly necessary to say that in the magical use of the names of the archangels that of Mīkāʾīl is on the same level as that of his companions (e.g. Zwemer, *The Influence of Animism on Islam*, p. 193, 197).

Bibliography: al-Yaʿḳūbī, *Taʾrīkh*, ed. Houtsma; al-Kisāʾī, *Ḳiṣaṣ al-anbiyā*, ed. Eiwenberg, Leyden 1922; al-Ṭabarī, de Goeje, i. 329 *sq.*; *Lisān*, xx. 159 (on the form of the name and its meaning); Ibn Hishām, ed. Wüstenfeld, p. 328, 624; Rhodokanakis, in *WZKM*, xvii. 282; Umaiya d. Abī Ṣalt, ed. Schulthess, in *Beiträge z. Assyriologie*, vii., No. lv., l. 8 (spurious); Horovitz, *Koranische Untersuchungen*, Leipzig—Berlin 1926, p. 143.

MĪĶĀT (A., *mifʿāl-form* from *w-ḳ-t*, plural *mawāḳīt*) appointed or exact time. In this sense the term occurs several times in the Ḳurʾān (Sūra ii. 181; vii. 142, 143, 155; xxvi. 38; xliv. 40; lvi. 50; lxxviii. 17).

In *ḥadīth* and *fiḳh* the term is applied to the times of prayer and to the places where those who enter the *ḥaram* are bound to put on the *iḥrām*. For the latter meaning of the term cf. IḤRĀM, I.

Although some general indications for the times at which some *ṣalāts* are to be performed occur in the Ḳurʾān (cf. sūra ii. 238; xi. 114; xvii. 78; xxiv. 58), it may be considered above doubt that during Muḥammad's lifetime neither the number of the daily *ṣalāts* nor their exact times had been fixed and that this happened in the first decades after his death.

A reminiscence of that period of uncertainty may be preserved in those traditions which apply a deviating nomenclature to some of the *ṣalāts*. The *ṣalāt al-ẓuhr* e.g. is called *al-hadjir al-ūlā*; the *ṣalāt al-maghrib*, *ʿishāʾ*; the *ṣalāt* al-*ʿishāʾ*, *ʿatama*; the *ṣalāt al-fadjr*, *ghadāt* (Bukhārī, *Mawāḳīt al-ṣalāt*, bāb 13, 19). In other traditions the term *al-ʿatama* as applied to the *ṣalāt al-ʿishāʾ* is ascribed to the Beduins and prohibited (Muslim, *Masādjid*, trad. 228, 229; Abū Dāwūd, *Ḥudūd*, bāb 78; Aḥmad b. Ḥanbal, *Musnad*, ii. 10 etc.); cf. on the other hand Bukhārī, *Mawāḳīt*, bāb 20; Muslim, *Ṣalāt*, trad. 129 etc., where the term *ʿatama* is used without censure.

From some traditions so much may be gathered, that the — or at least some of the — Umaiyads showed a predilection for postponing the times of the *ṣalāt* (Bukhārī, *Mawāḳīt*, b. 7; Muslim, *Masādjid*, trad. 166. 167; al-Nasāʾī, *Imāma*, b. 18, 55; Zaid b. ʿAlī, *Madjmūʿ al-fiḳh*, No. 113).

In opposition to this a *ṣalāt* in due time is declared the best of works (Bukhārī, *Djihād*, b. 1; *Mawāḳīt*, b. 5; Muslim, *Īmān*, trad. 138, 139; Tirmidhī, *Ṣalāt*, b. 13; *Birr*, b. 2). In other traditions this is said of a *ṣalāt* at its earliest time (Tirmidhī, *Ṣalāt*, b. 13).

This early state of things is reflected in several respects in a tradition according to which ʿUmar b. ʿAbd al-ʿAzīz once postponed one of the *ṣalāts* and was rebuked for this by ʿUrwa b. al-Zubair, who related to him that al-Mughīra b. Shuʿba had once been rebuked for the same reason by Abū Masʿūd al-Anṣārī, on account of the fact that Gabriel himself had descended five times in order to perform the five *ṣalāts* at their exact times in the presence of Muḥammad. Thereupon ʿUmar admonished ʿUrwa to be careful in his statements (Bukhārī, *Mawāḳīt*, b. 1; Muslim, *Masādjid*, trad. 166, 167; al-Nasāʾī, *Mawāḳīt*, b. 10).

Some early groups of traditions affect to reproduce reminiscences of the practice in Madīna in Muḥammad's time.

a. The *ṣalāt al-ẓuhr* was performed at noon, when the sun was beginning to decline (Bukhārī, *Mawāḳīt*, b. 11);

b. the *ṣalāt al-ʿaṣr* when the sun was shining into ʿĀʾisha's room, no shadows being yet cast there (Bukhārī, *Mawāḳīt*, b. 13; Muslim, *Masādjid*, trad. 168). After this *ṣalāt* people had still time to visit the remotest parts of the town, while the sun was still "alive" or "pure" (Bukhārī, *Mawāḳīt*, b. 1, 13, 14, 18, 21);

c. the *ṣalāt al-maghrib* was finished at a time when people could still perceive the places where their arrows fell down (Bukhārī, *Mawāḳīt*, b. 21);

d. the *ṣalāt al-ʿishāʾ* was sometimes postponed till a late hour, sometimes till the first third of the night had passed (Bukhārī, *Mawāḳīt*, b. 11, 20, 21, 24);

e. the *ṣalāt al-fadjr* was performed by Muḥammad at a time when a man could discern his neighbour (Bukhārī, *Mawāḳīt*, b. 13); but the women on their way home could not yet be recognized (Bukhārī, *Mawāḳīt*, b. 27).

In a second layer of traditions these general indications are specified by the mention of the first and the last limits allowed for the different prayers (cf. e.g. Muslim, *Masādjid*, trad. 176, 177). On one day Muḥammad performed.

a. the *ṣalāt al-ẓuhr* when the sun began to decline;

b. the *ṣalāt al-ʿaṣr* when the sun was still high bright and pure;

c. the *ṣalāt al-maghrib* immediately after sunset;

d. the *ṣalāt al-ʿishāʾ* when the twilight had disappeared;

e. the *ṣalāt al-fadjr* at daybreak.

On the following day Muḥammad performed:

a. the *ẓuhr* later than the day before;

b. the *ʿaṣr* later than the day before, the sun being still high up

c. the *maghrib* before the twilight had disappeared;

d. the *ʿishāʾ* when the first third of the night had passed;

e. the *fadjr* when sunrise was near (*asfara bihā*).

In a tradition communicated by al-Shāfiʿī (*Kitāb al-umm*, i. 62) the fixing of the mawāḳīt just mentioned is ascribed to the example of Gabriel (cf. Zaid b. ʿAlī, *Madjmūʿ al-fiḳh*, No. 109). These mawāḳīt have for the most part passed into the books of *fiḳh*. We cannot reproduce all details here. The following scheme may suffice:

a. ẓuhr: from the time when the sun begins to decline till the time when shadows are of equal length with the objects by which they are cast, apart from their shadows at noon. The Ḥanafites alone deviate in one of their branches in so far as they replace the ultimate term by the time when the shadows are twice as large as their objects. In times of great heat it is recommended to postpone the *ẓuhr* as late as possible;

b. ʿaṣr: from the last time allowed for *ẓuhr* till before sunset. According to Mālik the first term begins somewhat later;

c. maghrib: from the time after sunset till the time when the red twilight had disappeared. Small deviations only, in connection with a predilection for the first term;

d. ʿishāʾ: from the last term mentioned for the *ṣalāt al-maghrib* till when a third, or half of the night has passed, or: till daybreak;

e. fadjr: from daybreak till before sunrise.

Side by side with these mawāḳīt we find in the books of Tradition and of Law the times on which it is not allowed to perform prayer, viz. sunrise, noon, and sunset (Bukhārī, *Mawāḳīt*, b. 30—32; Muslim, *Ṣalāt al-musāfirīn*, trad. 285—294; cf. al-Nawawī's commentary for controversies regarding this point, and further Wensinck, *Handbook*, p. 192a). According to ʿĀʾisha it is only forbidden to await sunrise and sunset for prayer (Muslim, *Musāfirīn*, trad. 296). In Mecca prayer is allowed at all times (Bukharī, *Ḥadjdj*, b. 73; Tirmidhī, *Ḥadjdj*, b. 42).

Bibliography: Apart from the works cited: Zaid b. ʿAlī, *Madjmūʿ al-fiḳh*, ed. Griffini, Milano 1919, p. 23—26; Abu 'l-Ḳāsim al-Muḥaḳḳiḳ, *Kitāb sharāʾiʿ al-islām*, Calcutta 1255, p. 26; A. Querry, *Droit musulman*, Paris, 1871, p. 50 *sqq.*; Mālik, *al-Muwaṭṭaʾ*, ch. *Wuḳūt al-ṣalāt*, i. 12 *sqq.*; Khalīl b. Isḥāḳ, *al-Mukhtaṣar fi 'l-fiḳh*, Paris 1318/1900, p. 13 *sq.*, trans. I. Guidi and D. Santillana, Milano 1919, i. 45 *sqq.*; al-Shāfiʿī, *Kitāb al-umm*, Cairo 1321—25, i. 61 *sqq.*; Th W. Juynboll, *Handleiding tot de kennis van de Moh. Wet*, Leyden 1925, p. 53 *sq.*; Burhān al-Dīn Abu 'l-Ḥasan ʿAlī b. Abī Bakr al-Marghinānī, *al-Hidāya wa 'l-kifāya*, Bombay 1280, i. 83—89; al-Shaʿrānī, *al-Mīzān al-kubrā*, Cairo 1279, i. 158—160.

MILLA (A.), religion, rite. However obvious it may be to connect this word with the Hebrew and Jewish- and Christian-Aramaic *milla*, *mella*, "utterance, word", it has not been satisfactorily proved how and where it received the meaning which is taken for granted in the Ḳurʾān: religion or rite. Nor is it known whether it is a purely Arabic word or a loanword adopted by Muḥammad or others before him (Nöldeke, *ZDMG*, lvii. 413 seems to hold that it is Arabic for he refers to the 4th form *amalla* or *amlā* "to dictate"). In the Ḳurʾān it always means (even in the somewhat obscure passage, Sūra xxxviii. 7) "religion" and it is used of the heathen religions (vii. 88 *sq.*; xiv. 13; xviii. 20) as well as of those of the Jews and Christians (ii. 120), and of the true religion of the fathers (xii. 38). The word acquired a special significance in the Madīna sections where the Prophet in his polemic against the Jews speaks of "Abraham's *milla*", by which he means the original revelation in its purity, which it was his duty to restore (ii. 130; iii. 95; xvi. 123; xxii. 78 *sq.*; cf. iv. 125; vi. 161; xii. 37). Muslim literature follows this Ḳurʾānic usage but the word is not in frequent use. With the article, *al-milla* means the true religion revealed by Muḥammad and is occasionally used eliptically for *ahl al-milla*, the followers of the Muḥammadan religion (Ṭabarī, iii. 813, 883), just as its opposite *al-dhimma* is an abbreviation for *ahl al-dhimma*, the non-Muḥammadans who are under the protection of Islām; e.g., Ibn Saʿd, iii./1, 238; cf. also the derivative *millī* opposed to *dhimmī*, client (Baihaḳī, ed. Schwally, p. 121 infra).

Bibliography: Nöldeke, *Orientalische Skizzen*, p. 40; do., *ZDMG*, lvii. 413; Ṭabarī, ed. de Goeje, *Glossar*, s.v.; Snouck Hurgronje, *Het Mekkaansche Feest*, p. 30 *sqq.*; see also the art. IBRĀHĪM.

MINĀ, later often pronounced Munā, a place in the hills east of Mecca on the road from it to ʿArafa (q.v.]. The distance between the two is given by al-Maḳdisī as one parasang, while Wavell calls it five miles and says the continuation to ʿArafa is nine miles. Minā lies in a narrow valley running from west to east, 1,500 paces long according to Burckhardt, surrounded by steep barren granite cliffs. On the north side rises a hill called Thabīr. Travellers from Mecca come down into the valley by a hill path with steps in it; this is the ʿAḳaba which became famous in connection with Muḥammad's negotiations with the Madinians. The town consists of stone houses of fair size which form two long streets. Close beside the ʿAḳaba is a rudely hewn short pillar leaning against a wall: this is the "great djamra" or the "ʿAḳaba djamra", at which the pilgrims cast stones [cf. DJAMRA]. A little to the east in the middle of the street is the "middle djamra" also marked by a pillar and lastly at a similar distance the third (the so-called "first djamra"). As one approaches the east end of the valley, there is on the right of the road a square mosque surrounded by a wall, the Masdjid al-Khaif, which was rebuilt by Saladin and in 874/1467 reconstructed by the Mamlūk Sulṭān Ḳāʾit Bey. Along the west side of the surrounding wall is a colonnade with three rows of pillars, but there is none on the other sides. It was different earlier, for Ibn Rusteh (c. 300/913) tells us that the mosque had 168 pillars of which only seventy-eight supported the west wing. The north side of the wall is pierced by several doors. In the centre of the court of the mosque is a little domed building with a minaret built over a fountain. There is another dome over the colonnade on the west side.

The most striking feature of Minā is the very great difference, noted already by al-Maḳdisī, between the quiet and empty streets of the greater part of the year and the tremendous throng and bustle of the pilgrimage month when, as Wavell says, half a million people with heavily laden beasts of burden hope to cover nine miles in the period between sunrise and 10 a.m. Every spot in the valley is then covered with tents in which the pilgrims spend the night. Al-Maḳdisī speaks of fine houses built of teak and stone (among them was a frequently mentioned Dār al-Imāra), and large stone buildings are still to be found in Minā; but these are usually empty and are only let at the pilgrimage to the more wealthy pilgrims and even among these many prefer to live in tents. This depopulation of the city has been a subject for discussion among the legists, for some held that this curcumstance enables Minā and Mecca to be regarded as one city (*miṣr*), a view which others reject. But another circumstance must have contributed to prevent a permanent settlement of the town, which is also true of other places on the pilgrim's route, namely the incredible filth and dreadful stench which is caused by such masses of humanity at the Ḥadjdj. Complaints are made even of the uncleanness of the Masdjid al-Khaif and at Minā there are further the decomposing remains of the countless animals sacrificed.

The Ḥadjdj cremonies in Minā date back to the old pagan period [cf. ḤADJDJ], for Muḥammad, as usual in taking over old customs, contented himself with cutting out the too obviously pagan elements, the result being that we can no longer reconstruct the old forms with certainty. The old poets make only passing references to them [cf. DJAMRA]; that they were similar to the Muslim practices is evident, for example, from an interesting passage in the Madīna poet Ḳais b. Khaṭīm (ed. Kowalski, No. 4, p. 1 *sqq.*) where there is a reference to the "three days in Minā" and where we further learn that the festival held there offered an occasion for entering into and carrying on love-affairs. The stone throwing is certainly very ancient; its significance is quite unintelligible in Islām, although it is doubtful if there were already three heaps of stones in the pre-Islāmic period [cf. DJAMRA]. It is also clear that the ceremonies in Minā formed the conclusion of the Ḥadjdj even in ancient times. Muḥammad however made some serious alterations here, for he inserted a visit to Mecca before the stay in Minā, whereby the ceremony first received its legitimate Muḥammadan character; but the old elements remained the important factors, for the Ḥadjdj ends not in Mecca but, as before, in Minā, to which the pilgrims return after the digression to Mecca. A survival of the pagan period probably exists in the slaughtering place preferred by the majority on the southern slopes of Thabīr "the place of sacrifice of the ram" (cf. Sūra xxxvii. 102 *sqq.*), as its association with the story of Abraham probably enabled an old pagan sacred spot to be adopted into Islām. From Burton's description it is a square rocky platform reached by a few steps. Muḥammad himself did not directly forbid the use of the pagan place of slaughter, but deprived it of its importance by saying that all Minā is a place of sacrifice: a clever procedure which he also followed at ʿArafāt and Muzdalifa.

According to the law of Islām, the pilgrims who arrive in Mecca on the 8th Dju 'l-Ḥidjdja should leave this town in time to be able to perform the mid-day ṣalāt in Minā and remain there till sunrise on the 9th and only then go on to ʿArafāt. The majority however do not do this but go on the 8th straight on to ʿArafāt where they arrive in the evening. After performing the ceremonies of the pilgrimage in ʿArafāt and Muzdalifa they go before sunrise on the 10th to Minā to celebrate the day of the great sacrifice (*yawm al-aḍḥā* or *yawm al-naḥr*) (in contrast to the pre-Islāmic practice, which was to start only after sunrise). Here the concluding rites are gone through, the slaughtering, the clipping of the hair and nails and the lapidation. There is not complete agreement on the order of these ceremonies, which one tradition (Wāḳidī, transl. Wellhausen, p. 429) makes Muḥammad declare to be quite irrelevant. The modification of the stone throwing is noteworthy, for on the day of sacrifice it is only done at the ʿAḳaba heap, while on the three following days each pilgrim daily throws seven little stones on all three heaps. The conclusion of the whole pilgrimage is the three Minā or *tashrīḳ* days, the 11th, 12th and 13th Dhu 'l-Ḥidjdja. They are days of rejoicing which are celebrated with great jubilation, illumination and the firing of shots. All the pilgrims however do not wait for these three days but many set off on their return journey before then.

Bibliography: Wāḳidī, transl. Wellhausen, p. p. 423, 426, 428; Ibn Saʿd, II/i. 125; al-Maḳdisī, *BGA*, iii. 76; Ibn Rusteh, *ibid.*, vii. 55; Yāḳūt, *Muʿdjam*, ed. Wüstenfeld, iv. 642 *sq.*; Burckhardt, *Reisen in Arabien*, p. 415—431; R. Burton, *A Pilgrimage to al-Madīnah and Meccah*, London 1893, ii. 203—222; al-Batanūnī, *al-Riḥla al-Ḥidjāzīya*, Cairo 1329; Wavell, *A modern Pilgrim*, p. 153—171; E. Rutter, *The Holy Cities of Arabia*, i. 168—187; Wellhausen, *Reste arabischen Heidentums* [2], p. 80, 88; Snouck Hurgronje, *Het Mekkaansche Feest*, Leiden 1880, esp. p. 158—167 (= *Verspr. Geschr.*, i. 1—124); Juynboll, *Handbuch*, p. 151—157; Glaudefroy-Demombynes, *Le pèlerinage à la Mekke*, 1923, p. 238—295; cf. the Bibl. to the article DJAMRA, and add: Houtsma, *Het Skopelisme en het Steenwerpen te Minā*, in *Versl. Med. Ak. Amst.*, *Afd. Letterkunde*, 4. Reeks, vi. 104—217; Chauvin, *Le jet de pierres et le pèlerinage de Mecque*, in *Annales de l'Acad. d'Archéologie de Belgique*, ser. v., vol. 4, p. 272 *sqq.*; Wensinck, *Handbook*, s.v.

MINARET. [See MANĀRA].

MINBAR (A.), pulpit [MASDJID, D, 2*d*.].

MIʿRĀDJ (A.), originally ladder, later "ascent", especially Muḥammad's ascension to heaven. In the Ḳur'ān, Sūra lxxxi. 19—25 and liii. 1—12, a vision is described in which a heavenly messenger appears to Muḥammad and Sūra liii. 13—18 deals with a second vision of a similar kind. In both cases the Prophet sees a heavenly figure approach him from the distance but there is no suggestion that he himself was carried off. It is otherwise with the experience alluded to in Sūra xvii. 1: "Praise him, who travelled in one night with his servant from the Masdjid al-Ḥarām to the Masdjid al-Aḳṣā, whose surroundings we blessed, in order to show him our signs". That Muḥammad is meant by the "servant" is generally assumed and there is no reason to doubt it (Schrieke, *Islam*, vi. 13, note 6; Bevan, *ZATW*, xxvii. 53 *sq.*); that the Masdjid al-Ḥarām is the Meccan sanctuary is certain from Ḳur'ānic usage (Horovitz, *Koran. Unters.*, p. 140); but what is the Masdjid al-Aḳṣā [q.v.]? According to the traditional explanation, but not the only one recognized in Ḥadīth (see Schrieke, *op. cit.*, p. 12, 14 and above, s.v. ISRĀ') it would mean Jerusalem, but how could Muḥammad, who in Sūra xxx. 1 speaks of Palestine as *adna 'l-arḍ*, call a sanctuary situated in Jerusalem *al-masdjid al-aḳṣā*? The age of this explanation is not quite certain; perhaps it was already known to ʿUmar b. Abī Rabīʿa (ed. Schwarz, xci.) and Abū Ṣakhr (*Lieder der Hudhailiten*, ed. Wellhausen, cclxiv. 24); but even these belong only to the Umaiyad period (contrary to Lammens, *Sanctuaires*, p. 72, this is true also of Abū Ṣakhr, who according to *Aghānī*, xxi. 94 was a partisan of the Banū Marwān and panegyrist of ʿAbd al-Malik). Muḥammad probably meant by al-Masdjid al-Aḳṣā a place in heaven, such as the place in the highest of the seven heavens in which the angels sing praises of Allāh and we would then have in Sūra xvii. 1, evidence from the Prophet himself about his nocturnal ascension into the heavenly spheres (Schrieke, *op. cit.*, p. 13 *sqq.*; Horovitz, *Isl.*, ix. 161 *sqq.*), testimony which is however content with the mention of the experience itself and says nothing about its course. The question of the possibility of an ascent to heaven is several times touched on in the Ḳurʾān. In Sūra xl. 36 Firʿawn gives Hāmān orders to build a palace so that he can reach the cords of heaven and climb up to the god of Mūsā (cf. also Sūra xxviii. 4). In Sūra lii. 38, the calumniators are asked whether they had perchance a ladder (*sullam*) so that they could hear the heavenly voice and in Sūra vi. 35 the consequences are considered which the signs brought by the Prophet with the help of a ladder to heaven might have on his hearers. The old poets also talk of ascending to heaven by a ladder, as a means of escaping something one wants to avoid (Zuhair, *Muʿallaḳa*, p. 54; Aʿshā, xv. 32).

Ḥadīth gives further details of the Prophet's ascension. Here the ascension is usually associated with the nocturnal journey to Jerusalem, so that the ascent to heaven takes place from this sanctuary. We also have accounts preserved which make the ascension start from Mecca and make no mention of the journey to Jerusalem. In one of these the ascension takes place immediately after the "purification of the heart" (see Bukhārī, *Ṣalāt*, bāb 1; *Ḥadjdj*, bāb 76; *Manāḳib*, bāb 42; Aḥmad b. Ḥanbal, *Musnad*, iv. 207, v. 143; Ṭabarī, ed de Goeje, i. 1157 *sq.*). In the last mentioned passage we read: "When the Prophet had received his revelation and was sleeping at the Kaʿba, as the Ḳuraish used to do, the angels Gabriel and Michael came to him and said: With regard to whom have we received the order? Whereupon they themselves answered: With regard to their lord. Thereupon they went away but came back the next night, three of them. When they found him sleeping they laid him on his back, opened his body, brought water from the Zamzam well and washed away all that they found within his body of doubt, idolatry, paganism and error. They then brought a golden vessel which was filled with wisdom and belief and then his body was filled with wisdom and belief. Thereupon he was taken up to the lowest heaven". The other versions of the same story show many additions and variants; according to one, for example, Gabriel came to Muḥammad through the roof of his house which opened to receive him; according to another, it was Gabriel alone who appeared to him and there are many similar variants. All these versions however put Muḥammad's ascension at an early period and make it a kind of dedication of him as a Prophet, for which the purification of the heart had paved the way. Ethnographical parallels (Schrieke, *op. cit.*, p. 2—4) show other instances of a purification being preliminary to an ascension. Similar stories are found in pagan Arabia (Horovitz, *op. cit.*, p. 171 *sqq.*) and also in Christian legends (*op. cit.*, p. 170 *sqq.*). Another story (Ibn Saʿd, 1/i. 143) says that the ascension took place from Mecca although it does not associate it with "the purification of the heart" which had in the meantime been put back to the childhood of the Prophet.

How did it come about however that this, obviously the earlier, tradition of Mecca as the starting point of the ascension was ousted by the other which made it take place from Jerusalem? The localisation of the Ḳurʾānic Masdjid al-Aḳṣā in Jerusalem is by some connected with the effoıts of ʿAbd al-Malik to raise Jerusalem to a place of special esteem in the eyes of believers (Schrieke, *op. cit.*, p. 13; Horovitz, *op. cit.*, p. 165 *sqq.*; do., in *Islamic Culture*, ii. 35 *sqq.*) and in any case it cannot be proved that this identification is older than the time of ʿAbd al-Malik. It might all the easier obtain currency as Jerusalem to the Christians was the starting point of Christ's ascension and from the fourth century Jesus's footprint had been shown to pilgrims in the Basilica of the Ascension; as now, perhaps as early as the time of ʿAbd al-Malik, that of their Prophet was shown to Muslim pilgrims (Horovitz, *op. cit.*, p. 167 *sq.*). The idea of the "heavenly Jerusalem" may have had some influence on the development of the *isrāʾ* legends; when Muḥammad meets Ibrāhīm, Mūsā and ʿĪsā in Jerusalem, the presence of these prophets in the earthly Jerusalem is not at once intelligible, but it loses any remarkable features if Bait al-Maḳdis (Ibn Hishām, p. 267) from the first meant the "Heavenly Jerusalem" (Horovitz, *op. cit.*, p. 168; for another explanation cf. the art. ISRĀʾ). Perhaps also the phrase *alladhī bāraknā ḥawlahu* was taken to support the reference to Jerusalem; when these words occur elsewhere in the Ḳurʾān they refer to sites in the holy land (Lammens, *op. cit.*, p. 72, note). While the stories quoted above only say that Gabriel took the Prophet up to the heights of heaven, but are silent as to how, others add that a ladder (*miʿrādj*) was used for the ascent (see Ibn Hishām, p. 268; Ṭabarī, *Tafsīr*, xv. 10; Ibn Sʿad, 1/i. 143); this ladder was of splendid appearance; it is the one to which the dying turn their eyes and with the help of which the souls of men ascend to heaven. The ladder is probably identical with Jacob's ladder in Genesis, xxviii. 12; the Ethiopic Book of Jubilees xxvii. 21 calls this *maʿāreg* and Sūra lxx. 3, 4 calls Allāh *Dhu 'l-maʿāridj* "to whom the angels and the spirit ascend" (*taʿrudj*). According to Sūra xxxii. 5, the *amr* rises to Allāh; according to Sūra lvii. 4 and xxxiv. 2, Allāh knows "what descends from heaven and what ascends to it", and in Sūra xliii. 33 there is a reference to steps (*maʿāridj*) in the houses of men. Muḥammad therefore already knew the word, which is presumably taken from Ethiopic (Horovitz, *op. cit.*, p. 174 *sqq.*). Among the Mandaeans also the ladder (*sumbilta*) isthe means of ascending to heaven (*Ginza*, transl. Lidzbarski, p. 49, 208, 490) and there are parallels to the ladder of the dead in the mysteries of Mithras (see Andrae, *Die Person Muhammeds*, p. 45; Wetter, *Phos*, p. 114, note 2); the Manichaean *ʿamūd al-sabḥ* (*Fihrist*, p. 335) by means of which the dead man is taken to the sphere of the moon is a more distant parallel (Bevan, *op. cit.*, p. 59).

Just as the miʿrādj is associated with the ascension, so Burāḳ [q.v.] is originally connected with the night journey to Jerusalem; it found its way however at an early date into the legend of the ascension (see Bukhārī, *Manāḳib*, bāb 42; Aḥmad b. Ḥanbal, *Musnad*, iv. 207; v. 387; Ṭabarī, *Tafsīr*, xv. 12). The prophets earlier than Muḥammad had used Burāḳ as their steed (Ibn Hishām p. 263; Diyārbakrī, *Taʾrīkh al-khamīs*, i. 349), in particular Ibrāhīm (ʿAdjdjādj, ed. Ahlwardt, xlv. 48—52;

Ṭabarī, *Tafsīr*, xv. 5; Thaʿlabī, *ʿArāʾis*, p. 63; Ḥalabī, i. 369). This idea of one animal used by the different prophets is borrowed; according to the Midrashic statement, late it is true (*Yalḳūṭ* on Zachariah, ix., No. 875; *Pirḳē de R. Eliʿezer*, xli.), the ass which Abraham rode (Genesis xxii. 3) is the same as that used by Zipporah and her sons (Exodus, iv. 10) and is that on which the Messiah will make his entrance (cf. also Ibn Saʿd, 1/ii. 176). The recollection that this steed was an ass survives in Muslim tradition so that Burāḳ is described as "smaller than a mule and larger than an ass' (Bukhārī, *Manāḳib*, bāb 43; similarly Ibn Hishām, p. 264; Ibn Saʿd, 1/i. 143). Ibn Saʿd already describes Burāḳ as a female beast and, as early as a story attributed by Ibn Isḥāḳ to al-Ḥasan al-Baṣrī, Burāḳ is given wings (Ibn Hishām, *loc. cit.*). Thaʿlabī seems to be the first who speaks of Burāḳ's human face (in Ḥalabī, i. 370); in the miniatures dealt with fully by Arnold, *Painting in Islam*, p. 113 *sqq.*, al-Burāḳ usually has a woman's head.

At the gate of each of the seven heavens through which he wanders with the Prophet, Gabriel is asked for his own name and that of his companion (Bukhārī, *Ṣalāt*, bāb 1, Ṭabarī, *Tafsīr*, xv. 4; *Annales*, ed. de Goeje, i. 1157). After he gives these he is next asked if Muḥammad has already been sent as a prophet (*awaḳad buʿitha ilaihi*, correction for the original *awaḳad buʿitha* found in Ṭabarī, *Annales*, i. 1158; see Snouck Hurgronje, *Isl.*, vi, 5, note 4); this also indicates that the ascension originally belonged to the period immediately after his call (Schrieke, *op. cit.*, p. 6). In each heaven they meet one of the earlier messengers of God, usually Adam in the first, Yaḥyā and ʿĪsā in the second, Yūsuf in the third, Idrīs in the fourth, Hārūn in the fifth, Mūsā in the sixth and Ibrāhīm in the seventh heaven; there are also variations and Adam appears as judge over the spirits of the dead (Andrae, p. 44 *sq.*; Schrieke, p. 17; Aḥmad b. Ḥanbal, *Musnad*, v. 143; cf. *Apoc. Mosis*, p. 37). Of the other messengers of God we are only told — in addition to being given a description of their personal appearance — that they greeted Muḥammad; Mūsā is an exception who expressly says that Muḥammad is higher in the esteem of Allāh than himself and that the number of his followers surpasses his own (Ṭabarī, *Tafsīr*, xv. 11). On another occasion, Muḥammad engages in a conversation with Mūsā after Allāh had imposed upon him 50 ṣalāts a day as obligatory prayers for the faithful. On Mūsā's advice, Muḥammad asks several times for an alleviation and each time Allāh grants it; but when Mūsā says 5 ṣalāts are still too many, the Prophet refuses to ask for less (on *Genesis*, xviii. 23 *sqq.* as the prototype of this episode; cf. Goldziher, *Studien*, i. 36; Schrieke, p. 19; Andrae, p. 82). According to some versions, Mūsā dwells in the seventhhe aven and the conversation seems to be more natural there. To the ascension belong the visits to paradise and to hell. Paradise according to many versions is in the seventh heaven, according to others in the first; in some it is not mentioned at all. The statements about its rivers are contradictory (Schrieke, p. 19; cf. above KAWTHAR), the *Sidrat al-muntahā* is usually placed in the seventh heaven (Bevan, p. 59; Schrieke, p. 18). In one description hell is put below the first heaven (Ibn Hishām, p. 269; Ṭabarī, *Tafsīr*, iv. 10). According to another, the place of punishment of the damned is on the way between heaven and earth and Muḥammad sees it on his journey to the Bait al-Maḳdis (Ṭabarī, *Tafsīr*, xv. 101, also Aḥmad b. Ḥanbal, *Musnad*, i. 257; ii. 353; iii. 120, 182, 224, 231, 239). On the punishment in hell cf. Schrieke, p. 17; Andrae, p. 44; Horovitz, p. 173; Reitzenstein, *Das mandäische Buch des Herrn der Grösse*, p. 81 *sqq.*; Lidzbarski, *Johannisbuch*, p. 98 *sqq.*; *Ginza*, p. 183.

That Muḥammad appeared before Allāh's throne in the seventh heaven and that the conversation about the obligatory prayers took place there, is already recorded in the oldest stories (see above) but only rarely do they extend the conversation between Allāh and the Prophet to other subjects (Ṭabarī, xxvii. 26; *Musnad*, iv. 66 as a dream; Andrae, p. 70). But objection was raised to the assertion that Muḥammad on this occasion saw Allāh face to face (Andrae, p. 71 *sqq.*), and the question was also raised at an early date whether the ascension was a dream or a reality, whether only the soul of the Prophet was carried up or also his body (Caetani, *Annali*, Intr. § 320; Andrae, p. 72; Bevan, p. 60; Schrieke, p. 13, note 1).

The Ḥadīth contains, besides these, other details which Asín (*Escatologia*, Madrid 1919, p. 7—52; do., *Dante y el Islam*, Madrid 1927, p. 25—71) has discussed. In developing the story of the Prophet's ascension Muḥammadan writers have used models afforded them by the Jewish and Christian Apocalypses. A few features may also come from the Parsees from the Arda Viraf; cf. the works already mentioned by Andrae, Bevan, Schrieke, Horovitz and W. Bousset, in *ARW*, iv. 136—169.

Later accounts (Chauvin, *Bibliographie*, xi. 207 *sqq.*: Asín, *Escatologia*, p. 53 *sqq.*; do., *Dante* etc., p. 72 *sqq.*; Nallino, in *RSO*, viii. 802) collect and systematize the material scattered in the older sources; they only increase the matter without however increasing the depth of its thought. Among the Miʿrādj-books which have become popular in modern times that of al-Ghaiṭī may be mentioned (this is the correct form, see Nallino, *op. cit.*, p. 813) on which Dardīr (d. 1201/1786) wrote a *ḥāshiya*; also that of Barzandjī (d. 1179/1765). In the non-Arab lands of Islām, Persian, Turkish, Hindustānī and Malay versions of the legend have contributed to its dispersion (see Chauvin, *loc. cit.*).

The ascension of the Prophet later served as a model for the description of the journey of the soul of the deceased to the throne of the divine judge (Asín, *Escatologia*, p. 59 *sq.*); for the Ṣūfīs however, it is a symbol of the rise of the soul from the bonds of sensuality to the heights of mystic knowledge. Ibn al-ʿArabī thus expounds it in his work *Kitāb al-isrāʾ ilā maḳām al-asrā* (Asín, p. 61 *sqq.*; Andrae, p. 81 *sq.*), and in his *Futūḥāt*, ii. 356—375 he makes a believer and a philosopher make the journey together but the philosopher only reaches the seventh heaven, while no secret remains hidden from the pious Muslim (Asín, p. 63 *sqq.*). Abu 'l-ʿAlāʾ al-Maʿarrī's *Risālat al-ghufrān* is a parody on the traditional accounts of the Miʿrādj (Asín, p. 71 *sqq.*). Asín in his two books quoted has dealt with the knowledge of Muslim legends of the ascension possessed by the Christian middle ages and their influence on Dante. See also the edition by E. Cerulli of the Latin and French translations made c. 1270 by Ibrāhīm "al-ḥakīm", *Il "Libro della Scala"* (Città del Vaticano 1949).

According to Ibn Saʿd, 1/i. 147 the *isrāʾ* took place on the 17th Rabīʿ I, the ascension on the 17th Ramaḍān. For centuries however, the night before the 27th Radjab — a date also significant in the history of Mecca (see Snouck Hurgronje, *Mekka*, ii. 71) — has been regarded by the pious as the *Lailat al-miʿrādj*, and the eve is like the *mawlid al-nabī* devoted to reading the legend of the feast (see Ibn al-Ḥādjdj al-ʿAbdarī, *Madkhal*, i. 143 *sqq.*; Herklots, *Qanoon e Islam* ², p. 165; Lane, *Manners and Customs*, London 1896, p. 474 *sq.*; Snouck Hurgronje, *The Achehnese*, i. 219; Asín, *Escatologia*, p. 97).

Bibliography: is given in the article; cf. also R. Hartmann, in *Bibliothek-Warburg, Vorträge* 1928—1929 (Leipzig 1930), p. 42—65; G. Levi della Vida, *Nuove luce sulle fonti islamiche della Divina Commedia*, in *Andalus* 1949, 377—407.

MĪRĀTH (A.), Inheritance (pl. *mawārīth*); *wārith* the heir, *mūrith* the person leaving the estate. This branch of Muḥammadan law is also called *'ilm al-farāʾid* "the science of the ordained quotas" (cf. Sūra iv. 11) after its most important and most difficult part.

1. In keeping with the patriarchal system prevailing among the Arabs, the estate of a deceased tribesman went ab intestato to the nearest male relative(s); the order of succession in which these relatives, the so-called *ʿaṣaba* (corresponding to *agnati*), were called upon to inherit survives systematized in Muslim law. Minors were, as incapable of bearing arms, excluded from the succession as were female relatives; widows also were not entitled to inherit, and originally presumably themselves formed a part of the estate, a view which survived in the levirate marriage usual among the Arabs, to which Sūra iv. 19 refers in forbidding it. There is no evidence of any preferential treatment of the first-born, which we find elsewhere in Semitic law. This, the original legal position, had by Muḥammad's time certainly altered somewhat in favour of women; in cases where the deceased left no male relatives his daughters seem frequently to have obtained the estate; but woman had by no means equal treatment with man, as is clear from the Ḳurʾānic regulations. In addition to these principal heirs the pre-Islāmic Arabs had also secondary heirs who correspond to the later socalled quota-heirs (*dhawu 'l-farāʾiḍ*) and received a part of the estate, the bulk of which went to the *ʿaṣaba*. From Sūra ii. 180 and iv. 33 which confirm this arrangement, we can see that these included the parents, the "relatives" — apparently so far as they were not *ʿaṣaba* — and the so-called confederates (*ḥalīf*, plur. *ḥulafāʾ*); the settlement of the portions falling to them was done — at least in part — according to the last will of the testator. All this has its parallels in the development of a 'mitigated agnatic succession' among other peoples.

2. The Ḳurʾān modified this system considerably in details, the main point being the improvement in the treatment of women here as well as with regard to the laws of family life generally; at the same time there is a clear endeavour to fix in legal form the practice which had varied considerably in heathen times. One provision which had been made under special circumstances was abandoned later on: immediately after the *hidjra*, it had been ordered that those who migrated with the Prophet (the *muhādjirūn*) and the believers in Madīna (the *anṣār*) should regard themselves as brethren and therefore inherit from one another, while all bonds of relationship between the *muhādjirūn* and their relatives left in Mecca, even if they were believers, were to be regarded as broken (Sūra viii. 72, with the limitation imposed in viii. 75); but this was expressly revoked by Sūra xxxiii. 6. Tradition regards this fraternization as a special case of confederacy (*ḥalīf*dom). For the rest, the Ḳurʾān in the first Madīna period confirmed the system of secondary heirs and the whole general practice in regard to inheritance (Sūra ii. 180 is probably to be dated before Ramaḍān of the year 2, and iv. 33 cannot be much later); that Sūra ii. 180 expressly makes the fair treatment of the secondary heirs a duty, already reveals the direction which later ordinances were to take. Connected with this is the probably contemporary ii. 240 which secures the wife, if she survives her husband, a legacy of maintenance for a year. Not much later, about the year 3, is Sūra iv. 19: "Ye who believe, it is not lawful for you to inherit women against their will"; this is not meant as a regular legal ordinance but is part of the Ḳurʾānic endeavour to improve the position of women. Very soon after the battle of Uhud, when numerous Muslims had fallen, we have — as a result of it — the final Ḳurʾānic ordinance of Sūra iv. 7—14. "To the men belongs a share of what their parents and kindred leave, and to the women belongs a share of what their parents and kindred leave — whether it be little or much — as a determined share. 8. If the next of kin (not entitled to inherit), the orphans and the poor are present at the division, give them some of it and speak kindly to them (verses 9 *sq.* go on to deal with the treatment of orphans). 11. Allāh ordains for you, concerning your children, (as follows): for the male the like of the portion of two females; but if there are (only) females (and) more than two, two-thirds of the estate belongs to them and if there is (but) one (female) to her belongs the half. And the parents shall each have a sixth of the estate if (the deceased) has children, and if he has no children and (only) his parents inherit from him, his mother shall have a third. But if he has brothers, his mother shall have a sixth. (All this) after deducting a bequest he may have made or a debt. Ye know not whether your parents or your children be nearest to you in usefulness. (This is) an ordinance of Allāh and Allāh is knowing and wise. 12. To you belongs the half of the estate of your wives, if they have no children; but if they have children a fourth of their estate belongs to you — after deducting a bequest they may have made or a debt. To them belongs a fourth of your estate, if you have no children; but if you have children an eighth of your estate belongs to them — after deducting a bequest you may have made or a debt. If distant relatives inherit from a deceased male or female, and he has a brother or a sister, each shall have a sixth; but if there are more then that, they shall share in a third after deducting a bequest he may have made or debt, without prejudice. (This is) an ordinance of Allāh, and Allāh is knowing and gracious" (Verse 13 *sq.* contain promises and threats). As the settlement of the succession in indirect lines left questions undecided, Sūra iv. 176 supplemented the above: "They will ask thee for a decision. Say: Allāh gives you the following decision for remoter kinship: if a man die and have no children, but have a sister, half of the estate belongs to her and he is her heir if she have no children; if there be two sisters, two thirds of the estate belongs to them; but if there be both brothers and sisters, the male shall have like the portion of two females".

The object of these regulations is simply to supplement the law regarding the rights of the *ʿaṣaba*; they are not a reorganisation of the whole law. Each of the persons named is therefore only allotted a definite portion; the remainder, and this is as a rule the major portion, of the estate falls as before to the *ʿaṣaba*. Female relatives thus generally receive half the share of male relatives of the same degree. The quotas here given abolished the testamentary settlement of the portions usual in the heathen period, which was still approved by Sūra ii. 180; this is the historical starting point for the tradition — early interpreted in another sense — that a legacy in favour of the heirs is not valid. Sūra ii. 240 is probably rightly regarded as abrogated by the settling of the widow's portion. There is a slight difficulty in interpretation only in iv. 12; but there can be no doubt that this passage refers to half-sisters on the mother's side, as indeed it has always been interpreted; the text of Ubaiy even inserts an addition to this effect. The verse iv. 176 on the other hand refers to full sisters. In iv. 11 "more than two" is to be interpreted, as the sense requires, as "two and more".

3. The full details which tradition is able to give regarding the causes of the revelation of the regulations on the law of inheritance are not historical; on internal grounds all we can say is that it took place soon after the battle of Uḥud. The numerous *ḥadīths* which simply repeat the Ḳur'ānic regulations may be neglected here. Tradition can only record very few actual divergences from the prescriptions of the Ḳur'ān: one of these is that a woman received back as her inheritance a slave whom she had presented to her mother and who represented the latter's whole estate. According to another story, the Prophet is said to have laid it down that the wives of the *muhādjirūn* should inherit the house of their husbands. While nothing can be quoted in favour of the first *ḥadīth*, the second, which does not seem to be intended as a foundation for any legal clause, may have a kernel of historical truth in it.

4. The prescriptions of the Ḳur'ān are supplemented and developed in countless traditions among which a comparatively large number relate not decisions of the Prophet himself, but of his Companions; in reality they must not even be regarded as that, but only as anonymous evidence of the first developments of the Ḳur'ānic law of inheritance. At this stage of development it is already firmly established that an unbeliever cannot inherit from a Muslim; the right of a Muslim to inherit from an unbeliever is finally also denied, although there is some opposition to this view. Excluded from the right of inheritance is also one who has killed the proprietor of the estate, at least if the slaying was deliberate (with *ʿamd*; cf. ḲATL). That a slave has no right of inheritance is taken for granted. Legal relationship is necessary for the right of inheritance; thus illegitimate children or those whose paternity has been disputed by *liʿān* have no legal claim on the estates of their father and his relations. The *mawlā* [q.v.] is annexed to the *ʿaṣaba*: the patron and the manumitted slave inherit from one another and according to one view, the same right is even granted to the man before whom the person concerned has adopted Islām, who is also called *mawlā*. After the *mawlā* come — although some oppose this — the *dhawu 'l-arḥām*, i.e. persons related to the legator in the female line, whose representative is usually the *khāl* or maternal uncle. In case all these heirs should not exist, the fellow-tribesmen are named. With certain modifications which occur again in the later teaching, a son's daughters are treated like daughters and grandparents like parents, but this regulation only won recognition after opposition and varying practice in details. There arises the problem of the share of the grandfather beside the brothers, which goes back to his varying position in the series of the *ʿaṣaba*; along with other views we find quoted also the one that later prevailed but it does not seem to be the earliest. The Ḳur'ān lays it down that before dividing the estate the amount of any legacies and debts should be deducted; in early times — probably in literal interpretation of the Ḳur'ānic passages — the legacies often were given preference to debts; after some opposition the opposite teaching prevailed. The *diya* [q.v.] to be paid for a slain man should be subject to the usual rules as part of his estate; but in early times the wife was not allowed a share in the *diya* of her slain husband, which goes back to old Arab conceptions of the family; the other view ultimately prevailed. The eager interest taken in early Islām in the law of inheritance is reflected in *ḥadīth*; there are traditions in which the Prophet orders the law of inheritance to be taught and learned, calls it "the half of knowledge" on account of its difficulty and expresses the fear that this subject, so difficult to remember, might disappear from the memory of his community.

5. The following are the principles of the law of inheritance in the fully developed *fiḳh* according to the Shāfiʿī teaching.

a. The law of intestacy in general. There is no fusion between the property of the deceased and that of the heir; the creditors of the estate can therefore only assert their claims against the estate. In addition to obligations entered into by the deceased, the debts of the estate include the funeral expenses and the religious duties omitted by the deceased so far as they consist of concrete things (e.g. unpaid *zakāt*) or can be atoned for by payment (e.g. neglected fasts [*ṣawm*]) or can be carried through at the expense of the estate by a deputy (e.g. the *ḥadjdj* omitted without good reason). After the debts any legacies have to be paid [cf. WAṢĪYA]; the remainder passes to the heirs. A necessary condition for inheriting is that the heir has survived the deceased; in doubtful cases, when persons who would inherit from one another have died without its being certain which died first, as a rule no inheritance passes between them. The heir must also have existed when the testator died; only in the case where a man leaves a pregnant widow or *umm al-walad*, is a child's share reserved for the unborn child. Excluded from succession are the following: one who has caused the death of the deceased, the *murtadd*, an unbeliever from the succession to a Muslim and vice versa, the *ḥarbī* (the unbelieving member of a state with which the Muslim stands in no treaty relation) and the slave. The *ʿaṣaba* are the normal heirs; inheritance by others is only an exception; so the *ʿaṣaba* receive the whole estate after the deduction of the portions for the quota-heirs. If there are no *ʿaṣaba*, the remainder of the estate goes to the state treasury (*bait al-māl*; a notable change from the view found in traditions), on the condition that this is administered according to law for the benefit of the Muslims; otherwise the quota-heirs receive the remainder of the estate in proportion to their quotas by the so-called law of reversion (*radd*), with the exception of the widower or widow. Only if there are neither *ʿaṣaba* nor quota-heirs and the state treasury is not being administered in accordance with the law are the *dhawu 'l-arḥām* — i.e. persons related to the deceased in the female line as well as those female relatives who cannot be quota-heirs — called upon to inherit. If there are none of these relatives, any Muslim may take possession of the estate, if he is capable and ready to administer it for the general good of Muslims.

b. Succession of the *ʿaṣaba*. The *ʿaṣaba* are called upon to inherit in the following order: 1. The male descendants of the deceased in the male line, a nearer excluding the more distant relatives from the succession. 2. The nearest male relative in the ascending male line with the provision that the father, but not the grandfather (and the remoter ascendant) of the deceased inherits before his brothers. 3. The nearest male relative in the male line among the descendants of the father: first the full brother, then the half-brother on the father's side, then the descendants of the full brother, then those of the half-brother on the father's side. 4. The nearest male relative in the male line among the descendants of the grandfather (as under 3) etc. 5. Lastly the *mawlā*, i.e. the patron (or patroness), if the deceased was a freed man, and then his *ʿaṣaba*. — The brothers of the deceased inherit along with the grandfather as *ʿaṣaba* in equal shares, but if there are more than two brothers, the grandfather receives not less than one-third of what is to be divided between him and the brothers. If there are also quota-heirs, the grandfather is allowed in addition at least a sixth of the estate (which he would inherit as a quota-heir; cf. *c*). He can then choose the most favourable of the three arrangements. — Female *ʿaṣaba*. If the deceased left sons as well as daughters they inherit jointly, the share of a son being twice as large as that of a daughter while the quota allotted to the daughters is dropped, as is intended by the spirit of the Ḳurʾānic law. The daughter who inherits along with a son is therefore also called *ʿaṣaba*. The daughter of a son of the legator is similarly treated, inheriting along with the son of a son; and likewise the full sister who inherits along with a full brother; finally also the half-sister on the father's side who inherits with a half-brother on the father's side. — If the full sister and the half-sister on the father's side inherit along with a daughter of the deceased or of his son, they do not receive their quota which in this case goes to the daughter or son's daughter, but the rest of the estate after deduction of all quotas that have to be paid.

c. Shares of the quota-heirs (*dhawu 'l-farāʾiḍ*; cf. FARĀʾIḌ). It is true that in the Ḳurʾān only the daughters, parents, husband and wife, and brothers and sisters are allotted a quota but the rules holding for the daughters have been extended to the daughters of the son and those for the parents to the grandparents; in addition, a distinction has been made among the sisters between the full sister, the half-sister on the father's side and the half-sister on the mother's side. The total number of quota-heirs has thus been raised to twelve: 1. The daughter is entitled to half the estate, two or more daughters get two-thirds, but if daughters inherit along with sons, they become *ʿaṣaba* (cf. *b*). 2. The daughter of a son is subject to the same rules as a daughter and takes her place in default of her; inheriting along with the son of a son she becomes *ʿaṣaba*. As the son's daughter is related to the deceased through his son, she is excluded from participation when a son of the deceased inherits. A daughter on the other hand does not exclude directly a son's daughter from the succession; as however daughters and son's daughters together have only two-thirds of the estate as their quota, a son's daughter has only a sixth if there is one daughter, and nothing if there are two or more, unless she inherits in these cases along with a son's son as *ʿaṣaba*. 3. The father's quota is always a sixth of the estate; in addition he is *ʿaṣaba* and receives also any residuum of the estate after deducting all quotas, unless there are male descendants of the deceased. 4. The paternal grandfather (in default of him, the remoter ascendant) also receives one sixth of the estate as his quota, but is excluded by the father; he is also *ʿaṣaba* if there are no male descendants nor father of the deceased. But if, in this case, there are also brothers of the legator, he becomes *ʿaṣaba* along with them (on the share which falls to the grandfather in this case and in the case where there are also quota-heirs cf. *b*). 5. The mother receives one-sixth of the estate if there are children, son's children or two or more brothers or sisters of the deceased; otherwise a third (in practice the father in this case as a rule receives two-thirds, i.e. one sixth as quota-heir and the rest as *ʿaṣaba*; on an exceptional case cf. *d*). 6. The quota of the grandmother is always a sixth; from this the mother's mother is excluded by the mother, and the father's mother by the father and mother; in default of grandmother their place is taken by the remoter female ascendants of the deceased, so far as they are not related to him by a male descendant not entitled to inherit. 7. A full sister receives half, two or more such sisters receive together two-thirds of the estate; along with a full brother or the grandfather she becomes *ʿaṣaba* and receives the half of the brother's share; along with the daughter or son's daughter she becomes also *ʿaṣaba* (cf. *b*); sons, sons' sons and the father exclude her from succession. 8. The treatment of the half-sister on the father's side is similar to that of the full sister; along with a half-brother on the father's side or the grandfather, she becomes *ʿaṣaba*, and likewise with the daughter or son's daughter (cf. *b*).; sons, sons' sons, father and full brothers exclude her from the succession. Full sisters exclude her only so far as daughters exclude son's daughters (cf. no. 2). 9 and 10. Each of the half-brother on the mother's side and of the half-sister on the mother's side receives a sixth, two or more together share a third among them; they are excluded from the succession by descendants and male ascendants. 11. The widower receives half of the estate, but only a quarter if there is a child or son's child; it is indifferent whether these are his own descendants or not. 12. The widow receives the half of what a widower would receive under the same circumstances; if the deceased leaves more than one widow they share equally the quota allotted to the widow. During the *ʿidda* (period of waiting; q.v.) after a revocable *ṭalāḳ* a man and woman are still regarded as man and wife for purposes of inheritance.

d. Exceptions from the general rules. Although the quota-heirs can never all inherit together and in particular most of the collateral relatives are excluded by those in the direct line, the number of qualified quota-heirs may sometimes be so large that the sum of their shares is larger than the whole estate; in this case their shares are proportionately reduced. Otherwise the concurrence of a number of heirs necessitates no change from the main rules, except in a few particular cases which have special names; these are cases in which, if the main rules were strictly carried through, the inheritances would be in a proportion to one another which would be contrary to the spirit of the law. E.g. in the case of the so-called *gharībatān*: if some one dies leaving a husband or wife and both parents, the mother would receive in any case a third, the father's share however, which is usually two-thirds (cf. *c* 5), would be here reduced by the quota either of the widow or of the widower; according to tradition, it was

ʿUmar who decided in this case that father and mother should share, in the proportion of two to one, what remains after deducting the portion of the widow or widower. Another case, the so-called *mushatraka*, is that in which a wife leaves her husband, her mother, two or more half-brothers on the mother's side and also one or more full brothers; as the quotas in this case make up the whole estate, nothing would be left for the full brothers as *ʿaṣaba* in this case, which is also said to have been decided by ʿUmar; the law lays down that the full brothers have the same rights as the half-brothers so that all inherit in equal shares the third originally set aside for the half-brothers.

6. The most important points of difference among the *maḏhāhib* are the following. Unbelievers who belong to different religions cannot inherit from one another according to Mālik and Ibn Ḥanbal, but they can according to Abū Ḥanīfa and al-Shāfiʿī. There are contradicting views regarding inheritance from the *murtadd*. One who has deliberately (with *ʿamd*) and illegally killed the proprietor of the estate, is, by unanimous agreement excluded from inheriting. Abū Ḥanīfa, al-Shāfiʿī and Ibn Ḥanbal, but not Mālik, also exclude one who has killed him without design (with *khaṭaʾ*; q. v.). One who is partially a slave can, according to Abū Ḥanīfa, Mālik and al-Shāfiʿī, neither inherit nor be inherited from; according to Ibn Ḥanbal, Abū Yūsuf, al-Shaibānī and al-Muzanī he does so in the proportion he is free. The so-called law of reversion to the quota-heirs if there are no *ʿaṣaba* (cf. 5*a*) as well as the precedence of the *dhawu ʾl-arḥām* and the treasury if there are no quota-heirs either, are disputed among the *madhāhib*. The paternal grandmother is not excluded from the succession by the father, according to Ibn Ḥanbal only; in his view, in this case she inherits a sixth either alone or shared equally with the mother. There are delicate points of difference regarding the succession of the remoted female ascendents. One who is entitled to receive a quota from more than one side inherits, according to Mālik and al-Shāfiʿī, only on ground of "stronger" relationship, according to Abū Ḥanīfa and Ibn Ḥanbal on ground of both respects; in the case of two cousins on the father's side, of which one is also the brother on the mother's side, the latter, it is unanimously agreed, receives a sixth and the remainder falls to the two as *ʿaṣaba* in equal portions, while Abū Thawr makes him inherit the whole. In the special case of the socalled *mushatraka*, Mālik's view agrees with that of al-Shāfiʿī (cf. 5*d*); according to Abū Ḥanīfa and his fellows, Ibn Ḥanbal and Dāwūd al-Ẓāhirī, the full brothers actually receive nothing.

7. *a*. The law of inheritance with the Imāmīs (Twelver-Shīʿīs) is based on the same principles as that of the Sunnīs but in its final development shows a number of quite important features of its own, which for the greatest part are but the consequences of their dogmatic-political doctrines (ʿAlī and Fāṭima had to be the only heirs of the Prophet, excluding Ibn ʿAbbās), and partly already expressed in the traditions or result from the rejection of certain *ḥadīths* by the Shīʿa. Among the main divergences are the ignoring of the *ʿaṣaba* and the constitution of one group of "heirs by relationship", which is divided into three classes: 1. the ascendants in the first degree and the descendants; 2. the other ascendants and the descendants of the ascendants in the first degree; 3. the maternal and paternal uncles and aunts. Each of these classes excludes the following ones from the succession and within the two categories of the two first classes the relative of the nearer degree excludes all others of a remoter degree of relationship, i.e. for example the daughter excludes the son's son; within the third class a distinction into degrees is made between the uncles and aunts of the deceased himself and their descendants, the uncles and aunts of his parents and their descendants etc., and here also the member of a nearer degree excludes those of a remoter degree. An exception which finds its explanation only in the individual case of the heirs of the Prophet, is that the son of the father's full brother excludes one (but not more than one) half-brother (on the father's side) of the father, if there are no other uncles. Within the same degree the full relatives (male or female) exclude all relatives on the father's (not the mother's) side, e.g. full sisters exclude halfbrothers; the relatives on the mother's side are excluded by all other relatives of the same degree only from a share in the 'reversion' of the estate. If relatives whose relationships with the deceased are traced through different persons inherit jointly, the proportion of their shares is settled by the (hypothetical) shares of the persons through whom they are related to the deceased; if, for example, paternal and maternal uncles inherit together, the former divide two-thirds of the estate (i.e. the father's hypothetical share), the latter a third (i.e. the mother's hypothetical share). This idea of 'representation' reappears in one of the Sunnite theories on the succession of the *dhawu ʾl-arḥām*. The rules applying to the brothers and sisters of the deceased are also applied to his father's brothers and sisters and so on, if the latter are called upon to inherit; if, for example, father's full brothers and sisters, and father's brothers and sisters on the mother's side exist together, the latter are not excluded by the former but receive a third which is divided equally among them (if there is only one, a sixth), and the former receive the remaining two-thirds (or five-sixths as the case may be) of which each uncle gets twice the share of an aunt; the process is similar when their children take the place of uncles and aunts. The grandfather (and if the case arises the remoter ascendants) always inherits equally with the brothers of the legator. Within homogeneous groups the male inherits double as much as the female, so far as there are no special regulations to the contrary; for the rest the male relative on the father's side is not especially privileged before the others, as among the Sunnīs. Besides these "heirs by relationship", there are "heirs for special reasons", i.e. husband and wife, and the patron (*mawlā*), namely 1. a patron who has freed the deceased from slavery; 2. a patron before whom the legator has become a Muslim, or who has pledged himself to pay the *diya* for him (this idea is also attested in the traditions and is to be found sporadically among the Sunnī authorities); 3. the *imām*, who here takes the place of the state treasury, and who, as the general patron of all Muslims, is entitled to inherit in the last resort. — In both main groups there are "simple" heirs and such as have a claim to a Ḳurʾānic quota. If the estate does not suffice to satisfy all the quotas, the shares are correspondingly reduced to the paternal relatives only, never to the maternal. What is left over after satisfying the quotas is given to the simple "heirs by relationship" according to the above rules; if they do not exist, the quota-heirs, with the exception of the husband or wife, receive the residuum also; if there are no "heirs by relationship" at all, the patrons come in, in the order given.

These general rules are sufficient to cause the distribution of an estate to look often very different among the Shīʿīs from among the Sunnīs. There are in addition differences in detail, of which the most important are the following: The Muslim does inherit from the unbeliever; unbelievers of all sects inherit from one another. In determining the portion of the childless widow, the landed property of the deceased is not taken into account. If the sole existing heir is a slave, he is purchased at the expense of the estate (his owner cannot refuse to sell him), thus becomes free and inherits what is left; if the parents of the deceased are slaves, they must in all cases be purchased at the expense of the estate, according to some the children also. The part-slave inherits to the degree in which he is free. One who has a claim to an inheritance from two sides inherits on both grounds. There are no legal relationships between an illegitimate child and his mother and her relatives, only between him and his descendants; if there are none, the estate goes to the *imām*. In the special case of the so-called *gharībatān* (cf. above 5 *d*), there is no divergence from the general principles. — On the whole the Shīʿa law of inheritance diverges further from the old Arab pre-Islāmic principles than the Sunnī doctrine in opposition to which it has been elaborated.

b. The law of inheritance of the Shīʿīte Zaidīs resembles rather closely the system of the Sunnīs, which has influenced its origins.

c. The most important peculiarities of the law of inheritance among the Khāridjī Ibāḍīs are the following: the paternal grandfather inherits as quota-heir a sixth of the estate if there are descendants of the deceased; otherwise he inherits as *ʿaṣaba*, thus excluding the brothers. The half-sister on the mother's side is assimilated to the half-sister on the father's side if neither this relative nor a full sister exist. The grandmother is only excluded by the mother. Female descendants, like husband or wife, have no share in the 'reversion' of the estate. Manumission confers no rights of inheritance. If there are no heirs at all, the estate is given away in charity. The special case of the so-called *musharraka* is settled as among the Shāfiʿīs (cf. 5 *d*). — The dependence of this system on the Sunnī is apparent.

8. The law of inheritance, as a branch of family law and as possessing a peculiarly religious character from its very full regulation in the Ḳurʾān, has always been one of the chapters of Muslim law most carefully observed in practice [cf. ʿĀDA and SHARĪʿA]. As in the long run it must lead inevitably to the splitting up of even the largest estates, various endeavours have been made to avoid this result, which was considered undesirable. A method, frequently adopted, was to constitute considerable portions of the estate religious endowments [cf. WAḲF] the proceeds of which could be disposed of by the grantor as he pleased; but most endowments in course of time became much broken up or were completely alienated. Another way adopted for instance in Indonesia is, in keeping with the local *ʿāda*, to admit only a portion of the actual estate to division among the heirs; sometimes an estate is divided already during the lifetime of its possessor by gift or friendly arrangement, and not infrequently some member of the family, according to circumstances, simply takes over the estate and obligations of the deceased. Especially landed property is often taken out of the control of Muslim law. Women are excluded from inheritance by customary law in many Muslim countries, as among the Berbers, in parts of India, in China; in Algeria, this state of things has only in recent times been modified by the French administration. Different expedients (*ḥiyal*) which may serve to evade the Muslim rules of inheritance have found their way into literature already at an early period. So far only a very few Indian modernists (notably Khudā Bukhsh) have dared to criticize openly the Muslim law of inheritance and demand its abolition. It is actually valid in Muslim countries (with the exceptions indicated above) and is applied by the *sharīʿa* tribunals, which also undertake the distribution of the estate, a thing too difficult for a layman to attempt. The Muslim law of inheritance is also applied to members of other creeds, when they come to the Sharīʿa tribunals, which often happens in Muslim countries.

Bibliography: For section 1: Robertson Smith, *Kinship and Marriage*, 2nd ed., p. 65 *sqq.* — For section 2 (chronology of the Ḳurʾān verses): Nöldeke-Schwally, *Geschichte des Qorāns*, vol. 1 (partly different from the explanations given above); Peltier and Bousquet, *Les successions agnatiques mitigées* (also for the subsequent development). — For section 3 and 4: Wensinck, *Handbook of Early Muhammadan Tradition*, s.v. HEIRS; Peltier, *Le Livre des Testaments du „Çaḥîḥ" d'el-Bokhâri*; al-Shawkānī, *Nail al-awṭār*, in the *Kitāb al-farāʾiḍ*. — For section 5 and 6 (for the older period, the two recensions of Mālik's *al-Muwaṭṭaʾ* are an especially valuable source): Juynboll, *Handleiding tot de kennis van de mohammedaansche wet* (3rd ed.), p. 241 *sqq.*; Sachau, *Muhammedanische Recht*, p. 181 sqq. (Shāfiʿite); Baillie, *The Moohummudan Law of Inheritance*; do., *A Digest of Moohummudan Law*, vol 1 (2nd ed.); G. Bergsträsser, *Grundzüge des islamischen Rechts*, p. 90 *sqq.* (Ḥanafite); Khalīl b. Isḥāḳ, *Mukhtaṣar*, trans. Guidi and Santillana; Sánchez Pérez, *Partición de herencias entre los Musulmanes* (Mālikite); Hirsch, *Abd ul Kadir Muhammed*: *Wissenschaft des Erbrechts* (Ḥanafite and Shāfiʿite). — For section 5—7: Vesey-Fitzgerald, *Muhammadan Law*, p. 111 *sqq.* — For section 7 *a*: Querry, *Droit musulman*, vol. ii. p. 326 *sqq.*; Baillie, *Digest*, vol. ii. — For section 7*b*: Bergsträsser, in *OLZ*, xxv. 124; Strothmann, in *Isl.* xiii. 36 *sqq.* — For secton 7*c*: Sachau, *SB Pr. Ak. W.*, 1894, p. 159 *sqq.* — For section 8: Juynboll, *Handleiding*, p. 250 *sqq.*; *REI*, i. 47 *sqq.*; ii. 502 *sqq.*; v, 1 *sqq.*; vi, 158 *sq.*; *OM*, 1937, p. 541; Hamid Ali, in *Islamic Culture*, xi, 354 *sqq.*, 444 ff.

MĪRZĀ GHULĀM AḤMAD. [See AḤMADĪYA].

MISWĀK (A.), a term denoting the toothbrush as well as the tooth-pick. The more usual term is *siwāk* (plural *suwuk*) which means also the act of cleansing the teeth, the verbal expression being *istāka*. Neither of the two terms occurs in the Ḳurʾān. In Ḥadīth miswāk is not used, siwāk on the other hand, frequently. In order to understand its use, it is necessary to know that the instrument consists of a piece of smooth wood, the end of which is incised so as to make it similar to a brush to some extent. The piece of wood used as a tooth-pick must have been smaller and thinner, as appears e.g. from the tradition in which it is related that Muḥammad one day received a visitor and kept the tooth-pick "at the end of his tongue" (Muslim, *Ṭahāra*, trad. 45).

Concerning Zaid b. Khālid it is related that he used to sit in the mosque keeping the tooth-pick behind his ear, "just as a writer will keep his pen" (Abū Dāwūd, *Ṭahāra*, bāb 25; al-Tirmidhī, *Ṭahāra*, bāb 18). When Muḥammad was in his last hours, there entered a man with a piece of wood fit for a siwāk; ʿĀʾi<u>sh</u>a took and chewed it, so as to make it smooth (Bu<u>kh</u>ārī, *Ma<u>gh</u>āzī*, bāb 83).

In general Ḥadī<u>th</u> emphasizes the value attached by Muḥammad to the siwāk. When he entered his house, his first movement was towards it (Muslim, *Ṭahāra*, trad. 43; Abū Dāwūd, *Ṭahāra*, bāb 27). His servant ʿAbd Allāh b. Masʿūd has received the epithet of *ṣāḥib al-siwāk* "he who used to take care of Muḥammad's siwāk" (Bu<u>kh</u>ārī, *Faḍāʾil al-ṣaḥāba*, bāb 20). When Muḥammad awoke at night, he cleansed his mouth by means of the siwāk before he washed himself and performed night-prayer (Bu<u>kh</u>ārī, *A<u>dh</u>ān*, bāb 8; *Wuḍūʾ*, bāb 73; *Taha<u>dj</u>djud*, bāb 9; Abū Dāwūd, *Ṭahāra*, bāb 30; Muslim, *Ṭahāra*, trad. 46, 47). When fasting Muḥammad also made use of the siwāk (Aḥmad b. Ḥanbal, iii. 445, 446).

The miswāk is chiefly used before *wuḍūʾ* as preparation before the *ṣalāt*. It is said that this was the practice of Muḥammad (Muslim, *Ṭahāra*, trad. 48) who attached so great a value to it, that he would have declared it obligatory before every *ṣalāt*, were it not that he feared thereby to overburden his community (Bu<u>kh</u>ārī, *A<u>dh</u>ān*, bāb 8; Muslim, *Ṭahāra*, trad. 42; Abū Dāwūd, *Ṭahāra*, bāb 25; Tirmi<u>dh</u>ī, *Ṭahāra*, bāb 18). In one tradition it is said, as a matter of fact, that the obligatory use of the siwāk before every *ṣalāt* was introduced by Muhammad as a compensation for the abolition of the obligatory *wuḍūʾ* before every *ṣalāt* (Abū Dāwūd, *Ṭahāra*, bāb 25). In another tradition (Nasāʾī, *<u>Dj</u>umʿa*, bāb 66) the use of the siwāk is called obligatory before the Friday-service.

The appreciation of the miswāk which appears from all these traditions culminates in the view that it belongs to the customs of the "natural religion" (*fiṭra*: Abū Dāwūd, *Ṭahāra*, bāb 29) or to the ordinances of the Apostles (Tirmi<u>dh</u>ī, *Nikāḥ*, bāb 1).

Nevertheless Fiḳh does not declare the use of the miswāk obligatory in any case. There is general agreement on this point. According to some traditions, however, the Ẓāhirites did declare the use of the miswāk obligatory before the *ṣalāt*, but these traditions are not generally accepted. According to Fiḳh the use of the miswāk is recommended at all times, especially in 5 cases: in connection with the *ṣalāt*, under all circumstances; in connection with the *wuḍūʾ*; with the recitation of the Ḳurʾān; after sleep; and as often as the mouth has lost its freshness, e.g. after long silence.

According to the school of <u>Sh</u>āfiʿī the use of the miswāk is blamable (*makrūh*) between noon and sunset at the time of fasting; for the nasty smell (*<u>kh</u>ulūf*) of the faster's breath is beloved by Allāh (cf. Nasāʾī, *Ṭahāra*, bāb 6).

It is recommended to use a miswāk of *arāk*-wood of medium hardness, neither too dry nor too moist; to cleanse the palate as well as all sides of the teeth, beginning from the right side of the mouth, moving the miswāk upwards and downwards in order not to hurt the alveoles.

Bibliography: Wensinck, *Handbook*, s.v. Toothbrush; the juridical points of view in al-Nawawī's commentary on the *Ṣaḥīḥ* of Muslim, Būlāḳ 1290, i. 325; Wellhausen, *Reste arab. Heidentums*, 2nd ed., p. 172; Goldziher, in *RHR*, xliii. 15 *sq.*; Buhl, *Das Leben Muhammeds*, p. 354, note 94.

MOLLA. [See MAWLĀ].

MUʾA<u>DDH</u>IN. [See A<u>DH</u>ĀN, MANĀRA, MAS<u>DJ</u>ID G. 4.].

MUʿARRAB. [See MUSTAʿRIBA].

MUBĀḤ. [See ḤUKM, <u>SH</u>ARĪʿA].

MUʿ<u>DJ</u>IZA (A.), part. act. iv. of *ʿ-<u>dj</u>-z*, lit. "the overwhelming" has become the technical term for miracle. It does not occur in the Ḳurʾān, which denies miracles in connection with Muḥammad, whereas it emphasizes his "signs", *āyāt*, i.e. verses of the Ḳurʾān; cf. the art. KURʾĀN. Even in later literature Muḥammad's chief miracle is the Ḳurʾān (cf. Abū Nuʿaim, *Dalāʾil al-nubuwwa* p. 74); Ra<u>sh</u>īd Riḍā, *al-Waḥy al-muḥammadī*, passim). Muʿ<u>dj</u>iza and *āya* have become synonyms; they denote the miracles performed by Allāh in order to prove the sincerity of His apostles. The term *karāma* [q.v.] is used in connection with the saints; it differs from muʿ<u>dj</u>iza in so far as it denotes nothing but a personal distinction granted by Allāh to a saint.

Miracles of Apostles and Prophets, especially those of Muḥammad, occur in the *sīra* and in *ḥadī<u>th</u>*. Yet in this literature the term muʿ<u>dj</u>iza is still lacking, as it is in the oldest forms of the creed. The *Fiḳh Akbar*, ii., art. 16, mentions the *āyāt* of the prophets and the *karāmāt* of the saints. Muʿ<u>dj</u>iza occurs in the catechism of Abū Ḥafṣ ʿUmar al-Nasafī (ed. Cureton, p. 4; ed. Taftāzānī, p. 165): "And He had fortified them (the apostles) by miracles contradicting the usual course of things".

Taftāzānī explains it in this way: A thing deviating from the usual course of things, appearing at the hands of him who pretends to be a prophet, as a challenge to those who deny this, of such a nature that it makes it impossible for them to produce the like of it. It is Allāh's testimony to the sincerity of His apostles.

A very complete and systematic description occurs in al-Īdjī's *Mawāḳif*. He gives the following definition of muʿ<u>dj</u>iza: It is meant to prove the sincerity of him who pretends to be an apostle of Allāh. Further he enumerates the following conditions: 1. It must be an act of Allāh; 2. it must be contrary to the usual course of things; 3. contradiction to it must be impossible, 4. it must happen at the hands of him who pretends to be an apostle, so that it appears as a confirmation of his sincerity; 5. it must be in conformity with his announcement of it; 6. the miracle itself must not be a disavowal of his claim (*daʿwā*); 7. it must follow on his *daʿwā*.

Further, according to al-Īdjī, the miracle happens in this way that Allāh produces it at the hands of him whose sincerity He wishes to show, in order to realize His will, viz. the salvation of men through the preaching of His apostle. Finally, as to its effect, it produces, in accordance with Allāh's custom in those who witness it, the conviction of the apostle's being sincere.

Bibliography: Abū Ḥanīfa, *Fiḳh Akbar* with the commentary of ʿAlī b. Sulṭān Muḥammad al-Ḳārī, Cairo 1327, p. 69; Abu 'l-Barakāt ʿAbd Allāh b. Aḥmad al-Nasafī, *ʿUmda*, ed. Cureton, p. 15 *sqq.*; Abū Ḥafṣ al-Nasafī, *ʿAḳāʾid*, with the commentary of Taftāzānī, Constantinople 1313, p. 165—167; Muḥammad Aʿlā al-Tahānawī, *Ka<u>shsh</u>āf iṣṭilāḥāt al-funūn*, Calcutta 1862, p. 975 *sqq.*; Abū Nuʿaim Aḥmad b. ʿAbd Allāh al-Iṣbahānī, *Dalāʾil al-nubuwwa*, Haidarābād 1320; al-Īdjī, *Mawāḳif*, ed. Sörensen, p. 175; Wensinck, *The Muslim Creed*, p. 224; A. S. Tritton, *Muslim Theology*, London 1947, see Index s.v. Miracles.

MU<u>DJ</u>TAHID. [See I<u>DJ</u>TIHĀD].

MUFTĪ. [See FATWĀ].

AL-**MUHĀ<u>DJ</u>IRŪN**, the emigrants, a name often applied in the Ḳurʾān to those followers of Muḥammad who had migrated from Mecca to Madīna with him. The word is derived from *hid̲j̲ra*, which does not mean "flight" but breach, dissolution of an association based on descent, in the place of which a new connection is formed. The term *muhād̲j̲ir* is not applied to the Prophet himself but only to those who migrated with him before him or after him and later made up a considerable portion of the population of Madīna. The followers of the Prophet who were natives of Madīna were given the name Anṣār [q.v.] to distinguish them from the Muhād̲j̲irūn, because the immigrants were mainly dependent on their help and active support after they had given up their homes and livelihoods in Mecca. With the greatest eloquence Muḥammad describes them as the particular favourites of Allāh who will receive a splendid reward for their sacrifices "when those who have adopted the faith, who have migrated and fought for Allāh's cause may hope for his grace" (Sūra ii. 218); "the sins of the emigrants and of those driven from home are forgiven" (iii. 195). Those who remained in Mecca and feared to migrate although the earth was large enough to afford them shelter are severely censured. He who emigrates finds a home on the earth and if he dies Allāh will reward him (iv. 101). This was however at first only an indication of a future which had not yet materialized, and in addition to these exhortations (cf. viii. 74; xvi. 41; xxii. 58) the Prophet made more practical efforts to help those who were living in dificult circumstances. A portion of the plunder taken in fighting was given to the poor emigrants who had been driven from their possessions in order to aid Allāh: "they are the trustworthy" (lix. 8). In order to make the bond between them and the Madīnese as close as possible it is announced in Sūra viii. 72 that the emigrants who had left their homes to fight for the true religion and those who gave them shelter (cf. Ibn His̲h̲ām, p. 321 *sqq.*) and assistance (the Anṣār) should enjoy rights of kinship with one another while, on the other hand, those who while adopting Islām had not migrated, should not have any rights of kinship. According to the usual interpretation, this passage refers to the peculiar bond of brotherhood which Muḥammad instituted between each emigrant and a Madīnese believer, an explanation which is however not quite certain as the passage perhaps only expresses a general principle (cf. Fr. Buhl, *Leben Muhammeds*, p. 109). Besides, the usual exegesis sees in the regulations for inheritance (Sūra iv. 12) a proof that this special bond was very early abolished again.

The high esteem in which the emigrants were held finds expression in Sūra ix. 20, where we read "those who believed and migrated and expended blood and treasure in fighting for the cause of Allāh, occupy a higher position (than other believers); they are the fortunate ones". Muhād̲j̲ir in this way became a title of honour (cf. Sūra xxix. 26 where Lot is so called). Individuals who had migrated not to Madīna but to Abyssinia also proudly called themselves muhād̲j̲ir (see Fr. Buhl, *op. cit.*, p. 172). But the real "migration" was that to Madīna in which the Prophet himself took part. The number of the Muhād̲j̲irūn gradually grew as the increasing power of Muḥammad from time to time induced Meccans to leave their heathen city and go to Madīna. It is to them that Sūra viii. 75 refers, where those who adopted Islām later than the first emigrants who migrated and afterwards fought alongside of the older Muhād̲j̲irūn are acknowledged as belonging to the community ("they are of you"). After the treaty of Ḥudaibīya in particular, we hear of Meccan women who left their pagan husbands and went to Madīna where in accordance with Muḥammad's interpretation of the treaty they were not surrendered if they offered the so-called women's pledge (see Sūra lx. 11 *sqq.*). Thus the Muhād̲j̲irūn, later and earlier, formed an increasing element in the population of Madīna, whom Muḥammad often mentions along with other sections of the community as possessing equal rights with them (e.g. Sūra xxxiii. 6, 50), in which connection it should be noted that Muhād̲j̲irūn is never, as was the case among the Anṣār, used in genealogies.

With the occupation of Mecca, the migration ceased while the Muhād̲j̲irūn remained as a separate highly honoured body. It is natural to suppose that a certain amount of rivalry might easily arise between them and the other elements of the community, and that there was actually a certain amount of friction between the emigrants and the Madīnese is evident from the fact that in the troubles after the Prophet's death the Madīnese endeavoured to set up one of of their number, Saʿd b. ʿUbāda, as successor to the Prophet. The attempt failed through the energetic action of ʿUmar, Abū Bakr and Abū ʿUbaida, and the leadership of the community remained in the hands of the Muhād̲j̲irūn until the descendants of Muḥammad's old opponents in Mecca seized power for themselves.

In the Ḥadīt̲h̲ the question who is a muhād̲j̲ir is discussed and answered in general in two ways. The first declares that the Hid̲j̲ra finds its term in the year 8 A.H. (*lā hid̲j̲ra baʿd al-fatḥ*); the second connects it with the participation in the holy war (see Wensinck, *Handbook*, s.v. *Hid̲j̲ra*). — The K̲h̲ārid̲j̲ites called muhād̲j̲irūn those who joined their camp (*muʿaskar*); and mysticism has spiritualized the term.

Bibliography: The biography of Muḥammad, especially Ibn His̲h̲ām, ed. Wüstenfeld, p. 341 *sqq.*

MUḤAMMAD, the founder of Islām, was a native of the city of Mecca, out of which the energetic Ḳurais̲h̲ had in the sixth century created a flourishing centre of commerce by exploiting the much visited places of pilgrimage there. In consequence of the unreliability of the sources at our disposal the very first question a biographer has to ask, namely when was his hero born, cannot be answered with certainty. That Muḥammad's activity in Madīna covered ten years (622—632) is certain; but we have no certain data for the Meccan period. There is however no cogent reason to doubt the statement in a poem ascribed sometimes to Abū Ḳais b. Abī Anas and sometimes to Ḥassān b. T̲h̲ābit (ed. Hirschfeld, No. 19) to the effect that his prophetic activity in Mecca lasted "ten and some years". The parellelism between the two periods which might be brought forward as a ground of suspicion, is not complete, and on the other hand, the annual recurrence of the great pilgrimage at Mecca must have made it easy for the inhabitants to reckon by them, so that a chronological statement originating there deserves more confidence than others. The Meccan period in any case must not be put too short, for according to ʿUrwa's story mentioned below (Ṭabarī i. 1181). "several years" passed after the migration of his followers to Abyssinia before they returned, after which new difficulties arose which produced the migration to Madīna. — For the period before he came forth as a religious reformer we have only the indefinite expression *ʿumr* (Sūra x. 16). The Muslim historians make him usually 40, sometimes 43 years old at the time of his call, which, taken with the already mentioned data, would put the date of his birth at about 570 A.D. When however tradition puts the date of his birth in the "year of the Elephant" (see Sūra cv.) this is a result of an unhistorical combination, for Abraha's attack on Mecca must have taken place considerably before 570. But Lammens has cast various, not unfounded doubts on the whole chronological calculation itself; in particular the fact that Muḥammad's migration to Madīna and his resultant activities there do not give the impression that he was then a man already in the fifties. In reality 580 or one of the years immediately following would suit very well as the date of the Prophet's birth, so that the Ḳur'ānic expression *ʿumr* would mean about 30 years.

The name "Muḥammad" occurred previously among the Arabs (e.g. Ibn Duraid, ed. Wüstenfeld, p. 6 *sq.*; Ibn Saʿd, 1/i. 111 *sq.*) and therefore need not be regarded as an epithet only adopted later in life by the Prophet; the name Muḥammada for women occurs several times in the Syrian *Book of the Himyarites*. As to Muḥammad's descent several old poems (e.g. Ḥassān b. Thābit, ed. Hirschfeld, No. 25; Aʿshā in Ibn Hishām, p. 256; cf. also on Djaʿfar: Ḥassān b. Thābit, No. 21; Kaʿb b. Mālik in Ibn Hishām, p. 800; on Ḥamza: Ibn Hishām, p. 630; on Abū Lahab: Ḥassān b. Thābit, No. 217) confirm the statement of tradition that he belonged to the family of Hāshim; and that he was recognized by them as one of themselves is evident from the fact that only the protection of a fairly powerful family could have made it possible for him to stay so long in Mecca in face of the hostility of his fellow-citizens (cf. the words put in the mouth of the enemies of Shuʿaib (Sūra xi. 91): "Had we not had consideration for thy family, we would have stoned thee"). The Hāshim family related to the Banū Muṭṭalib (Ibn Hishām, p. 536) was apparently one of the better class families of Mecca (cf. Ibn Hishām, p. 821 and the words of the poetess Ḳutaila, *ibid.*, p. 539, which however might be interpreted merely as a polite formula; cf. Song of Solomon, vii. 2; Dalman, *Palästinischer Diwan*, p. 190, 255 *sq.*; E. Littmann, *Neuarabische Volkspoesie*, p. 141). On the other hand, the Meccan enemies of the Prophet say in Sūra xliii. 31 that they would believe in him more readily if he had been one of the prominent men of the two cities (Mecca and Ṭā'if). The Hāshim family in any case could not compare with the most prominent families like the Makhzūm and Umaiya; and what is recorded of the needy circumstances of Muḥammad and some of his relatives suggests that the Hāshim family must have been exceedingly poverty stricken at this time. On his mother's side he had connections, which are not clear to us, with Madīna; according to Mūsā b. ʿUḳba the Madīnese called al-ʿAbbās their "sister's son" (cf. Ibn Saʿd, iv/i. 8, 12). We know nothing more that is definite about his ancestry, for most of what is related is legend. His father, who is said to have died before his birth, is quite a colourless figure, whose name ʿAbd Allāh is perhaps only a later improvement on a heathen name. His grandfather is called Shaiba or ʿAbd al-Muṭṭalib; the connection between these two names is however as obscure as is that between ʿAbd al-Muṭṭalib and the oft mentioned family of Muṭṭalib (Ḥassān b. Thābit, No. 184; Ibn Hishām, p. 230, 536) or the Banū Shaiba (Ibn Saʿd, 1/i. 94, 11/i. 124). The only thing certain from the Ḳur'ān is that Muḥammad grew up as an orphan in very miserable circumstances (Sūra xciii. 6 *sq.*). The first tangible historical figures among his relatives are his uncles: Abū Ṭālib, with whom tradition records that he found a kindly reception, ʿAbbās, Ḥamza [q.v.] and ʿAbd al-ʿUzzā [cf. ABŪ LAHAB]. The story of the cleansing of his breast (a similar story is related of Umaiya b. Abi 'l-Ṣalt; cf. Goldziher, *Abh. z. Arab. Phil.* i. 213) is a materialization of Sūra xciv. 1.

In Sūra xciii. already quoted, we are told that Allāh made the poor orphan prosperous. Corresponding to this in tradition is the marriage of Muḥammad with a rich merchant's widow, in whose service he had been [cf. KHADĪDJA]. She bore him four daughters, who play a part in later history, and several sons all of whom died in infancy; one of them at least must be historical as his pagan name ʿAbd Manāf (Sprenger, i. 199 *sq.*; Caetani, i. 173) could not be invented by later writers; such a fiction in any case, as posthumous comfort to alleviate the disgrace of the lack of male heirs (Lammens), would be very inadequate, if it had to make the sons die again soon after their birth. The interest in business matters apparent in the Ḳur'ān (Sūra ii. 198; lxii. 9 *sq.*) as well as his fondness for business expressions (cf. however similar expressions in the Wisdom of Solomon, iv. 20; Pirqe Abot, iii. 16; iv. 22; Horn, *Gesch. d. Pers. Lit.*, p. 10) are very natural if Muḥammad took part in business transactions as Khadīdja's assistant and husband. On the other hand, it would be wiser to set aside the alleged trading journeys into neighbouring lands, which he is said to have made even as a child with Abū Ṭālib and later in Khadīdja's service; in the form in which they are given they have distinctly apologetic tendencies (cf. BAḤĪRĀ] and are quite unnecessary to explain his later religious development. Sūra xxxvii. 137 *sq.* in any case is no clear proof that he himself had passed by Lot's dwellings on a journey. Nor did Khadīdja equip trading caravans independently. Equally little confidence is to be placed in the story, which is given in the usual *märchen* style, of the part played by Muḥammad in rebuilding the Kaʿba.

While the questions already raised are really of no great importance, the problems which concern Muḥammad's emergence as a religious reformer are of the utmost importance but offer the greatest difficulties to the student in view of the insufficient material available in the sources. The main question is: whence did Muḥammad, who everywhere betrays a great receptivity for foreign matter, get his ideas? That he originally shared the religious conceptions of his milieu is in every way the most natural supposition — his uncle Abū Lahab was an ardent defender of paganism and Abū Ṭālib, who was like a father to him, died without adopting Islām — and is confirmed not only by the name of his son already mentioned but also by Sūra xciii. 3: "God found thee wandering and guided thee" (cf. also xlii. 52: "Thou didst not know what book or belief was" and the statement of Ibn al-Kalbī that he once brought a sheep as a sacrifice to al-ʿUzzā). Distinct traces of his early beliefs survived in his later life. He shared the belief of his fellow countrymen in *djinn* and *shayāṭīn*, in evil omens etc. Mecca with its sanctuary was a sanctified place in his eyes (Surā xxvii. 91; xxviii. 57; xxix. 67; cv. 1 *sqq.*; cvi. 1 *sqq.*); he admitted the sacrifices offered there into the true worship (cviii. 2) and allowed his followers to take part in the pilgrimage (vii. 31 *sq.*) so that it was all the easier for him later to accept it as one of the main features of his religion (see below). We shall later discuss a relapse into paganism, which however was speedily overcome, as well as the fact that he was only gradually led to attack on principle the gods of Mecca.

He was also influenced by the manner of the old Arab inspired soothsayers (cf. on the modern Ruwala: Musil, *Die Kultur*, 1910, p. 10 and *EI*, *Suppl.*, s.v. RUWALA) to the extent that he adopted their peculiar form of speech with mysterious oaths and rhymed prose (*sad̲j̲ʿ*; cf. Goldziher, *Abhandlungen z. arab. Philol.*, i. 59 *sqq.*; Masʿūdī, *Murūd̲j̲*, iii. 381 *sq.*), when he began to announce his revelations. All his earlier conceptions were however driven out except for such trifling residua as these, when a new world of ideas began to fill him to an ever increasing extent, until he was finally compelled with irresistible force to come forth and proclaim them. These new ideas point mainly to the religions of the "possessors of a scripture" — Judaism and Christianity — and he was conscious of this, in as much as he repeatedly emphasizes the agreement between his teaching and these older religions of revelation as i. . .utable evidence of its truth (cf. the significant passage: "If thou art in doubt about what We have revealed, ask them who read the scripture before thee", Sūra x. 94). The only question is, in what way did he become possessed of these new ideas. This much only is certain that he did not get them from his own reading of the holy scriptures of the Jews and Christians. The word *ummī* [q.v.], applied to him (Sūra vii. 157) signifies, without committing us to anything about his ability in reading or writing — as a merchant he must have had a certain knowledge of these arts — that he was an illiterate layman, who was not able to read the Hebrew or Greek Bible, and that this was actually the case the Ḳurʾān shows on every page. For this explanation of the term Wensinck, *Acta orient.*, ii. 191 and (citing the Hebrew *ummōt ha-ʿolām*) Horovitz, *Kuranische Untersuchungen*, p. 52 would put "pagan", ἐθνικός, but although this might fit some passages, it could hardly suit Sūra ii. 78 where there is a reference to a difference between the "possessors of a scripture" and the *ummīyūn* among the Jews. The usual explanation suits well enough, as it is certain and it is confirmed by the Ḳurʾān everywhere that, while Muḥammad had some notion of the books of the Bible, the Hebrew and Greek Bibles were closed books to him. Utterances like the saying that Jesus "received" the Gospels (iii. 58; v. 46; lvii. 27) and that it should be "observed" like the law (v. 66, 68) clearly show that he did not know its real contents. Sūra xxi. 150 contains a quotation from the Psalms, but this is quite an isolated instance and he knew nothing of the Psalms as a part of the Old Testament (xvii. 55). The parable of the camel and the eye of a needle (vii. 40) proves of course no literary dependence and the alleged description of Muḥammad and his followers in the Gospels (xlviii. 29) shows what he could build up on a vague recollection of something he had heard. On the other hand the stories reproduced, e.g. the long account of Joseph (Sūra xii.), show that he was indirectly dependent on the Bible and not only on the Old but also on the New Testament (cf. what he relates of Mary, Joseph, Zacharia and John); the story of the Seven Sleepers (cf. AṢḤAB AL-KAHF and M. Huber, *Die Wanderlegende von den Siebenschläfern*, 1910) also presupposes Christian authorities. One therefore cannot blame his enemies when they said that he had foreign teachers (xvi. 103; xxv. 4 *sq.*; xliv. 14), which is certainly not refuted by the reply in xvi. 103. Further it is clear from the Ḳurʾān that he did not come into contact in this indirect way with the books of the Bible in their simple form but that his authorities had drawn on Midrashic and Apocryphal works, which is easily explained by the varied and luxuriant character of the religious tendencies in Arabia. In particular what he tells of the birth and childhood of Jesus (xix. 22 *sqq.*; iii. 46; v. 110 *sq.*) comes from Apocryphal sources, and his account of the death of Jesus (iv. 157) has parallels among the Manichaeans and Basilidians.

To state exactly what religion exercised particular influence on Muḥammad's ideas is hardly possible in view of the scanty information available about conditions in these days, especially as many things indicate that he was influenced from various sides, primarily by Christian sects, but later also by the Jews. There was ample opportunity to become acquainted with both these religions from caravans passing through to Syria or the lands of the Euphrates, from communication by sea with Abyssinia, and from foreign merchants visiting the great markets; and not only in the more advanced districts of South Arabia, but also among several Beduin tribes (e.g. Bakr, Tag̲h̲lib, Ḥanīfa, Ṭaiy), Christianity had established itself, while Jewish colonies had settled in Madīna and the oases north of it. But a citizen of Mecca in particular had repeated opportunities of coming into contact with Christians and Jews. The great festivals attracted people from all districts and it is expressly recorded that Christians also took part in the pilgrimage (Snouck Hurgronje, *Het Mekkaansche Feest*, p. 28, 128, 159); in addition there were Christians captured in war and immigrant G̲h̲assānids living in Mecca (Azraḳī, ed. Wüstenfeld, p. 97, 458, 466; cf. the Christian slave in Ṭāʾif: Ibn His̲h̲ām, p. 280 *sq.*). In the Ḳurʾān, alongside of expressions coming from the Aramaic, several Ethiopic loanwords are evidence of religious influence from Abyssinia (cf. Nöldeke, *Neue Beiträge zur semitischen Sprachwissenschaft*, p. 47). Some scholars have been inclined to seek a main source of Muḥammad's ideas and their formulation in the religious development which is alleged to have taken place in South Arabia. This is certainly a possibility to be reckoned with, but so long as we know so little of South Arabian religious history and in particular so long as no intermediate South Arabian forms are found for the Abyssinian loanwords in the Ḳurʾān we are better to set it aside. It should also be noted that Muḥammad in his stories of the prophets frequently mentions the Arab tribes of ʿĀd and T̲h̲amūd [q.v.] but only rarely touches on the older history of South Arabia (Sūra xxvii. 20 *sqq.*; xxxiv. 15 *sq.*; xliv. 25; l. 14, on the other hand hardly lxxxv. 1 *sqq.*; cf. M. Hartmann, *Die arabische Frage*, p. 474). In the utterance ascribed to the Prophet (Buk̲h̲ārī, *Mag̲h̲āzī*, bāb. 74): "Belief and wisdom are Yamanī", Yamanī as the context shows, only means "of Yamanī fashion", i.e. cultured, human, in contrast to Beduin uncouthness. The main objection however, is that the hypothesis would only mean an unnecessarily circuitous route, for Muḥammad always appeals directly to his agreement with Christianity, without suggesting any remodeling of these religions through a South Arabian medium. And the stronger one endeavours to make Yemenite influence on religious matters in Mecca, the more unintelligible becomes the stubborn opposition of the Meccans to Muḥammad. Much greater weight should be given to Tor Andrae's treatment of the question of Muḥammad's dependence on Christianity. After calling attention to the wide dissemination and dominating position of Nestorianism in the Persian empire, which is of importance as it must have been much more accessible to Muḥammad than Monophysitism, he points out the close relationship between Muḥammad's ideas and the ecclesiastical writings of the Syrians: the contempt for worldly possessions, the strong condemnation of the arrogance and frivolity of the unbelievers, the warnings against laughing, joking and careless speech, the emphasis on the significance of almsgiving as an atonement for sin, the descriptions of Paradise (we even find the houris in Ephraim the Syrian) etc. Alongside of these very instructive similarities, there is however one point to be remembered in which the relationship is somewhat modified namely Muḥammad's Christology. It is, in any case, remarkable in several respects for it is distinguished from his other accounts of prophets and approximates to the teaching of the Church in striking fashion e.g. in the account of the birth of Jesus and his miraculous gifts and in the undeniable echoes of the doctrine of the Logos (Sūra iii. 39; iv. 171). But already in the Meccan period (e.g. xliii. 57 *sqq.*) Muḥammad vigorously rejects the idea of Christ being the son of God and definitely denies that he had ever asserted anything of the kind of himself. Here it is not sufficient to point to the Nestorians since they did not deny that Christ was the son of God. When Muḥammad from the first insists on the complete agreement of his teaching with the old revealed religions, i.e. with Christianity also, he seems to have been influenced by a form of Christianity where this dogma occupied a very unimportant position.

What one can deduce in this way from the Ḳurʾān about Muḥammad's development is supplemented in an important way by tradition, according to which he was not alone in his search for a purer religion. Various individuals are named who, dissatisfied with old Arab religion, were seeking for a more intellectual faith, in particular a cousin of K͟hadīd͟ja, Waraḳa b. Nawfal. Even if these traditions cannot be utilised in the form in which we have them, as they have been influenced by later Muslim ideas, yet they certainly have a historical basis, because they are not taken from the Ḳurʾān and are not intended to show Muḥammad in a more favourable light. In addition there are the Ḥanīfs [q.v.] of whom the traditions of the Arabs have preserved only a very hazy picture, and Umaiya b. Abi 'l-Ṣalt whose poems often have points of contact with the Ḳurʾān, which would be of great importance if they could even in part be regarded as genuine [cf. also the article MUSAILIMA].

While Muḥammad was in a state of great spiritual excitement as a result of contact with the religious ideas that had penetrated into Arabia, something happened which suddenly transformed his whole consciousness and filled him with a spiritual strength which decided the whole course of his life: he felt himself called to proclaim to his countrymen as a prophet the revelations which were communicated to him in a mysterious way. When Caetani wishes to see in this the result of a long development and continued reflection, this is certainly not correct. We have much rather every reason to trust the tradition which tells of a sudden outburst of conviction that he was called to proclaim the word of God. For this view we have the analogy of prophets in general, from the Old Testament prophets down to Joseph Smith; and no long drawn reflections but only an overwhelming spiritual happening could give him the unshatterable conviction of his call. This is also confirmed by several passages in the Ḳurʾān, which point to a deciding moment, definite in time (xliv. 3 *sq.*; xcvii., 1; ii. 185), in which connection it is of minor importance whether it is possible to identify the revelation of the call itself among the Sūras of the Ḳurʾān (according to a common opinion, xcvi. 1 *sqq.*; according to some, on the other hand, lxxiv. 1 *sqq.*), especially as one must reckon with the possibility that the very earliest revelations were not written down. If this really was the case, however, the reason certainly was not that they were deliberately suppressed, since a revolutionary change of his world of ideas into its diametrical opposite while retaining the earlier apparatus of inspiration would be quite an untenable hypothesis.

The Ḳurʾān gives only a few hints about the manner of these inspirations; a veil lay over them which the Prophet either could not or would not raise completely. Perhaps the wrapping up (lxxiii. 1; lxxiv. 1) refers to a preparation for the reception of the revelations in the manner of the old Arab *kāhins*; but we are taken further in an indirect way by the oft recurring accusation of his enemies that Muḥammad was possessed (*mad͟jnūn*), a soothsayer (*kāhin*), a magician (*sāḥir*), for they show that in his moments of inspiration he made an impression similar to those figures well known in ancient Arabia. In addition there are several traditions which describe his condition in such moments more fully and may undoubtedly be regarded as genuine, since they are the last thing later Muḥammadanism might be expected to invent, while these mysterious seizures afforded to those around him the most valid evidence for the superhuman origin of his inspirations. In Byzantine authors we find it stated that the Prophet was an epileptic (e.g. Theophanes, *Chronographia*, ed. de Boor, i. 334); modern psychiatrists recognize the correctness of these descriptions of his attacks and we must of course leave it to them to define the exact nature of his condition. From the scientific point of view the fact is that the voice heard by him only uttered what he had from time to time heard from others and which now cropped up out of his subconscious. The scientific student therefore does not see in Muḥammad a deceiver but fully agrees with the impression of sincerity and truthfulness which his utterances in the older revelations make (e.g. Sūra, x. 17, 21; xxviii. 85 *sq.*; lxix. 44; lxxv. 16 *sq.*; cf. vii. 203; xvi. 98; the cogent imperatives lxxix. 2; xcvi. 1; the self-denunciation lxxx. 1 *sqq.* etc.) along with the fact that he unselfishly endured years of hostility and humiliation in Mecca in the unshakable conviction of his lofty task. It is more difficult with the later Madīnese revelations, in which it is often only too easy to detect the human associations, to avoid the supposition that his paroxysms (e.g. at the battle of Badr: Ibn His͟hām, p. 444; in the slandering of ʿĀʾis͟ha, p. 736) could sometimes be artificially brought on, and there is even a tradition which makes ʿĀʾis͟ha say to the Prophet: "Thy Lord seems to have been very quick in fulfilling thy prayers". It must not be forgotten however that natures like this, without actually being conscious of it, are able to provoke the same states of excitation which earlier arose without their assistance; and so probably not only were his followers in Madīna (cf. Kaʿb b. Mālik in Ibn His͟hām, p. 614) but he himself was convinced, that the spirit was continually hovering about him to communicate the revelations to him. By this we do not of course mean that in his ecstatic condition he received the divine communications *in extenso*, as we now have them in the Ḳurʾān; only the foundations were given him, which he afterwards developed into discourses of greater length. Since in doing this he used the external forms of the old Arab soothsayers it is natural that the Meccans took him for one, but it does not follow that he was spiritually akin from the first to those soothsayers who were inspired by *d̲j̲inns*.

While it is in this way possible with the help of the Ḳur'ān and Tradition to get an on the whole satisfactory picture of Muḥammad's development and his condition when prophesying, he himself gives in the Ḳur'ān quite a different interpretation of the revelations that came to him, which is based on a peculiar theory which he apparently did not invent himself but adopted from others. The fundamental idea in it is the conception of a divine book existing in heaven, *al-kitāb*, a well guarded book, which only the pure may touch (lvi. 79), a well guarded tablet (lxxxv. 21 *sq.*), the mother of the book (xliii. 3 *sq.*), on honourable leaves, exalted and pure, by the hands of noble and pious scribes (lxxx. 13 *sqq.*). He himself did not read this book, as E. Meyer erroneously thinks, but it was communicated to him orally piece by piece, not in its original form but in an Arabic version intelligible to him and his countrymen (cf. xii. 1; xiii. 37; xx. 113; xxvi. 192 *sqq.*; xli. 3; xliv. 58 and especially xli. 44: "If we had made it a Ḳur'ān in a foreign tongue, they would say: Why are its *āyāt* ["signs", from the small sections of the text] not expounded intelligibly?, a foreign text and an Arab reader!"]. In addition there is the fact that Muḥammad was aware that the complete contents of the book were not communicated to him, as he expressly states, e.g. of the stories of the prophets, not all of which were related to him (xl. 78; iv. 164). He received the communications orally, Allāh rehearsing to him the substance of the separate sections (lxxv. 16 *sqq.* etc.), while in several passages it is stated more precisely that the revelations were communicated through the Spirit (xxvi. 192 *sq.*; xvi. 102; xlii. 52) or the Angel (xvi. 2; xv. 8; cf. liii. 5 *sqq.*; lxxxi. 23 *sqq.*); a late passage of the Madīna period (ii. 97) is even more precise in saying that they were communicated by Gabriel. References to visions are rare (e.g. the encouraging apparitions in Sūra viii. 43; xvliii. 27; the night journey must also have been a vision) and even in such cases the main thing is not what he heard (liii. 10; lxxxi. 19). These communications were the great miracle that was granted him, while he expressly and repeatedly says that the ability to perform miracles in the usual sense was denied to him (unlike Jesus).

From this book in heaven, the all-comprising contents of which are not by any means exhausted in the extracts forming the Ḳur'ān, also came the older religions of revelation "of the possessors of a scripture", whose religions therefore in his view coincide with his and, as he often says, were confirmed by it (cf. Ḥassān b. T̲h̲ābit, No. 134). This again is connected with a theory expounded by him of a line of prophets which began with Adam, and of which he was the last representative. His source for this idea was not Judaism, for he does not know of the great prophets who wrote books of the Old Testament; on the other hand the fact that Jesus and John the Baptist are the last links in the chain of prophets clearly suggests a Christian origin, and certain parallels in more or less heretical early Christian literature can be demonstrated. Of the prophets Muḥammad relates a number of stories, which do not begin to appear in any number until the middle Meccan period when the Meccans were beginning sharply to reject his mission.

The ideas in the oldest, passionately excited inspirations, developed under a baroque power of imagination rarely reached later, are very simple. They are based not on the dogmatic conception of monotheism but on the strong general religious and moral impression which contact with older religions had made upon him, which was bound finally to lead to a breach with polytheism. In particular he was filled with the idea of the moral responsibility of man created by Allāh, and with the idea of the judgment to take place on the day of resurrection, which again points undoubtedly more to Christian than Jewish influence (cf. especially the introductory sounding of trumpets, not found among the Jews). To this are added vivid descriptions of the tortures of the damned and seductive pictures of the joys of Paradise (cf. what is said above, p. 393). Gradually monotheism was emphasized as an overruling basic idea and at the same time his conception of the character of Allāh was widening under the inflnences of Old Testament teaching, probably transmitted partly through a Christian medium. With all the vigour of an elemental religious nature, he points to the wonders of everyday life, especially to the marvellous phenomenon of man (in this connection cf. the poem of the Jew Samaw'al, *al-Aṣmaʿiyāt*, ed. Ahlwardt, No. 20). The religious duties which he imposes on himself and others are simple and few in number; one should believe in God, appeal to Him for forgiveness of sins (xxiii. 1—11), offer prayers frequently on the model of the Jews and Christians, in the night also (xi. 114; lxxiii. 20; cf. lxxvi. 25 *sq.*), assist one's fellow-men, especially those who are in need, free oneself from the love of delusive wealth and — what is significant for the commercial life of Mecca — from all forms of cheating (xxvi. 182 *sq.*; lv. 9 *sq.*), lead a chaste life and not expose new-born girls, as the barbarous custom of the time was (according to Sūra vi. 151; xvii. 31 from poverty, cf. al-Mubarrad, *Kāmil*, ed. Wright, p. 277; originally perhaps a kind of magic to procure sons, when only girls had been born, cf. Musil, *Ḳuṣair ʿAmra*, p. 38; even before Muḥammad's time there had been people who fought against this barbaıous custom, cf. al-Mubarrad, *Kāmil*, *loc. cit.*). This is the ideal of the truly pious man who is called by the name of *muslim* (lxviii. 35; xxi. 108 etc.) or *ḥanīf* (x. 105; xxx. 30; xcviii. 4; cf. vi. 79 and the article). Cf. in this connection the list of Muḥammad's precepts in Aʿs̲h̲ā's poem (Ibn His̲h̲ām, p. 255; *Morgenländische Forschungen*, p. 25 *sq.*).

From all this, it is quite evident that Muḥammad had at this time no thought of founding a new religion. His task was only to be a "warner" (li. 50; lxxiv. 2; lxxix. 45; lxxx. 11; lxxxviii. 21 *sqq.*), in view of the approach of the day of judgment, to his countrymen, to whom no prophet had yet been sent (vi. 157; xxviii. 46; xxxii. 3; xxxiv. 44; xxxvi. 6; no notice is taken here of Hūd and Ṣāliḥ) and as a result of the revelations granted him to give them, in the form of a lucid Arabic Ḳur'ān (see above), what the "possessors of a scripture" had in their scriptures, which were not accessible to the Arabs and thereby to save them from the divine wrath. The Jews and Christians also must therefore testify to the truth of his preaching (x. 94; xvi. 43; xxi. 7; xxvi. 197; xxviii. 52 etc.).

On the account of the insufficiency of the sources, it is very difficult to ascertain in detail how Muḥammad's relations with the Meccans developed. The

Ḳur'ān contains only vague hints, which permit no chronological arrangement, while the traditions are very full but little reliable. Only one report, which ʿUrwa composed for the caliph ʿAbd al-Malik (Ṭabarī, i. 1180 *sq.*, 1224 *sq.*), the value of which has already been indicated by Sprenger, gives a brief but apparently trustworthy glimpse of the main events (cf. also al-Zuhrī in Ibn Saʿd, 1/i. 133). At first Muḥammad met with no serious opposition and in not a few cases his preaching fell on fruitful soil; indeed in the words addressed to Ṣāliḥ (xi. 62) we may find a hint that he had at first aroused considerable expectations among the Meccans. All traditions agree that Khadīdja was the first believer, while they differ as to who was his first male adherent. In any case Abū Bakr, the manumitted slave Zaid b. Ḥāritha, Zubair b. al-ʿAwwām, Ṭalḥa b. ʿUbaid Allāh, ʿAbd al-Raḥmān b. ʿAwf, Saʿd b. Abī Waḳḳās, and Muḥammad's cousin ʿAlī [q.v.] were among his earliest followers. The majority of those who were won over by his preaching were however young and of no great social standing, while the well-to-do and influential held back (xix. 73; xxxiv. 31 *sqq.*; xxxviii. 62 *sq.*; lxxiii. 11; lxxx. 1 *sqq.*; cf. the veiled references in vii. 75; xi. 27; xvii. 16; xxvi. 111). This became still more the case when the full consequences of his ideas became clear to him and he openly attacked the religion of his native town; for the Meccans, to the majority of whom such devotional meetings had been a matter of complete indifference, now discovered that a religious revolution might be dangerous to their fairs and their trade. That this was the salient feature of their resistance to Muḥammad is evident from the fact that he frequently endeavours to calm the fears of the Ḳuraish on this point: the Meccan sanctuary, he said, belonged to his god Allāh, whom the Meccans also recognized as the highest god (xxxi. 25; xxxix. 35; cf. Ḳais b. al-Khaṭīm, ed. Kowalski, v. 14; xiii. 12 where Allāh is the lord of the Kaʿba) and he will protect and bless his sanctuary, if they submit to him (xxvii. 91; xxviii. 57; xxix. 67; cvi. 1 *sqq.*). In addition there was the conservative attitude of these merchants in the field of religion and their animosity to new and fantastic ideas, particularly to that of the resurrection of the dead.

Traditions record at great length the persecution and ill-treatment which Muḥammad and his followers suffered at the hands of the Meccans [see KHUBAIB]. These descriptions are undoubtedly much exaggerated, for the object was to glorify the self-sacrifice of the believers and no doubt also to put the old patrician families of Mecca in an unfavourable light. But it is equally certain that there is some foundation for these stories. ʿUrwa speaks of two persecutions (*fitna*) which twice forced the believers to migrate, and in the Ḳur'ān there is mention of "trials" which their opponents inflicted upon the believers, men and women (lxxxv. 10), and it is expressly mentioned that the influential wished to prevent Muḥammad from praying (xcvi. 9 *sq.*; cf. the veiled account vii. 86), while on the other hand the complaints about what they would have liked to do should not be taken at their face value (viii. 26; xxxvi. 17; cf. xi. 91). The peculiar feature, repeatedly found in stories of the prophets, that their opponents threaten them and their followers with stoning (Sūra xi. 91 and frequently) might suggest the hypothesis that Muḥammad was actually threatened in this way by the Meccans, but this would probably only have been in a momentary outburst of passion and in any case the quarrel was mainly conducted in endless wordy disputations in which the spiritual advantage lay with Muḥammad. His strength lay in the consciousness that he lived in a higher intellectual world which was closed to the Meccans and that he proclaimed ideas, "the equal of which neither men nor djinn with combined efforts could produce" (xvii. 88). Very pertinently he often points to the lack of logic in his enemies, when they recognize Allāh as the real true God but will not draw the logical deductions from this. But even his most crushing arguments rebounded from the impregnable wall of their prejudices which were based on their material interest. This circumstance now began to influence the matter of his preaching in a very remarkable way. When his opponents mocked him because the divine judgment threatened by him did not come (xxxviii. 16; lxx. 5) he began to describe in an increasing degree in his stories how the contemporaries of earlier prophets had met them with incredulity and had therefore brought on their heads dreadful punishments. That he did not use such means at the very beginning of his mission is evident from the fact that his preaching, according to the already mentioned credible tradition, at first gave no offence, and indeed this feature is lacking in the sūras which are certainly the oldest. It was the hardness of heart of his countrymen which made him take to this weapon in order to stir them. At first it proved by no means ineffective, as the Arabs knew of old trading peoples like the Thamūd [q.v.], whose destruction might well give them cause for reflection. But gradually this line of attack lost its effect. To Muḥammad however this resistance to the obvious truth was something so unintelligible that he could only find solace in an idea, which was to be of far-reaching importance in the further development of Muḥammadan dogmatics: Allāh, the immeasurably exalted and almighty, could of course not be impeded by the resistance of mortals; the unbelief of the Prophet's opponents was therefore an effect of the divine will: "Allāh makes to err whom he will and guides whom he will" (x. 99; xxxii. 12 *sqq.*; xxxv. 8; lxxiv. 34 etc.), a view which his enemies endeavoured not unskilfully to turn against himself (xvi. 35; xxxvi. 47).

Several episodes stand out in the Meccan period which are unfortunately more or less obscure and may be interpreted in various equally uncertain ways. It is certain, in spite of the silence maintained about it in the Ḳur'ān (even xvi. 47 *sq.* does not refer to it), that Muḥammad's community was at one time in so great distress that a considerable section of them migrated to Abyssinia. The later view was that participation in this flight became a patent of nobility similar to that conferred by the great Hidjra to Madīna, which was actually granted as a titular distinction (Wellhausen, *Skizzen*, iv. 113); but the Prophet gave the advice to seek protection among the Abyssinian Christians only to those of his followers of whom he was afraid that they had not sufficient strength to maintain their faith under the difficult conditions in Mecca (cf. the significant story of the cool reception which some of the exiles later received on their return to Madīna; Bukhārī, *Maghāzī*, bāb. 38). M. Hartmann's view that the emigrants were to conduct political propaganda in Abyssinia is not capable of proof. According to ʿUrwa, these emigrants (i.e. probably the greater number of them) returned to their native town, when Islām had become strengthened by the accession to its ranks of a number of individuals of positions. At the same time there is a different story of their return, which it would not be difficult to combine with ʿUrwa's story if we assume that they gradually drifted back. We are told that Muḥammad proclaimed in one of his sermons that the favourite deities of the Meccans, al-Lāt, al-ʿUzzā and Manāt [see these articles], might be regarded as divine beings whose intercession was effectual with Allāh. This led to a general reconciliation, news of which reached Abyssinia and induced a number of the Muslims there to return home. Here however they learned to their horror that the agreement had been of short duration, as the Prophet had very soon recognized these words as interpolations of Satan and had substituted for them the words which we now have in Sūra liii. 19—23. The credibility of this story has been doubted, certainly wrongly; for in view of the absolute impossibility of such a story being a later invention, any possible objections to the reliability of the authorities cited (Ṭabarī, i. 1192, 1195; Ibn Saʿd, 1/i. 137 *sq.*) hardly deserve consideration and passages like vi. 56, 67; xvii. 75 *sq.* (cf. iv. 113) amply show that the incident was quite possible from the psychological point of view.

It is much more difficult to elucidate another episode of the Meccan period, the story of the boycott of the Hās̲h̲imids. That Muḥammad's whole position during his struggle with the Meccans was only made possible by the support given him by his own family has already been indicated. All members of the family of Hās̲h̲im with the exception of Abū Lahab [q.v.], who on this account is perpetually damned in the Ḳurʾān along with his wife, chivalrously fulfilled their duty in this respect, although only a few of them believed in his call. It would therefore be not unnatural in itself for the Meccans in the end to attempt to make the whole family innocuous without bringing on themselves the guilt of bloodshed by an open attack. The story, however, which tells how they forced the Hās̲h̲imids to withdraw into their own part of the town and pledged themselves to refrain from intermarriage or commerce with them, is confirmed neither by the Ḳurʾān nor by ʿUrwa, but sounds in itself somewhat suspicious and is probably much exaggerated. That the effort finally failed is conceded by the story itself. On the other hand, it is quite possible that K̲h̲adīd̲j̲a's fortune may have suffered considerably from Muḥammad's obligations to his necessitous followers and from the enmity of the influential merchant princes.

To the last portion of the Meccan period most probably belongs Muḥammad's nocturnal journey, later so celebrated, to the "remotest place of prayer" to which xvii. 1 (perhaps also verse 60) briefly refers, no doubt a vision, which however made upon him an impression of reality [cf. ISRĀʾ]. According to the prevailing opinion, the terminus of this journey was the temple in Jerusalem, and conclusions are drawn from this about the great significance which this city then had for him. Schrieke (*Isl.* vi. 1 *sqq.*) and Horovitz (*ibid.*, ix. 159 *sqq.*) have however sought to show that *al-masd̲j̲id al-aḳṣā* refers to the place of prayer of the angels in heaven (cf. vii. 206; xxxix. 75), for which view several cogent arguments can be produced, notably that the nocturnal journey is associated with the journey to heaven as early as in the tradition given by Ibn Isḥāḳ and that in the Ḳurʾān there is several times a reference to an ascent into heaven (vi. 35; xvii. 93; xv. 14 *sq.*).

Of other details we may further recall that Muḥammad, who, as already remarked, was firmly convinced that his preaching agreed with the religion of the "possessors of a scripture", nevertheless had already begun in Mecca to reject the christological dogmas of the church. This is certain from the conversation with his pagan opponents (xliii. 57 *sqq.*) which can only have taken place in Mecca. This however does not affect his idea of the fundamental identity of his with the older revelations but only the false doctrine later adopted in the church, for he makes Jesus vigorously reject the doctrine of his divinity; but this limitation of his theory was not without importance and was able to serve him as a model in his later criticism of Judaism.

The sources are somewhat fuller for the close of the Meccan period, although late tendencious historiography has coloured everything in the traditions. According to ʿUrwa's account, Muḥammad did, it is true, succeed in winning a few notables in Mecca (including probably ʿUmar) for his teaching, after the emigration of a number of his followers to Abyssinia. But on the whole his attempt at a religious reformation could be regarded as having failed; and when K̲h̲adīd̲j̲a and Abū Ṭālib died, his position gradually became more and more hopeless. An attempt to establish himself in Ṭāʾif brought him into considerable danger, according to the narrative, although the approval of his preaching expressed by some d̲j̲inn (cf. xlvi. 29; lxxii. 1) certainly raised his drooping spirits. It was probably at this period that Mutʿim b. ʿAdī took him under his protection, which is corroborated by Ḥassān b. T̲h̲ābit (No. lxxxviii.). He could now have consoled himself with the reflection that he had done his duty as a "warner" and could regard it as the will of Allāh that his countrymen were not to be saved (cf. x. 99; xliii. 89). But the consciousnes of being a chosen instrument of Allāh had gradually become so powerful within him that he was no longer able to sink back into an inglorious existence with his object unachieved. His astonishing gift of being able to exert a powerful religious suggestion even on men who were intellectually superior to him imperiously demanded a wider sphere of activity than a small number of adherents, mostly without influence. In addition, there was a factor of which he himself was certainly unconscious but which is apparent on every page of the Meccan sūras, namely his mental exhaustion and his lack of new ideas. All this brought him to the idea of looking for a new sphere of activity outside Mecca, however difficult it must have been for an Arab to break the links that bound him to his tribe and family. The congress of people from all parts at the pilgrimage gave him good opportunities to attempt to find one. After several unsuccessful negotiations he found a favourable soil for his scheme with some men from Madīna. Unfortunately we know very little about conditions at this time in this town but we may safely assume that the large number of Jews in it had contributed to make the peasant population of Madīna somewhat familiar with religious ideas (cf. Ibn His̲h̲ām, p. 178). There is however no question that the Madīnese did not so much want to attract an inspired preacher to themselves as to get a political leader, who would readjust their political relations, which had been shattered in the tribal conflicts culminating in the battle of Buʿāth. With this we are faced with one of the most difficult problems in the biography of Muḥammad, the double personality which he presents to us. The inspired religious enthusiast, whose ideas mainly centred around the coming last judgment, who had borne all insults and attacks, who only timidly touched on the possibility of active resistance (xvi. 126) and preferred to leave everything to Allāh's intervention, with the migration to Madīna enters upon a secular stage and at one stroke shows himself a brilliant political genius. That Muḥammad's eye in Mecca took in the wider political situation is evident from the prophecy in Sūra xxx. 1 *sq.*; but the passage is quite isolated there and in any case M. Hartmann's effort (*Die arabische Frage*, p. 53), to make him play the part of a far-seeing diplomat in international politics is based on fanciful arguments with no basis in the sources. Nevertheless in the despatch of a section of his followers to Abyssinia and in the attempt to reach a compromise with the polytheists in Mecca, we have hints which to some extent bridge over the gulf between the two figures. The decisive point however is that the Madīnese would certainly not have thought of seeking in him a saviour from their social and political difficulties, if they had not been much impressed by his abilities in this direction.

After Muḥammad had entered into relations with some Madīnese who had come as pilgrims to Mecca, the latter began to spread Islām in their native town along with men whom he had sent there and thus he was able after a preliminary conference in al-ʿAḳaba to conclude at the pilgrimage next year (622) at the same place a formal agreement with a considerable number of Madīnese, in which they pledged themselves in the name of their fellow-citizens, to take him into their community and to protect him as one of their own citizens, which, as the further history shows, was also to hold for his Meccan followers if they moved to Madīna. Tradition, and no doubt rightly, here mentions only the promise of the Madīnese to take Muḥammad under their protection and not any further obligations. On the other hand according to Ibn Hishām, p. 287, at the first conference at ʿAḳaba Muḥammad is said to have imposed a series of commands upon them; but this so-called "women's homage" is, as the very name shows, taken from the later Sūra lx. 12 and is clearly adapted to Meccan conditions (cf. especially the vow not to kill children). These negotiations, which could not remain unknown to the Meccans, produced great bitterness, and a second *fitna*, as ʿUrwa says, began for the believers, which must have still more confirmed them in their resolution to migrate to Madīna. They slipped away in larger or smaller bodies, so that finally only Muḥammad with Abū Bakr and, according to the story ʿAlī, was left. That the Prophet did not go with the others was certainly due to the fact that the Meccans otherwise would have prevented the whole emigration. They knew him well enough to see the danger if he were to ally himself with another tribe and there is therefore no reason to doubt Tradition when it relates, although with much legendary embellishment (cf. on David's flight Ṭabarī, i. 556), how he had to be the last to flee from the town. Tradition is also confirmed by Sūra ix. 40 where there is mention of Muḥammad and his companion (Abū Bakr) stopping in the cave.

The migration of the Prophet, the Hidjra [q.v.], has been with justice taken by the Muslims as the starting-point of their chronology, for it forms the first stage in a movement which in a short time became of significance in the history of the world. According to the usual calculation, he arrived in Ḳubāʾ, a suburb of Madīna, on the 12th Rabīʿ I of the first year, i.e. Sept. 24, 622 and shortly after went into his new home. The tasks which awaited him placed the greatest strain on his diplomatic and organizing abilities. He could only rely with absolute certainty on those who had migrated with him (the *muhādjirūn*, q.v.), for their whole future existence depended entirely on him and of course only those had migrated who were firmly convinced of the truth of his mission. In addition, there were those Madīnese who had already adopted Islām or did so soon after his arrival, the so-called *anṣār* [q.v.] or "helpers", who however formed only a portion of the inhabitants of Madīna. He only found direct opposition in a few families, like the Aws Allāh; but at the same time there were a number who while they did not exactly oppose him only reluctantly accepted the new relations, the so called *munāfiḳūn* [q.v.], who were to cause him much anxiety. Fortunately for him, they were led by a man, the Khazradjī ʿAbd Allāh b. Ubaiy, who possessed the *munāfiḳ* quality of irresolution to such an extent that he regularly let slip every occasion on which he might have offered successful opposition. A further danger lay in the fact that the old and bitter feud between the two chief parties, the Aws and Khazradj, had by no means died down, but might easily break out again on any occasion. Finally there were the Jews (in the first place *al-kāhinān*, i.e. the Naḍīr and Ḳuraiẓa; cf. Ḳais b. al-Khaṭīm, ed. Kowalski, xx.; Ḥassān b. Thābit, No. 216; Ibn Hishām, p. 660 and Ibn Saʿd, viii. 86, 91) and the judaicized tribes in Madīna, who played an important part because of their wealth and the support they had in the Jewish colonies in Khaibar etc. For Muḥammad they were on the whole a plus factor in his calculations for, according to his theory already mentioned, he might expect that they would champion the truth of his preaching. His relations with the Christians in Madīna (cf. Ḥassān b. Thābit, No. 133) were no longer absolutely unstrained, since he had begun in Mecca to reject the orthodox ecclesiastical Christology; but they were insignificant and could be ignored. He also had a much greater sympathy with them than with the Jews (v. 82; lvii. 27).

Muḥammad had to form a united community out of these heterogeneous elements. The first problem to be tackled was how to procure the necessary means of subsistence for the emigrants, who were for the most part without means or work, which could for the time being only be done through the self-sacrifice of the Anṣār and certainly only very inadequately. To strengthen their claims for protection, he ordered the relationship of brotherhood to be created between each emigrant and a man of Madīna. This arrangement, to which was added brotherhood between every two emigrants, was abolished after the battle of Badr by Sūra xxxiii. 6 and left only a few traces (see Ibn Saʿd, iii. xxxiv.). On the other hand, we possess for a somewhat later period, when relations between Muḥammad and the Jews had begun to be strained, a very valuable document in Muḥammad's constitution of the community which has been preserved by Ibn Isḥāḳ. It reveals his great diplomatic gifts, for it allows the ideal which he cherished of an *umma* definitely religious in outlook to sink temporarily into the background and is shaped essentially by practical considerations. It is true that the highest authority is with Allāh and Muḥammad, before whom all matters of importance are to be laid; but the *umma* included also Jews and pagans, so that the legal forms of the old Arab tribes are substantially preserved. This scheme had however no considerable practical importance; it is nowhere mentioned in the Ḳurʾān (hardly even in viii. 56), because it was soon rendered obsolete by the rapidly changing conditions.

It is a proof of the Prophet's political wisdom that he endeavoured to attach the Jews to himself by taking over several features of their worship. Thus he made the 10th Muḥarram a fast-day, obviously in imitation of the Jewish fast on the 10th Tis̲h̲ri, the day of atonement, which is particularly obvious in its name, taken from the Aramaic (*ʿās̲h̲ūrāʾ*, q.v.). On Jewish practice are probably also based the introduction of the midday ṣalāt, which was now (ii. 230) added to the morning and evening ṣalāts and the easier rule about purification before the ṣalāt (iv. 43; v. 96). On the other hand, Friday as the day of the common ṣalāt, which probably goes back to the Jewish day of preparation (cf. Becker's correction to Ibn Saʿd, III/i. 83, 23, in *Isl.*, iii. 379), is said to have been already introduced before the Hid̲j̲ra by Muṣʿab b. ʿUmair (according to others, Asad b. Zurāra). Whether the choice of Jerusalem as the *ḳibla* [q.v.] was one of the concessions made to the Madīnese Jews is uncertain as the statements about his attitude in Mecca on this point differ. But it is improbable that he should have turned towards the Kaʿba there, otherwise it is difficult to understand how the different stories could have arisen. But whether he then used Jerusalem as the *ḳibla*, which need not necessarily mean a borrowing from the Jews as this direction of prayer was elsewhere found in the east, e.g. among the Ebionites and Elkesaites, whether he turned to the east like many Christians, or whether he had a *ḳibla* at all (the Ḳurʾān is silent on the point) is uncertain, but in any case the balance of probability is in favour of the Jerusalem *ḳibla* having been one of the alterations made to gratify the Madīnese Jews. If some writers have seen in the immediate erection of a place of prayer (Ibn His̲h̲ām, p. 336) a copying of the Jewish synagogues, Caetani has with weighty reasons argued that this was not a building definitely assigned to the worship of God, since the alleged masd̲j̲id was also used for all kinds of secular purposes, because in reality it was simply the court-yard (*dār*) occupied by Muḥammad and his family, while the assemblies for regular worship were held on the *muṣallā* [cf. this art. and MADĪNA]. But nevertheless the "mosque of opposition" so called by the Prophet with horror (Sūra ix. 107; see below) seems to have been an actual building recalling the Jewish synagogues. In spite of these concessions to the Jews, it soon became obvious that he had seriously miscalculated with regard to them. Although they undoubtedly cherished lively expectations of the coming of the Messiah (Ibn His̲h̲ām, p. 286, 373 *sq.*) they could not possibly recognize an Arab as the expected Messiah and he had soon reason to lament that only a few among them believed in him (iii. 110). In particular, the misunderstandings in his reproduction of the Old Testament stories or laws aroused the notorious Jewish love of ridicule and thus brought him into an unfortunate position. His conviction of the divine origin of his mission and his position among the believers would not allow him to confess that he had made a mistake and on the other hand he had too often himself appealed to the testimony of the older religions of revelation to be able to ignore this criticism. He rescued himself from this dilemma by asserting that the Jews had only received a portion of the revelation (iv. 44; cf. iii. 119) and even this included a number of special laws adapted to a particular age (iv. 160; vi. 146; xvi. 118) but they had also concealed all sorts of things in their holy scriptures (ii. 42, 146, 159, 174; iii. 77 etc.) and indeed had even falsified their scriptures (ii. 59; iv. 46; v. 13, 47; vii. 162; cf. Ḥassān b. T̲h̲ābit, No. 96; and the article TAḤRĪF), in short they obtained hardly more benefit from their scriptures than an ass from the books which he is carrying on his back (lxii. 5). The Jews were not able to refute these assertions for, although he challenged them to produce these scriptures (iii. 93) neither he nor his followers could read a word of them. He therefore now poured forth the vials of his wrath upon the Jews in many speeches and awaited the time when he would be able to refute their criticism and malicious witticisms and tergiversations in convincing fashion (e.g. iii. 181 *sqq.*; iv. 46). As he had now already begun to regard the church doctrine of the Christians as a corruption of the true teaching of Jesus, he felt himself called upon to reform the degenerate religions of revelation, each of which asserted it was the only true one (ii. 113). As a result he now claimed a special place among the prophets: he is seal of the prophets (xxxiii. 40; a metaphorical expression which Mani among others applied to himself and which indicates the conclusion of the series), he is the last prophet, to whom Jesus himself had pointed under the name Aḥmad (lxi. 6; cf. iii. 87). Still he is not thinking any more than before of introducing a new religion but only of restoring the religion proclaimed by the prophets from the beginning. But nevertheless the early years after the migration were the period when Muḥammadanism was born as an independent religion for parallel with his criticisms of the religions of revelation and in particular opposition to Judaism ran a positive shaping of Islām, through which he was emancipating himself in important points from his previous models. He gave his religion a pronounced national character by taking over various elements from the worship of the old Arabs and associating them with his religious ideas. In the second year of the Hid̲j̲ra (July 623—June 624) after some hesitation, he ordered that Jerusalem should not longer be the *ḳibla* at prayer but the ancient sanctuary of the Black Stone at Mecca (ii. 142—150 for it "is a gathering-place and a safe retreat for men" (ii. 125). His native town was thus made the centre of the true religion. As a substitute for the pilgrimage which he now adopted into his religion as one of the main rites, but from which he and his followers were temporarily cut off, he had an animal sacrificed in this year on the 10th D̲h̲u 'l-Ḥid̲j̲d̲j̲a on the *muṣallā* in Madīna (Ṭabarī, i. 1362; according to Ibn Saʿd, I/ii., 9 he continued this after the occupation of Mecca) and in the following year he calls the ḥad̲j̲d̲j̲ one of the obligations of believers towards Allāh (iii. 96 *sq.*). Friday retained its significance but was not to be a day of rest like the Jewish Sabbath (lxii. 9 *sq.*), which is connected with his rejection of the Old Testament idea of God resting after the creation (l. 38). In place of the fasting on ʿĀs̲h̲ūrāʾ, he substituted quite a new particular rite, according to which his followers were to fast throughout Ramaḍān, the month in which he had received the fundamental revelation (ii. 185), as long as the sun was visible in the heavens. The Manichaeans had a similar custom; but whether he took the new revelation from them or from another sect cannot be ascertained [cf. RAMAḌĀN].

This nationalisation of Islām, which was to have so many results, gave Muḥammad a final legitimation, which brought it into harmony with his earlier appeal to the religions of revelation, as he came forward as the restorer of the religion of Ibraham (*millat Ibrāhīm*) which had been corrupted by the Jews and Christians. Abraham, whom Jews and Christians alike regarded as the great type of faith and whom he had himself emphatically indicated as the true *ḥanīf* (e.g. vi. 79), now becomes the great *ḥanīf*, not only in contrast to the heathen but also to the possessors of a scripture (neither polytheist, nor Jew nor Christian [ii. 135; iii. 67, 95] wherefore, as Snouck Hurgronje has shown, vi. 161 and xvi. 123 must also be Madīnese). He and his son Ishmael, the ancestor of the Arabs, founded the Meccan sanctuary and the rites celebrated here, now corrupted by the heathen, which Muḥammad is to restore (ii. 124 *sq.*; xxii. 26 *sqq.*). Whether this bold idea, which according to Sūra iii. 65 met with opposition from the possessors of a scripture, was an original one and in this case a really brilliant invention of Muḥammad's or whether it was already in existence, for example among arabicized Jews, cannot be decided. The only thing certain is that he cannot have been acquainted with it in Mecca for we meet it nowhere in connection with mentions of the Kaʿba and it is actually excluded by the passages mentioned above.

While his religion was being transformed in this way, Muḥammad's personal position was being gradually changed by the altered conditions. According to the already mentioned constitution of the community, all important matters were to be laid before Allāh and himself. It now became a fundamental duty of the believers to be obedient to Allāh and to himself (iii. 132, 172; iv. 13 *sq.*, 59 [where it is added: "and to those among you who have to exercise authority"]; v. 92; xxiv. 52, 62; cf. also lx. 12, the "women's homage" which is inserted in the account of the second conference at ʿAḳaba, Ibn Hishām, p. 289) and those who are disobedient are threatened with the tortures of hell (ix. 63). Alongside of the belief in Allāh now appears belief in the Prophet (xlviii. 9; lxiv. 8 etc.). Allāh is his protector, as is Gabriel, and the angels are at his disposal (lxvi. 4). He claims certain privileges, which suggest a worldly mortal rather than a spiritual leader (xxiv. 62; xlix. 2 *sqq.*; xxiv. 63; lviii. 12 *sq.*; xxxiii. 53) but which however must be judged as quite moderate demands.

The elevation of Mecca to be the centre of his religion imposed on Muḥammad new tasks, which were soon to lead to unexpected results. If visiting the holy places in and around Mecca was a duty of the Muslims, who were excluded from the town (xxii. 25 *sq.*), the result was the inevitable necessity of forcing admission to them. In addition the Prophet had an account to settle with the Meccans, for by his expulsion they had triumphed over him in the eyes of the world and the punishment repeatedly threatened them had not materialized, unlike the stereotyped punishments of the godless in the stories of the prophets. This led to a new command, that of the holy war ("war on the path of Allāh", *al-djihād*, q.v.), and to set such a war in motion now became the object of his endeavour, which he tenaciously pursued. There were however considerable difficulties in the way of achieving this object. The Madīnese had only pledged themselves to defend him like one of their number if he were attacked, and the anything but warlike merchants of Mecca were not inclined to oblige him by beginning. The emigrants were, it is true, not bound in this way, but it went nevertheless very much against their feelings as Arabs openly to fight members of their tribe and blood relations. How much their resistance vexed him is shown by the vigorous reproaches which he makes to his followers in this connection (ii. 216; xxii. 38 *sqq.* etc.). He succeeded however in finding a way out of the difficulty, which might be able to pave the way for military enterprises without injuring these feelings too much. After he had sent different men with small armed forces who did not succeed in encountering the enemy, in Radjab, one of the sacred months in which all fighting was forbidden, he sent some of his followers to Nakhla, where a caravan was expected and gave their leader sealed orders in which he left it to their judgment what they should do. They did not disappoint him for they fell upon the caravan which felt secure until the end of the month and one of the Meccans was killed. The rich plunder was sent to Madīna, where in the meanwhile a storm of indignation had broken out. Muḥammad however gave the people time to recover and finally calmed them, by the revelation ii. 217. The success of the coup had such an effect in Madīna that not only emigrants but also a number of Anṣār offered their services, when he appealed for followers in Ramaḍān 2 A.H. in a new raid, which he himself would lead. On this occasion chance came to his aid in unexpected fashion. He had learned that a rich caravan was on its way from Syria and he decided to ambush it at Badr. The very cautious Abū Sufyān who was leading the caravan got wind of his plan however and sent messengers express to Mecca for help. But when by a diversion to the coast he had reached safety, he soon afterwards sent other messengers to Mecca to cancel the first message. The angered Meccans had however already collected an army which was three times the size of Muḥammad's little handful of men and were unwilling to let the opportunity escape of properly chastising their troublesome enemy. They went to Badr where soon afterwards Muḥammed arrived with his men, expecting to meet Abū Sufyān's helpless caravan. When they discovered their mistake they were filled with terror (viii. 5 *sqq.*; cf. the continuation of ʿUrwa's story: Ṭabarī, i. 1284 *sq.*); but the Prophet saw in the encounter the wonderful dispensation of Allāh, who wished to force them to a battle and his remarkable power of suggestion was able so to inspire his men that they completely routed the far superior enemy. A number of the Meccans, including the leader of the aristocrats Abū Djahl, were slain and several, including Muḥammad's uncle ʿAbbās, were brought prisoners to Madīna, where Muḥammad had two of them, al-Naḍr and ʿUḳba b. Abī Muʿaiṭ, put to death, while the others were held to ransom. This in our eyes very insignificant fracas, which however must be judged in light of the observation by Doughty who knew the country (*Travels*, ii. 378), became of the utmost significance for the history of Islām, for Muḥammad saw in the victory a powerful confirmation of his belief in the susperiority of Allāh (viii. 17, 65; iii. 123; cf. Kaʿb b. Mālik, in Ibn Hishām, p. 520 *sq.*) and in his own call, and besides the commercial city of Mecca enjoyed such great prestige in Arabia that its conqueror was bound to attract all eyes to himself. He therefore displayed even greater energy and was able to utilise the advantages he had won. After he had drawn up the programme given in Sūra viii. 55 *sqq.* he began to besiege the Jewish tribe of Ḳainuḳāʿ in their forts. The Munāfiḳūn did not dare to oppose him seriously and the other Jews left their co-religionists in the lurch in shameful fashion (cf. lix. 14) so that the latter were forced to migrate to Transjordania.

In order to protect himself while fighting from attacks from another foe, Muḥammad at this time adopted a plan which is a further proof of his outstanding political ability. He concluded, as a number of letters that have been preserved show (cf. J. Sperber, *Mitteilungen des Seminars für orient. Sprachen*, 1916), as lord of Madīna. alliances with a number of Beduin tribes in which the two parties pledged themselves to assist one another.

In the year 3/624—5 Muḥammad continued his attacks on the Meccan caravans so that the Ḳur'aish finally saw the necessity of taking more vigorous measures and revenging themselves for Badr. An army of 3,000 men was equipped and set out with much display for Madīna under the leadership of Abū Sufyān, who was little suited for the task. Although several of his followers advised Muḥammad to make his defence within the town, he decided to go out with his forces, which had been much reduced by the departure of the Munāfiḳūn, and took up a position at the foot of the hill of Uḥud. In spite of the numerical superiority of the Meccans, the fighting at first went in favour of the Muslims, until a number of archers who had been placed to defend his flank joined against Muḥammad's express orders in the battle, which promised to yield rich booty and this at once enabled Khālid b. al-Walīd to fall upon Muḥammad's flank. The tables were now turned and many of the Muslims began to flee, especially when the rumour spread that the Prophet had fallen (cf. iii. 144). In reality he was only wounded and escaped with a few faithful followers through a ravine on to the south side of the hill. Fortunately for him, the Meccans were quite incompetent to follow up their victory and as they thought that Muḥammad had been punished and their honour saved, they turned quietly back to Mecca. The Prophet was thus saved from the worst, but he had to lament many fallen friends including Ḥamza [q.v.] and his newly acquired prestige naturally also suffered. With all the eloquence in his power he endeavoured to raise the morale of his followers by exhortation and censure alike (iii. 118 *sq.*, 139—160, 165—200) but the consequences of his reverse did not fail to materialize. The Jews who had taken no part in the fighting (according to Ibn Hishām, they were observing the Sabbath), made no secret of their delight at his misfortune, and several Beduin tribes next year (4/625—6; the eclipse of the moon which took place in Djumādā II of this year was that visible in Madīna in the night of Nov. 19—20, 625, cf. Rhodokanakis, in *WZKM*, xiv. 105; Caetani, i. 598 *sq.*) showed how much his prestige with them had sunk. It was therefore all the more necessary to make an example and another Jewish tribe in Madīna, the Naḍīr, seemed a suitable object after Kaʿb b. Ashraf's (cf. Ḥassān b. Thābit, No. 97) murder had served as a prelude. It is made a charge against them in Sūra lix. 4 that they defy Allāh and his messenger, on which account Tradition imputes all sorts of crimes to them. After a siege of several weeks (Ṭabarī, i. 1850; cf. Euting, *Tagebuch*, p. 111) they were forced to emigrate to Khaibar or Syria. They left behind them their weapons and their gold and silver as a rich booty, the distribution of which on this occasion Muḥammad reserved for himself (lix. 6 *sqq.*).

To this period most probably belongs the prohibition of the drinking of wine which is characteristic of Islām (v. 90 *sq.*; cf. the instructive gradation in lxxxiii. 25; xvi. 67; iv. 43; ii. 219, where the word "great" is to be deleted as Schwally proposes). It has been connected with a number of features of life in the old Semitic east but the main reason should rather be sought in the connection with the *maisir* games [q.v.]. Drinkingbouts with feasting on a specially slain camel and games of chance, which were in the eyes of the old Arabs the bright spots in their hard struggle for existence, and in which they endeavoured to display their nobility and hospitality, brought the Muslims into suspicious relations with pagans and with Christian and Jewish wine-sellers, which might easily lead to their faltering in their new religion (cf. Wāḳidī, transl. Wellhausen, p. 100; Bukhārī, *Farḍ al-khums*, bāb 1); and this might explain why he forbade both at the same time, which of course does not exclude the possibility that forms of abstinence for other reasons may have been known to him (Musailima's prohibition of wine was obviously intended as asceticism; cf. the article). While Muḥammad was endeavouring to restore his weakened authority, a new and threatening storm came upon him and Madīna from Mecca. The Ḳuraish, whose caravans were being continually harassed by him (cf. Ḥassān b. Thābit, No. 16 *sq.*) and who were urged on by the Jews of Khaibar, recognized that the victory at Uḥud had only been a blow in the air and realized the necessity of occupying Madīna, which they had then neglected to do. Conscious of their slight military skill, they negotiated vigorously with various Beduin tribes and thus raised a large army — said to have been 10,000 men — with which they set out against Madīna in the year 5/626—7. The various accounts of the season of the year (sometimes a month after the barley harvest, sometimes cold winter storms, the latter in agreement with Sūra xxxiii. 9; cf. Ḥassān b. Thābit, No. 14) may be reconciled by the possibility that the siege lasted a considerable time (cf. Doughty's description, *Travels*, ii. 429 *sqq.* of the siege of ʿAnēze, which in general illustrates this war excellently). The advance of this imposing army produced great consternation in Madīna, which was still further increased by the vacillating attitude of the Munāfiḳūn and by the discovery or perhaps only the suspicion that the Jews were conspiring with the enemy (xxxiii. 10 *sqq.*, 26). Muḥammad in order to strengthen the defences had a ditch (*khandaḳ*, a Persian word) dug in front of the unprotected parts of the town. According to several stories, he did this on the advice of a Persian named Salmān, but J. Horovitz (cf. *Isl.* xii. 178—183) would reject this as a later accretion. Modest as the defences were — about 150 years later ʿĪsā b. Mūsā bridged the ditch which had been restored by Muḥammad b. ʿAbd Allāh, by throwing a few doors across it — they seem to have imposed upon the enemy who had little experience in the art of war and the siege gradually dragged on. The able lord of Madīna used the time for secret negotiations with the Ghaṭafān and cleverly stirred up distrust of one another among his opponents and when at the same time the weather conditions became unfavourable the besiegers lost heart and gradually began to retire so that the last effort of the Ḳuraish to destroy their sinister foe came to nothing. For one section of the participants however, the comedy of the "War of the Ditch" was to become a bloody tragedy. Hardly had the besiegers retired than the Prophet declared war on the last Jewish tribe of any size, the Ḳuraiẓa [q.v.], and began to besiege their quarter of the town. The Jews no doubt hoped to escape in the same easy fashion as the Naḍīr had, especially as their allies, the Aws, were very actively trying to induce Muḥammad to clemency; but this time he was inexorable and carried out seriously a threat that he had previously made (lix. 3). Tradition has however endeavoured to put the responsibility for the massacre of the Ḳuraiẓa on Saʿd b. Muʿādh (cf. Ḥassān b. Thābit, No. clxvii., who asserts Saʿd's sincerity). But there are various indications that it was the Prophet himself who made the decision and perhaps induced the Jews to surrender.

By these amputations, which however did not remove all the Jews from Madīna (cf. Ibn Hishām, p. 895; Wāḳidī—Wellhausen, p. 264, 309, 393; Ḥassān b. Thābit, No. 133), the Prophet had come nearer his goal, the organisation of an *umma* on a purely religious basis, which hitherto he had to keep somewhat in the background for political reasons. For the present he continued his attacks on the Meccan caravans far into the year 6/627—8 and his raids, usually punitive expeditions, on Beduin tribes; of these expeditions, which have no particular interest, mention may be made of that against the Banū Muṣṭaliḳ which must have taken place about this time, as it gave rise to a serious conflict between the Muhādjirūn and the Anṣār and involved ʿĀʾishā [q.v.] in the celebrated adventure which nearly cost her her position as the wife of the Prophet, until finally a revelation saved her (xxiv. 4 *sq.*, 11—20).

Towards the end of the year 6 Muḥammad thought that his position in Madīna was so firmly established that he could risk a step, which would bring him nearer the desired goal. He and the emigrants were still excluded from Mecca and its holy places, but through secret confidential agents, among whom we may certainly include his carefully calculating uncle ʿAbbās, he knew that feeling in the town had been gradually coming round (cf. xlviii. 15; lx. 7). An increasing number had become tired of the hopeless wars and thought it would be much more advantageous for the commerce of Mecca to make peace with their indefatigable enemy, especially after he had adopted into his programme the pilgrimages to their fairs, the source of the city's wealth. Trusting to this revulsion of feeling he gave his followers in Dhu 'l-Ḳaʿda of the year 6, i. e. March 628 (the news of the death of the Persian king Khusraw Parwēz on the Feb. 29 of this year reached him on the way) orders to provide themselves with sacrificial victims and undertake an ʿumra [q.v.] with him to Mecca, as Allāh in a vision had promised him a successful fulfilment of the visit (xlviii. 27). He probably chose an ʿumra deliberately (Ibn Hishām, p. 740; Wāḳidī-Wellhausen, p. 249 *sq.*, 253; cf. Sūra, xxii 29, 33) instead of the great pilgrimage which was soon due, as the consequences of an encounter with all manner of tribes, with whom he might possibly have been waging war, were too incalculable for him; but perhaps he cherished also the hope that, if all went well, he might remain there in the following month also (cf. ii. 196 which perhaps belongs to this connection). The step was nevertheless a risky one, so that he asked several Beduin tribes to accompany him in case they met with resistance. To his disappointment however, they refused (xlviii. 11 *sq*) so that he decided to abandon the military character of the march and make his followers go as harmless pilgrims. In Mecca many were inclined to meet his wishes but the belligerent party was still strong enough to get a body of armed men sent to meet him to prevent him entering the town. He therefore encamped at al-Ḥudaibīya where he began to negotiate with the Meccans, and when this led to no result he sent ʿUthmān, who was protected by his family connections, into the town as his representative. But when the latter showed no signs of returning and finally a rumour got about that he had been murdered, the situation became critical and Muḥammad dropped all negotiations, collected his followers under a tree, probably one long held sacred, and made them swear to fight for him to the last, which they did with enthusiasm (xlviii. 10, 18). But soon afterwards a number of Meccans arrived and offered a compromise, which is very characteristic of the aimless Meccan policy, by which he was to retire this time but to be allowed to perform an ʿumra next year. He agreed to the proposal, concluded a ten years' truce with the Ḳuraish and further promised to surrender all Meccans of dependent status who came to him. His followers, whom he had worked up into a state of great excitement by his promises and the taking of the oath, heard these conditions with scarcely concealed anger; but Muḥammad calmly ordered the sacrificial animals brought with them to be slain, which was to have been done at an ʿumra in the town (see Lane, *Lexicon*, s.v. *maḥill*), and had his hair cut, and by his authority forced his grumbling followers to do the same. Only later did they discover that he had made a brilliant stroke of policy for he had induced the Meccans to recognize the despised fugitive as an opponent of equal rank and had concluded a peace with them which promised well for the future.

He and the participants received ample compensation for the apparently frustrated ʿumra at the beginning of the year 7/628—9 by the capture of the fertile oasis of Khaibar which was inhabited by Jews. It was the first actual conquest by the Prophet and he instituted on this occasion a practice which became regular afterwards, when Jews or Christians capitulated: he did not put the people to death or banish them but let them remain as tenants, as it were, who had to pay dues every year. This expedition, which also brought the Jewish colonies of Wādi 'l-Ḳurā into his power, made the Muslims rich (xlviii. 18—21).

In this period, although the exact date is variously given, tradition puts the despatch of letters from the Prophet to Muḳawḳis, governor of Alexandria, the ruler of Abyssinia, the Byzantine emperor, the Persian king etc., in which he demanded that they should adopt Islām. The alleged original manuscript of the first of these has however proved not to be genuine (see *JA*, 1854, p. 482 *sqq.*; Zaidān, in *Hilāl*, 1904, p. 103 *sq.*; Becker, *Papyri Schott-Reinhardt*, i. 3). But even what is related about these epistles hardly deserves the faith most people have put in it. Even if we disregard the many apocryphal details, we must surely consider it very unlikely that so sober a politician as Muḥammad, who had at this time a very definite object, the conquest of Mecca, before his eyes, should have thought of indulging so fantastic an idea as the conversion of Heraclius or the Persian king, to whom the "lucid Arabic Ḳurʾān" was no less unintelligible than the Bible to the Prophet and his countrymen, and whom he could neither compel by force nor entice with proferred advantages. It is very doubtful if Muḥammad ever thought at all of his religion as a universal religion of the world, as for example Nöldeke, in *WZKM*, xxi. 307, Goldziher, *Vorlesungen über den Islam*, p. 25, and T. W. Arnold, *The Preaching of Islam*, p. 23 *sqq.* hold (against them, see Snouck Hurgronje, *Mohammedanism*, p. 48 *sqq.*; H. Lammens, *Études sur le règne du calife Moʿâwia*, i. 422). The passages in the Meccan sūras which can be quoted in favour of this theory (vi. 90; xii. 104; xxi. 107; xxv. 1; xxxiv. 28; xxxvi. 70; xxxviii. 87; lxviii. 52; lxxxi. 27; cf. from the later period: iii. 96; xxii. 25) are limited by their context or by unambiguous parallels (like vi. 92; xlii. 7 [the mother of towns, i.e. Mecca]; cf. xxvi. 214). Besides, in the Madīna period, the place of persuasion and proof ("no compulsion in religion": ii. 256; cf. xvi. 125) was taken by the spread of Islām by force of arms, which, although based on the supremacy of Islām over other religions (iii. 85; ix. 33; lxi. 9), was confined to the lands inhabited by Arabs. If after the conquest of Mecca he also declared war on the possessors of a scripture (see below), the campaigns undertaken by him prove that he was only thinking of Arabs under Byzantine or Persian rule, and it cannot be proved that he ever went beyond this in his schemes (the gift of Hebron, Balādhurī, ed. de Goeje, p. 129 may be confidently asserted to be a forgery). The decisive consideration however is that Muḥammad at the height of his power never demanded from Jews or Christians that they should adopt Islām but was content with political subjection and the payment of tribute. The correct conclusion is therefore to reject these stories and to look for the real historical basis in negotiations of a purely political nature, e.g. with the friendly Muḳawḳis (cf. Butler, *The Arab Conquest of Egypt*. 1902), and to assume that the idea of a great missionary enterprise arose later under the influence of Christian traditions, notably of the miracle of Pentecost.

On the other hand, the character of the genuine letters of the Prophet to the Arab tribes changes at this time, for he was no longer content with a purely political agreement but, relying on his now consolidated power, also demanded that they should adhere to his religion, which involved performing the ṣalāt and paying "alms"; he even gave the Djudhām on the Syrian coast a respite (*amān*) of two months after which they were to decide (see Sperber, *op. cit.*, p. 14 *sqq.*).

In March 629, Muḥammad performed the ʿumra stipulated for him by the peace of Ḥudaibīya (the ʿumra of the "contract" or "recovery"). For him who had been driven out of his native city it was undoubtedly a great satisfaction to be able to visit Mecca as the acknowledged lord of Madīna; but otherwise the significance of the occasion was more symbolical and the efforts of the practised diplomat to prolong his stay by his marriage with a sister-in-law of his secret ally ʿAbbās were politely but firmly resisted by the Meccans. On the other hand, it was of great significance that some of the most important Meccans, like ʿAmr b. al-ʿĀṣī and the military genius Khālid b. al-Walīd, who saw he was the coming man, openly joined him, while his uncle ʿAbbās and the very patriotic (Ibn Hishām, p. 275) but cautious Abū Sufyān endeavoured in secret negotiations to prepare in the most favourable way for the inevitable result. In the meanwhile he continued his military expeditions. His forces suffered a serious reverse in the first considerable effort to extend his authority over the Arabs on Byzantine soil, at Muʾta in Transjordania; this is also recorded by Theophanes (*Chronographie*, ed. de Boor, i. 335). But several Beduin tribes now began to see what advantages they would procure not only for the next but also for this world by joining him, and large groups like the Sulaim voluntarily adopted Islām and placed themselves under his flag.

That it was Muḥammad's intention to break the truce with the Ḳuraish at the first opportunity may be taken as certain; for it must have been intolerable for him that the heathen should still have Allāh's sanctuary in their control (ix. 17 *sq.*; cf. iii. 4). The tactlessness of the Meccans now gave him his opportunity. Much against the advice of Abū Sufyān, the belligerent party in Mecca had supported the Bakr against the Khuzāʿa, who were Muḥammad's allies, and thus given a plausible casus belli (cf. perhaps ix. 12 *sq.*). In Ramaḍān of the year 8/Dec. 629 he set out at the head of an army of Muhādjirūn, Anṣār, and Beduins. The news produced considerable anxiety in Mecca where the number of those who wanted to fight shrank daily so that the more prudent now could take control. Abū Sufyān, who was sent out with several others (including the Khuzāʿī Budail b. Waraḳa who was a friend of the Prophet's) met Muḥammad not far from the town, paid homage to him and obtained an amnesty for all the Ḳuraish who abandoned armed resistance (cf. ʿUrwa, Ṭabarī, i. 1634 *sq.*). Except for a few irreconcilables (cf. *Diwan der Hudhailiten*, No. 183; Mubarrad, *al-Kāmil*, ed. Wright, p. 365), they acquiesced and thus the Prophet was able to enter his native city practically without a struggle and almost all its inhabitants adopted Islām. He acted with great generosity and endeavoured to win all hearts by rich gifts (*taʾlīf al-ḳulūb*, a new use of the alms; cf. ix. 60). Only he demanded ruthlessly the destruction of all idols in and around Mecca. Only Sūra cx. seems to preserve an echo of the exaltation with which this victory filled him; here as in the unusually touching passage xlviii. 1 *sq.*, he sees in the success of this plans a sign that Allāh has forgiven him all his sins.

Muḥammad did not rest long upon his laurels for not only was Ṭāʾif, which was closely associated with Mecca, still ubsubdued, but the Hawāzin tribes in Central Arabia were preparing for a decisive fight. A battle was fought with these Beduins at Ḥunain on the road to Ṭāʾif which at first threatened to be a fatal disaster to the Prophet, mainly because of the unreliability of a number of the new converts, until some of his followers succeeded in recalling the fugitives and routing the enemy (ix. 25 *sq.*). On the other hand, his inexperienced troops were unable to take Ṭāʾif with its defences (cf. the description of impregnable fortresses in *Diwan der Hudhailiten*, No. 66 *sq.*). The people of Ṭāʾif however afterwards fell in with the spirit of the time and adopted Islām. When Muḥammad, after raising the siege, was distributing the booty of Ḥunain, the Anṣār, who as soon as he entered Mecca had expressed the fear that he would take up his residence again in his native town, became very indignant about the rich gifts that he made to his former opponents in order "to win their hearts", while they themselves went empty-handed (cf. Ḥassān b. Thābit, No. xxxi.) but he spoke so kindly to them that they burst into tears and declared themselves satisfied.

The characteristic feature of the year 9/630—1 in the memory of the Muslims was the many embassies which came from different parts of Arabia to Madīna, to submit on behalf of their tribes to the conqueror of Mecca (cf. cx. 3) and the letters which he sent to the tribes, to lay down the conditions of their adoption of Islām. In the autumn of his year, he made up his mind to conduct a campaign against Northern Arabia on a considerable scale, probably because the defeat in Transjordania required to be avenged and because the Ghassānid king was adopting a hostile attitude (cf. Ibn Hishām, p. 911; Bukhārī, *Maghāzī* b. 78, 79). But his appeal for followers met with little support. Munāfiḳūn as well as Beduins held back and even among his devoted followers there were some who put forward all sorts of objections out of fear of a campaign so far away in the glowing heat (cf. ix. 45, 81—90, 98 *sqq.*). In particular he seems to have had to face at this time a considerable opposition in Madīna (ix. 58—72, 125) so that he had to have recourse to his old instrument of intimidation and his words recall in a remarkable way the period of passion in Mecca (ix. 70, 128 *sq.*) Matters came to such a pitch that some of the opposition, behind whom is said by one tradition to have been his old inexorable opponent, the ascetic Abū ʿĀmir ʿAbd ʿAmr, founded a house of prayer of their own "for division among the faithful and a support for those who had formerly fought against God and his Prophet" (ix. 107 *sqq.*). Unfortunately the expressions in the Ḳurʾān and in the traditions are quite insufficient to enable us to get a clear picture of this very remarkable affair. In spite of all opposition however, he carried through his plan; but when after great hardships he had reached Tabūk on the frontier (in the land of the Byzantines; cf. Ibn Hishām, p. 956), he stayed there some time and then returned to Madīna. The campaign was however not without success. His prestige had now become so great that the petty Christian and Jewish states in the north of Arabia submitted to him during his stay in Tabūk, for example the Christian king Yuḥannā in Aila, the people of Adhruḥ and the Jews in the port of Makna. Khālid also occupied the important centre of Dūmat al-Djandal (cf. for a criticism of the account: Caetani, II/i. 261—268; Sperber, *op. cit.*, p. 44 *sqq.*; on the alleged letter from Muḥammad to the Jews in Makna, see also Wensinck, in *Isl.*, ii. 290).

Unfortunately we do not know how the matters which were rapidly coming to a head in Madīna actually developed; but we may safely assume that the death of ʿAbd Allāh b. Ubaiy, which took place not long after the expedition to Tabūk, must have contributed to slacken the tension. These years showed a marked increase in the prestige of the lord of Madīna abroad. Mecca was in his hands and among the Beduins an inclination was noticeable in several places to submit to the will of the conqueror of this town, to be safe against his attacks and to have a share in his rich booty. This was for example the case with the group of tribes of ʿĀmir b. Ṣaʿṣaʿa, with portions of the great tribe of Tamīm and the neighbouring Asad and further north with the Bakr and Taghlib. Even in regions so remote as Baḥrain and ʿUmān within the Persian sphere of influence and among the chiefs of South Arabia, the new teaching and order of things penetrated and found ardent followers in some places. But we must not allow ourselves to be deceived by the representations of the historians, from which it appears as if all the people in these lands adopted Islām. Caetani and Sperber in particular have shown that these accounts are not in keeping with reality and that it was only little groups that submitted, while there was a not inconsiderable number who rejected the Prophet's demands. As regards open opponents the question was quite simple: when they were heathen, adhered to their paganism and would not abandon their polytheism, they were to be threatened by Muḥammad with the "holy war". He had not only to deal with such as those in Arabia, but there were also in addition to the Jews who had already felt his strength, a considerable number of Christians, and some Parsis in the eastern and southern districts. Muḥammad was thus faced with a problem which he had to solve. From his words in Sūra ix. 29 *sqq.* where he includes the Christians and even the Jews, the people of such strict monotheism, among the polytheists, who give Allāh a son and honour men as lords beside him, one would expect that he would have fought them like the heathen, if they did not adopt Islām (cf. also the attack on the Christians, verse 76 *sqq.*). But in contrast to such utterances we have another (Sūra v. 82) where he mentions the Christians very sympathetically because they, unlike the Jews, show themselves kindly towards true believers and are not arrogant, which he ascribes to the fact that they have priests and monks (cf. his judgment on monasticism: Sūra lvii. 27). These remarkable contradictions may be explained, as pointed out by Tor Andrae, by the difference between the Monophysites and the Nestorians. The former aroused his unqualified displeasure by their Christology, while the latter, who were then predominant in the Persian empire, attracted him much more, and this attitude was shared by his followers after his death, as the letter of the Catholicos Ishōʿyahb, quoted by Tor Andrae, shows. On the other hand, his remarks about the Jews are always very severe. It is therefore all the more remarkable that the distinction between Jews and Christians completely disappears when their position is finally settled. They were included together as "peoples of a scripture" and they were allowed to retain their religion if they recognized the political suzerainty of the Prophet by paying a tax (*djizya*, q.v.); if they did not they were to be fought without mercy. The memory of the agreement between Muḥammad's teaching and that of the "peoples of a scripture", earlier so much emphasized, must have contributed to this rather illogical settlement and in addition there was the fact that treating the Jews as tax-paying tenants, and allowing them to practise their religion, as had been already done at Khaibar, was much more practical for the Muslims than fighting them till they gave in. A further compromise with the "peoples of a scripture" was that believers were allowed to marry the daughters of the "peoples of a scripture" and to eat food prepared by them (v. 5). It is noteworthy that the Parsis (xxii. 17, see MADJŪS) were included among the "peoples of a scripture", which made a difficulty for later better informed generations (Ṭabarī, i. 1005 *sq.*; Balādhurī, p. 79): probably Muḥammad did not dare for political reasons to demand that they should give up their religion. This extended application of the term "peoples of a scripture" is found not in the Ḳurʾān but in a letter of Muḥammad's to the Parsis in Hadjar (Ibn Saʿd, I/ii. 19) but with the limitation that the Muslims are forbidden to marry their women and eat meat killed by them.

With these exceptions, the Prophet had approached nearer the object which was always before him, although it had hitherto eluded him, the formation of an *umma* on a definitely religious basis, for the inhabitants of a number of parts of Arabia were now actually bound together by religion. The old differences between the tribes with their endless feuds, their blood-vengeance and their lampoons which continually stirred up new quarrels, were to disappear at the will of Muḥammad and all believers were to feel themselves brethren (ix. 11; xlix. 10). There was to be no distinction among believers except in their degree of piety (xlix. 13). The Prophet certainly had an ideal before him, but it was realized only in a very incomplete way. The very rapid extension of Islām had been accompanied by a considerable diminution in its religious content. Alongside of the older adherents, who were really carried away by his preaching and whose faith had been tried by privations and dangers, there were now the many new converts who had been gained mainly by fear (cf. the well-known poem of Kaʿb b. Zuhair; the poem of the Hudhailī Usaid b. Abī Iyās in Kosegarten, *Carmina Hudsail.*, No. 127) or by the prospect of material advantages. In spite of the teachers sent out to them there could be no question of any deep-seated conversion among these Arabs and how the old Arab spirit continued to flourish among them unweakened is shown for example by the boasting and abuse in the poems in Ibn Hishām, p. 934 *sqq.*, which are in no way inferior to the old poems. The Prophet himself in Sūra xlix. 14 has recorded very definitely how far the Beduins were from the true faith: they cannot say that they believe but only that they have adopted Islām. Commandments relating to religion and worship, which had considerably occupied Muḥammad in the early Madīnese period, give way in striking fashion to social and political regulations, a natural result of the fact that the new members were not ripe for the former. Uncertainty on these matters was still great and even at headquarters much seems still to have been in an embryonic state. This is true even of so fundamental a law as the rule for the times of daily prayer, as the five prayers later obligatory are nowhere laid down in the Ḳurʾān (see above; cf. also the expression "morning and evening" in Aʿshā's poem: *Morgenländ. Forsch.*, p. 259; see MĪḲĀT). That they were introduced by Muḥammad himself at the end of his life is possible, but not very probable in view of the silence on the point in the Ḳurʾān, and in any case it is not certainly proved by the mention of the five times of prayer in a letter of the Prophet's (Ibn Hishām, p. 962) as we are not justified in expecting absolutely literal accuracy in the transmission of such documents.

Only one or two religious institutions are dealt with at all fully in the Ḳurʾān, the great pilgrimage to the sanctuaries at Mecca and the ʿumra in the town itself, but the ḥadjdj was indeed the crown of his endeavours begun in Mecca and carried through with tenacity. The Prophet, although he was now lord of Mecca, did not take part in the pilgrimage in the year 8, which was so inexplicable to later generations that they invented an ʿumra unknown to many of his followers (Ibn Hishām, p. 886; Ṭabarī, i. 1670 [ʿUrwa], 1685; Wāḳidī, p. 380; Ibn Saʿd, II/ii. I, 123 *sq.*; III/i. 103; cf. II/i. 123 *sq.*; Snouck Hurgronje, *Het Mekkaansche Feest*, p. 58 *sq.*). Nor did he come in the year 9 to Mecca to the ḥadjdj; he showed his interest in it however by sending Abū Bakr as his representative and making him read a proclamation which had momentous results (Bukhārī, *Maghāzī*, bāb 66, *Tafsīr al-Ḳurʾān*, Sūra ix. bāb 2; according to the usual tradition, it was ʿAlī who acted as his deputy; but this is probably a tendencious alteration; cf. Ṭabarī, i. 1760 *sq.* where Abū Bakr complains about being passed over and is comforted by Muḥammad; there is also another tradition, according to which Abū Bakr commissioned Abū Huraira to proclaim the exclusion of the heathen from the pilgrimage: Ibn Saʿd, II/i. 121 *sq.*). This was what is known as the *barāʾa* in which Muḥammad, who had been for so many years excluded from the pilgrimage, forbade all heathen any participation in it and gave them a period of four months, after the expiry of which they had the choice between the adoption of Islām and merciless warfare (Sūra ix.). This explains his absence from the celebration in the two preceding years; he wished to wait until he could celebrate it as sole ruler and completely in agreement with his intentions or, as he said, with the ceremonies introduced by Abraham (ii. 125 *sq.*). Finally all was prepared and at the end of the year 10/March 632 he was able to carry through the first reformed pilgrimage (the "Farewell Pilgrimage" or the "Pilgrimage of Islām"), which became the standard for all time. It is remarkable that the regulations for the ceremonies of the ḥadjdj, the object of which was to remove all that was too obviously pagan in the old ceremony (cf. e.g. the *awthān* in Minā in Farazdaḳ, in *ZDMG*, lix. 604; Azraḳī, ed. Wüstenfeld, p. 402) and to give it an Islāmic colouring, are found mainly in traditions, where later details can of course easily have been inserted, and only in fragments and more or less incidentally in the Ḳurʾān; but broadly speaking, the later form is undoubtedly based on what the Prophet laid down on this memorable occasion [cf. the article ḤADJDJ].

The Farewell Pilgrimage, at which an effective address, of which somewhat variant versions have been handed down, is put in the Prophet's mouth, marks the culminating point in his career. His feelings at this time are probably expressed in Allah's words in Sūra v. 3: "To-day I have perfected your religion, and completed my favours for you and chosen Islām as a religion for you". There is therefore a touch of the dramatic in the fact that his career closed a few months later. He himself hardly expected this, for only a month before his death he was preparing an expedition, which was to set out under the leadership of the young Usāma against Transjordania (not as in some traditions to West of the Jordan), in order to avenge the death of his father. The situation was such in other respects also that it required a man in full vigour to deal with it; in several places the appearance of different "prophets" had provoked disturbances [cf. AL-ASWAD, ṬULAIḤA and MUSAILIMA]. Then Muḥammad suddenly fell ill, presumably of the ordinary Madīna fever (Farazdaḳ, ix. 13); but this was dangerous to a man physically and mentally overwrought. He rallied a little but then died on the 13th Rabīʿ I of the year 9 (i.e. June 8, 632; only this date suits the statement in Ḥassān b. Thābit, No. cxxxiii. and all traditionists that it was a Monday) on the bosom of his favourite wife ʿĀʾisha, according to the story with the words: "The highest friend (*rafīḳ*, for which Goldziher once proposed *raḳīʿ*, "the vault of heaven") of Paradise!". He left — fortunately however for his community — no legal successor, for even the little Ibrāhīm whom the Coptic slave Māriya bore to him had died shortly before (on Jan. 27, 632, if the statement is right that there was an eclipse of the sun on the day he died; cf. Rhodokanakis, in *WZKM*, xiv. 78 *sqq.*; Mahler, *op. cit.*, p. 109 *sqq.*). The wild confusion which party passions let loose in Madīna when his death became known had the remarkable result that his corpse remained neglected for a whole day until it was finally buried under ʿĀʾisha's hut (Ṭabarī, i. 1817; Ibn Saʿd, II/ii. 57 *sqq.*, 71).

The great difficulty which the biographer of Muḥammad feels on every page is this, that the real secret of his career, the wonderful strength of his personality and his power of influencing those around him by suggestion, is not recorded in the early sources and indeed could not be recorded. From the Ḳurʾān, it is true, one becomes acquainted with his earliest remarkable inspirations, which even now are not without effect, and with his eminent political gift later in Madīna. We do of course find instances in the battle of Badr or the agreement of Ḥudaibīya where his intellectual superiority is overwhelmingly evident; but these are only isolated flashes and for the most part we have to read the essentials between the lines. The really powerful factor was his unshakable belief from beginning to end that he had been called by Allāh, for a conviction such as this, which does not admit of the slightest doubt, exercises an incalculable influence on others; and the certainty with which he came forward as the executor of Allāh's will gave his words and ordinances an authority which proved finally compelling. His real personality was revealed quite openly with its limitations; his strength and his knowledge were limited, the ability to perform miracles was denied him and he speaks quite frankly of his faults (xxxiv. 50; xl. 55; xlvii. 19; xlviii. 1 *sq.*; lxxx. 1 *sqq.*; ix. 43). Apart from the revelation with which he was favoured, he is a man like any other and several times refers to the fact that he will die (xxxix. 30; xxi. 34 *sq.*; iii. 144; the episode in Ibn Hi<u>sh</u>ām, p. 1012 *sq.* is not historical but a tendencious story directed against the tendency becoming apparent to apotheosize the Prophet). This is exactly the field in which later ages have felt dissatisfied, so that they quite early, driven mainly by their disputations with the Christians (see M. Schreiner, in *ZDMG*, xlii. 594), wove around the person and life of the Prophet a network of superhuman features (see Tor Andrae's work quoted below). Apart from the traditions which are clearly confirmed by the Ḳurʾān we can only have certainty in the strictest sense of the word in cases where the stories place the Prophet in an unfavourable light, not only from our point of view but also from that of the Muslims, e.g. in the story of his temporary recognition of the three Meccan goddesses or of his being censured by ʿUmar for putting off the *iḥrām* between the ʿumra and ḥad<u>j</u>d<u>j</u> on the Farewell Pilgrimage, for it is quite incredible that such features should be later inventions and as a rule in such cases the compromising stories are confirmed by the existence of variant traditions which endeavour to dispose of the offensive features by glossing them over or altering them.

Bibliography: E. Sachau, *Das Berliner Fragment des Mūsā b. ʿUḳba*, in *S B Pr A*, 1904, p. 445—470; Wüstenfeld, *Das Leben Muhammeds v. Muhammad b. Isḥāḳ*, ed. by Ibn Hi<u>sh</u>ām, 1858—1860 (German transl. by Weil, 1864); Wellhausen, *Muhammed in Medina; das ist Vāḳidīs Kitāb al-Ma<u>gh</u>āzi in verkürzter deutscher Wiedergabe*, 1882; Muḥammad b. Saʿd, ed. by E. Sachau, 1/i., ii.; II/i., ii.; Ibn Wāḍiḥ al-Yaʿḳūbī, *Historiae*, ed. Houtsma, ii. 1 *sqq.*; al-Balā<u>dh</u>urī, ed. de Goeje, 1866; Ṭabarī, *Annales*, i. 1073 *sqq.*; works on ḥadī<u>th</u>, esp. al-Bu<u>kh</u>ārī, ed. L. Krehl (vol. iv., ed. Juynboll). — Of later date: Nūr al-Dīn al-Ḥalabī, *al-Sīra al-Ḥalabīya*, Cairo 1308. See also SĪRA and MAWLID.

J. Gagnier, *La vie de Mahomet*, 3 vols. 1758; G. Weil, *Mohammed der Prophet, sein Leben und seine Lehre*, 1843; W. Muir, *Life of Mahomet*, 4 vols. 1858; A. Sprenger, *Leben und Lehre des Mohammed*, 3 vols. 1861—65; Th. Nöldeke, *Das Leben Muhammeds nach den Quellen populär dargestellt*, 1863; R. Dozy, *Essai sur l'histoire de l'Islamisme*, 1879, p. 18 *sqq.*; L. Krehl, *Das Leben des Muhammed*, 1884; A. Müller, *Der Islam im Morgen- und Abendlande*, 1885, i. 44 *sqq.*; H. Grimme, *Mohammed*, 2 vols. 1892—5; Lamaitresse et Dujarric, *Vie de Mahomet d'après la tradition*, 1897—8; F. Buhl, *Muhammeds Liv*, 1903; do. *Muhammeds religiöse Forkyndelse efter Quranen*, 1924; do. *Das Leben Muhammeds*, Leipzig 1934; D. S. Margoliouth, *Mohammed and the Rise of Islam*, 1905; H. Reckendorf, *Mohammed und die Seinen*, 1907; Caetani, *Annali dell' Islam*, i and i/ii.

Of further literature we may mention: Wellhausen, *Skizzen und Vorarbeiten*, iv. (on Madīna, Muḥammad's constitution of the community and the embassies and letters); Sperber, *Die Schreiben Muhammeds an die Stämme Arabiens* (in *MSOS*, xix.); Snouck Hurgronje, *Het Mekkaansche Feest*, 1880 (= *Verspr. Geschr.* i, 1 *sqq.*); do. *Verspr. Geschr.* i, 183 *sqq.*; H. Lammens, *Mahomet fut-il sincère*, 1911; do., *Qoran et Tradition*, 1910; do., *Fāṭima et les filles de Mahomet*, 1912; Wensinck, *Mohammed en de Joden te Medina*, 1908; H. Hirschfeld, *Essai sur l'histoire des Juifs à Medina*, in *REJ*, x. 26; R. Leszynsky, *Die Juden in Arabien z. Zeit Mohammeds*, 1910; A. Geiger, *Was hat Mohammed aus dem Judentum aufgenommen*, 1833; Rudolph, *Die Abhängigkeit des Qorans v. Juden- und Christentum*, 1922; J. Goldziher, *Muhammedanische Studien*, 1889—1890; Tor Andrae, *Die Person Muhammeds in Lehre und Glauben seiner Gemeinde* (in *Archives d'Études Orientales*, xvi. 1918); do., *Mohammed, sein Leben und Glaube*, Göttingen 1932; K. Ahrens, *Muhammed als Religionsstifter*, Leipzig 1935; Ph. K. Hitti, *History of the Arabs*, London 1937, p. 111 *sqq.*

MUḤAMMAD B. **ʿABD** AL-**WAHHĀB**. [See WAHHĀBĪS].

MUḤAMMAD ʿABDUH, Muslim theologian, founder of the Egyptian modernist school.

Muḥammad ʿAbduh belonged to an Egyptian peasant family and was born in 1849 in Lower Egypt. Having learned the Ḳurʾān by heart, he was sent in 1862 to the theological school of Ṭanṭā but he left this discouraged and was only induced to resume his studies through the influence of a great-uncle who aroused in him an interest in mysticism. In 1865 he returned to Ṭanṭā but the next year proceeded to Cairo to the Azhar mosque. There Muḥammad ʿAbduh at once devoted himself entirely to mysticism, practised ascetism and retired from the world. It was again his great-uncle who persuaded him to give this up. In 1872, Muḥammad ʿAbduh came into contact with Saiyid <u>D</u>jamāl al-Dīn al-Af<u>gh</u>ānī [q.v.] who revealed traditional learning to Muḥammad ʿAbduh in a new light, called his attention to European works accessible in translations and attracted his interest finally to Egyptian and Muslim problems of the day. Muḥammad ʿAbduh soon became his most ardent disciple; this appears already from his two first publications on mysticism and dogmatics. The influence of Saiyid <u>D</u>jamāl al-Dīn caused Muḥammad ʿAbduh in 1876 to take to journalism, which he practised henceforth. After concluding his studies at the Azhar mosque and acquiring the certificate of an *ʿālim* (scholar), he first of all gave private tuition; in 1879 he was appointed as teacher in the Dār al-ʿUlūm, but in the same year dismissed for unknown reasons and sent to his native village, while Saiyid <u>D</u>jamāl al-Dīn was banished from Egypt. A liberal ministry very soon recalled Muḥammad ʿAbduh (1880) and appointed him chief editor of the official gazette *al-waḳāʾiʿ al-miṣrīya*; under Muḥammad ʿAbduh's control it became the mouthpiece of the liberal party. In spite of a common ultimate goal: the liberation of the Muslim peoples and a renaissance of Islām by its own strength, there was an essentiel difference between Muḥammad ʿAbduh's programme and that of Saiyid Djamāl al-Dīn; the latter was a revolutionary who aimed at a forcible upheaval; Muḥammad ʿAbduh, on the other hand, held that no political revolution could take the place of a gradual transformation of mentality. ʿArābī Pāshā's rebellion put an end to Muḥammad ʿAbduh's activity on these lines. His part in this movement has not yet been sufficiently elucidated; after its suppression he was condemned to banishment from Egypt at the end of 1882. He first went to Bairūt and then to Paris where in the beginning of 1884 he met Saiyid Djamāl al-Dīn. The two founded a society called *al-ʿurwa al-wuthḳā* and published a paper with the same name, which had to cease publication after eight months but exercised a very profound influence on the development of nationalism in the Muslim east; it expressed the views of Saiyid Djamāl al-Dīn entirely. In Tunis Muḥammad ʿAbduh continued propaganda for the society, but then cut himself off from it and settled in Bairūt at the beginning of 1885. Here he taught at a theological school and engaged in Muslim and Arabic studies. In this period he produced his translation from the Persian of the *Risālat at-radd ʿala 'l-dahrīyīn*, the only considerable work of Saiyid Djamāl al-Dīn [1303/1886], and two valuable philological treatises (*Sharḥ Nahdj al-balāgha* [1302/1885] and *Sharḥ Maḳāmāt Badīʿ al-zamān al-Hamadhānī* [1306/1889]). When in 1889 he was allowed to return, he at once went to Cairo and was immediately appointed a judge on the Tribunaux Indigènes, two years later Conseiller at the Cour d'Appel. One result of his work in the courts was his request *Taḳrīr fī iṣlāḥ al-maḥākim al-sharʿīya* (1318/1900) which gave the stimulus to important reforms in the administration of the *sharīʿa*. In 1899 he attained the highest religious post in Egypt, that of state *muftī*, an office he held till his death. The most remarkable among his *fatwā*'s are those permitting the eating of meat of animals slaughtered by Jews or Christians, and legalizing loans on interest. In the same year, 1899, he became a member of the Conseil Législatif, which marked the first stage of constitutional representation in Egypt. Finally in 1894 he became a member of the Conseil supérieur of the Azhar, which had been constituted at his suggestion, and in this capacity not only acquired great renown by his reforms but himself took an active and far-reaching part in the teaching. In addition to this many-sided activity he found time to publish his two most important books: his principal theological work the *Risālat al-tawḥīd* [1315/1897], and a defence of Islām against Christianity entitled *al-Islām wa 'l-naṣrānīya maʿa 'l-ʿilm wa 'l-madanīya* [1320/1902], and to write a commentary upon a work on logic: *Sharḥ Kitāb al-baṣā'ir al-nāṣirīya, taṣnīf al-Ḳāḍī Zain al-Dīn* [1316/1898]). On the contrary, he was not able to finish his commentary on the Ḳur'ān, on which he laid great importance and of which only portions appeared in his lifetime; it was revised and completed by his disciple and friend Shaikh Muḥammad Rashīd Riḍā, and published first of all in *al-Manār*. Of Muḥammad ʿAbduh's numerous articles by which, along with his lectures, he most influenced public opinion, two (of 1900) were published in a French translation entitled *L'Europe et l'Islām* by Muḥammad Ṭalʿat Ḥarb Bey (1905). The advanced ideas put forward by Muḥammad ʿAbduh provoked the most vigorous hostility in orthodox and conservative circles, which manifested itself not only in serious refutations but also in a whole literature of lampoons. But his teaching met with remarkable support among many seriously minded Muslims. The principal organ of his views was the monthly *al-Manār*, which had appeared since 1897 under the editorship of Muḥammad Rashīd Riḍā, who also produced an extensive literary monument to his master. Muḥammad ʿAbduh died in 1905; but his teaching has retained its influence steadily to the present day. Ḥāfiẓ Ibrāhīm composed an elegy on him; the house in which he was born has been declared a historical monument; since 1931 a scholarship foundation for Azhar students bears his name.

Muḥammad ʿAbduh's programme according to his own statement was: 1. the reform of the Muslim religion by bringing it back to its original condition, 2. the renovation of the Arabic language, 3. the recognition of the rights of the people. Besides, he was dominated by the idea of patriotism, which he was the first to champion enthusiastically in Egypt. As an opponent equally of political control by Europe and of Oriental despotism in Muslim lands he favoured an inner assimilation of western civilization, without abandoning the fundamental Muslim ideas, and a synthesis of the two factors. From this programme, which assures Muḥammad ʿAbduh an important place among the founders of modern Egypt, must be distinguished his effort to carry it through in the field of theology. Here his main aim was to establish and maintain Islām as a religion against the onslaught of the west, while he abandoned without a struggle those aspects of Muslim Oriental life in which religion was of less moment. The actual foundations of his teaching came primarily from the school of Ibn Taimīya and Ibn Ḳaiyim al-Djawzīya, who favoured reform on conservative lines, and from al-Ghazzālī's ethical conception of religion. He was thus brought to attack the *madhhab*'s and *taḳlīd* [q.v.], to demand freedom for *idjtihād* [q.v.] and a new *idjmāʿ* [q.v.], in keeping with modern conditions, based on the Ḳur'ān and the true sunna; he was also brought to reject the hairsplitting of the *fuḳahā'*, the worship of saints (regarding whose alleged miracles he is sceptical), and all *bidʿa*s. The antiquated system of Fiḳh, against which Muḥammad ʿAbduh claimed in theory full freedom, while in practice retaining its method and most of its positive doctrines, was to be replaced by new laws capable of development in which consideration for the common good (*maṣlaḥa*) and the times should have if necessary preference even to the literal text (*naṣṣ*) of revelation. There was in Muḥammad ʿAbduh the conviction that knowledge and religion, properly understood, could not come into conflict at all; but reason must, after it has tested the proofs of the truth of religion, accept its dogmas. In dogmatics he adopts essentially the most rational conception that could still be reconciled with orthodoxy. He interiorises the conception of revelation (to him it is an intuitive knowledge caused by God and accompanied by a consciousness of its origin, but this kind of religious experience is limited to the prophets) and softens that of religion (to him it is an intuitive feeling for the paths to happiness in this and the next world, which cannot be clearly grasped by the reason). The task of prophecy for him is the moral education of the masses; religious teaching and commandments are therefore intended for the masses and not for the élite. Muḥammad

ʿAbduh regards the Ḳurʾān as created and endeavours to weaken the rigidly opposed point of view of orthodoxy. In spite of the denial of causality and laws of nature by orthodoxy, he finds a basis for explaining nature by causal laws but by quite scholastically formal reasoning. As regards the positive commandments of religion, Muḥammad ʿAbduh adheres to the main four duties: ritual prayer, almstax, fasting and pilgrimage; only he shifts them, as usual in mysticism, from the sphere of worship to that of ethics. On the question of freewill Muḥammad ʿAbduh decides for indetermination, preaches vigorous activity by every one and, following the ethics of the mystics, mutual support. The sending of prophets was a gradual process of education of step by step; the last and highest stage, that of absolute religion, is the sending of Muḥammad. If the Muslim peoples of the present do not correspond to the Muslim ideal, this is only the result of the fact that they have lost the old purity of the teaching; an improvement is possible by return to it. This primitive Islām of Muḥammad ʿAbduh is however not the historical Islām but a very much idealised one. The superiority of Islām over Christianity in substance lies, according to Muḥammad ʿAbduh, in its rationalism and its closeness to reality and its avoidance of unattainable ideals of life.

In this theology, the religious content may be resumed as humility before God, reverence for the Prophet, enthusiasm for the Ḳurʾān. There is no place for piety of the S̲h̲īʿa type nor for mysticism apart from its ethics. On the contrary, the genuinely old Muslim rationalism is for Muḥammad ʿAbduh the main weapon of defence of Islām and actually takes the place of a deepening of religion so that his theology has the character of an apologetic compromise. There remains as his achievement to have opened the door to Western ideas for orthodox Muslims and to have conducted them on their road for a certain distance; although the general development of modernism had already partly outdistanced him and has by now left him far behind, it still remains true that he contributed considerably to creating a place for Islām in the modern world.

Bibliography: Bergsträsser, *Islam und Abendland*, in *Auslandsstudien*, iv., Königsberg 1929, p. 15 *sqq.*; Goldziher, *Richtungen der islamischen Koranauslegung*, p. 320 *sqq.*; R. Hartmann, *Krisis des Islām*, p. 13 *sqq.*; Horten, *Mohammed Abduh*, in *Beiträge zur Kenntnis des Orients*, xiii., xiv.; B. Michel and Cheikh Moustapha Abdel Razik, *Cheikh Mohammed Abdou, Rissalat al-Tawhid, Esposé de la Religion Musulmane* (translation with introduction on the life and teaching of Muḥammad ʿAbduh and bibliography). Adams, *Islam and Modernism in Egypt* (with bibliography); do., *Muḥammad ʿAbduh and the Transvaal Fatwā*, in *Macdonald Presentation Volume*, p. 12 *sqq.*; Cromer, *Modern Egypt*, iii. 179—180. On the life story of Muḥammad ʿAbduh is based the trilogy of novels by F. Bonjean and A. Deyf: *Mansour, El Azhar* and *Cheikh Abdou l'Égyptien.*

MUḤAMMAD AḤMAD B. **ʿABD ALLĀH**, the Mahdī of the Sūdān, was born about 1258/1834 on the island of Ḍarār in Dongola among the Argū islands north of el-ʿOrde. A member of the Kunūz family of the Nubian Arab Berābera, in later life when Mahdī, to prove his kinship and mystical relationship with ʿAlī and the Prophet, he traced his genealogy on his father's side to Ḥasan and on the mother's to Ḥasan and ʿAbbās. He was the second son of a ship's carpenter and had an older sister and three brothers. Mystic tendencies early revealed themselves in him; after the usual early education he therefore in 1277/1861 entered the order of the Sammānīya with S̲h̲aik̲h̲ Muḥammad S̲h̲arīf; after a seven years' noviciate Muḥammad S̲h̲arīf appointed him a S̲h̲aik̲h̲ of the order. After a short stay in K̲h̲arṭūm where he married, he went to the island of Abbā (in the White Nile, north of Kosti), built a *d̲j̲āmiʿ* there and a *k̲h̲alwa* and collected pupils around him. His master Muḥammad S̲h̲arīf, with whom he maintained a constant connection, settled near him in 1288/1872 which seems to have been unwelcome to Muḥammad. Shortly after this event there awoke in Muḥammad the consciousness that he was the *mahdī al-muntaẓar*, under the influence of the traditional ideas of the Mahdī, which brought about a breach between him and his master. He now joined the enemy of his former leader, the S̲h̲aik̲h̲ al-Ḳuras̲h̲ī, and in 1297/1880 became his successor. In his wanderings (*siyāḥa*) from Dongola to Sennār, from the Blue Nile to Kordūfān, he convinced himself of the discontent of the people, who were oppressed by the Egyptian government; the turbulent, mixed population of the Sūdān, the religious fanaticism, the dissension between Turks and Arabs, the old opposition of the S̲h̲īʿa to the Turkish ruling official classes, all formed a fruitful soil for his claims to be the Mahdī; the movement begun by Muḥammad Aḥmad which, as his letters and proclamations show, was based on a religious experience in which he earnestly believed, became from the first mixed up with political and social ideas, which in the east cannot be separated from religion, and in which finally deception and cunning played an evil part. According to the traditional formula, Muḥammad Aḥmad felt himself called "to purify the world from wantonness and corruption". For this purpose he summoned the people to fight in the first place against "the infidel Turks". He had previously bound a number of chiefs in Kordūfān and Dārfūr to him by *baiʿa* (oaths of fealty, after the model of the Prophet; for the text see Dietrich, in *Islām*, 1925, p. 39) and had been cleverly able to attach men of action like the unscrupulous ʿAbdullāhi al-Ṭaʿāyis̲h̲ī, later his K̲h̲alīfa, to him; at the same time he practised a shameless nepotism. He further incited the people by numerous pamphlets and edicts, which contained his visions of the Prophet, who had appointed him Mahdī, of al-K̲h̲iḍr, Gabriel, the *aḳṭāb*, summons "to purify religion", to "emigrate", to swear fealty, to imitate the Mahdī, to the *d̲j̲ihād* etc. The hill of Gadīr in Dār Nūba became the centre of this secret propaganda; in S̲h̲aʿbān 1298/July 1881 be made his first public appearance as Mahdī. Negotiations begun by the government in K̲h̲arṭūm with Muḥammad Aḥmad proved fruitless. Two companies sent against him under Abu 'l-Saʿūd were destroyed; this secured further victories for him. The Egyptian government was moreover prevented by the rebellion of ʿArābī Pās̲h̲ā from taking vigorous action. The expeditions of the governor of Fas̲h̲ōda, Ras̲h̲īd Pās̲h̲ā, Yūsuf Pās̲h̲ā al-S̲h̲allālī (at Gadīr May 1882) and of Hicks Pās̲h̲ā (at S̲h̲aikān or Kas̲h̲gil) all ended unsuccessfully. The Mahdīya thus spread unhindered from Kordūfān via Baḥr al-G̲h̲azāl to the eastern Sūdān; there in Sawākin, ʿOt̲h̲mān Digna, a former slave dealer, soon to be the ablest Mahdist general, entered Muḥammad Aḥmad's service. Attempts by the Mahdī to extend his power to the west and with this object to conclude alliances with Muḥammad al-Sanūsī in Djaghbūb and with Morocco came to nothing. At the height of his power the campaign of 1301/1884 took him to Kharṭūm, which after a heroic defence by Gordon, fell into the Mahdī's hands on Jan. 30, 1885; Gordon was killed. Muḥammad Aḥmad dit not however long survive his victory; he died, probably of typhus, on 9th Ramaḍān 1302/June 22, 1885 at Omdurmān near Kharṭūm, where a *ḳubba* was erected to him by his successor, the Khalīfa ʿAbdullāhi; it was henceforth the Mahdist capital until Kitchener put an end to ʿAbdullāhi's rule and to the Mahdīya in 1898.

The organisation of the Mahdīya under Muḥammad Aḥmad, which was primarily to follow the *sunna* of the Prophet, was early developed; it was quite military in character, for the *djihād* was considered more important than the *ḥadjdj*. He had four khalīfas beside him, of whom al-Taʿāyishī was the most intimate and undoubtedly had the most pernicious influence on him. Particular attention was devoted to the distribution of booty and to the administration of the treasury (*bait al-māl*).

Muḥammad Aḥmad's teaching shows some of the features of the extreme popular Ṣūfism and some of those of an idealised primitive Islām. His asceticism was hostile to progress; the contempt for learning in the Mahdīya and the order to burn all books on *sunna* and *tafsīr* alienated the educated classes from him. The only things that had validity in addition to the Ḳurʾān were the proclamations of the Mahdī, the *Rātib* (a collection of *dhikr* exercises) and the *Madjlis*, a work that contained Muḥammad Aḥmad's own *sunna* as a substitute for the previous one but remained incomplete. In the abolition of the four *madhhabs* we see the *ikhtilāf* tendencies frequent among the Ṣūfīs. Wahhābī influences are very probable in a number of regulations, for example in the prohibition of adornment, music, extravagance at weddings, tobacco and wine; particularly however in the zeal against the worship of saints and sorcery; as a matter of fact Muḥammad Aḥmad himself became an object of worship among his followers even before his death.

The only really new thing in Muḥammad Aḥmad is the addition to the *shahāda*: "... *wa-anna Muḥammad*^{an} *Aḥmad*^{a} *'bn*^{a} *ʿAbd*^{i} *'llāh*^{i} *huwa Mahdīy*^{u} *ʾllāh*^{i} *wa-khalīfat*^{u} *rasūlihi*. Where the traditions of the Mahdī did not suit him, he did not hesitate to alter them. He laid down the following 6 *arkān* instead of the *arkān* of the *sunna*: 1. *ṣalāt*, on the congregational performance of which the greatest stress was laid; 2. *djihād*, in express opposition to the *sunna* practice and in place of the *ḥadjdj*; 3. obedience to God's commandments; 4. the extended *shahāda*; 5. recitation of the Ḳurʾān and; 6. of the *Rātib*.

A few extremist ideas, like that of equality between rich and poor, come partly from the revolutionary character of the old Shīʿa, partly from the political and social conditions of the time; the social ideas were however not his central ones but only incidentally used cunningly to attract the masses. In practice the Mahdīya had an exceedingly unifying and equalising effect: slaves and slave-dealers fought under one banner, the humblest often rose in a short time to the highest offices.

Muḥammad Aḥmad's eschatology centres round the world domination of the Mahdī. The conquest of the Sūdān was to be followed by that of Egypt, Mecca, Syria and Constantinople.

The formation of legends around Muḥammad Aḥmad's personality began very early, sometimes deliberately encouraged by him and his inmediate followers and sometimes actually believed by them. Under pressure from him his court chronicler Ismāʿīl ʿAbd al-Ḳādir composed a highly coloured *sīra* entitled *Kitāb al-Mustahdī illā Sīrat al-Imām al-Mahdī*. It covered the years 1298 to 1302 A.H. but was burned in the time of the Khalīfa ʿAbdullāhi. The Egyptian writer Shuḳair (see below) claims to have had in his hands a copy that was said to have survived.

Bibliography: Naʿūm Shuḳair Bey, *Taʾrīkh al-Sūdān*, Cairo 1903 (in the third part Shuḳair, utilizing the edicts of Muḥammad Aḥmad and the Khalīfa ʿAbdullāhi which were collected and printed under the Khalīfa, as well as the above mentioned *Sīra* and his own experiences in the Anglo-Egyptian army, gives a very full account of the Mahdīya under Muḥammad Aḥmad and ʿAbdullāhi; Djirdjī Zaidān, *Riwāyāt asīr al-mutamahdī*, Cairo 1892. — ʿAbd al-Raḥmān al-Rāfiʿī, *Al-thawra al-ʿarabīya wa'l-iḥtilāl al-Inglīzī*, Cairo 1937. F. R. Wingate, *Mahdiism in the Egyptian Sudan*, London 1891; do., *The Rise and Wane of the Mahdi Religion*, London 1893; Jos. Ohrwalder, *Aufstand u. Reich des Mahdi*, Innsbruck 1892; Slatin Pasha, *Fire and Sword in the Sudan*, London 1896; Hasenclever, *Geschichte Ägyptens im 19. Jahrhundert*, Halle 1917; Ernst L. Dietrich, *Der Mahdi Mohammed Ahmed nach arabischen Quellen*, in *Isl.*, 1925, p. 1—90 (with further literature); *Neue Rundschau*, Juli—August 1931; A. v. Tiedemann, *Mit Kitchener gegen den Mahdi*, Berlin 1906; R. A. Bermann, *The Mahdi of Allah*, London 1931; B. M. Allen, *Gordon and the Sudan*, London 1933; P. Crabitès, *Gordon, the Sudan and Slavery*, London 1933; do., *The Winning of the Sudan*, London 1934; Fr. Charles-Roux, *L'Egypte de 1801 a 1882*, and H. Deherain, *Le Soudan égyptien de Mohammed Aly à Ismail Pacha*, Paris 1936; A. Sammarco, *Histoire de l'Egypte moderne*, 3 vols., Cairo 1937.

MUḤAMMAD B. AL-HANAFĪYA. [See KAISĀNĪYA; SHĪʿA].

AL-**MUḤAMMADĪYA**, a name of several heretical schools, notably the ultra-Shīʿī Muḥammadīya.

As the example of the Kaisānīya [q.v.] shows, at an early date some Shīʿīs transferred the imāmate to ʿAlids who were not descendants of the Prophet's daughter Fāṭima and then to men who were not ʿAlids at all. The Manṣūrīya revered such a one in Abū Manṣūr al-ʿIdjlī, whom Yūsuf b. ʿUmar al-Thaḳafī, governor of the ʿIrāḳ, executed in the reign of the Caliph Hishām, i.e. before 125/743. Abū Manṣūr, rejected by the Imām Djaʿfar al-Ṣādiḳ for Shīʿī exaggeration, thrust the ʿAlids aside by still further increasing this tendency; Muḥammad's family, he said, was heaven, the Shīʿa the earth and he himself the "fragment falling from heaven" mentioned in Sūra lii. 44, as he had been personally touched and taught by God on a journey to heaven; he is said to have abolished the religious laws. While one group, the Ḥusainīya, recognized the Imām in his son al-Ḥusain after the death of Abū Mansūr, another, the Muḥammadīya, recognized Muḥammad b. ʿAbd Allāh b. al-Ḥasan b. al-Ḥasan b. ʿAlī b. Abī Ṭālib. He is the pretender celebrated as *al-Nafs al-Zakīya* ("the pure soul"), who in 145/762 fell at Madīna fighting the troops of the ʿAbbāsid Caliph al-Manṣūr. The Muḥammadīya quoted as authority for again recognizing an ʿAlid again an alleged testamentary disposition of Abū Manṣūr and compared the following order of succession: testament of the Ḥusainid

Muḥammad Bāḳir for Abū Manṣūr and of the latter for the Ḥasanid Muḥammad b. ʿAbd Allāh, with the Jewish line: first Moses, then Joshua, son of Nun, then the sons of Aaron (the later priesthood is meant). This arrangment was chosen in both cases so that conflict might not arise between the two lines of brothers (*baṭnān*). — We cannot be certain that the Muḥammadīya formed a definite sect. Al-Nawbakhtī, *Firaḳ al-Shīʿa*, does not mention the name. The name rather records the fact that the rising of al-Nafs al-Zakīya, which was of great extent, attracted all circles of the Shīʿa to its ranks, even those who belonged to the Ḥusainid camp; likewise members of the Mughī.īya, the followers of Mughīra b. Saʿīd, killed in the year 119/737 by Yūsuf b. ʿUmar's predecessor Khālid b. ʿAbd Allāh al-Ḳasrī, probably under the leadership of Djābir b. Yazīd al-Djuʿfī supported al-Nafs al-Zakīya with their good wishes at least.

Quite a different group is the ultra-Islāmic Muḥammadīya or Mīmīya. It took its name from the belief in the divinity of the Prophet Muḥammad in reply to an ʿUlyānīya or ʿAinīya who regarded ʿAlī as God. Its principal representative al-Faiyāḍ b. ʿAlī was executed between 279/892 and 289/902.

The Khāridjī Muḥammadīya was a separate party within the strictly Khāridjī sub-group of the ʿAdjārida; it is called after a certain Muḥammad b. Zuraḳ.

Bibliography: al-Ashʿarī, *Maḳālāt al-Islāmiyīn*, ed. H. Ritter, Constantinople, 1928, i. 8 *sq.* 22 *sq.*; al-Baghdādī, p. 42 *sq.*, 214 *sq.*, 234 *sq.*; Ibn Ḥazm, iv. 186 *sq.*; cf. al-Īdjī, *Mawāḳif*, ed. Soerensen, Leipzig, 1848, p. 353 *sq.*; Masʿūdī, *Murūdj*, cf. Index; I. Friedländer, *The Heterodoxies of the Shiites*, in *JAOS*, xxviii. and xxix., cf. Index; Th. Haarbrücker (on Shahrastānī's) *Religionspartheien und Philosophenschulen*, ii. 409.

MUḤAMMADĪYA.

(1) Reformist Muslim organisation in Indonesia, founded Nov. 18, 1912, by Kyahi Haji Aḥmad Dahlan, in Jogjakarta, after the example of reformist movements in Egypt and India. Non-political. Mainly spread amongst middle-class Muslims throughout Indonesia. Membership in 1925: 4.000, in 1930: 24.000, not counting members of affiliated organisations. During Japanese occupation its activities were paralysed; in the post-war period reconstruction was very incomplete.

Main objectives: to stimulate Muslim religious education and studies in Indonesia, and to promote Muslim religious life amongst the members. Organisatory aspects: religious propaganda (tablegh); primary and secondary schools of several types (1925: 55 schools throughout Indonesia; 1929: 126 schools in Jogjakarta, Surakarta and Jakarta, not counting other schools throughout the archipelago); several periodicals and other publications; polyclinics; social welfare institutions (e.g. orphanages). Affiliated organisations: women's organisation "ʿA'ishīyah", and boy scout movement "Hizb ul-Watan". Before the war many congresses and mass-meetings were held.

Bibliography: Lothrop Stoddard, *The New World of Islam* (1921); B. J. O. Schrieke, *Bijdrage tot de bibliografie van de huidige godsdienstige beweging ter Sumatra's Westkust (Tijdschrift Indische Taal-, Land- en Volkenkunde*, vol. lix); H. Kraemer (Zendingstijdschrift *De Opwekker*, 1923, p. 183, 1927, p. 293); G. F. Pijper, *Fragmenta Islamica* (1934); C. A. O. van Nieuwenhuijze, *Moslims leven en Indonesische levenssfeer (Wending*, vol. 4).

(2) Muslim mystical brotherhood (tarekat) in Southern Celebes.

AL-MUḤARRAM (A.), the first month of the Muḥammadan year. The name is originally not a proper name but an adjective, as the article shows, qualifying Ṣafar. In the pre-Muḥammadan period the first two months of the old Meccan year were Ṣafar I and II [see TAʾRĪKH], which is reflected in the dual "a potiori" *al-Ṣafarāni* for al-Muḥarram and Ṣafar; in the old Arab year the first half year consisted of "three months of two months each" (Wellhausen), as the two Ṣafars were followed by two Rabīʿs and two Djumādās. The first of the two Ṣafars, as the one that belonged to the sacred months, was given the adjectival epithet *al-muḥarram* which gradually became the name of the month itself. As Dhu 'l-Ḥidjdja also belonged to the sacred months, three of the four sacred months came together except in leap years. The month intercalated to equate the year to the solar year was inserted after Dhu 'l-Ḥidjdja and was not sacred. It thus came about that learned Muslims described the intercalation as renaming the Muḥarram concerned Ṣafar, i.e. as making Muḥarram not sacred; they mean that the month after the pilgrimage, which they consider as al-Muḥarram, following the custom, is not sacred, i.e. is "*Ṣafar*" and the second month i.e. in their view Ṣafar, is "al-Muḥarram". In doing this they of course overlook the fact that Ṣafar proper now only comes third; but when the intercalary month was abolished in Islām, the proper conception of the state of affairs was lost.

In the early period when an attempt was made to equate with the solar year by inserting intercalary months — which was not successful on account of the ignorance of the old Arabs in astronomical matters — al-Muḥarram introduced the winter half year as the names of the first six months show. The Arab year began, like the Jewish, in autumn. After Muḥammad had forbidden the insertion of the intercalary months in Sūra ix. 37, 1st Muḥarram, the beginning of the year, went through all the seasons as the year, which now consisted of 12 lunar months, had always only 354 or 355 days, as it still has. Whether the first month of the year was originally marked by a festival we do not know. Wellhausen has endeavoured to show that the *ḥadjdj* originally fell in the first month of the year, so that Muḥarram was *ḥarām* in its quality as "Dhu 'l-Ḥidjdja". This also suggests that there was originally only one sacred month, but it was observed at different times in different parts of Arabia. Muḥammad in the Ḳurʾān always speaks only of *the* sacred month (ii. 194, 217; v. 2, 97); only in Sūra ix. 36 in laying down the method of reckoning time does he speak of four sacred months, in which it was sought to recognize a later declaration of the equal sanctity of four different sacred months of different districts, which was however illusory, as within Islām the peace of God reigns without this and, according to Sūra ii. 217, the defence of the faith takes preference over the sacred month. What the sacred month referred to in the Ḳurʾān is, we do not know; in Sūra v. 2, at any rate, the month of the pilgrimage must be meant, which fits Wellhausen's theory excellently. The commentators think Radjab or Dhu 'l-Ḳaʿda is meant, at any rate not al-Muḥarram.

Al-Muḥarram has 30 days of which, in addition to the 1st as the beginning of the year, the following are specially noted: the 9th as the fast-day of the Shīʿī ascetics; the 10th as the anniversary of Karbalāʾ (60/680), on which al-Ḥusain b. ʿAlī b. Abī Ṭālib [q.v.] fell fighting against the Caliph Yazīd b. Muʿāwiya and therefore the great day of mourning of the Shīʿa (on the significance of the 10th Muḥarram for the Sunnis see ʿĀSHŪRĀʾ), celebrated by pilgrimages to the sacred places of the Shīʿa, especially to Karbalāʾ (see MASHHAD ḤUSAIN), in which the passion play, representing the death of ʿAlī's sons [see TAʿZIYA], plays the most important part; also the 16th as the day of the selection of Jerusalem as the Ḳibla [q.v.] and the 17th as the day of the arrival of the "people of the elephant" (Sūra cv.).

Bibliography: Wellhausen, *Reste arab. Heidentums*² (1897), p. 94—101; Moberg, *An-Nasīʾ (Koran IX, 37) in der islamischen Tradition (Lunds Universiteits Årsskrift*, N. F., Avd. 1, vol. xxvii., No. 1, 1931); Buhl, *Das Leben Muhammeds* (1930), p. 57, note 129, p. 350 *sq.*; al-Bīrūnī, *Āthār*, ed. Sachau, p. 60, 62, 196, 201, 328 *sqq.*; al-Ḳazwīnī, *ʿAdjāʾib al-makhlūḳāt*, ed. Wüstenfeld, p. 66, 68 (where further events that happened on the 10th Muḥarram are given); on the "people of the elephant" cf. Buhl, *op. cit.*, p. 12 *sq.*

AL-**MUḤĀSIBĪ**, ABŪ ʿABD ALLĀH ḤĀRITH B. ASAD AL-ʿANAZĪ, called Muḥāsibī, i.e. "he who examines his conscience", was born in Baṣra about 165/781; he died in Baghdād in 243/857. A legist of the Shāfiʿī school, a theologian who advocated the use of reason (*ʿaḳl*), using the dialectic vocabulary of the Muʿtazilīs, which he was the first to turn against them, he finally adopted a life of ascetic renunciation after a moral conversion long meditated which is described at the beginning of his *Waṣāyā*. Involved with the Muʿtazilīs in a general persecution as a result of Ibn Ḥanbal's attack on the dialecticians, he had to give up all teaching in 232/846 and died in retirement.

His principal works are: *Riʿāya li-ḥuḳūḳ Allāh*; *Waṣāyā* (more accurately: *Naṣāʾiḥ*); *Kitāb al-tawahhum*; *Māʾiyat al-ʿaḳl wa-maʿnāhu*; *Risālat al-ʿaẓama*; *Fahm al-ṣalāt*; The *Kitāb al-riʿāya*, his principal work, was edited in 1940 by Margaret Smith (Gibb. Mem. New Ser. 15), while the *Kitāb al-tawahhum* appeared in 1937 in Cairo, edited by A. J. Arberry. The *Dawāʾ dāʾ al-nufūs*, which Sprenger attributes to him, is of an earlier date; it was arranged by his chief teacher Aḥmad b. ʿĀṣim Anṭāḳī.

Muḥāsibī is the first Sunnī mystic whose works reveal a complete theological education; they combine in a very original way a keen concern for exact philosophical definitions, and a fervid reverence for the most naive traditions with the rigorous search for an increasing moral purification.

In his *Riʿāya* he discards the foundations of that "method" of introspection which Anṭāḳī had envisaged; he shows that a correlation is possible between two series of human happenings, the external actions of the members and the intentions of the heart (against this: ʿAllāf and the majority of contemporary *mutakallimūn*); he proves in detail that the enchainment of the states of conscience (*aḥwāl*) can be guided progressively towards a perfect purity, provided an ascetic and moral rule of life is observed, the true *rahbānīya* mentioned in Sūra lvii. 27.

His adversaries (*muḥaddithūn*), especially Ḥanbalīs, attacked him for having differentiated the concepts of *ʿilm* and *ʿaḳl* (parable of the "sower"), *īmān* and *maʿrifa* (like Ibn Karrām); admitted the created character of the *lafẓ* (our pronunciation of Ḳurʾānic verses); held that the elect, in Paradise, would be summoned to enjoy directly familiarity with the divine being; chosen his proofs from traditions not by following the formal correctness of their *isnāds*, but on account of their intrinsic significance, and their moral weight (*ʿibra*), for the reader.

The *Riʿāya* is his main work; it forms in 61 chapters, in the shape of advice given to a pupil, a complete manual of the inner life. Ghazzālī used it before writing his *Iḥyāʾ*; and in spite of periodical attacks, its reputation among Arabic-speaking Muslim mystics lasted for a long time and may be compared with that of the *Imitatio Jesu Christi* among Christian mystics using Latin; the Shādhilīya brotherhood, with Mursī, Ibn ʿAbbād, Rundī and Zarrūḳ Burnūsī, have always recommended its use; and one of them, ʿIzz al-Dīn Maḳdisī, has made a summary of it. The Ashʿarī theologians also esteem Muḥāsibī as a precursor.

Bibliography: Margaret Smith, *An early Mystic of Baghdad, a Study of the Life and Teaching of Hārith b. Asad al-Muhāsibī*, London 1935; Hudjwīrī, *Kashf al-maḥdjūb*, ed. Zhukovski, Leningrad 1926, p. 134, 219; transl. Nicholson, p. 108, 176; Ghazzālī, *Munḳidh*, ed. Cairo, p. 28—29; Samʿānī, *Kitāb al-ansāb*, in *GMS*, 1912, fol. 509ᵇ *sqq.*; Subkī, *Ṭabaḳāt*, ii. 37—42; L. Massignon, *Essai sur les origines ... de la mystique musulmane*, Paris 1922, p. 210—225 and 126—127; do., *Passion d'al-Hallaj*, index, s.v.; do., *Textes inédits concernant ... la mystique musulmane*, Paris 1929, p. 15—23; Abd al-Halim Mahmoud, *al-Mohasibi*, Paris 1940; Brockelmann, *GAL*, *S.*i. p. 351 *sqq.*

MUKĀTAB. [See ʿABD].

MUʾMIN. [See ĪMĀN].

AL-**MUNĀFIḲŪN** (A.), the term applied in the Ḳurʾān to those Madīnese upon whose fidelity and zeal Muḥammad could not absolutely rely. The Arabs (e.g. Mubarrad, *Kāmil*, ed. Wright, p. 153) derive the word from *nāfiḳāʾ* ("one of the entrances to the hole of a fieldmouse"), but it is certainly the borrowed Ethiopic *manāfeḳ* "heretic" from *nafaḳa* to "split", *nāfaḳa* "to be divided, irresolute". The meaning "waverer", "doubter" quite fits the usual use of the word in the Ḳurʾān, while the usual translation "hypocrite" only suits a few passages. Another description of the same people in the Ḳurʾān is: "those in whose hearts there is sickness (weakness, doubt)", again in contrast to the unshakably firm believers. Sometimes (ix. 67 *sq.*; xxxiii. 73; xlviii. 6; lvii. 13) there are references to women of this type (*munāfiḳāt*) in addition to the male munāfiḳūn. A closer consideration of the passages in question shows we have not to think of a regular, rigidly defined party; sometimes the reference is to such Madīnese as had only joined the Prophet under compulsion or reluctantly, and sometimes to those who had quite honestly joined him but had not been able to retain their belief and enthusiasm (ix. 66; lxiii. 3). Muḥammad also on one occasion speaks of munāfiḳūn among the Beduins. The first group found their leader in ʿAbd Allāh b. Ubaiy who would have been the chosen head of the Ḳaila tribes, if a new and superior force, which he could not meet, had not opposed him in Muḥammad. Nevertheless these grumblers, joined by other unreliable elements, were strong enough to cause the greatest embarrassment to the Prophet in critical moments e.g. before the battle of Uḥud (iii. 166 *sq.*), in the War of the Ditch (xxxiii. 1, 12—24, 60, 73) and before the march on Tabūk (ix. 65—69, 74, 78), as he had always to be careful not to drive them over into the enemy's camp. It is no wonder then that his utterances about them are always made in a tone of great irritation. He describes them as hypocrites, who say something different from what they mean in their hearts (iii. 167; xiii. 1); in their irresolution they join, according to their view of the future, sometimes the Muslims and sometimes the enemy (iv. 138—143; v. 52); if it goes badly with the believers, they think that their religion has deceived them (viii. 49). When they are together among themselves they revenge themselves for the restraint which they must put upon themselves by malicious remarks about the Prophet and his revelations, but are in great anxiety, lest Allāh may communicate their secret conversations (ix. 64 *sqq.*, 78, 124 *sqq.*). They are indolent at prayer (iv. 142), refuse to take part in the fighting or to contribute from their means (xlvii. 20, 29; lxiii. 1 *sq.*; cf. iv. 36 *sqq.*); they hope for a weakening of his power so that the more worthy may expel the meaner (lxiii. 8). As representatives of the true Madīnese aristocracy, their attitude and eloquence made a certain impression on the Prophet but on closer examination they are nothing but "propped timbers" (lxiii. 4). In a word, they are not better than the unbelievers. God makes them err (iv. 47 *sqq.*) and their abode shall be hellfire (ix. 73; lvii. 13 *sq.*). We cannot help feeling in some ways a certain sympathy for these men who were deprived of their rights; but in the end they deserved their fate for their complete lack of ideas and courage at decisive moments, and their conduct with regard to the Jews in Madīna, whom they incited to resist Muḥammad and then left in the lurch (cf. lv. 11), makes a very unfavourable impression. With the death of ʿAbd Allāh they lost their leader and their opposition was forced to be silent before the great successes of Muḥammad's last years.

The word munāfiḳ remained however and like other Ḳurʾānic terms was used in the fighting between the various parties as a term of abuse; cf. e.g. its application to Ibn Zubair (Ṭabarī, ii. 467) and his party (Ahlwardt, *Anonyme arab. Chronik*, p. 73).

In the Ḳurʾān Sūra lxiii. is called after the Munāfiḳūn; it is connected by most commentators with the campaign against the Banū Muṣṭaliḳ.

Bibliography: Wellhausen, *Reste arabischen Heidentums* [2], p. 232; Nöldeke, *Neue Beiträge zur semitischen Sprachwissenschaft*, p. 48 *sq.*; Nöldeke-Schwally, *Geschichte des Qorāns*, i. p. 88 *sq.*, 167 *sq.* 209; Ibn Hishām, ed. Wüstenfeld, p. 411—413, 546 *sq.*, 558—560, 651, 670, 688, 726, 734, 894; F. Buhl, *Das Leben Muhammeds*, p. 206 *sqq.*

MUNKAR WA-NAKĪR (the forms with the article are also found), the names of the two angels who examine and if necessary punish the dead in their tombs. To the examination in the tomb the infidels and the faithful — the righteous as well as the sinners — are liable. They are set upright in their tombs and must state their opinion regarding Muḥammad. The righteous faithful will answer that he is the Apostle of Allāh; thereupon they will be left alone till the Day of Resurrection. The sinners and the infidels, on the other hand, will have no satisfactory answer at hand. In consequence of this the angels will beat them severely, as long as it will please Allāh, according to some authorities till the Day of Resurrection, except on Fridays.

In some sources a distinction is made between the punishment and the pressure (*ḍaghṭa*) in the tomb, the righteous faithful being exempt from the former, not from the latter, whereas the infidels and the sinners suffer punishment as well as pressure (Abū 'l-Muʿīn Maimūn b. Muḥammad al-Nasafī, as cited in the commentary on the *Waṣīyat Abī Ḥanīfa*, Ḥaidarābād 1321, p. 22).

The punishment in the tomb is not plainly mentioned in the Ḳurʾān. Allusions to the idea may be found in several passages, e.g. Sūra xlvii. 27: "But how when the angels, causing them to die, shall smite them on their faces and backs"; Sūra vi. 93: "But couldst thou see, when the ungodly are in the floods of death, and the angels reach forth their hands, saying, Yield up your souls: this day shall ye be recompensed with a humiliating punishment"; Sūra viii. 50: "And if thou wert to see when the angels take the life of the unbelievers; they smite their faces and their backs, and taste ye the torture of burning" (cf. further Sūra ix. 101; xxxii. 21; lii. 47).

The punishment of the tomb is very frequently mentioned in Tradition (see *Bibliography*), often, however, without the mention of angels. In the latter group of traditions it is simply said that the dead are punished in their tombs, or why, e.g. on account of special sins they have committed, or on account of the wailing of the living.

The names of Munkar and Nakīr do not appear in the Ḳurʾān, and once only in canonical Tradition (Tirmidhī, *Djanāʾiz*, bāb 70). Apparently these names do not belong to the old stock of traditions. Moreover, in some traditions one anonymous angel only is mentioned as the angel who interrogates and punishes the dead (Muslim, *Īmān*, trad. 163; Abū Dāwūd, *Sunna*, bāb 39[b]; Aḥmad b. Ḥanbal, iii. 233, 346; iv. 150; Ṭayālisī, No. 753).

So there seem to be four stages in the traditions regarding this subject: the first without any angel being mentioned, the second mentioning "the" angel, the third two angels, the fourth being acquainted with the names Munkar and Nakīr.

This state of things as reflected in *ḥadīth* finds a similar reflex in the early forms of the creed. In the *Fiḳh Akbar* i., which may date from the middle of the viii[th] century A.D., the punishment of the tomb appears as the only eschatological representation (art. 10). In the *Waṣīyat Abī Ḥanīfa*, which may represent the orthodox views of the middle of the ix[th] century, we find, apart from an elaborate eschatology, the two following articles (art. 18, 19): "We confess, that the punishment in the tomb shall without fail take place. We confess, that in view of the traditions on the subject, the interrogation by Munkar and Nakīr is a reality". The term "reality" is apparently intended to oppose the allegorical interpretation of eschatological representations as taught by the Muʿtazilīs.

The *Fiḳh Akbar* ii., which may represent the new orthodoxy of the middle of the xth century A.D., is still more elaborate on this point (art. 23): "The interrogation of the dead in the tomb by Munkar and Nakīr is a reality and the reunion of the body with the spirit in the tomb is a reality. The pressure and the punishment in the tomb are a reality that will take place in the case of all the infidels, and a reality that may take place in the case of some sinners belonging to the faithful". In the later creeds and works on dogmatics the punishment and the interrogation in the tomb by Munkar and Nakīr are expressed in similar ways.

The Karrāmīya [q.v.] taught the identity of Munkar and Nakīr with the two guardian angels who accompany man (ʿAbd al-Ḳāhir al-Baghdādī, *Uṣūl al-dīn*, Stambul 1928, p. 246). Ghazzālī admits the idea that eschatological representations are a reality that takes place in the *malakūt.*

The origin of the names is uncertain; the meaning "disliked" seems doubtful. The idea of the examination and the punishment of the dead in their tombs is found among other peoples also. The details to be found in Jewish sources (*ḥibbūṭ hak-ḳeber*) are strikingly parallel to the Muslim ones.

Bibliography: The passages from *ḥadīth* in Wensinck, *Handbook*, s.v. Grave(s); further E. Sell, *The Faith of Islam*, London 1880, p. 145; Mouradgea d'Ohsson, *Tableau de l'Empire othoman*, Paris 1787, i. 46; Wensinck, *The Muslim Creed*, Cambridge 1932, General Index, s.v. Punishment and Munkar and Nakir; J. C. G. Bodenschatz, *Kirchliche Verfassung der heutigen Juden*, Erlangen 1748, iii. 95 *sq.*; al-Ṭaḥāwī, *Bayān al-sunna wa 'l-djamāʿa*, Ḥalab 1344, p. 9; Abū Ḥafs ʿUmar al-Nasafī, *ʿAḳāʾid*, Stambul 1313, with the commentary of Taftāzānī, p. 132 *sqq.*; al-Ghazzālī, *Iḥyāʾ*, Cairo 1302, iv. 451 *sqq.*; do., *al-Durra al-fākhira*, ed. Gautier, p. 23 *sqq.*; *Kitāb aḥwāl al-ḳiyāma*, ed. M. Wolff, p. 40 *sq.*

AL-**MURDJIʾA**, name of one of the early sects of Islām, the extreme opponents of the Khāridjites [q.v.]. The latter thought that a Muslim by committing a mortal sin becomes a *kāfir*. The Murdjiʾa, on the other hand, were of opinion that a Muslim does not lose his faith through sin. This doctrine led them to a far-reaching quietism in politics; according to their doctrine, the *imām* who was guilty of mortal sins did not cease to be a Muslim and must be obeyed. The *ṣalāt* performed behind him was valid.

Occidental and Oriental explanations of the name show considerable divergencies (cf. e.g. Sale, *Preliminary Discourse*, p. 229 *sqq.*; Goldziher, *Richtungen der islam. Koranauslegung*, p. 179; v. Kremer, *Gesch. d. herrschenden Ideen*, p. 20; Houtsma, *Strijd over het dogma*, p. 34). It seems that the origin of the name must be sought in the term *irdjāʾ*, and that Murdjiʾa thus meant adherents of the doctrine of *irdjāʾ* (ʿAbd al-Ḳāhir al-Baghdādī uses the term for their doctrine), fnrther that this term goes back to verse 106 of Sūra ix. The context of this verse not only explains the term *irdjāʾ*, but may also give an insight into the evolution of the ideas of the Murdjiʾites. In the preceding verses Muḥammad makes a distinction between two groups among the Madīnese who had forsaken him in the expedition to Tabūk. Some had shown *nifāḳ* without penitence; they were to receive punishment in this and in the other world (verse 101). Others had shown penitence (*tawba*); they were left to Allāh's mercy (verse 102). The third group, who had not made penitence, were left in suspense (*murdjaʾūnā*, or according to a different reading, *murdjawna*).

The situation in Madīna after the expedition to Tabūk was generalized by later sects. As a matter of fact, the third group mentioned in the passage discussed — viz. sinners who did not show penitence — was relegated to Hell by the Khāridjites. In opposition to this, the Murdjiʾites taught the doctrine of *irdjāʾ* mentioned in Sūra ix. 106 and therefore they were called Murdjiʾa, i.e. the adherents of the doctrine of respite or hope. This is how the term *irdjāʾ* is to be understood; the variants *murdjaʾūna* and *murdjawna* are irrelevant in this respect.

In the course of time the doctrine of the Murdjiʾa assumed a double aspect. Their chief thesis was the indelible character of faith, in opposition to the Khāridjites. Their second thesis was of an eschatological nature: where there is faith, sins will do no harm. On account of the latter doctrine they were called the adherents of promise (*ahl al-waʿd*), in contra-distinction to the Muʿtazila [q.v.] who were called the adherents of threats (*ahl al-waʿīd*). So the doctrine of *irdjāʾ* had acquired a triple aspect — which accounts for the divergent explanations of the name —, viz. the doctrine of faith bearing an indelible character, an indulgent attitude towards sinners in the Muslim community, and a hopeful prospect for them in the Last Judgment.

These are the chief tenets of the Murdjiʾa as they appear to us as well as to later Muslim writers such as al-Shahrastānī. Earlier authors enumerate a number of divergences among the different groups of Murdjiʾites. Al-Ashʿarī mentions their variety of opinion regarding faith, unbelief, sins, *tawḥīd*, interpretation of the Ḳurʾān, eschatology, mortal and venial sins, forgiveness of mortal sins, the impeccability of the Prophets, punishment of sins, the question whether there were infidels among the early generations of Islām, redress of wrongs, the beatific vision, the nature of the Ḳurʾān, the *quidditas* of Allāh, His names and *ṣifāt*, predestination.

ʿAbd al-Ḳāhir al-Baghdādī mentions three groups of Murdjiʾa: *a.* those who taught *irdjāʾ* regarding faith and free-will; to this group belonged Ghailān Abū Marwān al-Dimashḳī, Abū Shāmir, Muḥammad b. Abī Shabīb al-Baṣrī; *b.* those who taught *irdjāʾ* regarding faith and compulsion (*djabr*); *c.* those who gave faith the pre-eminence before works and belonged neither to the adherents of the doctrine of free will nor to those of predetermination; to the latter group belonged the followers of Yūnus b. ʿAwn, Ghassān, Abū Thawbān, Abū Muʿādh al-Tawmanī, Bishr b. Ghaiyāth al-Marīsī. The followers of Ghassān reckoned Abū Ḥanīfa as one of their friends, not, however, quite rightly, according to al-Baghdādī. That Abū Ḥanīfa shared the general views of the Murdjiʾa appears from his (unedited) letter to al-Battī, which is preserved in a MS. in the library of Cairo.

Although al-Baghdādī mentions a *ḥadīth* in which the Murdjiʾa are cursed, the high esteem in which Abū Ḥanīfa stood as a dogmatist and as a doctor of the law would be in itself sufficient proof of the fact that the "sect" was not too eccentric. As a matter of fact, their political quietism was largely practised by orthodoxy itself. As regards eschatological punishment, the *Fiḳh Akbar II* (art. 14) rejects the Murdjiʾī doctrine of our good deeds being accepted and of our sins being forgiven, Allāh being free to punish the sinner or to grant him forgiveness. — The same *ʿaḳīda*, however, shares the Murdjiʾī doctrine of the constancy of faith (art. 18).

Bibliography: M. Th. Houtsma, *De strijd over het dogma in den Islâm tot op al-Ashʾari*, Leiden, 1875, p. 34 *sqq.*; I. Goldziher, *Vorlesungen über den Islam*, Heidelberg 1910, Index s.v. Murdschi'a; G. van Vloten, *Irdschâ*, *ZDMG*, xlv, 161 *sqq.*; A. J. Wensinck, *The Muslim Creed*, Cambridge 1932, General index, s.v. Murdjites; al-Ashʿarī, *Maḳālāt al-Islāmīyīn*, ed. Ritter, Stambul 1929, i. 132 *sqq.*; ʿAbd al-Ḳāhir al-Baghdādī, *Kitāb al-farḳ bain al-firaḳ*, ed. Muh. Badr, Cairo 1328, p. 190 *sqq.*; al-Shahrastānī, *Kitāb al-milal wa 'l-niḥal*, ed. Cureton, p. 103 *sqq.*; Ibn Ḥazm, *Kitāb al-faṣl*, ii. 112 *sqq.*; iv. 44 *sqq.*, 204 *sqq.*; Ibn al-Athīr, ed. Tornberg, x. 29; Muir, *The Life of Mohammad*, 3rd ed., Edinburgh 1914, p. 431; A. S. Tritton, *Muslim Theology*, London 1947, p. 43 *sqq.* and passim; W. M. Watt, *Free will and predestination in early Islam*, London 1948.

MURĪD. [See ṬARĪḲA].

MURTADD (A.), "one who turns back", especially from Islām, an apostate. Apostasy is called *irtidād* or *ridda*; it may be committed verbally by denying a principle of belief or by an action, for example treating a copy of the Ḳur'ān with disrespect.

1. In the Ḳur'ān the apostate is threatened with punishment in the next world only; the "wrath of God" will fall upon him according to a Sūra of the latest Meccan period (xvi. 106 *sq.*) and severe punishment (*ʿadhāb*) "except he did it under compulsion and his heart is steadfast in belief". Similarly it is written in the Madīna Sūra iii. 86 *sqq.*: "... This is the punishment for them, that the curse of Allāh, the Angels and of men is upon them (87) for all time; the punishment shall not be lightened for them and they shall not be granted allevation, (88) except for those who later repent and make good their fault, for Allāh is forgiving and merciful. (89) Those who disbelieve after believing and increase in unbelief, shall not have their repentance accepted; they are the erring ones. (90) Those who are unbelievers and die as unbelievers, from none of them shall be accepted the earth-full of gold even if he should wish to ransom himself with it; this is a painful punishment for them and there will be no helpers for them" (91); (cf. also iv. 137; v. 54; ix. 67). Sūra ii. 217 is to be interpreted in the same way although it is adduced by Shāfiʿī as the main evidence for the death penalty: "... He among you who falls away from his belief and dies as an unbeliever — these, their works are fruitless in this world and the next, and they are the companions of the fire for ever".

2. There is little echo of these punishments in the next world in the Traditions (cf. Ibn Mādja, *Ḥudūd*, bāb 2; Ibn Ḥanbal, i. 409, 430, 464 *sq.*; v. 4, 5). Instead we have in many traditions a new element, the death penalty. Thus Ibn ʿAbbās transmits an utterance of the Prophet: "Slay him, who changes his religion" or "behead him" (Ibn Mādja, *Ḥudūd*, bāb 2; Nasā'ī, *Taḥrīm al-dam*, bāb 14; Ṭayālisī, No. 2689; Mālik, *Aḳḍiya*, tr. 15; cf. also Bukhārī, *Murtaddīn*, bāb 2; Tirmidhī, *Ḥudūd*, bāb 25; Abū Dāwūd, *Ḥudūd*, bāb 1; Ibn Ḥanbal, i. 217, 282, 322). According to another tradition of Ibn ʿAbbās and ʿĀ'isha, the Prophet is said to have permitted the blood to be shed of him "who abandons his religion and separates himself from the community (*djamāʿa*)" (Bukhārī, *Diyāt*, bāb 6; Muslim, *Ḳasāma*, tr. 25, 26; Nasā'ī, *Taḥrīm al-dam*, bāb 5, 14; *Ḳasāma*, bāb 6; Ibn Mādja, *Ḥudūd*, bāb 1; Abū Dāwūd, *Ḥudūd*, bāb 1; Tirmidhī, *Diyāt*, bāb 10; *Fitan*, bāb 1; Ibn Ḥanbal, i. 382, 444). But there was no agreement from the first on the nature of the death penalty; thus ʿIkrima (d. 106/724) and Anas b. Mālik (d. 91/710) criticise ʿAlī for having burned apostates (Bukhārī, *Murtaddīn*, bāb 2; Tirmidhī, *Ḥudūd*, bāb 25; Abū Dāwūd, *Ḥudūd*, bāb 1; Ibn Ḥanbal, i. 217; according to a variant the reference is to Zindīḳs or Zuṭṭ who served idols; Nasā'ī, *Taḥrīm al-dam*, bāb 14; Ibn Ḥanbal, i. 282, 322). According to a tradition of ʿĀ'isha, apostates are to be slain, crucified or banished (Nasā'ī, *Taḥrīm al-dam*, bāb 11; *Ḳasāma*, bāb 13; Abū Dāwūd, *Ḥudūd*, bāb 1).

On the question whether the apostate should be given an opportunity to repent, traditions differ. According to one tradition of Abū Burda (d. 104/722), Muʿādh b. Djabal refused to sit down until an apostate brought before him had been slain "in accordance with the decision of God and of his apostle" (Bukhāri, *Maghāzī*, bāb 60; *Murtaddīn*, bāb 2; *Aḥkām*, bāb 12; Muslim, *Imāra*, tr. 15; Abū Dāwūd, *Ḥudūd*, bāb 1; Ibn Ḥanbal, v. 231). In the same tradition in Abū Dāwūd however, it is added that they had tried in vain for 20 nights to convert the apostate. The caliph ʿUmar is also represented as disapproving of this proceeding with the words: "Did you then not shut him up for three days and give him a round loaf (*raghīf*) daily and try to induce him to repent. Perhaps he would have repented and returned to obedience to God. O God! I was not there, I did not order it and I do not approve; see, it was thus reported to me" (Mālik, *Aḳḍiya*, tr. 15). There are also traditions according to which God does not accept the repentance of an apostate (Ibn Ḥanbal, v. 2 *sqq.*) and others according to which even the Prophet forgave apostates (Nasā'ī, *Taḥrīm al-dam*, bāb 14, 15; Abū Dāwūd, *Ḥudūd*, bāb 1; Ibn Ḥanbal, i. 247; Ṭabarī, *Tafsīr*, iii. 223).

3. *a.* In the Fiḳh there is unanimity that the male apostate must be put to death, but only if he is grown up (*bāligh*) and compos mentis (*ʿāḳil*) and has not acted under compulsion (*mukhtār*). A woman on the other hand is imprisoned, according to Ḥanafī and Shīʿī teaching, until she again adopts Islām, while according to al-Awzāʿī, Ibn Ḥanbal (Tirmidhī, *Ḥudūd*, bāb 25), the Mālikīs and Shāfiʿīs (cf. *Umm*, i. 131, where Shāfiʿī vigorously attacks Abū Yūsuf who is not mentioned by name) she also is put to death (a pregnant woman however only after her confinement; *Umm.*, vi., 149). Although this punishment is not properly *ḥadd* (cf. thereon Shāfiʿī, *Umm*, vii. 330) it is regarded as such by some jurists, as it is a question of a *ḥaḳḳ Allāh* (cf. e.g. Sarakhsī, *Siyar*, iv. 162); therefore the execution of the punishment lies with the imām; in the case of a slave however, the *mawlā* can carry it out, as with any other *ḥadd* punishment. Execution should be by the sword. According to the above traditions, apostates must sometimes have been tortured to death. The caliph ʿUmar II had them tied to a post and a lance thrust into their hearts (Abū Yūsuf, *Kharādj*, p. 112). Bādjūrī expressly forbids any form of torture, like burning, drowning, strangling, impaling, flaying; according to him, Sulṭān Baibars (708—709/1309—1310) was the first to introduce torture (Snouck Hurgronje, *Verspr.Geschriften*, ii. 198). Lane (*Manners and Customs*, ch. iii., near the end) records the case of a woman who had apostatized and was led through the streets of Cairo on an ass, then strangled in a boat in the middle of the Nile and thrown into the river (the throwing of the corpse into the Nile was already usual in Cairo in the Fāṭimid period; cf. Mez, *Renaissance d. Isl.*, p. 29). In quite recent times followers of the Ḳādyānī or Aḥmadīya sect in Afghānistān were stoned to death (*OM*, v. [1925], 138). In former Turkish territory and Egypt as well as in Muslim lands under European rule since the middle of the xix^th^ century, under European influence the execution of an apostate on a ḳāḍī's sentence has been abolished, but we still have imprisonment and deportation (cf. Isabel Burton, *The inner Life of Syria*, London 1875, i. 180 *sqq.*); nevertheless renegades are not sure of their lives as their Muslim relatives endeavour secretly to dispose of them by poison or otherwise. Occasionally modern Islāmic writers (Aḥmadīya movement) endeavour to prove that Islām knows of no death penalty for apostasy; the Indian apologist Muḥammad ʿAlī lays great stress on the fact that there is not once an indication of the death penalty in the

Ḳur'ān (Zwemer, *The Law of Apostasy in Islam*, London 1924, p. 17, 37 *sq.*; *OM*, v. [1925], 262).

b. Whether attempts at conversion must be made is a question of *ikhtilāf*. A number of jurists of the first and second (viith and viiith) centuries deny this (as do the Ẓāhirīs), or like ʿAṭā' (d. 115/733) make a distinction between the apostate born in Islām and one converted to Islām; the former is to be put to death at once (so also the Shīʿīs). Others insist on three attempts at conversion (relying on Sūra iv. 137; cf. Ṭabarī, *Tafsīr*, v. 193 *sq.*) or have him in the first place imprisoned for three days (cf. above 2). According to others again one should await the round of the five times of prayer and ask him to perform the *ṣalāt* at each; only when he has refused at each is the death punishment to be enforced. If however he repents and professes Islām once more, he is released (cf. thereon Shāfiʿī, *Umm*, i. 228; Abū Yūsuf, *Kharādj*, p. 109). In later times *istitāba* was always applied. A Christian or a Jew who is converted to Islām has not only to pronounce the *shahāda*, but must also abjure his former creed.

c. Apart from the fact that apostasy deprives the murtadd of burial with Muslim rites it has certain civil consequences. The property of the murtadd is *fai'* according to Shāfiʿī and Mālik; if the fugitive murtadd returns penitent, he is given back what remains (cf. *Umm*, i. 231 *sqq.*, where Shāfiʿī opposes the contrary Ḥanafī view). Others, especially later Shāfiʿīs, regard the rights of ownership of the apostate as suspended (*mawḳūf*) and treat him as one who is under guardianship (*maḥdjūr*); only if the fugitive apostate dies in the *dār al-ḥarb*, does his property become *fai'* (Shīrāzī, *Muhadhdhab*, Cairo 1343, ii. 240; cf. Shāfiʿī, *Umm*, vi., 151; vii. 355). Among the Ḥanafīs and Shāfiʿīs the estate is allotted by the ḳāḍī to the legal heirs (cf. also the traditions in Dārimī, *Farā'iḍ*, bāb 40), the *mudabbar* and *umm walad* are set free, even when the apostate escapes into the *dār al-ḥarb*, for this is equivalent to his death. If he comes back penitent, however, he receives of his property what still exists; the heirs however are not liable for compensation. — The marriage of the murtadd is void (*bāṭil*). Of his legal undertakings the *istīlād* is effective (*nāfidh*), i.e. the *umm walad* becomes free; the *kitāba* also continues. Other legal activities, like manumission, endowment, testament, sale are suspended (*mawḳūf*) according to Abū Ḥanīfa; according to Abū Yūsuf they are effective as in the case of a person in good health, according to Muḥammad al-Shaibānī, however, only as in the case of an invalid i.e. they cannot deal with more than one third of the estate. In the case of the female apostate however, they are always effective. If the apostate makes such legal arrangements after his flight into the *dār al-ḥarb*, they are invalid (Sarakhsī, *Siyar*, iv. 152; cf. also Abū Yūsuf, *Kharādj*, p. 111). But since according to Shāfiʿī and Mālik his whole estate becomes *fai'*, such legal arrangements are invalid; only the manumission of a slave remains suspended until his possible return penitent; in the case of his death also this slave becomes *fai'* (cf. however above the view of later Shāfiʿīs).

He is punished for crimes committed before apostasy, if he returns penitent; for crimes committed during *ridda*, no notice is taken of the *ḥuḳūḳ Allāh* (i.e. no *ḥadd*) but only of the *ḥuḳūḳ al-ʿibād*, and he must for example pay the *diya* (Sarakhsī, *Siyar*, iv. 163, 208 *sq.*; cf. Shāfiʿī, *Umm*, i. 231; vi. 153).

Bibliography: In addition to the books on Tradition and Fiḳh see especially: Shāfiʿī, *Kitāb al-umm*, Cairo 1321, i. 227—234; v. 51; vi. 154—156; vii. 330 *sqq.*, 355; Abū Yūsuf, *Kitāb al-kharādj*, Cairo 1302, p. 109—112; Sarakhsī, *Sharḥ al-siyar al-kabīr*, Ḥaidarābād 1336, iv. 146—219; Dabūsī, *Ta'sīs al-naẓar*, Cairo n.d., p. 22; Goldziher, *Muh. Studien*, Halle 1890, ii. 215 *sq.*; Santillana, *Istituzioni di diritto musulmano malichita*, Rom. 1926, i. 131—134; Zwemer, *The Law of Apostasy in Islam*, London 1924; G. F. Pijper, *Echtscheiding en Apostasie*, in *Fragmenta Islamica*, Leiden 1934; cf. also KATL.

MŪSĀ, the prophet Moses of the Bible. A Coptic etymology of the name (*mū* = "water" and *shā* = "trees") is given by Sharīshī in his *Sharḥ al-maḳāmāt*, Būlāḳ 1284, p. 89.

1. In the Ḳur'ān. Muḥammad regards Mūsā as his predecessor, his model, and believes he had already been foretold by Mūsā (vii. 157); his religion is also Mūsā's religion (xlii. 13). Mūsā is also conceived in Muḥammad's image. Charges are brought against him similar to those made against Muḥammad: he is said to want to pervert people from the faith of their fathers, (x. 78); he practises magic (xxviii. 19). Mūsā and Hārūn seem rather to be sent to the stubborn Pharaoh than to the believing Israelites. Revelation is granted him: *tawrāt*, *kitab*, *furḳān*, *ṣuḥuf* (ii. 53; xxi. 48; liii. 38; lxxxvii. 19), illumination, instruction and guidance. The picture of him is made up of Biblical, Haggadic and new elements. Mūsā is exposed, watched by his sister, refuses the milk of other nurses and is suckled by his own mother. Coming to the assistance of a hard pressed Israelite he kills an Egyptian but repents of this crime to which Satan had tempted him. He is pursued and escapes to Madyan. At a well there he waters the flocks of the two daughters of a shaikh. One of them invites him home modestly. He receives her as his wife at the price of 8—10 years service. This preliminary history is told in Sūra xxviii. 1—28; the mission itself is often mentioned.

Mūsā receives from the burning bush in the holy valley of Ṭuwā (xx. 12; lxxix. 16) orders to take off his shoes, the message to Pharaoh, the signs of his mission, the rod, the snake, the hand that becomes white. His speech is difficult to understand (xliii. 52); Hārūn accompanies him as wazīr (xx. 31; xxv. 37). Pharaoh reproaches Mūsā with ingratitude, saying he had been brought up by them (xxvi. 18). Pharaoh assembles his magicians but their rods are devoured by Mūsā's. The magicians profess their belief in God and are mutilated in punishment (vii. 109—126; xx. 57—76; xxvi. 35—51). Pharaoh wishes prayers to be offered to him as God, and orders Hāmān to build him a tower so that he can reach the God of Mūsā (xxviii. 38; xi. 36). Mūsā performs nine miracles (xvii. 101; xx. 57—76; xxvii. 12). These are: 1. the rod and snake; 2. white hand; 3. deluge; 4. locusts; 5. lice; 6. frogs; 7. blood; 8. darkness; 9. dividing the sea (cf. e.g. Ṭabarī ed. de Goeje, i. 485).

Mūsā spends 30 and 10 nights with God (vii. 142). He brings instruction and admonition on the tablets. In his absence Sāmirī makes the lowing golden calf (vii. 148; xx. 77—98). Mūsā breaks the tablets. He desires to see God. God crumbles the hill to dust (vii. 143). Israel fears war and has to wander 40 years in the wilderness (v. 21—26). Mūsā's enemies, Ḳārūn (Korah), Pharaoh and Hāmān, perish (xxix. 39).

Some details differ from the Biblical story. Instead of Pharaoh's daughter, it is his wife who rescues the infant; instead of seven shepherdesses Mūsā assists two. Instead of ten plagues, Muḥammad speaks of nine miracles. Mūsā strikes twelve springs out of the rock, one for each tribe (ii. 60, a memory of the twelve springs of Elim, Exodus xv. 27). The divergence is greater when Hāmān is made minister to Pharaoh. Then there are new features: Mūsā repents of having slain the Egyptian. Mūsā sees the burning bush at night and desires to take a brand from its fire for this house (xx. 9; xxviii. 29). Pharaoh's magicians die for their belief in God.

The following seems to originate in Haggada: God forbids the infant to be suckled by an Egyptian mother (xxviii. 12). In the Haggada Moses is offered to all Egyptian suckling mothers; but the mouth that is to speak with God cannot imbibe anything impure (*Sōṭa*, 12b). That God tilts the mountain over Israel (ii. 63, 93; vii. 171) is explained from the Haggada: Israel hesitated to accept the Tora and God tilted Sinai over them: Tora or death (*Sabbath*, 80[a]; *ʿAboda Zara*, 2b). The turning of the sabbath breakers into apes (ii. 65; iv. 53; v. 60; vii. 166) recalls the Haggada in which the builders of the tower of Babel become apes (*Sanhedrin*, 109[a]). Ḳārūn is represented as an exceedingly rich man the keys of whose treasure can hardly be carried by many strong men (xxviii. 76, 79); the Haggada says that Korah found a hidden Egyptian treasure; 300 mules carried the keys of his treasury (*Pessachim*, 119[a]; *Sanhedrin*, 110[a]; Pal. *Sanh.*, x.27[d]; Ginzberg, *Legends*, vi. 99, 560). — The Ḳurʾānic story of a believer at the court of Pharaoh who wants to save Mūsā is not quite clear (xl. 28). Ought we to compare Jethro in the Haggada who advises clemency at Pharaoh's court? (*Sōṭa*, 11[a]; *Sanhedrin*, 106[a]; Ginzberg, v. 392, 21; v. 412, 101).

The story of Mūsā accompanying a wise man on a journey seems without parallel (xviii. 60—82). The attempt is often made to distinguish this Mūsā of Khaḍir as Mūsā b. Manasse from Mūsā b. ʿImrān [cf. the article KHAḌIR].

2. Mūsā in post-Ḳurʾānic legend. The histories of the prophets (especially Thaʿlabī's) supplement the Ḳurʾānic story with much from the Bible, Haggada and folklore.

Much is added from Haggada. Pharaoh's sick daughters are cured as soon as they touch Moses's cradle. *Exodus Rabba*, i. 23 makes Pharaoh's daughter be cured of leprosy. — The infant Mūsā scratches Pharaoh's chin. Pharaoh wants to slay him. On the intercession of Āsiya he tests him by putting gold and jewels on one side and burning coals on the other. Mūsā reaches for the gold but Gabriel directs his hand to the burning coal. Mūsā puts his burned hand on his tongue and therefore becomes a stammerer (Ginzberg, v. 402; Hamilton, *Zeitschr. f. romanische Philologie* xxxvi. 125—159).

Elements of other legends are woven into the legend of Mūsā. The Ibrāhīm-Namrūd legend supplies the following features: Pharaoh frightened by dreams persecutes the infants; Mūsā is hidden from the assassins in the burning oven but the fire becomes cool and does him no harm. Pharaoh orders prayers to be offered to him self as to a god, has a tower built, shoots an arrow against heaven; the arrow comes back blood-stained and Pharaoh boasts he has slain God (Ṭabarī, i. 469). — From the story of Jacob and Laban come the following: Mūsā serves 8—10 years for his wife (xxviii. 27). His father-in-law offers him the spotted lambs born in his flock and the ewes from the watering troughs bear spotted lambs (Thaʿlabī, p. 112). There are frequent references to a pious Egyptian woman who is martyred by Pharaoh with her seven children, the youngest of whom is still at its mother's breast (Thaʿlabī, p. 118, 139); this is of course modelled on the martyr mother of the Maccabees.

There are many fanciful embellishments, e.g. the miracle of the snakes, the plagues, the scenes on the Red Sea; Moses's rod in particular plays a great part. It came from Paradise; Ādam, Hābil, Shīth, Idrīs, Nūḥ, Hūd, Ṣāliḥ, Ibrāhīm, Ismāʿīl, Isḥāḳ and Yaʿḳūb had previously used it (Kisāʾī, p. 208). In Ṭabarī (p. 460 *sq.*) an angel brought the rod. Mūsā obtained it from his wife; his father-in-law quarrels with him about its ownership and an angel decides in favour of Mūsā. It is a miraculous rod and Thaʿlabī (p. 111—112) in particular relates the wonders it performs. It shines in the darkness; it gives water in a drought, and placed in the ground it becomes a tree bearing fruit; it produces milk and honey and fragrant scent; against an enemy it becomes a double dragon. It pierces mountains and rocks; it leads over rivers and sea; it is also a shepherd's staff and keeps beasts of prey from the herds of Moses. When Mūsā was asleep on one occasion the rod slew a dragon, on another occasion seven of Pharaoh's assassins.

The varied Biblical, Haggadic, legendary and fairy tale features in the Islāmic legend of Mūsā are thus blended into a very full picture and in Thaʿlabī form a regular romance.

See also the articles: HĀRŪN, ḲĀRŪN, AL-SĀMIRĪ, TAWRĀT, YUSHAʿ.

Bibliography: Ṭabarī, i. 414—449; Thaʿlabī, *Ḳiṣaṣ al-anbiyāʾ*, Cairo 1325, p. 105—156; Kisāʾī, *Ḳiṣaṣ al-anbiyāʾ* ed. Eisenberg, p. 194—240; Ibn al-Athīr, *al-Kāmil*, Būlāḳ, i. 61—78; Abr. Geiger, *Was hat Mohammed...*, 1902, p. 149—177; J. Eisenberg, *Moses in der arabischen Legende*, 1910; M. Grünbaum, *Neue Beiträge*, p. 153—185; J. Horovitz, *Koranische Untersuchungen*, p. 141—143; R. Basset, 1001 *Contes, Récits et légendes arabes*, iii. 67, 85; D. Sidersky, *Les Origines des Légendes musulmanes dans le Coran et dans la Vie des Prophètes*, Paris 1933, p. 73—103; J. Walker, *Bible Characters in the Koran*, p. 84—111; Speyer, *Die bibl. Erzählungen im Qoran*, p. 225—363.

MUṢʿAB B. ʿUMAIR, a follower of Muḥammad of the Ḳuraish family of ʿAbd al-Dār. The son of rich parents, this handsome young man had attracted attention by his elegant appearance when Muḥammad's preaching made so deep an impression upon him that he abandoned the advantages of his social position to join the despised adherents of the Prophet. Tradition dilates on the contrast between his former luxurious life and later poverty but these, like such stories in general, are somewhat suspicious, although not impossible, since the people in Muṣʿab's time had not yet acquired wealth and could not have been accustomed to luxury.

When his parents endeavoured to prevent him taking part in the worship of the believers, he went with several of the faithful to Abyssinia from which he returned however before the Hidjra. The Prophet thought highly of him and sent him after the first meeting at ʿAḳaba as a missionary to Madīna where he won a number of followers for Islām. According to some traditions, he on this occasion, following the practice of the Jews [see MUḤAMMAD], introduced the common Friday ṣalāt, which, however, as was noted as early as by Mūsā b. ʿUḳba, others ascribe to the Madīnese Asʿad b. Zurāra, while others in an effort at harmonising say that Asʿad conducted the common ṣalāt during the absence of Muṣʿab.

At Badr and at Uḥud he carried the Prophet's banner in memory of the old privilege of the ʿAbd al-Dār; he met his death in the latter battle. With what ardour he adopted the new teaching is seen from his attitude to his mother who is depicted as a most lovable character and particularly from his words at the capture of his brother in the battle of Badr. His wife was Ḥanna bint Djaḥsh of the Asad.

Bibliography: Mūsā b. ʿUḳba, ed. Sachau in *SBPr. Ak. W.*, 1904, p. 451; Ibn Hishām, p. 208, 241, 289 *sq.*, 459 *sq.*, 487, 560, 566, 586; Ṭabarī, i. 1182, 1214 *sqq.*, 1337, 1386, 1394, 1404, 1425; al-Wāḳidī, transl. Wellhausen, p. 49, 68, 79, 106, 114, 135, 143; Ibn Saʿd, III/i., 81—86; III/ii., 139; Nawawī, ed. Wüstenfeld, p. 556 *sq.*; Ibn Ḥadjar al-ʿAsḳalānī, *Iṣāba*, ed. Sprenger, iii. 861; Wensinck, *Mohammed en de Joden te Medina*, p. 111 *sq.*; Buhl, *Das Leben Muḥammad's*, Leipzig 1930, p. 186, 214, 257; Caetani, *Annali dell' Islām*, i and ii index s.v.

MUSAILIMA (a contemptuous diminutive from Maslama, which is the form of his name given in Mubarrad, *Kāmil*, ed. Wright, p. 443; Balādhurī, ed. de Goeje, p. 422; cf. Ṭulaiḥa [q.v.] for Ṭalḥa), a prophet of the Banū Ḥanīfa in Yamāma contemporary with Muḥammad. His genealogy is variously given but always contains the name Ḥabīb; his *kunya* was Abū Thumāma. According to the usual account, he appeared as a prophet soon after the death of Muḥammad, after having visited the latter in Madīna with a deputation. There is however another tradition according to which he began his prophetic career before Muḥammad did, and D.S. Margoliouth has given very cogent reasons for accepting this. According to Ibn Isḥāḳ (Ibn Hishām, ed. Wüstenfeld, p. 200), Muḥammad's enemies reproached him with having obtained his wisdom from a man of Yamāma named Raḥmān. Now we have ample evidence (Wāḳidī, transl. Wellhausen, p. 28; Ṭabarī, i. 1935; Balādhurī, p. 105; Baghawī on Sūra xxv. 60) that Musailima, who preached in the name of Raḥmān, was himself called Raḥmān. Further the story recurring in all traditions that Musailima proposed to the Madīnese prophet a division of authority or a transfer of his power to him on his death (a similar story is told of the Ḥanīfa chief Hawdha) becomes more intelligible if this prophet already occupied in Yamāma a position similar to that of Muḥammad in Madīna. It is also worthy of note that the prophetic utterances attributed to Musailima recall the earliest Meccan sūras with their short rhyming sentences and curious oaths and have no resemblance at all to the later Madīnese sūras. In particular the fact that all the Banū Ḥanīfa followed him into battle against the Madīnese shortly after the death of Muḥammad shows that he must have been active for a considerable time and was no upstart imitator of Muḥammad. That the latter was the usual method of explaining the "liar" Musailima is readily intelligible, nor is it to be wondered at that orthodox tradition could not deny itself the pleasure of depicting his relations with the Tamīm prophetess Sadjāḥ [q.v.] in the most scurrilous fashion. Fortunately however, the otherwise little reliable Saif gives quite a different story, which although influenced by later ideas (Musailima in order to gain followers reduces the five daily *ṣalāts* to three; he has a *muʾadhdhin* and a *muḳīm*; he tries in vain to imitate Muḥammad's miracles etc.), gives a picture of him which is in the main correct and we can agree with Wellhausen that his utterances have a distinctly Yamāma colouring. According to Saif's account, he must have been considerably influenced by Christianity for he speaks of the kingdom of heaven and of him who will come from heaven. Like several other men of the time in Arabia of deep religious feelings he favoured asceticism. He forbade wine and marital intercourse after the birth of a son. It is interesting that Palgrave on his journey into Nadjd found a number of sayings still current under Musailima's name; unfortunately he did not trouble to record them so that we cannot compare them with what is recorded of his utterances in literature. This rival community in the heart of Arabia meant a serious danger to the young faith of Islām. Therefore when the first attempts to repress it had failed, Abū Bakr sent his ablest leader Khālid b. al-Walīd against Musailima and the Banū Ḥanīfa. A battle was fought at ʿAḳrabāʾ in 12 A.H. which at first went against the Muslims, but Khālid's superior strategy finally prevailed and Musailima and many of his followers fell martyr for their faith. The battle was unusually fierce and the Muslims also suffered heavily, among the fallen being a number of the best authorities on the revelations of Muḥammad.

Bibliography: Ibn Hishām, p. 945 *sq.*, 964 *sq.*, 971, 996 *sq.*; al-Balādhurī, p. 86 *sqq.*; Ṭabarī, i. 1737—1739, 1748—1750, 1795—1797, 1871, 1880, 1915—1921, 1929—1957; Ibn Ḳutaiba, *Kitāb al-maʿārif*, ed. Wüstenfeld, p. 206; Masʿūdī, *Tanbīh*, in *BGA*, vii. 275, 284 *sq.*; Baihaḳī, *Kitāb al-maḥāsin*, ed. Schwally, p. 32; Muir, *Annals of the Early Caliphate*, p. 31, 38—46; Wellhausen, *Skizzen und Vorarbeiten*, iv. 102, 115, 156 *sq.*; vi. 15—19; Caetani, *Annali dell' Islām*, ii. 450 *sq.*, 635—648, 727—738; Hirschfeld, *New Researches*, p. 25; D. S. Margoliouth, in *JRAS*, 1903, p. 485 *sqq.*; against him Lyall, *ibid.*, p. 771 *sq.*; Palgrave, *Narrative of a Year's Journey through Central and Eastern Arabia*, i. 382; F. Buhl, *Das Leben Muhammeds*, p. 303.

MUṢALLĀ (A.), part. pass. II of *ṣ-l-w*, place where the ṣalāt is performed on certain occasions. When Muḥammad had fixed his abode in Madīna, he performed the ordinary *ṣalāt*'s in his *dār*, which was also his *masdjid* (not in the sense of temple). The extraordinary *ṣalāt*'s, however, were performed on a place situated southwest of the city in the territory of the Banū Salima, outside the wall, northeast of the bridge on the wādī, where at present the street from the suburb al-ʿAnbarīya reaches the market-place Barr al-Munākha (cf. Burton, *Personal Narrative*, plan opp. i. 256; picture of the muṣallā as well as of the mosque of ʿUmar situated on the place, opp. i. 329; al-Batanūnī, *al-Riḥla al-Ḥidjāzīya*, 2th ed., plan of Madīna opp. p. 252; part of the Barr al-Munākha, *ibid.*, opp. p. 264; Caetani, *Annali*, vol. II/i., opp. p. 72).

On this spot the *ṣalāt* was performed on the 1st Shawwāl and on the 10th Dhu 'l-Ḥidjdja (Ṭabarī, i. 1281, 1362). On the latter day the *ṣalāt* was combined with the slaughtering of two spotted rams (Bukhārī, *Aḍāḥī*, bāb 6). On the two days of festival Muḥammad and his followers on their way to the muṣallā were preceded by Bilāl who bore the spear (*ʿanaza*).

It is also said that the *ṣalāt* for rain was held on the muṣallā (copious *data* in Tradition, cf. Wensinck *Handbook*, s.v. Rain; and do., *Mohammed en de*

Joden, p. 141). Further it is related that the service for the dead was performed on this spot (Bu<u>kh</u>ārī, *D<u>j</u>anā'iz*, bāb 4, 61; Wensinck, *Mohammed en de Joden*, p. 140). Finally the muṣullā is mentioned as the place where executions took place (Bu<u>kh</u>ārī, *Ṭalāḳ*, bāb 11; Ṭabarī, i. 1903). The sacred character of the place appears from the fact that menstruating women were taught to avoid it (Bu<u>kh</u>ārī. *Ḥaiḍ*, bāb 23). According to Caetani (*Annali*, A. H. 11, § 55, note 3; cf. A.H. 2, § 24, note 1), the muṣallā was used more frequently.

It was not only in Madīna but in a large number of other places that the rites mentioned, or some of them, were performed on a muṣallā. According to al-Nawawī (commentary on Muslim's *Ṣaḥīḥ*, Cairo 1283, ii. 296), this was the practice of most of the capitals. The custom prevails up to the present day. According to Doutté, the North-African muṣallā is used for the rites of the 10th <u>Dh</u>u 'l-Ḥid<u>dj</u>a. It is a large space like a threshing-floor, with a wall provided with a *miḥrāb*; there is also an elevated place for the *<u>kh</u>aṭīb*. This is the form of the muṣallā in many towns of Morocco.

To the doctors of the law it was questionable whether the festival ceremonies should be performed on the muṣallā or in the mosque. There was divergency of opinion on this point, even within the *ma<u>dh</u>hab*'s (Abū Isḥāḳ al-<u>Sh</u>īrāzī, *Tanbīh*, ed. Juynboll, p. 41, where "the field" (*al-ṣaḥrā'*) is mentioned side by side with the mosque; Zurḳānī, comm. on the *Muwaṭṭa'*, i. 328; <u>Kh</u>alīl b. Isḥāḳ, *Mu<u>kh</u>taṣar*, Paris 1318, p. 33 *sq.*; al-Nawawī, *op. cit.*, ii. 296).

Wensinck has conjectured that even in pre-Islāmic times rites of several kinds were performed on an open area, threshing-floor, muṣallā or the like. The connection between all those rites and the special place is sought by him therein, that they had a special connection with the fertile earth, of which the threshing-floor and the like were symbols.

Bibliography: Caetani, *Annali dell' Islam*, A.H. 2, § 7, 24, note 1, 67, 91, 101; A.H. 6, § 19; A.H. 11, § 55, note 3, 159; Buhl, *Das Leben Muhammads*, transl. Schaeder, Leipzig 1930, p. 205, 233; R. Burton, *Personal Narrative of a Pilgrimage* ..., London 1857, i. 378; Wensinck, *Mohammed en de Joden te Medina*, Leiden 1908, p. 25, 138—142; do., *Handbook*, s.v.; do., *Rites of Mourning and Religion*, in *Verh. Ak. Amst.*, N. R., vol. xviii./i., p. 1 *sqq.*; Doutté, *Magie et religion dans l'Afrique du Nord*, Algiers 1908, p. 462; Samhūdī, *<u>Kh</u>ulāṣat al-wafā'*, Cairo 1285, p. 187 *sqq.*; Wüstenfeld, *Gesch. der Stadt Medina*, in *Abh. G. W. Gött.*, ix. (separate ed., Göttingen 1860, p. 127 *sqq.*); Ibn al-A<u>th</u>īr, ed. Tornberg, ii. 89; al-Ya'ḳūbī, ed. Houtsma, ii. 47; al-Diyārbakrī, *Ta'rī<u>kh</u> al-<u>kh</u>amīs*, ii. 14; Yāḳūt, *Mu'<u>dj</u>am*, iii. 104, 703; iv. 51 (poetic references); Yule and Burnell, *Hobson-Jobson*, s.v. *mosellay*.

MU<u>SH</u>RIK. [See <u>SH</u>IRK].

MUSLIM (A.), part. IV of *s-l-m*, denotes the adherent of Islām. The term has become current in some European languages (also in the forms *moslim, moslem*), as a noun or as an adjective or as both, side by side with *Muhammadan* (in different forms). It has replaced *Musulman* (in different forms), except in French, where the latter term is used as a noun and as an adjective. The origin of *musulman* is probably *muslim* with the ending *ān* of the adjective in Persian. In Arabic literature the term Muslim is and has always been used to denote the adherents of Islām. See further the artt. ĪMĀN, AMĪR AL-MUSLIMĪN.

Bibliography: H. Yule and A. C. Burnell, *Hobson-Jobson*, s.v. *Musulman*; H. Lammens, *Remarques sur les mots français dérivés de l'arabe*, Beyrouth 1890, p. 176; E. Littmann, *Morgenländischen Wörter im Deutschen*, 2nd ed., Tübingen 1924, p. 61 *sq.*; R. Dozy, *Oosterlingen*, 's-Gravenhage—Leyden—Arnhem 1867, p. 44; D. Künstlinger, „*Islām*", „*Muslim*", „*aslama*" im *Ḳurān*, in *Rocznik Orjent.* xi (1936), p. 128 *sqq.*; H. Ringgren, *Islam, aslama and muslim*, Uppsala 1949.

MUSLIM B. AL-**ḤA<u>DJDJ</u>Ā<u>DJ</u>**, ABU 'L-ḤUSAIN AL-ḲU<u>SH</u>AIRĪ AL-NAISĀBŪRĪ was born at Naisābūr in 202/817 or in 206/821. He died in 261/875 and was buried at Naṣrābād, a suburb of Naisābūr. An anecdote regarding the cause of his death is related by Ibn Ḥa<u>dj</u>ar (see *Bibliography*). His fame is based upon his *Ṣaḥīḥ*, which, along with Bu<u>kh</u>ārī's book of the same name, enjoys the highest fame among the collections of traditions.

Muslim travelled widely to collect traditions, in Arabia, Egypt, Syria and 'Irāḳ, where he heard famous authorities such as Aḥmad b. Ḥanbal, Ḥarmala, a pupil of <u>Sh</u>āfi'ī, and Isḥāḳ b. Rāhūya. His *Ṣaḥīḥ* is said to have been composed out of 300,000 traditions collected by himself. He wrote a large number of other books, on *fiḳh*, traditionists and biography, none of which seems to have survived.

The *Ṣaḥīḥ* differs from the other collections of canonical *ḥadī<u>th</u>* in that the books are not subdivided into chapters, whereas in Bu<u>kh</u>ārī's work the traditions serve as examples of the *tar<u>dj</u>ama*'s. Still, it is not difficult to trace in the order of the traditions in Muslim's *Ṣaḥīḥ* a close connection with corresponding ideas of *fiḳh*. As a matter of fact the groups of traditions have been provided with superscriptions which may be compared with Bu<u>kh</u>ārī's *tar<u>dj</u>ama*'s; this was not, however, done by Muslim himself, as appears from the fact that the headings are not uniform in the different editions of the *Ṣaḥīḥ*.

A second difference between Muslim and the other collections consists in the fact that he pays peculiar attention to the *isnād*'s, to such an extent that a tradition in his work is often followed by several different *isnād*'s which serve as an introduction to either the same or to a slightly different *matn*. Such a new *isnād* is indicated in the text by the letter *ḥ* (*taḥwīl* or *ḥawāla* "change"). Muslim is praised for his accuracy regarding this point; in other respects, however, Bu<u>kh</u>ārī is superior to him, as is even recognized by a man so devoted to him as al-Nawawī, who wrote upon the *Ṣaḥīḥ* a commentary, which in itself is a work of immense value for our knowledge of Muslim theology and *fiḳh*.

Muslim has prefixed to his work an introduction to the science of tradition. The work itself consists of 52 books which deal with the common subjects of *ḥadī<u>th</u>*: the five pillars, marriage, slavery, barter, hereditary law, war, sacrifice, manners and customs, the Prophets and the Companions predestination and other theological and eschatological subjects. The book closes with a chapter on the Ḳur'ān (*Tafsīr*), the shortness of which is several times outweighed by the value of the *Kitāb al-īmān*, which opens the work, and which is a complete survey of the early theology of Islām.

On the commentaries upon the *Ṣaḥīḥ* see Brockelmann, *GAL*, i. 167, *S.* i. 265 *sq.*

Bibliography: Al-Nawawī, *Tah<u>dh</u>īb*, ed. Wüstenfeld, p. 548 *sq.*; Ibn <u>Kh</u>allikān, *Wafayāt al-a'yān*, ed. Wüstenfeld, No. 727, 19, 152; Ibn Ḥa<u>dj</u>ar al-ʿAsḳalānī, *Tahdhīb al-ahdhīb*, Ḥaidarābād 1327, x. 126—128; Ḥādjdjī Khalīfa, ed. Flügel, Index auctorum, s.v. Abū 'lhosein Moslim Ben Ḥajjáj; Nöldeke-Schwally, *Geschichte des Qorāns*, ii. 149 *sq.*; Goldziher, *Muh. Studien*, ii. 245 *sqq.*; J. E. Sarkīs, *Muʿdjam al-maṭbūʿāt al-ʿarabīya wa 'l-muʿarraba*, Cairo 1346 (1924), col. 1746.

MUSNAD. [See ḤADĪTH].

MUSTAḤABB. [See ḤUKM, SHARĪʿA].

MUSTAʿRIB(A) (A.), "arabicized", the name of one of the groups into which the Arab genealogists divide the population of Arabia. The first is the *ʿarab ʿāriba*, the original Arabs of pure stock; they numbered nine (some say seven) tribes which are regarded as the descendants of Aram b. Sām b. Nūḥ [q.v.] and the first settlers in Arabia: ʿĀd, Thamūd, Umaiyim, ʿAbīl, Ṭasm, Djadīs, ʿImliḳ, Djurhum, and Wabār. These are extinct except for a few remnants incorporated in other tribes. The second group comprises the *mutaʿarriba* [q.v.] who are not pure blooded Arabs. They are regarded as descendants of Ḳaḥṭān (the Yokṭān of the list of nations in Gen. x. 25 *sq.*) and live in southern Arabia. The third group is called *mustaʿriba*; this name is also applied to tribes who were not originally Arabs; they trace their descent from Maʿadd b. ʿAdnān, a descendant of Ismāʿīl [q.v.]. The latter is said to have lived with the *ʿarab ʿāriba* and to have learned their language. All the north Arabian tribes are included among the *mustaʿriba*, so that the Banū Ḳuraish to which Muḥammad belonged is one of them; his genealogy is in this way traced back to Abraham and thus provided for him a direct connection with the Biblical prophets. The old term *mustaʿriba*, for tribes not originally of Arab descent, obtained a new meaning after the conquest of Spain. It was applied to the Christian Spaniards who adopted Islām; the word *mustaʿriba* was corrupted to Mozarab.

Bibliography: Caetani, *Annali dell' Islām*, i., § 43; do., *Studi di Storia Orientale*, i. 306 *sq.*; Caussin de Perceval, *Essai sur l'Histoire des Arabes*, i. 6 *sqq.*; C. Ritter, *Arabien*, i. 57; al-Suyūṭī, *Muzhir*, first Nawʿ; *Tādj al-ʿarūs*, i. 371; cf. Lane, *Lex.*, s.v.

MUTʿA (A.), temporary marriage (according to the Arab lexicographers "marriage of pleasure"), a marriage which is contracted for a fixed period on rewarding the woman.

I. Before Islām. According to Ammianus Marcellinus, xiv. 4, temporary marriage was in use among the Arabs already in the fourth century A.D.; but this can hardly be a reference to mutʿa as the woman brings a lance and tent to the man and can leave him if she likes after the period has elapsed. It is also doubtful if there is a distinct mutʿa character in the marriage of Hāshim with Salma bint ʿAmr, whom he married during a temporary stay in Yathrib and left with her family there after the birth of her child (Caetani, i. 111, § 92). From the passage *Aghānī*, xvi. 63 (*mattiʿūnī biha 'l-laila*) as well as from Muslim traditions it may be concluded that mutʿa was known in the Djāhilīya. If we remember that the same kind of temporary marriage as the mutʿa was known in Erythraea (Conti Rossini, *Principi di diritto consuetudinario*, Rome 1916, p. 189, 249) it seems that mutʿa is an old Arabian institution.

II. In the Ḳurʾān there is undoubtedly a reference to this form of marriage in the Madīna Sūra iv. 24 although the orthodox explanation of this passage as early as the first century refers it to the ordinary *nikāḥ*; after giving a list of the classes of women with whom marriage is forbidden, it goes on: "And further you are permitted to seek out wives with your wealth, in decorous conduct but not in fornication; but give them their reward (*udjūr*) for what you have enjoyed of them (*istamtaʿtum*) in keeping with your promise". After *istamtaʿtum*, Ubaiy b. Kaʿb and Ibn ʿAbbās read the words *ilā adjalin musammaan* "for a definite period" (Ṭabarī, *Tafsīr*, v. 9), a reading which naturally has not found its way into Sunnī circles but is often added in Shīʿa books.

III. The traditions are contradictory on the question of mutʿa. According to some, it was in use in the time of the Prophet and he was even said to have practised it (*mattaʿahā*: Ṭabarī, *Annales*, i. 1775, 1776; cf. Caetani, ii. 748, No. 17 and 19). In return for a robe or a handful of dates one could take an unmarried woman (*uyyām*) for a period of cohabitation (Muslim, *Nikāḥ*, tr. 13, 17; Ṭayālisī, No. 1637). Especially when a man came to a strange town he could marry a woman there for the period of his stay so that she could look after him (Tirmidhī, *Nikāḥ*, bāb 28).

On the other hand, according to one tradition related by ʿAlī, it was forbidden by the Prophet on the day (or in the year) of Khaibar (Wensinck, *Handbook*, p. 145).

According to other traditions, he is said to have permitted it for a short time on particular occasions. In this connection we have a group of traditions which goes back to Sabra b. Maʿbad; the various accounts of this, some long, some short, which supplement one another, are in part given without date, in part referred to the conquest of Mecca and in part to the farewell pilgrimage (*Handbook*, l.c.). Their substance is as follows: The Prophet permitted mutʿa; Sabra therefore went with a companion to a woman and each offered her his cloak. She chose the younger with the shabbier cloak and slept three nights with him; thereupon the Prophet forbade it. According to the stories associated with the farewell pilgrimage, the woman wished mutʿa only for a fixed period so that ten days or nights was agreed upon, but the Prophet forbade it after the first night, saying: "Whoever of you has married a woman for a period, shall give her what he promised and claim nothing of it back and he shall separate from her; for God had forbidden this up to the day of resurrection".

According to a second group of traditions, which goes back to Djābir b. ʿAbd Allāh and Salama b. al-Akwaʿ, the Prophet permitted mutʿa for three days on a campaign. In Bukhārī (*Nikāḥ*, bāb 31) we have at the end: "The partnership of the two parties lasted three nights; and if they agreed to extend it, they did so, and if they wished to separate, they did so". A prohibition is given only in two versions in this group.

According to other traditions, mutʿa was first forbidden by the caliph ʿUmar at the end of his caliphate; (Muslim, *Nikāḥ*, tr. 16—18; Aḥmad b. Ḥanbal, iii. 304, 380 and iii. 325, 356, 363, where there is a reference to the two kinds of mutʿa, i.e. *tamattuʿ* on the pilgrimage and *mutʿat al-nisāʾ*). ʿUmar threatened the punishment of stoning so that he regarded mutʿa as fornication. Cf. the angry exclamation of Ibn ʿUmar when he was asked about mutʿa: "By Allāh, we were not unchaste in the time of the Prophet of Allāh nor fornicators".

What then is at the bottom of these contradictory traditions? While Wellhausen regards mutʿa as simply prostitution and not an old Arabian custom,

Caetani points out that the traditions agree in connecting mutʿa with an entrance of the Prophet into Mecca and sometimes even with the *ḥadjdj* and that a three days' duration is a feature of the mutʿa; taking account of other considerations, he concludes that mutʿa in the pagan period was religious prostitution on the occasion of the Meccan festival. However tempting this explanation may be, there is a complete lack of evidence for any religious prostitution in Mecca. With Wilken and Robertson Smith, we must rather regard mutʿa as the survival into Islām of an old Arabian custom. The Prophet gives this custom sanction in the Ḳur'ān and also practised it himself. The traditions, if examined carefully, only mention two cases of prohibition by the Prophet: Khaibar and Mecca. As both these are later than the above Ḳur'ānic passage (years 3—5, according to Nöldeke-Schwally, i. 198) this prohibition would be quite possible. But since on the other hand the caliph ʿUmar prohibited mutʿa, which there is no reason to doubt, we might regard the tradition of prohibition as representing later views, which, as is often the case, are put back to the time of the Prophet.

IV. Attitude of the fuḳahā'. ʿIbn Abbās (d. 68) was an ardent champion of mutʿa (Bukhārī, *Nikāḥ*, bāb 31; Muslim, *Nikāḥ*, tr. 18; Ṭayālisī, No. 1792; Rāzī, *Mafātīḥ al-ghaib*, Cairo 1324, iii. 195). In Mecca and the Yaman, according to Ibn Rushd (*Bidāya*, Cairo 1339, ii. 54), he also had followers; but before his death he is said to have been converted to the opposite view (Tirmidhī, *Nikāḥ*, bāb 28; Rāzī, *loc. cit.*). In later times, people still spoke derisively of a marriage by a *fatwā* of Ibn ʿAbbās. In the second half of the first century in Mecca, *fatwās* were still given permitting mutʿa (Muslim, *Nikāḥ*, tr. 29). The Ḳur'ān commentators Mudjāhid (d. 100), Saʿīd b. Djubair (d. 95), and al-Suddī (d. 127) also referred the above verse of the Ḳur'ān to mutʿa. Suddī says that it is a marriage for a fixed period and that it should be concluded with the permission of the *walī* and with two witnesses; that after the expiry of this period the man has no longer any claim on the woman, that she, however, should wait until she knew whether she was pregnant and that the two parties cannot inherit from one another (Ṭabarī, *Tafsīr*, v. 8). With the second century, the contrary view begins to predominate; although individuals like ʿAmr b. Dīnār (d. 126), Ibn Djuraidj (d. 150) and the Zaidī sect of the Djārūdīya permit mutʿa (Ibn Rushd, *loc. cit.*; van Arendonk, *Opkomst* etc., Leyden 1919, p. 72, note 9), al-Thawrī (d. 161), Ibn al-Mubārak (d. 181) [Tirmidhī, *Nikāḥ*, bāb 28] and all the Sunnī schools of law as well as the Zaidīs (al-Nāṭiḳ bi 'l-Ḥaḳḳ, *Taḥrīr*, Berlin MS., Glaser 74, fol. 53b) consider mutʿa forbidden. Its recognition was now limited to the Shīʿa. And if the caliph Ma'mūn tried to introduce mūtʿa again this was certainly due to his Shīʿī tendencies (Ibn Khallikān, *Wafayāt*, ii. 218).

At the same time, we still have in the second century the opinions of a period of transition. According to Zufar (d. 158), the marriage concluded under the form of mutʿa was valid as a marriage but its limitation in time was invalid (Sarakhsī, *Mabsūṭ*, v. 153; cf. also Bukhārī, *Ḥiyal*, bāb 4). According to al-Ḥasan b. Ziyād al-Lu'lu'ī (d. 204), the mutʿa was valid if the partners could not survive the time fixed, e.g. 100 years or more (Sarakhsī, *loc. cit.*).

But in spite of their refusal to recognize mutʿa, the Sunnīs made concessions by which mutʿa gained a footing in another form. It became the practice not to insert a definite period in the contract; any agreement made outside the contract was not affected by the law. Al-Shāfiʿī (*Umm*, v. 71) for example, declared a marriage valid when it was concluded with the unuttered resolution (*nīya*) to observe it only for the period of stay in a place or for a few days only, so long as this was not expressly stipulated in the contract. Similarly if agreement to this effect (*murāwaḍa*) had been previously made and even if made on oath; but he describes such an agreement as *makrūh*. There are also traces in later literature of a decision by Mālik by which he permitted mutʿa (Sarakhsī, v. 152; Badā'ūnī, *Muntakhab al-tawārīkh*, ed. Lees, ii. 208 *sqq.*) although only the contrary is recorded in the *Muwaṭṭa'* and *Mudawwana* (iv. 46).

A good exposition of the two opposite points of view is given from the Sunnī side by Kāsānī (d. 587), *Badā'iʿ al-ṣanā'iʿ*, Cairo 1327, ii. 272—274 and in Rāzī, *op. cit.*, iii. 193—198 and from the Shīʿī side by ʿAlam al-Hudā al-Murtaḍā, *Intiṣār*, Teheran 1315, p. 60—65. The Sunnīs refer the verse above mentioned from the Ḳur'ān to regular marriage and declare the *adjr* to be *mahr*, while the Shīʿīs base their view on this verse and consider the traditions of prohibition not to be abrogatory and do not consider ʿUmar authoritative for a prohibition. The Imāmīs even go so far as to say: "The believer is only perfect when he has experienced a mutʿa" (al-Ḥurr al-Āmilī, v. 69, [2]).

V. The teachings of the Imāmīs. 1. Form. Mutʿa is an irrevocable (*lāzim*) contract which, like every contract, comes into existence through *ḳabūl* and *īdjāb*. It may be concluded with the words *nikāḥ*, *tazwīdj* or *tamattuʿ*, but must always contain a precise statement of the period (*adjal*) and a definite recompense (*adjr* or *mahr*). This recompense may be the dowry usual in other marriages or a handful of corn, a dirham or such like. The period may vary from a day to months or even years. Witnesses are not necessary; nor need it be concluded before the ḳāḍī, if the partners are capable of using the formulae correctly. If the *mahr* is not given, the contact is invalid. If the period is not given, according to some it is a regular marriage if the word *tamattuʿ* was not used at the conclusion of the marriage-contract; in the latter case the contract is again invalid.

2. The two partners must naturally fulfil the usual conditions for the conclusion of an agreement. The woman must further be unmarried and chaste (*ʿafīfa*) and if possible ought to know about mutʿa, i.e. be a Shīʿī, and can only contract a temporary marriage with a Muslim. According to Ibn Bābūya (d. 381) and al-Mufīd (d. 413), mutʿa with an unbeliever is forbidden, even with a member of the possessors of a scripture (*kitābīya*). The *nawāṣib* (extreme Khāridjīs) are included among the unbelievers. According to most Imāmīs, (and Ṭūsī also) however, mutʿa with a Christian or Jewish woman is permitted but *makrūh* with a *madjūsīya*. Mutʿa with a slave-girl is only admitted with the consent of her master. Usually the woman contracts the marriage without a *walī*; only a virgin (*bikr*), according to some, requires her father's consent (Abū 'l-Ṣalāḥ, 5th century, Ibn Bābūya, d. 381; Ibn al-Barrādj, d. 481; cf. Ḥillī, iii. 92). The man may in this way take other wives in addition to his four legal wives, especially on journeys. He must not, however, take two sisters at the same time, not even during the *ʿidda*.

3. The mutʿa ends on the expiry of the period agreed upon. It cannot be prolonged by arrangement

between the two parties; a new temporary marriage with a new *mahr* must rather be contracted at the end of the period. Divorce is impossible; according to some, however, *liʿān* and *ẓihār* are permitted.

4. There is no obligation on the man to provide food and home for the woman. The two partners cannot inherit from one another; but according to some, inheritance may be provided for in the contract. The *ʿidda* after the expiry of the mutʿa is two periods or 45 days, i.e. the *ʿidda* of a slavegirl. The children go with the father.

VI. Modern practice. Although these Shīʿī views have a certain amount of moral support, the mutʿa in many cases can only be described as legalized prostitution. It is true that in Persia such marriages are made for very long periods, e.g. 99 years, but the Persian, when on a journey, temporarily marries in any place where he is stopping for some time and in the towns and caravanserais mollahs and other brokers offer a wife to each new arrival. To make this business more profitable, the *ʿidda* period is evaded by concluding a second temporary marriage with the same man after the expiry of the first, for in the case of such a marriage not being consummated the *ʿidda* is not necessary. This marriage and a woman of this kind is called in Persia *ṣīghe* (lit. "form" i.e. of the contract) Cf. Olearius [1637], *Muscowit. u. pers. Reyse*, Schlesswig 1656, p. 609; Chardin [1673], *Voyages*, Paris 1811, ii. 222—223, 225—227; Polak, *Persien*, Leipzig 1865, i. 107 *sq.*; E. G. Browne. *A Year amongst the Persians*, Cambridge 1927, p. 505 *sq.*; H. Norden, *Persien*, 1929, p. 148, 167; and the novel of the traveller James Morier, *The adventures of Hajji Baba of Isaphan*, 1824, part iii., chap. 6—8.

In Mecca, in modern as well as ancient times (for the middle ages cf. *Lisān al-ʿArab*: *wa-mutʿat al-tazwīdj bi-Makka minhu*), temporary marriages were concluded among the Sunnīs but nothing is said of this in the marriage contract, otherwise this would make it invalid; everything necessary is arranged previously by word of mouth. On the conclusion of the contract, the man utters the *ṭalāḳ* formula with a time limit. Such agreements are as a rule kept (Snouck Hurgronje, *Mekka*, ii. 156; do., *Verspr. Geschriften*, vi. 150). The same artifice is used in such cases as Shāfiʿī indicated long ago (cf. above). In the xx[th] century marriages of this kind were still concluded at Deir es-Zōr by Beduins who came there temporarily for reasons of trade (V. Müller, *En Syrie avec les Bédouins*, Paris, 1931, p. 231 *sq.*).

Bibliography: Early History: G. A. Wilken, *Matriarchat*, Leipzig 1884, p. 9—25; W. Robertson Smith, *Kinship and Marriage*, London 1903, p. 82 *sqq.*; Wellhausen, *Die Ehe bei den Arabern*, in *NGW Gött.*, 1893, p. 464 *sq.*; Caetani, *Annali*, Milan 1910, iii. 894—903; Griffini in Zaid, *Corpus iuris*, Milan 1919 p. 324—332; Gertrude H. Stern, *Marriage in early Islam*, London 1939, p. 155 *sqq.* — In addition to the usual works on Fiḳh and Tradition: al-Mufīd (d. 413/1022), *Muḳniʿa*, Tabrīz 1274, p. 77 *sqq.*; commentary thereon: Ṭūsī (d. 459/1067), *Tahdhīb al-aḥkām*, Teheran 1318, ii. 183 *sqq.*; al-Muḥaḳḳiḳ (d. 676/1277—1278), *Sharāʾiʿ al-islam*, transl. Querry as *Droit Musulman*, Paris 1871, i. 689 *sqq.*; Ibn al-Muṭahhar al-Ḥillī (d. 726/1326), *Mukhtalaf al-shīʿa fi aḥkām al-sharīʿa*, Teheran 1323—1324, iv. 8—14; al-Ḥurr al-ʿĀmilī (d. 1099/1688), *Wasāʾil al-shīʿa*, Teheran 1288, v. 68—76; ʿAlī b. Muḥammad ʿAlī al-Ṭabāṭabāʾī (written in 1192/1778), *Riyāḍ al-masāʾil*, Teheran 1267, ii. 133—141. — Tornauw, *Moslem. Recht*, Leipzig 1855, p. 80; P. Kitabgi Khan, *Droit musulman schyite. Le marriage et le divorce*, Lausanne 1904, p. 79 *sqq.*; R. K. Wilson, *Anglo-Muhammadan Law*, London 1912, p. 452—658; Juynboll, *Handleiding*, Leyden 1925, p. 193 *sq.*; Goldziher, *Vorlesungen*, Heidelberg 1910, p. 238; R. Levy, *Sociology of Islam*, London 1931—33, ii. 164 *sqq.*; J. Schacht, *The origins of Muhammadan Jurisprudence*, Oxford 1950, p. 266.

MUTAʿARRIB(A) (A.) "arabicized", the term applied to the descendants of Ḳaḥṭān (the Biblical Yoḳṭān) who were regarded by the genealogists as "having become Arabs" in contrast to such tribes as ʿĀd, Thamūd, etc. alleged to be "pure" Arabs. They settled in South Arabia and adopted Arabic from the "pure" Arabs. The latter had learned it through Djurhum, the only man who spoke Arabic in Noah's ark (all the rest spoke Syriac), and whose son-in-law Aram b. Sām b. Nūḥ was the ancestor of the ʿĀd and Thamūd etc. From South Arabia, their main centre, tribes of the Banū Ḳaḥṭān migrated to the north so that there are in Northern Arabia also tribes which, according to their genealogy belong to the Banū Ḳaḥṭān [cf. the article MUSTAʿRIB(A) where the literature is given].

MUTAKALLIM. [See KALĀM].

MUTAWĀLĪ (pl. MATĀWILA, popularly "Metoualis"). This name, which means "those who profess to love (ʿAlī)" has been applied since the beginning of the xviii[th] century to those elements of the population of Lebanon who belong to the Shīʿa Twelver sect; at this date they liberated themselves from the suzerainty of the emīrs of Lebanon under the leadership of three families: the Āl Naṣṣār in the Djabal ʿĀmil, the Āl Ḥarfūsh at Baʿlabakk and the Āl Ḥamāde in northern Lebanon. There is a tendency at the present day to extend the name *matāwila* to the imāmīs of the Djaʿfarī sect of other parts of Syria, notably to the 15,000 Shīʿīs of Aleppo, of Idlib (Fūʿa, Nubbul, Nughāwila; the Banū Zuhra family, formerly *nuḳabāʾ al-ashrāf* at Aleppo), of Iṣlāḥīye and the banks of the Euphrates; in the region of Damascus these Shīʿīs pass themselves off as Sunnīs. In the Lebanon on the other hand, the "metoualis" (105,000 in 1924) form an officially recognized minority having deputies in parliament. They are concentrated in the south (Djabal ʿĀmil, Merdj-ʿayūn, Ṣūr and Ṣaidā), Kesrawān and Hermil. They are peasants and traders, formerly backward but with a certain gift for Arabic poetry; one of their number, Shaikh ʿĀref al-Zain of Ṣaidā, has worked for 30 years through his printing press and his magazine *al-ʿIrfān* with success in spreading education and modern culture among them, while remaining an ardent Shīʿī.

With the extremist Shīʿīs of the north (the bloc of 250,000 Nuṣairīs), the Mutawālīs of the south represent the remnants of the old Shīʿa population of Syria, which had its great poets (Dīk al-Djinn). They claim to go back to the preaching of Abū Dharr (cf. his *maḳām* at Ṣarafend, the ancient Sarepta) and are undoubtedly connected with certain Yaman tribes (ʿĀmila > ʿĀmil) and the *Ḥamrā*, those arabicized Īrānians of the ʿIrāḳ whom Muʿāwiya transplanted to Syria for their military qualities and also to weaken the ʿAlid party in ʿIrāḳ to which they belonged.

Bibliography: Kurd ʿAlī, *Khiṭaṭ al-Shām*, 1928, vi. 251—258; Aḥmad ʿĀref al-Zain, *Taʾrīkh Ṣaidā*, 1331 (1913), 176 p., and *Mukhtaṣar taʾrīkh al-Shīʿa*, Ṣaidā 1914, 42 p.; H. Lammens, *Les*

"*Perses*" *du Liban et l'origine des Métoualis*, in *MFOB*, xiv./2., 1929, p. 23—39; al-Ḥurr al-ʿĀmilī (d. 1099/1688), *Amal al-āmil fī ʿulamāʾ Djabal ʿĀmil*, the classical manual of Imāmī bio-bibliography, of which the first part deals with the Shīʿī ʿulamāʾ born in Syria, like the "first martyr", born at Djezzin, Muḥammad b. Makkī al-ʿĀmilī (d. 782/1382) and the "second martyr", born at Djubaʾ near Djezzin, Zain al-Dīn al-ʿĀmilī (d. 966/1558), Kafʿamī al-Djabāʾī, author of the *Djunnat al-aman* and the author himself (born at Mashghara); Tannūs b. Yūsuf al-Shidyāḳ *Akhbār al-aʿyān fī Djabal Lubnān*, Bairūt 1859, p. 359—361. — The old Imāmī mutawālī authors belong rather to the conservative school of the Akhbārīs than to that of the Uṣūlīs.

MUTAWĀTIR (A.), part. act. vi. from *w-t-r*, "that which comes successively". It is used as a technical term in two senses:

a. In the theory of cognition it is applied to historical knowledge (*khabar*), if the latter is generally acknowledged; e.g. the knowledge that there is a city called Makka and that there has existed a king called Alexander.

Definitions of the term show slight differences. According to al-Djurdjānī knowledge is mutawātir, when it is supplied by so many persons that either their number or their trustworthiness excludes doubt of its truth (*Taʿrīfāt*, ed. Flügel, p. 210; cf. Sprenger, *Dictionary of Technical Terms*, p. 1471).

According to Abū Ḥafṣ ʿUmar al-Nasafī (d. 537/1142) reports are mutawātir when handed down without deviation by persons who cannot be supposed to have plotted a lie. Taftāzānī in his commentary (p. 33 *sq.*) mentions two objections. The first is, that Jews and Christians accept as mutawātir reports that are rejected by Muslims. To this objection Taftāzānī simply replies that the possibility that these reports should be mutawātir is excluded. The second objection is, that the reports of every single reporter (*āḥād*) represent an opinion only and that an accumulation of opinions cannot be said to afford certainty. To this Taftāzānī replies that often plurality has a power of which singleness is devoid, e.g. a cord made of hair.

For the place of this source of knowledge within the theory of cognition, cf. ʿILM.

b. In prosody the terms is applied to the rhyme in which one moving letter intervenes between the quiescents.

Bibliography: *a*. ʿAbd al-Ḳāhir al-Baghdādī, *Uṣūl al-dīn*, Stambul 1928, p. 11 *sqq.*; *Wasīyat Abī Ḥanīfa*, art. 16; Abū Ḥafṣ ʿUmar al-Nasafī, *ʿAḳīda*, ed. Cureton, p. 1 *sq.*; Abu 'l-Barakāt al-Nasafī, *ʿUmda*, ed. Cureton, p. 1; Taftāzānī, commentary on Nasafī's *ʿAḳīda*, Stambul 1313, p. 33 *sqq.*; *Lisān al-ʿArab*, vii. 137; Goldziher, *Le livre d'Ibn Toumert*, p. 47 *sqq.*; A. J. Wensinck, *The Muslim Creed*, index, s.v.

b. Freytag, *Darstellung der arab. Verskunst*, Bonn 1830, p. 303, 305; W. Wright, *Arabic Grammar*, 3rd ed., new impression, Cambridge 1933, ii. 355.

MUṬAWWIF, Meccan pilgrims' guide. The word literally means one who gives instruction in the *ṭawāf* [q.v.]. The task of the *muṭawwifs* is however by no means limited to assisting pilgrims from foreign lands, who entrust themselves to their guidance, to go through the ceremonies required at the circumambulation of the Kaʿba. On the contrary they act as guides at the *saʿy* also and at all other ceremonies which are prescribed or only recommended for the *ḥadjdj* or *ʿumra* [q.v.]. The muṭawwifs also cater very completely for the physical welfare of the pilgrims. As soon as the pilgrims arrive in Djidda, their agents are ready on the arrival of the steamers to provide all the services they require from disembarkment to departure for Mecca. In Mecca the muṭawwifs or members of their families and servants take charge of the pilgrims. During the whole of their stay they provide the pilgrims with lodging, service, food, purchases (necessary and unnecessary), attend them if they fall ill and in case of death take charge of what they leave behind them.

The muṭawwifs of course do not do all this for nothing. They are appropriately paid for their trouble and see that, if the pilgrim is rich, their friends and relations also make something out of him. Of the money which they themselves receive, they have to hand over a considerable part in the form of fees, presents etc. to the shaikh of the gild and to the treasury, — another reason for getting as much as possible out of those entrusted to their care. It is therefore no wonder that many pilgrims have complained bitterly about the covetousness of these particularly prominent representatives of the Meccan pilgrim industry. In later times the fees for guides have been fixed by a legal enactment of the government (*OM*, xii. [1932], 249).

Reference has already been made to the fact that the muṭawwifs are organized in gilds; they are divided up into separate groups each of which has the right to exploit the pilgrims from one definite area only (e.g. Lower Egypt). All these groups together form the gild with a chief shaikh officially recognized at their head. The gild is very exclusive. Independent guides (*djarrārs*) have to be content with the scanty pickings left over for them by the organized muṭawwifs.

Bibliography: Snouck Hurgronje, *Mekka*, The Hague 1888, ii. 28—38, 98—101, 295 *sqq.* (English transl. by Monahan, Leyden and London 1931, pp. 23 *sqq.*, 78 *sqq.*, 238 *sqq*); Juynboll, *Handbuch des islamischen Gesetzes*, Leiden-Leipzig 1930, p. 140; Gaudefroy-Demombynes, *Le pèlerinage à la Mekke*, Paris 1923, p. 200—4; F. Durguet, *Le pèlerinage à la Mecque au point de vue religieux, social et sanitaire*, Paris 1932, p. 70 *sq.*, 82 *sq.*; J. L. Burckhardt, *Travels in Arabia*, London 1829, i. 354—60; in modern times: E. Rutter, *The holy cities of Arabia*, New York—London 1928, i. 80 *sq.*, 113 *sq.*, ii. 143—148; Shekīb Arslān, *al-Irtisāmāt al-liṭāf fī khāṭir al-ḥādjdj ilā aḳdas maṭāf*, Cairo 1350, p. 71—80.

AL-**MUʿTAZILA** is the name of the great theological school which created the speculative dogmatics of Islām. The meaning of the name is clear from al-Masʿūdī, *Murūdj*, vi. 22: the Muʿtazilīs are those who profess the doctrine of *iʿtizāl*, i.e. the doctrine of the *manzila baina 'l-manzilatain* or the state intermediate between belief and unbelief, the fundamental doctrine of the school (see below). A tradition which emanates from the *ahl al-ḥadīth* derives the name Muʿtazila from a schism which took place in the circle of al-Ḥasan al-Baṣrī: after laying down their doctrine of the *manzila baina 'l-manzilatain*, Wāṣil b. ʿAṭāʾ and ʿAmr b. ʿUbaid are said to have separated (*iʿtazala*) from al-Ḥasan's circle to found an independent school, or rather to have been expelled from it by the latter. These traditions are not entirely without historical foundation, but the interpretation of the name deduced from them is certainly wrong. The Muʿtazilīs were proud of their name, which they certainly would not have been if it had been a nickname invented by their enemies. We have here, as the variety of versions also shows, a tendencious invention of the *ahl al-sunna wa 'l-djamāʿa* anxious to rehabilitate al-Ḥasan and brand the Muʿtazilīs as heretics.

Origins and political history. There are quite definite indications that the Muʿtazila was of political origin and that it arose under the same constellation as the Shīʿī and Khāridjī movements. The accession of ʿAlī (Dhu 'l-Ḥidjdja 35) is the great watershed in the currents of the history of Islām. It is well known that several notable Companions of the Prophet refused to pay ʿAlī the homage which he demanded, or offered it reluctantly. The most frequently mentioned were Ṭalḥa and al-Zubair, but the names of many others have been preserved: Saʿd b. Abī Waḳḳāṣ, ʿAbd Allāh b. ʿUmar, Muḥammad b. Maslama, Usāma b. Zaid, Ṣuhaib b. Sinān and Zaid b. Thābit (al-Ṭabarī, i. 3072). Of these Ṭalḥa and al-Zubair openly rebelled against ʿAlī, but the majority remained neutral. The Madīnese in general followed the example of the latter, and in Baṣra al-Aḥnaf b. Ḳais with 6,000 Tamīmīs and a group of Azdīs under Ṣabra b. Shaimān also stood aside from the quarrel (al-Ṭabarī, i. 3169, 3178). In speaking of the latter the text uses the verb *iʿtazala*, which still has its proper sense of "to separate from", but which is already on the way to become a political term meaning "to take up a neutral attitude in the quarrel between ʿAlī and his adversaries". Now al-Nawbakhtī mentions (*Kitāb Firaḳ al-Shīʿa*, ed. Ritter, p. 5) a party which on the accession of ʿAlī separated and followed Saʿd b. Abī Waḳḳāṣ, ʿAbd Allāh b. ʿUmar, Muḥammad b. Maslama and Usāma b. Zaid. "These separated (*iʿtazalū*) from ʿAlī and refused either to fight against him or to take his side, although they had paid homage to him and had received him favourably; they were called *al-Muʿtazila*, and are the ancestors of all the later Muʿtazila". The Muʿtazila as a theological school must therefore have been preceded by a political Muʿtazila, which determined its structure.

This hypothesis seems to be confirmed if we analyse carefully what is recorded of the founders of the theological school. According to a unaminous tradition, this school originated with two natives of Baṣra, Wāṣil b. ʿAṭāʾ [q.v.] and ʿAmr b. ʿUbaid [q.v.]. The period of their activity covers practically the reign of the caliph Hishām and his Umaiyad successors, i.e. the years 105—131 / 723—48. We have a good deal of quite early information about them, not always free from lacunae, but sufficient to enable us to grasp the leading ideas in their theological work (see *Bibl.*). It is clear from all these traditions that the doctrine of *iʿtizāl* formed the starting point for the creation of the school, that Wāṣil was the first to formulate it and that he later won over ʿAmr to his teaching. This is how al-Khaiyāṭ records the origin of the idea of *iʿtizāl*. Muslims were agreed that he who committed a grave sin deserved the name of *fāsiḳ* and of *fādjir*, but opinions varied as to the character of the individual who received these epithets. The Khāridjīs said he was an infidel. The Murdjiʾīs said he was a believer in spite of his *fisḳ* and his *fudjūr*; al-Ḥasan al-Baṣrī and his circle described him as a hypocrite (*munāfiḳ*). Wāṣil demonstrates that the description given in the Ḳurʾān of a believer and an infidel cannot be applied to a believer who has committed a grave sin; the latter is therefore neither believer nor infidel. Now it is impossible to regard him as a hypocrite as al-Ḥasan wants to do, for a hypocrite must pass as a believer until his hypocrisy is brought to light. The only possible course then is to put the *fāsiḳ* in a special category of those who are in an intermediate state (*manzila baina 'l-manzilatain*). These same ideas are found in the conversation by which Wāṣil is said to have won ʿAmr over to the doctrine of *iʿtizāl* (al-Saiyid al-Murtaḍā, *Amālī*, i. 114 *sq.* = Ibn al-Murtaḍā, *al-Muʿtazila*, p. 22 *sq.*; source probably al-Khaiyāṭ).

There are political problems concealed behind these speculations. The doctrine of *manzila baina 'l-manzilatain* is not the result of interest in pure speculation, but arose out of a clearly defined opinion on the individuals who took part in the quarrels that raged round the caliphate of ʿAlī. It is striking how much space is occupied by the question of ʿAlī, of Ṭalḥa, of al-Zubair and of ʿĀʾisha in the rather scanty information which we possess regarding the theology of Wāṣil and ʿAmr; we cannot doubt that here they were dealing with a central problem. Wāṣil and ʿAmr took neither side in the dispute (*Kitāb al-Intiṣār*, p. 97—98). According to them, ʿAlī, Ṭalḥa, al-Zubair and ʿĀʾisha were originally true and pious believers. But the war which broke out among them divided them into two parties who could not both be right; one of these parties committed a sin, but we do not know which. We must therefore leave their cause to Him who knows it, but in their relations with one another we cannot regard them as true believers in the strict sense of the word. As a result, if one of these individuals bears witness against another of the opposite party, we cannot accept this evidence; relatively to the one, the other is *fāsiḳ* and vice-versa (cf. also Baghdādī, *Kitāb al-Farḳ*, p. 100). If we may believe the *ahl al-ḥadīth*, ʿAmr showed himself more severe than Wāṣil; he is said to have refused to accept the deposition made by any member of these parties against any member of the community on any matter whatever (*Taʾrīkh Baghdād*, xii. 178; al-Baghdādī, *Kitāb al-Farḳ*, p. 100); for he declared guilty (*fussāḳ*) *per se* both the parties engaged in the battle of the Camel. It is therefore not surprising that Wāṣil and ʿAmr have sometimes been confused with the Khāridjīs (verse of Isḥāḳ b. Suwaid al-ʿAdawī, al-Djāḥiẓ, *Bayān*, i. 13).

However, the opinion of the leaders of the Muʿtazila on ʿAlī is based on quite a different foundation. To understand the position correctly it is important to note that 1. Wāṣil and the whole Muʿtazila were definitely enemies of the Umaiyads and that 2. Wāṣil adopted a somewhat ambiguous attitude regarding ʿUthmān and his murderers (*Kitāb al-Intiṣār*, p. 97—98). This tacitly implies a declaration in favour of the ʿAlids, the first actors in the drama played at Mecca in the year 35. Indeed Wāṣil was on somewhat intimate terms with the ʿAlids of Madīna (Ibn al-Murtaḍā, *al-Muʿtazila*, p. 20); the Zaidīya revere him as one of their leaders, and Zaidī theology is essentially based on that of Wāṣil. This is true not only of the speculative theology; there is agreement also on political doctrines. The Zaidīs do not say that the first caliphs Abū Bakr and ʿUmar were usurpers, as the extreme Shīʿīs do; Wāṣil and with him the whole Muʿtazila regards the caliphate of Abū Bakr as legitimate (commentary of Ibn Abī Ḥadīd on *Nahdj al-balāgha*, Cairo 1329, i. 3); he left undecided the question of knowing who had the superior claim, Abū Bakr, ʿUmar or ʿAlī, but he credited ʿAlī with a superior claim to ʿUthmān.

This attitude, a little complicated as regards ʿAlī, and therefore prudent towards the extreme S͟hīʿīs, at the same time unreservedly hostile to the Umaiyads, can only be interpreted in one way. All these apparently dissimilar lines converge on a common centre: the ʿAbbāsid movement. It is precisely Wāṣil's attitude which we must regard as characteristic of the partisans of the ʿAbbāsids. The latter regarding themselves as the true *ahl al-bait*, it was evidently in their interest to lower somewhat the preponderating position attributed to ʿAlī by the extreme S͟hīʿīs in order themselves to profit by the prestige enjoyed by the family of the Prophet; but on the other hand they had every reason not to cut the links with the S͟hīʿīs who were indispensable as allies to them. It is obvious that in these circumstances it was particularly important for them to win over the relatively moderate Zaidī faction to their cause. In a general way the teaching of Wāṣil on *al-manzila* can only be perfectly understood if we see in it the theoretical crystallisation of the political programme of the ʿAbbāsids before their accession to power. Everything leads us to believe that the theology of Wāṣil and the early Muʿtazila represents the official theology of the ʿAbbāsid movement. This gives an unforced explanation of the fact that it was the official doctrine of the ʿAbbāsid court for at least a century. It seems even probable that Wāṣil and his disciples took direct part in the ʿAbbāsid propaganda. In his *ḳaṣīda* mentioned below Ṣafwān al-Anṣārī tells us that Wāṣil had emissaries (*duʿāt*) in all parts of the Muslim world. Ṣafwān describes them as ardent believers and ascetics who were distinguished from other men in physiognomy and dress; they were the supports (*awtād*) of God in all lands and centres in which his commandments were made manifest and in which the art of disputation (with the enemies of the faith) flourished. The period of this activity coincides exactly with that of the most intense ʿAbbāsid propaganda, in which all the forces working for the ruin of the Umaiyads were cooperating; it is impossible not to believe there was a connection between the two. That Wāṣil did actually extend his propaganda very far to the west is proved by the fact that there existed long after the fall of the Umaiyads a Wāṣilī community at Tāhert (Yāḳūt, i. 815), numbering about 3,000 members who had allied themselves with the Ibāḍīs. They had rebelled against Manṣūr under Idrīs b. ʿAbd Allāh al-Ḥasanī (al-S͟hahrastānī, p. 31; on these happenings see Ṭabarī, iii. 561); they were therefore reckoned among the enemies of the first ʿAbbāsid caliphs. It is interesting to note that the connection between Wāṣil and the K͟hāridjīs, supposed by Isḥāḳ b. Suwaid al-ʿAdawī to exist (see above) was here an actuality.

The quarrels of Wāṣil and his followers with Djahm b. Ṣafwān [q.v.] form a difficult problem which has not yet been solved. On the one hand Djahm's theology left distinct traces on that of the Muʿtazila; the doctrine of the created Ḳurʾān which was later to become a fundamental Muʿtazila thesis was probably formulated by Djahm and in the doctrine of the divine attributes there are coincidences on both sides which cannot be accidental. On the other hand, there are many serious differences which are probably practical and political in their nature. Djahm professed in the most extreme form the doctrine of predestination (*djabr*). All the actions of man are involuntary. Wāṣil maintained the opposite thesis of free will. Now once again we have political problems hidden behind these theological controversies; the Umaiyads in general preferred the dogma of predestination, while the opposition accepted the dogma of free will in its widest interpretation; in Damascus, G͟hailān al-Dimas͟hḳī, who figures among the fathers of the Muʿtazila (Ibn al-Murtaḍā, *al-Muʿtazila*, p. 15—17), was put to death by the caliph His͟hām for holding the doctrine of free will (al-Ṭabarī, iii. 1733).

Once the hypothesis of a definite connection between the Muʿtazila and the ʿAbbāsids is admitted, the question of the relations between the Muʿtazila founded by Wāṣil and the early Muʿtazila of the period of ʿAlī presents itself in a new aspect. It will be admitted that there is a striking resemblance between the attitude of these former companions of the Prophet and that of the ʿAbbāsids. It is true that ʿAbd Allāh b. al-ʿAbbās entered the service of ʿAlī after the death of ʿUt͟hmān, but his true sentiments were somewhat ambiguous; he was a great friend of ʿUt͟hmān, but a rather lukewarm partisan of ʿAlī, and after the latter's death he placed himself at the service of the Umaiyads. His descendants did not remain at Madīna, probably because the ʿAlids were their rivals there; after a stay in Damascus, his son went to Humaima near Ad͟hruḥ and here a formal rapprochement took place in 98 between the ʿAbbāsids and the ʿAlids (Wellhausen, *Das arabische Reich*, p. 312 *sq.*). Before this event, we may regard the ʿAbbāsids as a kind of Muʿtazila in the old sense of the word.

With ʿAmr b. ʿUbaid a new element enters the Muʿtazila as founded by Wāṣil. ʿAmr originally was one of the *ahl al-ḥadīt͟h*; brought up in the circle of al-Ḥasan al-Baṣrī, he transmitted a large number of ḥadīt͟hs from his master and he is remembered as one of the *muḥaddit͟hūn*. His conversion to the doctrine of *iʿtizāl* brought about a rupture between him and these circles; but with him a considerable section of the Ḳadarīs of the *ahl al-ḥadīt͟h* joined the Muʿtazila, thus reinforcing the more politically inclined Ḳadarīya, of which Wāṣil was the champion. *Ḳadarī* and *muʿtazilī* were soon to become synonymous terms. ʿAmr seems to have been decidedly anti-ʿAlid (see above), in any case he preferred Abū Bakr to ʿAlī (Ibn Abī Ḥadīd on *Nahdj al-balāg͟ha*, i. 3). This attitude implies a certain predilection for ʿUt͟hmān, which is foreign to Wāṣil; indeed, a section of the old Baṣrīs, among them al-Djāḥiẓ, is said to have belonged to the party called *al-ʿUt͟hmānīya*. ʿAmr's point of view was of great importance for the development of the Muʿtazila. After their final triumph, the ʿAbbāsids immediately dissolved the alliance with the S͟hīʿa, which had only been a political instrument for them. As regards the extreme S͟hīʿa, the Rawāfiḍ, the Muʿtazila unreservedly followed the direction of their new masters; but it is fairly evident that some of them did not decide to break so abruptly with the moderate S͟hīʿa. This resulted in a schism. One section remained faithful to the alliance with the moderate S͟hīʿa; this section was later to form a special Muʿtazila school in Bag͟hdād. But the Muʿtazilīs of Baṣra with ʿAmr at their head seem to have attached themselves without protest to the ʿAbbāsid cause. ʿAmr even became the intimate friend of Manṣūr and so to speak his spiritual father. In the west, the Muʿtazilīs allied with the K͟hāridjīs rebelled against the ʿAbbāsids (see above).

Let us sum up the characteristic features of the Muʿtazila at the beginning of the ʿAbbāsid period. The Muʿtazila was: 1. in general devoted to the cause of the ʿAbbāsid caliphs, only a faction being opposed to them; 2. decidedly hostile to the extreme Shīʿa, the Rāfiḍa; 3. hostile to the Djahmīya, by which however it was a little influenced; 4. *ḳadarī* in reuniting several of the old factions of this name; 5. in serious disagreement with the *ahl al-ḥadīth*, who soon declared it heretical. This position had a decisive influence in determining the structure of the Muʿtazila theology. The beginnings of this theology go back to Wāṣil and ʿAmr and are connected with the fight against the Rāfiḍa. The extreme Shīʿīs had quite early assimilated a good number of non-Muslim beliefs; we need not doubt that Manichaeism played a part in them; in any case certain gnostic and dualist ideas had found a way into Islām through the intermediary of these Shīʿīs. These tendencies, very marked in Kūfa, were also represented at Baṣra; in the house of an Azdī who was a *sumanī* or Buddhist, Wāṣil and ʿAmr had frequent meetings with ʿAbd al-Karīm b. Abi 'l-ʿAwdjāʾ and Ṣāliḥ b. ʿAbd al-Ḳuddūs, who professed dualist doctrines (read *al-thanawīya* instead of *al-tawba*; we should probably understand by this Manichaean views) and the poet Bashshār b. Burd (*Kitāb al-Aghānī*, iii. 24). A serious schism broke up this curious *madjlis*. This even decided the whole future of the Muʿtazila. Henceforth the fight against *zandaḳa* and *thanawīya* is a cardinal point in the programme of the Muʿtazila. Wāṣil himself composed a refutation of Manichaeism which al-Bāhilī (c. 300 A.H.) was still able to peruse (*al-Muʿtazila*, p. 21). But they also found themselves compelled to combat these heresies in a positive fashion; to the doctrine of fire professed by Bashshār they offered a theology of earth, so to speak, a theology based on the natural philosophy of the time. The poems of Ṣafwān al-Anṣārī (al-Djāḥiẓ, *Kitāb al-Bayān*, i. 16—19) afford us a specimen of this theology; here we have one of the fundamental documents for the history of Muʿtazila dogmatics. It is not yet clear whence came the philosophy put at the service of theology, but its general character is apparent; it is philosophy of the alchemists and physicists of late antiquity, a kind of *summa* of the scientific principles which seem to have been accepted everywhere in Asiatic Hellenism. Ṣafwān perhaps gives us a hint as to the circles from which it came to the Muʿtazila, when he tells us that Bashshār called Wāṣil and his friends *Daiṣānīs*; this is in any case worth noting. In a general way those who handed on this natural philosophy seem to have been the school called *Dahrīya* by Muslims. The Muʿtazila fought these Dahrīs with a vigour which reveals the dependence on this heretical philosophy of which they were conscious. The true founder of the dogmatic system of the Muʿtazila was Abu 'l-Hudhail Muḥammad b. al-Hudhail al-ʿAllāf (d. 840). Abu l'Hudhail, his friends and pupils, continued on a large scale the polemic against Manichaeism, a polemic which is certainly not unconnected with the persecution begun by the ʿAbbāsids against the open or secret adherents of this religion. On the other hand, he fought the Rāfiḍa most vigorously, then represented by the very remarkable theologian Hishām b. al-Ḥakam; and it was through his disputes with the latter that he was led to study the books of the philosophers, which furnished him with a system of dogmatics, a little bold, but full of fertile new ideas. Alongside of him there was a crowd of important theologians at Baṣra: Muʿammar, an independent mind whose ideas have not yet been sufficiently analysed; Hishām b. ʿAmr al-Fuwaṭī and al-Aṣamm, adversaries of Abu 'l-Ḥudhail and several others. Among Abu 'l-Hudhail's pupils mention must first be made of Ibrāhīm b. Saiyār al-Naẓẓām [q.v.]. These theologians gave Muʿtazila dogmatics its essential character. This theology is: 1. apologetic; it aims at defending the revelation of the Prophet; as a result it is 2. strictly Ḳurʾānic: the sacred book is the only source of the theological denominations (*asmāʾ*) and of the precepts of religion (*aḥkām*); it is 3. polemical: it vigorously invaded the domains of other religions and other Muslim parties to fight them on their own ground; it is 4. speculative: it has recourse to philosophical means to refute its adversaries and formulate its dogmas; consequently it is 5. intellectualist: it envisages the problem of religion under the purely intellectual aspect. Nothing could then be less justifiable than to regard the Muʿtazila as philosophers, free thinkers or liberals. On the contrary, they are theologians of the strictest school; their ideal is dogmatic orthodoxy; philosophy for them is only an *ancilla fidei*; they are nothing less than tolerant. What they created was Muslim scholasticism.

Parallel to the school of Baṣra, a Muʿtazila school was founded in Baghdād by Bishr b. al-Muʿtamir (d. 210/825—826). This school was pro-ʿAlid (ʿAlī preferable to Abū Bakr), and Bishr was persecuted by Hārūn al-Rashīd. But under Maʾmūn (198—218/813—833), a decidedly pro-ʿAlid caliph, the school of Bishr gained a preponderating influence mainly through the theologians Thumāma b. Ashras (d. in 210/825—826) and Ibn Abī Duʾād (d. in 240/854—855). This school particularly attacked those who held the doctrine of the uncreated Ḳurʾān [q.v.]. This attack however had disastrous consequences for the Muʿtazila. Abandoned by the caliph al-Mutawakkil (232—247) who adopted the doctrine of the uncreated Ḳurʾān, it rapidly fell from its influential position and soon found itself surrounded by implacable enemies. In the second half of the third century, Ibn al-Rāwandī, a partisan of the Baghdād school, made a stir when he left the Muʿtazila for the most advanced Rāfiḍa; a man of violent temperament, he criticized the Muʿtazila in a scathing way which did it much damage. Towards the end of the third century, the Ḳarmaṭian movement came on the scene, reinforcing the extreme Rāfiḍa and causing trouble in every secular and spiritual sphere. In the struggle against the Ḳarmaṭians it is no longer the Muʿtazila who appear at the head of the defenders of orthodoxy, but the *ahl al-ḥadīth*. In the year 300, al-Ashʿarī broke with the Muʿtazila of Baṣra, of which he had been a convinced supporter, to introduce speculative dogmatics among the *ahl al-ḥadīth*, who were soon to give its character to Sunnī theology.

Among the Muʿtazila theologians of the third century we may mention the following. At Baṣra the tradition of Abu 'l-Hudhail al-ʿAllāf was propagated by a flourishing school represented by Yūsuf b. ʿAbd Allāh al-Shaḥḥām, Abū ʿAlī al-Aswārī and others. ʿAbbād b. Sulaimān was the pupil of Hishām al-Fuwaṭī. Ibrāhīm b. Ismāʿīl known as Ibn ʿUlaiya (d. 218/833) was the pupil of al-Aṣamm. The school of al-Naẓẓām developed certain special doctrines which the later Muʿtazila rejected (Faḍl al-Ḥadhdhāʾ and Aḥmad b. Ḥāʾiṭ, *Kitāb al-Intiṣār*, p. 222—223); but among the disciples of al-Naẓẓām we also find al-Djāḥiẓ. In the second half of the century, the most important Baṣra theologian was undoubtedly Abū ʿAlī Muḥammad b. ʿAbd al-Wahhāb al-Djubbāʾī. In Baghdād we find in addition to the theologians already mentioned ʿĪsā b. Ṣubaiḥ al-Murdār, contemporary of Bi͟shr b. al-Muʿtamir; then "the two D͟jaʿfars": D͟jaʿfar b. Muba͟sh͟shir (d. 234/849) and D͟jaʿfar b. Ḥarb (d. 236/850), at a later date Muḥammad b. S͟haddād al-Mismaʿī Zurḳān (d. 278/891) and Abu 'l-Ḥusain ʿAbd al-Raḥīm b. Muḥammad al-K͟haiyāṭ, the great authority on the history of the Muʿtazila (d. at the end of the third century). On the Muʿtazila of Syria we are not well informed; and only a little better on that of Egypt. The first Muʿtazilī here was Ibn ʿUlaiya (cf. above), who had disputations with al-S͟hāfiʿī; with him Ḥafṣ al-Fard came to Cairo; this last represented the official theology in Cairo during the *miḥna* of al-Wāt͟hiḳ. Ḥafṣ was declared a heretic by al-K͟haiyāṭ (*Kitāb al-Intiṣār*, p. 133—134). — In Spain the Muʿtazilī teaching was disseminated by Abū Bakr Faraḏi al-Ḳurṭubī who had visited the east and studied there with al-D͟jāḥiẓ; it was therefore al-D͟jāḥiẓīya — at bottom al-Naẓẓāmīya — that was known in Spain; very soon the Muʿtazila seems to have become undistinguishable from the Bāṭinīya (Asin Palacios, *Abenmasarra y su escuela*, Madrid 1914, p. 21—22).

The fourth century saw the S͟hīʿa flourishing and ʿAbbāsid power disappearing; the favour of several Būyid governors now to some degree made good the loss of prestige which had been suffered by the Muʿtazila. The schools continued their work and the Muʿtazila spread to the east. At Baṣra, al-D͟jubbāʾī had left a large number of disciples, but his school was soon surpassed by that of his son Abū Hās͟him; representatives of the latter were among others Abū ʿAbdAllāh al-Ḥusain b. ʿAlī al-Baṣrī (d. 369/970); Abu 'l-Ḥusain al-Azraḳ (Aḥmad b. Yūsuf b. Yaʿḳūb) al-Tanūk͟hī (d. 377/979), member of the well known al-Tanūk͟hī family; Abū Isḥāḳ Ibrāhīm b. ʿAiyās͟h al-Baṣrī and his pupil the Ḳāḍī ʿAbd al-D͟jabbār b. Aḥmad al-Hamad͟hānī. The latter, the most remarkable of the Baṣra theologians of the period, migrated in 360/971 to Raiy where he founded an influential school and died in 415/1025. In Bag͟hdād the school of Abū Bakr Aḥmad b. ʿAlī al-Ik͟hs͟hīd͟h (d. 320/932) dominated the whole century. A very celebrated Bag͟hdādī, Abu 'l-Ḳāsim ʿAbd Allāh b. Aḥmad al-Balk͟hī al-Kaʿbī, a pupil of al-K͟haiyāṭ, founded a school at Nasaf, where he died in 319/931; among his pupils we find al-Aḥdab Abu 'l-Ḥasan. We also find the Muʿtazila in Iṣfahān, where Abū Bakr Muḥammad b. Ibrāhīm al-Zubairī of the school of Abu 'l-Hud͟hail had introduced Muʿtazila doctrines; at Ḳirmisīn (school of Abū Hās͟him), Gurgān, Nīs͟hāpūr and in several other towns of K͟hurāsān. During the fifth century it was the theology of ʿAbd al-D͟jabbār which dominated at Baṣra; one of his pupils, Abū Muḥammad al-Ḥasan b. Aḥmad b. Mattawaihi, handed down the great work on dogmatics of his master, *al-Muḥīṭ bi 'l-taklīf*; another theologian, Abū Ras͟hīd Saʿīd b. Muḥammad al-Naisābūrī (d. about 460/1068), compiled a resumé of the questions disputed in the schools of Baṣra and Bag͟hdād. Several theologians of Bag͟hdād are known; some of them must have belonged to the Zaidīya, and generally speaking the Bag͟hdād school becomes more and more merged in the Zaidīya. The last great theologian of the Muʿtazila was al-Zamak͟hs͟harī [q.v.] (d. 538/1144), but the schools continued to exist long after him, especially in K͟hwārizm. It was probably the invasion of the Mongols that put an end to them; the Muʿtazila has however survived to our day in the Zaidīya.

It was not speculative dogmatics alone that formed the subject of Muʿtazila activity. Their part in the history of the exegesis of the Ḳurʾān is a very considerable one; it was they who introduced the strictly grammatical method. There is a very close connection between them and the philological school of Baṣra, the representatives of which in general taught Muʿtazila doctrines (e.g. al-Aṣmaʿī). The exegetical works of the Muʿtazila, for the most part now lost, were utilized to a large extent by their adversaries, e.g. Fak͟hr al-Dīn al-Rāzī. — All questions of *fiḳh* were vigorously discussed in the Muʿtazila schools; the influence of the Muʿtazila on the *uṣūl al-fiḳh* and the *mad͟hāhib* has still to be examined. — Lastly the science of *ḥadīt͟h* certainly received various stimuli from the Muʿtazila criticism of the *ahl al-ḥadīt͟h*.

Mad͟hhab. Muʿtazila theology is summed up under five principles (*uṣūl*) or fundamental doctrines which one must accept in their integrity to be recognized as a Muʿtazilī (al-Masʿūdī, *-Murūd͟j*, vi. 22). Being probably in origin the principal points in the programme of Muʿtazilī propaganda, these *uṣūl* later became a kind of framework of speculative dogmatics.

I. *Aṣl al-tawḥīd*: the strictest profession of monotheism (against any kind of dualism); denial of all resemblance between Allāh and his creatures (against the anthropomorphisms of the *muḥaddit͟hūn* on the one hand and those of the Rāfiḍa and Manichaeans, on the other); the divine attributes recognized (against the D͟jahmīya) but deprived of their real existence: they are not entities added to the divine being (this would be *s͟hirk*; against the *Ṣifātīya* among the *ahl al-ḥadīt͟h*) but identical with the being (Wāṣil, Abu 'l-Hud͟hail); allegorical interpretation of the anthropomorphisms of the Ḳurʾān; denial of the beatific vision; vigorous affirmation of a personal God and creator (against the Dahrīya); integral affirmation of the revelation of the Prophet, but distinction between a natural theology and a revealed theology. Problems discussed here: 1. The nature of God and his attributes: a. omnipresence: God is in all places, in the sense that he directs everything (Abu 'l-Hud͟hail; al-D͟jubbāʾī) — he is not in any place (thesis generally adopted); b. perceptibility: he is not perceived by the senses (thesis generally adopted) — he is perceived by the heart (Abu l'-Hud͟hail) — he has a hidden *māhīya* which will be perceived in another world with the help of a sixth sense which God will then create (Ḥafṣ al-Fard and others; thesis declared heretical); c. the attributes (eternal; names of the essence): identical with the essence (Abu l'-Hud͟hail; thesis generally adopted) — inherent in the essence through *maʿānī* (Muʿammar) — through *aḥwāl* (Abū Hās͟him); expressing positive aspects (Abu 'l-Hud͟hail and generally) — negative (knowledge: negation of ignorance etc.; al-Naẓẓām). 2. The structure of the created world: a. starting-point: anthropology treated in a positive way (exact definition of religious duties) and negative (refutation of *t͟hanawīya*): man is the empirical phenomenon which we see, the body (*d͟jism*) which is composed of a certain number of indivisable entities (atoms) and which supports the accidents: life, the senses, colours etc.; *nafs* is *maʿnā* and distinct from *rūḥ* (Abu 'l-Hud͟hail) — al Naẓẓām taught the following doctrines: man is composed of body (*badan*) and *rūḥ* (identical with *nafs*) which are mutually interpenetrant (*mudāk͟hala*); the colours, senses, sensations forms and spirits form different categories of *d͟jawāhir* (not accidents; not atoms); all that is living forms a single category (*mud͟jānasa*) — other doctrines: man is an indivisible entity (*djawhar*) characterized by *ḥayāt, ʿilm, ḳudra*; the body is the instrument of this *djawhar*; the accidents (movement, rest, colours etc.) are inherent in it through *maʿānī* which are inherent in other *maʿānī* etc. *in infinitum* (Muʿammar) — man is *bashar* (ʿAbbād b. Sulaimān); the *nafs* is an instrument which the body uses; the *rūḥ* is an accident (Djaʿfar b. Ḥarb) — the *rūḥ* is a body and distinct from the life which is an accident (al-Djubbāʾī); b. the physical world: dead nature is distinct from that which is living in as much as nature acts through *ḍarūra* while living beings act through their free will (*ikhtiyār*); for the rest, the one and the other category are of the same structure, the problems of physics being those of anthropology (substance, accidents, bodies, atoms etc.); theory of *ẓuhūr* and *kumūn* formulated by al-Naẓẓām and which correspond to his theory of interpenetration (*mudākhala*): things are hidden one in the other, physical development consists in the hidden things becoming manifest (e.g. the fire hidden in the stone). 3. The relation between God and the created world: a. *laisa ka-mithlihi shaiʾun*: a rigorous distinction between *ḳadīm* and *muḥdath* (no *ḥulūl*); b. the activities of God, expressed by his attributes, have for their objects the things of the created world. If these activities are eternal, the things ought to be so also; now these things are created i.e. put into existence after having been non-existent; several solutions of the problem: "thing" is only what exists and before the creation the thing was not thing, which implies that divine knowledge is born with the things (Djahmī thesis adopted by Hishām al-Fuwaṭī) — before the creation things were posited (*thābit*) as non-existent in God's eternal knowledge, but without the accidents which characterize them in existence (al-Shaḥḥām and others) — with these accidents (al-Khaiyāṭ, al-Kaʿbī and several theologians of Baghdād [school of *maʿdūmīya*]) — God created all things at one time, one in the other and these things are manifested in the created world one after the other (al-Naẓẓām); c. are the objects of divine knowledge and power limited? Yes (Abu 'l-Hudhail) — no (the others); d. divine power does not extend to the accidents (Muʿammar) — to the phenomena resulting spontaneously from human action (*tawallud*, see below under *aṣl al-ʿadl*). 4. Revelation: a. prophecy: a prophet is *maʿṣūm*, i.e. free from grave sins; b. the Ḳurʾān: created; God creates the word in a substratum (*lawḥ al-maḥfūẓ*; the Prophet; the bush etc.). The Ḳurʾān is miraculous in composition and style — denied by al-Naẓẓām; distinction (which goes back to Wāṣil) between *muḥkam*, the precepts of the Ḳurʾān which are clear and without ambiguity and *mutashābih*, the precepts which are not immediately clear and evident; distinction between *nāsikh* and *mansūkh*.

II. *Aṣl al-ʿadl*: God is just; all that he does aims at what is best for his creation (*aṣlaḥ*); he does not desire evil and does not ordain it (*amr* and *irāda* identical). He has nothing to do with man's evil deeds; all human actions result from man's free will; man has a *ḳudra* and an *istiṭāʿa ḳabla 'l-fiʿl*; man will be rewarded for his good deeds and punished for his evil ones. Problems discussed here: 1. Divine power: a. can God commit an injustice? No: al-Naẓẓām — yes, but he does not: thesis generally adopted; b. theodicy: could God prevent evil? yes, for he possesses a store of hidden grace (*luṭf*) which would be sufficient to destroy evil completely at once: Bishr b. al-Muʿtamir and several Baghdād theologians — no, for he always does what is best and wisest for his creation: thesis generaly adopted. 2. Human power: created by God; physical evils, diseases etc. are not subject to the human will; man's actions are movements; distinction between *afʿāl al-ḳulūb* and *afʿāl al-djawāriḥ*; problem of *tawallud* stated by Abu 'l-Hudhail and particularly discussed in the school of Baghdād: the effects of an action are attributed to him who performs it, and even after his death he remains responsible for it.

III. *Aṣl al-waʿd wa 'l-waʿīd* (or *al-asmāʾ wa 'l-aḥkām*): practical theology. Problems here discussed: a. belief and unbelief: belief consists in all the acts of obedience, obligatory or supererogatory; sins (*maʿāṣī*) are divided into grave (*kabāʾir*) and petty (*ṣaghāʾir*); the following are *kabāʾir*: *tashbīh Allāh bi khalḳihi, tadjwīruhu fī ḥukmihi* and *takdhībuhu fī khabarihi, radd al-idjmāʿ ʿan al-nabī*; God of his grace may forgive *ṣaghāʾir*; he who is not a Muslim obeys God if he does something which God has commanded in the Ḳurʾān (*ṭāʿa lā yurād allāh bihā*): Abu 'l-Hudhail (thesis rejected by al-Naẓẓām and the Baghdād school); distinction between *īmān bi'llāh* and *īmān li'llāh* from Hishām al-Fuwaṭī onwards; belief consists in avoiding *kabāʾir* i.e. acts regarding which God has laid down a threat (*waʿīd*): al-Naẓẓām; b. *al-asmāʾ wa 'l-aḥkām*: the good (*al-ḥasan*) is what God has ordained in the Ḳurʾān, evil (*al-ḳabīḥ*) what he has forbidden; questions of *fiḳh* in general; c. Tradition: the authenticity of a tradition is only guaranteed by 20 believers one of whom is predestined to Paradise; there are in each generation 20 believers who are free from grave sins (*maʿṣūm*): Abu 'l-Hudhail and Hishām al-Fuwaṭī; the *tawātur* does not necessarily presuppose believers; the Muslim community can agree upon what is an error or a mistake: al-Naẓẓām and others.

IV. *Aṣl al-manzila baina 'l-manzilatain* 1. Problems of theocracy: a. the caliphate of Abū Bakr was legitimate, but not based on a divine revelation: thesis generally adopted; b. superiority of Abū Bakr over ʿAlī (Abū Bakr superior to ʿUmar, the latter to ʿUthmān, the latter to ʿAlī): the old Baṣrīs and Thumāma; superiority of ʿAlī to Abū Bakr: the other Baghdādīs and some later Baṣrīs (al-Djubbāʾī towards the end of his life; ʿAbd al-Djabbār); neutral attitude (*tawaḳḳuf*) on all that concerns the question of knowing who was entitled to the superiority: Abū Bakr, ʿUmar or ʿAlī, but ʿAlī regarded as superior to ʿUthmān: Wāṣil, Abu 'l-Hudhail, Abū Hāshim. 2. The problems of fāsiḳ; the old problem being no longer a live one, petty sins (*al-ṣaghāʾir*) were discussed under this head.

V. *Aṣl al-amr bi 'l-maʿrūf wa 'l-nahy ʿan al-munkar*: programme of Muʿtazila activity before the coming of the ʿAbbāsids; the faith must be spread by the tongue, the hand and the sword; later this *aṣl* is little discussed; al-Aṣamm denied its obligatory character.

Bibliography: Steiner, *Die Muʿtaziliten oder die Freidenker im Islam*, Leipzig 1865; v. Kremer, *Gesch. d. herrschenden Ideen des Islams*, Leipzig 1868; Houtsma, *De strijd over het dogma* etc., Leyden 1875; Duncan B. Macdonald, *Development of Muslim Theology* etc., London 1903; Galland, *Essai sur les Moʿtazélites*, Paris n.d. ((1906); Horovitz, *Über den Einfluss der griechischen Philosophie auf die Entwicklung des Kalām*, Breslau 1909; Horten, *Die philosophischen Probleme der spekulativen Theologie im Islam*, Bonn 1910; do., *Die philosophischen Systeme der spekulativen Theologen im Islam*, Bonn 1912; do., *Die Modus-Theorie des Abū Hāschim*, in *ZDMG*, lxiii. (1909), 303—24; do., *Die Lehre vom Kumūn bei Naẓẓām*, *ibid.*, p. 774—792; do., *Was bedeutet maᶜnā als philosophischer Terminus?*, *ibid.*, lxiv. (1910), 391—396; Goldziher, *Aus der Theologie des Fachr al-Dīn al-Rāzī*, *Islam*, iii. (1912), 213—347; do., *Vorlesungen über den Islam*, 2nd ed., Heidelberg 1923, ch. 3; do., *Die Richtungen der islamischen Koranauslegung*, 1920; Nallino, *Di una strana opinione attribuita ad al-Ǧāḥiẓ intorno al Corano*, in *RSO*, vii. (1916—1918), 421—428; do., *Sull' origine del nome dei Muᶜtaziliti*, *ibid.*, p. 429—454; do., *Rapporti fra la dogmatica muᶜtazilita e quella degli Ibāḍiti dell' Africa settentrionale*, *ibid.*, p. 455—560; do., *Sul nome di "Qadariti"*, *ibid.*, p. 461—466; Andrae, *Die Person Muhammeds*, Stockholm 1917, p. 108—116, 139—145; v. Arendonk, *De opkomst van het Zaidietische Imamaat in Yemen*, Leyden 1919, introduction; Massignon, *La passion d'al-Hallaj*, Paris 1922, *passim*; Snouck Hurgronje, in Chantepie de la Saussaye, *Lehrbuch der Religionsgeschichte*, Tübingen 1925, i., p. 722—738; Nyberg, introduction to the *Kitāb al-intiṣār* (s. below); do., *Zu den Grundideen und zur Geschichte der Muᶜtazila*, in *Ephémérides Orientales* publ. by O. Harrassowitz, no. 31 (1927), 10—12; do., *Zum Kampf zwischen Islam und Manichäismus*, in *OLZ*, 1929, p. 426—441; Pretzl, *Die frühislamische Atomenlehre*, in *Isl.* xix. (1931), 117—130; Strothmann, *Islamische Konfessionskunde und das Sektenbuch des Aśᶜarī*, *ibid.*, p. 193—242; Wensinck, *The Muslim Creed*, Cambridge 1932; E. Mainz, *Muᶜtazilitische Ethik*, in *Isl.* xxii (1935); Pines, *Beiträge zur islamischen Atomenlehre*, Berlin 1936; al-Khaiyāṭ, *Kitāb al-Intiṣār wa 'l-Radd ᶜalā Ibn al-Rāwandī al-mulḥid. Le livre du triomphe*, ed. H.S. Nyberg, Cairo 1925; al-Ashᶜarī, *Maḳālāt al-islāmīyin*, ed. Ritter, Istanbul 1929—1933 (*Bibliotheca Islamica*, i., a—c); *Kitāb al-Fihrist*, in *WZKM*, iv. (1890), p. 217—235; al-Baghdādī, *Kitāb al-farḳ*, Cairo 1910, p. 93—189; do., *Uṣūl al-dīn*, Istanbul 1928; al-Saiyid al-Murtaḍā, *Amālī*, Cairo 1325, i. 113—143; do., *Kitāb al-Shāfī fi 'l-imāma wa 'l-naḳḍ ᶜalā kitāb al-mughnī li 'l-Ḳāḍī ᶜAbd al-Djabbār*, lith. Teheran 1301; Ibn Ḥazm, *al-Fiṣal*; al-Shahrastānī, *al-Milal*, ed. Cureton, p. 29—60; al-Īdiī, *Mawāḳif*, Cairo 1327, viii. 277—384; Saᶜīd al-Anṣārī, *Multaḳaṭ djāmiᶜ al-ta'wīl li-muḥkam al-tanzīl*, *Shibli Academy Series*, vol. 14, London 1921 (fragments of the *Tafsīr* of the Muᶜtazilī Abū Muslim Muḥ. b. Baḥr al-Iṣfahānī, d. in 322; selections from the *Mafātīḥ* of Fakhr al-Dīn al-Rāzī); ᶜAbd al-Djabbār, *Tanzīh al-Ḳur'ān ᶜan al-maṭāᶜin*, Cairo (al-Azharīya press) 1329; Abū Rashīd, *al-Masā'il fi 'l-khilāf baina 'l-Baṣrīyin wa 'l-Baghdādīyin*, ch. i., ed. by Biram (*Die atomistische Substanzenlehre aus dem Buch der Streitfragen* etc., Berlin 1902); T. W. Arnold, *al-Muᶜtazilah: Being an Extract from the Kitābu-l Milal wa 'n-Nihal by al-Mahdī li-din Aḥmad b. Yaḥyā b. al-Murtaḍā*, Leipzig 1902; A. S. Tritton, *Muslim Theology*, London 1947, p. 79—112; W. M. Watt, *Free will and predestination in early Islam*, London 1948, index; also the works mentioned in the text.

AL-MUZDALIFA, a place roughly halfway between Minā and ᶜArafat where the pilgrims returning from ᶜArafat spend the night between the 9th and 10th Dhu 'l-Ḥidjdja, after performing the two evening ṣalāts. On the next morning they set off before sunrise and climb up through the valley of Muḥassir to Minā. Other names for this place are *al-mashᶜar al-ḥarām*, from Sūra ii. 198 and Djamᶜ (cf. *lailat Djamᶜ*: Ibn Sᶜad, II/i. 129); but Djamᶜ, according to another statement, comprises the whole stretch between ᶜArafat and Minā, both included, so that *yawm Djamᶜ* (*Kitāb al-aghānī*, vi. 30) is explained as the day of ᶜArafat and *aiyām Djamᶜ* as the days of Minā. The rites associated with the night of Muzdalifa go back to the old pagan period, which the Arabs themselves recognize when they make Ḳuṣaiy introduce the kindling of the sacred fire in this night and say that guiding of the departure for Minā is a privilege of the family of Adwān.

The sacred place in Muzdalifa was the hill of Ḳuzaḥ. Even after Muḥammad in deliberate contrast to the pagan practice had declared all Muzdalifa to be *mawḳif* [cf. HADJDJ, I, *c.*), this hill retained its ancient sanctity. According to Azraḳī, there was a thick round tower upon it on which the Muzdalifa fire was kindled; in the time of Hārūn al-Rashīd it was a fire of wood; later it was illuminated with wax-candles. In the Muslim period a mosque was built about 400 yards from the tower, of which Azraḳī gives a detailed description while Muḳaddasī speaks of a place of prayer, a public fountain and a minaret. Burton also mentions a high isolated tower at Muzdalifa but the illumination in the night of Muzdalifa now takes place on the mosque.

Bibliography: Ibn Hishām, p. 77; Ibn Saᶜd, I/i. 41; II/i. 125, 129; Ṭabarī, i. 1105, 1755; Azraḳī, ed. Wüstenfeld, p. 36, 130, 411 *sqq.*, 415 *sqq.*; *BGA*, i. 17; ii. 24; iii. 76 *sq.*; Bakrī, ed. Wüstenfeld, p. 243 *sq.*, 509 *sq.*; Yāḳūt, ed. Wüstenfeld, iv. 519 *sq.*; Burckhardt. *Reisen in Arabien*, p. 412 *sq.*; Burton, *Personal Narrative of a Pilgrimage to el-Medinah and Meccah*, iii., 1856; Snouck Hurgronje, *Het Mekkaansche Feest*, p. 154—158 (= *Verspr. Geschr.* i. 101—104); Wellhausen, *Reste arabischen Heidentums*, p. 81 *sq.*, 120; Juynboll, *Handbuch des islamischen Gesetzes*, p. 157; E. Rutter, *Holy cities*, i. 165.

N

NABĪ (A.), prophet, borrowed from Hebr. *nabī* or Aram. *nᵉbī'ā*, is found in the Ḳur'ān from the second Meccan period in the singular and plural *nabīyūn*; in the Madīna period we find also the broken plural *anbiyā'*. Lists of the *nabīyūn* are given in Sūra vi. 83—86; iii. 39; iv. 163 *sqq.*; further information about them is given in several passages of Sūra xix, and in xvii. 55. The list consists exclusively of names from the Old and New Testaments (if we leave out Idrīs in Sūra xix. 56, whose name Muḥammad had however also learned from a Christian source; see the art. IDRĪS; Horovitz, *Koran. Unters.*, p. 88 *sqq.*); while messengers of God (*rasūl* [q.v.], plur. *rusul*; *mursalūn*) had also been sent to other peoples of the past — e.g. Hūd or Ṣāliḥ —, according to the Ḳur'ānic idea "prophets" had appeared only among the *ahl al-kitāb* [q.v.]. Only a minority of the individuals called prophets in the Ḳur'ān are so described in the Bible, and Yūnus b. Mattai [q.v.] is the only one of the *anbiyā'* of the Ḳur'ān who appears among the literary prophets of the Bible. Muḥammad himself did not claim the name nabī until he was in Madīna when he was addressed as the Prophet (*yā aiyuha 'l-nabī*) and, as finally closing the series of prophets, is called their "seal" (*khātam*). When Muḥammad in Sūra vii. 157 and 158 is called *al-nabī al-ummī*, this is to distinguish him as the prophet who has arisen among the heathen; the Jews called the heathen *ummōt hā-ʿōlam* ("peoples of the world") and also recognized prophets who has arisen among them: among these they included e.g. Balaam and Job. This Jewish name for the heathen became the *al-ummīyūn* of the Ḳur'ān (Sūra lxii. 2; iii. 20, 75); that *ummīyūn* refers to the heathen in quite clear from Sūra iii. 20, where they are contrasted with those who have received the scripture. When Sūra ii. 78 refers to the *ummīyūn min ahl al-kitāb*, the reference is most probably (with Wellhausen, *Skizzen*, iv. 13, note 2) to originally pagan Arabs who had adopted Judaism. The derivation of *ummī* from Hebrew *ummōt hā-ōlam* therefore fits all the Ḳur'ānic passages, while that most generally adopted from Hebrew *ʿam hā-āreṣ* "people of the country", a term for Jews who did not know the Jewish law, would at best fit only Sūra ii. 78 but even for this passage is not absolutely essential.

The post-Ḳur'ānic ideas about the prophethood of Muḥammad are discussed in the article MUḤAMMAD (cf. also Tor Andrae, *Die Person Muhammeds in Lehre und Glaube seiner Gemeinde*, Stockholm 1918). The accounts of the other prophets which found a way into Islām in the post-Ḳur'ānic period are collected in the works on the *ḳiṣaṣ al-anbiyā'*. These, however, are not confined to the prophets proper who appear in the Ḳur'ān by name or anonymously, and to other figures of Jewish and Christian Biblical and post-Biblical tradition, but deal also with the history of such personalities as Djirdjīs and Buluḳyā to whom there is not the slightest reference in the Ḳur'ān.

Bibliography: Wensinck, in *Acta Orientalia*, ii. 173 *sqq.*; Lidzbarski, *De propheticis quae dicuntur legendis*; Horovitz, in *ZDMG.*, lv. 519 *sqq.*; do., *Koranische Untersuchungen*, Berlin and Leipzig 1926, p. 44 *sqq.*

NABĪDH (A.), a comprehensive designation for intoxicating drinks, several kinds of which were produced in early Arabia, such as *mizr* (from barley), *bitʿ* (from honey: Bukhārī, *Maghāzī*, bāb 60; *Ashriba*, bāb 4; *Adab*, bāb 80; or from spelt; Aḥmad b. Ḥanbal, iv. 402), *fadīkh* (from different kinds of dates: Bukhārī, *Ashriba*, bāb 3, 21).

Grapes being scarce in Arabia, it is said that in al-Madīna "wine" was usually prepared from kinds of dates, exceptionally from grapes (Bukhārī, *Ashriba*, bāb 2, 3; Muslim, *Ashriba*, trad. 3, 6). This may be true. Yet even these traditions betray a tendency connected with the question whether the prohibition of wine included that of intoxicating drinks. Generally speaking *ḥadīth* favours the affirmative answer and is consequently anxious to point out that the *khamr* which was prohibited by Muḥammad included nabīdh.

The question was difficult in so far as these kinds of drinks were intoxicating to degrees which partly depended upon the duration of the process of fermentation. This appears e.g. from the copious traditions in which ʿĀ'isha relates how nabīdh was prepared for Muḥammad and at what time the beverage was done away with [cf. KHAMR], as well as from the traditions in which the previous prohibition of certain vessels (*ḥantam, muzaffat*, etc.) was abrogated and all kinds of vessels declared allowed, provided the drinks prepared in them were not intoxicating (Muslim, *Djanā'iz*, trad. 106; *Ashriba*, trad. 63—65, 67—75 etc.). A series of traditions which could be adduced by the Ḥanafites in favour of their view, according to which nabīdh is not included in the prohibition of wine, is to be found in al-Nasā'ī's collection, *Ashriba*, bāb 48. Cf. further the art. KHAMR.

Side by side with milk and honey nabīdh was also the beverage that was offered to the pilgrims in Mecca. The institution, *al-siḳāya* (also the name of the building, close to Zamzam, where the distribution took place), was an office held by the ʿAbbāsids (Aḥmad b. Ḥanbal, *Musnad*, i. 372; Muslim, *Ḥadjdj*, trad. 347; Abū Dāwūd, *Manāsik*, bāb 90). The descriptions by Ibn Saʿd (d. 230/845) and al-Azraḳī (d. 244/858) give the impression of referring to the present state of things; in the time of al-Maḳdisī (d. about 1000 A.D.) the instititution had already passed into desuetude. For details, cf. the work of Gaudefroy-Demombynes.

Bibliography: cf. the *Bibliography* of the article KHAMR; further: *Fatāwā ʿĀlamgīrī*, Calcutta 1251 (1835), vi. 607; Khalīl b. Isḥāḳ, *Mukhtaṣar*, trans. Santillana, ii. 739 *sqq.*; Ibn Ḥadjar al-Haitamī, *Tuḥfa*, Cairo 1282, iv. 118 *sqq.*; Abu 'l-Ḳāsim al-Muḥaḳḳiḳ, *Kitāb sharā'iʿ al-islām*, Calcutta 1255, p. 522; Querry, *Recueil de lois conc. les musulmans schyites*, Paris 1872, ii. 237 *sqq.*; Th. W. Juynboll, *Handleiding tot de kennis van de moh. wet*, Leyden 1925, p. 173; Snouck Hurgronje, *Het mekkaansche Feest*, Leyden 1880, p. 169 (*Verspr. Geschr.* i., 111); Gaudefroy-Demombynes, *Le pèlerinage á la Mekke*, Paris 1923 (*Annales du Musée Guimet, Bibl. d'études*, No. 23), p. 71 *sqq.*; al-Azraḳī, ed. Wüstenfeld, p. 335 *sqq.*

NADHR, vow, was taken over into Islām from the pre-Muḥammadan Arabs and underwent modification by the new religion. The idea of dedication is associated with the root *n-dh-r* which is also found in South Arabic, Hebrew and Aramaic and to some extent in Assyrian. An animal could be the object of dedication among the Arabs. For example, they dedicated by nadhr certain of their sheep etc., for the *ʿatīra* feast in Radjab (*Lisān al-ʿArab* and Djawharī, s.v.); the dedication which was expressed in solemn formulae signified that the animals were removed from the mundane sphere and placed in the sacred one.

As a rule, a sacrifice was dedicated in order to obtain good fortune in a particular respect. The promise to dedicate an animal when the herd had reached the number of a hundred (*op. cit.*) had an effect on the prosperity of the animals because the word anticipated the fact. According to the story, ʿAbd al-Muṭṭalib similarly dedicated a son to be slain beside the Kaʿba if he should have ten sons and they grew up (Ibn Hishām, p. 97 *sq.*) but for his nadhr 100 camels were substituted. — A childless woman could also vow if she had a son to dedicate him to the sanctuary (*ibid.*, p. 76; perhaps this story is a literary borrowing). According to the *ḥadīth* of Maimūna bint Kardam, her father promised to sacrifice 50 sheep if he had a son (Yāḳūt, i. 754; Abū Dāwūd, *Aimān*, bāb 19; Ibn Mādja, *Kaffārāt* bāb 18). If a child was sick, its mother could dedicate it by a vow as *aḥmas* (from *ḥums*) if it recovered (Azraḳī, p. 123 *sqq.*). Escape from every difficulty was sought by a *nadhr*. During a battle a camel could be dedicated as a sacrifice (Wāḳidī-Wellhausen, p. 39). The traveller in the desert used to make a vow on account of the danger (see the verse in Lane and *Lisān al-ʿArab*, s.v.). In distress at sea one promised offerings to God or a saint or vowed to do something oneself, such as fasting (Sūra x. 22; xxix 65; Abū Dāwūd, *Aimān*, bāb 20; see also Goldziher, *Muh. Stud.*, ii. 311). During a drought ʿUmar vowed to taste neither *samn*, nor milk nor meat till the rain fell (Ṭabarī, i. 2573).

Even if a sacrifice were promised, the vow also affected the person concerned, as we see from the fact that he had his hair shorn not only on the ḥadjdj but also, for example, when sacrificing after a journey (Ibn Hishām, p. 15, 749; Wāḳidī-Wellhausen, p. 324, 381, 429 *sq.*; Bukhārī, *Ḥadjdj*, bāb 125); for the cutting of the hair ended, as in the case of the Israelite Nazirite, the state of consecration. The vow therefore had always more or less the character of a self-dedication. This aspect was often quite prominent. Ordinary sacred duties such as participation in the ḥadjdj were assumed as a consecration by nadhr (Sūra xxii. 29) at which special obligations were assumed e.g. to go to the sanctuary on foot, or barefooted (Bukhārī, *Djazāʾ al-ṣaid*, bāb 27; Tirmidhī, *al-Nudhūr wa 'l-aimān*, bāb 17). The sacred condition of *iʿtikāf* was assumed as a nadhr; thus before his conversion ʿUmar vowed to make a nightly *iʿtikāf* in the Meccan sanctuary (Bukhārī, *Maghāzī*, bāb 54; *Aimān*, bāb 29). Such a vow to separate oneself from everyday life in some special way was very frequent among the ancient Arabs; for Labīd (17, 17) compares an antelope buck alone among the bushes to one fulfilling his vow (*ḳāḍī 'l-nudhūr*).

This isolation had the definite object of spirutal concentration and strengthening the soul and thereby influencing the deity. Abstinence was therefore practised in preparation for great deeds, especially in war. The Arabs "touched no perfume, married no woman, drank no wine and avoided all pleasures when they were seeking vengeance, until they attained it" (*Ḥamāsa*, p. 447, v. 5 schol.) These abstentions like the ḥadjdj rites and the *iʿtikāf* are also the objects of a nadhr. The form of this vow is for example "wine and women are *ḥarām* to me until I have slain 100 Asadīs" (*Aghānī*, viii. 68; 2nd ed., p. 65). A definite term may be fixed, such as drinking no wine for 30 days in order to obtain vengeance (Ḳais b. al-Khaṭīm, ed. Kowalski, iv. 28). When a man fights well it is therefore said that he fulfils nadhr or (synonymous) *naḥb* (Sūra xxxiii, 23; Wāḳidī—Wellhausen, p. 120). Forms of abstention are refraining from meat, or all kind of food, wine, ointment, washing and sexual intercourse (*Aghānī*, vi. 99; 2nd ed. p. 97; viii. 68; 2nd ed., p. 66; xv, 161; 2nd ed., p. 154; *Ḥamāsa*, p. 237, v. 4 *sqq.*; Ibn Hishām, p. 543, 980; Wāḳidī-Wellhausen, p. 73, 94, 105, 201; 402). After a wish has been fulfilled a vow of gratitude may also be taken (Waḳīdī, p. 290).

The consecration placed the person making the vow in connection with the divine powers, the nadhr was an *ʿahd* (Sūra ix. 75; xxxiii 23; xlviii. 10), whereby he pledged himself. A neglect of the *nadhr* was a sin against the deity (Imraʾ al-Ḳais, 51, 10). The sacred obligation of living made this a nadhr which one should fulfil (*ḳaḍā*), instead of wandering aimlessly (Labīd, 41, 1). The importance of the binding pledge gradually becomes more prominent (cf. *Lisān al-ʿArab*, where *nadhara* is explained by *awdjaba*, ironically *Aṣmaʿīyāt*, 7, 2); the emphasis on the material dedication gradually became less. The abstinences mentioned get the sense on the one hand of works meritorious to the deity, on the other of unpleasant deprivations, by which the person taking the vow compels himself. This strict obligation inherent in the nadhr makes it closely related to the oath [see ḲASAM].

One can also bind one's family by a vow. A mother swears not to comb her hair or to seek shade until her son or daughter fulfils her wish (*Aghānī*, xviii. 205; 2nd ed., p. 205; Ibn Hishām, p. 319; ii. 90). The strength of this kind of "conjuration" is based on the relationship between the two partners. If a dying man vows that his tribe shall slay 50 to avenge him, this binds the tribe (*Ḥamāsa*, p. 442 *sq.*). There thus arose in Islām the problem of how far unfulfilled vows had to be fulfilled by the descendants (Muslim, *Nadhr*, trad. 1; Bukhārī, *Waṣāyā*, bāb 19; cf. Goldziher, *Zàhiriten*, p. 80).

In Islām the vow and the oath are treated together. In the Ḳurʾān it is prescribed that unconsidered expressions (*laghw*) in an oath may be broken and expiated (Sūra ii. 225; v. 91). The context shows that the reference is to vows of abstinence, especially relating to food and women. Special cases of this kind are known as *ilāʾ* and *ẓihār* [see ḲASAM]. Though it is probable in this case that we have Jewish influence, the principle of releasing oneself from a vow by doing something else is certainly also originally Arab. But with Islām comes the view that *nudhūr* are useless because they cannot influence God (Bukhārī, *Aimān*, bāb 26; *Ḳadar*, bāb 6; Muslim, *Nadhr*, trad. 2). Thus we find ḥadīths which urge the fulfilment of vows as well as those that forbid them. Following hints in the ḥadīths, we find a systematic division into vows of piety (*nadhr al-tabarrur*), which are intended to acquire merit by a pious deed (*ṭāʿa*), and vows of oaths which, since they are conditioned, serve to incite, prevent or strengthen. The latter are called *nadhr al-ladjādj wa 'l-ghaḍab*. They are deprecated but must be treated like oaths. Their matter must not be sinful; according to some, such a vow is invalid, according to others, it is valid but must be broken. Their matter must not in itself be an individual duty (*wādjib ʿainī*). The person taking the vow must, like him taking an oath, be *mukallaf* and be acting of his own free-will.

Bibliography: J. Wellhausen, *Reste arabischen Heidentums*, Berlin 1897, p. 122 *sqq.*; W. Robertson Smith, *Religion of the Semites*, ed. S. A. Cook (1927), p. 332, 481 *sqq.*; Th. W. Juynboll, *Handbuch des islamischen Gesetzes*, Leyden 1930, p. 273 *sq.*; Khalīl b. Isḥāḳ, *Mukhtaṣar*, transl. I. Guidi (1919), p. 371—383; D. Santillana, *Istituzioni di diritto Musulmano Malichita*, i., Rome 1925, p. 212—15; Johs. Pedersen, *Der Eid bei den Semiten*, Strassburg 1914, index, s.v. Gelübde; W. Gottschalk, *Das Gelübde nach älterer arabischer Auffassung*. Berlin 1919; the ḥadīth-material in Wensinck, *Handbook*, s.v. Vow.

NAḌĪR (BANU 'L-), one of the two main Jewish tribes of Madīna, settled in Yathrib from Palestine at an unknown date, as a consequence of Roman pressure after the Jewish wars. Al-Yaʿḳūbī (ii. 49) says they were a section of the Djudhām Arabs, converted to Judaism and first settled on Mount al-Naḍīr, whence their name. According to the *Sīra Ḥalabiya* (Cairo, iii. 2) they were a truly Jewish tribe, connected with the Jews of Khaibar.

This seems the more probable, but a certain admixture of Arab blood is possible; like the other Jews of Madīna they bore Arabic names, but kept aloof from the Arabs, spoke a peculiar dialect, and had enriched themselves with agriculture, money-lending, business in armour and jewels.

They were clients of the Aws, siding with them in their conflicts with the Khazradj, and entering with them into the compact with Muḥammad known as the Constitution of Madīna in 1 A.H. Their most important chief at this time was Ḥuyaiy b. Akhṭab, whose daughter Ṣafīya became Muḥammad's wife in 7 A.H. For a list of Muḥammad's worst enemies among the Banu 'l-Naḍīr see Ibn Hishām, *Sīra*, p. 351—352.

Their fortresses were half a day's march from Madīna, and they owned land in Wādī Buṭhān and Buwaira; their dwelling places were south of the city.

The Banu 'l-Naḍīr seem to have been in (commercial?) relations with Abū Sufyān before the battle of Uḥud. In 4 A.H., in Rabīʿ I, owing to difficulties about the Banu 'l-Naḍīr's contribution to certain blood-money which was being collected from the whole Muslim community in Madīna, Muḥammad, who had personally negotiated the matter with their chiefs, became convinced of their enmity towards himself and suspected them of intending to kill him. He decided to get rid of such dangerous neighbours, and ordered them through Muḥammad b. Maslama al-Awsī to leave the city within ten days, under penalty of death, allowing them to take with them all their movable goods and to return each year to gather the produce of their palm-groves.

The tribe, having no hope of help from the Aws, agreed to leave, but ʿAbd Allāh b. Ubaiy al-Khazradjī, chief of the *munāfiḳūn*, persuaded them to resist in their fortresses, promising to send 2,000 men to their aid. Ḥuyaiy b. Akhṭab, hoping the Banū Ḳuraiẓa would also help them, prepared to resist, in the face of opposition from moderate elements in the tribe.

The siege lasted about a fortnight, help from the *munāfiḳūn* was not forthcoming, and when the Muslims began to cut down their palms the Banu 'l-Naḍīr surrendered. Muḥammad's conditions were much harder than formerly; their immovable property was forfeited, and nothing left them but what they could take away on camels, arms alone excepted. After two day's bargaining the tribe departed with a caravan of 600 camels; some went to Syria, others to Khaibar.

The Banu 'l-Naḍīr's booty Muḥammad did not divide in the usual manner; the land was distributed among the *muhādjirūn* [q.v.] so as to relieve the *anṣār* [q.v.) of their maintenance; part of it the Prophet kept for himself.

The *Sūrat al-Ḥashr* (lix.) was revealed upon the expulsion of the Banū 'l-Naḍīr.

From Khaibar the exiles planned with the Ḳuraish the siege of Madīna in Dhu 'l-Ḳaʿda 5 A.H. The treasure of the Banu 'l-Naḍīr was captured by Muḥammad in Khaibar in 7 A.H.

Bibliography: Caetani, *Annali dell' Islam*, 1 A.H., § 38, 39, 58; 4 A.H., § 10—14; Ibn Hishām, p. 652—661; Nöldeke—Schwally, *Geschichte des Qorāns*, i. 206; Yāḳūt, *Muʿdjam*, ed. Wüstenfeld, i. 662—663, 756; Wensinck, *Mohammed en de Joden te Medina*, p. 22, 23 *sqq.*, 156 *sqq.*; R. Leszynski, *Die Juden in Arabien*, Berlin 1910; F. Buhl, *Das Leben Muhammeds*, p. 264 *sqq.*

AL-**NADJAF** (MASHHAD ʿALĪ), a town and place of pilgrimage in the ʿIrāḳ, 6 miles west of al-Kūfa. It lies on the edge of the desert on a flat barren eminence from which the name al-Nadjaf has been transferred to it (A. Musil, *The Middle Euphrates*, p. 35).

According to the usual tradition the Imām ʿAlī b. Abī Ṭālib [q.v.] was buried near Kūfa, not far from the dam which protected the city from flooding by the Euphrates, at the place where the town of al-Nadjaf later arose (Yāḳūt, *Muʿdjam*, ed. Wüstenfeld, iv. 760), also called Nadjaf al-Kūfa (Zamakhsharī, *Lexicon geographicum*, ed. Salverda de Grave p. 153). Under Umaiyad rule the site of the grave near al-Kūfa had to be concealed. As a result it was later sought in different places, by many in al-Kūfa itself in a corner above the *ḳibla* of the mosque, by others again 2 farsakhs from al-Kūfa (al-Iṣṭakhrī, ed. de Goeje, *BGA*, i. 82 *sq.*; Ibn Ḥawḳal, *ibid.*, ii. 163). According to a third story, ʿAlī was buried in al-Madīna near Fāṭima's grave (al-Masʿūdī, *Murūdj al-dhahab*, ed. Barbier de Meynard, viii. 289), according to a fourth, at Ḳaṣr al-Imāra (Caetani, *Annali dell' Islām*, x., 1926, p. 967 *sq.*; A.H. 40, § 99). Perhaps then the sanctuary of al-Nadjaf is not the real burial-place but a tomb held in reverence in the pre-Islāmic period, especially as the graves of Adam and Noah were also shown there (Ibn Baṭṭūṭa, *Tuḥfa*, ed. Defrémery and Sanguinetti, i. 416; G. Jacob in A. Nöldeke, *Das Heiligtum al-Husains zu Kerbelâ*, Berlin 1909, p. 38, note 1). It was not till the time of the Ḥamdānid of al-Mawṣil Abu 'l-Haidjāʾ that a large *ḳubba* was built over ʿAlī's grave, adorned with precious carpets and curtains; also a citadel was built there (Ibn Ḥawḳal, *op. cit.*, p. 163). The Shīʿī Būyid ʿAḍud al-Dawla in 368/979—980 built a mausoleum which was still in existence in the time of Ḥamd Allāh Mustawfī, and was buried there, as were his sons Sharaf and Bahāʾ al-Dawla. Al-Nadjaf was already a small town with a circumference of 2,500 paces (Ibn al-Athīr, ed. Tornberg, viii. 518; Ḥamd Allāh Mustawfī, *Nuzhat al-ḳulūb*, ed. Le Strange, p. 32: in the year 366/976—977). Ḥasan b. al-Faḍl, who died about 414/1023—24 built the defensive walls of Mashhad ʿAlī (Ibn al-Athīr, ix. 154). The Mashhad was burned in 443/1051—1052 by the fanatical populace of Baghdād, but must have been soon rebuilt. The Saldjūḳ sulṭān Malikshāh and his vizier Niẓām al-Mulk who were in Baghdād in 479/1086—1087 visited the sanctuaries of ʿAlī and Ḥusain (Ibn al-Athīr, x. 103). The Īlkhān Ghāzān (1295—1304) according to Ḥamd Allāh Mustawfī built in al-Nadjaf a Dār al-Siyāda and a dervish monastery (*khānḳāh*). The Mongol governor of Baghdād in 1263 led a canal from the Euphrates to al-Nadjaf but it soon became silted up and was only cleared out again in 1508 by order of Shāh Ismāʿīl. This canal was originally called Nahr al-Shāh (now al-Ḳenāʾ) (*Lughat al-ʿArab*, Baghdād, ii., 1930— 1931, p. 458). This Shīʿī Ṣafawid himself made a pilgrimage to the *mashhadān* of Karbalāʾ and al-Nadjaf. Sulaimān the Magnificent visited the holy places in 941/1534—1535. A new canal made in 1793 also soon became silted up, as did the Zerī al-Shaikh and al-Ḥaidarīya canals, the latter of which was made by order of ʿAbd al-Ḥamīd II. In 1912 iron pipes were laid to bring water from the Euphrates to al-Nadjaf (*Lughat al-ʿArab*, ii. 458 *sq.*, 491).

According to the Arab geographers, al-Ḥīra lay on the eminence of al-Nadjaf (al-Yaʿḳūbī, *Kitāb al-buldān*, ed. de Goeje, *BGA* vii. 309). Massignon thinks (*MIFAO*, xxviii. 28, note 1) that al-Ḥīra lay on the site of the present al-Nadjaf, while Musil

(*The Middle Euphrates*, p. 35, note 26) places the centre of the ruins of al-Ḥīra S.E. of the *tell* of al-Knēdre which lies halfway between al-Kūfa and al-Khawarnaḳ. Ibn Baṭṭūṭa entered Mashhad ʿAlī, which he visited in 726/1326, through the Bāb al-Ḥadra which led straight to the Mashhad. He describes the town and sanctuary very fully. According to al-Yaʿḳūbī (*loc. cit.*), the ridge on which al-Nadjaf stands once formed the shore of the sea which in ancient times came up to here. For the number of its inhabitants and its architectural beauty, Ibn Baṭṭūṭa reckoned the town among the most important in the ʿIrāḳ. It has now about 20,000 inhabitants (Persians and Arabs), has a Shīʿī college and celebrated cemetery in the Wādī al-Salām. Near al-Nadjaf were the monasteries of Dair Mār Fāthyūn (Yāḳūt, *Muʿdjam*, ii. 693) and Dair Hind al-Kubrā᾽ (Yāḳūt, ii. 709), also al-Ruhba (5 hours S.W. of the town; Yāḳūt, ii. 762; Musīl, *The Middle Euphrates*, p. 110, note 61) and Ḳaṣr Abi ᾿l-Khaṣīb (Yāḳūt, iv. 107). The lake of al-Nadjaf marked on many older maps has long since completely dried up (Nolde, *Reise nach Innerarabien*, p. 105).

Bibliography: Ibn al-Athīr, *Kāmil*, ed. Tornberg, index, vol. ii., p. 808 (*Mashhadʿ ʿAlī*), 817 (*al-Nadjaf*); al-Ṭabarī, ed. de Goeje, Indices, p. 784; Abu ᾿l-Faradj al-Iṣfahānī, *Kitāb al-aghānī* Būlāḳ 1323, ii. 116; v. 88, 121; viii. 161; ix 117; xi. 24; xxi. 125—127; al-Iṣṭakhrī, *BGA* i. 82; Ibn Ḥawḳal, *BGA* iii. 163; al-Maḳdisī, *BGA* iii. 130; Ibn al-Faḳīh, *BGA* v. 163, 177, 187; Ibn Rusta, *BGA* vii. 108; al-Yaʿḳūbī, *BGA* vii. 309; Abu ᾿l-Fidā᾽, ed. Reinaud, p. 300, transl. Guyard, II/ii. 73; al-Idrīsī, *Nuzha*, iii. 6; Ibn Djubair, ed. de Goeje, p. 210; Yāḳūt, *Muʿdjam*, ed. Wüstenfeld, iv. 760; al-Bakrī, *Muʿdjam*, ed. Wüstenfeld, p. 164, 302, 354, 364, 573; Ibn Baṭṭūṭa, *Tuḥfa*, ed. Defrémery-Sanguinetti, i. 414—416; Ḥamd Allāh Mustawfī al-Ḳazwīnī, *Nuzhat al-ḳulūb*, ed. Le Strange, p. 9, 31, 165 *sq.*, 267; Niebuhr, *Reisebeschreibung nach Arabien u.a. umliegenden Ländern*, Copenhagen 1778, ii. 254—264 (inscriptions: 263); J. B. L. J. Rousseau, *Description du pachalik de Bagdad*, Paris, 1809, p. 75—77; Nolde, *Reise nach Innerarabien*, Braunschweig 1895, p. 103—111; M. v. Oppenheim, *Vom Mittelmeer zum Persischen Golf*, Berlin 1900, ii. 137, 274, 281; G. Le Strange, *The Lands of the Eastern Caliphate*, Cambridge 1905 [repr. 1930), p. 76—78; A. Nöldeke, *Das Heiligtum al-Husains zu Kerbelâ*, Berlin 1909 (= *Türk. Bibl.*, xi.), *passim*; H. Grothe, *Geographische Charakterbilder aus der asiatischen Turkei*, Leipzig 1906, p. xiii and table lxxv.—lxxix. with illustr. 132—134, 137; L, Massignon, *Mission en Mesopotamie* (1907—1908). Cairo 1910, i. 50—51; ii. 88, note, 1, 114, 138, note (= *MIFAO*, xxviii, xxxi.); G. L. Bell, *Amuraᵗʰ to Amurath*, London 1911, p. 160, 162; St. H. Longrigg, *Four Centuries of Modern Iraq*, Oxford 1925, index, p. 372 (*Najf*); A. Musil, *The Euphrates*, New York 1927, p. 35, note 26 (= *American Geographical Society, Oriental Explorations and Studies*, no. 3); D. M. Donaldson, *The Shi᾽ite Religion*, London 1933, p. 54 *sqq.*

AL-**NADJDJĀR**, AL-ḤUSAIN B. MUḤAMMAD ABŪ ʿABD ALLĀH, a Murdji᾽ī and Djabarī theologian of the period of al-Ma᾽mūn, a pupil of Bishr al-Marīsī, whose views were combatted by Abu ᾿l-Hudhail al-ʿAllāf and al-Naẓẓām. He probably lived in Bamm where he was a weaver. According to him, the divine attributes are identical with the essence and express its negative aspects. Vision of God is only possible through a divine act which transforms the eye into a heart by giving it the power of recognition. The word of God is created, accident when it is read, body when it is written. God who knows from all eternity all worldly things, wills them all, good as well as evil, faith as well as unbelief. God has a hidden essence (theory of *māhīya*); there is in him a hidden fund of grace (*luṭf*) which would suffice to bring all the infidels back to him. Problems of the body and accidents: atom = accident; the body then consists of a conglomerate of accidents (= Ḍirār) which are in juxtaposition without interpenetrating one another (against the *mudākhala* of al-Naẓẓām); momentariness of the accidents. This orientation of the problem is due to the theocentric tendencies of al-Nadjdjār. All that takes place in the world comes from the incessant and unrestrained activity of God, beside whom there is neither reality nor agent. God creates the actions of man. He gives his assistance to every good action and shows his desertion of every bad one; this assistance and desertion constitute the faculty of doing which accompanies the action (*al-istiṭāʿa maʿa ᾿l-fiʿl*, against the Muʿtazila). The activity of man consists in his appropriation of the divine will (*kasb*). Man carries out one action only by one *istiṭāʿa*: the secondary effects (*al-muwalladāt*) do not depend on man but on God (against the Muʿtazila theory of *tawallud*). Faith consists in the knowledge of God, of his apostles and his commandments and in the profession of this knowledge by the mouth. Faith consists of several qualities (*khiṣāl*), each of which is an act of obedience (*ṭāʿa*); complete faith is the sum of all *ṭāʿāt*. Faith may increase but not diminish; it can be completely lost only through unbelief. He who commits a heinous sin and dies impenitent is doomed to hell, from which he will emerge however, unlike the complete infidel. Al-Nadjdjār denied the punishment of the tomb (*ʿadhāb al-ḳabr*), probably as a result of his determinism. — Al-Nadjdjār like his master Bishr represents the reformed and modified Djahmīya. The influence of Muʿtazila theology on this school is manifest; on the other hand, the Muʿtazila itself, especially that of Baghdād, seems to have received certain quite important stimuli from his school in spite of its opposition to it. Several of al-Nadjdjār's doctrines are found at a later date in al-Ashʿarī,. — The Nadjdjārīya flourished in Raiy and Gurgān. It was divided into three schools: 1. the Burghūthīya, the followers of Muḥammad b. ʿĪsā Burghūth; 2. the Zaʿfarānīya, the followers of a certain Abū ʿAbd Allāh b. al-Zaʿfarānī; 3. the Mustadrika, a reforming party which taught paradoxical doctrines on the divine word.

Bibliography: *al-Fihrist*, ed. Flügel, p. 179 (with a list of his writings); al-Maḳdisī, *BGA*, iii. 37—38, 126, 365, 394—395; al-Samʿānī, *Ansāb*, fol. 554; al-Khaiyāṭ, *Kitāb al-Intiṣār*, ed. Nyberg, s. index; al-Ashʿarī, *Maḳālāt al-Islāmīyin*, ed. Ritter, s. index; al-Baghdādī, p. 195—198, 201; al-al-Shahrastānī, p. 61—63; A. S. Tritton, *Muslim Theology*, London 1947, p. 71 *sqq.*; W. M. Watt, *Free will and predestination in early Islam*, p. 106 *sqq.*

NADJIS (A.), impure, opp. *ṭāhir*, cf. ṬAHĀRA. According to the Shāfiʿī doctrine, as systematized by al-Nawawī (*Minhādj*, i. 36 *sqq.*; cf. Ghazzālī, *al-Wadjīz*, i. 6 *sq.*), the following are the things impure in themselves (*nadjasāt*): wine and other spirituous drinks, dogs, swine, *maita*, blood and excrements; milk of animals whose flesh is not eaten.

Regarding these groups the following may be remarked. On wine and other spirituous drinks cf.

the artt. KHAMR and NABĪDH. — Dogs are not declared impure in the Ḳur'ān; on the contrary, in the description of the sleepers in Sūra xviii. the dog is included (verses 18, 22). In *ḥadīth*, however, the general attitude against dogs is very strong, as may be seen in the art. KALB. Goldziher considers this change due to an attitude of conscious contrast (*mukhālafa*) to the estimate of dogs in Parsism. It must not, however, be forgotten that the Jews also declared dogs impure animals, just as swine. The latter are already declared forbidden food in the Ḳur'ān (Sūra xvi. 115; vi. 146; v. 3; ii. 173). — As to *maita*, cf. the article. — Blood is mentioned in the Ḳur'ān (Sūra xvi. 115; vi. 146; v. 3; ii. 173) as prohibited food. As to the religious background of this prohibition cf. the art. MAITA. — As for excrements and several kinds of secretions of the body, the theory and practice of Jews and Christians sufficiently explain the attitude of Islām in this respect. It must also be admitted, though data are very scarce, that in early Arabia religious impurity included some of these things. — Details are to be found in the large legal works of each of the *madhhabs* (cf. *Bibl.*).

Of the differences of the schools regarding this subject the most important only may be mentioned. Spirituous drinks are not impure according to the Ḥanafīs [cf. NABĪDH]. Living swine are not impure according to the Mālikīs. — The Shī'a adds to the things mentioned above the human corpse and the infidels. The human corpse was one of the chief sources of impurity according to Jewish ideas (cf. already *Numbers*, ch. xix.). A current in early Islām tending to follow the Jewish customs in ceremonial law was very strong; the Shī'ī view regarding the human corpse may be a residuum of it. — The impurity of infidels is based upon Sūra ix. 28, where the polytheists are declared to be filth (*nadjas*). The Sunnī schools do not follow the Shī'a in the exegesis of this verse.

The *nadjāsāt* enumerated above cannot be purified, in contradistinction to things which are defiled only (*mutanadjdjis*), with the exception of wine, which becomes pure when made into vinegar, and of hides, which are purified by tanning. On purification cf. the artt. ṬAHĀRA, GHUSL., WUḌŪ'.

Bibliography: *al-Fatāwā al-'Ālamgīrīya*, Calcutta 1828, i. p. 55—67; al-Marghīnānī, *Kifāya*, Bombay 1863, i. p. 15 *sqq.*, 41; Khalīl b. Isḥāḳ, *Mukhtaṣar*, Paris 1318 (1900), p. 3 *sqq.*; transl. I. Guidi, Milan 1919, i. p. 9—12; al-Ghazzālī, *al-Wadjīz*, Cairo 1317, i. 6 *sq.*; al-Nawawī, *Minhādj al-ṭālibīn*, Batavia 1882, i. p. 36 *sqq.*; al-Ramlī, *Nihāya*, Cairo 1304, i. 166 *sqq.*; Ibn Ḥadjar al-Haitamī, *Tuḥfa*, Cairo 1282, i. 71 *sqq.*; 'Abd al-Ḳādir b. 'Umar al-Shaibānī, *Dalīl al-ṭālib*, with comm. by Mar'ī b. Yūsuf, Cairo 1324—1326, i. 11 *sqq.* (Ḥanbalī); Abu 'l-Ḳāsim al-Muḥaḳḳiḳ, *Sharā'i' al-islām*, Calcutta 1255, i. 92 *sqq.*; A. Querry, *Recueil de lois concernant les musulmans schyites*, Paris 1871, i. p. 42 *sqq.*; al-Sha'rānī, *Mīzān*, Cairo 1279, i. 123—128; Th. W. Juynboll, *Handleiding tot de kennis d. mohammedaansche wet*, Leyden 1925, p. 56, 165 *sq.*; Goldziher, *Die Ẓāhiriten*, p. 61 *sqq.*; do., *Islamisme et Parsisme*, in *RHR*, xliii. 17 *sqq.*; do., *Lā misāsa*, in *RA*, 1908, No. 268, p. 23 *sqq.*; A. J. Wensinck, *Die Entstehung der muslimischen Reinheitsgesetzgebung*, in *Isl.*, v. 62 *sqq.*; do., *Handbook*, s.v. Dogs.

NĀFI' B. AL-AZRAḲ AL-ḤANAFĪ AL-ḤANẒALĪ, Abū Rāshid, according to some sources the son of a freed blacksmith of Greek origin (Balādhurī, ed. de Goeje, p. 56), chief of the extreme Khāridjites [q.v.], who after him are called Azraḳites. At first, after his secession to Ahwāz, Nāfi' joined 'Abd Allāh b. al-Zubair in Mecca. Soon, however, he and his followers turned their backs on the holy city and arrived before Baṣra, where they spread terror among the inhabitants, who left the town in multitudes. Al-Muhallab however succeeded in driving them back to Persia. They made a halt in Ahwāz, where they practised *isti'rāḍ*, in keeping with their doctrine. The bloody battle of Dūlāb, fought against Muslim b. 'Ubais, put an end to his life (64 or 65/683—684).

His special doctrine comprised the following points: 1. secession (*barā'a*) from the quietists (*al-ḳa'ada*); 2. examination (*miḥna*) of those who wanted to join his encampment; 3. declaring infidels those who did not perform *hidjra* to him; 4. declaring it allowed to kill the wives and children of opponents (*isti'rāḍ*). This is al-Ash'arī's enumeration, which differs slightly from that of al-Shahrastānī (p. 90).

Bibliography: al-Ash'arīk, *Maḳālāt al-Islāmiyīn*, ed. Ritter, Istanbul 1929, p. 86 *sqq.*; 'Abd al-Ḳāhir al-Baghdādī, p. 62—67; Ibn Ḥazm, iv. 189; al-Shahrastānī, ed. Cureton, p. 89—91; al-Ṭabarī ed. de Goeje, indices, s.v.; Ahlwardt, *Anonyme arabische Chronik*, p. 78 *sqq.*, 90 *sqq.*; Balādhurī, ed. de Goeje, p. 56; Abū Ḥanīfa al-Dīnawarī, ed. Guirgass and Kratchkovsky, p. 279, 282, 284; Mas'ūdī, *Murūdj*, v. 229; Yāḳūt, ed. Wüstenfeld, ii. 574, 623; al-Mubarrad, *al-Kāmil*, ed. Wright, index, s.v. (p. 943); Ibn al-Athīr, *Kāmil*, ed. Tornberg, index, s.v.; al-Ya'ḳūbī, ed. Houtsma, ii. 317, 324; M. Th. Houtsma, *De strijd over het dogma in den Islam*, Leyden 1875, p. 28 *sq.*; Wellhausen, *Die religiös-politischen Oppositionsparteien*, in *Abh. G. W. Gött.*, N.S., v. 2, 1901, p. 28 *sq.*, 32; R. E. Brünnow, *Die Charidschiten unter den ersten Omaiyaden*, Leyden 1884; Caetani, *Chronographia islamica*, p. 762; G. Weil, *Geschichte der Chalifen*, index, s.v.

NĀFILA (A.), plur. *nawāfil*, part. act. fem. I from *n-f-l*, supererogatory work.

1. The word occurs in the Ḳur'ān in two places. Sūra xxi. 72 runs: "And we bestowed on him [viz. Ibrāhīm] Isaac and Jacob as additional gift" (*nāfilat^an*). In Sūra xvii. 79 it is used in combination with the vigils, thus: "And perform vigils during a part of the night reciting the Ḳur'ān, as a nāfila for thee".

In *ḥadīth* it is frequently used in this sense. "Forgiveness of sins past and future was granted him [Muḥammad] and his works were to him as supererogatory works" (Aḥmad b. Ḥanbal, vi. 250). — In another tradition it is said with reference to the month of Ramaḍān, that Allāh "writes down its reward and its *nawāfil* even before its beginning" (Aḥmad b. Ḥanbal, ii. 524). Of peculiar importance, also in a different respect is the following *ḥadīth ḳudsī*: "When My servant seeks to approach to Me through superogatory works, I entirely love him. And when I love him I become the hearing through which he heareth, the sight through which he seeth, the hand with which he graspeth, the foot with which he walketh" etc. (al-Bukhārī, *Riḳāḳ*, bāb 38).

Finally the following tradition may be translated: "Whoso performs the *wuḍū'* [q.v.] in this way [viz. in the way described in the foregoing part of the tradition] receives forgiveness of past sins, and his *ṣalāt* and his walking to the mosque are for him as a nāfila" (Muslim, *Ṭahāra*, trad. 8; Mālik, *Ṭahāra*, trad. 30). In the parallel tradition (Muslim, *loc. cit.*, trad. 7), the term used is *kaffāra* "expiation". — This parallelism is an indication of the effect ascribed to supererogatory works in Muslim theology, viz. the expiation of light sins (cf. al-Nawawī on Muslim, Cairo 1283, i. 308).

Further in the theological terminology the term nāfila is often applied to works which are supererogatory in the plain sense of the word, in contra-distinction to other works which have become a regular practice. These latter are called *sunna mu'akkada*, the former *nāfila* or *sunna zā'ida* (cf. *infra*, sub 2).

The place of superogatory works in theology is defined in the *Waṣīyat Abī Ḥanīfa*, art. 7 in the following way: "We confess that there exist three categories of works: obligatory, supererogatory and sinful works. The first category is in accord with Allāh's will, desire, pleasure, decision, decree, creation, knowledge, guidance and writing on the Preserved Table. The second category is not in accord with Allah's commandment, but in accord with His will, desire" etc.

The term designing supererogatory works in the above citation is not nāfila but *fāḍila*.

2. In *ḥadīth* nāfila denotes in the first place supererogatory ṣalāt (Bukhārī, *ʿĪdain*, b. 11; *Tahadjdjud*, b. 5, 27). Often it is found in combinations such as *ṣalāt al-nāfila* (Ibn Mādja, *Iḳāma*, b. 203) and *ṣalāt al-nawāfil* (Bukhārī, *Tahadjdjud*, b. 36). In *fiḳh* we find this terminology often, not always; another term denoting the supererogatory *ṣalāts* is *ṣalāt al-taṭawwuʿ* (e.g. Abū Isḥāḳ al-Shīrāzī, ed. Juynboll, p. 26), an expression which goes back to the Ḳur'ān (Sūra ii. 158, 184; ix. 79) and occurs also in canonical *ḥadīth* (Abū Dāwud has a *kitāb al-taṭawwuʿ* in his *Sunan*). The whole class of supererogatory *ṣalāt*'s is called *nawāfil* and also *sunan*. *Nawāfil*, as a general designation of supererogatory *ṣalāts* has three subdivisions. The following table gives a survey of the terminology:

Nawāfil (*Fatāwī ʿĀlamgīrīya*, i. 156, Ḥanafī)	*sunna* / *mandūba* / *taṭawwuʿ*
Sunan (Fagnan, *Additions*, p. 23, Mālikī)	*mu'akkada* / *raghība* / *nāfila*
Nawāfil (Khalīl, transl. Guidi, p. 95, Mālikī)	*sunna* / *mu'akkada* / *mandūba*
Nāwafil, (Ghazzālī, *Iḥyā'*, i. 174, Shāfiʿī)	*sunna* / *mustaḥabba* / *taṭawwuʿ*

It may be added that the term *rawātib* is used especially for the supererogatory *ṣalāts* preceding or following the *maktūba*; they belong to the first subdivision.

In Shīʿī *fiḳh* nawāfil is the widest term; by *muraghghabāt* the daily and non-daily supererogatory prayers are designated.

Bibliography: *Waṣīyat Abī Ḥanīfa*, Ḥaidarābād 1321, p. 8—10; Sell, *The Faith of Islam*, London 1888, p. 199; Wensinck, *The Muslim Creed*, Cambridge 1931, p. 126, 142 *sqq.*; Th. W. Juynboll, *Handleiding tot de kennis v. d. Moh. wet*, Leyden 1925, p. 382 *sq.*; al-Ghazzālī, *Iḥyā' ʿulūm al-dīn*, Cairo 1302, i. 174 *sqq.*; al-Nawawī, *Minhādj al-ṭālibīn*, Batavia 1882, i. 121 *sqq.*; Khalīl b. Isḥāḳ, *Mukhtaṣar*, transl. I. Guidi, Milan 1919, i., p. 20, note 55; p. 95; Fagnan, *Additions aux dictionnaires arabes*, Algiers-Paris 1923, s.v.; Abu 'l-Ḳāsim al-Muḥaḳḳiḳ, *Kitāb sharā'iʿ al-islām*, Calcutta 1255, i. 25, 51; transl. Querry, i. 49 *sq.* 52 *sq.*, 100 *sqq.* Further the artt. KHAṬĪ'A; ṢALĀT III.

NAFS (A.), soul. Nafs, in the early Arabic poetry, is used reflexively to refer to the self or person, while *rūḥ* meant breath and wind. Beginning with the Ḳur'ān nafs also means soul, and rūḥ means a special angel messenger and a special divine gift. Only in post-Ḳur'ānic literature are nafs and *rūḥ* used interchangeably and both applied to the human spirit, angels and *djinn*.

I. The Ḳur'ānic uses. *A*. Nafs and its plurals *anfus* and *nufūs* have two uses: 1. Reflexive: *a*. In most cases they refer to the human self or person, e.g., iii. 61: "Let us call... ourselves and yourselves"; also xii. 54; li. 20, 21. *b*. In six verses nafs refers to Allāh: v. 116*b*: "Thou [Allāh] dost know what is in myself [says ʿĪsā], but I do not know what is in Thyself (*nafsika*)"; also iii. 26, 30; vi. 12, 54 and xx. 41. *c*. One reference, xxv. 3 (cf. xiii. 16), is to gods: "They [*āliha*] do not possess for themselves (*anfusihim*) any harm or benefit at all!" *d*. in vi. 130 the plural is used twice to refer to the company of men and *djinn*: "We have witnessed against ourselves (*anfusinā*)". 2. It means the human soul: vi. 93: "While the angels stretch forth their hands [saying], Send forth your souls (*anfus*)"; also l. 16; lxiv. 16; lxxix. 40, etc. This soul has three characteristics: *a*. It is *ammāra*, commanding to evil (xii. 53). Like the Hebrew *nefesh* the basal idea is "the physical appetite", in Pauline usage ψυχή, and in the English New Testament "flesh". It whispers (l. 16), and is associated with *al-hawā*, which, in the sense of "desire", is always evil. It must be restrained (lxxix. 40) and made patient (xviii. 28) and its greed must be feared (lix. 9*b*). *b*. The nafs is *lawwāma*, i.e., it upbraids (lxxv. 2); the souls (*anfus*) of deserters are straitened (ix. 118). *c*. The soul is addressed as *mutma'inna*, tranquil (lxxxix. 27). These three terms form the basis of much of the later Muslim ethics and psychology. It is noteworthy that nafs is not used in connection with the angels (cf. R. Blachère, *Notes sur le substantif „nafs" dans le Coran*, in *Semitica* i, 1948).

B. Rūḥ has five uses: 1. Allāh blew (*nafakha*) of His rūḥ, *a*. into Adam, giving life to Adam's body (xv. 29; xxxviii. 72; xxxii. 9), and *b*. into Maryam for the conception of ʿĪsā (xxi. 91 and lxvi. 12). Here rūḥ equates with *rīḥ* and means the "breath of life" (cf. *Gen*. ii. 7), the creation of which belongs to Allāh. 2. Four verses connect rūḥ with the *amr* of Allāh, and the meanings of both rūḥ and *amr* are disputed. *a*. In xvii. 85, it is stated: "They ask thee [O Muḥammad] about al-rūḥ; say: *al-rūḥ min amr rabbī*, and ye are brought but little knowledge". *b*. In xvi. 2. Allāh sends down the angels with *al-rūḥ min amrihi* upon whomsoever He wills of His creatures to say: "Warn that the fact is, There is no God but Me, so fear". *c*. In xl. 15, Allāh "casts *al-rūḥ min amrihi* upon whomsoever He wills of His creatures to give warning". *d*. In xlii. 52: "We revealed (*awḥainā*) to thee [O Muḥammad] *rūḥan min amrinā*; thou knewest not what the book was, nor the faith, but We made it to be a light by which We guide whomsoever We will of Our creatures". Whatever meanings *amr* and *min* may have, the contexts connect al-rūḥ in *a*. with knowledge; in *b*. with angels and creatures, to give warning; in *c*. with creatures, for warning, and in *d.* with Muḥammad, for knowledge, faith, light and guidance. Therefore this rūḥ is special equipment from Allāh for prophetic service. It reminds forcibly of Bezalel, who was "filled with the spirit of God in wisdom, in understanding and in knowledge" (*Exodus* xxxv. 30, 31). 3. In iv. 171, ʿĪsā is called a rūḥ from Allāh. 4. In xcvii. 4, lxxviii. 38 and lxx. 4, al-rūḥ is an associate of the angels. 5. In xxvi. 193, *al-rūḥ al-amīn*, the faithful rūḥ, comes down upon Muḥammad's heart to reveal the Ḳurʾān. In xix. 17, Allāh sends to Maryam "Our rūḥ", who appears to her as a well-made man. In xvi. 102, *rūḥ al-ḳudus* sent the Ḳurʾān to establish believers. Three other passages state that Allāh helps ʿĪsā with *rūḥ al-ḳudus* (ii. 87; ii. 253 and v. 110). This interrelation of service and title imply the identity of this angelic messenger, who may be also the rūḥ of 4. Thus in the Ḳurʾān rūḥ does not mean angels in general, nor man's self or person, nor his soul or spirit. The plural does not occur.

C. Nafas, breath and wind, cognate to nafs in root and to rūḥ in some of its meanings, does not occur in the Ḳurʾān, but is used in the early poetry (F. Krenkow, *The Poems of Ṭufail and aṭ-Ṭirimmāḥ*, London 1927, p. 32). The verb *tanafassa* (Sūra lxxxi. 18) is derived from that meaning, while the only other Ḳurʾānic forms from the same radicals are *falyatanāfasi 'l-mutanāfisūn* (lxxxiii. 26) and are derived in al-Ṭabarī, *Djāmiʿ al-baiyān*, Cairo 1321, xxx. 57, probably correctly, from *nafisa*, "he desired".

II. The poetry of the Umaiyad period first uses rūḥ for the human soul (*Kitāb al-aghānī*, ed. 1285, xvi. 126, last line; Cheikho, *Le Christianisme*, Bairūt 1923, p. 338) where the Ḳurʾān had used nafs as in No. 2 above.

III. Of the early collections of traditions, Mālik's *al-Muwaṭṭaʾ*, *Ṭalāḳ*, 95 uses *nasama*, which does not occur in the Ḳurʾān, and nafs (ed. Cairo 1339, ii. 262) for the soul or spirit, while Ibn Ḥanbal's *Musnad* uses *nasam* (vi. 425), nafs (i. 297; ii. 364; vi. 140) and nafs and rūḥ (iv. 287, 296). Muslim's *al-Ṣaḥīḥ* (Constantinople 1331), viii. 44, 162 *sq.* and al-Bukhārī's *al-Ṣaḥīḥ*, Cairo 1314, iv. 133, both use rūḥ and *arwāḥ* for the human spirit. Cf. further *CTM* s.v.

IV. The *Tādj al-ʿArūs* (iv. 260) lists 15 meanings for nafs and adds two others from the *Lisān al-ʿArab*, as follows: spirit, blood, body, evil eye, presence, specific reality, self, tan, haughtiness, self-magnification, purpose, disdain, the absent, desire, punishment, brother, man. It states that most of these meanings are metaphorical. The *Lisān* (viii. 119—126) finds examples of these meanings in the poetry and the Ḳurʾān. Lane's *Lexicon* faithfully reproduces the material (p. 2827*b*). The lexical treatments of nafs disclose these facts: 1. Any attribution to Allāh of nafs as "soul" or "spirit" is avoided. 2. In man, *a.* nafs and rūḥ are synonymous, or *b.* nafs applies to the mind and rūḥ to life, or *c.* man has *nafsāni*, two souls, one vital and the other discriminative, or *d.* the discriminative soul is double, sometimes commanding and sometimes forbidding.

V. The influences that affected the post-Ḳurʾānic uses of both nafs and rūḥ were the Christian and Neo-Platonic ideas of rūḥ with human, angelic and divine applications, and the more specifically Aristotelian psychological analysis of nafs. Al-Kindī is the one who introduced the Neo-Platonic doctrine of the soul into the earliest Arabic philosophy. He revised ʿAbd al-Masīḥ al-Nāʿima's translation of the treatise called "The Theology of Aristotle", which quotes and paraphrases Books iv—vi of the *Enneads* of Plotinus. Here the Muslims were taught the theory of the emanation of the human soul from the One Absolute Cause, first through the Spirit or Intelligence and then through the Universal Soul to which it belongs. Man's soul is thus an immortal spiritual or intelligible substance. Its salvation consists in freeing itself from the corporeal stains of the sensible world and returning to the eternal world of spiritual substances. This is the theory of the soul's origin, nature and destiny which underlies the later Muslim mysticism.

The doctrines of the soul and spirit that influenced the Muslims are clearly shown in the records of the religious controversies.

A. Al-Ashʿarī (H. Ritter, *Die dogmatischen Lehren der Anhänger des Islam von Abu 'l-Ḥasan ʿAlī bin Ismāʿīl al-Aśʿarī*, Istanbul 1929) reports the Rāfiḍīya doctrines of the incarnation of *rūḥ Allāh* in Adam and its transmigration through the prophets and others (p. 6, 46), as well as the conflicting positions that man is body (*djism*) only, body and spirit, and spirit (rūḥ) only (p. 61, 329 *sqq.*). His creed of the orthodox (p. 290—297) omits any statement about the nature of man.

B. Al-Baghdādī [q.v.] (*al-Farḳ bain al-firaḳ*, Cairo 1328) records the same heretical doctrines about man's nature (p. 28, 117 *sqq.*, 241 *sqq.*), says the transmigration theories were held by Plato and the Jews (p. 254) and describes the incarnation beliefs of the Ḥulūlīya sects [cf. ḤULŪL] among whom he includes the Ḥallādjīya (p. 247). His position is: "The life of Allāh is without rūḥ and nourishment and all the *arwāḥ* are created, in opposition to the Christian doctrine of the eternity of the Father, Son and Spirit" (p. 325).

C. Ibn Ḥazm [q.v.] uses nafs and rūḥ interchangeably of man's soul (*Kitāb al-faṣl fi 'l-milal*, 5 parts, Cairo 1317—1321; v. 66). He excludes from Islām all who hold metempsychosis views, among whom he includes the physician-philosopher Muḥammad b. Zakarīyāʾ al-Rāzī (i. 90 *sqq.*; iv. 187 *sq.*). He rejects absolutely the doctrine of some of the Ashʿarīya of the continual re-creation of the rūḥ (iv. 69). He taught that Allāh created the spirits of all Adam's progeny before the angels were commanded to prostrate to him (Sūra vii. 171), and that these spirits exist in al-Barzakh [q.v.] in the nearest heaven until the angel blows them into embryos (iv. 70).

D. Al-Shahrastānī [q.v.] (*Kitāb al-milal wa 'l-niḥal*, ed. Cureton, part. i., London 1842) in his description of the belief of the pagan Arabs concerning survival after death does not use the terms nafs or rūḥ, but says the blood becomes a wraith bird that visits the grave every hundred years. One of his most important sections (p. 203—240) deals with the orthodox and heterodox doctrines of al-rūḥ. Al-Ḥunafāʾ, or true believers, debate with al-Ṣābiʾa [q.v.], who are dualists, emanationists and gnostics. His account of the views of the Ṣābiʾa faithfully reflects the doctrines of the Ikhwān al-Ṣafāʾ (*Rasāʾil*, 4 vols., Bombay 1305), who taught that man is a whole compounded of a corporeal body and a spiritual nafs (I/II., 14), and that the substance (*djawhar*) of the nafs descended from the spheres (*al-aflāk*). He applies the term *rūḥānī* to all spirits, good and evil (p. 213). His description of the nature of man (p. 216 *sqq.*) with three souls, vegetative, animal and human, each with its own source, need, place and powers, resembles that of the Ikhwān al-Ṣafāʾ (*Rasāʾil*, I/II., 48 *sqq.*). But al-

Shahrastānī rejects the Neo-Platonic idea that human souls (*nufūs*) are dependent upon the souls of the superhuman spirit world (*al-nufūs al-rūḥānīyāt*) (p. 210, 224 *sq.*), and the Hermetic doctrines that the *nafs* is essentially evil (p. 236) and that salvation consists in the release of the rūḥ from material bodies (p. 226 *sq.*). Indeed, the Aristotelian analysis of the human soul as given in *De Anima*, and handed on by Alexander of Aphrodisias and Porphyry, had been adopted with little modification by the Arabic philosophers, such as al-Kindī, al-Fārābī, each of whom wrote a *Kitāb al-nafs*, Ibn Sīnā who wrote two, and Ibn Miskawaih, whose *Tahdhīb al-akhlāḳ* has the same immaterial (p. 1) and functional (p. 7) psychology for its ethical basis. Al-Shahrastānī achieved the long needed interpretation of the conflicting usages of nafs and rūḥ in the Greek and Christian heritage, and in the Ḳurʾān and Muslim tradition. But the philosophers, even with his support, were not able to force the Greek psychology upon orthodox Islām. The *Mutakallims* [s. art. KALĀM] and the great majority of Muslims broadened the Ḳurʾānic terminology, but retained the traditional views of the nature of the soul as a direct creation of Allāh having various qualities.

VI. Aristotle's principle of the incorporeal character of spirit had nevertheless found a permanent place in Muslim doctrine through the influence of Islām's greatest theologian, al-Ghazzālī [q.v.]. In al-Tahānawī's *Dictionary of the Technical Terms* (ed. Sprenger, Calcutta 1862) are extracts of the doctrines of al-Ghazzālī on man's rūḥ and nafs. He defines man as a spiritual substance (*djawhar rūḥānī*), not confined in a body, nor imprinted on it, nor jointed to it, nor separated from it, just as Allāh is neither without nor within the world, and likewise the angels. It possesses knowledge and perception, and is therefore not an accident (p. 547 at top; cf. *Tahāfut al-falāsifa*, Cairo 1302, p. 72). He devotes the second section of *al-Risāla al-laduniya* (Cairo 1327, p. 7—14) to explain the words nafs, rūḥ and ḳalb (heart), which are names for this simple substance that is the seat of the intellectual processes. It differs from the animal rūḥ, a refined but mortal body in which reside the senses. He identifies the incorporeal rūḥ with *al-nafs al-muṭmaʾinna* and *al-rūḥ al-amrī* of the Ḳurʾān. He then uses the term nafs also for the "flesh" or lower nature, which must be disciplined in the interests of ethics.

VII. This position of al-Ghazzālī's was that of the theistic philosophers in general, as well as some of the Muʿtazila and the Shīʿa, but it has never dominated Islām. The great analytical philosopher and theologian, Fakhr al-Dīn al-Rāzī, could not bring himself to accept it. In his *Mafātīḥ al-ghaib*, v. 435, commenting on Sūra xvii. 87, he quotes as the opinion of al-Ghazzālī the statement that is in the latter's *Tahāfut* (p. 72; cf. also al-Rāzī's *Muḥaṣṣal*, Cairo 1323, p. 164), but on p. 434 (l. 9 and 8 from below) of the *Mafātīḥ* he acknowledges the strength of the corporeal doctrine, and in his *Maʿālim uṣūl al-dīn*, on the margin of the *Muḥaṣṣal*, p. 117 *sq.*, he definitely rejects as baseless (*bāṭil*) the view of the philosophers that the *nafs* is a substance (*djawhar*) which is not a body (*djism*) and not corporeal.

VIII. Al-Baiḍāwī's [q.v.] system of cosmogony and psychology is given in his *Ṭawāliʿ al-anwār* (lithograph ed. with commentary of Abu 'l-Thanāʾ al-Iṣfahānī and glosses by al-Djurdjānī, Istanbul 1305, p. 285 *sqq.*). He discusses 1. The classes of incorporeal substances, 2. the heavenly intelligences, 3. the souls of the spheres, 4. the incorporeality of human souls, 5. their creation 6. their connection with bodies and 7. their survival. His cosmogony follows: Allāh, because of his unity, created only one Intelligence (*ʿaḳl*). This Second Intelligence, that emanated first (*al-ṣādir*) from Allāh, is the cause (*ʿilla*) of all other potentialities and is not body (*djism*), nor original matter (*hayūlī*) nor form (*ṣūra*). It is the secondary cause (*sabab*) of another intelligence with soul (*nafs*) and sphere (*falak*). There emanates from the second a third intelligence and so on to the tenth (p. 288) who is the rūḥ of Sūra lxxviii. 38 (cf. al-Baiḍāwī's *Anwār al-tanzīl*, ed. Fleischer, ii. 383, l. 4) whose effective influence is in the world of the elements and who is the producer of the spirits (*arwāḥ*) of mankind. Below these intelligences are the high or heavenly angels, which the philosophers call *al-nufūs al-falakīya*, and the low *nufūs*, which are in two classes: earthly angels, in control of the simple elements and the earthly souls, such as the reasoning souls (*anfus nāṭiḳa*) controlling particular persons. In addition (p. 285) there are the incorporeal substances, without effect or control, who are angels, some good (*al-kurūbīyūn*) and some evil (*al-shayāṭīn*) and the *djinn*, who are ready for both good and evil. This is the classification he refers to in his comment on Sūra ii. 28 (= 26; ed. Fleischer, i. 47). His psychology resembles that of al-Ghazzālī, whom he mentions (p. 294). For the incorporeality of the soul (*tadjarrud al-nafs*) he presents five arguments from reason, four Ḳurʾān verses and one tradition. His commentator remarks (p. 300) that these prove only that the soul differs from the body. He then argues that all *nufūs* are created when their bodies are completed. The nafs (p. 303) is not embodied in and is not close to the body, but is attached as the lover to the beloved. It is connected with that rūḥ which comes from the heart and is generated of the finest nutritive particles. The reasoning nafs produces a force that flows with that rūḥ through the body, producing in every organ its proper functions. These functional powers are perceptive, which are the five external senses, and the five internal faculties of the *sensus communis*, imagination, apprehension, memory and reason, and the active (*al-muḥarrika*) which are voluntary (*ikhtiyārīya*) and natural (*ṭabīʿīya*, p. 308).

IX. The dominant Muslim doctrine concerning the origin, nature and future of al-rūḥ and al-nafs is most fully given in the *Kitāb al-rūḥ* of Ibn Ḳaiyim al-Djawzīya (Ḥaidarābād, second ed., 1324). Of his 21 chapters Ibn al-Ḳaiyim devotes the 19th to the problem of the specific nature of the nafs (p. 279—342). He quotes the summaries given by al-Ashʿarī (*op. cit.*, p. 331—335), and by al-Rāzī (*Mafātīḥ al-ghaib*, v. 431—434). He denies al-Rāzī's statement that the *mutakallims* consider man to be simply the sensible body, and says all intelligent people hold man to be both body and spirit. The rūḥ is identified with the nafs, and is itself a body, different in quiddity (*al-māhiya*) from this sensible body, of the nature of light, high, light in weight, living, moving, interpenetrating the bodily members as water in the rose. It is created, but everlasting; it departs temporarily from the body in sleep; when the body dies it departs for the first judgement, returns to the body for the questioning of Munkar and Nakīr, and, except in the cases of prophets and martyrs, remains in the grave foretasting bliss or punishment until the Resurrection. He rejects (p. 256) Ibn Ḥazm's doctrine that Adam's progeny are in al-Barzakh awaiting their time to be blown into embryos. He presents 116 evidences for the corporeality of the rūḥ, 22 refutations of opposing arguments and 22 rebuttals of objections. He represents traditional Islām.

X. The earlier Ṣūfīs had accepted the materiality of the rūḥ. Both al-Ḳushairī [q.v.] (*al-Risāla*, with commentary of Zakarīyā' al-Anṣārī and gloss of al-ʿArūsī, Būlāḳ 1290, ii. 105 *sqq.*) and al-Hudjwīrī (*Kashf al-maḥdjūb*, ed. Nicholson, London 1911, p. 196, 262) call the rūḥ a fine, created substance (*ʿain*) or body (*djism*), placed in the sensible body like sap in green wood. The nafs (*al-Risāla*, p. 103 *sqq.*; *Kashf al-maḥdjūb*, p. 196) is the seat of the blameworthy characteristics. All together make the man.

In addition to the philosophical position of the immateriality of al-rūḥ that al-Ghazzālī had made orthodox, another interpretation of spirit developed which is essentially theosophical. Ibn al-ʿArabī [q.v.] (H. S. Nyberg, *Kleinere Schriften des Ibn al-ʿArabī*, Leyden 1919, p. 15, 11 *sqq.*) divides "things" into three classes: Allāh, Who is Absolute Being and Creator, the world, and an undefinable *tertium quid* of contingent existence that is joined to the Eternal Reality and is the source of the substance and the specific nature of the world. It is the universal and common reality of all realities. Man likewise is an intermediate creation, a *barzakh* (p. 22, 42) between Allāh and the world, bringing together the Divine Reality and the created world (p. 21, 42) and a vicegerent connecting the eternal names and the originated forms (p. 96). His animal spirit (*rūḥ*) is from the blowing of the divine breath (p. 95) and his reasoning soul (*nafs nāṭiḳa*) is from the universal soul (*al-nafs al-kullīya*), while his body is from the earthly elements (p. 95 *sq.*). Man's position as vicegerent (p. 45 *sq.*) and his resemblance to the divine presence (p. 21) come from this universal soul, which has various other names, holy spirit (*rūḥ al-ḳudus*), the first intelligence (p. 51), vicegerent (*khalīfa*), the perfect man (p. 45) and the rūḥ of the world of command (*ʿālam al-amr*), which al-Ghazzālī held to be Allāh's direct creation (p. 122). In his *Fuṣūṣ* (lithograph ed. with commentary by al-Ḳāshānī, Cairo 1309, p. 12 *sqq.*) he says that Allāh appears to Himself in a form which thus becomes the place of manifestation of the Divine essence. This place receives a rūḥ, who is Adam, the *khalīfa* and the perfect man. He discusses (Nyberg, *op. cit.*, p. 129 *sqq.*) the essence and properties of the rūḥ, quoting among others the view he says is "attributed" to al-Ghazzālī which is in *al-Tahāfut* (as above). He finds the differences of doctrine harmless since all agree that the rūḥ is originated. In his tractate on the nafs and rūḥ (M. Asín Palacios, *Tratado acerca del Conocimiento del Alma y del Espiritu*, in *Actes du XIVème Congrès international des Orientalistes*, Paris 1906, iii. 167—191) he describes how men may reach the distinction of "the perfect man" through the cultivation of the qualities of the rūḥ and the suppression of the nafs.

Ibn al-ʿArabī's contemporary, the poet Ibn al-Fāriḍ (Nicholson, *Studies in Islamic Mysticism*, Cambridge 1921, chap. iii.), at times identifies his own rūḥ with that from which all good emanates (*al-Tā'iya al-kubrā*, on margin of his *Dīwān*, Cairo 1319, ii. 4 *sq.*) and with the "pole" (*ḳuṭb*) upon which the heavens revolve (p. 113, 115). Al-Ḳāshānī, the commentator of *al-Tā'īya*, explains that this identity is with the greatest spirit (*rūḥ al-arwāḥ*) and the greatest "pole". The compiler of the commentaries on the *Dīwān* states (ii. 196) that incarnation (*ḥulūl*) and identification (*ittiḥād*) with Allāh are impossible, but there is real "passing away" (*fanā'*) and union (*waṣl*) of the rūḥ and nafs in the *nafs* of Allāh, for His nafs is their nafs.

ʿAbd al-Karīm al-Djīlānī [q.v.] carries this position of existential monism on to straight animistic pantheism. In *al-Insān al-kāmil* [q.v.] (Cairo 1334) the terms *rūḥ al-ḳudus*, *rūḥ al-arwāḥ* and *rūḥ Allāh* stand for a special one of the aspects of the Divine Reality (*al-Ḥaḳḳ*), not to be embraced under the command "be" nor created. This spirit is the divine aspect in which stand the created spirits of all existences or beings, sensible and intelligible (p. 94). Existence itself subsists in the nafs of Allāh, and His nafs in His Essence (*dhāt*). Moreover, every sensible thing has a created spirit (rūḥ) (p. 94). One of the aspects of the angel of Sūra xlii. 52, who is named the command (*amr*) of Allāh, and who is an aspect of Allāh as above, is given to the rūḥ of Muḥammad, which is identified as the rūḥ mentioned in the verse. That angelic and divine rūḥ thereby becomes the Idea (*ḥaḳīḳa*) of Muḥammad (p. 95 *sq.*) and he thereby becomes the "perfect man" (p. 96, 131 *sqq.*). The rūḥ which is the specific nature of the human nafs has five names: animal, commanding to evil, instinctive (*al-mulhama*), reproving, and tranquil. When the divine qualities actually describe the nafs, then the names, qualities and essences of the gnostic (*ʿārif*) are those of the One Known (*Maʿrūf*) (p. 130 *sq.*).

XI. In geomancy (*ʿilm al-raml*) the first "house" (*bait*) of the *ummāhat* is called nafs because it guides to problems concerning the soul and spirit of the inquirer, and to the beginning of affairs (Muḥammad al-Zanātī, *Kitāb al-faṣl fī ʿilm al-raml*, Cairo n. d., p. 7; cf. Henr. Corn. Agrippae, *Opera*, Lyons, n.d., but early xvii[th] cent., p. 412: *Nam primus domus personam tenet quaerentis*).

Bibliography: In addition to the references in the article see especially D. B. Macdonald, *The Development of the Idea of Spirit in Islam*, in *Acta Orientalia*, 1931, 307—351 (reprinted in *MW*, 1932, 25—42, 153—168) upon which much of the present article is based; Muslim philosophical psychology goes back to Aristotle's *De Anima* (best ed. by R. D. Hicks, Cambridge 1907); for the early metempsychosis beliefs see I. Friedländer, *The Heterodoxies of the Shiites* etc., in *JAOS*, xxviii. 1—80; xxix. 1—183; for the relation between Aristotle and Ibn Sīnā see S. Landauer, *Die Psychologie des Ibn Sînâ*, in *ZDMG*, xxix. 335—418; English trans. by A. E. van Dyck, Verona 1906; F. Rahman, *Avicenna's Psychology*, Oxford 1952; M. Horten, *Die philosophischen Systeme im Islam*, Bonn 1912; T. J. De Boer, *The History of Philosophy in Islam*, London 1903.

NAKĪR. [See MUNKAR].

NAḲSHBAND, MUḤAMMAD B. MUḤAMMAD BAHĀ' AL-DĪN AL-BUKHĀRĪ (717—791/1317—1389), founder of the Naḳshbandī Order. His name, which signifies "painter" is interpreted as "drawing incomparable pictures of the Divine Science" (J. P. Brown, *The Darvishes*, 2nd ed., p. 142) or more mystically as "holding the form of real perfection in the heart" (*Miftāḥ al-maʿīya* quoted by Ahlwardt, Berlin Catalogue, No. 2188). The title *al-Shāh* which is given him in a dirge cited in the *Rashaḥāt* means "spiritual leader". The *nisba* al-Uwaisī implies that his system resembled that of Uwais al-Ḳaranī. His *Acta* were collected by one of his adherents, Ṣalāḥ b. al-Mubārak in a work called *Maḳāmāt Saiyidinā al-Shāh Naḳshband*, which furnished material to the author of *Rashaḥāt ʿain al-ḥayāt* (893/1488), and from which large citations, apparently in the words of Naḳshband himself, but translated from Persian into Arabic, are given in the modern work *al-Ḥadā'iḳ al-wardīya fī ḥaḳā'iḳ adjillā' al-Naḳshbandīya* by ʿAbd al-Madjīd b. Muḥammad al-Khānī (Cairo 1306). He was born in a village at the distance of one *farsakh* from Bukhārā, called Kushk Hinduwān, but afterwards Kushk ʿĀrifān. At the age of 18 he was sent to Sammās, a village one mile from Ramīthan and three from Bukhārā, to learn Ṣūfism from Muḥammad Bābā al-Sammāsī. In this person's system the *dhikr* was recited aloud; Naḳshband preferred that of ʿAlā al-Dawla ʿAbd al-Khāliḳ al-Ghudjdawānī (d. 575 A.H.), who recited it to himself; and this led to ill-feeling between him and the other adherents of al-Sammāsī, who however, it is stated, ultimately confessed that Naḳshband was right, and on his deathbed appointed him his *khalīfa*. After this person's death he went to Samarḳand, and thence to Bukhārā, where he married, and whence he returned to his native village; thence he went to Nasaf, where he continued his studies under a *khalīfa* of al-Sammāsī, Amīr Kulāl. He then lived for a time in villages near Bukhārā given as Zewartūn and Anbīkta, then studied with a *khalīfa* of Amīr Kulāl named ʿĀrif al-Dīk-kirānī for seven years; after this he spent twelve years in the service of the Sulṭān Khalīl, whose rise to sovereignty is described by Ibn Baṭṭūṭa (iii. 49), and whose capital appears to have been Samarḳand. After this monarch's fall (747/1347) he returned to Zewartūn, where he practised philanthropy and the care of animals for seven years, and roadmending for another seven. The last years of his life appear to have been spent in his native village, where according to the *Rashaḥāt* he was buried. Vámbéry (*Travels in Central Asia*, 1864) gives Baveddin, two leagues from Bukhārā, as the name of the village which contains his tomb, "whither pilgrimages are made even from the most remote parts of China, while it was the practice in Bukhārā to go thither every week, intercourse with the metropolis being maintained by means of some 300 asses plying for hire".

The biographies bring him into connection with various places and persons. At Herāt a banquet was given in his honour by the Amīr Ḥusain (b. Ghiyāth al-Dīn al-Ghūrī; cf. Ibn Baṭṭūṭa, *loc. cit.*), where in spite of the Amīr's assertion that the food had been honestly obtained Naḳshband refused it, and it had to be given away in charity. He was with this prince also at Sarakhs. Two or three pilgrimages and visits to Baghdād, Naisābūr and Tāyābād are mentioned. His sayings were collected by Muḥammad b. Muḥammad al-Ḥāfiẓī al-Bukhārī at the request of ʿAlā' al-Din ʿAṭṭār al-Bukhārī (d. 802 A.H.) (Brit. Mus. Add. 26294). Persian writings by him are mentioned in the *Ḥadā'iḳ*.

Bibliography: Besides those mentioned above: *Nafaḥāt al-uns*, No. 442; *al-Shaḳā'iḳ al-nuʿmānīya*, transl. Rescher, p. 165.

NĀḲŪS (A.), pl. *nawāḳīs*, a kind of rattle used and in some parts still used by Christians in the east to summon the community to divine service. It is a board pierced with holes which is beaten with a rod. The name, which comes from the Syriac *nāḳōshā*, is not infrequently found with the verbs *ḍaraba* or *ṣakka* in the old Arabic poets especially when early morning is to be indicated, e.g. ʿAntara, app.; Labīd, No. 19, 6; *ZDMG*, xxxiii. 215; Mutalammis, ed. Vollers, p. 178, v. 6; al-Aʿshā in Nöldeke's *Delectus*, p. 26; *Kitāb al-aghānī*, xix. 92. According to tradition, Muḥammad hesitated between this instrument and the Jewish trumpet before deciding on the call to prayer by the mu'adhdhins [s. ADHĀN].

Bibliography: Paine Smith, *Thesaurus Syriacus*, col. 2466; Fraenkel, *Die aramäischen Fremdwörter*, p. 276; G. Jacob, 6. *Jahresbericht d. geogr. Gesellsch. zu Greifswald*, 1896, p. 4; do., *Altarabisches Beduinenleben*, 1897, p. 22, 233; Ibn Hishām, ed. Wüstenfeld, p. 346 *sqq.*; Ibn Saʿd, ed. Sachau, III/ii. 87.

NAMRŪD, also NAMRŪDH, NIMRŪD, the Nimrod of the Bible, is associated in Muslim legend, as in Haggada, with the story of the childhood of Abraham. The Ḳur'ān, it is true, does not mention him but probably, as in many other cases, only from dislike of mentioning names. That Muḥammad was acquainted with the legend of Namrūd is evident from the following verse "Do you not see how he disputed with Ibrāhīm about the Lord who had granted him dominion? When Ibrāhīm said: It is my Lord who gives life and death, the other replied: I give life and I slay. When Ibrāhīm said: God makes the sun rise in the east; do you make it rise in the west; then the liar was humbled" (ii. 258). The Ḳur'ān exegists are probably right when they see Namrūd here disputing with Ibrāhīm. The Ḳur'ān alludes also to the legend, that N. would punish Ibrāhīm for his refusing to adore his idols or to adore N. himself as divinity; N. threw him in the fire. "They (the adherents of N.) said: burn him and save your gods, if you will not rest idle; and we (God) said: fire, become cool, peace with Ibrāhīm" (xxi. 68, 69); "What did Ibrāhīm's people answer? They only said: kill him, burn him; but God saved him from the fire (xxix. 24); "They (the adherents of N.) said: make for him a building (a pile of fuel) and cast him in the glowing flame" (xxxvii. 97).

The legend of the construction of the tower to assault heaven, ordinarily connected with N., is in the Ḳur'ān transposed to Firʿawn and Hāmān: Firʿawn charges his counsellor Hāmān to construct the heaven-reaching tower (xxviii. 38, xl. 36, 37).

The legend is already richly developed in Ṭabarī, but it is at the beginning of the romance of ʿAntar in the Abraham midrāsh that we find its most luxurious development.

Ṭabarī already numbers Namrūd among the three or (with Nebuchadnezzar) four kings who, like Sulaimān b. Dāwūd and Dhu 'l-Ḳarnain, ruled the whole world. His astrologers told him that a child would be born who would overthrow his kingdom and destroy his idols. Ibrāhīm thus becomes one of those heroes of legend who are persecuted from the moment of birth by a tyrant, to whom they are destined to prove fatal. Ūsha, the wife of Āzar or Tārikh (Terakh), is able to deceive N. and his seachers. Ibrāhīm is born in concealment; maturing rapidly, he engages in a religious dispute with Namrūd; N. cannot be God, for God gives life and death. N. replies that he can do this also for he can execute or pardon a man condemned to death. N. has Ibrāhīm thrown into the fire; it becomes a cool health-resort. An angel keeps Ibrāhīm cool at which N. marvels like Nebuchadnezzar at the preservation of the three young men in the fiery furnace (Daniel iii. 24 *sq.*). N. resolves to attack the God of Ibrāhīm in his heaven. He feeds four young eagles on meat and wine till they are of a great size, ties them to the four corners of a chest, fastens a spear at each corner with a piece of meat on the point and sits in the chest; the eagles, trying to reach the meat, fly higher and higher. The mountains appear like antheaps and later the whole world looks like a ship in the water. It is in vain however for he falls to earth. Next he builds a tower in order to reach the god of Ibrāhīm, then the tongues are confused; in place of one Syriac tongue, 73 arose. God's angels admonish Namrūd. But he equips his armies against God. God sends an army of gnats against him, who eat the flesh and drink the blood of Namrūd's men. A gnat enters Namrūd's brain through his nose. For 400 years he had exercised his tyrannical rule and for 400 years he was tortured by the gnat until he died.

Muslim legend derives the name Namrūd from *tamarrada*: he who rebelled (against God). But there is another derivation, viz. from *namra* "tigress" in that version of the N. legend in which Namrūd is suckled by a tigress. This version resembles the Romulus and Remus story (Jean de l'Ours) and culminates in the Oedipus story, for Namrūd, brought up unknown, kills his father and marries his mother. Al-Kisā'ī has preserved this version and it is given at greater length in the introduction to the romance of ʿAntar.

Namrūd's father Kanaʿān b. Kūsh has a dream which troubles him; it is interpreted to mean that his son will kill him. The child is born, a snake enters his nose, which is an ominous sign. Kanaʿān wants to kill the child, but his mother Sulkhā' entrusts him secretly to a herdsman; the latter's flocks scatter at the sight of the black flat-nosed infant. The shepherd's wife throws the child into the water; the waves wash him to the bank where he is suckled by a tigress. Already dangerous when quite a boy, as a young man he becomes a robber leader, attacks Kanaʿān with his band, kills him (without knowing that he is killing his father), marries his own mother and becomes king of the country and later lord of the world. Āzar (already in the Ḳur'ān the father of Ibrāhīm) builds him a marvellous palace flowing with milk, oil and honey, with mechanical singing birds — in the mediaeval epic the wonderful feature of the Chrysotriklinium in Byzantium. The lore of astrology, the inheritance of Idrīs and Hermes, he acquires by force from the pupils of Idrīs. Iblīs teaches him magic. He has himself worshipped as a god. Then dreams, voices, omens frighten him. In spite of all Namrūd's cruel orders, Ibrāhīm is born, brought up and soon shatters the belief in Namrūd. N. throws those who believe in God to the wild animals but they do not touch them. He denies them food; the sand of the desert becomes corn for them; on every grain of it is written: "gift of God". N. throws Ibrāhīm into the fire but he is unharmed. N. builds up a pile of fuel, the flames of which burn the birds for miles round — it is impossible to approach it. Iblīs then designs a ballista which hurls Ibrāhīm on to the flaming pile. Ibrāhīm spends the finest days of his life there under blooming trees and amid rippling brooks. N. then decides to attack the God of Ibrāhīm in heaven. Starved eagles fly up with his litter, until he hears a voice saying the first heaven is 500 years in width, it is 500 years between heaven and heaven, then comes infinity. N. shoots an arrow against God; the arrow comes back stained with blood. N. suddenly becomes grey and old and falls to the ground. But he plumes himself on having slain God. Then a gnat puts an end to his life.

The history of the Namrūd legend. Very little can have been taken from the Bible. Ḳur'ān expositors and collectors of legends call Namrūd *djabbār* (tyrant) no doubt after the *gibbor* applied to Namrūd in the Bible (Gen. x. 6); Geiger also sees in *djabbār ʿanīd* (xi. 62) an allusion to Namrūd. Ṭabarī (i. 217) also describes Namrūd as a *mutadjabbir*. Muslim legend and Haggada (*Targ. Sheni* on Esther I, i.; *Midr. Hagādōl*, ed. Schechter, p. 180—181; Gaster, *Example of the Rabbis*, N. I) make Namrūd ruler of the world. From Haggada comes the association of N. with the Tower of Babel and in particular with the childhood of Abraham, and with the latter's rescue from the fire (*Gen. Rabba*, xlix., 1). The death of Namrūd caused by the gnat is also based on Haggada, which makes Titus, the destroyer of the Temple, die in this way; Nebuchadnezzar comes to a similar end (see Grünbaum, *Neue Beiträge*, p. 97—99). The flight to heaven especially in the romance of ʿAntar with the intervals of 500 years recall the ascent of Nebuchadnezzar in the Talmud (*Chagiga*, p. 13ᵃ). But the flight has far more resemblance to that of Shāh Kai-Kā'ūs as described by Firdawsī (ed. Mohl, ii. 31—34). The Namrūd legend borrows from many directions. Ṭabarī mentions that N. had been identified as the Persian Ḍaḥḥāk (*Annales*, i. 253) but he refutes this idea (*Annales*, i. 323, 324). Bible, Haggada and Persian epic were further developed, the marvels increased, an early history invented, N. made an Oedipus, and in the *Sīrat ʿAntar* he becomes the hero of a romance. The Muslim Namrūd legend then found its way into the late Jewish legend of Abraham. Bernard Chapira (see below) has published one such in Hebrew and Arabic. He is certainly wrong in taking seriously the authorship of Kaʿb al-Aḥbār; this is one fiction out of many thousands. But the mutual influence of Haggada and Muslim legend is indisputable. The later *Midrāsh*, as M. Grünbaum has clearly shown, *Pirke R. Elieser, Tanna de bē Eliyahu, Midrāsh Haggādōl, Sēfer haiyāshār, Shēbeṭ Mūsār* of R. Eliyah Hakkohen from Smyrna, is influenced in the sections on Abraham and Nimrod by Muslim literature.

Bibliography: The commentaries on Sūra ii. 260; xxix. 23; Ṭabarī, ed. de Goeje, i. 217, 219, 220, 252—265, 319—325; Ibn al-Athīr, *Ta'rīkh*, i. 29, 37—40; Thaʿlabī *Ḳiṣaṣ al-anbiyā'*, Cairo 1325, p. 46—49; al-Kisā'ī, *Ḳiṣaṣ al-anbiyā'*, ed. Eisenberg, i. 141; *Sīrat ʿAntar*, Cairo 1291, i. 9—79 (1306, i. 4—34); Damīrī, *Ḥayāt al-ḥayawān*, s.v. *nasr*; Geiger, *Was hat Mohammad...*², 1902, p. 112 *sq.*, 115 *sq.*, 121; M. Grünbaum, *Neue Beiträge*, p. 90—99, 125—132; Bernard Chapira, *Légendes bibliques attribuées á Kab el-ahbar*, in *REJ*, 1919, lxix. p. 86—107, Arabic and Hebrew text 1920, lxx. 37—44; B. Heller, *Die Bedeutung des arabischen ʿAntar-Romans für die vergl. Litteraturkunde*, Leipzig 1921, p. 16—21; S. Sidersky, *Les origines des légendes musulmanes*, Paris 1933, p. 31—35; Speyer, *Die bibl. Erzählungen im Qoran*, 1931, p. 116—118, 263, 283, 356, 475, 477.

NĀR. [See DJAHANNAM].

AL-**NASAFĪ**, *nisba* of several eminent persons of whom the following may be mentioned:

I. ABU 'L-MUʿĪN MAIMŪN B. MUḤAMMAD B. MUḤAMMAD... B. MAKḤŪL... AL-ḤANAFĪ AL-MAKḤŪLĪ (d. 508/1114), one of the *mutakallimūn* whose scholastic position is between that of the early period as represented by ʿAbd al-Ḳāhir al-Baghdādī [q.v.], who is still endeavouring to find a convenient arrangement and an adequate formulation of the contents of *kalām*, and the younger mutakallims who have at hand the necessary formulas for ready use. His best known works are:

1. *Tamhīd li-ḳawāʿid al-tawḥīd* (Cairo, MS. 2417, fol. 1—30; cf. *Fihrist... Miṣr*, ii. 51), a treatise in which the contents of the creed are proved according

to the scholastic method. The first chapter consists of an exposition of the doctrine of cognition, the last of the doctrine of the imāmate. The work closes with a *murshida* which contains the doctrina de Deo in an abridged form; 2. *Tabṣirat al-adilla* (Cairo, MSS. 2287, 6673; cf. *Fihrist... Miṣr*, ii. 8), an elaborate work on dogmatics of nearly the same scheme as the *Tamhīd*; 3. *Baḥr al-kalām*, printed at Cairo 1329 (1911), differs from the two foregoing works in so far as it deals with heresies and is polemical. It is identical with *Mubāhathat ahl al-sunna wa 'l-djamā'a ma'a 'l-firaḳ al-ḍālla wa 'l-mubtadi'a* (Leyden, cod. or. 862). The work is preserved in several libraries under one of these titles (Brockelmann, *GAL*, i. 547, *Suppl.* i. 757).

Bibliography: in the art.; cf. also Ḥādjdjī Khalīfa, ed. Flügel, index, No. 6453.

II. ABŪ ḤAFṢ 'UMAR NADJM AL-DĪN (d. 537/1142), jurist and theologian. Of his works the only one edited is the *'Aḳā'id*, which has the form of a catechism. It became popular and was much commented, probably because it was the first abridged form of the creed according to the scholastic method of the new orthodoxy. In Europe it became known as early as 1843 through the edition by Cureton (*The Pillar of the Creed*, No. 2).

Bibliography: Brockelmann, *GAL*, i. 548, *Suppl.* i. 758—760, and the references given there.

III. ḤĀFIẒ AL-DĪN ABU 'L-BARAKĀT 'ABD ALLĀH B. AḤMAD B. MAḤMŪD, an important Ḥanafī legist and theologian, born in Nasaf in Sogdiana, was a pupil of Shams al-A'imma al-Kardarī (d. 642/1244—1245), Ḥamīd al-Dīn al-Ḍarīr (d. 666/1267—1268) and Badr al-Dīn Khwāherzāde (d. 651/1253). He taught in the Madrasa al-Ḳuṭbīya al-Sulṭānīya in Kirmān, came in 710 to Baghdād and died in Rabī' I 710/August 1310 (according to Ḳurashī and Ibn Taghrībirdī: 701) apparently on his way back to Īdhadj (in Khūzistān), where he was buried. His pupils were Muẓaffar al-Dīn Ibn al-Sā'ātī, author of the *Madjma' al-baḥrain* (d. 694/1294—1295), and Ḥusām al-Dīn al-Sighnāḳī, a commentator on the *Hidāya* (d. 714/1314—1315).

The best of his works is thought to be the *Kitāb al-manār fī uṣūl al-fiḳh*, a concise account of the foundations of law; there are numerous later commentaries but he himself wrote two, one of which is entitled *Kashf al-asrār* (2 vols., Būlāḳ, 1316). Out of his original plan of writing a commentary on the *Hidāya* of al-Marghīnānī there came the lawbook modelled on it *Kitāb al-wāfī*, on which he composed in 684 a special commentary, the *Kitāb al-kāfī* (delivered in lectures in Kirmān in 689). He had previously prepared a synopsis of the *Wāfī* entitled *Kanz al-daḳā'iḳ* (Cairo 1311, Lucknow 1294, 1312, etc.) which Ibn al-Sā'ātī in 683 (this is no doubt the correct reading for 633 in Kaffawī) heard him deliver in Kirmān. This synopsis was used as late as the xixth century in Damascus and at al-Azhar in Cairo (v. Kremer, *Mittel-Syrien u. Damaskus*, Vienna 1853, p. 136; do., *Ägypten*, Leipzig 1863, ii. 51). The best known printed commentaries on the *Kanz* are: *a. Tabyīn al-ḥaḳā'iḳ* of al-Zaila'ī (d. 743/1342—1343) in 6 vols., Būlāḳ 1313—1315; *b. Ramz al-ḥaḳā'iḳ* of al-'Ainī (d. 855/1451) in 2 vols. Būlāḳ 1285 and 1299; *c. Tabyīn al-ḥaḳā'iḳ* of Mollā Miskīn al-Harawī (written in 811/1408—1409), Cairo 1294, 1303, 1312; *d. Tawfīḳ al-raḥmān* of al-Ṭā'ī (d. 1192/1778), Cairo 1307 etc.; *e.* the most important: *al-Baḥr al-rā'iḳ* of Ibn Nudjaim (d. 970/1562—1563) in 8 vols., Cairo 1334.

He also wrote a series of commentaries, e.g. two on the *Kitāb al-nāfi'* of Nāsir al-Dīn al-Samarḳandī (d. 656/1258) entitled *al-Mustaṣfā* and *al-Manāfi'*; on the *Manẓūma* of Nadjm al-Dīn Abū Ḥafṣ al-Nasafī (d. 537/1442—43) on the differences of opinion between Abū Ḥanīfa, his two pupils, and al-Shāfi'ī and Mālik entitled *al-Mustaṣfā*, as well as a synopsis entitled al-*Muṣaffā* (finished on 20th Sha'bān 670); cf. Brockelmann, *GAL*, i. 550; also on the *Muntakhab fī uṣūl al-dīn* of Akhsīkatī (d. 644/1246—1247; Ibn Taghrībirdī, Ḥādjdjī Khalīfa, No. 13095). On the other hand, he did not write a commentary on the *Hidāya*, as Ibn Ḳuṭlūbughā and Ḥādjdjī Khalīfa, vi. 484 say (cf. the story of the origin of his *Wāfī* according to al-Itḳānī (d. 758/1357) in Ḥādjdjī Khalīfa, vi. 419). He also wrote a commentary on the Ḳur'ān, *Madārik al-tanzīl wa-ḥaḳā'iḳ al-ta'wīl* (printed in 2 vols., Bombay 1279, Cairo 1306, 1326).

In his confession of faith *al-'Umad fī uṣūl al-dīn* (apparently also called *al-Manār fī uṣūl al-Dīn*: Ḳurashī, Ibn Duḳmāḳ) he closely follows the *'Aḳīda* of Nadjm al-Dīn al-Nasafī (see above) and also wrote a special commentary on it; *al-I'timād fi 'l-i'tiḳād*.

Bibliography: The following biographies borrow from the same unknown source: al-Ḳurashī, *al-Djawāhir al-muḍī'a*, Ḥaidarābād 1332, i. 270; Ibn Duḳmāḳ, *Naẓm al-djumān fī ṭabaḳāt aṣḥāb al-nu'mān*, Ms. Berlin Pet, ii. 24, fol. 147r; Ibn Ḳuṭlūbughā, *Tādj al-tarādjim*, ed. Flügel, Leipzig 1862, No. 86; Ibn Taghrībirdī, *al-Manhal al-ṣāfī*, Ms. Paris, Bibl. Nat., Arabe 2071, fol. 16r. Also al-Kaffawī, *I'lām al-akhyār*, Ms. Berlin, Sprenger, 301, fol. 282r—283v (extract: al-Laknawī, *al-Fawā'id al-bahīya*, Cairo 1324, p. 101); Ḥādjdjī Khalīfa, *Kashf al-ẓunūn*, ed. Flügel, index; Flügel, *Classen d. hanafit, Rechtsgelehrten*, Leipzig 1860, p. 276, 323, where the date of death is wrongly given; Brockelmann, *GAL*, ii. 250 *sqq.*; *Suppl.* ii. 263—268; Sarkīs, *Dictionnaire de bibliogr. arabe*, col. 1852 *sq.*; Nicolas P. Aghnides, *Mohammedan theories of finance*, New York 1917, p. 176, 181.

AL-NASĀ'Ī ABŪ 'ABD AL-RAḤMĀN AḤMAD B. SHU'AIB B. 'ALĪ B. BAḤR B. SINĀN, author of one of the six canonical collections of traditions [cf. ḤADĪTH], d. 303/915. Very little is known about him. He is said to have made extensive travels in order to hear traditions, to have settled in Egypt, afterwards in Damascus, and to have died in consequence of ill-treatment to which he was exposed at Damascus or, according to others, at Ramla, in consequence of his feelings in favour of 'Alī and against the Umaiyads. On account of this unnatural death he is called a martyr. His tomb is at Mecca. Al-Nasā'ī's collection of traditions has been used in editing the *CTM*. It is divided into 51 chapters, each of which is subdivided into *bābs*. As to the subjects, considerable space is given to traditions dealing with the ceremonial duties (*'ibādāt*); the chapters *iḥbās*, *nuḥl*, *ruḳbā* and *'umrā* (forms of bequest, donation etc.) do not occur in any of the other collections, although a part of the materials contained in them appears under different heads. On the other hand, chapters on eschatology (*fitan*, *ḳiyāma*, etc.), on hero-worship (*manāḳib* etc.), on the Ḳur'ān are lacking.

Brockelmann (*GAL*, i. 170; *Suppl.* i. 269 *sq.*). mentions two other works by al-Nasā'ī: *Fī faḍl 'Alī*, published at Cairo 1308, under the title *Kitāb Khaṣā'iṣ amīr al-mu'minīn 'Alī b. Abī Ṭālib*, and *Kitāb al-Ḍu'afā'*; lith. Agra 1323; Allāhābād 1325, as an appendix to Bukhārī, *al-Ta'rīkh al-ṣaghīr*).

Bibliography: Ibn Khallikān, No. 28; al-Dhahabī, *Ṭabaḳāt al-ḥuffāẓ*, ii. 266 *sqq.*; Ibn Ḥadjar al-ʿAsḳalānī, *Tahdhīb al-tahdhīb*, Ḥaidarābād 1325, i. 36 *sqq.*; al-Samʿānī, *Kitāb al-ansāb*, *GMS*, xx. fol. 559; Goldziher, *Muhammedanische Studien*, ii. 141, 249 *sqq.*; do., in *ZDMG*, l. 112; Wüstenfeld, *Der Imam el-Schâfiʿi und seine Anhänger*, in *Abh. GW Gött.*, xxxvii. 108 *sq.*

NAṢĀRĀ (A.), Christians, especially members of the eastern churches living under Muslim rule.

A. Before Islām.

Little is known of the early history of Christianity in Arabia. It spread naturally from Syria and al-ʿIrāḳ but its history really begins with the conversion of Ghassān. Al-Ḥārith b. Djabala was an ardent monophysite and in A.D. 542 or 543 he persuaded the empress to appoint bishops in Edessa and Buṣrā. Nestorian Christianity came early to Ḥira where a monastery was built in A.D. 410; a bishop is recorded in the same year. Al-Mundhir III (d. 554) was a pagan though he had a Christian wife and some of the notables were also Christian. Religious strife in the Greek empire drove monophysite exiles to Ḥīrā; in A.D. 518 they had a monastery, and a bishop is recorded in 551. The Nestorians converted al-Nuʿmān c. 593. Their missions followed the trade routes. Bishops are recorded in ʿUmān in 424 and in the district of Baḥrain in 575. Two stories say that Nadjrān was evangelized from Ḥīrā and a third brings the missionary from Syria, probably before 400. The Abyssinians conquered south Arabia early in the sixth century. As soon as they had withdrawn, a Jewish chief attacked and persecuted the Christians in Nadjrān and Ḥadramawt. A second expedition defeated him and established Abyssinian rule. Probably this was part of Greek policy with regard to Persia and crusading motives were secondary. When the Persians conquered south Arabia they favoured the Nestorians; there was a bishop of Ṣanʿā' as late as *c.* 800. From the borders Christianity filtered through into the interior. There were bishops at Aila, Dūma, and Taimā', and most of the tribes of the north had some knowledge of the faith; it is said that drinking wine was all they knew of the faith.

B. Under Islām (the middle ages).

1. History. At first Muḥammad favoured the Christians as shown by Ḳur'ān ii, 62; v. 69 and xxii. 17, where they are praised together with the Jews and the Ṣābians. Later he turned against them, probably as a result of his contact with Christian states. He attacked their belief that Masīḥ was God's son (ix. 30) and points to the division of the Christians amongst themselves (v. 14). The Christian dogma of the Trinity is especially denounced. (iv. 17 and v. 73) Muḥammad's relation with the Christians of Nadjrān is, according to the commentaries, alluded to in iii. 61, where he invites them to an ordeal between himself and them by means of stating their claims with oaths (*ibtihāl*). But most often the Christians are mentioned together with the Jews as "People of the Book", while their claim of possessing the true religion is refuted (ii. 111, 114, 135, 140; ix. 29); they will be punished by God (v. 18) and no community with them will be tolerated (v. 51). Ibrāhim was neithers a Jew nor a Christian (iii. 67). On the other hand the enmity between Jews and Christians did not escape the Prophet (ii. 113). During his life there were no subject Christians and relations with tribes and settlements were fixed by treaty. That with Nadjrān gave the Christians freedom of religion and the control of their own affairs so long as they paid tribute and gave some services to the Muslims. To this period belongs the command in the Ḳur'ān (ix. 29) to fight against the people of the book until they pay tribute. The sudden expansion of the state under ʿUmar made the problem acute. He settled it in a rough and ready way, usually copying the Nadjrān treaty. In Asia the cities made treaties with the Muslim commanders, the terms varied but always included tribute. In Egypt the fall of the capital was followed by that of the whole country. Muslim governors were set over the provinces and big towns, the people paid much the same taxes as before, and there was little interference with their social and religious life. Sometimes a church was turned into a mosque but property rights were usually respected. It seems that part of al-ʿIrāḳ was given to the tribe of Badjīla but the grant was soon revoked, and the inhabitants were left to cultivate their lands for the benefit of the Muslims as a whole. The Christians of Nadjrān were exiled to al-ʿIrāḳ though individuals continued to live in al-Madīna itself. ʿUmar was, even according to Christian sources, kindly disposed to the *dhimmīs*. During the following decades the treatment and status of Christians shows many contradictions, due to the caprice of individuals. Churches were built in Arab towns, the caliph helped to restore that at Edessa, but many were destroyed, and the Muslims had twice tried to seize the cathedral at Damascus before al-Walīd incorporated it in the mosque. Christians continued to hold high offices in the state; Muʿāwiya had a Christian secretary, the state accounts were kept in Greek in Syria and Egypt till the reign of ʿAbd al-Malik, and local accounts in Egypt were kept in Greek till much later. Christians served in the Muslim armies, some giving military service instead of tribute. There was persecution and also forced conversions. Jews were settled in some of the conquered towns because they were hostile to the Christians. The caliph sometimes interfered in the election of the patriarch. The Christian Arabs of al-ʿIrāḳ formed a class apart, paying double *zakāt* instead of tribute. Muslims were often friendly with Christians and the caliph did not disdain to employ Christian poets, especially al-Akhṭal. Then came a change for the worse, ʿAbd al-Malik changed the system of taxation in Egypt, Syria, and al-ʿIrāḳ, introducing the personal tax on the *dhimmīs*. Often the form of receipt was a leaden seal tied to the neck or wrist. ʿUmar II tried to dismiss all *dhimmīs* from government service but such confusion resulted that the order was ignored. He was also the author of the "ordinances", which were later ascribed to ʿUmar I, prescribing the restrictions to be placed on *dhimmīs* and the wearing of the *zunnār*. By the end of the iind/viiith century the laws governing the *dhimmīs* were fixed in their main outlines but they were not always enforced. Thus it was generally accepted that no new churches might be built though the old might be repaired; but a governor's fancy or a riot might destroy a church and there was no redress. At least six rebellions of the Copts took place during the century. Hārūn al-Rashīd re-enacted the "ordinances", forbidding Christians to dress like Muslims; but in the reign of Ma'mūn a Christian headman, dressed in black, rode in state on Fridays to the mosque and then left his deputy to attend the prayers. Men began to object to their riding on horses and restrictions were placed on religious processions. Taxation became heavier and the patriarch often had to bribe the caliph to get elected.

Christian doctors became prominent as court favourites and did not always use their influence well. Many Christians were in places of trust and al-Mutawakkil himself had a Christian secretary. On the other hand there were written in the ixth century several polemical treatises against the Christians such as those of ʿAlī b. Sahl Rabban al-Ṭabarī (d.c. 860) and of Abū ʿĪsā Muḥammad al-Warrāḳ (d. 909). In 236/850 al-Mutawakkil intensified the repressive laws. A Christian had to wear a yellow *ṭailasān* and the *zunnār* and a woman had to wear a yellow wrap out of doors. If he rode he must have wooden stirrups and two balls behind the saddle. Men (or slaves) had to wear the *ghiyār*. They were dismissed from the civil service. All new churches were to be pulled down and the cross might not be displayed at festivals. Graves had to be flush with the ground. The tithe was levied on their houses and wooden devils fixed to them. Four years later they were forbidden to ride horses and were told to wear two yellow *durrāʿas*. These laws are the limit of legal persecution but were not always enforced, for Christians were always to be found in the civil service and sometimes even in the army. The Būyids and Fāṭimids were the first to appoint Christians as *wazīr*, but this was exceptional. Still complaints were always made of the dishonesty of the Christian secretaries; especially in the finance department where they held a quasi-monopoly, which lasted in Egypt till the nineteenth century. In later times rulers were often more tolerant than the mob, though taxes were sometimes made heavier. In Egypt between 1260 and 1280 a *dīnār* over and above the poll tax was imposed on them. Their request to be allowed to wear white turbans with a badge was refused at the instance of Ibn Taimīya. They were worse off than their Muslim fellow-subjects for, while both were oppressed by the ruler, the Christians were liable to be attacked by the mob. Mass conversions still occurred, but the disappearance of the Christians of north Mesopotamia, which was the chief centre of Christianity in the Muslim dominions down to the late middle ages, is probably connected with the decay of agriculture there.

2. Legal status. Here as elsewhere the facts of history do not fit the systems of the theorists, who condemned the laxity of the people and also the highhandedness of the rulers. The law puts the *dhimmī* below the Muslim in nearly every way; it protects his life and property but will not accept his evidence. One authority says that eight acts put a *dhimmī* outside the law: an agreement to fight the Muslims, fornication with a Muslim woman, an attempt to marry one, an attempt to turn a Muslim from his religion, robbery of a Muslim on the highway, acting as a spy or guide to unbelievers, or the killing of a Muslim.

3. Social status. The fact that Christians were citizens as it were at second remove, was of course reflected in their social position. The consequences of this disability were to some extent mitigated by their numbers and influence in the administration, and by the hold they had on some important professions, especially medicine. In many towns the only doctor was a *dhimmī*. The prohibition of usury to Muslims worked in favour of the *dhimmīs* as merchants and money-changers, and gave them the monopoly of the trades of goldsmith and jeweller. Some were rich and it was often their imprudent display which drove the mob to violence. Apart from friendships between individuals the universal celebration of the festivals of the Christian year and those of the patron saints of the great monasteries shows that Christians and Muslims were usually on good terms. Books written by Christians are mentioned with approval by Muslim historians. At times the Muslim murderer of a *dhimmī* was executed. Even an apostate sometimes found mercy on the ground that a forced conversion was not valid. Christians acted for Muslims in business and kept Muslim slaves, both male and female; fornication with a Muslim woman was not always punished with death. But still the stigma of inferiority remained. The humiliating regulations, the need for constant watchfulness, the constant recourse to intrigue and influence to circumvent the law, the segregation of *dhimmīs* in many cities, inevitably sapped their morale. Still more serious were their legal disabilities; there could be no true justice for the *dhimmī* when his evidence was excluded from the Muslim courts, even though *ḳāḍīs* were enjoined not to discriminate against them in other respects, not could there by any permanent social relationship in the absence of intermarriage. It is not surprising therefore that the Christian communities of the East gradually dwindled not only in numbers, but also in vitality and moral tone.

See also: DHIMMA, DJIZYA, KHARĀDJ, FAIʾ.

C. The Ottoman Empire.

From the beginning of the period of the *Tanẓīmāt* (1839) the Ottoman Empire gradually abandoned the governmental traditions of Muḥammadan states, and this change fundamentally affected the treatment of its Christian subjects.

Up to the beginning of the xixth century the treatment of Christians in the Empire was, on the whole, in accordance with the prescriptions of the *sharīʿa* after the Ḥanafī *madhhab* as to the treatment of *dhimmīs*. Christians were subject to the payment of the *djizye-i geberān*, more often called *kharādj* in Turkey [cf. these two articles], whence the expression *kharādj-guzār*. This tax was levied in three classes, according to the financial capacity of the payers. D'Ohsson (*Tableau*, iii. 4 *sqq.*) says that in his time (about 1800) each year 1,600,000 tax-forms were issued for the non-Muslims, of which 30,000 were in the capital. The regulations as to the building and restoration of Christian churches were observed in principle; the Ḥanafī *madhhab* allows the restoration of decayed churches but not of churches deliberately demolished; Sheikhī Zāde, however, in his commentary on the *Multaḳā* (*Madjmaʿ al-anhur*, printed Constantinople 1276, p. 415) complains that this distinction was not duly observed in his time (1666). From the xvith century indeed the building and rebuilding of churches was a subject of frequent intervention by the representatives of foreign Christian powers. The turning of churches into mosques by the Ottoman conquerors — such as the case of the Aya Sofia — was generally in concordance with Islāmic laws of war. Likewise the prescriptions about clothing were observed and from time to time reinforced; as late as the xviiith century certain sulṭāns such as ʿUthmān III and Muṣṭafā III are known to have given special attention to this point.

We also find in the *ḳānūn-nāmes* — the contents of which were declared in accordance with the *sharīʿa* by the Shaikh al-Islām — some special clauses about non-Muslims (*kāfirs*). A *ḳānūn-nāme* of the time of Sulaimān I prescribes that, in the case of certain crimes that are punished by fines, the fines of non-Muslims shall amount to only half the sum inflicted on a Muslim in each case (cf. the second *ḳānūn-nāme*, published as appendix to *TOEM*, iii. 3, 4, 6). The same *ḳānūn-nāme* gives directions with regard to the inheritance of non-Muslims.

The Christians thus constituted in the Ottoman Empire, just as in other Muḥammadan states, a section of the population which, so far as their relations with the Government went, had minor rights compared to Muḥammadans and to which the high functionnaries of the state never belonged. They were improperly designated by the term *raʿāyā*. Hence the use of the term *rayas* in European works when speaking of the Christian subjects of the sulṭān. *Gʿaur* was a more or less contemptuous expression in the idiom of Muslim circles.

There had been, however, since the coming into existence of the Ottoman Empire, several circumstances that presented the problem of the Christian subjects in forms quite different from those prevailing in contemporary Muḥammadan states. The beginnings of the Ottoman state itself had been anything but orthodox. ʿUthmān and Orkhān, the founders of the state, had many dealings with the Christian aristocracy of Bithynia, some of whom joined readily the cause and the creed of the new conquerors. Christianity was at that time still widely spread in Asia Minor and was at first adapted to the rather unorthodox mystic form in which the Turcomans of Rūm had made acquaintance with Islām. Large parts of the population adhered for centuries to a Christian-Islāmic mixture of religious convictions, such as appeared in the derwīsh revolt under Simawna Oghlu Badr al-Dīn (cf. Babinger, in *Isl.*, xi.), and as survived in the beliefs and practices of the Bektāshīs and the mixed worship of certain saints by both the Islāmic and the Christian population (cf. Hasluck, *Christianity and Islam under the Sultans*, Oxford 1929). Survivals of this mixed creed were also observed among the so-called Crypto-Christians of Trebizond (cf. Hasluck, in *Journal of Hellenic Studies*, xli. 199 *sqq.*). It was only after the restoration of the Empire in the xv^th^ century that the orthodox Islāmic attitude prevailed in the government of the sulṭāns, who repeatedly had to take strong measures against the heterodox elements.

During this same period it was of no less importance that the Ottoman Empire came to incorporate more and more territories in Europe exclusively inhabited by Christians. With the exception of eastern Thrace, northern Macedonia, Bosnia and Crete, the new subjects were never islamized in great numbers; in the Empire they came to form a very considerable minority, which was counterbalanced only by the large Muḥammadan population of the Asiatic territories. So long as the government and the Muḥammadan ruling class were strong, this did not affect the political system. But this ruling class itself, as well as their powerful military instrument, the Janissaries, were recruited in a large measure from the Greek and Slavonic Christian population of the European provinces and often kept up friendly relations with their non-converted kinsmen (one of the many instances is that of Djandarlï Khalīl Pasha under Muḥammad II). Accordingly much consideration was shown to large parts of the Christian population, and the more so as many Christians served in the state chanceries, where they performed important administrative duties (Crusius, *Turcograecia*, p. 14). Besides, many high-placed persons, including the sulṭāns themselves, had, through their ḥarems, many Christian relations without and within the Empire. So the domestic and foreign policy of the state often brought about measures of toleration, which were not altogether in accordance with the strict demands of Muḥammadan law. An outstanding example is the way in which Constantinople and its Christian inhabitants were treated after the excesses of the first days of the conquest were over. Muḥammad II did all that he could to repopulate his new capital, even with Greeks, when the Muḥammadan element proved insufficient; he even had a new Oecumenical Patriarch chosen not long after the conquest (cf. Fr. Giese, *Die Stellung der christlichen Untertanen im Osmanischen Reich*, in *Isl.*, xix., 1931, p. 264 *sqq.*). Only afterwards, in the first half of the xvi^th^ century, when Muḥammadan fanaticism had increased, there was a party which, invoking the fact that the town had been taken by force (*ʿanwatan*), claimed the destruction of all churches that were left to the Christians, and only with great difficulty was evidence constructed to prove that Constantinople was really taken by a capitulation (cf. J. H. Mordtmann, *Die Kapitulation von Konstantinopel im Jahre* 1453, in *Byzantinische Zeitschrift*, xxi., 1912, p. 129 *sqq.*). Other signs of fanaticism in the same period are i.a. the intention attributed to Selīm I to convert all Christians to Islām, the wish of Murād III to turn all churches into mosques, and the alleged oath of Murād IV to exterminate all Christians. Still, apart from these occasional outbursts, tolerance prevailed. In the capital a Greek Christian aristocracy and plutocracy was permitted to live in the quarter of Phanar; from their midst came influential persons such as Michael Kantakuzenos, the "pillar of the Christians" (Jorga, *GOR*, iii. 211) in the xvi^th^ century, and the well-known Phanariote families who later supplied dragomans to the Porte and the princes of the Danube principalities.

The official attitude towards the Christians was complete abstinence from their domestic religious and secular affairs so long as this did not affect the public order. This explains also the tolerance towards the activities of the Roman Catholic missionaries who were sent from the xvi^th^ century onwards to convert the eastern Christians. The government took no interest in the different denominations of Christians, while their internal divisions reinforced its authority. R. Gragger in his article *Türkisch-Ungarische Kulturbeziehungen* (*Literaturdenkmäler aus Ungarns Türkenzeit*, in *Ungarische Bibliothek*, i., no. 14, Berlin 1927) depicts the tolerant attitude and the sometimes amused interest of the Turkish Pashas in Hungary in the religious disputes between Roman Catholics and Protestants. On the other hand, the serious domestic troubles amongst the Greeks belonging to the much decayed Oecumenical Patriarchiate as the result of which the party of the patriarch Cyrillus Lucaris took in the first half of the xvii^th^ century a definite anti-Roman Catholic attitude could not be wholly indifferent to the Porte because from that time on the only political protector of the Greeks was the Ottoman government. Arbitrary measures such as occasional executions of the patriarch (for the first time in 1657; v. Hammer, *GOR*², iii. 474) and excesses in war time are not sufficient to refute the statement that the attitude of the government was on the whole tolerant.

What, at length, came to influence most deeply this attitude was the interest shown in the lot of the Christians by the governments of the Christian powers with whom the Porte began to enter into peaceful relations. In the early centuries those foreign Christians who were allowed to reside in the seaport towns fell within the category of *mustaʾmin*. Legal conceptions of that time did not distinguish sharply between religious denomination and nationality, both being designated by the word *millet*; therefore a foreigner who embraced Islām was entirely assimilated to the Muḥammadan subjects of the sulṭān. In course of time *millet* came to be used also for the different "national" denominations of the Christians within the Empire. The first foreign power to be interested in the Christians of Turkey was the Vatican, as was manifested several times by the inevitable participation of the Popes in the preparation of anti-Turkish crusades. The Cardinal Protettore di Levante in Rome exercised, through his vicar, considerable influence on the Latin Roman Catholic community of Pera, which, since the conquest of Constantinople, had enjoyed, like the other Christian communities, administrative independence. This "religious protection" was not altogether in conformance with the wishes of the Christians themselves (G. Young, *Corps de Droit Ottoman*, Oxford 1905, ii. 124), but at those times the Porte followed a policy of non-intervention and did not seize the opportunity of placing these Christian inhabitants of her territory under her more direct control. The same policy made her accept without difficulty the remonstrances of a second, more powerful, protector, the King of France, who already before the conclusion of the treaty of 1535 had begun to act as intermediary between the Catholics in Jerusalem and other places in the Levant and the Porte. This intervention of France — which, in the eyes of Christian Europe, served her as an excuse for her entering into diplomatic relations with the Porte — was tolerated equally in favour of other than French ecclesiastics and missionaries, and of non-French Christian prisoners. Occasionally France's protection was also invoked by other than Roman Catholics; in 1639, the Oecumenical Patriarch himself asked the French King to declare himself protector of the Eastern Church. The French capitulation of 1673 recognized at last the protectorate of the King of France over the Roman Catholic foreign Christians, though a general protectorate over all the Christians in the Empire had been demanded originally; the famous capitulation of 1740 confirmed the dispositions of that of 1673 (cf. G. Pelissié du Rausas, *Le Régime des Capitulations dans l'Empire Ottoman*, Paris 1911, i. 80 *sqq*.). A third powerful protector of Christian interests, this time of the Greek Orthodox Christians, arose in the xviii[th] century in the person of the Russian Czar. Shortly after the fall of Constantinople Ivan the Great had begun to regard himself as successor of the Byzantine Emperors and, as the power of Russia increased, the Greek orthodox Christians in the western and eastern parts of the Empire came to look upon the Czar as their natural protector. Especially the Christian institutions in Jerusalem and the much impoverished patriarchate of that town benefited by the Russian religious interest. On the other hand, Russia learnt to use her influence with the Orthodox Christians as a powerful political instrument. The peace treaty of Küčük Ḳainard̲j̲e (1776) recognized at last the right of the Russian diplomatic representatives to interfere in favour of the Christians in the Empire.

With the weakening of the Empire in the xviii[th] century the so-called "religious protection" became a heavy burden on Turkey's inner political conditions. Especially after the disastrous happenings under Maḥmūd II's reign, it became clear that the old Muḥammadan conception of the state, which left the non-Muslims entirely to themselves, or to others, could no longer be maintained. It was one of the chief stimuli to the introduction of the *Tanẓīmāt*. In order to retain as much control as possible over her Christian subjects the Porte now had to apply her governmental activity equally to non-Muslims and Muslims. Accordingly the *K̲h̲aṭṭ-i S̲h̲erīf* of Gül-K̲h̲āne (1839) declared that perfect security was guaranteed to all subjects, Muslims or *raʿāyā*, as to their lives, their honour and their possessions. Still in the following years no important administrative measures were taken, while on the other hand the intervention of foreign powers in Christian affairs continued and led amongst other incidents to the outbreak of the Crimean War in 1853. An incident of 1843, in the meantime, had made the Porte give a formal assurance to the French and English ambassadors with regard to the non-application of capital punishment to persons who had renounced the Muḥammadan creed (Young, *op. cit.*, ii. 11 *sqq*.).

The law of May 10, 1855 is an important landmark in the history of Ottoman policy towards the Christian subjects; this law abolished the capitation tax for non-Muslims and envisaged the possibility of their service in the army [cf. D̲J̲IZYA and the *Bibliography* of this art.]. This legislative measure was completed by the *K̲h̲aṭṭ-i Humāyūn* of February 18, 1856, which may be regarded as the Magna Carta of the rights of the non-Muslim subjects of the Empire; in this memorable edict the rights and privileges of the different religious denominations and their members were proclaimed in fuller detail; as to their military service the edict laid down the principle that it could be replaced by the payment of an exemption tax, which, under the name of *bedel*, came to be regularly applied to all non-Muslims. In accordance with the contents of the *K̲h̲aṭṭ-i Humāyūn*, the Ottoman legislation now began for the first time to take notice officially of the existence of the great number of Christian communities existing in the Empire. Organic statutes were elaborated for the more important of these communities (called *millet*): in 1860 for the Armenian Gregorian community and in 1862 for the Greek Orthodox community. In 1870 followed the institution, with the cooperation of the Porte, of the Bulgarian Exarchate, while in course of time a host of laws, decrees and regulations were issued, containing more detailed provisions with regard to these and the minor communities: Patriarchates of Antioch and Jerusalem, Mount Athos, the Serbian Church, the Nestorians, the Latin communities, and the different churches united with Rome (Armenians, Chaldaeans, Maronites, Melkites). This highly complicated legislation aimed at making these Christians Ottoman subjects in the full sense of the word, but met with great difficulties created by the existence of an age-old system of autonomy and by the frequent intervention of the foreign powers. The leading principle of the government was to divest the purely religious authorities as much as possible of their power and to reinforce the power of the lay institutions. This policy led to endless troubles in which new regulations continually tried to restore order. In the constitution of Midḥat Pas̲h̲a (1876) Islām was proclaimed as the State religion, but immediately afterwards there follows the declaration that the profession of all recognized religions in the Empire is free and that all privileges granted to the different religious communities shall be maintained (art. 11). Art. 9 guarantees the personal freedom of all Ottoman subjects and art. 17 their complete equality before the law.

All the time during the period of reforms the

Turkish government had to reckon with reactionary feelings against the giaurs in large sections of the Muḥammadan population, which in many instances made the application of equal treatment before the law and elsewhere illusory. This justified to a certain extent the never-ending remonstrances of the European powers, who lost no opportunity of insisting on new reforms in favour of the Christians. Art. 62 of the treaty of Berlin (July 13 1878) stipulated again for the equal treatment by the Ottoman government of all non-Muslim subjects, amongst others that every one, without difference of religion, should be admitted as a witness before the law courts.

The effect of the foreign intervention in their favour encouraged on the other hand large sections of the Christian population to disloyal feelings and actions against their legal government. While the latter did what it could do to assimilate the different groups of the population the factors of dissolution became at the same time ever stronger. Even the peaceful relations that had hitherto characterized on the whole the intercourse between Muḥammadans and Christians — especially in the cities — began to make way for religious hatred between group and group, in which the government officials were often unable to observe the required neutral attitude. Amongst many other symptoms the Armenian troubles which began in 1889 in the Armenian wilāyets — where a racial antagonism between Muḥammadan Kurds and Christian Armenians had existed for centuries — were the most disastrous. They led to repeated Armenian attempts at revolt and to the notorious massacres in Constantinople of 1897.

By this development the treatment of the Christian subjects ceased to be a religious problem; it became a problem of nationality (*millet* in the new acceptation of the word) and of race, and at the same time one of the vital problems for the Empire. After the revolution of 1908 and the re-establishment of Midḥat's constitution, these facts were not yet fully recognized. The Ottomanization of all subjects of the Empire was seriously attempted; the new representative bodies included a number of Christian members; occasionally there were Christian ministers. Then the world war of 1914 precipitated the inevitable course of events. This time non-Muslims were for the first time incorporated in the Turkish army, but only for service behind the front. At the same time, the domestic policy of the Young Turks took a pan-Turkish turn, from which religious motives were quite absent. National Turkish feeling prevailed. The measures of deportation of Christian inhabitants from the frontier zones — measures from which the Armenians especially suffered terribly — were inspired by fear of disloyalty towards Turkey, though in their execution remnants of religious fanaticism, notably on the side of the Kurds, certainly played a large part.

The events after the armistice of Mudros have proved that a great part of Christian population preferred independence or incorporation into a Christian state to remaining with Turkey. And the Turks themselves also were ready to part with their Christian subjects. Under these circumstances were concluded at Lausanne, in 1923, the agreements with Greece for the exchange of the Greek population of the new Turkish state against Turks established on Hellenic territory; only Constantinople and some islands were excluded from his measure. Since by the events of the war the number of Armenians and other Christians in Asiatic Turkey had already been reduced to a very small minority, the result was that the present Turkish republic has only to deal with a Christian population of no numerical importance, most of whom live in Constantinople. The Lausanne Treaty of 1923 contains in its articles 37—45 only the obligation on Turkey to treat the minorities on an equal basis with the Turkish subjects; it provides for their right to live after a personal legal statute of their own. Finally the treatment of Christians in Turkey has definitely ceased to be a legal problem in the old sense of the word since, by the alteration of the Constitution on April 5, 1928 the state has been completely secularized (cf. *Tarih*, Istanbul 1931, iv. 213) by cancelling the article declaring that the state religion is Islām.

Bibliography: Tor Andrae, *Der Ursprung des Islams und das Christentum*, 1926; Rothstein, *Die Dynastie der Laḫmiden in Ḥīra*, 1899; Nöldeke, *Geschichte der Araber und Perser zur Zeit der Sassaniden*, 1879; Cheikho, *Christianisme en Arabie avant l'Islam*, 1919; Nau, *Arabes Chrétiens*, 1933; Moberg, *The Book of the Ḥimyarites*, 1924; Dussaud, *Les Arabes en Syrie avant l'Islam*, 1907; Lammens, *Les Chrétiens à la Mecque* (*BIFAO*, 1918); Tritton, *The Caliphs and their non-Muslim subjects*, 1930; Mez, *Die Renaissance des Islams*, 1922; Arnold, *The Preaching of Islam*, 1913; Gottheil, *Dhimmis and Muslims in Egypt* (*Harper Studies*, ii. 353), 1908; Belin, *Une Fetoua*, in *JA* 1851; Margoliouth, *The early Development of Mohammedanism*, 1914; Hirschberg, *Jüdische und Christliche Lehren im vor- und frühislamischen Arabien*, Cracow 1939.

AL-NAWAWĪ (or AL-NAWĀWĪ), MUḤYĪ AL-DĪN ABŪ ZAKARĪYĀʾ YAḤYĀ AL-ḤIZĀMĪ AL-DIMASHḲĪ, a Shāfiʿī jurist, born in Muḥarram 631/Oct. 1233 in Nawā south of Damascus in Djawlān. The ability of the boy very early attracted attention and his father brought him in 649 to the Madrasa al-Rawāḥīya in Damascus. There he first of all studied medicine but very soon went over to Islāmic learning. In 651 he made the pilgrimage with his father. About 655 he began to write and was called to the Ashrafīya school of tradition in Damascus in succession to Abū Shāma who had just died. Although his health had suffered severely during his life as a student, he lived very frugally and even declined a salary. His reputation soon became so great that he even dared to approach Sulṭān Baibars to ask him to restore the confiscated gardens of the Damascenes, to free the people of Syria from the war-taxes imposed upon them, or to protect the teachers in the madrasas from a reduction in their income. All this was in vain however, and Baibars expelled al-Nawawī from Damascus when he alone refused to sign a *fatwā* approving the legality of these exactions. (This action of al-Nawawī's is commemorated in the popular romance *Sīrat al-Ẓāhir Baibars*, Cairo 1326, xli. 38 *sqq.* in which the Sulṭān, cursed by al-Nawawī, becomes blind for a time). He died unmarried in his father's house in Nawā on Wednesday 24th Radjab 676/Dec. 22, 1277. His tomb is still held in honour there.

Al-Nawawī has retained his high reputation to the present day. He had an exceptional knowledge of Tradition and adopted even stricter standards than later Islām; for example he admits only five works on Tradition as canonical, while he expressly puts the *Sunan* of Ibn Mādja on a level with the *Musnad* of Aḥmad b. Ḥanbal (cf. his *Sharḥ Muslim*, i. 5; *Adhkār*, p. 3). In spite of his fondness for Muslim, he gives a higher place to Bukhārī (*Tahdhīb*, p. 550). He wrote the principal commentary on Muslim's

Ṣaḥīḥ (pr. in 5 volumes, Cairo 1283); as an introduction to this, he wrote a history of the transmission of this work and a sketch of the science of Tradition. He gives not only observations on the *isnāds* and a grammatical explanation of the traditions but he also comments on them, mainly from the theological and legal aspect, quoting when necessary not only the founders of the principal schools but also the older jurists like al-Awzāʿī, ʿAṭāʾ, etc. He also inserted headings (*tardjama*) in Muslim's work. We may also mention his frequently annotated *Kitāb al-arbaʿīn* (pr. Būlāḳ 1294 and often since) and portions of commentaries on al-Bukhārī (*GAL, Suppl.* i. 261) and Abū Dāwūd (Ibn al-ʿAṭṭār, fol. 10); and an extract from Ibn al-Ṣalāḥ, *ʿUlūm al-ḥadīth* with the title *al-Taḳrīb wa 'l-taisīr*, partly transl. by Marçais, in *JA*, ser. 9, xvi.—xviii. and printed at Cairo 1307, with a commentary by al-Suyūṭī, *Tadrīb al-rāwī*.

Al-Nawawī's importance as a jurist is perhaps even greater. In Shāfiʿī circles he was regarded with his *Minhādj al-ṭālibin* (finished 669; pr. Cairo 1297 and frequently; ed. van den Berg with French transl., Batavia 1882—1884; cf. thereon Snouck Hurgronje, *Verspr. Geschr.*, vi. 3—18) as the highest authority along with al-Rāfiʿī and since the tenth (xvi^th^) century the two commentaries on this work, Ibn Ḥadjar's *Tuḥfa* and al-Ramlī's *Nihāya*, have been regarded almost as the law books of the Shāfiʿī school. The book consists of excerpts from the *Muḥarrar* of Rāfiʿī and, as the author himself says, is intended to be a kind of commentary on it. It certainly owes the estimation in which is it held also to the fact that it goes back via al-Rāfiʿī and al-Ghazzālī to the Imām al-Ḥaramain. We should also mention the *Rawḍa fī mukhtaṣar sharḥ al-Rāfiʿī* (on Ghazzālī's *Wadjīz*; pr. Dehli 1307) finished in 669, on which commentaries have often been written, and the commentaries on Shīrāzī's *al-Muhadhdhab* and *al-Tanbīh* (pr. Cairo 1329) and al-Ghazzālī's *al-Wasīṭ*, which do not seem to have survived, and a collection of *fatwā*'s put together by his pupil Ibn al-ʿAṭṭār (Cairo 1352).

His biographical and grammatical studies resulted in the *Tahdhīb al-asmāʾ wa 'l-lughāt* (Part 1 on the names, ed. Wüstenfeld, Göttingen 1842—1847; Part 2 pr. Cairo n. d., cf. Levi della Vida, *Elenco dei Ms. arabi islamici della Bibl. Vaticana*, p. 99; included by Ibn al-ʿAṭṭār among the unfinished works and there are certainly gaps in it) and *al-Taḥrīr fī alfāẓ al-tanbīh* finished in 671. To his mystical tendencies — he had attended lectures on the *Risāla* of al-Ḳushairī and transmitted it — we owe works like the *Kitāb al-adhkār* on the prayers, finished in 667 (pr. Cairo 1331 and frequently), the *Riyāḍ al-ṣāliḥīn* (finished in 670; pr. Mecca 1302, 1312) and the incomplete *Bustān al-ʿārifīn fī 'l-zuhd wa 'l-taṣawwuf* (pr. Cairo 1348). A complete list of his some 60 works is given in Heffening, *l.c.*, p. 171—88, those that are still in MSS. are given in Brockelmann, *GAL*, i. 496 *sqq.*, *Suppl.* i. 680 *sqq.* and index.

Bibliography: Ibn al-ʿAṭṭār (d. 724/1324), *Tuḥfat al-ṭālibīn fī tardjamat shaikhinā al-imām al-Nawawī* [with many *marthiya*'s], MS. Tübingen, No. 18; al-Sakhāwī (d. 902/1496—1497), *Tardjamat ḳuṭb al-awliyāʾ ... al-Nawawī*, Ms. Berlin, Wetzstein, ii. 1742, fol. 140—207 (Ahlwardt, No. 10125); al-Suyūṭī, *al-Minhādj fī tardjamat al-Nawawī*, MS. Berlin Wetzstein ii. 1807, fol. 53^r^—68^r^ (Ahlwardt, No. 10126); al-Subkī, *Ṭabaḳāt al-shāfiʿiya al-kubrā*, Cairo 1324, v. 165—168; al-Dhahabī, *Tadhkirat al-ḥuffāẓ*, Ḥaidarābād n.d., iv. 259—264; al-Yāfiʿī, *Mirʾāt al-djanān*, Ḥaidarābād 1339, iv. 182—186; the other sources are printed in Wüstenfeld, *Über das Leben und die Schriften des Scheich Abu Zakarija Jahja el-Nawawi*, Göttingen 1849; Snouck Hurgronje, *Verspr. Geschriften*, ii. 387 *sq.*; Heffening, *Zum Leben u. zu den Schriften al-Nawawī*'s in *Isl.* xxii. (1935), p. 165—90; xxiv. (1937), p. 131—50.

AL-NAẒẒĀM, IBRĀHĪM B. SAIYĀR B. ḤĀNIʾ B. ISḤĀḲ, a Muʿtazilī theologian of the Baṣra school. Brought up in Baṣra, he spent the latter part of his life in Baghdād, where he died between 220 and 230 (835—845) while still, it seems, at the height of his powers. A brilliant poet, a philologist of note, and above all an extremely perspicacious and subtile dialectician, he is one of the most interesting figures in the culture of the ʿAbbāsid period. He occupies a most important place in the development of Muslim ideas. He studied speculative theology in the *madjlis* of Abu 'l-Hudhail al-ʿAllāf, from which he soon separated to found an independent school. In Baṣra he vigorously continued the struggle waged by his teacher against Manichaeism, but devoted his abilities mainly to the refutation of the Dahrī philosophy, with which he was thoroughly acquainted. So far as we can judge, it was al-Naẓẓām who began the struggle, which was continued by Islām for centuries, against the philosophy of Asiatic Hellenism — the struggle the classic document in which is the *Tahāfut* of al-Ghazzālī. In Baghdād he engaged in lively disputations with Murdjiʾī and Djabrī theologians, the traditionists and the *fuḳahāʾ*, submitting their views to a searching criticism which had considerable repercussions in the history of Sunnī theology. On the other hand, his ideas seem to have had a considerable influence on the Muʿtazilī school of Baghdād in spite of the resistance which it offered to him. Al-Naẓẓām was above all a theologian. Two tendencies dominate his thought: zeal for *tawḥīd*, the strictest monotheism, and zeal for the Ḳurʾān, which compelled him to set aside any other source of theology and ethics. His interest in religion was purely intellectual, and emotion seems to have played a very limited part in it. Hiw opponents described him as a Dahrī; this is to misconceive completely the fundamental idea of his theological work; nevertheless it is quite true that it was the dispute with the Dahrīya which imposed upon him the first principles of his dogmatics and which determined their structure, so much so that Islām in his hands assumed a rather strange form. His dogmatic extravagances brought down upon him the condemnation of al-most the whole of the Muslim community and even of the Muʿtazila; it was however he who was the first to state several of the principal problems of Sunnī theology. His writings are lost, but considerable fragments have been preserved, mainly in the works of his pupil al-Djāḥiẓ. Many of the teachings which are attributed to him in the books on heresies were handed down by his pupils, not always correctly, as al-Khaiyāṭ tells us. The exposition of his theology given by al-Baghdādī in his *Kitāb al-Farḳ* probably goes back to Ibn al-Rāwandī; it is a typical example of misrepresentation and deliberately false interpretation. — On the main features of his theology and of his school, cf. the article AL-MUʿTAZILA. Here we give a few observations on the problems of his theology.

1. *Aṣl al-tawḥīd*. Al-Naẓẓām's main interest here is to defend the Ḳurʾānic doctrine of the creation against the Dahrīya which teaches the perpetual circulation of the elements and therefore the eternity of the material world. It is with this object

that he develops the doctrine of the *ẓuhūr* and the *kumūn*, a strictly anti-Dahrī thesis and one already adopted by Abu 'l-Hudhail al-ʿAllāf. His ideas regarding the body and its relations are the logical result of this teaching. The structure of these ideas is however strongly influenced by the polemic against Manichaeism, the fundamental problems of which al-Naẓẓām had studied deeply. In his positive demonstration of the dogma of the creation one occasionally thinks there are traces of Aristotelianism: the creation was a setting in motion and the created world is in a continual state of movement (even rest is defined as a form of movement). God is then himself immobile, but at the same time the primordial moving power. The *tanzīh*, the distinction between the creator and creation, is carried a considerable distance. The divine attributes are represented to us by negations. The divine word is a body (therefore created), but that of man is an accident. The Ḳurʾān is miraculous because of the information it gives about the past and on account of the secrets which it reveals, but not on account of its style, which men could have imitated if God had not prevented them (in reality there is no *muʿāraḍa* in al-Naẓẓām). Al-Naẓẓām fundamentally rejects the arbitrary interpretations of the Ḳurʾān given by the great authorities on Tradition, an ʿIkrima, a Kalbī, a Suddī or a Muḳātil b. Sulaimān; he demands a strictly literal exegesis. Prophethood had always been universal, i.e. all the prophets and not Muḥammad alone have been sent to the whole of humanity (against the traditionists; al-Naẓẓām thus did not deny the prophethood of Muḥammad).

2. *Aṣl al-ʿadl*. The freedom of the human will is restricted, according to al-Naẓẓām, in a way that anticipates the Ashʿarī theology. All the actions of a man are movements, therefore accidents, and movements which relate only to the man himself; the effects which are realized outside of the man are not due to him, but to the natural forces which God has placed in his body (denial of *tawallud*). Man is the *rūḥ*, which penetrates the body; the body in its turn represents an infirmity (*āfa*) of the *rūḥ*. Now it is the body, different from man in the strict sense, which sets in motion the action of which man (i.e. the *rūḥ*) is capable. It follows that man (the *rūḥ*) is capable of the action before it is realised (*al-istiṭāʾ ḳabla 'l-fiʿl*), but at the moment when it is realized, the man is not capable of it.

3. *Aṣl al-waʿd wa 'l-waʿīd*. Al-Naẓẓām is very keenly interested in practical problems of *fiḳh*; we know his views and those of his school on the *ṣalāt*, on fraud and on ritual purity (in which connection he gives some very curious psychological explanations). But he is particularly concerned with the *uṣūl*. He waged a passionate campaign against the *aṣḥāb al-raʾy wa 'l-ḳiyās*, therefore against the Ḥanafīs who were the representatives of the Murdjiʾīs. He flatly refused to admit *raʾy* and *ḳiyās* and did not shrink even from attacking the great men among the *ṣaḥāba* who in his opinion had been guilty of using them. He was in this way led to criticize violently the institution of the *idjmāʿ*, which however he admitted to a certain extent. Through all this he prepared the way for Dāwūd al-Ẓāhirī and the Ẓāhirīya school.

Bibliography: al-Djāḥiẓ, *Kitāb al-ḥayawān*, Cairo 1323, *passim* (esp. i. 167—169, on the exegesis of the Ḳurʾān, and v. 1—31, on the *ẓuhūr* and the *kumūn*); al-Khaiyāṭ, *Kitāb al-intiṣār*, ed. Nyberg, Cairo 1925, index; Ibn Ḳutaiba, *Taʾwīl mukhtalif al-ḥadīth*, Cairo 1326, p. 20—53; al-Ashʿarī, *Maḳālāt*, ed. Ritter, index; al-Saiyid al-Murtaḍā, *Kitāb al-amālī*, Cairo 1325, i. 132—134; al-Baghdādī, *Kitāb al-farḳ*, Cairo 1910, p. 113—136; *Kitāb al-Fihrist*, in *WZKM*, iv. 220—221; Ibn Ḥazm, *Kitāb al-faṣl*, Cairo 1317, *passim*; al-Shahrastānī, *Kitāb al-milal wa 'l-niḥal*, ed. Cureton, p. 37—41; Ibn Abi 'l-Ḥadīd, *Sharḥ nahdj al-balāgha*, Cairo 1329, ii. 48—50 (with some fragments of the treatise *Kitāb al-nukat* by al-Naẓẓām); al-Khaṭīb al-Baghdādī, *Taʾrīkh Baghdād*, Cairo 1349, vi. 97—98; Ibn al-Murtaḍā, *al-Muʿtazila*, ed. Arnold, Leipzig 1902, p. 28—30; Ibn Ḥadjar al-ʿAskalānī, *Lisān al-mīzān*, Ḥaidarābād 1329, i. 67; cf. also the *Bibliography* to the article AL-MUʿTAZILA; A. S. Tritton, *Muslim Theology*, London 1947, p. 89 *sqq*.

AL-NIFFARĪ, MUḤAMMAD IBN ʿABD AL-DJABBĀR. This mystic, whom the principal Ṣūfī biographers fail to mention, flourished in the iv^th^/x^th^ century, and, according to Ḥādjdjī Khalīfa, died in the year 354/965. His *nisba* refers to the town of Niffar in Mesopotamia, and one MS. of his works asserts that it was during his residence at Niffar and Nīl that he committed his thoughts to writing. Niffarī's literary reliquiae consist of two books, the *Mawāḳif* and the *Mukhāṭabāt*, together with a number of fragments. It is improbable that Niffarī himself was responsible for the editing of his writings; according to his principal commentator, ʿAfīf al-Dīn al-Tilimsānī (d. 690/1291), either his son or his grandson collected his scattered writings and published them according to his own ordering. The *Mawāḳif* consists of 77 sections of varying length, made up for the most part of brief apothegms touching on the main aspects of Ṣūfī teaching, and purporting to be inspired and dictated by God; the *Mukhāṭabāt* is similar in content, and is divided into 56 sections. Niffarī's most characteristic contribution to mysticism is his doctrine of *waḳfa*. This term, which would appear to be used by him in a peculiarly technical sense, implies a condition in the mystic which is accompanied by direct divine audition, and perhaps even automatic script. *Mawḳif* is the name given to the state of the mystic in which *waḳfa* is classed higher than *maʿrifa*, and *maʿrifa* is above *ʿilm*. The *wāḳif* is nearer to God than any other thing, and almost transcends the condition of *basharīya*, being alone separated from all limitation. Niffarī definitely maintains the possibility of seeing God in this world; for he says that vision (*ruʾya*) in this world is a preparation for vision in the world to come. In several places Niffarī distinctly touches on the theory of the Mahdī, and indeed appears to identify himself with the Mahdī, if these passages are genuine; and this claim is seemingly in the mind of Zabīdī, when he describes Niffarī as *ṣāḥib al-daʿāwā wa 'l-ḍalāl*. Tilimsānī however interprets these passages in an esoteric and highly mystical sense; and it does not accord with the general character of the author that he should make for himself such extravagant claims. Niffarī shows himself in his writings to be a fearless and original thinker. While undoubtedly influenced by his great predecessor al-Ḥallādj, he acknowledges no obligations, and has a thorough conviction of the reality of his own mission. Ibn ʿArabī, who mentions him several times in his *al-Futūḥāt al-Makkiya*, certainly owes much to him. The collected works were published in 1935 with an English translation (*GMS*, n.s. ix) by A. J. Arberry.

Bibliography: D. S. Margoliouth, *Early Development of Muhammedanism*, p. 186—198; R. A. Nicholson, *The Mystics of Islam*, *passim*.

NIKĀḤ (A.), marriage (properly: sexual intercourse, but already in the Ḳur'ān used exclusively of the contract). Here we deal with marriage as a legal institution; for marriage customs see ʿURS.

1. Some essential features of the Muslim law of marriage survive from the old customary law of the Arabs. In this, although there were differences according to districts and to the individual cases, the regulations governing marriage were based upon the patriarchal system, which permitted the man very great freedom and still bore traces of old matriarchal ideas. It is true that before the coming of Islām a higher conception of the marriage state had already begun to exist but the position of the woman was still a very unfavourable one. The marriage contract was made between the suitor and the "guardian" i.e. the father or the nearest male relative of the bride, the latter's consent not being regarded as necessary. But even before Islām it had already become generally usual for the bridal gift to be given to the woman herself and not to the guardian. In marriage the woman was under the unrestricted authority of her husband, the only bounds to which were consideration for her family. Dissolution of the marriage rested entirely on the man's opinion; and even after his death his relatives could enforce claims upon his widow.

2. Islām reformed these old marriage laws in far-reaching fashion, while retaining their essential features; here as in other fields of social legislation the chief aim of the Ḳur'ān was the improvement of the woman's position. The regulations regarding marriage which are the most important in principle are laid down in Sūra iv. (of the period shortly after the battle of Uḥud): "3. If ye fear that ye cannot act justly to the orphans marry the women whom ye think good (to marry), by twos, threes or fours; but if ye fear (even then) not to be equitable, then only one or (the slaves) whom you possess;... 4. Give the women their dowries freely; but if they voluntarily remit you any of it, enjoy it and may it prosper you. 22. Marry not the women whom your fathers have married, except bygones; for this is shameful and abominable and an evil way. 23. Forbidden to you are your mothers, your daughters, your sisters, your aunts paternal and maternal, the daughters of your brother and sister, your foster-mothers and foster-sisters, the mothers of your wives and your step-daughters who are in your care, born of your wives, with whom ye have had intercourse — but if ye have not had intercourse with them, it is no sin for you — and the wives of your sons, who are your offspring, also that ye form a connexion between two sisters, except bygones; Allāh is forgiving and merciful. 24. Further decorous women except (slaves) that you possess. That is prescribed to you by Allāh. But permitted to you is all besides this, to seek them with your money in decency and not in fornication. To those of them that ye have enjoyed give their reward as a due, but it is no sin for you to make an agreement between you beyond the due. Allāh is knowing and wise. 25. If however any one of you cannot produce the means of marrying free believing women (let him marry) among your believing handmaids whom you possess; Allāh best knows (to distinguish) your faith. Marry them then with the permission of their people, and give them their reward in kindness, they being decorous and not fornicating and not receivers of paramours. There is, further, in Sūra ii. 221 (uncertain date) the prohibition of marriage with infidels, male or female (cf. Sūra lx. 10), in Sūra xxxiii. 50. (probably of the year 5) an exception in favour of the Prophet, and in Sūra v. 5 (of the farewell pilgrimage in the year 10) the permission of marriage with the women of the possessors of a sacred scripture. Other passages of the Ḳur'ān which emphasize the moral side of marriage are Sūra xxiv. 3, 26, 32 and Sūra xxx. 20. In tradition various attitudes to marriage find expression; at the same time the positive enactments regulating it are supplemented in essential points. The most important is the limitation of the number of wives permitted at one time to four; although Sūra iv. 3 contains no such precise regulation, this interpretation of it must have predominated very early, as in the traditions it is assumed rather than expressly demanded. The co-operation of the "guardian", the dowry and the consent of the woman is regarded as essential and competition with a rival whose suit is still pending is forbidden.

3. The most important provisions of Muslim law (according to the Shāfiʿī school) are the following. The marriage contract is concluded between the bridegroom and the bride's *walī* (guardian), who must be a free Muslim of age and of good conduct (*ʿadl*; the Ḥanafīs and Mālikīs dispense with this last quality); the Ḥanafīs alone recognize a marriage concluded by the woman herself without *walī* as valid. The *walī* is in his turn bound to assist in concluding the contract of marriage demanded by the woman, if the bridegroom fulfils certain legal conditions. The *walī* is to be one of the following in this order: 1. the nearest male ascendant in the male line; 2. the nearest male relative in the male line among the descendants of the father; 3. do. among the descendants of the grandfather etc.; 4. in the case of a freed woman the *mawlā* (manumitter) and if the case arises his male relatives in the order of the *ʿaṣaba* [cf. MĪRĀTH]; 5. the representative of the public authority (*ḥākim*) appointed for the purpose; in many countries it is the *ḳāḍī* or his deputy. In place of the *ḥākim* the future husband and wife may agree to choose a *walī* and must do so if there is no authorized *ḥākim* in the place. The *walī* can only give the bride in marriage with her consent but in the case of a virgin silent consent is sufficient. Only the father or grandfather has the right to marry his daughter or granddaughter against her will, so long as she is a virgin (he is therefore called *walī mudjbir*, *walī* with power of coercion); the exercise of this power is however strictly regulated in the interest of the bride. As minors are not in a position to make a declaration of their wishes which is valid in law, they can only be married at all by a *walī mudjbir*. According to the Ḥanafīs on the other hand, every blood relative acting as *walī* is entitled to give a virgin under age in marriage without her consent; but a woman married in this way by another than her ascendant is entitled on coming of age to the right of option called *khiyār al-bulūgh*, i.e to demand the divorce by *faskh* through the *ḳāḍī*. A bridegroom who is a minor may also be married by his *walī mudjbir*. As a kind of equivalent for the rights which the husband acquires over the wife, he is bound to give her a bridal gift (*mahr*, *ṣadāḳ*) which is regarded as an essential part of the contract. The contracting parties are free to fix the *mahr*; it may consist of any object or service that has value in the eyes of the law; if it is not fixed at the conclusion of the contract and if the parties cannot agree upon it, we have a case for the *mahr al-mithl*, the average bridal gift according to the circumstances which is fixed by the *ḳāḍī*. It is not necessary to pay the

mahr at once; frequently a portion is paid before the consummation of the marriage and the remainder only at the dissolution of the marriage by divorce or death. The claim to the full *mahr* or the full *mahr al-mit̲h̲l* arises only when the marriage is consummated; if the marriage is previously dissolved the wife can only claim half the *mahr* or a present (*mutʿa*) fixed arbitrarily by the man; these regulations go back to Sūra ii. 236 *sq.* (cf. xxxiii. 49). In form the marriage contract, which is usually prefaced by a sollicitation (*k̲h̲iṭba*), follows the usual scheme in Muslim contracts with offer and acceptance; the *walī* of the bride is recommended to deliver a pious address (*k̲h̲uṭba*) on the occasion. The marriage must be concluded in the presence of at least two witnesses (*s̲h̲āhid*), who possess the legal qualifications for a witness; their presence is here not simply, as in other contracts, required for evidence, but an essential element in the validity of the marriage; for the Mālikīs, the essential point is the public notoriety of the marriage which can also be achieved by other means than by the presence of witnesses. On the other hand, no collaboration by the authorities is prescribed. But since great importance is generally attached to fulfilling the formalities of the marriage contract, upon which the validity of the marriage depends, it is usual not to carry through this important legal matter without the assistance of a qualified specialist. We therefore everywhere find men whose profession this is and who as a rule act under the supervision of the *ḳāḍī*. The part they take is to prompt the necessary formulae to the parties or to act directly as representatives of one of them, usually the *walī* of the bride. Those professional experts have developed, in most of the contemporary Muslim countries, into government officials (called in Egypt, for instance, *maʾd̲h̲ūn*) whose collaboration is necessary for contracting a legal marriage. The most important impediments to marriage are the following: 1. blood relationship, namely between the man and his female ascendants and descendants, his sisters, the female descendants of his brothers and sisters as well as his aunts and great-aunts; 2. foster-relationship (*raḍāʿ*) which by extension of the Ḳurʾānic wording (Sūra iv. 23) by tradition is regarded as an impediment to marriage in almost the same degrees as blood relationship; 3. relationship by marriage, namely between a man and his mother-in-law, daughter-in-law, step-daughter etc. in the direct line; marriage with two sisters or with an aunt and niece at the same time is also forbidden; 4. the existence of a previous marriage, in the case of a woman without limitation (inclusive of the period of waiting after the dissolution of the marriage, *ʿidda*, q.v.) and in the case of a free man with the provision that he cannot be married to more than four women at once; 5. the existence of a threefold *ṭalāḳ* [q.v.] or of a *liʿān* [q.v.]; 6. social inequality: the man must not be by birth, profession etc. below the woman (unless both the woman and the *walī* agree); further, a free Muslim can only marry another's slave girl if he cannot provide the bridal gift for a free woman, and the marriage between a master (or mistress) and his slave (or her slave) is quite impossible (a master is however permitted concubinage with his slave girls); 7. difference of religion: there is no exception to the prohibition of marriage between a Muslim woman and an infidel man, while the permission given in theory for marriage between Muslim men and the women of the possessors of a scripture is at least by the S̲h̲āfiʿīs so restricted by conditions as to be prohibited in practice; 8. temporary obstacles such as the state of *iḥrām* [q.v.]. On the other hand, the law knows no minimum age for a legal marriage. If a marriage contract does not fulfil the legal requirements, it is invalid; the Ḥanafīs and especially the Mālikīs but not the S̲h̲āfiʿīs distinguish in this case between void (*bāṭil*; q.v.) and incorrect (*fāsid*) according as the error affects an essential or unessential element in the contract; in the former case there is no marriage at all, in the second its validity may be attacked but (according to the Mālikīs) consummation removes any defect. Marriage does not produce any community of property between husband and wife and the woman retains her complete freedom of dealing; this is somewhat restricted by the Mālīkīs who place her under the guardianship" (*wilāya*) of the husband; but husband and wife inherit from each other [cf. MĪRĀT̲H̲]. The man alone has to bear the expense of the household and is obliged to support (*nafaḳa*) his wife in a style befitting her station; if he should not be in a position to do so his wife may demand divorce by *fask̲h̲*. The man can demand from his wife readiness for marital intercourse and obedience generally; if she is continually disobedient, she loses her claim to support and may be chastised by the man. The latter in his turn is expressly forbidden to take upon himself vows of continence (*īlāʾ* and *ẓihār*). Children are regarded as legitimate if they are born at least six months after consummation of the marriage and not more than 4 years (the predominant S̲h̲āfiʿī view) after its dissolution; it is presumed that such children are begotten by the husband himself; the latter has the right to dispute his paternity by *liʿān*. Parentage can also be established by *iḳrār* [q.v.], while both adoption and recognition of illegitimate children are impossible. A slave may marry only with the consent of the owner who thereby becomes liable for the financial obligations arising out of the contract; the male slave is allowed only two wives according to the Ḥanafīs, S̲h̲āfiʿīs and Ḥanbalīs, but four according to the Mālikīs; the children of a married slave woman are slaves and property of the owner of their mother.

4. The prescriptions of the law regarding the rights and duties of husband and wife cannot be modified by the parties in the contract. This can however be effected by the man pronouncing a conditional *ṭalāḳ* immediately after the conclusion of the marriage contract; this expedient to secure the position of the woman is particularly common among Indian and Indonesian Muslims. For the rest the couple are left to private agreements which need not be mentioned in the marriage contract. The actual position of the married woman is in all Muslim countries entirely dependent on local conditions and on many special circumstances. It is not a contradiction of this to say that the legal prescriptions regarding marriage are most carefully observed as a rule. In spite of certain ascetic tendencies Islām as a whole has been decidedly in favour of marriage. — In modern Islām the problem of the woman's position in marriage and polygamy is especially discussed between conservatives and adherents of the different trends of modernism. Attempts in India to legalize free sexual relationships by an extension of the idea of concubinage with slave girls consented by the Muslim law, have been repelled [cf. however, UMM AL-WALAD]. On the other hand, modern Egyptian legislation shows a certain tendency of bringing the Muḥammadan marriage under a closer control by the state and to adopt,

although with orthodox Muslim arguments, some of the leading western ideas on this subject. Nevertheless marriage, at least between Muslims, remains governed here as elsewhere by the *sharīʿa*, and Turkey and Albania are so far the only Muḥammadan countries which have regulated this institution, together with the whole family law, by the wholesale adoption of western codes.

5. Alongside of the usual form of the old Arabian marriage which in spite of its laxity aimed at the foundation of a household and the procreation of children, there existed the temporary marriage in which the pair lived together temporarily for a period previously fixed. Such temporary marriages were entered upon mainly by men who found themselves staying for a time abroad. It is by no means certain that these are referred to in Sūra iv. 24, although the Muslim name of this arrangement (*mutʿa* [q.v.]. "marriage of [sexual] pleasure") is based on the wording of the verse; it is however certain from Tradition that the Prophet really permitted *mutʿa* to his followers especially on the longer campaigns. But the caliph ʿUmar strictly prohibited *mutʿa* and regarded it as fornication (*zinā*ʾ; a group of traditions already ascribes this prohibition to the Prophet). As a result, *mutʿa* is permitted only among the Shīʿīs but prohibited by the Sunnīs. The latter have however practically the same arrangement; those who wish to live as husband and wife for a certain period simply agree to do so without stipulating it in the marriage contract.

Bibliography: For the pre-Muḥammadan Arabs: G. A. Wilken, *Het matriarchaat bij de oude Arabieren* (German translation: *Das Matriarchat bei den alten Arabern*, Leipzig 1884); W. Robertson Smith, *Kinship and Marriage in Early Arabia*; Wellhausen, *Die Ehe bei den Arabern* (*NGW Gött.*, 1893); Lammens, *Le Berceau de l'Islam*, p. 276 *sqq.* — For the traditions: Wensinck, *Handbook*, s.v. MARRIAGE; Gertrude H. Stern, *Marriage in early Islam*, London 1939. — For the doctrines of the *fiḳh*: Snouck Hurgronje, *Verspreide Geschriften*, vol. iv, Index, s.v. Huwelijk; Juynboll, *Handleiding tot de kennis van de mohammedaansche wet* (3rd ed.) p. 174 *sqq.*; Santillana, *Istituzioni di diritto musulmano malichita*, vol. i., p. 150 *sqq.*; J. López Ortiz, *Derecho musulmán*, p. 154 *sqq.*; J. Schacht, *The Origins of Muhammadan Jurisprudence*, Oxford 1950. — For the social aspect of marriage: Lammens, *Moʿâwia Ier*, 306 *sqq.*; R. Levy, *Sociology of Islam*, vol. i, p. 131 *sqq.*; Snouck Hurgronje, *Mekka in the Latter Part of the 19th Century*, Index, s.v. Marriage; *id.*, *Verspreide Geschriften*, vol. iv/i., p. 218 *sqq.*; Polak, *Persien*, vol. i., p. 194 *sqq.* — For the modernism: Goldziher, *Richtungen der islamischen Koranauslegung*, p. 360 *sqq.*; Paret, *Zur Frauenfrage in der arabisch-islamischen Welt*, Stuttgart, 1934; Kernkamp, *De Islām en de vrouw*, Amsterdam 1935. — For the ethics of marriage: H. Bauer, *Islamische Ethik*, fasc. ii.; Mez, *Die Renaissance des Islàms*, p. 276 *sq.*; do., *El Renacimiento del Islam*, p. 355 *sq.*; C. H. Becker, *Islamstudien*, vol. i., p. 407.

NĪYA (A.), intention. The acts of ceremonial law, obligatory or not, require to be preceded by a declaration by the performer, that he intends to perform such an act. This declaration, pronounced audibly or mentally, is called nīya. Without it, the act would be *bāṭil* [q.v.].

The nīya is required before the performance of the *ʿibādāt*, such as washing, bathing, prayer, alms, fasting, retreat, pilgrimage, sacrifice. "Ceremonial acts without nīya are not valid", says Ghazzālī (*Iḥyā*ʾ, Cairo 1282, iv. 316). Yet a survey of the opinions of the lawyers regarding the nīya in connection with each of the *ʿibādāt* would show that there is only unanimity about the nīya as required before the *ṣalāt*.

Further the nīya must immediately precede the act, lest it should lose its character and become simple decision (*ʿazm*). It must accompany the act until the end (Abū Isḥāḳ al-Shīrāzī, *Tanbīh*, ed. Juynboll, p. 3). Its seat is the heart, the central organ of intellect and attention. Lunatics, therefore, cannot pronounce a valid nīya.

So the nīya has become a legal act of its own. It is usually called obligatory, but in some cases, e.g. the washing of the dead, commendable. It can even be asked what the intention of the nīya is. According to al-Bādjūrī (i. 57), four conditions must be fulfilled in a nīya: who pronounces it, must be Muslim, *compos mentis*, well acquainted with the act he wants to perform, and having the purpose to perform this act. In some instances *adjmaʿa* is used, where the later language has *nawā* (e.g. Nasāʾī, *Ṣiyām*, bāb 68; Tirmidhī, *Ṣawm*, bāb 33).

The term does not occur in the Ḳurʾān. It is found in canonical *ḥadīth*, but the passages show that is has not yet acquired in this literature the technical meaning and limitation described above. The development of this technical use appears to have taken place gradually, probably aided by Jewish influence. In Jewish law the *kawwānā* has a function wholly analogous to the nīya. Al-Shāfiʿī (d. 204/820) appears to be acquainted with the nīya in its technical sense (*Kitāb al-umm*). In canonical *ḥadīth* — i.e. the literature which, generally speaking, reflects the state of things up to the middle of the eighth century A.D. — neither the verb *nawā* nor the noun nīya appears to have any special technical connection with the *ʿibādāt*. On the contrary, nīya has here the common meaning of intention.

In this sense it is of great importance. Bukhārī opens his collection with a tradition, which in this place is apparently meant as a motto. It runs: "Works are in their intention only" (*innama 'l-aʿmāl bi 'l-nīya* or *bi 'l-nīyāt*). This tradition occurs frequently in the canonical collections. It constitutes a religious and moral criterion superior to that of the law. The value of an *ʿibāda*, even if performed in complete accordance with the precepts of the law, depends upon the intention of the performer, and if this intention should be sinful, the work would be valueless. "For", adds the tradition just mentioned", "every man receives only what he has intended"; or "his wages shall be in accordance with his intention" (Mālik, *Djanāʾiz*, trad. 36). In answer to the question how long the *hidjra* is open, tradition says: "There is no *hidjra* after the capture of Mecca, only holy war and intention" (Bukhārī, *Manāḳib al-Anṣār*, bāb 45; *Djihād*, bāb 1, 27; Muslim, *Imāra*, trad. 85, 86 etc.). This higher criterion, once admitted, may suspend the law in several cases (cf. Snouck Hurgronje, *Islam und Phonograph*, in *Verspr. Geschriften*, ii. 419 *sqq.*). So the intention, in this sense, becomes a work of its own, just as the intention in its juridical application. Good intention is taken into account by Allāh, even if not carried out; it heightens the value of the work. On the other hand, refraining from an evil intention is reckoned as a good work (Bukhārī, *Riḳāḳ*, bāb 31). In this connection the (post-canonical) tradition can be understood, according to which the intention of the faithful is better than his work (*Lisān al-ʿArab*, xx. 223; cf. Ghazzālī, *Iḥyāʾ*, iv. 330 *sqq.* where this tradition is discussed). In similar instances nīya comes near to the meaning of *ikhlāṣ*.

Bibliography: al-Bādjūrī, *Ḥāshiya*, Cairo 1303, i. 57; al-Shaʿrānī, *al-Mīzān al-kubrā*, Cairo 1279, i. 135, 136, 161; ii. 2, 20, 30, 42; al-Ghazzālī, *Kitāb al-wadjīz*, Cairo 1317, i. 11, 12, 40, 87, 100 *sq.*, 106, 115; do., *Iḥyāʾ*, vol. iv., book vii.; also transl. into German by H. Bauer, Halle a.d. Saale 1916; C. Snouck Hurgronje, *Verspreide Geschriften*, i. 50; ii. 90; Th. W. Juynboll, *Handleiding*, index, s.v.; Wensinck, *Handbook*, s.v. Intention; do., *De intentie ... der semietische volken*, in *Versl. Med. Ak. Amst.*, ser. v., vol. iv., p. 109 *sqq.*

NŪḤ, the Noah of the Bible, is a particularly popular figure in the Ḳurʾān and in Muslim legend. Thaʿlabī gives 15 virtues by which Nūḥ is distinguished among the prophets. The Bible does not regard Noah as a prophet. In the Ḳurʾān the gift of *waḥy* (inspiration) is bestowed upon Nūḥ (xi. 36) and he is the first prophet of punishment, followed by Hūd, Ṣāliḥ, Lūṭ, Shuʿaib and Mūsā. Ibrāhīm is one of his following (*shīʿa*) (Sūra xxxvii. 83). He is the perspicuous admonisher (*nadhīr mubīn*, xi. 25; lxxi. 2) the *rasūl amīn* "the true messenger of God" (xxvi. 107), the *ʿabd shakūr*, "the grateful servant of God" (xvii. 3). Allāh enters into a covenant with Nūḥ just as with Ibrāhīm, Mūsā and ʿĪsā (xxxiii. 7). Peace and blessings are promised him (xi. 48), *salām* in the two worlds (xxxvii. 79), like Ibrāhīm, Mūsā, Hārūn, Ilyās (S. Speyer, *Die bibl. Erzählungen im Qoran*). Muḥammad is fond of seeing himself reflected in the earlier prophets. In the case of Nūḥ, the Muslim Ḳurʾān exegetes have already noticed this (see Grünbaum, *Neue Beiträge*, p. 90). The mission of Nūḥ is put on the same level with the mission of Ibrāhīm, Mūsā, ʿĪsā, and even with the revelation to Muḥammad (xlii. 13). Just as Ibrāhīm, Mūsā, Muḥammad, Nūḥ is also considered to be a Muslim (x. 72). Muḥammad often passes himself off as *nadhīr mubīn* (see Speyer, p. 93, note 7). When Nūḥ asks forgiveness for his parents and for the visitors of his house (lxxi. 29), this applies better to Muḥammad. Muḥammad puts into the mouth of Nūḥ things that he would himself like to say and into the mouths of his opponents what he himself has heard from his. Nūḥ is reproached with being only one of the people (x. 71—73). God should rather have sent an angel (xxiii. 24). Nūḥ is wrong (vii. 60), is lying, deceiving (vii. 64), is possessed by *djinn* (liv. 9), only the lowest join him (xi. 27; xxvi. 111). When Nūḥ replies: "it is grievous to you that I live among you, I seek no reward, my regard is with Allāh (x. 71—73; xi. 29); I do not claim to possess Allāh's treasures, to know his secrets, to be an angel and I cannot say to those whom ye despise, God shall not give you any good" (xi. 29—31), we have here an echo of Muḥammad's defence and embarrassment about many of his followers. Muḥammad pictures events as follows: Allāh sends Nūḥ to the sinful people. Sūra lxxi. which bears his name, gives one of these sermons threatening punishment for which other analogies can be found. The people scorn him. Allāh commands him to build an ark by divine inspiration. Then the "chaldron boils" (xi. 40; xxiii. 27). The waters drown everything; only two of every kind of living creature are saved and the believers whom Nūḥ takes into the ark with him. But there were very few who believed. Nūḥ appeals even to his son in vain; the latter takes refuge on a mountain but is drowned. When Nūḥ bids the waters be still, the ark lands on mount Djūdī (xi. 25—49). Not only Noah's son but also his wife (with Lūṭ's wife) are sinners (lxvi. 10). From the *Haggada* are developed, as Geiger shows, the following elements of this Ḳurʾānic legend of Nūḥ: 1. Nūḥ appears as a prophet and admonisher; 2. his people laugh at the ark; 3. his family is punished with hot water (main passages: *Talm. Sanhedrin*, 108; *Gen. Rabba*, xxix.—xxxvi. *Tanḥūma Noah*).

The post-Ḳurʾānic legend of Nūḥ as in other cases fills up the gaps, gives the names of those not mentioned in the Ḳurʾān, makes many links e.g. connects Nūḥ with Feridūn of the Persian epic although it is pointed out that the Magi (Persians) do not know the story of the flood. Nūḥ's wife is called Wāliya and her sin is that she described Nūḥ to his people as *madjnūn*. The names of Nūḥ's sons. Sām, Ḥām, Yāfith are known to Ḳurʾān exegesis from the Bible but it also gives the name of Nūḥ's sinful son who perished in the flood: Kanʿān, "whom the Arabs call Yām". Muḥammad's statement that Nūḥ was 950 years of age at the time of the flood (*ṭūfān*) (xxix. 14) is probably based on Gen. ix. 39 which says Nūḥ lived 950 years in all, but on the other hand, it serves as a basis for calculations which make Nūḥ the first *muʿammar*; according to the *Kitāb al-muʿammarīn* of Abū Ḥātim al-Sidjistānī (ed. Goldziher, p. 1), who begins his book with Nūḥ, he lived 1,450 years. Yet in his dying hour he describes his life as a house with two doors in which one goes in through one and out through the other. Muslim legend knows the Biblical story of Nūḥ, his times and his sons, but embellishes it greatly and in al-Kisāʾī it becomes a romance. From the union of Ḳābil's and Shīth's descendants arises a sinful people which rejects Nūḥ's warnings. He therefore at God's command builds the ark from trees which he has himself planted. As he is hammering and building the people mock him: "once a prophet, now a carpenter?" "a ship for the mainland?". The ark had a head and tail like a cock, a body like a bird (Thaʿlabī). How was the ark built? At the wish of the apostles, Jesus arouses Sām (or Ḥām) b. Nūḥ from the dead and he describes the ark and its arrangements: in the lower storey were the quadrupeds, in the next the human beings and in the top the birds. Nūḥ brought the ant into the ark first and the ass which was slow because Iblīs was clinging to his tail, last. Nūḥ called out impatiently: "come in even if Satan is with thee"; so Iblīs also had to be taken in. The pig arose out of the tail of the elephant and the cat from the lion. How could the goat exist alongside of the wolf, or the dove beside the birds of prey? God tamed their instincts. The number of human beings in the ark varies in legend between seven and eighty. ʿŪdj b. ʿAnaḳ was also saved along with the believers. Ḳābil's race was drowned. Nūḥ also took Adam's body with him which was used to separate the women from the men. For in the ark continence was ordered, for man and beast. Only Ḥām transgressed and for this was punished with a black skin. The whole world was covered with water and only the Ḥaram (in al-Kisāʾī also the site of the sanctuary in Jerusalem) was spared; the Kaʿba was taken up into heaven and Djibrīl concealed the Black Stone (according to al-Kisāʾī the stone was snow-white until the Flood). Nūḥ sent out the raven but finding some carrion it forgot Nūḥ; then he sent the dove which brought back an olive leaf in its bill and mud on its feet; as a reward it was given its collar and became a domestic bird. On the day of ʿĀshūrāʾ every one came out of the ark, men and beasts fasted and gave thanks to Allāh.

Later the legend of the different degrees of drunkenness was also connected with Nūḥ. On the vine planted by Nūḥ Iblīs pours the blood of several animals; who drinks the wine is afflicted with their qualities. Damīrī quotes the legend from the book *Rawḍat al-ʿulamāʾ*. The older Ḳurʾān-exegesis, Ṭabarī, Thaʿlabī and others, still seems ignorant of it.

The feature that Nūḥ is considered to be a prophet, is already found in the Tannaitic *Seder ʿOlām* xxi. The *Vetus Itala* on Tobit iv. 13 (Neubauer, *The book of Tobit*, lxxiv.) says: Noe prophetavit prior.

Bibliography: Ṭabarī i. 174—201; Ibn al-Athīr, *al-Kāmil*, i. 27—29; Thaʿlabī, *Ḳiṣaṣ al-anbiyāʾ*, Cairo 1325, p. 34—38; al-Kisāʾī, *Ḳiṣaṣ al-anbiyāʾ*, ed. Eisenberg, i. 85—102; Geiger, *Was hat Mohammed ...*, 1902², p. 106—111; M. Grünbaum, *Neue Beiträge*, p. 79—90; J. Horovitz, *Hebrew Union College Annual*, ii., 1925, p. 151; do., *Koranische Untersuchungen*, 1926, esp. p. 146; J. Walker, *Biblical Characters in the Koran*, p. 113—121; Sidersky, *Les origines des légendes musulmanes*, Paris 1933, p. 26 *sq.*; Speyer, *Die Bibl. Erzählungen im Qoran*, p. 84—115. — On the name Nūḥ: Goldziher, in *ZDMG*, xxiv. (1870), 207—211; on Nūḥ as Muʿammar; Goldziher, *Abhandlungen zur arabischen Philologie*, ii., Leyden 1899, p. lxxxix. and p. 2.

NŪR (A.), light. The doctrine that God is light and reveals himself as such in the world and to man is very old and widely disseminated in Oriental religions as well as in Hellenistic gnosis and philosophy. We cannot here go into the early history; it will be sufficient to refer to some parallels in the Old and New Testaments, e.g. Gen. i. 3; Isaiah, lx. 1, 19; Zach., iv.; John, i. 4—9; iii. 19; v. 35; viii. 12; xii. 35 and Rev., xxi. 23 *sq.*

How Muḥammad became acquainted with this teaching we do not know, but the Ḳurʾān has its "light" verses [notably Sūra xxiv. 35, the" light verse" proper; cf. with it Sūra xxxiii. 46 (Muḥammad as lamp); lxi. 8 *sq.* (Allāh's light); lxiv. 8 (the light sent down = revelation)]. The light verse runs (as translated by Goldziher, in *Richtungen*, p. 183 *sq.*): "Allāh is the light of the heavens and of the earth; his light is like a niche in which there is a lamp; the lamp is in a glass and the glass is like a shining star; it is lit from a blessed tree, an olive-tree, neither an eastern nor a western one; its oil almost shines alone even if no fire touches it; light upon light. Allāh leads to his light whom he will, and Allāh creates allegories for man, and Allāh knows all things".

From the context it is clear that we have to think of the light of religious knowledge, of the truth which Allāh communicates through his Prophet to his creatures especially the believers (cf. also Sūra xxiv. 40). It is pure light, light upon light, which has nothing to do with fire (*nār*), which is lit from an olive tree, perhaps not of this world (cf. however A. J. Wensinck, *Tree and Bird as cosmological Symbols in Western Asia*, in *Verh. Ak. Amst.*, 1921, p. 27 *sq.*). Lastly it is Allāh as the all-knowing who instructs men and leads them to the light of his revelation (cf. Sūra lxiv. 8). It is clear that we have here traces of gnostic imagery but those rationalist theologians, who — whether to avoid any comparison of the creature with God or to oppose the fantastic mystics — interpreted the light of Allāh as a symbol of his good guidance probably diverged less from the sense of the Ḳurʾān than most of the metaphysicians of light. Passages are very frequent in the Ḳurʾān in which Allāh appears as the Knowing (*ʿalīm*) and the Guiding (*hādī*). One did not need to look far for an exegesis on these lines. As al-Ashʿarī observes (*Maḳālāt*, ed. Ritter, ii. 534) the Muʿtazilī al-Ḥusain al-Nadjdjār interpreted the light verse to mean that God guides the inhabitants of heaven and earth. The Zaidīs also interpreted the light as Allāh's good guidance [cf. the article SHĪʿA].

From ca. 100 A.H. we find references to a prophetic doctrine of *nūr*, and gradually to a more general metaphysics of light, i.e. the doctrine that God is essentially light, the prime light and as such the source of all being, all life and all knowledge. Especially among the mystics in whose emotional thinking, being, name and image coalesced, this speculation developed. Meditation on the Ḳurʾān, Persian stimuli, gnostic-Hermetic writings, lastly and most tenaciously, Hellenistic philosophy provided the material for new ideas. Kumait (d. 743) had already sung of the light emanating through Adam via Muḥammad into the family of ʿAlī [cf. the article SHĪʿA]. The doctrine of light was dialectically expounded by Sahl al-Tustarī (d. 896) (see also Massignon, *Textes inéd.*, p. 39 and the article SAHL AL-TUSTARĪ).

The first representatives of a metaphysics of light in Islām readily fell under the suspicion of Manichaeism, i.e. of the dualism of *nūr* and *ẓulma* (darkness) as the eternal principles. The tradition of Tirmidhī that Allāh created in darkness [cf. the article KHALḲ] must have aroused misgivings. The physician Rāzī (d. 923 or 932), although a Hellenistic philosopher, adopted ideas from Persia and was for this refuted or cursed by various theologians and philosophers. Many mystics also (e.g. Ḥallādj; according to Massignon, *Passion*, p. 150 *sq.* wrongly) were accused of this dualism.

But the speculations about *nūr* found a powerful support from the ninth century in the monistic doctrine of light of the Neo-Platonists (we do not know of any Persian monism of light) which was compatible with the monism of Islām. The father of this doctrine is Plato, who in his *Politeia*, 506 D *sqq.* compares the idea of the good in the supersensual world with Helios as the light of the physical world. The contrast is not therefore between light and darkness but between the world of ideas or mind and its copy, the physical world of bodies, in the upper world pure light, in the lower world light more or less mixed with darkness. Among the Neo-Platonists the idea of the good = the highest God = pure light. This identification was also facilitated by the fact that according to Aristotle's conception light is nothing corporeal (*De anima*, ii. 7, 418). From the context which is however not all clear, it appears that Aristotle regarded light as an effective force. This is however of no importance here. Many Aristotelian forces and Platonic ideas are described by Neo-Pythagoreans and Neo-Platonists sometimes as forces and sometimes as substance (spiritual). With Aristotle darkness was conceived not as something positive but as the absence of light.

From this developed the doctrine which we find in the Arabic "Theology of Aristotle". Not far from the beginning (ed. Dieterici, p. 3) it is said: the power of light (*ḳuwwa nūriya*) is communicated by the prime cause, the creator, to the *ʿaḳl* and by the *ʿaḳl* to the world soul, then from the *ʿaḳl* through the world soul to nature and from the world soul through nature to things which originate and decay. The whole process of this creative development proceeds without movement and timelessly. But God who causes the force of light to pour forth is also light (*nūr*; occasional synonyms: *ḥusn, bahāʾ*), the "prime light" (p. 51) or (p. 44) the "light of lights". Light (p. 51) is essentially in God not a quality (*ṣifa*) for God has no qualities but works through his being (*huwīya*) alone. The light flows through the whole world, particularly the world of men. From the supersensual original (p. 150), the first man (*insān ʿaḳlī*), it flows over the second man (*insān nafsānī*) and from him to the third (*insān d̲j̲ismānī*). These are the originals of the so-called real men. Light is of course found in its purest form in the souls of the wise and the good (p. 51). It should be noted also that *nūr* as a spiritual force (*rūḥānī, ʿaḳlī*) is distinguished from fire (*nār*) which is said to be only a force in matter with definite quality (p. 85). Fire of course like everything else has its supersensual original. But this is more connected with life than with light.

The elevation of the soul to the divine world of light corresponds to the creative descent of light (p. 8). When the soul has passed on its return beyond the world of the *ʿaḳl*, it sees there the pure light and the beauty of God, the goal of all mystics.

Although the author of the *Liber de causis* is of the opinion that nothing can be predicated regarding God, yet he has to call him the prime cause and more exactly pure light (§ 5, ed. Bardenhewer, p. 69) and as such the origin of all being and all knowledge (in God is *wud̲j̲ūd* = *maʿrifa*; see § 23, p. 103).

The light emanated by God may, if it is regarded as an independent entity, be placed at various parts of the system. Most philosophers and theologians connect it with the *rūḥ* or *ʿaḳl* or identify it with them, sometimes also with life (*ḥayāt*), but this must be more closely investigated.

The great philosophers in Islām, al-Fārābī and Ibn Sīnā, connected the doctrine of light with the *ʿaḳl* in metaphysics as well as in psychology. Al-Fārābī is fond of using many synonyms for the light of God and the *ʿaḳl* (*bahāʾ* etc.; see e.g. *Der Musterstaat*, ed. Dieterici, p. 13 *sqq.*). In the biography of al-Fārābī in Ibn Abī Uṣaibiʿa (*ʿUyūn*, ed. Müller, ii. 134—140) a prayer is attributed to him in which God is invoked as the "prime cause of things and light of the earth and of heaven". Ibn Sīnā like al-Fārābī takes up the doctrine of light in theology and further develops it. In his psychological writings he regards the light as a link of the soul and body (cf. Sahl al-Tustarī who places *nūr* between *rūḥ* and *ṭīn* in the four elements of man). In the *Kitāb al-is̲h̲ārāt* (ed. Forget, Leyden 1892, p. 126 *sq.*) he even reads the whole metaphysical doctrine of the *ʿaḳl* of the Aristotelians into the light verse of the Ḳurʾān. Light is the *ʿaḳl bi 'l-fiʿl*, fire the *ʿaḳl faʿʿāl* and so on. Allāh's *nūr* is therefore like the *nous* of Aristotle! This discovery of Ibn Sīnā's was incorporated in the pious reflections of G̲h̲azzālī (in *Maʿārid̲j̲ al-ḳuds fi madārid̲j̲ maʿrifat al-nafs*, Cairo 1927, p. 58 *sq.*).

The best expositions of the further developments of speculation on *nūr*, especially among the gnostics and mystics, are in the articles KARMAṬIANS and TAṢAWWUF.

Bibliography: Clermont-Ganneau, *La lampe et l'olivier dans le Coran* (in *RHR*, lxxxi., 1920, p. 213—259); W. H. T. Gairdner, *al-G̲h̲azālī*'s *Mis̲h̲kāt al-Anwār and the G̲h̲azāli-Problem* (in *Isl.*, v., 1914, p. 121—153); do., *al-G̲h̲azālī*'s *Mis̲h̲kāt al-Anwār*, transl. with introduction, London 1924; cf. also the articles ʿAḲL and AL-INSĀN AL-KĀMIL.

NŪR MUḤAMMADĪ, the technical term for the pre-existence of the soul of the Prophet Muḥammad; the predestined essence of the last of the prophets is said to have been created first of all, in the form of a dense and luminous point; all the predestined souls are said to have emanated from this.

Among the Sunnīs, the idea first appears among the mystics in the third century A.H., then gradually begins to dominate popular worship (cf. Sahl Tustarī and Ḥakīm Tirmid̲h̲ī, in Massignon, *Recueil*. . ., 1929, p. 34, No. 39 and p. 39); Abū Bakr Wāsiṭī, whose *Ḥāmīm al-ḳidam* should be identified with ch. i. of the *Ṭawāsīn* of Ḥallād̲j̲ (cf. Massignon, *Passion*, p. 830—840) expounds it. According to Kīlānī, Muḥammad is "the image in the pupil which is in the centre of the eye of creation" (*insān ʿain al-wud̲j̲ūd*); this is what Ibn ʿArabī calls the *ḥaḳīḳa muḥammadīya* the pre-eternal conception of which is celebrated by the poets Ṣarṣarī, Witrī and the mystic D̲j̲azūlī, hence Muḥammad's immaculate pedigree since Adam (cf. the poems on the *mawlid*). Orthodoxy has always carefully placed the doctrine of the uncreated Ḳurʾān above this cult. Popular legend among the *ḥas̲h̲wīya* has reduced and materialized this devotion: in showing the model of the body of the Prophet kneaded from a handful of earth from Paradise with water from the spring Tasnīm which makes it shine like a white pearl. But it is certain that it is a question here primarily of a gnostic pre-existence, an intellectual substance of the nature of the angels as is evident from the antiquity of the equation (*nūr* = *ʿaḳl*, borrowed by Tirmid̲h̲ī from the Ismāʿīlīs [cf. ʿAḲL].

Among the S̲h̲īʿīs, this doctrine appears earlier and with more logical coherence; among the extremists, who explain this "prophetic light", either as a "spirit" transmitted from age to age and from elect to elect, or as spermatic germ (traducianism) inherited from male to male. At the beginning of the second century Mug̲h̲īra and D̲j̲ābir taught the primogeniture of the luminous shadow (*ẓill*, opposed to *s̲h̲abaḥ* "dark body") of Muḥammad. It is a fundamental dogma of Ismāʿīlism from its beginning (*al-sābiḳ nūr maḥḍ* = *al-mīm*); it is found again extended through solidarity to all the ʿAlids or to all the Ṭālibīs with the gift of sinlessness among the Nuṣairīs and even among many pious Imāmī writers (Kulīnī, *Kāfī*, p. 116).

The authors of this doctrine derive it from the Ḳurʾān (*āyat al-nūr*: xxiv. 35; the *taṣliya*; the connexion between the two terms of the *s̲h̲ahāda*) effectively interpreted by the old ḥadīt̲h̲s (*durra baiḍā*; *lawlāka*) as proving that Muḥammad is "the first (by *taḳdīr, waṣla, k̲h̲alḳ*) and the last" (by *īd̲j̲ād, nubuwwa, baʿt̲h̲*). But it certainly required for its development the stimulus of Christian, gnostic and Manichaean antecedents.

Bibliography: Goldziher, *Neuplatonische und gnostische Elemente im Ḥadīt̲h̲*, in *ZA*, xxii. (1908), p. 317—344; T. Andrae, *Die Person Muhammads* . . ., 1917, p. 313—326; V. Ivanow, *L'Ummu 'l-kitāb*, in *REI*, 1932, p. 444—451.

NŪRBAK̲H̲S̲H̲ĪYA, religious sect or order called after Muḥammad b. Muḥammad b. ʿAbd Allāh, called Nūrbak̲h̲s̲h̲ (795—869/1393—1465).

1. Life of the founder. Of this person there is a detailed biography in the work *Mad̲j̲ālis al-muʾminīn* of Nūr Allāh al-S̲h̲us̲h̲tarī (Bodleian, MS., Ous. 366; see also Brit. Mus. Catalogue of Persian MSS), chiefly based on a work (*tad̲h̲kira*) by Mu-

ḥammad b. Muḥammad al-Samarḳandī. His father was born in Ḳaṭīf, and his grand father in al-Ḥasā, whence in some *ghazals* he styles himself Laḥsawī. His father migrated to Ḳā'in in Ḳuhistān, where his son was born. The latter became a disciple of Isḥāḳ al-Khutlānī, himself a disciple of Saiyid ʿAlī al-Hamadhānī (whose biography is published in *Khazīnat al-aṣfiyā'*, Lucknow 1322, ii. 293). Isḥāḳ in obedience to a dream gave his pupil the name Nūrbakhsh ("light-gift"), and conferred on him the *khirḳa* of ʿAlī al-Hamadhānī. In virtue of his supposed descent from the Imām Mūsā al-Kāẓim he received the title Mahdī, and was proclaimed Caliph by a number of followers; indeed in the heading of his *Ghazals* (Brit. Mus. Add. 16779) he is styled "Imām and Caliph over all the Muslims". In a letter to a disciple (Brit. Mus. Add. 7688) he claims mastery of all sciences, religious and secular; he could have taught Plato mathematics, etc. He calls on the people of his time to take pride in such a contemporary and display activity in his cause. These pretensions were taken seriously by the Sulṭān Shāh-rukh (Tīmūrid, 807—850), whose viceroy Bāyazid arrested him at Kuh-Tīrī "a fortress in the neighbourhood of Khutlān", whither he had gone in 826; he was sent to Herāt and thence to Shīrāz, where he was released by Ibrāhīm Sulṭān; after traveling to Baṣra, Ḥilla, Baghdād and the (Shīʿī) Sanctuaries, he went to Kurdistān, where he was again proclaimed Caliph, and coins were struck in his name. He was again arrested by Shāh-rukh's order, and brought to Ādharbāidjān; he made his escape and after much suffering reached Khalkhāl, where he was recaptured, and sent back to Shāh-rukh, who despatched him to Herāt, where he had to mount the pulpit and abjure the caliphate. In 848 he was released on condition that he confined his activities to teaching; but, having incurred suspicion he was sent to Tabrīz, thence to Shirwān, and thence to Gīlān.

After Shāh-rukh's death he was set free, and took up his residence in a village Sulfan in the neighbourhood of Raiy, where he died.

2. His doctrines. In his poems (*ghazal*, *mathnawī* and *rubāʿī*), he insists on his personal importance, but also emphasizes the Ṣūfī pantheism, e.g. "We have washed away the impress of other from the tablet of existences; we have seen that the world has qualities and an identical substance". Prose works by him were a *Risāla-i ʿaḳīda* probably in Persian, and a treatise on Law, in Arabic, called *al-Fiḳh al-aḥwaṭ*. Neither of these appears to have reached Europe. The extracts from the latter given in the *Madjālis* are Shīʿī in character. The *imām* besides possessing numerous virtues must be a descendant of ʿAlī and Fāṭima; this is sufficient for "the lesser *djihād*", but for "the greater" he must also be a *walī* perfect in the *maḳāmāt* of that dignity. The *mutʿa* marriage is lawful, since it was so certainly in the Prophet's time, and the writer had been commanded to abolish innovations and revive the practice of the Prophet's time. He rejects the expedient called *ʿawl* in dealing with deceased persons' estates, as being neither in the Ḳur'ān nor the Sunna.

3. Later history of the sect. The *Madjālis* names two successors (*khalīfa*) of Nūrbakhsh: Shams al-Dīn Muḥammad b. Yaḥyā al-Lahdjānī al-Gīlānī, called Asīrī, the author of a *Dīwān* of which there is a copy in the Brit. Mus.; this person built a *khānḳāh* in Shīrāz; and Nūrbakhsh's son Shāh Ḳāsim Faiḍbakhsh, first heard of in ʿIrāḳ, whence by permission of the Aḳ-Ḳoyunlu Sulṭān Yaʿḳūb (884—896) he was allowed to go to Khurāsān to cure Ḥusain Mīrzā, the governor, of an ailment by his *baraka*. His religious opinions won him the favour of Ismāʿīl the Ṣafawid (907—930). According to Firishta, who cites the *Ẓafarnāme*, a disciple of Shāh Ḳāsim, named Mīr Shams al-Dīn went from ʿIrāḳ to Kashmīr about 902, where he was received with high honour by Fatḥ Khān, who made over to him the confiscated lands which had formerly fallen to the crown. In a short time many of the Kashmīrīs, particularly those of the tribe Čuk, became converts to the Nūrbakhshī sect (Firishta, transl. Briggs, Calcutta 1910). The Kashmīrīs had previously been Sunnī of the Ḥanafī rite according to Mīrzā Ḥusain (author of *Ta'rīkh-i rashīdī*, transl. E. D. Ross, London 1895, p. 435), who when he came into possession of the country asked the opinion of the *ʿulamā'* of Hindustān about *al-Fiḳh al-aḥwaṭ*; as they condemned it as heretical, he persecuted and endeavoured to extirpate the sect (about 950). His confused and fanatical account of it has misled some European writers. It survived his persecution, and according to J. Biddulph (*Tribes of the Hindoo Koosh*, Calcutta 1880) it numbers over 20,000 followers, most of whom are to be found in Shigar and Khapolor of Baltistān. A few of the sect, he adds, are now to be found in Kishtwar, to which place they were deported by Golab Sing when he conquered Baltistān.

The work last cited contains some details about their practices; its account is, however, mixed with fables, and without access to the *Fiḳh aḥwaṭ* it is difficult to estimate the justice of the assertion that the system is "an attempt to form a *via media* between Shīʿī and Sunnī doctrines".

NUṢAIRĪ, the name of an extreme Shīʿa sect in Syria.

I. The etymology of the name is disputed; the most probable explanation is that it is a *nisba* from Ibn Nuṣair, i.e. Muḥammad b. Nuṣair Namīrī ʿAbdī (= of the ʿAbd al-Ḳais, a Bakr clan), whom we will find below as the first theologian of the sect.

As a matter of fact this name adopted from the time of Khaṣībī (d. 346/957) by these sectarians, previously called Namīrīya (Nawbakhtī, *Firaḳ*, p. 78; Ashʿarī, *Maḳālāt*, i. 15) and who called themselves *mu'minūn*, has been applied since Samʿānī and ʿUmāra (ed. Derenbourg, p. 145, 286) not to a district only partly converted in the north of Syria, but to an extreme Shīʿa sect also found in Egypt and along the Euphrates. This etymology is that of all the Muslim heresiographers, from the Shīʿī Ibn al-Ghaḍā'irī (d. 411 A.H.) and the Sunnī Ibn Ḥazm.

II. The term has three acceptations: administrative, social and religious.

a. Administration: it is the "mountain of the Anṣārīye" of Syria (formerly Djabal Lukkām), the former *liwā* of Lādhiḳīya to the east of the Orontes which has been extended to the south and from 1920 to 1945 has been the state of the Alawīs (6,500 sq. km.; 334,173 inhabitants end of 1933 of whom 213,066 are Nuṣairīs, 61,817 Sunnīs in the north of Ṣahyūn and at Bāniyās, 5,669 Ismāʿīlīs at Ḳadmūs and Maṣyaf, 53,604 Christians mainly Orthodox at al-Ḥiṣn and to the north of Ṭarṭūs), capital Lādhiḳīya (22,000); a country of patient and industrious agriculturalists (tobacco, silkworms). Its place-names studied by M. Hartmann (*ZDPV*, xiv. [1891], 151—255) show an old stratum of names in part Aramaic and later vocational Arabic without any definite local religious traits except for modern S̲h̲īᶜa influences, beneath which one can hardly see the pagan or Christian culture of the substratum (cf. on the contrary the Lebanon). The study of the district from the point of view of ethnology and folklore has hardly begun; certain prohibitions regarding food have been noted (Niebuhr, *loc. cit.*; Dupont, in *JA*, 1824, p. 134; *Bākūra*, p. 57), some general (camels, hares, eels and catfish) and others special to the S̲h̲amsiya (female or maimed animals, gazelles, pig, crab, shellfish, pumpkins, *bāmiya*, tomatoes). The only domestic art is basket-making.

b. Socially, the name covers tribes of different origins, almost all speaking Arabic, who have adopted the Nuṣairī teaching:

1. in the state of the Alawīs (213,000): the nucleus seems to be descended from Yemen clans of Hamdān and Kinda (Yaᶜḳūbī, in *BGA*, vii. 324), G̲h̲assān, Bahrā and Tanūk̲h̲ (Hamdānī, *Ṣifa* p. 132) early converted to the S̲h̲īᶜa, from Tiberias and the D̲j̲abal ᶜĀmil (where are still Mutawālīs) to Aleppo, increased by immigrants from Ṭaiy (end of the ninth century A.D.) and from G̲h̲assān who at the time the crusaders were being driven back came with their amīr Ḥasan b. Makzūn (d. 638/1240, ancestor of the Ḥaddādīn), from Mount Sind̲j̲ār, and imposed on the district their ruling families, their clans and ethnical structure (M. E. G̲h̲ālib Ṭawīl, p. 356). The following is the present day list of the principal clans (ᶜas̲h̲āᵓir) (map in *RMM*, xlix. 6; cf. *ibid.*, xxxvi. 278; and Ṭawīl, p. 349—52) grouped in 4 confederations: Kalbīya (at Ḳardāḥa; with Nawāṣira, Ḳarāḥila, D̲j̲ullaiḳīya, Ras̲h̲āwina, S̲h̲alāhima, Rasālina, D̲j̲urdīya, Bait al-S̲h̲ilf, Bait Muḥammad and Darāwisa); K̲h̲aiyāṭīn (at Marḳab with Ṣarāmita, Mak̲h̲āliṣa, Faḳāwira, ᶜAmāmira [mixed with ᶜAbd al-Ḳais]); Ḥaddādīn (clan of the amīr Ḥasan b. Makzūn: with Mahāliba, Banī ᶜAlī Yas̲h̲ūtīya, ᶜAtārīya Mas̲h̲āliba); and Matāwira (with Numailātīya, Sawārik of Aleppo, Ṣawārima, Mahāriza who claim to be Hās̲h̲imīs and Bas̲h̲ārig̲h̲a). From the xiiᵗʰ century their political history has been a series of persecutions by invaders (the Crusades; Baibars who covered the country with mosques; legend of Durrat al-Ṣadaf, daughter of Saᶜīd al-Anṣār [tomb at Aleppo] who instigated Tīmūr to sack Damascus; massacres under Selīm I) and civil wars, both among the clans themselves and against the Ismāᶜīlīs of Ḳadmūs (lost, and retaken for a brief period in 1808 by the Mahāriza) and of Maṣyaf allied with the Turks;

2. in the sand̲j̲aḳ of Alexandretta (58,000: at Antioch 1/3), D̲j̲uwaidīye, Suwaidīye, ᶜAidīye, D̲j̲illīye;

3. in the State of Syria (29,693): at Ḥamāh and at Ḥomṣ; in two quarters of Aleppo; near D̲j̲isr, and to the north of lake Ḥūle (ᶜAin Fīt: 3,060);

4. in Palestine (2,000): to the north of Nāblus;

5. in Cilicia from the xvᵗʰ century (at Ṭarsūs and Adana: 80,000 in 1921, now turkicized);

6. along the Euphrates. In Kurdistān and in Persia, there are ultra-S̲h̲īᶜa elements who have similar views and are called Nuṣairīs (among the ᶜAlī-Ilāhīs or Ahl-i Ḥaḳḳ; q.v.);

7. in Lebanon, there were some down to the xviᵗʰ century (in Kisrawān).

III. *c.* Religion: it is the religious teaching of the Nuṣairī sect that we have to study more particularly here.

Cosmogony and eschatology. According to the Nuṣairīs there is immediately below the ineffable divinity a spiritual world of heavenly beings (or stars) which emanates from him in the following hierarchy: *ism*, *bāb* and other *ahl al-marātib* (of the first seven classes); it is the "great luminous world" (ᶜālam kabīr nūrānī); when they appear here below it is to lead back gradually to heaven the "little luminous world", fallen beings, half materialized, imprisoned in the bodies which are their tombs; this operation revives them and brings them back to heaven to form the seven last classes of the *ahl al-marātib* (119,000 out of a total of 124,000 = the traditional number of the prophets); next comes the "little world of darkness" (ẓulmānī), extinguished lights, souls whose damnation materializes (ḳumṣān al-masūk̲h̲īya) in the bodies of women and animals; and lastly the "great world of darkness" composed of all the "adversaries" (aḍdād) of the great luminous world; demons, who after innumerable metamorphoses in corpses of murdered men or slaughtered animals still quivering after death, are reduced to inert or passive matter (forged metals etc.). Just as the fall takes place through seven stages (doubts about divine appearances), so does the return to the heaven of the elect go through seven cycles or *adwār* of divine emanations.

Theory of revelation. The pure divinity (g̲h̲aib), the object of adoration, being ineffable, his first emanation is the Name (*ism*), the articulating prophetic voice (nāṭiḳ), the signification (maᶜnā) of divine authority; such was the primitive teaching, that of Abu 'l-K̲h̲aṭṭāb, the common teacher of the Ismāᶜīlīs and the Nuṣairīs. But his disciple Maimūn Ḳaddāḥ, thinking that the enunciation by the divinity of an object which manifests him, is of greater importance than its signification which is a mute idea, detached the *maᶜnā* from pure divinity, identified it with the ṣāmit (the "silent" imām; opposed to nāṭiḳ) and placed it as a mere accident, below the substance, the *ism*. Then, by reaction, other K̲h̲aṭṭābīya, like Bas̲h̲s̲h̲ār, S̲h̲aᶜīrī retaining the equation *maᶜnā = ṣāmit*, reestablished the *maᶜnā* before the *ism*. And, as Abu 'l-K̲h̲aṭṭāb had taught that in the Muḥammadīya cycle, the signification (maᶜnawīya) of the ineffable divinity was expressed through five privileged asmāᵓ (Muḥammad, ᶜAlī, Fāṭim [= the masculine form of Fāṭima, for as we have seen women have no souls; this explains why they may form part of the offering of hospitality among initiates], Ḥasan and Ḥusain, announcing equivalently its mysterious Unity), this group of Five equals, in which we recognize the Five of the *mubāhala* (cf. Massignon, *Salmān Pāk*, No. 7 of the *Publ. de la Soc. des Etudes Iraniennes*, 1933, p. 40—42) became in the hands of his pupil Maimūn a descending series of five terrestrial terms (symmetrical with the five spiritual terms, and inferior to them, the Druzes say): nāṭiḳ (= mīm), asās (= ᶜain), dāᶜī maᵓd̲h̲ūn, mukāsir: whence the mīm, the K̲h̲ārid̲j̲ī Ward̲j̲alānī remarks, has the priority [cf. NŪR MUḤAMMADĪ]. While according to Bas̲h̲s̲h̲ār, the five were equal and became Muḥammad, Fāṭim, Ḥasan, Ḥusain, Muḥ(as)sin: ᶜAlī being thought to surpass them was identified by hyperbolism and against all logic with the *maᶜnā*. It is this last list that the Nuṣairīs have adopted. And this is the origin of their "god ᶜAlī" for whom there is no need to seek antecedents in the Syrian pagan pantheon or in a Druze emanation. Bas̲h̲s̲h̲ār and the ᶜulyāᵓīya (or ᶜainīya), copied by the Nuṣairīs, have simply copied the Ḳarmaṭian list of Maimūn, by inverting the order of priority between *mīm* and *ʿain*, and making the *ṣāmit* (= *maʿnā*) the superiors of the *nāṭiḳ* (= *ism*). The following is the double list (*ism* in italics): *a.* in the seven cycles (*adwār*, *ḳibāb* personified by women among the poets) of the *ẓuhūrāt dhātīya*: 1. Hābīl, *Adam*; 2. Nūḥ, *Shīth* (sic!); 3. Yūsuf, *Yaʿḳūb*; 4. Yūshaʿ, *Mūsā*; 5. Aṣaf, *Sulaimān*; 6. Shimʿūn, *ʿĪsā*; 7. ʿAlī (= Abū Turāb, Amīr al-Naḥl), *Muḥammad*. Khaṣībī allows that there were 44 (= 63—19) other *ẓuhūrāt* (*mithlīya*) during these seven cycles; *b.* in the *saṭr al-aʾimma* (= the twelve classical imāms substituted for the early list of Ibn Nuṣair [which we shall see later] by Khaṣībī) each imām is promoted *maʿnā* after having been the *ism* of his predecessor. The mode of appearance of the two divine emanations localised behind the screen (*taghyīb*, *iḥtidjāb*) of a phantomlike body (*ḳamṣ al-ẓuhūr*, *maʿdin al-ishāra*), is a reality for the faith of the Nuṣairīs; this body is the support of a momentary illumination for the believer; while for the Druze nominalism it is only a mirage (*sarāb*) and for the Isḥāḳīya, a real body, transfigured by a gradual sanctification.

Theory of catechesis. Abu 'l-Khaṭṭāb had taught that the Five persons of the *ism* were pointed out to the believers by one or more inspired angelic intermediaries (*asbāb*, *rūḥānīyūn*; of whom the first was Salsal or al-Sīn = Salmān in the Muḥammadīya cycle; cf. *Salmān Pāk*, p. 36). These initiators became, with his disciple Maimūn, the five spiritual symmetricals of the *asmāʾ* (*ʿaḳl* = Salmān; *nafs* = Miḳdād; *djadd* = Abū Dharr; *fatḥ* = [ʿUthmān b.] Maẓʿūn; *khayāl* = [ʿAmmār] b. Yāsir: corr. thus No. 60 of the Druze catechism). While among the Nuṣairīs, these five initiators which remained equal and far below the *ism*, became the five *aitām* (Miḳdād, Abū Dharr, ʿAbd Allāh b. Rawāḥa, ʿUthmān b. Maẓʿūn and Ḳanbar), Salmān being thought to be above them was placed third as *Bāb* after the *maʿnā* and the *ism*. Such was the origin of the Nuṣairī triad, *ʿain-mīm-sīn* (= *maʿnā-ism-bāb*) in which there is no need to see an original pagan Syrian triad of Sun, Moon and Sky; this astrological correspondence, a favourite subject with Nuṣairī poets, found its way into the Shīʿa catechism of Kūfa under the influence of the Sabaeans of Ḥarrān; the assimiliation, in the spiritual, of the sun to Muḥammad and of the moon to ʿAlī (the moon, like the imām, is the regulator of canonical acts; cf. *Salmān*, p. 36, note 4) appears at Kūfa with Mughīra (d. 119). In any case if pagan survivals are at the basis of astral gnosticism, as Dussaud suggests, it is not among the uneducated peasants of Djabal Lukkām but among the town-dwellers in Ḥarrān that they have been able to survive.

The following is a list of the personifications of the *bāb*: *a.* in the seven cycles (they are really only six, Salmān, the long-lived = Rūzbih): the *maḳāmāt*: 1. Djibrāyīl; 2. Yāyīl; 3. Ḥām b. Kūsh; 4. Dān b. Aṣbawūṭ; 5. ʿAbd Allāh b. Simʿān; 6. Rūzbih. *b.* In the *saṭr al-aʾimma* (here are only eleven): the *maṭāliʿ*: 1. Salmān; 2. Ḳais b. Waraḳa Riyāḥī (= Safīna); 3. Rushaid Hadjarī (d. ca. 58); 4. Ḳankar b. Abī Khālid Kābilī; 5. Yaḥyā b. Muʿammar b. Umm al-Ṭawīl (d. ca. 83); 6. Djābir b. Yazīd Djuʿfī (d. 128); 7. Abu 'l-Khaṭṭāb Muḥammad b. Abī Zainab Miḳlāṣ Asadī Kāhilī (d. 138; cf. Kashī, p. 191); 8. Mufaḍḍal b. ʿUmar Djuʿfī (d. ca. 170); 9. Muḥammad b. Mufaḍḍal Djuʿfī; 10. ʿUmar b. al-Furāt (Djuʿfī; killed in 203 by Ibrāhīm b. al-Mahdī); 11. Muḥammad b. Nuṣair ʿAbdī (*bāb* ca. 245, d. 270). Beginning with No. 7, these individuals have actually played the part of party leaders (Nrs. 9—10 had as rival Muḥammad b. Sinān). A nephew of No. 10, grandfather of the vizier Ibn al-Furāt, was the principal supporter of Ibn Nuṣair.

Below the *bāb* are the five *aitām*, whom he associates as lords of the elements (*muwakkalūn bi-maṣāliḥ al-ʿālam*) with his role of Demiurge engendering souls by initiation. The list of Nuṣairī *aitām* given above should be compared (as well as that of the Druze *ḥudūd* "wise virgins" of Salmān; like the Nuṣairī *aitām* are the *dadjadjāt* of the *dīk al-ʿarsh* = Salmān) with the lists of Garmī (Astarābādī. *Manhadj*, p. 225) and of the Khaṭṭābīya of the Pamirs (*REI*, 1932, p. 442, transl. Ivanow).

IV. Initiation. This has three degrees (*nadjīb*, *naḳīb*, *imām*); the first consists of a solemn pledge (*ʿiḳād*, *khiṭāb* with *ṭalāḳ muʿallaḳ*; to reveal nothing of this spiritual marriage (*nikāḥ al-samāʿ*) in which the word of the initiator fertilizes the soul of the initiate in three seances, the ritual of which is related to that of the other extreme Shīʿa sects (and of the *futuwwat-nāme*) and through them and the Sabaeans of Ḥarrān to the old mysteries of Asia (cf. SHADD; Dussaud, p. 106—119; *Bākūra*, p. 2—7, 82). The cup of wine (called *ʿabd al-nūr*, Cat. No. 91) the anticipation of Paradise, is partaken of at it.

The initiatory teaching is essentially an ultra-Shīʿa symbolism (*taʾwīl*) of the seven canonical rites (*daʿāʾim*) of Islām, which are personified: 1. *ṣalāt*: the five *awḳāt* by Muḥammad (= *ẓuhr*; same among the Isḥāḳīya), Fāṭim, Ḥasan, Ḥusain and Muḥsin (= *fadjr*; among the Druzes as among the Khaṭṭābīya of the Pamirs: by the *nudjabāʾ*, the *nuḳabāʾ*, Abū Dharr, Miḳdād, Salmān). Similarly the 17 (then 51) *rakʿa*; 2. *ṣawm*: the secret guarded regarding 30 names of men (days) and thirty of women (nights of Ramaḍān); 3. *zakāt*: by Salmān; 4. *ḥadjdj*: the "sacred land 12 miles around", this is the sect; Bait = the *ism*; the Black Stone = Miḳdād; the 7 *ashwāṭ* = the 7 cycles; 5. *djihād* = the maledictions upon the *aḍdād* (*Bākūra*, p. 44) and the discipline of the mystery; 6. *walāya* = devotion to the ʿAlids and hatred of their adversaries; 7. the *shahāda*: referred to the formula *ʿain-mīm-sīn*. The Ḳurʾān is an initiation to devotion to ʿAlī; it was Salmān (under the name of Djibrāyīl) who taught it to Muḥammad.

The annual festivals include: the Shīʿa lunar festivals: Fiṭr, Aḍḥā, Ghadīr, Mubāhala, Firāsh, ʿĀshūrāʾ, 9th Rabīʿ I (martyrdom of ʿUmar) and 15th Shaʿbān (death of Salmān); then certain solar festivals: Nawrūz and Mihrdjān, Christmas and Epiphany, 17th Adhār, St. Barbara. Certain liturgies (*ḳuddās*) pertain to these festivals and are wrongly called "masses" (*ḳuddās al-ṭīb*, *al-bakhūr*, *al-ishāra*).

V. History of the Sect. All the initiatory isnāds of the sect go back from Khaṣībī to Ibn Nuṣair through two intermediaries, Muḥammad b. Djundab and Muḥammad al-Djannān al-Djunbulānī. Of Ibn Nuṣair, a notable of Baṣra, teacher of ʿAiyāshī, we know that in 245 A.H. he proclaimed himself the *bāb* of the tenth Shīʿī imām ʿAlī Naḳī and of his eldest son Muḥammad who died before him in 249, the year of the *ghaiba* of the Mahdī, according to Ibn Nuṣair (Ibn Babawaih, *Ghaiba*, p. 62, l. 12, taken from Nawbakhtī, *Firaḳ*, p. 77, 83; such was still the belief of the Ḥamdānid amīr Abū Firās, *Dīwān*, 1873, p. 39). It is only Khaṣībī who says that Ibn Nuṣair joining the eleventh imām (Nūrī, *Nafas*, p. 144) had taken for mahdī his son Muḥammad b. Ḥasan.

Of the two successors of Ibn Nuṣair we only know that the second, like Khaṣībī, belonged to Djunbulā between Kūfa and Wāsiṭ, the centre of the Zandj and Ḳarmaṭian rebels (Ṭabarī, iii. 1517, 1925, 2198; Mas'ūdī ,*Tanbīh*, p. 391), native place of Ibn Waḥshīya. Ḥusain b. Ḥamdān Khaṣībī (vocalisation attested by Dhahabī, *Mushtabih*; in Persia and the 'Irāḳ wrongly now pointed Ḥaḍinī) died in 346/957 or 358/968 at Aleppo (tomb to the north called Shaikh Bairāḳ); he was the real founder of the Nuṣairīs; he lived, like his patrons the Ḥamdānids, between Kūfa (in 344, according to Astarābādī; *loc. cit.*, p. 112) and Aleppo; he dedicated to them his *Hidāya*; cf. his *Risāla Rāstbāshīya* (*Ṭawīl*, p. 196 *sqq.*, 240 257). Among his 51 disciples the best known is Muḥammad b. 'Alī Djillī of Djillīye near Antioch where the chief of the Ḥaidarīs still lives. His direct disciple was Sa'īd Maimūn Ṭabarānī (d. 427/1035) a prolific polemicist against the chief of the Isḥāḳīya of Latakia, Abū Dahība Ismā'īl b. Khallād. After him mention is made of 'Iṣmat al-Dawla, Ḥātim Ṭawbānī (c. 700/1300; Paris MS. 1450, fol. 112*a*; Ṭawīl, p. 315), author of the *Risāla Ḳubrūsiya*, Ḥasan Adjrūd of 'Āna, died at Latakia in 836/1432 (Ṭawīl, p. 317); lastly several heads of parties, the Ḳamarī poet Muḥammad b. Yūnus Kalāzī (1011/1602), who lived near Antioch, 'Alī Mākhūsī, Nāṣir Naiṣāfī, Yūsuf 'Ubaidī. In this connection we may note that the four alleged Nuṣairī sects reduce themselves to two; that of the north (Shamsīya because it is Mīmīya, Shamālīya = Ḥaidarīs, from the name of 'Alī Ḥaidarī, its head in the ixth/xvth century = Ghaibīya) and that of the south (Ḳiblīya, for it is dominant there), which is 'Ainīya, then Ḳamarīya.

The spiritual organisation is quite distinct from the political among the Nuṣairīs. The four *mukaddams* mentioned by Niebuhr in 1780 (at Bahlūlīye near Latakia, Simerian-Khᵂābī, Ṣāfītā and Djabal Kalbīye) were temporal rulers. In 1914, there were two spiritual leaders, the *baghčibashi* (Shamsī) in Cilicia and the *khādim ahl al-bait* (Ḳamarī) at Ḳardāḥa (in 1933: Sliman al-Aḥmad of the Numailātīya). From 1920 the Dja'farī Shī'ī ḳāḍīs of the south have found their way among the Nuṣairīs. In the last ten years a shepherd of the 'Amāmira, Sliman Murshid, has been trying to found a new sect to the north of Maṣyaf.

Bibliography: 1. Nuṣairī and Muḥammadan sources: there is no canon of the Nuṣairī initiatory writings as for the Druzes (cf. de Sacy and Seybold); but Catafago has given a list (*JA*, 1876) of 40 esoteric works, of which 29 are theological und 11 poetical (specimens translated by Huart, in *JA*, 1879); we may mention No. 20, *Kitāb al-madjmū'* = 16 liturgical sūras; text in *Bākūra*, p. 7—34 and Dussaud, p. 181—189 with transl.) and No. 19, *Kitāb madjmū' al-a'yād* of Ṭabarānī: analysed in *JA*, 1848 and in *RMM*, xlix. 57—60. This list might be supplemented (apocrypha in Paris MSS. 1449—1450 etc.) for there is a bio-bibliographical collection of the writers of the sect, similar to that of the Ismā'īlī writers published by Ivanow. Nuṣairī writers make free use of moderate Shī'a works (Mufīd is quoted by Ṭabarānī) and have even written some; e.g. the *Hidāya* of Khaṣībī which is still read in Persia. Two Nuṣairī catechisms have been studied: *Ta'līm diyānat al-Nuṣairīya*, in 101 questions (Paris MS. 6182; anal. by Wolf, *ZDMG*, iii. 302— 309 where No. 88 is lacking), modern, directed against the Christians; and the old formulary by A. Baiṭār (anal. by Niebuhr, *Reisen*, ii. 440—444). An invaluable disclosure (but not without more or less biassed errors) of the Nuṣairī rites was published in 1863 at Bairūt by a convert to Christianity, Sulaimān of Adana (he was assassinated): the *Bākūra Sulaimānīya* (119 pp.; part transl. Salisbury in *JAOS*, 1868, p. 227—308; cf. Ṭawīl, p. 386; the first part is taken from an authentic manual used where there is not a lodge of initiation; cf. MS. Taimūr, *'Aḳ.*, No. 564). A popular history, in places conaining a good deal of romance but documented (without exact references), was published by Meḥmed Emīn Ghālib (d. 1932), of the Āl al-Ṭawīl of Adana: *Ta'rīkh al-'Alawīyīn*, pr. Taraḳḳī, Latakia 1343/1924, 478 pp. Two refutations are well known; a Druze one by Ḥamza (*Risāla dāmigha*, No. xvi. of the canon; perhaps refuting No. 9 of Catafago's list) and a Sunnī by Ibn Taimīya (*fatwā*, p. 94—102 of the *Madjmū'*, Cairo 1323; transl. Guyard, in *JA*, ser. 6, vol. xviii., 1871, p. 158).

2. Western works: The fundamental work is that of R. Dussaud, *Histoire et religion des Noṣairis* Paris 1900, 35—213 pp. (cf. Goldziher, in *ARW*, 1901, p. 85—96), the excellent bibliography in which comes down to 1899. There are also important articles by H. Lammens (in *Etudes religieuses*, Paris 1899, p. 461; *ROC*, 1899, p. 572; 1900, p. 99, 303, 423; 1901, p. 33; 1902, p. 442; 1903, p. 149; *JA*, 1915, p. 139—159; cf. his *Syrie*, 1921, i. 184), a resumee of Dussaud by R. Basset (in Hasting's, ix. [1917], 417—419), maps, lists and photos, especially by General Nieger, publ. by L. M(assignon), in *RMM*, xxxvi. (1920), p. 271—280 and xlix. [1922], p. 1—69; G. Samné, *La Syrie*, 1921, p. 337—342; J. de la Roche (in "*La Géographie*", xxxviii, 1922], p. 279, and "*Asie française*", 1931, p. 166); A. Brun (in "*La Géographie*", xliii. [1925], p. 153); P. May, *L'Alaouite* (plate, Bairūt, [1931]); Paul Jacquot, *L'Etat des Alaouites* (second ed., 1931, 264 pp.); E. Janot, *Des croisades au mandat*, Lyons 1934; J. Weulersse, in *BEtOr*. 1934; do., *Le pays des Alaouites*, Paris 1940; L. Massignon, in *Eranos-Jahrbuch* 1937; do., in *ZDMG* 1938; do., in *Mélanges Dussaud*; R. Strothmann, in *Isl.* 1946 and *NGW. Gött*, 1950.

3. In Arabic the only recent studies are: Kurd 'Alī, *Khiṭaṭ al-Shām*, vol. vi. (1928), p. 258—268; and Kāmil Ghazzī, *Nahr al-Dhahab* (Aleppo 1342, vol. i., p. 204—205); cf. also the Bairūt press (*Aḥrār*, Sept. 19, 1930) and that of Damascus (*Aiyām*, March 29; 2933).

O see U

P

PĀNDJ PĪR (Pānchōn Pīr, Paj Piriya sect) "Five Elders", objects of a cult spread widely in India. It seems certain that the name first signified the Holy Family of Islām: Muḥammad, ʿAlī, Fāṭima, Ḥasan, and Ḥusain. For these various other names are substituted, indeed according to R. C. Temple, "the Five Saints are any five the author may remember or worship". In the small district of Benares W. Crooke discovered five different lists with eleven names. According to E. A. H. Blunt most Indian Muslims reckon five lesser saints: Bahāʾ al-Ḥaḳḳ, S̲h̲āh S̲h̲amsī Tabrīz, Mak̲h̲dūm D̲j̲ahānīya D̲j̲ahānkus̲h̲t, all of Multan, S̲h̲āh Rukn ʿĀlam Ḥadıat of Lucknow, Bābā S̲h̲aik̲h̲ Farīd al-Dīn of Pāk Patān; others give four: ʿAlī, K̲h̲ʷād̲j̲ā Ḥasan Baṣrī, K̲h̲ʷād̲j̲ā Ḥabīb ʿAzmī and ʿAbd al-Wāḥid Kūfī. Other names will be mentioned below.

According to Blunt the Five are worshipped by some 53 castes, of which some 44 are wholly or partly Hindu. At the census of 1901 Hindu devotees were put at one and three-quarter millions; but he (1931) puts the whole numbers of the members of Hindu castes who worship the Five at thirteen and a half millions. Twenty-eight castes of the sort are enumerated by W. Crooke in his *Tribes and Castes of Bengal*. R. Greeven gives two theories as to the origin of the worship: 1) that low-caste converts to Islām degraded its purer doctrines into a species of more intelligibe idolatry; 2) that the Hindu low castes, under the influence of terror, deified certain of the earlier Muslim conquerors, into whose worship the humbler converts, never wholly emancipated from idolatry, relapsed by an easy passage. Two facts are apparently not disputed; 1) that the worshippers belong to low castes — indeed according to one authority they are almost entirely "sweepers". 2) That even among Hindu devotees the Muslim origin of the cult is not forgotten. "Thus the villagers speak of the quintette as the Mussulman deities (*Mussulmani deotar*) and without exception have the ceremonies performed by Muslim drummers (*daffālis*) who constitute a professional and hereditary priesthood".

The cult generally centres round G̲h̲āzī Miyān, identified with Saiyid Sālār Masʿūd, nephew of Maḥmūd G̲h̲aznawī, who in 1034 A.D. was killed on the day of his wedding during a popular rising of Hindus at Bahraich, at the age of eighteen, and has since been revered under the title "Prince of Martyrs" (Greeven). Though usually included among the Five he is in some places worshipped independently. An interesting list in Crooke's collection is that of the Kalwar of Allahabad. "According to them the Panchon Pir consist of Ghazi Miyan, Parihar, Athile or Hathile, Brahma Deota, and the Bare Purukh, personified ancestor of the tribe. Parihar is the son of the giant Ravana of the Ramayana; Hathile sister's son of G̲h̲azi Miyan; Brahma Deota was a Brahmin who died as a follower of G̲h̲azi Miyan, whose spiritual guide was Bare Purukh". This writer enumerates the offerings presented to these deities at different places, the needs which they are supposed to serve, and the days of celebration. Thus "the Luniya present the Five with fowls, goats, and pigs, also pulse cakes cooked in oil or butter (*mālida*) and rice milk (*khir*). Some prescribe a special offering for each of the quintette: for Subhan some sweets and a castrated goat (*khassi*): for Ghazi Miyan sweets and a goat: for Baba Barahna a delicacy known as *tosha* made of wheat flour, sugar and clarified butter: for Palihar liquor and a cock: for Amina Sati a cloth (*patau*) with a red border: for Bibi Fatima sweets". (This gives six names; two are female, evidently the Prophet Muḥammad's mother and daughter. With the Churihar, who are Sunnī Muslims, the feminine element in the quintette is Sahja Mai).

The Beldar offer the Five a turban (*patuka*) and a sheet (*patau*) made of coarse country cloth and occasionally a fowl. The sheets before being offered are marked by a streak of red. Other offerings mentioned are sherbet, garlands of flowers, perfumes, a mixture of pepper and sugar (*mirchwan*) which is poured on the shrine and the remainder drunk by the worshippers (the Dabgar), parched barley-flour, cucumber, and melon (the Rangrez). "The Dhuniya have one special usage, known as the *Piyala* or Cup, when on a Tuesday in the month of Aghau the men and women go to the riverside and offer up some spirits and sweetmeats to Sahjanai, one of the quintette of the Panchon Pir". With the Pasi "the household worship of the P.P. is often represented by an iron spear (*sang*) with three points or by five wooden pegs buried in the floor of the courtyard". With the Rangrez "Ghazi Miyan is worshipped after marriage with an offering of boiled rice, curds, and a fowl, known as *Kanduri*, properly a term for the special worship of Gatima; no male is ever allowed to see this food".

With the Kurmis in Behar their altar is a platform of earth erected outside the dwellinghouse. The Halwais place their offerings on seven stones near the family shrine.

Specimens of the ballad poetry of the sect are given by R. Greeven, *The Heroes Five, an attempt to collect some of the songs of the Pachpiriya Balladmongers in the Benares Division*, Allahabad 1898. They are very largely adaptations of tales found in the Indian Epics to Muslim ideas, and the glorification of Saiyid Sālār and his family.

Bibliography: R. C. Temple, *Legends of the Panjab*, Bombay 1884; W. Crooke, *Tribes and Castes of Bengal*, Calcutta 1896; J. N. Battacharya, *Hindu Castes and Sects*, Calcutta 1896; E. A. H. Blunt, *The Caste System of Northern India*, Oxford 1931.

PANGULU (Jav.), *panghulu* (Sund.), *pangòlò* (Madur.), literally "headman, director" used in Indonesia as the name for secular and religious chief administrators, in the islands of Java and Madura the name of a mosque official, namely the chief in his area. The official representatives of religion are organized there on the same scheme as the native administrative officials. Alongside of the regent, the highest administrative official, is the pangulu of the regency, alongside of the head of the district is the pangulu of the district, called the *pangulu naib* or briefly *naib*, and so on. The officials of the mosque are graded in a hierarchy; the pangulu at the capital of the regency is at the head of all the personnel of the mosques of the regency. The village official in charge of the divine services is of a different origin. He is a member of the village authority for attending to the religious requirements of the village and does not belong to the staff of the mosque. This man is exceptionally called pangulu in Bantĕn (Western Java); elsewhere he is known by other names.

The pangulu is the director of the mosque and the chief of its personnel; according to *adat* law, he is appointed, like the rest of the staff of the mosque, by the regent, usually being chosen from the staff of his own or another mosque. This procedure does not always guarantee that the man appointed is specially qualified (see below).

The functions of the pangulu are very varied, but not uniform throughout the whole regency. The office of director of the mosque has already been mentioned; in larger villages, especially at the capital of the regency, the staff is large: there the pangulu has charge of marriages which are concluded in his presence: *ṭalāḳ* and *rudjūʿ* are pronounced by him and marriages are registered by him. The pangulu of a regency only performs this office in the case of very prominent families: in this case it is the custom to conclude the marriage in the house of the family. The pangulu also performs the ceremony when the *walī* of the bride appoints him *wakīl*, a regular custom, observed by the majority without the reason being quite clear to them; to the popular mind the pangulu is the person who binds in marriage. It is therefore a very old custom to have the marriage performed in the mosque by the pangulu: this unwritten custom has now been given the force of law by a government enactment (since 1895, the law in question is of 1929). This law also regulates the fees to be paid at marriages, proclamations of *ṭalāḳ* and *rudjūʿ*, taking the old customs as the guiding principle. These fees form the most important part of the income of the pangulu and his staff; the latter also receive their share; if properly qualified they frequently act as deputy for the pangulu at marriages. Women who have no *walī* are married by the pangulu as *walī ḥākim*. The number of pangulus with this qualification is always less than the number of officials appointed to perform marriages. In some districts the regent appoints himself *walī ḥākim* but in practice he leaves the exercise of his rights to the pangulu.

The *djakat* (Ar. *zakāt*) is of course not collected in Java and Madura by the authorities; it is, if it is levied at all, a free-will offering and in many places insignificant. Only in Western Java was the collection at one time organized and in the hands of the mosque officials. The revenue went to them. To this day the *djakat* is still a considerable source of revenue for the pangulus, especially in Western Java.

The pangulu — this is true only of the pangulu of the regency — is also the *ḳāḍī*; but his jurisdiction is limited to family law and the *wakap* (Ar. *waḳf*) estates. The office of *ḳāḍī* is his main sphere of activity. These judicial functions of the pangulu have a curious history. The colonial authorities thought from the official position of the mosque officials that they were priests; they further thought that they had to deal with a *collegium* because the pangulu sits with some of his subordinates to assist him when in legal session. This misunderstanding was perpetuated fifty years ago in colonial legislation. The pangulu was made president of a bench of judges; his assessors were appointed by the authorities and chosen from the subordinates of the pangulu and private individuals learned in law. In this way a pangulu of lower rank may be a member of a "priestly college". It is now intended to restore the old state of affairs. The "college" is to be abolished and the pangulu's court i.e. one in which the pangulu, sitting with assistants, will be sole judge, will take its place. The law is prepared but has not yet been put into operation. The "priestly college" holds its meetings in a room in the mosque. Most of the cases are brought by women. In Western and Central Java it is the regular custom for the husband immediately after the wedding to be forced to pronounce the *taʿlīḳ* in a way which, from the legal point of view, is not quite free from objection. If he does not fulfil the obligations which he takes upon himself in the *taʿlīḳ* formulae and if the wife is not satisfied she brings the matter before the "college" and the latter pronounces that a *ṭalāḳ* has taken place. These are the most common cases. In Eastern Java and Madura a facilitated *fas<u>kh</u>* takes the place of the *taʿlīḳ*. We also find cases in the rest of Java where the "priestly college" decides questions of *fas<u>kh</u>*. Women who are refused *nafaḳa* also apply to the "college". If there are difficulties after a divorce about the division of property acquired during marriage, or if the the heirs to a property are dissatisfied with the decisions of an ordinary pangulu, the matter is referred to the "college" for decision. The method of procedure is as follows. The "college' gives its verdict as to how the property should be divided according to the *<u>sh</u>arīʿa*. If the parties prepare to carry this out but all are not ready to do so, the scheme can only be legally enforced when the secular court has given authority. This is always done if the verdict of the "priestly college" is formally in order; no test is made of its material correctness. Fees have to be paid whenever application is made to the "college"; a considerable revenue is gained from the division of estates as in such cases the "college" gets a percentage of the objects in dispute, often 10% — hence the name *usur*. The "college" is consulted also in other matters of family law but these are of less importance.

Finally there are *wakap* foundations the founders of which intended the revenues for mosques, schools of religion, or cemeteries. It is the task of the "priestly college" to decide according to the *<u>sh</u>arīʿa* such disputes as arise and in general to supervise the administration.

The pangulus in the native states are appointed by the princes; their sphere of activity is the same. Whenever a new pangulu is appointed he is given his appointment as *ḳāḍī* by an edict "in confirmation of my oral command", as the phrase is, in order to comply with the demands of the *<u>sh</u>arīʿa*. In this edict the phraseology suggests that the ruler hands over his jurisdiction to the pangulu.

The Netherlands Indies colonial law required the presence of the pangulu when Muslims appear in the government courts as accused in civil or criminal cases. A number of such assessors are attached to each court according to its requirements. They are appointed by the government and chosen from the personnel of the mosques. It is arranged that the director of the mosque is at the same time an assessor. As the pangulu is usually chosen from the lower staff, the government has been able to secure influence over the appointment of these minor officials so far as they are capable of being pangulus. The object is to choose as competent men as possible, so that the prestige of the pangulu has increased in the Muslim community. This is less true of their position as assessors at the courts; the colonial law intended that the court should be advised regarding the *adat* (traditional) law. The choice of the pangulu was therefore a mistake, as the latter goes by the *fiḳh* books.

The word pangulu as the name of a mosque official is not unknown outside the islands of Java and Madura. In some place there are pangulus whose work resembles that of the pangulus of Java, e.g. in the centre of the former sultanate of Palembang (Sumatra). The colonial authorities have retained the name; they have also given the name to the court assessors appointed by them in districts where the name was not previously in use.

Bibliography: C. Snouck Hurgronje, *Verspreide Geschriften*, iv/i. 279 *sqq.*, 89 *sqq.*; iv/ii. 366 *sqq.*; C. van Vollenhoven, *Het Adatrecht van Nederlandsch-Indië*, ii. 160 *sqq.*

PĀRSĪS. Under this name (Pahl. *pārsīk*, Mod. Pers. *pārsī* literally "inhabitant of Fārs") are known the Zoroastrian Īrānians, who, after the Arab conquest, refusing to adopt Islām fled and after various vicissitudes finally settled in India in Gudjarāt, where they now form an ethnical and religious group of 100,000 persons (101,778 according to the census of 1921). At the present day the name Pārsī is beginning to be used also for the Zoroastrians remaining in Īrān instead of *geber*, the somewhat contemptuous significance of which [cf. MADJŪS] is no longer in keeping with the spirit of tolerance which is increasing every day in Īrān.

What we know of the wanderings of the Pārsīs before their arrival in their present abode in India is based principally on two narratives: *Ḳiṣṣah-i Sandjān*, written in verse by a Zoroastrian priest named Bahman Kai Kabad of Nawsāri in the year of Yazdagird 969 (1600 A.D.) and *Ḳiṣṣah-i zartushtyān-i Hindūstān wa-bayān-i ātash Bahrām-i nawsārī*, a work written at the end of the xviii^th^ century by the Dastur Shapurdji Manockdji Sandjana (1735—1805).

According to these sources, the first group was composed of Zoroastrians who about a century after the Arab conquest went from Khurāsān, where they had sought refuge, to the south, reaching the island of Hormuz at the mouth of the Persian Gulf (751 A.D.). After a short sojourn there they crossed to Diu on the Gulf of Cambay to the south of the coast of Kāthiāwār (766) and remained there 19 years. Continuing their journey southwards they landed at Sandjān (785) and installed the sacred fire there. According to the tradition of the Pārsī priests, before obtaining permission to settle there they drew up for the lord of Diu, Djādi Rānāh, in a series of 16 *shlokas* the principal articles of their faith. In these *shlokas*, of which several versions exist in Sanskrit and Gudjarātī, several points of contact between Hinduism and Zoroastrianism are cleverly brought out. At Sandjān they were twice joined by other bodies of refugees and these formed a community which prospered rapidly and spread to Cambay, Bariāw, Bānkāner and Ankleswar. After the year 1000 Pārsīs are also found in upper India, but it is probable that these were isolated bodies who came directly from Īrān.

In 1490 A.D. the Pārsīs who had made common cause with the Hindus were forced by the troops of Sulṭān Maḥmūd Bīgara to abandon Sandjān and take refuge with their sacred fire among the mountains of Barhūt. When the Muslim pressure ceased the Zoroastrian community resumed its development According to the date given in *Ḳiṣṣah-i Sandjān* the sacred fire was installed at Nawsāri in 1491 after the sack of Sandjān, and after a brief period at Barhūt and Bansdah it was brought back in 1516.

The sacred fire was installed at Sūrat in 1733 as a result of the raids of the Pindarris but the settlement of the Pārsīs in the town dates from the second half of the xvi^th^ century. We do not know the exact date when the Pārsīs went to Bombay, which is now the principal centre of the Pārsī community in India.

The Pārsīs were able to settle in India without meeting any opposition mainly owing to the excellence of the moral principles of the Mazdaean religion observed in the threefold rule of *humata, hūxta, hwarshta* — "good thougths", "good word", "good works" — which is found in the Avesta. Although they have always abstained from any proselytizing activities, they had the good fortune to attract the great emperor Akbar to the Mazdaean religion. Trustworthy and active, assisted by the fact that the social character of their religion does not prevent adaptation to the forms of western life, they are at the present day a flourishing and well organized community much appreciated for the high standard and dignity of their lives.

The old religious inheritance of Zoroastrianism has been preserved by the Pārsīs with remarkable piety. In the xvi^th^ century on the initiative of the *desai* Čāngā Asā of Nawsāri a mission was sent to Persia to obtain from the Zoroastrians who had remained there information regarding certain details of the religion. As a result the study of the manusscripts of the Avesta and of the exegetic literature was intensified and at the present day Pārsī scholars are displaying a laudable activity in the publication of the old texts.

The sacerdotal class still occupies a predominant place in the community; its hierarchy (*dastūr, mōbadh, hērbadh*) is a hereditary one.

The interests of the community are managed by a committee (*pancāyat* composed of 6 *dastūrs* and 12 *mōbadh*) but with incorporation in the public life of India the functions of such a committee are gradually diminishing.

The mass of the faithful (*behadīn*) conform — with a few concessions to the demands of modern life — fully to the ritual prescription of Zoroastrianism. Birth must take place on the floor of the house to show detachment from the things of the world. At the age of 7 there is the investiture with the *kustī*, the sacred cord formed of 72 threads which winds three times round life. The funeral rites consist of exposure of the corpse on the tower of silence which is frequented by vultures (*dakhm*). In the ceremony of marriage, which tends more and more to monogamy with the marriage of full rights (Pahl. *žanīh-i pātikhshāyīhāh*) to the exclusion of secondary marriages, Hindu customs have prevailed.

The prohibitions regarding contamination of the sacred elements of fire, water, earth are still scrupulously observed and the greatest care taken in purification after contact with impure objects, especially corpses. The Zoroastrian principles of morality are faithfully observed in all activities of life; hatred of falsehood, honesty in all dealings, assistance of the poor are the regular rules of piety.

The Zoroastrian community in India is keenly interested in the lot of their co-religionists in Īrān and it was through the intervention of the Pārsī "Persian Zoroastrian Amelioration Fund" that the djizya paid by the Zoroastrians of Yazd and Kirmān was abolished in 1882 by the Persian government. As a result of the decline of religious intolerance in Persia, there has been increasing intercourse with the Zoroastrian communities still existing in Īrān and the Pārsī community has frequently sent appeals to the Muslims of Persia to ask them to return to the ancient religion.

While as regards doctrine perfect harmony still exists in the community, as regards ritual controversies have not been wanting and are not lacking within it. In 1686 the question of precedence was raised between the priests of Nawsāri and those of Sandjān. Another question which has been a subject of controversy even since the xviii[th] century, is the question whether the use of the *padān* — i.e. a kind of veil placed in front of the mouth to prevent the sacred fire from being contaminated by the breath — should also be put on the dying, thus violating the laws of piety.

Much more serious however is another controversy, that regarding the calendar; it goes back to the xviii[th] century and divides the community into two sects: the Shahenshāhīs and the Ḳadīmīs.

According to the Avestic calendar adopted by the Pārsīs, to make up for the loss of a quarter of a day each year, a month is added every 120 years but this system was not observed during the period of persecution following the Muslim conquest. In 1745 a group of the faithful felt the need for a reform of the calendar; but this group, which took the name of Ḳadīmīs, was opposed by those who wished to adhere to the Hindu system of calculating the months and who took the name of Shahenshāhīs. The result is that the calendar adopted by the latter is a month behind that adopted by the Ḳadīmīs. The Pārsīs follow the era of Yazdigird which dates from the accession of the last Sāsānid (June 16, 632).

Bibliography: For the *Ḳiṣṣah-i Sandjān*, cf. E. B. Eastwick, in *JRAS*, *Bombay Branch*, i. (1842), p. 167—191 and J. J. Modi, *A few Events in the Early History of the Parsis and their Dates*, in *Zartoshti I* (1273 Yazdigird), ii. (1274 Yazdigird). — For the *Ḳiṣṣah-i Zartushtyān-i Hindūstān*, cf. J. J. Modi, *Journal of the KR Cama Oriental Institute*, xvii. (1930), p. 1—63; xix. (1931), p. 45—57; xxv. (1933), p. 1—155; Bomandji Byramdji Patell, *Pārsī Prakāsh, being a Record of important Events in the Growth of the Parsi Community in Western India*, Bombay 1878—1888 (Gudjarātī), ser. ii., 1891; *The Gujarāt Parsis from their Earliest Settlement to the Present Time*, Bombay 1898; D. Menant, *Les Parsis: histoire des communautés zoroastriennes de l'Inde*, *Annales du Musée Guimet*, Paris 1898; *Parsis et Parsisme*, *ibid.*, Paris 1904; art. *Parsis*, in Hastings, *Encyclop. of Rel. and Ethics*; J. J. Modi, *Parsees at the Court of Akbar and Dastur Meherji Rana*, Bombay 1903; Menant, *Les Parsis à la Cour d'Akbar*, in *RHR*, l. (1904), p. 38 *sqq.*; G. Bonet-Maury, *La religion d'Akbar et ses rapports avec l'islamisme et le parsisme*, in *RHR*, li. (1905), p. 153 *sqq.*; K. Inostrantsev, *The Emigration of the Parsis to India and the Musulman World in the midst of the viii[th] century*, transl. by L. Bogdanov, in *Journal of the KR Cama Oriental Institute*, i. (1922), p. 33 *sqq.*; J. J. Modi, *A Parsee High Priest (Dastur Āzar Kaiwān 1529—1614 a.D.) with his Zoroastrian Disciples in Patna, in the 16th and 17th Century a.C.*, *ibid.*, xx. (1932), p. i. *sqq.*

PASANTREN. Javanese "*santri*-place", seminary for students of theology (*santri*) on the islands of Java and Madura, Madur. *panjantren*, Sund. usually *pondok*, i.e. the lodgings of the students of the school ("to go to the *pondok*" = to attend a pasantren). — Elementary education i.e. reciting the Ḳur'ān and the elements of a knowledge of ceremonial law is given in the East Indian Archipelago wherever there are Muḥammadans by teachers, who confine themselves to these subjects, in their own houses. In the larger villages and towns of Java and Madura there are also teachers who collect pupils around them in a mosque, in their own house or in a special building. If their reputation increases it often happens that students come from a distance and live in the place for a time to enjoy their instruction.

The pasantrens however are institutions for advanced theological training. They consist of several buildings and when they are not built out in the country, form at least a separate quarter of the village. Javanese princes have from time to time issued edicts making villages "free" i.e. the taxes and services which they have to yield are given in perpetuity to the teacher of the pasantrens founded there. Pious individuals have also endowed *waḳf* in favour of pasantren. The others are private institutions which owe their origin to the initiative of a learned man who establishes himself as a teacher. Their foundation and propserity or decline is therefore bound up with the personality of the teacher and the estimation in which his learning is held; even pasantrens which are regularly endowed are influenced by this factor.

The pasantren consists in the first place of the houses of the teacher and his assistants, then of lecture-rooms, a chapel, rarely a Friday Mosque, the lodgings of the students (*pondok*), rice-barns, all of which occupy a considerable space. The *pondok* alone possess a peculiar form of architecture not found in other buildings. A *pondok* is a quadrangular building built of the usual materials. The interior is divided by two walls into three long compartments of about equal breadth, the central one of which forms a corridor running from an end of the building to the other. The two outer ones form the living rooms; each of them is divided into cells of equal size by partitions. The door of the *pondok* is in the centre of one of the shorter outer walls; it opens into the corridor. Only blank walls are seen on right and left as one enters; then it is noticed that very low little doors are let into these walls, made of the same material as they are; these admit to the cells. The little doors are at regular intervals in the two walls, two always being opposite one another. The cells are lit from the outside by little windows in the wall; they are so low that the occupant can only sit or lie on the floor; for the students study in a recumbent position. Several students live in one cell; in very popular pasantrens, the *pondok* may have two stories. The number of students may amount to several hundreds. It may also be quite small. There are hundreds of pasantren in existence. In each *pondok* discipline is maintained by one of the older students or by a junior teacher. In spite of this, cleanliness leaves much to be desired. The head of the *pondok* is at the same time tutor and assists the students under him in every way. We also find women sharing in the instruction given in a pasantren but it is very rare for them to live in one.

The pasantrens have a life of their own. Great

activity prevails even before dawn. After the *ṣalāt al-ṣubḥ* which the teacher himself conducts and which is followed by a *dhikr*, the lectures begin. The teacher takes the beginners one after the other and after their lesson they return to the *pondok*; here they go over what they have learned by themselves or with a more advanced student or with the head of the *pondok* until noon. The students then have their midday meal, the *santri* of each *podok* forming one mess; this is practically speaking their only meal. All then go to chapel to the *ṣalāt al-ẓuhr*. They are summoned to three further *ṣalāts* in the course of the day. The intervals between them are devoted to lectures and study. The more advanced students are taken together by the teacher; he reads the Arabic text, translates it and adds any necessary notes of explanation. After the *ṣalāt al-ʿishāʾ* the day's work is over and the students retire for the night. Some *santri* may still be engaged on little tasks which may bring them in something, soon these also stop and quiet reigns over all. — Friday brings a variation in this monotonous round; all go to the nearest Friday mosque to attend the *ṣalāt al-djumʿa*. Harvest is also a busy time for the *santri*; they work in the rice-fields or beg for *zakāt*. Many *santri* go home in the months of the fast.

Fiḳh is the primary subject of study in the pasantrens; the Arabic works used are those in use in other Shāfiʿī lands. There are also a large number of Javanese works; those based on Arabic sources or theological works taken from Arabic are known as *kitāb*. Javanese is the language of the pasantrens; in the Sundanese speaking districts (western Java) Javanese works are more and more replaced by Sundanese. At the same time dogmatics are also studied. Here no particular *madhhab* is followed, nor are the works used written only by Shāfiʿīs. Orthodox mysticism is less studied. There is, it is true, a popular form of mysticism tinged with pantheism; but this is less and less taught in the pasantrens. The *santri* calls the main *fiḳh* book used by him in the pasantren *kitab pĕkih* without further qualification (he hardly knows its title) and work on dogmatics *kitab usul*. Small books for elementary instruction on the duties of religion and dogmatics are also called *kitab usul*.

The method of instruction is one peculiar to the pasantren. As soon as he has finished the elementary text-books, the student is introduced to more important Arabic texts. He reads them, sentence by sentence, under the supervision of the teacher who himself has perhaps never studied Arabic properly and has only his memory to rely upon for the vocalisation. The sentence is translated into Javanese and paraphrased by the teacher. Finally the student is so far advanced that he can translate easy texts from Arabic into Javanese (a list of the texts most used [at the time] is given in *TBGKW*, xxxi. [1886], p. 518 *sqq*.). This takes a long time; the joy however at seeing his knowledge steadily increasing and the pleasant feeling of being able to read texts in the original spurs the student on. Under Meccan and Ḥaḍramawt influence, however, this method is being gradually driven out by another which begins with Arabic grammar. It certainly seems the more logical; one disadvantage, however, is that the study of Arabic offers so many difficulties to the Indonesian that many lose heart before they succeed in reading texts.

Study at the pasantrens is quite free. Diplomas are neither sought nor given. The student comes and goes as he pleases. The majority when they enter the pasantren have already had an elementary education at home. The desire to increase their knowledge of the faith, the wish among rich and prominent families to see one of their sons devoting himself to the study of religion and among others the hope of gaining a livelihood, bring young men into the pasantren. The *santri* endeavour to attend the lectures of a number of teachers, each on his special subject. They therefore go from one school to another; some indeed travel about all their lives studying. Others when they think they have acquired sufficient learning settle somewhere, but not in their own districts, as teachers or become assistant teachers in a pasantren or they may prefer to remain "independent scholars". There are no offices for which study in a pasantren is a requisite preliminary; in general the theologians are averse from anything official or belonging to the state but the higher mosque officials have usually studied for a time in a pasantren.

It is considered very reprehensible to give instruction in sacred learning for an agreed fee. Nevertheless, most of the teachers are well to do. Pious gifts are liberally given to them on account of the blessing they bring. The teacher is a most welcome guest at religious feasts, of which there are many in Javanese life. All appeal at all times to his learning or for his intercession; gifts accompany these appeals. New arrivals among the students, if they can afford it, make their offering; sons of the better situated parents bring back presents when they go home, and poor students work in the teacher's fields.

The majority of the students are poor and indeed live by begging. On certain days they go round the district; their begging is not considered a nuisance; they are assisted readily for they are acquiring sacred learning; to give to them brings a blessing. Work on the land, the copying of Ḳurʾāns etc. also bring them in the little they require for their frugal life. The government only troubles about the pasantren in so far as it exercises a general supervision over them; the foundations of new ones are reported to the authorities and the principal has to keep a register of the names of the students and of the titles of the books used.

The spread of schools on the European model has dealt a blow to the pasantrens in recent years. Only the pasantrens could give religious instruction as the public schools instituted by the government authorities gave none. On the other hand, only the latter prepared for everyday life. This has resulted in the growth of private schools intended to do both. These are called *madrasas* and are intended to be schools for all. Attached to the *madrasas* are schools for higher education; in these religious instruction plays a very prominent part. In these schools, which owe their origin to circles influences by modern ideas, the method of instruction is taken from European models; but their outlook is not by any means broader than that of the old pasantrens. The name *madrasa* points to Egypt or perhaps Arabia; the organization, apart from the religious instruction, is modelled exactly on the government schools.

In the country of the Minangkabau Malays (Central Sumatra) there are theological seminaries which correspond on the whole with the pasantren; they are called *surau*, a name also given to elementary schools, chapels, houses for men, and also to the separate buildings of the institution called *surau*. The students' houses are not divided into cells; the occupants have a common lecture- and sleeping-room.

Atjeh also has seminaries comparable with the Javanese. The method of instruction however, which in Java may be called the new one, is the only one here; Malay takes the place of Javanese there; a knowledge of this language is therefore indispensable for students in Atjeh. The lodgings of the students (*rangkang*) have the same plan as the *pondok* of Java; just as the pasantrens are also called *pondok*, so the name *rangkang* in Atjeh is also applied to the whole institution.

Bibliography: C. Snouck Hurgronje, *De Atjèhers*, Batavia 1894, ii. 1 *sqq.*; do., *De Islam in Nederlandsch-Indië*, in *Verspr. Geschriften*, iv/ii 377 *sqq.*; *De masdjids en inlandsche godsdienstscholen in de Padangsche bovenlanden*, in *Ind. Gids* 1888, 318 *sqq.*; G. F. Pijper, *Fragmenta islamica*, Leiden 1934, p. 19 *sqq.*, 107 *sqq.*

PHARAOH [See FIRʿAWN].

POTIPHAR. [See ḲITFĪR].

R

RABB (A.), lord, God, master of a slave. Pre-Islāmic Arabia probably applied this term to its gods or to some of them. In this sense the word corresponds to the terms like Baʿal, Adon in the Semitic languages of the north where rabb means "much, great". — In one of the oldest sūras (cvi. 3) Allāh is called the "lord of the temple". Similarly al-Lāt bore the epithet al-Rabba, especially at Ṭāʾif where she was worshipped in the image of a stone or of a rock. — In the Ḳurʾān rabb (especially with the possessive suffix) is one of the usual names of God. This explains why in Ḥadīth the slave is forbidden to address his master as *rabbī*, which he must replace by *saiyidī* (Muslim, *al-Alfāẓ min al-adab*, trad. 14, 15, etc.). — The abstract *rubūbīya* is not found in either Ḳurʾān or Ḥadīth; it is in common use in mystic theology.

Bibliography: The Arabic dictionaries; Flügel, *Concordantiae Corani*.

RĀBIʿA AL-ʿADAWĪYA, a famous mystic and saint of Baṣra, a freedwoman of the Āl ʿAtīk, a tribe of Ḳais b. ʿAdī, known also as al-Ḳaisīya, born 95/713—714 or 99, died and was buried at Baṣra in 185/801. A few verses of hers are recorded: she is mentioned, and her teaching quoted, by most of the Ṣūfī writers and the biographers of the saints.

Born into a poor home, she was stolen as a child and sold into slavery, but her sanctity secured her freedom, and she retired to a life of seclusion and celibacy, at first in the desert and then in Baṣra, where she gathered round her many disciples and associates, who came to seek her counsel or prayers or to listen to her teaching. These included Mālik b. Dīnār, the ascetic Rabāḥ al-Ḳais, the traditionist Sufyān al-Thawrī and the Ṣūfī Shaḳīḳ al-Balkhī. Her life was one of extreme ascetism and otherworldliness. Asked why she did not ask help from her friends, she said, "I should be ashamed to ask for this world's goods from Him to Whom it belongs, and how should I seek them from those to whom it does not belong"? To another friend she said: "Will God forget the poor because of their poverty or remember the rich because of their riches? Since He knows my state, what have I to remind Him of? What He wills, we should also will". Miracles were attributed to her as to other Muslim saints. Food was supplied by miraculous means for her guests, and to save her from starvation. A camel which died when she was on pilgrimage, was restored to life for her use; the lack of a lamp was made good by the light which shone round about the saint. It was related that when she was dying, she bade her friends depart and leave the way free for the messengers of God Most High. As they went out, they heard her making her confession of faith, and a voice which responded, "O soul at rest, return to thy Lord, satisfied with Him, giving satisfaction to Him. So enter among My servants into My Paradise" (Sūra lxxxix. 27—30). After her death Rābiʿa was seen in a dream and asked how she had escaped from Munkar and Nakīr, the angels of death, when they asked her, "Who is your Lord?", and she replied, "I said, return and tell your Lord, 'Notwithstanding the thousands and thousands of Thy creatures, Thou hast not forgotten a weak old woman. I, who had only Thee in all the world, have never forgotten Thee, that Thou shouldst ask, Who is thy Lord?'"

Among the prayers recorded of Rābiʿa is one she was accustomed to pray at night upon her roof: "O Lord, the stars are shining and the eyes of men are closed and kings have shut their doors, and every lover is alone with his beloved, and here am I alone with Thee". Again she prayed, "O my Lord, if I worship Thee from fear of Hell, burn me therein, and if I worship Thee in hope of Paradise, exclude me thence, but if I worship Thee for Thine own sake, then withold not from me Thine Eternal Beauty". Of Repentance, the beginning of the Ṣūfī Path, she said, "How can anyone repent unless his Lord gives him repentance and accepts him? If He turns towards you, you will turn towards Him". She held that Gratitude was the vision of the Giver, not the gift, and one spring day, when urged to come out to behold the works of God, she rejoined, "Come rather inside to behold their Maker. Contemplation of the Maker has turned me aside from contemplating what He has made". Asked what she thought of Paradise, Rābiʿa replied, "First the Neighbour, then the house" (*al-djār thumma 'l-dār*) and Ghazzālī, commenting on this, says she implied that no one who does not know God in this world will see him in the next, and he who does not find the joy of gnosis here will not find the joy of the Vision there, nor can anyone appeal to God in that world if he has not sought His friendship in this. None may reap who has not sown (*Iḥyāʾ*, iv. 269). The otherworldliness of her teaching is shown in her declaration that she had come from that world and to that world she was going, and she ate the bread of this world in sorrow, while doing the work of that world. One who heard her said derisively, "One so persuasive in speech is worthy to keep a rest-house" and Rābiʿa responded, "I myself am keeping a rest-house; whatsoever is within, I do not allow it to go out and whatever is without, I do not allow to come in. I do not concern myself with those who pass in and out, for I am contemplating my own heart, not mere clay". Asked how she had attained to the rank of the saints, Rābiʿa replied, "By abandoning what did not concern me and seeking fellowship with Him Who is eternal".

She was famed for her teaching on mystic love (*maḥabba*) and the fellowship with God (*uns*) which is the pre-occupation of His lover. Every true lover, she said, seeks intimacy with the beloved, and she recited the lines:

"I have made Thee the Companion of my [heart,
But my body is present for those who seek [its company,
And my body is friendly towards its guests.
But the Beloved of my heart is the guest of [my soul".
Iḥyā', iv. 358, margin)

She demonstrated the need for disinterested love and service by taking fire in one hand and water in the other and saying, when asked the meaning of her action, "I am going to light fire in Paradise and to pour water on to Hell, so that both veils may be taken away from those who journey towards God, and their purpose may be sure and they may look towards their Lord without any object of hope or motive of fear. What if the hope of Paradise and the fear of Hell did not exist? Not one would worship his Lord or obey Him" (Aflākī, *Manāḳib al-ʿārifīn*, India Office, No. 1670, fol. 114*a*). Questioned about her love for the Prophet she said, "I love him, but love of the Creator has turned me aside from love of His creatures", and again. "My love to God has so possessed me that no place remains for loving any save Him". Of her own service to God and its motive-force she said, "I have not served God from fear of Hell, for I should be but a wretched hireling if I did it from fear; nor from love of Paradise, for I should be a bad servant, if I served for the sake of what was given me, but I have served Him only for the love of Him and desire of Him". Her verses on the two types of love, that which seeks its own ends and that which seeks only God and His glory, are famous and much quoted:

"In two ways have I loved Thee, selfishly,
And with a love that worthy is of Thee.
In selfish love my joy in Thee I find,
While to all else, and others, I am blind.
But in that love which seeks Thee worthily,
The veil is raised that I may look on Thee.
Yet is the praise in that or this not mine,
In this and that the praise is wholly Thine".

Ghazzālī again comments, "She meant, by the selfish love, the love of God for His favour and grace bestowed and for temporary happiness, and by the love worthy of Him, the love of His Beauty which was revealed to her, and this is the higher of the two loves and the finer of them" (*Iḥyā'*, iv. 267). Like all mystics, Rābiʿa looked for union with the Divine (*waṣl*). In certain of her verses she says, "My hope is for union with Thee, for that is the goal of my desire", and again she said, "I have ceased to exist and have passed out of self. I have become one with God and am altogether His".

Rābiʿa, therefore, differs from those of the early Ṣūfīs who were simply ascetics and quietists, in that she was a true mystic, inspired by an ardent love, and conscious of having entered into the unitive life with God. She was one of the first of the Ṣūfīs to teach the doctrine of Pure Love, the desinterested love of God for His own sake alone, and one of the first also to combine with her teaching on love the doctrine of *kashf*, the unveiling, to the lover, of the Beatific Vision.

Bibliography: Chief biographes: ʿAṭṭār, *Tadhkirat al-awliyā'*, ed. Nicholson, i. 59 *sqq.*; Taḳī al-Dīn al-Ḥiṣnī, *Siyar al-ṣāliḥāt*, Paris No. 2042, fol. 26a *sqq.*; M. Zihnī, *Mashāhīr al-nisā'*, Lahore 1902, p. 225; Ibn Khallikān, *Biographical Dictionary*, transl. de Slane, iii. 215; al-Munāwī, *al-Kawākib al-durrīya*, Br. Mus. Add. 23,369, fol. 50 *sqq.*; al-Shaʿrānī, *al-Ṭabaḳāt al-kubrā*, Cairo 1299, p. 56; Djāmī, *Nafaḥāt al-uns*, ed. Nassau-Lees, p. 716 *sqq.* — Chief references to teaching: al-Ghazzālī, *Iḥyā'*, Cairo 1272, iv. 267, 269, 291, 308 second ed. 1340, ii. 211; Kalābādhī, *Kitāb al-Taʿarruf*, ed. Arberry, Cairo 1934, p. 73, 121; al-Ḳushairī, *Risāla*, Būlāḳ 1867, p. 86, 173, 192; al-Makkī, *Ḳūt al-ḳulūb*, Cairo 1310, i. 103, 156 *sqq.*; ii. 40, 57 *sq.* — For a detailed account of life and teaching, with full references, cf. Margaret Smith, *Rābiʿa the Mystic and her Fellow-saints in Islām*, Cambridge 1928.

RĀBIṬA. [see RIBĀṬ, ZĀWIYA].

RAḌĀʿ or RIḌĀʿ, also RAḌĀʿA (A.), suckling; as a technical term, the suckling which produces the impediment to marriage of foster-kinship. It is to be supposed that the idea of foster-kinship was already prevalent among the ancient Arabs (cf. Robertson Smith, *Kinship and Marriage in Early Arabia* [2], p. 176, 196, note 1); this is evident from, among other things, the way in which the prescription of the Ḳur'ān regarding this is interpreted in Tradition. In Sūra iv. 23, among the female relatives with whom marriage is forbidden are the foster-mother and the foster-sister. This must correspond nearly to the old Arab usage, which regarded blood-relationship also only in these two degrees as an impediment to marriage (cf. Robertson Smith, *loc. cit.*). But as the Ḳur'ān in the passage quoted extends the circle of prohibited relationships beyond that of blood-relationship, foster-kinship was treated accordingly contrary to the unambiguous language of the passage. To justify this, it is frequently laid down in traditions, in keeping with the principle of the old Arab attitude, that foster-kinship is an impediment in the same degrees as blood-relationship. The isolated case, which is decisive for the principle, that of the prohibition of marriage with the Daughter of a foster-brother, is brought into close personal relationship with the Prophet. Through the prohibition of marriage laid down in Tradition between the foster-children of two wives of the same man, relationship by marriage becomes included in foster-relationship, and in the tradition which expounds the verse of the Ḳur'ān quoted, foster-kinship is given among the impediments to marriage on the ground of relationships in law. As a justification for this prohibition it is stated that the *semen genitale* (which the milk has procuced) is the same; against the view that bloodrelationship is not to be combined with foster-kinship, so that the brother of the husband of the foster-mother is not to be regarded as a foster-relation, there is a polemic in a tradition (*Kanz al-ʿummāl*, iii., No. 3911). The question of the amount of suckling necessary to produce foster-relationship is a very old point of dispute; some traditions do not consider isolated sucks by the suckling or one or two acts of suckling as sufficient, others demand not less than seven acts of suckling, others again say that the child must be fed entirely; on the other side, one group of traditions says the prohibition of marriage is the same whatever the amount of suckling that has been given. There is even said to have been a passage in the Ḳurʾān which in the older, later abrogated, version demanded ten feedings and in the later version five. This story which was obviously only intended to support this view is not trustworthy (cf. Nöldeke-Schwally, *Geschichte des Qorāns*, i. 253 *sqq.*; *Kanz al-ʿummāl*, No. 3923 *sqq.*). That the practice of suckling adults in order to establish an artificial foster-kinship existed is certain; it is recognized by several traditions and by others directly or indirectly denied (by the legal maxim: *al-raḍāʿa min al-madjāʿa*, "suckling demands hunger"). The chief case for the validity of such an act of suckling is described as a privilege granted by the Prophet personally (*Kanz al-ʿummāl*, No. 3919) and even the suckling of children to establish an impediment to marriage is in an isolated case described as illegal (*ibid.*, No. 3885). To prove foster-kinship many traditions are content with the testimony of the foster-mother with or even without oath or with the testimony of a woman simply or with that of a man and of one woman; in refutation of this anomaly, obviously at one time permitted, another group of traditions demands the normal testimony of two men or of one man and two women. These points of difference found in traditions are continued in the differences of opinion among the older jurists. The views of the principal authorities are given in al-Shawkānī, *Nail al-awṭār*, Cairo 1345, vii. 113 *sqq.* The most important new point in dispute, discussed in this later period but scarcely touched upon in the traditions, is the period within which foster-kinship can be established by a child; sometimes it is said to be the period till weaning, sometimes the whole of childhood without an exact limitation, sometimes the fixed period of two years, or 2½ or 3 or 7 years; for the period of two years the authority of the Ḳurʾān is quoted, Sūra ii. 233 ("Mothers shall suckle their children two full years if they wish to carry through the suckling to its end") (on the details cf. al-Shawkānī, *op. cit.*, p. 120). The four regular Sunnī law-schools are agreed that foster-relationship exists between a man and all his descendants on the one side and his nurse, all her foster- and blood-relatives, her husband and all his foster- and blood-relations on the other; on the other hand, no foster-relationship is assumed between a man and the ascendants or lateral relatives of his foster-brothers and sisters and between the nurse and the ascendants or lateral relatives of her foster-child. The Ḥanafīs and the Mālikīs demand no definite minimum period, the Shāfiʿīs however five acts of suckling. The period for feeding is with the Mālikīs (unless previously weaned), the Shāfiʿīs and Ḥanbalīs two years, with the Ḥanafīs 2½ years; the Ẓāhirīs also recognized the suckling of an adult. To establish the foster-relationship the Shāfiʿīs are content with the testimony of four women, the Mālikīs with the evidence of two, if the fact is well known, and the Ḥanafīs with the evidence of one woman.

Prominent Meccans have retained since before Islām to the present day the custom of having Beduin nurses for their children (cf. Lammens, *La Mecque à la veille de l'hégire*, p. 101). The custom very common in the early period of Islām of hiring nurses in return for food and clothing has resulted in this arrangement, which is not in itself in accordance with the demands of the law, becoming recognized. In one tradition it is recommended that gratitude should be shown to a nurse by giving her a slave, male or female. The suckling of children by the mother or a hired nurse in a case where the marriage is dissolved is fully regulated on the basis of the Ḳurʾānic passage, Sūra ii. 233.

Bibliography: Wensinck, *Handbook*, s.v. Nursing; Juynboll, *Handbuch des islāmischen Gesetzes*, p. 219; do., *Handleiding* ², p. 185; Santillana, *Istituzioni di diritto musulmano malichita*, i. 161; for the Imāmīs: Querry, *Droit musulman*, i. 657 *sqq.*

RADJAB (A.), the name of the seventh month in the Muslim calendar. In the Djāhilīya it introduced the summer half year until, as a result of the abolition of the intercalated months, the months ceased to fall regularly at the same season of the year [see AL-MUḤARRAM]. The month was a sacred one; in it the ʿumra [q.v.], the essentially Meccan part of the pre-Muḥammadan ceremonies of pilgrimage, took place. The peace of Allāh therefore prevailed in it; the forbidden war which was fought in Radjab between Ḳuraish and Hawāzin and in which the young Muḥammad took part is called *Fidjār* (perfidy).

In the Ḳurʾān, as recorded in the article AL-MUḤARRAM, only "the" holy month is mentioned and not the four which have become traditional from the sole reference ix. 36. If the reference in Sūra v. 2, is to the ʿumra we can therefore understand why the commentators in part identify the holy month mentioned in this verse with Radjab.

In Islām the month attained great importance through the memory of the Prophet's night journey to heaven which in later times was transferred to the 27th of the month (on the original dates see MIʿRĀDJ). This night is therefore called *Lailat al-miʿrādj* and is celebrated with readings of the legends of the ascension.

Bibliography: Wellhausen, *Reste arab. Heidentums* ², p. 97 *sq.*; al-Bīrūnī, *Āthār*, ed. Sachau, p. 60 *sqq.*; Juynboll, *Handbuch des islāmischen Gesetzes*, 1910, p. 131 *sq.*, the works mentioned in the books and articles quoted.

RADJM (A.), the casting of stones. *R-dj-m* is a Semitic root, derivatives from which are found in the Old Testament with the meaning of "to stone, to drive away or kill by throwing stones" an abominable creature: *radjma* is "a heap of stones, an assembly of men, cries, tumult". — In Arabic, the root means "to stone, to curse"; *radjam*ᵘⁿ, "heap of stones", also means simply the stones placed upon tombs either as flagstones or in a heap, a custom which ḥadīth condemns and recommends that a grave should be level with the surface of the ground. On the ḥadīth of ʿAbd Allāh b. Mughfal, it is discussed whether *lā turadjdjimū ḳabrī* means "do not build my grave in a mound" or "do not utter imprecations there". — The lapidation and heaps of stones at Minā are called *djamra*, and *djamarāt al-ʿarab* means the groups of Beduin tribes; we find there the two old meanings of the root which can be taken back to *dj-m*, in Arabic *djamma* and *djamaʿa* "to reunite". The Arab grammarians derive djamra "lapidation" from *djamarāt al-ʿarab*; and we have to remember the double meaning of *radjm* and a metathesis from *djamr(a)* = *radjm.*

In addition to the meaning of "ritual stoning as a punishment for fornication", radjm means the casting of stones at Minā, which is one of the pre-Muḥammadan rites preserved by Muḥammad and inserted among the ceremonies of the pilgrimage (see the articles DJAMRA, ḤADJDJ and MINĀ with their bibliographies).

The Ḳurʾān does not mention this rite; but it knows *radjama* in its Biblical sense of "stoning of prophets by unbelievers", and also *radjīm* (= *mardjūm*) as an epithet of Satan, "driven away and struck with projectiles of fire by the angels", and lastly (xviii. 22) in an abstract sense which indicates a long semantic evolution.

The rite of casting stones at Minā was regulated by ḥadīths in the classical collections. There is a model *ḥadjdj*, that of the Prophet, which we find in the manuals of *manāsik al-ḥadjdj*, e.g. in the *Risāla* of Ibn Taimīya (cf. Rifʿat, i. 89 *sqq.*). Some ḥadīths of archaic form (e.g. Bukhārī, *Nikāḥ*, b. 2; *Salam*, b. 1 and 2; al-ʿAinī, *ʿUmda*, viii. 489) show that Muḥammad had to lay down rules for the essential question of the *wuḳūf*, the culmination of the *ḥadjdj*. The *Ḥums*, i.e. the Ḳuraish and their allies, observed it at Djamʿ (Muzdalifa), in the *ḥaram*; the others, the *ʿArab*, at ʿArafa, outside of the *ḥaram* of Mecca. Having to choose between his companions of two different origins, the *Muhādjirūn* and the *Anṣār*, Muḥammad decided with the latter for ʿArafa; but he retained a secondary *wuḳūf* at Muzdalifa, and the two *ifāḍa*, the new combination of rites culminating in the throwing of stones at ʿAḳaba.

Situated at the bottom of the valley of Minā, on the slope of the defile towards Mecca, al-ʿAḳaba is "not in Minā but it is its boundary on the side of Mecca" (*ʿUmda*, iv. 770). On the morning of the 10th Dhu 'l-Ḥidjdja the pilgrim goes down into the valley, passes without saluting them in front of the great *djamra*, 500 yards farther on the middle one, and 400 yards beyond he comes to *djamrat al-ʿAḳaba* (Rifʿat, i. 328). There he throws 7 stones and this is one of the four ceremonies which on the tenth day are intended to remove his state of sanctity. He must also have his hair shaved (*ḥalḳ*), sacrifice a victim (*naḥr*) and return in procession to Mecca (*ifāḍa*). This last rite prepares the sexual deconsecration; the three others together abolish the prohibitions of the *ḥadjdj* but the legists are not agreed on the order in which they have to be accomplished. The ḥadīths say that the Prophet replied to the pilgrims who were dismayed, not having followed the order in which he had himself followed them: *lā ḥaradja*: "no harm (in that)" (Bukhārī, *Ḥadjdj*, b. 125, 130 etc.). It is explained that the Prophet on this day of rejoicing did not wish to hurt the feelings of the ignorant Beduins. We may imagine that these ʿArab did not follow the customs of the Ḳuraish and that Muḥammad had neither the time nor the inclination to impose his own choice between the varying customs.

Muḥammad began with the lapidation at al-ʿAḳaba. After the *ḥalḳ*, the sacrifice and the *ifāḍa*, he returned to spend the night in Minā. Then on the 11th, 12th and 13th, he cast 7 stones at the three *djamarāt* ending with that of al-ʿAḳaba. The pilgrims imitating him ought therefore to throw 7 + (7 × 3) 3 = 70 stones. But in general they take advantage of the liberty (*rukhṣa*) given them by the ḥadīth to leave Minā finally on the 12th and therefore only to throw 7 + (7 × 2) 3 = 49 stones. It is probable that there was no ancient usage; the presence of the bodies of the sacrificial victims made Minā a horrible place. It is difficult to see how Wavell (*Pilgrim*, p. 202) threw 63 stones, i.e. (7 × 3) 3; this is however the number of victims which, according to tradition, Muḥammad sacrificed with his own hand, one for each year of his life.

The stoning of al-ʿAḳaba is done on the 10th by the pilgrims in *iḥrām*; those of the three days following by the deconsecrated pilgrims. The whole business is not a fundamental element (*rukn*) of the pilgrimage.

Little stones are thrown, larger than a lentil, but less than a nut, what the old Arabs called *ḥaṣa 'l-khadhf* (Tirmidhī, *Ḥadjdj* b. 55), which were thrown either with the fingers or with a little lever of wood forming a kind of sling (*mikhdhafa*). A ḥadīth forbids this dangerous game, which might knock out an eye but is not strong enough to kill an enemy: it must therefore have had something magical or pagan in its character. The stones have to be collected of the proper size and not broken from a rock. Gold, silver, precious stones etc. are condemned; but some texts allow, in addition to date-stones, a piece of camel-dung or a dead sparrow, which we find are the means used by the women of the Djāhilīya at the end of their period of isolation to remove the impurity of their widowhood and prepare a new personality. — It is recommended that the 7 stones for the lapidation of al-ʿAḳaba should be gathered at the *mashʿar al-ḥaram* at Muzdalifa, outside of Minā. As a rule the 63 others are gathered in the valley of Minā, but outside of the mosque and far from the *djamarāt* to avoid their having already been used (Ibn Taimīya, p. 383). Besides it is thought that stones accepted by Allāh are carried away by angels. — Stones collected but not used should be buried; they have assumed a sacred character which makes them dangerous.

The model pilgrimage of the Prophet fixed the time of the *djamrat al-ʿAḳaba* for the day of the 10th. It shows him beginning the *ifāḍa* of Muzdalifa after the prayer at dawn (*fadjr*) and casting the stones after sunrise. But by survival of an ancient custom more than for reasons of convenience other times are allowed by law. Al-Shāfiʿī, against the three other imāms, permits the ʿAḳaba ceremony before sunrise (Rifʿat, i. 113); in general, the time is extended to the whole morning (*ḍuḥā*), till afternoon (*zawāl*), till sunset, till night, till the morning of the day following: these infractions of the normal routine are atoned for by a sacrifice or alms, varying with the different schools. — The *djamarāt* of the three days of the *tashrīḳ* take place in the *zawāl*: here again there are various opinions (Bukhārī, *Ḥadjdj*, b. 134). — In fixing the time of the lapidations the law has always endeavoured to avoid any Muslim rite, e.g. prayer, coinciding with one of the three positions of the sun by day, rising, noon, setting. A. J. Wensinck has shown the probability of the solar character of the pagan *ḥadjdj*. [ḤADJDJ II].

Muḥammad made his lapidation at al-ʿAḳaba from the bottom of the valley, mounted on his camel, turned towards the *djamra*, with the Kaʿba on his left and Minā on his right, standing at a distance of five cubits (eight feet). But there are other possible positions. — Rifʿat (i. 328) gives the *djamra* the following dimensions: 10 feet high and 6 feet broad on a rock 5 feet high (see the photographs, *ibid.*). It is said to have been removed at the beginning of Islām and replaced in 240/854—5 (Azraḳī, p. 212). — Muḥammad made the lapidations of the other two *djamarāt* on foot turning towards the *ḳibla*. In brief, the stones are cast in the attitude one happens to be in. The position facing the Great Devil is explained by the nature of the ground, but it would also be in keeping with the idea of a curse cast in the face of a fallen deity. The position which makes the pilgrim turn towards the Kaʿba is due to the Muslim legend of the tempter Satan and to the rule of the *takbīr* which will be explained below.

According to the *sunna*, the stones are placed on the thumb and bent forefinger and thrown, one by one, as in the game of marbles. However the possibility of the stones having been thrown together in a handful has been foreseen, and it was decided that this should only count as one stone and that the omission could be made good. — The stone should not be thrown violently nor should one call "look out! look out!" (Tirmidhī, *Ḥadjdj*, bāb 65, a pagan custom which the modern Beduins still retained quite recently (Rifʿat, i. 89). It seems that Muḥammad put some strength into it for he raised his hand "to the level of his right eyebrow" (Tirmidhī, *Ḥadjdj*, bāb 64) and showed his armpit (Bukhārī, *Ḥadjdj*, b. 141).

In Islām the casting of each stone is accompanied by pious formulae. It is generally agreed that the *talbiya* is no longer pronounced at ʿArafa or at least before the lapidation of al-ʿAḳaba (Bukhārī, *Ḥadjdj*, b. 101); some writers however approve of it after al-ʿAḳaba. The *tahlīl* and *tasbīḥ* are permitted, but it is the *takbīr* which is recommended (Ibn Taimīya, p. 382; Bukhārī, *Ḥadjdj*, b. 138 and 143). The spiritual evolution of the rites even sees in this the essential feature of the rite, the throwing of the stone and the figure formed in throwing it by the thumb and forefinger forming an *ʿuḳd* which represents 70, being no more than symbolical and mnemonical gestures. "The throwing of the stones was only instituted to cause the name of God to be repeated" (Tirmidhī, *Ḥadjdj*, bāb 67). To Ghazzālī (*Iḥyāʾ*, i. 192) it is an act of submission to God and of resistance to Satan who seeks to turn man away from the fatigues of the *hadjdj* but the rite is without rational explanation (*min ghair ḥaẓẓ li 'l-ʿaḳl wa 'l-nafs fīhi*, cf. Goldziher, *Richtungen*, p. 252). — The devout man adds a prayer (*duʿāʾ*) which is as a rule quasi-ritual. The usual one is: *Allāhumma 'djʿalhu ḥadjdjan mabrūran wa-dhanban maghfūran wasaʿyan mashkūran* "Lord, make this pilgrimage a pious one, pardon our sins and recompense our efforts!". There is, as matter of fact, after the stoning a halt, a *wuḳūf*, before the two higher *djamarāt*, that at the second being especially long: the duration is calculated by the recitation of the Sūra of the Cow (ii.), or of Joseph (vii.), or of the family of ʿImrān (iii.) by altering the indication in the ḥadīth (Bukhārī, *Ḥadjdj*, b. 135, 136 and 137). This would take the place of an ancient ceremony of imprecation.

Breaches of the rules for the performance of these diverse ceremonies, especially as regards the number of stones thrown and the time when they are thrown (*ʿUmda*, iv. 767 *sqq.*; Rifʿat, i. 113), are punished by atonements the exact nature of which the legists delight to vary from the sacrifice of a victim to the giving of a *mudd* of food in alms.

The Muslim teachers have sought to explain the lapidations of Minā. Some exegists (e.g. Ṭabarī, *Tafsīr*, xxx. 167) have seen quite clearly that they represent ancient rites and have compared the *ramy* of the tomb of Abū Ridjāl. Others are known, for example at the well of Dhu 'l-Ḥulaifa (Lammens, *Bétyles*, p. 94). The works quoted in the other articles show the spread of this rite and the cases in which we are certain that it is a question of the driving away or the expulsion of evil; they might be further added to. Stones used to be thrown behind an individual whom one wished never to return (Hamadhānī, *Maḳāmāt*, ed. Bairūt, p. 23). At Alexandria, tired people used to go and lie down on a fallen pillar, throw 7 stones behind them on a pile "like that of Minā", then go away quite recuperated (Ḳalḳashandī, *Ṣubḥ al-aʿshā*, iii. 322). But comparisons would take us out of Arabia (Lods, *Prophètes d'Israël*, p. 354).

Popular legend has connected the lapidation like many other rites with Abraham. It was Abraham or Hagar or Ishmael or even Muḥammad that Satan wished to deter from accomplishing the rites of the *ḥadjdj* and who chased him away with stones. If we conclude that he is *radjīm*, we are contradicted by the explanation of Sūra lxvii. 5 (cf. above).

One would like to be able to locate the lapidations among the rites of the pre-Islāmic pilgrimage. One would first have to have a clear idea of the meaning and details of the ceremonies and of the part played by lapidations and sacred piles of stones in Semitic and Mediterranean antiquity. — Stoning seems to have been a rite of expulsion of evil which coincided with the deconsecration of the pilgrim and seems to protect his return to everyday life. It is possible that lapidations at one time followed the sacrifices which perhaps took place at ʿArafa and Muzdalifa.

Bibliography: Add to the *Bibliographies* of the articles quoted: Ibrāhīm Rifʿat Pasha, *Mirʾāt al-Ḥaramain*, Cairo 1344, 2 vols.; Ibn Taimīya, *Risālat manāsik al-ḥadjdj*, in *Madjmūʿat al-rasāʾil al-kubrā*, Cairo 1323, ii. 355; Snouck Hurgronje, *Het Mekkaansche feest* (*Verspr. Geschr.*, i. 17, 105, 113).

RĀFIḌITES, in Arabic AL-RĀFĪḌA or AL-RAWĀFĪḌ, is one of the names given to the Shīʿa [q.v.]. Al-Ashʿarī (*Maḳālāt al-Islāmīyīn*, ed. Ritter, p. 16, 54—55) explains this denomination as those who rejected the imāmate of Abū Bakr and ʿUmar (*rafaḍa*); he mentions them, however, alongside the Ghulāt and the Zaidites, as one of the three main groups of the Shīʿa. According to him al-Rāfiḍa is only another name for the Imāmīya. Van Arendonk, (*De opkomst van het Zaidietische Imamaat in Yemen*, Leiden 1919, p. 28) has pointed to a narrative by Abū Mikhnaf in Ṭabarī (ii. 1699), according to which the Shīʿites in Kūfa were called *rāfiḍa*, because they rejected Zaid ibn ʿAlī, when the latter refused to condemn Abū Bakr and ʿUmar. This, however, is possibly an ancient polemic device against the Rāfiḍites, for otherwise the *rafḍ al-shaikhain* is one of their distinctive marks. Al-Malaṭī (*K. al-tanbīh wa 'l-radd ʿalā ahl al-ahwāʾ wa 'l-bidaʿ*, ed. Dedering in *Bibliotheca Islamica* 9, 1936, p. 14) likewise gives to Rāfiḍa the same meaning as to Imāmīya, but he mentions the Zaidīya as the last of their eighteen subsections (cf. also Snouck Hurgronje, *Mekka* i. 33 sq.). Also ʿAbd al-Ḳāhir al-Baghdādī counts the Zaidīya with the Rāfiḍa, together with the Imāmīya, the Kaisānīya and the Ghulāt (*K. al-farḳ baina 'l-firaḳ*, ed. Muḥ. Badr, Cairo 1328/1910, p. 15). According to the latter author the Sabāʾīya, the followers of ʿAbd Allāh b. Sabāʾ, were the first Rāfiḍites. From all this it may be concluded that Rāfiḍa was a general abusive name for people considered as Shīʿites (cf. al-Maḳdisī, p. 126 infra: *khudhū hādha 'l-rāfiḍīya*) and never was applied exclusively to any special subdivision of the Shīʿa.

RAHBĀNĪYA (A.), monasticism. The term is derived from *rāhib* [q.v.]; it occurs in the Ḳurʾān once only, in a passage (Sūra lvii. 27) that has given rise to divergent interpretations: "And we put in the hearts of those who followed Jesus, compassion and mercy, and the monastic state, they instituted the same (we did not prescribe it to them) only out of a desire to please God. Yet they observed not the same as it ought truly to have been observed. And we gave unto such of them as believed their reward; but many of them were evildoers".

According to some of the exegists the verb "we put" has two objects only, viz. compassion and mercy, whereas the words "and the monastic state" are the object of "they instituted". Accordingly the monastic state appears here as a purely human institution, which moreover has been degraded by evildoers.

According to others, however, the object of the words "and we put" is: compassion, mercy and the monastic state. According to this exegesis monasticism is called a divine institution. Massignon has pointed out that this exegesis is the older one; the younger one expresses a feeling hostile to monasticism, which coined the tradition "No rahbānīya in Islām".

This tradition does not occur in the canonical collections, but the way is already prepared for it there. When the wife of ʿUthmān b. Maẓʿūn complained of being neglected by her husband, Muḥammad took her part, saying: Monasticism (rahbānīya) was not prescribed to us (Aḥmad b. Ḥanbal, vi. 226; Dārimī, *Nikāḥ*, bāb 3). The following tradition is less exclusive: Do not trouble yourselves and God will not trouble you. Some have troubled themselves and God has troubled them. Their successors are in the hermitages and monasteries, "an institution we have not prescribed to them" (Abū Dāwūd, *Adab*, bāb 44).

Islām, thus rejecting monasticism, has replaced it by the holy war: "Every prophet has some kind of rahbānīya; the rahbānīya of this community is the holy war" (a tradition ascribed to Muḥammad in Aḥmad b. Ḥanbal, iii. 266; to Abū Saʿīd al-Khudrī, *ibid.*, iii. 82). Cf. also ṬARĪḲA, ZUHD.

Bibliography: L. Massignon, *Essai* etc. p. 123 *sqq.*; the commentaries of the Ḳurʾān on Sūra lvii. 27; Ibn Saʿd, III/i. 287; Ḥarīrī, *Maḳāmāt*, ed. de Sacy, p. 570—571; Zamakhsharī, *al-Fāʾiḳ*, Ḥaidarābād 1324, i. 269; Ibn al-Athīr, *Nihāya*, s.v.; Sprenger, *Das Leben und die Lehre des Moḥammad*, i. 389; Goldziher, *Muhammedanische Studien*, ii. 394; do., in *RHR*, xviii. 193—194; xxxvii. 314; Pautz, *Mohammeds Lehre von der Offenbarung*, p. 194; Tor Andrae, *Zuhd und Mönchtum*, in *MO* 1931.

RĀHIB (A., plur. *ruhbān, rahābīn, rahābina*), a monk. The figure of the monk is known to pre-Islāmic poetry and to the Ḳurʾān and Tradition. The pre-Islāmic poets refer to the monk in his cell the light of which the traveller by night sees in the distance and which gives him the idea of shelter.

In the Ḳurʾān the monk and the *ḳissīs*, sometimes also the *aḥbār*, are the religious leaders of the Christians. In one place it is said that rabbis and monks live at the expense of other men (Sūra ix., 34) and that the Christians have taken as their masters instead of God their *aḥbār* and their monks as well as al-Masīḥ b. Maryam (Sūra ix. 31). In another passage the Christians are praised for their friendship to their fellow-believers which is explained from the fact that there are priests and monks among them (Sūra v. 82). In Ḥadīth the rāhib is frequently encountered in stories of the nature of the *ḳiṣaṣ al-anbiyāʾ* (cf. Bukhārī, *Anbiyāʾ*, bāb 54; Muslim, *Zuhd*, tr. 73; *Tawba*, tr. 46, 47; Tirmidhī, *Tafsīr*, Sūra 85, bāb 2; *Manāḳib*, bāb 3; Nasāʾī, *Masādjid*, bāb 11; Ibn Mādja, *Fitan*, bāb 20, 23; Dārimī, *Faḍāʾil al-Ḳurʾān*, bāb 16; Aḥmad b. Ḥanbal, i. 461; ii. 434; iii. 337, 347; v. 4; vi. 17 *bis*).

From the fact that in Muslim literature of the early centuries A.H. the epithet *rāhib* was given to various pious individuals it is evident that there was nothing odious about it then. Cf. however the article RAHBĀNĪYA.

Bibliography: see that of RAHBĀNĪYA.

RĀḤĪL, in the Bible Rachel, wife of Jacob, mother of Joseph and Benjamin, is not mentioned in the Ḳurʾān. There is however a reference to her in Sūra iv. 23: "Ye may not have two sisters to wife at the same time; if it has been done formerly God now exercises pardon and mercy". This is said to allude to Jacob's marriage with Liyā and Rāḥīl; before Moses revealed the Torah, such a marriage was valid. Ṭabarī gives this explanation in the *Annals*, i. 356, 359 *sq.* Ibn al-Athīr, p. 90, adopts it. But already in *Tafsīr*, iv. 210, Ṭabarī explains the verse correctly: Muḥammad forbids for the future marriage with two sisters but he does not dissolve such marriages concluded before the prohibition. — Islāmic tradition generally adopts the view that Yaʿḳūb only married Rāḥīl after Liyā's death. So already in Ṭabarī, i. 355, Zamakhsharī, Baiḍāwī, Ibn al-Athīr etc. Al Kisāʾī even thinks that Yaʿḳūb only married Rāḥīl after the death of Liyā and of his two concubines. Here again Muslim legend differs from the Bible, in making him not marry Rāḥīl until after 14 years of service; in the Bible, Jacob serves seven years, married Leah and after the wedding week Rachel and serves another seven years. — Yaʿḳūb's wooing and Laban's trick by which he substitutes Liyā for Rāḥīl as "neither lamp nor candle-light" illuminate the bridal chamber, is embellished in Muslim legend.

Rāḥīl is also of importance in the story of Yūsuf. Yūsuf inherits his beauty from Rāḥīl; they had half of all the beauty in the world, according to others two-thirds, or even according to the old Haggadic scheme (*Ḳiddushin*, 49b), nine tenths (Thaʿlabī, p. 69). — When Yaʿḳūb left Lāban, he had no funds for the journey; at Rāḥīl's suggestion, Yūsuf steals Lāban's idols. — As Yūsuf, sold by his brothers, passes the tomb of Rāḥīl he throws himself from his camel on the grave and laments: "O mother, look on thy child, I have been deprived of my coat, thrown into a pit, stoned and sold as a slave". Then he hears a voice: "Trust in God". The old Haggada does not know this touching scene. But it has found its way into the late mediaeval book of stories *Sefer Hayashar* (ed. Goldschmidt, p. 150). The Jewish-Persian poet Shahīn (xivth century) adapts this motif from Firdawsī's *Yūsuf u-Zulaikhā* in his book of Genesis.

Bibliography: Ṭabarī, i. 355—360, 371; do., *Tafsīr*, iv. 210; Thaʿlabī, *Ḳiṣaṣ al-anbiyāʾ*, Cairo 1325, p. 69, 74; Ibn al-Athīr, ed. Tornberg, i. 90; al-Kisāʾī, *Ḳiṣaṣ al-anbiyāʾ*, ed. Eisenberg, p. 155 *sq.*, 160; Neumann Ede, *A muhammedán József monda*, Budapest 1881, p. 12, 39 *sq.*; Grünbaum, *Gesammelte Aufsätze zur Sprach- und Sagenkunde*, ed. F. Perles, Berlin 1901, p. 523, 534—538, 548; W. Bacher, *Zwei jüdisch-persische Dichter, Schahin und Imrāni*, Budapest 1907, p. 119; s. also the articles YAʿḲŪB, YŪSUF.

RAḤĪM. [See ALLĀH].

RAḤMA, compassion [see ALLĀH].

RAḤMĀN. [See ALLĀH].

RAḤMĀNĪYA, Algerian Order (*ṭarīḳa*) called after Muḥammad b. ʿAbd al-Raḥmān al-Gushtulī al-Djurdjurī al-Azharī Abū Ḳabrain, who died 1208

/1793—1794. It is a branch of the Khalwatīya and is said to have at one time been called Bakrīya after Muṣṭafā al-Bakrī al-Shāmī. At Nefta, in Tunisia, and some other places it is called ʿAzzūzīya after Muṣṭafā b. Muḥammad b. ʿAzzūz.

Life of the Founder. His family belonged to the tribe Ait Smāʿīl, part of the confederation Gashtula in the Ḳābilīya Djurdjura; having studied at his home, and then in Algiers, he made the pilgrimage in 1152/1739—1740, and on his return spent some time as a student at al-Azhar in Cairo, where Muḥammad b. Sālim al-Ḥafnawī (d. 1181: *Silk al-durar*, iv. 50) initiated him into the Khalwatī Order, and ordered him to propagate it in India and the Sudan; after an absence of thirty years he returned to Algeria, and commenced preaching in his native village, where he founded a *zāwiya*; he seems to have introduced some modifications into Khalwatī practice, and in his Seven Visions of the Prophet Muḥammad made some important claims for his person and his system; immunity from hell-fire was to be secured by affiliation to his order, love for himself or his order, a visit to himself, stopping before his tomb, hearing his *dhikr* recited. His success in winning adherents provoked the envy of the local *murābiṭs*, in consequence of which he migrated to Ḥamma in the neighbourhood of Algiers. Here too his activities met with opposition from the religious leaders, who summoned him to appear before a *madjlis* under the presidency of the Mālikite Muftī ʿAlī b. Amīn; through the influence of the Turkish authorities, who were impressed by the following which he had acquired, he was acquitted of the charge of unorthodoxy, but he thought it prudent to return to his native village, where shortly afterwards he died, leaving as his successor ʿAlī b. ʿĪsā al-Maghribī. His corpse is said to have been stolen by the Turks and buried with great pomp at Ḥamma with a *ḳubba* and a mosque over it. The Ait Smāʿīl however maintained that it had not left its original grave, whence it was supposed to have been miraculously duplicated, and the title *Abū ḳabrain* "owner of two graves" was given him.

History and propagation of the Order. ʿAlī b. ʿĪsā al-Maghribī was undisputed head from 1208/1703—1794 to 1251/1836—1837; his successor died shortly after, and from the following year, though the Order continued to win adherents, it divided into independent branches. This was owing to the objections raised by the Ait Smāʿīl to the succession of al-Ḥādjdj Bashīr, another Maghribī; in spite of the support of ʿAbd al-Ḳādir (the famous enemy of the French) he had to quite his post, which was held for a time by the widow of ʿAlī b. ʿĪsā, who, however, owing to the dwindling of the revenues of the *zāwiya* had ultimately to summon Bashīr back. Meanwhile the founders of other *zāwiyas* were assuming independence. After the death of Bashīr in 1259/1843—4, ʿAlī b. ʿĪsā's son-in-law al-Ḥādjdj ʿAmmār succeeded to the headship. Finding his influence waning owing to his failure to participate in the attack on the French organized by Bū Baghla he in August 1856 called his followers to arms and obtained some initial successes; he was however compelled to surrender in the following year, and his wife (or mother-in-law) at the head of a hundred *khwān* shortly after. ʿAmmār retired to Tunis, where he endeavoured to continue the exercise of his functions, but he was not generally recognized as head of the order, and his place among the Ait Smāʿīl was taken by Muḥammad Amziān b. al-Ḥaddād of Ṣaddūḳ, who at the age of 80 on April 8, 1871 proclaimed *djihād* against the French, who had recently been defeated in the Franco-Prussian War. The insurrection met with little success, though it spread far, and on July 13 Ibn al-Ḥaddād surrendered to General Saussier, who sent him to Bougie. The original *zāwiya* was closed as a precautionary measure.

His son ʿAzīz, who had been transported to New Caledonia, succeeded in escaping to Djidda, whence he endeavoured to govern the community; but various *muḳaddams* who had been appointed by his father, as well as other founders of *zāwiyas*, asserted their independence. Lists are given by Depont and Coppolani of these persons and their spheres of influence, which extend into Tunisia and the Sahara. In their work the numbers of the adherents to the Order are reckoned at 156,214 (1897). Rinn notices that the Raḥmānīya of Tolga regularly maintained good relations with the French authorities.

Practices of the Order. The training of the *murīd* consists in teaching him a series of seven "names", of which the first is the formula *lā ilāhᵃ illa 'llāhᵘ*, to be repeated from 12,000 to 70,000 times in a day and night, and followed by the others, if the shaikh is satisfied with the neophyte's progress; these are 2. *Allāh* three times; 3. *huwa*; 4. *ḥaḳḳ* three times; 5. *ḥaiy* three times; 6. *ḳaiyūm* three times; 7. *ḳahhār* three times (Rinn's list differs slightly from this). Rinn states that the *dhikr* of the Order consists in repeating at least 80 times from the afternoon of Thursday to that of Friday the prayer ascribed to Shādhilī, and on the other weekdays the formula *lā ilāhᵃ illa 'llāhᵘ*. Favourite lessons are the "Verse of the Throne" followed by Sūras i., cxii.—cxiv. (prescribed in the founder's diploma, translated by A. Delpech, in *RA*, 1874) and the Seven Visions mentioned above (translated by Rinn, p. 467).

Literature of the Order. Most of this would seems to be still in MS.; the founder is credited with several books. A. Cherbonneau, in *JA*, 1852, p. 517 describes a catechism called *al-Raḥmāniya* by Muḥammad b. Bakhtarzī with a commentary by his son Muṣṭafā, perhaps identical with a work called by French writers *Présents dominicaux*. Another work belonging to the Order which they mention is called *al-Rawḍ al-bāsim fi manāḳib al-Shaikh Muḥammad b. al-Rāsim*.

Bibliography: Private communication obtained from Caid Benhassine Larba of Khanga Sidi Nadji by favour of M. P. Geuthner; E. de Neveu, *Les Khouan*, Paris 1846; L. Rinn, *Marabouts et Khouan*, Alger 1884; O. Depont and X. Coppolani, *Les Confréries religieuses musulmanes*, Algiers 1897; H. Garrot, *Histoire générale de l'Algérie*, Algiers 1910.

RAKʿA. [See ṢALĀT].

RAMAḌĀN (A.), name of the ninth month of the Muḥammadan calendar. The name from the root *r-m-ḍ* refers to the heat of summer and therefore shows in what season the month fell when the ancient Arabs still endeavoured to equate their year with the solar year by intercalary months.

Ramaḍān is the only month of the year to be mentioned in the Ḳurʾān (Sūra ii. 185): "The month of Ramaḍān (is that) in which the Ḳurʾān was sent down" in connection with the establishment of the fast of Ramaḍān. The discussion on the origin of this edict cannot yet be considered ended; to what has been said in the article ṢAWM have to be added the researches of F. Goitein, *Zur Entstehung des Ramaḍān*, in *Isl.* xviii. (1929), p. 189 *sqq.*, who in connection with the above mentioned verse of the Ḳur'ān calls attention to the parallelism between the mission of Muḥammad and the handing of the second tablets of the law to Moses, which according to Jewish tradition took place on the Day of Atonement (*ʿāshūrā'*, the predecessor of Ramaḍān!) and actually was the cause of its institution. Goitein suggests that the first arrangement to replace the ʿĀshūrā' [q.v.] was a period of ten days (*aiyām maʿdūdāt*, Sūra ii. 184), not a whole month, which ran parallel with the ten days of penance of the Jews preceding the Day of Atonement and survives to the present day in the 10 days of the *iʿtikāf* [q.v.]. If we consider further that the Muslim ideas of the *Lailat al-ḳadr*, which falls in Ramaḍān, in which according to Ḳur'ān xcvii. 1, the Ḳur'ān was sent down, coincide in many points with the Jewish on the Day of Atonement, we must concede a certain degree of probability to Goitein's suggestions in spite of the undeniable chronological difficulties (alteration of the length of the period of the fast, within a very short time) and although the final settlement of the term as a whole month is not thereby satisfactorily explained. On the other hand to strengthen Goitein's position, it ought perhaps to be pointed out that the *Lailat al-barā'a* precedes Ramaḍān in the middle of the preceding month of Shaʿbān. The ideas and practices described in the article SHAʿBĀN, which are associated with this night really to some extent resemble Jewish conceptions associated with the New Year — which precedes the Day of Atonement by a rather shorter interval than the *Lailat al-barā'a* Ramaḍān — that the connection between the latter and the Day of Atonement is thereby strengthened. If we try to connect the hitherto unexplained word *barā'a* with the Hebrew *beri'ā* "creation" and reflect that according to the Jewish idea the world was created on New Year's Day (numerous references in the liturgy of the festival) we have perhaps a further link in the chain of proof; but first of all the age of the ideas associated with the *Lailat al-barā'a* must be ascertained.

The legal regulations connected with the fast of Ramaḍān are given in the article ṢAWM [cf. also TARĀWĪḤ]. Of important days of the month, al-Bīrūnī, among others, mentions the 6th as birthday of the martyr Ḥusain b. ʿAlī, the 10th as the day of death of Khadīdja, the 17th as the day of the battle of Badr, the 19th as they day of the occupation of Mecca, the 21st as the day of ʿAlī's death, and of the Imām ʿAlī al-Riḍā's, the 22nd as birthday of ʿAlī and finally the night of the 27th as *Lailat al-ḳadr*.

The name of this night is Ḳur'ānic; Sūra xcvii. is dedicated to it. It is there described as a night, "better than 1,000 months" in which the angels descend free from every commission (*bi-idhn Allāh min kull amr*) and which means blessing till the appearance of the red of dawn. The revelation of the Ḳur'ān, as already mentioned, is expressly located in it. The same night is obviously referred to in Sūra xliv. 2 as a "blessed" one. The date, the 27th, is however not absolutely certain, the pious therefore use all the odd nights of the last ten days of Ramaḍān for good works, as one of them at any rate is the *Lailat al-ḳadr* [cf. IʿTIKĀF].

Trade and industry are largely at a standstill during Ramaḍān, especially when it falls in the hot season. The people are therefore all the more inclined to make up during the night for the deprivations of the day. As sleeping is not forbidden during the fast, they often sleep a part of the day; and the night, in which one may be merry, is given up to all sorts of pleasures. In particular the nights of Ramaḍān are the time for public entertainments, the shadow play and other forms of the theatre.

On the termination of the fast by the "little festival", cf. ʿĪD AL-FIṬR.

Bibliography: Wellhausen, *Reste*², p. 97; al-Bīrūnī, *Āthār*, ed. Sachau, p. 60, 325, 331 *sqq.*; Snouck Hurgronje, *Mekka*, ii.; do., *The Achehnese*, i.; Lane, *Manners and Customs*, chap. 25; Mehmed Tevfiq, *Ein Jahr in Konstantinopel*. 4. *Die Ramazan-Nächte*, transl. by Th. Menzel (*TB*, iii. 1905); Wensinck, *Arabic New-Year*, in *Verh. Ak. Amst.*, NS., xxv. 2; do., *The Muslim Creed*, p. 219 *sqq.*; Pijper, *Fragmenta Islamica*; Littmann, *Über die Ehrennamen* etc., in *Isl.*, viii. 228 *sqq.*

RASŪL (A., plur. *rusul*), messenger, apostle. The word is found in Arabic literature with the profane sense of envoy, messenger. Here we are only concerned with its religious acceptance. According to the Ḳur'ān, there is a close relation between the apostle and his people (*umma*; q.v.). To each *umma* God sends only one apostle (Sūra x. 47; xvi. 36; cf. xxiii. 44; xl. 5). These statements are parallel to those which mention the witness whom God will take from each *umma* at the Day of Judgment (Sūra iv. 41; xxviii. 75 and cf. the descriptions of the rasūl who will cross the bridge to the other world at the head of his *umma*: Bukhārī, *Adhān*, bāb 129; *Riḳāḳ*, bāb 52).

Muḥammad is sent to a people to whom Allāh has not yet sent an apostle (Sūra xxviii. 46; xxxii. 3; xxxiv. 44). The other individuals to whom the Ḳur'ān accords the dignity of rasūl are Nūḥ, Lūṭ, Ismāʿīl, Mūsā, Shuʿaib, Hūd, Ṣāliḥ and ʿĪsā.

The list of the prophets [cf. NABĪ] is a longer one; it contains, besides the majority of the apostles, Biblical or quasi-Biblical characters like Ibrāhīm, Isḥāḳ, Yaʿḳūb, Hārūn, Dāwūd, Sulaimān, Aiyūb, Dhu 'l-Nūn. Muḥammad in the Ḳur'ān is called sometimes rasūl, sometimes *nabī*. It seems that the prophets are those sent by God as preachers and *nadhīr* to their people, but are not the head of an *umma* like the rasūl. One is tempted to imagine a distinction between rasūl and *nabī* such as is found in Christian literature: the apostle is at the same time a prophet, but the prophet is not necessarily at the same time an apostle. But this is not absolutely certain, the doctrine at the basis of the Ḳur'ānic utterances not being always clear.

As to the close relation which exists between the rasūl and his *umma*, it may be compared with the doctrine of the *Acta apostolorum apocrypha*, according to which the twelve apostles divided the whole world among them so that each one had the task of preaching the Gospel to a certain people.

As regards the term rasūl, account must be taken of the use of the word apostle in Christianity, as well as of the use of the corresponding verb (*shalaḥ*) in connection with the prophets in the Old Testament (Exodus, iii. 13 *sq.*; iv. 13; Isaiya, vi. 8; Jeremiah, i. 7). The term *rasūl Allāh* is used in its Syriac form (*sheliḥeh dalaha*) *passim* in the aprocryphal Acts of St. Thomas.

Post-Ḳur'ānic teaching has increased the number of apostles to 313 or 315 without giving the names of all (Ibn Saʿd, ed. Sachau, 1/i. 10; *Fiḳh Akbar III*, art. 23; Reland, *De religione mohammedica*, sec. ed., Utrecht 1717, p. 40).

The doctrine that they were free from mortal sin is part of the faith [see ʿIṢMA]. For the rest, the difference between rasūl and *nabī* — apart from the considerable difference in point of numbers — seems in later literature to disappear in the general teaching about the prophets. Thus, in the *ʿAḳīda* of Abū Ḥafṣ ʿUmar al-Nasafī the two categories are treated together and the author makes no difference between rasūl and *nabī*. Similarly al-Īdjī deals with prophets in general, so far as can be seen, including in them the rasūls. If one difference can be pointed out, it is that the rasūl, in contrast to the prophet, is a law-giver and provided with a book (commentary on the *Fiḳh Akbar II* by Abu ʾl-Muntahā, Ḥaidarābād 1321, p. 4). According to the catechism published by Reland (p. 40—44), the rasūl-lawgivers were Ādam, Nūḥ, Ibrāhīm, Mūsā, ʿĪsā and Muḥammad.

In the catechism of Abū Ḥafṣ ʿUmar al-Nasafī, the sending of the apostles (*risāla*) is called an act of wisdom on the part of God. Al-Taftāzānī's commentary calls it *wādjib*, not in the sense of an obligation resting upon God but as a consequence arising from his wisdom. This semi-rationalist point of view is not however shared by all the scholastics: according to e.g. al-Sanūsī (cf. his *Umm al-barāhīn*) it is *djāʾiz* in itself but belief in it is obligatory.

Bibliography: A. Sprenger, *Das Leben und die Lehre des Moḥammed*, ii. 251 *sqq.*; Snouck Hurgronje, *Verspreide Geschriften*, index, under "gezanten Gods"; J. Horovitz, *Koranische Untersuchungen*, Berlin-Leipzig 1926, p. 44 *sqq.*; Pautz, *Muhammeds Lehre von der Offenbarung*, index; A. J. Wensinck, in *AO*, ii. 168 *sqq.*; do., *The Muslim Creed*, Cambridge 1932, p. 203—204; al-Īdjī, *Mawāḳif*, ed. Soerensen, p. 169 *sqq.* — Cf. also the *Bibliography* to the art. NABĪ.

RĀTIB (A., plur. *rawātib*), a word meaning what is fixed and hence applied to certain non-obligatory ṣalāts or certain litanies. The term is not found in the Ḳurʾān nor as a technical term in Ḥadīth. On the first meaning see the article NĀFILA. As to the second, it is applied to the *dhikr* which one recites alone, as well as to those which are recited in groups. We owe to Snouck Hurgronje a detailed description of the *rawātib* practised in Atchin.

Bibliography: C. Snouck Hurgronje, *De Atjehers*, Batavia—Leyden 1893—1894, ii. 220 *sqq.*; English transl. by O'Sullivan, *The Achehnese*, Leyden, 1906, ii. 216 *sqq.*

AL-**RĀZĪ**, Fakhr al-Dīn Abū ʿAbd Allāh Muḥammad b. ʿUmar b. al-Ḥusain, famous theologian and philosopher of religion. He was born 543/1149 — or 544 — in al-Raiy where his father, Ḍiyāʾ al-Dīn ʿUmar, was khaṭīb (his biography in Subkī, *Ṭabaḳāt* iv. 285). For this reason the son is also called Ibn Khaṭīb al-Raiy. After studying in his native town and in Marāgha under excellent teachers, he acted himself as a Shāfiʿite and Ashʿarite scholar. He went to Khwārizm in order to combat the Muʿtazilite doctrines prevailing there, but later on was compelled to leave the country, and went to Bukhārā and Samarḳand. About the year 582/1185 he worked in Ghazna and Hind (Pandjāb) and finally settled in Herāt, under the protection of the Ghōrid sultans and the Khwārizmshāh ʿAlāʾ al-Dīn. At a more advanced age he also worked in the latter's capital al-Djurdjānīya (Tashköprüzāde, *Miftāḥ al-saʿāda*, Ḥaidarābād 1329 i. 447). In Herāt a madrasa was founded for him, where he, as a famous scholar with the title Shaikh al-Islām, attracted great masses of disciples. He had, however, many enemies, among whom was his own brother Rukn al-Dīn, and in 585/1189 he came into great danger by an attack of the Karrāmīya (q.v.), who charged him with having betrayed Islām. He died in Herāt in 606/1209, poisoned, it is said, at the instigation of the Karrāmīya.

Al-Rāzī's life-work is of importance by his attempt at reconciliation of philosophy and religious traditions, in which he displayed a rationalism uncommon for his time. To the first period of his life belong his well-known treatise *Sharḥ al-ishārāt*, a commentary to Ibn Sīnā, and *al-Mabāḥith al-mashriḳīya*. In these writings he continues in a way the work of the earlier philosophers and shows himself an admirer of al-Fārābī and Abū Bakr Muḥ. b. Zakarīyā al-Rāzī. His commentary on Abū ʾl-ʿAlāʾ al-Maʿarrī's dīwān, *Sharḥ Saḳṭ al-zand*, gives evidence of his admiration for this poet.

The opposition which al-Rāzī met with on the part of many scholars of his time, was due as much to his bold opinions as to his aggressive personality of which we get an impression in the *Munāẓarāt al-ʿallāma Fakhr al-Dīn*, a sort of autobiography, in which he describes his meetings and discussions with the scholars of Transoxania. It is quite possible that this very personal work was meant to serve as a justification of the author against the attacks of his contemporaries. On this important treatise — the only known MS of which is in the Egyptian Library — cf. P. Kraus, *The "Controversies" of Fakhr al-Dîn Râzî*, in *Islamic Culture* xii. (1938) p. 131. As it appears in particular from the *Munāẓarāt*, al-Rāzī on several occasions made a stand against al-Ghazzālī, who in his rejection of the *falsafa* could not fail to come into conflict with his own ideas.

To his later writings belong the *Kitāb Muḥaṣṣal afkār al-mutaḳaddimīn wa ʾl-mutaʾakhkhirīn*, a manual of metaphysics (abridged translations by M. Horten, *Die philosophischen Ansichten von Rāzī und Ṭūsī*, Bonn 1912, and *Die spekulative und positive Theologie des Islam und ihre Kritik durch Ṭūsī*, Leipzig 1912) and the famous Ḳurʾān-commentary *Mafātīḥ al-ghaib*, also called *al-Tafsīr al-kabīr*. This work is not only an Ashʿarite answer to the Muʿtazilite Ḳurʾān-exegesis which had found its exponent in the *Kashshāf* of Zamakhsharī, but provides him also with a means to expose his philosophical views. That al-Rāzī was nevertheless, in some respects, under Muʿtazilite influence, is proved by Goldziher (*Isl.* 1912). He left his commentary unfinished; it was completed by his disciple Shams al-Dīn Aḥmad b. al-Khalīl al-Khuwaiyī, chief ḳāḍī of Damascus (d. 639/1242) and also by Nadjm al-Dīn Aḥmad b. Muḥ. al-Ḳamūlī (d. 777/1375). There exist several Oriental editions: Būlāḳ 1278, Cairo 1308, Istanbul 1278; cf. R. P. Mc. Neile, *An Index to the Commentary of Fakhr al-Razi*, London 1933. An abridgement is to be found in *al-Tanwīr fi ʾl-Tafsīr mukhtaṣar al-Tafsīr al-kabīr* by Muḥ. b. Abī ʾl-Ḳāsim al-Rīghī (d. 1307).

Among the other writings of al-Rāzī are the *Manāḳib al-Imām Shāfiʿī*, and several works on fiḳh (as the Shāfiʿītic uṣūl-work *K. al-Maḥṣūl*), and on astrology, rhetorics and encyclopaedia.

At the end of his life al-Rāzī excelled as a preacher. By that time he had come to reject the dialectic methods of the *kalām* as being of no use, and he declared that he found his highest satisfaction and peace of mind in the reading of the Ḳurʾān.

Bibliography: Biographical notes are to be found in Ibn Abī Uṣaibiʿa, Ibn al-Ḳifṭī, Ibn Khallikān, al-Ṣafadī, al-Dhahabī, Yāḳūt, al-Subkī and Ibn al-Sāʿī; cf. also Barhebraeus, *Mukhtaṣar al-duwal*, p. 419. Further I. Goldziher, *Aus der*

Theologie des Fachr al-Dîn Râzî, in *Isl.* iii. (1912) p. 213—47; do., *Vorlesungen über den Islam*, 1910, Index s.v. Fachr al-Din al-Razi; do., *Die Richtungen der Muh. Koranauslegung*, p. 123; Brockelmann, *GAL* i. 666 *sqq.*, *Suppl.* i. 920 *sqq.*; T. J. de Boer, *Geschichte der Philosophie im Islam.*

RIBĀ (A.), lit. increase, as a technical term, usury and interest, and in general any unjustified increase of capital for which no compensation is given. Derivatives from the same root are used in other Semitic languages to describe interest.

1. Transactions with a fixed time limit and payment of interest as well as speculations of all kinds formed an essential element in the highly developed trading system of Mecca (cf. Lammens, *La Mecque à la veille de l'hégire*, p. 139 *sqq.*, 155 *sqq.*, 213 *sq.*). Among the details given by the Muslim sources we may believe at least the statement that a debtor who could not repay the capital (money or goods) with the accumulated interest at the time it fell due, was given an extension of time in which to pay, but at the same time the sum due was doubled. This is clearly referred to in two passages in the Ḳur'ān (Sūra iii. 130; xxx. 39) and is in keeping with a still usual practice. As early as Sūra xxx 39 of the third Meccan period (on the dating cf. Nöldeke-Schwally, *Geschichte des Qorāns*, i.) the Ḳur'ān contrasts ribā with the obligation to pay *zakāt* but without directly forbidding it: "What ever ye give in usury to gain interest from men's substance shall not bear interest with Allāh, but what ye give as *zakāt* in seeking the face of Allāh, these shall gain double". The express prohibition follows in Sūra iii. 130 (Madīna, obviously earlier than the following passage): ,"Believers, devour not the ribā with continual doubling; fear God, perhaps it will go wel with you". This prohibition had to be intensified in Sūra ii. 275—280 (evidently of the earlier Madīnese period; cf. on the following passage): "Those who devour ribā shall only rise again as one whom Satan strikes with his touch; this because they say, 'selling is like usury'; but Allāh has permitted selling and forbidden usury. He therefore who receives a warning from his Lord and abstains shall have pardon for what is past and his affairs is with Allāh; but they who relapse to usury, are the people of Hell, they shall remain in it for ever. Allāh abolishes usury and makes alms bring interest; Allāh loveth no sinful unbeliever ... Believers, fear Allāh and remit the balance of the ribā if ye be believers. But if ye do not, be prepared for war from Allāh and his apostle. If ye repent ye shall receive your capital without doing an injustice or suffering injustice. If any one is in difficulty, let there be a delay till he is able to pay, but it is better for you to remit if ye be wise". To evade the dogmatic difficulty, of an eternal punishment for the sin of a believer, the passage in question has been interpreted (already presupposed in Ṭabarī) to mean that by relapse is meant the holding lawful and not the taking of interest; in any case the Ḳur'ān regards ribā as a practice of unbelievers and demands as a test of belief that it should be abandoned. It comes up again in Sūra iv. 161 (of the period between the end of the year 3 and the end of the year 5; this also gives a clue to the date of the preceding passage) in a passage which sums up the reproaches levelled against the Jews: "and because they take ribā, while it was forbidden them, and devour uselessly the substance of the people". The fact that the principal passages against interest belong to the Madīna period and that the Jews are reproached with breaking the prohibition suggests that the Muslim prohibition of ribā owes less to conditions in Mecca than to the Prophet's closer acquaintance with Jewish doctrine and practice in Madīna. In the later development of the teaching on the subject as we find it in tradition, Jewish influence is in any case undeniable (cf. Juynboll, *Handleiding*, p. 286).

2. The traditions give varying answers to the question what forms of business come under the Ḳur'ānic prohibition of ribā, none of which can be regarded as authentic. The ignorance of the correct interpretation is emphasized in a tendencious tradition, obviously put into circulation by interested individuals (the tradition is probably older than Lammens, *op. cit.*, p. 214, thinks); according to this view, the principal passage in Sūra ii. is the latest in the whole Ḳur'ān, which the Prophet could not expound before his death. That the rigid prohibition of usury in Muḥammadan law only developed gradually is clear from many traditions. Alongside of the view repeatedly expressed, but also challenged, that ribā consists only in (the increase of substance in) a business agreement with a fixed period (*nasī'a, naẓira, dain*) we have the still more distinct statement that there is no ribā if the transfer of ownership takes place immediately (*yad^an bi-yad*). But even in arrangements with a time limit, a number of traditions pre-suppose a general ignorance of the later restrictions; for example we are told that in Baṣra under Ziyād gold was sold on credit for silver (this may have an anti-Umaiyad bias — cf. below on Mu'āwiya —, but it is illuminating); but at a later date such forms of the traditions against ribā were to some extent dropped. What was generally understood in the earliest period as the ribā forbidden in the Ḳur'ān, seems only to have been interest on loans (chiefly of money and foodstuffs); anything that goes beyond this is to be regarded as a later development. The reason for such prohibitions is at different times said to be the fear of ribā and sometimes we have underlying the recognition that there is no tradition of the Prophet relating to this. This is also expressed in the form that nine-tenths of the permitted is renounced or that ribā was conceived as going as far as ten times the capital. The view which later became authoritative is laid down in a group of traditions of which one characteristic example is as follows: "gold for gold, silver for silver, wheat for wheat, barley for barley, dates for dates, salt for salt, the same thing for the same thing, like for like, measure for measure; but if these things are different, sell them as you please if it is (only) done measure for measure". Another common tradition expressly forbids the exchange of different quantities of the same thing but of different quality (cf. below). Other traditions demand equality of quantity even in the sale of manufactured precious metals. This last case seems to have been especially discussed, and on more than one occasion Mu'āwiya appears as champion of the opposite view and practice (this again has a distinctly anti-Umaiyad bias). Particularly conscientious people went even further in their limitation of ribā than the generality and would only exchange wheat for barley in equal quantities. Still stricter was the view that the exchange of even the same quantities of the same thing, especially of precious metals, was ribā. This view must be older than a difference from the usual opinion (e.g. Muslim, *Bāb bai' al-ṭa'ām mithl^an bi-mithl*), which is based on the secondary interpretation of an already recognized tradition, which obviously only forbade the exchange of different quan-

tities of the same thing but of different quality (cf. above). This same general prohibition of exchange is also given for dates. The question whether one party to an agreement can voluntarily give the other a bonus, is denied for an exchange, but affirmed for a loan. The reduction of the amount of the debt if the loan is voluntarily paid before it falls due, is sometimes approved as the opposite of ribā, sometimes disapproved, sometimes forbidden as being equivalent to ribā; in any case it is clear that the practice existed. On the sale of an animal for an animal on credit, opinion is also not unanimous.

Numerous traditions forbid ribā without defining it more closely; the Prophet is said to have uttered this prohibition at his farewell pilgrimage (scarcely historical). Ribā is one of the gravest sins. Even the least of its many forms is as bad as incest and so on. All who take part in a transaction involving ribā are cursed, the guilty are threatened with hell, various kind of punishment are described; in this world also gains from ribā will bring no good. In spite of all this tradition foresees that ribā will prevail.

In connection with ribā tradition mentions various antiquated forms of sale of special kinds, like *muḥāḳala*, *mukhābara*, *muzābana* etc., which concern the exchange of different stages in the manufacture or development of the same thing, or of different qualities, and which are forbidden: an exception is made, obviously because of its undeniable practical and social necessity, of what is known as *ʿarīya* (plur. *ʿarāyā*), fresh dates on trees intended to be eaten, which it is permitted to exchange in small quantities for dried dates.

3. While the existence of the Ḳurʾānic prohibition of ribā has never been doubted, the difference of opinion that finds expression in tradition regarding the relevant facts is continued in the earliest stage of development of Muḥammadan law. Unanimity prevails regarding the main lines of the limitations to be imposed upon the exchange of goods capable of ribā (*māl ribawī*); it is only permitted if transfer of ownership takes place at once and, so far as goods of the same kind are concerned, only in equal quantities. In the case of a loan it is forbidden to make a condition that a larger quantity shall be returned without regard to the kind of article. Gold and silver are generally regarded as *māl ribawī* (only quite exceptionally are coins of small denomination included). All the greater are the differences of opinion as to what things outside of the precious metals are liable to the ribā ordinances. In isolated cases one still finds views that show themselves uninfluenced in principle by the authoritative group of traditions (cf. above), e.g. when everything realisable is subjected to the ribā ordinances (Ibn Kaisān) or all business dealing in things of the same kind (Ibn Sīrīn, Ḥammād) or when everything liable to *zakāt* is considered capable of ribā (Rabīʿa b. ʿAbd al-Raḥmān). Other opinions differ in the treatment of property capable of ribā from that group of traditions, although it is not known what they understand by this; possibly if at an exchange of the same kind of thing not equality of quantity but equality of value in two quantities is demanded (Ḥasan al-Baṣrī) or equality of quantity also in the exchange of different kinds apparently within a limited circle of goods capable of ribā (Saʿīd b. Djubair). The old interpretation that there is no ribā if the transfer of possession takes place at once is ascribed to ʿAṭāʾ and the jurists of Madīna. The views of most authorities however and in particular those which survive later in the law schools assume the literal acceptance of the text of that group of traditions and differ only in its interpretation. Thus there are mentioned as precursors of the later Ẓāhirī doctrine: Ṭāwūs, Masrūḳ, al-Shaʿbī, Ḳatāda, ʿUthmān al-Battī; as precursors of the Ḥanafī view: al-Zuhrī al-Ḥakam, Ḥammād (cf. however above), Sufyān al-Thawrī; as precursors of the earlier view of al-Shāfiʿī: Saʿīd b. al-Musaiyib and others; as precursors of his later view: al-Zuhrī (cf. however above) and Yaḥyā b. Saʿīd. On the questions whether a loan can be repaid in another kind and what is to be done if defects are revealed in an exchange of *māl ribawī* after it has changed hands, there are old differences of opinion.

4. In the above mentioned group of traditions the following goods in addition to gold and silver are expressly mentioned as bearing the prohibition of ribā at their exchange: wheat, barley, dates and salt (sometimes also raisins, butter and oil). The Ẓāhirīs, as a result of their refusal on principle to accept analogy (*ḳiyās*), assume that the prohibition applies only to the six things especially named (the other kinds are rejected as not well attested). The other schools of law, on the other hand, consider the kinds mentioned in tradition only as examples of the variety of things that come under *māl ribawī*, but differ from one another in their lists of these things. According to the Ḥanafīs and Zaidīs (also al-Awzāʿī), gold and silver represent examples of the class of things defined by weight (*mawzūn*) and the four other things those sold by measure (*makīl*). The Imāmī teaching is practically the same. According to the Mālikīs and Shāfiʿīs, gold and silver represent the class of precious metals and the four other things the class of foodstuffs: the latter, in the Mālikī view, including actual estables so far as they can be preserved according to the older view of al-Shāfiʿī, provisions which are sold by weight and measure; according to his later view, which is also that of his school, foodstuffs without any qualification. The teaching of the Ḥanbalīs corresponds to that of the Ḥanafīs; as regards the "four kinds", two further opinions of Aḥmad b. Ḥanbal are handed down which correspond to the two views held by al-Shāfiʿī. In these, wheat and barley are regarded as two different kinds by the Ḥanafīs, the Shāfiʿīs and the better known tradition of the Ḥanbalīs (as well as Ẓāhirīs, Zaidīs and Imāmīs); as one kind according to the Ḥanbalīs (also according to al-Laith b. Saʿd and al-Awzāʿī). The Ḥanafīs and the Imāmīs, in contrast to the other schools, are content, in so far as it is not a question of the exchange of precious metals, with fixing the quantities, and do not demand actual change of ownership during the negotiation (*madjlis*). The Ẓāhirīs, in the strict interpretation of the text of one tradition, in every case demand a change of ownership in the fullest sense at once. The sale of fresh dates for dried dates is forbidden by all schools except the Ḥanafīs on the authority of one tradition, the barter of *ʿarāyā* on the other hand is not permitted by the Ḥanafīs but regulated by the other schools, without any uniformity; as regards exchange of the same material in different stages of manufacture there are many differences of opinion. As regards the exchange of goods of the same kind which are not *māl ribawī*, the difference of quantity is generally permitted, postponement (*nasīʾa*, *nasāʾ*) of the single payment still forbidden by the Ḥanafīs and Zaidīs but permitted by the other schools (with differences in detail). At the sale of wares, also of those which are

māl ribawī, for precious metal, the payment at later date (*salam*) and sale on credit (*baiʿ al-ʿīna*) with postponement of delivery or of payment is permitted. The apparent contradiction of analogy in the *salam*, which forms a type of transaction by itself, has given rise to discussions on principle. The postponement of both sides of the transaction is regarded on the authority of a tradition as entirely forbidden in all agreements regarding sale or exchange.

5. The prohibition of ribā plays a considerable part in the system of Muḥammadan law. The structure of the greater part of the law of contract is explained by the endeavour to enforce prohibition of ribā and *maisir* (i.e. risk; q.v.) to the last detail of the law (Bergsträsser, in *Isl.*, xiv. 79). Ribā in a loan exists not only when one insists upon the repayment of a larger quantity but if any advantage at all is demanded. Therefore even exchange (*suftadja*) is sometimes disapproved (as by the Ḥanafīs), sometimes actually forbidden (as by the Shāfiʿīs) because the vendor, who is regarded as the creditor, reaps the advantage of avoiding cost of transport. This did not prevent the wide spread of this arrangement in the Arabic middle ages and its influence upon European money-changing. But they were always conscious that a direct breach of the prohibition of ribā was a deadly sin. Pious Muslims to this day therefore not infrequently refuse to take bank interest. The importance of the prohibition of ribā on the one hand deeply affecting everyday life and the requirements of commerce on the other have given rise to a number of methods of evasion. Against some of these there is nothing formally to object from the standpoint of the law; they are therefore given in many lawbooks and expressly said to be permitted. The Shāfiʿīs, the later Ḥanafīs and the Imāmīs have recognized such methods of evasion while the Mālikīs, the Ḥanbalīs and the Zaidīs reject them. The recognition of these methods of evasion is not contrary to the strict enforcement of the prohibition in the *fiḳh*. The inner significance of decrees of the divine law naturally cannot be understood by the mind of man. This is shown in the case of ribā in the limitation to certain kinds of goods. The Ẓāhirīs are thus among the most energetic defenders of evasions of the prohibition of ribā. Their line of argument is based not only on their formal negative rejection of deduction by analogy but also upon their positive estimation of the intention underlying the evasions. One of the oldest transactions of the kind, against which several traditions are already directed, is the double contract of sale (from one of its elements it is called *baiʿ al-ʿīna*, credit sale *par excellence*): one sells to someone who wants to lend money at interest something against the total sum of capital and interest which are to be due at a fixed date, and at the same time buys the article back for the capital which is at once handed over. This transaction was taken over in mediaeval Europe under the name of *mohatra* (from the Ar. *mukhāṭara*; cf. Juynboll, *Handleiding*, p. 289, note 1, and E. Bussi, in *Rivista di storia del diritto italiano*, v., part 2). Another method of evasion consists of handing over to the creditor the use of a thing as interest by a fictitious agreement to sell or to pledge. All these practices are still in use and in spite of the prohibition of ribā money-lending is a flourishing business in most Muslim countries (50% is often regarded as moderate interest).

Bibliography: On the traditions cf. in addition to the references in Wensinck, *Handbook* s.v. Usury, especially the collection of material in *Kanz al-ʿummāl*, ii. No. 4623 *sqq.*, 4951 *sqq.* The material of tradition is dealt with from the point of view of the respective authors in Ibn Ḥazm, *al-Muḥallā*, No. 1478 *sqq.*; al-Ṣanʿānī, *Subul al-salām*, Cairo 1345, iii. 45 *sqq.*; al-Shawkānī, *Nail al-awṭār*, Cairo 1345, v. 295 *sqq.* — Discussion of the various views in the authors mentioned and in al-Nawawī, *al-Madjmūʿ*, Cairo 1348, ix. 390 *sqq.* — A survey of the differences among the great schools is given in Ibn Hubaira, *Kitāb al-ifṣāḥ*, Aleppo 1928, p. 164 *sqq.* — On ribā as a grave sin cf. Ibn Ḥadjar al-Haitamī, *Kitāb al-zawādjir*, Būlāḳ 1284, i. 231 *sqq.* — European treatment, generally: Goldziher, *Die Zâhiriten*, p. 41 *sqq.*; Snouck Hurgronje, *Verspreide Geschriften*, ii. 141 *sq.*, 152 *sq.*, 244 *sq.*; Amedroz, in *JRAS* 1916, p. 299 *sqq.*; Ḥanafīs: Bergsträsser-Schacht, *Grundzüge des islamischen Rechts*, p. 62 *sq.*; Dimitroff, *Asch-Schaibānī*, in *MSOS*, xi/ii. 105 *sq.*, 156 *sqq.*; Shāfiʿīs: Juynboll, *Handbuch des islāmischen Gesetzes*, p. 270 *sqq.*; do., *Handleiding* [3], p. 285 *sqq.*; Sachau, *Muhammedanisches Recht*, p. 279 *sqq.*; Mālikīs: Guidi-Santillana, *Sommario del diritto malechita*, ii. 186 *sqq.*, 282 *sqq.*; Imāmīs: Querry, *Droit musulman*, i. 402 *sqq.* — On methods of evasion cf. Juynboll, *op. cit.*; Schacht, *Das Kitāb al-ḥiyal wa 'l-makhāridj des al-Khaṣṣāf*, chap. 2 and 3 with transl. and commentary (this text is supposed to belong to ʿIrāḳ, c. 400 A.H.). — On the practice of taking interest cf. Juynboll, *op. cit.*, and the travellers, e.g. Snouck Hurgronje, *Mekka in the latter part of the 19th century*, p. 4 *sq.*; Polak, *Persien*, i. 345.

RIBĀṬ (A.), a fortified Muḥammadan monastery. Of the various explanations that have been given of this word from the root *rabaṭa*: "to bind, attach", the most reasonable is that which refers to the Ḳurʾān, viii. 60: "Prepare against them (the enemies of Allāh) all that ye possess of strength and places for horses..." (*min ribāṭⁱ 'l-khailⁱ*). The ribāṭ is originally the place where the mounts are assembled and hobbled to be kept in readiness for an expedition. Ribāṭ also has the closely related meanings of relay of horses for a courier, caravanserai. The word however was early applied to an establishment at once religious and military which seems quite specifically Islamic.

The institution of the ribāṭ is connected with the duty of the holy war [see DJIHĀD], the defence of the lands of Islām and their extension by force of arms. The Byzantine empire was acquainted with the fortified monastery, like Mandrakion built at Carthage near the sea, mentioned by Procopius: but it seems doubtful whether the monks living in it played any military part. The regular or occasional occupants of the ribāṭ are essentially fighters for the faith. The ribāṭs are primarily fortresses, places of concentration of troops at exposed points on the Muḥammadan frontier. Like western castles, they offer a refuge to the inhabitants of the surrounding country in time of danger. They serve as watch-towers from which an alarm can be given to the threatened populace and to the garrisons of the frontier and interior of the country who could support the efforts of the defenders. The structure of the ribāṭ therefore consisted of a fortified surrounding wall with living rooms, magazines of arms and storehouses for provisions and a tower for signalling. This architectural scheme, the development of which will be indicated below, was of course often very summarily treated. The ribāṭ in many cases was reduced to a watch-tower and a little fort like those the Byzantines built on their frontiers. This explains the considerable number of ribāṭs mentioned by the geographers. We are told that in Transoxiana alone there were no less than 10,000 (Ibn Khallikān, transl. de Slane, i. 159, No. 3). The coasts were also amply provided for. There were ribāṭs all along the coast of Palestine and of Africa. The fire-towers, attached to the ribāṭ or isolated, enabled messages, we are told, to be sent in one night from Alexandria to Ceuta. This is clearly an exaggeration. Nevertheless we may note a fairly rapid system of signalling and the mention of Alexandria, the pharos of which seems to have served as a ribāṭ. The Spanish coast also had its ribāṭs, as had the frontier against the Christian kingdoms, especially after the coming of the Almoravids, which saw an intensification of the *djihād*. For Sicily, Ibn Ḥawḳal gives some curious information about the ribāṭs near Palermo and we know the little town of Rabato in the island of Gozo in the Maltese archipelago.

Devotion to religion stimulated individuals to multiply their foundations, notably in Ifrīḳiya in the vicinity of towns like Tripolis and Sfax. It was a work of piety to build a ribāṭ at one's own expense or strengthen its defences. It was equally meritorious to urge men to go there to serve the cause of Islām, to revictual the garrison, lastly and above all to go there oneself. For the coast of Palestine, al-Maḳdisī tells us of another use of the ribāṭ equally pleasing to Allāh. Their fires were used to signal the approach of Christian vessels bringing Muslim prisoners to be ransomed. Everyone endeavoured to contribute to this according to his means.

The building of the large ribāṭs and of many of the smaller ones was naturally the task of the sovereigns of the country. In Ifrīḳiya the first was that of Monastir built by the ʿAbbāsid governor Harthama b. Aʿyān (179/795). The third (ninth) century was the golden age: the Aghlabids all along the eastern coasts multiplied ribāṭs in the strict sense and *maḥras*; this word means a fortified area containing a small garrison or a watch-tower. Monastir retained the preeminence which the Prophet himself is said to have foretold for it. In the xiith century the dead were brought from al-Mahdīya to enjoy the blessing of being buried there. But the ribāṭ of Sūs founded by the Aghlabid Ziyādat Allāh in 206/821 had assumed considerable importance. We know that Sūs was the port from which the troops embarked for the conquest of Sicily.

Compared with the east coast of Ifrīḳiya, which was directly threatened by attacks of the Rūm or which was the base for expeditions across the sea, the rest of the Barbary coast was less well supplied. There were however ribāṭs on the coast of the extreme Maghrib, at Nakūr and Arzila to prevent raiding by the Norman pirates, and at Salé to facilitate the war against the Barghawāṭa heretics.

If the majority of the ribāṭs were official foundations, the service done by the combatants in them does not seem to have been in any way compulsory. The men of the ribāṭ, the *murābiṭūn*, were volunteers, pious individuals who had taken a vow to devote themselves to the defence of Islām. Some may have entered the ribāṭ like a monastery, to end their days in it, but the great majority only stayed in them for longer or shorter periods, and the garrisons were changed completely several times a year. In the ribāṭ of Arzila, this change in the garrison took place al the festival of *ʿāshūrāʾ* (10th Muḥarram), the beginning of Ramaḍān and *al-ʿīd al-kabīr*. An important fair was held on the occasion. In case of alarm the garrisons were reinforced by able-bodied men from the country round, summoned by the beating of drums (Palestine, according to al-Maḳdisī).

Life in the ribāṭ was spent in military exercises and on guard, but also in devotional exercises. The murābiṭs prepared themselves for martyrdom by long prayers under the direction of a venerated shaikh. The traveller Ibn Ḥawḳal however reveals a dark side to this edifiying picture. Speaking of the ribāṭs of Palermo in the fourth (tenth) century, he tells us that they were the rendezvous of the bad characters of the country who thus found a means of livelihood outside of regular society and at the expense of the pious and charitable.

The double character — military and religious — of the life of the murābiṭs found expression in the architecture of the old ribāṭs that have survived. Tunisia has preserved those of Monastir and Sūs. The first is still very imposing but the frequent restorations have complicated the original plan. The second which is more simple may be taken as typical. With its high square wall flanked with semi-circular towers at the corners and the middle of the sides, it recalls the Byzantine forts of the country. The only entrance was by one of the salients in the middle of the wall. A staircase went down in the interior into the central court surrounded by covered galleries and very simple cells. The first storey, reached by two staircases, also consisted of cells on three sides of the court. Along the fouth side was a hall with a *miḥrāb*. This was the oratory of the ribāṭ. The *ḳibla* wall was pierced with embrasures. On the level of the terraces which are above this first storey, is the door of the signal tower, cylindrical in form, which rises from the square base of a salient at one corner and dominates the fortress from a height of about 60 feet. A little dome which also rises above the terraces crowns, as in the mosque of the period, the square area in front of the *miḥrāb* in the oratory.

The ribāṭ of Sūs takes us back to the heroic times when the institution had distinctly a warlike character and these frontier posts played a strategic role on the borders of the lands of Islām. They retained this character in the xith—xiith century in the extreme Maghrib where the struggle with the Christians in Spain kept alive the tradition of the *djihād*. We know that a ribāṭ built on an island in the Lower Senegal was the starting place of the career of the Lamtūna Berbers and gave them the name of Almoravids (*al-murābiṭūn*) under which they became famous in history. The Almohads who succeeded them had also their ribāṭs, two of which at least are worth mentioning. The ribāṭ of Tāzā was fortified in 528/1138 by ʿAbd al-Muʾmin at the time when he was conducting against the Almoravids a campaign which had all the appearance of a *djihād*. The Ribāṭ al-Fatḥ, the name of which survives in that of the town of Rabat, was, if not the port of embarkation, at least the great camp of concentration for the armies preparing to cross to Spain. The prestige of this Almohad foundation survived the dynasty which built it. Rabat, or rather the adjoining little town of Shālla, which also ranked as a ribāṭ, became the necropolis of the Marīnid princes, who in being buried there hoped to share in the merit of the warriors of the faith.

In the xivth century, to anticipate landings by the Christians on the coast, *maḥras* and signal towers were still being built "to serve as ribāṭs". Ibn Marzūḳ, the historiographer of the Marīnid Abu 'l-Ḥasan, who tells of them, says however that these posts were occupied by paid soldiers. They were not true ribāṭs, the garrison of which consisted of volunteers. While however we find down to the xvi[th] century, in the extreme Maghrib, a ribāṭ like that of Asfi playing a military part in the struggle with the Portuguese, in the east, in the lands where the infidels no longer threatened Islām, the institution had changed its character or rather the ascetic discipline and the pious recitations which were the regular practices in the old ribāṭs, had entirely taken the place of military exercises. From the vi[th]/xii[th] century, and perhaps even earlier, the development of mysticism and the grouping of the Ṣūfīs into communities gave these barracks a new *raison d'être* by transforming them into monasteries. From Persia, where it originated, this evolution of the ribāṭs rapidly spread through the Muslim world. In the east the ribāṭ merged into the Persian *khānaḳā*. Ibn Djubair (ed. Wright and de Goeje, p. 243) refers to a *khānaḳā* founded by Ṣūfīs which was also called a ribāṭ, at Rās al-ʿAin to the north of the Syrian desert. When however a writer like Ibn al-Shiḥna describing Aleppo seems to distinguish the *khānaḳās* from the ribāṭs, the difference between them escapes us. It may be supposed that the *khawānik* were inhabited by permanent residents who spent their whole lives there and that the ribāṭs, as before, received devout men for limited periods, but one cannot assert definitely that this was the distinction. In any case the four ribāṭs within the city of Aleppo (one attached to a *madrasa* and the mausoleum of its founder with Ḳurʾān-readers and Ṣūfīs) had no longer anything of a military character. It was the same with the two ribāṭs of Mecca mentioned by Ibn Baṭṭūṭa. In Cairo the only inscription found by Van Berchem in which a ribāṭ is mentioned is that of the convent of Malik Ashraf ʿInāl (860/1455).

In Barbary, which the wave of eastern mysticism had reached in the xi[th]—xii[th] century, the term ribāṭ was likewise retained but applied to the *zāwiya* [q.v.] in which ascetics gathered round a shaikh or his tomb. As a matter of fact Ibn Marzūḳ in this connection makes a distinction which nevertheless still remains obscure. Speaking of the *zāwiyas* founded by Abu 'l-Ḥasan, his master, he tells us first that *khānaḳā*, a Persian word, has the same meaning as ribāṭ and adds: "In the terminology of the *faḳīrs* one understands by ribāṭ the act of devoting oneself to the holy war and to guarding [the frontiers]. Among the Ṣūfīs it means on the contrary the place in which a man shuts himself up to worship the divinity". This last use of the word seems to be the usual one in his time. The Ribāṭ al-ʿUbbād is the group of pious foundations near Tlemcen that have grown up around the tomb of the famous mystic Sīdī Bū Madyan. The ribāṭ of Taskedelt to the south west of Oran is dedicated to a saint of the Banū Iznāsen; the ribāṭ of Tāferṭast on the borders of the Wādī Sbū contains the tomb mosque of two Marīnid princes and apartments for *ṭulbāʾ* (Ḳurʾān readers).

With this improper use of the old Arabic word we might connect the parallel change undergone by the word *murābiṭ* (marabout). This is applied to a saint, an individual who by his own merits or the mystic initiation which he had received or his relationship with a *walī* [q.v.] enjoys the veneration of those around him.

In Muslim Spain, the last land of the *djihād*, we may suppose that the ribāṭs continued to stud the successive frontiers which the "reconquista" imposed on the lands of Islām; but to be certain we must wait until the study of the texts and the enquiry being conducted by F. Hernández and H. Terrasse into the military architecture of Muslim Spain give us precise details regarding the dates of the castles and their object. The evolution in meaning of the word ribāṭ would lead one to think it had ceased to mean a fortress. Among the Arabic authors of Spain and al-Maḳḳarī, as among the *faḳīrs* mentioned by Ibn Marzūḳ, ribāṭ is often used to mean a holy war, generally defensive, and it passed into Spanish in the form *rebato* with the meaning as J. Oliver Asín has shown of "sudden attack executed by a body of horsemen in keeping with Muslim tactics". If the Arabic term had lost its original meaning, however, another word derived from it was commonly used in a slightly different meaning. Spain saw the *rābiṭas* multiplying and their memory is preserved in place-names in the forms Rápita, Rávita, Rábida. The word *rābiṭa* was also known in Barbary. It meant "a hermitage to which a holy man retired and where he lived surrounded by his disciples and his religious servitors" (cf. al-Bādisī, *Maḳṣad*, transl. Colin, p. 240 and the article ZĀWIYA). Everything points to its having been the same in the Peninsula. The multiplication of *rābiṭas* in Spain and their possible confusion with ribāṭs are connected with the great movement of mystic piety which, starting in Persia, had brought about the substitution of monasteries — *khānaḳā* in the east, *zāwiya* in Barbary — for the foundations, more military than religious, of the heroic age of Islām.

Bibliography: Abu 'l-ʿArab, *Classes des savants de 'l-Ifrīḳiya*, ed. and transl. Bencheneb, Algiers 1920; Al-Bakrī, *Description de l'Afrique septentrionale*, ed. and transl. de Slane, Algiers 1911—1913; al-Idrīsī, *Description de l'Afrique et de l'Espagne*, ed. and transl. Dozy and de Goeje, Leyden 1866; Ibn Ḥawḳal, transl. de Slane, in *JA*, 1842, i. 168; do., *Description de Palerme*, transl. Amari, in *JA*, 1845, i. 96; Ibn Khallikān, transl. de Slane, i. 159, No. 3; al-Maḳdisī, in Le Strange, *Palestine under the Moslems*, p. 23—24; Ibn al-Shiḥna, *Les perles choisies*, transl. Sauvaget, Bairūt 1933, i. 107; Ibn Marzūḳ, *Musnad*, ed. and transl. E. Lévi-Provençal, in *Hespéris*, v., 1925; Dozy, *Supplément aux dictionnaires arabes*, s.v. *ribāt*, *maḥras*; Van Berchem, *Matériaux pour un Corpus* etc., Paris 1894, p. 162, No. 3; 408, No. 4; Doutté, *Les Marabouts*, in *RHR*, xl.—xli., pr. in part 1900; H. Basset and E. Lévi-Provençal, *Chella*, Paris 1923; G. Marçais, *Note sur les ribāṭs en Berbérie*, in *Mélanges René Basset*, Paris 1925, ii. 395—430; do., *Manuel d'art musulman*, i. 45—46; Jaime Oliver Asín, *Origen árabe de rebato, arrobda y sus homónimos*, Madrid 1928; H. Basset and H. Terrasse, *Sanctuaires et forteresses almohades*, in *Hespéris*, 1932 (the ribāṭ of Ṭīt), p. 337—376.

RIDDA, apostasty, especially from the faith. For the position of apostates in theology and in fiḳh cf. the article MURTADD.

Al-Ridda is also the name given to the defection of the Arab tribes after the death of the Prophet. At this time several so-called false prophets rose into prominence (see the articles AL-ASWAD, MUSAILIMA, ṬULAIḤA). Caetani has, however, shown it to be probable that in reality only the Arabs of Central Arabia fell away whereas the rest of Arabia was conquered for the first time by Abū Bakr (*Annali dell' Islam*, 2, ii. pp. 850 *sqq.*

AL-**RIFĀʿĪ**, AḤMAD B. ʿALĪ ABU 'L-ʿABBĀS,

founder of the Rifāʿī ṭarīḳa, died 22nd Djumādā I, 578/Sept. 23, 1183 at Umm ʿAbīda, in the district of Wāsiṭ. The date of his birth is given by some authorities as Muḥarram 500/Sept. 1106, but others say Radjab 512/Oct.—Nov. 1118, at Ḳaryat Ḥasan, a village in the district of Baṣra. These places being in the region called al-Baṭāʾiḥ he has the further *nisba* al-Baṭāʾiḥī; al-Rifāʿī is usually explained as referring to an ancestor Rifāʿa, but by some is supposed to be a tribal name. This ancestor Rifāʿa is said to have migrated from Mecca to Seville in Spain in 317, whence Aḥmad's grandfather came to Baṣra in 450. Hence he is also called al-Maghribī.

Ibn Khallikān's notice of him is meagre; more is given in Dhahabī's *Taʾrīkh al-islām* (Bodleian MS.), taken from a collection of his *Manāḳib* by Muḥyi 'l-Dīn Aḥmad b. Sulaimān al-Ḥammāmī recited by him to a disciple in 680. This work does not appear in the lists of treatises on the same subject furnished by Abu 'l-Hudā Efendi al-Rifāʿī al-Khālidī al-Ṣaiyādī in his works *Tanwīr al-abṣār* (Cairo 1306) and *Ḳilādat al-djawhar* (Bairūt 1301), the latter of which is a copious biography, frequently citing *Tiryāḳ al-muḥibbīn* by Taḳī al-Dīn ʿAbd al-Raḥmān b. ʿAbd al-Muḥsin al-Wāsiṭī (d. 744; known to Ḥādjdjī Khalīfa), *Umm al-barāhīn* by Ḳāsim b. al-Ḥādjdj, *al-Nafḥa al-miskīya* by ʿIzz al-Dīn al-Fārūthī (d. 694), and others. Al-Ḥammāmī's statements are cited from one Yaʿḳūb b. Kurāz, who acted as *muʾadhdhin* for al-Rifāʿī. Great caution is required in the use of such materials.

Whereas according to some accounts he was a posthumous child, the majority date his father's death 519 in Baghdād, when Aḥmad was seven years old. He was then brought up by his maternal uncle Manṣūr al-Baṭāʾiḥī, resident at Nahr Daḳlā in the neighbourhood of Baṣra. This Manṣūr (of whom there is a notice in Shaʿrānī's *Lawāḳiḥ al-anwār*, i. 178) is represented as the head of a religious community, called by Aḥmad (if he is correctly reported by his grandson, *Ḳilāda*, p. 88) al-Rifāʿīya; he sent his nephew to Wāsiṭ to study under a Shāfiʿī doctor Abu 'l-Faḍl ʿAlī al-Wāsiṭī and a maternal uncle Abū Bakr al-Wāsiṭī. His studies lasted till his 27th year, when he received an *idjāza* from Abu 'l-Faḍl, and the *khirḳa* from his uncle Manṣūr, who bade him establish himself in Umm ʿAbīda, where (it would seem) his mother's family had property, and where her father Yaḥyā al-Nadjdjārī al-Anṣārī was buried. In the following year (540) Manṣūr died and bequeathed the headship of his community (*mashyakha*) to Aḥmad to the exclusion of his own son.

His activities appear to have been confined to Umm ʿAbīda and neighbouring villages, whose names are unknown to the geographers; even Umm ʿAbīda is not mentioned by Yāḳūt, though found in one copy of the *Marāṣid al-iṭṭilāʿ*. This fact renders incredible the huge figures cited by Abu 'l-Hudā for the number of his disciples (*murīdīn*) and even deputies (*khulafāʾ*), the princely style and the colossal buildings in which he entertained them. Sibṭ ibn al-Djawzī in *Mirʾāt al-zamān* (Chicago, 1907, p. 236) says that one of their shaikhs told him he had seen some 100,000 persons with al-Rifāʿī on a night of Shaʿbān. In *Shadharāt al-dhahab* the experience is said to have been Sibṭ ibn al-Djawzī's own, though this person was born in 581, three years after al-Rifāʿī's death. In *Tanwīr al-abṣār* (p. 7, 8) his grandfather as well as himself is credited with the assertion.

His followers do not attribute to him any treaties, but Abu 'l-Hudā produces 1. two discourses (*madjlis*) delivered by him in 577 (3rd Radjab) and 578 respectively; 2. a whole *dīwān* of odes; 3. a collection of prayers (*adʿiya*), devotional exercises (*awrād*), and incantations (*aḥzāb*); 4. a great number of casual utterances, sometimes nearly of the length of sermons, swollen by frequent repetitions. Since in 1, 2 and 4 he claims descent from ʿAlī and Fāṭima, and to be the substitute (*nāʾib*) for the Prophet on earth, whereas his biographers insist on his humility, and disclaiming such titles as *ḳuṭb*, *ghawth*, or even *shaikh*, the genuineness of these documents is questionable.

In *Shadharāt al-dhahab* (iv. 260) it is asserted that the marvellous performances associated with the Rifāʿīs, such as sitting in heated ovens, riding lions, etc. (described by Lane, *Modern Egyptians*, i. 305) were unknown to the founder, and introduced after the Mongol invasion; in any case they were no invention of his, since the like are recorded by Tanūkhī in the fourth century A.H. The anecdotes produced by Dhahabī (repeated by Subkī, *Ṭabaḳāt*, iv. 40) imply a doctrine similar to the Indian *ahinsā*, unwillingness to kill or give pain to living creatures, even lice and locusts. He is also said to have inculcated poverty, abstinence and non-resistance to injury. Thus *Mirʾāt al-zamān* records how he allowed his wife to belabour him with a poker, though his friends collected 500 dīnārs to enable him to divorce her by returning her marriage gift. (The sum mentioned is inconsistent with his supposed poverty).

Inconsistent accounts are given of his relations with his contemporary ʿAbd al-Ḳādir al-Gīlānī. In *Bahdjat al-asrār* it is recorded by apparently faultless *isnāds* on the authority of two nephews of al-Rifāʿī, and a man who visited him at Umm ʿAbīda in 576 that when ʿAbd al-Ḳādir in Baghdād declared that his foot was on the neck of every saint, al-Rifāʿī was heard to say at Umm ʿAbīda "and on mine". Hence some make him a disciple of ʿAbd al-Ḳādir. On the other hand, Abu 'l-Hudā's authorities make ʿAbd al-Ḳādir one of those who witnessed in Madīna in the year 555 the unique miracle of the Prophet holding out his hand from the tomb for al-Rifāʿī to kiss; further, in the list of his predecessors in the discourse of 578 al-Rifāʿī mentions Manṣūr, but not ʿAbd al-Ḳādir. It is probable therefore that the two worked independently.

Details of his family are quoted from the work of al-Fārūthī, grandson of a disciple named ʿUmar. According to him, al-Rifāʿī married first Manṣūr's niece Khadīdja; after her death, her sister Rabīʿa; after her death Nafīsa, daughter of Muḥammad b. al-Ḳāsimīya. There were many daughters; also three sons, who all died before their father. He was succeeded in the headship of his order by a sister's son, ʿAlī b. ʿUthmān.

Bibliography: The sources of this account have been cited above.

RŪḤ. [See NAFS].

RUḲAIYA, name of one of the daughters of Muḥammad and Khadīdja, born in Mecca, where she married or was betrothed to a son of Abū Lahab. Whether this marriage was soon dissolved, or the whole episode is unhistorical, we know Ruḳaiya as the wife of ʿUthmān b. ʿAffān, who married her shortly before or after his conversion. With him she made the first *hidjra* to Abyssinia (Ibn Hishām, p. 208); she bore to him ʿAbd Allāh b. ʿUthmān, who died young. She died during the battle of Badr, so that her husband, who nursed her, had to be absent from that exploit. He subsequently married her sister Umm Kulthūm [q.v.], whence his epithet *dhu 'l-nūrain* "the man with the two lights".

The chronological questions related to Rukaiya's age and the date of her marriage are so narrowly related to those regarding Khadīdja, Fāṭima and Umm Kulthūm, that for an exposé of them reference may be made to those articles.

Bibliography: Ibn Hishām, p. 121, 208 *sq.*, 241; Ibn Saʿd, *Ṭabaḳāt*, viii, 24 *sq.*; Ṭabarī, iii, 2430; Wāḳidī, trans. Wellhausen, p. 66, 71, 83; Caetani, *Annali dell' Islām*, index at the end of vol. ii.; F. Buhl, *Das Leben Muhammeds*, p. 120, 151, 172, 243, 378; Lammens, *Fâtima et les filles de Mahomet*, p. 3 *sqq.*

RUKŪʿ. [See ṢALĀT, II].

S

AL-**ṢĀBIʾA**. the Sabaeans. This name has been given to two quite distinct sects. 1. the Mandaeans or Subbas, a Judaeo-Christian sect practising the rite of baptism in Mesopotamia (Christians of John the Baptist); 2. the Sabaeans of Ḥarrān, a pagan sect which survived for a considerable period under Islām, of interest for its doctrines and of importance for the scholars whom it has produced.

The Sabaeans mentioned in the Ḳurʾān (ii. 62; v. 69; xxii. 17), who are on three occasions placed along with the Jews and Christians among the "people of the book", i.e. possessors of a revealed book, have sometimes been identified with the Mandaeans or with the Elkasaites. The name must come from the Hebrew root *ṣ-b-ʿ* "to plunge, to immerse", by loss of *ʿain*, and must mean 'baptists', those who practise baptism by immersion. The pagan Sabaeans, who did not know this rite at all, may have adopted this name as a measure of precaution to secure the advantages of the toleration accorded by the Ḳurʾān to Jews and Christians.

Arab writers from the fourth century A. H. onwards very frequently mention the Sabaeans of Ḥarrān and always with interest. Al-Shahrastānī devotes a very long section to them and the exposition of their doctrines. He classes them among those who admit spiritual substances (*al-rūḥāniyūn*), especially the great astral spirits. They recognize as their first teachers two philosopher-prophets, ʿAdhimūn (Agathodemon = the good spirit) and Hermes who have been indentified with Seth and Idrīs respectively. Orpheus was also one of their prophets. They believe in a creator of the world, wise, holy, not produced, and of inaccessible majesty, who is reached through the intermediary of the spirits. The latter are pure and holy in substance, in act and state; as regards their nature, they have nothing corporeal, neither physical faculties nor movements in place nor changes in time. They are our masters, our gods, our intercessors with the sovereign Lord; by purifying the soul and chastising the passions, one enters into relations with them. As to their activities they produce, renew and change things from state to state; they cause the force of the divine majesty to flow down towards the lower beings and lead each of them from its beginning to its perfection. Among them are the administrators of the seven planets, which are like their temples. Each spirit has a temple, each temple has a sphere, and the spirit is to his temple as the soul is to the body. Sometimes the Ṣābiʾa call the planets fathers and the elements mothers. The activity of the spirits consists in moving these spheres and in acting upon the elements and the physical world through them; from this result the mixtures in composite things, and also the corporeal faculties. The general beings proceed from the general spirits and the particular from the particular spirits, thus rain in general has its spirit, its spiritual master, and every drop of rain has its own. They preside over the phenomena of the world, winds, storms, earthquakes, and give to each being its faculties and lay down laws for it; their condition is entirely spiritual and analogous to that of the angels.

Al-Shahrastānī distinguishes between the Sabaeans who worshipped the stars, called temples, directly, and those who worshipped idols made with hands (*ashkhās*, persons), representing the stars, in temples made by man. There is a very remarkable section on the temples and idols of the Sabaeans as well as on their ceremonies in al-Dimashḳī (*Cosmographie*, ed. A. F. Mehren, 1866); the shape of the temples, the number of the steps, the colour of the ornaments, the material of the idols and the nature of the sacrifices varied with the planets, and this is interesting for the history of the cult. Here and elsewhere we find the accusation of human sacrifices made, which undoubtedly is not to be maintained. The Jewish philosopher Maimonides says he had seen idols which resembled those of which al-Dimashḳī speaks. Al-Shahrastānī further tells us that all the Sabaeans had three prayers; they purified themselves by ablution after contact with a corpse, forbade the flesh of swine, dogs, birds with talons and pigeons. They did not have circumcision, allowed divorce only by decree of the judge and forbade bigamy.

The Sabaeans were at first scattered throughout the north of Mesopotamia and had their principal centre at Ḥarrān, the ancient Carrhae; their liturgical language was Syriac. The Caliph Maʾmūn thought of persecuting and destroying them; but their intellectual merits gained them toleration. Towards 259/872 the celebrated Thābit b. Ḳurra, after a quarrel with his co-religionists, was excommunicated at Ḥarrān and came to Baghdād, where he founded another branch of Sabaeanism. The Sabaean community in Baghdād lived for some time in peace; but the Caliph al-Ḳāhir began to persecute them and forced Sinān, son of Thābit, to embrace Islām. In about 364/975 the Sabaean Abū Isḥāḳ b. Hilāl, who was secretary to the Caliphs al-Mutīʿ and al-Ṭāʾiʿ, caused an edict of toleration to be issued in favour of his coreligionists of Ḥarrān, Raḳḳa and Diyār Muḍar and protected those of Baghdād. In the ivth/xth century there were still many Sabaeans at Baghdād and at Ḥarrān. In 424/1033 there was left only a temple of the moon, which formed a citadel at Ḥarrān; this temple was at that date taken by the Fāṭimids of Egypt. After the middle of the vth/xith century all trace of the Sabaeans of Ḥarrān is lost; we still find them at Baghdād till the end of this century.

The great men who have rendered this sect illustrious are: Thābit b. Ḳurra, the eminent geometrician, original astronomer, translator and philosopher; Sinān b. Thābit, physician and meteorologist; other physicians and astronomers of the same family; Thābit b. Sinān and Hilāl b. al-Muḥassin, historians; Abū Isḥāḳ b. Hilāl, vizier, and other members of the family; al-Battānī (Albategnus), the celebrated astronomer; Abū Djaʿfar al-Khāzin, mathematician. Ibn al-Waḥshīya, the author of the *K. al-Filāḥa al-Nabaṭīya*, although professing to be a Muslim, in every way belonged to the Sabaean school. Finally it may be mentioned that these scholars are quoted on mineralogy by al-Dimashḳī.

Bibliography: On the Ṣābiʾa in the Ḳurʾān: Horovitz, *Koranische Untersuchungen*, 121—2. On the Mandaeans see W. Brandt, *Die mandäische Religion* (Leipzig 1889); do., *Mandäische Schriften* (Göttingen 1893); do., *Die Mandäer* (*Verh. Ak. Amst.*, new Series, xvi., No. 3); F. Scheftelowitz, *Die Entstehung der manichäischen Religion und des Erlösungsmysteriums* (Giessen 1922) and H. H. Schaeder in *Isl.*, xiii. (1923), p. 320—333; Pedersen in *Oriental Studies presented to E. G. Browne* (Cambridge 1922). On the Elkasaites: W. Brandt, *Elchasai* (Leipzig 1912). On the Sabaeans of Ḥarrān: D. Chwolsohn, *Die Ssabier und der Ssabismus*, 2 vols. (St. Petersburg 1856); de Goeje, *Mémoire posthume de Dozy contenant de nouveaux documents pour l'étude de la religion des Harraniens* (Travaux de la 6e session du Congrès int. des Orientalistes, tenu en 1883 à Leyde), ii. 291—366; Muḥammad al-Shahrastānī, ed. Cureton, 1846, ii. 202—251; al-Dimashḳī, *Cosmographie*, ed. A. F. Mehren (St. Petersburg 1866), p. 39—48; al-Masʿūdī, *Murūdj*, iv. 61—71.

SABĪL ALLĀH. [See DJIHĀD].

SABʿĪYA "Seveners", the name of various Shīʿa groups who restrict the number of visible Imāms to seven. — The legitimist Shīʿa, who believe that the character of Imām is transmitted by divine providence from father to son, were thrown into confusion when about 145/762 Ismāʿīl, the (eldest?) son of the sixth Imām Djaʿfar al Ṣādiḳ [q.v.] died before his father. While the majority replaced Ismāʿīl by another son of Djaʿfar, Mūsā al-Kāẓim, the seventh in the series of the twelve visible Imāms of the Ithnā-ʿasharīya [q.v.], "twelvers", and others attached themselves to the otherwise less prominent sons, Muḥammad, ʿAbd Allāh and ʿAlī, the strictests legitimists remained faithful to Ismāʿīl. They denied that he died before his father's death. The evidence brought forward in support of this view seems to have impressed even their opponents, for the latter found it necessary, in order to dispose of Ismāʿīl, to attack his character; they said that, on account of his evil life, his father had withdrawn from him the right of succession at first intended for him. These accusations, particularly that of wine-drinking, may well be explained as an attack on the slackening of the legal ordinances by the Seveners directed back against the Imām who gave them their name.

From the first the Sevener movement was not a united one. A Mubārakīya sect "stood fast" by Ismāʿīl, so that for them he is the last Imām and the Mahdī [q.v.]. But the majority continued the imāmate down to his son Muḥammad, who becomes *ḳāʾim al-zamān* with the official title of al-Tāmm "finisher", a title which, in some of the minor systems, seems to be prejudiced by the fact that he is in turn followed by invisible Imāms, known only to the initiated. In spite of the position of Muḥammad al-Tāmm, however, the name of Ismāʿīl remains attached to the main groups. In their hierarchic view therefore the Seveners belong to the many "Wāḳifīya" "those who stand fast". This is, in part, explained by the political conditions of the period. In 145/762—3 the ʿAbbāsid Caliph al-Manṣūr had put down the rising at Madīna led by al-Nafs al-Zakīya Muḥammad b. ʿAbd Allāh b. al-Ḥasan b. al-Ḥasan b. ʿAlī; in the following year, the latter's brother Ibrāhīm also fell. The ʿAlid question was thus disposed of for the time and with such success that even in these activist circles who chose their Imāms from those vigorous ʿAlids that actually took to the sword, a "Djārūdīya" sect "stood" by al-Nafs al-Zakīya as the concealed Mahdī. The tendency to hope for a return increased still further among the legitimists, who were bound by their dogma to definite persons, as it would have been useless to carry on into active history an imāmate which had really become hopeless. There were some "who stood fast" by each of Ismāʿīl's brothers; the Mūsawīya, nicknamed Mamṭūra, "rained upon", often called simply the Wāḳifīya, became of some importance. Strictly speaking, such groups also come under the head of Seveners. But, as a rule, Sabʿīya is used identically with Ismāʿīlīya [q.v.]. For them steadfastness did not develop into the abandonment of political aims — although it was over a century before this became apparent — but rather into the very skilful plan of retaining the most effective idea of an Imām given by sacred birth and yet rejecting the individual that chance brought forward in the person of the often very incapable firstborn of the seed of ʿAlī and Ḥusain. The Sevener movement thus attained considerable importance in secular history also, through men who appeared as *dāʿī* [q.v.] of the hidden seventh Imām Muḥammad b. Ismāʿīl, like Ḥamdān Ḳarmat, or as his successor who had come forth from concealment, like the Fāṭimid Saʿīd b. ʿAbd Allāh b. Maimūn, or as his "return" himself; cf. in Ṭabarī iii. 2218, the puzzle about the Ḳarmaṭian missionary Yaḥyā b. Dhikrawaih. Karmaṭians, Fāṭimids, Assassins and the Ismāʿīlīs of India, Persia and Central Asia are the groups through which the Sevener movement finds its place in secular history, but the Druses too and in some respects the Matāwila and Nuṣairīs also may be traced back to the old Sabʿīya.

The Sabʿīya itself, however, is quite as much a religious, and an independent religious, movement as a political one. The remarkable feature that the number of Imāms was fixed at seven simultaneously in the names of the different sons of Djaʿfar is more simply understood if we assume that the political reasons already mentioned were further supported by a point of view which regarded all cosmic and historical happenings as occurring in periods characterized by the sacred number of seven. The example of the Khaṭṭābīya, who worshipped Ismāʿīl's father, Djaʿfar, as a god, shows that in the early days of development of the Sabʿīya the deification of Imāms was not entirely unimaginable. We cannot, of course, in the circumstances deal with the theology of the Seveners. We only know of some details out of the different systems and even these are often obscure, through being known chiefly from hostile representations. We may claim for the Seveners as their individual contribution to theology a gnostic cosmogony in which names and things are often, however, not used consistently. The steps of emanation are (1) God, (2) universal intelligence (*ʿaḳl*), (3) universal soul (*nafs*), (4) primeval matter, (5) space or the pleroma, (6) time or the kenoma, (7) the world of earth and man. This number seven recurs in the lower world in the 7 prophets or *nāṭiḳ* "speakers" in the history of redemption: Adam is the first *nāṭiḳ*, but as a rule not the first man; then follow Noah, Abraham, Moses, Jesus, Muḥammad and Muḥammad al-Tāmm. Between each two of these *nāṭiḳ* there are inserted seven "silent ones", *ṣāmit*, of whom the first, as special helpers of the *nāṭiḳ*, under titles like *fātiḳ*, "releaser", or *asās*, "foundation", are particularly important, because it is only through the esoteric exposition attributed to them the teachings and laws of the *nāṭiḳ* receive their true meaning or are completely dissolved. These *fātiḳ* are Seth — which reminds one of the gnosis of the Sethians — Shem, Ishmael (son of Hagar), Aaron, Peter, ʿAlī and the seventh is the inaugurator of the particular Sevener group in question, e.g. ʿAbd Allāh b. Maimūn. Alongside of the *ṣāmit*, there is a further lower hierarchy arranged in sevens or twelves, notably to *ḥudjdja* and the *dāʿī*. The system is, however, confused by a theory of incarnation which actually equates the seventh Imām with God; thus ʿAbd al-Kāhir al-Baghdādī, p. 288, reports, on the authority of a man who had been for a period engaged in Ismāʿīlī propaganda, that the latter had been expected to see in Muḥammad al-Tāmm Him who had revealed himself to Moses. In several groups, e.g. the Indian Ismāʿīlīs, the cosmogony and with it the periodicity of the sacred number seven has fallen into the background and ʿAlī has become God as the first Imām. The way thus leads from the Seveners on to the Ahl-i Ḥaḳḳ [q.v.]. Starting with ʿAlī, the Khōdjas [q.v.] count right down to the 47th Imām, the present Agha Khān Muḥammad Shāh. Next to the Imām, and in history often surpassing him in importance, comes the *ḥudjdja*. Muḥammad the Prophet often appears as the *ḥudjdja* of ʿAlī. But he is for political reasons substituted for Salmān al-Fārisī, who is really intended.

For salvation the recognition of the concealed Imām known only to the initiated is absolutely necessary; consequently the "instruction" attains increased importance and they are accordingly also called Taʿlīmīya. Initiation into the esoteric religion takes place through 7 or 9 initiatory stages. Al-Baghdādī, 282 *sqq.* mentions (1) the *tafarrus*, the "exact investigation", a psychological method, particularly skilful, or almost a means of working oneself entirely into him who is to be won and of placing oneself on common ground with him. Then the adept is "shown" (2) in the *taʾnīs* the whole "beauty" of his previous belief with the suggestion that it is much more splendid than he has suspected hitherto, after which (3) in the *tashkīk* he becomes "shaken by doubt" that he is not yet fully conscious of his belief. After such anthroposophical spiritual guidance, the moment arrives at which the novice is "bound" and "attached" to the secret authority with the formula that real knowledge only exists in the Concealed One and his organs through (4) the *rabṭ*, and (5) the *taʿlīḳ*. In (6) the *tadlīs* the real esoteric meaning is by allegorical explanations brought out of the external covering of the letter, under which all historical prophecies and laws are "obscured". (7) The "grounding" (*taʾsīs*) can now begin in a novitiate proper of some length, after the expiry of which the disciple subscribes himself body and soul by "agreements sealed by oaths". (8) *mawāthīḳ biʾl-aimān*, to the bond, in return for which he is "released" in the (9) *khalʿ* and *sulkh* from all earlier dogmatic restraints and all external legislation outside these obligations.

The whole system is assiduously supported for form's sake on Ḳurʾān passages, which is the more easily done in consequence of the frequently obscure allusions made in the sacred book. Thus the adept's attention is caught when he learns from Ḳurʾān xv. 99, "serve thy Lord till certainty comes to thee", that his previous worship of God has only a preliminary step. The passages in which the word *bāṭin* "inner" occurs are made to supply *dicta probantia* for an extravagant, and of its kind not exactly original, system of allegory, including an extensive alphabetic kabbala, which is not limited to the mysterious letters of the Sūras, and to names of Imāms or dogmatic formulae. — It has not contributed to the elucidation of the relations of Muslim sects that a particular group is called after many features and that, for example, the Seveners are also included as Bāṭinīya [q.v.] along with other bodies of quite different tendencies, like the Khurramīs (see KHURRAMĪYA) and Mazdakīs, and often even described as the Bāṭīniya and on this account called by their opponents by the corresponding nickname Muʿaṭṭila, "emptiers, nihilists".

The actual origin of the speculative ideas of the Seveners is, so far, hardly better known to us than to the Muslim authors, whose opinions must be taken with particular caution as their point of view was vitiated by hatred of the heretics. The Sunnī symbolists usually insist on Jewish or Christian, still more Ṣābiʾan and especially Parsi, origin; but they also, it is true, suspect a connection with Hellenistic philosophy and Hermetic writings. The point still requires investigation as to how Neo-Platonic speculations, Parsi mysteries and such myths as are found in the Christian "Treasure-Cave" came to be clothed with a Ḳurʾānic covering and developed into Islāmic gnosis. To wider circles of Muslim intellectuals Sabʿīya philosophical tendencies have been propagated by the tracts of the "Pure Brethren", *Ikhwān al-Ṣafāʾ*.

All classes of Seveners are very unfavourably criticized by the Muslims, even by the Shīʿīs. They are regarded as extreme "exaggerators", *ghulāt* [see GHĀLĪ], and usually are considered to be beyond the pale of Islām, so that some symbolists do not quote them at all. The main reason is that they weaken the divinity of Allāh and the finality of Muḥammad's prophecy. It is, however, due to the great elasticity of Muslim names of sects, and to a polemical rather than matter-of-fact frame of mind that they are also called Dahrīya [q.v.] and associated with the materialists, who are essentially different from them. A contributory cause of the unfavourable opinion held of them was, of course, the bitterness felt at their revolutionary aims and their underground political propaganda in the name of the seventh Imām; but still more their casting off the external law of religion is usually judged and dismissed as sheer libertinism; the accusations commonly made against secret sects of sodomy and nightly orgies with wine and community of women also play a great part in the attacks made against them. The charges of religious, moral and political nihilism framed against them have also found a way into the European literature on the subject. Further investigation, which does not exclude the possibility of syncretism, recognizing that every religious system that has become concrete is a syncretic formation with ramifications, will alone be able to show how far the theology, or, if one prefers the term, the theosophy of the Sevener movement represents an intelligible reaction against the theology of the God of Islām, and in how far the libertinism, said to be general and certainly existing among many, is an attempt to meet the disjointed total of the prescriptions of the S͟harīʿa with a system of ethics, such as is taught by Nāṣir i-Khusraw, for example, in verses 374 *sqq.* of his *Rus͟hhannāī nāma* (*ZDMG* xxxiv, 1880, p. 459 *sq.*) regarding the seven sins of character and the seven cardinal virtues. In this investigation it will not much matter whether the "Book of Illumination" was written when the poet had already attained a very important place in the hierarchy of the Seveners as *ḥud͟jd͟ja* of the Ismāʿīlīs, or whether it was written before he joined them, and reveals the attitude of mind which definitely decided him to join this body. Certain groups of the Seveners, like the Assassins and Ḳarmaṭians, were certainly extremely intolerant to other Muslims; but in contrast to this we have the tolerant and wise administration of many of the Fāṭimids in Egypt. Some groups are occasionally said to have been communist, but this is certainly not a general feature. While in the fourth and fifth centuries the Muslim writers report their spread and their propagandist activities in the whole Muḥammadan wo:ld, the old groups had long become stereotyped. But their ideas continued to be effective and were carried from Persia far to the north and from India especially to East Africa. In spite, however, of the consciousness of connection with the old Seveners, the nature of their beliefs has been essentially transformed. The political aspect has disappeared and the religious attitude is not so aggressive. It is noteworthy that the modern Sabʿīya are often just those who are the strongest supporters of the feeling of solidarity in Islām.

Bibliography: ʿAbd al-Ḳāhir b. Ṭāhir al-Bag͟hdādī, *al-Farḳ bain al-firaḳ* (Cairo 1328), p. 265 *sqq.*; Ibn Ḥazm, *al-Milal wa 'l-niḥal* (Cairo 1321), ii. 116; Ibn al-D͟jawzī, *Naḳd al-ʿilm wa-'l-ʿulamāʾ aw Talbīs Iblīs* (Cairo 1340), p. 102—108; Nawbak͟htī, *Firaḳ al-S͟hīʿa* (ed. Ritter), p. 57 *sqq.*; S͟hahrastānī (ed. Cureton), p. 16, 126 *sqq.*, 145 *sqq.*; cf. also the translation by Haarbrücker, ii. 415; S͟huhfur b. Ṭāhir al-Isfarāʾinī (MS. Berl. 2801) under Imāmīya in Chap. 8, Ismāʿīlīya, Mubārakīya... and in Chap. 13, Bāṭinīya; al Īdjī, *Mawāḳif* (ed. Soerensen), p. 348 *sq.*; Guyard, *Fragments relatifs à la doctrine des Ismaélis* in the *NE*, xxii (1874), 177 *sqq.*; Ivanow, *Ismaelitica* in the *Memoirs of the Asiatic Society of Bengal*, viii (1922), 1—76; do., *A Guide to Ismaili Literature* (London 1933); do., *A Creed of the Fatimids* (Bombay 1936); do., *Ummu 'l-kitāb*, in *Isl.*, xxiii (1936), p. 1—132; Ḥusain Hamdānī, *Rasāʾil Ik͟hwān aṣ-Ṣafā in literature of the Ismāʿīlī Ṭaiyibi-Daʿwat*, in *Isl.* xx (1932), p. 218—300; B. Lewis, *The Origins of Ismaʿilism* (Cambridge 1940); al-G͟hazzālī, *Faḍāʾiḥ al-Bāṭinīya* in Goldziher, *Streitschrift des Ġazālī gegen die Bāṭinijja-Sekte* (Leiden 1916); do., *Vorlesungen über den Islam*, p. 247 *sqq.*; De Boer, *Geschichte der Philosophie im Islam*, p. 76 *sqq.*; cf. also De Sacy, *Exposé de la religion des Druzes* i. pl. xiii *sqq.*, as well as the bibliographies to the articles quoted in the text.

ṢABR (A.). The significance of this conception can hardly be conveyed in a West-European language by a single word, as may be seen from the following. According to the Arabic lexicographers, the root *ṣ-b-r*, of which *ṣabr* is the *nomen actionis*, means to restrain or bind; thence *ḳatalahu ṣabr^an^* "to bind and then slay someone". The slayer and the slain in this case are called *ṣābir* and *maṣbūr* respectively. The word has a special technical application in the expression *yamīnu ṣabr^in^*, by which is meant an oath imposed by the public authorities and therefore taken unwillingly (e.g. al-Buk͟hārī, *Manāḳib al-Anṣār*, bāb 27; *Aimān*, bāb 17; Muslim, *Īmān*, trad. 176).

In the Ḳurʾān derivations from the root *ṣ-b-r* frequently occur, in the first place with the general meaning of being patient. Muḥammad is warned to be patient like the Apostles of God before him (xxxviii. 17; xlvi. 35: "for Allāh's threats are fulfilled", is added in xxx. 60). A double reward is promised to the patient (xxiii. 111; xxviii. 54; cf. xxv. 75). In xxxix. 17, it is even said that the *ṣābirūn* shall receive their reward without *ḥisāb* (which in this case is explained as measure or limitation). The conception is given a special application to the holy war (e.g. iii. 146; viii. 65); in such connections it can be translated by endurance, tenacity.

The word is next found with the meaning resignation, e.g. in the Joseph sūra (xii. 18) where Jacob, on hearing of the death of his son, says: "Now goodly resignation is fitting" (*faṣabr^un^ d͟jamīl^un^*).

Sometimes *ṣabr* is associated with *ṣalāt* (ii. 45, 153). According to the commentators, it is in these passages synonymous with fasting and they quote in support the name *s͟hahr al-ṣabr* given to the month of Ramaḍān.

As an adjective we find *ṣabbār* in the Ḳurʾān, associated with *s͟hakūr* (Sūra xiv. 5 etc.); cf. thereon al-Ṭabarī, *Tafsīr*: "It is well with the man who is resigned when misfortune afflicts him, grateful when gifts of grace become his"; and Muslim, *Zuhd*, trad. 64: "Wonderful is the attitude of the believer; everything is for the best with him; if something pleasant happens to him, he is thankful and this proves for the best with him; and if misfortune meets him, he is resigned and this again is for the best with him".

The later development of the conception is, of course, also reflected in the commentaries on the Ḳurʾān; it is difficult to say in how far these interpretations are already inherent in the language of the Ḳurʾān. In any case, the conception *ṣabr*, in all its shades of meaning, is essentially Hellenistic in so far as it includes the ἀταραξία of the Stoic, the patience of the Christian and the self-control and renunciation of the ascetic; cf. below. In place of many other explanations of the commentators, we will give here only that of Fak͟hr al-Dīn al-Rāzī (*Mafātīḥ al-g͟haib*, Cairo 1278, on Sūra iii. 200). He distinguishes four kinds of *ṣabr*: (1) endurance in the laborious intellectual task of dealing with matters of dogma, e.g. in the doctrine of *tawḥīd*, *ʿadl*, *nubuwwa*, *maʿād* and disputed points; (2) endurance in completing operations one is bound or recommended by law to do; (3) steadfastness in refraining from forbidden activities; (4) resignation in calamity, etc. *Muṣābara* is, according to him, the application of *ṣabr* to one's fellow-creatures (like neighbours, people of the Book), refraining from revenge, the *amr bil-maʿrūf wa'l-nahy ʿani 'l-munkar*, etc.

The high value laid upon *ṣabr* is also seen in the fact that *ṣabūr* is included among the beautiful names of Allāh. According to the *Lisān* (s.v. *ṣ-b-r*), *ṣabūr* is a synonym of *ḥalīm*; — with the difference that the sinner need not fear any retribution from the *ḥalīm*, but he is not sure of such leniency from the *ṣabūr*. Allāh's *ṣabr* is in the Ḥadīth increased to the highest degree in the saying that no one is more patient than He towards that which wounds His hearing (al-Bukhārī, *Tawḥīd*, bāb 3).

In the Ḥadīth, *ṣabr* is, in the first place, found in general connections like: to him who practises *ṣabr* Allāh will grant *ṣabr*, for *ṣabr* is the greatest charisma (al-Bukhārī, *Zakāt*, bāb 50; *Riḳāḳ*, bāb 20; Aḥmad b. Ḥanbal, iii. 93); in the Ḥadīth also, *ṣabr* is applied to endurance in the holy war. (Aḥmad b. Ḥanbal, iii. 325); the word is found in other passages in the sense of enduring, (al-Bukhārī, *Riḳāḳ*, bāb 53; *Fitan*, bāb 2; cf. *Aḥkām*, bāb 4; Muslim, *Imāra*, trad. 53, 56 etc.). The word here usually has the meaning of resignation as in the oft-recurring saying: "The (true) *ṣabr* is revealed at the first blow, (al-Bukhārī, *Djanā'iz*, bāb 32, 43; Muslim, *Djanā'iz*, trad. 15; Abū Dā'ūd, *Djanā'iz*, bāb 22 etc.). The word is often found in this connection associated with the proper word for resignation, viz. *iḥtisāb* (e.g. al-Bukhārī, *Aimān*, bāb 9; Muslim, *Djanā'iz*, trad. 11); with this should be compared the following *ḥadīth ḳudsī*: "If my servant is deprived of the light of both his eyes, I grant him paradise in compensation" (al-Bukhārī, *Marḍā*, bāb 67; Aḥmad b. Ḥanbal, iii. 283).

In conclusion we may remark that in the canonical Ḥadīth the meaning renunciation, which receives so great an importance in ethico-ascetic mysticism, is exceedingly rare, (cf. what has already been said above on Sūra ii. 45, 153). Al-Bukhārī, *Riḳāḳ*, bāb 20 (which, like the chapter *zuhd* in the other collections of traditions, represents the oldest stage of this tendency in Islām) has in the *tardjama*... ʿUmar said: We have found the best of our life in *ṣabr*." Here we already can trace the Hellenistic sphere of thought for which renunciation was the kind of life fitting the true man, the wise man, the martyr.

What the Ḳur'ān and Ḥadīth say about *ṣabr* recurs in part again in ethico-mystical literature; but the word has here become, so to speak, a technical term and to a very high degree, as *ṣabr* is the cardinal virtue in this school of thought. As with order fundamental conceptions (see the series of definitions of Ṣūfī and Ṣūfism in Nicholson's essay in the *JRAS*, 1905), we find numerous definitions of *ṣabr*, definitions which often point rather to fertility of imagination than give an exhaustive exposition of the idea, but are of great value for the light they throw upon the subject like lightning flashes. Al-Ḳushairī in his *Risāla* (Būlāḳ 1287, p. 99 *sq.*) gives the following collection: — "The gulping down of bitterness without making a wry face" (al-Djunaid); — "the refraining from unpermitted things, silence in suffering blows of fate, showing oneself rich when poverty settles in the courts of subsistence"; — "steadfastness in fitting behaviour (*ḥusn al-adab*) under blows of fate" (Ibn ʿAṭā'); — "bowing before the blow without a sound or complaint"; — "the *ṣabbār* is he who has acccustomed himself to suddenly meeting with forbidden things" (Abū ʿUthmān); — "*ṣabr* consists in welcoming illness as if it were health"; — "steadfastness in God and meeting His blows with a good countenance and equanimity" (ʿAmr b. ʿUthmān); — "steadfastness in the ordinances of the Book and of the Sunna" (al-Khawwāṣ); — the *ṣabr* of the mystics (literally: lovers) is more difficult than that of the ascetics" (Yaḥyā b. Muʿādh); — "refraining from complaint" (Ruwaim); — "seeking help with God" (Dhu 'l-Nūn); — *ṣabr* is like His name (Abū ʿAlī al-Daḳḳāḳ); — "there are three kinds of *ṣabr*, *ṣabr* of the *mutaṣabbir*, of the *ṣābir* and of the *ṣabbār* (Abū ʿAbd Allāh b. Khafīf); — "*ṣabr* is a steed that never stumbles" (ʿAlī b. Abī Ṭālib); — *ṣabr* is: not to distinguish between the condition of grace and that of trial, in peace of spirit in both; *taṣabbur* is calm under blows, while one feels the heavy trial" (Abū Muḥammad al-Djurairī; cf. ἀταραξία.

Al-Ghazzālī treats of *ṣabr* in the fourth part of the *Iḥyā'*, which describes the virtues that make blessed, Book II. We have seen that already in the Ḳur'ān *ṣabr* and *shukr* are found in association. Al-Ghazzālī discusses the two conceptions in the second book separately, but in reality in close connection. He bases the combination, not on the Ḳur'ānic phraseology, but on the maxim: "belief consists of two halves: the one *ṣabr* and the other *shukr*". This again goes back to the tradition: "*ṣabr* is the half of belief" (cf. the traditions given above which also associate *ṣabr* and *shukr*).

Only the following outline of his treatment can be given here. *Ṣabr*, like all religious *maḳāmāt*, consists of three parts, *maʿrifa*, *ḥāl* and *ʿamal*. The *maʿārif* are like the tree, the *aḥwāl* the branches and the *aʿmāl* the fruits. Out of the three classes of beings man alone may possess *ṣabr*. For the animals are entirely governed by their desires and impulses; the angels, on the other hand, are completely filled by their longing for the deity, so that no desire has power over them and as a result no *ṣabr* is necessary to overcome it. In man, on the contrary, two impulses (*bāʿith*) are fighting: the impulse of desires and the impulse of religion; the former is kindled by Satan and the latter by the angels. *Ṣabr* means adherence to the religious as opposed to the sensual impulse.

Ṣabr if of two kinds: (a) the physical, like the endurance of physical ills, whether active, as in performing difficult tasks, or passive, as in suffering blows, etc.; this kind is laudable; (b) the spiritual, like renunciation in face of natural impulses. From this wide range of meaning we can understand that Muḥammad, when asked, could answer: "*īmān* is *ṣabr*". This kind is absolutely laudable (*maḥmūd tāmm*).

As regards the greater or less strength of their *ṣabr*, three classes of individuals are distinguishable: (a) the very few in whom *ṣabr* has become a permanent condition; these are the *ṣiddīḳūn*, the *muḳarrabūn*; (b) those in whom animal impulses predominate; (c) those in whom a continual struggle is going on between the two impulses: these are the *mudjāhidūn*; perhaps Allāh will turn towards them.

In section VI, al-Ghazzālī shows how the believer requires *ṣabr* under all circumstances; (a) in health and prosperity; there the close connection between *ṣabr* and gratitude is seen; (b) in all that does not belong to this category, as in the performance of legal obligations, in refraining from forbidden things, in whatever happens to a man against his will, either from his fellow-men or by God's decree.

As *ṣabr* is an indication of the struggle between the two impulses, its salutary effect consists in all that may strengthen the religious impulse and weaken the animal one. The weakening of the animal impulse is brought about by asceticism, by avoiding whatever increases this impulse, e.g. by withdrawal (*ʿazla*), or by the practice of what is permitted, e.g. marriage. The strengthening of the religious impulse is brought about (a) by the awakening of the desire for the fruits of the *mudjāhada*, e.g. by means of the reading of the lives of saints or prophets; (b) by gradually accustoming this impulse to the struggle with its antagonist, so that finally the consciousness of superiority becomes a delight.

Bibliography: Besides the references in the text, see also: Sprenger, *Dict. of the Techn. Terms*, i. 823 *sqq.*; M. Asín Palacios, *La mystique d'al-Gazzali*, in *MFOB*, vii. 75 *sqq.*; R. Hartmann, *al-Ḳuschairîs Darstellung des Ṣufîtums*, *Türk. Bibl.*, xviii., Berlin 1914, Index; L. Massignon, *Al-Hallaj, martyr mystique de l'Islam*, Paris 1922, Index; do., *Essai sur les origines...de la mystique musulmane*, Paris 1922, Index.

SAʿD b. Abī Waḳḳāṣ, an Arab general. His father's full name was Mālik b. Wuhaib b. ʿAbd Manāf b. Zuhra b. Kilāb b. Murra. Saʿd, who had become a convert to Islām at the age of seventeen, was one of the oldest companions of the Prophet, being a special favourite of his and one of those who had been promised Paradise; he took part not only in the battles of Badr and Uḥud but also in the campaigns that followed. When al-Muthannā b. Ḥāritha, who assumed command in al-Ḥīra after the departure of Khālid b. al-Walīd, asked the Caliph ʿUmar for reinforcements, the latter at first appeared inclined to take command of the army himself, probably simply in order to stir up the enthusiasm of the Muslims; in the end, however, he did not do so but gave the post of commander-in-chief to Saʿd. Saʿd advanced against the Persians with a large army and encamped at al-Ḳādisīya on the frontiers of Persia and Arabia. Here — probably in the first half of the year 16 (summer of 637) — a great battle was fought, which is said to have lasted several days; the details of it have been much elaborated by the Arab historians. Illness prevented Saʿd from taking part in the battle personally and he had to confine himself to directing the operations, which, however, was not quite in accordance with the traditional Arab custom. After the Sāsānian leader Rustam had fallen, the struggle ended in the complete defeat of the Persians and Saʿd was now master of the whole of ʿIrāḳ al-ʿArabī; nor were the Persians able to hold permanently al-Madāʾin, the capital of the provinces east of the Tigris. The young Sāsānian king Yezdedjird had to flee and abandon his capital to Saʿd. When the latter entered the city, he obtained countless booty and made al-Madāʾin his headquarters for the time being.

To this period also belongs the foundation of Kūfa. To Saʿd likewise is due the credit of having made a strong military camp here, which in course of time grew into an important city, and he was appointed first governor of the rapidly growing settlement. He seems, however, not to have paid due attention to the Caliph's insistence on the maintenance of old-fashioned simplicity. At any rate we are told that Saʿd built a splendid palace in Kūfa modelled on the Ṭāḳ-i Khusraw at al-Madāʾin; but when ʿUmar, who feared the injurious influence of Persian luxury on the simple habits of the Arabs, heard of this, he is said to have administered a sharp rebuke to Saʿd and even to have had the palace burned by Muḥammad b. Maslama. Saʿd was dismissed from his post as early as the year 20/640—1, because the fickle and turbulent inhabitants of Kūfa — of all possible elements, Arabs and Persians, Jews and Christians — accused him of being unjust and tyrannical. When, however, Muḥammad b. Maslama appeared in Kūfa by the Caliph's order to investigate Saʿd's conduct in his office, only one or two individuals dared to appear against him. Nevertheless Saʿd was dismissed and ʿAmmār b. Yāsir appointed his successor; but the latter only remained a short time in office and was followed by al-Mughīra b. Shuʿba. The great military and administrative services of Saʿd were, however, later fittingly recognized by ʿUmar. When on his deathbed the latter empowered six of Muḥammad's most trusted companions to choose a new ruler within three days, he chose Saʿd as one of this group and is even said to have added that if Saʿd was not given the office himself, he would recommend the future Caliph to compensate him with a governorship, because he had been removed from his post neither for incompetence nor for treacherous conduct. Following this suggestion, ʿUthmān in 25/645—6 restored to him the governorship of Kūfā; again, however, he was dismissed after a short period of office. After the assassination of ʿUthmān, Saʿd was requested to come forward as a claimant to the throne but declined, because he wished to live in peace; nor was he inclined to take any steps to take vengeance on the murderers. When ʿAlī was chosen Caliph, Saʿd declined to pay homage to him and retired to his estate in al-ʿAḳīḳ, where he lived till his death remote from politics, which one of his sons made a reproach against him. According to the usual statement he died in 50/670—1 or 55/674—5, aged about 70. He is said to have left vast wealth behind him and was buried in Madīna.

Bibliography: Ibn Saʿd, III/i. 97 *sqq.*, vi. 6; Ibn Hishām, *passim*; al-Balādhurī (ed. de Goeje), see Index; al-Ṭabarī (ed. de Goeje), *passim*; Ibn al-Athīr, *al-Kāmil* (ed. Tornberg), see Index; do., *Usd al-ghāba*, ii. 290 *sqq.*; Ibn Ḥadjar, *al-Iṣāba*, ii. No. 4086; al-Nawawī (ed. Wüstenfeld), p. 275 *sq.*; al-Yaʿḳūbī (ed. Houtsma), see Index; al-Wāḳidī, transl. Wellhausen, see Index; Muḥibb al-Dīn al-Ṭabarī, *al-Riyāḍ al-nāḍira* (Cairo 1327), i. 17 *sqq.*, ii. 292 *sqq.*; al-Bukhārī, *Manāḳib al-Anṣār*, bāb 31; Ibn Mādja, *Sunan*, introductory chapter, bāb 11; Muslim, *Zuhd*, trad. 11; Aḥmad b. Ḥanbal, *Musnad*, i. 168, 177—193; ii. 222. Wellhausen, *Skizzen und Vorarbeiten*, vi. 70 *sqq.*, 95 *sqq.*; Caetani, *Annali dell' Islām*, see Index.

SAʿD b. Muʿādh b. al-Nuʿmān b. Imruʾ al-Ḳais b. Zaid b. ʿAbd al-Ashhal al-Anṣārī al-Awsī, a contemporary of Muḥammad's. He was head of the great clan of the Banū ʿAbd al-Ashhal in Madīna. Saʿd was won over to the new faith by a Meccan, Muṣʿab b. ʿUmair, who went to Madīna after the first meeting at al-ʿAḳaba and made a successful propaganda for Islām. From the very first he showed great zeal for the faith and when Muḥammad undertook an expedition against Buwāṭ, he appointed Saʿd, according to the usual report, to be his deputy in Madīna. Saʿd carried the standard in the battle of Badr and with Saʿd b. ʿUbāda [q.v.] he went to the assistance of the Prophet when the latter was wounded in the battle of Uḥud. Like Saʿd b. ʿUbāda and Usaid b. Ḥuḍair, he protested against the negotiations with the Ghaṭafān in the "war of the ditch", but was soon afterwards severely wounded in the hand by the arrow of a Ḳuraishī. After the retreat of the confederates Muḥammad decided to rid himself of the troublesome Banū Ḳuraiẓa and began to besiege them in Madīna, although their only crime lay in the fact that they had remained neutral during the "war of the ditch". The negotiations, which they were soon forced to begin with the Prophet, ended in their surrendering unconditionally, probably in the hope that they could save themselves through the intervention of their former allies, the Awsīs. When Muḥammad asked them whether they would leave the decision to a man of the tribe of Aws they declared their readiness to do so. Saᶜd, who lay mortally wounded in the mosque where he was being tended by a woman, was then asked for his opinion and after he had secured a promise from the Prophet and all present that they would obey his decision implicitly, he declared that the men should be killed, the women and children sold as slaves and their property divided. The verdict was put into execution the next day. Over 600 Jews are said to have sacrified their lives for their faith and soon afterwards Saᶜd also died of his wound; he is represented in Tradition as a glorified hero of the faith.

Bibliography: Ibn Saᶜd, III/ii. 2—13; Ibn Hishām, p. 290, 322, 344, 433, 439, 445, 674, 697; al-Ṭabarī, *passim*; Ibn al-Athīr, *Kāmil* (ed. Tornberg), see Index; the same, *Usd al-ghāba*, ii, 296 *sqq.*; Ibn Ḥadjar, *Iṣāba*, ii. No. 4096; al-Nawawī (ed. Wüstenfeld), p. 276 *sqq.*; al-Yaᶜḳūbī (ed. Houtsma), ii. 52 *sq.*; al-Wāḳidī (transl. Wellhausen), see index; Caetani, *Annali dell' Islam*, see index; A. J. Wensinck, *Mohammed en de Joden te Medina* (Leiden 1908), p. 171 *sqq.*; F. Buhl, *Das Leben Muhammeds*, p. 186, 275.

SAᶜD b. ᶜUbāda b. Dulaim b. Ḥāritha b. Abī Ḥazīma b. Thaᶜlaba b. Ṭarīf al-Khazradjī, a contemporary of Muḥammad's. The distinguished and prosperous Saᶜd was one of the few people who were able to write in Arabia in his time; he was also celebrated as a fine swimmer and archer. In the history of Islām we first meet with his name in the accounts of the second meeting at al-ᶜAḳaba where he is mentioned among the nine Khazradjīs who were chosen to be guarantors (*naḳīb*) of the new converts. He then fell into the hands of the Meccans and was severely handled by them; it was only through the intervention of two Meccan friends, to whom he had once done valuable service, that he succeeded in escaping. During Muḥammad's expedition against al-Abwāʾ Saᶜd remained behind as his deputy in Madīna. In the battle of Badr, according to the most reliable authority, he did not take part; on the other hand he was at the battle of Uḥud where with Saᶜd b. Muᶜādh [q.v.] he tended the wounded Prophet. In the other military enterprises of Muḥammad also he proved himself an exceedingly energetic champion of Islām, and several times acted as standardbearer. In particuliar he distinguished himself by great liberality. During the siege of the Banū Naḍīr he distributed dates among the Muslims at his own expense; the troops besieging the Banū Ḳuraiẓa were likewise supplied with provisions by him. He supported the expedition to Tabūk by a particularly handsome contribution. When the Prophet began secret negotiations with the two chiefs of the Ghaṭafān in the "war of the ditch", ᶜUyaina b. Ḥiṣn and al-Ḥārith b. ᶜAwf, and promised them a third of the next date-harvest of Madīna if they would retire and the Ghaṭafān declared their readiness to do so, his plan met with opposition from those Muslims who were ardent to fight; the strongest opponents of the attempt to bring about an agreement are said to have been Saᶜd b. ᶜUbāda, Saᶜd b. Muᶜādh and Usaid b. Ḥuḍair. In the intended campaign against Mecca which led to the treaty of al-Ḥudaibiya Saᶜd's energy and thirst for fighting were clearly seen. Although he insisted that Muḥammad should take the necessary precautions and provide the Muslims with weapons, the Prophet declined to follow his advice. After the death of ᶜAbd Allāh b. Ubaiy Saᶜd became undisputed head of the Khazradjīs and it need cause no surprise that he was proposed as successor to the Prophet. As soon as the news of Muḥammad's death had spread through Madīna, the Aws and Khazradj assembled; Saᶜd addressed them and recommended some one among the Anṣār. The majority of those present were already inclined to pay homage to him at once. Then other Muslims appeared, notably Abū Bakr and ᶜUmar, and after fairly heated negotiations which threatened to end in open fighting, Abū Bakr received homage as Caliph. Henceforth Saᶜd retired from public life and later went to al-Ḥawrān where he died "two and a half years after the accession of ᶜUmar" i.e. about the year 15/636—7.

Bibliography: Ibn Saᶜd, iii/II, 142—145; vii/II, 115 *sq.*; Ibn Hishām, *passim*; Ṭabarī (ed. de Goeje), *passim*; Ibn al-Athīr, *al-Kāmil* (ed. Tornberg), see Index; do., *Usd al-ghāba*, ii. 283—285; Ibn Ḥadjar, *al-Iṣāba*, ii. No. 4066; Nawawī (ed. Wüstenfeld), p. 274 *sq.*; Waḳidī, transl. Wellhausen, see Index; Yaᶜḳūbī (ed. Houtsma), i. 267; ii. 136, 137; Caetani, *Annali dell' Islām*, see Index.

ṢADAḲA, alms. According to Arabic authors this word is derived from the verb *ṣadaḳa*, "to speak the truth", which is explained by pointing to the fact that the giving of alms by a Muslim is a witness to the truthfulness of his religion. In reality the word is a transliteration of the Hebrew word *ṣĕdāḳā*, which meant originally "honesty", but was used by the Pharisees for what they considered the chief duty of the pious Israelite, namely almsgiving, a meaning which it still retained at the time of the coming of Islām and afterwards. Its proper sense is, therefore, voluntary or spontaneous almsgiving or what we call "charity".

Arabic authors, however, use the word *ṣadaḳa* in two different senses. In the first place it is frequently employed as synonymous with *zakāt* [q.v.], that is, the legal poor-rate, which is obligatory, and of which the amount is fixed. It is so used in the Ḳurʾān, ix. 58 *sqq.*, 103 *sq.* (see Lane, s.v.). It is so used also in the *Muwaṭṭaʾ* of Mālik ibn Anas, in which, in the *Kitāb al-zakāt*, *ṣadaḳa* is substituted for *zakāt*. He does this apparently when it is a case of *zakāt* upon quadrupeds (*mawāshī*, camels, flocks and herds), but also in other cases. In Bukhārī, on the other hand, *ṣadaḳa* seems to be put for *zakāt* quite indiscriminately, and the two words are used simultaneously as synonyms. Bukhārī uses *zakāt* where Mālik uses *ṣadaḳa* (e.g. *Zakāt*, bāb 43); he quotes the tradition "There is no *ṣadaḳa* on less than five *dhawd* of she-camels" in the same form as Mālik, yet speaks of the *ṣadaḳat al-fiṭr* where Mālik uses the usual *zakāt al-fiṭr*. The same failure to distinguish between the two words is found also in later writers, both legal and historical (e.g. Ibn al-Athīr, *al-Kāmil*, iii. 42, after Ṭabarī). If there were any doubt as to the identity of this *ṣadaḳa* and *zakāt*, it would be removed by the fact that the six or seven classes of persons who are entitled to benefit by them are the same in each case, namely, the poor and needy, those engaged in the work of distributing the *ṣadaḳa or zakāt*, Muslim captives in enemy hands, debtors, those engaged in the *d̲j̲ihād*, travellers, and (originally) the *muʾallafa ḳulūbuhum.*

The proper use of the word *ṣadaḳa* is, however, as has been said, in the sense of voluntary almsgiving. In this sense it is, for the sake of distinction, called *ṣadaḳat al-taṭawwuʿ* ("alms of spontaneity"). Ibn al-ʿArabī thus defines this *ṣadaḳa*: "Voluntary *ṣadaḳa* is an act of worship arising from free choice mixed with authority; and if it be not so then is it not voluntary *ṣadaḳa*, for the man makes it obligatory upon himself, just as God makes mercy obligatory upon Himself towards those who repent, and corrects those who do ill in ignorance". *Ṣadaḳa* appears to be used in this sense in the remaining passages of the Ḳurʾān where it occurs, other than the two cited above (cf. ii. 263, 264, 271, 276; iv. 114; ix. 79; lviii. 12). These Ḳurʾānic passages supply a natural basis for many expositions by later writers.

Mālik treats of the *ṣadaḳa* in its etymological sense along with a variety of other matters in the closing paragraphs of his work. He does not use any distinctive term such as *ṣadaḳat al-taṭawwuʿ*. What he says is as follows. Under the heading "Inciting to almsgiving" he records a saying of Muḥammad: "Whoever gives an alms out of honest gain (and God accepts only the honest) is only placing it in the palm of the Merciful, and He will make it grow for him, just as one of you lets his weanling foal or camel grow until it becomes like a mountain". Anas ibn Mālik [q.v.] used to tell how Abū Ṭalḥa, who was the richest Anṣārī in Madīna, prized above all his wealth a well beside the mosque, from which Muḥammad was in the habit of drinking. When the verse "You shall never win piety until you spend of what you love" (iii. 92) came down, he wished to give this well. Muḥammad, however, persuaded him to keep it in his own family. To some who were ever begging Muḥammad gave, but with the reproof that "the best of gifts is endurance". It was when speaking from the pulpit about almsgiving and about refraining from begging that the Prophet used the oft-quoted saying: "The upper hand is better than the lower hand". Mālik interprets that the upper hand is the hand that spends and the under hand is the hand that asks. Muḥammad also said: "By Him in whose hand my life is, it were better for one of you to take a rope and gather fuel upon his back, than to beg from one to whom God has given of his bounty, whether he give or refuse". Under the heading "What is disliked in regard to alms" Mālik notes that the family of Muḥammad may not accept alms, which are only "the offscouring of mankind" (*awsāk̲h̲ al-nās*). It was not lawful for Muḥammad to give alms out of the *ṣadaḳa* (that is, the *zakāt*). He might give only of his own.

Al-Buk̲h̲ārī in the following century deals with *ṣadaḳa* in both its senses in the xxiv^th^ book of the *Ṣaḥīḥ*, on *zakāt*, without perhaps being aware that he is speaking of two different things. Of the voluntary almsgiving he says in various *bābs*, that alms is the duty of a Muslim. If he lack the means to give alms, he must work and gain them. If he cannot find work, he must at least refrain from ill, and this will be counted to him for alms. The alms given should be according to his means, out of the surplus of his possessions. They must be given with the right hand, and not given to the wrong person. A wife may give alms out of her husband's substance, and a slave out of his master's. Begging is not to be indulged in; but alms may be taken from the rich and given to the poor. Almsgiving atones for sin.

Al-G̲h̲azzālī discusses almsgiving in the *Kitāb asrār al-zakāt* of the *Iḥyāʾ*, especially in the 8th *waẓīfa*, in which he defines the proper recipient of alms. He must be ascetic, learned, truthful, uncomplaining, necessitious and related to the giver. In the 4th *faṣl* he takes up *ṣadaḳat al-taṭawwuʿ*. After recounting sayings ascribed to Muḥammad and others, he comes to the question raised in the Ḳurʾān, whether it is better to do alms in secret or openly, but decides that much may be said on both sides, and that all depends on circumstances and motives. He then turns to the question whether it is better to accept *zakāt* or *ṣadaḳa* but again declines to make a general rule. Cases differ.

Ibn al-ʿArabī deals with this matter in the *Futūḥāt al-Makkīya*, in bāb 70, on "the secrets of the *zakāt*". He also discusses the question of secret or open alms. His definition of voluntary alms has been given above.

The S̲h̲īʿite views of *ṣadaḳa* and *zakāt* are similar to those of the Sunnīs, but, while both debar the family of the Prophet from benefit of *zakāt*, the S̲h̲īʿites permit them to share in the *ṣadaḳa*.

Bibliography: The Tradition works s.v. *Zakāt* (see Wensinck, *Handbook* s.v. Alms); al-G̲h̲azzālī, *Iḥyāʾ ʿulūm al-dīn* (Cairo 1326), i. 149 *sqq.*; Ibn al-ʿArabī, *al-Futūḥāt al-Makkīya* (Cairo 1329), i. 562 *sqq.*; al-Marg̲h̲inānī, *The Hidayah with its commentary called the Kifayah*, ed. by Abdool Mujeed and others (Calcutta 1834), i. 481 *sqq.* (*Bāb ṣadaḳat al-sawāʾim*); transl. by Charles Hamilton, 1791, iii. 310 *sq.*; al-Nawawī, *Minhād̲j̲ al-Ṭālibīn*, (ed. v. d. Berg), i. 288 *sqq.*; transl. van den Berg and E. C. Howard (London 1914), p. 277 *sq.*; T. W. Juynboll, *Handbuch des islamischen Gesetzes* (Leiden and Leipzig 1910), p. 109 *sq.*; A. Querry, *Recueil de lois concernant les musulmans schyites* (Paris 1871).

SAʿDĪYA or D̲J̲IBĀWĪYA, an order of dervishes named after the founder SAʿD AL-DĪN AL-D̲J̲IBĀWĪ, i.e. of D̲j̲ibā, "between the Ḥawrān and Damascus". His death-date is variously given as 700 and 736 A.H.; and the accounts which we have of him are clearly fabulous. According to the *K̲h̲ulāṣat al-at̲h̲ar*, i. 34, his father was the S̲h̲aik̲h̲ Yūnus al-S̲h̲aibānī, a pious man, whom in his youth he disobeyed, becoming a leader of banditti in the Ḥawrān; owing, however, to his father's prayers he was favoured with a vision which resulted in his conversion. The authority followed by Depont and Coppolani makes him practice severe asceticism, and visit various sanctuaries, including Mecca; after this he returned to Syria, and founded in Damascus the order which bears his name, but which is traced by a *silsila* through D̲j̲unaid, Sarī Saḳaṭī and Maʿrūf al-Kark̲h̲ī to the Imāms of the Prophet's house.

In the *K̲h̲ulāṣat al-at̲h̲ar*, the author of which died in 1092 A.H., the Banū Saʿd al-Dīn appear as a society (*ṭāʾifa*) in Damascus, noted for their piety; there they held a service in the Umaiyad Mosque after the Friday prayer, and they possessed a *zāwiya* in the district Ḳubaibāt, whence the descendants of the founder took the name Ḳubaibātī (i. 33 and ii. 208). The biography of Muḥammad known as Ibn Saʿd al-Dīn, who became s̲h̲aik̲h̲ of the society in 986 A.H. (*ibid.*, iv. 160), seems to suggest that the institution began with him, for it records how having begun life as a trader he was miraculously converted at Mecca. With him one of his brothers was associated, and the two divided the duties of the headship between them; presently domestic disputes arose, and thus Muḥammad became sole head of the society, in which capacity he acquired vast wealth, and became the most influential personage in Damascus. He died in 1020, and was succeeded by his son Saʿd al-Dīn, who died on pilgrimage in 1036.

In this account the Banū Saʿd al-Dīn specialized in the cure of insanity. "On a scrap of paper they draw some lines anyhow, and the patient is cured thereby (i.e. by drinking the water in which the scrap has been immersed). In order to drink it he must abstain from everything spirituous; they then write an amulet which the patient is to use (wear on his person) after he has drunk the potion. The words which they signify by the lines and which they write on the amulet are the *basmala*".

At some time — possibly later than this period — the society spread to Egypt and Turkey; Depont and Coppolani give a long list of its meeting-places in Constantinople and the neighbourhood. They regard the Saʿdīya as a branch of the Rifāʿīya; but the authorities of J. P. Brown make it an original order, and, indeed, second in the list. He states (p. 56) that the Saʿdī's have twelve *terks* in their cap, wear turbans of a yellowish colour and perform their ceremonies on foot. The cloth of the cap which covers the head is in six gores (p. 214); and they wear long hair. They are supposed to possess special powers over snakes.

In Lane's time the order was well represented in Egypt, and on the day preceding the night of the Mawlid practised the ceremony called *dōsa*, wherein the shaikh of the order rode on horseback over the backs of the dervishes, who lay flat on the ground with their faces downwards for the purpose. It was supposed that none of them suffered any harm in consequence. This ceremony was forbidden by the khedive Tawfīḳ. After the *dōsa* there used to be an assembly wherein some of the dervishes ate live serpents; according to Lane, the serpents had first been deprived of their poisonous teeth or rendered incapable of biting; all that was eaten of the serpent was the head to the point about two inches further back where the thumb of the dervish pressed. By the time of Lane's second visit this practice had been forbidden by the shaikh of the order on the ground that such food was unlawful. The *dōsa* was then followed by a *dhikr*, where in the formulae employed were *Allāhu ḥaiy* and *Yā dāʾim*.

The *dōsa* resembles performances by Ṣūfīs of a much earlier period, who were supposed to override natural laws in a variety of ways. Egyptian historians do not appear to allude to it, unless al-Djabartī may have it in mind when he commends the Khalwatīya system for not enforcing on its members more than they can bear (i. 294 ult.). It does not therefore seem possible at present to say when or whence it was introduced. The practice of snake-charming, whereby followers of the order are said to make their living still in Egypt, is attributed to the founder and explained by fables connected with his conversion.

Writers on Ṣūfism pay little attention to this order, though it is just mentioned in the *Djāmiʿ al-uṣūl*, without any specification of its doctrines or practices. The founder is mentioned neither in the *Ṭabaḳāt* of al-Shaʿrānī, nor in the *Nafaḥāt al-uns* of al-Djāmī, who suggests that one Saʿd al-Dīn al-Ḥamawī, d. 650 A.H., was the founder of a society.

Bibliography: al-Muḥibbī, *Khulāṣat al-athar*, Cairo 1284; Depont and Coppolani, *Confréries religieuses musulmanes*, Algiers 1897; E. W. Lane, *Manners and Customs of the modern Egyptians*, London 1871; J. P. Brown, *The Dervishes*, London 1886.

SADJĀḤ, Umm Ṣādir bint Aws b. Ḥikk b, Usāma, or bint al-Ḥārith b. Suwaid b. ʿUḳfān, prophetess and soothsayer, one of several prophets and tribal leaders who sprang up in Arabia shortly before and during the *ridda*. The genealogy, which her history proves to be a true one, shows that she belonged to the Banū Tamīm. On her mother's side she was related to the Taghlib, a tribe which comprised many Christians. She was a Christian herself, or at least had learnt much concerning Christianity from her relatives. Next to nothing is known concerning the import of her revelations and doctrines; she delivered her messages from a *minbar*, in rhymed prose, and was attended by a *muʾadhdhin* and a *ḥādjib*. Her name, or one of her names, for God was "the Lord of the clouds" (*rabb al-saḥāb*).

Sadjāḥ came to the fore in 11 A.H., after Muḥammad's death. One account of her exploits describes her as a Taghlib upstart, who had arrived from Mesopotamia at the head of a band of followers belonging to Rabīʿa, Taghlib, the Banū al-Namr, the Banū Iyāḍ, the Banū Shaibān; she found the Tamīm divided, in consequence of the Prophet's death, by deep internal strife between apostates, Muslims, and those who wavered between revolt and allegiance to Madīna, and succeeded in converting by her revelations and uniting under her command both branches of Ḥanẓalah (the Banū Mālik and the Banū Yarbūʿ), which she intended to lead against Madīna. The extent of her influence on the Tamīm seems, however, to have been much greater than this version, intended to minimize their share in the *ridda*, would have us believe. The prophetess was no outsider, she really belonged to the Tamīm, as the end of her career implies, and had gained, probably for some time before Muḥammad's death, the support of her whole tribe, whose conversion Islām had been mainly a matter of expediency, easily shaken off.

Sadjāḥ's forces began by attacking the Banū Ribāb, in obedience to one of her revelations, and were severely beaten. Retreating to al-Nibādj (in Yamāma) they suffered a second defeat at the hands of the Banū ʿAmr, and Sadjāḥ had to promise that she would leave the territory of the Tamīm. Followed by the Yarbūʿ, she decided to join the prophet Musailima [q.v.], who still controlled most of Yamāma, in order to unite their fortunes or to restore her own. Their encounter happened at al-Amwāh or at Ḥadjr. Musailima was menaced by the Muslim army and the neighbouring tribes threatened to shake off his authority, so that the arrival of a vanquished, ambitious and desperate colleague, accompanied by many armed followers, proved a trying, indeed a dangerous visitation. There is no reliable account of the meeting: according to one version, the strange couple came to an understanding, recognized each other's mission and decided to unify their two religions and their worldly interests; they were actually married, and the prophetess stayed by Musailima to the hour of his tragic death. Al-Ṭabarī preserves obscene and very probably fictitious details concerning this union, which must have been rather a political alliance than a lustful orgy; the wedding, according to these legends, was celebrated in the same walled garden where Musailima was to meet his death.

Other accounts of the meeting are that Musailima,

after having married Sadjāḥ, cast her off, and that she returned to her people; a third version does not mention the marriage, and says that the prophet tried to persuade his rival and would-be ally to attack the Muslims, hoping thus to get rid of her; on her refusal he offered, if she consented to depart, half the year's crops of Yamāma; she declined to go unless he promised half of the next year's harvest as well, set off with the first part of the booty, and left her representatives with Musailima to wait for the rest, repairing to her kinsfolk. The second part of the ransom was never collected, as Musailima was vanquished and massacred by Khālid before the next harvest.

Whatever the outcome of Sadjāḥ's relations with Musailima was, her own career was either merged into his, or cut short by repulse, and we hear nothing more of her mission. According to all accounts, she went back to her native tribe, and lived obscurely amongst them. On Ibn al-Kalbī's authority we learn that she embraced Islām when her family decided to settle in Baṣra, which had become the principal centre of the Tamīm under the Umaiyads, lived and died there a Muslim, and was buried with the customary prayers and ceremonies.

Bibliography: al-Ṭabarī (ed. de Goeje), i. 1911—1920; al-Balādhurī (ed. de Goeje), p. 99—100; *Kitāb al-aghāni*, xviii. 165; Ibn Khaldūn, *ʿIbar*, Būlāḳ 1284, ii., App., p. 73; Wellhausen, *Skizzen und Vorarb.*, vi. 13—15; Caetani, *Annali dell' Islam*, A. H. 11, § 160—164, 170—173, A. H. 12, § 92—93; Fānī, *Dābistān*, transl. Shea and Troyer (London 1843), vol. iii.

SADJDJĀDA (A., plural *sadjādjid, sadjādjīd, sawādjid*), the carpet on which the *ṣalāt* is performed. The word is found neither in the Ḳurʾān nor in the canonical Ḥadīth; the article itself, however, was known at quite an early period, as may be seen from the traditions about to be mentioned. In the Ḥadīth we are often told how Muḥammad and his followers performed the *ṣalāt* on the floor of the mosque in Madīna after a heavy shower of rain with the result that their noses and heads came in contact with the mud (e.g. al-Bukhārī, *Adhān*, bāb 135, 151; Muslim, *Ṣiyām*, trad. 214—216, 218 etc.). This shows that at the time when such traditions arose the use of these carpets was not so general that people dated their origin as far back as the time of the Prophet. With this may be compared the fact that in a series of traditions the saying is put into Muḥammad's mouth that it was his privilege in contrast with the other prophets that the earth was for him *masdjid wa-ṭahūr* (e.g. al-Bukhārī, *Tayammum*, bāb 1; *Ṣalāt*, bāb 56, etc.). Al-Tirmidhī (*Ṣalāt*, bāb 130) also tells us that some faḳīhs prefer the *ṣalāt* on the bare earth and in modern Egypt and Morocco persons of the lowers orders do not use these mats at all.

The canonical Ḥadīth gives us the following picture. Muḥammad performs the *ṣalāt* on his own garment, protecting his arms against the heat of the soil during prostration with one of its sleeves, his knees with one end and his fore-head with the *ʿimāma* or *ḳalansuwa* (al-Bukhārī, *Ṣalāt*, bāb 22, 23; Muslim, *Masādjid*, trad. 191; Aḥmad b. Ḥanbal, *Musnad*, i. 320). On the passage quoted from Muslim, al-Nawawī observes that, according to al-Shāfiʿī, it is forbidden to prostrate oneself on the garment one is wearing. Al-Bukhārī (*Ṣalāt*, bāb 22) tells us that Muḥammad performed the *ṣalat* on his quilt (*firāsh*).

The Ḥadīth also informs us that the *ṣalāt* was performed on mats; e.g. al-Tirmidhī, *Ṣalāt*, bāb 131, where a *bisāṭ* is mentioned (so also Ibn Mādja, *Iḳāmat al-ṣalawāt*, bāb 63; Aḥmad b. Ḥanbal, i. 232, 273; iii. 160, 171, 184, 212); in the latter passage it is observed that this *bisāṭ* was made out of palm-leaves, *djarīd al-nakhl*. Al-Tirmidhī adds that most scholars permit the *ṣalāt* on *ṭunfusa* or *bisāṭ*. A similar mat of palm-leaves on which the *ṣalāt* was performed is called *ḥaṣīr* (e.g. al-Bukhārī, *Ṣalāt*, bāb 20; Aḥmed b. Ḥanbal, iii. 52, 59, 130 *sq.*, 145, 149, 164, 179, 184 *sq.*, 190, 226, 291). This tradition is also found in Muslim, *Masādjid*, trad. 266; al-Nawawī observes on this passage that the faḳīhs generally declared the performance of the *ṣalāt* permitted on whatever grows out of the earth. It is, however, evident from Abū Dāʾūd, *Ṣalāt*, bāb 91, that at the end of the third (ninth) century dressed skins of animals were already being used (*farwa maṣbūgha*).

At the same time we frequently find it mentioned that Muḥammad performed the *ṣalāt* on a *khumra* (al-Bukhārī, *Ṣalāt*, bāb 21; Muslim, *Masādjid*, trad. 270; al-Tirmidhī, *Ṣalāt*, bāb 129; Aḥmad b. Ḥanbal, i. 269, 308 *sq.*, 320, 358; ii. 91 *sq.*, 98; al-Nasāʾī, *Masādjid*, bāb 43; Ibn Saʿd, I/II. 160). The distinction between *khumra* and *ḥaṣīr* appears to have lain not in the material of which they were made but in the size. According to Muḥammad b. ʿAbd Allāh al-ʿAlawī's marginal glosses to Ibn Mādja, *Iḳāma*, bāb 63, 64, the *khumra* afforded just sufficient room for the prostration, while the *ḥaṣīr* was of the length of a man.

The word *sadjdjāda* is found a century after the conclusion of the canonical Ḥadīth literature. Al-Djawharī, *Ṣaḥāḥ*, s.v., declares *sadjdjāda* to be synonymous with *khumra*. In his *Supplément*, Dozy quotes passages from the 1001 Nights and Ibn Baṭṭūṭā. The latter mentions among the customs of the inmates of a certain *zāwiya* in Cairo that the whole body went to the mosque on Friday, where a servant had laid his *sadjdjāda* ready for each one (ed. Paris, i. 73; cf. 72). The same traveller tells us something similar regarding Māllī, where everyone sent his servant with his *sadjdjāda* to the mosque to lay it ready on his place. He adds that they were made out of the leaves of a palm-like tree (iv. 422).

In modern Mecca every one in the great mosque performs the *ṣalāt* on a *sadjdjāda*, usually a small carpet, just large enough for the *sudjūd*. After use it is rolled up and carried off on the shoulder. The lower orders believe that it is not advisable to leave the *sadjdjāda* unrolled after use as Iblīs would seize the opportunity to perform the *ṣalāt* on it. Well-to-do people sometimes had their *sadjdjāda* kept by a servant of the mosque but even among them this was not at all general. In place of a carpet a towel is sometimes used, for example the one which has been used for drying oneself after the *wuḍūʾ*. The lines woven in the carpet are not symmetrical but run to a point on one of the short sides which is placed in the direction of the *ḳibla* [q.v.]; cf. below Lane's "niche".

In Morocco the common people do not make any use of the *sadjdjāda*; the middle classes favour small felt carpets (*labda*) like saddle cushions, just large enough for performing the sudjūd. They are especially used by the faḳīhs, so that they have almost become one of their distinctive marks. In Algeria the *sadjdjāda* is very rarely used, except among the heads of the ṭarīḳa's and various *marabout*'s. Here the *sadjdjāda*'s usually consist of simple skins of goats or gazelles. The common people ascribe miraculous powers to these skins; in legends the *marabout*'s are often represented as using them in order to have themselves transferred thereon to Mecca or to walk on the waves. Occasionally the pilgrims bring home from Mecca sadjdjāda's analogous to those described above; these rugs are nowadays often imported from Europe.

According to Lane, sadjdjāda's (carpets) were imported from Asia Minor into Egypt and used there only by the rich for the *ṣalāt* and also as saddle-covers. They were about the size of a wide hearth-rug. A "niche" was represented upon it, the point of which was turned towards the *ḳibla*. Persons of the lower orders oftens perform the *ṣalāt* upon the bare ground simply; and they seldom immediately wipe off the dust which adheres to the nose and forehead as a result of prostration (cf. the well-known traditions regarding the traces of the *sudjūd*); but when a person has a cloak or any other garment, which he can decently take off, he spreads it upon the ground.

The usual practice in Indonesia is described by Snouck Hurgronje. A number of long narrow mats and carpets are placed broadwise on the floor of the mosque before the beginning of the services. After the service these are rolled up and laid aside (*De Islam in Nederlandsch-Indië*, Baarn 1913, p. 10 = *Verspreide Geschriften*, iv/ii. 366). But it is usual here also to bring one's own mat to the mosque.

In Istanbul, the carpet which formerly covered the floor of the Aya Ṣofya was divided up by patterns into separate sadjdjāda's, but in performing the *ṣalāt* this separation was not observed.

In the chapel in the Seraglio in Constantinople, in which are preserved the relics of the Prophet, the alleged sadjdjāda of Abū Bakr is preserved (d'Ohsson, *Tableau de l'Empire Othoman*, Paris 1787—1820, i. 267). In Barbier de Meynard, *Dict. Turc-français*, we find, s.v., a number of Turkish phrases in which the sadjdjāda plays a part.

The sadjdjāda has assumed special significance in the religious societies and in the Dervish orders. Among the latter — at least in Egypt — the word has become synonymous with order in the expression *shaikh al-sadjdjāda*, which is applied to the head of an order. The corresponding terms in Persian is *sadjdjāda-nishīn*.

In the terminology of these societies, sadjdjāda alternates with *bisāṭ* (cf. above) and expressions borrowed from other languages. According to the hierarchic legend, Gabriel brought Adam a sadjdjāda made out of the skins of the sheep of Paradise, on which he was made to kneel during the *shadd* ceremony. This *sadjdjādat al-khilāfa* was the one used by all succeeding generations in the same ceremony; Muḥammad, Abū Bakr, ʿUmar, ʿUthmān and ʿAlī are especially mentioned. From ʿAlī it has been passed on to the shaikhs of the order down to the present day. The Shaikh therefore sits on this sadjdjāda during the *shadd* ceremony and the expression *bisāṭ al-ṭarīḳ(a)* makes the sadjdjāda in a certain sense the throne of the whole order. Before the beginning of the *shadd* ceremony it is spread by the *naḳīb* whose duty this is. The Shaikh sits down ceremonially after its seal, as it were, has been broken by its being spread out. The candidate on whose account the ceremony is being performed stands, on the other hand, on the *bisāṭ al-djamʿ*. From the descriptions it is not always clear, whether by candidate is meant an oridinary novice or rather a *naḳīb*.

A whole series of mystical interpretations is associated with the *sadjdjāda* or *bisāṭ*. Head, feet, etc. are ascribed to it as to a living animal; it has four letters, which are connected with the elements; references are found to the *sadjdjāda* of the paths of salvation, and the *tawḥīd* profession is called the *sadjdjāda* of the faith. Accounts are given of the material of which the *sadjdjāda*'s of various people were made or are made, as well as of their colour (cf. the picture in *Isl.*, vi. 1916, 170.

Bibliography: In addition to the works quoted in the text cf. also: Lane, *Manners and Customs of the Modern Egyptians*, Index (s.v. *seggádeh*); J. P. Brown, *The Dervishes*, London 1868, p. 196; H. Thorning, *Beitr. zur Kenntnis des islam. Vereinswesens, Türk. Bibl.*, xvi., Berlin 1913, Index; P. Kahle, *Zur Organisation der Derwischorden in Egypten* in *Isl.*, vi. 1916, 194 *sqq.*; F. Taeschner, *Aufnahme in eine Zunft, op. cit.*, p. 169; illustrations of sadjdjāda's in F. Sarre and F. R. Martin, *Die Ausstellung von Meisterwerken Muhammedanischer Kunst in München* 1910 (München 1912). See also A. Upham Pope, *A Survey of Persian Art*, London and New York, iii. (1939), vi. (1939).

AL-ṢAFĀ, a mound at Mecca which now barely rises above the level of the ground. The meaning of the name is like that of the name of the eminence al-Marwa, which lies opposite to it: "the stone" or "the stones" (cf. al-Ṭabarī, *Tafsīr* to Sūra ii. 153).

As is well known, Muslims perform the *saʿy* between al-Ṣafā and al-Marwa in memory, as the legend relates (e.g. al-Bukhārī, *Anbiyāʾ*, bāb 9), of the fact that Hādjar ran backwards and forwards seven times between these two eminences to look for a spring for her thirsty son. — It is certain that cults were located at al-Ṣafā and al-Marwa even in the pagan period. According to most traditions there were two stone idols there, Isāf on al-Ṣafā and Nāʾila on al-Marwa, which the pagan Arabs on their *saʿy* used to touch. On the origin of these images the following story is given in the commentary of Naisābūrī on Sūra ii. 158, and al-Shāfiʿī gives his approval to it: Isāf and Nāʾila were guilty of indecent conduct in the Kaʿba and were therefore turned into stones, which were placed on the two pieces of raised ground al-Ṣafā and al-Marwa to be a warning to all. In course of time the origin of the stone figure was forgotten and people began to pay them divine worship. — According to another tradition there were copper images there (cf. Snouck Hurgronje, *Het Mekkaansche Feest*, p. 26); according to a third story demons lived on the two hills who shrieked at night (given in al-Ṭabarī, *Tafsīr*).

Bibliography: Yāḳūt, *Muʿdjam* (ed. Wüstenfeld), iii. 397; Juynboll, *Handbuch des islāmischen Gesetzes* (Leiden—Leipzig 1910), p. 136—37; Snouck Hurgronje, *Het Mekkaansche Feest* (Leiden 1880), p. 114 = *Verspr. Geschriften*, i. 76 *sq.*; Wellhausen, *Reste arabischen Heidentums*, Berlin 1897, p. 77.

ṢAFĪYA Bint Ḥuyaiy b. Akhṭab, Muḥammad's eleventh wife, was born in Madīna and belonged to the Jewish tribe of the Banu 'l-Naḍīr; her father and her uncle Abū Yāsir were among the Prophet's most bitter enemies. When their tribe was expelled from Madīna in 4 A.H., Ḥuyaiy b. Akhṭab was one of those who settled in Khaibar, together with Kināna b. al-Rabīʿ, to whom Ṣafīya was married at the end of 6 or early in 7 A.H.; her age at this time was about 17. There is a tradition that she had formerly been the wife of Sallām b. Mas͟hkam, who had divorced her.

When K͟haibar fell, in Ṣafar 7, Ṣafīya was captured in a fortress, al-Ḳamūs or Nīzār, together with two of her cousins. In the division of the spoils she had been assigned, or actually given, to Diḥya b. K͟halīfa al-Kalbī, but when Muḥammad saw her he was struck by her beauty, and threw his mantle over her as a sign that he had chosen her for himself. He redeemed her from Diḥya against seven head of cattle, and induced her to embrace Islām. Her husband was condemned to death by Muḥammad for having refused to give up the treasure of the Banu l'-Naḍīr; the desire of marrying Ṣafīya may have influenced the Prophet, for the nuptials were celebrated with uncommon haste, either in K͟haibar itself or at al-Ṣabhā', some 8 miles from it, on the way back to Madīna. Ṣafīya's dowry consisted in her emancipation, and she assumed the veil (*ḥid̲j̲āb*), thus establishing her position as a wife, which at the beginning appears to have been questioned.

In Madīna Ṣafīya received a cold welcome: ʿĀ'is͟ha and Muḥammad's other wives showed their jealousy with slights upon her Jewish origin. She seems to have lived aloof from her surroundings, for we find no further mention of her in the years preceding Muḥammad's death, except in an episode that shows how, during his last illness, she expressed her devotion to him, and was criticized by the other wives. With the Prophet's daughter Fāṭima she was, however, on good terms.

In 35 A.H. Ṣafīya sided with ʿUt͟hmān; while he was besieged in his house she made an unsuccessful attempt to reach him, and she used to bring him food and water by means of a plank placed between her dwelling and his. When ʿĀ'is͟ha asked her to be present at ʿUt͟hmān's last interview with ʿAlī, Ṭalḥa and al-Zubair, which took place in her house, Ṣafīya went, and tried to defend the unfortunate Caliph.

She died in 50 or 52, during Muʿāwiya's caliphate, leaving a fortune of 100,000 dirham in land and goods, one third of which she bequeathed to her sister's son, who still followed the Jewish faith. Her dwelling in Madīna was bought by Muʿāwiya for 180,000 dirham.

In Cairo there is a xvii. century mosque dedicated to Sitt Ṣafīya, which gives its name to the surrounding quarter.

Bibliography: Ibn His͟hām, ed. Wüstenfeld, p. 354, 653, 762, 766; Ibn Saʿd, viii. 85—92; L. Caetani, *Annali dell' Islām*, i. 379, 415; ii/i. 29, 34; viii. 223; al-Ṭabarī, i. 73; Lammens, *Moʿâwia*, p. 246; G. H. Stern, *Marriage in Early Islam*, 1939, index, s.v.

ṢAḤĀBA, "Companions"; as technical term of Islām it has the sense of "Companions of the Prophet". In earlier times the term was restricted to those who had enjoyed intercourse with the Prophet. Later the circle of the ṣaḥāba was extended to the faithful who had seen him even if only for a short time, or at an early age (cf. Goldziher, *Muh. Stud.* ii. 240). ʿĀmir b. Wāt͟hil al-Kinānī Abu 'l-Ṭufail who died shortly after 100 A. H. is styled the last of the Companions (*Usd al-g͟hāba*, iii. 97; v. 233); he must have been quite a little child when he saw Muḥammad.

The ṣaḥāba occupy high rank in the estimation of Sunnī Islām, Ḥadīt͟h being handed down from them. Attested accounts of their own procedure are regarded as evidences for the correct *sunna*. This importance which they have in the establishing of Islām made them from the beginning objects of piety to the orthodox. To revile them is considered an execrable crime, to be punished by scourging or even by death-penalty in case of obstinacy.

In precedence among the ṣaḥāba the first four caliphs occupy the highest places; with six other ṣaḥāba they share the pre-eminance of being promised Paradise by Muḥammad [see the article AL-ʿAS͟HARA AL-MUBAS͟HS͟HARA]. Other categories among the ṣaḥāba are determined by the different nature of their share in the Prophet's enterprises: *Muhād̲j̲irūn* [q.v.], *Anṣār* [q.v.], *Badrīyūn* (who took part in the battle of Badr), etc. The opinion on their qualitative gradation have been collected in al-Nawawī's commentary on Muslim (*Ṣaḥīh*, v. 161).

The contemptuous attitude arising out of a hatred for the ṣaḥāba, because with their approval the first four caliphs wrested away the rights of ʿAlī and his family, forms an outstanding feature of the S͟hīʿa in contrast to Sunnī Islām. The adherents of the latter constantly make the *tarḍiya*-eulogy (*raḍiya 'llāhᵘ ʿanhu*, "Allāh be pleased with him!") follow the mention of any one of the Aṣḥāb in speech or writing. In the theological literature of the Sunnīs the collection of the traditions concerning their virtues (*faḍā'il* or *manāḳib al-aṣḥāb*) receives assiduous attention, most systematic works on ḥadīt͟h contain a section on such. The earliest biographical source for the Companions is the *Kitāb al-ṭabaḳāt* by Ibn Saʿd [q.v.]. There are, besides, several works in which the names of all the companions have been collected with biographical notices and communications regarding the ḥadīt͟h they have handed down. They display many variations from one another. Of ʿAbd al-Bāḳī Ibn Ḳāniʿ, (d. 351/962), a *Muʿd̲j̲am al-ṣaḥāba* is mentioned (Brockelmann, *S.* i. 279). The authors of the most famous of these works dealing with the Companions are: Abū ʿAbd Allāh b. Manda (d. 395/1004—5), Abū Nuʿaim al-Iṣfahānī (d. 430/1038—9), Abū ʿUmar b. ʿAbd al-Barr al-Namarī al-Ḳurṭubī (d. 463/1070—1), *Kitāb al-istiʿāb fī maʿrifat al-aṣḥāb* (2 vols., Haidarābād 1318; cf. the critical notes on this in Subkī, *Ṭabaḳāt al-S͟hāfiʿīya*, vi. 135), Abū Mūsā Muḥammad b. Abī Bakr al-Iṣfahānī (d. 581/1185—6). The material of these predecessors has been critically compiled, corrected and supplemented by Ibn al-At͟hīr (d. 630/1232—3) in his comprehensive *Usd al-g͟hāba fī maʿrifat al-ṣaḥāba* (5 vols., Cairo 1286), also D͟hahabī, *Tad̲j̲rīd usd al-g͟hāba* (2 vols., Ḥaidarābād 1315; 8809 biographies). Still fuller material is given by Ibn Ḥad̲j̲ar al-ʿAsḳalānī (d. 852/1448—9) in his *al-Iṣāba fī tamyīz al-ṣaḥāba* (4 vols. Calcutta 1853—1894; 8 vols., Cairo 1323—1325).

SAHL AL-TUSTARĪ, ABŪ MUḤAMMAD SAHL B. ʿABD ALLĀH B. YŪNUS, a Sunnī theologian and mystic, born at Tustar (al-Ahwāz) in 203/818 and died in exile at Baṣra in 283/896.

A pupil, through his master Ibn Sawwār, of strict Sunnīs like al-T͟hawrī and Abū ʿAmr b. al-ʿAlā', Sahl was above all an ascetic of a very strict moral discipline. He was also a theologian with a vast store of intellectual knowledge.

Of his life, apparently quiet and solitary, only one detail is known: his exile to Baṣra at the time of the revolt of the Zand̲j̲ (about 261/874) when the ʿulamā' of al-Ahwāz condemned his doctrinal treatise on the obligatory character of contrition (*tawba farḍ*).

Sahl wrote nothing, but his "thousand sayings", collected and edited by his pupil, Muḥammad Ibn

Sālim (d. 297/909), presented sufficient dogmatic coherence to give rise to a theological school, the Sālimīya [q.v.]. It is from Sahl that this school derives its characteristics: with a conscious inwardness practising the rites of worship and a technical semi-gnostic vocabulary tending to monism.

Sahl's argumentation is purely dialectic (*istidlāl; aṣl, farʿ*) like that of the mutakallimūn; he does not yet argue in syllogisms in the Greek fashion as his old pupil Ḥallādj [q.v.] was to do after leaving him. In psycho-physics he teaches that man is composed of four elements (*ḥayāt, rūḥ, nūr, ṭīn*), that the *rūḥ* is superior to the *nafs* (against the view of the Hellenisers) and that it survives after death (against the view of Mubarrad).

In Ḳurʾānic exegesis each verse has four meanings, literal (*ẓāhir*), allegorical (*bāṭin*), moral (*ḥadd*) and anagogical (*muṭṭalaʿ*); he admits the Imāmī theory of *djafr* [q.v.]. The examples of the prophets should be meditated upon in order that we may gradually attain their state of soul.

For Sahl, as for Ibn Karrām and al-Ashʿarī, the "Islāmic community" comprises all believers, provided they turn towards the *ḳibla* (the Sunnī view; opposed to that of the Muʿtazilīs and Imāmīs). The word "faith" (*īmān*) signifies at once acquiescene with the lips (*ḳawl*), conformity of conduct (*ʿamal*), identity of intention (*nīya*) and inner enjoyment of the real (*yaḳīn*).

The true worshipper of God ought first to obey the state and strictly observe the rites: "to love is to extend obedience" (al-Tustarī, also, said "*perinde ac cadaver*"). He is bound to produce actions, in imitation of the Prophet (semi-Muʿtazilī notion of *iktisāb*, opposed to the quietist *tawakkul* of Shaḳīḳ and Ibn Karrām), but he ought continually to turn towards God (*Allāh ḳiblat al-nīya*) with incessant contrition (*tawba farḍ fī kull waḳt*). The analysis that Sahl makes of the stages of the voluntary act, derived from that of al-Muḥāsibī and adopted by al-Ghazzālī, remains classic. In the supreme degree the ascetic "expatriated" from the world ought to possess the essential reality of God (*yaḳīn*) beyond rites of worship (*ghayba bi 'l-madhkūr ʿan al-dhikr*); an adumbration of the Ḥallādjī doctrine of mystic union.

In eschatology Sahl uses with discretion the semi-gnostic data of Imāmī origin; the "column of light" (*ʿamūd al-nūr, ʿadl makhlūḳ bihi*), a kind of "mass of primordial adoration", composed of all the souls of saints to be (as opposed to ordinary men, *adamīyūn*), an adumbration of the *nūr muḥammadīya* of the later mystics. The saints alone are predestined to possess *sirr al-rubūbīya* or *sirr al-anā*, "mystery of the sovereign personality", or "divine right to say 'I'". This idea is an adumbration of the *huwa huwa*. From it Sahl deduced the probability of final rehabilitation for Satan; an idea later developed by Ibn al-ʿArabī and ʿAbd al-Karīm Djīlī [q.v.].

Bibliography: Sahl al-Tustarī, *Tafsīr*, ed. Naʿsānī, Cairo 1326 (artificial compilation); Abu 'l-Ḳāsim al-Saḳallī (who wrote in Ḳairawān in 390/999 and also left a *Ṣifat al-awliyāʾ*), *Sharḥ wabayān limā ashkal min kalām Sahl*, and *Kitāb al-muʿāraḍa wa'l-radd ʿalā ahl al-firāḳ min kalām Sahl*, MS. Köpr. 727; al-Hudjwīrī, *Kashf al-maḥdjūb*, transl. Nicholson, London 1911, Index, s.v.; R. Hartmann, *al-Kuschairīs Darstellung des Ṣūfītums*, Berlin 1914, Index, s.v.; L. Massignon, *Essai sur les origines... de la mystique musulmane*, Paris 1922, p. 264—70; do., *La passion d'al-Hallaj*, Paris 1922, Index, s.v.

SAIYID (A.; plur. *sāda*), a prince, lord, chief, or owner: one who is eminent by virtue of his personal qualities, his possessions, or his birth. In this last sense it is used throughout the Muslim world almost exclusively of the descendant of Muḥammad (see the art. SHARĪF). It occurs only twice in the Ḳurʾān, where it is used once (iii. 39) of John the Baptist, and once (xii. 25) of the husband of Zulaikhāʾ. By the Arabs it is applied not only to men, but to the *djinn*, to animals, and to inanimate objects. A verse refers to "*djinn*, who are aroused by night, summoning their chief (saiyid)", the wild ass is called the saiyid of his female, and al-Zadjdjādj calls the Ḳurʾān *saiyid al-kalām*, "the paragon of speech". Of its application to non-Muslims the best known instance is Rodrigo Diaz, "el Cid Campeador".

Bibliography: E. W. Lane, *Lexicon*, s.v.

SAKĪNA is a loan-word borrowed from the Hebrew (*shekīnā*). There it signifies the presence of God, in the purely spiritual sense, sometimes made clear by a sign like fire, cloud, or light, which can be appreciated by the senses. Muḥammad was apparently not quite clear regarding the true meaning of the word, when he says (Sūra ii. 248) that the *sakīna* along with some relics was in the sacred ark of the Israelites. Possibly he associated with this Hebrew loan-word conceptions from pagan demonology; many Ḳurʾānic exegists at any rate give here quite a djinn-like description of *sakīna* (cf. al-Ṭabarī, *Tafsīr*, ii. 385 *sq.*; it is noteworthy that on this point Wahb b. Munabbih relies on a Jewish source; he also confuses the ark of the covenant with the oracle of the *ʾūrīm wetummīm*). In other passages where the word is found in the Ḳurʾān, it is generally explained by the commentators as the subjective condition of peace of soul and security (see the commentaries on ix. 26, 40, and xlviii. 4, 18, 26). Side by side with these meanings, a secular one is found in Arabic: *sakīna* means the quality of calm and dignity in character (e.g. al-Bukhārī, *Badʾ at-khalḳ*, bāb 15) and then simply: to keep quiet, e.g. at the *ṣalāt* (al-Bukhārī, *Djumʿa*, bāb 18) or at the *ifāḍa* (al-Bukhārī, *Ḥadjdj*, bāb 94). Besides this there is a change of meaning of the word in its religious use as the Jewish meaning of the word gradually penetrates into Islām. Thus the *sakīna* is said to come benevolently down when the Ḳurʾān is recited (al-Bukhārī, *Faḍāʾil al-ḳurʾān*, bāb 11 and 15). As among the Jews the *rūah haḳḳōdesh*, which rests on the Prophets, gradually develops out the *shekīnā*, so we find in Islāmic writers also *sakīna* occasionally used with the meaning "Holy Ghost" (see Goldziher, p. 194 *sq.*).

Bibliography: A. Geiger, *Was hat Mohammad aus dem Judentume aufgenommen?* [2], Leipzig 1902, p. 53 *sq.*; I. Goldziher, *Über den Ausdruck "sakīna"*, in *Abhandlugen zur arabischen Philologie*, Leiden 1896; do. in *RHR*, xxviii. 1—12.

SALĀM (A.), verbal noun from *salima* "to be well, uninjured", used as a substantive in the meaning of "peace, health, salutation, greeting".

The word is of frequent occurrence in the Ḳurʾān, especially in the Sūras which are attributed to the second and third Meccan periods. The oldest passage that contains *salām* is Sūra xcvii. 5, where it is said of the *Lailat al-Ḳadr*: "It is peace until the coming of the dawn". *Salām* is also to be taken in this meaning in Ḳurʾān, l. 34, xv. 46, xxi. 69, xi. 48. *Salām* means peace in this world as well as in the next. In the latter meaning we find it used in the expression *Dār al-Salām*, "the abode of bliss" for Paradise (Sūra x. 25, vi. 127).

But *salām* is most frequently used in the Ḳur'ān as a form of salutation. Thus in Sūra lvi. 89 (first Meccan period) the people of the right hand are greeted by their companions in bliss with *Salām laka* "Peace be upon thee". *Salām* (Sūra xxxvi. 58, xiv. 23; x. 10; xxxiii. 44) or *Salām ʿalaikum* (xvi. 32; xxxix. 73, xiii. 24) is the greeting which is given the blessed in Paradise or on entering Paradise (cf. also xxv. 75). *Salām* is also the greeting of the guests of Ibrāhīm and his reply (li. 25, xi. 69; cf. xv. 52). In Sūra xx. 47 Mūsā in his address to Firʿawn is made to use the expression *al-salām ʿalā man ittabaʿa 'l-hudā* "peace be on him who follows the right guidance". *Salām ʿailakum* "peace be upon you" is found in Sūra vi. 54 at the beginning of the message which the Prophet has to deliver to the believers. As a benediction *salām* is also used repeatedly in Sūra xxxvii. where at the end of the mention of each prophet a *salām* is uttered over him (verses 79, 109, 120, 130, 181; cf. also xix. 15, 33). In Sūra lix. 23 (Madīnese) *al-salām* occurs as one of the names of Allāh, which al-Baiḍāwī interprets as *maṣdar* used as *ṣifa* in the meaning of "the Faultless" (for other explanations cf. *Lisān al-ʿArab* xv. 182 and the article ALLĀH, b. 1). The word has even been taken to mean Allāh in the formula *al-salām ʿalaikum* (Fakh̲r al-Dīn al-Rāzī, *Mafātīḥ al-gh̲aib* on Sūra vi. 54, ed. Cairo 1278, iii. 54; *Lisān al-ʿArab*, xv. 182).

At quite an early period the view became established among the Muslims that the *salām* greeting was an Islamic institution. This, is however, only correct in so far as the Ḳur'ān recommends the use of this greeting in a late Meccan passage and in two Madīna passages: in vi. 54 it is commanded to the Prophet: "If those come to you who believe in our signs say: "Peace be upon you" (*Salām ʿalaikum*). Your Lord has laid down a law of mercy for himself"; and in xxiv. 27: "O ye believers, enter not into dwellings which are not your own before you have asked leave and said *salām* (*wa-tusallimū*) on its inhabitants, etc."; similarly xxiv. 61: "If ye enter dwellings, say *salām* upon one another (*fasallimū*) etc." (cf. a similar prescription Matth. x. 12, Luk. x. 5). But Goldziher has pointed out (*ZDMG*, xlvi. 22 *sqq.*) and quoted passages from poets in support of the view that *salām* was already in use as a greeting before Islām. The corresponding Hebrew and Aramaic expressions *S̲h̲ālōm lᵉḵā*, *S̲h̲ᵉlām lāḵ* (*lᵉḵon*), *S̲h̲ᵉlāmā ʿᵉlāḵ*, which go back to Old Testament usage (cf. Judges, xix. 20, 2 Sam., xviii. 28, Dan. x. 19, 1 Chron., xii. 19), were also in use as greetings among the Jews and Christians. A very great number of Nabataean inscriptions further show the use of *s̲h̲-l-m* to express good wishes in North-west Arabia and the Sinai peninsula (*CIS*, ii. *Inscriptiones Aramaeae*, i. No. 288 *sqq.*, twice repeated in No. 244, 339, thrice repeated in No. 302), and the Arabic *s-l-m* frequently occurs in the Safaitic inscriptions as a benedictive term. Cf. E. Littmann, *Zur Entzifferung der Safa-Inschriften*, Leipzig 1901; do., *Semitic Inscriptions*, New York-London 1905, *Safaitic inscriptions*. Lidzbarski has suggested that *salām* reproduces the idea expressed by σωτηρία (*ZS*, i. 85 *sqq.*).

Muḥammad must have placed a high religious value on the *salām* formula as he considered it the greeting given by the angels to the blessed and used it as an auspicious salutation on the prophets who had preceded him. A *salām*, like that in the *tas̲h̲ahhud* (see below) or like the salutation of peace which closes the *ṣalāt* and has its parallel in the Jewish *tᵉphillā* (cf. E. Mittwoch, *Zur Entstehungsgeschichte des islam. Gebets und Kultus*, in the *Abh. Pr. Ak. W.*, ph.-h. Kl., 1913, No. 2, p. 18), may have been from the first an essential feature of the ritual of divine service.

In the ritual of the *ṣalāt* as legally prescribed, the benediction on Allāh and the *salām* on the Prophet, on the worshipper and those present and on Allāh's pious servants, precede the confession of faith in the *tas̲h̲ahhud*: *al-Salām ʿalaika aiyuha 'l-nabī wa-raḥmat Allāh wa-barakātuhu*; *al-salām ʿalainā wa-ʿalā ʿibād Allāh al-ṣāliḥīn*. Among the compulsory ceremonies of the *ṣalāt* there is also at the end of it the *taslīma al-ūlā*, the fuller form of which consists in the worshipper in a sitting position turning his head to right and left and saying each time: *al-salām ʿalaikum wa-raḥmat Allāh.*

The preference of the Ḳur'ān for the *salām* formula and its liturgical use may have contributed considerably to the fact that it soon became considered an exclusively Muslim greeting (*taḥīyat al-salām*). As already mentioned above, the Ḳur'ān prescribes the *salām* on the Prophet to follow the *taṣliya*. Tradition reports that the latter endeavoured to introduce it (Ibn His̲h̲ām, ed. Wüstenfeld, p. 472 *sq.*; Ṭabarī, ed. de Goeje, i., 1335 *sqq.*). Those around him are also said to have been eager to introduce this greeting (Ibn Saʿd, *Ṭabaḳāt*, v. 369; Sprenger, *Das Leben...des Mohammad*, iii. 482, 485; Goldziher, *Moh. Stud.*, i. 264). The Jews are said to have distorted this greeting with respect to Muḥammad to *al-sām ʿalaika*, "death to you", whereupon the Prophet answered *wa-ʿalaikum* "and to you" (Buk̲h̲ārī, *Isti'd̲h̲ān*, bāb 22, *Adab*, bāb 38; *Lisān al-ʿArab*, xv. 206).

The expressions which could be used were *salām* or *salām ʿalaikum* (*-ka*) or *al-salām ʿalaikum*. In the Ḳur'ān the use of *salām ʿalaikum* preponderates. Fak̲h̲r al-Dīn al-Rāzī endeavours to explain that the indefinite form is preferable and expresses the conception of perfect greeting (*op. cit.*, ii. 500, iii. 512). The formula *al-salām ʿalaikum* was, however, much used as a greeting. The undetermined form is expressly prescribed in the *taslīma* (al-Rāzī, *op. cit.*, ii. 501, Bād̲j̲ūrī, i. 170, *Lisān al-ʿArab*, xv. 182). As a return greeting *wa-ʿalaikum al-salām* became usual (for further details on this inversion see Fak̲h̲r al-Dīn al-Rāzī, *op. cit.*, ii. 500, iii. 512).

According to some traditions, Muḥammad had described the expression *ʿalaika 'l-salām* as the salutation to the dead and insisted on being greeted with *al-salām ʿalaika* (Ṭabarī, iii. 2395; Ibn al-At̲h̲īr, *al-Nihāya fi g̲h̲arīb al-ḥadīt̲h̲ wa 'l-āt̲h̲ār*, Cairo 1311, ii. 176 below). But there are also traditions in which the Prophet greets the dead in the cemetery with an expression beginning with (*al-*)*salām* (Ṭabarī, iii. 2402; Ibn al-At̲h̲īr and *Lisān al-ʿArab*, *loc. cit.*).

The *salām* formula was very early extended by the addition of the words *wa-raḥmat Allāh* or *wa-raḥmat Allāh wa-barakātuhu*. The first extension became used in the *taslīma* and the second in the *tas̲h̲ahhud* (cf. above). Applying the Ḳur'ānic commandment iv. 86: "when ye are saluted with a salutation, salute the person with a better than his or at least return it", it is recommended (*sunna*) in the return greeting to add the wish of blessing and benediction or occasionally, when replying to a simple *salām*, only the former (cf. Buk̲h̲āri, *Isti'd̲h̲ān*, bāb 16, 18, 19). According to Lane (*Manners and Customs* [3], i. 229, note) the threefold formula was very common as a return greeting in Egypt;

cf. also Nallino, *L'arabo parlato in Egitto*², Milan 1913, p. 121. In Mecca it is comparatively rarely used; the reply usual there is *weᶜalēkum essalām war-raḥma* (*we-raḥmatu'llāh* or *wal-ikrām*); cf. Snouck Hurgronje, *Mekkanische Sprichwörter und Redensarten, Verspr. Geschr.* v. 112).

At the conclusion of a letter the expression *wa 'l-salām* (*ᶜalaika, -kum*) is often used, e.g. Ibn Saᶜd, *op. cit.*, i/ii. 27, 28, 29. *Wa 'l-salām* has occasionally the meaning of "and that is the end of it" (cf. Snouck Hurgronje, *op. cit.*, p. 88).

In keeping with Ḳur'ān xx. 46, it became usual to use the form *al-salām ᶜalā man ittabaᶜa 'l-hudā* to non-Muslims when necessary. It is found, for example, in letters ascribed to Muḥammad. Papyri of the year 91/710 bear early testimony to its use (*Papyri Schott-Reinhardt*, i., ed. by C. H. Becker, Heidelberg 1906, i. No. 29, ii. 40; iii. 87; x. 11; xi. 7; xviii. 9). A letter from Muḥammad to the Jews of Maḳnā concludes, however, with *wa 'l-salām* (Ibn Saᶜd, *op. cit.* i/ii. 28); similarly a letter to the Christians in Aila (*ibid.*, p. 29).

Salām means also a *ṣalawāt* litany, which is pronounced from the minarets every Friday about half an hour before the beginning of the midday service before the *adhān*. This part of the liturgy is repeated inside the mosque before the beginning of the regular ceremonies by several people with good voice standing on a *dikka* (Goldziher, *Über die Eulogien, etc.* in *ZDMG*, l. 103 *sqq.*; cf. Lane, *op. cit.*, i. 117). The same name is given to the benedictions on the Prophet which are sung during the month of Ramaḍān about half an hour after midnight from the minarets (Lane, *op. cit.*, ii. 264).

The auspicious formula *ᶜalaihi 'l-salām*, which, according to the strictly orthodox opinion, like the *taṣliya*, should only follow the names of prophets but was more freely used in the earlier literature, was used by the Shīᶜa without limitation of ᶜAlī and his descendants also.

The Sunnīs of India make a magical use of the so-called seven *salām*'s which refer to Sūra xxxvi. 58; xxxvii. 79, 109, 120, 130; xxxix. 73; xcvii. 5. In the morning of the festival of Akhir-i Čahārshamba they write the seven *salām*'s or have them written with saffronwater, ink or rosewater on the leaf of a mango-tree or a sacred fig-tree, or of a plantain. They then wash off the writing in water and drink it in the hope that they may enjoy peace and happiness (Djaᶜfar Sharīf-Herklots, *Islam in India or the Qānūn-i Islām*, new ed. by W. Crooke, London 1921, p. 186 sq.).

On coins *salām* (sometimes abridged to *s*) means "of full weight, complete"; cf. J. G. Stickel, *Das grossherz. orientalische Münzkabinett zu Jena* (*Handb. der Morgenl. Münzkunde*), Leipzig 1845, i. 43 *sq.*; O. Codrington, *A Manual of Musulman Numismatics*, London 1904, p. 10.

Bibliography: In addition to that mentioned in the article: Ibn ᶜAbd Rabbihi, *al-ᶜIḳd al-farīd*, Būlāḳ, 1293, i. 276 *sq.*; Lane, *op. cit.*, i. 298 *sqq.*; Landberg, *Etudes sur les dialectes de l'Arabie méridionale*, Leiden 1905—1913, ii. 776—781, 786—789; D. Künstlinger, "*Islām*", "*Muslim*", "*aslama*" *im Ḳurān*, in *RO*. xi. (1936), p. 130 *sq.*; H. Ringgren, *Islam, aslama and muslim*, Uppsala 1949.

ṢALĀT, the usual name in Arabic for the ritual prayer or divine service. The translation "prayer" without further definition is not accurate; the Arabic word *duᶜā'* corresponds to the concept of prayer (Snouck Hurgronje has several times drawn attention to this distinction; *Verspreide Geschriften*, i. 213 *sq.*, ii. 90, iv. 56, 63 *sq.*, etc.). The word does not seem to occur in the pre-Ḳur'ānic literature. Muḥammad took it, like the ceremony, from the Jews and Christians in Arabia. In many Kūfic copies of the Ḳur'ān and often in later literature also in connection with the sacred book it is written صلوة It is very often assumed that this orthography represents a dialectic pronunciation (Nöldeke, *Geschichte des Qorans*, p. 255; Wright-de Goeje, *Arabic Grammar*, i. 12 A; Brockelmann, *Arabische Grammatik*⁶, p. 7). The writing of a *wāw* in place of the *alif* which one would expect is found, it is true, in several other words belonging to the language of the Ḳur'ān; but with the exception of *ribā* (ربوا) only in the termination *āt* (or *ōt*), so frequent in Aramaic. The view that in forms like زكوة, صلوة etc. Aramaic influence may be seen (cf. Fränkel, *De vocabulis in antiquis Arabum carminibus et in Corano peregrinis*, p. 21) is, however, doubtful (see C. Rabin, *Ancient West-Arabian*, pp. 105 *sq.*).

The etymology of the Aramaic word *ṣᵉlōtā* is quite transparent. The root *ṣ-l-'* in Aramaic means to bow, to bend, to stretch. The substantive *ṣᵉlōtā* is the *nomen actionis* from this and means the act of bowing, etc. It is used in several Aramaic dialects for ritual prayer, although it can also mean spontaneous individual prayer, which in Syriac at least is usually called *bāᶜūtā*. Muḥammad took over the word *ṣalāt* in this sense from his neighbours and the Muslim ṣalāt shows in its composition a great similarity to the Jewish and Christian services, as will be shown in greater detail below. — The verb *ṣallā* is a denominative derived from the substantive *ṣalāt* with the meaning "to perform the ṣalāt".

It is clear that at first Muḥammad had not the material available in ample measure for the ritual. The texts which were recited and sung in the solemn litanies of the Christians and Jews in their services were lacking to him. This fact may still be deduced from the celebrated tradition regarding the revelation of Sūra xcvi., which, according to the common view, was the first revealed to him. To the command of the angel urging him to recite he replied: "I have nothing to recite". The divine part of this dialogue, which so troubled Muḥammad, is then said to have at once become the first text for recitation, and it was followed by others with longer or shorter pauses.

Although the ṣalāt is nowhere described or exactly regulated in the Ḳur'ān, it can be assumed that its characteristic features have not changed in the course of development of the worship. The indications in the Ḳur'ān of its various component parts lead us to believe this. The standing position is everywhere presupposed in the ṣalāt, alternating with inclinations (*rukūᶜ*) and prostrations (*sudjūd*). How closely the ṣalāt was bound up even in the Meccan period with the recitation of the Ḳur'ān is seen from the fact that in Sūra xvii. 78 the morning ṣalāt is called *Ḳur'ān al-fadjr*. On the other hand we find the recitation of the Ḳur'ān by itself also associated with prostration (Sūra lxxxiv. 21).

That at this period praises already constituted a very considerable part of the ṣalāt is clear from Ḳur'ānic passages like Sūra xx. 130 and xxiv. 41, where *taḥmīd* and *tasbīḥ* are mentioned in the closest connection with the ṣalāt.

From the mention of the *ṣalāt* and the verb *ṣallā* in the oldest Sūra's (e.g. lxxv. 31, lxx. 23, cvii. 5, lxxiv. 43, cviii. 2) it may be further seen that we can assert that this rite was an accompaniment of Islām from the earliest times and that Caetani's sceptical reflexions and hypotheses do not give sufficient weight to the Ḳur'ānic evidence (cf. *Annali, Introduzione*, § 219 note — in part in connection with similar views of Grimme). How much Muḥammad disturbed the Meccans with his new religion may be seen from Sūra xvii. 110, where he is recommended by Allāh not to perform the ṣalāt too loudly, which is interpreted by tradition — and, no doubt, rightly — to mean that his unbelievings fellow-citizens molested him for holding his services too noisily. This is in agreement with the fact that in the period during which Muḥammad is continually advised to imitate the example of the earlier prophets and model himself on the patience, attention is regularly called to their also having summoned those around them to hold the ṣalāt (e.g. Sūra xxi. 73, xix. 31, xiv. 37, xix. 55, xx. 132).

In the Ḳur'ān the ṣalāt is very frequently mentioned along with the *zakāt*; the two are obviously considered the manifestations of piety most loved by Allāh (e.g. Sūra ii. 83, 110, 172, 277, iv. 77, 162, v. 12, 55 etc.). In Sūra ii. 45, 153 the believers are exhorted to seek help in *ṣalāt* and *ṣabr*. *Ṣabr* [q.v.] is interpreted in this connection as fasting. There is further in the Ḳur'ān no trace so far of the five "pillars" which later attained such an important position. The ṣalāt is an expression of humility (Sūra xxiii. 2) which latter was considered throughout the Hellenistic world as the attitude to the deity most befitting man. Punctual observance (*muḥāfaẓa*) of the ṣalāt is repeatedly enjoined (vi. 92, xxiii. 9, lxx. 34; cf. lxx. 22) and neglect (*sahw*) is censured (cvii. 5). In Sūra iv. 103 a similar injunction is given the following justification: "for the ṣalāt is a *kitāb mawḳūt* i.e. "a regulated ordinance of religion". It is blamed in the Munāfiḳūn [q.v.] that they perform the ṣalāt without zeal and with eye-service only (Sūra iv. 142). The limitation and later interdiction of the use of wine owed its origin to the fact that over-indulgence disturbed order at divine service (Sūra iv. 43).

As has already been observed, we may assume that the essential features of the later ṣalāt were in existance from the very beginning. We know very little about the peculiarities of the ṣalāt and its accompanying phenomena in the oldest period of Islām. A ritual ablution (cf. the articles GHUSL, ṬAHĀRA, WUḌŪ') before the ṣalāt is prescribed in Sūra v. 6; the *nidā'* for the ṣalāt is mentioned in v. 58 and in lxii. 9 for the Friday ṣalāt. A special ṣalāt in case of imminent danger is described in Sūra iv. 102 (see below under *Ṣalāt al-khawf*). Praises of Muḥammad and the *taslīm* form the conclusion of the later ṣalāt. This practice can be justified by Sūra xxxiii. 56, where it is written: "Allāh and his angels bless the Prophet; ye who believe, bless him and bring him salutations of peace". The Friday ṣalāt is mentioned in lxii. 9 in the words: "O believers, when the call to the ṣalāt occurs in Fridays, haste ye to the invocation (*dhikr*) of Allāh and quit trafficking. This is better for ye when ye know".

In these circumstances it is intelligible that Muḥammad laid great stress on those who showed themselves ready to adopt Islām being at once initiated into practice of the ṣalāt. Tradition thus reports that he sent As'ad b. Zurāra or Muṣ'ab b. 'Umair to the Madīnese for this express purpose and that the latter was the first to hold the Friday service with them (see A. J. Wensinck, *Mohammad en de Joden te Medina*, p. 111 *sqq.*, and C. H. Becker in *Der Islam*, iii. 378 *sq.*). In Muḥammad's messages to the tribes of Arabia the ṣalāt is frequently inculcated as Muslim duty (see J. Sperber, *Die Schreiben Muḥammads an die Stämme Arabiens* in *MSOS As.*, xix., reprint, p. 16, 19, 38, 58, 77 etc.). According to Muslim tradition the establishment of five daily observances of the ṣalāt dates back to the beginnings of Islām. It is connected with Muḥammad's ascension to heaven (see the article ISRĀ'). When Muḥammad is taken up to the highest heaven fifty ṣalāts daily are imposed on his community by Allāh; Muḥammad leaves the presence of Allāh with this commission; on his way back he meets Mūsā who asks him what Allāh has imposed on his community. When Mūsā hears the orders he says: "Return to thy Lord for the community is not able to bear this". Allāh then alters the fifty to twenty-five. On his way back Muḥammad tells Mūsā of the alteration and receives the same reply. The same processes are repeated until finally the number remains at five (al-Bukhārī, *Ṣalāt*, bāb 1; Muslim, *Imān*, trad. 259, 263; al-Tirmidhī, *Mawāḳīt al-ṣalāt*, bāb 45: al-Nasā'ī, *Ṣalāt*, bāb 1; Ibn Mādja, *Iḳāma*, bāb 194; Aḥmad b. Ḥanbal, i. 315 (ter), iii. 148 *sq.*, 161; cf. Ibn Sa'd, 1/i. 143 etc.). On the other hand, in a widely disseminated tradition we are told that Gabriel came down five times in one day and performed the ṣalāt in Muḥammad's presence and the latter on each occasion imitated the angel (al-Bukhārī, *Mawāḳīt*, bāb 1; Muslim, *Masādjid*, trad. 166, 167; Abū Dā'ūd, *Ṣalāt* bāb 2; al-Tirmidhī, *Mawāḳīt*, bāb 1; al Nasā'ī, *Mawāḳīt* bāb 1, 10, 17; Ibn Mādja, *Ṣalāt*, bāb 1; al-Dārimī, *Ṣalāt*, bāb 2; Mālik, *Wuḳūt*, trad. 1; etc.). This idea cannot, however, survive literary and historical criticism. In a short but searching study Houtsma has come to the following conclusions (*Iets over den dagelijkschen çalat der Mohammedanen* in *Theologisch Tijdschrift*, 1890, xxiv. 127 *sqq.*). How the Meccan practice was regulated is seen from Sūra xi. 114: "And hold the ṣalāt at the two ends of the day as well as at the ends (?) of the night". With this Sūra xvii. 78 agrees, where a morning ṣalāt, a ṣalāt when the sun declines and the night ṣalāt (*tahadjdjud*) are prescribed; cf. Sūra xxiv. 58, where the *ṣalāt al-fadjr* and the *ṣalāt al-'ishā'* are mentioned. Then we find appearing suddenly in the Madīna Sūra ii. 238 the "middle ṣalāt" (*al-wusṭā*). This must therefore have been added in Madīna to the two usual ṣalāts and probably after the example of the Jews, who also performed their *t'fillā* three times a day.

We thus arrive at three daily ṣalāts in Muḥammad's life-time. The question how the number five came to be fixed upon is answered by Houtsma, who says that the two midday ṣalāts (*ẓuhr* and *'aṣr*) and the two evening ṣalāts (*maghrib* and *'ishā'*) are duplications of the *wusṭā* and *'ishā'* respectively, duplications which are easily explained from the lack of accurate means of defining the times for the ṣalāt in Muḥammad's life-time (cf. E. Mittwoch, *Zur Entstehungsgeschichte des islamischen Gebets und Kultus*, *Abd. Pr. Ak. W.*, 1913, No. 2, p. 10 *sqq.*). Goldziher on the contrary (*Islamisme et Parsisme* in *RHR*, 1901, xliii. 15), assumes Persian influence in settling the number at five. When the theory of the five obligatory daily ṣalāts became firmly established cannot be exactly settled as yet. According to Ibn 'Abbās, Muḥammad "combined" in Madīna several ṣalāts, e.g. the *ẓuhr* and *'aṣr* ṣalāt on the one hand and the *maghrib* and *'ishā'* ṣalāt on the other, without his being on a journey or threatened by danger (Muslim, *Musāfirīn*, trad. 49). Asked for

Muḥammad's presumed reason, Ibn ʿAbbās replied that he did not wish to expose any members of his community to (the danger of) sinning (by overburdening them) (ibid., trad. 50; cf. 54, 55). In another version of the same ḥadīth we read: "We were wont in Muḥammad's life-time to combine ṣalāts in twos (ibid., trad, 58). Al-Nawawī's commentary on the passages quoted (ed. Cairo 1282 ii. 196 *sq.*) is instructive for the difficulties which these traditions held in store for the ʿulamāʾ and how they were able to overcome them. To us, such traditions are an indication that the number of daily ṣalāts had not yet been fixed at five in Muḥammad's lifetime.

In the canonical Ḥadīth the number five is found in numerous traditions. In the schools of law there is no difference of opinion on this point. We shall therefore have to place the origin of this theory before the end of the first century.

The five compulsory ṣalāts are named as follows, according to the time of day at which they are observed (see the article MĪḲĀT): *ṣalāt al-ṣubḥ*, often also called *ṣalāt al-fadjr*; *ṣalāt al-ẓuhr*; *ṣalāt al-ʿaṣr*; *ṣalāt al-maghrib*; *ṣalāt al-ʿishāʾ*, often also called *ṣalāt al-ʿatama*, but the latter name is often condemned as improper (Muslim, *Masādjid*, trad. 228, 229; Abū Dāʾūd, *Ḥudūd*, bāb 78; al-Nasāʾī, *Mawāḳīt*, bāb 23; etc.).

II.

Every Muslim who has attained his majority and is *compos mentis* is bound to observe the five daily ṣalāts (*al-maktūba*, in contrast to the voluntary ṣalāts, which are called *nāfila* or *ṣalāt al-taṭawwuʿ*). The obligation is suspended for the sick. Omitted ṣalāts must be made up (*ḳaḍāʾ*). The theories of the Shāfiʿī school on this point are given in al-Nawawī's commentary on Muslim, *Musāfirīn*, trad. 309—316 (ii. 178 *sqq.*). According to the strict theory (which in Islām has in very many cases little or nothing to do with practice) any one who deliberately omits the ṣalāt because he does not recognize it as a legal duty is to be regarded as *kāfir*. Even deliberate neglect without any such theoretical basis makes him liable to the death penalty (cf. ḲATL] (see al-Nawawī, *Minhādj al-ṭālibīn*, ed. v. d. Berg, i. 202; cf. Abū Isḥāḳ al-Shīrāzī, *K. al-tanbīh fi 'l-fiḳh*, ed. Juynboll, p. 15).

Several preliminary conditions must be fulfilled for the performance of a valid ṣalāt. The requisite ritual purity must be restored, if necessary, by *wuḍūʾ* [q.v.], *ghusl* [q.v.] or *tayammum* [q.v.]. The dress worn should fulfil the legal regulations which aim at the "covering of the privy parts" (*satr al-ʿawra*). This means that in men the body must be covered from the navel to the knees, in free women the whole body except the face and hands. The latter regulation is remarkable, because it is in striking contrast to the popular European opinion regarding the compulsory veiling of Muslim women (cf. Snouck Hurgronje, *Twee populaire dwalingen*, in *Verspreide Geschriften*, i. 295 *sqq.*). In the Ḥadīth the question of dress, like so many others, has not yet reached a uniform formulation. Sometimes only the covering of the privy parts is mentioned (e.g. al-Bukhārī, *Ṣalāt*, bāb 10), and sometimes the saying is ascribed to Muḥammad that the shoulders also should be covered (e.g. Muslim, *Ṣalāt*, trad. 175); sometimes the use of the scanty *ṣammāʾ* is expressly mentioned in this connection (e.g. Aḥmad b. Ḥanbal, *Musnad*, iii. 322 etc.) and at the same time we are told that the ṣalāt in one *thawb* is permitted or even quite common (e.g. Abū Dāʾūd, *Ṣalāt*, bāb 77, 80—82); on the other hand it is said that one who owns two *thawb* should put them on at the ṣalāt (e.g. Abū Dāʾūd, *Ṣalāt*, bāb 82; Aḥmad b. Ḥanbal, ii. 148).

The ṣalāt need not be held in a mosque but may be celebrated in a dwelling-house and any other place; the authority given for this is the saying of Muḥammad that he was granted the privilege that for him the earth was *masdjid wa-ṭahūr* (e.g. al-Bukhārī, *Ṣalāt*, bāb 56). Tombs are excepted (e.g. Muslim, *Ṣalāt al-musāfirīn*, trad 208, 209) and unclean places, like slaughterplaces etc. (e.g. al-Tirmidhī, *Mawāḳīt al-ṣalāt*, bāb 141).

The place where the ṣalāt is performed is marked off in some way from the surrounding area by a *sutra*; on this cf. the article SUTRA. A *sadjdjāda* [q.v.] is used as a rule. Care must be taken also that the worshipper faces in the direction of Mecca; cf. the article ḲIBLA.

The ṣalāt proper consists of the following elements, our description of which is based on the Shāfiʿī practice.

The *nīya* (= intention; q.v.) is pronounced aloud or in a low voice, with an announcement of the ṣalāt which one intends to perform: it corresponds to the Jewish *kawwānā* (cf. Mittwoch, *op. cit.*, p. 16; A. J. Wensinck, *De intentie in recht, ethiek en mystiek der semietische volken* in *VMAW*, series 5, vol. iv.). Then are pronounced the words *Allāhu akbar*, the *takbīrat al-iḥrām*, with which begins the consecrated state (cf. the arcticle IḤRĀM). Mittwoch has compared this formula with the benedictions of the Jewish *tᵉfillā* (*op. cit.*, p. 16 *sq*). The ṣalāt is performed standing. Mittwoch points out that the Jewish *tᵉfillā* is called *ʿamīdā* (*op. cit.*, p. 16). It is sunna to utter a *duʿāʾ* or a *taʿawwudh* after the *takbīra* (see *Minhādj*, i. 78). Then follows the recitation which usually consists of the *Fātiḥa*. In the Ḥadīth the importance of this *ḳirāʾa* is expressed in the maxim: *lā ṣalāt liman lam yaḳraʾ bi-fātiḥati 'l-kitāb* (e.g. al-Bukhārī, *Adhān*, bāb 95; Muslim, *Ṣalāt*, trad. 34—36, 42). In a congregational ṣalāt it is the custom for only the *Fātiḥa* to be recited along with the Imām; if the latter begins with the second *ḳirāʾa*, those present have to listen (cf. *Minhādj*, i. 80). In the Ḥadīth there are numerous statements as to whether recitation should be loud or low; e.g. al-Bukhārī, *Kusūf*, bāb 19; Abū Dāʾūd, *Ṭahāra*, bāb 89; al-Nasāʾī, *Iftitāḥ*, bāb 27—29, 80, 81, etc.; cf. al-Bukhārī, *Adhān*, bāb 96, 97, 108; Muslim, *Ṣalāt*, trad. 47—49.

Next comes the *rukūʿ* which consists in bending the back till the palms of the hands are on a level with the knees (the Jewish *kerīʿā*; see Mittwoch, *op. cit.*, p. 17 *sq.*; cf. also the pictures of the various attitudes in the ṣalāt in Lane's *Manners and Customs*, in the chapter on *Religion and Laws*, and in Juynboll, *Handbuch*, p. 76). The upright position is then resumed (*iʿtidāl*); as soon as the head is raised after the *rukūʿ*, the hands are uplifted and the worshipper pronounced the words "Allāh heeds him who praises him". This is found quite early, even in Ḥadīth (e.g. al-Bukhārī, *Adhān*, bāb 52, 74, 82; Muslim, *Ṣalāt*, trad. 25, 28, 55, 62—64 etc.).

There have been differences of opinion regarding the raising of the hands in *ṣalāt* and *duʿāʾ*. Some say that Muḥammad used to lift up his hands at the ṣalāt (e.g. al-Bukhārī, *Adhān*, bāb 83—86; Muslim, *Ṣalāt*, trad. 21—26; Abū Dāʾūd, *Ṣalāt*, bāb 114—126; al-Nasāʾī, *Iftitāḥ*, bāb 1—6, 85—87; Aḥmad b. Ḥanbal, i. 93, 255, etc.). Importance is attached (as may be seen in the passages just quoted) to giving the height to which it is permitted to raise the hands. Besides raising the hands the spreading out of them also occurs (al-Bukhārī, *Adhān*, bāb 130). It is also evident from the passages of Ḥadīth quoted that the raising of the hands took place not only after the *rukūʿ* but also in other parts of the ṣalāt. This ritual gesture was made with special preference at the ṣalāt for rain (e.g. al-Bukhārī, *Djumʿa*, bāb 34, 35; Muslim, *Istisḳāʾ*, trad. 5—7; Aḥmad b. Ḥanbal iii. 104, 153, 181 etc.). Occasionally the *rafʿ al-yadain* is declared permitted for no *duʿāʾ* except the *istisḳāʾ* (e.g. al-Nasāʾī, *Ḳiyām al-lail*, bāb 52; Aḥmad b. Ḥanbal, ii. 243). What value was given to this rite may be seen, for example, from the fact that Muḥammad is made to perform the *wuḍūʾ* before raising the hands in the *duʿāʾ* (al-Bukhārī, *Maghāzī*, bāb 55). This all becomes quite clear when we reflect that the raising of the hands is as it were a measure of coercion used by man towards the Deity, as Goldziher has shown in his *Zauberelemente im islamischen Gebet* (*Nöldeke-Festschrift* i. 320). The Sunna further associates with the *rukūʿ* the *ḳunūt* [q.v.], which in parts falls into the same category as the raising of the hands, as Goldziher has also shown in the essay just mentioned.

The next "pillar" of the ṣalāt in orders is the prostration (*sudjūd*), which was also one of the rites of the Jewish (Mittwoch, *op. cit.*, p. 17 *sq.*, *hishtahawāyā*) and of the Christian service (Wensinck, *Mohammad en de Joden te Medina*, p. 104 *sq.*). Next the worshipper assumes the half-kneeling, half-sitting position, which in Arabic terminology is usually called *djulūs* (cf. Juynboll, *op. cit.*, p. 76, fig. 7). Then comes another *sudjūd*.

The ceremonies from the recitation of the *Fātiḥa* to the second *sudjūd* inclusive constitute a *rakʿa*. It is to be noted that in the Ḥadīth literature at least this terminology still varies a good deal. Sometimes *rakʿa* seems to be used in the same sense as *sadjda*, sometimes (and this is the regular usage later) *rakʿa* is the more comprehensive term, applied to the middle part just described of the whole ṣalāt. Only the history of the Muslim ritual, which has still to be written, will make clear the exact state of affairs. The most usual terminology (in Ḥadīth also) gives the number of *rakʿa's* for each ṣalāt, viz. for the *ṣalāt al-fadjr*, 2; for the *ṣalāt al-ẓuhr*, 4; for the *ṣalāt al-ʿaṣr*, 4; for the *ṣalāt al-maghrib* 3; for the *ṣalāt al-ʿishāʾ*, 4. Muslim tradition even says that the ṣalāt originally consisted of two *rakʿa*'s, that this number was retained for the ṣalāt on journeys, but four was fixed for the normal ṣalāt (e.g. al-Bukhārī, *Ṣalāt*, bāb 1; Muslim, *Ṣalāt al-musāfirīn*, trad. 1—3, etc.). Mittwoch (*op. cit.*, p. 18 *sq.*) assumes Jewish influence on the original choice of two *rakʿa*'s.

The statement that this or that ṣalāt consists of so many *rakʿa*'s means that the introductory rites which precede the first *ḳirāʾa* and those which follow the second *sudjūd* (see below) need only occur once in the ṣalāt in question while, on the other hand, the ceremonies in between are repeated so many times.

The rites which follow the second *sudjūd* are the *tashahhud*, the profession of faith, which is pronounced sitting. That the rule just mentioned for the repetition of certain parts of the ṣalāt only developed gradually is evident from a tradition which ascribes to Muḥammad the pronouncement that the *tashahhud* should be repeated after every two *rakʿa*'s (Aḥmad b. Ḥanbal, i. 211).

Then comes the ṣalāt on the Prophet which consists of eulogies in which occurs the much discussed formula *ṣallā 'llāhu ʿalaihi wa-sallama*. These formulae are pronounced sitting. The worshipper remains seated for the concluding ceremony, the *salām* or *taslīmat al-taḥlīl*, which ends the consecrated state. The fullest version of it is, according to al-Nawawī (*op. cit.*), p. 91 *sq.*: *al-salām ʿalaikum wa-raḥmatu 'llāhi*; but it may also be abbreviated. It is pronounced twice, once looking to the right and a second time to the left. If is considered a salutation to the believers; but it is also referred to the guardian angels present (cf. Sūra xvii. 80). On analogies in the Jewish service see Mittwoch, *op. cit.*, p. 18.

The different ceremonies of the ṣalāt are classified according to their importance or their obligatory or sunna character. Al-Nawawī (*op. cit.*, p. 74 *sqq.*) numbers the following among the *arkān al-ṣalāt*: *nīya, takbīrat al-iḥrām, ḳiyām, ḳirāʾa, rukūʿ, iʿtidāl, sudjūd, djulūs, tashahhud, ḳuʿūd, al-ṣalāt ʿala 'l-Nabī, salām* and (13) the correct order of succession (*tartīb*). The other ceremonies — some of which are mentioned above — are considered sunna by him. Cf. Abū Isḥāḳ al-Shīrāzī, *Tanbīh*, p. 25.

It is the many sunna ceremonies which, according as they are abbreviated or carried through in great detail, give each ṣalāt its peculiar character and in particular affect its length. This is true especially of the eulogies interspersed (see Maulvi Muḥammad ʿAlī, *The Holy Qurʾān*, 2nd ed., Lahore 1920, p. II) and of the *ḳirāʾa*; for the recitation of the *Fātiḥa* may be followed by the recitation of further chapters from the Ḳurʾān. The Ḥādīth has much to say on this subject. It appears that the great zeal of many imāms in this respect has often been a burden to the faithful. Complaints on the subject are said to have been made to Muḥammad and he is said to have readily admitted their justice. "Reflect", he is said to have warned the imāms, "that there are weak and old men among you" (e.g. al-Bukhārī, *ʿIlm*, bāb 28; Muslim, *Ṣalāt*, trad. 179—190; Abū Dāʾūd, *Ṣalāt*, bāb 122, 123 etc.). We even find him quoted as describing the imām concerned as a *fattān* (tempter) (e.g. al-Bukhārī, *Adhān*, bāb 60; Aḥmad b. Ḥanbal, iii. 308). Praise is also given to Muḥammad because no one went through the ṣalāt more completely and in a shorter time than he did (Aḥmad b. Ḥanbal, iii. 279, 282 and many other passages).

It is natural that the correct order of the ceremonies in the ṣalāt is considered one of its pillars by the faḳīhs. But we are justified in supposing that there was still considerable variation in this long after Muḥammad's death. Such unintentional deviations from the usual number and order of the ceremonies are discussed in the Fiḳh, and Ḥadīth — the *enfant terrible* of the Fiḳh — supplies the historical background for them. Both say that these unintentional deviations in minor points are made good by the performance of additional *rakʿa*'s or *sadjda*'s. With what painful accuracy the Fiḳh deals with this subject may be seen, for example, from al-Nawawī (*op. cit.*, p. 90 *sqq.*). Ḥadīth, on the other hand, is content, as a rule, to say that Muḥammad, who was later also credited with such deviations, in these cases used to perform two additional *sadjda*'s, which are called *sadjdatā 'l-sahw* (e.g. Muslim, *Masādjid*, trad. 85; Aḥmad b. Ḥanbal, iii. 12, 37, 42; al-Bukhārī, *Ṣalāt*, bāb 88; *Sahw*, bāb 4 etc.). Al-Bukhārī in the heading to bāb 32 of the chapter *Ṣalāt* preserves the memory of less minutely regulated conditions.

The Fiḳh also defines quite minutely what actions

and contingent states of body destroy the validity of the ṣalāt (al-Nawawī, *op. cit.*, p. 103 *sqq.*; Abū Isḥāḳ al-Shīrāzī, p. 28 *sq.*). The Ḥadīth records that at first the believers used to talk freely with each other during the ṣalāt and greeted Muḥammad and one another, but that the Prophet put an end to this licence (al-Bukhārī, *al-ʿAmal fi 'l-ṣalāt*, bāb 2—4). The old state of affairs is strikingly illuminated in the oft-told story of how Muḥammad performed the ṣalāt with Zainab's little daughter hanging round his neck; when he came to the *sudjūd* he, it is said, put down the child and took her up again when he arose (e.g. al-Bukhārī, *Ṣalāt*, bāb 106; Muslim, *Masādjid*, trad. 41—44; al-Nasāʾī, *Masādjid*, bāb 19). In another tradition it is related how Ḥasan and Ḥusain jumped on Muḥammad's back during his *sudjūd* (e.g. Aḥmad b. Ḥanbal, ii. 513). These were the good old days which the faḳīhs clearly did not wish back again.

III

Besides the five daily ṣalāts there are some that are not compulsory; al-Ghazzālī divides them into three categories: *sunna*, *mustaḥabb* and *taṭawwuʿ* (*Iḥyāʾ*, Cairo 1302, i. 174); some of them may have come into use after Muḥammad's death and were therefore never given legal force, others had already fallen somewhat into desuetude in Muḥammad's lifetime.

The latter is true of the night-ṣalāt (*ṣalāt al-lail*). This name is the most usual in the Ḥadīth, while in the Ḳurʾān *tahadjdjud* (Sūra xvii. 79) is used. The etymology of this word (the "waking") suggests a close connection with the Christian vigils and especially with the custom of keeping awake (Syriac *shahrā*), which was much cultivated among ascetics and mystics of Western Asia. We have detailed knowledge of this rite from Syriac ascetic literature; in it the keeping awake is in itself a very meritorious work; it is usually combined with the reading of scripture, meditation and ritual prayer. We must imagine the *tahadjdjud* to have been something similar. In the description of the nightly exercises in the *Lailat al-Ḳadr*, and in the nights of Ramaḍān in general, the name *ḳiyām* is preferably used, which shows that great value was put upon standing and waking in themselves.

That such nightly exercises were zealously carried through in the oldest Muslim community is clear from the Ḥadīth. For further details see the article TAHADJDJUD. Here we shall only say that even in Muḥammad's lifetime these exercises had been deprived of their obligatory character (Abū Dāʾūd, *Taṭawwuʿ*, bāb 17, 26; al-Nasāʾī, *Ḳiyām al-lail*, bāb 2; al-Dārimī, *Ṣalāt*, bāb 165).

The night-ṣalāt is closely connected with the *witr*. This word means "uneven" and the rite really consists in the addition of one *rakʿa* to the even number of *rakʿa*'s in the night-ṣalāt. For further information see the article WITR. How varying the practice was in the oldest community with regard to the daily ṣalāts may be seen from the statements regarding the *ṣalāt al-ḍuḥā*, the only one in the forenoon. In Aḥmad b. Ḥanbal, i. 147, the time is fixed in the following way: Muḥammad used to perform the *ḍuḥā* when the sun had risen the same distance from its starting point as it is distant from its place of setting at the *ṣalāt al-ʿaṣr*. Some make Muḥammad recommend the *ṣalāt al-ḍuḥā* (al-Nasāʾī, *Ḳiyām al-lail*, bāb 28; *Ṣiyām*, bāb 81; al-Dārimī, *Ṣalāt*, bāb 151; Aḥmad b. Ḥanbal, ii. 175, 265 bis, 271, etc.) and perform it regularly (Aḥmad b. Ḥanbal, i. 89, ii. 38); it is even said that it was *farīḍa* for him and *sunna* for the Muslims (do., i. 231, 232, 317 bis). Others again say that Muḥammad only performed this ṣalāt once or that the authority in question only saw him do it once (al-Bukhārī, *Adhān*, bāb 41; Muslim, *Ṣalāt al-musāfirīn*, trad. 80, 81; Abū Dāʾūd, *Taṭawwuʿ*, bāb 12; Aḥmad b. Ḥanbal, iii. 156); or that Muḥammad only performed it on returning from a journey (Muslim, *Ṣalāt al-musāfirīn*, trad. 75, 76). Such statements are supported by the traditions which say that the great authorities like Abū Bakr, ʿUmar and Ibn ʿUmar did not perform the *ṣalāt al-ḍuḥā* (al-Bukhāri, *Tahadjdjud*, bāb 31; al-Dārimī, *Ṣalāt*, bāb 152). The last named goes so far as to call it a *bidʿa* (= innovation; a strong word) (Muslim, *Ḥadjdj*, trad. 220; Aḥmad b. Ḥanbal, ii. 128 *sq.*, 155).

The ṣalāts before and after the obligatory ones, usually consisting of two *rakʿa*'s, are very numerous. Before and after the *Ṣalāt al-fadjr*: al-Bukhārī, *Adhān*, bāb 15; Abū Dāʾūd, *Taṭawwuʿ*, bāb 6. Before and after the *Ṣalāt al-ẓuhr*: al-Bukhārī, *Tahadjdjud*, bāb 25; Muslim, *Ṣalāt al-musāfirīn*, trad. 150, 106. Before and after the *Ṣalāt al-ʿaṣr*, but care should be taken to avoid coinciding with the sunset (see the article MIḲĀT): Abū Dāʾūd, *Taṭawwuʿ*, bāb 8; al-Bukhārī, *Mawāḳīt*. bāb 53; cf. *Maghāzī*, bāb 69. Before and after the *Ṣalāt al-maghrib*: al-Bukhārī, *Tahadjdjud*, bāb 35, 25 (six *Rakʿa*'s after the *Ṣalāt al-maghrib*: al-Tirmidhī, *Mawāḳīt*, bāb 203). After the *Ṣalāt al-ʿishāʾ*: al-Bukhārī, *Tahadjdjud*, bāb 25. But it is reported even of Muḥammad that he did not observe all these voluntary ṣalāts every day; the number is usually fixed at 16 or 12 (Aḥmad b. Ḥanbal, i. 111, 142, 143, 146, 147 *sq.*). In addition there are such *rawātib* on different days of the week and month (see al-Ghazzālī, *Iḥyāʾ*, i. 174 *sqq.* in bāb 7 of the chapter *Ṣalāt*) and on different occasions, such as on entering a mosque, returning from a journey (al-Bukhārī, *Ṣalāt*, bāb 60; Muslim, *Musāfirīn*, trad. 74).

IV

One may perform the daily ṣalāt by oneself; but it is recommended to perform it with the community (on differences of opinion on this question see al-Nawawī, *op. cit.*, i. 126 *sq.*). In any case, according to al-Nawawī, there is no obligation on women; it is even not recommended for them. In the Ḥadīth the advantages of the congregational ṣalāt are strongly emphasized (e.g. al-Bukhārī, *Adhān*, bāb 29—31, 34; Muslim, *Masādjid*, trad. 245—259, 271—282; al-Nasāʾī, *Aʾimma*, bāb 42, 45, 48—50, 52). The mosque is at the same time recommended as the place of assembly, although not obligatory, nor does the validity depend on a certain number of participants being present. In Abū Isḥāḳ al-Shīrāzī (*Tanbīh*, p. 31; cf. Ibn Mādja, *Iḳāma*, bāb 5) it is said that two persons can hold a *djamāʿa*. Very often ṣalāts performed by three individuals are described (e.g. Muslim, *Masādjid*, trad. 269).

One is recommended to go quietly to the ṣalāt (al-Bukhārī, *Adhān*, bāb 20, 21, 23; Muslim, *Masādjid*, trad. 151—155). It is also considered particularly meritorious to take one's place some time before the commencement of the ṣalāt and to wait some time after its conclusion (Aḥmad b. Ḥanbal, ii. 266, 277, 289 *sq.*, 301). If anyone comes so late that he can only take part in one *rakʿa* he has nevertheless "achieved the ṣalāt" (al-Bukhārī, *Mawāḳīt*, bāb 29; Muslim, *Masādjid*, trad. 161—165 etc.; the opposite view is held by Mālik, *Wuḳūt*, trad.

16). Even if one enters the mosque after already performing the ṣalāt concerned by oneself, one should take part in the ṣalāt with the congregation (Abū Dā'ūd, *Ṣalāt*, bāb 56; al-Tirmidhī, *Mawāḳīt*, bāb 49). The opposite view, however, has also its supporters (Abū Dā'ūd, *Ṣalāt*, bāb 57). The frequently mentioned rule is that one should make up in private for what one has missed in the *djamā'a* (Aḥmad b. Ḥanbal, ii. 237, 238, 239, 270, etc.).

The worshippers arrange themselves in rows (*ṣaff*) on the closed and good order of which much stress is laid (al-Bukhārī, *Adhān*, bāb 71, 72, 74—76, 114; Muslim, *Ṣalāt*, trad. 122—128; Abū Dā'ūd, bāb 93—100; Aḥmad b. Ḥanbal, iii. 3, 112 *sq.*, 114, 122, etc.). The places in the front row have special advantages (al-Bukhārī, *Adhān*, bāb 9, 73; Muslim, *Ṣalāt*, trad. 129—132); within this row again the places on the right of the *Imām* are especially recommended (Ibn Mādja, *Iḳāma*, bāb 34). This, however, is true only of men; women are advised to take their places in the last row (Aḥmad b. Ḥanbal, ii. 247, 336, 354, 370). The *ṣalāt al-djamā'a* is conducted by an imām who takes up a position before the front row, or, if there are only two individuals present besides him, between the two or so that one is on his right and the other behind him (Abū Dā'ūd, *Ṣalāt*, bāb 98; al-Nasā'ī, *Taṭbīḳ*, bāb 1; Aḥmad b. Ḥanbal, i. 451).

It is laid down that one should copy the imām exactly (al-Bukhārī, *Adhān*, bāb 51—53, 74, 82 etc.). Anyone who neglects this rule exposes himself to punishment from God (Aḥmad b. Ḥanbal, ii. 425; Mālik, *Nidā'*, trad. 57).

Mittwoch (*op. cit.*, p. 22; cf. thereon Becker in *Der Islam*, iii. 386 *sqq.*) has pointed out that the imām corresponds to the *sh^elī^aḥ has-ṣibbūr* at the Jewish service. At the latter as in Islām the duties can be carried through by any member of the community qualified to do so. In Muḥammad's lifetime the position in Madīna was that it only happened exceptionally that the Prophet did not conduct the ṣalāt. During his last illness and also on other occasions when he was absent Abū Bakr is said to have usually represented him. The Ḥadīth loves to expand itself on this point; in this we have probably to consider many things as reflections of the events after Muḥammad's death. The conducting of the ṣalāt was then of tremendous importance, as is clear from the manifold meanings of the word imām. The leader of the *djamā'a* in the mosque of the Prophet was naturally also the leader of the community in political matters. Gradually there came about a separation of the functions but the Caliph and the leader of the smallest village *djamā'a* alike retain the title of *imām*.

While the imām — at least in the days of the early Caliphs — was appointed to the mosque of the Prophet, in the provinces an alternation in the exercise of the duties was more to be expected. In the canonical Ḥadīth we look in vain for a regular usage in the provinces. Perhaps it may be concluded from this that in the first century of the Hidjra no regular usage had yet developed. If a number of persons assemble for the *djamā'a*, sometimes it is said that the oldest (al-Bukhārī, *Adhān*, bāb 17, 18, 35, 49, 140; *Djihād*, bāb 42; al-Nasā'ī, *Adhān*, bāb 7 etc.), sometimes the one with the best knowledge of the Ḳur'ān should conduct the ṣalāt (Muslim, *Masādjid*, trad. 289—291; al-Nasā'ī, *Adhān*, bāb 8; Aḥmad b. Ḥanbal, iii. 24, 34, 36 etc.). Slaves and freedmen could perform the duties (al-Bukhārī, *Adhān*, bāb 54). In a Zaidī tradition there is even a mention of women as imām ("*Corpus Juris*" *di Zaid ibn 'Alī*, ed. Griffini, No. 189). The question behind whom one may perform the ṣalāt is also discussed in the Fiḳh books and in the collections of traditions (al-Nawawī, *op. cit.*, p. 131 *sqq.*; al-Bukhārī, *Adhān*, bāb 56; Abū Dā'ūd, *Ṣalāt*, bāb 63).

The responsibility of the imām (Aḥmad b. Ḥanbal, ii. 232, 284, 377 *sq.*, etc.) as well as his heavenly reward are emphasized (Abū Dā'ūd, *Ṣalāt*, bāb 58; Ibn Mādja, *Iḳāma*, bāb 47). One should retire if someone is there who has greater authority in religious matters (al-Nasā'ī, *A'imma*, bāb 3, 6). No one should thrust himself on the people (Abū Dā'ūd, *Ṣalāt*, bāb 62; al-Tirmidhī, *Mawāḳīt*, bāb 149). The imām is not to be a stranger but a local man (Abū Dā'ūd, *Ṣalāt*, bāb 65; al-Tirmidhī, *Mawāḳīt*, bāb 147; Mālik, *Ṣalāt al-djamā'a*, trad. 15).

The direction of the *djamā'a* gradually developed into a more or less definite office. In Egypt the imām was often a small tradesman or a schoolmaster (Lane, *Manners and Customs*, p. 96 *sq.*). In the larger mosques there are two imāms appointed who are paid out of the funds of the mosque. In Mecca we find the most distinguished scholars and quite insignificant individuals alike acting as imām (Snouck Hurgronje, *Mekka*, ii. 234, note). In Indonesia the duties are often performed by the *pangulu*, who also holds juridical offices (cf. that article and Snouck Hurgronje *Verspr. Geschr.*, ii. 116 *sq.*, 177; *De Atjèhers*, i. 89). See further the article MASDJID G, 1.

Besides the five daily ṣalāts there are special services to be held by the community on certain occasions. The first place among these is occupied by the Friday ṣalāt; for a description of which see the article DJUM'A. For the ṣalāt on the two feasts see the article 'ĪD, for the ṣalāt for rain see ISTISḲĀ' and for the *Ṣalāt al-kusūf* see KUSŪF. Here we shall only say that much ancient and popular matter has survived in these divine services.

Of quite another kind, i.e. special or short forms of the true Muslim ṣalāt, is the ṣalāt on journeys, which consists of two *rak'a*'s. The jurists naturally devote much attention to the question of what is meant by a journey. Another alleviation on journeys consists in the combination of two or more ṣalāts into one (*djam'*). The Ḥadīth has much information on the subject (e.g. al-Bukhārī, *Taḳṣīr al-ṣalāt*, bāb 6, 13—19; Muslim, *Ṣalāt al-musāfirīn*, trad. 42—58 etc.). As mentioned in section I, it is said that Muḥammad combined several ṣalāts in Madīna; on the significance of such statements cf. what is said there and also al-Nawawī, *op. cit.* p. 159 *sq.*

A special ṣalāt already described in the Ḳur'ān is that which is held when danger threatens from the enemy (Sūra iv. 101—103). The deviation from the usual ritual consists mainly in the fact that the believers are arranged in two rows of which one keeps watch with weapon in hand during the *sudjūd* of the other; they repeat this in turn until all have performed the *sudjūd*. The *tashahhud* is then recited by them all together. If the enemy is to be expected from another direction than that of the *ḳibla* the ritual is modified as conditions demand (for further information see e.g. al-Nawawī, *op. cit.*, p. 181 *sqq.*). In this case also the ṣalāt may be abbreviated (Muslim, *Ṣalāt al-musāfirīn*, trad. 4, 5; al-Nasā'ī, *Ṣalāt al-khawf*, bāb 4, 7, 23, 24, 26, 27). There is even mention of a *ṣalāt al-khawf* of only one *rak'a* (Aḥmad b. Ḥanbal, i. 237, 243).

In conclusion we must here deal briefly with the ṣalāt for the dead (*al-ṣalāt 'ala 'l-maiyit*, *ṣalāt al-*

dj̲ināza). It is a common duty (*farḍ al-kifāya*) which can only be omitted in exceptional cases (cf. Snouck Hurgronje, *Verspr. Geschr.*, i. 138, note 3). In some traditions the ṣalāt is ordered for every dead Muslim (Ibn Mād̲j̲a, *Dj̲anāʾiz*, bāb 31; al-Nasāʾī, *Dj̲anāʾiz*, bāb 57). In the Ḥadīt̲h̲ (al-Buk̲h̲ārī, *Dj̲anāʾiz*, bāb 23, 85; *Tafsīr*, Sūra 9, bāb 12, 13; Muslim, *Faḍāʾil al-Ṣaḥāba*, trad. 25 etc.) it is related how Muḥammad held the ṣalāt for the dead ʿAbd Allāh b. Ubaiy, the arch-munāfiḳ, and was reproved by ʿUmar for doing so. Therefore Sūra ix. 84 was revealed: "and never perform the ṣalāt for one of them who dies and stand not at his grave, for they are unbelievers against Allāh and His Messenger and they die as *fāsiḳ*" (on the legal definition of the conception of *fāsiḳ* see Snouck Hurgronje, *Verspr. Geschr.*, ii. 97).

In the Ḥadīt̲h̲ it is further related that Muḥammad omitted the ṣalāt in cases where the deceased had committed suicide (Muslim, *Dj̲anāʾiz*, trad. 107; Abū Dāʾūd, *K̲h̲arād̲j̲*, bāb 46). Al-Nawawī, *op. cit.*, p. 225, says, however, that no exception was made in this case. The Ḥadīt̲h̲ also tells us that Muḥammad refused to hold this ṣalāt unless the debts of the deceased had already been paid (al-Buk̲h̲ārī, *Ḥawālāt*, bāb 3; Abū Dāʾūd, *Buyūʿ*, bāb 9; Aḥmad b. Ḥanbal, ii. 290, 399). In law therefore the mourners are recommended to settle this matter quickly (al-Nawawī, i. 221). In the Ḥadīt̲h̲ we find contradictory statements regarding the question whether Muḥammad held the *ṣalāt al-dj̲ināza* on behalf of those who had been legally executed (Abū Dāʾūd, *Dj̲anāʾiz*, bāb 47; al-Nasāʾī, *Dj̲anāʾiz*, bāb 63, 64). We shall hardly be wrong if we suppose that this ṣalāt also retained certain pre-Muḥammadan customs (cf. A. J. Wensinck, *Some Semitic Rites of Mourning and Religion* in *Verh. AW.* New Series, vol. xviii. No. 1, Chap. 2 and 3). According to Abū Isḥāḳ al-S̲h̲īrāzī (ed. Juynboll, p. 47 *sq.*), the following is the order of the ṣalāt for the dead: the imām stands at the top of the bier in the case of a man, at the bottom in the case of a woman (this is the old tradition; cf. al-Buk̲h̲ārī, *Dj̲anāʾiz*, bāb 63; Muslim, *Dj̲anāʾiz*, trad. 87, 88 etc.); he pronounces the *nīya* and utters four *takbīr*'s with hands raised; at the first he recites the *Fātiḥa*, at the second he utters the eulogy on Muḥammad, at the third he pronounces the *duʿāʾ* for the dead man, at the fourth a *duʿāʾ* for those who take part in the service, the two *taslīma*'s conclude the ceremony.

Difference of opinion prevails regarding the place where the *ṣalāt al-dj̲ināza* should be held. There are indications that in ancient Madīna the *muṣallā* [q.v.] was used, for example in the case of the service for Nad̲j̲ās̲h̲ī, who died in Abyssinia (al-Buk̲h̲ārī, *Dj̲anāʾiz*, bāb 4; Muslim, *Dj̲anāʾiz*, trad. 63, 64). In Ibn Saʿd, I/ii. 14, it is said that the *ṣalāt* was held by Muḥammad in the home of the deceased. People therefore thought it an innovation when the body of Saʿd b. Abī Waḳḳāṣ was brought into the mosque at the request, it is said, of ʿĀʾis̲h̲a or of the widows of the Prophet. ʿĀʾis̲h̲a is said to have replied to the complaints that were made: "How short is the memory of the people. Muḥammad was indeed wont to hold this ṣalāt in the mosque" (Muslim, *Dj̲anāʾiz*, trad. 99—101). Muslim's commentator, al-Nawawī, gives on this passage (as al-Zurḳānī does on Mālik, *Dj̲anāʾiz*, trad. 22) the points of view of the different schools with reference to the legal category in which they place the holding of this ṣalāt in the mosque (on the question cf. also *Semitic Rites of Mourning and Religion*, p. 2—4). In any case it is the custom in various parts of the Muslim world to-day to perform this ṣalāt in a mosque (Lane, *Manners and Customs*, p. 526; Snouck Hurgronje, *Mekka*, ii. 189). In Atjeh, on the other hand, as in usually also the case in Java, it takes place in the front part of the enclosure before the house of the deceased (Snouck Hurgronje, *The Achèhnese*, i. 423; do., *Verspr. Geschr.*, iv/i. 242). This is at least permitted by the law although not recommended (it depends on the *mad̲h̲hab*).

The body is not necessarily present at the ṣalāt. In Mecca it is the custom to hold the *ṣalāt al-dj̲ināza* for residents who have died away from home (*Mekka*, ii. 189). Justification may be claimed for this practice in the widespread tradition according to which Muḥammad held a service in Madīna for the dead Nad̲j̲ās̲h̲ī (cf. above).

See further the article DJ̲INĀZA.

V

The question of the significance of the ṣalāt is usually approached in a one-sided fashion by European critics. They like, it must be admitted, to follow Ranke in placing a high value on the ṣalāt as a disciplinary measure and certainly it is difficult to appreciate this too highly. A considerable part of the life of the community must have centred in and around the ṣalāt in Madīna in Muḥammad's life-time and through it the transformation of the old Arab mind into the Muslim must have taken place. The same phenomenon was afterwards repeated in the provinces of the Caliphate. The ṣalāt must have been one of the most effective formative elements in the communities.

The European, on the other hand, usually forms his judgment of the ṣalāt from his own point of view; the Protestant misses the intensification, the Roman Catholic the imposing ceremonial.

Both attitudes are wrong from a scientific standpoint. Whoever wishes to gain a clear idea of the significance of the ṣalāt must ask the question: "what does it mean to the Muslim?"

This question may be partly answered by observing the enthusiasm for the ṣalāt displayed by Muslims in different countries. The results of such observations almost everywhere go to suggest that there are few Muslims who regularly observe the five daily ṣalāts (Lane, *op. cit.*, p. 84; Snouck Hurgronje, *Verspr. Geschr.*, iv/i. 8, 16). In Indonesia the Achehnese, who were so prominent in the *dj̲ihād* [q.v.], only take part in small numbers in the congregational ṣalāt; in Banten (Java), in Palembang (Sumatra) and in isolated parts of the Archipelago on the other hand we find it much more religiously observed (Snouck Hurgronje, *Verspr. Geschr.*, iv/ii. 343 *sq.*; *The Achèhnese*, i. 86).

Lane's remarks regarding the ṣalāt in Egypt (*Manners and Customs*, p. 98) are important: "The utmost solemnity and decorum are observed in the public worship of the Muslims. Their looks and behaviour in the mosques are not those of enthusiastic devotion, but of calm and modest piety. Never are they guilty of a designedly irregular word or action during their prayers. The pride and fanaticism which they exhibit in common life, in intercourse with persons of their own or of a different faith, seem to be dropped on their entering the mosque, and they appear wholly absorbed in the adoration of their Creator — humble and downcast, yet without affected humility or a forced expression of countenance".

A rich source for the study of the significance of the ṣalāt in the religious life of the Muslims is to be found in literature. For the first two centuries it is mainly the Ḥadīth that we have to use. In the enumeration of the five pillars of Islām the ṣalāt always appears in the second place (al-Bukhārī, *Īmān*, bāb 2; Muslim, *Īmān*, trad. 19—22; in passing it may be noted that the first pillar is variously given). In the so frequently recurring story of the untutored Beduin who suddenly asks Muḥammad the question: "How shall I be saved?" the latter answers with a list of the duties imposed by Islām upon the believers, viz.: five ṣalāts daily, fasting in Ramaḍān and zakāt (al-Bukhārī, *Īmān*, bāb 34; Muslim, *Īmān*, trad. 8). In other traditions also, which enumerate the obligations of a Muslim, as, for example, in the commission given to Muʿādh b. Djabal when he was sent by Muḥammad to Yaman, we find mentioned besides the *tawḥīd* or the service of Allāh the five ṣalāts and the zakāt (e.g. al-Bukhārī, *Zakāt*, bāb 1; Muslim, *Īmān*, trad. 29—31). Here the ḥadjdj and the fasting in Ramaḍān are omitted. In the scale of the most meritorious works the ṣalāt often appears in the first place (al-Bukhārī, *Mawāḳit*, bāb 5; cf. Ibn Mādja, *Ṭahāra*, bāb 4; al-Dārimī, *Wuḍūʾ*, bāb 2). The strict observation of the five daily ṣalāts secures admission into Paradise (al-Nasāʾī, *Iḳāma*, bāb 6; Mālik, *Ṣalāt al-lail*, trad. 14 etc.). The omission of the ṣalāt is a bridge to unbelief and heathenism: "between man and polytheism and unbelief lies the neglect of the ṣalāt" (Muslim, *Īmān*, trad. 134; cf. al-Nasāʾī, *Ṣalāt*, bāb 8).

The cleansing power of the ṣalāt is allegorically described in Tradition: "The ṣalāt is like a stream of sweet water which flows past the door of each one of you; into it he plunges five times a day; do ye think that anything remains of his uncleanness after that?" (Mālik, *Ḳaṣr al-ṣalāt fi 'l-safar*, trad. 91; cf. Aḥmad b. Ḥanbal, i. 71 *sq.*, 177, ii. 375, 426, 441, iii. 305, 317 etc.). It is described without allegory in the equally well-known tradition: "an obligatory ṣalāt is a cleansing for the sins which are committed between it and the following one" (*op. cit.*, ii. 229; as is well known grievous sins are usually excluded from the cleansing effect of pious exercises (*op. cit.*, ii. 359).

We have just quoted the tradition according to which the observation of the daily ṣalāts secures entrance into Paradise. The following utterance goes still further: "He who knows that the ṣalāt is a compulsory duty will enter Paradise" (*op. cit.*, i. 60). At the final reckoning on the Day of Resurrection the more or less faithful observance of the ṣalāt will be a consideration of the first importance: "The first thing to be dealt with is the ṣalāt; if this point is in order, the man has attained bliss; if not then he is lost (cf. al-Nasāʾī, *Ṣalāt*, bāb 9; al-Tirmidhī, *Mawāḳit*, bāb 188; Aḥmad b. Ḥanbal, i. 161 *sq.*, 171, ii. 290 etc.).

The ṣalāt should be performed devoutly with concentrated attention. It is often related how Muḥammad put away one of his garments because figures woven on it distracted his attention at the ṣalāt (al-Bukhārī, *Ṣalāt*, bāb 14; al-Nasāʾī, *Ḳibla*, bāb 20; cf. bāb 12).

That the ṣalāt does not, as is sometimes said, imply only the performance of a duty but that the heart is in it too is seen from the following tradition; Muḥammad said: "Of worldly things women and perfume are dearest to me and the ṣalāt is the comfort of my eyes" (Aḥmad b. Ḥanbal, iii. 128 bis, 285). Weeping at the ṣalāt is also sometimes mentioned (Abū Dāʾūd, *Ṣalāt*, bāb 156; al-Nasāʾī, *Sahw*, bāb 18; Aḥmad b. Ḥanbal, ii. 188, iv. 25 bis, cf. 26).

By far the most significant characteristic of the ṣalāt is the one which we find in two different settings, namely that the ṣalāt is intimate conversation with Allāh. On the one hand it is found in the Ḥadīth, in which spitting in the direction of the *ḳibla* during the ṣalāt is forbidden, the reason given being that the ṣalāt is intimate conversation with Allāh (al-Bukhārī, *Ṣalāt*, bāb 39; *Mawāḳit*, bāb 8; Muslim, *Masādjid*, trad. 54; Aḥmad b. Ḥanbal, ii. 34 *sq.*, 144, iii. 176, 188, 199 *sq.*, 234, 273, 278, 291 etc.). On the other hand we find it expressed in the following form: "If one of you performs the ṣalāt he is in confidential converse with his Lord; at that time he ought to know exactly what he says in this way with his Lord; therefore no one should drown the voice of another at the recitation" (Aḥmad b. Ḥanbal, ii. 36, 67, 129). An illustration of this utterance is given in the following *ḥadīth ḳudsī*: Allāh says: "I have divided the ṣalāt into two halves between Myself and My servant, one of which belongs to Me while the other is for My servant and My servant obtains what he asks". The Messenger of God said: "recite!": when the servant says: "Praise be to Allāh, the Lord of the Worlds!", Allāh says: "My servant hath praised Me"; when the servant says: "to the Merciful and Compassionate", Allāh says: "My servant hath glorified Me"; when the servant says: "to the Lord of the Day of Judgment", Allāh says: "My servant hath praised Me"; when my servant says: "Thee do we serve and Thee do we beseech for help", Allāh says: "this verse is between Me and My servant and he receives what he has prayed for"; when the servant says: "lead us the right way, the way of those whom Thou favourest, with whom Thou art not angry and who do not err", Allāh says: "This belongs to My servant and he receives what he has prayed for" (Aḥmad b. Ḥanbal, ii. 460).

That the ṣalāt was also used as a means of healing is not remarkable in view of similar phenomena in other religions (Ibn Mādja, *Ṭibb*, bāb 10; Aḥmad b. Ḥanbal, ii. 390, 403). At the same time we may mention the *ṣalāt al-ḥādja*, which is observed to secure the attainment of some ardently desired object (al-Tirmidhī, *Witr*, bāb 17), and the *ṣalāt al-istikhāra* [see ISTIKHĀRA] before a more or less important decision (al-Bukhārī, *Tahadjdjud*, bāb 25; Abū Dāʾūd, *Witr*, bāb 31; al-Tirmidhī, *Witr*, bāb 18; Aḥmad b. Ḥanbal, iii. 344 etc.).

The description of the ṣalāt as *munādjāt* is characteristic of the meditative tendency found even in the oldest period of Islām (on this see especially L. Massignon, *Essai sur les origines du lexique technique de la mystique musulmane*, Paris 1922); it has certainly been one of the main avenues by which mysticism entered Islām from without.

One of the oldest Muslim mystics, al-Muḥāsibī (d. 243/857), wrote a tractate on the significance of the ṣalāt (cf. Massignon, *op. cit.*, p. 259, note 1) and the philosopher al-Tirmidhī (d. 285/898) expounded the mystical side of the ṣalāt in 42 aphorisms (quoted in Massignon, *op. cit.*, p. 259). Among the more modern mystics the ṣalāt gives place in importance to *dhikr* and *wird*. Al-Ḳushairī does not devote a separate chapter to it in his *Risāla*. In al-Hudjwīrī it appears as especially suitable for novices, who are to recognize in it to some extent a reflection of the whole mystic way. To them the *ṭahāra* represents the conversion, the *ḳibla* the dependence on spiritual leadership, the recitation the *dhikr*, the *rukūʿ* humility, the prostration self-knowledge, the *tashahhud* the *uns*, the *taslīm* renunciation of the world. Of the real mystics everyone sees something different in the ṣalāt: to one it is a means to *ḥuḍūr* with God, to another *g͟haiba* (al-Hud͟jwīrī, *Kas͟hf al-maḥd͟jūb*, transl. Nicholson, p. 301 *sqq.*). Al-Hud͟jwīrī, however, also emphasizes the affection of various Ṣūfīs for the ṣalāt.

Of the philosophers, Ibn Sīnā (Avicenna) is the only one to be mentioned. He wrote a short treatise on the ṣalāt (*Fi 'l-kas͟hf ʿan māhīyat al-ṣalāt wa-ḥikma tas͟hrīʿihā* in *D͟jāmiʿ al-badāʾiʿ*, Cairo 1335 (1917), p. 2—14). According to him, the essence of the ṣalāt is the recognition of God in His existence and necessity of it. It is exoteric or esoteric according to the character of the believer who performs it. The law-giver knew that not all men can ascend the steps of the spirit. Such men therefore require corporal discipline and compulsory mortification, to keep their natural impulses in check. This is the exoteric side of the ṣalāt. Its true esoteric significance is the *mus͟hāhadat al-Ḥaḳḳ* with pure heart and a soul which is liberated and purified from desires (*amānī*). Ibn Sīnā then proceeds to deal with the saying that a man at prayer is in intimate converse with his Lord (see above). This can, he says, only happen outside of the material world. Those who are in this state of mind are spiritually in the presence of God and the gaze upon the deity (*al-Ilāh*) in a real vision. The ṣalāt is therefore a real *mus͟hāhada* and a pure worship, i.e. the real divine love and spiritual vision.

Al-G͟hazzālī's chapter *ṣalāt* has in the *Iḥyāʾ* in the *rubʿ al-ibādāt* a position between *ṭahāra* and *zakāt* (as in the Fiḳh). As with the other *ʿibādāt* it should be observed in this case also with what meticulous accuracy he describes the legal regulations (ed. Cairo 1302, i. 140 *sqq.*) and how on the other hand he raises the ṣalāt to an ethico-mystical level which sufficiently meets all the demands of intensification. After what has been said above in II and III, we need only briefly survey here the latter side of his exposition. The inward *maʿānī* which bring the life of the ṣalāt to perfection are the six following: the presence of the heart (*ḥuḍūr al-ḳalb*), understanding, respect (*taʿẓīm*), reverence (*haiba*), hope and humility (*ḥayāʾ*).

Particularly significant are his remarks on the presence of the heart (p. 145). The faḳīhs demand the presence of the heart only at the *takbīr*; according to the *fuḳahāʾ al-mutawarriʿūn* and the *ʿulamāʾ al-āk͟hira*, on the other hand, the heart should be present at the whole ṣalāt. But only very few succeed in achieving this. The ideal ṣalāt is that of Ḥātim al-Aṣamm, who said: "When the time for the ṣalāt arrives, I perform a copious *wuḍūʿ* and go to the place where I want to perform the ṣalāt. There I sit till my limbs are rested, then I stand up, the Kaʿba straight in front of me, the *ṣirāṭ* under my feet, Paradise on my right, Hell on my left and the Angel of Death behind me; and I think that this ṣalāt is my last. I then stand wavering between hope and fear, join in the *takbīr* and *taḥḳīḳ*, recite with *tartīl*, perform the *rukūʿ* in submission and the *sud͟jūd* in humility, sit on my left thigh, spread out the upper part of the left foot and fix the right one on the great toe and accompany this with *ik͟hlāṣ*. Then I do not know whether my ṣalāt has been graciously accepted by Allāh or not (p. 139, 7 *sqq.*).

Al-G͟hazzālī lays down his ethical point of view in the sentence: If his ṣalāt does not restrain a man from evil and wrong-doing, he only obtains estrangement from God by it (cf. Sūra vi. 92).

In the chapter on "the useful remedies for securing the *ḥuḍūr al-ḳalb*" distracting thoughts are given as the principal obstacles which divert attention at the ṣalāt. These enemies are to be overcome by fighting their causes. These are of two kinds, external and internal. The external causes of distraction (*g͟hafla*, in the Syriac mystics *fehyā*) come from the organs of sense. One therefore ought to prevent these from being distracted. The *mutaʿabbidūn* therefore perform the ṣalāt in a dark cell with only sufficient room for the *sud͟jūd*. Ibn ʿUmar is said not to have allowed a single object in this cell. The internal causes of distraction exercise a much stronger effect. They have their root in earthly cares, thoughts and occupations. But desires have the most powerful influence. They are to be fought by meditation on the future world. All preparations for the ṣalāt and all its parts should be connected with the *āk͟hira*. At the *ad͟hān* one should think of the *nidāʾ* on the Day of the Resurrection. At the covering of the *ʿawra* one should enquire whether there is no internal *ʿawra* etc.

The highest goal of the ṣalāt is complete absorption in the Deity by humiliating oneself. Sufyān al-T͟hawrī is reputed to have said: "If a man does not know humility, his ṣalāt is invalid". This is laid down in two special sections (*Bayān is͟htirāṭ al-k͟hus͟hūʿ wa-ḥuḍūr al-ḳalb*, p. 145 *sq.*, and *Ḥikāyāt wa-ak͟hbār fi ṣalāt al-k͟hās͟hiʿin*, p. 157 *sqq.*). In the latter he shows by several examples how much the great leaders used to be absorbed in their ṣalāt.

ṢĀLIḤ, a prophet who was sent to the Arab people T͟hamūd. He is, as usual, depicted as a sign and a warning in the style of Muḥammad; he demanded that his countrymen should turn to him and pray to Allāh alone (Sūra vii. 73; xi. 61; xxvi. 141); he called their attention to the benefits received from God (vii. 74; li. 43) and prided himself on seeking for no reward from them (xxvi. 145). But they rejected him abruptly, called him bewitched (xxvi. 153), a man like themselves, who could make no claim to revelations (liv. 24); they could not surrender the religion of their fathers (xi. 62) and scorned the idea of a day of judgment (lxix. 4). His appearance produced a schism in the people (xxvii. 45) for only the weak believed in him, while the strong scoffed at him (vii. 75). The only new feature was that they had placed their hope in him before he irritated them by his preaching (xi. 66), which, if based on some corresponding incident, would be an interesting contribution to the history of Muḥammad. Then follows the special story of this prophet. Allāh sent them as a sign a she-camel (xvii, 59) and Ṣāliḥ begged them to allow it to feed unharmed and to share water with it (vii. 73; xxvi. 155; liv. 28). But they lamed it and killed it (vii. 77; xi. 65; xxvi. 157) by the hand of a particularly godless individual among them (xci. 12; liv. 29) and scornfully asked Ṣāliḥ to inflict the threatened punishment (vii. 77). He told them to hide three days in their houses (xi. 65); then a tremendous storm broke out (xi. 67; li. 44; according to vii. 78 an earthquake; cf. also liv. 31; lxix. 5) and on the following morning they lay dead in their houses. In the later Muslim stories of prophets these brief features are elaborated in various ways.

This story has a certain amount of foundation in fact in as much as the T͟hamūd according to vii. 74 the successors of the ʿĀd, were an ancient Arab tribe known also from other sources (see the art. T͟HAMŪD). The dwellings which the T͟hamūd had hewn out of the rocks (lxxxix. 9; vii. 74; xxvi. 149), often mentioned in the texts, the remains of which were still visible (xxix. 38), are undoubtedly the tombs, containing remains of human bones, hewn in the rocks of al-ʿÖla, which led Philippe Berger to the further supposition that the word *kafrā* (tomb) found in the inscriptions there may have been explained as *kufr* (unbelief). But whence Muḥammad got the name Ṣāliḥ and the story of the camel cannot be ascertained. It is further remarkable that the stories of Ṣāliḥ and Hūd [q.v.] are in contradiction to the usual teaching of Muḥammad in the Meccan period to the effect that no prophet had been sent to the Arabs before him (xxviii. 46; xxxii. 3; xxxiv, 44; xxxvi. 6). The stories of these two prophets are found in the earliest Meccan Sūras e.g. liii. 50 *sq.*; lxxxv, 17 *sq.*; lxxxix. 9; xci. 11 *sqq.*, and frequently recur in the following sections; on the other hand they disappear in the Madīna revelations except for the brief enumeration in ix. 70.

Bibliography: The Ḳurʾān commentaries on Sūra vii; al-Ṭabarī, ed. de Goeje, I, 244—251; al-Masʿūdī, *Murūdj al-dhahab* (Paris, 1861—1877), iii. 85—90; al-Thaʿlabī, *Ḳiṣaṣ al-anbiyāʾ* or *ʿArāis al-madjālis*, Cairo 1290, p. 58 *sqq.*; Grimme, *Mohammed*, Münster 1892—95, ii. 80; Philippe Berger, *L'Arabie avant Mahomet d'après les inscriptions*, Paris 1885; Caetani, *Annali dell' Islām*, ii/i. A.H. 9 § 34; cf. Register; J. Horovitz, *Koranische Untersuchungen*, p. 123.

SĀLIMĪYA, school of dogmatic theologians, which was formed among the Mālikite Sunnites in Baṣra in the iiith—ivth century.

Founded by Sahl al-Tustarī [q.v.], who died in 283/896, it takes its name from his principal disciple, Abū ʿAbd Allāh Muḥammad Ibn Sālim (d. 297/909), and his son Abu 'l-Ḥasan Aḥmad Ibn Sālim (d. 350/960) who succeeded one another at its head. The second Ibn Sālim, a friend of the Ḳurʾān exegesist Ibn Mudjāhid, is well known from the eulogies of his pupil and successor Abū Ṭālib al-Makkī (d. 380/990) in his *Ḳūt al-ḳulūb* and from the criticisms of his adversary Abū Naṣr al-Sarrādj (d. 377/987) in his *Lumaʿ* (ed. Nicholson).

The main theses of the Sālimīya have been preserved for us by their Ḥanbalī adversaries, particularly Abū Yaʿlā Ibn al-Farrāʾ (d. 458/1066) who enumerates sixteen of them (ten were given in the *Ghunya* attributed to al-Djīlānī):

(a) God never ceases for a moment to be creating; his uncreated efficiency (*tafʿīl*) makes him thus equivalently present everywhere, especially in the elocution of every reader reading the Ḳurʾān.

(b) God has an uncreated will (*mashīʾa*) and created decisions (*irāda*) by which the faults of created beings are produced without his wishing their culpability; Satan in the end obeyed God; at the Day of Judgment God will appear in a human form, transfigured, immediately perceptible by all creatures (*tadjallī*).

(c) The practice of the law is realised by an effort of voluntary adaptation (*iktisāb*, opposed to the quietism of the Karrāmīya); endurance is superior to enjoyment; the prophets are superior to the saints; wisdom is synonymous with faith.

(d) Mystical union consists for the believer in gaining consciousness of his personality, of the divine "ego" in the proportion in which he has been pre-eternally invested with it (*sirr al-rubūbīya*).

The Ḥanbalī polemicists, from Ibn al-Farrāʾ to Ibn al-Djawzī and Ibn Taimīya, with perspicacity denounced the semi-Muʿtazilī affinities and the monistic tendencies of these theses, which al-Ḥallādj, al-Ashʿarī and Ibn Khafīf had criticized from the first in different degrees. Nevertheless since the Sālimīya were with the Karrāmīya the only Sunnī theologians to support belief in the personal survival of the soul (between death and the resurrection), it is to them that the majority of Sunnī mystics, from Abū Bakr al-Wāsiṭī, have attached themselves. Al-Ghazzālī in the second period of his life designed his *Iḥyāʾ* on the lines of the *Ḳūt* of a Sālimī, Abū Ṭālib al-Makkī. The semi-Ismāʿīlī school of Andalusian mystics of the sixth century — from Ibn Barradjān (d. 536/1141) and Ibn Ḳasyī to Ibn ʿArabī [q.v.] — owes, as Ibn Taimīya has pointed out, several of its monist formulae to the Sālimīya. Other Sālimīya theses have been traditionally preserved in the order of the SHĀDHILĪYA [q.v.].

Bibliography: Abū Ṭālib Muḥammad al-Makkī, *Ḳūt al-ḳulūb*, Cairo 1310, 2 volumes (the text seems to have been purified at an early period); Ibn al-Farrāʾ, *Muʿtamad fī uṣūl al-dīn*, MS. Damascus, Ẓāhirīya Library, Part "Tawḥīd", No. 45; ʿAbd Ḳādir al-Djīlānī, *Ghuniya li-ṭālibī ṭarīḳ al-ḥaḳḳ*, Cairo 1288, i. 83—84; al-Maḳdisī, in the *BGA*, iii. 126; Ibn al-Dāʿī, *Tabṣirat al-ʿawāmm*, lith. Teheran 1313, p. 391; Goldziher, *ZDMG*, 1907, lxi. 73—80; Amedroz, *JRAS*, 1912, p. 572—575; Massignon, *Essai sur les origines...de la mystique musulmane*, 1922, p. 264—270; do. *Passion d'al-Ḥallādj*, Index, s.v.; A. S. Tritton, *Muslim Theology*, 1947, p. 136.

SALMĀN AL-FĀRISĪ, a companion of the Prophet and one of the most popular figures of Muslim legend. According to one tradition, the most complete version of which among the many that exist goes back to Muḥammad b. Isḥāḳ, he was the son of a *dihḳān* of the Persian village of Djaiy or old-Iṣfahān. According to other stories, he belonged to the vicinity of Rāmhurmuz and his Irānian name was Māhbeh (Māyeh) or Rūzbeh (cf. Justi, *Iran. Namenbuch*, p. 217, 277). Attracted by Christianity while still a boy he left his father's house to follow a Christian monk and having changed his teachers several times arrived in Syria; from there he went right down to the Wādi 'l-Ḳurā in Central Arabia seeking the prophet who was said to have restored the religion of Ibrāhīm, the imminence of whose coming had been predicted to him by his last teacher on his deathbed. Betrayed by Kalbī Beduins, who were acting as his guides through the desert, and sold as a slave to a Jew, he had occasion to go to Yathrib where soon after his arrival the *hidjra* of Muḥammad took place. Recognizing in the latter the marks of the prophet which the monk had described to him, Salmān became a Muslim and purchased his liberty from his Jewish master, after being miraculously aided by Muḥammad himself to raise the sum necessary to pay his ransom.

The name of Salmān is associated with the siege of Madīna by the Mekkans for it was he who on this occasion advised the digging of the ditch (*khandaḳ*) by means of which the Muslims defended themselves from the enemy. Horovitz (see the *Bibliography*) in 1922 put forward the thesis that, as the earliest accounts of the *yawm al-khandaḳ* make no mention of Salmān's intervention, the story was probably invented in order to attribute to a Persian the introduction of a system of defence the name of which is of Persian origin. Massignon, on the other hand, has come in 1934, after a careful consideration of the sources, to the conclusion that the legend of Salmān contains elements of historic truth; as a *Mawlā* of the Prophet he may have earned at an early time the sympathy of the *mawālī* in Kūfa and thus have become, although his name was Arabic — or in any case Semitic —, the prototype of the converted Persians (just as the Abyssinians and the Greeks are represented by Bilāl and Ṣuhaib respectively), who played such a part in the development of Islām; as such he has become the national hero of Muslim Persia and one of the favourite personages of the *Shuʿūbīya* (cf. Goldziher, *Muh. Studien*, i. 117, 136, 153, 212).

In the tradition of the Persian Shīʿites Salmān is particularly notable for two features, firstly his intimacy with the family of the Prophet, expressed by Muḥammad's words: *Salmān minnā ahl al-bait*, and secondly by his defence of the principle of legitimacy, by his enunciation: *kardīd wa-nakardīd*, which is said to refer to the election of Abū Bakr after the Prophet's death. Salmān approved of Abū Bakr as an able leader, but he disapproved because ʿAlī had not been chosen. It is also reported that the annuity assigned to Salmān was equal to that of Ḥasan and Ḥusain.

The sources do not agree as to the date of Salmān's death. The greatest probability is for the first years of ʿUthmān's caliphate; he is said to have received from ʿUmar the governorship of al-Madāʾin and to have died there. Massignon supposes that the reason why he came to ʿIrāḳ was his alliance (*ḥilf*) with the Rabīʿa tribe of the ʿAbd al-Ḳais, who were later established in Kūfa. In any case his tomb is still pointed out in Madāʾin, to the north-west of the Ṭāḳ-i Kisrā; it is called after him Salmān Pāk (Salmān the Pure) and is already mentioned by al-Yaʿḳūbī in the third century (*BGA*, vii. 322). His sepulchral mosque, which was seen in its older form by Pietro della Valle in 1617 (*Viaggi*, ed. Gancia, Brighton 1843, i. 394), was renovated by Sulṭān Murād IV (1623—1640) and restored in 1322/1904—1905 (Herzfeld-Sarre, *Archäol. Reise im Euphrates- und Tigrisgebiet*, ii. 262). It is the object of numerous pilgrimages, especially on the part of Shīʿis, who do not fail to visit it in returning from Karbalāʾ (cf. Aubin, *La Perse d'aujourd'hui*, Paris 1908, p. 426—428). Other traditions locate the tomb of Salmān elsewhere: near Iṣbahān (Yāḳūt, *Muʿdjam*, ii. 170), Dāmaghān, Sudūd, Jerusalem, Lydda in Palestine. On the other hand, Salmān, like other persons who are said to have embraced Islām after long experiences with other religions, is also credited with an extraordinary long life (Goldziher, *Abhandlungen*, ii).

The figure of Salmān appears as one of the founders of Ṣūfism, along with the *aṣḥāb al-ṣuffa* (*K. al-lumaʿ*, ed. Nicholson, p. 134 sq.). He is also one of the principal links in the mystic chain (*silsila*) of various religious orders (Depont et Coppolani, *Les confréries religieuses*, p. 91). Still more important is the part played by him in the traditions of the workmen's corporations and the *futuwwa*-rites practised by the latter [see FUTUWWA]. Salmān is the patron of all corporations, the fourth "initiated" (*mashdūd*), who shaved the heads of the Prophet's companions as a sign of their initiation (cf. H. Thorning, *Studien zu Basṭ madad et-taufīq*, diss. Kiel 1913 = *Türkische Bibliothek*, vol. xvi. p. 33—37 and 85—90).

He has risen to a still higher rank in the gnostic speculations of the extreme Shīʿites. Here the historic figure of Salmān is lost in the divine emanation which was represented by him on earth during a certain time. As such he is called *Sīn* (after the first letter of Salmān) and a member of the divine trinity, the other two members being *ʿAin* (ʿAlī) and *Mīm* (Mūḥammad). While *ʿAin* stands for the static, central element of the divinity, and *Mīm* for the dynamic and self manifesting element, *Sīn* represents the necessary connection between both (the *sabab ila 'l-samāʾ* of Sura xxii. 15). The different sects have a different conception of the gradation of these divine emanations; thus the Nuṣairī's [q.v.] consider *Sīn* as the third member of the trinity, of which he constitutes the gate (*bāb*). With the Ahl-ī Ḥaḳḳ [q.v.] the *Sīn* is on the same degree as the *Mīm*, below the *ʿAin*; Salmān is here the first and Muḥammad the third person of the pentad in the second of their seven cycles.

Bibliography: (besides that mentioned in the article): Ibn Hishām, p. 136—142 (= Ibn Saʿd, iv. 1, 53—57; Ibn Ḥanbal, *Musnad*, v. 441—444; al-Maḳdisī, *Kitāb al-badʾ wa'l-taʾrīkh*, ed. by Cl. Huart, p. 110—113, 345, 673, 677; al-Ṭabarī, ed. de Goeje, Index s.v.; Ibn al-Athīr, *Usd al-ghāba*, ii. 328—332, and other collections of biographies of the Companions; L. Caetani, *Annali dell' Islām*, v. 399—419 (35 A.H., §§ 541—598) and index to vols. i.—ii., iii.—v.; do., *Chronographia Islamica*, i. 383 (35 A.H., § 73); C. Huart, *Selmân du Fârs* in *Mélanges H. Derenbourg*, Paris 1909, p. 297—310; do., *Nouvelles recherches sur la légende de Selmân du Fârs* in the *Annuaire de l'Ecole pratique des Hautes Etudes*, Section des sciences religieuses, 1913; J. Horovitz in *Isl.*, 1912, xii. 178—183; L. Massignon, *Salmân Pâk et les prémises spirituelles de l'Islam Iranien* (= *Publications of the Société des Etudes Iraniennes*, No. 7), Tours 1934.

SALSABĪL is the name of a fountain in Paradise, mentioned only once in the Ḳurʾān, in Sūra lxxvi. 18. The passage runs: "And there shall they (the just) be given to drink of the cup tempered with ginger, from the fount therein whose name is Salsabīl".

Grammarians differ as to the derivation of the word. Some refer it to the triliteral root *s-b-l* while others derive it from a quinqueliteral root of which it is, except in its own feminine form, the sole derivative. Some explain it as meaning "that which slips or steals (*yansallu*) into the throat", as though the only radical letters wer *s* and *l*. The derivation from *sal-sabīlan* as in the comment *sal rabbaka sabīlan ilā hādhihi 'l-ʿain* is condemned as erroneous. The word is explained as meaning "easy" or "smouth" (as a beverage), "in which is no roughness", "easy of entrance into the throat", and is applied as an epithet to milk, water and wine, but in the Ḳurʾān it is understood to refer to wine, which will be lawful to Muslims in Paradise.

Some grammarians take it to be the proper name of the fountain, and therefore imperfectly declined, without *tanwīn*, but it is given *tanwīn* in the verse quoted in order that it may conform with زَنْجَبِيلًا, but others understand it as an epithet applied to the fountain, and therefore perfectly declined, with *tanwīn*. That the conception of the word as of a proper name was popular in the Muslim community, appears from a tradition in Muslim, *Ḥaiḍ*, No. 37, where it is said that the fountain in Paradise from which the faithful will drink is called Salsabīl.

Bibliography: The standard lexica and the commentaries on the Ḳurʾān.

AL-**SĀMIRĪ**, "the Samaritan", is the name in Ḳurʾān, xx. 85, 87, 95 of the man who tempted the Israelites to the sin of the golden calf. This sin is alluded to in the late Madīnan Sūra ii. 45—48 to illustrate God's clemency. The late Meccan Sūra vii. 148—149, relates further that the people of Mūsā made from their ornaments a corporeal calf, which lowed". A more detailed version is given in Sūra xx. 79—89, the time of composition of which is disputed (cf. Nöldeke-Schwally, *Geschichte des Qorāns*, i. 124 *sq.*); Goldziher ascribes it to a later period than Sūra vii, but Speyer (*Die biblische Erzählungen im Qoran*, p. 482) puts it earlier. Here al-Sāmirī tempts the children of Israel to cast their ornaments into the fire and so there came into existence a corporeal calf, which lowed. When challenged by Mūsā, al-Sāmirī justified himself by saying that he saw what the others did not see, the footsteps of the messenger (according to Muslim tradition: the tracks of the hoof of Gabriel's horse). Mūsā then announced his punishment to him: "so long as thou livest, thoug shalt call out to those that meet thee: *lā misāsa* "touch me not"."

The figure of al-Sāmirī was first put into its true light by Goldziher (see below) who explains him as the representative of Samaritanism through the story of the Samaritan secession. We have already evidence of this secession in Sirach, l. 25, and the Gospels Luke, ix. 52, John, iv. 9. Goldziher collects Jewish, Christian and Muslim references, which show that the Samaritans considered contact with those not of their stock as impurity. What Muḥammad or rather his presumed Jewish source knew as a ritual principle of the Samaritans is put back into earlier times and explained as a punishment of al-Sāmirī for having incited the Israelites to make and worship the calf.

Goldziher's convincing arguments can be reinforced by the early Muslim interpretation of the Ḳur'ān. Al-Ṭabarī (*Tafsīr* on xx. 85—97), himself following an earlier tradition, sees in al-Sāmirī a prominent Israelite of the Samaritan tribe; as a punishment for his sin Mūsā forbade the Israelites to have social or commercial relations with him and "this has remained the case". Similarly al-Zamakhsharī: al-Sāmirī belonged to a Jewish tribe called Sāmira whose religion differed somewhat from the Jewish. Al-Sāmirī was forbidden to have social and commercial intercourse with men; it is said that his people still observe the prohibition.

Post-Ḳur'ānic legend embellishes the story of al-Sāmirī, as already in Ṭabarī (*Annales*, i. 489). Al-Sāmirī makes the people believe that booty is not allowed to them. Thereupon they bring the ornaments captured from the Egyptians; in it al-Sāmirī throws dust which he has taken from under the hoofs of Djibrīl; the calf comes forth and lows. — Much more detailed is Thaʿlabī (Cairo 1325, p. 131—133). Al-Sāmirī takes the dust from under the hoofs of the horse by means of which Djibrīl causes confusion among the stallions of the Egyptians. Al-Sāmirī alone recognizes the archangel, for when in Egypt the Hebrews concealed their new-born sons in caves, these were educated by angels, al-Sāmirī by Djibrīl himself. Al-Sāmirī throws the handful of dust in the calf, this becomes flesh and blood, lows and goes away. According to some authorities Iblīs speaks from inside the calf. Al-Sāmirī makes the people believe that Allāh speaks to them from inside the calf, just as he has spoken to Mūsā from the thorn-bush. Mūsā forces al-Sāmirī to soil the calf and curses him: *lā misāsa*. On the prohibition of touching cf. Lev. xiii. 45; Is. liv. 11; Lam. iv. 15.

The Islamic legend has penetrated into the later Midrash: in the *Pirkē R. Elieser*, in *Tanḥūma Ki Tisza*, with which Thaʿlabī shows remarkable connections.

The story of al-Sāmirī in the Ḳur'ān thus has also an aetiological tendency; it gives the reason why the Samaritans are secluded from the others ,namely by way of punishment, — just as the food-prohibitions are inflicted on the Jews (Sūra iv. 156); the sin of al-Sāmirī was the golden calf.

Bibliography: al-Ṭabarī: *Tafsīr*, and al-Zamakhsharī, *al-Kashshāf* on Ḳur'ān xx. 85—95; al-Thaʿlabī, *Ḳiṣaṣ al-anbiyā'*, Cairo 1282, p. 82; Geiger, *Was hat Mohammed aus dem Judenthume aufgenommen?*, Frankfurt 1902, p. 162—165; S. Fraenkel, *Der Sāmirī*, in *ZDMG*, 1902, lvi. 73; I. Goldziher, *La Misāsa*, in *Revue Africaine*, No. 268, Algiers 1908, p. 23, 28; Speyer, *Die bibl. Erzählungen im Qoran*, p. 330.

AL-**SANŪSĪ**, SĪDĪ MUḤAMMAD B. ʿALĪ AL-SANŪSĪ AL-MUDJĀHIRĪ AL-ḤASANĪ AL-IDRĪSĪ, born in 1206/1791 at Tursh near Mustaghānem (Algeria) in a duar of the Khaṭāṭiba (Ūlād Sīdī Yūsuf) of Zaiyānī Berber stock, and died in 1276/1859 at Djaghbūb (Cyrenaica), the founder of the celebrated modern brotherhood of the Sanūsīya (the "Senusis").

Taught at first by Abū Rās (d. 1823) and Belganduz (d. 1829) in his native country, he went to live at Fās from 1821 to 1828 where he studied Ḳur'ānic exegesis, tradition, the principles of law and jurisprudence. He then performed the pilgrimage, going via Southern Tunisia and Cairo to Mecca where he lived from 1830 to 1843 (except for a sojourn in Sabia); there in 1837 he founded the first zāwiya of his order on the Abū Ḳubais.

Returning to the west he did not stay in Cairo but settled in Cyrenaica, where he founded first the zāwiya of Rafāʿa, then of al-Baiḍā near Cyrene (Dj. Akhdar), then Temessa, lastly Djaghbūb (1855), which he peopled with liberated slaves. There he died and was buried.

He had two sons: Sīdī Muḥammad al-Mahdī (born 1844, d. 1901 at Guro), his successor, and Sīdī Muḥammad al-Sharīf (b. 1846, d. 1896). The elder left two sons: Sīdī Muḥammad Idrīs (b. 1883, given an estate in the west in 1909; Amīr under Italian protection from 1916 to 1923) and Sīdī al-Riḍā. The younger had six sons, Sīdī Aḥmad Sharīf (b. 1880; head of the brotherhood from 1901 to 1916; he took the side of Germany, went to Turkey and for a time conducted a pan-Islāmic campaign from Ankara), Sīdī Muḥammad al-ʿĀbid (given an estate in the south, in Fezzān; he directed the Saharan rising against France in 1916—1918), Sīdī ʿAlī al-Khaṭṭāb, Sīdī Ṣafī al-Dīn (president of the Italian Parliament of Cyrenaica in 1921), Sīdī al-Ḥallāl and Sīdī al-Riḍā.

The headquarters of the order were first at Djaghbūb (1855—1895), then transferred to Kufra (1895), Guro (1899), then back to Kufra (1902), while the number of *zāwiya*'s rose from 22 in 1859 to 100 (1884).

Sīdī Muḥammad b. ʿAlī al-Sanūsī left, in addition to instructions regarding initiation into his order (types of *wird*; *sirr*: *yā Laṭīf*, repeated a thousand times), four works; one on the *uṣūl*, one on a harmony between the Ḳur'ān and the Ḥadīth (established without taking account of the *taḳlīd* of any of the four rites; although the author calls himself a Mālikī, he postulates *idjtihād*) and two on mysticism, *Fahrasa*, the enumeration of his "chains of support" (canonical; 150, of whom 64 were mystics) guaranteeing the orthodoxy of his order, and *al-Salsabīl al-muʿīn fi 'l-ṭarā'iḳ al-arbaʿīn* containing the *dhikr* formulae of the "forty" previous orders [see ṬARĪḲA] of which his order was to give the quintessence. This last work is the most curious. Although the statements in it are represented as received by oral initiatory transmission, they are, he confesses, taken from the *Risāla* of Ḥasan ʿUdjaimī, (1113/1702), imitated by Sīdī Murtaḍā al-Zabīdī, in his *ʿIḳd al-djumān*; the chapter on the *dhikr* of the Ḥallādjīya is found word for word in the *Adab al-dhikr* of Abū Saʿīd al-Ḳādirī, written in India in 1097/1686 (MS. Calcutta 1280, cf. the Catalogue by Ivanov), which betrays a common source, probably the *Idrākāt* of the Aḥmadī al-Shinnāwī (d. 1028/1619).

His claims to juridical *idjtihād* were dismissed as *kufr* at Cairo in 1843 by the learned Mālikī Muḥammad al-ʿAish; the followers of al-Sanūsī do not observe the Mālikī *isbāl* (the hanging down of the arms at the *tasmīʿ* in the *ṣalāt*).

Initiated into mysticism at Mustaghānem (Ḳādirīya) and at Fās (Tidjānīya, Ṭaibīya), al-Sanūsī's ideas took definite shape at Mecca, under the influence of his teacher Aḥmad b. Idrīs al-Fāsī (d. 1837 at Sabia), founder of the Khaḍirīya-Idrīsīya, and teacher of two other founders of modern brotherhoods (Rashīdīya and Amīrghanīya).

Bibliography: For the order see the standard works of H. Duveyrier, *La confrérie musulmane de Sīdī Muhammed ben ʿAlī es-Senousi*, in *Bull. de la Soc. Géogr. de Paris*, 7th series, V. (1884), p. 145—226 (separate ed. 1886 and Rome 1918), and Rinn, *Marabouts et Khouans*, 1884, p. 481—515. On the founder and his family: Muḥammad ben-Otomane el Hachaichi, *Voyages au pays des Senoussia*, Paris 1912; A. Le Châtelier, *Les confréries musulmanes du Hedjaz*, Paris 1887, p. 257—258; E. Insabato, *Rassegna contemporanea*, VI/ii., Rome 1913; E. Graefe in *Der Isl.*, iii. 141—150, 312—313; C. A. Nallino, *Raccolta di Scritti*, vol. ii (Rome 1940), pp. 387—410; E. E. Evans-Pritchard, *The Sanusī of Cyrenaica*, Oxford 1949.

AL-SANŪSĪ, ABŪ ʿABD ALLĀH MAḤAMMAD (for Muḥammad) B. YŪSUF B. ʿUMAR B. SHUʿAIB, a learned Ashʿarī theologian of Tlemcen, where he was born and died at the age of about 63 on Sunday, Djumādā II 18, 895/May 9, 1490; his epitaph, however, gives neither day of the week nor day of the month.

He studied Muslim lore as well as mathematics and astronomy in his native town with such teachers as his father Abū Yaʿḳūb Yūsuf, his half-brother ʿAlī al-Tallūtī, Abū ʿAbd Allāh al-Ḥabbāk, Abu 'l-Ḥasan al-Ḳalasādī, the famous Ibn Marzūḳ, Ḳāsim al-ʿUḳbānī, etc. He is said to have gone to Algiers where he studied under ʿAbd al-Raḥmān al-Thaʿālibī. The scholars of the Maghrib, in whose eyes he was the reviver of Islām at the beginning of the ixth century A.H., all agree in praising his merit, his learning, especially theological, his fear of God and his zeal.

Among his disciples may be mentioned Ibn al-Ḥādjdj al-Yabdarī, Ibn al-ʿAbbās al-Ṣaghīr, Ibn Ṣaʿd, Abu 'l-Ḳāsim al-Zawāwī. Of his many works the following are the best known:

1. *ʿAḳīdat ahl al-tawḥīd al-mukhridja min ẓulumat al-djahl wa-ribḳat al-taḳlīd* or *al-ʿAḳīdat al-kubrā*; 2. *ʿUmdat ahl al-tawfīḳ wa 'l-tasdīd*, commentary on the preceding, publ. with it at Cairo in 1317; 3. *ʿAḳīdat ahl al-tawḥīd al-ṣughrā* or *Umm al-barāhīn* and, more briefly, *Al-Sanūsīya*, published several times in Cairo and Fās, transl. into German by Ph. Wolff, *El Senusi's Begriffsentwicklung d. mohammedanischen Glaubensbekenntnisses, ar. u. deutsch mit Anm.*, Leipzig 1848; into French by Luciani, *Petit traité de théologie musulmane*, Algiers 1896; cf. Delphin, *La philosophie du Cheikh Senousi d'après son aqida es-sor'ra*, *JA*, Ser. 9, x. 356; Luciani, *A propos de la trad. de la Senoussia*, in the *Revue Afr.*, 1898, xlii., No. 231.

Bibliography: al-Mallālī Muḥammad b. ʿUmar al-Tilimsānī, *al-Mawāhib al-ḳaddūsīya fi 'l-manāḳib al-Sanūsīya*, ms. Algiers, No. 1706; Ibn ʿAskar, *Dawḥat al-nāshir*, Fās 1309, p. 89; Aḥmad Bābā, *Nail al-ibtihādj*, Fās 1309, p. 346, art. reproduced by al-Ḥafnāwī, *Taʿrīf al-khalaf bi ridjāl al-salaf*, Algiers 1907, i. 176; do., *Kifāyat al-muḥtādj* (ms. of the Madrasa of Algiers), f. 181 v.; Ibn Maryam, *al-Bustān*, Algiers 1910, p. 270; Brosselard, *Tombeau de Cid Mohammed es-Senouci et de son frère le Cid et-Tallouti* in the *Rev. afr.*, 1858, iii. 245; do., *Retour à Sidi Senouci* in the *Rev. afr.*, 1861, v. 241; Abbé Bargès, *Compl. de l'Histoire des Beni-Zeiyan*, Paris 1887, p. 366; Cherbonneau, *Documents inédits sur El-Senouci, son caractère et ses écrits*, *JA*, 1854, p. 175, 442, 443; Brockelmann, *GAL* 2, ii. 323, *Suppl.* ii. 352 *sqq.*; Moh. Ben Cheneb, *Etude sur les pers. mentionnées dans l'Idjāza du Cheikh ʿAbd el-Ḳadir el-Fasy*, Paris 1907, No. 55.

SAWDA BINT ZAMʿA B. ḲAIS, Muḥammad's second wife, was one of the first women who embraced Islām. She accompanied her first husband al-Sakrān b. ʿAmr and her brother Malik to Abyssinia, with the second party of Muslims who repaired thither. The pair returned to Mecca before the *Hidjra*, and al-Sakrān, who had become a Christian in Abyssinia, died there. By this union Sawda had a son, ʿAbd al-Raḥmān, who was killed in the battle of Djalūlā.

Sawda's marriage to Muḥammad was arranged by Khawla bint Ḥakīm, who wished to console him for the loss of Khadīdja, and took place about a month after the latter's death, in the tenth year of Muḥammad's mission, in Ramaḍān, before his journey to al-Ṭāʾif.

In the first year of the *Hidjra* Sawda, together with Muḥammad's daughters, joined him in Madīna; her dwelling and ʿĀʾisha's were the first to be built in the Mosque.

Sawda was no longer young at the time of her second marriage, and, as she grew older, became fat and ungainly to such a point that Muḥammad, during a pilgrimage, allowed her the privilege of reaching Minā for the morning prayer before the crowd's arrival, to avoid being jostled. As she grew older Muḥammad neglected her, while he spent a great deal of his time with the youthful ʿĀʾisha; in 8 A.H. he divorced her, but Sawda stopped him in the street and begged him to take her back, offering to yield her day to ʿĀʾisha, as "she was old, and cared not for men; her only desire was to rise on the Day of Judgement as his wife". The Prophet consented; on this occasion Sūra iv. 128 was revealed.

Sawda was charitable and good-natured; in one of his utterances Muḥammad seems to have alluded to her as the "longest-handed", i.e. the most charitable of his wives, who would be the first to join him in Heaven, and ʿĀʾisha used to say: "There is no woman in whose skin I had rather be than Sawda's, except that she is somewhat envious".

Together with Zainab bint Djaḥsh, Sawda did not take part in the last pilgrimage. Of her life after Muḥammad's death there is no record, except that that she received a gift of money from ʿUmar; this, together with the fact that no mention is made of her dowry, may mean that she was in straitened circumstances, though she had received her share of the spoils of Khaibar. She died in Madīna, in Shawwāl 54 A.H., during the caliphate of Muʿāwiya, who bought her house in the Mosque, together with that of Ṣafīya, for 180,000 dirham.

Bibliography: Ibn Hishām, ed. Wüstenfeld, p. 214, 242, 459, 787, 1001; Ibn Saʿd, viii. 35—39; al-Ṭabarī, ed. de Goeje, i. 1767, 1769; iii. 2437—2440; *Aghānī*, iv. 32; Caetani, *Annali dell' Islām*, i. 378—379; F. Buhl, *Das Leben Muhammeds*, p. 198; G. H. Stern, *Marriage in Early Islam*, 1939, index, s.v.

ṢAWM (A.), with ṢIYĀM, *maṣdar* from the root *ṣ-w-m*; the two *maṣdar* are used indiscriminately. The original meaning of the word in Arabic is "to be at rest" (Th. Nöldeke, *Neue Beiträge zur sem. Sprachw.*, Strassburg 1910, p. 36, note 3; cf. previously S. Fränkel, *De vocab. . . . . in Corano peregrinis*, Leiden 1880, p. 20; "quiescere"). The meaning "fasting" may have been taken from Judaeo-Aramaic usage, when Muḥammad became better acquainted with the institution of fasting in Madīna. The word has this meaning in the Madīna sūras; in the Mecca sūras it occurs only once, in Sūra xix. 26, where the commentators explain it by *ṣamt* "silence" (this is therefore given as one of the translations of the word in the dictionaries); but perhaps *ṣawm* has simply to be translated "fasting" here (see below). The verb is followed by the accusative of the time spent in fasting.

Origin of the rite of Fasting. In favour of the occurrence of fasting as a voluntary practice of mortification among the first Muslims in Mecca is the probability that Muḥammad on his many and varied journeys had observed the rite among Jews and Christians. But we can say nothing definite on this point; anything told us on this subject in the *Sīra* and Muslim tradition may be biased. In the Mecca sūras, as above mentioned, there is a reference to *ṣawm* in xix. 26: a voice commands Mary to say "I have made a vow of *ṣawm* to the Merciful, wherefore I speak to no one this day". There is some possibility that *ṣawm* here simply means "fasting", because observing silence as a Christian fasting practice (cf. Afrāhāṭ, ed. Parisot, in *Patrol. Syriaca*, i., p. 97) may have been known to Muḥammad. Muḥammad was in any case not acquainted with the details, because it was only after the Hidjra that he ordered the *ʿĀshūrāʾ*-day [q.v.] to be spent in fasting, when he saw the Jews doing it in Madīna. In the year 2. A.H., according to unanimous reliable Muslim tradition (cf. A. J. Wensinck, *Mohammed en de Joden te Medina*, Diss. Leiden 1908, p. 136—137, in contradiction to e.g. A. Sprenger, *Das Leben und die Lehre des Mohammad*, iii. 53—59), the revelation of Sūra ii. 183—185 again abolished the *ʿĀshūrāʾ*-fast as an obligation by the institution of the fast of Ramaḍān. On the question why Muḥammad chose this particular month and whence he took the arrangement of the Muslim fast cf. A. J. Wensinck in his essay *Arabic New-Year and the Feast of Tabernacles* in *Verh. Ak. W. Amst.*, New Series, 1925, vol. xxv/ii. 1—13 and the article RAMAḌĀN.

The first regulations concerning the manner of the Muslim fasting are given in Sūra ii. 183—185, which probably belong together (Nöldeke-Schwally, i., p. 178; in opposition to Th. W. Juynboll, *Handbuch des islāmischen Gesetzes*, Leiden-Leipzig 1910, p. 114, who considers 185 a later revelation; al-Baiḍāwī also assumes that it was revealed in separate parts): one ought to fast during a definite number of days, to be precise, in the month of Ramaḍān, "in which the Ḳurʾān was sent down"; special dispensations were granted to invalids and travellers on condition that they made restitution for it. In obedience to these divine commands the Muslims fasted in Ramaḍān and the devout among them followed the Jewish custom of fasting from one sunset to the next until a new revelation (ii. 187) limited the period of fasting to the day (cf. al-Bukhārī, *Ṣawm*, bāb 15, etc.). The fast is also mentioned elsewhere in the Ḳurʾān: in Sūra ii. 196, where it is prescribed as a substitute for the *ḥadjdj* in certain circumstances; in iv. 92, where fasting during two successive months is ordered as an atonement when someone has killed a believer of an allied nation by accident (cf. the article ḲATL); v. 89: one should fast three days (as a substitute) if one has broken an oath; v. 95: one should fast (as a substitute) if one has killed game on the pilgrimage; lviii. 4: one should fast (as a substitute) for two successive months if one wants to make the *ẓihār* invalid (cf. the regulations of the *kaffāra*, below). *Ṣāʾim* is further used in xxxiii. 35 to describe the devout Muslim, along with other epithets, while in Sūra ii. 45 and 153 *ṣabr* [q.v.] is explained as *ṣawm*.

The ordinances in Sūra ii. 183—185, 187, form the basis of the detailed regulation by the *fuḳahāʾ* of the law regarding fasting; many minor details were taken from tradition. What follows here is a résumé of the law on fasting according to the Shāfiʿī school, as contained in the treatise by Abū Shudjāʿ al-Iṣfahānī (v[th] century A.H.) *Mukhtaṣar fi 'l-fiḳh*, annotated by Ibn Ḳāsim al-Ghazzī (d. 918/1522) and glossed by Ibrāhīm al-Bādjūrī (d. 1278/1861).

How the fast should be observed and who is bound to fast. Fasting in the legal sense is abstinence (*imsāk*) from things which break the fast (*mufṭirāt*), with a special *nīya* (intention) for each of the statutory fasts, and for the whole day; the *ṣāʾim* must be a Muslim in full possession of his senses (*ʿāḳil*) and, if a woman, free from menstruation and the bleeding of childbed. The fast may be valid (*ṣaḥīḥ*) under these conditions; there is an obligation to fast on every one who is full-grown (*bāligh*) if he is physically fit (*ḳādir*). It is to be noted that the actual profession of Islām at the time is necessary for the *ṣiḥḥa*, while for the *wudjūb* the Islām of a *murtadd* is also valid, who is thus after his conversion obliged to make up for the fast days he has omitted (*ḳaḍāʾ*); one who was born a *kāfir*, who is pledged to Islām, and ought, therefore, to obey its laws also, need not, however, make up for his omissions. The fasting of a non-*bāligh*, who is *mumaiyiz* (has power of discrimination), is valid (one ought to compel a child to fast from the tenth year), as is that of a non-*ḳādir*.

The *arkān* (pillars) of the fast are, besides the *ṣāʾim*, the nīya and abstinence from the *mufṭirāt*. One ought to formulate the nīya before dawn on each day of fasting (*tabyīt*); by *taḳlīd* [q.v.], however, the Shāfiʿī can follow the Mālikī madhhab, which allows one to formulate the *nīya* for the whole of the month of Ramaḍān in the night before the first of Ramaḍān; if one fasts voluntarily, the *nīya* may still be formed before noon, if one has actually fasted during the preceding part of the day.

The Mufṭirāt are:

1. The entering into the body of any material substances in so far as it is done conscientiously and

is preventable, i.e. the swallowing of food and beverages, the inhaling of tobacco smoke, the swallowing of spittle which can be ejected; if one sprays or drops liquids or inserts instruments into the various orifices of the body; if one retains what the body in the course of nature would reject.

2. Deliberate vomiting, which is only permitted by doctor's orders and even then only with liability to *ḳaḍāʾ*.

3. Sexual intercourse.

4. Deliberate seminal emission, which is a consequence of sexual contact; in other cases a distinction is made as to whether it is caused by passion or not, whether the person causing it is a stranger or a *dhū maḥram*, a boy, a woman or a *ḥāʾil*. Nocturnal or similar emissions (*iḥtilām*) are not *mufṭir*.

5. Menstruation; this even makes the fast *ḥarām* (this rule is not clear to al-Bād̲j̲ūrī, because the fast does not demand ritual purity otherwise).

6. The bleeding of a woman in child-bed.

7. Unsound mind.

8. Intoxication (7 and 8 make any *ʿibāda* impossible), to which a ninth may be added, childbirth, but only in the view of some *fuḳahāʾ*.

The *ifṭār* occurs, *casu quo*, only in case of deliberateness (*taʿammud*), knowledge (*ʿilm*) and free will (*ik̲h̲tiyār*), i.e. not by neglect, in ignorance of the obligations if this is to be excused, or under compulsion. "If one eats by an oversight", says the tradition, "he may continue the fast because God himself has caused him to eat" (Buk̲h̲ārī, *Ṣawm*, bāb 26; *Aymān*, bāb 15; Muslim, *Ṣiyām*, tr. 171).

It is to be commended if the *ṣāʾim* 1) takes the *faṭūr* as soon as possible after he is certain the sun has set; he ought preferably to use ripe dates for this, or (zamzam-)water or otherwise something tasty; 2) eats the *saḥūr* (what is eaten after midnight) as late as possible and uses for it the same as is recommended for the *faṭūr*; 3) refrains from indecent talk, slander, calumnies, lies and insults; 4) avoids such actions as, although not actually forbidden, might arouse passion in oneself or in others; 5) refrains from being cupped or bled; 6) tastes no food; 7) chews nothing edible; 8) thanks God after the day of fasting; 9) recites the Ḳurʾān for oneself or others, and 10) observes the *iʿtikāf* in the month of Ramaḍān [q.v.] (in accordance with Sūra ii. 187). Al-G̲h̲azzālī adds to these charity in the month of Ramaḍān.

Arranged according to the five legal categories, the fast may be:

I. Obligatory (*wād̲j̲ib*, *farḍ*) (*a*) in the month of Ramaḍān; (*b*) if one has to make up for days omitted in Ramaḍān (*ḳaḍāʾ*); (*c*) on account of a vow; (*d*) in definite circumstances to atone for a transgression (*kaffāra*, q.v.), and (*e*) when the *Imām* prescribes the *istisḳāʾ*-ceremonies [q.v.] in season of drought. In the case of inexcusable *ifṭār* one is bound, according to al-G̲h̲azzālī, to fast during the remainder of the day, *tas̲h̲bīhan bil-ṣāʾimīn*.

Fasting in the month of Ramaḍān is the fourth pillar of Islām; whoever denies the obligation to fast is a *kāfir*, unless he has only recently come in contact with Islām, or has grown up remote from the ʿulamāʾ. Whoever omits to fast without good cause, without, however, denying the compulsion to fast, is to be locked up and brought to formulate the *nīya* by forced abstinence. The general obligation to fast (*ʿalā sabīl al-ʿumūm*) begins on the first of Ramaḍān, after the 30th S̲h̲aʿbān, or after the 29th if the *ḥākim* (*ḳāḍī*) has then accepted the evidence of one *ʿadl* that he has seen the new moon; the personal obligation (*ʿalā sabīl al-k̲h̲uṣūṣ*), in the case of an unaccepted *ruʾyā* of one's own or that of another person whom one believes in this respect, even if he should not be *ʿadl*, after the 29th S̲h̲aʿbān; if only one *ʿadl* has seen the new moon on the 29th S̲h̲aʿbān, fasting etc. only becomes due on the 2nd Ramaḍān. The beginning of Ramaḍān has to be announced to the people in a way settled by the local custom (gun-shot, the hanging of lamps on the *manāra*, in Java by beating the *bĕdug*). Special regulations hold regarding *nīya* and *ḳaḍāʾ* if it is impossible for one to hear of the announcement or if he is wrongly informed. The observations of an astronomer, the calculations of a mathematician, or the dream of one who has received in his sleep information regarding the beginning of Ramaḍān from the Prophet, etc., can only allow Ramaḍān to begin for the astronomer, mathematician or dreamer themselves and those who firmly believe in them.

The law permits relaxations in the following circumstances:

A. Such as have reached a certain age (men 40; not exactly defined for women) and sick people for whom there is no hope of recovery, if they are unable to fast, may omit the fast without being bound to the *ḳaḍāʾ* should their strength or health be restored.

B. If pregnant or nursing women fear it would be dangerous for them if they should fast, *ifṭār* is *wād̲j̲ib* for them and *ḳaḍāʾ* is obligatory.

C. Sick persons who are likely to recover and those who are overcome by hunger and thirst may break the fast on condition that the *ḳaḍāʾ* is performed.

D. Travellers who set out before sunrise may, if necessary, break the fast, but not if they begin their journey during the day.

E. Those who have to perform heavy manual labour should formulate the *nīya* in the night but may break the fast if need be.

When the justification for relaxing the rules disappears during the day of fast, it is *sunna* to pass the rest of the day fasting.

II. Voluntary fasting (*ṣawm al-taṭawwuʿ*), is meritorious for a married woman only with the consent of her husband; it may be broken without any penalty; the *nīya*, which can be formulated any time up till noon, need not be definitely specified, although some fuḳahāʾ consider it desirable for the *sunan rawātib*. The *sunan rawātib* in the *ṣawm* are fasting (*a*) on the ʿĀs̲h̲ūrāʾ-day [q.v.]; (*b*) on the ʿArafa-day, the 9th D̲h̲u 'l-Ḥid̲j̲d̲j̲a; (*c*) on six days of S̲h̲awwāl. Fasting on the day of ʿArafa applies specially to those who do not spend this day in ʿArafa. Whether Muḥammad fasted on this day is disputed in Tradition (cf. Wensinck, *Mohammed en de Joden te Medina*, p. 126—130, and Nöldeke-Schwally, *Gesch. d. Qorans*, i. 159).

Six separate days can be taken for the fast on the six days of S̲h̲awwāl; but it is best to take six successive days immediately after the festival, i.e. from the 2nd to the 7th S̲h̲awwāl.

The following days are further recommended for voluntary fasting: the day before and after the ʿĀs̲h̲ūrāʾ-day; the Yawm al-Miʿrād̲j̲ (27th Rad̲j̲ab); Monday and Thursday (*sunna muʾakkada*, according to al-Bād̲j̲ūrī), because on these days, says Tradition, the works of men are offered to God. Wednesday, "out of gratitude", says al-Bādjūrī, "that God on this day did not lead this *umma* to destruction, like the other *umam*"; the days of the white nights, i.e. the 13th, 14th, 15th and best of all also the 12th of each month; as a counterpart, presumably after the example of the white nights, the days of the black nights, i.e. the 28th, 29th, 30th (or 1st) and best of all also the 27th of each month; every day on which one has nothing to eat; all other days if they are proper for fasting.

Al-Ghazzālī gives as additional days recommended for fasting the first, the middle and the last day of every month, speaks of the superiority of fasting in the sacred months (*al-ashhur al-ḥurum*: Muḥarram, Radjab, Dhu 'l-Ḥidjdja and Dhu 'l-Ḳaʿda), but more important is what he says regarding life-long fasting (*ṣawm al-dahr*) which, as he tells us, was practised by the mystics (*al-sālikūn*) of his time in various ways (as had already been done by ascetics in the earliest days of Islām). It is highly recommended, however, to fast on alternate days (*niṣf al-dahr*), which achievement al-Ghazzālī considers even more difficult; Muḥammad said: "The most excellent fasting is that of my brother Dā'ūd, who fasteth one day and not the next" (cf. al-Bukhārī, *Ṣawm*, bāb 54, 56; cf. 58, 59; *Anbiyā'*, bāb 37, 38, etc.; Muslim, *Ṣiyām*, trad. 181, 182, 186, 187, 189—193, 196 etc.). To fast every third day is also very meritorious. To fast voluntarily for more than four days in succession is considered wrong by the ʿulamā' and (as a general rule) also by al-Ghazzālī.

III. Fasting is forbidden (*ḥarām*) on the days of the two great festivals, on the *tashrīḳ*-days and for a woman during menstruation: in definite cases when danger threatens, as already mentioned above.

IV. It is reprehensible to fast on Friday because it distracts the attention from the Friday service (but according to al-Ghazzālī it is meritorious); on Sunday or Saturday, at least if one has no particular reason for fasting, because the Christians and Jews observe these as holy days. One also should not fast if one fears he will suffer in any way on account of the fast. It is very wrong to fast without special reason on the "doubtful day" (*yawm al-shakk*) and in the second half of the month of Shaʿbān. The "doubtful day" is the day following the 29th Shaʿbān if one does not know, with a clear sky, whether an *ʿadl* has seen the new moon of Ramaḍān.

The three other madhhabs differ in details from the Shāfiʿī school; the differences are collected in the *Ikhtilāf*-books. The following is taken from the *Kitāb al-mīzān* of ʿAbd al-Wahhāb al-Shaʿrānī (ii. 20—30; Cairo 1279).

1. Abū Ḥanīfa teaches that the fasting of a young boy or girl is not valid, but valid is that of a *murāhiḳ*, and that a *murtadd* is not bound to a *ḳaḍā'* after his conversion.

2. Abū Ḥanifa teaches that the fast need not be definitely specified in the *nīya*, that even the intention of doing a good work is sufficient.

3. Abū Ḥanīfa does not consider deliberate swallowing of fragments of food one of the *mufṭirāt* any more than one of the opinions said to have been held by Mālik regards the application of a poultice as one.

4. Vomiting does no harm, according to Abū Ḥanīfa and Aḥmad b. Ḥanbal, up to a certain point, which they calculate differently.

5. Mālik teaches that seminal emission spoils the fast if it is a result of sensual images, even without preceding sexual contact.

6. In spite of the above-mentioned tradition, Mālik teaches that anyone who deliberately eats, drinks, or has sexual intercourse breaks the fast and is liable to *ḳaḍā'*; Aḥmad b. Ḥanbal, only in the last case, *kaffāra* then being also necessary.

7. Mālik says that kissing is always *ḥarām*; Aḥmad b. Ḥanbal that the cupper and his patient both break the fast; both Imāms say that the taking of *kuḥl* is to be deprecated and, if the fragrance enters the throat, is actually *mufṭir*.

8. Mālik demands for the settlement of the beginning of Ramaḍān the evidence of two *ʿadl*, Abū Ḥanīfa only the testimony of one, but of a large number when the sky is unclouded.

9. Like al-Shāfiʿī, Abū Ḥanīfa also teaches that the weak-minded is not bound to perform *ḳaḍā'* in the event of his recovery; Mālik teaches the contrary; both views are credited to Aḥmad b. Ḥanbal.

10. The four Imāms impose the major *kaffāra* only on one who breaks the fast in Ramaḍān; some fuḳahā' also on those who break the *ḳaḍā'* fast of Ramaḍān. Aḥmad b. Ḥanbal imposes a *kaffāra* for every breach of the regulations in question, even if several are committed on the same day; in the second transgression the obligation is imposed on the guilty woman also. Abū Ḥanīfa, however, is less severe.

11. Aḥmad b. Ḥanbal imposes, in addition, the (minor) *kaffāra* on pregnant and nursing women, if they thave broken the fast out of fear of injuring themselves; Abu Ḥanīfa, however, only *ḳaḍā'*, others only *kaffāra* and no *ḳaḍā'*.

12. Sick people for whom there is no hope and old people are, according to Abū Ḥanīfa and a section of the Shāfiʿīs, liable to *fidya* only; Mālik denies this also.

13. Travellers may, as Aḥmad b. Ḥanbal teaches, break the fast, even if they have set out after the beginning of the fast, but this relaxation does not include, according to him, permission for sexual intercourse; the *kaffāra* regulations hold, therefore, also with him.

14. Mālik teaches that fasting on six Shawwāl-days is not recommendable; both he and Abū Ḥanīfa say that one is bound to complete (*itmām*) a voluntary fast day also.

15. One ought to fast on the doubtful day, according to Aḥmad b. Ḥanbal, when the sky is clouded; otherwise it is reprehensible.

16. Lastly it is to be mentioned that, according to the Ḥanafī and Mālikī view, fasting during the *iʿtikāf* [q.v.] is obligatory; cf. e.g. Abū Dā'ūd, *Ṣawm*, bāb 80 (see A. J. Wensinck in his treatise *Arabic New-Year*).

The Shīʿa law regarding fasting differs in various details from the *Sunna* (according to A. Querry's edition of the *Sharā'iʿ al-Islām fī masā'il al-ḥalāl wa 'l-ḥarām* of Nadjm al-Dīn al-Muḥaḳḳiḳ, entitled *Recueil de Lois concern. les Musulmans Schyites*, Paris 1871—72, i. 182—209, ii. 75—77, 197—199, 203—205).

Al-Ghazzālī gives at the beginning of his *Kitāb asrār al-ṣawm* in the *Iḥyā'* some considerations on the value of fasting. He points out, referring to some well-known traditions, the high esteem in which fasting stands with God; he gives as a reason for this that fasting is a passive act and no one sees men fast except God; secondly it is a means of defeating the enemy of God, because human passions, which are the Shaiṭān's means of attaining his ends, are stimulated by eating and drinking. The passions "are the places where the Shaiṭān live in abundance and where they feed; so long as they are fruitful, they continue to visit them often, and so long as they visit them frequently, the majesty of God is concealed from His servant and he is shut off from meeting with Him. The Prophet of God even says: "If the Shaiṭān did not fly around the hearts of men they would readily think of heaven" Fasting is therefore "the gateway to divine service"."

In the first *faṣl* al-Ghazzālī details the legal obligations and recommended actions of the fast, according to Shāfiʿī doctrine, and in the third the recommended fast days, just as a faḳīh would do. But he says in the second *faṣl* that the most punctilious observation of the external law of the fast is not the essential of the fast. He distinguishes three steps in the fast. The first step is that of the *fiḳh*, the third that of the Prophets, the *ṣiddīḳūn* and those who have been brought into the proximity (of God) (*al-muḳarrabūn*), whose fast consists in refraining from all mean desires and wordly thoughts. The second step suffices for the pious, however; it consists in keeping one's organs of sense and members free from sin and from all things that detract from God. Everything should be avoided which might affect the result of the fast; for example, at the *ifṭār* one should not eat more or far better than usual (this is contrary to the *fiḳh* regulation) and one should not sleep during the day to avoid feeling hunger or thirst, for they are the *rūḥ* and *sirr* of fasting because they fight the power of the passions. Subjection of the passions, whereby the soul is brought nearer to God, is the real object of fasting, not mere abstinence; and he deduces the worthlessness of the fast of those whose conduct at the *ifṭār* destroys the results of the fast day, of whom the tradition says: "How many fasters there are for whom only hunger and thirst are the results of their fast" (Aḥmad b. Ḥanbal, ii. 373).

The ethical conception of the fast which al-Ghazzālī gives in this second *faṣl* supplements, he says, the barren law of the fuḳahāʾ, but to us it appears often to contradict it. In the Ḥadīth we find already various traditions with ethical tendencies and al-Ghazzālī does not fail to quote them in support of his view. Besides we find in the works on Ḥadīth a mass of traditions relating to the fast, which will be found classified under the separate subjects in Wensinck's *Handbook of Early Muhammadan Tradition*, under the word FASTING. Here we can only quote a few traditions which refer to the estimation in which fasting was held in the early Muslim world. As it is to this day a widespread view that fasting, especially the fast of Ramaḍān, is the most fitting atonement for sins committed in the course of the year — which is why the fast is fairly generally observed, although not always so strictly as the fuḳahāʾ desire; cf. the article RAMAḌĀN —, so it was with the early Muslims (cf. al-Bukhārī, *Īmān*, bāb 28; *Ṣawm*, bāb 6; al-Tirmidhī, *Ṣawm*, bāb 1, etc.). Various traditions compare the value of fasting at one time with its value at another, as, for example, "fasting on one day in the holy months (see above) is better than 30 days at another time, and fasting on one day in Ramaḍān is better than 30 days in the holy months". "If anyone fasts three days in a holy month, Thursday, Friday and Saturday, God considers one day equal to 900 years for him". Similar traditions refer to fasting on the ʿĀshūrāʾ-day, the ten days in Dhu 'l-Ḥidjdja and especially in Ramaḍān [q.v.]. Other traditions tell how dear to God is the person of the faster or his characteristics; even is "the scent of the breath of a fasting man more pleasant to God than the scent of musk" (Aḥmad b. Ḥanbal, ii. 232, etc.). God compares one who denies his passions for His sake with His angels and says to him: "Thou art with Me like one of My angels", and He urges His angels to regard those who fast. The joys of the faster in Paradise are described and how he is honoured there; he will enter by a special gate (*al-Raiyān*) and meet God (al-Bukhārī, *Ṣawm*, bāb 4; Muslim, *Ṣiyām*, tr. 166, etc.). This is his heavenly joy; his joy on earth is the *ifṭār* (al-Bukhārī, *Tawḥīd*, bāb 35; Aḥmad b. Ḥanbal, i. 446, etc.). One should, therefore, not deny this joy, because one has a right to it. To continue fasting after twilight is, moreover, not necessary, for "the sleep of the faster is (already) *ʿibāda*".

Bibliography: A comprehensive work on fasting among the Muslims has not yet appeared. An outline of the law on the subject according to the Shāfiʿī school is given by Th. W. Juynboll, *Handbuch des islāmischen Gesetzes*, Leiden-Leipzig 1910, p. 113 *sqq.* (Dutch: Leiden 1903 and 1925; in the edition of 1925 the most recent bibliography is given). The main sources are the pertinent sections in the books of *Ḥadīth*, *Fiḳh* and *Ikhtilāf*. For Tradition cf. Wensinck, *Handbook*; al-Ghazzālī, *Iḥyāʾ ʿulūm al-dīn*, Cairo 1346, i. 207—214.

SAʿY. When the pilgrim who is making the *ʿumra* or the *ḥadjdj* has performed the circumambulation (*ṭawāf*) of the Kaʿba, kissed the Black Stone for the last time and drunk of the well of Zamzam, he goes out, taking care to put his left foot first, of the sacred mosque by the Bāb al-Ṣafāʾ, pronouncing the formula of salutation to the mosque, then a second formula indicating his intention (*nīya*) to accomplish the ceremony of *saʿy*. He ascends the steps of al-Ṣafāʾ about 50 yards from the gate and standing there he makes an invocation, looking towards the Kaʿba, with his hands raised to the level of his shoulders and the palms turned towards the sky. Between al-Ṣafāʾ and another little hill, al-Marwa, lies a broad street with houses and shops on either side; this is the *masʿā* where the pilgrims have to accomplish the ritual course. Walking at a normal rate he descends towards the former bottom of the valley (*masīl*), marked by four pillars, two along the mosque on the left and two others opposite it; to cross it, he assumes a more rapid pace, called *harwal* or *khabab*, like the *ramal* of the *ṭawāf*, and runs. Then walking slowly he reaches al-Marwa which is marked by an arch of stone like al-Ṣafāʾ and he again prays there. He has now completed one of the seven elements of the ceremony for, except for one isolated opinion, the authorities agree that the *saʿy* consists of seven such courses. It is usually followed by a desanctification by shaving or cutting the hair, which explains the large number of barbers' shops on the *masʿā*.

The *saʿy* has not the value of an independent rite like the circumambulation of the Kaʿba, the accomplishment of which, without the *ʿumra* and the *ḥadjdj*, is reckoned to the spiritual credit of the believer. The *saʿy* is an appendage to the circumambulation (*ṭawāf*) of the *ʿumra* or of the arrival (*ḳudūm*) or of the desanctification (*ifāḍa*), and the authorities are not agreed as to its importance, whether essential, obligatory or traditional. The law does not impose on the faithful who accomplish it the strict necessity of ritual purity that it demands for the *ṭawāf*.

The *saʿy* is an ambulatory rite with a brief period of running, analogous to the *ṭawāf*, to the *ifāḍa* of ʿArafa and Muzdalifa etc.; undoubtedly it was actually a separate ancient rite, which became combined with those of the Kaʿba, as the *ifāḍa* did to the ceremonies of ʿArafa and Muzdalifa. Tradition has retained the memory of the cult of two divinities, Isāf and Nāʾila, but only in the story that they were a man and a woman who were turned into stone for fornicating in the sanctuary and later came to be worshipped. Later Muslim tradition turned them into Adam and Eve, who sat on either of the hills to take a rest. But tradition has made special efforts, not without hesitation, to connect the rite with the story of Abraham: Hādjar, cast off by Abraham and seeing Ismāʿīl perishing of thirst, ran in despair seven times from one hill to the other; or it is said that Abraham instituted the *saʿy* for the worship of Allāh and quickened his pace (the *harwal*) to escape Satan who was lying in wait for him at the bottom of the ravine.

Bibliography: See the art. ḤADJDJ and KAʿBA, and add: Gaudefroy-Demombynes, *Le Pèlerinage de la Mekke*, p. 225—234, with references especially to al-Azraḳī, Ḳutb al-Dīn, Ibn Djubair, Nāsir Khusraw, Muḥammad al-Ṣādiḳ, al-Batanūnī, Burckhardt, etc.

SHAʿBĀN, name of the eighth month of the lunar year. In classical *ḥadīth* it has already its place after Radjab Muḍar. In Pakistan and India it has the name of *Shab-i barāt* (see below), the Atchehnese call it *Kandūri bu*, the Javanese *ruah* (from *arwāḥ*, cf. Juynboll, *Handleiding*[4], 160) and among the Tigrē tribes it is called *Maddāgen*, i.e. which follows upon Radjab.

In early Arabia the month of Shaʿbān (the name may mean "interval") seems to have corresponded, as to its significance, to Ramaḍān. According to the *ḥadīth* Muḥammad practised supererogatory fasting by preference in Shaʿbān (Bukhārī, *Ṣawm*, b. 52; Muslim, *Ṣiyām*, trad. 176; Tirmidhī, *Ṣawm*, b. 36). ʿĀʾisha recovered in Shaʿbān the fastdays which were left from the foregoing Ramaḍān (Tirmidhī, *Ṣawm*, b. 65).

In the early-Arabian solar year Shaʿbān as well as Ramaḍān fell in summer. Probably the weeks preceding the summer-solstice and those following it, had a religious significance which gave rise to propitiatory rites such as fasting. This period had its centre in the middle of Shaʿbān, a day which, up to the present time, has preserved features of a New-Year's day. According to popular belief, in the night preceding the 15th the tree of life on whose leaves are written the names of the living is shaken. The names written on the leaves which fall down indicate those who are to die in the coming year. In *ḥadīth* it is said that in this night Allāh descends to the lowest heaven; from there he calls mortals in order to grant them forgiveness of sins (Tirmidhī, *Sunan*, b. 39).

Among a number of peoples the beginning or the end of the year is devoted to the commemoration of the dead. This connection can also be observed in the Muslim world. For this reason Shaʿbān bears the epithet of *al-muʿaẓẓam* "the venerated". In Pakistan and India in the night of the 14th people say prayers for the dead, distribute food among the poor, eat *ḥalwa* (sweetmeats) and indulge in illuminations and firework. This night is called *lailat al-barāʾa* which is explained by "night of quittancy" i.e. forgiveness of sins.

In Atcheh this month is likewise devoted to the dead; the tombs are cleansed, religious meals (*kandūri*), are given and it is the dead who profit from the merits of these goods work. The night of the middle of Shaʿbān bears a particularly sacred character as is testified by the *kandūris* and the *ṣalāts* which are called *ṣalāt al-ḥādja* or, on account of certain eulogies, *ṣalāt al-taṣābīḥ*. During the last days of the month, a market is held in the capital.

At Mecca Radjab, not Shaʿbān, is devoted to the dead. Here, in the night of the 14th Shaʿbān, religious exercises are held; in the mosque circles are formed which under the direction of an *imām* recite the prayer peculiar to this night.

In Morocco on the last day of Shaʿbān a festival is celebrated which resembles a carnival. A description of it is to be found in L. Brunot, *La mer dans les traditions et les industries indigènes à Rabat et Salé* (Paris 1921), p. 98 *sq.*

Bibliography: E. Littmann, *Die Ehrennamen und Neubenennungen der isl. Monate*, in *Isl.*, viii. 1918, 228 *sq.*; Herklots, *Qanoon-i Islam*; C. Snouck Hurgronje, *The Achehnese*, i. 221 *sqq.*; do., *Mekka*, ii. 76, 291; A. J. Wensinck, *Arabic New-Year* (*Verh. Ak. Amst.*, new ser. xxv. No. 2), p. 6 *sq.*; G. F. Pijper, *Lailat al-niṣf min shaʿbān op Java*, in *TTLV* 1933.

SHADD (or RABṬ AL-MIḤZAM), "ligature", "girdle which is bound on"; this is the most important rite in the initiation ceremony practised since at least the twelfth century A.D. in the guilds of artisans (*ḥirfa*) as well as in certain mystical congregations (cf. ṬARĪḲA). At his initiation before the body of initiates, the candidate (*mashdūd*) if he is a Muslim, takes part if required in the recitation of the *Fātiḥa*, the 7 *salām*'s, the *nashāʾid* in honour of the Prophet, the latter preceded by his taking a preliminary oath. Then comes the *shadd*; the novice bends down and is "bound" by the initiator (*naḳīb*, *shādd*), either on the body, the head, or the shoulder (cf. the Turkish miniature in *Islam*, vi. 171), with a knot of material, a shawl of silk or wool (*miḥzam*), a cloth handkerchief (*fūṭa*, *mandīl*, *ghaiba*, *zunnār*), or a simple piece of string (*maftūl*). Several successive twists, knots or turns are made in the cord, usually 4 (sometimes 3, 7 or 8); prayers are recited at each twist invoking some patron saint: when there are four of them, the prayer is in honour of the *mashdūd*, Gabriel, Muḥammad, ʿAlī and Salmān; in this case, two supplementary knots are added (called *gharsa*, *shakla*) in honour of Ḥasan and Ḥusain.

The shadd is characteristic of the solemn initiation *ʿalā bisāṭ Allāh, fī maidān ʿAlī, bayn al-fityān*; it binds the initiate, whether he be Muslim, Christian or Jew to the corporation as a body, as the *ʿahd al-khirḳa* of the mystics binds one to the whole brotherhood; on the other hand, the *takhāwī*, called "pact without a knot" is a private pact of brotherhood binding to a single individual only by a kind of foster-brotherhood (cf. *ʿahd al-yad wa 'l-iḳtidā* or *talḳīn*, for the novice mystic).

After the *shadd*, the initiate is sometimes partially shaved (forelock, moustache or beard); then he puts on a special dress (*libās*, *sarāwīl*) in the old guilds; *khirḳa* on the shoulders and *tādj* (*kulāh* or *ḳurmus*, according to Baḳlī as early as 570/1174 or *tāḳiya*) on the head, in the congregations. The initiate's solemn pledge is then taken (*ʿahd*, *bayʿa*, *mubāyaʿa*, *mīthāḳ al-ikhā*), certain esoteric instruction on his new duties is given him with permission to make use of it (*idjāza*). He then takes his place with this brethren on the carpet of initiation (*bisāṭ*, *sadjdjāda*), for the traditional meal (*tamlīḥ*, *walīma*).

During the last forty years this rite has begun to disappear with the gradual disappearance of the old guilds. Some congregations (*Rifāʿīya* and *Beḳtāshīya*), however, have still preserved the solemn *shadd*.

Thorning was the first to study and classify methodically the esoteric manuscripts relating to the guilds, or *kutub al-futuwwa*, which describe this ritual (they are a kind of catechism of initiation, like the masonic handbooks, compiled in vulgar Arabic with some Persian terms: *dastūr* "by your leave", *pīr*, *kār*); the earliest manuscript is dated 844/1440 but the text is of the xiii[th] century; an inscription found by van Berchem in Egypt alludes to them as early as 771/1369; the Caliph Nāṣir (d. 622/1225) is remembered for having based his attempt at an order of chivalry (*libās al-futuwwa*) on the rite of *shadd*, which is found even earlier in 578/1182 among the *Nubuwīya* of Damascus, and in 535/1140 in a guild of thieves of Baghdād (cf. also Ibn al-Djawzī, *Talbīs Iblīs*, ed. Cairo 1340, p. 421).

Its origins are still more remote, if we remember the significance from the fourth century A.H. among the mystics of the words already mentioned *bisāṭ*, *fūṭa*, and especially *futuwwa* [q.v.], this "knightly honour" which no threat nor prayer could turn from regarding their oaths (like Satan damned for his fidelity to the monotheistic pact, which he had taken, according to Ḥallādj, *Ṭawāsīn*, vi. 20—25, Abū Ṭālib al-Makkī, *Ḳūt al-ḳulūb*, Cairo 1310, ii., p. 82, Aḥmad al-Ghazzālī, quoted in Ibn al-Djawzī, *Ḳuṣṣāṣ*, Leiden MS., cod. Warn. 998, f. 117[a] *sqq.*). The appropriation to the *shadd* of Ḳur'ān, vii. 172 and xlviii. 10 seems to be more modern. But certain elements of the ritual itself are ancient, probably of extremist Shīʿa origin. It is not by chance that the sect of the Nuṣairīs who practise initiation as reformed by Khaṣībī and Ṭabarānī in the fourth century A.H., already credits Salmān with the same qualities as initiator as do the guild catechisms describing the *shadd*; moreover, the oath of secrecy and the right to initiate non-Muslim monotheists point to the Ḳarmaṭians.

Bibliography: H. Thorning, *Beiträge zur Kenntnis des islamischen Vereinswesens auf Grund von "Basṭ madad et taufīq* (*Türkische Bibliothek*, xvi.), Berlin 1913, p. 1—7, 123—164 and 197—199; this is the standard work; cf. also v. Kremer, *Culturgeschichte*, ii. 187; Elia Ḳoudsī, in *VI*[e] *Congrès des orientalistes*, Leiden 1884, ii., p. 134; Goldziher, *Abhandlungen zur arabischen Philologie*, 1899, ii., p. lxxvii.—lxxxix; Köprülüzade, *Türk Adabiyātende ilk Mutaṣawwifler*, Istanbul 1919, p. 412; see also under FUTUWWA.

SHĀDHILĪYA, or SHĀDHALĪYA, pronounced in Africa Shādulīya, order of dervishes called after Abu 'l-Ḥasan ʿAlī b. ʿAbd Allāh al-Shādhilī, whose title is variously given as Tādj al-Dīn and Taḳī al-Dīn (593—656 A.H.).

His system. Al-Shādhilī does not appear to have composed any large work, but many sayings, spells and an ode are ascribed to him, and since some of the first are recorded in the work of his disciple's disciple, Tādj al-Dīn al-Iskandarī, composed in 694, they may be to some extent genuine. The best known of his productions is the *Ḥizb al-baḥr* "Incantation of the Sea", which was reproduced by Ibn Baṭṭūṭa (i. 41), whence the translation is copied by L. Rinn (*Marabouts et Khouan*, p. 229). Extraordinary powers are ascribed to it by Ḥādjdjī Khalīfa (iii. 58), and its author thought it might have prevented the fall of Baghdād; several commentaries on it are enumerated. Several other incantations and prayers are given in the *Laṭā'if* (ii. 47—66) and the *Mafākhir* (p. 135 *sqq.*). The latter of these works also contains fairly lengthy discourses, in some of which the stages through which the *murīd* should pass are described in detail, though the language is, as usual in such cases, not intelligible to the ordinary reader. It would appear from these that al-Shādhilī's aim was in the main the inculcation of the higher morality, such as is found in the works which he approved, viz. the *Iḥyā' ʿulūm al-dīn* and the *Ḳūt al-ḳulūb*; and indeed the five principles (*uṣūl*) of his system are given as (1) fear of Allāh in secret and open; (2) adherence to the Sunna in words and deeds; (3) contempt of mankind in prosperity and adversity; (4) resignation to the will of Allāh in things great and small; (4) having recourse to Allāh in joy and sorrow.

It would seem unlikely that it was his intention to found an order in the sense which afterwards became attached to the word *ṭarīḳa*. He desired his adherents to pursue the trades and professions in which they were engaged, combining, if possible, their normal activities with acts of devotion. Anecdotes are recorded of men who offered to abandon their employments and follow the saint, who urged them to continue working at the same. Mendicancy was discouraged and even government subsidies for their meeting-houses were, it is asserted, refused. Indeed the erection of *zāwiya*'s and similar buildings does not seem to have been contemplated by al-Shādhilī or his successor Abu 'l-ʿAbbās, who is praised by his biographer for never placing stone on stone. Even the holding of high office with ample emoluments and a luxurious mode of living was not discouraged; and this doctrine, as will be seen, survived till recent times among adherents of the system.

Doubtless the ultimate aim of al-Shādhilī was, as with other Ṣūfīs, *al-fanā'*, and the method pursued was the usual one of the religious exercises called *awrād* and *adhkār*. Formulae, as usual, were selected and their repetition a stated number of times enjoined. Lists of these with the ritual appertaining to them are given in the *Mafākhir* (p. 125, 126). The shaikh, indeed, is said to have adapted his recommendations to the needs of each *murīd* and to have given each permission to follow some other shaikh, if he found his methods more effective. The use of such formulae, however, is not easily separated from the supposed acquisition of miraculous powers, which are described in the *Mafākhir* (*loc. cit.*): "The least of their (the Shādhilīs') messengers are blindness, crippling and desolation", but there was some doubt whether they were justified in sending them on their enemies.

Apart from their mysterious knowledge the leaders of the system claimed to be strictly orthodox, and, indeed, when a revelation which one of the adherents received conflicted with a *sunna* he was told to reject the former in favour of the latter. In spite of this some of al-Shādhilī's assertions incurred the censure of Ibn Taimīya, whose supporters in this matter in their turn incurred the censure of the historian al-Yāfiʿī (iv. 142).

The three specialties which the members of the sect claimed were: (1) that they are all chosen from the "well-guarded Tablet", i.e. have been predestined from all eternity to belong to it; (2) that ecstasy with them is followed by sobriety, i.e. does not permanently incapacitate them from active life; (3) that the *ḳuṭb* will throughout the ages be one of them.

Spread of the system. The absence at the first of religious buildings renders it difficult to trace the progress of the community. It seems clear that the first group of adherents was formed in Tunis; al-Shādhili's successor, however, Abu 'l-ʿAbbās al-Mursī (d. 686) lived 36 years in Alexandria, "without once seeing the face of the governor or sending to him" (*Laṭāʾif*, i. 128), and, as has been seen, did not lay stone on stone; still ʿAlī Pasha Mubārak (*Khiṭaṭ djadīda*, vii. 69) records the existence there of a mosque bearing his name (restored 1189/1775—1776), doubtless built by his disciples; also of one called after his disciple Yāḳūt al-ʿArshī (d. 707) and a third called after their joint disciple Tādj al-Dīn b. ʿAṭā al-Iskandarī (d. 709; author of the *Laṭāʾif*). The first of these is called a *djāmiʿ* and is richly endowed. There are *mawlid* celebrated in honour of the first two of these persons. ʿAlī Pasha states that the mosques are chiefly frequented by Maghrebines; he mentions a mosque belonging to the order in Cairo, which, however, is in ruins. It is probable that the adherents of al-Shādhilī were at all times to be found chiefly to the West of Egypt; but H. H. Jessup (*Fifty-three years in Syria*, ii. 537) asserts that they were in his time numerous in Syria and advocated the reading of the Old and New Testaments and fraternization with Christians. In 1892 a lady adherent, "from Koraun in the Bukaa, North of Mt. Hermon", set out on a preaching tour in Syria; she advocated reform and an upright life and insisted that all, Muslims, Christians and Jews, are brothers. She preached in the mosques in Damascus, Ḥāṣbīyā, Sidon, Tyre and other cities, rebuking the sins of the people. It would seem certain that religious toleration of this sort by no means coincided with the views of the founder of the order.

It was reported by C. Niebuhr (*Reisebeschr. nach Arabien*, i. 439; French transl., i. 350) that in Moshā in S. Arabia Shaikh al-Shādhilī was regarded as the patron saint of the place and, indeed, the originator of coffee-drinking; and S. de Sacy afterwards (*Chrest. Arabe*, ii. 274) produced from the *Djihān-numā* a passage relating how al-Shādhilī came to Arabia in 656, and the series of miracles which led to the production of coffee becoming the staple industry of Mokhā. It is more probable that the patron of Mokhā is a later member of the sect, ʿAlī b. ʿUmar al-Ḳurashī (whose verses are cited in the *Mafākhir*, p. 7), a disciple (and probably cousin) of Nāṣir al-Dīn Muḥammad b. ʿAbd al-Dāʾim b. al-Mailaḳ (d. 797), head of the order in his time (Ritter, *Erdkunde, Arabien*, ii. 572). It is not clear from Niebuhr's account how far the people of Mokhā in his time observed the Shādhilī ritual or belonged to the community.

The main seat of the Shādhilī community appears then to have been Africa west of Egypt, and chiefly Algeria and Tunisia. Materials for the religious history of this region are at present scanty; from a MS. called *Ṭabaḳāt Wad Ḍaifulla*, written 1805 A.D., MacMichael produces the following excerpt relating to a shaikh who died A.H. 1155 (*A History of the Arabs of the Sudan*, ii. 250):

"It was characteristic of him (Khogali b. ʿAbd al-Raḥmān b. Ibrāhīm) that he held to the Book and the Law [*sunna*] and followed [the precepts and example of] the Shádhalía Sayyids as to word and deed. And he used to wear gorgeous raiments, such as a green robe of Baṣra, and upon his head a red fez [*ṭarbūsh*], and round it as a turban rich muslin stuffs. For footwear he wore shoes [*ṣarmūga*]; and he fumigated himself with India-wood [*el ʿūd el hindī*], and perfumed himself, and put Abyssinian civet on his beard and on his clothes. All this he did in imitation of Sheikh Abu el Ḥasan el Shádhalí . . . And it was remarked to him that the Ḳádiría only wear cotton shirts and scanty clothes, and he replied 'My clothes proclaim to the world "We are in no need of you", but their clothes say "We are in need of you"'.

The same notice contains the names of some important members of the order; the shaikh's conduct, as will be seen, agrees exactly with the anecdotes recorded in the *Laṭāʾif*, and the same is the case with what is told in the next paragraph:

"It was also characteristic of him that he never rose up to salute any of the great ones of the earth, neither the Awlad ʾAgib, the rulers of his country nor the kings of Gaʾal, nor any of the nobility, excepting only two men, the successor [*Khalífa*] of Sheikh Idrís and the successor of Sheikh Ṣughayerūn".

In the nineteenth century the order received considerable extension through the efforts of one "Si Maisum" (= al-Miʿṣūm) Muḥammad b. Muḥammad b. Aḥmad, born about 1820 among the Gharīb, a tribe located halfway between Bogar and Miliana, whose biography is given in detail by A. Joly in the *Revue Africaine*, 1906, 1907. After studying under certain provincial teachers he went to Mazouma, the centre of Muslim studies in Algeria. Having acquired what was to be learned there, he went back to the Gharīb among whom he founded two mosques, in one of which he taught the Ḳurʾān and Fiḳh, in the other Grammar and Logic. Having associated with members of different orders, he hovered between the Madanīya and the Shādhilīya; in 1860 he visited the shrine of ʿAbd al-Raḥmān al-Thaʿālibī near Algiers, and this saint having been a Shādhilī, Si Maisum became attracted to their doctrine; a member of the order advised him to join it and visit the Shaikh of the order, ʿAdda, at Djabal al-Luḥ in Walad Lakreud. There he stayed for a time, after which he returned to the Gharīb. By special providence he had been spared the preliminary trials imposed on other aspirants, and instead of starting his career in the order as a *muḳaddim*, he was elevated shortly after joining to the dignity of Shaikh. About 1865 he founded a *zāwiya* at Boghari and divided his time between the Gharīb and Boghari, to the latter of which he ultimately withdrew. In 1866 owing to the death of ʿAdda he became Shaikh of the Shādhilīya in Central Algeria, though at first he had to contest it with ʿAdda's son. He was offered the headship of a government madrasa at Algiers, but declined. This invitation, however, brought him the acquaintance of European officials, whose respect he enjoyed till his death in 1883. By this time his sphere of influence had extended over the greater part of the Tell Oranais and the whole of Western Algeria. Places where he had *khulafāʾ* were Mustaghanem, Mascara, Relizane, Nedroma, Oran, Tlemcen. After his death some of these *khulafāʾ* made themselves independent and the unity of control which he had established came to an end.

Statistics for the end of the last century are given by Depont and Coppolani (p. 454), whence it appears that the number of adherents in Algiers and Constantine did not reach 15,000, with 11 zāwiya's. The communities which split off from the Shādhilīya are there given as 13 in number, and among these the Shaikhīya, Ṭaibīya and Derḳāwīya are said to be the most numerous.

Although when the community started there appears to have been little in the way of organization contemplated and the connection between adherents was loose, it is evident that in course of time the normal organization of a *ṭariḳa* was introduced.

Literature of the Order. It is noticed that neither Shādhilī himself nor his successor Abū 'l-ʿAbbās al-Mursī published any treatises, whereas his disciple Yāḳūt al-ʿArshī seems to have composed *Manāḳib*, and their joint disciple Tādj al-Dīn al-Iskandarī was the author of several works, of which two, *Laṭāʾif al-minan*, dealing with the first two heads of the sect, and *Miftāḥ al-falāḥ wa-miṣbāḥ al-arwāḥ*, are printed on the margin of the *Laṭāʾif al-minan* of al-Shaʿrānī (Cairo 1321). The former of these is the main source of our knowledge of al-Shādhilī's career. A biography of al-Shādhilī which cannot have been much later was the *Durrat al-asrār* of Muḥammad b. al-Ḳāsim al-Ḥimyarī b. al-Ṣabbāgh, which is excerpted in the *Mafākhir*. Another biography called *al-Kawākib al-zāhira*, by Abu 'l-Faḍl ʿAbd al-Ḳādir b. Muʿaizil (d. 894), was excerpted by Haneberg (*ZDMG*, vii. 14 *sqq*.). The general account of the system called *al-Mafākhir al-ʿalīya fi 'l-maʿāthir al-Shādhilīya* (printed Cairo 1314) by Ibn Iyāḍ is later than al-Suyūṭī. For doctrine this work refers to two *Risāla*'s called respectively *al-Uṣūl* and *al-Ummahāt* by Sīdī Zarrūḳ (Shihāb al-Dīn Aḥmad al-Fāsī, d. 896). Haneberg, *loc. cit.*, mentions the Shādhilī poet ʿAlī b. Wafāʾ (d. 807) and his father Muḥammad Wafāʾ, author of certain mystical works, and a "diwan, of which the odes breathe for the greater part the spirit of joyous devotion to Allah, without disturbing admixture". A poem called *Ḥāl al-sulūk* by the Nāṣir al-Dīn who has already been mentioned is noticed by Ḥādjdjī Khalīfa. A Shādhilī writer, Dāwūd b. ʿUmar b. Ibrāhīm of Alexandria (d. 733), is mentioned by al-Suyūṭī in *Bughyat al-wuʿāt*, p. 246. Biographies of Shādhilī saints are collected in *Kitāb ṭabaḳāt al-Shādhilīya al-kubrā* by al-Ḥasan b. al-Ḥādjdj Muḥammad al-Kawhan al-Fāsī, Cairo 1347.

To the European literature noticed in the text should be added Asín Palacios, *Šādilīes y alumbrados*, in *Andalus*, 1944 *sqq.*

SHAFĀʿA (A.), intercession, mediation. He who makes the intercession is called *Shāfiʿ* and *Shafīʿ*. The word is also used in other than theological language, e.g. in laying a petition before a king (*Lisān*, s.v.), in interceding for a debtor (Bukhārī, *Istriḳrād*, bāb 18). Very little is known of intercession in judicial procedure. In a ḥadīth it is said: "He who by his intercession puts out of operation one of the *ḥudūd Allāh* is putting himself in opposition to Allāh" (Ibn Ḥanbal, *Musnad*, ii. 70, 82; cf. Bukhārī, *Anbiyāʾ*, bāb 54; *Ḥudūd*, bāb 12).

The word is usually found in the theological sense, particularly in eschatological descriptions; it already occurs in the Ḳurʾān in this use. Muḥammad became acquainted through Jewish and more particularly Christian influences with the idea of eschatological intercession. In Job xxxiii., 23 *sqq.* (the text is corrupt) the angels are mentioned who intercede for man to release him from death. In Job v. 1, there is reference to the saints (by whom here also angels are probably meant), to whom man turns in his need. Abraham is a mortal saint whom we find interceding in the Old Testament (in the story of Sodom and Gormorrah).

In the apocryphal and pseudepigraphical literature we again find the same classes of beings with the same function. The angels (*Test. Adam*, ix. 3), the saints (2. *Maccab.*, xv. 14; *Assumptio Mosis*, xii. 6). In the early Christian literature the same idea repeatedly occurs, but here we have two further classes of beings; the apostles and the martyrs (cf. Cyril of Jerusalem in Migne, *Patrologia Graeca*, vol. xxxiii., 1115; patriarchs, prophets, apostles, martyrs; cf. vol. xlvi., 850; lxi. 581).

In the Ḳurʾān intercession occurs mainly in a negative context. The day of judgment is described as a day on which no shafāʿa will be accepted (Sūra ii. 48, 254). This is directed against Muḥammad's enemies as is evident from Sūra x. 18: "they serve not Allāh but what brings them neither ill nor good and they say these are our intercessors with Allāh"; cf. also Sūra lxxiv. 48: "the intervention of those who make shafāʿa will not avail them".

But the possibility of intercession is not absolutely excluded. Sūra xxxix, 44 says: Say: the intercession belongs to Allāh, etc. Passages are fairly numerous in which this statement is defined to mean that shafāʿa is only possible with Allāh's permission: "Who should intervene with Him, even with His permission" (Sūra ii. 255, cf. x. 3). Those who receive Allāh's permission for shafāʿa are explained as follows: The shafāʿa is only for those who have an *ʿahd* with the Merciful (Sūra xix. 87) and xliii. 86: "They whom they invoke besides Allāh shall not be able to intercede except those who bear witness to the truth". xxi., 28 is remarkable in that it evidently credits the power of intercession to the angels: "they say the Merciful has begotten offspring. Nay, they are but His honoured servants who .... and they offer not to intercede save on behalf of whom it pleaseth Him". It appears that the angels are meant by the honoured servants. Sūra xl. 7 (cf. xlii. 5) is more definite: "Those who bear the throne and surround it sing the praises of their Lord and believe in Him and implore forgiveness for those who believe (saying) "Our Lord; who embracest all things in mercy and knowledge; bestow forgiveness on them that repent and follow Thy path and keep them from the pains of Hel."

Such utterances paved the way for an unrestricted adoption by Islām of the principle of *shafāʿa*. In the classical Ḥadīth which reflects the development of ideas to about 150 A.H. we already have ample material. Shafāʿa is usually mentioned here in eschatological descriptions. But it should be noted that the Prophet even in his lifetime is said to have made intercession. ʿĀʾisha relates that he often slipped quietly from her side at night to go to the cemetery of Baḳīʿ al-Gharḳad to beseech forgiveness of Allāh for the dead (Muslim, *Djanāʾiz*, trad. 102; cf. Tirmidhī, *Djanāʾiz*, bāb 59). Similarly his *istighfār* is mentioned in the *ṣalāt al-djanāʾiz* (e.g. Ibn Ḥanbal, *Musnad*, iv. p. 170) and its efficacy explained (*ibid.*, p. 388). The prayer for the forgiveness of sins then became or remained an integral part of this *ṣalāt* (e.g. Abū Isḥāḳ al-Shīrāzī, *Kitāb al-Tanbīh*, ed. J. W. T. Juynboll, p. 48) to which a high degree of importance was attributed. Cf. Muslim, *Djanāʾiz*, trad. 58: "If a community of Muslims, a hundred strong, perform the *ṣalāt* over a Muslim and all pray for his sins to be forgiven him, this prayer will surely be granted"; and Ibn Ḥanbal, iv. 79, 100, where the number of hundred is reduced to three rows (*ṣufūf*).

Muḥammad's intercession at the day of judgment is described in a tradition which frequently occurs (e.g. Bukhārī, *Tawḥīd*, bāb 19; Muslim, *Īmān*, trad. 322, 326—329; Tirmidhī, *Tafsīr*, Sūra xvii., trad. 19; Ibn Ḥanbal, i. 4) the main features of which are as follows: On the day of judgment Allāh will assemble the believers; in their need they turn to Adam for his intercession. He reminds them, however, that through him sin entered the world and refers them to Nūḥ. But he also mentions his sins and refers them to Ibrāhīm. In this way they appeal in vain to the great apostles of God until ʿĪsā finally advises them to appeal to Muḥammad for assistance. The latter will gird himself and with Allāh's permission throw himself before Him. Then he will be told "arise and say, intercession is granted thee". Allāh will thereupon name him a definite number to be released and when he has led these into Paradise, he will again throw himself before his Lord and the same stages will again be repeated several times until finally Muḥammad says: "O Lord, now there are only left in hell those who, according to the Ḳurʾān, are to remain there eternally".

This tradition is in its different forms the locus classicus for the limitation of the power of intercession to Muḥammad to the exclusion of the other apostles. In some traditions it is numbered among the charismata allotted to him (e.g. al-Bukhārī, *Ṣalāt*, bāb 56).

Muḥammad's *shafāʿa* then is recognized by the *idjmāʿ*; it is based on Sūra xvii. 79: "Perhaps the Lord shall call thee to an honourable place"; and on xciii. 5: "and thy Lord shall give a reward with which thou shalt be pleased" (al-Rāzī's commentary i. 351; cf. earlier, Muslim, *Īmān*, trad. 320). Muḥammad is said to have been offered the privilege of *shafāʿa* by a message from his Lord as a choice; the alternative was the assurance that half of his community would enter paradise. Muḥammad, however, preferred the right of intercession, doubtless because he thought he would get a considerable result from it (Tirmidhī, *Ḳiyāma*, bāb 13; Ibn Ḥanbal, iv. 404).

The traditions describe very vividly how the "people of hell" (*djahannamīyūn*) are released from their fearful state. Some have had to suffer comparatively little from the flames; others on the other hand are already in part turned to cinders. They are sprinkled with water from the well of life and they are restored to a healthy condition (e.g. Muslim, *Īmān*, trad. 320).

In another class of traditions it is said that every prophet has a "supplication" (*daʿwā*) and that Muḥammad keeps his secret in order to intercede with Allāh for his community on the day of judgment (cf. e.g. Ibn Ḥanbal, ii. 313; Muslim, *Īmān*, trad. 334 *sqq.*).

Quite in keeping with the Christian view already mentioned, Islām, however, was not content with Muḥammad as the advocate. Along with him we find the angels, the apostles, the prophets, the martyrs and the saints (Bukhārī, *Tawḥīd*, bāb 24; Ibn Ḥanbal, iii. 94 *sq.*, 325 *sq.*, v. 43; Abū Dāʾūd, *Djihād*, bāb 26; al-Ṭabarī, *Tafsīr*, iii. 6 on Sūra ii. 255; xvi. 85 on Sūra xix. 87; xxix. 91 on Sūra lxxiv. 48; Abū Ṭālib al-Makkī, *Ḳūt al-ḳulūb*, i. 139).

Finally after all these classes have said their word, there is still Allāh's *shafāʿa* (Bukhārī, *Tawḥīd*, bāb 24; cf. Sūra, xxxix. 45). Muḥammad's pre-eminence remains inasmuch as he is the first to intercede for his community (Muslim, *Īmān*, trad. 330, 332; Abū Dāʾūd, *Sunna*, bāb 13).

Finally the question for whom intercession is effective is discussed. While it is generally said 70,000 will enter paradise through the intercession of one man of Muḥammad's community (e.g. Dārimī, *Riḳāḳ*, bāb 87; cf. Ibn Ḥanbal, iii. 63, 469 *sq.*), the answer is already given as early as classical Tradition that *shafāʿa* holds good for those who ascribe no associate to Allāh (Bukhārī, *Tawḥīd*, bāb 19; Tirmidhī, *Ḳiyāma*, bāb 13). To this group also belong those who have committed great sins (*ahl al-kabāʾir*). "The prophet of God said: My intercession is for the great sinners of my community" (Abū Dāʾūd, *Sunna*, bāb 20; Tirmidhī, *Ḳiyāma*, bāb 11). This view, however, is not shared by the Muʿtazila (cf. Zamakhsharī, *Kashshāf* on ii. 48; no *shafāʿa* for the *ʿuṣāt*). Al-Rāzī deals very fully with the Muʿtazilī view in his commentary on the Ḳurʾān (i. 351 *sqq.*, vi. 404) according to which there is no such thing as *shafāʿa*, as no one is released from hell who is once thrown into it. For the denial of *shafāʿa* they appeal to some of the verses of the Ḳurʾān already quoted above.

Bibliography: Besides the works quoted in the text cf. Ghazzālī, *al-Durra al-fākhira*, ed. and transl. by Gautier (Geneva, Basle and Lyons 1878), text p. 66; transl. p. 56; M. Wolff, *Mohammedanische Eschatologie* (1872), p. 100 *sqq.*; R. Leszynski, *Mohammedanische Traditionen über das letzte Gericht*, Diss. Heidelberg, 1909, p. 50 *sqq.*; cf. also Goldziher, *Muhammedanische Studien*, ii. 308 *sqq.*; Ibn Ḥazm, *Kitāb al-faṣl fi 'l-milal wa 'l-ahwāʾ wa 'l-niḥal*, Cairo 1317—1321, iv. 64 *sqq.*; *Dictionary of the technical Terms*, ed. Nassau Lees and Sprenger, Calcutta 1862, p. 762; T. Huitema, *De voorspraak (shafâʿa) in den Islam*, Leiden 1936.

AL-**SHĀFIʿĪ**, ABŪ ʿABD ALLĀH MUḤAMMAD B. IDRĪS, the founder of the Shāfiʿī school of law. A great deal of legend has gathered round the story of his life and it is difficult to disentangle the historical element in it. The chronology in particular offers great difficulties. The early sources are very scanty. The first historian to mention him is al-Masʿūdī (d. 345). The only authentic material is the document making *waḳf* his two houses in Mecca of Ṣafar 203/Aug. 818 (*Umm*, vi. 179 = Kern in *MSOSA*s, 1904, p. 55), his will of Shaʿbān 203/Febr. 819 (*Umm*, iv. 48 = Kern, in *MSOSA*s, 1904, p. 59) and that of his house in Fusṭāṭ (*Umm*, iii. 281) in which it is true the name and date are omitted, but there is no doubt it is of al-Shāfiʿī himself. His later biographers use old manāḳibs like those of Dāʾūd al-Ẓāhirī (d. 270), al-Sādjī (d. 307), Ibn Abī Ḥātim (d. 327) among others, but there is already a great deal of legend here. For example, al-Khaṭīb al-Baghdādī, p. 59 already tells the story from Ibn ʿAbd al-Ḥakam (d. 257) of his birth, which connects him with the planet Jupiter rising over Egypt.

Al-Shāfiʿī belonged to the tribe of Ḳuraish. He was a Hāshimī and distantly related to the Prophet. His mother belonged to the tribe of Azd, but some say she was an ʿAlid. Born in 150/767 in Ghazza (al-Iṣṭakhrī, p. 58; al-Khaṭīb, p. 59) he early lost his father and was brought up ' , his mother in poor circumstances in Mecca. He spent much time among the Beduins and acquired a thorough knowledge of the old Arab poetry (for example he quotes verses from Zuhair, Imru'l-Ḳais, Djarīr, etc. in the *Kitāb al-Umm*; cf. Heffening, *Islam. Fremdenrecht*, p. 147, note 1). The philologist al-Aṣmaʿī heard from the boy the poetry of the Banū Hudhail (cf. also *Umm*, ii. 167; iv. 133) and the *Dīwān* of Shanfarā. He studied *Ḥadīth* and *Fiḳh* in Mecca with Muslim al-Zandjī (d. 180) and Sufyān b. ʿUyaina (d. 198). He knew the whole of the *Muwaṭṭaʾ* by heart. When about 20 he went to Madīna to Mālik b. Anas and remained there till the latter's death in 179/796. Al-Khaṭīb (p. 56) gives a list of his other teachers. He then went to fill an office in the Yaman. Here he became involved in ʿAlid intrigues — he was secretly a follower of the Zaidī Imām Yaḥyā b. ʿAbd Allāh (cf. v. Arendonk, *Opkomst van het zaiditische Imamaat*, p. 60 and 290), — and was brought prisoner with other ʿAlids to the caliph Hārūn al-Rashīd in Raḳḳa in 187/803. He was pardoned and through this incident brought into closer contact with the famous Ḥanafī Muḥammad b. al-Ḥasan al-Shaibānī (d. 189/805) whose books he had copied. But as he did not yet dare to take up position against al-Shaibānī who was an influential man at court, he went in 188/804 via Ḥarrān and Syria to Egypt where as pupil of Mālik he was at first well received. It was not till 194/810—1 that he returned to Baghdād and set up as a teacher there. Here he attached himself to ʿAbd Allāh, the son of the newly appointed governor of Egypt ʿAbbās b. Mūsā, and came to Egypt on the 26th Shawwāl 198/June 21, 814 (al-Kindī, ed. Guest, p. 154). As a result of unrest, he soon went to Mecca, returning finally to Egypt in 200/815—6. He died on the last day of Radjab 204/Jan. 20, 820 in Fusṭāṭ and was buried in the vault of the Banū ʿAbd al-Ḥakam at the foot of the Muḳaṭṭam. The text of his epitaph is given in al-Khaṭīb, p. 70. Ṣalāḥ al-Dīn had a large and commodious madrasa built there (Ibn Djubair, *Riḥla*, p. 48). The ḳubba still in existence was built by the Aiyūbid al-Malik al-Kāmil in 608/1211—2. It was always a prominent place of pilgrimage (cf. e.g. al-ʿAiyāshī, [d. 1090/1679], *Riḥla*, Fās 1316, i. 151).

Al-Shāfiʿī may be described as an eclectic, who took an intermediate path between independent invention of laws and the traditionalism of his period. He not only worked through the whole material of the law but in his *Risāla* (pr. Cairo 1321; summary of contents by L. B. Graf, *al-Shāfiʿī's verhandeling over de "wortelen" van den Fikh*, Amsterdam 1934) also investigated the methods and principles of jurisprudence. He is regarded as the founder of the *uṣūl al-fiḳh*. In contrast to the Ḥanafīs he endeavours to lay down rigid rules for *ḳiyās* *Risāla*, p. 66 and 70) while he rejects *istiḥsān* [q.v.]. The principle of *istiṣḥāb* [q.v.] seems only to have been introduced by the later Shāfiʿīs (cf. Goldziher, *Ẓāhiriten*, p. 20 *sqq.*; Bergsträsser, *Anfänge und Charakter des juristischen Denkens im Islām*, in *Isl.*, xiv. [1924], 76—80). Two periods of creative activity may be distinguished in al-Shāfiʿī, an earlier (in the ʿIrāḳ) and a later (in Egypt). Al-Ḥākim (d. 405) for example says this of the *Risāla* (al-ʿAsḳalānī, p. 77) which however only survives in the later recension. These two periods are frequently apparent in the *Kitāb al-Umm* as well as in the tenets of the later Shāfiʿīs. Four pupils are regarded as the transmitters of the older teaching: al-Zafarānī (d. 260), Abū Thawr (d. 240), Aḥmad b. Ḥanbal (d. 241) and al-Karābīsī (d. 245), and of the later six pupils: al-Muzanī (d. 264), al-Rabīʿ b. Sulaimān al-Djīzī (d. 256), al-Rabīʿ b. Sulaimān al-Murādī (d. 270), al-Buwaiṭī (d. 231), Ḥarmala (d. 243) and Yūnus b. ʿAbd al-Aʿlā (d. 264) [Ibn Khallikān, *Wafayāt*, i. 129].

His writings in which he handles dialogue with opponents, usually unnamed, in masterly fashion have, so far as they survive, been handed down by the above mentioned al-Rabīʿ b. Sulaimān al-Murādī. A list is given in the *Fihrist*, p. 210, another by al-Baihaḳī (d. 458) in al-Asḳalānī, p. 78 and a third in Yāḳūt, p. 396—8. The most of the titles mentioned there are parts of the *Kitāb al-Umm*. a collection of the writings and lectures of Shāfiʿī (Cairo 7 vols. 1321—25). The title of this collection can hardly be the original one and only established itself in course of time. Ibn Ḥadjar (d. 852) is still aware of this (cf. Murtaḍā al-Zubaidī, *Itḥāf*, vi. 239). While the author of the *Fihrist* and even Yāḳūt do not know this title, Abū Ṭālib al-Makkī (d. 386: *Ḳūt al-ḳulūb*, Cairo 1310, ii. 228) already mentions if (from him comes the same but abbreviated statement in al-Ghazzālī, *Iḥyā*, Cairo 1327, ii. 131); al-Baihaḳī similarly knows it (d. 458; in al-ʿAsḳalānī, p. 78 and al-Nawawī, *Tahdhīb* p. 67). In the work itself it only occurs in passages which prove to be glosses that have found their way into the text (e.g. *Umm*, i. 158; iii. 286). According to Abū Ṭālib al-Makkī (*op. cit.*; cf. al-Ghazzālī, *op. cit.*; Ḥādjdjī Khalīfa, *Kashf*, v. 52), al-Buwaiṭī prepared the collection which afterwards went under the name of Rabīʿ b. Sulaimān al-Murādī without naming himself in it, and al-Rabīʿ b. Sulaimān al-Murādī published it with his own additions.

This must have taken place shortly after al-Shāfiʿī's death, for al-Rabīʿ was transmitting the collection as early as 207 in Egypt, (*Umm* ii. 93). The printed edition is based on al-Rabīʿ al-Murādī's recension, although in a different arrangement: parts of it in the original arrangement are, however, known from manuscript tradition (cf. the editor's note in *Umm*, ii. 227). As late as the vth/xith century al-Baihaḳī had access to another recension, which agreed in arrangement with neither that of al-Rabīʿ nor with that of the later predominant Shāfiʿī arrangement (that of al-Muzanī's *Mukhtaṣar*). Perhaps this should be identified as the arrangement made by Buwaiṭī, which al-Rabīʿ used along with that of Ibn Abī Djārūd (cf. *Umm*, i. 96, 157; ii. 52; vii. 389 *et pass.*). Brockelmann's statement (*Suppl.*, i. 304) that Buwaiṭī's recension is preserved in Mss in Constantinople, is infortunately not correct. Still later various scholars arranged the *Umm*, e.g. Ibn al-Labbān (d. 749/1348—9) and Sirādj al-Dīn al-Bulḳīnī (d. 805/1402—3).

The latter's arrangement and edition of al-Rabīʿ's recension is available in the Cairo edition. But this edition is not sufficient for a definitive study of the origin and history of the text; for the editor has based his work on the arrangement of the Mss. by Bulḳīnī without noting the divergences in the other Mss. Moreover in the existing text of the *Umm*, glosses of varying length have found their way into the text (e.g. iii. 226, [19]); for example also al-Ghazzālī, Ibn al-Ṣabbāgh (d. 477), al-Māwardī and others are quoted (cf. *Umm*. i, 114 *sqq.*, 158). Only a careful study of the Mss. can throw further light on this point. The quotations in al-Ṭabarī, *Ikhtilāf al-fuḳahāʾ*, as the earliest evidence for al-Rabīʿs text, are of essential help for this: al-Ṭabarī had available a better form of the text of the *Umm* than the printed version (cf. Heffening, in *Festschrift P. Kahle*, Leyden, 1935, p. 104 *sq.* and discussion of Schacht's edition of Ṭabarī, in *Deutsche Literatur-Zeitung*, 1935, col. 181 *sq.*). Zakī Mubārak has recently disputed al-Shāfiʿī's authorship and puts forward the thesis that al-Buwaiṭī composed the work based on the teaching of his master, and that in addition Abū Muḥammad al-Rabīʿ b. Sulaimān al-Murādī and Abū Muḥammad al-Rabīʿ b. Sulaimān al-Djīzī were responsible and that the al-Rabīʿ b. Sulaimān mentioned by al-Ghazzālī as publishing the book is al-Djīzī. The arguments for this thesis, which naturally has met with much resistance in al-Azhar circles, are however untenable. In the first place from the existing text al-Buwaiṭī can only have been the collector and editor of the various works of al-Shāfiʿī; secondly the varying use of *ism* and *kunya* for the same man is nothing unusual in Arabic literature (the examples quoted may equally well refer to one and the same man; the passages *Umm*, v. 7, is undoubtedly a gloss), and lastly that the publisher of the work is not identical with al-Rabīʿ al-Murādī generally described as the *rāwī* of al-Shāfiʿī's works is not proved and incredible.

The works quoted by al-Baihaḳī as separate are really parts of the *Umm*: *Djimāʿ al-ʿilm* (*Umm*, vii. 250 *sqq.*). *Kitāb Ibṭāl al-istiḥsān* (vii. 267 *sqq.*), *K. Bayān al-farḍ* (vii. 262 *sqq.*), *K. Ṣifat al-amr wa 'l-nahy* (vii. 265?), *K. Ikhtilāf Mālik wa 'l-Shāfiʿī* (vii. 177 *sqq.*), *K. Ikhtilāf al-ʿIrāḳīyain* (vii. 87 *sqq.*), i.e. Abū Ḥanīfa and Ibn Abī Laila; d. 148), *K. Ikhtilāf maʿa Muḥammad b. al-Ḥasan* (vii. 277 *sqq.* = *K. al-Radd ʿalā Muḥ. b. al-Ḥasan*) and *K. Ikhtilāf ʿAlī wa-ʿAbd Allāh b. Masʿūd* (vii. 151 *sqq.*). The *K. Ikhtilāf al-ḥadīth* is printed on the margin of the *Umm*, vol. vii., the *Musnad* on the margin of vol. vi.

The latter contains traditions from his different works, for example from the no longer existing *K. Aḥkām al-Ḳur'ān*, *K. Faḍā'il Ḳuraish*, among others, mentioned in the *Fihrist* and by Yāḳūt. It exists in the recension handed down by Abū 'l-Abbās al-Aṣamm (d. 346), who took it down from al-Rabīʿ b. Sulaimān in 266 (cf. *Umm*, vi. 274). The *K. al-Mabsūṭ fi 'l-fiḳh* (*Fihrist*, p. 210) must have been another large legal work, which was still accessible to al-Baihaḳī, and was also known as *al-Mukhtaṣar al-kabīr wa' l-manthūrāt*; al-Shīrāzī (*Ṭabaḳāt*, No. 128) mentions a *K. al-Amālī* transmitted by Ibn Abi'l-Djārūd. There also survives a profession of faith by Shāfiʿī entitled *K. Waṣiyat al-Shāfiʿī* (mentioned in Yāḳūt, ed. by Kern in *MSOSAs*, 1910), while the *K. al-Fiḳh al-Akbar* ascribed to him (Cairo 1324, and often) is a brief dogmatical works of the Ashʿarī period (cf. now Wensinck, *The Muslim Creed*, Cambridge 1932, p. 264 *sqq.*). A few poems are evidence of his literary power (al-Masʿūdī, *Murūdj*, viii. 66; al-Ghazzālī, *Iḥyā'*, ii. 130; Ibn Khallikān, i. 448; al-ʿAsḳalānī, p. 73 *sqq.*).

Baghdād and Cairo were the chief centres of his work as a teacher. The names of his most important pupils have already been given. From these two cities Shāfiʿī teaching spread in the course of the third and fourth (ninth and tenth) centuries gaining more and more adherents, although from the first the Shāfiʿīs had a difficult position in Baghdād, the centre of the *ahl al-ra'y*. In the fourth (tenth) century. Mecca and Madīna were regarded as its chief centres outside of Egypt. In the beginning of the tenth century they were successfully disputing Syria with the Awzaʿīs so that they held the office of ḳāḍī of Damascus continuously from Abū Zurʿa (302/915). In the time of Maḳdisī Shāfiʿīs exclusively held the offices of ḳāḍī in Syria, Kirmān, Bukhārā and the greater part of Khurāsān; they were also strongly represented in northern Mesopotamia (Aḳūr) and Dailam (Egypt by this time was Shīʿī). In the vth—vi[th] (xi[th]—xii[th]) century there was often fighting in the streets with the Ḥanbalīs in Baghdād, with the Ḥanafīs in Iṣfahān, while on the other hand they won to their side the Ghūrid princes of Ghazna (Snouck Hurgronje, *Verspr. Geschr.*, ii. 306). In Yāḳūt's time (d. 624/1227; *Muʿdjam*, ii. 893) they gained the upperhand in al-Raiy after fighting with the Shīʿīs and Ḥanafīs. In Egypt they again became the predominant *madhab* under Ṣalāḥ al-Dīn (564/1169). But al-Malik al-Ẓāhir Baibars on 28th Dhu 'l-Ḳaʿda 663/11th Sept. 1265 for Cairo and on the 6th Djumādā I 664/13th Feb. 1266 for Damascus appointed a Ḥanafī, Ḥanbalī and Mālikī chief judge alongside of the Shāfiʿī (according to al-Nuwairī, in *Isl.*, xxiv., 1937, p. 131, note 4; cf. al-Subkī, v. 134). In the last centuries before the Ottoman conquest the Shāfiʿīs had won undoubted supremacy in the central lands of Islām. Already in Ibn Djubair's time (*Riḥla*, p. 102) the Shāfiʿī imām was leading prayer in Mecca. It was only under the Ottoman sulṭāns at the beginning of the tenth (xvi[th]) century that they were supplanted by Ḥanafīs, who were given the judgeships in Constantinople, while the Central Asian lands with the rise of the Ṣafawids (1501) passed to the Shīʿa. In spite of this, the people in Egypt, Syria and the Ḥidjāz continued to follow the Shāfiʿī *madhhab* (Snouck Hurgronje, *Verspr. Geschr.*, ii. 378/9). To this day in the Azhar mosque, the imām of which from 1724—1870 was always a Shāfiʿī, Shāfiʿī teaching is industriously studied along with that of the other schools. It is still predominant in South Arabia, Baḥrain, the Malay Archipelago, the East Africa, Daghistān and several parts of Central Asia.

Among notable and important Shāfiʿīs were: the traditionist al-Nasā'ī (d. 303/915), al-Ashʿarī (d. 324/935), al-Māwardī (d. 450/1058), al-Shīrāzī (d. 476/1083), the Imām al-Ḥaramain (d. 478/1085), al-Ghazzālī (d. 505/1111), al-Rāfiʿī (d. 623/1226), al-Nawawī (d. 676/1277) among others.

Al-Nawawī (*Tahdhīb*, p. 4) describes five books as standard works in his time: 1. al-Muzanī's (d. 264/877) *al-Mukhtaṣar*, a synopsis of the writings of the founder of the school, 2. *al-Tanbīh*, 3. *al-Muhadhdhab*, both by al-Shīrāzī (d. 470/1083), 4. *al-Wasīṭ* and 5. *al-Wadjīz* (both by al-Ghazzālī; d. 505/1111). The two last are synopses of al-Ghazzālī's *al-Basīṭ*, which again is based on the *Nihāyat al-maṭlab* of his teacher Imām al-Ḥaramain (d. 478/1085). All these works however were more or less driven out of use by later works based upon them. The shortest compendium is the *Taḳrīb* of Abū Shudjāʿ (d. shortly before 500/1106); ed. with translation by S. Keyser, Leyden 1859, with the commentary *Fatḥ al-ḳarīb* by Ibn Ḳāsim al-Ghazzī (d. 918/1512), ed. with transl. by L. C. van den Berg, Leyden 1895 and glosses by al-Bādjūrī (d. 1277/1861). Standard works of the later period were the *Muḥarrar* of Rāfiʿī (d. 623/1226), based on Ghazzālī and Nawawī's (d. 676/1277) synopsis of it *Minhādj al-ṭālibīn*, ed. with transl. by L. W. C. van den Berg, 3 vols., Batavia 1882/84, and the two commentaries on the *Minhādj*: al-Ramlī's (d. 1004/1596) *Nihāya*, and the *Tuḥfa* of Ibn Ḥadjar al-Haitamī (d. 973/1565). We should further mention: Ibn al-Khaṭīb al-Sharbīnī's (d. 977/1569) *al-Mughnī*, a commentary on the *Minhādj*, and Zakarīyā al-Anṣārī's (d. 926/1520) *Manhadj al-ṭullāb*, a synopsis of the *Minhādj* with the author's commentary *Fatḥ al-wahhāb*. On al-Ghazzālī also is based the *Ḥāwī* of al-Ḳazwīnī (d. 665/1266) with a synopsis *al-Irshād* by Ibn al-Muḳri' (d. 837/1433) and two commentaries on this synopsis by Ibn Ḥadjar: *Fatḥ al-djawād* and *al-Imdād*. A further synopsis of the *Muḥarrar* is the *Rawḍa* of Nawawī of which al-Muḳri' in turn made a synopsis, the *Rawḍ* on which a commentary was written by Zakarīyā al-Anṣārī, entitled *Asnā al-maṭālib* (on the dependence of these works on al-Ghazzālī see the table in Snouck Hurgronje, *Verspr. Geschr.*, iv/i., p. 105).

Of the numerous collections of *fatwās* the most important are those by al-Nawawī, Ibn al-Firkāḥ (d. 690/1291), al-Zarkas͟hī (d. 794/1392) and particularly al-Ramlī and Ibn Ḥad͟jar (*Al-Fatāwā al-kubrā*).

Of works on *Uṣūl* Ibn K͟haldūn mentions the following four as standard: *al-ʿAhd* by ʿAbd al-D͟jabbār (d. 415/1024) with the commentary *al-Muʿtamad* by Abu 'l-Ḥusain al-Baṣrī (d. 436/1044), *al-Burhān* by the Imām al-Ḥaramain (d. 478/1085) and *al-Mustaṣfā* by al-G͟hazzālī (d. 505/1111). Fak͟hr al-Dīn al-Rāzī (d. 606/1209) summed up these works in his *Maḥṣūl*, on which was based the *Minhād͟j al-wuṣūl* of Baiḍāwī (d. 682/1286) with a commentary by al-Asnawī (d. 772/1370); a later esteemed work was the *D͟jamʿ al-d͟jawāmiʿ* of Tād͟j al-Dīn al-Subkī (d. 772 /1370).

Muslim law according to the S͟hāfiʿī school has been expounded by L. W. C. van den Berg, *De beginselen van het mohammed. recht* [3], Batavia 1883 (cf. thereon Snouck Hurgronje, *Verspr. Geschr.*, ii. 59—221), French transl. by R. de France de Tersant: *Principes du droit musulman...* (Algiers 1886); Ed. Sachau, *Muham. Recht* (Stuttgart and Berlin 1897; cf. thereon Snouck Hurgronje, *Verspr. Geschr.* ii. 367—414); Th. W. Juynboll, *Handbuch des islāmischen Gesetzes* (Leyden 1910), Italian transl. with notes by G. Baviera: *Manuale di diritto musulmano ...* (Milan 1916); do., *Handleiding tot de kennis van de mohammed. wet*, Leyden 1930.

Bibliography: al-K͟haṭīb al-Bag͟hdādī, *Taʾrīk͟h Bag͟hdād*, Cairo 1931, ii. 56—73; al-Samʿānī, *Kitāb al-Ansāb*, in *GMS* xx., fol. 325v; Yāḳūt, *Irs͟hād al-ʿarīb*, in *GMS*, VI/vi., p. 376—98 (cf. thereon Bergsträsser, in *ZS*, ii., 1924, p. 201); al-Nawawī, *Biograph. Dictionary*, ed. Wüstenfeld, p. 56—76; Ibn K͟hallikān, No. 569; *Fragmenta hist. arab.*, i. 359 *sq.*; al-ʿAsḳalānī, *Tawāli 'l-taʾnīs bi-maʿālī b. Idrīs fī manāḳib... al-S͟hāfiʿī* (Būlāḳ 1301); Wüstenfeld, *Der Imām al-S͟hāfiʿī*, in *Abh. Gött. Ak. W.*, xxxvi. (1890); de Goeje, *Einiges über den Imām aš-Šafiʿī*, in *ZDMG*, xlvii. (1893), 106—17; Goldziher, *Ẓāhiriten*, p. 20—26; Brockelmann, *GAL*, i. 188 *sq.* *Suppl.*, i. 303 *sq.*; Heffening, *Islam. Fremdenrecht* (Hannover 1925), p. 145 *sq.*, 149; Schacht, *Origins of Muhammadan Jurisprudence* (Oxford 1950); Zakī Mubārak, *Iṣlāḥ as͟hnaʿ k͟haṭaʾ fī taʾrīk͟h al-tas͟hrīʿ al-islāmī, Kitāb al-Umm lam yuʿallifhu al-S͟hāfiʿī wa-innamā allafahu al-Buwaiṭī*, Cairo 1934. — Spread of the S͟hāfiʿī's: al-Subkī, *Ṭabaḳāt al-S͟hāfiʿīya al-kubrā* (Cairo 1324), i. 172—5; Ibn K͟haldūn, *Muḳaddima*, Cairo 1327, p. 500 *sqq.* (de Slane, in *NE*, xxi/l [1868], p. 10 *sqq.*); A. Mez, *Renaissance des Islam* (Heidelberg 1922), p. 202—6; Aḥmad Taimūr, *Naẓra taʾrīk͟hīya fī ḥudūt͟h al-mad͟hāhib al-arbaʿa*, Cairo 1344, p. 28 *sqq.*

S͟HĀFIʿĪS [s. AL-S͟HĀFIʿĪ, at the end.]

S͟HAHĀDA (A.), testimony, whether in the ordinary sense of the word, the statement of an eye-witness (from *s͟hāhada* "to see"), or in the religious and legal sense.

1. In the religious use of the word *s͟hahāda* is the Muslim profession of faith: "there is no god but God; Muḥammad is the Prophet of God" (cf. TAS͟HAHHUD); and by extension it is the testimony one gives in fighting for Islām, and more particularly in dying for it in the holy war. The Muslim who falls on the battlefield is called *s͟hahīd* [q.v.] "witness, martyr".

2. In the civil and legal sense, the witness is called *s͟hāhid*: e.g. the witnesses of a marriage who accompany the relatives before the Imām; the witnesses in a case of adultery; Sūra, iv. 19: "If your wives commit the act of infamy, call four witness".

On the theory of evidence in law consult the article S͟HĀHID.

Bibliography: See the handbooks of law; d'Ohsson, *Tableau général de l'Empire Othoman*, Paris 1778, i. p. 176; ii., p. 319—324, 348—350; Carra de Vaux, *Les Penseurs de l'Islam*, iii., Paris 1923, chap. on Tradition; Wensinck, *The Muslim Creed*, index.

S͟HAHĪD (A.), witness, martyr (pl. *s͟huhadāʾ*) is often used in the Ḳurʾān (as is *s͟hāhid* [q.v.], plur. *s͟huhūd*, from which it is not definitely distinguished) in the primary meaning of witness. The following examples are typical of the various contexts in which it occurs: Sūra ii. 133: "Or were ye eye-witnesses when Jacob was at the point of death and he said to his sons" ... Sūra xxiv. 6: "Those who slander their wives and have not witness except themselves" ... Sūra ii. 143: "And thus we have made you a people in the middle that ye may be witnesses in regard to you"; Sūra l. 21: "(On the day of judgment) every soul shall come, with an urger and a witness". (On the expression: to give evidence from belief, etc., see the articles S͟HAHĀDA and TAS͟HAHHUD). *S͟hahīd* frequently occurs as referring to God, e.g. Sūra iii. 98: "God is the witness of your deeds"; Sūra v. 117: "Thou art the witness of all things". *S͟hahīd* is therefore also one of "the most beautiful names" (*al-asmāʾ al-ḥusnā*, cf. the article ALLĀH).

The meaning martyr is not found for *s͟hahīd* in the Ḳurʾān. It is only later commentators that have tried to find it in Sūra iv. 69. The Ḳurʾān always uses circumlocutions to express this conception, e.g. Sūra iii. 156: "If ye be slain or die on the path of God, then pardon from God and mercy is better than what ye have amassed". Sūra iii. 166: "Consider not those slain on God's path to be dead, nay, alive with God; they are cared for". Sūra xlvii. 4—6: "And those who fight for the cause of God, their works He will not suffer to miscarry. He will guide them and bring their heart to peace and lead them into Paradise which He whas made known to them".

The development of meaning of *s͟hahīd* to martyr (there is not the parallel development in *s͟hāhid*; this never means anything but witness, namely in a court of justice, cf. the article S͟HĀHID), took place under Christian influence, cf. the Syriac *sāhdā* for the N. T. Greek μάρτυς.

Wensinck's monograph on martyrdom in the east shows that the development in Christianity and in Islām runs parallel down to minor details and that the doctrine of martyrdom in both religions in the last resort goes back to old oriental (Jewish) and Hellenistic ideas. The old meaning *s͟hahīd* = witness, later became so forgotten in Islām that false etymologies are regularly given for it (e.g. from *s͟h-h-d* to look, etc.).

The martyr who seals his belief with his death in battle against the infidels is *s͟hahīd* throughout the Ḥadīt͟h literature, and the great privileges which await him in heaven are readily depicted in numerous ḥadīt͟hs. By his sacrifice the martyr escapes the examination in the grave by the "interrogating angels" Munkar and Nakīr [q.v.], nor does he need to pass through the "Islamic purgatory", *barzak͟h* [q.v.]. Martyrs receive the highest of the various ranks in Paradise, nearest the throne of God; the Prophet sees in a vision the most beautiful abode in Paradise, the *Dār al-s͟huhadāʾ*. The wounds of the *s͟hahīd* received in the *d͟jihād* become red like blood on the day of judgment, and shine and smell of musk. None of the dwellers in Paradise would ever come back to earth, except the *shahīd*: for on account of the very special privileges which are granted him in Paradise he wishes to suffer martyrdom another ten times. Martyrs are freed by their death from the guilt of all sins so that they do not require the intercession of the Prophet, and indeed in later traditions we even find them interceding for other men. They are already pure, and therefore alone among men are not washed before their burial, a view which has found a place in the Fiḳh (cf. A. J. Wensinck, *Handbook*, s.v. *Martyrs*).

In the Fiḳh books the *shahīd* is dealt with in the section on *ṣalāt* in connection with the prayer for the dead, and the differences of opinion in the schools (the reasons for them are sometimes very interesting) centre mainly round the question whether the *shahīd* is washed, whether the prayer for the dead is uttered over him, whether he is to be buried in his bloodstained garments, or not, etc. In them we find the distinction made whether the *shahāda* has been for this world, for the next or for both, for as an ethical action it must be judged according to its *nīya*; on the other hand we find the different kinds of *shuhadā'* in the wider sense, detailed below. The case of shahīd in the legal sense does not occur if the man concerned survived the battle in spite of his wounds and was able to arrange his affairs before his death. We sometimes find sections *fī faḍl al-shahāda* in the book of *djihād*, where martyrdom is praised quite in the style of the Ḥadīth.

The praise of *shahāda* led to a real longing to meet a martyr's death and according to some traditions, even Muḥammad and ʿUmar longed for it. This *ṭalab al-shahāda*, however, was by no means encouraged by orthodox theology but rather deprecated, perhaps — following a suggestion of Wensinck — because this kind of self-sacrifice looked very like suicide, always condemned in Islām. Therefore peaceful moral duties are represented as equal to or even better than voluntary death, such as fasting, regularity in prayer, reading the Ḳur'ān, gratitude to one's parents, honesty as a tax-collector, learning: these are all deeds on the path of God, *fī sabīl Allāh* (this expression with the gradual cessation of the wars of conquest undergoes the same change from a warlike to a peaceful ethical meaning as *shahīd*) and may enable men to share in the rewards otherwise promised for the *shuhadā'*. [Cf. also the later distinction between the *djihād al-akbar*, the fight against one's own self, and the *djihād al-aṣghar*, the "holy war"; cf. *WJ*. iii. (1916) p. 200 note]. But the conception of shahīd itself underwent an important extension which may be partly already seen in Ḥadīth, so that in the end almost anyone who had died any violent death and aroused pity was considered by the general public to be a martyr and soon was actually regarded as a saint. An important factor in bringing about this development was the very old tendency of the people to worship holy men generally, cf. the article WALĪ. In this sense, for example, anyone who dies of disease, like the plague and the "diseases of the stomach", is considered a shahīd; anyone who dies a violent death, e.g. from starvation, thirst, drowning, being buried alive, burning, poison, a lightning stroke, being killed by robbers or wild beasts, or a mother who dies in child-bed; also one who dies during the performance of a meritorious action, e.g. in the pilgrimage or in a foreign land, where no friend or relative is with him, or on a journey which is *sunna* or while visiting a saint's tomb or while in the act of prayer, or as a result of continuous ablutions, or on a Friday night, or in the search for the knowledge of the faith: *fī ṭalab ʿilm al-dīn*, or in defending the right against injustice: the *amr bi 'l-maʿrūf wa 'l-nahy ʿan al-munkar* against the *ẓālim*; whoever loves and remains chaste and does not betray his secret and dies, dies a shahīd, and anyone who meets his death fighting against his own impulses in the *djihād akbar* is shahīd.

The tomb of such a shahīd is regarded as a *mashhad*, enjoys the reverence of the pious and becomes an object of pilgrimage. At many of these *mashāhid* it can be proved that they relate to pre-Islāmic local cults which have been continued in this form under Islām. This aspect of the survival of the ancient in the nearer East has been illuminated by van Berchem's study of the inscriptions, but only after further material is available will a final verdict be possible. The phrase found as early as tombs of the third century A.H.: *hādhā mā yashhadu bihi wa ʿalaihi*, with which the term *mashhad* might perhaps be connected (according to a suggestion by M. Hartmann, *ZDPV*, xxvi. 65 [2]; cf. however, Ritter in *Isl.*, xii. 148—150), is interesting. When we further find Sulṭāns called *shahīd* in inscriptions, the word here has lost its real significance and is no more than a pious term for deceased. In many cases the name *mashhad* was transferred to local cult-centres, which have nothing to do with a shahīd and in Turkish *shehīdlik* and *meshhed* (also pronounced *meshaṭ*) is a name for cemetery in general (see Mordtmann, in *Isl.*, xii. 223). The inscriptions also show that frequently the Muslim builders of *mashāhid* built them in their own lifetime, apparently in order to share in the blessings of their good deed while still here on earth.

In Cairo there used to be celebrated on 8 May a Christian festival in commemoration of martyrs, in which Muslims took part up to the viiith century (Maḳrīzī, *Khiṭaṭ*, i. 68 *sq.*; Mez, *Die Renaissance des Islam*, p. 399 *sqq.*).

In contrast to orthodoxy the various sects often kept rigidly to the original sense of shahīd; for example the Khawāridj fanatically sought death fighting against the government, which they considered unrighteous, while the orthodox theologians taught that rebellion against the government was not a *djihād* with a view to martyrdom.

Martyrdom plays a special role of peculiar importance for the Shīʿa. For them Ḥusain is the *shahīd* par excellence, the king of martyrs, *shāh-i shuhadā* (much as the favourite martyr of the Ṣūfīs is al-Ḥallādj). In keeping with the character of the Shīʿa, Ḥusain is sometimes endowed with features which almost recall the passion of Christ or sufferings of St. Francis (conscious self-sacrifice, transmission and inheritance of the divine light in the family of the Prophet, immortality etc., cf. the articles SHĪʿA MUḤARRAM, ḤUSAIN). There is a rich literature of martyrologies describing very fully the sufferings of Ḥusain and other members of the family of the Prophet, a speciality of the Shīʿa; for example there is a famous work entitled *Rawḍat al-shuhadā'* by Ḥusain b. ʿAlī al-Wāʿiẓ al-Kāshifī, which has been translated into Turkish (by Fuẓūlī with the title: *Ḥadīḳat al-suʿadā'*) and into Eastern Turkish and several times also abbreviated.

The worship of shahīds has attained noteworthy developments in parts of India where there is a gigantic *Shahīd gandj* said to be the tomb of no fewer than 150,000 *shuhadā'*.

Bibliography: A. J. Wensinck, *The Oriental Doctrine of the Martyrs. Med. Akad. Amsterdam*, 1921, liii., Ser. A, No. 6; Goldziher, *Muhammedanische Studien*, ii. 387—391; Muḥ. Aʿlā, *Dict. of Techn. Terms*, s.v.; J. Horovitz, *Koranische Untersuchungen*, Berlin 1926, p. 50; in the Fiḳh: Ḥanafī: Ibn al-Ḥalabī, *Multaḳā al-abḥur*, with the commentaries *Madjmaʿ al-anhur* und *al-Durr al-muntaḳā*, Constantinople 1328, i. 188; Shāfiʿī: Bādjūrī, *Ḥāshiya*, Cairo 1321, i. 265; Mālikī; Khalīl b. Isḥāḳ, *Mukhtaṣar*, transl. of Guidi and Santillana, Milan 1919, i. 153; Zaidī: Zaid b. ʿAlī, *Madjmūʿ al-fiḳh*, ed. Griffini, p. 70, 237; Shaʿrānī, *Mīzān*, Cairo 1317, i. 197; Ibn al-Ḥādjdj, *Mudkhal*, ii. 116 *sqq.*; Haneberg, *Das muslimische Kriegsrecht*, p. 239 *sq.*; Van Berchem, *Corpus Inscriptionum Arabicarum*, Jerusalem ville, ii. p. 84 etc.; do. in Diez, *Churasanische Baudenkmäler*, i. 89 *sqq.* On the Shīʿa: Goldziher, *Vorlesungen*, p. 123; van Berchem, *La Chaire de la Mosque d'Hébron*, in *Festschrift Eduard Sachau*, Berlin 1915, p. 301 *sqq.*; E. G. Browne, *Hist. of Persian Liter. in Modern Times*, p. 172 *sqq.*; Ivar Lassy, *The Muharram mysteries among the Azerbeijan Turks of Caucasia*, Diss. Helsingfors, 1916, p. 132 *sqq.*; Geiger-Kuhn, *Grundriss der iranischen Philologie*, ii. 358; A. Nöldeke, *Das Heiligtum des Husain zu Kerbela*, 1909, p. 37, 43.

SHĀHID (A., pl. *shuhūd*), witness. The statement (*shahāda*) of a witness, is a declaration on a legal claim in favour of a second person against a third, which is based on an accurate knowledge of the state of affairs and is made before the judge in prescribed form (*ashhadu bi-kadhā wa-kadhā*). The following main principles have grown up, based on the Ḳurʾān and Tradition and perhaps also influenced by the legal opinions in the Talmud and are in the main common to all *madhāhib*; there are of course numerous differences in points of detail which cannot be dealt with here.

The taking and giving of evidence (*shahāda*) is a *farḍ ʿala 'l-kifāya*; but if only one person was present on the scene, there is an absolute obligation on him to give evidence (*farḍ al-ʿain*). In the case of a *ḥaḳḳ Allāh* it is, however, left to the discretion of the witness whether he cares to bring the culprit before the *ḳāḍī* or spare his Muslim co-religionist and remain silent; the latter course is usually recommended as the more meritorious. The witness must: 1. have accurate knowledge (*ʿilm*) of what he is talking of and have perceived it with his own eyes and ears (cf. Sūra v. 8); 2. be *mukallaf* (of age and responsible); 3. be a free man; 4. be a Muslim (if he is giving evidence in a case brought against a Muslim); 5. be able to observe and to speak; 6. be *ʿadl* [q.v.] (cf. Sūra v. 106, and lxv. 2: *dhawā ʿadlin*); he must also not have been previously punished with *ḥadd* for slander (cf. Sūra xxiv. 4); 7. lead a decent and moral life (*muruwwa*); thus for example a witness is rejected, if he enters the bath without a shift or is devoted to gambling (chess, *nard*) or eats in public; 8. be above suspicion; he must not for example get any advantage for himself from his evidence or avert any injury to himself; he must not be on bad terms with the accused, if he is giving evidence against him. Nor can those who have a claim for maintenance give evidence against one another, like parents and children, husband and wife, master and slave.

The following regulations concern the number and sex of the witnesses: 1. In *zināʾ* four male witnesses are required (cf. Sūra xxiv. 2 *sq.* and iv. 15). 2. In all other cases, which do not concern *māl*, like theft, murder, marriage and divorce, release of slaves etc., two male witnesses are required (cf. Sūra ii. 282 *sq.* and v. 106 *sqq.*); in cases which, as a rule, women alone are competent to deal with (child-birth, physical defects in women, etc.), four women are sufficient according to the Shāfiʿī teaching (two for the Mālikis and only one for the Ḥanafīs and Zaidīs). 3. In cases which concern *māl*, like claims arising out of contracts and bonds or accidental homicide, two men or one man and two women are required as witnesses (cf. Sūra ii. 282 *sq.*). In these cases one male witness is usually sufficient along with the oath of the accuser.

Except in criminal cases, it is allowed to replace one original witness (*shāhid al-aṣl*) by two male deputy witnesses (*shuhūd al-farʿ*), the so-called *shahāda ʿalā shahāda*; but only when the original witness is dead or cannot appear before the court on account of severe illness or is three days' journey or more from the place of trial.

The witnesses may withdraw their evidence before the judge; but if sentence has alredy been passed, they are liable for the injury done. If a statement which affirmed *zināʾ* is withdrawn, the witnesses are punished with *ḥadd* for slander (*ḳadhf*). False witness (*shahādat al-zūr*) is already censured in the Ḳurʾān (Sūra xxv. 72; ii. 283) and Tradition. The venality of witnesses in the east has often been noted by observers (cf. E. Lane, *Manners and Customs of the Modern Egyptians*[5], 1860, p. 100, 114; Ch. White, *Three Years in Constantinople*, 1845. i, 103).

The most difficult point in the above rules is undoubtedly the question of *ʿadāla*; the witnesses must either be personally known as *ʿadl* to the ḳāḍī or their *ʿadāla* must first of all be established. From the end of the second (eighth) century an assistant to the ḳāḍī, the *ṣāḥib al-masāʾil* or *muzakkī*, was appointed to conduct these often lengthy investigations. As Muslim procedure does not recognize documentary evidence as proof but only the oral evidence of eye-witnesses, such people were preferred for the verification of legal matters whose *ʿadāla* had already been proved. Thus permanent "witnesses" came into existence: at times their numbers rose to thousands but usually there were only a few. They were officials of the ḳāḍī, and were appointed and dismissed by him. Thus arose the body of notaries, who were called *shuhūd* in Cairo and Baghdād, in the east and the Maghrib *ʿudūl*. Besides verifying legal matters they also decided smaller disputes independently. They were as a rule young lawyers who later received judicial appointments. Muslim writers frequently complain of the corruption among these people. This development began in the ii[th]/viii[th] century (the first reference is in Cairo in 174 A.H.: al-Kindī, *Governors and Judges*, ed. Guest, p. 386) and reached its final stage in the iv[th]/x[th] century. These "witnesses" are properly to be regarded as a revival of the Roman-Byzantine notaries. — For the present conditions see Lane, *op. cit.*, ch. iv.; Vassel, *Über marokkanische Processpraxis* in *MSOS As.*, 1902, v., p. 175 *sq.*

Bibliography: The pertinent chapter of the books of Tradition and Fiḳh, especially: al-Kāsānī, *K. Badāʾiʿ al-ṣanāʾiʿ*, Cairo 1910, vi. 266—90; Khalīl, *Mukhtaṣar*, transl. D. Santillana, Milan 1919, ii. 616 *sqq.*; Ed. Sachau, *Muh. Recht*, Stuttgart 1897, p. 690 *sq.*, 737 *sqq.*; van den Berg, *Principes du droit musulman*, Algiers 1896, p. 216 *sq.*; Th. W. Juynboll, *Handbuch des islam. Gesetzes*, Leiden 1910, p. 315 *sqq.*, fourth

(Dutch) ed., 1930, p. 318 *sqq.*; M. Moraud, *Etudes de droit musulman*, Algiers 1910, p. 313 *sqq.*; W. Heffening, *Islam. Fremdenrecht*, Hanover 1925, § 26; G. Bergsträsser, *Grundzüge des islamischen Rechts*, 1935, Index s.v.; Schacht, *Origins of Muhammadan Jurisprudence*, p. 167 *sqq.*, 187 *sqq.*, 311 *sqq.* — On the development of the *Shuhūd* to notaries cf. in addition to the literature quoted in Juynboll, *op. cit.*, p. 317: Amedroz, *The office of kadi*, in *JRAS*, 1910, p. 779, *sqq.*; Bergsträsser in *ZDMG*, lxviii. 1914, p. 409 *sq.*; Mez, *Renaissance des Islams*, Heidelberg 1922, p. 218—220; É. Tyan, *Le Notariat et le Régime de la preuve par écrit* (Annales de l'Ecole francaise de Droit de Beyrouth, 1945, no. 2).

SHAIBA (Banū), the name of the keepers of the Kaʿba (*sadana, hadjaba*) whose authority does not, however, extend over the whole of the sanctuary (*masdjid al-harām*), nor even as far as the well of Zamzam and its annexes. They are the *Banū Shaiba* or *Shaibīyūn* and have as their head a *zaʿīm* or *shaikh*.

Modern works only give brief references to them. Snouck Hurgronje gives the days on which they open the door of the Kaʿba. He notes that they only admit the faithful on payment of a fee and quotes the witty Mecca saying: "The B. Shaiba are wreathed in smiles; this must be a day for opening the Kaʿba". — They find a further source of revenue in the sale of scraps of the covering of the holy house, which is replaced every year by their care. The embroidered parts reserved in theory for the sovereign are given more or less gratuitously to the great personages who represent him at Mecca and on the *hadjdj*. The remainder in accordance with custom (*Chroniken d. Stadt Mekka*, iii. 72) is the perquisite of the *Shaibīyūn*, who sell it in the little booths at the Bāb al-Salām (Batanūnī, p. 139), the ancient Bāb B. Shaiba, the principal gate of the mosque. They also sell there the little brooms made of palm leaves, which are all alleged to have been used for cleaning the floor of the Kaʿba, a solemn ceremony in which the greatest personages glory in participating (Ibn Djubair, p. 138; Batanūnī, p. 109). They also have the charge and care of the offerings made by the faithful, which adorn the interior of the holy house. This treasure comprises the most diverse objects, articles of gold and of silver, precious stones, lamps richly adorned, foreign idols, the offerings of converts in distant lands. This treasure has regularly been plundered by the Amīrs of Mecca, by the governors, by its guardians and even by the Shaibīyūn themselves (Gaudefroy-Demombynes, *Le Pèlerinage*, p. 57) although according to tradition, the grand-master Shaiba is said to have defended it against the attempts of the Caliph ʿUmar (*Usd al-ghāba*, iii. 8). They have charge of the interior curtains of the Kaʿba. They had at one time the care of the *Maḳām Ibrāhīm*.

The possession of these diverse functions by the Shaibīyūn is now so generally recognized that it attracts no attention. They evoked a more lively interest from earlier authors and especially from the pilgrims. The principal narratives are those of Ibn Djubair in 1183 and of Nāṣir-i Khosraw in 1276.

The privilege of the B. Shaiba is very old; the historians of the ninth century Ibn Hishām, Ibn Saʿd, Yaʿkūbī and the compilers of collections of ḥadīths confirm this; but they pile up proofs of its legitimacy in a way that makes one think it was recent and disputed.

Traditions do not agree as to the way in which, on the day of the surrender of Mecca, the Prophet received the keys of the Kaʿba from the hands of ʿUthmān b. Ṭalḥa, who is said to have been converted previously at al-Ḥudaibīya (Ṭabarī, *Taʾrīkh*, i. 1604, ii. 2348; Ibn Sa'd, *Ṭabaḳāt* v. 331; al-Azraḳī, *Chroniken*, i. 187). The real guardian of the Kaʿba seems to have been at the time Shaiba b. ʿUthmān b. Abī Ṭalḥa, a cousin of the ʿUthmān b. Ṭalḥa mentioned. This Shaiba probably had not yet been converted to Islām at the time of the conquest of Mecca, but it is clear that he possessed great local authority up to the reign of Yazīd b. Muʿāwiya (cf. a.o. Ibn Hishām, p. 845; *Chroniken*, i. 67, ii. 46, iii. 15).

The tradition which gave to the Shaibīyūn the *hidjāba* of the Holy House is an ancient one. It is still perpetuated in the name of the archway, which, beside Zamzam, marks the ancient boundary of the wall of the *masdjid al-harām*. When the former had been enlarged, the new gate, called at the present time Bāb al-Salām, which was in a line with the Kaʿba and the ancient arcade, was called in its turn Bāb Banī Shaiba. On the entire subject cf. Gaudefroy-Demombynes, *Le pèlerinage à la Mecque*, Paris 1923, p. 57 *sqq.*

AL-**SHAIBĀNĪ**, Abū ʿAbd Allāh Muḥammad b. al-Ḥasan b. Farḳad, mawlā of the Banū Shaibān, a Ḥanafī jurist, born at Wāsiṭ in 132/749—50. Brought up in al-Kūfa, he studied at the early age of fourteen under Abū Ḥanīfa, from whom he learned the principles of legal reasoning. At twenty he is said to have lectured in the mosque of al-Kūfa. He extended his knowledge of ḥadīth under Sufyān al-Thawrī (d. 161), al-Awzāʿī (d. 157) and others and especially Mālik b. Anas (d. 179), whose lectures he attended for over three years in Madīna. His training in Fiḳh, however, he owed mainly to Abū Yūsuf, but he soon began to threaten the latter's prestige by his own lectures, so that Abū Yūsuf tried to get him a judgeship in Syria or Egypt, which, however, al-Shaibānī declined. In 176/792—3 he was consulted by the Caliph Hārūn al-Rashīd in the affair of the Zaidī imām Yaḥyā b. ʿAbd Allāh. On this occasion he lost the Caliph's favour through his own fault and became suspected of being a supporter of the ʿAlids (Ṭabarī iii., 619; Kardarī, ii. 163 *sqq.*) He was, it is true, like some of his teachers a Murdjiʾī (Ibn Ḳutaiba, *Maʿārif*, p. 301; Shahrastānī, ed. Cureton, p. 108), but he seems to have kept clear of Shīʿa activities (*Fihrist*, p. 204). It was not till 180/796 at the earliest — in this year Hārūn made al-Raḳḳa his capital (Ṭab., iii. 645) — that Hārūn made him ḳāḍī of al-Raḳḳa. After his dismissal (187/803) he stayed in Baghdād till the Caliph commanded him to accompany him on his journey to Khurāsān (189/805) and appointed him ḳāḍī of Khurāsān (according to Abū Ḥāzim (d. 292) in Kardarī, ii. 147). He died there in the same year at Ranbūye, near al-Raiy.

He belonged to the moderate school of *raʾy* and sought to base his teaching wherever possible on ḥadīths. He was also considered an able grammarian. Among his pupils are mentioned the imām al-Shāfiʿī [q.v.], who nevertheless wrote a polemic against him (*Kitāb al-radd ʿalā Muḥammad b. al-Ḥasan* in *K. al-Umm*, Cairo 1325, vii. 277 *sqq.*). It is to Shaibānī and Abū Yūsuf that the Ḥanafī *madhhab* owes its first spread of popularity. His writings, which have had frequent commentaries made on them, are the oldest that enable us to judge the teachings of Abū Ḥanīfa, although they differ in many points from the ideas of Abū Ḥanīfa. The most important are: *Kitāb al-aṣl fi ʾl-furūʿ* or *al-Mabsūṭ*; *K. al-Ziyādāt*, *K. al-djāmiʿ al-kabīr* (pr. Cairo 1356); *K. al-djāmiʿ*

al-ṣaghīr (pr. Būlāḳ 1302 on the margin of Abū Yūsuf, *K. al-kharādj*); *K. al-siyar al-kabīr* (pr. with the commentary of al-Sarakhsī in 4 vol., Ḥaidarābād 1335—1336), *K. al-āthār* (lith. in India); *K. al-makhāridj fi 'l-ḥiyal* (ed. J. Schacht, Leipzig 1930; his authorship, however, was contested already in the third century; cf. also Pröbster in *Isl.* v. 581 *sq.*, vi. 260 *sqq.*).

We also owe to him an edition, with many critical additions, of the *Muwaṭṭa'* of his teacher Mālik b. Anas, which differs widely from the usual version (cf. Goldziher, *Muh. Studien*, ii. 222, *sq.*; now printed in Kazan, 1909).

Bibliography: Ibn Saʿd, *Ṭabaḳāt*, ed. Sachau, VII/ii. 78 (synopsis in: Ibn Ḳutaiba, *K. al-maʿārif*, ed. Wüstenfeld, p. 251; al-Ṭabarī, ed. de Goeje, iii. 2521; al-Nawawī, *Biograph. dictionary*, p. 104); *Fihrist*, p. 203 *sq.* — The later sources are more legendary in character: al-Khaṭīb al-Baghdādī, *Ta'rīkh* (his biography is lacking in the Cairo edition), in al-Samʿānī, *K. al-Ansāb*, *GMS*, xx. fol. 342v and al-Nawawī, p. 103 *sqq.*; al-Sarakhsī, *Sharḥ al-siyar al-kabīr*, Introduction; Ibn Khallikān, No. 578; al-Ḳurashī, *al-Djawāhir*, Ḥaidarābād 1332, ii. 42—44; al-Kardarī, *Manāḳib al-imām al-aʿẓam*, Ḥaidarābād 1321, ii. 146—167 (uses old sources); Ibn Ḳuṭlūbughā, ed. Flügel, No. 159 — Barbier de Meynard, *Notice sur Moh. b. Hasan* in *JA*, 4th Ser., xx. 1852, p. 406—419; Flügel, *Classen der hanafit. Rechtsgelehrten*, p. 283; Dimitroff, *Asch-Schaibānī und sein corpus iuris* in *MSOSAs.*, xi. 1908, p. 75—98; Brockelmann, *GAL*, i. 178 *sq.*, *Suppl.* i. 288; Schacht, *Origins of Muhammadan Jurisprudence*, Oxford 1950.

SHAIKH. This word means one who bears the marks of old age, who is over fifty (cf. *Lisān*, iii. 509). It is applied to aged relatives; the Shaikh is the patriarch of the tribe or family.

In pre-Islāmic antiquity the title *Saiyid*, the chief of the tribe, was frequently given the epithet *Shaikh* meaning full maturity in years and therefore of mental powers. The moral influence of the Shaikhs over the Beduins was considerable and the term came to mean chiefs having a long and renowned career behind them.

In the history of the Muslim period, it has frequently the sense of supreme chief, especially among the royal pretenders seeking to revive Arab traditions. Thus in the fourth (tenth) century the reformer Abū Yazīd calls himself *Shaikh al-Mu'minīn*, i.e. Shaikh of the Believers (Ibn al-ʿAdhārī, *Bayān*, ed. Dozy, i. 225, transl. Fagnan, i. 315). Ibn Baṭṭūṭa (ii. 288—289) mentions a governor of a town with this title. It is also the title of the governor of Madīna, *Shaikh al-Ḥaram*. Ibn Khaldūn (*Muḳaddima*, ii. 14 and 165 of the transl.) tells us that at the Hafṣid court of Tunis the first minister, regent of the empire, who appointed all the officials was called Shaikh of the Almohads. Muḥammad, the founder of the Waṭṭāsid dynasty took the title al-Shaikh as did Muḥammad al-Mahdī founder of the dynasty of Saʿdī Sharīfs.

The title, at the present day, at once a term of polite address and a sign of importance, respected, venerated, which all who govern, administer or hold a share of public authority are happy to have, whether in the spiritual or political sphere, in the mystic as well as the social life, is borne with unconcealed pride. It is given to the head of a family, to the political head of the section of a tribe called *dwar* (in North Africa) and comprising a group of common origin. It is given to high dignitaries of religion, to teachers, scholars, to men of religion without distinction of age, to all persons respected for their office, their age or their morals. Thus we have the *Shaikh al-Islām* [q.v.], the title of the Grand Muftī, the highest religious dignitary of Islām, the *Shaikh al-Dīn*, Minister of Religion, *Shaikh al-Madīna*, Chief of police, *Shaikh al-Balad*, the mayor of a town. Al-Bukhārī and Muslim are the two Shaikhs par excellence (Ibn Khaldūn, *Muḳaddima*, ii. 165); the official leader of the pilgrimage is called in Egypt *Shaikh al-Djamal* (Perron, *Précis de jurisprudence Musulmane*, ii. 641). In the Muslim religious brotherhood or *ṭarīḳa* [q.v.] the title Shaikh is particularly significant.

SHAIKH AL-ISLĀM is one of the honorific titles which first appear in the second half of the fourth century A.H. While other honorific titles compounded with *Islām* (like *ʿIzz-*, *Djalāl-*, *Saif al-Islām*) were borne by persons exercising secular power (notably the viziers of the Fāṭimids, cf. van Berchem, *ZDPV*, xvi., p. 101), the title of Shaikh al-Islām has always been reserved for *ʿulamā'* and mystics, like other titles of honour whose first part is *Shaikh* (e. g. *Shaikh al-Dīn*; the surname of *Shaikh al-Futyā* is given by Ibn Khaldūn to the jurist Asad b. al-Furāt; cf. *Muḳaddima*, transl. de Slane, i., p. lxxviii.). Of all these titles only that of Shaikh al-Islām has been extensively used. Thus in the fifth century the head of the Shāfiʿī theologians in Khurāsān, Ismāʿīl b. ʿAbd al-Raḥmān, was called by the Sunnīs the Shaikh al-Islām par excellence (cf. also Djuwainī, *Djihān-gushā*, ii. 23, where there is a reference to the *Shaikh al-Islām-i Khurāsān*), while at the same period the partisans of the mystic Abū Ismāʿīl al-Anṣārī (396—481/1006—1088) claimed this title for him (al-Subkī, *Ṭabaḳāt*, Cairo 1324, iii. 117; Djāmī, *Nafakhāt al-uns*, ed. Lees, Calcutta 1859, p. 33, 376). In the sixth century Fakhr al-Dīn al-Rāzī [q.v.] was called Shaikh al-Islām. Other examples in the centuries following are the mystic Shaikh Ṣafī al-Dīn of Ardabīl (cf. Browne, *Persian Literature in Modern Times*, p. 33), and the theologian al-Taftāzānī. In Syria and in Egypt, however, Shaikh al-Islām had become a title of honour (but not an official one) which could only be given to jurists and more particularly to those who by their *fatwā*'s had attained a certain fame or the approval of a great body of jurists, especially at the beginning of the Mamlūk period. Thus in the polemics provoked by the teachings of Ibn Taimīya, his adversaries refused him the title of Shaikh al-Islām, given him by his partisans. The modernists of our day who are under the influence of Ibn Taimīya and Ibn Ḳaiyim al-Djawzīya, represent these two jurists as religious leaders who really deserve the title Shaikh al-Islām (*al-Manār*, ix. 34, according to Goldziher, *Die Richtungen der islamischen Koranauslegung*, p. 339). Towards 700/1300 Shaikh al-Islām had thus become a title which each *muftī* of some authority could claim for himself. Maḥmūd b. Sulaimān al-Kafawī (d. 990/1582) in his biographies of Ḥanafī jurists, *al-Aʿlām al-akhyār min fuḳahā' madhhab al-Nuʿmān al-Mukhtār* (Brockelmann, *GAL*, ii. 572) says that among the *muftī*'s those are called Shaikh al-Islām who settle differences and decide questions of general discipline (according to ʿAlī Emīrī in *ʿIlmiye Sālnāmesi*, p. 306). We thus find that in Egypt and in Russia down to the present day, and in Turkey till the xviiith century (cf. Ewliyā Čelebi, *Siyāḥatnāma*, passim) *muftī*'s (Shīʿīs as well as Sunnīs) of any importance may be given this title. In Persia the development of the title has been different;

here the Shaikh al-Islām has become a judicial authority who presides in each important village over the ecclesiastical tribunal, composed of Mollas and Mudjtahids. In the time of the Ṣafawids he was appointed by the Ṣadr al-Ṣudūr (cf. Tavernier, *Les six voyages*, Paris 1767, i. 598, who calls him Scheik el-Selom; Curzon, *Persia*, London 1892, i. 452, 454).

But the title gained its greatest lustre after it had become applied more particularly to the Muftī of Constantinople, whose office in the Empire of the Ottoman Sulṭāns in time acquired a religious and political importance without parallel in other Muslim countries. In the early centuries of the Ottoman Empire the influence of the ʿulamāʾ had been greatly surpassed by that of the mystic shaikhs and after the reconstitution of the empire by Muḥammad I, we see a furious struggle between the new Sunnī orthodox influences and mystic-Shīʿa influences (e.g. the incident of Badr al-Dīn Maḥmūd), a struggle ending in the victory of orthodoxy under Selīm I. Historical pragmatic tradition seems to have ignored this development and must be accepted with a good deal of reserve, while the older sources give but little information. Thus the collection of biographies *al-Shaḳāʾiḳ al-Nuʿmānīya* (written under Sulaimān I) is compiled from an entirely orthodox point of view, but it is quite evident from it that the majority of the older jurists in Ottoman countries had studied in Egypt or Persia or had Arab or Persian teachers; some of the first *muftī*'s of Constantinople were themselves foreigners like Fakhr al-Dīn al-ʿAdjamī (*muftī* from 1430—1460) and ʿAlāʾ al-Dīn al-ʿArabī. Later tradition makes Shaikh Ede Bālī, father-in-law of ʿOthmān, already the first *muftī* of the Ottoman lands (*ʿIlmīye Sālnāmesi*, p. 315). They also claim that a Muftī Al-Anām was appointed as early as under Murād II, with authority over all the other *muftī*'s (*Sidjill-i ʿOthmānī*, i. 6), and that Muḥammad II after the taking of Constantinople gave the official title of Shaikh al-Islām to the *muftī* of the new capital, Khiḍr Beg Čelebi, who was at the same time given authority over the two *ḳāḍī ʿasker* (d'Ohsson, von Hammer), but there is nothing to show that the *muftī* was already so important a personage at this time. According to the *Shaḳāʾiḳ*, this Khiḍr Beg was only ḳāḍī of Stambūl, while Fakhr al-Dīn al-ʿAdjamī was the *muftī* (*op. cit.*, p. 111, 81). Although at a later date the biographer of the Shaikh al-Islām in the *Dawḥat al-mashāʾikh* (see *Bibl.*) begins his biographies with the *muftī* Muḥammad Shams al-Dīn Fenārī (d. 1430), this seems to be purely conventional. It is only under Selīm I that the great influence of the *Muftī* of Constantinople begins to manifest itself during the 24 years in which the office was held by the famous Zembilli ʿAlī Djemālī Efendi. In the time of the latter the was *Muftī* from 1501 to 1525), the two *ḳāḍī ʿasker* still had precedence over him because they sat in the Imperial *Dīwān*, while the *Muftī* did not (*Shaḳāʾiḳ*, p. 305), but on the other hand we are told that the same Djemālī Efendi refused to accept from Sulṭān Sulaimān I the two *ḳāḍī-ʿaskerliks* combined which were offered him (*Shaḳāʾiḳ*, p. 307). It is in the reign of Sulaimān that the *Muftī* of Constantinople first seems to have acquired undisputed authority over all the *ʿulamāʾ* of the empire, including all grades of judges. According to d'Ohsson and von Hammer, this *muftī* was Čiwi Zāde Muḥyī al-Dīn Efendi; it should be noted, however, that the latter was also the first *Muftī* who was relieved of his office by the Sulṭān (in 1541).

The growth in importance of the *Muftī* of Constantinople was in any case spontaneous and not caused by the sovereign will of the Sulṭāns, expressed by the conferring on his part of the title of Shaikh al-Islām, which at this period was borne by many *muftī*'s (see below). The explanation of this development may the sought in various directions. There is the tempting hypothesis of Gaudefroy-Demombynes who sees a striking analogy between the position of *Muftī* of Constantinople and that of the ʿAbbāsid caliph at the court of the Mamlūks, before the conquest of Egypt by the Turks (*La Syrie*, Paris 1923, p. xxii.). On the other hand, the organisation of the *ʿulamāʾ* of the Ottoman empire under a religious chief may have been in some way influenced by that of the Christian hierarchy in the empire under the Oecumenical patriarch. Lastly we may perhaps see in the Shaikh al-Islāmat a survival of the ancient mystical religious tradition in the Ottoman state, a tradition which demanded, alongside of the secular power, a religious authority having no judicial powers but representing, so to speak, the religious conscience of the people.

This last hypothesis would explain the tenacity with which the Shaikh al-Islāmat maintained its position through the centuries that followed, in spite of the power of the Sulṭān to dismiss the holder of the title, a power of which they made frequent use. ʿOthmān II (1618—1622) went so far as to deprive the *muftī* of all his prerogatives — on account of his refusal to issue a *fatwā* legalizing the fratricide — but under his successor all these prerogatives were restored. Murād IV had the *muftī* Akhī Zāde Ḥusain (1632) put to death, without the dignity of the office itself being compromised. Sixteen years later it was the *muftī* ʿAbd al-Raḥīm Efendi who took the initiative in the dethronement and execution of Ibrāhīm I, although this cost him his office. The last *muftī* who was able to retain his position for a long series of years was Abu 'l-Ṣuʿūd (1545—1574). After this time they succeeded one another at intervals averaging three to four years. From the end of the xvi[th] century it became possible for the same person to become *muftī* several times. The frequent change of *muftī*'s became more and more connected with the political intrigues of the Grand Viziers, of the imperial ḥarem, of the Janissaries, intrigues by which the *muftī*'s themselves were sometimes gravely compromised, e.g. the famous Ḳara Čelebi Zāde; the majority, however, were men of integrity, although their political independence became for the most part quite illusory.

Since the beginning of the xvi[th] century, the *muftī*'s have all been natives of Ottoman countries and, like all *ʿulamāʾ*, have belonged to Muslim families; in this they have been distinguished from the high officers of state and of the army who were frequently children of Christian parents, recruited by the *dewshirme*. Later the *muftī*'s sometimes belonged to different generations of one family. They usually acquired the *mashyakhat-i islāmīye* (the usual Turkish pronunciation, however, is *mashīkhat*) after having gone through the higher offices of the judicature; the majority of the *muftī*'s therefore had been *ḳāḍī ʿasker* before their appointment. This custom gave rise to an esprit de corps among the *ʿulamāʾ* and their chief which often comes out in history. Unlike the usage which gradually became established for the high judicial offices, the title of Shaikh al-Islām was not given to an individual without his actually accepting the office (there are only two exceptions).

The eminence of the Shaikh al-Islām's position

in the state found its expression in the ceremonial. As, according to the *Ḳānūn* on ceremonial, he was regarded as the Abū Ḥanīfa of his time, only the Grand Vizier was higher in rank than he. In addition to Shaikh al-Islām he had several more titles, the oldest of which *Muftī al-Anām* was the most used.

The political function of the Shaikh al-Islām was formally confined to his power of issuing *fatwā*'s. In supplying the demand for *fatwā*'s to private individuals, he was soon replaced by the Fetwā Emīnī (see below) but enormous importance was attached to *fatwā*'s relating to questions of policy and public discipline. To the first category belong for example the *fatwā* of ʿAlī Djemālī on the war against Egypt (1516) and that of Abu 'l-Ṣuʿūd on the war against Venice (1570). Under ʿOthmān II the *muftī* Esʿad Efendi declined to authorize by *fatwā* the fratricide of the Ottoman princes. *Fatwā*'s regarding public discipline were for example, that of Abu 'l-Ṣuʿūd authorizing the drinking of coffee, that of ʿAbd Allāh Efendi on the establishing of a printing-press (in 1727, cf. Babinger, *Stambuler Buchwesen*, Leipzig 1919, p. 9) and that of Esʿad Efendi authorizing the Niẓām-i Djedīd of Selīm III. By their *fatwā*'s the *muftī*'s also collaborated in imperial legislation by legalizing by their *fatwā*'s the different *Ḳānūn-nāme*'s (e.g. the *Ḳānūn*'s of Sulaimān I all had the approbation of Abū 'l-Ṣuʿūd, cf. *Millī tetebbüʿler medjmūʿasi*, 1331, i., Nos. 1 and 2). Besides, it was the custom to consult the Shaikh al-Islām on all political matters of any importance. In the majority of cases the *muftī*'s thus exercised a beneficial influence on public affairs, although by their personal interference they had often to suffer from the Sulṭān's arbitrary measures.

Although in the Ottoman empire of the xix^th^ and xx^th^ centuries the Shaikh al-Islām no longer played this important political role, appeal was occasionally made to the traditional authority of this institution when policy required it, as on the occasion of the deposition of ʿAbd al-Ḥamīd in 1909, the proclamation of the *djihād* in 1914 and the *fatwā* against the nationalists of Ankara in 1920. The *fatwā*'s of 1914 are not only concerned with the policy of the Ottoman empire but are addressed to the whole Muslim world. This fact reveals a new, and more general, pan-islamic conception of the function of the Ottoman Shaikh al-Islāmat. It is a conception which seems to have developed in Turkey in the course of the xix^th^ century, probably in connection with new theories on the caliphate. And just as is the case with these latter theories, the idea of the central importance of the Shaikh al-Islām for all the Muslim world is first found in Christian European authors. The xvi^th^ century travellers (e.g. Ricaut) already compare him with the Pope. Volney (*Voyage en Syria*, Paris 1789/1790, ii. 371) regards him as the representative of the spiritual power of the Caliph to the whole Muslim world. Legally speaking, it is true, the *fatwā* of a *Muftī* is addressed to every Muslim who wishes to follow it, but it was only in 1914 that the attempt was made to take advantage of the universal spiritual authority, which was attributed at the time by Christians as well as by Muslims to the Shaikh al-Islām in Constantinople (cf. Snouck Hurgronje, *Verspreide Geschriften*, iii. 272).

As head of the hierarchy of the *ʿulamā*ʾ, the *Muftī* had acquired the right of recommending to the sulṭān persons, who should be nominated to the six higher grades of the judicature. He himself only very rarely acted as a judge.

When towards the end of the xviii^th^ century the administration of the Ottoman empire began to be modernized, there was gradually formed an administrative department with the Shaikh al-Islām at its head. By this time there were already several personages who assisted the Muftī in his many duties, such as the *ketkhoda* or *kʿāya* who could represent the muftī, the *tel-khīṣdji*, who was his agent in the government, the *mektūbdji* or general secretary and the *fetwā emīnī* whose duty it was to prepare and distribute the *fatwā*'s asked for by the public. All these functionaries had their own offices. In the period of the *tanẓīmāt* (after 1839), this departmental organisation was consolidated. The Shaikh al-Islām was given as his official residence the former residence of the Agha of Janissaries; it was in this office, henceforth called Shaikh al-Islām Ḳapīsī or Bāb-i Fetwā, that the offices of his department were housed till its abolition. The department dealt with the administration and management of all institutions having a religious basis, except the administration of the *awḳāf*. The Shaikh al-Islām thus became the colleague of the heads of the other ministerial departments, which were created in the course of the xix^th^ century. He became a member of the Ministry and as such his tenure of office was limited by the life of the cabinet of which he was a member. He retained his precedence over the other ministers; this priority was laid down in Art. 27 of the Constitution of Midḥat Pasha of 1876, in which it is enacted that the Sulṭān is to choose the Grand Vizier and Shaikh al-Islām directly while the other ministers are appointed by the Grand Vizier. As early as the xviii^th^ century the Grand Vizier and the Shaikh al-Islām were the only officials who received their investiture in the presence of the Sulṭān.

In proportion as the secularisation of the institutions of the Ottoman empire advanced, the influence of the Shaikh al-Islām in the State declined. The institution in 1839 of a Council of State (*Shūrā-yī Dewlet*) deprived him of much of his influence on domestic politics; then the creation in 1879 of new civil and penal tribunals under a new Minister of Justice (*ʿAdliye Neẓāreti*) took away another large share of his influence. A series of legislative measures was passed which defined the competence of jurisdiction according to the *sharīʿa* and *niẓāmīya* tribunals. This development filled a prominent part in the religious reforms of the Young Turks (cf. e.g. the poem *Meshīkhat* of Ziā Gök Alp, p. 62 of *Aus der religiösen Reformbewegung in der Türkei*, by Dr. A. Fischer, Leipzig, 1922) and was brought to its logical conclusion, when in 1916 the Young Turkish government removed the administration of all the *maḥākim-i sharʿīye* to the Ministry of Justice and that of the *madrasas* to the Ministry of Education. This step was justified by appeals to modern public law. The declared object was to avoid the mistakes made at the time of the *tanẓīmāt* and to make the *mashīkhat-i islāmīye* a department for purely religious matters (cf. e.g. the *Ṭanīn* of Oct. 31 and Nov. 2, 1916). It was in the same spirit that an office was established in 1917 at the Shaikh al-Islāmat, the *dār al-ḥikma al-islāmīya*, of a propagandist character. After the armistice of Mudros (Nov. 2, 1918) the Young Turkish reforms were revoked by the new government. But by this time, however, the life of the Shaikh al-Islāmat was nearing its end, for in November 1922 after the victory of Turkish nationalisation all that remained in Constantinople of the old government institutions of the Ottoman empire was abolished. Their functions were taken over by the officers of the new government at Ankara. This government no longer included the Shaikh al-Islāmat. At the constitution of the new government, it is true, a *sharʿīya wekālcti* had been instituted but the anti-clerical spirit of the Grand National Assembly did not allow this imitation of the Shaikh al-Islāmlik to survive; it was replaced by a modest *diyānet ishleri reʾīsliyi*, by a law passed on March 3, 1924, the day on which the Ottoman caliphate was abolished.

The fullest description of the office of Shaikh al-Islām towards the end of his existence is found in the *ʿIlmīye Sālnāmesi* published in 1334/1916 by the Shaikh al-Islāmat which was then under the vigorous direction of Muṣṭafā Khairī Efendi.

Bibliography: The biographies of 108 Shaikh al-Islām are given in *Dawḥat al-mashāʾikh* by Rifʿat Efendi, lithogr. at Stambul n.d.; the last biography is that of ʿOmer Ḥusām al-Dīn Efendi (d. 1288/1871). A *dhail* has been written by ʿAlī Emīrī Efendi. Following these two sources the *ʿIlmīye Sālnāmesi*, p. 322—641 gives the biographies of 124 Shaikh al-Islām down to Muṣṭafā Khairī Efendi (held office till Nov. 1916), edited by the historians Aḥmad Refīḳ and ʿAlī Emīrī Efendi. The latter contributed to the same *Sālnāme*, p. 304—320, a *Mashyakhat-i Islāmīye taʾrīkhčesi*. At Vienna there is a manuscript of the *Dawḥat al-mashāʾikh* of Mustaḳīm Zāde (Flügel, ii., p. 409 *sqq.*). Many western writers on Turkey have notices in their books of the Shaikh al-Islāmat: Ricaut, *The history of the present state fo the Ottoman empire*, [6], London 1686, p. 200 *sqq.*; D'Ohsson, *Tableau Général de l'Empire Othoman*, ii., Paris 1790, p. 256 *sqq.*; J. von Hammer, *Des osmanischen Reiches Staatsverfassung*, Vienna 1815 ii. 373 *sqq.*; other descriptions: Dr. Stephan Kekule, *Uber Titel, Amter, Rangstufen und Anreden in der offiziellen osmanischen Sprache*, Halle 1892, p. 16 *sqq.*; G. Young, *Corps de droit ottoman*, Oxford 1905, i. 285 *sqq.*; A. H. Lybyer, *The Government of the Ottoman Empire in the Time of Suleiman the Magnificent*, Cambridge 1913, p. 207 *sqq.*

SHAIKHĪ, followers of Aḥmad Aḥsāʾī, dissenting Shīʿa theologians of Persia. Their teachers are the pupils and successors of the founder: Saiyid Kāẓim of Resht, teacher of Ḥādjdjī Muḥammad Karīm Khān of Kirmān and Mollā Muḥammad Māmaḳānī, a theologian who was one of the commission which tried and condemned the Bāb at Tabrīz towards the end of 1847. Their doctrines definitely prepared the way for those of the Bāb. They are opposed to those of the Akhbārī, who follow pure tradition; they protest against the immoderate number of traditions and the complete absence of criticism with which they are adopted; from this particular point of view they approach the Sunnī way of thinking.

They give new explanations of the principles of religion and of ḥadīth. The twelve Imāms are the effective cause of creation, being the scene of the manifestation of the divine will, the interpreters of God's desire. If they had not existed, God would not have created anything; they are therefore the ultimate cause of creation. All the acts of the divinity are produced by them but they have no power in or of themselves; they are only organs of transmission. Hence the charge of *tafwīḍ* (delegation of God's powers) was wrongly brought against the Shaikhī by the Shīʿa theologians. God being incomprehensible and escaping the thought of every created being, He can only be understood through the intermediary of the Imāms, who are in reality hypostases of the supreme being; to sin against them is to sin against God. The *lawḥ maḥfūẓ* is the heart of the Imām, which embraces all the heavens and all the worlds. The Imāms are the first of created beings and have preceded them all.

In eschatology the Shaikhī have been charged with denying the resurrection of the material body. They reply that man possesses two bodies; one is formed by temporal elements: "like a robe which a man sometimes puts on and sometimes takes off"; it is this which dissolves in the grave; the other which subsists when the first has crumbled to dust, is a subtle body which belongs to the invisible world (*djism huwarḳiliyāʾī*); it is this which is resurrected on this earth and then goes into paradise or hell.

Their thought became later more definite, for they admitted two *djasad* and two *djism* (these Arabic words both mean "body"); the first *djasad* is composed of the four visible elements, it is it which is perceptible in this world below and does not share in the future life; the second *djasad* persists and reappears in the other life; the first *djism* is the body which the spirit reclothes in *barzakh* (purgatory) from the moment of death till the first sound of the trumpet; the second *djism* continues to subsist: it is in it that the spirit becomes incarnate which directs itself towards the second *djasad*; it is it and the latter which come out of the grave entirely purified.

Knowledge of God. For God there exist two kinds of knowledge; one is essential knowledge and has no connection with contingencies: the other is a new knowledge created (*muḥdath*); this knowledge is the actual being of the known and the Imāms are the gates (*bāb*) which give access to this knowledge. The world is eternal in time and new in essence, for accidents without substances, forms without any substratum cannot come into existence. Accidents are transitory novelties, sometimes they exist, sometimes they disappear; they were nothing and they return to nothing. Substance on the contrary is not a transitory novelty; in consequence matter is a novelty in essence; it is eternal in the future, but not in the past; otherwise the future life would have an end; paradise and hell would disappear. Paradise is the love of the people of the House, the members of the family of the Prophet, the Imāms. Paradise and hell are created by the acts of men.

The material bodies of the Imāms after their death fall into decay in the grave; while it is true that these bodies are subtle, they show themselves under the human form, created of the four elements; as soon as their human body is no longer useful to men, they return it whence they have taken it and each of its molecules returns to its source: while the Shīʿīs believe that the bodies of the Imāms are not subject to the injuries of time.

It is not possible for known things to be eternal; they must therefore then be new and contingent; they are different from the essence of God but knowledge existed before the objects of knowledge. There are two kinds of knowledge; essential knowledge and newly created knowledge, the latter being of two kinds, that of possibility (*ʿilm imkānī*) and that of beings (*ʿilm akwānī*); the first is used of things before their existence, and the second once they exist. This second acquired knowledge is not an attribute of God, but is present with Him.

They attribute particular importance to the order given by God (*amr*) which is the first class of created things and precedes the creation in the strict sense of the word (*khalḳ*); the first *amr* constitutes a fixed world without change: it is through it that time exists and in consequence the latter can exert no influence on it. The knowledge of other creatures is preceded by ignorance, while this is not the case with God; this knowledge is new in the creature, it cannot be so for God. It is by the reflection of phenomena that man gains the apperception of the world which surrounds him. This reflection does not exist for God who knows beings by their essence. Just as beings are manifold and varied as regards their existence, so there exists in God's knowledge of beings plurality and multiplicity.

They condemn Ṣūfism and its pantheism with such sayings as: "It is impossible for the essence of God to be the being of multiple things". They explain the miracles of the Prophet (ascension by night, the split moon) not in a material sense but figuratively and with rationalistic interpretation.

At the beginning of the reign of Nāṣir al-Dīn Shāh, troubles broke out in Tabrīz in 1266/1850 because a Shaikhī was forbidden to enter the public baths as a result of a decision of the *Mudjtahid*. The governor succeeded in quieting the disturbance and made peace between the two parties. Later persecutions were several times directed against the members of the sect.

Bibliography: Riḍā-ḳuli-khān, *Rawḍat al-Ṣafā-i Nāṣirī*, Teheran 1274, x., p. 93; A. L. M. Nicolas, *Essai sur le Chéikhisme*, iii. (= *R M M* 1911) and iv., Paris 1911; E. G. Browne, *A History of Persian Literature in Modern Times*, Cambridge 1924, p. 150, 403; do., *Travellers' Narrative*, ii., Paris 1900, p. 236, 278; Gobineau, *Religions et philosophies* [3], Paris 1900, p. 30—32; Brockelmann, *GAL.*, *Suppl.* ii. 844—845.

SHAIṬĀN, Satan. (See also DJINN, IBLĪS). "Every proud and rebellious one among *djinn*, men and animals" is the meaning given in the dictionaries. As applied to spirits shaiṭān has two distinct meanings with separate histories. The sense of devil goes back to Jewish sources and that of superhuman being has its roots in Arab paganism, though the two meanings interact. In the stories about Solomon a shaiṭān is nothing more than a *djinn* superior in knowledge and power to other *djinn*. But even their powers are limited. Closely connected with this is the use of the word in the sense of genius. "He made up his mind, when they died, to hunger and disappointment, but his Demon said to him — Thou hast the charge of a household to meet" (*Mufaḍḍaliyāt*, xvii. 68). Belonging to the same order of idea is the belief that a poet was possessed by a shaiṭān who inspired his words. Later writers know the names of these familiar spirits. There is some evidence that the pagan gods of Arabia were afterwards reduced to the rank of demons. Ṭabarī says (*Tafsīr*) that the shaiṭān are those whom the infidels obeyed while disobeying God. The bow of Ḳuzaḥ was afterwards called the bow of Shaiṭān and the two horns of Shaiṭān is a name for a phenomenon accompanying sunrise. Similarly old superstitions are preserved in the belief that a shaiṭān eats excrement and all manner of filth and frequents the borderline between shade and sunlight.

The word is common in the Ḳur'ān but in the Sūras of the first Meccan period the indefinite singular alone is found and that only once. It is not till the second period that the definite form occurs, suggesting that the Prophet had found or remembered another idea. Shaiṭān is tacitly identified with Iblīs who is obviously borrowed from Judaism. Thus al-Shaiṭān is the chief of the evil spirits and shaiṭān is a spirit, though not necessarily evil. There is no fixed tradition as to the relation of al-Shaiṭān with the shaiṭāns and other *djinn*. One account says that he is their father; another makes him produce eggs from which they were hatched and another says that God first created the devil then his wife and from the union came three eggs from which the various sorts of *djinn* were hatched. The Ḳur'ān says that Shaiṭān is made of fire (vii. 12, xxxviii. 76); the commentators refine on this and say that the angels are made of light, Shaiṭān of fire or of the smoke of fire. It is not settled whether the shaiṭāns have no bodies at all or have bodies of some very subtle substance. The punishment of Shaiṭān for resisting God is postponed to the end of the world when he will receive his reward in hell-fire. He is not the lord of hell; according to the Ḳur'ān Mālik is lord of hell. His standing epithet *radjīm* is derived by tradition from the stoning of the devil by Ibrāhīm at Minā; according to Nöldeke it is derived from the Abyssinian word meaning accursed. Other names for Shaiṭān are *Ṭāghūt* and *Djānn*, which is said to mean the father of the *djinn*. The serpent which helped Shaiṭān to tempt Adam was punished by being deprived of its legs but the peacock, the intermediary, seems to have escaped scot-free. Perhaps there is some connection with the Mālik Tā'ūs of the Yazīdīs [q.v.].

In religious thought Shaiṭān is the power that opposes God in the hearts of men. He whispers his insidious suggestions in their ears and makes his proposals seductive to them. The Ḳur'ān ascribes this activity now to one shaiṭān now to several. Later it is said that one shaiṭān is attached to each man so that it is possible for everyone to speak of "my shaiṭān". There are no exceptions to this rule for even Yaḥyā b. Zakārīyā (the Baptist) had his shaiṭān though he was too good to listen to its insinuations. The union between a man and his shaiṭān is as close as that between a man and his blood. But there is no hint of dualism for a shaiṭān has no real power over man, he owes his success to craft alone. He cannot exploit that success for he is afraid of God and leaves men in the lurch as soon as he has persuaded them to sin. The popular view is that every man is attended by an angel and a shaiṭān who urge him to evil and good deeds respectively. Ḥasan al-Baṣrī is reported to have said: — "They are two thoughts that rush into the minds of men." He thus reduced these spirit forces to mental states.

Shaiṭāns were of both sexes and ugly. They could appear in human form without anything unnatural betraying their identity. Their feet were hoofs. Many had names. Those of the familiars of some poets were known. Farazdaḳ's demon was *ʿAmr*. The shaiṭāns of India and Syria were among the most powerful and the names of their chiefs are given. Diseases, particularly the plague, were their weapons. Some said that the shaiṭāns were bound during the month of Ramaḍān and a cock was supposed to be a protection against them.

Attempts were made to reduce these ideas to some system. An unbelieving *djinn* was a shaiṭān; one strong enough to move buildings and overhear the divine plans was a *marīd* (rebel) and one capable of more than that was an *ʿifrīt*. Spirits who attacked boys were called *arwāḥ*. Some men had power over the various kinds of spirits, but this power was not for all. The body of the *makhdūm* had to be a fit temple (*haikal*) for spirits if a man was to control them.

As the idea of the shaiṭān is obviously borrowed,

it is probable that the word — a regular Arabic form — is also borrowed from the Ethiopic which is in turn derived from Hebrew.

Bibliography: The passages of the Ḳurʾān and the commentaries thereon; Goldziher, *Abhandlungen zur arabischen Philologie*, i. 106 *sqq.*; Nöldeke, *Neue Beiträge*, p. 34; al-Djāḥiẓ, *Kitāb al-ḥayawān* (cf. v. Vloten, in *WZKM*, viii.); Thaʿlabī, *Ḳiṣaṣ al-anbiyāʾ*; Ṭabarī, i. 78; al-Ghazzālī, *Iḥyāʾ*, iii. 20 *sqq.*; al-Ḳazwīnī, *ʿAdjāʾib al-makhlūḳāt*; al-Masʿūdī, *Murūdj al-dhahab*, iii. 321; J. Horovitz, *Koranische Unters.*, p. 120; A. Jeffery, *Foreign Vocabulary of the Qurʾān*, pp. 187—190.

SHAMSĪYA, order of dervishes called after Shams al-Dīn Abu 'l-Thanāʾ Aḥmad b. Abi 'l-Barakāt Muḥammad Sīwāsī or Sīwāsī-zāde, also called Ḳara Shams al-Dīn and Shamsī (d. 1009/1600—1601). He is mentioned by the historians Naʿīmā (Constantinople 1281, i. 372) and Pečewī (Constantinople 1283, ii. 290) among the saints of the reign of Muḥammad III, and they state (probably on the authority of this sovereign, whose letter is cited by von Hammer, *Geschichte der osmanischen Dichtkunst*, iii. 286) that he fought at the taking of Erlau (1005/1596). He was the author of numerous works in Turkish, enumerated by Ḥādjdjī Khalīfa, who, however, confuses him with other persons; of one called *Manāzil al-ʿĀrifīn* there is a copy in the British Museum, and another called *Gulshanābād* is preserved in the Vienna Library. Notices of this order in European works are mainly derived from d'Ohsson, who mentions it in his list (*Tableau*, iv. 625), whence von Hammer obtains his information in the *Geschichte des osmanischen Reiches*, iv. 236, adding that the founder lived and died at Madīna in the odour of sanctity. In his later work on Ottoman Poetry, *loc. cit.*, he states that this person was head of the Khalwatī order in Sīwās; and in the *Ḳāmūs al-aʿlām* he is called the restorer of the Khalwatī order. In a pedigree of orders made by a Naḳshbandī and cited by Le Châtelier, *Confréries*, p. 50, the Shamsīya is represented as a branch of the Khalwatīya and appears to be confined to Sīwās. It does not figure in the list of *tekye* at Sīwās drawn up by Cuinet (*La Turquie d'Asie*, i. 666), whence it was probably a local name for the Khalwatī order which speedily became obsolete. Le Châtelier, *loc. cit.*, p. 179, mentions an order of this name as a branch of the Badawīya in Egypt.

SHARĀB (A., plur. *ashriba*), beverage. The collections of traditions deal with two subjects in the chapter on *ashriba*: beverages and the laws to be observed in drinking. Here we only deal with the latter as the former has been dealt with in the article KHAMR.

Blessings should be uttered before and after drinking (Abū Dāʾūd, *Ashriba*, bāb 21; Dārimī, *Aṭʿima*, bāb 3; Ibn Ḥanbal i. 225, 284; iii. 100, 117). The cup should be held in the right, not the left hand. The Prophet of God said: "When one of you eats, let him eat with the right hand and if he drinks, he should drink with the right for Satan eats and drinks with the left hand" (Muslim, *Ashriba*, trad. 105; cf. 106).

Opinions differ on the question whether it is permitted to drink standing. On the one hand there are a large number of utterances which represent this attitude in drinking as forbidden (e.g. Muslim, *Ashriba*, trad. 112—116).

On the other hand Ibn ʿAbbās says that he gave the Prophet Zemzem water and that he drank it standing (Muslim, *Ashriba*, trad. 117—120). ʿAlī abolished any misgivings on this point by saying that he had seen Muḥammad drink standing (e.g. Ibn Ḥanbal, i. 101 *sq.*).

It is further considered forbidden to drink out of the mouth of the water-skin (cf. Abū Dāʾūd, *Ashriba*, bāb 14) or to bend the latter inwards to drink (Ibn Mādja, *Ashriba*, bāb 20); but this is also allowed (Tirmidhī, *Ashriba*, bāb 18).

In drinking one should not lap like a dog (Ibn Mādja, *Ashriba*, bāb 25) or blow or snort on the drink (Muslim, *Ashriba*, trad. 121; Abū Dāʾūd, *Ashriba*, bāb 16, 20); on the other hand one should inhale and exhale the breath (Abū Dāʾūd, *Ashriba*, bāb 10; Ibn Saʿd, *Ṭabaḳāt*, ed. Sachau, I/ii. 103) and not drink the whole at one draught (Abū Dāʾūd, *Ṭahāra*, bāb 18). If one is drinking in company the cup should be passed to the right (Bukhārī, *Sharb*, bāb 1).

The knowledge of these matters distinguishes the believer from the infidel. The latter "drinks in seven stomachs, the former in one" (Mālik, *Muwaṭṭaʾ*, *Ṣifat al-Nabī*, bāb 10). See also Ibn Ḳutaiba, *K. al-Ashriba* (pr. Damascus 1947).

SHARĪʿA (A.), also SHARʿ, the road to the watering place, the clear path to be followed, as a technical term, the canon law of Islām; the plural *sharāʾiʿ* which, properly speaking, denotes all the individual prescriptions composing it, is used in practically the same sense; *shirʿa*, which also designs custom and later became obsolete, is synonymous. *Shāriʿ* is used as a technical term for the Prophet as the preacher of the *sharīʿa*, but more frequently it is applied to Allāh as the law-giver. *Mashrūʿ* is what is regulated and provided for by the *sharīʿa*. Anything connected with the canon law, or anything in keeping with it, or legal is called *sharʿī*. *Sharʿī* is also used in opposition to *ḥissī* ("purely sensible"); the former means the outward perceptible actions, which come under the cognisance of the law; the latter, all those in which this is not the case and which, consequently, have no significance in the *sharīʿa* (offer and acceptance are, for example, in concluding a contract, *sharʿī*, in other circumstances *ḥissī*). Similarly *sharʿ* and *ḥukm* (see below) are in contrast to *ḥaḳīḳa*, the actual relations, from which those created by the law may be divergent.

1. The technical use goes back to some passages in the Ḳurʾān: xlv. 18 (of the late Meccan period): "Then we gave thee a *sharīʿa* in religion; follow it and do not follow the lusts of those who do not know"; xlii. 13 (the same period, perhaps somewhat later): "He hath enjoined on you (*sharaʿa*) the religion which", etc.; ibid. 21: "(false gods) who have enjoined on them (*sharaʿū*) a religion which Allāh hath not approved"; v. 48 (Madīna, perhaps of the first Madīna period); "To every one (people) of you, we have given a *shirʿa* and a *minhādj* (a clear way)." Here *sharīʿa* and *shirʿa* are not yet technical terms.

An old definition of *sharīʿa* is given by Ṭabarī on Ḳurʾān, xlv. 18: the *sharīʿa* comprises the law of inheritance (*farāʾiḍ*), the *ḥadd*-punisments, the commandments and prohibitions. In the later system by *sharīʿa* and *sharʿ* is understood the totality of Allāh's commandments relating to the activities of man, apart from those relating to ethics (*akhlāḳ*) which are treated separately. *Fiḳh* (along with its auxiliary sciences) is the science of the *sharīʿa* (cf. FIḲH) and can sometimes be used as synonymous with it, and the *uṣūl al-fiḳh* (cf. UṢŪL) are also called *uṣūl al-sharʿ*. According to the orthodox view, the *sharīʿa* is the basis (*manshaʾ*) for the judgment of actions as good or bad, which accordingly can only come from Allāh, while according to the Muʿtazila, it only confirms the verdict of the intelligence which has preceded it.

The *sharīʿa*, as *forum externum*, regulates only the external relations of the subject to Allāh and his fellow-men and ignores his inner consciousness, his attitude to the *forum internum*. Even the *nīya* (intention) which is required, for example in many religious exercises, implies no impulse from the heart. The *sharīʿa* demands and is only concerned with the fulfilment of the prescribed duties. Thus the *sharīʿa*, its legal judgment (*ḥukm*) of actions and the judicial verdict (*ḳaḍāʾ*) which is only concerned with the external circumstances, are in contrast to the conscience and religious feeling of responsibility (*diyāna, tanazzuh*) of the individual and his inner relation to Allāh (*mā bainahū wabaina 'llāh*). Religious minds like al-Ghazzālī therefore protested against the over-estimation of the legal point of view and the *faḳīh*'s themselves say that it is not sufficient simply to fulfil the commandments of the *sharīʿa*. With this is connected the position of the *sharīʿa* among the Ṣūfīs (cf. TAṢAWWUF): the law is a starting-point on the path of the Ṣūfī; on the one hand, it can be regarded as an indispensable basis for the further religious life, by which the fulfilment of the law has to be refined (*sharīʿa* and *ḥaḳīḳa*, the "mystical reality", then form a correlated pair), on the other hand, only as a symbolical parable and allegory, finally even as superfluous and dangerous formalism which one has to cast off entirely. On the whole, the *sharīʿa* is the most characteristic phenomenon of Islamic thought and forms the nucleus of Islām itself. Moreover, it represents a highly interesting type of "holy law".

2. Allāh's law is not to be penetrated by the intelligence, it is *taʿabbudī*, i.e. man has to accept it without criticism, with its apparent inconsistencies and its incomprehensible decrees, as wisdom into which it is impossible to enquire. One must not look in it for causes in our sense, nor for principles; it is based on the will of Allāh which is bound by no principles, therefore evasions are considered as a permissible use of means put at one's disposal by Allāh himself. Muslim law which has come into being in the course of time through the interworking of many factors, which can hardly be exactly appreciated, has always been considered by its followers as something elevated, high above human wisdom, and as a matter of fact human logic or system has little share in it. A modest enquiry into the meaning of the divine laws so far as Allāh himself has indicated the path of enquiry is, however, not prohibited. There is therefore frequent reference to the deeper meaning and suitability (*ḥikma*) of a law. But one must always guard against placing too much stress on such theoretical considerations.

For this very reason, the *sharīʿa* is not "law" in the modern sense of the word, any more than it is on account of its subject matter. It comprises, withouth restriction, as an infallible doctrine of duties the whole of the religious, political, social, domestic and private life of those who profess Islām, and the activities of the tolerated members of other faiths so fas as they may not be detrimental to Islām. In the result, the *sharīʿa* applies to non-Muslims only within the Islamic territory to a limited extent, and even Muslims are not bound by some of its prescriptions outside it; it therefore restricts its own validity at once by a personal and a territorial standard. The prescriptions of the *sharīʿa* may be classed in two main groups according to their subject: (1) Regulations relating to worship and ritual duties; (2) regulations of a juridical and political nature. These are absolutely similar from the Muslim point of view (although it is of course felt that the former, the so-called *ʿibādāt*, are more closely connected with religion), and this is also true of the numerous regulations scattered everywhere through the *fiḳh* books regarding the most varied matters, which can hardly be brought under the heads of the two main groups, e.g. permitted and forbidden musical instruments, the use of gold and silver vessels, the social intercourse between the two sexes, racing and shooting contests, the copying of living things, clothing and ornaments for men and women, etc. The fundamental tendency in the growth of the *sharīʿa* was the religious evaluation of all affairs of life and juridical considerations, such as the granting of subjective rights in consequence to objective happenings, were only secondary. This point of view which is quite characteristic of the *sharīʿa*, is already plainly appearing once and for all in its first stage, the Ḳurʾānic period, although the regulations enacted by the Ḳurʾān are still far from covering the whole field traced above. The Ḳurʾān was primarily concerned with prescribing what to do and what not to do regarding given contracts and situations, not with putting down legal rules for those contracts and situations and their consequences. As to the material sources of Islamic law, many elements of widely differing derivation (old Arabic Beduin ideas; commercial law of the trading town Mecca; agrarian law of the oasis Madīna; customary law of the conquered countries, some of it of Roman provincial origin; Jewish law) have been unhesitatingly retained and adopted, only to become subject to that common religious appreciation, which in its turn did not fail to produce quite a number of highly original juridical creations. By this general commanding and forbidding tendency the variegated contents of the *sharīʿa* have been forged into one indissoluble unit. A systematic division of the *sharīʿa* was never reached. The Sunnīs sometimes classify it quite formally into *ʿibādāt* (obligations regarding worship), *muʿāmalāt* (civil and legal matters) and *ʿuḳūbāt* (punishments), without any special stress being laid on this; the Shīʿī Twelver Imāmites use an equally formal division, which is not even logically carried through, into *ʿibādāt*, *ʿuḳūd* (contracts), *īḳāʿāt* (onesided dispositions) and *aḥkām* (the remaining prescriptions).

3. The knowledge of Allāh's commands was originally, after the death of the Prophet, obtained directly from the Ḳurʾān and Tradition (hence, also the sciences of *tafsīr* and *ḥadīth* belong to the *fiḳh*); but later among the Sunnīs (in contrast to some Ḥanbalīs, the Wahhābīs and the Shīʿīs) no one was considered qualified to investigate these sources independently (cf. IDJTIHĀD, TAḲLĪD). To later generations the knowledge of the *sharīʿa* is authoritatively communicated through the system of *fiḳh*, which has been worked out by the four orthodox schools (*madhhab*, pl. *madhāhib*) to the most trifling details, and the authority of which is ultimately based on the infallible *idjmāʿ*. Every orthodox Muslim is bound to accept it, but in recent times the so-called modernist movement has been gaining strength; it challenges the authority of the traditional form of the *sharīʿa* and claims the right to reform it in accordance with modern ideas and modern needs, not without an arbitrary choice of its authorities and forcible interpretations of fundamental texts.

A result of the development of the *fiḳh* has been that there is no codification of the law in the modern sense nor can there be one; the several "codifications" of the last and the present centuries have been made under the influence of European ideas and for the use of non-specialists, and are not applied by any of the *sharīʿa* law courts. At the same time the *fiḳh* books, especially those of later date and recognized as authoritative in wide circles (by *idjmāʿ*), are practically "law books" for the orthodox Muslim; in them he finds Allāh's *sharīʿa* expounded in the way in which it is binding to him, and according to the particular *madhhab* which he follows while the Ḳurʾān and Ḥadīth have no direct legal importance for him. But it is not everyone's affair to ascertain from the *fiḳh* books with sufficient technical knowledge how the law affects a particular case; the non-specialists rather require instruction from experts. This is done through *fatwā*'s (legal opinions; cf. the art.), and a scholar who gives *fatwā*'s is called *mufti*.

4. During the early period of Islām, no unanimity prevailed as to what were the main duties of Muslims. The Ḳurʾān had laid special weight on the *ṣalāt* (ritual worship), *zakāt* (charity) and *ṣawm* (fasting). Many further regarded participation in the *djihād* (holy war) as one of the first duties of a Muslim, a view still held among the Khāridjīs (also adopted by the Sūdānese *Mahdī* Muḥammad Aḥmad). The Shīʿīs in general regard recognition of the imāmate and attachment (*wilāya*) to their *imāms* as one of the main duties; the Ismāʿīlīs add also the *djihād*. But according to the view that has come to prevail among the Sunnīs, Islām is based on five "pillars" (*arkān*, sg. *rukn*): *shahāda* (the profession of faith), *ṣalāt, zakāt, ḥadjdj* (pilgrimage to Mecca), *ṣawm* (during the month of Ramaḍān). The profession of faith is as a rule not dealt with in the *fiḳh* books. Questions connected with the creed were so numerous that the teaching of the first pillar soon became a special branch of study, the science of *kalām* [q.v.]. The other four *arkān* are sometimes classed together with *ṭahāra* (ritual purification), which by the Ismāʿīlīs is regarded as a further "pillar", as the five *ʿibādāt*. In the traditional arrangement of the *fiḳh* and *ḥadīth* books, the first chapters are always devoted to these *ʿibādāt*, followed by the other subjects: contracts, inheritance, marriage and family law, criminal law, war against unbelievers and attitude to unbelievers generally, laws regarding food, sacrifice and killing of animals, oaths and vows, judicial procedure and evidence, liberation of slaves. This is the arrangement usual with the Shāfiʿīs; for the different sequence of chapters adopted by the earlier Ḥanafīs which rather agrees with that of the Mishna, Jewish influence has been suggested. Nevertheless, all systems of arrangement have much in common, and this must go back to the 2nd century A.H.

As regards religious appreciation, all actions are classified by the *sharīʿa* under one of the following five categories (*al-aḥkām al-khamsa*) (1) "duty" (*farḍ*) or "obligatory" (*wādjib*), i.e. actions the performance of which is rewarded and omission punished; of the further divisions of *farḍ* (*wādjib*), the most important is that into *farḍ ʿain* and *farḍ kifāya* (cf. FARḌ), a similar division being made in the following category; (2) meritorious (*sunna* "the usual custom"; [*sunna* in this meaning is not to be confounded with the "*sunna* of the Prophet", one of the *uṣūl al-fiḳh*], *mandūb* "recommended", *mustaḥabb* "desirable", *nafl* or *nāfila* "voluntary meritorious action"; the performance of such is called *taṭawwuʿ*), i.e. actions the neglect of which is not punished, but the performance of which is rewarded; its contrary is *kifāya*, "the sufficient minimum"; (3) "indifferent" (*mubāḥ* or *murakhkhaṣ*), i.e. actions the performance or neglect of which the law leaves quite open and for which neither reward nor punishment is to be expected; *mubāḥ* should be differentiated from *djāʾiz* "permissible" (see below) and from *ḥalāl* "lawful", i.e. all that is not *ḥarām* (see below); (4) "reprehensible" (*makrūh*), i.e. actions which although not punishable are disapproved of from the religious point of view; the later Shāfiʿīs further distinguish a milder form of *makrūh*, the *khilāf al-awlā*, "diverging from the obvious"; correspondingly there is also an *awlā* "obvious" which lies between the indifferent and the meritorious; (5) "forbidden" (*ḥarām*, also *maḥẓūr*), i.e. actions punishable by Allāh; different aspects here are "sin" (*maʿṣiya, ithm*) "grave sins" (*kabāʾir*) "venial sins" (*ṣaghāʾir*) and "trespass" (*taʿaddī*). Something the law likes is called *maṭlūb*; this may be *farḍ*, *sunna* or *awlā*. There are still further subdivisions and intermediate grades between the categories mentioned.

The reasons which lead to an action being classed under one of these categories may be of the most varied kind and here there is a wide field for difference of opinion (*ikhtilāf*) among jurists. What one party considers absolutely forbidden or an absolute duty, the others often regard as reprehensible or meritorious or even indifferent. Here, however, the catholic tendency of Islām makes itself felt. Thus it may happen that something is considered *sunna* by one *madhhab* simply because the latter is unwilling to differ too much from the view of another school of *fiḳh*, which considers it a duty. That the same action according to circumstances can be sometimes forbidden, sometimes reprehensible, sometimes indifferent, sometimes meritorious, sometimes a duty is general recognized.

A second scale of qualifications is applied to the juridically relevant actions with regard to their legal significance; it has been developed most in detail by the Ḥanafīs as follows: (1) valid (*ṣaḥīḥ*), if both the essence (*aṣl*) and the qualities (*waṣf*) of an action correspond to the standards of the law; (2) reprehensible (*makrūh*), if the same is the case, but the action is connected with something forbidden; (3) incorrect (*fāsid*), if its essence corresponds to the law but not its qualities; (4) (*bāṭil*), if neither its essence nor its qualities correspond to the law. In the cases of (1) and (2) ,the legal effects come fully into force, in the case of (3) only under certain conditions or with certain restrictions; in the case of (2) an additional liability may be incurred; in the case of (4), there is no legal effect at all. The other *madhāhib* do not differentiate *fāsid* from *bāṭil* [q.v.]. *Ṣaḥīḥ* is often used in the sense of "legally effective", so as to include also *makrūh*; direct terms for this larger conception are *nāfidh* ("objectively effective"), *lāzim* (in its primary meaning: "subjectively binding") and *wādjib* ("irrevocable" to be distinguished from the meaning of *wādjib* mentioned above). In this wider sense, *ṣaḥīḥ* is practically synonymous with *djāʾiz* (see above); both terms denote all that is permissible from the religious point of view and therefore legally valid. In quite a parallel meaning, *idjāza* ("declaration that something is *djāʾiz*", "ratification") is employed withing the purely juridical sphere; if the person concerned declares his approval of the transaction in question, it becomes thereby valid. This mutual interference of both scales of qualifications, which is evident also from the common term *makrūh*, is, however, not complete; even "forbidden" actions are not always, as to their legal consequences, "void", but sometimes only "incorrect" or even "valid". Thus the possibility of applying the second scale forms an objective criterium for the still somehow independent existence of the juridical subject-matter within the *sharīʿa*.

5. After the death of the Prophet his successor, the first caliph, although taking over quite naturally his role as the supreme judge of the Muslim community, could not pretend to continue his activity as the transmitter of divine revelation. This has actually been the case, according to the tenents of the Shīʿīs, with their *imāms*; but this idea has remained here a mere dogmatic theory and has not influenced the development of the law. As to the Sunnīs, during the first generation of Islām after the Prophet, the authority for deciding how the law should be and the authority for enforcing it, were vested in the same persons, the companions of Muḥammad, centring in the caliphs; there was therefore little danger of utterly impractical ideas forcing their way in. During this whole period the law for its greater part still remained indifferent to the religious point of view. The regulations of the Ḳurʾān and the other prescriptions of the Prophet were of course complied with, and the new decisions were to be according to his intention; but the legal institutions as found in the recently conquered territories were freely adopted, so far as no religious criticism could be raised against them. After the coming of the Umaiyads, however, those pious men lost their position of authority. They and their successor then began — being no longer bound by realities — to devote themselves to developing their doctrine of duties in an ideal direction in a way which became more and more irreconcilable with practical life. They were busy with subjecting the whole of life, and with it law in its entirety, to religious standards; they drew the juridical consequences not only from the prescriptions of the Ḳurʾān, but also from authentic or alleged relations about the sayings and actions of the Prophet. Thus a learned body developed out of the council of the first caliphs. The early ʿAbbāsids tried in vain to bridge the gulf between the holy law and the political reality. The only lasting result was a kind of truce between the representatives of religious learning and the temporal powers, the terms of which are nowhere expressly formulated but which was observed by both sides under the pressure of circumstances. The pious men obeyed the government in practice — the *sharīʿa* itself, as an early concession to things as they were, enjoining the acknowledgement of any established Muslim authority —, but retained full liberty to censure theoretically, and thus we find everywhere laments about "the present age" and warnings against "the princes of this world". The latter in their turn recognized the religious law in theory and did not claim for themselves the right of legislation within the *sharīʿa*, but when they thought fit, put the latter practically out of action by issuing independent regulations (*ḳānūn* [q.v.], sometimes also called *siyāsa*) on legal matters and instituting administrative courts of laws. This did not prevent them when they wished to be considered particularly pious, from sometimes enforcing some prescriptions of the *sharīʿa*, especially penal laws, without much regard for the necessary procedure. Of this state of affairs the pious scholars themselves draw the consequence. To brand almost all Muslims as sinners or worse, because they had continually to disregard the religious law if they were not prepared to withdraw from the world entirely, was not feasible; on the contrary, these things had rather to be taken as inevitable and willed by Allāh. Thus the *sharīʿa* continued to claim unconditioned theoretical acknowledgment, and everyone who fails in this respect, is to be considered as an infidel (*kāfir*, q.v.); but at the same time it virtually ceased to demand actual observance in so far as it could not be enforced in practice. This tendency appears already in the qualification of certain actions only as recommended or reprehensible and in the lack of penal sanction for the omission of most religious duties; furthermore, appeal was made to the principle that necessity breaks the laws, and the way was even pointed out so evade the rules of the *sharīʿa* (by means of the so-called *ḥiyal* which often consist in fictitious transactions). The conviction that the Muslim community would steadily become worse after its golden age until the coming op the *mahdī* [q.v.] which had been deduced from the course of events, was expressed in traditions which were put in the mouth of the Prophet; these conditions were thus sanctioned as a fulfilment of his prophecy. So the *sharīʿa* in the convinced opinion of its representatives themselves could be strictly enforced only in the ideal community in the early decades of Islām and in the time of the *mahdī*; this was a confession of the impotence of the pious in face of the circumstances of the age. The *sharīʿa*, essentially academic in character, has at the same time always been a considerable educational force and is still ardently studied; in spite of the advice of al-Ghazzālī [q.v.] and others to the contrary, it is still regarded in wide circles of Islām as the only subject of true learning. But as it was held up as an unattainable ideal and because the doctrine of the infallibility of the *idjmāʿ* [q.v.] together with the conviction of cessation of the *idjtihād* [q.v.] forbade any divergence from what had been settled once for all, it has become quite rigid: its representatives are opponents of all change; even yet many prescriptions are carried along which only referred to the early Arab society and can have no longer any practical significance even for the most orthodox Muslim of to-day.

6. One should, however, not draw too sharp a line between the doctrine of the *sharīʿa* and the law as enforced by the state. This is particularly evident in the office of *ḳāḍī* [q.v.], the religious judge who is at the same time a state official; the Muslim princes have never ceased to appoint *ḳāḍīs* and to grant them, in principle at least, the necessary organs for enforcing their decisions. The early *ḳāḍīs* rendered their judgments according to their own discretion, basing themselves — besides on the prescriptions of the Ḳurʾān and the directives of the caliphs — on equity and on customary law with more or less stress laid on the religious points of view. During the whole first period, the administration of justice had made most important contributions to the development of the *sharīʿa*. But once this had arrived at its definite form — a fact which roughly coincident with the coming to power of the ʿAbbāsids —, the *ḳāḍī* remained exclusively bound by this authoritative doctrine, in complete independence of the government. This is the theory; in practice, the *ḳāḍīs* could not but take notice of the wishes of the authority by which they were appointed and dismissed and on which they depended for the execution of

judgments; moreover, the hearing of certain claims could be withheld from the *ḳāḍī*'s competence, so as to make prescriptions of the law inapplicable. Although under the Umaiyads occasional attempts at direct interference by the political authorities were mostly rejected, this completely changed, in spite of the theory, early under the ʿAbbāsids. The *sharīʿa* itself recognizes, to a certain extent, the courts of the *nāẓir al-maẓālim* and of the *muḥtasib* which rather soon became over a long period fixed institutions besides the tribunal of the *ḳāḍī*; the former had to deal with offences which the *ḳāḍī* had not the means to repress, whilst the latter may be described as a police court. Thus everywhere in Islām a twofold legal practice has grown up, which may be called the religious and the secular; criminal and financial law as well as the law regarding landed property were more and more monopolised by the temporal power; furthermore, the *sharīʿa* has never been actually in practice as regards the constitution of the Muslim state, international relations and war. To the jurisdiction of the *ḳāḍī* there was finally left only public worship and purely religious obligations, the law regarding marriage, family and inheritance, in part also pious foundations (*waḳf*, q.v.,), all fields which in the popular mind are more closely connected with religion, and in which the *sharīʿa* always prevailed. It was during the flourishing period of the Ottoman empire in the 16th and 17th centuries that the *sharīʿa* reached at last, under the auspices of "pious" rulers, the peak of its practical application, even in the fields of civil and commercial law; uniformity of jurisdiction all over the territory was achieved, the *ḳāḍīs* were organized in a kind of hierarchy, the supreme *muftī*, the *shaikh al-islām* [q.v.], had to superintend the proper application of the *sharīʿa*; but even then the criminal, financial and landed property law was ruled by the temporal legislation of the so-called *ḳānūn-nāmas*, which actually were, although they pretended not to be, contrary to the *sharīʿa*. The reform movement starting in the 19th century (see TANẒĪMĀT) brought about the introduction of codes conceived on European lines, at first for the commercial, then for the penal law, but still as late as 1876 the civil law of the *sharīʿa* was codified in the *medjelle*; this however, being a code, quite apart from the modifications contained in it, did not correspond to the strict requirements of the doctrine, and was not to be used by the *sharīʿa* tribunals themselves but by secular courts. The last step was taken in 1926 by the introduction of the Swiss civil (and the Italian penal) code which replaced the *sharīʿa* even for the law of marriage, family and inheritance, followed in 1928 by the omission of the last mention of the *sharīʿa* from the constitution and the radical secularisation of the state. Albania has so far been the only Islamic country to follow the example of Turkey by completely abandoning the *sharīʿa*. In Egypt, the adoption of codes after the European model for the field abandoned by the *sharīʿa* in practice, began only in 1883; some modifications of the doctrine regarding procedure, comparable to those contained in the *medjelle* but binding the *sharīʿa* tribunals themselves, were first introduced in 1910; at last, the material rules regarding some points of family law have been modified, cautiously at first in 1920, more boldly in 1929 and 1931 (here also Turkey had taken the lead in 1917).

7. All this regards the relation between the *sharīʿa* and the state; the following remarks concern the kindred problem of its place in popular mind and practice. Here it should always be remembered that there may be considerable differences in detail in different periods and countries and that strictness and slackness in following the *sharīʿa* have nothing to do with tolerance or intolerance. Even in ritual and the religious duties in the narrower sense, which mean most to Muslims, ignorance and gross neglect is general, but nevertheless throughout the whole Muslim world there is perceptible a striving to perform some at least of the main obligations as closely as possible. The usages especially, by which Muslims are externally distinguished from members of other creeds, are in general very closely observed and considered very important even if they are not according to the law, while, on the other hand, many religious obligations imperative in theory are quite neglected in practice. The law relating to marriage, family and inheritance is usually quite closely followed, but even here the *sharīʿa* is occasionally encroached upon by the local customary law (*ʿāda*, *ʿurf*, *desturi* [Suaheli for *dustūrī*]). The other parts of the law have for popular conscience long since lost any practical significance, although everywhere and in every period are to be found conscientious men who endeavour to take account as far as possible of the doctrine of the *sharīʿa* even in commercial affairs (even nowadays, bank interest is often refused). Offences against positive commands of the law were much more strictly avoided than, for instance, invalidity of contracts; thus, in the field of commercial law, practice went its course unencumbered; here the *sharīʿa* never really prevailed. This customary law, to which the *ḥiyal* belong, is not in direct contradiction to the *sharīʿa*, but accords to its main rules a greater flexibility and has developed large complements to some of its institutions (especially in the law of real property), together with an elaborate system of written documentation (*shurūṭ*). In addition to the *ḥiyal* and *shurūṭ*, also the collections of *fatwā*'s are valuable for ascertaining the actual practice: they show in what parts of the law the people of a country are most interested, what "abuses" are most prevalent and what conditions arouse misgivings regarding their legality. This *ʿāda*, differing widely according to circumstances, is the direct successor of the old customary law which, during the whole early period, was freely admitted into the *sharīʿa*, although it did not finally succeed in gaining theoretical recognition as the fifth of the *uṣūl* [q.v.] *al-fiḳh*. But to the popular mind only the *ʿadā* is present; even the prescriptions of the law, which are actually observed, are observed simply because they belong to use and wont, and in Indonesia for example (apart from the religious scholars proper), the *ʿāda* is recognized among authoritative Muslim circles as being even in theory equal in every way to the *sharīʿa*.

Bibliography: Sprenger, *Dictionary of the Technical Terms*, s.v.; Goldziher, *Vorlesungen über den Islam*, 2nd ed., p. 30 *sqq.*; Snouck Hurgronje, in: Bertholet-Lohmann, *Lehrbuch der Religionsgeschichte*, 4th ed., p. 695 *sqq.*; Macdonald, *Development of Muslim Theology, Jurisprudence and Constitutional Theory*; Santillana, in: Arnold and Guillaume, *The Legacy of Islam*, p. 284 *sqq.*; R. Levy, *An Introduction to the Sociology of Islam*, 2 vols.; art. LAW in: T. P. Hughes, *A Dictionary of Islam*. Also the relevant chapters in M. Guidi, *Storia della Religione dell'Islam*, in: P. Tacchi Venturi, *Storia delle Religioni*, vol. 2; Lammens, *L'Islam*; Snouck Hurgronje, *Mohammedanism*.

A. A. Fyzee, *Outlines of Muhammadan Law*, Oxford 1949. — Important monographic investigations: Goldziher, *Die Ẓâhiriten*; do., *Muhammedanische Studien*, vol. 2; do., in *Zeitschr. f. vergl. Rechtswissensch.*, viii. p. 406 *sqq.*; do., *Das muslimische Recht und seine Stellung in der Gegenwart*, Budapest 1916 (reprinted from *Pester Lloyd*, 31st October 1916); Snouck Hurgronje, *Verspreide Geschriften*, especially vols. ii and iv. 1, 2; Bergsträsser, in *Isl.*, xiv. p. 76 *sqq.*; do., in *Islamica*, iv, p. 283 *sqq.*; Schacht, *Origins of Muhammadan Jurisprudence.* — Manuals: Juynboll, *Handbuch des islāmischen Gesetzes*; id., *Handleiding*, 3rd ed.; López Ortiz, *Derecho musulmán*; Santillana, *Istituzioni di diritto musulmano malichita*, 2 vols.; G. Bergsträsser, *Grundzüge des islamischen Rechts*. — Translations of arabic works: Baillie, *A Digest of Moohummudan Law*, 2 vols.; Sachau, *Muhammedanisches Recht nach schafiitischer Lehre*; I. Guidi and D. Santillana, *Il "Muḫtaṣar" o sommario del diritto malechita di Ḫalīl ibn Isḥāq*, 2 vols.; Querry, *Droit musulman, recueil de lois concernant les musulmans schyites*, 2 vols. — For the modernism: Snouck Hurgronje, *Mohammedanism*; R. Hartmann, *Die Krisis des Islam.* — For the actual practice, see ʿĀDA — Bibliographies: for European works: Juynboll, *ll.cc.*; Pfannmüller, *Handbuch der Islam-Literatur*; for oriental sources: Aghnides, *Mohammedan Theories of Finance*.

SHARĪF (A.) (plur. *ashrāf*, *shurafāʾ*) "noble, exalted", the root of which expresses the idea of elevation and prominence, means primarily a freeman, who can claim a distinguished position because of his descent from illustrious ancestors (cf. *LA.*, xi. 70 *sq.*). It is of course assumed here that the meritorious qualities of the fathers are transmitted to their descendants. The possession of several illustrious ancestors is the requisite condition for a *sharaf* (also *ḥasab*) *ḍakhm*, a "solid" nobility. (Goldziher, *Muh. Stud.*, i. 41 *sq.*; Lammens, *Le Berceau de l'Islam*, 1914, p. 289 *sqq.*). Although in Islām the doctrine — based on Ḳurʾān xlix, 13 "Verily the noblest among you in the eyes of God is he that fears God most" — of the equality of all Arabs and ultimately of all believers grew up (Goldziher, *op. cit.*, i. 50 *sqq.*, 69 *sqq.*), it never quite displaced the old reverence for a distinguished genealogy.

The *ashrāf* were the heads of the prominent families, to whom were entrusted the administration of the affairs of the tribe or alliance of towns; cf. Ibn Hishām, *Sīra*, ed. Wüstenfeld, p. 237 l z.; 295, $_{17}$; al-Ṭabarī, *Akhbār al-rusul wa 'l-mulūk*, ed. Leiden, i. 1191; the *Ashrāf* of al-Ḥīra, ibid., i. 2017; the *Ashrāf al-ḳabāʾil*, ibid., ii. 541, $_{17}$; the *Ashrāf* in Kūfa, ibid., ii. 631 *sqq.* passim; the *Ashrāf* of Khurāsān, ibid., iii. 714, $_{1}$; the *Ashrāf al-aʿādjim*, al-Yaʿḳūbī, ed. Houtsma, ii. 176, $_{8}$. The *ashrāf* regarded themselves as the aristrocrats (*ahl al-faḍl*) with whom were contrasted the rude and untutored masses (*arādhil*, *sufahāʾ*, *akhissāʾ*) (al-Ṭabarī, ii. 631, $_{7}$). *Sharīf* also means a person of importance in contrast to one of low social status (*ḍaʿīf*, *waḍīʿ*; al-Bukhārī, *Badʾ al-waḥy*, b. 6, *al-Ḥudūd*, b. 11, 12). In this sense the word frequently found in the older literature of Islām, e.g. in the very title of al-Balādhurī's history, *Ansāb al-Ashrāf*.

In Islām under the influence of Shīʿa views and the increasing veneration for the Prophet, membership of the house of Muḥammad became a mark of special distinction. The expression *ahl al-bait* comes from Ḳurʾān xxxiii. 33*b*: "God will remove the stains from you, O people of the house and purify you completely" which the Shīʿīs applied to ʿAlī and Fāṭima and their sons (cf. already al-Kumait, *al-Hāshimīyāt*, ed. Horovitz, Leiden 1904, text, p. 38, verse 30, cf. p. 92, verse 67) by interpreting it through the well known tradition of the mantle (*ḥadīth al-kisāʾ*, *ḥ. al-ʿabāʾ*) also adopted in orthodox tradition. The explanation of the phrase as referring to the "women", which is more in keeping with the context, said to have been put forward by Ibn ʿAbbās and ʿIkrima is found in some versions of this tradition, in which Umm Salama is recognized by the Prophet as belonging to the *ahl al-bait*. The current orthodox view is based on the harmonising opinion, according to which the term *ahl al-bait* includes the *ahl al-ʿabāʾ*, i.e. the Prophet, ʿAlī, Fāṭima, al-Ḥasan and al-Ḥusain as well as the women of the Prophet. But even the ʿAbbāsids relied on the verse of purification and therefore, we have the counterpart of the *ḥadīth al-kisāʾ* which includes al-ʿAbbās and his sons in the *ahl al-bait*.

Ahl al-bait is given a still wider interpretation in a version of the so-called *ḥadīth al-thaḳalain*, where the term is referred to those to whom the sharing in *ṣadaḳa* is forbidden; among such are definitely mentioned the Āl ʿAlī, the Āl ʿAḳīl, the Āl Djaʿfar and the Āl al-ʿAbbās. According to this, the *ahl al-bait* includes the Ṭālibids and ʿAbbāsids, historically the most important families of the Banū Hāshim; cf. Lammens, *Fāṭima*, Rome 1912, p. 95 *sqq.*; Strothmann, *Das Staatsrecht der Zaiditen*, Strassburg 1912, p. 19 *sq.*; van Arendonk, *De Opkomst van het Zaidietische Imamaat in Yemen*, Leyden, p. 65 *sqq.*

The clan of the Banū Hāshim was put in the forefront by the editors of the *Sīra* of the Prophet. God's deliberate choice after a gradual process of elimination of families finally selected the Hāshim as the family to produce the Prophet. A tradition which occurs in several versions runs as follows: The Prophet of Allāh said: "Allāh chose Ismāʿīl from the sons of Ibrāhīm and from the sons of Ismāʿīl the Banū Kināna and from the Banū Kināna the Ḳuraish and from the Ḳuraish the Banū Hāshim" (Ibn Saʿd, *Ṭabaḳāt*, ed. Sachau, i/$_{1}$, 2). One of these versions concludes with the words: "consequently I (i.e. Muḥammad) am the best of you as regards family and the best of you as regards genealogy" (Ibn ʿAbd Rabbihi, ii. 247).

To al-Kumait who lauded the noble blood of the Prophet in exuberant language (*op. cit.*, text, p. 14, $_{45}$ *sqq.*) the Banū Hāshim are "the peaks of splendid nobility" (ibid., p. 5, $_{14}$), who are granted "a pre-eminence over all men" (p. 58, $_{37}$). To be able to show kinship with the Prophet was thus an important claim to *sharaf*.

This special position of the Banū Hāshim, among whom the Ṭālibids are already celebrated by al-Kumait as *ashrāf* and *sāda* (*op. cit.*, text, p. 10, $_{29}$, p. 56, $_{80}$), led in the later ʿAbbāsid period (about the ivth/xth century) to a limitation of the title of honour *al-sharīf*, which is also said to have been a *laḳab* of ʿAlī (Muḥibb al-Dīn al-Ṭabarī, *al-Riyāḍ al-naḍira*, Cairo, 1327, ii. 155, $_{18}$) to the descendants of al-ʿAbbās and Abū Ṭālib. Al-Ṭabarī (iii. 635, $_{6}$) also mentions the *ashrāf* as a special group alongside of the Banū Hāshim.

In al-Māwardī (*al-Aḥkām al-sulṭānīya*, ed. Enger, Bonn 1853, p. 165, $_{7}$) the *ashrāf* are divided into Ṭālibīyūn and ʿAbbāsīyūn. From the literary history of the second half of the ivth/xth) century we know of the two brothers al-Sharīf al-Raḍī and al-Sharīf al-Murtaḍā (cf. Brockelmann, *GAL*, i. 81). According to al-Suyūṭī, *Ris. al-Sulāla al-Zainabīya*, f. 4*a sq.* (= al-Ṣabbān, p. 112 *sq.*) the name al-Sharīf was used in the earlier period (*al-ṣadr al-awwal*) of all who belonged to the *ahl al-bait*, whether a Ḥasanī, Ḥusainī or ʿAlawī, i.e. a descendant of Muḥammad b. al-Ḥanafīya or of another of ʿAlī's sons, or a Djaʿfarī, ʿAḳīlī or ʿAbbāsī. He points out that in the chronicle of al-Dhahabī we often meet with titles like *al-Sharīf al-ʿAbbāsī*, *al-Sharīf al-ʿAḳīlī*, *al-Sharīf al-Djaʿfarī*, *al-Sharīf al-Zainabī*, which however proves very little for the older period. The Fāṭimids however, as he observes, restricted the name *al-Sharīf* to the descendants of al-Ḥasan and al-Ḥusain and this had remained the custom in Egypt down to his time. We may assume that the word *al-sharīf* in the strict sense was at that time applied only to a Ḥasanī or Ḥusainī. For ,as al-Suyūṭī notes in another connection (p. 6*a*/*b*, al-Ṣabbān, p. 190 *sq.*, similarly Ibn Ḥadjar al-Haitamī, *al-Fatāwī al-ḥadīthīya*, p. 124 *sqq.*), a *waḳf* or a testamentary deposition in favour of the *ashrāf* is only awarded to the descendants of al-Ḥasan and al-Ḥusain for such depositions are decided by local usage (*ʿurf*) and according to the usage in Egypt, dating from the Fāṭimid period, this term was applied only to the Ḥasanids and Ḥusainids. In conclusion al-Suyūṭī observes that according to the linguistic usage of Egypt the noble blood (*sharaf*) was divided into different classes, namely a grade which included the whole of the *ahl al-bait*, another which contained only the *dhurrīya*, i.e. the descendants of ʿAlī which included the Zainabīs, the descendants of Zainab bint ʿAlī and also all sons of ʿAlī's daughters, and finally a still smaller class the *sharaf al-nisba* which only admitted the descendants of al-Ḥasan and al-Ḥusain.

Among the historians the title *Sharīf* is first used for the ʿAlids in the period of the dissolution of the ʿAbbāsid empire, when the ʿAlids were rebelling everywhere and attaining power in Ṭabaristān and Arabia (Snouck Hurgronje, *Mekka*, i. 56 *sq.*).

The case of *saiyid* "lord" was similar to that of *sharīf*. *Saiyid* means the master in contrast to the slave (cf. e.g. al-Bukhārī, *al-Aḥkām*, b. 1, etc.; al-Tirmidhī, *al-Birr*, b. 53), and the husband as opposed to the wife (e.g. Ḳurʾān, xii. 25). *Saiyid* was also the usual name for the head of a tribe or clan (cf. Ḳurʾān xxxiii. 67; Ibn Hishām, p. 295, $_{17}$), whose authority was based mainly on personal qualities like discretion (*ḥilm*), liberality and command of language (cf. Ibn Ḳutaiba, *ʿUyūn al-akhbār*, i. 223 *sqq.*). Certain physical qualities are also said to mark a man as a *saiyid* (Ibn Ḳutaiba, *loc. cit.*; Mez, *Die Renaissance des Islâms*, p. 144). The Ḳurʾān praises the prophet Yaḥyā as a *saiyid* (iii. 39). *Saiyid* may have become particularly used as a title for ʿAlids and Ṭālibids at about the same time as *sharīf*. This development was probably not unaffected by traditions which describe al-Ḥasan and al-Ḥusain and their parents as *saiyid(a)*. The Prophet is recorded to have said of al-Ḥasan, "this my son is a *saiyid* and perhaps Allāh will bring about reconciliation between the two parties of Muslims through him" (al-Bukhārī, *Fitan*, b. 20, No. 2, *Faḍāʾil al-Ṣaḥāba*, b. 22; al-Tirmidhī, *Manāḳib*, b. 30). Al-Ḥusain appears in the Ḥadīth as *saiyid shabāb ahl al-djanna*, "lord of young men among the inhabitants of Paradise" (al-Nabhānī, p. 64, $_{17}$ *sqq.*) and along with his brother he is celebrated as *saiyidā shabāb* etc. "the two lords of the young men" etc. (al-Tirmidhī, *loc. cit.*; al-Nasāʾī, *Khaṣāʾiṣ Amīr al-Muʾminīn ʿAlī b. Abī Ṭālib*, Cairo 1308, p. 24, 26), while their mother Fāṭima is lauded by the Prophet as "mistress of the women of my (this) community" or "mistress of the women of the worlds", "mistress of the women of the dwellers in Paradise" (*Saiyidat nisāʿ ummatī*, and *hādhihi 'l-umma*, *S. n. al-ʿālamīn*, *S. n. ahl-djanna*, cf. Ibn Saʿd, *Ṭabaḳāt*, viii. 17, $_{7}$ *sqq.*; al-Bukhārī, *Faḍāʾil Aṣḥāb al-Nabī*, b. 29; al-Nasāʾī, *op. cit.*, 23 *sq.*; al-Nabhānī, p. 54, $_{8}$ *sqq.*). The Prophet is said to have called ʿAlī *Saiyid al-ʿArab* and *Saiyid al-Muslimīn* and to have once said to him "Thou art a *saiyid* in this world and a *saiyid* in the next" (Muḥibb al-Dīn al-Ṭabarī, *op. cit.*, ii. 177).

In the beginning the term *saiyid* may have been first applied to those who possessed some authority in their own sphere. In the genealogical work of the Ḥasanid Ibn Muhannā, *ʿUmdat al-ṭālib fī ansāb āl Abī Ṭālib*, individual ʿAlids are often described as *saiyid* (Bombay edition 1318, e.g. p. 51, $_{16}$, 52, $_{2}$). Al-Dhahabī, *Taʾrīkh al-Islām*, MS. Leyden 1721, f. 65[a] gives this title to the Twelver Imām ʿAlī b. Muḥammad. We also find the combination *al-Saiyid al-Sharīf* or vice versa (al-Nuwairī, *Nihāyat al-ʿArab*, Cairo 1342, ii., p. 277, $_{12}$; al-Khazradjī, *al-ʿUḳūd al-Luʾluʾīya*, i., *GMS.*, iii. 4, Leyden—London 1913, p. 314, $_{11}$). The word *saiyid* also came to be applied to Ṣūfī authorities, saints and notable theologians, e.g. *al-Sāda* (*al-Ṣūfīya*), *al-Sādāt al-awliyāʾ* (al-Shardjī, *Ṭabaḳāt al-khawāṣṣ*, Cairo 1321, p. 2, $_{9}$, 3, $_{1}$, 195, $_{3}$); *al-Sāda al-aʿlām* (Ibn Ḥadjar al-Haitamī, *al-Fatāwī al-ḥadīthīya*, p. 124,). The term *Saiyidī* or *Sīdī* (frequently in al-Shaʿrānī, *Lawāḳiḥ al-anwār fī ṭabaḳāt al-akhyār*, Cairo 1315), became very popular for persons regarded as holy, and is the expression used by the slave in addressing his master.

Like *al-sharīf*, *al-saiyid* came in many Muslim lands to be applied only to Ḥasanids and Ḥusainids. Thus in Ḥaḍramawt their usual title is *saiyid* (Snouck Hurgronje, *Verspr. Geschr.*, iii. 163). To judge from al-Khazradjī (*op. cit.*, i. 315 *sqq.* passim) *sharīf* was in his day the usual name for them, now according to Amīn al-Raiḥānī (*Mulūk al-ʿArab*, Bairūt 1924, i. 92, note 1) it is *saiyid*. In the Ḥidjāz it was the custom to call *sharīf* only those Ḥasanids whose ancestors had lived in Mecca and to give the name *saiyid* only to the Ḥusainids. But the Meccan talks of the Grand Sharīf as *saiyidanā* and the latter gives the members of his family the title *saiyid* (Snouck Hurgronje, *Mekka*, i. 57; do., *Verspr. Geschr.*, iii. 163, v. 31, 40; al-Nabhānī, p. 41). The names *saiyid* and *mīr* (*amīr*) used in Persia were also current in Turkey and India. Along with the title *saiyid* usual in the Malay Archipelago we also find in Atjeh the honorific *ḥabīb* (beloved) also used in Arabia (Snouck Hurgronje, *The Achehnese*, i. 155).

In the ʿAbbāsid period, the *Ashrāf*, ʿAbbāsids and Ṭālibids, were usually under the authority of a *naḳīb* "marshal of nobility" chosen by them. The history of this office has so far been little investigated. That it already existed under the Umaiyads as von Kremer (*Culturgeschichte d. Orients unter den Chalifen*, Vienna 1875, i. 449, note 1) supposes from Ibn Khaldūn, *al-ʿIbar*, Būlāḳ 1284, ii. 134, $_{8}$ from below, is very doubtful as the passage quoted is probably corrupt (cf. al-Ṭabarī, ii. 16, ult., 17, $_{1}$). The two branches of the Banū Hāshim were from the first probably under a marshal as was the case about 301/913—4 (ʿArīb, ed. de Goeje, p. 47, $_{10}$). The ʿAlid ʿAlī b. Muḥammad b. Djaʿfar al-Ḥimmānī who died in 260/873—4 was *naḳīb* in Kūfa (al-Masʿūdī, *Murūdj al-dhahab*, Paris 1861—1877, vii.

338). Perhaps at this date there were in the larger towns as at a later date, marshals of the nobles, who were under a grand marshal (*naḳīb al-nuḳabā'*). In general theory it was the duty of the *naḳīb* who had to possess a good knowledge of genealogical matters, to keep a register of nobility, enter births and deaths in it and to examine the validity of alleged ʿAlid genealogies (cf. thereon ʿArīb, p. 49 *sq.*, 167). He had to keep a watch on the behaviour of the *as͟hrāf*, to restrain them from excesses, to remind them to do their duty and avoid anything which might injure their prestige. He had also to urge their claims, especially those on the treasury, to endeavour to prevent the women of noble blood from making mésalliances and to see that the waḳf's of the *as͟hrāf* were properly administered. The chief naḳīb had other special duties, including certain judicial powers. Cf. al-Māwardī, *op. cit.*, p. 164 *sqq.*; von Kremer, *op. cit.*, i. 448 *sq.*; Mez, *op. cit.*, p. 145.

The green turban (q.v.] which became usual as a mark of the *as͟hrāf*, especially in Egypt, owes its origin to an edict of Sulṭān al-As͟hraf S͟haʿbān (764—778/1363—1376) who ordered in 773/1371—2 that the *As͟hrāf* should wear a green badge (*s͟huṭfa*) fastened to their turbans to distinguish them from other people and as an honour for their rank (Ibn Iyās, *Badā'iʿ al-zuhūr*, Cairo 1311, i. 227; ʿAlī Dede, *Muḥāḍarat al-awā'il wa-musāmarat al-awāk͟hir*, Būlāḳ 1300, p. 85; Dozy, *Dict. des noms des vêtements chez les Arabes*, p. 308; Mez, *op. cit.*, p. 59). This edict which is commemorated by the poets of the time recalls that of al-Ma'mūn which replaced in Ramaḍān 201/817 the black colour of his house by green, when he designated the Ḥusainid ʿAlī b. Mūsā al-Riḍā as his successor (al-Ṭabarī, iii. 1012 *sq.*). According to the work *Durar al-aṣdāf* which is quoted by al-Kattānī (in *al-Diʿāma li maʿrifat sunnat al-imāma*) the wearing of an entirely green turban dates from an edict of the Pas͟ha of Egypt al-Saiyid Muḥammad al-S͟harīf (cf. al-Isḥāḳī, *Ak͟hbār al-uwal fī-man taṣarrafa fī Miṣr min arbāb al-duwal*, Cairo 1311, p. 164 infra) of the year 1004 /1596: when he had the *kiswa* for the Kaʿba exhibited, he ordered the *as͟hrāf* to come before him, every one wearing a green turban. Al-Suyūṭī observes that the wearning of this badge is a permissible innovation (*bidʿa mubāḥa*) which no one, whether a *s͟harīf* or not a *s͟harīf* can be prevented from following, if he wishes to do so, and which cannot be forced upon any one who wishes to omit it, as it cannot be deduced from the law. At most it can be said that the badge was introduced as a distinction for the *as͟hrāf*: it is therefore equally permissible to limit it to the Ḥasanids and Ḥusainids or to allow it to the Zainabīya also and to the still wider circle of the remaining ʿAlids and the Ṭālibids. An endeavour is made to connect this custom with Ḳur'ān xxxiii. 59. With regard to this Ḳur'ānic verse, it should, according to al-Ṣabbān (p. 191), be held that the wearing of the green badge or green turban is recommended for the *as͟hrāf*, and blameworthy for others than them, because the latter by wearing it would put themselves into another than their real genealogical category, which is not permitted. On this account according to al-Kattānī, even the Mālikī authorities considered the wearing of a green turban as forbidden to a non-s͟harīf. Other authorities like to insist that green is the colour of the garments of the dwellers in Paradise (cf. Ḳur'ān xviii. 31, lxxvi. 21), and that it was the Prophet's favourite colour (al-Kattānī p. 95 *sq.*, with references to Ḥadīt͟h).

The green turban did not become the general headgear of the *as͟hrāf* throughout the Muslim world. In Arabia they rarely wear other than white turbans (Snouck Hurgronje, *Verspr. Geschr.*, IV/i. 63). The green colour was preferred in Persia (Chardin, *Voyages*, v. 290); according to P. M. Sykes. *Ten Thousand Miles in Persia*, London 1902, p. 24, note 1, the *saiyid* is distinguished there by a blue turban and a green loin-cloth. In India *sayid*'s wear green; they are therefore occasionally called: *sabzpūs͟h*: "green-robed". According to al-Nabhānī (p. 42 *sq.*) the green turban is not a mark of noble blood in Constantinople. It is worn there not only by learned men and students but also by artisans and street merchants, especially in winter as it does not show dirt so quickly. On this account many *as͟hrāf* are said to avoid the colour green.

Those of the Prophet's blood are also distinguished in other ways according to orthodox views. For example the sharing in the *ṣadaḳa* (*zakāt*, q.v.) is forbidden them. The Prophet is recorded to have frequently said of the *ṣadaḳa*: "It is the filth of men (cf. Ḳur'ān, ix. 103) and permitted neither to Muḥammad or the family (*āl*) of Muḥammad". The legal authorities differ on the question whether this rule applies not only to the Banū Hās͟him but also to the Banu 'l-Muṭṭalib and the clients of these families, and whether also free-will offerings (*ṣadaḳat al-nafl*, *ṣ. al-taṭawwuʿ*) are included in it (al-Nabhānī, p. 33 *sqq.*).

The sons of Fāṭima have the privilege of being called "sons of the Prophet of God" and thus having their descent traced directly to the Prophet. They are therefore frequently addressed as *Ibn Rasūl Allāh*. From the work of al-Ṭabarānī sayings of the Prophet are quoted in justification such as: "All the sons of one mother trace themselves back to an agnate, except the sons of Fāṭima, for I am their nearest relative and their agnate" (*walīyuhum wa-ʿaṣabatuhum*. Cf. Ibn Ḥad͟jar al-Haitamī, *al-Fatāwī al-ḥadīt͟hīya*, p. 123, $_{24}$ *sqq.*; al-Nabhānī, p. 48 *sq.*).

From the fact that the *ahl al-bait* are the noblest in descent it results that the female members of the family have no one of equal birth to them (*kuf'*). According to al-Suyūṭī (f. 3*a sq.*, = al-Ṣabbān, p. 188; cf. Ibn Ḥad͟jar al-Ḥaitamī, *op. cit.*, p. 123, $_{31}$) it is a very old opinion that the son of the marriage of a *s͟harīfa* woman with a man who is not a *s͟harīf*, is not a *s͟harīf*. As al-Ṣabbān, p. 192, points out there are many however who consider him a *s͟harīf*. In practice however marriages of a saiyid's daughter with men not their equals are extremely rare (Snouck Hurgronje, *The Achehnese*, Leyden 1906, i. 158; do., *Verspr. Geschr.*, IV/i. 297 *sqq.*; Mrs. Meer Hasan Alī, *Observations on the Mussulmans of India*², with notes by W. Crooke, London 1917, p. 4 *sq.*).

The following saying of the Prophet refers particularly to the *ahl al-bait*: "Every bond of relationship and consanguinity (*sabat wa-nasab*) will be severed on the day of resurrection except mine". They are therefore the only ones whose relationship can avail them (al-Nabhānī, p. 22, 30, 39 *sq.*, 47).

A weak tradition makes the Prophet say: "The stars are a security (*amān*) for the dwellers in the heavens and my *ahl al-bait* are a security for the dwellers on earth" (or "for my community"). According to the commentators by the *ahl al-bait* are here meant the descendants of Fāṭima. Their existence on the earth is a security for its inhabitants in general and for the community of the Prophet in particular against punishment or against overwhelming by "temptations" (*fitan*).

None of the *ahl al-bait* will suffer the punishment

of Hell (al-Maḳrīzī, f. 190[b]; al-Nabhānī, p. 21, 17 *sqq.*, 33, 5 *sq.*, 45) and ʿAlī, al-Ḥasan, and al-Ḥusain with their families will be the first to enter Paradise along with the Prophet (al-Nabhānī, p. 48, 11 *sqq.*).

The "sons of the Prophet of God" may be certain of divine forgiveness and any wrong inflicted by them must be accepted like a dispensation of Allāh, if possible with gratitude. Cf. Ibn al-ʿArabī, who takes the verse of purification in connection with Ḳurʾān xlviii. 2, in which the Prophet is promised pardon for his sin (*Futūḥāt*, Cairo 1329, i. 196 *sqq.*).

A *sharīf* who has received *ḥadd* punishment for incontinence, taking intoxicating liquor or theft may be compared with an *amīr* or *sulṭān* whose feet have become soiled but are wiped clean by one of his servants. He is also likened to a refractory son, who is however not deprived of his inheritance (Ibn Ḥadjar al-Haitamī, *op. cit.*, p. 122, 20 *sqq.*; al-Nabhānī, p. 46).

The duty of love for the *ahl al-bait* is based on Ḳurʾān xlii. 23, where *ḳurbā* is referred to relationship with the Prophet. It is further pointed out that the conclusion of the *tashahhud* [see ṢALĀT] contains a prayer for the Āl Muḥammad (Ibn Ḥadjar al-Haitamī, *al-Ṣawāʿiḳ*, p. 143; al-Nabhānī, p. 75 below). There are further a large number of traditions, which urge this affection, represent it as a proof of belief, and promise in return for it the *shafāʿa* of the Prophet on the day of the resurrection and a heavenly reward, forbid signs of hatred and even describe the latter as infidelity (Ibn Ḥadjar al-Haitamī, *al-Ṣawāʿiḳ*, p. 141 *sq.*; al-Shabrāwī, p. 3 *sq.*; al-Nabhānī, p. 81 *sqq.*).

Reverence and respect ought therefore always to be shown to the *ashrāf*, especially to the pious and learned among them; this is a natural result of reverence for the Prophet. One should be humble in their presence: the man who injures them should be an object of hatred. Unjust treatment from them should be patiently borne, their evil returned with good; they should be assisted when necessary; one should refrain from mentioning their faults, on the other hand their virtues should be lauded abroad; one should try to come nearer to God and his Prophet through the prayers of the devout among them (al-Shabrāwī, 7, 17, *sqq.*). According to al-Shaʿrānī, one should treat a *sharīf* with the same distinction as a governor or a *ḳāḍī al-ʿaskar*. One should not take a seat if a *sharīf* is without one. Special reverence should be paid to the *sharīfa*; one hardly dare look at them. Any one who really loves the sons of the Prophet will present them with anything they wish to buy. Whoever has a daughter or sister to give in marriage with a rich dowry, should not refuse her hand to a *sharīf* even if he has no more than the bridal gift for her and can only live from hand to mouth. If one meets a *sharīf* or *sharīfa* on the street, who asks for a gift, one should give him what one can (al-Nabhānī, p. 89 *sqq.*).

One should not refuse marks of respect even to a *sharīf* whose conduct is contrary to the law (*fāsiḳ*), because one knows his sin will be forgiven him. This high esteem is his due on account of his pure origin (*al-ʿunṣur al-ṭāhir*) and *fisḳ* does not affect his genealogy (al-Nabhānī, p. 45). If it is doubtful whether a man is a *sharīf* but there is nothing to object to in his genealogy from the legal point of view he should be treated with the proper respect.

The numerous saiyids and sharīfs are represented throughout the whole Muslim world. Several families have attained ruling power for longer or shorter periods, e.g. in Ṭabaristān and Dailam, in western Arabia, Yemen and Morocco. Other families have exercised local influence but by far the great majority lived and live in poor circumstances. The genuineness of an ʿAlid pedigree has for long not been unassailable. The genealogical tradition has survived in its greatest purity in western Arabia and Ḥaḍramawt. The family of ʿAlawī's in Ḥaḍramawt, which has produced many notable jurists, theologians and mystics, regard only the west Arabian sharīfs as their equals in birth.

The saiyid, who distinguishes himself by a pious life, readily becomes reverenced as a saint. His blessing is expected to bring good fortune, while his wrath brings misfortune. By vows and gifts it is hoped to secure his auspicious intercession and his tomb becomes a place of pilgrimage. On the much visited tombs of saiyids and saiyidas in Cairo cf. al-Shablandjī's work cited below.

In the Yemen as in Ḥaḍramawt, the saiyid who is to be distinguished there from the armed *sharīf* carrying a staff (*ʿukkāz*) and rosary, acts as intermediary between two disputing parties. He also drives away the locusts and his prayer puts an end to infertility while his curse makes it continue. Many saiyids are also visited for their healing powers. Reverence for the saiyid frequently finds expression in presenting him with lands (H. Jacob, *Perfumes of Araby*, London 1915, p. 45, 173, *sqq.*).

For a fuller description of the sharīfs and saiyids and the reverence paid to them see Snouck Hurgronje, *Mekka*, i. 32 *sqq.*, 70 *sqq.*; on the saiyids of Ḥaḍramawt, who are also strongly represented in the Malay Archipelago and to whom belong the founders of the sultanates of Siak and Pontianak, cf. do., *Verspr. Geschr.* iii. 162 *sqq.*, and *The Atchehnese*, i. 153 *sqq.*; v. d. Berg, *Le Ḥadramout* etc., Batavia 1886; D. v. d. Meulen, *Ḥaḍramaut*, Leiden 1932.

For the history of the Sharīfs who ruled in Mecca and the Ḥidjāz from the iv[th]/x[th] century till 1924, see Snouck Hurgronje, *Mekka*, i. and the article MEKKA (history); cf. also the sketch in al-Batanūnī, *al-Riḥla al-Ḥidjāzīya*², Cairo 1329, p. 73 *sqq.* — Information on the families of *ashrāf* in Arabia is given in *A Handbook of Arabia*, i., comp. by the Geogr. Sect. of the Naval Intelligence Division, London n.d., Ind. s.v. *Ashrāf*.

The genealogy of the Ṭālibids is discussed in Aḥmad b. ʿAlī . . . Ibn Muhannā al-Dāʾūdī al-Ḥasanī, *ʿUmdat al-ṭālib fī ansāb āl Abī Ṭālib*, Bombay 1318.

Bibliography: al-Nasāʾī, *Khaṣāʾiṣ Amīr al-Muʾminīn ʿAlī b. Abī Ṭālib*, Cairo 1308; Yaḥyā b. al-Ḥasan . . . Ibn al-Biṭrīḳ al-Ḥillī, *Kit. Khaṣāʾiṣ waḥy al-mubīn fī manāḳib Amīr al-Muʾminīn* lith. s. l. 1311; do., *Kit. al-ʿumda*, lith. Bombay 1309; al-Maḳrīzī, *Kitāb fīhi maʿrifat ma yadjibu li-āl al-bait, min al-ḥaḳḳ ʿalā man ʿadāhum*, Leiden MS. 560, xiii. (*Cat. Cod. Arab.*, ii. 50); al-Suyūṭī, *Risālat al-sulāla al-Zainabīya*, Leyden MS. 2326 (*Cat. Cod. Arab.*, ii. 65); do., *Iḥyāʾ al-mayyit fi 'l-aḥādīth al-wārida fi āl al-bait*, on the margin of al-Shabrāwī, *al-Itḥāf*, see below; Ibn Ḥadjar al-Haitamī, *al-Ṣawāʾiḳ al-muḥriḳa fi 'l-radd ʿalā ahl al-bidaʿ wa 'l-zandaḳa*, Cairo 1308; do., *al-Fatāwī al-ḥadīthīya*, Cairo 1329; al-Shabrāwī, *al-Itḥāf bi-ḥubb al-ashrāf*, Cairo 1318; Muḥammad al-Ṣabbān, *Isʿāf al-rāghibīn fī sīrat al-muṣṭafā wa-faḍāʾil ahl baitihi al-ṭāhirīn*, on the margin of al-Shablandjī, *Nūr al-abṣār fī manāḳib āl bait al-Nabī al-mukhtār*, Cairo 1322; Yūsuf b. Ismāʿīl al-Nabhānī, *al-Sharaf al-muʾabbad li-āl Muḥammad*, Cairo 1318; Niebuhr, *Beschreibung von Arabien*, Copenhagen 1722, p. 11 *sqq.*; E. W. Lane, *An*

Account of the Manners and Customs of the Modern Egyptians, 3rd ed., London 1842, i. 42, 46, 197, 210, 366; E. Westermarck, *Ritual and Belief in Morocco*, 1926, Ind. s.v. *Sherifs*, *Sīdi*, *Siyed*.

SHAṬḤ (A., pl. *shaṭaḥāt* or [*kalimāt*] *shaṭḥīyāt*) a technical term in mysticism, signifying an "ecstatic phrase", or more exactly a "divinely inspired utterance".

Etymology: This term, which was probably a Syriac loan-word (*shaṭṭaḥ* = expands) is derived from the root *sh-ṭ-ḥ* in Arabic: "disturb, agitate" (*mishṭāḥ* = place where flour is ground). Adopted in the tenth century A.D. by the Ṣūfīs it is applied to the perturbation of the consciousness, into which divine grace suddenly penetrates, then to the "divinely inspired utterance" which this supernatural commotion extracts from the subject.

The Muslim mystics are unanimous in seeing in the *shaṭḥ*, following preparatory anagogic graces (*khaṭarāt*, *fawāʾid*, *nukat*), the sign of a perfect purification reaching the soul of the mystic. But the majority of theorists — at first from scruples of orthodoxy, later from anomic, monistic conviction — consider that this state is transitory and is only a stage before the definitive annihilation of personality in the divine silence. Some, notably Muḥāsibī and Ḥallādj [q.v.], on the other hand consider that these divine touches transfigure the faltering voice of the lover, give him an intermittent divine investiture, which will make him consent for ever to the dialogue of love (*muḥādatha*) "between Thee and me".

The first "ecstatic sayings" were incorporated by tradition in the classical collections of *Ḥadīth*, not as utterances of the mystics but as "words of God" (*ḥadīth ḳudsī*).

From the third century A.H. Muslim orthodoxy excluded this source of traditions and the *shaṭḥīyāt* circulate under the names of those responsible for uttering them. Here we give the most famous, arranged according to two tendencies, the one class referring rather to an immediate psychological commotion, the other which betrays a scholarly reconstruction, or at least a retrospection influenced by the prejudices of the school, sometimes showing an insolent and cynical familiarity.

a. Abū Yazīd al-Bisṭāmī (d. 261/875): "Praise be to Me! (*Subḥānī*). My intercession is greater than that of Muḥammad! Thou obeyest me more than I obey Thee. Adam sold his God for a mouthful. Thy Paradise is only a children's game". — Al-Ḥallādj (d. 309/922): "I am the Truth (*ana 'l-ḥaḳḳ*). It is Thou, or it is I? That would make two gods. Ah! for mercy's sake take away this *annī* ("it is I") from between us two! I do not desire thee for my joy but for my hurt. Pardon them and do not pardon me. For the perfect lover prayer becomes impiety". — Abū Bakr Nassādj al-Ṭūsī (d. 487/1094): "Guide of those who have gone astray, lead me still further astray". — Aḥmad al-Ghazzālī (d. 517/1123): "God alone understands God. There is no master more persuasive than Desire! The call for the union is the essence of the beloved; the call for separation is the essence of the lover whether We torture him with desire, whether We kill him by severing him from contemplation".

Ibn Sahl al-Tustarī (d. 283/896): "I am the Proof of God, in face of the saints of my time. Divine omnipotence has a secret; if it is revealed there is an end of the prophetic mission." — Al-Wāsiṭī (d. 320/932): "Ritual acts are only impurities". Al-Shiblī (d. 334/945): "I am the diacritical point under the letter *bā*! In Paradise there is no person except God. Mysticism is only polytheism, since it is engaged in purifying the heart of that which is not God, when God alone is." — Al-Khurḳānī (d. 426/1034): "I am only two years younger than God. God is my instant (my unity of psychological time)." — Ibn Abi 'l-Khair (d. 440/1048): "Under my robe there is only God". — Abū Ḥāmid al-Ghazzālī (d. 505/1111): "There is nothing more in the possible than in the created". — Ibn ʿArabī (d. 638/1240): "The slave is the lord and the Lord is the slave; ah; how can one tell which of the two is the debtor?" — ʿAlī al-Ḥarīrī (d. 645/1247): "The perfect poor man has no longer a heart, nor a lord." — Ibn Sabʿīn (d. 668/1269): "There is nothing but God" (*laisa illa'llāh*, the *dhikr* of his order). — ʿAfīf al-Tilimsānī (d. 690/1291): "The whole Ḳurʾān is simply polytheism."

Whole monographs have been devoted to elucidating, criticizing or justifying one or other of these ecstatic utterances. Dūrī and Sarrādj were the first to perceive their theological importance, and we possess in three books by Rūzbihān Baḳlī (d. 606/1209) a full treatise on the question.

Bibliography: Sarrādj, *Lumaʿ*, ed. Nicholson, London 1914, p. 375—409 (with an extract from the commentary of Djunaid on the *shaṭaḥāt* of Bisṭāmī, probably from Dūrī); Khargūshī, *Tahdhīb*, MS. Berlin, Sprenger 832, f. 230a; Sulamī, *Ghalaṭāt*, MS. Cairo vii. 228; Baḳlī, *Shaṭḥīyāt*, MS. Shahīd ʿAlī Pāshā 1342 (extr. in Ḥallādj, *Kitāb al-Ṭawāsīn*, ed. Massignon, Paris 1913); Kawrānī, *Maslak djalī fī ḥukm shaṭḥ al-walī*, MS. Stambul, Walī al-Dīn 1815 (cf. MS., 1821 § ix. of the same library); Dārā Shikūh, *Shaṭaḥāt* (alias: *Ḥasanāt al-ʿārifīn*), written in 1062/1652, lith. in India; L. Massignon "*Ana'l ḥaḳḳ*" (in *Der Islam*, 1912, 248—257); do, *Passion d'al Ḥallāj*, Paris 1922, p. 713, 935.

On the *Ḥadīth Ḳudsī* cf. Rāghib Pāshā, *Safīna*, Cairo 1282, p. 162; L. Massignon, *Essai sur les origines de la mystique musulmane*, Paris 1922, p. 100—108; and S. Zwemer, in *Moslem World*, 1922, p. 263—275.

SHAṬṬĀRĪYA, Ṣūfī order included in the list of 161 orders furnished to S. Anderson by the Imperial Board of Derwishes at Constantinople (*Moslem World*, 1922, p. 56). It is called *madhhab-i shuṭṭār* (or *shaṭṭār*) in the Persian work cited below; since a person named Shaṭṭār is not mentioned in the chief biographical dictionaries of saints, the former vocalization may be correct, as the plural of *shāṭir*, according to Redhouse "a mystic who has broken with the world", though this sense is not recognized by Sāmī Pasha (see, however, a biography of the supposed founder in Ghulām Sarwar, *Khazīnat al-aṣfiyāʾ*, Cawpore 1893, lith., ii. 306—8). The order is mentioned by Abu 'l-Faḍl (*Āīn-i Akbarī*, transl. Jarrett, iii. 422) as one which provided his father with instructors, though he does not deal with it in his list of orders (*ibid.* 349—360), and he suggests that its headquarters in India were at Djawnpūr (*ibid.* 373). Allusions to it in Ṣūfī literature are rare.

Some notice of its doctrines is to be found in the *Irshādāt al-ʿārifīn* of Shaikh Muḥammad Ibrāhīm Gazur-i Ilāhī, contemporary of Awrangzēb. The following are the chief passages: The sect of the Shuṭṭārī's dispenses with negation and adheres to affirmation. It is waste of time in *murāḳaba* (meditation) to attend to negation, for it is negativing a nonentity. In the Shuṭṭārī religion there is no self-effacement. There is nothing in it except "I am I".

Tawḥīd is understanding one, saying one, seeing one, and being one. "I am one and no partner with me".

With the Shuṭṭārī's there is neither opposition to *nafs*, nor *mudjāhada*; neither is there *fanāʾ* nor *fanāʾ al-fanāʾ*; for *fanāʾ* requires two personalities; one that is to be annihilated, and the other one is the one in which this one is to be annihilated, which is opposed to *tawḥīd*. The Shuṭṭārī's affirm *tawḥīd* and observe the *dhāt* with its *ṣifāt* in all stages and *tadjalliyāt*.

The Shuṭṭārī's do not complain, they eat whatever they get, keeping the real Gift-giver in view.

Consider your *dhāt*, *ṣifāt* and *afʿāl* as the *dhāt*, *ṣifāt* and *afʿāl* of God and become one. This is the way of the Shuṭṭārī's and not of the other gnostics (*abrār* and *akhyār*), who adopt the practices and *mudjāhadāt*, and say "consider your *nafs* in the way of *fanāʾ*, and God's in the way of *baḳāʾ*; your *nafs* in the way of *ʿubūdīyāt* (servantship) and His in the way of *rubūbīyāt* (rulership)".

So this doctrine claims to carry through the consequences of the formula *ana 'l-ḥaḳḳ* more strictly than the others. For the Shaṭṭārīya in Indonesia cf. Snouck Hurgronje, *The Achehnese*, ii. 18 *sq.*; do. in *Meded. Ned. Zendelingengenootschap*, xxxii. 186; D. A. Rinkes, *Abdoerraoef van Singkel*, Dissert. Leiden 1909, register.

SHĪʿA, the general name for a large group of very different Muslim sects, the starting point of all of which is the recognition of ʿAlī as the legitimate caliph after the death of the Prophet.

The motives of the Shīʿa and the earlier period

Islām is a religious and a political phenomenon as its founder was a prophet and statesman. The development of the community of Islām into separate sectional groups was therefore determined by the different possible relations which the political constitution and religious belief might bear to one another. Three main schools may be distinguished. The middle line was taken by the Sunnīs. Their leading principle that the "imāmate belongs to the Ḳuraish" is a simple expression of recognition of the historical fact that the world of Islām in the early centuries was ruled by Meccan families. The intelligible demand that the rulers who represented the state which was founded upon religion should be really religious personalities very early led among the Sunnīs also to the unhistorical glorification of the first "four pious caliphs" and further faced them with the problem of finding formulae to explain that it was also a religious duty to owe obedience to caliphs of little worth and even to foreign Sulṭāns, so long as the exercise of religion and the maintenance of order was afforded by them. How little, however, such principles arose out of wholehearted assent is best shown by the constant warnings, not only from pious circles, to be careful in dealing with secular, though Sunnī rulers. If we have here on the Sunnī side less a clear theory than rather the attempt to reconcile a religious ideal with political reality, there appeared on the other hand on the two flanks of Islām two fundamental theories. The one demands clean-cut separation of the constitutional question from the religious one, the other has interwoven the two. The former view, although already in existence, only obtained greater publicity in the first civil war among the Khāridjīs [q.v.] for whose salvation the question of the person of the caliph was a matter of such indifference that he might "even be an Abyssinian slave". The Shīʿīs on the other hand lay religious value on the question of the imāmate and their dogmatic books contain a special section, the leading idea of which is the traditional principle "whosoever dies without knowing the true Imām of his time dies the death of an unbeliever".

There was a political Shīʿa, more accurately a *Shīʿat ʿAlī* i.e. a party of ʿAlī [q.v.] at the very latest immediately after the death of the Prophet. If we may believe the Shīʿa accounts the original Shīʿa consisted of three men: Salmān al-Fārisī, Abū Dharr and al-Miḳdād b. al-Aswad al-Kindī. They were the only ones — some stories give a few more names — who championed ʿAlī's succession on the death of the Prophet and therefore did not fall away from the faith. For the other companions of the Prophet are credited by the majority of the Shīʿīs with *ridda* [q.v.] for paying homage to Abū Bakr. But the stories, especially about Salmān al-Fārisī [q.v.], are quite legendary. A large number of the later Shīʿa traditions and many prophecies regarding the future of ʿAlids are associated with his name.

The desire that the imāmate in Islām should be kept for the ʿAlids [q.v.] as the family of the house (of the Prophet; *Ahl al-Bait*) was never fulfilled. The brief reign of ʿAlī from 35—40/656—661 was only a strongly contested partial caliphate while his son Ḥasan [q.v.] can hardly be seriously reckoned as a caliph. The first ʿAlid independent principality was founded in 172/789 in Morocco by the Ḥasanid Idrīs I b. ʿAbd Allāh. But his territory was entirely Sunnī, that is to say we have not here a Shīʿa state but simply an ʿAlid kingdom. At the present day there still exist a few states with ʿAlid chiefs, of whom however the Imām of Ṣanʿāʾ in Yemen alone is Shīʿī and in particular a Zaidī (see below).

As the energies of the Shīʿa forces met with too much resistance in the political field they devoted themselves to the religious. The political experiences of the Shīʿa had been particularly suitable to further this development. The martyr's death of one ʿAlid succeeded that of another. Much more than the blood of ʿAlī who was murdered by a single Khāridjī, it was the blood of Ḥusain [q.v.] who perished under the swords of the government troops that was the seed of the Shīʿa church. The passion motive was thus restored to religion again among the Shīʿa; it had been lost to official Islām since the turn of fortune which after the Hidjra set the Prophet's career on the path of worldly prosperity and excluded all possibility of it by a peaceful death, devoid of any tragedy that might have borne fruit in this direction. The insistence on the idea of a passion has so thoroughly penetrated the Shīʿa that it has formed legends full of difficult historical problems, which make even the lives of ʿAlids, who never attained any prominence, end in martyrdom, usually through poison at the instigation of the caliphs, as in the cases of Ḥasan I, Djaʿfar al-Ṣādiḳ, ʿAlī al-Riḍā, and on the whole of each Imām of the "Twelvers" (see below).

That this feeling of passion, which can remain worldly and among the Zaidīs, who are closest to the Sunnīs, has remained very worldly, was transformed to something completely religious in the majority of Shīʿīs, i.e. that to the Shīʿīs the death of Ḥusain paved the way to Paradise, is a result of the fact that another religious idea came into play, which is, as the history of religions shows, often associated with the passion motive, namely the idea of the manifestation of the divine in man (epiphany). It was not strange to Muḥammad, indeed to him for example Jesus was "a word of God" (Ḳurʾān

iii. 45). But he had not placed the mediation between God and man in a person and certainly not in his own (Ḳurʾān, xviii. 110; xli. 6; xvii. 93) but in a revelation, the Ḳurʾān. From this point of view the characteristic of the Shīʿa can be thus defined: — to the First Article: "I believe in God the One" — and the Second Article "I believe in the revelation of the Ḳurʾān which is uncreated from all eternity" — is added a Third Article: — "I believe that the Imām especially chosen by God as the bearer of a part of the divine being is the leader to salvation". But if such an Imām possesses in the eyes of his believers any quality or more frequently a substance of divine origin, then when faced with his decease, they do not console themselves with the thought of his living on in paradise, which he only shares, although in a higher degree, with all believers, but to them the death of an Imām is rendered void by the idea of *radjʿa*, belief in "concealment" and parousia. The Imām becomes the Mahdī [q.v.]. Many indeed abandon the earthly part of the Imām but make his divine element pass into the next Imām, after the manner of the doctrine of transmigration. The mutual interaction of the idea of passion and epiphany again shows that the expectation of parousia arising from the latter, which, as the example of the hidden Mahdī Muḥammad b. al-Ḥanafīya shows, can also arise independently of a martyrdom, was increased by martyrdom.

The state of our sources does not allow us to obtain a reliable insight into the history of the confluence of the various Shīʿa motives. It must for example remain an open question how far the Shīʿa ideas of epiphany and the intercession of the Imām are the direct continuation of the similar ideas which, according to Ibn Isḥāḳ, certain singers of primitive Islām already associated with the person of Muḥammad: i.e. the question arises how far these religious ideas of the Shīʿa were within Islām before the year 11/632. Under ʿAlī, however, they appear in strongly dogmatic form. If the tradition about ʿAbd Allāh b. Sabā is still obscure, we find it somewhat clearer in the many poets of Shīʿī mentality. Abu 'l-Aswad al-Duʾalī, who fought by the side of ʿAlī at Ṣiffīn, praised him with more than ordinary infatuation: "When I looked into the face of Abu 'l-Ḥusain, I saw the full moon, which filled the spectators with reverent wonder. The Ḳuraish now know, wherever they may be, that thou art their noblest in merit and religion". His attitude to ʿAlī is therefore already religious. In accordance with traditions referring to him, therefore already current (see below), he calls him "our *mawlā* and *waṣī*". Phrases like "I seek God and the future abode through my love to ʿAlī" are frequently found. Kuthaiyir, d. 105/723, expects the *radjʿa* of Muḥammad b. al-Ḥanafīya; Kumait, d. 126/743, sings of the light emanating from Adam through Muḥammad to the holy family. In the ʿAbbāsid period political disillusionment increased still further this religious attachment. Saiyid al-Ḥimyarī devotes his poems to it. In Diʿbil, the "panegyrist of the holy house", the coarse attacks on the ruling family, in which "one sinner inherits the caliphate after another", are explained by his belief in the unique claim of ʿAlī al-Riḍā to the imāmate at the time. In a poem on the death of Ḥusain, often lamented previously by him, he looks for the *ḳāʾim*. "If it were not for what I hope for to-day or to-morrow, my heart would break for woe: the "arising" of an Imām, who will without doubt arise, who will appear in the name of God and with all blessings".

The ʿAlids at this time as a rule had not the leadership in the political field in their own hands. They were urged on by their followers, just as Ḥusain and Zaid b. ʿAlī had been used for political purposes and as Muḥammad b. al-Ḥanafīya had been a pawn in the hands of al-Mukhtār, and Muḥammad b. Ṭabāṭabā and Muḥammad b. Muḥammad b. Zaid in the hands of Abu 'l-Sarāya. It was the same in the sphere of religion. Religious fanatics gathered round every prominent ʿAlid. Of those around ʿAlī we may mention his client Ḳanbar, who is said to have recognized the "tongue of the word of God" in his master. That this was considered mild language is seen from the legend in which Ḳanbar himself figures as opposing those extravagant Shīʿīs who had attributed *rubūbīya* (divinity) to ʿAlī and who are therefore condemned to fire by both ʿAlī and Ḳanbar.

Djābir b. ʿAbd Allāh al-Anṣārī attached himself to Ḥusain's son Zain al-ʿĀbidīn and his son Muḥammad al-Bāḳir; the former had paid homage to the Prophet in the "first Aḳaba" along with the first Madīnese to do so. He influenced the young ʿAlid as the preserver of the continuity of Shīʿa belief, and had intercession assured him by Muḥammad al-Bāḳir on the Last Day. With Bāḳir and his successors Djaʿfar al-Ṣādiḳ and Mūsā al-Kāẓim were found theologians like Djābir b. Yazīd al-Djuʿfī, Hishām b. al-Ḥakam, Hishām b. Sālim al-Djawālīḳī, a former prisoner of war, and Yūnus b. ʿAbd al-Raḥmān, a client of the Āl Yaḳṭīn b. Mūsā. Yūnus also belonged to the great circle of ʿAlī Riḍā.

The literary form of this theory is of course of the general Muslim type, which means the form of Tradition, *sunna*. Shīʿīs are to a much greater degree "Sunnīs" than the so-called Sunnīs. We must not place the origin of their *ḥadīth*'s too late, since some are as early as Duʾalī. The most celebrated are: ʿAlī is Aaron; ʿAlī is the *waṣī* who is designated by the Prophet and Allāh. He is the *Mawlā*; the holy family is the ark of Noah; the holy family and the Ḳurʾān are the two treasures of the earth; Muḥammad, ʿAlī, Fāṭima, Ḥasan and Ḥusain are the five companions of the cloak. Similar principles also underlie their exegesis of the Ḳurʾān, which regards a vast number of verses (e.g. xxxiii. 33; lvii. 26; xi. 74; xxiv. 35) as evidences for the Shīʿa claims.

The particular character of the Shīʿa offered so much incentive to dogmatic speculation and religious fantasy that it never, like the Sunna, attained any far-reaching uniformity. Three main forms may be distinguished within the Shīʿa: The Zaidīs [q.v.] who are nearest akin to the Sunnīs, limit the manifestation of God in the Imām quite rationalistically to mere divine "right' guidance' and deny the miraculous influx of the divine portion of light into a definite ʿAlid individual. The martyrdom of the Imāms finds expression among them mainly in the political field in constant endeavours to attain with the sword of man and help of God the goal of ʿAlid supremacy. They have successfully resisted various chiliastic expectations of the Mahdī that have appeared among them. On the other wing, the epiphany becomes completely indwelling, absolute *ḥulūl* [q.v.]; the mortal in the Imām is entirely swallowed up; in the end God himself has no place beside him. The representatives of this school are ardently combatted by the Zaidīs and Imāmīs, the representatives of the middle school, as people who have brought the Shīʿa into discredit and have fallen away from Islām — they call them Ghulāt (sg. ghālī, q.v.). To the

Imāmīs the Imām remains mortal but a divine light-substance is inherent in him by partial *ḥulūl*. The death of the Imām, which among the Ghulāt, e.g. the Druses, is simply the withdrawal of the deified, becomes with them the religious force which makes it a joy to die. Its voluntariness is emphasized with dogmatic intention. In the battle of Karbalā' God sent the angel of victory to Ḥusain; but he preferred "to approach to God".

In the course of history each of the three divisions had perforce to divide into many subdivisions, simply on account of the specifically Shīʿite ideas of each. Thus, as a result of the Zaidī agitations, small principalities arose in Ṭabaristān and Dailam from 250/864 and in Yemen from 284/897 which from the distance between them could not form a political unity nor maintain a complete dogmatic uniformity. The Zaidīs of the ʿIrāḳ, who never attained independence in a kingdom of their own, but were often able to make up for this by exerting considerable influence in the Caliph's empire, had to adapt themselves to conditions there by a greater use of the *taḳīya* [q.v.] or the *kitmān*. The school of the Ghulāt, who went furthest beyond Muḥammad's inheritance and so gave the greatest play to individual initiative, found very varied expression in the Karmaṭian groups, the Ismāʿīlīs, the Druses and ultimately in the Nuṣairīs and ʿAlī Ilāhīs (Ahl-i Ḥaḳḳ). These groups also to great degree cut themselves away from the members of the holy family. This is already seen in the Kaisānīya [q.v.] whose Imām, Muḥammad b. al-Ḥanafīya, is not a descendant of the Prophet; it is also expressed in a tradition: "Salmān al-Fārisī belongs to the family of the house". It led for example in the ixth/xvth century among the Ḥurūfīs [q.v.] to the exclusion of the ʿAlid Imāms in favour of the deity incarnate in Faḍl Allāh al-As arābādī. But the very principle of the Imāmīya had the seeds of dissension within it. For the contact between God and man is not at a point of intersection but in a continuous line, not in a single individual but in an uninterrupted series of Imāms, among whom the divinely inspired father appoints the son in every generation or — according to others — the divine element is transmitted directly to the eldest son, whose mother also comes from the holy family. But religious adherence to an Imām might become so fervent that one could not abandon him even after his death, i.e. believe that he is really dead; or the successor might be a person of very doubtful character; he might be an infant child, or he might be quite defective. Thus arose the subordinate groups of the *wāḳifīya* and *ḳiṭṭīʿīya* or *ḳaṭʿīya*. The former "hesitate" regarding the death of the Imām, therefore "stand" by him and see in him the Mahdī; the latter regard the death of the Imām as "definite" and therefore continue the line. There are a whole series of such Wāḳifīya, like the Djaʿfarīya with Djaʿfar al-Ṣādiḳ, the Mūsawīya, the Riḍawīya etc.; in the narrower sense the term applies only to the Djaʿfarīya. For the reasons mentioned, however, the line could not be continued endlessly even among the Ḳiṭṭīʿīya. It is very doubtful whether the eleventh Imām Ḥasan al-ʿAskarī left a child at all at his death in 260/873, but the belief has prevailed among the Imāmīs in the existence, the mysterious disappearance and the Mahdī character of a son Muḥammad Ḥudjdjat Allāh. Thus the Imāmīs become "Twelvers", *Ithnā ʿAshariya* [q.v.], although it was for a period still disputed whether there was not a thirteenth Imām.

If we thus see among the Shīʿa denominations, simply in so far as they are Shīʿī, a range which corresponds to that in Christian church history which separates the Theopaschites from the Socinians, nevertheless, we have so far considered only one of its formative principles. For the Shīʿa belongs to Islām and is therefore faced with all the problems that agitate Islām generally. Islām looks at the world not from the point of view of religion only, but has its cultural, economic, social, and beyond the question of the *khalīfa* its political problems also. Their effects among the Shīʿa can only be briefly indicated here. In dogmatics we find besides the Muʿtazilīs [q.v.] predestinarians like the Zaidī Sulaimān b. Djarīr, and anthropomorphists like the already mentioned Imāmī Hishām b. Sālim al-Djawālīḳī; and how much the dispute common to all Islām regarding the nature of the Ḳur'ān was also a disintegrating danger for the Shīʿa is shown by the tradition attributed to Djaʿfar al-Ṣādiḳ, said to have been uttered to the above mentioned Yūnus b. ʿAbd al-Raḥmān, a saying which suggests a provisional formula: "The Ḳur'ān is neither creator nor created; it is the word of a creator". In relation to philosophy both attraction and repulsion were considerably stronger than among the Sunnīs. For on the one hand their richer theological speculation required to a greater extent the categories of philosophy and its dialectic for dogmatic stabilisation, on the other hand the Shīʿa were here particularly sensitive, indeed vulnerable, like every religious community which sets out from such strong metaphysical postulates, as it does with the belief in the Imāmate. Apart from epistemological antagonistic principles which philosophy, called in to its aid, introduced into the Shīʿa, the latter had also to settle the well known disputed points within Islām on the fundamentals, the *uṣūl al-dīn* and the *uṣūl al-fiḳh*, for example on the binding force of a single tradition or on *ḳiyās* [q.v.]. In this way there were in Shīʿa law such disputed points as were found in the Sunnī schools from Ẓāhirīs to Ḥanafīs. In worship there was in all groups a strong impulse to satisfy the tendency towards adoration by the reverencing of Imāms and places of pilgrimage at the graves of their martyrs, which was in conflict with the conservative tendency still to remain Muḥammadans.

The line where the Shīʿa creed and domestic politics i.e. nationalism meet is very intricate and much broken. It is not simply that the conquered people like the Persians had sided from the first with the Shīʿa opposition. The oldest of the principal leaders were genuine Arabs, of the south, is it true. Among those mentioned around the Imāms Yūnus and the two Hishām's were clients but Diʿbil a raceproud South Arabian and an opponent of the Northern Arabs. Two hundred years later we still find Mufīd (see below) priding himself on his South Arabian descent "from Yaḳṭān, the first man to speak Arabic". Social disputes were brought into the Shīʿa as early as al-Mukhtār when he mobilised the clients and slaves. Among some Ghulāt, like the Karmaṭians, socialistic demands were heightened to the point of communism, which however here too in view of the authoritative attachment to an imām or his representative was only a mask for a despotic oligarchy. A more obvious aristocracy was formed by those circles of higher administrative officials at the ʿAbbāsid court, who, for the most part Iranians, were bound together by ardent devotion to the Imāmate, among these, for example were the family of the Nawbakht.

As regards women also the Shī^ca had to deal with all aspects of the problem. Some of the Ḳarmaṭians are accused — at least — of having community of women; the Imāmīs allow temporary marriages (see MUT^cA); the Zaidīs confine themselves to polygamy as defined by the Sunna; the ^cAlī Ilāhīs decided on monogamy.

As the numbers of possibilities in the fields of dogma, epistemology, law, worship, politics and social sciences are not additional to but multipliers of the figures of possibilities in the question of the Imāms, the result is that, although we do not have in practice all the possible combinations, we have a number of Shī^ca subdivisions, which far exceeds the well known number "72". At the same time this possibility of variation explains the many discrepancies in the usual Muslim books on the various sects, because the latter, as can easily be understood, divide one and the same community into several groups according to the special feature they emphasize.

In view of the elemental force with which the Shī^ca creed, in itself full of problems, made its appearance in the world of Islām which was already full of its own problems, we can understand that the personalities who are considered heads of schools in the present Shī^ca communities were less creators than circumscribers, but we can also see that the consensus each time became limited to a smaller circle. In the language of the Shī^ca, the *idjmā^c* affects only the individual *ecclesiola*, which alone will be blessed. In dogmatics this effort of limiting has attained no small success: Zaidīs, as well Imāmīs, finally joined the Mu^ctazila. This is not mere accident, as the example of the Ḳur'ān already shows: of the above mentioned articles of belief, the third was bound to drive out the second. The *homoousia* of an uncreated Ḳur'ān had in the long run no place beside an imām as a guarantor of the true faith. It is also logical that the Imāmīya for the purpose of its classification below the belief in the imāmate subjected the Revealed Book to allegorical explanation and that on the extreme wings the Ghulāt disputed it, made interpolations or even rejected parts and became themselves Bāṭinīs (cf. BĀṬINĪYA). The Mu^ctazila was perhaps the first step; but through these borrowings from philosophy, though primarily devoted to the search for the formal, philosophy penetrated into the space left vacant by the supernatural belief in revelation; theology thus became theosophy and gnosis.

The origin of the Shī^ca motives is not explained if we again emphasize the fact, in itself illuminating after what has been said above, that Gnostic, Neo-Platonic, Manichaean and old Iranian ideas have intermingled. But in the present state of our knowledge, we cannot go far beyond this statement, as the literary doors of approach to the details have not yet been opened. With the echoes of Christianity also, one must for the time be content with the general remark that Islām spread over countries formerly Christian and made many converts whose forefathers had been Christians. Still more general but not less important is the observation that motives so fertile from the religious point of view like passion and divine epiphany could not be lost at the foundation of a new religion like Islām.

The later period

The consolidation of the separate groups begins in the second half of the third (ixth) century. The outlines of this process were first noticeable among the Zaidīs. Al-Ḳāsim b. Ibrāhīm b. Ṭabāṭabā al-Rassī (d. 246/860) selected the dogmatic and legal foundations for an ecclesiastical state, which his grandson Yaḥyā b. al-Ḥusain brought into existence in Yemen in 284/897. His teaching also became partly current in the territory of the older Zaidī state which had been founded in 250/864 on the Caspian Sea. In 297/909 the state of the Ismā^cīlī Fāṭimids arose in Africa and at the same time bodies of Ḳarmaṭians held small tracts in N.E. and S. Arabia. Here we may refer the reader to the special articles for the lateral branches but we shall consider the main branch somewhat more fully, the Imāmīs or "Twelvers". It is of them one usually thinks when using the term Shī^cīs generally. They form also numerically by far the majority of Shī^cīs, viz. the majority of the population of Persia and more than the half in ^cIrāḳ, and in addition to sporadic groups also considerable bodies in India and in Syria. Their literature, which is still the most easily accessible of all Shī^cite literature, also forms the best approach to Shī^cī problems, on account of the intermediate position of the Imāmīya.

Even the old ^cAlids like Dja^cfar al-Ṣādiḳ and ^cAlī al-Riḍā often had not themselves been the real leaders. Plenipotentiaries (*wakīl*, plur. *wukalā'*) acted on their behalf — or alleged behalf. When the Imām had disappeared the office of envoy (*safīr*, plur. *sufarā'*) became highly important. He claimed to be the only one who knew the concealed Imām. Four men have succeeded since 260/873 in establishing this claim for themselves. When the fourth, ^cAlī b. Muḥammad al-Samurrī died about 329/940 the so-called "Little *Ghaiba*" came to an end and has been succeeded to the present day by the "Great *Ghaiba*", in which for example the Friday service dependent on the cooperation of the Imām should be in abeyance. A clerical aristocracy took over the leadership, many representatives of which claimed to base their teachings on miraculous meetings with the hidden "Lord of the Age". It is true that the modern Persian theologian can still be a *mudjtahid* (q.v. and below); but in all essentials he too remains like the Sunnī bound by what that aristocracy has made canonical. The literary deposit of the process of forming a canon, in the usual Muslim way, produced a large number of books on the criticism of the authorities and theological authors. They formed a kind of clerical censorship, long before the Ṣafawids instituted a Shaikh al-Islām for the state church.

Political aspirations were opened up to the Shī^cīs by the rise of the tolerant Sāmānids — not themselves Shī^cīs however — especially after the conquest of Khurāsān by Ismā^cīl in 290/903, and by the rise of the Ḥamdānids of Mawṣil from 317/929. When the Būyid Aḥmad Mu^cizz al-Dawla entered Baghdād in 334/945, a great period began for the Shī^cīs who had for long been in the capital, occupying, for example, the whole Karkh quarter. To this external consolidation corresponded an inner one. The canonical collections of traditions arose, the so-called "Four Books": 1. *al-Kāfī* (pr. Teheran, 1312—1318) of Kulainī, d. 328/939 or 329/940); of over 16,000 ḥadīths on the *uṣūl* and *furū^c* chapters, 5072 are considered "sound" by later authorities, 140 "good" and 1118 as "established", 302 as "strong" and 9488 as "weak"; a popular commentary is *al-Shāfī* of Khalīl b. Ghāzī al-Ḳazwīnī, begun at Mecca in 1057/1647 and also published by him in Persian with the title *al-Ṣāfī*. Smaller in extent than *al-Kāfī* is 2.

Man la yaḥḍuruhu 'l-faḳīh (pr. Teheran 1324) by Ibn Bābūya the younger (d. 381/991—2). Of about 6,000 ḥadīths some 4,000 have a complete *isnād*; in recent times a commentary was written on this collection by Muḥammad Tāḳī al-Madjlisī, father of the author of the *Biḥār al-anwār* (see below) in two editions, Arabic (*Rawḍat al-muttaḳīn*) and Persian (*Lawāmiʿ-i Ṣāḥib-Ḳirānī*), while the commentary *Man la yaḥḍuruhu 'l-nabīh* of ʿAbd Allāh b. Ṣāliḥ al-Samāhīdjī (d. 1135/1722—3) was never finished; 3. *al-Istibṣār fīma 'khtulifa min al-akhbār* (Lucknow, n. d.) and the more comprehensive 4. *Tahdhīb al-aḥkām* (Teheran 1314) are both by the celebrated author of the Shīʿī *Fihrist* (see *Bibl.*) Abū Djaʿfar Muḥammad b. al-Ḥasan al-Ṭūsī and were originally intended as commentaries on *al-Muḳniʿa fi 'l-fiḳh* of Mufīd (d. 413/1022). In both the attempt is made to sort out the huge mass of material that had been handed down, of course not in a critical fashion but according to the degree of agreement with the doctrines that had come to prevail. This *Tahdhīb* is not to be confused with the lawbook *Tahdhīb al-Shīʿa* of Muḥammad b. Aḥmad b. al-Djunaid al-Iskāfī (d. 381/991—2) which fell into neglect because he went too far in the application of *ḳiyās*. Only very rarely do we find the larger collection of Ibn Bābūya, *Madīnat al-ʿilm*, recognized as the "Fifth Book".

Among the Shīʿī-Imāmī leaders of the fourth and fifth centuries may be mentioned Kulainī (Muḥammad b. Yaʿḳūb al-Rāzī). He is celebrated as the "renovator" at the beginning of the fourth century just as the year 100 was hallowed by the fifth Imām Muḥammad Bāḳir, 200 by the eighth Imām ʿAlī al-Riḍā and later 400 by the Sharīf al-Murtaḍā, while for 500 there is no one of equal importance to place alongside of al-Ghazzālī who is also esteemed by many Shīʿīs. A maternal uncle of Kulainī, ʿAllān, had been one of the leading Shīʿīs of Raiy-Ṭihrān. He himself worked in Baghdād where his grave enjoyed the reverence paid to that of an Imām. Ibn Bābūya Muḥammad b. ʿAlī, called al-Shaikh al-Ṣadūḳ, claimed to have been born to his father on the intercession of the hidden twelfth Imām. His father had been Shaikh of the Shīʿīs in Ḳumm, which was already strongly ʿAlid in sentiment in the second century, but down to late in the fourth century remained an exception in Persia which was mainly Sunnī. Of his works the *Risāla fi 'l-sharāʾiʿ* to his son was used by the latter in his *Man la yaḥḍuruhu 'l-faḳīh*. In Baghdād the son became associated with the Būyid Rukn al-Dawla, who was able to make good use of his teaching on the imāmate for political purposes. Among the many pupils of the younger Ibn Bābūya was the father of Nadjāshī (see *Bibl.*). Raiy is mentioned as the place of his death, but the tomb now honoured in Ṭihran was only discovered in 1238/1823 by the members of the court of Fatḥ ʿAlī Shāh after an alleged miracle. There was a necessity for graves of saints in Persia proper, besides those in Meshhed, Ṭūs and Ḳumm, especially as Nadjaf, Karbalāʾ, and the great Shīʿī cemeteries of al-Kāẓimain near Baghdād lay in foreign lands. The tomb of the father in Ḳumm beside the tomb of the saint Fāṭima the Second, sister of the eighth Imām al-Riḍā, was, we know, very much visited even in ancient times. Of the some 300 writings of the son a considerable number have been printed, e.g. *al-Khiṣāl* on good and bad qualities (Teheran 1302), the *ʿIlal al-sharāʾiʿ* and the book on the concealment of the Mahdī *Kamāl al-dīn wa-tamām al-niʿma* (ibid. 1301; on the latter cf. E. Möller, *Beiträge zur Mahdilehre des Islams*, Heidelberg 1901). His *Madjālis* are very popular and likewise his *ʿUyūn akhbār al-Riḍā* (Teheran 1317). While these already contain beside theological, legendary, edifying and polemical matter, many questions of law, a special comprehensive *Fiḳh al-Riḍā* (2 vols., Tabrīz 1274) was first compiled by Mufīd Muḥammad b. Muḥammad b. al-Nuʿmān b. ʿAbd al-Salām al-ʿUkbarī al-ʿArabī. His conscious pride in his Arab descent did not prevent his close association with the Būyid ʿAḍud al-Dawla. His funeral service was conducted by Sharīf al-Murtaḍā ʿAlam al-Hudā Abu 'l-Ḳāsim ʿAlī b. al-Ḥusain. In the latter the Shīʿa in Baghdād reached its zenith. A direct descendant of the seventh Imām Mūsā al-Kāẓim, he was, as official *naḳīb*, the recognized representative of the ʿAlids and also held the offices of chief secretary and leader of the pilgrim-caravan. His authority gave his lectures and his participation in the business of the court great theological and political importance. He conducted a vigorous correspondence with the faithful in Mawṣil, Dailam, Djūrdjān, and as far as Syria in Ḥalab and Tripolis, the latter of which was wholly Shīʿī according to the testimony of the contemporary Nāṣir-i Khosraw (*Safar-Nāme*, ed. Schefer, 12 ult.). The discourses with his pupils held at the halting-places on a journey to Mecca, *Ghurar al-farāʾiḍ wa-durar al-ḳalāʾid* were printed at Teheran in 1312; the *Intiṣār*, dedicated to the vizier ʿAmīd al-Dīn, ibid. 1315; the *Amālī* also at Cairo in 1325. On the fundamental question of the Shīʿa he published his attack on the three first caliphs in *al-Shāfī* (Teheran 1301).It was al-Nadjāshī who washed the body of Murtaḍā before it was laid to rest in the burial-place of his ancestors in al-Kāẓimain. For 28 years the pupil of Murtaḍā and of Mufīd, al-Ṭūsī Abū Djaʿfar Muḥammad b. Ḥasan, called the "Shaikh" or the "Shaikh of the (Shīʿa) people (Shaikh al-Ṭāʾifa)", had worked in Baghdād alongside of Murtaḍā, who lived to be over 80. When the Saldjūḳ Toghril Beg entered Baghdād (447/1055), the position of the Shīʿa became more difficult. This and the desire of being buried near the holy Meshhed ʿAlī induced Ṭūsī to move to Nadjaf, where he died in 458 or 460 (1065—1068).

The enormous Shīʿī literature of the fourth and fifth centuries, of which only a few authors and books have been mentioned here, seems at the first glance to be very one-sided. The same traditional themes crop up again and again: the imāmate; the estimation from the theological and legal point of view of the earliest caliphs and of the opponents in the battles of the "camel" and of Ṣiffīn; the *ghaiba* and all that is connected with the concealed Imām; then along with Fiḳh in general, special Imāmī subjects like the *mutʿa* marriage or the *mutʿatān*, i.e. the *mutʿa* marriage and the *tamattuʿ* form of pilgrimage; besides complete exegesis of the Ḳurʾān, special interpretations of favourite Shīʿa passages like Sūra xlii. 23 and xxxiii. 33 and notably the "light-verse" xxiv. 35; finally, constantly recurring polemics against opponents within the Shīʿa. But a development cannot be denied, as a reference to the main problem may show. Ibn Bābūya the younger had still granted the possibility in Prophets and Imāms of *sahw* ("inadvertence") in secondary matters and even described the opposite view as the first step to *ghulūw* (heretical exaggeration). Against him for example Mufīd urged in a special pamphlet their absolute infallibility (*ʿiṣma*), although later the position is still often discussed. But that on the other hand the gates were not at once closed against extremes is shown by the estimation in which the principal book of the Ismāʿīlīs, the *Daʿāʾim al-Islām* long continued to be held. The author, Nuʿmān b. Muḥammad b. Manṣūr Ibn Ḥaiyān (d. 363/973), the "Abū Ḥanīfa of the Shīʿa" mentions no later authorities than the sixth Imām Djaʿfar al-Ṣādiḳ. His omission of later authorities might seem excusable on the ground of an alleged *taḳīya* of this Fāṭimid Ḳāḍī of Cairo, as the special Imām of the Seveners was also left out. But Ibn Shahrāshūb al-Māzandarānī (d. 588/1192) (see *Bibl.*) says simply "he is not an Imāmī" (no. 826) and he is followed by later writers like Tafrīshī (see *Bibl.*).

In the following centuries there appeared among other works the great commentaries on the Ḳurʾān (printed in Teheran) by Abū ʿAlī al-Faḍl al-Ṭabarsī, died between 548 and 552 (1153—1158), *Madjmaʿ al-bayān* and *Djāmiʿ al-djawāmiʿ* which are still in use along with the concise *Tafsīr* of ʿAlī b. Ibrāhīm b. Hāshim al-Ḳummī (Teheran 1301), which dates from the time of Kulainī and gives the special Shīʿa features in moderate compass. Al-Faḍl, who belonged to a family with literary traditions, was in Ṭūs the centre of a learned Shīʿa circle which included for example Ibn Shahrāshūb and Abū Faḍl Shādhān b. Djibrīl, author of one of the many Shīʿī *K. al-Faḍāʾil wa 'l-manāḳib* (Tabrīz 1304). By moving to Sabzawār al-Faḍl contributed to the spread and consolidation of the Shīʿa in Persia; but he is buried in the sanctuary of Riḍā in Ṭūs. A leading personality in the next century was Djaʿfar b. al-Ḥasan b. Yaʿḳūb b. Saʿīd al-Ḥillī, called al-Muḥaḳḳiḳ (d. 676/1277). His influence in Baghdād extended to the immediate entourage of the last ʿAbbāsid al-Mustaʿṣim. His circle included several members of the Saiyid family of the Banū Ṭāʾūs, much distinguished for its literary activity. To this family also belonged the then *naḳīb* Abu 'l-Ḳāsim ʿAlī b. Mūsā al-Ṭāʾūsī, the author of the still very popular little books of prayers, passion-mournings, amulets and guides for pilgrims, like *al-Mudjtana min al-duʿāʾ* (Bombay 1317) and *al-Iḳbāl* (Teheran 1314). To Djaʿfar al-Ḥillī also the modern Shīʿa owes one of its most popular handbooks, *Sharāʾiʿ al-Islām*, which has been continuously commented on in Persian and Arabic (Calcutta 1839, Teheran 1274, part i., ed. and transl. by Kasembeg, St. Petersburg 1862). While Djaʿfar al-Ḥillī secured permanent importance by his work on *furūʿ*, his countryman Ḥasan b. Yūsuf Ibn al-Muṭahhar al-Ḥillī, called al-ʿAllāma for short, is regarded as the great authority on *uṣūl*. His father before him had been represented as such in the presence of Djaʿfar to the philosopher, mathematician, astronomer and ardent Shīʿī Naṣīr al-Dīn al-Ṭūsī (d. 672/1274) when this confidant of Hūlāgū went to Ḥilla near Babel, which had long been strongly Shīʿī. Naṣīr al-Dīn himself, the "Khwādja", is not exactly renowned for his theological writings although these are still studied among the Shīʿīs, in spite of the fact that they are not easy to understand; but he is one of the most dazzling figures in Shīʿa politics. He assisted in winning the Assassin strongholds of Alamūt and Maimundīz for the Mongol Khān, entered Baghdād with the latter's army and induced this pagan to execute the last caliph. He thus still has in the eyes of the Shīʿa the merit of having destroyed two of its worst enemies, the *ghulāt* and the "insolent" ʿAbbāsids, the betrayers of the holy family. His constructive work for the Shīʿa was taken over by Ibn al-Muṭahhar, who was brought by him into contact with the family of the Khān and later attached himself to Khān Uldjaitū as leader of the Shīʿīs. He disputed before the latter with the Ashʿarites and "sophists", wrote pamphlets against them and against the Sunnī law-schools, and converted to the Imāmīya the Khān himself who had been baptised when a prince, later became a Ḥanbalī, then a Shāfiʿī. Some twenty of the works of Ibn Muṭahhar are still in use, for example the *Nahdj al-mustarshidīn* on theological principles (Bombay 1303) with the commentary of al-Miḳdād b. ʿAbd Allāh al-Suyūrī, who was trained in philosophy; the *Kashf al-fawāʾid* (Teheran 1305) is a commentary on the *Ḳawāʿid al-ʿaḳāʾid* of Naṣīr al-Dīn al-Ṭūsī who was his teacher. For the fuller understanding of the middle school of Shīʿa his two volumes *Mukhtalaf al-Shīʿa* (Teheran 1324) are most important.

Ibn al-Muṭahhar was neither the first nor the last to thrust the fundamental *uṣūl* into the foreground. They generally play a more essential part among the Shīʿīs than among the Sunnīs, for the gate of *idjtihād* is not closed to the former. While the *muftī* chooses his fatwā's among those of the old authorities, the learned faḳīh in Persia claims the title of a *mudjtahid* who bases his decision on the Ḳurʾān and Sunna through the formal factors of analogy, the search for connections and usefulness, and by recognition of the above mentioned consensus of the spiritual aristocracy. There is thus at all times a kind of invigorating unrest in the Imāmī theology and jurisprudence, the matter of which otherwise has a tendency to rigidity. Ibn al-Muṭahhar formulated his doctrines in the course of the disputes which he waged, especially against a daughter's son of the old Shaikh al-Ṭūsī, Muḥammad b. Aḥmad Ibn Idrīs al-Ḥillī al-ʿIdjlī, who by rejecting all Sunna appeared to him to pervert the *idjtihād* into arbitrariness. In the xi^th^/xvii^th^ century a reaction came from the opposite side through Mullā Muḥammad Amīn al-Astarābādī (d. about 1036/1626), whose views are still much disputed. As he allows only the Shīʿī Sunna as a source of law beside the Ḳurʾān and consequently also worked on commentaries to the "Four Books", he and his followers accomplished the method of the Akhbārīs in opposition to the Uṣūlīs who favour the method of the *idjtihād*. In his polemics which he conducted from Mecca he was very severe. He refuses to rate *idjmāʿ* higher than the consensus of the Jews, Christians or philosophers. His activities however enlivened the discussion on *ḳiyās, istiḥsān, istiṣḥāb* and on the legal force of a unique tradition in the same way as the attacks of Ibn Ḥanbal or Dāʾūd al-Ẓāhirī had done among the Sunnīs. The matter of the disputed principles among the Shīʿīs is of course modified in keeping with their system; thus the recognition which he demands of the authority of the dead, *taḳlīd al-maiyit*, is the subjection to the principles of the holy Imāms laid down in the Sunna.

The conception of the passion has always remained alive in the Shīʿa. Out of the multitude of Shīʿī learned men special honour is therefore given to those who combine the fame of an author with the glory of a martyr. Four martyrs are particularly famous. The first *shahīd* is Muḥammad b. Makkī al-ʿĀmilī al-Djizzīnī, the author of the Fiḳh book *al-Lumaʿ al-Dimashḳīya*. Betrayed by seceders, he was imprisoned in Damascus and executed with the sword on the fatwā of the Shāfiʿī and notably also of the Mālikī ḳāḍī, impaled and burned, according to most authorities in 786/1384. The second *shahīd* is Zain al-Dīn b. ʿAlī b. Aḥmad b.

Taḳī al-ʿĀmilī al-Shāmī. After fruitful activity in Damascus, Baalbek and Ḥaleb and after much travelling, he was put to death about 966/1558 in Constantinople or on the way there for delivering a Shīʿī legal opinion. In addition to several legal, eschatological and edifying writings his commentary on the *Lumaʿ* (2 vols.) has been printed (Tabrīz 1287). The third shahīd is usually held to be Saiyid Nūr Allāh (also Nūr al-Dīn) b. Sharīf al-Dīn al-Marʿashī al-Shushtarī. His well known biographies, the Persian *Madjālis al-muʾminīn* (Teheran 1268 etc.), have been used by Ethé and Horn for the *Grundriss der iranischen Philologie* (vol. ii. 214, 252). His *Iḥḳāḳ al-Ḥaḳḳ* (Teheran 1273) was destined to be fatal for him, on account of its polemics or more accurately apologetics directed against Sunnī writings like *al-Ṣawāʿiḳ al-muḥriḳa ʿalā Ahl al-Rafḍ wa 'l-Zandaḳa* (Cairo 1307, 1308) of the Shāfiʿī Ibn Ḥadjar al-Haitamī. The fanatical Emperor Djahāngīr had him whipped to death in 1019/1610 (cf. also Horovitz in *Isl.* iii. 63); his co-religionists used quite recently to visit his tomb in Akbarābād (Agra). The honour of being the fourth shahīd is given to Muḥammad Mahdī b. Hidāyat Allāh al-Iṣfahānī, but he is surpassed in importance by his pupil Saiyid Dildār ʿAlī b. Muʿīn al-Naṣrābādī, d. 1235/1819—20, who expounded his theology in *ʿImād al-Islām* (printed in India in 1319). In more recent times Mullā Muḥammad Taḳī al-Ḳazwīnī attained martyrdom, an opponent of Shaikh Aḥmad al-Aḥsāʾī (see below) and of the Bābīs, from among whom came his murderer in 1263/1847.

The first two shahīds were Syrians, the third lived in India. But Persia had become the centre of the Shīʿa under the Ṣafawids since 907/1502. The temporary persecutions under the Afghāns from 1135—1142/1722—1729 and under Nādir (1148—1160/1736—1747) made no difference to this. A man whose family had the same native place and the same Ṣūfī tendencies as the ancestor of the new ruling house, Ḥusain b. ʿAbd al-Ḥaḳḳ al-Ardabīlī al-Ilāhī (the theologian) had under Ismāʿīl I appealed directly to Persian sentiment by writing his tractates and commentaries in Persian. In the still mainly Sunnī country he was often forced to lead the life of a *muhādjir* (emigrant) between Tabrīz, Shīrāz, Herāt etc. The necessary vitality was, however, imported into the Persian Shīʿā from outside, a point which is also important for the problem: Persia and the Shīʿa. Those concerned were mainly Shīʿīs from the Syrian mountains of ʿĀmila (cf. Maḳdisī, p. 161, $_{12}$; 162, $_{3}$; 184, $_{8}$; also called ʿĀmil). The last Serbedār ʿAlī Muʾaiyad of Sabzawār is said to have offered an asylum to an ʿĀmilī, the First Shahīd. These rustic scholars came into the Ṣafawid kingdom in increasing numbers. They settled there and through continual accessions to their numbers retained the traditions of their home. Further Shīʿīs came from Baḥrain. This is why among the nisbas of Persian Shīʿīs we frequently find ʿĀmilī or Baḥrānī, or names showing the origin more definitely like Karakī in the one and Aḥsāʾī in the other. We can mention very few names for this later period here. Muḥammad b. Ḥasan b. al-Ḥurr al-ʿĀmilī al-Mashgharī had a great success with his first book *al-Djawāhir al-saniya* (Teheran 1302) because in it he collected, for the first time it is said, the Shīʿī "ḥadīth ḳudsī" (utterances of God not in the Ḳurʾān). But later the extravagance, volume and speed of his literary output, brought upon him sharp criticism even from theologians used to wholesale production; his six-volume *Tafṣīl wasāʾil al-Shīʿa ilā masāʾil al-sharīʿa* (Teheran 1288) with a special index *Man lā yaḥduruhu 'l-Imām* is still however of value on account of the great mass of tradition he has worked into it and the fact that he gives the authors. He emigrated only at the age of 40 and after long pilgrimages settled in Ṭūs and Iṣfahān. Among natives of Persia the leading family in its day were the Madjlisī. Their most notable representative Muḥammad Bāḳir b. Muḥammad Taḳī, d. 1110 or 1111 (1698—1700), was appointed Shaikh al-Islām by Shāh Sulaimān I. He aimed at reaching the people and wrote about half his works in Persian; he also translated edifying books written in Arabic by Abu 'l-Ḳāsim al-Ṭāʾūsī. His own largest work is called *Biḥār al-anwār*, a great encyclopaedia of law and theology in 25 volumes, which has been printed in Tabrīz and Teheran. Several were translated into Persian, for example the thirteenth on the Mahdī, by order of Shāh Nāṣir al-Dīn.

The attitude to the Ṣūfīs, who do not require an imām as mediator, and to whom the spiritual union with God attainable by every believing lover is something at the opposite pole from the inherence of the "divine part" in the chosen imām, is naturally a hostile one, and also the reverencing of saints in the two schools is of course very different in origin and aim. The most notable encounter between the two was the active part taken by the Imāmī Abū Sahl al-Nawbakhtī (d. 311/923) in the execution of Ḥallādj, who indeed had severely offended the Shīʿīs by his claim to be the wakīl of the hidden lord of the age (see the article ḤALLĀDJ and L. Massignon, *al-Hallaj, martyr mystique de l'Islam*, Paris 1922, i. 138 *sqq.*). The attitude to the philosophers is at least one of suspicion, since, as the case of the *Ghulāt* warned the Imāmīs, scholasticism might undermine them. But there are many offshoots, mystics and philosophers, who profess to be conscientious Shīʿīs and are not to be disposed of simply by the usual polemics. All the centuries therefore show examples of a fundamental revulsion alongside those of mutual attraction. Khwādja Naṣīr al-Dīn, himself the author of the mildly Ṣūfī work *Awṣāf al-Ashrāf* (Teheran 1320) is in spite of the verdict of Ibn Bābūya, Mufīd, Shaikh Ṭūsī and Ibn al-Muṭahhar, an admirer of Ḥallādj; Radjab b. Muḥammad al-Ḥāfiẓ al-Bursī is, it is true, censured as the "renewer of Ṣūfism" since he built up his system on "deceitful fanciful interpretations" and ultra-Shīʿī "exaggerations", but his *Mashāriḳ al-amān* or *al-anwār* written about 800/1397 were used even by such an enemy of the Ṣūfīs as Madjlisī, although with caution, for the *Biḥār*; and the fair-minded concede to Mullā Ṣadrā i.e. Muḥammad b. Ibrāhīm al-Shīrāzī, d. between 1040/1630 and 1050/1641, that in the "Explanation of the Throne-Verse" (Sūra ii. 255) he has kept himself free from Ṣūfī fancies; his commentary on the *Uṣūl al-Kāfī* of Kulainī, the *Mafātīḥ al-ghaib* (Teheran, n.d.), is also used and his version of the fourfold ascent to God in *al-Asfār al-arbaʿa* or *al-Ḥikma al-mutaʿāliya* (Teheran 1282) is tolerated, but it is always objected to him that his commentary on the *Ḥikmat al-ishrāḳ* of the mystic Suhrawardī has too much of the language and sentiments of the mystics. His pupil Muḥammad b. Murtaḍā al-Kāsh(ān)ī, called Muḥsin-i Faiḍ, author of the Shīʿī commentary on the Ḳurʾān *al-Ṣāfī* (Teheran 1276) vigorously defended himself against similar reproaches in *al-Inṣāf fī bayān ṭarīḳ al-ʿilm li-asrār al-dīn* (in the collected *Rasāʾil*, Teheran 1301) and as a matter of fact he is cited by his pupil Saiyid Niʿmat Allāh al-Djazāʾirī against the Ṣūfīs. There is a better foundation for the orthodoxy of the two teachers of Mullā Ṣadrā, the two friends at the court of ʿAbbās I, Muḥammad b. Ḥusain Bahāʾ al-Dīn or al-Bahāʾī al-ʿĀmilī (d. 1030/1620 and Muḥammad Bāḳir al-Astarābādī (d. 1040 /1630) called Mīr Dāmād, as son of the "son-in-law" of ʿAlī b. ʿAbd al-ʿAlī al-Karakī, i.e. also an ʿĀmilī and one of the numerous commentators on *Sharāʾiʿ al-Islām*. In spite of his many-sided interests, al-Bahāʾī, who was also Shaikh al-Islām, as a true Shīʿī revived a very old Shīʿī feature, the ritual interdiction of meat slaughtered by "people of a book" in the *Risāla fī Taḥrīm dhabāʾiḥ ahl al-kitāb*. His *Djāmiʿ-i ʿAbbāsī* (Tabrīz 1309, Bombay 1319) contains decisions in the vernacular on all heads of the law relating to worship. Mīr Dāmād, although he also reverenced Ḥallādj showed himself a good Shīʿī in his *al-Rawāshiḥ al-samawīya fī sharḥ al-aḥādīth al-Imāmīya* (pr. 1311), and in *al-Ḳabasāt* (Teheran 1314) he reconciled his philosophy with orthodoxy, acknowledging that God had existed from all times and is eternal and that the world is transitory. Philosophical discussions were further enlivened by the fact that they were interwoven with specifically theological problems. There were therefore both Uṣūlīs and Akhbārīs among the scholastic Mutakallimūn. The conflict occasionally became so fierce, as recently as last century, that, for example in Karbalāʾ, books were only handled in a wrapper of cloth lest a member of another school might have used them. One of the chief leaders in the feud was Shaikh Aḥmad b. Zain al-Dīn al-Aḥsāʾī, a Baḥrānī as his name shows. A theologian, poet, astronomer, and mathematician, he fought against Ṣūfīs and philosophers and especially for *idjtihād* and *idjmāʿ* against the Akhbārīs (cf. his *Djawāmiʿ al-kalām* or *Ḥaiyāt al-nafs*, Tabrīz 1276). A much too philosophical doctrine of the resurrection, which to the rigidly orthodox seemed ill founded, brought on him and his school, the Shaikhīya (cf. SHAIKHĪ), the reproach of sectarianism, and also, as subsequently with Radjab (see above), the charge of responsibility for the heresy of the Bābīs. These themselves like their offshoot, the Bahāʾīs, saw to it that even in quite recent times, the feud was vigorously maintained by deed and pen. Nor was there a lack of other polemics. Madjlisī was not the last to write against the Jews. War was waged on Christianity after the arrival of missionaries beginning with H. Martyn in 1195/1781 and later against C. G. Pfander's missionary pamphlet *Mīzān al-ḥaḳḳ* and in recent years the activities of the societies for distributing the Bible.

Popular expression of the Shīʿa creed is found in the legends of martyrs, *maḳātil*, almanacs for pilgrimage, *djannāt al-khuld*, and passion-plays, *taʿziyāt*. The apocrypha are also numerous; we are not concerned here with those popular in all Islām like the frequently printed songs and sayings of ʿAlī (cf. Fleischer, *Alis 100 Sprüche*, Leipzig 1837) and the collection of his utterances in the *Nahdj al-balāgha* of Muḥammad al-Riḍā, a brother of Shaikh Murtaḍā; but there are also many little books of prayers like the *Ṣaḥīfa* of ʿAlī, that of the fourth Imām ʿAlī Zain al-ʿĀbidīn and that of the eighth Imām ʿAlī al-Riḍā; also the *Ḥadīth ḳudsī* of ʿAlī collected by Bahāʾī al-ʿĀmilī and finally commentaries on the Ḳurʾān, which are attributed to the sixth Imām Djaʿfar al-Ṣādiḳ or the eleventh like the *Tafsīr al-ʿAskarī* (Teheran 1315), which the younger Ibn Bābūya still used freely, though many later authorities express doubts as to their authenticity.

Bibliography: Besides the works here quoted and those mentioned in the articles referred to, the catalogues of Arabic and Persian manuscripts should be consulted; also Brockelmann, *Gesch. d. Arab. Litt.*; E. G. Browne, *A History of Persian Literature in modern Times*, 1924, p. 353 *sqq.*, where also Shīʿī biographies and bibliographies are utilised; Strothmann, *Die Zwölfer-Schīʿa*, Leipzig 1926; Goldziher, *Vorlesungen* [2], ed. Babinger, Heidelberg 1925, p. 196 *sqq.*; Gobineau, *Les religions et les philosophies dans l'Asie Centrale* [2], Paris 1866, p. 63 *sqq.*; Mez, *Die Renaissance des Islâms*, Heidelberg 1922, p. 55 *sqq.*; Babinger in *ZDMG*, lxxvi. 126 *sqq.*; Nöldeke in *Isl.* xiii. 70 *sqq.*; Andrae, *Die Person Muhammeds in Lehre und Glauben seiner Gemeinde*, 1918, see Index; Buhl, *Alidernes Stilling til de Shiʿitiske Bevaegelser under Umajjaderne* (*Kgl. Danske Vidensk. Selskabs Forhandlinger*, 1910, No. 5). — As a systematic introduction the following are recommended in additon to sources mentioned in the text: al-Nawbakhtī, *Firaḳ al-Shīʿa*, ed. Ritter (Bibliotheca Islamica 4); Muḥ. b. ʿUmar al-Kashshī, *Maʿrifat Akhbār al-ridjāl* as selected by Shaikh Ṭūsī, Bombay 1317; al-Nadjāshī (d. 450/1058), *Maʿrifat ʿilm al-ridjāl*, Bombay 1317; al-Ṭūsī, *Asmāʾ al-ridjāl*, Teheran 1271; *Fihrist kutub al-Shīʿa*, ed. by Sprenger and Mawlawī ʿAbd al-Ḥaqq, Calcutta 1853—1855; Ibn Shahrāshūb (d. 588/1192), *Maʿālim al-ʿulamāʾ*, ed. by Abbas Eghbal, Teheran 1353/1934; Ibn al-Muṭahhar al-Ḥillī, *Khulāṣat al-maḳāl* (also called *K. al-Ridjāl*), Teheran 1310; Mīrzā Muḥammad b. ʿAlī al-Astarābādī (d. about 1028/1619), *Manhadj al-maḳāl*, Teheran 1307; Muḥ. b. al-Ḥurr al-ʿĀmilī, *Amal al-āmil fī dhikr ʿulamāʾ Djabal ʿĀmil*, ibid. 1307; Khwāndamīr, *Ḥabīb al-siyar* (Pers.; written 929/1523), Bombay 1273 etc.; al-Tafrīshī, *Naḳd al-ridjāl* (written 1015/1606), Teheran 1318; Yūsuf b. Aḥmad al-Baḥrānī (d. 1187/1773), *Luʾluʾat al-Baḥrain*, Teheran 1269, Bombay n.d.; Muḥ. Bāḳir al-Khwansārī, *Rawḍāt al-djannāt* (written 1287/1870), Teheran 1306; Muḥammad b. Ṣādiḳ b. Mahdī, *Nudjūm al-samāʾ* (Pers.), Lucknow 1313; Iʿdjāz Ḥusain al-Kentūrī (d. 1286/1870), *Kashf al-ḥudjub wa 'l-astār*, ed. by Hidāyet Ḥusain, Calcutta 1330. — On the Imāms: Abu 'l-Faradj al-Iṣbahānī, *Maḳātil al-Ṭālibīyīn*, Teheran 1307; first half also on the margin of Fakhr al-Dīn Aḥmad b. ʿAlī al-Nadjafī, *al-Muntakhab fī 'l-marāthī wa 'l-khutab*, Bombay 1314; Aḥmad b. ʿAlī b. Muhannā (d. 828/1424), *ʿUmdat al-ṭālib fī ansāb Āl Abī Ṭālib*, Bombay 1318; ʿAbd Allāh b. Nūr Allāh (wrote in 1240/ 1824), *Maḳtal al-ʿawālim*, pr. 1295. — Traditions: Yaḥyā b. al-Ḥasan b. al-Biṭrīḳ (d. 600/1204), *Khaṣāʾiṣ waḥy al-mubīn fī manāḳib Amīr al-Muʾminīn*, pr. 1311; do., *al-ʿUmda fī ʿuyūn ṣiḥāḥ al-akhbār*, Bombay 1309. — Recent works on the doctrine of Nūr: Al-Ḥusain b. Murtaḍā al-Yazdī al-Ṭabāṭabāʾī, *al-Raḳḳ al-manshūr wa-lawāmiʿ al-ẓuhūr*, Bombay 1303. — Sunnī polemics with reference to internal disputes; Maḥmūd Shūkrī al-Ālūsī (d. 1270/1853), *Mukhtaṣar al-tuḥfa al-ithnā ʿashariya*, pr. 1301; C. van Arendonck, *De opkomst van het Zaidietische Imamaat in Yemen*, Leiden 1919; Dwight M. Donaldson, *The Shiʿite Religion*, London 1933.

AL-**SHIBLĪ**, ABŪ BAKR DULAF B. DJAḤDAR, a Sunnī mystic. Born in Baghdād (of a family which came from Transoxiana) in 247/861 he died there in 334/945. At first an official (and *walī* of Demāwend), at the age of 40 he became a convert to asceticism under the influence of Khair Nassādj, a friend of Djunaid [q.v.]; he brought into mystic circles in Baghdād the enthusiasm, at times cynical, of a dilettante, bolder in words than deeds. The tragic end of the trial of his friend al-Ḥallādj [q.v.] frightened him; he denied him before the vizier and went, it is said, to accuse him at the foot of the scaffold (309/922); in the end whether deliberately (through remorse or to avoid possible persecution) or unconsciously (through an excess of asceticism) Shiblī affected a bizarre mode of life, cultivating eccentricities of speech and action which caused his internment in the lunatic asylum in Baghdād; there he used to discourse readily on mysticism in presence of distinguished visitors.

He left no works, but his sayings (or "allusions" *ishārāt*) figure in the classical collections on *shaṭḥ* [q.v.] as do his deliberate eccentricities, his ricidulous penances, humiliating or painful, such as putting salt in his eyes to prevent himself from sleeping. In the legend of al-Ḥallādj the part attributed to Shiblī is very important. He seems to have revered him in secret after denying him in public. In dogma, his ideas are those of Djunaid; in law he followed the Mālikī school, which saved him in his lifetime and caused him to be canonised after his death in legal circles, as a rule very hostile to Ṣūfism. In the classical *silsila* (cf. ṬARĪḲA) Shiblī figures as a link in the chain, between Djunaid and Naṣrābādhī, the latter having in fact been his pupil.

His tomb is still venerated at the Aʿẓamīya in Baghdād, near the *madfan* of Abū Ḥanīfa.

Bibliography: Sarrādj, *Lumaʿ*, ed. Nicholson, p. 395—406 and index (cf. Baḳlī, *Shaṭḥiyāt*); al-Ḳushairī, *Risāla*, Cairo 1318, p. 30 and transl. R. Hartmann, index; al-Maʿarrī, *Ghufrān*, Cairo, p. 206; al-Hudjwīrī, *Kashf*, transl. Nicholson, p. 155—156 and index; Ibn al-Djawzī, *Talbīs Iblīs*, Cairo 1340, p. 216, 268, 361—362, 383—386; ʿAṭṭār, *Tadhkira*, ed. Nicholson, ii. 160—182; L. Massignon, *Passion d'Al-Hallaj*, p. 41—43, 306—310 and index; do., *Mission en Mésopotamie*, Cairo 1912, ii. p. 80—81 (for the present state of the tomb).

SHIRK (also *ishrāk*, A.), association, especially associating a companion with God, i.e. worshipping another besides God, polytheism. In the oldest sūras of the Ḳurʾān, during the so-called first Meccan period, the conceptions *shirk* and *mushrikūn* do not occur. In the later parts of the Ḳurʾān they are often mentioned, and regular disputations with the mushrikūn sometimes occur; in particular they are continually threatened with the Last Judgment; the mushrikūn will then receive their punishment (Sūra xxviii. 62 *sqq.*). They think their idols will intercede for them with Allāh, but these cannot do this (Sūra vi. 94; x. 18; xxx. 13; xxxix. 3 and 38); quite the contrary, for they will accuse their worshippers on the Last Day (Sūra xix. 81 *sq.*; x. 28 *sq.*) and they will become fuel for hell together with them (Sūra xxi. 98 *sq.*). The mushrikūn are not grateful to God for saving them from the perils of the sea (Sūra xxix. 65). The believers are to keep away from them and not to marry the mushrikāt (Sūra ii. 221) but they are not to revile the unbelievers but endure them unless the latter in their turn attack Allāh (Sūra vi. 108). In the year 9, however, Muḥammad finally casts off the mushrikūn (Sūra ix. 3, cf. however earlier Sūra xv. 94 *sq.*); the mushrikūn are unclean (Sūra ix. 28). The believers are not to pray for them, even if they are their nearest relatives (Sūra ix. 113 *sq.*). Muḥammad had already earlier expressly declared shirk to be the sin for which God has no forgiveness (Sūra vi. 51, 116; xxxi. 13) and rejected it as absurd (Sūra xxi. 22).

This development is very similar to that of the conception of the *kāfir* [q.v.] in the Ḳurʾān. Kāfir is the most usual term for the unbelievers, and comprises both mushrikūn and the "people of a book". Thus Sūra xcviii. 6 says "those who are unbelievers, the possessors of a scripture as well as the worshippers of gods, will dwell eternally in Hell-fire". The commentators on this passage differ in their views. Some hold the view that the people of a book are to be included among the mushrikūn and that here we have the narrower term used first, and then the more comprehensive one. Other commentators have distinguished the people of a book from the idolators in the narrower sense and this corresponds to the use of the phrase which later became predominant. But everywhere in the Ḳurʾān shirk is used in direct contrast to the profession of the oneness of God, which has been given its most pregnant expression in Sūra cxii. (*Sūrat al-Tawḥīd* or *Sūrat al-Ikhlāṣ*) and according to one somewhat artificial explanation, a definite variety of *shirk* is made impossible by each single verse of this sūra.

In the Ḥadīth literature, shirk has usually the same meaning of "an external obscuring of the belief in the oneness of God". The mushrikūn are — as in the above mentioned Ḳurʾānic passage — ungrateful to God and say in their vain boasting, "if we had not our gods we would be robbed", and so on. For the rest, the hostile feeling against the mushrikūn in the period of the great conquests is reflected in the rest of the Ḥadīth literature. Before the battle the mushrikūn received the demand to adopt Islām; on one occasion Muḥammad even prays to God for right guidance for them; on another he curses them and calls down fire on their houses and tombs, and subsidences and earthquakes. According to one ḥadīth the believer very rarely falls away into shirk, and the Prophet says, full of confidence, "Shirk is in my community more difficult to find than a black seed on a hard rock in the darkest night" — or he says to Abū Bakr, "I will tell a word to thee, the utterance of which protects thee against any shirk: O God, I take refuge with Thee, lest I wittingly give thee a companion, and beseech Thy pardon if I have done it unwittingly".

In the Fiḳh books, mushrik is the proper legal term for unbeliever, although *kāfir* is often also found. The unbeliever according to the Fiḳh is in general regarded as an outlaw and of little value. Unbelievers, especially if hostile, can be killed without punishment, while on no account can a believer be put to death for the sake of an unbeliever (Dārimī, *Diyāt* b. 5). On this point in general, cf. the article KĀFIR and on special points DJIHĀD and DĀR AL-ḤARB for the laws of warfare, and the articles DHIMMA, KHARĀDJ and DJIZYA for the constitutional law. On some points the unbelievers are allowed to make legal arrangements among themselves, as for example in the law of marriage: — Unbelievers are at liberty to arrange the marriage of their children as they please; unbelievers can be witnesses at a marriage between believers; unbelieving husband and wife must be divorced if one of the two adopts Islām. Law of inheritance: — Bequests from one unbeliever to another, even of different religions, are quite as valid as in the case when either the testator or legatee is a Muslim; but in no case can anything be bequeathed to an enemy unbeliever.

The ḳāḍī has to prevent the appointment of an unbeliever as executor to a will. On the law of slaves cf. the article ʿABD; and the article TAḲĪYA on the cases of urgent necessity in which a believer is permitted to conceal his faith.

The broadening of the Muslim outlook in the wars of conquest had naturally quite early brought about a recognition of the fact that all mus̲h̲rikūn are not the same and are not to be treated alike. In the books on *milal wa-niḥal* we find more or less full accounts of the different foreign religious systems, which term includes also the philosophers, star-worshippers and atheists, and in the apologetic literature we occasionally find systematic expositions of the various foreign religions. Attempts are not wanting which explain psychologically the origin of idolatry. From such considerations the conception of s̲h̲irk came to be divided into many varieties, with which we cannot deal here. But these researches had a practical legal significance insomuch as through them the oaths came to be formulated by which members of strange religions were sworn, to get a binding promise from them, especially in the case of recognition of the authority of Muslim State. An interesting collection of such formulae for oaths for the Mamlūk period is given by Ḳalḳas̲h̲andī, *Ṣubḥ al-aʿs̲h̲ā*, xiii. 200 *sqq.*

In the course of the dogmatic development of Islām the conception of s̲h̲irk received a considerable extension through the circumstance that the adherents of many sects had no compunction about reproaching their Muslim opponents with s̲h̲irk, as soon as they saw in them any obscuring of monotheism, although only in some particular respect specially emphasized by themselves; and in the later systematized dogmatic works, which, as a rule in connection with *tawḥīd*, go into its opposite s̲h̲irk, one can trace in almost any sentence what sectarian view is referred to or refuted, and then trace the path by which the present formulation has come about. S̲h̲irk has thus become no longer simply a term for the unbelief prevailing outside of Islām, but a reproach hurled by one Muslim against another inside of Islām.

The Muʿtazilīs, for example, called their opponents mus̲h̲rikūn in as much as they, by adopting eternal attributes of the Deity, postulated their existence as eternal beings beside God. The attributes rather, they say, do not exist for themselves but are inseparably one with God and not different from Him, and expressions like "God is all-knowing", "God is mighty", "God is living", simply mean "God is".

Quite in the same spirit, the Almohads, whose special programme was the *tawḥīd*, accused their opponents of s̲h̲irk, because they held the doctrine of the non-creation of the Ḳurʾān, and their *tawḥīd* includes the demand to recognize its uncreatedness; only in this way is it possible to exclude the Ḳurʾān from being a second eternal being besides God. Mus̲h̲rikūn to them also are the anthropomorphists who make God possess physical human qualities and thus affect his *waḥdānīya*. According to their strict view, they alone are professors of the oneness of God (*muwaḥḥidūn*) in the true sense, the whole of the rest of the Muslim world is *mus̲h̲rikūn* to them and the Christians *ahl al-kufr*. (The Ismāʿīlīya also were fond of calling themselves *muwaḥḥidūn* but this was not a distinctive name for them; for them every one who associates another with his Imām is like one who associates another with God or the Prophet, i.e. is unclean).

The s̲h̲irk theory of the Wahhābīs goes to the greatest extreme. Their hostility is directed against s̲h̲irk which in their view infects the whole of orthodox Islām in the form of the cult of prophets, saints, and tombs. Besides, there have not been wanting in orthodoxy and elsewhere (cf. e.g. Goldziher, *Zahiriten*, p. 189; cf. Strothmann, *Kultus der Zaiditen*, p. 67 *sq.*) those who condemn the cult of saints for reasons of *tawḥīd*, and at bottom it is only tolerated as a concession to the overwhelming practice of the people. The Wahhābīs also consider themselves the only *muwaḥḥidūn*, all other Muslims are mus̲h̲rikūn and they themselves are called to the *iḥyāʾ al-sunna*. The old sunna and the picture of the character of the Prophet and therefore the very heart of Islam has indeed been falsified by the worship of saints. Therefore they attack the very holiest places of Islām of the Sunnīs and S̲h̲īʿis, because these in their eyes are regular strongholds of idolatry.

According to the theorists of the Wahhābīs, their opposition is directed in detail against 1. *s̲h̲irk al-ʿilm*: prophets and saints have no *ʿilm al-g̲h̲aib* except when it is revealed to them by God, who alone possesses it. It is s̲h̲irk to credit or ascribe knowledge to them or to soothsayers astrologers and interpreters of dreams. 2. *s̲h̲irk al-taṣarruf*; the assumption that any one except God has power. Whoever then regards a saint as an intermediary with God commits s̲h̲irk, even if it only, he thinks, serves to bring him nearer to God. Any kind of intercession (*s̲h̲afāʿa*, q.v.) is therefore rejected on the authority of Sūra xxxix. 44; the Prophet himself will receive from God permission to intervene only on the Last Day and not before. 3. *s̲h̲irk al-ʿibāda*: the reverencing of any created thing, the grave of the Prophet, the tomb of a saint, by prostration, circumambulation, giving of money, vows, fasting, pilgrimage, mentioning the name of a saint, praying at his grave, kissing certain stones, etc. 4. *s̲h̲irk al-ʿāda*: superstitious customs like *istik̲h̲āra* [q.v.], belief in omens, in good or bad days, etc., in personal names like ʿAbd al-Nabī, asking soothsayers for advice, etc. 5. *s̲h̲irk fi 'l-adab*: swearing in the name of the Prophet, of ʿAlī, of the Imāms, or Pīrs.

S̲h̲irk has a special meaning in Muslim ethics, notably in al-G̲h̲azzālī. To the refined ethical conscience "every kind of worship of God which is not absolutely disinterested" is s̲h̲irk. Thus the hypocritical practice of religion which is performed for the sake of reward, i.e. to gain the admiration or applause of men, is s̲h̲irk, because it associates consideration for men with the thought of God. Similarly arrogance and egoism are a kind of s̲h̲irk. Numerous grades of this s̲h̲irk are further distinguished, and it is called also *s̲h̲irk ṣag̲h̲īr* or *s̲h̲irk aṣg̲h̲ar* in contrast to crude and obvious polytheism, *s̲h̲irk ʿaẓīm*; the ethical value of an action is based on the degree of admixture or omission that clouds the pure intention, *ik̲h̲lāṣ* [q.v.].

Just as the term *ik̲h̲lāṣ* for the Ṣūfīs now has the meaning "exclusive devotion to God", so s̲h̲irk has for them come to have the meaning "being prevented by something from exclusive devotion to Him". For example the mere illusion of the soul (*nafs*) that it has something good in it and has a certain worth is a secret idolatry (*s̲h̲irk k̲h̲afī*). It is the same with the assertion "I know God", because here we have an admission of the duality between the subject which knows and the object of knowledge. For the Ṣūfī seeking union with the deity, difference of rites and religions loses all significance, and this does not exclude Islām, and the following bold saying is ascribed to Tilimsānī, a pupil of Ibn ʿArabī, that "the Ḳurʾān is absolute shirk; profession of oneness is found only in our (i.e. Ṣūfī) speech" (Goldziher, *Vorlesungen*, p. 171).

Bibliography: Goldziher, *Vorlesungen*, index s.v.; do., *Muh. Studien* ii. 280 *sqq.*; Wensinck, *Handbook* s.v. Polytheism; Muḥ. Aʿlā, *Dict. of Techn. Terms*, ii. 770 *sqq.*; Fagnan, *Additions*, p. 88; Nöldeke-Schwally, *Geschichte des Qorāns*, i. 129, 225, 229; Weitbrecht-Stanton, *The Teaching of the Qoran*, index under Idolatry and Idols; Horovitz, *Koranische Untersuchungen*, p. 60 *sqq.*; Hamilton, *Hidāya*, index s.v. Infidels; Abū Yūsuf, *Kit. al-Kharādj*, Būlāḳ 1302, p. 73 *sqq.*, 118 *sqq.*; Khalīl, *Mukhtaṣar*, transl. Guidi-Santillana, index s.v. guerra santa, kitābī; *"Corpus Iurus" di Zaid ibn ʿAlī*, ed. Griffini, index s.v. Mušrik; al-Nafūsī, *Ḳanāṭir al-khairāt*, i. 227, 231, 252, 289; al-Maḳrīzī, *Tadjrīd at-tawḥīd* Cairo 1343; Houtsma, *De Strijd over het Dogma in den Islam tot op el-Ash'ari*, p. 16 *sqq.*; Goldziher, *Materialien zur Kenntnis der Almohadenbewegung, ZDMG*, xli. 68; Hughes, *Dict. of Islam*, s.v. Mushrik, Shirk, Wahhābī; R. Hartmann, *al-Qoshairī's Darstellung des Ṣûfîtums*, p. 15 *sqq.*, 59 and 77; H. Bauer, *Islamische Ethik*, i. p. 45 *sqq.*, 64 *sqq.*, 68 *sqq.*; Obermann, *Der ... Subjektivismus al-Ghazālī's*, p. 154 [3], 263; Pedersen, *Der Eid* ... p. 208, 228.

SHĪTH (Hebr. *Shēth*), Seth, the third son of Adam and Eve (*Gen.*, iv. 25, 26 and v. 3—8) was born when his father was 130 years of age, five years after the murder of Abel. When Adam died, he made him his heir and executor of his will. He taught him the hours of the day and of the night, told him of the Flood to come and taught him to worship the divinity in retirement at each hour of the day.

It is to him that we trace the genealogy of mankind, since Abel did not leave any heirs and Cain's heirs were lost in the Flood. It is said that he lived at Mecca performing the rites of pilgrimage until his death; that he collected the leaves revealed to Adam and to himself (numbering fifty) and regulated his conduct by them; that he built the Kaʿba of stone and clay. On his death he left as his successor his son Anūsh (Enoch); he was buried beside his parents in the cavern of Mount Abū Ḳubais; he had attained the age of 912 years. According to Ibn Isḥāḳ he married his sister Ḥazūra.

Ṭabarī, *Annales*, writes Shath and Shāth (i. 153) and says that Shīth is a Syriac form (*sūryānī*). The name signifies "in place of, gift (of God)" because he was given in place of Abel (*Gen.*, iv. 26).

Al-Muḳannaʿ, who came forward about 780 as a prophet in Khurāsān, held that the spirit of God was transferred from Adam to Seth (Muṭahhar b. Ṭāhir al-Maḳdisī, *Livre de la Création*, ed. and transl. by Huart, vi. 96). This idea comes from a Gnostic sect, the Sethites who were found in Egypt from the fourth century, and who possessed a "*Paraphrase of Seth*", to be more precise, seven books by this patriarch and seven others by his children, whom they called the "Strangers" (Epiphanes, *Haer.*, xxxix. 5). The Gnostics possessed the books of Jaldabaoth, the Demiurge, attributed to Seth (Epiphanes, *op. cit.*, xxvi. 8). The Ṣābiʾūn of Ḥarrān had several writings attributed to Seth, and the latter was associated with Adam by the Manichaeans (Prosper Alfaric, *Les Ecritures manichéennes*, Paris 1918, p. 6, 9, 10). Seth is always associated with Adam by the Druzes (Philipp Wolff, *Drusen*, Leipzig 1845, p. 151, 193, 372 *sqq.*).

Bibliography: Ṭabarī, *Annales*, i. 152—168, 1122, 1123; Ibn al-Athīr, *al-Kāmil*, ed. Tornberg, i. 35, 39; Thaʿlabī, *ʿArāʾis al-madjālis*, ed. lith. 1277, p. 42; Mirkhond, *Rawḍāt al-ṣafā*, Bombay 1271, i. 12 *sqq.*

SHUʿAIB, a prophet mentioned in the Ḳurʾān who, according to Sūra xi. 89, came later than Hūd, Ṣālih and Lot; according to Sūra xxvi. 176—189 which belongs to the middle Meccan period, he was sent to the "people of the thicket" (*al-Aika*) who are again mentioned in l. 13; xv. 78; xxxviii. 13. In the later Meccan Sūras, xi. 84—95; xxix. 36 *sq.*; vii. 85—93, he appears among the inhabitants of Madyan as their brother. Only later commentators identify him with the unnamed father-in-law of Moses, the Old Testament Jethro, who lived in Madyan mentioned in xxviii. 22 *sqq.* (cf. v. 41), but there is no foundation for this in the Ḳurʾān. From the passages mentioned, it is evident that Muḥammad had no very clear conception of Shuʿaib and it is not worth while enquiring whence he got the name, which does not occur elsewhere. What Muḥammad tells of him follows the stereotyped scheme in his stories of the prophets and reflects his own experiences and struggles. Besides preaching monotheism he urges his countrymen mainly to honesty in weights and measures, and warns them against destroying the order restored in the land and against driving the believers who follow him from the path of Allāh. But the notables among the people reject him and threaten to expel him and his followers; he had no prestige among them and if they had not had consideration for his family they would have stoned him (xi. 91). An earthquake overtakes them as a punishment, so that they are all found dead in their dwellings.

That a much later tradition moves Shuʿaib's grave to Ḳarn Ḥattīn in Syria is perhaps to be explained by the confusion of the adjacent Khirbet Midyan, the ancient Madon, with Madyan.

Bibliography: Thaʿlabī, *Ḳiṣaṣ al-anbiyāʾ*; Dalman, *Palästina Jahrbuch*, x. 41 *sqq.*; J. Horovitz, *Koranische Untersuchungen*, Berlin and Leipzig 1926, p. 119 *sq.*

SHURĀT (A., sg. SHĀRĪ), the name which the extreme Khāridjīs [q.v.] give themselves. This name of a religious denomination is taken from the Ḳurʾān (iv. 74) and means, "those who sell their life to God" by vowing to fight to the death against his enemies.

The first Shurāt were exterminated by ʿAlī at the battle of Nukhaila. The most celebrated of their martyrs was Abū Bilāl Mirdās b. Djawdar, of the Rabīʿa tribe. They swore to fight, even when hope had gone, for the cause of justice "until only three amongst them should remain".

This state of extreme political feeling or *shirā* is contrasted in Khāridjī terminology to the state of "triumph" (*ẓuhūr*), of "defence" (*dafʿ*) and of "secret" (*kitmān*).

The name of Shurāt has been applied by extension to a group of Khāridjī jurists, natives of ʿUmān, Sidjistān, Ādharbāidjān, Shahrizōr, and ʿUkbarā, like Djubair b. Ghālib and Ḳarṭalūsī, who have written in justification of the attitude of *shirā*.

The Malay custom of *amok* sometimes takes the form of *shirā* among Muslim Filipinos.

Bibliography: Mubarrad, *Kāmil*, ed. Wright, p. 577; Ibn al-Nadīm, *Fihrist*, ed. Flügel, p. 236—237; Abū Zakarīyā Shammākhī, *Chronique*, transl. Masqueray, Algiers 1878, p. 272—335; Ibn ʿAbd Rabbihi, *al-ʿIḳd al-farīd*, Cairo 1316, ii. 138.

SHUSHTARĪ, SAIYID NŪR ALLĀH B. SHARĪF MARʿASHĪ, a Shīʿite writer who defended imāmism against Sunnī polemists and at the same time mysticism against the anti-mysticism of the majority of the Imāmī doctors. Ḳāḍī of Lahore, he was condemned as a heretic by orders of Djahāngīr and whipped to death in 1019/1610. He is the third martyr (*shahīd thālith*) of the Imāmīs. He left two important works, in Persian the *Madjālis al-Muʾminīn* (finished at Lahore in 1073/1604), a biographical collection based on good sources on the principal martyrs of Imāmī and mystic Islām; and in Arabic the *Iḥḳāḳ al-Ḥaḳḳ*, a treatise on Imāmī apologetics.

Bibliography: Rieu, *Catal. Persian MSS. British Museum*, London 1879, i., p. 337; Goldziher, *Beiträge zur Literaturgeschichte der Shīʿa und der sunnitischen Polemik*, Vienna 1874; *GAL.*, *Suppl.* ii. 607 sq.

AL-**ṢIDDĪḲ** (probably the Aramaic *ṣaddīḳ*), surname of the first caliph Abū Bakr, means "the eminently veracious" and "he who always accepts, or confirms, the truth".

According to Ibn Isḥāḳ, Abū Bakr received this surname because when the Muslims' faith in Muḥammad had been shaken by his account of the *miʿrādj*, Abū Bakr testified that the Prophet's description of Jerusalem was strictly truthful, thereby restoring their belief in him. Another tradition relates that Muḥammad had complained to Gabriel of his people's lack of faith; the Archangel replied: "Abū Bakr believes in thee (*yuṣaddiḳuka*), for he is *al-ṣiddīḳ*".

The saying: *wa-'lladhī djāʾa bi 'l-ṣidḳi wa-ṣaddaḳa bihi*, in Sūra xxxix. 34, which has been rendered: "But he who brought the truth and he who accepted it as the truth", is referred, in a tradition attributed to ʿAlī b. Abī Ṭālib, to Muḥammad and Abū Bakr respectively; this explanation seems to owe something to the latter's surname.

In the Ḳurʾān the epithet *al-ṣiddīḳ* is given only to Joseph (xii. 46), in the sense of veracious. *Ṣiddīḳ*, in conjunction with *nabī*, is applied to Idrīs (xix. 56) and Abraham (xix. 41); the virgin Mary is called *ṣiddīḳa* (v. 75), and true believers in general are called *al-ṣiddīḳūn* (lvii. 19 and iv. 69).

Those who claim descent from Abū Bakr are usually styled *al-Bakrī al-Ṣiddīḳī*; when only one of these *ansāb* is used for brevity's sake, al-Ṣiddīḳī is preferred.

Bibliography: Ibn Hishām, p. 264; Ṭabarī, i. 2133; Ibn Saʿd, *Ṭabaḳāt*, iii. 1, 120; Lane, *Lexicon*, iv. 1667, *a* and 1668, *b*, *c*; Barbier de Meynard, *Surnoms et sobriquets dans la littérature arabe*, in *JA.*, series 10, x. 62; J. Horovitz, *Koranische Untersuchungen*, Berlin and Leipzig 1926, p. 49; A. Jeffery, *Foreign Vocabulary of the Qurʾān*, pp. 194 *sq.*

ṢIFA does not occur in the Ḳurʾān but the infin. *waṣf* is used once and the impf. of the first stem 13 times in the meanings: "to ascribe or assert as a description, to attribute" and always with an implication of falsehood. Thus of Allāh in Ḳurʾān vi. 100; xxiii. 91; xxxvii. 159, 180; xliii. 82 — all similar, fixed phrases; this standing implication is used in the *Mufradāt* of Rāghib al-Iṣbahānī (p. 546, *s.v.*) to suggest that all descriptions of Allāh are unsound.

The *ṣifāt* of Allāh are to be distinguished from his Names (*asmāʾ*). The Names are the epithets applied to him as descriptives in the Ḳurʾān, following the wide use of such epithets in the old poetry. On these Names see especially al-Ghazzālī, *Al-maḳṣad al-asnā*. But his *ṣifāt* are strictly the abstract qualities which lie behind these epithets, as *ḳudra* behind *ḳadīr* and *ʿilm* behind *ʿalīm*. A very important problem in theology is the relation of these *ṣifāt* to his *dhāt*. The resultant orthodox statement, after long controversy, is that they are eternal, subsisting in his essence, and that they are not He, nor are they other than He (*lā huwa wa-lā ghairuhu*); see Taftāzānī on Nasafī's *ʿAḳāʾid* with super-commentaries, Cairo 1321, pp. 67 *sqq.* and the commentary of Djurdjānī on the *Mawāḳif* of al-Īdjī, Būlāḳ 1266, pp. 479 *sqq.* The struggle was, in part, to maintain the internal unity of the personality of Allāh; in part, to do justice to the Ḳurʾānic descriptives of him; in part, to determine what were primary and necessary of these and what could be regarded as merely relations and connectives of these with the material world. It was a struggle with unbelieving philosophers, with Muʿtazilite heretics and, within orthodox Islām, between Ashʿarites and Māturīdites; see Louis Massignon, *La Passion d'al-Hallaj*, pp. 568, 571 and especially 645 *sqq.* and the translations from Nasafī and Faḍālī in Macdonald, *Development of Muslim Theology*, pp. 309, 319 *sqq.* Also Sanūsī's *Prolégomènes Théologiques*, ed. and transl. by Luciani, pp. 162—216. Through it all ran the position of the *Mufradāt* [see above] that descriptions of Allāh must be, at the best, inadequate and misleading, and, at the worst, impossible. On Allāh's mystical manifestation of himself by means of his *ṣifāt* see Massignon, p. 514 and R. A. Nicholson, *Studies in Islamic Mysticism*, pp. 90, 98.

Bibliography: has been given above.

SIḤR, glamour, magic. Islām is a system of frank supernaturalism; for it there is our material world of the senses and behind that a world of spirits, into relation with which we can enter by means of either magic or religion. From the Islamic point of view, the question is whether the intercourse with this world of spirits may affect man's relation to Allāh and imperil his eternal salvation. In the Arabia of Muḥammad's time, if we leave out the elements affected by Christianity and Judaism, the spirit-world consisted of Allāh, the tribal gods and the djinn; and the links between it and men were *kāhin*'s, magicians and soothsayers, poets and madmen. Murtaḍā al-Zabīdī in his commentary on the *Iḥyāʾ* (i. 217 foot) quotes Tādj al-Dīn al-Subkī as saying, "*Siḥr* and *kahāna* and astrology and *sīmiyāʾ* (science of talismans) are all of the same *wādī*". Further, when Islām spread out of Arabia it entered into contact with all the supernatural beliefs and magical arts and rituals of the different races and countries which it conquered, and these were blended with the Ḳurʾānic and Arabian conceptions and usages. The confusion worked in two directions: (i.) the superstitions and nomenclature of Arabia were imposed on non-Arab and even non-Semitic peoples, and (ii.) even fundamental Islām was deeply affected by completely alien beliefs.

Siḥr in its exact etymology suggests the limited form of magic called "glamour". The lexica assert that it is the turning (*ṣarf*) of a thing from its true nature (*ḥaḳīḳa*) or form (*ṣūra*) to something else which is unreal or a mere appearance (*khayāl*). For the mind of Muḥammad and for his environment, however, *siḥr* was a real thing, although the message given in and through it might, in great part, be false. By far the most important Ḳurʾānic verse for the whole subject is ii. 102: "And they [unbelievers in general and Jews in particular] followed what the *shaiṭān*'s used to recite in the reign of Sulaimān [or against the reign of Sulaimān] — and Sulaimān was never an unbeliever but the *shaiṭān*'s were unbelievers — teaching mankind magic (*siḥr*); and [they followed] what was revealed to [or by means of] the two angels in Bābil, Hārūt and Mārūt; and they do not teach any one until they say to him: We are only a temptation (*fitna*); so do not disbelieve. So they [the learners] learn from the two that by which they may divide a man from his wife, but they do not harm by it any one except by the permission of Allāh. They learn that which harms them and does not aid them, having knowledge, indeed, that he who purchases it has no portion in the world to come."

In spite of al-Baiḍāwī's compact style his exposition occupies more than a page and there is a page and a half in the *Kashshāf* of al-Zamakhsharī. In the greater commentaries it is treated at length as the *locus classicus* on magic; thus al-Ṭabarī's *Tafsīr*, i. 334—353 and Fakhr al-Dīn al-Rāzī's *Mafātīḥ*, i. 427—440 in ed. Cairo 1307. The *shaiṭān*'s, say these commentators, are the source of magic; they listened at the walls of heaven and added lies to what they heard there; they brought this to the *kāhin*'s and made books of it. The Jews even said that Sulaimān was not a prophet but a magician (Rāzī, p. 428). This verse is an answer to them. Elsewhere in the Ḳur'ān (xxxvii. 6; xli. 12; lxvii. 5; lxxii. 8, 9) we are told that the djinn used to sit beside the nearer sky and listen there to the Heavenly Host (*al-mala' al-a'lā*) and that they are chased away from it by lamps set in it for adornment but thrown at them as missiles by the angels on guard. They used to listen thus regularly, but now (*al-āna*, lxxii. 9) — apparently since Muḥammad was sent — they have found the angels especially vigilant against them. In xxvi. 221—225 there is a significant passage telling how the *shaiṭān*'s come down to every great liar (*affāk*) and that these receive what the *shaiṭān*'s have heard. The straying poets, too, follow them, wandering in every *wādī* and never doing what they say. On poetry as thus inspired by the *djinn* see Goldziher, *Abh. zur arab. Philologie*, i., pp. 1—121 and on this passage especially, p. 27, note 2.

Later Islām traced all licit or "white" magic back to Sulaimān (see above). The other occurrences of *siḥr* and its cognates are connected with the stories of Mūsā, 'Īsā, and Muḥammad himself. To the story of Mūsā [q.v.] and his contests with the magicians of Pharaoh belong all references in certain Sūras. Many other passages, however, relate to Muḥammad, such as vi. 7; x. 2; etc. There are certain significant phrases and usages: *siḥr* is opposed to *al-ḥaḳḳ*, "reality", in xx. 75, 76; xliii. 30; xlvi. 7, and to the reality of Hell in lii. 15. In xxi. 3 *sqq.* various accusations are brought against Muḥammad — that his message is *siḥr*, that it is "bundles of dreams", etc., and in lxxiv. 24 (the oldest occurrence in the Ḳur'ān) the message of Muḥammad is called *siḥr yu'thar*, "a magic derived or learned" from someone else. Several times the Ḳur'ān, its message and proofs are called magic: xi. 7; xxxiv. 43; xliii. 30; etc. But Muḥammad did not show any other signs of being a magician or wonder-worker. In the case of two passages in this context of magic (x. 2; xxxvii. 15) the commentators, e.g. Zamakhsharī and Baiḍāwī, are quite sure that the reference is to miracles, but the whole drift of the Ḳur'ān and even the passages themselves show that the reference is to the revelations. It was necessary for the early Muslim interpreters to make as firm a distinction as possible between the phenomena of Muḥammad and those of the other links with the spirit-world. This they did by emphasizing revelation through Djibrīl as opposed to automatic speech through a possessing spirit. For Muḥammad *siḥr* was heathen revelation, coming from the spirit-world and in so far real, but perverted and amplified by its intermediaries, spirit and human, and in so far false.

In the traditions on the subject it is impossible to say what goes back to Muḥammad and what arose in later controversy. Reference may be made to a miscellaneous farrago in the *Ṣaḥīḥ* of Muslim (*Salām*, tr. 40 *sqq.*), on medicine (*ṭibb*) and spells (*ruḳwa*), lawful and unlawful magic, poison, *shaiṭān*'s, *ghūl*'s, *kahāna*, *ṭaira*, *fa'l*, all jumbled together. On seeing the Prophet in dreams and on dreaming generally see Muslim, *Ru'yā*, tr. 1 *sqq.* All these subjects were, and are, in close association in the Muslim mind.

But though Muḥammad was perfectly assured as to the reality of these phenomena, whether as glamour or as perverted revelation from unbelieving spirits, the early rationalistic theologians, the Mu'tazila [q.v.], had many doubts. This comes out very clearly in the book of Ibn Ḳutaiba (d. 276/889), *Mukhtalif al-ḥadīth* (ed. Cairo 1326, pp. 220—235); see on it Goldziher, *Moh. Stud.*, ii. 136 *sqq.* The Mu'tazila attacked the traditions which tell that Muḥammad was bewitched; that was impossible in a prophet who was under the protection of Allāh (*ma'ṣūm*). Also the magic spoken of in the Ḳur'ān, e.g. in the story of Mūsā and in Sūra ii. 102, was nothing but juggling (*takhyīl*).

In the *Fihrist* (written between 377 and 400/987—1010) we find the magical system fully developed and with a rich literature behind it. The principal passage is in the second *fann* of the 8th *maḳāla* (ed. Flügel, 308 *sqq.*). Magicians, licit and illicit, according to the author, all assert that magic is worked by the obedience of spirits to the magician. Licit magicians (*al-mu'azzimūn*) assert that they control the spirits by obeying and supplicating Allāh and by bringing adjurations by Allāh to bear on the spirits. Illicit magicians (*al-saḥara*) assert that they enslave the spirits by offerings and by evil deeds displeasing to Allāh. He records several kinds of magic, in particular those practised in Egypt (the Bābil of the magicians), and mentions also the philosophers and star-worshippers, the Indians, Chinese, and Turks.

Licit magic (*al-ṭarīḳa al-maḥmūda*) is traced back to Sulaimān b. Dāwūd, who was the first to enslave the spirits. The same is said for Persian magic of Djamshīd; for an account of his place in Persian myth and of his confusion with Solomon see especially E. G. Browne, *Lit. Hist. of Persia*, i. 112—114. Details on the magical literature ascribed to Sulaimān are given in al-Djawbarī's *Kitāb fī kashf al-asrār* (cf. de Goeje in *ZDMG*, xx. 486 *sqq.* and Fleischer in *ZDMG*, xxi. 274). The *Fihrist* then gives a list of 70 names of spirits. Further lists and descriptions are in Ḳazwīnī's *'Adjā'ib al-makhlūḳāt* (ed. Wüstenfeld, 371 *sqq.*) and in Damīrī's *Ḥayāt al-ḥayawān* (ed. Cairo 1313, i. 177—187). Illicit magic (*al-ṭarīḳa al-madhmūma*) is traced similarly to Iblīs through his daughter or his son's daughter, Baidakh, and the *Fihrist* adds the names of individuals and of some books by them.

If the author of the *Fihrist* was in evident doubt as to there being any real magic and simply recorded biographical and bibliographical facts as he found them, al-Ghazzālī (d. 505/1111) had no such doubts. The spirit-world was very real to him; throughout the *Iḥyā'* he enters on full details as to the *djinn* and the *shaiṭān*'s and their activities (see Macdonald, *Religious Attitude ... in Islam*, 274 *sqq.*), and he wrote also on the interpretation of dreams (*al-taḥbīr fi ʿilm al-taʿbīr*, Aleppo 1328). See further for this side of al-Ghazzālī, Goldziher's introduction to his *Livre d'Ibn Toumert*, Alger 1903, p. 15 *sqq.* His philosophical pragmatism led him to accept all those workings in nature and in man for which he found good evidence. The *budūḥ* square had "worked"; therefore he accepted it and all that it implied. But as a moral philosopher he had to consider and classify the practiser of magic. This he does early in the *Iḥyāʾ* (ed. Cairo 1334, i. 15, 26). Among the sciences that do not go back to the prophets some are blameworthy; and the example of the blameworthy is the twin sciences of magic, including talismans, and juggling. They are blameworthy, he explains, inasmuch as they are more hurtful than useful to men (in accordance with the wellknown Muslim utilitarianism). Against al-Ghazzālī the scholastics pointed out that, on the one hand, it was only the practice of magic for evil purposes which could be called blameworthy, and, on the other, that a knowledge of magic was essential to anyone who had to distinguish between the results of magic and the evidentiary miracles (*muʿdjizāt*) of prophets, and still more, the *karāmāt* [q.v.] of the saints (al-Baiḍāwī, ed. Fleischer, i. 76).

A noteworthy exposition is given by Fakhr al-Dīn al-Rāzī in his commentary on Sūra ii. 102 (*Mafātīḥ*, ed. Cairo 1307, i. 427 *sqq.*), in which he characterizes magic as a psychical working with physical effects. Ibn Khaldūn develops the psychical position of al-Rāzī still further and clarifies it until it practically coincides with the modern psychological doctrine of automatisms (*Muḳaddima*, ed. Quatremère, i. 191—195, and iii. 129 *sqq.*). In his view the essential force of magic lay in the *nafs* of the magician. In regard to the magical work of al-Būnī (d. 622/1225), *Shams al-maʿārif* (see *GAL*, i. 655) — still much studied today —, in which the author tried to draw up a system of licit magic, Ibn Khaldūn held that it was illicit magic, because it professed to derive its forces from natural powers and not from Allāh.

In orthodox Islām the confusion of old Arabia between the *kāhin* and the *nabī* has never died out. Thus the way was open to the continuance among orthodox Muslims of the study and even the practice of magic. Among the other means by which magic has survived among the Muslim masses was its association with saints (for which see E. Doutté, *Les Marabouts*, Paris 1900, and *Magie et Religion dans l'Afrique du Nord*, Alger 1909; E. Westermarck, *The Moorish conception of Holiness*, Helsingfors 1916; T. H. Weir, *The Shaikhs of Morocco*, Edinburgh 1904; Emily, Shareefa of Wazan, *My Life Story*, London 1911), the numerous popular stories in which unbelieving djinn and the magic and talismans of unbelieving magicians are overcome by the stronger talismans handed down from the earlier prophets, and the popular classification of philosophers as magicians, especially in the case of Ibn Sīnā (cf. Chauvin, *Bibl. Ar.*, v. 143).

Thus in Ḳurʾān and *ḥadīth*, in orthodox theology, in mystical theology of all phases stretching to pantheistic theosophy, in philosophy and natural science of all kinds from almost experimental psychology to the speculations of the pseudo-Ibn Sīnā, in primitive animistic devotion, the existence of magic as a reality, though it may be a dangerous one, has been perpetuated.

Bibliography: In addition to the work of al-Būnī (see above) many works on magic are still in circulation. See also A. Guillaume, *Prophecy and Divination* (London 1938); Bousquet, *Fiqh et sorcellerie*, in *AIEO*, viii. and the articles DJAFR, DJINN, GHŪL, ḤAMĀʾIL, HĀRŪT WA-MĀRŪT, ʿIFRĪT, KĀHIN, SHAIṬĀN.

SĪRA, the traditional biography of Muḥammad. The word seems to be used for the first time as the title of a special treatise in Ibn Hishām's work, but there is already earlier testimony to its use in the sense of biography of Muḥammad (Ibn Saʿd, *Ṭabaḳāt* ii/i; cf. also iii/ii. 152). Besides, the word *sīra* at this time had already the sense of biography in general (e.g. *Sīrat Muʿāwiya*). It seems that at first the plural form *siyar* was used by preference in connection with the biography of the Prophet, having been probably applied to the narrative of the life of Muḥammad in the style of the *siyar al-mulūk* of Middle Persian origin. This term *siyar*, in the majority of references which we possess to the early production of Arab literature relating to the biography of Muḥammad, is constantly found associated with the term *maghāzī* "military expeditions" (cf. A. Fischer, in Nöldeke-Schwally, *Gesch. des Qorans*, ii. 221).

The earliest interest in the biography of the Prophet was concerned, on one hand, with fixing the regular practice of worship and religious law according to the teaching and example of the Prophet; this motive has brought about the development of the literature of the Ḥadīth. On the other hand the early Muslims wanted to celebrate, after the fashion of pre-islamic Arabia, the warlike exploits of their chief; these narratives are simply the continuation or development of the literature of the *aiyām al-ʿArab*. The collection of these dispersed materials for a biography of the Prophet properly so called owes its origin to the transformation undergone by the personality of Muḥammad in the religious consciousness of Islām. It was above all contact with Judaism and Christianity which encouraged the development of the legend with which the person of Muḥammad has been surrounded (cf. the fundamental work of T. Andrae, *Die Person Mohammeds in Lehre und Glaube seiner Gemeinde*, Stockholm 1918, especially ch. i).

The main question, therefore, is whether this Sīra of Muḥammad, which was completed in its main lines barely a century after his death, contains still elements which are based on a tradition worthy of credence. Influence of Jewish and Christian tradition was long ago suspected by Sprenger; Nöldeke (*ZDMG*, lii. 16—22) was the first to point out, by analysing the stories of the conversion of the first believers, that very often the Sīra, far from reflecting an authentic tradition, only represents an anticipation of a state of affairs much later than the events related. It was however Goldziher's brilliant essay on the character of the narrative ḥadīth (*Muhammedanische Studien*, ii) that marked a decisive turning-point in the critical study of the Sīra (cf. also Caetani, *Annali*, i. 28—58). The analysis of Lammens in his well-known works (*Recherches de science religieuse*, 1910 No. 1; 1911 No. 1 and 2; *L'âge de Mahomet* in *JA*, 1911; *Fatima et les filles de Mahomet*, Rome 1912; *Le berceau de l'Islam*, Rome 1914) goes to prove that the whole structure of Muslim tradition regarding the life of the Prophet, at least for the phase preceding the Hidjra, is quite without foundation, each alleged historical detail being only the result of a subjective exegesis of a verse of the Ḳurʾān. The Sīra would thus be in substance only a great "Ḳurʾānic midrash". This radicalism has seemed extreme to many scholars; cf. de Goeje in *Centenario Amari*, 1910; Nöldeke in *WZKM*, 1906; the same in *Isl.* 1913; Becker in *Isl.* 1913 = *Islamstudien*, Leipzig 1924, i., 520—7; a popular account of the question is given by Levi della Vida, *Storia e religione nell 'Oriente semitico*, Rome 1924, p. 11—37. Detailed investigation has revealed however, from particular passages of the Sīra, the midrash-like method which governed its formation (cf. Schrieke in *Isl.* 1915, 1—30; Horovitz in *Isl.* 1914, p. 41—53, 1919, p. 159—83, 1922, p. 178—89; Vacca in *RSO* 1923, p. 87—209).

We are to infer that the material collected in this way became organized and systematized in the schools of the Madīna *muḥaddithūn*. Religious pragmatism also seized upon stories relating to the Madīna period and modified their character, often quite profoundly, but in this field it encountered more precise historical statements, which had already been elaborated after the custom and style of dealing with stories relating to pre-islamic military expeditions.

The first literary redactions of the Sīra have grown up from the stories as told by the *ḳuṣṣāṣ*, the professional story-tellers. A specimen of this sort of literature was the *Kitāb al-Maghāzī* of Wahb b. Munabbih (654—728). The oldest author of a book on the biography of Muḥammad, ʿUrwa b. al-Zubair (643—712) was a son of the famous companion of the Prophet. Quotations of this work are found in Ṭabarī (cf. Caetani, *Annali*, index to vol. i and ii). He also communicated to his pupils oral information guaranteed by *isnād*. The same rule was adopted by Abān b. ʿUthmān (642—723), the son of the Caliph. These earliest literary productions are given the name of *maghāzī*; this name *maghāzī* is also regularly borne by the works of the second and third generation of historians, such as ʿĀṣim b. ʿUmar b. Ḳatāda (died between 737 and 746), Ibn Shihāb al-Zuhrī (671—751) and Mūsā b. ʿUḳba (d. 758). A fragment of the *maghāzī* of Mūsā has become known by a publication of Sachau (*SBPr. Ak. W.*, 1904).

At the same period the *ʿilm al-maghāzī* was also cultivated outside of Madīna (Sulaimān b. Tarkhān in Baṣra; Maʿmar b. Rashīd in Ṣanʿāʾ), but such success as these works attained was eclipsed by that of Muḥammad b. Isḥāḳ (d. 767 or 768). Ibn Isḥāḳ was the first to place Islām and its founder in the scheme of universal history; the rise of Islām, according to him, is the continuation and conclusion of Jewish and Christian "sacred history", while Muḥammad appears at the same time as the most glorious representative of Arabism, through whom the age of Arab domination in the world is to be opened. The "Sīra of Ibn Isḥāḳ", as it lies before us in the well-known recension of Ibn Hishām, was however only a part of the complete historiographic activity of Ibn Isḥāḳ, such as it existed in the form of oral teaching put down in writing. As is generally recognized, Ibn Hishām has conserved nearly intact the original text of Ibn Isḥāḳ. As Ibn Isḥāḳ wished to compile a work of greater scope than the *maghāzī* of his predecessors, his use of the *isnād* was corrupted in such a way that the scholastic tradition of the *ʿilm al-ḥadīth* was deeply shocked by it and unanimously refused him the title of a *muḥaddith* worthy of credence. This verdict was already pronounced in the lifetime of Ibn Isḥaḳ by Anas b. Mālik; it marks the clear separation between historical and purely doctrinal *ḥadīth*, as this is found in the chapters on the *maghāzī* and *manāḳib* in the collections of Bukhārī and Muslim.

Ibn Isḥāḳ takes care to give the source, not always particularly reliable, of some of his information, especially when it goes back to Jewish or Christian informants. He does not neglect, contrary to what seems to have been the case with his predecessors, to use poetry to supplement his sources, and he introduces the narrative of the life of the Prophet with abundant genealogical and antiquarian notes. All this justifies the immense success which his work has enjoyed through the centuries, a success which has not only overshadowed similar previous works and some which closely followed him (as the *maghāzī* of Abū Maʿshar, d. 786, and of Yaḥyā b. Saʿīd b. Abān, d. 809) but made him a decisive influence on the future development of the Sīra. Ibn Isḥāḳ's biography was reproduced for the most part by al-Ṭabarī in his two great compilations, the *Taʾrīkh* and the *Tafsīr*.

Only one other writer has a position of hardly less importance than Ibn Isḥāḳ, namely Muḥammad b. ʿUmar al-Wāḳidī (797—874), whose work as a biographer of the Prophet has come down to us by three different channels: 1. by his *Kitāb al-Maghāzī* (abridged translation by Wellhausen, Berlin 1882), which was transmitted by Muḥammad b. Shudjāʿ al-Thaldjī (797—874), 2. by the Sīra which precedes the *Ṭabaḳāt* of his pupil Muḥammad b. Saʿd (d. 845), 3. by the *Ṭabaḳāt* themselves, especially in vols. iii. and iv. Al-Wāḳidī's work — though its author composed also a *Kitāb al-Taʾrīkh wa'l-mabdaʾ wa'l-maghāzī* (*Fihrist*, p. 68) assumes for the most part (in contrast to the work of Ibn Isḥāḳ) the form of a collection of detached monographs, of which the most elaborate are those devoted to the public life of Muḥammad, his expeditions, his correspondence, the embassies which he received or sent. He shows a great interest in the chronology, the systematic treatment of which, as we know, goes back to him. On the other hand, in collecting the statements of traditions regarding the companions of the Prophet, he founded the new subsidiary study of the *ʿilm al-ridjāl*, the biography and criticism of the traditionists. The Sīra in al-Balādhurī's *Ansāb al-ashrāf* goes almost entirely back to al-Wāḳidī.

After al-Wāḳidī the Sīra is not dealt with again for some centuries in works of great importance; the attention of the historians was attracted to the *dalāʾil al-nubuwwa* and to the *shamāʾil*, a branch which broke off from the Sīra to assume a development of its own. The numerous collections of biographies of the Prophet's companions — such as the *Istiʿāb* of Ibn ʿAbd al-Barr, the *Usd al-ghāba* of Ibn al-Athīr and the *Iṣāba* of Ibn Ḥadjar — contain however some deviating statements on the Sīra. Most of the material found in the commentaries to Ibn Hishām's Sīra — the best known of which is the *Rawḍ* of Suhailī (1114—85), see *GAL, Suppl.* i. 206 — consists only of legends of late origin or gives simply variants of stories already known. Among the many later compilations of the Sīra it is sufficient to name the following: *ʿUyūn al-āthār*, by Ibn Saiyid al-Nās (1273—1334; *GAL.* ii. 85); *al-Mawāhib al-laduniya* by al-Ḳasṭallānī (1448—1517; *GAL*, ii. 87) *al-Sīra al-Shaʾmīya* by Shams al-Dīn al-Shaʾmī (died 1536; *GAL*, ii. 392); *al-Sīra al-Ḥalabīya* by Nūr al-Dīn al-Ḥalabī (1567—1635; *GAL*, ii. 395); and the commentaries to the two first-named works: *Nūr al-nibrās* by Sibṭ ibn al-ʿAdjamī (died 1438) and *Sharḥ al-Mawāhib* by al-Zarḳānī (died 1710).

Bibliography: Ḥādjdjī Khalīfa, ed. Flügel, iii. 634—6; Wüstenfeld, *Die arabischen Geschichts-*

schreiber (*Abh. Gött. Ges.*, xviii—xix. 1882) passim; Sprenger, *Das Leben und die Lehre des Muhammed*, Berlin 1869, iii; Caetani, *Annali dell 'Islam* (Milan 1905); Nöldeke-Schwally, *Geschichte des Qorans*, Leipzig 1919, ii. 129—144; Ibn Saᶜd, *Ṭabaḳāt*, ed. Sachau, ii/i Introduction, iii/ii Intr.; Buhl, *Das Leben Muhammeds*, Berlin 1930, p. 366 *sq.*; Nallino, *Il prof. Gabrieli e una inedita dissertazione di laurea intorno ad una fonte arabica del la biografia di Maometto.* Rome 1918; G. Gabrieli, *Ancora intorno alla primitiva biografia di Maometto*, Rome 1919; J. Fück, *Muḥammad ibn Isḥāḳ, Literarhistorische Untersuchungen*, Frankfurt a/M. 1925.

SUBḤA (A.), also pronounced *sebḥa* (in Turkish *tesbīḥ*) the rosary, which at present is used by nearly all classes of Muslims, except the Wahhābīs who disapprove of it as a *bidᶜa*. There is evidence for its having been used at first in Ṣūfī circles and among the lower classes (Goldziher, *Le Rosaire dans l'Islam*, in *RHR*, xxi. p. 296); opposition against it made itself heard as late as the xvth century A.D., when Suyūṭī composed an apology for it (Goldziher, *Vorlesungen über den Islam*, 1st ed., p. 165). At present it is usually carried by the pilgrims (cf. Mez, *Die Renaissance des Islâms*, p. 441) and the darwīshes.

The rosary consists of three groups of beads made of wood, bone, mother of pearl, etc. The groups are separated by two transversal beads of a larger size (*imām*), while a much larger piece serves as a kind of handle (*yad*; Snouck Hurgronje, *Verspr. Geschr.* iii. 135). The number of beads within each group varies (e.g. 33 + 33 + 34 or 33 + 33 + 31); in the latter case the *imāms* and the *yad* are reckoned as beads. The sum total of a hundred is in accordance with the number of Allāh and his 99 beautiful names. The rosary serves for the enumeration of these names; but it is also used for the counting of eulogies, *dhikr*'s and the formulae at the end of the *ṣalāt*. Lane (*Manners and Customs*, Register) makes mention of a *sebḥa* consisting of a thousand beads used in funeral ceremonies for the thrice one thousand repetitions of the formula *Lā ilāha illa 'llāh.*

Masābiḥ (plur. of *misbaḥa*) are mentioned as early as the 8th century A.D. (cf. A. Mez, *Die Renaissance des Islâms*, p. 318). Goldziher (*Vorlesungen*, p. 165) thinks it certain that the rosary came from India to Western Asia. Still, Goldziher himself has pointed to traditions mentioning the use of small stones, date-kernels, etc. for counting eulogies such as *takbīr, tahlīl, tasbīḥ.*

From such traditions the following may be mentioned: "on the authority of Saᶜd b. Abī Waḳḳāṣ ... that he accompanied the Apostle of Allāh who went to visit a woman, who counted her eulogies by means of kernels or small stones lying before her. He said to her: Shall I tell you what is easier and more profitable? "Glory to Allāh" according to the number of what he has created in the earth; "glory to Allāh" according to what he has created in the heaven; "glory to Allāh" according to the number of what is between these; "glory to Allāh" according to what he will create. And in the same way *Allāh akbar, al-ḥamdu lillāhi* and "there is no might nor power except in Allāh" (Abū Daʾūd, *Witr*, bāb 24; Tirmidhī, *Daᶜawāt*, bāb 113).

The tendency of this tradition is elucidated by the following one: Ṣafīya said: the Apostle of Allāh entered while there were before me four thousand kernels which I used in reciting praises. I said: I use them in reciting praises. He answered: I will teach thee a still larger number. Say: "Glory to Allāh" according to the number of what he has created (Tirmidhī, *Daᶜawāt*, bāb 103).

To a different practice points the tradition according to which the Apostle of Allāh "counted the *tasbīḥ*" (Nasāʾī, *Sahw*, bāb 97). The verb used here is *ᶜaḳada*; its being translated by "to count" is based upon the fact that the lexicons give it among others this meaning. Probably this is based in its turn upon traditions like the one just mentioned, and like the following: "The Apostle of Allāh said to us (the women of al-Madīna): Practise *tasbīḥ, tahlīl* and *taḳdīs*, and count these praises on your fingers, for these will have to give account" (Abū Dāʾūd, *Witr*, bāb 24; Tirmidhī, *Daᶜawāt*, bāb 120). According to Goldziher, in these traditions the counting of praises on the fingers is contrasted with their being counted by means of stones etc. There, is however, a tradition that makes it a matter of doubt whether *ᶜaḳada* in connections like those mentioned has always the meaning of counting and not its proper sense of tying. This is a tradition preserved by Ibn Saᶜd (viii. 348) according to which Fāṭima bint Ḥusain used to say praises aided by threads in which she made knots (*bi-khuyūṭ maᶜḳūd fīhā*).

The term *subḥa* does not occur in classical tradition in the meaning of rosary; it is often used in the sense of supererogatory *ṣalāt*, e.g. *subḥat al-ḍuḥā* (Muslim, *Musāfirūn*, trad. 81). Al-Nawawī explains the term by *nāfila* (Commentary on Muslim's *Ṣaḥīḥ*, Cairo 1283, ii. 204). Ibn al-Athīr, *Nihāya*, s.v. asks how it is that the ideas of *nāfila* and *subḥa* coincide. He answers: Praises (*subḥa*) are supererogatory additions to the obligatory *ṣalāt*'s. So supererogatory *ṣalāt*'s came to be called *subḥa*.

If Ibn al-Athīr's opinion is right, the semasiological evolution of *subḥa* took two directions:

praises
- supererogatory praises in *ṣalāt* → supererogatory *ṣalāt*
- counted praises → instrument used for counting praises

SUDJŪD. [See ṢALĀT, ii).

ṢŪFĪ. [See TAṢAWWUF].

AL-**ṢUFRĪYA.** [See AL-IBĀḌĪYA; KHĀRIDJITES].

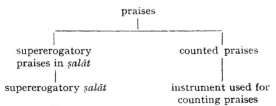

SULAIMĀN B. DĀWŪD, the biblical King Solomon, is an outstanding personality in Muhammadan legends. There were, as the Arab histories recount, four great world-rulers, two of whom were infidels, Nimrod and Nebuchadnezzar; and two of whom were believers, Alexander the Great and Solomon. Of these the last was the most resplendent figure. Special emphasis was placed on his wonderful powers of magic and divination. The most puzzling riddles and the most abstruse subjects were within his ken. Perspicacity and discernment dwelt in his eyes; wisdom and justice were graven on his forehead. His knowledge was deeper than the Jordan Valley. In the Ḳurʾān itself he is frequently mentioned, and along with Alexander enjoys the distinction of being designated a true Apostle of Allāh, a divine messenger and prototype of Muḥammad. The Ḳurʾānic passages tell how at an early age he even surpassed his father David in skilful administration of justice (xxi. 78, 79). And when David died Solomon was chosen from amongst the other sons as successor (xxvii. 16). He had admirable endowments. God had granted him esoteric knowledge. He was acquainted with the speech of birds and animals (xxvii. 16, 19), a tradition based on I Kings iv. 33. A strong wind was subjected to him (xxi. 81; xxxviii. 37). It blew in the morning for a month, and in the evening for a month, while a fountain of molten brass was made to flow for his benefit (xxxiv. 13). At his command were legions of satans to do whatever he wished. They were employed, for example, in diving for pearls (xxi. 82; xxxviii. 37). The *dj̲inn* were forced to work his will. If they disobeyed they were threatened with the pains of hell (xxxiv. 12). They constructed for him shrines and statues and costly vessels (*ibid.*, 13). His armies were recruited from men and *dj̲inn* and birds. The hoopoe (*hudhud*) was the first to bring him tidings of the kingdom of Saba and of its illustrious queen, Bilḳīs [q.v.]. Solomon, as a prophet, corresponded with her and summoned her to Islām. And after an exhibition of his strength and wisdom, she submitted (xxvii. 20—44). The devils frequently sought to convict him of infidelity, but in vain (ii. 101). On a certain occasion he failed in the observance of his religious duties, and that was when his admiration for his stud of horses led him to forget his prayers. In atonement he sacrificed them, cutting their legs and necks (xxxviii. 30—33). For a time he seems to have lapsed into idolatry. As a punishment he lost his kingdom, his throne being occupied by some one in his own likeness. When he had asked forgiveness, he was restored to his place, and promised divine favour in Paradise (xxxviii. 34, 35, 40). When he died he was resting on his staff, and no one knew of his death until a worm bored its way through the prop and the body collapsed. Then the *dj̲inn* were released from their labours (xxxiv. 14).

Later legendary lore has magnified all this material, which is chiefly Rabbinic in origin. Solomon's control over the *dj̲inn* and his use of them in his building operations are derived from the *Midras̲h̲* on Ecclesiastes, ii. 8. His kingdom is even made universal, perhaps after the analogy of that of the 40 (or 72) kings of the Pre-Adamite *dj̲inn*, who were each named Solomon (Lane, *Arabian Nights*, Introd., note 21; d'Herbelot, *Bibliothèque Orientale*, v. 372). His renowned wisdom included "the wisdom" for which Egypt was famous, i.e. occult science. Pythagoras is said to have received his knowledge from Solomon in Egypt (Suyūṭī, *Ḥusn al-muḥāḍara fī akh̲bār Miṣr*, i. 27). Solomon is said to have been the pupil of Mambres the Egyptian Theurgist (G. R. S. Mead, *Thrice-Greatest Hermes*, iii. 283, note). Hence his reputation in tales as a magician. This magic power of his was effected by means of a talismanic ring engraved with "the most great name" of God. Permission to use this was also vouchsafed to his wazīr, Āsaf b. Bark̲h̲īya, who transported the throne of Bilḳīs from S̲h̲eba to Jerusalem in the twinkling of an eye. Solomon was in the habit, when he performed his ablutions, of laying aside this ring from his finger, and entrusting it to one of his wives, Amīna. Ṣak̲h̲r, one of the Satanic spirits, assumed the form of the king, purloined the magic seal, and for forty days ruled, while Solomon was forced to wander as an outcast. The demon, however, lost the ring in the sea, whence Solomon recovered it when he cut open a fish which had swallowed it. Thus he regained his throne. It is said he was punished in this way because of the idolatry of the royal consort, D̲j̲arāda, the daughter of the king of the Sidonians. Some say the counterfeit body that occupied his throne was his son who died. The 13th of the month is regarded as unlucky because on that day Solomon was exiled by God. The Persian *Nawrōz* festival and its customs are said to date from the restoration of Solomon to his kingdom (al-Bīrūnī, *Chronology*, ed. Sachau, p. 199). Because he boasted that 1,000 wives would bear him 1,000 warrior sons, he had one son only who was misshapen, with one hand, one eye, one ear, and one foot. Then in humility he prayed to God, and his son was made whole. In his capacity of warrior, he conquered many kingdoms (Baiḍāwī, v. 19).

Some of the marvellous works of Solomon may be briefly mentioned. Shortly after his accession he was in a valley between Hebron and Jerusalem, when he received his authority over winds, water, demons and animals from the four guardian angels in charge of these spheres. Each one gave him a jewel which he placed in a ring composed partly of brass and iron. With the brass he sealed his orders for the good *dj̲inn*, while with the iron he sealed his orders for the evil *dj̲inn*. The seal is said to have held a mandrake (Frazer, *Folk-Lore in the Old Testament*, ii. 390). Solomon's seal (*K̲h̲atam Sulaimān*) is a common charm, in the form of a six-pointed star, often inscribed on drinking cups as well as occasionally on Muḥammadan coins from early Umaiyad times. The Table of Solomon (*Mā'idat Sulaimān*) and other marvellous relics, according to legend, found their way to Spain where they were discovered by Ṭāriḳ at the capture of Toledo. They had been taken from Jerusalem as booty (Ibn al-At̲h̲īr, *Annales du Maghreb*, ed. Fagnan, p. 37 *sqq.*; Ṭabarī, *Chronique*, ed. Zotenberg, iv. 183; Dozy, *Recherches* [3], i. 52). The Table was made of green beryl, had 360 legs, and was inlaid with pearls and rubies. There was also a magic mirror which revealed all places in the world (Carra de Vaux, *Abrégé des Merveilles*, p. 122).

The blocks of stone for the building of the Temple were hewn by means of the miraculous pebble Samur (*S̲h̲amir*) which the demon Ṣak̲h̲r procured from the sea-eagle. Solomon sheltered himself from the heat of the sun under a canopy composed of all the birds of the air. A magic carpet of green silk for aerial transportation was woven for him. On this he could leave Syria with all his equipment in the morning, and reach Afghanistan by evening. Untold wealth of precious stones and gold and silver was accumulated with the help of the servile dj̲inn. They also assisted him in erecting palaces, fortresses, baths and reservoirs. Various relics of these operations are pointed out in Palestine, Arabia and elsewhere (see *Revue des traditions populaires*, ix. 190; Nāṣir-i K̲h̲osraw, *Sefer-Nāma*, p. 56, 76, 84, 85). He had 1,000 glass-roofed houses containing 300 couches and 700 wives (T̲h̲aʿlabī, *Ḳiṣaṣ*, p. 204). Besides the building of the Temple, during which he outwitted the dj̲inn, the Masdj̲id al-Aḳṣā is likewise claimed as his work (Mirk̲h̲ond, *Rawḍat al-ṣafā*, ii./i. 76). He is even credited with founding a mosque in Alexandria (Suyūṭī, *op. cit.*, i. 37). Part of his leisure time was spent in acquiring the art of basket-weaving, that he might have some means of earning a livelihood if the need arose (Mirk̲h̲ond, *op. cit.*, p. 79). The tradition seems Rabbinic in character. His throne was constructed of pure gold. The whole natural world was so completely under his sway that on one occasion the sun stood still to enable him to say his evening prayers. The evil dj̲inn he imprisoned in vessels of lead (cf. *Zechariah*, v. 8). ʿAid̲h̲āb, on the Red Sea, was assigned by him as a place of incarceration for the demons (Nāṣir-i K̲h̲osraw, *op. cit.*, p. 297). His knowledge of the speech of the animal world enabled him at times to display his clemency. Once he turned aside his armed hosts in order to avoid smashing the eggs of a bird; while on another occasion, he had compassion on a colony of ants (Bīrūnī, *op. cit.*, p. 199; Sūra xxvii. 17, 18).

A claim is put forward that he invented the Arabic and Syriac scripts, and that he was the author of many Arabic treatises on magic. He is compared with Djamshīd, and there were, undoubtedly, Iranian influences at work in the Solomon Saga. His personal appearance is variously given, e.g. as "a large-headed man riding on a horse" (Mirkhond, *op. cit.*, ii./i. 83), and as being "fair, well-built, of lustrous beauty, with a plentiful supply of hair, and clothed in white garments" (Thaʿlabī, *op. cit.*, p. 254). When he died he was aged 53, having reigned for forty years. The exact location of his tomb is uncertain. Some place it in Jerusalem, in the Ḳubbat al-Ṣakhra, others near the Sea of Tiberias. The Prophet said (according to Ṭabarī, *Chronique*, i. 60) it was "in the midst of the sea ... in a palace excavated in a rock. This palace contains a throne on which Solomon is placed with the royal ring on his finger appearing as though he were alive, protected by twelve guardians, night and day. No one hath arrived at his tomb except two persons, Affān and Bulukiya" (Lane, *op. cit.*, xx. 96; see Mirkhond, *op. cit.*, p. 102—103). The tomb is placed also in the Andaman Islands (*Les Merveilles de l'Inde*, p. 134). Solomon has found his way into Malayan folklore. Fowlers use his name for snaring pigeons (Frazer, *Golden Bough*, iii. 418; *Folk-Lore in the O.T.*, ii. 476 *sq.*). Regarding Solomon and the Evil Eye, see W. B. Stevenson in *Studia Semitica et Orientalia*, Glasgow 1920, p. 104 *sq.* and the references therein. The Ethiopic Legends of Solomon and Mākedā, Queen of ʿAzēb, may be found in Bezold, *Kebra Negast*, and in Wallis Budge, *The Queen of Sheba and her only Son Menyelik* (see art. BILKĪS). Examples of the Solomonic riddles may be seen in Thaʿlabī, *op. cit.*, p. 202; Jacques de Vitry, *PPTS*, p. 17.

Bibliography: besides the works mentioned in the text, consult the Ḳurʾān commentaries; a great many Solomonic legends are contained in Thaʿlabī, *Ḳiṣaṣ al-anbiyāʾ*, p. 200 *sqq.*; see also Ṭabarī, ed. de Goeje, index; *Chronique*, ed. Zotenberg, index; Idrīsī, *Description de l'Afrique*, p. 140, 173, 188; Masʿūdī, *Murūdj* i. 110 *sqq.*; Dīnawarī, *Kitāb al-akhbār al-ṭiwāl*, ed. Guirgass p. 9, 14, 22—26, 29, 43; Damīrī, *Ḥayāt al-ḥayawān*, trans. Jayakar, i. p. 106, 494—6, 746—9; al-Ḥamdānī, *Ṣifa*, ed. Müller, p. 141; Abu 'l-Fidāʾ, *Taʾrīkh*, p. 25, 67; Weil, *Biblische Legenden der Musulmänner*, p. 247 *sqq.*; Grünbaum, *Neue Beiträge zur semitischen Sagenkunde*, p. 189 *sqq.*; Salzberger, *Die Salomo-Sage in der semit. Lit.*; do. *Salomos Tempelbau und Thron in der semit. Sagenliteratur*; R. Färber, *König Salomon in der Tradition*; A. Geiger, *Was hat Mohammed aus dem Judenthume aufgenommen*? Bonn, 1833, p. 184—189; W. A. Clouston, *Flowers from a Persian Garden*, p. 125 *sqq.*; Baring-Gould, *Myths of the Middle Ages*, index; Hanauer, *Folklore of the Holy Land*; Wallis Budge, *Alexander the Great*, index; Seymour, *Tales of Solomon*; J. C. Mardrus, *The Queen of Sheba*; John Freeman, *Salomon and Balkis*; De Vogüé, *Le Temple de Jerusalem*, p. 13; R. Basset, *Mille et Un Contes, Récits et Légendes Arabes*, i. 356; do., *Contes populaires berbères*, p. 27; J. Horovitz, *Koranische Untersuchungen*, p. 82, 102, 116—118, 167; A. J. Wensinck, *Handbook*, p. 222; Speyer, *Die biblischen Erzählungen im Qoran*, p. 372 *sqq.*; J. Walker, *Bible Characters in the Koran*, p. 123—129; F. Lexa, *La Magie dans l'Egypte antique*; D. G. Marta, *Les Tombeaux de David et de Salomon d'après les auteurs arabes*, in al-Mashriḳ 1909, pp. 897—906; G. Le Strange, *Lands of the Eastern Caliphate*, p. 68; *Numismatic Chronicle*, 1933 p. 263; C. C. Torrey, *Jewish Foundation of Islam*, p. 49, 70, 113—115; D. Sidersky, *Les Origines des Légendes Musulmanes*, p. 112—126; M. Asín Palacios, *Abenmasarra y su Escuela*, Madrid 1914, p. 42; T. Canaan, *Mohammedan Saints and Sanctuaries in Palestine*, p. 37—38, 52, 81.

AL-**SULAMĪ**, ABŪ ʿABD AL-RAḤMĀN MUḤAMMED B. AL-ḤUSAIN B. MŪSĀ AL-AZDĪ AL-NĪSĀBŪRĪ, author of several important works on Ṣūfism, was born in 330/941, studied under his maternal grandfather Ibn Nudjaid (d. 366/976), and received the cloak of initiation from Abu 'l-Ḳāsim al-Naṣrābādhī: he died in Shaʿbān 412/November 1021. His *nisba* al-Sulamī has been derived by M. Hartmann (who writes al-Sullamī) from *sullam* = κλῖμαξ (sc. scala perfectionis): this derivation is, however, not generally admitted, and al-Samʿānī's statement (*Kitāb al-Ansāb*, fol. 303*a*), that the name refers to the great Arabian tribe of Sulaim [b. Manṣūr], is quite feasible. For a list of his extant works — Ibn al-ʿImād, *Shadharāt al-dhahab*, iii. 196, states that his total output amounted to 100 volumes — see Brockelmann, *GAL*, i. 218, *Suppl.* 361. Of his voluminous commentary on the Ḳurʾān (*Ḥaḳāʾiḳ al-tafsīr*), a work of the greatest importance for the study of Ṣūfī exegesis — which Ibn Nāṣir al-Dīn, in Ibn al-ʿImād, iii. 197, describes as containing "great nonsense" — selections, relating to al-Ḥallādj, have been published by L. Massignon, *Essai sur les origines*, appendix, p. 23—76. His greatest work on the history of Ṣūfism is the *Ṭabaḳāt al-Ṣūfiyīn* (the first pages published by J. Pedersen, Paris 1938); this book was the foundation of Anṣārī's Persian *Ṭabaḳāt*, for which see W. Ivanow, *Catalogue of the Persian Manuscripts in the Collection of the Asiatic Society of Bengal*, p. 78—83; *JRAS*, 1923, p. 1—34, 337—382; Anṣārī's *Ṭabaḳāt* in its turn formed the basis of Djāmī's *Nafaḥāt al-uns*. The monograph on the Malāmatīs (*Uṣūl al-Malāmatīya*) has been fully analysed by R. Hartmann, in *Isl.*, viii. 157—204: the Cairo manuscript of this tract contains an appendix, which is a mere plagiarism of al-Sarrādj; see *JRAS*, 1937, p. 461—5. A popular handbook of spiritual discipline is his *ʿUyūb al-nafs*, on the sins of the soul, on which a metrical paraphrase was written by Ibn Zarrūḳ (d. 899/1493), and a commentary by al-Kharrūbī (d. 963/1556). There can be no doubt that al-Sulamī, as initiate and hagiographer, is a most important figure in the history of Ṣūfism, and he has not yet received the attention which he deserves.

SULŪK (A., "journeying") is a term used by Ṣūfīs to describe the mystic's progress in the Way to God, beginning with his entrance into the *ṭarīḳa* (Way) under the direction of a Shaikh and ending with his attainment of the highest spiritual degree within his capacity. *Sulūk* implies a quest deliberately undertaken, methodically pursued; he who prosecutes it (*sālik*) must pass through, and make himself perfect in, each of the "stages" or "stations" (*maḳāmāt*) — *dhikr*, trust in God, poverty, love, knowledge and so on — before he can become united with God (*wāṣil*). Hence *sulūk* is contrasted with *djadhba*.

Bibliography: Djāmī, *Nafaḥāt al-uns*, Calcutta 1859, p. 7 *sq.*; R. A. Nicholson, *The Mystics of Islam*, p. 28 *sq.*; E. H. Palmer, *Oriental Mysticism*, p. 65 *sq.*

SUNNA (A.), custom, use and wont, statute. The word is used in many connections. Here only the following will be dealt with. In the Ḳur'ān sunna usually occurs in two connections: *sunnat al-awwalīn*, "the sunna of those of old" (viii. 38; xv. 13; xviii. 55; xxxv. 43) and *sunnat Allāh*, "the sunna of Allāh" (xvii. 77; xxxiii. 62; xxxv.43; xlviii. 23). The two expressions are synonymous in so far as they refer to Allāh's punishment of earlier generations, who met the preaching of prophets sent to them with unbelief or scorn. The expressions are therefore found mainly in the Meccan sūras of which the main subjects are stories of the prophets. In Sūra iii. 137, the plural *sunan* occurs meaning judgments. *Sunnat Allāh* is found in Sūra xxxiii. 38, where it means the privileges which Allāh granted to earlier prophets.

In Ḥadīth by sunna is usually understood Muḥammad's sunna; Allāh is connected with the community by his Book and Muḥammad by his sunna (cf. Muslim, *Īmān*, trad. 246: "Allāh's book and your Prophet's sunna").

According to the usual explanation Muḥammad's sunna comprises his deeds, utterances and his unspoken approval (*fiʿl*, *ḳawl*, *taḳrīr*). Observance of the sunna might in a way be called: "Imitatio Muhammadis".

In itself however the word is colourless. One speaks of good and bad sunna's, e.g. of the bad sunna of the *djāhilīya* (Bukhārī, *Diyāt*, bāb 9). Muḥammad prophesies: "Verily ye shall imitate the sunan of those who were before you, inch for inch, ell for ell, span for span; if they were to crawl into a lizard's hole, you would follow after them" (Aḥmad b. Ḥanbal, *Musnad*, ii. 327).

The contrast between good and bad sunnas finds its classical expression in the following ḥadīth: "He who institutes a fair sunna in Islām, so that it is practised after his death, to him a reward shall be given equal to that of all who have practised it, without anything being deducted from their reward. But he who institutes a bad sunna in Islām, so that it is practised after his death, against him a sin shall be debited, like that of all who have practised it without anything being subtracted from their sins" (Muslim, *ʿIlm*, trad. 15).

Al-Sunna has however become the characteristic term for the theory and practice of the catholic Muḥammadan community. *Ahl al-sunna wa 'l-djamāʿa*, "The people of the sunna and of the community", are those who refrain from deviating from dogma and practice. The expression is particularly used in this sense in opposition to Shīʿa [q.v.]. Great stress is therefore put upon following Muḥammad's sunna. "He who tires of my sunna, does not belong to me" (Bukhārī, *Nikāḥ*, bāb 1). "The prescribed *ṣalāt*, Friday and Ramaḍān are an atonement for the period till the next *ṣalāt*, the next Friday and the nest Ramaḍān, except in the case of polytheism, breach of agreement and neglect of the sunna..., and neglect of the sunna is secession from the community" (*djamāʿa*; Aḥmad b. Ḥanbal, ii. 229). Among the six categories of those who are cursed by Allāh, Muḥammad and all the prophets are those who have abandoned Muḥammad's sunna (Tirmidhī, *Ḳadar*, bāb 17). Knowledge of the sunna is one of the criteria in deciding who will act as imām at the ṣalāt (Tirmidhī, *Ṣalāt*, bāb 60; Nasā'ī, *Imāma*, bāb 3).

The companions are the propagators of the sunna (Muslim, *Īmān*, trad. 80); the word is occasionally referred to the example of the companions and the oldest generations of Islām; in Bukhārī, *Aḥkām*, bāb 43, the sunna of Allāh, his Prophet and the two khalīfas is mentioned; in Tirmidhī, *ʿIlm*, bāb 16, there is a reference to the sunna of Muḥammad and the rightly guided caliphs.

The word thus acquires the meaning of standard; it is recorded that Muḥammad said when drawing up such prescriptions: "at discretion lest any sunna (burdensome to the community) arise" (Bukhārī, *Tahadjdjud*, bāb 35).

The opposite of sunna in the sense of the theory or practice consecrated by Muḥammad's example or the tradition of the community is *bidʿa* [q.v.] (cf. e.g. Tirmidhī, *ʿIlm*, bāb 16).

Muḥammad's sunna in the sense of his words, actions and silent approval is fixed orally and in writing in the Ḥadīth [q.v.]. In theory the conceptions of sunna and ḥadīth are separate but in practice they often coincide, which may be due to the fact that some of the collections of ḥadīth have the title *Sunan* (e.g. the collections of Abū Dā'ūd, Ibn Mādja and al-Nasā'ī).

If we are to understand the theoretical and practical significance of the sunna in Islām we must remember that while the Ḳur'ān was a source from which a considerable part of the practice was deduced, on the other hand Muḥammad had settled many questions, not by revelation but by decision from case to case and that the words and deeds of the Prophet even in his lifetime were recognized as a "fine example" and as a result of this recognition the sunna of the Prophet was drawn up and fixed in writing, although not in a form equally canonical with the Ḳur'ān. The Ḥadīth itself illuminates this side of Muḥammad's sunna in traditions: People came to the Prophet and asked him: "Send us men to teach us the Ḳur'ān and Sunna" (Muslim, *Imāra*, trad. 147). "The faith has settled in the depths of the hearts of men. They have thus learned Ḳur'ān and Sunna" (Bukhārī, *Riḳāḳ*, bāb 35). ʿUmar b. al-Khaṭṭāb said: "People will come to dispute with you over doubtful points in the Ḳur'ān. Answer them with the sunan, for the people of the Sunan are best able to decide about the Ḳur'ān" (Dārimī, *Muḳaddima*, bāb 16).

In the Ḳur'ān itself references to the importance of Muḥammad's sunna are found, like the command to believe in Allāh and Muḥammad (Sūra vii. 158; lxiv. 8) and Ibrāhīm's prayer, when he founded the temple at Mecca: "O Lord send to them a prophet from their midst, to read out to them thy verses and to teach them the book and wisdom and to purify them" (Sūra ii. 129 and similar passages).

It is clear then that in the system of Islām the Sunna became a standard of conduct alongside of the Ḳur'ān, and that the representatives of the system also sought to answer the question of the mutual relation of the two elements. This question is also discussed in traditions. At first Ḳur'ān and Sunna appear as of equal authority. Khālid b. Usaid said to ʿAbd Allāh b. ʿUmar: "We find the *ṣalāt al-ḥaḍar* and the *ṣalāt al-khawf* in the Ḳur'ān but not however the *ṣalāt al-safar*". Ibn ʿUmar answered: "My cousin, Allāh sent us Muḥammad when we were in complete ignorance; therefore we do as we saw Muḥammad do" (Aḥmad b. Ḥanbal, ii. 94). Another tradition is still more definite: "a prohibition by the Prophet of Allāh is equal to a prohibition by Allāh" (Dārimī, *Muḳaddima*, bāb 48). Ranking the Sunna equal to the Ḳur'ān led to the idea that the Sunna also was revealed: "Djibrīl used to come down with the Sunna to Muḥammad just as he used to come down with the Ḳur'ān" (Dārimī, *Muḳaddima*, bāb 48). They even went further and said: "the highest standard is not the Ḳur'ān but the Sunna" (l.c.: *al-sunna ḳāḍiya ʿala 'l-Ḳur'ān, wa-laisa 'l-Ḳur'ān bi-ḳāḍin ʿala 'l-sunna*).

The question of the relation between Ḳur'ān and Sunna is fully discussed in the Uṣūl books. Shāfiʿī in his *Risāla* explains that there are prescriptions in the Ḳur'ān, the general form of which was only made precise in the Sunna (p. 12), e.g. the punishment of the thief prescribed in the Ḳur'ān (Sūra v. 38) by the tradition that the punishment is not to be applied when it is a question of the theft of an insignificant amount (see e.g. Bukhārī, *Ḥudūd*, bāb 13). It is known that Muḥammad punished *zinā'* of a *thaiyib* with stoning (cf. e.g. Bukhārī, *Djanā'iz*, bāb 61), while Sūra xxiv. 2 prescribes 100 lashes as the punishment for the *zānī* and the *zāniya*.

The Sunna's relation to the Ḳur'ān may be of three kinds: (1) in entire agreement with the Ḳur'ān; (2) an explanation of the sacred text; (3) not directly connected with the sacred text (*Risāla*, p. 16). — The last named is however not recognized by those who always give the Sunna a direct connection with the sacred text.

The relation between Ḳur'ān and Sunna is illustrated by the doctrine of *nāsikh wa-mansūkh*, "the abrogating and the abrogated", and by other examples relating to Ḳur'ānic commands and prohibitions. Here we shall only point out that al-Shāfiʿī in contrast to other scholars does not agree that the Ḳur'ān can be abrogated by Sunna. In his view, Ḳur'ān can only be abrogated by Ḳur'ān and Sunna by Sunna (p. 16 *sq.*). But there are verses of the Ḳur'ān the abrogating character of which is only made clear by Sunna (p. 18—21) or by Sunna and *Idjmāʿ* (p. 21 *sq.*).

The *uṣūl al-fiḳh* are of course not confined to Ḳur'ān and Sunna; nevertheless in wide circles protests were made against any attempt to add to the two historical objective norms such subjective elements as *idjmāʿ* [q.v.] or *ḳiyās* [q.v.]. In Ḥadīth we find traces of this opposition: "When Ibn Masʿūd and Ḥudhaifa one day were together, a man propounded a question to them. Then Ibn Masʿūd said to Ḥudhaifa: Why do you think that people ask us about these things? He replied: As soon as they are told they neglect it. Then Ibn Masʿūd said to the questioner: If you ask us about a Ḳur'ānic matter, which we know, we will give you information, likewise about a sunna of Muḥammad, but we have no advice to give about your innovations" (Dārimī, *Muḳaddima*, bāb 16). Bukhārī has significantly given a chapter of his *Ṣaḥīḥ* the title: "On the observance of Ḳur'ān and Sunna".

This attitude is however abandoned by the four *madhāhib*; *idjmāʿ* and *ḳiyās* have obtained their place among the *uṣūl al-fiḳh*. The four roots were never recognized by the Khāridjīs and Wahhābīs, in addition to the Shīʿa.

With the term Sunna in the theory of the Uṣūl must not be confused the second of the five categories, under which actions are considered from the legal point of view and which is also called Sunna. On this see the article SHARĪʿA.

In common parlance of many Islamic peoples — e.g. among the Turks and in Indonesia — *sunna* means also "circumcision"; see the art. KHITĀN.

Bibliography: Th. W. Juynboll, *Handleiding tot de kennis van de mohammedaansche wet*, Leiden 1925, p. 34 *sqq.*; I. Goldziher, *Hadîth und Sunna*, in *Muh. Studien*, ii. 1—27; C. Snouck Hurgronje, *Verspreide Geschriften*, i. 249; ii. 36 *sqq.*, 72 *sq.*; Mawlawī Muḥ. Aʿlā b. ʿAlī, *Dictionary of Techn. Terms*, p. 703 *sqq.*; A. J. Wensinck, *Handbook of Early Muhammadan Tradition*, Leiden 1927, s.v.; Ibn al-Subkī, *Djamʿ al-djawāmiʿ* with the commentary of Banānī, Cairo 1318, ii. 58—109; Mullā Khusraw, *Mir'āt al-uṣūl*, p. 182—226; Ibn Amīr al-Ḥadjdj, *al-Taḳrīr wa 'l-taḥbīr fī sharḥ Kitāb Taḥrīr Ibn Hammām*, Būlāḳ 1316, ii. 223 *sqq.*; on the margin of this work: Baiḍāwī, *Minhādj al-uṣūl*, ii. 23 *sqq.*

SŪRA, the name given to the chapters of the Ḳur'ān. In the Ḳur'ān itself, the word means, in the Meccan as well as the Madinese parts, the separate revelations which were revealed to Muḥammad from time to time. Thus he challenges his opponents to produce a sūra like his own (ii. 23; x. 38) or to bring ten sūras like his of their own devising (xi. 13). As a superscription we have in xxiv. 1: "(this is) a sūra which we have sent down and sanctioned and in it we have revealed clear signs (*āyāt*)". The Munāfiḳūn, we are told (ix. 64), fear that a sūra may be sent down that will tell them what is in their hearts; cf. ix. 86: "when a sūra was sent down which commanded them to believe and to fight etc.". In ix. 124, 127; xlvii. 20, mention is made of the different effects of a sūra upon believers and unbelievers. As far as contents are concerned the word thus coincided with the word "Ḳur'ān" in its original meaning, but in later usage they became separated; Ḳur'ān became the name of the collected revelations in book form while sūra was used of the chapters of the sacred book, which consisted originally each of a single revelation but later were formed of the combination of several revelations or fragments.

Where Muḥammad took the word from is still uncertain in spite of the attempts made to trace its origin. Nöldeke thinks it is the modern Hebrew *shūrā* "order, series" but even if this could be explained as "line" it would not take us to the original meaning of the word, and against it is the fact that one sūra, according to xxiv. 1, contained several *āyāt*. Perhaps the word is in some way connected with Muḥammad's conception of a book in heaven (*al-Kitāb*), the contents of which were revealed to him piecemeal. "Piece, section" or a similar meaning would make good enough sense and would also explain the later usage, but linguistically it cannot be proved, for H. Hirschfeld's supposition that it is a corruption of the Hebrew *seder* is not at all probable. *Sāra*, to mount, fall upon, overcome (e.g. with wine) might possibly yield a meaning like *impetus*, sudden overwhelming inspiration etc., but *sawra* and not *sūra* is the derivative found from it.

The authorized Ḳur'ān contains 114 sūras of which the first (*al-Fātiḥa*, q.v.) and the two last conjurations are loosely connected as introduction and conclusion to the rest. This agrees with the fact that these three sūras are said to have been lacking in the Ḳur'ān as edited by Ibn Masʿūd. There was a certain amount of freedom at first in this respect so that Ubaiy for example had two sūras in addition to those usually accepted. The order of the sūras also was not definitely fixed, although the same principle of arrangement may be recognized in the different editions. The reader may be referred to the article KUR'ĀN on this point, as well as on the names of the sūras, their separation in the manuscripts and the letters which are found in the superscriptions to some of them.

Bibliography: Nöldeke, *Geschichte des Qorans*, second edition by Schwally, i. 30 *sq.*, ii./i., 30 *sqq.*; H. Hirschfeld, *New Researches into the Composition and Exegesis of the Qoran*, 1902, p. 2; A. Jeffery, *Materials for the History of the Text of the Qur'ān*, Leiden 1937; D. Künstlinger, *Eine rabbinische Parallele zu Sūra*, *BSOS*, 1934, p. 599 *sq.*

ṢŪRA, image, form, shape (*ṣūrat al-arḍ* means a world map) or face, countenance (see below). *Taṣwīr*, pl. *taṣāwīr* is rather a picture.

The biblical idea according to which man was created in God's *ṣelem* (Gen. i. 27) has most probably passed into Ḥadīth. In Bukhārī, *Isti'dhān*, bāb 1 (cf. Muslim, *Djanna*, trad. 28) it is said: "Allāh created man after his *ṣūra*: his length was 60 ells". On this Ḳasṭallānī (ix. 144) says: "the suffix 'his' refers to Adam; the meaning therefore is: Allāh created Adam according to his, i.e. Adam's form, that is perfect and well-proportioned". But there are also other explanations. The second passage in which the tradition occurs is Muslim, *Birr*, trad. 115: "If a man fights with his brother, he ought to spare his face, for Allāh created man after his *ṣūra*". Nawawī's commentary on this tradition coincides in part with the already quoted section in Ḳasṭallānī. He quotes a.o. al-Māzinī, who says: "Ibn Ḳutaiba has interpreted this tradition wrongly by taking it literally. He says: 'Allāh has a *ṣūra*, but not like other *ṣuwar*'. This interpretation is obviously wrong, for the conception *ṣūra* involves composition and what is put together is created (*muḥdath*); but Allāh is not created, therefore is not composed; therefore he is not *muṣawwar*".

We have further to deal with the conception *ṣūra* in connection with the prohibition of images, which, in so far as it is known in the West, is erroneously traced to the Ḳur'ān like most Muslim institutions. We cannot deny, however, that the prohibition of images is based on a view which finds expression in the Ḳur'ān. In Ḳur'ānic linguistic usage *ṣawwara* "to fashion" or "form" is synonymous with *bara'a* "to create", cf. Sūra iii. 3; vii. 11; xl. 66. In Sūra lix. 24 Allāh is called *al-khāliḳ*, *al-bāri'*, *al-muṣawwir*, i.e. according to Baiḍāwī: "He who takes the resolution to create things according to His wisdom, who creates them without error, who calls their forms and qualities into existence, according to his will".

If then Allāh according to the Ḳur'ān is the great fashioner, it follows in Ḥadīth that all human fashioners are imitators of Allāh and as such deserving of punishment: "Whosoever makes an image him will Allāh give as a punishment the task of blowing the breath of life into it; but he is not able to do this" (Bukhārī, *Buyū'*, bāb 104; Muslim, *Libās*, trad. 100). "Those who make these pictures will be punished on the Day of Judgment by being told: Make alive what you have created" (Bukhārī, *Tawḥīd*, bāb 56). Houses which contain images, dogs and ritually impure people are avoided by the angels of mercy (Bukhārī, *Bad' al-khalḳ*, bāb 17 etc.). The latter statement is illuminated by the story of how 'Ā'isha once purchased a cushion (*numruḳa*) on which were pictures; when Muḥammad saw it from outside the house, he stood at the door without coming in. When asked for the reason of this, he replied: "The makers of these images will be punished and they will be told: Make alive what you have created". And further he said: "A house which contains images is not entered by the angels" (Muslim, *Libās*, tr. 96; cf. 85, 87, 91—99; Bukhārī, *Libās*, bāb 92; Aḥmad b. Ḥanbal, vi. 172). Muḥammad is also said to have removed the images and statues out of the Ka'ba (Bukhārī, *Maghāzī*, bāb 48). A remarkable tradition on this subject, which has some resemblance to the Christophorus legend, is found in Aḥmad b. Ḥanbal, i. 84; cf. 151.

According to the Law it is forbidden to copy living beings, those that have a *rūḥ*. As appears from Nawawī's commentary on Muslim's *Ṣaḥīḥ*, *Libās*, tr. 81 (Cairo 1283, iv. 443) it makes no difference whether the image is put upon a cloth, carpet, coin, vessel or wall, etc. The copying of trees, camel-saddles, and other things apart from living creatures is not forbidden. As regards the use of articles which have on them images of living creatures, if these are hung on a wall or are on a garment which is worn or on a turban or other article which is not treated lightly, they are *ḥarām*. If the reproductions however are on carpets which are walked upon, on cushions and pillows etc. which are in use, they are not *ḥarām*. The opinion of some of the older jurists that only what has a shadow is forbidden, is rejected by Nawawī. According to al-Zuhrī images are without exception forbidden as well as the use of articles on which there are images or the entering of a house in which there are images. Others say: What is embroidered on a cloth whether for humble use or not, whether hung on a wall or not is permitted. The *idjmā'* forbids all representations which have shadows and declares their defacement *wādjib*. Some make an exception for the playing of little girls with dolls. The casuistic treatment of similar cases is still further persued by Nawawī.

In spite of the opinions of theologians and jurists, breaches are not rare as in the case of the prohibition of wine; as for example the frescoes in the bath-house of Ḳuṣair 'Amra, the pictures of dancing girls, animals, birds, etc. at Samarra, the miniatures in Persian and Turkish manuscripts, Turkish and Egyptian stamps. At the end of the tenth century Khumarawaih, the ruler of Egypt, had statues of himself, his wives and singing-girls made, and in Spain 'Abd al-Raḥmān III set up a statue of his favorite wife al-Zahrā' in the palace he called after her name. There have even been pictures of Muḥammad in recent times. But this does not affect the fact that among Muslim peoples there has been neither painting or sculpture to any considerable extent. Objections were for long made to photography (see Snouck Hurgronje, *Verspreide Geschr.* ii. 432 *sq.*); now these seem, in certain circles at least, no longer to be so strong or even to have been quite overcome. Chauvin gives examples of the horror of being copied, examples which still have their counterpart in the modern western world. Here also we find people objecting to being photographed because they feel as if something were being stolen from their persons.

It may be asked whether the Muslim interdiction of images was influenced by the Jewish interpretation of the second commandment. From the literature (Flavius Josephus) on the one hand and the coins on the other, it is evident that the Jewish extension of the prohibition of images was exactly the same as the Muslim: no living creatures, only plants and other objects.

Bibliography: Th. W. Juynboll, *Handleiding*, Leiden 1925, p. 157 *sqq.*; Chauvin, *La défense des images chez les Musulmans*, in *Annales de l'Ac.*

d'arch. de Belgique, 4. série, viii. 229 *sq.*; Snouck Hurgronje, *Ḳuṣair ʿAmra und das Bilderverbot*, in *ZDMG*, lxi. 186 *sqq.* = *Verspr. Geschr.* ii. 449 *sqq.*; do. *Mekka*, ii. 219 and note 3; A. J. Wensinck, *The second commandment*, in *Med. Ak. Amst.* vol. lix. Ser. A. Nr. 6; Lammens, *L'attitude de l'Islam primitif en face des arts figurés*, in *JA*, 1915, 239–79; Goldziher, *Zum islamischen Bilderverbot*, in *ZDMG*, lxxiv (1920), 288; the material of classical Ḥadīth in Wensinck's *Handbook*, under IMAGES; legal: Abū Isḥāḳ al-Shīrāzī, *K. al-Tanbīh*, ed. Juynboll, Leiden 1879, p. 206.

SUTRA, covering, protection, shelter, especially at the *ṣalāt*, where *sutra* means the object which the worshipper places in front of him or lays in the direction of the *ḳibla* whereby he shuts himself off in an imaginary area within which he is not disturbed by human or demoniacal influences. "The fictitious fencing off of an open place of prayer, the *sutra*, seems to have had among other objects that of warding off demons" (Wellhausen, *Reste* ², p. 158). In one tradition the man who deliberately penetrates into this imaginary area is actually called a *shaiṭān* (Bukhārī, *Ṣalāt*, bāb 100; cf. Aḥmad b. Ḥanbal, *Musnad*, iv. 2; Ṭayālisī, *Musnad*, Ḥaidarābād 1321, N⁰. 1342).

The word is not found in the Ḳurʾān. In Ḥadīth it often occurs in the expression *satara* (*tasattara*, *istatara*) *bi-thawb* in traditions which describe the ritual ablution, in which one conceals one's nakedness or causes it to be concealed by a cloak or curtain (e.g. Bukhārī, *Ṣaid*, bāb 14; *Ghusl*, bāb 21; Muslim, *Ḥaiḍ*, trad. 70, 79; Abū Dāʾūd, *Ṭahāra*, bāb 123; *Manāsik*, bāb 37). Similarly *sitr* is the name given to the curtain by which Muḥammad concealed his women from the gaze of the world (Bukhārī, *Maghāzī*, bāb 56; *Nikāḥ*, bāb 67). We are further told that one performs the *ṣalāt* in the direction of an object which isolates him from the multitude (*yasturuhu min al-nās*) so that he is not disturbed by them (e.g. Bukhārī, *Ḥadjdj*, bāb 53; Muslim, *Ṣalāt*, trad. 259; Abū Dāʾūd, *Manāsik*, bāb 53).

Muḥammad is said to have been quite unrestricted in his choice of a *sutra*: baggage-camels, horses, trees, saddles (Bukhārī, *Ṣalāt*, bāb 98), a couch (*ibid.*, bāb 99), lance (*ḥarba*, bāb 92), stick (*ʿanaza*, bāb 93), the pillars of the mosque (bāb 95) are mentioned. Ḥadīth has preserved the memory of two opinions regarding the *sutra*: one gives minute rules and the other opposes this.

The former endeavours to lay down accurately what distance should be preserved between the *sutra* and him who performs the *ṣalāt* (*mamarr al-shāt*, "space to allow a sheep to pass"; Bukhārī, *Ṣalāt*, bāb 91; Muslim, *Ṣalāt*, trad. 263, 264 etc.); it makes Muḥammad explain that no one is to be allowed to pass between anyone and his *sutra* (Bukhārī, *Ṣalāt*, bāb 100, 101; Muslim, *Ṣalāt*, trad. 258—262 etc.), that passers-by, especially dogs, asses and women, intercept the *ṣalāt*: the Apostle of God said: "If one performs the *ṣalāt* without having in front of him something, such as the end or central part of a saddle, his *ṣalāt* is intercepted by a passing dog, ass or woman" (Tirmidhī, *Mawāḳīt*, bāb 136; Aḥmad b. Ḥanbal, vi. 86).

The other view holds that the *ṣalāt* is never intercepted by passers-by (this is also Shāfiʿī's view according to Tirmidhī's note on *Mawāḳīt*, bāb 135). ʿĀʾisha exclaims indignantly: "you place us on the same level as asses and dogs; by Allāh, the Prophet used to perform the *ṣalāt* while I lay on the couch between him and the *ḳibla*" (Bukhārī, *Ṣalāt*, bāb 105). The same tendency is seen in an anecdote by Ibn ʿAbbās: "I was riding behind al-Faḍl on a she-ass; we came up to the Prophet just as he was performing the *ṣalāt* with his companions in Minā. We dismounted and took our places in the row, while the animal ran among the people without intercepting the *ṣalāt*" (Tirmidhī, *Mawāḳīt*, bāb 135; cf. Aḥmad b. Ḥanbal, ii. 196).

The Shāfiʿīs call the sutra *sunna*. The various views of the jurists are given in al-Nawawī in his commentary on Muslim's *Ṣaḥīḥ*, Cairo 1283, ii. 76 sq.; cf. also Tirmidhī's remarks on bāb 133—136 in his chapter *Mawāḳīt al-ṣalāt*.

Abū Isḥāḳ al-Shīrāzī, ed. Juynboll, p. 29, writes as follows: "If anyone passes a man who is performing the *ṣalāt* and there is a *sutra* or stick between them of about an arm's length in size, it is not *makrūh*; nor is it *makrūh* if there is no stick but a line which the worshipper has drawn at a distance of 3 ells; if on the contrary there should be nothing of the kind at all then it (passing by) would be *makrūh*. The *ṣalāt* would however remain valid".

It may be mentioned in conclusion that the *sutra* of the *imām* at the *ṣalāt* serves for those with whom he performs the *ṣalāt* (Bukhārī, *Ṣalāt*, bāb 90).

Bibliography: The material of the classical ḥadīth in A. J. Wensinck, *Handbook*, s.v.; Ibn Ḥadjar al-Haitamī, *Tuḥfa*, Cairo 1282, i. 180 *sq.*; Rhodokanakis, in *Wörter und Sachen*, 1912, p. 124 *sq.*

T

ṬAʿĀM (A.), food. Eating is part of religion; a grateful eater is as one who fasts patiently. So food is controlled by law and the rules connected with it codified by the moralists. Excessive fasting is forbidden because it unfits a man for performing his religious duties. The Ḳurʾān says that all good things of the earth may be eaten; the earliest passage (Sūra xxxvi. 33) mentions grain (vegetarian diet) as the main food. Bad things are forbidden (vii. 157); al-Shāfiʿī explains bad as meaning those things which the Arabs naturally did not eat. Some other things are forbidden, *maita* [q.v.], blood, pork, and what has been sacrificed to idols (xvi. 115). *Maita* means first the carcass of an animal which has died a natural death, and then one from which the blood has not been drained off. In another passage, blood is qualified by shed (vi. 145), thus forbidding the Arab practice of eating blood. Al-Ṭabarī says that blood which is more or less flesh (the liver and spleen), and that which remains in the body without draining away, is lawful; the Muslims on this point being less strict than the Jews. Again, *maita* is further defined as what has been strangled, clubbed to death, killed by a fall, gored by another beast, or killed by a beast of prey.

The lawyers tried to classify those things which were not expressly forbidden. There was one general rule; all that the Arabs approve may be eaten. A strange animal should be shown to Arabs; if they give it the name of a clean animal, it may be eaten; if they have no name for it, it may be eaten or not as it is more like a clean or an unclean animal. Classes of unclean animals are birds and beasts of prey, crawling things, those animals which men are commanded to kill, and those which they are forbidden to kill. (Men are forbidden to kill the hoopoe because it obeyed a prophet.) Al-Baiḍāwī admits that custom had a share in fixing these rules. They are not quite accurate and the schools differ in details. Domesticated asses and mules may not be eaten. Al-Shāfiʿī allowed foxes and hyenas; he also allowed horseflesh though Abū Ḥanīfa and the school of Mālik forbid it. Mālik himself did not forbid it though he disapproved of it because the practice of eating it would diminish the supply of horses for the army. Tradition says that the Prophet would not eat a lizard though he did not object to others doing so. Locusts are permitted. Mālik held that all that lives in or on water is allowed but the others permitted fish only. The elephant is lawful (it is said to be eaten in Abyssinia) but perhaps this is a joke, like al-Shaʿbī's judgment that the flesh of a *shaiṭān* may be eaten in moderation and flies by those who like them. All other animals may be eaten if they have been properly killed. The method is that the name of God is pronounced as the beast faces the *ḳibla* and then its throat is cut. Al-Shāfiʿī held that any Muslim kills in the name of God even if he forgets to say the words. The schools differ. In the throat are four main vessels, the windpipe, gullet, and two arteries. Mālik said that all four must be cut; al-Shāfiʿī held it enough to cut the windpipe and gullet; Abū Ḥanīfa said that any three must be divided. This is *dhakāt*, ritual slaughter. Facts of anatomy made it necessary to kill a camel by cutting the neck where it joins the trunk; this was called *naḥr*. It is better for a woman to do her own butchering than to ask one of the "people of the Book" to act for her. If an animal falls into a pit, where it is impossible to cut the throat, any method of killing is lawful so long as the blood drains out of the carcass. Food prepared by the "people of the Book" is lawful though it is better not to eat it. (Muslims in England usually get their meat from Jewish butchers.) Food prepared by Magians is not lawful. Fish does not need to be killed, the catching of it is equivalent to ritual slaughter. Those that die a natural death and are found floating on the surface are forbidden; Mālik, however, allowed them and tradition tells of an army which lived for a month on a fish it found cast up on the beach. Locusts found dead may not be eaten; they have to be killed by pulling off their heads or throwing them alive on the fire.

Hunting gave room for casuistry but there is no need to mention all the hair-splitting. If the hunter said the name of God when he shot his arrow or set his hound on the game, the bird or animal was lawful food. If the dog was not trained, the prey was lawful only if the hunter cut its throat before it died. Under any circumstances it was and is customary to cut the throat. If a Muslim hunts with a dog trained by a Magian, the game is clean; if a Magian hunts with a dog trained by a Muslim, it is unclean; the dog is only an instrument like an arrow. Some said that game taken by a Magian was lawful. Fish, even if caught by an idolater, is clean. Complaint was made that the Christian demand for fish on their fast days raised the price. All unclean things, except intoxicants, may be used as medicine or, in dire necessity, as food. This raised the question whether a man might eat his fill of the unclean or only so much as would enable him to reach a place where he would find clean. Some said that it was better to take the food of another than to eat unclean.

Rigorists were particular about food; it must have been lawfully prepared and bought with money which had been honestly gained. One man would not let a woman from a neighbouring house suckle his child for a few minutes lest her milk should be tainted. Some made themselves objectionable by accepting invitations and then asking searching questions about the food. So it was ruled that food in the house of another was to be eaten without question; if the guest could not do this, he should stay away. Aḥmad b. Ḥanbal forbade the eating of black dogs because they are *djinn*.

Eating has to be decent and orderly; a man was rebuked for eating by the roadside. The meal begins and ends with the name of God. A man must sit to eat and not recline. The right hand only is used and a man should take what is nearest to him, except that he may pick and choose fruit. Formerly, and still among the bedouin, all ate from the common dish. A meal should begin and end with salt. Edifying talk should accompany food. Among the bedouin, where the company often eats in relays, there is little talk. The sexes eat separately. The table-manners inculcated by al-Ghazzālī are the dictates of common-sense and kindliness; he says "practise good manners when alone so that you are not artificial in company". After eating, the fingers should be licked before washing them; where the company remains seated, the basin should pass to the right. Among bedouin the hands are wiped on the tent wall. The servant who prepares and serves the food should not be forgotten.

AL-ṬABARĪ, ABŪ DJAʿFAR MUḤAMMAD B. DJARĪR, the Arab historian, was born probably in 839 (end of 224 or beg. 225 A.H.) at Āmul in the province of Ṭabaristān. He began to devote himself to study at a precociously early age, and is said to have known the Ḳurʾān by heart by the time he was seven. After receiving his early education in his native town, he received from his father who was quite well off the necessary means of visiting the centres of the Muslim learned world. He thus visited Raiy and its vicinity, then Baghdād, where Aḥmad b. Ḥanbal under whom he had intended to study had died shortly before his arrival there. After a brief stay in Baṣra and Kūfa he again returned to Baghdād where he remained for some time. He then set out for Egypt but stopped in the Syrian towns to study *ḥadīth*. When he was in Egypt he must already have been regarded as a celebrated scholar. From there he returned to Baghdād where except for two journeys to Ṭabaristān (the second in 289—91/902—903) he lived till his death in 310/923.

Ṭabarī seems to have been of a quiet scholarly disposition but full of character. In his earlier years he devoted his whole energy to acquiring the material of Arab and Muslim tradition; later he spent his time mainly in teaching and writing. Although he had only a modest competence, he rejected all financial advantages and even refused lucrative official positions which were offered him. In this way he was able to devote himself to an extremely prolific and versatile literary activity. Apart from his main subjects, history, *fiḳh*, the recitation and exegesis of the Ḳurʾān, he devoted himself also to poetry, lexicography, grammar and ethics and even mathematics and medicine. For ten years after his return from Egypt he followed the Shāfiʿī *madhhab* and then founded a school of his own, whose followers called themselves *Djarīriya* after his father's name. But it seems to have differed less in principle than in practice from the Shāfiʿī school and fell comparatively quickly into oblivion. His break with Aḥmad b. Ḥanbal however was more fundamental. He recognized the latter only as an authority on *ḥadīth* but not on *fiḳh*. He thus brought upon himself the hostility of the Ḥanbalīs. He is said to have attracted the particular hostility of the latter by attacking their interpretation of Sūra xvii. 81.

Ṭabarī's works have not come down to us by any means completely. For example those writings have been completely lost in which he laid down the principles of his new school of law. On the other hand his great commentary on the Ḳurʾān (*Djāmiʿ al-bayān fī tafsīr al-Ḳurʾān* or briefly *Tafsīr*) has survived. In this work Ṭabarī collected for the first time the ample material of traditional exegesis and thus created a standard work upon which later Ḳurʾānic commentators drew; it is still a mine of information for historical and critical research by western scholars. Ṭabarī's own position with regard to the traditions collected by him is mainly defined by linguistic (lexicographical and grammatical) criteria. But he also deals with dogmatic and legal deductions which can be obtained from the Ḳurʾān and sometimes permits himself to express a rather candid opinion without however in any way basing it on historical criticism.

Ṭabarī's most important work is his history of the world (*Taʾrīkh al-rusul wa ʾl-mulūk*). The well known Leyden edition gives only an abbreviated text of the huge work which is said to have been ten times as long but even so it fills 12½ volumes. Even this synopsis is not complete but had to be supplemented in various passages from later writers who had used Ṭabarī's history of the world.

The work begins after an introduction with the history of the patriarchs, prophets and rulers of the earliest period (i. 1). Then comes the history of the Sāsānian period (i. 2) and of the period of Muḥammad and the first four caliphs (i. 3—6); the history of the Umaiyads (ii. 1—3); lastly the history of the ʿAbbāsids (iii. 1—4, middle). From the beginning of the Muḥammadan era the material is arranged annalistically under the years of the Hidjra. The work stops in Muḥarram 303/July 915.

Ṭabarī's *Taʾrīkh al-ridjāl* gives the most necessary facts about the persons whom he has used as authorities in *ḥadīth*. The work was originally current as an appendix (*dhail*) to Ṭabarī's *Annals*. A synopsis, not however complete, was published at the end of the Leyden edition of Ṭabarī (iii, p. 2295—2501).

Bibliography: Brockelmann, *GAL*, i, 148 *sq.*, *Suppl.* i, 217—219; Yāḳūt, *Irshād al-arīb*, ed. Margoliouth, vi, 423.62 (*GMS* vi, 6); Samʿānī, *Kitāb al-Ansāb*, fol. 367 a (*GMS* xx); Ibn Khallikān, No. 542, transl. de Slane, Paris-London 1843, ii. p. 597 *sq.*; *Fihrist*, ed. Flügel, p. 234 *sq.*; I. Goldziher, *Die literarische Tätigkeit des Ṭabari nach Ibn ʿAsākir*, in *WZKM* ix, 1895, p. 359—371; his great commentary on the Ḳurʾān is printed at Cairo 1331, 30 parts; O. Loth, *Ṭabarī's Korankommentar*, in *ZDMG* xxxv., 1881, p. 588—628; Nöldeke-Schwally, *Geschichte des Qorans*, ii., Leipzig 1919, p. 139—142, 171—173, 184; I. Goldziher, *Die Richtungen der islamischen Koranauslegung*, Leyden 1920, p. 85—98, 101 *sq.*

TĀBIʿ (A.), pl. *tābiʿūn*, follower, follower of a prince, disciple of a teacher, adherent of a doctrine; the verbal form is *tabiʿa* or *tābaʿa*, e. g. *tābaʿa Djālīnūs*, he followed Galen (in medicine).

The word is of special significance in Tradition where the name *tābiʿ* is given to those who came after the Companions of the Prophet, the *ṣaḥāba* [q.v.] The *ṣaḥāba* are the people who saw and were directly acquainted with the Prophet; the *tābiʿūn* are those of the next generation or contemporaries of the Prophet, who did not know him personally but who knew one of his Companions. The "followers" of the second generation (*tābiʿū ʾl-tābiʿīn*) are those who knew one of the first *tābiʿūn* and so on. Traditions are of more or less value according as they go back to a "follower" of a more or less early generation and according as the *tābiʿ* who is the first transmitter of it is more or less esteemed and famous. Thus the *mashhūr* or wide-spread tradition is that which goes back to a *tābiʿ* of the first generation and which has been disseminated and handed down by several *tābiʿūn* of the second generation and their successors (cf. ḤADĪTH). There are in the same way generations of transmitters for traditions regarding the reading of the Ḳurʾān and for those of Ṣūfism. One of the most celebrated "followers" of the first generation is Ḥasan al-Baṣrī.

Bibliography: The traditionists Bukhārī, Muslim, etc.; Carra de Vaux, *Les Penseurs de l'Islam*, Paris 1923, vol. iii., p. 176, 282 *sqq.*; al-Hudjwīrī, *Kashf al-maḥdjūb*, transl. R. A. Nicholson, Leyden-London 1911.

TADJWĪD (A.) is the art of reciting the Ḳurʾān, giving each consonant its full value, as much as it requires to be well pronounced without difficulty or exaggeration: strength, weakness, tonality, softness, emphasis, simplicity (*tarḳīḳ*). There are three kinds of *tadjwīd*: 1. *tartīl*, slow recitation; 2. *ḥadr*, rapid recitation; 3. *tadwīr*, medium recitation. — Tadjwīd, "the adornment of recitation", has for its object to prevent the tongue making any mistake in the recitation of the divine words. Besides the study of the articulation of consonants it deals with the knowledge of the laws which regulate the pause, the *imāla* or inclination of the vowel *ā* to the sound *ī* and contraction. The consonants fall into two groups:

1. *Mustaʿliya* "elevated" so called because in pronouncing them, the tongue is raised to the palate. These are *kh*, *ṣ*, *ḍ*, *ṭ*, *ẓ*, *gh* and *ḳ*. They are all emphatic and *ṣ*, *ḍ*, *ṭ*, *ẓ* more so than the others.

2. *mustafila* "depressed", so called because the tongue is below the palate when they are pronounced. They are called simple; i. e. they are not emphatic, except *rāʾ* and *lām* in the following cases: *rāʾ* is emphatic when it is vocalized with a *ḍamma* or a *fatḥa*. The *rāʾ* is not emphasized if it is vocalized with an original or accidental *kasra*, if it is quiescent and preceded by an original *kasra*, and lastly if the *rāʾ* and the *kasra* belong to the same word, provided the *rāʾ* is not followed by an elevated consonant. *Lām* is only emphatic

in Allāh and Allāhumma when they are preceded by a consonant modified by a *fatḥa* or a *ḍamma*: *ḳāla 'llāh, ḳāla 'llāhumma, yaḳūlu 'llāh, yaḳūlu 'llāhumma*. At the end of a word the *nūn* and *tanwīn* retain their natural pronunciation when they are followed by one of the six guttural letters *ḥ, kh*, ʿ, *gh, h*, ʾ. The quiescent *nūn* and *tanwīn* are assimilated to the letter which follows them if the latter is *y, r, l, w, n*. The assimilation takes place with nasalization except for the *r*. When the word that they affect ends in another consonant the *nūn* and *tanwīn* have not their natural pronunciation; they are assimilated but not completely. It is the same with the quiescent *mīm* which is contracted with the *mīm* which follows it. It is modified when it is followed by a vocalized *bāʾ*. In other cases it retains its ordinary pronunciation.

There are two kinds of contractions:

1. Great, when the consonants are both vocalized like *mā salakakum* (Sūra lxxiv. 42) to be pronounced *mā salakkum*.

2. Little, when the first of the consonants is quiescent and the second vocalized.

It should also not be forgotten that the *lām* of the article is only assimilated if the consonant following is solar; the sound should be prolonged when the word contains an *alif*, a *wāw* or a *yāʾ* preceded by a vowel of the same nature. If the *wāw* or *yāʾ* are preceded by a *fatḥa* they become softening letters. The *hamza* may be retained or suppressed; in the latter case, its vowel is carried back to the preceding quiescent consonant. If the *hamza* is quiescent, not by apocope, it may be changed into a letter of prolongation of the same nature as its support. The pronunciation of *hamza* is incompletely softened when it is not preceded by a vocalized and non-quiescent *hamza*; the vowel of the second *hamza* then resembles a *sukūn*, a *wāw* when the *hamza* is preceded by a *ḍamma* (*aʾunabbiʾukum*), a *yāʾ* when it is preceded by a *kasra* (*aʾidhā*), an *alif* when it is preceded by a *fatḥa* (*aʾanta*). The second *hamza* "falls" when the two *hamza* are affected by the same vowel and belong to two words which follow them (*djāʾa adjalukum*).

The verses of the Ḳurʾān, although separated by a sign, are not to be recited with a stop at the end of each of them. The pause is only to be made if the sense of the verse or verses is complete and forms a homogeneous whole. As a rule in good copies of the Ḳurʾān, the places where the pause is not allowed are indicated by لا (= no pause). If a pause is made after words like *ʿamma, mimma, hunna*, a quiescent *h* should he added (called silent *h*). Some readers restore the suppressed final *y* in the middle of the discourse like *wāḳin, hādin* etc. ...; others drop the *sukūn* and its vowel and say *wāḳ, hād* etc. ... When a word ends in a *hamza* preceded by a *yāʾ* or a *wāw*, the *hamza* is assimilated to the letter which precedes and one says *barīy* for *barīʾ*, especially after *hamza*. The *-an* of the accusative is changed to *alif*. The final *t* of feminine singular nouns is changed to quiescent *h*. A vocalized final consonant loses its vowel; this vowel is sometimes only weakened (by *rawm*) or rather it is pronounced like a final French *e* (*ishmām*). However this last method of pronunciation is not allowed in words ending in *kasra*; some even say that *rawm* and *ishmām* only affect *ḍamma*.

Bibliography: Suyūṭī, *al-Itḳān*, Cairo 1306, i. 87—105; Tahānāwī, *Kashshāf al-iṣṭilāḥāt*, Constantinople, i. 216; ʿAlī b. Sulṭān al-Ḳāriʾ, *al-Minaḥ al-fikrīya ʿalā matn al-Djazarīya*, and in the margin: Zakarīyāʾ al-Anṣārī, *al-Daḳāʾiḳ al-muḥkama fī sharḥ al-muḳaddima[t al-Djazarīya]*, Cairo 1344; Sulaimān al-Djamzūrī, *Fatḥ al-aḳfāl bi-sharḥ Tuḥfat al-aṭfāl*, and following it: anonym, *Fatḥ al-Raḥmān fī tadjwīd al-Ḳurʾān*, Cairo 1343; Shaikh Ṭāhir al-Djazāʾirī, *Tadrīb al-lisān ʿalā tadjwīd al-Bayān*, finished in 1321, Beyrouth n.d.; Shaikh Mutawallī, *Fatḥ al-muʿṭī wa-ghunyat al-muḳrī fī sharḥ muḳaddimat Warsh al-Miṣrī*, Cairo 1309; Abū Rīma, *Hidāyat al-mustafīd fī aḥkām al-tadjwīd*, Cairo 1344; Djurdjānī, *Taʿrīfāt*, s.v. *tartīl*; Bustānī, *Muḥīṭ al-muḥīṭ*, s.v., i. 314; ʿAbd al-Nabī b. ʿAbd al-Rasūl, *Djāmiʿ al-ʿulūm*, Ḥaidarābād 1329, i. 274; Ibn al-Ḳāṣiḥ, *Sirādj al-ḳāriʾ al-mubtadī wa-tadḳār al-ḳāriʾ al-muntahī, sharḥ Ḥirz al-amānī wa-wadjh al-tahānī li 'l-Shāṭibī*, Cairo 1341, especially p. 36—120; O. Pretzl, *Die Wissenschaft der Koranlesung*, *Islamica* vi (1933—4); G. Bergsträsser, *Koranlesung in Cairo*, in *Isl.* xx, xxi (1932—3); J. Cantineau et L. Barbès, *La Récitation Coranique à Damas et à Alger*, in *AIEO* vi (Alger 1942—7), 66—107.

TAFSĪR (A.), p. *tafāsīr*, explanation, commentary, a term applied to commentaries on scientific and philosophical works, as an alternative to *sharḥ*, e.g. for the Greek and Arabic commentaries on Aristotle.

In Islām the word means particularly the commentaries on the Ḳurʾān and the science of interpreting the sacred book. This branch of learning, entitled *ʿilm al-Ḳurʾān wa'l-tafsīr*, is a special and important branch of ḥadīth, and is taught in the madrasas and universities. Included under the heading of *tafsīr* are a few general works on the Ḳurʾān, but the majority are continuous commentaries, in which the text of the sacred book is explained phrase by phrase, and sometimes even word by word. Of the many such commentaries the most famous are those of Ṭabarī, Zamakhsharī, (Fakhr al-Dīn) al-Rāzī, and Baiḍāwī (see these articles).

The science of tafsīr seems to date from the beginnings of Islām. Ibn Abbās (d. 68), for example, became renowned as an authority on the subject, and a work on it is attributed to him. Recent criticism (Goldziher, Lammens, etc.) has raised the question of the real value of the traditions contained in these enormous compilations. The answer so far has not been very favourable; the majority of the traditions seem to have been invented, either to settle a point of law or with some theological object, or simply to explain the occasion or the allusions of the text. There is, these critics say, no hope of finding much exact information in these commentaries about the circumstances in which the Ḳurʾān was composed and made public; nevertheless they are important for the minute study of Muslim law and theology, as well as for the legends and philology. Of recent years, beginning with Shaikh Muḥammad ʿAbduh (q.v.), a number of new commentaries have been written to serve as vehicles for various modernizing or reforming tendencies.

Originally the term *taʾwīl* was synonymous with *tafsīr*; in course of time, however, it became the technical term for the material interpretation of the Ḳurʾān, relating to its content, whereas *tafsīr* was applied rather to the external philological exegesis. Several less orthodox schools, such as the Ikhwān al-Ṣafā, the Ṣūfīs and the Shīʿites, saw in *taʾwīl* a means by which the text of the Ḳurʾānic revelation could be brought into agreement with their own tenets. Alongside the interpretation according to the meaning of the text there grew up a tendentious allegorical explanation which smuggled the most far-fetched ideas into the literal text. Certain features in this use of allegorical *ta'wīl* may go back, as Goldziher has pointed out (*Richtungen*, p. 210), to influences deriving from the Alexandrians, and in particular from Philo.

Bibliography: Suyūṭī, *Itḳān* ii (Cairo 1287), 204-6; Goldziher, *Muhammedanische Studien* ii. (Halle 1890), 206; do., *Die Richtungen der islamischen Koranauslegung* (Leiden 1920); do., *Streitschrift des Ġazālī gegen die Bāṭinīya-Sekte* (Leiden 1916), p. 50; Carra de Vaux, *Les Penseurs de l'Islam*, vol. iii. (Paris 1923), chap. xi; Nöldeke-Schwally, *Gesch. d. Qorans*, vol. ii.; Blachère, *Introduction au Coran* (Paris 1947), pp. 221—240; A. Jeffery, *Islam* xx, pp. 301—8.

TAHADJDJUD (A.), infinitive V from the root *h-dj-d* which is one of the roots with opposed meanings (*aḍdād*), as it signifies "sleep" and also "to be awake", "to keep a vigil", "to perform the night ṣalāt or the nightly recitation of the Ḳur'ān". The latter two meanings have become the usual ones in Islām. The word occurs only once in the Ḳur'ān, Sūra xvii. 79: "And in a part of the night, perform a ṣalāt as a voluntary effort" etc., but the thing itself is often referred to. We are told of the pious (li. 17) that they sleep little by night and pray to Allāh for forgiveness at dawn. In Sūra xxv. 64, there is a reference to those who spend the night prostrating themselves and standing before their Lord.

From the Ḳur'ān it may be deduced that the old practice in Mecca was to observe two ṣalāts by day and one by night (Sūra xvii. 78 *sq.*); Sūra lxxvi. 25: "And mention the name of thy Lord in the morning and in the evening [26] and in the night prostrate thyself before Him and praise Him the livelong night"; Sūra xi. 114: "And perform the ṣalāt at both ends of the day and in the last part of the night". Tradition is able to tell us — and there is no real reason for scepticism — that for a shorter or longer period (mention is actually made of a "period of ten years", Ṭabarī, *Tafsīr*, xxix. 68), vigils were so ardently observed that Muḥammad and his companions began to suffer from swollen feet. The old practice is said to be based on Sūra lxxiii.: "1. O thou enfolded one, 2. stand up during the night, except a small portion of it, 3. the half or rather less, 4. or rather more and recite the Ḳur'ān with accuracy"; but its origin cannot be dissociated from the example of Christian ascetics. In the end, however, this form of asceticism became too much for Muḥammad's companions. The revelation of verses 20 ff. of Sūra lxxiii. brought an alleviation: "See, thy Lord knoweth that thou standest praying about two thirds, or the half or a third of the night, thou and a part of thy companions. But Allāh measureth the night and the day; he knoweth that ye are not able for this; therefore he turneth mercifully to you with permission to recite as much of the Ḳur'ān as is convenient for you". By the institution of the five daily ṣalāts the obligatory character of the tahadjdjud was then abolished (cf. Abū Dā'ūd, *Taṭawwu'*, bāb 17 and Baiḍāwī on Sūra lxxiii. 20).

Nevertheless Muḥammad is said not to have abandoned the vigils (Abū Dā'ūd, *Taṭawwu'*, bāb 18b); in Ḥadīth and Fiḳh it is considered blameworthy to omit them for those who were wont to perform these ṣalāts (Muslim, *Ṣiyām*, trad. 185; Nasā'ī, *Ḳiyām al-lail*, bāb 59; Bādjūrī, *Ḥāshiya*, i. 165). The performance is in general regarded as *sunna*. David is said to have spent a third of the night in these exercises (Muslim, *Ṣiyām*, trad. 189; Abū Dā'ūd, *Ṣawm*, bāb 67); another reason given in justification of it is that the *tahadjdjud* loosens one of the knots which Satan ties in the hair of a sleeper (Abū Dā'ūd, *Taṭawwu'*, bāb 18). The *tahadjdjud* is particularly meritorious in Ramaḍān and in the night before each of the two feasts (Ibn Mādja, *Ṣiyām*, bāb 68: Nasā'ī, *Ḳiyām al-lail*, bāb 17, where the term *iḥyā' al-lail* is used [see also TARĀWĪḤ]).

Even at the present day the *mu'adhdhin* in some lands summons to a night ṣalāt (consisting of an even number of *rak'as* and therefore called *shaf'*; cf. WITR) shortly after midnight by an *adhān* to which special formulae are added (Lane, *Manners and Customs*, chapter iii. "Religion and Laws"; cf. Snouck Hurgronje, *Mekka*; Juynboll, *Handleiding*, p. 74).

Bibliography: Besides the works quoted cf. Sprenger, *Das Leben und die Lehre des Moḥammad*, i. 321 *sqq.*; M. Th. Houtsma, *Iets over den dagelijkschen çalât der Mohammedanen*, in *Theol. Tijdschrift*, 1890, p. 137 *sqq.*; R. Bell, *The Origin of Islam in its Christian Environment*, London 1926, p. 143.

For the views of the different law schools cf. also Khalīl, *Mukhtaṣar*, transl. Guidi, Milan 1919, i. 97; Abū Isḥāḳ al-Shīrāzī, *al-Tanbīh*, ed. A. W. T. Juynboll, p. 27; al-Ramlī, *Nihāyat al-muḥtādj*, i. 488 *sqq.*; Ibn Ḥadjar al-Haitamī, *Tuḥfa*, i. 201 *sqq.*; Abu 'l-Ḳāsim al-Ḥillī, *Kitāb Sharā'i' al-Islām*, Calcutta 1839, i. 27; A Querry, *Droit Musulman*, Paris 1871, i. 52 *sq.*; Niẓām, *al-Fatāwā' 'l-'Ālamgīrīya*, Calcutta 1243, i. 157.

ṬAHĀRA (A.); grammatically *ṭahāra* is a *maṣdar* and means purity; it has also the technical sense of ceremonial, levitical purity and purification. It holds an important place in Islām, for "purity is half the faith", a saying attributed to Muḥammad (Muslim, *Ṭahāra*, trad. 16). Theologians divide defilements into material and mental; lawyers divide them into actual (*ḥaḳīḳī*) and religious (*ḥukmī*). *Fiḳh* deals with bodily, material impurity only. Sexual intercourse, menstruation, and childbirth are religious impurities. Actual impurities (*nadjis*, q.v.) have a perceptible body. They are wine, pigs and dogs and what is begotten of them, dead bodies (except those of men, animals used for food, fish, and creatures that have no blood, i.e. insects), and certain discharges from the body. There are five things that are not unclean: any dirt left after defecation, dust or mud on the roads, the soles of shoes, the blood squashed out of a full-fed flea, and the blood or pus from a boil or pimple or from cupping. Tears, sweat, spittle and mucus are clean. The laws of purity are not meant to be burdensome. The usual means of purification is cold water but after defecation stones are also used. Water is pure if running, if from a pool above 100 sq. cubits (*dhirā'*) in area, or from smaller quantities so long as the colour, taste and smell are not changed. Elaborate rules are laid down for the various cases. After micturition or defecation there is a preliminary cleansing with stones or earth (*istidjmār*) and one with water (*istindjā'*). On ablutions and baths, see WUḌŪ', GHUSL. When no water is to be had or, by reason of illness or some other cause, the use of it is feared, sand or dust may be employed [see TAYAMMUM]. The rules of the Shī'a differ in detail from those of the Sunnīs. After helping to carry a corpse to the grave an ablution is necessary, not merely approved; and according to them a quantity of water amounting to two *ḳulla* (the meaning is uncertain, but it is generally taken to be a large jar) is clean.

Popular practices do not always agree with canonical rules; it is said that round ʿAden the defilement of micturition can be removed by helping to carry a bier on its way to the cemetery.

These processes must not be just mechanical; purpose (*nīya*) must come first, and they must be accompanied by the thought of God and special prayers, which vary at different times and places. The theologians develop this side of the idea and say that purification consists of four stages: purification of the body from physical dirt; of the members from offences; of the heart from evil desires; of the spirit (*sirr*) from all that is not God.

Ṭahāra has become the common name for circumcision and the ceremonies that accompany it [see KHITĀN].

Bibliography: The chapters *Ṭahāra* and *Nadjāsa* in the books of *Fiḳh*; Ghazzālī, *Iḥyā*ʾ, vol. 1, book 3; Abū Ṭālib al-Makkī, *Ḳūt al-ḳulūb*, vol. 2, p. 91; Th. W. Juynboll, *Handleiding tot de kennis van de Moh. wet*, Leyden 1925, p. 165 *sqq.*; A. J. Wensinck, *Der Ursprung der musl. Reinheitsgesetzgebung*, in *Isl.*, v. 62 *sqq.*; do., *Handbook* s.v. Purity.

ṬĀHIR, or SHĀH ṬĀHIR DAKKANĪ ḤUSAINĪ, a learned Persian theologian and politician who came to India in 926/1520, spent his life in the diplomatic service of Burhān Niẓām Shāh of Aḥmadnagar (1508—1553), and died there between 952 and 956 (1545—1549). He was the author of several learned works, and of many poems, but at present apparently only his work on *inshā*ʾ, i.e. a collection of epistolary models, remains.

His most extraordinary achievement was the conversion of Burhān Niẓām Shāh, who was a Sunnī, to the *ithnā-ʿasharī* school of the Shīʿa [q.v.]; moreover, the Shāh proclaimed in 1537 this form of Islām as the official religion of his state.

Some documents recently discovered in Badakhshān reveal quite unexpected circumstances in Shāh Ṭāhir's life. It appears that he was regarded by his followers as a Nizārī Ismāʿīlī Imām, the legitimate successor of the Imāms of Alamūt [cf. ISMĀʿĪLIYA]. The great majority of the Nizārī Ismāʿīlīs, however, regarded this line as schismatic; it apparently became extinct soon after Awrangzīb's time.

According to the tradition of this sect, the last Imām of Alamūt, Rukn al-Dīn Khūrshāh, was followed by his son Shams al-Dīn Muḥammad; he was succeeced by Muʾmin Shāh, who probably flourished before the middle of the fourteenth century. The Imāms after him were: Shams al-Dīn Muḥammad II; ʿAlāʾ al-Dīn Muʾmin Shāh II; ʿIzz al-Dīn Shāh Ṭāhir I; Raḍī al-Dīn Muḥammad; ʿIzz al-Dīn Ṭāhir II; Raḍī al-Dīn ʿAlī; and Shāh Ṭāhir Dakkanī, who is the subject of this note. He himself was succeeded by his son Ḥaidar (Raḍī al-Dīn); then by Ṣadr al-Dīn Muḥammad; Khudābakhsh; ʿAzīz; ʿAbd al-ʿAzīz; and, possibly, Shāh Mīr Muḥammad Musharraf, who flourished about 1700, though it is not certain whether he really was an Imām. Nothing is known as to what has ultimately happened with the line, and whether their followers still exist in India. In Aḥmadnagar, Bīdjāpūr and Gulbarga there is at present no memory of the saint. Apparently there are no followers of his sect in India, but there are about four thousands of them in Syria, namely in Maṣyāf and Ḳadmūs, with some adjacent hamlets. Formerly all Ismāʿīlīs of Syria belonged to this branch of the Nizārīs, but the majority joined the other branch about sixty years ago.

The doctrine of the sect forms a link between the Mustaʿlian dogma and the Persian Nizārī. Their religious books almost entirely perished in their wars with Nuṣairīs in 1919 and 1920. In India apparently the only existing work is the *Lamaʿāt al-ṭāhirīn*, a voluminous versified treatise, in which the doctrine is hidden under the guise of Ṣūfic and *ithnā-ʿasharī* terminology. In the Upper Oxus region the sect apparently had centuries ago a large following. Only one short treatise in Persian is known, namely the *Irshād al-ṭālibīn* by ʿAlī Ḳunduzī, who wrote about 924/1518.

TAḤRĪF (A.), corruption of a document, whereby the original sense is altered. It may happen in various ways, by direct alteration of the written text, by arbitrary alterations in reading aloud the text which is itself correct, by omitting parts of it or by interpolations or by a wrong exposition of the true sense. The Muslims found occasion to deal with this conception in connection with those passages in the Ḳurʾān where Muḥammad accused the Jews of falsifying, *ḥarrafū* [cf. ḲURʾĀN, sub 4], the books of revelation given them, i.e. the Torah. He had from the beginning appealed to the evidence of the "peoples of a scripture", i.e. the Jews and the Christians, as he was firmly convinced that the teachings of the former prophets coincided with what he preached on the basis of his revelations. At Madīna his claims were received with so much criticism and ridicule from the Jews that he seemed to be put in a false position. But as his consciousness of his prophetic inspiration was unassailable, the Ḳurʾān declares that the Jews had maliciously corrupted their sacred books. In this connection Muḥammad uses the expression *ḥarrafa* (Sūra ii. 75; iv. 46; v. 13, 41), more rarely the synonym *lawā* (iii. 78; iv. 46) or *baddala* the meaning of which is narrower, "to exchange", "to put in the place of something" (ii. 59; vii. 17). There is a direct charge of having falsified the text in Sūra ii. 78: "Woe to them, who write the Scripture with their hands and say: this comes from Allāh". On the other hand in iii. 78 there seems to be a reference to an alteration in the text while it is being read: "A part of them twist their tongue in the scripture so that you think that it is out of the scripture, but it is not out of the scripture; they say: it comes from Allāh, but it does not come from Allāh"; cf. iv. 46: "they twist with their tongue". In other passages the Jews are charged with concealing and suppressing all sorts of things in their scripture (Sūra ii. 159, 174). This is expressed in a peculiar fashion in vi. 91 where it is said "you make the scripture of Moses into leaves which you display and suppress much of it"; which can only mean that they removed the passages attesting the truth of Muḥammad's mission from the copies which they used in the disputations. He gives in ii. 58 and vii. 161 a specimen of their alterations which is unfortunately not clear; they are said to have used another word instead of the word *ḥiṭṭa* which brought a heavy punishment upon them. The examples quoted in ii. 104; iv. 46 are hardly meant as quotations from scripture. Among the suppressed passages, the traditions make special mention of the law which punishes incontinence with stoning (Ibn Hishām p. 394 *sq.*) and the descriptions of Muḥammad as the expected Prophet (*ibid.*, p. 353). Muḥammad naturally extended this charge of taḥrīf to the Christians, of whom he also asserted that they likewise concealed the passages in their holy scriptures which contained evidence of the truth of his mission; cf. the appeal to the "possessors of a scripture" in Sūra ii. 146; iii. 71 and with reference to the prophecy of Muḥammad's coming, Ibn Hishām, p. 388. This attitude naturally led to counter-charges of *tabdīl* by Muḥammad's opponents, and in Sūra x. 15 he vigorously defends himself against the charge that he had substituted another revelation in place of the one given him. But the not rare abrogations of earlier legal prescriptions [cf. KUR'ĀN] caused him no misgiving, and xvi. 101 clearly refers to his having occasionally substituted one verse for another, a thing with which his enemies did not forget to reproach him.

The vague way in which Muḥammad in the Ḳur'ān speaks of falsifications of scriptures by the "possessors of a scripture" resulted in the Muḥammadan scholars who gradually became better acquainted with the Old and New Testaments and were fond of dealing in their polemical works with the charge of *taḥrīf*, *tabdīl* and *taghyīr*, coming to hold very divergent views in their opinions of the facts lying at the basis of the charge. Some continued to hold the opinion usual in the early centuries after Muḥammad that the Jews had actually altered the text. A vigorous champion of this view was the Spanish Arab Abū Muḥammad ʿAlī b. Ḥazm (d. 456/1064). Diametrically opposed to this was the view held by others that the texts of the "possessors of a scripture" were intact and that the divergent opinions of Jews and Christians were simply due to erroneous interpretations of the passages concerned. One of the earliest representatives of this view was the Zaidī of the Yemen, al-Ḳāsim b. Ibrāhīm (d. 246/860), in his polemical treatise directed against the Christians; among his later followers, special mention may be made of the great historian Ibn Khaldūn. As is usual in such controversies there was also a middle school, for some conceded the actual falsifications of the text by the "peoples of a scripture" but limited them to a minimum. Of these different opinions, the first was decidedly the simplest and most logical, for it was based on the first impression which the words of the Ḳur'ān naturally made and had made in the early days of Islām, but it led to rather serious consequences which gradually came to be appreciated. When one had always to deal with the possibility that the texts of the earlier books of revelation had been falsified, they lost considerably in value and indeed the holders of this theory frequently speak slightingly of them and disapprove of their use. But in this way one came up against a question of apologetics, to which the theologians were devoting themselves with ardour, namely the prophecy of Muḥammad's coming as the expected Prophet in the Bible (e.g. Deut., xviii. 15), for this naturally presupposed the authenticity of the passage in question. This factor had such an influence that only a minority took seriously the charge of *taḥrīf* in its strictest form. But in its milder form it continued to play a principal part in Muslim polemics against Jews and Christians, as may be seen for example from Doughty's statement that in his conversations with Arabs he frequently heard this accusation made (*Travels in Arabia*, i. 298; Snouck Hurgronje, *Mekka*, ii. 204).

In the disputations between the different Muslim sects the charge of *taḥrīf* is also made, as the Shīʿīs have often insisted that in the orthodox Ḳur'ān many things have been omitted or inserted with the object of disposing of or refuting evidence of the truth of their doctrine. The orthodox naturally reply by making the same charge against the Shīʿīs.

Bibliography: Goldziher, *ZDMG*, xxxii. 341 *sqq.*, on Steinschneider, *Polemische u. apologetische Literatur in arabischer Sprache* (*Abhandlungen für die Kunde des Morgenlandes*, vol. vi., N⁰. 3); M. Schreiner, *Z. Gesch. der Polemik zw. Juden u. Muhammedanern*, *ZDMG* xlii. 591 *sqq.*; Di Matteo, *Taḥrīf od alterazione della Biblia secundo il Muselmani*, *Bessarione*, Anno xxvi., vol. xxxviii. 64—111. — On *taḥrīf* within Islām cf. Goldziher, *Muh. Stud.*, ii., 158, 382 *sq.*; do., *Die Richtungen der islamischen Koranauslegung*, p. 272, 281.

TAKBĪR (A.), the pronouncing of the formula *Allāhu Akbar*. [See ṢALĀT, ii].

TAḲDĪR [See ḲADAR].

TAḲĪYA (A.), caution, fear (see *Glossarium* to Ṭabarī, s.v. *t-ḳ-a*) or *kitmān*, "disguise", is the technical term for dispensation from the requirements of religion under compulsion or threat of injury.

Muḥammad himself avoided the Passion motive in religion: in dogmatics by docetism (Sūra iv. 157), in his own life by the *Hidjra* and further by allowing in case of need the denial of the faith (Sūra xvi. 106), friendship with unbelievers (iii. 28) and the eating of forbidden foods (vi. 119; v. 3). This point of view is general in Islām. But, as he at the same time asserted the proclamation of his mission to be a duty and held up the heroic example of the old saints and prophets as a model (lxxiv. 7; v. 67; iii. 152 etc.), no definite general rule came to be laid down, not even with the separate sects. Minor questions, which are very fully discussed, are whether taḳīya is a simple permitted alleviation (*rukhṣa*) or a duty, whether it is valid in private interest or only in that of the community.

The taḳīya was not rejected even by the extreme wing of the strict Khāridjīs [q.v.], although among the Azraḳīs in the similar question of divine worship when danger threatens (*ṣalāt al-khawf*), the example is often given that one should not interrupt the ṣalāt even if his horse or his money be stolen from him during it. But the advice is old: "God gave the believers freedom of movement (*wassaʿa*) by the taḳīya; therefore conceal thyself!" The principle adopted by the Ibāḍīs went as far as to say that "the taḳīya is a cloak for the believer: he has no religion who has no taḳīya" (Djumaiyil, xiii. 127 *sq.*).

Among the Sunnī authorities the question was not such a burning one. Nevertheless Ṭabarī says on Sūra xvi. 106 (*Tafsīr*, Būlāḳ 1323 *sqq.*, xxiv. 122): "If any one is compelled and professes unbelief with his tongue, while his heart contradicts him, to escape his enemies, no blame falls on him, because God takes his servants as their hearts believe". The reason for this verse is unanimously said to have been the case of ʿAmmār b. Yāsir, whose conscience was set at rest by this revelation when he was worried about his forced worshipping of idols and objurgation of the Prophet. It is more in the nature of theoretical speculation, when in this connection the question of *hidjra* is minutely investigated, that in certain circumstances e.g. threat of death, a Muslim who cannot live openly professing his faith may have to migrate "as God's earth is wide". Women, children, invalids and one who is tied by considerations for them, are permitted *muwāfaḳa* ("connivance"); but an independent individual is not justified in *taḳīya* nor bound to *hidjra* if the compulsion remains within endurable limits, as in the case of temporary imprisonment or flogging which does not result in death. The endeavour, however, to represent the *taḳīya* as only at most permitted and not under all circumstances obligatory, as even some Sunnīs endeavour to hold on the basis of Sūra ii. 195, has resulted in the invention of admonitory traditions, e.g. *ra'ʾs al-fiʿl al-mudārāt* "to be good friends (with unbelievers) is the beginning of actual (unbelief)". To prove that steadfast martyrdom is a noble thing, the story is told of the two Muslim prisoners of Musailima, one of whom allowed himself to be forced to acknowledge the anti-prophet, while the other died for the Prophet. The latter is reported to have said: "The dead man has departed in his righteousness and certainty of belief and has attained his glory, peace be with him! But God has given the other an alleviation, no punishment shall fall upon him".

The *taḳīya* is of special significance for the Shīʿa. Indeed it is considered their distinguishing feature, not however always with justice, as Naṣīr al-Dīn Ṭūsī in the *Talkhīṣ al-Muḥaṣṣal* protests against Rāzī (see at the foot of Rāzī's *Muḥaṣṣal afkār al-mutaḳaddimīn wa 'l-mutaʾakhkhirīn*, Cairo 1305, p. 182, on 281). The peculiar fate of the Shīʿa, that of a suppressed minority with occasional open not always unheroic rebellions, gave them even more than the Khāridjīs occasions and examples for extreme taḳīya and its very opposite; even the Ismāʿīlīs, usually masters in the art of disguising their creed, made the challenge to their leaders: "He who has 40 men at his disposal and does not seek his rights is no Imām". The Zaidīs give as the number of helpers which removes the necessity of taḳīya from the Imām, that of those who fought at Badr. It is a common polemical charge of the Sunnīs, quoted from the writings of the Shīʿīs themselves, that the latter, as followers of fighting martyrs, are not justified in taḳīya, whereas the Twelvers in particular, while representing the Imāms as examples compelling one to resoluteness, appeal on the other hand to the conduct of ʿAlī during the reign of the three first Caliphs and to the *Ghaiba* of the Mahdī as the typical taḳīya. Belief is expressed by heart, tongue and hand; a theory of probabilities developed with considerable dialectic skill calculates under what real or expected injuries, "the permitting of what is pleasing to God and the forbidding of what is displeasing to God" is made void. Observance with the heart is absolutely neccessary. But if it is probable to any one (*law ghalaba ʿalā ẓannihi*) or if he is certain that an injury will befall him, his property or one of his co-religionists, then he is released from the obligation to intercede for the faith with hand or tongue.

In Shīʿī biographies concealment is a regular feature; we are told, and not at all in an apologetic way, that the hero broke the laws of religion like the prohibition of wine under compulsion. But since for them also Muḥammad is the Prophet, and since as among the Sunnīs a Prophet may not practice taḳīya in matters of his office, because otherwise one could not be certain of the revelation, we have, in view of the double example of the Imāms, in the code of morals for the ordinary pious men of the Shīʿa, the following sayings of ʿAlī in juxtaposition: "It is the mark of belief to prefer justice if it injures you, to injustice if it is of use to you"; and as an explanation of Sūra xlix. 13: "He among you who is most honoured before God is the most fearful (of God)", that is "he who uses the taḳīya most (*aʿḳākum = aktharukum taḳīyat^{an}*)"; and it is also said: "The *kitmān* is our *djihād*", but at the same time the *djihād* chapters are to be read with the implied understanding that the fighting is primarily against other Muslims. It is also to be noted that the taḳīya of the Shīʿīs is not a voluntary ideal (cf. Khʷānsārī, *Rawḍāt al-djannāt*, Teheran 1306, iv. 66 *sq.*), but one should avoid a martyrdom that seems unnecessary and useless, and preserve oneself for the faith and one's co-religionists.

Ultimately the taḳīya is based on the intention and so we continually find the appeal made to the *nīya* in this connection. The validity of the profession of faith as an act of worship is not only settled by the correct formulation of the intention to do it, but this is the essential of it, so that the intention alone counts if under compulsion a profession of unbelief is made with the lips or worship performed along with unbelievers. God's rights alone may be injured by the taḳīya. He has the power to punish the constrainer, and only in certain circumstances will a slight portion of the punishment fall upon the constrained. The wiles (*ḥiyal*) used in this connection, especially in oaths with mental reservations, give however ample opportunities to injure one's fellow-creatures.

The moral dangers of taḳīya are considerable, but it may be compared with similar phenomena in other religions and even among mystics. The ethical question whether such forced lies are nevertheless lies, such a forced denial of the faith nevertheless a denial, is not put at all by the one "who conceals himself", as he is not in a state of confidence which would be broken by lies or denial.

Bibliography: Goldziher, in *ZDMG*, lx. (1906), p. 213—226, where further references are given. — Sunnīs: Bukhārī, *K. al-ikrāh*; al-Ḳudūrī, *Mukhtaṣar*, Kasan 1880, p. 162; al-Nawawī, *Minhādj al-ṭālibīn*, ed. van den Berg, Batavia 1882—1884, ii. 433. — Khāridjīs: al-Basīwī, *Mukhtaṣar*, Zanzibar 1304, p. 123; Djumaiyil b. Khamīs, *Ḳāmūs al-sharīʿa*, Zanzibar 1297 — 1304, xiii. 127 *sqq.*, 157. — Zaidīs: Mss. Berlin 9665, fol. 35ᵃ; 4878, fol. 96ᵇ; van Arendonk, *De opkomst van het Zaidietische Imamaat in Yemen*, Leyden 1919, s. Index; Strothmann, *Das Staatsrecht der Zaiditen*, Strassburg 1912, p. 90 *sqq.* — Imāmīs: Djaʿfar b. al-Ḥusain al-Ḥillī, *Sharāʾiʿ al-Islām*, St. Petersburg 1862, p. 149 *sqq.*; Ibn al-Muṭahhar al-ʿAllāma al-Ḥillī, *Mukhtalaf al-Shīʿa*, Teheran 1323 *sqq.*, ii. 158 *sq.*; Horovitz, in *Isl.*, iii. 63—67. — Druses: Manuscr. Berlin, Mg 814 (not in Ahlwardt), fol. 11ᵇ; Ibn Ḥazm, *al-Fiṣal fi 'l-milal*, Cairo 1317, iii. 112 *sqq.*; iv. 6; al-Shaʿrānī, *Mīzān*, transl. Perron, Algiers 1898, p. 456 *sq.* — Modern general survey of the question: Maḥmūd Shukrī Ālūsī, *Mukhtaṣar al-Tuḥfa al-Ithnāʿasharīya*, Baghdād 1301, p. 188–194.

TAḲLĪD (A.), "to hang something upon the neck or the shoulder", used as a technical term in three meanings:

1. *Taḳlīd* is the name of the old Arab custom surviving in the ancient practice of Islām and in *fiḳh*, of hanging certain objects (the so-called *ḳilāda*, plur. *ḳalāʾid*) around the neck of the animals to be slain as a sacrifice (*hady*) in the sacred territory (*ḥaram*) of Mecca. The *ḳalāʾid* are mentioned along with the *hady* in Ḳurʾān v. 2 and 97 among the customs of the pilgrimage instituted by Allāh. The object of this rite was, along with the *ishʿār* (marking by an incision in the skin), to destine the animal for sacrifice in the *ḥaram* and to give it a kind of *iḥrām* [q.v.] analogous to that of the pilgrim. Connected with this, although not identical, is the custom

of the pilgrim hanging round his neck and that of his riding animal on the return journey from Mecca the bark of certain plants of the *ḥaram*, which is also called *ḳilāda*; this custom is also found in Islām but is opposed to, and ignored by the *fiḳh*. The *ḳilāda* on the sacrificial animal is unlike this, for it consists of one or both sandals of the pilgrim or in default of them of a piece of leather; the animal so marked goes through all the essential ceremonies of the *ḥadjdj* along with the pilgrim and is slain at Minā. The practice of early Islām was not unanimous as to the consequences of sending such an animal to Mecca, without the sender at the same time performing the *ḥadjdj*, a practice which may be specifically Muslim. There is a group of traditions which impose upon the sender the obligations of the *iḥrām* from the time of the *taḳlīd* until the time of slaying the animal; but the traditions are far more numerous which — some with an obvious polemical intention — say that the Prophet did not assume the *iḥrām* in this case; finally there is also an intermediate *ḥadīth* which leaves the assumption of the *iḥrām* to the choice of the individual, and the essential alleviation forbidding only sexual intercourse on the Friday night. In the fully developed *fiḳh* there is no longer any place for this *iḥrām* and it must have dropped out of use quite early. A further proof of the close connection between *iḥrām* and *taḳlīd* is the view reported of Sufyān al-Thawrī, Aḥmad b. Ḥanbal and others, that the pilgrim becomes *muḥrim ipso facto* by practising the *taḳlīd*, and the allied view that the *taḳlīd* made by a pilgrim binds him to adopt also the *iḥrām*; Mālik b. Anas says at least that it is undesirable for the pilgrim to separate the *taḳlīd* from the assumption of the *iḥrām*. — The *fiḳh* regards the hanging on of a *ḳilāda* as desirable (*mustaḥabb*) in the case of camels or cattle, and according to the Shāfiʿīs, Ḥanbalīs and Abū Thawr and Dāwūd in the case of sheep and goats also; of the Ḥanafīs and Mālikīs who do not allow this, the Mālikīs do not recognize sheep and goats as a *hady* at all. When the pilgrims no longer brought the sacrificial animals with them from home and a market for them was instituted at Minā, the *taḳlīd* fell into oblivion.

In addition, we may note that a leather neck band, also called *ḳilāda*, on the camel to avert the evil eye, especially if a bell hang from it, is reproved by a *ḥadīth*.

Bibliography: Lane, *Arab.-Engl. Lexicon*, s.v.; Wensinck, *Handbook*, s.v.; Mālik b. Anas, *al-Muwaṭṭaʾ* in both recensions; al-Zurḳānī, *Sharḥ al-Muwaṭṭaʾ*; al-Ṭaḥāwī, *Sharḥ Maʿānī ʾl-Āthār*; Gaudefroy-Demombynes, *Le pèlerinage à la Mekke*, p. 279—285 differing in minor points from the sketch given above).

2. *Taḳlīd* also means installation in a military office, which was done by girding on a sword; it then comes to mean investiture with any administrative office, including that of *ḳāḍī*.

Bibliography: Lane, l.c.; Sprenger, *Dictionary of the Technical Terms*, s.v.

3. *Taḳlīd* lastly means "clothing with authority" in matters of religion: the adoption of the utterances or actions of another as authoritative with faith in their correctness without investigating his reasons. In this sense *taḳlīd* is the opposite of *idjtihād* [q.v.]. The historical beginnings of the *taḳlīd* coincide with the formation of the juridical *madhāhib* (cf. MADHHAB), which in part at least arose through adhesion to particularly notable jurists. Al-Shāfiʿī in his *Risāla*, 8, 18, uses the word in a sense very close to the later technical use, but al-Ṭaḥāwī still applies it to the recognition of traditions and their use for the deduction of precepts of *fiḳh*. When definite conceptions had been formed about the *mudjtahid* i.e. the person qualified for independent derivation of *fiḳh* rules from the sources, and at the same time the conviction of the cessation of unlimited *idjtihād* from the third century on, and of the other kinds of *idjtihād* correspondingly later, all later scholars or laymen had to acknowledge *taḳlīd* with regard to the earlier authorities. According to the general orthodox Muslim view, everyone is now and has been for centuries bound to what has been authoritatively laid down by his predecessors, no one may any longer consider himself qualified to give a verdict of his own in the field of *fiḳh*, independent of that of an earlier *mudjtahid*. All later persons are called *muḳallids* i.e. those who have to exercise *taḳlīd*. In support of this view it is argued that the *faḳīhs* only in the early centuries of Islām had possessed the real perspicuity and sufficient learning to deduce *fiḳh* from its sources and to form an opinion of their own about it; this is quite in keeping with the way in which orthodox Islām regards the history of its own development. The *taḳlīd* has contributed to maintain the differences between the separate *madhāhib* but is not to be held responsible for the deadening of the stimulus to the development of *fiḳh* in later times.

While it is the unanimous view that the layman as well as the scholar is bound to *taḳlīd*, it is occasonally demanded of the scholar that he should be aware of the correctness of the *idjtihād* of his *mudjtahid*. If there are several *mudjtahids*, as is actually the case, the *muḳallid* may follow any one of these he pleases (presuming of course that he remains within the bounds of the *idjmāʿ* i.e. does not choose a *mudjtahid* whose teachings are no longer recognized by the *idjmāʿ*, the obligation to *taḳlīd* itself being based on the *idjmāʿ*); according to Aḥmad b. Ḥanbal, he has to decide to whom the preference is to be given and then to follow him (this divergence of opinion is really confined to terminology). In theory the *muḳallid* can make a new choice of a *mudjtahid* with each question that arises for him, but in practice he usually joins once and for all the *madhhab* of one of the four recognized *mudhtahids*. There are a fair number of cases of transference from one *madhhab* to another; opinions are divided as to whether such a transfer is admissible in theory. More frequently it happens that on a particular question the more convenient rules of another *madhhab* are followed; the *fiḳh* books themselves occasionally hint at the possibility of this *taḳlīd*, but in such a case it is demanded that the affair should be carried through to its conclusion according to this particular *madhhab* once it has been chosen.

This all holds of *taḳlīd* in questions of *fiḳh*; with regard to the *ʿaḳlīyāt*, the fundamental questions of dogma, e.g. the existence of Allāh, besides the opinions that *taḳlīd* is obligatory or that it is admissible, the view that it is inadmissible is also strongly represented as on these questions knowledge is demanded which cannot be obtained by *taḳlīd* alone. It was the school of the Ashʿarīs which gave this originally Muʿtazilī view wide dissemination in Islām.

Even the principle of *taḳlīd* in law has not been enforced in orthodox Islām without opposition. Also in later generations there have been scholars who held that there must always be a *mudjtahid*, like Ibn Daḳīḳ al-ʿĪd or al-Suyūṭī, or who were inclined to claim for themselves unlimited *idjtihād*, like al-Djuwainī and again al-Suyūṭī. But there came also protests against the *taḳlīd* on grounds of principle from several quarters. This, it is true, is not the case with al-Ghazzālī who only fought against the *taḳlīd* of the Bāṭinīs (Ismāʿīlīs) with whom it was still more pronounced than with the Twelver-Shīʿīs; according to him, their dogmatical recognition of a certain person, the *imām*, as infallible, is in opposition to the choice of a trustworthy guide as practised by the Sunnīs. (The Ismāʿīlīs, however, argue that the *imām* issues an unequivocal declaration, *naṣṣ*, of his will, and that obedience to this makes *taḳlīd* superfluous). It is, however, the case with Dāwūd b. ʿAlī, Ibn Ḥazm and other authorities of the Ẓāhirīs, who condemned *taḳlīd* and established the obligation, even for the later scholars, to practise *idjtihād*. For this very reason the Ẓāhirī *madhhab* numbers among its sympathisers not a few famous mystics whose aversion from *taḳlīd* was a consequence of a position common to many Ṣūfīs with regard to the *sharīʿa* in general (cf. SHARĪʿA). Some later Ḥanbalīs, like Ibn Taimīya and Ibn Ḳaiyim al-Djawzīya, were led by the consistent reference to the authorities of the "good old times" (*al-salaf al-ṣāliḥ*) to the rejection of numerous elements incorporated by the later *fiḳh*, and therefore to the condemnation of *taḳlīd* in its traditional form. The Wahhābīs, whose views go back to these Ḥanbalīs, beginning with their founder Ibn ʿAbd al-Wahhāb, equally reject *taḳlīd*, and the *idjtihād-taḳlīd* question forms the main controversial topic between them and their adversaries. The same holds true of the reformatory *Salafīya* movement. Like the Wahhābīs, their extreme opponents, the modernists in Islām, for whom those, it is true, paved the way, condemn *taḳlīd* and demand and exercise a new *idjtihād* which in its lack of restrictions far surpasses even its most liberal exercise in the early period of legal development. On the other hand, the recent Egyptian legislation modifying directly the *sharīʿa*, although quite modernistic in outlook, claims, as far as possible, to be based on the opinions of old authorities; this procedure is, however, widely different from the traditional use of *taḳlīd*. For reasons similar to those of the Wahhābīs the Ibāḍīs also reject *taḳlīd*; the decisions arrived at by their *mudjtahid*'s in common deliberation are considered as sanctioned by *idjmāʿ* [q.v.]. Lastly the Shīʿīs differ from the orthodox doctrine of *taḳlīd*; according to the Twelvers, during the period when the "hidden *imām*" is concealed, there are *mudjtahids* who have to guide the faithful as his agents; as these have thus living teachers always in view in religious matters, *taḳlīd* towards a dead man is forbidden; the details are eagerly discussed down to quite modern times. (For the Ismāʿīlīs see above).

Bibliography: Lane, l.c.; Sprenger, l.c. (not wholly reliable); Juynboll, *Handleiding*, 3rd ed., p. 23 *sqq.* and note 13; Snouck Hurgronje, *Verspreide Geschriften*, ii. passim; Goldziher, *Vorlesungen über den Islam* (cf. the index); do., *Streitschrift des Gazālī*, p. 1 *sqq.*; Asín Palacios, *Abenhazam*, i. p. 141 *sqq.*; R. Hartmann, *Die Krisis des Islam*; for the Ibāḍīs: Milliot and Giacobetti, in *REI*, 1930, p. 222; for the Twelver-Shīʿīs: C. Frank, in *Islamica*, ii. p. 171 *sqq.*

TAKLĪF is imposing a requisition or constraint upon any one; it requires an action in which there is difficulty and trouble (Lane, *Suppl.*, p. 3002c; *Lisān*, xi. 218: *amarahu bi-mā yashuḳḳu ʿalaihi*). The verb is used in several forms seven times in the Ḳurʾān (ii. 233, 286; iv. 84; vi. 152; vii. 42; xxiii. 62; lxv. 7) to express that Allāh does not require of any one what is beyond his capacity (*wusʿ*). As a theological term it means the necessity which lies on the creatures of Allāh to believe and act as He has revealed to them. It is therefore defined legally by the majority of canonists as the requiring (*ilzām*) of an action in which is difficulty and trouble. On this definition, it applies only to things necessarily required and to things forbidden (*al-wādjib, al-ḥarām*). But some canonists define it as an assertion of a belief that the action is one of the legal rulings (*al-aḥkām al-sharʿīya*). On this definition, *taklīf* applies also to the recommended (*al-mandūb*), the disliked (*al-makrūh*) and the permitted (*al-mubāḥ*). Further, there is dispute as to who is *mukallaf*, i.e. under this divine requirement. It is accepted that every sane, human adult (*ʿāḳil, insī, bāligh*) is thus *mukallaf* (Juynboll, *Handbuch*, p. 69). But the *djinn* are also under this *taklīf* so far as the prophetship of Muḥammad is concerned; he was sent to the *djinn* and the other prophets were not. Similarly of the angels, although this applies only to their acts of obedience, as faith (*īmān*) exists of necessity (*ḍarūrī*) in them. Yet some assert that as their created nature is obedience, the prophetic mission of Muḥammad to them was only to glorify them (*li-tashrīfihim*; cf. al-Baidjūrī on the *Kifāya* of al-Faḍālī, ed. Cairo 1315, p. 13). Some further extend this *taklīf* of the prophetic mission of Muḥammad even to inanimate things (*al-djumādāt*), on the ground that in some of the miracles (*muʿdjizāt*) of Muḥammad reason was created in some inanimate things to the point that these believed in him. Another matter of controversy as to *taklīf* is the allowability of Allāh's requiring of a creature that which the creature has not power to do (*taklīf mā lā yuṭāḳ*). The Māturīdites asserted, in the language of the Ḳurʾān as above, that the creature is not required to do what is not in his capacity (*mā laisa fī wusʿihi*; *ʿAḳāʾid* of al-Nasafī, ed. Cairo 1321 with commentary of al-Taftāzānī, p. 103). Al-Īdjī in his *Mawāḳif* (ed. Būlāḳ 1266, p. 535 middle, 537 middle), as an Ashʿarite, brings the question back under the general ruling that Allāh's will and action cannot be limited in any way; nothing is incumbent upon him and nothing is evil that proceeds from him. It is a general agreement of the Muslim people (*al-umma*) that Allāh does not do an evil thing (*ḳabīḥ*) and does not leave undone a necessary thing (*wādjib*). He adds that the Ashʿarites put it that the *ḳabīḥ* and the *wādjib* have no relationship to Allāh at all, while the Muʿtazilites hold that what would be *ḳabīḥ* from Him he does not do and what is incumbent on Him he does. See, further, in the passages cited above, long scholastic discussions of these points by al-Taftāzānī and al-Īdjī.

Bibliography: Add to passages cited above the general discussion in *Dictionary of technical terms*, under "Taklīf", p. 1255.

ṬALĀḲ (A.), the repudiation of a wife by the husband. The root idea of the word is: "getting free (from a bond), being set loose".

I. Under this head the different kinds of divorce in Muslim law will be treated, first of them the *ṭalāḳ* proper.

1. The right to a one-sided dissolution of a marriage belonged to the man exclusively, among the pre-Muḥammadan Arabs. Long before the Prophet this ṭalāḳ was in general use and meant the immediate definite abandonment by the man of all rights over his wife, which he could insist upon as a result of

his marriage (the opposite view on this point was held by Robertson Smith and by Wellhausen).

2. The Ḳurʾān lays down regulations which go into the ṭalāḳ with comparative thoroughness. From their fullness, and still more from the many admonitions to observe them exactly, it is evident that it was here introducing new rules which had been previously quite unknown to the contemporaries. The Ḳurʾān found particularly repulsive the apparently not uncommon exploitation in its milieu of the wife by the *walī* as well as by the husband, which took place especially in connection with the ṭalāḳ. So the first Muslim regulation about the ṭalāḳ is the prohibition to use it for extortions from the woman: Sūra iv. 20 (of the years 3—5; the preceding verse is directed against encroachments by the relatives of the deceased): "If ye wish to exchange one wife for another and have given one of them even a great sum (as *mahr*, or bridal gift) do not take from it anything; would ye take it by manifest slander and sin?" (here the Ḳurʾān recognizes the ṭalāḳ as such as legitimate). The next passage which deals with the ṭalāḳ introduces an important innovation, namely the period of waiting (*ʿidda*), which is on the one hand intended to leave no doubt about the real paternity of a child born from the divorced woman and on the other to give the man an opporunity of rectifying a too hurried pronunciation of the ṭalāḳ by withdrawing it; thus it is laid down in Sūra ii. 228: "The women who have been given the ṭalāḳ shall wait three *ḳurʾ*-periods (this expression which is variously explained means in any case phenomena connected with menstruation); it is not lawful for them to conceal what Allāh creates in their bodies, if they believe in Allāh and the last day; their husbands have the full right to take them back during this period, if they wish for reconciliation; they have right to the same fairness to which they are bound, but the men are above them in rank" (the man is here given the right to take back the wife during the period of waiting even against her will). But this right now given to the man for the first time was very soon abused; the wife was taken back near the end of the period of waiting and a new ṭalāḳ at once pronounced over her so that she was permanently in a state of waiting, in order to induce her to purchase her freedom by giving back the *mahr* or making some other financial sacrifice; verse 229 *sq.* was therefore revealed: "The ṭalāḳ may be pronounced twice, and he may still keep her in fairness or let her go with good treatment; it is not lawful for you to take away anything of what ye have given them.... 230. If he then still pronounces the ṭalāḳ over her she shall not be lawful for him until afterwards she marries another husband; if the latter pronounce the ṭalāḳ over her, it is no sin for the two to return to one another if they think they can observe Allāh's commands" (it is probable that the second part of verse 230 was induced by a concrete case in which a thrice divorced woman who had married another husband and received the ṭalāḳ from him also, desired bona fide to marry her first husband again). A further extension made necessary by the practice, which was intended to prevent abuses of the right of taking back the wife during the period of waiting, is given in verse 231: "When ye give women the ṭalāḳ and they reach their time, retain them with you in fairness or let them go in fairness; but do not keep them to harm them in order to transgress; he who does so thereby only injures himself; make not a jest of Allāh's words!" (here it is forbidden to take back the wife under a show of reconciliation, simply with the object of making her life uncomfortable and forcing her to purchase her release by the payment of a sum of money; the perhaps contemporary verse 232 contains warning admonitions to the *walī*'s of divorced women). Later than Sūra ii. 228, which is presupposed, but still before the end of the year 5 are the regulations of Sūra lxv. 1 *sqq.*: "O Prophet, when ye pronounce the ṭalāḳ over women, do it with regard to their period of waiting (the meaning, not quite clear, of the Arabic expression seems to be that the ṭalāḳ is to be pronounced in such a way that the period of waiting can be easily calculated, i.e. not during menstruation), and calculate the term exactly and fear Allāh your Lord; put them not out of their houses and they are not to depart (of their own accord) unless they do manifestly something shameful (i.e. commit adultery); ... thou knowest not whether Allāh after this may not bring about a change (in the attitude of the man to the woman so that he may take her back). 2. When they have reached their term, then either keep them in fairness or separate from them in fairness, and take upright people from among you as witnesses and bear witness for the sake of Allāh. This is an admonition for him who believes in Allāh and the last day .... 3. (further exhortations to observe the precepts). 4. If your wives can no longer expect a menstruation and ye are in doubt (about the period of waiting) their period of waiting shall be three months, and for those which have not yet menstruated, too; and if they are pregnant, their term shall be their delivery; ... 5. (further exhortations). 6. Let them dwell where ye dwell according to your means and do not harm them, to make their lives unpleasant; if they are pregnant, maintain them till they are delivered..." (here follow rules for nursing by the divorced woman). In these verses certain obligations are laid upon men regarding the housing and maintainance of their wives during the period of waiting; this completes the work of protecting the woman against financial exploitation by the man in connection with the ṭalāḳ, which Sūra iv. 20 had begun. Sūra xxxiii. 49 belongs to the end of the year 5: "O believers! when ye marry believing women and then pronounce the ṭalāḳ over them before ye have touched them, ye have not to make them wait a period; provide for them and dismiss them in a suitable fashion". The general rule here given is stated more fully in Sūra ii. 236 *sq.*: "It is no sin for you if ye pronounce the ṭalāḳ over your women before ye have touched them or made a settlement (as bridal gift) upon them; provide fairly for them, the well-to-do according to his means and the straitened in circumstances according to his means; this is a duty for those who do what is right. 237. If ye pronounce the ṭalāḳ over them before ye have touched them and have already made a settlement upon them (as bridal gift), (ye shall give them) half of what ye have settled unless they remit it, or he in whose hand is the marriage tie (i.e. the husband) remits it; but that you should remit is nearer to piety" (this rule also seems to owe its origin to a concrete case in which doubts had arisen). In the case of a quarrel between the spouses, Sūra iv. 35 provides for the appointment of two referees, one from the family of the husband and the other from that of the wife, who have to mediate between them.

In addition there are Sūra xxxiii. 28 (of the end of the year 5) and Sūra lxvi. 5 (of the late Madīna period) in which Muḥammad threatens his own wives with the ṭalāḳ.

3. The ṭalāḳ is treated hardly less fully in the *ḥadīth*. Besides numerous traditions which simply repeat the well-known precepts of the Ḳurʾān and therefore need not be dealt with here, there are also some which further develop the doctrine of ṭalāḳ. A group of traditions which endeavour to limit as much as possible the ṭalāḳ, deserves particular attention: "Among permitted things the ṭalāḳ is the most hated by Allāh"; the wife cannot demand from the husband that he should pronounce the ṭalāḳ over another wife on her account; Allāh punishes the woman who seeks the ṭalāḳ from her husband without sufficient reason. A question not yet conceived in the Ḳurʾān is that of the effect of a ṭalāḳ pronounced thrice at one time; the traditions are divided regarding this; alongside of the approval of such a thing, there is the strongest disapproval, sometimes it is even held to be invalid; in the same direction points the *ḥadīth* that down to the caliphate of ʿUmar such a ṭalāḳ was considered to be a single one and that ʿUmar was the first to introduce into jurisprudence its threefold validity, in order to restrain people by the fear of the undesirable consequences of this abuse. The traditions further mention as requirements for the ṭalāḳ which is to be *sunna* i.e. in keeping with the prescriptions of the Ḳurʾān and of the Prophet, that the man must not pronounce it during the woman's menstruation (Sūra lxv. 1 is unanimously interpreted in this sense) and must have had no intercourse with her during the period of purity in which he pronounces it. The so-called *taḥlīl* which consists in marrying a thrice divorced woman and at once pronouncing the ṭalāḳ over her, simply with the object of enabling her to remarry her first husband is strongly disapproved of and even cursed. Besides, the woman is only considered to be "lawful" for the first husband when the second marriage is actually completed. To check frivolous pronunciation of the ṭalāḳ, a ṭalāḳ pronounced in jest is considered legal and binding. As, on the other hand, the ṭalāḳ means the dissolution of the marriage, a ṭalāḳ pronounced before the conclusion of the marriage is of no importance. Whether a woman who has thrice received the ṭalāḳ has a claim during the period of waiting on her husband for lodging and maintenance is not evident from the Ḳurʾān; the earliest differences of opinion are enshrined in a group of traditions, some of which completely deny any such claim, some of which recognize it only for lodging and some for maintenance also. Ṭalāḳ between slaves is not regulated in the Ḳurʾān; the *ḥadīth* gives the slave also the right to the ṭalāḳ but (in analogy with other legal enactments) only twice, and similarly puts the period of waiting of a slave-woman at two *ḳurʾ*-periods. Anyone who becomes a convert to Islām and has more than four wives is bound to keep only four and pronounce the ṭalāḳ on the others; if he is married to two sisters, he must pronounce the ṭalāḳ on one of them. Finally it should be mentioned that, according to tradition, the Prophet at once gave the ṭalāḳ to women who took their refuge with Allāh from him and is said to have induced ʿAbd Allāh b. ʿUmar to separate from his wife by a ṭalāḳ out of consideration for his father's dislike of her.

4. The oldest jurists (down to the beginning of the formation of the *madhhab*'s), some of whom go back to the time of the origin of the traditions, develop the doctrine of ṭalāḳ on the lines indicated above; the most important views to be mentioned here are the following. The doctrine of *ṭalāḳ al-sunna* and its requirements is further developed; it is even applied to the case when a woman is pregnant. The ṭalāḳ pronounced thrice at one time is considered as a sin but thrice valid, by the overwhelming majority; sometimes the view is even described as the only valid one, against which no contradictory opinion is alleged to be known; but even at a somewhat later date there were nevertheless champions of the view that the ṭalāḳ of this kind is to be considered as only once valid. While according to the view of the majority, the wife becomes forbidden to the man after a threefold ṭalāḳ and can only marry him again after completing and dissolving a marriage with another man, these consequences, according to a view which is still followed by al-Ṭabarī, and which goes back to a divergent interpretation of Sūra ii. 229 *sq.*, come into force already after a twofold ṭalāḳ, if the man does not withdraw it, but "allows the woman to go". That the second marriage must be actually consummated if the woman is to be lawful again to the first man, is unanimously demanded. The validity of the ṭalāḳ pronounced in jest is expressly affirmed, and is regarded as generally recognized. The principle is unanimously affirmed that in the case of ambiguous expressions the opinion of the speaker decides, but here is much difference of opinion as to whether certain expressions are to be considered ambiguous or not, and also whether the ṭalāḳ pronounced under pressure or under the influence of intoxication is valid or not. All this is a question of the application of principles, important in other cases also, in a field which on account of its practical importance had a great influence on their development. The validity of the ṭalāḳ pronounced before the consummation of the marriage is denied, in agreement with the traditions, by many authorities. The ṭalāḳ pronounced on condition that the marriage takes place ("if I marry thee, thou art divorced"), is on the other hand recognized as valid by some, while others deny it. Any ṭalāḳ pronounced before the consummation of the marriage is irrevocable; this rule is undoubtedly in the spirit of the Ḳurʾān. The different views found in the *ḥadīth* regarding the claims of the thrice divorced woman to lodging and maintenance are also found here. Some authorities allow the slave only the possibility of the twofold ṭalāḳ, whether in respect of a female slave or a free woman; according to others on the other hand, the deciding factor is the status of the woman, so that every husband of a slave, whether slave or freeman, has only the possibility of a twofold ṭalāḳ. The Ḳurʾānic expression *ḳurʾ* (Sūra, ii. 228) is sometimes interpreted as menstruation and sometimes as period of purity. Less important differences of opinion are associated with the interpretation of different Ḳurʾānic expressions in Sūra ii. 228 and lxv. 1, 2, 4. There is unanimity on the point that the man has the right to withdraw the ṭalāḳ even against the will of the woman.

5. The teachings of the developed *fiḳh* on ṭalāḳ, which are based on the above, can be briefly summarized as follows. The husband has the right to pronounce the ṭalāḳ on his wife even without giving the reasons, but his pronouncing it without good grounds is considered *makrūh* (reprehensible) and by the Ḥanafīs even as *ḥarām* (forbidden); the *ṭalāḳ al-bidʿa* also, i.e. one in which the requirements of the *ṭalāḳ al-sunna* (cf. above) are not observed, is regarded as *ḥarām*; the validity of the ṭalāḳ is not in any way affected thereby. To be able to pronounce the ṭalāḳ the husband must have attained his majority and be *compos mentis*; the ṭalāḳ of a

minor is regarded as valid only by one tradition from Aḥmad b. Ḥanbal; the guardian acts for the legally disqualified husband. The ṭalāḳ is a personal right which the husband must exercise by himself or through a mandatory specially appointed by him; he may also entrust this mandate to his wife, who can then pronounce the ṭalāḳ on herself.

The ṭalāḳ presupposes a valid marriage; the ṭalāḳ pronounced on condition that the marriage takes place (cf. above) is invalid according to the Shāfiʿīs and Ḥanbalīs, but valid according to the Ḥanafīs and Mālikīs (according to the latter, however, not if it is expressed in quite general terms, e.g. "every woman that I marry is divorced").

The ṭalāḳ pronounced in delirium or by a lunatic is invalid. The ṭalāḳ of an intoxicated man has given rise to lively discussions in all the *madhhabs*; in the case of culpable intoxication it is regarded as valid by the majority. The ṭalāḳ pronounced under pressure is valid according to the Ḥanafīs, but not according to the Mālikīs, Shāfiʿīs and Ḥanbalīs.

Words referring unambiguously and directly to the ṭalāḳ bring it into operation, whatever may have been the intention of the speaker who uttered them; if the speaker uses unambiguous circumlocutions, the Ḥanafīs, Shāfiʿīs and Ḥanbalīs demand also a corresponding intention, while the Mālikīs pay no heed to the intention; in the case of ambiguous expressions or gestures the intention of the speaker is the only deciding factor. There is a great difference of opinion among the *madhhabs* on all these questions, when it comes to the individual case. The question of the validity of a conditionally pronounced ṭalāḳ (apart from the above mentioned case) is also much disputed; the Ḥanafīs and Shāfiʿīs make such a ṭalāḳ, in general, come into operation on the fulfilment of the condition; the Mālikīs regard it, according to the nature of the condition, as sometimes at once effective and sometimes void.

The woman's period of waiting begins at once after the ṭalāḳ unless it is a question of a ṭalāḳ before consummation of the marriage, which is always definite: in this case the woman does not need to have a period of waiting and has only a claim to half the bridal gift, if it was already fixed (if it was already paid, she has to pay back half of it), or to a gift at the discretion of the man, the so-called *mutʿa*. In the other cases, a distinction has to be made between a revocable and a definite ṭalāḳ. In the first contingency the marriage is still considered legally in existence with all its consequences and the woman has a claim upon the man for lodging and maintenance for the whole period of waiting; on the other hand, the man has the right to revoke the ṭalāḳ throughout the period of waiting. If he allows the period to pass without exercising this right, the marriage is definitely dissolved at its expiry; if the bridal gift was not yet paid, it is now due unless some later date was agreed upon for its payment. If a reconcilation then still takes place between the two parties and they wish to marry again, they must draw up a new contract of marriage with a new bridal gift.

With a definite ṭalāḳ on the other hand, the marriage is at once finally dissolved (with the single exception that a definite ṭalāḳ pronounced by a man during his mortal illness does not abolish the wife's rights of inheritance: so the Ḥanafīs, Mālikīs and Ḥanbalīs with differences of opinion on details, while the Shāfiʿīs consider the opposite view the better). The woman has however in this case also to pass the period of waiting, during which she cannot conclude a new marriage; during this period she has a claim on the husband for lodging, but for maintenance only if she is pregnant. The husband's payment of the bridal gift is the same as in a revocable ṭalāḳ. The conclusion of a new contract of marriage between the former partners is impossible, unless the woman has in the meanwhile contracted and completed marriage with another man; but even this way out is only open to them twice.

The third ṭalāḳ is considered definite among freemen and the second among slaves; it is a matter of indifference whether the separate repudiations were made in one marriage or in several, not separated by *taḥlīl*. In mixed marriages between freemen and slaves the status of the man is decisive according to the Mālikīs, Shāfiʿīs and Ḥanbalīs, and that of the woman according to the Ḥanafīs. Among the Ḥanafīs also a single ṭalāḳ, in which especially strong expressions are used, is considered final, but does not exclude remarriage.

The period of waiting for a free woman is three *ḳurʾ* periods i.e. according to the Mālikīs and Shāfiʿīs three periods of purity, and according to the Ḥanafīs three menstruations; if she has not menstruated or no longer menstruates, three months; if she is pregnant, the period lasts till her confinement. For a slave woman the period of waiting is in the first case two *ḳurʾ* and in the second a month and a half; if she is pregnant, the period of waiting again lasts till her confinement.

Sexual intercourse with a not definitely divorced woman during the period of waiting is permitted according to the Ḥanafīs and the better accredited view of the Ḥanbalīs; according to the Mālikīs, Shāfiʿīs and the other Ḥanbalī view, it is forbidden. In keeping with the views of the first class, it is regarded by them as revoking the ṭalāḳ in every case, according to the Mālikīs only if the man intends it to have this meaning, while the Shāfiʿīs only regard a statement by the man as revoking the ṭalāḳ.

6. The Shīʿa rules concerning ṭalāḳ only differ in unimportant details from the Sunnī with which we have so far dealt. By a more strict interpretation of Sūra lxv. 2 the presence of two legal witnesses is regarded as absolutely necessary for the validity of a ṭalāḳ, while the Sunnīs dispense with them. All circumlocutions, ambiguous expressions and gestures are neglected, whatever may have been the intention of the speaker.

7. As an institution of family law, the ṭalāḳ has had in practice to follow closely the lines dictated by the principles of Muslim law. The very frequent pronunciation of the ṭalāḳ, often on the most trivial grounds and thrice at one time has brought about the following usage: if the couple wish to marry one another again after the third ṭalāḳ, they seek a suitable individual who is ready for a certain reward to go through the ceremony of marriage with the woman and at once repudiate her; the woman is then again lawful (*ḥalāl*) for her first husband; this practice is therefore called *taḥlīl*, and he who undertakes it *muḥallil*. For this purpose a minor or a slave is used by preference. Nothing can be urged against the validity of such a procedure providing that at the conclusion of the intervening marriage the word *taḥlīl* is not used; its permissibility is defended by the Ḥanafīs but disputed by the Mālikīs and Shāfiʿīs; the Ḥanbalī Ibn Taimīya regarded the *taḥlīl* as invalid and attacked it in

a special work, but he seems to be practically alone in this view.

The conditional pronunciation (*taʿlīḳ*) of the ṭalāḳ may have different objects: a man may pronounce such a ṭalāḳ, for example, to drive his wife or himself to doing something or to refrain from something by threatened separation, or to give force to some statement made by him. In parts of India, the Straits Settlements and a large portion of Indonesia, this *taʿlīḳ* of the ṭalāḳ has become a regular custom at the conclusion of a marriage; it is hardly ever omitted and serves to impose upon the man certain obligations towards his wife, on the non-fulfilment of which the marriage is dissolved automatically.

On the practice of the ṭalāḳ as it has developed in different countries under the influence of the *sharīʿa* and under native customary law, the ethnological works and travel descriptions should be consulted.

Turkey and likewise Albania are so far the only Muḥammadan countries which have abolished the ṭalāḳ with the introduction of western civil codes, whereas in modern Egyptian legislation there is a strong tendency towards its limitation.

II. The KHULʿ is a special form of divorce by which the wife purchases her freedom. The name comes originally from the symbolical act of "taking off" and throwing away a piece of clothing, but already in the pre-Islamic period it had long become an expression for the dissolution of legal relations in general. In Muḥammad's time it obviously happened often that the wife had to purchase ṭalāḳ from her husband by returning a portion of the bridal gift: this kind of extortion is forbidden by the Ḳurʾān in Sūra iv. 20 and ii. 229 (cf. above). Soon, however, the necessity arose for affording separation to the pair after a bona fide agreement in return for compensation: this was done by the insertion of the following in Sūra ii. 229: "unless both fear that they cannot observe Allāh's commands; so if ye fear that they cannot observe Allāh's commands there is no sin on their part if she ransoms herself". The classical traditions regarding *khulʿ* deals with the case of Thābit b. Ḳais, whose wife desired to purchase her freedom. The basic fact with the details, which cannot be derived from elsewhere and are not utilized in *fiḳh*, that the Prophet ordered the husband to release the wife and imposed on her a period of waiting of one *ḳurʾ* only, may be historical, although the differences in the name of the wife and in other points prevent us from accepting any one of the different versions of this tradition as the authentic one. In the oldest period of *fiḳh* the most prominent question is whether *khulʿ* is to be considered as repudiation (ṭalāḳ) or as the rescission, annulment (*faskh*) of the marriage, a difference which is not irrelevant in law. The first view, for which (without historical justification) most of the earliest authorities of Islām are quoted, survives in the teaching of Abū Ḥanīfa and Mālik and their schools, of Zaid b. ʿAlī and his followers and of Ibn Abī Lailā, as well as in one view of al-Shāfiʿī and of Aḥmad b. Ḥanbal, the second in the teaching of Abū Thawr, of Dāwūd al-Ẓāhirī and his school and further in one view of al-Shāfiʿī and the better known opinion of Aḥmad b. Ḥanbal; the teaching of the Shāfiʿī school varies. With regard to the wording of the tradition, many were reluctant to recognize a *khulʿ* as being in keeping with the *sunna* if the wife's contribution amounted to more than the *mahr* had been: accordingly an agreement of this kind is regarded by the Ḥanafīs and Ḥanbalīs as reprehensible (*makrūh*) but nevertheless valid (*ṣaḥīḥ*).

The system of *fiḳh* regards the *khulʿ* as a *muʿāwaḍa* contract (exchange of property or rights) but with limitations: the full legal capacity is asked from the woman only; less strict demands are laid down regarding the compensation (known as *badal*, *ʿiwaḍ* or also *khulʿ*) than in the full *muʿāwaḍa* contract; it may also be paid by a third party for the woman; if the compensation of the *khulʿ* was inadmissible the divorce nevertheless holds. With those who regard the *khulʿ* as a ṭalāḳ, it has the effect of a single final repudiation; according to the Shāfiʿīs, the final or revocable character of the divorce by *khulʿ* depends mainly on the nature of the compensation. The right of recalling a ṭalāḳ which is not yet final may also be given up in return for compensation.

Alongside of this we have the possibility of a divorce by agreement without compensation, while abandoning the mutual claims on property, which is known as *mubāraʾa* (i.e. mutual release), as well as by empowering (*tafwīḍ*) the wife, if she wishes, to pronounce the ṭalāḳ. This is the Ḥanafī teaching and terminology; the Mālikīs limit the term *mubāraʾa* to the special case of the *khulʿ* in a marriage not completed, and for the other cases of divorce by agreement without compensation (which according to them are *makrūh* because not based on the *sunna*), use the expression *tamlīk al-ṭalāḳ*, i.e. transference of the right of divorce to the wife. The Shāfiʿīs recognize the *khulʿ* also without compensation and make it then revocable. Like the ṭalāḳ, the *khulʿ* has remained in practice down to the present day. For the practice of *khulʿ* in India and Indonesia, see Bousquet in *REI*, 1938, p. 231, 237 and the art. UMM AL-WALAD, § 7.

III. To divorce in the modern sense FASKH alone corresponds: i.e. "the rescinding, annulling" of the marriage (the term *faskh* is also used of the annulling of contracts in general), also called TAFRĪḲ, i.e. "the separation" of the husband and wife. It is done in exceptional cases by one of the parties: not by the husband who possesses the right of ṭalāḳ but rather by the *walī* in the exercise of his right of intervention if the husband is not of equal birth, or by a wife, who had been married as a slave, at the manumission. As a rule the dissolution of the marriage is done by the *ḳāḍī* on petition after evidence of the reason for divorce, in certain circumstances after the fruitless expiry of a term fixed by him for redress. This divorce which, according to circumstances, may be either revocable or final is distinguished from ṭalāḳ by its consequences as regards property: if the marriage was not completed, no *mahr* has to be paid, or that already paid has to be given back; if it was completed and the divorce is to the husband's charge the *mahr* has to be paid, if it is at the woman's charge no *mahr* has to be paid, or that already paid, returned. The most important grounds for divorce which give an option (*khiyār*, q.v.) for dissolution of the marriage (with many differences of opinion among the schools in details) are: 1. certain grave chronic diseases (leprosy, elephantiasis, lunacy) and physical defects which prevent marital intercourse (also impotence of the man); the field of cases is, at least with the Ḥanafīs, larger in favour of the woman than in favour of the man, again in view of his right to ṭalāḳ; 2. non-payment of the *mahr* before completion of the marriage (after completion of the marriage this is a ground of separation only with the Ḥanafīs and the Ḥanbalīs, not with the Mālikīs and the S͟hāfiʿīs); 3. inability of the man to provide support (for simple non-fulfilment of this duty in the first place only the order to provide it is made); this separation is not final so long as the woman's *ʿidda* runs: 4. non-fulfilment of special conditions and obligations of the marriage contract (not in all cases); 5. ill-treatment (*ḍarar*) of the wife by the husband, but only if repeatedly done and in more serious cases; this separation may be either revocable or final; 6. refractoriness (*nus͟hūz*) in the woman or incompatibility in the man, and in general discord (*s͟hiḳāḳ*) between husband and wife; this case has special rules based on Sūra iv. 35 (cf. above I, 2): the *ḳāḍī* appoints two referees, one from the family of each consort; they first of all attempt a reconciliation and if their efforts are fruitless they decide the question of guilt: if the fault is on the woman's side, the husband is empowered to use the Ḳurʾānic means of compulsion (admonishment, confinement, beating); if it is on the side of the man, the marriage is annulled by the referees; if the fault is on both sides the marriage is again annulled and the referees decide about the payment or return of the *mahr*; the verdict of the referees is confirmed by the *ḳāḍī*. This case brings us to separation *ex officio judicis*; this happens also when there are impediments to marriage and differences of opinion between the husband and wife regarding the *mahr*, without proof being possible. — In general then the grounds for which a woman can seek a divorce are small in number and difficult of proof.

IV. The LIʿĀN (A.) an oath by which a husband may allege, without legal proof, adultery by his wife without becoming liable to the punishment by which *ḳad͟hf* [q.v.] is threatened, and deny the paternity of a child borne by the wife, is in itself not a divorce proper but has the dissolution of the marriage as a consequence.

1. The basis for the regulations regarding the *liʿān* is Sūra xxiv. 6 *sqq.*: "As to those who accuse their wives (of adultery) without having other witnesses than themselves, the man concerned shall testify four times by Allāh that he is speaking the truth, 7. and the fifth time that the curse of Allāh shall be on him if he is lying; 8. but she may avert the punishment from herself if she testifies four times by Allāh that he is lying, 9. and the fifth time that the wrath of Allāh shall be on her if he is speaking the truth." These verses belong to a part of the Ḳurʾān, apparently revealed at one time, containing various regulations about adultery and consisting of xxiv. 1—10, 21—26; verses 11—20, which certainly belong to the year 5, were inserted later; our verses must therefore be older. They form an exception, in favour of the husband, to the severe punishment laid down in Ḳurʾān xxiv. 4 (cf. also verses 23—25) for *ḳad͟hf*, and are therefore, like this penalty, primarily Muslim and have no affinities in Arab paganism in which an institution like the *liʿān* had no place at all (contrary to Santillana). The word *liʿān*, which comes from the Ḳurʾān, is unknown to the pre-Muḥammadan poetry.

The traditions concerning *liʿān* are almost entirely (the oldest probably exclusively) exegetical and profess to give the occasion of the revelation of the Ḳurʾānic verses in question; they are to some extent contradictory and unreliable. Four types may be distinguished among them: 1. the husband (unnamed) laments his sad case to the Prophet in covert language whereupon the verses are revealed (oldest form); 2. ʿUwaimir b. Ḥārit͟h asks in the same way, first through the intermediary of a friend and then directly of the Prophet (a development of the first type); 3. Hilāl b. Umaiya accuses his wife of adultery and is to be punished with *ḥadd* for this, when Allāh saves him by the revelation of the verses (this type, probably likewise a development of the first has of the three the most schematic and not original appearance); 4. some one marries a young woman and finds her not a virgin while she disputes his assertion; the Prophet therefore orders *liʿān* (not exegetic). In so far as the traditions yield nothing new about *liʿān*, this brief outline is sufficient; they are only of importance when they afford evidence for the oldest juristic adaptation of this Ḳurʾānic institution.

2. The first subject of the earliest legal speculation was the question, not touched upon in the Ḳurʾān, whether *liʿān* makes separation between the husband and wife necessary. In many traditions this question is so expressly (sometimes polemically) affirmed that there must have been a school which approved the continuity of the marriage after the *liʿān*. Among the oldest representatives of the other view which later became predominant, that a continuance of the marriage was impossible after *liʿān*, may be included with certainty al-Zuhrī in whose time it was already *sunna*, and Ibrāhīm al-Nak͟haʿī (*Kitāb al-Āt͟hār*). Next arises the question how this annulment of the marriage as a result of *liʿān* is to take place, whether by a triple ṭalāḳ which the husband has to pronounce against his wife, or by the decision of the *ḳāḍī* before whom the *liʿān* is taken, or by the *liʿān* itself. The first view is undoubtedly represented by a large number of traditions, while no trace of its use in law has survived; these traditions are rather interpreted in favour of the second view. The second opinion survives in the later legal *ik͟htilāf*, apart from the ample testimony to it in *ḥadīt͟h*; its oldest representatives known with certainty are again al-Zuhrī, in whose time it appears as *sunna*, and Ibrāhīm al-Nak͟haʿī (*Kitāb al-Āt͟hār*). For the third there is no evidence in tradition; it is only found after the rise of the *mad͟hhabs*. We seem therefore to have a tendency to development in a particular direction.

Other prescriptions about *liʿān* in tradition, going beyond what is laid down in the Ḳurʾān, are of less importance. Thus, when the question is raised at all, it is unanimously laid down that the husband can never marry the wife again at a later date, that a *liʿān* may take place during pregnancy (legal *ik͟htilāf* is later attached to the interpretation of this *ḥadīt͟h*), that the child has only relationship with its mother as regards kinship or inheritance, i.e. is considered illegitimate. Other traditions say that the *liʿān* must be taken in a mosque and attribute the formulae to be spoken there by the *ḳāḍī* to the Prophet.

3. The teachings of the separate *mad͟hhabs* develop the views of their earliest representatives, not entirely on the same lines (e.g. from the *Muwaṭṭaʾ* it is to be assumed with probability that Mālik followed the second view regarding the element in *liʿān* which annulled the marriage [cf. above], while his school later held the third opinion entirely). The most important regulations of the *fiḳh* regarding *liʿān* are as follows: if the husband accuses the wife of adultery (*zināʾ*) or denies the paternity of her child without being able to prove it in the legally prescribed fashion and she denies his charge, recourse

is had to the process of *liʿān*. If the husband refuses to pronounce the formulae prescribed for him, he is punished with the *ḥadd* for *ḳadhf*, according to Abū Ḥanīfa, however, imprisoned until he pronounces the formulae, whereby he is set free, or declares to have lied, whereupon he is liable to *ḥadd*. If the wife refuses to pronounce the corresponding formulae, she is punished with the *ḥadd* for adultery, according to Abū Ḥanīfa and the better tradition of Aḥmad b. Ḥanbal, however, imprisoned until she pronounces the formulae, whereupon she is set free, or confesses her transgression and is then liable to *ḥadd*. On the question whether *liʿān* is possible if one partner is or both are not Muslims or not free or not *ʿadl*, there is wealth of *ikhtilāf*; the same applies to the possibility of *liʿān* during the pregnancy of the woman, with the object of denying the paternity of the child. On this point the strength of the principle that the marriage decides the descent of the child, is remarkable, as is the distinction between two objects of *liʿān* (accusation of the wife of adultery and denial of paternity); this is only a result of later developments, for in the whole of the earlier period these two objects coincide from the juristic point of view. The divorcing element in *liʿān* is, according to the Mālikīs (on their presumed divergence from Mālik himself on this question, cf. above) and a tradition of Aḥmad b. Ḥanbal, the *liʿān* of the wife, according to al-Shāfiʿī that of the husband, according to Abū Ḥanīfa and the better tradition of Aḥmad b. Ḥanbal however the verdict of the *ḳāḍī* pronounced after the *liʿān* of both. Opinions also differ regarding the legal consequences of a later withdrawal of the *liʿān* by the husband: according to Abū Ḥanīfa and one tradition of Aḥmad b. Ḥanbal, a new marriage of the two people is possible in this case, according to Mālik, al-Shāfiʿī and the better tradition of Aḥmad b. Ḥanbal it is not; among older authorities only Saʿīd b. Djubair is quoted as in favour of the first view, the majority in favour of the second, which was also held by al-Awzāʿī and Sufyān al-Thawrī. Finally it is a disputed question whether the *liʿān* can only be performed orally or (in the case of a dumb person) by gestures; al-Bukhārī devotes chapter 25 of his *Kitāb al-ṭalāḳ* to the discussion of the question and the reasons for his attitude to it. The doctrines of the Shīʿa on *liʿān* do not offer any remarkable peculiarities.

4. It is easy to understand that resort was only had to the *liʿān* in extreme cases. Thus we find a scholar of Cordova in the fourth (tenth) century pronouncing the *liʿān* against his wife simply in order to revive this *sunna* of the Prophet, which had fallen into oblivion (I. Goldziher, *Muhammedanische Studien*, ii. 21). But it has not yet fallen completely into desuetude, as Muslim law has no other means of disputing the paternity of a child. The ruling of Anglo-Muḥammadan jurisprudence in India amounts to no more than that an accusation of adultery by the husband may, if persisted in, be cruelty, thus giving the wife a right to obtain divorce; thus, the original character of the *liʿān* has been reversed into its contrary.

Bibliography: (in addition to the above): Sprenger, l.c., s.v.; Dozy, *Suppl. aux Dict. Arabes*, s.v.; al-Ṭabarī, *Tafsīr*; al-Ḳasṭallānī, Commentary on al-Bukhārī, *Ṭalāḳ*, 25 and 30; al-Zurḳānī, *Sharḥ al-Muwaṭṭaʾ, Bāb mā djāʾa fi ʾl-liʿān*.

V. An ancient special form of repudiation was the ĪLĀʾ, i.e. the oath taken by the man to cease marital intercourse. In the endeavour to prevent too hasty repudiation, Sūra ii. 266 *sqq.* (perhaps contemporary with the adjoining verses) gives the husband a period for reflection: "Those who swear off from their women may wait four months: if they break their vow — Allāh is forgiving and merciful. 227. But if they are determined upon the divorce — Allāh is hearing and knowing". In Islāmic law the *īlāʾ* is regarded from another point of view: as the abandonment of the marital relationship by the man as a consequence of which divorce takes place. If a man takes on oath to avoid marital intercourse for more than four months (or without stating a period) and keeps his oath (or keeps it for longer than four months) this, according to the Ḥanafīs, has the effect of a final repudiation; but he can break this oath like any other before the expiry of the period, and is then bound to atone for it either by the legal penalty (*kaffāra*, q.v.) or by the fine (*djazāʾ*) fixed in the oath itself in case of non-fulfilment; according to the three other schools, the husband after the expiry of the period is given the choice of breaking his oath or pronouncing a (revocable) divorce. According to the Mālikīs and one tradition of Aḥmad b. Ḥanbal, actual omission of marital intercourse for over four months from dislike of the wife has the same effect as the fulfilment of the oath. On the cases in which the oath of continence has no effect on account of the special condition of the husband or wife, on the rules valid for slaves and on details of procedure, there are differences of opinion. In any case this pagan custom, which was early dropped in Islām, is considered a sin.

VI. Another old Arabian method of repudiation was the ẒIHĀR, i.e. the pronouncement of the formula: "Thou art as to me (as untouchable) as the back (*ẓahr*) of my mother". The Ḳurʾān refers to this in Sūra lviii. 1 *sqq.* (from the later Madīna period): "Allāh has heard the speech of her who is wrangling with you about her husband, and complaining to Allāh. ... 2. As to those of you who separate from their wives by *ẓihār*, they are not their mothers; their mothers are only those who gave them birth; they speak an objectionable and false speech.... 3. As to those who separate from their wives by *ẓihār* and then (would) come back to what they have said: the liberation of a slave before they touch each other.... 4. But when they do not find (the means), then a fast of two consecutive months, before they touch each other; and when they are unable (to fast), then the feeding of sixty poor folk". Similarly to verse 2, the *ẓihār* is again condemned in the later passage xxxiii. 4. Sūra lviii. 1 *sqq.* is obviously inspired by an individual case; tradition pretends to know details (the name of the husband is unanimously given as ʿAws b. al-Ṣāmit). According to Islāmic law, the *ẓihār* is a sinful pronouncement in consequence of which any marital intercourse between husband and wife becomes forbidden, until the special atonement provided for in the Ḳurʾān is made, the details of which are minutely specified. According to the Ḥanafīs, the *ẓihār* has no further legal effect on the marriage, and the man who wishes to continue the marriage can be forced by the *ḳāḍī* to make the atonement; the Mālikīs and Shāfiʿīs deal with *ẓihār* as *īlāʾ* (with slight differences in detail) when the man will not withdraw it. This pagan practice also very early fell into disuse in Islām.

VII. A marriage ceases of itself if it becomes null and void (*bāṭil*), either because one party as a slave becomes the property of the other, or because he becomes an apostate (*murtadd*) from Islām. This provision of the law has in India and Indonesia, i.e. countries where under European rule the severe punishments of the *s͟harīʿa* for apostasy cannot be applied, taken advantage of by women to procure, by a temporary apostasy, a dissolution of the marriage for which otherwise they have only slight opportunities (cf. above III). This subterfuge has obviously been suggested by legal experts; in Indonesia where full records are available, we even find cases of divorce by apostasy with the complicity of the *s͟harīʿa* law courts. On the other hand, we have in Indonesia a disinclination supported by more or less sound reasons on the parts of the religious courts to accept such declarations.

Bibliography: Robertson Smith, *Kinship and Marriage in early Arabia*, 2nd ed. p. 112 *sqq.*; Wellhausen, *Die Ehe bei den Arabern* (*Nachr. d. Kgl. Ges. d. Wiss. Göttingen* 1893) p. 452 *sqq.*; Gertrude H. Stern, *Marriage in early Islam*, London 1939, p. 127 *sqq.*; Wensinck, *Handbook*, s.v. Divorce; Sprenger, *Dictionary of the technical terms*, s.v.; Juynboll, *Handleiding*, 3rd ed. p. 203 *sqq.*; Santillana, *Istituzioni*, i. 201 *sqq.*; G. Bergsträsser, *Grundzüge*, p. 84 *sqq.*; Ubach u. Rackow, *Sitte und Recht in Nordafrika*, passim; Lane, *Manners and customs of the modern Egyptians*, ch. iii. and iv.; Jaussen, *Coutumes des Arabes au pays de Moab*, § 3; do., *Coutumes des Fuqarâ*, § 4; Snouck Hurgronje, *De Atjehers*, i. 382 *sqq.*; do., *Verspr. Geschr.* iv./i. 300 *sq.*, iv./ii. 380; G. F. Pijper, *Fragmenta Islamica*, p. 74—94.

TALBIYA (A.), infinitive of form II of the verb *labbā*, which is formed from the term *labbaika* to mean "to pronounce the formula *labbaika*" etc. *Labbaika* is connected — and probably rightly — by the Arab lexicographers with *labb*[un] which means "offering devoted service" as *labbaika* does "at your service". According to the native grammarians *labbai* is a "frequentative" dual. It is difficult to say what is the significance of the element *ai* in this and similar forms like *saʿdaika*. The explanation from the Hebrew proposed by Dozy (*De Israëlieten te Mekka*, Haarlem 1864, p. 120) may be said to be now generally abandoned.

The formula is used in various forms and on different occasions. The talbiya of the Prophet is said to have been: *Labbaika allāhumma labbaika labbaika lā s͟harīka laka inna 'l-ḥamda wa 'l-niʿmata laka wa 'l-mulka la s͟harīka laka* (Buk͟hārī, *Ḥad̲j̲d̲j̲* b. 26), but shorter forms are given like: *labbaika allāhumma, labbaika wa-saʿdaika* etc. It is usually referred to Allāh, in Ḥadīt͟h also to Muḥammad, or to his helpers but only in its briefest form *labbaika* (e.g. Buk͟hārī, *K͟huṣūmāt*, b. 4; Muslim, *Zakāt*, tr. 32; Tirmid͟hī, *Ḳiyāma*, b. 36) and *yā labbaika* (Muslim, *D̲j̲ihād*, tr. 76). It is also placed in the mouths of pious men of the past like Ādam and Nūḥ. According to a tradition in Muslim (*Ḥad̲j̲d̲j̲*, tr. 22) the heathen in Muḥammad's time used it in a false form. The talbiya is especially pronounced on the *ḥad̲j̲d̲j̲* [q.v.], at an early stage at the *iḥrām* which Muḥammad and others assumed with the formula *labbaika bi-ḥad̲j̲d̲j̲at*[in] *wa-ʿumrat*[in] (Buk͟hārī, *Ḥad̲j̲d̲j̲*, b. 34) or *labbaika bi-ʿumrat*[in] *wa-ḥad̲j̲d̲j̲at*[in] (Tirmid͟hī, *Ḥad̲j̲d̲j̲*, b. 11) or with the exclusive mention of the *ḥad̲j̲d̲j̲* (Buk͟hārī, *Ḥad̲j̲d̲j̲*, b. 35). At the beginning of the *ʿumra* ʿĀʾis͟ha is said to have used the formula *labbaika bi 'l-ʿumrat*[i] (Abū Dāʾūd, *Manāsik*, b. 23).

The talbiya is continually pronounced during the *ḥad̲j̲d̲j̲* up to the lapidation (e.g. Aḥmad b. Ḥanbal, i. 114) and in a loud voice (Aḥmad b. Ḥanbal, v. 192).

On the question whether the talbiya is obligatory or sunna, see al-Nawawī on Muslim, *Ḥad̲j̲d̲j̲*, tr. 22.

TALISMAN [See ḤAMĀʾIL; SIḤR].

ṬĀLŪT is the name given in the Ḳurʾān (ii. 247, 249) to the Israelite king Saul. Ṭālūt seems to be (with the doubtful case of S͟huʿaib) the only name in the Ḳurʾān which differs entirely from its biblical form. It is apparently derived from the verb *ṭāla*, "to be long" (alluding to the high stature of Saul: I. Sam., x. 23), by assonance with D̲j̲ālūt, the name of the biblical Goliath in the Ḳurʾān (ii. 249—251), Ṭālūt-D̲j̲ālūt constituting a pair of rhyming names like Hārūt-Mārūt, Hābil-Ḳābil, Yād̲j̲ūd̲j̲-Mād̲j̲ūd̲j̲, and perhaps Hārūn-Ḳārūn.

In the Ḳurʾān (ii. 246—252) the following is told of Ṭālūt. After the time of Moses Israel demanded a king. God appointed Ṭālūt king but the people did not find him worthy of the throne. Ṭālūt was distinguished for the greatness of his knowledge and for his great physique also; it was a sign of his fitness to rule that angels brought back the ark (*tābūt*) with the *sakīna* [q.v.] and with the relics of the families of Moses and Aaron. Ṭālūt tested his people at a river; whoever drank from it did not follow him. Israel took the field against D̲j̲ālūt; David slew D̲j̲ālūt and became king.

The divergences from the Biblical story in this version are obvious. The first book of Samuel relates that Israel demanded a king (viii.) but no respect was shown to the new king (x. 27; xi. 12). The sacred ark which Muḥammad regards as a token of Saul's worth was recaptured in the Bible before his accession. The test by drinking water is made in the Bible not by Saul but by Gideon (Judges, vii. 5—7).

Nöldeke sees in this Ḳurʾānic story an effort by Muḥammad to arouse the Muslims to courage and obedience by examples from Jewish history. Later Muslim tradition (Ṭabarī, T͟haʿlabī, al-Kisāʾī) often mentions that the number of the faithful who fought by Muḥammad's side in the battle of Badr was the same as those who passed Ṭālūt's test by water.

Muslim legend has more to say, explains every feature of the Ḳurʾān story, and adds many new details. Later writers (Ṭabarī, T͟haʿlabī, Ibn al-Athīr, Abu 'l-Fidā also know the name Saul, son of Ḳīs͟h, (شاول بن قيش). In explanation of the name Ṭalūt, we are told that at this time the future king of Israel was to be recognized by his height (T͟haʿlabī); Samuel set up a measure, but no one in Israel reached its height, except Ṭālūt. As a miracle which took place to show the rightness of their choice, we are told that when Ṭālūt went to consult Samuel (S͟hamwīl) about his lost she-asses, the coronation oil began to boil. Ṭabarī's *Tafsīr* mentions inspiration as another token. In explanation of the story in the Ḳurʾān, that Ṭālūt appeared unworthy to the people, it is said that Saul was descended from Benjamin, that is neither from Judah, the tribe of kings, nor from Levi, the tribe of priests (T͟haʿlabī). On the ark, the token of Ṭālūt's worthiness, Muslim legend has much that is marvellous to tell. This sacred ark had been handed down from the time of Adam from generation to generation through Ismāʿīl to Ḳaidar. Ḳaidar gave it to Jacob. Within the ark were kept the *sakīna*, the hearts of the prophets, the tables of the law, the rod of Moses, Aaron's turban and rod (T͟haʿlabī). This ark had fallen into the hands of D̲j̲ālūt, the king of the Amalekites. When plagues fell upon the Amalekites, they sent back the ark on the advice of a captured Jew. Two cattle led by angels brought the ark to Ṭālūt and returned. According to another legend, the angels themselves brought it to Ṭālūt between heaven and earth. The people were then convinced of Ṭālūt's worthiness.

Ṭālūt's relations with Dā'ūd are fully described. Ṭālūt promised his daughter and one third of the kingdom to whoever should kill Djālūt. Nevertheless he next demanded a nuptial gift of 200 slain giants. When the affections of the people turned to Dā'ūd, Ṭālūt wanted to slay his son-in-law. Warned by his wife, Dā'ūd put a wine-skin in his bed and Ṭālūt stabbed it. Dā'ūd on one occasion was saved by a spider spinning a web at the entrance to a cave. Dā'ūd showed his magnanimity by once leaving four (in Ibn al-Athīr: two) arrows besides Ṭālūt; on another occasion he took from Ṭālūt his cup, his jar, his arms, a piece of his garment and hair from his beard.

Saul's raising of the dead (I Sam. xxviii) is completely transformed in Muslim legend. Sometimes it is Joshua and sometimes Samuel that is called up. Ṭālūt learns that there is only atonement for him, he must fight with all his family and die for Allāh. Ṭālūt abdicates and suffers with his sons the "death on the path of Allāh".

Bibliography: Ṭabarī, ed. de Goeje, i. 549, 559, 1297, 1298 (Badr); Ṭabarī, *Tafsīr*, Cairo 1321, ii. 357—375; Thaʿlabī, *Ḳiṣaṣ al-anbiyā'*, Cairo 1325, p. 167—173; Ibn al-Athīr, *Ta'rīkh al-Kāmil*, i. 150 *sqq.*; Kisā'ī, *Ḳiṣaṣ al-anbīyā'*, ed. Eisenberg, Leyden 1923, ii. 250—258; Weil, *Biblische Legenden der Muselmänner*, Frankfurt a/M. 1845, p. 192—208; Grünbaum, *Neue Beiträge*, Leyden 1893, p. 185—189, 192—195; Nöldeke-Schwally, *Gesch. des Qorāns*, i. 184. Speyer, *Die bibl. Erzählungen im Qoran*, p. 363—371. — On the name: Goldziher, *Der Mythos bei den Hebräern*, p. 232—234; Joseph Horovitz, in *Hebrew Union College Annual*, ii., Cincinnati 1925, p. 162, 163; do., *Koranische Untersuchungen*, 1926, p. 81—84, 106, 123. — On the spider's web which saved David: R. Basset, *La Bordah du Cheikh el Bousiri*, Paris 1897, p. 81—86.

TAMATTUʿ. [See IḤRĀM; MUTʿA].

TANĀSUKH, transmigration, metempsychosis; a belief widespread in India and among several sects of the Muslim world. Muḥammadan authors who deal with it attribute it to the Indians rather than to the Pythagoreans.

Al-Bīrūnī in his *India* has a good chapter on metempsychosis, of which he says that it is the shibboleth of the Hindu religion, as the belief in the unity of God is that of Islām. He cites Vāsudeva, Patanjali, compares their opinions with those of Plato, Proclus and the Ṣūfīs, and quotes this view of the Indian philosophers: a single life is too short for the soul to comprise the multiplicity of things comprised in the world.

Shahrastānī in his article on the "people of metempsychosis" takes the word in a wider sense: to him it means the doctrine of the successive lives and rebirths of the world. The Indians, he says, are of all nations those who believe most in metempsychosis. They tell the story of the phoenix and then say it is the same with the universe; after a certain number of revolutions, the celestial spheres, the stars, all come back to the same point and the life of the universe is repeated. The length of this period of revolution is 30,000 years according to some and 360,000 according to others. Masʿūdī (*Murūdj*, i. 163) also talks of this great revolution and gives the cycle a duration of 70,000 years. This idea was known to the Greek astronomers who called it the "great year".

In another sense *tanāsukh* means the diffusion and distribution of the divine spirit among the beings of our world. The Ghulāt, who were extreme Shīʿīs, admitted, says Shahrastānī, *tanāsukh* and the descent or incarnation (*ḥulūl*) of all or part of the divine principle in certain men. Belief in this kind of *tanāsukh* is found among many peoples, who received it from the Mazdakite Magi, Brahmans of India, philosophers and Sabaeans. Hudjwīrī is acquainted with a sect of Ṣūfīs whom he calls Ḥulūlīs; they assert that there is only a single spirit, eternal and divine, which is diffused and passes into different bodies. This view, says Hudjwīrī, is that of many Christians, although they do not confess it, of the generality of Indians, Tibetans, Chinese, and it is found among the Shīʿīs, Ḳarmaṭians and the Ismāʿīlīs. There are four degrees of metempsychosis: *naskh*, *maskh*, *faskh* and *raskh*.

In the popular sense, of passing from one body to another, the belief in metempsychosis is held by several Shīʿī sects. Among the Muʿtazilīs, according to Shahrastānī, the disciples of Aḥmad b. Ḥā'iṭ taught that God first created beings in a kind of Paradise; then those who were guilty of some disobedience were sent by Him into our world in the form of men or animals according to the gravity of their sins; they then migrate from form to form until the effects of their sins have ceased.

The Ismāʿīlīs did not admit the passage of the soul into the bodies of animals; but they did admit successive lives in which the souls pass to and fro in the world of birth and death until they have recognized the *Imām*; they then rise to the world of light.

The Nuṣairīs believe that the sinner of their religion will return to the world as a Jew, Sunnī Muslim or Christian; the infidels who have not known ʿAlī become camels, mules, asses, dogs or other similar animals. There are seven degrees of metempsychosis, according to the Nuṣairīs; the faithful soul which has passed through the seven degrees rises into the stars from which in the beginning it had descended. Anz and Dussaud have connected this theory with the doctrine of the ascension of the soul through the seven heavens, which, originating on Babylonian soil, spread into Persian beliefs and then into those of the Neo-Platonists and the Gnostics. The Druses have taken some of their popular beliefs from the Nuṣairīs, although their founder Ḥamza was opposed to them; they believe that the souls of the enemies of ʿAlī will enter the bodies of dogs, monkeys and swine. The Kurds and the Yazīdīs believe in transmigration into the bodies of men and animals and in successive existences separated by an interval of 72 years. According to Saiyid Sharīf Djurdjānī (*Taʿrīfāt*) the *tanāsukh* is the passing of the soul to a new body without intervals on account of the inclination of the spirit for the body.

Al-Samarḳandī quotes curious legends about *maskh* (a variant of *naskh*), according to which the monkey, the pig and other animals are descended from people who have been metamorphosed. The star Suhail and the planet Zuhra (Venus) are in the same way said to have been a king and a princess punished by God for their crimes and placed — somewhat illogically — among the stars. Finally we may mention the stories of metamorphosis found in the *Arabian Nights* and other tales.

Bibliography: *Alberuni's India*, tr. Sachau, London 1910, chap. V; Shahrastānī, *Kitāb al-milal wa 'l-niḥal*, ed. Cureton, London 1842, ii, 297 and *passim*; Hudjwīrī, *Kashf al-maḥdjūb*.

transl. R. A. Nicholson, in *GMS*, Leyden and London 1911, p. 260 *sqq.*; R. Dussaud, *Histoire et religion des Noṣairîs*, Paris 1900, p. 120 *sqq.*; W. Anz, *Zur Frage nach dem Ursprung des Gnostizismus*, in *Texte und Untersuchungen* by v. Gebhardt und Harnack, xv., Leipzig 1897; St. Guyard, *Un grand Maître des Assassins au temps de Saladin*, *JA*, Paris 1877 (tales); Naṣr b. Muḥammad b. Ibrāhīm al-Samarḳandī, *Bustān al-ʿārifīn*, Mecca 1300, p. 240; J. Menant, *Les Yézidis*, in *Annales du Musée Guimet*, Paris 1892, p. 87.

TANZĪL. [See WAḤY].

TARĀWĪḤ (A.), plural of the rare sing. *tarwīḥa*, the ṣalāts which are performed in the nights of the month of Ramaḍān. Tradition says that Muḥammad held these ṣalāts in high esteem, with the precaution, however, that their performance should not become obligatory (Bukhārī, *Tarāwīḥ*, trad. 3). ʿUmar is said to have been the first to assemble behind one *ḳāriʾ* those who performed their prayers in the mosque of al-Madīna singly or in groups (*loc. cit.*, trad. 2); he is also said to have preferred the first part of the night for these pious exercises.

Canon law recommends the performance of the tarāwīḥ shortly after the *ṣalāt al-ʿishāʾ*. They consist of 10 *taslīma*'s, each containing 2 *rakʿa*'s; after every four *rakʿa*'s a pause is made; hence the name *tarāwīḥ* "pauses". In the Mālikite rite they consist of 36 *rakʿa*'s. They belong to the *ṣalāt*'s that are *sunna* and are as popular as any rite connected with Ramaḍān [q.v.]. Shīʿa *fiḳh* prefers the performance of a thousand supererogatory *rakʿa*'s throughout the month of Ramaḍān.

In Mecca people assemble in groups varying from 10 to 150 persons, behind one *imām* [q.v.], who acts in this case unofficially, even if he should be an appointed official. The recitation of the Ḳurʾān has a prominent place in these *ṣalāt*'s. Although busy people may make these devotions as short as possible, other groups remain behind their *imām*'s reciting the Ḳurʾān once or several times in the nights of Ramaḍān. Even after the tarāwīḥ many people stay for pious exercises.

In Atchin every night large crowds assemble in order to perform the tarāwīḥ. Usually, however, it is the *tönku* alone who takes the active part in them, the others limiting their part to a loudly audible joining in with the *āmīn* and the eulogies on the Prophet. The *tönku* receives the *zakāt al-fiṭr* as a remuneration for his endurance. In his *Arabic New-Year* (*Verh. Ak. Amst.*, new ser., xxv., No. 2) Wensinck traces the rites of Ramaḍān back to pagan times.

Bibliography: Bukhārī, *Tarāwīḥ*, with the commentaries; Mālik, *Muwaṭṭaʾ*, *Ṣalāt fī Ramaḍān* with Zurḳānī's commentary; Abū Isḥāḳ al-Shīrāzī, *Tanbīh*, ed. Juynboll, p. 27; al-Ramlī, *Nihāya*, Cairo 1286, i. 503 *sqq.*; Ibn Ḥadjar al-Haitamī, *Tuḥfa*, Cairo 1282, i. 205 *sq.*; Abu 'l-Ḳāsim al-Ḥillī, *Sharāʾiʿ al-Islām*, Calcutta 1255, p. 51; Caetani, *Annali*, A.H., 14, § 229 *sq.*; Juynboll, *Handleiding*, Leyden 1925, register; Snouck Hurgronje, *Mekka*, ii. 81 *sqq.*; do., *Mekkanische Sprichwörter*, No. 49; do., *De Atjèhers*, i. 247 *sqq.*; d'Ohsson, *Tableau général de l'empire othoman*, Paris 1787, i. 214 *sq.* (to be used with caution); Lane, *Manners and Customs of the Modern Egyptians*, London and Paisley 1899, p. 481.

ṬARĪḲA (pl. *ṭuruḳ*). This Arabic term, meaning "road, way, path", has acquired two successive technical meanings in Muslim mysticism:

1. In the ninth and tenth centuries A.D. it was a method of moral psychology for the practical guidance of individuals who had a mystic call; 2. after the xi[th] century, it becomes the whole system of rites for spiritual training laid down for communal life in the various Muslim religious orders which began to be founded at this time.

In the first sense (cf. texts by Djunaid, Ḥallādj, Sarrādj, Ḳushairī, Hudjwīrī), the word *ṭarīḳa* is still vague and means rather a theoretical and ideal method (*riʿāya*, *sulūk* are stronger) to guide each one who has had a call by tracing an *itinerarium mentis ad Deum* leading through various psychological stages (*maḳāmāt*, *aḥwāl*) of the literal practice of the revealed law (*sharīʿa*) to divine reality (*ḥaḳīḳa*). Since this bold claim provoked criticism and even persecution from the canonists, the teachers of mysticism devoted themselves to defining and restraining their activities on more orthodox lines compiling rules calculated to avert suspicion (*ādāb al-Ṣūfīya*), from Sulamī and Makkī to Ibn Ṭāhir Maḳdisī (*ṣafwa*) and Ghazzālī. In practice, while keeping as the goal direct access (*fatḥ*) to reality, they gradually abandoned the freedom of musical assemblies (*samāʿ*), which stimulated not only ecstasy but also often reprehensible theopathic utterances [cf. SHAṬḤ), for regular recitations of litanies founded on the Ḳurʾān (*dhikr*): thus preparing the adept for a state of mental concentration (*tafakkur*) through which, in quiet aloneness, he seeks to experience a state in which the successive perception of differently coloured lights (*anwār*) gradually denudes from its covering of words the "clarity" (of the recited litany) and "substantialises" it in the heart; which then participates in the divine essence of its prayer (*dhikr al-dhāt bi-tadjawhur nūr al-dhikr fi 'l-ḳalb*, says Suhrawardī on chap. xxvii. of the *ʿAwārif*, ii. 191).

Thus *ṭarīḳa* comes finally to mean a common life (*muʿāshara*), founded on a series of special rules in addition to the ordinary observances of Islām: to become an adept (*faḳīr*, Pers. *darwish*) the novice (*murīd*, *gandūz*) receives initiation (*baiʿa*, *talḳīn*, *shadd*) before a hierarchy of witnesses (*shaikh al-sadjdjāda* = Pers. *pīr* = Turk. *bābā*; *murshid*, *muḳaddam*, *naḳīb*, *khalīfa*, *turdjumān*, Pers. *rind*, *rāhpar* etc.); even if he is of an order allowing a wandering life (*siyāḥa*), he has to make periodic retreats (*ʿuzla*, *khalwa*, *arbaʿīnīya* = Pers. *čihil*) with them in a monastery (*ribāṭ*, *zāwiya* = Pers. *khanḳa* = Turk. *tekkiye*) of the order, supported by expiatory alms (*hadya*) and generally built near the tomb of a venerated saint whose anniversary (*mawlid*, *ʿurs*) is celebrated and whose blessing (*ziyāra*, *baraka*) is invoked.

In the interior of the monastery the common life of the brethren (*ikhwān* = Turk. *ākhīler*, an Anatolian term since the xii[th] century; there were attempts to found convents of sisters only in Egypt and Syria in the xiii[th] and xiv[th] centuries) is at the same time distinguished by supererogatory exercises, vigils (*sahr*), fasts (*ṣiyām*), invocations (*wird*; e.g. *yā laṭīf*, repeated 100 or 1,000 times), litanies (*dhikr*, *ḥizb*) especially at certain festivals (a kind of liturgical office for the vigils, *barāʾa*, *raghāʾib*, *ḳadr*), also by dispensations (*rukhaṣ*), like the collections of alms (*ḳasama*, collected in the *kashkūl*) and private assemblies (*ḥadra*, *waẓīfa*, *zerda*) in which in addition to litanies, platonic glances (*naẓar ila 'l-murd*), jesting (*mizāḥ*) even going as far as horseplay, dancing (*raḳṣ*) and the rending of garments (*tamzīḳ*) are allowed.

The actual ritual initiation, identical to that of initiation into trade-guilds of Ḳarmaṭian origin, as Kahle has observed, was probably borrowed from them in the xii^th^ century (Taeschner, *Islām*, vi. 169—172, published a Turkish miniature of the xvii^th^ century representing the scene). The diploma of initiation (*idjāza*) in use since 1227 (cf. Ibn Abī Uṣaibiʿa, *ʿUyūn al-anbā*, ii. 250) reproduces the *isnād* of the traditionists to give the new initiate his double chain of affiliation (*silsila, shadjara*). At the same time he is given a double frock (*khirḳat al-wird, khirḳat al-tabarruk*) to show his twofold taking of an oath (*ʿahd al-yad wa 'l-iḳtidā'* = *talḳīn* and *ʿahd al-khirḳa*), his double adopted genealogy, instruction (oral transmission of the rule) and inspiration (individual illumination), to which his vow of obedience entitles him.

The orthodox canonists (*fuḳahā'*) have constantly attacked the innovations (*bidʿa*) propagated by the *ṭarīḳa*'s: their supererogatory exercises and their dispensations, their special costumes (characteristic headdresses with strips of colour, *kulāh, tādj* etc.), their use of stimulants (coffee, *ḥashīsh*, opium), their jugglery, their belief in the supernatural efficacy of the *talḳīn* and the *baraka* (blind submission to the individual and anarchical enlightenment of an irresponsible leader). They have devoted special attention to the critical history of the *isnād* of initiation, exposing the lacunae and the improbability of their chains [cf. TAṢAWWUF] and they have protested against the *isnād ilhāmī* (spiritual) which bases the privileges of the order on the apparitions of a holy being, mysterious and immortal, al-Khaḍir [q.v.], whom all the orders revere as the "master of the path" (*ṭarīḳa*), since, having been the guide of Moses (Ḳur'ān, xviii. 65—82), he is superior to the law (*sharīʿa*) and the prophets and capable of guiding the soul of the mystic to the supreme reality (*ḥaḳīḳa*).

In Turkey the government has often persecuted the orders on account of their Shīʿa associations; and after a brief truce during which the pan-Islām of ʿAbd al-Ḥamīd endeavoured to make use of them, they were dissolved in 1925 for reactionary conspiracy. In the other Muslim countries, in spite of some attempts at reform interesting from the moral (India) or intellectual (Algeria) point of view, they are in a state of complete decline. The acrobatics and juggling practised by certain adepts of the lower classes, and the moral corruption of too many of their leaders has aroused against almost all of them the hostility and contempt of the elite of the modern Muslim world.

The *ṭarīḳas* however cannot be completely neglected: and although their average moral level is very far below that of the great examples of the first *Ṣūfiya*, the great part that they have never ceased to play in the everyday life, humble but profound, of the Muslim community promises important results to those who will undertake a thorough study of their rules and writings. Ethnologists like Tremearne and Westermarck have already shown that several of their rites, incorporated in an Islāmic liturgic structure, in which they play an unexpected part, are in reality pre-Islāmic survivals (e.g. in the East Indies and in Java) or animistic infiltrations (e.g. *zār* of the Gülshanīya of Cairo borrowed from the Azande; sacrifices of the ʿĪsawīya of Meknes, modelled on the *bori* of the Hausa; cf. *RMM*, xliv. 1—52). Comparative folklore and psychology will also have something to learn from the hagiographic documentation of the great Muslim orders (cf. *Mél. R. Basset*, 1923, i. 259—270 and *Journal de Psychologie*, 1927, p. 163—168).

Introduction to the list of the ṭarīḳa's of Islām.

To get the data in this list into their proper historical setting let us recall briefly that the isolated attempts at a common life in Islām [cf. TAṢAWWUF] earned their adepts a generic name only in 814 (Alexandria, Kūfa), that of *Ṣūfiya*. After 857 (Muḥāsibī) this name begins to be applied in a rather loose way to all who had received a mystic call in the ʿIrāḳ (where some denser nuclei were called Sālimīya, Ḥallādjīya); this name was then contrasted for over two centuries with the name *Malāmatīya*, applied to the more active and more strict mystics of Khurāsān, who professed "indifference to censure" and reproached the *Ṣūfiya* with their aesthetic quietism and their fondness for the *samāʿ*.

For this primitive period, the list below only gives anachronistic names, artificially revived from the xiii^th^ century by Muslim hagiographers, along with the names of authentic doctrinal schools, incorrectly described as religious orders, and names of heresies imagined by the Imāmī theologians.

After the xii^th^ century on the other hand, the list reflects with sufficient accuracy the different foundations of orders, the history of which may be briefly summed up as follows: birth among the *Ṣūfiya-Khafīfīya* of a secondary order, the *Kāzarūnīya* (1304), and among the *Ṣūfiya-Djunaidīya* of a larger order, directed by regular superiors (Djurdjānī, Fārmadhī, Nassādj, Aḥmad Ghazzālī), which finally divided in the xiii^th^ century into three branches: *Khwādjagān* (Yūsuf Hamadhānī, d. 1140), the *Kubrāwīya* (Kubrā, d. 1221) and the *Ḳādirīya* (although their founder died in 1166, their rule was not organized till half a century later). To these two last orders, Aḥmad Ibn al-Ḳāḍī (*Ḳawāʿid wafīya*, cf. Laleli MS. 1478) adds: the *Rifāʿīya, Madanīya* (the future *Shādhilīya*) and *Čishtīya* to form the group of "five primitive *khirḳa*'s".

Others were soon added: in the xiii^th^ century *Ḳalandarīya, Aḥmadīya, Mawlawīya*; in the xiv^th^ century *Bekṭāshīya, Naḳshabandīya, Ṣafawīya, Khalwatīya* with their numerous later subdivisions; in the xv^th^ century we have the reformation by Djazūlī in the Maghrib and rise of the *Shaṭṭārīya* in India and Sumatra; finally in the xix^th^ century in the Maghrib we have with the reformation of the *Ḳādirīya* and of the *Shādhilīya*, the foundation of the *Tidjānīya, Darḳāwa* and *Sanūsīya*.

None of the great orders is at the present day centralized except the Sanūsīya and the Mawlawīya; the bond which binds the adepts, being neither perpetual nor exclusive, becomes often extremely loose. As a rule the number of persons affiliated to the brotherhoods in any particular Muslim country is not over 3% of the population, the most widely disseminated orders at present are: the *Ḳādirīya* (ʿIrāḳ, Turkey, India, Turkistān, China, Nubia, Sūdān, Maghrib); *Naḳshabandīya* (Turkistān, China, Turkey, India, Malayan Archipelago); *Shādhilīya* (Maghrib, Syria); *Bekṭāshīya* (Turkey, Albania); *Tidjānīya* (Maghrib, Fr. W. Africa; Tchad); *Sanūsīya* (Ṣaḥarā, Ḥidjāz); *Shaṭṭārīya* (India, Malayan Archipelago).

Several attempts at the federation of various brotherhoods were made in the Ḥamīdī period; they took the form of a curious syncretist hierarchy associating a permanent body of four universal intercessors: Rifāʿī (president), Djīlānī, Badawī and Dasūḳī, with the *abdāl* and the *ḳuṭb* of the present hour.

The Muslim orders not all having special articles in the present publication, the list below gives in alphabetical order the names of the principal *ṭarīḳa*'s with a brief note on its origin and its subdivisions, its geographical position and the date (A.D.) of death of its founder. The principal orders are in small capitals and those that still exist are preceded by an asterisk. The main sources for the list are: Hudjwīrī, *Kashf al-maḥdjūb*, ed. Shukovski, 1926, p. 218—340, and transl. Nicholson, 1911, p. 176—266 (11 names); ʿUdjaimī, (d. 1702) *Fahrasa*, MS. M. Fasi (40 names); Sanūsī (d. 1859) *Salsabīl muʿīn*, MS. Massignon (40 names); Maʿṣūm ʿAlī Shāh, *Ṭarāʾiḳ al-ḥaḳāʾiḳ*, lith. Teheran 1319, ii. 136 *sqq.* (17 names); d'Ohsson, *Tableau genéral de l'empire othoman*, Paris 1788, ii. 294—316 [in Hughes, *Dictionary of Islam*, p. 117; Brown, *Darwishes*, ed. Rose, 1927, p. 267—271 (32 names)]; Gümüshkhānī, *Djāmiʿ uṣūl...*, Cairo 1319, p. 3 *sqq.* (40 names); L. Rinn, *Marabouts et Khouan*, Algiers 1885 (31 names) (cf. also: Le Chatelier, *Confréries musulmanes du Hedjaz*, Paris 1887; Depont-Coppolani, *Confréries religieuses musulmanes*, Algiers 1897; Montet in *Encyclopaedia of Religion and Ethics*, X, 719—26); Malcolm, *History of Persia*, 1815, ii. 271 (5 names); Massignon, *Annuaire du Monde Musulman*, 2nd ed., 1926.

LIST

Adhamīya. — artificial Turco-Syrian isnād of the xvth century, referring to a saint (d. 776).
AḤMADĪYA. — Egyptian order (Ṭanṭā — Badawī d. 1276). Numerous branches: Shinnāwīya, Marāziḳa, Kannāsīya, Anbābīya, Ḥammūdīya, *Manāʾifīya, Sallāmīya, Ḥalabīya, Zāhidīya, Shuʿaibīya, Tasḳiyanīya, ʿArabīya, *Suṭūḥīya, Bundārīya, Muslimīya (= Shurunbulālīya), *Baiyūmīya.
ʿAidarūsīya. — Yemenite branch of the Kubrāwīya (xvth century).
Akbarīya. — = Ḥātimīya.
ʿAlawīya — artificial isnād referring to the 4th khalīfa.
*ʿAllawīya. — Algerian branch of the Darḳāwa (Mostaganem — Ben Alioua, since 1919).
*Amīrghanīya. — Nubian branch of the Idrīsīya — (d. 1853).
*ʿAmmārīya. — Algero-Tunisian branch of the Ḳādirīya (xixth century).
*ʿArūsīya. — Tripolitan branch of the Ḳādirīya (Zliten, xixth century).
ʿĀshiḳīya. — heresy.
Ashrafīya. — Turkish branch of the Ḳādirīya (Iznik) — (d. 1493) — = Wāḥidīya.
*ʿAwāmirīya. — Tunisian branch of the ʿĪsawīya (xixth century).
*ʿAzzūzīya. — small Tunisian order (xixth century).

Bābāʾīya. — Turkish order (Adrianople) — (d. 1465).
Badawīya. — = Aḥmadīya.
*Bairamīya. — Turkish branch of the Ṣafawīya (Angora) — (d. 1471). Sub-branches: Ḥamzāwīya, Shaikhīya, Khwādja-Himmatīya.
Baiyūmīya. — cf. Aḥmadīya.
*Bakkāʾīya. — Sudanese branch of the Ḳādirīya (d. 1505). Branches (Kunta): Faḍlīya, Āl Sīdīya.
Bakrīya. — cf. Ṣiddīḳīya.
Bakrīya. — name sometimes given to the Bait al-Bakrī (Shuyūkh al-Ṣūfīya of Cairo since the xvith century).
Bakrīya. — Syro-Egyptian branch of the Shādhilīya — (d. 1503).
Bakrīya. — Egyptian reformed Khalwatīya (d. 1709).
*Banāwa. — branch of the Ḳādirīya in the Dekkan (xixth century).
*BEKTĀSHĪYA. — Anatolian (since before 1336) and Balkan order (Albanian branch autonomous since 1922; centre at Aḳčé Ḥiṣār).
*Bībarīya. — small Cilician order (in 1924).
Bisṭāmīya. — artificial Turkish isnād of the xvth century (cf. Taifūrīya).
*Būʿalīya. — Algero-Egyptian branch of the Ḳādirīya (xixth century).
*Būnūḥīya (= Būniyīn). — small order in Southern Morocco (cf. *RMM*, lviii. 141).
*BURHĀNĪYA (or Burhamīya). — Egyptian order (Ibr. Dasūḳī d. 1277). Branches: Shahāwīya, Sharāniba.

Dardīrīya. — Egyptian branch of the Khalwatīya († 1786).
*DARḲĀWA. — Algero-Moroccan branch of the Djazūlīya. — (d. 1823). Various branches: Būzīdīya, Kittānīya, Ḥarrāḳīya, ʿAllawīya.
Dasūḳīya. — = Burhānīya.
Dhahabīya. — Persian name of the Kubrāwīya.
Djahrīya. — Yemenite order (xvth century).
*Djahrīya. — orders authorizing the dhikr in public, in China and Turkistān (Ḳādirīya); cf. Khafīya. — (xixth century).
*Djalālīya-Bukhārīya. — Hindu branch of the Suhrawardīya (Makhdūm-i-djahānīyān, d. 1383).
DJALWATĪYA. — Turkish branch of the Ṣafawīya (Brussa, Pīr Uftāda d. 1580). Branches: Hāshimīya, Rawshanīya, Fanāʾīya, *Hudāʾīya.
Djamālīya. — Persian branch of the Suhrawardīya. — (Ardistānī d. xvth century).
Djamālīya. — Turkish order — Stambul. — (d. 1750).
*Djarrāhīya. — Turkish branch of the Khalwatīya. — (d. 1733).
DJAZŪLĪYA. — Moroccan reformed Shādhilīya. — (d. 1465). Its branches are: Darḳāwa, Ḥamādisha, ʿĪsawīya, Sharḳāwa, Ṭaibīya.
Djibāwīya = Saʿdīya.
Djilāla. — Moroccan name for the Ḳādirīya.
Djunaidīya. — doctrinal Baghdād school (d. 909) which was evolved in the Ṣūfīya in the xith century —, and gave rise to the Khwādjagān, Kubrāwīya and Ḳādirīya — name revived in the xvith century for the artificial isnād of a *dhikr*.

Firdawsīya. — Hindu name of the Kubrāwīya.

*Ghawthīya. — Hindu branch of the Shaṭṭārīya (Ghawth, d. 1562 at Gwalior).
Ghazzālīya. — doctrinal school of Ghazzālī (d. 1111).
*Ghāzīya. — branch of the Shādhilīya in South Morocco — (d. 1526).
*Gülshanīya. — = Rawshanīya.
*Gurzmar. — Hindu branch of the Ḳādirīya.

*Ḥabībīya. — branch of Shādhilīya in Tafilelt (d. 1752).
*Haddāwa. — wandering Moroccan order: at Tagzirt. — (xixth century).
*Ḥafnawīya. — Egyptian branch of the Khalwatīya. — (d. 1749).
Ḥaidarīya. — Persian branch of the Ḳalandarīya (xiith century).
*Ḥaidarīya. = Khāksār. — Persian artisan brotherhood (xixth).
Ḥakīmīya. — doctrinal school of Ḥakīm Tirmidhī (d. 898).

Ḥallādjīya. — doctrinal school of Ḥusain b. Manṣūr Ḥallādj (d. 922); name revived in the xiii[th] century for the artificial isnād of a *dhikr*.
Hamadhānīya. — Kashmir branch of the Kubrāwīya. — (ʿAlī Hamadhānī d. 1385).
*Ḥamādisha. — Moroccan branch of the Djazūlīya in the Zerhoun (xviii[th] century) with sub-branches: Daghūghīya, Ṣaddāḳīya, Riyāḥīya, Ḳāsimīya, — at Meknès and at Salé.
Ḥamzāwīya. — mixture of Bairamīya and Malāmīya.
*Ḥanṣalīya. — small Orano-Moroccan order. — (d. 1702).
Ḥanṣalīya. — Chleuh branch of the Nāṣirīya. — (xix[th] century).
Ḥarīrīya. — Hauranian branch of the Rifāʿīya. — (d. 1247).
Ḥātimīya. — doctrinal school of Ibn ʿArabī (d. 1240).
Hudāʾīya = Djalwatīya.
Ḥulmānīya. — Ḥulūlīya sect of the xth century.
Ḥulūlīya. — heresy.
Ḥurūfīya. — heresy.

Ibāḥīya. — heresy.
*Idrīsīya. — branch of the Khāḍirīya settled in ʿAsīr (xix[th] century).
Ighit-Bāshīya. — Turkish branch of the Khalwatīya (d. 1544).
Ightishāshīya. — Khurāsān branch of the Kubrāwīya (Isḥāḳ Khattalānī, d. xv[th] century).
*ʿĪSAWĪYA. — Moroccan branch of the Djazūlīya at Meknès (d. 1524).
Ishrāḳīya. — doctrinal school of Suhrawardī Ḥalabī (d. 1191).
*Ismāʿīlīya. — Nubian order in Kurdufān (xix[th] century).
Ittiḥādīya. — heresy.

*ḲĀDIRĪYA. — Baghdād order developed from the school of the Djunaidīya (ʿAbd al-Ḳādir Djīlānī d. 1166). — Many branches: in Yemen and Somalia, Yāfiʿīya (xiv[th] century), Mushāriʿīya, ʿUrābīya; in India, Banāwa and Gurzmar; in Anatolia, Ashrafīya, Hindīya, Khulūṣīya, Nābulūsīya, Rūmīya and Waṣlatīya; in Egypt, Fāridīya and Ḳāsimīya (xix[th] century); in Maghrib, ʿAmmārīya, ʿArūsīya, Būʿalīya and Djilāla; in western Sūdān, Bakkāʾīya.
ḲALANDARĪYA. — itinerant order founded in Persia (Sāwidjī d. 1218), spread to Syria and India (xiv[th] century—xvi[th] century) now extinct.
*Karrāʾīya. — small Tunisian order (xix[th] century)
*Karzāzīya. — Shādhilīya branch in Tafilelt (xix[th] century).
Ḳaṣṣārīya. — doctrinal school of the ix[th] century: = Malāmatīya.
Kāzarūnīya. — Persian order descended from the doctrinal school of the Khafīfīya, at Shīrāz. — (d. 1034)
Khāḍirīya (= Khiḍrīya). — Moroccan order (Ibn al-Dabbāgh d. 1717) whence are derived the Amīrghanīya, Idrīsīya and Sanūsīya.
Khafīfīya. — doctrinal school of Ibn Khafīf (d. 982). name revived in the xiv[th] century for an artificial isnād.
*Khafīya. — surname of the Naḳshabandīya in China and Turkistān (xix[th] century); cf. Djahrīya.
*Khalīlīya. — small Tunisian order (xix[th] century).
*KHALWATĪYA. — branch of the Suhrawardīya which arose in Khurāsān (Ẓahīr al-Dīn d. 1397) and spread into Turkey. — Numerous branches: in Anatolia, Djarrāḥīya, Ighitbāshīya, ʿUshshāḳīya, Niyāzīya, Sünbülīya, Shamsīya, Gülshanīya and Shudjaʾīya; in Egypt, Ḍaifīya, Hafnawīya, Sabāʿīya, Ṣāwīya-Dardīrīya, Maghāzīya, in Nubia, in Ḥidjāz and in Somaliland, Ṣāliḥīya; in Kabylia, Raḥmānīya.
*Khammūsīya. — Tunisian order (xix[th] century).
Kharrāzīya. — doctrinal school of Abū Saʿīd Kharrāz (d. 899); then artificial Turkish isnād of the xv[th] century.
Khawāṭirīya. — Ḥidjāzi order of Madanīya (Ibn ʿArrāḳ d. 1556).
Kh[w]ādjagān. — Persian order descended from the school of the Djunaidīya and spread in Turkestān (= Yasawīya). — (Yūsuf Hamadhānī d. 1140).
KUBRĀWĪYA. — Khurāsān order descended from the school of the Djunaidīya (Nadjm Kubrā d. 1221). Branches: ʿAidarūsīya, Hamādhānīya, Ightishāshīya, Nūrbakhshīya, Nūrīya, Ruknīya.
Ḳūniyāwīya. — doctrinal school of Ṣadr Rūmī (d. 1273), descended from the Ḥātimīya.
Ḳushairīya. — artificial isnād of the xvi[th] century, refering to Ḳushairī (d. 1074).

Madanīya. — first name of the Shādhilīya.
*Madanīya. — Tripolitan branch of the Darḳāwa at Misurata (d. 1823).
*MADĀRĪYA. — wandering Hindu order (Shāh Madār, d. 1438 at Makanpur).
Maghribīya. — perhaps to be identified with the disciples of the Persian poet Maghribī (d. 1406).
Malāmatīya. — doctrinal school of Khurāsān (ix[th]—xi[th] century), opposed to the Ṣūfīya of the ʿIrāḳ — name revived in the xvi[th] century for an artificial isnād.
Malāmīya. — (= Ḥamzāwīya) — branch of the Bairamīya of Turkey (d. 1553).
Manṣūrīya = Ḥallādjīya.
Marāziḳa. — branch of the Aḥmadīya (xiv[th] century)
Mashīshīya. — disciples of the Moroccan saint Ibn Mashīsh (d. 1226), at first united with the Shādhilīya, then regrouped in the xvi[th] century.
*Matbūlīya. — small Egyptian order (d. 1475).
*MAWLAWĪYA. — Anatolian order (Djalāl al-Dīn Rūmī, d. 1273 at Koniya). Branches: Pūstnishīnīya, Irshādīya.
Miṣrīya = Niyāzīa.
Muḥammadīya. — devotional artificial isnād refering to the Prophet without intermediary: utilised in the xvi[th] century by ʿAlī Khawwāṣ and Shaʿrānī; also used in connection with the recitation of *Dalāʾil* of Djazūlī.
Muḥāsibīya. — doctrinal school of Ḥārith Muḥāsibī (d. 859).
Murādīya. — Turkish order in Stambul. — (d. 1719).
Mushāriʿīya. — Yemenite branch of the Ḳādirīya (xv[th] century).
Muṭāwiʿa = Aḥmadīya.

*NAḲSHABANDĪYA. — order in Turkestān, claiming descent from the school of the Ṭaifūrīya. — Branches in China, Turkestān, Kazan, Turkey, India and Java. — (Bahāʾ al-Dīn d. 1388).
NAḲSHABANDĪYA. = Khālidīya. — reformed Turkish (xix[th] century).
*Nāṣirīya. — South Moroccan branch of the Shādhilīya, at Tamghrūt (xvii[th] century) with Tunisian sub-branch (Shabbīya).
*NIʿMATALLĀHĪYA. — the only order of the Persian Shīʿa in Kirmān: descended from the Ḳādirīya-Yāfiʿīya. — (d. 1430).

Niyāzīya. — Turkish branch of the Khalwatīya (d. 1693).
Nubuwīya. — artisan brotherhood in Syria (xiith century).
Nūr al-Dīnīya. — = Djarrāḥīya.
Nūrbakhshīya. — Khurāsān branch of the Kubrāwīya (Muḥammad Nūrbakhsh d. 1465).
Nūrīya. — doctrinal school of Nūrī (d. 907).
Nūrīya. — dissenting branch of the Ruknīya (xivth century).
Nūrīya. — heresy.

Pīr-Ḥādjāt. — Afghān order professing to be that of Anṣārī Harawī (d. 1088).

*Raḥḥālīya. — order of Moroccan jugglers (xvith century).
*Raḥmanīya. — branch of the Khalwatīya in Kabylia. — (1793).
*Rashīdīya. — small Algerian order formed dissenting from the Yūsufīya (xixth century).
*Rasūlshāhīya. — Hindu order of Gudjarāt (xixth century).
Rawshanīya. — branch of the Khalwatīya, in Turkey and Cairo (Gülshanī d. 1533).
Rawshanīya. — Afghān branch of the Suhrawardīya (Bāyazīd Anṣārī, d. end of the xvith century).
*Rifāʿīya. — South ʿIrāḳ order — (d. 1175) — spread from its centre in Baṣra to Damascus and Stambul. — Syrian branches: Ḥarīrīya, Saʿdīya, Saiyādīya; — Egyptian: Bāzīya, Mālikīya, and Ḥabībīya (xixth century).
Ruknīya. — Baghdād branch of Kubrāwīya (ʿAlāʾ al-Dawla Simnānī d. 1336).
Rūmīya. — = Ashrafīya.

Sabʿīnīya. — doctrinal school and wandering order of Ibn Sabʿīn (d. 1268).
*Saʿdīya. — Syrian branch of the Rifāʿīya (Saʿd al-Dīn Djibāwī d. 1335). — Branches: ʿAbd al-Salāmīya, Abu ʾl-Wafāʾīya.
Ṣafawīya. — Azéri branch of Suhrawardīya at Ardabīl. — (d, 1334). It gave rise to the sect of the Ḳizilbāshīya, to the Persian dynasty of the Ṣafawids, and to several Turkish orders.
Sahlīya. — doctrinal school (Sahl Tustarī d. 896); name revived in the xvith century for an artificial isnād.
Saḳaṭīya. — Turkish artificial isnād of the xvith century. — (Saḳaṭī d. 867).
Salāmīya = ʿArūsīya.
Sālimīya = Sahlīya (in the first sense).
*Sammānīya. — Egyptian branch of Shādhilīya (xixth century).
*Sanānīya. — minor order (xixth century).
*Sanūsīya. — military order, descended from the Khādirīya, at Djagbub then Cufra, in the oriental Ṣaḥarā. — (d. 1859).
Sāsānīya. — artisan brotherhood in Syria and Anatolia (xiith—xvith centry).
Saiyārīya. — doctrinal school of the xth century.
*Shaʿbānīya. — Turkish branch of the Khalwatīya at Kastamuni. — (d. 1569).
*Shādhilīya. — order founded by Abū Madyan of Tlemcen (d. 1197) and ʿAlī Shādhilī of Tunis (d. 1256). — Maghrib branches: Ghāzīya, Ḥabībīya, Karzāzīya, Nāṣirīya, Shaikhīya, Suhailīya, Yūsufīya, Zarrūḳīya and Ziyānīya —; Egyptian: Bakrīya, Khawāṭirīya, Wafāʾīya, Djawharīya, Makkīya, Hāshimīya, Sammānīya ʿAfīfīya, Ḳāsimīya, ʿArūsīya, Handūshīya, Ḳawūḳdjīya —; there are some at Stambul, in Rumania, in Nubia and in the Comores.

Shāhmadārīya = Malang = Madārīya.
*Shaikhīya. — name given to the Shādhilīya Ulād Sīdī Shaikh of Orania (xixth century).
Shamsīya. — Turkish branch of Khalwatīya. — (d. 1601) = Nūrīya-Sīwāsīya.
*Sharḳāwa. — Moroccan branch of the Djazūlīya at Bujad (1599).
Sharḳāwīya. — Egyptian order of the Khalwatīya (xviiith century).
*Shaṭṭārīya. — Hindu, Sumatra and Javanese order (ʿAbdallāh Shāṭṭār d. 1415 or 1428). — Branches: Ghawthīya, ʿUshaiḳīya.
Shūdhīya. — wandering Spanish order of the xiith century based on the Sabʿīnīya.
Ṣiddīḳīya. — artificial isnād referring to the second khalīfa (invented by Ibn ʿAṭā ʾllāh, xiiith century).
Sinān-Ummīya. — Turkish order (d. 1668).
Suhailīya. — Algerian branch of Shādhilīya (xixth century).
*Suhrawardīya. — Baghdād order founder by ʿAbd al-Ḳāhir Suhrawardī (d. 1167) and ʿUmar Suhrawardī (d. 1234) who were called "Ṣiddīḳīya" = descendants of the second khalīfa; found in Afghānistān and in India. — Branches: Djalālīya, Djamālīya, Khalwatīya, Rawshanīya, Ṣafawīya and Zainīya.
*Sulṭānīya. — order of Turkestān (xixth century).
*Sünbülīya. — Turkish branch of the Khalwatīya (d. 1529).

*Tabbāʾīya. — Tunisian order (xixth century).
*Ṭaibīya. — Moroccan branch of the Djazūlīya at Ouezzan (d. 1727).
Ṭaifūrīya. — doctrinal school of Dāsitānī and Khurḳānī (xith century), descended from Abū Yazīd Ṭaifūr Bisṭāmī (d. 877).
*Ṭālibīya. — small Moroccan order at Salé (xixth century; cf. *RMM*, lviii. 143).
Ṭalḳīnīya. — heresy.
*Tidjānīya. — Algero-Moroccan order (d. 1815). From Temacin and ʿAin Mahdī it has spread through Eastern and Western Sūdān.
*Tshishtīya. — Indo-Afghān order: centre at Adjmir (d. 1236).
Tuhāmīya = Ṭaibīya.

ʿUlwānīya. — Turkish artificial isnād of the xvith century, referring to a saint of Djidda of the viiith century.
Ummī-Sinānīya. — Turkish order — (d. 1552).
ʿUrābīya. — branch of the Ḳādirīya (xvith century).
ʿUshaiḳīya. — Hindu branch of the Shaṭṭārīya. (Abū Yazīd ʿIshḳī d. xvth century).
*ʿUshshāḳīya. — Turkish branch of the Khalwatīya (d. 1592).
Uwaisīya. — Turkish artificial isnād of the xvith century, referring to a Ṣaḥābī.

*Wafāʾīya. — reformed Syro-Egyptian of the Shādhilīya (d. 1358).
Waḥdatīya. — heresy = Wudjūdīya = Ḥātimīya.
*Wārith ʿAlīshāhīya. — Hindu order (end of the xixth century); founded in Oude.
Wuṣūlīya. — heresy.

Yasawīya. — branch of the Khwādjagān in Turkestān (Yasawī d. 1167).
Yūnusīya. — wandering Syrian order (Shaibānī d. 1222).

*Yūsufīya. — Maghrib branch of Shādhilīya at Miliana (xvi[th] century).
Zarrūḳīya. — branch of the Shādhilīya of Fès (d. 1493).
Zainīya. — Turkish branch of Suhrawardīya at Brussa (Khwāfī d. 1435).
*Ziyānīya. — Maghrib branch of the Shādhilīya (xix[th] century).

Bibliography: The principal sources areenumerated at the head of the table given above. One may add those given by G. Pfannmüller, in *Handbuch der Islam-Literatur*, 1923, p. 292—315. — Cf. also the articles BEKTĀSHĪYA, ČISHTĪYA, DERḲĀWĀ, DERWĪSH, DHIKR, FUTUWWA, ḤALLĀDJ, ḲĀDIRĪYA, ḲALANDARĪYA, KAZARŪNĪ, MAWLAWĪYA, NAḲSHBAND, NŪRBAKHSHĪYA, RAḤMĀNĪYA, RIFĀʿĪ, SAʿDĪYA, SĀLIMĪYA, SANŪSĪYA, SHADD, SHĀDHILĪYA, SHAṬḤ, SHAṬṬĀRĪYA, TĪDJĀNĪYA, ZĀWIYA.

TA'RĪKH, era, chronology. The word originally means "dating" and has acquired also the meaning of "chronicle, historical work, history" and likewise that of "chronogram". In this article the Muḥammadan Calendar will be dealt with.

Our knowledge of the early Arab method of reckoning time, which is based on scattered references in what remains of the old poetry is still very incomplete and cannot by any means be regarded as satisfactory on all points. There is much in favour of the view — especially the meaning of most of the old names of the months (Ṣafar I, II, Rabīʿ I, II, Djumādā I, II, Ramaḍān) — that the old Arab year was lunisolar in character and resembled in some degree the Jewish year ("Tishrī year"). It cannot, however, be safely assumed that in the whole of Arabia there was a uniform system of time-reckoning in the early period. Among the Arab Beduin tribes as well as among other nomad peoples, there was originally a calendar based on the moon only — a so-called "pure lunar year", and the adaptation to the solar year only took place later. This assumption is also supported by the statements of various Muslim scholars (used by Mahmoud Effendi in his article in *JA*, 1858, ser. v., vol. xi); for example al-Bīrūnī (*Āthār*, ed. Sachau, Leipzig 1878), agreeing with Abū Maʿshar Djaʿfar b. Muḥammad al-Balkhī (*Kitāb al-Ulūf fī buyūt al-ʿibādāt*) with whose work he was acquainted, mentions that the transition from pure lunar years to lunisolar years took place about two centuries before the Hidjra under the influence of the Jewish year. The later theory, adopted by F. K. Ginzel (*Chronologie*, i. 248) from Mahmoud Effendi (*Mém. des savants étrangers de l'Académie royale de Belgique*, xxx., 1861), which assumes the existance of a pure lunar year in the period immediately before the Hidjra cannot be quoted as a sound argument against the preceding, as it is not sufficiently established that the conjunction of Jupiter and Saturn in March 571 — the "conjunction of religion" (*ḳirān al-dīn*) — actually took place immediately before the birth of the Prophet and that we have not here to deal with a later conjunction. The Arab lunisolar year, like the Jewish, began in autumn; the year itself consisted of 12, in leap years 13 months, which were reckoned from *hilāl* to *hilāl* (new moon). The intercalation of the thirteenth month which was necessary to fix the beginning of the year at a definite period in the solar year was done empirically from time to time, on the average every two or three years. The much disputed word *nasī'* (Sūra ix. 37) indicates, as Moberg has conclusively shown (Axel Moberg, *An-Nasī' in der islāmischen Tradition*, Lund 1931), this intercalation of the extra month; this was first expressly prohibited by Muḥammad in the year 10 A.H. (Ḳur'ān, *loc. cit.*). The time of the *ḥadjdj* (q.v.), originally associated with autumn — i.e. fixed by the solar year —, was fixed presumably by the cosmic setting (*naw'*, pl. *anwā'*) of one of the 28 stations of the moon (*manāzil*); this method of fixing solar dates is also found at a later period (cf. the "*Calendrier de Cordoue de l'année* 961", ed. Dozy, Leyden 1873) and we find it also in early periods in other parts of the world (China, India, Egypt). In Muḥammad's time however, as a result of insufficient skill in observing and intercalating, the lunisolar year had advanced so far in front of the solar year that the beginning of the year, with the month Dhu 'l-Ḥidjdja which preceded it and the time of the ḥadjdj, fell in the spring.

In the later period of the Djāhilīya the names of the months were already fixed as we know them in the Muslim period, except that al-Muḥarram [q.v.] in the latter took the place of Ṣafar I; they were Ṣafar I, Ṣafar II, Rabīʿ I, Rabīʿ II, Djumādā I, Djumādā II, Radjab, Shaʿbān, Ramaḍān, Shawwāl, Dhu 'l-Ḳaʿda, Dhu 'l-Ḥidjdja; it is to be noted that the first half year consisted of three double months. The names of the early Arab months as given us by al-Bīrūnī are quite different; these, supplanted by those just mentioned, were al-Mu'tamir (= Ṣafar I), Nādjir, Khawwān, Buṣṣān, Ḥantam or Ḥanam (vocalisation uncertain), Zabbā' or Zubbī, al-Aṣamm, ʿĀdil, Nāfiḳ, Waghl, Huwāʿ, Burak; some of them are still occasionally found later as epithets of the corresponding Muḥammadan months, e.g. al-Aṣamm for Radjab, ʿĀdil for Shāʿbān. In addition to these, al-Bīrūnī, al-Masʿūdī and the Sabaean inscriptions give many other names of months, which differ so considerably with the different tribes and sources that no deductions can be made from them about the earliest period of the Arab calendar.

According to Wellhausen (*Reste arabischen Heidentums*, Berlin 1897, p. 96 *sq.*), the year was originally divided into three seasons: The period of rain, of drought and of heat. In the old Arab poetry we find a division into four; Kharīf or Rabīʿ, Shitā', Ṣaif and Ḳaiẓ, roughly corresponding to our autumn, winter, spring and summer; it is possible there was also a sixfold division into Rabīʿ (late harvest), Kharīf (autumn), Shitā' (winter), al-Rabīʿ al-thānī (early harvest), Ṣaif (early summer) and Ḳaiẓ (summer).

The use of the week of seven days can be proved to have existed at a very early period among the pagan Arabs. According to al-Bīrūnī (*Āthār*, p. 64), the old names of the days of the week were: Awwal (Sunday), Ahwan, Djubār, Dubār, Mu'nis, ʿArūbā and Shiyār. It should not however be assumed that the seven-day week was an original invention of the Arabs; on the contrary, many things point to its having been taken over from Babylonia or the Jews, among whom it was established at a very early period.

The days were grouped within the month into ten groups of three each, the names of which, reckoned from the new moon (*hilāl*) were Ghurar, Nufal, Tusaʿ, ʿUshar, Bīḍ, Duraʿ, Ẓulam, Ḥanādis or Duhm, Da'ādi' and Miḥāḳ (cf. al-Bīrūnī, *op. cit.*, p. 63 *sq.*). The day itself began at sunset, as among the Jews and as was later the custom in Islām. There is no evidence of the division of the day into 24 hours in the pre-Muḥammadan period.

The fixed points or epochs used in the pre-

Muḥammadan period from which to reckon years seem to have been very numerous. Al-Bīrūnī mentions battles, memorable events, the year of the restoration of the Kaʿba etc. as epochs of the different tribes (*op. cit.*, p. 34). More general seems to have been the reckoning from the "days of treason", *aiyām al-fidjār* (probably between 585 and 591 A.D.), and from the "year of the Elephant", *ʿām al-fīl* (probably about 570 A.D.), the latter being, according to some authors, the year of Muḥammad's birth (571).

The Calendar in Islām. By the already mentioned prohibition of the *nasīʾ* in the year 10 A.H. by Muḥammad there came into use the system of reckoning by pure lunar months which is characreristic of Islām (one pure lunar month = 12 synodical months of 29d 12h 44m 3s = 354d 8h 47m 36s; the term lunar year is really absurd). An adaptation to the annual course of the sun was now no longer possible and the beginning of the Muḥammadan year therefore falls about 11 days behind each solar year, coming back to the same solar time in about 33 years; 33 lunar years are therefore almost equivalent to 32 solar years. From this proportion we get the approximation formulae for transforming years A.H. into years A.D. and vice versa:

A.D. = $^{32}/_{33}$ (A.H. + 622) or A.H. = $^{33}/_{32}$ (A.D. — 622).

For exact calculations the *Vergleichungstabellen* by Wüstenfeld and Mahler are indispensable (see Bibl.).

According to the Ḳurʾān (Sūra x. 5, etc.) which expressly makes the moon the measurer of time, the beginning of the month and of the year must be established as in ancient times by actual observation of the new moon, and as a matter of fact the popular calendar still does this at the present day. For reasons which are readily intelligible, at quite an early period a cyclic reckoning established itself which, starting from the fact that the period of two lunations is approximately 59 days, gave the months alternately a length of 30 and 29 days so that 1 (Muḥarram), 3, 5, 7, 9, 11 have each 30 days and 2, 4, 6, 8, 10, 12 have 29 days. The ordinary year thus has 354 days. The difference of 8h 48m 36s (almost exactly $^{11}/_{30}$ days) by which the astronomic lunar year is longer was made good by intercalating 11 days (*yawm al-kabs*) in every 30 lunar years. The most widely disseminated method in Muslim lands is the practice of making years 2, 5, 7, 10, 13, 16, 18, 21, 24, 26 and 29 in the cycle of 30 leap years (*sana kabīsa*). The intercalated day itself is always given to the month Dhu 'l-Ḥidjdja, which in the ordinary year has 29, in leap year 30 days (on other systems of intercalation, especially the Turkish eight cycles, see Ginzel, *Chronologie*, i. 255).

The day (i.e. νυχθήμερον, *al-yawm bi-lailatihi*) in the period of the Djāhilīya was reckoned from sunset; as al-Farghānī emphasizes, this method of counting comes from the fact that the first day of the month is fixed by the *hilāl* (first light of new moon), which is always to be observed at sunset. The division of the νυχθήμερον into 24 hours is however to be traced to Greek influence. In ordinary reckoning of time temporal hours (i.e. the light day and night respectively divided by 12) alone are used, on the other hand the astronomers very often use equinoctial hours (day and night together divided by 24) and always expressly describe them as such.

Instead of the old names of the days of the week, we find in Islām simply the cardinal numbers in altered form (from Sunday to Thursday), Frida· becomes "the day of assembly" and Saturday the "Sabbath", as follows: Yawm al-Aḥad (Sunday), Yawm al-Ithnain (Monday), Yawm al-Thalāthāʾ (Tuesday), Yawm al-Arbaʿā (Wednesday), Yawm al-Khamīs (Thursday), Yawm al-Djumʿa (Friday), Yawm al Sabt (Saturday). (In the days of the week it should be remembered, as already explained, that Yawm al-Aḥad begins on the evening of our Saturday, Yawm al-Ithnain on the evening of Sunday, and so on, so that the Arabic and European names do not cover exactly the same 24 hours).

In Muslim chronology the year begins on 1st Muḥarram of the year in which the Prophet made his Hidjra from Mecca to Yathrib (not the day of the Hidjra itself or of the arrival in Madīna, which is usually taken to be the 8th Rabīʿ I, i.e. Sept. 20, 622). It was Thursday (Yawm al-Khamīs) July 15, 622 A.D., called *Taʾrīkh al-Hidjra* (in the Julian reckoning by days, day 1, 948, 439). The introduction of this era took place under the Caliph ʿUmar. See also the art. HIDJRA).

Along with the numbering according to years after the Hidjra, different foreign eras were in use, as the Alexandrian era (*taʾrīkh al-Ḳibṭ* or *taʾrīkh al-shuhadāʾ*) and the Seleucid era (*taʾrīkh al-Rūm* or *taʾrīkh Dhi 'l-Ḳarnain*). In several Islāmic countries the administration was obliged from an early date to introduce a land-tax-year (*sana kharādjiya*) as in Egypt. By the Ottoman Turks on similar grounds the financial year (*sene-i mālīye*) came into use since 1087/1677. In 1926 the Gregorian calender was officially introduced in Turkey.

Bibliography: al-Battānī, *Kitāb al-zīdj al-ṣābiʾ* (*Opus Astronomicum*) ed. A. Nallino, i—iii. (Milan 1899—1907); al-Bīrūnī, *Āthār* (*Chronology of ancient nations*), ed. Sachau, Leipzig 1878; F. K. Ginzel, *Handbuch der mathematischen und technischen Chronologie*, 1. Leipzig 1906; R. Dozy, *Le Calendrier de Cordoue de l'année 961*, Leyden 1873; Wüstenfeld—Mahler, *Vergleichungstabellen der muhammedanischen und christlichen Zeitrechnung*, Leipzig 1926; J. Mayr, *Osmanische Zeitrechnungen*, in F. Babinger, *Die Geschichtsschreiber der Osmanen*, Leipzig 1927; do., *Umrechnungstafeln für Wandeljahre* (*Astron. Nachr.* ccxlvii. 2/3, Kiel 1932); S. B. Burnaby, *The Jewish and Muhammadan Calender*, London 1931.

TARWIYA. [See HADJDJ].

TAṢAWWUF. 1. Etymology. — *Maṣdar* of form V, formed from the root *ṣūf*, meaning "wool", to denote "the practice of wearing the woollen robe (*labs al-ṣūf*)", hence the act of devoting oneself to the mystic life on becoming what is called in Islām a *ṣūfī*.

The other etymologies, ancient and modern, proposed for this name of *ṣūfī* may be rejected: such are *ahl al-ṣuffa* (devotees seated on the "bench" of the mosque at Madīna in the time of the Prophet), *ṣaff awwal* (first row of the faithful at prayer), *banū Ṣūfa* (a Beduin tribe), *ṣawfāna* (a kind of vegetable), *ṣafwat al-ḳifā* (a lock of hair on the nape of the neck), *ṣūfiya* (passive of form III, of the root *ṣafā*, to be purified; at a very early date — the eight century A.D. —, this passive is found in puns on the word *ṣūfī* "mystic clothed in wool"), and the Greek σοφός (the attempt has even been made to derive taṣawwuf from θεοσοφία); Nöldeke (*ZDMG*, xlviii., p. 45) refuted this last etymology by showing that the Greek *sigma* regularly became *sīn* (and not *ṣād*) in Arabic and that there is no Aramaic intermediary between σοφός and *ṣūfī*.

The individual surname *al-ṣūfī* first appeared in history in the second half of the eighth century with Djābir Ibn Ḥaiyān, a Shīʿī alchemist of Kūfa, who professed an ascetic doctrine of his own (cf. Khashīsh Nasāʾī, d. 253/867, *Istiḳāma*, s.v.) and Abū Hāshim of Kūfa, a celebrated mystic. As to the plural *ṣūfīya* which appears in 199/814 in connection with a minor rising in Alexandria (al-Kindī, *Ḳuḍāt Miṣr*, ed. Guest, p. 162, 440), it was applied about the same date, according to Muḥāsibī (*Makāṣib*, Pers. MS., p. 87) and Djāḥiẓ (*Baiyān*, i. 194), to a semi-Shīʿī school of Muslim mysticism which originated in Kūfa, the last head of which, ʿAbdak al-Ṣūfī, a vegetarian legitimist, died in Baghdād about 210/825. The name *ṣūfī* is then at first clearly confined to Kūfa.

It was destined to have a remarkable future. Within fifty years it denoted all the mystics of the ʿIrāḳ (in contrast to the Malāmatīya mystics of Khurāsān) and two centuries later, *ṣūfīya* was "applied to the whole body of Muslim mystics as our terms Ṣūfī" and "Ṣūfism" still are to-day. In the interval the wearing of the *ṣūf* or "cloak of white wool", considered in 100/719 as a foreign and reprehensible fashion of Christian origin (with which Farḳad Sabakhī, a disciple of Ḥasan al-Baṣrī, is reproached), had become what it henceforth remained, an eminently orthodox Muslim fashion; numerous ḥadīths (handed down and probably invented by Djawbiyārī) even make it Muḥammad's favourite dress for a religious man.

2. Origins. The mystical *tafsīr*'s on the Ḳurʾān and the mystical ḥadīths of the inner life of Muḥammad, about which we know so very little, are comparatively late and therefore suspect. But the tendencies to mystical life, which are of all countries and of all nations, were not lacking in the Islām of Arabia of the first two centuries A.H.; and when once the later legends are eliminated, Djāḥiẓ and Ibn al-Djawzī (*Ḳuṣṣāṣ*) have preserved for us the names of over forty authentic ascetics of this period, among whom the "interiorisation" of the rites of worship show distinct features of the mystic life. It cannot, however, be any longer asserted that Muḥammad *a priori* excluded mystics from the Muslim community, for it is now known that the famous ḥadīth: *Lā rahbānīyata fi 'l-Islām*: "no monasticism in Islām" to which Sprenger had given this meaning, is apocryphal, and that it must have been invented at latest in the third century A.H. to encourage and strengthen a new, deprecatory and interdictive interpretation of a famous verse of the Ḳurʾān (lvii. 27) where *rahbānīya* (monastic life, vows of chastity and seclusion) is mentioned: a verse unanimously interpreted in a permissive and laudatory sense by the exegists of the first three centuries, like Mudjāhid and Abū Imāma Bāhilī (cf. Massignon, *Essai*, p. 123—131), and by the most learned of the old mystics (cf. Djunaid, *Dawā*) before the opposite interpretation became disseminated and Zamakhsharī made it predominant.

Muslim mysticism may claim among the *Ṣaḥāba* two real precursors in Abū Dharr and Ḥudhaifa (the cases of Uwais and Ṣuhaib are not conclusively proved). After them came ascetics (*nussāk*, *zuhhād*), penitents or "weepers" (*bakkāʾūn*) and popular preachers (*ḳuṣṣāṣ*). At first isolated, they gradually tend to fall into two individual schools, like the adepts in other branches of Muslim thought, schools which had their headquarters on the Mesopotamian frontier of the Arabian desert, one at Baṣra and the other at Kūfa.

The Arab colony at Baṣra, of Tamīmī origin, realist and critical by nature, enamoured of logic in grammar, realism in poetry, criticism in Ḥādīth, and of the sunna with Muʿtazilī and Ḳadarī tendencies in dogmatics, had as teachers of mysticism: Ḥasan al-Baṣrī (d. 110/728), Mālik b. Dīnār, Faḍl al-Raḳḳāshī, Rabāḥ b. ʿAmr al-Ḳaisī, Ṣāliḥ al-Murrī and ʿAbd al-Wāḥid b. Zaid (d. 177/793), founder of the famous caenobitic group of ʿAbbādān.

The Arab colony of Kūfa, of Yamanī origin, idealist and traditionalist by temperament, enamoured of *shawādhdh* in grammar, Platonism in poetry, Ẓāhirism in Ḥadīth, and of the Shīʿa with Murdjiʾī tendencies in dogmatics, had as teachers of mysticism: Rabīʿ b. Khaitham (d. 67/686), Abū Isrāʾīl Mulāʾī (d. 140/757), Djābir b. Ḥaiyān, Kulaib al-Ṣaidāwī, Manṣūr b. ʿAmmār, Abu 'l-ʿAtāhiya and ʿAbdak. The three last-named spent the latter part of their lives in the capital of the empire, Baghdād, which became the centre of the Muslim mystic movement after 250/864: the date when the first meeting-places for religious discussions and sacred concerts (*ḥalḳa*) were opened, with the first public lectures on mysticism in the mosques.

This was also the period in which the mystics had their first open encounter with the theologians, the trial of Dhu 'l-Nūn al-Miṣrī (240/854), Nūrī and Abū Ḥamza (between 262/875 and 269/882, according to Ibn al-Djawzī, *Talbīs*, p. 183) and Ḥallādj, before the ḳāḍīs of Baghdād.

3. The part played by Ṣūfism in the Muslim community. The early Muslim mystics had not foreseen that they would come into conflict with the administrative authorities of the Muslim community. If they lived rather retired lives in voluntary poverty (*faḳr*) it was in order to be the better able to meditate on the Ḳurʾān (*taḳarraʾa* is the old synonym of *taṣawwafa*) by seeking to draw near to God in prayer. The mystic call is as a rule the result of an inner rebellion of the conscience against social injustices, not only those of others but primarily and particularly against one's own faults: with an intense desire after inner purification to find God at any price; this which is already clearly seen in the life, examples and sermons of Ḥasan al-Baṣrī (cf. Schaeder, *Isl.*, xiv. 1—72, and Massignon, *Essai*, p. 152—179), is magnificently expounded in the moving autobiographies of the two great mystics, Muḥāsibī in his *Waṣāyā* (transl. in Massignon, p. 216—218) and Ghazzālī in his *Munḳidh* (transl. Barbier de Meynard), but does not yet directly threaten the established order, however unrighteous may be the conduct of the ruler. But it was the canonists and professional theologians, *fuḳahāʾ* and *mutakallimūn*, who, very displeased at seeing people speak of searching their consciences and judging one another by this inner tribunal — since the Ḳurʾānic law had only legislated for an external tribunal and punished public sins and had no weapon against religious hypocrisy (*nifāḳ*) — tried to show that the ultimate results of the life led by the mystics were heterodox, since they held that the intention is more important than the act, that practical example (*sunna*) is better than strict letter of the law (*farḍ*) and that obedience is better than observance.

Among the Muslim schools, the Khāridjīs were the first to display their hostility to Ṣūfism, in the case of Ḥasan al-Basrī; then the Imāmīs (Zaidīs, Twelvers and *ghulāt*) in the third century A.H. condemned all calls to the mystic life as introducing among believers an unusual kind of life (*ṣūf*, *khanḳa*), finding expression in the search for a state of grace (*riḍā'*) and dispensing with devotion to the twelve Imāms, and a body of doctrine contrary to their custom of *taḳīya*.

The Sunnīs were slower in declaring their attitude and there was never unanimity among them in condemning mysticism. The attacks on mysticism came from two sections among them: on the one hand from conservative circles (*ḥashwīya*): Ibn Ḥanbal accuses mysticism of developing meditation at the expense of oral prayer and of seeking for the soul a state of personal friendship with God (*khulla*), henceforth freeing it from the observances prescribed by law (*ibāḥa*); his immediate disciples, Khashīsh and Abū Zur'a, put it in a special subsection (*rūḥānīya*) of the heresy of the *zanādiḳa*.

On the other hand, the Mu'tazilīs and Ẓāhirīs denounce as absurd the idea of a common love (*'ishḳ*) uniting the Creator to his creatures, for it implies in theory anthropomorphism (*tashbīh*) and in practice, contact and mutual permeation (*mulāmasa* and *ḥulūl*).

As a matter of fact, however, moderate Ṣūfism has never been excommunicated by Sunnī Islām, which has always borrowed its practical morality and its life of prayer, from the popular little books of Ibn Abi 'l-Dunyā (d. 281/894) to masterpieces like the *Ḳūt al-ḳulūb* of Abū Ṭālib al-Makkī (d. 386/996) and especially the *Iḥyā'* of Ghazzālī; learned Sunnīs, who were hostile to mysticism, like Ibn al-Djawzī, Ibn Taimīya and Ibn al-Ḳaiyim, respected the great moral authority of Ghazzālī and it was only against the monism of the disciples of Ibn 'Arabī that the fulminations of the late Sunnī canonists were thundered, without much success however. The founder of the Wabhābīs, prejudiced against mysticism as he was, himself wrote a commentary on the *Waṣīya* of the Ṣūfī Shaḳīḳ to Ḥātim al-Aṣamm.

4. The history of the evolution of the conception of mystic union. Primitive Ṣūfism was based on the two following postulates: *a.* the fervent practice of worship engenders in the soul graces (*fawā'id*), immaterial and intelligible realities (a postulate rejected by the Ḥashwīya); *b.* the "science of hearts" (*'ilm al-ḳulūb*) will procure the soul an experimental wisdom (*ma'rifa*), which implies the assent of the will to the graces received (a postulate rejected by the Mu'tazilīs, who are content with a theoretical psychology). The Ṣūfīs assert that there is a dynamic character in the "science of hearts"; it traces their itinerary (*safar*) to God, marks it by a dozen stages (*maḳāmāt*) and steps (*aḥwāl*), some virtues acquired, other graces received, as in the *Scala Sancta* of St. John Climacus; their double list varies with different authors (cf. Sarrādj, Ḳushairī, Ghazzālī) but contains almost always well known terms like *tawba, ṣabr, tawakkul, riḍā*. Without laying stress on the individual variants of this mystic itinerary the Ṣūfīs aimed especially at defining the ultimate goal when, triumphing over its attachment to the flesh, the soul finds the true God to whom it is aspiring, the Real (*al-Ḥaḳḳ*, a word used as early as the third century A.H. and perhaps borrowed from the pseudo-theology of Aristotle). But how could there be defined in orthodox terms this supreme state in which the soul enters with God into this ecstatic dialogue of which the first revelations are made by Rābi'a, Muḥāsibī and Yaḥyā al-Rāzī, a state which raises the difficult question of theopathic utterances (*shaṭḥ* [q.v.])?

It was a serious step for the mystics to seek recourse henceforth to the theological vocabulary of their time; they borrow from it here and there technical terms of which they twist the sense a little, without giving a fixed meaning to them. Thus Shaḳīḳ introduces *tawakkul*, Miṣrī and Ibn Karrām *ma'rifa*, Miṣrī and Bisṭāmī *fanā'* (opp. *baḳā* = cf. Ḳur'ān lv. 26—27), Kharrāz *'ain al-djam'*, Tirmidhī *wilāya*, etc. In doing this, primitive Muslim mysticism involved itself in the snares of the metaphysics of the first *mutakallimūn*, atomism, materialism and occasionalism in metaphysics, denying the spirituality and even the immortality of the soul, confounding ontological unity with arithmetical unity; precisely for this reason the attempts at explanation of the first Muslim mystic schools are necessarily classified with the heresy of the Ḥulūlīya. In the case of the Karrāmīya who desire to emphasize the actual interest which God has in the souls, the Ash'arites accuse them of inserting accidents into the being of the Eternal; of the Sālimīya who wish to assert that ardent souls became capable of cohering to the divine presence, the Ḥanbalīs say that they introduce God into the tongue of the reciter; finally when the Ḥallādjīya conclude from the ecstatic dialogue, from the continual change in subject which is then produced in the depth of the soul, that God has made living testimonies (*shawāhid*) out of the saints, this view is accused of being a blasphemous impossibility, of implying the usurpation of the divinity by the humanity of a perishable body, since two substances cannot occupy the same place at one and the same time.

From the fourth century A.H. infiltrations from Greek philosophy, which had been continually increasing since the early Ḳarmaṭian gnostics and the physician Rāzī down to Ibn Sīnā, brought into existence a more correct metaphysical vocabulary implying the immateriality of the spirit (*rūḥ*) and of the soul, the consideration of general ideas, the chain of secondary causes. But this vocabulary became amalgamated with the pseudo-theology of Aristotle, with Platonic idealism and the Plotinian doctrine of emanation, which influenced profoundly the further development of Ṣūfism. The learned mystics of this period hesitate between three explanations of mystic union: *a.* the *ittiḥādīya*, from Ibn Masarra and the Ikhwān al-Ṣafā to Fārābī and Ibn Ḳasyī, explaining this union as the formation of concepts by an inner operation of the active intellect, a divine emanation (identified with the *nūr muḥammadī* of the Ḳarmaṭians and the Sālimīya) on the passive soul; *b.* the *ishrāḳīya* from Suhrawardī, Ḥalabī and Djildakī to Dawwānī and Ṣadr al-Dīn Shīrāzī, teaching the substantialisation (*tadjawhur*) of the soul, the divine spark reviving under the illuminations of active intellect; *c. wuṣūlīya* from Ibn Sīnā to Ibn Ṭufail and Ibn Sab'īn, confining themselves to stating that the soul having attained to God, then takes on consciousness of a total indifferentiated existence in which there is no longer number nor discrimination of any sort. We may note in passing that Ghazzālī (*Maḳṣad*, p. 74) refuted the thesis of the *ittiḥādīya*, a thesis which Ibn Sīnā had admitted into his *Nadjāt* (Cairo, p. 402, 481) but rejected in his *Ishārāt* (ch. ix., p. 118; cf. Ibn 'Arabī, *Tadjalliyāt*), and that Ibn Sab'īn, a convinced hylomorphist, sees in God only the form (*ṣūra*) or principle of individuation (*annīya*) of all created beings.

The third and last period in the development of Ṣūfī doctrine begins in the vii[th]/xiii[th] century; its predominant school has been justly given by its adversaries the name of *Waḥdatīya* (or *Wudjūdīya*) as professing the doctrines of existentialist monism (*waḥdat al-wudjūd*). The doctrine of the *Wudjūdīya* claims a long descent: it turns to its advantage Ḳur'ān verses (ii. 115; xxviii. 88; l. 16), the primitive Ashʿarī *kalām* regarding every spiritual happening as an immediate act of God, and extravagances of language of the early mystics like Bisṭāmī and Ḥallādj (in those that ʿAin al-Ḳuḍāt al-Hamadhānī collected in his *Tamhīdāt*, the word *wudjūd*, derived from *wadjd*, ecstasy, still means the empowerment of a creature by God in opposition to *kawn*, his extension in space). It is however really derived from the identification, proposed as early as the third century A.H., of the *nūr muḥammadī* of Muslim gnosticism with the active intellect of the Hellenistic doctrine of emanation (from which Ibn Rushd himself is not free, since he asserts in the *Tahāfut* that divine prescience is the superior degree of the existence of things and that souls ought to unite in it like a single passive intellect in the active intellect). Ibn ʿArabī (d. 678/1240) was the first to formulate the doctrine of existentialist monism; for him at bottom "the existence of created things is nothing but the very essence of the existence of the Creator" (*wudjūd al-makhlūḳāt ʿain wudjūd al-khāliḳ*, Ibn Taimīya justly remarks). He teaches in fact that things emanate from divine prescience in which they pre-existed (*thubūt*) as ideas, by a flux evolving in five periods and that the souls by a logically constructed inverse involution reintegrate the divine essence. Farghānī and Djīlī only add a few touches of detail to this main theory, which to this day has remained that of all Muslim mystics. It is the one which the Persian poets have sung interminably in the simplified form which Ḳuniyawī, putting into order the ideas of ʿAṭṭār, expresses thus: "God is existence in as much as it is general and unconditional"; it is that which flows, like the sea under its waves, through the fleeting forms of individual beings; and at the end of the xvii[th] century of our era, Kawrānī and Nābulusī aroused the indignation of orthodox Sunnīs by concluding that this pantheistic monism is the only correct interpretation to give to the monotheistic profession of faith of Islām (cf. Massignon, *Ḥallāj*, p. 784—90); in their eyes, the *shahāda* by which Islām had thought to affirm the pure transcendence of the one God signifies the absolute immanence of God in his creation, in other words that the totality of all beings in all their actions is divinely adorable. This quietism, which established the supremacy of the divine decree over legal precept, led the Ṣūfīs among other paradoxes to the rehabilitation of Iblīs (supported by Djīlī) and of the Pharaoh of the Exodus (the celebrated thesis of Ibn ʿArabī).

5. The other characteristic features of Ṣūfism and the study of its sources.

The other doctrinal peculiarities still to be noted are.

a. The *isnād* or spiritual genealogy invented to link up, as is done in the case of ḥadīths, the chain of teachers of mysticism to the direct teaching of the Prophet. The earliest known *isnād* (*Fihrist*, p. 183) is that of Khuldī (d. 348/959) which claims to go back to the Prophet by the following links: Djunaid (7), Saḳaṭī (6), Maʿrūf al-Karkhī (5), Farḳad (4), Ḥasan al-Baṣrī (3), and Anas b. Mālik (2). Twenty years later Daḳḳāḳ (d. 405/1014; cf. Ḳushairī, p. 158) goes back to the same names except that he gives only the name of Dāwūd al-Ṭā'ī (4), before Karkhī. Finally the classic *isnād* fixed in the xiii[th] century (Ibn Abī Uṣaibiʿa, *ʿUyūn*, ii. 250) and since adopted by all the great religious orders, gives after Djunaid (7), Rūdhbārī (8), Abū ʿAlī Kātib or Zadjdjādjī (9), Maghribī (10) and Gurgānī (11), and, going back before Dāwūd al-Ṭā'ī (4), Ḥabīb ʿAdjamī (3), Ḥasan al-Baṣrī (2), ʿAlī (1). Ibn al-Djawzī and Dhahabī have shown that the four oldest links in this *isnād* are false, since these men never met one another. Some religious orders utilize an *isnād* which goes back (before Maʿrūf al-Karkhī) to the nine first Shīʿī Imāms and is still more apocryphal.

b. The invisible hierarchy of believing souls in the world (*ridjāl al-ghaib*); the world is supposed to endure, thanks to the intercessions of a concerted hierarchy of "averting" saints, fixed in number, the place of one who dies being immediately filled. These are the 300 *nuḳabā'*, the 40 *abdāl*, the 7 *umanā'*, the 4 *ʿamūd* and their *ḳuṭb* (pole or mystic axis of the world = *ghawth*).

c. The privileges and dispensations (*rukhaṣ*) on which is founded the communal life of the Ṣūfīs, [cf. ṬARĪḲA]: privileges frequently of an anarchical and unusual character from the distant days of Bisṭāmī, Shiblī and Abū Saʿīd down to the more or less irresponsible and scandalous *madjdhūbīn* of modern times. At their assemblies the Ṣūfīs recite special poems; this literature, which is very characteristic of Islām, has developed everywhere in extreme profusion and as a rule has not escaped either monotony or dullness; it is intended to provoke among listeners a psychic excitement by aesthetic means so as to release a sort of artificial ecstasy.

This literature extols in mystical language wine (*khamr*) interdicted by the law in this world and reserved for the Paradise of the elect, the lovingcup (*ka's al-maḥabba*) which the cup-bearer (*sāḳī* = *shammās al-dair* = *tersabeče*) causes to circle amongst them, such allegorical descriptions being frequently developed with a certain delight in titillating detail which the majority of western translations prudently slur over. Among such poems the following are specially famous: in Arabic, those of Ibn Fāriḍ and of Shushtarī; in Persian, the quatrains of Abū Saʿīd, the long *methnewī*'s of ʿAṭṭār and Rūmī (cf. his monistic apologue: "Who is there? — It is Thou" etc.), the *ghazal* of Ḥāfiẓ and the various poems of Djāmī, in Turkish the works of Nesīmī and Niyāzī. This kind of literature has become naturalized in Urdu and in Malay, where it still survives at the present day although it has now disappeared in the nearer East; the modern Muslim élite are more and more abandoning it.

The critical study of the sources of Ṣufism is far from being completed. Surprised at the profound dogmatic difference which lies between its present monism and strict orthodoxy, the early students of Islām thought Ṣūfism could be explained as a doctrine of foreign origin, derived either from Syrian monachism (Merx) or Greek Neo-Platonism or Persian Zoroastrianism, or from the Vedānta of India (Jones). Nicholson has shown that in this simple form the hypothesis of borrowing is untenable; indeed from the very beginning of Islām, it can be observed that the formation of the theses peculiar to Muslim mystics went on from within in the course of assiduous recitations of and meditations on the Ḳur'ān and Ḥadīth, under the influence of social and individual crises in the very centre of the Muslim community. But if the initial framework of Ṣūfism was specifically Muslim and Arab, it is not exactly useless to identify the foreign decorative elements which came to be added to this framework and flourished there; in this way it has been possible for recent students to discover several devotional elements derived from Christian monachism (Asín Palacios, Wensinck, T. Andrae) and several Greek philosophical terms translated from the Syriac; the Iranian analogies (suggested by Blochet) have hardly been examined; as to the Indian elements (Horten's theory) few arguments have been added to the old similar conjectures of al-Bīrūnī and Dārā Shikūh on the parallels between the Upanishāds or the Yōga Sūtra and the ideology of primitive Ṣūfism. On the other hand, it is probable that the critical student of the rhythmical movements of the body producing the *dhikr* of the modern congregations [cf. TARĪḲA] would establish the infiltration of certain methods of Hindu asceticism.

Bibliography: The list of western sources to be consulted on Ṣūfism has been prepared with much care by G. Pfannmüller in his *Handbuch der Islam-Litteratur*, Leipzig 1923, p. 265—292. From this long list the best general works are those of R. A. Nicholson, *The Mystics of Islam*, London 1914; *Studies in Islamic Mysticism*, Cambridge 1921; and *The Idea of Personality in Sufism*, Cambridge 1923; further A. J. Wensinck, *Oostersche Mystiek*, 1930; A. J. Arberry, *Sufism*, 1950. — On special points may be consulted: on the origins, acute articles by Goldziher (*RHR*, xxxvii. 314; *WZKM*, xiii. 35; *ZA*, xxii. 317; *ZDMG*, lxviii. 544; *Isl.*, ix. 144); Massignon, *Essai sur les Origines du Lexique technique de la mystique musulmane*, Paris 1922; and *La Passion d'al-Ḥalāj, martyr mistique de l'Islam*, Paris 1922. On Ghazzālī: Asín Palacios, *Algazel*, Saragossa 1901 and in *Cultura española*, 1901, p. 209, and *MFOB* 1914, p. 67; Obermann, *Der philosophische und religiöse Subjektivismus Ghazalis*, Vienna 1921. On Ibn al-Fāriḍ: Nallino (in reply to Di Matteo, in *RSO*, 1919—1920). On Ibn ʿArabī: Asín Palacios, *El mistico Murciano Abenarabi*, in *Bol. Ac. Hist.*, Madrid 1925—8. On Hindu Ṣūfism of the xvii[th] century, see von Kremer, *JA*, 1869, p. 105, and on the general psychological methods of Ṣūfism, the documents of Eflākī (translated by Huart in *Les Saints des derviches tourneurs*, Paris 1918) and the remarks by D. B. Macdonald, *The Religious Attitude and Life in Islam*, Chicago 1908. — As to the original texts, we have the fine editions by Nicholson of Sarrādj, ʿAṭṭār, Ibn ʿArabī and Rūmī, the translations by Richard Hartmann (of Ḳushairī) and Huart (Dārā Shikūh, in *JA*, 1926, p. 285), the commentaries of Gairdner on Ghazzālī (*Al-Ghazzālīs mishkāt al-anwār*, London 1924), of Horten on Suhrawardī Ḥalabī (*Die Philosophie der Erleuchtung nach Suhrawardi*, Halle 1912), of Köprülüzāde Meḥmed Fūʾād on the early Turkish mystics (*Türk Edebiyatendé ilk mutaṣawwifler*, Stambul 1919), of Nyberg on Ibn ʿArabī (*Kleinere Schriften des Ibn al-ʿArabi*, Leyden 1919) etc. The fundamental sources in Arabic are the works of Muḥāsibī, Makkī, Ghazzālī and Ibn ʿArabī, favourable to Ṣūfism; and those of its two great opponents: Ibn al-Djawzī (*Talbīs Iblīs*, Cairo 1340) and Ibn Taimīya.

TASHAHHUD. [See ṢALĀT, iii].

TASHBĪH, assimilating, comparing (God to man), anthropomorphism, and TAʿṬĪL, emptying, divesting (God of all attributes), are the names of two opposite views within the Islāmic doctrine of the nature of God; both are regarded as heresies and grave sins in dogma. The fierce dispute over these conceptions, by which even the dogma of the Ḳurʾān is influenced, is explained by the central position of the doctrine of the nature of God in Islām. The formal cause is to be found in the Ḳurʾān, which strongly emphasizes the absolute uniqueness of God and yet at the same time plainly describes him in the language of anthropomorphism, giving him a face, eyes and hands and talking of his speaking and sitting. The commentaries, such as, for example, Ṭabarī on the Throne-verse ii. 255 (cf. also Goldziher, *Vorlesungen*², Heidelberg 1925, p. 102 *sqq.*; *Die Richtungen der islamischen Koranauslegung*, Leiden 1920, passim) enumerate the most diverse interpretations, most of which can no longer be verified; these vary from crude emphasis of the literal meaning to its explanation as allegorical. Instead of the name *tashbīh*, which came very early into use and with reference to God means not merely a phraseology which is ambiguous because generally used of man, but which had, one might say, the sanction of the Ḳurʾān, we find *tamthīl* also used in connection with Sūra xlii. 11, where the possibility of anything like God is excluded, while the verb *sh-b-h* II is found only in Sūra iv. 157, applied to the docetic description of the death of Jesus. *Taʾwīl* by degrees became a special term for the allegorical and the rational interpretation of the anthropomorphic literal expressions as a means and first step to *taʿṭīl*, although the root *ʾ-w-l* in the Ḳurʾān has not a censorious sense. The Sunna here again plays its double part. There are ḥadīths which are devoted to the question, not only purely tendencious sayings, which originated in this dispute and were coined for the purpose, but also such as are quite free from dogmatic prejudice, as e.g. in certain Ṣūfī circles the longing aroused in the mystic worship of youth may have found expression in the strongly anthropomorphic visions of God in the form of a noble-looking youth (Ritter in *Isl.*, xvii. [1928], p. 257; cf. also his references to manuscripts in the preceding pages). Other ḥadīths again were cited as arguments in the dispute on the strength of their accidental wording, e.g. that of the nightly descent of God to earth, in itself really soteriological and edifying, in which the exact point actually lies in the hearing of prayer.

It is exceedingly difficult for us to approach the question, since, so far as we can see, none of the Muslim theologians declares frankly for one of the two views of God, but rather every one asserts that he stands for *tanzīh*, keeping (God) pure, against *tashbīh*, and for *tathbīt*, positive determination on the basis of *tanzīl*, recognition of the revealed text, against *taʿṭīl*. All the more eagerly however, do they accuse one another of one or even both transgressions. The use of these terms is quite relative and the grouping of their alleged representatives is equally relative. There are no definite *muʿaṭṭila* and *mushabbiha* sects; on the contrary, the differences in the teaching about God's nature and attributes do not run parallel with any other statements about God and still less do they coincide with other differences in dogma and religio-political theory. Little is known of Djaʿd b. Dirham, said to have been the first *muʿaṭṭil*, whom even Ibn Taimīya, in *al-Furḳān* (cf. *Madjmūʿat al-rasāʾil al-kubrā*, Cairo 1323, i. 137, 14 *sqq.*) still makes responsible for the fall of the last Umaiyad, who is definitely called a Djaʿdī, and in remarkable contrast also responsible for the Bāṭinīya of the Assassins and the Rāfiḍīya of Syria. The exponent of *taʿṭīl* most frequently mentioned, the somewhat younger Djahm b. Ṣafwān al-Rāsibī, put to death in 128/745, was described by the Shīʿī Ibn al-Rāwandī as a Muʿtazilī Unitarian (*muʾaḥḥid*) but was rejected from the Muʿtazila as the *imām* of the *mus̲h̲abbiha* by the Muʿtazilī Abu 'l-Ḥusain al-K̲h̲aiyāṭ in the *Kitāb al-intiṣār* (*Le Livre du triomphe*, ed. Nyberg, Cairo 1925, p. 133 ult., 134, $_4$) on the authority of a poem cursing him by Bis̲h̲r b. al-Muʿtamir and, on account of the one principle in common, — that God's knowledge of things only comes into existence at their creation — was classed (p. 126, $_{10}$) with the S̲h̲īʿī Ibn al-Ḥakam (see below), as the chief of anthropomorphism; al-K̲h̲aiyāṭ as a rule attributes anthropomorphic views particularly to the Nābita, i.e. the ʿUt̲h̲mānic-Umaiyad party (p. 145, $_9$ *sq.*); Ibn Ḥazm (*Faṣl*, Cairo 1320, iv. 205, $_{15}$) classes D̲j̲ahm among the Murd̲j̲iʾīs along with al-As̲h̲ʿarī; S̲h̲ahrastānī (ed. Cureton, p. 60 *sq.*) and the Ibāḍī Abū Sitta Muḥammad al-Ḳaṣbī (on the margin of D̲j̲anāwunī, *Kitāb al-waḍʿ*, Cairo 1305, p. 70) put him with the D̲j̲abarīs who believe in predestination. Although the description of D̲j̲ahm as a *muʿaṭṭil* seems to be general, the writers on heresies can only be used as authorities with the greatest caution. While K̲h̲as̲h̲īs̲h̲ al-Nasāʾī (d. 253/867; see Massignon, *al-Hallaj, martyr mystique de l'islam*, Paris 1922, p. 635 and note 2) calls the dogmatics of D̲j̲ahm *tak̲h̲mīm* (purifying from any attributes of a created being), and As̲h̲ʿarī, *Maḳālāt al-Islāmīyīn* (ed. Ritter, p. 280, $_2$ *sq.*) and similarly Bag̲h̲dādī in *Farḳ bain al-firaḳ* (Cairo 1328, p. 199, $_{11}$) only point out that D̲j̲ahm from fear of *tas̲h̲bīh* did not teach "God is a something", Ibn Ḥazm also quotes the negative denial: but also "not a not-anything", which reveals the same anxiety about *taʿṭīl* or its intenser from *ibṭāl*, destruction, annihilation, nihilism. Of the numerous pamphlets against D̲j̲ahm that of Ibn Ḥanbal is accessible in *al-Radd ʿala 'l-zanādiḳa wa 'l-D̲j̲ahmīya* (see *Ilahiyat Fakültesi mecmuasi*, 1927, p. 313—327). Ibn Ḥanbal allows his opponent to say very little and the latter's arguments must not be taken as authentic without further evidence; the subject of the dispute and arguments from Ḳurʾān and Sunna are however clear. D̲j̲ahm is said to have denied that God can be seen by the blessed in Paradise, that he talked with Moses and that he sits on a throne. Here however Ibn Ḥanbal interprets D̲j̲ahm's fear of fixing God to a definite place in such a literal and anthropomorphic manner that he says the logical consequence for the D̲j̲ahmīs is to believe that God is in their bodies, in the bellies of swine and in latrines. He himself has however to explain God's being among men in Sūra lviii. 7; xx. 46; ix. 40 etc. as metaphorical *taʾwīl*, which shows how little it is possible to draw a dividing line: on the one side Sunnīs with verbal exegesis and on the other Muʿtazilīs with *taʾwīl*! At the same time Ibn Ḥanbal earns from D̲j̲ahm the reproach of hypostasizing after the fashion of the Christian Trinity for his dogma that God is eternal with all his eternal attributes, for which he unhesitatingly uses the metaphor of the palm-tree consisting of root, trunk, branch, twigs, leaves, and sap.

Aḥmad b. Ḥanbal has become the great orthodox authority against *tas̲h̲bīh* and *taʿṭīl*. Al-As̲h̲ʿarī [q.v.] relies on him for his confession of faith (s. Spitta, *Zur Geschichte Abu 'l-Ḥasan al-Aš'ari's*, Leipzig 1876, p. 133 *sqq.*; Macdonald, *Development of Muslim Theology, Jurisprudence and Constitutional Theory*, New York 1903, p. 293 *sqq.*; cf. also *Maḳālāt*, p. 290—297) and gave his own views on the subject in many special treatises particularly on the possibility of seeing God. That by simply recognizing the hands, the face and the sitting down of God "without a how" (*bi-lā kaif*) he struck the happy mean is constantly asserted by his followers. It has however been brought against him as "the entrance to the doctrine of the anthropomorphists" by Ibn Ḥazm, who at the same time regards Ibn Ḥanbal as an authority (ii. 166, $_{17-19}$); Ibn Ḥazm for his part attacks the Muʿtazilite toning down of the conception with equally colourless *taʾwīl* (cf. ii. 166, $_{16}$ *sq.* to 167, $_6$ *sqq.*). That As̲h̲ʿarī's doctrine of the nature of God was always considered *tas̲h̲bīh* by the Ibāḍīs is shown quite recently by al-Ḳāsim b. Saʿīd al-S̲h̲ammāk̲h̲ī in *al-Ḳawl al-matīn fi 'l-radd ʿala 'l-muk̲h̲ālifīn* (Cairo 1324, cf. esp. p. 67 *sqq.*). His verdict is no more lenient than that of the Almohad Ibn Tūmart (see *Le Livre de Mohammed Ibn Toumert*, ed. Goldziher, Algiers 1903, p. 261, $_3$, 232, $_8$) on the *tas̲h̲bīh* of the Almoravids. For al-Kātib al-K̲h̲ʷārizmī (*Mafātīḥ al-ʿulūm* [ed. van Vloten], p. 27) the As̲h̲ʿarites are plainly *mus̲h̲abbih*.

In the effort to keep as near to Ibn Ḥanbal as possible while averting the suspicion of *tas̲h̲bīh* the Māturīdites rather emphasized the negative: God is not bounded, not numbered, not divided, not compounded; e.g. Abū Ḥafṣ al-Nasafī (cf. Macdonald, *op. cit.*, p. 309). This brought upon them, as it had on their fore-runner Bis̲h̲r al-Marīsī from ʿUt̲h̲mān b. Saʿīd al-Dārimī, and on G̲h̲azzālī from strict Ḥanbalīs like Ibn Taimīya (*op. cit.*, i. 425 *sqq*) the reproach of the "divesting" *taʾwīl*. But the Ḥanbalī school of theologians did not remain at one. In *Dafʿ s̲h̲ubhat al-tas̲h̲bīh wa 'l-radd ʿala 'l-mud̲j̲assima* (ed. Ḥusām al-Dīn al-Ḳudsī, Damascus 1345, esp. p. 5 *sqq.*) Ibn al-D̲j̲awzī attacks three fellow Ḥanbalīs for lack of purity of conception. On the other hand it is Ibn al-D̲j̲awzī's celebrated pupil Ibn Taimīya who is regarded, along with men like Abū ʿĀmir M. b. Saʿdūn al-Ḳuras̲h̲ī, as a pure anthropomorphist since the statement of Ibn Baṭṭūṭa (ed. Paris 1893, i. 217) that he said: "God comes down just as I am now coming down (from the pulpit)". More serious than the striking note on this by Ḥusām al-Dīn (in Ibn D̲j̲awzī, *op. cit.*, p. 48, note) may be the attack in his own works on the formula "Look like my look, hand like my hand!" (*Furḳān*, i. 119, $_{13}$); also his explanation of God's being among men, which may with equal justice be called rationalistic *taʾwīl* (i. 456 *sqq.*); then the constant endeavour to transfer anthropomorphic expressions applied to God to a sphere *sui generis*, but particularly his opinion on all grossly material ḥadīt̲h̲s of God's coming down to earth as deliberate forgeries of the zindīḳs, invented to make the Sunnīs appear ludicrous (i. 280, $_2$) and in general his continual attacks on *tas̲h̲bīh* and *taʿṭīl* (i. 270, $_{14}$ *sqq.*; 395, $_2$ *sqq.* etc.) which at least reveal his aim and his personal conviction.

The case is worse with Abū Muḥammad His̲h̲ām b. al-Ḥakam (d. 179/795 or 199/814) since we possess none of his writings. As̲h̲ʿarī however in *Maḳālāt*, p. 31, $_{11}$ *sqq.*, reveals the lack of agreement among the notices of him when collected. Among them is a definite testimony that this His̲h̲ām was free from actual *tas̲h̲bīh* and a concise positive indication of the view held, of an affinity and correspondence (*tas̲h̲ābuh*; in D̲j̲urd̲j̲ānī on Īd̲j̲ī, *Mawāḳif*, ed. Soerensen, Leipzig 1848, p. 347 $_6$ and $_{11}$: *mus̲h̲ābaha*), which first of all makes possible the relation of God to what is created and only makes his knowledge possible by his emanating penetration, which is only to be conceived in this way. When then in spite of this, As̲h̲ʿarī opens his section on anthropomorphism with this His̲h̲āmīya "who took the object of their adoration to be a body", we have a glimpse of the origin of this careless labelling such as became common among the later historians of heresies. The very full special expositions of the Shīʿīs are themselves contradictory. Among them another Hishām, Ibn Sālim al-Djawālīḳī, seems to be the crudest because he talked of God's hair and sides, citing the ḥadīth "God created man in his own image" and referring the "his" to God (Kashshī, *Maʿrifat akhbār al-ridjāl*, Bombay 1317, p. 183; Astarābādī, *Manhadj al-maḳāl fī taḥḳīḳ al-ridjāl*, Teheran 1306, p. 367). Hishām b. al-Ḥakam on the other hand with all his care for *ithbāt* and anxiety about *ibṭāl*, which made him choose the term "body" (*djism*) beside the vague expression "a something" (*shaiʾ*), yet made a serious attempt to keep his distance from anthropomorphism. Generally speaking *tadjsīm*, i.e. attributing to God a body, should not without more ado be ranked with *tashbīh* as its crudest form, since the very phrase "not like our body" is expressly added, for example even by Hishām b. al-Ḥakam. In spite of the efforts of later Shīʿīs to clear their ancestors from the stain of heresy, Astarābādī (p. 366, $_8$) still knows the damning verdict upon him as the pupil of the "Daiṣānī" Abū Shākir (v. art. THANAWĪYA). Perhaps the most suggestive remark is that of Ashʿarī (p. 33, $_8$) who says that Hishām b. al-Ḥakam expressed five different opinions on the nature of God in the space of one year. This is quite possible in one who, as Shīʿī sources record, was a man of highly strung temperament, a member of the circle of the Imām Djaʿfar al-Ṣādiḳ at a time when dogmatics were still in a very unsettled state, as is shown by the many polemics of the circle which include some of the two Hishāms against one other. The Shīʿīs themselves therefore have drifted widely apart. The Nuṣairīs under Ibn Ḥamdān al-Khaṣībī are classed by their opponents as Mushabbihīs on account of their doctrine of divine emanation. The Bāṭinīs, e.g. Nāṣir-i Khusraw, strictly separate the other creative world from this created one. The Creator (*ṣāmiʿ* or *bārī*), a fine substance (*djawharī laṭīf*), is the Universal Soul (*nafs-i kull*), but may also be called by "another name"; he is below the Universal Intelligence (*ʿaḳl-i kull*) and there is "kindred and familiarity" between him and the corporeal world. But "God (*Khudāy*) is too high for anything to be conform or akin (*mushākil u mudjānis*) to Him" (*Zād-i musāfirīn*, Berlin 1341, p. 168 *sqq.* 174 *sq.* 178; *Wadjh-i dīn*, Berlin 1343, p. 27 *sq.* 37). Poetically however Nāsir-i Khusraw glorifies Man: "Thy qualities are of God's qualities. Thou seest God when thou seest thyself" (*Rūshanāī nāma*, annexed to *Sefer nāma*, Berlin 1341, p. 17 and 22).

The Twelvers have waged a vigorous war on *taʿṭīl* and *tashbīh* with due emphasis, it is true, on *ithbāt*, but with especial Muʿtazilite suspicion against degrading *tashbīh*. Their views will be found under the rubrics (with reference to God) "denial of a body, of a form and of *tashbīh*" and "denial of time, space, movement, change of place" in the encyclopaedia of Madjlisī, *Biḥār al-anwār*, book ii., Teheran 1306, p. 89—105. It is only in the later authors since Kulainī, Ibn Bābūya, and Ṭūsī that we can verify the statements attributed to them.

The dangers, which Hishām b. al-Ḥakam sought to avoid in such varied ways, show the immanent dogmatic difficulty felt between "the two limits (*ḥadd*)". The problem is not so simple that it could be clearly defined in general terms as a twofold struggle over the recognition of God as a purely spiritual being on the one hand and over His in some way personal reality on the other. For where in that case would be put Ashʿarī, for example? The one thing certain from the history of Muslim dogma is that every Ashʿarite would object to the classification of his master in one of two so distinct classes. *Tashbīh* is dreaded as a transition to idolatry and paganism, *taʿṭīl* as a preliminary to atheism and pantheism, but both are felt to be originally cognate. It was because Djahm imagines God's speaking only as coming from a stomach, a tongue and two lips, i.e. anthromorphically, that, according to Ibn Ḥanbal, he fell into his "divesting" interpretations of the passages in question in the Ḳurʾān; Ibn Taimīya 127, $_{10}$ calls him an "anthropomorphizing divester" (*muʿaṭṭil mumaththil*).

Bibliography: The sections mentioned in the historians of heresies and the anecdotes of theologians are, in regard to the relativity of the points of view, not simply to be dismissed as malevolent inventions; at the same time they can only give indications of some value as to what views were considered to be particularly expounded on one side or the other. The value of the polemics also as authority for the doctrines of those they attacked is in the same way only preliminary. They can only be regarded as authentic sources for the views of the authors of the polemics, just as for any one the only criterion is his own exegesis of the Ḳurʾān and dogmatics, e.g. Ghazzālī, *Iḥyāʾ ʿulūm al-dīn*, i. 2: *Ḳawāʿid al-ʿaḳāʾid* iv., 5 and 6: *al-Tawḥīd wa 'l-tawakkul* and *al-Maḥabba*; cf. H. Bauer, *Die Dogmatik al-Ghazālīs*, Halle 1912, 48 *sqq.*; J. Obermann, *Der philosophische und religiöse Subjecktivismus Ghazālīs*, Vienna 1921, 197—200, 127; al-Ashʿarī, *Maḳālāt al-Islāmīyīn*, (*Bibl. Isl.* I); Abū Manṣūr ʿAbd al-Ḳāhir al-Baghdādī, *Uṣūl al-dīn*, Stambul 1928, i. 73—130 (not so much a systematic treatise as an account of *ikhtilāf* on the lines of his above mentioned *Farḳ bain al-firaḳ*).

TASHRĪḲ. [See ḤADJDJ, ic].

TAʿṬĪL. [See TASHBĪH].

ṬAWĀF (A.) from *ṭāfa* with *bi* of place) encircling; in the language of ritual the running round or circumambulation of a sacred object, a stone, altar, etc. There are traces of the rite having existed among the Israelites, cf. expecially Ps. xxvi. 6 (xxvii. 6, lxx.) and the ceremony of the feast of booths in the time of the Second Temple, where the altar is circumambulated once on the first six days and seven times on the seventh. The rite however was also found among Persians, Indians, Buddhists, Romans and others and is therefore very ancient. It played a very important part in the religious ceremonial of the ancient Arabs. We find the synonymous *dawār* (from *dāra*) also used. Thus Imru 'l-Ḳais, *Muʿallaḳa*, 63, compares the wild cows with young women in long trailing robes, who perform the circumambulation (*duwār*, a circumambulated idol like *dawār* in ʿAntara 10, $_2$, if *diwār* is not to be read here). In Mecca the Kaʿba which enclosed the Black Stone sacred from very ancient times used to be circumambulated and Muḥammad adopted this old custom when he established the rites of his religion and centred them round the Kaʿba. When, in the year 8, he made his victorious entry into his native town, he is said by Ibn Hishām, p. 820 and Ṭabarī, i. 1642 to have performed the ṭawāf riding on his camel, touching with his crooked staff the *rukn* (the eastern corner of the Kaʿba where the stone was). This was however something exceptional and according to Ibn Hishām, it was only shortly before his death at the "farewell pilgrimage" that he laid down the authoritative rules for the circumambulation. It may however be assumed with certainty that he observed ancient traditional forms ("handed down from Abraham": cf. Ibn Hishām, p 51, 10) so that we can deduce from Muslim practice what the ancient pagan custom was; one feature of the latter was that the circumambulation had to be performed seven times in succession (cf. above on the feast of booths) the three first at a greater speed, beginning at the black stone and ending there and during the course keeping the Kaʿba on the right; one should make a special effort to kiss the stone or at least touch it. On the contrary, if Wellhausen is correct, it was an innovation that the ṭawāf which previously took place only at the *ʿumra* [q.v.] was inserted by Muḥammad in the great ḥadjdj when the pilgrims visited Mecca. This suggestion is however disputed, cf. HADJDJ, II, where Sūra iii. 97 is quoted against it, but the expression *ḥadjdj al-bait* is hardly decisive, since Muḥammad may have decided on the expansion of the rites of the ḥadjdj when he conceived the verse, if the expression was not inserted in the text later. The following special courses are certainly Muslim innovations: the *ṭawāf al-taḥīya* or *al-ḳudūm* (circumambulation of greeting or arrival) and the *ṭawāf al-wadāʿ* (circumambulation of departure, cf. Burckhardt, *Reisen in Arabien*, p. 439) which are, it is worth noting, not obligatory. Of the old pagan customs, one at least was strictly forbidden by the Prophet, making the *ṭawāf* naked; see Sūra vii. 31; Ibn Hishām, p. 921; cf. Ibn Saʿd, III/i. 6, 12, where there is a reference to a wooden object at the Kaʿba, where the heathen laid their clothes at the circumambulation. The pavement surrounding the Kaʿba on which the course was run is called *al-Maṭāf*. At the al-Ḥaṭīm wall (see KAʿBA, II) they run close to the outer side of it, not as usual along the Kaʿba.

The ṭawāf, except for the special forms above mentioned, is strictly compulsory and therefore it became an important factor in Islām. It is therefore significant that the caliph ʿAbd al-Malik, when the rule of the anti-caliph ʿAbd Allāh b. al-Zubair made the visits of the faithful to Mecca difficult, proclaimed that a ṭawāf around the Dome of the Rock in Jerusalem would have the same value as that around the Kaʿba (cf. Goldziher, *Muhammedanische Studien*, ii. 35). The complete omission of this rite would have meant a serious gap in Muḥammadanism. But the innovation soon disappeared with its cause and in orthodox Islām any ṭawāf except that around the Kaʿba became more and more pointless. That the old ritual custom survived in the lower strata of Arab life is revealed in an interesting fashion by ʿUdjaimī, who says the Beduins endeavoured to perform the ṭawāf not only around the graves of their ancestors but also around the tomb of Ibn al-ʿAbbās in Ṭāʾif.

Bibliography: Robertson Smith, *Lectures on the Religion of the Semites*, 1889, p. 321; Scheftelowitz, in *MGWJ*, lxv. (1921), p. 118 *sqq.*; Wellhausen, *Reste arab. Heidentums* ², p. 67, 47, 141; Snouck Hurgronje, *Het Mekkaansche Feest*, p. 108; Juynboll, *Handbuch des islamischen Gesetzes*, 1910, p. 148, 150, 156 *sq.*; Azraḳī, ed. Wüstenfeld, in *Die Chroniken der Stadt Mekka*, i., *passim*; Wensinck, *Handbook of Early Muhammadan Tradition*, s.v.; Gaudefroy-Demombynes, *La pèlerinage à la Mekke*, 1923.

TAWBA (A.), repentance, originally meaning "return", is a verbal noun derived from *tāba*; the verb is often used in the Ḳurʾān (iv. 17, 18; ix. 104; xlii. 25), either absolutely or with *ilā*, of one who turns to God with repentance, and also with *ʿalā* of God, who turns with forgiveness to the penitent, for He is *tawwāb raḥīm*, "very forgiving and merciful" (Sūra ii. 37 *sqq.*). The validity of tawba depends on three things: 1. a conviction of sin, 2. remorse (*nadam*), 3. a firm resolution to abstain from sin in the future (Ghazzālī, *Iḥyāʾ*, book iv., where the subject is discussed in detail). If these conditions are fulfilled, God always accepts repentance, not from obligation (*wudjūb*) as the Muʿtazilites hold, but in virtue of His eternal will; on the other hand "a deathbed repentance" is unavailing (Sūra iv. 18). Sin being an offence against God, tawba is indispensable for salvation, though Aḥmad b. Ḥanbal and others deny this (Massignon, *La Passion d'al-Hallaj*, p. 666). The Ṣūfīs, rising above the legal notion of sin, attach a correspondingly higher significance to tawba. Amongst them the term denotes the spiritual conversion which is the necessary starting-point for those entering on the Path (*ṭarīḳa*), and which is represented as an act of divine grace. In its most profound sense tawba is not so much an acknowledgement and renunciation of sin as a new orientation of the entire personality, so that the penitent is wholly turned towards God. Any recollection of sin or thought of remorse is wrong; for to remember sin is to forget God, and self-consciousness is the greatest sin of all; hence, according to a well-known tradition, the Prophet sought forgiveness of God seventy times a day.

Bibliography: Hudjwīrī, *Kashf al-maḥdjūb*, ed. Schukovski, p. 378 *sqq.*; transl. Nicholson, in *GMS*, xvii., 294 *sqq.*; R. Hartmann, *al-Ḳuschairis Darstellung des Ṣûfîtums*, p. 107—110; M. Smith, *Rābiʿa the mystic*, 1928, p. 53—58; R. A. Nicholson, *Mystics of Islam*, p. 20—22.

TAWḤĪD (A.), infinitive II of *w-ḥ-d*, means literally "making one" or "asserting oneness" (Lane, p. 2927ᵃ). In consequence, it is applied theologically to the oneness (*waḥdānīya, tawaḥḥud*) of Allāh in all its meanings. The word does not occur in the Ḳurʾān, which has no verbal form from this root nor from the kindred *ʾ-ḥ-d*, but in the *Lisān* (iv. 464, 16 to 465, 4 from below) there is an elaborate philological statement of the usages of the different forms from these roots as applied to Allāh and to men. Technically "the science of *tawḥīd* and of the Qualities" (*ʿilm al-tawḥīd wa ʾl-ṣifāt*) is a synonym for "the science of *kalām*" [see article KALĀM] and is the basis of all the articles of the belief of Islām (Introduction by Taftāzānī to the *ʿAḳāʾid* of Nasafī, ed. Cairo 1321, p. 4 *sq.* and the marginal commentaries thereon; *Dict. of techn. terms*, p. 22). In this definition the Muʿtazilites would exclude the qualities and make the basis *tawḥīd* alone. But unity is far from being a simple idea; it may be internal or external; it may mean that there is no other god except Allāh, who has no partner (*sharīk*); it may mean that Allāh is a Oneness in himself; it may mean that he is the only being with real or absolute existence (*al-ḥaḳḳ*), all other beings having merely a contingent existence; it may even be developed into a pantheistic assertion that Allāh is All. Again, knowledge of this unity may be reached by the methods of systematic theology (*ʿilm*) or by religious experience (*maʿrifa, mushāhada*); and the latter, again, may be pure contemplation or philosophical speculation. In consequence, *tawḥīd* may mean simply "There is no god but Allāh", or it may cover a pantheistic position. There is a good statement of these developments in *Dict. of techn. terms*, p. 1468—1470; cf. also, p. 1463—1468.

TAʾWĪL. [See TAFSĪR].

TAWRĀT, Hebr. *Tōrā*, is in the Ḳurʾān of the Madīna period (cf. also an alleged verse of the Jewish poet Sammāk in Ibn Hishām, p. 659) the name of a holy scripture revealed after the time of Ibrāhīm (iii. 65) and Isrāʾīl (= Jacob; iii. 93) and afterwards confirmed by ʿĪsā (iii. 50; v. 46; lxi. 6) which contains the *ḥukm Allāh* (v. 46). While obedience to it brings a reward in Paradise to the "people of the book" (v. 65), those who do not take upon themselves the Tawrāt imposed upon them are "like asses who carry books" (lxii. 5). The Tawrāt also contains a prophecy of the coming of the *Nabī al-ummī* (vii. 157) i.e. Muḥammad, and in it Paradise is promised to the faithful who "fight on the path of Allāh" (ix. 111). A sentence from the Tawrāt is quoted in v. 45, which repeats approximately the text of Exodus xxi. 25 *sq.*, while the parable quoted in xlviii. 29 from Tawrāt and Indjīl comes not from the Torah but, although only in its gist, from the *Psalms*; cf. for example, Psalm i. 3; lxxii. 16; xcii. 14. In iii. 93[b] the Jews are challenged to read from the Tawrāt the law (Genesis, xxxii. 33) which corresponds to the substance of iii. 93[a]. On the other hand the sentence quoted in v. 32 comes not from the Tawrāt but the *Mishnā Sanhedrīn*, iv. 5. Besides such express references to the Tawrāt, the Ḳurʾān contains, frequently repeated, a number of stories from the Pentateuch — usually in their Haggada form and not infrequently adapted to Muḥammad's special purposes — and many laws from the Pentateuch, both without mentioning their origin. Of the books of the Old Testament, in addition to the Tawrāt, Muḥammad only knows the *Zabūr* [q.v.], i.e. the *Psalms*; perhaps, as the Jews themselves sometimes do, he meant by Tawrāt the whole of their holy scriptures (see Bacher, *Exegetische Terminologie*, i. 197).

In Ḥadīth the Tawrāt is also frequently mentioned and in several passages Mūsā is named as he who observed it (Bukhārī, *Tafsīr*, Sūra ii. bāb 1; do., *Tawḥīd*, bāb 19, 24: Muslim, *Īmān*, trad. 322: Ibn Mādja, *Zuhd*, bāb 37). While the Jews pride themselves on having a great treasure in the Tawrāt (Tirmidhī, *Tafsīr*, Sūra xvii., trad. 12; cf. for example *Prov.* iv. 2) it is on the other side pointed out (Tirmidhī, *ʿIlm*, b. 5) that its possession has availed them nothing and the Tawrāt contains nothing equal to the *Umm al-Ḳurʾān* i.e. the *Sabʿ min al-Mathanī* (Tirmidhī, *Tafsīr*, Sūra xvii., trad. 3; *Faḍāʾil al-Ḳurʾān*, bāb 1). The description which the Tawrāt gives of Muḥammad and which according to Bukhārī (*Tafsīr*, Sūra xlviii., bāb 3; do., *Buyūʿ*, bāb 50) has passed in part into Sūra xxxiii. 34; xlviii. 8, in the form given, *loc. cit.* proves to be only a rather inaccurate paraphrase of *Is.*, xlii. 1—4 (cf. similar passages in Ibn Saʿd, 1/ii. 87 *sqq.*). In Bukhārī, *Tawḥīd*, bāb 32, 47; *Manāḳib al-ṣalāt*, bāb 17, the *ahl al-Tawrāt* in a ḥadīth modelled on the parable of the labourers and their hire, complain that the reward of those who obey the Ḳurʾān is larger than theirs, although the former are "less in work" *aḳall*[u] *ʿamal*[an] than they, a reference to the greater number of the Jewish prescriptions. In explanation of Sūra iii. 93, Bukhārī (*Manāḳib*, bāb 26; *Tafsīr*, Sūra iii., bāb 6; *Tawḥīd*, bāb 51) says that the Prophet put the question to the Jews asking how they dealt with adulterers. They tried to give him a wrong answer and to conceal from him the passage in the Tawrāt, in which the punishment of stoning is prescribed (*Deuteron.* xxii. 23 *sq.*) but they did not succeed. According to Ibn Mādja, *Aṭʿima*, bāb 39, it is said in the Tawrāt "The *wuḍūʾ* is the *baraka* of meals", a statement which ascribes the Jewish command to wash the hands before meals to the Torah, in wich the Jewish students of the scriptures also claim to find it indicated (*Ḥullin*, fol. 106[a]).

The Ḳurʾānic allusions early aroused in Muslim scholars the desire to have a closer acquaintance with the contents of the Tawrāt, a knowledge which was however not without its dangers because it brought out certain contradictions which existed between the Ḳurʾānic and the Biblical revelation. How this danger was to be met, the Prophet himself gives a hint in an utterance several times quoted by Bukhārī (*Tawḥīd*, bāb 51; *Iʿtiṣām*, bāb 21; *Tafsīr*, Sūra ii., bāb 11): the *ahl al-Kitāb* were in the habit of explaining the Hebrew text of the Tawrāt to the Muslims in Arabic, whereupon the Prophet commanded the latter "Declare ye the statements of the *ahl al-Kitāb* neither true nor false but say 'we believe in Allāh and what He has revealed'", an utterance, which Bukhārī, as the title of his paragraph shows, wants to be able to apply to the decision on the question whether the translation of the holy scriptures of foreign religions into Arabic is permitted. While in Bukhārī, *Shahāda*, bāb 29, asking members of another faith about the substance of their revelations is deprecated, just as they should put no questions to Muslims about the contents of the Ḳurʾān, there is no lack of references to distinguished men of piety (Ibn Saʿd, VII/i. 79) who studied the Tawrāt in the original or even (*op. cit.*, p. 161) had read it through to the end in a week. The numerous quotations from the Tawrāt, which cannot be identified in the Pentateuch, preserved in Ḥadīth, canonical and extra-canonical, as well as in edifying literature, have tempted Cheikho (*MFOB*, iv. 39 *sq.*) to the untenable thesis that there was a book called Tawrāt different from the Hebrew Torah, from which these quotations were taken; in reality the passages in question are either pure invention or inaccurately modelled on sayings in the Bible or the Talmud.

An intimate knowledge of the text of certain parts of the Torah is shown by some chronological or genealogical statements about the Biblical period, such as are given by Ibn Isḥāḳ (d. 150/767) in his *Maghāzī*, while Ibn Hishām (d. 213/828) in his *Kitāb al-tīdjān*, quoting Wahb b. Munabbih (d. 110/728), gives certain Biblical names not only in their Hebrew but also in their Syriac form. That he checked the statements of Muslim tradition by the Biblical text is recorded in his *Kitāb al-maʿārif*, p. 13, by Ibn Ḳutaiba (d. 276/889) who also gives in this work word for word quotations from Genesis; the Biblical quotations in others of his works do not always correspond exactly to the original and the same is true of the quotations in Djāḥiẓ, *al-Radd ʿala ʾl-Naṣārā*. On the other hand in another contemporary of Ibn Ḳutaiba, the convert to Islām, ʿAlī b. Rabban al-Ṭabarī, we have many literal quotations from all parts of the Old Testament canon in his "Book of Religion and Empire" written about 240/854—855 (ed. by A. Mingana; if this work really belongs to him; cf. Bouyges, in *MFOB*, x. 242 *sqq.*); some also are to be found in the *Risāla* of ʿAbd al-Masīḥ b. Isḥāḳ al-Kindī. While the text of the Bible was accessible without difficulty to converts like ʿAlī b. Rabban, the Biblical quotations in authors born Muslims were either learned orally from Jews or Christians or from another Arabic translation of the Bible. Aḥmad b. ʿAbd Allāh b. Salām al-Indjīlī (whose relationship to ʿAbd Allāh b. Salām, the Jewish convert of the time of the Prophet, cannot be certainly established) is said to have made one such, notably a translation of the Tawrāt, and according to the *Fihrist*, p. 22 in the reign of Hārūn al-Rashīd. Three further translations are mentioned by Masʿūdī (*Tanbīh*, p. 112): that of the Nestorian Ḥunain b. Isḥāḳ (d. 260/873—4) based on the Septuaginta and two by the learned Jews Abū Kathīr (d. between 321/933 and 329/941) and Saʿīd b. Yūsuf al-Faiyūmī, best known under the name of Saʿadyā Gāʾōn (d. 331/943) from the original Hebrew. Of all these translations only that of Saʿadyā has survived (ed. Derenbourg, Paris 1893) and the only other of the period in existence is one made in Spain in 345/956 from the Latin. Of all later translations from the Coptic, Syriac or Hebrew by Christians and Samaritans, bibliographical details are given in the article "*Bibelübersetzungen, Arabische*", in Herzog: *Realenzyklopädie*.

Sūra vii. 155 firmly convinced believers that the Tawrāt contained a prophecy of the coming of Muḥammad. Attempts to prove this go back to the earliest period of Islām (see below) but it is not till the middle of the third century that definite verses of the Pentateuch and other books of the Old Testament are quoted in a literal translation and interpreted as prophecies of Muḥammad's coming. From an unnamed work of Ibn Ḳutaiba, Ibn al-Djawzī in his *Kitāb al-wafāʾ* quotes several passages of this kind and many others are given about the same time by ʿAlī b. Rabban al-Ṭabarī (see above); these recur again and again in the apologetics and polemics of the following centuries with greater or less completeness, From the Pentateuch the verses *Genesis*, xvi. 9—12; xvii. 20; xxi. 21; *Deut.*, xviii. 18; xxxiii. 2, 12, play a prominent part in these polemics. Since according to *Gen.*, xxi. 21, Faran was the abode of Ishmael, and according to Sūra ii. 125 he stayed in Mecca, Faran is identified with Mecca. On the basis of the same identification, *Deut.* xxxiii. 2 is referred to Muḥammad, as is xviii. 18, and in xxxiii. 12 a reference to the *khātam al-nubuwwa* is found.

Even in the Ḳurʾān we find the Jews reproached with "displacing phrases from their context" (iv. 41; v. 13, 41) and an example is given in iv. 41; further they are charged with having forgotten or concealing a part of what had been revealed to them (v. 13; iii. 69; vi. 91). We have already had from Ḥadīth an example of this concealing: the Jews wished to keep from Muḥammad the verse of the Tawrāt which prescribes the punishment of stoning for adultery. The reproach of "altering the words" is more precisely defined by Bukhārī, *Shahāda*, bāb 29, who says that the "possessors of the scripture" had altered the book of Allāh with their own hands and said it was Allāh's. Not all Muslim apologists go so far, however, as to assert deliberate falsification of the text; the milder school ascribes to the Jews only distortions of the meaning. The most distinguished representative of the stronger view is Ibn Ḥazm (d. 456/1064) who raises objections to no less than 57 passages in the Tawrāt and collects the impossibilities and contradictions which he had found in it. See also the art. TAḤRĪF.

Bibliography (so far as not given in the article): W. Rudolph, *Die Abhängigkeit des Qorans vom Judentum und Christentum*, p. 13, 52 *sq.*; J. Horovitz, *Koranische Untersuchungen*, Berlin-Leipzig 1926, p. 71; do., in *Isl.*, xii. 298; M. Steinschneider, *Die polemische und apologetische Literatur in arabischer Sprache*; I. Goldziher, in *ZDMG*, xxxii. 341 *sqq.*; do., in *REJ*, xxviii. 79; xxx. 1 *sqq.*; do., in *ZATW*, xiii. 315 *sqq.*; Grünbaum, *Neue Beiträge zur semitischen Sagenkunde*, p. 100 *sq.*; M. Lidzbarski, *De propheticis quae dicuntur legendis*, Leipzig 1893; G. Rothstein, *De chronographo arabe anonymo*, p. 49 *sqq.*; A. Sprenger, *Leben und Lehre Muhammads*, i. 56; G. Graf, *Die christlich-arabische Literatur*; M. Steinschneider, *Die arabische Literatur der Juden*, § 23; M. Schreiner, in *ZDMG*, xlii. 591 *sqq.*; do., in *Kohut Memorial Volume*, p. 496 *sqq.*; C. Brockelmann, in *ZATW*, xv. 138 *sqq.*; H. Hirschfeld, in *JQR* xiii. 230 *sqq.*; W. Bacher, *op. cit.*, p. 543; Graf, in *Biblische Zeitschrift*, xv. 193 *sqq.*, 291 *sqq.*; Di Matteo, in *RSO*, ix. 301 *sqq.*; *Bessarione*, xxxviii. 64 *sqq.*

TAYAMMUM (A.), the recommendation, or permission to perform the ritual ablution with sand instead of water in certain cases, is based on two passages in the Ḳurʾān, Sūra iv. 43 and v. 6. The latter passage runs as follows: "And if ye be impure, wash yourselves. But if ye be sick, or on a journey or if ye come from the privy or ye have touched women and ye find no water, take fine clean sand and rub your faces and hands with it. Allāh will not put a difficulty upon you but He will make you pure and complete His favour upon you, perhaps that ye may give thanks". Sūra iv. 43 is somewhat more briefly expressed but the law is formulated there in almost identical words except that the phrase "with it" is lacking from the sentence "and rub your faces and hands with it". According to the Shāfiʿīs (see Baiḍāwī on Sūra iv. 43) "with it" means that there must be some sand in the hand. The Ḥanafīs on the other hand consider the rite valid even if the hand has only been touched by a smooth stone.

In his *Mīzān al-kubrā*, Cairo 1279, i. 143 *sqq.*, al-Shaʿrānī gives 14 such points of difference between the *madhhab*'s; they refer to *a.* the material (earth, sand etc.); *b.* the obligation to look for water; *c.* the question how far face and hands are to be rubbed and in o what legal categories these rubbings fall; *d.* the question what one should do if he finds water after he has already begun the *ṣalāt*; *e.* the question whether a single *tayammum* suffices for two *farḍ* rites; *f.* the question whether one who has performed the *tayammum* before his *ṣalāt* may act as *imām* for persons who have performed the ablution with water; *g.* the question whether *tayammum* is permitted before the *ṣalāt* at festivals and for the dead, if one is not on a journey; *h.* the question whether one who is not travelling, and has difficulty in getting water for a *ṣalāt* the legal time for which is about to expire, should repeat the *ṣalāt* performed after *tayammum* as soon as he has found water; *i.* the question whether it is permitted to use the little water one has for a partial washing and do *tayammum* for the rest; *k.* the question what is to be done in cases of injury; *l.* the question whether the *ṣalāt* is to be repeated in four cases, in which it has been performed after *tayammum*.

There is agreement among the *madhhabs* on the point that *tayammum* is only done for the face or hands, whether after a minor or major *ḥadath* [q.v.], whether in place of a washing of all or any parts of the body is a matter of indifference (al-Nawawī, on Muslim, *Ṣaḥīḥ*, Cairo 1283, i. 406).

From various traditions it is evident that ʿAbd Allāh b. Masʿūd and ʿUmar had misgivings about declaring the *ṣalāt* valid after *tayammum* in cases of *djanāba* (cf. e.g. Bukhārī, *Tayammum*, bāb 7; Muslim, *Ḥaiḍ*, tr. 110). On the other hand the saintly Abū Dharr, who had similar misgivings, is made to say that the Prophet had disposed of them by saying: "fine sand is a means of purification when one cannot find water, even if he should look ten years for it" (Aḥmad b. Ḥanbal, *Musnad*, v. 146 *sq.*).

The permission is said to have been revealed when an expedition of Muḥammadans was held up so long looking for a necklace of ʿĀʾisha's that its water became exhausted.

In the *Talmud* (*Berakot*, fol. 15ᵃ) a permit to use sand in case of want of water similar to that of the Ḳurʾān is given and Cedrenus, *Annales*, ed. Hylander, Basle 1566, p. 206, tells how on an occasion in a journey through the desert, Christian baptism was performed with sand.

Bibliography: Cf. also the commentaries on Ḳurʾān, Sūra iv. 43 and v. 6; Nöldeke-Schwally, *Geschichte des Korāns*, i. 199; A. Geiger, *Was hat Moh. aus dem Judenthume aufgenommen?*, p. 86; Th. W. Juynboll, *Handleiding* etc., Leyden 1925, p. 58; A. J. Wensinck, *A Handbook of Early Muhammadan Tradition*, s.v. Tayammum.

TAʿZĪR (A.), punishment, intended to prevent the culprit from relapsing, to purify him (*li 'l-taṭhīr*). — The Ḳurʾān does not know this kind of punishment; on the contrary it classifies several transgressions afterwards punished with taʿzīr merely as sins, e.g. slander, for which there is no *ḥadd* punishment (Sūra iv. 112) and the bearing of false witness (Sūra ii. 283; iv. 135). Tradition has very little to record about it. According to one tradition of ʿAbd Allāh b. ʿUmar, those who bought provisions wholesale without measures or weights in order to sell them again were punished in the time of the Prophet by whipping (Bukhārī, *Ḥudūd*, bāb 43); in spite of the juristic utilization of this tradition by the commentators, it is clearly one of the many traditions which attack speculation in the necessities of life (cf. C. H. Becker, *Papyri Schott-Reinhardt*, Heidelberg 1906, p. 51); it is in any case based on later commercial usage. According to another tradition of Ibn ʿAbbās, the Prophet is said to have threatened with 20 lashes any man who insulted another by calling him soft or effeminate (Ibn Mādja, *Ḥudūd*, bāb 15). Very frequently on the other hand we find a tradition (of Abū Burda, of ʿAbd al-Raḥmān b. Djābir, of Abū Huraira), according to which the maximum that can be inflicted except for *ḥadd* is 10 lashes (Bukhārī, *Ḥudūd*, bāb 43; Muslim, *Ḥudūd*, tr. 39; Ibn Mādja, *Ḥudūd*, bāb 32; Ibn Ḥanbal, iii. 466; iv. 45). These traditions however can only have arisen later owing to divergences of opinion about the amount of taʿzīr, especially as the later law-schools admit a much larger number of lashes. In any case taʿzīr is a kind of punishment which only found its way into Muslim law at a comparatively late date. For this view it is noteworthy that tradition does not connect the later technical sense with the verb *ʿazzara*. It is true that it occurs in the above mentioned tradition in Ibn Mādja, *Ḥudūd*, bāb 32: *lā tuʿazzirū*; but in a tradition of Anas b. Mālik the verb *ʿazzara* is used with reference to the *ḥadd* punishment for drinking wine in contrast to its later technical sense. (Ibn Ḥanbal, iii. 180; a duplicate of this tradition in Ibn Ḥanbal, iii. 115 uses *djalada* in this passage).

According to the *fiḳh*-books, taʿzīr is inflicted for such transgressions as have no *ḥadd* punishment and no *kaffāra* prescribed for them, whether it is a question of disobedience of God such as neglect of the fivefold *ṣalāt* or of fasting, or a question of crime against man such as deceit, bearing false witness, theft of an article of trifling value etc. In the second group however there is also a breach of the divine law (*ḥaḳḳ Allāh*) as well as the breach of man's law (*ḥaḳḳ al-nās*).

The most remarkable condition for the application of taʿzīr is that the delinquent must be in full possession of his mental faculties (*ʿāḳil*). The kind and amount of taʿzīr is left entirely to the discretion of the judge: he may administer a public reprimand, expose him in a public place, banish him, confiscate his property (but there is a difference of opinion on this point, for the goods and chattels of a Muslim are regarded by some as inviolable in this case also), throw him into prison or have him whipped. Except in the Mālikī school however, the number of lashes must not be more than in the *ḥadd* punishment; according to the Shāfiʿī school, the maximum for a freeman is 39, for a slave 19; according to the Ḥanafīs, the maximum is 75 (some take the *ḥadd* for drinking wine, others the *ḥadd* for slander [*ḳadhf*] as the maximum); the Ḥanbalīs on the other hand only allow 10 lashes, relying on the above tradition. There are also very minute and varying rules regarding the administering of the lashes in the different schools.

As the primary object of the taʿzīr is reformation, and the degree of punishment to cause this varies with each individual, men are classified systematically by some jurists for this purpose. Al-Kāsānī, for example, distinguishes four classes: 1. the most distinguished of the upper classes, i.e. officials and officers of the highest rank; for them a personal communication from the judge through a confidential messenger is sufficient; 2. the notables, i.e. the intellectual elite and *fuḳahāʾ*; they are summoned before the judge and admonished by him; 3. the middle classes, i.e. the merchants; they are punished by imprisonment; 4. the lower strata of the people; they are punished with imprisonment or flogging. Other jurists however reject this external classification according to social status and lay stress on the inner worth of the individual, his attitude to religion and his mode of life.

If it seems advisable to the judge, he can completely remit the taʿzīr, in so far as it concerns the divine law; but the portion of the punishment which relates to human rights is not dropped unless the injured person renounces it.

The process of trial is simple in contrast to that for *ḥadd*. Taʿzīr is inflicted on a confession, which however cannot be withdrawn, or on a statement of two witnesses, one of whom may even be a woman; *shahāda ʿalā shahāda* [cf. SHĀHID] is also admitted. According to some, it is even enough if the judge alone has knowledge of the transgression.

How these cases for punishment left by the *sharīʿa* to unfettered judgment were dealt with by those in authority is very clearly seen from the stories in the *1001 Nights* (cf. Rescher in *Isl.*, ix. [1919], 68 *sqq.*). On the other hand the attempt was made to escape this arbitrary punishment by bribery. Frequently also the secular legislation of rulers interfered, regulating the sentence left to the ḳāḍī's discretion by laying down definite punishments for a series of transgressions, as is the case in the *Ḳānūn-nāme*'s of the Turkish Sulṭāns, where moreover a fine is always provided for besides the flogging (cf. Meḥmed II's *Ḳānūn-nāme* in *MOG*, i. [1922], 13 *sqq.*).

Bibliography: The *Kitāb al-ḥudūd* in the books on Tradition and Fiḳh; esp. Kāsānī, *Badāʾiʿ al-ṣanāʾiʿ*, Cairo 1910, vii. 63 *sqq.*; Khalīl, *Mukhtaṣar*, transl. Santillana, Milan 1919, ii. 742; Māwardī, *al-Aḥkām al-sulṭānīya*, ed. Enger, Bonn 1853, p. 399 *sqq.*; transl. Fagnan, Algiers 1915, p. 469 *sqq.*; Shaʿrānī, *Mīzān*, Cairo 1925, ii. 175 *sq.*; Juynboll, *Handbuch des islam. Gesetzes*, Leyden 1910, § 65; 3rd ed. (Dutch), 1925, § 68; Krcsmárik, *Beiträge zur Beleuchtung des islam. Strafrechts*, in *ZDMG*, lviii. (1904), 65, 556 *sqq.*; J. P. M. Mensing, *De bepaalde straffen in het Ḥanbalietische recht*, Leiden 1936; G. Bergsträsser, *Grundzüge des islamischen Rechts*, 1935, index. — For the traditions see Wensinck, *Handbook of Early Muḥammadan Tradition*, Leyden 1927, s.v. Punishment.

TAʿZIYA (A.), *a.* expression of condolence in general, *b.* the passion play of the Shīʿīs. The word, a verbal noun from *ʿaziya* II, is not found in the Ḳurʾān (but cf. *ʿizīn* in lxx. 37), yet occurs in all schools of fiḳh at the end of the book on public worship in the section, or in the separate book, *al-djanāʾiz* = burial, where Muslims are exhorted to condole with the relatives. Among the Shīʿīs it means in the first place the lamentation for the martyred imāms, which is held at their graves and also at home. In particular, however, it is mourning for Ḥusain. The *tābūt* or *naʿsh*, a copy of the *ḍarīḥ*, i.e. Ḥusain's tomb at Karbalāʾ, in popular language is also called *taʿziya*. Such models, often richly executed, are exhibited in the ceremonies of mourning for Ḥusain (see Mrs. Meer Hassan Ali, *Observations on the Mussulmanns of India*, ed. Crooke, 1917, pp. 18 *sqq.*) *Taʿziya* however means more especially the mystery play itself. The time for its performance is the first third of the month of Muḥarram, especially the 10th, *Rōz-i Ḳatl*, the day of the murder of Ḥusain and of the ʿĀshūrāʾ festival [q.v.]. The local usages in Persia and in the Shīʿī regions of Mesopotamia and India are very varied. In a wider sense the plays include the street processions such as the cavalcade with Ḥusain's horse, the marriage procession of Ḥasan's son al-Ḳāsim with Ḥusain's daughter Fāṭima (see below), the procession to the cemetery with the *tābūt*, all popular celebrations of a kind at which the deepest grief does not exclude a part being played by comic figures.

Lastly *taʿziya* means the actual performance of the passion play itself. In ʿIrāḳ it is usually called *shabīh*, because the actors make themselves "like" the dramatis personae. The stage is erected in public places, in caravanserais, even in mosques and in *imām-bāra*'s specially erected for the festival. The chief properties required for the stage are a large *tābūt* with receptacles for holding lights, also Ḥusain's bow, lance, spear and banner. The performers in addition to the players are the *rawẓa-khwān*, the poet, lit. he who pronounces the eulogy for the dead. He speaks the introduction and with gestures indicative of lamentation chants a *khuṭba* [q.v.] with many ḥadīths evocative of grief, surrounded by a choir of boys called *pesh-khwān*, lit. announcers, while the *nūwah* or *ḥannāna*, dressed as mourning women utter the lamentations of the women and mothers. The spectators are separated according to sexes. They are given *muhr* or *turba*, "stamped" cakes of "earth" from Karbalāʾ steeped in musk, on which they press their foreheads in abject grief. While on the stage the hunger and particularly the thirst of the martyrs is most realistically expressed, water and other refreshments are provided for the spectators. The gratuitous provision of the whole spectacle and everything connected with it including payment of the poet is not only an obligation on the well-to-do but a meritorious pious work "for he builds himself a palace in Paradise" when he builds the stage. The Saiyids play a prominent part in these festivals, for their descent from Ḥusain gives them a special claim to gifts from the charitable.

In spite of the similarity of their motives and to a great extent of their language, there is a large number of such plays, which are often touched up and expanded by the poets (cf. the catalogues of MSS.). The most widely used are in Persian but they also exist in Arabic and Turkish. The term drama can only be applied with reservation to the series of sometimes 40—50 independent tableaus which constitute the performance. The events, especially the actual death of Ḥusain, are prophesied from the beginning in all details by Gabriel, by the early prophets and Muḥammad himself, foreseen in dreams, foretold and afterwards narrated again and again.

The characters in the play are, in addition to the angels, principally taken from the history of redemption including the Old and New Testament. Their fate is often symbolically compared with that of the martyr. Jacob and Joseph confess that Ḥusain and his children have suffered more than they have; Eve, Rachel and Mary understand the mother's anguish of Fāṭima; Muḥammad, given by the angel of death the choice of surrendering to him his little son Ibrāhīm or the little Ḥusain, abandons to him the former so that the latter may be preserved to die as a redeemer. Muḥammad and ʿAlī are only brought in as subsidiary to Ḥusain, who even as a child plays the principal part in their thoughts and hours of death. The brother Ḥasan and his relation to Ḥusain is strongly idealised. Of the latter's nearer relations, there appear in addition to the spirit of his dead mother Fāṭima, his sisters Umm Kulthūm and Zainab, his wife Shahrabānū, daughter of Yezdegird III, and his son ʿAlī Akbar, who falls in battle. Very popular is the wedding of his and Shahrabānū's daughter Fāṭima with Ḥasan's son al-Ḳāsim celebrated just before the catastrophe, in which the bridegroom is almost immediately killed. The death of a little son and a young nephew, who are struck by an arrow while clasped to his bosom, aims at producing a special effect on the spectators, whereas the surviving son ʿAlī Zain al-ʿĀbidīn plays the main part in the mournful procession which brings the head and the captured women and children to the caliph Yazīd I. When this procession spends a night on the way in a Christian monastery, the prior pronounces the Muslim confession of faith before the head. Similar scenes are introduced with Jews and pagans and with Christian ambassadors at the caliph's court. Another affecting episode is the humility of a lion which pays homage to the head of the martyr.

More important, and also more serious, is the fact that these spectacles produce a completely biassed view of the figures of early Muslim history upon the Shīʿīs; such are Salmān-i Fārisī, Abū Dharr, Bilāl, al-Ḥurr who goes over to Ḥusain, all on the Shīʿa side and of the enemies: Abū Bakr and ʿUmar who are represented as depriving Fāṭima of her inheritance, the oasis of Fadak, with cruel blows. No distinction is made among the non-Shīʿīs; ʿAlī's slayer Ibn Muldjam is not for example branded as a Khāridjī [q.v.]; his murder likewise is laid to the charge of the Sunnīs. ʿUmar b. Saʿd, the leader of the hostile force, Shimr (Shamir), who is said to have dealt the fatal blow, and especially Yazīd I are painted in the blackest colours. The fury against the Sunnīs is so pronounced that non-Muslims might be tolerated as spectators but scarcely non-Shīʿa Muslims. National hatred of Arabs (and also Turks) is seen in such scenes as that in which Ḥusain's widow Shahrabānū returns to her home in Persia or the young Fāṭima is rescued by a Persian king.

The scenes, mainly written in the radjaz-metre, have grown out of various sources, but the material and the words are often old: verses of the Ḳurʾān, interpreted from the Shīʿa point of view, and particularly old traditions with a Shīʿa bias, which are clothed in a form calculated greatly to impress the hearers; sentences from the khuṭbas are found as early as Ṭabarī. Whole sermons, curses and prayers are already found in the earliest Shīʿite literature [cf. SHĪʿA], in Ibn Bābūya, Kulainī, Shaikh Ṭūsī, especially in the chapters *Ziyārāt* (visits to tombs), in the books on pilgrimage and the imāmate, and also in the *maḳātil* works. There also are found many hymns, while on the other hand songs of lamentation are still written in modern times. As a solemn epilogue to the passion-play may be regarded the pilgrimage to Karbalāʾ with a ceremonial procession on the 20th of Ṣafar "the fortieth day" called *rōz-i arbaʿīn* or *maradd al-raʾs* "Returning the (image of Ḥusain's) head" (to his body).

Judged from the effect on the spectators the *taʿziya* is a most impressive spectacle. Strangers, who cannot appreciate the inner significance of it, may find its broad realism repulsive, especially in the closing scenes where the decapitated head is the principal speaker and actor. They might easily get the idea that the spectators are simply revelling in the pain and cruelty of the spectacle. The real significance can only be ascertained from an unprejudiced examination of what is actually said. As already indicated the plays are full of dogmatics with emphasis on Shīʿite ḥadīths. It is possible that with the primitive nature of the production, touching and exciting scenes are introduced simply for their own sake. But the leading idea is a soteriology that rules everything and is brought out, in harmony with the text books but in much clearer fashion. Here we will only refer the reader to one of these mysteries easily accessible in Chodzko (see *Bibl.*). In the very first scene "The Messenger of God" Gabriel, representing Ḥasan as sharing his brother's fate, announces to Muḥammad: "Thy two grandchildren shall fall under the blows of a contemptible enemy, not because they have in some way transgressed God's laws; no, the filth of sin has never smirched a member of thy family, o Phoenix of the Universe! Rather are they sacrificed for the salvation of the peoples who adopt Islām so that the brow of the martyrs shall eternally reflect the brilliance of the elect of God. If thou desirest the forgiveness of the sins of these evildoing peoples, do not oppose the two roses of thy garden being plucked before the time!" (p. 5 *sq.*) And after this theme of the vicarious death for the forgiveness of sins has been again and again clearly formulated, the mystery comes to its logical conclusion in the last scene, in which the whole hierarchy of patriarchs from Adam to Ḥusain's mother Fāṭima is assembled round the sacred head. To Fāṭima her father Muḥammad (p. 215) says: "Thou art right to weep for thy slain child soaked in his noble blood; but there is a secret about the true reason of his martyrdom; as the price of this martyrdom God on the Day of Judgment will give into our hands the keys of Paradise and of Hell!" How old such ideas of this saving intercession are, is seen from the prayers of those "penitents" under Sulaimān b. Ṣurad who fortified themselves to fight to the death against the Umaiyads by doing penance at Ḥusain's grave four years after the battle of Karbalāʾ; they wanted to atone for their guilt which they had brought upon themselves by not having fought or died with the dead Ḥusain. One of them, ʿAbd Allāh b. Wālī al-Taimī, calls Ḥusain and his brother and father the "bond (of reconciliation) (*wa-ṣīla*) with God on the Day of Judgment". Ṭabarī, ii. 547, records this from Abū Mikhnaf on the authority of an ʿAlid, Ḥusain's grandson Muḥammad al-Bāḳir, through a Shīʿī authority Salama b. Kuhail; but the latter, generally considered a Zaidī, does not belong to an ultra-Shīʿī school.

In their elaborate form the taʿziya are recent and at one time could not be carried through without opposition from the mollas on account of their crude dogma and irreligious accompaniment of dances and processions. Adam Olearius who witnessed great celebrations in Ardabil in 1637 does not mention taʿziya, nor does J. B. Tavernier (cf. *Vierzig-Jährige Reisebeschreibung*, Nürnberg 1681, p. 178 *sqq.*) mention any special play among the Muḥarram ceremonies in Isfahan in 1667; on the other hand it was noted for example by J. Morier in 1811 in Teheran. It is probable that ancient rites of earlier mythological festivals like the Tammuz and Adonis cults have survived in the subsidiary plays, which in India have been adapted even by some Sunnīs and Hindus: the banners for the processions, a large staff, the hand which is carried round by those who summon to the festival and is now interpreted as the hand of Ḥusain which was cut off, have thus their ancient prototypes. That the significance of the sacred properties has altered is shown by the fact that among the Shīʿī Tatars the *tābūt* is called the "marriage house of Ḳāsim". In many places there are accompanying rites with water, which were originally indigenous; the throwing of the *tābūt* into water among the Indian Shīʿīs may be due to Hindu influence. Even the style of the mourning garments is partly influenced by earlier forms. But the passion play itself is the popular expression of that religious feeling which has its roots in the historic fact of Karbalāʾ.

Bibliography: W. Litten, *Das Drama in Persien*, Berlin 1929 (with reproductions of lithographed texts); A. Chodzko, *Théatre persan*, Paris 1878; Lewis Pelly, *The Miracle Play of Hasan and Husain*, 2 vols., London 1879; Ch. Virolleaud, *La passion de l'imam Hosseyn*, Paris 1927; J. Morier, *Second Voyage en Perse*, Paris 1818; M. de Gobineau, *Les religions et les philosophies dans l'Asie Centrale*², Paris 1866; J. Lassy, *The Muharram Mysteries among the Azerbeijan Turks of Caucasia*, Helsingfors 1916; E. G. Browne, *A History of Persian Literature in Modern Times*, Cambridge 1924, p. 172 *sqq.* and thereon H. Ritter in *Isl.*, xv. (1926), 107; B. D. Eerdmans, *Der Ursprung der Ceremonien des Hosein-Festes* (*ZA*, ix., 1894); G. van Vloten, *Les drapeaux en usage à la fête de Huçein à Téhéran* (*Internationales Archiv für Ethnographie*, v. [1892], 3); E. Aubin, *Le chiisme et la nationalité persane* (*RMM*, iv., 1908).

TEKE, TEKIYE. [See ṬARĪḲA].

THAMŪD, the name of one of those old Arabian peoples, which like the ʿĀd, Iram (Aram), Wibār (Jobaritae?) had disappeared some time before the coming of the Prophet. A series of older references, not of Arabian origin, confirm the historical existence of the name and people of Thamūd. Thus the inscription of Sargon of the year 715 B.C. mentions the Tamud among the people of eastern and central Arabia subjected by the Assyrians. We also find the Thamudaei, Thamudenes mentioned in Aristo, Ptolemy, and Pliny. The latter mentions as settlements of the Thamudaei Domatha and Hegra, which are probably to be identified as the modern Dūmat al-Djandal in Djōf and al-Ḥidjr on the Ḥidjāz railway north of al-ʿElāʾ. Old Arab tradition also locates the Thamūd at the last named place. The older poets mention the Thamūd with the ʿĀd as examples of the transitoriness of worldly glory, e.g. al-Aʿshā and Umaiya b. Abi ʾl-Ṣalt who quotes several legendary features of their story. In the Ḳurʾān the fate of the Thamūd along with that of the ʿĀd serves as a warning from native history along with the foreign ones from the Bible: for example in Sūra vii. 73—79; xi. 61—68; xv. 80—86; liv. 23—31. Arab tradition of the fall of the Thamūd, which was further developed by the earliest exegists from the references in the Ḳurʾān is in its main lines as follows. Just as there was a prophet named Hūd among the ʿĀd so there was one called Ṣāliḥ (b. ʿUbaid b. ʿĀmir b. Sām) among the Thamūd. Challenged by his opponents, whose leader is said to have been Djundaʿ b. ʿAmr, to give a sign of his divine mission, he conjured up a pregnant she-camel out of a rock. The tendons of this animal, sacred and inviolable as "Allāh's camel", were however cut along with those of its foal by the scoffers. In punishment the whole people was doomed to destruction. The manner of their destruction is said in Sūra vii. 74 to have been *radjfa*, earthquake, in Sūra xli. 13, 17, *ṣāʿiḳa*, a thunderbolt. These expressions make it probable that tradition associated the fall of the Thamūd with one of the volcanic outbreaks which led to the formation of more or less extensive fields of lava called *ḥarra* in Arabia. West of al-Ḥidjr lies one of the largest of these *ḥarra* (cf. B. Moritz, *Arabien*, Hanover 1923, p. 28). E. Glaser thinks the Thamūd are closely connected with the Liḥyān, the Lechieni of Pliny, that Thamūd was the older, Liḥyān the later name of the people still surviving in the two Liḥyān clans of the Hudhailīs, and that the decline of the Thamūd coincided with the end of the Liḥyān kingdom, somewhere between 400 and 600 A.D. The rock inscriptions found by Huber, Euting and others in al-ʿElāʾ, al-Ḥidjr and neighbourhood are called by epigraphists Liḥyān or Thamūdene.

Bibliography: The commentaries on the Ḳurʾān passages quoted; Ṭabarī, i. 219 *sqq.*, 244 *sqq.*; al-Maḳdisī, *Badʾ al-khalḳ*, ed. Huart, iii. 39 *sqq.*; Masʿūdī, *Murūdj*, iii. 84 *sqq.*; Abu ʾl-Fidāʾ, *Historia anteislamica*, ed. Fleischer, register; Caussin de Perceval, *Histoire des Arabes*, i. 24 *sqq.*; Sprenger, *Alte Geographie Arabiens*; E. Glaser, *Skizze zur Geschichte und Geographie Arabiens*, vol. ii.; J. Horovitz, *Koranische Untersuchungen*, p. 103—106.

THANAWĪYA, Dualism, means the doctrine that light and darkness are the two equal eternal creative principles. There is not a regular Thanawīya sect or school in Islām. The term, as the characteristic name of a school of thought, is limited to three non-Muslims and their adherents: Ibn Daiṣān, Mānī and Mazdak.

A danger arose to Islām through the tendency to dualism within its ranks from the mass conversions of Persians, as was seen for example at the beginning of the ʿAbbāsid period in the disturbing figure of Ibn al-Muḳaffaʿ. He was attacked for example by the Muʿtazilī Zaidī al-Ḳāsim b. Ibrāhīm Ṭabāṭabā, *al-Radd ʿala ʾl-zindīḳ al-laʿīn Ibrāhīm al-Muḳaffaʿ* (ed. M. Guidi, Rome 1927). In the further course of dogmatic development, the charge of dualism is often raised by controversialists, even reciprocally against one another. Several ultra-Shīʿīs of the third (ninth) century had this particular made against them: Abū Ḥafs al-Ḥaddād, Ibn Dharr al-Ṣairafī and Abū ʿĪsā al-Warrāḳ, the authority on heresies, who himself, originally a Mazdaean, even after his conversion is said to have "supported the Thanawīya by his writings". But the classification, for example, of the latter among the Manichaeans is based on his agreement with them on other, not metaphysical points, for example the prohibition of killing. Even the heretic who gets his usual epithet from a Thanawīya group, the Rāfiḍī Abū Shākir al-Daiṣānī got the name, so far as we can see, because he attributed a body to God, i.e. an opinion not in itself dualistic, and the *Fihrist* (ed. Flügel, 338, $_8$) classifies him more generally among the "secret Zindīḳs". In fact the distinctive Daiṣānī dogma, the derivation of bodies from the black and the white element (see Ashʿarī, *Maḳālāt al-Islāmīyīn* [ed. Ritter], p. 349) seems so far not to be traceable in Abū Shākir; besides the branding of an opponent on the ground of single, often quite subsidiary *tertium comparationis* is an all too frequent and confusing habit of the Muslim champions of orthodoxy.

The above charges against the three last-named are taken from al-Khaiyāṭ, *Kitāb al-intiṣār*, "Le Livre du Triomphe" (ed. Nyberg, Cairo 1344, p. 150, $_4$, 149, $_9$, 155, $_{10, 14}$; cf. also the index under the names mentioned here and below). To appreciate his opinions properly, one must remember that they are counter-attacks on Ibn al-Rāwandī, who in his *Kitāb faḍīḥat al-Muʿtazila* had branded several leaders of the Muʿtazila [q.v.] as dualists. It is true that these circles produced many polemics against Thanawīya, Manichaeans and Daiṣānīs; but Ibn al-Rāwandī seized upon the Muʿtazilite endeavour to make God not the originator of evil. Even al-Djāḥiẓ is said to have endangered monotheism by the assertion that "the bodies develop out of their nature" and that "God cannot destroy them" (*op. cit.*, p. 168). Ibn al-Rāwandī particularly characterized Ibrāhīm al-Naẓẓām, the teacher of Djāḥiẓ, although he wrote against the Thanawīya (*op. cit.*, p. 17, $_{12}$), as a downright dualist Manichaean and Daiṣānī (*op. cit.*, p. 38, $_3$, 40, $_{6}$, $_{17}$ *sq.*, 43, $_{17}$ *sq.* and pass.) chiefly on account of a view of the absolute opposition between good and evil, as between light and heavy. So long as the original works are not available we must accept with caution the distorted reproduction of his opponents' views by Ibn al-Rāwandī and the evasive exposition by al-Khaiyāṭ. It is, however, not only these opponents that suspect the Muʿtazilīs, who take pride in calling themselves the people of true monotheism; and it is not only the Muʿtazilīs mentioned who have become suspect, but several others like ʿAlī al-Aswārī and Abū Bakr al-Aṣamm (cf. also de Boer, *Geschichte der Philosophie im Islam*, Stuttgart 1901, p. 47; Horten, *Die philosophischen Systeme der spekulativen Theologen im Islam*, Bonn 1912, and his other works by index under Dualismus). The Muʿtazilite counter-attack however was able to reproach the Sunnīs with their assertion that the Ḳurʾān had existed from the beginning alongside of God.

Dualism is said to have been distinctly taught

by some disciples of al-Naẓẓām. Just as they are said to have intensified his Shīʿī tendencies till they became ultra-Shīʿa, so they are said to have developed his christianizing logos-theory into the doctrine of two creators: God and God's word. The latter however, identified with the Messiah, does not imply complete incompatibility with monotheism, as it is only a created creator, an intermediary. Even the names of these heretics are, it must be confessed, uncertain. In Shahrastānī (ed. Cureton), p. 42, 6, whose authority is Ibn al-Rāwandī, they are called al-Faḍl al-Ḥadathī and Aḥmad b. Khāʾiṭ. The latter is also the name given in Masʿūdī, *Murūdj* (ed. Barbier de Meynard), iii. 266, but in another classification; in Ibn Ḥazm, *Faṣl* (Cairo 1331), iv. 197, 20 *sq.*: Aḥmad b. Khābiṭ and al-Faḍl al-Ḥarbī (cf. Nyberg, p. 222 *sqq.*, on Khaiyāṭ, p. 148 and Friedländer, *The Heterodoxies of the Shiites*, in *JAOS*, xxix. [1909], p. 10 and Index). The ultra-Shīʿī al-Bayān b. Simʿān al-Tamīmī is said to have interpreted Sūra xliii. 84 to mean that there is one God of heaven and another, inferior however, of the earth, and Abu 'l-Khaṭṭāb Bazīgh and a certain al-Surrī are said to have agreed with him (al-Kashshī, *Maʿrifat akhbār al-ridjāl* [Bombay 1317], p. 196, 8 *sqq.*). This seems to lean towards those Ghulāt [cf. NUṢAIRĪ] who see in ʿAlī not so much the incarnate identity with God as the demiurge under the highest God. It is often insisted by theologians and philosophers (cf. Ibn Ḥazm, *Faṣl*, iv. 37; see also Schreiner, in *ZDMG*, lii. [1898], p. 479 *sqq.* and Nallino in the *Encyclopaedia of Religion and Ethics*, ii. 91 *sqq.*) that the participation in rule by the stars as second forces in addition to God, because it is dualism, is no less infidelity than the purely atheistic paganism of an absolute astrology.

To Islām with its striving after monotheism, duality means the abolition of the very idea of God (cf. on Sūra xvi. 51: al-Rāzī, *Mafātīḥ al-ghaib* [Cairo 1308], v. 327, 24, 36; al-Baiḍāwī, *Anwār al-tanzīl* [ed. Fleischer], p. 517, 12; al-Naisabūrī, *Tafsīr* [on the margin of Ṭabarī, *Tafsīr*, Būlāḳ 1323 *sqq.*], xiv. 74). Thanawīya thus became a term of contempt; consequently in this use, it is not absolutely free from ambiguity but occurs to some extent synonymously with the commoner and broader term applied to heretics, *zindīḳ*. Of the philosophical systems the Peripatetic brought a dualistic idea of metaphysics into the *kalām*. Ghazzālī very strongly emphasizes its halfway position, full of contradictions, between the true belief in tawḥīd on the one hand and complete infidelity on the other, as taught by the Dahrīya [q.v.], naturalism, erroneous it is true, but quite conceivable: "the philosophers think that the world is eternal, but in spite of this they assume a creator; this is a self-contradictory proposition which requires no refutation"; Ghazzālī insists that it is only hiding and not bridging over the difficulty when the empiricism of the Peripatetics summons to its assistance, from the Neo-Platonic doctrine of emanation, after the fashion of the Ikhwān al-Ṣafāʾ, a being intermediate between God and the universe: "a caused (creative intermediary) alongside of the prime cause gives two creators and those eternal" (cf. *Tahāfut al-falāsifa* [ed. with the works of the same name by Ibn Rushd and Khwādjazāde, Cairo 1319], p. 33, 27, and thereon J. Obermann, *Der philosophische und religiöse Subjektivismus Ghazālīs* [Vienna-Leipzig 1921], p. 43 *sq.*, 57 *sqq.*, 63 *sqq.*). Ghazzālī at the same time (p. 35) strongly emphasizes that from the Aristotelian Neo-Platonic point of view of Fārābī or Ibn Sīnā a proof of tawḥīd cannot be given. He is therefore not impressed in any way by the fact that the latter tries to remove the danger, evident to himself, of a "second Necessarily Existing One" (see Horten, *Die Metaphysik Avicennas* [Halle 1907], p. 542 *sqq.*; esp. p. 551 on Ibn Sīnā, *Kitāb al-shifāʾ*, iv., treatise 9). Even more insecure is the effect of the monotheistic protestations of Ibn Sīnā in the narrower scope of his *Kitāb al-nadjāt* (Cairo 1331), p. 327 *sqq.*, 356 *sqq.*, 374 *sqq.* etc., in view of the granting of the independence of the hylic substratum of creation, as it is reflected in his dualistic anthropology also.

How the contamination of Muslim monotheism by dualism from outside Islām presents itself to the Sunnī Ashʿarīs may be seen, for example, in ʿAbd al-Ḳāhir al-Baghdādī. In *Farḳ bain al-firaḳ* (Cairo 1328) he expresses even more ironical surprise than Ibn al-Rāwandī (see in Khaiyāṭ, p. 30, 1) at the fact that al-Naẓẓām in his archdualism (*Farḳ*, p. 120, 121: *taḥḳīḳ* [*bi-ʿainihi*] *ḳawl al-Thanawīya*) wrote against the Thanawīya and the Manichaeans (p. 117, 5, 120, 12, 123 ult., 124, 8). Al-Baghdādī in *Uṣūl al-dīn* (Istanbul 1928, p. 54) associates al-Naẓẓām directly with the Thanawīya outside Islām, among whom he, unlike the other heresiologists, carelessly includes the Marcionites. He describes the Bāṭinīs [q.v.] without qualification as dualists (p. 323): "They were originally Madjūs and Thanawī, then in the time of al-Maʾmūn their prophets like ʿAbd Allāh b. Maimūn al-Ḳaddāḥ and Ḥamdān b. Ḳarmaṭ preached that there were two creators whom they called the first and the second; but this is in substance the teaching of the Thanawīya about light and darkness and the substance of the teaching of the Madjūs about Yazdān and Ahraman". Who are meant by the "two creators" cannot be established with certainty from the brief general observation. It might be thought that al-Baghdādī had arbitrarily emphasized only the *nūr shaʿshāʿānī* and the *nūr ẓulāmī* out of the series of emanations [see KARMAṬIANS] in order to assert the Madjūs character of the Bāṭinīya. The known monotheistic tendency of the Bāṭinī Nāṣir-i Khusraw (*Zād-i Musāfirīn*, Berlin 1923, p. 74 *sqq.*, 150 *sqq.*, 160 *sqq.*) does not support the idea of a duality of this kind (cf. also Schaeder, *Die islamische Lehre vom vollkommenen Menschen*, in *ZDMG*, N.S., iv. [1925], p. 222 *sqq.*, esp. p. 231). The subordination of the second god would, it is true, fit this comparison with the Madjūs made by al-Baghdādī, but it is just this point that would not be regarded as proper dualism in the usual language of the Muslim heresiologists. They expressly excluded the Madjūs from the Thanawīya, distinguishing them from the three groups mentioned at the beginning of the article, because, according to their dynamic monarchianism, Ahraman-Darkness was a secondary creation of Yazdān-Light or, as the sub-group of the Zoroastrians (Zarādushtīya) teach, both are equal to each other, but are subordinate to a supreme God as the first things created by him.

Bibliography: Besides the books mentioned in the text, cf. the works quoted in the articles cited.

TIDJĀNĪYA (the forms TIDJDJĀNĪ, TIDJĪNĪ occur also), order founded by Abu 'l-ʿAbbās Aḥmad b. Muḥammad b. al-Mukhtār b. Sālim al-Tidjānī (1150—1230/1737—1815).

1. Life of the Founder. This person was born at ʿAin Māḍī, a village 72 kil. W. of Laghuat, 28 E. of Tahmut. His family were the Awlād Sīdī Shaikh Muḥammad, and his parents both died of plague in 1166/1753. After pursuing his studies at his native place, he went to Fez in 1171/1758

to continue them, thence to Abyaḍ, where he stayed five years, thence in 1181/1768 to Tlemsen, whence in 1186/1773 he went to Mecca and Madīna; thence to Cairo. At all these places he heard shaikhs, and at the last of these at the suggestion of one Maḥmūd al-Kurdī he founded a new order, having previously been admitted to the Ḳādirīya, Ṭaibīya and Khalwatīya; of the last of these his own is regarded as a branch. He then returned to the Maghrib, and after visiting Fez and Tlemsen went to Bu Semghun in the Ṣaḥara in 1196/1782, an oasis S. of Geryville, where he believed himself to have received a commission from the Prophet to proceed with the propagation of his Order. A disciple, ʿAlī al-Ḥarāzim, suggested to him to return to Fez, whither he went in 1213/1798, and was given possession of the palace Ḥawsh al-Marāyāt. Though much of the remainder of his life was spent in travelling, in order to regulate the affairs of his order, Fez remained his headquarters till his death, and he was buried in his *zāwiya* in that city.

2. Doctrines and practices of the order. The members of the order are called *aḥbāb* "friends", and they are strictly forbidden to join any other *ṭarīḳa*. Their *dhikr* consists (as usual) in the repetition (usually a hundred times) of certain formulas, at particular times of day; these are translated by Depont et Coppolani, p. 417. Their most important doctrine is that of submission to the established government, whence ever since the French conquest of Algeria they have been ordinarily on good terms with the French authority.

3. History of the order. On the death of the founder in 1230 his two sons (Muḥammad al-Kabīr and Muḥammad al-Ṣaghīr) were left in charge of one Maḥmūd b. Aḥmad at-Tūnisī, who was succeeded as guardian by al-Ḥādjdj ʿAlī b. ʿĪsā, himself head of a Tidjānī *zāwiya* at Temasin and nominated by the founder chief of the order. They were brought by the latter to ʿAin Māḍī, the palace which had been occupied by their father in Fez having been seized by a new Amīr, Yazīd b. Ibrāhīm. After a time ʿAlī b. ʿĪsā left the two sons in charge of the *zāwiya* at ʿAin Māḍī, and returned to Temasin. It would seem however that a split had occurred in the order even in the founder's time, the dissidents, who were called Tadjādjina, having been expelled by him from ʿAin Māḍī. In 1235/1820 these dissidents invoked the aid of Ḥasan, Bey of Oran, who besieged ʿAin Māḍī, but was induced by a heavy payment and the failure of an attempted storm to retire. Two years later the Bey of Titteri attacked the settlement, but unsuccessfully. These military achievements encouraged the two sons of the founder to take the offensive against the Turks in Mascara; they failed however both in 1241/1826 and 1242, and on the latter occasion Muḥammad the Elder lost his life.

Under the direction of Sīdī ʿAlī b. ʿĪsā, who remained at Temasin, the younger Muḥammad, now in sole charge at ʿAin Māḍī, proceeded with the propagation of the order, especially in the Ṣaḥara and the Sūdān. Great success attended these efforts, but though the power and wealth of the community increased, neither ʿAlī nor Muḥammad ventured on any military operations. Hence when after the French invasion of Algeria the Derḳāwī *muḳaddam* desired the aid of the Tidjānīs in the Sacred War, it was refused.

In 1251/1836 the Amīr ʿAbd al-Ḳādir, who aimed at the expulsion of the French, endeavoured to enlist their services; the Tidjānī chief replied that it was his purpose to live in the calm of a religious life, and after a long and fruitless correspondence the Amīr in 1254/1838 presented himself at the head of an army before the walls of ʿAin Māḍī, and demanded the submission of the Tidjānī chief. This was refused, and in spite of the inequality of the numbers the latter held out for eight months, wherein various expedients for reducing the place were tried by the Amīr and frustrated by the astuteness of the Tidjānī and his advisers. When the Tidjānī found the place no longer defensible, he took refuge in Laghuat. The reputation of the order was vastly increased owing to the length of their resistance, and in the following year (1840) he offered his moral and material aid against the Amīr ʿAbd al-Ḳādir to the French Marshal Valée. ʿAlī b. ʿĪsā, who remained at Temasin, also declined to join resistance to the French, and on his death in 1844 left the control of the order to the surviving son of the founder, who died in 1853, when the grandson of ʿAlī b. ʿĪsā, Muḥammad al-ʿĀʾid, succeeded.

The sons of the third Master of the order, Aḥmad and al-Bashīr, were of tender years at the time of his death, and fell under the charge of one Raiyān al-Masharī, who aimed at rendering the *zāwiya* of ʿAin Māḍī independent of Temasin, a policy which caused the relations between the two *zāwiya*ʾs to be strained, though it did not result in a definite split. In 1869 the two became suspected of disloyalty to the French, and were arrested and sent to Algiers. They succeeded however in making their peace with the French authorities, and the heads of the order have ever since maintained a friendly attitude towards them.

4. Distribution of the order. Although the missionaries of the order in the period of its greatest prosperity obtained adherents in Egypt, Arabia and other parts of Asia, its main expansion has been in French Africa. One Muḥammad al-Ḥāfiẓ b. Mukhtār b. Ḥabīb, called Baddī, who visited the founder in Fez about 1780, received instructions to spread it among the Ṣaḥarians of the extreme South of Morocco: "Returning home via Shingueti and Tijikja, he conducted the most active propaganda in favour of the Tidjānī order, and by 1830, about the time of his death, he had the satisfaction of leaving the whole tribe Ida Ou ʿAlī affiliated to it" (Paul Marty, *RMM*, xxxi. 239). Under his successor, who died in 1907, this attachment steadily increased. To the Meccan pilgrimage, faithfully observed by this community, there was added the practice of pilgrimage to Fez, to visit the tomb of the founder, and this is ordinarily performed before the visit to Mecca. The order was propagated in French Guinea by one Ḥādjdj ʿUmar after his return from Mecca to Dinguiray, which in consequence became one of the most important religious cities in this region; "the Tidjānī doctrine supplanted almost everywhere the Ḳādirīya traditions" (*ibid.*, xxxvi. 202).

5. Literature of the Order. The most important collection of their doctrines and practices is called *Djawāhir al-maʿānī wa-bulūgh al-amānī fī faiḍ al-Shaikh al-Tidjdjānī* known also as *al-Kunnāsh* (Cairo 1345). This work, which is said to have been dictated by the founder to Ḥarāzim, is the chief source of the former's biography; other works are enumerated by Depont and Coppolani, p. 418 n., and Lévi-Provençal, *Les Historiens des Chorfa*, Paris 1922, p. 377. A biographical dictionary of eminent members of the order called *Kashf al-ḥidjāb ʿan man*

talāḳā maʿa 'l-Tidjdjānī min al-aṣḥāb was composed by Abu 'l-ʿAbbās Aḥmad b. Aḥmad al-ʿAiyāshī Sukairidj (Fez 1325 and 1332). The commentary *Bughyat al-mustafīd* by Muḥammad b. Muḥammad al-Shawdjīṭī on the poem *Munyat al-Murīd* of Muḥammad al-ʿArabī (Cairo, 1347) contains biographies of the founder and many of his disciples, with other matter appertaining to the Order.

Bibliography: *RA*, 1861 and 1864 (articles by Arnaud); L. Rinn, *Marabouts et Khouan*, p. 416—451; Depont et Coppolani, *Confréries*, p. 413—441; Abbé Rouquette, *Les Sociétés secrètes chez les Musulmans*, 1899, p. 311—372; P. Marty, in *RMM* (cited above); Henry Garrot, *Histoire générale de l'Algérie*, Algiers 1910; F. G. Pijper, *Fragmenta Islamica*, Leiden 1934, p. 97 *sqq.*

AL-**TIRMIDHĪ**, ABŪ ʿĪSĀ MUḤAMMAD B. ʿĪSĀ B. SAWRA B. SHADDĀD, the author of one of the canonical or semi-canonical collections of traditions. The *nisba* al-Tirmidhī connects him with Tirmidh, a place on the upper Āmū Daryā, at a distance of 6 leagues from Balkh, where he is said to have died in 279/892—3; according to other reports, he died at Būgh, one of the boroughs of Tirmidh, in 275/888—9, or in 270/883—4.

Of his life very little is known. It is said that he was born blind but also that he lost his eyesight in his later years. He travelled widely, in Khurāsān, ʿIrāḳ and Ḥidjāz, in order to collect traditions. Among his masters were Aḥmad b. Muḥammad b. Ḥanbal [q.v.], al-Bukhārī [q.v.] and Abū Dāwūd al-Sidjistānī.

Two of his works have been printed: his collection of traditions and his *Shamāʾil*, a collection of traditions concerning the person and the character of the Prophet (for editions and commentaries, see Brockelmann, *GAL*, i. 169; *Suppl.* i, 268). Brockelmann mentions also a collection of forty traditions; it does not appear whether this was made by himself or by others. In Arabic sources other works on various subjects — asceticism, names and *kunya*'s, law, history — are ascribed to him, none of which seems to have come down to us.

His collection of traditions bears the title of *Ṣaḥīḥ* in the edition printed at Cairo, 1292; elsewhere it is called *Djāmiʿ*; it deserves the latter qualification (cf. Goldziher, *Muhammedanische Stud.*, ii. 231, note 2), as it comprises, besides traditions on law, also some concerning other topics. A glance at the list of chapters shows that nearly one half of the work is devoted to such subjects as dogmatic theology (*Ḳadar, Ḳiyāma, Djanna, Djahannam, Īmān, Ḳurʾān*), popular beliefs (*Fitan, Ruʾyā*), devotion (*Zuhd, Thawāb al-Ḳurʾān, Daʿawāt*), manners and education (*Istiʾdhān, Adab*), hagiology (*Manāḳib*).

The work contains far fewer traditions than those of Bukhārī or Muslim, but also less repetitions. Two of the chapters are particularly extensive, viz. *Manāḳib* and *Tafsīr al-Ḳurʾān*; they are lacking in the other three *Sunan* (by this title the four collections of Abū Dāwūd, al-Tirmidhī, Nasāʾī and Ibn Mādja are sometimes denoted). Though traditions showing a predilection for ʿAlī are not rare, those which favour Abū Bakr, ʿUmar and ʿUthmān are not lacking.

Tirmidhī's work is distinguished, however, by two features: the critical remarks concerning the *isnād*'s and the points of difference between the *madhhab*'s, which follow every tradition. On account of the latter feature, Tirmidhī's *Djāmiʿ* may be called the oldest work on *ikhtilāf* that has come down to us; the remarks on this subject found in Shāfiʿī's *Kitāb al-umm* are much less complete and not always authentic.

According to the *Taḳrīb*, as cited by Goldziher (*Muhamm. Stud.*, ii. 252, note 1), the MSS. are not uniform in reproducing Tirmidhī's remarks on the *isnād*'s (*ṣaḥīḥ, ḥasan, gharīb, ḥasan ṣaḥīḥ, ḥasan gharīb, ṣaḥīḥ gharīb*). The author gives no explanation of the principles upon which his distinctions are based. The work opens with an enumeration of the authorities who handed it down to the final redactor. It closes with a brief eulogistic formula.

Bibliography: al-Samʿānī, *Kitāb al-ansāb*, *GMS*, xx., fol. 106[a]; Dhahabī, *Ṭabaḳāt al-ḥuffāẓ*, ed. Wüstenfeld, part iii., p. 57, No. 3; do., *Mīzān al-iʿtidāl*, Cairo 1325, iii. 117, No. 1021; Ibn Khallikān, No. 624; Ibn Ḥadjar al-ʿAsḳalānī, *Tahdhīb al-tahdhīb*, Ḥaidarābād 1326, ix. 387—389, No. 236; do., *Taḳrīb al-tahdhīb*, lithogr. Delhi, no year, p. 230[b]; Ibn Khaṭīb al-Dahsha, *Tuḥfat dhawi 'l-ʿArab*, ed. T. Mann, p. 143; I. Goldziher, *Muhammedanische Studien*, ii. 250 *sqq.* The traditions of al-Tirmidhī have been completely used for Wensinck's *CTM*.

ṬULAIḤA B. KHUWAILID B. NAWFAL AL-ASADĪ AL-FAḲʿADĪ, one of the tribal leaders who headed the *ridda* as prophets.

In 4 A.H., being in command of the Banū Asad with his brother Salama, he was defeated by the Muslims in the expedition of Ḳaṭan. The following year he took part in the siege of Madīna. Early in 9 A.H. Ṭulaiḥa, as one of ten Asadīs, probably representing only a section of the tribe, came to Madīna and submitted to Muḥammad; Sūra xlix. 14—17 is said to rebuke their arrogance, but a tradition that Ṭulaiḥa alone embraced Islām points to political submission rather than conversion, he alone being considered a convert only because the *ridda* was explained as religious apostasy. The whole story may have been invented as a parallel to Musailima's visit to Madīna.

Ṭulaiḥa rebelled in 10 A.H.; he concentrated his forces at Samīrā, assumed the role of prophet, and is said to have offered terms to Muḥammad, who sent Ḍirār b. al-Azwar to keep him in check. No encounter of any consequence followed until after Muḥammad's death, when Ṭulaiḥa succeeded in gaining the support of the Banū Fazāra and an important portion of Ṭaiy, and joined the revolt in central Arabia, sending troops to the battle of Dhu 'l-Ḳaṣṣa.

In Radjab 11 Khālid b. al-Walīd marched against Ṭulaiḥa, and with threats persuaded most of the Banū Ṭaiy to follow him. The battle took place at Buzākha; Ṭulaiḥa's defeat was due to the defection of ʿUyaina b. Ḥiṣn, chief of the Banū Fazāra, disappointed, it is said, by his failure to obtain an encouraging revelation. Ṭulaiḥa fled with his wife; many of his followers, refusing Islām, were burnt alive, and his mother sought death in the flames.

After Buzākha, Ṭulaiḥa lived for a time in obscurity, near Ṭāʾif or in Syria. He was eventually converted after the submission of the Asad, Ghaṭafān and ʿĀmir; passing through Madīna on the *ʿumra* some time later, his presence was pointed out to Abū Bakr, who mercifully refused to molest the convert. On ʿUmar's election, Ṭulaiḥa went to do homage to him; the Caliph reproached him for slaying ʿUkkāsha b. Miḥṣan and Thābit b. Aḳram at Buzākha, and asked him what was left of his divination. "One or two puffs of the bellows", Ṭulaiḥa modestly answered.

His subsequent military career was long and creditable: he performed acts of valour at Ḳādisīya, at the head of his tribesmen, led the Muslim infantry at Djalūlā, and the victory of Nihāwand was credited to his plan of attack. He is generally reported killed in this action (21 A.H.), but we find him mentioned in 24, one of 500 Muslims who garrisoned Ḳazwīn, and the date of his decease remains uncertain; 21 was probably fixed upon because it was the year in which Khālid, Nuʿmān b. al-Muḳarrin and ʿAmr b. Maʿdīkārib also died.

His real name was Ṭalḥa; the diminutive is contemptuous (cf. Maslama—Musailima). Of his revelations, which he claimed to receive from an angel (Gabriel or Dhu 'l-Nūn), very little is known; one is a prophecy of conquest in Syria and ʿIrāḳ, another mentions the millstone, a common metaphor for victorious military action. He appears rather as a soothsayer than a prophet, for his few known utterances concern actual events, and no religious system is discernible.

Bibliography: al-Ṭabarī, ed. de Goeje, i. 1687, 1795, 1882, 1891; Yāḳūt, *Muʿdjam*, ed. Wüstenfeld, i. 602; vi. 487; Ibn al-Athīr, *Usd al-ghāba*, iii. 65; al-Dhahabī, *Tadjrīd*, i. 299; Ibn Hishām, ed. Wüstenfeld, p. 452; Balādhurī, ed. de Goeje, p. 95, 96, 258, 261, 264, 322; Caetani, *Annali dell' Islām*, A.H. 10, § 67; A.H. 11, § 127—146; A.H. 12, § 98; A.H. 16, § 21, 27, 31, 53, 69, 78, 157, 162; A.H. 21, § 46, 63, 337—338; Wellhausen, *Skizzen und Vorarbeiten*, vi. 9—11, 97.

TURBAN, the headdress of males in the Muslim east, consisting of a cap with a length of cloth wound round it. The name turban is found in this form in European languages only (English turban, turband; French turban, tulban; German Turban; Italian, Spanish and Portuguese, turbante; Dutch tulband; Rumanian tulipan; all going back to older forms with o: tol(l)iban, tolipan, tolopan, tourbant, tourban, torbante) and is usually traced to the Persian *dulband*, from which is also said to be derived the word tulip (cf. Meyer-Lübke, *Romanisches etymologisches Wörterbuch*, Heidelberg 1911, p. 682, where also is cited from the *Revue des Langues Romanes*, liii. 54 the Spanish name of the hammer-headed shark, torbandalo). It should be remembered however that the word *dulband* is by no means so widely disseminated in the east as one would have expected from the general use of the word turban in Europe, but is limited to the Persian (and to a smaller extent Turkish) speaking area and even here is not the only name in use. The commonest word in Arabic is *ʿimāma*, which properly means only the cloth wound round the cap and then comes to be used for the whole headdress, and in Turkish *ṣarıḳ* is the usual name for the turban. Besides these, however, there are a large number of other names for what we often loosely call turban and for its parts in different Muslim countries.

The origin of this form of headdress ought probably to be sought in the ancient east; a turban-like cap seems to be found represented on certain Assyrian and Egyptian monuments (cf. Reimpell, *Geschichte der babylonischen und assyrischen Kleidung*, p. 40; Josef von Karabacek, *Abendländische Künstler zu Konstantinopel*, *Denkschr. Ak. Wien*, lxii., 1918, p. 87 *sq.* and von Hammer, *GOR*, vii. 268 and *Staatsverfassung*, p. 441). In Arabia the pre-Muḥammadan Beduins are said to have worn turbans, and it has been supposed that the high cap is the Persian and the cloth wound round it the true Arab element of the turban (Jacob, *Altarabisches Beduinenleben*, p. 44, 237).

In Islām in course of time the turban has developed a threefold significance, a national for the Arabs, a religious for the Muslims and a professional for civil professions (later divided into religious and administrative offices, *waẓāʾif dīnīya wa-dīwānīya*) in contrast to the military.

Many details about the Prophet's turban have been handed down by tradition but most of these ḥadīths bear obvious traces of a late date. They therefore prove nothing for the time of the Prophet but only show what later ages wanted to believe. To the latter the turban, as succinctly expressed in a ḥadīth, signified "dignity for the believer and strength for the Arab", *waḳār li 'l-Muslim waʿizz li 'l-ʿArab* and the Prophet to them is the owner of the turban par excellence (*ṣāḥib al-ʿimāma*). The makers of turbans in Turkey (*dulbenddjiān*) actually chose the Prophet as their patron saint, for he is said to have traded in turbans in Syria before his call and to have exported them from Mecca to Boṣrā (Ewliyā, i. 590). The only reliable ḥadīth is negative: the *muḥrim* is not allowed to wear the turban, nor *ḳamīṣ, sarāwīl* etc. This ḥadīth is also found in Bukhārī in the *Bāb al-ʿamāʾim* (*Libās*, bāb 15) contrasted with the following, mostly weak, ḥadīths. According to one, for example, Adam is said to have worn a turban which Gabriel wound round his head on his expulsion from Paradise; previously he wore a crown (*tādj*). The next was Alexander (Dhu 'l-Ḳarnain) who wore a turban to conceal his horns. A much quoted ḥadīth runs "turbans are the crowns of the Arabs" (*al-ʿamāʾim tīdjān al-ʿArab*), which is variously explained to mean, either that turbans are as rare among the Arabs as crowns among other peoples for most Beduins only wear caps (*ḳalānis*) or no headdress at all, or that the Arabs wear turbans as the Persians wear crowns, so that the turban would be a national badge of the Arabs as the crown of the Persians. A similar ḥadīth runs "wear turbans and thus be different from earlier peoples" (*iʿtammū khālifū 'l-umam ḳablakum*).

Still more numerous are the ḥadīths which describe the turban as a badge of Muslims to distinguish them from the unbelievers; turbans are a mark of Islām (*al-ʿamāʾim sīmā al-Islām*); the turban divides the believers from the unbelievers (*al-ʿimāma ḥādjiza bain al-kufr wa 'l-īmān* or *bain al-Muslimīn wa 'l-mushrikīn*); the distinction between us and the unbelievers is the turban on the cap (*farḳ mā bainanā wa-bain al-mushrikīn al-ʿamāʾim ʿala 'l-ḳalānis*); or the prophecy: my community will never decay so long as they wear turbans over their caps (*lā tazālu ummatī ʿala 'l-fiṭra mā labisū 'l-ʿamāʾim ʿala 'l-ḳalānis*); and on the day of judgment a man will receive light for every winding of the turban (*kawra*) round his head or round his cap. Thus "to put on the turban" means "to adopt Islām". Nevertheless the stage was never reached where it was a religious duty (*farḍ*) to wear the turban; it is however recommended (*mustaḥabb, sunna, mandūb*) and a general recommendation runs: "wear turbans and increase your nobility" (*iʿtammū tazdādū ḥilm^{an}*).

Especially at the *ṣalāt* and on going to the mosque or tombs is the wearing of the turban recommended, and it is said: two rakʿas (or one rakʿa, or the ṣalāt) with a turban are better than seventy without; for it is not proper to appear before one's king with head uncovered. Or: God and the angels bless him who wears a turban on Fridays. In great heat and after the prayer however, it is permitted to take off the turban, but not during the prayer itself, on the other hand the want of a turban is no reason for absenting oneself from prayer. At other times also — in great heat or at home or while washing — the turban may be removed, and as a rule the Arabs always wore the turban "until the ascension of the Pleiades", i.e. until the beginning of the great heat (cf. Wensinck, *Handbook*, s.v. Turban, Clothes and Headdresses). Even in later times the turban played an important role in the spreading of Islām, e.g. in the Sudan (cf. A. Brass, in *Isl.*, x. 22, 27, 30, 33; *MSOS As.*, vi. 191 *sq.*).

It has not always been the custom in Islām for none but Muslims to wear turbans. The later regulations for dress demand, it is true, that only believers may wear turbans while unbelievers are only to wear a cap (*ḳalansuwa*). But in earlier times unbelievers were only to wear turbans of another colour or with some distinguishing mark. Rulers who were not generally well disposed to members of other faiths were always distinguished by strict regulations about dress; but with a change of attitude the observation of the prescriptions became slacker until it again became necessary to enforce them more strictly. In later days appeal was frequently made to an alleged dress regulation by ʿUmar I, which is however probably a later invention and was probably transferred from ʿUmar II to ʿUmar I. The latter is said to have been the first to forbid Christians to wear the turban or dress resembling that of the Muslim (cf. Tritton, *Islam and the protected Religions*, *JRAS*, 1927, p. 479—484). Further laws about dress are attributed to Hārūn al-Rashīd who, like ʿUmar II, is said to have issued a general order forbidding Christians to wear the same dress as Muslims. Mutawakkil is said to have prescribed yellow for the unbelievers, including the turbans if they wore any, and the Fāṭimid Ḥākim black because this was the colour of the hated ʿAbbāsids. At one time Christians were forbidden to wear red, at another any one who wore white was to be punished by death. In Egypt and Syria in the eighth century A.H. Christians wore blue, Jews yellow and the Sāmira red and they might also wear silk, turbans, and neck-veil (*ḥarīr*, *ʿimāma*, *ṭailasān*) of these colours (Ḳalḳashandī, *Ṣubḥ al-aʿshā*ʾ, xiii. 364).

Turkey has had a whole series of dress regulations of its own: the earliest was enforced by ʿAlāʾ al-Dīn Pasha (d. 732/1331) in the reign of Orkhan. He introduced a cone-shaped cap of white felt but only for officials in the Sulṭān's service; other subjects apparently had freedom of choice in their dress. In the reign of Meḥmed the Conqueror (1451—81), further laws about rank, titles and dress of the officials were issued. Under Sulaimān the Legislator, ranks and professions were carefully graded as described in the *Shamāʾilnāme-i Āl-i ʿOthmān* of Luḳmān b. Saiyid Ḥusain about 1580 (v. Hammer, *GOR*, iii. 17; Karabacek, p. 4). Sulaimān also regulated the use of the turban, hitherto apparently quite arbitrary, and issued regulations about the trade of turban-makers, *ṣarıḳdjıllar* (v. Hammer, *Staatsverfassung*, i. 443). Unbelievers were given red, yellow and black, while white was restricted to the Ottomans.

In other countries also the colour of the turban was not at all uniform and for every colour authority was given from alleged ḥadīths of the life of the Prophet, which of course are all weak. The commonest colour for the turban is white. The Prophet is said to have been fond of this colour and it is considered the colour of Paradise. There is not actually a ḥadīth telling us that the Prophet's turban was white, and the belief arose probably only because white was the normal colour. The angels who helped the believers at Badr are said to have worn white turbans. If other references speak of turbans of other colours, they are not in direct contradiction with white, for the colours in question are connected with the events and have therefore a special reason. For example another tradition says that at Badr the angels wore yellow turbans with the object of encouraging the fighting Muslims.

The Prophet is said to have worn a black cloak and a black turban on entering Mecca and at the address at the gate of the Kaʿba, also on other occasions at addresses from the minbar, on the day of Ḥudaibīya and during his illness. In black there is said to be a subtle allusion to sovereignty (*suʾdad*); moreover, black is the foundation of all colours. The ʿAbbāsids claimed that the black turban of the Prophet worn at the entry to Mecca had been handed down to them, and in a tendencious ḥadīth in which Gabriel prophesies the coming of the ʿAbbāsids, he of course wears a black turban. Turbans of black silk (*khazz*) are said to have been at first permitted but later forbidden by the Prophet; the so-called *ḥarḳānīya* turbans are black (the derivation of the word is uncertain, according to Suyūṭī from *ḥ-r-ḳ*, to burn) and the Prophet is said to have worn them on his campaigns. Many great men in Islām are also said to have worn black turbans, such as Ḥasan al-Baṣrī, Ibn al-Zubair, Muʿāwiya etc. and Suyūṭī wrote a whole book on black dress (*Thaladj al-fuʾād fī lubs al-sawād*). Later writers often claim the black turban as the special headdress of the *khaṭīb* and the *imām*.

The Prophet is said to have at first liked to wear blue but then forbade it because the unbelievers wore it. On behalf of red, it is urged that the angels at Uḥud (or also at Ḥunain) wore red turbans. According to others, Gabriel wore red at Badr and on one occasion appeared to ʿĀʾisha in a red turban. The so-called *ḳiṭrīya* turban which the Prophet wore is also said to have been red. Sometimes also striped material has been used as turban cloth, e.g. yellow and red or green and red (Fesquet).

In the history of religion the green turban is important, as the well known badge of the descendants of Muḥammad. Tradition is unanimous that the Prophet never wore a green turban, and there is no support for the colour green in law or tradition. But green is the colour of Paradise and it is also said to have been the Prophet's favourite colour and some say that the angels at Ḥunain (or also at Badr) had green turbans. The green turban as a badge of the sharīfs is however of much later origin: the ʿAbbāsid al-Maʾmūn in Ramaḍān 201 is said to have clothed the eighth Shīʿī Imām ʿAlī al-Riḍā in green, when he designated him his successor; the latter died before he could succeed, the ʿAbbāsids went back to black and there were even persecutions to compel the ʿAlids to wear black (cf. Ibn ʿAbdūs, *K. al-wuzarāʾ*, ed. Mžik, p. 395 *sq.*). They seem however for a period at least to have worn a piece of green cloth in the turban as a special badge (*shaṭfa*) and to have been fond of wearing green, especially in times of liberty of conscience. In 773 A.H. the Mamlūk Sulṭān Ashraf Shaʿbān ordered that the turban cloths (*al-ʿaṣāʾib ʿala ʾl-ʿamāʾim*) of the ʿAlids should be green and from 1004 A.H. the whole turban became green by order of the Ottoman governor of Egypt al-Saiyid Muḥammad al-Sharīf. This fashion spread from Egypt to other Muslim countries, at first regarded as a late innovation and sometimes disputed, but has now become generally approved. It is now regarded as a law that no non-ʿAlid should wear the green turban nor strictly anyone who is only connected with the Prophet on the mother's side but this last point is frequently disregarded.

Not only the colour but other *ādāb* of the turban are regulated by religion: 1. When should a boy be first given a turban? When his beard begins to grow, when he reaches maturity or at the age of say 7 to 10 years. One should go by the practice of the country; but in any case it shows shamelessness to wear a turban before one's beard begins to grow. 2. How should a turban be wound? Here again the answer is given by stories of how the Prophet wound his. It should be wound standing (trousers on the other hand are put on sitting), with the right hand, twisted to the right around the head and not simply laid upon it and in doing this, one should act according to the sunna, as regards pulling the loose end (*ʿadhaba*) under the chin (*taḥnīk*) and the size of the turban. As in putting on any other garment, one should utter a *basmala*, while the *ḥamdala* is only used for new articles of clothing. A new turban should if possible be put on for the first time on a Friday. It should be carefully done before a looking-glass but one should not spend too much time over it. People of position may have their turban wound by two servants. There are countless ways in which a turban may be wound; 66 are mentioned but these are not all. 3. The question whether gold and silver ornaments may be worn in the turban is usually answered in the negative. In the course of the development of the headdress, it was the women in particular who adorned their turban-like headdress in this way. Silk on the other hand is allowed with certain restrictions. 4. The turban has acquired considerable religious significance as a symbol of investiture, since there is no crown or coronation proper as symbols of sovereignty in the Muslim east. The prototype is again an act of Muḥammad's; he is said to have put a turban on ʿAlī at the pond of Khumm and again when in Ramaḍān of the year 10 he appointed him governor of the Yemen; he is next said to have wound the turban on every governor in order to teach him fine manners (*tadjammul*) and to give him dignity. Following this example, the caliphs, the successors of the Prophet, put the turban on their viziers and later on sulṭāns. For example Ḳalḳashandī, iii. 280 *sq.* describes the investiture of the Egyptian Mamlūk Sulṭān Abū Bakr b. al-Nāṣir in 742 by the Egyptian ʿAbbāsid caliph Ḥākim II. The caliph wore a black neck-veil (*ṭarḥa*) with white stripes (*marḳūma bi 'l-bayāḍ*) and placed on the head of the sulṭān a black turban (*ʿimāma sawdāʾ*) with white stripes round the edge (*marḳūmat al-ṭaraf bi 'l-bayāḍ*). Then we have a description of the investiture of Nāṣir Faradj by Mutawakkil in 801 A.H. where we are told *ʿimāma sawdāʾ marḳūma, fawḳahā ṭarḥa sawdāʾ marḳūma*. The turban is also an essential feature of the robe of honour (*khilʿa*) which Muslim rulers used to bestow upon their viziers and emīrs and this is the origin of the differences in the turbans of the different classes, which were such that the initiated could at once tell an individual's profession by his turban. In general it may be said that the largest turbans belonged to the highest and most respected ranks, especially of the clerical profession, and the differences in sizes of the turban are, according to some, more important than those of colour. With this is connected the endeavour to give oneself as large a turban as possible and against this religion has had to fight: a warning is uttered against wearing too large a turban as it is an extravagance — but not among learned men; on the contrary, they ought to be recognizable at once by some external feature to attain success in their labours. Hence the dress of the scholar is not a censurable innovation (*bidʿa*), although earlier men of learning did not wear it. All other statements about the sizes of turbans, including definite lengths like seven or ten ells, are again defended from the example of the Prophet.

The turban, generally speaking, has, as we have said, become the badge of the civilian professions. Turban-wearer (*ṣāḥib al-ʿimāma*: Ibn Shīth, *Maʿālim al-kitāba*, p. 34, or *rabb al-ʿimāma*) is synonymous with civilian and there is the expression: he abandoned the turban of men of the law and assumed in its stead the cap (*sharbush*) and the dress of the emīrs (Maḳrīzī-Blochet, p. 335, note). To distinguish the various officers, the officials in Turkey under the old regime had different badges on their turbans, clusters of feathers and egrettes (*süpürge* and *balıḳdjıl*), and soldiers wore on them decorations awarded for bravery (*sorghuč* and *čelenk*; v. Hammer, *Staatsverfassung*, i. 446). Fesquet says that secretaries and scholars wore the turban high with many windings, merchants and artificers loose and broad and slaves very small.

It is on this point that we find the differences in the various countries and especially between the east (Syria, the ʿIrāḳ, Egypt, Persia) and the west (Spain, North Africa). This is noticeable in the description of western dress in Ḳalḳashandī and in the *Masālik al-abṣār*, and vice-versa in the accounts of eastern customs as given by the Moroccan Kattānī. In Muslim Spain very few turbans were worn at all; the neck-veil (*ṭailasān*; *Masālik*, p. 42; Ḳalḳashandī, v. 271) was rather worn instead; the loose end (*ʿadhaba*) and the chinstrap (*taḥnīk*) are, originally at least, apparently western fashions. In 1596 we find the Turks being struck by the narrow turban of striped silk worn by the Persian ambassador (*GOR*, iv. 275).

In modern times there has arisen a movement against the turban, which is more or less apparent through the whole of the east. Men are reluctant to wear a turban and the young people and the women laugh at it and say: *al-daffa khair min al-laffa*, "the board for washing the dead is better than winding a turban". But the conservative classes vigorously attack the *bidʿa* implied in this and declare that contempt for the turban is heresy and unbelief. Associated with this we often find abandonment of the old Muslim style of hair-dressing with clean upper lip and a beard on the chin. These two things are essential features of emancipation and are regarded by many as signs of the Day of Judgment (*ashrāṭ al-sāʿa*). This modern development is attacked in a number of special treatises on the turban mentioned below, notably the last one by Kattānī, and according to them, any one who succeeds in restoring the turban to a country acquires the merit of reviving a good tradition (*iḥyāʾ al-sunna*). The modern development however can hardly be checked, and in Turkey a hundred years ago the turban was officially replaced by the fez, which in its turn had to give way in 1925 to the modern European hat (*shapḳa*) (cf. *Oriente Moderno*, v. 630 *sq.*), just as in modern Persia the turban has been driven out by the *kulāh*.

The turban could also be used for many purposes other than that for which it was primarily intended. We give a few examples: in Saʿdī,

Būstān, p. 156, a man in the desert giving a dog dying of thirst water uses his cap (*kulāh*) to get water out of the well and his turban-cloth (*destār* or *maizar*) as a rope. The turban was often used as a pocket, also as a rope to tie up criminals, or to tie firmly in the saddle or to strangle. In 1623 the rebel Turkish *ʿulamāʾ* chose the turban of Shaikh Aḳ Shams al-Dīn as their standard (*GOR*, iv. 590).

Bibliography: Arabic works dealing especially with the Turban:

1. Abū ʿAbd Allāh M. b. al-Waddāḥ al-Andalusī al-Mālikī, *Kitāb faḍl libās al-ʿamāʾim*, a contemporary of Baḳī b. Makhlad, d. 276/889, *GAL*, i. 172; 2. Nāṣir al-Dīn M. b. Abī Bakr ʿAlī b. Abī Sharīf al-Maḳdisī al-Shāfiʿī, *Ṣawb al-ghimāma fī irsāl ṭaraf al-ʿimāma*, d. 906/1500, *GAL*, ii. 122, Berlin, No. 5433; 3. Djalāl al-Dīn al-Suyūṭī, *al-Aḥādīth al-ḥisān fī-mā warada fi 'l-ṭailasān*, or: ... *fī Faḍl al-ṭailasān*, d. 911/1505, cf. *GAL*, S. ii. 189; 4. do., *Ṭaiy al-lisān ʿan dhamm al-ṭailasān*; 5. do., *Djawāb fī sīmat al-malāʾika wa- fi 'l-ʿadhaba* (*wa-hal yadjūz an yuḳāl li 'l-Aḥādīth Kalām Allāh*), *GAL*, ii. 190, 118, Berlin, No. 2509; 6. M. b. Yaḥyā al-Bukhārī, *Risāla fī faḍīlat al-ʿimāma wa-sunaniha*, d. 934/1527, Berlin, No. 5459; 7. ʿAlwān al-Ḥamawī, *Manẓūma fi 'l-kalām ʿala 'l-ʿimāma*, d. 936/1530, *GAL*, ii. 437; 8. Shihāb al-Dīn Aḥmad b. Ḥadjar al-Haitamī al-Makkī, *Kitāb darr al-ghimāma fī durr al-ṭailasān wa 'l-ʿadhaba wa 'l-ʿimāma*, d. 973/1565, *GAL*, ii. 509; 9. M. b. Sulṭān M. al-Ḳārī, *Risāla fī masʾalat al-ʿimāma wa 'l-ʿadhaba*, d. 1014/1606, Berlin, No. 5460; 10. M. Ḥidjāzī b. M. b. ʿAbd Allāh "al-Wāʿiẓ" (al-Shaʿrāwī Ṭarīḳat^an, al-Ḳalḳashandī Balad^an, al-Shāfiʿī Madhhab^an), *al-Mawārid al-mustaʿdhaba bi-maṣādir al-ʿimāma wa 'l-ʿadhaba*, d. 1035/1626; 11. A. b. M. b. A. al-Makkarī, *Azhār al-kumāma fī akhbar al-ʿimāma*, d. 1041/1632, cf. *GAL*, ii. 381; 12. Abu 'l-Faḍl M. b. A. "Ibn al-Imām", *Tuḥfat al-umma bi-aḥkām al-ʿimma*, d. 1062/1652, Ḥādjdjī Khalīfa, No. 2551; 13. Shihāb al-Dīn A. b. M. al-Khafādjī al-Efendi (Shāriḥ al-Shifā), *al-Thimāma fī ṣifat al-ʿimāma*, d. 1069/1659, cf. *GAL*, ii. 368; 14. al-Saiyid M. b. Mawlāya Djaʿfar al-Kattānī, *al-Diʿāma li-maʿrifat aḥkām sunnat al-ʿimāma*, modern, printed Damascus 1342.

No. 14 is the most detailed monograph on the turban and has been much used for the above article. Of other writings he mentions No. 1, 2, 3, 8, 10, 12, 13, but has himself only seen and used No. 8. In addition to No. 14 for this article No. 2 has been used.

Of European literature in addition to the works of Dozy (*Les noms des vêtements en Arabe*), Karabacek and Brunot cited above a few general works on costume may be mentioned: Rosenberg, *Geschichte des Kostüms*, 5 vols, plates with brief descriptions, pl. 297 on the turban; J. v. Falke, *Kostümgeschichte der Kulturvölker*; Alb. Kretschmer, *Die Trachten der Völker*; *Katalog der Lipperheideschen Kostümbibliothek*. — 16 forms of turban are illustrated by Fesquet, 44 different ones by Niebuhr, and no less than 286 are given by Michael Thalman, *Elenchus librorum or. mss.*, Vienna 1702, vi. 29 *sq.* on Cod. turc., vii., Bologna; cf. Victor Rosen, *Remarques sur les mss. orientaux de la Collection Marsigli à Bologne* (*Atti della Real Acc. dei Lincei*, 281, 1883—1884), p. 182.

U

ʿULAMĀʾ is strictly the plural of *ʿalīm*, one who possesses the quality *ʿilm* [q.v.], knowledge, learning, science in the widest sense, and in a high degree (*mubālagha*). In usage, however, the accepted singular of *ʿulamāʾ* is *ʿālim*. Both singulars are Ḳurʾānic and can be used of Allāh and of man; but the plural *ʿulamāʾ* occurs only twice in the Ḳurʾān and there of men (xxvi. 197; xxxv. 28). The plural *ʿālimūn* occurs four times: twice of Allāh (xxi. 51, 81) and twice of men (xii. 44; xxix. 43). On all this see *Mufradāt* of al-Rāghib al-Iṣfahānī, Cairo 1324, p. 348 *sqq.* and *Lisān*, xv. 310 *sqq.*

Inasmuch as *ʿilm* in the first instance was knowledge of traditions and of the resultant canon law and theology, the *ʿulamāʾ*, as peculiarly custodians of that tradition, were canonists and theologians. They, thus, as a general body, represented and voiced the Agreement [cf. article IDJMĀʿ] of the Muslim people, and that Agreement was the foundation of Islām. In consequence the *ʿulamāʾ*, in whatever stated form they functioned, came to have, in a wide and vague fashion, the ultimate decision on all questions of constitution, law and theology. Whatever the *de facto* government might be, they were a curb upon it, as a surviving expression of the Agreement and of the right of the People of Muḥammad to govern itself. The different governments might try to control them by giving them official status and salaries, and to some extent might succeed in that. If the success were too glaring the people would re-act by contempt for such government agents and would give their respect and devotion to private scholars who refused thus to be muzzled. This was a constantly recurring situation under all Muslim governments. The *ʿulamāʾ*, therefore, might be government functionaries, either controlled by the government or keeping the government in a certain awe; or they might be private and independent students of canon law and theology.

The term *ʿālim* is applied at the present day in its literal meaning to any one who is evidently a scholar in our sense. For this situation in Egypt in the early xix^th century see Lane's *Modern Egyptians* chaps. iv. and ix. and by index. For a similar situation under the Mamlūks see Gaudefroy-Demombynes, *La Syrie à l'époque des Mamlouks*, passim and especially p. lxxvi. *sqq.* It is plain that the organization of the *ʿulamāʾ* was the solid framework of permanent government behind those changing dynasties. For the Ottoman Empire see E. J. W. Gibb, *History of Ottoman Poetry*, ii., p. 394 *sqq.* For the same situation in the Muslim world generally see W. Arnold, *The Caliphate*, by index under ʿUlamāʾ. For the distinction between the *ʿālim*, canon lawyer and systematic theologian, and the *ʿārif*, the mystic who knows Allāh by religious experience and vision, see article ʿilm above; so, too, for the distinction between the *ʿālim* who was at first a knower of definite facts (Ḳurʾānic texts and traditions and their meanings) and the *faḳīh* [q.v.] who was at first the independent thinker about these by his intelligence (*fiḳh*). It is, perhaps, hardly necessary to notice the error of western writers who frequently use *ʿulamāʾ*, in many spellings, as a singular.

ʿUMAR Ibn al-Khaṭṭāb, the second Caliph, one of the greatest figures of the early days of Islām and the founder of the Arab empire. Religious legend has naturally in the case of ʿUmar, as with other heroes and saints of Islām filled his biography with a mass of apocryphal details. Nevertheless the main characteristics of his personality are revealed to historical research with sufficient clearness for it to be possible to understand his character and assign him his place in the formation of Islām. Like many other people whose strongest characteristic is an energy of will, ʿUmar began by being the declared enemy of the cause which he was later to support with all his strength. Legend has perhaps somewhat coloured the stories of ʿUmar's persecution of the early Muslims and exaggerates in representing his conversion as the sudden result of his having overheard some verses of the Ḳurʾān read in the house of his sister Fāṭima, who with her husband, Saʿīd b. Zaid, had early given ear to the Prophet's preaching. It is from this sudden reversal of his attitude as well as perhaps from the fact that it was under ʿUmar that Islām became a world phenomenon, from the simple incident in Arab history that it originally was, that ʿUmar has earned the epithet of the "St. Paul of Islām" which the west has given him. In reality there is nothing in common between the two, except the stubborn energy with which they later championed the cause against which they originally fought.

Tradition places the conversion of ʿUmar in his 26th year, four years before the Hidjra. It is probable that the round figure of 30 which we thus get as the age of ʿUmar at the beginning of the new era has something artificial about it. But he was in any case certainly in the flower of his vigour when he began his new career of apostle of Islām. Besides, at first his support was only personal and legend has no doubt exaggerated its importance. ʿUmar was not able to assist the new religion through the power of his clan (he belonged to the Banū ʿAdī b. Kaʿb who being only Ḳuraish al-Ẓawāhir enjoyed no influence in the political life of the merchant republic) and his position with regard to his fellow-citizens was in no way outstanding. It is only in Madīna alongside of the Prophet and apparently through the prestige of his initiative and strength of will that ʿUmar, without holding any official position, began to be the real organizer of the new theocratic state. His part was that of councillor rather than of soldier; although he took part in Badr, Uḥud and later battles, practically nothing is recorded of his military exploits, accounts of which are so abundant in the case of ʿAlī and other Companions. Tradition which traces to his initiative no less than three Ḳurʾānic revelations (ii. 125: on the worship of the *maḳām Ibrāhīm* beside the Kaʿba; xxxiii. 53: on the veiling of the Prophet's wives: lxvi. 6: on the threat of punishment to the same women) is probably not only true but may even record only a few of the cases in which a suggestion from ʿUmar stimulated the Prophet's inspiration. What is remarkable about ʿUmar in the Madīna period is his perfect agreement with Abū Bakr, a concord which — a surprising thing and one which is a tribute to the two great champions of Islām — was never disturbed by jealousy. The fact that ʿUmar, like Abū Bakr, also became the father-in-law of the Prophet through the marriage of his daughter Ḥafṣa, did not arouse the slightest feelings of rivalry in him; on the contrary it was he who on the death of Muḥammad thrust the caliphate upon Abū Bakr.

The question whether the dying Abū Bakr designated ʿUmar as his successor has been the subject of much discussion by the theorists of Muslim constitutional law. As a matter of fact, there does not seem to have been any formal act of investiture which would in any case have been of no value for it would have been quite out of keeping with Arab custom. ʿUmar assumed power *de facto* and the recognition which was at once given him by the majority of the Companions assured him the exercise of it in a way quite similar to that in which the nomination of the amīr in the tribes took place. Such a system however primitive gave no trouble, except when the feeling between two parties was acute; this is what happened at the election of ʿAlī. Against ʿUmar there was only the dissatisfaction of the "legitimist" party of ʿAlī and the Anṣār, who had however been defeated too recently when Abū Bakr had become caliph to feel like organizing a regular opposition.

ʿUmar at the beginning of his rule found that the great expansion by conquest had already begun; he had perhaps contributed more than any other to its beginning in his capacity as adviser to his predecessor. If the military victories were not due directly to ʿUmar it was certainly to him that the credit should go of never having lost control of his generals and above all of having been able to make use of the powerful and talented family of the Umaiyads, without however allowing them to have a free hand. His quarrel with Khālid b. al-Walīd [q.v.] who, after having won the most brilliant victories for Islām, was dismissed and died in oblivion, gives us an idea of the political talent of ʿUmar and the extent of his authority. The knowledge of the limits of his power (which is the mark of political genius) caused him to treat the wily ʿAmr b. al-ʿĀṣ [q.v.] with tact and to leave him the initiative in the conquest of Egypt. But he was careful at the same time to put at his side an old Companion of the Prophet, al-Zubair, as a check upon him. He was careful in general (and the appointment of al-Zubair was no exception to the rule) not to appoint to high commands respected Companions whose ambition he had cause to fear. He preferred to watch them from close at hand and to satisfy their parvenu desires with the revenues of the great royal domains of the ʿIrāḳ and Syria which he assigned to them.

The caliphate of ʿUmar which is marked by the complete transformation of the Muslim state, is regarded by tradition as the period in which all the political institutions by which it was later ruled had their origin. That there has been in tradition a process of idealisation which centred in a single individual a complicated development extending over several generations is what historical criticism has not failed to recognize. But the part played by ʿUmar was nevertheless a great one. The regulations for his non-Muslim subjects, the institution of a register of those having the right to military pensions (the *dīwān*), the founding of military centres (*amṣār*) out of which were to grow the future great cities of Islām, the creation of the office of ḳāḍī were all his work, and it is also to him that a series of ordinances goes back, religious (the prayer of the month of Ramaḍān, the obligatory pilgrimage) as well as civil and penal (the era of the Hidjra, the punishment of drunkenness, and stoning as a punishment for adultery; in connection with the last it looks as if he did not hesitate to interpolate a verse in the text of the Ḳur'ān; cf. Nöldeke-Schwally, *Geschichte des Qorāns*, i. 248—251).

In spite of the autocratic character of ᶜUmar's rule, his caliphate has nothing of the monarchical character about it. It is further distinguished from that of Abū Bakr by a deeper feeling of its permanent character. Thus for the title of *khalīfa* which conveyes the idea of deputy there was substituted that of *amīr al-mu'minīn* (which ᶜUmar is said to have assumed in the year 19), in which the character of sovereign is more marked. Tradition makes Muḥammad say: "If God had wished that there should have been another prophet after me, ᶜUmar would have been he" (cf. al-Muḥibb al-Ṭabarī, *Manāḳib al-ᶜashara*, i. 199).

Tradition shows us ᶜUmar feared rather than loved. This feeling must have been a real one but it should be pointed out that it was only to his high moral character that ᶜUmar owed the respect which he inspired, for the physical force at his command was not great. The opposition to him (to that of ᶜAlī there was later added that of a number of the old Companions) did not dare to display itself publicly. The man in whom ᶜUmar confided, perhaps his successor *in pectore*, was the third member of the "triumvirate", Abū ᶜUbaida. When he died, a victim of the great plague of the year 18, it does not seem that ᶜUmar had thought of the question of the succession. He was still, besides, at the height of his powers (53, according to the age accepted by tradition) when he fell on the 26th Dhu 'l-Ḥidjdja 23/Nov. 3, 644 by the dagger of Abū Lu'lu'a, a Christian slave of al-Mughīra b. Shuᶜba, governor of Baṣra. The motive which tradition gives to the murder is the very heavy tax against which the slave had appealed in vain to the caliph; according to Caetani, the murderer was only the unconscious instrument of a conspiracy of the Companions tired of the caliphs' tyranny. It is certain that one of the latter's sons, the unstable ᶜUbaid Allāh who fell in the battle of Ṣiffīn (in 37 A.H.), cherished this suspicion but there is really no reason to believe that it was well founded (cf. the remarks made by Levi della Vida on Caetani's views in *RSO*, iv., 1912, p. 1059—1061). We may suppose that if he had lived to a greater age ᶜUmar would have provided for the succession. He was not spared to do this and the plan of an elective council formed of the six oldest Companions (*shūrā*) which resulted in the election of ᶜUthmān, even if ᶜUmar had nominated this council on his deathbed, could only be a temporary expedient.

While orthodox tradition reveres in ᶜUmar not only the great ruler but also one of the most typical models of all the virtues of Islām (cf. a list of his merits in the work of al-Muḥibb al-Ṭabarī, *al-Riyāḍ al-nādira fī manāḳib al-ᶜashara*, Cairo 1327), the Shīᶜa has never concealed its antipathy to him who was the first to thwart the claims of ᶜAlī (cf. Goldziher, in *WZKM*, xv. 321 *sqq*.). The *ṣūfī* teaching, although it exalts the ascetic austerity of the life of ᶜUmar, has very little to do with him: besides this type of puritan lends itself very little to mystical speculations whether in its historical reality or in its idealisation in legend.

Bibliography: All the historical material is to be found collected in L. Caetani, *Annali dell' Islām*, iii.—vi. (Milan 1909—1912); vol. v. contains the historical synthesis of his caliphate and vi. the general Index. The material contained in the works on Ḥadīth, which has only been partly utilised by Caetani, is collected by A. J. Wensinck, *A Handbook of early Muhammadan Tradition*, Leyden 1927, p. 234—236, s.v. *ᶜUmar*.

UMM AL-KITĀB, the original copy of the Book with Allāh in heaven, from which the revelations of the Ḳur'ān come and from which Allāh "abrogates and confirms what He pleases" (Sūra xiii. 39). This original copy, called *aṣl al-Kitāb* in Ḥadīth (e.g. Ṭabarī, *Tafsīr*, xxv. 26), is according to Sūra lxxxv. 21 written in a "carefully preserved table" (*fī lawḥ maḥfūẓ*; cf. Enoch 93, $_2$; Book of Jubilees 5, $_{13}$; 16, $_9$; 32, $_{21}$). In the Madīna period Umm al-Kitāb is used in another sense: according to Sūra iii. 7, the book revealed by Allāh to Muḥammad, i.e. the Ḳur'ān, consists of verses "clearly expressed" (*āyāt muḥkamāt*) and of "others ambiguous" (*mutashābihāt*); only the first however constitute the Umm al-Kitāb. In keeping with this expression post-Ḳur'ānic linguistic usage calls the *Fātiḥa*, as containing the essential content of the Book, *Umm al-Kitāb* or *Umm al-Ḳur'ān*.

Bibliography: Lane, *Lexicon*, s.v. *Umm*; Horovitz, *Koranische Untersuchungen*, Berlin-Leipzig 1926, p. 65.

UMM KULTHŪM, daughter of Muḥammad. Tradition knows even less of her than of her sister Ruḳaiya and this little consists mainly of a repetition of what is told of the latter. Umm Kulthūm is said to have married a son of Abū Lahab but to have been divorced by him by his father's orders before the marriage was consummated; what this means is discussed in the article RUḲAIYA. The view there expressed that Umm Kulthūm was really married to a son of Abū Lahab is supported by the usual and literal interpretation of her *kunya* (her real name is nowhere recorded). That at a later date efforts should have been made to suppress all record of such a grandson of the Prophet is only natural. Otherwise we are only told of her that her brother-in-law ᶜUthmān married her after Ruḳaiya's death during the Badr campaign. She died in Shaᶜbān of the year 9 without having borne a son to him.

Bibliography: Ibn Hishām, ed. Wüstenfeld, p. 121; Ibn Saᶜd, viii., p. 25 *sq*.; Ṭabarī, ed. de Goeje, iii. 2302; H. Lammens, *Fāṭima et les Filles de Mahomet*, 1912, p. 3 *sqq*.

UMM AL-WALAD (A.), a female slave who has borne her master a child.

1. The master's right to take his slaves as concubines is the continuation of a general practice among the pagan Arabs. In the period just before the coming of Islām, children of such unions were as a rule called only after their mother and not after their father, and only received their freedom when expressly recognized by their father, and the position of their slave mother was not at all a privileged one. Even her designation *umm al-walad* ("mother of children") is in contrast to *umm al-banīn* ("mother of sons") as the name for a free woman.

2. This state of affairs was continued under Islām without any essential change at first. The Ḳur'ān permits concubinage with a man's own slaves in several passages dealing with the limits of lawful sexual intercourse (iv. 3, 24 *sq*.; xxiii. 6, 50—52;

lxx. 30, all Madīnese). In the Ḳur'ān the position of the *umm al-walad* is not defined, nor is the Prophet known to have issued a decree altering her position or that of her children. That he is said to have set free the slave-girl Māriya, when she had borne him his son Ibrāhīm, should not be taken as a general rule; this episode is not at all prominent in the material of tradition relating to the *umm al-walad*. There is every reason to believe in the genuineness of a *ḥadīth* transmitted by Abū Dāwūd (*ʿAtāḳ*, bāb 8) and Ibn Ḥanbal (vi. 360). According to this, a woman, who had been sold in the heathen period by her uncle as a slave and had borne her master a son and now on the death of her master was to be sold again to pay his debts, complained to the Prophet; the latter ordered the administrator of the estate to manumit the woman and gave him a slave in compensation. Again, there is no doubt that it was a decision for this one case only.

3. That an *umm al-walad* should become free *ipso iure* on the death of her master, and during his lifetime no longer liable to be sold (or given away etc.) was first ordained by the caliph ʿUmar. This is certain from numerous accounts, although the details vary and are embellished with legends. But ʿUmar's decree in no way made a final settlement; it gave trouble under ʿUthmān and ʿAlī again diverged from it. Ibn ʿAbbās is specially mentioned as another opponent of ʿUmar's view among the Companions of the Prophet. In the dispute that now arose between the different opinions, the attempt was made on the one side to ascribe ʿUmar's decision to the Prophet and to ascribe the same opinion even to ʿAlī and Ibn ʿAbbās; on the other hand, it was insisted that the Prophet had approved the sale of the *umm al-walad*; against this, evidence was quoted to show that the Companions of the Prophet gave approval to ʿUmar's ordinance. From the point of view of the Muslim criticism of tradition, none of these *ḥadīths* is unimpeachable in its *isnād* with the exception of the one quoted above in paragraph 2, so that it is usually preferred simply to quote ʿUmar and his *ra'y* as authority for the view that later prevailed. Al-ʿAinī is thus able to give a list of seven different opinions on the *umm al-walad* in addition to ʿUmar's from the period of the earliest jurists before the rise of the schools: 1. The master may release her for money (i.e. as *mukātaba*); 2. she may be sold without restriction; 3. the master may sell her at any time during his life-time and when he dies she becomes free (she is thus regarded as *muddabbara*); 4. she may be sold to pay a debt due by the estate; 5. she may be sold, but if her child is alive at the death of his father and her master, she is manumitted at the expense of his share in the estate and inherits with him; 6. she can only be sold on condition that she is to be set free; 7. even if she is contumacious and runs away, she cannot be sold, but only if she commits fornication or becomes an unbeliever. But even by this time the thesis that the *umm al-walad* could not be sold but became free on the death of her master, had won most supporters, among whom al-Ḥasan al-Baṣrī, ʿAṭā', Mudjāhid, al-Zuhrī, Ibrāhīm al-Nakhaʿī and others are specially mentioned.

4. In the time of the formation of the schools the view that the *umm al-walad* cannot be sold is held by Abū Ḥanīfa with Abū Yūsuf, Zufar, al-Shaibānī and their companions, al-Awzāʿī, al-Thawrī, al-Ḥasan b. Ṣāliḥ, al-Laith b. Saʿd, Mālik and his companions, Abū Thawr and Ibn Ḥanbal. This is also the final opinion of al-Shāfiʿī and therefore that of his companions and pupils, while he, according to a reliable tradition, had previously sanctioned the sale of the *umm al-walad*. According to Dāwūd and the Ẓāhirīs, the Zaidīs and the Twelver-Imāmīs (here however with the qualification that she becomes free if she was still in the possession of her master at his death and her child is alive) as well as the Muʿtazilīs she can be sold.

5. In order to prevent the birth of a child the practice of *ʿazl* was frequent, especially in intercourse with slaves, and it is therefore often discussed in connection with the *umm al-walad*. Here it is sufficient to say that *ʿazl* was in general considered to be permitted with a slave. — To prevent a slave becoming *umm al-walad* the master had also the possibility of not acknowledging the paternity of her child. While this was never so seriously regarded as in the case of disputing the paternity of a wife's child (cf. ṬALĀḲ, section iv.), nevertheless an effort was made to restrict the right of disputing the paternity in the case of the *umm al-walad* also. *Ḥadīths* are quoted from ʿUmar and Ibn ʿUmar to the effect that no one who has had intercourse with his slave may dispute the paternity of her child, even if he says he used *ʿazl* or if there is another paternity possible. The Mālikīs and Shāfiʿīs agree with this. The Ḥanafīs on the other hand hold the view that the paternity of the child and the character of the slave as *umm al-walad* in this case depends entirely on an acknowledgment by the master. — That the child borne by a slave to her master (on the assumption that his paternity is established) is free, has always been recognized in Islām without any difference of opinion, and in the discussion of the position of the *umm al-walad* is even regarded as an argument for her not being sold. The deduction is natural that the father's recognition of children born in concubinage must have been the rule in the days just before Islām.

6. The details of the teaching of the *fiḳh* about the *umm al-walad* are as follows. Every, even non-Muslim, slave who has borne her master (even after his death) a child is considered *umm al-walad*; on the death of her master she becomes *ipso iure* free (so that she can neither be sold to pay off debts on the estate [cf. however below] nor falls under the limit of the third of the estate applicable to legacies); a legacy set aside by her master in her favour is valid; all legitimate and illegitimate children she may have had from other men after becoming pregnant by her master become likewise free. Even in the case of a stillborn child, the mother becomes *umm al-walad*; opinions differ regarding a miscarriage. From the *umm al-walad*'s expectancy of freedom, it follows that she cannot be sold, given away or pledged; if she commits a crime the master cannot evade his responsibility for her by cession as in the case of another slave. In other respects she remains a slave; the master has the right to her body and to her labour, but the Mālikīs allow him only to demand light service from her and prohibit him hiring her out. — Apart from the fact that the *umm al-walad* can be sold to pay debts which her master had incurred before she became pregnant, she loses her expectancy of freedom only, in the opinion of the Ḥanafīs and Mālikīs, if she deliberately kills her master. — The opinions of the Shīʿa differ essentially from all this (cf. above, § 4).

7. In Muslim law a most rigid distinction is made between marriage and concubinage, so much so that

the master cannot enter into marriage with his own slaves at all. Divergences from this rule are extraordinarily rare. There was a tendency in India in the last century to assimilate concubinage with a free woman to that with a slave, but this has not been recognized by the doctrine. On the other hand, a kind of morganatic marriage with free women besides the four legal spouses is in use even now among the princes and other persons of high position in India and Indonesia; in order to ensure the legitimacy of the children from these unions, one of the legal spouses is temporarily divorced by khulʿ and the pregnant concubine married instead; but this again has no foundation in Islāmic law. — Notwithstanding all the ameliorations which the development of Muslim law brought to the position of the *umm al-walad*, the old contemptuous feeling towards a union with a slave and the children born from it remained for a certain time; but under completely changed social conditions, the absolute equality of the children born from a marriage with a free woman and in legal concubinage was at last completely established in Islām (cf. ʿABD § d).

Bibliography: Lammens, *Le Berceau de l'Islām*, p. 276—306; Robertson Smith, *Kinship and Marriage in Early Arabia*, 2nd ed., p. 89—91; Wellhausen, in *NGW Gött.*, 1893, p. 435 *sq.*; Wensinck, *Handbook*, s.v. Manumission, Slaves, Intercourse; *Kanz al-ʿummāl*, vol. v.; al-ʿAinī, commentary on al-Bukhārī, *ʿItḳ*, b. 8; Juynboll, *Handleiding*, 3rd ed., p. 236, 238; Sachau, *Muhammedanisches Recht*, p. 127, 168 *sqq.*; Santillana, *Istituzioni*, i. 123 *sq.*; Querry, *Droit Musulman*, ii. 147 *sqq.* (for the Shīʿīs). — For paragraph 7: ʿAbd al-Ḳādir, *al-Djawāhir al-muḍīʾa*, i. no. 668; *al-Fihrist*, p. 207, 15; Snouck Hurgronje, *Mekka in the Latter Part of the 19th Century*, p. 109; Bousquet, in *REI*, 1938, p. 231.

UMMA, the Ḳurʾānic word for people, community, is not to be derived from the Arabic root *ʾmm*, but to be explained as a loanword from the Hebrew (*ummā*) or Aramaic (*ummethā*). It has therefore no direct connection with the homonyms also found in the Ḳurʾān, which mean "a period" (Sūra xi. 8; xii. 45) and "conduct" (Sūra xliii. 22 *sq.*). Perhaps the loanword found its way into Arabic at a comparatively early period (see Horovitz's citation of the Ṣafā inscription, li. 407, in *Koranische Untersuchungen*, Berlin-Leipzig 1926, p. 52). In any case the word was taken up by Muḥammad and henceforth becomes a specifically Islāmic term.

The passages in the Ḳurʾān, in which the word *umma* (plur. *umam*) occurs are so varied that its meaning cannot be rigidly defined. This much however seems to be certain, that it always refers to ethnical, linguistic or religious bodies of people who are the objects of the divine plan of salvation. Even in passages like Sūra vii. 164 and xxviii. 21, where *umma* is used in quite a colourless fashion, there is a hint of this significance. The term is in isolated cases applied to the Djinn (Sūra vii. 38; xli. 25; xlvi. 18), indeed to all living creatures (Sūra vi. 38) but always with the implication that these creatures are to be included in the divine scheme of salvation and are liable to judgment. *Umma* is exceptionally applied in one passage (Sūra xvi. 120) to an individual, Abraham. Here the term either has the meaning of *imām* (so the Arab lexicographers), or Abraham is so called in his capacity as head of the community founded by him (Horovitz), by a use of the part for the whole. Otherwise *umma* always refers to whole groups or at least to groups within large communities.

God has sent to each umma a messenger (Sūra vi. 42; x. 47; xiii. 30; xvi. 34, 63; xxiii. 44; xxix. 18; xl. 5) or admonisher (Sūra xxxv. 24, 42) to guide them on the right path. But like Muḥammad, these messengers of God have often been attacked and called liars (Sūra xxiii. 44; xxix. 18; xl. 5). They will therefore appear on the day of judgment as witnesses against them (Sūra iv. 41; xvi. 84, 89; xxviii. 75; cf. ii. 143). For each umma is brought to judgment (Sūra vi. 108; vii. 33; x. 49; xv. 5; xxiii. 43; xxvii. 85; xlv. 28). In contrast to those who could not be converted, a number within the individual ummas however heeded the appeal of God's messenger and thus came on to the right path (Sūra xvi. 36). This is particularly true of the *ahl al-Kitāb*. The companies of the righteous among the *ahl al-Kitāb* are also called ummas (Sūra iii. 115 *sq.*; v. 66; vii. 159; cf. ii. 134, 141; vii. 168, 181; xi. 48). They are relatively small groups within larger communities.

Muḥammad frequently discusses the question why mankind consists of a plurality of ummas and has not remained a unit. He sees the ultimate reason for this in God's inscrutable decree. "Men were a single umma. Then they became disunited. If a word had not previously gone out from thy Lord, the matter would have been decided between them, about which they disagreed" (Sūra x. 19; cf. v. 48; xi. 118; xvi. 93; xlii. 5). Sometimes he traces this disruption to the malevolence of mankind (Sūra ii. 213; xxi. 92 *sq.*; xxiii. 52 *sq.*). In another passage it is traced to the division of the Israelites into 12 tribes (Sūra vii. 160; cf. 168). These rhetorical rather than logical utterances of Muḥammad are most likely to be taken as replies to objections raised by his opponents (of the *ahl al-Kitāb*). The Prophet would hardly have come to tackle this difficult problem of his own accord.

As regards Muḥammad's umma in particular, we can trace a number of variations and changes in the meaning of the term. But the question is simpler here as we are dealing to some extent with a historical phenomenon.

In the first period of his prophetic activity Muḥammad regarded the Arabs in general or his Meccan countrymen as a closed umma. Just as the earlier messengers and admonishers of God had been sent to the ummas of the past (see above), so he had now been given the task of transmitting the divine message to the Arab umma which had hitherto been neglected, in order to show it the way to salvation. Like the earlier messengers (see above), he also was fiercely attacked by his umma and accused of lying. After he had finally broken off relations with the pagan Meccans and migrated with his followers to Madīna, he created a new community there. He went beyond the circle of Muslims proper and included those citizens of Madīna who had not yet heeded his religious appeal in one political combination. "The constitution of the community of Madīna", in which this unification is laid down in writing, expressly states that the citizens of the town, including the Jews, now form an umma (Ibn Hishām, p. 341, 3 *sq.*, 342, 18 *sqq.*). The predominantly political character of this new umma was however only a makeshift. As soon as Muḥammad felt himself firmly established and had successfully attacked the pagan Meccans, he was able to exclude from his politico-religious community the Madīnese (especially the Jews) who had not yet adopted his religion. As time went on, his umma came more and more to consist only of his proper followers, the Muslims. In contrast to the *ahl al-Kitāb*, with whom he had previously been in alliance, he now described the Muslims as an umma and laid stress on their religious and ethical qualities (Sūra iii. 104, 110). His final breaking away from the *ahl al-Kitāb* had as a result that he turned more and more to the Meccans and their centre of worship, the Kaʿba (cf. in this connection Sūra ii. 125 *sqq.*, esp. 128, and Sūra xxii. 34, 67). He only apparently resumed with this his original idea of an umma embracing all the Arabs. In reality the final result was fundamentally different from the starting-point. The Arab umma, which Muḥammad had originally taken for granted, was only created by him after much hard work. If it at first represented a community of Arabs, this was more or less a secondary phenomenon. The essential thing was the religious foundation on which it was based. The umma of the Arabs was transformed into an umma of the Muslims. It is no wonder then that it spread very soon after Muḥammad's death far beyond the bounds of Arabia and in course of time brought together very different stocks and nations to form a higher unit.

Bibliography: E. W. Lane, *An Arabic English Lexicon*, i. 90; J. Horovitz, *Koranische Untersuchungen*, Berlin-Leipzig 1926, p. 51—53; do., *Jewish Proper Names and Derivatives in the Koran* (*Hebrew Union College Annual*, vol. ii., Cincinnati 1925, p. 145—227), p. 190; K. Ahrens, in *ZDMG*, NF, ix. 37; Buhl-Schaeder, *Das Leben Muhammeds*, Leipzig 1930, p. 209—212 (see further literature, note 24), 277, 343—345; Snouck Hurgronje, *Der Islam* (Chantepie de la Saussaye, *Lehrbuch der Religionsgeschichte*), p. 658—660, 672 *sq.*; on umma in the literature of Tradition see the references under *Community* in A. J. Wensinck, *A Handbook of Early Muhammadan Tradition*, Leyden 1927.

UMMĪ, an epithet of Muḥammad in the Ḳurʾān, connected in some way with the word *umma* [q.v.]. It does not seem however to be a direct derivative, as it only appears after the Hid̲j̲ra and has a different meaning from *umma*, which is already common in the period before the Hid̲j̲ra. In Sūra iii. 20, Muḥammad invites the *ahl al-Kitāb* and the ummīs to adopt Islām (*ḳul li 'llad̲h̲īna ūtu 'l-kitāb wa 'l-ummīyīn . . .*). *Ummīyūn* here means "heathen", as it does in the same Sūra, verse 75, where the word is put with this meaning into the mouths of the *ahl al-Kitāb*. The latter passage makes it probable that *ummī* or *ummīyūn* is a word coined by the *ahl al-Kitāb* (probably the Jews especially) to describe the heathen. This explanation is all the more probable since Horovitz in his *Koranische Untersuchungen* (Berlin-Leipzig 1926, p. 52) has shown that it has an equivalent in the Hebrew *ummōt hā-ʿōlām* (Greek = τὰ ἔθνη τοῦ κόσμου).

In Sūra lxii. 2 there is an allusion to God having sent an apostle to the *ummīyūn* from amongst themselves. As Muḥammad here is unmistakably called an apostle from the heathen and for the heathen, it is natural to assume that he also refers to himself as the heathen prophet in the words *al-nabī al-ummī* (Sura vii. 157, 158) and presents himself "to the Jews as one of the *nᵉbīʾē ummōt hā-ʿōlām*" (Horovitz; cf. Sūra vii. 157: "whom they find written with them in the *Tawrāt* and the *Ind̲j̲īl*"). What further shades of meaning Muḥammad himself gave to this epithet is however very difficult to ascertain. If we compare the words of Sūra vii. 157 with the praise which Muḥammad gives in Sūra iii. 104, 110 to his *umma* we cannot help thinking that he might possibly also have been making a play on the etymology *ummī* $<$ *umma*. In any case, he did not in the least consider the epithet *al-nabī al-ummī* as derogatory.

Frants Buhl (Buhl-Schaeder, *Das Leben Muhammeds*, Leipzig 1930, p. 131) put forward the thesis that *ummī* means not "heathen" (ἐθνικός) but "untaught" (λαϊκός). In spite of the fact that this could very well fit the text of Sūra ii. 78, there is on the whole more against than for it. *Ummīyūn* in Sūra ii. 78 can, if necessary, be translated "heathen", if one does not want to try something else (see Horovitz). On the other hand, the same word in Sūra iii. 75 cannot from the context possibly be translated "untaught", even if we really understand the heathen by it. *Ummī* would also on etymological grounds be difficult to explain as "layman", for neither the Arabic *umma* nor the Hebrew *ummā* nor the Aramaic *ummᵉt̲h̲ā* means people in the sense of the laity. Finally Buhl's objection to the Prophet calling himself a "heathen prophet" loses weight when we remember that Muḥammad was perhaps not quite clear about the full significance of the Jewish conception of "heathen" and that he, as above indicated, may have given it a new significance.

The application of the term *ummī* to Muḥammad was often quoted as evidence that he could not read or write. In reality the expression has no bearing on the question. For the text of Sūra ii. 78 which gives rise to this assumption does not charge the *ummīyūn* with ignorance of reading and writing, but with a deficient knowledge of the holy scriptures. Nevertheless, this misinterpretation was generally adopted with the result that the Arabic word *ummī* now has the meaning of "illiterate".

Bibliography: A. J. Wensinck, in *Acta Orientalia* ii. (Leiden 1924), p. 191 *sq.*; J. Horovitz, *Koranische Untersuchungen*, Berlin-Leipzig 1926, p. 51—53; do., *Jewish Proper Names and Derivatives in the Koran* (*Hebrew Union College Annual*, ii., Cincinnati 1925, p. 145—227), p. 190 *sq.*; K. Ahrens, in *ZDMG*, *NF*, ix. 37; Buhl-Schaeder, *Das Leben Muhammeds*, Leipzig 1930, p. 56, 131 (cf. Horovitz, *OLZ*, 1931, 148 *sq.*).

ʿUMRA, "the little pilgrimage". 1. The ceremonies of the (Muslim) ʿumra. The ʿumra, like the ḥad̲j̲d̲j̲ [q.v.], can only be performed in a state of ritual purity (*iḥrām* [q.v.]). On assuming the *iḥrām*, the pilgrim (*muʿtamir*) must make up his mind whether he is going to perform the ʿumra by itself or in combination with the ḥad̲j̲d̲j̲ and express his intention in an appropriate *nīya* [q.v.]. If he combines the ʿumra with the ḥad̲j̲d̲j̲ (see below) he can assume the *iḥrām* for both pilgrimages at once; in the other case the *iḥrām* must be specially assumed for the ʿumra in the unconsecrated area (*ḥill*) outside of the ḥaram of Mecca. This holds also for native Meccans who, when they are going to perform the ḥad̲j̲d̲j̲, can assume the *iḥrām* within Mecca. Three places are preferred for the assumption of the *iḥrām* for the ʿumra: D̲j̲iʿrāna, Ḥudaibiya and especially Tanʿīm. The latter place was therefore also known as al-ʿUmra. With the utterance of the *labbaika* formula [see TALBIYA], the actual ceremony of the pilgrimage begins. The muʿtamir goes to Mecca in order first of all to go around the Kaʿba [cf. ṬAWĀF]. He enters the mosque through the north door of the north-east side (Bāb al-Salām), goes under the portal of the Banū S̲h̲aiba to the Black Stone built into the wall of the Kaʿba and, turning right, begins the sevenfold circumambulation of the Kaʿba, saying prayers all the while. The first three circumambulations are performed at a rapid pace (*ramal*), the four last at an ordinary rate. After this is finished, in order to acquire a special blessing he presses himself against the part of the Kaʿba wall which lies between the Black Stone and the door of the Kaʿba. In conclusion he prays two rakʿas behind the Maḳām Ibrāhīm, drinks a draught of the holy Zemzem water and touches once again in farewell the Black Stone (these last ceremonies are however not considered absolutely necessary). The muʿtamir now leaves the mosque through the great al-Ṣafā door in order to perform the second essential part of the ʿumra, the running between al-Ṣafā and al-Marwa [cf. the article SAʿY]. He goes to the hill al-Ṣafā and utters a few prayers there. He then goes to the hill al-Marwa, over four hundred yards farther north, passing the north-east side of the mosque. A short low-lying stretch at the east corner of the mosque is covered at a more rapid pace (*harwal* or *khabab*). Reaching al-Marwa, the muʿtamir again utters a prayer. He then returns the same way in the reverse direction and so on until he has covered the distance seven times and ends at al-Marwa. He has thus completed the ceremony of the ʿumra, and has only to have his hair cut or be shaved by one of the barbers waiting there. If he is making the ʿumra in combination with the ḥadjdj, he only has his hair trimmed and has the proper cutting done on the 10th Dhu 'l-Ḥidjdja at the end of the ḥadjdj.

2. The History of the ʿUmra and its relation to the Ḥadjdj. The ceremonies which make up the Muslim ʿumra are undoubtedly for the most part taken over from the pre-Islāmic period. They completely lack any close connection with the religion preached by Muḥammad, except for the Muḥammadan prayers and the monotheistic interpretation of the ceremony. The Prophet did not inaugurate these practices but only assimilated them to his teaching. This he could do all the more readily as their original significance seems to have become but obscurely understood by his contemporaries. That he allowed them to persist at all is probably less to be attributed to his personal reverence for them than to his political instinct which made him respect the traditions of his conservative fellow-countrymen.

On the parts played by the separate ceremonies of the Muslim ʿumra in the pre-Islāmic period see the articles IḤRĀM, SAʿY and ṬAWĀF. The Muslim ʿumra as a group of ceremonies forming a single whole also appears to go back to a pre-Muḥammadan institution. This is shown by the very fact that Muḥammad refers to it by a name which in his time seems already to have been a special term and enables us to assume that the thing itself was well-known. This however does not mean that the separate parts of the pre-Islāmic ʿumra exactly corresponded to those of the Muslim ʿumra. The two institutions, so far as we can see, by no means coincide. It is however very difficult to make out in what the difference lay, as we do not even know the earliest form of the Muslim ʿumra, much less that of the Djāhilīya. We have therefore to make up for the lack of authentic sources by deductions from material which even itself is not above reproach.

The pre-Muḥammadan ʿumra probably also consisted of ritual acts, which were performed in a state of *iḥrām* within Mecca and included the *ṭawāf* of the Kaʿba. On the other hand, the course between al-Ṣafā and al-Marwa (*saʿy*) does not seem to have been included. This follows from the text of Sūra ii. 158, which clearly distinguishes between ḥadjdj and ʿumra on the one hand and the course between al-Ṣafā and al-Marwa on the other and describes the performance of the latter in connection with the ḥadjdj or ʿumra as irreproachable, indeed even meritorious, but still as a work of supererogation. Muḥammad himself performed it in 632 following the *ṭawāf* and thus by his example gave a further stimulus to the incorporation of the *saʿy* into the Muslim ʿumra. If the Muslim ʿumra in this respect shows an accretion compared with that of the pre-Muḥammadan period, it seems also to have lost something. For the ʿumra in the Djāhilīya can hardly have consisted of the *ṭawāf* only. Probably an additional essential element in it was the sacrifice of animals brought for the special purpose, a custom which was later mainly confined to the ḥadjdj. Muḥammad himself brought sacrificial animals to the unfortunate ʿumra of al-Ḥudaibiya and a year later to the so-called *ʿumrat al-ḳaḍā'*.

As to the relation of the ʿumra to the ḥadjdj, the very similarity of these two institutions has contributed to confuse them and to blend their distinguishing features. Their reciprocal fusion had already begun in the last years of the Prophet. Muḥammad began the only ḥadjdj in which he took part as head of the Muslim community shortly before his death, by performing the *ṭawāf* and *saʿy* after his arrival in Mecca, ceremonies which did not originally form the beginning of the ḥadjdj but were elements of the Muslim ʿumra. He thereupon put off the *iḥrām* and said that the ceremonies so far performed formed an ʿumra. When moreover ʿUmar and others of those with him did not approve of putting off the *iḥrām* and did not follow him, this clearly shows how closely the ceremonies of the ʿumra were associated with those of the ḥadjdj for them and that in their view these holy acts should be performed in one and the same *iḥrām*. If we reflect that the revelation announced on this occasion (Sūra ii. 196) laid down a penance for using the ḥadjdj for the ʿumra in this way and that thereby Muḥammad to someext entac knowledged himself guilty, then it is natural to suppose that Muḥammad had only put off the *iḥrām* in order to be able to associate with his wives who were there and not with the object of keeping ʿumra and ḥadjdj absolutely distinct (see Snouck Hurgronje, *Het Mekkaansche Feest*, p. 83—102). In any case, Muḥammad in the year 632 made the ʿumra precede the performance of the ḥadjdj and thus put his approval on the combination of ḥadjdj and ʿumra. This combination had a deeper cause: Muḥammad on the one hand proclaimed Mecca with the Kaʿba as the centre of the worship of Islām and on the other took over the ḥadjdj, which originally had very little, if anything at all, to do with Mecca, into Islām. He had indeed every reason to bring the Muslim ḥadjdj into connection with the sanctuary of Mecca. The more he succeeded, however, the more the ʿumra lost its *raison d'être* as a special pilgrimage to Mecca. It was therefore quite a natural development when the Muslim ʿumra became more associated with the Muslim ḥadjdj and original elements of the ʿumra were absorbed by the corresponding elements of the ḥadjdj, as was presumably the case with the sacrifices (see above). The ʿumra and the ḥadjdj did not however absolutely combine into one. This was prevented by, amongst other things, the fact that Muḥammad in the pilgrimage above mentioned drew a line of separation between the two by discarding the *iḥrām*.

In the consensus (*idjmāʿ*) of Muslim opinion, two ways of combining the ʿumra with the ḥadjdj came to be recognized in course of time: *tamattuʿ* and *ḳirān*. The former term was applied, following Sūra ii. 196 (*man tamattaʿa bi 'l-umrati ila 'l-ḥadjdji*), to the way which Muḥammad had actually followed, namely combining ʿumra and ḥadjdj with a break in the *iḥrām*. ʿUmar certainly threatened during his caliphate to punish its observance with the punishment of stoning and even under the early Umaiyads it does not seem to have been usual. *Ḳirān* is the name given to the combination of ʿumra and ḥadjdj without breaking the *iḥrām*. In this the *iḥrām* is assumed for the ʿumra and the ḥadjdj at the same time. As in the Muslim ḥadjdj the ceremonies which consitute an ʿumra are also performed, according to the prevailing view an ʿumra is completely carried out when the ceremonies of the ḥadjdj have been performed (with the *nīya* of *ḳirān*). Some authorities however demand that the ceremonies of the ʿumra should be carried through separately. But the *iḥrām* must on no account be broken.

The ʿumra, in spite of its partial absorption in the ḥadjdj, has however retained its independence, although only to a limited degree. When the ḥadjdj is performed alone in the *ifrād*, i.e. by itself (in contrast to *tamattuʿ* and *ḳirān*), the ʿumra also must be performed separately. Pilgrims who come from outside to Mecca seem as a rule in this case to perform the ʿumra after the completion of the ḥadjdj ceremonies so that they naturally have to assume the *iḥrām* again. In the course of time this independent ʿumra ceremony seems to have become gradually confined to such Muslims as were permanently or for a considerable time resident in Mecca or came there at a time other than that of the ḥadjdj. But it was just this local limitation of the independent ʿumra that favoured the survival of traditions from the pre-Muḥammadan period. If we therefore learn that the ʿumra for centuries was celebrated as an independent ceremony, preferably in the month of Radjab, we can probably see in this a survival of pre-Islāmic tradition: the ʿumra in the time of Djāhilīya was presumably a ceremony observed annually in Radjab and therefore had nothing to do with the ḥadjdj, the pilgrimage in Dhu ʾl-Ḥidjdja (cf. also the tradition according to which ʿUkkāsha had his hair cut in Radjab of the year 2 to make himself look like a pilgrim). As Muḥammad could only prepare the way for the combination of the ʿumra with the ḥadjdj but not complete it, the old tradition of performing it in Radjab survived for centuries later. It is only in comparatively modern times that Radjab seems to have lost its significance for the performance of the ʿumra. The custom of the Meccans of journeying to the holy places of Madīna in Radjab perhaps broke it down. When ʿumras are now performed in dissociation from the ḥadjdj (i.e. in *ifrād*), the nights of the months of the fast (Ramaḍān) are specially favoured for this purpose and especially the last ten which are connected with the *lailat al-ḳadr*.

3. The significance of the pre-Islāmic and the Islāmic ʿumra. If the pre-Islāmic ʿumra was annually performed in Radjab and also if the calculation is correct which places Radjab originally in the spring, its similarity with the Jewish passover strikes one at once. The animals sacrificed were perhaps, as in the Jewish ceremony, originally first-borns (cf. Wellhausen, *Reste*², p. 98 *sq.*; W. Robertson Smith, *Lectures on the Religion of the Semites*³, p. 227 *sq.*, 464). In Muḥammad's time however, the original significance of the ʿumra seems to have been practically forgotten and it no longer fell in the spring.

The Islāmic ʿumra is an expression of piety, mainly of a personal nature, especially if it is undertaken separately and not with the ḥadjdj, the ceremony observed annually by the Muslim community together. Probably this individual character is the result of the fact that it lost its independence in time and so far as it was not associated with the ḥadjdj constituted a work of supererogation. Before Islām the ʿumra had probably a more collective character.

The question, answered differently by the different madhāhib, whether the Muslim is bound to the same degree to perform the ʿumra as he is the ḥadjdj is of little significance, in as much as every Muslim who performs the ḥadjdj as a rule performs the ʿumra at the same time. The case of a pilgrim who has begun a ḥadjdj and for any reason cannot complete it, is a special one. Under these circumstances he is bound to perform an ʿumra in order to be able to put off the *iḥrām* for a time. The omission is however not made good by this. The ḥadjdj on the contrary must be made good in the following year.

Bibliography: Th. W. Juynboll, *Handbuch des islamischen Gesetzes*, Leyden-Leipzig 1910, p. 138 *sqq.*; [Wizārat al-Awḳāf, Ḳism al-Masādjid], *al-Fiḳh ʿala ʾl-madhāhib al-arbaʿa, Ḳism al-ʿibādāt*, Cairo 1928, p. 664—669, 676—686, 692—698; Bukhārī, *Ṣaḥīḥ, K. al-ʿUmra*; Muslim-Nawawī, iii. 216—218; Nāṣir-i Khosraw, *Sefer-nāme*, ed. Schefer, p. 66 *sq.*; Ibn Djubair, *Riḥla*, ed. Wright-de Goeje (*GMS*, v.), p. 80 *sq.*, 128—137; Ibrāhīm Rifʿat Bāshā, *Mirʾāt al-Ḥaramain*, Cairo 1925, i. 99, 101, 337; Burton, *Personal Narrative of a Pilgrimage to Mecca and Medina*, iii., Leipzig 1874, p. 122—128; E. Rutter, *The Holy Cities of Arabia*, London-New York 1928, i. 96—114; Snouck Hurgronje, *Mekka*, ii., Haag 1889, p. 55, 70, 75 *sq.*, 83 *sq.*; do., *Het Mekkaansche Feest*, Leyden 1880 (= *Verspreide Geschriften*, i. 1 *sqq.*); Wellhausen, *Reste arabischen Heidentums*, p. 78 *sq.*, 84, 98; Gaudefroy-Demombynes, *Le pèlerinage à la Mekke*, Paris 1923, esp. p. 192 *sqq.* and 304 *sqq.*; H. Lammens, *Le culte des bétyles et les processions religieuses chez les Arabes préislamites* (*BIFAO*, Cairo 1910, p. 39—101), esp. p. 64 and 78; do., *Les sanctuaires préislamites dans l'Arabie occidentale* (*MFOB*, xi. 2), Bairūt 1926, esp. p. 119, 129—133; C. Clemen, *Der ursprüngliche Sinn des ḥaǧǧ* (*Isl.*, x., 161—177), p. 165—167.

ʿURF. [See ʿĀDA; UṢŪL, 8].

ʿURS, ʿURUS (A., Pl. *aʿrās* and *ʿurusāt*), originally the leading of the bride to her bridegroom, marriage, also the wedding feast simply. *ʿArūs* means both bridegroom and bride; in modern linguistic usage this term has however been supplanted by *ʿarīs* "bridegroom" and *ʿarūsa* "bride" (as early as the *1001 Nights*, cf. Dozy, *Supplément*). Two kinds of weddings have to be distinguished: *ʿurs* is the wedding performed in the tribe or the house of the man, and *ʿumra* is the wedding performed in the house or tribe of the woman. The two forms agree for the most part in practice; they only differ in the choice of place for the main ceremonies and in the fact that in the *ʿumra* the *zaffa* of the bride is omitted.

a. "We learn little from the poems" says G. Jacob "of the wedding customs" of the pre-Muḥammadan Arabs. They seem to have been very simple in the Arabian Peninsula itself, as is still the case among the Beduins. The pomp and display of later centuries, especially in the bridal procession, was probably unknown. The wedding lasted a week, whence it is also called *usbūʿ* (cf. *Aghānī*, xii. 145). The bride is adorned, perfumed and painted with *kuḥl*. There is an old proverb which says: "The scent behind a bride cannot be concealed" (Nöldeke, *Delectus*, p. 48, 9; Maidānī, *Proverbia*, ed. Freytag, xxiii. 269). The bride is called "the conducted one" (cf. ʿAntara, xxvii. 1); she was therefore conducted to the bridegroom, usually by a number of women without any pomp, but very quietly and simply. Sometimes she was brought in a litter (*mizaffa*), as is still the case in Mecca (Snouck Hurgronje, *Mekka*, ii. 182). A special tent was always put up for the young couple. About the bridegroom there is an old proverb: "The bridegroom wants little to be an amīr (or king)" (D̲j̲awharī, *Ṣaḥāḥ*, s.v. *ʿ-r-s*; Maidānī, *Proverbia*, xii. 143).

b. The records in Tradition are on the whole in keeping with the simple usages of the Arab pagan period. ʿĀʾis̲h̲a wore at her wedding with the Prophet a robe of red striped material which came from Baḥrain and "every woman in Madīna, when dressing (for her *zifāf*), used to borrow it from her" (Buk̲h̲ārī, *Hiba*, bāb 34). For Fāṭima's wedding with ʿAlī, ʿĀʾis̲h̲a and Umm Salama made the preparations at home; they scattered soft dust from the Baṭḥāʾ over the ground and filled two cushions with fibre (*līf*) and teased it out. They laid out dates and figs to eat and sweet-tasting water to drink; they also put up at one side of the room a stand for the clothes and the water-skin (Ibn Mād̲j̲a, *Nikāḥ*, bāb 24). Fāṭima's trousseau consisted of a silken robe with fringes (*k̲h̲amīl*), a water-skin (*ḳirba*) and a cushion filled with rushes (*id̲h̲k̲h̲ir*; Nasāʾī, *Nikāḥ*, bāb 81). In another tradition the Prophet allows considerable expenditure on large carpets with fringes (*anmāṭ*; Nasāʾī, *Nikāḥ*, bāb 83). From numerous traditions it is evident that the bride was conducted by her mother and other female relatives to the house of the bridegroom. When the Prophet married ʿĀʾis̲h̲a who was then six years old, she was brought by her mother Umm Rūmān to the Prophet's house; there women were awaiting her and greeted her with "For good, and bliss, and good fortune". The women then washed her hair and adorned her while the Prophet stood smiling by. She was then handed over by the women to the Prophet (Muslim, *Nikāḥ*, bāb 69; cf. Buk̲h̲ārī, *Nikāḥ*, bāb 58). Tradition gives no further details of the toilet; but the men seem also to have been perfumed. According to a tradition transmitted by Abū Huraira the Prophet uttered the following blessings at weddings: *Bāraka 'llāhu lakum* (var. *laka*) *wa-bāraka ʿalaikum* (var. *ʿalaika*) *wa-d̲j̲amaʿa bainakumā fī* (var. *ʿalā*) *k̲h̲airin* or instead of the third part: *wa-bāraka laka fīhā* (Ibn Mād̲j̲a, *Nikāḥ*, bāb 23), while he forbade the wish from the period of the D̲j̲āhilīya *bi 'l-rifāʾ wa 'l-banīn* "in harmony and with sons!" (Nasāʾī, *Nikāḥ*, bāb 73; Ibn Mād̲j̲a, *Nikāḥ*, bāb 23; Dārimī, *Nikāḥ*, bāb 6; Aḥmad b. Ḥanbal, i. 201; iii. 451). The bride was conducted to the bridegroom by young girls who sang *g̲h̲azals*; two opening lines of such a *g̲h̲azal* are preserved: *Atainākum atainākum fa-ḥaiyānā wa-ḥaiyākum* "we come to you, we come to you, may (God) give us long life and give you long life" (Ibn Mād̲j̲a, *Nikāḥ*, bāb 21; cf. also Buk̲h̲ārī, *Nikāḥ*, bāb 64) or *atainākum atainākum fa-ḥaiyūnā nuḥaiyīkum* (so it should be read!) "We come to you, we come to you, then greet us, we greet you" (Aḥmad b. Ḥanbal, iv. 78). The participation of women and children in the wedding ceremonies is according to Anas b. Mālik expressly approved by the Prophet (Buk̲h̲ārī, *Nikāḥ*, bāb 76; *Manāsik al-Anṣār*, bāb 5). On these occasions young girls used to beat tambourines (*duff*) and sing of the death of the champions of Badr, which the Prophet is definitely said to have permitted (Buk̲h̲ārī, *Nikāḥ*, bāb 49; *Mag̲h̲āzī*, bāb 12; Ibn Mād̲j̲a, *Nikāḥ*, bāb 20, 21; Tirmid̲h̲ī, *Nikāḥ*, bāb 6; Nasāʾī, *Nikāḥ*, bāb 72, 80; Ṭayālisī, No. 1221; Aḥmad b. Ḥanbal, iii. 418).

A wedding feast (*walīma* or *ṭaʿām*) for the men was part of the wedding (Buk̲h̲ārī, *Nikāḥ*, bāb 69; Aḥmad b. Ḥanbal, v. 359; Zaid, *Mad̲j̲mūʿ*, No. 949; etc.). A feast is obligatory (*ḥaḳḳ*) for the first day and commendable (*maʿrūf*; for the second (Tirmid̲h̲ī regards it also as *sunna*), and on the third day ostentation (*sumʿa wa-riyāʾ*, i.e. done in order that people may hear and see it; Tirmid̲h̲ī, *Nikāḥ*, bāb 10; Abū Dāʾūd, *Aṭʿima*, bāb 5; Dārimī, *Aṭʿima*, bāb 28; Ibn Mād̲j̲a, *Nikāḥ*, bāb 25; Aḥmad b. Ḥanbal, v. 28, 371). Saʿīd b. al-Musaiyab (according to Dārimī: the Prophet) is said to have accepted the invitation for the first two days, but refused that for the third (Abū Dāʾūd, *Aṭʿima*, bāb 5; Dārimī, *Aṭʿima*, bāb 28). Buk̲h̲ārī, in the superscription to *Nikāḥ*, bāb 72, speaks of a week's feasting and says that the Prophet did not limit it to one or two days. The feast at the Prophet's wedding with Ṣafīya consisted of *ḥais*, a dish of dates, curds (*aḳiṭ*) and fat, to which according to some traditions was added meal of roasted barley (*sawīḳ*); according to another tradition, the Prophet used on this occasion another $1^1/_2$ *mudd* of the best kind of dates (*ʿad̲j̲wa*). At the Prophet's wedding with Zainab and at the wedding of Rabīʿa al-Aslamī bread and meat were given, which seems to have been usual along with *ḥais* as in some cases it is specially mentioned that there was no bread and meat. In other passages 2 *mudd* of barley is mentioned, or a sheep and millet; but for the *walīma* at least a sheep should be slaughtered. — As a rule the traditions give no information about the time of the *walīma*. In the few passages which admit a definite time, the *walīma* took place after the bride had been taken to the bridegroom's house but before the wedding night (Buk̲h̲ārī, *Tafsīr*, Sūra xxxiii., bāb 8; Aḥmad b. Ḥanbal, iii. 196 and the other traditions about Zainab's wedding); but the *walīma* at Ṣafīya's wedding seems to have taken place next day, probably as a result of the special conditions, as the Prophet married her on the return of the expedition to K̲h̲aibar. — An invitation to a wedding feast ought always to be accepted (Muslim, *Nikāḥ*, tr. 100, 101; Abū Dāʾūd, *Aṭʿima*, bāb 1; Aḥmad b. Ḥanbal, ii. 22). People of all conditions, rich and poor, should be invited; in one tradition given by Abū Huraira, we read: "The wedding feast at which the rich eat and from which the poor are kept away is an evil feast" (Aḥmad b. Ḥanbal, ii. 494). For further references see Wensinck, *Handbook of Early Muhammadan Tradition*, Leyden 1927, s.v. *Walīma*.

The following two traditions presumably refer to the procedure in the bridal chamber: "If any one of you marry a woman... he shall take her by her forelock and pray (to God) for blessing (*baraka*)... and pray to God for refuge from the accursed Satan" (Mālik, *Nikāḥ*, bāb 52) and "If any one of you marry a woman... he shall say: O God, I pray Thee for her good and for her good inclinations which Thou hast created, and I seek refuge with Thee from her evil and from her evil inclinations which Thou hast created" (Abū Dāʾūd, *Nikāḥ*, bāb 44). According to many traditions (Anas b. Mālik, among others), it is a *sunna* for the young husband to spend seven days and nights with his young wife if she is a virgin (*bikr*) and only three days and nights if she is not (*t̲h̲aiyib*); only after this does the regular rotation with the other wives begin. According to another tradition, the young husband should only stay three days even with a virgin and only two with a bride who is not.

As to the season of the year, the month of Shawwāl is expressly mentioned in Tradition as the month in which the Prophet celebrated his wedding with ʿĀʾisha (Nasāʾī, *Nikāḥ*, bāb 18, 77; Muslim, *Nikāḥ*, tr. 73; etc.).

c. In the Fiḳh, the Mālikīs pay special attention to wedding customs, since most of them are primarily intended to call public attention to the conclusion of the marriage. According to Mālik b. Anas as well as Ibn Abī Lailā (cf. Sarakhsī, *Mabsūṭ*, v. 30) in contrast to other schools, making the wedding public (*iʿlān*) is a necessary condition for the validity of a marriage. Witnesses are not essential for the conclusion of a contract of marriage, although with the Mālikīs it is usual to have them in practice; if the two witnesses were not present at the conclusion of the contract they must be present on the night of the wedding and for example push the bridegroom into the bridal chamber (Ḳairawānī, *Risāla*, Cairo 1338, p. 66; Khalīl, ii. 1, 59; Kāsānī, *Badāʾiʿ al-ṣanāʾiʿ*, Cairo 1327, ii. 252; Ibn Rushd [Averroes], *Bidāyat al-mudjtahid*, Cairo 1349, ii. 16 where we already find witnesses mentioned among the essentials). On the same grounds of publicity, Khalīl (ii. 1) also recommends congratulations to the bridal pair. The doors of the house should therefore not be closed at the *walīmat al-ʿurs* (Khalīl, ii. 117). This *walīma* is considered praiseworthy (*mustaḥabb*) among the Mālikīs, Ḥanafīs and Ḥanbalīs while the Shāfiʿīs hold a stricter view: according to one view, it is *sunna muʾakkada*, according to the others, it is even *wādjib* (cf. Shīrāzī, p. 205; Ghazzālī, ii. 22; Nawawī, p. 90; Ardabīlī, ii. 94). According to Khalīl, it should be held the day after the wedding, according to other Mālikīs, however, before, so that the wedding is only consummated after its public proclamation (Tīdjānī, *Tuḥfa*, p. 35). A wealthy man should kill at least a sheep, a poorer man provide as much as he can afford (Shīrāzī, Ardabīlī). To accept an invitation to a *walīma* is according to the Ḥanafīs praiseworthy (*mustaḥabb*), among the Mālikīs, Ḥanbalīs and Shāfiʿīs on the other hand a duty (*wādjib*; Shāfiʿī, *Umm*, vi. 178 says: *ḥaḳḳ*). Among the Shāfiʿīs it is praiseworthy to accept the invitation for the second day also; on the other hand, it is best to refuse it for the third day (Nawawī describes acceptance for the third day as *makrūh*). If the person invited is fasting, he should nevertheless accept the invitation; he need not however eat anything; it is best however if he breaks his fast unless he is pledged to observe it. If an intoxicated man is at the *walīma* or wine or anything else forbidden, it is best to stay away; similarly if there are in the room representations of living creatures, even if one tramples on them (e.g. on carpets). According to Shīrāzī, one should also stay away from the *walīma* where songs are sung, even if one does not listen to them and only pays attention to *ḥadīth* and eating. Music is on the other hand permitted to some extent — for example that of the tambourine (*duff*) already mentioned in tradition; Khalīl gives a list of permitted instruments: another kind of tambourine (*ghirbāl*), an older kind of lute (*mizhar*; cf. H. G. Farmer, *History of Arabian Music*, London 1929, p. 46—47), a kind of flute (*zummāra*) and horns (*būḳ*).

The question is much discussed whether one should scatter among the crowd at weddings nuts, almonds, sweets (Ardabīlī also mentions dates, dirhams and dīnārs). According to Dimashḳī (ii. 76), Abū Ḥanīfa and Aḥmad b. Ḥanbal had no objections, while Mālik, Shāfiʿī and Aḥmad b. Ḥanbal in a second opinion declare the practice *makrūh*. The views of the later Shāfiʿīs are however divided.

The considerable mass of references to marriage customs in mediaeval Islāmic literature (e.g. in the writings of belle-lettrists, preachers and moralists, popular poetry and tales — especially *Alf laila wa-laila* — and in the narratives of travellers and geographers such as Ibn al-Mudjāwir) have not yet been fully assembled and studied. Since the xv[th] century the writings of European travellers supply additional, though not always trustworthy, information. It is only with the collection of dialect texts and the systematic compilation of folklore in recent years (e.g., by Westermarck in Morocco and Jaussen in Nāblus) that there has been made available on this subject an immense quantity of material, of which only a selection is given in the bibliography below.

In general, wedding customs vary considerably from country to country. This is most clearly seen on the periphery of the Muslim world, e.g. in the Malay Archipelago, in Central Africa or among the Ḳirghiz and Turkomans. Here Islām has taken over old local customs and sometimes adapted them to its point of view. For the original lands of Islām, however, the same observation can be made, except that the process was completed earlier. In modern Syria and Egypt the customs among Muslims and Christians are almost identical except in their ecclesiastical and religious aspects. This fact shows that both go back to old customs of the Near East, at any rate not to specifically Muslim practices. Moreover, customs differ in different levels of society. Therefore, three groups at least have to be distinguished: townsmen, fellāḥīn, and beduins. The usages of the two latter are essentially simpler, and in closer agreement with the old Arab practices than those of the townsmen.

Bibliography: (cf. the article NIKĀḤ) Shāfiʿī, *K. al-umm*, Būlāḳ 1324, vi. 178; Muzanī, *Mukhtaṣar*, on the margin of the preceding, iv. 39—41; Shīrāzī, *Tanbīh*, ed. Juynboll, Leyden 1879, p. 205 *sq.*; Ghazzālī, *Wadjīz*, Cairo 1318, ii. 22; Nawawī, *Minhādj*, Cairo 1329, p. 90; Ardabīlī, *Kitāb al-anwār li-aʿmāl al-abrār*, Cairo 1328, ii. 94—96; Khalīl, *Mukhtaṣar*, transl. Santillana, Milan 1919, ii. 63 *sqq.*; Ibn Rushd, *Muḳaddimāt*, on the margin of the *Mudawwana al-kubrā*, Cairo 1324, ii. 58; Shaʿrānī, *Mīzān*, Cairo 1925, ii. 124; Dimashḳī, *Raḥmat al-umma*, on the margin of the preceding, ii. 76; Tornauw, *Das moslemische Recht*, Leipzig 1855, p. 70 *sq.*; Juynboll, *Handbuch des islamischen Gesetzes*, Leyden 1910, p. 162 *sqq.*; Gertrude H. Stern, *Marriage in early Islam*, London 1939.

For wedding-customs in general: Westermarck, *The History of Human Marriage*[5], 3 vols., London 1925; Tīdjānī [written c. 710/1310], *Tuḥfat al-ʿarūs*, Cairo 1301; *Alf Laila wa-Laila*, transl. Littmann, 6 vols., Leipzig 1921—1928; *Sīrat Saif b. Dhī Yazan*, Būlāḳ 1294; Ibn Iyās, *Badāʾiʿ al-zuhūr fī waḳāʾiʿ al-duhūr*, ed. Kahle, Istanbul 1931, vol. iv. (*Bibliotheca islamica*, v.). — For local customs: — Mecca and Madīna: J. L. Burckhardt [1814], *Travels in Arabia*, London 1829, i. 361, 399, 401—402; R. F. Burton [1853], *Personal narrative of a pilgrimage to Mecca and Medina*, Leipzig 1874, ii. 167, 253; Snouck Hurgronje, *Mekka*, Hague 1888—1889, ii. 155—187; E. Rutter, *The Holy Cities of Arabia*, London 1928, ii. 67—69.

— South-Arabia: C. Niebuhr [1763], *Reisebeschreibung nach Arabien*, Copenhagen 1774, i. 402—403; Ad. von Wrede [1843], *Reise in Ḥadhramaut*, Braunschweig 1870, p. 262 *sq.*; C. von Landberg, *Études sur les dialects de l'Arabie méridionale*, Leyden 1909, II/i. 192—202; II/ii. 717—869. — Zanzibar: E. Ruete, *Memoirs of an Arabian Princess*, New York 1888, p. 146—170. — Syria and Palestine: J. van Ghistele [1485], *Voyage*, Ghent 1557, p. 15; Joh. Cotovicus [1598—1599], *Itinerarium Hierosolymitanum et syriacum*, Antwerp 1619, p. 475—476 (reprinted in Gabriel Sionita, *Arabia*, Amsterdam 1633, p. 194—195); d'Arvieux [1659], *Mémoires*, Paris 1735, i. 447; do., *Die Sitten der Beduinen-Araber*, transl. Rosenmüller, Leipzig 1789, p. 120—124; A. Russell [c. 1750], *The Natural History of Aleppo*, London 1756, p. 110—113, 125—139; do., *Naturgeschichte von Aleppo*, transl. Gmelin, Göttingen 1797, i. 399 [rather Turkish customs], ii. 110 *sqq.* [Maronites]; J. L. Burckhardt [c. 1810], *Bemerkungen über die Beduinen und Wahaby*, Weimar 1831, p. 86 *sqq.*, 212 *sqq.*; Wetzstein, *Syrische Dreschtafel*, in *Zeitschrift f. Ethnologie*, v. (1873), 288 *sqq.*; H. H. Jessup, *The Women of the Arabs*, London 1874, p. 27 [Druses]; Klein, *Mitteilungen über Leben, Sitten und Gebräuche der Fellachen in Palästina*, in *ZDPV.*, vi. (1883), 81—101; E. Littmann, *Neuarabische Volkspoesie*, Berlin 1902, p. 94 *sqq.*, 119 *sqq.*, 137 *sqq.* [Christian]; C. T. Wilson, *Peasant life in the Holy Land*, London 1906, p. 110—115; Rothstein, *Muslimische Hochzeitsgebräuche in Lifta bei Jerusalem*, in *Palästinajahrbuch*, vi. (1910), 102—136 (with pictures); Al. Musil, *Arabia Petraea*, Vienna 1908, iii. 186 *sqq.* [Fellāḥīn], 196 *sqq.* [Beduins]; G. Bergsträsser [1914], *Zum arabischen Dialekt von Damaskus*, Hanover 1924, i. 64—67; Chémali, *Marriage et noce au Liban*, in *Anthropos*, x./xi. (1915—1916), 913—941 (with pictures); K. Daghestani, *La Famille musulmane contemporaine en Syrie*, Paris n.d.; Spoer and Haddad, *Volkskundliches aus el-Qubêbe bei Jerusalem*, in *ZS*, iv. (1926), 199—126, v. (1927), 95—134; A. Jaussen, *Coutumes Palestiniennes*, i., *Naplouse et son district*, Paris 1927, p. 67 *sqq.*; Al. Musil, *The Manners and Customs of the Rwala Bedouins*, New York 1928, p. 135 *sqq.*; T. Canaan, *Unwritten laws affecting the Arab Women of Palestine*, in *Journal of the Palestine Oriental Society*, xi. (1931), 190, 192, 199; Hilma Granqvist, *Marriage Conditions in a Palestinian village*, Helsingfors 1931-35 [Muslims]. — Mesopotamia: Br.Meissner, *Neuarab.Geschichten aus dem ʿIrâq*, Leipzig 1903, p. 107. — Egypt: Nic. Christ. Radzivil [1583], *Jerosolymitana peregrinatio*, Antwerp 1614, p. 186 *sq.*; Cl. Savary [1777], *Zustand des alten und neuen Egyptens*, Berlin 1788, iii. 261—264; *Description de l'Egypte*², Paris 1826, xviii. 85—89; J. L. Burckhardt [1817], *Arabische Sprichwörter*, Weimar 1834, p. 171 *sqq.*, No. 422; E. Lane [1835], *Manners and Customs of the Modern Egyptians*⁵, London 1871, i. 197—222; E. Lane, *Arabic society in the middle ages*, p. 232 *sqq.*; Alf. von Kremer, *Ägypten*, Leipzig 1863, i. 58 *sqq.* [Fellāḥīn]; Klunzinger [1872—1875], *Bilder aus Oberägypten*², Stuttgart 1878, p. 193 *sqq.* [Ḳuṣair], p. 260 [Beduins]; W. S. Blackman, *The Fellâḥîn of Upper Egypt*, London 1927, p. 90 *sqq.*; Out el Kouloub, *Harem*, Paris 1937, 45—71. — Tripolitania: O. Gabelli, *Usanze nuziali in Tripolitania*, in *Riv. della Tripolitania*, 1926; Curotti, *Gente di Libia*, in *La Quarta Sponda*, 1927; Pfalz, *Arabische Hochzeitsgebräuche in Tripolitanien*, in *Anthropos*, xxiv. (1929), 221—227; Bertarelli, *Guida d'Italia. Possedimenti e Colonie*, Milan 1929, 221—223. — Tunis: Ch. de Peyssonel and Desfontaines [xviiith century], *Voyages dans les régences de Tunis et d'Alger*, Paris 1838, i. 175, ii. 42—43; Maltzan, *Reise in den Regentschaften Tunis und Tripolis*, Leipzig 1870, iii. 88—92; K. Narbeshuber, *Aus dem Leben der arab. Bevölkerung in Sfax*, Leipzig 1907, p. 11—16; L. Bertholon and E. Chantre, *Recherches anthropologiques sur les indigènes de la Berbérie Orientale*, Paris 1913, i. 575—586; W. Marçais and Abderrahmân Guiga, *Textes arabes de Takroûna*, Paris 1925, i. 355 *sqq.*, 381 *sqq.*; W. Reitz, *Bei Berbern und Beduinen*, Stuttgart 1926, p. 142 *sqq.* — Algeria: Haëdo [xvith century], *Topographie et histoire générale d'Alger*, in *R. Afr.*, xv. (1871), 96—101; d'Arvieux [1674], *Mémoires*, Paris 1735, v. 287; J. P. Bonnafont [1830—1842], *Pérégrination en Algérie*, Paris 1884, p. 152 *sqq.*; F. Mornand, *La vie arabe*, Paris 1856, p. 57 *sq.*; L. Féraud, *Moeurs et coutumes Kabiles*, in *R. Afr.*, vi. (1862), 280, 430—432; Villot, *Moeurs, coutumes...des indigènes de l'Algérie*³, Algiers 1888, p. 97 *sqq.*; Gaudefroy-Demombynes, *Notes de sociologie maghrébine. Cérémonies du mariage chez les indigènes de l'Algérie*, Paris 1901; Bel, *La population musulmane de Tlemcen*, in *Revue des études ethnograph. et sociologiques*, i. (1908), 215 *sqq.*; A. M. Goichon, *La vie féminine au Mzab*, Paris 1927, p. 73 *sqq.*, 280 *sqq.* — Morocco: Leo Africanus [1526], *Description de l'Afrique*, ed. Ch. Schefer, Paris 1897, ii. 120—125; J. Mocquet [1605], *Voyages*, Rouen 1685, p. 204—205; Diego de Torres, *Histoire des Cherifs*, Paris 1667, p. 144; G. Hoest [1760—1768], *Nachrichten von Marókos und Fes*, Copenhagen 1781, p. 102—104; Edm. Westermarck, *Marriage ceremonies in Morocco*, London 1914; Legey, *Essai de Folklore marocain*, Paris 1926, p. 134 *sqq.*; M. Gaudry, *La femme Chaouia de l'Aurès*, Paris 1928, p. 78—83; Jérome and Jean Tharaud, *Fez*, Paris 1930, p. 130 *sqq.*; L. Brunot, *Textes arabes de Rabat*, Paris 1931, No. 16 and 17. — Sūdān: Zain al-ʿĀbidīn al-Tūnisī [c. 1820], *Das Buch des Sudan*, transl. Rosen, 1847, p. 28 *sqq.*; Ing. Pallme, *Travels in Kordofan*, London 1844, p, 81—86; Seligman, *Kabâbîsh*, in *Harvard African Studies*, ii. (1918), 131 *sqq.*; J. S. Trimingham, *Islam in the Sudan*, London 1949, 182 *sq.* — Turkey: H. Dernschwam [1553—1555], *Tagebuch einer Reise nach Konstantinopel u. Kleinasien*, ed. Babinger, Munich 1923, p. 135—133; Salomon Schweigger [1578], *Newe Reyssbeschreibung nach Konstantinopel*, Nürnberg 1608, p. 205 *sqq.*; P. della Valle [1615], *Reiss-Beschreibung*, Geneva 1674, i. 43; Thevenot [1657], *Voyages*, Paris 1689, i. 171 *sq.*; de Tournefort, *Relation d'un voyage de Levant*, Paris 1717, ii. 364—366; Olivier [1793—1797], *Voyage dans l'empire othoman*, Paris 1800, i. 154—157; Ch. White, *Three years in Constantinople*, London 1845, iii. 6—14; do., *Häusliches Leben und Sitten der Türken*, transl. Reumont, Berlin 1845, ii. 309 *sqq.*; Osman Bey, *Les Femmes en Turquie*, Paris 1883; L. N. J. Garnett, *The women of Turkey*, London 1891, esp. ii. 480—489; Th. Löbel, *Hochzeitsgebräuche in der Türkei*, Amsterdam 1897. — Persia: Olearius [1637], *Muscovitische u. Persische Reyse*², Schleswig 1656, p. 605—608; J. B. Tavernier [1664], *Les six voyages*, Paris 1779, i. 719—720; Chardin [1673], *Voyages*, ed. Langlès, Paris 1811, ii. 233 *sqq.*; John Fryer [1678], *A new Account of East India* *and Persia*, London 1915 (*Hakluyt Society*), iii. 129, 138; (*Kitāb-i Kulthūm-nane*), *Customs and manners of the women of Persia*, transl. Atkinson, London 1832, p. 42 *sqq.*, 70 *sqq.*; Ed. Polak, *Persien*, Leipzig 1865, i. 210 *sqq.*; C. J. Wills, *Persia as it is*, London 1886, p. 57 *sqq.*; S. G. Wilson, *Persian Life and Customs* [3], New York 1899, p. 237—239 [ʿAlī Ilāhī's]; Ritter, *Aserbeidschanische Texte zur nordpersischen Volkskunde*, in *Isl.*, xi. (1921), 189 *sqq.*; H. Norden, *Persien* Leipzig 1929, p. 86—89. — Russia: W. Radloff [1860—1870], *Aus Sibirien*, Leipzig 1893, i. 476—484 [Kirgiz]; H. Vámbéry [1863], *Reise in Mittelasien*, Leipzig 1865, p. 258—259 [Turkomans]; E. Schuyler, *Turkistan* [5], London 1876, i. 42—43 [Kirgiz], i. 142 *sqq.* [Tashkent]; H. Lansdell [c. 1880], *Russisch-Central-Asien*, Leipzig 1885, p. 248—252 [Kirgiz], p. 831—832 [Khīwa]; H. Vámbéry, *Das Türkenvolk*, Leipzig 1885, p. 229—250 [Kirgiz], p. 433—434 [Kazan Tartars], p. 540—542 [Krim-Tatars]; R. Karutz, *Unter Kirgisen und Türkmenen*, Leipzig 1911, p. 101 *sqq.*; Pelissier, *Mischärtatarische Sprachproben*, Berlin 1919 (*Abh. Pr. Ak. W.*, 1918), p. 3 *sqq.*, 28; Sciatskaya, *Antiche cerimonie nuziali dei Tatari di "Crimea Vecchia" e dei dintorni*, in *OM.*, viii. (1928), 542—548; Essad Bey, *Zwölf Geheimnisse im Kaukasus*, Leipzig 1930, p. 52 *sqq.* — India: P. della Valle [1629 in Surat], *Reissbeschreibung*, Geneva 1674, iv. 12; Thevenot [1666 in Surat], *Voyages*, Paris 1689, iii. 66 *sqq.* [with illustr.]; John Fryer [1674 in Surat], *op. cit.*, i. 237; Hassan Ali, *Observations of the Musulmans of India*, London 1832, i., letter xiii./xiv.; C. A. Herklots [1832], *Islam in India*, Oxford 1921, p. 57 *sqq.* — Indonesia: Wilken, *Plechtigheden en gebruiken bij verlovingen en huwelijken bij de volken van den Ind. Archipel*, in *BTLV*, series v., i. (1886), 167—219; iv. (1889), 380—462; Snouck Hurgronje, *Verspreide Geschriften*, Bonn 1924, IV/i. 226 *sqq.*; do., *The Achehnese*, Leyden 1906, i. 329 *sqq.*

ʿUSHR, the tenth or tithe levied for public assistance, is frequently used in the sense of *ṣadaḳa* and *zakāt* (Abū Yūsuf, p. 31; Yaḥyā b. Ādam, p. 79, 83, 121, 123) and indeed there is no very strict line drawn in the Sharīʿa books between zakāt and ʿushr dues (cf. Tornauw, p. 318). The term ʿushr is not found in the Ḳurʾān but Sūra vi. 141 is taken to refer to the tithe or half tithe (Abū Yūsuf, p. 32; Yaḥyā b. Ādam, p. 88 *sq.*). Etymologically ʿushr is the same as the Assyrian *ish-ru-u* (E. Schrader, *Keilinschriftl. Bibliothek*, iv. 192, 205) which means tribute paid in kind (corn, dates) or in gold, and with the Hebrew *maʿashēr* (Gen. xiv. 20; xxix. 20—22), the tenth which the sanctuaries received but which was also levied by kings and which the Mosaic law wished to introduce as compulsory (Lev. xxvii. 30—33; Num. xviii. 21—26).

An investigation of the significance of the tenth as a tax among neighbouring peoples is therefore important and necessary because light is thereby thrown on Arab conditions. Of great significance is the fact recorded by Pliny, *Hist. Nat.*, xii. 63 especially for South Arabia (*Arabia felix*) that the tenth part of the frankincense harvest was collected by the priests for the god Sin (MS. SABIN) out of which to meet public expenses and the maintenance of guests. In the inscriptions we find *ʿushr* and *ʿshwrt* along with *frʿ* as a tax and both are taken by N. Rhodokanakis, *Studien zur Lexikographie und Grammatik des Altsüdarabischen* ii., *SB Ak. Wien*, clxxxv./3, 1917, p. 58 to be taxes on land, which however came under the temple taxes. According to Sūra iv. 138, the pagan Arabs, even the Ḳuraish, both Beduins and Fellāḥīn offered a gift from their fruits of the field and animals to Allāh or other gods, which in practice of course went to the guardians of the sanctuary. Muḥammad, probably deliberately, deprived the tenth of any connection with worship and, perhaps on the analogy of South Arabian customs, made the tithe a kind of tax. Thus, in his letter to the Khathʿam in Bīshr (J. Wellhausen, *Skizzen und Vorarbeiten*, iv., Berlin 1889, No. 68, p. 130), it is laid down that a tenth is to be paid on all lands irrigated by running streams and a half tenth on lands artificially irrigated. This also held for the oasis of Dūmat al-Djandal (*ibid.*, No. 119, p. 173) and the Ḥimyar (Yaḥyā b. Ādam, p. 83); in the letter to the latter the tithe is called *ṣadaḳa*. For the nomads around Ṣuḥār for example a tax of one in ten loads of dates is fixed for their palmgroves (J. Wellhausen, *op. cit.*, No. 69, p. 130).

Mecca, Madīna, the Ḥidjāz, the Yaman and the Arabian territory were thus regarded as ʿushr land (E. Fagnan, p. 89) from which alone the tenth was to be raised (*op. cit.*, p. 79) and this was contrasted with the *kharādj* land on which the land tax was levied. With the gradual expansion of the Islāmic empire, the ʿushr land increased considerably in area. For example at the conquest of al-Raḳḳa (18 A.H.) the lands which the protected people (*ahl al-dhimma*) did not use were given to Muslims on payment of the tithe (*Annali dell' Islām*, iv. 40). The lands acquired by peace treaties, on which no land tax was levied became ʿushr land in so far as they belonged to new converts (Yaḥyā b. Ādam, p. 15). Further all land on which no land tax was levied became ʿushr land on the conversion of its owner, if the cultivator dug a well or an irrigation channel (Fagnan, p. 99).

A considerable increase in ʿushr land also resulted from the transference of land by sale or gift. If for example a Muslim bought land from the Banū Taghlib he paid the tithe, according to others the double *ṣadaḳa*; the same held of every member of this tribe or Christians generally who became converts to Islām, since the land thereby became ʿushr land (Yaḥyā b. Ādam, p. 12, 16, 46 *sq.*). Land in areas acquired by treaties of peace became ʿushr land in so far as it had been acquired by Muslims by purchase, even if the payment of land tax was expressly laid down in the treaty (*op. cit.*, p. 37). The tithe was also to be levied on naturally irrigated *ḳaṭāʾiʿ* lands in Sawād (Fagnan, p. 79). C. H. Becker, *Islāmstudien*, p. 230 *sqq.*, has shown how ʿushr land developed in Egypt. Gifts of land to meritorious Muslims and purchase by Muslims from Copt landowners here made the land ʿushr land, which in Egypt certainly developed to a considerable extent out of the old domains. On the other hand, the practice of allowing new converts to pay only the tenth frequently created ʿushr land. Of the rules which were in force regarding the transference of ʿushr land it may be mentioned that allies (*muʿāhid*) who acquired ʿushr land by purchase had to pay *kharādj*, which remained a burden on the land if it was sold again to a Muslim. This at any rate is the Ḥanafī teaching (Yaḥyā b. Ādam, p. 16). If on the other hand a Christian buys ʿushr land from a Muslim he has to pay the double tithe (*khums*), which is regarded as a double *ṣadaḳa*. The land is further treated as *ʿushrī* if the owner becomes converted to Islām (*op. cit.*). This had of course great disadvantages for the treasury, as had the sale of *kharādj* land to a Muslim, and therefore ʿUmar II laid it down that in the latter case the land tax fell upon the new owner, who had also to pay the tithe or half tithe on the produce and agricultural land, as the *kharādj* was due upon the soil and the tithe or half tithe was due as *zakāt* from the Muslims (Yaḥyā b. Ādam, p. 1.). This regulation was however in contradiction to the principle that (according to ʿIkrima) *kharādj* and ʿushr could not be levied at the same time, any more than *ʿushr* with *zakāt* or *djizya* (poll-tax), and ʿUmar I had already prohibited the collection of the tithe from a Muslim or ally when he paid *kharādj* (*ibid.*, p. 10, 32, 46). How far this limitation was actually observed is impossible to say. How greatly the practice varied is clear from Māwardī (p. 104) according to whom an ally who owns ʿushr land has to pay neither ʿushr nor *kharādj* according to the Shāfiʿīs, *kharādj* according to the Ḥanafīs, *ṣadaḳa* according to others, while according to Yaḥyā b. Ādam, p. 15, the ally of the tribe of Taghlib who bought ʿushr land had to pay the double tithe, but if he belonged to a tribe which had been adopted into the Islāmic state as an ally, he paid neither ʿushr nor *kharādj*. Further it was open to the Imām — in practice the financial administrator of the province and the machinery of collection — to turn *kharādj* land into ʿushr land (Fagnan, p. 89) so that in later times the rule as to what land paid *kharādj* and what paid ʿushr was treated quite arbitrarily and at most we can observe a certain tendency to observe principles generally regarded as valid and sanctified by custom. In the letting of lands and *muzāraʿa* agreements the rule was probably that the cultivator of ʿushr land should pay a tenth or twentieth of the yield, according to the kind of ground (Yaḥyā b. Ādam, p. 121). If a Muslim takes over the land of an ally to till it he pays a tenth of the yield, the *dhimmī* the land-tax; if he has leased untilled land out of the *kharādj* land, the landlord pays the *kharādj* but the cultivator no tithe (Yaḥyā b. Ādam, p. 120).

If the untilled land is *ʿushrī* the cultivator has to pay $^1/_{10}$ or $^1/_{20}$ of the yield as *zakāt* (*op. cit.*, p. 116, 123). If a Muslim has leased *ʿushrī* untilled land, he pays the tenth while the landlord pays nothing (*ibid.*, p. 124). The Muslim also pays on rented *kharādj* land $^1/_{10}$ or $^1/_{20}$ of the yield as *zakāt*, the landlord the *kharādj* (this is the Shāfiʿī practice) while the Ḥanafīs make the landlord pay tithe (Māwardī, p. 105). The same thing holds if owner and occupier are the same individual (Yaḥyā b. Ādam, p. 118—120). According to Māwardī, p. 104, however, the Muslim occupier, as having contracted an agreement to cultivate a piece of *kharādj* land has to pay tithe and *kharādj* (Shāfiʿī), only the *kharādj* according to the Ḥanafīs.

According to Abū Yūsuf (Fagnan, p. 79), the tithe was only to be paid on durable products of the land but not on vegetables, fodder or fuel, according to Yaḥyā b. Ādam (p. 84, 105) on palms, wheat, barley, grapes, raisins, while (*op. cit.*, p. 79, 101) it is laid down that the tithe is to be levied as *zakāt* on all that the earth produces, even if it be only a bundle of green stuff. The latter is according to Yaḥyā b. Ādam (p. 103) along with walnuts, almonds, and all fruit, only liable to tithe in the form of *zakāt* if it is over 200 dirhams in value. For dates the limit of exemption is 5 *wasḳ* (Fagnan, p. 80). ʿUmar levied no tax on vines, peaches and pomegranates, while wine and oil are regarded as liable to tithe (*ibid.*, p. 50, 111). According to some, ʿushr is levied on honey, according to others, only when it is produced on ʿushr land (*op. cit.*, p. 17); this also holds of saffron. As a kind of trade-tax, the ʿushr was levied on merchants coming into Islāmic territory and the ally paid a twentieth but a tenth on wine and pigs (*op. cit.*, p. 32—49 *sq.*). Muslims under age are according to some jurists exempt from the tithes, according to others not (*op. cit.*, p. 48).

The half, single, one and a half and double tenth are the rates for the ʿushr; we even have higher ones, for they are fixed quite at the discretion of the Imām (Fagnan, p. 90). It is however a principle and it is in keeping with the old practice that the tenth is levied on all land which is irrigated by running water, brooks and streams or by rain, the half tenth on land which is irrigated by carried water, by water-wheels or water drawn by camels (Yaḥyā b. Ādam, p. 78, 80—86).

The income from the tithes could be used for other than benevolent purposes. Thus for example, the administrator of the provincial revenues in Egypt, ʿUbaid Allāh b. Ḥabḥāb, gave the Ḳais who were settled here funds to buy beasts of burden out of the tithes (Maḳrīzī, *Abhandlung*, p. 488). Echoes of the ancient pre-Islāmic practice have survived in South Arabia where the *raʿīye* pay ʿushr to the sulṭān or amīr; here it is also called *ʿashīra* but it is worth noting that it is mainly levied on the fruits of the field, corn, dates coffee, indigo etc. Among the Barkān and the people of ʿAryab, the corn is piled up, measured and $^1/_{10}$ of the wheat set aside, of which the poor of the sanctuary receive the half and the other half goes to the *mashāʾikh*, a custom which has analogies with the conditions in the Bible and also with those recorded by Pliny.

Bibliography: Yaḥyā b. Ādam al-Ḳurashī, *Kitāb al-kharādj*, ed. T. W. Juynboll, Leyden 1896; Abū Yūsuf Yaʿḳūb b. Ibrāhīm, *Kitāb al-kharādj*, Būlāḳ 1302; transl. by E. Fagnan, *Le livre de l'impot foncier* (*Kitâb el-Kharâdj*), Paris 1921; Abu 'l-Ḥasan ʿAlī b. Muḥammad b. Ḥabīb al-Māwardī, *Kitāb al-aḥkām al-sulṭānīya*, Cairo 1909, p. 104 *sq.*; F. Wüstenfeld, *el-Macrizi's Abhandlung über die in Agypten eingewanderten arabischen Stämme*, in *Göttinger Studien*, 1847, p. 488; J. von Hammer, *Über die Länderverwaltung unter dem Chalifate*, Berlin 1835, p. 113, 119 *sq.*, 122 *sq.*; A. v. Kremer, *Culturgeschichte des Orients unter den Chalifen*, i., Vienna 1875, i. p. 55; v. Tornauw, *Das Eigentumsrecht nach moslemischem Rechte*, in *ZDMG*, xxxvi., 1882, p. 294, 318; M. van Berchem, *La propriété territoriale et l'impot foncier sous les premiers califes, étude sur l'impot du kharâg*, Geneva 1886, p. 9, 14, 31, 40 *sq.*, 69; C. H. Becker, *Islamstudien*, i., Leipzig 1924, p. 230 *sq.*; A. Grohmann, *Südarabien als Wirtschaftsgebiet*, i., Vienna 1922, p. 74, note 2, 80, 81, 85, 101; iii. 6, 35, note 1.

UṢŪL (A.), roots, principles, pl. of *aṣl*. Among the various terminological uses of this word, three are prominent as terms for branches of Muslim learning: *uṣūl al-dīn*, *uṣūl al-ḥadīth* and *uṣūl al-fiḳh*. *Uṣūl al-dīn* is synonymous with *kalām* [q.v.]; by *uṣūl al-ḥadīth* is meant the treatment of the terminology and methods of the science of Tradition [see ḤADĪTH]; the *uṣūl al-fiḳh*, frequently called simply (science of the) *Uṣūl*, are the doctrine of the "principles" of Muslim jurisprudence, *fiḳh* [q.v.].

1. In the usual classification of Muslim sciences, the *uṣūl al-fiḳh* are generally defined as the methodology of Muslim jurisprudence, as the science of the proofs which lead to the establishment of legal standards in general. Its existence is justified by the consideration that man was not created without

a purpose (Sūra xxiii. 115) and is not aimlessly left to himself (Sūra lxxv. 36) but that all his actions are regulated by legal standards; as there cannot be a special standard for every individual case, one has to depend for the derivation on proofs. These proofs, according to the view which finally prevailed, are four: *Ḳur'ān*, *sunna*, *idjmā*ʿ and *ḳiyās* [q.v.]. In the *uṣūl al-fiḳh*, therefore, we are not so much concerned with the material sources of Islāmic law as with the formal basis of the individual prescriptions. Thus the four *uṣūl* include in addition to two material sources, *Ḳur'ān* and *sunna*, which are regarded from the point of view, not of their substance but of their legal force, the general condition of *idjmā*ʿ and the method of *ḳiyās*, while other historically no less important sources of Muslim law are not recognized. The development of these and other *uṣūl* which did not attain full recognition is somewhat as follows.

2. The logically first and most highly esteemed source of law in Islām is of course the Ḳur'ān; there could be no doubt of its final authority and infallibility — even if the devil might have attempted to falsify it (cf. the commentaries on Sūra xxii. 52 and Nöldeke-Schwally, *Gesch. d. Qorāns*, i. 100), nor could there be any doubt that it had been handed down essentially intact (cf. *ibid.*, i. 261; ii. 93) — even if the Prophet had forgotten some verses (Sūra ii. 106; lxxxvii. 6 *sq.*). The fact that the Ḳur'ān itself describes several of its sections as abrogated (*mansūkh*) by later revelations (Sūra ii. 106; xvi. 101 *sq.*; cf. Nöldeke-Schwally, *op. cit.*, ii. 52 *sqq.*), is not in contradiction to this. It was the task of later interpretation to eliminate the numerous contradictions within the Ḳur'ān, which reflect the development of Muḥammad's prophetical mission, by harmonising them or in extreme cases by assuming that the later revelation abrogated the earlier. It was in no way the Prophet's intention to create, even in its main outlines, a "system" which was to regulate the whole life of his followers; on the contrary, the old Arab customary law, which already included many elements of foreign origin, remained in force in Islām as a matter of course with its variations reflecting the local and social conditions (Beduins, the commercial town Mecca, the agrarian oasis Madīna); the new legislation contained in the Ḳur'ān does not go farther than to correct isolated points out of considerations of religion — for even the modifications affecting social life have a religious basis — from case to case, mostly with regard to concrete happenings. Including the verses dealing with questions of ritual and worship and those of a military or political nature, the total number of verses of legal importance known as *al-āyāt al-sharʿīya* is only about 500—600; but essential parts of the legislation affecting worship, e.g. the ritual of the *ṣalāt*, were not regulated by the Ḳur'ān, but simply by the example and guidance of the Prophet, and also a number of prescriptions given by Muḥammad, usually of minor importance and not intended for general application, although having prophetic authority, are not in the Ḳur'ān (cf. Nöldeke-Schwally, *op. cit.*, i. 260). From the beginning, the authority of the Prophet, even apart from transmitting the Ḳur'ānic revelation, has never been doubted in Islām; at the same time, however, his actions as a mere mortal were not considered infallible even in religious matters and on several occasions he was sharply criticized by his companions. The abolition of certain practices in which Muḥammad had found no harm, in the first period after his death, points in the same direction. The Prophet himself made no claim to infallibility; the Ḳur'ān expressly states (e.g. Sūra xviii. 110; xli. 5) that, although he was the transmitter of revelation, in other respects he was a man "like others" and sometimes even condemns his attitude (e.g. Sūra lxi. 1).

3. With the death of Muḥammad, legislative activity through Ḳur'ānic revelation and prophetic authority of course came to an end. It was natural that the early caliphs should endeavour to guide the Islāmic community on the lines of its founder, in consultation with the leading Companions of the Prophet. The guiding principles were to be found in the Ḳur'ān and in authoritative decisions of Muḥammad outside it. The endeavour to extend these comparatively narrow foundations led very early to their interpretation being broadened beyond the original meaning and probably even then to the rise of alleged traditions from the Prophet. At the same time the caliphs, as heads of their state and representatives of the Prophet, did not refrain from legislative activity of their own and from sometimes even altering decisions of Muḥammad. It may be historical that according to tradition Abū Bakr is represented as modelling himself exactly on the Prophet in this connection and ʿUmar rather as showing more tendency to interfere and change. The relationship to customary law continued unchanged, even after the latter had been more than ever exposed to foreign influence as a result of the great conquests in the ʿIrāḳ, Syria and Egypt.

4. With the coming of the Umaiyads and the transference of the seat of government to Damascus the circles of the devout in Madīna, hitherto the centre, lost all actual influence on the business of government. They therefore began to devote themselves with all the more zeal to preparing an ideal picture of things as they ought to be, in contrast to the actual practice. While in reality the customary law continued to exist undisturbed in the various provinces of the caliphate, and developed in combination with the actual administration of justice — for the Umaiyad caliphs, with the exception of ʿUmar II, had in general little inclination to interfere and establish standards based on religion — the foundations of Muslim law were laid in Madīna and also in the ʿIrāḳ and Syria. The object of those pious men who at first worked without any thought of theory or method, was to correct and adjust the material of the laws they found in existence, according to Muslim religious principles, and to systematize it. They took their religious standards from the Ḳur'ān and those traditions which they recognized as binding; the (real and alleged) sayings and actions of the Companions of the Prophet, of whom as a body they were the successors, had also high authority with them. It was of special importance when a majority of the Companions had acted in the same way and the same majority principle did a great deal to cause individual views gradually to approximate to one another. The results of these reflections were for the most part formulated in traditions and put in the mouth of the Prophet. This considerable increase in the material of Tradition, from other sources also, again introduced into Muslim law numerous new elements, amongst which those of Jewish origin deserve special mention. That activity resulted in establishing once and for all certain characteristic peculiarities of Muslim law: its character as the interpretation and unfolding of the prescriptions, given in essence at least, by Allāh

through his Prophet, the denial of the possibility of development and of legislative activity after the death of the Prophet in contrast to the historical facts, the recognition of the usage of the Prophet, the *sunnat al-nabī*, as the second main standard occupying a place inferior to the Ḳurʾān only in rank, not in power and authority. It was just because the teaching was based for a very large part on Muḥammad's (real or fictitious) *sunna* that thisw as regarded as an infallible standard for the Muslim community, a view which was with difficulty read into the Ḳurʾān (e.g. iii. 32; iv. 59; xvi. 44; xxxiii. 21; liii. 3) but was distinctly laid down in Tradition. The contradictions, which naturally appeared much more frequently in Tradition than in the Ḳurʾān, were to be disposed of by the same means as in the latter, and also by criticism of the *isnāds*, behind which criticism of the subject matter had, it is interesting to note, usually to conceal itself. On the other hand, the free use, openly avowed, of individual reasoning, especially in the ʿIrāḳ, should not be underestimated (cf. the beginning of the next paragraph). The more or less strongly islāmicized customary law still remained quite naturally the basic material for the juridical activity of this period, especially when it aroused no misgivings from the religious point of view. As its Muslim equivalent, the "*sunna* of pious men" is sometimes given particular authority. During this whole time, the office of the *ḳāḍī* acted as an important intermediary between legal doctrine and practice.

5. The first reflections on theory were provoked towards the end of this period, at the beginning of the second (eighth) century, by the coming into existence of a special science of *ḥadīth* alongside of *fiḳh*. The representatives of the former reproached the "jurists", those who were mostly engaged in developing the positive law, with bringing by their use of reason a human element into the law which ought rather to be based exclusively on the Ḳurʾān and on Tradition as representing the *sunna* of the Prophet. The opponents replied to this by saying that one's own intelligence (*raʾy*) was indispensable for the deduction of legal precepts, and both parties cited traditions to support their views. From the first, the dispute was more concerned with form than matter and frequently was simply a quarrel over words; the result of it was the general recognition in principle of the place of *raʾy* in the *fiḳh*, the various schools laying varying emphasis on *ḥadīth*; at any rate the results obtained are everywhere of much the same kind. As early as the first half of the second (eighth) century three different shades of *fiḳh* had developed in the three centres of the Ḥidjāz, the ʿIrāḳ and Syria, in the origin and spread of which geographical conditions had played an essential part, on the one hand through developing life and doctrine uniformly within closed areas and on the other through the original differences of the basic legal material in the different regions; these variants were the precursors of the later *madhhabs* of Mālik, Abū Ḥanīfa and al-Awzāʿī; the Ḥidjāz school laid most emphasis on Tradition and the ʿIrāḳ school on *raʾy*. In these circumstances the views held by the majority of learned men in Madīna (or Mecca and Madīna) or in Kūfa or in Baṣra carried particular weight. To about the middle of the second (eighth) century belong the first writings of any length by important representatives of these three schools, especially of the Ḥidjāz and the ʿIrāḳ, which enable us to see the character of their arguments; this sketch is based on the results of the study of Mālik's *al-Muwaṭṭaʾ*, the only work that has been at all studied in this connection. Mālik devotes great care to establishing the *idjmāʿ* of the learned men of Madīna; this conception, which originally had simply meant the majority (just as in the science of Ḳurʾānic readings which borrowed the term from the *fiḳh*), has here already become the qualified majority, approaching unanimity. At the same time Mālik recognizes as authoritative the *sunna*, i.e. legal use and wont in Madīna, which is not yet at all identical with the *sunnat al-nabī*. Both *idjmāʿ* and *sunna* of Madīna are to him closely connected; his work represents the degree of islāmicization of the customary law attained in his time in Madīna and — as is evident from a comparison with the later period — this process was now fairly complete. The great works of al-Shaibānī were undoubtedly something similar for the ʿIrāḳ.

6. In al-Shāfiʿī (d. 204/820) we have the founder of Muslim jurisprudence. It is his great achievement that in him legal thought becomes conscious of itself and thus becomes a science, that he argues not only occasionally and *ad hoc* but throughout and on principle and that he also discusses the starting points and methods of argumentation in jurisprudence. The most important steps in advance which he made in the *uṣūl al-fiḳh*, based on the results of previous development, are as follows. He finally defines *sunna* as a source of law as being the usage of the Prophet, as the ʿIrāḳ school had already done before him. He further defines the *idjmāʿ* as the view held by the majority of Muslims and uses it as a secondary source of elucidation on questions which cannot be decided from the Ḳurʾān and the *sunna* of the Prophet; he justifies its authority by general considerations and by traditions which order adhesion to the community of Muslims, but he does not yet know the *ḥadīth* later often quoted: "My community will never agree upon an error". While the islāmicization of law had in general been already completed before Mālik, al-Shāfiʿī did a great deal to advance its systematization. To attain this object, he to some extent abandoned the method, which had already made its first appearance before him, of laying down exact juridical definitions, and if he did not invent the process of *ḳiyās* (analogy), he considerably developed the principle and applied it extensively. It is essentially the old method of *raʾy* which he adopts here under this less ominous name, which at the same time points to a certain restriction in its application. (Among the old representatives of the ʿIrāḳ school *ḳiyās* seems to have been used to dispose of isolated abnormal traditions). Al-Shāfiʿī further endeavoured to lay down definite rules for its use; he only succeeded to a very small extent however and even in later times, in spite of some limitations in method, *ḳiyās* still had not overcome the vagueness which causes it to lack cogent power of conviction. In al-Shāfiʿī it still appears as synonymous with *idjtihād* [q.v.] in the old sense in which the latter as a synonym of *raʾy* means the jurist's use of his intelligence. Among the representatives of the ʿIrāḳ school and also among those of the Ḥidjāz, *istiḥsān* [q.v.] was used as a variety of *raʾy*. It consisted in diverging from the result properly to be expected by analogy (*ḳiyās*) out of considerations of equity, out of regard for the practice etc. Al-Shāfiʿī vigorously challenged this process as purely subjective and held that only *ḳiyās* was valid. Al-Shāfiʿī in this way carried through a deliberate islāmicization of the *uṣūl*.

7. The development after al-Shāfiʿī resulted in the Ḳurʾān, *sunna, idjmāʿ* and *ḳiyās* being classed together, according to the prevalent doctrine, as the four *uṣūl al-fiḳh*, a fact which is only intelligible from their history, and in further developments in detail. Among the latter are the settlement of the mutual relations of Ḳurʾān and *sunna*: while al-Shāfiʿī taught that the precepts of the Ḳurʾān were given greater precision by the *sunna* but that the Ḳurʾān could only be abrogated by the Ḳurʾān and the *sunna* by the *sunna*, it was already recognized in part before and certainly generally after him, that it was possible for the Ḳurʾān to become abrogated by the *sunna*, which was thus ranked in fact not only equal to but above the Ḳurʾān; the practical legal results were however hardly affected by this theoretical differentiation. As to the *idjmāʿ*, in later times they were not content with the majority of Muslims, but demanded the general agreement of the scholars living at the same time in a certain period, which was to be permanently binding, but unanimity in the literal sense was never demanded. The *idjmāʿ* in this sense did not remain merely supplementary to the Ḳurʾān and *sunna*, but was regarded as confirming them, on the ground of the general conviction of its infallibility, which had developed quite naturally and found expression in the above quoted *ḥadīth* (Ḳurʾānic passages like iii. 103; iv. 83, 115 are also quoted in support). Finally it was even allowed the power of cancelling prescriptions of the Ḳurʾān and *sunna*, as was actually done for example in the case of the worship of saints and the doctrine of the infallibility of the Prophet (cf. above § 2); but this, at least as far as theory is concerned, was reproved as an unauthorized innovation (*bidʿa*) by Aḥmad b. Ḥanbal (d. 241/855) and the traditionalist school represented by him in general. Important sections of the system of Muslim law are based on the *idjmāʿ* alone, e.g. the caliphate, the recognition of the *sunna* of the Prophet as an obligatory standard, the authorization of *ḳiyās* etc. In the last resort, in this view the whole of Muslim law owes its authority to the infallible *idjmāʿ*, which guarantees its correctness and agreement with the true meaning of the divine sources; this conception of *idjmāʿ* is in its essentials already found in al-Ṭabarī (d. 310/923). This is the common orthodox doctrine; only the Mālikīs define *idjmāʿ* as the agreement, firstly of the Companions of the Prophet, then of the two generations following them (the so-called "successors" and "successors of the successors"), then as the *sunna* of Madīna, the home of the true *sunna*, but grant this *idjmāʿ* the same authority as the others do. Only some Ḥanbalīs and the Wahhābīs, as well as the Ẓāhirīs, to be mentioned below, limit *idjmāʿ* to the agreement of the Companions of the Prophet, which has resulted in considerable differences in doctrine. The Khāridjīs (Ibāḍīs) recognized only *idjmāʿ* within their own community and here they demand unanimity. At the same time, there were various divergent views on *idjmāʿ* in the early period. — Even after al-Shāfiʿī a vigorous opposition to *ḳiyās* was raised by Dāwūd al-Ẓāhirī (d. 270/883) and his school, who rejected all *ḳiyās* and *raʾy* and pretended, in the interpretation of the Ḳurʾān and *sunna*, to follow the outward sense (*ẓāhir*) only; but even they could not get along without making deductions, which they endeavoured to represent at being already inherent (*mafhūm*) in the words of the text. But this school, which survived down to the xi^th^/xv^th^ century, was not destined to have a lasting influence. We also still find other isolated opponents of *ḳiyās* and *raʾy*, even among the Shāfiʿīs, e.g. al-Bukhārī (d. 256/870) and al-Ghazzālī (d. 505/1111), who — at least in his mystic period — applies it in practice, but in theory does not recognize it as having equal force with the traditional sources; in the end however, *ḳiyās* won undisputed recognition and also the Ḥanbalīs and Wahhābīs as well as the Khāridjīs (Ibāḍīs) recognize it. The Shāfiʿīs and with certain limitations also the Ḥanafīs use in *istiṣḥāb* [q.v.] a special variety, surer in method, of the usual *ḳiyās*, which is regarded, especially by the Shāfiʿīs, as an independent *aṣl*. The Ḥanafīs followed the other *madhhabs* in taking over the term *ḳiyās* for the old *raʾy*, but in contrast to al-Shāfiʿī they retained *istiḥsān*. Also the Mālikīs continue to recognize this, but in general they prefer the process or rather the name *istiṣlāḥ* [q.v.], a variety of *ḳiyās* which decides in favour of the public welfare. This *istiṣlāḥ* is also found among the Shāfiʿīs, who following their master vigorously reject *istiḥsān*. As a matter of fact, the two processes are practically identical. On account of the arbitrariness with which the results of *ḳiyās* were often simply thrust aside, when it was considered necessary or simply desirable to diverge from the strict demands of theory, both methods are disputed by many and have never been generally included among the *uṣūl* of the *fiḳh*. The Twelver Shīʿīs (Imāmīs) agree with the Sunnīs in recognizing the Ḳurʾān and *sunna* as *uṣūl* of the *fiḳh*; with them however not only the *sunna* of the Prophet is authoritative but also that of the divinely guided twelve *imāms*, whose infallible authority guarantees the correctness of the law in a similar fashion to the *idjmāʿ* in the Sunnī system. For the documentation of the *sunna* the Shīʿīs have works of their own on tradition, the contents of which differ to a considerable degree from those of the Sunnīs; in particular all traditions and decisions are rejected which go back to the authority of the first three caliphs before ʿAlī or in which ʿAlī appears as their representative and successor. Under the guidance of an *imām* further *uṣūl* are unnecessary; during the concealment of the last *imām*, however, there are still two others which correspond to the two last Sunnī *uṣūl*. But even in this period the school of the *Akhbārī* regards the *sunna* along with the Ḳurʾān as alone authoritative and seeks to trace back all decisions to traditions from the *imāms*, limiting as far as possible rational deductions, and even demands for the elucidation of each verse of the Ḳurʾān a tradition relating to it. The school of the *Uṣūlī*, on the other hand, which enjoys greater prestige as the more widely disseminated, recognizes reason (*ʿaḳl*) as the third of the *uṣūl*, but rejects *ḳiyās* (this variation from the Sunnīs is however limited to terminology). Lastly the fourth among the *uṣūl* with them is the agreement of the majority of jurists since the beginning of the concealment of the last *imām*. While the *sunna* here can abrogate another *sunna* and even the Ḳurʾān, the *idjmāʿ* can only dispose of traditions, the correctness of the transmission of which it disputes. At the same time, the Shīʿīs recognize as secondary *uṣūl* the *istiṣḥāb*, the similar methods of deduction known as *barāʾa* and *ishtighāl*, as well as the choice of the judge between several possible views.

8. Although the *idjmāʿ* is strongly rooted in customary law and has actually gained official recognition for important elements in practice even against the Ḳurʾān and Tradition, its fitness for the further development of Islāmic law, the rejection of old prescriptions and the assimilation of new elements must

not be overestimated, as it is, in its final function, as likely to prevent as to encourage innovations; the numerous foreign elements which Muslim law contains had for the most part entered it before *idjmāʿ* had begun to prevail over *fiḳh* as a whole. On the other hand, *istiḥsān* and *istiṣlāḥ* afford the possibility of paying consideration to customary law, though to a gradually diminishing extent in course of time. Occasionally the attempt was even made to place *ʿurf*, the general usage, as a fifth *aṣl* of the *fiḳh* alongside of the four generally recognized, even as late as the vth/xi[th] century; in general it is regarded as meritorious not to let the laws derived from the Ḳurʾān and *sunna* come into conflict with actual practice and to legitimate the latter as far as possible, in order to "escape the danger of sinning"; but a general direct recognition of *ʿurf*, even in a subordinate position, by the *fiḳh* never came about. The discussions which we find about *ʿurf ʿāmm* (general usage) and *ʿurf khāṣṣ* (local custom or custom observed for a time only), their relation to the *idjmāʿ* and their legal authority, are purely theoretical; in the cases in which the *sharīʿa* itself refers to *ʿurf* or *ʿāda* (custom), the reference is hardly ever to legal practice; customary law is in theory not recognized as binding even for the cases for which the *fiḳh* gives no rule. The view prevailing in Indonesia for example, of the equality of *sharīʿa* and *ʿāda* [cf. SHARĪʿA, section 7] takes us quite outside of the doctrine of the *fiḳh*, which can leave almost all practice to customary law, but not give it a place at all in its theoretical system. Even the later Mālikī jurists, especially in North Africa, who have made particular efforts to adapt themselves closely to actual practice, make no exception on this question of principle. However important and natural the influence of customary law and of foreign legal elements in general was in the early period of Islāmic law, all the more difficult has been its further advance, especially since the theoretical recognition of the *uṣūl* in their final form. The different shades of the modernist movement treat the established *idjmāʿ* with a more or less marked indifference; the general recognition won by the Wahhābī state in the Muḥammadan world has also contributed to weakening a little the predominant hold of the *idjmāʿ* in its traditional form, even on the learned circles.

9. As the *fiḳh* had already developed in all essentials before the theory of the *uṣūl* was established, the elements which led to its origin cannot be represented by them in their correct historical perspective. But even from the point of view of the Muslim system, they have for long had only a purely theoretical position as regards the positive *fiḳh*. Only the *mudjtahid* is qualified to apply them, that is to say to derive independently legal rules from them; now, according to the orthodox *idjmāʿ*, *idjtihād* has long ceased and all jurists are obliged to use the lowest degree of *taḳlīd* [cf. the articles]. Many jurists are therefore content, without going deeper into the study of the *uṣūl*, with the occasional brief notes on them which most of the *fiḳh* books add to the discussion of different prescriptions. There are however numerous special works on the *uṣūl* and these form the subject of one of the traditional Muslim sciences. The Sunnī works on *uṣūl* deal *inter alia*, according to the author's point of view, with Ḳurʾān, *sunna* and *idjmāʿ* as regards their respective authority for the purposes of *fiḳh*, the rules — usually given very fully — for their interpretation with regard to form and legal substance, also the so-called legal categories [cf. the article SHARĪʿA, section 4], the reconciliation of contradictions among the sources by harmonizing or assuming abrogation, the use of *ḳiyās*, dispensation etc. and lastly, as a rule, the questions of *idjtihād* and *taḳlīd*. The first work of this kind, which however does not yet fall into the scheme given, is al-Shāfiʿī's *Risāla*. Among especially important and much annotated works of a later period are the following: Imām al-Ḥaramain al-Djuwainī (d. 478/1085), *al-Waraḳāt fī uṣūl al-fiḳh* (translated and explained by L. Bercher, in *Revue Tunisienne*, N.S., i. 93 *sqq.*; 185 *sqq.*); al-Pazdawī (d. 482/1089), *Kanz al-wuṣūl ilā maʿrifat al-uṣūl*; Ṣadr al-Sharīʿa al-Thānī (d. 747/1346), *al-Tanḳīḥ* and *al-Tawḍīḥ*; al-Subkī (d. 771/1369), *Djamʿ al-djawāmiʿ*; Mollā Khosraw (d. 885/1480), *Mirḳāt al-wuṣūl* and *Mirʾāt al-uṣūl*.

Bibliography: The fundamental works for the history of the *uṣūl* are: Goldziher, *Die Ẓāhiriten*; Snouck Hurgronje, *Verspreide Geschriften*, vol. 2; Schacht, *Origins of Muhammadan Jurisprudence*. — Macdonald, *Development of Muslim Theology*, p. 65 *sqq.* gives an older historical view; concise accounts of the prevailing theory with historical notes are given by Juynboll, *Handleiding*, 3rd ed., p. 32 *sqq.* and more fully by Santillana, *Istituzioni*, p. 25 *sqq.*; further literature is also given there. — Lists of the best known Arabic works on *uṣūl* are given in Ḥādjdjī Khalīfa, ed. Flügel, i., No. 835 *sqq.* and in Ṭāshköprüzāde, *Miftāḥ al-saʿāda*, Ḥaidarābād, 1910, ii. 53 *sqq.*

ʿUTHMĀN B. ʿAFFĀN, the third caliph (23—35/644—655). He belonged to the great Meccan family of the Banū Umaiya and to the branch descended from Abu ʾl-ʿĀṣī, whose grandson he was (cf. the genealogy in Wüstenfeld, *Geneal. Tabellen*, U, 23). This makes his prompt acceptance of the teaching of Muḥammad quite noteworthy; he became a convert, if not at the very beginning of the Prophet's mission, at least at a very early date, several years before the Hidjra. ʿUthmān was a rich merchant and an accomplished man of the world; tradition, which likes to represent him as a model of beauty and elegance and deals to a degree which borders on exaggeration with his toilet, may be correct, simply because it is unusual. One set of historical traditions connects his conversion with his marriage to Muḥammad's daughter Ruḳaiya but other sources, probably with more justice, put this marriage after his conversion. ʿUthmān is believed to have taken part in the two migrations to Abyssinia and then joined the *muhādjirūn* in Madīna; but he did not take part in the battle of Badr. After the death of Ruḳaiya the Prophet's alliance with ʿUthmān was renewed by his marriage with another daughter, Umm Kulthūm; the doubts raised by Lammens (*Fāṭima et les filles de Mahomet*, Rome 1912, p. 3—5) regarding the actuality of this marriage do not seem to be justified.

During the lifetime of the Prophet and those of the caliphs Abū Bakr and ʿUmar, the part played by ʿUthmān was a very humble one; how did it happen then that the council (*shūrā*) appointed by ʿUmar on his deathbed chose him as successor to the second caliph? What it seems possible to affirm is that the most outstanding candidates ruled one another out; for example ʿAlī whose election would have meant the negation of ʿUmar's policy; or al-Zubair and Ṭalḥa, also it seems opponents of ʿUmar and whose ambition and covetousness was feared. If among the three who remained, Saʿd b. Abī Waḳḳāṣ, ʿAbd al-Raḥmān b. ʿAwf and ʿUthmān, it was the latter who was chosen, it may be thought that even more than his relationship to the Prophet it was his being a member of the Umaiyad clan that proved the decisive argument in his favour.

Nevertheless, as Wellhausen pointed out and Caetani has expounded at length, ʿUthmān only followed and developed the policy of ʿUmar. The difficulties he encountered were only the results of the policy laid down by his predecessor. But it was just here that the difference in their talents became apparent.

The tragedy which put a bloody end to the reign of ʿUthmān and opened up the period of civil wars has caused the greatest embarrassment to the Arab historians, forced to record the series of grievances which the adversaries of ʿUthmān raised against his rule. There has been preserved for us the long list of these grievances (which are given in great detail for example in Muḥibb al-Dīn al-Ṭabarī, *al-Riyāḍ al-nāḍira fī manāḳib al-ʿashara*, Cairo 1327, ii. 137—152). The first and perhaps the gravest charge against him is that he appointed members of his family to the governorhsips in the provinces. It cannot be denied that these measures of ʿUthmān were not entirely free from nepotism; but we must recognize in them a deeper motive: the intention of establishing unity of government and administration, which was being threatened by the excess of independence which the governors enjoyed. It was practically the same end that ʿUmar had had in view but the latter had succeeded by his energy and prestige in imposing his authority even on governors who belonged to other tribes and clans. Under ʿUthmān, on the other hand, the parts were reversed and it was the caliph who was under the influence of his relatives (perhaps however to a less extent than the official historians say). Indeed (and it is one of Caetani's great merits that he has called attention to this) the *dīwān* system instituted by ʿUmar demanded that the plunder taken in war should increase steadily in perpetuity, the regular receipts from the taxation of the *ahl al-dhimma* not sufficing for the new recruits who hastened to the provinces from the depths of Arabia. From this came the stimulus to the expeditions which in the caliphate of ʿUthmān never ceased to push forward the frontiers of the Arab empire.

Nevertheless the booty produced by these expeditions was perhaps not so great as had been hoped; besides, ʿUthmān — this is another of the grievances against him — instead of assigning it entirely to the soldiers, reserved a share for his governors and for the members of his family, by developing the system of fiefs (*ḳaṭāʾiʿ*), which ʿUmar had already made great use of. Besides, the economic crisis, the inevitable consequence of the sudden enriching of the Arab masses, very soon forced the state to make economies and to cut down the military pensions; this not unnaturally increased the number of malcontents.

One of the steps which contributed very greatly to stirring up against ʿUthmān the religious element was the official edition of the Ḳurʾān (cf. Nöldeke-Schwally, *Geschichte des Qorāns*, ii. 47—119). What was found most odious in this process was the destruction of the provincial copies. The *ḳurrāʾ*, who were the receptacles and of course also the expositors of the sacred text, exercised for this reason a tremendous influence on the masses, which made them to some degree independent of the central power, the latter having no way of checking whether the Ḳurʾānic passages used by the *ḳurrāʾ* were authentic or not. In depriving them of this weapon and making itself the monopolist of divine revelation, the government was endeavouring to realise unity and to establish its absolute power over the state.

The course of development of events can only be briefly indicated here. Tradition divides quite artificially the caliphate of ʿUthmān into two periods of equal length: six years (23—29) of good government and six (30—35) of illegality and confusion. The change is represented symbolically by the loss of the seal of the Prophet which ʿUthmān, according to the story, dropped into the well of ʿArīs in the year 30. It is in any case a fact that it was just at this period that the first movements of rebellion began in the ʿIrāḳ, the region which was suffering most from the economic crisis and the one where the turbulent elements were the most numerous. Much more serious troubles broke out in Kūfa in 32—33, led by the *ḳurrāʾ*, who combined a religious character with political activity and gathered round them a number of doubtful elements. In spite of severe measures taken against them, the recalcitrant elements succeeded in procuring the deposition of Saʿīd b. al-ʿĀṣ who was replaced by the former governor of Baṣra, Abū Mūsā al-Ashʿarī, himself a pietist and opponent of ʿUthmān; Kūfa was henceforth no longer under the central government. Similarly in Egypt, Ibn Abī Sarḥ had to yield to the violence of a group led by the young Muḥammad b. Abī Ḥudhaifa who although an adopted son of ʿUthmān took the side of his opponents. It seems that the wily ʿAmr b. al-ʿĀṣ who had retired to Palestine after his dismissal was secretly encouraging the revolutionary movement in Egypt. The storm which had been brewing for some time burst at the end of the year 35 when bodies of rebels advanced on Madīna from the provinces. The first to arrive were Egyptians; dramatic interviews took place between them and the caliph; the grievances against ʿUthmān were expounded with great bitterness of language. But the rebels were disarmed by the humble and conciliatory attitude of the caliph who gave in to all their demands, promised to annul his previous measures and to change his governors; the Egyptians left satisfied. But suddenly, on the way back at the halting-place of al-ʿArīsh, a messenger of ʿUthmān's was seized and a letter found upon him from ʿUthmān to Ibn Abī Sarḥ confiscated which contained an order to put to death or mutilate the leaders of the movement on their return. The latter turned back furious and retraced their steps to Madīna, determined on vengeance. ʿUthmān denied that the letter was genuine, and even insinuated that it had been forged by his enemies in order to ruin him. A regular siege of ʿUthmān's house was set up, while the old Companions, ʿAlī in particular, maintained an attitude of malevolent neutrality. ʿĀʾisha, the widow of the Prophet, who had conducted a violent campaign against ʿUthmān, preferred to slip away at the last moment on the pretext of a pilgrimage to Mecca. Reduced to the last extremity, ʿUthmān mustered all his dignity and refused to abdicate. After a siege, the length of which is given differently in the different sources, a number of men penetrated into the house in the last days of 35 (June 656) led by Muḥammad b. Abī Bakr who raised his hand against ʿUthmān. His blood flowed, it is said, upon the copy of the Ḳurʾān which he was reading when attacked; his wife, the Kalbite Nāʾila bint al-Furāfiṣa, was wounded. The house was pillaged. During the night the body was buried with the greatest secrecy by his wife and some friends. The troops sent by Muʿāwiya from Syria received the news of the murder when half way there and quickly returned home.

Political unity, and soon also the religious unity, of Islām was now at an end and the period of schisms and civil wars had begun. The caliphate of ʿUthmān and its bloody end mark a turning point in Muslim history and give to the third caliph an importance which his true personality, a somewhat mediocre one at best, would never have merited.

Bibliography: The sources and earlier works are collected and summed up in Caetani, *Annali dell' Islām*, vii. and viii., Milan 1914—1918 (cf. also by the same author *Chronographia Islamica*, p. 279—388). Further: al-Balādhurī, *Ansāb al-ashrāf*, vol. v. ed. Goitein, Jerusalem 1936—8. For the long biography of ʿUthmān in the *Taʾrīkh Dimashk* of Ibn ʿAsākir, vol. viii, see the edition of Damascus 1951— . The *ḥadīths* relating to ʿUthmān are given in A. J. Wensinck, *A Handbook of early Muhammadan Tradition*, Leyden 1927, p. 239—240.

ʿUZAIR is mentioned once in the Ḳurʾān: "The Jews said: ʿUzair is the son of God; the Christians said: Christ is the son of God" (Sūra ix. 30). ʿUzair is generally identified with Ezra. But as such a belief among the Jews that Ezra was the son of God can hardly be imagined, much less proved to exist, Casanova (*JA*, 1924, ccv, 356—360) made the attractive suggestion that ʿUzair is Uzail-Azael, Azazel, one of the fallen angels (on him see Heller, in *REJ*, 1910, lx. 201—212; Jung, in *JQR*, 1925, 1926, *NS*, xvi. 202—205, 287 *sqq.*). Ezra, on the other hand, Casanova recognizes in Idrīs (Sūra xix. 56; xxi. 25). But Muslim Tradition unhesitatingly sees Ezra in ʿUzair and quotes legends in support of the belief that he was the son of God (see also Horovitz, *Koranische Unters.*, 127—8, 167).

The commonest explanation of this belief is as follows: ʿUzair is one of the *ahl al-Kitāb*, the possessors of the Torah. When they sin, God deprives them of the *tābūt* (sacred ark) and punishes them with a sickness which makes them forget the Torah. ʿUzair mourns. Then a flame from God enters ʿUzair's body so that he is filled with knowledge of the Torah. He teaches his people. God then sends down the sacred ark to Israel again; the Torah is compared with ʿUzair's teaching and they are found to agree; the Jews therefore believe that ʿUzair must be the son of God.

Bibliography: For this and other legends see Ṭabarī, ed. de Goeje, i. 669—671; the commentaries on Sūra ii. 259 and ix. 30, esp. Ṭabarī, Cairo 1321, iii. 18—20; x. 68—69; al-Damīrī, *Ḥayāt al-ḥaiyawān*, s.v. *Ḥimār al-ahlī*; al-Thaʿlabī, *Ḳiṣaṣ al-anbiyāʾ*, Cairo 1325, p. 217—219. Further: Geiger, *Was hat Mohammed aus dem Judenthume aufgenommen?*, Leipzig 1902 ², p. 191, 192; B. Heller, in *Encyclopaedia Judaica*, vi. 783 *sq.*; D. Künstlinger, *ʿUzair ist der Sohn Allāh's*, in *OLZ*, 1932, 381—83.

AL-**ʿUZZĀ**, an old Arabian goddess, whose name means "the Strong, the Powerful". She was especially associated with the Ghaṭafān (cf. Yāḳūt, i. 296) but her principal sanctuary was in the valley of Nakhla on the road from Ṭāʾif to Mecca (cf. Yāḳūt, iv. 765 *sqq.*) to which Ḥassān b. Thābit (ed. Hirschfeld, xci. 3, where *nakhla* is to be read) refers. It consisted of three *samura* (acacia) trees in one of which the goddess revealed herself. It also included the sacred stone (Wāḳidī, transl. Wellhausen, p. 351) and the so-called Ghabghab, a cave into which the blood of animals sacrificed was poured (Ibn Hishām, p. 55, ₆). There are also references (e.g. Ibn Hishām, p. 389) to a "house" which Wellhausen takes to be a confusion with another sanctuary of al-ʿUzzā. From these centres her cult spread among a number of Beduin tribes, the Khuzāʿa, Ghanm, Kināna, Balī, Thaḳīf and especially the Ḳuraish, among whom she gradually acquired a predominant position. Here she formed with al-Lāt [q.v.] and Manāt [q.v.] a trinity in which she was the youngest but came in time to overshadow the others. The Meccans called the three "Allāh's daughters", which produced a vigorous polemic from Muḥammad after he had retracted a compromise [see MUḤAMMAD]. The way in which Ḳurʾān, liii. 19 *sq.*, mentions the three suggests that Manāt was subordinate to the other two, and in keeping with this is the fact that al-ʿUzzā and al-Lāt are several times mentioned alone (Ṭabarī, i. 185; Ibn Hishām, p. 145, ₇, 206, ₂, 871, ₆, where Wadd is also mentioned). When in the year 3, Abū Sufyān set out to attack Muḥammad he took the symbols of al-ʿUzzā and al-Lāt with him (Ṭabarī, i. 1395). That of the two al-ʿUzzā was the more important as the patron deity of Mecca is shown from Abū Sufyān's war-cry: al-ʿUzzā is for us and not for you (Ṭabarī, i. 1418; cf. on the other hand: arise Hubal!: Ibn Hishām, p. 582) and the same thing is seen in Ibn Hishām's poem, p. 145, where Zaid b. ʿAmr talks of "ʿUzzā and her two daughters", if by them are meant al-Lāt and Manāt.

Outside of Arabia proper, ʿUzzā was worshipped especially by the Lakhmids of Ḥīra. Mundhir IV swears by her (*Kitāb al-aghānī*, ii. 21, ₅ from below) and according to *Ḥamāsa*, p. 116, a Lakhmid prince Nuʿmān sent men to her so that she might settle a dispute. Her worship here had a particularly cruel character. Mundhir IV sacrificed to her 400 captured nuns and on another occasion a son of the Djafnid Ḥārith, whom he had taken prisoner.

The name ʿUzzā is also, although rarely, found among the Syrians. As a rule, they use instead the name *Kawkabtā* "the (female) star", which they, like the Jews, apply especially to the morning star. It agrees very well with this that the Saracens who stormed the Sinai monastery according to Nilus wanted to sacrifice the young Theodulos to the morning star. The nature of ʿUzzā could be defined in this way but the question arises whether we would yet have the true Arab conception of her and whether some syncretism had not taken place in the frontier lands. The same question is raised by the identification of ʿUzzā with the "Queen of the Heavens" (Jer. vii. 18; xliv. 17—19 in Isaac of Antioch, *Opera*, ed. Bickell, i. 210, 220, 244). This name occurs among the Syrians, and according to Isaac the sacrifice of the women upon the roofs mentioned by Jeremiah was known among the Arabs; the baking of cakes in honour of the goddess can also be proved to have existed among the Arabs (see also Wellhausen, *Reste*, p. 41). But this may all be due to foreign influence (just as the word *kawwānīm* used by Jeremiah goes back to the Assyrian *kamanu* connected with the worship of Istar) so that the true Arab significance of al-ʿUzzā still remains uncertain.

After the taking of Mecca, Muḥammad sent Khālid b. al-Walīd to the sanctuary of al-ʿUzzā to destroy it. According to Wāḳidī, the last priest was Aflaḥ b. Naṣr al-Shaibānī, according to Ibn al-Kalbī, Dubaiya b. Ḥarma. Her cult disappeared after this as did the numerous proper names, combinations of al-ʿUzzā, while the masculine counter-part ʿAbd al-ʿAzīz remained because ʿAzīz was one of the names of Allāh. But Doughty's statement that the Arabs still seek the help of the three goddesses in cases of illness is therefore very interesting [see AL-LĀT].

Bibliography: Ibn al-Kalbī, transl. Wellhausen, in *Reste arabischen Heidtentums*, p. 34—37; Ibn Hishām, ed. Wüstenfeld, p. 55, 145, 206, 839, 871 (cf. vol. ii. 46); Wāḳidī, transl. Wellhausen, p. 350 *sq.*; Ibn Saʿd, ed. Sachau, i. 5, 99; Ṭabarī, ed. de Goeje, i. 1648 *sq.*; Yāḳūt, *Muʿdjam*, ed. Wüstenfeld, i. 296; iii. 644; iv. 769 *sq.*; Land, *Anecdota Syriaca*, iii. 24, 247; Procopius, *De bello Pers.*, ii. 28; Wellhausen, *Reste arab. Heidentums*, p. 34—45; Rothstein, *Die Dynastie der Lakhmiden in Ḥīra*, p. 81 *sq.*, 141 *sq.*

W

AL-**WAHBĪYA**. [See AL-ʿIBĀḌĪYA].

WAHHĀBĪYA, Islāmic community founded by Muḥammad b. ʿAbd al-Wahhāb (1115—1201/1703—1787). This name was given to the community by its opponents in the founder's lifetime, and is used by Europeans; it is not used by its members in Arabia, who call themselves *Muwaḥḥidūn* "unitarians" and their system (*ṭarīḳa*) "Muḥammadan"; they regard themselves as Sunnīs, following the school of Ibn Ḥanbal, as interpreted by Ibn Taimīya, who attacked the cult of saints in many of his writings, especially in a *Risāla* condemning the visitation of tombs (in his *Rasāʾil*, Cairo 1323).

§ 1. Life of the Founder. He was of the Banū Sinān, a branch of Tamīm and was born at ʿUyaina (written by travellers *Ayainah, el-Ayenah, al-Ajjena, Ayana*), a place now in ruins, but which (according to L. P. Dame, in *MW*, xix. 356) "at one time must have had a population of nearly 25,000". He studied at Madīna under Sulaimān al-Kurdī and Muḥammad Ḥayāt al-Sindī, both of whom (according to Daḥlān) detected in him signs of heresy (*ilḥād*). Many years of his life seem to have been spent in travel; according to the *Lamʿ*, he lived four years in Baṣra, where he was tutor in the house of a ḳāḍī Ḥusain; five years in Baghdād, where he married a wealthy woman, who died leaving him "2,000 dīnārs"; a year in Kurdistān, two years in Hamadhān, after which he went to Iṣfahān at the commencement of Nādir Shāh's reign (1148/1736); here he is said to have studied for four years peripatetic philosophy, the Ishrāḳīya and the Ṣūfī systems; for a year he attracted students as an exponent of Ṣūfism, then went to Ḳumm, after which he became an advocate of Ibn Ḥanbal's school. Returning to ʿUyaina, where he had property, he spent eight months in retirement, and then publicly preached his doctrines, as set forth in his *Kitāb al-tawḥīd*. He met with some success, but also with much opposition, and indeed from his own relations, such as his brother Sulaimān, who wrote a tract against him, and his cousin ʿAbd Allāh b. Ḥusain. It appears from his correspondence that his views attracted attention outside ʿUyaina before he left the place. Different reasons are assigned for his expulsion; according to the *Lamʿ*, his dispute with his cousin led to bloodshed between the Tamīm clans of Yamāma, in consequence of which Sulaimān b. Shāmis, al-ʿAnazī, prince of Ḥasā, wrote to the governor of the place demanding that he be expelled. He departed with his family and property, said to be considerable, and was received at Darʿīya (at the time a village of 70 houses) where the chieftain Muḥammad b. Saʿūd accepted his doctrine and undertook its defence and propagation. Possibly later events originated the statement that the two came to an arrangement whereby, should they succeed in enforcing their system on their neighbours, the sovereignty should rest with Ibn Saʿūd, whereas the religious headship should belong to Muḥammad b. ʿAbd al-Wahhāb; this in any case represents the relations between the two. The founder's subsequent history belongs to that of the fortunes of the community.

§ 2. Doctrines of Muḥammad b. ʿAbd al-Wahhāb. His general aim was to do away with all innovations (*bidaʿ*) which were later than the third century of Islām; thus the community are able to acknowledge the authority of the four *sunnī* law-schools, and the six books of tradition. His written polemic and that of his followers is almost entirely aimed at the cult of saints, as exhibited in the building of mausoleums, their employment as mosques, and their visitation. The following list which is taken from the *Lamʿ* seems to agree with what is known of Wahhābī practice.

1. All objects of worship other than Allāh are false, and all who worship such are deserving of death.

2. The bulk of mankind are not monotheists, since they endeavour to win God's favour by visiting the tombs of saints; their practice therefore resembles what is recorded in the Ḳurʾān of the Meccan *mushrikūn*.

3. It is polytheism (*shirk*) to introduce the name of a prophet, saint, or angel, into a prayer.

4. It is *shirk* to seek intercession from any but Allāh.

5. It is *shirk* to make vows to any other being.

6. It involves unbelief (*kufr*) to profess knowledge not based on the Ḳurʾān, the Sunna, or the necessary inferences of the reason.

7. It involves unbelief and heresy (*ilḥād*) to deny *ḳadar* in all acts.

8. It involves unbelief to interpret the Ḳurʾān by *taʾwīl*.

His system is said to have departed from that of Ibn Ḥanbal in the following matters:

1. Attendance at public *ṣalāt* is obligatory.

2. Smoking of tobacco is forbidden and punished with stripes not exceeding forty; the shaving of the beard and the use of abusive language are to be punished at the ḳāḍī's discretion.

3. Alms (*zakāt*) are to be paid on secret profits, such as those of trading, whereas Ibn Ḥanbal exacted them only from manifest produce.

4. The mere utterance of the Islāmic creed is not sufficient to make a man a believer, so that animals slaughtered by him are fit for food. Further inquiry must be made into his character.

The list given by S. Zwemer in *The Mohammedan World of to-day* (New York 1906, p. 106) does not differ materially from the above, but contains the following item which may be noticed:

They forbid the use of the rosary, and count the names of God and their prayers on the knuckles of the hand instead.

Wahhābī mosques are built with the greatest simplicity, and no minarets nor ornaments are allowed.

The *Rawḍat al-afkār* devotes a long section to a list of the practices savouring of paganism current in Arabia in Muḥammad b. ʿAbd al-Wahhāb's time; besides the visitation of tombs, reverence was paid to sacred trees and gifts of food were placed on graves. It is clear that the two latter were not "innovations", but survivals of pre-Islāmic usage. Charges brought against him of burning theological works on a great scale are treated both by himself and his followers as calumnies; the latter admit the burning of the work *Rawḍ al-rayāḥīn*, but not (apparently) that of the *Dalāʾil al-k͟hairāt*. The charge of rejecting the Sunna altogether (repeated by Nolde) is certainly erroneous. On the other hand, the destruction of tombs on a great scale was practised both by Muḥammad b. ʿAbd al-Wahhāb and his followers. The former destroyed that of Zaid b. al-Khaṭṭāb at D̲j̲ubaila, and it has recently been carried on on a great scale at al-Baḳīʿ of Madīna, as a comparison of the photographs in Rifʿat Pas̲h̲a's *Mirʾāt al-Ḥaramain* (1925) with Eldon Rutter's *Holy Cities of Arabia* (1928) shows.

Various minor points of ritual, in which they claim to have abolished innovations are enumerated in *al-Hadīya al-sunnīya*, p. 47—49; such are: raising the voice in places of *ad̲h̲ān* with matter other than the *ad̲h̲ān*; reciting the Tradition of Abū Huraira before the Friday sermon; special gatherings to hear the *Sīrat al-Nabī* recited, etc.

It would appear that under the Banū Ras̲h̲īd the founder's precepts were followed less rigorously than under the Banū Saʿūd; yet Philby in confining the name Wahhābī to the followers of the latter differs from the other travellers, who regarded Ḥāʾil as for a time the metropolis of the community. As has been seen, the community does not itself recognize the appellation.

§ 3. Early history of the movement. It is asserted that within a year of Muḥammad b. ʿAbd al-Wahhāb's arrival at Darʿīya he had won the assent of all the inhabitants except four, who left the place; he proceeded to build a mosque with a floor of uncarpeted gravel; there he gave instruction in his *Kitāb al-tawḥīd*, punishing those who failed to attend. But he also gave instruction in the use of fire-arms. The new sect soon became involved in war with the s̲h̲aik̲h̲ of Riyāḍ, Dahhām b. Dawwās, which, commencing in 1160/1747, lasted 28 years. During this period Ibn Saʿūd and his son ʿAbd al-ʿAzīz, who proved a capable general, were steadily winning ground, with occasional reverses; it became the practice of Ibn Saʿūd and his son, when they captured a place to build a fort at some distance from the original citadel, with a moat round it, if the soil were suitable. These forts were garrisoned with men called *umanāʾ*, who were well paid. In the larger places a ḳāḍī and a muftī were installed, in the smaller only a ḳāḍī. The series of raids whereby the power of Ibn Saʿūd gradually grew is sketched by Philby, and need not be reproduced. In 1718/1765 Ibn Saʿūd died, and was succeeded by ʿAbd al-ʿAzīz, who retained Muḥammad b. ʿAbd al-Wahhāb as his religious guide. In the following year a deputation was sent to Mecca, which was honourably entertained by the S̲h̲arīf, and satisfied the theologians appointed to discuss matters with it, that the Wahhābī doctrine accorded with the system of Ibn Ḥanbal. In 1187/1773 the most stubborn opponent of the sect, Dahhām, fled from Riyāḍ, which was occupied by ʿAbd al-ʿAzīz, who was now master of "the whole of Nad̲j̲d from Ḳaṣīm in the north to K̲h̲ard̲j̲ in the south" (Philby). The son of ʿAbd al-ʿAzīz, Saʿūd, also displayed some military capacity, and was employed by his father in various expeditions. Meanwhile relations had become strained with the new S̲h̲arīf of Mecca, Surūr, who forbade the Wahhābīs access to the city as pilgrims: but owing to the difficulties which resulted to pilgrims from ʿIrāḳ and Persia, this prohibition was withdrawn in 1199/1785.

In 1792 Muḥammad b. ʿAbd al-Wahhāb died, at the age of 89; in the years that followed (1792—1795) the Wahhābīs advanced eastwards, subduing the Banū K̲h̲ālid in Ḥasā; but even before 1790 they had made casual raids into the grazing grounds of the Muntafiḳ and other tribes on the borders of ʿIrāḳ; and representations having been made to the Porte of the danger from the new power that was arising in Arabia, the Pas̲h̲a of Bag̲h̲dād received instructions to deal with it. In 1797, T̲h̲uwainī, chief of the Muntafiḳ, who had for a time been exiled, but was now officially in control of Baṣra, collected a force with the object of crushing the Wahhābīs, but was assassinated by a negro slave at S̲h̲ibāk on July 1, 1797, in consequence of which the force dispersed. Meanwhile the new S̲h̲arīf of Mecca, G̲h̲ālib, after some attempts at compromise, had been attacking the Wahhābī communities from the west, with very little success. In 1798 a fresh expedition was organized from Bag̲h̲dād on a great cale, but this also proved abortive, and in the following year a treaty between the opponents was ratified in Bag̲h̲dād. It had little efect, as the Wahhābī tribes continued to raid, and in 1802 invaded and sacked Karbalāʾ, and massacred the inhabitants. In 1803 G̲h̲ālib found it necessary to evacuate Mecca, which was entered by Saʿūd, who proceeded to purge the city of all that in Wahhābī opinion savoured of idolatry, and to execute persons suspected of favouring such practices. His attempts on D̲j̲idda and Madīna failed, and in the same year he left the Ḥid̲j̲āz, where the garrison which he had established in Mecca was massacred by the inhabitants. On Nov. 4 of this year (1803), the Wahhābī Imām, ʿAbd al-ʿAzīz I, was assassinated at Darʿīya by a S̲h̲īʿī from Karbalāʾ, who had come to the capital as a pretended convert to Wahhābism; Saʿūd, who had previously been declared heir-apparent, succeeded him without opposition, and employed his son ʿAbd Allāh as commander of the army. A fresh attack on the Wahhābīs was organized from Bag̲h̲dād, but petered out, as the previous expeditions had done; Saʿūd was thus left free to renew his invasion of the Ḥid̲j̲āz, where Madīna capitulated in 1804, Mecca in February 1806, and D̲j̲idda somewhat later. In the following years his raiders advanced beyond the bounds of Arabia, attacking Nad̲j̲af, and Damascus, which successfully resisted. "The Wahhabi empire extended in 1811 from Aleppo in the north to the Indian Ocean(?) and from the Persian Gulf and the Iraq frontier in the east to the Red Sea" (Philby). The alarm felt by the Ottoman government was now so serious that Muḥammad ʿAlī Pas̲h̲a, ruler of Egypt, was authorized to deal with it. This he proceeded to do with his usual energy, and although his army, commanded by his son Tūsūn, suffered an initial defeat, it was after reinforcement able to take Madīna in 1812, and recover Mecca in the following year. Muḥammad ʿAlī himself took the command in the latter half of 1813, and suffered a serious defeat, but the death of Saʿūd on May 1, 1814, was a blow to the Wahhābī cause, since ʿAbd Allāh, who succeeded him, was far less capable. Tūsūn, whom Muḥammad ʿAlī left in command, found it necessary to make a treaty with ʿAbd Allāh, who was to acknowledge the suzerainty of the Ottoman Sulṭān, while the Egyptians were to evacuate Nadjd; but this treaty was denounced by Muḥammad ʿAlī, who in 1816 organized a fresh expedition under the command of the able Ibrāhīm Pasha. Ibrāhīm fought with varied fortune, but on April 6, 1818 reached Darʿīya, and on Sep. 9 took the capital. ʿAbd Allāh himself surrendered and was sent to Constantinople, where he was beheaded. This terminated the first Wahhābī empire.

§ 4. Restoration of the Wahhābī state after Ibrāhīm Pasha's departure. While the Ḥidjāz after the conquest was securely garrisoned by Turkish troops, less importance was attached to the security of Nadjd, where a revolt was organized by Turkī, a cousing of Saʿūd, who chose Riyāḍ for the capital of the reviving community, and established himself there in 1821. "By 1833 the whole coast of the Persian Gulf acknowledged Wahhabi rule and paid tribute" (Sir A. Wilson), and several of the inland provinces which had formerly been held by Saʿūd were recovered. During the absence of Turkī's son Faiṣal at the head of his army the former was assassinated in 1834 by a pretender of the royal family, who shortly afterwards met the same fate at the hands of Faiṣal, aided by a Shammar chieftain, ʿAbd Allāh b. Rashīd, who was rewarded for his service by the governorship of Ḥāʾil.

§ 5. The Rashīd dynasty of Ḥāʾil. ʿAbd Allāh b. Rashīd, a capable ruler, contrived to maintain amicable relations with both the Egyptian overlord and the Wahhābī ruler of Riyāḍ till his death in 1847, when he was succeeded by his son Ṭalāl, known to Europeans from Palgrave's travels, who calls him "a warrior even more energetic than his father, and infinitely his superior in the arts of statesmanship". His military skill was displayed in his conquest of the Djawf, of Khaibar, and of Taimāʾ; the province of Ḳaṣīm, which belonged to the sovereign of Riyāḍ, voluntarily transferred its allegiance to Ṭalāl; and steps were taken to pacify the Bedouin raiders on all sides. "Henceforth no Bedouin in Jebel Shammar, or throughout the whole kingdom, could dare to molest traveller or peasant" (Palgrave). Ṭalāl further encouraged the presence of traders in Ḥāʾil by offering liberal terms and security to members of different religious communities. In 1868 this ruler took his own life, through fear of losing his reason; he was followed by his brother Mitʿab. shortly afterwards murdered by Ṭalāl's sons Badr and Bandar, of whom the latter assumed the sovereignty; he was shortly afterwards slain by another brother of Ṭalāl, Muḥammad, who inaugurated his rule with a massacre, described by Doughty (ii. 16). Doughty's statistical computation of the populations under the rule of Ibn Rashīd at this time at 30,000 and of his revenue at £ 30,000 and expenditure at 13,000, is critized by Philby as an understatement. About the same time Faiṣal died at Riyāḍ (Dec. 25, 1869) and was succeeded by his son ʿAbd Allāh, who had endeavoured to obtain poison from Palgrave for his brother Saʿūd. The latter obtained allies who helped him to dethrone his brother in 1870; his reign was marked by the loss of Ḥasā to the Turks, and other losses on the west; and on his death in 1877 ʿAbd Allāh returned to Riyāḍ as ruler, it is said through the influence of Muḥammad b. Rashīd. Relations between the two soon became strained, and in 1883 a pitched battle took place between the forces of the two, wherein Ibn Rashīd won a complete victory; peace was made but a revolt of Saʿūd's sons in 1884 gave Ibn Rashīd the opportunity to invade Riyāḍ, despatch ʿAbd Allāh to Ḥāʾil, and place a governor of his own in Riyāḍ. "Ultimately in the spring of 1891 events occurred which seemed to settle the fate of Nadjd for a long time" (E. Nolde, *Reise in Innerarabien*, 1895, p. 69); a great alliance was formed against the too powerful Emīr of Ḥāʾil, consisting of 1. ʿUnaiza under its warlike chieftain Zāmil; 2. the whole royal family of Riyāḍ; 3. the towns Buraida, Raʾs and Shaḳra; 4. the united tribes ʿUtaiba and Muṭair. According to Nolde, who gives the most detailed account of this campaign, the forces on either side numbered about 30,000; in the struggle, which lasted a whole month, the initial results were in favour of the allies; but at the end of the month (March) Ibn Rashīd succeeded by a mass attack of 20,000 camels in spreading panic among the allies' infantry, and won a complete victory (battle of Mulaida). Riyāḍ had been governed during this rising by ʿAbd al-Raḥmān, another son of Faiṣal; after the defeat of the allies he sought refuge in various places and finally received protection in Kuwait. Muḥammad b. Rashīd was ruler of desert Arabia till his death in 1897.

§ 6. Restoration of the Saʿūd dynasty. Muḥammad was succeeded by his nephew ʿAbd al-ʿAzīz son of Mitʿab, and ere long this ruler was involved in a struggle with the Shaikh of Kuwait, who was harbouring ʿAbd al-Raḥmān b. Saʿūd and his family. In January of 1901 ʿAbd al-ʿAzīz, son of ʿAbd al-Raḥmān, at the head of a small force succeeded in entering Riyāḍ, and reestablishing the old dynasty there, after an interval of eleven years spent in exile. The succeeding years were spent by him in recovering provinces which had belonged to the old Wahhābī empire, and by 1904 "he was master of all that his grandfather had ruled effectively in Najd" (Philby). The campaigns which he conducted in the following years against Ibn Rashīd, the Turks, disaffected tribes, pretenders of his own family, and finally the rulers of the Ḥidjāz, are recorded in detail by Philby, but only a few events of importance need be mentioned here. On Nov. 2, 1921 Ibn Saʿūd obtained possession of Ḥāʾil, and put an end to the Rashīd dynasty. In October 1924 his forces occupied Mecca; on Dec. 5, 1925 they obtained possession of Madīna, and on Dec. 23 of Djidda. Thus the whole of the Ḥidjāz was added to Ibn Saʿūd's realm. In 1926 he took ʿAsīr under his protection, against the menaces of the Imām of Yaman, who had taken possession of Hodeida. In 1934 war broke out between Ibn Saʿūd and Imām Yaḥyā, and Ibn Saʿūd took Hodeida, but retroceded it after the treaty of Ṭāʾif.

§ 7. Institution of the Ikhwān. In 1912 Ibn Saʿūd commenced the foundation of agricultural colonies, whose residents were to be devotees, who took the title *ikhwān* "brethren", indicating that the religious tie had superseded that of the tribe. The first of these colonies was Arṭawīya (so called by Philby, but by Rīḥānī Irṭawīya) in the Ḳaṣīm, and its inhabitants were mainly drawn from the Muṭair tribe. The able-bodied were provided with arms to be used in the *djihād*, but they were also told to cultivate the land, which in each case was near a source of water, and the accumulation of wealth was encouraged. Mud huts were built to serve the Bedouin in lieu of their tents, and they were told to sell their camels. "About seventy *hidjras* (the name for these colonies) with a population of from 2,000 to 10,000 each sprang up after the Wahhābī revival in about ten years" writes Amīn Rīḥānī, who adds that the population of a *hidjra* consists of three classes: Bedouins who have become farmers, missionaries called *muṭawwiʿ* and the merchant class; but for military purposes the division is into those who are at all time ready to respond to the call to the *djihād*; the reserves, who in time of peace are herdsmen and journeymen; while the third class are those who remain in the colonies to keep up trade and agriculture, though not exempt from military service if necessary. The first two classes can be called out by the ruler; but the *nafīr*, or calling out of the civil population requires an announcement by the *ʿulamāʾ* that this is necessary. A list of the *hidjar* with their population and the tribes represented is given by him (*Ibn Saoud of Arabia*, 1928, p. 198). Dame (*l.c.*) declared that the agriculture of these *hidjar* was exceedingly primitive, and that the movement was on the wane.

§ 8. Wahhābism in India. Wahhābī doctrine was introduced into India by one Saiyid Aḥmad, a native of the British District of Rai Bareli, born 1786; having already adopted puritan views, during his pilgrimage to Mecca in 1822—1823 he incurred the hostility of the authorities by the similarity of his doctrines to those of the Wahhābīs, and having been expelled from the holy city, became an adherent of the Wahhābī system. He had already acquired a large following in India, and established a permanent centre in Patna, where he appointed four *khalīfas*, and an *imām*; visits to Bombay and Calcutta swelled the numbers of his followers, and in 1824 he was at the head of an army at the Peshawar frontier, preaching a *djihād* against the Sikh cities of the Pandjāb. Djumādā II, 1242/Dec. 31, 1826 was fixed as the date for the commencement of the war, which all Muslims were called upon to join, in a proclamation called *targhīb al-djihād*; and though the Sikhs put up a fierce resistance, Saiyid Aḥmad's army took Peshawar towards the end of 1830. He proceeded to take the title Khalīfa and to strike coins in his own name. His reign was ephemeral, as he was killed by a Sikh army in the following year. His adherents however found a refuge at Sittana in the mountains beyond the Indus, whither those Muslims who were unwilling to live under non-Muslim rule flocked, and two of his *khalīfas* from Patna circulated the doctrine that Saiyid Aḥmad was not dead, but was merely hiding with a view to reappearance at a suitable time. They extended the *djihād* to Hindus and British, and started an insurrection in Lower Bengal, under a disciple of Saiyid Aḥmad, Titu Miyān, who after some successes was defeated and killed by government forces (Nov. 17, 1831). In spite of these defeats the *khalīfas* continued energetic propaganda among the Muslim population of India, and while maintaining the puritan doctrines of the Wahhābīs of Arabia concentrated attention on the duty of the *djihād*. The Wahhābī movement thus became a constant source of trouble to the government of India, since a system was devised whereby funds were collected and men selected and trained to be sent first to the headquarters of the community at Patna, and thence to the frontier camp of Sittana, and thereafter employed in fighting against the non-Muslim rulers of India. After a great deal of trouble, destruction of property, and bloodshed had been caused by their efforts, and a series of trials had revealed the ramifications of the conspiracy, the older Muslim communities of India, both Shīʿa and Sunna, in 1870 and 1871 issued official declarations dissociating themselves from the Wahhābī doctrine of *djihād*. Since that time, the sect, though it still exists in India, has attracted little attention and indeed one portion of it is said to have abandoned the doctrine of *djihād*. As late, however, as 1890, according to E. A. Oliver (*Across the Border*, p. 29), it had not ceased to be formidable.

§ 9. Wahhābism in other countries. Schuyler in his *Turkestan* (London 1867, ii. 254) mentions the presence of Wahhābī preachers in Khoḳand; in 1871 an attack was made on the Russian station Ḳaraṣu, on the high road between Tashkent and Hodjent, led by Ishan Ish Muḥammad Ḳul, disciple of a Khoḳandian Wahhābī preacher, Ṣūfī Badal. Here then, as in India, the aim of the community was to throw off non-Muslim authority, but the forces collected were too exiguous to accomplish anything of consequence. The presence of the community in Afghānistān was connected with their aim in India.

§ 10. Wahhābī Literature. Prior to Ibn Saʿūd's recent conquest of the Ḥidjāz there appears to have been no printing office in Wahhābī territory; the works of Muḥammad b. ʿAbd al-Wahhāb circulated in MS. The Wahhābīs of India, on the other hand, appear to have employed the printing or lithographic press on a considerable scale. Hunter, p. 66, enumerates 13 works in Arabic, Persian, and Urdu by Wahhābī authors of this country, and adds that "even the briefest epitome of the Wahhābī treatises in prose and verse on the duty to wage war against the English would fill a volume". A work by Muḥammad Ismāʿīl, nephew of Saiyid Aḥmad, *al-Ṣirāṭ al-mustaḳīm*, is said to be "the Ḳurʾān of the Wāhhābīs of India". For the principal Arabic works of or relating to Wahhābī doctrine and history see Brockelmann, *Suppl.* ii. 530—2.

Bibliography: Ḥusain b. Ghannām, *Rawḍat al-afkār* (history of the founder and of Wahhābī campaigns down to 1212/1797-8); ʿUthmān b. ʿAbd Allāh b. Bishr, *ʿUnwān al-madjd fī taʾrīkh Nadjd*; *Lamʿ al-shihāb fī sīrat Muḥammad b. ʿAbd al-Wahhāb* (somewhat, but not excessively, hostile); H. St. John Philby, *Arabia* (London 1930: a complete history of the community to date of publication); A. Musil, *Northern Nejd* (New York 1928: p. 256—304 furnish a continuous history); Ameen Rihani, *Ibn Saoud of Arabia and his Land* (London 1928); S. B. Mills, *The Countries and Tribes of the Persian Gulf* (London 1919: treats especially of the dealings of the Wahhābīs with ʿUmān); S. H. Longrigg, *Four Centuries of Modern Iraq* (Oxford 1925: treats especially of their dealings with ʿIrāḳ) — For the Indian community: W. W. Hunter, *The Indian Musulmans* (London 1871); *Calcutta Review*, vol. l. and li. (Calcutta 1870); R. W. van Diffelen, *De leer der Wahhabieten*, Leyden 1927; R. Hartmann, *Die Wahhabiten*, in *ZDMG*, *NF*, iii. (1924), 176—213; W. Caskel, *Altes und neues Wahhābitentum*, in *Ephemerides Orientales*, Nr. 38, Leipzig 1929: J. Schacht, *Zur Wahhabītischen Literatur*, in *ZS*, vi. (1928), 200—12; J. P. M. Mensing, *De bepaalde straffen in het Hanbalietische recht*, Leiden 1936. — See further the bibliography to the art. IBN TAIMĪYA.

WAḤY (A.), revelation [cf. also ḲUR᾿ĀN, MUḤAMMAD]. As to the etymology of the word, cf. Jewish-Aramaic אוחי "to hasten", Ethiopic *waḥaya*, "to go round, to recognize", and the non-religious meaning *ilhām bi-surʿa*, given by the *Dictionary of Technical Terms*, ed. Sprenger; on the use of the verb by the poets, cf. *Lisān*, s.v. As a religious technical term it is distinguished from inspiration (*ilhām*, q.v.) of saints, artists and others, from *tanzīl*, which chiefly denotes the object of revelation and from *inzāl* which denotes the sending down of revelation from heaven and from its heavenly archetype [see UMM AL-KITĀB], in so far as it denotes revelation as transmitted to the prophets.

Use in the Ḳur᾿ān. *a.* In the early passage Sūra xcix. 5 the earth is the object of divine revelation: On that day shall she (the earth) tell out her tidings, because thy Lord hath inspired her. In Sūra xxviii. 7 the object of revelation is the mother of Moses; here al-Baiḍāwī explains the term by inspiration or vision, in order to distinguish it from waḥy proper. Likewise in Sūra xix. 11 the subject of *awḥā* is Zakarīyā and its object his people; here it is explained by *awma᾿a*. In a peculiar way the term is used in Sūra vi. 112: Even thus have We given an enemy to every prophet, Satans among men and among djinn: tinsel discourses do they suggest (*yūḥī*) the one to the other, in order to deceive.

The technical term for daemoniac inspiration is *wiswās*. The means of communication between God and man is waḥy, either directly, or indirectly through the intermediary of the angels: It is not for man that God should speak with him but by revelation, or from behind a veil, or He sendeth a messenger to reveal by Him, or he sendeth a messenger to reveal by His permission, what He will (Sūra xlii. 51 *sq.*). — Allāh's communications to the angels are also called waḥy, Sūra viii. 12: When the Lord revealed unto the angels: I will be with you etc.

b. In many passages waḥy and the verb *awḥā* refer to the prophets before Muḥammad: Nūḥ (Sūra xxiii. 27), Mūsā (Sūra xx. 13 etc.; xxi. 7; vii. 160), Yūsuf (Sūra xii. 15) etc. — All those who were sent before Muḥammad, were men to whom We granted revelations (Sūra xxi. 7).

c. The chief object of revelation in the Ḳur᾿ān is Muḥammad. Sūra xiii. 30: Thus have We sent thee to a people whom other peoples have preceded, that thou mightest rehearse to them our revelations to thee. — Sūra xxxiv. 50: But I have guidance, it is of my Lord's revealing. Muḥammad's contemporaries are astonished at his receiving revelations: A matter of astonishment to the men (of Mecca) that to a man among themselves We revealed etc. (Sūra x. 2). But he says: I say not to you, "In my possession are the treasures of God"; nor "I know things secret"; neither do I say to you, "Verily, I am an angel": only what is revealed to me do I follow (Sūra vi. 50). — The words of Allāh thus revealed to him may not be changed: And publish what hath been revealed to thee of the book of the Lord, none may change his words (Sūra xviii. 27).

The divine character of Muḥammad's revelations is emphasized in Sūra liii. 4: Verily, it is no other than a revelation revealed; his honesty in Sūra vi. 93: But is any more wicked than he who deviseth a lie of God, or saith, "I have had a revelation", when nothing was revealed to him. — Muḥammad therefore is ordered to follow nothing but what was revealed to him by his Lord (Sūra xxx. 3; xliii. 43). He does not forbid any food, because he does not find such a prohibition among his revelations (Sūra vi. 145).

d. The contents and the aim of revelation are described in various ways [see also MUḤAMMAD]. The story of the Āl ʿImrān is interrupted by the verse (Sūra iii. 44): This is one of the announcement of things by thee unseen: To thee do we reveal it. — The story of Yūsuf is introduced to him with the verse: In revealing to thee this Ḳur᾿ān, one of the most beautiful narratives will We relate to thee, of which thou hast verily aforetime been regardless (Sūra xii. 3). — Muḥammad's following "the religion of Ibrāhīm" is ascribed to divine inspiration (Sūra xvi. 123); likewise his knowledge about the djinn listening to the recitation of the Ḳur᾿ān (Sūra lxxii. 1), as well as about the disputations of the angels at the creation of man is due to waḥy (Sūra xxxviii. 69 *sqq.*).

The aim of the revelation of the Ḳur᾿ān is mentioned in Sūra vi. 19: And this Ḳur᾿ān hath been revealed to me, that I should warn you by it and all whom it shall reach.

Various terms are used in the Ḳur᾿ān in order to denote the contents of revelation. Sūra v. 48: And to thee We have sent down the book with truth (cf. Sūra xxxix. 2, 41; xxxii. 3; xxiii. 73; xvii. 105, etc.), confirmatory of previous scripture and its safe-guard (cf. vi. 92). — Sūra xxxi. 1 *sq.*: These are the signs of the wise book, a guidance and a mercy to the righteous. — Sūra xxvii. 2: These are the signs of the Ḳur᾿ān and of the lucid book; guidance and glad tidings to the believers. — Sūra vii. 52: And now We have brought them the book: with knowledge have we explained it: a guidance and mercy to them that believe. — Sūra xlii. 52: And thus we have sent the spirit to thee with a revelation by our command. Thou knewest not, ere this, what the book was, or what the faith. But we have ordained it for a light. — Further the contents of revelation are called knowledge (*ʿilm*: Sūra iii. 61; ii. 120, 145), wisdom (Sūra xvii. 39), guidance (Sūra xlv. 11, vii. 52 etc.), healing (Sūra xli. 44), light (Sūra iv. 174; xlii. 52).

Regarding the forms of revelation recorded in the biographies of Muḥammad the following may be said. The beginning of revelation consisted in dreams anticipating real events (Ibn Hishām, p. 151; Ṭabarī, *Tafsīr*, xxx. 138; Ibn Saʿd, 1/i. 129). Also afterwards such dream visions are said to have occurred. When ʿĀ᾿isha was under suspicion, she hoped that Allāh would reveal her innocence to Muḥammad in a dream vision (Aḥmad b. Ḥanbal, vi. 197; Bukhārī, *Tafsīr*, Sūra 24, bāb 6).

The first revelation in which Djibrīl appeared to Muḥammad took place on mount Ḥirā᾿, when the angel said to him: I am Djibrīl. Thereupon Muḥammad hastened to Khadīdja, crying: Wrap me up (Sūra lxxiii. 1 or lxxiv. 1).

The first portion of the Ḳur᾿ān revealed was Sūra xcvi., when the angel, in the month of Ramaḍān, during his retreat, showed him a piece of cloth, on which this sūra was written, saying: recite! When Muḥammad protested that he could not recite, the angel pressed him so strongly that he was nearly suffocated. At the third repetition the angel pronounced the verses which Muḥammad retained.

After this there came a pause (*fatra*) in revelation. During this time Muḥammad was in such depression that the thought of suicide came upon him (Ṭabarī, i. 1150; Ibn Hishām, p. 156, 166; Ibn Saʿd, 1/i.

131). The pause ended with the revelation of Sūra lxxiv or xciii.

The angel who transmitted revelation was visible to Muḥammad and to others (Bukhārī, *Faḍā'il al-Ḳur'ān*, bāb 1; Ibn Hishām, p. 154, cf. 156; Abū Nuʿaim, p. 69). To some extent the ascension [cf. MIʿRĀDJ] and the night journey may also be reckoned as revelations. Visions are also mentioned in the Ḳur'ān. Sūra liii. 3 *sqq.*: Verily, it is no other than a revelation revealed: one terrible in power taught it him, endued with understanding. With even balance stood he. And he was in the highest point of the horizon. Then came he nearer and approached closely, and was at the distance of two bows and even closer. And he revealed to his servant what he revealed, his heart falsified not what he saw. Will ye then dispute with him what he sees? And he saw him once again, near the *sidra*-tree, which marks the boundary... His gaze turned not aside, nor did it wander, for he saw the greatest of the signs of the Lord.

Sūra lxxxi. 19 *sqq.*: Verily this is the word of an illustrious messenger, powerful with the Lord of the throne, of established rank ... faithful also to his trust. And your compatriot is not one possessed by djinn; for he saw him in a clear horizon.

In other sūras, however, revelation is said to have taken place by audition. Sūra lxxv. 16 *sqq.*: Move not thy tongue that thou mayest hurry over the revelation; we verily will see to the collecting and the recital of it; when therefore we recite, then follow thou the recital. Afterwards, verily it shall be Ours to make it clear. — Moreover the whole form of the Ḳur'ān with its often repeated *ḳul* "say" on the part of Allāh, supposes revelation by the way of audition.

Particulars regarding Muḥammad's auditive revelations are to be found in the *sīra* and chiefly in *ḥadīth*.

a. How they were perceived by Muḥammad. 1. "Sometimes it comes as the ringing of a bell; this kind is the most painful. When it ceases I retain what was said. Sometimes it is an angel who speaks to me as a man, and I retain what he says" (Bukhārī, *Bad' al-waḥy*, bāb 2; *Bad' al-khalḳ*, b. 6; Muslim, *Faḍā'il*, trad. 87; Tirmidhī, *Manāḳib*, b. 7; Nasā'ī, *Iftitāḥ*, b. 37; Mālik, *Muwaṭṭa'*, chap. *al-Wuḍū' li-man massa al-Ḳur'ān*, trad. 7; Aḥmad b. Ḥanbal, ii. 222; vi. 158, 163, 256 *sq.*).

2. In a different form of this tradition Muḥammad says: Sometimes it approaches me in the form of a young man (*al-fatā*) who hands it down to me (Nasā'ī, *Iftitāḥ*, bāb 37).

3. The Apostle of Allāh heard a sound like the humming of bees near his face; thereupon Sūra xxiii. 1 *sqq.* was revealed to him (Tirmidhī, *Tafsīr*, Sūra 23, trad. 1; Aḥmad b. Ḥanbal, i. 34).

4. The Apostle of Allāh used to move his lips from pain, as soon as revelation began. After the revelation of Sūra lxxv. 16, however, he listened till Djibrīl had withdrawn; thereupon he recited what he had heard (Bukhārī, *Tawḥīd*, b. 43; al-Nasā'ī, *Iftitāḥ*, b. 37; Ṭayālisī, No. 2628).

5. "...on the authority of ʿAbd Allāh b. ʿUmar: I asked the Prophet: Do you perceive the revelation? He answered: Yes, I hear sounds like metal being beaten (cf. above, under 1). Then I listen, and often I think to die (from pain) (Aḥmad b. Ḥanbal, ii. 222).

b. How they were perceived by others. 1. Even on cold days sweat appeared on his forehead (Bukhārī, *Bad' al-waḥy*, b. 2; *Tafsīr*, Sūra 24, b. 6; Muslim, *Faḍā'il*, trad. 86; Aḥmad b. Ḥanbal, vi. 58, 103, 197, 202, 256 *sq.*; cf. iii. 21; cf. further above under *a.* 1.).

2. Muḥammad covers his head, his colour grows red, he snores as one asleep, or rattles like a young camel; after some time he recovers (*surriya ʿanhu*) (Bukhārī, *Ḥadjdj*, b. 17; *ʿUmra*, b. 10; *Faḍā'il al-Ḳur'ān*, b. 2; Muslim, *Ḥadjdj*, trad. 6; Aḥmad b. Ḥanbal, iv. 222, 224).

3. Muḥammad's colour grows livid (*tarabbada lahu wadjhuhu*: Muslim, *Ḥudūd*, trad. 13, 14; *Faḍā'il*, trad. 88; Aḥmad b. Ḥanbal, v. 317, 318, 320 *sq.*, 327; *mutarabbid^{an}*: Ṭabarī, *Tafsīr*, xviii. 4; *tarabbud^{u} djildihi*: Aḥmad b. Ḥanbal, i. 238 *sq.*; *tarrabbada li-dhālika djasaduhu wa-wadjhuhu*: Ṭayālisī, No. 2667)

4. He falls into a lethargy or a trance (*subaṭ*: Aḥmad b. Ḥanbal, vi. 103).

5. "Thereupon the Apostle of Allāh sat down, turning towards him (ʿUthmān b. Maẓʿūn). When they talked, the Apostle of Allāh let his gaze swerve towards heaven; after a while he looked down to his right side and turned away from his companion, following his gaze and began to shake his head as if he tried to understand what was said to him, while ʿUthmān sat looking on. When Muḥammad had reached his aim, his gaze turned anew towards heaven, etc." (Aḥmad b. Ḥanbal, i. 318).

6. "When Muḥammad received a revelation... this caused him much pain, so that we perceived it. That time he separated himself from his companions and remained behind. Thereupon he began to cover his head with his shirt, suffering intensely, etc." (Aḥmad b. Ḥanbal, i. 464).

"When the Apostle of Allāh received a revelation, he began to cover his face with his shirt. When he had swooned, we took it away, while etc." (Aḥmad b. Ḥanbal, vi. 34; cf. above *b.* 2.).

7. Zaid b. Thābit said: "I was at Muḥammad's side, when the *sakīna* [q.v.] came upon him. His thigh fell upon mine so heavily, that I feared it would break. When he recovered, he said to me: Write down, and I wrote down Sūra iv. 95" (Aḥmad b. Ḥanbal, v. 184, 190 *sq.*; Abū Dā'ūd, *Djihād*, b. 19).

8. ʿAbd Allāh b. ʿAmr said: "The Sūra al-Mā'ida was revealed to the Apostle of Allāh, while he was riding on his camel. The beast could not bear him any longer, so that he had to descend from it" (Aḥmad b. Ḥanbal, ii. 176). A similar tradition on the authority of Asmā' bint Yazīd: Aḥmad b. Ḥanbal, vi. 455, 458; another tradition of the same type: Ibn Saʿd, 1/i., 131.

c. The circumstances under which revelation came upon Muḥammad. 1. Muḥammad is directly or indirectly asked for his opinion or decision, when the answer is revealed to him, e.g. concerning the use of perfumes during the *ʿumra* (Bukhārī, *Ḥadjdj*, b. 17; see above *b.* 2.); concerning excuses for staying at home during an expedition (Abū Dā'ūd, *Djihād*, b. 19; Aḥmad b. Ḥanbal, v. 184); concerning the question whether evil may proceed from good (Aḥmad b. Ḥanbal, iii. 21; Ṭayālisī, No. 2180); concerning the question whether his wives were allowed to relieve a want near town (Aḥmad b. Ḥanbal, vi. 56); concerning ʿĀ'isha's being or not being guilty (Bukhārī, *Tafsīr*, Sūra 24, b. 6; Aḥmad b. Ḥanbal, vi. 103, 197); concerning divorce in case of adultery witnessed by one witness

(Ṭayālisī, No. 2667); concerning *ẓihār* (Ṭabarī *Tafsīr*, xviii. 2).

2. Revelation comes upon Muḥammad while he is riding (above, *b.* 8.; Ṭabarī, *Tafsīr*, xxvi. 39), while his head is being washed (Ṭabarī, *Tafsīr*, xviii. 2), while he is at table, holding a bone in his hand (Aḥmad b. Ḥanbal, vi. 56), while he is on the pulpit (Aḥmad b. Ḥanbal, iii. 21).

d. The contents of these revelations are not always communicated, and, if so, they are not always parts of the Ḳur'ān (cf. Nöldeke-Schwally, *Geschichte des Qorans*, i. 256—261), e.g. Muḥammad's answer to the question whether evil may proceed from good (Aḥmad b. Ḥanbal, iii. 21; Ṭayālisī, No. 2180); the permission granted to his wives to leave the town (Aḥmad b. Ḥanbal, vi. 56), the punishment of fornication (Aḥmad b. Ḥanbal, v. 317, 318, 320 *sq.*, 327, not the *āyat al-radjm*), the permission of *liʿān* (Ṭayālisī, No. 2667).

In Muslim literature the idea of revelation has not called forth discussions of importance. Al-Īdjī and his commentator al-Djurdjānī combat the views of philosophers according to whom it is a charisma peculiar to the prophets that "they see the angels in their corporeal forms and hear their speech by revelation; it is not to be rejected that they being awake see what common people see when asleep, i.e. that they see persons who speak to them poetical words, which point to ideas corresponding to what really happens, since their soul is free from bodily occupations and can easily come into contact with the divine world (*ʿālam al-ḳuds*). Often this peculiarity becomes in them a settled faculty which is easily set working". This theory of revelation is, according to al-Īdjī, misleading, not being in harmony with the views of the philosophers themselves, according to whom the angels cannot be seen, being merely psychic beings, who do not produce audible speech, which belongs expecially to corporeal beings. So the theory of philosophers explains revelation as the imagining of what has no basis in reality, as little as what comes from the lips of ailing and lunatic people. Yet if any of us should command and prohibit on his own authority what is salutary and sensible, he would not on account thereof be a prophet. How much the less then would be a prophetic utterance what is based upon imaginations which have no foundation and often are contrary to reason (*Mawāḳif*, p. 217 *sq.*).

Bibliography: Ibn Hishām, p. 150 *sqq.*; Ibn Saʿd, 1/i. p. 126 *sqq.*; Ṭabarī, i. 1146 *sqq.*; Nöldeke-Schwally, *Geschichte des Qorāns*, i. 21 *sq.*; J. Horovitz, *Koranische Untersuchungen*, p. 67 *sq.*; for the collections of Tradition, cf. Wensinck, *Handbook*, p. 162ᵇ, 163ᵃ; Sprenger, *Das Leben und die Lehre des Muḥammad*, i. Berlin 1861, p. 207 *sqq.*; iii. 1865, p. xviii. *sqq.*; W. Muir, *The Life of Mohammad*, Edinburgh 1912; F. Buhl, *Das Leben Muhammeds*, Leipzig 1930, p. 134 *sqq.*; T. Andrae, *Die Person Muhammeds*, Upsala 1917, p. 311; G. Hölscher, *Die Propheten*, Leipzig 1914; O. Pautz, *Muhammeds Lehre von der Offenbarung*, Leipzig 1898; T. Andrae, *Mohammed*, Göttingen 1932, p. 77 *sqq.*; Abū Nuʿaim, *Dalā'il al-nubuwwa*, Ḥaidarābād 1320, p. 68 *sqq.*; al-Rāghib al-Iṣbahānī, *al-Mufradāt fī gharīb al-Ḳur'ān*, Cairo 1324, p. 536 *sq.*; ʿAḍud al-Dīn al-Īdjī, *Kitāb al-mawāḳif*, ed. Soerensen, Leipzig 1848, p. 172 *sqq.*; Muḥammad ʿAlā' b. ʿAlī al-Tahānawī, *Kitāb kashshāf iṣṭilaḥāt al-funūn*, Calcutta 1862, p. 1523.

WAḲF or HABS (A.) is properly an Arabic *maṣdar* meaning "to prevent, restrain". In Muslim legal terminology it means primarily "to protect a thing, to prevent it from becoming the property of a third person (*tamlīk*)" (Sarakhsī, *Mabsūṭ*, xii. 27). By it is meant 1. state land, which on being conquered passed to the Muslim community either by force or by treaty and remained in possession of the previous owners on payment of the *kharādj* and could neither be sold nor pledged by them (cf. Pröbster, in *Islamica*, iv. 421 *sqq.*) and 2. commonly a pious foundation, which is defined in various ways in the Sharīʿa according to the school. Following up these definitions we may say that by *waḳf* (plur. *awḳāf*) is meant a thing which while retaining its substance yields a usufruct and of which the owner has surrendered his power of disposal with the stipulation that the yield is used for permitted good purposes. Waḳf really means however the legal process by which one creates such an endowment (synonymous with *taḥbīs*, *tasbīl* or *taḥrīm*) and in popular speech became transferred to the endowment itself, which is properly called *mawḳūf*, *maḥbūs*, *muḥabbas* or *ḥabīs*. Among the Mālikīs and therefore in Morocco, Algiers and Tunis the name *ḥubus* (plur. of *ḥabīs*) or the syncopated form *ḥubs* (pl. *aḥbās*) predominates (hence in French legal language: *habous*).

I. The main principles of Fiḳh

1. The founder (*wāḳif*) must have full right of disposal over his property; he must therefore be in full possession of his mental faculties, be of puberty and a free man (*ʿāḳil, bāligh, ḥurr*). He must further have unrestricted ownership in the subject of the endowment. Endowments by non-Muslims are therefore only valid if they are intended for a purpose not incompatible with Islām (e.g. they must not be intended for Christian churches or monasteries; yet this took place in practice; cf. e.g. Saarisalo, *Waqf documents from Sinai*, in *Studia Orientalia*, v. 1934).

2. The object of the endowment (*mawḳūf*) must be of a permanent nature and yield a usufruct (*manfaʿa*), so that it is primarily real estate. There is a diference of opinion about movables. One section of the Ḥanafīs regards the granting of movables in an endowment as inadmissible but the majority, like the Shāfiʿīs and Mālikīs, grant the principle, when it is a case of things which can be the subject of an agreement legal in the Sharīʿa, e.g. animals for their milk and wool, trees for their fruits, slaves for their labour, books for study. There are however here also differences of opinion on points of detail (thus Shīrāzī does not permit a slave to be made a waḳf). Provisions, money (prohibition of usury!) etc. are in general not admitted as their substance is consumed; they can only be the object of a *ṣadaḳa*. Among the Mālikīs a *manfaʿa* can also be made a waḳf, e.g. the yield of a piece of ground which is let for the period of the lease (Khalīl, ii. 553). Cf. to this question the passages collected by Suhrawardy, *The waqf of movables* (*JASB*, NS. vii [1915], p. 323 *sqq.*). Nowadays in Egypt bankcredits also are made waḳfs (*OM*, xv, 1934, s. 311).

3. The purpose of the endowment must be a work pleasing to God (*ḳurba*) although this is not always apparent on the surface. Two kinds are distinguished: *waḳf khairī*, endowments of a definitely religious or public nature (mosques, madrasas, hospitals, bridges, waterworks), and *waḳf ahlī* or *dhurrī*, family endowments, for example for children or grand-children

or other relations, or for other persons; the ultimate purpose of such a foundation must however always be *ḳurba*, for the poor for example.

An endowment for oneself is however invalid (except in Abū Yūsuf). The Shāfiʿīs give a subterfuge (*ḥīla*) to evade this condition: the thing which is to be the subject of the endowment is to be presented or sold at a low price to a third person; the latter can then create an endowment in favour of the original owner.

4. The form need not be a written one, although this is usually the case. The founder must clearly express his wishes either by *waḳaftu*, *ḥabbastu*, *sabbaltu* or if he uses other formulae by an addition that "it must neither be sold nor given away nor bequeathed", (otherwise it would only be a *ṣadaḳa*). The founder must further describe the object accurately and state exactly for what purpose and in whose favour the endowment is made. The fiḳh works deal very fully with the interpretation of the separate expressions describing those for whom the foundation is intended.

5. The following conditions are further necessary for the completion of a valid waḳf:

a. It must be made in perpetuity (*muʾabbad*), which in the case of foundations for definite individuals is managed by allotting the proceeds after their death to the poor. It is therefore also inalienable.

b. It must come into force at once and there must be no condition for postponing it (*munadjdjaz*), except the death of the founder; but in this case as in the case of a will the founder can only make one third of his property waḳf.

c. It is an irrevocable legal transaction (*ʿaḳd lāzim*); but according to Abū Ḥanīfa (not however his pupils and the later Ḥanafīs), the foundation may be revoked except when it is connected with the death of the founder (Sarakhsī, *Mabsūṭ*, xii. 27). The Ḥanafī founder therefore always brings a formal suit against the administrator for the restoration of his property; the judge, who then has the choice between the teaching of Abū Ḥanīfa and that of Abū Yūsuf, decides according to Abū Yūsuf, since the latter teaches irrevocability, and confirms the waḳf by rejecting the petition.

d. Among the Ḥanafīs (also in Ibn Abī Lailā; Sarakhsī, xii. 35) and the Imāmīs there is further required the conveyance (*taslīm*) of the endowment to those for whom it is intended or rather to the administrator; but according to Abū Yūsuf, as in the other schools, the endowment is already complete by the declaration of the founder's wishes (*ḳawl*). In the case of a foundation for the common good (mosque or cemetery) the conveyance is completed by its being used, even if only by one person.

Among the Mālikīs on the other hand, the points mentioned here are not essential, e.g. it can be revoked not only by the founder but also by his heirs (Khalīl, transl. Santillana, ii. 560—61).

6. As Muslim law does not know the conception of the legal person, opinions differed regarding the position of the waḳf in the law of property. According to one view (Shaibānī, Abū Yūsuf and the later Ḥanafīs; Shāfiʿī and his school), the founder's right of ownership ceases; it is usually said that it passes to Allāh; this however only denies the right of ownership of the founder and that of all other mortals. According to a second view (Abū Ḥanīfa [cf. thereon also Shāfiʿī, *Umm*, iii. 275 *sq.*] and the Mālikīs) the founder and his heirs retain the right of ownership; he is however prevented from exercising it. According to a third view (some Shāfiʿīs, Aḥmad b. Ḥanbal), the ownership passes to the beneficiaries (*mawḳūf ʿalaihi*) (cf. e.g. Shīrāzī, *Tanbīh*, ed. Juynboll, p. 164, 7). The ownership in the yield (*manfaʿa*) belongs however, according to all jurists, to the *mawḳūf ʿalaihi*.

7. The administration of the waḳf is in the hands of a *nāẓir*, *ḳaiyim* or *mutawallī* who receives a salary for his services. The first administrator is usually appointed by the founder; frequently he is the founder himself (among the Mālikīs this invalidates the foundation). The ḳāḍī has a right of supervision; he appoints the administrators and if necessary dismisses them (e.g. for neglect of duty). The form of the administration and the use to which the revenues are put depend on the conditions laid down by the founder. The revenues must however be used primarily for the maintainance of the buildings etc.; only the surplus goes to the beneficiaries. Agreements to lease the lands and buildings can only be made for three years as a maximum.

8. Extinction of the waḳf. If the founder secedes from Islām, the foundation becomes invalid and passes to his heirs. Endowments which have lost their object fall, according to the view held of the position with regard to the law of property, to the legitimate heirs (among the Mālikīs only if they are poor) or they must be used for the poor or for the common good; in no case may they be confiscated by the temporal authorities.

II. Origin, history and significance

According to the general opinion of the Muslims there were no waḳfs in Arabia before Islām, neither in houses or lands (cf. Shāfiʿī, *Umm*, iii. 275, 280). The fuḳahāʾ trace the institution to the Prophet although there is no evidence of this in the Ḳurʾān. In comparison with other things the support for this institution in traditioni s very slight, although it is always said by the legists that the companions of the Prophet and the first caliphs used to make waḳfs. In a tradition of Anas b. Mālik it is said that the Prophet wished to purchase gardens from the Banū 'l-Nadjdjār in order to build a mosque; they refused to take the purchase money however and gave the land for the sake of God (Bukhārī, *Waṣāyā*, bāb 28, 31, 35). According to a tradition of Ibn ʿUmar, on which the legists lay chief stress, ʿUmar, later caliph, at the partition of Khaibar acquired lands which were very valuable to him and asked the Prophet whether he should give them away as *ṣadaḳa*. The Prophet replied: "Retain the thing itself and devote its fruits to pious purposes". ʿUmar did this with the provision that the land should neither be sold nor bequeathed; he gave it as *ṣadaḳa* for the poor, (needy) relatives, slaves, wanderers, guests and for the propagation of the faith (*fī sabīl Allāh*); it is not to be a sin for the administrator to eat of it in moderation or feed a friend if he does not enrich himself from it (Bukhārī, *Shurūṭ*, bāb 19 and other places). In another version of this tradition the reference is to a palm-garden called Thamgh (Bukhārī, *Waṣāyā*, bāb 23 etc.). In both cases however, the reference is to one and the same piece of ground in Khaibar which was called Thamgh (cf. Nawawī, *Sharḥ Muslim*; Sarakhsī, *Mabsūṭ*, xii. 31). A third tradition of Anas b. Mālik concerns a family endowment. In keeping with the pronouncement in Sūra iii. 92, Abū Ṭalḥa gave the Prophet his favourite piece of ground, the Bairuḥā' garden (in Madīna) where the Prophet used to go to to enjoy the shade and drink the water. The Prophet however gave it back to him with the observation that he should make it an endowment for his relatives. Abū Ṭalḥa thereupon gave the garden as a *ṣadaḳa* for Ubaiy and Ḥassān (Bukhārī, *Waṣāyā*, bāb 17). In other traditions quoted by Bukhārī and others regarding the making waḳf of movables it is only a case of simple *ṣadaḳa*.

The legists seek to trace the institution of waḳf back to the Prophet through these traditions. It is remarkable however that the oldest legists are not agreed on essential points of the waḳf. In this connection Shāfiʿī's polemics against unnamed opponents, certainly including Abū Ḥanīfa, are interesting (*Umm*, iii. 275 *sqq.*, 280). There the view of Shuraiḥ (d. 82/701) is refuted, which challenges the admissibility of waḳf at all by quoting a saying of the Prophet not found in the canonical collections: "No withholding from the quotas ordained by God" (*lā ḥabsᵃ ʿan farāʾiḍ Allāh*). Shāfiʿī attacks the view that the waḳf remains the property of the founder and his heirs. The inalienability of the waḳf was disputed by Shuraiḥ as the Prophet was said to have sold things which had been made waḳf (*ḥabīs*) (Kāshānī, *Badāʾiʿ al-ṣanāʾiʿ*, vi. 219). Shāfiʿī seems to have contributed to the success of the views on waḳf which later became predominant. Abū Yūsuf is said to have first declared for the irrevocability of the waḳf, when on a pilgrimage he saw in Madīna the numerous waḳfs of the Muslims (Sarakhsī, *Mabsūṭ*, xii. 28). All this suggests that the institution of the waḳf arose only after the death of the Prophet in the course of the first century A.H. and only assumed rigid legal forms in the second century. Its origin is to be sought in the strongly marked impulse to charitable deeds which is characteristic of Islām; thus we find it associated in a tradition (see above) with an appropriate verse of the Ḳurʾān, and Shāfiʿī (*Umm*, iii. 275) calls it a *ṣadaḳa muḥarrama*. In addition there was the fact that the Arabs found in the conquered lands foundations for the public benefit for churches, monasteries, orphanages and poorhouses (*piae causae*) and may have adopted this form for the practice of the charity recommended by their religion. These endowments of the Byzantine period were inalienable, and managed by *administratores* and were under the supervision of the bishops (cf. especially Justinian, *Novelle* 7 and 131; Duff, *The charitable foundations of Byzantium*, in *Cambridge legal essays*, 1926, p. 83 *sqq.*). C. H. Becker (*Isl.*, ii. 404) had already come to the same conclusion when he showed that the custom of making sites in the towns (*ribāʿ*) waḳf and not agricultural land (*arāḍī*), which existed in Egypt down to the Ṭūlūnid period, goes back to a Greek original. But already in this early period agricultural land must elsewhere have been made waḳf; Shāfiʿī already speaks of this and Bukhārī (*Waṣāyā*, bāb 27) has a chapter: "If anyone makes agricultural land (*arḍ*) waḳf and does not give the boundaries". This was not unknown to the Byzantines also (cf. Justinian, *Novelle* 65).

On the further history of the waḳfs in Egypt Maḳrīzī (*Khiṭaṭ*, ii. 295 *sq.*) gives interesting notes. Abū Bakr Muḥammad b. ʿAlī al-Madharāʾī (d. 345/956) was the first to make agricultural land waḳf for the holy cities and other purposes. The Fāṭimids however at once forbade the making waḳf of country estates and entrusted the Ḳāḍī 'l-Ḳuḍāt with the supervision, assisted by a *dīwān al-aḥbās*. In 363/974 al-Muʿizz ordered the property of the endowments and the waḳf documents (*sharāʾiṭ*) to be handed over to the state treasury (*bait al-māl*); the revenues from the waḳfs were then farmed out for 1,500,000 dirhams annually; out of this sum the beneficiaries were paid while the rest went to the treasury. As a result of this system of farming them out, the waḳf possessions had so sunk in value by the time of al-Ḥākim that the revenues in the case of many mosques no longer sufficed for their maintenance. In 405/1014 he therefore created a large new foundation and had the condition of the mosques regularly examined.

In the Mamlūk period the foundations were divided into three groups: 1. *Aḥbās*. These were under the supervision of the *dawādār al-sulṭān* and were administered by a *nāẓir* with a special *dīwān*; they comprised extensive estates (in 740/1339, 130,000 *faddān*) in the provinces of Egypt and were used to keep up mosques and zāwiyas. Maḳrīzī (d. 845/1442) complains bitterly about the abuse and neglect of these endowments; they had come through corrupt practices into the hands of the emīrs; the beneficiaries, who were called *faḳīh* or *khaṭīb* but knew nothing of fiḳh or of preaching, were registered in the name of some ruined mosque. 2. *Awḳāf ḥukmīya*. These consisted of town lands in Miṣr and Ḳāhira; their revenues were earmarked for the two holy cities as well as for charities of all kinds. They were under the control of the Ḳāḍi 'l-Ḳuḍāt and were administered by a *nāẓir* (sometimes by two, one for each part of the city); there was a special *dīwān* for each part of the town. In this connection Maḳrīzī again makes a touching complaint about the conditions which were becoming worse and worse. 3. *Awḳāf ahlīya*, family endowments, each of which had their own administrator. These were monasteries (*khānḳāh*) madrasas, mosques, türbas, which owned extensive estates in Egypt and Syria, some of which were originally state lands, which had been acquired and made waḳf.

Conditions in other lands must have been similar to those in Egypt. A hundred years before Maḳrīzī we find the Ḥanafī Ṣadr al-Sharīʿa al-Thānī (d. 747/1346) in Transoxania complaining that the ḳāḍīs made the waḳfs void by a *ḥīla* (Snouck Hurgronje, *Verspr. Geschriften*, ii. 163).

The waḳf inscriptions afford many valuable details. In point of numbers, business premises were most frequently made waḳf, usually small shops (*ḥānūt*) which often belonged in scores to a waḳf, but also warehouses (*khān, funduḳ*) and stables (*ruwāʾ*), tenements (*dār*) or even smaller dwellings. Alongside of these we have various industrial premises: baths, mills, bakeries, oil and sugar presses, soap works, paper works, looms (*ṭirāz*), post-houses (*yam*). In the third place are agricultural establishments, most frequently gardens, but also farms and even whole villages. The use to which the produce, sometimes in money and sometimes in kind, was to be put was minutely prescribed in the foundation document. In addition to benefiting the poor the revenues were primarily used to pay the staffs of mosques, madrasas, Ḳurʾān schools, libraries, hospitals or to be used for the benefit of the inmates of a monastery etc. (cf. for details C. H. Becker, *Islamstudien*, i. 264 *sq.*). The income was also used in some way for the two holy cities.

The inscriptions are also eloquent about abuses, embezzlements, and exploitation of the waḳfs. Thus we frequently find edicts which free the waḳf from unjust burdens and taxes. The founders themselves endeavoured to prevent embezzlement etc. by dividing the lands among a number of endowments in small portions so that the several administrators could keep a check on one another, or the supervision is put by the founder in the hands of an administrative commission, to which the ḳāḍī, the khaṭīb and the prominent citizens of the town belong (e.g. in Mostaganem of the year 742/1340 in *JA*, ser. 11, xiii. 81).

The wakf system was very beneficial in ameliorating poverty and misery and in furthering learning, but it had disadvantages morally as well as economically. On the one hand, considerable sections of the populace were taken from industry by the continual creation of new sinecures and supported at the expense of the country; on the other hand, the capital for these great endowments had to be supplied by the wealthy and this was acquired not by productive labour but by extortion and unprecedented exploitation of the people. Further, the immense accumulation of landed property in the possession of the Dead Hand was economically injurious, although from time to time confiscations by the state and illegal disposal by the administrators had a regulating effect. One consequence of this accumulation very frequently was that the soil was not used to the best advantage; these great *latifundia* are even often an impediment to the introduction of modern agricultural methods. They often deteriorated so much that the yields were not even sufficient for the necessary upkeep and improvements. To avert this evil and to arouse the personal interest of the tenants perpetual leases have been granted, apparently since the xvi[th] century, which differ somewhat in the different countries but are the same in their main lines. Originally only used in case of lands that had gone out of cultivation, they gradually came into use for other wakf estates also.

The most widely distributed type of agreement of this kind (throughout the whole of the former Turkish empire including Egypt and Tripolis) is the *idjāratain* (in contrast to this the short term lease is called *idjāra wāḥida*) so called from the two sums in it: the tenant pays a lump sum according to the value of the land on the conclusion of the agreement (*idjāra muʿadjdjala*) and an annual fixed rent (*idjāra muʾadjdjala*) so that the right of ownership in the endowment may not lapse. He is bound to keep the land in order and make it productive. He can bequeath it and sell his rights in the land with the approval of the administrator of the endowment. If the tenant dies or the tenant following him without leaving heirs the land as *maḥlūl* goes back to the endowment. New buildings are regarded as increment.

Another kind of agreement usual in Syria and Egypt is the *ḥikr* which corresponds to the *kirdār* in Tripolis and Tunis but has a rent which rises or falls with alterations in the value of the piece of ground. The tenant can only bequeath it, but has unrestricted rights in his new buildings and new plantations. The agreement only becomes void on non-payment of rent. In Turkey the *muḳāṭaʿa* is similar and in Tunis the *enzel* (*inzāl*) agreement, but with a fixed annual rent and in Algiers down to the French occupation the *ana* (*ʿanāʾ*) agreement and in Morocco the *guelza* (*djilsa* or *djulsa* in the case of business houses and factories) and *gza* (*djazāʾ*: in case of agricultural lands), (cf. Michaux Bellaire, in *RMM*, xiii [1911], 197-248), as well as throughout the Maghrib the *khalw* [or *khulū*] *al-intifāʿ*. In all these agreements it is a question of the usufruct (*ḥuḳūḳ al-manāfiʿ*). The thing itself (*raḳaba*) remains the property of the endowment, which is recognized by the payment of rent; while the *manfaʿa* became the property of the lessee.

These varieties of agreement were not however created specially for the letting of wakf estates but were rather older forms of lease adapted to the wakf. They probably originated in cases in which a piece of land had been made wakf in this way, and are ultimately a survival of the ancient emphyteusis, which was already usual in the Byzantine period for churches and monasteries and their lands.

Family endowments are almost as old as those for the public good. The earliest example is the wakf document in which Shāfiʿī makes his house in Fusṭāṭ with everything belonging to it wakf for his descendants (*Umm*, iii. 281—283). Such foundations while being a charitable object in keeping with religion, primarily secure the descendants an income for all emergencies and in particular protect the property in times of insecurity from unscrupulous rulers, although in practice they did not always have the desired result. In addition it was a legal means of evading the Ḳurʾānic law of inheritance, whether in order to exclude particular heirs or to include those not entitled to inherit (cf. Hacoun, *Etude sur l'évolution des coutumes Kabyles*, p. 11), or in order to keep the estate intact, when it would be broken up by the application of the law of inheritance. The institution of the family endowment was also abused for other purposes: a man would make his property wakf for his descendants in order to put it out of reach of his creditors, which however is forbidden in a *fatwā* of Abu 'l-Suʿūd (d. 928/1474; cf. P. Horster, *Zur Anwendung des islam. Rechts*, Stuttgart 1935, p. 42). Family endowments are very numerous and economically harmful from their great extent. In Egypt for example, the income from these endowments in 1928—1929 was higher than that from all the other wakfs together (over £ 1,000,000; cf. *REI*, iii. 295).

III. Modern Conditions

The estates of the Dead Hand in the former Turkish empire were estimated at three quarters of the whole arable land and in modern Turkey they have recently been calculated at T £ 50,000,000 in value (in the Budget for 1928 the revenues were entered as T £ 3,489,000). Towards the middle of the xix[th] century, they comprised in Algiers the half, in 1883 in Tunis $^1/_3$ and in 1935 in Egypt $^1/_7$ and in 1930 in Iran about 15% of the cultivated soil. The accumulation of such extensive possessions in the Dead Hand meant serious injury to the economic life of the country; but apart from anything else a piece of ground that is wakf cannot be burdened by a mortgage. In addition there were everywhere abuses in the management of these estates and frequently there was uncertainty in law regarding their ownership. The wakf system thus everywhere became a problem in the course of the last century. The European Powers (France) were the first to see in it an impediment to the economic development of their Muslim colonies but Muslims themselves (Turkey, Egypt) are now no longer blind to this point of view.

France was the first to try to tackle the problem in Algiers; at length, after several experiments, by the law of July 26, 1873, the legal position of land was brought completely under French law and all conditions contradictory to it were abolished. The sale of the *habous* was thus recognized in practice, but in order not to interfere further with the religious sentiments of the Muslims or with their family life, the institution was left in existence as a means to circumvent the Muslim law of inheritance, although in this mutilated form.

In Tunesia *enzel* agreements were made legally valid by the decree of 22 June, 1888, and successive subsequent decrees have facilitated the alienation of *habous*. Since 1908 a *Conseil Supérieur des Habous* has controlled their administration, alongside the central office (*djamʿiya*) for the administration of public *habous* set up by Khair al-Dīn in 1874. In Morocco a *Direction des Habous* was created in 1912, which also supervises family endowments, and new regulations for the leasing of *habous* were promulgated in 1913.

In Turkey a central administration of the *ewḳāf* was created in the early part of the xix[th] century and made a Ministry in 1840. A distinction was made between regular *ewḳāf* (*waḳf-i ṣaḥīḥ*) in *mulk* lands and irregular *ewḳāf* (*waḳf-i ghairi ṣaḥīḥ*) in *mīrīye* or state lands, or according to the method of administration, between *ewḳāf-i mazbūṭa*, which were in the possession of the Ewḳāf Ministry and administered by it, *ewḳāf-i mulḥaḳa*, which were only under the supervision of the Ministry, and *ewḳāf-i mustethnā*, which were completely independent (e.g. Christian foundations). By one of the secularizing laws of 3 March, 1924 (no. 429), the Ewḳāf Ministry was abolished, and waḳf affairs were transferred to a general directory subordinate to the Premier, which was given the task of liquidating waḳf estates by selling them to the communes and other undertakings for the public benefit.

In Egypt, all waḳf agricultural land (*rizḳa*) was confiscated by Muḥammad ʿAlī, and only waḳfs consisting of houses and gardens were left in existence. In 1851 a central administration of waḳfs was set up, and after various transformations was made into a Ministry in 1913. By decree of 13 July, 1895, all waḳfs for the common good were placed under its administration, as well as family waḳfs which for any reason were transferred to its supervision by legal decision or arrangement. After various unsuccessful projects for reform, a Committee was set up in 1936 to propose draft legislation relating to waḳfs amongst other matters, and its proposals were passed into law in 1946 after some amendment. The major innovation of the new law was to decree that all family waḳfs must henceforth be temporary, and that even public waḳfs might also be temporary, unless in favour of a mosque or a cemetery.

In Palestine, Syria and ʿIrāḳ, it was provided in the mandates that the waḳfs should be administered by the mandatory in keeping with the Sharīʿa and the conditions laid down by the founder. In Palestine waḳf affairs were placed under the control of a *Supreme Muslim Sharia Council*, and in ʿIrāḳ a Ministry of Waḳfs was set up under the constitution of 1924. In the French mandated territories, on the other hand, the waḳfs were placed under the direct supervision of the mandatory power (see Rabbath, *L'évolution politique de la Syrie sous mandat*, Paris 1928, p. 297 *sqq.*), replaced by Ministries in the independent States of Syria and Lebanon. In Lebanon family waḳfs were reformed by a law of 1947, following the general lines of the Egyptian law of 1946; in Syria they were prohibited by a law of 1949, which also provided for the liquidation of existing waḳfs of this nature.

Bibliography: In addition to the well known collections of traditions and the Fiḳh books there are numerous special works of which the following have been printed: Hilāl al-Raʾy (d. 245/859), *Aḥkām al-waḳf*, Haidarābād 1355; al-Khaṣṣāf (d. 261/875), *Aḥkām al-waḳf*, Cairo 1904; Ibrāhīm b. Mūsā al-Ṭarābulusī (d. 922/1516), *al-Isʿāf fī aḥkām al-awḳāf*, Cairo 1292; transl. B. Adda and E. D. Ghalioungui as *Le Wakf*, Alexandria 1893; Ḳadrī Pasha, *Ḳānūn al-ʿadl wa 'l-inṣāf li 'l-Ḳaḍāʾ ʿalā mushkilāt al-awḳāf*, Būlāḳ 1311. — Of the extensive literature only the more important need be mentioned: Tornauw, *Das moslem. Recht*, Leipzig 1885, p. 155 *sqq.*; Th. W. Juynboll, *Handbuch des islam. Gesetzes*, Leyden 1910, § 60; 3rd (Dutch) ed. 1925, § 62; Krcsmárik, *Das Wakfrecht vom Standpunkte des Šarīʿatrechtes nach der Ḥanafit. Schule*, in *ZDMG*, xlv. (1891), 511—576; E. Clavel, *Le Wakf ou Habous (Rites hanafite et malékite)*, 2 vols., Cairo 1896; E. Mercier, *Le Hobous ou Ouakof, ses règles et sa jurisprudence*, Algiers n.d. (from *Revue algérienne et tunisienne de législation et de jurisprudence*); do., *Le Code des hobous*, Constantine 1899; M. Morand, *Etudes de droit musulman*, Algiers 1910, p. 225 *sqq.*; O. Pesle, *La théorie et la pratique des Habous dans le rite malékite*, Casablanca n.d.; Santillana, *Istituzioni di diritto musulmano malichita*, Rome 1926, i. 246 *sqq.* (on long term agreements); M. del Nido y Torres, *Derecho musulmán*, 2. ed., Tetuan 1927, p. 163 *sqq.*; Pröbster, *Privateigentum u. Kollektivismus*, in *Islamica* iv (1931), p. 471 *sqq.* (*Manfaʿa-Berechtigungen*). — Egypt: Ahmed Zaki Saad, *Le "Wakf" de famille. Etude critique*, Paris 1928; A. Sékaly, *Le problème des wakfs en Egypte*, in *REI*, iii. (1929); S. Messina, *Traité de droit civil égyptien mixte*. T. iv.: *Traité du wakf*, P.i. 2. Alexandria 1934 (with bibliography); M. F. al-Sanhūrī, *Ḳānūn al-waḳf*, Cairo 1949; J. N. D. Anderson, *Recent Developments in Sharīʿa Law* (*MW* 1952, pp. 257—276) (relates also to Lebanon). — Syria: J. Chaoui, *Le régime foncier en Syrie*, Aix 1928 (Th. dr.), p. 57—69, 180—182. — Tripolis: Gius. Califano, *Il regime dei beni Auqâf nella storia e nel diritto dell' Islam*, Tripolis 1913; E. Cucinotta, *Istituzioni di diritto coloniale italiano*, Roma 1930, p. 309 *sq.*, 384 *sq.* (with further references). — Tunis: H. de Montety, *Une loi agraire en Tunisie*, Cahors 1927 (Toulouse, Th. dr.); E. Sultan, *Essai sur la politique foncière en Tunisie*, Paris 1930, p. 309 *sqq.*; E. Fitoussi and A. Benazet, *L'état Tunisien et le protectorat Français*, Paris 1931, ii. 393 *sq.*; A. Scemla, *Le contrat d'Enzel en droit Tunisien*, Paris 1935. — Algiers: E. Larcher, *Traité élémentaire de législation algérienne*[3], Paris 1923, iii. 203—213; J. Terras, *Essai sur les biens habous en Algérie et en Tunisie*, Lyon 1899 (with earlier literature); Hacoun, *Etude sur l'évolution des coutumes Kabyles spéc. en ce qui concerne l'exhérédation des femmes et la pratique des Hobous*, Algiers 1921 (Th. dr.); M. Mercier, *Etude sur le wakf Abadhite et ses applications au Mzab*, Algiers 1927 (Th. dr.). — Morocco: Pröbster gives earlier literature in *Islamica* iv. 373 notes, 374 note 1; Michaux-Bellaire, Paris 1914, *Les Habous de Tanger*, in *AM*, xxii.—xxiii.; L. Milliot, *Démembrements du Habous*, Paris 1918; Ch. Ader, *Le régime foncier Marocain*, Toulouse 1920, p. 52 *sqq.*; A. Mesureur, *La propriété foncière au Maroc*, Paris 1921, p. 53 *sqq.*, 75 *sqq.*; P. L. Rivière, *Traités, codes et lois du Maroc*, Paris 1925, iii. 839 *sqq.* — Persia: K. Sandjabi, *Essai sur l'économie rurale et le régime agraire de la Perse*, Paris 1934, p. 111 *sqq.* — Indonesia: C. van Vollenhoven, *Het adatrecht van Ned. Indië*, ii. Leiden 1931, p. 166; Koesoemah Atmadja, *De Mohammedanische vrome stichtingen in Indië*, 1922.

AL-**WĀḲIDĪ** (See SĪRA].

WALĪ (A.) 1. From the Arabic root *walā*, to be near, and *waliya*, to govern, to rule, to protect someone. In ordinary use this word means protector, benefactor, companion, friend and is applied also to near relatives, especially in Turkish.

When used in a religious connection walī corresponds very much to our title "saint"; but the idea behind it has given rise to a regular theory and in practice has attained sufficient importance for it to be necessary to explain the use of the term. In the Ḳur'ān this theory does not yet exist; the term *walī* is found there with several meanings: that of near relative, whose murder demands vengeance (xvii. 33), that of friend of God (x. 62) or ally of God; it is also applied to God himself: ii. 257: "God is the friend of those who believe": The same title was given to the Prophet and it is one of the names of God in the Muslim rosary.

2. According to Djurdjānī, *Ta'rīfāt*, the term walī is equivalent to that of *'ārif bi'llāh* "he who possesses mystic knowledge", "he who knows God". The Muslim saint who is important enough to merit this title is believed to possess several privileges. Not only is he delivered from the 'yoke of the passions' as Hudjwīrī says, not only has he influence with God and can 'bind and loose' but he also has the gift of miracles (*karāmāt*). He can transform himself, transport himself to a distance, speak diverse tongues, revive the dead; he can produce various phenomena, often mentioned to-day in psychic studies: thought-reading, telepathy, prophecy; he can raise himself from the ground (levitation) or summon objects from a distance. He can make a dry stick put forth leaves, check a flood, control rains and springs etc. Hudjwīrī goes even farther and attributes to the saints 'the government of the universe'. It is by their blessing, (*baraka*) that the rain falls and by their purity that plants come up again in the spring. Their spiritual influence gives victory in battles.

This conception resembles that of Indian poems of the great ascetics of Brahmanism who by power of penance succeeded in gaining complete power over nature; but in Islām this power is rather the result of a gift from God than the result of the personal merit or ascetic practices of the saints. Popular belief has however not extended the power of the saints in this way: it has rather inclined to specialise it, each of them having in the eyes of the multitude the power of performing a special miracle, like curing a particular disease, bringing success in a particular kind of business, guiding travellers, discovering secrets etc. These miracles of saints (*karāmāt*) are distinguished from the miracles of the prophet, which are called *mu'djizāt* and are besides few in number, and the theologians discuss in an interesting fashion their evidential value. It is not absolute, whereas the miracles of the prophet count as proofs of religion. — The Mu'tazilīs denied that there were men like this having special gifts; they reject the privileges and miracles of the saints and teach that every faithful Muslim who obeys God is a 'friend of God, walī'.

3. The saints have been classed in a hierarchy according to a system which is found in much the same form in different authors. There are always saints on the earth; but their sanctity is not always apparent; they are not all nor always visible. It is sufficient that their hierarchy goes on and that they are replaced on their death so that their number is always complete. 4,000 live hidden in the world and are themselves unconscious of their state. Others know one another and act together. These are in ascending order of merit: the *akhyār* to the number of 300; the *abdāl*, 40; the *abrār*, 7; the *awtād*, 4; the *nuḳabā'*, 3 and the Pole, *ḳuṭb* or *ghawth* who is unique. A number of mystics have actually been given the title of Pole. Djunaid for example was the Pole of his time; Ibn Masrūḳ was one of the 'pillars' (*awtād*). Every night the *awtād* traverse the universe in thought and inform the Pole of any defects in order that he may remedy them.

Another variant of this theory is given by Doutté from Algeria. The hierarchy consists of 7 degrees. In the lowest there are the *nuḳabā'* to the number of 300, each of whom is at the head of a group of saints without special titles. Next come the *nudjabā'*; then the *abdāl*, from 40 to 70 in number; the *khiyār*, the chosen, 7, who continually move about and spread the Muslim faith in the world; the *awtād*, pillars, 4, living at the four cardinal points of the compass with reference to Mecca; the *ḳuṭb*, the Pole, the greatest saint of his time, and quite at the top the *ghawth*, here distinct from the Pole, capable of taking upon his shoulders a portion of the sins of the believers.

D'Ohsson gives the following theory for Turkey; here also there are 7 degrees. There are always 356 saints living on the earth. The first is the *ghawth a'ẓam* or 'great refuge'; the second, his vizier, the Pole, *ḳuṭb*. Then come the 4 *awtād*, the pillars. The rest are known by their numbers: *üčler*, the 3; *yediler*, the 7; *kirkler*, the 40 and *üčyüzler*, the 300.

These seven classes correspond to the 7 degrees of beatitude in Paradise. The saints of the first three classes are present invisibly in Mecca at the hours of prayer. When the *ghawth* dies, the *ḳuṭb* replaces him and there is a moving up all through the series, the purest soul of each class rising to the next degree.

This classification of the walīs was made, according to Hudjwīrī, by Abū 'Abd Allāh Muḥammad al-Tirmidhī, who lived shortly before him (vth/xith century). This individual, also called Muḥammad Ḥakīm, wrote a work entitled *Khatm al-wilāya*, the "seal of sanctity", and founded a sect called the Ḥakīmī. One of his disciples, Abū Bakr Warrāḳ, was surnamed the "instructor of the saints", *mu'addib al-awliyā'*.

Some difficulty may be found in reconciling this system with the pure spirit of orthodox Islām; it was admitted by the theologians only with the express reservation that however great the saints, the walīs, may be, they are always inferior in rank to Muḥammad and the prophets.

4. The worship of saints is not Ḳur'ānic. Without being expressly prohibited by the Ḳur'ān it is sufficiently contrary to its spirit, Muḥammad having forbidden the worship of standing stones, tombs and every kind of superstition. But Islām had to yield on this point to the pressure of popular sentiment, which by its traditions, its tendency to the marvellous and other psychological factors, is strongly inclined to this way of expressing its religious feelings. Numerous saints, differing in different areas, are held in honour in Muslim lands, Sunnī and Shī'ī. These saints are of different origins. Some are great mystics, often founders of orders or of religious brotherhoods; others are ancestors or chiefs of tribes, princes and founders of dynasties. Some are of humbler origin, *illuminati*, half-deranged persons, *madjdhūb*, whose peculiar or incoherent utterances are often regarded as inspired, or even the simple-minded,

bahlūl. Other saints are transformations or survivals of ancient cults, heroes of old days, gods of woods and springs; we find such among the Beduins. As in the Roman Catholic worship, saints are patrons of towns, villages, trades and corporations.

In the Turkey of the sulṭāns, each province had its saint. The most venerated were: Shaikh ʿUbaid Allāh in Samarḳand; Mawlānā Djāmī, the great poet, in Bukhārā; Khōdja Aḥmad Nesefī in Turkestān; Mawlānā Djalāl al-Dīn Rūmī, the famous author of the *Methnewī* and founder of the Mawlawī order (dancing dervishes) in Ḳonya; Shaikh Ṣadr al-Dīn Ḳonawī in the same town; Pīr Naḳshbandī, founder of an order, in Ḳaṣr ʿArifān in Persia, also venerated in Egypt and Turkey; Shaikh Aḥmad Rifāʿī, founder of the order of "howling" dervishes, in Asia Minor; Aḳ Shams al-Dīn, Aḳ Bīyīk Dede, Shaikh Abu 'l-Wafāʾ, Saiyid Aḥmad Bukhārī, Ḥādjdjī Bektāsh, founder of the Bektāshīs, Ḥadjdjī Bairām Walī in Aḳ Serāi in Anatolia.

Baghdād has been called the "city of saints" on account of the great number of saints who lived in the town or whose tombs are there. The most famous is Sīdī ʿAbd al-Ḳādir al-Djīlānī, whose prestige is very great throughout the whole Muslim world. Djunaid is also an illustrious saint of Baghdād, as is Shihāb al-Dīn al-Suhrawardī who has a magnificent mausoleum in the centre of the town. Near Damascus is the tomb of Ibn al-ʿArabī, the famous mystic and prolific writer, who is honoured in Syria and elsewhere. The greatest saint of Constantinople and its patron is Abū Aiyūb al-Anṣārī, the standard-bearer of the Prophet, who fell as a "martyr" (*shahīd*) at the fort of the Golden Horn and was buried on the spot where the famous mosque that bears his name stands. A son-in-law of Bāyazīd I, Emīr Sulṭān, was regarded as a saint. Several Ottoman sulṭāns are also venerated but the title of walī has actually only been given to Bāyazīd II, on account of his piety. Other princes of the Imperial house have been regarded as saints and miracles attributed to them. Among the Arabs the only caliph who is reputed a saint — excepting of course the first four who occupy a special position — is the Umaiyad ʿUmar b. ʿAbd al-ʿAzīz, a very pious ruler.

In Egypt the most popular saints are Ibrāhīm al-Dasūḳī and Shaikh Aḥmad al-Badawī whose tombs are at Ṭanṭā. To these we may add Sīdī al-Shādhilī who died at Ḥumaithira in the mountains of Upper Egypt; his tomb is much visited. The festival of Saiyid Marzūḳ al-Aḥmadī in Cairo is the cause of one of the most picturesque processions. A very popular saint in Egypt is Sitt Nafīsa.

In Arabia various individuals were honoured in the holy cities and their tombs visited, in addition to the usual rites of the pilgrimage. At Madīna in the cemetery of Baḳīʿ are the tombs of several imāms, that of the caliph ʿUthmān and that of the amīr Ḥamza, uncle of the Prophet. The "tomb of Eve" destroyed by the Wahhābīs, as well as many others, was a few minutes from Djidda and much visited. The tomb had the peculiarity of being in several parts: the head, the navel and the feet were separated by a short distance from each other. In Mecca, in the cemetery of al-Muʿallā, the pilgrims used to visit the tombs of Āmina and Khadīdja, the mother and wife of the Prophet.

In North Africa the worship of saints and marabouts is highly developed. The road to Tripoli along the sea and the vicinity of the town are fringed with numerous tombs of marabouts, elegant in style, shaded by palm-trees, decorated with gaily coloured cloths and ex-votos placed there by the devout. In the desert at Djerbūb is the tomb of Shaikh al-Sanūsī, founder of a well known order.

The patron saint of Tunis is Sīdī Makhlaṣ and its other saints are Sīdī Ben ʿArūs, Sīdī Ben Ḳāsim, Sīdī Ben Saʿīd. The Tunisians hold in reverence the caves to which these pious men retired. This region includes the sacred city of Ḳairawān which has many tombs and the famous mosque of Sīdī ʿOḳba and that called "of the Barber" in which the barber of the Prophet is said to be buried. — In Algeria in the first rank is Sīdī Abū Madyan, a great miracle-worker whose mausoleum near Tlemcen is still much visited. No less important is Sīdī ʿAbd al-Ḳādir al-Djīlānī, the saint of Baghdād, to whom are dedicated a vast number of mosques, chapels, and cemeteries in Algeria. Over 200 *ḳubba*'s are dedicated to him in the province of Oran alone. Next come Sīdī Ben Mashīsh, successor to Sīdī Abū Madyan of the tribe of the Benī ʿArūs, assassinated in 625 A.H., whose tomb is in the Djebel ʿAlem near Tetwān; Mawlāy al-ʿArbī al-Darḳāwī of Fās, a modern saint who died not long after 1822, and was buried in his *zāwiya* near Fās; Shaikh al-Tīdjānī, founder of the order, died in 1230/1815 and also buried in his *zāwiya* near Fās. In Morocco the principal patron saints are Mawlāy Idrīs, the founder of the dynasty, venerated at Volubilis, and the sharīfs of Wezzān, even during their lifetime, on account of the blessing they bring (their *baraka*) which is much esteemed by the people; even their women are believed to possess this virtue. Several women in Morocco like Lālla Marnia, and Umm ʿAbd Allāh have been given, like Sitt Nafīsa, the title of saint (*walīya*). Marrākush has seven patron saints called "the 7 men", *sabʿat al-ridjāl*; among them are Sīdī bel ʿAbbās and Sīdī Slimān al-Djazūlī, author of a wide-spread book of prayers. In Tangiers there is Sīdī Bū al-Raḳya, a miracle-worker of the xviiith century whose festival (*mawsim*) is celebrated on the seventh day of the Prophet's *mawlid*; at Meknes, Muḥammad b. ʿĪsā, founder of the ʿĪsāwīya order. In this town a strange story is recorded of a living saint who kept standing leaning against a wall; pious people had a penthouse built above him, then a *ḳubba* without disturbing him. — In Timbuktu Sīdī Yaḥyā, a miracle-worker of the xvth century, and Sīdī Ben Sāssī are held in honour.

Bibliography: Oriental works: Among the most famous works are: Abū Nuʿaim al-Iṣbahānī, *Ḥilyat al-awliyā*, 10 vols., Cairo 1932; al-Hudjwīrī, *Kashf al-maḥdjūb*, transl. R. A. Nicholson, in *GMS*, xvii., London 1911; Farīd al-Dīn ʿAṭṭār, *Tadhkira-i awliyāʾ*, transl. Pavet de Courteille, Paris 1889. This book gives the biographies of 97 shaikhs. A similar work by Djāmī, *Nafaḥāt al-uns*, "The breathings of the esoteric life", ed. Nassau Lees, Calcutta, 1859, contains 600 biographies; Muḥammad ʿAlī ʿAinī, *Ḥādjdjī Beirām Walī*, Constantinople 1343. The various brotherhoods also have books which tell of the lives and miracles of their saints, and there are numerous works on local saints, e.g. Ibn al-ʿArabi, *Vidas de santones Andaluces*, tr. M. Asín Palacios, Madrid 1933; al-Bādisī, *El-Maqṣad* (*vies des saints du Rîf*), tr. G. S. Colin, Paris 1926.

Western works: M. d'Ohsson, *Tableau général de l'Empire Othoman*, Paris 1788, i. 306 *sqq.*; Kremer, *Geschichte der herrschenden Ideen des Islams*; Trumelet, *Les Saints de l'Islam*, Paris 1881; L. Rinn, *Marabouts et Khouan*, Algiers 1884; Goldziher, *Muhammedanische Studien*, Halle 1888,

ii. 275—378; Bargès, *Vie du célèbre Marabout Cidi Abou-Médien*, Paris 1884; Doutté, *L'Islam Algérien en l'an* 1900, Algiers 1900; do., *Les Marabouts*, in *RHR*, xl.—xli. Paris 1900; Asín Palacios, *El Mistico Murciano Abenarabi*, ii., Madrid 1926; J. W. McPherson, *The Movlids of Egypt*, Cairo 1941; and various books by travellers.

WALĪMA. [See ʿURS].

WARAḲA B. NAWFAL B. ASAD AL-ḲURASHĪ, cousin of Khadīdja, who encouraged and possibly influenced Muḥammad in the first years of his mission.

All that we know concerning him has the colour of legend: he is classed with the (artificial?) group of Meccans known to tradition as the *ḥanif*, who, abandoning paganism, resolved to seek for the true religion of Abraham. Waraḳa became a Christian; he was abstemious, knew Hebrew, studied the Bible, and had written down the Gospels in Hebrew (in the Hebrew alphabet?).

In his relations with Muḥammad he is endowed with supernatural powers, like the hermit Baḥīra. The fictitious woman who offered herself to ʿAbd Allāh in order to become the future Prophet's mother, is described as a sister of Waraḳa, who had seen on ʿAbd Allāh's forehead the sign of his son's mission. It was Waraḳa who found the infant Muḥammad when he strayed from his nurse. Khadīdja consulted him on her marriage, of which Waraḳa warmly approved. One of the earliest confidants of the first revelation, he told Muḥammad that Jesus had predicted his mission, that he had been visited by the *Nāmūs* who came to Moses, and foretold his career and final triumph. It was also Waraḳa who consoled Bilāl, tormented by his pagan master.

Tradition however admits that Waraḳa was never converted; this is rather feebly explained by making him die in the second or third year of the mission, before Muḥammad had been ordered to preach and make converts. He was probably an independent religious thinker, unlikely to follow a younger and less learned enthusiast. In the last years of his life Waraḳa became blind. After his death Muḥammad had a dream of him in white robes, meaning that he was in heaven.

Waraḳa died too early to transmit any traditions; Muslims authors on *ḥadīth* denounce as apocryphal the brief account of Gabriel's appearance which Ibn ʿAbbās claimed to have heard from him.

Bibliography: Ibn Hishām, p. 100—101, 107, 143, 149, 153—154, 205; al-Ṭabarī, i. 1147—1152; Ibn Saʿd, 1/i. 58, 130; Ibn al-Athīr, *Usd al-ghāba* v. 88; Ibn Ḥadjar, *Iṣāba*, Cairo 1325, vi. 317; *Kitāb al-aghānī*, iii. 14—15; Sprenger, *Leben und Lehre*, i. 128—134; Caetani, *Annali dell' Islām*, Introduzione, p. 129, 156, 180, 182, 183, 208, 210, 227, 231, 251, 262; Lammens, *Les Juifs de la Mecque à la veille de l'Hégire*, in *Recherches de Science des Religions*, viii. (1918), 18; M. Guidi, *Storia della religione dell'Islam*, Turin, 1935, p. 16—18; F. Buhl, *Das Leben Muhammeds*, p. 97.

WĀṢIL B. **ʿAṬĀʾ**, ABŪ ḤUDHAIFA AL-GHAZZĀL, the chief of the Muʿtazila [q.v.]. Biographical facts concerning this personality are meagre, especially from early sources, yet without considerable divergences. Born in Madīna in 80/699—700, where he was a client of the Banū Ḍabba, or of the Banū Makhzūm, he migrated to Baṣra, where he belonged to the circle of Ḥasan al-Baṣrī [q.v.], and entered into friendly relations with notable personalities such as Djahm b. Ṣafwān and Bashshār b. Burd. With none of these three men, however, these relations remained undisturbed. His wife was a sister of ʿAmr b. ʿUbaid Abū ʿUthmān, next to himself the most celebrated of the earliest Muʿtazila. He had the guttural pronounciation of the *r*; on account of his mastery of the language he succeeded in avoiding this letter, in *khuṭba*'s and sayings, specimens of which are preserved. Further he was conspicuous for his giraffe-like neck, an object of satirical lines by his former friend Bashshār.

He received the *laḳab* al-Ghazzāl because of his frequenting the spinners' market in order to bestow alms upon the poor women who exercised that métier. He was praised for being very scrupulous in touching money.

Wāṣil's deviation from the views of Ḥasan is said to have become the starting point of the Muʿtazila. The origin of the name of the sect cannot, however, be based on that fact [see MUʿTAZILA].

Four theses are ascribed to Wāṣil: Denial of Allāh's eternal qualities [cf. the art. ṢIFA]; the doctrine of free will, which he shared with the Ḳadarites; the doctrine that the Muslim who commits a mortal sin enters into a state intermediate between that of a Muslim and that of a *kāfir*; the doctrine that one of the parties who took part in the murder of ʿUthmān, in the battle of the Camel and that of Ṣiffīn was wrong, just as in the case of *liʿān* [q.v.] one of the parties must be considered to swear a false oath.

The last doctrine is made by the author of the *Kitāb al-intiṣār* the starting point of Wāṣil's system. He represents it in this form: The intention to kill a *ṣaḥābī* does not render a Muslim *fāsiḳ* (p. 170). Yet he admits to having been rebuked for this representation, on the ground that Wāṣil considered the intention to kill one of the *ṣaḥāba* as *kufr* [cf. KĀFIR].

In this connection it may be noted that the passage on Wāṣil in Djāḥiẓ' *Bayān* suggests more important deviations from orthodox Islām than those mentioned in later sources. Lack of contemporary information prevents fuller investigation of his position.

It is said that Wāṣil propagated his ideas through missionaries whom he sent to different parts of the Muslim world. Al-Shahrastānī states that in his days a sect called *al-Wāṣilīya* was living in the Maghrib. Yet the *Wāṣilīya* are not mentioned in al-Ashʿarī's *Maḳālāt*, where the name of Wāṣil occurs once only (ed. Ritter, i. 222). — He is said (see e.g. Ibn Khallikān) to have written several books or pamphlets on the theological and political questions of his day. He died in 131/748—749.

Bibliography: Abu 'l-Ḥusain ʿAbd al-Raḥīm b. Muḥammad b. ʿUthmān al-Khaiyāṭ, *Kitāb al-intiṣār*, ed. Nyberg, Cairo 1344, index; al-Masʿūdī, vii. 234; al-Djāḥiẓ, *Kitāb al-bayān*, Cairo 1311, i. 8 *sqq.*; Ibn Ḳutaiba, *Adab al-kātib*, ed. Grünert, p. 15 *sq.*; *Kitāb al-aghānī*, iii. 24, 61; al-Baghdādī, index; al-Shahrastānī, p. 31—34; al-Mubarrad, *al-Kāmil*, ed. Wright, index; al-Īdjī, *Mawāḳif*, ed. Soerensen, p. 290, 330; Ibn Khallikān, No. 791; Yāḳūt, *Irshād*, ed. Margoliouth, *GMS*, vii. 223 *sqq.*; al-Mahdī li-Dīn Allāh Aḥmad b. Yaḥyā b. al-Murtaḍā, *Kitāb al-munya*, ed. Arnold, Ḥaidarābād 1316—Leipzig 1902, index; al-Dhahabī, *Mīzān al-iʿtidāl*, No. 2301; Pococke, *Spec. hist. arabum*, ed. White, Oxford 1806, p. 214 *sq.*; Weil, *Geschichte der Chalifen*, i. 193; ii. 261, 262; A. v. Kremer, *Kulturgeschichte des Orients unter den Chalifen*, ii. 410 *sq.*; H. Steiner, *Die Muʿtaziliten*, Leipzig 1865, p. 25, 49 *sqq.*; Houtsma, *De strijd over het dogma in den Islam tot op el-Ashʿari*, Leyden 1875, p. 51 *sqq.*; Goldziher, *Vorlesungen über den Islam*, Heidelberg 1910, p. 101; H. Galland, *Essai sur les Moʿtazelites*, Geneva 1906, p. 39 *sqq.*; M. Horten, *Die philosophischen Systeme der spekulativen Theologen im Islam*, Bonn 1912, index; Houtsma, in *WZKM*, iv. 219 *sq.* A. J. Wensinck, *The Moslim Creed*, Cambridge 1932, index.

WAṢĪYA (A.), commission, mandate; as a technical term, last will, testament, legacy; *waṣī*, the commissioner, particularly the executor of a will.

1. The *waṣīya* of the pre-Islāmic Arabs was less concerned with the distribution of the estate than with orders and instructions to the survivors; it is the spiritual testament of the dying man which is to hand on obligations and secure the continuity of tradition. In this sense, according to the Shīʿa, ʿAlī is the *waṣī* of the Prophet and every imām the *waṣī* of his predecessor, i.e. the continuer of his religious task and the steward of his doctrine. The literary form known as *waṣīya* for transmitting instruction and advice, especially from devout men and scholars, goes back to the same source.

2. In so far as the *waṣīya* was concerned with property in the Prophet's milieu, it must have consisted in something between a testament and a legacy by which other persons were given a share alongside of the ʿ*aṣaba* who are normally called upon to inherit [cf. MĪRĀTH]. According to Sūra xxxvi. 50 (of the second Meccan period) to draw it up before death was a matter of course for a Ḳuraish merchant. Such a *waṣīya* is expressly ordered the believers by Sūra ii. 180 *sqq.* in favour of parents and "relatives" (Sūra iv. 33, which, without using the term demands the same thing, adds also the so-called confederates); at the same time a falsifying alteration is forbidden but a friendly interference in the interests of equity is allowed; Sūra ii. 240 going decidedly beyond the old Arab usage, makes provision for the widow by a *waṣīya* a duty. These three passages date from about the same time, the year 2 A.H. Sūra v. 106 *sqq.*, apparently later, prescribes for the *waṣīya*, which it presumes to be usual, two witnesses, the method of swearing them and the manner of challenging their evidence.

3. The later thorough regulation of the law of inheritance was doubtless intended to replace the earlier rules for the *waṣīya* [cf. MĪRĀTH]; a tradition which expressly states this was very early interpreted to mean that a legacy in favour of an heir-at-law is inadmissible at all; the former verses were therefore considered abrogated by the latter. Along with this prohibition the restriction of the legacies to one third of the estate is prominent in the traditions. Neither of these rules can be traced back to the Prophet himself, but they have obtained recognition so early and so generally that only the slightest traces of divergent views are to be found in tradition (e.g. al-Dārimī, *Waṣāyā*, bāb 8, 14, 26; *Kanz al-ʿummāl*, viii., No. 5409). The question was more disputed, in connexion with Sūra vi. 12—15, whether the legacies should have precedence of the payment of debts or vice versa; the second alternative predominated and quite early too. Further traditions reveal two opposite views on the making of a *waṣīya*: on the one hand it is urgently recommended and on the other one is advised against it; in any case, an unjust *waṣīya* is regarded as a grievious sin and a just one as a good deed. To insert pious advice in the *waṣīya* (cf. section 1) is regarded as commendable. — Stress is laid upon the statement that the Prophet died without making a waṣīya, in opposition to the Shīʿa view.

4. According to the doctrine of the *fiḳh*, every Muslim may make arrangements by will that: *a.* one or more individuals shall settle the business of the estate as *waṣī*; this *waṣī* represents the estate, actively and passively, may not however burden it with an acknowledgment (*iḳrār*) and enjoys the privileged position of a trustee (*amīn*); that *b.* he or another *waṣī* as *walī al-māl* is to administer the property of the infant children (or grandchildren) of the deceased; for this office the mother usually comes first, although according to the Shāfiʿīs, she has no legal claim to it; the *waṣī* as administrator of property is empowered to transact all business of his ward but may only pledge or dispose of his real estate in a case of obvious advantage or absolute necessity, and when the latter reaches his legal majority he must render an account; in both cases *a.* and *b.* the persons named are urgently recommended to accept the appointment as *waṣī* (the so-called *īṣāʾ*) and if possible to do the work of the office without payment; in case of necessity the *ḥākim*, the public authority, represented by the *ḳāḍī*, sees to the appointment of a *waṣī*, who in this case is usually called *ḳaiyim*; the *ḳāḍī* is also empowered to supervise the *waṣī* and if necessary to dismiss him; that *c.* legacies (*waṣīya*, plur. *waṣāyā*) which in all must not amount to more than a third of the estate after payment of debts are to be paid; if it turns out that they amount to more than a third of the estate they are cut down *pro rata* unless the heirs *ab intestato*, to whom the remaining two thirds go, confirm the provision of the deceased after his death. Under the same limitation come all gratuitous business transactions which one has undertaken in a condition of severe illness (*maraḍ al-mawt*; also, according to the Shāfiʿīs and Mālikīs, under any other serious threat to one's life) if death results from it; a legacy in favour of a person who is also one's heir, to be valid needs in every case the approval of the other heirs. It is further demanded that the person who makes the will be capable of doing business (with the exception of the spendthrift who has been deprived of this capacity) and act under no pressure; that the legatee at the time of making the will be in a position to accept the legacy (except an unborn child, which is born within the next six months) and survive the testator; further that a transfer of property in the subject of the legacy be possible (but it need not yet be in existence at the death of the testator, for example the produce of a piecc of land). The *waṣīya* can be made not only for individuals and groups of individuals but also for public purposes or even assume the form of a foundation (*waḳf*), but in this case its purpose must be one allowed by law; notwithstanding Sūra v. 106 *sqq.* (cf. Section 2), a definite form is not prescribed for making a will but the Muḥammadan law of evidence requires two witnesses even in the case of a written *waṣīya*; lastly, for validity, acceptance by the legatee after the death of the legator is necessary; the legator on the other hand retains while alive the power to alter the *waṣīya*. According to the *fiḳh*, the *waṣīya* is no real testament, but merely a legacy.

5. The limitation of gratuitous disposal of property in case of mortal illness to a third of the estate is the answer of the *fiḳh* to attempts to obtain real liberty of bequest by evasions; other plans however, which are still in practical use at the present day,

could not so easily be prohibited. Among these is the acknowledgment (*iḳrār*) which may refer to all kinds of obligations, is irrevocable, admits no counterproof and is fully valid even during a mortal illness as well as, at least according to the Shāfiʿīs, in favour of an heir; only in case of obvious impossibility is it invalid. The next two evasions are only effective before being overtaken by mortal illness. They are the so-called *hiba bi 'l-ʿiwaḍ*, i.e. a gift, in return for which another, even if insignificant, gift is stipulated or given (this gift is complete and irrevocable even if the giver does not hand it over until his death), and the foundation (*waḳf*) the yield of which the founder can allot quite freely to any one and (but this is only according to the Ḥanafīs) earmark during his own lifetime for his own support or the payment of his debts. A simple gift (*hiba*) may also be used to circumvent the restriction of legacies to a third of the estate and sometimes the *waṣīya* is actually put in the form of a *hiba*, for which as far as possible the approval of the nearest blood relations is obtained (both usual in Indonesia). Further possibilities of evasion by fictitious transactions are given in the *ḥiyal*-literature. In many Muslim countries however, in contrast to these endeavours there is a decided objection to the *waṣīya*, e.g. in Somaliland.

Bibliography: General: Peltier et Bousquet, *Les Successions agnatiques mitigées*, Paris 1935. — For section 1: Wellhausen, *Reste arabischen Heidentums* ², p. 191; Lammens, *L'Arabie occidentale avant l'Hégire*, p. 200. — For section 3: Wensinck, *Handbook* s.v. WILL; Peltier, *Le Livre des Testaments du "Çaḥiḥ" d'el-Bôkhari*, Algiers 1909. — For section 4: Juynboll, *Handleiding*, 3rd ed., p. 229, 260 *sqq.* (further literature is given there); M. Abdel Gawad, *L'Exécution testamentaire en droit musulman*, Paris 1926; Pesle, *Le testament dans le rite malékite*, Paris 1933. — For the doctrine of the Shīʿīs: M. Mossadegh, *Le testament en droit musulman* (*Secte Chyite*), Paris 1914; A. A. A. Fyzee, *The Ismaili Law of Wills*, Oxford 1933; for the doctrine of the Ibāḍīs: Milliot, in *Revue des Etudes Islamiques*, 1930, p. 188 *sqq.*

WILĀYA (A.), a general term for any legal competence.

I. In constitutional law it means the sovereign power (= sulṭān; Ibn al-Sikkīt [d. 243/857], in *Lisān*, s.v.) or the power delegated by the sovereign, the office of a governor, a *wālī*. The *wilāya* is derived from Sūra iv. 59: "O ye who believe, obey God and obey the Prophet and those in authority amongst you". It is regarded as granted by God and is a *farḍ ʿala 'l-kifāya*. A distinction is made between a general and a special *wilāya*. The *imām* [q.v.] or *khalīfa* [q.v.] possesses the general *wilāya*. According to Māwardī, the vizier and governors of provinces also have the general *wilāya*, the latter for their provinces. On the other hand, military commanders, judges, imāms (i.e. the leaders of the *ṣalāt*), the leaders of the *ḥadjdj*, financial officials etc. have a special *wilāya*. The possessors of a *wilāya* must be males of full age (*bāligh*), be in full possession of their mental faculties, have no physical defects, must be *ʿadl* and be fitted by education and knowledge for the office in question; there are also still further conditions for particular offices (e.g. the *ḳāḍī* must be a free man).

Wilāya then comes to mean the appointment and certificate of appointment of an official and in later times an administrative district.

II. In personal law every freeman possesses *wilāya* (usually pronounced *walāya*; cf. *Lisān*, s.v.), the power of disposing of himself (cf. e.g. Sarakhsī, *Mabsūṭ*, xxiv. 157, 18 *sq.*). In certain cases this power can and must be transferred to another. But even then the Islāmic jurists speak simply of a *walāya*. We have this *walāya* in the case of the administrator of waḳf properties, the executor of a will, a father with respect to his infant children and particularly in the case of *walāyat al-nikāḥ* [see NIKĀḤ] and *walāyat al-māl*, guardianship. We shall deal only with the latter here.

a. Muḥammad, himself an orphan, was always interested in the protection of orphans, e.g. in the later Meccan period in Sūra xvii. 34 = vi. 152: "Touch not the property of the orphan, except for his good, until he is grown up". In the Madīna period we are told that one should deal fairly with orphans (iv. 127), be good to them (iv. 36; ii. 83, 215) and treat them as brothers (ii. 220) and support them for the love of God (ii. 177). Muḥammad set aside the fifth of the booty for orphans among other objects (viii. 41; cf. lix. 7). The principal passage however is Sūra iv. 2 *sqq.*: "And give to the orphans their property; substitute not worthless things for that which is good, and devour not their property after adding it to your own; for this is a great crime... (5) And entrust not to the incapable (i.e. in money matters; *sufahāʾ*) your substance which God has placed with you for a support; but maintain them therewith, and clothe them, and speak to them with kindly speech; (6) and make trial of orphans until they reach the age of marriage; and if ye perceive in them a sound judgment (*rushd*) then hand over their substance to them; but consume ye it not wastefully or hastily (out of fear that) they are growing up. And let the rich guardian abstain [from it]; and let him who is poor use it for his support (eat of it) with discretion. And when ye make over their substance to them, then take witnesses against them... (10) Behold, they who swallow the substance of the orphans wrongfully, shall swallow down only fire into their bellies, and shall burn in the flame".

The pertinent traditions only contain certain developments of the Ḳurʾānic idea (cf. Wensinck, *Handbook*, s.v. Walī and Orphans).

b. The main doctrines of the Fiḳh.

1. The ward (*maḥdjūr*, i.e. the "bound") is either an orphan minor or a mentally deficient person (*madjnūn*) or a spendthrift (*safīh* or *mubadhdhir*). The *safīh* was only added about the end of the first or beginning of the second century A.H. The Ḳurʾān (cf. above) speaks, it is true, of the *safīh* but not yet in the later technical sense; the oldest expositors of the Ḳurʾān (Mudjāhid [d. 100/718], al-Ḥakam [d. 115/733], Ḳatāda [d. 117/736], al-Suddī [d. 127/744]) only understand thereby women and children or one of these two. Ṭabarī still criticises this interpretation at considerable length and defines the *safīh* as "one who on account of the dissipation of his fortune, his immorality, his injury to and mismanagement of his fortune requires control (*ḥadjr*)" (*Tafsīr*, iv. 153). Abū Ḥanīfa still refused to put the *safīh* under a guardian.

2. The guardian to be appointed should by law be the paternal father or grandfather, who is also entitled to appoint a guardian by will, the so-called *waṣī* (who may also be the mother). In other cases the guardian (*ḳaiyim*) is appointed by the ḳāḍī. The guardian must be a Muslim, who has attained

years of discretion and is in full possession of his mental faculties, of good repute (*ʿadl*) and able to undertake the office. Guardianship is a religious duty and can only be declined for important reasons approved by the ḳāḍī.

3. The obligations imposed on a guardian. He has to administer the estate of his ward and act here as *wakīl*. Among his powers are not that of arranging marriage or divorce and making of a will etc. He has to champion the interests of his ward; he may invest his ward's estate in business enterprises but not in his own business. He can only dispose of lands or houses with the approval of the ḳāḍī. He cannot have any business dealing between himself and his ward and cannot give anything away of his ward's property.

4. The guardianship is ended by the death of the guardian or of the ward, by deposition of the guardian for faithless conduct or when the ward attains years of discretion (*bāligh*, as a rule at 14) or becomes *rashīd*, i.e. capable of administering his estate himself (and according to the Shāfiʿī view also possesses the ability to recognize the true faith). The guardian has then to give his ward an account of his stewardship.

Bibliography: On I: Māwardī, *al-Aḥkām al-sulṭānīya*, ed. Enger, Bonn 1853; transl. by E. Fagnan as *Les status gouvernementaux*, Algiers 1915; transl. Ostrorog, 2 vols. (unfinished), Paris 1901, esp. introd., p. 74 *sqq.* — On II: In addition to the *Kitāb al-Ḥadjr* in the Fiḳh works: Th. W. Juynboll, *Handbuch des islam. Gesetzes*, Leyden 1910, § 44; 3rd (Dutch) ed., Leyden 1925, § 52; D. Santillana, *Istituzioni di diritto musulmano malichita*, Rome 1926, i. 232 *sqq.*; M. Morand, *Etudes de droit musulman algérien*, Alger 1910, p. 135 *sqq.*

WIRD (A., pl. AWRĀD). The technical term *wird* (etymologically "to go down to a watering-place"; not to be vocalised *ward*) means the definite time (*waḳt*) of day or night which the pious believer devotes daily to God in private prayer (in addition to the five prescribed prayers). It also means the formula of prayer recited on this occasion, called properly *ḥizb* [q.v.] (plur. *aḥzāb*; cf. Makkī, *Ḳūt al-ḳulūb*, i. 81—84 and i. 4—22). The simplest *wird* consists of 4 rakʿas, with the recitation of a seventh of the Ḳurʾān; but, very early, in private devotional prayer (*duʿāʾ* [q.v.], Sunnī as well as Shīʿī, cf. Kulainī, *Kāfī*, at the end — and Khāridjī, cf. Djaiṭālī, *Ḳanāṭir al-khairāt*, iii. 397—416) there were added litanies, either isolated phrases (*basmala, tahlīl, takbīr, tasbīḥ, taṣliya, istighfār; istiʿādha*) or isolated words (Arabic names of God; *Allāh, huwa*, and invented or cabalistic names) because they were found to be "efficacious".

When in the xiith century, Islāmic congregations were formed which took up the Shīʿa idea of the initiatory *baiʿa*, they decided to teach the novice on the day of his admittance (*talḳīn* = *akhdh al-wird*) a special *wird* (cf. for the first appearance of this term L. Massignon, *Recueil*, 1929, p. 107, 6) which became the distinctive *dhikr* of each congregation.

In practice the *wird* is divided into two: *wird ʿāmm* (*dhikr djahrī*), an exoteric formula often of some length (several hundred *istighfār*, etc. several times a day: after the *fadjr* and *maghrib* among the ʿAlawīya), and *wird khāṣṣ* (*dhikr sirrī*), "secret" name of God (e.g. *yā Laṭīf*, among the Sanūsīya), which the Shaikh only communicates to the initiate as a great mystery (cf. Ḥasan Ḳādirī, *Irshād al-rāghibīn*, p. 27—28; publ. at the end of the *Ḳawl maḳbūl* of Ibn ʿAlīwa of Mostaganem, Tunis, Nahḍa, 1339). The term *ḥizb* or *dhikr* is used by preference for the assemblies of the brethren for common recitation (old term *samāʿ*; now *waẓīfa*).

Since the xivth century special collections have been put together, in the style of the *muḥaddithūn*, containing the *awrād* of the principal Sunnī *ṭarīḳa*'s with the *isnād* of the transmission of the initiation. The oldest, the *Risāla* of the *ḥāfiẓ kubrawī* Aḥmad b. Abi l'-Futūḥ Ṭāwūsī of Abarḳuh, compiled shortly after 822/1419 (cf. Ḳushāshī, *Simṭ*, p. 75, 109 and Kattānī, *Fihris*, i. 337; ii. 274—275, 306—311), remodelled and brought up to date successively by the *shaṭṭārī* Ghawth Hindī (d. 970/1562; in *Djawāhir* and *Daradjāt*), Abu 'l-Mawāhib Shinnāwī (d. at Madīna in 1028/1619; in *Sharḥ ʿala 'l-djawāhir*), Aḥmad Ḳushāshī (d. 1070/1661; cf. his *Simṭ madjīd*, lith. Ḥaidarābād 1327) and Ḥasan ʿUdjaimī (*Risāla*; cf. ʿAiyāshī, *Riḥla*, lith. Fās n.d., ii. 214—222; and Kattānī, *loc. cit.*, i. 336—337; ii. 150, 193—195, 396), culminated in the famous manual, still unpublished, of Sanūsī, called *al-Salsabīl al-muʿīn* (cf. the article ṬARĪḲA and L. Massignon, *Recueil*, 1921, p. 169—171) where everything is found down to the "*wird* of the Hindu Yogis". These collections of *awrād*, brought from Mecca by pilgrims with *idjāza*, have spread then throughout the Muslim world.

Bibliography: The essential work is ʿAbd al-Ḥaiy Kattānī, *Fihris al-fahāris*, Fās 1346, 2 vols.

WITR. In the treatment of ceremonial law in *ḥadīth* and *fiḳh* this term is applied to the odd number of *rakʿa*'s which are performed at night. For details see below.

I. *a*. Witr (*watr* is also admitted) does not occur in this sense in the Ḳurʾān, but frequently in *ḥadīth*, which in this case also discloses to us a piece of the history of the institution, which is probably a continuation of the history of the fixation of the daily *ṣalāt*'s, as the traditions on witr presuppose the five daily *ṣalāt*'s. Some traditions even go so far as to call witr an additional *ṣalāt* of an obligatory nature (see also below, II). When Muʿādh b. Djabal, at his arrival in Syria, perceived that the people of this country did not perform witr, he spoke to Muʿāwiya on this subject. When the latter asked him: Is then this *ṣalāt* obligatory? Muʿādh answered: Yes, the Apostle of Allāh said: My Lord has added a *ṣalāt* to those prescribed to me, namely witr, its time is between *ʿishāʾ* (cf. MĪḲĀT) and daybreak (Aḥmad b. Ḥanbal, *Musnad*, v. 242). In accordance with this tradition it is reported that witr, when it had been forgotten or neglected, had to be recovered (Aḥmad b. Ḥanbal, ii. 206; Ibn Mādja, *Iḳāma*, b. 122). ʿUbādā b. al-Ṣāmit, on the other hand, denied the obligatory character of witr, on account of a different tradition (Aḥmad b. Ḥanbal, v. 315 *sq.*, 319).

A second stage in the position of witr is expressed in those traditions in which Muḥammad admonishes his people to perform witr, "for Allāh is witr (viz. One), and He loves witr" (e.g. Aḥmad b. Ḥanbal, i. 110).

The third stage of *ḥadīth*, which was to become the point of view of all *madhhab*'s with one exception, is represented in those traditions which call this *ṣalāt sunna*. Many traditions of this kind expressly deny its obligatory character and are consequently of a polemical nature; they are frequently ascribed to ʿAlī (e.g. Aḥmad b. Ḥanbal, i. 86, 98, 100, 115, 120, 145, 148 etc.). It may be that this question, like other ceremonial points, belonged to the polemical repertory of the early Shīʿīs.

b. The time of witr is mentioned in *ḥadīth* in connection with different parts of the night. "Witr consists of pairs of *rakʿa*'s; whosoever fears *ṣubḥ*, has to add a *rakʿa* in order to make the total number odd" (Aḥmad b. Ḥanbal, ii. 5, 9, 10, 75). In other traditions three *rakʿa*'s are mentioned in order to avoid the *ṣubḥ* (*fa-bādir al-ṣubḥ bi-rakʿatain*, e.g. Aḥmad b. Ḥanbal, ii. 71). The number of thirteen *rakʿa*'s occurs also (Tirmidhī, *Witr*, b. 4), and in general witr is supposed not to be allowed after the *ṣalāt al-ṣubḥ* (cf. Mālik, *Muwaṭṭaʾ*, *Witr*, trad. 24—28, and Ṭayālisī, No. 2192: "No witr for him who has not performed it before *ṣubḥ*").

Witr is also frequently mentioned in connection with the first part of the night (cf. below, II). Abū Huraira performed it before going to sleep, on Muḥammad's order (Tirmidhī, *Witr*, b. 3). Muḥammad himself is said to have performed this *ṣalāt* in any part of the night (e.g. Tirmidhī, *Witr*, b. 4). The time between *ʿishāʾ* and daybreak appears as the largest space accorded to witr in *ḥadīth* (Aḥmad b. Ḥanbal, v. 242). It is prohibited to perform more than one *witr-ṣalāt* in one night (Aḥmad b. Ḥanbal, iv. 23 bis).

c. Tradition frequently mentions the *rakʿa*'s, prayers, invocations and formulas by which witr used to be followed (e.g. Nasāʾī, *Ḳiyām al-lail*, b. 51, 54; Aḥmad b. Ḥanbal, i. 199, 350).

II. The chief regulations of witr as fixed by the different *madhhab*'s show insignificant divergences only (see Shaʿrānī, p. 198 *sqq.*), with the single exception, that witr is declared obligatory by the Ḥanafīs, whereas in all the other *madhhab*'s it is *sunna* (cf. above, I. *a*). The rules of the Shāfiʿī school are as follows: the number of *rakʿa*'s may vary between the odd numbers from one to eleven; the *nīya* [q.v.] is required; after every two *rakʿa*'s and after the last a *salām* or *tashahhud* is performed. The best time is immediately after *tahadjdjud* [q.v.] for those who do not perform this *ṣalāt* in the first third of the night. In the second half of Ramaḍān [see TARĀWĪḤ], witr is prolonged by *ḳunūt* [q.v.].

Bibliography: A. J. Wensinck, *Handbook*, s.v.; al-Marghīnānī, *al-Hidāya wa 'l-kifāya*, Bombay 1863, i. 152 *sqq.*; *Fatāwī ʿĀlamgīrī*, Calcutta 1829, i. 155 *sqq.*; al-Shāfiʿī, *Kitāb al-umm*, Cairo 1321, i. 123 *sqq.*; Abū Isḥāḳ al-Shīrāzī, *Tanbīh*, ed. Juynboll, p. 27; al-Ghazzālī, *Kitāb al-wadjīz*, Cairo 1317, i. 54; do., *Iḥyāʾ*, Cairo 1302, i. 177 *sqq.*; Ibn Ḥadjar al-Haitamī, *Tuḥfat al-muḥtādj bi-sharḥ al-Minhādj*, Cairo 1282, i. 203—205; Abu 'l-Ḳāsim al-Muḥaḳḳiḳ, *Kitāb sharāʾiʿ al-Islām*, Calcutta 1255 (1839), p. 25; Abū Ṭālib al-Makkī, *Ḳūt al-ḳulūb*, Cairo 1310, i. 31; al-Shaʿrānī, *Kitāb al-mīzān al-kubrā*, Cairo 1219, p. 198 *sqq.*; Lane, *Manners and Customs*, index s.v. Taráweeh prayers; C. Snouck Hurgronje, *Mr. L. W. C. v. d. Berg's beoefening v. h. moh. recht*, p. 402 *sq.* (*Verspreide Geschriften*, ii. 101 *sq.*); Th. W. Juynboll, *Handleiding tot de kennis der mohammedaansche wet*, Leyden 1925, p. 75.

WUḌŪʾ (A.), the minor ritual ablution which gets rid of the condition of "minor" ritual impurity (*ḥadath*). Regulations for ritual ablutions based on a belief in demons and on animistic ideas were known to the Arabs as a survival from the older semitic period but in the time of the Prophet they were hardly any longer carefully observed. The regulation in Sūra v. 6, of the late Madīna period, already betrays Jewish influence: "Ye, who believe, when you prepare for the *ṣalāt*, wash your faces and your hands up to the elbows and rub your heads and your feet up to the ankles..." (the continuation is in part identical with iv. 43). Muslim regulations for purity based on this passage developed in all details under the influence of the corresponding regulations of Judaism but on the whole are less exacting than the Jewish system. The material for the study of their origins is contained in an unusually comprehensive body of traditions, in the transmission of which Aḥmad b. Ḥanbal had a particularly large share; in it we find on the one hand a, to some extent, antinomian tendency, on the other an endeavour to regulate everything in minute detail, and lastly the harmonising tendency of the moderate elements.

The text of the Ḳurʾān taken literally prescribes a ritual ablution before each *ṣalāt*. This is actually maintained to be obligatory by the Ẓāhirīs and Shīʿīs. The four orthodox schools however are agreed that a *wuḍūʾ* is indispensible for the validity of a *ṣalāt* in case of a "minor" *ḥadath* only. This view, which it was even endeavoured to support by an insertion in the text of the Ḳurʾān ("while ye are in the condition of *ḥadath*"), represented a concession to actual practice, which had already become very slack since ancient times. According to the law, a "minor" *ḥadath* is produced by: 1. touching the skin of the other sex (sexual intercourse itself causes "major" *ḥadath*) unless the two persons are related in a way that prohibits marriage; 2. relieving nature; 3. loss of consciousness and sleep, apart from a snooze while sitting; 4. touching the sexual organs and in several other ways.

The essential elements of the *wuḍūʾ* are according to the Shāfiʿī doctrine: 1. washing the face; 2. washing the hands and the forearms up to the elbows; 3. rubbing the wet hands on the head; 4. washing the feet; 5. observing this order in the process; 6. formulating the intention (*nīya*) of performing the *wuḍūʾ* before beginning it. Other actions recommended by the law as *sunna*, are: the previous washing of the hands, rinsing of the mouth and clearing the nose (before 1); stroking through the beard with the wet fingers, rubbing the ears and rubbing the neck (before 4); uttering certain formulae at the separate actions, beginning with the right side of the body and performing certain actions three times. As a rule the *wuḍūʾ* takes barely two minutes to perform; many people do it hurriedly and confine themselves to the essential points. The demands to which the water intended for ritual ablutions must conform are fully discussed in the *fiḳh* books. If the believer has no suitable water available or on account of illness or wounds cannot perform the usual *wuḍūʾ*, it is sufficient to rub the face, hands, and forearms with sand or dust (*tayammum*). — As a rule, mosques and places of *ṣalāt* in general are provided with facilities for performing the *wuḍūʾ*.

All the orthodox schools permit a man who is at a permanent abode, during twenty-four hours, and if he is on a journey, during seventy-two hours, to rub his foot-covering instead of washing the feet at the *wuḍūʾ*, if the feet when last covered were washed clean and put into clean shoes, which must be impermeable, fit tightly and cover the whole foot. This process of *masḥ ʿala 'l-khuffain* is not permitted by the Khāridjīs nor by the Shīʿīs; as one of the most important external distinctions between Sunna and Shīʿa, this has attained a considerable religious significance and among the Sunnīs its recognition is a standing feature in the professions of faith (*ʿaḳīda*'s).

The practice of *mash ʿala ʾl-khuffain* is very old and is perhaps one of the alleviations of ritual introduced by the Muslim armies. There is besides a difference of opinion regarding the normal treatment of the feet at the *wuḍūʾ*: all the Sunnīs, the Khāridjīs and the Zaidīs demand that they should be washed, the Twelver-Imāmīs, on the other hand, rubbed only; the former view, which is in easy keeping with the sense of Sūra v. 6, is no doubt the original one, while the latter represents an attempt to emend it on the basis of the literal text of the Ḳurʾān, which caused the representatives of the older view to produce tortuous explanations.

Bibliography: On the aspects of *wuḍūʾ* in the history of religion: Goldziher, in *Archiv für Religionswissenschaft*, xiii. 20 *sqq.*; Wensinck, in *Isl.*, iv. 219 *sqq.* — On tradition: Wensinck, *Handbook*, s.v. WUḌŪʾ. — On the development of Muslim legislation on purity: Wensinck, in *Isl.*, v. 62 *sqq.* — On the doctrines of the *fiḳh*: Juynboll, *Handleiding*, 3rd ed., p. 56 *sqq.* (where further references given); Goldziher, *Die Ẓahiriten*, p. 48 *sqq.*; Lane, *Manners and Customs of the modern Egyptians*, chapt. Religion and Laws. — On *mash ʿala ʾl-khuffain*: Strothmann, *Kultus der Zaiditen*, p. 21 *sqq.*; Goldziher, *Vorlesungen über den Islam*, p. 273 *sq.* (2nd ed., p. 368 *sqq.*); Wensinck, *The Muslim Creed*, general index, s.v. Shoes. — Cf. also ṬAHĀRA.

WUḲŪF or WAḲFA (A.), "halt", means in particular the halting of the pilgrims at any spot they choose within the plain of ʿArafa; it begins on the afternoon of the 9th Dhu ʾl-Ḥidjdja and lasts until after sunset. This *wuḳūf* is considered the most essential part of the ḥadjdj. The imām of the ḥadjdj usually introduces it (before the beginning of the combined *ẓuhr* and *ʿaṣr ṣalāt*) with a khuṭba; his words can of course only be heard by those in his immediate neighbourhood. The pilgrims for their part recite portions of the Ḳurʾān, say prayers — mainly for forgiveness of sins — and cry *labbaika* and other religious formulae. The ceremony ends with the running (*ifāḍa*) to Muzdalifa. A similar halt, spent in prayer and also called *wuḳūf*, is made in the early morning of the 10th Dhu ʾl-Ḥidjdja in Muzdalifa before the running to Minā, also on each of the 11th, 12th and 13th Dhu ʾl-Ḥidjdja after the throwing of stones on the "little" and "middle" heap. The stop, spent in prayer, on the elevations of al-Ṣafā and al-Marwa in the running (*saʿy*) between these two sacred places is also occasionally called *wuḳūf*.

The significance of the *wuḳūf* in the Muslim ḥadjdj is clear: it is a kind of common worship, a "standing before God" (cf. Ibrāhīm Rifʿat, *Mirʾāt al-Ḥaramain*, Cairo 1925, i. 141). But the form of the ceremony probably has its origins in the pre-Islāmic rites. For the monotheism preached by Muḥammad would in itself have had no reason to invent the sacred rite in ʿArafa and with it the most important part of the ḥadjdj. It might however be supposed that Muḥammad wished with the help of this act of worship to fill in gaps which may have arisen from the omission of some ceremonies of the pagan pilgrimage, and to this extent the *wuḳūf* may have in a way been a new creation of his. But this hypothesis loses its probability when we reflect that the *wuḳūf* (except in the last halt on al-Marwa, which follows the last *saʿy*) seems always to precede a ritual running and to be connected with it (cf. *Isl.*, xviii. 192: *wuḳūf* in contrast to *iʿtikāf*). Now, since the ceremony of ritual running certainly goes back to pre-Islāmic rites, the same may be presumed for the *wuḳūf*. The original significance of this custom is however not thereby explained. This much nevertheless seems to be probable, that the *wuḳūf* took place on holy ground or at least in the neighbourhood of such: the *wuḳūf* of ʿArafa was perhaps located at the foot of the hill later called Djabal al-Raḥma, the special sanctity of which continued under Islām although in a disguised form. The sojourn of the Israelites at the foot of Sinai described in Exodus xix. might in a way be compared with it. The Muslim theory, according to which the whole of ʿArafa (or Muzdalifa) is *mawḳif* (place of *wuḳūf*), perhaps points to the very fact that this was not the case before Islām. This statement, it is true, is easily explained as a concession to the multitude of Muslim pilgrims who could not all find a place on a restricted area. But it may also from the first have served the purpose of destroying the influence of an old pagan sanctuary within ʿArafa (or Muzdalifa). The supposition that the *wuḳūf* in its original form presupposed the making of a sacrifice cannot be maintained, so far as the present evidence goes.

Bibliography: Th. W. Juynboll, *Handbuch des isl. Gesetzes*, Leyden-Leipzig 1910, p. 152 *sqq.*; [Wizārat al-Awḳāf, *Ḳism al-masādjid*] *al-Fiḳh ʿalā ʾl-madhāhib al-arbaʿa, Ḳism al-ʿibādāt*, Cairo 1928, p. 638—641; Muḥammad Labīb al-Batanūnī, *al-Riḥla al-Ḥidjāzīya*[1], p. 135, 141, 153 *sq.*; Ibrāhīm Rifʿat Bāshā, *Mirʾāt al-Ḥaramain*, Cairo 1925, i. 45—47, 111 *sq.*; J. L. Burckhardt, *Travels in Arabia*, London 1829, p. 264—273; Burton, *Personal Narrative of a Pilgrimage to Mecca and Medina*, Leipzig 1874, iii. 73—79; J. F. Keane, *Six Months in Meccah*, London 1881, p. 149—153; E. Rutter, *The Holy Cities of Arabia*, London-New York 1928, i. 162 *sq.*; Muḥammad Saʿūd al-ʿŪrī, *al-Riḥla al-Saʿūdīya al-Ḥidjāzīya al-Nadjdīya*, Cairo 1349, esp. p. 44 *sqq.*, 90 *sqq.*; Snouck Hurgronje, *Het Mekkaansche Feest*, Leyden 1880 (= *Verspreide Geschriften*, i. 1 *sqq.*), p. 108, 146—152, 158, 172; Wellhausen, *Reste arabischen Heidentums*, p. 79—83, 120; Gaudefroy-Demombynes, *Le pèlerinage à la Mekke*, Paris 1923, p. 227, 241 *sqq.*, 259 *sqq.*, 273 *sqq.*; W. R. Smith, *Lectures on the Religion of the Semites*[3], 1927, p. 340—342; Houtsma, *Het Skopelisme en het steenwerpen te Mina* (*Versl. en Mededeel. der Koninkl. Akad. van Wetenschappen, Afd. Letterk., R.* iv., *Deel* 6, p. 185—127, Amsterdam 1904), p. 195—197; C. Clemen, *Der ursprüngliche Sinn des ḥağğ* (*Isl.*, x. 161—177), p. 167—169; see also the articles ʿARAFA and ḤADJDJ.

Y

YĀDJŪDJ WA-**MĀDJŪDJ** (the forms Ya'djūdj and Ma'djūdj occur also), Gog and Magog (cf. *Gen.* x. 2; *Ez.* xxxviii., xxxix), two peoples who belong to the outstanding figures of Biblical and Muslim eschatology. Magog in *Gen.* x. is reckoned among the offspring of Japheth; this notion is also found in Arabic sources (e.g. Baiḍāwī on Sūra xviii. 94 [93], where also different traditions are mentioned); this much only may be said here, that the Bible as well as the Arabic sources connect these peoples with the North-East of the ancient world, the dwelling-place of peoples who are to burst forth from their isolation in the Last Days, devastating the world southwards, until they will be destroyed in the land of Israel (cf. H. Gressmann, *op. cit.*).

In Muslim eschatology this picture is repeated with many, partly fresh, details, and connected with the reappearance of ʿĪsā on the earth. Yādjūdj and Mādjūdj will be so numerous that they will drink all the water of the Euphrates and Tigris or of the Lake of Tiberias. When they have killed the inhabitants of the earth they will shoot their arrows against heaven, whereupon God shall send worms into their nostrils, necks or ears, which will kill them to the last man in one night, so that the smell of their corpses will fill the earth (Muslim, *Fitan*, trad. 110; Ibn Mādja, *Fitan*, bāb 33, 59; Aḥmad b. Ḥanbal, i. 375; ii. 510 *sq.*; iii. 77; iv. 182; Ṭabarī *Tafsīr*, xvii. 62 *sq.*, 65). Or a host of birds will catch them and drown them in the sea (Ṭabarī, *Tafsīr*, xvii. 64). They are cannibals (Thaʿlabī, p. 320) and dwell behind the mountains of Armīniya and Ādharbāidjān (Ṭabarī, *Tafsīr*, xvi. 12).

The traditions of the Arabic sources are largely connected with Sūra xxi. 96:... "until Gog and Magog shall have a passage opened for them [in the Last Days] and they shall hasten from every high hill" etc. Here is an allusion to the connection of Gog and Magog with the dam which was built by Alexander the Great, as it is said in Sūra xviii. 93 *sqq.*: "And he [Alexander] prosecuted his journey from south to north, until he came between the two mountains, beneath which he found certain people, who could scarce understand what was said. And they said, O Dhu 'l-Ḳarnain, verily Gog and Magog waste the land; shall we therefore pay thee tribute, on condition that thou build a rampart between us and them? He answered, The power wherewith the Lord hath strengthened me is better than your tribute; but assist me strenuously, and I will set a strong wall between you and them" etc. Then the text goes on to relate how Alexander built the dam or gate behind which Yādjūdj and Mādjūdj should thenceforth be shut up till the Last Days. Every night they will try to dig under the wall in order to escape, and every night the sound of their tools is heard. But God repairs before the morning the breach they have made (Ṭabarī, *Tafsīr*, xvii. 64).

Yādjūdj and Mādjūdj are of three kinds: one as tall as cedars; the second are as broad as they are tall; the third can cover their bodies with their ears (Ṭabarī, *Tafsīr*, xvi. 16).

Tradition relates that one day Muḥammad came in a hurry into the room of Zainab bint Djaḥsh, saying: So much has been opened of the dam of Yādjūdj and Mādjūdj, making a sign with his thumb and index finger. She said: Shall we perish, there being so many good people? He answered: Ay, if evil be widespread (Bukhārī, *Anbiyā'*, b. 7; Tirmidhī, *Fitan*, b. 23; Ibn Mādja, *Fitan*, b. 9; Aḥmad b. Ḥanbal, ii. 341, 529 *sq.*; vi. 428, 429).

According to de Goeje, the story of the dam (which is found in the Syriac Legend of Alexander; cf. *Bibl.*) refers in reality to the wall which surrounded a part of the Chinese empire and which had a gate in the South, called the jasper gate. He mentions reports of travellers who visited the wall, especially in the times of the caliphate.

Bibliography: The commentaries on the Ḳur'ān, on Sūra xviii. 94 and xxi. 96; for the passages in *ḥadīth*, cf. Wensinck, *Handbook*, s.v.; Ṭabarī, i. 68 *sq.*, 211 *sq.*, 218, 223, 627; Masʿūdī, i. 267, 337; ii. 308; iii. 66; Yaʿḳūbī, i. 13, 93; Ibn Khurdādhbih, *BGA*, vi. 162—169; Ibn Rosteh, *BGA*, vii. 83, 98, 148 *sq.*; Masʿūdī, *BGA*, viii. 24, 26, 32; Idrīsī, transl. Jaubert, ii. 344, 349, 380, 431; Yāḳūt, *Muʿdjam*, ed. Wüstenfeld, i. 515; ii. 440; iii. 53, 131; iv. 591; al-Thaʿlabī, *Ḳiṣaṣ al-anbiyā'*, Cairo 1290, p. 320 *sqq.*; I. Friedländer, *Die Chadhirlegende und der Alexanderroman*, Leipzig-Berlin 1913, indices; de Goeje, *De muur van Gog en Magog*, in *Versl. Med. Ak. Amst.*, 3rd series, vol. 5, p. 87 *sqq.*; Nöldeke, *Beiträge zur Geschichte des Alexanderromans*, in *Denkschriften d. Kais. Ak. d. Wissensch.*, Vienna, vol. xxxvii., No. 5; H. Gressmann, *Der Ursprung der israelitisch-jüdischen Eschatologie*, Göttingen 1905, p. 180 *sqq.*; C. Hunnius, *Das syrische Alexanderlied* (Dissertation), Göttingen 1904; do., *Das syrische Alexanderlied*, in *ZDMG*, lx. 159 *sqq.*; E. A. Wallis Budge, *The History of Alexander the Great*, Cambridge 1889; Fr. Lenormant, *Gôg et Magôg*, in *Revue des sciences et des lettres*, Louvain 1882, p. 9 *sqq.*

YĀFITH, the Japheth of the Bible, is not mentioned in the Ḳur'ān; but the exegesis of the Ḳur'ān and legend are familiar with the names of the sons of Nūḥ: Sām, Ḥām, Yāfith (exceptionally Yāfit: Ṭabarī, i. 222). The Biblical story (Gen. ix. 20—27) of Ḥām's sin and punishment and the blessing given to Sām and Yāfith is known in Muslim legend but it is silent about Noah's planting the vine and becoming intoxicated. This variation only appears at a later time [see NŪḤ]. Al-Kisā'ī completely transforms it: in the Ark Nūḥ could not sleep from anxiety; when he came out he fell asleep on Sām's bosom; the wind revealed his nakedness, Sām and Yāfith covered him up but Ḥām laughed so loudly that Nūḥ was awakened; he uttered the following blessings and curse: prophets shall be born descendants of Sām, kings and heroes of Yāfith and black slaves of Ḥām (al-Kisā'ī, p. 99). But Ḥām's descendants intermarry with Yāfith's family; thus the Abyssinians, Hind and Sind were born to Kūsh b. Ḥām; the Copts are the descendants of the union of Ḳūṭ b. Ḥām with a descendant of Yāfith. Nūḥ divided the earth among his three sons: Yāfith received the district of Faisun (Pishon). His descendants are variously given, either exactly as in the Bible (Ṭabarī, i. 217 *sq.*) or partly (al-Kisāʾī, i. 101) or quite differently. He is usually regarded as the ancestor of Yādjūdj and Mādjūdj, often of the Turks and Khazars, more rarely of the Ṣaḳāliba. Persia and Rūm are sometimes traced to Sām, sometimes to Yāfith; to Yāfith also e.g. Cyrus, who killed Belshazzar b. Evilmerodach b. Nebuchadnezzar, and Yezdigird. Briefly Sām is said to be the father of the Arabs, Yāfith of Rūm (or Yādjūdj-Mādjūdj), Ḥām the father of the Sūdān. Of the three, Semitic tradition naturally prefers Sām. But Yāfith is rarely spoken of unfavourably as in Ṭabarī, i. 223 where we are told that nothing good comes from Yāfith and his descendants are deformed. On the other hand, the 72 languages are divided as follows: 18 to Sām, 18 to Ḥām and 36 to Yāfith. He is the blessed son of Nūḥ.

Bibliography: Ṭabarī, i. 211—225; Thaʿlabī, *Ḳiṣaṣ al-anbiyāʾ*, Cairo 1325, p. 38; al-Kisāʾī, *Ḳiṣaṣ al-anbiyāʾ*, ed. Eisenberg, i. 98—102.

YAHŪD(Ī), the Jews. The message which Muḥammad as an "admonisher" brought to his people was believed by him to come from the same source of revelation as the Torah and the Gospel. If the "Arabic version" of the new scriptures was only a confirmation of what preceding "scriptures" taught, the new Prophet was referred for instruction to the Jews and Christians. The idea of the "day of judgment" which continually recurs in the early Meccan period, makes him speak of the 19 guardians of hell in order to convince those "to whom the scripture was given" of the truth of the Ḳurʾān (lxxiv. 30 *sq.*), from which it may be deduced that Muḥammad at the beginning of the first Meccan period was already engaged in trying to win over the Jews. Of them he already knew that they "studied" their scriptures (lxviiii. 37: *darasa*). It is in keeping with this that he also speaks of the *ṣuḥuf Ibrāhīm wa-Mūsā* (lxxxvii. 19), i.e. he knows that Jews and Christians ascribed to Abraham the composition of sacred books (*Jubil.*, xii. 27; *ʿAbōdā-zārā*, 14ᵇ; Fabricius, *Cod. pseudepigr. Vet. Test.*, Hamburg 1722, i. 400). Hebrew expressions are already increasing; e.g. *li 'l-ʿālamīn* = *leʿōlāmīm*, *al-muʾtafika* for *mahpēkā* (liii. 53), *ʿilliyān* for *ʿelyōnīm* (lxxxiii. 18), *gan* for "garden", *sullam* for "ladder" and *maḳām* (lv. 46), which perhaps corresponds to the Talmudic epithet of God, *hammāḳōm*.

The desire to produce a book of revelation makes Muḥammad at the beginning of the second period frequently speak of "books" in which all that has happened is written down (liv. 43, 52—53). The first reference to the "children of Isrāʾīl" whom Allāh saved from Firʿawn and whom he chose "in his knowledge" in preference to all the world (cf. Amos, iii. 2; Aphraates, *Hom.*, 16, ed. Wright, p. 331) is in Sūra xliv. 30—33. The story of Mūsā in Sūra xx. which contains Jewish legends (e.g. verses 49—52; cf. *Exod. r.*, 5, 18) thrice mentions the "children of Isrāʾīl" (verses 47, 80, 94) whom Firʿawn is to release, who received the revelation and of whose sin of the calf Mūsā complains to Hārūn. Sūra xxvi. four times mentions the "children of Isrāʾīl" (verses 16, 21, 58, 197) in connection with the story of Firʿawn and the revelation of the Ḳurʾān which "the wise men among the children of Isrāʾīl" (*ʿulamāʾ Banī Isrāʾīl* = *ḥakmē Yisrāēl*) shall recognize. Sūra xix. 58 mentions "the descendants of Ibrāhīm and Isrāʾīl" whom Allāh guided in the right path and in this connection the *millat Ibrāhīm* is put alongside of the revelation as of equal worth. Just as Firʿawn and his people are an "example" in the bad sense for later generations (xliii. 56), ʿĪsā who desired to be nothing but a servant of Allāh is an "example" in a good sense for the "children of Isrāʾīl" (xliii. 57, 59). The conception of God, formulated by Muḥammad at this time (xxiii. 116 *sq.*), seems to be of purely Jewish origin and he at this time decisively rejects the idea of Christ being the son of God (xliii. 59; xxiii. 91; xxi. 26). The story of Ibrāhīm destroying the idols, which is now given in detail (xxi. 58 *sqq.*) and which is also occasionally found among Christians (*Apok. of Abraham*, ed. Bonwetsch, p. 10 *sqq.*; Philastrius, *De haeresibus*, p. 97) is therefore rather of Jewish origin (*Gen. r.*, 38, 39). Jewish expressions which now appear are *būr* (xxv. 18), with which we may compare *Ābōt*, ii. 5; *Yōmā*, 37ᵃ. The "children of Isrāʾīl" according to the revelation granted them are to recognize none except Allāh (xvii. 2), according to the scripture revealed to them they shall twice cause ruin (verse 4) on the earth, and once live in the holy land (verse 104). Perhaps it was also Jews who at this time wished to induce Muḥammad to leave his country (verse 76). According to Muḥammad's view however, only the Ḳurʾān could smooth over the disagreements among the "children of Isrāʾīl" (xxvii. 76). It is in keeping with this that the story of Mūsā in this Sūra (verse 7 *sqq.*) has a distinctly Jewish stamp as has the story of Sulaimān (verse 17 *sqq.*; cf. *Targum Shēnī*).

As late as the beginning of the third Meccan period Muḥammad was frequently reminding the "children of Isrāʾīl" of the revelation granted them through Mūsā (xxxii. 23; xlv. 16). Allāh gave them leaders and preferred them but the Israelites fell out among themselves when the "knowledge" came to them, and now Allāh has placed Muḥammad over them as arbiter in religious matters (xlv. 16—18). Jewish expressions in the story of Yūsuf which (Sūra xii.) like the story of Nūḥ (xi. 25 *sqq.*) can be proved to be of Jewish origin are *baʿīr* for "cattle" (xii. 65, 72) and *Yūsuf aiyuha 'l-ṣiddīḳ* for *Yōsēf haṣṣaddīḳ* (xii. 46). The Hebrew word *mishnā* was probably taken over by Muḥammad at this time with the meaning of "story" (xxxix. 23). The Meccans however are still only to dispute "in the best fashion" with the "people of the scriptures" to whom they are so closely bound as regards religion (xxix. 46). Allāh had indeed granted the "children of Isrāʾīl" a safe habitation, provided them with all good things (x. 93) and given them, the weak people, "the east and the west of the land" (vii. 137). Muḥammad however now calls himself the *ummī*, the prophet of the *ummōt hā-ʿōlām*, whose coming was foretold by Torah and Gospel. He now considers the food prohibitions of the Jews as a punishment for their secession (vi. 146).

The Madīna period made Muḥammad more acquainted with Jews and Jewish conditions and he gradually drew the barriers between the "peoples of the book" and the new community of Islām. Muḥammad then turned to the "children of Isrāʾīl" with the demand that they should keep their bond with Allāh (ii. 40 *sqq.*), be conscious of their having been chosen, remember they were saved from the hand of Firʿawn (ii. 49). The Jews, if they only believe in Allāh and the last judgment, are still mentioned along with believing Christians and Sabaeans (ii. 62) but we already have it indicated that their scriptures are forgeries (ii. 75). They write it down with their own hands and say: "it is from Allāh"

(ii. 79). But in reality there are uneducated people among them who do not know their scriptures at all (*ibid.*). The punishment of hell which must overtake them is regarded by them as being only temporary (ii. 80). The "children of Isrā'īl" have broken their bond with Allāh (ii. 83). They drive one another out of the country but on the other hand ransom their prisoners (ii. 85). Mockingly they say of themselves: "our hearts are uncircumcised" (ii. 88). They made ambiguous speeches when against their will they had to accept the Torah (ii. 93: *samiʿnā wa-ʿasainā* instead of *shāmaʿnū wa-ʿāsinū*). They cling to life and many would like to live a thousand years (ii. 96). Instead of the mocking *rāʾinā* with which they address the Prophet, they are to say clearly *unẓurnā* (ii. 104). At this time many Jewish ideas came to Muḥammad, e.g. *safaka 'l-dimāʾ* for *shafak dam* (ii. 30, 84) and *khalāḳ* for *ḥēleḳ le-ʿōlām habbā* (ii. 102). The Jews believe, as do the Christians, that they alone will enter Paradise, without being able to prove it (ii. 111). From this time onwards Muḥammad calls the Jews of his time al-Yāhūd, a term by which they were already known before his time (Abū Miḥdjan, ed. Landberg, p. 72; ʿUrwa, xiii. 1), or uses the root *hāda*, while by "children of Isrā'īl" he means their Old Testament ancestors. Muḥammad noticed how Jews and Christians reproached each other with the worthlessness of their religion (ii. 113) and he sees that neither creed will be satisfied with him until he follows t h e i r religion (ii. 120). But they are not to profess Judaism or Christianity but only the "religion of Ibrāhīm", who professed the true religion (ii. 135). But neither Ibrāhīm, Ismāʿīl, Isḥāḳ, Yaʿḳūb nor the tribes were Jews or Christians (ii. 140). The Jews now refuse to follow "on the path of Allāh", that is, to fight in battle for him, and the "children of Isrā'īl" acted similarly when they asked for a king after the death of Mūsā (ii. 246). Yet Allāh had always given the "children of Isrā'īl" many clear signs (ii. 211). An expression taken over from the Jews at this time is *furḳān* for "distinction" (ii. 185). Muḥammad had heard the Jews boasting of their scriptures although in his opinion they often did not know them (ii. 78). But "the simile" for those who are laden with the Torah and will not carry it is that of an "ass carrying books" (lxii. 5 = *ḥamōr nōsē sefārīm*). The Jews should desire death rather than assert they are the "friends of Allāh" (lxii. 6; cf. 1. Chr. xvi. 12 *sqq.*). Torah and Gospel are only confirmed by the Ḳur'ān which is to be regarded as *furḳān* (iii. 3). ʿĪsā has already taught the children of Isrā'īl Torah and Gospel "book" and "wisdom" (iii. 48) and Muḥammad is the confirmer of the Torah (iii. 50). The dispute about the *millat Ibrāhīm* is therefore meaningless. Torah and Gospel were only revealed after it (iii. 65) and Ibrāhīm was neither Jew nor Christian but a Muslim (iii. 67). His real followers are Muḥammad and his community (iii. 68). The reference is obviously to the Jews in Sūra iii. 75, where there is mention of those among the "people of the scripture" who will not readily give back property entrusted to them, saying "there is no obligation upon us towards the *ummīyūn* (*ummōt hā-ʿōlām*)". It is they also who are represented by Muḥammad as relying upon scriptures which do not belong to the "scripture" at all; the reference is probably to the so-called "oral Torah" (*Tōrā beʿal pē*) (iii. 78). In reality the prophets have already solemnly pledged themselves to recognize the "apostle" who will one day appear (iii. 81), and compared with the *millat Ibrāhīm* all previous revelations are alike (iii. 84). In the dispute with the "children of Isrā'īl" regarding what is forbidden or permitted Muḥammad actually challenges them: "Bring the Torah and read it if you are speaking the truth" (iii. 93). The Jews, however, distort the sense of the words of the scriptures (iv. 46,) and if the "people of the scripture" demand from Muḥammad as a sign of his mission that he should bring a book down from heaven (iv. 153) their ancestors once asked Mūsā to do an even greater thing as proof of his mission (*ibid.*). The laws regarding food were only given to the Jews because they left Allāh's way and practised usury although it was forbidden them (iv. 160—2). Muḥammad however holds out prospect of a great reward to those among them who believe in Allāh, the last judgment and in the new mission (iv. 162). In this period falls the fighting between Muḥammad and the Jewish tribes in which, in spite of their strongholds, numbers of them were forced to emigrate (lix. 2 *sqq.*) or were taken prisoners (xxxiii. 26). Their land became Muḥammad's booty (xxxiiii. 27). After he had laid down the boundaries between the new Islām and the "peoples of the scripture", he mentions as enemies of the believers Jews, Christians, Sabaeans, Magians and polytheists (xxii. 17). Muḥammad in this period attributes hateful things to the Jews. They worship ʿUzair as "Allāh's son" (ix. 30 *sq.*; cf. Ezra xiv. 9, 14), worship their rabbis as the Christians do their monks along with Allāh, who want to "extinguish Allāh's light with their mouth" (ix. 32). Jews and Christians are wrong in saying "we are the children of Allāh and his favourites" (v. 18), since Allāh punishes them for their sins (*ibid.*). The Jews to Muḥammad are "listeners to lies and listeners to others" (v. 41), who falsify the words of their scriptures (*ibid.*) and quote their Torah against Muḥammad's mission (v. 43). But all the apostles of God, who ever legislated truthfully according to the Torah, the prophets, rabbis and teachers, were Muslims (v. 44). Believers should therefore not accept the Jews and Christians as friends (v. 51). The Jews wrongly believe "that Allāh's hand is tied" (v. 64). Muḥammad finally turns to the "peoples of the scripture" and assures them that they have "nothing to stand upon" if they do not recognize the revelation thrice given in the Torah, Gospel and Ḳur'ān (v. 68). But "the children of Isrā'īl" have always followed the apostles of falsehood (v. 70), even ʿĪsā to them was only Allāh's servant (v. 72), and the infidels among them were once cursed by Dāwūd (v. 78). Muḥammad finally finds that the Jews and idolators are the greatest enemies of the believers, while the Christians are friendly to Muḥammad and his community (v. 82). — The Hebrew expressions and terms used by Muḥammad in the late Meccan period are: *ḳaddasa* from the Jewish liturgical *ḳiddēsh* (lix. 23); *bahīma* from *behēmā* (xxii. 34); *aḥbār* for *ḥabērīm* (ix. 31, 34); *minhādj* for *minhāg* (v. 22); *kaffāra* for *kappārā* (v. 45, 95); *rabbānīyūn* for *rabbānīm* (v. 44, 63) and frequently *tawrāt* for *tōrā* (v. 43 *sqq.*). — See also the article DHIMMA.

Bibliography: A. Geiger, *Was hat Mohammed aus dem Judentum aufgenommen?*, Bonn 1833; Hirschfeld, *Jüdische Elemente im Koran*, Berlin 1878; do., *Beiträge zur Erklärung des Koran*, Leipzig 1886; Schapiro, *Die haggadischen Elemente im erzählenden Teile des Koran*, Heft 1, Leipzig 1907; Nöldeke-Schwally, *Geschichte des Qorâns*, i.—ii., Leipzig 1909—1919; Wensinck, *Mohammad en de Joden te Medina*, Leyden 1908; Leszynsky, *Die Juden in Arabien zur Zeit Mohammeds*, Berlin 1910;

Horovitz, *Jewish proper Names and Derivatives in the Koran* (*Hebrew Union College Annual*, ii., Cincinnati 1925); do., *Koranische Untersuchungen*, Berlin and Leipzig 1926, p. 153 *sq.*; Goitein, in *Tarbiz*, Jerusalem, 1932, p. 410; J. W. Hirschberg, *Jüdische und christliche Lehren im vor- und frühislamischen Arabien*, Krakow; G. Vajda, in *JA*, 1937; Speyer, *Die bibl. Erzählungen im Qoran*; F. Buhl, *Das Leben Muhammeds*, p. 213 *sqq.*

YAḤYĀ, John the Baptist. This prophet plays a fairly prominent part in the Ḳur'ān, which mentions him with Jesus, Elijah and other prophets among the just persons who serve as arguments for the oneness of God (Sūra vi. 83). The history in the Gospels of his miraculous birth is twice given (iii. 38—40 and xix. 1 *sq.*); God gives him to his parents Zacharias and Elisabeth in spite of their years. There is a kind of annunciation to Zacharias: "O Zacharias, we announce a son to thee; his name shall be Yaḥyā; no one has borne this name before him" (xix. 7). Yaḥyā speaks in his cradle and, like Jesus, has wisdom from his childhood. God gives him the title of lord (*saiyid*) which according to the commentators means merciful. His characteristic qualities are gentleness and chastity. A point discussed is the phrase in Sūra xix. 12: "O Yaḥyā, take the book with steadfastness", which seems to mean that Muḥammad thought that John had received a revealed book. The commentators, however, do not admit this meaning; they are of the opinion that the book mentioned here is the *Torah*, the Pentateuch, and the Yaḥyā did not receive a special revelation but had as his mission only to "confirm the word of God" (iii. 39). Zamakhsharī simply says that God gave him understanding of the Torah. — The Ḳur'ān does not mention his role of Baptist, and does not tell the story of his death.

The legend of John the Baptist among the Arabs presents different features according to different authors. Ṭabarī says he was the first to believe in Jesus; he makes him survive Jesus and says that he was put to death at the request of Herodias, niece of Herod or daughter of his wife, for having said to the king that he could not marry her. A curious episode, developed at length by Ṭabarī, is that of the boiling of the blood of the decapitated Baptist. The blood boils not only in the dish on which the head is presented but on the tomb of the martyred prophet and can only be restored to its normal condition after great calamities. The blood and the decapitated head speak. — The legend is evidently in some way connected with the Neapolitan cult of the blood of St. Januarius.

Mas'ūdī relates of Elisabeth, John's mother, the story of the flight into Egypt which the Gospel tells of Mary. Elisabeth fled with her infant son to escape the wrath of a king. John sent as a prophet to the Jews is disowned by them and put to death. Later his "blood" is avenged by a king named Kherdūsh who massacres many of the Jews. Mas'ūdī knows the episode of the baptism of Jesus by John, the scene of which he puts in the Lake of Tiberias, or in the Jordan. Al-Bīrūnī mentions among the feasts of the Syrian calendar that of the "beheading" of John the Baptist on the 29th of the month Āb, and he records that, according to al-Harawī, there could be seen in front of the "Pillar Gate" at Jerusalem a pile of stones said to have been thrown by the passers-by to restore John's blood to a normal state, but the blood would not cease boiling and continued to do so until a Persian king had sent a general who put many men to death on the prophet's grave. Al-Bīrūnī thinks, like Ṭabarī, that this general was an Ashkanian.

At the present day there is still shown a tomb of John the Baptist in the great mosque of Damascus, where is also a tomb of Zacharias mentioned by Ibn Baṭṭūṭa.

As to the "Christians of St. John" or Mandaeans, the Ḳur'ān and the Arab writers hardly know them; if they do refer to them, it is not by these names but as "Ṣābi'a" [q.v.]. They regard them as a sect intermediary between the Jews and the Christians and admit that they have a "book"; they do not however give them John the Baptist as their prophet but Noah.

Bibliography: Ṭabarī, indices, s.v.; the Chronicle of Ṭabarī-Bal'amī, transl. H. Zotenberg, Paris 1867, i. 535, 568; Mas'ūdī, *Murūdj*, s. index; al-Bīrūnī, *Āthār*, ed. Sachau, p. 297, 301; Chwolsohn, *Die Ssabier und der Ssabismus*, St. Petersburg 1856.

YA'ḲŪB, the patriarch, the son of Isaac in the Bible, is in the early Meccan Sūras (vi. 84; xix. 49; xxi. 72; xxix. 27) the brother of Isḥāḳ, son of Ibrāhīm; the genealogy: Ibrāhīm, Ismā'īl, Isḥāḳ, Ya'ḳūb, the (12) tribes (ii. 136, 140), is more true to the Bible. Ya'ḳūb is numbered among the prophets (xix. 49). He is once or twice mentioned in the Yūsuf Sūra: Ya'ḳūb orders his sons not to go through a door (xii. 67); he becomes blind through sorrow and regains his sight when Joseph's coat touches his eye (xii. 93, 94).

Post-Ḳur'ānic legend relates that Ya'ḳūb and Esau fought already in their mother's womb, that Ya'ḳūb was to be born first but to spare his mother took second place: Ya'ḳūb was really entitled to the rights of the first-born (Ṭabarī, i. 350). Ya'ḳūb's journey to Haran and his stay with Laban are told as in the Bible, but in several versions Ya'ḳūb only marries Rāḥīl after Leah's death. The Yūsuf Sūra receives many embellishments. On hearing that a wolf has torn Yūsuf to pieces, Ya'ḳūb wishes to see the wolf; the brothers bring the first wolf they can find, but this beast miraculously begins to speak and exposes their deceit. Many reasons are given as to why Ya'ḳūb has to suffer. Ya'ḳūb writes a letter to the king of Egypt. After eighty years of separation, Ya'ḳūb recognizes at a distance of 80 parasangs the heavenly aura of Yūsuf. The haggada is known according to which Esau and Ya'ḳūb dispute about the burial-place in Machpelah: "thou hast made me lose the blessing, thou shall not make me lose the tomb" (Ṭabarī, i. 359, very similarly *Sōṭā* 13a; later parallels in Ginzberg, *Legends of the Jews*, v. 371, 422.

Bibliography: Ṭabarī, i. 354—413; al-Tha'labī, *Ḳiṣaṣ al-anbiyā'*, Cairo 1325, p. 67—89; al-Kisā'ī, *Ḳiṣaṣ al-anbiyā'*, ed. Eisenberg, p. 153—156; A. Geiger, *Was hat Mohammed* etc., 1902 2, p. 135—138; J. Horovitz, *Koranische Untersuchungen*, 1926, p. 152 *sq.*; Snouck Hurgronje, *Verspreide Geschriften*, i. 24.

YATĪM (A.), the orphan, i.e. fatherless minor child. The improvement of the social position of orphans, who were particularly numerous in ancient Arabia, played a large part in the Prophet's scheme of social reforms. The vigour with which he had to intervene on their behalf is significant of the conditions which he found. When relations did not take charge of them, the care of orphans fell upon the *saiyid* of the tribe; this obligation was also put upon the Prophet as leader of the community. In Sūra xciii. 6, 9 (of the first Meccan period) the Prophet is reminded that he himself as an orphan was protected by Allāh, and admonished on his part not to oppress the orphan. The Ḳur'ānic passages which make good treatment of orphans a duty and forbid their oppression cover a long period: Sūra cvii. 2; xc. 15; lxxxix. 17 (also of the first Meccan period); xvii. 34; lxxvi. 8; xviii. 82 (of the second Meccan period); vi. 152 (of the third Meccan period); ii. 83, 177, 215, 220 (of the year 2); iv. 8—10, 36 (of the years 3—5). In Sūra viii. 41, and lix. 7 (of the years 2 and 4 respectively) the orphans are allotted a share in the fifth part of the *ghanīma* [q.v.] or in the *fai'* [q.v.]. Illegal appropriation of the property of an orphan — apparently by his guardian — is specially condemned and in Sūra iv. 10 even threatened with the punishment of hell. Sūra iv. 2—6, 127 (also of the years 3—5) where we have the fullest reference to orphans, is particularly directed against such crimes: "2. And give the orphans their property; substitute not the vile (in exchange) for the good, and spend not their property in addition to your own; this is a great crime. 3. If ye fear that ye cannot act justly against orphans, then marry the women who seem good to you by twos, or threes, or fours; and if ye (still) fear that ye cannot act equitably, then (only) one or (the slaves) whom your right hand possess; that keeps you nearer to not being partial....; 6. Prove the orphans, and when they reach the (age of) marriage, if ye perceive in them a sound judgment, then hand over to them their property; but spend ye it not extravagantly and in anticipation of their growing up. Let the rich (guardian) abstain and let him who is poor spend in reason. When ye hand over to them their property, take witnesses before them; Allāh maketh a sufficient account". Verse 127 apparently refers to verse 3: "They will ask thee a decision about women; say: Allāh gives you a decision about them and that which is rehearsed to you in the Book, about orphan women to whom ye do not give what is prescribed for them, and whom ye want (or: want not) to marry; also about weak children; and that ye deal towards orphans with fairness. What ye do of good, verily Allāh knoweth it". It is probable from this that verse 3 also deals with orphan girls where marriage with their guardian is in prospect; the exact interpretation is uncertain. The two verses are interpreted in this sense also in a tradition ascribed to 'Ā'isha; but the details are not reliable. Another tradition not dependent on the wording of the Ḳur'ān (in Aḥmad b. Ḥanbal) forbids the guardian to force an orphan girl who is his ward to marry him. Other traditions simply repeat the substance of the Ḳur'ānic prescriptions. The idea of protecting the orphan is also at the basis of a *ḥadīth*, which makes the Prophet dissuade Abū Dharr, the type of the pious and inexperienced man, from undertaking a guardianship. In two points the tradition shows a development of the doctrine. In the first place the question is raised when the position of being an orphan may be considered to end (it is on this problem that Muḥammadan law has worked out its conception of majority); various answers, some emphasizing age, others discretion, are put in the mouth of Ibn 'Abbās and 'Alī; of the later *madhhabs* the Mālikīs and Shāfi'īs make the power of disposing of his own affairs in one who has attained his majority dependent also on his discretion, while the Ḥanafīs drop this condition after his 25th year. There were also differences of opinion as to whether the money of orphans (and of minors in general) was liable to *zakāt* or not; the latter view is still held by the Ḥanafīs and the former by the other schools; this is justified not only by the direct statement that 'Ā'isha in such a case paid *zakāt* but also by the demand attributed to the Prophet or to 'Umar that the guardian should trade with his ward's money so that the *zakāt* should not gradually consume it. On the doctrines of the *fiḳh* on orphans cf. WAṢĪYA and WILĀYA. It is worth noting that the right of the poor guardian to use the orphan's estate has been limited by the *fiḳh* to receiving compensation for his trouble; and the Ḳur'ānic command to take witnesses has lost most of its importance through the fact that the guardian is considered a trustee (*amīn*).

Bibliography: Wensinck, *Handbook*, s.v. ORPHANS.

YAZĪDĪ, YAZĪDĪYA, the name of a Kurd tribal group and of their peculiar religion which shows ancient characteristics.

Area of Distribution. The Yazīdīs are found scattered over a wide area usually leading a settled life but also split up into nomadic clans: 1. in the district of Mōṣul in the northern 'Irāḳ, in Assyria proper, in the district of Shaikhān. Special mention may be made of: Bā'adhrī (Bā'idhrī, Ba'idhrā) about 40 miles N. of Mōṣul, the residence of the chief emīr, their political head; three hours to the north at Lālesh in the valley Shaikh 'Adī is the tomb of their chief saint Shaikh 'Adī, their national sanctuary and the centre of their national and religious life; Baḥazanīye, north of Alḳosh at the foot of the hill on which is the Chaldaean monastery of Rabbān Hormuzd; and also Bā'shīḳā (Bā'ashīḳā, Ba Heshīke) N. E. of Mōṣul, the centre of the tombs of the shaikhs; 2. on the Djebel Sindjār, 100 miles west of Mōṣul, a range of hills in the middle of the desert, which is the great bulwark of their efforts for freedom and independence. The chief Sindjār-Shaikh lives in the Beled Sindjār (picture of the stronghold in P. Schütz, *Zwischen Nil und Kaukasus*, p. 135); formerly his residence was in Milik (Mirik); 3. in the district of Diyārbakr, N. and N. E. of the Tigris; 4. in the district of Aleppo, W. of the Euphrates, at Killīs and 'Aintāb; 5. in Russian Armenia (Kars, Eriwan) and in the Caucasus (at Tiflis) — There are also Yazīdīs in Persia. The total number of the Yazīdī's can only be approximately estimated; there can hardly be more than 60,000—70,000 altogether, while only half a century ago they numbered 120,000—150,000.

The name Yazīdī, which the Yazīdīs themselves feel to be modern, seems to have nothing to do with Yazīd b. Mu'āwiya or with Yazīd b. Unaisa, with whom it is connected, and as little with the name of the Persian city of Yazd. It probably comes from the modern Persian *ized* (angel, deity). The Azidi, Izidi, Izedi or Izdi would therefore be as they themselves say "worshippers of God", an etymology known to the Yazīdīs, and quoted as early as Campanile, *Storia della regione del Kurdistan*, Naples 1818, p. 148, as *Seguace di Jazad* (*Iddio*). The Yazīdīs call themselves Dāsin, Dasnī, Dasenī, plur. Dawāsīn, Duāsin, Dawāshim, probably from the name of an old Nestorian diocese. In 941/1534 Sulṭān Sulaimān gave the Yazīdī chief Ḥusain Beg Dāsinī, who was later executed, the sandjaḳ of Arbil and the wilāyet of Sohrān. Among the Syrians, the Yazīdīs are called Dasnāyē. The defamatory name given them quite unjustly is *shaiṭān-perest* or *'abede-i Iblīs* ("devil-worshipper") although they should rather be called "angel-worshippers", and *čiragh söndiren* ("light-extinguishers"). Another term of abuse for them is the Turkish *halta* ("dog-collar").

Although the Yazīdīs hold no communion with the neighbouring tribes and in particular do not intermarry with them, they look exactly like Kurds, even those who live in Syria in the centre of an Arabic speaking area, although two types are to be distinguished among them: one, their own traditional type, Assyrian-Semitic with particularly thick hair and beard, and the other more an Indo-Germanic type. In any case traces of the early inhabitants of the country still survive in them. They have some physiological similarities with the earlier Van Armenians: an Armenian intermixture is not to be denied. Their thick hair earned them from the Turks the nickname *sačli Kurd* ("hairy Kurds") and *sekiz bïyïklï* ("eightfold bearded") because hair grows on the lips, eye brows, nostrils and ears.

They are organised like the Kurdish tribes, with an emīr or chief of the tribe (*agha-e eʾe*) at the head. According to Karcew, the tribe is divided into bodies of elders (*ruspiti*). Every family or sept forms a unit by itself. On the tribal organisation, the taxes and labour given to the chiefs, on the law of inheritance (primogeniture, but restricted by the condition of worthiness), on the patriarchal life of the tribes, settled and nomadic, see Jegiazarow, *Kratkij etnografičeskij očerk Kurdov*, in *Zapiski*, xiii., Tiflis 1891, who gives very full data (Menzel, *op. cit.*, p. 108); also Minorsky, s.v. KURDS in *Encyclopaedia of Islam*, Isya Joseph and Empson.

The language of the Yazīdīs is almost without exception Kurdish, with a number of dialects which are particularly closely related to Kurmandjī Kurdish. The Yazīdīs of the Sindjār also speak Arabic.

The origin and evolution of their peculiar synthetic religion have not yet been fully explained but it seems to include old pagan elements (but no worship of the sun and moon), Iranian-Zoroastrian elements (echoes of Persian dualism), Manichaean (the Persian gnosis), Jewish elements (prohibition of certain foods), features from Christian sects, especially the Nestorians (baptism, a kind of eucharist, breaking of bread, visiting of Christian churches at weddings, permission to drink wine), also Muslim elements (circumcision, fasting, sacrifice, pilgrimage, Muslim inscriptions on tombs), Ṣūfī-Rāfiḍī features (secrecy of doctrine, ecstasy, reverence for a large number of Ṣūfī-Shaikhs), Sabaean (transmigration of souls) and Shamanistic features (burial, interpretation of dreams, dances).

The spoken language is used throughout in worship. It is therefore all the more remarkable that the text of the two sacred books, said to have been in existence before the Creation and to have been learned from the original copies, was in Arabic, although only the priests and the ḳawwāls learned some Arabic. These are the *Kitāb al-Djilwa* (*Kitēb-ī Djälwä*) "the Book of Revelation" and the *Maṣḥaf räsh* "the Black Book". "Black" seems to imply worthy of veneration. One cannot conceal a certain disappointment on becoming acquainted with the sacred books. A hymn in praise of Shaikh ʿAdī in 80 verses of considerable theological merit, written in Arabic, is also regarded as a kind of sacred book.

In the actual doctrinal system, the six minor deities (see below) seem to disappear completely and to be replaced by the dualism between God and Malak Ṭāʾūs, the peacock angel. God is only the Creator, not the preserver of the world. He is passive and does not trouble about the world. The active, executive organ of the divine will is Malak Ṭāʾūs, with whom Shaikh ʿAdī, who has risen to divinity through transmigration, seems to form one. Malak Ṭāʾūs is God's *alter ego* and is the active aspect of God's being. He is one with God and inseparably bound up with him. To this extent Yazīdism is monotheistic but there are also semi-divine and divine beings, intermediate between God and man. Malak Ṭāʾūs is a good deity. Yazīdism does not countenance the worship of Satan. Shaiṭān = Malak Ṭāʾūs is regarded as an angel who has fallen into disgrace and, according to the legend, for his repentance has been restored or will be restored to God's favour. The Yāzīdīs do not appear to believe in a hell, in a devil in our sense or in the punishment of hell, which would be an incorporation of the principle of evil. Evil is denied. According to legend, Malak Ṭāʾūs with his tears of repentance in hell filled 7 jars in 7,000 years and with them the fires of hell were extinguished. The triumph over hell by this theory of redemption is found in several variants in Yazīdī legend. Corresponding to the non-existence of an eternal hell is the belief in transmigration, which makes possible a gradual purification through continual rebirths. It is strictly forbidden to pronounce the name of Malak Ṭāʾūs: *Shaiṭān* even as the name of the deity (art. 5 of the creed). The white pearl is of the same nature and identical with the peacock. The peacock also plays a part in early Christian and other religions as a symbol of the sun and of immortality, as its flesh is said not to decay. The problem of the origin and nature of the worship of the divine angel Malak Ṭāʾūs, who is represented in the form of a bird, as a cock or peacock, is not yet solved.

The most concrete expressions of Yazīdism are the figures of peacocks made of bronze or iron, the so-called *sandjaḳ* (Yaz. *sindjaḳ*) pl. *sanādjiḳ*, sometimes quite crude figures, sometimes very fine products of Persian art. Pictures of them may be found in Layard, Menant, Guerinal, Isya Joseph, *Anthropos* VI, Empson, Ḥusnī etc. There are seven *sandjaḳ*, corresponding to the number of the angels who took part in the creation of the world; they have particular names, being called after individuals who have attained divinity through transmigration: Dāwūd, Shaikh Shams al-Dīn, Yazīd (b. Muʿāwiya), Shaikh ʿAdī, Shaikh Ḥasan al-Baṣrī, Manṣūr (al-Ḥallādj). The last named is the oldest *sandjaḳ*, weighs 679 lbs. and is called "caliph of the *sandjaḳ*". It remains always at the tomb of Shaikh ʿAdī. The seventh *sandjaḳ* is lacking in all the illustrations. Six *sandjaḳs* make the round of the various Yazīdī lands yearly. The travelling *sandjaḳs* are taken by the Ḳawwāl and Kočak in their own simple receptacles on the dangerous journey. If lost they seem to be replaced at once. They are kept in the treasury *Khazīnat al-Raḥmān* in Shaikh ʿAdī.

Here one may deal with the often mentioned snake, of the height of a man, painted black, which is cut into the wall at the entrance door of the sanctuary. On the same wall are carved a number of peculiar figures: rings, daggers, a peculiar kind of crozier or seven armed sceptre, hands, spoons, croziers, combs. They are probably family or tribal marks, as the little houses for pilgrims scattered all over the valley bear the same marks on the walls.

The idea of their complete separation from the rest of mankind held by the Yazīdīs is remarkable. They are convinced that they are descended from a child (Shahīd b. Djaiyār) or twins, developed from the seed of Adam only in a jar which was kept closed for nine months, while the jar with the seed of Eve who was disputing for priority produced only vermin. On this is based the belief of the Yazīdīs in their unique position which does not allow them to mix with the rest of mankind who are descended from Adam and Eve. One cannot become a Yazīdī, one must be born one. This strict isolation is intensified by a rigid caste system within the Yazīdīs. The most dreadful punishment for a Yazīdī, which can only be completely realised when we remember this fact, is excommunication, expulsion from his people, because this also settles the fate of his soul.

The prayers consist of a Kurdish main prayer and a morning prayer at sunrise, which has to be said at a distance from members of other creeds, and in the direction of the sun (Creed, art. 3). They ought at the same time to walk round a stone put up for the purpose. The principal prayer is addressed to Malak Ṭāʾūs and shows that the latter is regarded as identical with the Christian and Muslim God. The seven divine angels are addressed. A three days' fast is observed in December, the fast being broken by drinking wine with the proper Shaikh or Pīr. The performance of prayer, however, is — apparently under Ṣūfī influence — not regarded as a strict duty. According to the Yazīdī catechism, Saturday is the day of rest and Wednesday the holy day.

The annual pilgrimage to the tomb of Shaikh ʿAdī on Sept. 15—20 of the Greek Julian calendar is a strict religious duty. This pilgrimage to the national sanctuary is the principal expression of the national and religious isolation of the Yazīdīs. The feast of the pilgrimage is celebrated with ritual ablutions by bathing in the river, by washing or dipping the *sandjaks*, with processions, music (flute, drum and tambourine), hymns, esctatic songs and dances by the priests, which recall the Ṣūfī *dhikr* and Shamanistic rites, the lighting of hundreds of sesame oil-lamps at all the saints' graves, by offerings and special foods (*harisa, sawīḳ*), the cooking of a sacrificed ox (*kaldūsh*).

The blessing of Shaikh ʿAdī is important for the rites, i.e. little balls of earth or clay from the tomb of the saint, and consecrated water from the water in which the *sandjak* has been dipped for the living and the dead. The little balls of earth are used as talismans and as a medicine and as extreme unction for the dying. All eyewitnesses agree as to the devoutness and dignity of all these ceremonies in the outer court of the sanctuary. The ceremonies within the sanctuary, which seem to include the reading of sacred books, have never been witnessed by an outsider. Trees, at the sanctuary mulberry trees, are also honoured, surrounded with walls and visited by the sick. These trees have their own personal names. Non-obligatory pilgrimages are made to the tombs of several other saints, mostly Ṣūfī shaikhs. The most important festival of the year, the feast of the New Year: *sar-i sāl, sardalī, sarsalīye* on the first Wednesday in April, is celebrated with great solemnity, as among the Harranians, at the tomb of Shaikh ʿAdī but without music.

The obligatory institution of the brotherhood of the next world, which corresponds to our system of godfathers (each Yazīdī must have a brother and sister of the next world), binds one to a daily kiss of the hand and presence in the dying hour. The collar of a new shirt, which unlike other eastern shirts is always buttoned behind, must in any case be opened by a sister of the next world.

In marriage, endogamy is strictly observed and the limitations imposed by the caste system are very marked. Marriage is as a rule monogamous, except in the case of the emīr, who is allowed several wives. It is marriage by purchase with simple ceremonies performed by the local shaikh or pīr, who breaks a loaf in two and gives it to the two parties. The bride wears red clothes and has to visit all the places of worship including the Christian churches on the way. The bridegroom on her entering the house gives her a blow with a stone as a sign of her subjection. Drums and fifes are necessary. Here and there the old system of marriage by capture survives, but it is now forbidden. The punishment for adultery used to be death. Divorce is rendered difficult through the necessity of having three witnesses. The widow may be remarried six times. If a Yazīdī remains more than a year abroad, he cannot live with his wife again nor can he receive another Yazīdī woman to wife.

Baptism is a characteristic ceremony: it is performed by a shaikh or pīr plunging the child three times into the zemzem in a dark vault of the sanctuary in the first week after birth. In the case of Yazīdīs living at some distance away, consecrated water brought by the ḳawwāls is used. Circumcision, which takes place soon after baptism, seems to be more a matter of choice. In some Yazīdī tribes it is said to have fallen into disuse some time ago, probably to escape military service. The burial ceremonies are peculiar. The corpse is buried immediately after death with arms crossed and pointing to the east. In the case of persons of rank, a rough wooden figure is hung with the deceased's clothes and carried for three days in procession with music. The tomb is repeatedly visited by the mourners. On the 3rd, 7th and 40th day and the anniversary memorial services are held. After death an answer to the question of the rebirth of the soul of the deceased is sought from the interpretation of a dream of a priest or kočak.

The whole structure of this people, small and scattered but extremely well organised, is theocratic. The Yazīdīs fall into two very distinct classes:

I. The laity (*murīd*) who form one great caste without consideration of position or wealth and among whose members there is no distinction in principle, in spite of the division into common Yazīdīs and notables (emīrs), so that marriage between them is possible and frequent. Every Yazīdī is the novice or disciple of a definite shaikh or pīr, whose hand he must kiss every day, with whom he must break his fast by drinking wine and who has to perform the various rites of worship for him.

II. The clergy, priests, *rūḥān, kahana,* who enjoy extraordinary respect and reverence. The cleric must not cut his beard nor crop his hair. As regards duties the clergy are divided into six classes and as regards exclusiveness into three rigidly marked classes. Every one must live and die in the caste in which he is born

The *rūḥān* are divided into the following classes:

1. The *shaikhs* who are descended from only five families in all are believed to be descended from pupils or brothers of Shaikh ʿAdī. The houses of the shaikhs serve as the places of worship of their charges.

2. The *pīrs*, priests of less exalted descent. The shaikhs and pīrs are the regular clergy and pastors, they enjoy immunity of person and various privileges. The so-called *mollā* or *imām*, who claims descent from Ḥasan al-Baṣrī is said alone to have the right

to read and write. At one time he had charge of the sacred books but they are now kept for safety in Sindjār. Writing is strictly forbidden to the common Yazīdīs by custom, probably in order not to profane it, since according to the *Maṣḥaf*, xxxi., God himself puts creation on record.

3. The *faḳirs* or *ḳarabash* ("blackheads", on account of their black headgear), a kind of order, a voluntary brotherhood, recruited from the shaikhs and pīrs and under a head called *kāk* "master", who lives near Aleppo and receives the income of the *sandjaḳ* Yazīd.

4. The *ḳawwāls*: singers, clergy of minor rank. There is a gild of musicians said to number 50 men, which has to take part in all religious festivals by singing hymns (we have two of these hymns with the music), playing the flute, tamborine or drum. They also act as *missi dominici* of the chief shaikh and chief emīr. They are farmers of the sacred images, the *sandjaḳ*, for which they had to pay an annual rent and with which they went regular definite circuits through the different Yazīdī districts in order to strengthen the faith of the Yazīdīs and keep them together and to collect offerings.

5. The *kočak*, dancers, who serve in considerable numbers at the tomb of Shaikh ʿAdī (the estimates vary between 30 and 300) and as ministrants of the *ḳawwāls* carry the *sandjaḳs* to the villages on their circuits and dance at festivals in frenzied ecstacy with their long hair unbound.

6. The lowest class of clergy: the *awḥān* or *awān* (deacons) and *ghulām-e odjaḳh-e Shēkh ʿAde*, the servants at the tomb of Shaikh ʿAdī, together with a *ferrāsh* (sacristan to look after the oil-lamps) and 4 or 5 *shāwish* (*čawsh*): doorkeepers who serve in the sanctuary. Each Yazīdī village also has a *shāwish* to maintain order. The head of the servants at the tomb is the *ikhtiyār* of Merke (Menzel, *op. cit.*, p. 147, note 1).

At the top of this theocratic organisation there are a religious and a secular head:

1. The chief Shaikh: *mīr-i shaikhān*, known as *Shaikh Nāẓir*, who is said to be descended from the family of Ḥasan al-Baṣrī or from a brother of Shaikh ʿAdī and lives in Lālesh. He takes precedence of every one and the supreme spiritual power is in him. He is infallible on questions of belief. He is the chief authority on and expositor of the holy scriptures; he alone gives legal decisions, and — with the approval of the chief of the tribe — sentences to the severest punishment, excommunication. He can summon to the holy war — this recalls the *djihād* — but the leadership devolves on the chief emīr.

2. The Mīrzā Beg or *emīr al-umarāʾ*, the prince of the Yazīdīs, who according to the *Maṣḥaf* is regarded as a descendant of Shāpūr but is usually called a descendant of Yazīd and exercises the highest political and secular power. He lives in Bāʿadhrī. His person enjoys immunity and he receives voluntary offerings. His word is final on all secular matters. He alone represents the Yazīdīs to the outer world.

We are quite in the dark regarding the first appearance and early history of this people who reveal so many diverse elements. According to the chief shaikh, the Yazīdīs, Layard tells us, have a chronology of their own, an era beginning in 292 A.D. It is not clear what part the caliph Yazīd b. Muʿāwiya (60—64/680—683) really plays in Yazīdism; according to the origin of the name already given, he can have had nothing to do directly with their foundation. Guidi however holds — in contrast to views hitherto held by Eurpean scholars — that the connection of Yazīdism with Yazīd can no longer be doubted, and regards the Yazīdīs as having at one time been Muslims, a view which has always been held by Muḥammadan theologians. According to the Yazīdī view, Yazīd was not the real founder of the Yazīdīya, but only the restorer of the original sect, founded by Shāhid b. Djarrāḥ, the only son of Adam. By transmigration Yazīd became Shaikh ʿAdī, who will come to earth again and again. In *Maṣḥaf* xv., ʿAdī alone is mentioned, whom God sends from Syria to Lālesh, but not Yazīd.

It seems no less peculiar that the Yazīdīs should have chosen as a national saint a Ṣūfī Shaikh like ʿAdī b. Musāfir (d. in Lālesh 555 or 557/1160 or 1162), recognized without qualification throughout the whole Muḥammadan world, whose orthodoxy, as we find it in his works, could hardly have led to the foundation of a sect so heterodox and foreign to the nature of Islām as Yazīdism actually is. It appears impossible that a Muslim Ṣūfī order could diverge into a religion so different from Islām as Yazīdism is. Attempts to point to another ʿAdī as the originator of the religion have so far proved unconvincing.

According to the tradition still alive among them, they came from Baṣra and the lower Euphrates in time of Tīmūr at the end of the xivth century and gradually advanced into the Sindjār which they did not inhabit before the xvth century, and into Kurdistān and there became kurdicized. As, strange to say, unlike Muslims, the Yazīdīs never laid stress on their possession of sacred books, they were not regarded as privileged *Ahl al-Kitāb*. Down to recent times, they were connected from their name with the hated caliph Yazīd and branded as Muslim heretics.

It was from this point of view that the various authoritative *fatwās* were issued which unanimously declared the land of the Yazīdīs *dār al-ḥarb* and proclaimed the destruction of the Yazīdīs and the confiscation of all their property permitted and meritorious from the religious point of view. These served as justification for the numerous attempts at conversion and extermination by the Turkish pāshās and the Kurdish tribes.

The resolution and strength of character of the Yazīdīs is remarkable; in spite of centuries of persecution they have never abandoned their identity nor their faith.

Bibliography: Th. Menzel, Yazīdī-Bibliography, published in *Ein Beitrag zur Kenntnis der Yeziden*, in H. Grothe's *Vorderasienexpedition*, i., Leipzig 1911, p. 109—126, which comes down to 1910. See also Th. Menzel, *Yeziden*, in *Die Religion in Geschichte und Gegenwart*, iii. 171—173.

Additional works: J. W. Crowfoot, *A Yezidi rite*, in *Man*, i., 1901; J. de Morgan, *Mission scientifique en Perse*, vol. v., Paris 1904; Girīdī Muṣṭafā Nūrī Pasha, *ʿAbede-i Iblīs yakhod Ṭāʾifa-i bāghīye-i yezīdīyeye bir Naẓar*, Mōṣul 1323; do., *ʿAbede-i Iblīs. Yezīdī Ṭāʾifasīnīn iʿtiḳādāti, ʿādāti, ewṣāfi, ḥāṣilāti*, Istanbul 1328; H. Lammens, *Le Massif du Gebel Siman et les Yézidis de Syrie*, Bairūt 1906; L. Bouvat, *A propos des Yézidis*, in *RMM*, xxviii., 1908; Isya Joseph, *Yezidi Texts*, *AJSL*, xxv., 1909; do., *Devil-Worship: The sacred books and traditions of the Yezidis*, Boston 1918, 1924; A. V. Williams Jackson, *Yezīdīs*, in *New International Encyclopaedia*, xx., New York

1910; J. Menant, *Les Yézidis*, Paris 1910; Father Anastase Marie, *al-Yazīdīya*, in *Mach.*, ii., 1899; do., *La découverte récente des deux livres sacrés des Yezidis*, in *Anthr.*, vi., Vienna 1911; cf. on this: *RMM*, xxviii., 1914; M. Bittner, *Die beiden heiligen Bücher der Yeziden im Lichte der Textkritik*, in *Anthr.*, vi., 1911; do., *Die heiligen Bücher der Yeziden oder Teufelsanbeter (kurdisch und arabisch)*, in *Denkschriften d. K. Ak. d. Wiss. in Wien*, 1913; do., *Die kurdischen Vorlagen mit einer Schrifttafel*, in *Denkschriften*, Vienna 1913; cf. on this M. Grünert, in *WZKM*, Vienna 1913; R. Frank, *Scheich ʿAdī*, in *Türk. Bibl.*, xiv., Berlin 1911; W. B. Heard, *Notes on the Yezīdis*, in *J. Anthr. I.*, xli., 1911; R. Strothmann, *Analecta haeretica*, in *Isl.*, iv. 1913; do., *Yeziden (Kritische Bibliographie*, No. 228), *ibid.*, xiii., 1923; do., *Gegenwartsgeschichte des Islam.*, *ibid.*, xvii., 1928; Cl. Huart, *Geschichte der Araber*, Leipzig 1914; W. A. Wigram, *Our smallest Ally*, London 1920; F. Nau, *Note sur la date et la vie de Cheikh ʿAdī, chef des Yézides*, in *ROC*, series 2, ix., 1914; do., *Recueil de textes et de documents sur les Yézidis*, *ibid.*, xx., 1915—1917, reprinted Paris 1918; H. Pognon, *Sur les Yézides du Sindgar*, in *ROC*, 1915—1917; A. Mingana, *Devil Worshippers: Their beliefs and their sacred books*, in *JRAS*, ii., 1916; do., *Sacred books of the Yazīdī*, *ibid.*, vii., 1921; G. R. Driver, *Account of Religion of Yezīdī Kurds*, ii., *Studies in Kurdish history, Bulletin*, ii., 1922; A. Dirr, *Einiges über die Yeziden*, in *Anthr.*, xii.—xiii., Vienna 1917—1918; M. Horten, *Die Geheimlehre der Yezidi, der sog. Teufelsanbeter*, in *NO*, iii., Berlin 1918; Minorsky, in *RMM*, xl., 1920; numerous contributions to *OM*, i.—xii.; G. Buschan, *Illustrierte Völkerkunde*, ii., 2nd and 3rd ed., Stuttgart 1923; Lachuti, *Kurdistan i Kurdy*, in *Novyj Vostok*, iv., Moscow 1923; E. S. Stevens, *By Tigris and Euphrates*, London 1923; M. Tilke, *Orientalische Kostüme*, Berlin 1923 (plate 78); E. Klippel, *Als Beduine zu den Teufelsanbetern*, Dresden 1925; R. C. Temple, *The Yezidis or devil-worshippers of Mosul*, in *The Indian Antiquary*, liv., 1925; *Eine arabische risâle von Mollâh Çâlih... über die Jezîden* and *Über die Ansichten der Jeziden (Aus dem K. "umm el-ibar" des ʿAbdesselâm Efendi el-Mardînî)* in O. Rescher, *Orientalische Miszellen*, ii., Stambul 1926; Meḥmed Sheref al-Dīn, *Yezīdīler*, in *Dār ül-Fünūn Ilāhiyāt Fakültesi Medjmūʿasī*, i., No. 3, 4, Istanbul 1926; R. H. W. Empson, *The Cult of the Peacock Angel*, London 1928; W. B. Seabrook, *Adventures in Arabia: Among the Beduins, Druses, Whirling Dervishes and Yezidee Devil-worshippers*, London 1928; Aḥmad Taimūr, *al-Yazīdīya wa-manshāʾ niḥlatihim*, Cairo 1347 (1928), cf. *Isl.*, xix., 1930, p. 81; ʿAbd al-Razzāḳ al-Ḥusnī, *al-Yazīdīya aw ʿibādat al-shaiṭān*, Baghdād 1347; 2nd edition entitled: *ʿAbadat al-shaiṭān fi ʾl-ʿIrāḳ*, Ṣaidā (Syria) 1350; G. Furlani, *Testi religiosi dei Yezidi*, Bologna 1930; do., *Origine dei Yazidi*, in *RSO*, xiii., 1932; do., *Sui Yezidi*, *ibid.*; do., *Religione dei Yesidi*, Bologna 1932; do., in *Orientalia* 1936; ʿAbbās Azzāwī, *Aṣl al-Yazīdīya fi ʾl-taʾrikh, Les Yézidis dans l'histoire*, in *Lughat al-ʿArab*, ix., 1931; A. A. Semenov, *Küčük Asya Yezidilerinin šeytana tapmalarī*, in *Ilāhiyāt Fakültesi Mecmuasī*, No. 20, 1931; M. Guidi, *Origine dei Yazidi*, in *RSO*, xiii., 1932; do., *Nuove ricerche sui Yazidi*, *ibid.*; K. Hadank, *Haben die Jezīden Gotteshäuser?* in *OLZ*, 1933; Ismaël Bey Chol, *The Yazīdīs past and present*, ed. by Costi K. Zurayh, Beyrouth 1934; R. Lescot, *Enquête sur les Yézidis de Syrie*, 1938.

YŪNUS B. MATTAI, the prophet Jonah, son of Amittai (II Kings xiv. 25). In the Ḳurʾān he is four times mentioned as Yūnus, without his father's name being given, once as Dhu 'l-Nūn (xxi. 87), once (lxviii. 48) as *ṣāḥib al-ḥūt*, "he of the fish". This epithet explains also why Yūnus is the only one of the major and minor prophets who is mentioned in the Ḳurʾān; a prophet who is swallowed by a fish naturally attracts attention. Muḥammad numbers Yūnus among the apostles of God (iv. 163; vi. 86). Sūra x. is called after Yūnus, and tells of the town which comes to believe and therefore its fate is averted from it (x. 98). Yūnus, an apostle of God, fled on a ship which was overloaded. He was condemned by lot and a fish swallowed him. He was worthy of blame. If he had not praised God he would have remained in the fish's belly until the resurrection. So We threw him sick upon a barren shore, and caused a gourd to grow up over him, sent him to over a hundred thousand people; and they believed and We gave them respite for a further period (xxxvii. 139—148). Remember Dhu 'l-Nūn, how he departed in wrath and thought We could exercise no power over him; then he called out of the darkness: There is no God but Thee, praise be unto Thee, I was one of the sinners. Then We heard him and rescued him (xxi. 87—88). Await patiently the judgment of thy Lord; be not like him of the fish, who cried out when he was in distress; had the grace of his God not been granted to him, he would have been shamefully cast upon the barren shore but the Lord heard him and he became one of the righteous (lxviii. 48, 49)

Bukhārī and Nawawī also quote as divine revelation not put in the Ḳurʾān the utterance: "No one can say he is better than Yūnus b. Mattai, as long as his genealogy goes back to his father" (Nöldeke-Schwally, *Geschichte des Qorāns*, i. 257).

Muslim legend further develops this material. Yūnus serves Allāh in Niniveh. Why was he enraged? 1. He lived at a time when the $9^1/_2$ tribes were already made captive. It was him king Ḥizḳia sent to the exiled, though there were five prophets in Israel at the time. Yūnus is angry because the mission is entrusted precisely to him. 2. Yūnus is angry because his mission is so urgent that he has not even time to put on a shoe or to mount a riding animal. 3. Yūnus is enraged because he sees that his threat to Niniveh has not been fulfilled so that he appears to be a liar. Yūnus prophesies that the punishment will come after 40 days; on the 37th day the colour of the sinners changes. They repent, restore all they had unjustly acquired, even the objects immured in their houses (cf. *Mishnā Gittin* v. 5. t. 55a); men, women, children, animals, clothe themselves in sackcloth; sucklings, equally of men and of animals, are separated from their nurses. On the ʿĀshūrā' day Allāh grants his forgivenesses.

Urged by Satan Yūnus embarks in the ship. It becomes immovable in the open sea, which is a sign that a runaway slave is on board, The lot, arrow oracles, and his own confession point to Yūnus as the sinner. The fish which swallows Yūnus has been advised that Yūnus is not destined to be eaten but that the fish shall be his shelter (after Ṭabarī, i. 683 his mosque); none of his bones or members may be injured. The fish is swallowed by a second one and the latter by a third one. But all the three of them become so transparant that Yūnus can hear the songs of praise of the sea-monsters. The darkness of which Allāh speaks (Sūra xxi. 87) is the threefold darkness of the night, the depth of the sea, and the interior of the fish. It is disputed whether Yūnus remained 3, 7, 20 or 40 days in the fish. Yūnus is hurled on the shore, emaciated like a plucked chicken. An antelope, (Thaʿlabī), a goat (Ibn al-Athīr) or a gazelle (Kisāʾī) suckles him with her milk. Yūnus finds shade under a gourd. When the tree withers Yūnus laments, but Allah reproves him, saying that he has compassion with a gourd but not with 100,000 people. This admonition is impressed upon him by the example of a potter who is anxious about his pots, and of a sower who fears the grass-shoppers for his seed. Then Yūnus has a shepherd announce his approach; the earth, a tree, an animal of his herd miraculously bear witness to the truth of his message. The king cedes his throne to the shepherd, and himself goes to live with Yūnus as an ascetic.

The feature that Allāh forgives the sinful town on the ʿĀshūrāʾ day suggests Jewish influence; in the synagogue the book of Yona is recited precisely on the Day of Atonement, which in the early times of Islām coincided with the ʿĀshūrāʾ.

A legend, mentioned by al-Yāfiʿī in the *Rawḍ al-rayāḥīn*, originated probably at a very late time: Yūnus asks the angel Gabriel to show him the most pious of mankind. The angel shows him a man who loses feet, hands and eyes one after another and notwithstanding puts his confidence in God and gives himself up to him (R. Basset, 1001 *Contes*, iii. 172).

Al-Kisāʾī extends the miraculous to the earlier history of the prophet. His father was 70 when Yūnus was born. His mother, who became a widow soon after, had nothing left but a wooden spoon, which proves to be cornucopia. As a result of a miraculous dream he marries the daughter of Zakarīyāʾ b. Yaḥyā. He loses his wife, both his sons and his property. He therefore will not pray with the others on the ship. Everything is miraculously restored to him.

Bibliography: Ṭabarī, i. 782—789; do., *Tafsīr*, Cairo 1321, on sūra x. 98, vol. xiv. 109—111; on sūra xxi. 87, 88, vol. xvii. 54—58; on sūra lxviii. 48, vol. xxix. 25, 26; Ibn al-Athīr, Būlāḳ, i. 143—145; Thaʿlabī, *Ḳiṣaṣ al-anbiyāʾ*, Cairo 1325, p. 257—260; al-Kisāʾī, *Ḳiṣaṣ al-anbiyāʾ*, ed. Eisenberg, p. 296—311; Geiger, *Was hat Mohammed aus dem Judenthume aufgenommen?*, Leipzig 1902², p. 188, 189; Nöldeke-Schwally, *Geschichte des Qorāns*, i. 257; J. Horovitz, in *Hebrew Union College Annual*, ii., 1925, p. 170, 182, 183; do., *Koranische Untersuchungen*, p. 154 *sqq.*; Speyer, *Die bibl. Erzählungen im Qoran*, 407—410.

YŪSHAʿ B. NŪN, the Joshua of the Bible. The Ḳurʾān does not mention him by name but alludes to him. When Moses wished to lead his people into the holy land and Israel was afraid to fight with the giants, they were encouraged by two God-fearing men (Sūra v. 20—26), who may be recognized as Joshua and Caleb. Neither can it be doubted that the young man (*fatā* = *naʿar*, Exod. xxxiii. 11) who accompanies Moses on a journey to Khaḍir (not named) in Sūra xviii. 60—65 is no other than Joshua.

The excellently informed Ṭabarī was familiar with the Biblical history of Joshua: the crossing of the Jordan with the ark, the spies, the fall of Jericho, the dishonesty of ʿAchan, the artifice of the Gibeonites, the solstice, Bazaḳ. But already in Ṭabarī and after him in Muslim legend the figure of Yūshaʿ is supplied with features not found in the Bible but mostly derived from the Haggada. Yūshaʿ is given the task of summoning the Egyptians to the true faith. In order to enable Mūsā to quit this life without anxiety, Yūshaʿ is installed as prophet at Mūsā's death. Yūshaʿ is present at Mūsā's death. The garment of Mūsā remains in his hands (Elijah-Elisha motive). Yūshaʿ is suspected of having killed Mūsā; thereupon all Israelites have a dream in which Mūsā refutes the suspicion. Yūshaʿ conquers Amaleḳ — but Muslim tradition varies as to whether the victory was won in Mūsā's lifetime or after his death. Balaam supports Amaleḳ. In Ibn al-Athīr the story is embellished: Balaam's wife is bribed to incite him to evil. Sūra vii. 175—177 is also connected with Balaam. Yūshaʿ cannot cross the Jordan for 40 days; at his prayer the two hills on the banks become a bridge across which the people pass over (al-Kisāʾī). Jericho is besieged for 6 months and in the seventh the walls fall at the blowing of the trumpets. The miracle in which Yūshaʿ makes the sun stand still is mentioned sometimes in connection with the conquest of Jericho, and sometimes with the war against the united kings. Anyhow, it is the eve of the Sabbath; with sunset the Sabbath-rest would put an end to the fight. Yūshaʿ wishes to stop the sun; at fist the sun refuses, saying it is fulfilling divine orders (Haggadic motive, e.g. *Talmud Ḥullīn* 7a); finally the sun agrees. After the victory Yūshaʿ collects the booty and desires to offer a sacrifice, but no flame comes down from heaven to consume it (cf. Lev. ix. 24; 1 Kings xviii. 24 *sqq.*; 1 Chr. xxi. 26; 2 Chr. vii. 1). There has been some dishonesty. The lot points to ʿAchan as the sinner. According to another tradition, Yūshaʿ summons the heads of the tribes; the hand of the sinner sticks to the hand of Yūshaʿ. Al-Kisāʾī records another divine judgement: each tribe has his sign on Hārūn's robe and the sign of the guilty tribe becomes distorted. A bull's head studded with pearls and jewels is found in the sinner's possession and added to the booty. The flame now consume the booty along with the sinner.

Yūshaʿ roots out the inhabitants of Canaan, but a fraction of them migrate under the leadership of king Afrīḳīs to Africa; their king Djirdjīr (for Djirdjīs) is killed; from the others the North African Berbers are descended.

In Ṭabarī (i. 558) we have the isolated tradition that the dead man conjured up by Ṭālūt (Saul) was not Samuel but Yūshaʿ.

Bibliography: Ṭabarī, i. 414—429, 499, 503—528, 558; Ibn al-Athīr, Būlāḳ, i. 78, 79; Thaʿlabī, *Ḳiṣaṣ al-anbiyāʾ*, Cairo 1325, p. 155—157; al-Kisāʾī, *Ḳiṣaṣ al-anbiyāʾ*, ed. Eisenberg, p. 240—242; M. Grünbaum, *Neue Beiträge zur semitischen Sagenkunde*, Leyden 1893, p. 182—185; J. Horovitz, in *Hebrew Union College Annual*, ii., 1925, p. 179.

YŪSUF B. YAʿḲŪB, the Joseph of the Bible, is a favourite subject of Muslim legend. In Sūra xii. Muḥammad deals with the whole story of Yūsuf, which is described as the most beautiful of stories. It is the most beautiful, says Thaʿlabī, because of the lesson concealed in it, on account of Yūsuf's generosity and its wealth of matter, in which prophets, angels, devils, djinn, men, animals, birds, rulers and subjects play a part.

Yūsuf in the Ḳurʾān. Yūsuf is mentioned twice outside of Sūra xii. Once (vi. 84) as one of the pious ancestors; further in Sūra xl. 34: Yūsuf came with clear proofs but they doubted him and after his death it was thought that God would never send another prophet. Sūra xii. contains more and less than the Bible. Let us first consider the additions to the Biblical story.

Yūsuf is warned by Yaʿḳūb not to tell his dream to his brothers. The brothers ask their father to confide Yūsuf to their care. Yaʿḳūb is afraid for him on account of a wolf. The brothers lie to their father, saying that they had gone to run a race and had left Yūsuf near the baggage; then a wolf had torn him to pieces. Yaʿḳūb is blinded by his weeping. The caravan that passes sends a man to draw water; this man discovers Yūsuf. The Egyptian who buys Yūsuf proposes to his wife to adopt him. Yūsuf feels a strong desire for his temptress, but he resists, having received a clear sign from Allāh. The fact that Yūsuf's shirt is torn from behind proves his innocence. The temptress invites her friends at a banquet; when Yūsuf enters they cut their own fingers instead of the food, dazzled by Yūsuf's beauty. Though Yūsuf's innocence is clear, he is imprisoned. In prison he interprets the dreams of the court officials, but Satan makes the cupbearer forget Yūsuf. Yūsuf interprets Pharaoh's dreams while still in prison: there will come 7 fat and 7 lean years, then a year with a good rainfall. As a reward Yūsuf asks to be appointed over the store-houses of Egypt. The brothers come to Egypt, already accompanied by the youngest on the first occasion. Yaʿḳūb enjoins them not to enter all by one gate. The youngest brother is kept back in Egypt, while the others return to their father, who does not believe their narrative. The brothers go up to Egypt a second time; they apologize for bringing but little money, but ask all the same for full measure and charitable treatment. Yūsuf makes himself known and sends his father a shirt, which is to restore his eyesight. Yaʿḳūb recognizes its smell from a distance. His sons ask for forgiveness. He prays for them to Allāh.

Of these divergences from the Biblical story a Haggadic origin may be traced in the following: Yaʿḳūb enjoins his sons not to enter by one gate only. This is already found in the pre-Ḳurʾānic *Genesis Rabba* xci. 1, 6, as well as in several later Midra<u>sh</u>im with the explanation that they should not draw the evil eye upon themselves. — Yūsuf longs for the temptress, but Allāh sends him a sign and Yūsuf resists. What sign? The Haggada describes how Yūsuf is overcome with desire, but then there appears before him the image of his father or of his mother, by which his heated blood is cooled (*Gen. R.* lxxxvii. 7, ed. Theodor-Albeck 1372; xcviii, 20, ed. Th.-Alb. 1270).

Sūra xii. 74 seems to be less clear: when Yūsuf's cup is found in Benjamin's sack the brothers cry out: If he be a thief, his brother has already been a thief. The Ḳurʾān-commentators are at a loss to explain this (cf. in particular Ṭabarī, *Tafsīr* xiii. 17, 18; <u>Th</u>aʿlabī, 83); Yūsuf had stolen the idols of his grandfather and broken them; he had, at the instigation of Rāḥīl, stolen the idols of Laban; he had stolen food for the poor from his father's house during a famine; it is also said that Yūsuf's aunt, who could not part from him, had charged him with having stolen a belt of hers, and so she had a claim on him as a thief.

A Haggadic feature, though not supported by any source, seems to be the sign of Yūsuf's innocence: his coat is torn from behind, which proves that this happened in his flight, so he is innocent. Haggadic also is the story that the friends of the temptress, dazzled by Yūsuf's beauty, cut their own fingers instead of the food. The old Haggada has not preserved this poetical feature; in the younger *Tanḥūma* and the *Sefer hayā<u>sh</u>ār* it has probably been introduced from Islām.

It is worth while to point to what is lacking in the Ḳurʾān. We do not have the description of his character. Remarkable also is the omission of the dream of the brothers' sheaves which bow down before Joseph's sheaf (*Gen.* xxxvii. 5—7). This dream is also neglected in post-Ḳurʾānic legend. The Yūsuf Sūra is strikingly uncertain and hesitating in that it mentions no one by name except Yaʿḳūb and Yūsuf (*ʿAzīz* is not the name of the Biblical Potiphar but his rank) and gives no numbers or times. The only references are to one of the brothers or at best the eldest of the brothers, a king, a noble, his wife, a witness. Yūsuf is sold for a paltry sum; the number of his brothers is not given. This gives the expositors of the Ḳurʾān an opportunity to search for the anonymous and undefined (*mubhamāt*, see Goldziher, *Die Richtungen der islamischen Koranauslegung*, Leiden 1920, index, s.v. *Mubhamāt*).

Yūsuf in post-Ḳurʾānic legend. When the Ḳurʾān cautiously says "one of the brothers said or did something", in legend we find Reuben, Judah, Simeon and in Zama<u>kh</u><u>sh</u>arī and Baiḍāwī also Dan; in course of time we have Benjamin with his ten or three sons. Sometimes Judah, sometimes Reuben, sometimes Simeon is represented as possessing a terrible temper which can only be calmed by a hand of the house of Jacob. The man who buys Joseph from his brethren is called Mālik b. Daʿr and the Egyptian to whom he is sold Ḳiṭfīr [q.v.], Iṭfīr, Iṭfīn, Ḳutifar, Ḳiṭṭin, Ḳiṭṭifin; his wife is called Rāʿīl, later (as in Firdawsī, <u>D</u>jāmī, <u>Sh</u>āhīn, Kisāʾī and in the Hebrew *Sefer hayāshār*) Zalīka, Zulaika. The king of Egypt, whom Yūsuf converts to Islām, is called Raiyān b. Walīd, his cupbearer Nabū, his baker Mu<u>dj</u>lib. The <u>sh</u>āhid, the witness, becomes a relative of the temptress or even a baby who miraculously proves Joseph's innocence from his cradle. Even the names of the eleven stars which bow down before Joseph are given. Muslim legend knows how old Yūsuf was at the time of the dream, how long he was kept in the well. Who had dug the well? Sām b. Nūḥ. At what price was Yūsuf sold? For 20 dirhams or a pair of shoes (Haggada to *Amos* ii. 6). What was the offence of the cupbearer and the baker? They suspected each other of having planned to poison the king, a feature which partially occurs also in the later Midra<u>sh</u> and in *Pseudo-Jonathan* to *Gen.* xl. 1. How long was Yūsuf in prison? Seven years, as Job and Nebuchadnezzar also had a period of expiation of 7 years. His deed of purchase and also Yaʿḳūb's letter to Yūsuf are both given in full.

A reason is given for everything that is unexplained in the Ḳurʾān. Why does Yaʿḳūb suffer? Because he killed a calf before the eyes of its mother, because on one occasion he did not share his meal with a hungry man; because he separated a slave from her parents. — Why does Yūsuf suffer? Because of his vanity; later, because he appeals to the cupbearer instead of to God. — When Yūsuf is warned not to communicate his dream, how do the brothers learn of it nevertheless? From Yūsuf's aunt. By what did the brothers recognize Yūsuf? By a birth-mark, and so on.

Yūsuf is called in Islāmic legend al-Ṣiddīḳ. As such he is addressed by the cupbearer (Sūra xii. 46). In the Haggada and also in Jewish liturgy he is called *haṣ-ṣaddīḳ*, the just, the pious. Nöldeke (in

Schapiro, 36, note 1) states that Islām has borrowed this epithet from Judaism, but has given it another sense: the true one, one who truly explains dreams.

Yūsuf is remarkable for his beauty, which he has inherited from his mother Rāḥīl. All the beauty in the world was originally granted to Adam, but when he sinned two-thirds was taken from him and reserved for Yūsuf; according to others Yūsuf was possessed of nine-tenths of all the beauty (Haggadic feature, *Ḳiddushin* 49b). When the future generations defile before Adam he presses Yūsuf to his heart; Muḥammad also is dazzled by Yūsuf's beauty in Paradise (Thaʿlabī).

Haggadic is the following passage in Zamakhsharī: When the temptress tries to seduce Yūsuf she covers the idol in the room; it shall not be witness to her immorality. Yūsuf blames her: You are ashamed before an idol which cannot see nor hear, and should I not be ashamed before God, the all-seeing, the all-knowing? So already in *Gen. R.* lxxxvii. 5: Potiphar's wife covers the idol standing before her bed; Joseph warns her: Should I not rather fear him whose eyes go throughout the world? (Zach. iv. 10).

We also find the legend further developed by the story-teller's art without any foundation in Ḳurʾān or Haggada. Near Yaʿḳūb's house there grows a tree on which, as often as a son is born, a new twig sprouts; at Yūsuf's birth no new twig is forthcoming; on Yaʿḳūb's prayer Gabriel brings from Paradise a twig which surpasses all others by blooming and bearing fruit. Al-Kisāʾī relates also a first dream of Yūsuf's: he planted a slip which grew up, whereas his brothers' plantations wither. Yaʿḳūb sees in a dream how Yūsuf is torn to pieces by ten wolves; he touchingly recommends the little Yūsuf to the care of his brothers. They pretend to be very gentle when in sight of the father but very soon ill-treat him, break the jug out of which he wants to drink, tear his coat from his back which he begs as a shroud, and tell him to appeal to the sun, moon and stars of his dreams. Gabriel takes pity on the deserted boy, brings him the cloak with which Abraham was protected from the heat of the flames. Yaʿḳūb requires his sons to produce the wolf which has torn Yūsuf to pieces. The brothers catch the first wolf they meet and bring him to their father, but the wolf is miraculously given the power of speech and swears to his innocence: the flesh of prophets is forbidden to it. A caravan loses its way and comes to the well. The brothers ask the purchaser to put Yūsuf in chains, nevertheless Yūsuf takes leave of them with dignity. On the way he throws himself from his camel on the tomb of his mother Rachel, which they pass. — The efforts to seduce him are described in glowing language. In prison Yūsuf's fellow-prisoners tell him how they love him. But he is afraid of love: the love of his aunt (who charged him with theft), the predilection of his father who favoured him above his brothers, have brought him mischief; the love of his mistress has landed him in prison.

Yūsuf sells corn to the Egyptians. During the years of famine, however, Yūsuf starves also so that he may feel what it is like to be hungry; even to the banquets of Pharaoh he assigns a scanty measure. When Yūsuf is questioning the alleged magic cup, Benjamin asks him to enquire if Yūsuf still lives. — He lives; you will see him. When Yaʿḳūb receives a message from Yūsuf, he asks: How is it with Yūsuf? — He is king of Egypt. — That is not what I am asking; I mean how is it with his faith? — He is a Muslim. — Then my happiness is perfect. — Yūsuf enquires how his father could abandon himself completely to grief as if he did not believe in a reunion after the resurrection? — I believe in it but I was anxious lest you had abandoned your faith so that we should remain separated in the next world.

The Ḳurʾān tells nothing of Yūsuf's death and sarcophagus. Muslim legend, however, has taken stories of this from the Haggada. Yūsuf's sarcophagus was sunk in the Nile. At the Exodus Moses went to take it with him but could not find it until an old woman (Serach, daughter of Asher) showed it to him. In Islām, the legend seems to have been further developed, for we find the people living on the banks of the Nile disputing over the sarcophagus, which is finally sunk exactly in the middle of the river so that both sides may equally share its virtues.

Islām is very proud of its story of Yūsuf. Thaʿlabī declares that the Yūsuf Sūra surpasses the Torah. Kisāʾī tells us that God gave the Yūsuf Sūra to every prophet, but the Jews concealed it until Muḥammad revealed it as evidence that he was a prophet. —

Bibliography: Ṭabarī, i. 371—414; the commentaries on Sūra xii., esp. Ṭabarī, *Tafsīr*, Cairo 1321, vol. xii. 83—xiii. 53; Thaʿlabī, *Ḳiṣaṣ al-anbiyāʾ*, Cairo 1325, p. 67—89; Ibn al-Athīr, p. 54—61; Nöldeke-Schwally, *Geschichte des Qorāns*, i. 152, 153; Geiger, *Was hat Mohammed aus dem Judenthume aufgenommen?*, Leipzig 1902², p. 139—148; G. Weil, *Biblische Legenden der Musulmänner*, p. 100—125; M. Grünbaum, *Neue Beiträge zur semitischen Sagenkunde*, p. 148—152; Schapiro, *Die haggadischen Elemente im erzählenden Teil des Korans*, 1907; J. Walker, *Bible Characters in the Koran*, Paisly 1931, p. 67—75; Sidersky, *Les origines des légendes musulmanes dans le Coran*, Paris 1933, p. 52—68; Speyer, *Die biblische Erzählungen im Qoran*, p. 187—224; J. Horovitz, *Koranische Untersuchungen*, p. 154; Djāmī, *Yūsuf u-Zulaika*, ed. and transl. by Rosenzweig; Schlechta-Wssehrd, *Jussuf und Zuleicha, Romantisches Heldengedicht von Firdussi*, Vienna 1889; thereon M. Grünbaum, *Zu "Jusuf und Suleicha"*, in *ZDMG*, xli. 577; xliii. 1; do., *Gesammelte Aufsätze zur Sprach- und Sagenkunde*, ed. by Felix Perles, Berlin 1901, p. 515—593; Wilhelm Bacher, *Zwei jüdisch-persische Dichter, Schāhin und Imrāni*, Budapest 1907, p. 82, 117—124; on the women cutting their fingers see R. Köhler, *In die Hand nicht in die Speisen schneiden* (*Kleinere Schriften zur Märchenforschung*, ii. 83—87); B. Heller, *Die Sage vom Sarge Josefs* etc., in *MGWJ*, 1926, p. 271—276.

Z

ZABŪR (A.), probably a loanword from the South, but already used by pre-Islāmic poets in the sense of "writ"; in this sense it is still found in al-Farazdaḳ, *Naḳā'iḍ*, lxxv. 1. From the second Meccan period onwards, Muḥammad uses the plural *zubur* in order to denote the revealed books (Sūra xxvi. 196; iii. 184; xvi. 44; xxxv. 25) as well as the heavenly writings, in which human deeds are recorded (Sūra liv. 43, 52). The singular zabūr, on the other hand, occurs in the Ḳur'ān exclusively in connection with Dāwūd. In the early Sūra xvii. 55 Muḥammad says that Allāh has given Dāwūd one zabūr. The same zabūr he mentions another time, viz. in Sūra iv. 163, and in Sūra xxi. 105 he quotes from this zabūr Psalm xxxvii. 29, in an almost literal translation. Possibly the pre-Islāmic poets were already acquainted with Dāwūd as the author of the zabūr; it is e.g. not impossible that this is meant by Imra' al-Ḳais when he mentions a "zabūr in the books of the monks" (*ka-khaṭṭi zabūrin fī maṣāḥifi ruhbāni*, lxiii. 1). At any rate, this use of the term zabūr (apart from the question whether Muḥammad was the first to make use of it) is based on its affinity in sound with Hebrew *mizmōr*, Syriac *mazmōr* or Ethiopic *mazmūr*; it was this term that by Muḥammad or others before him, in analogy with Arabic zabūr, was identified with the latter's meaning "writ". Apart from Sūra xxi. 105 the Ḳur'ān contains other passages bearing a close resemblance to verses from the Psalms, especially from Psalm civ. Moreover the majority of the passages in the Ḳur'ān which remind us, by sense or sound, of the Bible, are from the Psalms. The commentaries on the Ḳur'ān recognize that the zabūr mentioned in Sūra iv. 163 is the book of Dāwūd bearing this name; it is only some of the Kūfan commentators who propose to read the plural *zubūr* in the sense of "writings". Ṭabarī rejects this view (Ṭabarī, *Tafsīr*, vi. 18). Aḥmad b. ʿAbd Allāh b. Salām, a *mawlā* of the caliph Hārūn, it is said, identifies the zabūr with "the *mazāmīr* which are in the hands of Jews and Christians", to the number of 150.

A fragment of an Arabic translation of the Psalms, dating from the iind/viiith century, the oldest known specimen of Christian-Arabic literature, was discovered in Damascus by B. Violet. It contains the Arabic translation of Psalm lxxviii., vss. 20—31, 51—61 in Greek majuscular writing. Al-Kindī, in his *Risāla* (composed about 204/819), and Ibn Ḳutaiba, as cited in Ibn al-Djawzī's *Wafā'*, quote verses from the Psalms in literal translation. The Nestorian renegade ʿAlī b. Rabban al-Ṭabarī who had the Syriac translation at hand, devotes to the Psalms an entire chapter of his "Book of Religion and Empire" (written about 240/854). Masʿūdī, *Tanbīh*, p. 112, mentions Arabic translations of the Bible which also contained the Psalms. Of these translations the one by Saʿīd al-Faiyūmī (*Fihrist*, p. 23, 7, 13; cf. also H. Malter, *Saadia Gaon*, p. 318 *sqq.*) has come down to us. Even a free translation of the Psalms in Arabic verses is still extant viz. the *Urdjūza* of Ḥafṣ b. al-Birr al-Ḳūṭī, which goes back at least to the vth/xith century. Muḥammadan apologists find the coming of Muḥammad prophesied in the *Zabūr* as they do in the *Tawrāt* [q.v.]. Ibn Ḳutaiba takes a number of verses in the Psalms to refer to Muḥammad; Alī b. Rabban in the section "Prophecies of David concerning the Prophet" collects similar references, some identical and others different (cf. G. Vajda, in *Memorial Blau*, Budapest 1938), and al-Sinhādjī adds a few more. On the other hand, Ibn Ḥazm criticises acutely the Psalms as well as other books of the Bible and says several passages are forgeries which he as a result of erroneous translation condemns as blasphemous. In contrast to the translations of the *ahlu 'l-alsinati 'l-mukhtalifati*, the *Kitāb al-Mazāmīr Tardjumat al-Zabūr* offers the translation said to have been made by the *ʿulamā' al-Islām*; it is preserved in several manuscripts, and Krarup and Cheikho have published selections. In reality however, this book has nothing to do with the Psalms, which only the two first sections recall; the author took the Ḳur'ān as his model and indeed calls his separate sections Sūras. The oldest MS. bears the date 666 A.H. and perhaps the *Kitāb Zabūr Dāwūd* ascribed to Wahb b. Munabbih in Ibn Ḥaiy's ***Fihrist*** (*Biblioteca Arabo-Hispana*, ix. 294) is identical with this work.

Bibliography: J. Horovitz, *Koranische Untersuchungen* (Berlin 1926), p. 69 *sqq.*; B. Violet, *Ein zweisprachiges Psalmfragment aus Damaskus* (Berlin 1902); C. Brockelmann, in *Beiträge z. Assyriologie*, iii. 46 *sqq.*; do., in *ZATW*, xv. 141 *sq.*; W. Bacher, *op. cit.*, p. 310; I. Goldziher, in *ZDMG*, xxxii., 351 *sq.*, 371, 377; M. Steinschneider, *Die arabische Litteratur der Juden*, § 66; O. Chr. Krarup, *Auswahl pseudodavidischer Psalmen* (Copenhagen 1909); L. Cheikho, in *MFOB*, iv. 40 *sqq.*, 47 *sqq.*; W. Rudolph, *Die Abhängigkeit des Korans*, p. 10 *sqq.* (Stuttgart 1922); C. Peters, *Arabische Psalmencitate bei Abu Nuʿaim*, in *Biblica* 1939.

ZACHARIAS. [See ZAKĀRĪYĀ].

AL-ẒĀHIRĪYA, a school of law, which would derive the law only from the literal text (*ẓāhir*) of the Ḳur'ān and Sunna. In the "branches" of law (*furūʿ al-fiḳh*) it still further increased the number of contradictory detailed regulations by many divergences, peculiar to it alone. More important is its significance for the principles of legislation (*uṣūl al-fiḳh*), the development and elucidation of which it considerably furthered by its uncompromising fight against *ra'y*, *ḳiyās*, *istiṣḥāb*, *istiḥsān* and *taḳlīd* [q.v.]. In the ʿIrāḳ the Ẓāhirī *madhhab*, also called Dā'ūdī after its founder Dā'ūd b. Khalaf, became organised as a regular school, the influence of which spread to Persia and Khurāsān, while in Spain Ibn Ḥazm remained practically isolated. Only in the reign of the Almohad Yaʿḳūb al-Manṣūr (580—594/1184—1199), were the official legal decisions after the Ẓāhirī form. But there had always been Ẓāhirīs in outlook, although not organised as a school or called one, and there continued to be such, after the Ẓāhirī method, in spite of all the concessions it was forced to make to the principles of its rivals, had failed in the solution of problems which had not cropped up in the circle of the Prophet or the earlier transmitters of the *Sunna*. As late as 788/1386 a Ẓāhirī outbreak is recorded in Syria, where the *madhhab* itself never prevailed; in Egypt we still find Maḳrīzī writing in the Ẓāhirī spirit. The Ẓāhirī attitude could be maintained, especially in theory, by people who were not in contact with the little matters of everyday life and disliking the casuistry and quarrels of the schools did not adhere to a particular school. It is therefore not remarkable that it is a mystic, Shaʿrānī [d. 973/1565], who has preserved many decisions of the historical Ẓāhirīya. It is true that commentators on the Ḳurʾān, notably Fakhr al-Dīn al-Rāzī, and on the collections of traditions frequently note the particular Ẓāhirī exegesis, but on the other hand, the later jurists no longer take their former rivals seriously and are silent about them, at least in the special literature of the *ikhtilāf al-fiḳh* that has survived. Shaʿrānī however puts Dāʾūd in the radiant rosette in his *Mīzān* (see *Bibl.*), p. 44, and on the parallel roads to the gate of Paradise (p. 47) between Abū Ḥanīfa and Ibn Ḥanbal respectively and al-Laith b. Saʿd. As no manuscripts of a Ẓāhirī lawbook are available we give as specimens of the distinctive features mentioned by Shaʿrānī from Book I those relating to ritual purity.

Details. P. 98, $_{12}$: Gold and silver vessels are not forbidden except for eating and drinking. According to Nawawī on the *Ṣaḥīḥ* of Muslim (Cairo 1284), iv. 416, and Abu 'l-Fidāʾ, *Annales* (ed. Reiske, ii. 262), the Ẓāhirīs on the authority of the *ḥadīth* in question, which only mentions drinking, permitted eating from such vessels. — P. 98, $_{23}$: The use of the toothstick (*miswāk*, q.v.) is obligatory; according to Isḥāḳ b. Rāhwaihi, Dāʾūd's teacher, deliberate neglect of this actually renders the prayer invalid. — P. 99, $_{12}$ *sqq.* and ii. 163, $_{15}$: Wine is not impure although forbidden. — P. 103, $_{17}$ and 107, $_{16}$: A person in a state of minor ritual impurity (*ḥadath*, q.v.) may take up and carry a copy of the Ḳurʾān. — P. 105, $_{33}$: Any contact of a man with a female of another family, even a new-born baby girl, produces *ḥadath* and the minor ablution (*wuḍūʾ*) is necessary. — P. 107, $_{26}$: There is no regulation that in relieving nature one should not turn the face or the back in the direction of the *ḳibla*; it is therefore permitted. — P. 108, $_{17}$ and 113, $_{10}$: 1. *Wuḍūʾ* is according to ʿUbaid Allāh al-Nakhaʿī, a Ẓāhirī ḳāḍī in Khurāsān (d. 376/986), only valid for 5 prayers (a certain ʿUbaid b. ʿUmair laid it down that it was only valid for one). — P. 109, $_{24}$: The mentioning of the name of God at the *wuḍūʾ* is not only recommended but obligatory. — P. 109, $_{33}$: According to some Ẓāhirīs, the previous washing of the hands is ordered whenever purification is obligatory. — P. 110, $_{30}$: Washing the hands does not extend to the elbows (Zufar b. Hudhail, d. 158/774, who was in close contact with Abū Ḥanīfa however, also held this view). — P. 113, $_{20}$: The major ritual ablution (*ghusl*, q.v.) is only obligatory after actual effluxus seminis. — P. 114, $_{21}$: If a woman is in a state of major ritual impurity (*djanāba*, q.v.) and then enters the *ḥaiḍ* [q.v.] she must perform two *ghusl*. — P. 114, $_{29}$ and 122, $_{22}$: In spite of *djanāba* any one, even a woman during *ḥaiḍ*, may recite the Ḳurʾān as he pleases. — P. 115, $_{11}$: Rubbing with sand (*tayammum*, q.v.) actually removes a *ḥadath*. — P. 120, $_{23}$: *Masḥ ʿala 'l-khuffain*, the wiping of only the foot-gear is valid even if it is much torn. — P. 122, $_{8}$: A partial washing suffices for the woman to fulfil the demands of Ḳurʾān ii. 222, so that intercourse is permitted even during the *ḥaiḍ* (so also Awzāʿī).

As these examples show, the Ẓāhirī *madhhab* cannot be briefly summed up as "light or heavy". Sharʿānī has sometimes to describe it as the mildest and sometimes as the strictest of all. The field in which many of the jurists found their main object, to make alleviations, was one into which it could not enter, and for example it insisted upon the literal text of the passages in the Ḳurʾān and Tradition against unbelievers to a degree of complete intolerance. It has not a systematical aspect, for it forbade inquiry into the reason for a regulation and did not allow it to be extended to an analogous case or from the individual to the class. It absolutely refused to weaken the words of the religious sources by parallels from passages in pagan poets, and aimed at creating the true *fiḳh al-ḥadīth* out of the religious texts with the assistance of a special Muslim philology and lexicography. Mālik's *fiḳh* seemed to it to be *raʾy* equally with that of Abū Ḥanīfa; Shāfiʿī, from whom it had itself started, had only disciplined, not abolished *raʾy*. *Idjmāʿ* [q.v.] could only be defined as the consensus of the early Companions. It made no distinction in degrees of prohibition or commandment; the imperative, in other systems not infrequently interpreted as mere permission and recommendation or simple disapproval, meant for it the absolutely obligatory or completely forbidden. It naturally used a great mass of Tradition and it has been charged with not examining carefully what it took over; on the other hand, it was itself forced to criticism of traditions against many *ḥadīths* favourable to *raʾy* which were finding recognition, or against that of difference of opinion as a grace; the Ẓāhirīya saw in this rather the disruptive influence of subjective methods against which it regarded itself as the champion of the lost unity of primitive Islām. In spite of Ibn Ḥazm, the Ẓāhirīya never attained theological unity. In general it maintained an attitude of cautious neutrality and aloofness in theological disputes and in keeping with its respect for the literal sacred text accepted the utterances about God without going into any exegesis.

Bibliography: Shaʿrānī, *al-Mīzān*², Cairo 1317, *passim*; Ibn al-Nadīm, *Fihrist*, ed. Flügel, i. 216—219; Samʿānī, *Kitāb al-ansāb* (in *GMS*, xx.), s.v. *Dāʾūdī*, fol. 220ʳ ult.—220ᵛ, further s.v. *Ẓāhirī*, fol. 376ᵛ; Ibn al-Athīr, *al-Kāmil*, ed. Tornberg, xii. 95 *sq.*; I. Goldziher, *Die Ẓâhiriten. Ihr Lehrsystem und ihre Geschichte*, Leipzig 1884.

ZAID B. **ʿALĪ**. [See AL-ZAIDĪYA].

ZAID B. **ʿAMR** B. NUFAIL, a Meccan and Ḳurashī, one of the religious seekers known as the *ḥanīf*, died before Muḥammad's mission, when the Prophet was about 35. He had abandoned the pagan religion without embracing either Christianity or Judaism, objected to female infanticide, refused to eat the flesh of animals sacrificed to idols or slaughtered without invoking God's name, and considered himself the only true believer in Mecca and a follower of Abraham's religion. A cousin of ʿUmar b. al-Khaṭṭāb, he was married to Ṣafīya bint al-Ḥaḍramī and to Fāṭima bint Baʿdja, and had a son, Saʿīd b. Zaid, who told traditions about him.

Persecuted by his family on religious grounds, he travelled in search of the true faith as far as Mawṣil, and visited Syria; in Maifaʿa, in al-Balḳāʾ, a learned monk (a double of Baḥīra?) predicted to him the rise of a true prophet in Mecca. Zaid hurried back, but was assaulted and killed while crossing the region inhabited by the Lakhm tribe. According to another tradition, Zaid had himself predicted Muḥammad's mission and career. Ibn Isḥāḳ quotes poetry attributed to him, but its authenticity is doubtful.

Though dead before Islām, Zaid was considered by *ḥadīth* a true believer; Muḥammad, declaring him to be in heaven, allowed prayers to be said for him.

Bibliography: Caetani, *Annali dell' Islām*, Introd., § 164, 180, 182, No. 2, 186, 187; Ibn Saʿd, I/i. 105; Ibn Isḥāḳ, ed. Wüstenfeld, p. 143—146, 149. See also WARAḲA B. NAWFAL.

ZAID B. **ḤĀRITHA** B. SHARĀḤĪL AL-KALBĪ, ABŪ USĀMA, was brought as a slave to Mecca by Ḥakīm b. Ḥizām b. Khuwailid, a nephew of Khadīdja's, who had bought him in Syria and sold him to her. Khadīdja made a gift of Zaid to Muḥammad before his mission. His father Ḥāritha came to Mecca to obtain his freedom, but Zaid refused to leave Muḥammad, who thereupon freed him and adopted him. He was thenceforward known as Zaid b. Muḥammad, and was often associated in his adopted father's commercial enterprises.

About ten years younger than Muḥammad, Zaid was one of the very first converts to Islām, perhaps the first. He came from a tribe settled near Dūmat al-Djandal, where converts to Christianity were plentiful and Jewish influence felt; his influence on the Prophet's religious development may have been considerable.

In Madīna Zaid was joined in brotherhood to Ḥamza b. ʿAbd al-Muṭṭalib. In 1 A.H. he went to Mecca to accompany Sawda bint Zamʿa and Muḥammad's daughters to Madīna. A brave warrior, Zaid fought at Badr, Uḥud, al-Khandaḳ, was at al-Ḥudaibiya, commanded several expeditions (al-Ḳarada in 2 A.H., al-Djamūn and al-ʿĪs in 6, etc.) and was often left in command at Madīna when Muḥammad was on some military expedition. For his marriage to, and divorce from, Zainab bint Djaḥsh see ZAINAB. Following this divorce, the verse in the Ḳurʾān abolishing adoption (xxxiii. 40) was revealed. After Zainab, Zaid married Umm Kulthūm bint ʿUḳba, who bore him Zaid and Ruḳaiya, and Durra bint Abī Lahab, both of whom he divorced; further Hind bint al-ʿAwwām and Muḥammad's freedwoman, the negroid Umm Aiman, who bore him Usāma.

Zaid died in 8 A.H., aged about 55, as commander and standard-bearer of the unfortunate expedition of Muʾta. Muḥammad mourned him and planned to avenge him. His place in *ḥādīth* is important, both on account of Muḥammad's affection for him, which induces orthodox tradition to set him up as the Prophet's favourite, against ʿAlī b. Abī Ṭālib, and by reason of his name being mentioned in the Ḳurʾān.

Bibliography: Ibn Saʿd, III/i. 26—31; Ibn Isḥāḳ, ed. Wüstenfeld, p. 160—161, 801—802; Ibn al-Athīr, *Usd al-ghāba*, ii. 224—227; Caetani, *Annali dell' Islām*, Introd., § 175, 223, 226, 227; 1 A.H., § 15, No. 50, § 50, 53; 5 A.H., § 201; 8 A.H., § 7—15; Lammens, *Fatima et les filles de Mahomet*, *passim*; F. Buhl, *Das Leben Muhammeds*, p. 150.

AL-**ZAIDĪYA**, the practical group of the Shīʿa, distinguished from the Ithnā ʿAsharīya [q.v.] and the Sabʿīya [q.v.] by the recognition of Zaid b. ʿAlī. This grandson of al-Ḥusain b. ʿAlī b. Abī Ṭālib was the first to try to wrest the caliphate from the Umaiyads by armed rebellion after the catastrophe at Karbalāʾ, when he placed himself at the disposal of the Kūfans as imām. After spending a year in Kūfa with secret preparations, he came forward openly, but was killed in street-fighting. This happened, according to most records, in the year 122/740; other dates are, however, also mentioned. Among the extant writings attributed to Zaid there is a complete compendium of fiḳh which, however, has not come down to us in its original form; it was edited by E. Griffini (*Corpus Juris di Zaid ibn ʿAlī*, Milan 1919).

After Zaid's death the Zaidīya took part in several ʿAlid risings but they were not a united body. Writers on heresy distinguish eight schools among them: from Abu 'l-Djārūd, who combined warlike activity with apotheosis of the imāms and belief in a Mahdī, to Salama b. Kuhail, whose Zaidism was watered down to a simple Shīʿa point of view. It was the same as regards theology. The Zaidīya only became a united community when ʿAlid claimants to the imāmate themselves took over the spiritual leadership. As far as can be ascertained this was the work of two men: 1. al-Ḥasan b. Zaid, founder about 250/864 of a Zaidī state in the south of the Caspian Sea, and 2. al-Ḳāsim al-Rassī Ibn Ibrāhīm Ṭabāṭabā b. Ismāʿīl al-Dībādj b. Ibrāhīm b. al-Ḥasan b. al-Ḥasan b. ʿAlī b. Abī Ṭālib (d. 246/860). While the works of al-Ḥasan b. Zaid are only known indirectly from quotations, we possess some by al-Ḳāsim, who was however quite unsuccessful in the political sphere, although his name has only recently become better known in connection with his polemica against the Christians (Di Matteo, in *RSO*, ix., 1921—1923, p. 301—364) and against Ibn al-Muḳaffaʿ (M. Guidi, *La lotta tra l'islām e il manicheismo*, Rome 1927). The school founded by al-Ḳāsim and developed by his successors, now the only surviving school, is Muʿtazilī in theology, in ethics anti-Murdjiʾite, with a puritanical trait in its rejection of mysticism; indeed Ṣūfī orders are forbidden in the modern Zaidī state. In worship it has certain "sectarian" features in common with the other Shīʿīs: the call to prayer "come to the best of works"; the fivefold *takbīr* in the funeral service; rejection of the *masḥ ʿala 'l-khuffain* (wiping the covered foot as a substitute for washing), of the impious leader at prayer and of the eating of the meat killed by a non-Muslim. In family law they prohibit mixed marriages, on the other hand they do not allow *mutʿa* [q.v.]. As their opponents were almost entirely Muslims they observed in theory at least the regulations for dealing with *bughāt*, those who refused obedience to the imām; but as there was in addition the distinction between Muʿtazilīs and Sunnīs, the Zaidīs often called themselves simply the believers in contrast to them, just as they called their wars *djihād* with the corresponding legal consequences. As a result of the scattered distribution of the original Zaidīs, we find the most diverse views on legal questions which were not fundamental for the sect as such. These are registered by later writers without the accusation of heresy out of simple delight in *ikhtilāf al-fiḳh*, and we find individual Zaidīs appearing with individual Sunnīs against other Zaidīs and other Sunnīs in changing combinations, so that the Zaidī *madhhab* in practice is a fifth alongside of the four. The Zaidī Abu 'l-Ḥasan ʿAbd Allāh b. Miftāḥ gives a vivid picture of this in his *al-Muntazaʿ al-mukhtār min al-ghaith al-midrār* (vol. i., Cairo 1328). In the present day Zaidī state there must of course be greater uniformity; this is brought about by the use of *al-Azhār fī fiḳh al-aʾimma al-aṭhār* (Brockelmann, *GAL*, ii. 239) of Aḥmad b. Yaḥyā b. al-Murtaḍā (see below) and *al-Rawḍ al-naḍīr* (see *Bibl.*) as official text-books.

The essential demands on the imām are: *a.* Membership of the *ahl al-bait*, without any distinction between Ḥasanids and Ḥusainids, i.e. no succession by inheritance; *b.* ability to resort to the sword if necessary for offence or defence so that neither a child nor a concealed Mahdī can be considered; *c.* the necessary learning: how seriously this is taken, is shown by the vast mass of writings of imāms at all times. As there could therefore be no dynastic tradition, and individual success was in the end the deciding factor, we have no series of imāms without a break; we find rather the possibility of "an age without an imām" recognized with a sense of the realities, while we also have the opposite: "several imāms at one time", i.e. the frequent appearance of an anti-imām; if the latter can oust his predecessor, the former's deposal or abdication is recognized as legal; if there is a turn in the tide he may however come back. If the qualifications for the imāmate are not completely possessed, he cannot be recognized as full imām; we thus have imāms of war of or learning only. Leaders whose strength is only sufficient to keep alive the Zaidī claim are called *dāʿī*, *muḥtasib*, *muḳtaṣid*, etc. The uncertainty as to who is really to be considered an imām is seen in the list of those among ʿAlid pretenders who have been chosen by the later Zaidīya as an organized state to preserve a connection with the original S͟hīʿa.

The political ambitions of the Zaidīya have been realized in two places: On the Caspian Sea about 20 imāms and *dāʿī* appeared from al-Ḥasan b. Zaid down to about 520/1126 at irregular intervals and sometimes also in opposition to one another. The Zaidīs there afterwards became merged in the little sect of Nuktawīs. The founder of the Zaidī state in the Yaman was al-Hādī ila 'l-Ḥaḳḳ Yaḥyā b. al-Ḥusain, grandson of al-Ḳāsim al-Rassī. It has survived all the kingdoms of the Yaman although it has frequently been driven back into its starting point Ṣaʿda, for example at the beginning of the fourth (tenth) century on the death of al-Nāṣir Aḥmad, son and second successor of al-Hādī, and in the course of this century only minor efforts at expansion could be made by sons and grandsons of this Aḥmad and also by collateral lines descended from al-Ḳāsim but not through al-Hādī; among the latter were the ʿAiyānī. One of these was the prolific writer the imām al-Mahdī al-Ḥusain b. al-Manṣūr al-Ḳāsim whose death in 404/1013 in view of the hopeless outlook produced a schism at which a group which expected the Mahdī at the end of a millenium broke off. About 447/1055 al-Nāṣir Abu 'l-Fatḥ b. al-Ḥusain fell in battle against the Ṣulaiḥids; he was called al-Dailamī because his original sphere of activity had been among the Caspian Zaidīs. He was a descendant of Zaid b. ʿAlī; it is therefore inaccurate to describe the Yaman imāms as Rassids. It was not till 533/1138 that a successor to him appeared (till 566/1170) in al-Mutawakkil Aḥmad b. Sulaimān of the family of al-Hādī; in addition to his military campaigns which took him as far as Nad͟jrān, he conducted a literary campaign against the theological heresy of the Muṭarrifīs. The disorder of the viith/xiiith century is seen in the fact that al-Mahdī Aḥmad b. al-Ḥusain of the family of Abu 'l-Barakāt b. Muḥammad b. al-Ḳāsim al-Rassī was murdered in 656/1258 by his own people after being imām for ten years. Al-Mahdī Ibrāhīm b. Tād͟j al-Dīn Aḥmad had a rival imām in Yaḥyā b. Muḥammad of a quite unknown Ḥasanid family of al-Sarād͟jī and he himself ended in the prison of the Rasūlid al-Muẓaffar Yūsuf in Taʿizz while al-Mutawakkil al-Muṭahhar b. Yaḥyā, again of al-Hādī's line (d. 699/1299), is famous as al-Muẓallal bi 'l-g͟hamāma, because a cloud enabled him to escape from the pursuing Rasūlid al-Muʾaiyad Dāwūd when he was on a dangerous retreat into K͟hawlān. The succession in the imāmate to his son al-Mahdī Muḥammad and his grandson al-Muṭahhar was interrupted by several strangers, for example al-Muʾaiyad Yaḥyā b. Ḥamza, descendant of the "Twelver" Imām ʿAlī al-Riḍā; his writings filled "as many sheets of paper as there were days in his life". No less prolific as a writer was al-Mahdī Aḥmad b. Yaḥyā b. al-Murtaḍā (d. 836/1432), imām for several days only. After several imāms had fought with one another and with the Ṭāhirids for D͟himār and Ṣanʿāʾ, his grandson al-Mutawakkil Yaḥyā S͟haraf al-Dīn had to retire for a time to T͟hulā before the invading generals of the Egyptian Mamlūks (in 933/1527). His son al-Muṭahhar was temporarily able to regain all land lost as far as al-Tihāma. In the meanwhile Ottoman suzerainty had been established and his grandson ended in prison in Istanbul, as did in 1004/1595 al-Nāṣir al-Ḥasan b. ʿAlī of a different line from al-Hādī, after maintaining himself in al-Ahnūm for seven years as imām.

In the following centuries the Zaidīs had to wage many wars with the Turks, during which in particular the town of Ṣanʿāʾ often changed rulers, whereas on the other hand — in a true Zaidī way — often several imāms acted at the same time. The present kingdom was established by the imām al-Mutawakkil Yaḥyā, who came forward in 1904 against the Turks and in November 1918 definitely occupied Ṣanʿāʾ. His record of warfare makes the imāmate of Yaḥyā recall, as in many other points, even the true Zaidī tenor of his encyclicals (see in ʿAbd al-Wāsiʿ, cf. *Bibl.*), that of the first Yaḥyā al-Hādī. He was reckoned — which may help to throw light on the theory of the imāmate — his descendant in the 26th generation, but counting partially recognized and anti-imāms about his 100th successor in office.

Bibliography: On the original sources cf. *Isl.*, i., p. 354—368 and ii., p. 49—78; since then there has been printed: al-Ḥusain b. Aḥmad al-Ḥaimī al-Ṣanʿānī, *al-Rawḍ al-naḍīr*, a commentary with glosses on *Mad͟jmūʿ al-fiḳh al-kabīr* (4 vol., Cairo 1347—1349). Of the collections, numbering many hundreds, of Zaidī manuscripts in Europe, a catalogue of MSS. in Vienna has not yet appeared and that of those in Milan by E. Griffini (in *RSO*, from vol. ii., 1908) has not been finished. — Further C. van Arendonk *De opkomst van het Zaidietische Imamaat in Yemen*, Leiden 1919; As͟hʿarī, *Maḳālāt al-Islāmīyīn*, ed. Ritter, index; S͟hahrastānī, p. 115—121; Ibn Ḥazm, *al-Faṣl fi 'l-milal*, Cairo 1325, iv. 179—188, and thereon J. Friedländer, in *JAOS*, xxviii., p. 1—80 and xxix., p. 1—183; R. Strothmann, *Das Staatsrecht der Zaiditen*, Strassburg 1912; do., *Kultus der Zaiditen*, Strassburg 1912; Amīn al-Raiḥānī, *Mulūk al-ʿArab*, Bairūt 1924, p. 69—196; M. Guidi, *Gli scrittori Zayditi e l'esegesi coranica Muʿtazilita*, Rome 1925; A. S. Tritton, *The Rise of the Imams of Sanaa*, Oxford 1925; ʿAbd al-Wāsiʿ b. Yaḥyā al-Wāsiʿī al-Yamānī (sic), *Taʾrīk͟h al-Yaman*, Cairo 1346; Muḥammad b. Muḥammad b. Yaḥyā Zubāra al-Ḥasanī al-Yamanī (sic) al-Ṣanʿānī, *Nail al-waṭar min tarād͟jim rid͟jāl al-Yaman fi 'l-ḳarn al-t͟hālit͟h ʿas͟har*, Cairo 1348.

ZAIN AL-DĪN ABŪ BAKR MUḤAMMAD B. MUḤAMMAD AL-K͟HAWĀFĪ, founder of an order called after him Zainīya, which traced itself to D͟junaid, was born in 757/1356 at K͟hawāf (between Būs͟hand͟j and Zūzan) in K͟hurāsān, and was buried in 838/1435 at the villages Mālīn (two parasangs from Herāt), whence his remains were transferred to Darwī<u>sh</u>ābād, and thence to the *ʿīdgāh* of Herāt, where a mosque was built over them. He obtained authorization (*i<u>dj</u>āza*) in Egypt from Nūr al-Dīn ʿAbd al-Raḥmān al-Miṣrī (*Nafaḥāt al-uns*, No. 505), and returned to Central Asia, but visited Egypt again, whence he sent in 822/1419 a gravestone for <u>Kh</u>ʷā<u>dj</u>a Muḥammad Pārsā, who died in Madīna, and from one of whose letters our authorities derive some of their information about him. In Egypt he made a disciple of ʿAbd al-Raḥīm b. al-Amīr al-Marzifūnī, who accompanied him to his home; in Jerusalem of ʿAbd al-Laṭīf b. ʿAbd al-Raḥmān al-Maḳdisī, and one ʿAbd al-Muʿṭī, a Ma<u>gh</u>ribī. A fourth disciple was <u>Kh</u>ʷā<u>dj</u>a Saʿd al-Dīn of Ka<u>sh</u><u>gh</u>ar, the most celebrated native of that place (d. 860/1456; *Relation de l'Ambassade au Kharezm*, transl. C. Schefer, 1879, p. 164). Zain al-Dīn was the author of several works: *Risālat al-waṣāyā al-Ḳudsīya*, composed in Jerusalem, *al-Awrād al-Zainīya*, and a treatise on asceticism. A grandson of his, also called Zain al-Dīn, was a courtier of Bābur, and translated his *Memoirs* into Persian.

Bibliography: <u>Dj</u>āmī, *Nafaḥāt al-uns*, No. 506; Ṭā<u>sh</u>köprüzāde, *al-<u>Sh</u>aḳāʾiḳ al-nuʿmānīya*, transl. O. Rescher, Istanbul 1927, p. 38—41; Brockelmann, *GAL*, ii. 265, *Suppl.* ii. 285.

ZAINAB BINT **<u>DJ</u>AḤ<u>SH</u>** B. RIʾĀB, AL-ASADĪYA, one of Muḥammad's wives, was the daughter of Umaima bint ʿAbd al-Muṭṭalib; her *kunya* was Umm al-Ḥakam and her name had been Barra. One of the first emigrants to Madīna, she was a virgin (some traditions say a widow) when the Prophet gave her in marriage to his freedman and adopted son Zaid b. Ḥāri<u>th</u>a.

In 4 A.H. Muḥammad, visiting Zaid in his home, saw Zainab alone and fell in love with her. Zaid divorced her in order that the Prophet might marry her; the latter's scruples were set at rest by the revelation of Ḳurʾān xxxiii. 36—39. Zainab received a dowry of 400 dirhams. She was proud of the circumstances of her marriage, and used to say that Muḥammad's other wives had been given to him by their fathers and brothers, while her union had been brought about by special divine revelation. The *āyat al-ḥi<u>dj</u>āb* (xxxiii. 53) is said to have been revealed on the occasion of Zainab's wedding feast, and Ḳurʾān lxvi. 1 is also referred by some to Zainab and to the other wives' envy of her.

Zainab was a friend of ʿĀʾi<u>sh</u>a's, and, next to her, Muḥammad's favorite. She accompanied him on the expedition against <u>Kh</u>aibar. Her charity is celebrated; Muḥammad's prediction "the longest-handed of my wives shall be the first to join me in paradise" is referred to her (but see SAWDA B. ZAMʿA). She had received 12,000 dirhams from ʿUmar in 20 A.H., but left no money, having given all to the poor.

Zainab was about 35 on her marriage to Muḥammad, and died at about 50, in 20 or 21 A.H.

The episode of the Prophet's infatuation with his adopted son's wife was made much of by Christian propaganda (see Marracci, *Refutatio Al-corani*, p. 562); modern Muslim biographers and commentators of the Ḳurʾān have tried to present the episode in a seemlier light, e.g. Muḥammad ʿAbduh in *Tafsīr al-Fātiḥa wa-mu<u>sh</u>kilāt al-Ḳurʾān*, Cairo 1330, in the chapter entitled *Tawḍīḥ masʾalat Zaid wa-Zainab*; and Mawlānā Muḥammad ʿAlī in his biography *Muḥammad the Prophet*, Lahore 1924, p. 249—250.

Bibliography: Ibn Saʿd, viii. 71—82; Caetani, *Annali dell' Islām*, 1 A.H., § 15, No. 25; 5 A.H., § 20—27; 8 A.H., § 15, No. 2; 10 A.H., § 139, No. 8; 20 A.H. § 267, 298, 400—406; Ibn Isḥāḳ, ed. Wüstenfeld, p. 1004; G. H. Stern, *Marriage in Early Islam*, London 1939, index; a literary portrait: Enrico Ruta, *Visioni d'Oriente e d'Occidente*, Milan 1924, p. 35—45: *Zainab*.

ZAINAB BINT **<u>KH</u>UZAIMA** B. AL-ḤĀRI<u>TH</u> AL-HILĀLĪYA, one of Muḥammad's wives, had borne the name of Umm al-Masākīn since the <u>Dj</u>āhilīya. Her first husband, al-Ṭufail b. al-Ḥāri<u>th</u>, had divorced her; the second, ʿUbaida b. al-Ḥāri<u>th</u>, was killed at Badr. Muḥammad married her in Ramaḍān 4 A.H. and gave her a dowry of 400 dirhams; she died 2 or 8 months later, the first of his Madīnese wives to die before him, and was buried in the cemetery of al-Baḳīʿ.

Bibliography: Ibn Saʿd, viii. 82; Caetani, *Annali dell' Islām*, 4 A.H., § 16 and § 22; al-Ṭabarī, i. 1775—1776; Ibn al-A<u>th</u>īr, *Usd al-<u>gh</u>āba*, v. 466—467; G. H. Stern, *Marriage in Early Islam*, London 1939, index.

ZAINAB BINT **MUḤAMMAD**, one of the Prophet's daughters, said to have been the eldest, was married before her father's mission to her maternal cousin Abu 'l-ʿĀṣī b. al-Rabīʿ.

She was in al-Ṭāʾif at the time of Muḥammad's *hi<u>dj</u>ra*, and did not follow him to Madīna; her husband, still a pagan, was taken prisoner at Badr. Zainab sent a necklace which had belonged to <u>Kh</u>adī<u>dj</u>a to ransom him, and Muḥammad freed him on condition that Zainab should come to Madīna. On her way thither she was maltreated by al-Ḥabbār b. al-Aswad and had a fall which caused her to miscarry (some authors place this accident in 8 A.H. and attribute her death to it).

Her husband was taken prisoner a second time in 6 A.H. in the expedition of al-ʿĪs, and freed by his wife's intercession. He became a Muslim in 7 and was reunited to his wife by a second marriage.

Zainab died in Madīna in 8 A.H. She had two children, ʿAlī who died in infancy, and Umāma, married to ʿAlī b. Abī Ṭālib after Fāṭima's death.

Bibliography: Ibn Saʿd, viii. 20—24; Caetani, *Annali dell' Islām*, Introd., § 160, No. 1; § 349, No. 1; 2 A.H., § 82; 6 A.H., § 9; 7 A.H., § 3; 8 A.H., § 80, 81, 201; al-Ṭabarī, iii. 2303—2307; H. Lammens, *Fatimah et les filles de Mahomet, passim*.

ZAKĀRĪYĀʾ, the father of John the Baptist, is reckoned in the Ḳurʾān (vi. 85) along with John, Jesus and Elias among the righteous. Muḥammad gives the substance of Luke i. 5—25 as follows: Zakārīyā guards the Virgin Mary in the niche (*miḥrāb*) and always finds fresh fruits there. He prays to God; angels announce to him that a son will be born to him, Yaḥyā, a name never previously given to anyone, a pious man, a prophet, Yaʿḳūb's heir, pleasing to God. Zakārīyā thinks he is too old. As a sign to him he is struck dumb for three days (Sūra iii. 37—41; xix. 1—15; xxi. 89—90).

Later legend expands the Gospel story and says that Gabriel was the announcer (Luke i. 19) and that Zakārīyā was struck dumb as a punishment for his doubts (i. 20). It elaborates the details as follows: 19 people anxious to take charge of Maryam write their names each on a reed; these are thrown into the pool of Siloam and the reed with Zakārīyā's name comes to the top. Zakārīyā grows old and resigns his office of custodian which a reed oracle gives to Joseph the carpenter (<u>Th</u>aʿlabī, p. 236). In Mary's niche there is winter fruit in summer and summer fruit in winter; this encourages Zakārīyā to pray that his aged body also may be fruitful out of season (Thaʿlabī, p. 237).

Muslim legend makes Zakārīyā as a prophet die the death of a martyr. After Yaḥyā's death he escapes into a tree which opens for him. But the hem of his cloak remains outside the tree. Iblīs betrays him, the tree is sawn down and with it Zakārīyā (Thaʿlabī, p. 240; Ibn al-Athīr, p. 120). This is modelled on the Haggada and the martyrdom of Isaiah (Pal. *Sanhedrin*, x. 28c; Bab. *Sanhedrin*, 101a; Kautzsch, *Apokryphen und Pseudepigraphen*, ii. 123: Isaiah, Djemshīd, Zakārīyā).

Muslim legend seems to identify the Zakārīyā of the Gospel with the prophet Zachariah of whom the Haggada records that his blood boiled until Nebuchadnezzar's general Nebuzaraddan came. The latter sought to calm it with the blood of the sacrificed victim and with the best of Israel, but in vain. Only his appeal calms it (many recordings in Ginzberg, *Legends of the Jews*, vi. 396, 3c). Muslim legend tells this of the blood of Yaḥyā b. Zakārīyā. Zechariah, son of the High Priest Jehoiada, who was martyred by king Joash (ii. Chron. xxiv. 21), is identified with Zacharias the father of John the Baptist not only in Muslim legend, but also in Christian apocryphal texts (*Protoevangelium Jacobi* xxiv).

Bibliography: Ṭabarī, i. 2, 213 *sq.*, 719 *sq.*; Thaʿlabī, *Ḳiṣaṣ al-anbiyāʾ*, Cairo 1325, p. 234—240; Ibn al-Athīr, Būlāḳ, 1290, i. 117—120; al-Ḳisāʾī, *Ḳiṣaṣ al-anbiyāʾ*, ed. Eisenberg, p. 297, 302, 303; Leo Baeck, *Secharja ben Berechja*, in *MGWJ*, 1932, p. 233—319; D. Sidersky, *Les Origines des légendes Musulmanes*, Paris 1933, p. 139 *sq.*; Ch. C. Torrey, *The Jewish Foundation of Islām*, New York 1933, p. 58, 67, 80; B. Heller, *Islamische Jesaja-Legende*; *Islamische Zacharija-Legende*, *MGWJ*, 1936, lxxx, 43 *sq.*

ZAKĀT (A.), the alms-tax, one of the principal obligations of Islām. By this the law means a tax which is levied on definite kinds of property and is distributed to eight categories of persons. The word, for which there is no satisfactory Arabic etymology, became known to the Prophet in a much wider sense from the usage of the Jews (Aramaic *zākūt*). Here among the religiously inclined, the giving away of worldly possessions was regarded as a particularly pious act, the possession of earthly riches on the other hand almost as an obstacle to salvation; the same word that denoted virtue and righteousness in general could therefore also be used for benevolence and charitable gifts. Muḥammad had become acquainted with this form of piety as one of the marks of the revealed religion, and the Ḳurʾān from the first lays stress on the practice of benevolence as one of the chief virtues of the true believer; cf. Sūra xiii. 22; xxxv. 29: "(those who) spend out secretly and openly of what we have bestowed on them" (many similar passages); Sūra lxx. 24 *sq.*: "those, who acknowledge a determined due from their possessions, to the beggar and the needy"; also Sūra lxxvi. 8 *sq.* (all of the Meccan period). Equally already to the Meccan period belongs the use of the word *zakāt* along with several derivatives of the root *zakā* "to be pure", which to the Arab mind were related to it. Even the latter have in the Ḳurʾān almost exclusively the meaning "to be pious", which is not pure Arabic, but going back to the Jewish religion. The term *zakāt* means virtue in general as well as, with an almost imperceptible transition of meaning (cf. Sūra lxxxvii. 14; xxiii. 4; xcii. 18), giving (e.g. Sūra xix. 31, 55) and the pious gift (e.g. Sūra vii. 156; xxi. 73; xxx. 39; xxxi. 4; xli. 7). During the whole Meccan period, in which the Prophet had only a few, but these enthusiastic, followers any regulation of private charity was unnecessary and indeed impossible. The Muslim view also places the introduction of the *zakāt* as a legal obligation in Madīna, but varies, as regards the date, between the year 2 and the year 9; the earlier general prescriptions are regarded as thereby abrogated. The uncertainty regarding date weakens the positive statements of this tradition; the following is the idea we get, mainly from the Ḳurʾān, of the further development of the *zakāt*. Charity, sometimes referred to in general terms and sometimes by the word *zakāt* (both in turn e.g. Sūra ii. 261—281), continues to be one of the chief virtues of the believer, and must be based on a corresponding frame of mind. In the term *zakāt* the general meaning of virtue gradually falls into the background to be replaced by that of gift. Ṣadaḳa [q.v.] occurs as practically synonymous with *zakāt*; the Prophet may have become acquainted with it from the Jews in Madīna. In this town altered conditions soon influenced the nature of the *zakāt*: the poor believers who had migrated from Mecca had to be supported, but private charity decreased as conversions to Islām took place from motives no longer purely religious. On the other hand, the Prophet was now able to introduce a kind of organisation for the reception and distribution of pious gifts, which is presupposed by Sūra ix. 60, but at first no change was made in the character of the *zakāt* as an individual offering, in spite of the obligatory character of certain *ṣadaḳa*'s (in Sūra ii. 177 both kinds of gifts are mentioned together). Finally Muḥammad used the yield of these collections not to support the needy only but also, and even preferably when the necessity arose, for his military enterprises and other political purposes. The raising of the considerable sums necessary for this caused great difficulties; therefore strong admonitions to give "for Allāh's purposes", supported by promises and threats of a religious nature and accompanied by complaints about the insufficient contributions, return again and again in the Ḳurʾān. The use made by the Prophet of the charitable gifts aroused the criticism of the believers; and there was an open conflict, when Muḥammad, after the surrender of Mecca, endeavoured to reconcile prominent Ḳuraishīs with the new order of things by gifts from the *zakāt* fund. The discontent had to be appeased by a special revelation (Sūra ix. 58—60): "There are some of them who make reproaches to thee with respect to the *ṣadaḳa*'s; if they are given from, they are satisfied, but if they are not given from them, they murmur... 60. The *ṣadaḳa*'s are for the poor, the needy, those who work on (collecting) them, those whose hearts are to be conciliated, for the slaves, the debtors and for Allāh's purposes and for the wayfarer, as an ordinance from Allāh". This passage became the basis for the later laws about the distribution of the *zakāt*. The agents here mentioned had to receive the *zakāt* of the Beduin tribes who had adopted Islām; for the latter the *zakāt* from the first was hardly anything but an obligatory impost, the amount of which was usually fixed exactly in the agreements made with the Prophet; the reluctance of many Beduins to pay it is fought in Sūra ix. 98 *sq.* The transformation of the *zakāt* into a fiscal institution, beginning herewith, was limited by the Prophet to the irreducible minimum; essential elements of the later regulation are unknown to the Ḳur'ān and a part of the traditions. The Ḳur'ān answers the question of the believers as to what they should give, without any limitation: "the superfluity" (Sūra ii. 219), and a revelation of the last year of the Prophet's life still threatens with the punishment of hell "those who hoard gold and silver and do not spend it for Allāh's purposes" (Sūra ix. 34 *sq.*). Tradition also ascribes to the Prophet utterances which imply no limitation to the obligation of *zakāt*; among the Companions of the Prophet, especially Abū Dharr is considered to have held the view that one should only keep as much property as one needs. ʿAlī is said to have fixed the maximum value of property allowed at 4,000 dirhams, and the opinion is even ascribed to so late an authority as Mālik b. Anas that all wealth is forbidden (*ḥarām*). The Ḳur'ān (e.g. Sūra ii. 215) and Tradition repeatedly describe as recipients of the *zakāt* parents, relatives, orphans, poor, travellers, beggars and slaves; but according to Tradition, a *zakāt* given to the rich, thieves and prostitutes can also be meritorious, since it is the mere fact of giving which is the first consideration. The nature of the objects liable to *zakāt* is not further defined in the Ḳur'ān; Tradition knows of cases of paying *zakāt*, which cannot be fitted into the later system. In any case, the character of *zakāt* in the time of the Prophet was still vague and it did not represent, properly speaking, a tax demanded by religion. After Muḥammad's death many Beduin tribes therefore refused to continue to pay *zakāt* as they considered their agreements cancelled by the death of the Prophet, and many believers, among them ʿUmar himself, were inclined to agree with this. Only the energy of Abū Bakr made the *zakāt* in its fiscal form a permanent institution, which through the establishment of a state treasury contributed greatly to the expansion of Muslim power. Ardent believers continued as before to regard it as their right to bestow their *zakāt* for themselves as they thought fit; but very soon the development and centralisation of the state made this impossible in practice. When the system of *fiḳh* came to be elaborated the *zakāt* was definitely maintained as a religious tax and regulated in all its details; the views put forward on this occasion have also left their effect in Tradition. Among them is prominent a detailed *zakāt* ordinance, which is usually ascribed to Abū Bakr, sometimes to the Prophet himself or to ʿUmar or ʿAlī.

According to the Shāfiʿī doctrine, the main prescriptions regarding *zakāt* are as follows. Only Muslims pay *zakāt* (according to the Ḥanafīs only those who are adults and in full possession of their faculties), and on the following kinds of property: 1. crops of the field, which are planted for food; 2. among fruits: grapes and dates especially mentioned in Tradition; 3. camels, cattle, sheep and goats (according to the Ḥanafīs also horses); 4. gold and silver; 5. merchandise. On the two first classes the *zakāt* is to be paid at once at the harvest, on the last three after one year's uninterrupted possession; a condition for liability to *zakāt* is the possession of a certain minimum (*niṣāb*). On the first and second class the *zakāt* is 10% (when artificial irrigation is used 5%), the *niṣāb* is 5 camel-loads (*wasḳ*). There are complicated rules for the third category, which are based mainly on the *zakāt* ordinance ascribed to Abū Bakr and take into consideration not only the number but also the kind of animals; the *niṣāb* is 5 camels; or 20 cattle, or 40 sheep or goats; the animals are only liable to *zakāt* if they have grazed freely during the whole year and not been used for any work. The *zakāt* on the fourth and fifth category is $2^1/_2$%; the *niṣāb* for precious metals is calculated according to the weight and amounts for gold to 20 *mithḳāls* (or *dīnārs* = c. 84 grammes = 1,320 grains), for silver seven times this, 200 dirhams (for gold and silver ornaments the commercial value is the deciding factor); the value of merchandise must be estimated at the end of the year in gold or silver; in this case also there is liability to *zakāt* only if the precious metal or merchandise has been kept for a full year unused "as treasure". Also outstanding debts and deposits are liable to *zakāt*, at least if their recovery is ensured. — Lastly the tax on precious metals obtained from mines as well as on treasure trove is regarded by the best authorities as *zakāt*. It is permitted to hand the *zakāt* direct to the persons who have claims to it; it is however preferable to hand it to the Muslim authorities for regulated distribution. If the *zakāt* is collected by the government, one is bound to pay it to the collector (*ʿāmil*) even if the character of the government is no guarantee of a proper distribution (according to some, especially Ḥanafī scholars, in this case to satisfy one's conscience, the *zakāt* should be given a second time and distributed direct). The right of the government to demand the *zakāt* is however limited to the so-called *ẓāhir* possessions, i.e. the 'openly visible' articles of the first three categories, in the case of which the *ʿāmil* can fix the amount of the *zakāt* from his own observation; the so-called *bāṭin* properties on the other hand, i.e. the 'hidden' articles of the two last catagories, are expressly withdrawn from this control and the *zakāt* is left entirely to the conscience of the individual. — The yield of the *zakāt* is destined only for the eight classes mentioned in Sūra ix. 60 (thus excluding the family of the Prophet, in contrast to the *ghanīma* and *fai'*): after deducting a fixed salary for the collectors it is to be distributed in equal parts to the other seven categories so far as they exist in the country (so according to the Shāfiʿīs, while according to the other schools the varying needs may be considered). The distinction that is made between "poor" and "needy" is quite an arbitrary one; at any rate, the legists usually interpret the definition in such a way that they themselves belong to one of these classes. Whether after the time of the Prophet there were still persons "whose hearts are to be conciliated" is disputed among the schools. By the slaves who have a claim to a share in the *zakāt* are understood (except by the Mālikīs) such as have concluded a contract to purchase their liberty (*mukātaba*), by debtors (with the Shāfiʿīs) especially such as have taken upon themselves to pay a debt for God's sake. The part set aside "for Allāh's purposes" is to be devoted to the fighters for the faith who voluntarily take part in the *djihād* without belonging to the regular troops. These categories have been drawn up as a result of a schematic interpretation of the passage in the Ḳur'ān. — The artifices (*ḥiyal*) to avoid payment of *zakāt* are according to the Mālikīs and Ḥanbalīs invalid, according to the Ḥanafīs and Shāfiʿīs sinful but valid. — The Bāṭinīs applied their allegorical interpretation of the whole law also to the *zakāt*.

Actual practice differed considerably from the theory of *zakāt* in the different Muslim countries. The high imposts and taxes (*mukūs*) not foreseen by the *sharīʿa* made the raising of *zakāt* usually difficult or impossible so that it, particularly on *bāṭin* property, was either not paid at all or not to the prescribed extent. Frequently its collection led to extortion and other abuses. Nor was the yield in the great majority of cases applied according to the law; the collectors themselves or the *ḳāḍīs* often kept the larger portion. Sometimes the *zakāt* on the crops of the field under the name of "tithe" (*ʿus̲h̲r*; q.v.) became a purely secular tax. Nevertheless the religious obligation to pay *zakāt* is everywhere recognized and where the peasant is not overburdened with other taxes, he pays it at least on *ẓāhir* property as far as circumstances permit, although with many abuses in details. *Zakāt* has also to be paid on banknotes (and bank deposits) as corresponding to first-class debts; quite recently, the abandonment of the gold standard in most countries has given rise to new problems.

By *zakāt al-fiṭr* (*zakāt* of the breaking of the fast) is meant the obligatory gift of provisions at the end of the month of Ramaḍān, which according to Tradition was ordered by the Prophet in the year 2 and fixed as regards the amount (the latter is however certainly not historical). There were differences of opinion regarding the relation of this *zakāt* to the general one and regarding the question whether it was obligatory. According to the view which finally prevailed, the *zakāt al-fiṭr* is obligatory (according to the Mālikīs only *sunna*) and has to be given by every free Muslim for himself and all persons whom he is legally bound to support at latest on the first of the month S̲h̲awwāl which follows Ramaḍān. A man is exempted only if he does not possess more than the bare necessities of life for himself and his family. The amount of this *zakāt* is 1 *ṣāʿ* (= $^1/_{60}$ *wasḳ*) or 4 *mudd* of the usual food-stuffs of the country for each member of the household. The recipients according to the S̲h̲āfiʿīs are the same as in the case of the general *zakāt*, while the other schools, more in keeping with the original character of the *zakāt al-fiṭr*, approve its limitation to the poor and needy. — Throughout the Muslim world the regulations about the *zakāt al-fiṭr* are observed with particular scrupulousness; the people consider it to be part of the duties of Ramaḍān and to serve as atonement for any involuntary negligence during this month.

In conclusion we may note that the voluntary, not obligatory charitable gifts (*ṣadaḳāt*) have been always considered very meritorious in Islām.

Bibliography: For the etymology: Nöldeke, *Neue Beiträge zur semitischen Sprachwissenschaft*, p. 25; Horovitz, in *Isl.*, viii. 137; Jeffery, *Foreign Vocabulary of the Qoran*, s.v. — For the Ḳurʾān: Snouck Hurgronje, *Verspreide Geschriften*, ii. 9 *sqq.*; i, 346 *sqq.* (review of H. Grimme, *Mohammed*, vol. i.). — For the tradition: Wensinck, *Handbook*, s.v. — For the *fiḳh*: Juynboll, *Handleiding*, 3rd ed., p. 77 *sqq.*; Hughes, *Dictionary of Islam*, s.v. — For the practice, especially in Indonesia: Snouck Hurgronje, *Verspr. Geschr.*, ii. 380 *sqq.*; Juynboll, *Handleiding*, p. 85, 89 *sqq.*; also, e.g., al-Ḳalḳas̲h̲andī, *Ṣubḥ al-Aʿs̲h̲ā*, iii. 461. — For the allegorical interpretation of the law of *zakāt* by the Bāṭinīs: Goldziher, *Streitschrift des Gazālī*, p. 23, n. 4.

AL-ZAMAK̲H̲S̲H̲ARĪ, ABU 'L-ḲĀSIM MAḤMŪD B. ʿUMAR, a Persian-born Arabic scholar, theologian and philologist. Born in K̲h̲wārizm on 27th Radjab 467/March 8,1075, in the course of his travels as a student he came to Mecca, where he stayed for some time as a pupil of Ibn Wahhās, hence his epithet *D̲j̲ār Allāh*. He must however have achieved a literary reputation before this; when he passed through Bag̲h̲dād on the pilgrimage he was welcomed there by the learned ʿAlid Hibat Allāh b. al-S̲h̲ad̲j̲arī. As a theologian he followed the teachings of the Muʿtazila; as a philologist, in spite of his Persian descent, he championed the absolute superiority of Arabic and used his mother tongue only in instructing beginners. He died at al-D̲j̲urd̲j̲ānīya in K̲h̲wārizm on the day of ʿArafāt 538 /June 14, 1144. Ibn Baṭṭūṭa (Paris ed., iii. 6) was still able to see his tomb there.

His principal work, completed in 528/1134, is his commentary on the Ḳurʾān, *al-Kas̲h̲s̲h̲āf ʿan Ḥaḳāʾiḳ al-Tanzīl*, which in spite of its Muʿtazilite bias — at the very beginning he declares the Ḳurʾān created — was widely read in orthodox circles. The author devotes most attention to dogmatic exegesis of a philosophical nature, paying only slight attention to tradition. Besides giving the purely grammatical exposition, he devotes special attention to pointing out rhetorical beauties and thus supporting the doctrine of the *iʿd̲j̲āz* of the Ḳurʾān. He gives particular care to the lexicographical side of his work, going fully into the readings and supports his explanations by ample extracts from the old poetry. His work still retained a place in literature when Baiḍāwī produced his own as the orthodox counterpart and tried to surpass him in the accuracy of the grammatical exposition and in quoting variant readings. Even in the western lands of Islām, where his dogmatic point of view gave particular offence to the Mālikīs, Ibn K̲h̲aldūn placed it high above other commentators; it is not however an accident that manuscripts of his work are rarer in the west than in the east. The first edition by W. Nassau Lees and the Mawlawīs K̲h̲ādim Ḥusain and ʿAbd al-Ḥaiy (Calcutta 1856, 2 vols.) was followed by the printed editions at Būlāḳ 1291, Cairo 1307, 1308, 1318, 1354. The *Kas̲h̲s̲h̲āf* has often been commentated and provided with glosses, for which cf. Brockelmann, *GAL*, i. 345 *sq.* and *Suppl.* i. 507 *sq.*

Of his grammatical works *al-Mufaṣṣal*, written in 513—515/1119—1121, has become celebrated for its succinct yet exhaustive and lucid exposition; it was published by J. B. Broch, Christiania 1859, 1879. For commentaries and glosses and his other philological works see Brockelmann on the quoted pages.

His wonderful knowledge of the language was shown in a series of collections and sayings which enjoy great popularity. A collection of old proverbs is contained in the still unprinted *al-Mustaḳṣā fi 'l-amt̲h̲āl*. In addition he made three collections of apophthegms, composed by himself with particular care and all the fine artifices of rhetoric; 1. *Nawābig̲h̲ al-kalim*, 2. *Rabīʿ al-abrār fīmā yasurr al-k̲h̲awāṭir wa'l-afkār*, 3. *Aṭwāḳ al-d̲h̲ahab*.

He composed also a series of moral discourses opening with the address *Yā Aba 'l-Ḳāsim* to himself and called *Maḳāmāt*, after the older meaning of this word; they are also known as *al-Naṣāʾiḥ al-kibār*, and he added 5 pieces of a different nature, on grammar, prosody and the *Aiyām al-ʿArab* after recovering from a severe illness in 512/1118; printed with the author's commentary Cairo 1313, 1325, transl. by O. Rescher, *Beiträge zur Maqâmenliteratur*, fasc. 6, Greifswald 1913. The *Kitāb Nuzhat al-muttaʾannis wa-Nahzat al-muḳtabis* also belongs to *adab* literature; it is a kind of "lexikographische Belletristik", preserved in the Aya Sofia No. 4331 (cf. Rescher, in *ZDMG*, lxiv. 508).

Of his poems, which were collected into a *Dīwān*, (*Fihrist*, Cairo², iii. 131), a *Mart̲h̲iya* on his teacher Abū Muḍar has been printed in al-ʿIzzī's *Maḍnūn*, ed. by Yahuda, p. 16 *sqq.*

He composed only two works on the field of Tradition: 1. *Mukhtaṣar al-muwāfaḳa baina Āl al-Bait wa 'l-ṣaḥāba*, Ms. in the library of Aḥmad Taimūr, see *RAAD*, x. 313; 2. *Khaṣā'iṣ al-ʿashara al-kirām al-barara*, see Ahlwardt, Berlin Ms. No. 9656; *Hespéris*, xii. 117, 991.

Bibliography: al-Anbārī, *Nuzhat al-alibbā'*, p. 469—473; Ibn Khallikān, *Wafayāt*, Būlāḳ 1299, ii. 107; Yāḳūt, *Irshād al-arīb*, ed. Margoliouth, vii. 147—151; Suyūṭī, *Bughyat al-wuʿāt*, p. 388; do., *Ṭabaḳāt al-mufassirīn*, ed. Meursinge, p. 41; Ibn Ḳuṭlūbughā, *Tādj al-tarādjim*, ed. by G. Flügel, No. 217; Muḥammad ʿAbd al-Ḥaiy al-Laknawī, *al-Fawā'id al-bahīya*, p. 87; Djamīl Bek, *ʿUḳūd al-Djawhar*, i. 294 *sqq.*; Ibn Taghrībirdī, ed. Popper, iii. 34, 7—17; Barbier de Meynard, in *JA*, 1875, ii. 314 *sqq.*; Brockelmann, *GAL*, i. 344 *sqq.*, *Suppl.* i 507—13; Sarkīs, *Muʿdjam al-maṭbūʿāt*, col. 973 *sqq.*; Nöldeke-Schwally, *Gesch. des Qorāns*, ii. 174; Goldziher, *Die Richtungen der islamischen Koranauslegung*, p. 117—177.

ZAMZAM, the sacred well of Mecca, also called the well of Ismāʿīl. It is in *al-ḥaram al-sharīf* S.E. of the Kaʿba opposite the corner of the sanctuary in which the Black Stone is inserted. It is 140 feet deep and is surmounted by an elegant dome. The pilgrims drink its water as health-giving and take it home with them to give it to the sick. Zamzam in Arabic means "abundant water" and *zamzama* "to drink by little gulps" and "to mutter through the teeth".

Muslim tradition connects the origin of this well with the story of Abraham. It was opened by the angel Gabriel to save Hagar and her son Ismāʿīl, who were dying of thirst in the desert. Hagar was the first to catch its water by building a wall of stone around it. It is at least certain that it was held in reverence at a very early period. In the pre-Islāmic period the Persians used to come there as a line of an old poet shows: "The Persians muttered their prayers around the well of Zamzam from the earliest times". According to another poet, the well was visited by Sāsān son of Bābak, the ancestor of the Sāsānids.

In the period of paganism, the Djurhumīs filled in Zamzam and threw all their treasure into it. Masʿūdī however remarks that the Djurhumīs were poor and that the treasures buried there must have been brought not by them, but by the Persians.

The well was rediscovered and dug out by ʿAbd al-Muṭṭalib, the ancestor of the Prophet, who provided it with walls of masonry; he took out of it two gazelles of gold, some "Ḳalʿīya" swords and some cuirasses. With the swords he made the door of the Kaʿba, which he covered with plates of gold made from one of the gazelles and he put the other inside the sanctuary. The water of the well was distributed to the inhabitants of Mecca.

In 297/909 Zamzam overflowed, a thing which had never been known before and several pilgrims were drowned.

Before leaving Mecca the pilgrims are in the habit of dipping the clothes in which they intend to be buried, in Zamzam.

Bibliography: Cf. the art. KAʿBA, i. and iii.; Masʿūdī, s. index; H. Kazem Zadeh, *Relation d'un Pèlerinage à La Mecque en* 1910—1911, Paris 1912; descriptions by various travellers: Snouck Hurgronje, *Verspr. Geschr.*, index s.v. Zamzam; picture in Snouck Hurgronje, *Bilder aus Mekka*, Leyden 1889, Nrs. i., iii.; *The Travels of Ali Bey*, ii., pl. lvii.; Gaudefroy-Demombynes, *Le pèlerinage à la Mekke*, Paris 1923, p. 71 *sqq.*

ZĀWIYA, properly the corner of a building, was at first applied to the cell of the Christian monk then to a small mosque or praying room; the word still has this meaning in the Muslim east in contrast to a more important mosque (*masdjid* or *djāmiʿ*). On the other hand the term zāwiya has retained a much more general meaning in North Africa and is applied to a building or group of buildings of a religious nature, which resembles a monastery and a school. An excellent definition of the Maghribī zāwiya was given as early as 1847 by Daumas (*La Kabylie*, p. 60) and it seems to be in essentials appropriate at the present day (cf. the quotation in Dozy, *Suppl.*, s.v.). All or several of the following are found in a zāwiya: a room for prayer with a *miḥrāb*; the mausoleum of a marabout or Sharīfan saint, which is surmounted by a dome (*ḳubba*); a room set aside exclusively for the recitation of the Ḳur'ān; a *maktab* or Ḳur'ān school; finally rooms for the guests of the zāwiya, pilgrims, travellers and students. The zāwiya is usually adjoined by a cemetery with the tombs of those who have during their lifetime expressed a wish to be buried here.

The conception of a zāwiya has, it seems, undergone a somewhat characteristic change since the middle ages, at least in the Muslim west; in the east on the other hand the term very soon acquired a definite meaning so that it was applied only to the more humble mosques and is not there used as an alternative for the more precise terms like *dair*, *khānḳāh* or *tekke*, which are used particularly for monastic institutions which as a rule owe their origin to Persian Muslim mysticism. In the Maghrib on the other hand the term *zāwiya* appears about the xiiith century as synonymous with *rābiṭa*, i.e. hermitage, to which a holy man retired and where he lived surrounded by his pupils and devotees (cf. G. S. Colin, transl. of al-Bādisī's *Maḳṣad*, in *AM*, xxvi. [1926], p. 240, s.v.). This *zāwiya* or *rābiṭa* is however not always identical with the *ribāṭ*, an institution which served another purpose and was primarily of a military character. In this connection however we may note a statement of Ibn Marzūḳ of Tlemcen (d. 781/1379), who in his monograph on the Marīnid Sulṭān Abu 'l-Ḥasan ʿAlī, *al-Musnad al-ṣaḥīḥ al-ḥasan*, devotes the 42nd chapter to the zāwiya; it corresponds to what in the east is called *ribāṭ* or *khānaḳāh*. It may be added that the word *ribāṭ* is also found in Morocco used for institutions in which the military activity was particularly directed to spreading Islām among heretics with the sword: this for example was the case with the *ribāṭ* Asfī and Sīdī-Shīker on the Wādī-Tansīft. The first zāwiya hermitages undoubtedly developed very quickly and became not only places of refuge from the world but also centres of religious and mystic life, where the *taṣawwuf*, hitherto the sole possession of urban scholars was to be brought nearer the masses. They now became centres of attraction, religious schools and to some extent free hostels for travellers in search of spiritual perfection. This explains how Ibn Marzūḳ could say when speaking of the zāwiyas of his time: "It is clear that with us in the Maghrib the zāwiyas serve to give shelter to wanderers and food to travellers" (cf. also RIBĀṬ).

In Muslim Spain we find no zāwiyas before the time of the Naṣrids of Granada. They therefore belong to the same time as those of the Marīnid sulṭān Abu 'l-Ḥasan and their foundation must have met the same needs. In 1903 W. and G. Marçais put forward the attractive hypothesis that the Maghribī *madrasas* were in the intention of their founders, the Marīnid and ʿAbd al-Wādid rulers of the xiv[th] century, only an "official recognition" of the schools attached to the zāwiyas. It is perhaps more possible that these rulers endeavoured by their foundations alongside of the great centres of religious instruction (notably the Djāmiʿ al-Ḳarawīyīn in Fās) to weaken to some degree the competition already caused in the towns and outside of them by the zāwiya schools.

At the present day the most important North African zāwiyas, whether they are now in the large towns or in the country — where little townships have almost always grown up around them — are the mother houses or branch settlements of the Marabout or Sharīfan religious brotherhoods [see ṬARĪḲA].

In addition to their religious and intellectual influence the zāwiyas of the Muslim west have exercised a direct political influence on the population of the country in areas remote from the seat of the central government. The most striking example of this is the Zāwiya al-Dilāʾ (in the district of Tādlā, in Central Morocco on the banks of the Umm Rabīʿ), the heads of which took advantage of the troubled times after the fall of the Saʿdian dynasty (in the second half of the xvii[th] century) to extend their secular power over the greater part of the district which was dependent on Fās. In more recent times the example of the Berber zāwiyas of Īligh in Tāzarwalt and Aḥanṣāl in the Central Atlas can be quoted.

Bibliography: M. van Berchem, *Matériaux pour un Corpus Inscriptionum Arabicarum*, p. I, *Egypte*, Paris 1903, p. 174, 244; W. and G. Marçais, *Les Monuments arabes de Tlemcen*, Paris 1903, p. 270—272; G. Marçais, *Note sur les ribāṭs en Berbérie*, in *Mélanges René Basset*, Paris 1925, ii. 395 *sqq.*; E. Levi-Provençal, *Le Musnad d'Ibn Marzūḳ*, Paris 1925, p. 70—71; R. Dozy, *Suppl. aux dict. arabes*, i. 615—616. — On the modern North African Zāwiyas there are a number of monographs, e.g.: E. Doutté, *Les Marabouts*, Paris 1900; L. Rinn, *Marabouts et Khouan*, Algiers 1884; O. Depont and X. Coppolani, *Les confréries religieuses musulmanes*, Algiers, 1897.

ZINĀʾ (A.), fornication, i.e. sexual intercourse between persons who are not in a state of legal matrimony or concubinage and cannot claim a *shubha* (see below). To the pre-Islāmic Arabs, *zināʾ* was not a sin but could become an injury to the rights of property of a fellow-tribesman. In the Ḳurʾān, however, evidently in keeping with Jewish or Christian ideas, warnings are uttered against *zināʾ* and chastity represented as a mark of the believer, e.g. Sūra xvii. 32; xxv. 68; xxxiii. 30. *Zināʾ* is then dealt with more fully in Sūra iv. (probably of the period after the battle of Uḥud in the year 3): "15. If your women commit something shameful, take four witnesses against them from among yourselves; and if they bear witness shut them up in their houses until death release them or Allāh give them a way. 16. If two of you commit it, then castigate them both; but if they repent and amend, leave them alone . . . 25. . . (The believing slave-girls whom you marry) shall be decorous and not dissolute and shall take no lovers. . .". Verse 16 is sometimes with less probability referred to sodomy. A new law was made as a result of ʿĀʾisha's notorious adventure in the year 6 in Sūra xxiv.: "2. The unchaste man and the unchaste woman, scourge each of them with a hundred stripes and do not let pity for them take hold of you in Allāh's religion, if you believe in Allāh and the last day; a party of believers shall witness their punishment. 3. The unchaste man shall only marry an unchaste woman or an idolatress and the unchaste woman shall only marry an unchaste man or an idolator; this has been forbidden to the believers". The end of Sūra iv. 25, continuing the prescriptions given there for slave-girls, must be later than Sūra xxiv. 2 which it presupposes: "But when they are decorously married, if they commit a disgrace then inflict upon them half the punishment for decorous (free) women". Sūra xxxiii. 30 (probably dating from the last part of 5 A.H.) where the wives of the Prophet who should commit a disgrace, are threatened with double punishment, seems to refer to the punishment in the other world. Not to be exactly dated but certainly Madīnese are Sūra xxiv. 33 ("Force not your slave-girls to prostitution, if they wish to remain decorous, in order to crave the goods of this life; if any one forces them, then after they have been compelled, Allāh will be forgiving and merciful"), and Sūra lxv. 1 (divorced women must not be driven out of their houses during the period of waiting "unless they do manifestly something shameful"). The so-called "verse of the stoning" is said to have been an original part of the Ḳurʾān and to have been acknowledged as such by the caliph ʿUmar: "If a full grown man and a full grown woman commit fornication stone them in every case, as Allāh's punishment". It is improbable that this verse is genuine, the traditions relating to it and the mention of ʿUmar are clearly tendencious; the stories that the Prophet punished by stoning are also unworthy of credence. This punishment, which must have entered Islām quite early, certainly comes from Jewish law (Deut. xxii. 22) as can still be seen in a *ḥadīth*. Other traditions emphasize the rules of the Ḳurʾān and develop them: *zināʾ* is a very grave sin and not compatible with belief; profit from *zināʾ* and prostitution is unlawful property; the flogging which remained as a punishment alongside of stoning is combined with a year's banishment. In the system of *fiḳh* and already in some traditions stoning and flogging are separated as *ḥadd* punishment for *zināʾ* in two categories of criminals, according as they are *muḥṣān* or not. By *muḥṣan* the law means in this case every individual who is adult, is in possession of his faculties, is free and has had sexual intercourse in a legal marriage; they however always remain *muḥṣan* even after their marriage is dissolved; the distinction is therefore not based on any moral grounds. According to Ḥanafīs and Ḥanbalīs, both the guilty parties must fulfil these conditions; the Ḥanafīs also demand that the *muḥṣan* should be a Muslim, while the Mālikīs consider neither of the punishments applicable to a non-Muslim. According to the Ḥanbalīs, the guilty *muḥṣan* is at first flogged, then stoned. The banishment for a year after the flogging is limited by the Mālikīs to the man, by the Ḥanafīs left to the discretion of the *imām*. Slaves are punished with fifty lashes, and, according to the Shāfiʿīs, banishment for six months. *Zināʾ* can only be proved by the evidence of four male, competent (*ʿadl*) witnesses; as they must report all the details of the incident and, if their evidence is not sufficient, are liable to the *ḥadd* for *ḳadhf* [q.v.], the *ḥadd* for *zināʾ* in practice can hardly ever be inflicted, unless the culprit himself confesses his guilt. According to the Ḥanafīs and Ḥanbalīs, this confession must also be made four times, and according to the general teaching can be withdrawn. The application of the *ḥadd* is excluded, on one side by compulsion, and on the other by the *shubha*, i.e. the "resemblance" of the criminal action to a permitted one from which the *bona fides* of the offender is presumed. Important cases (with differences of opinion about details) of *shubha* with *zināʾ* are: intercourse in most cases of invalid marriages (except those with the nearest relatives for which no excuse can be accepted); intercourse with a woman whom the man erroneously thinks to be his wife or slave; intercourse with a slave by her joint proprietor; intercourse with a slave owned by a descendant and with a slave whose master has permitted it. As a rule, a compensation — the bridal gift (*mahr*) for a free woman and the so-called *ʿuḳr* for a slave — has to be paid. If the *ḥadd* does not take place, there may be room for *taʿzīr* [q.v.]. Incest and violation are simply regarded as *zināʾ*. On sodomy (*liwāṭ*) and bestiality there are different views which more often than not tend to aggravate the punishment. If the husband kills the guilty couple *in flagrante delicto* he is not liable to punishment. In practice the place of the legal procedure was often taken by summary and usually secret action either by the authorities or, as frequently even nowadays, by the relatives of the guilty woman; in this case drowning was a common form of punishment.

Bibliography: Lammens, *Le Berceau de l'Islam*, p. 279; Nöldeke-Schwally, *Geschichte des Qorāns*, i. 248 *sqq.*; Wensinck, *Handbook*, s.v. ZINĀʾ; Juynboll, *Handleiding*, 3rd ed., p. 305 *sqq.*; Krcsmarik, *Beiträge zur Beleuchtung des islamischen Strafrechts*, in *ZDMG*, lvii. p. 101 *sqq.*; Hughes, *Dictionary of Islam*, s.v. ADULTERY and FORNICATION; Lane, *Manners and Customs of the Modern Egyptians*, ch. vii (end) and xiii (near the end).

ZINDĪḲ (pl. *zanādiḳa*; abstract *zandaḳa*), the term used in Muslim criminal law to describe the heretic whose teaching becomes a danger to the state; this crime is liable to capital punishment (by the application of Sūra v. 33; xxvi. 48; cf. *RMM*, 1909, ix. 99—103) and to damnation (the Mālikīs think it useless to ask the culprit to recant [*istitāba*] contrary to the Ḥanafīs; *takfīr*, often theoretical, is not so strong a term as *zandaḳa*).

The term was borrowed in the ʿIrāḳ from the Īrānian vocabulary of the Sāsānian administration; Schaeder, correcting Darmesteter, has shown that Masʿūdī (followed by Hudjwīrī) was right in saying that among the Mazdaeans, *zandīk* was the heretic who introduced a new gloss, an allegorical interpretation of a passage in the Awesta (cf. in the ninth century, the *zandīk* Abālīsh, studied by Barthélemy; cf. *Mēnōkēkhrat*, xxxvi. 16; *Shāyast nē Shāyast*, vi. 7); and more especially the Manichaean, follower of Mani (testimony of the Armenian writer on heresies Eznik, of the fifth century, transl. Schmidt, p. 95), or, in a more restricted sense still, the follower of the Manichaean schismatic Mazdak (according to Khwārizmī).

The term being Īrānian, A. Siddiqi has shown that we must reject the Aramaic etymology (*zaddīḳ*) suggested by Bevan as well as the Greek (γνωστικός) proposed by Vollers. The word *zindīḳ* must have become arabicized in the mixed Arabo-Īrānian society of the *mawālī Ḥamrā* of Ḥīra and Kūfa (cf. the exiling of the Mazdakīs to Ḥīra, in which we can see the explanation of the Shīʿī gnosticism of Kūfa in the following century). Indeed it appears for the first time in the ʿIrāḳ in 125/742, in connection with the execution of Djaʿd b. Dirham; then from 167/783 to 170/786 as an official inquisition was instituted by the ʿAbbāsid caliph under a special judge (*ʿarīf*); it was then that Bashshār b. Burd and Ṣāliḥ b. ʿAbd al-Ḳuddūs were executed. The term became a technical one and literary tradition designates three famous writers, Ibn al-Rāwandī, al-Tawḥīdī and al-Maʿarrī, as the "three *zanādiḳa* of Islām". But in general use, the term lost its precision and if the official definition of the *zindīḳ* (a dualist ascetic, then a Muslim who is secretly a Manichaean, according to the caliph Mahdī [Ṭabarī, iii. 588]) is already carelessly applied to the three first men executed mentioned above, it is clear that it does not at all explain the psychology of the three "*zanādiḳa* of Islām". In practice, the polemics of the conservatives describe as a *zindīḳ* or "free thinker" any one whose external profession of Islām seems to them not sufficiently sincere (cf. the poet Dj. S. Zahāwī in Baghdād or the critic Ṭaha Ḥusain in Cairo). This is the meaning in which it is already used by al-Maʿarrī in his *Risālat al-ghufrān*. This meaning denotes the radical doctrines of the free-thinkers, whose chief works, contained in Ismāʿīlī refutations, derive from authors as Erānshahrī, Abū ʿĪsā al-Warrāḳ, Ibn al-Rāwandī (*K. al-zumurrudh*, cf. *RSO*, xiv. 1933), the great physician al-Rāzī (*K. Makhāriḳ al-anbiyāʾ*) and al-Thughūrī, and have been edited by P. Kraus.

The evolution of the term is explained by its political character; it brands the heresy which imperils the Muslim state (this is already clear in the trial of al-Ḥallādj); and as the only crime systematically punished by the Prophet himself by death had been *sabb al-rasūl*, the jurists more and more made *zandaḳa* an intellectual rebellion insulting to the Prophet's honour (cf. Ibn Taimīya and Ibn Ḥadjar al-Haitamī).

The stages of this evolution can be brought closer together by summing up the definitions given of the word *zandaḳa* by the various Muslim schools.

The Ḥanbalīs, according to Khashīsh (d. 253/867), recognize five sects of *zanādiḳa*: *muʿaṭṭila*, who deny the creation and the Creator, reducing the world to an unstable mixture of the four elements; *mānawīya* (Manichaeans) and *mazdakīya* who are dualists; *ʿabdakīya* (vegetarian Imāmī ascetics of Kūfa; cf. Massignon, *Recueil*..., p. 11—12) and *rūḥānīya* (four ecstatic sects, who seek to free themselves from the constraint of observances and laws by an amorous union of the soul with God, a union denounced as implying identity of nature between the Creator and his creatures; in it Sunnī mystics like Rabāḥ and Rābiʿa are ranged alongside of an Imāmī alchemist like Ibn Ḥaiyān). Ibn Ḥanbal himself describes Djahm as a *zindīḳ* for having maintained that the spirit (*rūḥ*) is an immaterial emanation, therefore divine.

The Mālikīs of the west (Spain and Morocco) studied by Milliot and Lévi-Provençal instituted trials for *zandaḳa*, especially for "insults to the honour of the Prophet" (trial of Abu 'l-Khair at Cordova in the reign of al-Ḥakam II, of Ibn Ḥātim al-Azdī at Toledo in 457/1064 and later of Ibn Zakūr at Fās). Similarly the Ḥanafīs, especially during the Ottoman empire (*fatwās* against the Shīʿa; trial of Ḳābid in 934/1527; cf. Nābulusī, *Ghāyat al-maṭlūb*, Pers. MS., folio 77).

As to the theologians, the Muʿtazilīs at first saw in *zandaḳa* an amorous devotion seeking liberation from obligatory duties (cf. Thumāma, in al-Baghdādī, *Farḳ*, abbr. and ed. Hitti, p. 105), then a tendency to the *ibāḥa* of the Khurramīya; Ghazzālī defines it as a tendency to atheism.

The Ṣūfīs were early persecuted as *zanādiḳa* in view of their doctrine of the divine love (trial in the year 262/875 of Nūrī; execution of al-Ḥallādj); al-Ḥallādj (cf. *Ṭawāsīn*, v. 2) himself recognizes in a curious psychological analysis that on the threshold of transforming union, mysticism obtains a feeling of identity with God, which is *zandaḳa* (*Akhbār*, No. 52, p. 80*, l. 7).

The moderate S̲h̲īʿīs like to describe the extremist S̲h̲īʿīs, for an analogous reason, as *zanādiḳa* (emanations that give union with the divine: *daʿwā ila ʾl-rubūbīya*). The Zaidī imām Ḳāsim is credited with the authorship of a refutation of the *zindīḳ* Ibn al-Muḳaffaʿ which Guidi has edited and translated.

Lastly, in his *Fihrist* (ed. Flügel, p. 338), Ibn al-Nadīm has given a very heterogeneous list of *zanādiḳa* (the value of which is sometimes overestimated, it is rather imaginative [cf. G. Vajda, *Les Zindīqs en pays d'Islam au début de la période abbaside*, in *RSO* 1937]), showing Marwān II and the Barmakids alongside of Ismāʿīlīs, like Abū S̲h̲ākir and Djaihānī, an Imāmī like Nās̲h̲īʾ and an independent critic like Abū ʿĪsā al-Warrāḳ.

Bibliography: Ibn Ḥanbal, *Radd ʿala ʾl-zanādiḳa*, ed. Univ. Istanbul, 1931; K̲h̲as̲h̲īs̲h̲ al-Nasāʾī, *Istiḳāma*, ed. Malaṭī (descr. in Massignon, *Recueil de textes...*, p. 211—212); S. Dedering, in *Bibl. Islamica*, No. 9, Leipzig 1936; p. 5, 43, 71; Masʿūdī, *Murūdj*, ii. 167; K̲h̲wārizmī, *Mafātīḥ*, ed. van Vloten, p. 37; Sarrādj, *Lumaʿ*, ed. Nicholson p. 431; Hudjwīrī, *Kas̲h̲f*, transl. Nicholson, p. 404; G̲h̲azzālī, *Faiṣal al-tafriḳa bain al-Islām wa ʾl-zandaḳa*, ed. Ḳabbānī, p. 31, 54—55; Ibn al-Djawzī, *Talbīs Iblīs*, Cairo 1340, p. 118; Ibn Taimīya, *al-Ṣārim al-maslūl ʿalā s̲h̲ātim al-rasūl*, Ḥaidarābād 1322, p. 515, 529; Ibn Ḥadjar al-Haitamī, *al-Ṣawāʿiḳ al-muḥriḳa fi ʾl-radd ʿalā ahl al-bidaʿ wa ʾl-zandaḳa*, Cairo 1308; Ibn Kamāl Pās̲h̲a, *Fī tas̲h̲īḥ maʿna ʾl-zindīḳ* (MS. Köpr., No. 1580, descr. in Huart, *l.c.*, infra); Ronzevalle, in *Mach.*, i. 681; J. Darmesteter, in *JA*, 1884, p. 562—564; Goldziher, *Ṣāliḥ und das Zindīkthum*, in *Transactions IXth Orient. Congress*, 1892, ii. 104—129; Vollers, in *ZDMG*, l., 1896, p. 642; Huart, in *XIème Congrès Intern. Orientalistes*, 1897, p. 69—80; Massignon, *Passion d'al-Hallāj*, 1922, index, s.v.; Christensen, *Kāwadh I et le communisme mazdakite*, 1925, p. 71, 79; Nyberg, preface to his edition of the *Intiṣār* of al-K̲h̲aiyāṭ, 1925, p. 55—56; Mich. Guidi, *La lotta tra l'Islam e il manicheismo*, 1927; A. Siddiqi, in *Proceedings...IVth Or. Conf. Allahabad*, 1926—1928, ii. 228; H. H. Schaeder, *Iranische Beiträge*, i. 1930, p. 274—291; Ibn Sahl, *Aḥkām kubrā*, MS. Rabat, D. 264, fol. 243^b, 244^b, 246^b (cf. Milliot, *Recueil de jurisprudence chérifienne*, ii. 284, 287); Fück, in *Festschrift P. Kahle* (1935).

ZIYĀNĪYA, branch of the S̲h̲ād̲h̲ilī Order, has its headquarters at Ḳenād̲h̲ā; lists of the heads are given by Rinn, *op. cit.*, Depont and Coppolani, *Confréries*, p. 498, and Cour, *op. cit.*; in the second work a specimen is given of the diploma of *muḳaddam* conferred by the head of the order, with seal. Their practice is said to differ from those of the other S̲h̲ād̲h̲ilīs only in details; their ordinary *d̲h̲ikr* is reproduced by Rinn, *op. cit.*, p. 411, and consists in the repetition of certain formulae, a hundred, others a thousand times. Their speciality is the guiding and protection of caravans and travellers against brigands; in Rinn's time (1884) "no trader would venture to send a consignment of goods southwards" without having secured protection in the form of a Ziyānī rider bearing a letter with the seal of a *muḳaddam*, whom the brigands would be afraid to offend. Hence he calls them the pilots of the Sahara.

Much the same is said by A Bernard, writing in 1931 (*Le Maroc*, p. 205). The community appears to be little known outside French Africa; lists of their *zāwiyas* in Algeria with an account of their diffusion in Morocco are given by Depont and Coppolani, *op. cit.*

The order was founded by Muḥammad b. ʿAbd al-Raḥmān Ibn Abī Ziyān who died 1145/1733. In the *RMM*, xii. 360—379 and 571—590, A. Cour published in French some extracts from a MS. biography called *ṭahārat al-anfus wa ʾl-arwāḥ al-djismānīya fi ʾl-Ṭarīḳa al-Ziyānīya al-S̲h̲ād̲h̲ilīya*, itself an abridgment of an earlier work. This is chiefly a record of miracles, but furnishes certain details supplementing those collected by L. Rinn, *Marabouts et Khouan* (1884, p. 408—415). He was born at Thatha near Ḳenād̲h̲ā (S. W. of Figuig in Morocco), studied with Sīdī Mubārāk b. ʿAzza in Sidjilmāsa and after his death went to Fez, where he studied for eight years under Muḥammad b. ʿAbd al-Ḳādir al-Fāsī (died 1116/1704), Aḥmad b. al-Ḥādjdj (died 1109/1697), and others; according to Rinn, he was expelled from Fez by the emperor on the ground of sorcery, fled to Tāfīlālt, where the *muḳaddam* of the Naṣrīya branch of the S̲h̲ād̲h̲ilīya admitted him to the order, after which he made the pilgrimage to Mecca, and then on his return established himself at Ḳenād̲h̲ā, where he founded a *zāwiya*. Besides introducing some modifications into the S̲h̲ād̲h̲ilī ritual, and acquiring a reputation for saintliness, he appears to have dug wells and organized irrigation; his most celebrated miracle, which determined the future of his community, consisted in the suppression of brigands. His fame and talents attracted numerous visitors, who presently formed a flourishing colony. Like other Islāmic saints, he was the head of a family, and left the headship of his order to his son.

Bibliography: given in the article.

ZIYĀRA (A.), visit, in the religious sense the visit to a holy place or to the tomb of a saint, especially to Muḥammad's tomb in the mosque of al-Madīna, which even under the Wahhābī rule is paid by those who perform the *ḥadjdj*. The ziyāra paid to the tombs of the saints was among the *bidaʿ* which were combated by Muḥammad b. ʿAbd al-Wahhāb [cf. WAHHĀBĪYA]. For details cf. W. R. van Diffelen, *De leer der Wahhabieten*, Leyden 1927. That the Wahhābīs were not the first in Islām to question the legality of visiting tombs, and of the practices connected therewith, appears from the materials preserved in *ḥadīth* (cf. Wensinck, *Handbook*, s.v. Grave[s]) and from later literature [cf. IBN TAIMĪYA].

AL-ZUBAIR B. AL-ʿAWWĀM B. K̲h̲UWAILID B. ASAD B. ʿABD AL-ʿUZZĀ B. ḲUṢAIY B. KILĀB ABŪ ʿABD ALLĀH, with the surname of *al-Ḥawārī* (i.e. the Apostle, an Ethiopic loanword). His mother was Ṣafīya bint ʿAbd al-Muṭṭalib, so that he was a cousin of Muḥammad and a nephew of K̲h̲adīdja (bint K̲h̲uwailid).

Al-Zubair was one of the earliest converts to Islām; according to tradition, he was the fifth who, while still a child, recognized Muḥammad as a prophet; he is also one of the ten to whom Paradise was promised by Muḥammad.

Of his wives Asmā, the daughter of Abū Bakr, is renowned for her spartan attitude to her son ʿAbd Allāh. Another son she bore him was ʿUrwa. The third of al-Zubair's sons, who also plays a part in the history of Islām, is Muṣʿab. Al-Zubair is said to have remained faithful to Muḥammad under hardships and to have taken part in the two hidjras to Abyssinia. After the Hid̲j̲ra to Madīna he was united in brotherhood with Ibn Masᶜūd, or, according to other reports, with Ṭalḥa or with Kaᶜb b. Mālik. He further took part in all the great battles and campaigns during Muḥammad's career, being renowned for his gallantry. His epithet *al-Ḥawārī* (cf. above) was given him by Muḥammad on account of his services as a spy in the conflict with the Ḳuraiẓa [q.v.], with the words: "Every prophet has an apostle and my apostle is al-Zubair". For his attitude, exploits and death (the latter took place in the Battle of the Camel, at an age which is given with variations from 60 to 67) under the caliphate of Abū Bakr, ᶜUmar and ᶜUt̲h̲mān, we may refer to the relevant articles.

Tradition emphasizes the high esteem in which Muḥammad held him by pointing to the fact that Muḥammad, in speaking to him, once made use of the formula *fidāka abī wa-ummī*. He obtained, it is said, special permission to wear silk. For his testament, cf. Ibn Saᶜd, III/i. 75 *sqq.*; Buk̲h̲ārī, *K̲h̲ums*, bāb. 13.

Bibliography: Ibn Isḥāḳ, *Sīra*, ed. Wüstenfeld, index; Wāḳidī, transl. Wellhausen, Berlin 1882, index; Yaᶜḳūbī, index; Ṭabarī, indices; Ibn Saᶜd, III/i. 70—80; Balād̲h̲urī, index; Masᶜūdī, *Murūd̲j̲*, general index; Ibn Ḥad̲j̲ar al-ᶜAsḳalānī, *Iṣāba*, No. 2774; Ibn al-At̲h̲īr, *Usd al-g̲h̲āba*, Cairo 1286, ii. 196 *sqq.* The passages from Ḥadīt̲h̲ are registered in A. J. Wensinck, *Handbook*, s.v. — Sprenger, *Das Leben und die Lehre des Moḥammad*, i., Berlin 1861, p. 374 *sq.*, 422 *sqq.*; F. Buhl, *Das Leben Muhammeds*, Leipzig 1930, p. 151, 173; Caetani, *Annali*, indices in vols. II/ii., vi.; further vol. vii. § 70; viii. § 374 *sqq.*; ix., § 30—225 *passim*, 616—690; A. Müller, *Der Islam im Morgen- und Abendland*, Berlin 1885, p. 306 *sqq.*; Weil, *Geschichte der Chalifen*, index in vol. iii.; W. Muir, *The Caliphate*, ed. Weir, index; G. Levi della Vida, in *RSO*, vi. 440 *sq.*, 448 *sq.*

ZUHD, a technical term in Muslim mysticism, the virtue of a *zāhid* (pl. *zāhidūn*, *zuhhād*; Sūra xii. 19 seems very far from this meaning): abstinence: at first from sin, from what is superfluous, from all that estranges from God (this is the extreme that the Ḥanbalīs admit); then abstinence from all perishable things by detachment of the heart (and here we enter into the mystic), complete asceticism, renunciation of all that is created. Thus the term *zuhd*, taking the place of *nisk* (its synonym in the older texts), clearly means more not only than *ḳanāᶜa* (moderation and control of one's desires), but also than *waraᶜ*, scrupulous abstention from the use of everything doubtful in law (a Ḥanbalī virtue). In arranging the gradation of the virtues, Miṣrī notes that the "stage of *waraᶜ* brings one to *zuhd*" which G̲h̲azzālī places after *faḳr* and before *tawakkul*.

It was in the second—third century that the conception of *zuhd*, deepened from Ḥasan al-Baṣrī to Dārānī, became fixed: renunciation not only of dress, lodging, and pleasant food but also of women (Dārānī). Then as introspective analysis progresses with Muḥāsibī (and with the *Malāmatīya*), stress is laid on inner and subjective asceticism, renunciation of intentions and desires, which leads to the concept of *tawakkul*.

Interesting examples of *zuhd* taken from the biographies of the most illustrious Ṣūfīs will be found presented in an ironical and hostile way in Ibn al-D̲j̲awzī, and in the S̲h̲ād̲h̲ilī Ibn ᶜAbbād Rundī a carefully considered collection of cases of ascetic conscience. On the question of borrowing by Islām of ascetic observances from Christianity, Manichaeism or Hinduism, cf. L. Massignon, *Essai sur les origines du lexique technique*, Paris 1922, p. 45—80.

Bibliography: Makkī, *Ḳūt al-ḳulūb*, i. 242—271; K̲h̲argūs̲h̲ī, *Tahd̲h̲īb*, MS. Berlin, No. 2819, f. 53^{b}; Ḳus̲h̲airī, *Risāla*, p. 67 (and Hartmann, *Darstellung*, s.v.); Hud̲j̲wīrī, *Kas̲h̲f al-maḥd̲j̲ūb*, transl. Nicholson, index, s.v.; G̲h̲azzālī, *Iḥyāʾ*, ed. 1322, iv. 154—171 (résumé by Asín Palacios, in *MFOB*, vol. vii. [1914], p. 82—84); E. F. Tscheuschner, *Mönchsideale des Islam nach Ghazali's Abhandlung über Armut und Weltentsagung*, Gütersloh 1933; Ibn al-D̲j̲awzī, *Talbīs Iblīs*, ed. 1340, p. 312—315 (Dārānī), p. 374—388; Ibn ᶜArabī, *al-Futūḥāt al-Makkiya*[1], iii. 197; Ibn ᶜAbbād Rundī, *Rasāʾil*, lith. Fās (analysed by Asín Palacios, in *Etudes Carmélitaines*, April 1932, p. 113—167 and in *al-Andalus*, Madrid, i., 1933, p. 7—79); cf. esp. p. 122; cf. L. Massignon, *Recueil de textes inédits*, p. 146—148 and p. 17 (for Miṣrī); Tor Andrae, *Zuhd und Mönchtum*, *MO*, 1931.

Register of Subjects

RELIGION — Dīn, Ḥanīf, Islām, Milla, Muslim (see also *Worship*).
REPENTANCE — Tawba.
RESURRECTION — Ḳiyāma (see also *Eschatology*).
REVELATION — Djabrāʾīl, Indjīl, al-Ḳurʾān, Lawḥ, Muḥammad, Nabī, Rasūl, Shaṭḥ, Taḥrīf, Tawrāt, Waḥy.
ROSARY — Subḥa.

SAINTS — Ḳarāma, Marabout, Shirk, Taṣawwuf, Walī, Ziyāra;
Ḥabīb al-Nadjdjār, al-Khaḍir, Khwādja Khiḍr, Rābiʿa al-ʿAdawīya, Salmān al Fārisī.
SALUTATION — Salām.
SCRIPTURE — Ahl al-Kitāb, Indjīl, Ḳurʾān, Lawḥ, Tawrāt, Umm al-Kitāb, Zabūr.
SECTS — (Preislamic) Ṣābiʾa;
(Khāridjites) ʿAbd Allāh b. Wahb, al-Ibāḍīya, Khāridjites, Nāfiʿ b. al-Azraḳ, Shurāt;
(Shīʿites) Dāʿī, Fidāʾī, Ghālī, Imām, ʿIṣma, Khalīfa, Taḳīya, Taʿziya;
Ahl-i Ḥaḳḳ, ʿAlids, Assassins, Bāṭinīya, Bohoras, Dhammīya, Ḥurūfī, Ismāʿīlīya, Ithnā ʿAsharīya, Kaisānīya, Ḳarmaṭians, Khaṭṭābīya Khodjas, Muḥammadīya, Mutawālī, Rāfiḍites, Sabʿīya, Shīʿa, al-Zaidīya;
ʿAbd Allāh b. Maimūn, ʿAlī b. Abī Ṭālib, Darazī, Djaʿfar b. Muḥammad al-Ṣādiḳ, Ḥamdān Ḳarmaṭ, Ḥamza b. ʿAlī, al-Ḥasan b. al-Ṣabbāḥ, al-Ḥasan b. ʿAlī, al-Ḥusain b. ʿAlī, Imām Shāh, Salmān al-Fārisī, al-Shushtarī, Ṭāhir;
Mashhad, Mashhad Ḥusain, Nadjaf;
Aḥmadīya, Aḥmad Khān, Akbar, Bāb, Bābī, Bahāʾ Allāh, Druzes, Farāʾiḍiya, Nūrbakhshīya, Nuṣairī, al-Sanūsī, Wahhābīya, Yāzidī (see also *Dogmatics*).
SERMON — Khaṭīb, Khuṭba, Masdjid C 3 and G 2.
SEVEN SLEEPERS — Aṣḥāb al-Kahf, Kalb, Ḳiṭmīr.
SIN — Fāsiḳ, Khaṭīʾa, Murdjiʾa, Muʿtazila.
SLANDER — Ḳadhf.
SLAVES — ʿAbd, Mamlūk, Umm al-Walad.
SOOTHSAYER — Kāhin, Siḥr.
SOUL — Nafs.
SPIRITS — Djinn, Ghūl, Iblīs, ʿIfrīt, al Khaḍir, Khwādja Khiḍr, Nafs, Shaiṭān, Siḥr.
SUCKLING — Raḍāʿ.
SUPEREROGATORY WORKS — Kaffāra, Nāfila.

TAXES — Djizya, Kharādj, Maks, ʿUshr, Zakāt (see also *Alms-tax*).
TESTAMENT — Waṣīya (see also *Succession*).
THRONE — Kursī.
TITHE — ʿUshr.
TOOTH-PICK — Miswāk.
TRADITION — Ḥadīth, Isnād, Mutawātir, Sunna;
ʿAbd Allāh b. al-ʿAbbās, Abū Huraira, Anas b. Mālik, al-Bukhārī, al-Dārimī, Ibn Mādja, Ibn Masʿūd, al-Ḳasṭallānī, Muslim b. al-Ḥadjdjādj, al-Nasāʾī, al-Tirmidhī.

UNBELIEF — Dhimma, Kharādj, Kāfir, Shirk.
USURY — Ribā.

VIGILS — Tahadjdjud, Ṣalāt.
VOW — Nadhr.

WAITING PERIOD — ʿIdda.
WAR — Dār al-Ḥarb, Dār al Islām, Dār al-Ṣulḥ, Dhimma, Djihād, Djizya (see also *Booty*).
WEDDING — Masdjid II, Pangulu, ʿUrs (see also *Marriage*).
WINE — Khamr, Nabīdh.
WITNESS — Shāhid (see also *Justice*).
WOMEN — Ḥaiḍ, Ḥarīm, Ḥidjāb, Masdjid C I (see also *Marriage, Wedding*).
WORSHIP — Adhān, ʿAṣr, Bilāl, Djumʿa, Fātiḥa, ʿIbādāt, Iḥrām, Ikhlāṣ, Imām, Iʿtikāf, Khaṭīb, Khuṭba, Ḳibla, Ḳunūt, Ḳurba, Masdjid C, Mīḳāt, Muṣallā, Nāḳūs, Nīya, Rātib, Sadjdjāda, Salām, Ṣalāt, Sutra, Tahadjdjud, Tarāwīḥ, Tayammum, Witr (see also *Mosque, Pilgrimage, Prayer, Purification, Religion*).

ZOROASTRIANS — Madjūs, Pārsīs.

Origin of the articles

A

al-ʿAbbās (F. Buhl)
ʿAbd (Th. W. Juynboll)
ʿAbd Allāh b. al-ʿAbbās (F. Buhl)
ʿAbd Allāh b. Maimūn
ʿAbd Allāh b. ʿUmar (K. V. Zetterstéen)
ʿAbd Allāh b. Wahb (M. Th. Houtsma)
ʿAbd al-Ḳādir al-Djīlī (D. S. Margoliouth)
ʿAbd al-Karīm al-Djīlī (I. Goldziher)
ʿAbd al-Muṭṭalib (F. Buhl)
Abū Bakr (F. Buhl)
Abū Djahl (F. Buhl)
Abū Ḥanīfa (Th. W. Juynboll and A. J. Wensinck)
Abū Huraira (I. Goldziher)
Abū Lahab (J. Barth)
Abū Sufyān (F. Buhl)
Abū Ṭālib (F. Buhl)
Abū ʿUbaida (Anonymus)
ʿĀd (F. Buhl)
ʿĀda (I. Goldziher)
Ādam (M. Seligsohn)
Adat Law (R. A. Kern)
ʿAdhāb (Th. W. Juyboll)
Adhān (Th. W. Juynboll)
ʿAdl (Anonymus)
Ahl al-Kitāb (I. Goldziher)
Ahl al-Ṣuffa (A. J. Wensinck)
Ahl-i Ḥaḳḳ (V. Minorsky)
Aḥmad b. Muḥ. b. Ḥanbal (I. Goldziher)
Aḥmad al-Badawī (K. Vollers)
Aḥmadīya (M. Th. Houtsma)
Aḥmad Khān (Blumhardt)
ʿĀʾisha (M. Seligsohn)
Aiyūb (M. Seligsohn)
Akbar (A. S. Beveridge)
ʿAḳīda (A. J. Wensinck)
ʿAḳīḳa (Th. W. Juynboll)
ʿĀḳil (Th. W. Juynboll)
ʿĀḳila (Th. W. Juynboll)
ʿAlī b. Abī Ṭālib (Cl. Huart)
ʿAlids (Cl. Huart)
Allāh (D. B. Macdonald)
Amīr al-Muʾminīn (A. J. Wensinck)
ʿAmr b. al-ʿĀṣ (A. J. Wensinck)
ʿAmr b. ʿUbaid (Anonymus)
Anas b. Mālik (A. J. Wensinck)
al-Anṣār (H. Reckendorf)
ʿArafa (Anonymus)
ʿĀrīya (Th. W. Juynboll)
al-Arḳam (H. Reckendorf)
Aṣḥāb al-Kahf (A. J. Wensinck)
Aṣḥāb al-Ukhdūd (A. J. Wensinck)
al-ʿAshara al-Mubashshara (A. J. Wensinck)
al-Ashʿarī, Abu 'l-Ḥasan ʿAlī (A. J. Wensinck)
al-Ashʿarī, Abū Mūsā (K. V. Zetterstéen)
ʿĀshūrāʾ (A. J. Wensinck)
Assassins (Anonymus)
al-Aswad (F. Buhl)
Awtād (I. Goldziher)
Āzar (A. J. Wensinck)
Azhar (K. Vollers)

B

Bāb (Cl. Huart)
Bābī (Cl. Huart)
Badāʾ (I. Goldziher)
Badal (R. A. Nicholson)
al-Baghdādī (Anonymus)
Bahāʾ Allāh (Cl. Huart)
Baḥīrā (A. J. Wensinck)
Baiʿ (J. Schacht)
al-Baiḍāwī (C. Brockelmann)
Bairam (Cl. Huart)
Bairamīya (Cl. Huart)
Baiyūmīya (Cl. Huart)
Baḳīʿ al-Gharḳad (A. J. Wensinck)
Baḳlīya (Anonymus)
Bārā Wafāt (M. Hidayet Hosain)
Barṣīṣa (D. B. Macdonald)
Barzakh (B. Carra de Vaux)
Basmala (B. Carra de Vaux)
Basṭ (A. J. Arberry)
Bāṭil (J. Schacht)
Bāṭinīya (B. Carra de Vaux)
Bektāshīya (R. Tchudi)
Bidʿa (D. B. Macdonald)
Bilāl (F. Buhl)
Bilḳīs (B. Carra de Vaux)
Birgewī (Anonymus)
al-Bisṭāmī (R. A. Nicholson)
Bohoras (W. Ivanow)
al-Bukhārī (C. Brockelmann)
Burāḳ (B. Carra de Vaux)

C

Čishtī (Anonymus)
Čishtīya (D. S. Margoliouth)

D

al-Dadjdjāl (A. J. Wensinck and B. Carra de Vaux)
Dahrīya (I. Goldziher)
Dāʿī (B. Carra de Vaux)
Dār al-Ḥarb (D. B. Macdonald)
Dār al-Islām (D. B. Macdonald)
Dār al-Ṣulḥ (D. B. Macdonald)
Darazī (B. Carra de Vaux)
al-Dārimī (Moh. ben Cheneb)
Dasūḳī (D. S. Margoliouth)
Daʿwā (Th. W. Juynboll)
Dawsa (D. B. Macdonald)
Dāwūd (B. Carra de Vaux)
Derḳāwa (A. Cour)
Derwīsh (D. B. Macdonald)
al-Dhammīya (Anonymus)
Dhikr (D. B. Macdonald)
Dhimma (D. B. Macdonald)
Dhu 'l-Ḳarnain (E. Mittwoch)
Dhu 'l-Kifl (I. Goldziher)
Dhu 'l-Nūn (A. J. Arberry)
Dīn (D. B. Macdonald)
Diya (T. H. Weir)

Djabarūt (B. Carra de Vaux)
Djabrā'īl (B. Carra de Vaux)
Djabrīya (Anonymus)
Dja'far b. Muhammad (K. V. Zettersтéen)
Djafr (D. B. Macdonald)
Djahannam (B. Carra de Vaux)
Djāhilīya (T. H. Weir)
Djahm b. Ṣafwān (Anonymus)
Djā'iz (D. B. Macdonald)
Djalāl al-Dīn Rūmī (B. Carra de Vaux)
Djālūt (B. Carra de Vaux)
Djamāl al-Dīn al-Afghānī (I. Goldziher)
al-Djamra (F. Buhl)
Djanāba (Th. W. Juynboll)
Djanna (B. Carra de Vaux)
Djihād (D. B. Macdonald)
Djināza (A. J. W. Huisman)
Djinn (D. B. Macdonald)
Djizya (C. H. Becker)
Djum'a (Th. W. Juynboll)
al-Djunaid (A. J. Arberry)
al-Djuwainī (C. Brockelmann)
Druzes (B. Carra de Vaux)
Du'ā' (Anonymus)

F

al-Faḍālī (D. B. Macdonald)
Fai' (Th. W. Juynboll)
Faiḍ (Tj. de Boer)
Faḳīh (D. B. Macdonald)
Faḳīr (D. B. Macdonald)
Fanā' (B. Carra de Vaux)
Farā'iḍ (Th. W. Juynboll)
Farā'iḍīya (M. Hidayet Hosain)
Farḍ (Th. W. Juynboll)
Fāsiḳ (Th. W. Juynboll)
Fātiḥa (B. Carra de Vaux)
Fāṭima (H. Lammens)
Fatwā (D. B. Macdonald)
Fidā'ī (Cl. Huart)
Fidya (Anonymus)
Fiḳh (I. Goldziher)
Fir'awn (A. J. Wensinck)
Firdaws (D. B. Macdonald)
Fiṭra (D. B. Macdonald)
Furḳān (A. J. Wensinck)
Futuwwa (C. van Arendonk and Bichr Faris)

G

Ghaiba (D. B. Macdonald)
Ghālī (Anonymus)
Ghanīma (Th. W. Juynboll)
Ghawth (D. B. Macdonald)
al-Ghazzālī (D. B. Macdonald)
Ghūl (D. B. Macdonald)
Ghusl (Th. W. Juynboll)

H

Ḥabīb al-Nadjdjār (Anonymus)
Hābīl and Kābīl (J. Eisenberg)
Ḥadath (Th. W. Juynboll)
Ḥadd (B. Carra de Vaux)
Ḥadīth (Th. W. Juynboll)
Ḥadjdj (A. J. Wensinck)
Ḥaḍra (D. B. Macdonald)
Ḥafṣa (H. Lammens)
Ḥaiḍ (Anonymus)
Ḥaḳīḳa (D. B. Macdonald)
Ḥaḳḳ (D. B. Macdonald)
Ḥāl (D. B. Macdonald)
al-Ḥalabi (C. Brockelmann)
al-Ḥallādj (L. Massignon)
Ḥām (B. Heller)
Ḥamā'il (B. Carra de Vaux)
Hāmān (L. Eisenberg)
Ḥamdala (D. B. Macdonald)
Ḥamdān Ḳarmaṭ (Cl. Huart)
Ḥamza b. 'Abd al-Muṭṭalib (H. Lammens)
Ḥamza b. 'Alī (Anonymus)
Ḥanafites (W. Heffening)
Ḥanīf (F. Buhl)
Ḥaram (Anonymus)
Ḥarām (Anonymus)
Ḥarīm (Anonymus)
Ḥarrān (T. H. Weir)
Hārūn (J. Eisenberg)
Hārūt and Mārūt (A. J. Wensinck)
al-Ḥasan b. 'Alī (H. Lammens)
al-Ḥasan al-Baṣrī (Anonymus)
al-Ḥasan b. al-Ṣabbāḥ (Anonymus)
Ḥashwīya (Anonymus)
Ḥawāla (Cl. Huart)
Ḥawārī (A. J. Wensinck)
Ḥawḍ (A. J. Wensinck)
Ḥawwā' (J. Eisenberg)
Ḥidjāb (Cl. Huart)
al-Ḥidjr (J. Schleifer)
Hidjra (B. Carra de Vaux)
Ḥizb (D. B. Macdonald)
Ḥizḳīl (J. Eisenberg)
Hubal (Anonymus)
Hūd (A. J. Wensinck)
Ḥukm (T. H. Weir)
Ḥulūl (L. Massignon)
Ḥūr (A. J. Wensinck)
Ḥurūfī (Cl. Huart)
al-Ḥusain b. 'Alī (H. Lammens)

I

'Ibādāt (W. Heffening)
al-Ibāḍīya (T. Lewicki)
Iblīs (A. J. Wensinck)
Ibn 'Arabī (T. H. Weir)
Ibn 'Aṭā' Allāh (C. Brockelmann)
Ibn al-Fāriḍ (A. J. Arberry)
Ibn Ḥadjar al-Haitamī (C. van Arendonk)
Ibn Ḥazm (C. van Arendonk)
Ibn Isḥāḳ (C. Brockelmann)
Ibn Ḳaiyim al-Djawzīya (Anonymus)
Ibn al-Ḳāsim (Th. W. Juynboll)
Ibn Mādja (Anonymus)
Ibn Mas'ūd (A. J. Wensinck)
Ibn Sa'd (E. Mittwoch)
Ibn Taimīya (Moh. ben Cheneb)
Ibn Tūmart (R. Basset)
Ibrāhīm (J. Eisenberg and A. J. Wensinck)
Ibrāhīm b. Adham (R. A. Nicholson)
'Īd (E. Mittwoch)
'Īd al-Aḍḥā' (E. Mittwoch)
'Īd al-Fiṭr (E. Mittwoch)
'Idda (Th. W. Juynboll)
Īdjāb (Th. W. Juynboll)
al-Īdjī (Anonymus)
Idjmā' (D. B. Macdonald)
Idjtihād (D. B. Macdonald)
Idrīs (A. J. Wensinck)
'Ifrīt (D. B. Macdonald)
Iḥrām (A. J. Wensinck)
Iḳāma (Th. W. Juynboll)

Ikhlāṣ (C. van Arendonk)
Ikhtilāf (I. Goldziher)
Iḳrār (Th. W. Juynboll)
Ilāh (D. B. Macdonald)
Ilhām (D. B. Macdonald)
ʿIlm (D. B. Macdonald)
Ilyās (A. J. Wensinck)
Imām (W. Ivanow)
Imām-Bārā (Anonymus)
Imām-Shāh (W. Ivanow)
Īmān (D. B. Macdonald)
ʿImrān (J. Eisenberg)
Indjīl (B. Carra de Vaux)
al-Insān al-Kāmil (R. A. Nicholson)
Iram (A. J. Wensinck)
Iram Dhāt al-ʿImād (A. J. Wensinck)
Irmiyā (A. J. Wensinck)
ʿĪsā (D. B. Macdonald)
Isḥāḳ (J. Eisenberg)
al-Iskandar (Anonymus)
Islām (T. W. Arnold)
ʿIṣma (I. Goldziher)
Ismāʿīl (A. J. Wensinck)
Ismāʿīlīya (W. Ivanow)
Isrāʾ (B. Schrieke)
Isrāfīl (A. J. Wensinck)
Isrāʾīl (A. J. Wensinck)
Istiḥsān and Istiṣlāḥ (R. Paret)
Istikhāra (I. Goldziher)
Istindjāʾ (Th. W. Juynboll)
Istinshāḳ (Th. W. Juynboll)
Istiṣḥāb (Th. W. Juynboll)
Istisḳāʾ (A. Bel)
Ithnā ʿAsharīya (Cl. Huart)
Iʿtiḳād (D. B. Macdonald)
Iʿtikāf (Th. W. Juynboll)
Ittiḥād (R. A. Nicholson)
ʿIzrāʾīl (A. J. Wensinck)

K

Kaʿb b. Mālik (F. Buhl)
Kaʿba (A. J. Wensinck)
Ḳabḍ (A. J. Arberry)
Kabīr (T. W. Arnold)
Ḳaḍāʾ (D. B. Macdonald)
Ḳadar (D. B. Macdonald)
Ḳadarīya (D. B. Macdonald)
Ḳadhf (Th. W. Juynboll)
Ḳāḍī (Th. W. Juynboll)
Ḳādirīya (D. S. Margoliouth)
Kafāla (Th. W. Juynboll)
Kaffāra (Th. W. Juynboll)
Kāfir (W. Björkman)
Kāhin (A. Fischer)
Ḳainuḳāʿ (A. J. Wensinck)
Kaisānīya (C. van Arendonk)
Ḳaiṣar (A. Schaade)
al-Kalābādhī (A. J. Arberry)
Kalām (D. B. Macdonald)
Ḳalandarīya (F. Babinger)
Kalb (B. Joel)
Kanʿān (B. Joel)
Kanīsa (C. van Arendonk)
Karāma (D. B. Macdonald)
Karāmat ʿAlī (A. Yusuf Ali)
Ḳarmaṭians (L. Massignon)
Karrāmīya (D. S. Margoliouth)
Ḳārūn (D. B. Macdonald)
Ḳasam (J. Pedersen)
Kasb (D. B. Macdonald)
Kashf (D. B. Macdonald)
al-Ḳasṭallānī (C. Brockelmann)
Ḳatl (J. Schacht)
Kawthar (J. Horowitz)
Kāzarūnī (P. Wittek)
Khadīdja (F. Buhl)
al-Khaḍir (A. J. Wensinck)
Khwādja Khiḍr (M. Longworth Dames)
Khālid (K. V. Zettersteen)
Khalīfa (T. W. Arnold)
Khalḳ (Tj. de Boer)
Khamr (A. J. Wensinck)
Kharādj (Th. W. Juynboll)
al-Khargūshī (A. J. Arberry)
Khāridjites (G. Levi della Vida)
Khaṭaʾ (J. Schacht)
Khaṭīʾa (A. J. Wensinck)
Khaṭīb (J. Pedersen)
Khatm (F. Buhl)
Khaṭṭābīya (D. S. Margoliouth)
Khidhlān (A. J. Wensinck)
Khirḳa (Cl. Huart)
Khitān (A. J. Wensinck)
Khiyār (J. Schacht)
Khodja (W. Ivanow)
Khubaib (A. J. Wensinck)
Khurramīya (D. S. Margoliouth)
Khuṭba (A. J. Wensinck)
Ḳibla (A. J. Wensinck)
Ḳirāʾa (L. Massignon)
Ḳiṣāṣ (J. Schacht)
Ḳiṭfīr (B. Heller)
Ḳiṭmīr (J. H. Kramers)
al-Ḳiyāma (D. B. Macdonald)
Ḳiyās (A. J. Wensinck)
Ḳubbat al-Ṣakhra (J. Walker)
al-Ḳuds (F. Buhl)
Ḳunūt (A. J. Wensinck)
Ḳuraiẓa (V. Vacca)
al-Ḳurʾān (F. Buhl)
Ḳurbān (A. J. Wensinck)
Kursī (Cl. Huart)
al-Ḳushairī (L. Massignon)

L

al-Lāt (F. Buhl)
Lawḥ (A. J. Wensinck)
Lazarus (B. Heller)
Luḳaṭa (J. Schacht)
Luḳmān (B. Heller)
Lūṭ (B. Heller)

M

al-Madīna (F. Buhl)
Madjūs (V. F. Büchner)
Maḍmūn (O. Spies)
Madrasa (J. Pedersen)
al-Mahdī (D. B. Macdonald)
Maḥmal (F. Buhl)
Mahr (O. Spies)
Maimūna (F. Buhl)
Maisir (B. Carra de Vaux)
Maita (J. Schacht)
Maks (W. Björkman)
Malāʾika (D. B. Macdonald)
Mālik b. Anas (J. Schacht)
Mālikīs (W. Heffening)
Mamlūk (A. J. Wensinck)
Manāt (F. Buhl)
Marabout (E. Lévi-Provençal)
Māristān (J. Pedersen)

Shādhilīya (D. S. Margoliouth)
Shafāʿa (A. J. Wensinck)
al-Shāfiʿī (W. Heffening)
Shahāda (B. Carra de Vaux)
Shahīd (W. Björkman)
Shāhid (W. Heffening)
Shaiba (Gaudefroy-Demombynes)
al-Shaibānī (W. Heffening)
Shaikh (A. Cour)
Shaikh al-Islām (J. H. Kramers)
Shaikhī (Cl. Huart)
Shaiṭān (A. S. Tritton)
Shamsīya (D. S. Margoliouth)
Sharāb (A. J. Wensinck)
Sharīʿa (J. Schacht)
Sharīf (C. van Arendonk)
Shaṭḥ (L. Massignon)
Shaṭṭārīya (D. S. Margoliouth)
Shīʿa (R. Strothmann)
al-Shiblī (L. Massignon)
Shirk (W. Björkman)
Shīth (Cl. Huart)
Shuʿaib (F. Buhl)
Shurāt (L. Massignon)
al-Shushtarī (L. Massignon)
al-Ṣiddīḳ (V. Vacca)
Ṣifa (D. B. Macdonald)
Siḥr (D. B. Macdonald)
Sīra (G. Levi della Vida)
Subḥa (A. J. Wensinck)
Sulaimān b. Dāwūd (J. Walker)
al-Sulamī (A. J. Arberry)
Sulūk (R. A. Nicholson)
Sunna (A. J. Wensinck)
Sūra (F. Buhl)
Ṣūra (A. J. Wensinck)
Sutra (A. J. Wensinck)

T

Ṭaʾām (A. S. Tritton)
al-Ṭabarī (R. Paret)
Tābiʿ (V. Carra de Vaux)
Tadjwīd (Moh. ben Cheneb)
Tafsīr (B. Carra de Vaux)
Tahadjdjud (A. J. Wensinck)
Ṭahāra (A. S. Tritton)
Ṭāhir (W. Ivanow)
Taḥrīf (F. Buhl)
Taḳīya (R. Strothmann)
Taḳlīd (J. Schacht)
Taklīf (D. B. Macdonald)
Ṭalāḳ (J. Schacht)
Talbiya (A. J. Wensinck)
Ṭālūt (B. Heller)
Tanāsukh (B. Carra de Vaux)
Tarāwīḥ (A. J. Wensinck)
Ṭarīḳa (L. Massignon)
Taʾrīkh (W. Hartner)
Taṣawwuf (L. Massignon)
Tashbīh (R. Strothmann)
Ṭawāf (F. Buhl)
Tawba (R. A. Nicholson)
Tawḥīd (B. D. Macdonald)
Tawrāt (J. Horovitz)
Tayammum (A. J. Wensinck)
Taʿzīr (W. Heffening)
Taʿziya (R. Strothmann)
Thamūd (H. H. Bräu)
Thanawīya (R. Strothmann)
al-Tidjānīya (D. S. Margoliouth)
al-Tirmidhī (A. J. Wensinck)
Ṭulaiḥa b. Khuwailid (V. Vacca)
Turban (W. Björkman)

U

ʿUlamāʾ (D. B. Macdonald)
ʿUmar b. al-Khaṭṭāb (G. Levi della Vida)
Umm al-Kitāb (J. Horovitz)
Umm Kulthūm (G. Buhl)
Umm al-Walad (J. Schacht)
Umma (R. Paret)
Ummī (R. Paret)
ʿUmra (R. Paret)
ʿUrs (W. Heffening)
ʿUshr (A. Grohmann)
Uṣūl (J. Schacht)
ʿUthmān b. ʿAffān (G. Levi della Vida)
ʿUzair (B. Heller)
al-ʿUzzā (F. Buhl)

W

Wahhābīya (D. S. Margoliouth)
Waḥy (A. J. Wensinck)
Waḳf (W. Heffening)
Walī (B. Carra de Vaux)
Waraḳa b. Nawfal (V. Vacca)
Wāṣil b. ʿAṭāʾ (A. J. Wensinck)
Waṣīya (J. Schacht)
Wilāya (W. Heffening)
Wird (L. Massignon)
Witr (A. J. Wensinck)
Wuḍūʾ (J. Schacht)
Wuḳūf (R. Paret)

Y

Yādjūdj wa-Mādjūdj (A. J. Wensinck)
Yāfith (B. Heller)
Yāhūd(ī) (H. Speyer)
Yaḥyā (B. Carra de Vaux)
Yaʿḳūb (B. Heller)
Yatīm (J. Schacht)
Yazīdī (Th. Menzel)
Yūnus b. Mattai (B. Heller)
Yūshaʿ b. Nūn (B. Heller)
Yūsuf b. Yaʿḳūb (B. Heller)

Z

Zabūr (J. Horovitz)
al-Ẓāhirīya (R. Strothmann)
Zaid b. ʿAmr (V. Vacca)
Zaid b. Ḥāritha (V. Vacca)
al-Zaidīya (R. Strothmann)
Zain al-Dīn (D. S. Margoliouth)
Zainab bint Djaḥsh (V. Vacca)
Zainab bint Khuzaima (V. Vacca)
Zainab bint Muḥammad (V. Vacca)
Zakārīyāʾ (B. Heller)
Zakāt (J. Schacht)
al-Zamakhsharī (C. Brockelmann)
Zamzam (B. Carra de Vaux)
Zāwiya (E. Lévi-Provençal)
Zināʾ (J. Schacht)
Zindīḳ (L. Massignon)
Ziyānīya (D. S. Margoliouth)
Ziyāra (A. J. Wensinck)
al-Zubair b. al-ʿAwwām (A. J. Wensinck)
Zuhd (L. Massignon)